AAAI-02
Edmonton/Alberta
IAAI-02

Proceedings

AAAI-02
Edmonton/Alberta
IAAI-02

Proceedings

Eighteenth National Conference on
Artificial Intelligence (AAAI-02)

Fourteenth Innovative Applications of
Artificial Intelligence Conference (IAAI-02)

AAAI PRESS/THE MIT PRESS

MENLO PARK, CALIFORNIA • CAMBRIDGE, MASSACHUSETTS • LONDON, ENGLAND

Distributed by The MIT Press, Massachusetts Institute of Technology,
Cambridge, Massachusetts and London, England.

ISBN 0-262-51129-0

Printed on acid-free paper in the United States of America

Contents

AAAI-02 Technical Papers

Constraint Satisfaction

Knowledge Representation

Logic Programming

Learning

Markov Decision Processes

Multiagent Systems

Auctions

Satisfiability

Search

Vision

Web and Information Extraction

Innovative Applications of Artificial Intelligence Papers

Deployed Applications

Student Abstracts

SIGART/AAAI Doctoral Consortium

Intelligent Systems Demonstrations

Invited Talks

AAAI Organization

Officers

AAAI President
Tom M. Mitchell, *Carnegie Mellon University*

AAAI President-Elect
Ron Brachman

Past President
Bruce Buchanan, *University of Pittsburgh*

Secretary-Treasurer
Norman R. Nielsen, *The Enterprise*

Councilors

(through 2002):
Deborah McGuinness, *Stanford University*
Bart Selman, *Cornell University*
Reid G. Simmons, *Carnegie Mellon University*
Manuela Veloso, *Carnegie Mellon University*

(through 2003):
Craig Boutilier, *University of Toronto*
Rina Dechter, *University of California, Irvine*
Richard Doyle, *Jet Propulsion Laboratory,*
    California Institute of Technology
David Poole, *University of British Columbia*

(through 2004):
Marie desJardins, *University of Maryland,*
    Baltimore County
Craig Knoblock, *USC/ISI*
Daphne Koller, *Stanford University*
Peter Norvig, *Google, Inc.*

Standing Committees

Conference Chair
James A. Hendler, *University of Maryland*

Fellows/Nominating Chair
Bruce Buchanan, *University of Pittsburgh*

Finance Chair
Norman R. Nielsen, *The Enterprise*

Grants Chair
Manuela Veloso, *Carnegie Mellon University*

Membership Chair
Reid Simmons, *Carnegie Mellon University*

Publications Chair
David Leake, *Indiana University*

Symposium Chair
Holly Yanco, *University of Massachusetts Lowell*

Symposium Cochair
Daniel Clancy, *NASA Ames Research Center*

Symposium Associate Chair
David Poole, *University of British Columbia*

AAAI Press

Editor-in-Chief,
Kenneth Ford, *University of West Florida*
    Institute for Human and Machine Cognition

Press Editorial Board
Kenneth Ford, *University of West Florida*
    Institute for Human and Machine Cognition
Ken Forbus, *Northwestern University*
Patrick Hayes, *University of West Florida*
    Institute for Human and Machine Cognition

Janet Kolodner, *Georgia Institute of Technology*
George Luger, *University of New Mexico*
Robert Morris, *NASA Ames Research Center*
Alain Rappaport, *Carnegie Mellon University*
Brian Williams, *Massachusetts Institute of Technology*

AI Magazine

Editor
David Leake, *Indiana University*

Editor Emeritus
Robert Engelmore, *Stanford University*

Reports Editor
Robert Morris, *NASA Ames Research Center*

Book Review Editor
Michael Wellman, *University of Michigan*

Managing Editor
David M. Hamilton, *The Live Oak Press, LLC*

Production Editor
Sunny Ludvik, *Ludvik Editorial Services*

Magazine Editorial Board
James Allen, *University of Rochester*
Craig Boutilier, *University of Toronto*
Henrik Christensen, *Swedith Royal Institute of Technology*
Boi Faltings, *Swiss Federal Institute of Technology*
Usama Fayyad, *digiMine*
Kenneth Ford, *University of West Florida, Institute for Human and Machine Cognition*
Janice Glasgow, *Queen's University*
Kris Hammond, *Northwestern University*
Patrick Hayes, *University of West Florida, Institute for Human and Machine Cognition*
Henry Kautz, *University of Washington*
Janet Kolodner, *Georgia Institute of Technology*
Robert Milne, *Intelligent Applications, Ltd.*
Leora Morgenstern, *IBM Watson Research Labs*
Martha Pollack, *University of Michigan*
Jude Shavlik, *University of Wisconsin*
Moshe Tenneholtz, *Technion*
Sebastian Thrun, *Carnegie Mellon University*
Feng Zhao, *NASA Ames Research Center*

AAAI Staff

Executive Director
Carol McKenna Hamilton

Accountant/Office Manager
Colleen Boyce

Senior Conference Coordinator
Keri Vasser Harvey

Conference Coordinator
Elizabeth Ericson

Conference Assistant
Erin Hogan

Information Technology Manager
Richard A. Skalsky

Membership Assistant
Eve Garcia

Administrative Assistant
Ann Stolberg

Program Committees

Conference Chairs

Conference Committee Chair
James A. Hendler, *University of Maryland*

AAAI-02 Program Cochairs
Rina Dechter, *University of California, Irvine*
Michael Kearns, *University of Pennsylvania*
Richard S. Sutton

IAAI-02 Chair
Steve Chien, *Jet Propulsion Laboratory*

IAAI-02 Cochair
John Riedl, *University of Minnesota*

Intelligent Systems Demonstrations Chair
George Ferguson, *University of Rochester*

Student Abstract and Poster Cochairs
Mark Craven, *University of Wisconsin, Madison*
Sven Koenig, *Georgia Institute of Technology*

Robot Building Laboratory Chair
David Miller, *KISS Institute for Practical Robotics*

Robot Competition and Exhibition Cochairs
Holly Yanco, *University of Massachusetts Lowell*
Tucker Balch, *Georgia Institute of Technology*

SIGART/AAAI 2002 Doctoral Consortium Chair
Marie desJardins, *University of Maryland,
Baltimore County*

Tutorial Forum Chair
Michael L. Littman, *Stowe Research*

Workshop Chair and Cochair
Berthe Y. Choueiry, *University of Nebraska-Lincoln*
Janyce Wiebe, *University of Pittsburgh*

AAAI-02 Senior Program Committee

Fahiem Bacchus, *University of Toronto*
Jonathan Baxter, *Whizbang! Labs Research*
Roberto Bayardo, *IBM Almaden Research Center*
Chitta Baral, *Arizona State University*
Adnan Darwiche, *University of California, Los Angeles*
Tom Dietterich, *Oregon State University*
Oren Etzioni, *University of Washington*
Dieter Fox, *University of Washington*
Hector Geffner, *Universidad Simon Bolivar*
Leslie Kaelbling, *Massachusetts Institute of Technology*
Takeo Kanade, *Carnegie Mellon University*
Kevin Knight, *USC / Information Sciences Institute*
Alfred Kobsa, *University of California, Irvine*
Richard Korf, *University of California, Los Angeles*
David McAllester
Andrew Moore, *Carnegie Mellon University*
David Poole, *University of British Columbia*
Dan Roth, *University of Illinois, Urbana-Champaign*
Tuomas Sandholm, *Carnegie Mellon University*
Jonathan Schaeffer, *University of Alberta*
Bart Selman, *Cornell University*
Mark Steedman, *University of Edinburgh*
Peter Stone, *The University of Texas at Austin*
Peter van Beek, *University of Waterloo*
Weixiong Zhang, *Washington University*

AAAI-02 Program Committee

Steven Abney, *AT&T Laboratories - Research*
Gregory Abowd, *Georgia Institute of Technology*
Dimitris Achlioptas, *Microsoft Corporation*
James Allen, *University of Massachusetts*
Bruce D'Ambrosio, *Oregon State University*
Franz Baader, *RWTH Aachen*
Simon Baker, *Carnegie Mellon University*
Tucker Balch, *Georgia Institute of Technology*
Srinivas Bangalore, *AT&T Laboratories - Research*
Peter Bartlett, *University of California, Berkeley*

Dragomir Radev, *University of Michigan*
Jochen Renz, *Vienna University of Technology*
Jeff Rickel, *USC, Information Sciences Institute*
Irina Rish, *IBM T.J. Watson Research Center*
Amir Ronen, *Stanford University*
Jeffrey Rosenschein, *Hebrew University*
Francesca Rossi, *Università di Padova*
Nicholas Roy, *Carnegie Mellon University*
Thomas Schiex, *INRA (UBIA)*
Carsten Schuermann, *Yale University*
Dale Schuurmanns, *University of Waterloo*
Eddie Schwalb, *Schwalb Research LLC*
Fabrizio Sebastiani, *Consiglio Nazionale delle Ricerche*
Steven Seitz, *University of Washington*
Anup Kumar Sen, *Indian Institute of Management Calcutta*
John Shawe Taylor, *University of London*
Prakash Shenoy, *Kansas University*
Jianbo Shi, *Carnegie Mellon University*
Satinder Singh, *Syntek Capital*
Bill Smart, *Washington University in St. Louis*
Barbara Smith, *University of Huddersfield*
David Smith, *NASA Ames Research Center*
Tran Son, *New Mexico State University*
Robert St. Amant, *North Carolina State University*
Constantine Stephanidis, *Foundation for Research and Technology*
Matthew Stone, *Rutgers University*
Malcolm Strens, *QinetiQ*
Gaurav Sukhatme, *University of Southern California*
Subhash Suri, *University of California, Santa Barbara*
Moshe Tennenholtz, *Stanford University*
Sylvie Thiebaux, *The Australian National University*
Belinda Thom, *Harvey Mudd College*
Cindi Thompson, *University of Utah*
Jin Tian, *University of California, Los Angeles*
Paolo Traverso, *IRST*
Hudson Turner, *University of Minnesota, Duluth*
H. J. van den Herik, *Universiteit Maastricht*
Pascal Van Hentenryck, *Brown University*
Gérard Verfaillie, *ONERA*
Stephan Vogel, *Carnegie Mellon University*
Ellen Voorhees, *NIST*
Tom Wagner, *Honeywell Laboratories*
Toby Walsh, *The University of York*
William Walsh, *IBM T.J. Watson Research Center*
Janyce Wiebe, *University of Pittsburgh*
Bob Williamson, *Australian National University*
Peter Wurman, *North Carolina State University*
Qiang Yang, *Hong Kong University of Science*
David Yarowsky, *Johns Hopkins University*
Makoto Yokoo, *NTT Communication Science Laboratories*
Nevin Zhang, *Hong Kong University of Science & Technology*
Yan Zhang, *University of Western Sydney*
Shlomo Zilberstein, *University of Massachusetts*
Ingrid Zukerman, *Monash University*

AAAI-02 Auxiliary Reviewers

Dana Angluin
Dragomir Anguelov
Marta Arias
Andrew Arnt
Alessandro Artale
Chris Beck
Daniel Bernstein
Piergiorgio Bertoli
Darse Billings
Michael Brenner
Bret Browning
Diego Calvanese
Giuseppe Carenini
Amedeo Cesta
Alessandro Cimatti
Vincent Conitzer
Denver Dash
Sandip Debnath
Demetrios Demopoulos
Yannis Dimopoulos
Irina Dumitrescu
Esra Erdem
Wolfgang Faber
Zhengzhu Feng
Alan Fern
Jeremy Frank
David Furcy
Alfredo Gabaldon
Brian Gerkey
Yolanda Gil
Steven Greenberg
Emmanuel Guèrè
Andy Haas
Joe Halpern
Jason Hartline
Patrik Haslum
Langseth Helge
Johanna Hellemons
Malte Helmert
Ian Horrocks
Andrew Howard
G. Neelakanthan Kartha
Tomas Kocka
Ralf Küsters
Jonas Kvarnström
Michail Lagoudakis
Gerhard Lakemeyer
Nicola Leone
Uri Lerner
Reinhold Letz
Yaxin Liu
Derek Long
Tsai-Ching Lu
Thomas Lukasiewicz
Omid Madani
Jakob Mauss
Laurent Michel

Ion Muslea
XuanLong Nguyen
Romeo Sanchez Nigenda
Xavier Nodet
Angelo Oddi
Mushin Ozdemir
Maurice Pagnucco
Luis Paquete
Seung-Taek Park
Aarati Parmar
Mark Paskin
Vladimir Pavlovic
Terry Payne
Jose M. Pena
Erik Peterson
Gerald Pfeifer
Marco Pistore
Enrico Pontelli
Eric Postma
Marco Pranzo
Ganesh Ramesh
Jussi Rintanen
Jèrùme Rogerie
Nico Roos
Riccardo Rosati
Marco Roveri
Ulrike Sattler
Uday Savagaonkar
Richard Scherl
Renate Schmidt
Luciano Serafini
Jonathan Shapiro
Paul Shaw
Rajjog Singh
John Slaney
Alessandro Sperduti
Biplav Srivastava
Ashley W. Stroupe
Thomas Stuetzle
Gerd Stumme
Armando Tacchella
Ben Taskar
Mugur Tatar
Sergio Tessaris
Hans Tompits
Lorenzo Torresani
Iannis Vetsikas
Paul Vogt
Mark Wallace
Haiqin Wang
Lida Wang
Shengrui Wang
Emil Weydert
Floris Wiesman
Frank Wolter
Helen Yan
Dit-Yan Yeung
Neil Yorke-Smith

Mohammed Zaki
Klaus Zechner
Rong Zhou
Lin Zhu

IAAI-02 Program Committee

Bruce Buchanan, *University of Pittsburgh*
Steve Chien, *Jet Propulsion Laboratory*
Robert Engelmore, *KSL, Stanford University*
Randy Hill, *USC Institute for Creative Technologies*
Neil Jacobstein, *Teknowledge Corporation*
Craig Knoblock, *Information Sciences Institute*
David Kortenkamp, *NASA Johnson Space Center*
Ora Lassila, *Nokia Corporation*
Daniel Marcu, *Information Sciences Institute, University of Southern California*
David Opitz, *University of Montana*
John Riedl, *University of Minnesota*
Ted Senator, *DARPA/ISO*
Reid Smith, *Schulumberger Ltd.*
Ramasamy Uthurusamy, *GM Corporation*
Peter Wurman, *North Carolina State University*

Student Abstract Reviewers

Stephen Bay, *Stanford University*
Paul Bradley, *digiMine, Inc*
Michael Burl
Rich Caruana, *Cornell University*
Phil Chan, *Florida Institute of Technology*
Tina Eliassi-Rad, *Lawrence Livermore Laboratory*
Tara Estlin, *Jet Propulsion Laboratory*
Dayne Freitag
Lise Getoor, *University of Maryland*
Greg Grudic, *University of Colorado, Boulder*
Alexander Hartemink, *Levine Science Research Center*
Thomas Hofmann, *Brown University*
Thorsten Joachims, *Cornell University*
Terran Lane, *Massachusetts Institute of Technology*
Rich Maclin, *University of Wisconsin*
Amol Mali, *University of Wisconsin*
Dragos Margineantu, *The Boeing Company*
Marina Meila, *University of Washington*
Kamal Nigam, *Whizbang Labs*
Dave Opitz, *University of Montana*
David Parkes, *Harvard University*
Ted Pedersen, *University of Minnesota Duluth*
Drago Radev, *University of Michigan*
Bill Smart, *Washington University*
Matthew Stone, *Rutgers University*
Nick Street, *University of Iowa*
Cindi Thompson, *University of Utah*
Pete Wurman, *North Carolina State University*

AAAI-02 Outstanding Paper Award

This year, AAAI's National Conference on Artificial Intelligence honors one paper that exemplifies high standards in technical contribution and exposition.

During the blind review process, members of the Program Committee recommended papers to consider for the Outstanding Paper Award. A subset of the Senior Program Committee, carefully chosen to avoid conflicts of interest, reviewed all such papers and selected the winning paper:

On Computing All Abductive Explanations
Thomas Eiter, Technische Universität Wien and Kazuhisa Makino, Osaka University

AAAI-02
Edmonton/Alberta
IAAI-02

Sponsoring Organizations

- American Association for Artificial Intelligence
- ACM/SIGART
- Alberta Informatics Circle of Research Excellence (iCORE)
- Defense Advanced Research Projects Agency (DARPA)
- NASA Ames Research Center
- National Science Foundation
- Naval Research Laboratory

AAAI-02
Edmonton/Alberta
IAAI-02

Preface

The AAAI–02 Conference

This volume collects the papers accepted for presentation at AAAI-02, the Eighteenth National Conference on Artificial Intelligence. The traditionally high standards of submission and acceptance were in force once again this year, with the result being an exciting program reflecting the great variety and depth of modern AI research. Probabilistic and logical approaches to classical and recent problems seem to be not just peacefully coexisting, but benefiting from each other's presence. This year we had substantial numbers of submissions in all traditional areas of AI, including learning, knowledge representation and planning, probabilistic reasoning, constraint satisfaction, and satisfiability. There was also an impressive rise in areas such as multi-agent systems, electronic commerce, and algorithmic issues in game and auction theory.

The technical papers in this volume were selected from 470 submissions by a rigorous and blind review process. Each submission was reviewed by three members of the AAAI Program Committee, who were supervised by one member of the Senior Program Committee. Decisions were reached following discussions among the reviewers of each paper, and finalized in a meeting of the Senior Program Committee. We believe the reader will find these articles to be of the highest quality, representing a significant contribution to the field of AI in all its diversity.

The award for Outstanding Paper for AAAI-02 was selected by the Senior Program Committee, and chosen from a number of very strong candidates. We are pleased to present this award to the paper "On Computing All Abductive Explanations," by Thomas Eiter and Kazuhisa Makino. This work, along with other results, settles an open problem in classical abductive reasoning.

Apart from the presentations of accepted papers, and in addition to the presidential address by Tom Mitchell, we are very pleased to have four distinguished invited speakers: Hector Geffner, Michael Jordan, Raymond Kurzweil, and Naftali Tishby.

The National Conference on Artificial Intelligence relies on the generous help of many people. We extend our appreciation to the 180 members of the Program Committee, and the 25 members of the Senior Program Committee. Furthermore, we thank Carol Hamilton, Keri Harvey, Rick Skalsky, and the entire AAAI staff for their professionalism, organization, and courtesy. Finally, we thank the AAAI Executive Council for giving us this opportunity to cochair the conference.

- Rina Dechter, Michael Kearns, & Rich Sutton

The IAAI–02 Conference

The Fourteenth Annual Conference on Innovative Applications of Artificial Intelligence (IAAI-02) continues the IAAI tradition of case studies of deployed applications with measurable benefits from the use of AI technology. In addition, IAAI-02 also includes papers and invited talks that address emerging areas of AI technology or applications. IAAI is organized as an independent program within the National Conference, with schedules coordinated to allow attendees to move freely between IAAI and National Conference sessions. IAAI and the National Conference also jointly sponsor invited talks that fit the theme of both programs.

AI applications developers benefit from learning about the latest AI techniques that will enable the next generation of applications. Basic AI research benefits by exposure to the challenges of real-world domains and difficulties and successes in applying AI techniques to real business problems. IAAI-02 addresses the full range of AI techniques including knowledge-based systems, planning and scheduling, perception and monitoring, knowledge formation, knowledge management, learning, intelligent design, natural language processing, and diagnostic reasoning.

Deployed applications are case studies that provide a valuable guide to designing, building, managing, and deploying systems incorporating AI technologies. This year's papers address applications in a wide variety of domains, including large-scale scheduling, monitoring for terrorism response, text and language processing for customer support, engineering configuration, education, call-center scheduling, and quote generation. These applications provide clear evidence of the impact and value that AI technology has in today's world.

Papers on emerging applications and technologies describe efforts whose goal is the engineering of AI applications. They inform AI researchers about the utility of specific AI techniques for applications domains and also inform applications developers about tools and techniques that will enable the next generation of new and more powerful applications.

This year we are very pleased to have two invited talks. Robin Murphy's talk, "Robots for Urban Rescue," will describe the use of robots to facilitate rescue during both man-made and natural disasters and includes footage from efforts at the World Trade Center. In a talk jointly sponsored with AAAI, Ray Kurzweil will speak on "Human Level 'Strong' AI: The Prospects and Implications," in which he reflects on the accelerating pace of change in high technology areas.

New for IAAI in 2002 is a series of events focusing on AI businesses. We begin with the panel "AI Businesses: A 20 Year Review," chaired by Neil Jacobstein, President and CEO of Teknowledge. This panel will focus on the lessons learned from 20 years of AI businesses. Next, Craig Knoblock, Chief Scientist of Fetch Technologies, chairs the panel "Recent Startups." This panel will focus on how to overcome the hurdles in starting an AI business. Finally, Steve Chien and Minda Wilson chair the Entrepreneur's Forum, an informal event designed to enable Technologists, Legal Professionals, and Financiers to network during the AI Festival.

The Innovative Applications of Artificial Intelligence Conference could not take place without the generous help of many people. We extend our appreciation to the IAAI-02 program committee: Neil Jacobstein, Peter Wurman, Craig Knoblock, David Kortenkamp, Ted Senator, David Opitz, Bruce Buchanan, Randy Hill, Reid Smith, Sam Uthurusamy, Bob Engelmore, Ora Lassila, Daniel Marcu. Further, we thank Carol Hamilton, Keri Harvey, Rick Skalsky, and the entire AAAI staff for their professionalism, organization, and courtesy.

– Steve Chien & John Riedl

AAAI-02
Edmonton/Alberta
IAAI-02

Invited Talks and Panels

2002 AAAI Presidential Address:
AI and the Impending Revolution in Brain Science
Tom M. Mitchell, Carnegie Mellon University

AAAI-02 Keynote Address:
Probabilistic AI and Information Retrieval
Michael I. Jordan, University of California, Berkeley

Much progress has been made in recent years in the area of information retrieval, in particular as embodied in Internet search engine technology. Much progress has also been made in probabilistic, graph-theoretic AI. What are the possibilities for bringing these two lines of research together — for viewing large-scale information retrieval as a core enabling technology for AI systems, and for asking IR systems to exhibit true inferential capabilities? Jordan will discuss research aimed at bridging the AI/IR gap.

AAAI-02/IAAI-02 Joint Invited Talk:
Human Level "Strong" AI: The Prospects and Implications
Raymond Kurzweil, KurzweilAI.net (Kurzweil Accelerating Intelligence Network)

Three-dimensional molecular computing will provide the hardware for human-level "strong" AI well before 2030. The more important software insights will be gained in part from the reverse-engineering of the human brain, a process well under way. Once nonbiological intelligence matches the range and subtlety of human intelligence, it will necessarily soar past it because of the continuing acceleration of information-based technologies, as well as the ability of machines to instantly share their knowledge. The implication will be an intimate merger between the technology-creating species and the evolutionary process it spawned.

Perspectives on Artificial Intelligence Planning

Hector Geffner, ICREA - Universitat Pompeu Fabra (Barcelona)

Planning has always been a key area in artificial intelligence. In its general form, planning is concerned with the automatic synthesis of action strategies (plans) from a description of actions, sensors, and goals. Planning thus contrasts with two other approaches to intelligent behavior: the programming approach, where action strategies are defined by hand, and the learning approach, where action strategies are inferred from experience.

Different assumptions about the nature of actions, sensors, and costs lead to various forms of planning: (1) Planning with complete information and deterministic actions, (2) planning with non-deterministic actions and sensing, and (3) planning with temporal and concurrent actions, etc. Most

work so far has been devoted to "classical" planning (1. above), where significant changes have taken place in the last few years. On the methodological side, the area has become more empirical with experimental evaluation being routine; on the technical side, approaches based on heuristic or constrained-based search have taken over blind-search approaches.

In this talk, Geffner will provide a coherent picture of planning in AI while trying to convey some of the current excitement in the field. He'll make emphasis on the mathematical models that underlie various forms of planning, and the ideas that have been found most useful computationally.

Dimension Reduction that Preserves Information and Neural Coding

Naftali Tishby, The Hebrew University

Many cognitive functions, such as prediction, feature extraction, noise filtering, and learning, can be viewed as special cases of one principle: compression while preserving information. This information theoretic principle was turned into a computational paradigm: the information bottleneck method. This variational method yielded several novel learning and data analysis algorithms, with many applications to information retrieval as well as to analysis of neural coding in several neurobiological systems, that were carried in Tishby's lab. In this talk Tishby will focus on a new approach to data dimensionality reduction that stems from this

principle. Here he searches for low dimensional (nonlinear) reduction of co-occurrence (or contingency) tables that preserve the (mutual) information in the table. He gives a new alternate-projection algorithm for achieving such a reduction and show its convergence to an optimal set of information preserving features. This approach is particularly useful when the data is not naturally quantized but rather represented by low dimension continuous features. Such a reduction may have interesting biological implications. (Based on joint work with Amir Globerson and Noam Slonim.)

Robot-Assisted Urban Search and Rescue at the WTC: Where's the AI?

Robin R. Murphy, University of South Florida

On September 11, 2001, the Center for Robot-Assisted Search and Rescue responded within six hours to the WTC disaster; this is the first known use of robots for USAR. The University of South Florida was one of the four robot teams, and only academic institution. The USF team participated on-site in the search efforts from September 12 through 22, collecting and archiving data on the use of robots.

This talk will provide an overview of the use of robots for USAR as well as discuss what AI techniques were available, what was actually used, and why. It will also summarize the key lessons learned from the robotics efforts at the WTC.

The lessons learned cover the areas of platforms and mobility, sensors and sensing strategies, control, and human-robot interactions. Possibly the most pervasive lesson learned is that robots for USAR must be considered from an "information technology" perspective, where platforms, sensors, control schemes, networks, and interfaces must all be coevolved to ensure the information extracted by the robots is truly usable by the rescue community.

Extensive video footage of the site and "robot's eye" views will be shown.

IAAI-02 Invited Panel:

Pioneering AI Businesses I: A 20-Year Review

Panel Leader: Neil Jacobstein, Teknowledge Corporation

Several AI-based businesses started in the early 1980s. They underwent a classic boom and bust cycle. Hype exceeded expectations, and some investors and technologists lost patience. However, history shows that in cases of disruptive technological innovation, forecasts are usually too optimistic in the short run, and too conservative in the long run. Is that the case with AI businesses? This panel of AI entrepre-neurs will review the technology base and history of pioneering AI businesses, extract lessons learned, and identify future opportunities. Companies discussed will include IntelliCorp, Teknowledge, Inference, Syntelligence, Carnegie Group, Cycorp, and others. An interactive question and answer session with panel members will follow brief presentations from each panelist.

IAAI-02 Invited Panel:

Pioneering AI Businesses II: Recent Startups

Panel Leader: Craig Knoblock, University of Southern California and Fetch Technologies
Panelists: Tom Mitchell, Fredkin Professor of Computer Science, Carnegie Mellon University and Former Chief Scientist and VP at WhizBang; Yoav Shoham, Associate Professor, Stanford University and Cofounder and Chairman, TradingDynamics (ARBA) and Cariocas; Daniel Weld, Professor, University of Washington, Cofounder of Netbot, AdRelevance, Nimble Technology, and Asta Networks, and Venture Partner, Madrona Venture Group

This panel will focus on the process of starting an AI company. The challenges in creating a new company include how to apply a technology to address a specific market need and how to run a successful business. The speakers on this panel are AI researchers that have been involved in recent startups. Some of the issues the panelists will discuss include how to go from a technology to a business, how to get funding for a company, and what pitfalls to watch out for. An interactive question and answer session with panel members will follow brief presentations from each panelist.

IAAI-02 Invited Panel (Collocated with AI Festival):

PI Entrepreneurs Forum

This forum will provide an open and informal setting for AI pioneers, technologists, entrepreneurs, venture capitalists, legal, and intellectual property experts to network and discuss issues in starting and running AI-based companies.

AAAI-02
Edmonton/Alberta
IAAI-02

Technical Papers

AAAI-02
Edmonton/Alberta
IAAI-02

Constraint Satisfaction

The Yard Allocation Problem

Ping Chen and **Zhaohui Fu** and **Andrew Lim**
Department of Computer Science
National University of Singapore
3 Science Drive 2, Singapore 117543
{chenp,fuzh,alim}@comp.nus.edu.sg

Abstract

The Yard Allocation Problem (YAP) is a real-life resource allocation problem faced by the Port of Singapore Authority (PSA). We first show that YAP is NP-Hard. As the problem is NP-Hard, we propose several heuristics, including Tabu Search methods with short and long term memory, a "Squeaky Wheel" Optimization (SWO) method, and a new hybrid which combines SWO with TS to solve the problem. Extensive experiments show very favorable results for our new hybrid method.

Introduction

Singapore has one of the world's busiest ports in terms of shipping tonnage with more than one hundred thousand ship arrivals every year. One of the major logistical problems encountered is to use the minimum container yard necessary to accommodate all different requests. Each request consists of a single time interval and a series of yard space requirements during that interval. An interesting constraint applying to every request is that the length of the required space can either increase or remain unchanged as time progresses, and once yard space is allocated to a certain request, that portion of the yard space cannot be freed until the completion of the request. The major reason for such a constraint is that once a container is placed in the yard, it will not be removed until the ship for which it is bound arrives. As a result, the yard requirement can only increase. The current allocation is made manually, hence it requires a considerable amount of manpower.

Problem Definition

The objective of the Yard Allocation Problem (YAP) can be expressed in two ways:

1. Minimise the yard used to accomodate all the space requirements;

2. Maximise the number of requirements allocated on a fixed yard.

These two objectives are in fact similar to each other. We use the first one as our objective in this paper because

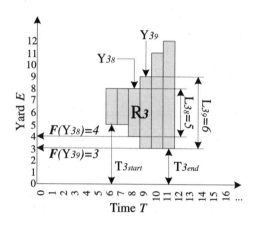

Figure 1: A *valid* request R_3.

the solution to the second problem requires the solution to the first one together with a partition routine. The formal definition of our problem can be described as follows:

Instance: A set R of n yard space requests and an infinite container yard E. $\forall R_i \in R$, R_i has a series of (continuous) space requirements Y_{i_j} with length L_{i_j}, $j \in [T_{i_{start}}, T_{i_{end}}]$.
Output: A mapping function F, such that $F(Y_{i_j}) = e_k$, where $e_k \in E$ is some position on E.
Constraint: $\forall p, q \in [T_{i_{start}}, T_{i_{end}}]$ such that $p = q - 1$, $F(Y_{i_p}) \geq F(Y_{i_q})$ and $F(Y_{i_p}) + L_{i_p} \leq F(Y_{i_q}) + L_{i_q}$.
Objective: To minimize:

$$\max_{\forall R_i \in R, \forall Y_{i_j} \in R_i} (F(Y_{i_j}) + L_{i_j})$$

We use an example to illustrate the definition. Figure 1 shows a layout with only one *valid* requests R_3. The yard E is treated as an infinite straight line. Time T becomes a discrete variable with a minimum unit of 1. R_3 has six space requirements within interval $[6, 11]$ ($T_{3_{start}} = 6, T_{3_{end}} = 11$). The final position for Y_{3_8} and Y_{3_9} are $F(Y_{3_8}) = 4$ and $F(Y_{3_9}) = 3$ respectively. The corresponding output for R_3 will then be $(5, 5, 4, 3, 3, 3)$. Note all our pre-defined constraints hold as $F(Y_{3_8}) \geq F(Y_{3_9})$ and $F(Y_{3_8}) + L_{3_8} \leq F(Y_{3_9}) + L_{3_9}$. The *max* comes from $Y_{3_{11}}$ with the value of $F(Y_{3_{11}}) + L_{3_{11}} = 12$.

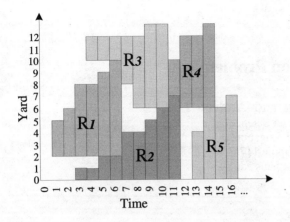

Figure 2: Five *valid* requests on yard

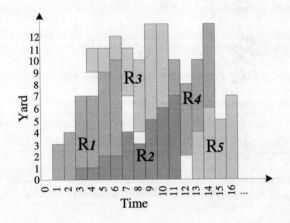

Figure 3: Five *invalid* requests on yard

We simply call each request a Stair Like Shapes (SLS) throughout this paper. Figure 2 shows five *valid* requests with the minimum yard required of 13. Though the packing in Figure 3 looks more compact, in fact, all allocations are *invalid* as the containment constraint is violated.

Theorem 1 *The Yard Allocation Problem (YAP) is NP-Hard.*

The Ship Berthing Problem (SBP) was first introduced in (Lim 1998). The SBP has a similar configuration except all the requests are of rectangular shape instead of SLS. (Lim 1999) has provided a NP-Hard proof for SBP by reducing the Set Partitioning Problem to SBP. As SBP is special case of YAP and YAP is in the class NP, YAP is NP-Hard.

Graph Transformation

Figure 2 illustrates the problem geometrically. However, the direct model may not be efficiently manipulated. We first transform the geometrical layout into a graph. Figure 4 is the corresponding graph transformation of the configuration in Figure 2. Each request R_i is represented by a vertex and there exists an edge E_{ij} connecting R_i and R_j iff R_i and

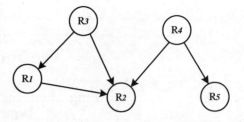

Figure 4: Graph Transformation of Figure 2

R_j have an overlap at some time. The direction of the edge determines the relative position of the two requests in the physical yard. Take Figure 2 again as an example, both R_1 and R_2 require some space at time 3,4,5 and 6, therefore in Figure 4 there is an edge between R_1 and R_2. Since R_1 is located above R_2, the direction of the edge is from R_1 to R_2. We name this edge E_{12}. Clearly, the transformed graph is a Direct Acyclic Graph (DAG). In a DAG, each vertex R_i can be assigned an Acyclic Label (AL) L_i and the edge E_{ij} implies $AL(R_i) < AL(R_j)$. Note that each $AL(R_i)(1 \leq i \leq n)$ is unique.

Lemma 1 *For each feasible layout of the yard, there exists at least one corresponding AL assignment of the vertices in the graph representation.*

A simple constructive proof can be obtained by the well-known Topological sorting algorithm. An AL assignment can also be interpreted as a permutation of $1, 2, \ldots, n$.

A "free" SLS is one with no other SLS above it, i.e. there is no obstacle blocking it from being popped out from the top of the layout. Again, use Figure 2 as an example. At the first iteration of the loop, R_3 and R_4 are the only two "free" SLSs. If we assign $AL(R_3) = 0$, in the second iteration, R_1 will become a new "free" SLS. The process continues until no more SLS are left in L.

The AL assignment only has the partial order property. Each physical layout may correspond to more than one AL assignments due to the lack of total order property. $[R_1 : 2, R_2 : 3, R_3 : 0, R_4 : 1, R_5 : 4]$ and $[R_1 : 2, R_2 : 4, R_3 : 1, R_4 : 0, R_5 : 3]$ are two possible AL assignments.

This one-to-many relationship between physical layout and AL assignments in the graph representation will incur a huge amount of confusion in heuristic searches, including Genetic Algorithms, etc. Heuristic methods tend to identify certain *good* patterns which may potentially lead to a better solution while exploring the search space. Two very different looking solutions, which may actually correspond to the same physical layout, will make it very difficult for the heuristic to identify the correct patterns.

We can avoid such confusion by normalizing the AL assignment. When there is more than one SLS to be popped out, we break the tie by selecting the SLS with the smallest label. Each un-normalized AL assignment is used to construct the corresponding DAG. Then a Topological Sort with above-mentioned tie-breaker will give the *unique* AL

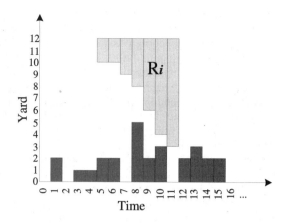

Figure 5: Before dropping: R_i is ceiling aligned

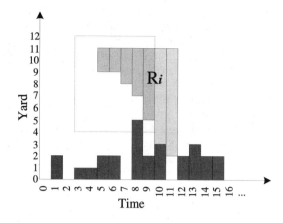

Figure 6: Each stair of R_i drop by 1. Stairs at times 10 and 11 are in their final positions. Those stairs which can drop further are in dark color surrounded by a rectangle

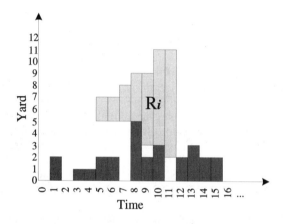

Figure 7: Final layout

assignment. From this point onwards, all our solutions are represented by their normalized unique AL assignments.

Each physical layout now has a unique AL assignment. Naturally, the optimal layout has an optimal AL assignment. Our goal is to find out such an optimal AL assignment. One of the major operations, the evaluation of a given AL assignment, turns out to be non-trivial. In SBP (Lim 1998) (Fu & Lim 2000), a longest path algorithm on a DAG was used to find the minimum berth length needed. However, YAP deals with SLS, whose relative position and distance cannot be calculated in a straight-forward way, unlike rectangles. We have to use a recursive procedure to find the minimum yard needed for a given AL assignment A.

Evaluate-Solution (A)
1 **while** exists unallocated SLS
2   pick SLS S with largest AL
3   Drop($S, S_{end}, 0$)
4   **foreach** time T_i
5   **if** $T_i > L$
6       $L := T_i$
7 **return** L

Drop (S, t, l)
1 $L :=$ lowest position to drop all stairs (time t')
2 **if** $L < l$
3   $L = l$
4 **forall** stair s after $t' - 1$
5   drop s to position L
6 Drop($S, t' - 1, L$)

The recursive function $Drop$ uses a greedy approach to drop a given SLS to a position as low as possible. We illustrate the details through Figures 5, 6 and 7: R_i has seven space requirements starting from time 5 to 11. R_i is first aligned to the ceiling before the process starts (Figure 5). Then from time 5 to 11, we find the maximum distance that each "stair" can drop, without exceeding a lower bound of 0. The minimum amongst all the maximum possible drop is used. In this case, the minimum distance of 1 is given at time 10 and hence every stair is shifted down by 1 (Figure 6).

Because of the initial ceiling alignment, no further shifting down is needed for all stairs at time 10 (inclusive) onwards. Note that the surface was touched at time 10.

Stairs from time 5 to 9, which are surrounded by a rectangle in Figure 6, can still be dropped further but this time with a lower bound of 3, which is the height of the previous touching surface at time 10. The dropping process completes after a few more recursions at times 8,7,6 and 5. The final layout is shown by Figure 7. Note the worst case time complexity for $Drop$ is $n \times T$, where n is the number of requests and T is the average time span for all requests.

Lemma 2 *For a given AL assignment, the greedy dropping approach always returns the layout with minimum yard used.*

Proof. The proof of the correctness of a greedy algorithm consists of two parts: First, the greedy choice always leads to an optimal solution, or any optimal solution can be transformed into a solution obtained by the greedy choice. Second, the problem has an optimal sub-structure, i.e. the global optimum implies a local optimum. The optimal sub-structure property is obvious for YAP. To show the greedy choice property, we compare the solution G obtained by the greedy dropping approach with any arbitrary optimal solution O. Consider the following algorithm:

Compact (A, G, O)
1 let $L :=$ set of SLSs;
2 while L is not empty
3   pick SLS S with largest AL
4   for $(i = S_{begin}; i \leq S_{end}; i++)$
5   let $G_{s_i} :=$ position of S_i in G
6   let $O_{s_i} :=$ position of S_i in O
7   if $O_{s_i} > G_{s_i}$
8       $O_{s_i} := G_{s_i}$

The algorithm *Compact* will transform any optimal solution into a corresponding solution that can be obtained by the greedy approach without increasing the amount of yard used. Note line 7 is based on the fact that no optimal solution can allocate S_i in a lower position than greedy approach.

Up to now, we have built a one-to-one relationship between physical layout and the AL assignment $(0, 1, \ldots, n-1)$. The problem is to find the optimal AL assignment.

Tabu Search

Tabu Search is a local search meta-heuristic that uses the best neighborhood move that is not "tabu" active to move out from a local optimum by incorporating *adaptive memory* and *responsive exploration* (Hammer 1993). According to the different usage of memory, conventionally, Tabu Search has been classified into two categories: Tabu Search with Short Term Memory (TSSTM) and Tabu Search with Long Term Memory (TSLTM) (Glover & Laguna 1997) (Sait & Youssef 1999).

TSSTM is the simpler method. Its usage of memory is via the Tabu List. Such an adaptation is also known as *recency* based Tabu Search. TSLTM uses more advanced Tabu Search techniques including intensification and diversification strategies. It archives total or partial information from all the solutions it has visited. This is also known as *frequency* based Tabu Search. It tries to identify certain potentially "good" patterns, which will be used to guide the search process towards possibly better solutions (Pham & Karaboga 2000).

Tabu Search with Short Term Memory

Our TSSTM implementation consists of two major components: a neighborhood search and a tabu list. The neighborhood solution can be obtained by swapping any two ALs in the AL assignment. For example: $[2, 3, 0, 1, 4]$ is a neighborhood solution of $[1, 3, 0, 2, 4]$ by interchanging the positions of 1 and 2. Neighbourhood solutions that are identical to the original solution after normalization are excluded for efficiency reasons.

Tabu Search with Long Term Memory

We implemented TSLTM in two phases: Diversification and Intensification. We used two kinds of diversification techniques, one used random re-starts and the other involved

randomly picking a sub-sequence and inserting it in a random position. For example, $[0, 1, 2, 3, 4]$ may be changed to $[0, 3, 2, 1, 4]$ if $[2, 3]$ is chosen as the sub-sequence and its reverse (or original, if random) is inserted back in the position in front of 1. Intensification is similar to TSSTM. TSLTM uses a *frequency* based memory by recording both the *residence* frequency and the *transition* frequency of the visited solutions. In our implementation, residence frequency is taken as the number of times that the $AL(R_i) < AL(R_j), 1 \leq i, j \leq n$ in the selected solution in each iteration. The transition frequency is taken as the summation of the improvements when $AL(R_i)$ is swapped with $AL(R_j)$. The sum can be either positive or negative.

Diversification and Intensification are interleaved and during either phase, the residence frequency and transition frequency are updated according to the current selected solution. The objective function has three contributors. Besides the length of the yard space required, both the residence frequency and the transition frequency are used to evaluate the solution. Higher residence frequency indicates that an attribute is highly attractive and encourages the solution towards such direction.

"Squeaky Wheel" Optimization

"Squeaky Wheel" Optimization (SWO) is a new heuristic approach proposed in (Clements *et al.* 1997a). Until now, this concept can only be found in a few papers: (Clements *et al.* 1997b), (Joslin & Clements 1998), (Joslin & Clements 1999) and (Draper *et al.* 1999). However, we found this approach very attractive because of its fitness to our problem and very encouraging results. In 1996, a "doubleback" approach was proposed to solve the Resource Constrained Project Scheduling (RCPS) problem (Crawford 1996), which motivates the development of SWO in 1998. Our YAP is similar to the RCPS except that YAP has no precedence constraints and the tasks (requirements) are Stair Like Shapes (SLS). Instead of Left-Shift and Right-Shift in "doubleback", we only use one "drop" routine similar to Left-Shift.

The idea of SWO is also very similar to how human beings solve problems by identifying the "trouble-spot" or the "trouble-maker" and trying to resolve problems caused by them. In SWO, a greedy algorithm is used to construct a solution according to certain priorities (initially randomly generated) which is then analyzed to find the "trouble-makers", i.e. the elements whose improvements are likely to improve the objective function score. The results of the analysis are used to generate new priorities that determine the order in which the greedy algorithm constructs the next solution. This Construct/Analyze/Prioritize (C/A/P) cycle continues until a certain limit is reached or an acceptable solution is found. This is similar to the Iterative Greedy heuristic proposed in (Culberson & Luo 1996). Iterative Greedy is especially designed for Graph Coloring Problem and may not be directly applicable to other problems, whereas SWO is a more general optimization heuristic.

From another perspective, SWO can be viewed as operating on two search spaces: solutions and prioritizations.

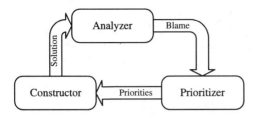

Figure 8: The CAP cycle in SWO

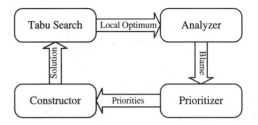

Figure 9: Modified SWO with Tabu Search

Successive solutions are only indirectly related via the re-prioritization that results from analyzing the prior solution. Similarly successive prioritizations are generated by constructing and analyzing solutions.

Figure 8 is the succinct illustration given in (Joslin & Clements 1999). Information such as solutions and priorities is passing around the C/A/P cycle. We implement the SWO system in our problem and it gives encouraging results. The system starts with a random solution, which is a random AL assignment. The normalization routine is applied before the solution is passed to the Analyzer, which evaluates the solution by applying the dropping routine. If the best known result (yard length) is B, then a threshold T is set to be $B - 1$. The blame factor for each request is the sum of the space requirements that exceed the threshold T, i.e. the total area of the SLS above the cutting line T. All the blame information is passed to the Prioritizer, which is a priority queue in our case. When the control has been handed over to the Constructor again, it continuously deletes the elements from the priority queue and immediately drops them in to the yard. A tie, i.e. more than one elements with the same priority, is broken by considering their relative positions in previous solution. This tie-breaker also helps avoid cycles in our search process. Experiments show that the normalization routine plays a very important role in SWO.

We also found that the performance of the SWO can be further improved if a "quick" Tabu Search technique, or TSSTM is embedded in the SWO. We call this modified algorithm SWO+TS, TS standing for Tabu Search. The flow chart now becomes Figure 9. The Constructor passes its solution to a TSSTM engine, which performs a quick local search and pass the local optimum to the Analyzer. Experiments shows a considerable improvement against the original SWO system. Similar ideas of SWO with "intensification" have been proposed in (Clements *et al.* 1997b), where the solution is partitioned and SWO is applied to each of the partitions.

Experimental Results

We conducted extensive experiments on randomly generated data [1]. The graph for each test case contains one connected component, in other words, the test cases cannot be partitioned into more than one independent sub-case. Due to the difficulties of finding any optimal solution in the experiments, a trivial *lower bound* is taken to be the sum of the

---

[1] All test data are available at the author's URL: http://www.comp.nus.edu.sg/~fuzh/YAP

space requirements at each time slot and used for benchmarking.

Data Set	LB	STM	LTM	SWO	SWO+TS
R126	21	28	26	25	24
R117	34	39	37	36	34
R145	39	50	45	45	40
R178	50	69	69	67	58
R188	74	105	98	98	82
R173	77	98	91	94	83
R250	83	141	119	113	94
R236	97	139	130	133	107
R213	164	245	246	246	190

Table 1: Experimental results (Entries in the table shows the minimum length of the yard required. Name of Data Set shows the number of SLSs in the file; LB:Lower Bound; STM:Tabu Search with Short Term Memory; LTM:Tabu Search Long Term Memory)

Table 1 illustrates the results. It is not surprising to see that SWO+TS outperforms all other heuristics in all test cases by a considerable margin. TSSTM gives the worst results though it has the simplest implementation. TSLTM has an obvious improvement from TSSTM, but the amount of improvement is not very stable. One of the major difficulties with Long Term Memory is the assignment of relative weights to yard length, residence frequency and transition frequency in the objective function. SWO is relatively easy to implement with comparable results to TSLTM. We believe that SWO has good *diversification* abilities and Tabu Search is good at *intensification*. Therefore combining the two methods gives the best results, which are within 10% of the trivial lower bound most of the time.

Data Set	STM	LTM	SWO	SWO+TS
R126	594	3423	1014	2719
R117	753	2521	956	2821
R145	1215	3693	1342	3375
R178	2568	5362	3474	5890
R188	2523	7822	2832	7832
R173	3432	6743	2764	7292
R250	4578	10239	3598	15632
R236	5027	11053	3486	17021
R213	4891	10476	3632	18983

Table 2: Experiment running time (seconds) for Table 1.

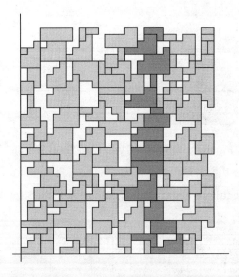

Figure 10: Physical layout of 117 SLSs (requests). Data Set: R117

Table 2 shows the running time for each of the test performed in Table 1 on a Dual-CPU (Pentium III 800MHz each) Linux machine. Although SWO and TSSTM are faster than the other two heuristics, SWO+TS is still the most cost-effective approach.

After a careful analysis of the normalization routine, it turns out that the normalization does not affect the Tabu Search very much, particularly in TSSTM. This is because TS focuses on neighborhood searches and does not pay too much attention to capturing solution patterns. An AL assignment identical to the original solution will have exactly the same value in the objective function and hence can only be identified as a non-improving move and is most unlikely to be selected. However, normalization is important to SWO by reducing the search space. When the *confusing* factors are removed, the search process becomes more stable and focused.

Figure 10 provides the solution obtained by SWO+TS for input file R117. The heavily-shaded SLSs contain the region that is the densest (lower bound). Due to the stair-like shapes, the packing layout looks sub-optimal. A closer look reveals further improvements are very unlikely.

Conclusion

In this paper, we have shown the Yard Allocation Problem (YAP) is NP-Hard by reducing the Ship Berthing Problem (SBP) to it. The geometrical representation of YAP is then transformed into a Direct Acyclic Graph (DAG) for efficient manipulation. A normalization procedure is proposed to guarantee a one-to-one relationship between geometric layout and Acyclic Label Assignment of the DAG. Finding the optimal layout is transformed into a search for the optimal Acyclic Label Assignment. Two heuristic methods are applied: first, the traditional Tabu Search, with both short and long term memory; second, the "Squeaky Wheel" Optimization (SWO) approach. The results obtained were not very attractive.

Observing that the SWO has good *diversification* abilities while the Tabu Search has good *intensification* abilities, we combined the two approaches together and named the new approach "Squeaky Wheel" Optimization with Tabu Search (SWO+TS). Extensive experiments showed that our new approach, SWO+TS, outperformed both original Tabu Search and SWO by a margin of 10%.

References

Clements, D.; Crawford, J.; Joslin, D.; Nemhauser, G.; Puttlitz, M.; and Savelsbergh, M. 1997a. Heuristic optimization: A hybrid AI/OR approach. In *Workshop on Industrial Constraint-Directed Scheduling*.

Clements, D.; Crawford, J.; Joslin, D.; Nemhauser, G.; Puttlitz, M.; and Savelsbergh, M. 1997b. Heuristic optimization: A hybrid ai/or approach. In *Proceedings of the Workshop on Industrial Constraint-Directed Scheduling. In conjunction with the Third International Conference on Principles and Practice of Constraint Programming (CP97)*.

Crawford, J. M. 1996. An approach to resource constrained project scheduling. In *Proceedings of the 1996 Artificial Intelligence and Manufacturing Research Planning Workshop*.

Culberson, J. C., and Luo, F. 1996. Exploring the k-colorable landscape with iterated greedy. *Johnson & Trick* 245–284.

Draper, D.; Jonsson, A.; Clements, D.; and Joslin, D. 1999. Cyclic scheduling. In *Proceedings of the Sixteenth International Joint Conference on Artificial Intelligence*.

Fu, Z., and Lim, A. 2000. A hybrid method for the ship berthing problem. In *Proceedings of the Sixth Artificial Intelligence and Soft Computing*.

Glover, F., and Laguna, M. 1997. *Tabu Search*. Kluwer Academic Publishers.

Hammer, P. L. 1993. *Tabu Search*. Basel, Switzerland: J.C. Baltzer.

Joslin, D. E., and Clements, D. P. 1998. Squeaky wheel optimization. In *Proceedings of the Fifteenth National Conference on Artificial Intelligence (AAAI-98), Madison, WI*, 340–346.

Joslin, D. E., and Clements, D. P. 1999. "squeaky wheel" optimization. *Journal of Artificial Intelligence Research* 10:353–373.

Lim, A. 1998. On the ship berthing problem. *Operations Research Letters* 22(2-3):105–110.

Lim, A. 1999. An effective ship berthing algorithm. In *Proceedings of the Sixteenth International Joint Conference on Artificial Intelligence*, 594–599.

Pham, D., and Karaboga, D. 2000. *Intelligent optimisation techniques: genetic algorithms, tabu search, simulated annealing and neural networks*. London; New York: Springer.

Sait, S., and Youssef, H. 1999. *Iterative Computer Algorithms with Applications in Engineering: Solving Combinatorial Optimization Problems*. IEEE.

Integrating Local Search and Network Flow
to Solve the Inventory Routing Problem

Hoong Chuin LAU
School of Computing
National University of Singapore,
3 Science Drive 2, Singapore 117543.
lauhc@comp.nus.edu.sg

Qizhang LIU
ASPrecise Pte Ltd,
11 Tampines Street 92,
Singapore 528872.
qizhang@asprecise.com

Hirotaka ONO
Graduate School of Information Science
and Electrical Engineering,
Kyushu University, Japan 812-8581.
ono@csce.kyushu-u.ac.jp

Abstract

The inventory routing problem is one of important and practical problems in logistics. It involves the integration of inventory management and vehicle routing, both of which are known to be NP-hard. In this paper, we combine local search and network flows to solve the inventory management problem, by utilizing the minimum cost flow sub-solutions as a guiding measure for local search. We then integrate with a standard VRPTW solver to present experimental results for the overall inventory routing problem, based on instances extended from the Solomon benchmark problems.

Keywords: Scheduling, Planning, Search, Applications, AI/OR integration, Hybrid methods

Introduction

Supply chain optimization involves decision-making processes to manage the production and flow of products and services from the source to the customers. Traditionally, the various activities along the supply chain are performed separately by different logistics operators. For example, goods are transported from the suppliers to the warehouses via one or more transport operators; the inventory control at each warehouse is handled by a warehouse operator; and the delivery of goods from the warehouses to the retailers are handled by some other transport operators.

An emerging industry trend is the formation of logistics operators that provide a one-stop point-to-point service for the entire distribution operation described above. Under this system, retailers need not manage their own inventory to ensure timely re-supply while the logistics operator achieves economies of scale by being able to co-ordinate deliveries to multiple retailers. Hence, a system-wide optimization can be achieved through an algorithmic integration of inventory and transportation.

In this paper, we consider *Inventory Routing Problem with Time Windows* (IRPTW). An IRPTW instance is given as a distribution system with multiple suppliers, capacitated warehouses, capacitated retailers, identical capacitated vehicles and unit-sized items. The items are to be transported from the suppliers to the warehouses, and subsequently delivered to the retailers by vehicles. Vehicles can combine deliveries to multiple retailers, provided that the items are delivered within stipulated time windows. Given the retailers' time-varying demand forecast over a finite planning horizon, the goal is to find a distribution plan so as to minimize the total operating cost, which comprises the (inventory) holding cost for amounts exceeding demand, backlog cost for amounts falling short of demand and transportation cost. Clearly, IRPTW is a complex problem, since it involves the integration of two classical optimization problems: dynamic capacitated lot-sizing problem (Florian *at al.* 80) and vehicle routing problem with time-windows (VRPTW) (Savelsbergh 86), both of which are NP-hard.

Many inventory models have been proposed by the OR community in the past (Campbell *et al.* 98; Carter *et al.* 96; Chan *at al.* 98; Caseau and Kokeny 98; Fredegruen and Zipkin 84; Graves *et al.*). In (Campbell *et al.* 98), a simplified version of IRP is considered. Even for that problem, the authors, who proposed an integer programming approach, reported that "This model is not very practical for two reasons: the huge number of possible delivery routes, and although to a lesser extent, the length of the planning horizon. To make this integer program computationally tractable, we only consider a small (but good) set of routes and aggregate time periods towards the end of the planning horizon."

Hence, to our knowledge, a logistics problem as complicated as IRPTW has not been extensively studied and experimented in the literature. The collaboration framework introduced in (Lau *et al.* 00) offered an attempt. There, IRPTW is divided into two sub-problems (distribution and routing) plus an interface mechanism to allow the two algorithms to collaborate in a *master-slave* fashion, with the distribution algorithm driving the routing algorithm. The overview of the framework is as follows: The Master will determine the flow amounts between the suppliers, warehouse and the retailers so as to minimize holding and backlog costs subject to warehouse and retailers' capacities. The Slave, based on the given flow amounts (or customer demands, in vehicle routing terminology), sequences the deliveries into routes so as to minimize transportation cost, subject to vehicle capacities and time windows. These routes in turn induce a re-partitioning of the retailers for the Master, and the process is repeated.

Since VRPTW is a well-studied NP-hard problem, conceivably one can use any existing standard algorithms as the

Slave. On the other hand, to our knowledge, there exists no efficient algorithm which can be used as the Master on this framework. (Lau *et al.* 00) proposed a simple algorithm based on tabu search, which does not seem to be effective, since it does not make use of the underlying network structure.

In this paper, we devise an elegant and rigorous local search approach to solve the Master problem. We demonstate how to perform efficient and effective neighborhood search in a complex local search space through the use of network sensitivity analysis. In essence, the choice of the next move is determined by solving an instance of minimum cost flow. Even though it is known that the minimum cost flow problem is polynomial-time solvable, since our algorithms make extensive use of minimum cost flow, we need to solve the minimum cost flow problem as efficiently as possible. Instead of solving each instance from scratch, by the nature of local search, it turns out that we can apply the theory of sensitivity analysis to obtain a solution by restarting from the previous solution (basis). For this purpose, we adopt the network simplex method whose strength lies in the ability to perform sensitivity analysis quickly.

As an example applying network flows to solve NP-hard problems, Xu and Kelly proposed a heuristic algorithm for VRP (Xu and Kelly 96). Their approach, an extension of ejection chains model (Glover 96), performs neighborhood searches approximately and efficiently by solving network flow problems. While there are significant differences between their approach and our model, both make use of a minimum cost flow problem, which can be solved quickly, as the background engine.

Preliminaries

Problem Definition

In this paper, we consider a basic version of IRPTW of a single item supplied by a single supplier. Our approach can be easily extended to the more general case involving multiple items and multiple suppliers. An IRPTW instance consists of the following inputs:

C: set of retailers (customers);

T: consecutive days in the planning period $\{1, 2, \cdots, n\}$;

d_{it}: demand of retailer i on day t;

q_V: vehicle capacity;

q_W: warehouse storage capacity;

q_i: storage capacity of retailer i;

W_{it}: time window of retailer i on day t;

c_i^h: holding cost per unit item per day at retailer i;

c_i^b: backlog cost per unit item per day at retailer i;

The outputs are as follows:

(1) the distribution plan, which is denoted by x_{it}: integral flow amount from the warehouse to retailer i on day t;

(2) the set of daily transportation routes Φ, which carry the flow amounts in (1) from the warehouse to the retailers such that the sum of the following linear costs is minimized:

a) holding costs and backlog costs

b) transportation cost from the warehouse to the retailers (T_{ik}).

We use indices i and t for retailers and days respectively.

The distribution plan must obey the demands and storage capacity constraints, and the transportation routes must obey the standard routing, vehicle capacities and time windows constraints. For notational convenience, we let Φ_t denote the set of routes for day t. Each route is an ordered list of retailers representing the delivery sequence performed by one particular vehicle per day.

IRPTW can be regarded either as a generalization of VRPTW or the dynamic lot-sizing problem. In the former case, IRPTW can be seen as a multi-day version of VRPTW, where the daily plans are related via holding and backlog quantities. In the latter case, IRPTW is a *constrained* version of the dynamic lot-sizing problem, whose set-up cost coefficients are defined by delivery (i.e. route) costs. Let this problem be denoted DLP.

Minimum Cost Flow Model for DLP

In this section, we explain our minimum cost flow model solving DLP.

Recall that VRPTWsolver outputs a set of routes Φ to DLP. The following variables can be derived directly from Φ: h_{ir}: 1 if retailer i is served by route $r \in \Phi_t$ on some day t, and 0 otherwise; c_r^r: cost of route $r \in \Phi_t$ on some day t, defined as the sum of transportation costs T_{ik} over all adjacent retailers i and k on route r.

The following intermediate variables are used:

z_{it}: integral amount held in retailer i on day t; b_{it}: integral amount of backlog for retailer i on day t; y_r: boolean variable, whether route $r \in \Phi_t$ on some day t is used;

The underlying model is a 4-layer network for warehouse V_1, days V_2, routes V_3 and retailers (customers) V_4 respectively. Each customer vertex is replicated n times for the n-day planning period. The day, route and customer vertices in the network are denoted by v^d, v^r and v^c respectively. Edges between vertices of different layers represent the flow amounts (warehouse to retailers), while edges between adjacent replicated vertices represent either inventory carrying over to the next day (E_4), or backlog from the previous day (E_5). Formally, the network model is defined as follows (see Fig. 1):

$$V = \bigcup_{i=1}^{4} V_i \text{ and } E = \bigcup_{i=1}^{5} E_i,$$

where

$$
\begin{aligned}
V_1 &= \{s\}, \\
V_2 &= \{v_t^d \mid t \in \{1, 2, \cdots, n\}\}, \\
V_3 &= \{v_r^r \mid r \in \Phi_t \text{ and } t \in \{1, 2, \cdots, n\}\}, \\
V_4 &= \{v_{it}^c \mid i \in C \text{ and } t \in \{1, 2, \cdots, n\}\}, \\
E_1 &= \{(s, v_t^d) \mid t \in \{1, 2, \cdots, n\}\}, \\
E_2 &= \{(v_t^d, v_r^r) \mid r \in \Phi_t \text{ and } t \in \{1, 2, \cdots, n\}\}, \\
E_3 &= \{(v_r^r, v_{it}^c) \mid h_{ir} = 1, r \in \Phi_t \text{ and } t \in \{1, 2, \cdots, n\}\},
\end{aligned}
$$

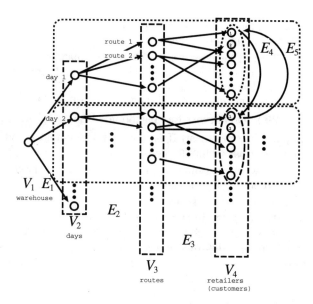

Figure 1: network flow model

$$E_4 = \{(v_{it}^c, v_{i,t+1}^c) \mid i \in C \text{ and } t \in \{1, 2, \cdots, n-1\}\},$$
$$E_5 = \{(v_{it}^c, v_{i,t-1}^c) \mid i \in C \text{ and } t \in \{2, 3, \cdots, n\}\}.$$

A demand of each vertex is defined as

$$d(v) = \begin{cases} -\sum_i \sum_t d_{it} & v \in V_1, \\ d_{it} & v_{it}^c \in V_4, \\ 0 & \text{otherwise.} \end{cases}$$

A lower bound of each edge is 0 and an upper bound (capacity) u_e is defined as

$$u_e = \begin{cases} q_W & e \in E_1 \\ M_{\text{big}} y_r & e \in E_2 \\ M_{\text{big}} & e \in E_3 \\ q_i & e = (v_{it}^c, v_{i*}^c) \in E_4 \cup E_5 \end{cases} \quad (1)$$

where M_{big} represents a very large value. The cost of each edge is defined as follows:

$$\text{cost}(e) = \begin{cases} c_r^r y_r & e = (v_t^d, v_r^r) \in E_2, \\ c_i^h z_{it} & e = (v_{it}^c, v_{i,t+1}^c) \in E_4, \\ c_i^b b_{it} & e = (v_{it}^c, v_{i,t-1}^c) \in E_5, \\ 0 & \text{otherwise.} \end{cases} \quad (2)$$

Hence, total costs of this network is

$$\sum_t \sum_i (c_i^h z_{it} + c_{it}^b b_{it}) + \sum_r y_r c_r^r,$$

and this flow satisfies quantity constraints obviously; i.e., this DLP is formulated as one kind of minimum cost flow problems.

Although this problem looks like a simple minimum cost flow problem, it is actually NP-hard since y_r's are 0-1 variables. On the other hand, for fixed y_r's, this problem becomes easy, i.e., polynomial solvable. Therefore, we can rewrite this problem as follows:

$$\min_y \quad \sum_{r \in \Phi_t} c_r^r y_r + \text{MCF}(y) \quad (3)$$
$$\text{subject to} \qquad y_r \in \{0, 1\},$$
$$r \in \Phi_t, t = 1, 2, \cdots, n,$$

where $\text{MCF}(y)$ is the optimal value of the above minimum cost flow network problem for a fixed y_r.

Network Simplex Method

To obtain $\text{MCF}(y)$ in (3), we use network simplex method originally proposed in (Dantzig 51) (see also (Ahuja *et al.* 93) for implementation). Since network simplex method is analogous to simplex method for linear programming problem, it is practically fast though it is not a polynomial time algorithm [1].

Another reason why we use network simplex method is that it is easy to implement sensitivity analysis. Since our heuristics algorithm to solve DLP is based on local search that uses the value of $\text{MCF}(y)$ as a guiding measure, we need to solve many minimum cost flow problem instances. Since these minimum cost flow problems usually have similar networks, we can solve new minimum cost flow problem by making use of solution of the *previous* minimum cost flow problem as the basis - hence, sensitivity analysis.

Now, we explain a basic idea of the network simplex method (for short NSM). (For details, see Chap. 11 of (Ahuja *et al.* 93), on which these explanations are based.)

NSM maintains a *spanning tree solution*, which partitions the edge set of network into three disjoint subsets: (1) T, the edges in the spanning tree; (2) L, the non-tree edges whose flow is restricted to value 0; and (3) U, the non-tree edges whose flow is restricted in value to the edges' flow capacities. We refer to (T, L, U) as a *spanning tree structure*.

Now we define the *reduced cost* $c_{uv}^\pi = c_{uv} - \pi(u) + \pi(v)$, where c_{uv} represents a cost of edge (u, v), and $\pi(u)$ represents a potential on vertex u. For for a spanning tree structure (T, L, U), we have optimal conditions

$$c_{uv}^\pi = 0 \quad \text{for all } (u, v) \in T, \quad (4)$$
$$c_{uv}^\pi \geq 0 \quad \text{for all } (u, v) \in L, \quad (5)$$
$$c_{uv}^\pi \leq 0 \quad \text{for all } (u, v) \in U. \quad (6)$$

For these conditions, the spanning tree solution in which all edges satisfy them is optimal. The reduced cost c_{uv}^π means the cost per unit flow intuitively. For example, if we were to add flow of x units on edge (u, v), then the total cost of this network increases by $(c_{uv} - \pi(u) + \pi(v))x$ units.

NSM proceeds as follows: It maintains a feasible spanning tree structure such that all tree edges satisfy condition (4) at each iteration and successively transforms it into an improved spanning tree structure until all non-tree also satisfy condition (5) and (6).

Algorithm NETWORK SIMPLEX METHOD:

Step 1: Find an initial feasible tree structure (T, L, U).

Step 2: If some non-tree edge violates the optimality condition (5) or (6), find an improved spanning tree structure and go to Step 2. Otherwise halt.

Next, we explain sensitivity analysis on edge costs. Consider that the cost of an edge (u, v) increases by λ. (Reducing λ also can be done similarly.) Let (T^*, L^*, U^*) denote

---

[1] Although there exist polynomial time algorithms to solve minimum cost flow problems (Ahuja *et al.* 93), network simplex method is still practical as simplex method for linear programming.

the spanning tree structure of the optimal solution and π^* denote the corresponding vertex potential. The analysis would be different when edge (u, v) is a tree or a non-tree edge.

Case 1. edge (u, v) is a non-tree edge.

Adding the cost of edge (u, v) does not affect the vertex potentials of the current spanning tree structure, since edges in T^* still satisfy optimal condition (4). The modified reduced cost of of edge (u, v) is $c_{uv}^{\pi^*} + \lambda$. If it cost satisfies condition (5) or (6), (T^*, L^*, U^*) remains optimal. Otherwise, we reoptimize the solution using NSM with (T^*, L^*, U^*) as the initial spanning tree structure.

Case 2. edge (u, v) is a tree edge.

We have to change some vertices' potentials in order to maintain the current spanning tree structure (T^*, L^*, U^*), satisfying optimal condition (4). If edge (u, v) is an upward-pointing edge on the current spanning tree, potentials of all the vertices in subtree whose root is u increase by λ, and if (u, v) is a downward-pointing edge, potentials of all the vertices in subtree whose root is v decrease by λ. If all non-tree edges still satisfy the optimality condition, the current spanning tree structure remains optimal; otherwise, we reoptimize the solution using NSM.

Local Search Algorithms for DLP

In this section, we present our local search algorithms for solving DLP. In general, local search starts from an initial feasible solution and repeats replacing it with a better solution in its *neighborhood* until no better solution is found in its neighborhood. Roughly speaking, a neighborhood is a set of solutions obtainable from the current solution by a slight perturbation.

In our problem, the solution is defined as an assignment of $y = (y_1, y_2, \cdots, y_k)$, and the cost, $cost(y)$, of solution y is defined as the value of equation (3). In our algorithm, we use the following neighborhoods:

Delete Neighborhood $N^{\mathrm{D}}(y)$ is defined as $N^{\mathrm{D}}(y) = \{y' \mid y' = y - e^{(j)}, j \in ON(y)\}$, where $ON(y) = \{j \mid y_j = 1\}$ and $e^{(j)}$ is j-th unit vector. This neighborhood represents transition that route j is deleted from the set of routes used in current solution.

Add Neighborhood $N^{\mathrm{A}}(y)$ is defined as $N^{\mathrm{A}}(y) = \{y' \mid y' = y + e^{(l)}, l \in OFF(y)\}$, where $OFF(y) = \{l \mid y_l = 0\}$ and $e^{(j)}$ is j-th unit vector. This neighborhood represents transition that route l is added into the set of routes used in current solution.

Swap Neighborhood $N^{\mathrm{S}}(y)$ is defined as $N^{\mathrm{S}}(y) = \{y' \mid y' = y - e^{(j)} + e^{(l)}, j \in ON(y) \text{ and } l \in OFF(y)\}$ where ON, OFF and e^* are as defined in Delete and Add neighborhood.

We apply moves to solutions in $N^{\mathrm{D}}(y)$, $N^{\mathrm{A}}(y)$ and $N^{\mathrm{S}}(y)$, *delete operation*, *add operation* and *swap operation*, respectively. Using these neighborhoods and operations, we propose the following LS (local search) algorithm:

Algorithm LS:

Step 1: (initialize) Find an initial solution σ_{init} (see below), and set $best:=cost(\sigma_{\mathrm{init}})$.

Step 2: (improve by LS) Improve σ by neighborhood search. set $improve:=$ **false**.

(2-a): If there exist $y' \in N^{\mathrm{A}}(y)$ such that $cost(y') < cost(y)$, set $y := y'$, $improve :=$ **true**, and return to (2-a). Otherwise go to (2-b).

(2-b): Do likewise for neighborhood N^{D}.

(2-c): Do likewise for neighborhood N^{S}

Step 3: (halt or repeat) If $improve=$ **false**, output y and stop; otherwise return to Step 2.

In Step 1, we use a simple heuristics algorithm *initial deletion* in order to find an initial solution y.

Algorithm INITIAL DELETION:

Step 1: Set $j := 0$, $y = (1, 1, 1, \cdots, 1)$, and an order $R_o = \{r_1 \preceq r_2 \preceq \cdots \preceq r_k\}$ of route $r \in \Phi_t$ for all t, according to the value c_r^r/w_r.

Step 2: Set $j := j + 1$. If $j = k + 1$, output y and halt. Otherwise go to Step 3.

Step 3: If $cost(y') < cost(y)$ where $y' = y - e^{(r_j)}$, set $y := y'$. Return to Step 2.

Since the value c_r^r/w_r in Step 1 can be considered the redundancy of route r, this algorithm is essentially a greedy algorithm.

Local search method has a disadvantage that it is impossible to escape from local optima; i.e., y does not have better solution in its neighborhood $N(y)$, but is not a global optimal. Therefore, we implement two meta-heuristics algorithms ILS and TS.

Iterated local search

Iterated local search (ILS) (Gu 92; Johnson 90) generates initial solutions of local search, by slightly perturbing a solution y_{seed}, which is a good (not necessarily the best) solution found during the search. This diversity of initial solutions lead us to escape from local optima. Our ILS works as follows:

Algorithm ILS

Step 0: (initialize) Generate an initial solution y_{seed} by Initial Deletion, and set $best:= cost(y_{\mathrm{seed}})$.

Step 1: (generate an initial solution) Generate a solution y by slightly perturbing y_{seed}.

Step 2: (improve by LS) Improve y by LS, i.e., set $y := LS(N, y)$.

Step 3: (update the best and seed solutions) If $cost(y) < best$, set $best := cost(y)$ and $y^* := y$. If some accepting criterion is satisfied, set $y_{\mathrm{seed}} := y$.

Step 4: (halt or random restart) If some stopping criterion (computational time or the number of iterations exceeded) is satisfied, output y^* and stop; otherwise return to Step 1.

In Step 1, the new solution y is generated by l-Jump Operation.

l-Jump Operation First, choose a set L of components from $\{1, 2, \cdots, k\}$ randomly, where $|L| = l$. For input y, flip values of components in L, i.e., for $i \in L$,

$$y_i := \begin{cases} 1 & y_i = 0, \\ 0 & y_i = 1. \end{cases}$$

Tabu search

Tabu search (Glover and Laguna 97) tries to enhance LS by using the memory of the previous search. The best solution in $N(y) \setminus (\{y\} \cup T)$ is chosen as the next solution, where the set T, called *tabu list*, is a set of solutions which includes those solutions most recently visited. Usually the size of tabu list $|T|$ is less than t_{tenure}, called *tabu tenure*. In tabu search, a move to a new solution is always executed even if the current solution is locally optimal. This causes cycling of solutions in general. Introducing T enables the algorithm to avoid cycling in a short period.

In our tabu search (TS), we keep tabu list as 1-array of size k, associated with routes, and put τ_j. τ_j is defined as the iteration number when an operation is done about route j most recently. For the current iteration number t_{it}, if $t_{\text{it}} - \tau_j < t_{\text{tenure}}$, all operations about j are forbidden, i.e., tabu. TS works as follows:

Algorithm TS

Step 1: (initialize) Generate a solution y by Initial Deletion, set $y^* := y$ and $T := \emptyset$.

Step 2: (decide a move) *improve* := **false**. Find the best solution y' in $N(y) \setminus (\{y\} \cup T)$ for (2-a),(2-b) and (2-c), and set $y := y'$.

   (2-a): Find the best solution $y' \in N^{\text{A}}(y)$ and set $y := y'$. If cost $(y') <$ cost (y), *improve* := **true**.

   (2-b): Do likewise for neighborhood N^{D}

   (2-c): Do likewise for neighborhood N^{S}

Step 3: (update the best cost) If cost $(y) <$ cost (y^*), set $y^* := y$ and $t_{\text{tenure}} := 0.9 \times t_{\text{tenure}}$.

Step 4: (update t_{tenure}) If *improve* = **false**, $t_{\text{tenure}} := 1.1 \times t_{\text{tenure}}$.

Step 5: (halt or further search) If some stopping criterion is satisfied, output y^* and stop; otherwise return to Step 2.

In general, more features such as *long term memory* and *aspiration level* are introduced in the framework of tabu search. For this paper, we adopt the above simple tabu search.

Sensitivity Analysis Induced by Local Search

In local search, we have to solve minimum cost flow problems many times, and it is quite time-consuming in general. However, since the computation is neighborhood search, these minimum cost flow problems have almost same structures (networks) except few edges coefficients. For example, a delete operation $y := y - e^{(r)}$ is considered changing 0 into M_{big} on the cost of the corresponding edge in the network. (We adopt sensitivity analysis about not the capacities coefficient but the cost one, since the cost one is a little simpler to implement and we can obtain the same effect.)

Changes about cost coefficient are (1) adding M_{big} (delete operation), (2) reducing M_{big} (add operation). A swap operation is performed as a combination of (1) and (2). Both of them can be performed by putting $\lambda = M_{\text{big}}$ (or $-M_{\text{big}}$) in the Network Simplex Method described above.

Numerical Experiments

In this section, we report experimental results. To our knowledge, no benchmark test data available in the literature matches our problem exactly. Hence, our experimental results are based on the test data generated from Solomon's VRPTW benchmark problems (Solomon 87), as follows.

We set the planning period $n = 10$. For each day in the planning period, we set the vehicle capacity, locations and time-windows of the retailers and warehouse (depot) to be equal to those specified in the Solomon instance. We create demand d_{it} of retailer i for day t from the demand d_i of Solomon instance, by partitioning $n \times d_i$ into n parts, i.e., $d_{i1}, d_{i2}, \cdots, d_{in}$ randomly such that d_{it} is within the range $[0.5 * d_i, 1.5 * d_j]$ for $t = 1, 2, \cdots, n$. The capacities of retailers and warehouse are set as vehicle capacity and M_{big} respectively. As for cost coefficients, holding cost of retailer (c_i^{h}) and backlog cost(c_i^{b}) are set to be 1 and 2 for all i respectively. The transportation cost of each route is set to be 10 times its total distance.

The DLPsolver is implemented by our algorithms described above. The VRPTWsolver is based on a standard two-phase heuristics. Both TS and ILS adopt the halting condition that CPU run time reaches 180 seconds.

We run our program on a Pentium 666MHz PC and the results are given as follows. In this table, we plot the different test instances against: (1)"VRPTW": initial objective value by using only VRPTW solver, (2)"ILS+VRP": final objective value where DLP is based on ILS and (3)"TS+VRP": final objective value where DLP is based on TS.

Data	VRPTW	ILS+VRP	TS+VRP
c201	178650	113263	112821
c202	192818	117483	124312
c203	200615	131920	122055
c204	216447	136384	142300
c205	175378	116147	109248
c206	177331	123978	127876
c207	177447	122204	117735
c208	175268	124110	125667
r201	304779	111330	116893
r202	291492	116982	114717
r203	247122	110215	115070
r204	227381	114118	114118
r205	284759	122333	123009
r206	260760	120928	123251
r207	223527	115438	115438
r208	228033	120011	117255
r209	249036	116840	120725

Table 1: Computational results of our algorithms

From Table 1, we observe that the improvement in the objective value of the final solution (2) over the VRPTW solution (1) is at least 29.1% in c208 and at best 39.0% in c202 (among C-instances). As for (3), the worst improvement is 27.9% in c206 and the best is 39.2% in c203. In case of R-instances, improvement ration is from 48.4% to 61.7% on TS, and from 47.4% to 63.5%.

Our approach seems useful for these instance. However, these improvement ratio seems to depend on the difficulty of the instances, as we can see the difference of the results between C- and R-instances. We also believe the difficulty of our IRPTW instances are influenced by cost coefficients.

Next, we show the effectiveness of sensitivity analysis. Recall that our algorithms need to invoke minimum cost flow many times. We implemented our algorithms in two ways: (a) solving each minimum cost flow problem from scratch; and (b) solving each minimum cost flow problem from the previous problem's solution (i.e., apply sensitivity analysis).

Table 2 shows the comparison between ways (a) and (b) for R2 Solomon instances. Each column shows the total number of pivots on NSM and total execution time. The third column shows the ratios of (a) to (b) rounded down to the nearest integer.

	(a) Scratch		(b) Sensitivity		Ratio	
	Pivots	Time	Pivots	Time	Pivots	Time
r201	19741024	113.83	423760	2.77	46	41
r202	11484659	65.9	300424	2.13	38	30
r203	4731487	25.86	280710	1.8	16	14
r204	3349778	18.51	264430	1.5	12	12
r205	10130292	57.57	346624	2.37	29	24
r206	3860581	21.83	281394	1.91	13	11
r207	5995470	34.94	230282	1.39	26	25
r208	5351521	31.49	281394	1.7	19	18
r209	8905561	51.43	326324	1.96	27	26

Table 2: Effectiveness of sensitivity analysis

From Table 2, the following observations can be made:

1. In terms of number of pivots, the ratio is at least 12.67, at most 46.59, and 25.514 on average. As for run time, the ratio is at least 12.34 times, at most 41.09 times, and 22.71 on average.

2. The pivot ratios are always slightly larger than time ratios.

Observation 1 shows sensitivity analysis on NSM is effective indeed. One reason for Observation 2 is as follows: In Step 1. of NSM, we add some artificial edges to the original network (see (Ahuja *et al.* 93)). These artificial edges make a new improved spanning tree structure simple, and make it easy to find a new improved spanning tree structure in the early iterations (pivots) on NSM. By contrast, sensitivity analysis use a network of the previous solution, which usually has more complicated form. Therefore, we suppose that one pivot in sensitivity analysis takes longer time than one pivot in original NSM.

Conclusion

In this paper, we propoed algorithms for solving IRPTW, based on the framework introduced in (Lau *et al.* 00). These algorithms are rigorous in the sense that they make use of the underlying network structure as a guidance measure for search. As a technical contribution, we demonstate how to perform efficient and effective neighborhood searches on local search through the use of network sensitivity analysis. We believe that our approach can be adapted quickly to solve other complex network optimization problems such as those arising in logistics and telecommunications applications.

References

R. K. Ahuja, T. L. Magnanti and J. B. Orlin, Network Flows : Theory, Algorithms and Applications, (Prentice-Hall, 1993).

A. Campbell, L. Clarke, A. J. Kleywegt, and M. W. P. Savelsbergh, The Inventory Routing Problem, in: T. G. Grainic and G. Laporte, eds., *Fleet Management and Logistics*, (Kluwer Academic Pub., 1998), 95–113.

M. W. Carter, J. M. Farvolden, G. Laporte, J. Xu, Solving an Integrated Logistics Problem Arising in Grocery Distribution, *INFOR*, **34:4** (1996), 290–306.

Y. Caseau and T. Kokeny, An Inventory Management Problem, *The Constraints Journal*, **3**, (1998), 363–373.

L. M. Chan, A. Fedegruen and D. Simchi-Levi, Probabilistic Analysis and Practical Algorithms for Inventory-Routing Models, *Oper. Res.*, **46:1** (1998) 96–106.

G. B. Dantzig, Application of the simplex method to a transportation problem, *Activity Analysis and Production and Allocation*, edited by T. C. Koopmans, (Wiley, 1951).

M. Florian, J. K. Lenstra, and A. H. G. Rinnooy Kan, Deterministic Production Planning: Algorithm and Complexity, *Management Sc.*, **26:7** (1980), 669–679.

A. Fedegruen and P. Zipkin, An Efficient Algorithm for Computing Optimal (s,S) Policies, *Operations Research*, **22** (1984), 1268–1285.

F. Glover, Ejection Chains, Reference Structures and Alternating Path Methods for Traveling Salesman Problems *Discrete Applied Mathematics*, **65**, (1996) 223–253.

F. Glover and M. Laguna, *Tabu Search*, (Kluwer Academic Publishers, 1997).

S. C. Graves, A. H. G. Rinnooy Kan and P. H. Zipkin eds., *Handbook in Operations Research and Management Science* Vol **4**: Logistics of Production and Inventory, (North-Holland, 1993).

J. Gu, Efficient Local Search for Very Large-Scale Satisfiability Problem, *SIGART Bulletin*, **3**, (1992), 8–12.

D. S. Johnson, Local Optimization and the Traveling Salesman Problem, *Proceedings of the 17th Colloquium on Automata, Languages and Programming* (1990) 446–461.

H. C. Lau, A. Lim and Q. Z. Liu, Solving a Supply Chain Optimization Problem Collaboratively, *Proc. 17th National Conf. on Artificial Intelligence (AAAI)*, (2000) 780–785.

M. W. P. Savelsbergh, Local Search for Routing Problems with Time Windows, *Annals of Operations Research*, **4**, (1986), 285–305.

M. M. Solomon, Algorithms for the Vehicle Routing and Scheduling Problem with Time Window Constraints, *Operations Research*, **35**, 1987, 254–265.

J. Xu and J. P. Kelly, A Network Flow-Based Tabu Search Heuristic for the Vehicle Routing Problem, *Transporation Science*, **30:4**, (1996) 379–393.

Generating Random Solutions for Constraint Satisfaction Problems

Rina Dechter   Kalev Kask
University of California, Irvine
{dechter, kkask}@ics.uci.edu

Eyal Bin   Roy Emek
IBM Research Laboratory in Haifa
{bin, emek}@il.ibm.com

Abstract

The paper presents a method for generating solutions of a constraint satisfaction problem (CSP) uniformly at random. The main idea is to transform the constraint network into a belief network that expresses a uniform random distribution over its set of solutions and then use known sampling algorithms over belief networks. The motivation for this tasks comes from hardware verification. Random test program generation for hardware verification can be modeled and performed through CSP techniques, and is an application in which uniform random solution sampling is required.

Introduction and Motivation

The paper presents a method for generating uniformly distributed random solutions for a CSP. The method we propose is based on a transformation of the constraint network into a belief network that expresses a uniform random distribution over the CSP's set of solutions. We then can use known sampling methods for belief networks to generate the desired solution samples. The basic algorithm we propose uses a variable elimination approach and its complexity is time and space exponential in the induced-width of the constraint problem. Because of this complexity the approach will not be practical in most real life situations and we therefore propose a general partition-based scheme for approximating the algorithm.

The random solution generation problem is motivated by the task of test program generation in the field of functional verification. The main vehicle for the verification of large and complex hardware designs is simulation of a large number of random test programs (Bergeron 2000). The generation of such programs therefore plays a central role in the field of functional verification.

The input for a test program generator is a specification of a test template. For example, tests that exercise the data cache of the processor and that are formed by a series of double-word `store` and `load` instructions. The generator generates a large number of *distinct* well-distributed test program instances, that comply with the user's specification. In addition, generated test programs must meet two inherent classes of requirements: (a) Tests must be *valid*. That is,

their behavior should be well defined by the specification of the verified system; (b) Test programs should also be of high *quality*, in the sense that they focus on potential bugs.

The number of potential locations of bugs in a system and the possible scenarios that can lead to their discovery is huge: In a typical architecture, there are from $10^{1,000}$ to $10^{10,000}$ programs of 100 instructions. It is impossible to exactly specify all the test programs that we would like to use out of the above combinations, and even harder to generate them. This means that users of test generators intentionally under-specify the requirements of the tests they generate, and expect the generators to fill in the gaps between the specification and the required tests. In other words, a test generator is required to explore the unspecified space and to help find the bugs for which the user is not directly looking (Hartman, Ur, & Ziv 1999).

There are two ways to explore this unspecified space, systematically or randomly. A systematic approach is impossible when the explored space is large and not well-understood. Therefore, the only practical approach is to generate pseudo-random tests. That is, tests that satisfy user requirements and at the same time uniformly sample the derived test space (Fournier, Arbetman, & Levinger 1999).

The validity, quality, and test specification requirements described above are naturally modeled through constraints (Bin *et al.* ; Chandra & Iyengar 1992). As an example of a validity constraint, consider the case of a translation table: $RA = trans(EA)$, where EA stands for the effective address and RA stands for the real (physical) address. For CSP to drive test program generation, the program should be modeled as constraint networks. The requirement to produce a large number of random, well-distributed tests is viewed, under the CSP modeling scheme, as a requirement to produce a large number of random solutions to a CSP. This stands in contrast to the traditional requirement of reaching a single solution, all solutions, or a 'best' solution (Dechter 1992; Kumar 1992).

Related work. The problem of generating random solutions for a set of constraints, in the context of hardware verification, is tackled in (Yuan *et al.* 1999). The Authors deal with Boolean variables and constraints over them, but do not use the CSP framework. Instead, they construct a single BDD that represents the entire search space, and develop a sampling method which uses the structure of the BDD. A BDD based constraint satisfaction engine imposes a restriction on the size of the problems that can be solved, since the BDD approach often requires exponential time and space. No approximation alternative was presented. As far as we know, in the CSP literature the task of random solution generation was not addressed.

Preliminaries

DEFINITION 1 (Constraint Networks) *A Constraint Network (CN) is defined by a triplet* (X, D, C) *where* X *is a set of variables* $X = \{X_1, ..., X_n\}$, *associated with a set of discrete-valued domains,* $D = \{D_1, ..., D_n\}$, *and a set of constraints* $C = \{C_1, ..., C_m\}$. *Each constraint* C_i *is a pair* (S_i, R_i), *where* R_i *is a relation* $R_i \subseteq D_{S_i}$ *where* $D_{S_i} = \bowtie_{X_j \in S_i} D_j$, *defined on a subset of variables* $S_i \subseteq X$ *called the scope of* C_i. *The relation denotes all compatible tuples of* D_{S_i} *allowed by the constraint. The constraint graph of a constraint network, has a node for each variable, and an arc between two nodes iff the corresponding variables participate in the same constraint. A solution is an assignment of values to variables* $x = (x_1, ..., x_n)$, $x_i \in D_i$, *such that no constraint is violated.*

EXAMPLE 1 *Consider a graph coloring problem that has four variables (A, B, C, D), where the domains of A and C are* $\{1, 2, 3\}$ *and the domains of B and D are* $\{1, 2\}$. *The constraint are not-equal constraints between adjacent variables. The constraint graph is given in Figure 4 (top, left).*

Belief networks provide a formalism for reasoning about partial beliefs under conditions of uncertainty.

DEFINITION 2 (belief network) *Let* $X = \{X_1, ..., X_n\}$ *be a set of random variables over multi-valued domains,* $D_1, ..., D_n$, *respectively. A belief network is a pair* (G, P) *where* $G = (X, E)$ *is a directed acyclic graph over the variables, and* $\mathcal{P} = \{P_i\}$, *and* P_i *denote Conditional Probability Tables (CPTs)* $P_i = \{P(X_i|pa_i)\}$, *where* pa_i *is the set of parents nodes pointing to* X_i *in the graph. The belief network represents a probability distribution* $P(x_1, ..., x_n) = \prod_{i=1}^{n} P(x_i|x_{pa_i})$ *where an assignment* $(X_1 = x_1, ..., X_n = x_n)$ *is abbreviated to* $x = (x_1, ..., x_n)$ *and where* x_S *denotes the restriction of a tuple* x *over a subset of variables* S. *The moral graph of a directed graph is the undirected graph obtained by connecting the parent nodes of each variable and eliminating direction.*

DEFINITION 3 (Induced-width) *An ordered graph is a pair* (G, d) *where* G *is an undirected graph and* $d = X_1, ..., X_n$ *is an ordering of the nodes. The width of a node in an ordered graph is the number of the node's neighbors that precede it in the ordering. The width of an ordering* d, *denoted* $w(d)$, *is the maximum width over all nodes. The induced width of an ordered graph,* $w^*(d)$, *is the width of the induced ordered graph obtained as follows: nodes are processed from last to first; when node* X *is processed, all its preceding neighbors are connected. The induced width of a graph,* $w*$, *is the minimal induced width over all its orderings (Arnborg 1985).*

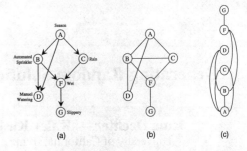

Figure 1: (a) Belief network (b) its moral graph (c) Induced width

EXAMPLE 2 *The network in Figure 1a expresses probabilistic relationship between 6 variables* A, B, C, D, F, G. *The moral graph is in Figure 1b and the induced-width along* $d = (A, B, C, D, F, G)$ *is 2, as shown in Figure 1c.*

The Random Solution Task

Given a constraint network $\mathcal{R} = (X, D, C)$ we define the uniform probability distribution $P_u(\mathcal{R})$ over X such that for every assignment $\vec{x} = (x_1, ..., x_n)$ to all the variables,

$$P_u(\vec{x}) = \begin{cases} \frac{1}{|sol|} & \text{if } \vec{x} \text{ is a solution} \\ 0 & \text{otherwise} \end{cases}$$

Where $|sol|$ is the number of solutions to $\mathcal{R}$. We consider in this paper the task of generating random solutions to a CSP, from a uniform distribution over the solution space. A *naive approach* to this task is to randomly generate solutions from the problem's search space. Namely, given a variable ordering, starting with the first variable X_1, we can randomly assign it a value from its domain (choosing each value with equal probability). For the second variable, X_2 we compute values that are consistent with the current assignment to X_1 and choose one of these values with equal probability, and so forth.

This approach is of course incorrect. Consider a constraint network over Boolean variables where the constraints are a set of implications: $\rho = \{A \rightarrow B, A \rightarrow C, A \rightarrow D, A \rightarrow E\}$. When applying the naive approach to this formula along the variable ordering A, B, C, D, E, we select the value $A = 1$ or $A = 0$ with equal probabilities of 1/2. If the value $A = 1$ is chosen, all the other variables must be set to 1, as there is a single solution consistent with $A = 1$. On the other hand, if $A = 0$ is generated, any assignment to the rest of the variables is a solution. Consequently, the naive approach generates solutions from the distribution:

$$P(a, b, c, d, e) = \begin{cases} 1/2 & \text{(a=1,b=1,c=1,d=1,e=1)} \\ 1/16 & \text{otherwise} \end{cases}$$

rather than from the uniform distribution $P_u(\rho)$. From the example it is clear that the naive method's accuracy will not improve by making the problem backtrack-free.

On the other extreme lies the *brute-force* approach. Namely, generate (by some means) all the solutions and subsequently uniformly at random select one. The brute-force approach is correct but impractical when the number of solutions is very large. We next present a range of schemes that lie between the *naive approach* and an exact approach, which permits trading accuracy for efficiency in anytime fashion.

Algorithm elim-count
Input: A constraint network $\mathcal{R} = (X, D, C)$, ordering d.
Output: Augmented output buckets including the intermediate count functions. The number of solutions.
1. **Initialize:** Partition C into $bucket_1, \ldots, bucket_n$, where $bucket_i$ contains all constraints whose latest (highest) variable is X_i. We denote a function in a bucket N_i, its scope S_i.)
2. **Backward:** For $p \leftarrow n$ downto 1, do
   Generate the function N^p: $N^p = \sum_{X_p} \prod_{N_i \in bucket_p} N_i$.
   Add N^p to the bucket of the latest variable in $\bigcup_{i=1}^{j} S_i - \{X_p\}$.
3. **Return** the number of solutions, N^1 and the set of output buckets with the original and computed functions.

Figure 2: Algorithm *elim-count*

Uniform Solution Sampling Algorithm

Our idea is to transform the constraint network into a belief network that can express the desired uniform probability distribution. Once such a belief network is available we can apply known sampling algorithms for belief networks (Pearl 1988). The transformation algorithm is based on a variable elimination algorithm that counts the number of solutions of a constraint network and the number of solutions that can be reached by extending certain partial assignments. Clearly, the task of counting is known to be difficult (#P-complete) but when the graph's induced-width is small the task is manageable.

We describe the algorithm using the bucket-elimination framework. *Bucket elimination* is a unifying algorithmic framework for dynamic programming algorithms (Bertele & Brioschi 1972; Dechter 1999). The input to a bucket-elimination algorithm consists of relations (functions, e.g., constraints, or conditional probability tables for belief networks). Given a variable ordering, the algorithm partitions the functions into buckets, where a function is placed in the bucket of its latest argument in the ordering. The algorithm processes each bucket, from the last variable to the first, by a variable elimination operator that computes a new function that is placed in an earlier bucket.

For the counting task, the input functions are the constraints, expressed as cost functions. A constraint R_S over scope S is a cost function that assigns 0 to any illegal tuple and 1 otherwise. When the bucket of a variable is processed the algorithm multiplies all the functions in the bucket and sums over the bucket's variable. This yields a new function that associates with each tuple (over the bucket's scope excluding the bucket's variable) the number of extensions to the eliminated variable. Figure 2 presents algorithm *elim-count*, the bucket-elimination algorithm for counting. The complexity of elim-count obeys the general time and space complexity of bucket-elimination algorithms (Dechter 1999).

THEOREM 1 *The time and space complexity of algorithm elim-count is $O(n \cdot exp(w^*(d)))$ where $n = |X|$ and $w^*(d)$ is the induced-width of the network's ordered constraint graph*

along d. $\square$

Let $\vec{x}_i = (x_1, \ldots, x_i)$ be a specific assignment to the first set of i variables and let N_k^j denotes a new function that resides in bucket X_k and was generated in bucket X_j, for $j > k$.

THEOREM 2 *Given an assignment $\vec{x}_i = (x_1, \ldots, x_i)$, the number of consistent extensions of $\vec{x}_i$ to full solutions is[1]*
$$\prod_{\{N_k^j | 1 \le k \le i, \; i+1 \le j \le n\}} N_k^j(\vec{x}).$$

EXAMPLE 3 *Consider the constraint network of Example 1 and assume we use the variable ordering (D, C, B, A), the initial partitioning of functions into buckets is given in the table below in the middle column.*

Processing bucket A we generate the function (We use the notation N^X for the function generated by eliminating variable X) $N^A(B, D) = \sum_A R(A, B) \cdot R(A, D)$ and place it in the bucket of B. Processing the bucket of B we compute $N^B(C, D) = \sum_B R(B, C) \cdot N^A(B, D)$ and place it in the bucket of C. Next we process C generating the function $N^C(D) = \sum_C R(C, D) \cdot N^B(C, D)$ placed it in bucket D and finally we compute (when processing bucket D) all the solutions $N^D = \sum_D N^C(D)$. The output buckets are:

Bucket	Original constraints	New constraints
$bucket(A)$	$R(A, B)$, $R(A, D)$	
$bucket(B)$	$R(B, C)$	$N^A(B, D)$
$bucket(C)$	$R(C, D)$	$N^B(C, D)$
$bucket(D)$		$N^C(D)$
$bucket(0)$		N^D

The actual N functions are displayed in the following table:

$N^A(b, d) : (b, d)$	$N^B(c, d) : (c, d)$	$N^C(d): (d)$	N^D
2: (1,1) or (2,2)	2 : (2,1) or (1,2)	5: (1)	10
1: (1,2) or (2,1)	3 : (3,1) or (3,2)	5: (2)	
	1 : (1,1) or (2,2)		

We next show, using the example, how we use the output of the counting algorithm for sampling. We start assigning values along the order D, C, B, A. The problem has 10 solutions. According to the information in bucket D, both assignments $D = 1$ and $D = 2$ can be extended to 5 solutions, so we choose among them with equal probability. Once a value for D is selected (lets say $D = 1$) we compute the product of functions in the output-bucket of C which yields, for any assignment to D and C, the number of full solutions they allow. Since the product functions shows that the assignment $(D = 1, C = 2)$ has 2 extensions to full solutions, $(D = 1, C = 3)$ has 3 extensions while $(D = 1, C = 1)$ has none, we choose between the values 2 and 3 of C with ratio of 2 to 3. Once a value for C is selected we continue in the same manner with B and A. Algorithm *solution-sampling* is given in Figure 3. Since the algorithm operates on a backtrack-free network created by elim-count, it is guaranteed to be linear in the number of samples generated.

The Transformed Belief Network

Given a constraint network $\mathcal{R} = (X, D, C)$ and its output-buckets generated by elim-count applied along ordering d,

---
[1] We abuse notation denoting by $N(\vec{x})$ the function $N(\vec{x}_S)$, where S is the scope of N.

Algorithm solution-sampling
Input: A constraint network $\mathcal{R} = (X, D, C)$, an ordering d. The output buckets along d, produced by elim-count.
Output: Random solutions generated from $P_u(\mathcal{R})$.
1. **While** not enough solutions generated, do
2.   For $p \leftarrow 1$ to n, do
        Given the assignment $\vec{x}_p = (x_1, ...x_p)$ and $bucket_p$ with functions $\{N_1, N_2, ...\}$, compute the frequency function of $f(X_{p+1}) = \prod_j N_j(\vec{x}_p, X_{p+1})$ and generate sample for X_{p+1} according to f.
3. **Endwhile**.
4. **Return** the generated solutions.

Figure 3: Algorithm *solution-sampling*

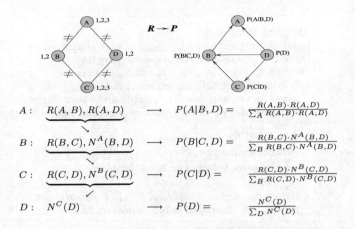

$$A: \quad \underbrace{R(A,B), R(A,D)} \quad \longrightarrow \quad P(A|B,D) = \frac{R(A,B) \cdot R(A,D)}{\sum_A R(A,B) \cdot R(A,D)}$$

$$B: \quad \underbrace{R(B,C), N^A(B,D)} \quad \longrightarrow \quad P(B|C,D) = \frac{R(B,C) \cdot N^A(B,D)}{\sum_B R(B,C) \cdot N^A(B,D)}$$

$$C: \quad \underbrace{R(C,D), N^B(C,D)} \quad \longrightarrow \quad P(C|D) = \frac{R(C,D) \cdot N^B(C,D)}{\sum_B R(C,D) \cdot N^B(C,D)}$$

$$D: \quad N^C(D) \quad \longrightarrow \quad P(D) = \frac{N^C(D)}{\sum_D N^C(D)}$$

Figure 4: The conversion process

$B_{(\mathcal{R},d)}$ is the belief network defined over X as follows. The directed acyclic graph is the induced graph of the constraint problem along d where all the arrows are directed from earlier to later nodes in the ordering. Namely, for every variable X_i the parents of X_i are the nodes connected to it in the induced-graph that precede it in the ordering. The conditional probability table (CPT) associated with each child variable X_i can be derived from the functions in the output-bucket by

$$P(X_i|pa_i) = \frac{\prod_j N_j(X_i, pa_i)}{\sum_{X_i} \prod_j N_j(X_i, pa_i)} \tag{1}$$

where N_j are both the original and new functions in the bucket of X_i.

EXAMPLE 4 *In our example, the parents of A are B and D, the parents of B are D and C, the parents of C is D and D is a root node (see Figure 4). The CPTs are given by the following table:*

$P(a|b,d)$	(d,b,a)	$P(b|c,d)$	(c,d,b)	$P(c|d)$	(d,c)
1/2	(1,1,2)	1	(1,1 or 2,2)	2/5	(1,2)
1/2	(1,1,3)	1	(2,1 or 2,1)	2/5	(2,1)
1/2	(2,2,1)	2/3	(3,1,1)	3/5	(1,3)
1/2	(2,2,3)	1/3	(3,1,2)	3/5	(2,3)
1	(1,2,3)	1/3	(3,2,1)		
1	(2,1,3)	2/3	(3,2,2)		

The conversion process is summarized in Figure 4. We can show

THEOREM 3 *Given a constraint network $\mathcal{R}$ and an ordering d of its variables, the Belief network $B_{(\mathcal{R},d)}$ (defined by Eq. 1), expresses the uniform distribution $P_u(\mathcal{R})$.*

Given a belief network that expresses the desired distribution we can now use well known sampling algorithms to sample solutions from the belief network. In particular, the simplest such algorithm that works well when there is no evidence, is *Logic sampling* (Henrion 1986). The algorithm samples values of the variables along the topological ordering of the network's directed graph. Given an assignment to the first $(i-1)$ variables it assigns a value to X_i using the probability distribution $P(X_i|pa_i)$, as the parents of X_i are already assigned. We can show that

Proposition 1 *Given a constraint network $\mathcal{R}$. Algorithm solution-sampling applied to the output-buckets of elim-*

count along d, is identical to logic sampling on the belief network $B_{(\mathcal{R},d)}$. □

Mini-bucket Approximation for Sampling

The main drawback of bucket elimination algorithms is that, unless the problem's induced-width is bounded, they are time and space exponential. *Mini-Bucket Elimination* is an approximation designed to reduce the space and time problem of full bucket elimination (Dechter & Rish 1997) by partitioning large buckets into smaller subsets called mini-buckets, which are processed independently. Here is the rationale. Let $h_1, ..., h_j$ be the functions in $bucket_p$ and let $S_1, ..., S_j$ be the scopes of those functions. When *elim-count* processes $bucket_p$, it computes the function $N^p = \sum_{X_p} \prod_{i=1}^j N_i$. The scope of N^p is $U_p = \bigcup_{i=1}^j S_i - \{X_p\}$. The Mini-Bucket algorithm, on the other hand, creates a partitioning $Q' = \{Q_1, ..., Q_t\}$ where the mini-bucket Q_l contains the functions $\{N_{l_1}, ..., N_{l_k}\}$. We can rewrite the expression for N^p as follows: $N^p = \sum_{X_p} \prod_{l=1}^t \prod_{l_i} N_{l_i}$. Now, if we migrate the summation inside the multiplication we will get a new function g^p defined by: $g^p = \prod_{l=1}^t \sum_{X_p} \prod_{l_i} N_{l_i}$. It is not hard to see that g^p is an upper bound on N^p: $N^p \leq g^p$. Thus, the approximation algorithm can process each mini-bucket separately (by using the summation and product operators), therefore computing g^p rather than N^p.

A tighter upper-bound for N^p can be obtained by bounding all the mini-buckets but one, by a maximization instead of summation, namely, $N^p \leq (\sum_{X_p} \prod_{l_1} N_{l_1}) \cdot (\prod_{l=2}^t \max_{X_p} \prod_{l_i} N_{l_i})$. Alternatively, we can minimize over the mini-bucket's variables, except one mini-bucket to yield a lower bound (replacing max by min), or apply averaging, yielding a mean-value approximation.

The quality of the approximation depends on the degree of partitioning into mini-buckets. Given a bounding parameter i, the algorithm creates an i-partitioning, where each mini-bucket includes no more than i variables[2]. The choice of

---

[2]We assume that i is at least as large as the size of scopes of

---

Algorithm MBE-count(i)

Input: A constraint network $\mathcal{R} = (X, D, C)$ an ordering d; parameter i

Output: A bound on (upper, lower or approximate value) of the count function computed by elim-count. A bound on the number of solutions

1. **Initialize:** Partition the functions in C into $bucket_1, \ldots, bucket_n$

2. **Backward** For $p \leftarrow n$ downto 1, do
- Given functions $N_1, N_2, \ldots, N_j$ in $bucket_p$, generate an (i)-partitioning, $Q' = \{Q_1, \ldots, Q_t\}$. For Q_1 containing $N_{1_1}, \ldots N_{1_t}$ generate $N^1 = \sum_{X_p} \prod_{i=1}^{t} N_{l_i}$. For each $Q_l \in Q'$, $l > 1$ containing $N_{l_1}, \ldots N_{l_t}$ generate function N^l, $N^l = \Downarrow_{U_l} \prod_{i=1}^{t} N_{l_i}$, where $U_l = \bigcup_{i=1}^{j} scope(N_{l_i}) - \{X_p\}$ (where $\Downarrow$ is max, min or mean). Add N^l to the bucket of the largest-index variable in its scope.

4. **Return** the ordered set of augmented buckets and number of solutions.

Figure 5: Algorithm, MBE-count(i)

i-partitioning affects the accuracy of the mini-bucket algorithm. Algorithm *MBE-count(i)* described in Figure 5, is parameterized by this i-bound. The algorithm outputs not only a bound on the number of solutions but also the collection of augmented buckets. It can be shown ((Dechter & Rish 1997)),

THEOREM **4** *Algorithm MBE-count(i) generates an upper (lower) bound on the number of solutions and its complexity is time $O(r \cdot exp(i))$ and space $O(r \cdot exp(i-1))$, where r is the number of functions.* □

EXAMPLE **5** *Considering our example and assuming $i = 2$, processing the bucket of A we have to partition the two functions into two separate mini-buckets, yielding two new unary functions: $N^A(B) = \sum_A R(A, B)$, $N^A(D) = \max_A R(A, D)$ placed in bucket B and bucket D, respectively (only one, arbitrary, mini-bucket should be processed by summation). Alternatively, we get $N^A(D) = 0$ if we process by min operator, $N^A(D) = 2$ by summation and $N^A(D) = \frac{1}{|D(A)|} \cdot \sum_A R(A, D) = 2/3$, by mean operator. Processing bucket B we compute $N^B(C) = \sum_B R(B, C) \cdot N^A(B)$ placed in bucket of C, and processing C generates $N^C(D) = \sum_C R(C, D) \cdot N^B(C)$ placed in bucket D. Finally we compute, when processing bucket D, an upper bound on the number of solutions $N^D = \sum_D N^C(D) \cdot N^A(D)$. The output buckets are given by the table below*

Bucket	Original constraints	New constraints
$bucket(A)$	$R(A, B)$, $R(A, D)$	
$bucket(B)$	$R(B, C)$	$N^A(B)$
$bucket(C)$	$R(C, D)$	$N^B(C)$
$bucket(D)$		$N^A(D)$, $N^C(D)$
$bucket(0)$		N^D

The actual N functions using the max operator are:

$$N^A(b) = 2 \quad N^B(c) = \begin{cases} 2 & \text{if } (c=1) \\ 2 & \text{if } (c=2) \\ 4 & \text{if } (c=3) \end{cases}$$

$$N^A(d) = 1 \quad N^C(d) = \begin{cases} 6 & \text{if } (d=1) \\ 6 & \text{if } (d=2) \end{cases} \quad N^D = 12$$

We see that the bound is quite good. Note that had we processed both mini-bucket by summation we would get a bound of 24 on the number of total solutions, 0 solutions using min and 8 solutions using the mean operator.

Given a set of output buckets generated by MBE-count(i) we can apply algorithm solution-sampling as before. There are, however, a few subtleties here. First we should note that the sample generation process is *no longer* backtrack-free. Many of the samples can get into a "dead-end" because the generated network is not backtrack-free. Consequently, the complexity of solution-sampling algorithm is no longer output linear. The lower the i-bound, the larger the time overhead per sample.

Can we interpret the sampling algorithm as sampling over some belief network? If we mimic the transformation algorithm used in the exact case, we will generate an *irregular* belief network. The belief network generated is irregular in that it is *not* backtrack-free, while by definition, all belief networks are backtrack-free, because regular CPTs must sum to 1.

An irregular belief network includes an irregular CPT $P(X_i|pa_i)$, where there could be an assignment to the parents pa_i such that $P(x_i|t_{pa_i}) = 0$ for *every* value x_i or X_i. An irregular belief network represent the probability distribution $P(x_1, \ldots, x_n) = \alpha \cdot \prod_{i=1}^{n} P(x_i|x_{pa_i})$ where α is a normalizing constant. It is possible to show that the sampling algorithm that follows MBE-count(i) is identical to logic sampling over such an irregular network created by the transformation applied to the output buckets generated by MBE-count(i).

EXAMPLE **6** *The belief network that will correspond to the mini-bucket approximation still has D, B as the parents of A, C is the parent of B and D is the parent of C. The probability functions that can be generated for our example are given below. For this example, sampling is backtrack-free. For variable A, after normalization, we get the same function as the exact one (see Example 4). The CPT for B, C and D are:*

$P(b|c)$	(c,b)	$P(c|d)$	(d,c)	$P(d)$	(d)
1	$(1,2)$ or $(2,2)$	$1/3$	$(1,2)$ or $(2,1)$	$1/2$	(1)
$1/2$	$(3,1)$ or $(3,2)$	$2/3$	$(1,3)$ or $(2,3)$	$1/2$	(2)

It is interesting to note that if we apply the sampling algorithm to the initial bare buckets, which can be perceived to be generated by MBE-count(0), we just get the naive-approach we introduced at the outset.

Empirical evaluation

We provide preliminary empirical evaluation, demonstrating the anytime behavior of the mini-bucket scheme for sampling. We used as benchmark randomly generated binary CSPs generated according to the well-known four-parameter

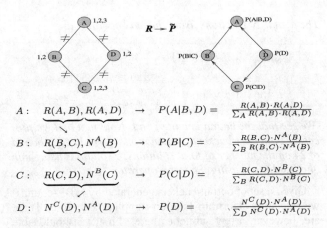

$$A : \underbrace{R(A,B), R(A,D)}_{} \rightarrow P(A|B,D) = \frac{R(A,B) \cdot R(A,D)}{\sum_A R(A,B) \cdot R(A,D)}$$

$$B : \underbrace{R(B,C), N^A(B)}_{} \rightarrow P(B|C) = \frac{R(B,C) \cdot N^A(B)}{\sum_B R(B,C) \cdot N^A(B)}$$

$$C : \underbrace{R(C,D), N^B(C)}_{} \rightarrow P(C|D) = \frac{R(C,D) \cdot N^B(C)}{\sum_B R(C,D) \cdot N^B(C)}$$

$$D : N^C(D), N^A(D) \rightarrow P(D) = \frac{N^C(D) \cdot N^A(D)}{\sum_D N^C(D) \cdot N^A(D)}$$

Figure 6: The conversion process

model (N, K, C, T) where N is the number of variables, K is the number of values, T is the tightness (number of disallowed tuples) and C is the number of constraints. We also tested the special structure of square grid networks.

Measures. We assume that the accuracy of the distribution obtained for the first variable is representative of the accuracy of the whole distribution. We therefore compare the approximated distribution associated with the first variable in the ordering (the probability of the first node in the ordering) computed by MBE-count(i) against its exact distribution, using several error measures. The primary measure is the KL distance which is common for comparing the distance between two probabilities (Chow & Liu 1968). Let $P(x)$ be a probability distribution and $P_a(x)$ its approximation. The KL-distance of P and P_a is defined as $KL(P, P_a) = \sum_x P(x) log(P(x)/P_a(x))$. It is known that $KL(P, Pa) \geq 0$, and the smaller $KL(P, P_a)$, the closer $P_a(x)$ is to $P(x)$, with $KL(P, P_a) = 0$ iff $P = P_a$. We also compute the absolute error[3] and the relative error[4]. Finally, for comparison we also compute the KL distance between the exact distribution and the uniform, KL_u of the first variable.

Benchmarks and results. We experimented with random problems having 40 and 50 variables with domains of 5 values and 8x8 grids with domains of 5 values. All problems are consistent. We had to stay with relatively small problems in order to apply the exact algorithm. The results with random CSPs are given in Tables 1 and 2, and results with 8x8 grids are given in Table 3. In the first column we have tightness T, in the second column the KL-distance between the exact distribution and uniform distribution (KL_u), and in the remaining columns various values of the i-bound. First we report the average time of MBE-count(i) per problem for each i. The remainder of the table consists of horizontal blocks, corresponding to different values of T. In columns corresponding to values of i-bound, we report, for each value of i, KL-distance between the exact probability and MBE(i) probability (KL_i), absolute error and relative error, aver-

---

$$^3 \epsilon_{abs} = \sum_i |P(x=i) - P_a(x=i)|/K.$$
$$^4 \epsilon_{rel} = \sum_i (|P(x=i) - P_a(x=i)|/P(x=i))/K.$$

$N = 40, K = 5, C = 90$. w^*=10.8. 20 instances.							
	i=4	i=5	i=6	i=7	i=8	i=9	i=10
time	0.05	0.09	0.33	1.3	5.2	20	86
T / KL_u	KL_i abs-e rel-e	KL_i abs-e rel-e	KL_i abs-e rel-e	KL_i abs-e rel-e	KL_i abs-e rel-e	KL_i abs-e rel-e	KL_i abs-e rel-e
8 0.398	0.223	0.184	0.144	0.086	0.091	0.063	0.020
	0.106	0.095	0.081	0.058	0.058	0.045	0.026
	1.56	1.13	0.86	0.65	0.64	0.48	0.21
9 0.557	0.255	0.323	0.303	0.132	0.109	0.082	0.085
	0.110	0.125	0.112	0.074	0.064	0.053	0.045
	37	28	23	5.16	1.76	0.99	0.61
10 0.819	0.643	0.480	0.460	0.340	0.295	0.401	0.228
	0.164	0.124	0.123	0.108	0.105	0.098	0.064
	28	7.51	9.41	5.41	4.31	2.69	0.81
11 1.237	0.825	0.803	1.063	0.880	0.249	0.276	0.193
	0.203	0.184	0.209	0.166	0.088	0.098	0.068
	1.33	1.65	2.71	1.15	0.88	1.24	0.33

Table 1: Accuracy and time on Random CSPs.

$N = 50, K = 5, C = 110$. w^*=12.7. 10 instances.						
	i=6	i=7	i=8	i=9	i=10	i=11
time	0.44	1.64	6.60	29	125	504
T / KL_u	KL_i abs-e rel-e	KL_i abs-e rel-e	KL_i abs-e rel-e	KL_i abs-e rel-e	KL_i abs-e rel-e	KL_i abs-e rel-e
10 1.044	0.372	0.599	0.442	0.631	0.295	0.278
	0.127	0.147	0.135	0.100	0.098	0.041
	52	120	81	79	8.12	0.91
10.5 0.923	0.502	0.285	0.137	0.215	0.214	0.464
	0.150	0.109	0.069	0.073	0.079	0.143
	1.97	1.93	0.44	1.60	1.28	3.73
11 1.246	0.781	0.851	0.550	0.490	1.670	-
	0.208	0.186	0.156	0.134	0.177	-
	116	81	44	91	100	-
11.5 1.344	0.577	0.660	0.333	0.231	0.088	-
	0.160	0.180	0.180	0.061	0.042	-
	5.69	3.40	3.02	2.70	0.94	-

Table 2: Accuracy and time on Random CSP.

aged over all problem instances.

The first thing to observe from the tables is that even the weakest (but most efficient) level of approximation is superior to the naive uniform distribution, sometimes substantially. We also see from Table 1 that as i increases, the running time of MBE(i) increases, as expected. Looking at each horizontal block, corresponding to a specific value of T, we see that as i increases, the KL-distance as well as absolute and relative error decrease. For large values of i, KL_i is as much as an order of magnitude smaller than KL_u, indicating the quality of the probability distribution computed by MBE-count(i). We see similar results from Table 2.

Conclusion

The paper introduces the task of generating random, uniformly distributed solutions for constraint satisfaction problems. The origin of this task is the use of CSP based methods for the random test program generation.

The algorithms are based on exact and approximate variable elimination algorithms for counting the number of solutions, that can be viewed as transformation of constraint networks into belief networks.

The result is a spectrum of parameterized anytime algorithms controlled by an i-bound that, starts with the naive approach on one end and the exact approach on the other. As i increases, we are likely to have more accurate sam-

8x8 grid, $K = 5$. $w^* = 10$. 25 instances.								
		$i=4$	$i=5$	$i=6$	$i=7$	$i=8$	$i=9$	$i=10$
	time	0.01	0.04	0.12	0.56	1.8	5.7	16
T	KL_u	KL_i / abs-e / rel-e	KL_i / abs-e / rel-e	KL_i / abs-e / rel-e	KL_i / abs-e / rel-e	KL_i / abs-e / rel-e	KL_i / abs-e / rel-e	KL_i / abs-e / rel-e
5	0.013	0.001 / 0.016 / 0.091	3e-4 / 0.008 / 0.044	2.3e-5 / 0.002 / 0.012	2.2e-5 / 0.002 / 0.010	1e-6 / 3.3e-4 / 0.002	0 / 4.6e-5 / 2.7e-4	0 / 1e-6 / 4e-6
7	0.022	0.002 / 0.021 / 0.133	7.2e-4 / 0.012 / 0.076	1.1e-4 / 0.005 / 0.026	1.2e-4 / 0.005 / 0.025	7e-6 / 0.001 / 0.006	0 / 2.1e-5 / 0.001	0 / 0.001 / 3e-5
9	0.049	0.009 / 0.045 / 0.440	0.002 / 0.022 / 0.215	4.1e-4 / 0.009 / 0.069	2.8e-4 / 0.007 / 0.056	3.8e-5 / 0.003 / 0.020	5e-6 / 0.001 / 0.006	0 / 6e-5 / 5e-4
11	0.073	0.020 / 0.060 / 1.63	0.005 / 0.031 / 0.342	0.003 / 0.021 / 0.265	0.002 / 0.017 / 0.223	6.8e-4 / 0.009 / 0.118	9.4e-5 / 0.003 / 0.039	1e-6 / 3e-4 / 0.003

Table 3: Accuracy and time on 8x8 grid CSPs.

ples that takes less overhead to generate during the sampling phase. Our preliminary evaluations show that the scheme provides substantial improvements over the naive approach even when using its weakest version. More importantly, it demonstrate the anytime behavior of the algorithms as a function of the i-bound. Further experiments clearly should be conducted on the real application of test program generation. In the future we still need to test the sampling complexity of the approximation and its accuracy on the full distribution.

Our approach is superior to ordinary OBDD-based algorithms which are bounded exponentially by the *path-width*, a parameter that is always larger than the induced-width. However, another variants of BDDs, known as tree-BDDs (McMillan 1994) extends OBDDs to trees that are also time and space exponentially bounded in the induced-width (also known as tree-width). As far as we know all BDD-based algorithms for random solution generation, use ordinary OBDDs rather than tree-BDDS.

The main virtue of our approach however is in presenting an anytime approximation scheme which is so far unavailable under the BDD framework.

Acknowledgement

This work was supported in part by NSF grant IIS-0086529 and by MURI ONR award N00014-00-1-0617.

References

Arnborg, S. A. 1985. Efficient algorithms for combinatorial problems on graphs with bounded decomposability - a survey. *BIT* 25:2–23.

Bergeron, J. 2000. *Writing Testbenches: Functional Verification of HDL Models*. Kluwer Academic Publishers.

Bertele, U., and Brioschi, F. 1972. *Nonserial Dynamic Programming*. Academic Press.

Bin, E.; Emek, R.; Shurek, G.; and Ziv, A. What's between constraint satisfaction and random test program generation. Submitted to IBM System Journal, Aug. 2002.

Chandra, A. K., and Iyengar, V. S. 1992. Constraint solving for test case generation. In *International Conference on Computer Design, VLSI in Computers and Processors*, 245–248. Los Alamitos, Ca., USA: IEEE Computer Society Press.

Chow, C. K., and Liu, C. N. 1968. Approximating discrete probability distributions with dependence trees. *IEEE Transaction on Information Theory* 462–67.

Dechter, R., and Rish, I. 1997. A scheme for approximating probabilistic inference. In *Proceedings of Uncertainty in Artificial Intelligence (UAI'97)*, 132–141.

Dechter, R. 1992. Constraint networks. *Encyclopedia of Artificial Intelligence* 276–285.

Dechter, R. 1999. Bucket elimination: A unifying framework for reasoning. *Artificial Intelligence* 113:41–85.

Fournier, L.; Arbetman, Y.; and Levinger, M. 1999. Functional verification methodology for microprocessors using the Genesys test program generator. In *Design Automation & Test in Europe (DATE99)*, 434–441.

Hartman, A.; Ur, S.; and Ziv, A. 1999. Short vs long size does make a difference. In *HLDVT*.

Henrion, M. 1986. Propagating uncertainty by logic sampling. In *Technical report, Department of Engineering and Public Policy, Carnegie Melon University*.

Kumar, V. 1992. Algorithms for constraint-satisfaction problems: A survey. *A.I. Magazine* 13(1):32–44.

McMillan, K. L. 1994. Hierarchical representation of discrete functions with application to model checking. In *Computer Aided Verification, 6th International conference, David L. Dill ed.*, 41–54.

Pearl, J. 1988. *Probabilistic Reasoning in Intelligent Systems*. Morgan Kaufmann.

Yuan, J.; Shultz, K.; Pixley, C.; Miller, H.; and Aziz, A. 1999. Modeling design constraints and biasing in simulation using BDDs. In *International Conference on Computer-Aided Design (ICCAD '99)*, 584–590. Washington - Brussels - Tokyo: IEEE.

Graph Coloring with Quantum Heuristics

Alex Fabrikant
EECS Dept., UC Berkeley
Berkeley, CA 94720

Tad Hogg
HP Labs
Palo Alto, CA 94304

Abstract

We present a quantum computer heuristic search algorithm for graph coloring. This algorithm uses a new quantum operator, appropriate for nonbinary-valued constraint satisfaction problems, and information available in partial colorings. We evaluate the algorithm empirically with small graphs near a phase transition in search performance. It improves on two prior quantum algorithms: unstructured search and a heuristic applied to the satisfiability (SAT) encoding of graph coloring. An approximate asymptotic analysis suggests polynomial-time cost for hard graph coloring problems, on average.

Introduction

To date, quantum computers [5, 7] appear to give substantial improvement for only a few problems, most notably integer factoring [21]. At first sight, this is puzzling since quantum computers can evaluate all combinatorial search states in about the same time a conventional machine evaluates just one. Hence one might expect high performance for problems having a rapid test of whether a state is a solution, i.e., NP problems, which are the main computational bottleneck in numerous AI applications.

Unfortunately, beyond the difficulties of building quantum computers, it appears impossible to reliably and rapidly extract an answer from this simultaneous evaluation for the worst cases of NP problems [1]. Of more practical interest is the average performance of quantum algorithms that use problem structure to guide search [11, 2, 13, 16, 6]. As with conventional heuristics, such algorithms are difficult to evaluate theoretically. Moreover, empirical evaluation is also limited because, currently, quantum algorithms must be simulated on conventional machines, exponentially increasing the required memory and run time. Hence, quantum heuristics can only be tested on much smaller problems than is possible for conventional algorithms.

Despite these difficulties, insights into the structure of NP problems, particularly when formulated as constraint satisfaction problems (CSPs), help understand the capabilities of quantum computers for typical searches. One significant insight is the analogy between CSPs and physical phase transitions [4, 23, 19], which has led to new heuristics for conventional machines [12, 8, 17]. However, conventional algorithms sample only a tiny, and deliberately unrepresentative, fraction of the search states. Thus insight into average properties can be difficult to exploit with conventional machines, particularly when the properties also have large variance, as is the case with phase transitions. On the other hand, quantum computers, by operating on the entire search space at once, can directly utilize knowledge of the average properties of search states. More broadly, quantum algorithms may motivate studies that provide new insight into typical search structure, particularly correlations among search state properties that hold on average over the whole space but not strongly enough on individual states for conventional heuristics to exploit. Gaining such insight is a fundamental concern for AI search applications, in contrast to the worst-case studies of theoretical computer science, including much of the work on quantum computation.

This paper illustrates these ideas with a quantum heuristic search algorithm for graph coloring. Graph coloring is an interesting problem for quantum algorithm design due to its structured constraints, solution invariance under permutation of colors, and nonbinary-valued variables. It thus provides additional symmetry and representational issues compared to prior studies for less structured problems such as satisfiability. Nevertheless, graph coloring is simple enough that its search space structure and phase transitions are well-understood. The operators and representations we introduce may also be useful for other, more structured, problems.

Graph Coloring

Graph coloring requires assigning one of k colors to each node in a graph so that no edge links nodes with the same color. We consider the NP-complete case of $k = 3$.

As with many search problems, graph coloring exhibits a phase transition in solubility. In our studies, we use the random graph ensemble where each graph with m edges and n nodes is equally likely to be selected. For large n the transition is near $m \sim 2.25n$, so the graphs have average degree 4.5. However, for smaller n the threshold occurs at somewhat smaller ratios of m/n. Thus, for each n we use m for which about 50% of random graphs are soluble.

Heuristics are often exponentially slower near this transition point than on either side. Generating instances near the transition gives a high concentration of hard instances for testing heuristics. While we adopt this procedure in this paper, a broader evaluation would also use hard instances found away from the transition and, more importantly, examples drawn from real-world applications. The latter include graphs with various forms of hierarchical clustering or small-world structure, which are not readily exhibited in the small graphs feasible for simulation in our studies.

Algorithm

Quantum computers operate on *superpositions* of all search states. A superposition corresponds to a *state vector*, consisting of a complex number, called an *amplitude*, for each search state. From an algorithmic perspective, a quantum computer is a device for performing some rapid operations on the state vector. These operations are matrix multiplications that have only polynomially growing cost even with exponentially many states. After a series of such operations, observing the machine (usually described as "measuring its state") probabilistically produces a single search state, with probability equal to the square of the magnitude of amplitude associated with that state. The measurement destroys the superposition, so obtaining another state requires repeating the quantum operations from scratch. A good quantum algorithm is a series of operations on the state vector giving large amplitudes for desired states (e.g., solutions to a search problem). Measurement will then be likely to produce one of these desired states.

Our graph coloring algorithm has the same general form as unstructured search [10] and heuristic methods [13, 16] for satisfiability (SAT) and traveling salesman (TSP) problems. The quantum computer acts as a coprocessor rapidly executing an inner loop, or *trial*, of the overall algorithm, while a conventional machine examines the trial result, continuing with additional trials until a solution is found. The algorithm is incomplete, i.e., cannot determine that no solution exists, so we focus on soluble problems.

Representing Graph Coloring

The operations available with quantum computers are most naturally treated as acting on superpositions of strings of N bits (each of which is called a "qubit"). Superpositions involve the 2^N possible values for these bits. Applying this framework to graph coloring requires choosing a representation for the search states, i.e., colorings for the graph, with such a bitstring. The representation should enable efficient implementation of the operations required for the heuristic. In our case, these operations evaluate the number of conflicts in a given state and mix amplitudes of different states by multiplication with a matrix based on a distance measure between search states.

A 3-coloring of an n-node graph has several natural representations. With 3^n possible colorings, the most compact bitstring representation uses $N = \lceil \log_2 3^n \rceil$ qubits. In this representation, the distance between states is not a simple function of their bitstrings so it is unclear whether distance-based mixing can be efficiently implemented.

A second representation consists of the powerset of all possible *(variable, value)* pairs, using $3n$ qubits. This representation easily encodes the property, used for pruning in backtrack-style searches, that a conflict in a partial coloring implies a conflict in all its extensions. Our limited evaluation of this encoding shows its potential benefit does not compensate for the disadvantage of its expanded search space.

We introduce a third representation, well-suited for 3-coloring. Specifically, we associate with each node one of four values, 0,1,2,3, where 0 indicates the node is uncolored, and the other values denote the assignment of a specific color to the node. These values need two bits per node, for a total of $N = 2n$ qubits. E.g., with four nodes, the bitstring 00 01 10 11 represents the state with node 1 uncolored, and nodes 2,3,4 assigned colors 1,2,3, respectively. While adding partial colorings expands the search space, it also allows the algorithm to use their conflict information. As detailed below, this representation readily implements mixing based on the *2-bit edit distance*, defined as the number of consecutive bit pairs (each representing a node coloring) that are distinct between two strings. For example, the distance between 00 01 10 11 and 00 10 10 01 is two, since the second and last pairs of the two bitstrings are different. This distance is a 2-bit version of Hamming distance.

In graph coloring, any permutation of a solution's colors gives another solution. In conventional search, this symmetry can reduce the size of the search space by fixing the color choices for two nodes linked by an edge. This could also be incorporated in the representations for the quantum heuristic, but treating two nodes differently from the others complicates the analysis, so is not included in our algorithm.

Trials

Let $\psi_s^{(h)}$ be the amplitude of state s after step h of a trial. A single trial consists of the following operations:

1. initialize the amplitude equally among the states, i.e., set the amplitude $\psi_s^{(0)} = 2^{-N/2}$ for each of the 2^N states s.

2. for steps 1 through j, adjust amplitude phases based on state costs and then mix the amplitudes giving

$$\psi^{(j)} = U^{(j)} P^{(j)} \ldots U^{(1)} P^{(1)} \psi^{(0)}, \qquad (1)$$

where $U^{(h)}$ and $P^{(h)}$ are the mixing and phase adjustment matrices for step h, described below.

3. measure the final superposition, giving state s with probability $p(s) = |\psi_s^{(j)}|^2$.

A conventional machine then tests whether the trial's result s is a solution and, if not, starts another trial. The probability of finding a solution with a single trial is $P_{\text{soln}} = \sum_s p(s)$ where the sum is over all solutions s. The expected number of trials to find a solution is $1/P_{\text{soln}}$, giving an expected cost of j/P_{soln} steps, each of which is comparable to a step in a conventional heuristic since it requires evaluating the conflicts in a state. This cost measure, used in the results given below, thus gives a good indication of the scaling of the cost with problem size and a relative comparison with conventional methods. More specific cost comparisons depend on the clock rates of quantum machines and how well compilers can optimize the operations, which remain open questions.

Phase Adjustment and Amplitude Mixing

The phase adjustment matrix P is diagonal and depends on the problem instance, with $P_{rr} = \exp(i\pi\rho(c(r)))$ where $c(r)$ is the cost associated with state r and $\rho(c)$ a function described below. We define a state's cost to be the sum of the numbers of 1) uncolored nodes and 2) edges connecting nodes of the same color. A solution is a zero-cost state.

The mixing matrix U is defined in terms of two simpler matrices: $U = WTW$. The Walsh transform W has entries

$$W_{rs} = 2^{-N/2}(-1)^{|r \wedge s|} \tag{2}$$

for states r and s, where $|r \wedge s|$ is the number of 1-bits the states have in common. The matrix T is diagonal with elements depending on the number of colored nodes in the state s. Viewed as a bitstring this is equivalent to the number of nonzero consecutive pairs $||s||$, e.g., $||00\,01\,10\,11|| = 3$. That is, $T_{ss} = \exp(i\pi\tau(||s||))$ with $\tau(b)$ a function described below. Quantum computers can efficiently compute the Walsh transform [2, 15], and hence U even though they involve exponentially many states. Using Eq. 2 shows the mixing matrix element U_{rs} for two states r and s has the form $u_{d(r,s)}$, i.e., depends only on the distance between the states, in analogy with conventional heuristics that examine neighbors of a given state to determine the next state to try. Because the representation allows for uncolored nodes, it is also analogous to dynamic backtracking [9] where variables can be instantiated in different orders. Unlike these conventional methods, however, U has contributions from all distances, not just neighbors. Thus the quantum operator incorporates information from the full search space in determining amplitudes for the next step.

Our 3-coloring algorithm uses the 2-bit edit distance, but generalizes to k-bit edit distance, allowing efficient implementation of mixing matrices based on distances between groups of k bits. This generalization is suitable for CSPs with more than four values per variable.

Tuning the Algorithm

Completing the algorithm requires explicit forms of $\rho(c)$ and $\tau(b)$ for each step, and a choice for the number of steps j. Ideally, these values would be selected to maximize a trial's success for the given problem instance. Unfortunately, this is not practical since it requires detailed prior knowledge about the solutions of that instance. Instead, as with conventional heuristics, we find choices that work well on average for the ensemble of hard random graphs discussed above.

$\rho(c)$ and $\tau(b)$ can be arbitrary efficiently-computable functions. As one example, the unstructured search algorithm [10] uses $\rho(0) = 1$, $\tau(0) = 1$ and all other $\rho(c)$ and $\tau(b)$ values equal to zero. Based on a sample of small problems, functions that vary linearly with cost, distance and step give performance almost as good as allowing arbitrary functions, a property also seen with the SAT heuristic [13]. Thus, for simplicity, we restrict attention to linear functions. An overall phase factor has no effect on the probability of finding a solution, so we drop the constant terms in the linear behavior as a function of cost and distance. Thus, for step h of the algorithm, we take $\rho(c) = \rho_h c$ and $\tau(b) = \tau_h b$ with $\rho_h = \frac{1}{j}R((h-1)/j)$ and $\tau_h = \frac{1}{j}T((h-1)/j)$ where

$$R(\lambda) = R_0 + (1 - \lambda)R_1 \tag{3}$$
$$T(\lambda) = T_0 + (1 - \lambda)T_1$$

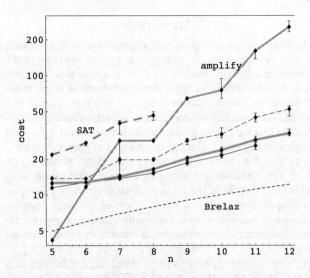

Figure 1: Median search costs vs. n. Quantum search using different phase parameter choices: optimized for each n (solid black), using $n = 6$ parameters (thick gray) and from the approximate theory (dashed black, see Section "Asymptotic Behavior"). Also shown, with labels next to the curves, are amplitude amplification on the smaller search space of the compact representation (thin gray), mapping to SAT (dashed gray, using $R_0 = 4.111$, $R_1 = -3.758$, $T_0 = 0.8288$ and $T_1 = 2.412$) and the Brelaz heuristic (dotted black), whose cost grows nearly linearly for these small problems. Graphs for $n = 5$ to 12 used 7, 10, 12, 14, 16, 18, 20 and 22 edges, respectively. Error bars show the 95% confidence intervals [22, p. 124]. For each n, the same sample of graphs was used for each method shown here.

vary linearly with the step. This choice allows explicit evaluation of the mixing matrix elements, giving

$$u_d = 2^{-2n} \left(1 - e^{i\pi\tau_h}\right)^d \left(1 + 3e^{i\pi\tau_h}\right)^{n-d} \tag{4}$$

for step h. We can determine good phase parameters, R_0, R_1, T_0, T_1, from numerical optimization on a sample of graphs or by applying the theory described below.

With exponentially many steps, each trial can have $P_{\text{soln}} \approx 1$ using the unstructured algorithm [10]. Empirical evaluation for small n shows using problem structure allows better performance with a fixed number of steps, so we use $j = 10$. However, somewhat fewer steps may give better performance for the smallest sizes we consider. The approximate theory described below indicates larger problems will likely require more steps for best performance, but growing only polynomially with n.

Behavior

We numerically optimized the phase parameters for each n for a sample of 10 random soluble graphs. We then tested the heuristic with an independent sample of 200 graphs for each n. Fig. 1 compares the resulting performance to the unstructured algorithm applied to the compact representation (i.e., the first one described in Section "Representing Graph Coloring"), without assuming the number of solutions is known a priori [2]. Even though our heuristic operates in

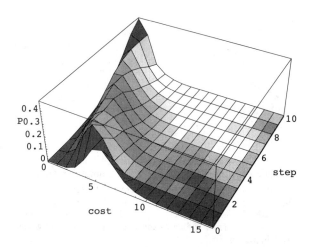

Figure 2: Amplitude shift for a graph with $n = 10, m = 18$ and 12 solutions. The plot shows the total probability in states with each cost for each step of a trial. Shading shows the relative deviation among the amplitudes for states with each cost, with lighter shadings indicating larger deviations. The deviation is relatively small for dominant cost values, i.e., near the peak in the probability for each step. This used the optimal parameters found for $n = 6$: $R_0 = 3.7032$, $R_1 = -2.12047$, $T_0 = 0.94955$ and $T_1 = 1.4052$.

a larger search space, it has lower cost and, significantly, the cost grows more slowly. The figure also shows a conventional backtrack search using the Brelaz heuristic [3]. For such small graphs, this heuristic almost always gives correct choices, avoiding any backtracking. A more significant comparison between the cost growth rates of classical and quantum methods requires larger problems to show the exponential growth of the Brelaz cost, beyond the current range of feasible quantum simulations.

Like quantum heuristics for SAT and TSP, the steps gradually shift the cost distribution toward lower costs (Fig. 2). Thus, if a trial does not yield a solution, it is still likely to yield a low-cost state, unlike unstructured search.

Numeric optimization of the phase parameters is costly, so it is useful to have a single set of parameters with reasonable performance for larger problems. Fig. 1 compares the performances using parameters optimized at each n and parameters optimized for $n = 6$ but used for all n. For all $n \neq 6$ tested, the drop in average performance is under 10%, with no visible divergence for larger problems.

SAT Mapping

Graph k-coloring has a natural mapping to k-SAT: each node maps to k variables, each denoting one color for that node, and constraints ensure each node has exactly one color and each edge connects nodes of different colors. Since quantum heuristics for k-SAT perform well on average [13], another approach to 3-coloring is mapping to 3-SAT and applying the 3-SAT heuristic. This map uses $N = 3n$, giving a larger search space than used with our graph-coloring heuristic.

The ensemble of random graphs does not map to the uniform random ensemble of SAT problems used to determine phase parameters for the quantum SAT heuristic. Thus we optimized the parameters for a sample of SAT problems created from coloring problems. Optimization became prohibitively expensive when $n > 6$. Considering the scaling results described above, we chose to compare performance of the coloring and SAT heuristics with parameters optimized at $n = 6$ for each. Fig. 1 shows the SAT heuristic lags behind the coloring heuristic. Thus our coloring heuristic uses graph coloring structure more effectively than is possible after transforming to SAT. Nevertheless, even the limited use of structure with the SAT mapping gives costs that appear to grow more slowly than unstructured search, again in spite of the larger search space.

Estimating Behavior for Large Problems

How well can quantum algorithms perform for large search problems? Ignoring problem structure gives only a quadratic improvement, far less than the improvement from exponential to polynomial cost for factoring [21]. Based on small cases, our graph coloring algorithm improves on the performance possible from unstructured algorithms but it is unclear how well it works for larger problems.

An Approximate Description

Observations with small problems indicate that states with given numbers of uncolored nodes and conflicts have similar amplitudes. This property becomes more pronounced as n increases for the states dominating the probability at each step. Among states with n_0 uncolored nodes and c conflicts, as $n \to \infty$ the overwhelming majority have nearly equal numbers of nodes with each color and about one-third of the conflicts involving each of the three colors. This motivates grouping the states according to the values $\hat{w} = (n_0, c)$ and approximating the amplitudes for such states as equal to their average value, i.e., $\psi_s^{(h)} \approx \Phi_{\hat{w}}^{(h)}$, where Φ is the average amplitude of all states with given $\hat{w}$.

Such "mean-field" approximations are often quite successful for large statistical systems [20]. In our case, the distribution of costs among states becomes narrower as problem size increases, leading to increasingly peaked versions of the distribution shift shown in Fig. 2. This approach also applies to a similar heuristic for random k-SAT [13].

The algorithm relies on the correlation of distance between states and their costs: nearby states tend to have many of the same conflicts and hence similar costs. We can exploit this by mixing amplitudes primarily among nearby states. Provided $j \gg 1$, Eq. 4 gives u_d equal to an irrelevant overall constant times $(-iv)^d$, with $v = \pi T/(4j)$, which decreases rapidly with d. Since the number of states at distance d from a given state is proportional to n^d, mixing is mainly among states at distances $d = O(1)$ when $j \sim n$ or larger. In particular, this means a polynomial growth in the number of steps is sufficient to ensure mixing mainly among nearby states.

With this approximation, up to an irrelevant overall normalization and phase, step h of Eq. 1 gives average amplitude of states with $\hat{W} = (N_0, C)$, namely $\Phi_{\hat{W}}^{(h)}$, in terms of the averages for the prior step as

$$\sum_{d,\hat{w}} (-iv)^d e^{i\pi\rho(c,n_0)} \Phi_{\hat{w}}^{(h-1)} Q(\hat{W},\hat{w},d) \qquad (5)$$

where Q is the average, over random 3-coloring problems with given m and n, of the number of states s with given $\hat{w}$ values at distance d from a state described by $\hat{W}$. Note ρ and T depend on the step h.

We allow the phase adjustment to depend separately on the number of conflicts c and number of uncolored nodes n_0 instead of just their sum. Again we find a linear form is sufficient to give good performance, i.e., for step h we take $\rho(c,n_0) = \rho_h c + \sigma_h n_0$ with $\sigma_h = \frac{1}{j}S((h-1)/j)$ a new parameter not necessarily equal to ρ_h and $S(\lambda)$ has the same linear form as $R(\lambda)$ in Eq. 3 with parameters S_0, S_1. In contrast, for the small problems described above, we treated both contributions to the cost the same way, i.e., we took $\sigma = \rho$, but the analysis described below suggests this is not the best choice for larger problems.

Q characterizes pairs of states and their conflicts for random graphs, independent of the quantum algorithm. It involves a product of binomial distributions, one for each of the 3 colors, of the number of edges linking nodes with the same colors. Evaluating Q is the key use of problem structure for analyzing the quantum algorithm, and is readily determined for random graphs. This approximation applies to any ensemble of graphs for which Q can be determined.

Asymptotic Analysis

Eq. 5 simplifies when mixing matrix elements decrease rapidly with d. In this case, those states giving the most contribution to $\psi_r^{(h)}$, with state r described by $\hat{W}$, have $n_0 \approx N_0$ and $c \approx C$. Hence, in Eq. 5 we can use a linearized expansion around the dominant values of N_0 and C to approximate $\Phi_{\hat{w}}^{(h-1)}$ by $\Phi_{\hat{W}}^{(h-1)} X^{c-C} Z^{n_0-N_0}$ where X and Z are complex numbers characterizing the behavior of the average amplitudes close to the dominant states at step $h-1$. The initial amplitudes, which are the same for all states, correspond to $X = Z = 1$. Small values of $|X|$ and $|Z|$ have amplitudes concentrated in states with few conflicts and few uncolored nodes, respectively. Thus good performance, i.e., $P_{\text{soln}} \approx 1$, in this approximation requires both X and Z to be small at the end of a trial, specifically $|X|, |Z| \ll 1/\sqrt{n}$.

With this linearization, Eq. 5 relates the values of X, Z at step h to those of the prior step. When j is large, the change in values from one step to the next is $O(1/j)$ so we can define smooth functions $X(\lambda), Z(\lambda)$ with $\lambda = h/j$ and the relation of values from one step to the next becomes a pair of differential equations for X and Z.

Asymptotic Behavior

For most phase parameter choices, numerical solution of the differential equations have $|X|$ and $|Z|$ nonzero for all steps, i.e., for $0 \leq \lambda \leq 1$. In such cases, the dominant states have a nonzero fraction of uncolored variables and conflicting

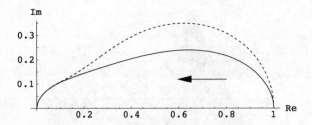

Figure 3: Behavior of $X(\lambda)$ (solid) and $Z(\lambda)$ (dashed) in the complex plane as λ ranges from 0 to 1. The initial condition is $X(0) = Z(0) = 1$ and both values approach 0 along the positive imaginary axis as $\lambda \to 1$. The parameters are $R_0 = 2.5467$, $R_1 = -2.1200$, $S_0 = 2.2521$, $S_1 = -1.1162$, $T_0 = 0.6531$ and $T_1 = 1.1759$. The arrow indicates direction of change along the curves as λ increases.

edges. However, for given μ, numerical evaluation identifies some phase parameters giving $X(1) = Z(1) = 0$. In this case, the discrete algorithm steps give final values for X, Z of size $O(1/j)$, which for $j \gg \sqrt{n}$ predicts the dominant states have the numbers of uncolored nodes and conflicts going to zero as n increases, so $P_{\text{soln}} \approx 1$ giving overall cost of $O(j)$ steps which is polynomial in n.

Fig. 3 shows the behavior for one such set of parameters. For small graphs, Fig. 1 shows the performance of the algorithm with these parameters and using the optimal number of steps for each n. That is, we examined the behavior for a few different values of j, in the range $n/2$ to n, and show the values giving the minimum median cost, i.e., j/P_{soln}. This gives $j = 4$ for $n = 5$, $j = 5$ for $n = 6, \ldots, 8$ and $j = 6$ for $n = 9, \ldots, 12$. Thus the best choice of j appears to grow somewhat slower than $j = O(\sqrt{n})$, a behavior also seen with solving SAT problems [14]. As one might expect, performance is worse than when using parameters optimized for small graphs. More significantly, the small sizes preclude a good evaluation of the asymptotic scaling behavior and the accuracy of the mean-field approximation.

By contrast, the unstructured search algorithm [10] gives a similar high concentration of amplitude in solutions but only after exponentially many steps. However, this result for the unstructured algorithm is exact, unlike the approximate evaluation of the heuristic method discussed here.

Discussion

Although the analysis predicts polynomial average cost, the accuracy of the mean-field approximation is an open question. Since the derivation requires $\sqrt{n} \gg 1$, empirical evaluation, limited to $n \approx 10$, does not effectively test the prediction. Nevertheless, this discussion indicates the possibility for polynomial average cost with suitable tuned parameters. The phase parameters giving $X(1) = Z(1) = 0$ according to the approximate theory are not unique and the number of steps, j, could be any power of n without precluding polynomial cost. With further analysis one could estimate the approximation error and select from among these possibilities those with the smallest error estimate. More broadly, instead of using only one choice for algorithm parameters, a portfolio of several choices gives better tradeoffs between expected performance and its variance [18].

Our mixing matrix uses the 2-bit distance, matching the structure of our problem representation. One could also try mixing matrices less directly connected to the structure. For instance, mixing based on the Hamming distance performs only slightly worse (with separately optimized parameters). Unstructured search [2] also shows this behavior. In our case, this can be understood from the heuristic's reliance on the correlation between state costs and distance, particularly for nearby states. The 2-bit and Hamming distances are strongly correlated for nearby states, leading to similar values for the mixing matrix. This highlights the possibility of designing algorithms based on matrices matching problem structure while still being free to use other matrices for the actual implementation, provided they have similar behaviors for nearby states. This flexibility may simplify eventual hardware implementations.

Our algorithm uses quantum coherence for only one trial at a time, reducing required hardware capabilities compared to the unstructured algorithm's need for exponentially long coherence. However, if sufficiently long coherence times become available, amplitude amplification operating on our algorithm gives a quadratic speedup to the results reported here [2]. In either case, algorithms using problem structure make significantly better use of the quantum machine.

In summary, we presented a quantum algorithm based on a generalized Hamming distance and using a simple representation including unassigned values. These features allow the algorithm to exploit more structure available in graph coloring than is possible by mapping it to satisfiability. Our approximate analysis for average behavior of large problems indicates the algorithm performs well by relying on statistical regularities throughout the search space. A definitive evaluation of this possibility for random and more structured graphs is an important open problem. More generally, this work illustrates how knowledge of problem structure from studies of CSPs can be incorporated in new quantum algorithms.

References

[1] Charles H. Bennett, Ethan Bernstein, Gilles Brassard, and Umesh V. Vazirani. Strengths and weaknesses of quantum computing. *SIAM Journal on Computing*, 26:1510–1523, 1997.

[2] Gilles Brassard, Peter Hoyer, and Alain Tapp. Quantum counting. In K. Larsen, editor, *Proc. of 25th Intl. Colloquium on Automata, Languages, and Programming (ICALP98)*, pages 820–831, Berlin, 1998. Springer. Los Alamos preprint quant-ph/9805082.

[3] Daniel Brelaz. New methods to color the vertices of a graph. *Communications of the ACM*, 22(4):251–256, 1979.

[4] Peter Cheeseman, Bob Kanefsky, and William M. Taylor. Where the really hard problems are. In J. Mylopoulos and R. Reiter, editors, *Proceedings of IJCAI91*, pages 331–337, San Mateo, CA, 1991. Morgan Kaufmann.

[5] D. Deutsch. Quantum theory, the Church-Turing principle and the universal quantum computer. *Proc. R. Soc. London A*, 400:97–117, 1985.

[6] Edward Farhi et al. A quantum adiabatic evolution algorithm applied to random instances of an NP-complete problem. *Science*, 292:472–476, 2001.

[7] Richard P. Feynman. *Feynman Lectures on Computation*. Addison-Wesley, Reading, MA, 1996.

[8] Ian P. Gent, Ewan MacIntyre, Patrick Prosser, and Toby Walsh. The constrainedness of search. In *Proc. of the 13th Natl. Conf. on Artificial Intelligence (AAAI96)*, pages 246–252, Menlo Park, CA, 1996. AAAI Press.

[9] Matthew L. Ginsberg. Dynamic backtracking. In Haym Hirsh et al., editors, *AAAI Spring Symposium on AI and NP-Hard Problems*, pages 64–70. AAAI, 1993.

[10] Lov K. Grover. Quantum mechanics helps in searching for a needle in a haystack. *Physical Review Letters*, 78:325–328, 1997. Los Alamos preprint quant-ph/9706033.

[11] Lov K. Grover. Quantum search on structured problems. *Chaos, Solitons, and Fractals*, 10:1695–1705, 1999.

[12] Tad Hogg. Exploiting problem structure as a search heuristic. *Intl. J. of Modern Physics C*, 9:13–29, 1998.

[13] Tad Hogg. Quantum search heuristics. *Physical Review A*, 61:052311, 2000. Preprint at publish.aps.org/eprint/gateway/eplist/aps1999oct19_002.

[14] Tad Hogg. Solving random satisfiability problems with quantum computers. Los Alamos preprint quant-ph/0104048, 2001.

[15] Tad Hogg, Carlos Mochon, Eleanor Rieffel, and Wolfgang Polak. Tools for quantum algorithms. *Intl. J. of Modern Physics C*, 10:1347–1361, 1999. Los Alamos preprint quant-ph/9811073.

[16] Tad Hogg and Dmitriy Portnov. Quantum optimization. *Information Sciences*, 128:181–197, 2000. Los Alamos preprint quant-ph/0006090.

[17] Eric Horvitz et al. A Bayesian approach to tackling hard computational problems. In *Proc. of the 17th Conference on Uncertainty and Artificial Intelligence*, 2001.

[18] Sebastian M. Maurer, Tad Hogg, and Bernardo A. Huberman. Portfolios of quantum algorithms. *Physical Review Letters*, 87:257901, 2001. Los Alamos preprint quant-ph/0105071.

[19] Remi Monasson, Riccardo Zecchina, Scott Kirkpatrick, Bart Selman, and Lidror Troyansky. Determining computational complexity from characteristic "phase transitions". *Nature*, 400:133–137, 1999.

[20] Manfred Opper and David Saad, editors. *Advanced Mean Field Methods: Theory and Practice*. MIT Press, Cambridge, MA, 2001.

[21] Peter W. Shor. Algorithms for quantum computation: Discrete logarithms and factoring. In S. Goldwasser, editor, *Proc. of the 35th Symposium on Foundations of Computer Science*, pages 124–134, Los Alamitos, CA, November 1994. IEEE Press.

[22] George W. Snedecor and William G. Cochran. *Statistical Methods*. Iowa State Univ. Press, Ames, Iowa, 6th edition, 1967.

[23] Colin P. Williams and Tad Hogg. Exploiting the deep structure of constraint problems. *Artificial Intelligence*, 70:73–117, 1994.

Reducing Search Space in Local Search for Constraint Satisfaction

H. Fang[*] and **Y. Kilani**[†] and **J.H.M. Lee**[†] and **P.J. Stuckey**[‡]

Abstract

Typically local search methods for solving constraint satisfaction problems such as GSAT, WalkSAT and DLM treat the problem as an optimization problem. Each constraint contributes part of a penalty function in assessing trial valuations. Local search examines the neighbours of the current valuation, using the penalty function to determine a "better" neighbour valuations to move to, until finally a solution which satisfies all constraints is found.

In this paper we investigate using some of the constraints, rather than as part of a penalty function, as "hard" constraints, that are always satisfied by every trial valuation visited. In this way the constraints reduce the possible neighbours in each move and also the overall search space.

The treating of some constraints as hard requires that the space of valuations that are satisfied is connected in order to guarantee that a solution can be found from any starting position within the region. Treating some constraints as hard also provides difficulties for the search mechanism since the search space becomes more jagged, and there are more deep local minima. A new escape strategy is needed.

We show in this paper how, for DIMACS translations of binary CSPs, treating some constraints as hard can significantly improve search performance of the DLM local search method.

Keywords: SAT, local search, binary CSP.

Introduction

A *constraint satisfaction problem* (CSP) (Mackworth 1977) is a tuple (Z, D, C), where Z is a finite set of variables, D defines a finite set D_x, called the *domain* of x, for each $x \in Z$, and C is a finite set of constraints restricting the combination of values that the variables can take. A *solution* is an assignment of values from the domains to their respective variables so that all constraints are satisfied simultaneously. CSPs are well-known to be NP-hard in general.

Local search techniques, for example GSAT (Selman, Levesque, & Mitchell 1992), WalkSAT (Selman & Kautz 1993; Selman, Kautz, & Cohen 1994), DLM (Wu & Wah 1999; 2000), the min-conflicts heuristic (Minton *et al.* 1992), and GENET (Davenport *et al.* 1994), have been successful in solving large constraint satisfaction problems. In the context of constraint satisfaction, local search first generates an initial variable assignment (or state) before making local adjustments (or repairs) to the assignment iteratively until a solution is reached. Local search algorithms can be trapped in a *local minimum*, a non-solution state in which no further improvement can be made. To help escape from the local minimum, GSAT and the min-conflicts heuristic use random restart, while Davenport *et al.* (1994), Morris (1993), and DLM modify the landscape of the search surface. Following Morris, we call these *breakout methods*. WalkSAT introduces noise into the search procedure so as to avoid and escape from local minima.

Local search algorithms traverse the search surface of a usually enormous search space to look for solutions using some heuristic function. The efficiency of a local search algorithm depends on three things: (1) the size of the search space (the number of variables and the size of the domain of each variable), (2) the search surface (the structure of each constraint and the topology of the constraint connection), and (3) the heuristic function (the definition of neighbourhood and how a "good" neighbour is picked). We propose the *Island Confinement Method* which aims to reduce the size of the search space. The method is based on a simple observation: a solution of a CSP P must lie in the intersection of the solution space of all constraints of P. Solving a CSP thus amounts to locating this intersection space, which could be either points or regions scattered around in the entire search space. In addition, the solution space of any subset of constraints in P must enclose all solutions of P. The idea of our method is thus to identify a suitable subset of constraints in P so that the solution space of the subset is "connected," and then restrict our search in only this region for solutions. By connectedness, we mean the ability to move from one point to any other point within the region without moving out of the region. Therefore, we are guaranteed that searching within this confined space will not cause

---

[*]Department of Computer Science Yale University New Haven, CT 06520-8285 USA. Email: hai.fang@yale.edu

[†]Department of Computer Science and Engineering, The Chinese University of Hong Kong, Shatin, N.T., Hong Kong, China. Email: {ykilani,jlee}@cse.cuhk.edu.hk

[‡]Department of Computer Science and Software Engineering, University of Melbourne, Parkville 3052, Australia. Email: pjs@cs.mu.oz.au

us to miss any solutions. The entire search space is trivially such a region but we would like to do better.

In this paper we illustrate one method for choosing a subset of the problem constraints which defines an island of connected solutions. We then show how, on encodings of binary CSPs into SAT problems, we can use this method to define an island that incorporates many of the problem constraints.

The introductions of island constraints complicates the search procedure because it may defeat the local minima escaping strategy of the underlying search procedure. We show how to modify DLM, a very competitive local search procedure for SAT problems so that it handles island constraints, and give empirical results showing where the island confinement method can give substantial improvements in solving some classes of SAT problems.

Background and Definitions

Given a CSP (Z, D, C). We use $var(c)$ to denote the set of variables that occur in constraint $c \in C$. If $|var(c)| = 2$ then c is a *binary* constraint. In a *binary CSP* each constraint $c \in C$ is binary. A *valuation* for variable set $\{x_1, \ldots, x_n\} \subseteq Z$ is a mapping from variables to values denoted $\{x_1 \mapsto a_1, \ldots, x_n \mapsto a_n\}$ where $a_i \in D_{x_i}$.

A *state* of problem (Z, D, C) (or simply C) is a valuation for Z (where $Z = \cup_{c \in C} var(c)$). A state s is a *solution* of a constraint c if s makes c true. A state s is a *solution* of a CSP (Z, D, C) if s is a solution to all constraints in C simultaneously.

SAT

SAT problems are a special case of CSPs. A *(propositional) variable* can take the value of either 0 (false) or 1 (true). A *literal* is either a variable x or its complement $\bar{x}$. A literal l is *true* if l assumes the value 1; l is *false* otherwise. A *clause* is a disjunction of literals, which is true when one of its literals is true. For simplicity we assume that no literal appears in a clause more than once, and no literal and its negation appear in a clause (which would then be trivial). A *satisfiability problem (SAT)* consists of a finite set of clauses (treated as a conjunction). Let $\bar{l}$ denote the complement of literal l: $\bar{l} = \bar{x}$ if $l = x$, and $\bar{l} = x$ if $l = \bar{x}$. Let $\bar{L} = \{\bar{l} \mid l \in L\}$ for a literal set L.

Since we are dealing with SAT problems we will often treat states as sets of literals. A state $\{x_1 \mapsto a_1, \ldots, x_n \mapsto a_n\}$ corresponds to the set of literals $\{x_j \mid a_j = 1\} \cup \{\bar{x}_j \mid a_j = 0\}$.

Local Search

A local search solver moves from one state to another using a local move. We define the *neighbourhood* $n(s)$ of a state s to be all the states that are reachable in a single move from state s. The neighbourhood states are meant to represent all the states reachable in one move, independent of the actual heuristic function used to choose which state to move to.

For the purpose of this paper, where we are interested in SAT problems, we assume the neighbourhood function $n(s)$ returns the states which are at a Hamming distance of 1 from the starting state s. The *Hamming distance* between states s_1 and s_2 is defined as

$$d_h(s_1, s_2) = |s_1 - (s_1 \cap s_2)| = |s_2 - (s_1 \cap s_2)|.$$

In other words, the Hamming distance measures the number of differences in variable assignment of s_1 and s_2. This neighbourhood reflects the usual kind of local move in SAT solvers: *flipping* a variable. In abuse of terminology we will also refer to flipping a literal l which simply means flipping the variable occurring in the literal.

A *local move* from state s is a transition, $s \Rightarrow s'$, from s to $s' \in n(s)$. A *local search procedure* consists of at least the following components:

- a neighbourhood function n for all states;
- a heuristic function b that determines the "best" possible local move $s \Rightarrow s'$ for the current state s; and
- possibly an optional "breakout" procedure to help escape from local minima.

We note that the notion of noise that has appeared in some solvers, such as WalkSAT (Selman & Kautz 1993; Selman, Kautz, & Cohen 1994), can be incorporated into the heuristic function b. We also decouple the notion of neighbourhood from the heuristic function since they are orthogonal to each other, although they are mixed together in the description of a local move in GSAT, WalkSAT, and others.

Island Constraints

We introduce the notion of island constraints, the solution space of which is connected in the following sense. Central to a local search algorithm is the definition of the neighbourhood of a state since each local move can only be made to a state in the neighbourhood of the current state. We say that a constraint is an *island constraint* if we can move between any two states in the constraint's solution space using a finite sequence of local moves without moving out of the solution space.

Let $sol(C)$ denote the set of all solutions to a set of constraints C, in other words the *solution space* of C. A set of constraints C is an *island* if, for any two states $s_0, s_n \in sol(C)$, there exist states $s_1, \ldots, s_{n-1} \in sol(C)$ such that $s_i \Rightarrow s_{i+1}$ for all $i \in \{0, \ldots, n-1\}$. That is we can move from any solution of C to any other solution using local moves that stay within the solution space of C.

We give a simple sufficient condition for when a set C of clauses results in an island. Let $lit(c)$ denote the set of all literals of a clause c. Let $lit(C) = \cup_{c \in C} lit(c)$. A set C of clauses is *non-conflicting* if there does not exist a variable x such that $x, \bar{x} \in lit(C)$.

Theorem 1 *A non-conflicting set C of clauses forms an island.*

Proof: Since C is non-conflicting $lit(C)$ can be extended to a state (it does not have both a literal and its complement). Any state $s \supseteq lit(C)$ clearly satisfies C. We show by induction that for any state s_0 satisfying C there is a path $s_0 \Rightarrow s_1 \Rightarrow \cdots \Rightarrow s_n = s$ where each s_i satisfies C. Since a path is reversible, there is a path between any two solutions

s_0 and s'_0 of C via s and hence C is an island. Let l be an arbitrary literal where s_i and s differ, that is $l \in s_i$ and $\bar{l} \in s$. Then $l \notin lit(C)$ and clearly $s_{i+1} = s_i - \{l\} \cup \{\bar{l}\}$ satisfies C since l does not occur in C and hence cannot be the only literal satisfying one of the clauses of C. □

We can map any CSP (Z, D, C) to a SAT problem, $SAT(Z, D, C)$. We illustrate the method for binary CSPs, which we will restrict our attention to, as follows.

- Every CSP variable $x \in Z$ is mapped to a set of propositional variables $\{x_{a_1}, \ldots, x_{a_n}\}$ where $D_x = \{a_1, \ldots, a_n\}$.

- For every $x \in Z$, $SAT(Z, D, C)$ contains the clause $x_{a_1} \vee \cdots \vee x_{a_n}$, which ensures that the any solution to the SAT problem gives a value to x.

- Each binary constraint $c \in C$ with $var(c) = \{x, y\}$ is mapped to a series of clauses. If $\{x \mapsto a \wedge y \mapsto a'\}$ is not a solution of c we add the clause $\bar{x}_a \vee \bar{y}_{a'}$ to $SAT(Z, D, C)$. This ensures that the constraint c holds in any solution to the SAT problem.

The above formulation allows the possibility that in a solution, some CSP variable x is assigned two values. Choosing either value is guaranteed to solve the original CSP. This method is used in the encoding of CSPs into SAT in the DIMACS archive.

When a binary CSP (Z, D, C) is translated to a SAT problem $SAT(Z, D, C)$ each clause has the form $\bar{x} \vee \bar{y}$ except for a single clause for each variable in Z. *The first class of clauses forms a non-conflicting set trivially.*

The Island Confinement Method in DLM

DLM (Wu & Wah 1999) is a discrete Lagrange-multiplier-based local-search method for solving SAT problems, which are first transformed into a discrete constrained optimization problem. Experiments confirm that the discrete Lagrange multiplier method is highly competitive with other SAT solving methods.

We will consider a SAT problem as a vector of clauses $\vec{c}$ (which we will often also treat as a set). Each clause c is treated as a penalty function on states, so $c(s) = 0$ if state s satisfies constraint c, and $c(s) = 1$ otherwise. DLM performs a search for a saddle point of the Lagrangian function

$$L(s, \vec{\lambda}) = \vec{\lambda} \cdot \vec{c}(s) \quad (\text{that is } \Sigma_i \lambda_i \times c_i(s))$$

where $\vec{\lambda}$ are Lagrange multipliers, one for each constraint, which give the "penalty" for violating that constraint. The saddle point search changes the state to decrease the Lagrangian function, or increase the Lagrange multipliers.

The core of the DLM algorithm can be extracted from Figure 1, by considering only lines without the "|" mark in addition to three slight modifications. First, the input to DLM is simply a set of clauses $\vec{c}$. Second, in the second line, s should be initialized to any random valuation for $var(\vec{c})$. Third, all occurrences of $\vec{c}_r$ and $\vec{\lambda}_r$ should be changed to $\vec{c}$ and $\vec{\lambda}$ respectively. Although DLM does not appear to examine all the neighbours at Hamming distance 1 in

each move, this is an artifact of mixing of the description of neighbourhood and the heuristic functions. Since only literals appearing in unsatisfied clauses (*unsat*) can decrease the Lagrangian function, (the heuristic function of) the DLM algorithm chooses to always ignore/discard neighbours resulting from flipping a variable not in one of these literals. We say such neighbours are *invalid*. The full DLM algorithm also includes a tabu list and methods for updating Lagrange multipliers; see (Wu & Wah 2000) for details.

Handling island constraints is simple at first glance. Given a problem defined by a set of clauses $\vec{c}_i \wedge \vec{c}_r$ partitioned into island constraints $\vec{c}_i$ and remaining clauses $\vec{c}_r$, we simply modify the algorithm to treat the remaining clauses as penalty functions and give an initial valuation s which is a solution of $\vec{c}_i$. For $SAT(Z, D, C)$, $\vec{c}_i$ consists of clauses of the form $\bar{x} \vee \bar{y}$. An arbitrary extension of $lit(\vec{c}_i)$ to all variables can always be such an initial valuation. We exclude literals $l \in unsat$ from flipping when $s' = s - \{\bar{l}\} \cup \{l\}$ does not satisfy $\vec{c}_i$. Hence we only examine states that are adjacent to s and satisfy $\vec{c}_i$. Let $n(s, \vec{c}_i) = \{s' \in n(s) \mid s' \in sol(\vec{c}_i)\}$. The rest of the algorithm remains unchanged. *A new problem arises.*

Example 1 Suppose we have the following clauses, where $\vec{c}_i = (c_1, c_2, c_3)$ and $\vec{c}_r = (c_4, c_5)$.

c_1	: $\bar{x}_1 \vee \bar{x}_4$	c_4	: $x_1 \vee x_2 \vee x_3$
c_2	: $\bar{x}_2 \vee \bar{x}_5$	c_5	: $x_4 \vee x_5$
c_3	: $\bar{x}_3 \vee \bar{x}_5$		

and the current state is $\{x_1, x_2, \bar{x}_3, \bar{x}_4, \bar{x}_5\}$, which satisfies c_1, c_2, c_3 and c_4. Three neighbours satisfy the island clauses c_1, c_2 and c_3: $\{\bar{x}_1, x_2, \bar{x}_3, \bar{x}_4, \bar{x}_5\}$, $\{x_1, \bar{x}_2, \bar{x}_3, \bar{x}_4, \bar{x}_5\}$, and $\{x_1, x_2, x_3, \bar{x}_4, \bar{x}_5\}$, all of which are invalid. Whatever the Lagrange multipliers for c_4 and c_5 is, none of the neighbours will be better than the current state. Hence DLM will always remain in this state no matter how the Lagrange multipliers are updated (in fact it will never consider the invalid moves), and cannot escape from this local minima. We call this an island trap. □

More formally an *island trap* for a problem $\vec{c}_i \wedge \vec{c}_r$ is a state s such that for all states $s' \in n(s, \vec{c}_i)$ whatever the value of the Lagrange multipliers $\vec{\lambda}_r$ no neighbour would be better than s, i.e. $\forall s' \in n(s, \vec{c}_i) \ \forall \vec{\lambda}_r > 0 \ L(s', \vec{\lambda}_r) \geq L(s, \vec{\lambda}_r)$. This holds if and only if $\{c \in \vec{c}_r \mid s \in sol(\{c\})\} \supseteq \{c \in \vec{c}_r \mid s' \in sol(\{c\})\}$ for all $s' \in n(s, \vec{c}_i)$.

In order to escape from an island trap, we need to flip some variable(s) to make uphill or flat move(s). We aim to stay as close to the current valuation as possible, but change to a state s' where at least one variable x, which cannot be flipped in the current state s since it would go outside of the island, can now be flipped in s'.

Let $makes(l, s, \vec{c}_i) = \{c \in \vec{c}_i \mid (s - \{l\} \cup \{\bar{l}\}) \notin sol(\{c\})\}$ be the island constraints that are satisfied in the current valuation s only by the literal l. If $makes(l, s, \vec{c}_i)$ is non-empty then we cannot flip the literal l in the current state without going outside the island.

Let $freeme(l, s, \vec{c}_i) = \{l' \mid (l \vee l') \in makes(l, s, \vec{c}_i)\}$ be the set of literals that need to be made true in order that we can flip literal l to $\bar{l}$, and stay within the island.

The base island trap escaping strategy we propose is thus: choose the literal l in an unsatisfied clause in $\vec{c}_r$ according to state s such that $|freeme(\bar{l}, s, \vec{c}_i)| > 0$ and minimal in size, and flip all literals in $freeme(\bar{l}, s, \vec{c}_i)$ and then continue. Note that we do not actually flip the literal l. We only move to a state where l can be flipped. In this state, however, we may find it preferable to flip another literal.

Example 2 Continuing Example 1, we find that in state $s = \{x_1, x_2, \bar{x}_3, \bar{x}_4, \bar{x}_5\}$, the unsatisfied clause is $x_4 \vee x_5$. Now $makes(\bar{x}_4, s, \vec{c}_i) = \{c_1\}$, and $makes(\bar{x}_5, s, \vec{c}_i) = \{c_2\}$. In addition $freeme(\bar{x}_4, s, \vec{c}_i) = \{\bar{x}_1\}$, and $freeme(\bar{x}_5, s, \vec{c}_i) = \{\bar{x}_2\}$. Suppose we choose randomly to free $\bar{x}_4$, then we flip all the literals in its freeme set ($\bar{x}_1$) obtaining the new state $\{\bar{x}_1, x_2, \bar{x}_3, \bar{x}_4, \bar{x}_5\}$. We can now flip $\bar{x}_4$ while staying in the island and also arriving at the solution $\{\bar{x}_1, x_2, \bar{x}_3, x_4, \bar{x}_5\}$. □

Unfortunately the simple strategy of simply flipping the minimal number of literals to make a currently unflippable literal (since it would go outside the island) flippable is not enough. It is easy for the local search to end up back in the same state, by choosing to reverse all the flips made to escape the trap. In order to prevent this we add an additional tabu list, $tabulit$, of length 1, to cope with the most common case that $freeme$ is of size 1. Unlike the regular tabu list, the literal in $tabulit$ is not allowed to be flipped under any circumstances (variables in the DLM tabu list can be flipped if the move is downhill). In order to get out of very deep traps, we occasionally need to flip many variables. To make this happen we add a parameter P which gives the probability of picking a literal to free which requires more than the minimal number of flips to free.

The DLM algorithm modified for islands (DLMI) is shown in Figure 1. Lines beginning in "|" are either different from their counterparts in the original DLM algorithm or new additions. For DLMI there are only Lagrange multipliers $\vec{\lambda}_r$ for the non-island clauses $\vec{c}_r$. A random valuation that satisfies the island clauses $\vec{c}_i$ is chosen (since $\vec{c}_i$ is non-conflicting this is straightforward). The candidate literals for flipping are restricted to those that maintain satisfiability of the island clauses and are not the literal in $tabulit$. If there are candidates then we proceed as in DLM; otherwise we are in an island trap. Note that $tabulit$ has introduced another kind of island trap where no flip will satisfy more clauses except flipping the literal in $tabulit$, which is disallowed. This trap is handled identically to the original island trap.

In an island trap we consider the literals ($free$) in the unsatisfied clauses which could not be flipped without breaking an island constraint. Note that $free \neq \emptyset$ otherwise we have a solution. We separate these into those requiring 1 other literal to be flipped to free them ($free\_1$), and those requiring two or more ($free\_2$). If the random number is greater than parameter P we choose a literal in $free\_2$ to free, and flip all the variables required to free it. Otherwise we choose, if possible, a variable in $free\_1$ whose $freeme$ is not the literal in $tabulit$ and flip the literal in that set.

Note that in both cases, the selection of l, the literal to free, may fail. In the first case when $free\_2$ is empty, in which case we perform nothing relying on randomness to

```
DLMI(c⃗_i, c⃗_r)
|  let s ∈ sol(c⃗_i) be a random valuation for var(c⃗_i ∪ c⃗_r)
   λ⃗_r = 1 %% a vector of 1s
|  tabulit := ∅
   while (L(s, λ⃗_r) > 0)
     unsat := ∪{lit(c) | c ∈ c⃗_r, s ∉ sol({c})}
|    candidate := {l ∈ unsat | (s − {l̄} ∪ {l}) ∈ sol(c⃗_i)}
|    if (candidate − tabulit ≠ ∅)
       %% not an island trap
       min := L(s, λ⃗_r)
       best := {s}
|      s_old := s
|      foreach literal l ∈ candidate − tabulit
         s' := s − {l̄} ∪ {l}
         if (L(s', λ⃗_r) < min)
           min := L(s', λ⃗_r)
           best := {s'}
         else if (L(s', λ⃗_r) = min)
           best := best ∪ {s'}
       s := a randomly chosen element of best
       %% a singleton set
|      tabulit := (s = s_old ? tabulit : s_old − s)
|    else %% island trap
|      free := unsat − candidate
|      free_1 := {l ∈ free | |freeme(l̄, s, c⃗_i)| = 1}
|      free_2 := free − free_1
|      r := random number between 0 and 1
|      if (free_1 = ∅ or r < P)
         %% free arbitrary literal
|        l := a randomly chosen element of free_2
|        s := s − ‾freeme(l̄, s, c⃗_i) ∪ freeme(l̄, s, c⃗_i)
|        tabulit := ∅
|      else if (free_1 ≠ ∅ and
|              ∪_{l∈free_1} freeme(l, s, c⃗_i) = tabulit)
|        %% fixed value detected
|        fix the value of the variable in tabulit
|      else %% free literal requiring single flip
|        l := a randomly chosen element of free_1
|            where freeme(l̄, s, c⃗_i) ≠ tabulit
|        s := s − ‾freeme(l̄, s, c⃗_i) ∪ freeme(l̄, s, c⃗_i)
|        tabulit := freeme(l̄, s, c⃗_i)
     if (Lagrange multipliers update condition holds)
       λ⃗_r := λ⃗_r + c⃗_r(s)
   return s
```

Figure 1: DLMI

eventually choose the other case. In the second case it may be that *every* literal in $free\_1$ has its freeme set equal to $tabulit$. In this case we have detected that $tabulit$ must hold, and we can eliminate the variable involved by unit resolution. In our code this is performed, we could avoid it by simplifying the original SAT formulation so that all such occurrences are removed, using SAT simplification methods such as (Brafman 2000).

Example 3 Modifying clause c_2 in Example 1 slightly.

$$
\begin{array}{llll}
c_1 & : & \bar{x}_1 \lor \bar{x}_4 & \qquad c_4 & : & x_1 \lor x_2 \lor x_3 \\
c_2 & : & \bar{x}_1 \lor \bar{x}_5 & \qquad c_5 & : & x_4 \lor x_5 \\
c_3 & : & \bar{x}_3 \lor \bar{x}_5 &
\end{array}
$$

We are in state $s = \{x_1, x_2, \bar{x}_3, \bar{x}_4, \bar{x}_5\}$ and $tabulit$ is $\{\bar{x}_1\}$. The literals in unsatisfied clauses are $unsat = \{x_4, x_5\}$, and $candidate = \emptyset$ since neither literal can be flipped. Hence $free = \{x_4, x_5\}$. Both of these literals are placed in $free\_1$, since $freeme(\bar{x}_4, s, \vec{c}_i) = freeme(\bar{x}_5, s, \vec{c}_i) = \{\bar{x}_1\}$. The selection of a literal l in $free\_1$ will fail. This provides a proof that $\{\bar{x}_1\}$ must hold in any solution of $\vec{c}_i \land \vec{c}$. We have $x_4 \lor x_5 \in \vec{c}$ and $\bar{x}_1 \lor \bar{x}_4$ and $\bar{x}_1 \lor \bar{x}_5$ in $\vec{c}_i$, then by resolution we obtain $\bar{x}_1$. In the context of CSP, x_1 corresponds to a value in the domain of a CSP variable (say u) which is incompatible with the two (all) values in the domain of the other CSP variable (say v). That is why the domain value of u corresponding to x_1 is arc inconsistent with respect to the constraint involving u and v. Fixing x_1 to 0 means removing the value from the domain of u. □

Experiments

We implemented DLMI by modifying the code of distribution of SAT-DLM-2000,[1] maintaining all the extra parts such as the tabu list, and penalty updating methods unchanged. We compare DLMI with DLM using the best parameter settings for DLM of the five (Wu & Wah 2000) included in the distribution. For the additional parameter P which we introduce, we use the setting 0.3 which performs the best overall. The results presented were obtained using a PC with Pentium III 800 Mhz and 256 MB memory.

Table 1 shows the comparison of DLM and DLMI on N-queens problems and a suite of binary CSPs from (Choi, Lee, & Stuckey 2000). We first transform the problem instances into SAT. Of the clauses in all instances, over 99% are island clauses. For each set of benchmark instances, we give the parameter settings (PS) from SAT-DLM-2000 used for DLM and also DLMI. Runs failing to find solution in one hour are aborted. The table shows number of variables (Vars), and number of clauses (Cls) in the SAT formulation, then the success ratio, average solution time (in seconds) and average flips on solved instances for DLM and DLMI.

DLMI shows substantial improvement over DLM using the same parameter set on the test suite. Generally DLMI traverses a smaller search space and needs to do less maintenance for island clauses and this is a significant saving. In many cases DLMI is one to two orders of magnitude better than DLM. DLMI is bettered marginally by DLM only in the hard graph coloring problem g125n-17c. DLMI is also slightly less robust in success rate with the phase transition random CSPs. This occurs because the search surface is now considerably more jagged. DLMI might appear to use more flips than DLM in a few cases, but many flips are used in escaping from island traps, and these are considerably cheaper since they do not require any computation of the Lagrangian function values.

---

[1]Downloadable from `http://www.manip.crhc.uiuc.edu/Wah/programs/SAT_DLM_2000.tar.gz`.

Conclusion

The island concept can significantly reduce the search space of a local search procedure, by treating some constraints as "hard" so that they are never violated during search process. We have shown one instance where we can define an island which encompasses a large part of the constraints in a problem: SAT formulations of binary CSPs. Interestingly in this case it corresponds to a local search on the original CSP where some CSP variables may not have values, but all constraints are always satisfied. We believe there is plenty of scope for using the island concept to improve other local search algorithms, such as WalkSAT and others. The difficulty lies in building an adequate island trap escaping strategy.

Acknowledgements

We thank the anonymous referees for constructive comments. The work described in this paper was substantially supported by a grant from the Research Grants Council of the Hong Kong Special Administrative Region (Project no. CUHK4204/01E).

References

Brafman, R. I. 2000. A simplifier for propositional formulas with many binary clauses. Technical report, Dept. of Computer Science, Ben-Gurion University.

Choi, K.; Lee, J.; and Stuckey, P. 2000. A Lagrangian reconstruction of GENET. *AI* 123:1–39.

Davenport, A.; Tsang, E.; Wang, C.; and Zhu, K. 1994. GENET: A connectionist architecture for solving constraint satisfaction problems by iterative improvement. In *Proc. AAAI-94*, 325–330.

Mackworth, A. K. 1977. Consistency in networks of relations. *AI* 8(1):99–118.

Minton, S.; Johnston, M. D.; Philips, A. B.; and Laird, P. 1992. Minimizing conflicts: a heuristic repair method for constraint satisfaction and scheduling problems. *AI* 58:161–205.

Morris, P. 1993. The breakout method for escaping from local minima. In *Procs. of AAAI-93*, 40–45.

Selman, B., and Kautz, H. 1993. Domain-independent extensions to GSAT: Solving large structured satisfiability problems. In *Procs. of IJCAI-93*, 290–295.

Selman, B.; Kautz, H. A.; and Cohen, B. 1994. Noise strategies for improving local search. In *Procs. of AAAI-94*, 337–343. AAAI Press/MIT Press.

Selman, B.; Levesque, H.; and Mitchell, D. G. 1992. A new method for solving hard satisfiability problems. In *Procs. of AAAI-92*, 440–446. AAAI Press/MIT Press.

Wu, Z., and Wah, B. W. 1999. Trap escaping strategies in discrete lagrangian methods for solving hard satisfiability and maximum satisfiability problems. In *Procs. of AAAI-99*, 673–678.

Wu, Z., and Wah, B. W. 2000. An efficient global-search strategy in discrete lagrangian methods for solving hard satisfiability problems. In *Procs. of AAAI-2000*, 310–315.

Instance	Vars	Cls	DLM			DLMI		
			Succ	Time	Flip	Succ	Time	Flip
N queens problem: PS = 2								
10queen	100	1480	100/100	0.01	413	100/100	0.00	110
20queen	400	12560	100/100	0.03	300	100/100	0.01	116
50queen	2500	203400	100/100	4.68	1471	100/100	0.12	175
100queen	10000	1646800	100/100	154.18	5482	100/100	0.88	244
Random permutation generation problems: PS = 4								
pp50	2475	159138	20/20	4.75	1496	20/20	0.13	204
pp60	3568	279305	20/20	12.75	2132	20/20	0.24	308
pp70	4869	456129	20/20	28.33	2876	20/20	0.36	323
pp80	6356	660659	20/20	54.97	3607	20/20	0.49	308
pp90	8059	938837	20/20	98.87	4486	20/20	0.73	311
pp100	9953	1265776	20/20	164.6	5378	20/20	0.94	269
Increasing permutation generation problems: PS = 3								
ap10	121	671	20/20	0.54	38620	20/20	0.03	6446
ap20	441	4641	20/20	563.75	14369433	20/20	33.39	3266368
ap30	961	14911	0/20	—	—	0/20	—	—
ap40	1681	34481	0/20	—	—	0/20	—	—
ap50	2601	66351	0/20	—	—	0/20	—	—
Latin square problems: PS = 4								
magic-10	1000	9100	20/20	0.05	899	20/20	0.02	401
magic-15	3375	47475	20/20	2.75	3709	20/20	0.11	1706
magic-20	8000	152400	20/20	24.19	14218	20/20	0.52	6824
magic-25	15625	375625	*	*	*	20/20	2.53	25240
magic-30	27000	783900	*	*	*	20/20	60.23	513093
magic-35	42875	1458975	*	*	*	3/20	723.42	3773925
Hard graph-coloring problems: PS = 3								
g125n-18c	2250	70163	20/20	5.06	**7854**	20/20	0.81	15314
g250n-15c	3750	233965	20/20	15.96	**2401**	20/20	0.47	2815
g125n-17c	2125	66272	20/20	**146.93**	**797845**	20/20	188.61	4123124
g250n-29c	7250	454622	20/20	331.91	**334271**	20/20	128.81	867396
Tight random CSPs: PS = 4								
rcsp-120-10-60-75	1200	331445	20/20	9.73	4857	20/20	1.33	2919
rcsp-130-10-60-75	1300	389258	20/20	12.52	5420	20/20	1.30	2528
rcsp-140-10-60-75	1400	451702	20/20	16.07	6125	20/20	2.08	3682
rcsp-150-10-60-75	1500	518762	20/20	20.21	6426	20/20	1.44	2102
rcsp-160-10-60-75	1600	590419	20/20	25.75	7575	20/20	2.33	3306
rcsp-170-10-60-75	1700	666795	20/20	28.68	6760	20/20	2.56	3435
Phase transition CSPs: PS = 3								
rcsp-120-10-60-5.9	1200	25276	**20/20**	158.03	**1507786**	19/20	28.71	1909746
rcsp-130-10-60-5.5	1300	27670	**20/20**	875.67	7304724	16/20	103.92	6445009
rcsp-140-10-60-5.0	1400	29190	20/20	109.89	888545	20/20	14.07	850886
rcsp-150-10-60-4.7	1500	31514	**20/20**	613.62	**3966684**	19/20	90.71	5273978
rcsp-160-10-60-4.4	1600	33581	**20/20**	382.84	2244334	19/20	31.129	1695978
rcsp-170-10-60-4.1	1700	35338	**20/20**	293.8	1383200	19/20	24.17	131357
Slightly easier phase transition CSPs: PS = 3								
rcsp-120-10-60-5.8	1200	24848	**20/20**	47.67	**443665**	18/20	9.61	641175
rcsp-130-10-60-5.4	1300	27168	**20/20**	155.75	1242907	19/20	16.82	1062060
rcsp-140-10-60-4.9	1400	28605	20/20	43.68	319386	20/20	3.28	195881
rcsp-150-10-60-4.6	1500	30843	20/20	60.5	**422370**	20/20	8.47	499480
rcsp-160-10-60-4.3	1600	32818	20/20	112.58	**554154**	20/20	10.36	574386
rcsp-170-10-60-4.0	1700	34476	**20/20**	46.73	244413	19/20	3.74	197758

Table 1: Comparative empirical results DLM versus DLMI: "*" indicates a segmentation fault, and bold entries show when DLM betters DMLI.

Preference-based Search and Multi-criteria Optimization

Ulrich Junker

ILOG
1681, route des Dolines
F-06560 Valbonne
ujunker@ilog.fr

Abstract

Many real-world AI problems (e.g. in configuration) are weakly constrained, thus requiring a mechanism for characterizing and finding the preferred solutions. Preference-based search (PBS) exploits preferences between decisions to focus search to preferred solutions, but does not efficiently treat preferences on defined criteria such as the total price or quality of a configuration. We generalize PBS to compute balanced, extreme, and Pareto-optimal solutions for general CSP's, thus handling preferences on and between multiple criteria. A master-PBS selects criteria based on trade-offs and preferences and passes them as optimization objective to a sub-PBS that performs a constraint-based Branch-and-Bound search. We project the preferences of the selected criterion to the search decisions to provide a search heuristics and to reduce search effort, thus giving the criterion a high impact on the search. The resulting method will particularly be effective for CSP's with large domains that arise if configuration catalogs are large.

Keywords: preferences, nonmonotonic reasoning, constraint satisfaction, multi-criteria optimization, search.

Introduction

In this paper, we consider combinatorial problems that are weakly constrained and that lack a clear global optimization objective. Many real-world AI problems have these characteristics: examples can be found in configuration, design, diagnosis, but also in temporal reasoning and scheduling. An example for configuration is a vacation adviser system that chooses vacation destinations from a potentially very large catalog. Given user requirements (e.g. about desired vacation activities such as wind-surfing, canyoning), compatibility constraints between different destinations, and global 'resource' constraints (e.g. on price) usually still leave a large set of possible solutions. In spite of this, most of the solutions will be discarded as long as more interesting solutions are possible. Preferences on different choices and criteria are an adequate way to characterize the interesting solutions. For example, the user may prefer Hawaii to Florida for doing wind-surfing or prefer cheaper vacations in general.

Different methods for representing and treating preferences have been developed in different disciplines. In AI,

preferences are often treated in a qualitative way and specify an order between hypotheses, default rules, or decisions. Examples for this have been elaborated in nonmonotonic reasoning (Brewka 1989) and constraint satisfaction (Junker 2000). Here, preferences can be represented by a predicate or a constraint, which allows complex preference statements (e.g. dynamic preferences, soft preferences, meta-preferences and so on). Furthermore, preferences between search decisions also allow to express search heuristics and to reduce search effort for certain kinds of scheduling problems (Junker 2000).

In our vacation adviser example, the basic decisions consist in choosing one (or several) destinations and we can thus express preferences between individual destinations. However, the user preferences are usually formulated on global criteria such as the total price, quality, and distance which are defined in terms of the prices, qualities, and distances of all the chosen destinations. We thus obtain a multi-criteria optimization problem.

We could try to apply the preference-based search (Junker 2000) by choosing the values of the different criteria before choosing the destinations. However, this method has severe draw-backs:

1. Choosing the value of a defined criterion highly constrains the remaining search problem and usually leads to a thrashing behaviour.

2. The different criteria are minimized in a strict order. We get solutions that are optimal w.r.t. some lexicographic order, but none that represents compromises between the different criteria. E.g., the system may propose a cheap vacation of bad quality and an expensive vacation of good quality, but no compromise between price and quality.

Hence, a naive application of preferences between decisions to multi-criteria optimization problems can lead to thrashing and lacks a balancing mechanism.

Multi-criteria optimization avoids those problem. In Operations Research, a multi-criteria optimization problem is usually mapped to a single or a sequence of single-criterion optimization problems which are solved by traditional methods. Furthermore, there are several notions of optimality such as Pareto-optimality, lexicographic optimality, and lexicographic max-order optimality (Ehrgott 1997). We can thus determine 'extreme solutions' where one criteria is favoured to another criteria as well as 'balanced solutions' where the different criteria are as close together as possible and that represent compromises. This balancing requires that the different criteria are comparable, which is usually achieved by a standardization method. Surprisingly, the balancing is not achieved by weighted sums of the different criteria, but by a new lexicographic approach (Ehrgott 1997). In order to find a compromise between a good price and a good quality, Ehrgott first minimizes the maximum between (standardized versions of) price and quality, fixes one of the criteria (e.g. the standardized quality) at the resulting minimum, and then minimizes the other criterion (e.g. the price).

In this paper, we will develop a modified version of preference-based search that solves a minimization subproblem for finding the best value of a given criterion instead of trying out the different value assignments. Furthermore, we also show how to compute Pareto-optimal and balanced solutions with new versions of preference-based search.

Multi-criteria optimization as studied in Operations Research also has draw-backs. Qualitative preferences as elaborated in AI can help to address following issues:

1. We would like to state that certain criteria are more important than other criteria without choosing a total ranking of the criteria as required by lexicographic optimality. For example, we would like to state a preference between a small price and a high quality on the one hand and a small distance on the other hand, but we still would like to get a solution where the price is minimized first and a solution where the quality is maximized first.

2. Multi-criteria optimization specifies preferences on defined criteria, but it does not translates them to preferences between search decisions. In general, it is not evident how to automatically derive a search heuristics from the selected optimization objective. Adequate preferences between search decisions provide such a heuristics and also allow to apply preference-based search to reduce the search effort for the subproblem.

In order to address the first point, we compare the different notions of optimal solutions with the different notions of preferred solutions that have been elaborated in non-monotonic reasoning. If no preferences between criteria are given, the Pareto-optimal solutions correspond to the G-preferred solutions (Grosof 1991; Geffner & Pearl 1992; Junker 1997) and the lexicographic-optimal solutions correspond to the B-preferred solutions (Brewka 1989; Junker 1997). Preferences between criteria can easily be taken into account by the latter methods. For balanced solutions, we present a variant of Ehrgott's definition that respects preferences between criteria as well. The different versions of preference-based search will also respect these additional preferences. We thus obtain a system where the user can express preferences on the criteria and preferences between the criteria and choose between extreme solutions, balanced solutions and Pareto-optimal solutions.

As mentioned above, the new versions of preference-based search solve a minimization subproblem when determining the best value for a selected criterion. We would like to also use preference-based search for solving the sub-

problems. However, the preferences are only expressed on the criteria and not on the search decisions. It therefore is a natural idea to project the preferences on the selected criterion to the search decisions. We will introduce a general method for preference projection, which we then apply to usual objectives such as sum, min, max, and element constraints. It is important to note that these projected preferences will change from one subproblem to the other. The projected preferences will be used to guide the search and to reduce search effort. Depending on the projected preferences, completely different parts of the search space may be explored and, in particular, the first solution depends on the chosen objective. Search effort can be reduced since the projected preferences preserve Pareto-optimality. We therefore adapt the new preference-based search method for Pareto-optimal solutions for solving the subproblems.

The paper is organized as follows: we first introduce different notions of optimality from multi-criteria optimization and then extend them to cover preferences between criteria. After this, we develop new versions of preference-based search for computing the different kinds of preferred solutions. Finally, we introduce preference projection.

Preferred Solutions

We first introduce different notions of optimality from multi-criteria optimization and then link them to definitions of preferred solutions from nonmonotonic reasoning.

Preferences on Criteria

Throughout this paper, we consider combinatorial problems that have the decision variables $\mathcal{X} := (x_1, \ldots, x_m)$, the criteria $\mathcal{Z} := (z_1, \ldots, z_n)$, and the constraints $\mathcal{C}$. Each decision variable x_i has a domain $D(x_i)$ from which its values will be chosen. For example, x_i may represent the vacation destination in the i-th of $m = 3$ weeks. The constraints in $\mathcal{C}$ have the form $C(x_1, \ldots, x_m)$. Each constraint symbol C has an associated relation R_C. In our example, there may be compatibility constraints (e.g., the destinations of two successive vacation destinations must belong to neighboured countries) and requirements (e.g., at least one destination should allow wind-surfing and at least one should allow museum visits). Each criterion z_i has a definition in form of a functional constraint $z_i := f_i(x_1, \ldots, x_m)$ and a domain $D(z_i)$. Examples for criteria are price, quality, and distance (zone). The price is a sum of element constraints:

$$price := \sum_{i=1}^{m} price(x_i)$$

The total quality is defined as minimum of the individual qualities and the total distance is the maximum of the individual distances. The individual prices, qualities, and destinations are given by tables such as the catalog in figure 1.

A solution S of $(\mathcal{C}, \mathcal{X})$ is a set of assignments $\{x_1 = v_1, \ldots, x_m = v_m\}$ of values from $D(x_i)$ to each x_i such that all constraints in $\mathcal{C}$ are satisfied, i.e. $(v_1, \ldots, v_m) \in R_C$ for each constraint $C(x_1, \ldots, x_m) \in \mathcal{C}$. We write $v_S(z_i)$ for the value $f_i(v_1, \ldots, v_m)$ of z_i in the solution S.

Destination	Price	Quality	Distance	Activities
Athens	60	1	4	museums, wind-surfing
Barcelona	70	2	3	museums, wind-surfing
Florence	80	3	3	museums
London	100	5	2	museums
Munich	90	4	2	museums
Nice ...	90	4	2	wind-surfing

Figure 1: Catalog of a fictive hotel chain

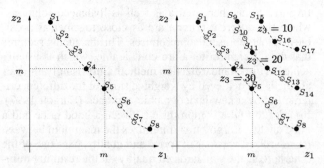

Figure 2: Pareto-optimal solutions for minimization criteria

Furthermore, we introduce preferences between the different values for a criterion z_i and thus specify a multi-criteria optimization problem. Let $\prec_{z_i} \subseteq D(z_i) \times D(z_i)$ be a strict partial order for each z_i. For example, we choose $<$ for price and distance and $>$ for quality. We write $u \preceq v$ iff $u \prec v$ or $u = v$. Multiple criteria optimization provides different notions of optimality. The most well-known examples are Pareto optimality, lexicographic optimality, and optimality w.r.t. weighted sums.

A Pareto-optimal solution S is locally optimal. If another solution S^* is better than S w.r.t. a criterion z_j then S is better than S^* for some other criterion z_k:

Definition 1 *A solution S of $(\mathcal{C}, \mathcal{X})$ is a Pareto-optimal solution of $(\mathcal{C}, \mathcal{X}, \mathcal{Z}, \prec_{z_i})$ iff there is no other solution S^* of $(\mathcal{C}, \mathcal{X})$ s.t. $v_{S^*}(z_k) \prec_{z_k} v_S(z_k)$ for a k and $v_{S^*}(z_i) \preceq_{z_i} v_S(z_i)$ for all i.*

Pareto-optimal solutions narrow down the solution space since non-Pareto-optimal solution do not appear to be acceptable. However, their number is usually too large in order to enumerate them all. Figure 2 (left) shows the Pareto-optimal solutions S_1 to S_8 for the two criteria z_1 and z_2.

From now on, we suppose that all the $\prec_{z_i}$'s are total orders. This simplifies the presentation of definitions and algorithms. A lexicographic solution requires to choose a ranking of the different criteria. We express it by a permutation of the indices:

Definition 2 *Let π be a permutation of $1, \ldots, n$. Let $V_S(\pi(\mathcal{Z})) := (v_S(z_{\pi_1}), \ldots, v_S(z_{\pi_n}))$. A solution S of $(\mathcal{C}, \mathcal{X})$ is an extreme solution of $(\mathcal{C}, \mathcal{X}, \mathcal{Z}, \prec_{z_i})$ iff there is no other solution S^* of $(\mathcal{C}, \mathcal{X})$ s.t. $V_{S^*}(\pi(\mathcal{Z})) \prec_{lex} V_S(\pi(\mathcal{Z}))$.*

Different rankings lead to different extreme[1] solutions which are all Pareto-optimal. In figure 2 (left), we obtain the extreme solutions S_1 where z_1 is preferred to z_2 and S_8 where z_2 is preferred to z_1. Extreme solutions can be determined by solving a sequence of single-criterion optimization problems starting with the most important criterion.

If we cannot establish a preference order between different criteria then we would like to be able to find compromises between them. Although weighted sums (with equal weights) are often used to achieve those compromises, they do not necessarily produce the most balanced solutions. If

---

[1]We use the term extreme in the sense that certain criteria have an absolute priority over other criteria.

we choose the same weights for z_1 and z_2, we obtain S_7 as the optimal solution. Furthermore, if we slightly increase the weight of z_1 the optimal solution jumps from S_7 to S_2. Hence, weighted sums, despite of their frequent use, do not appear a good method for balancing.

In (Ehrgott 1997), Ehrgott uses lexicographic max-orderings to determine optimal solutions. In this approach, values of different criteria need to be comparable. For this purpose, we assume that the preference orders $\prec_{z_i}$ of the different criteria are equal to a fixed order $\prec_D$. This usually requires some scaling or standardization of the different criteria. We also introduce the reverse order $\succ_D$ which satisfies $z_i \succ_D z_j$ iff $z_j \prec_D z_i$. When comparing two solutions S_1 and S_2, the values of the criteria in each solution are first sorted w.r.t. the order $\succ_D$ before being compared by a lexicographic order. This can lead to different permutations of the criteria for different solutions. We describe the sorting by a permutation ρ^S that depends on a given solution S and that satisfies two conditions:

1. ρ^S sorts the criteria in a decreasing order: if $v_S(z_i) \succ_D v_S(z_j)$ then $\rho_i^S < \rho_j^S$.

2. ρ^S does not change the order if two criteria have the same value: if $i < j$ and $v_S(z_i) = v_S(z_j)$ then $\rho_i^S < \rho_j^S$.

Definition 3 *A solution S of $(\mathcal{C}, \mathcal{X})$ is a balanced solution of $(\mathcal{C}, \mathcal{X}, \mathcal{Z}, \prec_D)$ iff there is no other solution S^* of $(\mathcal{C}, \mathcal{X})$ s.t. $V_{S^*}(\rho^{S^*}(\mathcal{Z})) \prec_{lex} V_S(\rho^S(\mathcal{Z}))$.*

Balanced solutions are Pareto-optimal and they are those Pareto-optimal solutions where the different criteria are as close together as possible. In the example of figure 2 (left), we obtain S_5 as balanced solution. According to Ehrgott, it can be determined as follows: first $max(z_1, z_2)$ is minimized. If m is the resulting optimum, the constraint $max(z_1, z_2) = m$ is added before $min(z_1, z_2)$ is minimized. Balanced solutions can thus be determined by solving a sequence of single-criterion optimization problems.

Preferences between Criteria

If many criteria are given it is natural to specify preferences between different criteria as well. For example, we would like to specify that a (small) price is more important than a (short) distance without specifying anything about the quality. We therefore introduce preferences between criteria in form of a strict partial order $\prec_{\mathcal{Z}} \subseteq \mathcal{Z} \times \mathcal{Z}$.

Preferences on criteria and between criteria can be aggregated to preferences between assignments of the form $z_i = v$. Let $\prec$ be the smallest relation satisfying following two conditions: 1. If $u \prec_{z_i} v$ then $(z_i = u) \prec (z_i = v)$ for all u, v and 2. If $z_i \prec_\mathcal{Z} z_j$ then $(z_i = u) \prec (z_j = v)$ for all u, v. Hence, if a criteria z_i is more important than z_j then any assignment to z_i is more important than any assignment to z_j. In general, we could also have preferences between individual value assignments of different criteria. In this paper, we simplified the structure of the preferences in order to keep the presentation simple.

In nonmonotonic reasoning, those preferences $\prec$ between assignments can be used in two different ways:

1. as specification of a preference order between solutions.

2. as (incomplete) specification of a total order (or ranking) between all assignments, which is in turn used to define a lexicographic order between solutions.

The ceteris-paribus preferences (Boutilier *et al.* 1997) and the G-preferred solutions of (Grosof 1991; Geffner & Pearl 1992) follow the first approach, whereas the second approach leads to the B-preferred solutions of (Brewka 1989; Junker 1997). We adapt the definitions in (Junker 1997) to the specific preference structure of this paper:

Definition 4 *A solution S of $(\mathcal{C}, \mathcal{X})$ is a G-preferred solution of $(\mathcal{C}, \mathcal{X}, \mathcal{Z}, \prec)$ if there is no other solution S^* of $(\mathcal{C}, \mathcal{X})$ such that $v_S(z_k) \neq v_{S^*}(z_k)$ for some k and for all i with $v_S(z_i) \prec_{z_i} v_{S^*}(z_i)$ there exists a j s.t. $z_j \prec_\mathcal{Z} z_i$ and $v_{S^*}(z_j) \prec_{z_j} v_S(z_j)$.*

Hence, a criterion can become worse if a more important criterion is improved. In figure 2 (right), S_1 to S_8 are G-preferred if $z_1 \prec_\mathcal{Z} z_3$ and $z_2 \prec_\mathcal{Z} z_3$ are given. Each G-preferred solution corresponds to a Pareto-optimal solution. If there are no preferences between criteria, each Pareto-optimal solution corresponds to some G-preferred solution. However, if there are preferences between criteria, certain Pareto-optimal solutions S are not G-preferred. There can be a G-preferred solution S^* that is better than S for a criterion z_i, but worse for a less important criterion z_j (i.e. $z_i \prec_\mathcal{Z} z_j$).

In general, we may get new G-preferred solutions if we add new constraints to our problem. However, adding upper bounds on criteria does not add new G-preferred solutions:

Proposition 1 *S is a G-preferred solution of $(\mathcal{C} \cup \{z_i \prec_{z_i} u\}, \mathcal{X}, \mathcal{Z}, \prec)$ iff S is a G-preferred solution of $(\mathcal{C}, \mathcal{X}, \mathcal{Z}, \prec)$ and $v_S(z_i) \prec_{z_i} u$.*

Although this property appears to be trivial it is not satisfied for the B-preferred solutions which will be introduced next. It will be essential for computing G-preferred solutions.

In the definition of lexicographic optimal solutions, a single ranking of the given criteria is considered. In the definition of B-preferred solutions, we consider all rankings that respect the given preferences between the criteria. Following definition has been adapted from (Brewka 1989; Junker 1997) to our specific preference structure:

Definition 5 *A solution S of $(\mathcal{C}, \mathcal{X})$ is a B-preferred solution of $(\mathcal{C}, \mathcal{X}, \mathcal{Z}, \prec)$ if there exists a permutation π such*

that *1. π respects $\prec_\mathcal{Z}$ (i.e. $z_i \prec_\mathcal{Z} z_j$ implies $\pi_i < \pi_j$) and 2. there is no other solution S^* of $(\mathcal{C}, \mathcal{X})$ satisfying $V_{S^*}(\pi(Z)) \prec_{lex} V_S(\pi(Z))$.*

The B-preferred solution for π can be computed by solving a sequence of minimization problems: Let $A_0 := \emptyset$ and

$$A_i := A_{i-1} \cup \{z_{\pi_i} = m\}$$
$$\text{where}$$
$$m = min_{\prec_{z_{\pi_i}}} \{v \mid \mathcal{C} \cup A_{i-1} \cup \{z_{\pi_i} = v\} \text{ has a solution}\}$$

In figure 2 (right), S_1 and S_8 are B-preferred (for $z_1 \prec_\mathcal{Z} z_3$ and $z_2 \prec_\mathcal{Z} z_3$). Each B-preferred solution corresponds to an extreme solution. If there are no preferences between criteria, each extreme solution corresponds to some B-preferred solution. If there are preferences between criteria certain extreme solutions may not be B-preferred. For example, S_{15} is an extreme solution, which is obtained if first the distance is minimized and then the price. However, this ranking of criteria does not respect the given preferences.

In (Junker 1997), it has been shown that each B-preferred solution is a G-preferred one, but that the converse is not true in general. In figure 2 (right), S_2 to S_6 are G-preferred, but not B-preferred. These solutions assign a worse value to z_1 than the B-preferred solution S_1, but a better value than S_8. Similarly, they assign a better value to z_2 than S_8, but a worse value than S_1. It is evident that such a case cannot arise if each criteria has only two possible values. Hence, we get an equivalence in following case, where no compromises are possible:

Proposition 2 *If there is no z_i such that $v_1 \prec_{z_i} v_2 \prec_{z_i} v_3$ and $\mathcal{C} \cup \{z = v_i\}$ has a solution for $i = 1, 2, 3$ then each G-preferred solution of $(\mathcal{C}, \mathcal{X}, \mathcal{Z}, \prec)$ is also a B-preferred solution of $(\mathcal{C}, \mathcal{X}, \mathcal{Z}, \prec)$.*

So far, we simply adapted existing notions of preferred solutions to our preference structure and related them to well-known notions of optimality. We now introduce a new kind of preferred solutions that generalizes the balanced solutions. We want to be able to balance certain criteria, e.g. the price and the quality, but prefer these two criteria to other criteria such as the distance. Hence, we limit the balancing to certain groups of criteria instead of finding a compromise between all criteria. For this purpose, we partition $\mathcal{Z}$ into disjoint sets $G_1, \ldots, G_k$ of criteria. Given a criterion z, we also denote its group by $G(z)$. The criteria in a single group G_i will be balanced. The groups themselves are handled by using a lexicographic approach. Thus, we can treat preferences between different groups, but not between different criteria of a single group. Given a strict partial order $\prec_G$ between the G_i's, we can easily define an order $\prec_\mathcal{Z}$ between criteria: if $G_1 \prec G_2$ and $z_i \in G_1$, $z_j \in G_2$ then $z_i \prec_\mathcal{Z} z_j$.

We now combine definitions 5 and 3. As in definition 5, we first choose a global permutation π that respects the preferences between groups. We then locally sort the values of each balancing group in a decreasing order. We describe this local sorting by a permutation θ^S that depends on a given solution S and that satisfies three conditions:

1. θ^S can only exchange variables that belong to the same balanced group: $G(z_i) = G(z_{\theta_i^S})$.

Algorithm *Extreme-PBS1*$(\mathcal{C}, \mathcal{Z}, \prec)$

1. $\quad A := \emptyset; U := \mathcal{Z}; Q := \emptyset;$
2. $\quad$ **while** $Q \cup U \neq \emptyset$ **do**
3. $\qquad$ **for all** $(z = q) \in Q$ **do**
4. $\qquad\quad$ let m be *minimize*$(\mathcal{C} \cup A, z, \prec_z)$
5. $\qquad\quad$ **if** $q \prec_z m$ **then** $Q := Q - \{z = q\};$
6. $\qquad$ **if** $U = \emptyset$ and $Q \neq \emptyset$ **then** fail;
7. $\qquad$ $B := \{y \in U \mid \nexists y^* \in U : y^* \prec_{\mathcal{Z}} y$ and
8. $\qquad\qquad\qquad \nexists (y = q) \in Q\};$
9. $\qquad$ **if** $B = \emptyset$ **then** fail **else**
10. $\qquad\quad$ select $z \in B;$
11. $\qquad\quad$ let m be *minimize*$(\mathcal{C} \cup A, z, \prec_z);$
12. $\qquad\quad$ **choose** $A := A \cup \{z = m\}; U := U - \{z\}$
13. $\qquad\qquad$ **or** $Q := Q \cup \{z = m\}$
14. $\quad$ return $A;$

Figure 3: Algorithm Extreme-PBS1

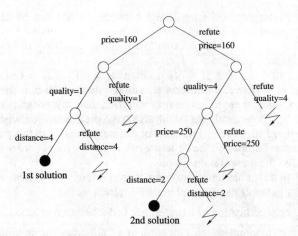

Figure 4: Finding extreme solutions

2. θ^S sorts the criteria of each group in a decreasing order: if $v_S(z_i) \succ_D v_S(z_j)$ and $G(z_i) = G(z_j)$ then $\theta_i^S < \theta_j^S$.

3. θ^S does not change the order if two criteria of the same group have the same value: if $i < j$, $v_S(z_i) = v_S(z_j)$, and $G(z_i) = G(z_j)$ then $\theta_i^S < \theta_j^S$.

Definition 6 *A solution S of $(\mathcal{C}, \mathcal{X})$ is an E-preferred solution of $(\mathcal{C}, \mathcal{X}, \mathcal{Z}, \prec)$ if there exists a permutation π such that 1. π respects $\prec_{\mathcal{Z}}$ (i.e. $z_i \prec_{\mathcal{Z}} z_j$ implies $\pi_i < \pi_j$) and 2. there is no other solution S^* of $(\mathcal{C}, \mathcal{X})$ s.t. $V_{S^*}(\theta^{S^*}(\pi(Z))) \prec_{lex} V_S(\theta^S(\pi(Z)))$.*

In figure 2 (right), S_5 is E-preferred ($z_1 \prec_{\mathcal{Z}} z_3$ and $z_2 \prec_{\mathcal{Z}} z_3$). Each E-preferred solution corresponds to a balanced solution. If there are no preferences between criteria, each balanced solution corresponds to an E-preferred solution.

Interestingly, we can map E-preferred solutions to B-preferred solutions if we introduce suitable variables and preferences. For each group G of cardinality n_G, we use following min-max-variables $y_{G,n_G}, \ldots, y_{G,1}$:

$$y_{G,i} := min\{max(X) \mid X \subseteq G \text{ s.t. } |X| = i\} \quad (1)$$

where $max(X) := max\{z \mid z \in X\}$. Let $\hat{\mathcal{Z}}$ be the set of all of these min-max-variables. Following preferences ensure that min-max-variables for larger subsets X are more important:

$$y_{G,i} \hat{\prec} y_{G,i-1} \text{ for } i = n_G, \ldots, 2 \quad (2)$$

A preference between a group G^* and a group G can be translated into a preference between the last min-max-variable of G^* and the first one of G:

$$y_{G^*,1} \hat{\prec} y_{G,n_G} \quad (3)$$

The E-preferred solutions then correspond to the B-preferred solutions of the translated criteria and preferences:

Theorem 1 *S is an E-preferred solution of $(\mathcal{C}, \mathcal{X}, \mathcal{Z}, \prec)$ iff S is a B-preferred solution of $(\mathcal{C}, \mathcal{X}, \hat{\mathcal{Z}}, \hat{\prec})$.*

We have thus established variants of Pareto-optimal, extreme, and balanced solutions that take into account preferences between criteria. On the one hand, we gain a better understanding of the existing preferred solutions by this comparison with notions form multi-criteria optimization. On

the other hand, we obtain a balancing mechanism that fits well into the qualitative preference framework.

Preference-based Search

We now adapt the preference-based search algorithm from (Junker 2000) to treat preferences on criteria and to compute Pareto-optimal solutions and balanced solutions as well.

Extreme Solutions

The algorithm in (Junker 2000) can easily be adapted to preferences on criteria. The resulting algorithm is shown in figure 3. We explain its basic idea for the small example shown in figure 4, where price and quality are preferred to distance. The algorithm maintains a set U of unexplored criteria, which is initialized with the set of all criteria (i.e. price, quality, and distance). In each step, the algorithm selects a best criterion z of U (e.g. the price). Instead of trying to assign different values to the total price, we determine the cheapest price by solving a minimization subproblem:

$$\begin{aligned} minimize(A, z, \prec_z) := \\ min_{\prec_z}\{v \mid A \cup \{z = v\} \text{ has a solution}\} \end{aligned} \quad (4)$$

In order to obtain a unique result, we assume that the orders $\prec_{z_i}$ are strict total orders throughout the entire section. In our example, the cheapest solution has a price of 160. We now add the assignment *price* $= 160$ to an initially empty set A of assignments. In figure 3, the elements of A occur as labels of the left branches. We then determine the best quality under this assignment. Once the price and quality have been determined we can determine a distance as well.

In order to find further solutions, *Extreme-PBS1* does not add the negation of assignments, but introduces a refutation query for each assignment $z = v$. We say that $z = v$ is refuted if it becomes inconsistent after assigning values to unexplored criteria that may precede z. The refutation queries are added to a set Q. We can remove an element from Q if it has been refuted by further assignments. The assignment to the distance cannot be refuted since there are no further unexplored criteria. The quality of 1 cannot be refuted since the single non-explored criterion distance cannot precede the quality. However, we can refute the price of 160 by first maximizing the quality. After this, we can again minimize the price and the distance, which leads to a new solution as shown in figure 3.

Theorem 2 *Algorithm Extreme-PBS1*$(\mathcal{C}, \mathcal{Z}, \prec)$ *always terminates. Each successful run returns a B-preferred solution of* $(\mathcal{C}, \mathcal{X}, \mathcal{Z}, \prec)$ *and each such B-preferred solution is returned by exactly one successful run.*

According to theorem 1, we can use this algorithm to also compute balanced solutions supposed we provide it with the adequately translated criteria and preferences.

Pareto-optimal Solutions

The algorithm for B-preferred solutions is thus relatively simple. Computing G-preferred solutions turns out to be more subtle. Interestingly, most operations of algorithm *Extreme-PBS1* are also valid for G-preferred solutions except for the rules in lines 6 and 8, where the algorithm backtracks since no B-preferred solution exists that is compatible with the given assignments and refutation queries. An algorithm for G-preferred solutions cannot backtrack in this case since there may be G-preferred solutions, which are not B-preferred. In order to obtain an algorithm for computing G-preferred solutions, we have to avoid such a situation. The basic idea is to add additional constraints that produce the equivalence between G-preferred and B-preferred solutions that is stated in proposition 2. We need to reduce the domain of each criterion z such that all values are either a best or a worst element of the domain. If there are intermediate values u between a best value q and a worst value v then we consider two possibilities: either we impose u as upper bound on z by adding a constraint $z \preceq_z u$ or we require that $z = u$ is refuted. In general, adding constraints can introduce new G-preferred solutions. Proposition 1 states that this is not the case if upper bounds are added.

The resulting algorithm is given in figure 5. It needs the set of values that have not yet been eliminated by some upper bound:

$$Pos(A, z) := \{v \mid \nexists (z \preceq u) \in A : u \prec_z v\} \quad (5)$$

The algorithm 5 determines all G-preferred solutions:

Theorem 3 *Algorithm Pareto-PBS1*$(\mathcal{C}, \mathcal{Z}, \prec)$ *always terminates. Each successful run returns a G-preferred solution of* $(\mathcal{C}, \mathcal{X}, \mathcal{Z}, \prec)$ *and each G-preferred solution is returned by exactly one successful run.*

Adding upper bounds thus helps to control the behaviour of PBS and to avoid that it jumps from one extreme solution to the other. In figure 4, minimizing the quality refutes the cheapest price of 160, as it was required. However, we now obtain a very high price of 250. In order to obtain compromises between price and quality, we constrain the price to be strictly smaller than 250 before minimizing the quality. This discussion indicates that we need not consider all upper bounds. We first determine an extreme solution that leads to a high price and we use this value to impose an upper bound on the price. Hence, we can extract the values of the upper bounds from the previous solutions found so far.

Algorithm *Pareto-PBS1*$(\mathcal{C}, \mathcal{Z}, \prec)$

1. $A := \emptyset; U := \mathcal{Z}; Q := \emptyset;$
2. **while** $Q \cup U \neq \emptyset$ **do**
3.   **for all** $(z = q) \in Q$ **do**
4.   let m be *minimize*$(\mathcal{C} \cup A, z, \prec_z)$
5.   **if** $q \prec_z m$ **then** $Q := Q - \{z = q\};$
6.   **if** $U = \emptyset$ and $Q \neq \emptyset$ **then** fail;
7. $B := \{y \in U \mid \nexists y^* \in U : y^* \prec_z y$ and
8. $\nexists (y = q) \in Q\};$
9.   **if** there is $(z = q) \in Q$ and $v, w \in Pos(A, z)$
10.   s.t. $q \prec_z v \prec_z w$ **then**
11.   select a $\prec_z$-minimal element u
12.   s.t. $u \in Pos(A, z)$ and $q \prec_z u \prec_z w;$
13.   **choose** $A := A \cup \{z \preceq_z u\};$
14.   **or** $Q := Q \cup \{z = u\};$
15.   **else if** $B = \emptyset$ **then** fail **else**
16.   select $z \in B;$
17.   let m be *minimize*$(\mathcal{C} \cup A, z, \prec_z);$
18. $A := A \cup \{z \succeq_z m\};$
19.   **choose** $A := A \cup \{z = m\}; U := U - \{z\}$
20.   **or** $Q := Q \cup \{z = m\};$
21. return $A;$

Figure 5: Algorithm Pareto-PBS1

Preference Projection

A multi-criteria optimization problem is often solved by a sequence of single-criterion optimization problems having different objectives. We can, for example, solve each of these subproblems by a constraint-based Branch-and-Bound which maintains the best objective value found so far. Now, when changing the objective, the search heuristics should be adapted as well. It is a natural idea to project the preference order of the objective to the decision variables that appear in its definition. We define preference projection as follows:

Definition 7 $\prec_{x_k}$ *is a projection of* $\prec_{z_j}$ *via* $f_j(x_1, \ldots, x_m)$ *to* x_k *if and only if following condition holds for all* $u_1, \ldots, u_m$ *and* $v_1, \ldots, v_m$ *with* $u_i = v_i$ *for* $i = 1, \ldots, k - 1, k + 1, \ldots, m$:

$$\begin{aligned} &\text{if } u_k \prec_{x_k} v_k \text{ then} \\ &f_j(u_1, \ldots, u_m) \preceq_y f_j(v_1, \ldots, v_m) \end{aligned} \quad (6)$$

Definition 8 $\prec_{x_1}, \ldots, \prec_{x_m}$ *is a projection of* $\prec_{z_1}, \ldots, \prec_{z_n}$ *via* $f_1, \ldots, f_n$ *to* $x_1, \ldots, x_m$ *if* $\prec_{x_i}$ *is a projection of* $\prec_{z_j}$ *via* $f_j(x_1, \ldots, x_m)$ *to* x_i *for all* i, j.

The projected preferences preserve Pareto-optimality:

Theorem 4 *Let* $\prec_{x_1}, \ldots, \prec_{x_m}$ *be a projection of* $\prec_{z_1}, \ldots, \prec_{z_n}$ *via* $f_1, \ldots, f_n$ *to* $x_1, \ldots, x_m$. *If* S *is a Pareto-optimal solution w.r.t. the criteria* $z_1, \ldots, z_n$ *and the preferences* $\prec_{z_1}, \ldots, \prec_{z_n}$ *then there exists a solution* S^* *that 1. is a Pareto-optimal solution w.r.t. the criteria* $x_1, \ldots, x_m$ *and the preferences* $\prec_{x_1}, \ldots, \prec_{x_m}$ *and 2.* $v_{S^*}(z_i) = v_S(z_i)$ *for all criteria* z_i.

Since extreme and balanced solutions are Pareto-optimal we can additionally use the projected preferences to reduce search effort when solving a sub-problem. For this purpose, we adapt the algorithm Pareto-PBS1 to the decision variables $x_1, \ldots, x_m$ and do consistency checks instead of minimize-calls.

We give some examples for preference projections:

1. The increasing order $<$ is a projection of $<$ via sum, min, max, and multiplication with a positive coefficient.

2. The decreasing order $>$ is a projection of $<$ via a multiplication with a negative coefficient.

3. Given an element constraint of the form $y = f(x)$ that maps each possible value i of x to a value $f(i)$, the following order $\prec_x$ is a projection of $<$ to x via $f(x)$:

$$u \prec_x v \quad \text{iff} \quad f(u) < f(v) \tag{7}$$

In our vacation example, the price, quality, and distance of a destination are all defined by element constraints. If we change the objective, we project preferences over a different element constraint. Since the projected preferences depend on the values f (e.g. price, quality), changing the objective will completely change the order of the value assignments $x_i = u$. Thus, the objective will have a strong impact on the search heuristics. On the one hand, the first solution detected is influenced by the projected preferences and thus may change when the objective is changed. On the other hand, search effort is reduced depending on the objective.

Conclusion

Although Preference-based Search (Junker 2000) provided an interesting technique for reducing search effort based on preferences, it could only take into account preferences between search decisions, was limited to combinatorial problems of a special structure, and did not provide any method for finding compromises in absence of preferences. In this paper, we have lifted PBS from preferences on decisions to preferences on criteria as they are common in qualitative decision theory (Doyle & Thomason 1999; Bacchus & Grove 1995; Boutilier *et al.* 1997; Domshlak, Brafman, & Shimony 2001). We further generalized PBS such that not only extreme solutions are computed, but also balanced and Pareto-optimal solutions. Surprisingly, balanced solutions can be computed by a modified lexicographic approach (Ehrgott 1997) which fits well into a qualitative preference framework as studied in nonmonotonic reasoning and qualitative decision theory.

Our search procedure consists of two modules. A master-PBS explores the criteria in different orders and assigns optimal values to them. The optimal value of a selected criterion is determined by a sub-PBS, which performs a constraint-based Branch-and-Bound search through the original problem space (i.e. the different value assignments to decision variables). We furthermore project the preferences on the selected criterion to preferences between the search decisions, which provides an adapted search heuristics for the optimization objective and which allows to reduce search effort further. Hence, different regions of the search space will be explored depending on the selected objective. Our approach has been implemented in ILOG JCONFIGURATOR V2.0 and adds multi-criteria optimization functionalities to this constraint-based configuration tool.

Other CSP-based approaches to multi-criteria optimization are doing a single Branch-and-Bound search for all criteria, which requires to maintain a set of non-dominated solutions (cf. (Boutilier *et al.* 1997), (Gavanelli 2002)) instead of a single bound. Dominance checking ensures that non-preferred solutions are pruned. Interestingly, the Master-PBS does not need dominance checking, but uses refutation queries to avoid non-preferred solutions.

Future work will be devoted to improve the pruning behaviour of the new PBS procedures by incorporating the conflict checking methods of (Junker 2000). We will also examine whether PBS can be used to determine preferred solutions as defined by soft constraints (Khatib *et al.* 2001).

Acknowledgements

For helpful comments and discussions, I would like to thank Olivier Lhomme, Xavier Ceugniet, Daniel Mailharro, Mark Wallace, as well as the anonymous reviewers.

References

Bacchus, F., and Grove, A. 1995. Graphical models for preference and utility. In *Proceedings of the Eleventh Conference on Uncertainty in Artificial Intelligence*, 3–10.

Boutilier, C.; Brafman, R.; Geib, C.; and Poole, D. 1997. A constraint-based approach to preference elicitation and decision making. In Doyle, J., and Thomason, R. H., eds., *Working Papers of the AAAI Spring Symposium on Qualitative Preferences in Deliberation and Practical Reasoning*.

Brewka, G. 1989. Preferred subtheories: An extended logical framework for default reasoning. In *IJCAI-89*, 1043–1048.

Domshlak, C.; Brafman, R.; and Shimony, E. 2001. Preference-based configuration of web-page content. In *IJCAI-2001*.

Doyle, J., and Thomason, R. H. 1999. Background to qualitative decision theory. *AI Magazine* 20(2):55–68.

Ehrgott, M. 1997. A characterization of lexicographic max-ordering solutions. In *Methods of Multicriteria Decision Theory: Proceedings of the 6th Workshop of the DGOR Working-Group Multicriteria Optimization and Decision Theory*, 193–202. Egelsbach: Häsel-Hohenhausen.

Gavanelli, M. 2002. An implementation of Pareto optimality in CLP(FD). In *CP-AI-OR'02*.

Geffner, H., and Pearl, J. 1992. Conditional entailment: Bridging two approaches to default reasoning. *Artificial Intelligence* 53:209–244.

Grosof, B. 1991. Generalizing prioritization. In *KR'91*, 289–300. Cambridge, MA: Morgan Kaufmann.

Junker, U. 1997. A cumulative-model semantics for dynamic preferences on assumptions. In *IJCAI-97*, 162–167.

Junker, U. 2000. Preference-based search for scheduling. In *AAAI-2000*, 904–909.

Khatib, L.; Morris, P.; Morris, R. A.; and Rossi, F. 2001. Temporal constraint reasoning with preferences. In *IJCAI*, 322–327.

Human-Guided Tabu Search

Gunnar W. Klau[1], Neal Lesh[2], Joe Marks[2], Michael Mitzenmacher[3]

[1] Vienna University of Technology, Austria
guwek@ads.tuwien.ac.at
[2] Mitsubishi Electric Research Laboratories, 201 Broadway, Cambridge, MA, 02139
{lesh,marks}@merl.com
[3] Harvard University, Computer Science Department
michaelm@eecs.harvard.edu

Abstract

We present a human-guidable and general tabu search algorithm. Our work expands on previous interactive optimization techniques that provide for substantial human control over a simple, exhaustive search algorithm. User experiments in four domains confirm that human guidance can improve the performance of tabu search and that people obtain superior results by guiding a tabu algorithm than by guiding an exhaustive algorithm.

Introduction

Interactive, or human-in-the-loop, optimization systems have been developed for a variety of applications, including space-shuttle scheduling, graph drawing, graph partitioning, and vehicle routing. While automatic algorithms typically solve an oversimplified formulation of a real-world problem, users can steer an interactive algorithm based on their preferences and knowledge of real-world constraints. Interactive optimization also leverages people's skills in areas in which people currently outperform computers, such as visual perception, strategic thinking, and the ability to learn. An additional advantage of interactive systems is that people can better trust, justify, and modify solutions that they help construct than they can automatically generated solutions.

Our work expands on the Human-Guided Simple Search (HuGSS) framework (Anderson *et al.*, 2000), which provides the user a greater degree of control than previous interactive optimization approaches, but employs a relatively weak optimization algorithm. With HuGSS, users can manually modify solutions, backtrack to previous solutions, and invoke, monitor, and halt an exhaustive breadth-first search. More significantly, users can constrain and focus the exhaustive search algorithm by assigning *mobilities*, which we describe below, to elements of the current solution. Experiments have shown that human guidance can improve the performance of the exhaustive search algorithm on the capacitated-vehicle-routing-with-time-windows problem to the point where the interactive algorithm is competitive with the best previously reported algorithms (Anderson *et al.*, 2000; Scott, Lesh, & Klau, 2002).

We present a general and human-guidable tabu search algorithm that serves as a superior alternative to the exhaus-

tive search algorithm in HuGSS. Tabu search is a powerful heuristic search algorithm that has proven effective for a wide variety of problems (for an overview see Glover & Laguna (1997)). While previous research on interactive optimization has generally addressed individual problems, we show the generality of our guidable tabu algorithm by applying it to four diverse optimization problems. The algorithm is guidable in that (1) it can be constrained and focused with the same mobilities metaphor used in HuGSS, (2) it controls its own search using mobilities, which provides a natural visualization of the tabu search, and (3) its control parameters are more easily understandable than the analogous ones used to fine-tune the performance of automatic tabu algorithms.

We describe two experiments designed to compare guided tabu search to guided exhaustive search and to unguided (i.e., fully automatic) tabu search. The first experiment included a total of seven test subjects, two domains, and 80 trials. The results indicate that 10 minutes of guided tabu search is comparable to, on average, 70 minutes of unguided tabu search. Furthermore, our experiments demonstrate that guided tabu search significantly outperforms guided exhaustive search. Our second set of experiments investigates if experienced users can improve highly optimized solutions produced by five hours of tabu-search precomputation. We show that half an hour of human-guided tabu search improves these solutions slightly more than 10 additional hours of unguided tabu search.

Background

Interactive Optimization

Interactive systems that leverage the strengths of both humans and computers must distribute the work involved in the optimization task among the human and computer participants. Existing systems have implemented this division of labor in a variety of ways.

In some interactive systems, the users can only indirectly affect the solutions to the current problem. For example, in interactive evolution, an approach primarily applied to design problems, the computer generates solutions via biologically inspired methods and the user selects which solutions will be used to generate novel solutions in the next iteration (Sims, 1991; Todd & Latham, 1992).

Other systems provide more interactivity by allowing the users to control search parameters or add constraints as the search evolves. Colgan *et al.* (Colgan, Spence, & Rankin,

1995) present a system which allows users to interactively control the parameters that are used to evaluate candidate solutions for circuit-design problems. Several constraint-based systems have been developed for drawing applications (Gleicher & Witkin, 1994; Ryall, Marks, & Shieber, 1997; Nelson, 1985). Typically, the user imposes geometric or topological constraints on an emerging drawing.

Some systems allow more direct control by allowing users to manually modify computer-generated solutions with little or no restrictions and then invoke various computer analyses on the updated solution. An early vehicle-routing system allows users to request suggestions for improvements after making schedule refinements to the initial solution (Waters, 1984). An interactive space-shuttle operations-scheduling system allows users to invoke a repair algorithm on their manually modified schedules to resolve any conflicts introduced by the user (Chien *et al.*, 1999).

The human-guided simple search (HuGSS) framework (Anderson *et al.*, 2000) also allows users to manually modify solutions, but in addition it allows them to explicitly steer the optimization process itself. In this approach, users invoke, monitor, and halt optimizations as well as specify the scope of these optimizations. Users control how much effort the computer expends on particular subproblems. Users can also backtrack to previous solutions. HuGSS was utilized in an interactive vehicle-routing system. Initial experiments with this system showed that human-guided optimization outperformed almost all reported vehicle-routing algorithms. A more focused study examined people's ability to guide search in the various ways allowed by HuGSS (Scott, Lesh, & Klau, 2002).

Following the HuGSS framework, do Nascimento and Eades developed an interactive layered graph-drawing system that provided most of the functionality of HuGSS and also allowed users to add constraints to the problem at run-time (Nascimento & Eades, 2001). Preliminary experiments have shown that people can improve automatically generated solutions using this system.

Tabu Search

Tabu search is a heuristic approach for exploring a large solution space (Glover & Laguna, 1997). Like other local search techniques, tabu search exploits a neighborhood structure defined on the solution space. In each iteration, tabu search evaluates all neighbors of the current solution and moves to the best one. The neighbors are evaluated both in terms of the problem's objective function and by other metrics designed to encourage investigation of unexplored areas of the solution space. The classic "diversification" mechanism that encourages exploration is to maintain a list of "tabu" moves that are temporarily forbidden, although others have been developed. Recent tabu algorithms often also include "intensification" methods for thoroughly exploring promising regions of the solution space (although our algorithm does not currently include such mechanisms). In practice, the general tabu approach is often customized for individual applications in myriad ways (Glover & Laguna, 1997).

Algorithm

Example applications

We applied our tabu search algorithm to the following four applications.

The *Crossing* application is a graph layout problem (Eades & Wormald, 1994). A problem consists of m levels, each with n nodes, and edges connecting nodes on adjacent levels. The goal is to rearrange nodes within their level to minimize the number of intersections between edges. A screenshot of the Crossing application is shown in Figure 1.

The *Delivery* application is a variation of the Traveling Salesman Problem in which there is no requirement to visit every location (Feillet, Dejax, & Gendreau, 2001). A problem consists of a starting point, a maximum distance, and a set of customers each at a fixed geographic location with a given number of requested packages. The goal is to deliver as many packages as possible without driving more than the given maximum distance. A screenshot of the Delivery application is shown in Figure 2.

The *Protein* application is a simplified version of the protein-folding problem, using the hydrophobic-hydrophilic model introduced by Dill (Dill, 1985). A problem consists of a sequence of amino acids, each labeled as either hydrophobic or hydrophilic. The sequence must be placed on a two-dimensional grid without overlapping, so that adjacent amino acids in the sequence remain adjacent in the grid. The goal is to maximize the number of adjacent hydrophobic pairs. A screenshot of the Protein application is shown in Figure 3.

The *Jobshop* application is a widely-studied task scheduling problem (Aarts *et al.*, 1994). In the variation we consider, a problem consists of n jobs and m machines. Each job is composed of m operations (one for each machine) which must be performed in a specified order. Operations must not overlap on a machine, and the operations assigned to a given machine can be processed in any order. The goal is to minimize the time that the last job finishes. A screenshot of the Jobshop application is shown in Figure 4.

Terminology

We introduce terminology for the abstractions in our framework. For each optimization problem, we assume there is some set of *problem instances*. For each problem instance, there is a set of candidate *solutions*. We assume that the solutions are totally ordered (with ties allowed); the function ISBETTER(s_1,s_2) returns true iff solution s_1 is strictly superior to s_2. The function INIT(p) returns an initial solution for problem p. A *move* is a transformation that can be applied to one solution to produce a new solution. Each move is defined as operating on one problem *element* and altering that element and possibly others. For example, moving a node from the 3rd to the 8th position in a list, and shifting the 4th through 8th nodes up one, would operate on the 3rd element and alter the 3rd through the 8th. The function MOVES(s,e) returns the set of transformations that operate on element e in solution s. The function ALTERED(m) returns the set of elements altered by m.

The definition of elements varies from application to application. The elements are customers, nodes, amino acids, and job operations in the Delivery, Crossing, Protein, and

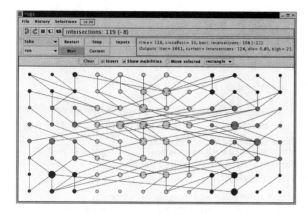

Figure 1: The Crossing Application.

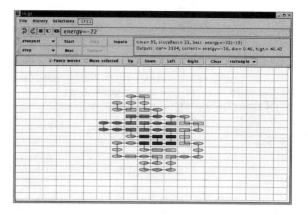

Figure 3: The Protein Application.

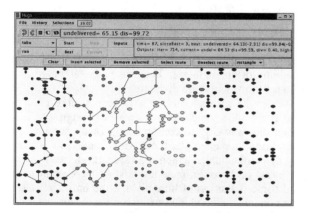

Figure 2: The Delivery Application.

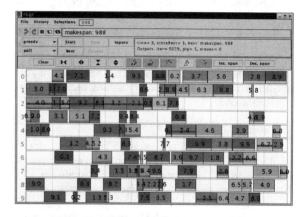

Figure 4: The Jobshop Application.

Jobshop applications, respectively. The definition of moves also varies from application to application. In fact, as with automatic optimization, which moves to include is an important design choice for the developer. Example moves are: swapping adjacent nodes within a level for Crossing; swapping adjacent operations on the same machine in Jobshop; and inserting a customer into the route in Delivery (among other moves). Our framework requires an additional decision by the developer: the elements that are altered by each tranformation. For example, in Delivery, the insertion move alters only the inserted customer. Alternatively, this move could be defined as altering nearby customers on the route. Initial experience with the application can help guide these decisions.

Mobilities

In our system, as with HuGSS, the system maintains and displays a single current solution, such as the ones shown in Figures 1, 2, 3, and 4. Mobilities are a general mechanism that allow users to visually annotate elements of a solution in order to guide a computer search to improve this solution. Each element is assigned a *mobility*: high, medium, or low. The search algorithm is only allowed to explore solutions that can be reached by applying a sequence of moves to the current solution such that each move operates on a

high-mobility element and does not alter any low-mobility elements.

We demonstrate mobilities with a simple example. Suppose the problem contains seven elements and the solutions to this problem are all possible orderings of these elements. The only allowed move on an element is to swap it with an adjacent element. Suppose the current solution is as follows, and we have assigned element 3 low mobility (shown in dark gray), element 5 and 6 medium mobility (shown in medium gray), and the rest of the elements have high mobility (shown in light gray):

A search algorithm can swap a pair of adjacent elements only if at least one has high mobility and neither has low mobility. It is limited to the space of solutions reachable by a series of such swaps, including:

```
GTABU (solution, mobilities, memSize, minDiv):
    best ← solution
    originalMobilities ← mobilities
    until halted by user
        m ← best move in LEGALMOVES(solution,mobilities)
        solution ← result of m applied to solution
        if ISBETTER(solution, best) then
            best ← solution
            mobilities ← originalMobilities
        else
            mobilities ← MEMORY(m,mobilities,memSize)
            mobilities ← DIVERSIFY(m,mobilities, minDiv)
    return best
```

Figure 5: Pseudo code for guidable tabu search.

Note that setting element 3 to low mobility essentially divides the problem into two much smaller subproblems. Also, while medium-mobility elements can change position, their relative order cannot be changed. Mobility constraints can drastically reduce the search space; for this example, there are only 12 possible solutions, while without mobilities, there are $7!=5040$ possible solutions.

We have found that this generalized version of mobilities is useful in a wide variety of applications, including the four described above.

Guidable Tabu

We now present GTABU, a guidable tabu search algorithm. The algorithm maintains a current solution and current set of mobilities. In each iteration, GTABU first evaluates all legal moves on the current solution given the current mobilities, in order to identify which one would yield the best solution. It then applies this move, which may make the current solution worse, and then updates its current mobilities so as to prevent cycling and encourage exploration of new regions of the search space. The pseudocode for GTABU is shown in Figures 5 and 6.

The algorithm updates the mobilities in two ways. First, the call to the MEMORY function prevents GTABU from immediately backtracking, or cycling, by setting elements altered by the current move to medium mobility. For example, in Crossing, if the current move swaps two nodes, then both nodes are set to medium mobility, so that these two nodes cannot simply be reswapped to their original locations. The nodes are restored to their original mobility after a user-defined number of iterations elapse, controlled by an integer $memSize$ which is an input to GTABU. Most tabu search algorithms have a similar mechanism to prevent cycling.

A second mechanism, performed by the DIVERSIFY function in Figure 6, encourages the algorithm to choose moves that alter elements that have been altered less frequently in the past. The algorithm maintains a list of all the problem elements, sorted in descending order by the number of times they have been altered. The *diversity* of an element is its position on the list divided by the total number of elements. The *diversity* of a move is the average diversity of the elements it alters. The *diversity* of a search is the average diversity of the moves it has made since the last time it has found a best solution. The user is allowed to indicate a target minimum diversity $minDiv$ between 0 and 1 for the search. Whenever the average diversity falls below this threshold,

```
LEGALMOVES (solution, mobilities):
    returns the set of all moves m in MOVES(solution,e)
    where e has high mobility in mobilities and every element
    in ALTERED(m) has high or medium mobility in mobilities

DIVERSIFY (move, mobilities, minDiv):
    restore any elements to high mobility that were set to
        medium mobility by previous call to DIVERSIFY
    compute average diversity of search (as defined in the paper)
    if average diversity is less than minDiv then set all
        elements with high mobility in mobilities and diversity
        less than minDiv to medium mobility
    return mobilities

MEMORY (move, mobilities, memSize):
    restore any elements to high mobility that were set to
        medium mobility memSize iterations ago by MEMORY
    set all high-mobility elements in ALTERED(move) to
        medium mobility
    return mobilities
```

Figure 6: Support functions for guidable tabu search.

then any element with a diversity less than $minDiv$ is set to medium for one iteration. This forces the tabu algorithm to make a move with high diversity.

Under the assumption that a system is more guidable if it is more understandable, we strove to design a tabu algorithm that was easy to comprehend. Many automatic tabu algorithms, for example, have a mechanism for encouraging diversification in which the value of a move is computed based on how it affects the cost of the current solution and some definition of how diverse the move is. The two components are combined using a control parameter which specifies a weight for the diversification factor. We originally took a similar approach, but found that users had trouble understanding and using this control parameter. Our experience from the training sessions described below is that users can easily understand the $minDiv$ control parameter.

The understandability of the algorithm is also greatly enhanced by the fact that the tabu algorithm controls its search by modifying mobilities. The users of our system learn the meaning of the mobilities by using them to control and focus the search. All four applications provide a color-coded visualization of the users' current mobility settings. This same mechanism can be used to display GTABU's mobilities. We provide several different visualization modes that allow the user to step through the search one iteration at a time or to view GTABU's current solution and mobility settings briefly at each iteration. During an optimization session, these visualizations are typically turned off because they reduce the efficiency of the system. However, while learning how to use the system, these visualization modes help users understand how the algorithm works.

Experimental Results

Implementation

We implemented domain-independent middleware for interactive optimization in Java and then implemented our four applications using this middleware. All applications use the same implementation of our tabu search algorithm. The middleware also includes a GUI and functions for managing

	greedy	Tabu									
		0.0	0.1	0.2	0.3	0.4	0.5	0.6	0.7	0.8	0.9
Delivery	79.8	72.2	70.6	67.6	65.6	**64.6**	65.2	66.9	68.8	70.3	70.9
Crossing	69.0	85.0	75.9	67.7	64.3	53.9	48.1	40.0	38.4	**37.9**	43.4
Protein	-31.5	-30.0	-31.3	-34.8	-36.1	**-36.6**	-36.1	-35.7	-34.1	-33.4	-29.3
Jobshop	2050.4	2167.4	2045.3	1922.2	1820.7	1821.9	**1779.5**	1846.9	1860.4	2059.0	2164.2

Table 1: Results of unguided greedy and unguided tabu with different minimum diversities. All results averaged over 10 problems, after five minutes of search. The best result in each row is shown in bold. All the problems are minimization problems, so lower numbers are better. Note that the numbers are negative for Protein.

the current working solution and mobilities, the history of past solutions, file Input/Output, and logging user behavior. This software is freely available for research or educational purposes. More details are described in Klau *et al.* (2002).

Our code follows the HuGSS framework. Users can manually modify solutions, backtrack to previous solutions, assign mobilities to problem elements, and invoke, monitor, and halt a search algorithm. Unlike HuGSS, however, our system provides a choice of search algorithms and visualization modes. In addition to tabu search, we also provide (a domain-independent) steepest-descent and greedy exhaustive search, similar to those in the original HuGGS system. Both exhaustive algorithms first evaluate all legal moves, then all combinations of two legal moves, and then all combinations of three moves and so forth. The steepest-descent algorithm searches for the move that most improves the current solution. The greedy algorithm immediately makes any move which improves the current solution and then restarts its search from the resulting solution.

Each application requires a domain-specific implementation of the problems, solutions, and moves. Essentially, all the functions described in the "Terminology" section above must be defined for each application. Each application also requires a visualization component to display the current solution and mobilities, as well as allow users to perform manual moves.

We generated problems as follows. For Delivery, we randomly distributed 300 customers on an 80×40 grid, and randomly assigned each customer between three and seven requests. The truck is allowed to drive a total of 400 units on the grid. For Crossing, we used ten 12×8 graphs with 110 edges which are publicly available from http://unix.csis.ul.ie/~grafdath/TR-testgraphs.tar.Z. We randomly generated similar graphs to train our test subjects. We also generated our own random 15×10 graphs, with between 213-223 edges, for the second set of experiments described below. For Protein, we created random sequences of amino acids of length 100 (each acid had 50% chance of being hydrophobic) and allowed them to be positioned on a 30×30 grid. For Jobshop, we used the "swv00"-"swv10" instances of size 20×10 and 20×15 (Storer, Wu, & Vaccari, 1992) and the four "yn1"-"yn4" instances of size 20×20 (Yamada & Nakano, 1992) available at http://www.ms.ic.ac.uk/info.html.

All experiments were performed with unoptimized Java code on a 1000 MHz PC. All user experiments were performed on a tabletop projected display, as was done in the original HuGSS experiments (Anderson *et al.*, 2000).

	Delivery		Crossing	
	10 min. guided tabu	10 min. guided greedy	10 min. guided tabu	10 min. guided greedy
unguided tabu	61	29	79	25
unguided greedy	>150	>150	>150	135

Table 2: Average number of minutes of unguided search required to match or beat the result produced by 10 minutes of guided search.

Experiments with unguided search

By *unguided search*, we mean running either the tabu or exhaustive algorithm without intervention and with all elements set to high mobility.

We performed experiments to evaluate our method for encouraging diversity of the tabu search. For each application, we ran the unguided tabu search with various minimum-diversity settings. We ran the search on 10 problems for five minutes with a fixed memory size of 10. The results, shown in Table 1 show that for each application, forcing the algorithm to make diverse moves improves the search, but that forcing too much diversity can hinder it.

We also compared exhaustive search to tabu search. We used the greedy variant of exhaustive search because the steepest-descent variant is ineffective when starting from a poor initial solution. As also shown in Table 1, with a reasonably well-chosen diversity setting, unguided tabu significantly outperforms unguided greedy search.

Finally, as an external comparison, we ran a suite of standard graph-layout heuristics (Gutwenger *et al.*, 2002) on the Crossing problem instances. The average best score was 36.63, which is slightly better than unguided tabu's best score of 37.9 from Table 1. (For these smaller instances, the optimal solutions have been computed (Kuusik, 2000) and average to 33.13.)

User studies

The goal of these experiments was to compare human-guided tabu search to unguided tabu search and to human-guided exhaustive search.

In our first set of experiments, we trained test subjects for 2-4 hours on how to use our system. We used the visualization modes to teach the subjects how the algorithms work and how tabu uses its minimum-diversity feature. Each subject performed five 10-minute trials using our system with only our GTABU algorithm and five 10-minute trials with only exhaustive search. The test subjects were students from

minutes	Delivery					Crossing				
	W	L	T	ave win	ave loss	W	L	T	ave win	ave loss
10	16	4	0	1.76	0.85	14	3	3	3.21	4.67
20	10	10	0	1.10	1.06	11	6	3	2.64	5.67
30	10	10	0	0.95	1.27	11	6	3	2.55	5.83
60	8	12	0	0.86	1.38	10	8	2	2.70	6.25
90	8	12	0	0.80	1.46	10	8	2	2.70	7.00
120	6	14	0	0.69	1.48	9	9	2	2.33	6.89
150	4	16	0	0.6	1.42	9	9	2	2.33	6.89

Table 3: The number of wins (W), losses (L), and ties (T) when comparing the result of 10 minutes of human-guided tabu search to 10 to 150 minutes of unguided tabu search, as well as the average difference of the wins and losses.

	num trials	initial solution	after 30 minutes guided	after 300 minutes unguided	after 600 minutes unguided
Delivery	4	61.46	60.86	60.97	60.94
Crossing	8	253.13	251.13	251.5	250.75
Jobshop	6	958	952.33	954	954

Table 4: The initial solution was computed with 5 hours of unguided tabu search. We compare a half hour of guided search to an additional 5-10 hours of unguided search.

nearby selective universities: our goal is to show that *some* people can guide search, not that most people can.

We used the same 10 problem instances for every subject. Half the subjects did the tabu trials first, and half did the exhaustive-search trials first. For each problem instance, half the subjects used tabu and half used exhaustive. For this first experiment, we fixed the minimum diversity of tabu to be the one that produced the best results in preliminary experiments on random problems for each application.

To evaluate each result, we compared it to 2.5 hours of unguided tabu search on the same problem. Table 2 shows the number of minutes required by unguided tabu and unguided greedy, on average, to produce an equal or better solution to the one produced by 10 minutes of guided search. As shown in the table, it took, on average, more than one hour for unguided tabu search to match or beat the result of 10 minutes of guided tabu search. Furthermore, the results of guided tabu were substantially better than those of guided greedy, as can be seen by the fact that unguided tabu overtakes the results of guided greedy search much more quickly.

Table 3 shows a detailed comparison of the result of 10 minutes of guided tabu search to between 10 and 150 minutes of unguided tabu search. The win and loss columns show how often the human-guided result is better and worse, respectively. The table shows that for Crossing, 10 minutes of guided search produced better results than 2.5 hours of unguided search in nine of 20 instances and tied in two. When guided search loses, however, it does so by more, on average, than it wins by. Incidentally, some test subjects consistently performed better than others. We plan to study individual performance characteristics more fully in future work.

We ran a second experiment on the larger instances to de-termine if experienced users could improve on highly optimized solutions produced by unguided search. Prior to the user sessions, we ran unguided tabu search for five hours to precompute a starting solution. The test subjects then tried to improve this solution using guided tabu for one half hour. The authors of this paper were among the test subjects for this experiment. Because the users were experienced, they were allowed to modify the minimum diversity setting. As shown in Table 4, users were able to improve upon the solutions more in half an hour than unguided tabu did in 10 hours, although by small amounts. (In Crossing and Delivery, the users outperformed or matched unguided tabu in all but one case. In that case, however, tabu found a significantly better solution.) We again ran the graph-layout heuristics on these larger Crossing problem instances. The average best score was 252.13; here guided search slightly outperforms the heuristics.

We also performed an initial investigation with the Protein application. As one anecdotal example, we applied our system to a hard instance with best known score of -49 (Bastolla et al., 1998). Five hours of unguided tabu produced a solution with score -47; one of the authors was able to guide tabu to improve this solution yielding a score of -48 in under an hour.

Informal observations

While each application had its own unique "feel," there were several common characteristics and general strategies for guiding tabu search in the four applications. A common pattern, for example, is for the user to try to escape a deep local minimum by making several manual moves. These moves often cause the score to become temporarily worse, but reinvoking the algorithm usually improves the solution. Mobilities are sometimes used to prevent the algorithm from returning to its previous local minimum. This approach fails to produce a new best solution more often than not, but a series of attempts often yields a new best solution. An efficient approach is to plan the next attempt while the computer is working on the current attempt.

In general, the user looks for combinations of moves that the computer would not consider at once. For example, in Delivery, it is a good strategy to remove a cluster of customers that are, as a whole, far from the route, set them to low mobility, and reinvoke the tabu search. The computer would not readily explore this option because removing one or two customers at a time would not significantly reduce the distance of the route. Similarly, in Crossing, the user often looks for nearly independent clusters of nodes which can all be moved to a new location. In Jobshop, it is common to move several operations earlier (or later) on their machines in order to give the machine more flexibility.

For the 10-minute user tests, an important strategy was to let the tabu search run uninterrupted for the first minute or two, since it would most often make its biggest improvements in the early part of the search. The test subjects had a harder time learning how to guide the search for the Crossing application than the Delivery application and uniformly spent more hours practicing before they felt comfortable to try the test cases. They seem to have reached a higher level of mastery, however.

Conclusions

We have presented GTABU, a guidable tabu search algorithm, and experiments to verify its effectiveness. To our knowledge, no previous human-guided tabu algorithm has been published previously.

GTABU represents a clear advance in interactive optimization. Because tabu search generally provides a more powerful search strategy than exhaustive search, a human-guidable tabu search can provide better solutions while still enjoying the advantages of involving people in the optimization process. Our experiments confirm that people can understand and control GTABU, and that guided tabu search outperforms guided exhaustive search.

GTABU also shows the potential for human interaction to improve on automatic optimization. Our experiments demonstrate that guided tabu outperforms unguided tabu in several domains; in particular, small amounts of human guidance can be as valuable as substantial amounts of unguided computer time.

Acknowledgements

We would like to thank all the participants in our study and Cliff Forlines for his help in designing the study. Michael Mitzenmacher's contribution was supported in part by NSF CAREER Grant CCR-9983832 and an Alfred P. Sloan Research Fellowship, and done while visiting Mitsubishi Electric Research Laboratories.

References

Aarts, E.; Laarhoven, P. v.; Lenstra, J.; and Ulder, N. 1994. A computational study of local search algorithms for job-shop scheduling. *ORSA Journal on Computing* 6(2):118–125.

Anderson, D.; Anderson, E.; Lesh, N.; Marks, J.; Mirtich, B.; Ratajczak, D.; and Ryall, K. 2000. Human-guided simple search. In *Proc. of AAAI 2000*, 209–216.

Bastolla, U.; Frauenkron, H.; Gerstner, E.; Grassberger, P.; and Nadler, W. 1998. Testing a new Monte Carlo algorithm for protein folding. *PROTEINS* 32:52–66.

Chien, S.; Rabideau, G.; Willis, J.; and Mann, T. 1999. Automating planning and scheduling of shuttle payload operations. *J. Artificial Intelligence* 114:239–255.

Colgan, L.; Spence, R.; and Rankin, P. 1995. The cockpit metaphor. *Behaviour & Information Technology* 14(4):251–263.

Dill, A. K. 1985. Theory for the folding and stability of globular proteins. *Biochemistry* 24:1501.

Eades, P., and Wormald, N. C. 1994. Edge crossings in drawings of bipartite graphs. *Algorithmica* 11:379–403.

Feillet, D.; Dejax, P.; and Gendreau, M. 2001. The selective Traveling Salesman Problem and extensions: an overview. TR CRT-2001-25, Laboratoire Productique Logistique, Ecole Centrale Paris.

Gleicher, M., and Witkin, A. 1994. Drawing with constraints. *Visual Computer* 11:39–51.

Glover, F., and Laguna, M. 1997. *Tabu Search*. Kluwer academic publishers.

Gutwenger, C.; Jünger, M.; Klau, G. W.; Leipert, S.; and Mutzel, P. 2002. Graph drawing algorithm engineering with AGD. In Diehl, S., ed., *Software Visualization: State of the Art Survey.*

Proc. of the International Dagstuhl Seminar on Software Visualization, Schloss Dagstuhl, May 2001, volume 2269 of *Lecture Notes in Computer Science*. Springer. To appear.

Klau, G. W.; Lesh, N.; Marks, J.; Mitzenmacher, M.; and Schafer, G. T. 2002. The HuGS platform: A toolkit for interactive optimization. *To appear in Advanced Visual Interfaces 2002.*

Kuusik, A. 2000. *Integer Linear Programming Approaches to Hierarchical Graph Drawing*. Ph.D. Dissertation, Department of Computer Science and Information Systems, University of Limerick, Ireland.

Nascimento, H. d., and Eades, P. 2001. User hints for directed graph drawing. *To appear in Graph Drawing.*

Nelson, G. 1985. Juno, a constraint based graphics system. *Computer Graphics (Proc. of SIGGRAPH '85)* 19(3):235–243.

Ryall, K.; Marks, J.; and Shieber, S. 1997. Glide: An interactive system for graph drawing. In *Proc. of the 1997 ACM SIGGRAPH Symposium on User Interface Software and Technology (UIST '97)*, 97–104.

Scott, S.; Lesh, N.; and Klau, G. W. 2002. Investigating human-computer optimization. *To appear in CHI 2002.*

Sims, K. 1991. Artificial evolution for computer graphics. *Comp. Graphics (Proc. of SIGGRAPH '91)* 25(3):319–328.

Storer, R.; Wu, S.; and Vaccari, R. 1992. New search spaces for sequencing instances with application to job shop scheduling. *Management Science* 38:1495–1509.

Todd, S., and Latham, W. 1992. *Evolutionary Art and Computers*. Academic Press.

Waters, C. 1984. Interactive vehicle routeing. *Journal of Operational Research Society* 35(9):821–826.

Yamada, T., and Nakano, R. 1992. A genetic algorithm applicable to large-scale job-shop instances. In *Parallel instance solving from nature 2*. North-Holland, Amsterdam: R. Manner, B. Manderick(eds). 281–290.

Node and Arc Consistency in Weighted CSP

Javier Larrosa

Department of Software
Universitat Politecnica de Catalunya
Barcelona, Spain
larrosa@lsi.upc.es

Abstract

Recently, a general definition of arc consistency (AC) for soft constraint frameworks has been proposed (Schiex 2000). In this paper we specialize this definition to weighted CSP and introduce a $O(ed^3)$ algorithm. Then, we refine the definition and introduce a stronger form of arc consistency (AC*) along with a $O(n^2d^3)$ algorithm. We empirically demonstrate that AC* is likely to be much better than AC in terms of pruned values.

Introduction

It is well known that *arc consistency* (AC) plays a preeminent role in efficient constraint solving. In the last few years, the CSP framework has been augmented with so-called *soft constraints* with which it is possible to express preferences among solutions (Schiex, Fargier, & Verfaillie 1995; Bistarelli, Montanari, & Rossi 1997). Soft constraint frameworks associate costs to tuples and the goal is to find a complete assignment with minimum combined cost. Costs from different constraints are combined with a domain dependent operator $*$. Extending the notion of AC to soft constraint frameworks has been a challenge in the last few years. From previous works we can conclude that the extension is direct as long as the operator $*$ is idempotent. Recently, (Schiex 2000) proposed an extension of AC which can deal with non-idempotent $*$. This definition has three nice properties: (i) it can be enforced in polynomial time, (ii) the process of enforcing AC reveals unfeasible values that can be pruned and (iii) it reduces to existing definitions in the idempotent operator case.

Weighted constraint satisfaction problems (WCSP) is a well known soft-constraint framework with a non-idempotent operator $*$. It provides a very general model with several applications in domains such as *resource allocation* (Cabon *et al.* 1999), *combinatorial auctions* (Sandholm 1999), *bioinformatics* and *probabilistic reasoning* (Pearl 1988). In recent years an important effort has been devoted to the development of efficient WCSP solvers (Freuder & Wallace 1992; Verfaillie, Lemaître, & Schiex 1996; Larrosa, Meseguer, & Schiex 1999).

In this paper, we specialize the work of (Schiex 2000) to WCSP and provide an AC algorithm with time complexity $O(ed^3)$ (e is the number of constraints and d is the largest domain size), which is an obvious improvement over the $O(e^2d^4)$ algorithm given in (Schiex 2000). Next, we introduce an alternative stronger definition of arc consistency (AC*) along with a $O(n^2d^3)$ algorithm (n is the number of variables). Our experiments on a real frequency assignment problem indicate that enforcing AC* is a promising filtering algorithm. An additional contribution of this paper is a slightly modified definition of the WCSP framework which allows the specification of a maximum acceptable global cost. As we discuss, this new definition fills an existing gap between theoretical and algorithmic papers on WCSP.

Preliminaries

CSP

A binary *constraint satisfaction problem* (CSP) is a triple $P = (\mathcal{X}, \mathcal{D}, \mathcal{C})$. $\mathcal{X} = \{1, \ldots, n\}$ is a set of variables. Each variable $i \in \mathcal{X}$ has a finite domain $D_i \in \mathcal{D}$ of values that can be assigned to it. (i, a) denotes the assignment of value $a \in D_i$ to variable i. A tuple t is a assignment to a set of variables. Actually, t is an ordered set of values assigned to the ordered set of variables $\mathcal{X}_t \subseteq \mathcal{X}$ (namely, the k-th element of t is the value assigned to the k-th element of $\mathcal{X}_t$). For a subset B of $\mathcal{X}_t$, the projection of t over B is noted $t \downarrow_B$. $\mathcal{C}$ is a set of unary and binary constraints. A unary constraint C_i is a subset of D_i containing the permitted assignments to variable i. A binary constraint C_{ij} is a set of pairs from $D_i \times D_j$ containing the permitted simultaneous assigments to i and j. Binary constraints are symmetric (*i.e.*, $C_{ij} \equiv C_{ji}$). The set of (one or two) variables affected by a constraint is called its *scope*. A tuple t is *consistent* if it satisfies all constraints whose scope is included in $\mathcal{X}_t$. It is *globally consistent* if it can be extended to a complete consistent assignment. A *solution* is a consistent complete assignment. Finding a solution in a CSP is an NP-complete problem. The task of searching for a solution can be simplified by enforcing arc consistency, which identifies globally inconsistent values that can be pruned.

Definition 1 (*Mackworth 1977*)

- Node consistency. (i, a) *is node consistent if a is permitted by C_i (namely, $a \in C_i$). Variable i is node consistent*

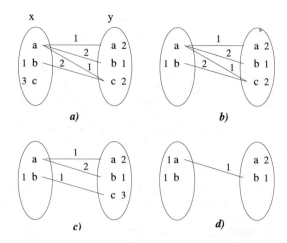

Figure 1: Four equivalent WCSPs.

if all its domain values are node consistent. A CSP is node
consistent *(NC) if every variable is node consistent.*

- Arc consistency. (i, a) *is arc consistent with respect constraint C_{ij} if it is node consistent and there is a value $b \in D_j$ such that $(a, b) \in C_{ij}$. Value b is called a* support *of a. Variable i is arc consistent if all its values are arc consistent with respect every binary constraint involving i. A CSP is* arc consistent *(AC) if every variable is arc consistent.*

Weighted CSPs

Valued CSP (as well as *semi-ring* CSP) extend the classical
CSP framework by allowing to associate *weights* (*costs*) to
tuples (Schiex, Fargier, & Verfaillie 1995; Bistarelli, Montanari, & Rossi 1997). In general, costs are specified by means
of a so-called *valuation structure*. A valuation structure is a
triple $S = (E, *, \succeq)$, where E is the set of costs totally ordered by $\succeq$. The maximum and a minimum costs are noted
$\top$ and $\bot$, respectively. $*$ is an operation on E used to combine costs.

A valuation structure is *idempotent* if $\forall a \in E, (a * a) = a$.
It is *strictly monotonic* if $\forall a, b, c \in E, s.t. (a \succ c) \wedge (b \neq \top), we\ have\ (a * b) \succ (c * b)$.

Weighted CSP (WCSP) is a specific subclass of valued
CSP that rely on specific valuation structure $S(k)$.

Definition 2 *$S(k)$ is a triple* $([0, \dots, k], \oplus, \geq)$ *where,*

- $k \in [1, \dots, \infty]$ *is either a strictly positive natural or infinity.*
- $[0, 1, \dots, k]$ *is the set of naturals bounded by k.*
- $\oplus$ *is the sum over the valuation structure defined as,*

$$a \oplus b = \min\{k, a + b\}$$

- $\geq$ *is the standard order among naturals.*

Observe that in $S(k)$, we have $0 = \bot$ and $k = \top$.

Definition 3 *A binary WCSP is a tuple* $P = (k, \mathcal{X}, \mathcal{D}, \mathcal{C})$.
*The valuation structure is $S(k)$. $\mathcal{X}$ and $\mathcal{D}$ are variables and
domains, as in standard CSP. $\mathcal{C}$ is a set of unary and binary
cost functions (namely, $C_i : D_i \to [0, \dots, k]$, $C_{ij} : D_i \times D_j \to [0, \dots, k]$)*

When a constraint C assigns cost $\top$ to a tuple t, it means
that C forbids t, otherwise t is permitted by C with the corresponding cost. The *cost* of a tuple t, noted $\mathcal{V}(t)$, is the sum
over all applicable costs,

$$\mathcal{V}(t) = \sum_{C_{ij} \in \mathcal{C},\ \{i,j\} \subseteq \mathcal{X}_t} C_{ij}(t \downarrow_{\{i,j\}}) \oplus \sum_{C_i \in \mathcal{C},\ i \in \mathcal{X}_t} C_i(t \downarrow_{\{i\}})$$

Tuple t is *consistent* if $\mathcal{V}(t) < \top$. It is *globally consistent*
if it can be extended to a complete consistent assignment.
The usual task of interest is to *find a complete consistent
assignment with minimum cost*, which is NP-hard. Observe
that WCSP with $k = 1$ reduces to classical CSP. In addition,
$S(k)$ is idempotent iff $k = 1$, and $S(k)$ is strictly monotonic
iff $k = \infty$.

For simplicity in our exposition, we assume that every
constraint has a different scope. We also assume that constraints are implemented as tables. Therefore, it is possible
to consult as well as to modify entries. This is done without
loss of generality with the addition of a small data structure
(see proof of Theorem 2 for details).

Example 1 *Figure 1.a shows a WCSP with valuation structure $S(3)$ (namely, the set of costs is $[0, \dots, 3]$, with $\bot = 0$
and $\top = 3$). It has two variables $\mathcal{X} = \{x, y\}$ and three values per domain a, b, c. There is one binary constraint C_{xy}
and two unary constraints C_x and C_y. Unary costs are depicted besides their domain value. Binary costs are depicted
as labelled edges connecting the corresponding pair of values. Only non-zero costs are shown. The problem solution
is the assigment of value b to both variables because it has
a minimum cost 2.*

The previous definition of WCSP differs slightly from
previous papers, which may require some justification. A
WCSP with $k = \infty$ has an important particularity: Since
the addition of finite costs cannot yield infinity, it is impossible to infer global inconsistency out of non-infinity costs.
Therefore, non-infinity costs are useless in filtering algorithms where the goal is to detect and filter out globally
inconsistent values. While theoretical papers on soft constraints (Schiex, Fargier, & Verfaillie 1995; Bistarelli, Montanari, & Rossi 1997) restrict WCSP to the $k = \infty$ case
(*i.e.*, they assume a strictly monotonic valuation structure),
most papers on algorithms use implicitly (and exploit intensively) our definition where a finite k is permitted. For instance, most *branch and bound*-based solvers keep the cost
of the best solution found so far as an upper bound ub of the
maximum acceptable cost in what remains to be searched.
When the algorithm detects that assigning a value to a future variable necessarily increases its cost up to ub, the value
is detected as unfeasible in the current subproblem and it is
pruned. Therefore, all these solvers are implicitly using the
valuation structure $S(ub)$ at every subproblem.

Node and Arc Consistency in WCSP

In this Section we define AC for WCSP. Our definition is essentially equivalent to the general definition given in (Schiex
2000). However, our formulation emphasizes the similarity with the CSP case. It will facilitate the extension of

AC algorithms from CSP to WCSP. Without loss of generality, we assume the existency of a unary constraint C_i for every variable (we can always define *dummy* constraints $C_i(a) = \bot, \forall a \in D_i$)

Definition 4 *Let $P = (k, \mathcal{X}, \mathcal{D}, \mathcal{C})$ be a binary WCSP.*

- *Node consistency. (i, a) is node consistent if $C_i(a) <$ $\top$. Variable i is node consistent if all its values are node consistent. P is node consistent (NC) if every variable is node consistent.*

- *Arc consistency. (i, a) is arc consistent with respect to constraint C_{ij} if it is node consistent and there is a value $b \in D_j$ such that $C_{ij}(a, b) = \bot$. Value b is called a support of a. Variable i is arc consistent if all its values are arc consistent with respect to every binary constraint affecting i. A WCSP is arc consistent (AC) if every variable is arc consistent.*

Clearly, both NC and AC reduce to the classical definition in standard CSP.

Example 2 *The problem in Figure 1.a is not node consistent because $C_x(c) = 3 = \top$. The problem in Figure 1.b is node consistent. However it is not arc consistent, because (x, a) and (y, c) do not have a support. The problem in Figure 1.d is arc consistent.*

Enforcing Arc Consistency

Arc consistency can be enforced by applying two basic operations until the AC condition is satisfied: pruning node-inconsistent values and forcing supports to node-consistent values. As pointed out in (Schiex 2000), supports can be forced by *sending* costs from binary constraints to unary constraints. Let us review this concepts before introducing our algorithm.

Let $a, b \in [0, \ldots, k]$, be two costs such that $a \geq b$. $a \ominus b$ is the *subtraction* of b from a, defined as,

$$a \ominus b = \begin{cases} a - b & : & a \neq k \\ k & : & a = k \end{cases}$$

The *projection* of $C_{ij} \in \mathcal{C}$ over $C_i \in \mathcal{C}$ is a flow of costs from the binary to the unary constraint defined as follows: Let α_a be the minimum cost of a with respect to C_{ij} (namely, $\alpha_a = \min_{b \in D_j} \{C_{ij}(a, b)\}$). The projection consists in adding α_a to $C_i(a)$ (namely, $C_i(a) := C_i(a) \oplus \alpha_a, \forall a \in D_i$) and subtracting α_a from $C_{ij}(a, b)$ (namely, $C_{ij}(a, b) := C_{ij}(a, b) \ominus \alpha_a, \forall b \in D_j, \forall a \in D_i$)

Theorem 1 *(Schiex 2000) Let $P = (k, \mathcal{X}, \mathcal{D}, \mathcal{C})$ be a binary WCSP. The projection of $C_{ij} \in \mathcal{C}$ over $C_i \in \mathcal{C}$ transforms P into an equivalent problem P'.*

Example 3 *Consider the arc-inconsistent problem in Figure 1.a. To restore arc consistency we must prune the node-inconsistent value c from D_x. The resulting problem (Figure 1.b) is still not arc consistent, because (x, a) and (y, c) do not have a support. To force a support for (y, c), we project C_{xy} over C_y. That means to add cost 1 to $C_y(c)$ and subtract 1 from $C_{xy}(a, c)$ and $C_{xy}(b, c)$. The result of this process appears in Figure 1.c. With its unary cost increased, (y, c) has lost node consistecy and must be pruned.*

After that, we can project C_{xy} over C_x, which yields an arc-consistent equivalent problem (Figure 1.d).

Figure 2 shows W-AC2001, an algorithm that enforces AC in WCSP. It is based on AC2001 (Bessiere & Regin 2001), a simple, yet efficient AC algorithm for CSP. W-AC2001 requires a data structure $S(i, a, j)$ which stores the current support for (i, a) with respect constraint C_{ij}. Initially, $S(i, a, j)$ must be set to **Nil**, meaning that we do not know any support for a. The algorithm uses two procedures. Function PruneVar(i) prunes node-inconsistent values in D_i and returns **true** if the domain is changed. Procedure FindSupports(i, j) projects C_{ij} over C_i or, what is the same, finds (or forces) a support for every value in D_i that has lost it since the last call. The main procedure has a typical AC structure. Q is a set containing those variables such that their domain has been pruned and therefore adjacent variables may have unsupported values in their domains. Q is initialized with all variables (line 11), because every variable must find a initial supports for every domain value with respect to every constraints. The main loop iterates while Q is not empty. A variable j is fetched (line 13) and for every constrained variable i, new supports for D_i are found, if necessary (line 15). Since forcing new supports in D_i may increase costs in C_i, node consistency in D_i is checked and inconsistent values are pruned (line 16). If D_i is modified, i is added to Q, because variables connected with i must have their supports revised. If during the process some domain becomes empty, the algorithm can be aborted with the certainty that the problem cannot be solved with a cost below $\top$. This fact was omitted in our description for clarity reasons.

Theorem 2 *The complexity of W-AC2001 is time $O(ed^3)$ and space $O(ed)$. Parameters e and d are the number of constraints and largest domain size, respectively.*

Proof 1 *TIME: Clearly, FindSupports(i, j) and PruneVar(i) have complexity $O(d^2)$ and $O(d)$, respectively. In the main procedure, each variable j is added to the set Q at most $d + 1$ times: once in line 11 plus at most d times in line 16 (each time D_j is modified). Therefore, each constraint C_{ij} is considered in line 14 at most $d + 1$ times. It follows that lines 15 and 16 are executed at most $2e(d + 1)$ times, which yields a global complexity of $O(2e(d + 1)(d^2 + d)) = O(ed^3)$*

SPACE: The algorithm, as described in Figure 2, has space complexity $O(ed^2)$, because it requires binary constraints to be stored explicitly as tables, each one having d^2 entries. However, we can bring this complexity down to $O(ed)$. The idea first suggested by (Cooper & Schiex 2002) is to leave the original constraints unmodified and record the changes in an additional data structure. Observe that each time a cost in a binary constraint is modified (line 5), the whole row, or column is modified. Therefore, for each constraint we only need to record row and column changes. Let $F(i, j, a)$ denote the total cost that has been substracted from $C_{ij}(a, v)$, for all $v \in D_j$ ($F(i, j, a)$ must be initialized to zero). The current value of $C_{ij}(a, b)$ can be obtained as $C_{ij}^0(a, b) \ominus F(i, j, a) \ominus F(j, i, b)$, where C_{ij}^0 denotes the

```
procedure FindSupports(i, j)
1.  for each a ∈ D_i if S(i, a, j) ∉ D_j do
2.      v := argmin_{b∈D_j}{C_ij(a, b)}; α := C_ij(a, v);
3.      S(i, a, j) := v;
4.      C_i(a) := C_i(a) ⊕ α;
5.      for each b ∈ D_j do C_ij(a, b) := C_ij(a, b) ⊖ α;
endprocedure
function PruneVar(i): Boolean
6.  change:=false;
7.  for each a ∈ D_i if C_i(a) = ⊤ do
8.      D_i := D_i − {a};
9.      change:=true;
10. return (change)
endfunction
procedure W-AC2001(X, D, C)
11. Q := {1, 2, ..., n};
12. while (Q ≠ ∅) do
13.     j := pop(Q);
14.     for each C_ij ∈ C do
15.         FindSupports(i, j);
16.         if PruneVar(i) then Q := Q ∪ {i};
17. endwhile
endprocedure
```

Figure 2: W-AC2001

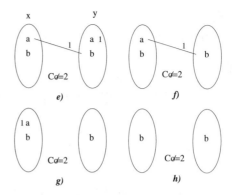

Figure 3: Four more equivalent WCSPs.

original constraint. There is an $F(i, j, a)$ entry for each constraint-value pair, which is space $O(ed)$.

It may look surprising that AC2001 has time complexity $O(ed^2)$ (Bessiere & Regin 2001), while W-AC2001 has complexity $O(ed^3)$. The reason is that AC enforcing in WCSP is a more complex task than in CSP. In classical CSP, domains are assumed to be *ordered* sets. AC2001 records in $S(i, a, j)$ the *first* support $b ∈ D_j$. When a loses its support, a new support is sought *after* b in D_j, because *new supports cannot have appeared before b*. Therefore, domain D_j is traversed only once during the execution looking for supports for a. In WCSP, binary constraints C_{ij} are projected over unary constraints C_i during the W-AC2001 execution with the purpose of finding new supports for values in D_i (lines 1-5). The projection of C_{ij} over C_i decreases the costs of the binary constraint (line 5), which may create, as a side-effect, new supports for values in D_j. Therefore, each time W-AC2001 searches for a new support for value a in D_j, it needs to traverse the whole domain, because *new supports may have appeared before a* since the last call (line 2). Therefore, domain D_j may be traversed up to d times during the execution looking for supports for a.

Node and Arc Consistency Revisited

Consider constraint C_x in the problem of Figure 1.d. Any assignment to x has cost 1. Therefore, any assignment to y will necessarily increase its cost in, at least 1, if extended to x. Consequently, node-consistent values of y are globally inconsistent if their C_y cost plus 1 equals $⊤$. For instance, $C_y(a)$ has cost 2, which makes (y, a) node consistent. But it is globally inconsistent because, no matter what value is assigned to x, the cost will increase to $⊤$. In general, the

minimum cost of all unary constraints can be summed producing a necessary cost of any complete assignment. This idea, first suggested in (Freuder & Wallace 1992), was ignored in the previous AC definition. Now, we integrate it into the definition of node consistency, producing an alternative definition noted NC*. We assume, without loss of generality, the existence of a zero-arity constraint, noted $C_∅$. A zero-arity constraint is a constant, which can be initially set to $⊥$. The idea is to project unary constraints over $C_∅$, which will become a global lower bound of the problem solution.

Definition 5 *Let $P = (k, X, D, C)$ be a binary WCSP. (i, a) is node consistent if $C_∅ ⊕ C_i(a) < ⊤$. Variable i is node consistent if: i) all its values are node consistent and ii) there exists a value $a ∈ D_i$ such that $C_i(a) = ⊥$. Value a is a support for the variable node consistency. P is node consistent (NC*) if every variable is node consistent.*

Example 4 *The problem in Figure 1.d (with $C_∅ = 0$) does not satisfy the new definition of node consistency, because neither x, nor y have a supporting value. Enforcing NC* requires the projection of C_x and C_y over $C_∅$, meaning the addition of cost 2 to $C_∅$, which is compensated by subtracting 1 from all entries of C_x and C_y. The resulting problem is depicted in Figure 3.e. Now, (y, a) is not node consistent, because $C_∅ ⊕ C_y(a) = ⊤$ and can be removed. The resulting problem (Figure 3.f) is NC*.*

Property 1

NC* reduces to NC in classical CSP.

NC* is stronger than NC in WCSP.

Algorithm W-NC* (Figure 4) enforces NC*. It works in two steps. First, a support is forced for each variable by projecting unary constraints over $C_∅$ (lines 1-4). After this, every domain D_i contains at least one value a with $C_i(a) = ⊥$. Next, node-inconsistent values are pruned (lines 5, 6). The time complexity of W-NC* is $O(nd)$.

An arc consistent problem is, by definition, node consistent. If we take the old definition of arc consistency (Definition 4) with the new definition of node consistency, NC*, we obtain a stronger form of arc consistency, noted AC*. Its higher strength becomes clear in the following example.

```
procedure W-NC*(X, D, C)
1.  for each i ∈ X do
2.      v := argmin_{a∈D_i}{C_i(a)}; α := C_i(v);
3.      C_∅ := C_∅ ⊕ α;
4.      for each a ∈ D_i do C_i(a) := C_i(a) ⊖ α;
5.  for each i ∈ X for each a ∈ D_i do
6.      if C_i(a) ⊕ C_∅ = ⊤ then D_i := D_i − {a};
endprocedure
```

Figure 4: W-NC*.

Example 5 *The problem in Figure 1.d is AC, but it is not AC*, because it is not NC*. As we previously showed, enforcing NC* yields the problem in Figure 3.f, where value (x, a) has lost its support. Restoring it produces the problem in Figure 3.g, but now (x, a) loses node consistency (with respect to NC*). Pruning the inconsistent value produces the problem in Figure 3.h, which is the problem solution.*

Enforcing AC* is a slightly more difficult task than enforcing AC, because: (i) $C_∅$ has to be updated after the projection of binary constraints over unary constraints, and (ii) each time $C_∅$ is updated all domains must be revised for new node-inconsistent values. Algorithm W-AC*2001 (Figure 5) enforces AC*. It requires an additional data structure $S(i)$ containing the current support for the node-consistency of variable i. Before executing W-AC*2001, the problem must be made NC*. After that, data structures must be initialized: $S(i, a, j)$ is set to **Nil** and $S(i)$ is set to an arbitrary supporting value (which must exist, because the problem is NC*). The structure of W-AC*2001 is similar to W-AC2001. We only discuss the main differences. Function PruneVar differs in that $C_∅$ is considered for value pruning (line 14). Function FindSupports(i, j) projects C_{ij} over C_i (lines 2-7). flag becomes **true** if the current support of i is lost, due to an increment in its cost. In that case C_i is projected over $C_∅$ (lines 9-12) to restore the support. The main loop of the algorithm differs in that finding supports and pruning values must be done independently, with separate **for** loops (lines 21 and 22). The reason is that each time $C_∅$ is increased within FindSupports(i, j), node-inconsistencies may arise in any domain.

Theorem 3 *The complexity of W-AC*2001 is time $O(n^2d^3)$ and space $O(ed)$. Parameters n, e and d are the number of variables, constraints and largest domain size, respectively.*

Proof 2 *Regarding space, there is no difference with respect to W-AC2001, so the same proof applies. Regarding time, FindSupports and PruneVar still have complexities $O(d^2)$ and $O(d)$, respectively. Discarding the time spent in line 22, the global complexity is $O(ed^3)$ for the same reason as in W-AC2001. The total time spent in line 22 is $O(n^2d^2)$, because the while loop iterates at most nd times (once per domain value) and, in each iteration, line 22 executes PruneVar n times. Therefore, the total complexity is $O(ed^3 + n^2d^2)$, which is bounded by $O(n^2d^3)$.*

The previous theorem indicates that enforcing AC and AC* has nearly the same worst-case complexity in dense problems and that enforcing AC can be up to n times faster in

```
procedure FindSupports(i, j)
1.   supported:=true;
2.   for each a ∈ D_i if S(i, a, j)) ∉ D_j do
3.       v := argmin_{b∈D_j}{C_{ij}(a, b)}; α := C_{ij}(a, v);
4.       S(i, a, j) := v;
5.       C_i(a) := C_i(a) ⊕ α;
6.       for each b ∈ D_j do C_{ij}(a, b) := C_{ij}(a, b) ⊖ α;
7.       if (a = S(i) and α ≠ ⊥) then supported:=false;
8.   if nosupported then
9.       v := argmin_{a∈D_i}{C_i(a)}; α := C_i(v)
10.      S(i) := v;
11.      C_∅ := C_∅ ⊕ α;
12.      for each a ∈ D_i do C_i(a) := C_i(a) ⊖ α;
endprocedure
function PruneVar(i): Boolean
13.  change:=false;
14.  for each a ∈ D_i if C_i(a) ⊕ C_∅ = ⊤ do
15.      D_i := D_i − {a};
16.      change:=true;
17.  return(change)
endfunction
procedure W-AC*2001(X, D, C)
18.  Q := {1, 2, . . . , n};
19.  while (Q ≠ ∅)do
20.      j := pop(Q);
21.      for each C_{ij} ∈ C do FindSupports(i, j);
22.      for each i ∈ X if PruneVar(i) do Q := Q ∪ {i};
23.  endwhile
endprocedure
```

Figure 5: W-AC*2001

sparse problems. Whether the extra effort pays off or not in terms of pruned values has to be checked empirically.

Experimental Results

We have tested W-AC2001 and W-AC*2001 in the frequency assignment problem domain. In particular, we have used instance 6 of the CELAR benchmark (Cabon *et al.* 1999). It is a binary WCSP instance with 100 variables, domains of up to 44 values and 400 constraints. Its solution has cost 3389. This value has been obtained using ad-hoc techniques, because the problem is too hard to be solved with a generic solver.

We generated random subproblems with the following procedure: A random tuple t is generated by randomly selecting a subset of variables $Q ⊂ X$ and assigning them with randomly selected values. $V(t)$ is the cost of t in the original problem. The resulting problem P_t has $X − Q$ as variables, each one with its initial domain. Constraints totally instantiated by t are eliminated, binary constraints partially instantiated by t are transformed into unary constraints by *fixing* one of its arguments to the value given by t, constraints not instanciated by t are kept unmodified. The valuation structure of P_t is $S(k)$, where $k = 3389 − V(t)$. In summary, we are considering the task of proving that a random partial assignment t cannot improve over the best solution.

We experimented with partial assigments of length k ranging from 0 to 30. For each k, we generated 10000 subproblems. For each subproblem, AC and AC* was enforced using W-AC2001 and W-AC*2001, respectively. Figure 6 reports average results for each value of k. The plot on the top shows the pruning power of AC *vs.* AC* as the ratio of pruned values. It can be observed that AC* prunes many more values than AC. For instance, with $k = 5$ AC* prunes 10% of values and AC prunes 1%; with $k = 10$ AC* prunes 70% of values and AC prunes 15%. AC* can prove unsolvability (i.e. there is no consistent solution) with 20 assigned variables, while AC requires 30. We observed that W-AC*2001 is more time consuming than W-AC2001 (it needs around 1.5-3 times more resources). However, this information ignores that W-AC*2001 is doing more work than W-AC2001 at each execution. A more comprehensive information is given in the second plot, which shows the tradeoff between cost and benefit. It depicts the CPU time (in miliseconds) required by each algorithm divided by the number of values that it prunes. It shows that W-AC*2001 prunes values with a lower per-value CPU cost than W-AC2001.

Conclusions and Future Work

We have presented two alternative forms of arc consistency for weighted CSP (AC (Schiex 2000) and AC*), along with their corresponding filtering algorithms (W-AC2001 and W-AC*2001). Although our algorithms may not be tuned to maximal efficiency, they could be a starting point towards an efficient branch and bound solver (BB) that maintains AC during search. Having seen the big advantage of maintaining AC in CSP (Bessiere & Regin 1996), we can expect even larger benefits in the WCSP case, because solving WCSP is much more time consuming than solving CSP. Comparing AC and AC*, our experiments seem to indicate that AC* presents a better cost-benefit trade-off.

Our definitions have the additional advantage of integrating nicely within the soft-constraints theoretical models two concepts that have been used in previous BB solvers: (i) the cost of the best solution found at a given point during search (upper bound in BB terminology) becomes part of the current subproblem definition as value k in the valuation structure $S(k)$, (ii) the minimum necessary cost of extending the current partial assignment (lower bound in BB terminology) can be expressed as the initial value of the zero-arity constraint $C_\emptyset$.

Acknowledgements

I would like to thank Pedro Meseguer, Thomas Schiex and the anonymous referees for their helpful comments. Supported work by the IST Programme of the Commission of the E.U. through the ECSPLAIN project (IST-1999-11969), and by the Spanish CICYT project TAP99-1086-C03.

References

Bessiere, C., and Regin, J.-C. 1996. MAC and combined heuristics: Two reasons to forsake FC (and CBJ?) on hard problems. *Lecture Notes in Computer Science* 1118:61–75.

Bessiere, C., and Regin, J.-C. 2001. Refining the basic constraint propagation algorithm. In *IJCAI-2001*, 309–315.

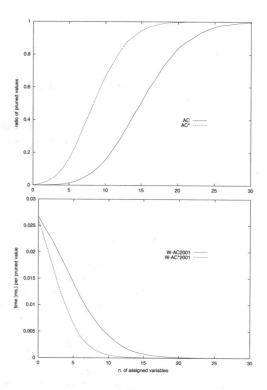

Figure 6: Experimental results on CELAR instance 6.

Bistarelli, S.; Montanari, U.; and Rossi, F. 1997. Semiring-based constraint satisfaction and optimization. *Journal of the ACM* 44(2):201–236.

Cabon, B.; de Givry, S.; Lobjois, L.; Schiex, T.; and Warners, J. 1999. Radio link frequency assignment. *Constraints* 4:79–89.

Cooper, M., and Schiex, T. 2002. Arc consistency for soft constraints. submitted.

Freuder, E., and Wallace, R. 1992. Partial constraint satisfaction. *Artificial Intelligence* 58:21–70.

Larrosa, J.; Meseguer, P.; and Schiex, T. 1999. Maintaining reversible DAC for max-CSP. *Artificial Intelligence* 107(1):149–163.

Mackworth, A. 1977. Consistency in networks of constraints. *Artificial Intelligence* 8.

Pearl, J. 1988. *Probabilistic Inference in Intelligent Systems. Networks of Plausible Inference*. San Mateo, CA: Morgan Kaufmann.

Sandholm, T. 1999. An algorithm for optimal winner determination in combinatorial auctions. In *IJCAI-99*, 542–547.

Schiex, T.; Fargier, H.; and Verfaillie, G. 1995. Valued constraint satisfaction problems: hard and easy problems. In *IJCAI-95*, 631–637.

Schiex, T. 2000. Arc consistency for soft constraints. In *CP-2000*, 411–424.

Verfaillie, G.; Lemaître, M.; and Schiex, T. 1996. Russian doll search. In *AAAI-96*, 181–187.

Model Induction: a New Source of CSP Model Redundancy

Y.C. Law and **J.H.M. Lee**
Department of Computer Science and Engineering
The Chinese University of Hong Kong
Shatin, N.T., Hong Kong SAR, China
{yclaw,jlee}@cse.cuhk.edu.hk

Abstract

Based on the notions of viewpoints, models, and channeling constraints, the paper introduces model induction, a systematic transformation of constraints in an existing model to constraints in another viewpoint. Meant to be a general CSP model operator, model induction is useful in generating redundant models, which can be further induced or combined with the original model or other mutually redundant models. We propose three ways of combining redundant models using model induction, model channeling, and model intersection. Experimental results on the Langford's problem confirm that our proposed combined models exhibit improvements in efficiency and robustness over the original single models.

Keywords: CSP, Problem Formulation, Model Redundancy

Introduction

The task at hand is to tackle *Constraint Satisfaction Problems* (CSPs) (Mackworth 1977), which are, in general, NP-hard. Much CSP research effort focuses on designing general efficient (systematic or local) search algorithms for solving CSPs, and exploiting domain-specific information to solve particular applications efficiently. A recent important line of research in the community investigates how problem formulation and reformulation affect execution efficiency of constraint-solving algorithms. Freuder (1997) lists problem modeling among the seven most important future directions of constraint research.

Selecting the most appropriate formulation or model for a problem is difficult in general. In fact, no objective and general notions of the "best" formulation exist to date. Different formulations of a problem do not compete. Cheng *et al.* (1999) introduce channeling constraints and present how these constraints can be used to connect mutually redundant CSP models to enhance constraint propagation in tree search. In this paper, we give another use of channeling constraints, namely to use them in generating additional model of a CSP through a process called *model induction*. Before we can present model induction, we define CSP models formally based on the notion of CSP viewpoints. We differentiate two different kinds of mutually redundant models, those sharing and those not sharing the same viewpoint. We give

three ways of combining the newly generated induced model with their redundant counterparts. To demonstrate the feasibility of our proposal, we compare our combined models against (1) the original models and (2) the redundant models proposed by Cheng *et al.* (1999) using the Langford's problem, which can be formulated as a Permutation CSP. We demonstrate improvement in terms of execution efficiency, number of failures, and robustness.

From Viewpoints to CSP Models

There are usually more than one way of formulating a problem P into a CSP. Central to the formulation process is to determine the variables and the domains (associated sets of possible values) of the variables. Different choices of variables and domains are results of viewing the problem P from different angles/perspectives. We define a *viewpoint*[1] to be a pair (X, D_X), where $X = \{x_1, \ldots, x_n\}$ is a set of variables, and D_X is a function that maps each $x \in X$ to its associated domain $D_X(x)$, giving the set of possibles values for x.

A viewpoint $V = (X, D_X)$ defines the possible assignments for variables in X. An *assignment* in V (or in $U \subseteq X$) is a pair $\langle x, a \rangle$, which means that variable $x \in X$ (or U) is assigned the value $a \in D_X(x)$. A *compound assignment* in V (or in $U \subseteq X$) is a set of assignments $\{\langle x_{i_1}, a_1 \rangle, \ldots, \langle x_{i_k}, a_k \rangle\}$, where $\{x_{i_1}, \ldots, x_{i_k}\} \subseteq X$ (or U) and $a_j \in D_X(x_{i_j})$ for each $j \in \{i_1, \ldots, i_k\}$. Note the requirement that no variables can be assigned more than one value in a compound assignment. A *complete assignment* in V is a compound assignment $\{\langle x_1, a_1 \rangle, \ldots, \langle x_n, a_k \rangle\}$ for all variables in X.

When formulating a problem P into a CSP, the choice of viewpoints is not arbitrary. Suppose $sol(P)$ is the set of all solutions of P (in whatever notations and formalism). We say that viewpoint V is *proper* for P if and only if we can find a subset S of the set of all possible complete assignments in V so that there is a one-one mapping[2] between S

---

[1] Geelan (1992) used the notion of viewpoint loosely and informally without actually defining it.

[2] A problem can contain identical objects, in which case we have to apply artificial markings to the objects to help differentiating these objects before we can model the problem as a CSP. We assume that the problem objects are already appropriately marked, if necessary, before we talk about such a mapping.

and $sol(P)$. In other words, each solution of P must correspond to a distinct complete assignment in V. We note also that according to our definition, any viewpoint is proper with respect to a problem that has no solutions.

A constraint c in V has two attributes. The *signature* $sig(c) \subseteq X$ defines the scope of c, while $rel(c)$ is the *relation* of c. For the purpose of this paper, we assume that $rel(c)$ is stored explicitly as a set of incompatible assignments in $sig(c)$. Suppose $sig(c) = \{x_{i_1}, \ldots, x_{i_k}\}$. An *incompatible assignment* $\{\langle x_{i_1}, a_1 \rangle, \ldots, \langle x_{i_k}, a_k \rangle\}$ for c is a compound assignment in $sig(c)$ that makes c false. Otherwise, it is a *compatible assignment*. It has the logical meaning that $\neg((x_{i_1} = a_1) \wedge \ldots \wedge (x_{i_k} = a_k))$. Therefore a constraint check amounts to a set membership check against $rel(c)$. We abuse terminology by saying that the incompatible assignment $\{\langle x_{i_1}, a_1 \rangle, \ldots, \langle x_{i_k}, a_k \rangle\}$ also has a signature: $sig(\{\langle x_{i_1}, a_1 \rangle, \ldots, \langle x_{i_k}, a_k \rangle\}) = \{x_{i_1}, \ldots, x_{i_k}\}$.

A *CSP model M* (or simply *model* hereafter) of a problem P is a pair (V, C), where V is a proper viewpoint of P and C is a set of constraints in V for P. Note that, in our definition, we allow two constraints to be on the same set of variables: $c_i, c_j \in C$ and $sig(c_i) = sig(c_j)$. We can *project* a compound assignment θ in U onto $U' \subseteq U$ using:

$$\pi_{U'}(\theta) = \{\langle x, a \rangle \mid x \in U' \wedge \langle x, a \rangle \in \theta\}.$$

A *solution* of $M = (V, C)$ is a complete assignment θ in V so that $\pi_{sig(c)}(\theta) \notin rel(c)$ for each $c \in C$. Since M is a model of P, the constraints C must be defined in such a way that there is a one-one correspondence between $sol(M)$ and $sol(P)$. Thus, the viewpoint V essentially dictates how the constraints of P are formulated (*modulo* solution equivalence).

Suppose M_1 and M_2 are two different models of the same problem P. By definition, there exists a one-one mapping between $sol(M_1)$ and $sol(M_2)$. We say that M_1 and M_2 are *mutually redundant* models. As we shall see, it is possible for mutually redundant models M_1 and M_2 to share the same viewpoint. In that special case, it is easy to verify that $sol(M_1) = sol(M_2)$.

Model Induction

In this section, we introduce *model induction*: a method for systematically generating a new model from an existing model, using another viewpoint and channeling constraints. The resulting model is called an *induced model*. The core of model induction is a meaning-preserving transformation for constraints, both implicit and explicit, from one model to constraints in another viewpoint. In the following, we describe channeling constraints, construction and properties of induced models, and a detailed example.

Channeling Constraints

Given two models $M_1 = ((X, D_X), C_X)$ and $M_2 = ((Y, D_Y), C_Y)$. Cheng *et al.* (1999) define a *channeling constraint* c to be a constraint, where $sig(c) \not\subseteq X$, $sig(c) \not\subseteq Y$, $sig(c) \subseteq X \cup Y$, and $c \notin C_X \cup C_Y$. Thus, c relates M_1 and M_2 by limiting the combination of values that their variables can take. Cheng *et al.* show how a collection of

channeling constraints can be used to connect two mutually redundant models of the same problem to form a combined model, which exhibits increased constraint propagation and thus improved efficiency.

We note in the definition that the constraints in the two models are immaterial. Channeling constraints relate actually the viewpoints of the models. In other words, channeling constraints set forth a relationship between the possible assignments of the two viewpoints. Not all arbitrary sets of channeling constraints can be used in model induction. Given viewpoints $V_1 = (X, D_X)$ and $V_2 = (Y, D_Y)$. A necessary condition is that the set of channeling constraints between V_1 and V_2 must collectively define a *total* and *injective* function f from the possible assignments in V_1 to those in V_2:

$$f : \{\langle x, a \rangle \mid x \in X \wedge a \in D_X(x)\}$$
$$\rightarrow \{\langle y, b \rangle \mid y \in Y \wedge b \in D_Y(y)\}$$

In other words, f maps every assignment in V_1 to a unique assignment in V_2.

Induced Models

Given a model $M = ((X, D_X), C_X)$, a viewpoint (Y, D_Y), and a set of channeling constraints defining a total and injective function f from the possible assignments in (X, D_X) to those in (Y, D_Y). We note that a CSP M contains two types of constraints: the explicit constraints as stated in C_X and the implicit constraints on variable assignments. The latter type of constraints can be further broken down into the restriction that (1) each variable must be assigned a value from its associated domain and (2) each variable cannot be assigned more than one value from its domain. The idea of *model induction* is to transform the constraints in model M, both implicit and explicit, using f to constraints C_Y in viewpoint (Y, D_Y), yielding the *induced model* $i(f, M) = ((Y, D_Y), C_Y)$. We show further that if M is a model for problem P and (Y, D_Y) is also a proper viewpoint of P, then M and $i(f, M)$ are mutually redundant.

- **Stated Constraints** The first type of constraints to transform is the constraints stated in C_X. Recall that a constraint c consists of a signature and a relation, which is simply a set of incompatible assignments for c. We apply f on the assignments in each incompatible assignments of all constraints in C_X, and collect the transformed assignments in a set S_Y:

$$S_Y = \{\{f(\langle x_{i_1}, a_1 \rangle), \ldots, f(\langle x_{i_k}, a_k \rangle)\} \mid$$
$$c \in C \wedge \{\langle x_{i_1}, a_1 \rangle, \ldots, \langle x_{i_k}, a_k \rangle\} \in rel(c) \wedge$$
$$cmpd(\{f(\langle x_{i_1}, a_1 \rangle), \ldots, f(\langle x_{i_k}, a_k \rangle)\}, (Y, D_Y))\}$$

where the predicate $cmpd$ ensures that the set of assignments $\theta = \{f(\langle x_{i_1}, a_1 \rangle), \ldots, f(\langle x_{i_k}, a_k \rangle)\}$ forms a compound assignment in (Y, D_Y). It is indeed possible for θ not being a compound assignment with, say, $f(\langle x_{i_u}, a_u \rangle)$ and $f(\langle x_{i_v}, a_v \rangle)$ being $\langle y, b_u \rangle$ and $\langle y, b_v \rangle$, where $y \in Y$ and $b_u \neq b_v$. Since we are transforming incompatible assignments from (X, D_X), the information conveyed in θ, including the restriction that the variable y cannot be assigned values b_u and b_v simultaneously, is correct. In fact, this information is already satisfied implicitly in viewpoint (Y, D_Y) so that we can ignore/discard θ.

- **No-Double-Assignment Constraints** Implicit in a CSP formulation, each variable should be assigned exactly one value. Part of this restriction can be translated to the requirement that no variables can be assigned two values from its domain at the same time. This corresponds to a set of (invalid) incompatible assignments of the form $\{\langle x, a \rangle, \langle x, b \rangle\}$ for all $x \in X$ and all $a, b \in D_X(x)$, which is satisfied implicitly and not represented in M. Their transformed counterparts, however, are needed in (Y, D_Y). We apply f on all these assignment sets, and collect the transformed assignments in a set N_Y:

$$N_Y = \bigcup_{x \in X} \{\{f(\langle x, a\rangle), f(\langle x, b\rangle)\} \mid$$
$$a, b \in D_X(x) \wedge a \neq b \wedge$$
$$cmpd(\{f(\langle x, a\rangle), f(\langle x, b\rangle)\}, (Y, D_Y))\}$$

- **At-Least-One-Assignment Constraints** The other part of the implicit variable constraint in M can be translated to the requirement that each variable must be assigned at least a value from its domain. This corresponds to the constraints $\bigvee_{b \in D_X(x_i)} x_i = b$ for all $x_i \in X$, which are satisfied implicitly and not represented in M. The other problem is that this unary constraint does not have any incompatible assignments. For each variable $x_i \in X$, we first apply f to every possible assignment of x_i. Suppose $D_X(x_i) = \{b_1, \ldots, b_r\}, f(\langle x_i, b_1\rangle) = \langle y_{k_1}, v_1\rangle, \ldots, f(\langle x_i, b_r\rangle) = \langle y_{k_r}, v_r\rangle$. These assignments form the compatible assignments of a constraint in $\{y_{k_1}, \ldots, y_{k_r}\}$. Using the closed world assumption, we compute the incompatible assignments by collecting all compound assignments θ with signature $\{y_{k_1}, \ldots, y_{k_r}\}$ such that every individual assignment in θ is not equal to $\langle y_{k_j}, v_j\rangle$ for all $j \in \{1, \ldots, r\}$:

$$A_Y = \bigcup_{x \in X} \{\theta \mid D_X(x) = \{b_1, \ldots, b_r\} \wedge$$
$$\forall j \in \{1, \ldots, r\} \cdot [f(\langle x, b_j\rangle) = \langle y_{k_j}, v_j\rangle]$$
$$\wedge \theta = \{\langle y_{w_1}, a_1\rangle, \ldots, \langle y_{w_s}, a_s\rangle\} \wedge$$
$$cmpd(\theta, (Y, D_Y)) \wedge$$
$$sig(\theta) = \{y_{k_1}, \ldots, y_{k_r}\} \wedge$$
$$\forall i \in \{1, \ldots, s\}, \forall j \in \{1, \ldots, r\} \cdot$$
$$[\langle y_{w_i}, a_i\rangle \neq \langle y_{k_j}, v_j\rangle]\}$$

We note that the incompatible assignments in a constraint $c \in C_X$ may be transformed to contribute to the incompatible assignments of more than one constraint in (Y, D_Y). Thus $S_Y \cup N_Y \cup A_Y$ consists of all the induced incompatible assignments with different signatures in (Y, D_Y). The next step is to extract incompatible assignments with the same signature from $S_Y \cup N_Y \cup A_Y$ and group them into a constraint in (Y, D_Y). Thus,

$$C_Y = \{c \mid sig(c) \subseteq Y \wedge rel(c) = \sigma_{sig(c)}(S_Y \cup N_Y \cup A_Y) \neq \emptyset\},$$

where $\sigma_U(\Theta) = \{\theta \mid \theta \in \Theta \wedge sig(\theta) = U\}$.

Due to limitation of space, we state without proof an important consequence of model induction: the transformation of incompatible assignments is meaning-preserving. In other words, if M is a model for problem P and the viewpoint of the induced model is proper with respect to P, then the induced model is also a model for P.

Theorem 1 *If $M = (V_1, C_1)$ is a model for problem P, and V_2 is a proper viewpoint of P, then M and $i(f, M)$ are mutually redundant models for all total and injective functions f (defined by channeling constraints connecting V_1 and V_2) mapping from possible assignments in V_1 to those in V_2.*

Corollary 1 *If $M_1 = (V_1, C_1)$ and $M_2 = (V_2, C_1)$ are mutually redundant models of P, and f is a total and injective function mapping from possible assignments in V_1 to those in V_2, then $sol(M_2) = sol(i(f, M_1))$.*

Corollary 2 *If $M = (V_1, C_1)$ is a model for problem P, V_2 is a proper viewpoint of P, and f is a total and bijective function (i.e., f^{-1} exists) mapping from possible assignments in V_1 to those in V_2, then $sol(i(f^{-1}, i(f, M))) = sol(M)$.*

Example

We illustrate the construction of induced model using the simple 4-queens problem, which is to place four queens on a 4×4 chessboard in such a way that no two queens can attack each other.

We give a textbook model $M = ((X, D_X), C_X)$ of the 4-queens problem. We use four variables $X = \{x_1, x_2, x_3, x_4\}$ and their associated domain function D_X. Each x_i denotes the column position of the queen on row i and $D_X(x_i) = \{1, 2, 3, 4\}$ for $i \in \{1, 2, 3, 4\}$. The constraints C_X enforce that no two queens can be on the same:

- column: $x_i \neq x_j$ for all $1 \leq i < j \leq 4$, and

- diagonal: $|x_i - x_j| \neq i - j$ for all $1 \leq i < j \leq 4$.

Next, we consider a 0-1 viewpoint (Z, D_Z) with sixteen variables $Z = \{z_{ij} \mid i, j \in \{1, 2, 3, 4\}\}$ and associated domain function D_Z. The assignment $\langle z_{ij}, 1\rangle$ denotes the fact that square position (i, j) (row i and column j) contains a queen; and $\langle z_{ij}, 0\rangle$ denotes otherwise. Therefore, $D_Z(z_{ij}) = \{0, 1\}$ for all $i, j \in \{1, 2, 3, 4\}$. The set of channeling constraints $x_i = j \Leftrightarrow z_{ij} = 1$ for all $i, j = 1, \ldots, 4$ defines the total and injective function

$$g(\langle x_i, j\rangle) = \langle z_{ij}, 1\rangle \text{ for all } i, j \in \{1, 2, 3, 4\}.$$

We first transform the stated constraints in C_X. The incompatible assignments for the diagonal constraints in M have the form $\{\langle x_i, k\rangle, \langle x_j, k \pm (i - j)\rangle\}$ for all $i, j, k \in \{1, 2, 3, 4\}, i < j$, and $1 \leq k \pm (i - j) \leq 4$. Hence, the induced incompatible assignments are $\{\langle z_{ik}, 1\rangle, \langle z_{j,k \pm (i-j)}, 1\rangle\}$. For example, the constraints $|x_1 - x_2| \neq 2 - 1$ generates the incompatible assignments $\{\langle z_{11}, 1\rangle, \langle z_{22}, 1\rangle\}, \{\langle z_{12}, 1\rangle, \langle z_{23}, 1\rangle\}, \{\langle z_{13}, 1\rangle, \langle z_{24}, 1\rangle\},$ $\{\langle z_{12}, 1\rangle, \langle z_{21}, 1\rangle\}, \{\langle z_{13}, 1\rangle, \langle z_{22}, 1\rangle\}, \{\langle z_{14}, 1\rangle, \langle z_{23}, 1\rangle\}$ for inclusion in S_Z. The column constraints can be transformed similarly.

The No-Double-Assignments constraints for (Z, D_Z) include incompatible assignments transformed from the implicit constraints that each $x_i \in X$ cannot be assigned two different values. Thus:

$$N_Z = \bigcup_{x_i \in X} \{\{g(\langle x_i, j_1 \rangle), g(\langle x_i, j_2 \rangle)\} \mid j_1, j_2 \in \{1, \dots, 4\}$$
$$\wedge \, j_1 < j_2\}$$
$$= \{\{\langle z_{ij_1}, 1 \rangle, \langle z_{ij_2}, 1 \rangle\} \mid i, j_1, j_2 \in \{1, \dots, 4\} \wedge j_1 < j_2\}$$

For example, the implicit requirement for $x_1 \in X$ will generate the following incompatible assignments $\{\langle z_{11}, 1 \rangle, \langle z_{12}, 1 \rangle\}$, $\{\langle z_{11}, 1 \rangle, \langle z_{13}, 1 \rangle\}$, $\{\langle z_{11}, 1 \rangle, \langle z_{14}, 1 \rangle\}$, $\{\langle z_{12}, 1 \rangle, \langle z_{13}, 1 \rangle\}$, $\{\langle z_{12}, 1 \rangle, \langle z_{14}, 1 \rangle\}$, $\{\langle z_{13}, 1 \rangle, \langle z_{14}, 1 \rangle\}$ to ensure that no more than one queen will be placed on row i of the chessboard.

Last but not least, we need to take care of the At-Least-One-Assignment constraints A_Z, which are obtained from the implicit constraints "each $x_i \in X$ must be assigned at least one value" in M. Applying g to the assignments $\langle x_i, 1 \rangle, \dots, \langle x_i, 4 \rangle$ for each $x_i \in X$ suggests that the incompatible assignments in (Z, D_Z) are among variables $z_{i1}, \dots, z_{i4}$. The incompatible assignments are those $\{\langle z_{i1}, q_1 \rangle, \dots, \langle z_{i4}, q_4 \rangle\}$ such that $q_1 \neq 1, \dots, q_4 \neq 1$. Since the domain of all variables z_{ij} is only $\{0, 1\}$, $\{\langle z_{i1}, 0 \rangle, \dots, \langle z_{i4}, 0 \rangle\}$ is the only incompatible assignment needed. Thus:

$$A_Z = \{\{\langle z_{11}, 0 \rangle, \langle z_{12}, 0 \rangle, \langle z_{13}, 0 \rangle, \langle z_{14}, 0 \rangle\},$$
$$\{\langle z_{21}, 0 \rangle, \langle z_{22}, 0 \rangle, \langle z_{23}, 0 \rangle, \langle z_{24}, 0 \rangle\},$$
$$\{\langle z_{31}, 0 \rangle, \langle z_{32}, 0 \rangle, \langle z_{33}, 0 \rangle, \langle z_{34}, 0 \rangle\},$$
$$\{\langle z_{41}, 0 \rangle, \langle z_{42}, 0 \rangle, \langle z_{43}, 0 \rangle, \langle z_{44}, 0 \rangle\}\}.$$

The intuitive meaning of these incompatible assignments is that there cannot be no queens in row i of the chess board.

The induced model $i(g, M) = ((Z, D_Z), C_Z)$ can be formed by extracting and grouping incompatible assignments of the same signatures to form constraints in C_Z. By Theorem 1, $i(g, M)$ and M are mutually redundant, and are both models of the 4-queens problem.

Exploiting Redundancy from Model Induction

Although model induction is an interesting and general model operator in its own right, we leave the study of its algebraic properties and interaction with other model operators as a topic of another paper. In this section, we focus our interest on induced models which are mutually redundant to their original models. We propose three ways of combining the redundant models so as to utilize the redundant information in enhancing constraint propagation.

Combining Redundant Models

Given a problem P, $M_1 = ((X_1, D_{X_1}), C_{X_1})$ and $M_2 = ((X_2, D_{X_2}), C_{X_2})$ are mutually redundant models of P with different viewpoints. Suppose there is a set C_c of channeling constraints connecting variables in X_1 and X_2. Following the redundant modeling approach (Cheng *et al.* 1999), we can form a combined model $M = M_1 \overset{C_c}{\bowtie} M_2 = (V, C)$, where

- $X = X_1 \cup X_2$ and $V = (X, D_X)$,

- for all $x \in X$,

$$D_X(x) = \begin{cases} D_{X_1}(x) & \text{if } x \in X_1 \wedge x \notin X_2 \\ D_{X_2}(x) & \text{if } x \notin X_1 \wedge x \in X_2 \\ D_{X_1}(x) \cap D_{X_2}(x) & \text{otherwise} \end{cases}$$

- $C = \{c \mid c' \in C_{X_1} \cup C_{X_2} \cup C_c\}$ with $sig(c) = sig(c')$ and $rel(c) = \{\theta \mid \theta \in c' \wedge cmpd(\theta, V)\}$.

The following theorems about the *modeling channeling* operation are straightforward to verify.

Theorem 2 $M_1 \overset{C_c}{\bowtie} M_2 = M_2 \overset{C_c}{\bowtie} M_1$

Theorem 3 M_1, M_2, and M are mutually redundant to one another.

When we are given two mutually redundant models that share the same viewpoint, the situation is simpler. We propose *model intersection* as a means to combine the models into one. Suppose $M_1 = (V, C_1)$ and $M_2 = (V, C_2)$. We can form $M = M_1 \cap M_2 = (V, C_1 \cup C_2)$. Again, we have the following theorems for model intersection.

Theorem 4 $M_1 \cap M_2 = M_2 \cap M_1$.

Theorem 5 $sol(M_1) = sol(M_2) = sol(M)$.

When intersecting two models, we have the option of *merging constraints* with the same signature into one constraint by taking the union of the constraints' sets of incompatible assignments. For example, suppose $sig(c_1) = sig(c_2)$, we can construct a merged constraint c' to replace c_1 and c_2 such that $sig(c') = sig(c_1) = sig(c_2)$ and $rel(c') = rel(c_1) \cup rel(c_2)$. The resultant constraint c', having a *more* global views on the variables in $sig(c')$, can potentially provide more constraint propagation than the individual constraints c_1 and c_2 when used separately. Note that constraint merging is applicable, not just in the context of model intersection, whenever we have more than one individual constraint with the same signature in a CSP.

Three New Forms of Model Redundancy

A viewpoint can greatly influence how a human modeler looks at a problem. Each viewpoint provides a distinct perspective emphasizing perhaps a specific aspect of the problem. Therefore, the modeler will likely express individual constraints differently under different viewpoints, although the constraints under each viewpoint should collectively give the same solutions to the problem being modeled. In particular, a constraint expressed for one viewpoint might not even have an (explicit) counterpart in the other viewpoint, and *vice versa*.

Suppose $M_1 = (V_1, C_1)$ and $M_2 = (V_2, C_2)$ are mutually redundant models with different viewpoints handcrafted by human modeler. We also have a set C_c of channeling constraints defining a total and injective function f from possible assignments of V_1 to those of V_2. Model induction essentially translates constraint information expressed in V_1 to V_2 via channeling constraints f. The transformed constraints express in V_2 the constraint information of the problem as viewed from V_1. These transformed constraints are likely different from constraints expressed directly using V_2 by the human modeler. Therefore, $i(f, M_1)$ and M_2 are redundant and yet complementary to each other.

Model channeling and intersection give various possibilities to combine M_1, M_2, and models induced from the two models. Model channeling is "collaborative" in nature. It allows the sub-models to perform constraint propagation on its own, and yet communicate their results (variable instantiation and domain pruning) to the other sub-models to possibly initiate further constraint propagation. Furthermore, model channeling allows constraint propagation to explore different variable spaces (viewpoints). Model intersection is "additive" in that it merges constraints to form stronger constraints, which is the source of increased constraint propagation.

Assuming f^{-1} exists, we propose three classes of interesting combined models.

- $i(f, M_1) \cap M_2$ and $M_1 \cap i(f^{-1}, M_2)$

- $M_1 \overset{C_c}{\bowtie} i(f, M_1)$ and $M_2 \overset{C_c}{\bowtie} i(f^{-1}, M_2)$

- $(i(f, M_1) \cap M_2) \overset{C_c}{\bowtie} (i(f^{-1}, i(f, M_1) \cap M_2))$ and $(i(f^{-1}, M_2) \cap M_1) \overset{C_c}{\bowtie} (i(f, i(f^{-1}, M_2) \cap M_1))$

We note that f^{-1} always exists for *Permutation CSPs* (Geelen 1992; Smith 2000; 2001). In a Permutation CSP $((X, D_X), C)$, we always have $D_X(x_i) = D_X(x_j)$ for all $x_i, x_j \in X$, and $|D_X(x_i)| = |X|$. In addition, any solution $\{\langle x_1, k_1 \rangle, \ldots, \langle x_n, k_n \rangle\}$ of a Permutation CSP must have the property that $k_i \neq k_j \Leftrightarrow i \neq j$.

Example

We give an example application where such application of model induction and model redundancy are possible. The Langford's problem, listed as "prob024" in CSPLib (Gent & Walsh 1999), can be modeled as a Permutation CSP having all the desired properties for experimenting with model induction and redundant modeling.

In the Langford's problem, there is an $m \times n$-digit sequence which includes the digits 1 to n, with each digit occurs m times. There is one digit between any consecutive pair of digit 1, two digits between any consecutive pair of digit 2, ..., n digits between any consecutive pair of digit n. The Langford's problem, denoted as (m, n) problem, is to find such a sequence (or all sequences).

Smith (2000) suggests two ways to model the the Langford's problem a CSP. We use the $(3, 9)$ instance to illustrate the two models. In the first model M_1, we use 27 variables $X = \{x_0, \ldots, x_{26}\}$, which we can think of as $1_1, 1_2, 1_3, 2_1, \ldots, 9_2, 9_3$. Here, 1_1 represents the first digit 1 in the sequence, 1_2 represents the second digit 1, and so on. The domain of these variables are the values that represent the positions of a digit in the sequence. We use $\{0, \ldots, 26\}$ to represent the domain. Hence, we have the viewpoint $V_1 = (X, D_X)$, where $D_X(x_i) = \{0, \ldots, 26\}$ for $i \in \{0, \ldots, 26\}$. Due to space limitation, we skip the description of constraints.

In the second model M_2, we again use 27 variables $Y = \{y_0, \ldots, y_{26}\}$ to represent each position in the sequence. Their domains are $\{0, \ldots, 26\}$, whose elements correspond

to the digits $1_1, 1_2, 1_3, 2_1, \ldots, 9_2, 9_3$. Hence, we have the viewpoint $V_2 = (Y, D_Y)$, where $D_Y(y_i) = \{0, \ldots, 26\}$ for $i \in \{0, \ldots, 26\}$.

We can write the channeling constraints C_c connecting V_1 and V_2 as $x_i = j \Leftrightarrow y_j = i$ for all $i, j = 0, \ldots, 26$. These constraints define a total and bijective function f where $f(\langle x_i, j \rangle) = \langle y_j, i \rangle$ for all valid i, j. With M_1, M_2, and f, we can construct the three proposed classes of combined models. We note that, for the special case of the Langford's problem:

- $i(f, M_1 \cap i(f^{-1}, M_2)) = i(f, M_1) \cap M_2$ and
- $i(f^{-1}, i(f, M_1) \cap M_2) = M_1 \cap i(f^{-1}, M_2)$.

It is thus only necessary to consider

$$(M_1 \cap i(f^{-1}, M_2)) \overset{C_c}{\bowtie} (i(f, M_1) \cap M_2)$$

for the third class of combined models.

Experiments

To verify the feasibility and efficiency of our proposal, we realize and evaluate the various models for the $(3, 9)$ and $(3, 10)$ instances of the Langford's problem using ILOG Solver 4.4 (1999) and running on a Sun Ultra 1/170 workstation with 512M of memory. We use the IlcTableConstraint function (ILOG 1999) to create constraints from sets of incompatible assignments. Full arc consistency is enforced in constraint propagation. Variables are chosen using the smallest-domain-first variable-ordering heuristic. Constraints are merged whenever possible, so that every constraint in a model has a different signature.

Table 1 shows our comparison results. Column 1 gives the models. In models with more than one viewpoint, it suffices to search/label variables of either viewpoint, although one may choose to search on both. In column 2, we give also the search variables. Columns 3 and 4 report the execution results of solving for only the first solution of the $(3, 9)$ and $(3, 10)$ instances respectively, while columns 5 and 6 report the results of solving for all solutions. Each cell contains both the number of fails and CPU time in sec (in bracket) of an execution. A cell labeled with "-" means that execution does not terminate within 20 minutes of CPU time. We also highlight in bold the best result of each column.

Each row corresponds to a particular model. We divide the models into five groups, the first two of which are used as control in the experiment. The first group consists of individual models, while the second group consists of combined models constructed using the redundant modeling approach (Cheng *et al.* 1999). The remaining groups correspond to our three proposed classes of combined models.

In analyzing the results, attention is sought not just on the CPU time, but also on the number of fails. In fact, the latter is more important and accurate as a measure of the robustness of a model. Combined models are bigger in size, and higher execution overhead is expected. The idea of combining redundant models is to spend more time in constraint propagation in the hope that the extra effort can result in substantial pruning of the search space. A model that gives more pruning has a higher possibility in solving problems that

Models	Search Variables	First Solution		All Solutions	
		(3, 9)	(3, 10)	(3, 9)	(3, 10)
M_1	X	192 (5.46)	569 (19.02)	938 (25.54)	3114 (101.83)
$i(f, M_1)$	Y	-	-	-	-
M_2	Y	-	-	-	-
$i(f^{-1}, M_2)$	X	-	-	-	-
$M_1 \overset{C_c}{\bowtie} M_2$	X	63 (6.49)	193 (18.80)	310 (25.73)	1109 (98.24)
$M_1 \overset{C_c}{\bowtie} M_2$	Y	44 (4.44)	20 (4.25)	322 (25.28)	980 (88.05)
$M_1 \overset{C_c}{\bowtie} M_2$	$X \cup Y$	39 (4.93)	104 (13.47)	225 (20.21)	697 (71.26)
$M_1 \cap i(f^{-1}, M_2)$	X	105 (4.87)	313 (14.34)	524 (**18.31**)	1650 (71.46)
$i(f, M_1) \cap M_2$	Y	-	-	-	-
$M_1 \overset{C_c}{\bowtie} i(f, M_1)$	X	73 (6.36)	207 (19.98)	401 (29.88)	1221 (112.14)
$M_1 \overset{C_c}{\bowtie} i(f, M_1)$	Y	47 (**4.19**)	21 (**3.21**)	338 (27.91)	1021 (96.85)
$M_1 \overset{C_c}{\bowtie} i(f, M_1)$	$X \cup Y$	42 (4.69)	113 (13.58)	239 (21.52)	730 (76.76)
$M_2 \overset{C_c}{\bowtie} i(f^{-1}, M_2)$	Y	589 (54.60)	475 (51.73)	1462 (126.45)	5547 (578.26)
$M_2 \overset{C_c}{\bowtie} i(f^{-1}, M_2)$	X	115 (14.49)	340 (48.73)	561 (62.51)	1812 (249.37)
$M_2 \overset{C_c}{\bowtie} i(f^{-1}, M_2)$	$X \cup Y$	113 (14.23)	338 (48.42)	550 (61.79)	1788 (246.65)
$(M_1 \cap i(f^{-1}, M_2)) \overset{C_c}{\bowtie} (i(f, M_1) \cap M_2)$	X	38 (6.53)	132 (17.80)	195 (22.49)	745 (84.91)
$(M_1 \cap i(f^{-1}, M_2)) \overset{C_c}{\bowtie} (i(f, M_1) \cap M_2)$	Y	31 (5.15)	**9** (5.12)	217 (22.27)	665 (78.57)
$(M_1 \cap i(f^{-1}, M_2)) \overset{C_c}{\bowtie} (i(f, M_1) \cap M_2)$	$X \cup Y$	**29** (5.72)	83 (14.18)	**156** (19.04)	**514** (**65.74**)

Table 1: Comparison Results Using the Langford's Problem

are otherwise computationally infeasible when expressed in weaker models.

The first and fifth groups of models represent the two ends of a spectrum, which indicates the amount of model redundancy utilized in the models. The single models in the first group use no redundancy, and thus performs the worst in terms of the number of fails. Their execution times are not among the worst since these models are the smallest in size, incurring the least execution overhead in constraint propagation. Note also that model M_2 is a poor model. Any model involving M_2 as a base model is bound to perform poorly, both in terms of CPU time and number of fails. In the following, we focus on only models using M_1 as a base model.

The second group makes use of only model channeling, which helps M_1 and M_2 share pruning and variable instantiation information. Constraint propagation also takes place in both viewpoints. Another advantage of this approach is that constraints in M_1 and M_2, constructed under different viewpoints, are complementary to each other. These characteristics are the source of increased constraint propagation, and thus drastic cut in the number of fails as compared to the models in the first group.

The third group of models uses only one viewpoint, but model intersection combines the constraints from the two models to form stronger constraints, thus entailing again more constraint propagation. We note, however, that the reduction in the number of fails is not as substantial as the case in the second group of models.

The fourth group of models employs both model induc-

tion and model channeling. The models inherit the good characteristics of model channeling, except that the constraints in both models are essentially from M_1. These models are deprived of the chance to share constraint information from M_2. Therefore, the performance of the fourth group is consistently and slightly worse than that of the second group.

The model in the fifth group enjoys the best of both worlds. Each of the sub-models is a combined model, encompassing strengthened constraints obtained from model intersection. The combined models are then connected via model channeling to take advantage of the sharing of pruning information and constraint propagation in different viewpoints. That explains why models in this group always give the lowest number of fails in all benchmarks. Their timings, although not the fastest, are also respectable compared to the fastest time of the respective benchmark, although these models are the largest in size.

Related Work

Rossi *et al.* (1990) propose a new definition of equivalence of CSPs, based on the concept of mutual reducibility. They believe that it is reasonable to consider two CSPs equivalent if it is possible to obtain the solution of one CSP from that of another, and vice versa. Geelen (1992) introduces two improved problem-independent value and variable ordering heuristics for solving CSPs. He also introduces a "dual-viewpoint" approach for Permutation CSPs. This approach allows suitable extensions to many heuristics including those introduced in his paper. Jourdan (1995) works on multiple modeling, in which models representing different but redundant views of the same problem are synchronized using the communication mechanisms of constraint logic programming and concurrent constraint languages. Weigel *et al.* (1998) introduces an algorithm to transform a CSP into its boolean form which is then used to find its reformulations. Reformulations differ with each other only in redundant constraints, and one can allow pruning in some situations which is not possible in other. Cheng *et al.* (1999) formally introduces redundant modeling. Two models of the same problem are combined together using channeling constraints. They show increased constraint propagation and efficiency by using this approach. Smith (2000; 2001) introduces the idea of minimal dual models for Permutation CSPs. It is similar to redundant modeling but the constraints in the second model is dropped. She shows that for the Langford's problem, the amount of propagation of the minimal dual model is equal to that of redundant modeling. However, it is not clear whether the same result can be transferred to Permutation CSPs in general. Walsh (2001) conducts an extensive theoretical and empirical study on using different models and combined models using channeling constraints. Smith and Walsh's works concentrate on the effect of different levels of constraint propagation on the constraints to ensure a permutation in Permutation CSPs.

Conclusion

Model induction gives a systematic way of generating alternate model in a different viewpoint from an existing model. Hand-crafting CSP model is an unamiable task performed daily by human modelers, who should find model induction a useful tool. An interesting application of model induction is to generate redundant models, which can be combined using modeling channeling and intersection. Benchmark results using the Langford's problem confirm that the proposed combined models are robust and efficient, both in terms of CPU time and number of fails.

Model redundancy is a relatively new concept. We take the work reported in this paper as a means to open up new possibilities to study, understand, and apply model redundancy in constraint satisfaction. There is plenty of scope for future work. First, model induction is applicable to general CSPs, although our empirical results are developed for only the Langford's problem. It will be interesting to check if the same techniques can be applied/generalized to other, not necessarily binary and/or Permutation, CSPs to obtain useful redundancy information. Second, we conjecture that our approach, as in the case of redundant modeling, is useful mainly for tight and highly connected CSPs. This property can be verified, perhaps, with the help of randomly generated CSPs. Third, model induction is defined in terms of extensional representation of constraints. There is no reason why we have to solve the resultant CSPs also in the extensional form. It would be worthwhile to study how the intensional (symbolic) representation of a constraint can be learned from its extensional counterpart. Fourth, it is also important to characterize the extra amount of constraint propagation provided by combining mutually redundant models.

Acknowledgements

We had fruitful discussions about minimal dual models, channeling constraints, and proper viewpoints with Barbara Smith. We thank also the anonymous referees for their constructive comments which help improve the quality of the paper. The work described in this paper was substantially supported by a grant from the Research Grants Council of the Hong Kong Special Administrative Region (Project no. CUHK4183/00E).

References

Cheng, B. M. W.; Choi, K. M. F.; Lee, J. H. M.; and Wu, J. C. K. 1999. Increasing constraint propagation by redundant modeling: an experience report. *Constraints* 4(2):167–192.

Freuder, E. 1997. In pursuit of the holy grail. *CONSTRAINTS* 2:57–62.

Geelen, P. A. 1992. Dual viewpoint heuristics for binary constraint satisfaction problems. In *Proceedings of the 10th European Conference on Artificial Intelligence*, 31–35.

Gent, I., and Walsh, T. 1999. CSPLib: A benchmark library for constraints. In *Proceedings of Principles and Practice of Constraint Programming (CP)*, 480–481. Available at http://www-users.cs.york.ac.uk/~tw/csplib/.

ILOG. 1999. *ILOG Solver 4.4 Reference Manual*.

Jourdan, J. 1995. *Concurrent constraint multiple models in CLP and CC languages: Toward a programming methodology by modelling*. Ph.D. Dissertation, Denis Diderot University, Paris VII.

Mackworth, A. 1977. Consistency in networks of relations. *AI Journal* 8(1):99–118.

Rossi, F.; Petrie, C.; and Dhar, V. 1990. On the equivalence of constraint satisfaction problems. In *Proceedings of the 9th European Conference on Artificial Intelligence*, 550–556.

Smith, B. M. 2000. Modelling a permutation problem. Research Report 2000.18, School of Computer Studies, University of Leeds.

Smith, B. M. 2001. Dual models in permutation problems. In *Proceedings of Principles and Practice of Constraint Programming (CP)*, 615–619.

Walsh, T. 2001. Permutation problems and channelling constraints. In *Proceedings of Logic for Programming, Artificial Intelligence and Reasoning (LPAR)*, 377–391.

Weigel, R., and Bliek, C. 1998. On reformulation of constraint satisfaction problems. In *Proceedings of 13th European Conference on Artificial Intelligence*, 254–258.

Knowledge Representation

On Computing all Abductive Explanations

Thomas Eiter

Institut für Informationssysteme,
Technische Universität Wien
Favoritenstraße 9–11, A-1040 Wien, Austria
e-mail: eiter@kr.tuwien.ac.at

Kazuhisa Makino

Division of Systems Science,
Graduate School of Engineering Science,
Osaka University, Toyonaka, Osaka 560-8531
makino@sys.es.osaka-u.ac.jp

Abstract

We consider the computation of all respectively a polynomial subset of the explanations of an abductive query from a Horn theory, and pay particular attention to whether the query is a positive or negative letter, the explanation is based on literals from an assumption set, and the Horn theory is represented in terms of formulas or characteristic models. We derive tractability results, one of which refutes a conjecture by Selman and Levesque, as well as intractability results, and furthermore also semi-tractability results in terms of solvability in quasi-polynomial time. Our results complement previous results in the literature, and elucidate the computational complexity of generating the set of explanations.

Introduction

Abduction is a fundamental mode of reasoning, which has been recognized as an important principle of common-sense reasoning (see e.g. (Brewka, Dix, & Konolige 1997)). It has applications in many areas of AI including diagnosis, planning, learning, natural language understanding and many others (see e.g. references in (Eiter & Gottlob 1995)). In a logic-based setting, abduction can be defined as the task, given a set of formulas Σ (the background theory) and a formula χ (the *query*), to find a smallest set of formulas E (an *explanation*) from a set of hypotheses such that Σ plus E is satisfiable and logically entails χ. For use in practice, the computation of abductive explanations is an important problem, for which well-known early systems such as Theorist (Poole 1989) or ATMS solvers have been devised. Since then, there has been a vastly growing literature on this subject, indicating the need for efficient abductive procedures.

Main problems considered. In this paper, we consider computing a set of explanations for queries from Horn theories. More precisely, we address the following problems:

• Computing *all* explanations of a query χ given by a letter q, with and without a set of assumption literals A from which explanations E must be formed, similar as in (Poole 1989; Selman & Levesque 1996). Note that the logical disjunction of all explanations is a weakest disjunctive form over the hypotheses explaining χ. It is easy to see that in general, there might be exponentially many explanations, and computing all explanations is inevitably exponential. However,

it is in this case of interest whether the computation is possible in *polynomial total time* (or *output-polynomial time*), i.e., in time polynomial in the combined size of the input and the output. Furthermore, if exponential space is prohibitive, it is of interest to know whether a few explanations (e.g., polynomially many) can be generated in polynomial time, as studied by Selman and Levesque (1996).

• We contrast formula-based (syntactic) with model-based (semantic) representation of Horn theories. The latter form of representation, where a Horn theory is represented by the *characteristic models*, was advocated by Kautz *et al.* (1993). As they showed, important inference problems are tractable in the model-based setting. Namely, whether a Horn theory Σ implies a CNF φ, and whether a query q has an explanation w.r.t. an assumption set A; the latter is intractable under formula-based representation. Similar results were shown for other theories by Khardon and Roth (1996).

• We investigate the role of syntax for computing abductive queries. In the framework of (Selman & Levesque 1996; Kautz, Kearns, & Selman 1993), the query is a positive letter q. However, it is of equal interest to consider *negative queries* as well, i.e., to explain the complement $\overline{q}$ of an atom q. Since the Horn property imposes semantic restrictions on theories, it is not straightforward to express such negative queries in terms of positive queries.

• Finally, we consider as a meaningful generalization the computation of *joint explanations*. That is, given a background theory Σ and observations $o_1, o_2, \ldots, o_l$, where $l \geq 2$, compute a *single* explanation E which is good for *each* o_i. Joint explanations are relevant, e.g., in diagnostic reasoning. We may want to know whether different observations allow to come up with the same diagnosis, given by an abductive explanation, about a system malfunctioning. Such a diagnosis is particularly strong, as it is backed up by several cases.

Main results. Our main results are summarized as follows.

• We refute Selman and Leveque's belief (1996, p. 266), that given a Horn theory Σ and a query letter q, it is hard to list all explanations of q from Σ even if we are *guaranteed* that there are only few explanations. More precisely, we disprove their conjecture that generating $O(n)$ many explanations of q is NP-hard, where n is the number of propositional letters in the language. This is a consequence of our result that generating *all* nontrivial explanations of q is possible in *total polynomial time* (Theorem 1).

- We give a detailed characterization of computing all explanations of a query from Horn theory in the formula- vs model-based setting, for both general explanations and explanations w.r.t. a set of assumption literals. In a nutshell, we obtain three kinds of results:

(1) A procedure which enumerates all nontrivial explanations of a query letter q from a Horn theory Σ with incremental polynomial delay. This is a positive result and trivially implies that all explanations can be found in polynomial total time. Moreover, it means that any polynomial number of explanations can be generated in polynomial time in the size of the input (Corollary 1).

(2) Intractability results for generating all explanations for a negative query $\overline{q}$ from a Horn theory Σ contained in a set of assumption literals A; this complements a similar result for positive queries in (Selman & Levesque 1996). Both results emerge from the fact that the associated problems of recognizing the correct output are co-NP-complete. Since some hard instances have only small (polynomial-size) output, they also imply that computing few (polynomially many) explanations is intractable.

(3) Under model-based representation, generating all explanations is polynomial-time equivalent to the well-known problem of dualizing a positive CNF (DUALIZATION), i.e., given a CNF φ in which no negative literal occurs, compute the (unique) prime DNF of φ. DUALIZATION is a well-known open problem in NP-completeness, cf. (Bioch & Ibaraki 1995; Fredman & Khachiyan 1996); it is known to be solvable in *quasi-polynomial* total time, i.e., in time $N^{o(\log N)}$ where N denotes the combined size of the input and output (Fredman & Khachiyan 1996); furthermore, polynomial total time algorithms are known for many special cases, and as recently shown, the decisional variant of recognizing the prime DNF of φ is solvable with limited nondeterminism, i.e., in polynomial time with $O(\log^2 N)$ many guesses (Eiter, Gottlob, & Makino 2002). Since DUALIZATION is strongly believed not to be co-NP-hard, our result thus provides strong evidence that under model-based representation, computing all explanations is not co-NP-hard. Interestingly, the equivalence result holds for both positive and negative queries, and whether arbitrary or explanations over a set of assumption literals A are admitted. This means that, in a sense, model-based representation, in contrast to formula-based representation, is not sensitive to these aspects. Furthermore, by resorting to respective algorithms for dualization, the result provides us with algorithms for enumerating all or polynomially many explanations with quasi-polynomial time delay between outputs.

- We show that deciding the existence of a joint explanation is intractable, for both formula- and model-based representation. Thus, the positive results for ordinary explanations do not extend to joint explanations.

Proofs of all results are given in (Eiter & Makino 2002).

Preliminaries

We assume a standard propositional language with letters $x_1, x_2, \ldots, x_n$ from a set P, where each x_i takes either value 1 (true) or 0 (false). Negated atoms are denoted by $\overline{x}_i$, and the opposite of a literal ℓ by $\overline{\ell}$. Furthermore, we use $\overline{A} = \{\overline{\ell} \mid \ell \in A\}$ for any set of literals A and set $Lit = P \cup \overline{P}$.

A clause is a disjunction $c = \bigvee_{p \in P(c)} p \vee \bigvee_{p \in N(c)} \overline{p}$ of literals, where $P(c)$ and $N(c)$ are the sets of atoms occurring positive and negated in c and $P(c) \cap N(c) = \emptyset$. Dually, a term is conjunction $t = \bigwedge_{p \in P(t)} p \wedge \bigwedge_{p \in N(t)} \overline{p}$ of literals, where $P(t)$ and $N(t)$ are similarly defined. We also view clauses and terms as sets of literals $P(c) \cup N(c)$ and $P(t) \cup N(t)$, respectively. A clause c is *Horn*, if $|P(c)| \leq 1$, and a CNF is *Horn*, if it contains only Horn clauses. A *theory* Σ is any set of formulas; it is *Horn*, if it is a set of Horn clauses. As usual, we identify Σ with $\varphi = \bigwedge_{c \in \Sigma} c$, and write $c \in \varphi$ etc.

Definition 1 Given a (Horn) theory Σ, called the background theory, a letter q (called query), and a set of literals $A \subseteq Lit$, an *explanation of q w.r.t. A* is a minimal set of literals E over A such that

(i) $\Sigma \cup E \models q$, and

(ii) $\Sigma \cup E$ is satisfiable.

If $A = Lit$, then we call E simply an *explanation of q*.

Observe that the above definition is slightly more general than the *assumption-based explanations* of (Selman & Levesque 1996), which emerge as $A = P' \cup \overline{P}'$ where $P' \subseteq P$ (i.e., A contains all literals over a subset P' of the letters). Furthermore, in some texts explanations must be sets of positive literals. As for Horn theories, the following is known, cf. (Khardon & Roth 1996):

Proposition 1 *Let E be any explanation of q w.r.t. $A \subseteq Lit$. Then $E \subseteq P$, i.e., E contains only positive literals.*

Example 1 Consider a theory $\Sigma = \{\overline{x}_1 \vee \overline{x}_4, \overline{x}_4 \vee \overline{x}_3, \overline{x}_1 \vee x_2, \overline{x}_4 \vee \overline{x}_5 \vee x_1\}$. Suppose we want to explain $q = x_2$ from $A = \{x_1, x_4\}$. Then, we find that $E = \{x_1\}$ is an explanation. Indeed, $\Sigma \cup \{x_1\} \models x_2$, and $\Sigma \cup \{x_1\}$ is satisfiable; moreover, E is minimal. On the other hand, $E' = \{x_1, \overline{x}_4\}$ satisfies (i) and (ii) for $q = x_2$, but is not minimal. $\square$

Horn theories have a well-known semantic characterization. A *model* is a vector $v \in \{0,1\}^n$, whose i-th component is denoted by v_i. For $B \subseteq \{1, \ldots, n\}$, we let x^B be the model v such that $v_i = 1$, if $i \in B$ and $v_i = 0$, if $i \notin B$, for $i \in \{1, \ldots, n\}$. The set of models of formula φ (resp. theory Σ), denoted by $mod(\varphi)$ (resp. $mod(\Sigma)$), is defined as usual.

For models v, w, we denote by $v \leq w$ the usual componentwise ordering, i.e., $v_i \leq w_i$ for all $i = 1, 2, \ldots, n$, where $0 \leq 1$; $v < w$ means $v \neq w$ and $v \leq w$. For any set of models $\mathcal{M}$, we denote by $\max(\mathcal{M})$, (resp., $\min(\mathcal{M})$) the set of all maximal (resp., minimal) models in M. Denote by $v \wedge w$ componentwise AND of vectors $v, w \in \{0,1\}^n$, and by $Cl_{\wedge}(S)$ the closure of $S \subseteq \{0,1\}^n$ under $\wedge$. Then, a theory Σ is Horn representable, iff $mod(\Sigma) = Cl_{\wedge}(mod(\Sigma))$.

Example 2 Consider $\mathcal{M}_1 = \{(0101), (1001), (1000)\}$ and $\mathcal{M}_2 = \{(0101), (1001), (1000), (0001), (0000)\}$. Then, for $v = (0101)$, $w = (1000)$, we have $w, v \in \mathcal{M}_1$, while $v \wedge w = (0000) \notin \mathcal{M}_1$; hence $\mathcal{M}_1$ is not the set of models of a Horn theory. On the other hand, $Cl_{\wedge}(\mathcal{M}_2) = \mathcal{M}_2$, thus $\mathcal{M}_2 = mod(\Sigma)$ for some Horn theory Σ.

As discussed by Kautz *et al.* (1993), a Horn theory Σ is semantically represented by its characteristic models, where $v \in mod(\Sigma)$ is called *characteristic* (or *extreme* (Dechter & Pearl 1992)), if $v \notin Cl_\wedge(mod(\Sigma) \setminus \{v\})$. The set of all such models, the *characteristic set of* Σ, is denoted by $char(\Sigma)$. Note that $char(\Sigma)$ is unique. E.g., $(0101) \in char(\Sigma_2)$, while $(0000) \notin char(\Sigma_2)$; we have $char(\Sigma_2) = \mathcal{M}_1$.

Generating Explanations

In this section, we consider the generation of all explanations for an atom q. We exclude in our considerations the trivial explanation $E = \{q\}$, which always exists if q belongs to the assumption literals A, $\Sigma \cup \{q\}$ is satisfiable and $\Sigma \not\models q$. These conditions can be efficiently checked under both formula- and model-based representations.

Recall that a prime implicate (res., prime implicant) of a theory Σ is a smallest (w.r.t. inclusion) clause c (resp., term t) such that $\Sigma \models c$ (resp., $t \models \Sigma$). As well-known, explanations can be characterized by prime implicates as follows.

Proposition 2 *For a theory Σ, E is a nontrivial explanation of q w.r.t. $A \subseteq Lit$ if and only if the clause $c = \bigvee_{p \in E} \overline{p} \vee q$ is a prime implicate of Σ such that $E \subseteq A$.*

We start with the generation of all nontrivial explanations under formula-based representation. For this problem, we present the following algorithm.

Algorithm EXPLANATIONS
Input: A Horn CNF φ and a positive letter q.
Output: All nontrivial explanations of q from φ.

Step 1. $\varphi^\star := \emptyset$, $S := \emptyset$, and $O := \emptyset$;

Step 2. **for each** $c \in \varphi$ **do**
    add any prime implicate $c' \subseteq c$ of φ to $\varphi^\star$;
    for each $c' \in \varphi^\star$ with $P(c') = \{q\}$ and $N(c') \notin S$ **do**
    begin output $N(c')$; $S := S \cup \{N(c')\}$;
        $O := O \cup \{(c, c') \mid c \in \varphi^\star\}$
    end;

Step 3. **while** some $(c_1, c_2) \in O$ exists **do**
    begin $O := O \setminus \{(c_1, c_2)\}$;
      if (1) $q \notin N(c_1)$, (2) $P(c_1) = \{r\} \subseteq N(c_2)$ and
        (3) $\varphi^\star \cup N(c_1) \cup N(c_2) \setminus P(c_1)$ is satisfiable
      then begin $c :=$ resolvent of c_1 and c_2;
        compute any prime implicate $c' \subseteq c$ of φ;
        if $N(c') \notin S$ **then**
        begin output $N(c')$; $S := S \cup \{N(c')\}$;
            $O := O \cup \{(c, c') \mid c \in \varphi^\star\}$
        end
      end
    end. $\square$

Example 3 We consider algorithm EXPLANATION on input of $\varphi = (\overline{x}_1 \vee \overline{x}_4)(\overline{x}_4 \vee \overline{x}_3)(\overline{x}_1 \vee x_2)(\overline{x}_3 \vee \overline{x}_5 \vee x_1)$, and $q = x_2$. As easily seen, each clause in φ is a prime implicate, and thus after Step 2, $\varphi^\star = \varphi$ and $S = \{\{x_1\}\}$. Furthermore, the explanation $E_1 = \{x_1\}$ was output.

In Step 3, (c_1, c_2), where $c_1 = \overline{x}_3 \vee \overline{x}_5 \vee x_1$ and $c_2 = \overline{x}_1 \vee x_2$, is the only pair in O satisfying (2) $P(c_2) = \{x_1\} \subseteq N(c_2)(= \{x_1\})$; moreover, (1) $q \notin N(c_1)(= \{x_3, x_5\})$ holds and (3) $\varphi^\star \cup \{x_3, x_5\}$ is satisfiable. Thus, in the body of the while-loop, its resolvent $c = \overline{x}_3 \vee \overline{x}_5 \vee x_2$ is computed.

Clause c is a prime implicate of φ, and thus $E_2 = \{x_3, x_5\}$ is output and added to S. Furthermore, O is updated.

In the next iterations, no pair $(c_1, c_2) \in O$ is found which satisfies condition (2), and thus the algorithm halts. Note that E_1 and E_2 are the nontrivial explanations of $q = x_2$. $\square$

The following result states that our algorithm works as desired. For any formula φ, denote by $\|\varphi\|$ its length, i.e., the number of literal occurrences in it.

Theorem 1 *Algorithm* EXPLANATIONS *incrementally outputs, without duplicates, all nontrivial explanations of q from φ. Moreover, the next output resp. termination occurs within $O(e \cdot m \cdot n \cdot \|\varphi\|)$ time, where m is the number of clauses in φ, n the number of atoms, and e the number of explanations output so far.*

Proof. (Sketch) Only pairs (c, c') are added to O such that c' is a prime implicate of φ. Furthermore, by condition (3) in Step 3, each such c' must have $P(c') = \{q\}$. Thus, by Props. 1 and 2, algorithm EXPLANATIONS outputs only nontrivial (clearly different) explanations $E_1, E_2, \ldots, E_k$ for q.

To show that it outputs all nontrivial explanations E for q, assume that such an E is not output, i.e., $E \neq E_i, i = 1, \ldots, k$. Let φ_N be the CNF of all negative prime implicates of φ, and let $\varphi' = \varphi_N \cup \{\bigvee_{p \in E_i} \overline{p} \vee q \mid i \in \{1, \ldots, k\}\}$. Since $c = \bigvee_{p \in E} \overline{p} \vee q$ is a prime implicate of φ and $c \notin \varphi'$, there exists a model $v \in mod(\varphi')$ such that $c(v) = 0$. Let w be a maximal such model, i.e., no model $u (> w)$ exists such that $u \in mod(\varphi')$ and $c(u) = 0$. Since $c(w) = 0$ implies $w \notin mod(\varphi)$, there exists a prime implicate c_1 in $\varphi^\star$ (when Step 2 is finished) such that $c_1(w) = 0$. Clearly $c_1 \notin \varphi'$, i.e., c_1 is of form $c_1 = \bigvee_{p \in N(c_1)} \overline{p} \vee x_i$ such that $x_i \neq q$. Moreover, we have $q \notin N(c_1)$ by $c(w) = c_1(w) = 0$. Consider now the model w' defined by $w'_i = 1$ and $w'_j = w_j$, for all $j \neq i$. Note that $c(w') = 0$, and by the maximality of w, there is a prime implicate $c_2 \in \varphi$ such that $c_2(w') = 0$. Since $c_2(w) = 1$ and $c_2(w') = 0$, we have $x_i \in N(c_2)$. Since $q \notin N(c_1)$, a resolvent $c^\star$ of c_1 and c_2 thus exists. It can be shown (Eiter & Makino 2002) that $c^\star$ creates a new prime implicate $c' = \bigvee_{p \in N(c')} \overline{p} \vee q \subseteq c^\star$ of φ in Step 3, i.e., $N(c') \neq E_i, i = 1, \ldots, k$. This contradicts our assumption.

Thus, EXPLANATION is correct, and it remains to verify the time bound. Computing a prime implicate $c' \subseteq c$ of φ in Steps 2 and 3 is feasible in time $O(n \cdot \|\varphi\|)$, and thus the outputs in Step 2 occur with $O(m \cdot n \cdot \|\varphi\|)$ delay. As for Step 3, note the O contains only pairs (c_1, c_2) where $c_1 \in \varphi^\star$ and $c_2 = N(c_2) \cup \{q\}$ such that $N(c_2)$ was output, and each such pairs is added to O only once. Thus, the next output or termination follows within $e \cdot m$ runs of the while-loop, where e is the number of solutions output so far. The body of the loop can be done, using proper data structures, in $O(n \cdot \|\varphi\|)$ time (for checking $N(c_1) \notin S$ efficiently, we may store S in a prefix tree). Thus, the time until the next output resp. termination is bounded by $O(e \cdot m \cdot n \cdot \|\varphi\|)$. $\square$

From this result, we obtain the following corollary.

Corollary 1 *Given a Horn CNF φ and a query q, computing $O(n^k)$ many explanations of q, where k is a constant, is possible in polynomial time.*

This corollary implies that Selman and Leveque's conjecture (1996, p. 266) that generating $O(n)$ many explanations of q is NP-hard, where n is the number of propositional letters in the language, is not true (unless P=NP). Note, however, that by the results of (Selman & Levesque 1996), computing $O(n)$ many or all assumption-based explanations from a Horn Σ is not possible in total polynomial time unless P $=$ NP.

Let us now consider computing all explanations in the model-based setting.

Theorem 2 *Given the characteristic set $\mathcal{M} = char(\Sigma) \subseteq \{0,1\}^n$ of a Horn theory Σ, a query q, and $A \subseteq Lit$, computing the set of all explanations for q from Σ w.r.t. A is polynomial-time equivalent to dualizing a positive CNF.*

Here, polynomial-time equivalence means mutual polynomial-time transformability between deterministic functions, i.e., A reduces to B, if there a polynomial functions f, g s.t. for any input I of A, $f(I)$ is an input of B, and if O is the output for $f(I)$, then $g(O)$ is the output of I, cf. (Papadimitriou 1994); we also request that O has size polynomial in the size of the output for I (if not, trivial reductions may exist). In our reduction, explanations correspond to clauses of the dual prime CNF and vice versa.

Proof. (Sketch) By Props. 1 and 2, we need only compute all nontrivial explanations $E \subseteq A$ corresponding to prime implicates c of Σ s.t. $P(c) = \{q\}$ and $N(c) = E \subseteq A \cap P$.

We describe how the problem can be transformed to dualization of polynomially many positive CNFs $\varphi_1, \ldots, \varphi_k$, such that the clauses of the dual prime CNFs ψ_i for φ_i correspond to the explanations of q w.r.t. $A \cap P$ (equivalently, w.r.t. A). Thus, the problem is polynomially reducible to dualizing (in parallel) several positive CNFs φ_i. By simple methods, we can combine $\varphi_1, \ldots, \varphi_k$ into a single CNF φ (using further variables) such that the clauses of the dual prime CNF for φ correspond to the explanations of q w.r.t. A. (This step is of less interest in practice, since dualization of the individual φ_i is at the core of the computation.)

To construct the φ_i, we proceed as follows. Let $q = x_j$.

(1) Define $\mathcal{M}_i = \{v \in \mathcal{M} \mid v_j = i\}$, $i \in \{0,1\}$.

(2) For every model $v \in \max(\mathcal{M}_1)$, let
$$F_v = \max(\{v \wedge x^A \wedge w \mid w \in \max(\mathcal{M}_0)\}).$$

We associate with F_v a monotone Boolean function f_v on the variables $P_v = A \cap \{x_i \mid v_i = 1\}$ such that $f_v(w) = 0 \Leftrightarrow w \le s$ for some vector s in the projection of F_v on P_v. That is, F_v describes the maximal false points of f_v.

(3) Finally, define for every $v \in \max(\mathcal{M}_1)$
$$\varphi_v = \{c \mid N(c) = \emptyset, P(c) = P_v \setminus S, x^S \in F_v\}.$$

Note that φ_v is a prime CNF for f_v.

It can be shown (Eiter & Makino 2002) that the nontrivial explanations of q w.r.t. A are given by the clauses in all dual prime CNFs ψ_v for φ_v where $v \in \max(\mathcal{M}_1)$ (equivalently, by all prime implicants t, i.e., a prime DNF representation of f_v, $v \in \max(\mathcal{M}_1)$). This proves one direction of the result.

For the converse, we show that, given a positive CNF φ on atoms P, computing an equivalent prime DNF ψ is reducible

to computing all explanations as follows. Let q be a fresh letter (for component $n + 1$), and define $\mathcal{M} = \{(v, 0) \mid v \in \max(\{w \mid \varphi(w) = 0\})\} \cup \{(11 \cdots 1)\}$ and $A = P$; note that $\max(\{w \mid \varphi(w) = 0\})$ is easily computed from φ. $\square$

Example 4 Let $\mathcal{M} = \{(11011), (11010), (10101), (01010), (00001)\}$, and suppose we want all explanations of $q = x_1$ w.r.t. $A = \{x_3, x_4, x_5\}$. According to above, we obtain:

(1) $\mathcal{M}_0 = \{(01010), (00001)\}$ and $\mathcal{M}_1 = \{(11011), (11010), (10101)\}$, thus $\max(\mathcal{M}_1) = \{(11011), (10101)\}$.

(2) We have two vectors $v^{(1)} = (11011)$ and $v^{(2)} = (10101)$:

$$
F_{v^{(1)}} = \max\left(\left\{\begin{array}{l}(11011) \wedge (00111) \wedge (01010), \\ (11011) \wedge (00111) \wedge (00001)\end{array}\right\}\right)
$$
$$
= \{(00010), (00001)\},
$$
$$
F_{v^{(2)}} = \max\left(\left\{\begin{array}{l}(10101) \wedge (00111) \wedge (01010), \\ (10101) \wedge (00111) \wedge (00001)\end{array}\right\}\right)
$$
$$
= \{(00001)\}.
$$

Thus, $P_{v^{(1)}} = \{x_4, x_5\}$ and $f_{v^{(1)}}(w) = 0$ iff $w \in \{(10), (01), (00)\}$, and $P_{v^{(2)}} = \{x_3, x_5\}$ and $f_{v^{(2)}}(w) = 0$ iff $w \in \{(01), (00)\}$.

(3) We obtain $\varphi^{(1)} = x_4 \wedge x_5$ and $\varphi^{(2)} = x_3$. The respective prime dual CNFs are $\psi^{(1)} = x_4 \vee x_5$ and $\psi^{(2)} = x_3$.

Thus, the explanations of q w.r.t. A are $E_1 = \{x_4, x_5\}$ and $E_2 = \{x_3\}$. It can be seen that this is the correct result.

Negative Queries

So far, we considered Horn theories Σ and queries given by a letter q. In a general setting, we might allow that the formulas in Σ and the query are any propositional formulas. As for computation, we can introduce for a query, given by any formula χ, a fresh letter q, add implications $q \rightarrow \chi$, $\chi \rightarrow q$ in Σ, and then ask for a nontrivial explanation of q. Thus, positive letter queries do not constrain the expressivity of the framework. However, this technique does not work for Horn theories, if one of the implications $q \rightarrow \chi$, $\chi \rightarrow q$ is not Horn. In the simplest case, χ is a negative literal $\overline{q}$.

The next result tells us that already in this case, abduction from a Horn CNF is intractable. Recall that a Horn CNF φ is *acyclic*, if the graph on P with arcs from $x_i \in N(c)$ to $x_i \in P(c)$, $c \in \varphi$, has no directed cycle.

Theorem 3 *Given a Horn CNF φ, a general query χ in CNF, and $A \subseteq Lit$, deciding if χ has a nontrivial explanation w.r.t. A is NP-complete. Hardness holds even if $\chi = \overline{q}$, φ is acyclic, and either (i) $A = P$ or (ii) $A = P' \cup \overline{P}'$ for some $P' \subseteq P$.*

Proof. (Sketch) The problem is in NP, since clearly an explanation E exists if some set $E \subseteq A$ exists such that $\Sigma \cup E$ is satisfiable and $\Sigma \cup E \models \chi$; such an E can be guessed and the conditions can be checked in polynomial time.

Hardness is shown by a reduction from 3SAT. Let $\gamma = c_1 \wedge \cdots \wedge c_m$ be a 3CNF over atoms $x_1, \ldots, x_n$, where $c_i = \ell_{i,1} \vee \ell_{i,2} \vee \ell_{i,3}$. We introduce for each clause c_i a new atom y_i, for each x_j a new atom x_j', and a special atom z. The Horn CNF φ contains the following clauses:

- $\overline{x}_i \vee \overline{x'_i}$, for all $i = 1, \ldots, n$;

- $\overline{z} \vee y_1$

- $\overline{y}_i \vee \overline{\ell_{i,j}} \vee y_{i+1}$ if $\ell_{i,j}$ is positive and $\overline{y}_i \vee \overline{\ell'_{i,j}} \vee y_{i+1}$ if $\ell_{i,j}$ is negative, for all $i = 1, \ldots, m-1$ and $j = 1, 2, 3$;

- $\overline{y}_m \vee \overline{\ell_{m,j}}$ if $\ell_{m,j}$ is positive and $\overline{y}_m \vee \overline{\ell'_{m,j}}$ if $\ell_{i,j}$ is negative, for $j = 1, 2, 3$.

As easily seen, φ is acyclic Horn. It can be shown (Eiter & Makino 2002) that the query $q = \neg z$ has a nontrivial explanation E consisting of positive literals iff γ is satisfiable, which proves NP-hardness under restriction (i). For (ii), we use a similar construction. $\square$

Note that this result contrasts the tractability result that a nontrivial explanation $E \subseteq P$ for a positive query q can be computed in polynomial time (Selman & Levesque 1996). Thus, the framework of Horn abduction is sensitive with respect to query representation. We also remark that we can find an arbitrary explanation E for a query $\overline{q}$ (which may contain negative literals), in polynomial time.

In the model-based setting, we obtain for computing all explanations for a negative query a similar result as for a positive query.

Theorem 4 *Given the characteristic set $\mathcal{M} = char(\Sigma) \subseteq \{0,1\}^n$ of a Horn theory Σ, a negative query $\overline{q}$, and $A \subseteq Lit$, computing all explanations for q from Σ w.r.t. A is polynomial-time equivalent to dualizing a positive CNF.*

Proof. (Sketch) Observe that since the query is not positive, explanations of q may involve negative literals.

Proposition 2 implies that the nontrivial explanations for $\overline{q}$ w.r.t. A correspond to the prime implicates c of Σ such that $q \in N(c)$ and $P(c) \cup N(c) \subseteq A \cup \{q\}$. Let $q = x_j$, and define sets $\mathcal{M}_0$ and $\mathcal{M}_1$ for $\mathcal{M}$ as in the proof of Theorem 2. Denote by A_+ (resp., A_-) the set of positive (resp., negative) literals in A. We consider the following two cases:

(1) *Positive explanations for $\overline{q}$*. I.e., all prime implicates c of Σ s.t. $\{q\} \subseteq N(c) \subseteq A_+ \cup \{q\}$ and $P(c) = \emptyset$.

Similarly as in the proof of Theorem 2, we construct dualization problems for functions f_v, but for $v \in \max(\mathcal{M}_0)$:

(1.1) For every $v \in \max(\mathcal{M}_0)$, let
$$F_v = \max(\{v \wedge x^{A+} \wedge w \mid w \in \max(\mathcal{M}_1)\}).$$

The associated monotone Boolean function f_v on $P_v = A \cap \{x_i \mid v_i = 1\}$ is defined by $f_v(w) = 0 \Leftrightarrow w \leq s$ holds for some vector s in the projection of F_v on P_v.

(1.2) We define, for $v \in \max(\mathcal{M}_0)$,
$$\varphi_v = \{c \mid N(c) = \emptyset, P(c) = P_v \setminus S, x^S \in F_v\}.$$

Similarly as in Theorem 2, we can show that the clauses in the dual prime CNFs for all φ_v, $v \in \max(\mathcal{M}_0)$, correspond to the positive explanations of $\overline{q}$ (Eiter & Makino 2002).

(2) *Non-positive explanations for $\overline{q}$*. These are all prime implicates c of Σ s.t. $\{q\} \subseteq N(c) \subseteq A_+ \cup \{q\}$ and $P(c) = \{r\}$, where $r \in A_-$.

For each $r = x_{j'}$ (where $j' \neq j$), we proceed as follows.

(2.1) For every $v \in \max(\mathcal{M}_0)$ and $i \in \{0, 1\}$, define
$$\mathcal{M}_i^r = \{v \in \mathcal{M}_i \mid v_r = i\}.$$

(2.2) For each $v^{(0)} \in \max(\mathcal{M}_0^r)$ and $v^{(1)} \in \max(\mathcal{M}_1^r)$, let
$$F_{v^{(0)}, v^{(1)}} = \max(\{v^{(0)} \wedge v^{(1)} \wedge x^{A+} \wedge w \mid$$
$$w \in \max(\{u \in \mathcal{M}_1 \mid u_{j'} = 0\})\}).$$

We associate with it a monotone Boolean function $f_{v^{(0)}, v^{(1)}}$ on $P_{v^{(0)}, v^{(1)}} = A \cap \{x_i \mid v_i^{(0)} = v_i^{(1)} = 1\}$ such that $f_{v^{(0)}, v^{(1)}}(w) = 0 \Leftrightarrow w \leq s$ for some s in the projection of $F_{v^{(0)}, v^{(1)}}$ on $P_{v^{(0)}, v^{(1)}}$.

(2.3) We define the CNFs
$$\varphi_{v^{(0)}, v^{(1)}} = \{c \mid N(c) = \emptyset, P(c) = P_v \setminus S, x^S \in F_{v^{(0)}, v^{(1)}}\}.$$

Then, it can be shown (Eiter & Makino 2002) that the clauses in the dual prime CNFs $\psi_{v^{(0)}, v^{(1)}}$ for all $\varphi_{v^{(0)}, v^{(1)}}$, where $v^{(0)} \in \max(\mathcal{M}_0^r)$ and $v^{(1)} \in \max(\mathcal{M}_1^r)$ and $r \in A_-$, correspond to the non-positive explanations of $\overline{q}$.

In total, computing all explanations of $\overline{q}$ is polynomial-time reducible to dualizing (in parallel) polynomially many positive CNFs. As mentioned in the proof of Theorem 2, this is polynomially reducible to dualizing a single CNF.

The converse is shown by a reduction similar to the one in the proof of Theorem 2; we just invert the polarity of q. $\square$

Joint Explanations

We call any set of $E \subseteq A$ of literals a *joint explanation* of observations $o_1, o_2, \ldots, o_l$ from a background theory Σ w.r.t. a set of assumptions $A \subseteq Lit$, if E is an explanation of each o_i from Σ w.r.t. A. The observations o_i may be letters, or in a generalized setting propositional formulas.

Note that any such E is also an explanation for the conjunction $\alpha = o_1 \wedge o_2 \wedge \cdots \wedge o_l$ of all observations, while the converse is not true in general: an explanation E of α may not satisfy minimality for o_1, say, i.e., some $E' \subset E$ may explain o_1. Thus, joint explanations are stronger than ordinary explanations. In case of multiple explanations, this may be used to single out those which match with each of the (possibly independently made) observations.

For example, the malfunctioning of a car may be explained by two car mechanics, based on observations o_1 and o_2, respectively. A match of their (individual) diagnoses E_1 and E_2 (i.e., $E_1 = E_2$) may be taken in favor of believing in their correctness. In fact, the diagnoses are robust in the sense that adding the other observation does not require a change; from another perspective, the same diagnosis is good for explaining different observations. If E_1 and E_2 are different, then we might want to know whether alternative diagnoses E_1' and E_2' do exist which coincide, i.e., whether a joint explanation is possible.

As it turns out, recognizing joint explanations for CNFs, i.e., deciding whether E is a joint explanation for observations $o_1, \ldots, o_l$ described by CNFs, from Σ w.r.t. assumptions A is tractable, for both formula- and model based representation. However, deciding existence is harder.

Theorem 5 *Given a Horn CNF φ, query CNFs $\chi_1, \chi_2, \ldots, \chi_l$, where $l \geq 2$, and $A \subseteq Lit$, deciding if a joint explanation exists from Σ w.r.t. A is NP-complete. Hardness holds even if $l = 2$, each χ_i is a letter, φ is acyclic, and $A = Lit$.*

Theorem 6 *Given the characteristic set $\mathcal{M} = char(\Sigma)$ of a Horn theory Σ, query CNFs $\chi_1, \chi_2, \ldots, \chi_l$, $l \geq 2$, and $A \subseteq Lit$, deciding if a joint explanation exists from Σ w.r.t. A is NP-complete. Hardness holds even if $l = 2$, each χ_i is a letter, and $A = Lit$.*

Thus, the tractability results in (Selman & Levesque 1996; Kautz, Kearns, & Selman 1993) do not generalize to joint explanations for positive queries. Similar intractability results hold for negative queries and combined positive and negative queries.

Related Works

Selman and Levesque (1990; 1996) were among the first to study the complexity of computing general and assumption-based explanations; Corollary 1 closes an open problem of them. The underlying algorithm EXPLANATIONS is a relative of a similar procedure by Boros *et al.* (1990) for computing all prime implicates of a Horn CNF in output-polynomial time. In fact, Theorem 1 can be seen as a strengthening of their result. For negative queries, a similar algorithm is not evident. del Val (2000) presented generation of implicates and prime implicates of certain clausal theories in a target language, which is formed on a subset of the atoms, using a procedure based on kernel resolution and derived exponential bounds on its running time. Furthermore, del Val described the use of this procedure for generating jointly all explanations of all literals not on a set of atoms V. However, neither is this method incremental in nature, nor is it clear whether it is total polynomial time. Moreover, it considers a letter q and its negation $\bar{q}$ at once.

Inoue (1992) considered, in the propositional and the first-order context, generating explanations and prime implicates using SOL-resolution. He proposed a strategy which processes, starting from the empty set, clauses from a theory incrementally. However, due to possible large intermediate results, this method is not total polynomial time in general. Khardon *et al.* (1999) show how computing all keys of a relational database schema, which is constrained by a Boolean formula φ, can be polynomially transformed into computing all explanations of a query q from $\varphi \wedge \psi$, where ψ is Horn. Thus, our algorithm EXPLANATIONS can be used for efficiently generating all keys of a database scheme where φ is a Horn CNF. This generalizes the result for φ consisting of non-negative Horn clauses, i.e., a set of functional dependencies (Lucchesi & Osborn 1978).[1] Note that Khardon *et al.* also show how to compute a single explanation of a query q from a theory φ polynomially, using repeatedly an oracle for computing a key of a database schema constrained by $\varphi \wedge \psi$, where ψ is Horn; however, this method is not usable for generating explanations from general Horn theories (cf. Footnote 1). Less related to our work is (Eiter & Gottlob 1995), which considered abduction from Horn and general propositional theories, but focused on existence of explanations and reasoning tasks about explanations.

Conclusion

We have presented a number of positive and negative results about generating all and some abductive explanations, re-

spectively, which complement previous work in the literature. In particular, we analyzed the role of positive vs negative abductive queries, under both formula- and model-based representation, and we considered the novel notion of joint explanation. Our positive results may be readily applied for efficiently computing (a subset of) all explanations. The results draw a complete picture for the model-based setting, and almost so for the formula-based setting; the complexity of generating all explanations for a negative query in it is currently open.

Acknowledgments

We thank the reviewers for helpful comments. This work was partly supported by the Austrian Science Fund (FWF) project Z29-INF, by TU Wien through a scientific collaboration grant, and by the Scientific Grant in Aid of the Ministry of Education, Science, Sports and Culture of Japan.

References

Bioch, C., and Ibaraki, T. 1995. Complexity of identification and dualization of positive Boolean functions. *Information and Computation* 123:50–63.

Boros, E.; Crama, Y.; and Hammer, P. L. 1990. Polynomial-time inference of all valid implications for Horn and related formulae. *Annals of Mathematics & Artificial Intelligence* 1:21–32.

Brewka, G.; Dix, J.; and Konolige, K. 1997. *Nonmonotonic Reasoning – An Overview*. Number 73 in CSLI Lecture Notes. CSLI Publications, Stanford University.

Dechter, R., and Pearl, J. 1992. Structure identification in relational data. *Artificial Intelligence* 58:237–270.

del Val, A. 2000. The complexity of restricted consequence finding and abduction. In *Proc. AAAI-00*, 337–342.

Eiter, T., and Gottlob, G. 1995. The complexity of logic-based abduction. *J. ACM* 42(1):3–42.

Eiter, T., and Makino, K. 2002. On computing all abductive explanations (preliminary report). Technical Report INFSYS RR-1843-02-04, Institut für Informationssysteme, TU Wien, Austria.

Eiter, T.; Gottlob, G.; and Makino, K. 2002. New results on monotone dualization and generating hypergraph transversals. In *Proc. 34th ACM Symp. on Theory of Computing (STOC 2002)*.

Fredman, M., and Khachiyan, L. 1996. On the complexity of dualization of monotone disjunctive normal forms. *Journal of Algorithms* 21:618–628.

Inoue, K. 1992. Linear resolution for consequence finding. *Artificial Intelligence* 56(2-3):301–354.

Kautz, H.; Kearns, M.; and Selman, B. 1993. Reasoning with characteristic models. In *Proc. AAAI-93*, 34–39.

Khardon, R., and Roth, D. 1996. Reasoning with models. *Artificial Intelligence* 87(1/2):187–213.

Khardon, R.; Mannila, H.; and Roth, D. 1999. Reasoning with examples: Propositional formulae and database dependencies. *Acta Informatica* 36(4):267–286.

Lucchesi, C. L., and Osborn, S. 1978. Candidate keys for relations. *J. Computer and System Sciences* 17:270–279.

Papadimitriou, C. H. 1994. *Computational Complexity*.

Poole, D. 1989. Explanation and prediction: An architecture for default and abductive reasoning. *Comp. Intelligence* 5(1):97–110.

Selman, B., and Levesque, H. J. 1990. Abductive and default reasoning: A computational core. In *Proc. AAAI-90*, 343–348.

Selman, B., and Levesque, H. J. 1996. Support set selection for abductive and default reasoning. *Artif. Intell.* 82:259–272.

---

[1] In fact, Khardon *et al.*'s transformation works only if φ has no negative prime implicate; otherwise, keys introduce inconsistency.

Measuring Inconsistency in Knowledge via Quasi-classical Models

Anthony Hunter

Department of Computer Science
University College London
Gower Street
London WC1E 6BT, UK
a.hunter@cs.ucl.ac.uk

Abstract

The language for describing inconsistency is underdeveloped. If a knowledgebase (a set of formulae) is inconsistent, we need more illuminating ways to say how inconsistent it is, or to say whether one knowledgebase is "more inconsistent" than another. To address this, we provide a general characterization of inconsistency, based on quasi-classical logic (a form of paraconsistent logic with a more expressive semantics than Belnap's four-valued logic, and unlike other paraconsistent logics, allows the connectives to appear to behave as classical connectives). We analyse inconsistent knowledge by considering the conflicts arising in the minimal quasi-classical models for that knowledge. This is used for a measure of coherence for each knowledgebase, and for a preference ordering, called the compromise relation, over knowledgebases. In this paper, we formalize this framework, and consider applications in managing heterogeneous sources of knowledge.

Introduction

Comparing heterogeneous sources often involves comparing conflicts. Suppose we are dealing with a group of clinicians advising on some patient, a group of witnesses of some incident, or a set of newspaper reports covering some event. These are all situations where we expect some degree of inconsistency in the information. Suppose that the information by each source i is represented by the set Φ_i. Each source may provide information that conflicts with the domain knowledge Ψ. Let us represent $\Phi_i \cup \Psi$ by Δ_i for each source i. Now, we may want to know whether one source is more inconsistent than another — so whether Δ_i is more inconsistent that Δ_j — and in particular determine which is the least inconsistent of the sources and so identify a minimal Δ_i in this inconsistency ordering. We may then view this minimal knowledgebase as the least problematical or most reliable source of information.

Current techniques for measuring the degree of inconsistency in a set of formulae are underdeveloped. Some approaches touch on the topic. In diagnostic systems, there are proposals that offer preferences for certain kinds of consistent subsets of inconsistent information (Kleer & Williams 1987; Reiter 1987); in proposals for belief revision, epistemic entrenchment is an ordering over formulae which re-

flects the preference for which formulae to give up in case of inconsistency (Gardenfors 1988); in proposals for drawing inferences from inconsistent information there is a preference for inferences from some consistent subsets (e.g. (Brewka 1989; Benferhat, Dubois, & Prade 1993)); in proposals for approximating entailment, two sequences of entailment relation are defined (the first is sound but not complete, and the second is complete but not sound) which converge to classical entailment (Schaerf & Cadoli 1995); and in proposals for partial consistency checking, checking is terminated after the search space exceeds a threshold which gives a measure of partial consistency of the data. However, none of these proposals provide a direct definition for degree of inconsistency.

In belief revision theory, and the related field of knowledgebase merging, there are some proposals that do provide some description of the degree of inconsistency of a set of formulae. For example, the Dalal distance (Dalal 1988), essentially the Hamming distance between two propositional interpretations, can be used to give a profile of an inconsistent knowledgebase. Let $dalal(w, w')$ denote the Dalal distance from w to w', let $[\alpha]$ denote the set of classical models of α, and let $d(w, \alpha)$ be the $w' \in [\alpha]$ such that $dalal(w, w')$ is minimized. Now suppose we have a knowledgebase $\{\alpha_1, .., \alpha_n\}$ where each α_i is consistent but the knowledgebase may be inconsistent. We can then obtain a value of $d(w, \alpha_i)$ for each world w and each formula α_i in the knowledgebase. Unfortunately, this does not provide a very succinct way of describing the degree of inconsistency in a given set of formulae, and it is not clear how we could compare sets of formulae using this approach. Furthermore, operators for aggregating these distances, such as the majority operator (Lin & Mendelzon 1998), egalitarist operator (Revesz 1997), or the leximax operator (Konieczny & Pino Perez 1998), do not seem to be appropriate summaries of the degree of inconsistency in the original knowledgebase since they seek to find the most appropriate model for particular kinds of compromise of the original knowledge. Related techniques for knowledgebase revision are similarly inappropriate.

Another approach to handling inconsistent information is that of possibility theory (Dubois, Lang, & Prade 1994). Let (ϕ, α) be a weighted formula where ϕ is a classical formula and $\alpha \in [0, 1]$. A possibilistic knowledgebase B is a set of weighted formulae. An α-cut of a possibilistic knowledgebase, denoted $B_{\geq \alpha}$, is $\{(\psi, \beta) \in B \mid \beta \geq \alpha\}$. The inconsistency degree of B, denoted $Inc(B)$, is the maximum value of α such that the α-cut is inconsistent. As presented, the problem with this measure is that it assumes weighted formulae. In other words, we need some form of preference ordering in addition to the set of classical formulae in the knowledgebase. The knowledgebase can be used to induce such an ordering as suggested in (Benferhat *et al.* 2000), where an ordering over inferentially weaker forms of the original formulae are generated. Again this does not offer a direct lucid view on the inconsistency in the original set of formulae.

Measuring the "amount of information" is related to the idea of measuring inconsistency. Information theory can be used to measure the information content of sets of inconsistent formulae. Applying Shannon's measure of information, Lozinskii proposes that the information in a set of propositional formulae Γ, that has been composed from n different atom symbols, is the logarithm of the number of models (2^n) divided by the number of models for the maximum consistent subsets of Γ (Lozinskii 1994). This information theoretic measure increases with additions of consistent information and decreases with additions of inconsistent information. However, as highlighted by Wong and Besnard, the measure by Lozinskii is syntax sensitive and it is sensitive to the presence of tautologies in Γ. To address this, they suggest the use of a normal form for the formulae in Γ that is obtained by rewriting Γ into conjunctive normal form, and then applying disjunction elimination and resolution exhaustively (Wong & Besnard 2001). However, this approach does not provide a direct measure of inconsistency since for example, the value for $\{\alpha\}$ is the same as for $\{\alpha, \neg\alpha, \beta\}$.

In this paper, we want to reflect each inconsistent set of formulae in a model, and then measure the inconsistency in the model. Obviously, this is not possible in classical logic, or indeed many non-classical logics, because there is no model of an inconsistent set of formulae. We therefore turn to quasi-classical logic, a form of paraconsistent logic, to model inconsistent sets of formulae. There are other paraconsistent logics that we could consider, for example Belnap's four-valued logic (Belnap 1977), or Levesque's 3-interpretations (Levesque 1984), or Grant's generalizations of classical satisfaction (Grant 1978), but these, as we will illustrate, involve the consideration of too many models. This increases the number of models that need to be analysed and it underspecifies the nature of the conflicts.

In this paper, we review the aspects of QC logic that we will require for the rest of the paper, we argue why QC models are more appropriate than those obtained from other paraconsistent logics, we define a new framework for measuring inconsistencies in models, and we extend this semantic framework to preference relations over sets of formulae.

Review of QC Logic

We review the propositional version of quasi-classical logic (QC Logic) (Besnard & Hunter 1995; Hunter 2000).

Definition 1 *The **language of first-order QC logic** is that of classical propositional logic. We let $\mathcal{L}$ denote a set of formulae formed in the usual way from a set of atom symbols $\mathcal{A}$, and the connectives $\{\neg, \vee, \wedge, \rightarrow\}$. If $\Gamma \in \wp(\mathcal{L})$, then Atoms$(\Gamma)$ returns the set of atom symbols used in Γ.*

Definition 2 *Let α be an atom, and let $\sim$ be a complementation operation such that $\sim \alpha$ is $\neg\alpha$ and $\sim(\neg\alpha)$ is α. The $\sim$ operator is not part of the object language, but it makes some definitions clearer.*

Definition 3 *Let $\alpha_1 \vee .. \vee \alpha_n$ be a clause that includes a literal disjunct α_i and $n > 1$. The **focus** of $\alpha_1 \vee .. \vee \alpha_n$ by α_i, denoted $\otimes(\alpha_1 \vee .. \vee \alpha_n, \alpha_i)$, is defined as the clause obtained by removing α_i from $\alpha_1 \vee .. \vee \alpha_n$.*

Example 1 *Let $\alpha \vee \beta \vee \gamma$ be a clause where α, β, and γ are literals. Hence, $\otimes(\alpha \vee \beta \vee \gamma, \beta) = \alpha \vee \gamma$.*

We now consider the essential idea behind QC logic. We describe it using the resolution proof rule. Resolution can be applied to clauses to generate further clauses called resolvents. For example, by resolution $\beta \vee \gamma$ is a resolvent of $\alpha \vee \beta$ and $\neg\alpha \vee \gamma$. Given a set of clauses as assumptions, each clause in the assumptions can be regarded as a belief, and each resolvent can be regarded as a belief. So resolution can be regarded as a process of focusing beliefs.

A useful property of resolution is that α is a resolvent only if all the literals used in α are literals used in the set of assumptions (assuming no introduction proof rules are used). This means that any resolvent, and hence any belief derivable from the assumptions, is a non-trivial inference from the assumptions. This holds even if the set of assumptions is classically inconsistent. As a result, resolution can constitute the basis of useful paraconsistent reasoning.

QC logic is motivated by the need to handle beliefs rather than the need to address issues of verisimilitude for given propositions. It is intended to be a logic of beliefs in the "real world" rather than a logic of truths in the "real world". Models are based on a form of Herbrand interpretation.

Definition 4 *Let $\mathcal{A}$ be a set of atoms. Let $\mathcal{O}$ be the set of objects defined as follows, where $+\alpha$ is a positive object, and $-\alpha$ is a negative object.*

$$\mathcal{O} = \{+\alpha \mid \alpha \in \mathcal{A}\} \cup \{-\alpha \mid \alpha \in \mathcal{A}\}$$

*We call any $X \in \wp(\mathcal{O})$ a **QC model**. So X can contain both $+\alpha$ and $-\alpha$ for some atom α.*

For each atom $\alpha \in \mathcal{L}$, and each $X \in \wp(\mathcal{O})$, $+\alpha \in X$ means that in X there is **a reason for** the belief α and that in X there is **a reason against** the belief $\neg\alpha$. Similarly, $-\alpha \in X$ means that in X there is **a reason against** the belief α and that in X there is **a reason for** the belief $\neg\alpha$.

Definition 5 *Let $\models_s$ be a satisfiability relation called **strong satisfaction**. For a model X, we define $\models_s$ as follows, where $\alpha_1, ..., \alpha_n$ are literals in $\mathcal{L}$, $n > 1$, and α is a literal in $\mathcal{L}$.*

$X \models_s \alpha$ iff there is a reason for the belief α in X

$X \models_s \alpha_1 \vee ... \vee \alpha_n$
iff $[X \models_s \alpha_1$ or ... or $X \models_s \alpha_n]$
*   and $\forall i$ s.t. $1 \leq i \leq n$*
* $[X \models_s \sim\alpha_i$ implies $X \models_s \otimes(\alpha_1 \vee ... \vee \alpha_n, \alpha_i)]$*

For $\alpha, \beta, \gamma \in \mathcal{L}$, we extend the definition as follows,

$$X \models_s \alpha \wedge \beta \text{ iff } X \models_s \alpha \text{ and } X \models_s \beta$$
$$X \models_s \neg\neg\alpha \vee \gamma \text{ iff } X \models_s \alpha \vee \gamma$$
$$X \models_s \neg(\alpha \wedge \beta) \vee \gamma \text{ iff } X \models_s \neg\alpha \vee \neg\beta \vee \gamma$$
$$X \models_s \neg(\alpha \vee \beta) \vee \gamma \text{ iff } X \models_s (\neg\alpha \wedge \neg\beta) \vee \gamma$$
$$X \models_s \alpha \vee (\beta \wedge \gamma) \text{ iff } X \models_s (\alpha \vee \beta) \wedge (\alpha \vee \gamma)$$
$$X \models_s \alpha \wedge (\beta \vee \gamma) \text{ iff } X \models_s (\alpha \wedge \beta) \vee (\alpha \wedge \gamma)$$
$$X \models_s (\alpha \rightarrow \beta) \vee \gamma \text{ iff } X \models_s \neg\alpha \vee \beta \vee \gamma$$
$$X \models_s \neg(\alpha \rightarrow \beta) \vee \gamma \text{ iff } X \models_s (\alpha \wedge \neg\beta) \vee \gamma$$

Definition 6 *For $X \in \wp(\mathcal{O})$ and $\Delta \in \wp(\mathcal{L})$, let $X \models_s \Delta$ denote that $X \models_s \alpha$ holds for every α in Δ. Let $\mathsf{QC}(\Delta) = \{X \in \wp(\mathcal{O}) \mid X \models_s \Delta\}$ be the set of QC models for Δ.*

A key feature of the QC semantics is that there is a model for any formula, and for any set of formulae.

Example 2 *Let $\Delta = \{\neg\alpha \vee \neg\beta \vee \gamma, \neg\alpha \vee \gamma, \neg\gamma\}$, where $\alpha, \beta, \gamma \in \mathcal{A}$, and let $X = \{-\alpha, -\beta, -\gamma\}$. So $X \models_s \neg\alpha$, $X \models_s \neg\beta$ and $X \models_s \neg\gamma$. Also, $X \models_s \sim\gamma$. Hence, $X \models_s \neg\alpha \vee \gamma$, and $X \models_s \neg\alpha \vee \neg\beta$, and so, $X \models_s \neg\alpha \vee \neg\beta \vee \gamma$. Hence every formula in Δ is strongly satisfiable in X.*

The following result from (Hunter 2000) provides a slightly different view on the semantics of disjunction.

Proposition 1 *Let $X \in \wp(\mathcal{O})$, and $\alpha_1, .., \alpha_n$ be literals in $\mathcal{L}$. We have $X \models_s \alpha_1 \vee .. \vee \alpha_n$ iff (1) for some $\alpha_i \in \{\alpha_1, .., \alpha_n\}$, $X \models_s \alpha_i$ and $X \not\models_s \sim\alpha_i$ or (2) for all $\alpha_i \in \{\alpha_1, .., \alpha_n\}$, $X \models_s \alpha_i$ and $X \models_s \sim\alpha_i$.*

Strong satisfaction is used to define a notion of entailment for QC logic. There is also a natural deduction proof theory for propositional QC logic (Hunter 2000) and a semantic tableau version for first-order QC logic (Hunter 2001). Entailment for QC logic for propositional CNF formulae is coNP-complete, and via a linear time transformation these formulae can be handled using classical logic theorem provers (Marquis & Porquet 2001).

Why measure inconsistency with QC models?

The definitions for QC models and for strong satisfaction provide us with the basic concepts for measuring inconsistency. QC logic exhibits the nice feature that no attention needs to be paid to a special form that the formulae in a set of premises should have. This is in contrast with other paraconsistent logics where two formulae identical by definition of a connective in classical logic may not yield the same set of conclusions. For example, in QC logic, β is entailed by both $\{(\neg\alpha \rightarrow \beta), \neg\alpha\}$ and $\{\alpha \vee \beta, \neg\alpha\}$ and γ is entailed by $\{\gamma \wedge \neg\gamma\}$ and $\{\gamma, \neg\gamma\}$. QC logic is much better behaved in this respect than other paraconsistent logics such as C_ω (da Costa 1974), and consistency-based logics such as (Benferhat, Dubois, & Prade 1993). Furthermore, the semantics of QC logic directly models inconsistent sets of formulae.

Whilst four-valued logic (Belnap 1977) also directly models inconsistent sets of formulae, QC logic is stronger in the sense that the number of non-tautological inferences obtained from a set of formulae is never less than with four-valued logic, and often it is greater. Consider the example $\{\alpha \vee \beta, \neg\alpha\}$ from which the inference β can be obtained

with QC logic but not with four-valued logic. This stronger notion of inference and entailment is reflected in the models and so more closely reflects the non-trivial aspects of classical reasoning.

Another way of viewing the weakness of Belnap's four-valued logic is that there are too many four-valued models in many situations. Consider for example $\{\alpha \vee \beta, \neg\alpha\}$. We have one minimal QC model $\{-\alpha, +\beta\}$, but with four-valued logic there are a number of models that satisfy this set. QC logic has a reduced number of models because of the constraint in the definition of strong satisfaction for disjunction that ensures that if the complement of a disjunct holds in the model, then the resolvent should also hold in the model. This strong constraint means that various other proposals for many-valued logic will tend to have more models for any given knowledgebase than QC logic.

Another approach that we should consider here is that of 3-interpretation by (Levesque 1984), and a similar proposal by (Grant 1978). A 3-interpretation is a truth assignment into {true,false} that does not map both a literal and its complement into false. This is extended to clauses so that a 3-interpretation satisfies a clause if and only if it satisfies some of the literals in the clause. As with Belnap's four-valued logic, there are too many models. First consider $\{\alpha, \neg\alpha \vee \neg\beta, \beta\}$. This has three 3-interpretations: (1) $\alpha, \neg\alpha, \beta$ are true and $\neg\beta$ is false; (2) $\alpha, \beta, \neg\beta$ are true and $\neg\alpha$ is false; and (3) $\alpha, \neg\alpha, \beta, \neg\beta$ are true. In contrast, there is just one minimal QC model $\{+\alpha, -\alpha, +\beta, -\beta\}$, and we argue that this QC model better describes the conflicts in the set of formulae. Now consider $\{\alpha, \neg\alpha \vee \neg\beta\}$. This has three 3-interpretations: (1) $\alpha, \neg\alpha, \neg\beta$ are true; (2) $\alpha, \neg\beta$ are true and $\neg\alpha$ is false; and (3) $\alpha, \neg\alpha$ are true and $\neg\beta$ is false. In contrast, there is just one minimal QC model $\{+\alpha, -\beta\}$.

Minimal QC models

For measuring inconsistency, we use minimal QC models.

Definition 7 *Let $\Delta \in \wp(\mathcal{L})$. Let $\mathsf{MQC}(\Delta) \subseteq \mathsf{QC}(\Delta)$ be the set of minimal QC models for Δ, defined as follows:*

$$\mathsf{MQC}(\Delta) = \{X \in \mathsf{QC}(\Delta) \mid \text{if } Y \subset X, \text{ then } Y \notin \mathsf{QC}(\Delta)\}$$

Example 3 *Consider the following sets of formulae.*

$$\mathsf{MQC}(\{\alpha \wedge \neg\alpha, \alpha \vee \beta, \neg\alpha \vee \gamma\})$$
$$= \{\{+\alpha, -\alpha, +\beta, +\gamma\}\}$$
$$\mathsf{MQC}(\{\neg\alpha \wedge \alpha, \beta \vee \gamma\})$$
$$= \{\{+\alpha, -\alpha, +\beta\}, \{+\alpha, -\alpha, +\gamma\}\}$$
$$\mathsf{MQC}(\{\alpha \vee \beta, \neg\alpha \vee \gamma\})$$
$$= \{\{+\beta, +\gamma\}, \{+\alpha, +\gamma\}, \{-\alpha, +\beta\}\}$$

Proposition 2 *Let $\mathsf{Atoms}(\Delta) = n$. If $X \in \mathsf{MQC}(\Delta)$, then $|X| \leq 2n$. Also, if $|X| = 2n$, and $X \in \mathsf{MQC}(\Delta)$, then $\mathsf{MQC}(\Delta) = \{X\}$.*

Increasing the number of inconsistencies in a knowledgebase tends to decrease the number of minimal QC models.

Definition 8 *Let $\Delta \in \wp(\mathcal{L})$, and $\mathsf{Incon}(\Delta) = \{\Gamma \subseteq \Delta \mid \Gamma \vdash \bot\}$ where $\vdash$ is classical consequence. The set of minimal inconsistent subsets of Δ, denoted $\mathsf{MI}(\Delta)$, is defined as,*

$$\mathsf{MI}(\Delta) = \{\Phi \in \mathsf{Incon}(\Delta) \mid \forall\Psi \in \mathsf{Incon}(\Delta) \; \Psi \not\subset \Phi\}$$

The following shows a simple relationship between the minimal QC models for a knowledgebase and those for the minimal inconsistent subsets of it.

Proposition 3 *Let $\Delta \in \wp(\mathcal{L})$. Let $\Gamma \in \mathsf{MI}(\Delta)$. If $X \in \mathsf{MQC}(\Delta)$, then $\exists Y \in \mathsf{MQC}(\Gamma)$ such that $Y \subseteq X$. However if $Y \in \mathsf{MQC}(\Gamma)$, then it is not necessarily the case that $\exists X \in \mathsf{MQC}(\Delta)$ such that $Y \subseteq X$.*

Finding minimal QC models is more expensive than finding just QC models. For any set of formulae Δ, let $X = \{+\alpha \mid \alpha \in \mathsf{Atoms}(\Delta)\} \cup \{-\alpha \mid \alpha \in \mathsf{Atoms}(\Delta)\}$. So X is a QC model that satisfies Δ, and it can be found in time that is a linear function of the size of the formulae, though X is not necessarily a minimal QC model. If $|X| = n$, then there are 2^n QC models that can be formed from X by taking subsets of X. This includes all minimal QC models of Δ.

Proposition 4 *Determining whether $X \in \mathsf{MQC}(\Delta)$ holds is a coNP-complete problem when all $\alpha \in \Delta$ are CNF.*

This result is based on the linear time transformation by (Marquis & Porquet 2001) that can be used to turn a QC satisfaction problem into a classical satisfaction problem, and on the coNP-complete property of checking whether a given classical interpretation is a minimal model of a given formula (Cadoli 1992).

Measuring coherence of QC models

We now consider a measure of inconsistency called coherence. The opinionbase of a QC model X is the set of atomic beliefs (atoms) for which there are reasons for or against in X, and the conflictbase of X is the set of atomic beliefs with reasons for and against in X.

Definition 9 *Let $X \in \wp(\mathcal{O})$.*

$$\mathsf{Conflictbase}(X) = \{\alpha \mid +\alpha \in X \text{ and } -\alpha \in X\}$$
$$\mathsf{Opinionbase}(X) = \{\alpha \mid +\alpha \in X \text{ or } -\alpha \in X\}$$

If $\mathsf{Opinionbase}(X) = \emptyset$, then X has no arguments for/against any beliefs, and hence X has no opinions. If $\mathsf{Opinionbase}(X) = \mathcal{A}$, then X is totally opinionated. If $\mathsf{Conflictbase}(X) = \emptyset$, then X is a conflictfree QC model. If $\mathsf{Opinionbase}(X) = \mathcal{A}$, and $\mathsf{Conflictbase}(X) = \emptyset$, then we describe X as omniscient.

In finding the minimal QC models for a set of formulae, minimization of the size of each model forces minimization of the conflictbase of each model. As a result of this minimization, there is a unique conflictbase that is common to all the minimal QC models for each set of formulae, though there is not necessarily a unique opinionbase.

Proposition 5 *Let $\Delta \in \wp(\mathcal{L})$. If $X, Y \in \mathsf{MQC}(\Delta)$, then (1) $\mathsf{Conflictbase}(X) = \mathsf{Conflictbase}(Y)$ and (2) either $\mathsf{Opinionbase}(X) = \mathsf{Opinionbase}(Y)$ or $\mathsf{Opinionbase}(X)$ is not a subset of $\mathsf{Opinionbase}(Y)$.*

This result is based on Proposition 1, and on the following observation, where Δ is a set of clauses: For all $X \in \mathsf{MQC}(\Delta)$, $+\alpha \in X$ and $-\alpha \in X$ iff there is a $\phi \in \cup\mathsf{MI}(\Delta)$ such that α is a disjunct in ϕ and there is a $\psi \in \cup\mathsf{MI}(\Delta)$ such that $\neg\alpha$ is a disjunct in ψ.

Increasing the size of the conflictbase, with respect to the size of the opinionbase, decreases the degree of coherence, as defined below.

Definition 10 *The $\mathsf{Coherence}$ function from $\wp(\mathcal{O})$ into $[0, 1]$, is defined below when X is non-empty, and $\mathsf{Coherence}(\emptyset) = 1$.*

$$\mathsf{Coherence}(X) = 1 - \frac{|\mathsf{Conflictbase}(X)|}{|\mathsf{Opinionbase}(X)|}$$

If $\mathsf{Coherence}(X) = 1$, then X is a totally coherent, and if $\mathsf{Coherence}(X) = 0$, then X is totally incoherent, otherwise, X is partially coherent/incoherent.

Example 4 *Let $X \in \mathsf{MQC}(\{\neg\alpha \wedge \alpha, \beta \wedge \neg\beta, \gamma \wedge \neg\gamma\})$, $Y \in \mathsf{MQC}(\{\alpha, \neg\alpha \vee \neg\beta, \beta, \gamma\})$, and $Z \in \mathsf{MQC}(\{\neg\alpha, \beta, \neg\gamma \wedge \gamma\})$. So $\mathsf{Coherence}(X) = 0$, $\mathsf{Coherence}(Y) = 1/3$, and $\mathsf{Coherence}(Z) = 2/3$.*

Different minimal QC models for the same knowledgebase are not necessarily equally coherent.

Example 5 *Let $\Delta = \{\alpha, \neg\alpha, \beta \vee \gamma, \beta \vee \delta\}$, and let $X = \{+\alpha, -\alpha, +\beta\}$ and $Y = \{+\alpha, -\alpha, +\gamma, +\delta\}$. So $\mathsf{MQC}(\Delta) = \{X, Y\}$, and $\mathsf{Coherence}(X) = 1/2$ and $\mathsf{Coherence}(Y) = 2/3$.*

We extend coherence to knowledgebases as follows.

Definition 11 *Let $\Delta \in \wp(\mathcal{L})$. Assign $\mathsf{Coherence}(\Delta)$ the maximum value in $\{\mathsf{Coherence}(X) \mid X \in \mathsf{MQC}(\Delta)\}$*

Example 6 *Let $\Delta = \{\alpha \wedge \neg\alpha, \beta \wedge \neg\beta, \alpha \vee \beta \vee (\gamma \wedge \delta)\}$ and $\Delta' = \{\alpha \wedge \neg\alpha, \alpha \vee \beta\}$. Here $\mathsf{Coherence}(\Delta) = \mathsf{Coherence}(\Delta') = 1/2$.*

Example 7 *Let $\Delta = \{\phi \wedge \neg\phi, \alpha \vee (\beta \wedge \gamma \wedge \delta)\}$ and $\Delta' = \{\phi \wedge \neg\phi, (\alpha \wedge \beta) \vee (\gamma \wedge \delta)\}$. Also let $X_1 = \{+\phi, -\phi, +\alpha\}$, $X_2 = \{+\phi, -\phi, +\beta, +\gamma, +\delta\}$, $Y_1 = \{+\phi, -\phi, +\alpha, +\beta\}$, and $Y_2 = \{+\phi, -\phi, +\gamma, +\delta\}$. So, $\mathsf{MQC}(\Delta) = \{X_1, X_2\}$ and $\mathsf{MQC}(\Delta') = \{Y_1, Y_2\}$. Also, $\mathsf{Coherence}(X_1) = 1/2$, $\mathsf{Coherence}(X_2) = 3/4$, $\mathsf{Coherence}(Y_1) = 2/3$, and $\mathsf{Coherence}(Y_2) = 2/3$. So $\mathsf{Coherence}(\Delta) > \mathsf{Coherence}(\Delta')$.*

The coherence function is not a monotonic function, as illustrated by the following example.

Example 8 *Let $\Delta = \{\alpha\}$ and $\Delta' = \{\alpha, \neg\alpha, \beta\}$. So $\Delta \subset \Delta'$, and $\mathsf{Coherence}(\Delta) > \mathsf{Coherence}(\Delta')$. Now let $\Delta'' = \{\alpha, \neg\alpha\}$. So $\Delta \subset \Delta'' \subset \Delta'$, and $\mathsf{Coherence}(\Delta'') < \mathsf{Coherence}(\Delta')$.*

The coherence function does not discriminate on the number or intersection of the minimal inconsistent subsets of a knowledgebase as illustrated by the following example.

Example 9 *Let $\Delta = \{\alpha \wedge \neg\alpha, \beta \wedge \neg\beta\}$ and $\Delta' = \{\alpha \wedge \beta, \neg\alpha \wedge \neg\beta\}$. Here Δ has two disjoint minimal inconsistent subsets whereas Δ' has one. Yet $\mathsf{Coherence}(\Delta) = \mathsf{Coherence}(\Delta') = 0$.*

Example 10 *Let $\Delta = \{\alpha \wedge \neg\alpha\}$ and $\Delta' = \{\beta \wedge \neg\beta\}$. Here $\mathsf{Coherence}(\Delta) = \mathsf{Coherence}(\Delta')$ even though Δ and Δ' are quite distinct as indicated by $\mathsf{Atoms}(\Delta) \cap \mathsf{Atoms}(\Delta') = \emptyset$.*

In the next section, we present an alternative to the coherence function for comparing knowledgebases. We aim to differentiate between knowledgebases such as Δ and Δ' given in Example 10.

Compromising on inconsistency

In the following, we define the compromise relation to prefer knowledgebases with models with a greater opinionbase and a smaller conflictbase.

Definition 12 *Let $\Delta, \Delta' \in \wp(\mathcal{L})$. The **compromise relation**, denoted $\preceq$, is defined as follows:*

$$\Delta \preceq \Delta' \text{ iff } \forall X \in \mathsf{MQC}(\Delta) \text{ and } \exists Y \in \mathsf{MQC}(\Delta')$$
$$\text{such that } \mathsf{Conflictbase}(X) \subseteq \mathsf{Conflictbase}(Y)$$
$$\text{and } \mathsf{Opinionbase}(Y) \subseteq \mathsf{Opinionbase}(X)$$

We read $\Delta \preceq \Delta'$ as Δ is a preferred compromise to Δ'. Let $\Delta \prec \Delta'$ denote $\Delta \preceq \Delta'$ and $\Delta' \not\preceq \Delta$. Also let $\Delta \simeq \Delta'$ denote $\Delta \preceq \Delta'$ and $\Delta' \preceq \Delta$.

Example 11 *If $\Delta = \{\alpha \wedge \beta \wedge \gamma\}$, and $\Delta' = \{\alpha \wedge \neg\alpha, \beta \vee \gamma\}$, then $\Delta \prec \Delta'$, since the following hold,*

$$\mathsf{MQC}(\Delta) = \{\{+\alpha, +\beta, +\gamma\}\}$$
$$\mathsf{MQC}(\Delta') = \{\{+\alpha, -\alpha, +\beta\}, \{+\alpha, -\alpha, +\gamma\}\}$$

Example 12 *If $\Delta = \{\alpha \wedge \neg\alpha \wedge \beta\}$ and $\Delta' = \{\beta\}$, then $\Delta \not\preceq \Delta'$, and $\Delta' \not\preceq \Delta$, since $\mathsf{MQC}(\Delta) = \{\{+\alpha, -\alpha, +\beta\}\}$ and $\mathsf{MQC}(\Delta') = \{\{+\beta\}\}$. Though $\mathsf{Coherence}(\Delta) < \mathsf{Coherence}(\Delta')$.*

Example 13 *If $\Delta = \{\alpha \vee \beta\}$ and $\Delta' = \{\alpha \vee \gamma\}$, then $\Delta \not\preceq \Delta'$, and $\Delta' \not\preceq \Delta$, since $\mathsf{MQC}(\Delta) = \{\{+\alpha\}, \{+\beta\}\}$ and $\mathsf{MQC}(\Delta') = \{\{+\alpha\}, \{+\gamma\}\}$. Though $\mathsf{Coherence}(\Delta) = \mathsf{Coherence}(\Delta')$.*

We now motivate the compromise relation. For checking whether $\Delta \preceq \Delta'$ holds, we want to compare the minimal QC models of Δ with the minimal QC models of Δ'. First, we want each minimal QC model of Δ to have a conflictbase that is a subset of the conflictbase of each minimal QC model of Δ'. We get this via Proposition 6. Second, we want for each minimal QC model X of Δ, for there to be a minimal QC model Y of Δ' such that the opinionbase of Y is a subset of the opinionbase of X. This is to ensure that Δ is not less conflicting than Δ' because Δ has less information in it. The reason we use the condition $\mathsf{Opinionbase}(Y) \subseteq \mathsf{Opinionbase}(X)$ rather than $Y \subseteq X$ is that if Y is more conflicting than X, then this will be reflected in the membership of Y but not in the membership of $\mathsf{Opinionbase}(Y)$. The reason we only seek one minimal QC model of Δ' for the comparison with all the minimal QC models of Δ is so that we can handle disjunction in Δ' as illustrated by Example 11. And according to Proposition 7, this is sufficient to ensure that there is no minimal QC model of Δ' that has a greater opinionbase than any minimal QC model of Δ.

Proposition 6 *If $\Delta \preceq \Delta'$, then $\forall X \in \mathsf{MQC}(\Delta)$, $\forall Y \in \mathsf{MQC}(\Delta')$, $\mathsf{Conflictbase}(X) \subseteq \mathsf{Conflictbase}(Y)$.*

Proposition 7 *If $\Delta \preceq \Delta'$, then it is not the case that $\exists X \in \mathsf{MQC}(\Delta)$, $\exists Y \in \mathsf{MQC}(\Delta')$, such that $\mathsf{Opinionbase}(X) \subset \mathsf{Opinionbase}(Y)$.*

Useful properties of the compromise relation include: (1) It is a pre-order relation; (2) It captures aspects of coherence (Propositions 8 and 9); and (3) It is syntax independent (Proposition 10).

Proposition 8 *If $\Delta \preceq \Delta'$, then $\forall X \in \mathsf{MQC}(\Delta)$ $\exists Y \in \mathsf{MQC}(\Delta')$ such that $\mathsf{Coherence}(X) \geq \mathsf{Coherence}(Y)$.*

Proposition 9 *If $\Delta \preceq \Delta'$, and $\Delta = \cup \mathsf{MI}(\Delta)$, and $\Delta' = \cup \mathsf{MI}(\Delta')$, and $\Delta \cup \Delta'$ is a set of clauses, then $\mathsf{Coherence}(\Delta) \geq \mathsf{Coherence}(\Delta')$.*

However, in general $\Delta \preceq \Delta'$ does not imply $\mathsf{Coherence}(\Delta) \geq \mathsf{Coherence}(\Delta')$. The converse does not hold either. This is illustrated by the following examples.

Example 14 *Let $\Delta = \{\alpha, \delta \wedge \neg\delta\}$ and $\Delta' = \{\alpha \vee (\beta \wedge \gamma), \delta \wedge \neg\delta\}$. So $\Delta \preceq \Delta'$ and $\mathsf{Coherence}(\Delta) < \mathsf{Coherence}(\Delta')$.*

Example 15 *Let $\Delta = \{\alpha, \beta \wedge \neg\beta\}$ and $\Delta' = \{\alpha, \gamma \wedge \neg\gamma\}$. So $\mathsf{Coherence}(\Delta) \geq \mathsf{Coherence}(\Delta')$. However, $\Delta \not\preceq \Delta'$ and $\Delta' \not\preceq \Delta$.*

We see that increasing the number of conjuncts in a formula tends to increase the size of the minimal QC models for that formula, whereas increasing the number of disjuncts in a formula tends to increase the number of the minimal QC models for that formula. We illustrate this in the following example, and see the effect on the compromise relation.

Example 16 *If $\Delta = \{\alpha \wedge \beta\}$ and $\Delta' = \{\alpha\}$ and $\Delta'' = \{\alpha \vee \beta\}$, then $\Delta \prec \Delta'$, and $\Delta' \prec \Delta''$, since $\mathsf{MQC}(\Delta) = \{\{+\alpha, +\beta\}\}$, $\mathsf{MQC}(\Delta') = \{\{+\alpha\}\}$, and $\mathsf{MQC}(\Delta'') = \{\{+\alpha\}, \{+\beta\}\}$.*

If Δ and Δ' are consistent sets of formulae, and $\Delta \simeq \Delta'$, then Δ and Δ' are not necessarily classically equivalent, as illustrated by the following example.

Example 17 *Let $\Delta = \{\neg\alpha\}$ and $\Delta' = \{\alpha\}$. So $\Delta \not\vdash \bot$, and $\Delta' \not\vdash \bot$ and $\Delta \simeq \Delta'$.*

The behaviour of the compromise relation illustrated above is the result of the opinionbase comparison within the compromise relation not differentiating between formulae and their complements. However, the compromise relation is syntax independent, which we formalize as follows.

Definition 13 *For $\Delta, \Delta' \in \wp(\mathcal{L})$, Δ is semantically equivalent to Δ' iff $\forall X \in \wp(\mathcal{O})(X \models_s \Delta$ iff $X \models_s \Delta')$. Let $\mathsf{SemanticEqual}$ be a function that gives the set of semantically equivalent knowledgebases for a knowledgebase.*

Example 18 *Let $\Delta = \{\alpha, \neg\alpha\}$. So $\{\alpha \wedge \neg\alpha\} \in \mathsf{SemanticEqual}(\Delta)$. Now let $\Delta' = \{\alpha, \neg\alpha \vee \neg\beta, \beta\}$. So $\{\alpha \wedge \neg\alpha, \beta \wedge \neg\beta\} \in \mathsf{SemanticEqual}(\Delta')$ and $\{\alpha, \neg\alpha \vee (\beta \wedge \neg\beta)\} \in \mathsf{SemanticEqual}(\Delta')$.*

Proposition 10 *Let $\Delta \in \wp(\mathcal{L})$. If $\Delta'' \in \mathsf{SemanticEqual}(\Delta)$, then $\Delta \simeq \Delta''$.*

Hence, $\preceq$ is syntax independent. As a result, if $\Delta \preceq \Delta'$ and $\Delta'' \in \mathsf{SemanticEqual}(\Delta)$, then $\Delta'' \preceq \Delta'$. And if $\Delta \preceq \Delta'$ and $\Delta'' \in \mathsf{SemanticEqual}(\Delta')$, then $\Delta \preceq \Delta''$.

Example 19 *Since $\{\alpha, \neg\alpha, \beta\} \preceq \{\alpha, \neg\alpha, \beta, \neg\beta\}$ holds, we can derive that $\{\alpha \wedge \neg\alpha \wedge \beta\} \preceq \{\alpha, \neg\alpha, \beta, \neg\beta\}$ holds.*

However, this syntax independence means that the compromise relation does not reflect the membership and cardinalities of the inconsistent subsets as illustrated by the following examples.

Example 20 *Let* $\Delta = \{\beta\}$ *and* $\Delta' = \{\alpha, \neg\alpha, \beta\}$. *So* $\mathrm{MI}(\Delta) = \emptyset$ *and* $\mathrm{MI}(\Delta') = \{\{\alpha, \neg\alpha\}\}$, *but* $\Delta \npreceq \Delta'$ *and* $\Delta' \npreceq \Delta$.

Example 21 *Let* $\Delta = \{\alpha, \neg\alpha \vee \neg\beta, \beta\}$ *and* $\Delta' = \{\neg\alpha, \alpha \vee \beta, \neg\beta\}$. *So* $\mathrm{MI}(\Delta) = \{\Delta\}$, *and* $\mathrm{MI}(\Delta') = \{\Delta'\}$, *and* $\Delta \simeq \Delta'$, *but* $\mathrm{MI}(\Delta) \not\subseteq \mathrm{MI}(\Delta')$ *and* $\mathrm{MI}(\Delta') \not\subseteq \mathrm{MI}(\Delta)$.

In general, the compromise relation is not monotonic so for instance, $\Delta \preceq \Delta'$ does not imply (1) $\Delta \cup \Gamma \preceq \Delta'$, (2) $\Delta \preceq \Delta' \cup \Gamma$, or (3) $\Delta \cup \Gamma \preceq \Delta' \cup \Gamma$. This is illustrated by the following example.

Example 22 *(1) Let* $\Delta_1 = \{\alpha, \beta\}$, $\Delta'_1 = \{\alpha\}$, *and* $\Gamma_1 = \{\neg\alpha\}$. *So* $\Delta_1 \preceq \Delta'_1$ *but* $\Delta_1 \cup \Gamma_1 \npreceq \Delta'_1$. *(2) Let* $\Delta_2 = \{\alpha\}$, $\Delta'_2 = \{\alpha\}$, *and* $\Gamma_2 = \{\beta\}$. *So* $\Delta_2 \preceq \Delta'_2$ *but* $\Delta_2 \npreceq \Delta'_2 \cup \Gamma_2$. *(3) Let* $\Delta_3 = \{\alpha \wedge \beta\}$, $\Delta'_3 = \{\alpha \vee \beta\}$, *and* $\Gamma_3 = \{\neg\alpha\}$. *So* $\Delta_3 \preceq \Delta'_3$ *but* $\Delta_3 \cup \Gamma_3 \npreceq \Delta'_3 \cup \Gamma_3$.

However, if have an update Γ, where $\mathrm{Atoms}(\Delta) \cap \mathrm{Atoms}(\Gamma) = \emptyset$ and $\mathrm{Atoms}(\Delta') \cap \mathrm{Atoms}(\Gamma) = \emptyset$, then $\Delta \preceq \Delta'$ implies $\Delta \cup \Gamma \preceq \Delta' \cup \Gamma$.

Analysing heterogeneous sources

Returning to the problem of comparing sources, discussed in the introduction, we briefly consider two types of analysis.

Definition 14 *Let* $\Phi_i, \Phi_j, \Psi \in \wp(\mathcal{L})$. *A* **qualified compromise relation** $\preceq_\Psi$ *is defined as follows, where* Φ_i *and* Φ_j *are sources and* Ψ *is background knowledge.*

$$\Phi_i \preceq_\Psi \Phi_j \text{ iff } \Phi_i \cup \Psi \preceq \Phi_j \cup \Psi$$

Example 23 *Let* $\Phi_1 = \{\neg\alpha, \neg\beta, \neg\gamma \vee \delta\}$, $\Phi_2 = \{\neg\alpha, \neg\beta, \delta, \neg\gamma\}$, *and* $\Psi = \{\alpha \vee \beta, \neg\delta \vee \gamma\}$. *So* $\Phi_1 \preceq_\Psi \Phi_2$.

When using a qualified compromise relation, there may be an assumption that the background knowledge is correct, and we rank sources by their conflicts with the background knowledge.

Another type of analysis assumes that the sources are all individually consistent with the background knowledge, but combinations of sources are inconsistent. The $\preceq$ or $\preceq_\Psi$ relations may then be used over all possible unions of sources.

References

Belnap, N. 1977. A useful four-valued logic. In Epstein, G., ed., *Modern Uses of Multiple-valued Logic*, 8–37. Reidel.

Benferhat, S.; Dubois, D.; Kaci, S.; and Prade, H. 2000. Encoding information fusion in possibilistic logic: A general framework for rational syntactic merging. In *Proceedings of the 14th European Conference on Artificial Intelligence (ECAI'2000)*, 3–7. IOS Press.

Benferhat, S.; Dubois, D.; and Prade, H. 1993. Argumentative inference in uncertain and inconsistent knowledge bases. In *Proceedings of Uncertainty in Artificial Intelligence*, 1449–1445. Morgan Kaufmann.

Besnard, Ph., and Hunter, A. 1995. Quasi-classical logic: Non-trivializable classical reasoning from inconsistent information. In *Symbolic and Quantitative Approaches to Uncertainty*, volume 946 of *LNCS*, 44–51.

Brewka, G. 1989. Preferred subtheories: An extended logical framework for default reasoning. In *Proceedings of the Eleventh International Joint Conference on Artificial Intelligence*, 1043–1048.

Cadoli, M. 1992. The complexity of model checking for circumscriptive formulae. *Information Processing Letters* 42:113–118.

da Costa, N. C. 1974. On the theory of inconsistent formal systems. *Notre Dame Journal of Formal Logic* 15:497–510.

Dalal, M. 1988. Investigations into a theory of knowledge base revision: Preliminary report. In *Proceedings of the 7th National Conference on Artificial Intelligence (AAAI'88)*, 3–7. MIT Press.

Dubois, D.; Lang, J.; and Prade, H. 1994. Possibilistic logic. In *Handbook of Logic in Artificial Intelligence and Logic Programming*, volume 3. Oxford University Press. 439–513.

Gardenfors, P. 1988. *Knowledge in Flux*. MIT Press.

Grant, J. 1978. Classifications for inconsistent theories. *Notre Dame Journal of Formal Logic* 19:435–444.

Hunter, A. 2000. Reasoning with conflicting information using quasi-classical logic. *Journal of Logic and Computation* 10:677–703.

Hunter, A. 2001. A semantic tableau version of first-order quasi-classical logic. In *Symbolic and Quantitative Approaches to Uncertainty*, volume 2143 of *LNCS*, 544–556.

Kleer, J. D., and Williams, B. 1987. Diagnosing mulitple faults. *Artificial Intelligence* 32:97–130.

Konieczny, S., and Pino Perez, R. 1998. On the logic of merging. In *Proceedings of the Sixth International Conference on Principles of Knowledge Representation and Reasoning (KR98)*, 488–498. Morgan Kaufmann.

Levesque, H. 1984. A logic of implicit and explicit belief. In *Proceedings of the National Conference on Artificial Intelligence (AAAI'84)*, 198–202.

Lin, J., and Mendelzon, A. 1998. Merging databases under constraints. *International Journal of Cooperative Information Systems* 7(1):55–76.

Lozinskii, E. 1994. Information and evidence in logic systems. *Journal of Experimental and Theoretical Artificial Intelligence* 6:163–193.

Marquis, P., and Porquet, N. 2001. Computational aspects of quasi-classical entailment. *Journal of Applied Non-classical Logics* 11:295–312.

Reiter, R. 1987. A theory of diagnosis from first principles. *Artificial Intelligence* 32:57–95.

Revesz, P. 1997. On the semantics of arbitration. *International Journal of Algebra and Computation* 7:133–160.

Schaerf, M., and Cadoli, M. 1995. Tractable reasoning via approximation. *Artificial Intelligence* 74:249–310.

Wong, P., and Besnard, Ph. 2001. Paraconsistent reasoning as an analytic tool. *Journal of the Interest Group in Propositional Logic* 9:233–246.

A Hoare-Style Proof System for Robot Programs

Yongmei Liu

Department of Computer Science
University of Toronto
Toronto, ON, Canada M5S 3G4
yliu@cs.toronto.edu

Abstract

Golog is a situation calculus-based logic programming language for high-level robotic control. This paper explores Hoare's axiomatic approach to program verification in the Golog context. We present a novel Hoare-style proof system for partial correctness of Golog programs. We prove total soundness of the proof system, and relative completeness of a subsystem of it for procedureless Golog programs. Examples are given to illustrate the use of the proof system.

Introduction

When it comes to building high-level robotic controllers, planning-based approaches suffer from computational intractability. A promising alternative is high-level programming. Given a particular domain, a high-level program can provide natural constraints on how to achieve a specific goal. The domain constraints then allow for replacing the unrestricted search for a sequence of actions achieving a goal by the more constrained task of finding a sequence of actions that constitutes a legal execution of some high-level program. The logic programming language Golog (Levesque *et al.* 1997) is designed to support such an approach.

As its full name (alGOl in LOGic) implies, Golog attempts to blend Algol programming style into logic. It provides a way of defining complex actions and procedures in terms of a set of primitive actions, by borrowing from Algol many well-known programming constructs such as sequences, conditionals, loops and recursive procedures. Primitive actions are domain-dependent actions in the external world, and their preconditions and effects, together with the initial state of the world, are axiomatized in the situation calculus (McCarthy & Hayes 1969). The formal semantics of Golog is defined by introducing an abbreviation $Do(\delta, s, s')$, where δ is a program, s and s' are situation terms. Intuitively, $Do(\delta, s, s')$ will expand into a (second-order) situation calculus formula saying that it is possible to reach situation s' from situation s by executing a sequence of actions specified by δ.

Needless to say, correctness of robot programs is of paramount importance. Hence we are concerned about verification of Golog programs. Due to the way the semantics of

Golog is defined, properties of Golog programs can be expressed as second-order situation calculus formulas. Thus theoretically, verification of Golog programs can be reduced to proof of such formulas. However, this is infeasible in practice: even though the semantic definition of Golog is very succinct, the whole formula to express the semantics of even a simple Golog program can be very complicated. In general, providing a formal semantics for a high-level robot programming language in a logic framework makes possible formal correctness proofs of robot programs, but does not furnish us with any systematic method for doing so.

In this paper, we explore the well-established axiomatic approach to program verification in the Golog context. This approach was initiated by Hoare (1969), and it was applied to Algol-like languages. In this approach, the relevant program properties are expressed as formulas in some mathematical logic. A proof system consisting of axioms and proof rules is given, which allows formal proofs of program properties. An important advantage of Hoare's approach is that the proof system is syntax-directed and hence makes proofs easier by induction on the structure of programs. Hoare's approach has received a great deal of attention, and many Hoare-style proof systems have been proposed for various programming constructs (Apt 1981; 1984).

However, the application of Hoare Logic to Golog is not routine due to the following differences between Golog and Algol-like languages. First, atomic Algol programs are assignments; while atomic Golog programs are user-defined primitive actions. Second, the semantics of Algol programs is interpretive, i.e., it is defined based on an interpretation for the first-order language in which the expressions in Algol programs are formed; while the semantics of Golog programs is defined by macro-expansion into situation calculus formulas.

In this paper, we present a novel Hoare-style proof system for partial correctness of Golog programs. We prove total soundness of the proof system, and relative completeness of a subsystem of it for procedureless Golog programs. Examples are given to illustrate the use of the proof system.

Failure to prove that a program satisfies a desired property may lead us to detect 1) errors in the program, or 2) inconsistency or incompleteness in the domain theory. So program verification can still be useful when the domain theory is itself inconsistent or incomplete.

Background

The Situation Calculus

The situation calculus as presented in (Reiter 2001) is a many-sorted second-order language for representing dynamic worlds. There are three disjoint sorts: *action* for actions, *situation* for situations, and *object* for everything else. A situation calculus language $\mathcal{L}$ has the following components: a constant S_0 denoting the initial situation; a binary function $do(a, s)$ denoting the successor situation to s resulting from performing action a; a binary predicate $s \sqsubseteq s'$ meaning that situation s is a subhistory of situation s'; a binary predicate $Poss(a, s)$ meaning that action a is possible in situation s; a countable set of action functions, e.g., $move(x, y)$; and a countable set of relational fluents, i.e., predicates taking a situation term as their last argument, e.g., $ontable(x, s)$. For simplicity of presentation, we ignore functional fluents in this paper.

We use $\mathcal{L}^-$ to denote the language obtained from $\mathcal{L}$ by removing the sort *situation* and removing the situation argument from every relational fluent. We call an $\mathcal{L}^-$-formula a pseudo-fluent formula (abbreviated "pff"). Let ϕ be a pff, and s be a situation term. We use $\phi[s]$ to denote the formula obtained from ϕ by restoring s as the situation arguments to all fluents mentioned by ϕ.

Frequently, we are interested only in executable situations, namely, action histories in which it is possible to perform the actions one after the other. This is formalized as follows:

$$executable(s) \overset{def}{=} (\forall a, s^*).do(a, s^*) \sqsubseteq s \supset Poss(a, s^*).$$

Any domain of application is axiomatized by a basic action theory $\mathcal{D}$ with the following components:

1. The foundational axioms for situations.

2. Action precondition axioms, one for each action function A, with syntactic form $Poss(A(\vec{x}), s) \equiv \Pi_A(\vec{x})[s]$, where $\Pi_A(\vec{x})$ is a pff.

3. Successor state axioms, one for each fluent F, with syntactic form $F(\vec{x}, do(a, s)) \equiv \Phi_F(\vec{x}, a)[s]$, where $\Phi_F(\vec{x}, a)$ is a pff. These embody a solution to the frame problem.

4. Unique names axioms for the primitive actions.

5. An initial database, namely a set of axioms describing S_0.

Golog

The formal semantics of Golog is specified by an abbreviation $Do(\delta, s, s')$, which is inductively defined as follows:

1. Primitive actions: For any action term α,
$$Do(\alpha, s, s') \overset{def}{=} Poss(\alpha, s) \wedge s' = do(\alpha, s).$$

2. Test actions: For any pff ϕ,
$$Do(\phi?, s, s') \overset{def}{=} \phi[s] \wedge s = s'.$$

3. Sequence:
$$Do(\delta_1; \delta_2, s, s') \overset{def}{=} (\exists s'').Do(\delta_1, s, s'') \wedge Do(\delta_2, s'', s').$$

4. Nondeterministic choice of two actions:
$$Do(\delta_1 \mid \delta_2, s, s') \overset{def}{=} Do(\delta_1, s, s') \vee Do(\delta_2, s, s').$$

5. Nondeterministic choice of action arguments:
$$Do((\pi\, x)\delta(x), s, s') \overset{def}{=} (\exists x)Do(\delta(x), s, s').$$

6. Nondeterministic iteration:
$$Do(\delta^*, s, s') \overset{def}{=} (\forall P).\{(\forall s_1)P(s_1, s_1) \wedge$$
$$(\forall s_1, s_2, s_3)[P(s_1, s_2) \wedge Do(\delta, s_2, s_3) \supset P(s_1, s_3)]\}$$
$$\supset P(s, s').$$

7. Procedure calls: For any $(n + 2)$-ary procedure variable (i.e., predicate variable whose last two arguments are the only ones of sort *situation*) P,
$$Do(P(t_1, \ldots, t_n), s, s') \overset{def}{=} P(t_1, \ldots, t_n, s, s').$$

8. Blocks with local procedure declarations: Let Env be an environment, i.e., a set of procedure declarations **proc** $P_1(\vec{v}_1)\; \delta_1$ **endProc**; $\ldots$; **proc** $P_n(\vec{v}_n)\; \delta_n$ **endProc**, where $P_1, \ldots, P_n$ are procedure variables. Then
$$Do(\{Env; \delta\}, s, s') \overset{def}{=}$$
$$(\forall \vec{P}).[\bigwedge_{i=1}^{n}(\forall \vec{v}_i, s_1, s_2).Do(\delta_i, s_1, s_2) \supset P_i(\vec{v}_i, s_1, s_2)]$$
$$\supset Do(\delta, s, s').$$

This says: when $P_1, \ldots, P_n$ are the smallest binary relations on situations that are closed under executing their procedure bodies $\delta_1, \ldots, \delta_n$, then any transition (s, s') obtained by executing the main program δ is a transition for executing $\{Env; \delta\}$.

Conditionals and loops are defined as abbreviations:

if ϕ **then** δ_1 **else** δ_2 **fi** $\overset{def}{=} [\phi?; \delta_1] \mid [\neg\phi?; \delta_2]$,

while ϕ **do** δ **od** $\overset{def}{=} [\phi?; \delta]^*; \neg\phi?$.

Hoare Logic

The basic formulas of Hoare Logic are constructs of the form $\{p\}\, S\, \{q\}$ (called Hoare triples), where S is a program, and p, q are first-order formulas. The intuitive meaning of $\{p\}\, S\, \{q\}$ is: if p holds before the execution of S and the execution of S terminates, then q holds afterwards. For example, the following are axioms and proof rules of a basic Hoare Logic for programs from a simple Algol-like language.

1. Assignment Axiom
$$\{p(x/t)\}\; x := t\; \{p\},$$

where $p(x/t)$ denotes the result of replacing all free occurrences of x in p by t.

2. Composition Rule
$$\frac{\{p\}\, S_1\, \{r\},\; \{r\}\, S_2\, \{q\}}{\{p\}\, S_1; S_2\, \{q\}}.$$

3. **if-then-else** Rule
$$\frac{\{p \wedge e\}\, S_1\, \{q\},\; \{p \wedge \neg e\}\, S_2\, \{q\}}{\{p\}\; \textbf{if } e \textbf{ then } S_1 \textbf{ else } S_2 \textbf{ fi}\; \{q\}}.$$

4. **while** Rule
$$\frac{\{p \wedge e\}\, S\, \{p\}}{\{p\}\; \textbf{while } e \textbf{ do } S \textbf{ od}\; \{p \wedge \neg e\}}.$$

5. Consequence Rule
$$\frac{p \supset p_1,\; \{p_1\}\, S\, \{q_1\},\; q_1 \supset q}{\{p\}\, S\, \{q\}}.$$

However, Hoare Logic is not complete; see (Apt 1981) for a discussion of the incompleteness results. Cook (1978) circumvented these incompleteness problems by defining the notion of relative completeness. The basic idea was to supply Hoare's system with an oracle which had the ability to answer questions concerning the truths of first-order formulas. In this way, he separated reasoning about programs from reasoning about the underlying domain, in his case, arithmetic.

The Proof System HG

In this section, we present a novel Hoare-style proof system HG for partial correctness of Golog programs.

Syntax and Semantics

A well-formed formula of HG (HG-wff) is either an invariant formula or a Hoare triple, which are defined as follows.

Definition 1 *An invariant formula is a construct of the form $\Box Q$, where Q is a pff; a Hoare triple is a construct of the form $\{Q\}\ \delta\ \{R\}$, where Q and R are pffs, and δ is a Golog program.*

In traditional work on Hoare Logic, the semantics of Hoare triples is defined with respect to an interpretation. In the Golog context, since the semantics of programs is defined by macro-expansion into situation calculus formulas, Hoare triples can be conveniently defined as abbreviations for situation calculus formulas.

Let ϕ be a formula. We use $(\forall).\phi$ to denote the first-order closure of ϕ, i.e., the result of prefixing to ϕ universal quantifiers for all free individual variables in ϕ.

Definition 2 *1. $\Box Q \stackrel{def}{=} (\forall).executable(s) \supset Q[s]$;*

2. $\{Q\}\ \delta\ \{R\} \stackrel{def}{=} (\forall).executable(s) \wedge Q[s] \wedge Do(\delta, s, s') \supset R[s']$.

Intuitively, $\Box Q$ means that Q is true in all executable situations; $\{Q\}\ \delta\ \{R\}$ means that if s is an executable situation satisfying Q and the execution of δ in s leads to a situation s', then s' satisfies R.

Axioms and Proof Rules

Let $\mathcal{D}$ be a basic action theory. The proof system $HG(\mathcal{D})$ is defined as follows. Abbreviations given in parentheses are used to refer to the axioms or rules.

Oracle Axioms
Invariant Oracle Axiom (Inv)

$$\Box Q, \text{ where } \mathcal{D} \models \Box Q.$$

Here we adopt Cook's idea in formulating the notion of relative completeness, and supply our proof system with an oracle which can answer questions concerning whether an invariant formula is entailed by a basic action theory. In this way, we can concentrate on reasoning about programs.

Axioms

1. Effect and Frame Axiom (EF)

$$\{\Phi_F(\vec{x}, A(\vec{y}))\}\ A(\vec{y})\ \{F(\vec{x})\},$$
$$\{\neg\Phi_F(\vec{x}, A(\vec{y}))\}\ A(\vec{y})\ \{\neg F(\vec{x})\},$$

where A is an action function, F is a relational fluent with successor state axiom $F(\vec{x}, do(a, s)) \equiv \Phi_F(\vec{x}, a)[s]$. Note that $\Phi_F(\vec{x}, A(\vec{y}))$ can be simplified using unique names axioms for actions.

2. Fluent-Free Axiom (FF)

$$\{Q\}\ \delta\ \{Q\},$$

where no fluent occurs in Q.

3. Test Action Axiom (TA)

$$\{\phi \supset R\}\ \phi?\ \{R\}.$$

Proof Rules

1. Primitive Action Rule (PAR)

$$\frac{\{Q \wedge \Pi_A(\vec{x})\}\ A(\vec{x})\ \{R\}}{\{Q\}\ A(\vec{x})\ \{R\}},$$

where A is an action function with action precondition axiom $Poss(A(\vec{x}), s) \equiv \Pi_A(\vec{x})[s]$.

2. Sequence Rule (Seq)

$$\frac{\{Q\}\ \delta_1\ \{S\},\ \{S\}\ \delta_2\ \{R\}}{\{Q\}\ \delta_1;\ \delta_2\ \{R\}}.$$

3. Nondeterministic Action Rule (NA)

$$\frac{\{Q\}\ \delta_1\ \{R\},\ \{Q\}\ \delta_2\ \{R\}}{\{Q\}\ \delta_1\ |\ \delta_2\ \{R\}}.$$

4. Nondeterministic Action Argument Rule (NAA)

$$\frac{\{Q\}\ \delta(x)\ \{R\}}{\{Q\}\ (\pi\ x)\ \delta(x)\ \{R\}},$$

where x does not occur free in Q or R.

5. Nondeterministic Iteration Rule (NI)

$$\frac{\{Q\}\ \delta\ \{Q\}}{\{Q\}\ \delta^*\ \{Q\}}.$$

6. Consequence Rule (Cons)

$$\frac{\Box(Q \supset Q_1),\ \{Q_1\}\ \delta\ \{R_1\},\ \Box(R_1 \supset R)}{\{Q\}\ \delta\ \{R\}}.$$

7. Conjunction Rule (Conj)

$$\frac{\{Q_1\}\ \delta\ \{R_1\},\ \{Q_2\}\ \delta\ \{R_2\}}{\{Q_1 \wedge Q_2\}\ \delta\ \{R_1 \wedge R_2\}}.$$

8. Disjunction Rule (Disj)

$$\frac{\{Q_1\}\ \delta\ \{R_1\},\ \{Q_2\}\ \delta\ \{R_2\}}{\{Q_1 \vee Q_2\}\ \delta\ \{R_1 \vee R_2\}}.$$

9. Quantification Rule (Quan)

$$\frac{\{Q(x)\}\ \delta\ \{R(x)\}}{\{\forall x Q(x)\}\ \delta\ \{\forall x R(x)\}},\quad \frac{\{Q(x)\}\ \delta\ \{R(x)\}}{\{\exists x Q(x)\}\ \delta\ \{\exists x R(x)\}},$$

where x does not occur free in δ.

10. **Recursion Rule (Rec)**

$$\frac{\{\{Q_i\}\ P_i(\vec{v}_i)\ \{R_i\}\}_{i=1}^n \vdash \{\{Q_i\}\ \delta_i\ \{R_i\}\}_{i=1}^n}{\{\{Q_i\}\ \{Env;\ P_i(\vec{v}_i)\}\ \{R_i\}\}_{i=1}^n},$$

where $\{\phi_i\}_{i=1}^n$ denotes the set $\{\phi_i \mid i = 1,\ldots,n\}$. Intuitively, this rule says that we can infer $\{Q_i\}\ \{Env;\ P_i(\vec{v}_i)\}\ \{R_i\}$, $i = 1,\ldots,n$ from the fact that $\{\{Q_i\}\ \delta_i\ \{R_i\}\}_{i=1}^n$ can be proved (using the other proof rules and axioms) from the hypotheses $\{\{Q_i\}\ P_i(\vec{v}_i)\ \{R_i\}\}_{i=1}^n$.

11. **Invocation Rule (IK)**

$$\frac{\{Q\}\ \delta_i\ {}^{P_j(\vec{t})}_{\{Env;\ P_j(\vec{t})\}}\ \{R\}}{\{Q\}\ \{Env;\ P_i(\vec{v}_i)\}\ \{R\}},$$

where $\delta_i\ {}^{P_j(\vec{t})}_{\{Env;\ P_j(\vec{t})\}}$ denotes the result of replacing each procedure call $P_j(\vec{t})$ in δ_i by its contextualized version $\{Env;\ P_j(\vec{t})\}$. Intuitively, to execute $\{Env;\ P_i(\vec{v}_i)\}$ is to execute $\delta_i\ {}^{P_j(\vec{t})}_{\{Env;\ P_j(\vec{t})\}}$.[1]

12. **Substitution Rule (Subs)**

$$\frac{\{Q(\vec{x})\}\ \{Env;\ P_i(\vec{x})\}\ \{R(\vec{x})\}}{\{Q(\vec{x}/\vec{t})\}\ \{Env;\ P_i(\vec{x}/\vec{t})\}\ \{R(\vec{x}/\vec{t})\}},$$

$$\frac{\{Q(\vec{x})\}\ P(\vec{x})\ \{R(\vec{x})\}}{\{Q(\vec{x}/\vec{t})\}\ P(\vec{x}/\vec{t})\ \{R(\vec{x}/\vec{t})\}},$$

where P is an action function or a procedure variable, and $Q(\vec{x}/\vec{t})$ denotes the result of simultaneously substituting terms from $\vec{t}$ for the corresponding variables from $\vec{x}$ in Q.

The following are derived rules:

1. **If Rule**

$$\frac{\{Q \wedge \phi\}\ \delta_1\ \{R\},\ \{Q \wedge \neg\phi\}\ \delta_2\ \{R\}}{\{Q\}\ \text{if } \phi \text{ then } \delta_1 \text{ else } \delta_2 \text{ fi } \{R\}}.$$

2. **While Rule**

$$\frac{\{Q \wedge \phi\}\ \delta\ \{Q\}}{\{Q\}\ \text{while } \phi \text{ do } \delta \text{ od } \{Q \wedge \neg\phi\}}.$$

Provability

Due to the recursion rule, the system $HG(\mathcal{D})$ is not a standard proof system. Let $BH(\mathcal{D})$ denote $HG(\mathcal{D})$ without the recursion rule. We first define provability in $BH(\mathcal{D})$, and then use it to define provability in $HG(\mathcal{D})$. In the sequel, we use Φ and Ψ to denote finite sets of HG-wffs.

Definition 3 *A formal proof of Ψ from Φ in $BH(\mathcal{D})$ is a finite sequence S of HG-wffs, each of which is either an axiom of $BH(\mathcal{D})$, an element of Φ, or is obtained from previous formulas of S by a proof rule of $BH(\mathcal{D})$. We write $\Phi \vdash_{BH(\mathcal{D})} \Psi$, if there is a proof of Ψ from Φ in $BH(\mathcal{D})$.*

---

[1] Note that this rule supports the compositional proof of properties of procedures. For example, suppose that P_1 only calls itself, and P_2 only calls P_1. We can first use the recursion rule to prove the property of P_1, and then use this property and the invocation rule to prove the property of P_2. Without the invocation rule, we can only prove properties of all procedures simultaneously.

Definition 4 *That Ψ is provable in $HG(\mathcal{D})$, written $\vdash_{HG(\mathcal{D})} \Psi$, is inductively defined as follows:*

1. $\vdash_{HG(\mathcal{D})} \varnothing$;

2. *If $\vdash_{HG(\mathcal{D})} \Phi$, and $\Phi \vdash_{BH(\mathcal{D})} \Psi$, then $\vdash_{HG(\mathcal{D})} \Psi$;*

3. *If $\vdash_{HG(\mathcal{D})} \Phi$, and $\Phi \cup \{\{Q_i\}\ P_i(\vec{v}_i)\ \{R_i\}\}_{i=1}^n \vdash_{BH(\mathcal{D})} \{\{Q_i\}\ \delta_i\ \{R_i\}\}_{i=1}^n$, then*
   $$\vdash_{HG(\mathcal{D})} \{\{Q_i\}\ \{Env;\ P_i(\vec{v}_i)\}\ \{R_i\}\}_{i=1}^n.$$

Example: A Blocks World

In this section, we demonstrate the use of our proof system by proving properties of robot programs in a simple domain: a blocks world. Despite its simplicity, this domain illustrates some important issues in verification of robot programs.

Action Precondition Axioms

$Poss(move(x, y), s) \equiv clear(x, s) \wedge clear(y, s) \wedge x \neq y$,
$Poss(moveToTable(x), s) \equiv$
     $clear(x, s) \wedge \neg ontable(x, s)$.

Successor State Axioms

$on(x, y, do(a, s)) \equiv a = move(x, y) \vee$
     $on(x, y, s) \wedge a \neq moveToTable(x) \wedge$
     $\neg(\exists z)a = move(x, z)$,
$above(x, y, do(a, s)) \equiv$
     $(\exists z)\{a = move(x, z) \wedge [z = y \vee above(z, y, s)]\} \vee$
     $above(x, y, s) \wedge a \neq moveToTable(x) \wedge$
     $\neg(\exists z)a = move(x, z)$,
$clear(x, do(a, s)) \equiv$
     $(\exists y)\{[(\exists z)a = move(y, z) \vee a = moveToTable(y)] \wedge$
          $on(y, x, s)\} \vee$
     $clear(x, s) \wedge \neg(\exists y)a = move(y, x)$,
$ontable(x, do(a, s)) \equiv a = moveToTable(x) \vee$
     $ontable(x, s) \wedge \neg(\exists y)a = move(x, y)$.

Initial Database

$\phi[S_0]$, where $\phi \in \mathcal{A}_{bw}$, which is the set of the following pffs:
$on(x, y) \equiv above(x, y) \wedge \neg(\exists z)(above(x, z) \wedge above(z, y))$,
$clear(x) \equiv \neg(\exists y)on(y, x)$,
$ontable(x) \equiv \neg(\exists y)on(x, y)$,
$\neg above(x, x)$,
$above(x, y) \wedge above(y, z) \supset above(x, z)$,
$above(x, y) \wedge above(x, z) \supset$
     $y = z \vee above(y, z) \vee above(z, y)$,
$above(y, x) \wedge above(z, x) \supset$
     $y = z \vee above(y, z) \vee above(z, y)$,
$ontable(x) \vee (\exists y)(above(x, y) \wedge ontable(y))$,
$clear(x) \vee (\exists y)(above(y, x) \wedge clear(y))$,
$above(x, y) \supset (\exists z)on(x, z) \wedge (\exists w)on(w, y)$.

Cook and Liu (2002) show that $\mathcal{A}_{bw}$ is complete in the following sense: if we model a state of blocks world by a finite collection of finite chains, then every sentence that is true in all such models is a consequence of $\mathcal{A}_{bw}$.

Let $\mathcal{D}_{bw}$ denote the basic action theory of this blocks world. We can prove that for each $\phi \in \mathcal{A}_{bw}$, $\mathcal{D}_{bw} \models \Box\phi$.

While Loop

Consider the following Golog program β, which nondeterministically moves a block onto another block, so long as there are at least two blocks on the table:

while $(\exists x, y)[ontable(x) \wedge ontable(y) \wedge x \neq y]$ **do**

$$(\pi\, u, v) move(u, v) \text{ **od**}$$

We want to prove that whenever this program terminates, there is a unique block on the table, provided there was some block on the table to begin with:

$$\{(\exists x)ontable(x)\}\ \beta\ \{(\exists! y)ontable(y)\}.$$

A proof consists of a sequence of lines. To justify a new line, we annotate it by an axiom or a proof rule, together with the lines that are used as rule premises.

In the following proof, to reduce length of formulas, we use $\phi(x, y)$ to denote $ontable(x) \wedge ontable(y) \wedge x \neq y$.

1. $\{ontable(x) \wedge u \neq x\}$
   $move(u, v)\ \{ontable(x)\}$ — EF
2. $\{\phi(x, y) \wedge u \neq x\}$
   $move(u, v)\ \{ontable(x)\}$ — Cons(1)
3. $\{ontable(y) \wedge u \neq y\}$
   $move(u, v)\ \{ontable(y)\}$ — EF
4. $\{\phi(x, y) \wedge u = x\}$
   $move(u, v)\ \{ontable(y)\}$ — Cons(3)
5. $\{\phi(x, y)\}\ move(u, v)$
   $\{ontable(x) \vee ontable(y)\}$ — Disj(2,4)
6. $\{\phi(x, y)\}\ (\pi\, u, v)move(u, v)$
   $\{ontable(x) \vee ontable(y)\}$ — NAA(5)
7. $\{(\exists x, y)\phi(x, y)\}\ (\pi\, u, v)move(u, v)$
   $\{(\exists x, y)[ontable(x) \vee ontable(y)]\}$ — Quan(6)
8. $\{(\exists x)ontable(x) \wedge (\exists x, y)\phi(x, y)\}$
   $(\pi\, u, v)move(u, v)\ \{(\exists x)ontable(x)\}$ — Cons(7)
9. $\{(\exists x)ontable(x)\}\ \beta\ \{(\exists! y)ontable(y)\}$ — While(8)

Recursive Procedure

Consider the following Golog procedure which puts all the blocks in the tower with top block b onto the table:

proc $flattenTower(b)$

$ontable(b)?\ |$

$(\pi\, c)[on(b, c)?;\ moveToTable(b);\ flattenTower(c)]$

endProc.

We want to prove its partial correctness:

$\{x = b \vee above(b, x)\}$

$\quad\{Env; flattenTower(b)\}\ \{ontable(x)\}.$

We will prove a stronger statement:

$\{ontable(x) \vee x = b \vee above(b, x)\}$

$\quad\{Env; flattenTower(b)\}\ \{ontable(x)\}.$

In what follows, we use $\psi(b, x)$ to denote $ontable(x) \vee x = b \vee above(b, x)$, and $\gamma(b, c)$ to denote $on(b, c)?;\ moveToTable(b);\ flattenTower(c)$.

By the recursion rule, it suffices to prove that

$\{\psi(b, x)\}\ flattenTower(b)\ \{ontable(x)\} \vdash_{BP(\mathcal{D}_{bw})}$

$\{\psi(b, x)\}\ ontable(b)?\ |\ (\pi\, c)\gamma(b, c)\ \{ontable(x)\}.$

We use blank lines to break the proof into paragraphs:

1. $\{\psi(b, x)\}\ flattenTower(b)$
   $\{ontable(x)\}$ — Hypothesis
2. $\{\psi(c, x)\}\ flattenTower(c)$
   $\{ontable(x)\}$ — Subs(1)
3. $\{ontable(x)\}\ flattenTower(c)$
   $\{ontable(x)\}$ — Cons(2)
4. $\{x = c \vee above(c, x)\}$
   $flattenTower(c)\ \{ontable(x)\}$ — Cons(2)

5. $\{\psi(b, x)\}\ ontable(b)?$
   $\{\psi(b, x) \wedge ontable(b)\}$ — TA
6. $\Box\{\psi(b, x) \wedge ontable(b) \supset$
   $ontable(x)\}$ — Inv
7. $\{\psi(b, x)\}\ ontable(b)?\ \{ontable(x)\}$ — Cons(5,6)

8. $\{ontable(x)\}\ on(b, c)?\ \{ontable(x)\}$ — TA
9. $\{ontable(x)\}\ moveToTable(b)$
   $\{ontable(x)\}$ — EF
10. $\{ontable(x)\}\ \gamma(b, c)\ \{ontable(x)\}$ — Seq(8,9,3)

11. $\{x = b\}\ on(b, c)?\ \{x = b\}$ — FF
12. $\{x = b\}\ moveToTable(b)\ \{x = b\}$ — FF
13. $\{true\}\ moveToTable(b)$
    $\{ontable(b)\}$ — EF
14. $\{x = b\}\ moveToTable(b)$
    $\{x = b \wedge ontable(b)\}$ — Conj(12,13)
15. $\{x = b\}\ moveToTable(b)$
    $\{ontable(x)\}$ — Cons(14)
16. $\{x = b\}\ \gamma(b, c)\ \{ontable(x)\}$ — Seq(11,15,3)

17. $\{above(b, x)\}\ on(b, c)?$
    $\{above(b, x) \wedge on(b, c)\}$ — TA
18. $\Box\{above(b, x) \wedge on(b, c) \supset$
    $x = c \vee above(c, x) \wedge b \neq c\}$ — Inv
19. $\{above(b, x)\}\ on(b, c)?$
    $\{x = c \vee above(c, x) \wedge b \neq c\}$ — Cons(17,18)
20. $\{x = c\}\ moveToTable(b)\ \{x = c\}$ — FF
21. $\{above(c, x) \wedge b \neq c\}$
    $moveToTable(b)\ \{above(c, x)\}$ — EF
22. $\{x = c \vee above(c, x) \wedge b \neq c\}$
    $moveToTable(b)$
    $\{x = c \vee above(c, x)\}$ — Disj(20,21)
23. $\{above(b, x)\}\ \gamma(b, c)\ \{ontable(x)\}$ — Seq(19,22,4)

24. $\{\psi(b, x)\}\ \gamma(b, c)\ \{ontable(x)\}$ — Disj(10,16,23)
25. $\{\psi(b, x)\}\ (\pi\, c)\gamma(b, c)\ \{ontable(x)\}$ — NAA(24)
26. $\{\psi(b, x)\}\ ontable(b)?\ |\ (\pi\, c)\gamma(b, c)$
    $\{ontable(x)\}$ — NA(7,25)

Soundness and Completeness Results

In traditional work on Hoare Logic, the soundness and completeness results explore the relationship between $I \models \phi$ and $H(I) \vdash \phi$, where I is an interpretation, ϕ is a Hoare triple, and $H(I)$ is a Hoare-style proof system with some set of formulas true in I taken as additional axioms. In our work, the soundness and completeness results will explore the relationship between $\mathcal{D} \models \phi$ and $G(\mathcal{D}) \vdash \phi$, where $\mathcal{D}$ is a basic action theory, ϕ is a Hoare triple, and $G(\mathcal{D})$ is a Hoare-style proof system with some set of formulas entailed by $\mathcal{D}$ taken as additional axioms.

Theorem 5 Total Soundness of HG. *For every basic action theory* $\mathcal{D}$, *if* $\vdash_{HG(\mathcal{D})} \Psi$, *then* $\mathcal{D} \models \Psi$.

The following are two important lemmas for the theorem. The fixpoint lemma handles the invocation rule, and the induction principle deals with the recursion rule.

Lemma 6 Fixpoint Lemma. *Let* $i = 1, \ldots, n$. *The following is a valid sentence:*

$$(\forall).Do(\{Env; P_i(\vec{v}_i)\}, s, s') \equiv Do(\delta_i \, {}^{P_j(\vec{t})}_{\{Env; P_j(\vec{t})\}}, s, s').$$

Lemma 7 Induction Principle for Recursive Procedures. *Let* $Q_1, \ldots, Q_n, R_1, \ldots, R_n$ *be pffs. The following is a valid second-order sentence:*

$$(\forall \vec{P})[\bigwedge_{i=1}^{n} \{Q_i\} \, P_i(\vec{v}_i) \, \{R_i\} \supset \bigwedge_{i=1}^{n} \{Q_i\} \, \delta_i \, \{R_i\}] \supset$$
$$\bigwedge_{i=1}^{n} \{Q_i\} \, \{Env; P_i(\vec{v}_i)\} \, \{R_i\}.$$

The notion of completeness applicable to HG is that of relative completeness. This is because HG has oracle axioms, which are not necessarily recursive. The relative completeness of HG remains open. Here we prove relative completeness of a subsystem of HG. Let WG be the set of Golog programs without procedures. Let HW be the restriction of HG to WG, i.e., programs appearing in Hoare triples are procedureless, and the recursion, invocation and substitution rules concerning procedures are removed. We will prove relative completeness of HW. We first define the notion of expressiveness, which is adapted from that in (Cook 1978).

Definition 8 *Let* $\mathcal{D}$ *be a basic action theory in language* $\mathcal{L}$ *and* Δ *be a set of Golog programs. We say that* $\mathcal{L}$ *is expressive relative to* $\mathcal{D}$ *and* Δ *if for any program* $\delta \in \Delta$ *and any pff* R, *there exists a pff* Q *such that*

$$\mathcal{D} \models (\forall).Q[s] \equiv (\forall s').Do(\delta, s, s') \supset R[s'];$$

we call Q *the weakest liberal precondition of* δ *wrt* R.

We first give an example of non-expressiveness by showing that the language of blocks world is not expressive relative to $\mathcal{D}_{bw}$ and WG. It is easy to write a program $\delta \in WG$ which makes a tower of even height with at most one block not in the tower. Then the weakest liberal precondition of δ wrt $(\exists!x)ontable(x)$ would assert that there are an even number of blocks, which we know is not expressible in the language of blocks world.

Theorem 9 Relative Completeness of HW. *For any basic action theory* $\mathcal{D}$ *in* $\mathcal{L}$ *such that* $\mathcal{L}$ *is expressive relative to* $\mathcal{D}$ *and* WG, *for any Hoare triple* $\{Q\} \, \delta \, \{R\}$ *such that* $\delta \in WG$, *if* $\mathcal{D} \models \{Q\} \, \delta \, \{R\}$, *then* $\vdash_{HW(\mathcal{D})} \{Q\} \, \delta \, \{R\}$.

Here we conjecture a sufficient condition for expressiveness relative to WG. For any basic action theory $\mathcal{D}$ in language $\mathcal{L}$, define $\mathcal{L}^+$ as the extension of $\mathcal{L}$ which contains a sort nat for natural numbers, the language of Peano arithmetic, and two function symbols (their intended interpretations are codings of objects and situations into natural numbers); define $\mathcal{D}^+ = \mathcal{D} \cup \mathcal{P} \cup \mathcal{C}$, where $\mathcal{P}$ is the second-order axiomatization of Peano arithmetic, and $\mathcal{C}$ asserts that the objects and situations are countable. We call $\mathcal{D}^+$ an arithmetical basic action theory. A nice property of models of

$\mathcal{D}^+$ is that by using Gödel's β-function we can encode finite sequences of elements from the domain by a pair of natural numbers. We say that $\mathcal{D}^+$ is finite-change if there are only finitely many fluents, and in each model of $\mathcal{D}^+$, each primitive action can only change the value of fluents at finitely many points. We conjecture that if $\mathcal{D}^+$ is finite-change, then $\mathcal{L}^+$ is expressive relative to $\mathcal{D}^+$ and WG.

Conclusions

Golog is a novel logic programming language for high-level robotic control. To establish a systematic approach for proving correctness of robot controllers written in Golog, we have explored Hoare's axiomatic approach to program verification in the Golog context. This is not a routine task due to the differences between Golog and Algol-like languages. Our technical contributions include the definition of the semantics of Hoare triples, and the formulation of the notions of soundness, completeness and expressiveness in the Golog context.

In summary, we have presented a novel Hoare-style proof system for partial correctness of Golog programs. We have proved total soundness of the proof system, and relative completeness of a subsystem of it for procedureless Golog programs. Using this proof system, we can obtain structured and compositional proofs for properties of Golog programs. An important future research topic is to investigate the completeness issue for procedures.

Acknowledgments

I thank Hector Levesque and Ray Reiter for many helpful discussions about this paper. I am grateful to Stephen Cook for his valuable help with this work. Thanks also to the anonymous referees for useful comments.

References

Apt, K. 1981. Ten years of Hoare's logic: a survey–Part I. *ACM Trans. Program. Lang. Syst.* 3(4):431–483.

Apt, K. 1984. Ten years of Hoare's logic: a survey–Part II: nondeterminism. *Theoret. Comput. Sci.* 28:83–109.

Cook, S., and Liu, Y. 2002. A complete axiomatization for blocks world. In *Seventh International Symposium on Artificial Intelligence and Mathematics*.

Cook, S. 1978. Soundness and completeness of an axiom system for program verification. *SIAM J. of Computing* 7(1):70–90.

Hoare, C. 1969. An axiomatic basis for computer programming. *Comm. ACM* 12(10):576–580, 583.

Levesque, H.; Reiter, R.; Lespérance, Y.; Lin, F.; and Scherl, R. 1997. Golog: A logic programming language for dynamic domains. *J. of Logic Programming* 31:59–84.

McCarthy, J., and Hayes, P. 1969. Some philosophical problems from the standpoint of artificial intelligence. In Meltzer, B., and Michie, D., eds., *Machine Intelligence 4*. Edinburgh University Press. 463–502.

Reiter, R. 2001. *Knowledge in Action: Logical Foundations for Specifying and Implementing Dynamical Systems.* MIT Press.

Representing and Reasoning about Mappings between Domain Models

Jayant Madhavan
University of Washington
jayant@cs.washington.edu

Philip A. Bernstein
Microsoft Research
philbe@microsoft.com

Pedro Domingos
University of Washington
pedrod@cs.washington.edu

Alon Y. Halevy
University of Washington
alon@cs.washington.edu

Abstract

Mappings between disparate models are fundamental to any application that requires interoperability between heterogeneous data and applications. Generating mappings is a labor-intensive and error prone task. To build a system that helps users generate mappings, we need an explicit representation of mappings. This representation needs to have well-defined semantics to enable reasoning and comparison between mappings. This paper first presents a powerful framework for defining languages for specifying mappings and their associated semantics. We examine the use of mappings and identify the key inference problems associated with mappings. These properties can be used to determine whether a mapping is adequate in a particular context. Finally, we consider an instance of our framework for a language representing mappings between relational data. We present sound and complete algorithms for the corresponding inference problems.

1 Introduction

The emergence of the World-Wide Web (WWW) and the promise of the Semantic Web have refocused our attention on building systems in which knowledge can be shared in an ad hoc, distributed environment. For example, information integration systems allow queries to be answered using a set of data sources on the WWW or across several databases in an enterprise. The Semantic Web goes a step further, and envisions a less centralized architecture where agents can coordinate tasks using rich ontologies.

A crucial element of all these system architectures is the ability to map between different models of the same or related domains. It is rare that a global ontology or schema can be developed for such a system. In practice, multiple ontologies and schemas will be developed by independent entities, and coordination will require mapping between the different models. Such a mapping will be a set of formulae that provide the semantic relationships between the concepts in the models. There will always be more than one representation of any domain of discourse. Hence, if knowledge and data are to be shared, the problem of mapping between models is as fundamental as modeling itself.

In current systems, mappings between models are provided manually in a labor-intensive and error-prone process,

which is a major bottleneck to scaling up systems to a large number of sources. Recently, several tools have been developed to provide support for constructing mappings. The approaches underlying these tools are usually based on heuristics that identify structural and naming similarities between models (Noy & Musen 2000; Rahm & Bernstein 2001) or on using machine learning to learn mappings (Doan, Domingos, & Halevy 2001; Lacher & Groh 2001; Doan *et al.* 2002; Berlin & Motro 2002). In both cases, the systems require feedback from a user to further refine a proposed mapping.

Our opening claim in this paper is that the study of mappings between models needs to be recognized as an important item on the research agenda. A robust tool for aiding users to generate mappings will need the ability to incorporate heuristics (domain dependent and independent), use machine learning techniques, and incorporate user feedback. To exploit all of these techniques in concert and in a principled fashion, we must have an *explicit* and well-defined representation of mappings that enables reasoning about mappings and evidence supporting these mappings, comparing between different mappings, and ultimately, learning mappings.

First, we must define semantics for such mappings. We therefore offer a framework for defining representations of mappings with associated semantics (Section 3). An instance of the framework is a particular mapping language, where the source and destination representation languages have been fixed. The framework makes three important contributions. First, it enables mapping between models in vastly different representation languages (e.g, relational data, XML, RDF, DAML+OIL (Horrocks, van Harmelen, & Patel-Schneider 2001)) *without* first translating the models into a common language. Second, the framework introduces a *helper model* in the mapping, which is needed in cases where it is not possible to map directly between a pair of models. Third, the framework enables representing mappings that are either incomplete or lose information.

While this paper focuses on the issue of representing mappings and reasoning about them, the problem of generating the mappings is still the ultimate goal. Our recent work on the problem of generating mappings (Doan, Domingos, & Halevy 2001; Madhavan, Bernstein, & Rahm 2001; Doan *et al.* 2002) has led us to the conclusion that in order to make further progress on the problem we need a well founded representation of mappings. With such a representation, we will be able to combine in a principled way different types of knowledge about mappings and make some inferences that will further help the process. Previous work has mostly avoided defining mapping semantics formally either because the focus was on how to obtain the mappings, or because finding mappings was a part of other application dependent goals (e.g., ontology merging, data migration), and hence the properties of mappings themselves were not investigated.

A mapping between models rarely maps all the concepts in one model to all the concepts in another, because models don't usually cover precisely the same domains. As a result, there are usually several possible mappings, so we need a way of determining whether a mapping is acceptable for a particular task. In Section 4 we identify a core set of properties that can be used to determine whether a mapping suffices for a particular context: (1) the ability to answer queries over a model, (2) inference of mapping formulas, and (3) compositionality of mappings.

As our final contribution, we demonstrate the application of the framework to a particular mapping language that maps between relational models. The mapping language we consider is the one used in several data integration systems (Levy, Rajaraman, & Ordille 1996; Duschka & Genesereth 1997; Friedman & Weld 1997; Lambrecht, Kambhampati, & Gnanaprakasam 1999; Gribble *et al.* 2001). However, the point of this section is not to argue for this particular language, but to illustrate our framework on one concrete (and important) case. We describe sound and complete algorithms for deciding each of the above properties. These results are also of independent interest in answering queries using views (Halevy 2001) and information integration.

2 Problem definition

In this section we first demonstrate the pervasive role that mappings between models play in several applications, and then outline the desiderata for formalisms specifying and manipulating such mappings.

Mappings between models are the foundation behind the following classes of applications:

Information integration and the Semantic Web: In many contexts, data resides in a multitude of data sources (e.g., many databases within an enterprise, data sources on the WWW, etc). Data integration enables users to ask queries in a uniform fashion, without having to access each data source independently (or even know about the existence of multiple sources). In an information integration system, users ask queries over a *mediated schema*, which captures only the aspects of the domain that are salient to the application. The mediated schema is solely a logical one (no data is stored in it), and mappings are used to describe the relationship between the mediated schema and the schemas of the data sources. The Semantic Web goes one step further. Here, there is no central mediated schema, tasks involve actions in addition to queries, and coordination is achieved using ontologies. Here too, mappings between ontologies are necessary for agents to interoperate.

Data migration: The goal of data migration is to take data/knowledge from an external source and merge it with some existing data stored using a different schema or ontology. In many cases, some information may be lost in the transformation since the external source does not necessarily represent the same aspects of the domain as the local one. Here too, the migration needs to be guided by a mapping between the external and internal representations. In *data warehousing*, several data sources are used to populate a data warehouse, which is later used for analysis queries. Here it is usually assumed that some information is lost during the loading of the warehouse (e.g., the warehouse may have only summary data, rather than detailed data).

Ontology merging: Several applications require that we combine multiple ontologies into a single coherent ontology (Noy & Musen 2000; Stumme & Maedche 2001). In some cases, these are independently developed ontologies that model overlapping domains. In others, we merge two ontologies that evolved from a single base ontology. The first step in merging ontologies is to create a mapping between them. Once the mapping is given, the challenge of a merge algorithm is to create a *minimal* ontology that covers the given ones.

The creation of mappings will rarely be completely automated. However, automated tools can significantly speed up the process by proposing plausible mappings. In large domains, while many mappings might be fairly obvious, some parts need expert intervention. There are several approaches to building such tools. The first (and more prevalent) uses a wide range of heuristics to generate mappings. The heuristics are often based on structure (e.g., if two classes match, then some of their sub-classes probably match), or based on naming (course and class may refer to the same concept). In some cases, domain-independent heuristics may be augmented by more specific heuristics for the particular representation language or application domain. A second approach is to learn mappings. In particular, manually provided mappings present examples for a learning algorithm that can generalize and suggest subsequent mappings.

Our ultimate goal is to build a system that uses a multitude of techniques to help users construct mappings. The system will combine different heuristics, hypotheses of learning modules and user feedback to guide the mapping process. Such a system needs a principled representation of mappings that it can manipulate in a well defined fashion. To fill this need, in the next section we offer a framework in which mappings between models can be defined. The framework can be instantiated to a particular context by considering a specific language (or set of languages) relevant to that context. The following example illustrates the issues involved.

Example 1 *Figure 1 includes two different models of a domain of students. The first model,* MyUniv, *is in DAML+OIL (Horrocks, van Harmelen, & Patel-Schneider 2001) (i.e., a description logic). The second one,* YourUniv, *is a relational schema.*

The ontology MyUniv *includes the concepts* STUDENT *with subclasses* ARTS-STD *and* SCI-STD *and* COURSE *with*

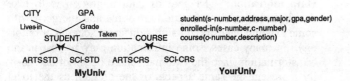

Figure 1: Models of the student domain

subclasses ARTS-CRS *and* SCI-CRS. *The binary relationship* Taken *represents the courses taken by students, and the relationships* Grade *and* Lives-in *represent properties of students.* Lives-in *is constrained to have the value "myCity".*

The schema YourUniv *includes the tables* student, course *and* enrolled-in. *In addition, the schema includes an integrity constraint specifying that the attribute* address *must contain the string "yourCity". Our goal is to specify a mapping between the two models.*

The first issue illustrated by this example is that we need to specify a mapping between models in different representation languages. The second issue is that not all concepts in one model exist directly in the other. For example, arts students in MyUniv are identified by a concept, while in YourUniv they can only be identified by a query (all students with major="arts"). A majority of works in the related literature have concentrated more on obtaining simple correspondences between concepts, and have ignored richer mappings such as this. Also note that some concepts in one model might not have corresponding ones in the other (gender of students in YourUniv).

A more subtle issue is that the mapping cannot simply equate MyUniv.STUDENT with YourUniv.student. The constraints on the addresses imply that these are disjoint sets (assuming that myCity and yourCity are distinct). The only way to relate the students in the different models is to define a *third* model that represents a set of students from (at least) both cities, and then relate MyUniv and YourUniv to the third model. □

To summarize our discussion, we pose the following desiderata for representations of mappings:

Clear semantics: The meaning of mappings should be formally defined. The semantics will provide a basis for reasoning about mappings (e.g., determining whether two mappings are equivalent or if a certain mapping formula is entailed by a mapping), combining evidence to propose likely mappings, and learning mappings.

Accommodate incompleteness: Incompleteness can arise in two ways: (1) because of loss of information when the two models cover different domains, and (2) when a certain concept can be mapped between the models, but the mapping is unknown or hard to specify. An example of the latter would occur if the two universities had different grading systems, and there is no direct mapping between them. The key point here is that even if the mapping is incomplete, it still may suffice for the task at hand. Detecting this is one of the important issues of interest to us.

Allow heterogeneity: By nature, mappings between models

will involve multiple representation languages. Therefore, a mapping language needs to be able to represent mappings between models in different languages. An alternative approach would be to first translate all the models into a common representation language, and then specify mappings as formulas in this language. However, it is often desirable to avoid the problems associated with designing a single representation language for all models (such as finding a suitably rich language in which inference is still tractable).

3 Mappings: syntax and semantics

We now define the basic terms we use for our framework. Unfortunately, the term "model" is overloaded. In our discussion we use the word *model* to denote a representation of a domain in a formal language, and use *logical model* to refer to an interpretation that satisfies all the formulas in a model. Our description considers mapping between a pair of models, but the framework can be extended in a straightforward way to multiple models.

Representation languages and models: We represent a domain of discourse using a set of expressions in some formal representation language. In this paper we consider languages with formal semantics (e.g., First-order logic, Description Logics, Horn rules, relational schemata, graph-structured data such as XML). We denote a language used in a representation by $\mathcal{L}$ possibly with a subscript. The set of expressions to represent a domain is called a *model*, and is denoted by T. We do not assume that the model is closed under logical deduction or even that reasoning in the representation language is decidable.

A model of a domain is often (but not always!) specified in two parts, terminological and extensional. The first part identifies the concepts in the domain and relations between them (or the set of relations in a relational schema). The second part populates the model with facts about specific individuals in the domain. The phrase *an extension of a model* T refers to a model in which we added an extensional component to the terminological component T. If T has a single component, then the phrase simply refers to T itself.

Expressions and formulas: A mapping between models consists of a set of relationships between expressions over the two models. An expression is built from the terms in the language and a set of operators. In order to be comparable, the expressions need to have compatible output types. For example, a SQL query produces a relation; a concept in a description logic represents a unary relation. An XML query language generates as output a nested XML document.

The expression language used in a mapping varies depending on the languages of the models being mapped. For our semantics to be well defined, we require the following: given a model T in a language $\mathcal{L}$ and an instance $\bar{a}$ of the data type of the output of an expression e, and an interpretation I of T, the question of whether I satisfies $e(\bar{a})$ (i.e., $I \models e(\bar{a})$) is well defined in $\mathcal{L}$ (and hence, $T \models e(\bar{a})$ is well defined as well). This essentially means that the set of outputs of an expression is well defined. Note that we don't require the entailment to be decidable. Also note that the output of an expression can be a constant.

A formula relates expressions over two models. Given two models T_1 (in language $\mathcal{L}_1$) and T_2 (in $\mathcal{L}_2$), *a formula over T_1 and T_2* is of the form e_1 **op** e_2, where e_1 and e_2 are expressions, and the operator **op** is well defined w.r.t. the output types of e_1 and e_2. For example, if both expressions have relations as output types, then **op** can be $=, \subseteq$, and if they both output numeric constants, then **op** can be $\geq, \leq, =$. If e_1 outputs a constant and e_2 outputs a unary relation, then **op** can be $\in$. Note that given an interpretation I_1 (I_2) for T_1 (T_2), $\{I_1, I_2\} \models e_1$ **op** e_2 is well defined.

This ability of a formula to relate expressions of different languages implies a measure of compatibility between the languages, namely that some of their types are in common. This aspect of formulas is what enables us to define mappings between models in different representation languages.

Syntax of mappings

We are now ready to define the syntax of a mapping between models T_1 and T_2.

Definition 1 *Let T_1 and T_2 be models in languages $\mathcal{L}_1$ and $\mathcal{L}_2$ respectively. A mapping between T_1 and T_2 may include a helper model T_3 (in language $\mathcal{L}_3$), and consists of a set of formulas each of which is over (T_1, T_2), (T_1, T_3) or (T_2, T_3).*

Example 2 *One possible mapping between* YourUniv *and* MyUniv *uses a helper model* Univ, *a relational schema with tables* Student, Course, Arts-Std, Sci-Std, Arts-Crs, *and* Sci-Crs. *The following are examples of the mapping formulae.*
Univ.Student(std,ad,gpa)$\supseteq$ MyUniv.STUDENT(std) $\wedge$
        MyUniv.Lives-in(std,ad) $\wedge$ MyUniv.Grade(std,gpa)
Univ.Student(std,ad,gpa)$\supseteq$YourUniv.student(std,ad,x,gpa,y)
Univ.Arts-Std(std)$\supseteq$MyUniv.ARTS-STD(std)
Univ.Arts-Std(std)$\supseteq$YourUniv.student(std,x,"arts",y,z)

The first two formulae map students in the two universities to the single student concept in the helper model. The other two formulae map art students and art majors to a single table for arts students. Other mappings can be defined similarly.

Semantics of mappings

The semantics of a model constrains its possible interpretations by specifying which ones are logical models. The semantics of a mapping between two models is a constraint on the pairs of interpretations (or triplets, when a helper model is used), and therefore specifies which pairs of interpretations can co-exist, given the mapping. Formally, satisfaction of a mapping is defined as follows:

Definition 2 *Let M be a mapping between the models T_1 and T_2, and assume that M also involves a helper model T_3. Let I_i be an interpretation of an extension of T_i for $i = 1, 2, 3$. The triplet (I_1, I_2, I_3) satisfies the mapping M if the following hold:*

- *I_i is a logical model of T_i, for $i = 1, 2, 3$, and*
- *For each formula $e \in M$, $\{I_1, I_2, I_3\} \models e$.*

In practice, it is often useful to restrict mappings to be *conservative augmentation* of the models being mapped. Intuitively, a mapping is a conservative augmentation if it does not entail new facts *within* the model, given the mapping. Formally, M is a conservative extension of T_1 if whenever $I_1 \models T_1$, there exist I_2 and I_3 such that $(I_1, I_2, I_3) \models M$.

Note that in examples 1 and 2, if the mapping formulae were simple equalities between expressions in the two models, their semantics would not be well-defined. There can be no interpretations of the two models over a common domain of discourse (body of students) since they have conflicting constraints on the city addresses of students. The use of the helper model enables a well-defined mapping.

There are a few points worth noting about our framework. First, the mapping formulae can be fairly expressive, and therefore it is possible to represent complex relationships between models. In particular, the expression language may even translate data elements in one model into schema elements in another (or vice versa), which is an important feature in practice. Second, though we have only emphasized mapping between concepts (or schema elements) here, the framework can also be used to map between data elements in the two models. Finally, our semantics are defined in terms of instances in the domain (interpretations map instances in the domain of discourse to elements in the models). However, that does not mean that we must have actual instances in the models; in fact, many ontologies do not have associated instances. Even in such cases, since these ontologies have well-defined semantics, there exists some implicit interpretation over their intended domains of discourse.

4   Important properties of mappings

In this section we identify several important properties of mappings that are worth studying. These properties are needed to decide whether a mapping is adequate for a particular task at hand. The first property is *query answerability*. A mapping between two models rarely maps all the concepts in one model to all concepts in the other. Instead, mappings typically lose some information and can be partial or incomplete. However, lossy mappings can be adequate for some tasks. Query answerability is a formalization of this property. The second property, *mapping inference*, provides a reasoning tool for determining whether mappings are equivalent. *Mapping composition* enables creating mappings between models that are related by intermediate models.

Query answerability: Mappings are typically required to enable a certain task. For example, in data integration a mapping is adequate if it enables the answering of queries over the mediated schema. For data migration, a mapping is adequate if we can populate the target schema, given an extension of the source schema. For ontology or schema merging, the merged ontology is adequate if we can use it to answer all the queries that were answerable in the original ontologies. Hence, it seems natural to consider a mapping adequate if it enables correct answering of a certain set of queries over the models at hand (note that the set of queries may be infinite!). We define the problem formally as follows. (The definition is written w.r.t. queries over T_1, but it can be defined similarly for queries over T_2).

Definition 3 *Let M be a mapping between models T_1, T_2 and an optional helper model T_3, and let Q be a query over T_1. We say that the mapping M enables query answering of Q if the following holds.*

Let T_2' be an extension of T_2. Let $\mathcal{I}$ be the set of interpretations of T_1 for which there exists an interpretation I_3 of T_3 and a logical model I_2 of T_2' such that $(I_1, I_2, I_3) \models M$. Then, for every tuple of constants $\bar{a}$, either $I_1 \models Q(\bar{a})$ for every $I_1 \in \mathcal{I}$ or $I_1 \not\models Q(\bar{a})$ for every $I_1 \in \mathcal{I}$.

Informally, the definition states that given an extension of T_2, it *uniquely* determines the answers for Q over T_1.

Example 3 *Consider the two models in example 1. For simplicity we ignore the constraints on the addresses, and hence, there is no need for a helper model. Instead, consider that the grades at the two universities are on different scales. Consider the mapping formula*

YourUniv.student(std,x,y,$\alpha\times$gpa,z) =
MyUniv.STUDENT(std)$\wedge$MyUniv.Grade(std,gpa)

where α is an unknown conversion factor between the grades. Consider the following two queries over MyUniv, *(1)* max-grade :- Max{ gpa | MyUniv.Grade(std,gpa)}, *and (2)* high-grade(std,gpa) :- MyUniv.Grade(std,gpa) $\wedge$ gpa $\geq$ 3.8

The mapping formula enables answering query (1) on YourUniv *because the max does not depend on the particular scale, i.e., given any database of students for* YourUniv*, the answer to* max-grade *will be uniquely determined. However the mapping does not enable answering query (2) because the answers to the query will differ depending on the value of α.*

Mapping Inference: A formal semantics for mappings enables a precise definition of several reasoning tasks. One particularly important task is determining whether a given mapping formula is entailed by a mapping (in which case, it doesn't provide new information). This, in turn, enables other reasoning tasks such as (1) whether two mappings are equivalent, and (2) whether a mapping is minimal (i.e., removing any formula from the mapping loses information). We formalize the mapping inference problem as follows:

Definition 4 *Let M be a mapping between models T_1 and T_2, and let e be a formula over T_1 and T_2. The mapping inference problem is to determine whether $M \models e$, i.e., whether whenever $(I_1, I_2, I_3) \models M$, then $(I_1, I_2, I_3) \models e$, where (I_1, I_2, I_3) are interpretations for T_1, T_2 and a helper model T_3, respectively.*

Mapping Composition: The need to compose mappings arises when we need to piece together a mapping given other mappings. In its simplest form, given two mappings from models T_0 to T_1 and T_1 to T_2, we might have to obtain a mapping directly between T_0 and T_2. Formally, the problem is defined as follows.

Definition 5 *Let M_{01} be a mapping between models T_0 and T_1, and M_{12} be a mapping between models T_1 and T_2. Let e be a formula over T_0 and T_2. The mapping composition problem is to determine whether $\{M_{01}, M_{12}\} \models e$, i.e., whether whenever a triple of interpretations (I_0, I_1, I_2) for T_0, T_1, T_2 respectively, satisfies $(I_0, I_1) \models M_{01}$ and $(I_1, I_2) \models M_{12}$ then $(I_0, I_1, I_2) \models e$.*

In section 5, we solve the problems of query answerability, mapping inference and mapping composition for a mapping language over relational representations.

5 Mappings between Relational Models

In this section we consider a specific instance in our framework, show that the properties discussed in the previous section can be decided, and specify the complexity of the decision problems. The language we consider expresses mappings between a pair of relational-database models (i.e., schemas). Formally, each model includes a set of relations, and an extension of the model includes a set of ground facts for each relation. The expressions in our language are of the following form:

$$q(\bar{X}) \Leftrightarrow p_1(\bar{X}_1) \wedge \ldots \wedge p_n(\bar{X}_n)$$

where the p_i's are database relations, $\bar{X}_i$ and $\bar{X}$ are tuples of variables (and $\bar{X} \subseteq \bar{X}_1 \cup \ldots \cup \bar{X}_n$). The variables in $\bar{X}$ are called *distinguished* and the other variables are called *existential*. The distinguished variables are assumed to be universally quantified, while the others are existentially quantified. We also use the same notation to describe queries, and the answer to the query is the set of tuples for $\bar{X}$. We note that although simple, this is a rather expressive language, since it enables defining relations in a very common subset of the SQL query language.

A formula in our language has the form $q_1(\bar{X}) = q_2(\bar{X})$, where q_1 (q_2) is defined by the left-hand side of a single expression over the relations in T_1 (T_2). We assume mappings that are conservative augmentations. Recall that this only means that a mapping cannot entail new conclusions about the *schema* but still allows to deduce new ground facts.

Our results assume the following restriction on mappings in our language: a mapping is said to be *variable-partitionable* if whenever a variable x appears in position i of relation R in one of the formulae in a mapping M, and is an existential variable in the formula, then there is no formula in M where a variable that appears in position i of R is distinguished. Note that this property holds trivially in the common case where the expressions in M do not contain existential variables.

Our first result concerns query answerability in our language. In the complexity analysis we are mostly concerned with the size of data in T_1 and T_2.

Theorem 1 *Let M be a variable-partitionable mapping between models T_1 and T_2, and let Q be a query in our language. The problem of deciding whether M enables answering Q is NP-complete.* □

The proof is based on showing that M enables answering Q if and only if there exists an *equivalent* rewriting of the query Q using the expressions over T_1 used in M. The latter problem is NP-complete (Halevy 2001). □

Our next result shows that reasoning about mappings is decidable:

Theorem 2 *Let M be a mapping between models T_1 and T_2, and let $u(\bar{X}) = v(\bar{X})$ be a mapping formula. If M is variable-partitionable, then the problem of deciding whether $M \models u(\bar{X}) = v(\bar{X})$ is NP-complete.* □

The proof of Theorem 2 is quite lengthy and omitted because of space limitations. Below we sketch the algorithm underlying the proof.

Suppose M is of the form $u_i(\bar{X}) = v_i(\bar{X})$ for $1 \leq i \leq k$, where the u_i's and the v_i's are defined using expressions in the language. The u_i's are defined over the schema of T_1 and the v_i's over T_2. We denote by Q_v (resp. Q_u) the rewriting of v (resp. u) using $v_1, \ldots, v_k$ (resp. $u_1, \ldots, u_k$). The rewriting can be found using the techniques in (Halevy 2001).

We denote by Q_v^u the result of substituting u_i for v_i in Q_v. Note that Q_v^u is an expression over the schema T_1. The algorithm checks that (1) Q_v is equivalent to v, and (2) Q_v^u is equivalent to u, and outputs that $M \models u(\bar{X}) = v(\bar{X})$ if and only if both (1) and (2) hold. Equivalence checking for these expressions is NP-complete (Sagiv & Yannakakis 1981). □

It should be noted that the above algorithm is sound even when M is not variable-partitionable.

Example 4 *Consider two relational models identical to YourUniv (from example 1) - Univ$_1$ and Univ$_2$. Model Univ$_i$ has tables student$_i$, enrolled-in$_i$ and course$_i$ (i=1,2). Consider the following view definitions,*

Major-Gender$_i$(std,mjr,gnd) :- student$_i$(std,x,mjr,y,gnd),
Some-Class$_i$(std) :- enrolled-in$_i$(std,x),
Some-Student$_i$(crs) :- enrolled-in$_i$(x,crs), *and*
Major$_i$(std,mjr) :- student$_i$(std,x,mjr,y,z).

Consider the mapping M = { course$_1$ = course$_2$, Some-Class$_1$ = Some-Class$_2$, Major-Gender$_1$ = Major-Gender$_2$}. Note that Major$_i$ is rewritable in terms of Major-Gender$_i$, but Some-Student$_i$ is not rewritable in terms of course$_i$, Some-Class$_i$ and Major-Gender$_i$. It follows that,

- *Given an extension of Univ$_2$, M enables answering of Major$_1$, but does not enable answering of Some-Student$_1$.*

- *M implies Major$_1$ = Major$_2$, but does not imply Some-Student$_1$ = Some-Student$_2$.*

Our final result shows that compositionality is also decidable for our language:

Theorem 3 *Let T_0, T_1 and T_2 be models, and let M_{01} (resp. M_{12}) be a variable-partitionable mapping between T_0 and T_1 (resp. T_1 and T_2). Let e be a formula over T_0 and T_2. Deciding whether $M_{01}, M_{12} \models e$ is NP-complete.*

The proofs for each of the results in this section are available in the full version of our paper.

6 Discussion and Related Work

Thus far, our discussion has focused on manipulating mappings mostly as a form of logical reasoning. The next steps are to incorporate *inaccurate* mappings and handle *uncertainty* about mappings. Inaccuracy arises because in many contexts there is no precise mapping. Reasoning about uncertainty of mappings is necessary because the generation of mappings often involves combining different heuristics and learned hypotheses. The two issues are highly intertwined, because heuristics are often used as a vehicle to choose the best mapping when no perfectly accurate one exists. We believe that some form of first-order probabilistic representation of mappings will be the appropriate tool for representing mappings, but none of the existing proposals (e.g. (Pfeffer *et al.* 1999)) provide sufficient expressive power for reasoning about formulas with variables and quantification.

In general, mappings may be inaccurate for multiple reasons: either the mapping language is too restricted to express more accurate mappings, or the concepts in the two models simply do not match up precisely. As an example of the former, in ontology mapping, it might not be possible to get an exact mapping when mapping formulae are restricted to be one-one correspondences between concepts.

When no accurate mapping exists, the issue becomes choosing the *best* mapping from the viable ones. A common heuristic is to restrict the language for expressing the mapping in order to prune the search space (of viable mappings). Mapping formulae or correspondences are produced in one of two ways: (1) applying a set of matching rules (Mitra, Wiederhold, & Jannink 1999; Noy & Musen 2000; Stumme & Maedche 2001), or (2) evaluating interesting similarity measures that compare and help choose from the set of all possible correspondences (Calvanese *et al.* 2001; Melnik, Garcia-Molina, & Rahm 2002; Lacher & Groh 2001; Doan *et al.* 2002). These heuristics often use syntactic information such as the names of the concepts or nesting relationships between concepts. They might also use semantic information such as the inter-relationship between concepts (slots of frames in (Noy & Musen 2000)), the types of the concepts, or the labeled-graph structure of the models (Calvanese *et al.* 2001; Melnik, Garcia-Molina, & Rahm 2002). Other techniques use data instances belonging to input models to estimate the likelihood of these correspondences (Doan, Domingos, & Halevy 2001; Lacher & Groh 2001; Stumme & Maedche 2001; Berlin & Motro 2002). Several systems also have powerful features for the efficient capture of user interaction (Noy & Musen 2000; McGuinness *et al.* 2000). In (Chalupsky 2000), an expressive rule language is proposed to support transformations between different symbolic representations. In (Rahm & Bernstein 2001) the authors survey the schema matching techniques in the database literature.

It should be noted that in some contexts there may be other factors than accuracy that affect the choice of mapping, such as the cost of applying the mapping to data. For example, in a data management application, mappings that result in more efficient query execution plans may be preferred.

The work of (Calvanese, Giuseppe, & Lenzerini 2001) describes a specialization of our framework to ontology integration. Their goal is to define the semantics of an ontology integration system whose sources are described by different ontologies. Since they focus on data integration, they require a global mediated ontology, whereas in our framework a mediated ontology will exist only if it makes sense for the task at hand. They do not address any of the inference questions that we outlined in Section 5.

The results we presented in Section 5 make use of the theory of answering queries using views (Friedman, Levy, & Millstein 1999; Halevy 2001), but extend the theory in important ways. We defined the notion of mappings enabling query answering, and showed the exact role that equivalent rewritings, which have been studied in that literature, play in this context. In addition, we presented results on equivalence and compositionality of mappings, which were not studied in previous work.

7 Conclusions

Mappings are crucial components of many applications. To reason simultaneously about multiple models, we need well-defined semantics for mappings. In addition to representing mappings and making inferences across models, this enables us to combine multiple techniques to mapping generation. In this paper we proposed a framework and associated semantics for mappings. We demonstrated an instantiation of our framework to answer questions about query answerability, mapping inference and composition for relational models.

Our work lays the foundation for research towards a broader goal of building a system that combines multiple techniques in helping users create mappings between models. The system should be able to improve over time and even transfer knowledge from one mapping task to another when appropriate. The next step in this work is to develop an appropriate probabilistic representation of mappings that enables capturing both inaccuracy and uncertainty.

Acknowledgments

We thank Corin Anderson, Rachel Pottinger, Pradeep Shenoy, and the anonymous reviewers for their invaluable comments. This work is supported by NSF Grants 9523649, 9983932, IIS-9978567, and IIS-9985114. The third author is also supported by an IBM Faculty Partnership Award. The fourth author is also supported by a Sloan Fellowship and gifts from Microsoft Research, NEC and NTT.

References

Berlin, J., and Motro, A. 2002. Database Schema Matching Using Machine Learning with Feature Selection. In *Proc. of the 14th Int. Conf. on Advanced Information Systems Engg. (CAiSE02)*.

Calvanese, D.; Castano, S.; Guerra, F.; Lembo, D.; Melchiorri, M.; Terracina, G.; Ursino, D.; and Vincini, M. 2001. Towards a Comprehensive Framework for Semantic Integration of Highly Heterogeneous Data Sources. In *Proc. of the 8th Int. Workshop on Knowledge Representation meets Databases (KRDB2001)*.

Calvanese, D.; Giuseppe, D. G.; and Lenzerini, M. 2001. Ontology of Integration and Integration of Ontologies. In *Proc. of the Int. Workshop on Description Logics (DL2001)*.

Chalupsky, H. 2000. Ontomorph: A Translation system for symbolic knowledge. In *Proc. of the 7th Int. Conf. on Principles of Knowledge Representation and Reasoning (KR2000)*.

Doan, A.; Madhavan, J.; Domingos, P.; and Halevy, A. 2002. Learning to Map between Ontologies on the Semantic Web. In *Proc. of the 11th Int. World Wide Web Conf. (WWW2002)*.

Doan, A.; Domingos, P.; and Halevy, A. Y. 2001. Reconciling Schemas of Disparate Data Sources: A Machine Learning Approach. In *Proc. of the ACM SIGMOD Conf.*

Duschka, O. M., and Genesereth, M. R. 1997. Answering recursive queries using views. In *Proc. of PODS*.

Friedman, M., and Weld, D. 1997. Efficient execution of information gathering plans. In *Proc. of the 15th Int. Joint Conf. on Artificial Intelligence (IJCAI)*.

Friedman, M.; Levy, A.; and Millstein, T. 1999. Navigational Plans for Data Integration. In *Proc. of the 16th National Conf. on Artificial Intelligence (AAAI)*.

Gribble, S.; Halevy, A.; Ives, Z.; Rodrig, M.; and Suciu, D. 2001. What can databases do for peer-to-peer? In *ACM SIGMOD WebDB Workshop 2001*.

Halevy, A. Y. 2001. Answering queries using views: A survey. *VLDB Journal* 10(4).

Horrocks, I.; van Harmelen, F.; and Patel-Schneider, P. 2001. DAML+OIL. http://www.daml.org/2001/03/daml+oil-index.html.

Lacher, M. S., and Groh, G. 2001. Facilitating the exchange of explixit knowledge through ontology mappings. In *Proc. of the 14th Int. FLAIRS conference*.

Lambrecht, E.; Kambhampati, S.; and Gnanaprakasam, S. 1999. Optimizing recursive information gathering plans. In *Proc. of the 16th Int. Joint Conf on Artificial Intelligence(IJCAI)*, 1204–1211.

Levy, A. Y.; Rajaraman, A.; and Ordille, J. J. 1996. Query answering algorithms for information agents. In *Proc. of the 13th National Conf. on Artificial Intelligence (AAAI)*.

Madhavan, J.; Bernstein, P. A.; and Rahm, E. 2001. Generic Schema Matching with Cupid. In *Proc. of the 27th Int. Conf. on Very Large Databases (VLDB)*.

McGuinness, D.; Fikes, R.; Rice, J.; and Wilder, S. 2000. The Chimaera Ontology Environment. In *Proc. of the 17th National Conf. on Artificial Intelligence (AAAI)*.

Melnik, S.; Garcia-Molina, H.; and Rahm, E. 2002. Similarity Flooding: A Versatile Graph Matching Algorithm. In *Proc. of the 18th Int. Conf. on Data Engg. (ICDE)*.

Mitra, P.; Wiederhold, G.; and Jannink, J. 1999. Semi-automatic Integration of Knowledge Sources. In *Proc. the 2nd Int. Conf. on Information FUSION*.

Noy, N., and Musen, M. 2000. PROMPT: Algorithm and Tool for Automated Ont. Merging and Alignment. In *Proc. of the 17th National Conf. on Artificial Intelligence (AAAI)*.

Pfeffer, A.; Koller, D.; Milch, B.; and Takusagawa, K. 1999. SPOOK: A system for probabilistic object-oriented knowledge representation. In *Proc. of the 15th Conf. on Uncertainty in Artificial Intelligence(UAI)*.

Rahm, E., and Bernstein, P. A. 2001. A survey on approaches to automatic schema matching. *VLDB Journal* 10(4).

Sagiv, Y., and Yannakakis, M. 1981. Equivalence among relational expressions with the union and difference operators. *Journal of the ACM* 27(4):633–655.

Stumme, G., and Maedche, A. 2001. FCA-MERGE: Bottom-Up Merging of Ontologies. In *Proc. of the 17th Int. Joint Conf. on Artificial Intelligence (IJCAI)*.

A Regression Based Adaptation Strategy for Case-Based Reasoning

David Patterson, Niall Rooney, Mykola Galushka
Northern Ireland Knowledge Engineering Laboratory (NIKEL)
School of Information and Software Engineering
University of Ulster at Jordanstown,
Newtownabbey, County Antrim,
Northern Ireland
e-mail: { wd.patterson, nf.rooney,mg.galushka}@ulster.ac.uk

Abstract

Adaptation is the least well studied process in case-based reasoning (CBR). The main reasons for this are the potentially complex nature of implementing adaptation knowledge and the difficulties associated with acquiring quality knowledge in the first place and competently maintaining it over time. For these reasons most CBR systems are designed to leave the adaptation component to the expert and therefore function simply as case *retrieval* systems as opposed to truly *reasoning* systems. Here we present a competent adaptation strategy, which uses a modified regression algorithm to automatically discover and implement locally specific adaptation knowledge in CBR. The advantages of this approach are that the adaptation knowledge acquisition process is automated, localised, guaranteed to be specific to the task at hand, and there is no adaptation knowledge maintenance burden on the system. The disadvantage is that the time taken to form solutions is increased but we also show how a novel indexing scheme based on k-means clustering can help reduce this overhead considerably.

Introduction

There was much enthusiasm within the Artificial Intelligence community during the early days of CBR systems development as it was widely regarded as a methodology which could successfully address many of the problems which had plagued classical expert (rule based) systems for so long. Firstly it could help relieve the knowledge acquisition bottleneck. Rather than acquiring knowledge as rules, which was a difficult process, now experts could recount cases of experience, which was seen as a much more intuitive and natural process. Secondly it could improve system maintenance. Rule based systems were notoriously difficult to maintain due to the 'ripple effect' that modifying one rule had on others. Updating an out of date case had no risk of knock on effects as cases were individually localised chunks of knowledge in their

own right and there was no need to worry about the effects that modifying one case would have on another. These arguments may have seemed valid at the time but unfortunately CBR has introduced new difficulties of its own. It has made knowledge acquisition easier on one level in that cases are more intuitive to acquire than rules but this is only one type of knowledge required for CBR. Other knowledge stores, or containers as they sometimes referred to, include similarity/retrieval knowledge, domain description knowledge, adaptation knowledge and maintenance knowledge [Richter 95]. Each container requires a dedicated acquisition process and a means to maintain that knowledge over time. Therefore it is reasonable to argue that the knowledge acquisition process for CBR has become more involved. This paper focuses on issues surrounding the acquisition and maintenance of adaptation knowledge. The CBR community has largely neglected this knowledge container over the years and as such it is the least well studied of all the CBR processes. The main reason for this neglect is due to difficulties with acquiring, storing and maintaining relevant adaptation knowledge and the potentially complex nature of applying it correctly to adapt retrieved cases [Hanney & Keane 1996]. Therefore to reduce the need for adaptation, knowledge engineers often opted to develop case *retrieval systems*, consisting of large densely packed case-bases consisting of as many conceivable cases as possible, as opposed to developing truly *reasoning* systems [Allen et al 1995]. The theory being that by increasing the chances of retrieving an exact match, the need for adaptation would be reduced. This approach has inevitably led to efficiency problems [Smyth 1995]. Other systems have been developed with limited hand coded, static adaptation knowledge built into them during system development [Simoudis & Miller 91]. As it is impossible (from both a time and operational perspective) to predetermine all the circumstances for adaptation a priori, this approach is too limited to be of practical use in real world systems. At best this approach could provide either very high level and generalised rules that could never take into consideration the task specific circumstances of individual retrievals, (something which is of vital importance to a competent case-based reasoner) or a limited number of very specific rules with much too narrow a scope to be applicable in all but a few retrieval circumstances. Additionally it takes no account of providing a learning mechanism whereby the knowledge can be maintained over time. Furthermore to rely on the expert for adaptation knowledge results inevitably in biased knowledge, in that not all experts solve problems in the same way and often there is much disagreement as to how a problem is best solved. Ideally what is required is an unbiased, automated, flexible, dynamic and intelligent method of acquiring and maintaining *locally* specific adaptation knowledge (and indeed all knowledge in CBR). This perspective was proposed initially by Patterson et al [Patterson et al 1999] where a framework was put forward to develop a Case-Based Reasoning Knowledge Base Management System which would assist in the automated acquisition and maintenance of knowledge for *all* the CBR containers. It is recognised that one knowledge type can often be converted into another in CBR [Richter 1995]. What we propose here is to use the knowledge present within case knowledge, coupled with data mining techniques, to discover and apply locally relevant adaptation knowledge independently from the expert. Leake [Leake 1996] has already recognised the potential of data mining techniques as a useful complement to CBR processes. Anand et al [Anand et al 1998a, Anand et al 1998b] and Patterson et al [Patterson et al 2000, Patterson et al 2002] have empirically shown them to be useful in acquiring and maintaining knowledge for various CBR processes such as similarity and retrieval.

A number of approaches, designed to automatically acquire flexible adaptation knowledge from case-knowledge, have been presented in the literature. For example Hanney [Hanney & Keane 1996] automatically discovered adaptation knowledge in the form of rules by generalising case knowledge. A disadvantage of this approach is that it moves adaptation knowledge maintenance back in the direction of a rule base and all the associated maintenance problems this introduces. McSherry [McSherry 1999a, McSherry 1999b], in order to discover adaptation rules to adapt a retrieved case to a target, discovered what he termed as an *adaptation triplet.* This is an engaging approach due to its implicit simplicity which does discover and use specific adaptation knowledge during adaptation but, unfortunately no empirical studies have been carried out using real world case-bases to validate its competency fully. Leake [Leake et al 1996] proposed a hybrid rule based/case-based approach to adaptation knowledge discovery and reuse. This approach is novel in that they proposed a *case-based* adaptation knowledge container, which although it requires a small set of rules to be engineered into the system to begin with, it learns, stores and reuses new adaptation knowledge in the form of cases during the lifetime of the system. This approach is attractive in that adaptation knowledge is stored as cases and therefore locally relevant

adaptation knowledge is available to solve problems but the newly discovered knowledge must be maintained over time and this can be a burden on the system. Lazy learning algorithms such as the nearest neighbour [Cover 1967] have also been used to adapt cases in CBR [Patterson et al 2000]. These generalise the solution through the variation of the parameter k (where k is the number of cases retrieved from an case-base). Using this as a basis for adaptation initially the most similar case (the primary case) is retrieved and then its solution is generalised (adapted) by modifying it as determined by the solutions of the other (k-1) cases (secondary cases) retrieved, based on a voting scheme. The contribution of the secondary cases solutions to the overall target solution is determined by their individual similarity to the target. For example, the k nearest neighbours could be assigned votes which are inversely proportional to their distances from the target [Dudani 1975], [Aha 1990]. The adaptation technique proposed here is a hybrid system, which combines knowledge from the nearest neighbour approach (lazy learning), with regression (eager learning), to dynamically discover specific and *locally relevant* adaptation knowledge, to adapt retrieved cases in real time. By locally relevant we mean the adaptation knowledge used is uniquely specific to the target problem in question. The competency of this approach is compared to k-nearest neighbour adaptation and shown to produce consistently better results over all four case-bases studied. The rest of the paper is organised as follows. The next section describes the hybrid adaptation strategy in detail. This is followed by a section which outlines the experiments implemented, and a section which describes and analyses the results obtained. Finally, in the last section conclusions are drawn and future research outlined.

Adaptation Strategy

The technique used for case adaptation was a hybrid approach based on the k nearest neighbour algorithm and regression analysis. The details of the approach are as follows. Ten fold cross validation [Kohavi 1995] was carried out within each case-base. Initially the k nearest (most relevant) neighbours to the target case were retrieved using the nearest neighbour algorithm. K was calculated as a percentage size of the whole case-base and was at least 30 cases (30 was experimentally found to be the minimum number of cases necessary to produce an accurate regression function). A generalised case was formed from the k cases. The input and output attribute values of the generalised case were created by combining the individual attributes of the k cases after inversely weighting them according to their Euclidean distance from the target case. Using the k nearest neighbours, a linear regression function was determined using standard methods which predicted the difference in the output attributes between two cases $C(x1,x2,..,xn)$ and $C'(x1',x2'..xn')$ based on a difference matrix where each entry was based on the difference between two case's attribute values[1] i.e. a function of the form shown in equation 1 was devised.

$$(y'- y) = a_1(x1'-x1) + a_2 (x2'-x2) + ... + a_n(xn'-xn) \quad ..1$$

Where n is the number of input attributes ,
$a_1..a_n$ are the regression coefficients and
$y'-y$ is the difference in output attributes between 2 cases.

Using the regression function the difference between the target attribute's solution field and the generalised case's solution field was then predicted ($y'-y$), using the differences in each input attribute for the target and generalised case as inputs to the function. This difference value was then added to the generalised case's output attribute field to give a final prediction to the target case's output attribute field. The mean absolute error (MAE) of the adaptation process was determined by comparing this predicted output value with the actual output value for the target case, and gave a measure of the competency of the system. It was hoped that this technique would provide competent adaptations as local regression has been shown to provide accurate approximations for diverse regression surfaces in machine learning [Torgo 2000].

Methodology

Four case-bases were used to evaluate the technique. As we were using a regression approach to adaptation case-bases were chosen which had continuous output fields.

House 1 case-base - consisted of 565 cases and ten attributes taken from a housing domain supplied by the Valuation and Lands Agency of Northern Ireland. Of these ten attributes five were numeric and five were categorical. The goal was to build a model for predicting house price.

House 2 case-base - consisted of 584 cases described using ten attributes taken from a different housing domain. Of these ten attributes eight were numeric and two were categorical. The goal was to build a model for predicting house price.

House 3 case-base obtained from the ML repository It consisted of 506 cases and 14 features, 12 of which were continuous, 1 was binary and one was categorical. The goal was to build a model for predicting house price.

Abalone case-base was obtained from the ML repository. It consisted of 4177 cases described using 8 fields. Of these 6 were continuous one was categorical and one was integer. The goal was to determine the age of the animal.

The object of the experiments was to investigate the competency of implementing the modified regression analysis as a method of automatically discovering locally

---

[1] For efficiency reasons, it is not necessary to calculate all the differences between all the case values; the differences between a case and random subset of other cases is sufficient.

specific adaptation knowledge to improve the adaptation process in CBR. A number of different experiments were carried out. Firstly the competency of using knn (k=5) to adapt cases was investigated (5nn). This was followed by using the proposed regression approach to adaptation (knnReg). As a large number of cases were retrieved and used in forming the regression function it was decided to investigate how using the same cases with knn alone would affect the competency of adaptation (knn Max). Feature irrelevancy and feature weighting are widely known to affect the competency of the nearest neighbour approach. Therefore the effects of feature subset selection (FSS) and feature weight optimisation were also investigated. This was a two-stage process whereby a genetic algorithm was initially used to reduce the feature subset and then to optimise the remaining feature weights to a value between 0 and 1. The effects of this on both 5nn (5nnOp) and the regression approach (knnRegOp) were investigated. As the regression approach inherently applies weights to features it is not expected that this will directly affect this approach greatly whereas it should improve the 5nn approach.

Results & Discussion

Figures 1 to 4 show how the MAE varies for each of the adaptation strategies across each of the four case-bases studied. From this it can be seen that when the number of cases considered for knn adaptation is large (knn Max) the results are poor. This is due to many irrelevant cases influencing the final solution. Knn Max always produced the least competent results of the five strategies investigated. Adaptation using 5nn produced significantly more competent solutions then knn Max across all case-bases. In every experiment this was the fourth most competent adaptation strategy. Feature optimisation through a process of FSS and feature weighting improved the 5nn strategy further. For three of the four case-bases 5nnOp proved to be the third most competent technique and once (House 3) it proved to be the second most competent technique, clearly demonstrating how feature optimisation improves the competency of the nearest neighbour approach. KnnRegOp proved to be the second most competent strategy with 3 of the case-bases and once (house 3) it proved to be the most competent. Finally the most competent strategy was knnReg. This provided the best results with 3 case-bases and once (house 3) it was third most competent behind knnRegOp and knn respectively. From this it can be seen that the hybrid adaptation strategy (knnReg or knnRegOp) is always more competent than knn (knn or knnOp). Therefore it can be advocated as a competent strategy for adaptation in CBR. It also negates the requirement for specific adaptation knowledge acquisition during system development as the required knowledge is obtained automatically, when required, in real time from the most appropriate cases in the case-base.

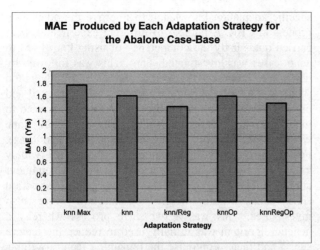

Figure 1 Affects of the adaptation strategies on MAE for Abalone case-base

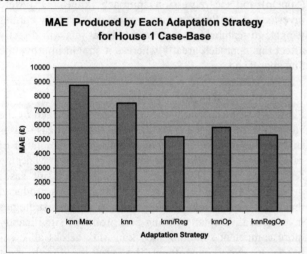

Figure 2 Affects of the adaptation strategies on MAE for House 1 case-base

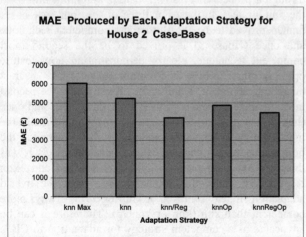

Figure 3 Affects of the adaptation strategies on MAE for House 2 case-base

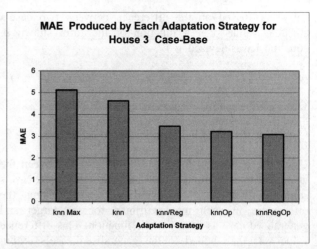

Figure 4 Affects of the adaptation strategies on MAE for House 3 case-base

This is an important benefit of the technique as human experts are no longer required during knowledge acquisition from whom to acquire knowledge. Additionally the need for adaptation knowledge maintenance is also not necessary as because no adaptation knowledge is stored (it is discovered each time it is required) then there is no requirement to maintain it. Where maintenance still has a crucial role is with case knowledge, as by carrying out case knowledge maintenance the adaptation knowledge discovered from it, is guaranteed to be optimal and current. Therefore case knowledge maintenance automatically subsumes adaptation knowledge maintenance at no additional cost to the system. Finally the most significant benefit of the approach is that the adaptation knowledge discovered is guaranteed to be locally relevant and specific to the task at hand. We believe this is why the technique provides such encouraging results. The results also confirm that FSS and weight optimisation has no positive effect on the competency of the adaptation technique.

Developing new strategies which improve one aspect of the CBR problem solving approach may cause limitations elsewhere. We have demonstrated that this approach improves problem-solving competency but how does it affect the efficiency of the problem solving process? It would be expected that the time taken to solve problems would be increased due to the extra time required to carry out the regression analysis after retrieval of the most relevant cases. From Table1 it can be seen that this is so.

Case-Base	knn sol. time (ms)	knn/Reg sol. time (ms)	Ratio
House 1	647	1421.1	2.2
House 2	705	1913.8	2.7
House 3	440.6	932.4	2.1
Abalone	21050.3	39009.1	1.9

Table 1 Solution times in ms

House 1 takes 2.2 times longer to adapt cases using the hybrid knn/reg strategy than with 5nn alone, house 2 takes 2.7 times longer, house 3 takes 2.1 times longer and abalone 1.9 times as long. These increased adaptation times reflect an improvement in competency of 31.0%, 19.7%, 25.1% and 10.2% respectively for house 1, house 2, house 3 and abalone when compared to knn and an improvement in competency of 11%, 13.6%, 4.3% (knnregOp) and 11.6% when compared to knnOp. Therefore the question arises - is the price of a decrease in efficiency worth paying for an improvement in competency? The answer to this depends on the goals of the system. If competency is paramount (as with most systems) then the decrease in efficiency is a small price to pay for such significant improvements in competency. Conversely if the system is time critical then the increased time costs associated with the improved competency may be too high and competency may have to be sacrificed to produce a less competent estimate of the solution in a faster time.

One possible solution to this trade off between competency and efficiency would be to use an indexing scheme to improve the speed cases are retrieved from the case-base. Indexes generally operate by identifying discriminatory features of cases and using these to partition the case-base into groups of cases with similar features. This is sometimes known as feature based recognition and a target case can be quickly matched with similar cases in the case-base through recognition of features they have in common. Examples of this type of indexing include k-d trees [Wess at al 1994], ID3 and C5.0 [Michalski et al 1999]. As only a selective portion of the case-base is made available during retrieval the efficiency of identifying a possible solution is increased dramatically. Unfortunately indexing cases correctly is not an easy task. The identification of a good feature for indexing is dependent on the retrieval circumstances. Therefore as circumstances change (as they inevitably will in a real world environment) the indexing structure of the case base must be maintained to reflect this. If the indexing scheme is poor or maintenance is ignored, cases with perfectly good solutions to the target problem may be overlooked as they reside in a different part of the case-base not accessible under the current indexing scheme. This can lead to the complex adaptation of less suited cases, the reduction in competency and in severe situations, problem-solving failures. Therefore, due to poor indexing and a lack of good maintenance, in an attempt to improve retrieval efficiency, competency is often sacrificed [Hunt et al 1995]. It has already been shown [Patterson et al 2002] how k-means clustering can define an efficient indexing strategy, which does not compromise on the competency of retrievals, while still providing an easily maintainable structure. Clustering is an unsupervised data mining technique, whereby groups of cases (clusters) are formed, based on their degree of similarity. The idea being that if they are similar they will have similar behaviours. When a target case, T, is presented, the cluster centroid it is closest to is identified. This thereby selects the cluster wherein T's

most similar cases most probably lie. Retrieval is carried out on this identified cluster to provide an estimate of a solution. The observed efficiency improvements are because the retrieval process only considers cases in one cluster at any time, thus ignoring cases in the other clusters. Here we examine how this indexing technique affects the efficiency and competency of the knnReg adaptation strategy. Clusters were formed and cases to be used to determine the adaptation knowledge for a target were retrieved from the most relevant cluster.

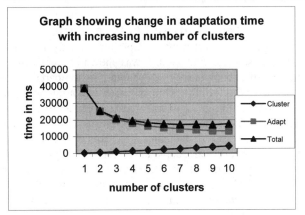

Figure 5 Time curves for the cluster based adaptation process

Figures 5 and 6 show the effect of k-means clustering on the knnReg adaptation process for the abalone case-base. From Figure 5 it can be seen that overall adaptation time (Total) decreases as the number of clusters formed increases. Also shown are times taken to form the individual clusters and the time for the regression based adaptation process itself (Adapt). Note total adaptation time is the cluster time plus the adaptation time and forming 1 cluster is equivalent to adaptation in the absence of clusters.

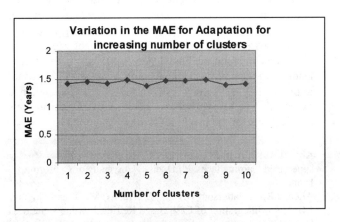

Figure 6 Showing how the MAE of adaptation varies with increasing cluster numbers

From this it can be seen how forming more than 7 clusters has little effect on efficiency of the adaptation process which takes 17174 ms at this point. If this is compared to the 5nn model, which takes 21050 ms (Table 1), it can be seen that the clustering process has in fact improved the efficiency of the adaptation strategy to the extent that it is now *more* efficient than 5nn retrieval by a factor of 1.3. Obviously this is only a useful approach if the competency of the adaptation process is not affected by clustering. From Figure 6 it can be seen that the competency of the adaptation process is stable as the number of clusters formed is increased. K-means clustering is therefore an efficient and competent indexing method to use to improve the speed of the adaptation process.

Conclusions and Future Work

In this paper a novel hybrid adaptation strategy for CBR was proposed and evaluated. It was shown to significantly improve the competency of adaptation compared to a standard knn approach. One possible limitation was the extra time required to adapt cases compared to knn. A novel indexing scheme based on k-means clustering was proposed as a way of reducing these effects and shown to provide more efficient adaptations than knn without loss of competency with one of the case-bases. This approach needs further experimentation in conjunction with the knnReg adaptation technique with more case-bases to verify its usefulness.

A drawback of this approach is that the regression strategy implemented is not very transparent, that is it is difficult to understand the adaptation knowledge the system uses to adapt the cases. A rule based adaptation knowledge base like Hanneys [Hanney & Keane 1996] would be easier to interpret but as pointed out can lead to maintenance problems which is something the hybrid approach will not cause.

In the future the technique should be extended to using nominal output features as opposed to just continuous as at present and the use of weighted regression. Additionally it could be applied to predicting missing values in data sets. Another interesting extension to this work would be to look at ways of storing the discovered adaptation knowledge for reuse in the future leading to a case-based adaptation process. This would improve the efficiency but increase the maintenance overhead. Finally we believe that this work has obvious implications for the machine learning community.

References

Aha, D. 1990. A study of instance-based algorithms for supervised learning tasks, Ph.D. diss., University of California, Irvine.

Allen, J.R.C., Patterson, D.W.R., Mulvenna, M. D. and Hughes, J.G. 1995. Integration of Case Based Retrieval with a Relational Database System in Aircraft Technical Support, 1st Intl Conference in Case Based Reasoning, pp 1-10.

Anand, S. S., Patterson, D. and Hughes, 1998. J. G. Knowledge Intensive Exception Spaces, Proceedings of 15th National Conference on Artificial Intelligence, pp 574-579.

Anand, S. S., Patterson, D., Hughes, J. G. and Bell, D. A. 1998. Discovering Case Knowledge Using Data Mining. Proceedings of

2nd Pacific-Asia Conference in Knowledge Discovery and Data Mining, pp 25- 35, LCNS Springer.

Cover, T.M. and Thomas, J.A. 1991. Elements of Information Theory. Wiley Series in Telecommunications. J. Wiley & Sons.

Dudani, S.A. 1975. Distance Weighted k-Nearest Neighbour rule. IEEE Trans on Systems, Man and Cybernetics, 6(4), pp 325-327.

Hanney, K. and Keane M. 1996. Learning Adaptation Rules from a Case-Base, Proc. Advances in Case-Based Reasoning, 3rd European Workshop, EWCBR, pp179-192.

Hanney, K. and Keane M. 1997. The Adaptation Knowledge Bottleneck. *Proc. Case-Based Reasoning: Research and Development, ICCBR-97*, pp359-370.

Hunt, J.E., Cooke, D.E. and Holstein, H. 1995. Case-memory and retrieval based on the immune system. 1st Int Conference on Case-Based reasoning (ICCBR-95), pp 205-216.

Kohavi, R. 1995. A study of cross validation and bootstrap for accuracy estimation and model selection. Proceedings of the 14th International Joint Conference on Artificial Intelligence (IJCAI-95), pp 1137-1145, Sam Mateo, CA: Morgan Kauffmann.

Leake, D. (ed.) 1996. *Case-Based Reasoning : Experiences, Lessons and Future Directions*, MIT Press, MA.

Leake, D. B., Kinley, A. and Wilson, D. 1996. Acquiring case adaptation knowledge: A hybrid approach. Proceedings of the 13th National Conference on Artificial Intelligence, AAAI Press, Menlo Park, CA.

McSherry, D. 1999. Relaxing Similarity Criteria in Adaptation Knowledge Discovery, Workshop Automating the Construction of Case-Based Reasoners, 16th International Joint Conference on Artificial Intelligence, Stockholm, pp 56-61.

McSherry, D. 1999. Automating case selection in the construction of a case library. Proceedings of ES99, the19th SGES International Conference on Knowledge-Based Systems and Applied Artificial Intelligence, Cambridge, pp 163-177.

Michalski, R., Bratko, I. And Kubat, M. 1999. Machine Learning & Data Mining: Methods & Applications. J. Wiley and Sons.

Patterson, D., Anand, S.S., Dubitzky, D. and Hughes, J. 1999. Towards Automated Case Knowledge Discovery in the M^2 Case-Based Reasoning System, Knowledge and Information Systems:An International Journal, (1), pp 61-82, Springer Verlag.

Patterson, D., Anand, S.S., Dubitzky, D. and Hughes, J. A 2000. Knowledge Light Approach to Similarity Maintenance for Improving Case-Based Competence. Workshop on Flexible Strategies for Maintaining Knowledge Containers 14th European Conference on Artificial Intelligence ECAI.

Patterson, D., Rooney, N., Galushka, M. and Anand, S. Towards Dynamic Maintenance of Retrieval Knowledge in CBR. 2002. Proceedings Fifteenth International FLAIRS Conference.

Richter, M. 1995. The Knowledge Contained in Similarity Measures. Invited Talk, The First International Conference in Case-Based Reasoning, Sesimbra, Portugal.

Simoudis, E. and Miller, J. 1991. The application of CBR to helpdesk Aapplications. In Bareiss, R. (Ed). Proceedings of the Case-Based Reasoning Workshop, pp 25-36. San Mateo. DARPA, Morgan Kaufmann, Inc.

Torgo, L. 2000. Efficient and Comprehensible Local Regression in Proceedings of the 4th Pacific-Asia Conference on Knowledge Discovery and Data Mining (PAKDD 2000). Terano et al. (eds.). LNAI 1805, p. 376-379. Springer-Verlag.

Wess, S., Althoff, K-D. and Derwand, G. 1994. Using k-d trees to improve the retrieval step in case-based reasoning. In topics in case-based reasoning. Lecture notes in artificial intelligence, Vol. 837. Springer-Verlag, Berlin Heidelberg New York, pp 167-181.

Cluster Ensembles – A Knowledge Reuse Framework for Combining Partitionings

Alexander Strehl and **Joydeep Ghosh**[*]
Department of Electrical and Computer Engineering
The University of Texas at Austin
Austin, TX 78712, USA
strehl@ece.utexas.edu and ghosh@ece.utexas.edu

Abstract

It is widely recognized that combining multiple classification or regression models typically provides superior results compared to using a single, well-tuned model. However, there are no well known approaches to combining multiple non-hierarchical clusterings. The idea of combining cluster labelings without accessing the original features leads us to a general knowledge reuse framework that we call *cluster ensembles*. Our contribution in this paper is to formally define the cluster ensemble problem as an optimization problem and to propose three effective and efficient combiners for solving it based on a hypergraph model. Results on synthetic as well as real data sets are given to show that cluster ensembles can (i) improve quality and robustness, and (ii) enable distributed clustering.

Introduction

The notion of integrating multiple data sources and/or learned models is found in several disciplines, for example, the combining of estimators in econometrics, evidences in rule-based systems and multi-sensor data fusion. A simple but effective type of such multi-learner systems are *ensembles*, wherein each component learner (typically a regressor or classifier) tries to solve the same task (Sharkey 1996; Tumer & Ghosh 1996).

But unlike classification and regression problems, there are no well known approaches to combining multiple clusterings which is more difficult than designing *classifier ensembles* since cluster labels are symbolic and so one must also solve a correspondence problem. In addition, the number and shape of clusters provided by the individual solutions may vary based on the clustering method as well as on the particular view of the data presented to that method.

A *clusterer* consists of a particular clustering algorithm with a specific view of the data. A *clustering* is the output of a clusterer and consists of the group labels for some or all objects. *Cluster ensembles* provide a tool for consolidation of results from a portfolio of individual clustering results. It is useful in a variety of contexts:

- *Quality and Robustness*. Combining several clusterings can lead to *improved quality and robustness* of results. Diversity among individual clusterers can be achieved by using different features to represent the objects, by varying the number and/or location of initial cluster centers in iterative algorithms such as k-means, varying the order of data presentation in on-line methods such as BIRCH, or by using a portfolio of diverse clustering algorithms.

- *Knowledge Reuse* (Bollacker & Ghosh 1998). Another important consideration is the *reuse of existing clusterings*. In several applications, a variety of clusterings for the objects under consideration may already exist. For example, in grouping customers for a direct marketing campaign, various legacy customer segmentations might already exist, based on demographics, credit rating, geographical region, or income tax bracket. In addition, customers can be clustered based on their purchasing history (e.g., market-baskets) (Strehl & Ghosh 2002). Can we reuse such pre-existing knowledge to create a single consolidated clustering? Knowledge reuse in this context means that we exploit the information in the provided cluster labels *without* going back to the *original features* or the algorithms that were used to create the clusterings.

- *Distributed Computing*. The ability to deal with clustering in a distributed fashion is useful to improve scalability, security, and reliability. Also, real applications often involve distributed databases due to organizational or operational constraints. A cluster ensemble can combine individual results from the distributed computing entities.

Related Work. As mentioned in the introduction, there is an extensive body of work on combining multiple classifiers or regression models, but little on combining multiple clusterings so far in the machine learning community. However, there was a substantial body of largely theoretical work on *consensus classification* during the mid-80s and earlier (Barthelemy, Laclerc, & Monjardet 1986). These studies used the term 'classification' in a very general sense, encompassing partitions, dendrograms and n-trees as well. In consensus classification, a profile is a set of classifications which is sought to be integrated into a single consensus classification. A representative work is that of (Neumann & Norton 1986), who investigated techniques for strict consensus. Their approach is based on the construction of a lattice over the set of all partitionings by using a refinement relation.

---

[*]This research was supported in part by the NSF under Grant ECS-9900353, by IBM and Intel.

Such work on strict consensus works well for small data-sets with little noise and little diversity and obtains solution on a *different* level of resolution. The most prominent application of strict consensus is for the computational biology community to obtain phylogenetic trees (Kim & Warnow 1999).

One use of cluster ensembles proposed in this paper is to exploit multiple existing groupings of the data. Several analogous approaches exist in supervised learning scenarios (class labels are known), under categories such as 'life-long learning', 'learning to learn', and 'knowledge reuse' (Bollacker & Ghosh 1999). Several representative works can be found in (Thrun & Pratt 1997).

Another application of cluster ensembles is to combine multiple clustering that were obtained based on only partial sets of features. This problem has been approached recently as a case of collective data mining. In (Johnson & Kargupta 1999) a feasible approach to combining distributed agglomerative clusterings is introduced. First, each local site generates a dendrogram. The dendrograms are collected and pairwise similarities for all objects are created from them. The combined clustering is then derived from the similarities.

The usefulness of having multiple views of data for better clustering has been recognized by others as well. In multi-aspect clustering (Modha & Spangler 2000), several similarity matrices are computed separately and then integrated using a weighting scheme. Also, Mehrotra has proposed a multi-viewpoint clustering, where several clusterings are used to semi-automatically structure rules in a knowledge base (Mehrotra 1999).

Notation. Let $\mathcal{X} = \{x_1, x_2, \ldots, x_n\}$ denote a set of objects/samples/points. A partitioning of these n objects into k clusters can be represented as a set of k sets of objects $\{\mathcal{C}_\ell | \ell = 1, \ldots, k\}$ or as a label vector $\lambda \in \mathbb{N}^n$. We also refer to a clustering/labeling as a model. A clusterer Φ is a function that delivers a label vector given an ordered set of objects. We call the original set of labelings, the *profile* and the resulting single labeling, the *consensus clustering*. Vector/matrix transposition is indicated with a superscript $\dagger$.

The Cluster Ensemble Problem

Illustrative Example

First, we will illustrate combining of clusterings using a simple example. Let the label vectors as given on the left of table 1 specify four clusterings. Inspection of the label vectors reveals that clusterings 1 and 2 are logically identical. Clustering 3 introduces some dispute about objects 3 and 5. Clustering 4 is quite inconsistent with all the other ones, has two groupings instead of 3, and also contains missing data. Now let us look for a good combined clustering with 3 clusters. Intuitively, a good combined clustering should *share as much information as possible* with the given 4 labelings. Inspection suggests that a reasonable integrated clustering is $(2, 2, 2, 3, 3, 1, 1)^\dagger$ (or one of the 6 equivalent clusterings such as $(1, 1, 1, 2, 2, 3, 3)^\dagger$). In fact, after performing an exhaustive search over all 301 unique clusterings of 7 elements into 3 groups, it can be shown that this clustering shares the maximum information with the given 4 label vectors (in terms that are more formally introduced in

the next subsection). This simple example illustrates some of the challenges. We have already seen that the label vector is not unique. In general, the number of clusters as well as each cluster's interpretation may vary tremendously among models.

Objective Function for Cluster Ensembles

Given r groupings with the q-th grouping $\lambda^{(q)}$ having $k^{(q)}$ clusters, a consensus function Γ is defined as a function $\mathbb{N}^{n \times r} \to \mathbb{N}^n$ mapping a set of clusterings to an integrated clustering: $\Gamma : \{\lambda^{(q)} | q \in \{1, \ldots, r\}\} \to \lambda$. The optimal combined clustering should share the most information with the original clusterings. But how do we measure shared information between clusterings? In information theory, mutual information is a symmetric measure to quantify the statistical information shared between two distributions. Suppose there are two labelings $\lambda^{(a)}$ and $\lambda^{(b)}$. Let there be $k^{(a)}$ groups in $\lambda^{(a)}$ and $k^{(b)}$ groups in $\lambda^{(b)}$. Let $n^{(h)}$ be the number of objects in cluster $\mathcal{C}_h$ according to $\lambda^{(a)}$, and n_ℓ the number of objects in cluster $\mathcal{C}_\ell$ according to $\lambda^{(b)}$. Let $n_\ell^{(h)}$ denote the number of objects that are in cluster h according to $\lambda^{(a)}$ as well as in group ℓ according to $\lambda^{(b)}$. Then, a [0,1]-normalized mutual information criterion $\phi^{(\mathrm{NMI})}$ is computed as follows (Strehl, Ghosh, & Mooney 2000):

$$\phi^{(\mathrm{NMI})}(\lambda^{(a)}, \lambda^{(b)}) = \frac{2}{n} \sum_{\ell=1}^{k^{(a)}} \sum_{h=1}^{k^{(b)}} n_\ell^{(h)} \log_{k^{(a)} \cdot k^{(b)}} \left(\frac{n_\ell^{(h)} n}{n^{(h)} n_\ell} \right)$$
(1)

We propose that the optimal combined clustering $\lambda^{(k-\mathrm{opt})}$ be defined as the one that has maximal average mutual information with all individual labelings $\lambda^{(q)}$ given that the number of consensus clusters desired is k. Thus, our objective function is Average Normalized Mutual Information (ANMI). Then, $\lambda^{(k-\mathrm{opt})}$ is defined as

$$\lambda^{(k-\mathrm{opt})} = \arg \max_{\hat{\lambda}} \sum_{q=1}^{r} \phi^{(\mathrm{NMI})}(\hat{\lambda}, \lambda^{(q)})$$
(2)

where $\hat{\lambda}$ goes through all possible k-partitions. The sum in equation 2 represents rANMI. For finite populations, the trivial solution is to exhaustively search through all possible clusterings with k labels (approximately $k^n/k!$ for $n \gg k$) for the one with the maximum ANMI which is computationally prohibitive. If some labels are missing one can still apply equation 2 by summing only over the object indices with known labels.

Efficient Consensus Functions

In this section, we introduce three efficient heuristics to solve the cluster ensemble problem. All algorithms approach the problem by first transforming the set of clusterings into a hypergraph representation.

Representing Sets of Clusterings as a Hypergraph

The first step for our proposed consensus functions is to transform the given cluster label vectors into a suitable hypergraph representation. In this subsection, we describe how any set of clusterings can be mapped to a hypergraph.

| | $\lambda^{(1)}$ | $\lambda^{(2)}$ | $\lambda^{(3)}$ | $\lambda^{(4)}$ | | | $\mathbf{H}^{(1)}$ | | | $\mathbf{H}^{(2)}$ | | | $\mathbf{H}^{(3)}$ | | | $\mathbf{H}^{(4)}$ | |
							$\mathbf{h}_1$	$\mathbf{h}_2$	$\mathbf{h}_3$	$\mathbf{h}_4$	$\mathbf{h}_5$	$\mathbf{h}_6$	$\mathbf{h}_7$	$\mathbf{h}_8$	$\mathbf{h}_9$	$\mathbf{h}_{10}$	$\mathbf{h}_{11}$
x_1	1	2	1	1		v_1	1	0	0	0	1	0	1	0	0	1	0
x_2	1	2	1	2		v_2	1	0	0	0	1	0	1	0	0	0	1
x_3	1	2	2	?	$\Leftrightarrow$	v_3	1	0	0	0	1	0	0	1	0	0	0
x_4	2	3	2	1		v_4	0	1	0	0	0	1	0	1	0	1	0
x_5	2	3	3	2		v_5	0	1	0	0	0	1	0	0	1	0	1
x_6	3	1	3	?		v_6	0	0	1	1	0	0	0	0	1	0	0
x_7	3	1	3	?		v_7	0	0	1	1	0	0	0	0	1	0	0

Table 1: Illustrative cluster ensemble problem with $r = 4$, $k^{(1,\dots,3)} = 3$, and $k^{(4)} = 2$: Original label vectors (left) and equivalent hypergraph representation with 11 hyperedges (right). Each cluster is transformed into a hyperedge.

For each label vector $\lambda^{(q)} \in \mathbb{N}^n$, we construct the binary membership indicator matrix $\mathbf{H}^{(q)} \in \mathbb{N}^{n \times k^{(q)}}$ in which each cluster is represented as a hyperedge (column), as illustrated in table 1. All entries of a row in the binary membership indicator matrix $\mathbf{H}^{(q)}$ add to 1, if the row corresponds to an object with *known* label. Rows for objects with unknown label are all zero. The concatenated block matrix $\mathbf{H} = (\mathbf{H}^{(1)} \dots \mathbf{H}^{(r)})$ defines the adjacency matrix of a hypergraph with n vertices and $\sum_{q=1}^{r} k^{(q)}$ hyperedges. Each column vector $\mathbf{h}_a$ specifies a hyperedge h_a, where 1 indicates that the vertex corresponding to the row is part of that hyperedge and 0 indicates that it is not. Thus, we have mapped each cluster to a hyperedge and the set of clusterings to a hypergraph.

Cluster-based Similarity Partitioning Algorithm (CSPA)

Essentially, if two objects are in the same cluster then they are considered to be fully similar, and if not they are fully dissimilar. This is the simplest heuristic and is used in the Cluster-based Similarity Partitioning Algorithm (CSPA) So, one can define similarity as the fraction of clusterings in which two objects are in the same cluster. The entire $n \times n$ similarity matrix $\mathbf{S}$ can be computed in one sparse matrix multiplication $\mathbf{S} = \frac{1}{r}\mathbf{H}\mathbf{H}^{\dagger}$. Now, we can use $\mathbf{S}$ to recluster the objects using any reasonable similarity based clustering algorithm. We chose to partition the induced graph (vertex = object, edge weight = similarity) using METIS (Karypis & Kumar 1998) because of its robust and scalable properties.

HyperGraph-Partitioning Algorithm (HGPA)

The second algorithm is another direct approach to cluster ensembles that re-partitions the data using the given clusters as indications of strong bonds. The cluster ensemble problem is formulated as *partitioning* the hypergraph by cutting a *minimal* number of hyper-edges. We call this approach the HyperGraph-Partitioning Algorithm (HGPA). All hyperedges are considered to have the same weight. Also, all vertices are equally weighted. Now, we look for a hyperedge separator that partitions the hypergraph into k unconnected components of approximately the same size. Equal sizes are obtained by maintaining a vertex imbalance of at most 5% as formulated by the following constraint: $k \cdot \max_{\ell \in \{1,\dots,k\}} \frac{n_\ell}{n} \leq 1.05$.

Hypergraph partitioning is a well-studied area. We use the hypergraph partitioning package HMETIS (Karypis *et al.* 1997), which gives high-quality partitions and is very scalable.

Meta-CLustering Algorithm (MCLA)

In this subsection, we introduce the third algorithm to solve the cluster ensemble problem. The Meta-CLustering Algorithm (MCLA) is based on clustering clusters. It also yields object-wise confidence estimates of cluster membership.

We represented each cluster by a hyperedge. The idea in MCLA is to group and collapse related hyperedges and assign each object to the collapsed hyperedge in which it participates most strongly. The hyperedges that are considered related for the purpose of collapsing are determined by a graph-based clustering of hyperedges. We refer to each cluster of hyperedges as a meta-cluster $\mathcal{C}^{(\mathrm{M})}$. Collapsing reduces the number of hyperedges from $\sum_{q=1}^{r} k^{(q)}$ to k. The detailed steps are:
- **Construct Meta-graph.** Let us view all the $\sum_{q=1}^{r} k^{(q)}$ indicator vectors $\mathbf{h}$ (the hyperedges of $\mathbf{H}$) as vertices of a regular undirected graph, the meta-graph. The edge weights are proportional to the similarity between vertices. A suitable similarity measure here is the binary Jaccard measure, since it is the ratio of the intersection to the union of the sets of objects corresponding to the two hyperedges. Formally, the edge weight $w_{a,b}$ between two vertices h_a and h_b as defined by the binary Jaccard measure of the corresponding indicator vectors $\mathbf{h}_a$ and $\mathbf{h}_b$: $w_{a,b} = \frac{\mathbf{h}_a^{\dagger}\mathbf{h}_b}{\|\mathbf{h}_a\|_2^2 + \|\mathbf{h}_b\|_2^2 - \mathbf{h}_a^{\dagger}\mathbf{h}_b}$. Since the clusters are non-overlapping (e.g., hard), there are no edges amongst vertices of the same clustering $\mathbf{H}^{(q)}$ and, thus, the meta-graph is r-partite.
- **Cluster Hyperedges**. Find matching labels by partitioning the meta-graph into k balanced meta-clusters. This results in a clustering of the $\mathbf{h}$ vectors in $\mathbf{H}$. Each meta-cluster has approximately r vertices. Since each vertex in the meta-graph represents a distinct cluster label, a meta-cluster represents a group of corresponding labels.
- **Collapse Meta-clusters**. For each of the k meta-clusters, we collapse the hyperedges into a single meta-hyperedge. Each meta-hyperedge has an association vector which contains an entry for each object describing its level of association with the corresponding meta-cluster. The level is

computed by averaging all indicator vectors **h** of a particular meta-cluster. An entry of 0 or 1 indicates the weakest or strongest association, respectively.

- **Compete for Objects**. In this step, each object is assigned to its most associated meta-cluster: Specifically, an object is assigned to the meta-cluster with the highest entry in the association vector. Ties are broken randomly. The confidence of an assignment is reflected by the winner's share of association (ratio of the winner's association to the sum of all other associations). Note that not every meta-cluster can be guaranteed to win at least one object. Thus, there are *at most* k labels in the final combined clustering λ.

In this paper, for all experiments *all three* algorithms, CSPA, HGPA and MCLA, are run and the clustering with the greater ANMI is used. Note that this procedure is still completely unsupervised. We call this the **supra-consensus function**.

Applications and Results

Consensus functions *enable* a variety of new approaches to several problems. After introducing the data-sets and evaluation methodology used, we illustrate how robustness can be increased and how distributed clustering clustering can be performed when each entity only has access to a limited subset of features.

Data-sets. We illustrate the cluster ensemble applications on two real and two artificial data-sets. The first data-set (2D2K) was artificially generated and contains 500 points each of two 2-dimensional (2D) Gaussian clusters. The second data-set (8D5K) contains 1000 points from 5 multivariate Gaussian distributions (200 points each) in 8D. Both are available from `http://strehl.com/`. The third data-set (PENDIG) is for pen-based recognition of handwritten digits from 16 spatial features (available from UCI Machine Learning Repository). There are ten classes of roughly equal size corresponding to the digits 0 to 9. The fourth data-set (YAHOO) is for news text clustering (available from `ftp://ftp.cs.umn.edu/dept/users/boley/`). The raw 21839×2340 word-document matrix consists of the non-normalized occurrence frequencies of stemmed words, using Porter's suffix stripping algorithm. Pruning all words that occur less than 0.01 or more than 0.10 times on average because they are insignificant or too generic, results in 2903. For 2D2K, 8D5K, PENDIG, and YAHOO we use $k = 2, 5,$ and 10, 40 respectively.

Quality Evaluation Criterion. Standard cost functions, such as the sum of squared distances from the cluster representative, depend on metric interpretations of the data. They cannot be used to compare techniques that use different distance/similarity measures or work entirely without them. However, when objects have already been categorized by an external source, i.e. when class labels are available, we can use information theoretic measures to indicate the match between cluster labels and class labels. Previously, average purity and entropy-based measures to assess clustering quality from 0 (worst) to 1 (best) have been used. While average purity is intuitive to understand, it is biased to favor small clusters (singletons, in fact, are scored as perfect). Also, a monolithic clustering (one single cluster for all objects) receives

a score as high as the maximum category prior probability. Using a measure based on normalized mutual information (equation 1) fixes both biases (Strehl, Ghosh, & Mooney 2000) and provides an unbiased and conservative measure as compared to purity and entropy. Given g categories (or classes), we use the categorization labels κ to evaluate the quality by normalized mutual information $\phi^{(\text{NMI})}(\kappa, \lambda)$, as defined in equation 1.

Robust Centralized Clustering (RCC)

A consensus function can introduce redundancy and foster robustness when, instead of choosing or fine-tuning a single clusterer, an ensemble of clusterers is employed and their results are combined. This is particularly useful when clustering has to be performed in a closed loop without human interaction.

In Robust Centralized Clustering (RCC), each clusterer has access to all features and to all objects. However, each clusterer might take a different approach. In fact, approaches *should* be very diverse for best results. They can use different similarity/distance measures (e.g., Euclidean, cosine) or techniques (graph-based, agglomerative, k-means) (Strehl, Ghosh, & Mooney 2000). The ensemble's clusterings are then integrated using the supra-consensus function.

To show that RCC can yield robust results in low-dimensional metric spaces as well as in high-dimensional sparse spaces *without* any modifications, the following experiment was set up: First, 10 diverse clustering algorithms were implemented: (1) self-organizing map; (2) hypergraph partitioning; k-means with distance based on (3) Euclidean, (4) cosine, (5) correlation, (6) extended Jaccard; and graph partitioning with similarity based on (7) Euclidean, (8) cosine, (9) correlation, (10) extended Jaccard. Implementational details of the individual algorithms are beyond the scope of this paper and can be found in (Strehl, Ghosh, & Mooney 2000).

RCC was performed 10 times each on sample sizes of 50, 100, 200, 400, and 800, for each data-set. Different sample sizes provide insight how cluster quality improves as more data becomes available. Quality improvement depends on the clusterer as well as the data. For example, more complex data-sets require more data until quality maxes out. We also computed a random clustering for each experiment to establish a baseline performance. The quality in terms of difference in mutual information as compared to the random clustering algorithm is computed for all 11 approaches (10 + consensus). Figure 1 shows learning curves for the average quality of the 10 algorithms versus RCC.

E.g., in case of the YAHOO data (figure 1(d)) the consensus function received three poor clusterings (Euclidean based k-means as well as graph partitioning; and self-organizing feature-map), four good (hypergraph partitioning, cosine, correlation, and extended Jaccard based k-means) and three excellent (cosine, correlation, and extended Jaccard based graph partitioning) clusterings. The RCC results are almost as good as the average of the excellent clusterers despite the presence of distractive clusterings. In fact, at the $n = 800$ level, RCC's average quality of 0.38 is 19% better than the average qualities of all the other algorithms (excluding random) at 0.32. This shows that for this scenario, cluster ensembles work well and also are robust!

Similar results are obtained for 2D2K, 8D5K and PENDIG. Figure 1 shows how RCC is consistently better in all four scenarios than picking a random / average single technique. The experimental results clearly show that cluster ensembles can be used to increase robustness in risk intolerant settings. Especially, since it is generally hard to evaluate clusters in high-dimensional problems, a cluster ensemble can be used to 'throw' many models at a problem and then integrate them using an consensus function to yield stable results.

Feature-Distributed Clustering (FDC)

In Feature-Distributed Clustering (FDC), we show how cluster ensembles can be used to boost quality of results by combining a set of clusterings obtained from partial views of the data. For our experiments, we simulate such a scenario by running several clusterers, each having access to only a restricted, small subset of features (subspace). Each clusterer has access to all objects. The clusterers find groups in their views/subspaces. In the combining stage, individual results are integrated to recover the full structure of the data (without access to any of the original features).

First, let us discuss results for the 8D5K data, since they lend themselves well to illustration. We create 5 random 2D views (through selection of a pair of features) of the 8D data, and use Euclidean-based similarity and graph-partitioning with $k = 5$ in each view to obtain 5 clusterings. Clustering in the 8D space yields the original generative labels and is referred to as the reference clustering. Using PCA to project the data into 2D separates all 5 clusters fairly well (figure 3). In figure 3(a), the reference clustering is illustrated by coloring the data points in the space spanned by the first and second principal components (PCs). Figure 3(b) shows the final FDC result after combining 5 subspace clusterings. Each clustering has been computed from a random feature pair. These subspaces are shown in figure 2. Each of the rows corresponds to a random selection of 2 out of 8 feature dimensions. For consistent appearance of clusters across rows, the dot colors/shapes have been matched using meta-clusters. All points in clusters of the same meta-cluster share the same color/shape amongst all plots. FDC (figure 3(b)) are clearly superior compared to any of the 5 individual results (figure 2(right)) and is almost flawless compared to the reference clustering (figure 3(a)).

We also conducted experiments on the other four datasets. Table 2 summarizes the results. The choice of the number of random subspaces r and their dimensionality is currently driven by the user. For example, in the YAHOO case, 20 clusterings were performed in 128-dimensions (occurrence frequencies of 128 random words) each. The average quality amongst the results was 0.17 and the best quality was 0.21. Using the supra-consensus function to combine all 20 labelings results in a quality of 0.38, or 124% higher mutual information than the average individual clustering. In all scenarios, the consensus clustering is as good or better than the best individual input clustering and always better than the average quality of individual clusterings. When

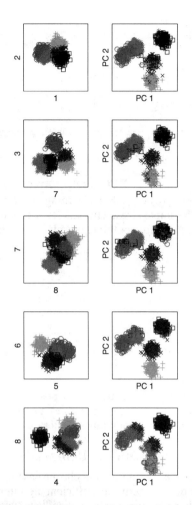

Figure 2: Illustration of feature distributed clustering (FDC) on 8D5K data. Each row corresponds to a random selection of 2 out of 8 feature dimensions. For each of the 5 chosen feature pairs, a row shows the clustering (colored) obtained on the 2D subspace spanned by the selected feature pair (left) and visualizes these clusters on the plane of the global 2 principal components (right). In any subspace, the clusters can not be segregated well due to strong overlaps. The supra-consensus function can combine the partial knowledge of the 5 clusterings into a far superior clustering (figure 3(b)).

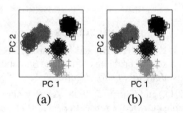

Figure 3: Reference clustering (a) and FDC consensus clustering (b) of 8D5K data shown in the first 2 principal components. The consensus clustering (b) is clearly superior compared to any of the 5 individual results (figure 2(right)) and is almost flawless compared to the reference clustering (a).

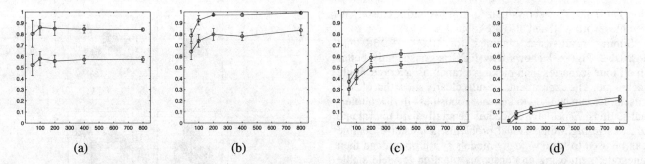

(a)	(b)	(c)	(d)

Figure 1: Summary of RCC results. Average learning curves and RCC learning curves for 2D2K (a), 8D5K (b), PENDIG (c), and YAHOO (d) data. Each learning curve shows the difference in mutual information-based quality $\phi^{(\text{NMI})}$ compared to random for 5 sample sizes. The bars for each data-point indicate ± 1 standard deviation over 10 experiments. The upper curve gives RCC quality for combining results of all other 10 algorithms. The lower curve is the average quality of the other 10.

data	subspace #dims	#models r	quality of consensus $\phi^{(\text{NMI})}(\kappa, \lambda)$	maximum quality in subspaces $\max_q \phi^{(\text{NMI})}(\kappa, \lambda^{(q)})$	average quality in subspaces $\text{avg}_q \phi^{(\text{NMI})}(\kappa, \lambda^{(q)})$	minimum quality in subspaces $\min_q \phi^{(\text{NMI})}(\kappa, \lambda^{(q)})$
2D2K	1	3	**0.68864**	0.68864	0.64145	0.54706
8D5K	2	5	**0.98913**	0.76615	0.69822	0.62134
PENDIG	4	10	**0.59009**	0.53197	0.44625	0.32598
YAHOO	128	20	**0.38167**	0.21403	0.17075	0.14582

Table 2: FDC results. The consensus clustering is as good as or better than the best individual subspace clustering.

processing on the all features is not possible but multiple, limited views exist, a cluster ensemble can boost results significantly compared to individual clusterings.

Concluding Remarks

In this paper we introduced the cluster ensemble problem and provide three effective and efficient algorithms to solve it. We conducted experiments to show how cluster ensembles can be used to introduce robustness and dramatically improve 'sets of subspace clusterings' for a large variety of domains. Selected data-sets and software are available from http://strehl.com/. Indeed, the cluster ensemble is a very general framework and enables a wide range of applications.

For future work, we desire a thorough theoretical analysis of the Average Normalized Mutual Information (ANMI) objective and its greedy optimization schemes. We also pursue work on comparing the proposed technique's biases. Moreover, we explore using cluster ensembles for object distributed clustering.

References

Barthelemy, J. P.; Laclerc, B.; and Monjardet, B. 1986. On the use of ordered sets in problems of comparison and consensus of classifications. *Journal of Classification* 3:225–256.

Bollacker, K. D., and Ghosh, J. 1998. A supra-classifier architecture for scalable knowledge reuse. In *Proc. Int'l Conf. on Machine Learning (ICML-98)*, 64–72.

Bollacker, K. D., and Ghosh, J. 1999. Effective supra-classifiers for knowledge base construction. *Pattern Recognition Letters* 20(11-13):1347–52.

Johnson, E., and Kargupta, H. 1999. Collective, hierarchical clustering from distributed, heterogeneous data. In Zaki, M., and Ho, C., eds., *Large-Scale Parallel KDD Systems*, volume 1759 of *Lecture Notes in Computer Science*, 221–244. Springer-Verlag.

Karypis, G., and Kumar, V. 1998. A fast and high quality multilevel scheme for partitioning irregular graphs. *SIAM Journal of Scientific Computing* 20(1):359–392.

Karypis, G.; Aggarwal, R.; Kumar, V.; and Shekhar, S. 1997. Multilevel hypergraph partitioning: Applications in VLSI domain. In *Proceedings of the Design and Automation Conference*.

Kim, J., and Warnow, T. 1999. Tutorial on phylogenetic tree estimation. In *Intelligent Systems for Molecular Biology, Heidelberg*.

Mehrotra, M. 1999. Multi-viewpoint clustering analysis (MVP-CA) technology for mission rule set development and case-based retrieval. Technical Report AFRL-VS-TR-1999-1029, Air Force Research Laboratory.

Modha, D. S., and Spangler, W. S. 2000. Clustering hypertext with applications to web searching. In *Proceedings of the ACM Hypertext 2000 Conference, San Antonio, TX, May 30-June 3*.

Neumann, D. A., and Norton, V. T. 1986. Clustering and isolation in the consensus problem for partitions. *Journal of Classification* 3:281–298.

Sharkey, A. 1996. On combining artificial neural networks. *Connection Science* 8(3/4):299–314.

Strehl, A., and Ghosh, J. 2002. Relationship-based clustering and visualization for high-dimensional data mining. *INFORMS Journal on Computing*. in press.

Strehl, A.; Ghosh, J.; and Mooney, R. 2000. Impact of similarity measures on web-page clustering. In *Proc. AAAI Workshop on AI for Web Search (AAAI 2000), Austin*, 58–64. AAAI/MIT Press.

Thrun, S., and Pratt, L. 1997. *Learning To Learn*. Norwell, MA: Kluwer Academic.

Tumer, K., and Ghosh, J. 1996. Analysis of decision boundaries in linearly combined neural classifiers. *Pattern Recognition* 29(2):341–348.

Knowledge Representation
Logic Programming

Logic Programming with Ordered Disjunction

Gerhard Brewka

Universität Leipzig
Institut für Informatik
Augustusplatz 10-11
04109 Leipzig, Germany
brewka@informatik.uni-leipzig.de

Abstract

Logic programs with ordered disjunction (*LPODs*) combine ideas underlying Qualitative Choice Logic (Brewka, Benferhat, & Le Berre 2002) and answer set programming. Logic programming under answer set semantics is extended with a new connective called ordered disjunction. The new connective allows us to represent alternative, ranked options for problem solutions in the heads of rules: $A \times B$ intuitively means: if possible A, but if A is not possible then at least B. The semantics of logic programs with ordered disjunction is based on a preference relation on answer sets. *LPODs* are useful for applications in design and configuration and can serve as a basis for qualitative decision making.

Introduction

In a recent paper (Brewka, Benferhat, & Le Berre 2002) a propositional logic called Qualitative Choice Logic (*QCL*) was introduced. The logic contains a new connective × representing ordered disjunction. Intuitively, $A \times B$ stands for: if possible A, but if A is impossible then (at least) B. This connective allows context dependent preferences to be represented in a simple and elegant fashion. As a simple example consider the preferences for booking a hotel for a conference. Assume the most preferred option is to be within walking distance from the conference site, the second best option is to have transportation provided by the hotel, the third best is public transportation. This can simply be represented as

$$walking \times hotel-transport \times public-transport$$

From a description of available hotels, a disjunction expressing that one of the hotels must be picked, and the above formula *QCL* is able to derive the hotel which satisfies best the given preferences (if there is more than one such hotel a corresponding disjunction is concluded).

The semantics of the logic is based on degrees of satisfaction of a formula in a classical model. The degrees, intuitively, measure disappointment and induce a preference relation on models. Consequence is defined in terms of most preferred models. It is argued in that paper that there are numerous useful applications, e.g. in configuration and design.

In this paper we want to combine ideas underlying *QCL* with logic programming. More precisely, we want to investigate logic programs based on rules with ordered disjunction in the heads. We call such programs logic programs with ordered disjunction (*LPODs*).

The semantical framework in which the investigation will be carried out is that of answer set semantics (Gelfond & Lifschitz 1991). Logic programs under answer set semantics have emerged as a new promising programming paradigm dubbed answer set programming. There are numerous interesting AI applications of answer set programming, for instance in planning (Lifschitz 2001) and configuration (Soininen 2000). One of the reasons for this success is the availability of highly efficient systems for computing answer sets like *smodels* (Niemelä & Simons 1997) and *dlv* (Eiter *et al.* 1998).

We think it is worthwile to investigate simple representations of context dependent preferences in the answer set programming paradigm. Our combination of ideas from *QCL* and answer set programming will lead to an approach which is less expressive than *QCL* in one respect: the syntax of *LPODs* restricts the appearance of ordered disjunction to the head of rules. On the other hand, we inherit from answer set programming the nonmonotonic aspects which are due to default negation. This allows us to combine default knowledge with knowledge about preferences and desires in a simple and elegant way.

The basic intuition underlying our approach can be described as follows: we will use the ordered disjunctions in rule heads to select some of the answer sets of a program as the preferred ones. Consider a program containing the rule

$$A \times B \leftarrow C$$

If S_1 is an answer set containing C and A and S_2 is an answer set containing C and B but not A, then - ceteris paribus (other things being equal) - S_1 is preferred over S_2. Of course, we have to give precise meaning to the ceteris paribus phrase. Intuitively ceteris paribus is to be read as S_1 and S_2 satisfy the other rules in the program equally well.

We will show that under certain conditions reasoning from most preferred answer sets yields optimal problem solutions. In more general decision making settings the preference relation on answer sets provides a basis for best possible choices given a specific decision strategy.

We will restrict our discussion in this paper to propositional programs. However, as usual in answer set programming, we admit rule schemata containing variables bearing in mind that these schemata are just convenient representations for the set of their ground instances.

The rest of the paper is organized as follows. In the next section we introduce syntax and semantics of *LPODs*. We define the degree of satisfaction of a rule in an answer set and show how to use the degrees to determine a preference relation on answer sets. Conclusions are defined as the literals true in all preferred answer sets. The subsequent section discusses some simple examples and potential applications. We then investigate implementation issues. The last section discusses related work and concludes.

Logic programs with ordered disjunction

Logic programming with ordered disjunction is an extension of logic programming with two kinds of negation (default and strong negation) (Gelfond & Lifschitz 1991). The new connective $\times$ representing ordered disjunction is allowed to appear in the head of rules only. A (propositional) *LPOD* thus consists of rules of the form

$$C_1 \times \ldots \times C_n \leftarrow A_1, \ldots, A_m, \text{not } B_1, \ldots, \text{not } B_k$$

where the C_i, A_j and B_l are ground literals.

The intuitive reading of the rule head is: if possible C_1, if C_1 is not possible then C_2, ..., if all of $C_1, \ldots, C_{n-1}$ are not possible then C_n. The literals C_i are called choices of the rule. Extended logic programs with two negations are a special case where $n = 1$ for all rules. As usual we omit $\leftarrow$ whenever $m = 0$ and $k = 0$, that is, if the rule is a fact. Moreover, rules of the form $\leftarrow body$ (constraints) are used as abbreviations for $p \leftarrow body, \text{not } p$ for some p not appearing in the rest of the program. The effect is that no answer sets containing *body* exist.

Before defining the semantics of *LPODs* a few observations are in order. As already mentioned in the introduction we want to use the ranking of literals in the head of rules to select some of the answer sets of a program as the preferred ones. But what are the answer sets of a program among which to make this selection?

Since ordered disjunction is a particular prioritized form of disjunction it seems like a natural idea to base the semantics of *LPODs* on one of the standard semantics for disjunctive logic programs, for instance Gelfond and Lifschitz's semantics (Gelfond & Lifschitz 1991).

Unfortunately, this doesn't work. The problem is that most of the semantics for disjunctive logic programs have minimality built in. For instance, according to Gelfond and Lifschitz, S is an answer set of a disjunctive logic program P iff S is a minimal set of literals which is logically closed, and closed under the S-reduct of P. The S-reduct of P is obtained from P by (1) deleting all rules r from P such that not B_j in the body of r and $B_j \in S$, and (2) deleting all default negated literals from the remaining rules. A set of literals S is closed under a rule r if one of the literals in the head of r is in S whenever the body is true in S (see (Gelfond & Lifschitz 1991) for the details).

In this approach answer sets are minimal: if S_1 and S_2 are answer sets of a disjunctive program P and $S_1 \subseteq S_2$, then $S_2 \subseteq S_1$.

Minimality is not always wanted for *LPODs*. Consider the following two facts:

1) $A \times B \times C$
2) $B \times D$

The single best way of satisfying both ordered disjunctions is obviously to make A and B true, that is, we would expect $\{A, B\}$ to be the single preferred answer set of this simple *LPOD*. However, since B is sufficient to satisfy both disjunctions, the set $\{A, B\}$ is not even an answer set of the corresponding disjunctive logic program (where $\times$ is replaced by $\vee$) according to the semantics of (Gelfond & Lifschitz 1991): the built in minimality precludes sets containing both A and B from consideration.

We thus have to use a semantics which is not minimal. Indeed, there is such a semantics, the possible models semantics proposed by Sakama and Inoue (Sakama & Inoue 1994). It is based on so-called split programs, that is, disjunction free programs which contain arbitrary subsets of single head rules obtained from disjunctive rules by deleting all but one alternatives in the head.

Unfortunately, also this semantics is inadequate, this time for opposite reasons: it admits too many literals in answer sets. Consider the disjunctive logic program

1) $A \vee B \vee C$

There are seven split programs corresponding to the nonempty subsets of the literals of the fact. The split program containing the facts A, B, C generates the possible model where A, B, C is true.

Let us replace disjunction by ordered disjunction in this formula. According to our intuitive discussion we want to read the rule as "if possible A, if this is not possible then B, and if also B is not possible then C". Under this reading models containing more than one of the literals in the head do not seem justified on the basis of a single rule (they may be justified by different rules, though).

For this reason we will not allow cases where a single rule of the original program gives rise to more than one rule in the split program. There is a further complication: consider the program:

1) $A \times B \times C$
2) A

We do not want to obtain $\{A, B\}$ as an answer set from the split program consisting of these 2 atomic facts since again this does not correspond to the intuitive reading of the first rule (B only if A is not possible). We therefore have to use slightly more complicated rules in split programs.

Definition 1 *Let* $r = C_1 \times \ldots \times C_n \leftarrow body$ *be a rule. For* $k \leq n$ *we define the kth option of r as*

$$r^k = C_k \leftarrow body, \text{not } C_1, \ldots, \text{not } C_{k-1}.$$

Definition 2 *Let* P *be an LPOD.* P' *is a split program of* P *if it is obtained from* P *by replacing each rule in* P *by one of its options.*

Here is a simple example. Let P consist of the rules

1) $A \times B \leftarrow \operatorname{not} C$
2) $B \times C \leftarrow \operatorname{not} D$

We obtain 4 split programs

$A \leftarrow \operatorname{not} C$ $A \leftarrow \operatorname{not} C$
$B \leftarrow \operatorname{not} D$ $C \leftarrow \operatorname{not} D, \operatorname{not} B$

$B \leftarrow \operatorname{not} C, \operatorname{not} A$ $B \leftarrow \operatorname{not} C, \operatorname{not} A$
$B \leftarrow \operatorname{not} D$ $C \leftarrow \operatorname{not} D, \operatorname{not} B$

Split programs do not contain ordered disjunction. We thus can define:

Definition 3 *Let P be an LPOD. A set of literals A is an answer set of P if it is a consistent answer set of a split program P' of P.*

We exclude inconsistent answer sets from consideration since they do not represent possible problem solutions. In the example above we obtain 3 answer sets: $\{A, B\}, \{C\}, \{B\}$. Note that one of the answer sets is a proper subset of another answer set. On the other hand, none of the rules in the original *LPOD* sanctions more than one literal in any of the answer sets, as intended.

Not all of the answer sets satisfy our most intended options. Clearly, $\{A, B\}$ gives us the best options for both rules, whereas $\{C\}$ gives only the second best option for 2) and $\{B\}$ the second best option for 1). To distinguish between more and less intended answer sets we introduce the degree of satisfaction of a rule in an answer set:

Definition 4 *Let S be an answer set of an LPOD P. S satisfies the rule*

$$C_1 \times \ldots \times C_n \leftarrow A_1, \ldots, A_m, \operatorname{not} B_1, \ldots, \operatorname{not} B_k$$

- *to degree 1 if $A_j \notin S$, for some j, or $B_i \in S$, for some i,*
- *to degree j $(1 \leq j \leq n)$ if all $A_j \in S$, no $B_i \in S$, and $j = \min\{r \mid C_r \in S\}$.*

Proposition 1 *If A is an answer set of P then A satisfies all rules of P to some degree.*[1]

Proof: Let r be a rule of P. If S is an answer set of P, then there is a split program P' such that S is an answer set of P'. Let r^i be the rule in P' generated from r. Since S is an answer set of P' either the body of r^i is satisfied in S and thus C_i is contained in S, in which case r is satisfied to degree i or smaller, or the body of r^i is not satisfied in S, in which case r is satisfied to degree 1 in S, or there is a better choice than C_k, $k < i$, in S and r is satisfied to degree k. $\square$

We use the degrees of satisfaction of a rule to define a preference relation on answer sets. There are different ways of doing this. For instance, we could simply add up the satisfaction degrees of all rules and prefer those answer sets where the total sum is minimal. Although this may be reasonable in certain applications, this approach makes quite strong assumptions about the commensurability of choices in different rule heads. In (Brewka, Benferhat, & Le Berre

---

[1]The other direction of the proposition does obviously not hold. For example, the set $\{A\}$ satisfies the rule $B \leftarrow \operatorname{not} A$, but is not an answer set for the program consisting of this single rule.

2002) a lexicographic ordering of models based on the number of premises satisfied to a particular degree was proposed. This lexicographic ordering has a highly syntactic flavour. Therefore, we will use here a somewhat more cautious preference relation (in the sense that fewer answer sets are considered better than others) based on set inclusion of the rules satisfied to certain degrees:

Definition 5 *For a set of literals S, let $S^i(P)$ denote the set of rules in P satisfied by S to degree i. Let S_1 and S_2 be answer sets of an LPOD P. S_1 is preferred to S_2 ($S_1 > S_2$) iff there is i such that $S_2^i(P) \subset S_1^i(P)$, and for all $j < i$, $S_1^j(P) = S_2^j(P)$.*

Definition 6 *A set of literals S is a preferred answer set of an LPOD P iff S is an answer set of P and there is no answer set S' of P such that $S' > S$.*

Definition 7 *A literal l is a conclusion of an LPOD P iff l is contained in all preferred answer sets of P.*

Consider again the program

1) $A \times B \leftarrow \operatorname{not} C$
2) $B \times C \leftarrow \operatorname{not} D$

As discussed before we obtain the 3 answer sets: $S_1 = \{A, B\}$, $S_2 = \{C\}$ and $S_3 = \{B\}$. S_1 satisfies both rules with degree 1, $\{C\}$ satisfies 1) to degree 1 but 2) to degree 2. $\{B\}$ satisfies 1) to degree 2 and 2) to degree 1. The single preferred answer set is thus S_1, as intended, and A and B are the conclusions of the program.

Examples

*LPOD*s allow us - like normal logic programs - to express incomplete and defeasible knowledge through the use of default negation. In addition, they provide means to represent preferences among intended properties of problem solutions. Moreover, these preferences may depend on the current context.

In this section we discuss several examples illustrating potential uses of *LPOD*s. The first example is about how to spend a free afternoon. You like to go to the beach, but also to the cinema. Normally you prefer the cinema over the beach, unless it is hot (which is the exception in the area where you live, except during the summer). If it is hot the beach is preferred over the cinema. In summer it is normally hot, but there are exceptions. If it rains the beach is out of question. This information can be represented using the following rules:

1) $cinema \times beach \leftarrow \operatorname{not} hot$
2) $beach \times cinema \leftarrow hot$
3) $hot \leftarrow \operatorname{not} \neg hot, summer$
4) $\neg beach \leftarrow rain$

Without further information about the weather we obtain the single preferred answer set $S_1 = \{cinema\}$. There is no information that it might be hot, so rule 1) will determine the preferences. S_1 satisfies all rules to degree 1.

Now assume the fact *summer* is additionally given. In this case we obtain $S_2 = \{summer, hot, beach\}$ as the single preferred answer set. Again this answer set satisfies all rules to degree 1.

Next assume that, in addition to *summer* also the literal ¬*hot* is given. The single preferred answer set now is $S_3 = \{summer, \neg hot, cinema\}$. All rules are satisfied to degree 1.

Finally, assume the additional facts are *summer* and *rain*. Now the single preferred answer set (and in fact the single answer set) is

$$S_4 = \{summer, rain, hot, \neg beach, cinema\}.$$

Note that this time it is not possible to satisfy all rules to degree 1: rule 2) is satisfied to degree 2 only. As often in real life, there are situations where the best options simply do not work out.

We think that *LPOD*s are well suited for representing problems where choices under preferences have to be made, for instance in cases where a number of components have to be chosen for a certain configuration task. The general idea would be to have

- for each component a set of rules describing its properties,
- rules describing which components are needed for the configuration to be complete; this may depend on other components chosen,
- rules describing intended properties of the solution we want to generate. The involved preferences may be context dependent, and
- a description of the case at hand.

In each case default knowledge can be used to describe what is normally the case. Consider the problem of configuring a menu. The menu should consist of a *starter*, a *main* course, a *dessert* and a *beverage*. As a *starter* you prefer *soup* over *salad*. As *main* course *fish*, *beef* and *lasagne* are possible (this is all you are able to cook) and your preferences are in this order. Of course, if the visitor is *vegetarian* the first two (as well as the *soup*) are out of the question. In case of *beef* you prefer *red* wine over *white* wine over mineral *water*, otherwise the order between wines is reversed. Only *ice-coffee* and *tiramisu* is available as a *dessert*. If *tiramisu* is chosen, then an extra *coffee* is necessary. You prefer *espresso* over *cappucino*.

The possible components thus are *soup*, *salad*, *fish*, *beef*, *lasagne*, *ice-coffee*, *tiramisu*, *espresso*, *cappucino*, *red*, *white* and *water*. The following properties of the components are relevant:

¬*vegetarian* ← *beef*	*alcohol* ← *white*
¬*vegetarian* ← *fish*	*alcohol* ← *red*
¬*vegetarian* ← *soup*	

The needed components are

starter	*beverage*
main	*coffee* ← *tiramisu*
dessert	

The preferences are as follows:

soup × *salad* ← *starter*
fish × *beef* × *lasagne* ← *main*
red × *white* × *water* ← *beverage, beef*
white × *red* × *water* ← *beverage*, not *beef*

espresso × *cappuccino* ← *coffee*
ice-coffee ← not *tiramisu, dessert*
tiramisu ← not *ice-coffee, dessert*

Now, given a description of the case at hand, e.g. whether the visitor is vegetarian or not, drinks alcohol or not, likes fish etc. the preferred answer sets will determine a menu which satisfies the preferences as much as possible. The last two rules are necessary to make sure that one of the desserts is picked. For the other courses this is implicit in the specified preferences. In the language of (Niemelä & Simons 2000) these rules can be represented as the cardinality constraint rule $1\{ice\text{-}coffee, tiramisu\}1 \leftarrow dessert$. Combinations of *LPOD*s and such constraints are a topic of further research.

Computation

The first question to ask is whether *LPOD*s can simply be reduced to standard logic programs with two kinds of negation. In that case standard answer set programming techniques would be sufficient for computing consequences of *LPOD*s. We will show that a seemingly natural translation does not yield the intended answer sets.

Definition 8 *The pseudo-translation* $trans(r)$ *of a rule*

$$r = C_1 \times \ldots \times C_n \leftarrow body$$

is the collection of rules

$$
\begin{aligned}
C_1 &\leftarrow body, \text{not } \overline{C_1} \\
C_2 &\leftarrow body, \text{not } \overline{C_2}, \overline{C_1} \\
&\ldots \\
C_{n-1} &\leftarrow body, \text{not } \overline{C_{n-1}}, \overline{C_1}, \ldots, \overline{C_{n-2}} \\
C_n &\leftarrow body, \overline{C_1}, \ldots, \overline{C_{n-1}}
\end{aligned}
$$

where $\overline{C}$ *is the complement of* C*, that is* ¬C *if* C *is an atom and* C' *if* $C = \neg C'$*. The pseudo-translation* $trans(P)$ *of an LPOD* P *is*

$$trans(P) = \bigcup_{r \in P} trans(r)$$

The pseudo-translation creates for each option C_i in the head of r a rule with head C_i which has the negation of the better options as additional body literals. In addition, the rule is made defeasible by adding the default negation of the complement of C_i to the body. There is an exception: the rule generated for the last option is not made defeasible this way since at least one of the options must be true whenever the body of the original rule is true.

Although this translation seems natural it does not work. Consider the following example:

1) $a \times b$
2) $p \leftarrow \text{not } p, a$

The single preferred answer set is $\{b\}$. The pseudo-translation is

1) $a \leftarrow \text{not } \neg a$
2) $b \leftarrow \neg a$
3) $p \leftarrow \text{not } p, a$

The resulting program has no answer set. In fact, we can prove the following proposition:

Proposition 2 *There is no translation trans from LPODs to extended logic programs (without ordered disjunction) such that for each program P the preferred answer sets of P and the answer sets of $trans(P)$ coincide.*

Proof: The proposition follows from the fact that preferred answer sets of $LPOD$s are not necessarily subset minimal. Consider the program $a \times b$; $c \times b \leftarrow a$; $\neg c$. The preferred answer sets are $S_1 = \{b, \neg c\}$ and $S_2 = \{a, b, \neg c\}$. Clearly, $S_1 \subset S_2$. There is thus no extended logic program with these answer sets. $\square$

Of course, this does not exclude the possibility of translations to programs containing some extra atoms. This is a topic of further study.

For the computation of preferred answer sets we suggest to search through the space of split programs. Fortunately, the split programs can be ordered according to the options they contain. Let us first introduce some notation. For an $LPOD$ P and a split program P' of P we let

$$P_{P'}^k = \{r \in P \mid k \text{ smallest integer such that } r^k \in P'\}.$$

Now consider the following preference relation on split programs:

Definition 9 *Let P_1 and P_2 be two split programs of the LPOD P. We define $P_1 > P_2$ iff there is a k such that $P_{P_2}^k \subset P_{P_1}^k$ and for all $j < k$, $P_{P_1}^j = P_{P_2}^j$.*

The split programs of P form a lattice whose top element is the program with all the best options and whose bottom element is the program with all the worst options. The *lub* of two programs picks for each rule in P the best option contained in one of the programs, the *glb* picks the worst option.

Among the split programs we are interested in consistent ones which are $>$-maximal. A program is consistent if it possesses at least one consistent answer set.

Definition 10 *A split program P' of P is called P-optimal iff P' is consistent, and there is no consistent split program P'' of P such that $P'' > P'$.*

We are able to prove the following proposition:

Proposition 3 *If S is a preferred answer set of an LPOD P then there is a P-optimal split program P' of P such that S is an answer set of P'.*

Proof: Sketch: Let S be a preferred answer set of P. Construct a split program P' as follows: for each rule $r = C_1 \times \ldots \times C_n \leftarrow body \in P$ choose r^1 if $body$ is false in S and r^k if $body$ is true in S and k is the smallest integer such that $C_k \in S$. The split program obtained this way has S as an answer set and can be shown to be optimal. $\square$

We can thus use the preference ordering on split programs to search for preferred answer sets, starting from the best split program. Whenever a split program possesses a consistent answer set we can eliminate all programs below from further consideration.

Conclusion

In this paper we introduced a new connective to logic programming. This connective - called ordered disjunction - can be used to represent context dependent preferences in a simple and elegant way. Logic programming with ordered disjunction has interesting applications, in particular in design and configuration.

There are numerous papers introducing preferences to logic programming. For an overview of some of these approaches see the discussion in (Brewka & Eiter 1999) or the more recent (Schaub & Wang 2001). Only few of these proposals allow for context dependent preferences. Such preferences are discussed for instance in (Brewka 1996; Brewka & Eiter 1999). The representation of the preferences in these papers is based on the introduction of names for rules, the explicit representation of the preference relation among rules in the logical language, and a sophisticated reformulation of the central semantic notion (answer set, extension, etc.) with a highly self-referential flavour. Alternative approaches (Delgrande, Schaub, & Tompits 2000; Grosof 1999) are based on compilation techniques and make heavy use of meta-predicates in the logical language. Nothing like this is necessary in our approach. All we have to do is use the degree of satisfaction of a rule to define a preference relation on answer sets directly.

Our approach is closely related to work in qualitative decision theory, for an overview see (Doyle & Thomason 1999). Poole (Poole 1997) aims at a combination of logic and decision theory. His approach incorporates quantitative utilities whereas our preferences are qualitative. Interestingly, Poole uses a logic *without* disjunction whereas we *enhance* disjunction. In (Boutilier *et al.* 1999) a graphical representation, somewhat reminiscent of Bayes nets, for conditional preferences among feature values under the *ceteris paribus* principle is proposed, together with corresponding algorithms. *LPODs* are more general and offer means to reason defeasibly. Several models of qualitative decision making based on possibility theory are described in (Dubois *et al.* 1999; Benferhat *et al.* 2000). They are based on certainty and desirability rankings. Some of them make strong commensurability assumptions with respect to these rankings. In a series of papers (Lang 1996; van der Torre & Weydert 2001), originally motivated by (Boutilier 1994), the authors propose viewing conditional desires as constraints on utility functions. Intuitively, $D(a|b)$ stands for: the b-worlds with highest utility satisfy a. Our interpretation of ranked options is different. Rather than being based on decision theory our approach gives a particular interpretation to the ceteris paribus principle.

In an extended version of this paper (available at www.informatik.uni-leipzig.de/~brewka) we show that *LPODs* can serve as a basis for qualitative decision models. In decision making it is not sufficient to consider the most preferred answer sets only since this amounts to an extremely optimistic view about how the world will behave. As is well-known in decision theory, for realistic models of decision making it is necessary to distinguish what is under the control of the agent (and thus may constitute the agent's decision) from what is not. This can be done by distinguishing a subset of the literals in a program as decision literals. The basic idea is to use *LPODs* to describe possible actions or decisions and their consequences, states of the world and desired outcomes. The necessary steps are:

1. Among the literals in the logical language distinguish a set of decision literals C the agent can decide upon. It's the agent's decision which makes them true. A decision is a consistent subset of C.

2. Represent the different alternative decisions which can be made by the agent. This can be done using standard answer set programming techniques. Note that certain options may lead to additional choices that need to be made.

3. Represent the different possible states of the world. Again standard answer set programming techniques apply.

4. Represent relationships between and consequences of different alternatives.

5. Represent desired properties. This is where ordered disjunction comes into play. Of course, desires may be context-dependent.

6. Use the preference relation on answer sets derived form the satisfaction degrees of rules to induce a preference relation on possible decisions. There are different ways to do this corresponding to different attitudes towards risk.

7. Pick one of the most preferred decisions.

We plan to investigate application methodologies for *LPODs* in decision making and other scenarios. An answer set programming methodology for configuration tasks was developed by Niemelä and colleagues at Helsinki University of Technology (Soininen 2000; Niemelä & Simons 2000). We plan to study possibilities of combining this methodology with *LPODs*. Finally, we are studying possibilities of implementing *LPODs* on top of the *smodels* system.

Acknowledgements

Thanks to S. Benferhat, R. Booth, T. Janhunen, I. Niemelä, T. Syrjänen and L. van der Torre for helpful comments.

References

Benferhat, S.; Dubois, D.; Fargier, H.; and Prade, H. 2000. Decision, nonmonotonic reasoning and possibilistic logic. In Minker, J., ed., *Logic-Based Artificial Intelligence*. Kluwer Academic Publishers.

Boutilier, C.; Brafman, R.; Hoos, H.; and Poole, D. 1999. Reasoning with conditional ceteris paribus preference statements. In *Proc. Uncertainty in Artificial Intelligence, UAI-99*.

Boutilier, C. 1994. Towards a logic for qualitative decision theory. In *Proc. Principles of Knowledge Representation and Reasoning, KR-94*, 75–86. Morgan Kaufmann.

Brewka, G., and Eiter, T. 1999. Preferred answer sets for extended logic programs. *Artificial Intelligence* 109:297–356.

Brewka, G.; Benferhat, S.; and Le Berre, D. 2002. Qualitative choice logic. In *Proc. Principles of Knowledge Representation and Reasoning, KR-02*. Morgan Kaufmann.

Brewka, G. 1996. Well-founded semantics for extended logic programs with dynamic preferences. *Journal of Artificial Intelligence Research* 4:19–36.

Delgrande, J.; Schaub, T.; and Tompits, H. 2000. Logic programs with compiled preferences. In *Proc. European Conference on Artificial Intelligence, ECAI-00*, 464–468. IOS Press.

Doyle, J., and Thomason, R. 1999. Background to qualitative decision theory. *AI Magazine* 20(2):55–68.

Dubois, D.; Berre, D. L.; Prade, H.; and Sabbadin, R. 1999. Using possibilistic logic for modelingqualitative decision: Atms-based algorithms. *Fundamenta Informaticae* 34:1–30.

Eiter, T.; Leone, N.; Mateis, C.; Pfeifer, G.; and Scarcello, F. 1998. The kr system dlv: Progress report, comparisons and benchmarks. In *Proc. Principles of Knowledge Representation and Reasoning, KR-98*. Morgan Kaufmann.

Gelfond, M., and Lifschitz, V. 1991. Classical negation in logic programs and disjunctive databases. *New Generation Computing* 9:365–385.

Grosof, B. 1999. Diplomat: Compiling prioritized rules into ordinary logic programs for e-commerce applications (intelligent systems demonstration abstract). In *Proc. AAAI-99*.

Lang, J. 1996. Conditional desires and utilities - an alternative logical approach to qualitative decision theory. In *Proc. 12th European Conference on Artificial Intelligence, ECAI-96*, 318–322. Wiley and Sons.

Lifschitz, V. 2001. Answer set programming and plan generation. available under www.cs.utexas.edu/users/vl/papers.html.

Niemelä, I., and Simons, P. 1997. Efficient implementation of the stable model and well-founded semantics for normal logic programs. In *Proc. 4th Intl. Conference on Logic Programming and Nonmonotonic Reasoning*. Springer Verlag.

Niemelä, I., and Simons, P. 2000. Extending the smodels system with cardinality and weight constraints. In Minker, J., ed., *Logic-Based Artificial Intelligence*. Kluwer Academic Publishers.

Poole, D. 1997. The independent choice logic for modelling multiple agents under uncertainty. *Artificial Intelligence Journal* 94(1-2):7–56.

Sakama, C., and Inoue, K. 1994. An alternative approach to the semantics of disjunctive logic programs and deductive databases. *Journal of Automated Reasoning* 13:145–172.

Schaub, T., and Wang, K. 2001. A comparative study of logic programs with preference. In *Proc. Intl. Joint Conference on Artificial Intelligence, IJCAI-01*.

Soininen, T. 2000. *An Approach to Knowledge Representation and Reasoning for Product Configuration Tasks*. Ph.D. Dissertation, Helsinki University of Technology, Finland.

van der Torre, L., and Weydert, E. 2001. Parameters for utilitarian desires in a qualitative decision theory. *Applied Intelligence* 14:285–301.

A Three-Valued Characterization for Strong Equivalence of Logic Programs

Pedro Cabalar

Dept. of Computer Science
University of Corunna
Corunna, Spain
cabalar@dc.fi.udc.es

Abstract

In this work we present additional results related to the property of strong equivalence of logic programs. This property asserts that two programs share the same set of stable models, even under the addition of new rules. As shown in a recent work by Lifschitz, Pearce and Valverde, strong equivalence can be simply reduced to equivalence in the logic of *Here-and-There* (HT). In this paper we provide an alternative based on 3-valued logic, using also, as a first step, a classical logic charaterization. We show that the 3-valued encoding provides a direct interpretation for nested expressions but, when moving to an unrestricted syntax, it generally yields different results from HT.

Introduction

There is no doubt that the application of logic programming (LP) as a tool for knowledge representation has influenced in the progressive evolution of LP towards a more logical-style orientation, avoiding the initial syntactic restrictions. Think, for instance, how the stable models semantics (Gelfond & Lifschitz 1988) has been successively modified to cope with explicit negation and disjunctive heads (Gelfond & Lifschitz 1991), default negation in the head (Lifschitz 1994; Inoue & Sakama 1998) or, finally, the full use of nested expressions (Lifschitz, Tang, & Turner 1999). Perhaps as a result of this evolution, the following question has become interesting: when can we consider that two (syntactically different) programs Π_1 and Π_2 *represent the same knowledge*?

From a traditional LP perspective, we would say that Π_1 and Π_2 are equivalent when they share the same set of stable models like, for instance, the programs $\{p\}$ and $\{p \leftarrow not\ q\}$ whose only stable model is $\{p\}$. However, nonmonotonicity may cause them to behave in a different way in the presence of additional rules (just add fact q to both programs). Thus, if we want to check whether Π_1 and Π_2 actually represent the *same knowledge*, we must require a stronger condition, talking instead about *strong equivalence*: for any Π, the stable models of $\Pi_1 \cup \Pi$ and $\Pi_2 \cup \Pi$ coincide.

An elegant solution to this problem is the recent characterization of stable models relying on Heyting's logic of *Here-and-There* (HT). In (Pearce 1997), Pearce first showed that

stable models can be simply seen as some kind of minimal HT models. Then, in (Lifschitz, Pearce, & Valverde 2000), Lifschitz, Pearce and Valverde proved that, in fact, this characterization fits with the semantics for nested operators independently proposed in (Lifschitz, Tang, & Turner 1999) and, what is more important, that two programs are strongly equivalent iff they have the same set of HT models.

In this paper we provide two closely related alternatives to HT that rely on classical logic and 3-valued logic (L_3), respectively. These alternatives present the advantage of using very well-known formalisms, which may help for a better insight of strong equivalence (the main emphasis of this paper), but can be useful for implementation purposes too. Unfortunately, we also show how, in both cases, their scope of applicability seems to be smaller than in the HT case. This is evident for the classical encoding we use as an introductory step, since it can only be understood as a "direct" semantics[1] for non-nested logic programs. As for the L_3 characterization, it properly handles nested expressions in a direct way, but loses some important properties when nesting is also allowed for rule conditionals.

The paper is structured as follows. The next section recalls the basic definition of stable models for general (non-nested) logic programs. The third section describes the classical encoding. In the fourth and fifth sections we respectively describe nested expressions and the 3-valued formalization. After that, we briefly comment the differences between the HT and L_3 interpretations. Finally, the last section contains a discussion and the conclusions. Proofs of theorems can be found in an extended version of this paper (Cabalar 2002).

Stable models

The syntax of logic programs is defined starting from a finite set of ground atoms Σ, called the *Herbrand base*, which will serve as propositional signature. We assume that all the variables have been previously replaced by their possible ground instances. Letters a, b, c, d, p, q will be used to denote atoms in Σ, and letters I, J to denote subsets of Σ. A *logic pro-*

---

[1] Application of the classical encoding to nested expressions is also possible, but only after a previous *syntactic* transformation.

gram is defined as a collection of rules of the shape:

$$a_1; \ldots a_m; not\ b_1; \ldots not\ b_n \leftarrow$$
$$c_1, \ldots c_r, not\ d_1, \ldots not\ d_s \quad (1)$$

We call *head* (resp. *body*) to the left (resp. right) hand side of the arrow in (1). The comma and the semicolon are alternative representations of conjunction $\wedge$ and disjunction $\vee$, respectively. When $m = n = 0$ we usually write $\bot \leftarrow B$ instead of $\leftarrow B$, whereas when $r = s = 0$ we directly write H instead of $H \leftarrow$ or $H \leftarrow \top$.

Sometimes, it will be convenient to think about program rules as classical propositional formulas, where $\leftarrow$ and *not* are respectively understood as material implication and classical negation. In this way, the usual expression $I \models R$ denotes that interpretation I satisfies rule R (seen as a classical formula), whereas $I \models \Pi$ means that I is a model of the program Π (seen as a classical theory).

The *reduct* of a program Π w.r.t. some set of atoms I, written Π^I, is defined as the result of replacing in Π any default literal *not p* by $\top$, if $p \notin I$, or by $\bot$ otherwise.

Definition 1 (Stable model) *A set of atoms $I \subseteq \Sigma$ is a stable model of a logic program Π iff I is a minimal model of Π^I.* □

Strong equivalence in classical logic

We can think about the definition of stable models as a try-and-error procedure which handles (propositional) interpretations for two different purposes. On the one hand, we start from some arbitrary interpretation I^a, we can call the initial *assumption*, used to compute the reduct Π^{I^a}. On the other hand, in a second step, we deal with minimal models of Π^{I^a} which, in principle, *need not to have any connection* with I^a. Each minimal model I^p can be seen as the set of propositions we can *prove* by deductive closure using the rules in Π^{I^a}. When the proved atoms coincide with the initial assumption, $I^p = I^a$, a stable model is obtained.

In order to capture this behavior, we reify all the atoms $p \in \Sigma$ to become arguments of two unary predicates, $assumed(p)$ and $proved(p)$, that respectively talk about I^a and I^p. Sort variable X will be used for ranging over any propositional symbol in Σ. When considering the models of any reified formula F, we will implictly assume that they actually correspond to $F \wedge$ UNA, where UNA stands for the unique names assumption for sort Σ. This allows us identifying any Herbrand model M of this type of formulas with a pair[2] (I^p, I^a) so that $M[assumed] = I^a$ and $M[proved] = I^p$. Expression $M \models F$ represents again satisfaction of reified formulas – ambiguity with respect to $I \models F$ is cleared by the shape of structures and formulas.

Given this simple framework, we provide two encodings: the first one is a *completely straightforward* translation to capture stable models, whereas the second one is a stronger translation to characterize strong equivalence.

---

[2] The superscripts p and a, which stand here for *proved* and *assumed*, respectively correspond to the worlds *here* and *there* in HT or to the sets of *positive* and *non-negative* atoms in L_3.

Definition 2 (First translation) *For any logic program rule R like (1), we define the classical formula $\dot{R}$ as the material implication:*

$$\left(\bigwedge_{i=1}^{r} proved(c_i) \right) \wedge \left(\bigwedge_{i=1}^{s} \neg assumed(d_i) \right) \supset$$
$$\left(\bigvee_{i=1}^{n} proved(a_i) \right) \vee \left(\bigvee_{i=1}^{m} \neg assumed(b_i) \right) \quad (2)$$

Given a logic program Π, the formula $\dot{\Pi}$ stands for the conjunction of all the $\dot{R}$, for each rule $R \in \Pi$. □

Intuitively, to obtain the minimal models I^p of Π^{I^a} we can use an ordering relation among pairs $(I^p, I^a) \preceq (J^p, J^a)$ that holds when both $I^a = J^a$ is fixed and $I^p \subseteq J^p$. The corresponding models $\preceq$-minimization have a simple syntactic counterpart[3]: predicate circumscription $\mathrm{CIRC}[\dot{\Pi}; proved]$.

After circumscription captures the minimal models, we must further require $I^p = I^a$, that is, we want pairs of shape (I, I) where what we assumed results to be exactly what we proved. These pairs of shape (I, I) will be called *total*. Clearly, forcing models to be total corresponds to including the formula:

$$\forall X. \left(proved(X) \equiv assumed(X) \right) \quad (3)$$

The intuitions above are not new. In fact, they were used in Theorem 5.2 in (Lin & Shoham 1992) which, adapted[4] to our current presentation, states the following result:

Proposition 1 *Let Σ be a propositional signature. A set of atoms $I \subseteq \Sigma$ is a stable model of a logic program Π iff $M = (I, I)$ satisfies the formula:*

$$\mathrm{CIRC}[\dot{\Pi}; proved] \wedge (3)$$

□

In order to capture strong equivalence of two programs, it seems that we should not only compare the final selected models, but also the set of non-minimal ones involved in the minimization. For instance, it is easy to see that, due to monotonicity of classical logic, the following proposition trivially applies:

Proposition 2 *Let Π_1 and Π_2 be two logic programs such that $\models \dot{\Pi}_1 \equiv \dot{\Pi}_2$. Then Π_1 and Π_2 are strongly equivalent.* □

Unfortunately, the opposite does not necessarily hold: Π_1 and Π_2 can be strongly equivalent while $\dot{\Pi}_1$ and $\dot{\Pi}_2$ have different models. This is because encoding in Definition 2 allows some models which are actually irrelevant for strong equivalence, as we will show next.

---

[3] See Section 2.5 in (Lifschitz 1993).

[4] In (Lin & Shoham 1992) they used a duplicated signature (atoms p and p') instead of reification and, therefore, they actually applied parallel circumscription. This result seems to have been first presented in (Lin 1991).

Definition 3 (Subtotal model) *For any reified theory T, a model (I^p, I^a) of T is called subtotal iff (I^a, I^a) is also model of T and $(I^p, I^a) \preceq (I^a, I^a)$.* □

Let $\mathrm{SUBT}(T)$ represent the set of subtotal models of T (note that total models are also included). It is clear that any model $M \notin \mathrm{SUBT}(\dot{\Pi})$ is irrelevant for selecting the total $\preceq$-minimal models, i.e., for obtaining the stable models of Π. The next theorem shows that the coincidence of subtotal models is a necessary condition for strong equivalence. The proof (available at (Cabalar 2002)) constitutes a direct rephrasing of that for the main theorem in (Lifschitz, Pearce, & Valverde 2000).

Theorem 1 *Two logic programs Π_1 and Π_2 are strongly equivalent iff* $\mathrm{SUBT}(\dot{\Pi}_1) = \mathrm{SUBT}(\dot{\Pi}_2)$ □

Theorem 1 points out that the $\dot{\Pi}$ encoding is still too weak for a full characterization of strong equivalence. We show next how, using a more restrictive translation (that is, adding more formulas) it is possible to obtain theories for which all their models are subtotal. To understand how to do this, consider the example program $\Pi_0 = \{p \leftarrow q\}$ where:

$$\dot{\Pi}_0 \stackrel{\text{def}}{=} proved(q) \supset proved(p)$$

This formula has 12 models: it restricts the extent of *proved* to 3 cases ($\emptyset$, $\{p\}$ and $\{p, q\}$) leaving free, in each case, the 4 possibilities for *assumed*.

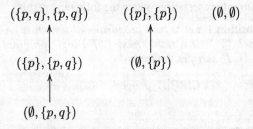

Figure 1: Subtotal models of $\dot{\Pi}_0$.

Figure 1 shows the 6 subtotal models of $\dot{\Pi}_0$, representing the $\preceq$-ordering relationships among them. Notice how subtotal models always satisfy $I^p \subseteq I^a$, that is, we can require:

$$\forall X.(proved(X) \supset assumed(X)) \tag{4}$$

Unfortunatley, the addition of this axiom is still not enough to rule out all the irrelevant models. For instance, $\dot{\Pi}_0 \wedge (4)$ has still one non-subtotal model: $(\emptyset, \{q\})$. This model, however, has the particularity that its assumed atoms $I^a = \{q\}$ do not satisfy the original program rule: $I^a \not\models p \leftarrow q$. As it is well-known, any stable model I of a program Π, is also a classical model: $I \models \Pi$. So, instead of starting from any arbitrary initial assumption I^a, we can begin requiring $I^a \models \Pi$. This can be easily incorporated into the encoding as follows. For each logic program rule R like

(1), we define $\ddot{R}$ as:

$$(\bigwedge_{i=1}^{r} assumed(c_i)) \wedge (\bigwedge_{i=1}^{s} \neg assumed(d_i)) \supset$$

$$(\bigvee_{i=1}^{n} assumed(a_i)) \vee (\bigvee_{i=1}^{m} \neg assumed(b_i)) \tag{5}$$

Again, $\ddot{\Pi}$ stands for the conjunction of $\ddot{R}$ for all $R \in \Pi$.

Definition 4 (Second translation) *For any logic program Π we define the formula* $\Pi^* \stackrel{\text{def}}{=} \dot{\Pi} \wedge \ddot{\Pi} \wedge (4)$. □

The proof for the following theorem uses well-known properties of circumscription (see (Lifschitz 1993)) to show that the additional formulas *do not affect* to the final set of stable models.

Theorem 2 *For any logic program Π:*
$$\mathrm{CIRC}[\Pi^*; proved] \wedge (3) \equiv \mathrm{CIRC}[\dot{\Pi}; proved] \wedge (3) \quad □$$

But, of course, the real interest of Π^* is that it finally rules out irrelevant models:

Property 1 *Let Π be a logic program. Then, any model $M = (I^p, I^a)$ of Π^* is subtotal.* □

Finally, this property, together with theorem 1, directly implies:

Theorem 3 *Two logic programs Π_1 and Π_2 are strongly equivalent iff* $\models \Pi_1^* \equiv \Pi_2^*$. □

Nested expressions.

The previous section has shown that strong equivalence of logic programs can be reduced to a simple equivalence test in classical logic, providing in this way a (we think) easier alternative to the HT characterization. Unfortunately, the applicability of the classical encoding is limited for rules of shape (1), whereas the HT formalization is still applicable to a more flexible rule syntax like, for instance, rules with nested expressions.

In (Lifschitz, Tang, & Turner 1999) a more general shape for program rules was considered. A *nested expression* is defined as any propositional combination of atoms with 0-ary operators $\bot$, $\top$, unary operator *not* and binary operators ',' and ';'. A logic program is now a set of rules $Head \leftarrow Body$ where $Head$ and $Body$ are nested expressions (notice that the rule conditional $\leftarrow$ is the only operator that cannot be nested). An example of rule could be, for instance:

$$a, b \leftarrow not\ (c; not\ d) \tag{6}$$

Stable models for this kind of programs can be easily described by a simple modification in the definition of program reduct. We define now Π^I as the result of replacing in Π every maximal occurrence[5] of *not F* by $\bot$ if $I \models F$ or by $\top$ otherwise. Note that the previous definition of reduct corresponds to the particular case in which F is an atom.

An interesting result derived from this modified semantics (proposition 7 in (Lifschitz, Tang, & Turner 1999)) is that

---

[5]That is, any *not F* that is not in the scope of an outer *not*.

any program with nested expressions is strongly equivalent to some (non-nested) program, just consisting of rules like (1). To obtain this non-nested program, the following transformations are defined. Let F, G and H represent nested expressions. By $\alpha \Leftrightarrow \beta$ we mean that we replace some regular occurrence of α by β. Then, we handle the following strongly equivalent transformations:

(i) $F, G \Leftrightarrow G, F$ and $F; G \Leftrightarrow G; F$.

(ii) $(F, G), H \Leftrightarrow F, (G, H)$ and $(F; G); H \Leftrightarrow F; (G; H)$.

(iii) $F, (G; H) \Leftrightarrow (F, G); (F, H)$ and $F; (G, H) \Leftrightarrow (F; G), (F; H)$.

(iv) $not\ (F; G) \Leftrightarrow not\ F, not\ G$ and $not\ (F, G) \Leftrightarrow not\ F; not\ G$.

(v) $not\ not\ not\ F \Leftrightarrow not\ F$.

(vi) $F, \top \Leftrightarrow F$ and $F; \top \Leftrightarrow \top$.

(vii) $F, \bot \Leftrightarrow \bot$ and $F; \bot \Leftrightarrow F$.

(viii) $not\ \top \Leftrightarrow \bot$ and $not\ \bot \Leftrightarrow \top$.

(ix) $(F, G \leftarrow H) \Leftrightarrow (F \leftarrow H), (G \leftarrow H)$.

(x) $(F \leftarrow G; H) \Leftrightarrow (F \leftarrow G), (F \leftarrow H)$.

(xi) $(F \leftarrow G, not\ not\ H) \Leftrightarrow (F; not\ H \leftarrow G)$.

(xii) $(F; not\ not\ G \leftarrow H) \Leftrightarrow (F \leftarrow not\ G, H)$.

For instance, rule (6) can be successively transformed as follows:

$a, b \leftarrow not\ c, not\ not\ d.$ By (iv)

$a \leftarrow not\ c, not\ not\ d,$
$b \leftarrow not\ c, not\ not\ d.$ By (ix)

$a; not\ d \leftarrow not\ c,$
$b; not\ d \leftarrow not\ c.$ By (xi)

This treatment of nested expressions exceeds the applicability of our previous classical logic representation. From a practical point of view, such a limitation is not very important, since we can always unfold nested expressions by applying (i)-(xii). Nevertheless, from a theoretical point of view, this clearly points out that the classical encoding fails as a real semantic characterization for LP connectives.

As shown in (Lifschitz, Pearce, & Valverde 2000), one of the important features of the HT formalization, apart from the result for strong equivalence, is that it preserves the above interpretation of nested expressions. We show next that a similar behavior can be obtained using standard 3-valued logic (L_3). Surprisingly, L_3 provides the same interpretation for nested expressions, but generally differs once free nesting of rule conditionals is allowed.

L_3: Three valued logic.

We will use propositional syntax plus Lukasiewicz's unary operator[6] l. Intuitively, a formula $l\ F$ is never unknown and points out that F is valuated to true. In this way, $\neg l\ F$ would mean that "F is not true," i.e., it is either false or unknown.

---

[6]For instance, see (Bull & Segerberg 1984), pag. 8, where l is denoted as $\Box$.

If F, G are L_3 formulas and p an atom of the signature Σ then:

$$p,\ \neg F,\ F \vee G,\ \top,\ \bot,\ l\ F$$

are also L_3 formulas. Propositional derived operators ($\wedge, \supset, \equiv$) are defined in the usual way.

A three valued interpretation M is a function $M : \Sigma \longrightarrow \{0, 1/2, 1\}$ assigning to each atom $p \in \Sigma$ a truth value $M(p)$ which can be 0 (false), 1/2 (unknown) or 1 (true). We will usually represent M as the pair of sets of atoms (I^p, I^a) respectively containing the *positive* (true) and *consistent* (non-false) atoms where, of course, we require consistence: $I^p \subseteq I^a$. Consequently:

$$M(p) = \begin{cases} 1 & \text{if } p \in I^p \\ 0 & \text{if } p \notin I^a \\ 1/2 & \text{otherwise} \end{cases}$$

Note that we use here the same notation as for the pairs we handled in the reified approach. This is not casual: the negative information of a 3-valued interpretation will be used to represent default negation, whereas the positive information will represent the set of proved atoms.

Definition 5 (L_3 **valuation of a formula**)
We extend the valuation function M to any formula F, $M(F) \in \{0, 1/2, 1\}$, so that:

1) $M(\top) = 1$ and $M(\bot) = 0$

2) $M(\neg F) = 1 - M(F)$

3) $M(F \vee G) = max(M(F), M(G))$

4) $M(l\ F) = \begin{cases} 1 & \text{if } M(F) = 1 \\ 0 & \text{otherwise} \end{cases}$

$\qquad\qquad\qquad\qquad\qquad\qquad\qquad\qquad\square$

An interpretation M *satisfies* a formula F, written $M \models_3 F$ when $M(F) = 1$. When F is satisfied by *any* interpretation, we call it an L_3-*tautology* and write $\models_3 F$. As usual, an interpretation is a *model* of a theory when it satisfies all its formulas. Maintaining the previous terminology, a 3-valued interpretation M is called *total* iff it has the shape $M = (I, I)$, that is, it contains no unknown atoms. Clearly, when considering total interpretations, the l operator can be simply removed, and L_3 collapses into 2-valued propositional logic.

LP connectives are simply defined among the following derived operators:

$$m\ F \stackrel{\text{def}}{=} \neg l\ \neg F$$
$$not\ F \stackrel{\text{def}}{=} \neg m\ F$$
$$G \leftarrow F \stackrel{\text{def}}{=} (l\ F \supset l\ G) \wedge (m\ F \supset m\ G)$$
$$F \leftrightarrow G \stackrel{\text{def}}{=} (F \leftarrow G) \wedge (G \leftarrow F)$$

It is easy to check that the derived semantics for each one of these operators corresponds to:

5) $M(m\ F) = \begin{cases} 1 & \text{if } M(F) \neq 0 \\ 0 & \text{otherwise} \end{cases}$

6) $M(not\ F) = \begin{cases} 1 & \text{if } M(F) = 0 \\ 0 & \text{otherwise} \end{cases}$

7) $M(G \leftarrow F) = \begin{cases} 1 & \text{if } M(F) \leq M(G) \\ 0 & \text{otherwise} \end{cases}$

8) $M(F \leftrightarrow G) = \begin{cases} 1 & \text{if } M(F) = M(G) \\ 0 & \text{otherwise} \end{cases}$

Operator m acts is the dual of l, ($m\,F$ can be read as "F is consistent") whereas implication $\leftarrow$ is the one proposed by Fitting (Fitting 1985) and Kunen (Kunen 1987). When we represent some program Π inside L_3, we will consider it as a single formula consisting in the conjunction of all the program rules. Note also that when $\models_3 F \leftrightarrow G$, we can apply uniform substitution in L_3 as we would do in classical propositional logic. For instance, $\models_3 (not\ F) \leftrightarrow (\bot \leftarrow F)$ means that we can replace any occurrence of $(not\ F)$ by $(\bot \leftarrow F)$ and vice versa. Let $\circ$ and $\bullet$ be two meta-operators, any of them indistinctly representing l or m. Then, the following formulas are also L_3 tautologies:

$$\circ(F \wedge G) \quad \leftrightarrow \quad \circ F \wedge \circ G \tag{7}$$

$$\circ(F \vee G) \quad \leftrightarrow \quad \circ F \vee \circ G \tag{8}$$

$$\bullet \circ F \quad \leftrightarrow \quad \circ F \tag{9}$$

$$\bullet \neg \circ F \quad \leftrightarrow \quad \neg \circ F \tag{10}$$

As m is defined in terms[7] of l, this means that we can unfold any L_3 formula until l is exclusively applied to literals. Using these properties, the following lemma can be easily proved:

Lemma 1 *Let R be a program rule like (1), and let the pair $M = (I^p, I^a)$ have the common shape of an L_3-interpretation and a classical interpretation for proved/assumed. Then, $M \models_3 R$ iff $M \models \dot{R} \wedge \ddot{R}$.* □

Besides, by inspection on L_3 semantics, we also have that:

Lemma 2 *For any transformation $\alpha \Leftrightarrow \beta$ in (i)-(xii): $\models_3 \alpha \leftrightarrow \beta$.* □

Theorem 4 *Let Π_1 and Π_2 be two logic programs possibly containing nested expressions. Then Π_1 and Π_2 are strongly equivalent iff: $\models_3 l\Pi_1 \equiv l\Pi_2$.* □

Notice that we check $l\Pi_1 \equiv l\Pi_2$ instead of the stronger condition $\Pi_1 \leftrightarrow \Pi_2$. To understand the difference, consider $\Pi_1 = \{a\}$ and $\Pi_2 = \{a \leftarrow \top\}$. The interpretation $M = (\{a\}, \{a\})$ is the only model of both programs and so, $\models_3 l\Pi_1 \equiv l\Pi_2$. However, $\Pi_1 \leftrightarrow \Pi_2$ is not a tautology, since $M' = (\emptyset, \{a\})$ makes $M'(\Pi_1) = 1/2 \neq 1 = M'(\Pi_2)$.

Differences with respect to HT

Theorem 4 shows that HT and L_3 coincide in their interpretations of programs with nested expressions. The next natural question is, do the HT and L_3 interpretations coincide for any arbitrary theory? The answer to this question is negative, as we will show with a pair of counterexamples. Of course, due to theorem 4, these counterexamples cannot be just programs with nested expressions, as defined in the fourth section. We study, for instance, a nested conditional, and the negation of a conditional.

---

[7]Of course, we could have equally chosen the dual operator m as the basic one.

Consider the theory consisting of the singleton formula $(a \leftarrow b) \leftarrow c$. In HT, this theory is equivalent to $(a \leftarrow b, c)$, which seems to be the most intuitive solution, whereas in L_3 it is actually equivalent to $(a; not\ c \leftarrow b)$. Both equivalences hold in classical propositional logic. However, for computing stable models, their behavior is quite different. For instance, the theory $\{b, (a \leftarrow c), (c \leftarrow a), ((a \leftarrow b) \leftarrow c)\}$ would have a unique stable model $\{b\}$ under the HT interpretation whereas, under L_3, an additional stable model $\{a, b, c\}$ is obtained.

The second example shows the most important problem of the L_3 interpretation: once we allow arbitrary theories, we may obtain non-subtotal models, something that does not happen[8] in HT. Let Π be the theory $\{b, not\ (a \leftarrow b)\}$. Its unique stable model is $\{b\}$ both in HT and L_3. However, while the pair $(\{b\}, \{b\})$ is the unique HT model[9] of Π, in L_3 there exists a second model $(\{b\}, \{a, b\})$ which is not subtotal. In other words, when using L_3 for this general syntax, the set of L_3 models does not fully characterize strong equivalence.

Discussion

The study of strong equivalence is probably one of the most active current topics in research in Logic Programming, as it becomes evident by the increasing amount of new results obtained recently (just to cite three examples (Turner 2001; Pearce, Tompits, & Woltran 2001; de Jongh & Hendriks 2001)).

In (Pearce, Tompits, & Woltran 2001), a classical logic characterization is also provided, which presents several similarities with the approach we present here. The main difference of Pearce et al's method is that it actually relies on a syntactic translation from HT into classical logic. This translation informally consists in a duplication of the atoms in the signature so that an atom p denotes our *proved* whereas an atom p' would denote *assumed*. In this paper, our initial motivation for using classical logic was to improve the presentation and the understanding. In this way, we have directly started from non-nested programs, trying to capture the definition of stable models in a way as direct as possible. As a result, our characterization does not provide an interpretation of nested connectives. In order to deal with them, we could apply a previous step, using transformations (i)-(xii). Pearce et al's encoding starts from HT logic, and so, deals with nested expressions (in the same way as HT does). Besides, the transformation presented in (Pearce, Tompits, & Woltran 2001) has the additional advantage of being linear, while (i)-(xii) are not polynomial in the general case. Despite of these two advantages of Pearce et al's approach, it must be noticed that none of the two classical encodings can actually be considered a full-semantics for nested logic programs, since *in both cases*, a previous syntactic transformation is required. Therefore, translation to classical logic is very interesting for practical purposes, but is limited from a purely semantic point of view.

---

[8]See for instance Fact 1 in (Lifschitz, Pearce, & Valverde 2000).

[9]In fact, the expression *not* $(a \leftarrow b)$ is HT-equivalent to the pair of constraints $(\bot \leftarrow not\ b)$ and $(\bot \leftarrow a)$.

Another similarity between our classical encoding with respect to (Pearce, Tompits, & Woltran 2001) is, not only how to decide strong equivalence, but how to obtain stable models. In our case, we simply used to that purpose the result presented by Lin and Shoham in (Lin & Shoham 1992) and then included slight variations that we proved to be sound. In (Pearce, Tompits, & Woltran 2001), a quantified boolean formula is used instead:

$$\phi' \wedge \neg \exists V((V < V') \wedge \tau_{HT}[\phi]) \qquad (11)$$

where V is the set of atoms, ϕ is the original program, ϕ' results from replacing any atom p by p' and finally $\tau_{HT}[\phi]$ is Pearce et al's translation from HT to classical logic. On the other hand, Lin and Shoham's result involving circumscription can be formulated[10] as:

$$(V = V') \wedge \mathcal{C}[\phi] \wedge \neg \exists V((V < V') \wedge \mathcal{C}[\phi]) \qquad (12)$$

where $\mathcal{C}[\phi]$ simply replaces each not p by $\neg p'$. Notice how, at least structurally, (12) is very similar to (11).

As for the L_3 encoding, it must also be noticed that other logical characterizations have been obtained apart from HT. In (de Jongh & Hendriks 2001), for instance, they use instead another logic, KC, and show that this is, in fact, the weakest intermediate logic (between intuitionistic and classical) that allows capturing strong equivalence of logic programs with nested expressions. An interesting open question is how logic KC deals with nested conditionals since, as we have shown, this is the case where HT and L_3 diverge.

Acknowledgements I want to thank Vladimir Lifschitz for his discussions and comments about a preliminary draft of the L_3 encoding, and to the anonymous referees for drawing my attention to part of the related work cited in this paper. This research is partially supported by the Government of Spain, grant TIC2001-0393.

References

Bull, R., and Segerberg, K. 1984. Basic modal logic. In Gabbay, D., and Guenthner, F., eds., *Handbook of Philosophical Logic*, volume 2. D. Reidel Publishing Company. 1–88.

Cabalar, P. 2002. Alternative characterizations for strong equivalence of logic programs. In *In Proc. of the Ninth Int'l Workshop on Non-monotonic Reasoning (NMR'2002)*.

D.H.J. de Jongh, A. Hendriks. 2001. Characterization of strongly equivalent logic programs in intermediate logics. Unpublished draft. http://turing.wins.uva.nl/~lhendrik/ .

Fitting, M. 1985. A kripke-kleene semantics for logic programs. *Journal of Logic Programming* 2(4):295–312.

Gelfond, M., and Lifschitz, V. 1988. The stable model semantics for logic programming. In Kowalski, R. A., and Bowen, K. A., eds., *Logic Programming: Proc. of the Fifth International Conference and Symposium (Volume 2)*. Cambridge, MA: MIT Press. 1070–1080.

Gelfond, M., and Lifschitz, V. 1991. Classical negation in logic programs and disjunctive databases. *New Generation Computing* 365–385.

Inoue, K., and Sakama, C. 1998. Negation as failure in the head. *Journal of Logic Programming* 35(1):39–78.

Kunen, K. 1987. Negation in logic programming. *Journal of Logic Programming* 4(4):289–308.

Lifschitz, V.; Pearce, D.; and Valverde, A. 2000. Strongly equivalent logic programs. *ACM Transactions on Computational Logic*. (to appear).

Lifschitz, V.; Tang, L. R.; and Turner, H. 1999. Nested expressions in logic programs. *Annals of Mathematics and Artificial Intelligence* 25:369–389.

Lifschitz, V. 1993. Circumscription. In D.M. Gabbay, C. H., and Robinson, J., eds., *Handbook of Logic in AI and Logic Programming*, volume 3. Oxford University Press. 298–352.

Lifschitz, V. 1994. Minimal belief and negation as failure. *Artificial Intelligence* 70:53–72.

Lin, F., and Shoham, Y. 1992. A logic of knowledge and justified assumptions. *Artificial Intelligence* 57:271–289.

Lin, F. 1991. *A Study of Nonmonotonic Reasoning*. Ph.D. Dissertation, Stanford.

Pearce, D.; Tompits, H.; and Woltran, S. 2001. Encodings of equilibrium logic and logic programs with nested expressions. In Bradzil, P., and Jorge, A., eds., *Lecture Notes in Artificial Intelligence*, volume 2258. Springer Verlag. 306–320.

Pearce, D. 1997. A new logical characterisation of stable models and answer sets. In *Non monotonic extensions of logic programming. Proc. NMELP'96. (LNAI 1216)*. Springer-Verlag.

Turner, H. 2001. Strong equivalence for logic programs and default theories (made easy). In *In Proc. of the Sixth Int'l Conf. on Logic Programming and Nonmonotonic Reasoning (LPNMR'01)*, 81–92.

---

[10]As described for instance in (Lifschitz 1993), propositional circumscription is nothing else but a quantified boolean formula.

ASSAT: Computing Answer Sets of A Logic Program By SAT Solvers

Fangzhen Lin and Yuting Zhao
Department of Computer Science
Hong Kong University of Science and Technology
Clear Water Bay, Kowloon, Hong Kong
{flin,yzhao}@cs.ust.hk

Abstract

We propose a new translation from normal logic programs with constraints under the answer set semantics to propositional logic. Given a logic program, we show that by adding, for each loop in the program, a corresponding loop formula to the program's completion, we obtain a one-to-one correspondence between the answer sets of the program and the models of the resulting propositional theory. Compared with the translation by Ben-Eliyahu and Dechter, ours has the advantage that it does not use any extra variables, and is considerably simpler, thus easier to understand. However, in the worst case, it requires computing exponential number of loop formulas. To address this problem, we propose an approach that adds loop formulas a few at a time, selectively. Based on these results, we implemented a system called ASSAT(X), depending on the SAT solver X used, and tested it on a variety of benchmarks including the graph coloring, the blocks world planning, and Hamiltonian Circuit domains. The results are compared with those by smodels and dlv, and it shows a clear edge of ASSAT(X) over them in these domains.

Introduction

Logic programming with answer sets semantics (Gelfond & Lifschitz 1988) and propositional logic are closely related. It is well-known that there is a local and modular translation from clauses to logic program rules such that the models of a set of clauses and the answer sets of its corresponding logic program are in one-to-one correspondence (You, Cartwright, & Li 1996; Niemelä 1999).

The other direction is more difficult and interesting. Niemelä (1999) showed that there cannot be a modular translation from logic programs to sets of clauses, in the sense that for any programs P_1 and P_2, the translation of $P_1 \cup P_2$ is the union of the translations of P_1 and P_2. However, the problem becomes interesting when we drop the requirement of modularity.

Ben-Eliyahu and Dechter (1996) gave a translation for a class of disjunctive logic programs, which includes all normal logic programs. However, one problem with their translation is that it may need to use quadratic (n^2) number of

extra propositions. While the number of variables is not always a reliable indicator of the hardness of a SAT problem, in the worst case, adding one more variable would double the search space.

In this paper we shall propose a new translation. It works by first associating a formula with each loop in the program, and then adding these formulas to the program's completion. The advantages of this translation are that it does not use any extra variables, and is intuitive and easy to understand as one can easily work it out by hand for typical "textbook" example programs.

Our work contributes to both the areas of answer set logic programming and propositional satisfiability. On the one hand, it provides a basis for an alternative implementation of answer set logic programming by leveraging on existing extensive work on SAT with a choice of variety of SAT solvers ranging from complete systematic ones to incomplete randomized ones. Indeed, our experiments on some well-known benchmarks such as graph coloring, planning, and Hamiltonian Circuit (HC) show that it has a clear advantage over the two popular specialized answer set generators, smodels (Niemelä 1999; Simons 2000) and dlv (Leone et al. 2001). On the other hand, this work also benefits SAT in providing some hard instances: we have encountered some relatively small SAT problems (about 720 variables and 4500 clauses) that we could not solve using any of the SAT solvers that we had tried.

This paper is organized as follows. We first introduce some basic concepts and notations used in the paper. We then define a notion of loops and their associated loop formulas, and show that a set is an answer set of a logic program iff it satisfies its completion and the set of all loop formulas. Based on this result, we propose an algorithm and implement a system called ASSAT for computing the answer sets of a logic program using SAT solvers. We then report some experimental results of running ASSAT on graph coloring, blocks world planning, and HC domains, and compare them with those using smodels and dlv.

Logical preliminaries

We shall consider fully grounded finite normal logic programs that may have constraints. That is, a logic program here is a finite set consisting of rules of the form:

$$p \leftarrow p_1, ..., p_k, \text{not } q_1, ..., \text{not } q_m, \qquad (1)$$

and constraints of the form:

$$\leftarrow p_1, ..., p_k, \text{not } q_1, ..., \text{not } q_m, \qquad (2)$$

where $k \geq 0, m \geq 0$, and $p, p_1, ..., p_k, q_1, ..., q_m$ are atoms without variables. Notice that the order of literals in the body of a rule or a constraint is not important under the answer set semantics, and we have written negative literals after positive ones. In effect, this means that a body is a set of literals. Thus we can use set-theoretic notations to talk about it. For instance, we may write $l \in G$ to mean that l is a literal in G.

Given a logic program P with constraints, a set S of atoms is its *answer set* if it is a stable model (Gelfond & Lifschitz 1988) of the program resulted from deleting all the constraints in P, and it satisfies all the constraints in P, i.e. for any constraint of the form (2) in P, either $p_i \notin S$ for some $1 \leq i \leq k$ or $q_i \in S$ for some $1 \leq i \leq m$.

Given a logic program P, its completion, written $Comp(P)$, is the union of the constraints in P and the Clark completion (Clark 1978) of the set of rules in P, that is, it consists of following sentences:

- For any atom p, let $p \leftarrow G_1, \cdots, p \leftarrow G_n$ be all the rules about p in P, then $p \equiv G_1 \vee \cdots \vee G_n$ is in $Comp(P)$. In particular, if $n = 0$, then the equivalence is $p \equiv false$.

- If $\leftarrow G$ is a constraint in P, then $\neg G$ is in $Comp(P)$.

Here we have somewhat abused the notation and write the body of a rule in a formula as well. Its intended meaning is as follows: if the body G is empty, then it is understood to be *true* in a formula, otherwise, it is the conjunction of literals in G with not replaced by $\neg$. For example, the completion of the program:

$$a \leftarrow b, c, \text{not } d. \quad a \leftarrow b, \text{not } c, \text{not } d.$$
$$\leftarrow b, c, \text{not } d.$$

is $\{a \equiv (b \wedge c \wedge \neg d) \vee (b \wedge \neg c \wedge \neg d), \neg b, \neg c, \neg d, \neg(b \wedge c \wedge \neg d)\}$.

In this paper, we shall identify a truth assignment with the set of atoms true in this assignment, and conversely, identify a set of atoms with the truth assignment that assigns a proposition true iff it is in the set. Under this convention, it is well-known that if S is an answer set of P, then S is also a model of $Comp(P)$, but the converse is not true in general.

In this paper we shall consider how we can strengthen the completion so that a set is an answer set of a logic program iff it is a model of the strengthened theory. The key concepts are loops and their associated formulas. For these, it is most convenient to define the *dependency graph* of a set of rules.

Given a set R of rules, the dependency graph of R is the following directed graph: the vertices of the graph are atoms mentioned in R, and for any two vertices p, q, there is a directed arc from p to q if there is a rule of the form $p \leftarrow G$ in R such that $q \in G$ (recall that we can treat the body of a rule as a set). Informally, an arc from p to q means that p is depended on q, Notice that not $q \in G$ does not imply an arc from p to q.

Recall that a directed graph is said to be *strongly connected* if for any two vertices in the graph, there is a (directed) path from one to the other. Given a directed graph, a *strongly connected component* is a set S of vertices such that for any $u, v \in S$, there is a path from u to v, and that S is not a subset of any other such set.

Loops and their formulas

It is clear that the reason a model of a logic program's completion may not be an answer set is because of loops. For instance, the logic program $\{a \leftarrow b.\ b \leftarrow a.\}$ has a unique stable model $\emptyset$. But its completion $\{a \equiv b, b \equiv a\}$ has two models $\emptyset$ and $\{a, b\}$. However, loops like this cannot always be deleted. For instance, if we add a fact a to this program, then the completion of the new program will have a unique model $\{a, b\}$, which is also an answer set. Notice here that in this new program, the rule $b \leftarrow a$ in the loop is used to derive b. The key point is then that a loop cannot be used to provide a circular justification of the atoms in the loop. The rules in a loop can be used only when there is an independent justification coming from outside of the loop. This is the information that we want to capture for a loop. Formally it is most convenient to define a loop as a set of atoms.

Definition 1 *A set L of atoms is called a loop of a logic program if the subgraph of the program's dependency graph induced by L is strongly connected.*

Given a logic program P, and a loop L in it, we associate two sets of rules with it:

$$R^+(L) = \{p \leftarrow G \mid p \in L, (\exists q).q \in G \wedge q \in L\}$$
$$R^-(L) = \{p \leftarrow G \mid p \in L, \neg(\exists q).q \in G \wedge q \in L\}$$

It is clear that these two sets are disjoint and for any rule whose head is in L, it is in one of the sets.

Intuitively, $R^+(L)$ contains rules *in the loop*, and they give rise to arcs connecting vertices in L in P's dependency graph; on the other hand, $R^-(L)$ contains those rules about atoms in L that are *out of the loop*.

Example 1 As a simple example, consider P below:

$$a \leftarrow b.\ b \leftarrow a.\ a \leftarrow \text{not } c.$$
$$c \leftarrow d.\ d \leftarrow c.\ c \leftarrow \text{not } a.$$

There are two loops in this program: $L_1 = \{a, b\}$ and $L_2 = \{c, d\}$. For these two loops, we have:

$$R^+(L_1) = \{a \leftarrow b.\ b \leftarrow a\}, R^-(L_1) = \{a \leftarrow \text{not } c\}$$
$$R^+(L_2) = \{c \leftarrow d.\ d \leftarrow c\}, R^-(L_2) = \{c \leftarrow \text{not } a\}$$

∎

While L_1 and L_2 above are disjoint, this is not always the case in general. However, if two loops have a common atom, then their union is also a loop.

For any given logic program P and any loop L in P, one can observe that $\emptyset$ is the only answer set of $R^+(L)$. Therefore an atom in the loop cannot be in any answer set unless it is derived using some other rules, i.e. those from R^-. This motivates our definition of *loop formulas*.

Definition 2 *Let P be a logic program, and L a loop in it. Suppose that we enumerate the rules in $R^-(L)$ as follows:*

$$p_1 \leftarrow G_{11}, \cdots, p_1 \leftarrow G_{1k_1},$$
$$\vdots$$
$$p_n \leftarrow G_{n1}, \cdots, p_n \leftarrow G_{nk_n},$$

then the (loop) formula associated *with L (under P) is the following implication:*

$$\neg [G_{11} \vee \cdots G_{1k_1} \vee \cdots \vee G_{n1} \vee \cdots \vee G_{nk_n}] \supset \bigwedge_{p \in L} \neg p. \quad (3)$$

Example 2 Consider again the program and loops in Example 1 above. The loop formula for L_1 is $c \supset (\neg a \wedge \neg b)$, and the one for L_2 is $a \supset (\neg c \wedge \neg d)$. Notice that the completion of P, $Comp(P)$, is:

$$a \equiv \neg c \vee b, \quad b \equiv a,$$
$$c \equiv \neg a \vee d, \quad d \equiv c,$$

which has three models: $\{a, b\}$, $\{c, d\}$, and $\{a, b, c, d\}$. However if we add the above two loop formulas to $Comp(P)$, it will eliminate the last model, and the remaining two are exactly the stable models of P. The following theorem shows that this is always the case. ∎

Theorem 1 *Let P be a logic program, $Comp(P)$ its completion, and LF the set of loop formulas associated with the loops of P. We have that for any set of atoms, it is an answer set of P iff it is a model of $Comp(P) \cup LF$.*

Computing loops

By Theorem 1, a straightforward approach of using SAT solvers to compute the answer sets of a logic program is to first compute all loop formulas, add them to its completion, and call a SAT solver. Unfortunately this may not be practical as in general there are exponential number of loops in a logic program. It seems more practical to add loop formulas one by one, selectively:

Procedure 1

1. Let T be $Comp(P)$.

2. Find a model M of T. If there is no such model, then terminate with failure.

3. If M is an answer set, then exit with it (go back to step 2 when more than one answer sets are needed).

4. If M is not an answer set, then find a loop L such that its loop formula Φ_L is not satisfied by M.

5. Let T be $T \cup \{\Phi_L\}$ and go back to step 2.

By Theorem 1, this procedure is sound and complete, provided a sound and complete SAT solver is used. The key question is step 4: given an M that satisfies $Comp(P)$ but is not an answer set of P, how can we find a loop whose loop formula is not satisfied by M? As it turns out, this can be done efficiently. The key lies in the following set:

$$M^- = M - Cons(P_M).$$

Here P_M is the Gelfond-Lifschitz reduct of the set of rules in P on M, and $Cons(P_M)$ is the set of atoms that can be derived from P_M. Notice that M is a stable model of the set of rules in P iff $M^- = \emptyset$.

Definition 3 *Let P be a program, and G_P its dependency graph. Let M be a model of $Comp(P)$. We say that a loop L of P is a maximal loop under M if L is a strongly connected component of the subgraph of G_P induced by M^-.*

A *maximal loop L under M is called a* terminating *one if there does not exist another maximal loop L_1 under M such that for some $p \in L$ and $q \in L_1$, there is a path from p to q in the subgraph of G_P induced by M^-.*

Notice that the set of strongly connected components of a graph can be returned in $O(n + m)$, where n is the number of vertices and m the number of arcs of the graph.

Theorem 2 *If M is a model of $Comp(P)$ but not an answer set of P, then there must be a terminating loop of P under M. Furthermore, M does not satisfy the loop formula of any of the terminating loops of P under M.*

ASSAT(X)

Based on Theorems 1 and 2, we have implemented a system called ASSAT along the line of Procedure 1:

ASSAT(X) – X a SAT solver

1. Instantiate a given program using lparse, the grounding system of smodels.

2. Compute the completion of the resulting program and convert it to clauses.[1]

3. **Repeat**

   (a) Find a model M of the clauses using X.

   (b) If no such M exist, then exit with failure.

   (c) Compute $M^- = M - Cons(M)$.

   (d) If $M^- = \emptyset$, then return with M for in this case it is an answer set.

   (e) Compute all maximal loops under M.

   (f) For each of these loops, compute its loop formula, convert it to clauses, and add them to the clausal set.

Notice that in the procedure above, when M is not an answer set, we will add the loop formula of every maximal loop under M to the current clausal set, instead of adding just the loop formula of one of the terminating loops if we want to follow Procedure 1 strictly using Theorem 2. The procedure above has the advantage of not having to check whether a loop is terminating. This is a feasible strategy as we have found from our experiments that there are not many such maximal loops.

Some experimental results

We experimented on a variety of benchmark domains. We report three here. They are graph coloring, the blocks world planning, and HC domains. For these domains, we

---

[1] When converting a program's completion, as well as loop formulas, to clauses, $O(r)$ number of extra variables may have to be used, where r is the number of rules. This may seem to compromise our claim earlier that our translation does not use any extra variables. But this is just a peculiarity of doing SAT using clauses. In principle, SAT does not have to be done on clauses. Practically speaking, this could be a potential problem as virtually all current SAT solvers take clauses as their input. So far, we do not find this to be a problem, though. For instance, for graph coloring and HC problems, no extra variables are needed. Notice that the approach in (Ben-Eliyahu & Dechter 1996) also needs a program's completion as the base case.

used Niemelä's (1999) logic program encodings that can be downloaded from smodels' web site.[2] Among the three domains, only HC requires adding loop formulas to program completions. The graph coloring programs are always loop-free, and while the logic programs for the blocks world planning problems have loops, Babovich *et al.* (2000) showed that all models of the programs' completions are answer sets. For graph coloring and blocks world planning, our results confirm the finding of (Huang *et al.* 2002), but we did it with many more and much larger problems.

The systems tested are as follows: For specialized answer set generators: smodels version 2.25[3] and dlv (Jun 11, 2001 version); for ASSAT, we tried the following SAT solvers: Chaff2 (Mar 23, 2001 version) (Moskewicz *et al.* 2001), walksat 3.7 (Selman and Kautz), relsat 2.0 (Bayardo), satz 2.13 (Li), and sato (Zhang).[4] For smodels and ASSAT, we use lparse 0.99.43, the grounding system of smodels, to ground a logic program (dlv has its own built-in grounding routine). All experiments were done on Sun Ultra 5 machines with 256M memory running Solaris. The reported times are in CPU seconds as reported by Unix "time" command, and include, for smodels the time for grounding, and for ASSAT the time for grounding, computing program completions, and checking that the returned assignment is indeed an answer set. We use 2 hours as the cut off limit. So in the following tables, if an entry is marked by "—", it means that the system in question did not return after it had used up 2 hours of the CPU time. Also in the following tables, if a system is not included, that means it is not competitive on the problems.

We want to emphasize that the experiments here were done using Niemelä's early encodings for these benchmark domains. They are not the optimal ones for smodels, and certainly not for dlv. As one of the referees pointed out, dlv is specialized in disjunctive logic programs. There are encodings of graph coloring and HC problems in disjunctive logic programs for which dlv will run faster. The newest version of smodels also has some special constructs such as mGn that can be used to encode the problems in a more efficient way. One can also certainly think of some encodings that are better suited for ASSAT. It is an interesting future work to see how all these systems fare with each other with each using its own "best possible" encodings.

The blocks world planning domain

We tested the systems on 16 large problems, ranging from the ones with 15 blocks and 8 steps to ones with 32 blocks and 18 steps. For these problems, dlv did badly, could not even solve the smallest one with 15 blocks and 8 steps within our time limit. Among the SAT solvers used with ASSAT, Chaff2 performed the best, followed by satz. Table 1 contains some run time data on five representative problems.

---

[2] http://www.tcs.hut.fi/Software/smodels/

[3] The current version of smodels is 2.26 which is slightly slower than 2.25 on the problems that we have tested.

[4] All these solvers can be found on the SATLIB web page http://www.satlib.org/solvers.html, except for Chaff2, which can be found at www.ee.princeton.edu/ chaff/index.php.

	steps	atoms	Smodels	ASSAT (Chaff2)	ASSAT (SATZ)
bw.19	9	12202	16.07	14.78	17.36
	10	13422	47.50	19.76	24.34
bw.21	10	16216	23.48	21.64	26.27
	11	17690	71.33	29.38	40.41
bw.23	11	21026	35.34	30.66	37.36
	12	22778	247.51	41.4	54.1
bw.25	13	28758	61.2	47.38	61.45
	14	30812	—	65.75	100.97
bw.32	17	59402	187.54	132.06	—
	18	62702	—	191.46	—

Table 1: The Blocks World Planning Domain. bw.n means that this problem has n blocks. In particular, bw.19 is the same as bw-large.e on smodels' web site.

Graph	3-Coloring			4-Coloring		
		Smodels	ASSAT (Chaff2)		Smodels	ASSAT (Chaff2)
p6e36	n	22.99	17.38	y	4714.28	309.41
p10e10	y	2929.92	33.79	y	7650.54	70.52
p10e11	y	2715.76	32.22	y	—	66.88
p10e15	y	2048.82	27.34	y	—	62.80
p10e20	y	1348.53	120.27	y	—	56.54
p10e21	n	19.69	16.49	n	29.50	24.20
p10e25	?	—	—	y	—	51.28
p10e30	?	—	—	y	—	44.74

Table 2: Graph Coloring. pnem – a graph with $n*1000$ nodes and $m*1000$ edges (p6e36 is the same as p6000 at smodels' web site.)

ASSAT(Chaff2) clearly was the winner here. We notice that for all problems that we had tested, if an optimal plan requires n steps, then smodels did very well in verifying that there does not exist a plan with $n-1$ steps. But it could not return an optimal plan after bw.24. ASSAT(satz) also did very well for problems with ≤ 25 blocks. After that, it suddenly degraded, perhaps because the problem sizes were too big for it to handle now.

The graph coloring domain

We tested both 3-coloring and 4-coloring problems. We tested the systems on over 50 randomly generated large graphs. Table 2 is the results for some of them. Again ASSAT(Chaff2) was the clear winner. Smodels was more competitive on 3-coloring problems. But on 4-coloring ones, it could not return within our time limit after p10e10, except for p10e21 which is not colorable. In general, we have observed that smodels and ASSAT(Chaff2) had similar performance on graphs which are not colorable.

The Hamiltonian Circuit (HC) domain

This is the only benchmark domain that we could find which requires adding loop formulas to program completions. We thus did some extensive testing on it. We test three classes of problems: randomly generated graphs, hand-coded hard graphs, and complete graphs. All these are directed graphs

	No.	Ave1	SD1	Ave2	SD2	Ave3	SD3
Smodels	33	1973	3201				
DLV	24	3623	3521				
Chaff2	43	481	1526	21	15	21	16
WC	43	330	1498	20	8	20	9

Table 3: HC on random graphs. Legends: No. – the number of problems solved; Ave1 – the average run time, with an unsolved instance counts as 2 hours; Ave2 – the average number of calls to a SAT solver; Ave3 – the average number of loop formulas added; SDi – the standard deviation on Ave*i*.

Graph	HC?	SM	ASSAT1	SAT	LF	ASSAT2
2xp30	n	1	1	2	2	2
2xp30.1	y	1	52	51	125	821
2xp30.2	y	—	51	66	120	1185
2xp30.3	y	—	51	66	120	1669
2xp30.4	n	—	5160	28	42	4047
4xp20	n	1	1	2	4	162
4xp20.1	n	—	9	2	4	9
4xp20.2	y	1	7	31	74	558
4xp20.3	n	1	15	15	19	20

Table 4: Hand-coded graphs. Legends: SM – smodels; ASSAT1 – ASSAT(Chaff2); ASSAT2 – ASSAT(WC); 2xp30 – 2 copies of p30; 2xp30.i – 2xp30 + two new arcs; 4xp20 – 4 copies of p20; 4xp20.i – 4xp40 + 3-4 new arcs; SAT – number of calls to SAT; LF – number of loop formulas added.

that do not have any arc that goes from a vertex to itself, as is usually assumed in work on HC. In this domain, we found walksat performed surprisingly well, even better than Chaff2. However, one problem with walksat is that it is incomplete. To address this, we invent WC (Walksat+Chaff2): given a SAT instance, try walksat on it first, if it does not return an assignment, then try Chaff2 on it. Another problem with walksat is that it is a randomized system, so its performance may vary from run to run. We address this problem by running it 10 times, and takes the average. Thus in all the tables below, the data on ASSAT(WC) are the averages over 10 runs.

Table 3 contains some statistics on 43 randomly generated Hamiltonian graphs (those with HCs). The numbers of nodes in these graphs range from 50 to 70 and numbers of arcs from 238 to 580. Smodels could not solve 12 of them (did not return after 2 hours of CPU time), which amounts to a 28% failure rate, dlv could not solve 19 of them (44%). It is interesting to notice that compared with the other two domains, dlv fared better here. While overall it was still not as good as smodels, there were 3 problems which smodels could not solve but dlv could in a few seconds. ASSAT with both Chaff2 and WC solved all of the problems. So far we had not run into any randomly generated graph which is Hamiltonian, either dlv or smodels could solve it, but ASSAT could not. It is interesting to notice that Ave2 and Ave3 are very close, so are SD2 and SD3. Indeed, we have found that for randomly generated graphs, if M is not an answer set, then often M^- is a loop by itself, i.e. M^- is the only maximal loop on M. Also the cost of ASSAT(X) is directly proportional to the number of calls made to X. One reason that ASSAT(WC) out-performed ASSAT(Chaff2) is that walksat (WC is really walksat here because it always returned a model for this group of graphs) is a bit luckier than Chaff2 in returning the "right" models. Also notice that on average, each call to Chaff2 took 23 seconds, and WC 16 seconds.

We have found that it was difficult to come up with randomly generated non-Hamiltonian graphs which are hard. Most of them were really easy for all the systems and occurred when the number of arcs is relatively small compared to that of vertices. For the systems that we have tested at least, the harder instances seem to be those graphs with more arcs, thus are likely to be Hamiltonian. We did stumble on two graphs which are not Hamiltonian, but none of

the systems that we tested (smodels, dlv, ASSAT(X)) could solve them. They are not Hamiltonian for the obvious reason that some of the vertices in them do not have an arc going out. They both have 60 vertices, and one has 348 arcs and the other 358. The completions of the logic programs corresponding to them, when converted to clauses, have only about 720 variables and 4500 clauses. But none of the SAT solvers that we tested could tell us whether they are satisfiable.

More interesting are some hand-coded hard problems. One strategy is to take the union of several copies of a small graph, and then add some arcs that connect these components. To experiment with this strategy, we took as bases p30 (a graph with 30 vertices) and p20 (a graph with 20 vertices), both downloaded from smodels' web site. The results are shown in Table 4. Notice that SAT No. and LF No. are not given for ASSAT(WC) in the table for lack of space. They are in general larger than the corresponding ones for ASSAT(Chaff2) as this time walksat was not as lucky as Chaff2. It is clear that ASSAT(Chaff2) was very consistent. It is interesting to notice that some of these graphs are also very hard for specialized heuristic search algorithm. For instance, for graph 2xp30.4, the HC algorithm (no.559, written in Fortran) in ACM Collection of Algorithms did not return after running for more than 60 hours.

Of special interest for ASSAT are complete graphs because for these graphs, Niemelä's logic programs for HC have exponential number of loops. So one would expect that these graphs, while trivial for heuristic search algorithms, could be hard for ASSAT. Our experiments confirmed this. But interestingly, these graphs are also very hard for smodels and dlv. This seems to suggest that while smodels and dlv do not explicitly compute loops, they also have to deal with them implicitly in their search algorithms. The results are given in Table 5. Again, the performance of ASSAT(WC) (ASSAT2 in the table) was sampled over 10 runs, and because of the randomized nature of walksat, it sometime ran faster on larger problems, as happened on $c90$, the complete graph with 90 nodes.

Complete graphs are difficult using Niemelä's encoding also because of the sheer sizes of the programs they produce. For instance, after grounding, the complete graph with 50

Graph	SM	ASSAT1	SAT	LF	ASSAT2	SAT	LF
c40	106	230	59	58	49	12	11
c50	417	857	97	96	435	41	40
c60	1046	72	4	3	1139	60	59
c70	2508	633	28	27	640	28	27
c80	4978	5833	122	121	6157	106	105
c90	—	—			4443	60	59

Table 5: HC on complete graphs. Legends: cn – a complete graph with n vertices; err – exit abnormally; the rest are the same as in Table 4;

nodes (c50) produces a program with about 5000 atoms and 240K rules, and needs 4.5M to store it in a file. For c60, the number of atoms is about 7K and rules about 420K.

Finally, we also compared ASSAT with an implementation[5] of Ben-Eliyahu and Dechter's translation (1996). As we mentioned earlier, theirs needs to use extra variables, and these extra variables seemed to exert a heavy toll on current SAT solvers. For complete graphs, it could only handle those up to 30 vertices using Chaff2. It caused Chaff2 to run into bus error after running for over 2 hours on graph 2xp30. Perhaps more importantly, while walksat was very effective on HC problems using our translation, it was totally ineffective with theirs as it failed to find an HC on even some of the simplest graphs such as p20. We speculate that the reason could be that the extra variables somehow confuse walksat and make its local hill-climbing strategy ineffective.

Conclusions

We have proposed a new translation from logic programs to propositional theories. Compared with the one in (Ben-Eliyahu & Dechter 1996), ours has the advantage that it does not use any extra variables. We believe it is also more intuitive and simpler, thus easier to understand. However, in the worst case, it requires computing exponential number of loop formulas. To address this problem, we have proposed an approach that adds loop formulas a few at a time, selectively. We have implemented a system called ASSAT based on this approach, and run it on many problems in some benchmark domains using various SAT solvers. While we were satisfied that so far our experimental results show a clear edge of ASSAT over smodels and dlv, we want to emphasize that the real advantage that we can see of ASSAT over specialized answer set generators lies in its ability to make use of the best and a variety of SAT solvers as they become available. For instance, with Chaff, we were able to run much larger problems than using others like sato, and while Chaff has been consistently good on all of the benchmark problems that we have tested, other SAT solvers, like the randomized incomplete SAT solver walksat, performed surprisingly good on HC problems.

We also want to emphasize that by no means do we take this work to imply that specialized stable model generators such as smodels are not needed anymore. For one thing, so far we have only considered the problem of finding one answer set of a logic program. It is not clear what would hap-

pen if we want to look for all the answer sets. Besides, there are special constructs such as mGn (at least m and at most n literals in G are true) in smodels one can use to write short and efficient logic programs. It is not immediately clear how these can be encoded efficiently in SAT. More importantly, we hope this work, especially our new translation of logic programs to propositional logic, will lead to a cross fertilization between SAT solvers and specialized answer set solvers that will benefit both areas.

Finally, ASSAT can be found at www.cs.ust.hk/faculty/flin/assat.html

Acknowledgments

We thank Jia-Huai You and Jicheng Zhao for many useful discussions about the topics and their comments on earlier versions of this paper. We especially thank Jicheng for suggesting to define loops as sets of atoms rather than sets of rules as we initially did, and for implementing a version of Ben-Eliyahu and Dechter's algorithm. We also thank Jia-Huai for making us aware of Chaff. Without it, we would not be able to make many claims that we are making in the paper. He also suggested us to try complete graphs for HC.

This work was supported in part by the Research Grants Council of Hong Kong under Competitive Earmarked Research Grants HKUST6145/98E and HKUST6061/00E.

References

Babovich, Y.; Erdem, E.; and Lifschitz, V. 2000. Fages' theorem and answer set programming. In *Proc. of NMR-2000*.

Ben-Eliyahu, R., and Dechter, R. 1996. Propositional semantics for disjunctive logic programs. *Annals of Mathematics and Artificial Intelligence* 12:53–87.

Clark, K. L. 1978. Negation as failure. In Gallaire, H., and Minker, J., eds., *Logics and Databases*. New York: Plenum Press. 293–322.

Gelfond, M., and Lifschitz, V. 1988. The stable model semantics for logic programming. In *Proc. Fifth International Conference and Symposium on Logic Programming*, 1070–1080.

Huang, G.-S.; Jia, X.; Liau, C.-J.; and You, J.-H. 2002. Two-literal logic programs and satisfiability representation of stable models: A comparison. In *Submitted*.

Leone et al., N. 2001. DLV: a disjunctive datalog system, release 2001-6-11. At http://www.dbai.tuwien.ac.at/proj/dlv/.

Moskewicz, M.; Madigan, C.; Zhao, Y.; Zhang, L.; and Malik, S. 2001. Chaff: engineering an efficient SAT solver. In *Proc. 39th Design Automation Conference*. Las Vegas, June 2001.

Niemelä, I. 1999. Logic programs with stable model semantics as a constraint programming paradigm. *Ann. Math. and AI* 25(3-4):241–273.

Simons, P. 2000. Smodels: a system for computing the stable models of logic programs, version 2.25. At http://www.tcs.hut.fi/Software/smodels/.

You, J.; Cartwright, R.; and Li, M. 1996. Iterative belief revision in extended logic programs. *Theoretical Computer Science* 170.

[5]Done by Jicheng Zhao.

Learning

State Abstraction for Programmable Reinforcement Learning Agents

David Andre and Stuart J. Russell
Computer Science Division, UC Berkeley, CA 94720
{dandre,russell}@cs.berkeley.edu

Abstract

Safe state abstraction in reinforcement learning allows an agent to ignore aspects of its current state that are irrelevant to its current decision, and therefore speeds up dynamic programming and learning. This paper explores safe state abstraction in hierarchical reinforcement learning, where learned behaviors must conform to a given partial, hierarchical program. Unlike previous approaches to this problem, our methods yield significant state abstraction while maintaining *hierarchical optimality*, i.e., optimality among all policies consistent with the partial program. We show how to achieve this for a partial programming language that is essentially Lisp augmented with nondeterministic constructs. We demonstrate our methods on two variants of Dietterich's taxi domain, showing how state abstraction and hierarchical optimality result in faster learning of better policies and enable the transfer of learned skills from one problem to another.

Introduction

The ability to make decisions based on only *relevant* features is a critical aspect of intelligence. For example, if one is driving a taxi from A to B, decisions about which street to take should not depend on the current price of tea in China; when changing lanes, the traffic conditions matter but not the name of the street; and so on. *State abstraction* is the process of eliminating features to reduce the effective state space; such reductions can speed up dynamic programming and reinforcement learning (RL) algorithms considerably. Without state abstraction, every trip from A to B is a new trip; every lane change is a new task to be learned from scratch.

An abstraction is called *safe* if optimal solutions in the abstract space are also optimal in the original space. Safe abstractions were introduced by Amarel (1968) for the Missionaries and Cannibals problem. In our example, the taxi driver can safely omit the price of tea in China from the state space for navigating from A to B. More formally, the value of every state (or of every state-action pair) is independent of the price of tea, so the price of tea is irrelevant in selecting optimal actions. Boutilier *et al.* (1995) developed a general method for deriving such irrelevance assertions from the formal specification of a decision problem.

It has been noted (Dietterich 2000) that a variable can be irrelevant to the optimal decision in a state *even if it affects the value of that state*. For example, suppose that the taxi is driving from A to B to pick up a passenger whose destination is C. Now, C is part of the state, but is not relevant to navigation decisions between A and B. This is because the value (sum of future rewards or costs) of each state between A and B can be *decomposed* into a part dealing with the cost of getting to B and a part dealing with the cost from B to C. The latter part is unaffected by the choice of A; the former part is unaffected by the choice of C.

This idea—that a variable can be irrelevant to *part* of the value of a state—is closely connected to the area of *hierarchical reinforcement learning*, in which learned behaviors must conform to a given partial, hierarchical program. The connection arises because the partial program naturally divides state sequences into parts. For example, the task described above may be achieved by executing two subroutine calls, one to drive from A to B and one to deliver the passenger from B to C. The partial programmer may state (or a Boutilier-style algorithm may derive) the fact that the navigation choices in the first subroutine call are independent of the passenger's final destination. More generally, the notion of *modularity* for behavioral subroutines is precisely the requirement that decisions internal to the subroutine be independent of all external variables other than those passed as arguments to the subroutine.

Several different partial programming languages have been proposed, with varying degrees of expressive power. Expressiveness is important for two reasons: first, an expressive language makes it possible to state complex partial specifications concisely; second, it enables irrelevance assertions to be made at a high level of abstraction rather than repeated across many instances of what is conceptually the same subroutine. The first contribution of this paper is an agent programming language, ALisp, that is essentially Lisp augmented with nondeterministic constructs; the language subsumes MAXQ (Dietterich 2000), options (Precup & Sutton 1998), and the PHAM language (Andre & Russell 2001).

Given a partial program, a hierarchical RL algorithm finds a policy that is consistent with the program. The policy may be *hierarchically optimal*—i.e., optimal among all policies consistent with the program; or it may be *recursively optimal*, i.e., the policy within each subroutine is optimized ig-

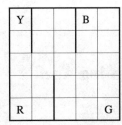

```
(defun root () (if (not (have-pass)) (get)) (put))
(defun get () (choice get-choice
                      (action 'load)
                      (call navigate (pickup))))
(defun put () (choice put-choice
                      (action 'unload)
                      (call navigate (dest))))
(defun navigate(t)
        (loop until (at t) do
              (choice nav (action 'N)
                          (action 'E)
                          (action 'S)
                          (action 'W))))
```

Figure 1: The taxi world. It is a 5x5 world with 4 special cells (RGBY) where passengers are loaded and unloaded. There are 4 features, x,y,pickup,dest. In each episode, the taxi starts in a randomly chosen square, and there is a passenger at a random special cell with a random destination. The taxi must travel to, pick up, and deliver the passenger, using the commands N,S,E,W,load,unload. The taxi receives a reward of -1 for every action, +20 for successfully delivering the passenger, -10 for attempting to load or unload the passenger at incorrect locations. The discount factor is 1.0. The partial program shown is an ALisp program expressing the same constraints as Dietterich's taxi MAXQ program. It breaks the problem down into the tasks of getting and putting the passenger, and further isolates navigation.

noring the calling context. Recursively optimal policies may be worse than hierarchically optimal policies if the context is relevant. Dietterich 2000 shows how a two-part decomposition of the value function allows state abstractions that are safe with respect to recursive optimality, and argues that "State abstractions [of this kind] cannot be employed without losing hierarchical optimality." The second, and more important, contribution of our paper is a three-part decomposition of the value function allowing state abstractions that are safe with respect to hierarchical optimality.

The remainder of the paper begins with background material on Markov decision processes and hierarchical RL, and a brief description of the ALisp language. Then we present the three-part value function decomposition and associated Bellman equations. We explain how ALisp programs are annotated with (ir)relevance assertions, and describe a model-free hierarchical RL algorithm for annotated ALisp programs that is guaranteed to converge to hierarchically optimal solutions[1]. Finally, we describe experimental results for this algorithm using two domains: Dietterich's original taxi domain and a variant of it that illustrates the differences between hierarchical and recursive optimality.

Background

Our framework for MDPs is standard (Kaelbling, Littman, & Moore 1996). An MDP is a 4-tuple, $(\mathcal{S}, \mathcal{A}, \mathcal{T}, \mathcal{R})$, where $\mathcal{S}$ is a set of states, $\mathcal{A}$ a set of actions, $\mathcal{T}$ a probabilistic transition function mapping $\mathcal{S} \times \mathcal{A} \times \mathcal{S} \to [0, 1]$, and $\mathcal{R}$ a reward function mapping $\mathcal{S} \times \mathcal{A} \times \mathcal{S}$ to the reals. We focus on infinite-horizon MDPs with a discount factor β. A solution to an MDP is an optimal policy π^* mapping from $\mathcal{S} \to \mathcal{A}$ and achieves the maximum expected discounted reward. An SMDP (semi-MDP) allows for actions that take more than one time step. $\mathcal{T}$ is now a mapping from $\mathcal{S} \times \mathbf{N} \times \mathcal{S} \times \mathcal{A} \to [0, 1]$, where $\mathbf{N}$ is the natural numbers; i.e., it specifies a distribution over both outcome states and action durations. $\mathcal{R}$ then maps from $\mathcal{S} \times \mathbf{N} \times \mathcal{S} \times \mathcal{A}$ to the reals. The expected discounted reward for taking action a in state s and then following policy π is known as the Q value, and is defined as

---

[1]Proofs of all theorems are omitted and can be found in an accompanying technical report (Andre & Russell 2002).

$Q^\pi(s, a) = E[r_0 + \beta r_1 + \beta^2 r_2 + ...]$. Q values are related to one another through the Bellman equations (Bellman 1957):

$$Q^\pi(s, a) = \sum_{s', N} \mathcal{T}(s', N, s, a)[\mathcal{R}(s', N, s, a) + \beta^N Q^\pi(s', \pi(s'))].$$

Note that $\pi \in \pi^*$ iff $\forall_s \pi(s) \in \arg\max_a Q^\pi(s, a)$.

In most languages for partial reinforcement learning programs, the programmer specifies a program containing choice points. A *choice point* is a place in the program where the learning algorithm must choose among a set of provided options (which may be primitives or subroutines). Formally, the program can be viewed as a finite state machine with state space Θ (consisting of the stack, heap, and program pointer). Let us define a joint state space Y for a program $\mathcal{H}$ as the cross product of Θ and the states, S, in an MDP $\mathcal{M}$. Let us also define Ω as the set of *choice states*, that is, Ω is the subset of Y where the machine state is at a choice point. With most hierarchical languages for reinforcement learning, one can then construct a joint SMDP $\mathcal{H} \circ \mathcal{M}$ where $\mathcal{H} \circ \mathcal{M}$ has state space Ω and the actions at each state in Ω are the choices specified by the partial program $\mathcal{H}$. For several simple RL-specific languages, it has been shown that policies optimal under $\mathcal{H} \circ \mathcal{M}$ correspond to the best policies achievable in $\mathcal{M}$ given the constraints expressed by $\mathcal{H}$ (Andre & Russell 2001; Parr & Russell 1998).

The ALisp language

The ALisp programming language consists of the Lisp language augmented with three special macros:

- (choice *<label> <form0> <form1>* ...) takes 2 or more arguments, where *<formN>* is a Lisp S-expression. The agent learns which form to execute.
- (call *<subroutine> <arg0> <arg1>*) calls a subroutine with its arguments and alerts the learning mechanism that a subroutine has been called.
- (action *<action-name>*) executes a "primitive" action in the MDP.

An ALisp program consists of an arbitrary Lisp program that is allowed to use these macros and obeys the constraint that

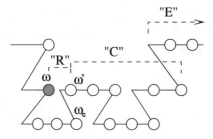

Figure 2: Decomposing the value function for the shaded state, ω. Each circle is a choice state of the SMDP visited by the agent, where the vertical axis represents depth in the hierarchy. The trajectory is broken into 3 parts: the reward "R" for executing the macro action at ω, the completion value "C", for finishing the subroutine, and "E", the external value.

all subroutines that include the choice macro (either directly, or indirectly, through nested subroutine calls) are called with the `call` macro. An example ALisp program is shown in Figure 1 for Dietterich's Taxi world (Dietterich 2000). It can be shown that, under appropriate restrictions (such as that the number of machine states Y stays bounded in every run of the environment), that optimal policies for the joint SMDP $\mathcal{H} \circ \mathcal{M}$ for an ALisp program $\mathcal{H}$ are optimal for the MDP $\mathcal{M}$ among those policies allowed by $\mathcal{H}$ (Andre & Russell 2002).

Value Function Decomposition

A value function decomposition splits the value of a state/action pair into multiple additive components. Modularity in the hierarchical structure of a program allows us to do this decomposition along subroutine boundaries. Consider, for example, Figure 2. The three parts of the decomposition correspond to executing the current action (which might itself be a subroutine), completing the rest of the current subroutine, and all actions outside the current subroutine. More formally, we can write the Q-value for executing action a in $\omega \in \Omega$ as follows:

$$
\begin{aligned}
Q^{\pi}(\omega, a) &= E\left[\sum_{t=0}^{\infty} \beta^t r_t\right] \\
&= E\left[\sum_{t=0}^{N_1-1} \beta^t r_t\right] + E\left[\sum_{t=N_1}^{N_2-1} \beta^t r_t\right] + E\left[\sum_{t=N_2}^{\infty} \beta^t r_t\right] \\
&= \quad Q_r^{\pi}(\omega, a) \quad + \quad Q_c^{\pi}(\omega, a) \quad + \quad Q_e^{\pi}(\omega, a)
\end{aligned}
$$

where N_1 is the number of primitive steps to finish action a, N_2 is the number of primitive steps to finish the current subroutine, and the expectation is over trajectories starting in ω with action a and following π. N_1, N_2, and the rewards, r_t, are defined by the trajectory. Q_r thus expresses the expected discounted reward for doing the current action ("R" from Figure 2), Q_c for completing rest of the current subroutine ("C"), and Q_e for all the reward external to the current subroutine ("E").

It is important to see how this three-part decomposition allows greater state abstraction. Consider the taxi domain,

x	y	pickup	dest	Q	Q_r	Q_c	Q_e
3	3	R	G	0.23	-7.5	-1.0	8.74
3	3	R	B	1.13	-7.5	-1.0	9.63
3	2	R	G	1.29	-6.45	-1.0	8.74

Table 1: Table of Q values and decomposed Q values for 3 states and action $a =$ (nav pickup), where the machine state is equal to {get-choice}. The first four columns specify the environment state. Note that although none of the Q values listed are identical, Q_c is the same for all three cases, and Q_e is the same for 2 out of 3, and Q_r is the same for 2 out of 3.

where there are many opportunities for state abstraction (as pointed out by Dietterich (2000) for his two-part decomposition). While completing the get subroutine, the passenger's destination is not relevant to decisions about getting to the passenger's location. Similarly, when navigating, only the current x/y location and the target location are important – whether the taxi is carrying a passenger is not relevant. Taking advantage of these intuitively appealing abstractions requires a value function decomposition, as Table 1 shows.

Before presenting the Bellman equations for the decomposed value function, we must first define transition probability measures that take the program's hierarchy into account. First, we have the SMDP transition probability $p(\omega', N | \omega, a)$, which is the probability of an SMDP transition to ω' taking N steps given that action a is taken in ω. Next, let S be a set of states, and let $F_S^{\pi}(\omega', N | \omega, a)$ be the probability that ω' is the first element of S reached and that this occurs in N primitive steps, given that a is taken in ω and π is followed thereafter. Two such distributions are useful, $F_{SS(\omega)}^{\pi}$ and $F_{EX(\omega)}^{\pi}$, where $SS(\omega)$ are those states in the same subroutine as ω and $EX(\omega)$ are those states that are exit points for the subroutine containing ω. We can now write the Bellman equations using our decomposed value function, as shown in Equations 1, 2, and 3 in Figure 3, where $o(\omega)$ returns the next choice state at the parent level of the hierarchy, $i_a(\omega)$ returns the first choice state at the child level, given action a [2], and A_p is the set of actions that are not calls to subroutines. With some algebra, we can then prove the following results.

Theorem 1 *If Q_r^*, Q_c^*, and Q_e^* are solutions to Equations 1, 2, and 3 for π^*, then $Q^* = Q_r^* + Q_c^* + Q_e^*$ is a solution to the standard Bellman equation.*

Theorem 2 *Decomposed value iteration and policy iteration algorithms (Andre & Russell 2002) derived from Equations 1, 2, and 3 converge to Q_r^*, Q_c^*, Q_e^*, and π^*.*

Extending policy iteration and value iteration to work with these decomposed equations is straightforward, but it does require that the full model is known – including $F_{SS(\omega)}^{\pi}(\omega', N | \omega, a)$ and $F_{EX(\omega)}^{\pi}(\omega', N | \omega, a)$, which can be found through dynamic programming. After explaining how

---

[2] We make a trivial assumption that calls to subroutines are surrounded by choice points with no intervening primitive actions at the calling level. $i_a(\omega)$ and $o(\omega)$ are thus simple deterministic functions, determined from the program structure.

$$Q_r^\pi(\omega, a) = \begin{cases} \sum_{\omega', N'} p(\omega', N | \omega, a) r(\omega', N, \omega, a) & \text{if } a \in A_p \\ Q_r^\pi(i_a(\omega), \pi(i_a(\omega))) + Q_c^\pi(i_a(\omega), \pi(i_a(\omega))) & \text{otherwise.} \end{cases} \tag{1}$$

$$Q_c^\pi(\omega, a) = \sum_{(\omega', N)} F_{SS(\omega)}^\pi(\omega', N | \omega, a) \beta^N [Q_r^\pi(\omega', \pi(\omega')) + Q_c^\pi(\omega', \pi(\omega'))] \tag{2}$$

$$Q_e^\pi(\omega, a) = \sum_{(\omega', N)} F_{EX(\omega)}^\pi(\omega', N | \omega, a) \beta^N [Q^\pi(o(\omega'), \pi(o(\omega')))] \tag{3}$$

$$\forall_{a \in A_p} Q_r^*(z_p(\omega, a), a) = \sum_{(\omega', N)} p(\omega', N | \omega, a) r(\omega', N, \omega, a) \tag{4}$$

$$\forall_{a \notin A_p} Q_r^*(z_r(\omega, a), a) = Q_r^*(z_r(\omega'), a') + Q_c^*(z_c(\omega'), a'), \text{ where } \omega' = i_a(\omega) \text{ and } a' = \arg\max_b Q^*(\omega', b) \tag{5}$$

$$\forall_a Q_c^*(z_c(\omega, a), a) = \sum_{(\omega', N)} F_{SS(\omega)}^*(\omega', N | \omega, a) \beta^N [Q_r^*(z_r(\omega', a), a') + Q_c^*(z_c(\omega', a), a')] \text{ where } a' = \arg\max_b Q^*(\omega', b) \tag{6}$$

$$\forall_a Q_e^*(z_e(\omega, a), a) = \sum_{(\omega', N)} F_{EX(z_e(\omega,a))}^*(\omega', N | z_e(\omega, a), a) \beta^N [Q^*(o(\omega'), a')] \text{ where } a' = \arg\max_b Q^*(o(\omega'), b) \tag{7}$$

Figure 3: Top: Bellman equations for the three-part decomposed value function. Bottom: Bellman equations for the abstracted case.

the decomposition enables state abstraction, we will present an online learning method which avoids the problem of having to specify or determine a complex model.

State Abstraction

One method for doing learning with ALisp programs would be to flatten the subroutines out into the full joint state space of the SMDP. This has the result of creating a copy of each subroutine for every place where it is called with different parameters. For example, in the Taxi problem, the flattened program would have 8 copies (4 destinations, 2 calling contexts) of the `navigate` subroutine, each of which have to be learned separately. Because of the three-part decomposition discussed above, we can take advantage of state abstraction and avoid flattening the state space.

To do this, we require that the user specify which features matter for each of the components of the value function. The user must do this for each action at each choice point in the program. We thus annotate the language with :depends-on keywords. For example, in the `navigate` subroutine, the (action 'N) choice is changed to

```
((action 'N)
 :reward-depends-on nil
 :completion-depends-on '(x y t)
 :external-depends-on '(pickup dest))
```

Note that t is the parameter for the target location passed into `navigate`. The Q_r-value for this action is constant – it doesn't depend on any features at all (because all actions in the Taxi domain have fixed cost). The Q_c value only depends on where the taxi currently is and on the target location. The Q_e value only depends on the passenger's location (either in the Taxi or at R,G,B, or Y) and the passenger's destination. Thus, whereas a program with no state abstraction would be required to store 800 values, here, we only must store 117.

Safe state abstraction

Now that we have the programmatic machinery to define abstractions, we'd like to know when a given set of abstraction

functions is safe for a given problem. To do this, we first need a formal notation for defining abstractions. Let $z_p[\theta, a]$, $z_r[\theta, a]$, $z_c[\theta, a]$, and $z_e[\theta, a]$ be abstraction functions specifying the set of relevant machine and environment features for each choice point θ and action a for the primitive reward, non-primitive reward, completion cost, and external cost respectively. In the example above, $z_c[nav, N] = \{x, y, t\}$. Note that this function z groups states together into equivalence classes (for example, all states that agree on assignments to x, y, and t would be in an equivalence class). Let $z(\omega, a)$ be a mapping from a state-action pair to a canonical member of the equivalence class to which it belongs under the abstraction z. We must also discuss how policies interact with abstractions. We will say that a policy π and an abstraction z are consistent iff $\forall_{\omega, a} \pi(\omega) = \pi(z(\omega, a))$ and $\forall_{a, b} z(\omega, a) = z(\omega, b)$. We will denote the set of such policies as Π_z.

Now, we can begin to examine when abstractions are safe. To do this, we define several notions of equivalence.

Definition 1 (P-equivalence) z_p is P-equivalent (Primitive equivalent) iff $\forall_{\omega, a \in A_p}$, $Q_r(\omega, a) = Q_r(z_p(\omega, a), a)$.

Definition 2 (R-equivalence) z_r is R-equivalent iff $\forall_{\omega, a \notin A_p, \pi \in \Pi_{z_r}}$, $Q_r(\omega, a) = Q_r(z_r(\omega), a)$.

These two specify that states are abstracted together under z_p and z_r only if their Q_r values are equal. C-equivalence can be defined similarly.

For the E component, we can be more aggressive. The exact value of the external reward isn't what's important, rather, it's the behavior that it imposes on the subroutine. For example, in the Taxi problem, the external value after reaching the end of the `navigate` subroutine will be very different when the passenger is in the taxi and when she's not – but the optimal behavior for `navigate` is the same in both cases. Let h be a subroutine of a program $\mathcal{H}$, and let Ω_h be the set of choice states reachable while control remains in h. Then, we can define E-equivalence as follows:

Definition 3 (E-equivalence) z_e is E-equivalent iff

1. $\forall_{h \in \mathcal{H}} \forall_{\omega_1, \omega_2 \in \Omega_h} z_e[\omega_1] = z_e[\omega_2]$ and

2. $\forall_\omega \arg\max_a Q_r^*(\omega, a) + Q_c^*(\omega, a) + Q_e^*(\omega, a) = \arg\max_a Q_r^*(\omega, a) + Q_c^*(\omega, a) + Q_e^*(z_e(\omega, a), a)$.

The last condition says that states are abstracted together only if they have the same set of optimal actions in the set of optimal policies. It could also be described as "passing in enough information to determine the policy". This is the critical constraint that allows us to maintain hierarchical optimality while still performing state abstraction.

We can show that if abstraction functions satisfy these four properties, then the optimal policies when using these abstractions are the same as the optimal policies without them. To do this, we first express the abstracted Bellman equations as shown in Equations 4 - 7 in Figure 3. Now, if z_p z_r, z_c, and z_e are P-, R-,C-, and E-equivalent, respectively, then we can show that we have a safe abstraction.

Theorem 3 *If z_p is P-equivalent, z_r is R-equivalent, z_c is C-equivalent, and z_e is E-equivalent, then, if Q_r^*, Q_c^*, and Q_e^* are solutions to Equations 4 - 7, for MDP $\mathcal{M}$ and ALisp program $\mathcal{H}$, then π such that $\pi(\omega) \in \arg\max_a Q^*(\omega, a)$ is an optimal policy for $\mathcal{H} \circ \mathcal{M}$.*

Theorem 4 *Decomposed abstracted value iteration and policy iteration algorithms (Andre & Russell 2002) derived from Equations 4 - 7 converge to Q_r^*, Q_c^*, Q_e^*, and π^*.*

Proving these various forms of equivalence might be difficult for a given problem. It would be easier to create abstractions based on conditions about the model, rather than conditions on the value function. Dietterich (2000) defines four conditions for safe state abstraction under recursive optimality. For each, we can define a similar condition for hierarchical optimality and show how it implies abstractions that satisfy the equivalence conditions we've defined. These conditions are leaf abstraction (essentially the same as P-equivalence), subroutine irrelevance (features that are totally irrelevant to a subroutine), result-distribution irrelevance (features are irrelevant to the F_{ss} distribution for all policies), and termination (all actions from a state lead to an exit state, so Q_c is 0). We can encompass the last three conditions into a strong form of equivalence, defined as follows.

Definition 4 (SSR-equivalence) *An abstraction function z_c is strongly subroutine (SSR) equivalent for an ALisp program $\mathcal{H}$ iff the following conditions hold for all ω and policies π that are consistent with z_c.*

1. *Equivalent states under z_c have equivalent transition probabilities:* $\forall_{\omega', a, a', N}$
   $F_{SS}(\omega', N | \omega, a) = F_{SS}(z_c(\omega', a'), N | z_c(\omega, a), a)$ [3]

2. *Equivalent states have equivalent rewards:* $\forall_{\omega', a, a', N}$
   $r(\omega', N, \omega, a) = r(z_c(\omega', a'), N, z_c(\omega, a), a)$

3. *The variables in z_c are enough to determine the optimal policy:* $\forall_a \pi^*(\omega) = \pi^*(z_c(\omega, a))$

The last condition is the same sort of condition as the last condition of E-equivalence, and is what enables us to maintain hierarchical optimality. Note that SSR-equivalence implies C-equivalence.

---

[3]We can actually use a weaker condition: Dietterich's (2000) factored condition for subtask irrelevance

The ALispQ learning algorithm

We present a simple model-free state abstracted learning algorithm based on MAXQ (Dietterich 2000) for our three-part value function decomposition. We assume that the user provides the three abstraction functions z_p, z_c, and z_e. We store and update $\hat{Q}_c(z_c(\omega, a), a)$ and $\hat{Q}_e(z_e(\omega, a), a)$ for all $a \in A$, and $\hat{r}(z_p(\omega, a), a)$ for $a \in A_p$. We calculate

$$\hat{Q}(\omega, a) = \hat{Q}_r(\omega, a) + \hat{Q}_c(z_c(\omega), a) + \hat{Q}_e(z_e(\omega, a), a).$$

Note that, as in Dietterich's work, $\hat{Q}_r(\omega, a)$ is recursively calculated as $\hat{r}(z_p(\omega, a), a)$ if $a \in A_p$ for the base case and otherwise as

$$\hat{Q}_r(\omega, a) = \hat{Q}_r(i_a(\omega), a') + \hat{Q}_c(z_c(i_a(\omega)), a'),$$

where $a' = \arg\max_b \hat{Q}(i_a(\omega), b)$. This means that that the user need not specify z_r. We assume that the agent uses a GLIE (Greedy in the Limit with Infinite Exploration) exploration policy.

Imagine the situation where the agent transitions to ω' contained in subroutine h, where the most recently visited choice state in h was ω, where we took action a, and it took N primitive steps to reach ω'. Let ω_c be the last choice state visited (it may or may not be equal to ω, see Figure 2 for an example), let $a' = \arg\max_b \hat{Q}(\omega', b)$, and let r_s be the discounted reward accumulated between ω and ω'. Then, ALispQ learning performs the following updates:

- if $a \in A_p$, $\hat{r}(z_p(\omega, a), a) \leftarrow (1 - \alpha)\hat{r}(z_p(\omega, a), a) + \alpha r_s$

- $\hat{Q}_c(z_c(\omega), a) \leftarrow (1 - \alpha)\hat{Q}_c(z_c(\omega), a) + \alpha\beta^N [\hat{Q}_r(z_c(\omega'), a') + \hat{Q}_c(z_c(\omega'), a')]$

- $\hat{Q}_e(z_e(\omega, a), a) \leftarrow (1 - \alpha)\hat{Q}_e(z_e(\omega, a), a) + \alpha\beta^N \hat{Q}_e(z_e(\omega', a'), a')$

- if ω_c is an exit state and $z_c(\omega_c) = \omega_c$ (and let a be the sole action there) then $\hat{Q}_e(z_e(\omega_c, a), a) \leftarrow (1 - \alpha)\hat{Q}_e(z_e(\omega_c, a), a) + \arg\max_b \hat{Q}(\omega', b)$ [4]

Theorem 5 (Convergence of ALispQ-learning) *If z_r, z_s, and z_e are R-,SSP-, and E- Equivalent, respectively, then the above learning algorithm will converge (with appropriately decaying learning rates and exploration method) to a hierarchically optimal policy.*

Experiments

Figure 5 shows the performance of five different learning methods on Dietterich's taxi-world problem. The learning rates and Boltzmann exploration constants were tuned for each method. Note that standard Q-learning performs better than "ALisp program w/o SA" – this is because the problem is episodic, and the ALisp program has joint states that

---

[4]Note that this only updates the Q_e values when the exit state is the distinguished state in the equivalence class. Two algorithmic improvements are possible: using all exits states and thus basing Q_e on an average of the exit states, and modifying the distinguished state so that it is one of the most likely to be visited.

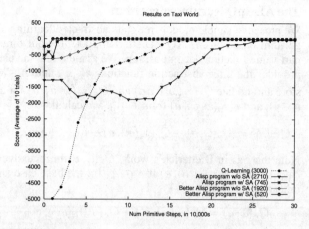

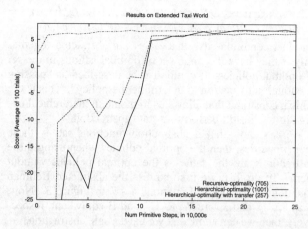

Figure 5: Learning curves for the taxi domain (left) and the extended taxi domain with time and arrival distribution (right), averaged over 50 training runs. Every 10000 primitive steps (x-axis), the greedy policy was evaluated for 10 trials, and the score (y-axis) was averaged. The number of parameters for each method is shown in parentheses after its name.

```
(defun root () (progn (guess) (wait)  (get) (put)))
(defun guess () (choice guess-choice
                        (nav R)
                        (nav G)
                        (nav B)
                        (nav Y)))
(defun wait () (loop while (not (pass-exists)) do
                     (action 'wait)))
```

Figure 4: New subroutines added for the extended taxi domain.

are only visited once per episode, whereas Q learning can visit states multiple times per run. Performing better than Q learning is the "Better ALisp program w/o SA", which is an ALisp program where extra constraints have been expressed, namely that the load (unload) action should only be applied when the taxi is co-located with the passenger (destination). Second best is the "ALisp program w/ SA" method, and best is the "Better ALisp program w/SA" method. We also tried running our algorithm with recursive optimality on this problem, and found that the performance was essentially unchanged, although the hierarchically optimal methods used 745 parameters, while recursive optimality used 632. The similarity in performance on this problem is due to the fact that every subroutine has a deterministic exit state given the input state.

We also tested our methods on an extension of the taxi problem where the taxi initially doesn't know where the passenger will show up. The taxi must guess which of the primary destinations to go to and wait for the passenger. We also add the concept of time to the world: the passenger will show up at one of the four distinguished destinations with a distribution depending on what time of day it is (morning or afternoon). We modify the root subroutine for the domain and add two new subroutines, as shown in Figure 4.

The right side of Figure 5 shows the results of running our algorithm with hierarchical versus recursive optimality. Because the arrival distribution of the passengers is not known in advance, and the effects of this distribution on reward are delayed until after the guess subroutine finishes, the recursively optimal solution cannot take advantage of the differ-

ent distributions in the morning and afternoon to choose the best place to wait for the arrival, and thus cannot achieve the optimal score. None of the recursively optimal solutions achieved a policy having value higher than 6.3, whereas every run with hierarchical optimality found a solution with value higher than 6.9.

The reader may wonder if, by rearranging the hierarchy of a recursively optimal program to have "morning" and 'afternoon" guess functions, one could avoid the deficiencies of recursive optimality. Although possible for the taxi domain, in general, this method can result in adding an exponential number of subroutines (essentially, one for each possible subroutine policy). Even if enough copies of subroutines are added, with recursive optimality, the programmer must still precisely choose the values for the pseudo-rewards in each subroutine. Hierarchical optimality frees the programmer from this burden.

Figure 5 also shows the results of transferring the navigate subroutine from the simple version of the problem to the more complex version. By analyzing the domain, we were able to determine that an optimal policy for navigate from the simple taxi domain would have the correct local sub-policy in the new domain, and thus we were able to guarantee that transferring it would be safe.

Discussion and Future Work

This paper has presented ALisp, shown how to achieve safe state abstraction for ALisp programs while maintaining hierarchical optimality, and demonstrated that doing so speeds learning considerably. Although policies for (discrete, finite) fully observable worlds are expressible in principle as lookup tables, we believe that the the expressiveness of a full programming language enables abstraction and modularization that would be difficult or impossible to create otherwise.

There are several directions in which this work can be extended.

- *Partial observability* is probably the most important outstanding issue. The required modifications to the theory are relatively straightforward and have already been investigated, for the case of MAXQ and recursive optimality, by Makar *et al.* (2001).

- *Average-reward learning* over an infinite horizon is more appropriate than discounting for many applications. Ghavamzadeh and Mahadevan (2002) have extended our three-part decomposition approach to the average-reward case and demonstrated excellent results on a real-world manufacturing task.

- *Shaping* (Ng, Harada, & Russell 1999) is an effective technique for adding "pseudorewards" to an RL problem to improve the rate of learning without affecting the final learned policy. There is a natural fit between shaping and hierarchical RL, in that shaping rewards can be added to each subroutine for the completion of subgoals; the structure of the ALisp program provides a natural scaffolding for the insertion of such rewards.

- *Function approximation* is essential for scaling hierarchical RL to very large problems. In this context, function approximation can be applied to any of the three value function components. Although we have not yet demonstrated this, we believe that there will be cases where componentwise approximation is much more natural and accurate. We are currently trying this out on an extended taxi world with continuous dynamics.

- *Automatic derivation of safe state abstractions* should be feasible using the basic idea of backchaining from the utility function through the transition model to identify relevant variables (Boutilier *et al.* 2000). It is straightforward to extend this method to handle the three-part value decomposition.

In this paper, we demonstrated that transferring entire subroutines to a new problem can yield a significant speedup. However, several interesting questions remain. Can subroutines be transferred only partially, as more of a shaping suggestion than a full specification of the subroutine? Can we automate the process of choosing what to transfer and deciding how to integrate it into the partial specification for the new problem? We are presently exploring various methods for partial transfer and investigating using logical derivations based on weak domain knowledge to help automate transfer and the creation of partial specifications.

Acknowledgments

The first author was supported by the generosity of the Fannie and John Hertz Foundation. The work was also supported by the following two grants: ONR MURI N00014-00-1-0637 "Decision Making under Uncertainty", NSF ECS-9873474 "Complex Motor Learning". We would also like to thank Tom Dietterich, Sridhar Mahadevan, Ron Parr, Mohammad Ghavamzadeh, Rich Sutton, Anders Jonsson, Andrew Ng, Mike Jordan, and Jerry Feldman for useful conversations on the work presented herein.

References

[1] Amarel, S. 1968. On representations of problems of reasoning about actions. In Michie, D., ed., *Machine Intelligence 3*, volume 3. Elsevier. 131–171.

[2] Andre, D., and Russell, S. J. 2001. Programmatic reinforcement learning agents. In Leen, T. K.; Dietterich, T. G.; and Tresp, V., eds., *Advances in Neural Information Processing Systems 13*. Cambridge, Massachusetts: MIT Press.

[3] Andre, D., and Russell, S. J. 2002. State abstraction in programmable reinforcement learning. Technical Report UCB//CSD-02-1177, Computer Science Division, University of California at Berkeley.

[4] Bellman, R. E. 1957. *Dynamic Programming*. Princeton, New Jersey: Princeton University Press.

[5] Boutilier, C.; Reiter, R.; Soutchanski, M.; and Thrun, S. 2000. Decision-theoretic, high-level agent programming in the situation calculus. In *Proceedings of the Seventeenth National Conference on Artificial Intelligence (AAAI-00)*. Austin, Texas: AAAI Press.

[6] Boutilier, C.; Dearden, R.; and Goldszmidt, M. 1995. Exploiting structure in policy construction. In *Proceedings of the Fourteenth International Joint Conference on Artificial Intelligence (IJCAI-95)*. Montreal, Canada: Morgan Kaufmann.

[7] Dietterich, T. G. 2000. Hierarchical reinforcement learning with the maxq value function decomposition. *Journal of Artificial Intelligence Research* 13:227–303.

[8] Ghavamzadeh, M., and Madadevan, S. 2002. Hierarchically optimal average reward reinforcement learning. In *Proceedings of the Nineteenth International Conference on Machine Learning*. Sydney, Australia: Morgan Kaufmann.

[9] Kaelbling, L. P.; Littman, M. L.; and Moore, A. W. 1996. Reinforcement learning: A survey. *Journal of Artificial Intelligence Research* 4:237–285.

[10] Makar, R.; Mahadevan, S.; and Ghavamzadeh, M. 2001. Hierarchical multi-agent reinforcement learning. In *Fifth International Conference on Autonomous Agents*.

[11] Ng, A.; Harada, D.; and Russell, S. 1999. Policy invariance under reward transformations: Theory and application to reward shaping. In *Proceedings of the Sixteenth International Conference on Machine Learning*. Bled, Slovenia: Morgan Kaufmann.

[12] Parr, R., and Russell, S. 1998. Reinforcement learning with hierarchies of machines. In Jordan, M. I.; Kearns, M. J.; and Solla, S. A., eds., *Advances in Neural Information Processing Systems 10*. Cambridge, Massachusetts: MIT Press.

[13] Precup, D., and Sutton, R. 1998. Multi-time models for temporally abstract planning. In Kearns, M., ed., *Advances in Neural Information Processing Systems 10*. Cambridge, Massachusetts: MIT Press.

Contentful Mental States for Robot Baby

Paul R. Cohen
Dept. of Computer Science.
University of Massachusetts,
Amherst
cohen@cs.umass.edu

Tim Oates
Dept. of Computer Science.
University of Maryland,
Baltimore County
oates@cs.umbc.edu

Carole R. Beal
Dept. of Psychology,
University of Massachusetts,
Amherst
cbeal@psych.umass.edu

Niall Adams
Dept. of Mathematics.
Imperial College,
London
n.adams@ic.ac.uk

Abstract

In this paper we claim that meaningful representations can be learned by programs, although today they are almost always designed by skilled engineers. We discuss several kinds of meaning that representations might have, and focus on a functional notion of meaning as appropriate for programs to learn. Specifically, a representation is meaningful if it incorporates an indicator of external conditions and if the indicator relation informs action. We survey methods for inducing kinds of representations we call structural abstractions. Prototypes of sensory time series are one kind of structural abstraction, and though they are not denoting or compositional, they do support planning. Deictic representations of objects and prototype representations of words enable a program to learn the denotational meanings of words. Finally, we discuss two algorithms designed to find the macroscopic structure of episodes in a domain-independent way.

Introduction

In artificial intelligence and other cognitive sciences it is taken for granted that mental states are representational. Researchers differ on whether representations must be *symbolic*, but most agree that mental states have *content* — they are *about* something and they *mean* something — irrespective of their form. Researchers differ too on whether the meanings of mental states have any causal relationship to how and what we think, but most agree that these meanings are (mostly) known to us as we think. Of formal representations in computer programs, however, we would say something different: Generally, the meanings of representations have no influence on the operations performed on them (e.g., a program concludes q because it knows $p \rightarrow q$ and p, irrespective of what p and q are about); yet the representations *have* meanings, known to us, the designers and end-users of the programs, and the representations are provided to the programs *because* of what they mean (e.g., if it was not relevant that the patient has a fever, then the proposition febrile(patient) would not be provided to the program — programs are designed to operate in domains where meaning matters.). Thus, irrespective of whether the contents of mental states have any causal influence on what and how *we* think, these contents clearly are intended (by us) to influence what and

how our programs think. The meanings of representations are not irrelevant but we have to provide them.

This paper addresses philosophical and algorithmic issues in what we might call robot intentionality or a philosophy of mind for robots. We adapt current thinking in philosophy of mind for humans, particularly that of Fred Dretske, reifying in algorithms otherwise abstract concepts, particularly the concept of meaning. If programs could learn the meanings of representations it would save us a great deal of effort. Most of the intellectual work in AI is done not by programs but by their creators, and virtually *all* the work involved in specifying the meanings of representations is done by people, not programs (but see, e.g., (Steels 1999; Pierce & Kuipers 1997; Kuipers 2000)). This paper discusses kinds of meaning that programs might learn and gives examples of such programs.

How do people and computers come to have contentful, i.e., meaningful, mental states? As Dennett (Dennett 1998) points out, there are only three serious answers to the question: Contents are learned, told, or innate. Lines cannot be drawn sharply between these, in either human or artificial intelligence. Culture, including our educational systems, blurs the distinction between learning and being told; and it is impossible methodologically to be sure that the meanings of mental states are innate, especially as some learning occurs in utero (de Boysson-Bardies 2001) and many studies of infant knowledge happen weeks or months after birth.

One might think the distinctions between learning, being told, and innate knowledge are clearer in artificial systems, but the role of engineers is rarely acknowledged (Cohen & Litch 1999; Utgoff & Cohen 1998; Dretske 1988). Most AI systems manipulate representations that mean what engineers intend them to mean; the meanings of representations are exogenous to the systems. It is less clear where the meanings of *learned* representations reside, in the minds of engineers or the "minds of the machines" that run the learning algorithms. We would not say that a linear regression algorithm knows the meanings of data or of induced regression lines. Meanings are assigned by data analysts or their client domain experts. Moreover, these people select data for the algorithms with some prior idea of what they mean. Most work in machine learning, KDD, and AI and statistics are essentially data analysis, with humans, not machines, assigning meanings to regularities found in the data.

We have nothing against data analysis, indeed we think that learning the meanings of representations *is* data analysis, in particular, analysis of sensory and perceptual time series. Our goal, though, is to have the machine do *all* of it: select data, process it, and interpret the results; then iterate to resolve ambiguities, test new hypotheses, refine estimates, and so on. The relationship between domain experts, statistical consultants, and statistical algorithms is essentially identical to the relationship between domain experts, AI researchers, and their programs: In both cases the intermediary translates meaningful domain concepts into representations that programs manipulate, and translates the results back to the domain experts. We want to do away with the domain expert and the engineers/statistical consultants, and have programs learn representations and their meanings, autonomously.

One impediment to learning the meanings of representations is the fuzziness of commonsense notions of meaning. Suppose a regression algorithm induces a strong relationship between two random variables x and y and represents it in the conventional way: $y = 1.31x - .03, R^2 = .86, F = 108.3, p < .0001$. One meaning of this representation is provided by classical inferential statistics: x and y appear linearly related and the relationship between these random variables is very unlikely to be accidental. Now, the statistician might know that x is daily temperature and y is ice-cream sales, and so he or his client domain expert might assign additional meaning to the representation, above. For instance, the statistician might warn the domain expert that the assumptions of linear regression are not well-satisfied by the data. Ignoring these and other cautions, the domain expert might even interpret the representation in causal terms (i.e., hot weather causes people to buy ice-cream). Should he submit the result to an academic journal, the reviews would probably criticize this semantic liberty and would in any case declare the result as meaningless in the sense of being utterly unimportant and unsurprising.

This little example illustrates at least five kinds of meaning for the representation $y = 1.31x - .03, R^2 = .86, F = 108.3, p < .0001$. There is the *formal* meaning, including the mathematical fact that 86 % of the variance in the random variable y is explained by x. Note that this meaning has nothing to do with the denotations of y and x, and it might be utter nonsense in the domain, but, of course, the formal meaning of the representation is not about weather and ice cream, it is about random variables. Another kind of meaning has to do with the *model* that makes y and x denote ice cream and weather. When the statistician warns that the residuals of the regression have structure, he is saying that a linear model might not summarize the relationship between x and y as well as another kind of model. The domain expert will introduce a third kind of meaning: he will interpret $y = 1.31x - .03, R^2 = .86, F = 108.3, p < .0001$ as a statement about ice cream sales. This is not to say that every aspect of the representation has an interpretation in the domain—the expert might not assign a meaning to the coefficient $-.03$—only that, to the expert, the representation is not a formal object but a statement about his domain. We could call this kind of meaning the *domain* semantics, or the *functional* semantics, to emphasize that the interpretation of a representation has some effect on what the domain expert *does* or thinks about.

Having found a relationship between ice cream sales and the weather, the expert will feel elated, ambitious, or greedy, and this is a fourth, *affective* kind of meaning. Let us suppose, however, that the relationship is not real, it is entirely spurious (an artifact of a poor sampling procedure, say) and is contradicted by solid results in the literature. In this case the representation is meaningless in the sense that it does not *inform* anyone about how the world really works.

To which of these notions of meaning should a program that learns meanings be held responsible? The semantics of classical statistics and regression analysis in particular are sophisticated, and many humans perform adequate analyses without really understanding either. More to the point, what good is an agent that learns *formal* semantics in lieu of *domain* or *functional* semantics? The relationship between x and y can be learned (even without a statistician specifying the form of the relationship), but so long as it is a *formal* relationship between random variables, and the denotations of x and y are unknown to the learner, a more knowledgeable agent will be required to translate the formal relationship into a domain or functional one. The denotations of x and y might be learned, though generally one needs some knowledge to bootstrap the process; for example, when we say, "x denotes daily temperature," we call up considerable amounts of common-sense knowledge to assign this statement meaning. [1] As to affective meanings, we believe artificial agents will benefit from them, but we do not know how to provide them.

This leaves two notions of meaning, one based in the functional roles of representations, the other related to the informativeness of representations. The philosopher Fred Dretske wrestled these notions of meaning into a theory of how meaning can have causal effects on behavior (Dretske 1981; 1988). Dretske's criteria for a state being a meaningful representational state are: the state must *indicate* some condition, have the *function* of indicating that condition, and have this function assigned as the result of a *learning* process. The latter condition is contentious (Dennett 1998; Cohen & Litch 1999), but it will not concern us here as this paper is about learning meaningful representations. The other conditions say that a reliable indicator relationship must exist and be exploited by an agent for some purpose. Thus, the relationship between mean daily temperature (the indicator) and ice-cream sales (the indicated) is apt to be meaningful to ice-cream companies, just as the relationship between sonar readings and imminent collisions is meaningful to mobile robots, because in each case an agent can do something with the relationship. Learning meaningful representations, then, is tantamount to learning reliable relationships between denoting tokens (e.g., random variables) and learning what to do when the tokens take on particular values.

The minimum required of a representation by Dretske's theory is an indicator relationship $\vec{s} \leftarrow I(\vec{S})$ between the external world state $\vec{S}$ and an internal state $\vec{s}$, and a function that exploits the indicator relationship through some kind of action a, presumably changing the world state: $f(\vec{s}, a) \rightarrow \vec{S}$. The problems are to learn representations $\vec{s} \sim \vec{S}$ and the functions f (the relationship $\sim$ is discussed below, but here means "abstraction").

These are familiar problems to researchers in the reinforcement learning community, and we think reinforcement learning is a way to learn meaningful representations (with the reservations we discussed in (Utgoff & Cohen 1998)). We want to up the ante, however, in two ways. First, the world is a dynamic place and we think it is necessary and advantageous for $\vec{s}$ to represent how the world changes. Indeed, most of our work is concerned with learning representations of dynamics.

---

[1] Projects such as Cyc emphasize the denotational meanings of representations (Lenat & Guha 1990; Lenat 1990). Terms in Cyc are associated with axioms that say what the terms mean. It took a collosal effort to get enough terms and axioms into Cyc to support the easy acquisition of new terms and axioms.

Second, a *policy* of the form $f(\vec{s}, a) \rightarrow \vec{s}$ manifests an intimate relationship between representations $\vec{s}$ and the actions a conditioned on them: $\vec{s}$ contains the "right" information to condition a. The right information is almost always an abstraction of raw state information; indeed, two kinds of abstraction are immediately apparent. Not all state information is causally relevant to action, so one kind of abstraction involves selecting information in $\vec{S}$ to include in $\vec{s}$ (e.g., subsets or weighted combinations or projections of the information in $\vec{S}$). The other kind of abstraction involves the *structure* of states. Consider the sequence AABACAABACAABA-CAABADAABAC. Its structure can be described many ways, perhaps most simply by saying, "the sequence AABAx repeats five times, and $x =$C in all but the fourth replication, when $x =$D." This might be the abstraction an agent needs to act; for example, it might condition action on the distinction between AABAC and AABAD, in which case the "right" representation of the sequence above is something like this $p_1 s_1 p_1 s_1 p_1 s_1 p_1 s_2 p_1 s_1$, where p and s denote *structural* features of the original sequence, such as "prefix" and "suffix'. We call representations that include such structural features *structural abstractions*.

To recap, representations $\vec{s}$ are meaningful if they are related to action by a function $f(\vec{s}, a) \rightarrow \vec{S}$, but f can be stated more or less simply depending on the abstraction $\vec{s} \sim \vec{S}$. One kind of abstraction involves selecting from the information in $\vec{S}$, the other is structural abstraction. The remainder of this paper is concerned with learning structural abstractions, with what AI researchers call "getting the representation right," a creative process that we reserve unto ourselves and to which, if we are honest, we must attribute most of the performance of our programs. Note that, in Dretske's terms, structural abstractions can be indicator functions but not all indicator functions are structural abstractions. Because the world is dynamic, we are particularly concerned with learning structural abstractions of time series.

Structural Abstractions of Time Series

As a robot wanders around its environment, it generates a sequence of values of state variables. At each instant t we get a vector of values $\vec{x_t}$ (our robot samples its sensors at 10Hz, so we get ten such vectors each second). Suppose we have a long sequence of such vectors $X = \vec{x_0}, \vec{x_1}, \ldots$. Within X are subsequences x_{ij} that, when subjected to processes of structural abstraction, give rise to *episode structures* that are meaningful in the sense of informing action. The trick is to find the subsequences x_{ij} and design the abstraction processes that produce episode structures. We have developed numerous methods of this sort and survey some of them briefly, here.

Figure 1 shows four seconds of data from a Pioneer 1 robot as it moves past an object. Prior to moving, the robot establishes a coordinate frame with an x axis perpendicular to its heading and a y axis parallel to its heading. As it begins to move, the robot measures its location in this coordinate frame. Note that the ROBOT-X line is almost constant. This means that the robot did not change its heading as it moved. In contrast, the ROBOT-Y line increases, indicating that the robot does increase its distance along a line parallel to its original heading. Note especially the VIS-A-X and VIS-A-Y lines, which represent the horizontal and vertical locations, respectively, of the centroid of a patch of light on the robot's "retina," a CCD camera. VIS-A-X decreases, meaning that the object drifts to the left on the retina, while VIS-A-Y increases, meaning the object

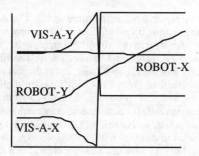

Figure 1: As the robot moves, an object approaches the periphery of its field of view then passes out of sight.

moves toward the top of the retina. Simultaneously, both series jump to constant values. These values are returned by the vision system when nothing is in the field of view.

Every time series that corresponds to moving past an object has qualitatively the same structure as the one in Figure 1. It follows that if we had a statistical technique to group the robot's experiences by the characteristic patterns in multivariate time series (where the variables represent sensor readings), then this technique would in effect learn a taxonomy of the robot's experiences. *Clustering by dynamics* (CBD) is such a technique (Tim Oates 2000a): A long multivariate time series is divided into segments, each of which represents an episode such as moving toward an object, avoiding an object, crashing into an object, and so on. The episodes are not labeled in any way. Next, a dynamic time warping algorithm (Kruskall & Liberman 1983) compares every pair of episodes and returns a number that represents the degree of similarity between the time series in the pair. The algorithm returns a degree of mismatch (conversely, similarity) between the series after the best fit between them has been found. Given similarity numbers for every pair of episodes, it is straightforward to cluster episodes by their similarity. Lastly, another algorithm finds the "central member" of each cluster, which we call the *cluster prototype* following Rosch (Rosch & Mervis 1975).

CBD produces structural abstractions (prototypes) of time series, the question is whether these abstractions can be meaningful in the sense of informing action. Schmill shows how to use prototypes as planning operators (Matthew Schmill 2000). The first step is to learn rules of the form, "in state i, action a leads to state j with probability p." These rules are learned by a classical decision-tree induction algorithm, where features of states are decision variables. Given such rules, the robot can plan by means-ends analysis. It plans not to achieve world states specified by exogenous engineers, as in conventional generative planning, but to achieve world states which are preconditions for its actions. This is called "planning to act," and it has the effect of gradually increasing the size of the corpus of prototypes and things the robot can do. In this way, clustering by dynamics yields structural abstractions of time series that are meaningful in the sense of informing action. There is also a strong possibility that CBD prototypes are meaningful in the sense of informing communicative actions. Oates, Schmill and Cohen (2000b) report a very high degree of concordance between the clusters of episodes generated by CBD and clusters generated by a human judge. The prototypes produced by CBD are not weird and unfamiliar to people, but seem to correspond to how humans themselves categorize episodes. Were this not the case, communication would be hard, because the robot would have an ontology of episodes unfamiliar to people.

A Critique of Sensory Prototypes

While the general idea of clustering by dynamics is attractive (it does produce meaningful structural abstractions), the CBD method described above has two limitations. First, it requires someone (or some algorithm) to divide a time series into shorter series that contain instances of the structures we want to find. The technique cannot accept time series of numerous undifferentiated activities (e.g., produced by a robot roaming the lab for an hour). A more serious problem concerns the kinds of prototypes produced by CBD, of which Figure 1 is an example. As noted earlier, this prototype represents the robot moving past an object, say, a cup. Can we find anything in the representation that denotes a cup? We cannot. Consequently, representations of this kind cannot inform actions that depend on individuating the cup; for example, the robot could not respond correctly to the directive, "Turn toward the cup." The abstractions produced by CBD contain sufficient structure to cluster episodes, but still lack much of the structure of the episodes. If one is comfortable with a crude distinction between sensations and concepts, then the structural abstractions produced by CBD are entirely sensory (Paul R. Cohen & Beal 1997). They do not represent objects, spatial relationships, or any other individuated entity.

Learning Word Meanings

Learning the meanings of words in speech clearly requires individuation of elements in episodes. To learn the meaning of the word "cup" the robot must first individuate the word in the speech signal, then individuate the object cup in other sensory series, associate the representations; and perhaps estimate some properties of the object corresponding to the cup, such as its color, or the fact that it participates as a target in a "turn toward" activity. In his PhD dissertation, Oates discusses an algorithm called PERUSE that does all these things (Oates 2001).

To individuate objects in time series PERUSE relies on *deictic markers* — functions that map from raw sensory data to representations of objects (Ballard, Hayhoe, & Pook 1997; Agre & Chapman 1987). A simple deictic marker might construct a representation whenever the area of colored region of the visual field exceeds a threshold. The representation might include attributes such as the color, shape, and area, of the object, as well as the intervals during which it is in view, and so on.

To individuate words in speech, PERUSE requires a corpus of speech in which words occur multiple times (e.g., multiple sentences contain the word "cup"). Spoken words produce similar (but certainly not identical) patterns in the speech signal, as one can see in Figure 2. (In fact, PERUSE's representation of the speech signal is multivariate but the univariate series in Fig. 2 will serve to describe the approach.) If one knew that a segment in Figure 2 corresponded to a word, then one could find other segments like it, and construct a prototype or average representation of these. For instance, if one knew that the segment labeled A in Figure 2 corresponds to a word, then one could search for similar segments in the other sentences, find A', and construct a prototype from them. These problems are by no means trivial, as the boundaries of words are not helpfully marked in speech. Oates treats the boundaries as

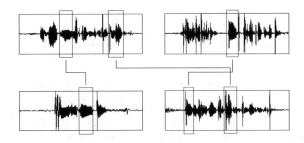

Figure 2: Corresponding words in four sentences. Word boundaries are shown as boxes around segments of the speech signal. Segments that correspond to the same word are linked by connecting lines.

hidden variables and invokes the Expectation Maximization algorithm to learn a model of each word that optimizes the placement of the boundaries. However, it is still necessary to begin with a segment that probably corresponds to a word. This problem is solved with two heuristics: In brief, the entropy of the distribution of the "next tick" spikes at episode (e.g., word) boundaries; and the patterns in windows that contain boundaries tend to be less frequent than patterns in windows that do not. These heuristics, combined with some methods for growing hypothesized word segments, suffice to bootstrap the process of individuating words in speech.

Given prototypical representations of words in speech, and representations of objects and relations, PERUSE learns associatively the *denotations* of the words. Denotation is a common notion of meaning: The meaning of a symbol is what it points to, refers to, selects from a set, etc. However, naive implementations of denotation run into numerous difficulties, especially when one tries to learn denotations. One difficulty is that the denotations of many (perhaps most) words cannot be specified as boolean combinations of properties (this is sometimes called the problem of necessary and sufficient conditions). Consider the word "cup". With repeated exposure, one might learn that the word denotes prismatic objects less than five inches tall. This is wrong because it is a bad description of cups, and it is more seriously wrong because no such description of cups can reliably divide the world into cups and non-cups (see, e.g., (Lakoff 1984; Bloom 2000)).

Another difficulty with naive notions of denotation is referential ambiguity. Does the word "cup" refer to an object, the shape of the object, its color, the actions one performs on it, the spatial relationship between it and another object, or some other feature of the episode in which the word is uttered? How can an algorithm learn the denotation of a word when so many denotations are logically possible?

Let us illustrate Oates' approach to these problems with the word "square," which has a relatively easy denotation. Suppose one's representation of an object includes its apparent height and width, and the ratio of these. An object will appear square if the ratio is near 1.0. Said differently, the word "square" is more likely to be uttered when the ratio is around 1.0 than otherwise. Let ϕ be the group of sensors that measures height, width and their ratio, and let x be the value of the ratio. Let U be an utterance and W be a word in the utterance. Oates defines the denotation of W as follows:

$$denote(W, \phi, x) = Pr(contains(U, W) | about(U, \phi), x) \quad (1)$$

The denotation of the word "square" is the probability that it is uttered given that the utterance is about the ratio of height to width and the value of the ratio. More plainly, when we say "square" we are talking about the ratio of height to width and we are more likely to use the word when the value of the ratio is close to 1.0. This formulation of denotation effectively dismisses the problem of necessary and sufficient conditions, and it brings the problem of referential ambiguity into sharp focus, for when an algorithm tries to *learn* denotations it does not have access to the quantities on the right hand side of Eq. 1, it has access only to the words it hears:

$$hear(W, \phi, x) = Pr(contains(U, W) | x) \quad (2)$$

The problem (for which Oates provides an algorithm) is to get $denote(W, \phi, x)$ from $hear(W, \phi, x)$.

At this juncture, however, we have said enough to make the case that word meanings can be learned from time series of sensor and speech data. We claim that the PERUSE algorithm constructs representations and learns their meanings by itself. PERUSE builds word representations sufficient for a robot to respond to spoken commands and to translate words between English, German and Mandarin Chinese. The denotational meanings of the representations are therefore sufficient to inform some communicative acts.

Although PERUSE is a suite of statistical methods, it is about as far from the data analysis paradigm with which we began this paper as one can imagine. In that example, an analyst and his client domain expert select and provide data to a linear regression algorithm because it means something to them, and the algorithm computes a regression model that (presumably) means something to them. Neither data nor model mean anything to the algorithm. In contrast, PERUSE selects and processes speech data in such a way that the resulting prototypes are likely to be individuated entities (more on this, below), and it assigns meaning to these entities by finding their denotations as described earlier. Structural abstraction of representations and assignment of meaning are all done by PERUSE.

Conclusion

The central claim of this paper is that programs can learn representations and their meanings. We adopted Dretske's definition that a representation is meaningful if it reliably indicates something about the external world and the indicator relationship is exploited to inform action. As this notion of meaning does not constrain what is represented, how it is represented, and how representations inform action, we have considerable freedom in how we gather evidence relevant to the claim. In fact, we imposed additional constraints on learned representations in our empirical work: They should be grounded in sensor data from a robot; the data should have a temporal aspect and time or the ordinal sequence of things should be an explicit part of the learned representations; and the representations should not merely inform action, but should inform two essentially human intellectual accomplishments, language and planning. We have demonstrated that a robot can learn the meanings of words, and construct simple plans, and that both these abilities depend on

representations and meanings learned by the robot. In general, we have specified *how* things are to be represented (e.g., as sequences of means and variances, multivariate time series, transition probabilities, etc.) but the *contents* of the representations (i.e., what is represented) and the relationship between the contents and actions have been learned.

Acknowledgments

This research is supported by DARPA under contract number USASMDCDASG60-99-C-0074. The U.S. Government is authorized to reproduce and distribute reprints for governmental purposes notwithstanding any copyright notation hereon. The views and conclusions contained herein are those of the authors and should not be interpreted as necessarily representing the official policies or endorsements either expressed or implied, of the DARPA or the U.S. Government.

References

Agre, P. E., and Chapman, D. 1987. Pengi: An implementation of a theory of activity. In *Proceedings of the Sixth National Conference on Artificial Intelligence*, 268–272. American Association for Artificial Intelligence.

Ballard, D. H.; Hayhoe, M. M.; and Pook, P. K. 1997. Deictic codes for the embodiment of cognition. Computer Science Department, University of Rochester.

Bloom, P. 2000. *How Children Learn the Meanings of Words*. MIT Press.

Cohen, P. R., and Litch, M. 1999. What are contentful mental states? dretske's theory of mental content viewed in the light of robot learning and planning algorithms. In *Proceedings of the Sixteenth National Conference on Artificial Intelligence*.

de Boysson-Bardies, B. 2001. *How Language Comes to Children*. MIT Press.

Dennett, D. 1998. Do it yourself understanding. In Dennett, D., ed., *Brainchildren, Essays on Designing Minds*. MIT Press and Penguin.

Dretske, F. 1981. *Knowledge and the Flow of Information*. Cambridge University Press. Reprinted by CSLI Publications, Stanford University.

Dretske, F. 1988. *Explaining Behavior: Reasons in a World of Causes*. MIT Press.

Kruskall, J. B., and Liberman, M. 1983. The symmetric time warping problem: From continuous to discrete. In *Time Warps, String Edits and Macromolecules: The Theory and Practice of Sequence Comparison*. Addison-Wesley.

Kuipers, B. 2000. The spatial semantic hierarchy. *Artificial Intelligence* 119:191–233.

Lakoff, G. 1984. *Women, Fire, and Dangerous Things*. University of Chicago Press.

Lenat, D. B., and Guha, R. V. 1990. *Building large knowledge-based systems: Representation and inference in the Cyc project*. Addison Wesley.

Lenat, D. B. 1990. Cyc: Towards programs with common sense. *Communications of the ACM* 33(8).

Matthew Schmill, Tim Oates, P. C. 2000. Learning planning operators in real-world, partially observable environments. In *Pro-*

ceedings Fifth International Conference on Artificial Planning and Scheduling, 246–253. AAAI Press.

Oates, J. T. 2001. *PhD: Grounding Knowledge in Sensors: Unsupervised Learning for Language and Planning*. Ph.D. Dissertation, Affiliation removed for blind review.

Paul R. Cohen, Marc S. Atkin, T. O., and Beal, C. R. 1997. NEO: Learning conceptual knowledge by sensorimotor interaction with an environment. In *Proceedings of the First International Conference on Autonomous Agents*, 170–177.

Pierce, D., and Kuipers, B. 1997. Map learning with uninterpreted sensors and effectors. *Artificial Intelligence Journal* 92:169–229.

Rosch, E., and Mervis, C. B. 1975. Family resemblances: Studies in the internal structure of categories. *Cognitive Psychology* 7:573–605.

Steels, L. 1999. *The Talking Heads Experiment: Volume I. Words and Meanings*. Laboratorium, Antwerpen. This is a museum catalog but is in preparation as a book.

Tim Oates, Matthew Schmill, P. C. 2000a. Identifying qualitatively different outcomes of actions: Gaining autonomy through learning. In *Proceedings Fourth International Conference, pp 110-111*. ACM.

Tim Oates, Matthew Schmill, P. C. 2000b. A method for clustering the experience of a mobile robot that accords with human judgments. In *Proceedings of Seventeenth National Conference, pp. 846-851*. AAAI Press/The MIT Press.

Utgoff, P., and Cohen, P. R. 1998. Applicability of reinforcement learning. In *The Methodology of Applying Machine leraning Problem Definition, Task Decompostion and Technique Selection Workshop, ICML-98*, 37–43.

Data Perturbation for Escaping Local Maxima in Learning

Gal Elidan and **Matan Ninio** and **Nir Friedman**
Hebrew University
{*galel,ninio,nir*}*@cs.huji.ac.il*

Dale Schuurmans
University of Waterloo
dale@cs.uwaterloo.ca

Abstract

Almost all machine learning algorithms—be they for regression, classification or density estimation—seek hypotheses that optimize a score on training data. In most interesting cases, however, full global optimization is not feasible and local search techniques are used to discover reasonable solutions. Unfortunately, the quality of the local maxima reached depends on initialization and is often weaker than the global maximum. In this paper, we present a simple approach for combining global search with local optimization to discover improved hypotheses in general machine learning problems. The main idea is to escape local maxima by perturbing the *training data* to create plausible new ascent directions, rather than perturbing hypotheses directly. Specifically, we consider example-reweighting strategies that are reminiscent of boosting and other ensemble learning methods, but applied in a different way with a different goal: to produce a *single* hypothesis that achieves a good score on training and test data. To evaluate the performance of our algorithms we consider a number of problems in learning Bayesian networks from data, including discrete training problems (structure search), continuous training problems (parametric EM, non-linear logistic regression), and mixed training problems (Structural EM)—on both synthetic and real-world data. In each case, we obtain state of the art performance on both training and test data.

Introduction

Training algorithms in machine learning are almost always optimization algorithms: that is, they search for a hypothesis that maximizes a score on the training data. This is true for regression, classification and density estimation, as well as most other machine learning problems. The most common scores used in machine learning are *additive* on training data, which means that the score of a hypothesis h on data $D = \{\mathbf{x}[1], ..., \mathbf{x}[M]\}$ is a sum of local scores on each individual example, plus an optional regularization penalty

$$\text{Score}(h, D) = \sum_m \text{score}(h, \mathbf{x}[m]) - \text{penalty}(h)$$

Such scores arise naturally in regression or classification problems, where the local score is typically negated prediction error, and in density estimation, where the local score is

typically log likelihood. Although we will apply our techniques to more general non-additive scores below, it will be useful to keep additive scores as a simple example.

Even for simple optimization objectives, in interesting hypothesis spaces like decision trees, neural networks, and graphical models, the problem of finding a globally optimal hypothesis is usually intractable. This is true whether one is searching for an optimal combination of hypothesis structure and parameters (e.g., decision tree learning), or just optimizing the parameters for a given structure (e.g., neural network training). Therefore, most training algorithms employ local search techniques such as gradient descent or discrete hill climbing to find locally optimal hypotheses (Bishop 1995). The drawback is that local maxima are common and local search often yields poor results.

A variety of techniques have been developed for escaping poor local maxima in general search, including random restarts, TABU search (Glover & Laguna 1993) and simulated annealing (Kirpatrick, Gelatt, & Vecchi 1994). However, these techniques do not exploit the particular nature of the training problem encountered in machine learning. Instead, they alter hypotheses in an oblivious fashion until this happens to provide an escape from a local basin of attraction.

In this paper, we consider strategies for escaping local maxima that perturb the *training data* instead of perturbing the hypotheses directly. In particular, we consider simple strategies for *reweighting* training examples to create useful ascent directions in hypothesis space. To do this we augment the score so that it considers a probability distribution w on the training examples, thus yielding

$$\text{Score}(h, D, \mathbf{w}) = \sum_m M \cdot \mathbf{w}_m \text{score}(h, \mathbf{x}[m]) - \text{penalty}(h)$$

An intuition for why example reweighting is effective for escaping local maxima is that it can cause "informed" changes to be made to the current hypothesis, rather than arbitrarily damage it: When a local maximum is reached, each training example contributes differently to the score. If the hypothesis is poor, then some training examples which contribute strongly to the score are likely to be outliers that should be down-weighted, whereas other examples that do not contribute strongly should be up-weighted to reflect their true importance in the underlying distribution. That is, a poor

```
procedure PerturbedSearch(D, w^0, h^0, τ^0, τ_final)
    t ← 0
    while τ^t > τ_final do
        w^{t+1} ← reweight(Score, w^t, τ^t, h^t, D)
        h^{t+1} ← optimize(Score, w^{t+1}, h^t, D)
        τ^{t+1} ← reduce(τ^t, t)
        t ← t + 1
    return h^t
```

Figure 1: Outline of the generic search procedure.

hypothesis will tend to fit outliers but under-represent examples that are actually important. Understanding how the score is influenced by training examples can therefore suggest plausible perturbations to the data which favor superior hypotheses.

Below, we consider two basic techniques for perturbing example weights to escape local maxima: *random reweighting*, which randomly samples weight profiles on the training data, and *adversarial reweighting*, which updates the weight profile to explicitly punish the current hypothesis, with the intent of moving the search quickly to a nearby basin of attraction. In both cases the weight profile is annealed toward uniform weights over time to ensure that the search eventually focuses on producing good solutions for the original distribution of training data.

Our basic approach has several benefits. First, these perturbation schemes are general and can be applied to a large variety of hypothesis spaces, either continuous or discrete. Second, our approach uses standard search procedures to find hypotheses, rather than employ the often wasteful "propose, evaluate, reject" cycle of simulated annealing approaches. Third, because a perturbation of the training data can generate a long chain of search steps in hypothesis space, a single reweighting step can result in a hypothesis that is very different from the one considered at the outset (although its score might not be that different). Finally, in the adversarial variant, the perturbations to the score are not arbitrary. Instead, they force the score to be more attentive to a subset of the training instances. Our experimental results show that substantial improvements are achieved in a variety of training scenarios.

Weight Perturbation for Escaping Maxima

Generic Search Procedure Our goal is to perturb the training data to allow local search to escape poor local maxima, under the constraint that we ultimately find a hypothesis that scores well on the original training distribution. Therefore, the perturbations should not move the training data too far from their original state, and eventually the data must be restored to its original form to ensure that the final hypothesis is optimized on the correct distribution. This suggests that we follow an annealing approach where we allow the weights to change freely early in the search, but then eventually "cool" the weights toward the original distribution.

Figure 1 outlines the generic search procedure we examine. The free parameters in this procedure are the an-

nealing schedule ($reduce(\tau, t)$), the local search method ($optimize(\text{Score}, w, h, D)$), and the example reweighting scheme ($reweight(\text{Score}, w, \tau, h, D)$), each of which we instantiate below. For the annealing schedule, we follow a standard initialization with standard decay, starting with temperature τ^0 and setting $\tau^{t+1} = \delta\tau^t$, with $\delta = 0.95$ in most runs. For local optimization, one issue is to note that local search can be interleaved with the example reweighting in many ways. For example, one could perform full local optimization between each reweighting step, or perform only a partial optimization between reweights. We apply both of these interleaving strategies in specific cases below, depending on what appears to be most advantageous for the problem at hand. The final component of our search procedure is the reweighting method, for which we propose the following two main strategies.

Random Reweighting The first approach we consider is a randomized method motivated by *iterative local search* methods in combinatorial optimization (Codenotti *et al.* 1996) and phylogenetic reconstruction (Nixon 1999). Instead of performing random steps in the hypothesis space, we perturb the score by randomly reweighting each training example around its original weight. Candidate hypotheses are then evaluated with respect to the reweighted training set and we perform standard optimization on the perturbed score. After each iteration is complete, we repeat the process by independently sampling new example weights, re-optimizing the hypothesis, etc., until the magnitude of the weight perturbation approaches zero.

For convenience, we require the weights to be a probability distribution over the M data instances. Thus, we sample with a *Dirichlet* distribution with parameter β, so that $P(W = w) \propto \prod_m w_m^{\beta-1}$ for legal probability vectors (see, for example (DeGroot 1989)). When β grows larger, this distribution peaks around the uniform distribution. Thus, if we use $\beta = 1/\tau^t$ the randomly chosen distributions will anneal toward the uniform distribution, since the temperature τ^t decreases with the number of iterations t. We refer to this random perturbation approach as **Random**.

Adversarial Reweighting The second approach we consider is to update weights to directly challenge the current hypothesis. This approach is motivated by the exponential gradient search of (Schuurmans, Southey, & Holte 2001) for constrained optimization problems. Here, we combine their technique with an annealing process and modify it for a machine learning context. Intuitively, one can challenge a local maxima by calculating the gradient of the score with respect to the weights and then updating the weights to *decrease* the hypothesis' score. For example, on a training item $\mathbf{x}[m]$ one could consider the adversarial weight update $w_m^{t+1} \leftarrow w_m^t - \eta \frac{\partial \text{Score}}{\partial w_m}$ which would explicitly make the current hypothesis appear less favorable and hence less likely to remain a local maximum. In this way, $\text{Score}(h, D, \mathbf{w})$ behaves somewhat like a Lagrangian, in the sense that the local search attempts to maximize the score over h whereas the weight update attempts to *minimize* the score over $\mathbf{w}$, in an adversarial min-max fashion.

This general approach still has to be adapted to our needs.

First, for reasons outlined above, we need to anneal the weight vector toward a uniform distribution. Therefore we add a penalty for divergence between $\mathbf{w}^{t+1}$ and uniform weights $\mathbf{w}^0$. We use the Kullback-Leibler measure (Kullback & Leibler 1951) to evaluate the divergence between the distribution of the weights with respect to the original weights. We heighten the importance of this term as time progresses and the temperature is cooled down by evaluating $\beta KL(\mathbf{w}^{t+1}\|\mathbf{w}^0)$ where $\beta \propto 1/\tau^{t+1}$. Second, to maintain positive weight values we follow an exponential gradient strategy and derive a multiplicative update rule in the manner of (Kivinen & Warmuth 1997) where a penalty term for the for the KL-divergence between successive weight vectors $\mathbf{w}^{t+1}$ and $\mathbf{w}^t$ is added. All of these adaptations to our general schema lead us to use the following penalized score to guide our weight updates

$$
\begin{aligned}
L(h, \mathbf{w}^{t+1}) &= \text{Score}(h, D, \mathbf{w}^{t+1}) \\
&+ \beta\, KL(\mathbf{w}^{t+1}\|\mathbf{w}^0) \\
&+ \gamma\, KL(\mathbf{w}^{t+1}\|\mathbf{w}^t)
\end{aligned}
$$

where $1/\beta$ and $1/\gamma$ are proportional to the temperature and enforce proximity to uniform weights and the previous weights respectively.

There are two ways to use this function to derive weight updates. The first is to explicitly minimize the penalized score by solving for $\mathbf{w}^{t+1}$ in $\nabla_{\mathbf{w}^{t+1}} L(h, \mathbf{w}^{t+1}) = 0$. If the score function is convex in $\mathbf{w}$ (as it often is) the solution can be quickly determined by iteration. A second, a more expedient approach is suggested by Kivinen and Warmuth (1997): Instead of doing full optimization, we heuristically fix the score gradient in $\nabla_{\mathbf{w}} L$ to its value at $\mathbf{w}^t$ and *analytically* solve for the minimum of the resulting approximation, up to a step size parameter η. This is tantamount to approximating the optimal update by taking a fixed step of size η in the exponential gradient direction from the current weight vector $\mathbf{w}^t$. Omitting the details, we recover the multiplicative update formula

$$
w_m^{t+1} = \alpha^{t+1}(w_m^0)^{\frac{\beta}{\beta+\gamma}}(w_m^t)^{\frac{\gamma}{\beta+\gamma}} e^{-\frac{\eta}{\beta+\gamma}\left(\frac{\partial \text{Score}}{\partial w_m}|_{w_m^t}\right)}
$$

where α^{t+1} is just a normalization constant. We refer to this approach as the **Adversary** strategy.

In sum, our second basic reweighting approach is to make adversarial weight updates by following the negative gradient in a well motivated function. This approach can be applied whenever the original weighted score is differentiable *with respect to the weights*, for any fixed hypothesis. Note this is a very weak requirement that is typically satisfied in machine learning scenarios. In particular, differentiability with respect to the weights has nothing to do with the discreteness or continuity of the hypotheses—it is a property of how the instance weights affect the score of a fixed hypothesis. Thus one could apply the adversarial reweighting approach to standard decision tree and neural network training problems without modification.

Although the adversarial strategy has many similar advantages to the randomized approach, one distinction is noteworthy: randomness is replaced by a guided methodology

where weights are perturbed to minimize an intuitive function. This loses some of the flexibility of a random approach, which may reach the optimal solution by chance, but promises a far better average solution since it benefits from superior guidance.

Relation to ensemble reweighting There are interesting relationships between these reweighting techniques and ensemble learning methods like boosting (Schapire & Singer 1999). However, our techniques are not attempting to build an ensemble, and although they are similar to boosting on the surface, there are some fundamental differences. On an intuitive level, one difference is that boosting attempts to build a weighted ensemble of hypotheses that achieves a good score, whereas we are deliberately seeking a single hypothesis that attains this. On a technical level, boosting derives its weight updates by differentiating the loss of an entire ensemble (Mason *et al.* 2000), whereas our weight updates are derived by taking only the derivative of the score of the most recent hypothesis. Interestingly, although we do not exploit a large ensemble, we find that our methods still produce hypotheses that generalize well to unseen *test data*. Although surprising initially, this phenomenon is explained by the fact that example reweighting discovers hypotheses that obtain good scores while simultaneously being robust against perturbations of the training data, which confers obvious generalization benefits.

Learning Bayesian Networks from Data

To illustrate our approach on a general density estimation learning task we consider several problems in learning Bayesian networks from data: learning Bayesian network structure from complete data (structure search), optimizing Bayesian network parameters from incomplete data but given a fixed structure (parametric EM), and learning Bayesian network structure from incomplete data (Structural EM). Although the scores we encounter in these cases are not all additive, they are still differentiable and we can apply our methodology without modification.

Consider a finite set $\mathcal{X} = \{X_1, \ldots, X_n\}$ of random variables. A *Bayesian network* is an annotated directed acyclic graph that encodes a joint probability distribution over $\mathcal{X}$. The nodes of the graph correspond to the random variables $X_1, \ldots, X_n$. Each node is annotated with a *conditional probability distribution* (CPD) that represents $P(X_i \mid \boldsymbol{U}_i)$, where $\boldsymbol{U}_i$ denotes the parents of X_i in G. A Bayesian network B specifies a unique joint probability distribution over $\mathcal{X}$ given by: $P(X_1, \ldots, X_n) = \prod_{i=1}^n P(X_i|\boldsymbol{U}_i)$.

Given a *training set* $D = \{\mathbf{x}[1], \ldots, \mathbf{x}[M]\}$ we want to learn a Bayesian network B that *best matches* D, for each of the above scenarios. (See (Heckerman 1998) for a comprehensive overview of Bayesian network learning.) We explore each of the problems noted above in more detail in the subsequent sections.

Perturbing Structure Search

Structure Scores In this scenario, we search for a network structure B that best matches our *training set* D. In order to

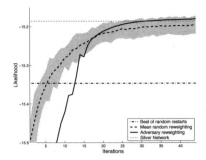

Figure 2: The progress of test set likelihood (log-loss/instance) during iterations while learning structure for the *Alarm* network. Compared are the golden model with parameters trained (**Silver** model), the best of random restarts search, the **Random** perturbation method and the **Adversary** method.

guide the search procedure, a scoring function for evaluating Bayesian network structures is used. A commonly used scoring function is the *BDe* score (Heckerman, Geiger, & Chickering 1995). A crucial property of the *BDe* (as well as other commonly used scores) is that it is a function of simple *sufficient statistics* of the data. For models in the exponential family, these sufficient statistics have a canonical form as a sum of functions applied to particular instances. Thus, if S is a sufficient statistic of interest, then

$$S(D) = \sum_m s(\mathbf{x}[m])$$

where $s()$ is a function of a particular training instance. For example, if $S(D)$ counts the number of times an event occurred in the data, then $s(\mathbf{x})$ is an indicator function that returns 1 if $\mathbf{x}$ satisfies the event, and 0 otherwise. When we perturb the score, we simply need to reweight the contribution of each instance. Thus, the perturbed statistic is

$$S(D, \mathbf{w}) = \sum_m M \cdot w_m \cdot s(\mathbf{x}[m])$$

Although the BDe score itself is not additive, it is nevertheless defined by sufficient statistics of the data and can therefore be easily adapted to the weighted case. (Details of the BDe score are given in the appendix.)

Once we specify the scoring function, the structure learning task reduces to a problem of searching over the combinatorial space of structures (i.e., DAGs) for the structure that maximizes the score. Since there are a super-exponential number of structures, an exhaustive search is infeasible. One common approach is to greedily follow local steps (add, remove or reverse an edge) using some search strategy (e.g. greedy hill-climbing) and incorporate a change into the current structure if it improves the score. Local search usually continues until convergence to a local maximum.

Note that the derivative of the *BDe* score with respect to w_m is straightforward (see appendix), and therefore both perturbation methods proposed above can be applied to this problem without change.

Experimental Evaluation We start by evaluating methods on the synthetic *Alarm* network (Beinlich *et al.* 1989) where

we can compare our results to the "golden" model that has the additional prior knowledge of the true structure. We compare our methods to a greedy hill-climbing procedure that is augmented with a TABU-search mechanism and performs several random restarts to try to improve the quality of the results.[1] We apply our perturbation methods following the outline specified in Figure 1 and allow the search procedure to fully optimize with respect to the perturbed weights at each iteration.

It is possible to evaluate the results both in terms of scores on training data and generalization performance on test data (average log-loss per instance). In all of our experiments the two measures correlate closely, and therefore due to lack of space we report only test set performance. Figure 2 shows the progress of the likelihood during iterations of the perturbed runs. Shown are the average performance of 100 runs of the **Random** perturbation method (with the 20/80% margin in gray) and the **Adversary** method, compared to the best of random re-starts with similar running times. Several conclusions are notable. First, both perturbation methods solidly outperform the random re-starts method. In fact, both methods are able to outperform the golden model with parameters retrained on the training set (**Silver** model). Second, the best model overall is found by **Random**. However, **Adversary** is significantly better than **Random**'s average performance. This allows one to either invest a lot of time and achieve a superior model by performing many random perturbation runs or obtain a near optimal structure with a single **Adversary** run.

To emphasize this point, Figure 3(a) shows the cumulative performance of **Random** for different temperatures and cooling factors. The less favorable line has a similar running time to **Adversary** while the superior **Random** takes an order of magnitude longer for each run. These runs often reach what appears to be the achievable global maximum.

We also evaluated the performance of our methods for structure search on a real-life data set. *Stock Data* (Boyen, Friedman, & Koller 1999) is a dataset that traces the daily change of 20 major US technology stocks for several years (1516 trading days). As shown in Table 1, a significant improvement in the models learned by the perturbed method.

Perturbing Parametric EM

Learning with Incomplete Data In many real life datasets learning is complicated by the fact that some of the variables are not always observed. In such cases we say that there are *missing values* in the data. An even more difficult situation is when certain variables are never observed, we call such variables *hidden* or *latent* variables. In these scenarios, the m'th training instance is not a complete instance $\mathbf{x}[m]$, but only a partial instance, which we denote by $\mathbf{o}[m]$.

---

[1] We also tried standard simulated annealing, as described by Heckerman *et al.* (1995). However, using the parameters proposed by Heckerman *et al.* we get worse results then the baseline search method. This is consistent with Chickering (1996), who showed that using multiple re-starts greedy hill-climbing is more effective than simulated annealing for this task.

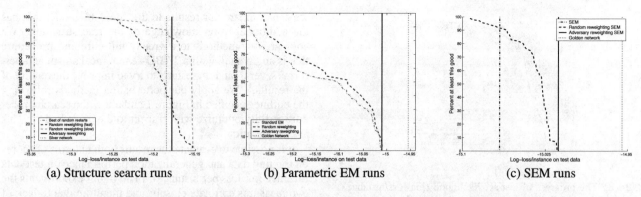

| (a) Structure search runs | (b) Parametric EM runs | (c) SEM runs |

Figure 3: Cumulative performance on test data of the *Alarm* network. The x-axis shows test-set likelihood (log loss/instance), the y-axis shows percent of runs that achieve that likelihood or higher. Compared are 100 runs each of baseline learning method, computationally intensive **Random** perturbations and **Adversary**. (a) Shows results for structure search with complete data. (b) Shows results for parameter estimation for data set with 4 central variables hidden, where the structure is fixed to the true structure. (c) Shows results for estimation of the parameters as well as the structure from the same dataset.

Since we do not have complete instances, we cannot estimate sufficient statistics and learning becomes more complicated. A common method to cope with such situations is to use the *expectation-maximization* (EM) algorithm (Dempster, Laird, & Rubin 1977). In this method, in each iteration, we use the previously found model $P_0(X_1, \ldots, X_n)$ to compute the *expected sufficient statistics*

$$E[S(D) \mid P_0] = \sum_m \sum_{\mathbf{x}[m]} s(\mathbf{x}[m]) P_0(\mathbf{x}[m] \mid \mathbf{o}[m])$$

where $P_0(\mathbf{x}[m] \mid \mathbf{o}[m])$ is the probability, according to the model P_0, of the complete instance $\mathbf{x}[m]$ given the partial observation $\mathbf{o}[m]$. Once we have computed these expected sufficient statistics, we can evaluate the score with respect to them. This score is referred to as the *expected score*. The main EM theorem shows that the improvement of the expected score between P_0 and the new model is a lower bound on the improvement between the (true) scores of the two models.[2] The simplest application of EM in graphical models is for parameter learning (Lauritzen 1995; Heckerman 1998). In this case our maximization objective is just the likelihood of the model on the training data. To do this we maximize the expected likelihood at each iteration of the EM algorithm.

Escaping Local Maxima One of the additional benefits of the ideas for perturbing the weights suggested above is that they are readily applicable for this problem as well. Instead of using expected sufficient statistics, we compute reweighted expected sufficient statistics using our current weight vector

$$E[S(D, \mathbf{w}) \mid P_0] = \sum_m M \cdot w_m \sum_{\mathbf{x}[m]} s(\mathbf{x}[m]) P_0(\mathbf{x}[m] \mid \mathbf{o}[m])$$

It is clear that the maximum point of the expected score is not the maximum point of the true score (for otherwise

---

[2]This statement of course depends on the score. It is true for the likelihood score (Dempster, Laird, & Rubin 1977; Lauritzen 1995) and for the MDL/BIC scores (Friedman 1997), and holds approximately for Bayesian structure scores (Friedman 1998).

one iteration suffices to get to the global maximum). Thus, the expected score is biased. In general, this bias is toward models that are in some sense similar to the one with which we computed the expected sufficient statistics. This suggests that we do not necessarily want to find the optimum of the expected score within EM iterations. Instead, we apply a limited number of EM iterations (i.e., one) within each *optimize* step of the **PerturbedSearch** procedure (Figure 1) and then reweight the instances. The general perturbation scheme is otherwise unchanged.

Experimental Evaluation We start by evaluating methods on the synthetic *Alarm* network. Figure 3(b) compares 100 runs of standard parametric EM, computationally intensive **Random** perturbation, and an **Adversary** run. Because of the limited number of EM iterations, **Adversary** takes only about 15 times longer than a single parametric EM run and **Random** takes around 50 times longer. We can clearly see the advantage of the **Adversary** method, which achieves what appears to be the global maximum. This maximum is reached by only a few of the random re-starts and **Random** perturbation runs, and is not far from the golden model that generated the test data.

Perturbing Structural EM

A more complex application of EM is the *Structural EM* (SEM) procedure for learning structures (Friedman 1997; 1998). Our problem is now two-fold: at each iteration we need to find an optimal structure and then optimize the parameters with respect to that structure. In order to do this, at each stage we compute the expected sufficient statistics for different structures, and use the structure score to compare them. By performing structure search *within* the EM iteration, the procedure attempts to optimize (or at least to improve) the expected score. Like standard EM, this procedure is guaranteed to improve at each iteration and typically converges to a local maxima. However, in practice the optimization problem now is much more complex with many local maxima, especially when *hidden* variables abound.

Experimental Evaluation The setting is identical to the one used in the EM runs, but we also attempt to learn the topology of the network. The starting point of the search is a structure where all the hidden variables are parents of all the observables. Figure 3(c) shows cumulative results 100 runs for the synthetic *Alarm* example. The standard structural EM (**SEM**) runs have a very low variance and are worse than over 90% of the **Random** perturbation runs. As with parametric EM, but more markedly, the **Adversary** method dominates random reweighting. Note that it halves the distance from the baseline performance to the golden model performance.

Experiments with real-life data Finally, we applied our perturbation methods to several real-life datasets: ¿From the UCI machine learning repository, we used the *Soybean* (Michalski & Chilausky 1980) disease database that contains 35 variables relevant for the diagnosis of 19 possible plant diseases, and the *Audiology* data set (Bareiss & Porter 1987) which explores illnesses relating to audiology dysfunctions. Both data sets have many missing values and comparatively few examples. We also used data from Rosetta's compendium (Hughes *et al.* 2000), using the preprocessing of (Pe'er *et al.* 2001), consisting of 300 examples over 6000 *Saccharomyces cerevisiae* genes. We chose 37 genes which participate in the *stationary phase* stress response.

For each data set we performed 5-fold cross validation and compared the log-loss performance on independent test data. Table 1 summarizes the results. Shown are results for best of multiple random restarts SEM, average and 80% values of **Random** perturbation runs, and the **Adversary** method. We can see that, as for the synthetic *Alarm* data, both perturbation methods achieve superior results to standard random restarts SEM. Similar to what was observed in structure search, it is sometimes possible to reach a superior model to **Adversary** by performing many **Random** perturbation runs.

As we see, in all domains, the perturbation methods improve over the baseline. Although the improvement per instances seems small, we stress that as one gets closer to the optimum, achieving additional improvements becomes more difficult. The results on synthetic data suggest that our methods are often very close to the global maximum achievable on the given training data.

Learning Sequence Motifs

All of our case studies so far have addressed unsupervised density estimation problems. We now examine a different learning situation where we consider discriminative learning. The problem here is to perform a non-linear logistic regression to find *regulatory motifs* in DNA promoter sequences; *i.e.*, short subsequences that regulate the expression of genes. In particular, a motif is defined as a relatively short signature of about 8-20 nucleotides (DNA letters) that appears somewhere in the DNA sequence—the exact location of which is unknown and can vary from sequence to sequence. An example of a motif might be the sequence

Table 1: Summary of results on independent test data for several data sets for the structure search and structural EM problems. Shown are log-loss/instance of improvement in performance with respect to the **Best** of random restarts baseline. Compared are the mean of the **Random** perturbation method (along with the **80%** mark) and the **Adversary** method.

	Domain	**Random**	**80%**	**Adv**
Search	Stock	-0.02	+0.01	+0.03
	Alarm	+0.15	+0.18	+0.17
SEM	Rosetta	-0.05	+0.27	+0.09
	Audio	0	+0.39	+0.23
	Soybean	+0.19	+0.32	+0.19
	Alarm	+0.254	+0.31	+0.33

ACGCGT for instance. Unfortunately, most known motifs are not preserved perfectly in DNA, and one generally has to allow for substitutions in one or several positions. Accordingly, the common representation of a motif is as a *weight matrix* (Durbin *et al.* 1998) which describes the weight of each of the four possible DNA letters for each position within the motif. Intuitively, a subsequence that has a large sum of letter weights is said to match the motif. We use the notation $w_i[x]$ to denote the weight of the letter x in the i'th position.

Following (Barash, Bejerano, & Friedman 2001; Segal *et al.* 2002) we define the basic training problem in discriminative terms. Given N promoter sequences $\mathbf{s}_1, \ldots, \mathbf{s}_N$, where the n'th sequence consists of K letters $s_{n,1} \ldots s_{n,K}$, and a set of of training labels $l_1, \ldots, l_N$, where l_i is 1 if the sequence is regulated by the motif and 0 if it is not (these labels can be obtained from different biological experiments), we wish to maximize the log-loss $\sum_i P(l_n \mid s_n)$ where

$$P(l_n = 1 \mid S_{n,1}, \ldots, S_{n,K})$$
$$= \text{logistic}\left(\log\left(\frac{v}{K}\sum_j \exp\{\sum_i w_i[S_{n,i+j}]\}\right)\right)$$

and $\text{logistic}(x) = \frac{1}{1+e^{-x}}$ is the logistic function and v is a threshold parameter; see Segal *et al* (2002) for more details.

Segal *et al.* (2002) address this problem in two stage. First, they search for high scoring seeds by considering all short words of length 6 using methods of Barash *et al* (2001). Then, for each seed they constructed a weight matrix of 20 positions that embodies the seed consensus sequence in the middle positions (the weights in flanking positions were initialized to 0), and then using conjugate gradient ascent (Price 1992) to maximize the log-likelihood score.

We adopt the same procedure augmented with our weight perturbation methods. After each weight perturbation, we perform a line search (Price 1992) in the direction of the gradient of the likelihood with respect to the reweighted samples. After the end of cooling schedule, we apply a final conjugate gradient ascent to find the local maxima in the vicinity of the final point of the search.

We applied this procedure to the 9 training sets generated during the analysis that Segal *et al.* performed on DNA-binding experiments of Simon *et al.* (2001). We report the

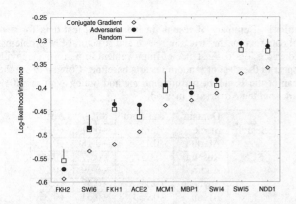

Figure 4: Performance of different methods in the motif finding task for 9 data sets. The x-axis corresponds to the different datasets, and the y-axis reports training log-likelihood per instance. We report the performance of the baseline conjugate ascent method, Adversarial reweighting, and Random reweighting. The box plot show the range between 20% to the 80% of 50 Random reweighting runs, and the narrow lines on top of the box show the best result of these 50 runs.

results in Figure 4. As one can see, both Random and Adversarial reweighting are consistently better than the baseline approach. In some cases (ACE2, SWI4, SWI5) the Adversarial reweighting achieves scores better than all the random runs, in others (FKH1, NDD1) it is better than at least 80% of the random runs, and only in two (FKH2, MBP1) it is worse than 80% of the random runs.

Discussion and Future Work

In this paper we proposed an annealing like method for escaping local maxima. The essence of our approach is to perturb the problem rather than the solution, and look for optimal solutions in the perturbed problems. As we show, such perturbations allow one to overcome local maxima in several learning scenarios. On both synthetic and real-life data, this approach seems to lead to significantly improved models in learning structure with complete data, learning parameters with hidden variables, and learning both parameters and structure with incomplete data. The improvements are particularly impressive for the complex problem of learning both structure and parameters from missing data. The Random reweighting approach we introduce here has been applied in Friedman *et al.* (2002) and Barash and Friedman (2002) for learning phylogenetic trees and context-specific clustering models, respectively. Both papers report dramatic improvements with this approach.

The perturbation of instance weights is particularly attractive for learning problems. It is easy to find reweighted versions of standard learning scores. Moreover, example weights are easily incorporated into non-trivial learning procedures such as EM. First, one can exploit the expected sufficient statistics for efficient search, and second, randomize the expected score to often find better scoring models.

In this paper, we compared two strategies for generating the sequences of weights during the annealing: *random-ized reweighting* and *adversarial reweighting*. Our results show that both approaches dominate the straw-man of multiple restart search. Randomized reweighting can sometimes achieve better performance, but this might require performing several annealing runs. The deterministic adversarial strategy has the advantage of achieving similar performance in a single run.

One class of approaches that might be related to the ones we describe here are the *deterministic annealing* methods (Rose 1998). These methods are similar in that they change the score by adding a "free energy" component. This component serves to smooth out the score landscape. Deterministic annealing proceeds by finding the (local) maxima at each iteration and then moves to a "colder" score that recovers more of the structure of the score of interest. Local ascent is then used to trace the maxima starting from the hypothesis of the previous iteration. At the outset the rationale for the scores used in deterministic annealing is quite different then our weight perturbation. It is unclear if there are deeper connections between the two methods.

One avenue that we did not explore in this paper is the combination of a randomized element within the adversarial strategy. It is also clear that for realistic applications, we need to tune the implementation to reduce the number of iterations. This can be done by incorporating more sophisticated cooling strategies from the simulated annealing literature (see (Laarhoven & Aarts 1987) for a review). It is also worth exploring improved ways to interleave the maximization and the reweighting steps. Finally, the empirical success of these methods raises the challenge of providing a better theoretical understanding of their effectiveness. This is particularly intriguing for the adversarial reweighting strategy. Although this strategy has similarities to boosting and multiplicative update strategies, the analysis of these methods does not seem to directly apply to our setting.

Acknowledgments The authors thank Yoseph Barash, Daphne Koller, Itsik Pe'er, Tal Pupko, and, in particular, Noam Lotner for useful discussions and comments on previous drafts of the paper. This research was supported in part by ISF grant 244/99 and Israeli Ministry of Science grant 2008-1-99. N. F. was supported by Alon Fellowship. D. S. was supported by NSERC and MITACS.

Appendix: Gradient of the Lagrangian

The Lagrangian used in the section for **Adversarial Reweighting** is of the form

$$
\begin{aligned}
L(h, \mathbf{w}^{t+1}) &= \text{Score}(h, D, \mathbf{w}^{t+1}) \\
&+ \beta\, KL(\mathbf{w}^{t+1} \| \mathbf{w}^0) \\
&+ \gamma\, KL(\mathbf{w}^{t+1} \| \mathbf{w}^t)
\end{aligned}
$$

The method suggested in that section requires the calculation of the derivative of the Lagrangian with respect to each instance weight.

The derivative of $KL(w^{t+1} \| w^0)$ is simply

$$
\frac{\partial \sum_m w_m^{t+1} \log \frac{w_m^{t+1}}{w_m^0}}{\partial w_m^{t+1}} = \log \frac{w_m^{t+1}}{w_m^0} + 1
$$

and similarly for the derivative of $KL(w^{t+1} \| w^t)$.

For Bayesian network structure learning, we use the BDe Score (Heckerman, Geiger, & Chickering 1995). This require defining a prior distribution P^0 over the domain, and a prior strength parameter N^0. For each event $\mathbf{x}$, we define $\alpha(\mathbf{x}) = N^0 \cdot P^0(x)$, and $\alpha'(\mathbf{x}) = \alpha(\mathbf{x}) + N(\mathbf{x})$, where $N(\mathbf{x})$ is the number of occurrences of $\mathbf{X} = \mathbf{x}$ in the training data. The BDE score is defined as

$$\text{Score}_{\text{BDe}} =$$
$$\sum_i \sum_{pa_i} \left(\log \frac{\Gamma(\alpha(pa_i))}{\Gamma(\alpha'(pa_i))} + \sum_{x_i} \log \frac{\Gamma(\alpha'(x_i, pa_i))}{\Gamma(\alpha(x_i, pa_i))} \right)$$

where x_i is an assignment to the i'th variable, pa_i is an assignment to the parents of the i'th variable, and $\Gamma(x)$ is the *gamma function*.

The only expressions that depend on the weights are $N(pa_i) = \sum_m w_m \cdot P(Pa_i = pa_i \mid e_m)$ and $N(x_i, pa_i)$, where e_m is the evidence of the m'th instance. Using the *digamma function* $\Psi(x) \equiv \frac{\Gamma'(x)}{\Gamma(x)}$ (DeGroot 1989), the derivative of $\text{Score}_{\text{BDe}}$ (for a specific value of pa_i) with respect to a specific weight w_m is given by

$$\frac{\partial \text{Score}_{\text{BDe}}}{\partial w_m} =$$
$$\sum_i \sum_{pa_i} \sum_{x_i} (\Psi(\alpha'(x_i, pa_i)) - \Psi(\alpha'(pa_i))) P(x_i, pa_i \mid e_m)$$

which can readily be evaluated using a numerical approximation to the digamma function.

References

Barash, Y., and Friedman, N. Context-specific Bayesian clustering for gene expression data. *J. Comp. Bio.* 9:169–191.

Barash, Y.; Bejerano, G.; and Friedman, N. 2001. A simple hyper-geometric approach for discovering putative transcription factor binding sites. In *Algorithms in Bioinformatics: Proc. First International Workshop*, 278–293.

Bareiss, R., and Porter, B. 1987. Protos: An exemplar-based learning apprentice. *Proceedings of the 4th International Workshop on Machine Learning* 12–23.

Beinlich, I.; Suermondt, G.; Chavez, R.; and Cooper, G. 1989. The ALARM monitoring system. In *Proc. 2'nd European Conf. on AI and Medicine*.

Bishop, C. M. 1995. *Neural Networks for Pattern Recognition*.

Boyen, X.; Friedman, N.; and Koller, D. 1999. Learning the structure of complex dynamic systems. In *UAI '99*.

Chickering, D. M. 1996. Learning equivalence classes of Bayesian network structures. In *UAI '96*. 150–157.

Codenotti, B.; Manzini, G.; Margara, L.; and Resta, G. 1996. Perturbation: An efficient technique for the solution of very large instances of the TSP. *INFORMS Journal on Computing* 8(2):125–133.

DeGroot, M. H. 1989. *Probability and Statistics*.

Dempster, A. P.; Laird, N. M.; and Rubin, D. B. 1977. Maximum likelihood from incomplete data via the EM algorithm. *Journal of the Royal Statistical Society* B 39:1–39.

Durbin, R.; Eddy, S.; Krogh, A.; and Mitchison, G. 1998. *Biological Sequence Analysis : Probabilistic Models of Proteins and Nucleic Acids*.

Friedman, N.; Ninio, M.; Peer, I.; and Pupko, T. 2002. A structural EM algorithm for phylogenetic inference. *J. Comp. Bio.* 9:331–353.

Friedman, N. 1997. Learning belief networks in the presence of missing values and hidden variables. In *ICML '97*. 125–133.

Friedman, N. 1998. The Bayesian structural EM algorithm. In *UAI '98*.

Glover, F., and Laguna, M. 1993. Tabu search. In *Modern Heuristic Techniques for Combinatorial Problems*.

Heckerman, D.; Geiger, D.; and Chickering, D. M. 1995. Learning Bayesian networks: The combination of knowledge and statistical data. *Machine Learning* 20:197–243.

Heckerman, D. 1998. A tutorial on learning with Bayesian networks. In *Learning in Graphical Models*.

Hughes, T. R.; Marton, M. J.; *et al* 2000. Functional discovery via a compendium of expression profiles. *Cell* 102(1):109–26.

Kirpatrick, S.; Gelatt, Jr., C.; and Vecchi, M. 1994. Optimization by simulated annealing. *Science* 220:671–680.

Kivinen, J., and Warmuth, M. 1997. Exponentiated gradient versus gradient descent for linear predictors. *Information and Computation* 132:1–63.

Kullback, S., and Leibler, R. A. 1951. On information and sufficiency. *Annals of Mathematical Statistics* 22:76–86.

Laarhoven, P., and Aarts, E. 1987. *Simulated Annealing: Theory and Applications*.

Lauritzen, S. L. 1995. The EM algorithm for graphical association models with missing data. *Computational Statistics and Data Analysis* 19:191–201.

Mason, L.; Baxter, J.; Bartlett, P.; and Frean, M. 2000. Functional gradient techniques for combining hypotheses. In *Advances in Large Margin Classifiers*.

Michalski, R., and Chilausky, R. 1980. Learning by being told and learning from examples. *International Journal of Policy Analysis and Information Systems* 4(2).

Nixon, K. C. 1999. The parsimony ratchet, a new method for rapid parsimony analysis. *Cladistics* 15:407–414.

Pe'er, D.; Regev, A.; Elidan, G.; and Friedman, N. 2001. Inferring subnetworks from perturbed expression profiles. *Bioinformatics* 17(Suppl 1):S215–24.

Price, W. H. 1992. *Numerical Recipes in C*.

Rose, K. 1998. Deterministic annealing for clustering, compression, classification, regression and related optimization problems. *Proc. IEEE* 80:2210–2239.

Schapire, R. E., and Singer, Y. 1999. Improved boosting algorithms using confidence-rated predictions. *Machine Learning* 37.

Schuurmans, D.; Southey, F.; and Holte, R. 2001. The exponentiated subgradient algorithm for heuristic Boolean programming. In *Proceedings IJCAI-01*, 334–341.

Segal, E.; Barash, Y.; Simon, I.; Friedman, N.; and Koller, D. 2002. From promoter sequence to expression:a probabilistic framework. In *RECOMB '02*.

Simon, I.; Barnett, J.; Hannett, N.; Harbison, C.; Rinaldi, N.; Volkert, T.; Wyrick, J.; Zeitlinger, J.; Gifford, D.; Jaakkola, T.; and Young, R. 2001. Serial regulation of transcriptional regulators in the yeast cell cycle. *Cell* 106:697–708.

Progressive Rademacher Sampling

Tapio Elomaa
Department of Computer Science
P. O. Box 26 (Teollisuuskatu 23)
FIN-00014 Univ. of Helsinki, Finland
elomaa@cs.helsinki.fi

Matti Kääriäinen
Department of Computer Science
P. O. Box 26 (Teollisuuskatu 23)
FIN-00014 Univ. of Helsinki, Finland
matti.kaariainen@cs.helsinki.fi

Abstract

Sampling can enhance processing of large training example databases, but without knowing all of the data, or the example producing process, it is impossible to know in advance what size of a sample to choose in order to guarantee good performance. Progressive sampling has been suggested to circumvent this problem. The idea in it is to increase the sample size according to some schedule until accuracy close to that which would be obtained using all of the data is reached. How to determine this stopping time efficiently and accurately is a central difficulty in progressive sampling.

We study stopping time determination by approximating the generalization error of the hypothesis rather than by assuming the often observed shape for the learning curve and trying to detect whether the final plateau has been reached in the curve. We use data dependent generalization error bounds. Instead of using the common cross validation approach, we use the recently introduced Rademacher penalties, which have been observed to give good results on simple concept classes.

We experiment with two-level decision trees built by the learning algorithm T2. It finds a hypothesis with the minimal error with respect to the sample. The theoretically well motivated stopping time determination based on Rademacher penalties gives results that are much closer to those attained using heuristics based on assumptions on learning curve shape than distribution independent estimates based on VC dimension do.

Introduction

Sampling can be a powerful technique for inductive algorithms to avoid unnecessary processing of the whole available data. It helps to circumvent memory limitations, gain efficiency, and can even result in increased accuracy (Fürnkranz 1998). Sampling is particularly useful in the data mining context, where the sheer abundance of the data may impair even the fastest algorithms (Kivinen and Mannila 1994, Toivonen 1996, Scheffer and Wrobel 2000). However, it is hard to know how large a sample to choose. Drawing a too small sample will not yield a good-enough performance and, on the other hand, choosing a too large sample will unavoidably mean wasting computational effort. An apparent solution is to use *progressive (or dynamic) sampling*;

taking gradually increasing portions of the available data as the sample (John and Langley 1996, Provost, Jensen, and Oates 1999). With a suitable sampling *schedule* — sample size selection scheme — and an efficient stopping time determination method progressive sampling is asymptotically as efficient as knowing the right sample size in advance (Provost, Jensen, and Oates 1999). Sampling schedules are theoretically well understood, but stopping time determination is not. Premature stopping will yield suboptimal results and too late stopping will mean unbeneficial wasting of resources. The obvious goal is to stop as soon as growing the sample will not yield any more advantage. Unfortunately, determining this stopping time is extremely difficult.

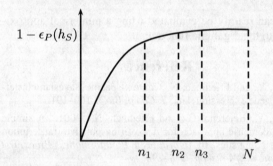

$$1 - \epsilon_P(h_S)$$

Figure 1: A common shape for a learning curve.

Previous studies on progressive sampling have relied on the empirically often observed common shape of the learning curves (Cortes et al. 1994, Oates and Jensen 1997, Frey and Fisher 1999): The classification accuracy of a learning algorithm first typically slopes steeply from the initial accuracy with the first few examples (see Fig. 1). After a while the accuracy growth diminishes before reaching a plateau, during which practically no accuracy gain is obtained. The optimal sample size to draw with this behavior would be the first one (the smallest one) giving an accuracy on the plateau.

It is hard to determine which sample sizes give accuracies belonging to the plateau and which do not. For example, which of the indicated subsample sizes, if any, in Fig. 1 is the first one giving an accuracy that belongs to the plateau? Furthermore, all domains do not have a plateau in their learning curve at all (Catlett 1991). One can approximate the steepness of the learning curve in the local neighborhood of a sample size in order to decide whether the expected plateau has been reached or not (Provost, Jensen, and Oates 1999), or one can try to approximate whether the accuracy with the sample size is with high probability close enough to that which will be reached eventually if all of the data is used (John and Langley 1996). In practice, though, learning curves are not always as well-behaving as the one depicted in Fig. 1 (Haussler at al. 1996, Provost, Jensen, and Oates 1999). Moreover, stopping time determination using the above-mentioned methods can be computationally costly.

Our approach, rather, is to rely on a data dependent bound on the generalization error of the learning algorithm in question. The idea is to stop sampling as soon as the generalization error of the hypothesis chosen by the learning algorithm can be guaranteed to be close to its error on the training set with high probability. Thus, we try to choose the smallest sample size that enables us to prove good results on the generalization capability of the hypothesis chosen by the learning algorithm. Instead of using distribution independent generalization error bounds based on, e.g., the Vapnik-Chervonenkis (VC) dimension (Vapnik 1998) we use the recently introduced approach based on *Rademacher penalization* (Koltchinskii 2001, Bartlett and Mendelson 2001). A related approach based on sequential statistical tests has been introduced by Schuurmans and Greiner (1995).

In the remainder of this paper we first review approaches to sampling large databases. Then data dependent bounds on the generalization error of a learning algorithm are recapitulated. In particular, Rademacher penalization is reviewed. Thereafter, progressive Rademacher sampling is introduced. We prove that it is possible to combine geometric sampling schedules efficiently with the Rademacher penalization approximation of the generalization error. Following that two-level decision trees and learning them (Auer, Holte, and Maass 1995) are briefly recapitulated. Our empirical experiments chart the utility and feasibility of progressive Rademacher sampling using two-level decision trees. We contrast the results to both theoretical and practical alternatives. Finally, some conclusions on the study are presented.

Static and Dynamic Sampling of Large Databases

Let $S = \{ (x_i, y_i) \mid i = 1, \ldots, N \}$ be an example set consisting of N independent examples $(x_i, y_i) \in X \times \{ 0, 1 \}$ each of which is drawn according to some unknown probability measure P on $X \times \{ 0, 1 \}$. We assume that N is finite, but so large that it cannot be exhausted in practice. For example, it may be impossible to keep N examples in main memory at one time. In such a situation the theoretical time complexities of learning algorithms do not necessarily hold.

Kivinen and Mannila (1994) have derived sample size bounds for approximate verification of the truth of first-order logical formulas represented in tuple relational calculus for a given database relation by considering only a random sample of the relation. The work of Toivonen (1996) was motivated by the need to reduce the number of expensive passes through the database in searching for the frequent association rules. One pass through the whole database can usually be avoided by inferring a (super)set of candidate rules with a lowered frequency threshold from a random sample of the database. Only one pass through the complete database is required to validate which of the candidates actually are frequent enough in the whole database. Scheffer and Wrobel's (2000) sequential sampling algorithm's main contributions are to return k best hypotheses instead of only one, work with many different utility functions, and to rank the candidate hypotheses already at an early stage.

The static sampling approaches require a lot of information in advance if results of guaranteed quality are desired. Dynamic approaches to sampling have also been proposed. An early dynamic sampling technique is Quinlan's (1983) *windowing*, in which a consistent decision tree is first grown on a random sample, falsely classified examples are then augmented to the data, and the process is repeated until convergence. Windowing can be beneficial in noise-free domains, but cannot cope well with noise (Fürnkranz 1998).

Successively increasing the sample size until it gives good enough results is the idea behind progressive sampling. The method of determining what size samples to choose next is called a *schedule*. John and Langley (1996) used an *arithmetic* schedule, in which the size of the sample is increased by a constant portion, n_Δ, at each step. Let n_0 be the number of examples in the initial sample S_0. Then the size of the ith sample S_i will be $|S_i| = n_i = n_0 + (i \cdot n_\Delta)$. The problem with this schedule is that one may need to iterate too many times before reaching the required accuracy.

An alternative to the arithmetic schedule is to use a *geometric* schedule, in which the initial sample size is multiplied according to a geometric sequence. In this case $n_i = a^i n_0$, where n_0 is the initial sample size and $a > 1$ is a constant. Provost, Jensen, and Oates (1999) showed that geometric schedule combined with an efficient stopping time detection is asymptotically optimal for superlinear learning algorithms in the sense that it gives the same asymptotic time complexity as knowing the optimal sample size in advance.

They also observed that it is in principle possible to compute the optimal schedule as well. However, that requires knowing the execution time $t(n)$ of the learning algorithm on n instances and the probability $\Phi(n)$ that convergence requires more than n instances. Then the expected cost of schedule $\Sigma = \{ n_1, \ldots, n_k \}$ can be computed as

$$C(\Sigma) = \sum_{i=1}^{k} \Phi(n_{i-1}) t(n_i),$$

where $n_0 = 0$ and $\Phi(0) = 1$, because convergence definitely requires more than 0 examples. Let $c[i, j]$ denote the cost of the minimum expected cost schedule, which includes samples of i and j instances, of all samples in the size range $[i, j]$. The cost of the optimal schedule $c[0, N]$ can be computed by the recurrence

$$c[i, j] = \min \left\{ \Phi(i)t(j), \min_{i < k < j} c[i, k] + c[k, j] \right\}.$$

Dynamic programming can be used to solve it in $O(N^3)$ time.

Provost, Jensen, and Oates (1999) based the approximation of the stopping time on learning curve analysis, where the underlying assumption is that machine learning algorithms perform on all domains with increasing sample sizes roughly as depicted in Fig. 1. However, as they also discuss, this well-behavedness assumption is not always true, even though many empirical studies have supported this view. If the learning curve does not behave well, there is no ground in trying to determine the stopping time by examining the learning curve's local slope. In John and Langley's (1996) work stopping time determination was, rather, based on trying to approximate the difference between the accuracy of the hypothesis chosen after seeing n examples and that of the one chosen after seeing all N examples. Approximating the accuracy on all of the data requires extrapolating the learning curve, and in this task an explicit power law assumption about the shape of the learning curve was also made.

Data Dependent Bounds on the Generalization Error of a Hypothesis

We now give up assumptions on the shape of the learning curve. However, if nothing is assumed about the learning algorithm or the hypotheses it may choose, it is impossible to prove any bounds on the generalization capability of a hypothesis. Therefore, we assume — as one usually does in the PAC and statistical learning settings — that the learning algorithm chooses its hypothesis from some fixed hypothesis class $\mathcal{H}$. Under this assumption generalization error analysis provides theoretical results bounding the generalization error of hypotheses $h \in \mathcal{H}$ that are based on the sample and the properties of the hypothesis class. We review next some results of generalization error analysis that will be useful in stopping time detection.

Given a hypothesis h, its *generalization error* is the probability that a randomly drawn example (x, y) is misclassified:

$$\epsilon_P(h) = P(h(x) \neq y).$$

The general goal of learning, of course, is to find a hypothesis with a small generalization error. However, since the generalization error of a hypothesis depends on the unknown probability distribution P, it cannot be computed directly based on the sample alone. We can try to approximate generalization error of the hypothesis h by its *training error* on n examples:

$$\hat{\epsilon}_n(h) = \frac{1}{n} \sum_{i=1}^{n} L(h(x_i), y_i),$$

where L is the 0/1 loss function

$$L(y, y') = \begin{cases} 1, & \text{if } y \neq y'; \\ 0, & \text{otherwise.} \end{cases}$$

Empirical Risk Minimization (ERM) is a principle that suggest choosing the hypothesis $h \in \mathcal{H}$ whose training error is minimal. In relatively small and simple hypothesis classes finding the minimum training error hypothesis is computationally feasible. To guarantee that ERM yields hypotheses with small generalization error, one can try to bound

$\sup_{h \in \mathcal{H}} |\epsilon_P(h) - \hat{\epsilon}_n(h)|$. Under the assumption that the examples are independent and identically distributed (i.i.d), whenever the hypothesis class $\mathcal{H}$ is not too complex, the difference of the training error of the hypothesis h on n examples and its true generalization error converge to 0 in probability as n tends to infinity. We take advantage of this asymptotic behavior, and base sampling stopping time determination on a data-dependent upper bound of the difference between generalization and training error.

The most common approach to deriving generalization error bounds for hypotheses is based on taking the VC dimension of the hypothesis class into account. The problem with this approach is that it provides optimal results only in the worst case — when the underlying probability distribution is as bad as can be. Thus, the generalization error bounds based on VC dimension tend to be overly pessimistic. Data dependent generalization error bounds, on the other hand, are provably almost optimal for any given domain (Koltchinskii 2001). In the following we review the foundations of a recent promising approach to bounding the generalization error.

A *Rademacher random variable* (Koltchinskii 2001) takes values $+1$ and -1 with probability 1/2 each. Let $r_1, r_2, \ldots, r_n$ be a sequence of i.i.d. Rademacher random variables independent of the data $(x_1, y_1), \ldots, (x_n, y_n)$. The *Rademacher penalty* of the hypothesis class $\mathcal{H}$ is defined as:

$$R_n(\mathcal{H}) = \sup_{h \in \mathcal{H}} \left| \frac{1}{n} \sum_{i=1}^{n} r_i L(h(x_i), y_i) \right|.$$

By a symmetrization inequality of the theory of empirical processes (Van der Vaart and Wellner 2000)

$$\mathbf{E} \left\{ \sup_{h \in \mathcal{H}} |\epsilon_P(h) - \hat{\epsilon}_n(h)| \right\} \leq 2\mathbf{E} \left\{ R_n(\mathcal{H}) \right\}, \quad (1)$$

where expectations are taken over the choice of examples on the left and over the choice of examples and Rademacher random variables on the right. Furthermore, the random variables $\sup_{h \in \mathcal{H}} |\epsilon_P(h) - \hat{\epsilon}_n(h)|$ and $R_n(\mathcal{H})$ are tightly concentrated around their expectations (Koltchinskii 2001). Thus, one can show using standard concentration inequalities that with probability at least $1 - \delta$

$$\epsilon_P(h) \leq \hat{\epsilon}_n(h) + 2R_n(\mathcal{H}) + \eta(\delta, n), \quad (2)$$

where

$$\eta(\delta, n) = 5\sqrt{\frac{\ln(2/\delta)}{2n}}$$

is a small error term that takes care of the fluctuations of the analyzed random variables around their expectations.

The usefulness of inequality (2) stems from the fact that its right-hand side depends only on the training sample and not on P directly. Furthermore, Koltchinskii (2001) has shown that computation of the Rademacher penalty is equivalent to the minimization of the training error on relabeled training data. This means that $R_n(\mathcal{H})$ can be computed with the algorithm used for ERM. To get the effects of Rademacher random variables r_i we define a new set of labels z_i for the training data as the flipping of the original label with probability 1/2.

Altogether, the computation of the Rademacher penalty entails the following steps.

- Flip the label of each example (x_i, y_i) with probability $1/2$ to obtain a new set of labels z_i.
- Find the functions $h_1, h_2 \in \mathcal{H}$ that minimize the empirical error with respect to the set of labels z_i and $-z_i$, respectively.
- Compute $|(1/n) \sum_{i=1}^{n} r_i L(h(x_i), y_i)|$ for $h = h_1, h_2$ and select the maximum out of these two values as the Rademacher penalty.

Progressive Rademacher Sampling

Koltchinskii et al. (2000) have applied Rademacher penalties to provide approximate solutions to difficult control problems. Dynamic sampling schedules with provable properties have been applied in this context as well. As sampling schedules the bootstrap approach as well as the geometric schedule $n_i = 2^i n_0$ were used. We now adapt the techniques introduced by Koltchinskii et al. (2000) to stopping time detection.

The least required sample size $n_{\min}^P(\varepsilon, \delta)$ over the class $\mathcal{H}$ with respect to P is the minimal number of examples needed to guarantee that the training error of the hypothesis h is within a distance ε from the generalization error of h for every $h \in \mathcal{H}$:

$$\arg \min_{n \geq 1} \left\{ \mathbf{Pr} \left\{ \sup_{h \in \mathcal{H}} |\epsilon_P(h) - \hat{\epsilon}_n(h)| \geq \varepsilon \right\} \leq \delta \right\}.$$

$n_{\min}^P(\varepsilon, \delta)$ can be thought of as an optimal sample size in the sense that a smaller sample size would not enable us to be confident that the training error of the hypothesis is a good approximation of its generalization error. However, $n_{\min}^P(\varepsilon, \delta)$ depends directly on P and, thus, cannot be computed. We show next how Rademacher penalties can be used to give computable approximations of $n_{\min}^P(\varepsilon, \delta)$.

Given $\varepsilon > 0$ and $\delta \in (0, 1)$, let $n_0(\varepsilon, \delta)$ denote the initial sample size of our learning algorithms. It is assumed to be a non-increasing function of both ε and δ. A random variable τ, taking positive integer values, is called a *stopping time* if, for all $n \geq 1$ the decision whether $\tau \leq n$, or not, depends only on the information available by time n; i.e., only on $(x_1, y_1), \ldots, (x_n, y_n)$. A stopping time τ is called *well-behaving* with parameters (ε, δ) if it is such that $\tau \geq n_0(\varepsilon, \delta)$ and

$$\mathbf{Pr} \left\{ \sup_{h \in \mathcal{H}} |\hat{\epsilon}_\tau(h) - \epsilon_P(h)| \geq \varepsilon \right\} \leq \delta.$$

An immediate consequence of this definition is that if τ is well-behaving with parameters (ε, δ) and $\hat{h}$ is a hypothesis that minimizes empirical risk based on the sample $\{ (x_i, y_i) \mid i = 1, \ldots, \tau \}$, then

$$\mathbf{Pr} \left\{ \epsilon_P(\hat{h}) \geq \inf_{h \in \mathcal{H}} \epsilon_P(h) + 2\varepsilon \right\} \leq \delta.$$

In other words, it is enough to draw τ examples in order to find, with high probability, a hypothesis in $\mathcal{H}$ that is almost as accurate as the most accurate one in $\mathcal{H}$.

The question, though, is how to construct the well-behaving stopping times on the basis of the available data only — without using the knowledge of P — and which of the stopping times from this set is the best used in the learning algorithms. Let us now define stopping times that are tied to a geometric sampling schedule and reduction of the Rademacher penalty.

Definition The *Rademacher stopping time* $\nu(\varepsilon, \delta)$ with parameters (ε, δ) for the hypothesis class $\mathcal{H}$ is

$$\nu(\varepsilon, \delta) = \min_{i \geq 1} \left\{ n_i = 2^i n_0(\varepsilon, \delta) \mid R_{n_i}(\mathcal{H}) < \varepsilon \right\}.$$

Koltchinskii et al. (2000) derived data dependent results that hold for any distribution that could have produced the sample S. Instead of considering the set of all probability distributions on S and its supremum upper bound (Koltchinskii at al. 2000), in the following results we examine the (unknown) true probability distribution P producing S.

Theorem 1 *Let*

$$n_0(\varepsilon, \delta) \geq \left\lfloor \frac{4}{\varepsilon^2} \log \left(\frac{4}{\delta} \right) \right\rfloor + 1.$$

Then, for all $\varepsilon > 0$ and $\delta \in (0, 1)$,

1. *$\nu(\varepsilon, \delta)$ is well-behaving with parameters $(5\varepsilon, \delta)$.*
2. *Moreover, if $n_{\min}^P(\varepsilon, \delta) \geq n_0(\varepsilon, \delta)$, then for all $\varepsilon > 0$ and $\delta \in (0, 1/2)$, the probability that $\nu(24\varepsilon, \delta) > n_{\min}^P(\varepsilon, \delta)$ is at most 3δ (for any class $\mathcal{H}$ of hypotheses and any distribution P).*

Theorem 2 *If*

$$n_0(\varepsilon, \delta) \geq \left\lfloor \frac{4}{\varepsilon^2} \log \left(\frac{4}{\delta} \right) \right\rfloor + 1$$

and $12/\varepsilon \leq n_{\min}^P(\varepsilon, \delta) \leq n_0(\varepsilon, \delta)$, then

$$\mathbf{Pr} \left\{ \nu(30\varepsilon, \delta) > 2n_0(\varepsilon, \delta) \right\} \leq \delta.$$

We omit the proofs of Theorems 1 and 2 because they are both simple modification of the corresponding proofs by Koltchinskii et al. (2000). The theorems show that, under certain mild conditions, $\nu(\varepsilon, \delta)$ is well-behaving and, furthermore, that it yields nearly as good sample sizes as knowing the unknown distribution-dependent sample complexity $n_{\min}^P(\varepsilon, \delta)$. This is in clear contrast with the stopping times that one could define based on the VC dimension of $\mathcal{H}$ which would be competitive with $n_{\min}^P(\varepsilon, \delta)$ only for worst-case P.

Learning Two-Level Decision Trees

Computation of the Rademacher penalty entails finding the hypothesis that minimizes the training error. Not many training error minimizing learning algorithms are known for hypothesis classes of reasonable size. Moreover, two executions of the learning algorithm are required to compute the Rademacher penalty of the underlying hypothesis class. Therefore, it is vital that the learning algorithm is

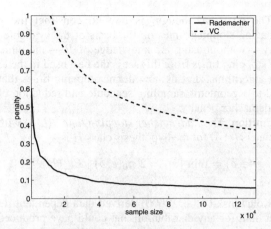

Figure 2: Development of the Rademacher penalty (solid line) and VC-based penalty (dashed line) with increasing sample size.

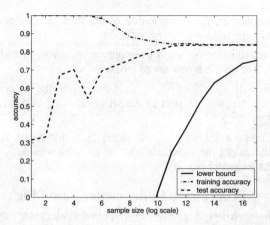

Figure 3: Training accuracy (dash-dotted line), test accuracy (dashed line), and the accuracy lower bound determined by Rademacher penalty (solid line) in progressive sampling.

efficient. Thus far the only practical experiments on using Rademacher penalties that we are aware of are those of Lozano (2000), who used real intervals as his concept class.

T2 (Auer, Holte, and Maass 1995) is an agnostic PAC-learning algorithm with guaranteed performance for any distribution of data. It learns two-level decision trees that minimize the training error within this class of hypotheses. Handling of numerical attributes is the main difficulty in learning concise representations; one cannot reiterate the splitting of a numerical value range like, e.g., C4.5 does (Quinlan 1993).

In the root of a decision tree produced by T2 a numerical value range can be split into two intervals using a threshold value. Missing attribute values, which are common in real-world data, are treated as an extra value in T2. Thus, if a numerical attribute is chosen to the root of a tree in T2, then the tree will have three subtrees rooted at the second level of the tree. At the second level the value range of a continuous attribute (even the one that was chosen to the root) can be split up to k intervals, where k is a prespecified parameter of the algorithm. A discrete attribute is handled, as usual, so that the node testing the value of such an discrete attribute will have as many subtrees as there are different values in the attribute's value range (plus one subtree for missing values).

The time complexity of T2 for n examples on m attributes is $O(k^2 m^2 n \log n)$. In other words, with respect to the sample size T2 only requires $O(n \log n)$ time. In experiments (Auer, Holte, and Maass 1995) the two-level decision trees produced by T2 have been observed to be highly competitive with the more complex decision tree hypotheses of C4.5 (Quinlan 1993).

Experiments

We have tested progressive Rademacher sampling combined with the T2 learning algorithm on some UCI (Blake and Merz 1998) domains. In the following results from the Adult (Census) domain, which was also used by Provost, Jensen, and Oates (1999), are reviewed.

Fig. 2 plots the penalties based on Rademacher penalization and VC dimension. For both penalties the confidence parameter δ equals 0.01. Rademacher penalty is the one given by (2). The VC dimension penalty is determined by the formula (Vapnik 1998):

$$2\sqrt{\frac{d(\ln(2n/d)+1)+\ln(9/\delta)}{n}},$$

where $d = 656$ is a lower bound of the VC dimension of the hypothesis class used by T2. The lower bound is determined by the maximal number of leaves in a single two-level tree for the Adult domain. The figure shows that the results obtained by Rademacher penalization are almost an order of magnitude smaller than those given by the VC method.

Fig. 3 plots the training and test accuracies of two-level decision trees on different sized samples. Observe that the x-axis in this figure is in logarithmic scale (with base 2). Thus, the points on the curves correspond to successive sample sizes of the geometric schedule that was used. The generalization error lower bound computed on the basis of Rademacher penalties is also displayed.

We chose $\varepsilon = 0.1$ and $\delta = 0.01$. With these values the initial sample size $n_0(\varepsilon, \delta)$ would be approximately 60,000, but for illustration we have plotted the accuracies and the lower bound starting from $n_0 = 2$. With these choices the stopping time $\nu(\varepsilon/5, \delta)$ evaluated to 65,536. If the sample size had been determined by the bounds based on VC dimension, a total of approximately 2,623,000 examples would have been needed.

On the other hand, the optimal sample size as determined empirically by Provost, Jensen, and Oates (1999) is approximately 8,000. Thus, although the sample size obtained by the method proposed in this paper is larger than the one suggested by heuristic stopping time detection methods, it dramatically outperforms the one based on VC dimension.

Conclusions

Sampling, in principle, is a powerful method for enhancing space and time efficiency as well as, on occasion, classifier accuracy in inductive learning. However, in static sampling we have to know a lot in advance, if results of guaranteed quality are desired. Progressive sampling has been proposed to circumvent the problems associated with static sampling. Nevertheless, it too has its problems, the most serious of which is the problem of determining the stopping time efficiently and accurately. To compute the optimal sampling schedule requires a lot of information. Also then the stopping time approximation can be computationally expensive.

In this paper we have studied combining data dependent Rademacher generalization error bound approximation with straightforward geometric sampling schedules. Computation of Rademacher penalties requires executing the learning algorithm two times and finding the minimum training error hypothesis within the hypothesis class. These requirements limit the applicable hypothesis classes to relatively simple ones. However, the two-level decision trees that were used in this study have been observed, in practice, to be competitive in their prediction accuracy with the more complex decision trees produced by C4.5.

Our experiments indicated that using Rademacher penalization gives orders of magnitude more realistic required sample size estimates than the ones based on VC dimension. However, the level attainable using direct learning curve estimation is hard to reach at least with the relatively small domain sizes and whenever the learning curve behaves at all well.

References

Auer, P.; Holte, R. C.; and Maass, W. 1995. Theory and Application of Agnostic PAC-Learning with Small Decision Trees. In *Proceedings of the Twelfth International Conference on Machine Learning*, 21–29. San Francisco, Calif.: Morgan Kaufmann.

Bartlett, P. L., and Mendelson, S. 2001. Rademacher and Gaussian Complexities: Risk Bounds and Structural Results. In *Computational Learning Theory, Proceedings of the Fourteenth Annual Conference*, 224–240. Lecture Notes in Artificial Intelligence **2111**. Heidelberg: Springer.

Blake, C. L., and Merz, C. J. 1998. UCI Repository of Machine Learning Databases. Univ. of California, Irvine, Dept. of Information and Computer Science.

Catlett, J. 1991. Megainduction: A Test Flight. In *Proceedings of the Eighth International Workshop on Machine Learning*, 596–599. San Mateo, Calif.: Morgan Kaufmann.

Cortes, C.; Jackel, L. D.; Solla, S. A.; Vapnik, V.; and Denker J. S. 1994. Learning Curves: Asymptotic Values and Rate of Convergence. In *Advances in Neural Information Processing Systems 6*, 327–334. San Francisco, Calif.: Morgan Kaufmann.

Frey, L. J., and Fisher, D. H. 1999. Modeling Decision Tree Performance with the Power Law. In *Proceedings of the Seventh International Workshop on Artificial Intelligence and Statistics*, 59–65. San Francisco, Calif.: Morgan Kaufmann.

Fürnkranz, J. 1998. Integrative Windowing. *Journal of Artificial Intelligence Research* **8**: 129–164.

Haussler, D.; Kearns, M.; Seung, H. S.; and Tishby, N. 1996. Rigorous Learning Curve Bounds from Statistical Mechanics. *Machine Learning* **25**(2–3): 195–236.

John, G., and Langley, P. 1996. Static versus Dynamic Sampling for Data Mining. In *Proceedings of the Second International Conference on Knowledge Discovery and Data Mining*, 367–370. Menlo Park, Calif.: AAAI Press.

Kivinen, J., and Mannila, H. 1994. The Power of Sampling in Knowledge Discovery. In *Proceedings of the Thirteenth ACM Symposium on Principles of Database Systems*, 77–85. New York, NY: ACM Press.

Koltchinskii, V. 2001. Rademacher Penalties and Structural Risk Minimization. *IEEE Transactions on Information Theory* **47**(5): 1902–1914.

Koltchinskii, V.; Abdallah, C. T.; Ariola, M.; Dorato, P.; and Panchenko, D. 2000. Improved Sample Complexity Estimates for Statistical Learning Control of Uncertain Systems. *IEEE Transactions on Automatic Control* **45**(12): 2383–2388.

Lozano, F. 2000. Model Selection Using Rademacher Penalization. In *Proceedings of the Second ICSC Symposium on Neural Networks*. Berlin, Germany: ICSC Academic.

Oates, T., and Jensen, D. 1997. The Effects of Training Set Size on Decision Tree Complexity. In *Proceedings of the Fourteenth International Conference on Machine Learning*, 254–261. San Francisco, Calif.: Morgan Kaufmann.

Provost, F.; Jensen, D.; and Oates, T. 1999. Efficient Progressive Sampling. In *Proceedings of the Fifth ACM SIGKDD International Conference on Knowledge Discovery and Data Mining*, 23–32. New York, NY: ACM Press.

Quinlan, J. R. 1983. Learning Efficient Classification Procedures and Their Application to Chess End Games. In Michalski, R. S.; Carbonell, J. G.; and Mitchell, T. M., eds., *Machine Learning: An Artificial Intelligence Approach*, 463–482. Palo Alto, Calif.: Tioga.

Quinlan, J. R. 1993. *C4.5: Programs for Machine Learning*. San Francisco, Calif.: Morgan Kaufmann.

Scheffer, T., and Wrobel, S. 2000. A Sequential Sampling Algorithm for a General Class of Utility Criteria. In *Proceedings of the Sixth ACM SIGKDD International Conference on Knowledge Discovery and Data Mining*, 330–334. New York, NY: ACM Press.

Schuurmans, D., and Greiner, R. 1995. Practical PAC Learning. In Proceedings of the Fourteenth International Joint Conference on Artificial Intelligence, 1169–1175. Menlo Park, Calif.: International Joint Conferences on Artificial Intelligence, Inc.

Toivonen, H. 1996. Sampling Large Databases for Association Rules. In *Proceedings of the Twenty-Second International Conference on Very Large Databases*, 134–145. San Francisco, Calif.: Morgan Kaufmann.

Van der Vaart, A. W., and Wellner, J. A. 2000. *Weak Convergence and Empirical Processes*. Corrected second printing. New York, NY: Springer-Verlag.

Vapnik, V. N. 1998. *Statistical Learning Theory*. New York, NY: Wiley.

Pruning and Dynamic Scheduling of Cost-sensitive Ensembles

Wei Fan
IBM T.J.Watson Research
Hawthorne, NY 10532
weifan@us.ibm.com

Fang Chu
Computer Science Department
University of California
Los Angeles, CA 90095
fchu@cs.ucla.edu

Haixun Wang and **Philip S. Yu**
IBM T.J.Watson Research
Hawthorne, NY 10532
{haixun,psyu}@us.ibm.com

Abstract

Previous research has shown that averaging ensemble can scale up learning over very large cost-sensitive datasets with linear speedup independent of the learning algorithms. At the same time, it achieves the same or even better accuracy than a single model computed from the entire dataset. However, one major drawback is its inefficiency in prediction since every base model in the ensemble has to be consulted in order to produce a final prediction. In this paper, we propose several approaches to reduce the number of base classifiers. Among various methods explored, our empirical studies have shown that the benefit-based greedy approach can safely remove more than 90% of the base models while maintaining or even exceeding the prediction accuracy of the original ensemble. Assuming that each base classifier consumes one unit of prediction time, the removal of 90% of base classifiers translates to a prediction speedup of 10 times. On top of pruning, we propose a novel dynamic scheduling approach to further reduce the "expected" number of classifiers employed in prediction. It measures the confidence of a prediction by a subset of classifiers in the pruned ensemble. This confidence is used to decide if more classifiers are needed in order to produce a prediction that is the same as the original unpruned ensemble. This approach reduces the "expected" number of classifiers by another 25% to 75% without loss of accuracy.

Introduction

Recently, cost-sensitive learning has been extensively studied due to its wide application in areas such as fraud detection and intrusion detection. In such applications where examples carry different benefits and incur different penalties when misclassified, it is simply not enough to maximize the accuracy based on the assumption that all examples are equally important. Credit card fraud detection, for example, seeks to maximize the total benefit - the transaction amount of correctly detected frauds minus the cost to investigate all (correctly and incorrectly) predicted frauds. The problem of cost-sensitive learning is made more difficult by the fact that most real-world cost-sensitive datasets are very large and potentially distributed. A typical

credit card company has millions of new transactions on a daily basis and numerous local authorization centers nationwide. However, most traditional learning algorithms are designed for centralized and memory-resident data. (Fan *et al.* 2002) introduced a scalable method that fits well into the large-sized and distributed scenario. Their method computes a number of base classifiers from partitions of the entire dataset. The predictions by the base classifiers are combined by averaging to compute the final prediction. Their approach achieves linear speedup and linear scaled speedup relative to the number of partitions while producing a similar or even higher benefit when compared to a single classifier computed from the entire dataset as a whole. Another difference from traditional heuristic-based ensemble approaches is that the accuracy of averaging ensemble can be estimated by statistical sampling techniques from a subset of base models, so the performance is known before learning every base model. However, the satisfactory performance and properties of averaging ensembles is discounted by elongated process of prediction, since all base classifiers have to be consulted before a final prediction can be made. This paper addresses the issue of averaging ensemble pruning and scheduling in a cost-sensitive context.

Our Contributions

In this paper, we focus on using pruning methods to reduce the size of averaging ensembles in order to increase system throughput. We also introduce a new strategy, *dynamic scheduling*, for further prediction speedup.

Previously proposed pruning methods choose either the most accurate or the most diverse classifiers. Those proposals work well for *cost-insensitive* applications where all examples are equally important. We have tested previously proposed accuracy-based method using mean square error and diversity-based method using KL-distance in *cost-sensitive* applications. However, none of these methods yield pruned ensembles with good total benefits (for example, the total recovered fraudulent transaction amount). In our work, we use total benefits directly as the criterion. We have applied greedy algorithm with and without backfitting to classifier selection. Empirical evaluations on several datasets have revealed that the benefit-based greedy approach with and without backfitting are both capable of pruning more than 90% of the ensemble while maintaining or exceeding the total benefits of the original unpruned ensemble on the test set. The more sophisticated backfitting does not lead to significantly higher benefits than greedy algorithm itself. We have also studied whether it helps to consider both diversity and total benefits at the same time. Experimental results show that total benefits is a good criterion by itself.

Another contribution is the proposal of dynamic scheduling. We find that not all the classifiers in the pruned ensemble are needed all the times for every example. Some examples are "easier" to predict than others. We propose a dynamic scheduling method that measures the confidence of a prediction by a subset of classifiers in the pruned ensemble and decides if more classifiers in the pruned ensemble need to be employed to generate a prediction that is likely to be the same as the original unpruned ensemble. In our experiment, the average or "expected" number of classifiers in the pruned ensemble is reduced by another 25% to 75% without loss of accuracy. Assuming each base classifier costs one unit of prediction time, the overall prediction throughput increases after pruning and dynamic scheduling is up to 40 ($=\frac{1}{10\%} \times \frac{1}{25\%}$) times at the best case. The complexity of benefit-based greedy algorithm is $O(k \cdot k' \cdot n)$, where n is the number of examples, k is the number of classifiers in the original ensemble and k' is the number of remaining classifiers in the pruned ensemble. More complicated methods (such as backfitting) and measures (such as KL-distance) will incur an additional term that is usually non-linear. The complexity of dynamic scheduling is $O(k' \cdot n)$.

Difference from Previous Work

Previous work mainly studies ensembles combined with either voting or meta-learning for cost-insensitive applications. (Margineantu & Dietterich 1997) first studied various pruning methods on AdaBoost ensembles. Their evaluation is mainly on *cost-insensitive* problems. We have adopted and tested several of their approaches for averaging ensemble in *cost-sensitive* applications; however, the results are not very satisfying. We have proposed new approaches using total benefits as a criterion and obtained significant improvement on both accuracy and efficiency. (Prodromidis 1999) proposed CART-like cost-based pruning methods to remove unnecessary classifiers in meta-learning trees.

The rest of the paper is organized as follows. Next we summarize the averaging method. We then discuss pruning criterion, classifier selection procedure, and scheduling. It is followed by experimental design and results.

Averaging Cost-Sensitive Ensembles

We briefly review how an averaging ensemble is constructed. Using credit card fraud detection for illustration. Each transaction x has a transaction amount of $y(x)$.

For undetected fraudulent transaction, the credit card issuer loses the whole transaction amount $y(x)$. Suppose that there is a fixed cost $90 to investigate and dispute a detected fraud. In this case, the *optimal decision policy* is to predict x being fraudulent or positive iff $(R(x) = P(fraud|x) \cdot y(x)) > \$90$, where $P(fraud|x)$ is the estimated probability that x is a fraud. $R(x)$ is called *risk*. Only those x's with $y(x) > \$90$ are worthy of being detected. The benefit for true positives is $y(x) - \$90$ and the "benefit" for false positives is $-\$90$. For some applications such as charity donation, the benefit for each example such as donation amount is not known. A separate dataset with different feature set is given to train a model to estimate the amount $Y(x)$ when someone does donate. The averaging ensemble method solves the problem of how to estimate $R(x)$ efficiently for large and possibly distributed datasets.

Assume that the dataset is partitioned into k disjoint subsets S_i and a base classifier C_i is trained from each S_i. Given an example x, C_i outputs a member probability $P_i(x)$. $R_i(x) = P_i(x) \cdot y(x)$ is the individual risk. If the benefit of x is not given, a separate dataset is available and partitioned similarly into k subsets and a model (eg. regression) $Y_i(x)$ is trained from each subset. Using *Simple Averaging*, the combined risk is $\frac{\sum_i R_i(x)}{k} = \frac{\sum_i P_i(x) \cdot Y_i(x)}{k}$. The training complexity of averaging ensembles is $k \cdot O(f(\frac{n}{k}))$ and the speedup and scaled speedup are both linear $O(k)$.

Pruning Methods

Given an averaging ensemble of k classifiers and an upper bound $k' < k$, pruning is used to identify a subset of "good" k' classifiers which give the same level of total benefits as the original ensemble. Primary issues include pruning criteria and procedures of classifier selection. We also introduce a strategy that schedules the selected classifiers based on estimated prediction confidence to reduce the expected number of classifiers used in prediction by a pruned ensemble.

Pruning Criteria

We start with some notations. x is an instance; it may be either *positive* or *negative*. $P(x)$ (and its variations with subscripts) is the estimated probability that x is positive. $B(x)$ is the benefit to predict x to be positive; it only depends on the example x, not on any methods. The total benefit of a method is the cumulative benefits for a data set, i.e., $\sum_x B(x)$. C_i is a classifier and outputs probability $P_i(x)$ for example x. $S = \{C_1, \cdots, C_k\}$ is the original ensemble, and S' is a pruned ensemble, $S' \subset S$, with k' base classifiers. The average probability estimate by an ensemble S for x is $P_S = \frac{\sum_{C_i \in S} P_i(x)}{|S|}$.

The first strategy is to choose a subset of classifiers that minimizes classification error. Probability estimate $P_{S'}(x)$ is compared with the true probability $P_T(x)$ (0 or 1). Use mean-square-error, the criterion is

$$MSE = \sqrt{\sum_x (P_{S'}(x) - P_T(x))^2}.$$

The second criterion directly uses total benefits. It chooses a subset of classifiers that maximizes the total benefits.

The third criterion favors diverse classifiers. KL-distance is a widely adopted measure. It may not be suitable for *cost-sensitive* learning as the difference between two classifiers is not reflected in the number of examples on which they disagree, but directly related to the benefits of those examples. We modify KL-distance for cost-sensitive scenarios. KL-distance is computed on *normalized* benefits, $\bar{B}(x) = \frac{B(x)}{\sum_x B(x)}$. Suppose the normalized benefits for x by two classifiers $\mathcal{C}_i$ and $\mathcal{C}_j$ are $\bar{B}_i(x)$ and $\bar{B}_j(x)$. The modified KL-distance is defined as $KL(\mathcal{C}_i, \mathcal{C}_j) = \sum_x \bar{B}_i(x) log \frac{\bar{B}_i(x)}{\bar{B}_j(x)}$.

Classifier Selection

Combinatorial search will be too costly. Instead, we have applied greedy algorithm both with and without backfitting to decide the sequence of classifiers to consider. Greedy by itself always starts with the classifier that maximizes or minimizes the chosen criterion (KL-distance starts with the one that has the highest total benefit.) At the following steps, it chooses one of the remaining classifiers in $S - S'$ to join with previously chosen classifiers to generate a candidate pruned ensemble that maximizes or minimizes the chosen measure. In both benefit and accuracy based greedy approaches, when a new classifier is considered, combined probabilities $P_{S'}(x)$ are incrementally updated for n examples. The complexity is $O(n \cdot \sum_1^{k'} (k-i)) \approx O(k \cdot k' \cdot n)$ for small k'. However, in diversity-based greedy algorithm, the KL-distance between the candidate and every previously chosen classifier have to be computed and summed up. The complexity is $O(n \cdot \sum_1^{k'} (k-i) \cdot i) \approx O(k \cdot k'^2 \cdot n)$ for small k'.

Greedy is a local-optimum algorithm. We tested to use backfitting to avoid local optimum. It greedily chooses a classifier at each step, then perturbs the chosen ensemble by replacing some randomly chosen classifiers. When perturbed ensemble generates a higher total benefit, it replaces the older ensemble.

Dynamic Scheduling

A pruned ensemble aims at reaching or exceeding the level of total benefits of the original ensemble. We may not need to use *every classifier* in a pruned ensemble to predict on *every example* to reach the same total benefits. For example, if the average probability estimate by 2 classifiers is 0.6 (such as $\frac{0.7+0.5}{2}$), and the average probability estimate by the original ensemble with 256 classifiers is 0.6, they will make exactly the same prediction and we don't need to consult any additional classifiers. Actually, probability estimates by the conjectured 2 classifiers and 256 classifiers

even need not be the same to make the same predictions due to the *error tolerance* property of optimal decision making policy. Let us re-write this policy for the credit card fraud detection dataset, $P(x) > \left(T(x) = \frac{\$90}{y(x)}\right)$. $T(x)$ is called *decision-threshold*. As long as, $P(x) > T(x)$ (or $P(x) \le T(x)$), the prediction will be the same. Assume that $y(x) = \$900$, consequently $T(x) = 0.1$, both $P(x) = 0.2$ and $P(x) = 0.4$ will produce the same prediction. This property actually helps reduce the "expected" number of classifiers consulted for prediction.

For a given pruned ensemble S' with size k', we first order the base classifiers into a "pipeline" according to their total benefits. To classify x, the classifier with the highest benefits will always be consulted first, followed by classifiers with decreasing total benefits. This pipeline procedure stops as soon as "a confident prediction" is made or there are no more classifiers in the pipeline. Assuming that $\mathcal{C}_1, \cdots, \mathcal{C}_{k'}$ is the ordered classifiers. The set of classifiers at pipeline stage i is $S'_i = \{\mathcal{C}_1, \cdots, \mathcal{C}_i\}$. Since the target is to reach the total benefits of the original ensemble, the confidence is calculated based on errors to the estimated probability $P_S(x)$ by the original ensemble. At pipeline stage i, the averaged probability for x is $P_{S'_i}(x)$. The error is simply $\epsilon_i(x) = P_{S'_i}(x) - P_S(x)$. In order to compute confidence, we divide the range of probability ($P_{S'_i}(x) \in [0, 1]$) into several bins and confidence is computed from examples in the same bin. We use $b(P_{S'_i}(x))$, or $\hat{b}_i(x)$ as a short form, to map $P_{S'_i}(x)$ to the bin it belongs to. We then calculate the average $\mu_i(\hat{b}_i(x))$ and variance $\sigma_i^2(\hat{b}_i(x))$ of error $\epsilon_i(x)$ for examples in the same bin $\hat{b}_i(x)$. These statistics measure the difference between $P_{S'_i}(x)$ and $P_S(x)$. To classify an unknown instance x, when $P_{S'_i}(x)$ is computed by the first i classifiers in the pipeline, we first determine the group it belongs to, $\hat{b}_i(x)$, then apply the following decision rules.

$$\begin{cases} (P_{S'_i}(x) - \mu_i(\hat{b}_i(x)) - \mathbf{t} \cdot \sigma_i(\hat{b}_i(x))) > T(x), & positive \\ (P_{S'_i}(x) - \mu_i(\hat{b}_i(x)) + \mathbf{t} \cdot \sigma_i(\hat{b}_i(x))) \le T(x), & negative \\ otherwise, & uncertain \end{cases}$$

$\mathbf{t}$ is a confidence interval parameter. Assuming normal distribution, $\mathbf{t} = 3$ has 99.7% confidence. When the prediction is uncertain, the next classifier in the pipeline ($\mathcal{C}_{i+1}$) has to be employed. If there are no more classifiers, the current prediction is returned. Thus, not all examples need to use all classifiers in the pipeline to compute a confident prediction, the "expected" number of classifiers can be reduced. Dynamic scheduling updates probabilities and group examples at each pipeline stage. The cost to compute confidence mainly comes from updating estimated probabilities for all n examples; the complexity to train a dynamic schedule is therefore $O(k' \cdot n)$. During classification, we map probabilities to confidence using a hash table. Decision trees output limited number of unique estimated probabilities since there are limited number of nodes. Besides binning, a more fine-grained approach is to group examples with the same value of $P_{S'_i}(x)$. However, some $P_{S'_i}(x)$ values computed at classification may not be seen at training time, the rea-

Dataset		rw	smth	ctl	ctl+smth
Donation	S	12489.6	14291.2	13292.7	14424.9
	E	**14138.9**	12483.0	**14907.3**	12994.4
Credit	S	552400	765009	733980	782545
	E	**817869**	705281	**791024**	730883
Adult	S	16225	15392	16443	15925
	E	**16432**	12764	16255	13695

Table 1: Total benefits by single model (S) and ensembles (E). If the result of the ensemble is higher than single model, it will be highlighted in **bold**.

Experiments and Results

We evaluate the ensemble pruning approaches on three cost-sensitive problems: credit card fraud detection, donation and adult. Details about these datasets can be found in (Fan *et al.* 2002). Credit card dataset has been discussed when introducing averaging ensembles. In donation dataset, suppose that the cost of requesting a charitable donation from an individual x is \$0.68 and the best estimate of the amount that x might donate is $Y(x)$. The optimal decision to solicit x iff $P(donate|x)Y(x) > \$0.68$. The total benefit is the total charity received minus the cost of mailing. In adult dataset, positive examples carry a benefit of 2 and negatives carry a benefit of 1. There is no penalty for misclassification. The optimal decision is to predict x to be positive iff $P(positive|x)\cdot 2 > (1 - P(positive|x))\cdot 1$.

The base classifiers in the ensembles are C4.5 decision trees that output calibrated probabilities (Zadrozny & Elkan 2001): raw (rw), smoothing (smth), curtailment (ctl) or curtailment plus smoothing (ctl+smth). The size of the original ensemble or the original number of base classifiers in the ensemble was chosen to be, $k \in \{64, 128, 256\}$. For each dataset, we apply different pruning techniques on the 12 ensembles (3 ensemble sizes (k) × 4 types of probability outputs.)

First, we report the baseline benefits that should be maintained after pruning. In Table 1, we cite the total benefits of both the averaging ensembles (E) and the single models (S). The ensemble's result (E) is the average total benefits over 3 ensembles with different sizes ($k \in \{64, 128, 256\}$). When the total benefit of the ensembles is higher than that of the single model, it will be highlighted in **bold** font. The averaging ensemble generally produces a higher total benefit with raw and curtailed probabilities, and their results are the highest among all three datasets.

Next, we discuss the experiments and results of the pruning methods. The number of classifiers selected k' by pruning is chosen to be $\frac{i}{32}$-th ($i \in \{1, 2, 3, 4\}$) (roughly 3%, 6%, 9% and 12%) of the original size of ensembles k, where $k \in \{64, 128, 256\}$. The pruning algorithm chooses

son is that some particular combination of leaf nodes from different trees are not encountered on training data. If this happens, the pipeline runs to the end.

Methods	rw	smth	ctl	ctl+smth
Accuracy	11812.8	13147.6	14120.4	14046.9
Diversity	8148.4	11295.3	12013.9	12048.5
Benefit	12965.2√	**13281.6**	14642.8√	**14171.6**

(a) Donation

Methods	rw	smth	ctl	ctl+smth
Accuracy	757382	715740	792291	735731
Diversity	752203	722291	799461	746575
Benefit	776838√	**730516**	809212√	**752473**

(b) Credit Card

Methods	rw	smth	ctl	ctl+smth
Accuracy	16362	12884	16242	15567
Diversity	16092	12611	15902	14973
Benefit	16362√	**13299**	**16381**	**15817**

(c) Adult

Table 2: Total benefits of pruning on different datasets. For each column of competitive methods, the highest result is highlighted. If the result is higher than the original unpruned ensemble (as shown in Table 1), it will be highlighted in **bold** font; otherwise if it is higher than at least the single classifier, it is marked with a √.

classifier based on their performance on training data, and the pruned ensembles are compared on their total benefits on test data. The results are shown in Table 2. Each number is the average benefits of 12 pruned ensembles (4 pruned ensemble sizes (k') × 3 original (k) ensembles.) In each column where competitive pruning methods were applied on the same data with the same probability outputs, the highest pruning result is highlighted as follows. If the result is higher than the respective unpruned ensemble baseline (as shown in Table 1), it will be shown in **bold** font; otherwise, if it is higher than the single classifier (Table 1), it will be followed by a √.

As we study the results, "benefit-based greedy" method consistently beats the other pruning methods; all the highlighted results in Table 2 are by benefit-based greedy algorithm. Every pruned ensemble produced by benefit-based greedy method has higher benefits than either the original ensemble or the single model or both. Comparing among different probability estimation methods (raw, smoothing and etc), pruning works the best with curtailment. For both donation and credit card dataset, the pruned curtailment ensemble has the second highest benefit (very close to the highest) among all ensembles and single models. One very interesting observation is that pruning significantly increases the benefits of ensemble with smoothing. In general, the ensemble method is able to increase benefits for ensembles with raw and curtailed probabilities, but this ability fails with smoothed probabilities. However, benefit-based greedy algorithm has the capability to choose the good set of classifiers to obtain high

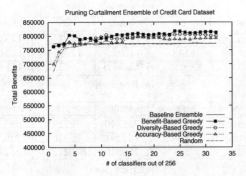

Figure 1: Pruning Effect on Credit Card Curtailment Ensembles

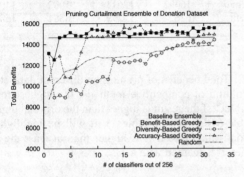

Figure 2: Pruning Effect on Donation Curtailment Ensembles

benefits. As a summary, benefit-based greedy approach can remove more than 90% of the base classifiers while maintaining or exceeding the accuracy of the unpruned ensemble.

One important study is to examine how well pruning works with ensembles containing a large number of base classifiers whose prediction is slower than ensembles with relatively smaller number of classifiers. We show result for credit card and donation datasets in Figures 1 and 2. (The result of adult is similar.) The original ensemble has $k = 256$ base classifiers. Pruning chooses continuously up to $k' = 32$ classifiers. As a comparison, we also plot the result of a "random selection" method that chooses classifiers arbitrarily. The random result is the average of 10 random choices. As we compare all the curves in Figures 1 and 2, an obvious observation is that random selection doesn't work well. The performance increase by benefit-based greedy method over baseline of the original ensemble and other pruning methods (accuracy and diversity) are shown clearly throughout the different choices of $k' \leq 32$. In the donation dataset, benefit-based greedy method already reaches the accuracy of the original ensemble when $k' = 3$ out of $k = 256$. The benefit still increases when more classifiers are chosen. When $k' = 31$, the total benefit is \$15573, which is significantly higher than the KDD98 Cup winning entry of \$14712.

Besides these basic methods and experiments, we experimented other variations. In one trial, we applied backfitting

to benefit-based greedy approach to seek further improvement. The maximal number of classifiers allowed to be replaced by backfitting is set to be 12. The additional effort on backfitting does not bring better results. In addition, we also try to consider both total benefits and diversity in the same time. To choose the next classifier in this new method, first the top 10 candidate classifiers (chosen from $k - k'$ remaining classifiers) are selected. At the second step, we select the one with the greatest KL-distance. However, this more sophisticated method brings no significant difference. These experiments strengthen our observation that benefit-based greedy algorithm is a promising pruning method for cost-sensitive ensembles.

When a subset of classifiers is chosen, we apply dynamic scheduling to reduce the "expected" number of classifier even further, as shown in Figure 3, where x-axis is the number of classifiers after pruning by benefit-based greedy method, or the expected or average number of classifiers consulted per example for dynamic scheduling. The curve for dynamic scheduling is obtained as follows. When dynamic scheduling is applied on a pruned ensemble with k' base classifiers, many examples from the test data uses $k'' < k'$ classifiers instead of k' classifiers. We calculate both the expected number of classifiers used when a prediction is confidently made and the resultant total benefits. These two numbers are plotted in Figure 3. The visual effect of dynamic scheduling is to "compress and shift" the curve of benefit-based greedy method towards the left or smaller number of classifiers. To see some detailed result, after dynamic scheduling is applied, on average, using 8 classifiers gives similar total benefits as using 32 classifiers all the time. Similar results are obtained on the other two datasets. As a summary, when there are totally 32 classifiers to be scheduled, dynamic scheduling cut the average number of classifiers to 75% for credit card dataset, 33% for adult and 25% for donation.

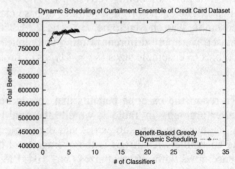

Figure 3: Total benefits of pruned credit card curtailment ensemble when dynamic scheduling is employed. X-axis is the number of classifiers after pruning for benefit-based greedy method, or the average number of classifiers consulted per example for dynamic scheduling.

Discussion and Future Work

As a sanity check, we ran the benefit-based greedy method up to $k' = k = 256$ for the credit card dataset as shown in

Figure 4. The curves on donation and adult are very similar. There are a few important observations. First, when $k' = 256$, the result is the same as the original ensemble. Second, even the most accurate base classifier (with x-axis value of 1) by itself is less accurate than the original ensemble, implying that ensemble is necessary. The curve resembles an "overfitting" curve that researchers in machine learning always use. It takes only three classifiers to reach the accuracy of the 256 classifier ensemble and the total benefit continues to increase as more classifiers are inserted, and begins to drop after about 50 classifiers until eventually it converges to the baseline. A conjectured reason for the shape of the curve is that there may be random noises from multiple sources. Averaging can cancel uncorrelated errors from the same source. Some classifiers may have errors from unique sources. In the beginning, errors from the same sources start to cancel out, and consequently the accuracy starts to increase. When more classifiers are introduced, more errors from unique sources that cannot be canceled by averaging are also added. These errors accumulate and decrease the overall accuracy eventually. More formal study is needed to explain this phenomenon and verify the conjecture. Nonetheless, the "overfitting" curve validates the necessity of pruning for both accuracy and efficiency reasons.

Both pruning and dynamic scheduling are performed after learning the complete ensemble. A possibly more efficient approach is to generate only the subset of classifiers that would not be pruned. One possibility is to apply boosting and bagging-like approaches that choose the subset of examples based on the performance of previously generated classifiers.

Related Work

Besides related work discussed in introduction, one of the first work to scale up learning by combining class labels is meta-learning (Chan 1996). Other incomplete list of significant contributions to scalable learning (mostly are on learning class labels or cost-insensitive learning) are scalable decision tree learner SPRINT (Shafer, Agrawl, & Mehta 1996), rule-based algorithm for multi-processor learning DRL (Provost & Hennesy 1996) among many others. There

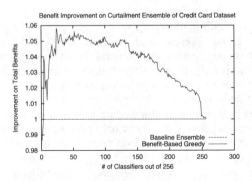

Figure 4: "Full spectrum" sanity check on credit card dataset with curtailed probabilities. Result is normalized over the total benefits of the original ensemble with 256 classifiers

are many recent publications on cost-sensitive learning, Domingos (Domingos 1999) converts a cost-sensitive problem into an equivalent cost-insensitive problem by mislabelling. A recent workshop on cost-sensitive learning can be found in (Dietterich *et al.* 2000).

Conclusion

Our studies have found that benefit-based greedy pruning can remove more than 90% of the base classifiers but with the same or higher accuracy than the original ensemble. We also found out that when dynamic scheduling is applied to a pruned ensemble, the expected number of classifiers used can be reduced by another 25% to 75% without loss of accuracy. Based on our studies, we conclude that benefit-based greedy approach plus dynamic scheduling is an effective and efficient approach to prune cost-sensitive averaging ensembles. In comparison with a single model trained from the entire dataset, pruned averaging ensemble achieves significantly higher learning efficiency, the same or better accuracy and comparable prediction efficiency.

References

Chan, P. 1996. *An Extensible Meta-learning Approach for Scalable and Accurate Inductive Learning*. Ph.D. Dissertation, Columbia University.

Dietterich, T.; Margineatu, D.; Provost, F.; and Turney, P., eds. 2000. *Cost-Sensitive Learning Workshop (ICML-00)*.

Domingos, P. 1999. MetaCost: a general method for making classifiers cost-sensitive. In *Proceedings of Fifth International Conference on Knowledge Discovery and Data Mining (KDD-99)*.

Fan, W.; Wang, H.; Yu, P. S.; and Stolfo, S. 2002. A framework for scalable cost-sensitive learning based on combining probabilities and benefits. In *Second SIAM International Conference on Data Mining (SDM2002)*.

Margineantu, D., and Dietterich, T. 1997. Pruning adaptive boosting. In *Proceedings of Fourteenth International Conference on Machine Learning (ICML-97)*.

Prodromidis, A. 1999. *Management of Intelligent Learning Agents in Distributed Data Mining Systems*. Ph.D. Dissertation, Columbia University.

Provost, F. J., and Hennesy, D. 1996. Scaling up: Distributed machine learning with cooperation. In *Proceedings of Thirteenth National Conference on Artificial Intelligence (AAAI-96)*.

Shafer, J.; Agrawl, R.; and Mehta, M. 1996. SPRINT: A scalable parallel classifier for data mining. In *Proceedings of Twenty-second International Conference on Very Large Databases (VLDB-96)*, 544–555. San Francisco, California: Morgan Kaufmann.

Zadrozny, B., and Elkan, C. 2001. Obtaining calibrated probability estimates from decision trees and naive bayesian classifiers. In *Proceedings of Eighteenth International Conference on Machine Learning (ICML'2001)*.

Specific-to-General Learning for Temporal Events[*]

Alan Fern and Robert Givan and Jeffrey Mark Siskind

Electrical and Computer Engineering, Purdue University, West Lafayette IN 47907 USA

{afern,givan,qobi}@purdue.edu

Abstract

We study the problem of supervised learning of event classes in a simple temporal event-description language. We give lower and upper bounds and algorithms for the subsumption and generalization problems for two expressively powerful subsets of this logic, and present a positive-examples-only specific-to-general learning method based on the resulting algorithms. We also present a polynomial-time computable "syntactic" subsumption test that implies semantic subsumption without being equivalent to it. A generalization algorithm based on syntactic subsumption can be used in place of semantic generalization to improve the asymptotic complexity of the resulting learning algorithm. A companion paper shows that our methods can be applied to duplicate the performance of human-coded concepts in the substantial application domain of video event recognition.

Introduction

In many domains, interesting concepts take the form of structured temporal sequences of events. These domains include: planning, where macro-actions represent useful temporal patterns; computer security, where typical application behavior as temporal patterns of system calls must be differentiated from compromised application behavior (and likewise authorized user behavior from intrusive behavior); and event recognition in video sequences, where the structure of behaviors shown in videos can be automatically recognized.

Many proposed representation languages can be used to capture temporal structure. These include standard first-order logic, Allen's interval calculus (Allen 1983), and various temporal logics (Clarke, Emerson, & Sistla 1983; Allen & Ferguson 1994; Bacchus & Kabanza 2000). In this work, we study a simple temporal language that is a subset of many of these languages—we restrict our learner to concepts expressible with conjunction and temporal sequencing of consecutive intervals (called "Until" in linear temporal logic, or LTL). Our restricted language is a sublanguage of

LTL and of the temporal event logic of Siskind (2001) as well as of standard first-order logic (somewhat painfully).

Motivation for the choice of this subset is developed throughout the paper, and includes useful learning bias, efficient computation, and expressive power. Here we construct and analyze a specific-to-general learner for this subset. This paper contains theoretical results on the algorithmic problems (concept subsumption and generalization) involved in constructing such a learner: we give algorithms along with lower and upper asymptotic complexity bounds. Along the way, we expose considerable structure in the language.

In (Fern, Siskind, & Givan 2002), we develop practical adaptations of these techniques for a substantial application (including a novel automatic conversion of relational data to propositional data), and show that our learner can replicate the performance of carefully hand-constructed definitions in recognizing events in video sequences.

Bottom-up Learning from Positive Data

The sequence-mining literature contains many general-to-specific ("levelwise") algorithms for finding frequent sequences (Agrawal & Srikant 1995; Mannila, Toivonen, & Verkamo 1995; Kam & Fu 2000; Cohen 2001; Hoppner 2001). Here we explore a specific-to-general approach.

Inductive logic programming (ILP) (Muggleton & De Raedt 1994) has explored positive-only approaches in systems that can be applied to our problem, including Golem (Muggleton & Feng 1992), Claudien (De Raedt & Dehaspe 1997), and Progol (Muggleton 1995). Our early experiments confirmed our belief that horn clauses, lacking special handling of time, give a poor inductive bias[1].

Here we present and analyze a specific-to-general positive-only learner for temporal events—our learning algorithm is only given positive training examples (where the event occurs) and is not given negative examples (where the event does not occur). The positive-only setting is of interest as it appears that humans are able to learn many event definitions given primarily or only positive examples. From a practical standpoint, a positive-only learner removes the often difficult task of collecting negative examples that are "representative" of what is not the event to be learned.

---

[*]This work was supported in part by NSF grants 9977981-IIS and 0093100-IIS, an NSF Graduate Fellowship for Fern, and the Center for Education and Research in Information Assurance and Security at Purdue University. Part of this work was performed while Siskind was at NEC Research Institute, Inc.

---

[1]A reasonable alternative approach to ours would be to add syntactic biases (Cohen 1994; Dehaspe & De Raedt 1996) to ILP.

A typical learning domain specifies an example space (the objects we wish to classify) and a concept language (formulas that represent sets of examples that they *cover*). Generally we say a concept C_1 is more general (less specific) than C_2 iff C_2 is a subset of C_1—alternatively, a generality relation that may not be equivalent to subset may be specified, often for computational reasons. Achieving the goal of finding a concept consistent with a set of positive-only training data generally results in a trivial solution (simply return the most general concept in the language). To avoid adding negative training data, it is common to specify the learning goal as finding the least-general concept that covers all of the data[2]. With enough data and an appropriate concept language, the least-general concept often converges usefully.

We take a standard specific-to-general machine-learning approach to finding the least-general concept covering a set of positive examples. Assume we have a concept language L and an example space S. The approach relies on the computation of two quantities: the least-general covering formula (LGCF) of an example and the least-general generalization (LGG) of a set of formulas. An LGCF in L of an example in S is a formula in L that covers the example such that no other covering formula is strictly less general. Intuitively, the LGCF of an example is the "most representative" formula in L of that example. An LGG of any subset of L is a formula more general than each formula in the subset and not strictly more general than any other such formula.

Given the existence and uniqueness (up to set equivalence) of the LGCF and LGG (which is non-trivial to show for some concept languages) the specific-to-general approach proceeds by: 1) Use the LGCF to transform each positive training instance into a formula of L, and 2) Return the LGG of the resulting formulas. The returned formula represents the least-general concept in L that covers all the positive training examples. This learning approach has been pursued for a variety of concept languages including, clausal first-order logic (Plotkin 1971), definite clauses (Muggleton & Feng 1992), and description logic (Cohen & Hirsh 1994). It is important to choose an appropriate concept language as a bias for this learning approach or the concept returned will be (or resemble) the disjunction of the training data.

In this work, our concept language is the AMA temporal event logic presented below and the example space is the set of all models of that logic. Intuitively, a training example depicts a model where a target event occurs. (The models can be thought of as movies.) We will consider two notions of generality for AMA concepts and, under both notions, study the properties and computation of the LGCF and LGG.

AMA Syntax and Semantics

We study a subset of an interval-based logic called event logic developed by Siskind (2001) for event recognition in video sequences. This logic is "interval-based" in explicitly representing each of the possible interval relationships given originally by Allen (1983) in his calculus of inter-

val relations (e.g., "overlaps", "meets", "during"). Event logic allows the definition of static properties of intervals directly and dynamic properties by hierarchically relating sub-intervals using the Allen interval relations.

Here we restrict our attention to a subset of event logic we call AMA, defined below. We believe that our choice of event logic rather than first-order logic, as well as our restriction to AMA, provide a useful learning bias by ruling out a large number of 'practically useless' concepts while maintaining substantial expressive power. The practical utility of this bias is shown in our companion paper (Fern, Siskind, & Givan 2002). Our choice can also be seen as a restriction of LTL to conjunction and "Until", with similar motivations.

It is natural to describe temporal events by specifying a sequence of properties that must hold consecutively; e.g., "a hand picking up a block" might become "the block is not supported by the hand and then the block is supported by the hand." We represent such sequences with *MA timelines*[3], which are sequences of conjunctive state restrictions. Intuitively, an MA timeline represents the events that temporally match the sequence of consecutive conjunctions. An AMA formula is then the conjunction of a number of MA timelines, representing events that can be simultaneously viewed as satisfying each conjoined timeline. Formally,

$$
\begin{aligned}
state &\;::=\; \textbf{true} \mid prop \mid prop \wedge state \\
MA &\;::=\; (state) \mid (state); MA \qquad \textit{// may omit parens} \\
AMA &\;::=\; MA \mid MA \wedge AMA
\end{aligned}
$$

where *prop* is a primitive proposition. We often treat states as proposition sets (with **true** the empty set), MA formulas as state sets[4], and AMA formulas as MA timeline sets.

A temporal model $\mathcal{M} = \langle M, \mathcal{I} \rangle$ over the set of propositions **PROP** is a pair of a mapping M from the natural numbers (representing time) to truth assignments to **PROP**, and a closed natural number interval I. The natural numbers in the domain of M represent time discretely, but there is no prescribed unit of continuous time alloted to each number. Instead, each number represents an arbitrarily long period of continuous time during which nothing changed. Similarly, states in MA timelines represent arbitrarily long periods of time during which the conjunctive state restrictions hold.[5]

- A state s is satisfied by model $\langle M, I \rangle$ iff $M[x]$ assigns P true for every $x \in I$ and $P \in s$.

- An MA timeline $s_1; s_2; \cdots; s_n$ is satisfied by a model $\langle M, [t, t'] \rangle$ iff $\exists t'' \in [t, t']$ s. t. $\langle M, [t, t''] \rangle$ satisfies s_1, and either $\langle M, [t'', t'] \rangle$ or $\langle M, [t''+1, t'] \rangle$ satisfies $s_2; \cdots; s_n$.

- An AMA formula $\Phi_1 \wedge \Phi_2 \wedge \ldots \wedge \Phi_n$ is satisfied by $\mathcal{M}$ iff each Φ_i is satisfied by $\mathcal{M}$.

---

[2]In some cases, there can be more than one such least-general concept. The set of all such concepts is called the "specific boundary of the version space" (Mitchell 1982).

[3]MA stands for "Meets/And", an MA timeline being the "Meet" of a sequence of conjunctively restricted intervals.

[4]Timelines may contain duplicate states, and the duplication can be significant. For this reason, when treating timelines as sets of states, we formally intend sets of *state-index pairs*. We do not indicate this explicitly to avoid encumbering our notation, but this must be remembered whenever handling duplicate states.

[5]We note that Siskind (2001) gives a continuous-time semantics for event logic for which our results below also hold.

The condition defining satisfaction for MA timelines may appear unintuitive, as there are two ways that $s_2; \cdots; s_n$ can be satisfied. Recall that we are using the natural numbers to represent arbitrary static continuous time intervals. The transition between consecutive states s_i and s_{i+1} can occur either within a static interval (i.e., one of constant truth assignment), that happens to satisfy both states, or exactly at the boundary of two static time intervals. In the above definition, these cases correspond to $s_2; \cdots; s_n$ being satisfied during the time intervals $[t'', t']$ and $[t''+1, t']$, respectively.

When $\mathcal{M}$ satisfies Φ we say $\mathcal{M}$ is a model of Φ. We say AMA Ψ_1 *subsumes* AMA Ψ_2 iff every model of Ψ_2 is a model of Ψ_1, written $\Psi_2 \leq \Psi_1$, and Ψ_1 *properly subsumes* Ψ_2 when, in addition, $\Psi_1 \not\leq \Psi_2$. We may also say Ψ_1 is *more general (or less specific) than* Ψ_2 or that Ψ_1 *covers* Ψ_2. Siskind (2001) provides a method to determine whether a given model satisfies a given AMA formula. We now give two illustrative examples.

Example 1. *(Stretchability)* *The MA timelines* $\overline{S_1; S_2; S_3,}$ $S_1; S_2; S_2; S_2; S_3,$ *and* $S_1; S_1; S_2; S_3; S_3$ *are all equivalent. In general, MA timelines have the property that duplicating any state results in an equivalent formula. Given a model* $\langle M, I \rangle$, *we view each* $M[x]$ *as a continuous time-interval that can be divided into an arbitrary number of subintervals. So, if state S is satisfied by* $\langle M, [x, x] \rangle$, *then so is the sequence* $S; S; \cdots; S$.

Example 2. *(Infinite Descending Chains) Given propositions A and B, the MA timeline* $\Phi = (A \wedge B)$ *is subsumed by each of* $A; B,$ $A; B; A; B,$ $A; B; A; B; A; B,$ $\ldots$ *This is clear from a continuous-time perspective, as an interval where A and B are true can always be broken into subintervals where both A and B hold—any AMA formula over only A and B will subsume* Φ. *This example illustrates that there are infinite descending chains of AMA formulas that each properly subsume a given formula.*

Motivation for AMA MA timelines are a very natural way to capture "stretchable" sequences of state constraints. But why consider the conjunction of such sequences, i.e., AMA? We have several reasons for this language enrichment. First of all, we show below that the AMA LGG is unique; this is not true for MA. Second, and more informally, we argue that parallel conjunctive constraints can be important to learning efficiency. In particular, the space of MA formulas of length k grows in size exponentially with k, making it difficult to induce long MA formulas. However, finding several shorter MA timelines that each characterize *part* of a long sequence of changes is exponentially easier. (At least, the space to search is exponentially smaller.) The AMA conjunction of these timelines places these shorter constraints simultaneously and often captures a great deal of the concept structure. For this reason, we analyze AMA as well as MA and, in our empirical companion paper, we bound the length k of the timelines considered.

Our language, analysis, and learning methods here are described for a propositional setting. However, in a companion paper (Fern, Siskind, & Givan 2002) we show how to adapt these methods to a substantial empirical domain (video event recognition) that requires relational concepts. There, we convert relational training data to propositional training data using an automatically extracted object correspondence between examples and then universally generalizing the resulting learned concepts. This approach is somewhat distinctive (compare (Lavrac, Dzeroski, & Grobelnik 1991; Roth & Yih 2001)). The empirical domain presented there also requires extending our methods here to allow states to assert proposition negations and to control the exponential growth of concept size with a restricted-hypothesis-space bias to small concepts (by bounding MA timeline length).

AMA formulas can be translated to first-order clauses, but it is not straightforward to then use existing clausal generalization techniques for learning. In particular, to capture the AMA semantics in clauses, it appears necessary to define subsumption and generalization relative to a background theory that restricts us to a "continuous-time" first-order–model space. In general, least-general generalizations relative to background theories need not exist (Plotkin 1971), so clausal generalization does not simply subsume our results.

Basic Concepts and Properties of AMA

We use the following conventions: "propositions" and "theorems" are the key results of our work, with theorems being those results of the most difficulty, and "lemmas" are technical results needed for the later proofs of propositions or theorems. We number the results in one sequence. Complete proofs are available in the full paper.

Least-General Covering Formula. A logic can discriminate two models if it contains a formula that satisfies one but not the other. It turns out AMA formulas can discriminate two models exactly when *internal positive* event logic formulas can do so. Internal positive formulas are those that define event occurrence only in terms of positive (non-negated) properties within the defining interval (i.e., satisfaction by $\langle M, I \rangle$ depends only on the proposition truth values given by M inside the interval I). This fact indicates that our restriction to AMA formulas retains substantial expressiveness and leads to the following result that serves as the least-general covering formula (LGCF) component of our learning procedure. The *MA-projection* of a model $\mathcal{M} = \langle M, [i, j] \rangle$ is an MA timeline $s_0; s_1; \cdots; s_{j-i}$ where state s_k gives the true propositions in $M(i + k)$ for $0 \leq k \leq j - i$.

Proposition 1. *The MA-projection of a model is its LGCF for internal positive event logic (and hence for AMA), up to semantic equivalence.*

Proposition 1 tells us that the LGCF of a model exists, is unique, and is an MA timeline. Given this property, when a formula Ψ covers all the MA timelines covered by another formula Ψ', we have $\Psi' \leq \Psi$. Proposition 1 also tells us that we can compute the LGCF of a model by constructing the MA-projection of that model—it is straightforward to do this in time polynomial in the size of the model.

Subsumption and Generalization for States. A state S_1 subsumes S_2 iff S_1 is a subset of S_2, viewing states as sets of propositions. From this we derive that the intersection of states is the least-general subsumer of those states and that the union of states is likewise the most general subsumee.

Interdigitations.   Given a set of MA timelines, we need to consider the different ways in which a model could simultaneously satisfy the timelines in the set. At the start of such a model, the initial state from each timeline must be satisfied. At some point, one or more of the timelines can transition so that the second state in those timelines must be satisfied in place of the initial state, while the initial state of the other timelines remains satisfied. After a sequence of such transitions in subsets of the timelines, the final state of each timeline holds. Each way of choosing the transition sequence constitutes a different "interdigitation" of the timelines.

Alternatively viewed, each model simultaneously satisfying the timelines induces a *co-occurrence relation* on tuples of timeline states, one from each timeline, identifying which tuples co-occur at some point in the model. We represent this concept formally as a set of tuples of co-occurring states that can be ordered by the sequence of transitions. Intuitively, the tuples in an interdigitation represent the maximal time intervals over which no MA timeline has a transition, giving the co-occurring states for each such time interval.

A relation R on $X_1 \times \cdots \times X_n$ is *simultaneously consistent* with orderings $\leq_1, \ldots, \leq_n$, if, whenever $R(x_1, \ldots, x_n)$ and $R(x'_1, \ldots, x'_n)$, either $x_i \leq_i x'_i$, for all i, or $x'_i \leq_i x_i$, for all i. We say R is *piecewise total* if the projection of R onto each component is total (i.e., every state in any X_i appears in R).

Definition 1.   *An interdigitation I of a set of MA timelines $\{\Phi_1, \ldots, \Phi_n\}$ is a co-occurrence relation over $\Phi_1 \times \cdots \times \Phi_n$ (viewing timelines as sets of states) that is piecewise total, and simultaneously consistent with the state orderings of the Φ_i. We say that two states $s \in \Phi_i$ and $s' \in \Phi_j$ for $i \neq j$ co-occur in I iff some tuple of I contains both s and s'. We sometimes refer to I as a sequence of tuples, meaning the sequence lexicographically ordered by the Φ_i state orderings.*

There are exponentially many interdigitations of even two MA timelines (relative to the timeline lengths). Figure 1 shows an interdigitation of two MA timelines.

We first use interdigitations to syntactically characterize subsumption between MA timelines. An interdigitation I of two MA timelines Φ_1 and Φ_2 is a *witness* to $\Phi_1 \leq \Phi_2$ if, for every pair of co-occurring states $s_1 \in \Phi_1$ and $s_2 \in \Phi_2$, we have $s_1 \leq s_2$. Below we establish the equivalence between witnessing interdigitations and MA subsumption.

Proposition 2.   *For MA timelines Φ_1 and Φ_2, $\Phi_1 \leq \Phi_2$ iff there is an interdigitation that witnesses $\Phi_1 \leq \Phi_2$.*

IS($\cdot$) and IG($\cdot$).   Interdigitations are useful in analyzing both conjunctions and disjunctions of MA timelines. When conjoining timelines, all states that co-occur in an interdigitation must simultaneously hold at some point, so that viewed as sets, the union of the co-occurring states must hold. A sequence of such unions that must hold to force the conjunction of timelines to hold (via some interdigitation) is called an "interdigitation specialization" of the timelines. Dually, an "interdigitation generalization" involving intersections of states upper bounds the disjunction of timelines.

Suppose $s_1, s_2, s_3, t_1, t_2,$ and t_3 are each sets of propositions (i.e., states). Consider the timelines $S = s_1; s_2; s_3$ and $T = t_1; t_2; t_3$. The relation

$$\{ \ \langle s_1, t_1 \rangle, \ \langle s_2, t_1 \rangle, \ \langle s_3, t_2 \rangle, \ \langle s_3, t_3 \rangle \ \}$$

is an interdigitation of S and T in which states s_1 and s_2 co-occur with t_1, and s_3 co-occurs with t_2 and t_3. The corresponding IG and IS members are

$$s_1 \cap t_1; \ s_2 \cap t_1; \ s_3 \cap t_2; \ s_3 \cap t_3 \ \in \ \text{IG}(\{S, T\})$$
$$s_1 \cup t_1; \ s_2 \cup t_1; \ s_3 \cup t_2; \ s_3 \cup t_3 \ \in \ \text{IS}(\{S, T\}).$$

If $t_1 \subseteq s_1, t_1 \subseteq s_2, t_2 \subseteq s_3,$ and $t_3 \subseteq s_3$, then the interdigitation *witnesses* $S \leq T$.

Figure 1: An interdigitation with IG and IS members.

Definition 2.   *An interdigitation generalization (specialization) of a set Σ of MA timelines is an MA timeline $s_1; \ldots; s_m$, such that, for some interdigitation I of Σ with m tuples, s_j is the intersection (respectively, union) of the components of the j'th tuple of the sequence I. The set of interdigitation generalizations (respectively, specializations) of Σ is called $\text{IG}(\Sigma)$ (respectively, $\text{IS}(\Sigma)$).*

Each timeline in $\text{IG}(\Sigma)$ (dually, $\text{IS}(\Sigma)$) subsumes (is subsumed by) each timeline in Σ. For our complexity analyses, we note that the number of states in any member of $\text{IG}(C)$ or $\text{IS}(C)$ is lower-bounded by the number of states in any of the MA timelines in C and is upper-bounded by the total number of states in all the MA timelines in C. The number of interdigitations of C, and thus of members of $\text{IG}(C)$ or $\text{IS}(C)$, is exponential in that same total number of states.

We now give a useful lemma and a proposition concerning the relationships between conjunctions and disjunctions of MA concepts (the former being AMA concepts). For convenience here, we use disjunction on MA concepts, producing formulas outside of AMA with the obvious interpretation.

Lemma 3.   *Given an MA formula Φ that subsumes each member of a set Σ of MA formulas, some $\Phi' \in \text{IG}(\Sigma)$ is subsumed by Φ. Dually, when Φ is subsumed by each member of Σ, some $\Phi' \in \text{IS}(\Sigma)$ subsumes Φ. In each case, the length of Φ' can be bounded by the size of Σ.*

Proof: (Sketch) Construct a witnessing interdigitation for the subsumption of each member of Σ by Φ. Combine these interdigitations I_Σ to form an interdigitation I of $\Sigma \cup \{\Phi\}$ such that any state s in Φ co-occurs with a state s' only if s and s' co-occur in some interdigitation in I_Σ. "Project" I to an interdigitation of Σ and form the corresponding member Φ' of $\text{IG}(\Sigma)$. Careful analysis shows $\Phi' \leq \Phi$ with the desired size bound. The dual is argued similarly. $\square$

Proposition 4.   *The following hold:*

1. *(and-to-or) The conjunction of a set Σ of MA timelines is equal to the disjunction of the timelines in $\text{IS}(\Sigma)$.*

2. *(or-to-and) The disjunction of a set Σ of MA timelines is subsumed by the conjunction of the timelines in $\text{IG}(\Sigma)$.*

Proof: $(\bigvee \text{IS}(\Sigma)) \leq (\bigwedge \Sigma)$ and $(\bigvee \Sigma) \leq (\bigwedge \text{IG}(\Sigma))$ are straightforward. $(\bigwedge \Sigma) \leq (\bigvee \mathrm{IS}(\Sigma))$ follows from Lemma 3 by considering any timeline covered by $(\bigwedge \Sigma)$. □

Using "and-to-or", we can now reduce AMA subsumption to MA subsumption, with an exponential size increase.

Proposition 5. *For AMA Ψ_1 and Ψ_2, $(\Psi_1 \leq \Psi_2)$ iff for all $\Phi_1 \in \mathrm{IS}(\Psi_1)$ and $\Phi_2 \in \Psi_2$, $\Phi_1 \leq \Phi_2$*

Subsumption and Generalization

We give algorithms and complexity bounds for the construction of least-general generalization (LGG) formulas based on an analysis of subsumption. We give a polynomial-time algorithm for deciding subsumption between MA formulas. We show that subsumption for AMA formulas is coNP-complete. We give existence, uniqueness, lower/upper bounds, and an algorithm for the LGG on AMA formulas. Finally, we give a syntactic notion of subsumption and an algorithm that computes the corresponding syntactic LGG that is exponentially faster than our semantic LGG algorithm.

Subsumption. Our methods rely on a novel algorithm for deciding the subsumption question $\Phi_1 \leq \Phi_2$ between MA formulas Φ_1 and Φ_2 in polynomial-time. Merely searching for a witnessing interdigitation of Φ_1 and Φ_2 provides an obvious decision procedure for the subsumption question—however, there are exponentially many such interdigitations. We reduce this problem to the polynomial-time operation of finding a path in a graph on pairs of states in $\Phi_1 \times \Phi_2$.

<u>Theorem 6.</u> *Given MA timelines Φ_1 and Φ_2, we can check in polynomial time whether $\Phi_1 \leq \Phi_2$.*

Proof: (Sketch) Write Φ_1 as $s_1, \ldots, s_m$ and Φ_2 as $t_1, \ldots, t_n$. Consider a directed graph with vertices V the set $\{v_{i,j} \mid 1 \leq i \leq m, 1 \leq j \leq n\}$. Let the (directed) edges E be the set of all $\langle v_{i,j}, v_{i',j'} \rangle$ such that $s_i \leq t_j$, $s_{i'} \leq t_{j'}$, and both $i \leq i' \leq i + 1$ and $j \leq j' \leq j + 1$. One can show that $\Phi_1 \leq \Phi_2$ iff there is a path in $\langle V, E \rangle$ from $v_{1,1}$ to $v_{m,n}$. Paths here correspond to witnessing interdigitations. □

A polynomial-time MA-subsumption tester can be built by constructing the graph described in this proof and employing any polynomial-time path-finding method. Given this polynomial-time algorithm for MA subsumption, Proposition 5 immediately suggests an exponential-time algorithm for deciding AMA subsumption—by computing MA subsumption between the exponentially many IS timelines of one formula and the timelines of the other formula. The following theorem tells us that, unless $P = NP$, we cannot do any better than this in the worst case.

<u>Theorem 7.</u> *Deciding AMA subsumption is coNP-complete.*

Proof: (sketch) AMA-subsumption of Ψ_1 by Ψ_2 is in coNP because there are polynomially checkable certificates to non-subsumption. In particular, there is a member Φ_1 of $\mathrm{IS}(\Psi_1)$ that is not subsumed by some member of Ψ_2, which can be checked using MA-subsumption in polynomial time.

We reduce the problem of deciding the satisfiability of a 3-SAT formula $S = C_1 \wedge \cdots \wedge C_m$ to the problem of recognizing non-subsumption between AMA formulas. Here,

each C_i is $(l_{i,1} \vee l_{i,2} \vee l_{i,3})$ and each $l_{i,j}$ either a proposition P chosen from $P_1, \ldots, P_n$ or its negation $\neg P$. The idea of the reduction is to view members of $\mathrm{IS}(\Psi_1)$ as representing truth assignments. We exploit the fact that all interdigitation specializations of $X; Y$ and $Y; X$ will be subsumed by either X or Y—this yields a binary choice that can represent a proposition truth value, except that there will be an interdigitation that "sets" the proposition to both true and false.

Let Q be the set of propositions

$$\{\mathrm{True}_k \mid 1 \leq k \leq n\} \cup \{\mathrm{False}_k \mid 1 \leq k \leq n\},$$

and let Ψ_1 be the conjunction of the timelines

$$\bigcup_{i=1}^{n} \{(Q; \mathrm{True}_i; \mathrm{False}_i; Q), (Q; \mathrm{False}_i; \mathrm{True}_i; Q)\}.$$

Each member of $\mathrm{IS}(\Psi_1)$ will be subsumed by either True_i or False_i for each i, and thus "represent" at least one truth assignment. Let Ψ_2 be the formula $s_1; \ldots; s_m$, where

$$s_i = \{\mathrm{True}_j \mid l_{i,k} = P_j \text{ for some } k\} \cup \{\mathrm{False}_j \mid l_{i,k} = \neg P_j \text{ for some } k\}.$$

Each s_i can be thought of as asserting "not C_i". It can now be shown that there exists a certificate to non-subsumption of Ψ_1 by Ψ_2, i.e., a member of $\mathrm{IS}(\Psi_1)$ not subsumed by Ψ_2, if and only if there exists a satisfying assignment for S. □

We later define a weaker polynomial-time–computable subsumption notion for use in our learning algorithms.

Least-General Generalization. The existence of an AMA LGG is nontrivial as there are infinite chains of increasingly specific formulas that generalize given formulas: e.g., each member of the chain $P; Q$, $P; Q; P; Q$, $P; Q; P; Q; P; Q$, $P; Q; P; Q; P; Q; P; Q, \ldots$ covers $P \wedge Q$ and $(P \wedge Q); Q$.

<u>Theorem 8.</u> *There is an LGG for any finite set Σ of AMA formulas that is subsumed by every generalization of Σ.*

Proof: Let Γ be the set $\bigcup_{\Psi' \in \Sigma} \mathrm{IS}(\Psi')$. Let Ψ be the conjunction of the finitely many MA timelines that generalize Γ while having size no larger than Γ. Each timeline in Ψ generalizes Γ and thus Σ (by Proposition 4), so Ψ must generalize Σ. Now, consider an arbitrary generalization Ψ' of Σ. Proposition 5 implies that Ψ' generalizes each member of Γ. Lemma 3 then implies that each timeline of Ψ' subsumes a timeline Φ, no longer than the size of Γ, that also subsumes the timelines of Γ. Then Φ must be a timeline of Ψ, by our choice of Ψ, so every timeline of Ψ' subsumes a timeline of Ψ. Then Ψ' subsumes Ψ, and Ψ is the desired LGG. □

Strengthening "or-to-and" we can compute an AMA LGG.

<u>Theorem 9.</u> *For a set Σ of MA formulas, the conjunction Ψ of all MA timelines in $\mathrm{IG}(\Sigma)$ is an AMA LGG of Σ.*

Proof: That Ψ subsumes the members of Σ is straightforward. To show Ψ is "least", consider Ψ' subsuming the members of Σ. Lemma 3 implies that each timeline of Ψ' subsumes a member of $\mathrm{IG}(\Sigma)$. This implies $\Psi \leq \Psi'$. □

Combining this result with Proposition 4, we get:

Theorem 10. $\mathrm{IG}(\bigcup_{\Psi \in \Sigma} \mathrm{IS}(\Psi))$ *is an AMA LGG of the set* Σ *of AMA formulas.*

Theorem 10 leads to an algorithm that is doubly exponential in the input size because both $\mathrm{IS}(\cdot)$ and $\mathrm{IG}(\cdot)$ produce exponential size increases. We believe we cannot do better:

Theorem 11. *The smallest LGG of two MA formulas can be exponentially large.*

Proof: (Sketch) Consider the formulas $\Phi_1 = s_{1,*}; s_{2,*}; \ldots ; s_{n,*}$ and $\Phi_2 = s_{*,1}; s_{*,2}; \ldots; s_{*,n}$, where $s_{i,*} = P_{i,1} \wedge \cdots \wedge P_{i,n}$ and $s_{*,j} = P_{1,j} \wedge \cdots \wedge P_{n,j}$. For each member $\varphi = x_1; \ldots; x_{2n-1}$ of the exponentially many members of $\mathrm{IG}(\{\Phi_1, \Phi_2\})$, define $\overline{\varphi}$ to be the timeline $P - x_2; \ldots; P - x_{2n-2}$, where P is all the propositions. It is possible to show that the AMA LGG of Φ_1 and Φ_2, e.g., the conjunction of $\mathrm{IG}(\{\Phi_1, \Phi_2\})$, must contain a separate conjunct excluding each of the exponentially many $\overline{\varphi}$. □

Conjecture 12. *The smallest LGG of two AMA formulas can be doubly-exponentially large.*

Even when there is a small LGG, it is expensive to compute:

Theorem 13. *Determining whether a formula Ψ is an AMA LGG for two given AMA formulas Ψ_1 and Ψ_2 is co-NP-hard, and is in co-NEXP, in the size of all three formulas together.*

Proof: (Sketch) Hardness by reduction from AMA subsumption. Upper bound by the existence of exponentially-long certificates for "No" answers: members X of $\mathrm{IS}(\Psi)$ and Y of $\mathrm{IG}(\mathrm{IS}(\Psi_1) \cup \mathrm{IS}(\Psi_2))$ such that $X \not\leq Y$. □

Syntactic Subsumption. We now introduce a tractable generality notion, syntactic subsumption, and discuss the corresponding LGG problem. Using syntactic forms of subsumption for efficiency is familiar in ILP (Muggleton & De Raedt 1994). Unlike AMA semantic subsumption, syntactic subsumption requires checking only polynomially many MA subsumptions, each in polynomial time (via theorem 6).

Definition 3. *AMA Ψ_1 is syntactically subsumed by AMA Ψ_2 (written $\Psi_1 \leq_{syn} \Psi_2$) iff for each MA timeline $\Phi_2 \in \Psi_2$, there is an MA timeline $\Phi_1 \in \Psi_1$ such that $\Phi_1 \leq \Phi_2$.*

Proposition 14. *AMA syntactic subsumption can be decided in polynomial time.*

Syntactic subsumption trivially implies semantic subsumption—however, the converse does not hold in general. Consider the AMA formulas $(A; B) \wedge (B; A)$, and $A; B; A$ where A and B are primitive propositions. We have $(A; B) \wedge (B; A) \leq A; B; A$; however, we have neither $A; B \leq A; B; A$ nor $B; A \leq A; B; A$, so that $A; B; A$ does not syntactically subsume $(A; B) \wedge (B; A)$. Syntactic subsumption fails to recognize constraints that are only derived from the interaction of timelines within a formula.

Syntactic Least-General Generalization. The *syntactic AMA LGG* is the syntactically least-general AMA for-

mula that syntactically subsumes the input AMA formulas[6]. Based on the hardness gap between syntactic and semantic AMA subsumption, one might conjecture that a similar gap exists between the syntactic and semantic LGG problems. Proving such a gap exists requires closing the gap between the lower and upper bounds on AMA LGG shown in Theorem 10 in favor of the upper bound, as suggested by Conjecture 12. While we cannot yet show a hardness gap between semantic and syntactic LGG, we do give a syntactic LGG algorithm that is exponentially more efficient than the best semantic LGG algorithm we have found (that of Theorem 10).

Theorem 15. *There is a syntactic LGG for any AMA formula set Σ that is syntactically subsumed by all syntactic generalizations of Σ.*

Proof: Let Ψ be the conjunction of all the MA timelines that syntactically generalize Σ, but with size no larger than Σ. Complete the proof using Ψ as in Theorem 8. □

Semantic and syntactic LGG are different, though clearly the syntactic LGG must subsume the semantic LGG. For example, $(A; B) \wedge (B; A)$, and $A; B; A$ have a semantic LGG of $A; B; A$, as discussed above; but their syntactic LGG is $(A; B; \mathbf{true}) \wedge (\mathbf{true}; B; A)$, which subsumes $A; B; A$ but is not subsumed by $A; B; A$. Even so, on MA formulas:

Proposition 16. *Any syntactic AMA LGG for an MA formula set Σ is also a semantic LGG for Σ.*

Proof: We first argue the initial claim $(\Phi \leq \Psi)$ iff $(\Phi \leq_{syn} \Psi)$ for AMA Ψ and MA Φ. The reverse direction is immediate, and for the forward direction, by the definition of $\leq_{syn}$, each conjunct of Ψ must subsume "some timeline" in Φ, and there is only one timeline in Φ. Now to prove the theorem, suppose a syntactic LGG Ψ of Σ is not a semantic LGG of Σ. Conjoin Ψ with any semantic LGG Ψ' of Σ—the result can be shown, using our initial claim, to be a syntactic subsumer of the members of Σ that is properly syntactically subsumed by Ψ, contradicting our assumption. □

With Theorem 11, an immediate consequence is that we cannot hope for a polynomial-time syntactic LGG algorithm.

Theorem 17. *The smallest syntactic LGG of two MA formulas can be exponentially large.*

Unlike the semantic LGG case, for the syntactic LGG we have an algorithm whose time complexity matches this lower-bound. Theorem 10, when each Ψ is MA, provides a method for computing the semantic LGG for a set of MA timelines in exponential time using IG (because $\mathrm{IS}(\Psi) = \Psi$ when Ψ is MA). Given a set of AMA formulas, the syntactic LGG algorithm uses this method to compute the polynomially-many semantic LGGs of sets of timelines, one chosen from each input formula, and conjoins all the results.

Theorem 18. *The formula $\bigwedge_{\Phi_i \in \Psi_i} \mathrm{IG}(\{\Phi_1, \ldots, \Phi_n\})$ is a syntactic LGG of the AMA formulas $\Psi_1, \ldots, \Psi_n$.*

Proof: Let Ψ be $\bigwedge_{\Phi_i \in \Psi_i} \mathrm{IG}(\{\Phi_1, \ldots, \Phi_n\})$. Each timeline Φ of Ψ must subsume each Ψ_i because Φ is an out-

---

[6]Again, "least" means that no formula properly syntactically subsumed by the syntactic LGG can subsume the input formulas.

Inputs	Subsumption		Semantic AMA LGG			Synt. AMA LGG		
	Sem	Syn	Low	Up	Size	Low	Up	Size
MA	P	P	P	coNP	EXP	P	coNP	EXP
AMA	coNP	P	coNP	NEXP	2-EXP?	P	coNP	EXP

Table 1: Complexity Results Summary. The LGG complexities are relative to *input plus output* size. The size column reports the largest possible output size. The "?" denotes a conjecture.

put of IG on a set containing a timeline of Ψ_i. Now consider Ψ' syntactically subsuming every Ψ_i. We show that $\Psi \leq_{\text{syn}} \Psi'$ to conclude. Each timeline Φ' in Ψ' subsumes a timeline $T_i \in \Psi_i$, for each i, by our assumption that $\Psi_i \leq_{\text{syn}} \Psi'$. But then by Lemma 3, Φ' must subsume a member of IG($\{T_1, \ldots, T_n\}$)—and that member is a timeline of Ψ—so each timeline Φ' of Ψ' subsumes a timeline of Ψ. We conclude $\Psi \leq_{\text{syn}} \Psi'$, as desired. □

This theorem yields an algorithm that computes a syntactic AMA LGG in exponential time. The method does an exponential amount of work even if there is a small syntactic LGG (typically because many timelines can be pruned from the output because they subsume what remains). It is still an open question as to whether there is an output efficient algorithm for computing the syntactic AMA LGG—this problem is in coNP and we conjecture that it is coNP-complete. One route to settling this question is to determine the output complexity of semantic LGG for MA input formulas. We believe this problem to be coNP-complete, but have not proven this; if this problem is in P, there is an output-efficient method for computing syntactic AMA LGG based on Theorem 18.

Conclusion

Table 1 summarizes the upper and lower bounds we have shown. In each case, we have provided a theorem suggesting an algorithm matching the upper bound shown. The table also shows the size that the various LGG results could possibly take relative to the input size. The key results in this table are the polynomial-time MA subsumption and AMA syntactic subsumption, the coNP lower bound for AMA subsumption, the exponential size of LGGs in the worst case, and the apparently lower complexity of syntactic AMA LGG versus semantic LGG. We described how to build a learner based on these results and, in our companion work, demonstrate the utility of this learner in a substantial application.

References

Agrawal, R., and Srikant, R. 1995. Mining sequential patterns. In *Proc. 11th Int. Conf. Data Engineering*, 3–14.

Allen, J. F., and Ferguson, G. 1994. Actions and events in interval temporal logic. *Journal of Logic and Computation* 4(5).

Allen, J. F. 1983. Maintaining knowledge about temporal intervals. *Communications of the ACM* 26(11):832–843.

Bacchus, F., and Kabanza, F. 2000. Using temporal logics to express search control knowledge for planning. *Artificial Intelligence* 16:123–191.

Clarke, E. M.; Emerson, E. A.; and Sistla, A. P. 1983. Automatic verification of finite state concurrent systems using temporal logic specifications: A practical approach. In *Symposium on Principles of Programming Languages*, 117–126.

Cohen, W., and Hirsh, H. 1994. Learnability of the classic description logic: Theoretical and experimental results. In *4th International Knowledge Representation and Reasoning*, 121–133.

Cohen, W. 1994. Grammatically biased learning: Learning logic programs using an explicit antecedent description lanugage. *Artificial Intelligence* 68:303–366.

Cohen, P. 2001. Fluent learning: Elucidation the structure of episodes. In *Symposium on Intelligent Data Analysis*.

De Raedt, L., and Dehaspe, L. 1997. Clausal discovery. *Machine Learning* 26:99–146.

Dehaspe, L., and De Raedt, L. 1996. Dlab: A declarative language bias formalism. In *International Syposium on Methodologies for Intelligent Systems*, 613–622.

Fern, A.; Siskind, J. M.; and Givan, R. 2002. Learning temporal, relational, force-dynamic event definitions from video. In *Proceedings of the Eighteenth National Conference on Artificial Intelligence*.

Hoppner, F. 2001. Discovery of temporal patterns—learning rules about the qualitative behaviour of time series. In *5th European Principles and Practice of Knowledge Discovery in Databases*.

Kam, P., and Fu, A. 2000. Discovering temporal patterns for interval-based events. In *International Conference on Data Warehousing and Knowledge discovery*.

Lavrac, N.; Dzeroski, S.; and Grobelnik, M. 1991. Learning nonrecursive definitions of relations with LINUS. In *Proceedings of the Fifth European Working Session on Learning*, 265–288.

Mannila, H.; Toivonen, H.; and Verkamo, A. I. 1995. Discovery of frequent episodes in sequences. In *International Conference on Data Mining and Knowledge Discovery*.

Mitchell, T. 1982. Generalization as search. *Artificial Intelligence* 18(2):517–542.

Muggleton, S., and De Raedt, L. 1994. Inductive logic programming: Theory and methods. *Journal of Logic Programming* 19/20:629–679.

Muggleton, S., and Feng, C. 1992. Efficient induction of logic programs. In Muggleton, S., ed., *Inductive Logic Programming*. Academic Press. 281–298.

Muggleton, S. 1995. Inverting entailment and Progol. In *Machine Intelligence*, volume 14. Oxford University Press. 133–188.

Plotkin, G. D. 1971. *Automatic Methods of Inductive Inference*. Ph.D. Dissertation, Edinburgh University.

Roth, D., and Yih, W. 2001. Relational learning via propositional algorithms: An information extraction case study. In *International Joint Conference on Artificial Intelligence*.

Siskind, J. M. 2001. Grounding the lexical semantics of verbs in visual perception using force dynamics and event logic. *Journal of Artificial Intelligence Research* 15:31–90.

Learning Temporal, Relational, Force-Dynamic Event Definitions from Video*

Alan Fern and **Jeffrey Mark Siskind** and **Robert Givan**

School of Electrical and Computer Engineering, Purdue University, West Lafayette IN 47907–1285 USA

{afern,qobi,givan}@purdue.edu

Abstract

We present and evaluate a novel implemented approach for learning to recognize events in video. First, we introduce a sublanguage of event logic, called k-AMA, that is sufficiently expressive to represent visual events yet sufficiently restrictive to support learning. Second, we develop a specific-to-general learning algorithm for learning event definitions in k-AMA. Finally, we apply this algorithm to the task of learning event definitions from video and show that it yields definitions that are competitive with hand-coded ones.

Introduction

Humans conceptualize the world in terms of objects and events. This is reflected in the fact that we talk about the world using nouns and verbs. We perceive events taking place between objects, we interact with the world by performing events on objects, and we reason about the effects that actual and hypothetical events performed by us and others have on objects. We also *learn* new object and event types from novel experience. In this paper, we present and evaluate novel implemented techniques that allow a computer to learn to recognize new event types from video input.

We wish the acquired knowledge of event types to support multiple modalities. Humans can observe someone *fax*ing a letter for the first time and quickly be able to recognize future occurrences of faxing, perform faxing, and reason about faxing. It thus appears likely that humans use and learn event representations that are sufficiently general to support fast and efficient use in multiple modalities. A long-term goal of our research is to allow similar cross-modal learning and use of event representations. We intend the same learned representations to be used for vision (as described in this paper), planning (something that we are beginning to investigate), and robotics (something left to the future).

A crucial requirement for event representations is that they capture the *invariants* of an event type. Humans clas-sify both picking up a cup off a table and picking up a dumbbell off the floor as *picking up*. This suggests that human event representations are *relational*. We have an abstract relational notion of *picking up* that is parameterized by the participant objects rather than distinct propositional notions instantiated for specific objects. Humans also classify an event as *picking up* no matter whether the hand is moving slowly or quickly, horizontally or vertically, leftward or rightward, or along a straight path or circuitous one. It appears that it is not the characteristics of participant-object motion that distinguish *picking up* from other event types. Rather, it is the fact that the object being picked up changes from being supported by resting on its initial location to be supported by being grasped by the agent. This suggests that the primitive relations used to build event representations are *force dynamic* (Talmy 1988). Finally, humans distinguish between picking up and putting down a cup despite the fact that both before putting down the cup and after picking up the cup the same state of affairs holds, namely the human is holding the cup. This suggests that event representations are *temporal*. The order of world states matters when defining event types.

Another desirable property of event representations is that they be *perspicuous*. Humans can introspect and describe the defining characteristics of event types. Such introspection is what allows us to create dictionaries. To support such introspection, the representation language should allow such characteristics to be explicitly manifest in event definitions and not be emergent consequences of distributed parameters as in neural networks or hidden Markov models.

We present a novel system that learns to recognize events from video input using temporal, relational, force-dynamic representations. This is not the first system to perform visual event recognition. We review prior work and compare it to the current work later in the paper. In fact, one of us has built two such prior systems. HOWARD (Siskind & Morris 1996) learns to classify events from video using temporal, relational representations. But these representations are not force dynamic. LEONARD (Siskind 2001) classifies events from video using temporal, relational, force-dynamic representations but does not learn these representations. It uses a library of hand-code representations. This work adds a learning component to LEONARD. We describe the representation language used to support learning and the algorithms used to learn representations in that language. We

---

*This work was supported in part by NSF grants 9977981-IIS and 0093100-IIS, an NSF Graduate Fellowship for Fern, and the Center for Education and Research in Information Assurance and Security at Purdue University. Part of this work was performed while Siskind was at NEC Research Institute, Inc.

also evaluate the performance of the approach and compare the performance of learned representations to the prior hand-coded representations. A companion paper (Fern, Givan, & Siskind 2002) addresses theoretical issues of the approach, elaborating on the algorithms, proving their correctness, and analyzing their complexity.

Representing Event Types

LEONARD uses *event logic* (Siskind 2001) to represent event types. An event-logic expression Φ is either a primitive event type or one of $\neg\Phi$, $\diamondsuit_R\Phi$, $\Phi_1 \vee \Phi_2$, $\Phi_1 \wedge_R \Phi_2$, Φ^+, $\forall x\Phi$, or $\exists x\Phi$, where x is a variable and R is a subset of interval relations (Allen 1983). In this paper, we use only the connective $\wedge_R$ with R being either $\{m\}$ or $\{=\}$. $\Phi \wedge_R \Psi$ denotes occurrence of Φ and Ψ during intervals related by a relation in R. $\Phi \wedge_{\{=\}} \Psi$, denoting simultaneous occurrence of Φ and Ψ, and $\Phi \wedge_{\{m\}} \Psi$, denoting occurrence of Φ followed immediately by occurrence of Ψ, are sufficiently common that we abbreviate them as $\Phi \wedge \Psi$ (without a subscript) and $\Phi; \Psi$ respectively.

LEONARD represents event types with definitions in event logic like the following:

$$\text{PICKUP}(x,y,z) \triangleq \begin{bmatrix} (\text{SUPPORTS}(z,y) \wedge \text{CONTACTS}(z,y)); \\ (\text{SUPPORTS}(x,y) \wedge \text{ATTACHED}(x,y)) \end{bmatrix}$$

This means that an event of x picking up y off of z is defined as a sequence of two states where z supports y by way of contact in the first and x supports y by way of attachment in the second. SUPPORTS, CONTACTS, and ATTACHED are primitive force-dynamic relations. These are recovered from video input by a force-dynamic model-reconstruction process (Siskind 2000). Events occurrences are inferred from these primitive force-dynamic relations using event definitions like the above (the actual definitions are more complex) by an event-classification process. Previously, these definitions were hand coded. In the work reported here, we learn these definitions by applying the same LEONARD force-dynamic model-reconstruction process to training videos and inducing definitions, using the novel techniques presented in this paper, from the primitive force-dynamic relations produced by model reconstruction. We then evaluate these definitions by using them to classify test videos processed with the standard LEONARD model-reconstruction and event-classification processes.

We determined that only a subset of the full event-logic language was used in the hand-coded definitions. This subset proved both to support a learning algorithm with certain properties (see the companion paper) and to be an effective restrictive learning bias (as demonstrated by the experimental results described later in this paper). We call this sub-language AMA. An *A formula* (intuitively 'and') is a conjunction $(L_1 \wedge \cdots \wedge L_l)$ of literals L_i. For now, these literals are primitive force-dynamic relations. The theoretical results in the companion paper are limited to positive literals. In the experimental results section, we discuss extensions to support negative literals. An *MA formula* (intuitively 'meets-and') is a sequence $(A_1; \ldots; A_m)$ of A formulas A_i. An *AMA formula* (intuitively 'and-meets-and')

is a conjunction $(M_1 \wedge \cdots \wedge M_n)$ of MA formulas M_i. The above definition for PICKUP is an MA formula (and hence an AMA formula). Intuitively, A formulas describe states of the world, MA formulas describe sequences of states, what we call *timelines*, and AMA formulas describe an event in terms of multiple timelines that it must satisfy.

Learning Event Definitions

We adopt a specific-to-general ILP approach to learning event definitions from positive-only data. The AMA language is suitable for this approach because of three key properties. First, the least general MA formula (and hence AMA formula) that covers any force-dynamic model produced by model reconstruction exists and is unique up to semantic equivalence. We call these *model covers*. Second, the least general AMA generalization (LGG) of two AMA formulas exists and is unique up to semantic equivalence. Third, we have a tractable syntactic notion of generalization for AMA, refining semantic generalization, for which the corresponding LGG of two formulas exists and is unique up to mutual syntactic generalization. (See the companion paper for discussion and proof of these properties.) We refer to this "syntactic LGG" as the "LGG" from here on[1]. Our learning algorithm operates by producing model covers for the training examples and folding the binary LGG operator over these to yield the least general AMA formula that covers the training set. This works because the binary LGG operator is commutative and associative.

A key characteristic of our domain that allows the above properties to hold is that our primitive event types are *liquid* (Shoham 1987), i.e. if a primitive holds of an interval, it holds of every subinterval of that interval. This means that for any A formula A, the MA formulas A, $A; A$, $A; A; A, \ldots$ are equivalent. We use this in finding model covers and computing the LGG of two AMA formulas.

Before presenting the algorithms to do so, we define some notation. An MA formula $(A_1; \ldots; A_m)$ has a set of $m + 1$ *transition points* t_i, one at the beginning, one between each pair of adjacent A formulas, and one at the end. This set is finite and totally ordered, yielding an adjacency relation. A *segment* $A_{t_i t_{i+1}}$ denotes the A formula between a pair $\langle t_i, t_{i+1} \rangle$ of adjacent transition points. An MA formula corresponds to a transition-point set and a set of segments between the pairs of adjacent transition points. And vice versa.

First, we show how to compute a model cover. The output of model reconstruction is a set of primitive event occurrences $L@[s_1, s_2]$ where L is a primitive event type and $[s_1, s_2]$ is a maximal interval during which it occurred. Because such primitive event types are liquid, occurrence during all subintervals of $[s_1, s_2]$ is implicit. Take the set of s_i that appear in such primitive event occurrences as a set of transition points, ordered by the $<$ relation on time instants. For every pair $\langle t_i, t_{i+1} \rangle$ of adjacent transition points, take $A_{t_i t_{i+1}}$ to be the conjunction of all primitive event types L where $L@[s_1, s_2]$ is a primitive event occurrence, $s_1 \leq t_i$,

---

[1]Our algorithm for syntactic LGG is exponentially more efficient than our best algorithm for the true semantic LGG.

and $t_{i+1} \leq s_2$. This yields a model cover. Note that constructing $A_{t_i t_{i+1}}$ requires primitive-event liquidity.

Next, we show how to compute the LGG of two AMA formulas. First, consider two MA formulas M_1 and M_2. Let T_1 and T_2 be the transition-point sets of M_1 and M_2 respectively. A *proto-interdigitation* T' of T_1 and T_2 is $T_1 \cup T_2$ along with a total, reflexive, transitive 'ordering' relation that satisfies the following: (a) the order on T' is consistent with the orders on T_1 and T_2, (b) no two elements of T_1 (T_2) are equated, and (c) the minimal (maximal) elements of T_1 and T_2 are equated. An *interdigitation* T of T_1 and T_2 is the partition of a proto-interdigitation under equality.

Given this, the LGG of two MA formulas M_1 and M_2 can be computed as follows. Let T_1 and T_2 be the transition point sets of M_1 and M_2 respectively. Let $A^1_{t^1_i t^1_{i+1}}$ be the segment in M_1 between transition points t^1_i and t^1_{i+1} in T_1. Similarly, let $A^2_{t^2_i t^2_{i+1}}$ be the segment in M_2 between transition points t^2_i and t^2_{i+1} in T_2. Let T be an interdigitation of T_1 and T_2. T can be interpreted as a transition-point set where the components are interpreted as transition points ordered by the interdigitation relation. Compute the segments of T as follows. For each transition point t_i in T, let $f_1(t_i)$ be the latest member of T_1 occurring in T no later than t_i. Define $f_2(t_i)$ similarly for T_2. Dually, define $g_1(t_i)$ to be the earliest member of T_1 occurring in T no earlier than t_i. Define $g_2(t_i)$ similarly for T_2. Now, for every pair $\langle t_i, t_{i+1} \rangle$ of adjacent transition points in T take $A_{t_i t_{i+1}}$ to be the intersection of $A^1_{f_1(t_i) g_1(t_{i+1})}$ and $A^2_{f_2(t_i) g_2(t_{i+1})}$. This yields an MA formula that generalizes M_1 and M_2. The conjunction of all such formulas derived from all interdigitations is the LGG of M_1 and M_2. The conjunction of the LGGs of all pairs of MA formulas M_1 and M_2 in the AMA formulas Φ_1 and Φ_2 respectively is the LGG of Φ_1 and Φ_2. Note that constructing $A_{t_i t_j}$, again, requires primitive-event liquidity. Timelines in the LGG that subsume other such timelines can be pruned in polynomial time using an algorithm presented in our companion paper.

This LGG computation is clearly exponential in the input size. The companion paper shows that the size of the *smallest* LGG of two AMA formulas, which may be smaller than the LGG computed here, can be exponential in the size of the input formulas, so no better worst-case bound can be achieved. This motivates restricting the AMA language to k-AMA: AMA formulas that contain only k-MA formulas, those with no more than k A formulas.

There is also a learning motivation for the k-AMA restriction: the hypothesis space grows exponentially as k is relaxed and yet the AMA conjunction of k-MA timelines can capture much of the structure that formulas with longer MA timelines capture. Thus, we study k-AMA rather than unbounded single MA timelines as hypotheses.

The k-*cover* of an AMA formula Φ is the least general k-AMA formula Φ' that covers Φ. We can compute the k-cover of Φ as follows. First consider MA formulas M with more than k A formulas. A k-*digitation* of M is a subset T' of the transition-point set T of M of size no greater than $k+1$ that contains the minimal and maximal elements

of T and is ordered by the same ordering relation as T. Form a new MA formula M' whose transition points are a k-digitation of M. Each segment $A'_{t'_i t'_{i+1}}$ of M' is the intersection of all segments $A_{t_j t_{j+1}}$ of M where $t'_i \leq t_j$ and $t'_{j'} \leq t_j$ in T. M' generalizes M and is k-MA. The k-cover of an MA formula M with no more than k A formulas is M itself. Otherwise, it is the conjunction of all such M' for all k-digitations of M. The k-cover of an AMA formula Φ is the conjunction of the k-covers of the MA formulas in Φ. We note that the k-cover of an AMA formula Φ may be exponentially larger than Φ. However, in practice, after pruning redundant k-MA formulas, we have found that k-covers do not exhibit undue size growth.

Given this, we restrict our learner to k-AMA by computing the k-cover of the output of both the model cover computation and the LGG computation each time it is performed.

Experiments Results

Prior to the work reported in this paper, LEONARD needed hand-coded event definitions. We have augmented LEONARD with the ability to learn definitions using our k-AMA learning algorithm and evaluated its performance.[2] LEONARD is a three-stage pipeline. The raw input consists of a video-frame sequence depicting events. First, a segmentation-and-tracking component transforms this input into a polygon movie: a sequence of frames, each frame being a set of convex polygons placed around the tracked objects in the video. Next, a model-reconstruction component transforms the polygon movie into a force-dynamic model. This model describes the changing support, contact, and attachment relations between the tracked objects over time. Finally, an event-recognition component determines which events, from a library of event definitions, occurred in the model and, accordingly, in the video. The learning process uses the early stages of the LEONARD pipeline to produce force-dynamic models from the training movies and applies the k-AMA learning algorithm to these models.

Relational Data

LEONARD produces relational models that involve objects and (force dynamic) relations between those objects. Thus event definitions include variables to allow generalization over objects. For example, a definition for PICKUP(x, y, z) recognizes both PICKUP(**hand**, **block**, **table**) as well as PICKUP(**man**, **dumbbell**, **floor**). Despite the fact that our k-AMA learning algorithm is propositional, we are still able to use it to learn relational definitions.

We take a straightforward object-correspondence approach to relational learning. We view the models output by LEONARD as containing relations applied to constants. Since we (currently) support only supervised learning, we have a set of distinct training examples for each event type. There is an implicit correspondence between the objects filling the same role across

[2]The code and data set reported here is available from
ftp://dynamo.ecn.purdue.edu/pub/qobi/ama.tar.Z.

the different training models for a given type. For example, models showing PICKUP(**hand**, **block**, **table**) and PICKUP(**man**, **dumbbell**, **floor**) have implicit correspondences ⟨**hand**, **man**⟩, ⟨**block**, **dumbbell**⟩, and ⟨**table**, **floor**⟩. We outline two relational learning methods that differ in how much object-correspondence information they require.

Complete Object Correspondence This first approach assumes that a complete object correspondence is given, as input, along with the training examples. Given such information, we can propositionalize the training models by replacing corresponding objects with unique constants. The propositionalized models are then given to our propositional k-AMA learning algorithm which returns a propositional k-AMA formula. We then lift this propositional formula by replacing each constant with a distinct variable. Lavrac, Dzeroski, & Grobelnik (1991) took a similar approach.

Partial Object Correspondence The above approach assumes complete object-correspondence information. While it is sometimes possible to provide all correspondences (for example, by color-coding objects that fill identical roles when recording training movies), such information is not always available. When only a partial (or even no) object correspondence is available, we can automatically complete the correspondence and apply the above technique.

For the moment, assume that we have an evaluation function that takes two relational models and a candidate object correspondence, as input, and yields an evaluation of correspondence quality. Given a set of training examples with missing object correspondences, we perform a greedy search for the best set of object-correspondence completions over the models. Our method works by storing a set P of propositionalized training examples (initially empty) and a set U of unpropositionalized training examples (initially the entire training set). For the first step, when P is empty, we evaluate all pairs of examples from U, under all possible correspondences, select the two that yield the highest score, remove them from U, propositionalize them according to the best correspondence, and add them to P. For each subsequent step, we use the previously computed values of all pairs of examples, one from U and one from P, under all possible correspondences. We then select the example from U along with the correspondence that yields the highest average score relative to all models in P. This example is removed from U, propositionalized according to the winning correspondence, and added to P. For a fixed number of objects, the effort expended is polynomial in the size of the training set. However, if the number of objects b in a training example grows, the number of correspondences grows as b^b. Thus, it is important that the events involve only a modest number of objects.

Our evaluation function is based on the intuition that object roles for visual events (as well as events from other domains) can often be inferred by considering the changes between the initial and final moments of an event. Specifically, given two models and an object correspondence, we first propositionalize the models according to the correspondence. Next, we compute ADD and DELETE lists for each model. The ADD list is the set of propositions that are true at the final moment but not the initial moment. The DELETE list is the set of propositions that are true at the initial moment but not the final moment. (These add and delete lists are motivated by STRIPS action representations.) Given such ADD$_i$ and DELETE$_i$ lists for models 1 and 2, the evaluation function returns the sum of the cardinalities of ADD$_1$ ∩ ADD$_2$ and DELETE$_1$ ∩ DELETE$_2$. This measures the similarity between the ADD and DELETE lists of the two models. We have found that this evaluation function works well in the visual-event domain.

Negative Information

The AMA language does not allow negated propositions. Negation, however, is sometimes necessary to adequately define an event class. It turns out that we can easily get the practical advantages of negation without incorporating negation into the AMA language. We do this by appending a new set of propositions to our models that intuitively represents the negation of each proposition. Assume the training examples contain the propositions $\{p_1, \ldots, p_n\}$. We introduce a new set $\{\bar{p}_1, \ldots, \bar{p}_n\}$ of propositions and add these into the training models. It is a design choice as to how we assign truth values to these new propositions.

In our experiments, we compare two methods for assigning a truth value to $\bar{p}_i$. The first method, called *full negation*, assigns true to $\bar{p}_i$ in a model iff p_i is false in the model. The second method, called *boundary negation*, differs from full negation in that it only allows $\bar{p}_i$ to be true in the initial and final moments of a model. $\bar{p}_i$ must be false at all other times. We have found that boundary negation provides a good trade-off between no negation, which often produces overly general results, and full negation, which often produces overly specific and much more complicated results. Both methods share the property that they produce models where p_i and $\bar{p}_i$ are never simultaneously true. Thus our learning methods will never produce formulas with states that contain both p_i and $\bar{p}_i$.

Data Set

Our data set contains examples of 7 different event classes: *pick up*, *put down*, *stack*, *unstack*, *move*, *assemble*, and *disassemble*. Each of these involve a hand and two to three blocks. For a detailed description of these event classes, see Siskind (2001). Key frames from sample video sequences of these event classes are shown in figure 1. The results of segmentation, tracking, and model reconstruction are overlaid on the video frames. We recorded 30 movies for each of the 7 event classes resulting in a total of 210 movies comprising 11946 frames. We replaced one movie, `assemble-left-qobi04`, with a duplicate copy of `assemble-left-qobi11`, because of segmentation and tracking errors.

Some of the events classes are hierarchical in that occurrences of events in one class contain occurrences of events in one or more simpler classes. For example, a movie depicting a MOVE(a, b, c, d) event (i.e. a moves b from c to d) contains subintervals where PICKUP(a, b, c) and PUTDOWN(a, b, d) events occur. In evaluating the learned definitions, we wish to detect both the events

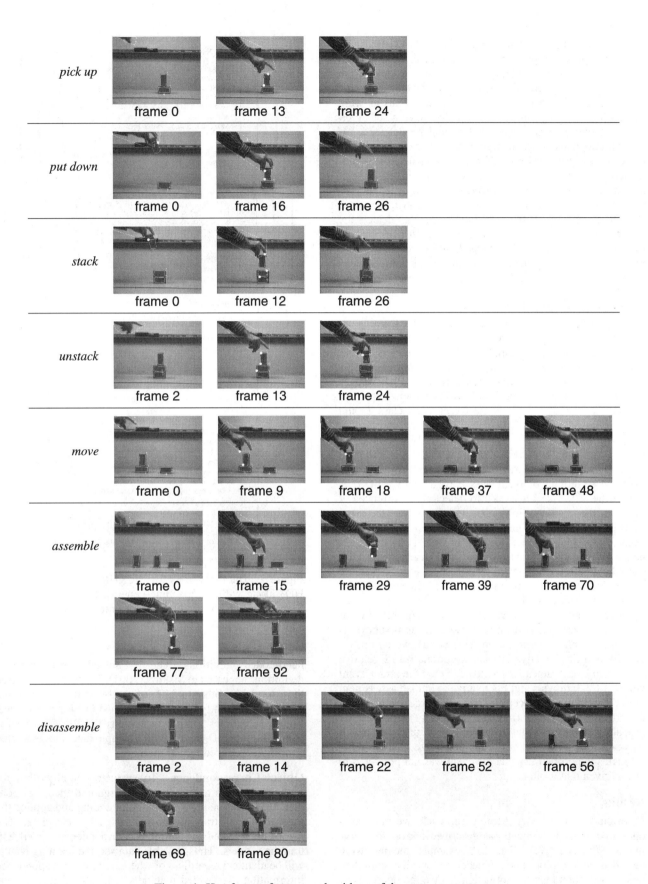

Figure 1: Key frames from sample videos of the seven event types.

that correspond to an entire movie as well as subevents that correspond to portions of that movie. For example, given a movie depicting $\textsc{Move}(a, b, c, d)$, we wish to detect not only the $\textsc{Move}(a, b, c, d)$ event but also the $\textsc{PickUp}(a, b, c)$ and $\textsc{PutDown}(a, b, c)$ subevents as well. For each movie type in our data set, we have a set of *intended* events and subevents that should be detected. If a definition does not detect an intended event, we deem the error a false negative. If a definition detects an untended event, we deem the error a false positive. For example, if a movie depicts a $\textsc{Move}(a, b, c, d)$ event, the intended events are $\textsc{Move}(a, b, c, d)$, $\textsc{PickUp}(a, b, c)$, and $\textsc{PutDown}(a, b, c)$. If the definition for *pick up* detects the occurrence of $\textsc{PickUp}(c, b, a)$ and $\textsc{PickUp}(b, a, c)$, but not $\textsc{PickUp}(a, b, c)$, it will be charged two false positives as well as one false negative. We evaluate our definitions in terms of false positive and negative rates as describe below.

Experimental Procedure

For each event class, we evaluate the k-AMA learning algorithm using a leave-one-movie-out cross-validation technique with training-set sampling. The parameters to our learning algorithm are k and the degree D of negative information used: either positive propositions only (P), boundary negation (NPN), or full-negation (N). The parameters to our evaluation procedure include the target event class E and the training-set size N. Given this information, the evaluation proceeds as follows: For each movie M (the held-out movie) from the 210 movies, apply the k-AMA learning algorithm to a randomly drawn training sample of N movies from the 30 movies of event class E (or 29 movies if M is one of the 30). Use LEONARD to detect all occurrences of the learned event definition in M. Based on E and the event class of M, record the number of false positives and false negatives in M, as detected by LEONARD. Let FP and FN be the total number of false positives and false negatives observed over all 210 held-out movies respectively. Repeat the entire process of calculating FP and FN 10 times and record the averages as $\overline{\text{FP}}$ and $\overline{\text{FN}}$.

Since some event classes occur more frequently in our data than others (because simpler events occur as subevents of more complex events but not vice versa), we do not report $\overline{\text{FP}}$ and $\overline{\text{FN}}$ directly. Instead, we normalize $\overline{\text{FP}}$ relative to the number of times LEONARD detected the target event within all 210 movies and $\overline{\text{FN}}$ relative to human assessment of the total number of occurrences of the target event within all 210 movies. The normalized value of $\overline{\text{FP}}$ estimates the probability that the target event did not occur, given that it was predicted to occur, while the normalized value of $\overline{\text{FN}}$ estimates the probability that the event was not predicted to occur, given that it did occur.

Results

To evaluate our k-AMA learning approach, we ran leave-one-movie-out experiments, as described above, for varying k, D, and N. The 210 example movies were recorded with color-coded objects to provide complete object-correspondence information. We compared our learned event definitions to the performance of two sets of

$$\left(\begin{array}{l}
\neg\Diamond x = y \wedge \neg\Diamond z = x \wedge \neg\Diamond z = y \wedge \\
\textsc{Supported}(y) \wedge \neg\Diamond\textsc{Attached}(x, z) \wedge \\
\left\{\begin{array}{l}
\left[\begin{array}{l}
\neg\Diamond\textsc{Attached}(x, y) \wedge \neg\Diamond\textsc{Supports}(x, y) \wedge \\
\textsc{Supports}(z, y) \wedge \\
\neg\Diamond\textsc{Supported}(x) \wedge \neg\Diamond\textsc{Attached}(y, z) \wedge \\
\neg\Diamond\textsc{Supports}(y, x) \wedge \neg\Diamond\textsc{Supports}(y, z) \wedge \\
\neg\Diamond\textsc{Supports}(x, z) \wedge \neg\Diamond\textsc{Supports}(z, x)
\end{array}\right]; \\
[\textsc{Attached}(x, y) \vee \textsc{Attached}(y, z)]; \\
\left[\begin{array}{l}
\textsc{Attached}(x, y) \wedge \textsc{Supports}(x, y) \wedge \\
\neg\Diamond\textsc{Supports}(z, y) \wedge \\
\neg\Diamond\textsc{Supported}(x) \wedge \neg\Diamond\textsc{Attached}(y, z) \wedge \\
\neg\Diamond\textsc{Supports}(y, x) \wedge \neg\Diamond\textsc{Supports}(y, z) \wedge \\
\neg\Diamond\textsc{Supports}(x, z) \wedge \neg\Diamond\textsc{Supports}(z, x)
\end{array}\right]
\end{array}\right\}
\end{array}\right)$$

$$\left(\begin{array}{l}
\neg\Diamond x = y \wedge \neg\Diamond z = x \wedge \neg\Diamond z = y \wedge \\
\textsc{Supported}(y) \wedge \neg\Diamond\textsc{Attached}(x, z) \wedge \\
\left\{\begin{array}{l}
\left[\begin{array}{l}
\neg\Diamond\textsc{Attached}(x, y) \wedge \neg\Diamond\textsc{Supports}(x, y) \wedge \\
\textsc{Supports}(z, y) \wedge \textsc{Contacts}(z, y) \wedge \\
\neg\Diamond\textsc{Supported}(x) \wedge \neg\Diamond\textsc{Attached}(y, z) \wedge \\
\neg\Diamond\textsc{Supports}(y, x) \wedge \neg\Diamond\textsc{Supports}(y, z) \wedge \\
\neg\Diamond\textsc{Supports}(x, z) \wedge \neg\Diamond\textsc{Supports}(z, x)
\end{array}\right] \wedge_{\{<, m\}} \\
\left[\begin{array}{l}
\textsc{Attached}(x, y) \wedge \textsc{Supports}(x, y) \wedge \\
\neg\Diamond\textsc{Supports}(z, y) \wedge \\
\neg\Diamond\textsc{Supported}(x) \wedge \neg\Diamond\textsc{Attached}(y, z) \wedge \\
\neg\Diamond\textsc{Supports}(y, x) \wedge \neg\Diamond\textsc{Supports}(y, z) \wedge \\
\neg\Diamond\textsc{Supports}(x, z) \wedge \neg\Diamond\textsc{Supports}(z, x)
\end{array}\right]
\end{array}\right\}
\end{array}\right)$$

$$\begin{array}{l}
\left\{\begin{array}{l}
\textsc{Supported}(y); \\
\left[\begin{array}{l}
\textsc{Supported}(y) \wedge \textsc{Attached}(x, y) \wedge \\
\textsc{Attached}(y, z)
\end{array}\right]; \\
[\textsc{Supported}(y) \wedge \textsc{Attached}(x, y)]
\end{array}\right\} \wedge \\
\left\{\begin{array}{l}
[\textsc{Supported}(y) \wedge \textsc{Contacts}(y, z)]; \\
[\textsc{Supported}(y) \wedge \textsc{Attached}(y, z)]; \\
[\textsc{Supported}(y) \wedge \textsc{Attached}(x, y)]
\end{array}\right\} \wedge \\
\left\{\begin{array}{l}
\left[\begin{array}{l}
\textsc{Supported}(y) \wedge \textsc{Supports}(z, y) \wedge \\
\textsc{Contacts}(y, z) \wedge \neg\Diamond\textsc{Supports}(x, y) \wedge \\
\neg\Diamond\textsc{Attached}(x, y) \wedge \neg\Diamond\textsc{Attached}(y, z)
\end{array}\right]; \\
[\textsc{Supported}(y) \wedge \textsc{Supports}(z, y)]; \\
[\textsc{Supported}(y) \wedge \textsc{Attached}(x, y)]
\end{array}\right\} \wedge \\
\left\{\begin{array}{l}
\left[\begin{array}{l}
\textsc{Supported}(y) \wedge \textsc{Supports}(z, y) \wedge \\
\textsc{Contacts}(y, z) \wedge \neg\Diamond\textsc{Supports}(x, y) \wedge \\
\neg\Diamond\textsc{Attached}(x, y) \wedge \neg\Diamond\textsc{Attached}(y, z)
\end{array}\right]; \\
\textsc{Supported}(y); \\
\left[\begin{array}{l}
\textsc{Supported}(y) \wedge \textsc{Supports}(x, y) \wedge \\
\textsc{Attached}(x, y) \wedge \neg\Diamond\textsc{Supports}(z, y) \wedge \\
\neg\Diamond\textsc{Contacts}(y, z) \wedge \neg\Diamond\textsc{Attached}(y, z)
\end{array}\right]
\end{array}\right\} \wedge \\
\left\{\begin{array}{l}
[\textsc{Supported}(y) \wedge \textsc{Supports}(z, y)]; \\
[\textsc{Supported}(y) \wedge \textsc{Attached}(x, y)]; \\
\left[\begin{array}{l}
\textsc{Supported}(y) \wedge \textsc{Supports}(x, y) \wedge \\
\textsc{Attached}(x, y) \wedge \neg\Diamond\textsc{Supports}(z, y) \wedge \\
\neg\Diamond\textsc{Contacts}(y, z) \wedge \neg\Diamond\textsc{Attached}(y, z)
\end{array}\right]
\end{array}\right\}
\end{array}$$

Figure 2: The definitions for $\textsc{PickUp}(x, y, z)$ in HD_1 and HD_2 along with the machine-generated definition for $k = 3$ and $D =$ NPN produced by training on all 30 *pick up* movies.

hand-coded definitions. The first set HD_1 of hand-coded definitions appeared in Siskind (2001). We manually revised these to yield another set HD_2 of hand-coded definitions that gives a significantly better $\overline{\text{FN}}$ at a cost in $\overline{\text{FP}}$ performance. Figure illustrates sample definitions for $\textsc{PickUp}(x, y, z)$ from HD_1 and HD_2 along with a sample machine-generated definition produced by our method.

Object Correspondence To evaluate our algorithm for finding object correspondences, we ignored the correspondence information provided by color coding and applied the algorithm to all training models for each event class. The algorithm selected the correct correspondence for all 210 training models. Thus, for this data set, the learning results will be identical regardless of whether or not correspondence information is provided manually. In light of this, the rest of our experiments use the manual correspondence informa-

k	D		pu	pd	st	un	mo	as	di
2	NPN	$\overline{FP}$	0	0.14	0	0	0	0.75	0
		$\overline{FN}$	0	0.19	0.12	0.03	0	0	0
3	NPN	$\overline{FP}$	0	0	0	0	0	0	0
		$\overline{FN}$	0	0.2	0.45	0.10	0.03	0.07	0.10
4	NPN	$\overline{FP}$	0	0	0	0	0	0	0
		$\overline{FN}$	0	0.2	0.47	0.12	0.03	0.07	0.17
3	P	$\overline{FP}$	0.42	0.5	0	0.02	0	0	0
		$\overline{FN}$	0	0.19	0.42	0.11	0.03	0.03	0.10
3	N	$\overline{FP}$	0	0	0	0	0	0	0
		$\overline{FN}$	0.04	0.39	0.58	0.16	0.13	0.2	0.2
3	NPN	$\overline{FP}$	0	0	0	0	0	0	0
		$\overline{FN}$	0	0.2	0.45	0.10	0.03	0.07	0.10
HD_1		$\overline{FP}$	0.01	0.01	0	0	0	0	0
		$\overline{FN}$	0.02	0.22	0.82	0.62	0.03	1.0	0.5
HD_2		$\overline{FP}$	0.13	0.11	0	0	0	0	0
		$\overline{FN}$	0.0	0.19	0.42	0.02	0.0	0.77	0.0

Table 1: $\overline{FP}$ and $\overline{FN}$ for both learned definitions, varying both k and D, and hand-coded definitions.

tion, provided by color-coding, rather than recomputing it.

Varying k The first three rows of table 1 show the $\overline{FP}$ and $\overline{FN}$ values for all 7 event classes for $k \in \{2, 3, 4\}$, $N = 29$ (the maximum), and $D = $ NPN. Similar trends were found for $D = $ P and $D = $ N. The general trend is that, as k increases, $\overline{FP}$ decreases and $\overline{FN}$ increases. Such a trend is a consequence of our k-cover approach. This is because, as k increases, the k-AMA language contains strictly more formulas. Thus for $k_1 > k_2$, the k_1-cover will never be more general than the k_2-cover. This strongly suggests (but does not prove) that $\overline{FP}$ will be non-increasing with k and $\overline{FN}$ will be non-decreasing with k.

Our results show that 2-AMA is overly general for *put down* and *assemble*, i.e. it gives high $\overline{FP}$. In contrast, 4-AMA is overly specific, as it achieves $\overline{FP} = 0$ for each event class but with a significant penalty in $\overline{FN}$. 3-AMA appears to provide with a good trade-off between the two, achieving $\overline{FP} = 0$ for each event class, while yielding reasonable $\overline{FN}$.

Varying D Rows four through sixth of table 1 show $\overline{FP}$ and $\overline{FN}$ for all 7 event classes for $D \in \{P, NPN, N\}$, $N = 29$, and $k = 3$. Similar trends were observed for other values of k. The general trend is that, as the degree of negative information increases, the learned event definitions become more specific. In other words, $\overline{FP}$ decreases and $\overline{FN}$ increases. This makes sense since, as more negative information is added to the training models, more specific structure can be found in the data and exploited by the k-AMA formulas. We can see that, with $D = $ P, the definitions for *pick up* and *put down* are overly general, as they produce high $\overline{FP}$. Alternatively, with $D = $ N, the learned definitions are overly specific, giving $\overline{FP} = 0$, at the cost of high $\overline{FN}$. In these experiments, as well as others, we have found that $D = $ NPN yields the best of both worlds: $\overline{FP} = 0$ for all event classes and lower $\overline{FN}$ than achieved with $D = $ N.

Experiments not shown here have demonstrated that, without negation for *pick up* and *put down*, we can increase k

arbitrarily, in an attempt to specialize the learned definitions, and never significantly reduce $\overline{FP}$. This indicates that negative information plays a crucial role in constructing definitions for these event classes.

Comparison to Hand-Coded Definitions The bottom two rows of table 1 show the results for HD_1 and HD_2. We have not yet attempted to automatically select the parameters for learning (i.e. k and D). Rather, here we focus on comparing the hand-coded definitions to the parameter set that we judged to be best performing across all event classes. We believe, however, that these parameters could be selected reliably using cross-validation techniques on a larger data set. In that case, the parameters would be selected on a per–event-class basis and would likely result in an even more favorable comparison to the hand-coded definitions.

The results show that the learned definitions significantly outperform HD_1 on the current data set. The HD_1 definitions were found to produce a large number of false negatives on the current data set. Manual revision of HD_1 yielded HD_2. Notice that, although HD_2 produces significantly fewer false negatives for all event classes, it produces more false positives for *pick up* and *put down*. This is because the hand definitions utilize *pick up* and *put down* as macros for defining the other events.

The performance of the learned definitions is competitive with the performance of HD_2. The main differences in performance are: (a) for *pick up* and *put down*, the learned and HD_2 definitions achieve nearly the same $\overline{FN}$ but the learned definitions achieve $\overline{FP} = 0$ whereas HD_2 has significant $\overline{FP}$, (b) for *unstack* and *disassemble*, the learned definitions perform moderately worse than HD_2 with respect to $\overline{FN}$, and (c) the learned definitions perform significantly better than HD_2 on *assemble* events.

We conjecture that further manual revision could improve HD_2 to perform as well as (and perhaps better than) the learned definitions for every event class. Nonetheless, we view this experiment as promising, as it demonstrates that our learning technique is able to compete with, and sometimes outperform, hand-coded definitions.

Varying N It is of practical interest to know how training set size affects our algorithm's performance. For this application, it is important that our method work well with fairly small data sets, as it can be tedious to collect event data.

Table 2 shows the $\overline{FN}$ of our learning algorithm for each event class, as N is reduced from 29 to 5. For these experiments, we used $k = 3$ and $D = $ NPN. Note that $\overline{FP} = 0$ for all event classes and all N and hence is not shown. We expect $\overline{FN}$ to increase as N is decreased, since, with specific-to-general learning, more data yields more-general definitions. Generally, $\overline{FN}$ is flat for $N > 20$, increases slowly for $10 < N < 20$, and increases abruptly for $5 < N < 10$. We also see that, for several event classes, $\overline{FN}$ decreases slowly, as N is increased from 20 to 29. This indicates that a larger data set might yield improved results.

Related Work

Prior work has investigated various subsets of the pieces of learning and using temporal, relational, and force-dynamic

N	pu	pd	st	un	mo	as	di
29	0.0	0.20	0.45	0.10	0.03	0.07	0.10
25	0.0	0.20	0.47	0.16	0.05	0.09	0.10
20	0.01	0.21	0.50	0.17	0.08	0.12	0.12
15	0.01	0.22	0.53	0.26	0.14	0.20	0.16
10	0.07	0.27	0.60	0.36	0.23	0.32	0.26
5	0.22	0.43	0.77	0.54	0.35	0.57	0.43

Table 2: $\overline{\text{FN}}$ for $k = 3$, $D = \text{NPN}$, and various values of N.

representations for recognizing events in video. But none, to date, combine all the pieces together. The following is a representative list and not meant to be comprehensive. Borchardt (1985) presents temporal, relational, force-dynamic event definitions but these definitions are neither learned nor applied to video. Regier (1992) presents techniques for learning temporal event definitions but the learned definitions are neither relational, force dynamic, nor applied to video. Yamoto, Ohya, & Ishii (1992), Starner (1995), Brand & Essa (1995), Brand, Oliver, & Pentland (1997), and Bobick & Ivanov (1998) present techniques for learning temporal event definitions from video but the learned definitions are neither relational nor force dynamic. Pinhanez & Bobick (1995) and Brand (1997a) present temporal, relational event definitions that recognize events in video but these definitions are neither learned nor force dynamic. Brand (1997b) and Mann & Jepson (1998) present techniques for analyzing force dynamics in video but neither formulate event definitions nor apply these techniques to recognizing events or learning event definitions.

Conclusion

We have presented k-AMA, a novel restrictive bias on event logic, along with a novel learning algorithm for that hypothesis space. This language is sufficiently expressive to support learning temporal, relational, force-dynamic event definitions from video. To date, however, the definitions are neither cross-modal nor perspicuous. And while the performance of learned definitions matches that of hand-coded ones, we wish to surpass hand coding. In the future, we intend to address cross-modality by applying k-AMA learning to the planning domain. And we believe that addressing perspicuity will lead to improved performance.

References

Allen, J. F. 1983. Maintaining knowledge about temporal intervals. *Communications of the ACM* 26(11):832–843.

Bobick, A. F., and Ivanov, Y. A. 1998. Action recognition using probabilistic parsing. In *Proceedings of the IEEE Computer Society Conference on Computer Vision and Pattern Recognition*, 196–202.

Borchardt, G. C. 1985. Event calculus. In *Proceedings of the Ninth International Joint Conference on Artificial Intelligence*, 524–527.

Brand, M., and Essa, I. 1995. Causal analysis for visual gesture understanding. In *Proceedings of AAAI Fall Symposium on Computational Models for Integrating Language and Vision*.

Brand, M.; Oliver, N.; and Pentland, A. 1997. Coupled hidden Markov models for complex action recognition. In *Proceedings of the IEEE Computer Society Conference on Computer Vision and Pattern Recognition*.

Brand, M. 1997a. The inverse hollywood problem: From video to scripts and storyboards via causal analysis. In *Proceedings of the Fourteenth National Conference on Artificial Intelligence*, 132–137.

Brand, M. 1997b. Physics-based visual understanding. *Computer Vision and Image Understanding* 65(2):192–205.

Fern, A.; Givan, R.; and Siskind, J. M. 2002. Specific-to-general learning for temporal events. In *Proceedings of the Eighteenth National Conference on Artificial Intelligence*.

Lavrac, N.; Dzeroski, S.; and Grobelnik, M. 1991. Learning nonrecursive definitions of relations with LINUS. In *Proceedings of the Fifth European Working Session on Learning*, 265–288.

Mann, R., and Jepson, A. D. 1998. Toward the computational perception of action. In *Proceedings of the IEEE Computer Society Conference on Computer Vision and Pattern Recognition*, 794–799.

Pinhanez, C., and Bobick, A. 1995. Scripts in machine understanding of image sequences. In *AAAI Fall Symposium Series on Computational Models for Integrating Language and Vision*.

Regier, T. P. 1992. *The Acquisition of Lexical Semantics for Spatial Terms: A Connectionist Model of Perceptual Categorization*. Ph.D. Dissertation, University of California at Berkeley.

Shoham, Y. 1987. Temporal logics in AI: Semantical and ontological considerations. *Artificial Intelligence* 33(1):89–104.

Siskind, J. M., and Morris, Q. 1996. A maximum-likelihood approach to visual event classification. In *Proceedings of the Fourth European Conference on Computer Vision*, 347–360. Cambridge, UK: Springer-Verlag.

Siskind, J. M. 2000. Visual event classification via force dynamics. In *Proceedings of the Seventeenth National Conference on Artificial Intelligence*, 149–155.

Siskind, J. M. 2001. Grounding the lexical semantics of verbs in visual perception using force dynamics and event logic. *Journal of Artificial Intelligence Research* 15:31–90.

Starner, T. E. 1995. Visual recognition of American Sign Language using hidden Markov models. Master's thesis, Massachusetts Institute of Technology, Cambridge, MA.

Talmy, L. 1988. Force dynamics in language and cognition. *Cognitive Science* 12:49–100.

Yamoto, J.; Ohya, J.; and Ishii, K. 1992. Recognizing human action in time-sequential images using hidden Markov model. In *Proceedings of the 1992 IEEE Conference on Computer Vision and Pattern Recognition*, 379–385. IEEE Press.

Structural Extension to Logistic Regression: Discriminative Parameter Learning of Belief Net Classifiers

Russell Greiner
Dept of Computing Science
University of Alberta
Edmonton, AB T6G 2H1 Canada
greiner@cs.ualberta.ca

Wei Zhou
Dept of Computer Science
University of Waterloo
Waterloo, ON N2L 3G1, Canada
w2zhou@math.uwaterloo.ca

Abstract

Bayesian belief nets (BNs) are often used for classification tasks — typically to return the most likely "class label" for each specified instance. Many BN-learners, however, attempt to find the BN that maximizes a different objective function (viz., likelihood, rather than classification accuracy), typically by first learning an appropriate graphical structure, then finding the maximal likelihood parameters for that structure. As these parameters may not maximize the classification accuracy, "discriminative learners" follow the alternative approach of seeking the parameters that maximize *conditional likelihood* (CL), over the distribution of instances the BN will have to classify. This paper first formally specifies this task, and shows how it relates to logistic regression, which corresponds to finding the optimal CL parameters for a naïve-bayes structure. After analyzing its inherent (sample and computational) complexity, we then present a general algorithm for this task, ELR, which applies to arbitrary BN structures and which works effectively even when given the incomplete training data. This paper presents empirical evidence that ELR works better than the standard "generative" approach in a variety of situations, especially in common situation where the BN-structure is incorrect.

Keywords: (Bayesian) belief nets, Logistic regression, Classification, PAC-learning, Computational/sample complexity

1   Introduction

Many tasks require producing answers to questions — *e.g.*, identifying the underlying fault from a given set of symptoms in context of expert systems, or proposing actions on the basis of sensor readings for control systems. An increasing number of projects are using "(Bayesian) belief nets" (BN) to represent the underlying distribution, and hence the stochastic mapping from evidence to response.

When this distribution is not known *a priori*, we can try to *learn* the model. Our goal is an *accurate* BN — *i.e.*, one that returns *the correct answer as often as possible*. While a perfect model of the distribution will perform optimally for any possible query, learners with limited training data are unlikely to produce such a model; moreover, this is impossible for learners constrained to a restricted range of possible dis-

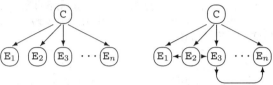

Figure 1: (a) NaïveBayes structure;   (b) TAN structure

tributions that excludes the correct one (*e.g.*, instantiations of a given BN-structure).

Here, it makes sense to find the parameters that do well with respect to the queries posed. This "discriminative learning" task differs from the "generative learning" that is used to learn an overall model of the distribution (Rip96). Following standard practice, our discriminative learner will seek the parameters that maximize the *conditional likelihood* (CL) over the data, rather than simple likelihood — that is, given the data $\{\langle c_i, \mathbf{e}_i \rangle\}$, we will try to find parameters Θ that maximize $\sum_i \log P_\Theta(c_i \mid \mathbf{e}_i)$, rather that the ones that maximize $\sum_i \log P_\Theta(c_i, \mathbf{e}_i)$ (Rip96).

Optimizing the CL of the root node of a *naïve-bayes* structure can be formulated as a standard logistic regression problem (MN89; Jor95). General belief nets extend naïve-bayes-structures by permitting additional dependencies between the attributes. This paper provides a general discriminative learning tool ELR that can learn the parameters for an arbitrary structure, even given incomplete training data. It also presents empirical evidence, from a large number of datasets, that ELR works effectively.

Section 2 provides the foundations — overviewing belief nets, then defining our task: discriminative learning the parameters (for an arbitrary fixed belief net structure) that maximize CL. Section 3 formally analyses this task, providing both sample and computational complexity; we also note how this compares with corresponding results for generative learning. Seeing that our task is NP-hard in general, Section 4 presents a gradient-descent discriminative learning algorithm for general BNs, ELR. Section 5 reports empirical results that demonstrate that our ELR often performs better than the standard learning algorithms (which maximize likelihood), over a variety of situations: In particular, when the learner has complete data, we show that ELR is often superior to the standard "observed frequency estimate" (OFE) approach (CH92), and when given partial data, we show ELR is often superior to the EM (Hec98) and APN (BKRK97) systems. We also demonstrate that the ELR is especially useful in the common situation where the given BN-structure is incorrect. (GZ02) provides the proofs of the theorems, as well as a comprehensive literature survey.

2 Framework

We assume there is a stationary underlying distribution $P(\cdot)$ over n (discrete) random variables $\mathcal{V} = \{V_1, \ldots, V_n\}$; which we encode as a "(Bayesian) belief net" (BN) — a directed acyclic graph $B = \langle \mathcal{V}, A, \Theta \rangle$, whose nodes $\mathcal{V}$ represent variables, and whose arcs A represent dependencies. Each node $D_i \in \mathcal{V}$ also includes a conditional-probability-table (CPtable) $\theta_i \in \Theta$ that specifies how D_i's values depend (stochastically) on the values of its parents. In particular, given a node $D \in \mathcal{V}$ with immediate parents $\mathbf{F} \subset \mathcal{V}$, the parameter $\theta_{d|\mathbf{f}}$ represents the network's term for $P(D = d \mid \mathbf{F} = \mathbf{f})$ (Pea88).

The user interacts with the belief net by asking *queries*, each of the form "$P(C = c \mid \mathbf{E} = \mathbf{e}) = ?$" where $C \in \mathcal{V}$ is a single "query variable", $\mathbf{E} \subset \mathcal{V}$ is the subset of "evidence variables", and c (resp., $\mathbf{e}$) is a legal assignment to C (resp., $\mathbf{E}$). We will focus on the case where all queries involve the same variable; *e.g.*, all queries ask about Cancer (but see the ALARM example in Section 5.6).

Following standard practice, we will assume there is a single distribution from which we can draw instances that correspond to queries with their labels, and let $sq(c; \mathbf{e})$ be the probability of the unlabeled query $\mathbf{e}$ being asked and c being the response. ((GGS97) explains the need to distinguish $sq(\cdot)$ from $P(\cdot)$; see also Section 5.6.)

Given any unlabeled query $\{\mathbf{E}_i = \mathbf{e}_i\}$, the belief net B will produce a distribution over the values of the query variable; our associated H_B classifier system will then return the value $H_B(\mathbf{e}) = \text{argmax}_c\{B(C = c | \mathbf{E} = \mathbf{e})\}$ with the largest posterior probability.

A good belief net classifier is one that produces the appropriate answers to these unlabeled queries. We will use "classification error" (aka "0/1" loss) to evaluate the resulting B-based classifier H_B

$$\text{err}(B) = \sum_{\langle \mathbf{e}, c \rangle} sq(\mathbf{e}; c) \times \mathcal{I}(H_B(\mathbf{e}) \neq c) \quad (1)$$

where $\mathcal{I}(a \neq b) = 1$ if $a \neq b$, and $= 0$ otherwise.[1]

Our goal is a belief net B^* that minimizes this score, with respect to the query+response distribution $sq(\cdot; \cdot)$. While we do not know this distribution *a priori*, we can use a sample drawn from this sq distribution, to help determine which belief net is optimal. (This sq-based "training data" is the same data used by other classifiers.) This paper focuses on the task of learning the optimal CPtable Θ for a given BN-structure $G = \langle \mathcal{V}, A \rangle$.

Conditional Likelihood: Our actual learner attempts to optimize a slightly different measure: The "(empirical) log conditional likelihood" of a belief net B is

$$\text{LCL}_{sq}(B) = \sum_{\langle \mathbf{e}, c \rangle} sq(\mathbf{e}; c) \times \log(B(c | \mathbf{e})) \quad (2)$$

---

[1] When helpful, we will also consider mean squared error: $MSE(B) = \sum_{\langle \mathbf{e}, c \rangle} sq(\mathbf{e}; c) \times [B(c | \mathbf{e}) - P(c | \mathbf{e})]^2$.

Given a sample S, we can approximate this as

$$\widehat{\text{LCL}}^{(S)}(B) = \frac{1}{|S|} \sum_{\langle \mathbf{e}, c \rangle \in S} \log(B(c | \mathbf{e})) \quad (3)$$

(MN89; FGG97) note that maximizing this score will typically produce a classifier that comes close to minimizing the classification error (Equation 1). Note also that many research projects, including (BKRK97), use this measure when evaluating their BN classifiers.

While this $\widehat{\text{LCL}}^{(S)}(B)$ formula closely resembles the "log likelihood" function

$$\widehat{\text{LL}}^{(S)}(B) = \frac{1}{|S|} \sum_{\langle \mathbf{e}, c \rangle \in S} \log(B(c, \mathbf{e})) \quad (4)$$

used by many BN-learning algorithms, there are some critical differences. As noted in (FGG97),

$$\widehat{\text{LL}}^{(S)}(B) = \frac{1}{|S|} \Big[\sum_{\langle c, \mathbf{e} \rangle \in S} \log(B(c | \mathbf{e})) + \sum_{\langle c, \mathbf{e} \rangle \in S} \log(B(\mathbf{e})) \Big]$$

where the first term resembles our $\text{LCL}(\cdot)$ measure, which measures how well our network will answer the relevant queries, while the second term is irrelevant to our task. This means a BN B_α that does poorly wrt the first "$\widehat{\text{LCL}}^{(S)}(\cdot)$-like" term may be preferred to a B_β that does better — *i.e.*, if $\widehat{\text{LL}}^{(S)}(B_\alpha) < \widehat{\text{LL}}^{(S)}(B_\beta)$, while $\widehat{\text{LCL}}^{(S)}(B_\alpha) > \widehat{\text{LCL}}^{(S)}(B_\beta)$.

3 Theoretical Analysis

How many "labeled queries" are enough — *i.e.*, given any values $\epsilon, \delta > 0$, how many labeled queries are needed to insure that, with probability at least $1 - \delta$, we are within ϵ to optimal? While we believe there are general comprehensive bounds, our specific results require the relatively benign technical restriction that all CPtable entries must be bounded away from 0. That is, for any $\gamma > 0$, let

$$\mathcal{BN}_{\Theta \succeq \gamma}(G) = \{ B \in \mathcal{BN}(G) \mid \forall \theta_{d|\mathbf{f}} \in \Theta, \ \theta_{d|\mathbf{f}} \geq \gamma \} \quad (5)$$

be the subset of BNs whose CPtable values are all at least γ; see (NJ01). We now restrict our attention to these belief nets, and in particular, let

$$B^*_{G, \Theta > \gamma} = \text{argmax}_B\{\text{LCL}_{sq}(B) \mid B \in \mathcal{BN}_{\Theta \succeq \gamma}(G)\} \quad (6)$$

be the BN with optimal score among $\mathcal{BN}_{\Theta \succeq \gamma}(G)$ with respect to the true distribution $sq(\cdot)$.

Theorem 1 *Let G be any belief net structure with K CPtable entries $\Theta = \{\theta_{d_i|\mathbf{f}_i}\}_{i=1..K}$, and let $\hat{B} \in \mathcal{BN}_{\Theta \succeq \gamma}(G)$ be the BN in $\mathcal{BN}_{\Theta \succeq \gamma}(G)$ that has maximum empirical log conditional likelihood score (Equation 3) with respect to a sample of*

$$M_{\gamma, K}(\epsilon, \delta) = O\left(\frac{K}{\epsilon^2} \ln(\frac{K}{\epsilon\delta}) \log^3(\frac{1}{\gamma}) \right)$$

labeled queries drawn from $sq(\cdot)$. Then, with probability at least $1 - \delta$, $\hat{B}$ will be no more than ϵ worse than $B^*_{G, \Theta > \gamma}$. ∎

A similar proof show that this same result holds when dealing with $\text{err}(\cdot)$ rather than $\text{LCL}(\cdot)$.

This PAC-learning (Val84) result can be used to bound the learning rate — i.e., for a fixed structure G and confidence term δ, it specifies how many samples M are required to guarantee an additive error of at most ϵ — note the $O(\frac{1}{\epsilon^2}[\log\frac{1}{\epsilon}])$ dependency.

As an obvious corollary, observe that the sample complexity is polynomial in the size (K) of the belief net even if the underbound γ is exponentially small $\gamma = O(1/2^N)$.

For comparison, Dasgupta (Das97, Section 5) proves that

$$O\left(\frac{nK}{\epsilon^2}\ln(\frac{K}{\epsilon\delta})\ln^3(n)\ln^2(\frac{1}{\epsilon})\right) \quad (7)$$

complete tuples are sufficient to learn the parameters to a fixed structure that are with ϵ of the optimal *likelihood* (Equation 4). This bound is incomparable to ours for two reasons: First, as noted above, the parameters that optimize (or nearly optimize) likelihood will not optimize our objective of *conditional* likelihood, which means Equation 7 describes the convergence to parameters that are typically inferior to the ones associated with Equation 1, especially in the unrealizable case; see (NJ01). Second, our Equation 1 includes the unavoidable γ term.[2] Nevertheless, ignoring this γ, our asymptotic bound is a factor of $O(n\ln^3(n)\ln^2(1/\epsilon))$ smaller; we attribute this reduction to the fact that our conditional-likelihood goal is more focused than Dasgupta's likelihood objective.[3]

The second question is computational: How hard is it to find these best parameters values, given this sufficiently large sample. Unfortunately...

Theorem 2 *It is NP-hard to find the values for the CPtables of a fixed BN-structure that produce the smallest (empirical) conditional likelihood (Equation 3) for a given sample.[4] This holds even if we consider only BNs in $\mathcal{BN}_{\Theta\succeq\gamma}(G)$ for $\gamma = O(1/N)$.* ∎

By contrast, note that there is an extremely efficient algorithm for the generative learning task of computing the parameters that optimize simple *likelihood* from complete data; see OFE, below. (Although the algorithms for optimizing likelihood from *incomplete* data are all iterative.)

---

[2]Unfortunately, we cannot use the standard trick of "tilting" the empirical distribution to avoid these near-zero probabilities (ATW91): Our task inherently involves computing *conditional* likelihood, which requires *dividing* by some CPtable values, which is problematic when these values are near 0. This also means our proof is *not* an immediate application of the standard PAC-learning approaches. See (GZ02).

[3]Of course, this comparison of upper bounds is only suggestive. Note also that our bound deals only with a single query variable; in general, it scales as $O(k^2)$ when there are k query variables.

[4]The class of structures used to show hardness are more complicated than the naïve-bayes and TAN structures considered in the next sections. Moreover, our proof relies on *incomplete* instances (defined below). While we do not know the complexity of finding the optimal-for-CL parameters for naïve-bayes structures given complete instances, the fact that there are a number of *iterative* algorithms here (for the equivalent task of logistic regression (Min01)) suggests that it, too, is intractable.

4 Learning Algorithm

Given the intractability of computing the optimal CPtable entries, we defined a simple gradient-descent algorithm, ELR, that attempts to improve the empirical score $\widehat{\text{LCL}}^{(S)}(B)$ by changing the values of each CPtable entry $\theta_{d|\mathbf{f}}$. To incorporate the constraints $\theta_{d|\mathbf{f}} \geq 0$ and $\sum_d \theta_{d|\mathbf{f}} = 1$, we used a different set of parameters — "$\beta_{d|\mathbf{f}}$" — where each

$$\theta_{d|\mathbf{f}} = \frac{e^{\beta_{d|\mathbf{f}}}}{\sum_{d'} e^{\beta_{d'|\mathbf{f}}}} \quad (8)$$

As the β_is sweep over the reals, the corresponding $\theta_{d_i|\mathbf{f}}$'s will satisfy the appropriate constraints. (In the naïve-bayes case, this corresponds to what many logistic regression algorithms would do, albeit with different parameters (Jor95): Find α, χ that optimize $P_{\alpha,\chi}(C = c \mid \mathbf{E} = \mathbf{e}) = e^{\alpha_c + \chi_c \cdot \mathbf{e}}/\sum_j e^{\alpha_j + \chi_j \cdot \mathbf{e}}$. Recall that our goal is a more general algorithm — one that can deal with *arbitrary* structures.)

Given a set of labeled queries, ELR descends in the direction of the total derivative wrt these queries, which of course is the sum of the individual derivatives:

Lemma 3 *For the labeled query* $[\mathbf{e};c]$, $\frac{\partial \widehat{\text{LCL}}^{([\mathbf{e};c])}(B)}{\partial \beta_{d|\mathbf{f}}} = \theta_{d|\mathbf{f}}[B(\mathbf{f} \mid c, \mathbf{e}) - B(\mathbf{f} \mid \mathbf{e})] - [B(d, \mathbf{f} \mid \mathbf{e}, c) - B(d, \mathbf{f} \mid \mathbf{e})]$.

Our ELR also incorporates several enhancement to speedup this computation. First, we use line-search and conjugate gradient (Bis98); Minka (Min01) provides empirical evidence that this is one of the most effective techniques for logistic regression. Another important optimization stems from the observation that this derivative is 0 if D and $\mathbf{F}$ are d-separated from $\mathbf{E}$ and C — which makes sense, as this condition means that the $\theta_{d|\mathbf{f}}$ term plays no role in computing $B(c \mid \mathbf{e})$. We can avoid updating these parameters for these queries, which leads to significant savings for some problems (GZ02).

5 Empirical Exploration

The ELR algorithm takes, as arguments, a BN-structure $G = \langle \mathcal{V}, A \rangle$ and a dataset of labeled queries (aka instances) $S = \{\langle \mathbf{e}_i, c_i \rangle\}_i$, and returns a value for each parameter $\theta_{d|\mathbf{f}}$. To explore its effectiveness, we compared the $\text{err}(\cdot)$ performance of the resulting Θ_{ELR} with the results of other algorithms that similarly learn CPtable values for a given structure.

We say the data is "complete" if every instance specifies a value for every attribute; hence "$E_1 = e_1, \ldots, E_n = e_n$" is complete (where $\{E_1, \ldots, E_n\}$ is the full set of evidence variables) but "$E_2 = e_2, E_7 = e_7$" is not. When the data is complete, we compare ELR to the standard "observed frequency estimate" (OFE) approach, which is known to produce the parameters that maximize likelihood (Equation 4) for a given structure (CH92). (E.g., if 75 of the 100 $C = 1$ instances have $X_3 = 0$, then OFE sets $\theta_{X_3=0|C=1} = 75/100$. Some versions use a Laplacian correction to avoid $0/0$ issues.) When the data is incomplete, we compare ELR

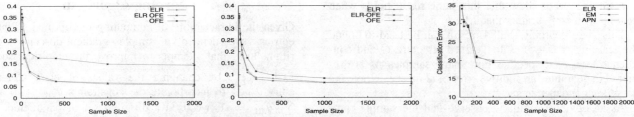

Figure 2: CHESS domain: (a) ELR vs OFE, complete data, structure is "Incorrect" (naïve-bayes); (b) ELR vs OFE, complete data, structure is "Correct" (POWERCONSTRUCTOR); (c) ELR vs EM,APN, complete data, structure is "Incorrect" (naïve-bayes)

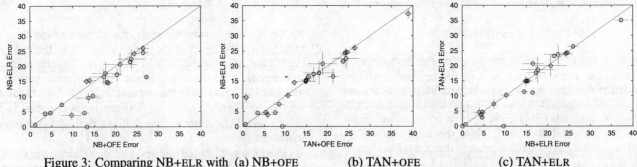

Figure 3: Comparing NB+ELR with (a) NB+OFE   (b) TAN+OFE   (c) TAN+ELR

to EM (Hec98) and APN (BKRK97),[5] which descends to parameter values whose likelihood is locally optimal.

This short article only reports on a few experiment, to illustrate the general trends; see (GZ02) for an exhaustive account of our experiments. Here we present only the results of the ELR=ELR_β algorithm, which used the β terms (Equation 8), as we found its performance strictly dominated the ELR_θ version which used θ directly

5.1 NaïveBayes — Complete, Real World Data

Our first experiments dealt with the simplest situation: learning the NaïveBayes parameters from complete data — which corresponds to standard logistic regression (NJ01).[6] Recall that the NaïveBayes structure requires that the attributes are independent given the class label; see Figure 1(a).

Here, we compared the relative effectiveness of ELR with various other classifiers, over the same 25 datasets that (FGG97) used for their comparisons: 23 from UCIrvine repository (BM00), plus "MOFN-3-7-10" and "CORRAL", which were developed by (KJ97) to study feature selection. To deal with continuous variables, we implemented supervised entropy discretization (FI93). Our accuracy values were based on 5-fold cross validation for small data, and holdout method for large data (Koh95). See (GZ02),(FGG97) for more information about these datasets.

We use the CHESS dataset (36 binary or ternary attributes) to illustrate the basic behaviour of the algorithms. Figure 2(a) shows the performance, on this dataset, of our NB+ELR ("NaïveBayes structure + ELR instantiation") sys-

tem, versus the "standard" NB+OFE, which uses OFE to instantiate the parameters. We see that ELR is consistently more accurate than OFE, for any size training sample. We also see how quickly ELR converges to the best performance. The ELR-*OFE* line corresponds to using OFE to initialize the parameters, then using the ELR-gradient-descent. We see this has some benefit, especially for small sample sizes.

Figure 3(a) provides a more comprehensive comparison, across all 25 datasets. (In each of these scatter-plot figures, each point below the $x = y$ line is a dataset where NB+ELR was better than other approach — here NB+OFE. The lines also express the 1 standard-deviation error bars in each dimension.) As suggested by this plot, NB+ELR is significantly better than NB+OFE at the $p < 0.005$ level (using a 1-sided paired-t test (Mit97)).

5.2 TAN — Complete, Real World Data

We next considered TAN ("tree augmented naïve-bayes") structures (FGG97), which include a link from the classification node down to each attribute and, if we ignore those class-to-attribute links, the remaining links, connecting attributes to each other, form a tree; see Figure 1(b).

Figure 3(b) compares NB+ELR to TAN+OFE. We see that ELR, even when handicapped with the simple NB structure, performs about as well as OFE on TAN structures. Of course, the limitations of the NB structure may explain the poor performance of NB+ELR on some data. For example, in the CORRAL dataset, as the class is a function of four interrelated attributes, one must connect these attributes to predict the class. As NaïveBayes permits no such connection, NaïveBayes-based classifiers performed poorly on this data. Of course, as TAN allows more expressive structures, it has a significant advantage here. It is interesting to note that our NB+ELR is still comparable to TAN+OFE, in general.

Would we do yet better by using ELR to instantiate TAN structures? While Figure 3(c) suggests that TAN+ELR is

---

[5]While the original APN_θ (BKRK97) climbed in the space of parameters θ_i, we instead used a modified APN_β system that uses the β_i values (Equation 8), as we found it worked better.

[6]While the obvious tabular representation of the CPtables involves more parameters than appear in this logistic regression model, these extra BN-parameters are redundant.

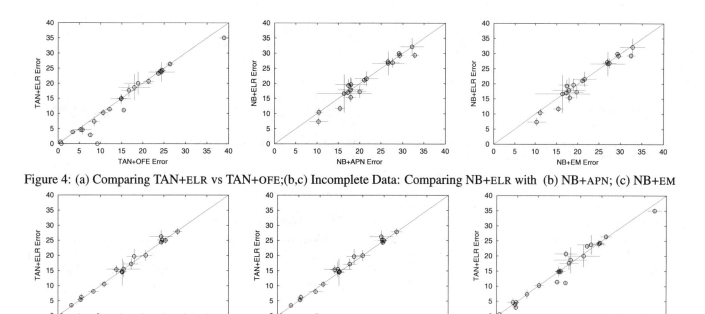

Figure 4: (a) Comparing TAN+ELR vs TAN+OFE;(b,c) Incomplete Data: Comparing NB+ELR with (b) NB+APN; (c) NB+EM

Figure 5: Incomplete data: Comparing TAN+ELR with (a) TAN+APN;   (b) TAN+EM;   (c) NB+ELR

slightly better than NB+ELR, this is not significant (only at the $p < 0.2$ level). However, Figure 4(a) shows that TAN+ELR does consistently better than TAN+OFE — at a $p < 0.025$ level. We found that TAN+ELR did perfectly on the the CORRAL dataset, which NB+ELR found problematic.

5.3   NB, TAN — Incomplete, Real World Data

All of the above studies used *complete* data. We next explored how well ELR could instantiate the NaïveBayes structure, using *incomplete* data.

Here, we used the datasets investigated above, but modified by randomly removing the value of each attribute, within each instance, with probability 0.25. (Hence, this data is missing completely at random, MCAR (LR87).) We then compared ELR to the standard "missing-data" learning algorithms, APN and EM. In each case — for ELR, APN and EM — we initialize the parameters using the obvious variant of OFE that considers only the records that include values for the relevant node and all of its parents.

Here, we first learned the parameters for the NaïveBayes structure; Figure 2(c) shows the learning curve for the CHESS domain, comparing ELR to APN and EM. We see that ELR does better for essentially any sample size.

We also compared these algorithms over the rest of the 25 datasets; see Figures 4(b) and 4(c) for ELR vs APN and ELR vs EM, respectively. As shown, ELR does consistently better — in each case, at the $p < 0.025$ level.

We next tried to learn the parameters for a TAN structure. Recall the standard TAN-learning algorithm computes the mutual information between each pair of attributes, conditioned on the class variable. This is straightforward when given complete information. Here, given *incomplete* data, we approximate mutual information between attributes A_i and A_j by simply ignoring the records that do not have values for both of these attributes. Figures 5(a) and 5(b) com-

pare TAN+ELR to TAN+APN and to TAN+EM. We see that these systems are roughly equivalent: TAN+ELR is perhaps slightly better than TAN+EM (but only at $p < 0.1$), but it is not significantly better than TAN+APN. Finally, we compared NB+ELR to TAN+ELR (Figure 5(c)), but found no significant difference.

5.4   "Correctness of Structure" Study

The NaïveBayes-assumption, that the attributes are independent given the classification variable, is typically incorrect. This is known to handicap the NaïveBayes classifier in the standard OFE situation (DP96).

We saw above that ELR is more robust than OFE, which means it is not as handicapped by an incorrect structure. We designed the following simple experiment to empirically investigate this claim.

We used synthesized data, to allow us to vary the "incorrectness" of the structure. Here, we consider an underlying distribution P_0 over the $k + 1$ binary variables $\{C, E_1, E_2, \ldots, E_k\}$ where (initially)

$$P(+C) = 0.9 \quad P(+E_i \mid +C) = 0.2 \quad P(+E_i \mid -C) = 0.8$$

(9)

and our queries were all complete; *i.e.*, each instance of the form $\vec{\mathbf{E}} = \langle \pm E_1, \pm E_2, \ldots, \pm E_k \rangle$.

We then used OFE (resp., ELR) to learn the parameters for the NaïveBayes structure from a data sample, then used the resulting BN to classify additional data. As the structure was correct for this P_0 distribution, both OFE and ELR did quite well, efficiently converging to the optimal classification error.

We then considered learning the CPtables for this NaïveBayes structure, but for distributions that were *not* consistent with this structure. In particular, we formed the $m-th$ distribution P_m by asserting that $E_1 \equiv E_2 \equiv \ldots \equiv$

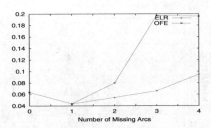 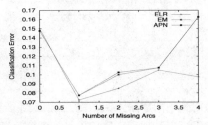 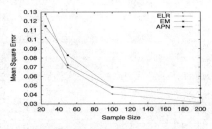

Figure 6: (a,b) Comparing ELR to OFE, on increasingly incorrect structures for (a) Complete Data; (b) Incomplete Data; (c) Using range of query values, and "incomplete" data on ALARM;

E_m (i.e., $P(+E_i \mid +E_1) = 1.0$, $P(+E_i \mid -E_1) = 0.0$ for each $i = 2..m$) in addition to Equation 9. Hence, P_0 corresponds to the $m = 0$ case. For $m > 0$, however, the m-th distribution cannot be modeled as a NaïveBayes structure, but could be modeled using that structure augmented with $m - 1$ links, connecting E_{i-1} to E_i for each $i = 2..m$.

Figure 6(a) shows the results, for $k = 5$, based on 400 instances. As predicted, ELR can produce reasonably accurate CPtables here, even for increasingly wrong structures. However, OFE does progressively worse.

5.5 "Correctness of Structure", Incomplete Data

We next degraded this training data by randomly removing the value of each attribute, within each instance, with probability 0.5. Figure 6(b) compares ELR with the standard systems APN and EM; we see that ELR is more accurate, in each case.

5.6 Nearly Correct Structure — Real World Data

We next asked whether ELR could find the best parameters for more complicated structures. Due to space limitation, this paper will report on only two situations; (GZ02) presents other examples. First, we considered the more-nearly-correct structures learned using the POWERCONSTRUCTOR system (CG02; CG99). We know that this system will converge to the correct belief net, given enough data (and some other relatively benign assumptions).

Figure 2(b) shows the results for CHESS: again ELR works effectively — and better than OFE. (Comparing Figure 2(a) to Figure 2(b) shows that ELR was not that hampered by the poorness of the NaïveBayes structure, but OFE was.)

To see how well ELR would perform on the correct structure, but given *incomplete* training data, we considered the ALARM network B_{alarm} (BSCC89), which has a known structure involving 36 nodes, 47 links and 505 parameters.

Here, we had to define the appropriate query distribution. From (HC91), we know that 8 of the ALARM variables typically appear as query variables, and a disjoint set of 16 variables can appear as evidence. We therefore generated queries by uniformly selecting, as query variable, one of the 8 query variables, and then, for each of the 16 evidence variables, including it with probability $1/2$ — hence on average a query will include $16/2$ evidence variables. (Note that different instances used different variables as the class label (CPT97); here it was critical to distinguish $sq(\cdot)$ from $P(\cdot)$ (GGS97).) We then specify values for these evidence variables based on the natural joint distribution for these ev-

idence variables. Figure 6(c) shows that ELR works more effectively here.

5.7 Other Experiments

The studies so far focus on the common situation where the model ("BN-structure") we are instantiating is likely simpler than the "truth" — e.g., we used naïve-bayes when there probably were dependencies between the attributes. Here, we have a great deal of evidence that our ELR algorithm, which tries to optimize conditional likelihood, works better than generative algorithms, which optimize likelihood. (GZ02) considers other (less typical) situations, where the model is more complex than the truth. In a nutshell, we observed, as expected, that discriminative learning (here ELR) will often over-fit in this situation, and so produce results that are often inferior to the generative learners. We were able to reduce this effect by initializing the parameters with the OFE values (in the complete data case); notice many discriminative learners do this, especially when (like here) these values are "plug-in parameters (Rip96).

5.8 Summary of Empirical Data

Our empirical studies using the UCI datasets suggest, when given complete training data,

TAN+ELR	>	TAN+OFE
NB+ELR	>	NB+OFE

and when dealing with incomplete data,

$$NB+ELR \quad > \quad \left\{ \begin{array}{c} NB+APN \\ NB+EM \end{array} \right\}$$

where ">" indicates statistical significance at the $p < 0.05$ level or better. (While many of the other comparisons suggest an ELR-based systems worked better, those results were not statistically significant.)

We see that ELR proved especially advantageous when the BN-structure was *incorrect* — i.e., whenever it is not a I-map of the underlying distribution by incorrectly claiming that two dependent variables are independent (Pea88). This is a very common situation, as many BN-learners will produce incorrect structures, either because they are conservative in adding new arcs (to avoid overfitting the data), or because they are considering only a restricted class of structures (e.g., naïve-bayes (DH73), poly-tree (CL68; Pea88), TAN (FGG97), etc.) which is not guaranteed to contain the correct structure.

6 Conclusions

This paper overviews the task of discriminative learning of belief net parameters for general BN-structures. We first describe this task, and discuss how it extends that standard logistic regression process by applying to arbitrary structures, not just naïve-bayes. Next, our formal analyses shows that discriminative learning can require fewer training instances than generative learning to converge, and that it will often converge to a superior classifier. The computational complexity is harder to compare: While we know our specific task — finding the optimal CL parameters for a given general structure, from incomplete data — is NP-hard, we do not know the corresponding complexity of finding the parameters that optimize likelihood. We suspect that discriminative learning may be faster as it can focus on only the relevant parts of the network; this can lead to significant savings when the data is incomplete. Moreover, if we consider the overall task, of learning both a structure and parameters, then we suspect discriminative learning may be more efficient that generative learning, as it can do well with a simpler structure.

We next present an algorithm ELR for our task, and show that ELR works effectively over a variety of situations: when dealing with structures that range from trivial (naïve-bayes), through less-trivial (TAN), to complex (Alarm, and ones learned by POWERCONSTRUCTOR). We also show that ELR works well when given *partial* training data, and even if different instances use different query variables. (This is one of the advantages of using a general belief net structure.) We also include a short study to explain why ELR can work effectively, showing that it typically works better than generative methods when dealing with models that are less complicated than the true distribution (which is a typical situation).

While statisticians are quite familiar with the idea of discriminative learning (*e.g.*, logistic regression), this idea, in the context of belief nets, is only beginning to make in-roads into the general AI community. We hope this paper will help further introduce these ideas to this community, and demonstrate that these algorithms should be used here, as they can work very effectively.

Acknowledgements

We thank Lyle Ungar, Tom Dietterich, Adam Grove, Peter Hooper, and Dale Schuurmans for their many helpful suggestions. Both authors were partially funded by NSERC; RG was also funded by Siemens Corporate Research; and WZ, by Syncrude.

References

[ATW91] N. Abe, J. Takeuchi, and M. Warmuth. Polynomial learnability of probablistic concepts with respect to the Kullback-Leibler divergence. In *COLT*, pages 277–289. 1991.

[Bis98] C. Bishop. *Neural Networks for Pattern Recognition*. Oxford, 1998.

[BKRK97] J. Binder, D. Koller, S. Russell, and K. Kanazawa. Adaptive probabilistic networks with hidden variables. *Machine Learning*, 29:213–244, 1997.

[BM00] C. Blake and C. J. Merz. UCI repository of machine learning databases. http://www.ics.uci.edu/~mlearn/MLRepository.html.

[BSCC89] I. Beinlich, H. Suermondt, R. Chavez, and G. Cooper. The ALARM monitoring system: A case study with two probabilistic inference techniques for belief networks. In *ECAI-Medicine*, August 1989.

[CG99] J. Cheng and R. Greiner. Comparing bayesian network classifiers. In *UAI'99* pages 101–107. August 1999.

[CG02] J. Cheng and R. Greiner. Learning bayesian networks from data: an information-theory based approach. *Artificial Intelligence*, 2002. to appear.

[CH92] G. Cooper and E. Herskovits. A Bayesian method for the induction of probabilistic networks from data. *Machine Learning*, 9:309–347, 1992.

[CL68] C. Chow and C. Liu. Approximating discrete probability distributions with dependence trees. *IEEE Trans. on Information Theory*, pages 462–467, 1968.

[CPT97] R. Caruana, L. Pratt, and S. Thrun. Multitask learning. *Machine Learning*, 28:41, 1997.

[Das97] S. Dasgupta. The sample complexity of learning fixed-structure bayesian networks. *Machine Learning*, 29, 1997.

[DH73] R. Duda and P. Hart. *Pattern Classification and Scene Analysis*. Wiley, New York, 1973.

[DP96] P. Domingo and M. Pazzani. Beyond independence: conditions for the optimality of the simple bayesian classier. In *ICML*, 1996.

[FGG97] N. Friedman, D. Geiger, and M. Goldszmidt. Bayesian network classifiers. *Machine Learning*, 29:131–163, 1997.

[FI93] U. Fayyad and K. Irani. Multi-interval discretization of continuous-valued attributes for classification learning. In *IJCAI*, pages 1022–1027, 1993.

[GGS97] R. Greiner, A. Grove, and D. Schuurmans. Learning Bayesian nets that perform well. In *UAI* 1997.

[GZ02] R. Greiner and W. Zhou. Beyond logistic regression. Technical report, UofAlberta, 2002.

[HC91] E. Herskovits and C. Cooper. Algorithms for Bayesian belief-network precomputation. In *Methods of Information in Medicine*, pages 362–370, 1991.

[Hec98] D. Heckerman. A tutorial on learning with Bayesian networks. In *Learning in Graphical Models*, 1998.

[Jor95] M. Jordan. Why the logistic function? a tutorial discussion on probabilities and neural networks, 1995.

[KJ97] R. Kohavi and G. John. Wrappers for feature subset selection. *Artificial Intelligence*, 97(1–2), 1997.

[Koh95] R. Kohavi. A study of cross-validation and bootstrap for accuracy estimation and model selection. In *IJCAI*, 1995.

[LR87] J. Little and D. Rubin. *Statistical Analysis with Missing Data*. Wiley, New York, 1987.

[Min01] Tom Minka. Algorithms for maximum-likelihood logistic regression. Technical report, CMU CALD, 2001. http://www.stat.cmu.edu/~minka/papers/logreg.html.

[Mit97] T. Mitchell. *Machine Learning*. McGraw-Hill, 1997.

[MN89] P. McCullagh and J. Nelder. *Generalized Linear Models*. Chapman and Hall, 1989.

[NJ01] A. Ng and M. Jordan. On discriminative versus generative classifiers: A comparison of logistic regression and naive bayes. In *NIPS*, 2001.

[Pea88] J. Pearl. *Probabilistic Reasoning in Intelligent Systems: Networks of Plausible Inference*. Morgan Kaufmann, 1988.

[Rip96] B. Ripley. *Pattern Recognition and Neural Networks*. Cambridge University Press, Cambridge, UK, 1996.

[Val84] L. Valiant. A theory of the learnable. *Communications of the ACM*, 27(11):1134–1142, 1984.

Bootstrap Learning for Place Recognition[*]

Benjamin Kuipers and Patrick Beeson

Computer Science Department
The University of Texas at Austin
Austin, Texas 78712
{kuipers,pbeeson}@cs.utexas.edu

Abstract

We present a method whereby a robot can learn to recognize places with high accuracy, in spite of perceptual aliasing (different places appear the same) and image variability (the same place appears differently). The first step in learning place recognition restricts attention to distinctive states identified by the map-learning algorithm, and eliminates image variability by unsupervised learning of clusters of similar sensory images. The clusters define *views* associated with distinctive states, often increasing perceptual aliasing. The second step eliminates perceptual aliasing by building a causal/topological map and using history information gathered during exploration to disambiguate distinctive states. The third step uses the labeled images for supervised learning of direct associations from sensory images to distinctive states. We evaluate the method using a physical mobile robot in two environments, showing high recognition rates in spite of large amounts of perceptual aliasing.

Introduction

It is valuable for a robot to know its position and orientation with respect to a map of its environment. This allows it to plan actions and predict their results, using its map.

We define *place recognition* as identifying the current position and orientation, a task sometimes called "global localization" (Thrun *et al.* 2001). However, not every location in the environment is a "place", deserving of independent recognition. Humans tend to remember places which are distinctive, for example by serving as decision points, better than intermediate points during travel (Lynch 1960). In fact, Polynesian navigators use distinctive places as representational devices even when they cannot be physically detected, such as on the open ocean (Hutchins 1995).

Real sensors are imperfect, so important but subtle image features may be buried in sensor noise. Two complementary problems stand in the way of reliable place recognition.

---

[*]This work has taken place in the Intelligent Robotics Lab at the Artificial Intelligence Laboratory, The University of Texas at Austin. Research of the Intelligent Robotics lab is supported in part by the Texas Higher Education Coordinating Board, Advanced Technology Program (grant 003658-0656-2001), and by an IBM Faculty Research Award.

- *Perceptual aliasing*: different places may have similar or identical sensory images.

- *Image variability*: the same position and orientation may have different sensory images on different occasions, for example at different times of day.

These two problems trade off against each other. With relatively impoverished sensors (e.g., a sonar ring) many places have similar images, so the dominant problem is perceptual aliasing. With richer sensors such as vision or laser range-finders, discriminating features are more likely to be present in the image, but so are noise and dynamic changes, so the dominant problem for recognition becomes image variability. We want to use real sensors in real environments, avoiding assumptions that restrict us to certain types of sensors or make it difficult to scale up to large, non-simply-connected environments.

Unique place recognition is not always possible using the current sensory image alone. If necessary, we will use active exploration to obtain history information to determine the correct place. However, when subtle features, adequate for discriminating between different places, are buried in the noise due to image variability, we want to recover those features.

We build on the *Spatial Semantic Hierarchy* (SSH) which provides an abstraction of the continuous environment to a discrete set of *distinctive states* (dstates), linked by reliable actions (Kuipers & Byun 1991; Kuipers 2000). We assume that the agent has previously learned a set of features and control laws adequate to provide reliable transitions among a set of distinctive states in the environment (Pierce & Kuipers 1997).

A Hybrid Solution

The steps in our solution to the place recognition problem apply several different learning and deductive methods (Figure 1).

1. Restrict attention to recognizing *distinctive states* (dstates). Distinctive states are well-separated in the robot's state space.

2. Apply an unsupervised clustering algorithm to the sensory images obtained at the dstates in the environment. This reduces image variability by mapping different images of

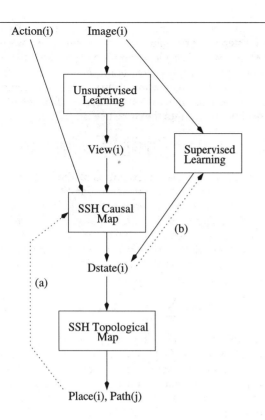

Action(i)   Image(i)

Unsupervised
Learning

View(i)

Supervised
Learning

SSH Causal
Map

(b)

Dstate(i)

(a)

SSH Topological
Map

Place(i), Path(j)

Figure 1: Bootstrap learning of place recognition. Solid arrows represent the major inference paths, while dotted arrows represent feedback.

the same place into the same cluster, even at the cost of increasing perceptual aliasing by mapping images of different states into the same cluster. We define each cluster to be a *view*, in the sense of the SSH (Kuipers 2000).

3. Build the SSH causal and topological maps — symbolic descriptions made up of dstates, views, places, and paths — by exploration and abduction from the observed sequence of views and actions (Kuipers 2000; Remolina & Kuipers 2001). This provides an unambiguous assignment of the correct dstate to each experienced image, which is feedback path (a) in Figure 1.

4. The correct causal/topological map labels each image with the correct dstate. Apply a supervised learning algorithm to learn a direct association from sensory image to dstate. The added information in supervised learning makes it possible to identify subtle discriminating features that were not distinguishable from noise by the unsupervised clustering algorithm. This is feedback path (b) in Figure 1.

We call this *bootstrap learning* because of the way a weak learning method (clustering) provides the prerequisites for a deductive method (map-building), which in turn provides the labels required by a stronger supervised learning method (nearest neighbor), which can finally achieve high performance.

Markov Localization

Markov localization has been used effectively by Thrun and his colleagues (Thrun, Fox, & Burgard 1998; Thrun *et al.* 2001) to build occupancy grid maps and to localize the robot in the grid, given observations from range sensors. The central equation for Markov localization is

$$p(x'|a, o, m) = \alpha \, p(o|x', m) \int p(x'|x, a, m) \, p(x|m) \, dx$$
$$(1)$$

which updates the prior probability distribution $p(x|m)$ over states x in the map m, to the posterior probability distribution $p(x'|a, o, m)$ after performing action a and observing sensory image o. $p(o|x', m)$ is the sensor model for the agent, $p(x'|x, a, m)$ is the action model, and α is a normalizing constant.

The Markov equation (1) applies whether m is an occupancy grid or a topological graph (Basye, Dean, & Kaelbling 1995), and its structure will help us compare the two representations.

Occupancy Grids

The occupancy grid representation has been popular and successful (Moravec 1988; Thrun, Fox, & Burgard 1998; Yamauchi, Schultz, & Adams 1998). Although the size of the occupancy grid grows quadratically with the size of the environment and the desired spatial resolution of the grid, this memory cost is feasible for moderate-sized environments, and modern Monte Carlo algorithms (Thrun *et al.* 2001) make the update computation tractable. Nonetheless, fundamental drawbacks remain.

- The occupancy grid assumes a single global frame of reference for representing locations in the environment. When exploring an extended environment, metrical errors accumulate. Reconciling position estimates after traveling around a circuit requires reasoning with a topological skeleton of special locations (Thrun *et al.* 1998).

- The occupancy grid representation is designed for range-sensors.[1] For a laser range-finder, an observation o consists of 180 range measurements r_i at 1° intervals around a semicircle: $o = \wedge r_i$. The scalar value stored in a cell of the grid represents the probability that a range-sensor will perceive that cell as occupied, making it relatively simple to define $p(r_i|x, m)$. Deriving a usable value of $p(o|x, m)$ is problematic, however.

The topological map representation (i) uses a set of dstates vastly smaller than an occupancy grid, (ii) does not assume a single global frame of reference, (iii) does not embed assumptions about the nature of the sensors in the representation, and (iv) clusters images o into views v giving a natural meaning to $p(v|x, m)$. We are particularly interested

---

[1] Minerva (Thrun *et al.* 2001, sect. 2.7) used Markov localization with particle filters using visual images from a vertically-mounted camera to localize in a "ceiling map." The ceiling map can be represented in an occupancy-grid-like structure because of the way nearby images share content. This trick does not appear to generalize to forward-facing images.

in a uniform framework for place recognition that will generalize from range-sensors to visual images (cf. (Ulrich & Nourbakhsh 2000)).

Abstraction to Distinctive States

The Spatial Semantic Hierarchy (Kuipers 2000) builds a topological map by abstracting the behavior of continuous control laws in local segments of the environment to a directed graph of *distinctive states* and actions linking them.

A distinctive state is the isolated fixed-point of a hill-climbing control law. A sequence of control laws taking the robot from one dstate to the next is abstracted to an *action*.

Starting at a given distinctive state, there may be a choice of applicable *trajectory-following* control laws that can take the agent to the neighborhood of another distinctive state. While following the selected trajectory-following control law, the agent detects a qualitative change indicating the neighborhood of another distinctive state. It then selects a *hill-climbing* control law that brings the agent to an isolated local maximum, which is the destination distinctive state. The error-correcting properties of the control laws, especially the hill-climbing step, mean that travel from one distinctive state to another is reliable, i.e., can be described as deterministic.

The directed link $\langle x, a, x' \rangle$ represents the assertion that action a is the sequence of trajectory-following and hill-climbing control laws that leads deterministically from x to x', both distinctive states. The directed graph made up of these links is called the *causal map*. The *topological map* extends the causal map with places, paths, and regions.

Since actions are deterministic, if the link $\langle x, a, x' \rangle$ is in the causal map, then $p(x'|x, a, m) = 1$, while $p(x''|x, a, m) = 0$ for $x'' \neq x'$. This lets us simplify equation (1) to get

$$p(x'|a, o, m) = \alpha \, p(o|x', m) \sum \{p(x|m) : \langle x, a, x' \rangle\} \quad (2)$$

A topological map represents vastly fewer values of x than an occupancy grid, so evaluating the sum in equation (2) will be very efficient.

Distinctive states are well-separated in the environment. Intuition suggests, and our empirical results below demonstrate, that sensory images collected at distinctive states are well-separated in image space, with the possibility of multiple states sharing the same cluster.

Unfortunately, one can construct counterexamples to show that this is not guaranteed in general. In particular, if sensory images are collected at states evenly distributed through the environment (Yamauchi & Langley 1997; Duckett & Nehmzow 2000), then image variability will dominate the differences due to separation between states, and well-separated clusters will not be found in image space. Restricting attention to a one-dimensional manifold or "roadmap" within the environment (Romero, Morales, & Sucar 2001) reduces image variability significantly, but not as much as our focus on distinctive states.

Cluster Images Into Views

A realistic robot will have a rich sensory interface, so the sensory image o is an element of a high-dimensional space,

and $p(o|x, m)$ is so small as to be meaningless. Therefore, we cluster sensory images o into a small set of clusters, called *views* v. The views impose a finite structure on the sensory space, so $p(v|x, m)$ is meaningful, and in fact can be estimated with increasing accuracy with increasing experience observing images o at position x. This lets us transform equation (2) into the more useful:

$$p(x'|a, v, m) = \alpha \, p(v|x', m) \sum \{p(x|m) : \langle x, a, x' \rangle\}$$

$$(3)$$

In addition, our place recognition method clusters images aggressively, to eliminate image variability entirely even at the cost of increasing perceptual aliasing. That is, for a given distinctive state x, there is a single view v such that, for every sensory image o observed at x, $o \in v$. We describe this situation by the relation $view(x, v)$. This means that $p(v|x, m) = 1$ and $p(v'|x, m) = 0$ for $v' \neq v$, allowing us to simplify equation (3) further:

$$p(x'|a, v, m) = \alpha \sum \{p(x|m) : \langle x, a, x' \rangle \wedge view(x', v)\}$$

$$(4)$$

Intuitively, this means that prior uncertainty in $p(x|m)$ is carried forward to $p(x'|a, o, m)$, except that alternatives are eliminated if the expected view v is not observed. The probability mass associated with that alternative is distributed across the other cases when the normalization constant α is recomputed.

Where does prior uncertainty come from, since this process can only decrease it? If the initial problem is global localization, then initial ignorance of position is reflected in the distribution $p(x|m)$. Alternatively, if the robot is exploring and building a map of an unknown environment, then sometimes it will be at a dstate x performing an action a such that $\langle x, a, x' \rangle$ is unknown. A view v is observed, but the resulting probability mass must be distributed across dstates x' such that $view(x', v)$.

How Many Clusters?

We cluster images using k-means (Duda, Hart, & Stork 2001), searching for the best value of k. We use two different metrics to assess the quality of clustering: one for the agent to use to select a value of k, and one for omniscient researchers to use to evaluate the agent's selection.

The *decision metric* M uses only information available to the agent, so the agent can select the value of $k > 1$ that maximizes M. After exploring several alternatives, we adopted the following formulation of this metric which rewards both tight clusters (the denominator in equation (5)) and clear separation between clusters (the numerator).

$$M = \frac{\min_{i \neq j}[min\{dist(x, y) : x \in c_i, y \in c_j\}]}{\max_i[max\{dist(x, y) : x, y \in c_i\}]} \quad (5)$$

The *evaluation metric* U uses knowledge of the true dstate x associated with each image o to allow the researchers to assess the quality of each cluster v. The agent, however, does not have access to U. The *uncertainty coefficient* $U(v|x)$ measures the extent to which knowledge of dstate x predicts the view v (Press *et al.* 1992, pp. 632–635). (Here,

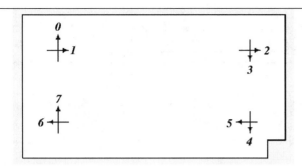

Figure 2: Simple environment for testing image variability, perceptual aliasing, and dstate disambiguation.

$p_{i,j}$ is the probability that the current view is v_i and the current dstate is x_j.)

$$U(v|x) = \frac{H(v) - H(v|x)}{H(v)}$$

$$H(v) = -\sum_i p_{i*} \ln p_{i*} \text{ where } p_{i*} = \sum_j p_{i,j}$$

$$H(v|x) = -\sum_{i,j} p_{i,j} \ln \frac{p_{i,j}}{p_{*j}} \text{ where } p_{*j} = \sum_i p_{i,j}$$

$U = 1$ means that image variability has been completely eliminated. As k increases, perceptual aliasing decreases, so the ideal outcome is for the value of k selected by the decision metric M to be the largest k for which $U = 1$.

A Simple Experiment

We begin testing our method in the simplest environment (Figure 2) with a distinguishing feature (the notch) small enough to be obscured by image variability.

Lassie is a RWI Magellan robot. It perceives its environment using a laser range-finder: each sensory image o is a point in R^{180}, representing the ranges to obstacles in the $180°$ arc in front of the robot. So that the Euclidean distance metric we use for clustering will emphasize short distances over long ones, we apply a "reciprocal transform", replacing each r_i in o with $1/r_i$.

Lassie explores a rectangular room (Figure 2) whose only distinguishing feature is a small notch out of one corner. Image variability arises from position and orientation variation when Lassie reaches a distinctive state, and from the intrinsic noise in the laser range-finder. Perceptual aliasing arises from the symmetry of the environment, and the lack of a compass. The notch is designed to be a distinguishing feature that is small enough to be obscured by image variability.

As Lassie performs clockwise circuits of its environment, it encounters eight distinctive states, one immediately before and one immediately after the turn at each corner. In 50 circuits of the notched rectangle environment (Figure 2), Lassie experiences 400 images. Applying the decision metric (5) of cluster quality, Lassie determines that $k = 4$ is the clear winner (Figure 3(top)). Figure 3(bottom) shows us that $k = 4$ is also optimal to the evaluation metric.

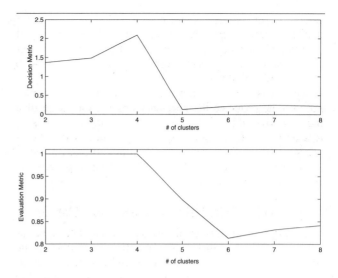

Figure 3: After Lassie explores the notched rectangle, $k = 4$ is selected as the best number of clusters by the decision metric M (top), and is confirmed as optimal by the evaluation metric U (bottom).

The notch in the rectangle is clearly being treated as noise by the clustering algorithm, so diagonally opposite dstates have the same views. In this environment, the four views correspond to the following eight dstates.

view	v_0	v_1	v_2	v_3
dstate	x_0, x_4	x_1, x_5	x_2, x_6	x_3, x_7

Build the Causal and Topological Maps

As the robot travels among distinctive states, its continuous experience is abstracted, first to an alternating sequence of images o_k and actions a_k, then images are clustered into views v_k, and finally views are associated with dstates x_k.

t_0		t_1		$\cdots$		t_n
o_0	a_0	o_1	a_1	$\cdots$	a_{n-1}	o_n
v_0		v_1		$\cdots$		v_n
x_0		x_1		$\cdots$		x_n

Clustering images into views eliminates image variability, but retains or increases perceptual aliasing:

$$view(x, v_1) \wedge view(x, v_2) \rightarrow v_1 = v_2$$
$$view(x_1, v) \wedge view(x_2, v) \not\rightarrow x_1 = x_2$$

The problem is to determine the minimal set of distinctive states x_i consistent with the observed sequence of views and actions. (Remolina & Kuipers 2001; Remolina 2001) provide a non-monotonic formalization of this problem and the axioms for the SSH causal and topological maps.

The approach is to assert that a pair of dstates is equal unless the causal or topological map implies that they are unequal. Of course, dstates with different views are unequal. But how do we conclude that $x_0 \neq x_4$ even though they share the same view v_0? When the topological map is constructed, dstate x_0 is at a place that lies on a path defined by dstates x_1 and x_2. x_4 is at a place that lies to the right of that same path, so $x_4 \neq x_0$. Similarly for the other pairs of diagonally opposite states in Figure 2. Lassie thereby determines that the four views are part of a topological map with eight dstates, four places, and four paths.

We were fortunate in this case that the prescribed exploration route provided the necessary observations to resolve the potential ambiguity. In general, it may be necessary to search actively for the relevant experience, using "homing sequences" from deterministic finite automaton learning (Rivest & Schapire 1989) or the "rehearsal procedure" (Kuipers & Byun 1991).[2]

Supervised Learning to Recognize Dstates

With unique identifiers for distinctive states (dstates), the supervised learning step learns to identify the correct dstate directly from the sensory image with high accuracy. The supervised learning method is the nearest neighbor algorithm (Duda, Hart, & Stork 2001). During training, images are represented as points in the sensory space, labeled with their true dstates. When a test image is queried, the dstate label on the nearest stored image in the sensory space is proposed, and the accuracy of this guess is recorded. Figure 6 shows the rate of correct answers as a function of number of images experienced. In two test environments, accuracy rises rapidly with experience to 100%.

The purpose of the supervised learning step is to resolve cases of perceptual aliasing,

$$view(x_1, v) \wedge view(x_2, v) \wedge x_1 \neq x_2,$$

by identifying a subtle distinction $v = v_1 \cup v_2$ such that $view(x_1, v_1) \wedge view(x_2, v_2)$. The effect of this in the Markov localization framework is that the probability distributions in equation (3) will be sharper and the sets in equations (4) will be smaller.

In general, of course, it is impossible to eliminate every case of perceptual aliasing, since there can be different dstates whose distinguishing features, if present at all, cannot be discerned by the robot's sensors. In this case, the robot must use historical context, via equation (4), to keep track of its location.

A Natural Office Environment

A natural environment, even an office environment, contains much more detail than the simplified notched-rectangle environment. To a robot with rich sensors, images at distinctive states are much more distinguishable. Image variability is the problem, not perceptual aliasing.

Lassie explored the main hallway on the second floor of Taylor Hall (Figure 4). It collected 240 images from 20 distinctive states. The topological map linking them contained seven places and four paths. When clustering the images, the

[2]We take comfort from the following qualified endorsement: *"Given a procedure that is guaranteed to uniquely identify a location if it succeeds, and succeeds with high probability, ... a Kuipers-style map can be reliably probably almost always usefully learned..."* (Basye, Dean, & Vitter 1997, p. 86).

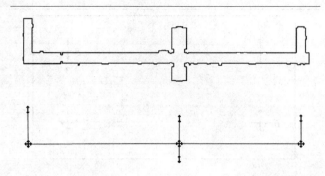

Figure 4: Taylor Hall, second floor hallway (top). The actual environment is 80 meters long and includes trash cans, lockers, benches, desks and a portable blackboard. The causal/topological map (bottom) has 20 dstates, 7 places, and 4 paths.

decision metric M had its maximum at $k = 10$. The evaluation metric U shows that higher values of k could still have eliminated all image variability (Figure 5). By building the causal and topological map the robot is able to disambiguate all twenty distinctive states, even though there are only ten different views. Given the correct labeling of images with dstates, the supervised learner reaches high accuracy (Figure 6(b)). In these environments, with rich sensors, perfect accuracy is achievable because sensory features are present with the information necessary to determine the dstate correctly, but supervised learning is required to extract that information from natural variation.

Conclusion and Future Work

We have established that bootstrap learning for place recognition can achieve high accuracy with real sensory images from a physical robot exploring among distinctive states in real environments. The method starts by eliminating image variability by focusing on distinctive states and doing unsupervised clustering of images. Then, by building the causal and topological maps, distinctive states are disambiguated and perceptual aliasing is eliminated. Finally, supervised learning of labeled images achieves high accuracy direct recognition of distinctive states from sensory images.

In future work, we plan to explore methods for robust error-recovery during exploration, by falling back from logical inference in the topological map to Markov localization when low-probability events violate the abstraction underlying the cognitive map. Once further exploration moves $p(v|x, m)$ and $p(x'|x, a, m)$ back to extreme values, the abstraction to a logical representation can be restored.

We are also exploring the use of local metrical maps, restricted to the neighborhoods of distinctive states, to eliminate the need for physical motion of the robot to the actual location of the locally distinctive state.

The current unsupervised and supervised learning algorithms we use are k-means and nearest neighbor. k-means will not scale up to the demands of clustering visual images. We plan to experiment with other algorithms to fill

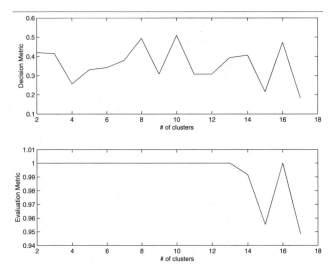

Figure 5: After Lassie's exploration of the Taylor hallway, $k = 10$ is selected as the best number of clusters by the decision metric M (top). The evaluation metric U (bottom) shows that larger numbers of views could have been selected, but $k = 10$ was still enough for supervised learning to converge to correct identification.

these roles in the learning method. Other representation and clustering techniques may be more sensitive to the kinds of similarities and distinctions present in sensor images. Supervised learning methods like backprop may make it possible to analyze hidden units to determine which features are critical to the discrimination and which are noise. Using methods like these, it may be possible to discover explanations for certain aspects of image variability, for example the effect of time of day on visual image illumination.

References

Basye, K.; Dean, T.; and Kaelbling, L. P. 1995. Learning dynamics: system identification for perceptually challenged agents. *Artificial Intelligence* 72:139–171.

Basye, K.; Dean, T.; and Vitter, J. S. 1997. Coping with uncertainty in map learning. *Machine Learning* 29(1):65–88.

Duckett, T., and Nehmzow, U. 2000. Performance comparison of landmark recognition systems for navigating mobile robots. In *Proc. 17th National Conf. on Artificial Intelligence (AAAI-2000)*, 826–831. AAAI Press/The MIT Press.

Duda, R. O.; Hart, P. E.; and Stork, D. G. 2001. *Pattern Classification*. New York: John Wiley & Sons, Inc., second edition.

Hutchins, E. L. 1995. *Cognition in the Wild*. Cambridge, MA: MIT Press.

Kuipers, B. J., and Byun, Y.-T. 1991. A robot exploration and mapping strategy based on a semantic hierarchy of spatial representations. *Journal of Robotics and Autonomous Systems* 8:47–63.

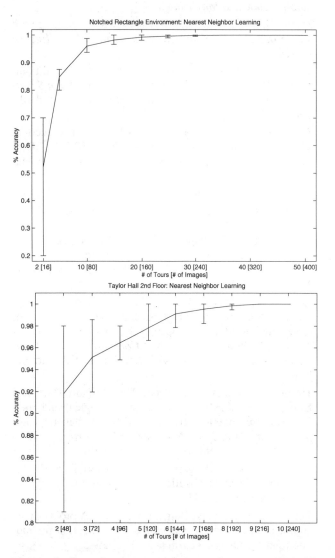

Figure 6: Learning curves (means and ranges using 10-fold cross validation) for nearest neighbor classification of dstates given sensory images for (a) the notched-rectangle environment (8 images/tour), and (b) second floor of Taylor Hall (24 images of 20 dstates/tour). Recognition rate rises rapidly to 100%, because even images of perceptually aliased dstates contain discriminating features that were averaged away by clustering, but can be identified by supervised learning.

Kuipers, B. J. 2000. The spatial semantic hierarchy. *Artificial Intelligence* 119:191–233.

Lynch, K. 1960. *The Image of the City*. Cambridge, MA: MIT Press.

Moravec, H. P. 1988. Sensor fusion in certainty grids for mobile robots. *AI Magazine* 61–74.

Pierce, D. M., and Kuipers, B. J. 1997. Map learning with uninterpreted sensors and effectors. *Artificial Intelligence* 92:169–227.

Press, W. H.; Teukolsky, S. A.; Vitterling, W. T.; and Flannery, B. P. 1992. *Numerical Recipes in C: The Art of Scientific Computing*. Cambridge University Press, second edition.

Remolina, E., and Kuipers, B. 2001. A logical account of causal and topological maps. In *Proc. 17th Int. Joint Conf. on Artificial Intelligence (IJCAI-01)*, 5–11. San Mateo, CA: Morgan Kaufmann.

Remolina, E. 2001. *Formalizing the Spatial Semantic Hierarchy*. Ph.D. Dissertation, Computer Science Department, University of Texas at Austin.

Rivest, R. L., and Schapire, R. E. 1989. Inference of finite automata using homing sequences. In *Proceedings of the 21st Annual ACM Symposium on Theoretical Computing*, 411–420. ACM.

Romero, L.; Morales, E.; and Sucar, E. 2001. An hybrid approach to solve the global localization problem for indoor mobile robots considering sensor's perceptual limitations. In *Proc. 17th Int. Joint Conf. on Artificial Intelligence (IJCAI-01)*, 1411–1416. San Mateo, CA: Morgan Kaufmann.

Thrun, S.; Gutmann, S.; Fox, D.; Burgard, W.; and Kuipers, B. J. 1998. Integrating topological and metric maps for mobile robot navigation: A statistical approach. In *Proc. 15th National Conf. on Artificial Intelligence (AAAI-98)*, 989–995. AAAI/MIT Press.

Thrun, S.; Fox, D.; Burgard, W.; and Dellaert, F. 2001. Robust Monte Carlo localization for mobile robots. *Artificial Intelligence* 128:99–141.

Thrun, S.; Fox, D.; and Burgard, W. 1998. A probabilistic approach to concurrent mapping and localization for mobile robots. *Machine Learning* 31(1–3):29–53.

Ulrich, I., and Nourbakhsh, I. 2000. Appearance-based place recognition for topological localization. In *IEEE International Conference on Robotics and Automation*, 1023–1029. IEEE Computer Society Press.

Yamauchi, B., and Langley, P. 1997. Place recognition in dynamic environments. *Journal of Robotic Systems* 14:107–120.

Yamauchi, B.; Schultz, A.; and Adams, W. 1998. Mobile robot exploration and map-building with continuous localization. In *IEEE International Conference on Robotics and Automation*, 3715–3720.

Papers from our research group are available at http://www.cs.utexas.edu/users/qr/robotics/.

Minimum Majority Classification and Boosting

Philip M. Long

Genome Institute of Singapore
1 Science Park Road
The Capricorn, #05-01
Singapore 117528, Republic of Singapore
gislongp@nus.edu.sg

Abstract

Motivated by a theoretical analysis of the generalization of boosting, we examine learning algorithms that work by trying to fit data using a simple majority vote over a small number of a collection of hypotheses. We provide experimental evidence that an algorithm based on this principle outputs hypotheses that often generalize nearly as well as those output by boosting, and sometimes better. We also provide experimental evidence for an additional reason that boosting algorithms generalize well, that they take advantage of cases in which there are many simple hypotheses with independent errors.

Introduction

Boosting algorithms (Schapire 1990; Freund 1995; Freund & Schapire 1997) work by repeatedly applying a subalgorithm to a dataset. Before each application, the examples are reweighted. The hypotheses returned are then combined by voting: for example, in the two-class case, each hypothesis is assigned a weight, and an item is classified as 1 if the total weight of the hypotheses classifying it as 1 is more than that of hypotheses classifying it as 0. Boosting has been successfully applied in a variety of domains (Drucker, Schapire, & Simard 1993; Freund & Schapire 1996a; Drucker & Cortes 1996; Abney, Schapire, & Singer 1999; Cohen, Schapire, & Singer 1999; Freund et al. 1998; Bauer & Kohavi 1999; Iyer et al. 2000; Schapire, Singer, & Singhal 1998).

The generalization observed by boosting algorithms appeared to run counter to the Occam's Razor principle which has been the bedrock of much of both theoretical and applied machine learning research. Loosely, Occam's Razor says that simpler hypotheses are to be preferred, because simple hypotheses are less apt to perform well on the training data by chance. But the hypotheses output by boosting algorithms are more complex than those output by the subalgorithm, and generalization is seen to improve as the number of rounds of boosting increases, even after all of the training data is classified correctly (Drucker & Cortes 1996; Quinlan 1996; Breiman 1998).

An influential theoretical analysis (Schapire et al. 1998) bounded the generalization error of the hypothesis output

by the boosting algorithm in terms of the *margin*.[1] This is the minimum, over all examples, of how much greater is the total weight of the hypotheses classifying the example correctly than the total weight of the incorrect hypotheses. (Grove and Schuurmans (1998) evaluated an algorithm that used linear programming to train weights to maximize the margin, and found that the resulting performance was often somewhat worse than obtained by Adaboost.)

The proof of the generalization bound in terms of the margin can be crudely paraphrased as follows: hypotheses that classify data correctly with a large margin generalize well because they can be accurately approximated by simple majority votes over few of the constituent hypotheses, which is a "simple" class of hypotheses. Continuing boosting for more rounds improves generalization even after the voting hypothesis has zero training error because, the resulting explanation goes, while the hypotheses generated are themselves more complex, they can be accurately approximated by simple hypotheses to an improved degree.

This observation motivates the following question. What if a learning algorithm worked by *directly* trying to find small collections of simple hypotheses for which a majority vote correctly classified much of the data? This is the subject of this paper. Our goals are both to better understand the reason that boosting algorithms generalize well, and to provide an approximation to boosting that outputs simpler hypotheses. (This problem was posed by Quinlan (1999) .)

The design of an algorithm applying this minimum majority principle gives rise to a nontrivial optimization problem. The author (Long 2001) previously proposed a polynomial-time algorithm for trying to minimize the size of a collection of hypotheses for which a simple vote yields correct classifications on all members of a dataset. The algorithm has a theoretical approximation bound, but it needed to be modified substantially to work well in practice. It makes use of a nonstandard variant (Pach & Agarwal 1995; Williamson 1999) of *randomized rounding* (Raghavan & Thompson 1987), a technique for solving integer programming problems in which, roughly

- the requirement that the variables are integers is removed,

---

[1] In fact, their analysis was more general, but the spirit of the analysis is captured in this simple case, and the below discussion also applies to their more general analysis.

- the resulting solution is used to generate a probability distribution over integer solutions, and

- an integer solution is sampled from this distribution.

Using this algorithm, we carried out a suite of experiments comparing its generalization with that obtained through boosting. As was done in some of the experiments in (Freund & Schapire 1996a), both algorithms used decision stumps (Iba & Langley 1992) as the hypotheses of the subalgorithm. (Decision stumps test the value of a single attribute, comparing it with a threshold if it is numerical, and base their classification on the result. Examples include "classify as 1 exactly when $x_3 \geq 2.2$" and "classify as 0 exactly when $x_7 = $ RED".) We compared them on a variety of datasets previously used for evaluating boosting (Freund & Schapire 1996a). In almost all cases, the minimum majority algorithm accurately approximated the generalization of boosting; sometimes it performed slightly better. However, in a few cases, it performed significantly worse.

Why? One possible explanation is as follows. The reweighting of the examples done by boosting tends to force the subalgorithm to return hypotheses whose errors are approximately independent (Ali & Pazzani 1996; Niyogi, Pierrot, & Siohan 2001), that is for example

$$\mathbf{Pr}(\text{first hypothesis right}$$
$$\text{AND second hypothesis wrong}$$
$$\text{AND ...}$$
$$\text{AND } k\text{th hypothesis right})$$
$$\approx \mathbf{Pr}(\text{first hypothesis right})$$
$$\times \mathbf{Pr}(\text{second hypothesis wrong})$$
$$\times ...$$
$$\times \mathbf{Pr}(k\text{th hypothesis right}).$$

If it is successful in finding a large number of different hypotheses that are fairly accurate and whose errors are mutually independent, then it can hurt generalization to only make use of a small number of them. This is because if there are many (approximately) independent hypotheses participating in a vote, the variance of the fraction of them that are correct on a random instance will be smaller, and thus the fraction will be less likely to dip below $1/2$.

This phenomenon is illustrated dramatically with a very simple artificial dataset. There are 100 attributes that are conditionally independent given the class label, agreeing with it with probability 2/3, and 100 examples. On this data, boosting decision stumps results in hypotheses using nearly all the attributes, which achieve 97.8% accuracy on independent test data, whereas the minimum majority algorithm chooses small subsets (averaging 6.6) of the attributes, and only gets 77.2% correct.

Another artificial dataset provides an example of where the minimum majority algorithm has the advantage. In this dataset, there are 111 boolean attributes. The first 100 are independent flips of a fair coin, and a majority vote over the first 11 of these determines the class label. The final 11 attributes are conditionally independent given the resulting class label, agreeing with it with probability $0.5 + 1/\sqrt{11} \approx$

0.8 (which a simple calculation shows is greater than the probability that a determiner agrees with the class label). When there are 6667 examples, the conditionally independent attributes that correlate with the class label feature prominently in the boosted hypothesis, whereas in ten runs with data sets of this type, the minimum majority algorithm always consisted of a majority vote over precisely the 11 attributes that determine the class label. (This is encouraging evidence of the effectiveness of the optimization routine. Note that any greedy algorithm would include the conditionally independent attributes that correlate better with the class label.) The generalization of minimum majority is of course 100%, where boosting yields 99.1%.

The above two artificial datasets demonstrate a clear separation between boosting and following the minimum majority principle, and suggest the following extended explanation of the generalization ability of boosting. It appears that in addition to finding hypotheses that can be approximated with sparse, simple majority votes, boosting also makes maximal use of large collections of hypotheses whose errors are independent when such opportunities arise.

The experiments on the UC Irvine data (see Table 1) suggest that the minimum majority principle leads to a learning algorithm that for many applications generalizes nearly as well as boosting, but outputs simpler hypotheses based on fewer attributes, and is based on basic, easily understood principles.

Algorithm

In this paper, we will concentrate on the two-class case. The two-class case is sufficient to bring up the points we wish to explore, and, besides, much of the work on multiclass prediction using boosting proceeds by reducing to the two-class case (Freund & Schapire 1995; Schapire & Singer 2000).

The algorithm is perhaps best described in stages. First, we will describe the basic algorithm, then describe a series of modifications.

Generating a list of decision stumps

For each numerical variable, we create a list of thresholds by sorting the values that the variable takes on the dataset, and then putting a threshold halfway between each consecutive pair of values in the resulting list. For example, if a variable took the values 0, 3, 4, and 6, then the thresholds created would be 1.5, 3.5 and 5. For each threshold, two decision stumps are created, one that predicts 1 if the variable is at least the threshold, and one that predicts 1 if the variable is at most the threshold. Boolean variables are treated as numerical variables taking the values 0 and 1.

For each nominal variable i, for each value y that it takes, two decision stumps are created: one which predicts 1 exactly when variable i takes the value y, and one which prediction 1 exactly when variable i doesn't take the value y.

Finally, decision stumps that always predict 1 and always predict 0 are added.

The basic algorithm

The basic algorithm addresses the problem of finding the smallest multiset of decision stumps for which a majority vote correctly classifies all the examples. This can be formulated as an integer program. Suppose there are n decision stumps and m examples, and let A be the $m \times n$ matrix in which $A_{i,j}$ is

- 1 if the ith decision stump is correct on the jth example,
- -1 if the ith decision stump is incorrect on the jth example,
- 0 if the variable queried has a missing value.

Then the problem can be phrased as that of setting nonnegative-integer-valued variables $x_1, ..., x_n$ to minimize $\sum_{i=1}^{n} x_i$ subject to the constraints that $Ax \geq (1, 1, ..., 1)^T$ (where $x = (x_1, ..., x_n)^T$). The ith variable is the number of times that ith decision stump gets to vote, and each constraint requires that the number of correct votes on a certain example is at least 1 more than the number of incorrect votes.

The basic algorithm

- solves the linear program obtained by removing the requirement that the variables are integers and gets the solution $(u_1, ..., u_n)$,
- sets

$$(p_1, ..., p_n) = (u_1, ..., u_n)/(u_1 + ... + u_n)$$

to be the probability distribution over decision stumps in which the probability of decision stump i is proportional to the value of u_i,

- repeatedly randomly picks a variable using the distribution $(p_1, ..., p_n)$ keeping track for each variable i of the number of times x_i that i has been picked, until
- $Ax \geq (1, 1, ..., 1)^T$, at which time it quits and outputs x.

This algorithm has been shown to approximate the optimal solution in polynomial time (Long 2001). Two facts help one imagine why. First, if a solution is feasible, then the solution obtained by scaling all components by a constant factor is also feasible; e.g., if a certain solution calls for a certain collection of decision stumps to each vote once, then if instead they all always vote twice, all the votes come out the same way. Second, if $Z = \sum_{i=1}^{n} u_i$ and $u = (u_1, ..., u_n)$, then, after the algorithm has randomly chosen ℓ variables, the expectation of the current solution x is $(\ell/Z)u$.

The system used in our experiments solves the linear program using PCx (Czyzyk *et al.* 1999), which implements an interior-point algorithm.[2]

Resolving

Note that after the algorithm has committed to its first choice of a decision stump, it is left with a subproblem of a similar

---

[2]PCx generally worked impressively well on the linear programs generated by this application. However, with the default parameter settings, PCx infrequently either incorrectly reported infeasiblity, or crashed – when either happened, the system used in our experiments would simply start another attempt to improve the best solution found. Increasing `opttol`, `prifeastol`, and `dualfeastol` to 0.00001 and setting `refinement` to `no` appeared to help.

form. It wants to add as few decision stumps as possible in subsequent iterations, subject to updated constraints. For examples on which the first decision stump is correct, only half of the remaining choices need to be correct. For examples on which the first decision stump is incorrect, the number of subsequent decision stumps that are correct must be at least two greater than the number that are incorrect, in order to overcome the error made by the first decision stump. These constraints lead to different priorities than were in effect at the beginning, so presumably solving the linear programming relaxation of this new integer program should lead to a more appropriate probability distribution to use for choosing the second decision stump. This continues for future iterations. Our algorithm does this. This had a major effect on its performance in practice: prior to this modification, it was effectively useless.

Committing to the integer parts

The above process can be viewed as making successive commitments that the values of various variables are at least certain integer values, and incrementing one of these values at each iteration. This can be seen by expressing the integer program formulated at each iteration in terms of the original variables. To see how, let us focus again on the second iteration. Suppose that the decision stump chosen in the first iteration is number i_1. Suppose we formulate the integer program faced at the beginning of the second iteration using the same variables as the original integer program, where each variable is the number of times one decision stump will be chosen overall. Then the new integer program can be obtained from the old simply by adding the constraint $x_{i_1} \geq 1$. In general, if after a certain number of iterations the decision stumps numbered 1 through n have been chosen a_1 through a_n times respectively, then the integer program to solve in the next iteration is

$$\text{minimize} \sum_{i=1}^{n} x_i, \text{ s.t.}$$

$$\sum_{i=1}^{n} A_{ij} x_i \geq 1, \text{ for all examples } j$$

$$x_i \geq a_i, \text{ for all decision stumps } i.$$

Sometimes, the solution $(u_1, ..., u_n)$ to the linear programming relaxation of an integer program of the above form has many variables for which $u_i \geq a_i + 1$. Rather than wait for those values to be committed to in future iterations, we went ahead and committed to the integer parts of all variables before making the next random selection. For example, suppose there were three decision stumps, and the linear program returned a solution of $(2.1, 3.2, 5.4)$. Then the algorithm would commit to making the first variable at least 2, the second variable at least 3 and the third variable at least 5, adding these constraints for use in the next and subsequent iterations. If $(2, 3, 5)$ was not a feasible solution, then it would sample from the distribution obtained by normalizing the fractional parts, (1/7,2/7,4/7), to decide which variable whose commitment to increase, update the constraints to respond to this choice, and continue. This also improved performance markedly. To see why, consider what happens if the linear programming relaxation has an integer solution, which happens fairly often on the benchmark data we have experimented with. With the change of this subsection, this is recognized immediately and handled appropriately. The random sampling process that would otherwise be used would often be unlikely to get this solution.

Feature selection

When the data has a large number of numerical attributes, the number of decision stumps can be prohibitively large. Since the decision stumps output by the minimum majority algorithm often were contained in those output in the first 100 rounds of Adaboost, we performed a feature selection step in which Adaboost was run for 100 rounds and the resulting decision stumps were gathered and passed to the minimum majority algorithm described above. This change does not affect the motivation derived from the analysis of Adaboost (Schapire *et al.* 1998): their argument showed that the hypothesis could be approximated using a simple majority vote of a few hypotheses, even if those hypotheses were restricted to be chosen from among those participating in the weighted voting hypotheses output by the boosting algorithm.

Feature selection is only performed when the number of decision stumps generated by the original process was more than 100. (In our experiments, it was not performed on the house dataset, but on all others.)

Ensuring feasibility

We ensure feasibility using a method analogous to the "soft margin" approach from Support Vector Machines (Cortes & Vapnik 1995; Klasner & Simon 1995; Rätsch, Onoda, & Müller 2001). For each example, we add a "slack variable" to the integer program. The variable for an example has a coefficient of 1 in the constraint corresponding to that example, and does not appear in any other constraints. By increasing the value of that variable enough, one can therefore satisfy the one constraint in which it appears. These extra variables are assigned a cost of $1/4$ in the objective function. Of course this cost could be made a parameter, to be set using cross-validation on the training set. (The same value of $1/4$ was used in all of the experiments reported in this paper. This was not carefully optimized – it was chosen based on a little tinkering with some simple artificial datasets and the ionosphere data set.)

Restarting

An obvious modification is to run the algorithm several times, and output the best solution found. Of course, later runs can halt when the number of decision stumps in the solution becomes as large as the best solution found so far. In fact, later runs can halt whenever a fractional solution has a value that, when rounded up, is at least the best solution found so far, because the value of the integer solution found will be at least the value of the fractional solution, and will be an integer.

Dataset	Minmaj test set accuracy	Adaboost 100 rounds test set accuracy	Adaboost 10 rounds test set accuracy	Minmaj hyp. size
promoters	0.883	0.900	0.883	4.4
hepatitis	0.799	0.833	0.838	1.2
ionosphere	0.851	0.904	0.867	8.8
house	0.952	0.965	0.961	1.0
breast-cancer	0.941	0.950	0.949	4.8
pima	0.734	0.751	0.744	1.0
hypothyroid	0.992	0.991	0.990	5.0
sick-euthyroid	0.972	0.966	0.965	5.8
kr-vs-kp	0.965	0.958	0.937	13.0
mushroom	0.9996	1.0000	0.971	10.6
vote-condind	1.000	0.991	0.975	11.0
condind	0.772	0.978	0.838	6.6

Table 1: Our experimental results. Datasets above the double line were used in Freund and Schapire's experimental evaluation of Adaboost. The entry "Minmaj hyp. size" gives the average number of decision stumps participating in the final vote output by the minimum majority algorithm on that dataset – the other entries should be self-explanatory.

Giving up

In our experiments, the system halted when either 1000 consecutive attempts failed to improve on the best solution found so far, or when a total of two hours of wallclock time (on a loaded, common use, Sun-Fire) had been expended trying.

Initial solution

In early versions of the system, sometimes the first run of the algorithm took a long time before finding a feasible solution. To combat this, the present system first finds the best solution possible by combining a single decision stump with the slack variables described above. Each run of the randomized rounding algorithm halts when it fails to improve on this.

Experiments

We did experiments using a collection of data sets used in Freund and Schapire's experimental evaluation of Adaboost (Freund & Schapire 1996a). The datasets we used were the two-class datasets from the UC Irvine Machine Learning repository that were easiest to put into a common form. We also experimented with two artificial datasets that we created ourselves. For each dataset, we repeated the following experiment 10 times: hold out a random $1/3$ of the dataset, train on the remaining $2/3$ and evaluate the hypothesis on the held out $1/3$. We then added up the results from the 10 runs and tabulated them in Table 1.

The implementation of Adaboost in our experiments used the same decision stumps as the minimum majority algorithm, and ran for 100 iterations. We also ran Adaboost for only 10 iterations, in order to obtain hypotheses with roughly the complexity of those output by the minimum majority algorithm (note that Adaboost's hypotheses are *weighted* majority votes, however).

Dataset	#examples	#attr
promoters	106	57
hepatitis	155	19
ionosphere	351	34
house	435	16
breast-cancer	699	9
pima	768	8
hypothyroid	3163	25
sick-euthyroid	3163	25
kr-vs-kp	3196	36
mushroom	8124	22
vote-condind	10000	111
condind	150	100

Table 2: Some characteristics of the data used.

One trend that is visible is that the comparative performance of the minimum majority algorithm improves as the number of examples increases. This is consistent with the view that the advantage of Adaboost is due to exploitation of groups of hypotheses with independent errors. If the errors of the individuals are not too small, as the number of examples gets large, all members of such a group must be included in a majority vote for it to fit the data well. Note that for three of the datasets, the minimum majority algorithm either always or almost always outputs a single decision stump.

The artificial datasets are generated as follows. The dataset vote-condind is the dataset described in the introduction, in which 11 attributes determine the class label by majority vote, 11 are conditionally independent given the class label, agreeing with it roughly with probability 0.8, and 89 attributes are irrelevant. The dataset described in the introduction with 100 conditionally independent attributes agreeing with the label with probability 2/3 is called condind.

Previous work

Perhaps the most closely related work is that of Grove and Schuurmans (1998), who compared the performance of Adaboost with an algorithm that explicitly tried to maximize the margin using linear programming. The linear program solved in our algorithm for use to determine the probability distribution for the choice of the first decision stump is the same as linear program used to train the hypothesis weights in their algorithm. Mason, et al (2000) designed an algorithm, called DOOM, that chose the weights of a weighted voting classifier to optimize a cost function inspired by the general upper bound on generalization error from (Schapire et al. 1998) (the more general bound was in terms of the margin obtained when a certain fraction of the training data was excluded, together with that fraction). They showed that DOOM often improved on the generalization of Adaboost.

A number of papers have given a variety of interpretations of boosting. Friedman, et al (1998) showed that an algorithm closely related to boosting is obtained from additive logistic regression. An interpretation of boosting as gradi-ent descent was given by Mason, et al (2000). Kivinen and Warmuth (1999) showed that reweighting of the examples used by boosting was the solution of an optimization problem involving a tradeoff between keeping the relative entropy between the new and old weightings small and choosing a weighting orthogonal to the vector indicating whether the previous hypothesis made mistakes on the various examples (thereby driving the new hypothesis to make errors approximately independent of the old). Niyogi, et al (2001) also described a way in which boosting could be viewed as trying to find hypotheses with independent errors, and described an alternative algorithm pursuing this goal in conjunction with having small errors. Ali and Pazzani (1996) had established an empirical relationship between the tendency of a base classifier to return hypotheses with independent errors and the ability of an ensemble method to improve it. Freund and Schapire (1996) described a connection between boosting and game theory. Kutin and Niyogi (2001) performed an analysis of the generalization of Adaboost using the notion of algorithmic stability (Bousquet & Elisseeff 2001).

The analysis of Winnow (Littlestone 1988) in (Littlestone 1989) suggests that the inductive bias of Winnow might be similar to that of the minimum majority algorithm proposed here.

Conclusion

We have provided experimental evidence that an algorithm based on the minimum majority principle can generalize like boosting, while returning simpler hypotheses. This appears especially to be the case when the dataset is large. Our experiments also suggest an extension to the explanation of why boosted hypotheses generalize well: in addition to generating hypotheses that can be approximated by hypotheses of a simple form, they take full advantage of occasions in which many simple hypotheses have independent errors.

Source code associated with this work is available at http://giscompute.gis.nus.edu.sg/~plong/minmaj.

Acknowledgements

I'd like to thank Edison Liu, Sayan Mukherjee, and Vinsensius Vega for valuable conversations about this work and related topics, and Shirish Shevade, Vinsensius Vega and anonymous referees for their comments on drafts of this paper.

References

Abney, S.; Schapire, R.; and Singer, Y. 1999. Boosting applied to tagging and pp attachment. In *Proceedings of the Joint SIGDAT Conference on Empirical Methods in Natural Language Processing and Very Large Corpora*.

Ali, K. M., and Pazzani, M. J. 1996. Error reduction through learning multiple descriptions. *Machine Learning* 24(3):173–202.

Bauer, E., and Kohavi, R. 1999. An empirical comparison of voting classification algorithm: Bagging, boosting and variants. *Machine Learning* 105–142.

Bousquet, O., and Elisseeff, A. 2001. Algorithmic stability and generalization performance. *Advances in Neural Information Processing Systems 13*.

Breiman, L. 1998. Arcing classifiers. *The Annals of Statistics*.

Cohen, W.; Schapire, R.; and Singer, Y. 1999. Learning to order things. In *Advances in Neural Information Processing Systems 11: Proc. of NIPS'98*. MIT Press.

Cortes, C., and Vapnik, V. 1995. Support-vector networks. *Machine Learning* 20(3):273–297.

Czyzyk, J.; Mehrotra, S.; Wagner, M.; and Wright, S. J. 1999. PCx: An interior-point code for linear programming. *Optimization Methods and Software* 11:397–430.

Drucker, H., and Cortes, C. 1996. Boosting decision trees. In *Advances in Neural Information Processing Systems 8*, 479–485.

Drucker, H.; Schapire, R.; and Simard, P. 1993. Boosting performance in neural networks. *International Journal of Pattern Recognition and Artificial Intelligence* 7:705–719.

Freund, Y., and Schapire, R. E. 1995. A decision-theoretic generalization of on-line learning and an application to boosting. *Proceedings of the Second European Conference on Computational Learning Theory* 23–37.

Freund, Y., and Schapire, R. 1996a. Experiments with a new boosting algorithm. *Proceedings of the Thirteenth International Conference on Machine Learning*.

Freund, Y., and Schapire, R. 1996b. Game theory, on-line prediction and boosting. In *Proc. 9th Annu. Conf. on Comput. Learning Theory*, 325–332. ACM Press, New York, NY.

Freund, Y., and Schapire, R. E. 1997. A decision-theoretic generalization of on-line learning and an application to boosting. *Journal of Computer and System Sciences* 55(1):119–139.

Freund, Y.; Iyer, R.; Schapire, R.; and Singer, Y. 1998. An efficient boosting algorithm for combining preferences. In *Proc. 15th International Conference on Machine Learning*.

Freund, Y. 1995. Boosting a weak learning algorithm by majority. *Information and Computation* 121(2):256–285.

Friedman, J.; Hastie, T.; and Tibshirani, R. 1998. Additive logistic regression: a statistical view of boosting. Technical report, Department of Statistics, Sequoia Hall, Stanford Univerity.

Grove, A., and Schuurmans, D. 1998. Boosting in the limit: Maximizing the margin of learned ensembles. In *Proceedings of the Fifteenth National Conference on Artifical Intelligence*.

Iba, W., and Langley, P. 1992. Induction of one-level decision trees. *Proc. of the 9th International Workshop on Machine Learning*.

Iyer, R.; Lewis, D.; Schapire, R.; Singer, Y.; and Singhal, A. 2000. Boosting for document routing. In *Proceedings of the Ninth International Conference on Information and Knowledge Management*.

Kivinen, J., and Warmuth, M. 1999. Boosting as entropy projection. In *Proc. COLT'99*.

Klasner, N., and Simon, H.-U. 1995. From noise-free to noise-tolerant and from on-line to batch learning. *Proceedings of the 1995 Conference on Computational Learning Theory* 250–257.

Kutin, S., and Niyogi, P. 2001. The interaction of stability and weakness in adaboost. Technical Report TR–2001–30, The University of Chicago.

Littlestone, N. 1988. Learning quickly when irrelevant attributes abound: a new linear-threshold algorithm. *Machine Learning* 2:285–318.

Littlestone, N. 1989. *Mistake Bounds and Logarithmic Linear-threshold Learning Algorithms*. Ph.D. Dissertation, UC Santa Cruz.

Long, P. M. 2001. Using the pseudo-dimension to analyze approximation algorithms for integer programming. *Proceedings of the Seventh International Workshop on Algorithms and Data Structures*.

Mason, L.; Bartlett, P. L.; and Baxter, J. 2000. Improved generalization through explicit optimization of margins. *Machine Learning* 38(3):243–255.

Mason, L.; Baxter, J.; Bartlett, P. L.; and Frean, M. 2000. Boosting algorithms as gradient descent. In *Advances in Neural Information Processing Systems 12*, 512–518. MIT Press.

Niyogi, P.; Pierrot, J.-B.; and Siohan, O. 2001. On decorrelating classifiers and combining them. Manuscript.

Pach, J., and Agarwal, P. 1995. *Combinatorial Geometry*. John Wiley and Sons.

Quinlan, J. 1996. Bagging, boosting and c4.5. In *Proceedings of the Thirteenth National Conference on Artifiicial Intelligence*, 725–730. AAAI/MIT Press.

Quinlan, J. R. 1999. Some elements of machine learning. *Proceedings of the Sixteenth International Conference on Machine Learning* 523–524.

Raghavan, P., and Thompson, C. 1987. Randomized rounding: a technique for provably good algorithms and algorithmic proofs. *Combinatorica* 7(4):365–374.

Rätsch, G.; Onoda, T.; and Müller, K.-R. 2001. Soft margins for AdaBoost. *Machine Learning* 42(3):287–320. also NeuroCOLT Technical Report NC-TR-1998-021.

Schapire, R., and Singer, Y. 2000. BoosTexter: A boosting-based system for text categorization. *Machine Learning* 39(2/3):135–168.

Schapire, R. E.; Freund, Y.; Bartlett, P.; and Lee, W. S. 1998. Boosting the margin: A new explanation for the effectiveness of voting methods. *The Annals of Statistics* 26(5):1651–1686.

Schapire, R.; Singer, Y.; and Singhal, A. 1998. Boosting and Rocchio applied to text filtering. In *Proceedings of the 21st Annual International Conference on Research and Development in Information Retrieval*.

Schapire, R. E. 1990. The strength of weak learnability. *Machine Learning* 5(2):197–226.

Williamson, D. P. 1999. Lecture notes on approximation algorithms. Technical Report RC–21409, IBM.

Content-Boosted Collaborative Filtering for Improved Recommendations

Prem Melville and **Raymond J. Mooney** and **Ramadass Nagarajan**

Department of Computer Sciences
University of Texas
Austin, TX 78712
{melville,mooney,ramdas}@cs.utexas.edu

Abstract

Most recommender systems use Collaborative Filtering or Content-based methods to predict new items of interest for a user. While both methods have their own advantages, individually they fail to provide good recommendations in many situations. Incorporating components from both methods, a hybrid recommender system can overcome these shortcomings. In this paper, we present an elegant and effective framework for combining content and collaboration. Our approach uses a content-based predictor to enhance existing user data, and then provides personalized suggestions through collaborative filtering. We present experimental results that show how this approach, *Content-Boosted Collaborative Filtering*, performs better than a pure content-based predictor, pure collaborative filter, and a naive hybrid approach.

Introduction

Recommender systems help overcome information overload by providing personalized suggestions based on a history of a user's likes and dislikes. Many on-line stores provide recommending services e.g. Amazon, CDNOW, BarnesAndNoble, IMDb, etc. There are two prevalent approaches to building recommender systems — Collaborative Filtering (CF) and Content-based (CB) recommending. CF systems work by collecting user feedback in the form of ratings for items in a given domain and exploit similarities and differences among profiles of several users in determining how to recommend an item. On the other hand, content-based methods provide recommendations by comparing representations of content contained in an item to representations of content that interests the user.

Content-based methods can uniquely characterize each user, but CF still has some key advantages over them (Herlocker *et al.* 1999). Firstly, CF can perform in domains where there is not much content associated with items, or where the content is difficult for a computer to analyze — ideas, opinions etc. Secondly a CF system has the ability to provide serendipitous recommendations, i.e. it can recommend items that are relevant to the user, but do not contain content from the user's profile. Because of these reasons, CF systems have been used fairly successfully to build recommender systems in various domains (Goldberg *et al.* 1992;

Resnick *et al.* 1994). However they suffer from two fundamental problems:

- *Sparsity*
  Stated simply, most users do not rate most items and hence the user-item rating matrix is typically very sparse. Therefore the probability of finding a set of users with *significantly* similar ratings is usually low. This is often the case when systems have a very high item-to-user ratio. This problem is also very significant when the system is in the initial stage of use.

- *First-rater Problem*
  An item cannot be recommended unless a user has rated it before. This problem applies to new items and also obscure items and is particularly detrimental to users with eclectic tastes.

We overcome these drawbacks of CF systems by exploiting content information of the items already rated. Our basic approach uses content-based predictions to convert a sparse user ratings matrix into a full ratings matrix; and then uses CF to provide recommendations. In this paper, we present the framework for this new hybrid approach, Content-Boosted Collaborative Filtering (CBCF). We apply this framework in the domain of movie recommendation and show that our approach performs better than both pure CF and pure content-based systems.

Domain Description

We demonstrate the working of our hybrid approach in the domain of movie recommendation. We use the user-movie ratings from the EachMovie[1] dataset, provided by the Compaq Systems Research Center. The dataset contains rating data provided by each user for various movies. User ratings range from zero to five stars. Zero stars indicate extreme dislike for a movie and five stars indicate high praise. To have a quicker turn-around time for our experiments, we only used a subset of the EachMovie dataset. This dataset contains 7,893 randomly selected users and 1,461 movies for which content was available from the Internet Movie Database (IMDb)[2]. The reduced dataset has 299,997 ratings for 1,408 movies. The average number of votes per user is

---

[1]http://research.compaq.com/SRC/eachmovie
[2]http://www.imdb.com

approximately 38 and the sparsity of the user ratings matrix is 97.4%.

The content information for each movie was collected from IMDb using a simple crawler. The crawler follows the IMDB link provided for every movie in the EachMovie dataset and collects information from the various links off the main URL. We represent the content information of every movie as a set of slots (features). Each slot is represented simply as a bag of words. The slots we use for the Each-Movie dataset are: movie title, director, cast, genre, plot summary, plot keywords, user comments, external reviews, newsgroup reviews, and awards.

System Description

The general overview of our system is shown in Figure 1. The web crawler uses the URLs provided in the EachMovie dataset to download movie content from IMDb. After appropriate preprocessing, the downloaded content is stored in the Movie Content Database. The EachMovie dataset also provides the user-ratings matrix, which is a matrix of users versus items, where each cell is the rating given by a user to an item. We will refer to each row of this matrix as a *user-ratings vector*. The user-ratings matrix is very sparse, since most items have not been rated by most users. The content-based predictor is trained on each user-ratings vector and a pseudo user-ratings vector is created. A pseudo user-ratings vector contains the user's actual ratings and content-based predictions for the unrated items. All pseudo user-ratings vectors put together form the pseudo ratings matrix, which is a full matrix. Now given an active user's[3] ratings, predictions are made for a new item using CF on the full pseudo ratings matrix.

The following sections describe our implementation of the content-based predictor and the pure CF component; followed by the details of our hybrid approach.

Pure Content-based Predictor

To provide content-based predictions we treat the prediction task as a text-categorization problem. We view movie content information as text documents, and user ratings 0-5 as one of six class labels. We implemented a bag-of-words naive Bayesian text classifier (Mitchell 1997) extended to handle a vector of bags of words; where each bag-of-words corresponds to a movie-feature (e.g. title, cast, etc.). We use the classifier to learn a user profile from a set of rated movies i.e. labeled documents. The learned profile is then used to predict the label (rating) of unrated movies. A similar approach to recommending has been used effectively in the book-recommending system LIBRA (Mooney & Roy 2000).

Pure Collaborative Filtering

We implemented a pure collaborative filtering component that uses a *neighborhood-based algorithm* (Herlocker *et al.* 1999). In neighborhood-based algorithms, a subset of users are chosen based on their similarity to the active user, and a weighted combination of their ratings is used to produce

---

[3]The active user is the user for whom predictions are being made.

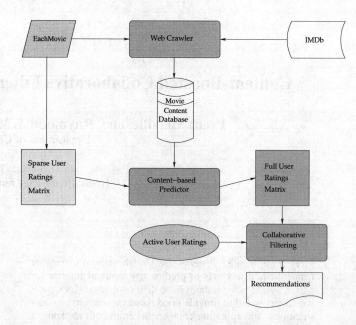

Figure 1: System Overview

predictions for the active user. The algorithm we use can be summarized in the following steps:

1. Weight all users with respect to similarity with the active user.
   - Similarity between users is measured as the Pearson correlation between their ratings vectors.

2. Select n users that have the highest similarity with the active user.
   - These users form the *neighborhood*.

3. Compute a prediction from a weighted combination of the selected neighbors' ratings.

In step 1, similarity between two users is computed using the Pearson correlation coefficient, defined below:

$$P_{a,u} = \frac{\sum_{i=1}^{m} (r_{a,i} - \overline{r}_a) \times (r_{u,i} - \overline{r}_u)}{\sqrt{\sum_{i=1}^{m} (r_{a,i} - \overline{r}_a)^2 \times \sum_{i=1}^{m} (r_{u,i} - \overline{r}_u)^2}} \quad (1)$$

where $r_{a,i}$ is the rating given to item i by user a; $\overline{r}_a$ is the mean rating given by user a; and m is the total number of items.

In step 3, predictions are computed as the weighted average of deviations from the neighbor's mean:

$$p_{a,i} = \overline{r}_a + \frac{\sum_{u=1}^{n} (r_{u,i} - \overline{r}_u) \times P_{a,u}}{\sum_{u=1}^{n} P_{a,u}} \quad (2)$$

where $p_{a,i}$ is the prediction for the active user a for item i; $P_{a,u}$ is the similarity between users a and u; and n is the number of users in the neighborhood. For our experiments we used a neighborhood size of 30, based on the recommendation of (Herlocker *et al.* 1999).

It is common for the active user to have highly correlated neighbors that are based on very few co-rated (overlapping) items. These neighbors based on a small number of overlapping items tend to be bad predictors. To devalue the correlations based on few co-rated items, we multiply the correlation by a *Significance Weighting* factor (Herlocker *et al.* 1999). If two users have less than 50 co-rated items we multiply their correlation by a factor $sg_{a,u} = n/50$, where n is the number of co-rated items. If the number of overlapping items is greater than 50, then we leave the correlation unchanged i.e. $sg_{a,u} = 1$.

Content-Boosted Collaborative Filtering

In content-boosted collaborative filtering, we first create a *pseudo user-ratings vector* for every user u in the database. The pseudo user-ratings vector, v_u, consists of the item ratings provided by the user u, where available, and those predicted by the content-based predictor otherwise.

$$v_{u,i} = \begin{cases} r_{u,i} : \text{if user } u \text{ rated item } i \\ c_{u,i} : \text{otherwise} \end{cases}$$

In the above equation $r_{u,i}$ denotes the actual rating provided by user u for item i, while $c_{u,i}$ is the rating predicted by the pure content-based system.

The pseudo user-ratings vectors of all users put together give the dense pseudo ratings matrix V. We now perform collaborative filtering using this dense matrix. The similarity between the active user a and another user u is computed using the Pearson correlation coefficient described in Equation 1. Instead of the original user votes, we substitute the votes provided by the pseudo user-ratings vectors v_a and v_u.

Harmonic Mean Weighting The accuracy of a pseudo user-ratings vector computed for a user depends on the number of movies he/she has rated. If the user rated many items, the content-based predictions are good and hence his pseudo user-ratings vector is fairly accurate. On the other hand, if the user rated only a few items, the pseudo user-ratings vector will not be as accurate. We found that inaccuracies in pseudo user-ratings vector often yielded misleadingly high correlations between the active user and other users. Hence to incorporate confidence (or the lack thereof) in our correlations, we weight them using the *Harmonic Mean weighting* factor (*HM weighting*).

$$hm_{i,j} = \frac{2m_i m_j}{m_i + m_j}$$

$$m_i = \begin{cases} \frac{n_i}{50} : \text{if } n_i < 50 \\ 1 : \text{otherwise} \end{cases}$$

In the above equation, n_i refers to the number of items that user i has rated. The harmonic mean tends to bias the weight towards the lower of the two values — m_i and m_j. Thus correlations between pseudo user-ratings with at least 50 user-rated items each, will receive the highest weight, regardless of the actual number of movies each user rated. On the other hand, even if one of the pseudo user-rating vectors is based on less than 50 user-rated items, the correlation will be devalued appropriately.

The choice of the threshold 50 is based on the performance of the content-based predictor, which was evaluated

using 10-fold cross-validation (Mitchell 1997). To test performance on varying amounts of training data, a learning curve was generated by testing the system after training on increasing subsets of the overall training data. We generated learning curves for 132 users who had rated more than 200 items. The points on the 132 curves were averaged to give the final learning curve. From the learning curve we noted that as the predictor is given more and more training examples the prediction performance improves, but at around 50 it begins to level off. Beyond this is the point of diminishing returns; as no matter how large the training set is, prediction accuracy improves only marginally.

To the HM weight, we add the significance weighting factor described earlier, and thus obtain the *hybrid correlation weight* $hw_{a,u}$.

$$hw_{a,u} = hm_{a,u} + sg_{a,u} \tag{3}$$

Self Weighting Recall that in CF, a prediction for the active user is computed as a weighted sum of the mean-centered votes of the best-n neighbors of that user. In our approach, we also add the pseudo active user[4] to the neighborhood. However, we may want to give the pseudo active user more importance than the other neighbors. In other words, we would like to increase the confidence we place in the pure-content predictions for the active user. We do this by incorporating a *Self Weighting* factor in the final prediction:

$$sw_a = \begin{cases} \frac{n_a}{50} \times max : \text{if } n_a < 50 \\ max \qquad : \text{otherwise} \end{cases} \tag{4}$$

where n_a is the number of items rated by the active user. Again, the choice of the threshold 50 is motivated by the learning curve mentioned earlier. The parameter max is an indication of the over-all confidence we have in the content-based predictor. In our experiments, we used a value of 2 for max.

Producing Predictions Combining the above two weighting schemes, the final CBCF prediction for the active user a and item i is produced as follows:

$$p_{a,i} = \overline{v}_a + \frac{sw_a(c_{a,i} - \overline{v}_a) + \sum_{\substack{u=1 \\ u \neq a}}^{n} hw_{a,u} P_{a,u}(v_{u,i} - \overline{v}_u)}{sw_a + \sum_{\substack{u=1 \\ u \neq a}}^{n} hw_{a,u} P_{a,u}}$$

In the above equation $c_{a,i}$ corresponds to the pure-content predictions for the active user and item i; $v_{u,i}$ is the pseudo user-rating for a user u and item i; $\overline{v}_u$ is the mean over all items for that user; sw_a, $hw_{a,u}$ and $P_{a,u}$ are as shown in Equations 4, 3 and 1 respectively; and n is the size of neighborhood. The denominator is a normalization factor that ensures all weights sum to one.

Experimental Evaluation

In this section we describe the experimental methodology and metrics we use to compare different prediction algorithms; and present the results of our experiments.

---

[4]Pseudo active user refers to the pseudo user-ratings vector based on the active user's ratings.

Methodology

We compare CBCF to a pure content-based predictor, a CF predictor, and a naive hybrid approach. The naive hybrid approach takes the average of the ratings generated by the pure content-based predictor and the pure CF predictor. For the purposes of comparison, we used a subset of the ratings data from the *EachMovie* data set (described earlier). Ten percent of the users were randomly selected to be the test users. From each user in the test set, ratings for 25% of items were withheld. Predictions were computed for the withheld items using each of the different predictors.

The quality of the various prediction algorithms were measured by comparing the predicted values for the withheld ratings to the actual ratings.

Metrics

The metrics for evaluating the accuracy of a prediction algorithm can be divided into two main categories: *statistical accuracy metrics* and *decision-support metrics* (Herlocker *et al.* 1999). Statistical accuracy metrics evaluate the accuracy of a predictor by comparing predicted values with user-provided values. To measure statistical accuracy we use the mean absolute error (MAE) metric — defined as the average absolute difference between predicted ratings and actual ratings. In our experiments we computed the MAE on the test set for each user, and then averaged over the set of test users.

Decision-support accuracy measures how well predictions help users select *high-quality* items. We use Receiver Operating Characteristic (ROC) sensitivity to measure decision-support accuracy. A predictor can be treated as a filter, where predicting a high rating for an item is equivalent to accepting the item, and predicting a low rating is equivalent to rejecting the item. The ROC sensitivity is given by the area under the ROC curve — a curve that plots *sensitivity* versus 1-*specificity* for a predictor. Sensitivity is defined as the probability that a good item is accepted by the filter; and specificity is defined as the probability that a bad item is rejected by the filter. We consider an item *good* if the user gave it a rating of 4 or above, otherwise we consider the item *bad*. We refer to this ROC sensitivity with threshold 4 as ROC-4. ROC sensitivity ranges from 0 to 1, where 1 is ideal and 0.5 is random.

The statistical significance of any differences in performance between two predictors was evaluated using two-tailed paired *t*-tests (Mitchell 1997).

Results

Algorithm	MAE	ROC-4
Pure content-based (CB) predictor	1.059	0.6376
Pure CF	1.002	0.6423
Naive Hybrid	1.011	0.6121
Content-boosted CF	**0.962**	**0.6717**

Table 1: Summary of Results

The results of our experiments are summarized in Table 1. As can be seen, our CBCF approach performs better than

the other algorithms on both metrics. On the MAE metric, CBCF performs 9.2% better than pure CB, 4% better than pure CF and 4.9% better than the naive hybrid. All the differences in MAE are statistically significant ($p < 0.001$).

On the ROC-4, metric CBCF performs 5.4% better than pure CB, 4.6% better than pure CF and 9.7% better than the naive hybrid. This implies that our system, compared to others, does a better of job of recommending high-quality items, while reducing the probability of recommending bad items to the user.

Interestingly, *Self Weighting* did not make significant improvements to our predictions. We believe that *Self Weighting* would play a more important role if the pure CB predictor significantly outperformed CF.

Discussion

In this section we explain how content-boosted collaborative filtering overcomes some of the shortcomings of pure CF; and we also discuss some ways of improving CBCF.

Overcoming the First-Rater Problem

In pure CF a prediction cannot be made for an item, for the active user, unless it was previously rated by other users. However, we can make such a prediction using a content-based predictor for the user. Using CBCF we can further improve the CB predictions by utilizing the content-based predictions of *other* users as well. If the neighbors of the active user are highly correlated to it, then their CB predictions should also be very relevant to the user. This is particularly true if neighbors have rated many more items than the active user; because their CB predictions are likely to be more accurate than the active user's. To verify this hypothesis we ran the following experiments. A set of 500 users were selected at random from the *EachMovie* data set. We randomly selected an item to be deleted from the user-ratings matrix. We then produced pure content-based and CBCF predictions for the users that had rated the selected item. We repeated this process for 55 items and averaged the MAE over all users and items. We found that the MAEs for the pure CB predictor and CBCF were 1.060 and 1.023 respectively; and that the difference is statistically significant ($p < 0.001$). So we can conclude that using collaborative information is beneficial even if no other user has rated the item in question. In this way, CBCF solves the first-rater problem, and produces even better predictions than the content-based predictor.

Tackling Sparsity

In CBCF, since we use a pseudo ratings matrix, which is a full matrix, we eliminate the root of the sparsity problem. Pseudo user-ratings vectors contain ratings for all items; and hence all users will be considered as potential neighbors. This increases the chances of finding similar users. Thus the sparsity of the user-ratings matrix affects CBCF to a smaller degree than CF. To verify this hypothesis we ran the following experiments. A set of 1000 users were selected at random from the *EachMovie* data set. We treated 500 of these users as test users, and produced predictions on 25% of the items they rated. We artificially increased the sparsity

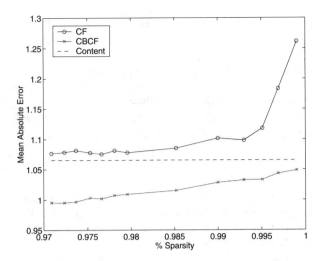

Figure 2: Effect of Sparsity on Prediction Accuracy

of the user-ratings matrix, by randomly dropping elements from the matrix. We compared the MAE of the different predictors at varying levels of sparsity. Figure 2 confirms our hypothesis that CBCF is more stable than CF with respect to sparsity. In fact, when sparsity exceeds 99%, the performance of CF drops precipitously, while CBCF is relatively unaffected. In the limit, CBCF will converge to pure content-based predictions.

Finding Better Neighbors

A crucial step in CF is the selection of a neighborhood. The neighbors of the active user entirely determine his predictions. It is therefore critical to select neighbors who are most similar to the active user. In pure CF, the neighborhood comprises of the users that have the best n correlations with the active user. The similarity between users is only determined by the ratings given to co-rated items; so items that have not been rated by both users are ignored. However, in CBCF, the similarity is based on the ratings contained in the pseudo user-ratings vectors; so users do not need to have a high overlap of co-rated items to be considered similar. Our claim is that this feature of CBCF, makes it possible to select a better, more representative neighborhood. For example, consider two users with identical tastes who have not rated any items in common. Pure collaborative filtering would not consider them similar. However, pseudo user-ratings vectors created using content-based predictions for the two users would be highly correlated, and therefore they would be considered neighbors. We believe that this superior selection of neighbors is one of the reasons that CBCF outperforms pure CF.

Improving CBCF

Due to the nature of our hybrid approach, we believe that improving the performance of the individual components would almost certainly improve the performance of the whole system. In other words, if we improved our pure content-based predictor or the CF algorithm, we would be able to improve our system's predictions. A better content-based predictor would mean that the pseudo ratings matrix generated would more accurately approximate the *actual* full user-ratings matrix. This in turn, would improve the chances of finding more representative neighbors. And since the final predictions in our system are based on a CF algorithm, a better CF algorithm can only improve our system's performance.

In our current implementation of the content-based predictor, we use a naive Bayesian text-classifier to learn a six-way classification task. This approach is probably not ideal, since it disregards the fact that classes represent ratings on a linear scale. This problem can be overcome by using a learning algorithm that can directly produce numerical predictions. For example, logistic regression and locally weighted regression (Duda, Hart, & Stork 2000) could be used to directly predict ratings from item content. We should be able to improve our content-based predictions using one of these approaches. In addition, the CF component in our system may be improved by using a *Clustered Pearson Predictor* (CPP) (Fisher *et al.* 2000). The CPP algorithm creates clusters of users based on k-means clustering. Collaborative predictions are made by only using the cluster centroids as potential neighbors. Fisher et al. claim that this approach is more accurate than the pure CF algorithm, with the added advantage of being more scalable.

Related Work

There have been a few other attempts to combine content information with collaborative filtering. One simple approach is to allow both content-based and collaborative filtering methods to produce separate recommendations, and then to directly combine their predictions (Cotter & Smyth 2000; Claypool, Gokhale, & Miranda 1999). In another approach (Soboroff & Nicholas 1999), the *term-document matrix* is multiplied with the user-ratings matrix to produce a *content-profile matrix*. Using Latent Semantic Indexing, a rank-k approximation of the content-profile matrix is computed. Term vectors of the user's relevant documents are averaged to produce a user's profile. Now, new documents are ranked against each user's profile in the LSI space. In Pazzani's approach (1999), each user-profile is represented by a vector of weighted words derived from positive training examples using the Winnow algorithm. Predictions are made by applying CF directly to the matrix of user-profiles (as opposed to the user-ratings matrix). An alternate approach, Fab (Balabanovic & Shoham 1997), uses relevance feedback to simultaneously mold a personal filter along with a communal "topic" filter. Documents are initially ranked by the topic filter and then sent to a user's personal filter. The user's relevance feedback is used to modify both the personal filter and the originating topic filter. In another approach, Basu et al. (1998) treat recommending as a classification task. They use *Ripper*, a rule induction system, to learn a function that takes a user and movie and predicts whether the movie will be liked or disliked. They combine collaborative and content information, by creating features such as *comedies liked by user* and *users who liked movies of genre X*. Good et al. (1999) use collaborative filtering along with a number of personalized information filtering agents. Predictions for a user are made by applying CF on the set of other users and the active user's personalized agents. Our method differs from this by also using CF on the personalized agents of the other users. In recent work, Lee (2001) treats the recommending task as the learning of a user's preference function that exploits item content as well as the ratings of similar users. They perform a study of several mixture models for this task. Popescul et al. (2001) extended Hofmann's aspect model to incorporate three-way co-occurrence data among users, items, and item content. They propose a method of dealing with sparsity that is similar to ours. They estimate the probability of a user accessing a document, that he has not seen before, by the average cosine similarity of the document to all the documents the user has seen. Our task differs from their's since we provide numerical ratings instead of just rankings. Also their approach is tied to the EM framework; whereas our approach is more modular and general, and as such it is independent of the choice of collaborative and content-based components.

Conclusions and Future Work

Incorporating content information into collaborative filtering can significantly improve predictions of a recommender system. In this paper, we have provided an effective way of achieving this. We have shown how Content-boosted Collaborative Filtering performs better than a pure content-based predictor, collaborative filtering, and a naive hybrid of the two.

CBCF elegantly exploits content within a collaborative framework. It overcomes the disadvantages of both collaborative filtering and content-based methods, by bolstering CF with content and vice versa. Further, due to the modular nature of our framework, any improvements in collaborative filtering or content-based recommending can be easily exploited to build a more powerful system.

Although CBCF performs consistently better than pure CF, the difference in performance is not very large (4%). The performance of our system can be boosted by using the methods described earlier. Experiments comparing the different approaches of combining content and collaboration, outlined in the previous section, are also needed.

Acknowledgments

We would like to thank Vishal Mishra for his web crawler and many useful discussions. We also thank Joydeep Ghosh and Inderjit Dhillon for their valuable advice during the course of this work. This research was supported by the National Science Foundation under grants IRI-9704943 and IIS-0117308.

References

Balabanovic, M., and Shoham, Y. 1997. Fab: Content-based, collaborative recommendation. *Communications of the Association of Computing Machinery* 40(3):66–72.

Basu, C.; Hirsh, H.; and Cohen, W. 1998. Recommendation as classification: Using social and content-based information in recommendation. In *Proceedings of the Fifteenth National Conference on Artificial Intelligence (AAAI-98)*, 714–720.

Claypool, M.; Gokhale, A.; and Miranda, T. 1999. Combining content-based and collaborative filters in an online newspaper. In *Proceedings of the SIGIR-99 Workshop on Recommender Systems: Algorithms and Evaluation*.

Cotter, P., and Smyth, B. 2000. PTV: Intelligent personalized TV guides. In *Twelfth Conference on Innovative Applications of Artificial Intelligence*, 957–964.

Duda, R. O.; Hart, P. E.; and Stork, D. G. 2000. *Pattern Classification*. New York: Wiley.

Fisher, D.; Hildrum, K.; Hong, J.; Newman, M.; Thomas, M.; and Vuduc, R. 2000. Swami: A framework for collaborative filtering algorithm development and evaluation. In *SIGIR 2000*. Short paper.

Goldberg, D.; Nichols, D.; Oki, B.; and Terry, D. 1992. Using collaborative filtering to weave an information tapestry. *Communications of the Association of Computing Machinery* 35(12):61–70.

Good, N.; Schafer, J. B.; Konstan, J. A.; Borchers, A.; Sarwar, B.; Herlocker, J.; and Riedl, J. 1999. Combining collaborative filtering with personal agents for better recommendations. In *Proceedings of the Sixteenth National Conference on Artificial Intelligence (AAAI-99)*, 439–446.

Herlocker, J.; Konstan, J.; Borchers, A.; and Riedl, J. 1999. An algorithmic framework for performing collaborative filtering. In *SIGIR '99: Proceedings of the 22nd Annual International ACM SIGIR Conference on Research and Development in Information Retrieval*, 230–237.

Lee, W. S. 2001. Collaborative learning for recommender systems. In *Proceedings of the Eighteenth International Conference on Machine Learning (ICML-2001)*, 314–321.

Mitchell, T. 1997. *Machine Learning*. New York, NY: McGraw-Hill.

Mooney, R. J., and Roy, L. 2000. Content-based book recommending using learning for text categorization. In *Proceedings of the Fifth ACM Conference on Digital Libraries*, 195–204.

Pazzani, M. J. 1999. A framework for collaborative, content-based and demographic filtering. *Artificial Intelligence Review* 13(5-6):393–408.

Popescul, A.; Ungar, L.; Pennock, D. M.; and Lawrence, S. 2001. Probabilistic models for unified collaborative and content-based recommendation in sparse-data environments. In *Proceedings of the Seventeenth Conference on Uncertainty in Artificial Intelligence*.

Resnick, P.; Iacovou, N.; Sushak, M.; Bergstrom, P.; and Reidl, J. 1994. GroupLens: An open architecture for collaborative filtering of netnews. In *Proceedings of the 1994 Computer Supported Cooperative Work Conference*. New York: ACM.

Soboroff, I., and Nicholas, C. 1999. Combining content and collaboration in text filtering. In Joachims, T., ed., *Proceedings of the IJCAI'99 Workshop on Machine Learning in Information Filtering*, 86–91.

Constructive Adaptive User Interfaces
— Composing Music Based on Human Feelings

Masayuki Numao, Shoichi Takagi, and **Keisuke Nakamura**

Department of Computer Science, Tokyo Institute of Technology

2-12-1 O-okayama, Meguro-ku, Tokyo 152-8552, Japan

numao@cs.titech.ac.jp

Abstract

We propose a method to locate relations and constraints between a music score and its impressions, by which we show that machine learning techniques may provide a powerful tool for composing music and analyzing human feelings. We examine its generality by modifying some arrangements to provide the subjects with a specified impression. This paper introduces some user interfaces, which are capable of predicting feelings and creating new objects based on seed structures, such as spectra and their transition for sounds that have been extracted and are perceived as favorable by the test subject.

Introduction

Music is a flow of information among its composer, player and audience. A composer writes a score that players play to create a sound to be listened by its audience as shown in Figure 1. Since a score, a performance or MIDI data denotes a section of the flow, we can know a feeling caused by a piece of score or performance. A feeling consists of a very complex elements, which depend on each person, and are affected by a historical situation. Therefore, rather than clarifying what a human feeling is, we would like to clarify only musical structures that cause a specific feeling. Based on such structures, the authors constructed an automatic arrangement and composition system producing a piece causing a specified feeling on a person.

The system first collects person's feelings for some pieces, based on which it extracts a common musical structure causing a specific feeling. It arranges an existing song or composes a new piece to fit such a structure causing a specified feeling. In the following sections, we describe how to extract a musical structure, some methods for arrangement or composition, and the results of experiments.

Extracting a musical structure

The system collects evaluation of some pieces in 5 grades for some adjective pairs via a web page as shown in Figure 2. The subject selects a music piece from the bottom menu containing 75 pieces, and evaluates it. The upper part

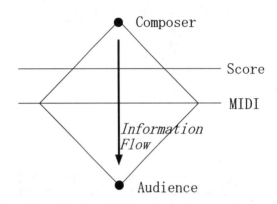

Figure 1: Information flow and authoring

is a MIDI player and a score. As well as the whole piece, it collects evaluation of each bar identified by $\boxed{1}$, $\boxed{2}$, ..., $\boxed{9}$. The middle part is a form to input evaluations, where the adjective pairs are written in Japanese.

To extract a structure that affects a feeling, the system analyzes some scores based on the theory of tonal music, i.e., ones with tonality, cadence, borrow chord structures, etc. For example, it automatically extracts rules to assign a chord to each function, or from two or three successive functions (Numao, Takagi, & Nakamura 2002). By using inductive logic programming — a machine learning method to find rules written in the programming language *PROLOG*, it is possible to find such a structure based on background knowledge, such as the theory of tonal music. Its procedure is as follows:

1. By using Osgood's semantic differential method in psychology, each subject evaluates 75 pieces by 6 adjective pairs[1], each of which is in 5 grades.

2. Find a condition to satisfy each adjective by using a machine learning method based on inductive logic programming. For the first stage, positive examples are structures in pieces whose evaluation is higher than or equal

---

[1](favorable, unfavorable), (bright, dark), (stable, unstable), (beautiful, ugly), (happy, unhappy), (heartrending, no heartrending).

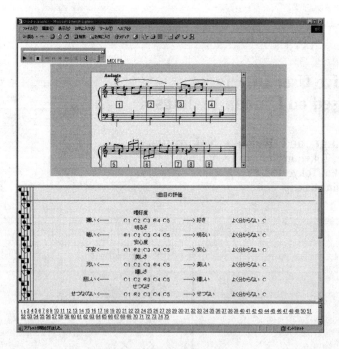

Figure 2: Gathering Evaluation

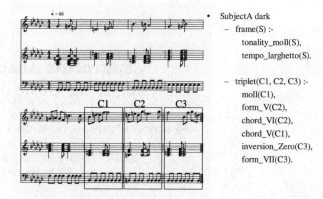

- SubjectA dark
  - frame(S) :-
    tonality_moll(S),
    tempo_larghetto(S).

  - triplet(C1, C2, C3) :-
    moll(C1),
    form_V(C2),
    chord_VI(C2),
    chord_V(C1),
    inversion_Zero(C3),
    form_VII(C3).

Figure 3: Acquiring predicates.

to 5. Other structures are negative examples. This gives a generalized structure whose evaluation is better than 5 by each adjective pair. This condition earns 5 points for the adjective pair.

3. Similarly, find a condition to accomplish evaluation better than 4. This condition earns 4 points.

The condition for the opposite adjective, such as *dark, unfavorable* and *unstable*, earns $6 - g$ points, where g is the grade given by the user. Since 75 pieces are too many to be evaluated in one session, the subjects evaluate them in multiple sessions by comparing a pair of some chosen pieces multiple times.

Each rule is described by a predicate rather than an attribute, since it is hard to describe a score by using only some attributes. PROLOG describes each condition, whose predicates are defined in background knowledge (Numao, Kobayashi, & Sakaniwa 1997). We prepare the following predicates in PROLOG to describe a musical structure, where frame is the name of predicate and /1 is the number of arguments:

1. frame/1 represents the whole framework of music, i.e., tonality, rhythm and instruments.

2. pair/2 represents a pattern of two successive chords.

3. triplet/3 represents a pattern of three successive chords.

For example, we can describe that a subject likes a piece whose tonality is E major or E minor, tempo is Allegretto, accompanying instrument is piano, rhythm is 4/4, and contains a specified pair of successive chords.

To acquire such conditions, we use Inductive Logic Programming (ILP), which is a machine learning method to find

a PROLOG program. A score is represented by a symbol, where a relation between two notes are important. These mean that ILP is a good tool for generalizing a score. Figure 3 shows a score and its generalization described in PROLOG. The variables C1, C2 and C3 represent successive bars. These clauses mean that *SubjectA* feels a piece dark when its tonality is moll (minor), its tempo is larghetto, the first chord is moll V, the second is triad (form_V) VI, and the third is 7th root position (inversion_Zero) chord.

Arrangement

The authors constructed the arranger and the composer separately, since arrangement is easier than composition, i.e., the composer is much slower than the arranger. The following method arranges a piece by minimally changing its chord sequence to cause the required feeling:

1. Analyze the original chords to recognize their function, e.g., tonic, dominant, subdominant, etc.

2. Modify each chord to satisfy the acquired conditions without changing its function.

3. Modify the original melody minimally to fit the modified sequence of chords.

This is accomplished by the following windowing procedure:

1. Set a window on the first three chords.

2. Enumerate the all chords with the same function to satisfy the acquired predicates pair and triplet. Sum up the points of acquired predicates to evaluate each chord sequence.

3. Shift the window by two, i.e., set a new window on the last chord and its two successors. Enumerate the chords similarly to the above.

4. Repeat the above to find a sequence with the most points.

5. Repeat the above for the all 12 tonality. Determine the tonality that earns the most points.

6. Determine the frame that earns the most points.

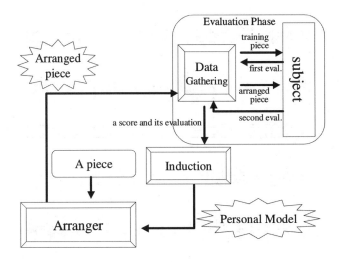

Figure 4: Arranger

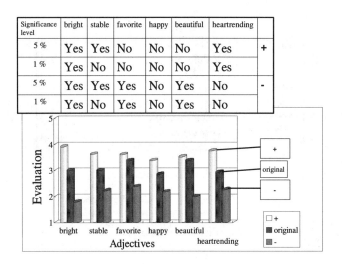

Significance level	bright	stable	favorite	happy	beautiful	heartrending	
5 %	Yes	Yes	No	No	No	Yes	+
1 %	Yes	No	No	No	No	Yes	
5 %	Yes	Yes	Yes	No	Yes	No	−
1 %	Yes	No	Yes	No	Yes	No	

Figure 5: Evaluation of arrangements

The authors prepared 75 well-known music pieces without modulation[2], from which they extracted 8 or 16 successive bars. For automatic arrangement they prepared other three pieces. The flow of experiment is shown in Figure 4. The subject evaluated each piece as one of 5 grades for 6 pairs of adjectives: *bright - dark, stable - unstable, favorable - unfavorable, beautiful - ugly, happy - unhappy, heartrending - no heartrending*. For each adjective pair the system constructed a personal model of feeling, based on which it tried to arrange the prepared three pieces into ones causing a specified feeling, which were evaluated by the same subject.

The system was supplied 3 original pieces, and alternatively specified 6 adjective pairs, i.e., 12 adjectives. Therefore, it produced $3 * 12 = 36$ arranged pieces, whose average evaluation by the subjects is shown in Figure 5. In the figure, '+' denotes a *positive arrangement (composition)*, which is a bright, stable, favorable, beautiful, happy or heartrending arrangement (composition). '−' denotes a *negative arrangement (composition)*, which is the opposite: dark, unstable, unfavorable, ugly, unhappy, no heartrending. The results show that the positive arrangements resulted in higher evaluation, and that the negative arrangements resulted in lower evaluation for all the adjective pairs. According to the table in Figure 5, many of the results are statistically significant.

After the experiments in (Numao, Kobayashi, & Sakaniwa 1997), the system has been improved in collecting evaluation of each bar, introducing `triplet/3` and `frame/1`, and the search mechanism for chord progression. The above results support their effects.

Composition

Based on a collection of conditions ILP derives, we have obtained a personal model to evaluate a chord progression. A genetic algorithm (GA) produces a chord progression by using the model for its fitness function. Such a chord progres-

---

[2]39 Japanese *JPOP* songs and 36 pieces from classic music or textbooks for harmonics.

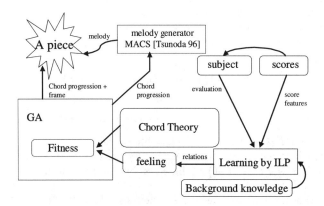

Figure 6: Composing system

sion utilizes a melody generator to compose a piece from scratch rather than to arrange a given piece. The procedure to compose music based on a personal feeling is described in Figure 6. The subject evaluates each piece as one of 5 grades for the 6 pairs of adjectives. The ILP system finds relations between a set of score features and its evaluation, which are described by the predicates defined in background knowledge. These relations describe a feeling, based on which a genetic algorithm produces a chord progression.

A genotype, operators and a fitness function are important in genetic algorithms. Figure 7 shows the genotype for producing a chord progression. To represent complicated parameters, a bit string in GA is extended to a matrix, where a bit is extended to a column in the matrix. Therefore, the crossover operator splits and exchanges a string of columns. The fitness function reflects a music theory and the personal model:

$$Fitness\_Function(M) =$$
$$Fitness\_Builtin(M) + Fitness\_User(M)$$

where M is a score described by a predicate `music/2`.

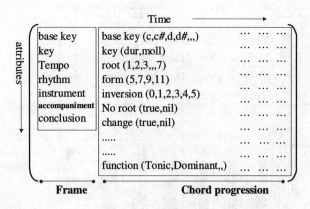

Figure 7: Genotype

Figure 8: A created bright piece

This makes possible to produce a chord progression that fits the theory and causes the required feeling. $Fitness\_Builtin(M)$ is a fitness function based on the theory of tonal music, which issues a penalty to a chord progression violating the theory. $Fitness\_User(M)$ is based on the extracted musical structures that reflect the subject's feelings:

$$Fitness\_User(M) = Fitness\_Frame(M)$$
$$+ Fitness\_Pair(M)$$
$$+ Fitness\_Triplet(M)$$

where $Fitness\_Frame(M)$ is fitness based on tonality, rhythm and instruments, etc. $Fitness\_Pair(M)$ and $Fitness\_Triplet(M)$ are based on two or three successive chords, respectively.

For producing a piece, the system uses MACS (Tsunoda 1996), which generates a melody from a chord progression and some rules for the duration. Since MACS is a black box containing complicated program codes, the authors start a new project to find simple rules describing the process, which clarifies the process of generating a melody.

Figure 8 and 9 show created pieces. Figure 8 is a piece the system tried to make bright. Figure 9 is one it tried to make dark. These examples show that the system composes a bright piece without handcrafted background knowledge on brightness and by automatically acquiring some musical structures that cause a bright feeling. Other created pieces are shown in (Numao, Takagi, & Nakamura 2002).

Figure 10 shows evaluation of the composed pieces. '+' shows the average result of pieces the system tried to make positive. '-' shows that it tried to make negative. According to Student's t-test, they are different for 4 adjective pairs at the level of significance $\alpha = 0.05$. They are different for 2 pairs at the level $\alpha = 0.01$. Figure 11 shows the effect of melody, which is dramatic in some adjective pairs.

This system is profoundly different from other composing systems in that it composes based on a personal model extracted from a subject by using a machine learning method. A composing system using an interactive genetic algorithm (IGA), such as GenJam (Biles 2002), may be similar method to ours in that it creates a piece based on the user interaction.

However, IGA generally requires far more interactions than ours, which reduces the number of interactions by utilizing a personal model generalized from examples, although the detailed comparison between GenJam and ours is a future work. Other advantages are that we can recycle a personal model in many compositions, and manually tailor a predicate in the system to improve its performance.

Related Work

In algorithmic music composition, a simple technique involves selecting notes sequentially according to a transition table that specifies the probability of the next note as a function of the previous context. Mozer (1994) proposed an extension of this transition table approach using a recurrent autopredictive connectionist network. Our system is more flexible than this in that the user specifies an adjective to change impressions of a created piece.

Wiggins (1999) proposed to apply genetic algorithms to music composition. Our method combines a genetic algorithm with a personal model acquired by machine learning.

Widmer (1994) proposed a method of accomplishing explanation-based learning by attaching harmonies — chord symbols to the notes of a melody. The present paper further discusses a means of controlling the process based on learned feelings.

Hirata (1999, 1996) constructed a reharmonizing and arranging system based on a knowledge representation in Deductive Object-Oriented Databases (DOOD). Our system is different in adaptation mechanism by acquiring a personal model.

Thom (2000) proposed to apply unsupervised learning to interactive Jazz/Blues improvisation. In contrast, our method is an application of inductive learning, i.e., supervised learning. Hörnell's system produces and harmonizes

Figure 9: A created dark piece

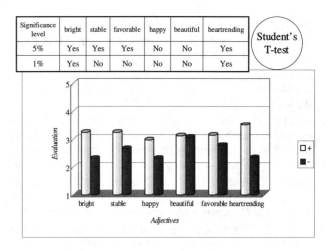

Significance level	bright	stable	favorable	happy	beautiful	heartrending	Student's T-test
5%	Yes	Yes	Yes	No	No	Yes	
1%	Yes	No	No	No	No	Yes	

Figure 10: Evaluation of Composition

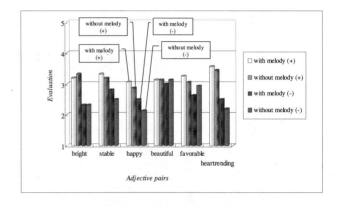

Figure 11: Effects of melodies

simple folk style melodies based on learned musical structure (Hörnel & Ragg 1996). Dannenberg, Thom and Watson (1997) apply machine learning techniques to musical style recognition. Our method is different from them in its emotional-driven generation of music.

The Wolfgang system utilizes emotions to enable learning to compose music (Riecken 1998). It is an interesting research topic to compare its cultural grammar and our PROLOG rules based on the semantic differential method. Emotional coloring (Bresin 2000) is an interesting research in the field of automatic music performance with a special focus on piano, although automatic composition is out of its scope.

Conclusion

Pat Langley (1998) proposed an adaptive user interface to be applied to a navigation system (Rogers, Fiechter, & Langley 1999). Our method extends the concept of adaptive user interfaces in a sense that it constructs a new description adaptively. That is why we call our system a *constructive* adaptive user interface.

Acknowledgements

The authors would like to thank Pat Langley and Dan Shapiro, who gave fruitful comments, when one of the authors gave a talk at Center for the Study of Language and Information, Stanford University.

References

Biles, J. A. 2002. Genjam. http://www.it.rit.edu/~jab/GenJam.html.

Bresin, R. 2000. *Virtual Virtuosity*. Ph.D. Dissertation, Kungl Tekniska Högskolan, Stockholm.

Dannenberg, R. B.; Thom, B. T.; and Watson, D. 1997. A machine learning approach to musical style recognition. In *Proc. ICMC97*.

Hirata, K., and Aoyagi, T. 1999. Musically intelligent agent for composition and interactive performance. In *Proc. ICMC*, 167–170.

Hirata, K. 1996. Representation of jazz piano knowledge using a deductive object-oriented approach. In *Proc. ICMC*.

Hörnel, D., and Ragg, T. 1996. Learning musical structure and style by recognition, prediction and evoloution. In *Proc. ICMC*. International Computer Music Association.

Langley, P. 1998. Machine learning for adaptive user interfaces. In *CSLI-Stanford University IAP Spring Tutorials*, 155–164.

Michalski, R. S., and Tecuci, G., eds. 1994. *Machine Learning: A Multistrategy Approach (Vol. IV)*. San Francisco, CA: Morgan Kaufmann.

Mozer, M. 1994. Neural network music composition by prediction: Exploring the benefits of psychoacoustic constraints and multiscale processing. *Connection Science*.

Numao, M.; Kobayashi, M.; and Sakaniwa, K. 1997. Acquisition of human feelings in music arrangement. In *Proc. IJCAI 97*, 268–273. Morgan Kaufmann.

Numao, M.; Takagi, S.; and Nakamura, K. 2002. CAUI demonstration — composing music based on human feelings. In *Proc. AAAI 2002*. AAAI Press.

Riecken, D. 1998. Wolfgang: "emotions" and architecture which enable learning to compose music. SAB'98 Workshop on Graounding Emotions in Adaptive Systems. http://www.ai.univie.ac.at/ paolo/conf/sab98/sab98sub.html.

Rogers, S.; Fiechter, C.-N.; and Langley, P. 1999. An adaptive interactive agent for route advice. In *Proc. the Third International Conference on Autonomous Agents*, 198–205.

Thom, B. 2000. Unsupervised learning and interactive Jazz/Blues improvisation. In *AAAI/IAAI*, 652–657.

Tsunoda, K. 1996. Computer-supported composition of music. Master Thesis, University of Mie.

Widmer, G. 1994. Learning with a qualitative domain theory by means of plausible explanations. In *(Michalski & Tecuci 1994)*. chapter 25, 635–655.

Wiggins, G., et al. 1999. Evolutionary methods for musical composition. *International Journal of Computing Anticipatory Systems*.

Reinforcement Learning for POMDPs based on Action Values and Stochastic Optimization

Theodore J. Perkins

Department of Computer Science
University of Massachusetts Amherst
140 Governor's Drive
Amherst, MA 01003
perkins@cs.umass.edu

Abstract

We present a new, model-free reinforcement learning algorithm for learning to control partially-observable Markov decision processes. The algorithm incorporates ideas from action-value based reinforcement learning approaches, such as Q-Learning, as well as ideas from the stochastic optimization literature. Key to our approach is a new definition of action value, which makes the algorithm theoretically sound for partially-observable settings. We show that special cases of our algorithm can achieve probability one convergence to locally optimal policies in the limit, or probably approximately correct hill-climbing to a locally optimal policy in a finite number of samples.

Introduction

Many intelligent agents face sequential decision problems that are naturally and realistically formulated as partially-observable Markov decision processes (POMDPs). Often, however, the dynamics of an agent's environment and observations are unknown. And even when these dynamics are known, finding optimal solutions is usually NP-hard or harder, depending on the type of solution required (Littman 1994; Madani, Condon, & Hanks 1999). For such problems, reinforcement learning (RL) methods are an attractive option for finding approximate solutions.

The simplest RL approach is to ignore the fact that the agent's environment is partially observable. Standard RL algorithms such as Q-Learning or Sarsa(λ) can be applied by treating observations as if they were states of a Markov decision problem (MDP). Researchers were quick to point out that this approach can lead to suboptimal behavior or, worse, that the parameters adjusted by the learning algorithm can fail to converge or even diverge (Whitehead 1992; Baird 1995). Allowing the agent to condition its learning on the recent history of observations (McCallum 1995) or to use an internal memory can sometimes alleviate these difficulties. And empirically, Sarsa(λ) and Monte Carlo approaches appear quite robust to partial observability (Pendrith & Ryan 1996; Loch & Singh 1998). However, Sarsa(λ) and Monte Carlo approaches can fail to converge even on some very simple problems (Gordon 1996). As long as the agent's representation of the environment is not fully Markov, the theoretical soundness of applying such action-value based RL algorithms is questionable.

Partly as a response to this situation, learning algorithms that perform various kinds of stochastic gradient descent on a fixed error function have been developed (Williams 1992; Baird & Moore 1999; Sutton *et al.* 2000). Usually, such algorithms search through a continuous space of stochastic policies which condition action choice on the agent's immediate observation, or on the immediate observation plus the state of an internal memory. Under appropriate conditions, these algorithms converge to a policy that is at least locally optimal. The evidence to date suggests that these algorithms learn much more slowly than action-value based RL algorithms such as Sarsa(λ), though this question is still under study.

Our aim is to provide an algorithm that is similar in design and empirical performance to the better action-value based RL algorithms, but which enjoys superior theoretical properties, similar to those of the gradient-based approaches. Our algorithm is most similar to the Monte-Carlo Exploring Starts algorithm for MDPs (Sutton & Barto 1998), and thus we call it Monte-Carlo Exploring Starts for POMDPs (MCESP). In its simplest version, MCESP maintains a table of observation-action values, which are updated based on Monte-Carlo samples of the return. Key to our algorithm is a new definition of action value, which is inspired by the fixed-point analyses of Pendrith and McGarity (1998). Under this definition, action values give information about the value of policies in a local neighborhood of the current policy. MCESP can be interpreted as a theoretically-sound algorithm for performing local search through the discrete space of policies that map observations to actions.

MCESP's free parameters can be chosen to incorporate a number of existing ideas from the stochastic optimization literature. Experiments reported in the final section, however, demonstrate that the strength of MCESP lies not only in its connections to stochastic optimization. The RL-style updating of action values can produce performance that is superior to existing, standard optimization approaches, and competitive with the best reported RL results, which are due to Sarsa(λ) (Loch & Singh 1998).

Problem Formulation

We assume the agent's environment is modeled as a POMDP (see, e.g., McCallum 1995) with an arbitrary underlying MDP, but with a finite observation set O. When the environment emits observation $o \in O$, the agent chooses an action a from a finite set $A(o)$. A deterministic, reactive policy, π, is a function that maps each $o \in O$ to some $a \in A(o)$. The agent's task is to learn a good deterministic, reactive policy, based on experience gathered in the POMDP.[1]

We consider episodic tasks, in which there is a start-state distribution and one or more terminal states, and we assume that episodes terminate with probability one under any policy. Let $\tau = \{o_0, a_0, r_0, o_1, a_1, r_1, o_2, a_2, r_2, \ldots, o_T\}$ denote a trajectory in the POMDP, where o_T is an observation corresponding to a terminal state. We assume that every policy, π, generates a well-defined probability measure, $\mu(\pi)$, over the set of all possible trajectories. This probability measure also depends on the start-state distribution of the POMDP and the underlying MDP, but we suppress these in the notation, since they are constant. Let $R(\tau) = \sum_{t=0}^{T} \gamma^t r_t$ denote the discounted return in trajectory τ, where $\gamma \in [0, 1]$ is a discount factor. We define the value of π as the expected discounted return:

$$V^\pi = E_{\tau \sim \mu(\pi)} \{R(\tau)\} ,$$

which we assume to be well-defined for all π. We can write the policy value more briefly as $V^\pi = E^\pi \{R(\tau)\}$.

An important aspect of MCESP is its interpretation as a local search algorithm. We consider policies π and π' neighbors if they assign the same action to all observations except one. π is locally optimal if $V^\pi \geq V^{\pi'}$ for all neighbors π'. More generally, π is ϵ-locally optimal if $V^\pi + \epsilon \geq V^{\pi'}$ for all neighbors π'.

Defining Action Value

In MDPs, the value of state-action pair (s, a) with respect to policy π is usually defined as the expected discounted return if the environment starts in state s, the agent takes action a, and then follows π afterward (Sutton & Barto 1998). Our definition of observation-action values for POMDPs differs in several key respects. We present our definition first, and then contrast it with the standard definition for MDPs.

Let τ be a trajectory and o an observation. We define $R_{pre-o}(\tau)$ to be the portion of $R(\tau)$ coming before the first occurrence of o in τ, if any; and we define $R_{post-o}(\tau)$ to be the portion of $R(\tau)$ following the first occurrence of o in τ, if there is one, and zero otherwise. For example, if o first occurs in τ at time step j, then $R_{pre-o}(\tau) = \sum_{i=0}^{j-1} \gamma^i r_i$ and $R_{post-o}(\tau) = \sum_{i=j}^{\infty} \gamma^i r_i$. Note that for any o, we can rewrite the value of a policy as:

$$
\begin{aligned}
V^\pi &= E^\pi \{R(\tau)\} \\
&= E^\pi \{R_{pre-o}(\tau)\} + E^\pi \{R_{post-o}(\tau)\} .
\end{aligned}
$$

[1] More generally, the POMDP's observation set can be infinite and the agent's actions can depend on the history of observations, rewards, and actions—as long the agent can be described as mapping each history to one of a finite number of table entries and associating to each entry a value for each action. That is, the agent aggregates the set of all histories into a finite number of partitions.

This motivates our definition of the value of observation-action pair (o, a) with respect to a policy π. Let $\pi \leftarrow (o, a)$ represent the policy that is identical to π except that observation o is mapped to action a. (Of course, $\pi \leftarrow (o, \pi(o))$ is just π.) Then we define:

$$Q_{o,a}^\pi = E^{\pi \leftarrow (o,a)} \{R_{post-o}(\tau)\} .$$

In words, $Q_{o,a}^\pi$ is the portion of the expected return that follows the first occurrence of o, if the agent takes action a whenever it observes o and adheres to π otherwise. This definition differs in three key respects from the standard state-action value definition for MDPs. First, the notion of starting in state s is replaced by a first occurrence of observation o. Second, the agent does not take action a and then follow π afterward. The agent takes action a and follows $\pi \leftarrow (o, a)$ afterward. In other words, the agent takes action a every time it sees observation o. Third, the observation-action value is the portion of the policy's expected discounted return that follows o, not the discounted return following o itself. This makes a difference in how the discount factor comes into play if o's first occurrence can happen at different times in different trajectories—the later o occurs, the less the return following o contributes to the overall policy value. Consider, for example, two trajectories, with reward sequences $\{r_0, r_1, r_2, \ldots, r_T\}$ and $\{r'_0, r'_1, r'_2, \ldots, r'_{T'}\}$. Suppose that in the first trajectory, o occurs on time step 2, and in the other, o occurs on time step 4. Then the first trajectory contributes $\gamma^2 r_2 + \gamma^3 r_3 + \ldots + \gamma^T r_T$ to the observation-action value, and the second trajectory contributes $\gamma^4 r'_4 + \gamma^5 r'_5 + \ldots + \gamma^{T'} r'_{T'}$. Under the standard definition, the trajectories would contribute $r_2 + \gamma r_3 + \ldots + \gamma^{T-2} r_T$ and $r'_4 + \gamma r'_5 + \ldots + \gamma^{T'-4} r'_{T'}$, respectively.

In MDPs, a policy is optimal if and only if it is greedy with respect to its action values (as normally defined). This is not necessarily true of the action values learned by Q-Learning or Sarsa(λ), for example, when applied to POMDPs. The theoretical motivation for our definition of action value is that it preserves this property, to some degree, in POMDPs.

Theorem 1 *For all π and $\pi' = \pi \leftarrow (o, a)$,*

$$V^\pi + \epsilon \geq V^{\pi'} \iff Q_{o,\pi(o)}^\pi + \epsilon \geq Q_{o,a}^\pi .$$

Proof: Let π be any policy and let $\pi' = \pi \leftarrow (o, a)$ be a neighboring policy. Then:

$$
\begin{aligned}
& V^\pi + \epsilon \geq V^{\pi'} \\
\iff & E^\pi \{R_{pre-o}(\tau)\} + E^\pi \{R_{post-o}(\tau)\} + \epsilon \\
& \qquad \geq E^{\pi'} \{R_{pre-o}(\tau)\} + E^{\pi'} \{R_{post-o}(\tau)\} \\
\iff & E^\pi \{R_{post-o}(\tau)\} + \epsilon \geq E^{\pi \leftarrow (o,a)} \{R_{post-o}(\tau)\} \\
\iff & Q_{o,\pi(o)}^\pi + \epsilon \geq Q_{o,a}^\pi .
\end{aligned}
$$

The middle equivalence holds because the portion of the expected discounted return before the first occurrence of o cannot depend on the action taken from observation o. $\square$

Corollary 1 *A policy is locally optimal if and only if it is greedy with respect to its action values (as we have defined them). A policy π is ϵ-locally optimal if and only if $Q_{o,\pi(o)}^\pi + \epsilon \geq Q_{o,a}^\pi$ for all o and a.*

```
MCESP(Q,π,α,ε)
```
Inputs: initial action values Q, policy π that is greedy w.r.t. Q, and learning rate and comparison threshold schedules α and ϵ.

```
 1:  c_{o,a} ← 0 for all o and a.
 2:  n ← 0
 3:  repeat
 4:      Choose some o and a ∈ A(o).
 5:      Generate a trajectory, τ, according to π ← (o, a).
 6:      Q_{o,a} ← (1 − α(n, c_{o,a}))Q_{o,a} + α(n, c_{o,a})R_{post−o}(τ)
 7:      c_{o,a} ← c_{o,a} + 1
 8:      if max_{a'} Q_{o,a'} − ε(n, c_{o,a'}, c_{o,π(o)}) > Q_{o,π(o)} then
 9:          π(o) ← a' ∈ arg max_{a'} Q_{o,a'} − ε(n, c_{o,a'}, c_{o,π(o)})
10:          n ← n + 1
11:          c_{o'',a''} ← 0 for all o'' and a''
12:      end if
13:  until Termination
```

Figure 1: The MCESP algorithm.

The MCESP Algorithm

In this section, we present the MCESP learning algorithm, which is based on the definition of action value above. The algorithm is displayed in Figure 1. It maintains a table of action values, Q, a current policy, π, a count of the number of times the current policy has changed, n, and counts, c, of the number of times each observation-action pair has been updated since the last policy change. At the beginning of each trial, the algorithm chooses some observation-action pair (o, a) to "explore." It follows the policy $\pi \leftarrow (o, a)$ for the whole trial, producing a trajectory, τ. The action value $Q_{o,a}$ is updated based on $R_{post−o}(\tau)$, and the algorithm checks if the current policy should change. The learning rates for action value updates follow a schedule, α, which depends on the number of policy changes since the algorithm began and on the number of updates the action value has received since the policy last changed. When checking whether the current policy should change as a result of an update, the algorithm compares the on-policy action value, $Q_{o,\pi(o)}$, with the off-policy action values $Q_{o,a'}$ for $a' \neq \pi(o)$. For a change to occur, it requires that $Q_{o,a'} > Q_{o,\pi(o)} + \epsilon$, where ϵ is a comparison threshold. (In Figure 1 this is written as $Q_{o,a'} − \epsilon > Q_{o,\pi(o)}$.) The ϵ allows one to express, for example, that an off-policy action must appear significantly better than the on-policy action before a change is made. Comparison thresholds are allowed to vary, depending on the number of policy changes so far and the number of times each of the action values involved in the comparison have been updated since the last policy change.

This general presentation of the algorithm leaves open a number of choices: how observation-action pairs are chosen for exploration, how learning rates and comparison thresholds are scheduled, and under what conditions the algorithm terminates. By making different choices for these, MCESP can incorporate various ideas from reinforcement learning and stochastic optimization. We begin by discussing a version of MCESP that estimates action values by taking a fixed number of samples and then comparing the sample averages. Next, we describe a version of MCESP based on Greiner's PALO algorithm which offers a PAC-style guarantee of hill-climbing to a local optimum. And lastly, we describe a set of conditions that ensure MCESP converges to a locally optimal policy in the limit. There are many other specializations of MCESP that might be of interest, and we mention some of these in the conclusion section.

The Sample Average Approximation

If the agent does not know the dynamics of the POMDP it must solve, then it cannot exactly evaluate any policy. But it can estimate a policy's value by generating some fixed number of trajectories, k, under the policy and computing the average discounted return. In the stochastic optimization literature, this has been called the sample average approximation (e.g., Kleywegt *et al.* 2001). The idea has also appeared in a number of PAC-style results in the RL literature (e.g., Ng and Jordan 2000).

A local search procedure based on this principle proceeds in stages, where at each stage k samples are taken of the value of a current policy and of each neighboring policy. If no neighbor has a better sample average than the current policy, the algorithm terminates. Otherwise, the neighbor with the best average becomes the current policy for the next stage. MCESP can reproduce this behavior by: 1) choosing observation-action pairs for exploration in simple round-robin fashion; 2) letting $\alpha(n, i) = \frac{1}{i+1}$, corresponding to simple averaging of the sample discounted returns; 3) letting $\epsilon(n, i, j) = +\infty$ if $i < k$ or $j < k$ and 0 otherwise, which effectively rules out comparison if fewer than k samples have been taken of either action value; 4) terminating if no policy changes are recommended after taking k samples of the value of each observation-action pair. If these particular choices are made, we call the resulting algorithm MCESP-SAA.

If k is small, then one expects the action-value estimates to be poor. MCESP-SAA could easily switch to a worse policy or stop erroneously at a policy that is not locally optimal. If k is large, then action-value estimates should be good, and MCESP-SAA should move strictly uphill and stop at the first locally-optimal solution it encounters. The next version of MCESP that we consider provides a PAC-style guarantee of the latter type of behavior.

PAC Hill-Climbing

Greiner's PALO algorithm is a general method for hill-climbing in the solution space of a stochastic optimization problem with finite local neighborhood structure (Greiner 1996). Given any ϵ and δ, PALO traverses, with probability at least $1 − \delta$, a sequence of solutions that is of strictly improving quality and terminates at a solution that is ϵ-locally optimal. At each stage, n, PALO determines a number, k_n, of samples that should be taken of the value of each solution in the current neighborhood. After k_n samples, PALO applies a simple threshold test based on Hoeffding's inequality to determine if any neighbor is sufficiently better than the current solution to warrant a switch. PALO also includes more stringent tests that allow it to move to a neighbor or terminate before a full k_n samples are taken, if the evidence is overwhelming. The number of samples taken at each step, k_n, is polynomial in $\frac{1}{\epsilon}$ and logarithmic in $\frac{1}{\delta}$ and n.

MCESP can implement PALO's strategy. As in the previous section, MCESP should sample observation-action pairs in round-robin fashion, and use learning rates that correspond to simple averaging (i.e., $\alpha(n, i) = \frac{1}{i+1}$). Suppose that N is an upper bound on the size of any policy's neighborhood, and suppose that all samples of observation-action values fall in some range $[x, y] \subset \Re$. Let $\delta_n = \frac{6\delta}{n^2\pi^2}$ and $k_n = \left\lceil 2\frac{(y-x)^2}{\epsilon^2} \ln \frac{2N}{\delta_n} \right\rceil$. Then MCESP reproduces PALO's comparison tests with the threshold schedule:

$$\epsilon(n, i, j) = \begin{cases} (y-x)\sqrt{\frac{1}{2i} \ln \left(\frac{2(k_n-1)N}{\delta_n} \right)} & \text{if } i = j < k_n \\ \frac{\epsilon}{2} & \text{if } i = j = k_n \\ +\infty & \text{otherwise} . \end{cases}$$

Note that thresholds are only finite when $i = j$. In PALO's formulation, "one sample" constitutes one sample from every member of the current neighborhood, thus there is never an issue of some members having been sampled more times than others. We could, of course, allow for comparisons when $i \neq j$. But to remain faithful to PALO as originally defined, we choose not to do so. The algorithm terminates if, after k_n samples, no policy change is triggered, or if, after i samples have been taken of each action value,

$$Q_{o,a} < Q_{o,\pi(o)} + \epsilon - (y-x)\sqrt{\frac{1}{2i} \ln \left(\frac{2(k_n-1)N}{\delta_n} \right)} ,$$

for all o and all $a \neq \pi(o)$. We call this version MCESP-PALO. The theorem below follows from Theorem 1 of Greiner (1996) and Corollary 1.

Theorem 2 *For any $\delta \in (0, 1)$ and $\epsilon > 0$, with probability at least $1 - \delta$, MCESP-PALO traverses a sequence of policies $\pi_0, \pi_1, \ldots, \pi_T$ and terminates, where each policy is of strictly greater value than the previous policy and π_T is ϵ-locally optimal.*

Probability One Convergence to Locally Optimal Policies

Because samples of action values are stochastic, it is not possible to guarantee that a policy is ϵ-locally optimal after any finite number of samples. Suppose, however, that MCESP takes samples of a particular policy's action values indefinitely. If the policy is not ϵ-locally optimal, then eventually the action value estimates should indicate that fact, prompting a switch to another policy. If, after n policy changes, MCESP delays comparing action values until k_n samples are taken, and if $\lim_{n\to\infty} k_n = \infty$, then MCESP should eventually converge to an ϵ-locally optimal policy. As n increases, the precision of the action value estimates by the time they start to be compared increases. For high enough n, MCESP should never mistakenly leave a strictly ϵ-locally

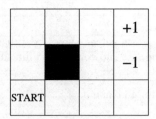

Figure 2: Parr's and Russell's Gridworld

optimal policy and should always leave a non-ϵ-locally optimal policy for some better one. Interestingly, it is not necessary to wait for increasing periods before comparing action values, nor is it necessary to combine samples using simple averaging, or to use "slow" learning rates so that data has a chance to accumulate before a change can occur.

Theorem 3 *If the initial action value estimates and all samples of action values are contained in some $[x, y] \subset \Re$; $\epsilon(n, i, j) = \epsilon_0$ for all n, i, j; $l_i \leq \alpha(n, i) \leq u_i$ for all n, where $\{l_i\}$ and $\{u_i\}$ are Robbins-Monroe sequences[2]; and observation-action pairs are selected for exploration at random with each pair having at least probability $p_{min} > 0$ of being selected on any trial; then with probability 1, MCESP converges to an ϵ_0-locally optimal policy (i.e., an ϵ_0-locally optimal policy becomes the current policy at some time, and remains the current policy forever).*

We call this version MCESP-CE, for "constant epsilon." This theorem does not follow directly from existing theory, and, unfortunately, our proof is rather detailed and does not fit the space available. A full proof will be available in a technical report.

Our theorems on MCESP-PALO and MCESP-CE discuss termination or convergence to ϵ-locally optimal policies. We note that, since the policy space is finite, for sufficiently small ϵ, all ϵ-locally optimal policies are simply locally optimal. However, that ϵ may not be known, and a more theoretically pleasing solution is to let comparison thresholds decrease over time, so that convergence to locally optimal policies is guaranteed. We are presently working on schedules for achieving this goal.

Experiments

We experimented with MCESP and Sarsa(λ) in Parr's and Russell's partially observable gridworld domain (Parr & Russell 1995). This problem is small enough that we were able to exactly evaluate every possible policy using off-line dynamic programming. This yields a deeper understanding of the problem and sheds light on the experimental results we obtained. At the same time, the problem is large enough to demonstrate interesting structure of the sort expected in larger, more realistic domains.

The domain is depicted in Figure 2. The 11 open squares represent possible locations of the agent. Each trial starts with the agent in the "START" square and ends after 100

[2] $\{x_i\}_{i=0}^{\infty}$ is a Robbins-Monroe sequence if $x_i \in [0, 1]$ for all i, $\sum_i x_i = \infty$, and $\sum_i x_i^2 < \infty$.

timesteps or when the agent enters the $+1$ or -1 squares, which give terminal rewards of $+1$ and -1 respectively. All other transitions receive a reward of -0.04. In each state, the agent may take one of four actions: Up, Right, Down, or Left, which move the agent in the named direction with probability 0.8, and in one of the perpendicular directions, each with probability 0.1. If one of these transitions would take the agent outside the maze or into the black square, the agent stays in place instead. The problem is partially observable because the agent only observes whether or not there is an open square to the left and whether or not there is on open square to the right. Thus, the POMDP has 11 states, 4 non-terminal observations, and just $4^4 = 256$ reactive policies.

Using dynamic programming to compute the values of all 256 reactive policies, we found that 118 have zero probability of reaching either of the terminal states. Such policies have value -4.0. 17 of those policies are non-strict local optima, being completely surrounded by other policies of their kind; we call these the bad locally optimal policies. There is a single globally-optimal policy with value 0.303470. Thus, the policy space is qualitatively characterized as having a plateau of minimal-value policies, some of them locally optimal, and a single peak corresponding to the unique, globally-optimal policy.

We experimented with various versions of MCESP: MCESP-SAA with $k \in \{1, 2, \ldots, 9\} \cup \{10, 20, \ldots, 90\} \cup \{100, 200, \ldots, 1000\}$; MCESP-PALO with $\epsilon = 0.01$ and $\delta = 0.99$; and MCESP-CE with uniformly random exploration, $\epsilon(n, i, j) = 0.01$ and $\alpha(n, i) = bi^{-p}$ for $b \in \{0.1, 0.25, 0.5, 1.0\}$ and $p \in \{0.51, 0.6, 0.8, 1.0\}$. The δ value for MCESP-PALO is quite high, but even at this level, $k_0 = 1,986,744$. The Hoeffding bound upon which PALO's equations are based is fairly loose, and MCESP-PALO tends to take a large number of samples before achieving the confidence to make a policy change. For MCESP-CE we report results just for $(b, p) = (1, 1)$, corresponding to simple averaging, and $(b, p) = (0.1, 0.6)$, which had the best asymptotic performance. We also ran Sarsa(λ) in the same manner as described in Loch and Singh (Loch & Singh 1998); We refer the reader to their paper for details. Loch's and Singh's results with Sarsa(0.9) are the best reported for model-free RL on a variety of problems, including the Parr and Russell gridworld. They found that Sarsa quickly and consistently found the optimal policy, so this is a high standard to compare to.

Figure 3 presents the result of our experiments. For MCESP-SAA and MCESP-PALO, which are terminating algorithms, we plot the mean value of the final policy against the time to termination, measured in total timesteps, or actions taken, in the POMDP. The set of white boxes corresponds to MCESP-SAA, with k increasing from left to right. For small k, the algorithm often erroneously terminates at policies that are not locally optimal, leading to poor average performance. For higher k, MCESP-SAA rarely moves to a lower-value policy, but often gets trapped in the set of bad locally-optimal policies. MCESP-PALO behaves essentially like MCESP-SAA with very large k. In the 1000 runs, we never observed MCESP-PALO making a change leading to a worse policy, although in theory there is some chance of

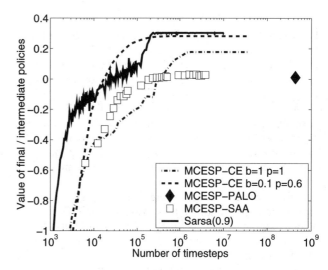

Figure 3: Results on Parr's and Russell's Gridworld

this happening. 932 runs ended at the optimal policy, with 68 ending at one of the bad locally-optimal policies.

For MCESP-CE and Sarsa we plot the mean current-policy value over the course of the runs. Every run of Sarsa converged to the optimal policy by around the $200,000^{th}$ step (about 10,000 trials). Encouragingly, MCESP-CE with $(b, p) = (0.1, 0.6)$ performed comparably. Asymptotic performance was slightly worse, as 5 of 1000 runs converged to one of the bad locally-optimal policies. Learning speed was comparable, which was surprising since MCESP updates only one action value per trial, which comes out to about once per twenty timesteps. These results are also encouraging because we spent little time hand-tuning the parameters of MCESP. By contrast, we spent approximately two days trying to get Sarsa(λ) to behave well before we gave up and implemented the exact design of Loch and Singh (1998). It turns out that Sarsa's behavior is very sensitive to how actions are chosen for exploration. Not knowing this, we spent a lot of time trying different choices for λ, different learning rates, and different versions of accumulating and replacing eligibility traces (Sutton & Barto 1998).

MCESP-CE with $(b, p) = (1, 1)$ did not fare as well as Sarsa(λ) or the other version of MCESP-CE, though performance was decent. 29 runs converged to one of the bad policies, with the rest converging to the optimal policy. Comparing the two versions of MCESP-CE it appears that using learning rate schedules other than simple averaging can be beneficial. Using simple averaging, the first update to an action value after a policy change completely wipes out the old action value. By contrast, the $(b, p) = (0.1, 0.6)$ schedule allows action value information to persist across policy changes—the first update, for example, is averaged in to the old action value with a learning rate of 0.1. This can be a good idea if, for example, changing the action associated to one observation is unlikely to affect the relative (or absolute) values of other observation-action values. Such a schedule might also be expected to reduce variance, which is often an issue with Monte Carlo algorithms.

Conclusion

We formulated a new definition of action value for reinforcement learning of reactive policies for POMDPs, and presented a general algorithm, MCESP, based on this definition. MCESP is similar in design to action-value based RL algorithms such as Q-Learning, Sarsa(λ), and especially Monte-Carlo Exploring-Starts (Sutton & Barto 1998). But, unlike those algorithms, MCESP is provably sound for application to partially observable settings. We have shown that MCESP can be specialized to achieve PAC hill-climbing to locally optimal policies, or probability one convergence in the limit to locally optimally policies.

Such theoretical guarantees are a double-edged sword. In experiments, we found that all versions of MCESP suffered to some degree from converging to locally-but-not-globally optimal policies. Encouragingly, though, one version of MCESP performed comparably in terms of learning speed and mean solution quality to Sarsa(λ), which was previously reported to be the best-performing model-free RL algorithm for learning reactive policies for POMDPs (Loch & Singh 1998). Further experimental work is needed to see how well this result generalizes, particularly for more complex domains than the one studied.

Our use of MCESP to date has been unrefined in many ways. For example, in all cases we have used simple round-robin or uniformly-random exploration. But there is every reason to believe that more sophisticated exploration strategies could be beneficial in identifying superior policies more quickly (Kaelbling 1993; Maron & Moore 1994). We are also interested in the possibility of letting comparison thresholds be negative at times, allowing occasional moves to policies that may seem worse. This idea has proven very successful in the simulated annealing algorithm for combinatorial optimization, and could be useful in RL as well.

Acknowledgments

This work was supported in part by the National Science Foundation under Grant Nos. ECS-0070102 and ECS-9980062. We thank Daniel Bernstein and Doina Precup for comments on drafts of this document.

References

Baird, L. C., and Moore, A. W. 1999. Gradient descent for general reinforcement learning. In *Advances in Neural Information Processing Systems 11*. MIT Press.

Baird, L. C. 1995. Residual algorithms: Reinforcement learning with function approximation. In *Proceedings of the Twelfth International Conference on Machine Learning*, 30–37. Morgan Kaufmann.

Gordon, G. 1996. Chattering in Sarsa(λ). CMU Learning Lab Internal Report. Available at www.cs.cmu.edu/~ggordon.

Greiner, R. 1996. PALO: A probabilistic hill-climbing algorithm. *Artificial Intelligence* 84(1–2):177–204.

Kaelbling, L. P. 1993. *Learning in embedded systems*. Cambridge, MA: MIT Press.

Kleywegt, A. J.; Shapiro, A.; and de Mello, T. H. 2001. The sample average approximation method for stochastic discrete optimization. *SIAM Journal of Optimization* 12:479–502.

Littman, M. L. 1994. Memoryless policies: Theoretical limitations and practical results. In *From Animals to Animats 3: Proceedings of the Third International Conference on Simulation of Adaptive Behavior*. Cambridge, MA: MIT Press.

Loch, J., and Singh, S. 1998. Using eligibility traces to find the best memoryless policy in a partially observable Markov decision process. In *Proceedings of the Fifteenth International Conference on Machine Learning*. San Francisco, CA: Morgan Kaufmann.

Madani, O.; Condon, A.; and Hanks, S. 1999. On the undecidability of probabilistic planning and infinite-horizon partially observable Markov decision process problems. In *Proceedings of the Sixteenth National Conference on Artificial Intelligence*. Cambridge, MA: MIT Press.

Maron, O., and Moore, A. 1994. Hoeffding races: Accelerating model selection search for classification and function approximation. In *Advances in Neural Information Processing Systems 6*, 59–66.

McCallum, A. K. 1995. *Reinforcement learning with selective perception and hidden state*. Ph.D. Dissertation, University of Rochester.

Ng, A., and Jordan, M. 2000. PEGASUS: A policy search method for large MDPs and POMDPs. In *Uncertainty in Artificial Intelligence, Proceedings of the Sixteenth Conference*.

Parr, R., and Russell, S. 1995. Approximating optimal policies for partially observable stochastic domains. In *Proceedings of the Fourteenth International Joint Conference on Artificial Intelligence (IJCAI-95)*. San Francisco, CA: Morgan Kaufmann.

Pendrith, M. D., and McGarity, M. J. 1998. An analysis of direct reinforcement learning in non-Markovian domains. In *Machine Learning: Proceedings of the 15th International Conference*, 421–429.

Pendrith, M. D., and Ryan, M. R. K. 1996. Actual return reinforcement learning versus temporal differences: Some theoretical and experimental results. In Saitta, L., ed., *Machine Learning: Proceedings of the 13th International Conference*, 373–381.

Sutton, R. S., and Barto, A. G. 1998. *Reinforcement Learning: An Introduction*. Cambridge, Massachusetts: MIT Press/Bradford Books.

Sutton, R. S.; McAllister, D.; Singh, S.; and Mansour, Y. 2000. Policy gradient methods for reinforcement learning with function approximation. In *Advances in Neural Information Processing Systems 12*. MIT Press.

Whitehead, S. D. 1992. *Reinforcement Learning for the Adaptive Control of Perception and Action*. Ph.D. Dissertation, University of Rochester.

Williams, R. J. 1992. Simple statistical gradient-following algorithms for connectionist reinforcement learning. *Machine Learning* 8:229–256.

Polynomial-Time Reinforcement Learning of Near-Optimal Policies

Karèn Pivazyan
pivazyan@stanford.edu
Management, Science and Engineering Department
Stanford University
Stanford, CA 94305

Yoav Shoham
shoham@stanford.edu
Computer Science Department
Stanford University
Stanford, CA 94305

Abstract

Inspired by recent results on polynomial time reinforcement algorithms that accumulate near-optimal rewards, we look at the related problem of quickly learning near-optimal policies. The new problem is obviously related to the previous one, but different in important ways. We provide simple algorithms for MDPs, zero-sum and common-payoff Stochastic Games, and a uniform framework for proving their polynomial complexity. Unlike the previously studied problem, these bounds use the minimum between the mixing time and a new quantity - the spectral radius. Unlike the previous results, our results apply uniformly to the average and discounted cases.

1 Introduction

Recent years have seen some groundbreaking results on reinforcement algorithms with polynomial running time. These include a PAC-based learning algorithm [Fiechter 1997] for discounted Markov Decision Problems (MDPs) with running time $poly(n, m, 1/\alpha)$, where n is the number of states, m the number of actions and α is the discount factor. More recently, the E^3 algorithm [Kearns & Singh 1998] was proposed for undiscounted (average return) MDPs with running time $poly(n, m, T)$, where T is the mixing time of the optimal policy. Most recently, the $R-max$ algorithm [Brafman & Tennenholtz 2001] was proposed for undiscounted zero-sum stochastic games (SGs), and thus also for undiscounted MDPs, with running time $poly(n, m, T)$. For the reader not familiar with these terms or results, we revisit them in later sections.

We continue this family of polynomial algorithms, but focus on a different goal. We distinguish between two goals of reinforcement learning - computing a near-optimal policy and accumulating a near-optimal reward. Following [Fiechter 1997], we call them *offline* and *online* problems, respectively. An example in which the offline model is appropriate is the training of a pilot on a flight simulator. An example in which the online model is appropriate is learning to fly on an actual plane.

The two problems are obviously related. For undiscounted setting, to accumulate good reward the agent must follow a good policy, while knowing a good policy lets the

agent accumulate good reward. The discounted setting is similar, except that to accumulate good reward the agent must follow a locally good policy, where the extent of locality depends on the discount factor. But offline and online problems also differ in one important aspect - complexity. For example, computing an optimal policy in a known MDP is polynomial time, whereas accumulating near-optimal reward by following that policy can be exponential. We exploit the lower complexity of the offline problem in this paper.

Most of the results to date - including the three mentioned at the beginning - concentrate on the online problem. In contrast, in this article we concentrate on the offline problem. Besides being interesting in its own right, understanding it well is conceptually prior to understanding the online problem. Indeed, although we do not pursue it further in this article for space reasons, the framework in this paper streamlines the existing approaches to the online problem.

In this paper we provide a simple uniform framework for offline reinforcement learning in polynomial time.

1. Show that for the known problem, near-optimal policies can be computed in polynomial time.

2. Show that policy value is continuous in the parameters of the problem, i.e., in the rewards and state transition probabilities.

3. Show that an approximate model with error ϵ can be computed in $poly(1/\epsilon)$ steps.

4. (SG only) Show that for some classes of SGs near-optimal value can be obtained regardless of opponent's actions or under reasonable assumptions on them.

We show that for undiscounted setting the complexity of our algorithms is $poly(n, m, \min(T, r_s))$, where the *spectral radius* r_s can be exponentially smaller than the mixing time. For discounted setting the complexity is $poly(n, m, r_s)$. Our results also improve on offline discounted PAC-algorithm [Fiechter 1994] by removing dependence on the discount factor. Finally, we are able to extend this framework to cover new classes of reinforcement learning problems, including learning in discounted zero-sum SGs, as well as in discounted and undiscounted common-payoff SGs.

The remainder of the article is organized as follows. In the next section we review the basic concepts of MDPs and SGs.

The following section proves complexity of offline learning in MDPs and presents an algorithm. Following that we extend the results and the algorithm to zero-sum and common-payoff SGs and discuss the complications that arise due to the opponent.

2 Background

Although the concepts in this section are likely well known by the reader, since part of our message is that there is much to be gained by being explicit about the setting, we want to err on the side of explicitness.

2.1 Markov Decision Processes

Definition 2.1 *A Markov Decision Process (MDP) is a tuple* $M = (S, A, p, r)$, *where*

- S *is a finite set of states of the world.* $|S| = n$.
- A *is a finite set of actions.* $|A| = m$.
- $p : S \times A \to \Delta(S)$ *is the probability transition function, giving for each state and action a probability distribution over next states.*
- $r : S \times A \to \Re$ *is the reward function, giving the expected immediate reward.*

Without loss of generality we will assume that the rewards lie in the $[-r_{max}/2, r_{max}/2]$ range.

Definition 2.2 *An MDP with known reward function and state transition probabilities is called a known MDP. Otherwise it is called an unknown MDP.*

A policy $\pi : S \to A$ prescribes which action to take in every state of the MDP. Associated with every policy π is a value $V^{\pi}(t) : S \to \Re$ which is the accumulated reward, either discounted or undiscounted, from following this policy for t steps. As $t \to \infty$, the value of t step policy approaches the value V^{π} of infinite-horizon policy. V^{π} can be computed by solving a system of linear equations. In this paper we are interested in discounted and undiscounted[1] (average return) problems, so we will use two definitions of V^{π}:

Definition 2.3 *(Discounted)*

$$V^{\pi}(s) = r(s, \pi(s)) + \alpha \sum_{s'} p(s, \pi(s), s') V^{\pi}(s').$$

Definition 2.4 *(Undiscounted)*

$$V^{\pi}(s) + h^{\pi}(s) = r(s, \pi(s)) + \sum_{s'} p(s, \pi(s), s') h^{\pi}(s').$$

Notice that because MDP is unichain, for undiscounted reward $V^{\pi}(s) = V^{\pi}(s')$, $\forall s, s'$.

We are interested in computing the optimal policy:

$$\pi^* = argmax_{\pi} V^{\pi}$$

---

[1]When speaking about undiscounted MDPs, we assume they are unichain [Bertsekas & Tsitsiklis 1996, Section 4.2].

2.2 Stochastic Games

Stochastic Games can be seen as either an extension of a normal form game to multiple states or as an extension of MDP to multi player setting. Both of these views will be useful to us. We confine ourselves to 2-player games.

Definition 2.5 *Stochastic Game (SG) is a tuple* $G = (S, A_1, A_2, p, r_1, r_2)$, *where*

- S *is a finite set of states of the world.* $|S| = n$.
- A_1 *is a finite set of player's actions.* $|A_1| = m_1$.
- A_2 *is a finite set of opponent's actions.* $|A_2| = m_2$.
- $p : S \times A_1 \times A_2 \to \Delta(S)$ *is the probability transition function, giving for each state, player's actions and opponent's actions, a probability distribution over next states.*
- $r_i : S \times A_1 \times A_2 \to \Re$ *is the reward function, giving the expected immediate reward for player i.*

Without loss of generality we will assume that the rewards lie in the $[-r_{max}/2, r_{max}/2]$ range. Also let $m = m_1 * m_2$.

The players have policies $\pi : S \to A_1$ and $\phi : S \to A_2$. A t-step value of a policy pair (π, ϕ) is $V^{\pi, \phi}(t) : S \to \Re$. The value of infinite-horizon policy is denoted by $V^{(\pi, \phi)}$. In a SG, every state s together with the sets of actions available to both players can be thought of as a normal form (or static) game g. We will work with zero-sum stochastic games (ZS-SG), where each static game is zero-sum (the players rewards sum to zero[2]) under discounted (DZS-SG) and undiscounted[3] (AZS-SG) reward formulations. Both DZS-SG and AZS-SG have an optimal value and there exist optimal stationary policies [Filar & Vrieze 1997]. We will also examine common-payoff (collaborative or cooperative) stochastic games (CP-SG) where each static game is common-payoff (the players' reward functions are equal) under discounted (DCP-SG) and undiscounted (ACP-SG) reward formulations. We define optimal value and optimal stationary policies in DCP-SG and ACP-SG by assuming that the players are able to coordinate in each stage game. Then these games can be solved as MDPs. We discuss our assumption further in Section 5.

3 Single Player Reinforcement Learning

In undiscounted setting traditional algorithms such as E^3 and $R - max$ have concentrated on the online problem. It is important to realize that this problem has two sources of difficulty - one having to do with the speed of learning the unknown parameters, and the other having to do with the speed of accumulating rewards. Unlike the former, the latter has nothing to do with the unknown nature of the problem - it is manifested already in fully known MDPs. The key insight of these algorithms is the identification of the mixing time.

Definition 3.1 *([Kearns & Singh 1998])* *The ϵ-return mixing time T_{ϵ} of policy π in undiscounted MDP M is the smallest T such that for all $t \geq T$, $|V^{\pi}(t, i) - V^{\pi}(i)| \leq \epsilon$ for all states i.*

---

[2]In fact, we can generalize slightly to constant-sum games.

[3]When speaking about undiscounted SGs, we assume they are irreducible [Filar & Vrieze 1997, Section 5.1].

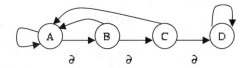

Figure 1: Exponential Mixing Time

In known MDPs, given a known optimal policy, the complexity of accumulating near-optimal rewards is linear in T_ϵ. The T_ϵ depends on the number of states, the connectivity of the graph and on the probability transition function. In general it can be exponential in the number of states. To see that, look at the Markov Chain in Figure 1. If the reward at state D is larger than at other states, the optimal return will be achieved after the system moves to state D. But starting from state A the number of transitions necessary to get to state D is proportional to $(1/\delta)^3$.

For discounted setting, a PAC-based algorithm addresses both offline [Fiechter 1994] and online [Fiechter 1997] problems. However, the algorithm learns good policies from a fixed initial state which is a reasonable assumption for online problem, but not for offline one. In addition, offline problem requires the presence of "reset" button.

In this paper we concentrate on the offline problem, making no assumptions on the initial state or special sampling procedures. In undiscounted setting we could use $E3$ or $R - max$ to compute a near-optimal policy, but does the mixing time give a satisfactory bound? Not always. To see that, consider any MDP with an exponential T_ϵ. Now add a new state which has actions leading to every state and add a new action to all states that leads to the new state. If the reward on going to and from the new state is very low, then T_ϵ will not change significantly. On the other hand, sampling the whole state space can be done very fast, since we basically have a reset button available. And having the whole model, we should be able to compute a near-optimal policy fast. In general, we can bound the sampling complexity by the spectral radius.

Definition 3.2 *Given an MDP, let $o(s, \pi, s')$ be some path $(s, i_1, ..., i_l, s')$ from state s to state s' under policy π. Let $P(s, \pi, s') = \max_{o(s,\pi,s')} \prod_k p(i_k, \pi(i_k), i_{k+1})$. Then for any MDP we define its* spectral radius r_s *as* $1/[\min_{s,s'} \max_\pi P(s, \pi, s')]$. *Similarly, for any SG we define its* spectral radius r_s *as* $1/[\min_{s,s',\varphi} \max_\pi P(s, \pi, \varphi, s')]$.

The complexity of sampling the whole state-space is polynomial in the spectral radius. The spectral radius depends on the number of states, the connectivity of the graph and on the probability transition function. In general it can be exponential in the number of states. However, it is not comparable to ϵ-return mixing time - it can be exponentially less or greater. We saw above the case when it is exponentially less. It is exponentially greater (see Figure 2) whenever there is a set of states with exponential sampling time (states A, B, C, D), whose low reward excludes them from the optimal policy (go directly to state E) and hence from affecting T_ϵ.

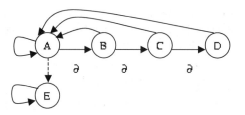

Figure 2: Exponential Spectral Radius

We will be interested in a complexity bound on learning a near-optimal policy that uses the minimum of T_ϵ and r_s for the undiscounted setting and uses r_s for the discounted setting. Our approach consists of three steps. First, we note that in known MDPs, the computation of an optimal policy - unlike the accumulation of optimal reward - can be done in fast.

Theorem 3.1 (MDP Complexity) *The optimal policy in discounted and undiscounted setting for known MDPs can be computed using linear programming in $poly(n, m)$ time [Bertsekas 1995].*

(Technically speaking, there is an extra term B, the maximum number of bits necessary to represent any parameter of MDP, in the complexity equation. But it is present in all our formulas and does not add new insight, so we omit it.)

Then we note that the optimal policy is continuous in the parameters of the MDP, i.e. rewards and probability transitions. To show that we first define a perturbed MDP.

Definition 3.3 *Let M be an MDP, and M_ϵ be an ϵ-perturbed MDP with the values of all its parameters differing from M by less than ϵ. Let π be some policy and V^π be its value (either discounted or undiscounted) in M, and V_ϵ^π its value (discounted or undiscounted respectively) in M_ϵ. Let π^* be the optimal policy in M and π_ϵ^* be the optimal policy in M_ϵ.*

Theorem 3.2 (MDP Continuity I) *The value of policy π is continuous in some neighborhood $\xi > 0$ w.r.t. perturbations in parameter space of the MDP for discounted and undiscounted settings. That is,*

$$|V^\pi - V_\epsilon^\pi| < C\epsilon, \text{ where } C \in \Re^+, \epsilon < \xi.$$

Proof: Follows from the fact that MDPs can be solved using linear programming, the solution of which is continuous in the inputs. For discounted MDPs, $\xi = \infty$. For undiscounted MDPs, ξ must be small enough to preserve unichain property of the MDP. It is easy to see that $\xi \geq \min_{s,a,s'} p(s, a, s')$. ∎

Corollary 3.3 (MDP Continuity II) *The optimal strategy in a perturbed game is nearly optimal in the original game. That is,*

$$\left|V^{\pi^*} - V^{\pi_\epsilon^*}\right| < C\epsilon, \text{ where } C \in \Re^+, \epsilon < \xi.$$

From this it follows that if we can sample the MDP in polynomial time, we can compute a near-optimal policy in polynomial time. First we need to determine how much we need to sample each unknown parameter. We estimate that using variants of the Chernoff bound.

Theorem 3.4 (Hoeffding) *Given a random variable r bounded by $[-r_{max}/2, r_{max}/2]$ and a set of its sampled values $r_1, \ldots, r_k$, for any $\epsilon > 0$,*

$$P\left\{\left|\frac{1}{k}\sum r_i - Er\right| \geq \epsilon\right\} \leq 2e^{-k\epsilon^2/r_{max}^2},$$

where Er is the expectation of r.

So the number of samples necessary for given levels of ϵ and δ is polynomial and given by

$$k(\epsilon, \delta) = \frac{r_{max}^2}{\epsilon^2}\left(-\ln\frac{\delta}{2}\right).$$

Similarly for probability transition functions.

Theorem 3.5 (Glivenko-Cantelli) *If $F(z)$ is the true pdf and $F_k(z)$ is the standard empirical pdf, then for any $\epsilon > 0$,*

$$P\left\{sup_{z \in \Re} |F(z) - F_k(z)| \geq \epsilon\right\} \leq 8ke^{-k\epsilon^2/32}.$$

We are now ready to state the main result of this section.

Algorithm 3.1 *The algorithm builds two MDPs, $\hat{M}$ and M_ϵ. Initially, both are empty. After each sample newly discovered states and actions are added to both MDPs. The probability transitions are also updated as standard empirical pdf. The MDPs differ in their updates of rewards. The M_ϵ is build using sampled rewards, while the $\hat{M}$ is assigned fictional rewards that facilitate exploration. In particular, given $\epsilon, \delta, r_{max}$ that specify model accuracy, the number of parameter samples required is computed via Theorems 3.4 and 3.5. Then, for MDP $\hat{M}$, $r(s, a)$ is set equal to the number of samples required minus the number of times that reward was actually sampled. The minimum value for $r(s, a)$ is 0.*

1. *Initialize T_s to some value for all states s.*

2. *From state s compute optimal T-step policy $\pi_T^*(s)$ in the MDP $\hat{M}$.*

3. *If reward from $\pi_T^*(s)$ is 0 then increase T_s.*

4. *Follow $\pi_T^*(s)$ for T steps, updating $\hat{M}$ and M_ϵ.*

5. *Goto step 2.*

We compare this algorithm to existing approaches. It explores strictly more than E^3 and $R - max$ in undiscounted MDPs, hence finding ϵ-optimal policy in $poly(n, m, 1/\epsilon, 1/\delta, T_\epsilon)$ time. It is also easy to see that after $poly(n, m, 1/\epsilon, 1/\delta, r_s)$ steps it will visit the whole state space and M_ϵ can be used to compute ϵ-optimal policy. Finally, for discounted MDPs, this result extends PAC-learning [Fiechter 1994] by removing dependence on the discount rate.

Theorem 3.6 (Main) *Using Algorithm 3.1 the ϵ-optimal policy for an unknown MDP can be computed with probability $1 - \delta$ in $poly(n, m, 1/\epsilon, 1/\delta, \min(r_s, T_\epsilon))$ for the undiscounted setting and in $poly(n, m, 1/\epsilon, 1/\delta, r_s)$ for the discounted setting.*

4 Reinforcement Learning in Zero-Sum Stochastic Games

The discussion of learning in stochastic games cannot be removed from the discussion of algorithms that react to the opponent behavior. In general SGs, even the notion of an optimal policy is suspect for a non-fixed opponent. However, in some classes of SGs we have a good definition of optimality, and for these classes we are able to extend the framework from the previous section. In particular, we cover zero-sum and common-payoff SGs. We start with the former in this section.

We are not aware of any existing results on offline reinforcement learning in DZS-SGs. For AZS-SGs we could use $R - max$, but as before we can improve upon the complexity bound by using spectral radius together with the mixing time. The first steps are the same as in the previous section. We start by showing that computing a near-optimal policy in a known ZS-SG is fast.

Theorem 4.1 (ZS-SG Complexity) *Value Iteration in ZS-SGs converges to an ϵ-optimal policy exponentially fast. For DZS-SG the convergence rate depends on n, m, α, while for AZS-SG it depends on n, m, r_s.*

Proof: See Chapters 11 and 13 of [Wal 1981] for convergence rates of value iteration in DZS-SG and AZS-SG respectively. We should note that for fixed α and r_s the ϵ-optimal policy in DZS-SG and AZS-SG respectively can be computed in time polynomial in these quantities. We also believe it is possible to remove the dependence on the α and r_s by using nonlinear programming, instead of value iteration (see, for example, Chapter 3 in [Filar & Vrieze 1997]). ■

Next we note that the optimal policy is continuous in the parameters of the ZS-SG. To show that we first define a perturbed ZS-SG.

Definition 4.1 *Let G be a ZS-SG. Then G_ϵ is called ϵ-perturbed ZS-SG if the values of all its parameters differ from G by less than ϵ. We use subscript $_\epsilon$ when referring to quantities of G_ϵ, for example $V_\epsilon^{(\pi^*, \phi^*)}$ or π_ϵ.*

Theorem 4.2 (ZS-SG Continuity I) *The optimal value $V^{(\pi^*, \phi^*)}$ of DZS-SG or AZS-SG is continuous in some neighborhood $\xi > 0$ w.r.t. perturbations in parameter space of that SG. That is,*

$$\left|V^{(\pi^*, \phi^*)} - V_\epsilon^{(\pi^*, \phi^*)}\right| < C\epsilon, \text{ where } C \in \Re^+, \epsilon < \xi.$$

Proof: See [Filar & Vrieze 1997], Theorem 4.3.7 for proof in DZS-SG case, with $\xi = \infty$. For AZS-SG we assume that parameter perturbations within some radius ξ do not change game irreducibility. It is easy to see from the definition of irreducible matrix that $\xi \geq \min_{s, a_1, a_2, s'} p(s, a_1, a_2, s')$. Let Θ denote all parameters of the game. Then we can write the value function explicitly as $V^{(\pi, \phi)}(\Theta)$. Now, we know that $V^{(\pi, \phi)}(\Theta)$ is continuous in Θ because it can be computed by solving a system of linear equations (Bellman's equations). Moreover, $V^{(\pi, \phi^*)}(\Theta)$ is also continuous in Θ since for a fixed π this game becomes an MDP. Finally, $V^{(\pi^*, \phi^*)}(\Theta) =$

$\max_\pi V^{(\pi,\phi^*)}(\Theta)$ is continuous in Θ as well because it is a composition of two continuous functions. ∎

Corollary 4.3 (ZS-SG Continuity II) *Optimal strategy π_ϵ^* in a perturbed game is nearly optimal in the original game. That is,*

$$\left| V^{(\pi^*,\phi^*)} - V^{(\pi_\epsilon^*,\phi^*)} \right| < C\epsilon, \text{ where } C \in \Re^+, \ \epsilon < \xi.$$

Proof: Neighborhood ξ is defined as in Theorem 4.2. See (Theorem 4.3.10, [Filar & Vrieze 1997]) for proof in DZS-SG case. For AZS-SG we have from Theorem 4.2

$$\left| V_\epsilon^{(\pi_\epsilon^*,\phi^*)} - V^{(\pi_\epsilon^*,\phi^*)} \right| < C\epsilon$$

$$\left| V^{(\pi^*,\phi^*)} - V_\epsilon^{(\pi_\epsilon^*,\phi^*)} \right| < C\epsilon$$

Therefore,

$$\left| V^{(\pi^*,\phi^*)} - V^{(\pi_\epsilon^*,\phi^*)} \right| <$$

$$\left| V^{(\pi^*,\phi^*)} - V_\epsilon^{(\pi_\epsilon^*,\phi^*)} + V_\epsilon^{(\pi_\epsilon^*,\phi^*)} - V^{(\pi_\epsilon^*,\phi^*)} \right| <$$

$$\left| V^{(\pi^*,\phi^*)} - V_\epsilon^{(\pi_\epsilon^*,\phi^*)} \right| + \left| V_\epsilon^{(\pi_\epsilon^*,\phi^*)} - V^{(\pi_\epsilon^*,\phi^*)} \right| < 2C\epsilon$$

∎

From this it follows that if we can sample the ZS-SG in polynomial time, we can compute a near-optimal policy in polynomial time. We know how much to sample each unknown parameter from Theorems 3.4 and 3.5. However, we run into a complication - the opponent can prevent the player from ever exploring some actions. We overcome this difficulty by showing that at any point in time the player always has a policy that is either better than the minimax or leads to fast sampling of unknown actions. In effect, by hiding information the opponent can either hurt himself or at best prolong the discovery of minimax policy for polynomial time. This is a special property of zero-sum games. First, we introduce subgames.

Definition 4.2 *A subgame $\hat{G}$ of stochastic game G is identical to G except that the opponent is limited to playing a nonempty subset of his actions in every state.*

Any SG is trivially a subgame of itself. So is any MDP formed by fixing opponent's policy. Such subgames are asymmetric for agents and there is an exponential number of them. Any subgame of a zero-sum SG is zero-sum. We note that by restricting his actions to a subgame, the opponent can only hurt himself.

Theorem 4.4 *The value $V^{(\hat{\pi}^*,\hat{\varphi}^*)}$ of the subgame $\hat{G}$ is at least as large as the value $V^{(\pi^*,\varphi^*)}$ of the ZS-SG G.*

Proof: Denote by Π and Φ policy spaces in G and by $\hat{\Pi}$ and $\hat{\Phi}$ policy spaces in $\hat{G}$. Then,

$$V^{(\hat{\pi}^*,\hat{\varphi}^*)} = \min_{\varphi\in\hat{\Phi}} \max_{\pi\in\Pi} V^{(\pi,\varphi)} \geq \min_{\varphi\in\hat{\Phi}} V^{(\pi^*,\varphi)} \geq$$

$$\geq \min_{\varphi\in\Phi} V^{(\pi^*,\varphi)} = V^{(\pi^*,\varphi^*)}$$

∎

Now we can show that in any partially known game, as long as the player knows all the rewards for one opponent action, the player always has a good strategy.

Corollary 4.5 *In a partially known ZS-SG the player always has a policy such that if the opponent plays only known actions, the player's reward will be at least minimax. If the partially known ZS-SG is actually a subgame, then the player's policy is best response versus that subgame.*

We omit the full presentation of the algorithm due to space constraints, but present an informal overview here. The algorithm has explicit, but alternating stages. The agent starts exploring, quickly finds ϵ-best response (guaranteed to be as good as ϵ-optimal) to the opponent's strategy by exploring all the actions that opponent plays, and starts exploiting. Then, once the opponent changes his strategy to include some previously unknown action, the agent immediately notices that, and once these unknown actions become known, he changes his strategy. The opponent can include previously unknown actions in his strategy only a polynomial number of times due to finite state and action spaces. The opponent can however prolong these changes indefinitely, therefore there is no finite time after which the algorithm can stop learning, unless the whole state-space has been explored. But we can guarantee that after each switch to unknown actions by the opponent, the agent learns ϵ-best response in polynomial time.

We compare this algorithm to existing approaches. It explores strictly more than $R - max$ in DZS-SGs, hence finding ϵ-best response policy in $poly(n, m, 1/\epsilon, 1/\delta, T_\epsilon)$ time. Also, for any opponent play, the agent finds this policy in $poly(n, m, 1/\epsilon, 1/\delta, r_s)$ time by exploring the whole state-space.

Theorem 4.6 (Main) *For any opponent play in ZS-SGs the agent can compute ϵ-best response, guaranteed to be at least as good as ϵ-optimal, with probability $1 - \delta$ in time $poly(n, m, 1/\epsilon, 1/\delta, \min(T_\epsilon, r_s))$ for AZS-SG and in time $poly(n, m, 1/\epsilon, 1/\delta, r_s, 1/\ln\alpha)$ for DZS-SG.*

Our results are similar in complexity to $R - max$ for AZS-SGs. The results on complexity of DZS-SGs are new to the best of our knowledge.

5 Reinforcement Learning in Common-Payoff Stochastic Games

In CP-SGs, assuming rational agents, optimal value is well defined together with a set of optimal policies. Rational agents try to coordinate in every stage game because that is in their best interest. We extend the framework from Section 3 for offline reinforcement learning. The first steps are the same. We note that assuming rational agents, optimal policies for a known CP-SG can be computed fast.

Theorem 5.1 (CP-SG Complexity) *The set of all optimal policy pairs for a CP-SG under discounted and undiscounted formulations can be computed in time $poly(n, m)$.*

Proof: Since the opponent will maximize his and therefore the agents' payoffs, it is sufficient to consider an MDP version of CP-SG formed by using the same state space S, same action space A_1, but with payoffs resulting from coordinated opponent behavior, $r(s, a) = \max_b r(s, a, b)$, and probabilities corresponding to that action choice, $p(s, a, s') =$

$p(s, a, b^*_{(s,a)}, s')$, where $b^*_{(s,a)} = \arg max_b r(s, a, b)$. The optimal policies in this MDP can be computed using linear programming. ∎

Next we note that the optimal policy is continuous in the parameters of the CP-SG. The perturbed CP-SG is defined similarly to Definition 4.1.

Theorem 5.2 (CP-SG Continuity I) *The optimal value $V^{(\pi^*, \varphi^*)}$ of DCP-SG or ACP-SG is continuous in some neighborhood $\xi > 0$ w.r.t. perturbations in parameter space of that SG. That is,*

$$\left| V^{(\pi^*, \varphi^*)} - V_\epsilon^{(\pi^*, \varphi^*)} \right| < C\epsilon, \text{ where } C \in \Re^+, \ \epsilon < \xi.$$

Corollary 5.3 (CP-SG Continuity II) *Optimal strategy in a perturbed game is nearly optimal in the original game. That is,*

$$\left| V^{(\pi^*, \varphi^*)} - V^{(\pi^*_\epsilon, \varphi^*)} \right| < C\epsilon, \text{ where } C \in \Re^+, \ \epsilon < \xi.$$

From this it follows that if we can sample the CP-SG in polynomial time, we can compute a near-optimal policy in polynomial time. We know how much to sample each unknown parameter from Theorems 3.4 and 3.5. Unlike zero-sum games, in common-payoff games the agents want to explore the whole state-space and do not hide parts of it from each other. There is only one difficulty - coordinating on the same optimal policy. If the agents do not coordinate, their actions can mismatch resulting in suboptimal rewards. If the agents have access to some coordination device (i.e. communications or coin flips) or the game has focal points, then the problem becomes simple. We will not use any such scheme. Instead we rely on action randomization and a suitable algorithm to make sure that the agents settle on the same optimum. We believe that because agents have common interest, it is reasonable to assume that they will use the same coordination algorithm.

Algorithm 5.1 *The algorithm builds two CP-SGs, $\hat{G}$ and G_ϵ, that are updated similarly to the MDPs in Algorithm 3.1. The value of a state is taken as the coordination optimum of the stage game.*

1. Initialize T_s to some value for all states s.

2. From state s compute optimal T-step policy $\pi^*_T(s)$ in the CP-SG $\hat{G}$. This policy is computed using dynamic programming.

3. If reward from $\pi^*_T(s)$ is 0 then increase T_s.

4. Follow $\pi^*_T(s)$ for T steps, updating $\hat{G}$ and G_ϵ.

5. Goto step 2.

At the end of the algorithm, once all near-optimal policies are computed, the agents enter into a coordination phase. They start randomizing among their optimal actions (derived from optimal policies) in each state. If in some state they have by chance played an optimal action pair (and they can detect this), then they settle on these actions in that state. If in a state with " settled" actions the opponent chooses some other action, the agent starts randomizing among optimal actions again (this could happen if the opponent is still exploring).

Theorem 5.4 (Main) *The agents can coordinate choosing ϵ-optimal policy pair in unknown CP-SGs with probability $1 - \delta$ in $poly(n, m, 1/\epsilon, 1/\delta, r_s)$ time for discounted setting and in $poly(n, m, 1/\epsilon, 1/\delta, \min(T_\epsilon, r_s))$ time for undiscounted setting.*

Proof: The proof is based on the same result for MDPs and on the fact that during coordination stage the probability of not playing any optimal action pair in l trials for any state decreases as $exp(l)$. ∎

All of the results in this section are new to the best of our knowledge.

6 Summary

In this paper we accent the distinction between online and offline reinforcement learning and present a simple, uniform framework for proving polynomial complexity in MDPs, zero-sum and common-payoff SGs. As in recent work our emphasis has been on the algorithms with provable properties, but we believe in the long run they will be useful for constructing practical algorithms. In the future paper we hope to show that our framework also provides a unifying simple view of the online problem.

7 Acknowledgements

This work was supported in part by DARPA grant F30602-00-2-0598. The authors would also like to thank members of Stanford University Multi-Agent Research Group.

References

Bertsekas, D. P., and Tsitsiklis, J. N. 1996. *Neuro-Dynamic Programming*. Belmont, MA: Athena Scientific.

Bertsekas, D. P. 1995. *Dynamic Programming and Optimal Control, Vols. I and II*. Belmont, MA: Athena Scientific.

Brafman, R., and Tennenholtz, M. 2001. R-max: A general polynomial time algorithm for Near-Optimal reinforcement learning. In *Proc. of the 17th International Conf. on Artificial Intelligence (IJCAI-01)*, 953–958. San Francisco, CA: Morgan Kaufmann Publishers, Inc.

Fiechter, C.-N. 1994. Efficient reinforcement learning. In *Proc. of the 7th Annual ACM Conf. on Computational Learning Theory*, 88–97. New Brunswick, New Jersey: ACM Press.

Fiechter, C.-N. 1997. Expected mistake bound model for on-line reinforcement learning. In *Proc. of the 14th International Conf. on Machine Learning*, 116–124.

Filar, J., and Vrieze, K. 1997. *Competitive Markov Decision Processes*. New York, NY: Springer-Verlag.

Kearns, M., and Singh, S. 1998. Near-optimal reinforcement learning in polynomial time. In *Proc. 15th International Conf. on Machine Learning*, 260–268. Morgan Kaufmann, San Francisco, CA.

Wal, J. V. D. 1981. *Stochastic Dynamic Programming*, volume 139 of *Mathematical Center Tracts*.

Constrained Formulations and Algorithms for Stock-Price Predictions Using Recurrent FIR Neural Networks

Benjamin W. Wah and **Minglun Qian**
Department of Electrical and Computer Engineering
and the Coordinated Science Laboratory
University of Illinois, Urbana-Champaign
1308 West Main Street, Urbana, IL 61801, USA
E-mail: {wah, m-qian}@manip.crhc.uiuc.edu

Abstract

In this paper, we develop new constrained artificial-neural-network (ANN) formulations and learning algorithms to predict future stock prices, a difficult time-series prediction problem. Specifically, we characterize stock prices as a non-stationary noisy time series, identify its predictable low-frequency components, develop strategies to predict missing low-frequency information in the lag period of a filtered time series, model the prediction problem by a recurrent FIR ANN, formulate the training problem of the ANN as a constrained optimization problem, develop new constraints to incorporate the objectives in cross validation, solve the learning problem using algorithms based on the theory of Lagrange multipliers for nonlinear discrete constrained optimization, and illustrate our prediction results on three stock time series. There are two main contributions of this paper. First, we present a new approach to predict missing low-pass data in the lag period when low-pass filtering is applied on a time series. Such predictions allow learning to be carried out more accurately. Second, we propose new constraints on cross validation that can improve significantly the accuracy of learning in a constrained formulation. Our experimental results demonstrate good prediction accuracy in a 10-day horizon.

I. Introduction

In this paper we study the following stock-price prediction problem. Given a sequence of daily closing prices $R(t)$ of a stock and the corresponding low-pass version $S(t)$ of $R(t)$, predict $S(t_0 + h)$ at *prediction horizon* h from the current time t_0 using only the history of closing prices $R(t_0), R(t_0 - 1), R(t_0 - 2), \ldots$ For simplicity, we only consider univariate time-series predictions in this paper.

The prediction problem as defined is difficult for the following reasons. First, the time series is noisy and non-stationary, making it difficult to use past information to predict future trends. We show in Section II that noise does not contribute to prediction accuracy and needs to be removed. Hence, the problem involves the prediction of a smoothed time series that may lag behind actual price changes. Second, many factors leading to price fluctuations cannot be captured precisely or may be too numerous and too difficult to be modeled. As a result, the prices of a single stock,

represented by a univariate time series, may not be enough to accurately predict its future prices.

We measure prediction quality by two metrics. The first metric is the widely used *normalized mean square error (nMSE)* defined as follows:

$$nMSE = \frac{1}{\sigma^2 N} \sum_{t=t_0}^{t_1} (o(t) - d(t))^2, \qquad (1)$$

where σ^2 is the variance of the true time series in period $[t_0, t_1]$, N is the number of patterns tested, and $o(t)$ and $d(t)$ are, respectively, the network and desired outputs at time t.

The second metric is the *hit rate* defined as follows. Let $D(t + h) = \text{sign}(S(t + h) - S(t))$ be the actual direction of change for $S(t)$, and $\hat{D}(t + h) = \text{sign}(\hat{S}(t + h) - \hat{S}(t))$ be the predicted direction change. We call a prediction for horizon h a *hit* iff $\hat{D}(t + h) \times D(t + h) > 0$. The hit rate $H(h)$ is defined to be

$$H(h) = \frac{\left| \left\{ t | D(t+h)\hat{D}(t+h) > 0, t = 1, \cdots, n \right\} \right|}{\left| \left\{ t | D(t+h)\hat{D}(t+h) \neq 0, t = 1, \cdots, n \right\} \right|} \qquad (2)$$

where $|E|$ represents the number of elements in set E. Figure 1 illustrates the definition. Assume that $S(t)$ lags behind and is only available up to $t = t_0 - m$. $\hat{S}(t)$, the predicted price in $t \in [t_2, t_3]$, is lower than $\hat{S}(t_0)$, the predicted price at t_0. This prediction is a hit because the actual price at t is also lower than $S(t_0)$. In contrast, $\hat{S}(t')$, the predicted price in $t' \in (t_1, t_2)$ is not a hit because it is lower than $\hat{S}(t_0)$, whereas $S(t')$ is higher than $S(t_0)$.

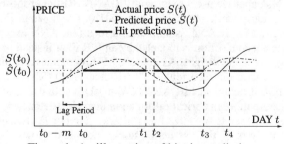

Figure 1: An illustration of hits in predictions.

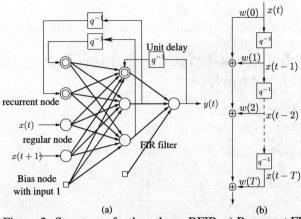

Figure 2: Structure of a three-layer RFIR: a) Recurrent FIR neural network; b) FIR filter. In a), double concentric circles indicate recurrent nodes, other circles are non-recurrent nodes, and small boxes are bias nodes with constant input 1. q^{-1} represents one unit time delay.

The hit rate is very useful when a trading decision is based solely on whether the predicted future price goes up or down as compared to the current price (Saad *et al.* 1998). Other metrics may be used, depending on the trading strategy. Without loss of generality, new metrics used can be added as constraints in cross validations in our formulation.

Existing models for time-series analysis can be classified into *linear* and *nonlinear models*(Chatfield 2001). Linear models such as Box-Jenkins' *ARIMA* and its variations (Box and Jenkins 1976) and *Exponential smoothing* (Brown 1963) work well for linear time series but fail to model complicated nonlinearity and trends in financial time series. *State-space models* (Aoki 1987) are another class of linear models that represent inputs as a linear combination of a set of state vectors that evolve over time according to some linear equations. In practice, state vectors and their dimensionality are hard to choose (Chatfield 2001). Nonlinear models, such as *time-varying parameter models* (Nicholls and Pagan 1985) and *threshold auto-regressive models* (Tong 1990), generally pre-specify a special nonlinear function to be used. These models are not effective for modeling financial time series because the nonlinear functions are hard to choose. Another class of nonlinear models are *artificial neural-network models* (ANN) that can model processes with unknown dynamics (Haykin 1999). They have been proved to be universal function approximators and do not require inside knowledge on the process under investigation. In this paper we use a recurrent FIR ANN (RFIR) proposed in our early work (Wah and Qian 2001b). As shown in Figure 2, an RFIR ANN is similar to a recurrent ANN except that each connection is modeled by an FIR filter instead of a single synaptic weight. As a result, RFIR combines a recurrent structure in recurrent ANNs (Elman 1990) (RNN) and an FIR structure in FIR ANNs (Wan 1993) (FIR-NN), and can store more historical information than either alone.

This paper is organized as follows. Section II presents the analysis of time series of stock prices and shows that low-pass filtering is needed to remove unpredictable high-frequency components. It further proposes schemes to overcome edge effects in low-pass filtering. Section III describes a constrained ANN formulation. By including new constraints to compensate for edge effects and on errors and hit rates in cross-validation, we apply violation-guided back-propagation to find suitable weights. Finally, Section IV compares the performance of different prediction methods.

II. Preprocessing of Time Series

Time series of most financial applications has been found to be non-stationary, noisy (Zheng *et al.* 1999) and behave like random walks (Hellstrom and Holmstrom 1997). To improve their predictability, they are preprocessed in order to remove unpredictable noise and enhance their stationarity.

A time series is said to be *stationary* if it has (near) constant mean and variance, where stationarity is often tested by computing its autocorrelations (Masters 1995). The autocorrelation of a stationary time series drops rapidly from a significant non-zero value to zero, whereas that of a non-stationary time series stretches out indefinitely. Two widely used methods to transform a non-stationary series to a stationary one are linear de-trending and differencing (Masters 1995), although such methods have not been found to work well on raw time series of stock prices. In particular, differencing may lead to accumulated errors when stock prices are reconstructed from the differenced time series.

On the other hand, unwanted noise can be removed by low-pass filtering or wavelet de-noising. There is a lot of recent interest in using wavelet transforms to decompose financial time series into bands in such a way that each band contains a set of near stationary signals and that the low-frequency band is smooth enough to be converted to stationary series. Unfortunately, de-noising introduces lags in the smoothed data because it uses future data in its computations. Such edge effects are not desirable because they reduce the number of most recent patterns that are critical for predictions, thereby introducing uncertainties in both $\hat{S}(t_0 + h)$ and $\hat{S}(t_0)$ in computing the hit rate.

Recently, a redundant Á *Trous* wavelet transform was proposed for de-noising instead of traditional decimated wavelet transforms (Zheng *et al.* 1999). It was argued that such transforms provide *shift invariance* and that the information at time t in each resolution reconstructs the original signal directly at time t with lags. Hence, the decomposition by wavelet transforms helps identify the properties of the signals at each resolution level. As an illustration, Figure 3 shows the autocorrelations (AC) of the closing prices of IBM, as well as the high-frequency channels w_1, W_2, W_3, W_4 and low frequency channel c_4 resulted from the Á *Trous* transform. The curves show that $R(t)$ and c_4 are non-stationary, whereas w_1 and w_2 are stationary.

Besides stationarity, we also need to consider the lag of a time series. A decomposed stationary time series that lags behind the original series is not useful for prediction unless future data beyond the lag period is correlated to the filtered series. Consider Table 1 that shows the lag and the number of autocorrelation coefficients that are larger than 0.5 for each resolution level of the decomposed IBM and Microsoft

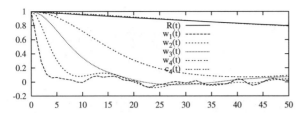

Figure 3: Autocorrelations (AC) of IBM's closing prices and their five decomposed channels using the Á *Tr ous* wavelet transform

Table 1: Low correlations for most channels beyond the lag period, based on the wavelet transforms in Figure 3.

Decomposed Signal	Days with $ACF > 0.5$		Lag
	IBM	MSFT	
w_1	1	1	0
w_2	3	2	2
w_3	7	6	6
w_4	14	15	14
c_4	50+	50	30

(MSFT) closing prices. The results show that, except for c_4, signals beyond the lag period are weakly correlated to signals available in the decomposed time series, making it difficult to predict beyond the lag period.

Due to a lack of correlation between signals in the high-frequency components and those beyond the lag period and the fact that high-frequency components generally have small magnitudes, we only consider in this paper the prediction of the low-frequency components of daily closing stock prices. Specifically, we use a 20-tap low-pass filter designed by Matlab function $firls(20, [0\ 0.1\ 0.2\ 1], [1\ 1\ 0\ 0])$. (Other low-pass filters will give similar results.) The low-pass filter will incur a 10-day lag in the smoothed time series. Further, for the same reason as in (Zheng *et al.* 1999), we do not use differencing to improve the stationarity of the low-frequency component because we do not want to introduce cumulative errors when stock prices are reconstructed from the differenced time series.

As mentioned before, another critical issue to be addressed in a low-pass time series is the edge effects incurred. Existing schemes handle these effects by extending the raw data $R(t)$ into the future in order to obtain low-pass data up to current time t_0. Some of these common techniques include *wrap-around, mirror extension, flat extension,* and *zero-padding* (Masters 1995) and are illustrated in Figure 4.

For example, suppose we use a 20-tap filter, and the current time is at t_0. Low-pass data is only available up to time $t_0 - 10$ because a 20-tap low-pass filter needs raw data $R(t_0 - 20)$ to $R(t_0)$ in order to generate $S(t_0 - 10)$. To obtain the missing low-pass data $S(t_0 - 9)$ to $S(t_0)$, flat extension assumes that future raw data $R(t_0 + h) = R(t_0)$ for all $h = 1, 2, \cdots, 10$ before the 20-tap low-pass filter is applied to obtain $S(t_0 - 9)$ to $S(t_0)$. Figure 4 clearly shows that, when a trend is present in the raw data, wrap-around and zero-padding do not work well because they may cause abrupt jumps at the transition point at t_0. In contrast, mirror and flat extensions work well in part of the lag period.

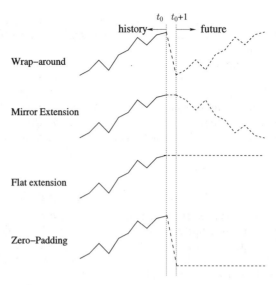

Figure 4: Four approaches for handling edge effect by extending raw data beyond t_0 in order to feed them to the low-pass filtering process. Solid lines represent raw data up to t_0, and dashed lines illustrate extensions to raw data made from $t_0 + 1$ and beyond.

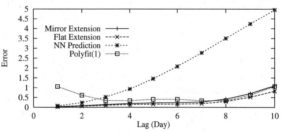

Figure 5: Average errors of IBM's closing prices between April 1, 1997, and March 31, 2002, on four approaches for handling edge effects ($m = 10, q = 7$).

Figure 5 shows that both methods have small average errors for the first seven estimated low-pass points in the lag period with respect to true low-pass data, and flat extensions perform slightly better. Other results (not shown) have similar behavior. This is a surprising result, as mirror extensions have traditionally been viewed as better.

We have also studied the approximation of raw data points in the lag period by a low-order polynomial curve using *polyfit*, a polynomial fitting procedure in Matlab. The objective is to find the coefficients of a polynomial function that minimizes the mean squared errors over the lag period between the raw and fitted smoothed data. Figure 5 shows that the average errors achieved by polynomial fits of degree one are generally larger (fits of higher degrees give worse errors). Note that the errors are particularly large at the beginning of the lag period because the fitted curve is not constrained to have small errors at the transition point.

Yet another method studied is to train an ANN using low-pass data available in order to predict the low-pass data in the lag period. Assuming a lag period of size m, we used a constrained ANN formulation but without the constraints on cross-validation proposed in Section III, trained the ANN to perform one-step predictions using patterns up to $t_0 - m$, and applied the ANN to perform iterative predictions on data in the lag period. The results in Figure 5 show clearly that such an approach performs poorly and justify the need for developing more powerful formulations.

Among all the methods tested, flat extensions achieve the smallest average errors for the first seven days of the lag period, but have considerably larger errors in the last three (Figure 5). Therefore, in our experiments, we use flat extensions to generate seven new training patterns (low-pass data) for the first seven days of the lag period, but include an additional constraint on the raw data in the last three (described in the next section).

III. ANNs for Predicting Filtered Stock Prices

The prediction problem studied in this paper is complex due to the non-stationarity of the time series, multiple objective measures that may not be in closed form, and missing training patterns in the lag period. As a result, it cannot be solved by conventional ANN training methods that perform local searches of a single unconstrained closed-form objective function. In this paper, we adopt a constrained formulation and training strategy we have developed recently (Wah and Qian 2001a), and propose new constraints on raw data in the lag period and on cross validations. By providing new information in constraints that leads a trajectory to reduced constraint violation, a search can overcome the lack of guidance in traditional unconstrained formulations when a trajectory is stuck in a local minimum of its weight space.

As proposed in (Wah and Qian 2001a), we introduce a constraint on the output error of each training pattern:

$$p_i^p(w) = (o(i) - d(i))^2 \leq \tau_i^p, \quad 1 \leq i \leq W, \qquad (3)$$

where $o(i)$ and $d(i)$ are, respectively, the ith actual and desired (target) outputs, τ_i^p is the error tolerance, and W is the window size of the time series used in learning.

We formulate the training objective to be the minimization of the sum of squared one-step prediction errors over a window of training patterns in a recurrent FIR ANN (RFIR) shown in Figure 2. We use the one-step error instead of the more complex iterative prediction error over a horizon because it allows gradients to be computed easily by back-propagation. The complex iterative prediction errors are formulated as constraints in cross validations.

Next, we introduce new constraints to limit errors from multiple validation sets in cross validations. In traditional approaches, cross validations involve the computation of a performance measure on a set of patterns available in training. Since the measure used in cross validations is the same as that in training, patterns used in cross validations and training must be different. The approach of formulating errors in cross validations as constraints not only allows measures that are different from those in learning to be used, but allows patterns in learning and cross validation to be shared. In our work, we avoid overfitting by using small networks along with constraints on iterative validation errors in the validation sets.

Our cross validation simulates as closely as possible the testing process after learning is completed and compares the results of iterative predictions by a trained ANN against

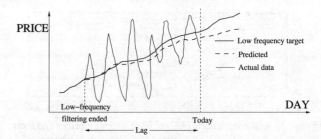

Figure 6: Illustration of constraints on lag period. Outputs of the network in the lag period is constrained to be centered by raw data.

known training patterns. Here, we define a *validation set* to be a collection of $L = m + h$ training patterns, where m is the size of the lag period and h is the horizon to be predicted. Starting from the first pattern in the validation set, we perform a flat extension of the patterns in the first q of the m patterns (described in the last section), perform q single-step predictions using the q extended patterns as inputs, and then perform iterative predictions on the next $h + m - q$ patterns. As training patterns have to be estimated in the lag period and substantial errors are incurred on patterns beyond the lag period, it is more difficult for cross-validation errors to converge. At this point, instead of summing the squares of all the h errors into a single error, as done in (Wah and Qian 2001a), we keep them separately, average the absolute error (MAE) at each horizon over multiple validation sets, and constrain each against a prescribed threshold. Based on the MAE and hit rate metrics defined in Section I, there are $2h$ additional constraints:

$$\begin{array}{ll} p_e^v(w) \leq \tau_e^v \\ p_e^r(w) \leq \tau_e^r \end{array} \qquad 1 \leq e \leq h, \qquad (4)$$

where $p_e^v(w)$ (resp. $p_e^r(w)$) is the average validation error (resp. residual hit rate $1 - H(e)$) at position e, and τ_e^v (resp. τ_e^r) is the corresponding tolerance. As we expect both validation errors and residual hit rates to increase with an increased horizon, we set τ_e^v and τ_e^r to be monotonically increasing functions with respect to e.

The last constraint to be added involves the $m - q$ patterns in the lag period that are not predicted accurately by flat extensions. As illustrated in Figure 6, the idea is to constrain the predictions of the trained ANN in such a way that its outputs (smoothed data) are centered around the raw data in the entire lag period.

$$p^s = \sum_{t=t_0-m+1}^{t_0-m+q} o(t) - R(t) + \sum_{t=t_0-m+q+1}^{t_0} \hat{S}(t) - R(t) \leq \tau^s, \quad (5)$$

where τ_e^s is the tolerance for this error.

Putting all the constraints together, we have:

$$\min_w \quad \sum_{i=1}^{W} \max \left\{ (o(i) - d(i))^2 - \tau, 0 \right\} \qquad (6)$$

$$\text{s.t.} \quad \begin{array}{l} p_i^p(w) \leq \tau_i^p, \quad 1 \leq i \leq W, \\ p_e^v(w) \leq \tau_e^v, \quad 1 \leq e \leq h, \\ p_e^r(w) \leq \tau_e^r \\ p^s = \sum(o(t) - R(t)) + \sum(\hat{S}(t) - R(t)) \leq \tau^s. \end{array}$$

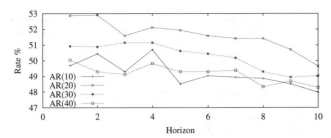

Figure 7: Hit rates of AR on 1,100 consecutive predictions between April 1, 1997, and March 31, 2002, using low-pass filtered data of Citigroup.

Since (6) is a constrained nonlinear programming problem (NLP) with *non-differentiable functions*, it cannot be solved by the traditional back-propagation algorithm or Lagrangian methods that require the differentiability of functions. To address this issue, we apply a new violation-guided back-propagation algorithm (VGBP) we have developed (Wah and Qian 2001a; 2001b) to solve this constrained problem. VGBP works on the Lagrangian function transformed from (6) and searches for discrete-space saddle points based on the *theory of Lagrange multipliers for nonlinear discrete constrained optimization* (Wah and Wu 1999). It does this by gradient descents in the original weight space and ascends in the Lagrange-multiplier space, using an approximate gradient of the objective function found by back-propagation and according to the violation of each constraint. Interested reader can refer to (Wah and Qian 2001b) for details about the VGBP algorithm.

The tolerances τ^p, τ^v, τ^r and τ^s are set by the *relax-and tighten* strategy in VGBP. This strategy is based on the observation that looser constraints are easier to satisfy, while achieving larger violations at convergence, and that tighter constraints are slower to satisfy, while achieving smaller violations at convergence. By using loose constraints in the beginning and by tightening the constraints gradually, learning converges faster with tighter tolerances.

IV. Experimental Results

In this section we compare the performance of our proposed constrained ANN with edge effects handled by flat extension (FE-NN) against four benchmark methods: simple Carbon Copy (CC), auto-regression (AR), ANN similar to FE-NN but without handling edge effects and no cross-validation (NN), and predictions using ideal data in the lag period (IP). CC is easy to implement because it always predicts future data to be same as the most recent available true data. AR was tested using the *TISEAN* implementation (Hegger and Schreiber 2002). We also constructed an ideal predictor (IP) in order to establish an upper bound on prediction accuracy. Based on true low-pass data in the first seven data points in the lag period (instead of predicting them based on flat extensions as in FE-NN), an ANN trained by VGBP is applied to predict the last three missing low-pass data in the lag period and future low-pass data. IP will give an approximate upper-bound accuracy that can be achieved, as it uses seven

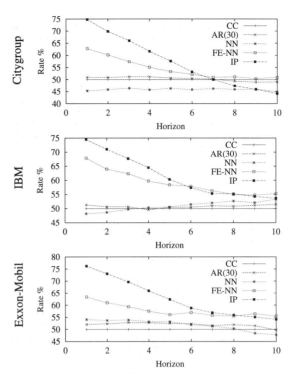

Figure 8: Hit rates on 1,100 consecutive predictions between April 1, 1997, and March 31, 2002, using predictors of Carbon copy (CC), auto-regression with order of 30 (AR(30)), traditional neural network (NN), neural network using constrained formulation coupled with flat extension technique (FE-NN), and ideal predictor (IP).

error-free low-pass data in the lag period that are unavailable otherwise. We tested the aforementioned predictors using three times series based on the closing prices of IBM (symbol **IBM**), Citigroup (symbol **C**) and Exxon-Mobil (symbol **XOM**) from April 1, 1997, to March 31, 2002.

Figure 7 shows the hit rates over different horizons by AR with a variety of orders over 1,100 predictions using low-pass filtered data of Citigroup. As there is a ten-day lag in the low-pass data, AR will need to predict data for ten days in the lag period before predicting into the future. Consequently, its first true prediction starts at the 11th day, and the prediction at horizon h is its $(h + 10)^{th}$ prediction. The results show that pure AR does not provide any useful prediction because its hit rate is always around 50%. Moreover, increasing its order does not improve the accuracy. Similar results have also been observed for the IBM and Exxon-Mobil stock prices. This poor performance may be attributed to the non-stationarity of the time series and the need to predict in the lag period. As AR(30) gives relatively better results, we use it in the remaining experiments on AR.

Figure 8 plots the hit rates for the five predictors. It shows that CC, AR(30) and NN behave like random walks over the ten-day horizon, as they always have around 50% chance to give the correct direction of price changes. On the other hand, our proposed FE-NN can achieve hit rates significantly higher than 50% over small horizons (one to five

Table 2: Normalized mean square errors ($nMSE$s) over 1,100 predictions made between April 1997 and March 2002 using five predictors: carbon copy (CC), autoregression with order 30 (AR(30)), traditional neural network (NN), neural network with constrained formulation and flat extension technique (FE-NN), and an ideal predictor (IP) which uses 7 true low-pass data in the lag period.

Stock	Citigroup			IBM			Exxon-Mobil		
Horizon	1	5	10	1	5	10	1	5	10
C.C	0.061	0.087	0.121	0.085	0.130	0.193	0.122	0.165	0.220
AR(30)	0.055	0.106	0.168	0.068	0.133	0.208	0.136	0.224	0.339
NN	0.086	0.173	0.253	0.095	0.310	0.541	0.183	0.362	0.657
FE-NN	0.010	0.052	0.128	0.013	0.063	0.153	0.019	0.094	0.210
IP	0.002	0.033	0.131	0.003	0.022	0.182	0.005	0.067	0.266

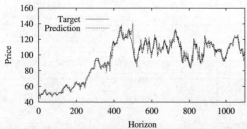

Figure 9: Predictions of FE-NN on a three-day horizon as compared to the actual low-pass data on the 1,100-day closing prices of IBM between April 1, 1997, and March 31, 2002.

days). For these horizons, IP performs better than FE-NN. However, at large horizons (six days and beyond), IP performs statistically the same as FE-NN.

Figure 9 plots the predictions of FE-NN for a three-day horizon, as compared to the actual low-pass data, on the 1,100-day closing prices of IBM between April 1, 1997, and March 31, 2002. The results show that the predictions track well with the actual low-pass data.

Table 2 shows the $nMSE$s of the five predictors over the 1,100 predictions. AR(30) and NN do not perform well because they need to predict iteratively in the ten-day lag period before predicting into the future. FE-NN improves significantly over CC and AR(30), especially for small horizons, and out-performs traditional NN over all horizons. Again, the table shows that FE-NN has errors closest to those of IP over small prediction horizons, and achieves slightly better $nMSE$ at longer horizons. (Note that IP only gives an *approximate* upper bound on prediction accuracy).

References

M. Aoki. *State Space Modeling of Time Series*. Springer-Verlag, Nerlin, 1987.

G. E. P. Box and G. M. Jenkins. *Time Series Analysis: Forecasting and Control, 2nd ed.* Holden-Day, San Francisco, 1976.

R. G. Brown. *Smoothing, Forecasting and Prediction*. Prentice Hall, Englewood Cliffs, NJ, 1963.

Chris Chatfield. *Time-series forecasting*. Chapman & Hall/CRC, Boca Raton, Florida, 2001.

J. L. Elman. Finding structure in time. *Cognitive Science*, 14:179–211, 1990.

S. Haykin. *Neural Networks: A Comprehensive Foundation*. Prentice Hall, NJ, 2 edition, 1999.

R. Hegger and T. Schreiber. The TISEAN software package. *http://www.mpipks-dresden.mpg.de/ tisean*, 2002.

T. Hellstrom and K. Holmstrom. *Predicting the Stock Market*. Technical Report Series IMa-TOM-1997-07, Malardalen University, Vasteras, Sweden, 1997.

T. Masters. *Neural, Novel and Hybrid Algorithms for Time Series Prediction*. John Wiley & Sons, Inc., NY, 1995.

D.F. Nicholls and A.R. Pagan. Varying coefficient regression. In E. J. Hannan, P. R. Krishnaiah, and M. M. Rao, editors, *Handbook of Statistics*, pages 413–449. North-Holland, Amsterdam, 1985.

E.W. Saad, D.V. Prokhorov, and D.C. Wunsch, II. Comparative study of stock trend prediction using time delay, recurrent and probabilistic neural networks. *IEEE Trans. on Neural Networks*, 9:1456–1470, 11 1998.

H. Tong. *Nonlinear Time Series: A Dynamical System Approach*. Oxford University Press, Oxford, 1990.

B. W. Wah and M.-L. Qian. Violation-guided learning for constrained formulations in neural network time series prediction. In *Proc. Int'l Joint Conference on Artificial Intelligence*. IJCAI, 771-776 Aug. 2001.

B. W. Wah and M.-L. Qian. Violation guided neural-network learning fo constrained formulations in time-series predictions. *Int'l Journal on Computational Intelligence and Applications*, 1(4):383–398, December 2001.

B. W. Wah and Z. Wu. The theory of discrete Lagrange multipliers for nonlinear discrete optimization. *Principles and Practice of Constraint Programming*, pages 28–42, October 1999.

E. A. Wan. *Finite Impulse Response Neural Networks with Applications in Time Series Prediction*. Ph.D. Thesis, Standford University, 1993.

G. Zheng, J.L. Starck, J.G. Campbell, and F. Murtagh. Multiscale transforms for filtering financial data streams. *J. of Computational Intelligence in Finance*, 7:18–35, 1999.

Rule-Based Anomaly Pattern Detection for Detecting Disease Outbreaks

Weng-Keen Wong
Dept of Computer Science
Carnegie Mellon University
Pittsburgh, PA, 15213
wkw@cs.cmu.edu

Andrew Moore
Dept of Computer Science
Carnegie Mellon University
Pittsburgh, PA, 15213
awm@cs.cmu.edu

Gregory Cooper
Ctr for Biomedical Informatics
University of Pittsburgh
Pittsburgh, PA 15213
gfc@cbmi.upmc.edu

Michael Wagner
Ctr for Biomedical Informatics
University of Pittsburgh
Pittsburgh, PA 15213
mmw@cbmi.upmc.edu

Abstract

This paper presents an algorithm for performing early detection of disease outbreaks by searching a database of emergency department cases for anomalous patterns. Traditional techniques for anomaly detection are unsatisfactory for this problem because they identify individual data points that are rare due to particular combinations of features. When applied to our scenario, these traditional algorithms discover isolated outliers of particularly strange events, such as someone accidentally shooting their ear, that are not indicative of a new outbreak. Instead, we would like to detect anomalous patterns. These patterns are groups with specific characteristics whose recent pattern of illness is anomalous relative to historical patterns. We propose using a rule-based anomaly detection algorithm that characterizes each anomalous pattern with a rule. The significance of each rule is carefully evaluated using Fisher's Exact Test and a randomization test. Our algorithm is compared against a standard detection algorithm by measuring the number of false positives and the timeliness of detection. Simulated data, produced by a simulator that creates the effects of an epidemic on a city, is used for evaluation. The results indicate that our algorithm has significantly better detection times for common significance thresholds while having a slightly higher false positive rate.

Introduction

Multidimensional data with a temporal component is available from numerous disciplines such as medicine, engineering, and astrophysics. This data is commonly used for monitoring purposes by a detection system. These systems inspect the data for anomalies and raise an appropriate alert upon discovery of any deviations from the norm. For example, in the case of an intrusion detection system, an anomaly would indicate a possible breach of security (Lane & Brodley 1999; Eskin 2000; Maxion & Tan 2001).

We would like to tackle the problem of early disease outbreak detection in a similar manner. In our situation, we have a database of emergency department (ED) cases from several hospitals in a city. Each record in this database contains information about the individual who was admitted to

the ED. This information includes fields such as age, gender, symptoms exhibited, home location, work location, and time admitted. (To maintain patient confidentiality, personal identifying information, such as patient names, addresses, and identification numbers were not in the dataset used in this research.) Clearly, when an epidemic sweeps through a region, there will be extreme perturbations in the number of ED visits. While these dramatic upswings are easily noticed during the late stages of an epidemic, the challenge is to detect the outbreak during its early stages and mitigate its effects. Different diseases cause different signals to appear in temporal, spatial and demographic data (Wagner *et al.* 2001). In order for any anomaly detection algorithm to be successful in early detection of disease outbreaks, it must be able to detect abnormalities in these three aspects of ED data.

Although we have posed our problem in an anomaly detection framework, the majority of anomaly detection algorithms are inappropriate for this domain. In this section, we will illustrate the shortcomings of traditional anomaly detection techniques in our task of early epidemic detection.

A simplistic first approach would be to report an ED case as an anomaly if it has a rare value for some attribute. As an example, we would signal an anomaly if we encountered a patient over a hundred years old. While this method detects the outliers for a single attribute, it fails to identify anomalies that occur due to combinations of features which by themselves might not be abnormal but together would certainly be unusual. For instance, the first technique would not find anomalies in cases where the patients were male and under the age of thirty but exhibited symptoms that were associated with a disease that affects primarily female senior citizens. Fortunately, there are plenty of anomaly detection algorithms that can identify outliers in multidimensional feature space. Typically these detection algorithms build a probabilistic model of the "normal" data using a variety of techniques such as neural nets (Bishop 1994) and a mixture of naive Bayes submodels (Hamerly & Elkan 2001)

However, even that kind of sophisticated outlier detection is insufficient for our purposes. Outlier detection succeeds at finding data points that are rare based on the underlying density, but these data points are treated in isolation from each other. Early epidemic detection, on the other hand, hinges on identifying anomalous groups, which we will refer to as *anomalous patterns*. Specifically, we want to know if the recent proportion of a group with specific characteristics is anomalous based on what the proportion is normally. Traditional outlier detection will likely return isolated irregularities that are insignificant to the early detection system.

We might then argue that aggregate daily counts of a single attribute or combination of attributes should be monitored in order to detect an anomalous group. For instance, we could monitor the daily number of people appearing in the ED with respiratory problems. A naive detector would determine the mean and variance of the monitored signal over a training set which is assumed to capture the normal behaviour of the system. Then, a threshold would be established based on these values. Whenever the daily count exceeds this threshold, an alert is raised. This technique works well if the monitored features are known. However, the spatial, temporal, and demographic signatures of diseases are simply too wide a space for us to know a priori what features to monitor. We could well miss some combination of features that would indicate an outbreak of a particular disease. Thus, we need an algorithm that is able to detect anomalous patterns rather than pre-defined anomalies.

Our approach to this problem uses a rule-based anomaly pattern detector. Each anomalous pattern is summarized by a rule, which in our current implementation consists of one or two components. Each component takes the form $X_i = V_i^j$, where X_i is the ith feature and V_i^j is the jth value of that feature. Multiple components are joined together by a logical AND. For example, a two component rule would be Gender = Male and Age_Decile = 4. One benefit to a rule-based system is that the rules are easily understood by a non-statistician.

However, we need to be wary of the pitfalls of rule-based anomaly pattern detection. Since we are finding anomalous patterns rather than isolated anomalies, we will be performing multiple hypothesis tests. When multiple hypothesis tests are performed, the probability of a false positive becomes inflated unless a correction is made (Benjamini & Hochberg 1995). In addition, as we add more components to a rule, overfitting becomes a serious concern. A careful evaluation of significance is clearly needed. Furthermore, temporal healthcare data used for disease outbreak detection, are frequently subject to "seasonal" variations. As an example, the number of influenza cases is typically higher during winter than summer. Additionally, the number of ED visits vary between weekends and weekdays. The definition of what is normal will change depending on these variations.

Rule-based Anomaly Pattern Detection

The basic question asked by all detection systems is whether anything strange has occurred in recent events. This question requires defining what it means to be recent and what it means to be strange. Our algorithm considers all patient records falling on the current day under evaluation to be recent events. Note that this definition of recent is not restrictive – our approach is fully general and recent can be defined to include all events within some other time period. In order to define an anomaly, we need to establish the concept of something being normal. Our algorithm is intended to be applied to a database of ED cases and we need to account for environmental factors such as weekend versus weekday differences in the number of cases. Consequently, normal behaviour is assumed to be captured by the events occurring on the days that are exactly five, six, seven, and eight weeks prior to the day under consideration. The definition of what is normal can be easily modified to another time period without major changes to our algorithm. We will refer to the events that fit a certain rule for the current day as C_{today}. Similarly, the number of cases matching the same rule from five to eight weeks ago will be called C_{other}.

From this point on, we will refer to our algorithm as WSARE, which is an abbreviation for "What's strange about recent events". WSARE operates on discrete data sets with the aim of finding rules that characterize significant patterns of anomalies. Due to computational issues, the number of components for these rules is two or less. The description of the rule-finding algorithm will begin with an overview followed by a more detailed example.

Overview of WSARE   The best rule for a day is found by considering all possible one and two component rules over events occurring on that day and returning the one with the best "score". The score is determined by comparing the events on the current day against events in the past. Following the score calculation, the best rule for that day has its p-value estimated by a randomization test. The p-value for a rule is the likelihood of finding a rule with as good a score under the hypothesis that the case features and date are independent. The randomization-based p-value takes into account the effect of the multiple testing that went on during the rule search. If we were running the algorithm on a day-by-day basis we would end at this step. However, if we were looking at a history of days, we would need the additional step of using the False Discovery Rate (FDR) method (Benjamini & Hochberg 1995) to determine which of the p-values are significant. The days with significant p-values are returned as the anomalies.

One component rules   In order to illustrate this algorithm, suppose we have a large database of 1,000,000 ED records over a two-year span. This database contains roughly 1000 records a day, thereby yielding approximately 5000 records if we consider the cases for today plus those from five to eight weeks ago. We will refer to this record subset as DB_i, which corresponds to the recent event data set for day i. The algorithm proceeds as follows. For each day i, retrieve the records belonging to DB_i. We first consider all possible one-component rules. For every possible feature-value combination, obtain the counts C_{today} and C_{other} from the data set DB_i. As an example, suppose the feature under consideration is the Age_Decile for the ED case. There are 9 possible Age_Decile values, ranging from 0 to 8. We start with the rule Age_Decile = 3 and count the number of cases for the current day i that have Age_Decile = 3 and those that have Age_Decile $\neq$ 3. The cases from five to eight weeks ago are subsequently examined to obtain the counts for the cases matching the rule and those not matching the rule. The four values form a two-by-two contingency table such as the one shown in Table 1.

Scoring each one component rule The next step is to evaluate the "score" of the rule using a hypothesis test in which the null hypothesis is the independence of the row and column attributes of the two-by-two contingency table. In effect, the hypothesis test measures how different the distribution for C_{today} is compared to that of C_{other}. This test will generate a p-value that determines the significance of the anomalies found by the rule. We will refer to this p-value as the *score* in order to differentiate this p-value from the p-value that is obtained later on from the randomization test. We use the Chi Squared test for independence of variables whenever the counts in the contingency table do not violate the validity of the Chi Squared test. However, since we are searching for anomalies, the counts in the contingency table frequently involve small numbers. In this case, we use Fisher's Exact Test (Good 2000) to find the score for each rule. Running Fisher's Exact Test on Table 1 yields a score of 0.00005058, which indicates that the count C_{today} for cases matching the rule Age_Decile = 3 are significantly different from the count C_{other}.

	C_{today}	C_{other}
Age_Decile = 3	48	45
Age_Decile ≠ 3	86	220

Table 1: A Sample 2x2 Contingency Table

Two component rules At this point, the best one component rule for a particular day has been found. We will refer to the best one component rule for day i as BR_i^1. The algorithm then attempts to find the best two component rule for the day by adding on one extra component to BR_i^1. This extra component is determined by supplementing BR_i^1 with all possible feature-value pairs, except for the one already present in BR_i^1, and selecting the resulting two component rule with the best score. Scoring is performed in the exact same manner as before, except the counts C_{today} and C_{other} are calculated by counting the records that match the two component rule. The best two-component rule for day i is subsequently found and we will refer to it as BR_i^2

BR_i^2, however, may not be an improvement over BR_i^1. We need to perform further hypothesis tests to determine if the presence of either component has a significant effect. This can be accomplished by determining the scores of having each component through Fisher's Exact Test. If we label BR_i^2's components as C_0 and C_1, then the two 2-by-2 contingency tables for Fisher's Exact Tests are as follows:

Records from Today matching C_0 and C_1	Records from Other matching C_0 and C_1
Records from Today matching C_1 and differing on C_0	Records from Other matching C_1 and differing on C_0

Table 2: First 2x2 Contingency Table 1 for a Two Component Rule

Records from Today matching C_0 and C_1	Records from Other matching C_0 and C_1
Records from Today matching C_0 and differing on C_1	Records from Other matching C_0 and differing on C_1

Table 3: Second 2x2 Contingency Table 2 for a Two Component Rule

Once we have the scores for both tables, we need to determine if they are significant or not. We used the standard α value of 0.05 and considered a score to be significant if it was less than or equal to α. If the scores for the two tables were both significant, then the presence of both components had an effect. As a result, the best rule overall for day i is BR_i^2. On the other hand, if any one of the scores was not significant, then the best rule overall for day i is BR_i^1.

Finding the p-value for a rule The algorithm above for determining scores is extremely prone to overfitting. Even if data were generated randomly, most single rules would have insignificant p-values but the best rule would be significant if we had searched over 1000 possible rules. In order to illustrate this point, suppose we follow the standard practice of rejecting the null hypothesis when the p-value is $< \alpha$, where $\alpha = 0.05$. In the case of a single hypothesis test, the probability of making a false discovery under the null hypothesis would be α, which equals 0.05. On the other hand, if we perform 1000 hypothesis tests, one for each possible rule under consideration, then the probability of making a false discovery could be as bad as $1 - (1 - 0.05)^{1000} \approx 1$, which is much greater than 0.05 (Miller *et al.* 2001). Thus, if our algorithm returns a significant p-value, we cannot accept it at face value without adding an adjustment for the multiple hypothesis tests we performed. This problem can be addressed using a Bonferroni correction (Bonferroni 1936) but this approach would be unnecessarily conservative. Instead, we turn to a randomization test in which the date and each ED case features are assumed to be independent. In this test, the case features in the data set DB_i remain the same for each record but the date field is shuffled between records from the current day and records from five to eight weeks ago. The full method for the randomization test is shown below.

Let UCP_i = Uncompensated p-value ie. the score
           as defined above.

For j = 1 to 1000
    Let $DB_i^{(j)}$ = newly randomized dataset
    Let $BR_i^{(j)}$ = Best rule on $DB_i^{(j)}$
    Let $UCP_i^{(j)}$ = Uncompensated p-value of $BR_i^{(j)}$ on DB_i^j
Let the compensated p-value of BR_i be CPV_i ie.

$$CPV_i = \frac{\text{\# of Randomized Tests in which } UCP_i^j > UCP_i}{\text{\# of Randomized Tests}}$$

It is clear from this procedure that CPV_i is an estimate of the chance that we would have seen an uncompensated p-value as good as UCP_i if in fact there was no relationship between date and case features. In practice, for computational reasons, we involve the old idea of "racing" (Maron & Moore 1997) during the randomization procedure. If BR_i is highly significant, we run the full 1000 iterations but we stop early if we can show with very high confidence that CPV_i is going to be greater than 0.05.

Using FDR to determine which p-values are significant
This algorithm can be used on a day-to-day basis similar to an online algorithm or it can operate over a history of several days to report all significantly anomalous patterns. When using our algorithm on a day-to-day basis, the compensated p-value CPV_i obtained for the current day through the randomization tests can be interpreted at face value. However, when analyzing historical data, we need to compare the CPV values for each day in the history. Comparison of multiple CPV values results in a second overfitting opportunity analogous to that caused by performing multiple hypothesis tests to determine the best rule for a particular day. As an illustration, suppose we took 500 days of randomly generated data. Then, approximately 5 days would have a CPV value less than 0.01 and these days would naively be interpreted as being significant. Two approaches can be used to correct this problem. Again, the Bonferroni method (Bonferroni 1936) aims to reduce the probability of making at least one false positive to be no greater than α. However, this tight control over the number of false positives causes many real discoveries to be missed (Miller *et al.* 2001). The other alternative is the False Discover Rate (FDR) method (Benjamini & Hochberg 1995; Miller *et al.* 2001), which guarantees that the fraction of the number of false positives over the number of tests in which the null hypothesis was rejected will be no greater than α. The FDR method is more desirable as it has a higher power than the Bonferroni method but still has reasonable control over the number of false positives. We incorporate the FDR method into our rule-learning algorithm by first providing an α value and then using FDR to find the cutoff threshold for determining which p-values are significant.

The Simulator

Validation of our algorithm is a difficult task due to the type of data required. Data consisting of ED cases during a disease outbreak is extremely limited and there are few available databases of ED cases during a bioagent release. To make matters more difficult, evaluation of our anomaly pattern detector requires a large amount of data that has records that are labeled as either anomalies or normal events. [1] In most cases, this task requires a human to perform the labelling by hand, resulting in an insufficient amount of data. As a result of these limitations, we resort to evaluating our algorithm using data from a simulator.

---

[1]Of course, labelled data is only needed for evaluation and validation. In regular deployment, WSARE is applied to unlabelled data

The simulator is intended to simulate (to a first approximation) the effects of an epidemic on a population. The world in this simulator consists of a grid in which there are three types of objects – places, people, and diseases. These three objects interact with each other in a daily routine for a fixed number of days. Each of these objects will be described in detail below.

Places The three types of places in the simulator include homes, businesses, and restaurants. Their roles are evident from what they represent in real life. People reside in homes, work in businesses and eat in restaurants.

People Each person in the simulation has a specified gender and age. Genders for the population are distributed uniformly between male and female while ages follow a normal distribution with mean 40 and standard deviation of 15. People have a home location, a work location, a list of restaurants that they eat at and a list of homes of friends that they like to visit. The locations of work, restaurants, and friends' homes are chosen to be in close proximity to a person's home. On each day, a schedule is generated for a person. In this schedule, people sleep at home until it is time to go to work. They go to work, stop for a lunch break at a restaurant, and then return to work. After work, they spend some time at home before going to a restaurant for dinner. Following dinner, they visit a random selection of friends at their houses. Finally they return home to sleep.

Diseases Diseases are the most complex objects in the simulator as they are designed to allow the creation of a large variety of disease models. People, places and grid cells can all serve as infection agents since they can all carry a disease. With infected places, we can create diseases that spread by a contaminated food supply while with infected grid cells, we can model airborne infections. Associated with each disease is a spontaneous generation probability which corresponds to how likely the disease is to appear in the population at each timestep. Typically, this probability is extremely small. Each disease also progresses through several stages at different rates. On each stage, the infected person can exhibit a variety of symptoms. The current simulation chooses randomly from a list of symptoms at each stage of the disease. At the final stage, an infected agent can either recover or die. The deceased are removed from the simulation.

The entire infection process revolves around the infection probability, which controls how easily an infected person can pass the disease on to another on each timestep. A radius parameter determines how close a person needs to be to catch the disease. The simulator only allows a person to have one disease at a time. Should more than one disease infect a person, the priority of an epidemic arbitrates which disease is assigned to the person. Diseases can be designed to spread from one particular type of agent to another for example place to person, person to person, or grid cell to person. Additionally, each disease has a specific demographic group that it infects. Whenever it has an opportunity to spread to a person outside of this demographic group, the infection probability is reduced to a small percentage of its original value.

We do not have hospitals in the simulation. Instead, when people exhibit a certain symptom, we create an ED case by adding an entry to a log file. This entry contains information such as the person id, the day, the time, the current location of the person, the home location of the person, and any demographic information about the individual. Most importantly, we add to each entry the actual disease carried by that person, though this last piece of information is hidden from the anomaly detector.

Results

Simulation Settings Our results were obtained by running the simulator on a 50 by 50 grid world with 1000 people, 350 homes, 200 businesses, and 100 restaurants. The simulation ran for 180 simulated days with the epidemic being introduced into the environment on the 90th day. There are nine background diseases that spontaneously appeared at random points in the simulation. At certain stages, these background diseases caused infected people to display the monitored symptom. These background diseases had low infection probabilities as they were intended to provide a baseline for the number of ED cases. The epidemic, on the other hand, had a higher priority than the background diseases and it had a relatively high infection probability, making it spread easily through its target demographic group.

The epidemic that we added to the system will be referred to as Epidemic0. This disease had a target demographic group of males in their 50s. Additionally, the disease is permitted to contaminate places. Epidemic0 had 4 stages with each stage lasting for two days. The disease was contagious during all four stages. At the final stage, we allowed the person to recover instead of dying in order to keep the total number of people in the simulation constant. Epidemic0 also exhibited the monitored symptom with probability 0.33 on the third stage, probability 1.0 on the final stage, and probability 0 on all other stages. This disease was designed to produce a subtle increase in the number of daily ED counts rather than causing extreme perturbations that could easily be picked up by the naive algorithm.

Evaluation of performance We treated our algorithm as if it ran on a day-by-day basis. Thus, for each day in the simulation, WSARE was asked to determine if the events on the current day were anomalous. We evaluated the performance of WSARE against a standard anomaly detection algorithm that treated a day as anomalous when the daily count of ED cases for the monitor symptom exceeded a threshold. The standard detector was allowed to train on the ED case data from day 30 to day 89 in the simulation to obtain the mean μ and variance σ^2. The threshold was calculated by the formula below, in which Φ^{-1} is the inverse to the cumulative distribution function of a standard normal.

$$\text{threshold} = \mu + \sigma * \Phi^{-1}(1 - \frac{\text{p-value}}{2})$$

In order to illustrate the standard algorithm, suppose we trained on the data from day 30 to 89. The mean and variance of the daily counts of the monitored symptom on this training set were determined to be 20 and 8 respectively. Given a p-value of 0.05, we calculate the threshold as $20 + 1.96 * \sqrt{8} = 25.54$. After training, the standard algorithm is run over all the days of data from day 0 to day 179. Any day in which the daily count of the particular symptom exceeds 25.54 is considered to contain anomalous events.

Both the standard algorithm and WSARE were tested using five levels of p-values (0.1, 0.05, 0.01, 0.005, and 0.001). In order to evaluate the performance of the algorithms, we measured the number of false positives and the number of days until the epidemic was detected. Note that there were two files used in this evaluation step. The first file is the database of ED cases produced by the simulator, which we will refer to as DB_{ED}. The second file is the list of anomalous days reported by the algorithm, which we will refer to as DB_{Anom}. We will call the subset of anomalies having a p-value below the ith p-value level as DB^i_{Anom}.

1. **Counting the number of false positives**
   The number of false positives for the ith p-value level was determined by checking each day in DB^i_{Anom} against DB_{ED}. If a case of the epidemic was not reported in DB_{ED} for that day, then the false positive count was incremented. However, since WSARE relies on data from five to eight weeks prior to the current day, detection does not begin until Day 56. In order to be fair, any false positives found before Day 56 in the standard algorithm were not included.

2. **Calculating time until detection**
   The detection time for the ith p-value level was calculated by searching for the first day in DB^i_{Anom} in which an epidemic case appeared in DB_{ED}. If no such days are found, the detection time was set to be 90 days ie. the maximum length between the introduction of the epidemic until the end of the simulation.

Figures 1 and 2 plot the detection time in days versus the number of false positives for five different p-value thresholds used in both the standard algorithm and WSARE. In Figure 1, the error bars for detection time and false positives are shown. Figure 2 fills in the lines to illustrate the asymptotic behaviour of the curves. These values were generated by taking the average over 100 runs of the simulation.

Results from Simulated Data

These results indicate that for p-value thresholds above 0.01, the detection time for WSARE is significantly smaller than that of the standard algorithm. On the other hand, as the p-value threshold decreases, the detection time for WSARE is somewhat worse than that of the standard algorithm. However, choosing an extremely low threshold would be unprofitable since all anomalies except those at an unusually high significance level would be ignored. For example, using a threshold of 0.01 corresponds to a 99% significance level.

The results also demonstrate that WSARE signals more false positives for higher p-value thresholds. While this behaviour is not desirable, it is tolerable since the number of false positives produced by WSARE differs by a small amount from the count generated by the standard algorithm. In this particular graph, there are at most 3 more false positives identified by WSARE that were not identified by the standard algorithm.

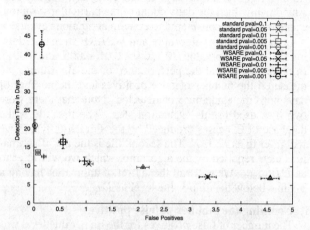

Figure 1: Scatterplot of Detection Time vs False Positives with Error Bars for Detection Time and False Positives

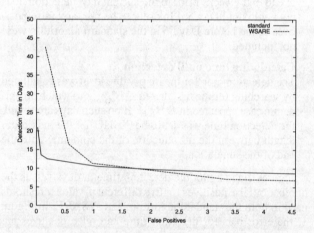

Figure 2: Plot of Detection Time vs False Positives

We now show some of the rules learned by WSARE. The rules below were obtained from one of the result generating simulations.

Rule 1: Sat Day97 (daynum 97, dayindex 97)
SCORE = -0.00000011 PVALUE = 0.00249875
33.33% (16/ 48) of today's cases have Age Decile = 5 and Gender = Male
3.85% (7/182) of other cases have Age Decile = 5 and Gender = Male

Rule 2: Tue Day100 (daynum 100, dayindex 100)
SCORE = -0.00001093 PVALUE = 0.02698651
30.19% (16/ 53) of today's cases have Age Decile = 5 and Col2 less than 25
6.19% (12/194) of other cases have Age Decile = 5 and Col2 less than 25

In rule 1, WSARE demonstrates that it is capable of finding the target demographic group that Epidemic0 infects. This rule proves to be significant above the 99% level. On

the other hand, Rule 2 discovers something that was not deliberately hardcoded into Epidemic0. Rule 2 states that on Day 100, there is an unusually large number of cases involving people in their fifties that were all in the left half of the grid. Since we had designed the people in the simulation to interact with places that are in close geographic proximity to their homes, we suspected that the locality of interaction of infected individuals would form some spatial clusters of ED cases. Upon further inspection of the log files, we discovered that 12 of the 16 cases from the current day that satisfied this rule were in fact caused by Epidemic0. This example illustrates the capability of WSARE to detect significant anomalous patterns that are completely unexpected.

Results from Real ED data

We also ran WSARE on an actual ED data collected from hospitals in a major US city. This database contained approximately 70000 records collected over a period of 505 days. Since we are looking at historical data, we need to use FDR to determine which of the p-values are significant. The results are shown below with α for FDR equal to 0.1.

Rule 1: Tue 05-16-2000 (daynum 36661, dayindex 18)
SCORE = -0.00000000 PVALUE = 0.00000000
32.84% (44/134) of today's cases have Time Of Day4 after 6:00 pm
90.00% (27/ 30) of other cases have Time Of Day4 after 6:00 pm

Rule 2: Fri 06-30-2000 (daynum 36706, dayindex 63)
SCORE = -0.00000000 PVALUE = 0.00000000
19.40% (26/134) of today's cases have Place2 = NE and Lat4 = d
5.71% (16/280) of other cases have Place2 = NE and Lat4 = d

Rule 3: Wed 09-06-2000 (daynum 36774, dayindex 131)
SCORE = -0.00000000 PVALUE = 0.00000000
17.16% (23/134) of today's cases have Prodrome = Respiratory and age2 less than 40
4.53% (12/265) of other cases have Prodrome = Respiratory and age2 less than 40

Rule 4: Fri 12-01-2000 (daynum 36860, dayindex 217)
SCORE = -0.00000000 PVALUE = 0.00000000
22.88% (27/118) of today's cases have Time Of Day4 after 6:00 pm and Lat2 = s
8.10% (20/247) of other cases have Time Of Day4 after 6:00 pm and Lat2 = s

Rule 5: Sat 12-23-2000 (daynum 36882, dayindex 239)
SCORE = -0.00000000 PVALUE = 0.00000000
18.25% (25/137) of today's cases have ICD9 = shortness of breath and Time Of Day2 before 3:00 pm
5.12% (15/293) of other cases have ICD9 = shortness of breath and Time Of Day2 before 3:00 pm

Rule 6: Fri 09-14-2001 (daynum 37147, dayindex 504)
SCORE = -0.00000000 PVALUE = 0.00000000
66.67% (30/ 45) of today's cases have Time Of Day4 before 10:00 am
18.42% (42/228) of other cases have Time Of Day4 before 10:00 am

Rule 1 notices that there are fewer cases after 6:00 pm quite possibly due a lack of reporting by some hospitals. Rule 6 correctly identifies a larger volume of data being collected before 10:00 am on Day 504. Since Day 504 was the last day of this database, this irregularity was the result of the database being given to us in the morning.

We are currently beginning the process of using input from public health officials of the city concerned to help us validate and measure WSARE's performance.

Future work

The algorithm described is computationally intensive, particularly when performing the many randomization tests required to obtain a good estimate of a rule's true p-value. Future research involves speeding up the randomization tests by using data structures that can be efficiently updated when the database is randomized. In addition, we would like to automatically model the "normal" database rather than using an arbitrary selection process of using data from five to eight weeks prior to the current date.

Related Work

Our approach is closely related to the work done by Bay and Pazzani (Bay & Pazzani 1999) in mining contrast sets. Contrast sets are conjunctions of attributes and values whose support differs significantly between groups. In (Bay & Pazzani 1999), the authors perform multiple hypothesis tests while searching for significant contrast sets. A Bonferroni correction is used to control the probability of a Type I error. The paper also prunes all contrast sets that cease to yield a valid chi-square test due to insufficient data points. Our approach is also somewhat similar to itemset mining (Brin et al. 1997). Other papers that deal with early disease outbreak detection include (Wagner et al. 2001) and (Goldenberg 2001).

Conclusion

WSARE has been demonstrated to be successful at identifying anomalous patterns in the data. From our simulation results, WSARE has significantly lower detection times than a standard detection algorithm provided the p-value threshold is not at at extremely low level. This condition should not be a problem since most anomalies are reported at a significance level of 95% or 99%, corresponding respectively to p-value thresholds of 0.05 and 0.01. WSARE also has a slightly higher false positive rate than the standard algorithm. However, this difference was shown to be about 3 more false positives in the worst case for our particular simulation.

We believe the three main innovations in this paper are:

1. Turning the problem of "detect the emergence of new patterns in recent data" into the question "is it possible to learn a propositional rule that can significantly distinguish whether records are most likely to have come from the recent past or longer past?"

2. Incorporating several levels of significance tests into rule learning in order to avoid several levels of overfitting caused by intensive multiple testing

3. Examining the interesting domain of early outbreak detection by means of machine learning tools

References

Bay, S. D., and Pazzani, M. J. 1999. Detecting change in categorical data: Mining contrast sets. In *Knowledge Discovery and Data Mining*, 302–306.

Benjamini, Y., and Hochberg, Y. 1995. Controlling the false discovery rate: a practical and powerful approach to multiple testing. *Journal of the Royal Statistical Society, Series B.* 57:289–300.

Bishop, C. M. 1994. Novelty detection and neural network validation. *IEEE Proceedings - Vision, Image and Signal Processing* 141(4):217–222.

Bonferroni, C. E. 1936. Teoria statistica delle classi e calcolo delle probabilità. *Pubblicazioni del R Istituto Superiore di Scienze Economiche e Commerciali di Firenze* 8:3–62.

Brin, S.; Motwani, R.; Ullman, J. D.; and Tsur, S. 1997. Dynamic itemset counting and implication rules for market basket data. In Peckham, J., ed., *SIGMOD 1997, Proceedings ACM SIGMOD International Conference on Management of Data, May 13-15, 1997, Tucson, Arizona, USA*, 255–264. ACM Press.

Eskin, E. 2000. Anomaly detection over noisy data using learned probability distributions. In *Proceedings of the 2000 International Conference on Machine Learning (ICML-2000)*.

Goldenberg, A. 2001. Framework for using grocery data for early detection of bio-terrorism attacks. Master's thesis, Carnegie Mellon University.

Good, P. 2000. *Permutation Tests - A Practical Guide to Resampling Methods for Testing Hypotheses.* New York: Springer-Verlag, 2nd edition.

Hamerly, G., and Elkan, C. 2001. Bayesian approaches to failure prediction for disk drives. In *Proceedings of the eighteenth international conference on machine learning*, 202–209. Morgan Kaufmann, San Francisco, CA.

Lane, T., and Brodley, C. E. 1999. Temporal sequence learning and data reduction for anomaly detection. *ACM Transactions on Information and System Security* 2:295–331.

Maron, O., and Moore, A. W. 1997. The racing algorithm: Model selection for lazy learners. *Artificial Intelligence Review* 11(1-5):193–225.

Maxion, R. A., and Tan, K. M. C. 2001. Anomaly detection in embedded systems. Technical Report CMU-CS-01-157, Carnegie Mellon University.

Miller, C. J.; Genovese, C.; Nichol, R. C.; Wasserman, L.; Connolly, A.; Reichart, D.; Hopkins, A.; Schneider, J.; and Moore, A. 2001. Controlling the false discovery rate in astrophysical data analysis. Technical report, Carnegie Mellon University.

Wagner, M. M.; Tsui, F. C.; Espino, J. U.; Dato, V. M.; Sittig, D. F.; Caruana, R. A.; McGinnis, L. F.; Deerfield, D. W.; Druzdzel, M. J.; and Fridsma, D. B. 2001. The emerging science of very early detection of disease outbreaks. *Journal of Public Health Management Practice* 7(6):51–59.

Extended Isomap for Pattern Classification

Ming-Hsuan Yang

Honda Fundamental Research Labs
Mountain View, CA 94041
myang@hra.com

Abstract

The Isomap method has demonstrated promising results in finding low dimensional manifolds from data points in the high dimensional input space. While classical subspace methods use Euclidean or Manhattan metrics to represent distances between data points and apply Principal Component Analysis to induce linear manifolds, the Isomap method estimates geodesic distances between data points and then uses Multi-Dimensional Scaling to induce low dimensional manifolds. Since the Isomap method is developed based on reconstruction principle, it may not be optimal from the classification viewpoint. In this paper, we present an extended Isomap method that utilizes Fisher Linear Discriminant for pattern classification. Numerous experiments on image data sets show that our extension is more effective than the original Isomap method for pattern classification. Furthermore, the extended Isomap method shows promising results compared with best methods in the face recognition literature.

Introduction

Subspace methods can be classified into two main categories: either based on reconstruction (i.e., retaining maximum sample variance) or classification principle (i.e., maximizing the distances between samples). Principal Component Analysis (PCA) and Multidimensional Scaling (MDS) have been applied to numerous applications and have shown their abilities to find low dimensional structures from high dimensional samples (Duda, Hart, & Stork 2001). These unsupervised methods are effective in finding compact representations and useful for data interpolation and visualization. On the other hand, Fisher Linear Discriminant (FLD) and alike have shown their successes in pattern classification when class labels are available (Bishop 1995) (Duda, Hart, & Stork 2001). Contrasted to PCA which finds a projection direction that retains maximum variance, FLD finds a projection direction that maximizes the distances between cluster centers. Consequently, FLD-based methods have been shown to perform well in classification problems such as face recognition (Belhumeur, Hespanha, & Kriegman 1997).

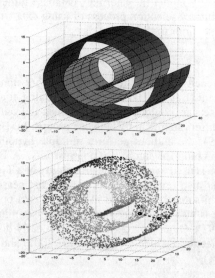

Figure 1: A complex manifold that shows why Euclidean distances may not be good metrics in pattern recognition.

Recently, two dimensionality reduction methods have been proposed for learning complex embedding manifolds using local geometric metrics within a single global coordinate system (Roweis & Saul 2000) (Tenebaum, de Silva, & Langford 2000). The Isomap (or isometric feature mapping) method argues that only the geodesic distance reflects the intrinsic geometry of the underlying manifold (Tenebaum, de Silva, & Langford 2000). Figure 1 shows one example where data points of different classes are displayed in distinct shaded patches (top) and data points sampled from these classes are shown (bottom). For a pair of points on the manifold, their Euclidean distance may not accurately reflect their intrinsic similarity and consequently is not suitable for determining intrinsic embedding or pattern classification. The Euclidean distance between circled data points (e.g., x_1 and x_2 in Figure 1) may be deceptively small in the three-dimensional input space though their geodesic distance on a intrinsic two-dimensional manifold is large. This problem can be remedied by using geodesic distance (i.e., distance metrics along the surface of the manifold) if one is able to compute or estimate such metrics. The Isomap method first constructs a neighborhood graph that connects each point to all its k-nearest neighbors, or to all the points within some fixed radius ϵ in the input space. For neighboring points, the input space distance usually provides a good approximation to their geodesic distance. For each pair of points, the shortest path connecting them in the neighborhood graph is computed and is used as an estimate of the true geodesic distance. These estimates are good approximations of the true geodesic distances if there are sufficient number of data points (See Figure 1). The classical multidimensional scaling method is then applied to construct a low dimensional subspace that best preserves the manifold's estimated intrinsic geometry.

The Locally Linear Embedding (LLE) method captures local geometric properties of complex embedding manifolds by a set of linear coefficients that best approximates each data point from its neighbors in the input space (Roweis & Saul 2000). LLE then finds a set of low dimensional points where each can be linearly approximated by its neighbors with the same set of coefficients that was computed from the high dimensional data points in the input space while minimizing reconstruction cost. Although these two methods have demonstrated excellent results in finding the embedding manifolds that best describe the data points with minimum reconstruction error, they are suboptimal from the classification viewpoint. Furthermore, these two methods assume that the embedding manifold is well sampled which may not be the case in some classification problems such as face recognition since there are typically only a few samples available for each person.

In this paper, we propose a method that extends the Isomap method with Fisher Linear Discriminant for classification. The crux of this method is to estimate geodesic distance, similar to what is done in Isomap, and use pairwise geodesic distances as feature vectors. We then apply FLD to find an optimal projection direction to maximize the distances between cluster centers. Experimental results on three data sets show that the extended Isomap method consistently performs better than the Isomap method, and performs better than or as equally well as some best methods in the face recognition literature.

Extended Isomap

Consider a set of m samples $\{\mathbf{x}_1, \ldots, \mathbf{x}_m\}$ and each sample belongs to one of the c class $\{Z_1, \ldots, Z_c\}$, the first step in the extended Isomap method is, similar to the Isomap method, to determine the neighbors of each sample $\mathbf{x}_i$ on the low dimensional manifold M based on some distance metrics $d_X(\mathbf{x}_i, \mathbf{x}_j)$ in the input space X. Such metrics can be Euclidean distance that is often used in face recognition (Turk & Pentland 1991) or tangent distance that has been shown to be effective in hand digit recognition (Simard, Le Cun, & Denker 1993). The assumption is that input space distance provides a good approximation to geodesic distance for neighboring points (See Figure 1). Consequently, input space distance metric can be utilized to determine whether two data points are neighbors or not. The k-Isomap method uses a k-nearest neighbor algorithm to determine neighbors while the ϵ-Isomap method includes all the points within

some fixed radius ϵ as neighbors. These neighborhood relationships are represented in a weighted graph G in which $d_G(\mathbf{x}_i, \mathbf{x}_j) = d_X(\mathbf{x}_i, \mathbf{x}_j)$ if $\mathbf{x}_i$ and $\mathbf{x}_j$ are neighbors, and $d_X(\mathbf{x}_i, \mathbf{x}_j) = \infty$ otherwise.

The next step is to estimate geodesic distance $d_M(\mathbf{x}_i, \mathbf{x}_j)$ between any pair of points on the manifold M. For a pair of points that are far away, their geodesic distance can be approximated by a sequence of short hops between neighboring data points. In other words, $d_M(\mathbf{x}_i, \mathbf{x}_j)$ is approximated by the shortest path between $\mathbf{x}_i$ and $\mathbf{x}_j$ on G, which is computed by the Floyd-Warshall algorithm (Cormen, Leiserson, & Rivest 1989):

$$d_G(\mathbf{x}_i, \mathbf{x}_j) = \min\{d_G(\mathbf{x}_i, \mathbf{x}_j), d_G(\mathbf{x}_i, \mathbf{x}_k) + d_G(\mathbf{x}_k, \mathbf{x}_j)\}$$

The shortest paths between any two points are represented in a matrix D where $D_{ij} = d_G(\mathbf{x}_i, \mathbf{x}_j)$.

The main difference between extended Isomap and the original method is that we represent each data point by a feature vector of its geodesic distance to any points, and then apply Fisher Linear Discriminant on the feature vectors to find an optimal projection direction for classification. In other words, the feature vector of $\mathbf{x}_i$ is an m dimensional vector $\boldsymbol{f}_i = [D_{ij}]$ where $j = 1, \ldots, m$ and $D_{ii} = 0$.

The between-class and within-class scatter matrices in Fisher Linear Discriminant are computed by:

$$\begin{aligned} S_B &= \sum_{i=1}^{c} N_i (\boldsymbol{\mu}_i - \boldsymbol{\mu})(\boldsymbol{\mu}_i - \boldsymbol{\mu})^T \\ S_W &= \sum_{i=1}^{c} \sum_{\boldsymbol{f}_k \in Z_i} (\boldsymbol{f}_k - \boldsymbol{\mu}_i)(\boldsymbol{f}_k - \boldsymbol{\mu}_i)^T \end{aligned}$$

where $\boldsymbol{\mu}$ is the mean of all samples $\boldsymbol{f}_k$, $\boldsymbol{\mu}_i$ is the mean of class Z_i, S_{Wi} is the covariance of class Z_i, and N_i is the number of samples in class Z_i. The optimal projection W_{FLD} is chosen as the matrix with orthonormal columns which maximizes the ratio of the determinant of the between-class scatter matrix of the projected samples to the determinant of the within-class scatter matrix of the projected samples:

$$W_{FLD} = \arg\max_{W} \frac{|W^T S_B W|}{|W^T S_W W|} = [\mathbf{w}_1 \ \mathbf{w}_2 \ \ldots \ \mathbf{w}_m]$$

where $\{\mathbf{w}_i | i = 1, 2, \ldots, m\}$ is the set of generalized eigenvectors of S_B and S_W, corresponding to the m largest generalized eigenvalues $\{\lambda_i | i = 1, 2, \ldots, m\}$. The rank of S_B is $c - 1$ or less because it is the sum of c matrices of rank one or less. Thus, there are at most $c - 1$ nonzero eigenvalues (Duda, Hart, & Stork 2001). Finally, each data point $\mathbf{x}_i$ is represented by a low dimensional feature vector computed by $\mathbf{y}_i = W_{FLD} \, \boldsymbol{f}_i$. The extended Isomap algorithm is summarized in Figure 2.

The computational complexity and memory requirement of the Isomap and the extended Isomap are dominated by the calculation of all pair shortest paths. The Floyd-Warshall algorithm requires $O(m^3)$ operations and stores $O(m^2)$ elements of estimated geodesic distances for straightforward implementations. On the other hand, the MDS procedure in the Isomap method can be time consuming as a result of its iterative operations to detect meaningful underlying dimensions that explain the observed similarities or dissimilarities (distances) between data points.

1. Constructing neighboring graph

First compute Euclidean distance, $d_X(\mathbf{x}_i, \mathbf{x}_j)$ between any two points $\mathbf{x}_i$ and $\mathbf{x}_j$ in the input space X. Next connect neighbors of any point $\mathbf{x}_i$ by finding its k-nearest neighbors or all the points that are within ϵ radius of $\mathbf{x}_i$. The procedure results in a weighted graph $d_G(\mathbf{x}_i, \mathbf{x}_j)$ where

$$d_G(\mathbf{x}_i, \mathbf{x}_j) = \begin{cases} d_X(\mathbf{x}_i, \mathbf{x}_j) & \text{if } \mathbf{x}_i \text{ and } \mathbf{x}_j \text{ are neighbors} \\ \infty & \text{otherwise.} \end{cases}$$

2. Computing shortest path between pairs of points

Compute shortest path between any pair of points $\mathbf{x}_i$ and $\mathbf{x}_j$ on d_G using Floyd-Warshall algorithm, i.e.,

$$d_G(\mathbf{x}_i, \mathbf{x}_j) = \min\{d_G(\mathbf{x}_i, \mathbf{x}_j), d_G(\mathbf{x}_i, \mathbf{x}_k) + d_G(\mathbf{x}_k, \mathbf{x}_j)\}$$

The shortest paths between any two points are represented in a matrix D where $D_{ij} = d_G(\mathbf{x}_i, \mathbf{x}_j)$.

3. Determining most discriminant components

Represent each point $\mathbf{x}_i$ by a feature vector $\boldsymbol{f}_i$ where $f_i = [D_{ij}]$, $j = 1, \ldots, m$. Determine a subspace where the class centers are separated as far as possible by using the Fisher Linear Discriminant method.

Figure 2: Extended Isomap Algorithm.

It can be shown that the graph $d_G(\mathbf{x}_i, \mathbf{x}_j)$ provides increasing better estimates to the intrinsic geodesic distance $d_M(\mathbf{x}_i, \mathbf{x}_j)$ as the number of data points increases (Tenebaum, de Silva, & Langford 2000). In practice, there may not be sufficient number samples at one's disposal so that the geodesic distances $d_G(\mathbf{x}_i, \mathbf{x}_j)$ may not be good approximates. Consequently, the Isomap may not be able to find intrinsic dimensionality from data points and not suitable for classification purpose. In contrast, the extended Isomap method utilizes the distances between the scatter centers (i.e., poor approximates may be averaged out) and thus may perform well for classification problem in such situations. While the Isomap method uses classical MDS to find dimensions of the embedding manifolds, the dimensionality of the subspace is determined by the number of class (i.e., $c - 1$) in the extended Isomap method.

To deal with the singularity problem of within-scatter matrix S_W that one often encounters in classification problems, we can add a multiple of the identity matrix to the within-scatter matrix, i.e., $S_W + \varepsilon I$ (where ε is a small number). This also makes the eigenvalue problem numerically more stable. See also (Belhumeur, Hespanha, & Kriegman 1997) for a method using PCA to overcome singularity problems in applying FLD to face recognition.

Experiments

Two classical pattern classification problems, face recognition and handwritten digit recognition, are considered in order to analyze the performance of the extended and original Isomap methods. These two problems have several interesting characteristics and are approached quite differently. In the appearance-based methods for face recognition in frontal pose, each face image provides a rich description of one's identity and as a whole (i.e., holistic) is usually treated as a pattern without extracting features explicitly. Instead, subspace methods such as PCA or FLD are applied to implicitly extract meaningful (e.g., PCA) or discriminant (e.g., FLD) features and then project patterns to a lower dimensional subspace for recognition. On the contrary, sophisticated feature extraction techniques are usually applied to handwritten digit images before any decision surface is induced for classification.

We tested both the original and extended Isomap methods against LLE (Roweis & Saul 2000), Eigenface (Turk & Pentland 1991) and Fisherface (Belhumeur, Hespanha, & Kriegman 1997) methods using the publicly available AT&T (Samaria & Young 1994) and Yale databases (Belhumeur, Hespanha, & Kriegman 1997). The face images in these databases have several unique characteristics. While the images in the AT&T database contain facial contours and vary in pose as well as scale, the face images in the Yale database have been cropped and aligned. The face images in the AT&T database were taken under well controlled lighting conditions whereas the images in the Yale database were acquired under varying lighting conditions. We used the first database as a baseline study and then used the second one to evaluate face recognition methods under varying lighting conditions. For handwritten digit recognition problem, we tested both methods using the MNIST database which is the *de facto* benchmark test set.

Face Recognition: Variation in Pose and Scale

The AT&T (formerly Olivetti) face database contains 400 images of 40 subjects (http://www.uk.research.att.com/ facedatabase.html). To reduce computational complexity, each face image is downsampled to 23×28 pixels for experiments. We represent each image by a raster scan vector of the intensity values, and then normalize them to be zero-mean unit-variance vectors. Figure 3 shows images of a few subjects. In contrast to images of the Yale database shown in Figure 5, these images include facial contours, and variations in pose as well as scale. However, the lighting conditions remain relatively constant.

Figure 3: Face images in the AT&T database.

The experiments were performed using the "leave-one-out" strategy (i.e., m fold cross validation): To classify an image of a person, that image is removed from the training set of $(m-1)$ images and the projection matrix is computed. All the m images in the training set are projected to a reduced space and recognition is performed using a nearest neighbor classifier. The parameters, such as number of principal components in Eigenface and LLE methods, were empirically determined to achieve the lowest error rate by each method. For Fisherface and extended Isomap methods, we project all samples onto a subspace spanned by the $c-1$ largest eigenvectors. The experimental results are shown in Figure 4. Among all the methods, the extended Isomap method with ϵ radius implementation achieves the lowest error rate and outperforms the Fisherface method by a significant margin. Notice also that two implementations of the extended Isomap (one with k-nearest neighbor, i.e., extended k-Isomap, and the other with ϵ radius, i.e., extended ϵ-Isomap) to determine neighboring data points) consistently perform better than their counterparts in the Isomap method by a significant margin.

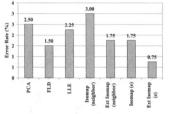

Method	Reduced Space	Error Rate (%)
Eigenface	40	2.50 (10/400)
Fisherface	39	1.50 (6/400)
LLE, # neighbor=70	70	2.25 (9/400)
Isomap, # neighbor=100	45	3.00 (12/400)
Ext Isomap, # neighbor=80	39	1.75 (7/400)
Isomap, ϵ=10	30	1.75 (7/400)
Ext Isomap, ϵ=10	39	0.75 (3/400)

Figure 4: Results with the AT&T database.

Face Recognition: Variation in Lighting and Expression

The Yale database contains 165 images of 11 subjects with facial expression and lighting variations (available at http://cvc.yale.edu/). For computational efficiency, each image has been downsampled to 29×41 pixels. Similarly, each face image is represented by a centered vector of normalized intensity values. Figure 5 shows closely cropped images of a few subjects which include internal facial structures such as the eyebrow, eyes, nose, mouth and chin, but do not contain facial contours.

Figure 5: Face images in the Yale database.

Using the same leave-one-out strategy, we varied the number of principal components to achieve the lowest error rates for Eigenface and LLE methods. For Fisherface and extended Isomap methods, we project all samples onto a subspace spanned by the $c-1$ largest eigenvectors. The experimental results are shown in Figure 6. Both implementations of the extended Isomap method perform better than their counterparts in the Isomap method. Furthermore, the extended ϵ-Isomap method performs almost as well as the Fisherface method (which is one of the best methods in the face recognition literature) though the original Isomap does not work well on the Yale data set.

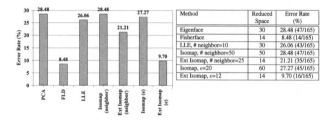

Method	Reduced Space	Error Rate (%)
Eigenface	30	28.48 (47/165)
Fisherface	14	8.48 (14/165)
LLE, # neighbor=10	30	26.06 (43/165)
Isomap, # neighbor=50	50	28.48 (47/165)
Ext Isomap, # neighbor=25	14	21.21 (35/165)
Isomap, ϵ=20	60	27.27 (45/165)
Ext Isomap, ϵ=12	14	9.70 (16/165)

Figure 6: Results with the Yale database.

Figure 7 shows more performance comparisons between Isomap and extended Isomap methods in both k-nearest neighbor as well as ϵ radius implementations. The extended Isomap method consistently outperforms the Isomap method with both implementations in all the experiments.

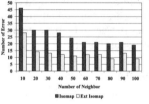

(a) Experiments of k-Isomap and extended k-Isomap methods on the AT & T database.

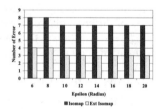

(b) Experiments of ϵ-Isomap and extended ϵ-Isomap methods on the AT & T database.

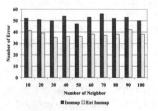

(c) Experiments of k-Isomap and extended k-Isomap methods on the Yale database.

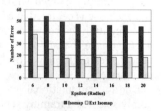

(d) Experiments of ϵ-Isomap and extended ϵ-Isomap methods on the Yale database.

Figure 7: Performance of the Isomap and the extended Isomap methods.

As one example to explain why extended Isomap performs better than Isomap, Figure 8 shows training and test samples of the Yale database projected onto the first two

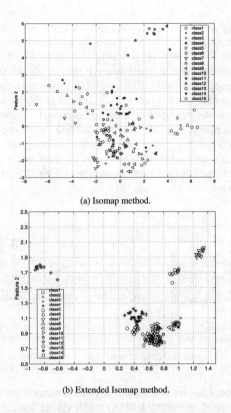

(a) Isomap method.

(b) Extended Isomap method.

Figure 8: Samples projected by the Isomap and the extended Isomap methods.

eigenvectors extracted by both methods. The projected samples of different classes are smeared by the Isomap method (Figure 8(a)) whereas the samples projected by the extended Isomap method are separated well (Figure 8(b)).

Handwritten Digit Recognition

The MNIST database of handwritten digits comprises a training set of 60,000 examples, and a test set of 10,000 examples (publicly available at http://www.research.att.com/~yann/exdb/mnist/index.html). The images are normalized while preserving their aspect ratio, and each one is centered in a 28×28 window of gray scales by computing the center of mass of the pixels, and translating the image so as to position this point at the center. Some handwritten digit images of the MNIST database are shown in Figure 9.

Due to computational and memory constraints, we randomly selected a training set of 1,500 MNIST images and a non-overlapping test set of 250 images for experiments. We repeated the same experiment five times and varied the parameters to achieve the lowest error rates in each run. As a baseline study, each image is represented by a raster scan vector of intensity values without applying any feature extraction algorithms. Figure 10 shows the averaged results by k-Isomap, ϵ-Isomap and our extended methods. The extended Isomap methods consistently outperform the original Isomap methods in our experiments with the MNIST data sets.

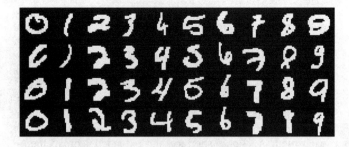

Figure 9: MNIST digit images.

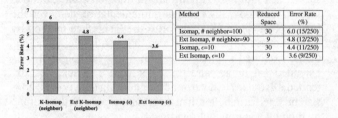

Method	Reduced Space	Error Rate (%)
Isomap, # neighbor=100	30	6.0 (15/250)
Ext Isomap, # neighbor=90	9	4.8 (12/250)
Isomap, ϵ=10	30	4.4 (11/250)
Ext Isomap, ϵ=10	9	3.6 (9/250)

Figure 10: Results with the MNIST database.

We note that the results achieved by the extended Isomap, shown in Figure 10, are not as competitive as the best methods in the literature (Burges & Schölkopf 1997) (LeCun *et al.* 1998) (Belongie, Malik, & Puzicha 2001), the reason being that no feature extraction algorithm is applied to the raw images which is in direct contrast to the best results reported in the literature (such as support vector machines, convolutional neural networks and shape contexts that use complex feature extraction techniques with nonlinear decision surfaces). Our MNIST digit recognition experiments serve as a baseline study to investigate the improvement of the extended Isomap over the original one in visual pattern recognition problems. The recognition rates can be improved by applying sophisticated feature extraction techniques or with k-nearest neighbor classifier in the lower dimensional subspace.

Discussion

The experimental results of two classical pattern recognition problems, face recognition and handwritten digit recognition, show that the extended Isomap method performs better than the Isomap method in the pattern classification tasks. On the other hand, we note that the Isomap method is an effective algorithm to determine the intrinsic dimensionality of the embedding manifolds and thus suitable for interpolation between data points (See (Tenebaum, de Silva, & Langford 2000) for examples).

The feature extraction issues that we alluded to in the handwritten digit recognition experiments can be addressed by combing kernel tricks to extract meaningful and nonlinear features of digit patterns. One advantage of kernel methods is that it provides a computationally efficient method that integrates feature extraction with large margin classifier. We plan to extend the Isomap method with kernel Fisher

Linear Discriminant (Mika *et al.* 2000) (Roth & Steinhage 2000) (Baudat & Anouar 2000) for pattern classification.

Conclusion

In this paper, we present an extended Isomap method for pattern classification when the labels of data points are available. The Isomap method is developed based on reconstruction principle, and thus it may not be optimal from the classification viewpoint. Our extension is based on Fisher Linear Discriminant which aims to find an optimal project direction such that the data points in the subspace are separated as far away as possible.

Our experiments on face and handwritten digit recognition suggest a number of conclusions:

1. The extended Isomap method performs consistently better than the Isomap method in classification (with both k nearest neighbor and ϵ radius implementations) by a significant margin.

2. Geodesic distance appears to be a better metric than Euclidean distance for face recognition in all the experiments.

3. The extended Isomap method performs better than one of the best methods in the literature on the AT&T database. When there exist sufficient number of samples so that the shortest paths between any pair of data points are good approximates of geodesic distances, the extended Isomap method performs well in classification.

4. The extended Isomap method still performs well while the Isomap method does not in the experiments with the Yale database. One explanation is that insufficient samples result in poor approximates of geodesic distances. However, poor approximates may be averaged out by the extended Isomap method and thus it performs better.

5. Though the Isomap and LLE methods have demonstrated excellent results in finding the embedding manifolds that best describe the data points with minimum reconstruction error, they are suboptimal from the classification viewpoint. Furthermore, these two methods assume that the embedding manifold is well sampled which may not be the case in face recognition since there are typically only a few samples available for each person.

Our future work will focus on efficient methods for estimating geodesic distance, and performance evaluation with large and diverse databases. We plan to extend our method by applying the kernel tricks, such as kernel Fisher Linear Discriminant, to provide a richer feature representation for pattern classification. We also plan to compare the extended Isomap method against other learning algorithms with UCI machine learning data sets, as well as reported face recognition methods using FERET (Phillips *et al.* 2000) and CMU PIE (Sim, Baker, & Bsat 2001) databases.

References

Baudat, G., and Anouar, F. 2000. Generalized discriminant analysis using a kernel approach. *Neural Computation* 12:2385–2404.

Belhumeur, P.; Hespanha, J.; and Kriegman, D. 1997. Eigenfaces vs. Fisherfaces: Recognition using class specific linear projection. *IEEE Transactions on Pattern Analysis and Machine Intelligence* 19(7):711–720.

Belongie, S.; Malik, J.; and Puzicha, J. 2001. Matching shapes. In *Proceedings of the Eighth IEEE International Conference on Computer Vision*, volume 1, 454–461.

Bishop, C. M. 1995. *Neural Networks for Pattern Recognition*. Oxford University Press.

Burges, C. J., and Schölkopf, B. 1997. Improving the accuracy and speed of support vector machines. In Mozer, M. C.; Jordan, M. I.; and Petsche, T., eds., *Advances in Neural Information Processing Systems*, volume 9, 375. The MIT Press.

Cormen, T. H.; Leiserson, C. E.; and Rivest, R. L. 1989. *Introduction to Algorithms*. The MIT Press and McGraw-Hill Book Company.

Duda, R. O.; Hart, P. E.; and Stork, D. G. 2001. *Pattern Classification*. New York: Wiley-Interscience.

LeCun, Y.; Bottou, L.; Bengio, Y.; and Haffner, P. 1998. Gradient-based learning applied to document recognition. *Proceedings of the IEEE* 86(11):2278–2324.

Mika, S.; Rätsch, G.; Weston, J.; Schölkopf, B.; Smola, A.; and Müller, K.-R. 2000. Invariant feature extraction and classification in kernel spaces. In Solla, S.; Leen, T.; ; K.-R; and Müller., eds., *Advances in Neural Information Processing Systems 12*, 526–532. MIT Press.

Phillips, P. J.; Moon, H.; Rizvi, S. A.; and Rauss, P. J. 2000. The FERET evaluation methodology for face-recognition algorithms. *IEEE Transactions on Pattern Analysis and Machine Intelligence* 22(10):1090–1034.

Roth, V., and Steinhage, V. 2000. Nonlinear discriminant analysis using kernel functions. In Solla, S.; Leen, T.; ; K.-R; and Müller., eds., *Advances in Neural Information Processing Systems 12*, 568–574. MIT Press.

Roweis, S. T., and Saul, L. K. 2000. Nonlinear dimensionality reduction by locally linear embedding. *Science* 290(5500).

Samaria, F., and Young, S. 1994. HMM based architecture for face identification. *Image and Vision Computing* 12(8):537–583.

Sim, T.; Baker, S.; and Bsat, M. 2001. The CMU pose, illumination, and expression (PIE) database of human faces. Technical Report CMU-RI-TR-01-02, Carnegie Mellon University.

Simard, P.; Le Cun, Y.; and Denker, J. 1993. Efficient pattern recognition using a new transformation distance. In Hanson, S. J.; Cowan, J. D.; and Giles, C. L., eds., *Advances in Neural Information Processing Systems*, volume 5, 50–58. Morgan Kaufmann, San Mateo, CA.

Tenebaum, J. B.; de Silva, V.; and Langford, J. C. 2000. A global geometric framework for nonlinear dimensionality reduction. *Science* 290(5500).

Turk, M., and Pentland, A. 1991. Eigenfaces for recognition. *Journal of Cognitive Neuroscience* 3(1):71–86.

Hierarchical Latent Class Models for Cluster Analysis

Nevin L. Zhang [*]
Department of Computer Science
Hong Kong University of Science and Technology
lzhang@cs.ust.hk

Abstract

Latent class models are used for cluster analysis of categorical data. Underlying such a model is the assumption that the observed variables are mutually independent given the class variable. A serious problem with the use of latent class models, known as local dependence, is that this assumption is often untrue. In this paper we propose hierarchical latent class models as a framework where the local dependence problem can be addressed in a principled manner. We develop a search-based algorithm for learning hierarchical latent class models from data. The algorithm is evaluated using both synthetic and real-world data.

Keywords: Model-based clustering, latent class models, local dependence, Bayesian networks, learning.

Introduction

Cluster analysis is the partitioning of similar objects into meaningful classes, when both the number of classes and the composition of the classes are to be determined (Kaufman and Rousseeuw 1990; Everitt 1993). In model-based clustering, it is assumed that the objects under study are generated by a mixture of probability distributions, with one component corresponding to each class. When the attributes of objects are continuous, cluster analysis is sometimes called *latent profile analysis* (Gibson 1959; Lazarsfeld and Henry 1968; Bartholomew and Knott 1999; Vermunt and Magidson 2002). When the attributes are categorical, cluster analysis is sometimes called *latent class analysis (LCA)* (Lazarsfeld and Henry 1968; Goodman 1974b; Bartholomew and Knott 1999; Uebersax 2001). There is also cluster analysis of *mixed-mode data* (Everitt 1993) where some attributes are continuous while others are categorical.

This paper is concerned with LCA, where data are assumed to be generated by a *latent class (LC)* model. An LC model consists of a class variable that represents the clusters to be identified and a number of other variables that represent attributes of objects [1]. The class variable is not observed

---

[*]This work is competed while the author is on leave at Department of Computer Science, Aalborg University, Denmark.
[1]Latent class models are sometimes also referred to as Naive

and hence said to be *latent*. On the other hand, the attributes are observed and are called *manifest variables*.

LC models assume *local independence*, i.e. manifest variables are mutually independent in each latent class, or equivalently, given the latent variable. A serious problem with the use of LCA, known as *local dependence*, is that this assumption is often violated. If one does not deal with local dependence explicitly, one implicitly attributes it to the latent variable. This can lead to spurious latent classes and poor model fit. It can also degenerate the accuracy of classification because locally dependent manifest variables contain overlapping information (Vermunt and Magidson 2002).

The local dependence problem has attracted some attention in the LCA literature (Espeland & Handelman 1989; Garrett & Zeger 2000; Hagenaars 1988; Vermunt & Magidson 2000). Methods for detecting and modeling local dependence have been proposed. To detect local dependence, one typically compares observed and expected cross-classification frequencies for pairs of manifest variables. To model local dependence, one can join manifest variables, introduce multiple latent variables, or reformulate LC models as loglinear models and then impose constraints on them. All existing methods are preliminary proposals and suffer from a number of deficiencies (Zhang 2002).

Our work

This paper describes the first systematic approach to the problem of local dependence. We address the problem in the framework of *hierarchical latent class (HLC) models*. HLC models are Bayesian networks whose structures are rooted trees and where the leaf nodes are observed while all other nodes are latent. This class of models is chosen for two reasons. First it is significantly larger than the class of LC models and can accommodate local dependence. Second inference in an HLC model takes time linear in model size, which makes it computationally feasible to run EM.

We develop a search-based algorithm for learning HLC models from data. The algorithm systematically searches for the optimal model by hill-climbing in a space of HLC models with the guidance of a model selection criterion. When

---

Bayes models. We suggest that the term "naive Bayes models" be used only in the context of classification and the term "latent class models" be used in the context of clustering.

there is no local dependence, the algorithm returns an LC model. When local dependence is present, it returns an HLC model where local dependence is appropriately modeled. It should be noted, however, that the algorithm might not work well on data generated by models that neither are HLC models nor can be closely approximated by HLC models.

The motivation for this work originates from an application in traditional Chinese medicine. In the application, model quality is of utmost importance and it is reasonable to assume abundant data and computing resources. So we take a principled (as opposite to heuristic) approach when designing our algorithm and we empirically show that the algorithm yields models of good quality. In subsequent work, we will explore ways to scale up the algorithm.

Related literature

This paper is an addition to the growing literature on hidden variable discovery in Bayesian networks (BN). Here is a brief discussion of some of this literature. Elidan *et al.* (2001) discuss how to introduce latent variables to BNs constructed for observed variables by BN structure learning algorithms. The idea is to look for structural signatures of latent variables. Elidan and Friedman (2001) give a fast algorithm for determining the cardinalities — the numbers of possible states — of latent variables introduced this way. Meila-Predoviciu (1999) studies how the so-called tree H models can be induced from data, where a tree H model is basically an LC model with each observed variable replaced by an undirected tree of observed variables. This work is based on the method of approximating joint probability distributions with dependence trees by Chow and Liu (1968).

The algorithms described in Connolly (1993) and Martin and VanLehn (1994) are closely related the algorithm presented in this paper. They all aim at inducing from data a latent structure that explains correlations among observed variables. The algorithm by Martin and VanLehn (1994) builds a two-level Bayesian network where the lower level consists of observed variables while the upper level consists of latent variables. The algorithm is based on tests of association between pairs of observed variables. The algorithm by Connolly (1993) constructs exactly what we call HLC models. Mutual information is used to group variables, a latent variable is introduced for each group, and the cardinality of the latent variable is determined using a technique called conceptual clustering. In comparison with Connolly's method, our method is more principled in the sense that it determines model structure and cardinalities of latent variables using one criterion, namely (some approximation) of the marginal likelihood.

The task of learning HLC models is similar to the reconstruction of phylogenetic trees, which is a major topic in biological sequence analysis (Durbin *et al.* 1998). As a matter of fact, phylogenetic trees are special HLC models where the model structures are binary (bifurcating) trees and all the variables share the same set of possible states. However, phylogenetic trees cannot be directly used for general cluster analysis because the constraints imposed on them. And techniques for phylogenetic tree reconstruction do not necessarily cover over to HLC models. For example, the structural

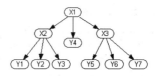

Figure 1: An example HLC model. The X_i's are latent variables and the Y_j's are manifest variables.

EM algorithm for phylogenetic tree reconstruction by Friedman *et al.* (2002) does not work for HLC models because we do not know, a priori, the number of latent variables and their cardinalities.

HLC models should not be confused with model-based hierarchical clustering (e.g. Hanson *et al.* 1991, Fraley 1998). In an LC model (or similar models with continuous manifest variables), there is only one latent variable and each state of the variable corresponds to a class. HLC models generalize LC models by allowing multiple latent variables. An HLC model contains a hierarchy of latent variables; In model-based hierarchical clustering, on the other hand, one has a hierarchy of classes. Conceptually there is only one latent variable. Classes at different levels of the hierarchy correspond to states of the variable at different levels of granularity.

Hierarchical latent class models

A *hierarchical latent class (HLC) model* is a Bayesian network where

1. The network structure is a rooted tree; and

2. The variables at the leaf nodes are observed and all the other variables are not [2].

Figure 1 shows an example of an HLC model. Following the LCA literature, we refer to the observed variables as *manifest variables* and all the other variables as *latent variables*. In this paper we do not distinguish between variables and nodes. So we sometimes speak also of *manifest nodes* and *latent nodes*. For technical convenience, we assume that there are at least two manifest variables.

We use θ to refer to the collection of parameters in an HLC model M and use m to refer to what is left when the parameters are removed from M. So we usually write an HLC model as a pair $M = (m, \theta)$. We sometimes refer to the first component m of the pair also as an HLC model. When it is necessary to distinguish between m and the pair (m, θ), we call m an *unparameterized HLC model* and the pair a *parameterized HLC model*. The term *HLC model structure* is reserved for what is left if information about cardinalities of latent variables are removed from an unparameterized model m. Model structures will be denoted by the letter S, possibly with subscripts.

---

[2]The concept of a variable being observed is always w.r.t some given data set. A variable is *observed* in a data set if there is at least one record that contains the state for that variable.

Parsimonious HLC models

In this paper we study the learning of HLC models. We assume that there is a collection of identical and independently distributed (i.i.d.) samples generated by some HLC model. Each sample consists of states for all or some of the manifest variables. The task is to reconstruct the HLC model from data. As will be seen later, not all HLC models can be reconstructed from data. It is hence natural to ask what models can be reconstructed. In this subsection we provide a partial answer to this question.

Consider two parameterized HLC models $M = (m, \theta)$ and $M' = (m', \theta')$ that share the same manifest variables $Y_1, Y_2, \ldots, Y_n$. We say that M and M' are *marginally equivalent* if the probability distribution over the manifest variables is the same in both models, i.e.

$$P(Y_1, \ldots, Y_n | m, \theta) = P(Y_1, \ldots, Y_n | m', \theta'). \quad (1)$$

Two marginally equivalent parameterized models are *equivalent* if they also have the same number of independent parameters. Two unparameterized HLC models m and m' are *equivalent* if for any parameterization θ of m there exists a parameterization θ' of m' such that (m, θ) and (m, θ') are equivalent and vice versa. Two HLC model structures S_1 and S_2 are *equivalent* if there are equivalent unparameterized models m_1 and m_2 whose underlying structures are S_1 and S_2 respectively.

A parameterized HLC model M is *parsimonious* if there does not exist another model M' that is marginally equivalent to M and that has fewer independent parameters than M. An unparameterized HLC model m is *parsimonious* if there exists a parameterization θ of m such that (m, θ) is parsimonious.

Let M be a parameterized HLC model and D be a set of i.i.d. samples generated by M. If M is not parsimonious, then there must exist another HLC model whose penalized loglikelihood score given D (Green 1998, Lanternman 2001) is greater than that of M. This means that, if one uses penalized loglikelihood for model selection, one would prefer this other parsimonious models over the nonparsimonious model M. The following theorem states that, to some extent, the opposite is also true, i.e. one would prefer M to other models if M is parsimonious.

Theorem 1 *Let M and M' be two parameterized HLC models with the same manifest variables. Let D be a set of i.i.d. samples generated from M.*

1. *If M and M' are not marginally equivalent, then the loglikelihood $l(M|D)$ of M is strictly greater than the loglikelihood $l(M'|D)$ of M' when the sample size is large enough.*

2. *If M is parsimonious and is not equivalent to M', then the penalized loglikelihood of M is strictly larger than that of M' when the sample size is large enough.*

The proofs of all theorems and lemmas in this paper can be found in Zhang (2002).

Model equivalence

In this subsection we give an operational characterization of model equivalence. Let X_1 be the root of a parameterized

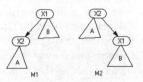

Figure 2: The operation of root walking.

HLC model M_1. Suppose X_2 is a child of X_1 and it is a latent node (see Figure 2). Define another HLC model M_2 by reversing the arrow $X_1 \rightarrow X_2$ and, while leaving the values for all other parameters unchanged, defining for $P_{M_2}(X_2)$ and $P_{M_2}(X_1|X_2)$ as follows:

$$P_{M_2}(X_2) = \sum_{X_1} P_{M_1}(X_1, X_2)$$

$$P_{M_2}(X_1|X_2) = \begin{cases} \frac{P_{M_1}(X_1, X_2)}{P_{M_2}(X_2)} & \text{if } P_{M_2}(X_2) > 0 \\ \frac{1}{|X_1|} & \text{otherwise,} \end{cases}$$

where $P_{M_1}(X_1, X_2) = P_{M_1}(X_1)P_{M_1}(X_2|X_1)$. We use the term *root walking* to refer to the process of obtaining M_2 from M_1. In the process, the root has walked from X_1 to X_2.

Theorem 2 [3] *Let M_1 and M_2 be two parameterized HLC models. If M_2 is obtained from M_1 by one or more steps of root walking, then M_1 and M_2 are equivalent.*

The two HLC models shown in Figure 3 are equivalent to the model in Figure 1. The model on the left is obtained by letting the root of the original model walk from X_1 to X_2, while the model on the right is obtained by letting the root walk from X_1 to X_3.

In general, the root of an HLC model can walk to any latent node. This implies the root node cannot be determined from data [4]. A question about the suitability of HLC models for cluster analysis naturally arises. We take the position that the root node can be determined from the objective in clustering and domain knowledge. Moreover we view the presence of multiple latent variables an advantage because it enables one to cluster data in multiple ways. Note that multiple clusterings due to multiple latent variables are very different from multiple clusterings in hierarchical clustering. In the latter case, a clustering at a lower level of the hierarchy is a refinement of a clustering at a higher level. The same relationship does not exist in the former case.

The inability of determining the root node from data also have some technical consequences. We can never induce HLC models from data. Instead we obtain what might be called unrooted HLC models. An *unrooted HLC model* is an

---

[3] A similar but different theorem was proved by Chickering (1996) for Bayesian networks with no latent variables. In Chickering (1996), model equivalence implies equal number of parameters. Here equal number of parameters is part of the definition of model equivalence.

[4] In the case of phylogenetic trees, this is a well-known fact (Durbin *et al.* 1998).

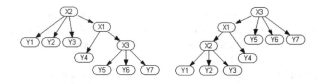

Figure 3: HLC models that are equivalent to the one in Figure 1.

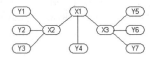

Figure 4: The unrooted HLC model that corresponds to the HLC model in Figure 1.

HLC model with all directions on the edges dropped. Figure 4 shows the unrooted HLC model that corresponds to the HLC model in Figure 1. An unrooted HLC model represents a class of HLC models; members of the class are obtained by rooting the model at various nodes and by directing the edges away from the root. Semantically it is a Markov random field on an undirected tree. The leaf nodes are observed while the interior nodes are latent. The concepts of marginal equivalence, equivalence, and parsimony can be defined for unrooted HLC models in the same way as for rooted models.

From now on when we speak of HLC models we always mean unrooted HLC models unless it is explicitly stated otherwise.

Regular HLC models

In this subsection we first introduce the concept of regular HLC models and show that all parsimonious models must regular. We then show that the set of unparameterized regular HLC models for a given set of manifest variables is finite. This provides a search space for the learning algorithm to be developed in the next section.

For any variable X, use Ω_X and $|X|$ to denote its domain and cardinality respectively. For a latent variable Z in an HLC model, enumerate its neighbors as X_1, X_2, ..., X_k. An HLC model is *regular* if for any latent variable Z,

$$|Z| \leq \frac{\prod_{i=1}^{k} |X_i|}{\max_{i=1}^{k} |X_i|}, \qquad (2)$$

and when Z has only two neighbors,

$$|Z| \leq \frac{|X_1||X_2|}{|X_1| + |X_2| - 1}. \qquad (3)$$

Note that this definition applies to parameterized as well as unparameterized models. The first condition was suggested by Kocka and Zhang (2002).

Theorem 3 *Irregular HLC models are not parsimonious*

In the rest of this section, we give three lemmas and one theorem that exhibit several interesting properties of regular HLC models.

A latent node in an HLC model has at least two neighbors. A *singly connected* latent node is one that has exactly two neighbors.

Lemma 1 *In a regular HLC model, no two singly connected latent nodes can be neighbors.*

This lemma inspires the following two definitions. We say that an HLC model structure is *regular* if no two singly connected latent nodes are neighbors. If there are no singly connected latent nodes at all, we say that the model structure is *strictly regular*.

Lemma 2 *Let S be an HLC model structure with n manifest variables. If S is regular, then there are fewer than $3n$ latent nodes. If S is strictly regular, then there are fewer than n latent nodes.*

Lemma 3 *There are fewer than 2^{3n^2} different regular HLC model structures for a given set of n manifest nodes.*

Theorem 4 *The set of all regular unparameterized HLC models for a given set of manifest variables is finite.*

Searching for optimal models

In this section we present a hill-climbing algorithm for learning HLC models. Hill-climbing requires a scoring metric for comparing candidate models. In this work we experiment with four existing scoring metrics, namely AIC (Akaike 1974), BIC (Schwarz 1978), the Cheeseman-Stutz (CS) score (Cheeseman and Stutz 1995), and the holdout logarithmic score (LS) (Cowell *et al.* 1999) .

Hill-climbing also requires the specification of a search space and search operators. According to Theorem 3, a natural search space for our task is the set of all regular (unparameterized) HLC models for the set of manifest variables that appear in data. By Theorem 4, we know that this space is finite.

Instead of searching this space directly, we structure the space into two levels according to the following two subtasks and we search those two levels separately:

1. Given a model structure, find optimal cardinalities for the latent variables.

2. Find an optimal model structure.

This search space restructuring is motivated by the fact that natural search operators exist for each of the two levels, while operators for the flat space are less obvious.

Estimating cardinalities of latent variables

The search space for the first subtask consists of all the regular models with the given model structure. To hill-climb in this space we start with the model where the cardinalities of all the latent variables are the minimum. In most cases, the minimum cardinality for a latent variable is 2. For a latent variable next to a singly connected latent node, however, the minimum possible cardinality is 4 because of the inequality (3). At each step, we modify the current model to get a number of new models. The operator for modifying a model is to increase the cardinality of a latent variable by one. Irregular new models are discarded. We then evaluate each of the new

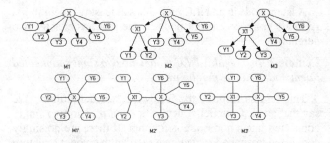

Figure 5: Illustration of structural search operators.

models and picks the best one to seed the next search step. To evaluate a model, one needs to estimate its parameters. We use the EM algorithm for this task.

Search for optimal model structures

The search space for the subtask of finding an optimal model structure consists of all the regular HLC model structures for the given manifest variables. To search this space, we start with the simplest HLC model structure, namely the LC model structure (viewed as an unrooted HLC model structure). At each step, we modify the current structure to construct a number of new structures. The new structures are then evaluated and the best structure is selected as the starting point for the next step. To evaluate a model structure, one needs to estimate the cardinalities of its latent variables. This issue is addressed in subtask 1.

We use three search operators to modify model structures, namely node-introduction, node-elimination, and neighbor-relocation.

Node introduction   To motivate the node-introduction operator, we need to go back to rooted models. Consider the rooted HLC model M_1 shown in Figure 5. Suppose variables Y_1 and Y_2 are locally dependent. A nature way to model this local dependence is to introduce a new parent for Y_1 and Y_2, as shown in M_2.

When translated to unrooted model structures, the new parent introduction operator becomes the *node-introduction* operator. Let X be a latent node in an unrooted model structure. Suppose X has more than two neighbors. Then for any two neighbors of X, say Z_1 and Z_2, we can introduce a new latent node Z to separate X from Z_1 and Z_2. Afterwards, X is no longer connected to Z_1 and Z_2. Instead X is connected to Z and Z is connected to Z_1 and Z_2. To see an example, consider the model structure M_1' in Figure 5. Introducing a new latent node X_1 to separate X from Y_1 and Y_2 results in the model structure M_2'.

In the case of rooted model structures, we do not consider introducing new parents for groups of three or more nodes for the sake of computational efficiency. This constraint implies that the model M_3 in Figure 5 cannot be reached from M_1 in one step. In the case of unrooted model structures, we do not allow the introduction of a new node to separate a latent node from three or more of its neighbors. This implies that we cannot reach M_3' from in Figure 5 cannot M_1' in one step.

Node-introduction is not allowed when it results in irregular model structures. This means that we cannot introduce a new node to separate a latent node X from two of its neighbors if it has only one other neighbor and that neighbor is a singly connected latent node. Moreover, we cannot introduce a new node to separate a singly connected latent node from its two neighbors. [5]

Node elimination   The opposite of node-introduction is *node-elimination*. We notice that a newly introduced node has exactly three neighbors. Consequently we allow a latent node be eliminated only when it has three neighbors. Of course, node elimination cannot be applied if there is only one latent node.

Neighbor relocation   In Figure 5, we cannot reach M_3' from either M_1' or M_2' using node-introduction and node-elimination. To overcome this difficult, we introduce the third search operator, namely *neighbor-relocation*. Suppose a latent node X has a neighbor Z that is also a latent node. Then we can relocate any of the other neighbors Z' of X to Z, which means to disconnect Z' from X and reconnect it to Z. To see an example, consider the model structure M_2' in Figure 5. If we relocate the neighbor Y_3 of X to X_1, we reach M_3'.

For the sake of computational efficiency, we do not allow neighbor relocation between two non-neighboring latent nodes. In Figure 4, for example, we cannot relocate neighbors of X_2 to X_3 and vice versa. Moreover neighbor relocation is not allowed when it results in irregular model structures. To be more specific, suppose X is a latent node that has a latent node neighbor Z. We cannot relocate another neighbor Z' of X to Z if X has only three neighbors and the third neighbor is a singly connected latent node. The relocation is not allowed, of course, if X has only two neighbors. Finally note that the effects of any particular neighbor relocation can always be undone by another application of the operator. [6]

Theorem 5 *Consider the collection of regular HLC model structures for a given set of manifest variables. One can go between any two structures in the collection using node-introduction, node-elimination, and neighbor-relocation.*

Empirical Results on Synthetic Data

Our algorithm for learning HLC models has been evaluated on both synthetic and real-world data. This section reports the results on synthetic data. The synthetic data were generated using the HLC model structure in Figure 1. The car-

---

[5]Node-introduction is similar to an operator that PROMTL, a system for inferring phylogenetic trees, uses to search for optimal tree topologies via star decomposition (Kishino *et al.* 1990). The former is slightly less constrained than the latter in that it is allowed to create singly connected nodes as by-products.

[6]Neighbor relocation is related to but significantly different than an operator called branch swapping that PAUP, a system for inferring phylogenetic trees, uses to search for optimal tree topologies (Swofford 1998). The latter includes what are called nearest neighbor interchange; subtree pruning and regrafting; and tree bisection/reconnection .

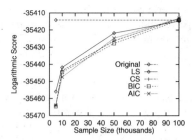

Figure 6: Logarithmic scores of learned models on testing data.

| | \multicolumn{4}{c}{50k} | | | | \multicolumn{4}{c}{100k} | | | |
	BIC	CS	LS	AIC	BIC	CS	LS	AIC
X_1	2	2	2	2	2	2	2	2
X_2	3	3	3	3	3	3	3	4
X_3	2	2	4	4	3	3	4	4

Table 1: Cardinalities of latent variables in learned models. In the original model all variables have 3 states.

dinalities of all variables were set at 3. The model was randomly parameterized. Four training sets with 5,000, 10,000, 50,000, and 100,000 records were sampled. A testing set of 5,000 records was also sampled. Each sample record consists of states for all the manifest variables.

We ran our learning algorithm on each of the four training sets, once for each of the four scoring metrics BIC, AIC, CS, and LS. There are hence a total number of 16 settings. For the LS scoring metric, 25% of the training data was set aside and used as validation data. Candidate models are compared using their logarithmic scores on the validation data. The EM termination threshold was set at 0.01 during model selection and at 0.0001 when estimating parameters for the final model. Irrespective of the threshold, EM was allowed to run no more than 200 iterations on any given model. For local maxima avoidance, we used the Chickering and Heckerman (1997) variant of the multiple-restart approach.

The logarithmic scores of the learned models on the testing data are shown in Figure 6. The scores are grouped into four curves according to the four scoring metrics. The score of the original model is also shown for the sake of comparison. We see that the scores of the learned models are quite close to that of the original model in the relative sense. This indicates that those models are as good as the original model when it comes to predicting the testing set. We also see that scores do not vary significantly across the scoring metrics.

The structures of the learned models do depend heavily on the scoring metrics. With either BIC or CS, our algorithm obtained, from the 50k and 100k training sets, models whose structures (unrooted trees) correspond precisely to the original structure. In this sense we say that the correct structure was recovered. From the 5k and 10k training sets, it obtained models with structures that differ from the original structure by only one or two search operations. With AIC and LS, our algorithm also recovered the correct structure from the 50k and 100k training sets. But the structures it produced for the 5k and 10k differ significantly from the original structures.[7]

Although the correct model structure was recovered from the 50k and 100k training sets regardless of the scoring metrics used, different scoring metrics gave different estimates for the cardinalities of the latent variables. As can be seen

---

[7]Structures and other details of the learned models are given in Zhang (2002).

from Table 1, BIC and CS have the tendency to underestimate while AIC and LS have the tendency to overestimate. Overall, BIC and CS seem to give better estimates.

In a second experiment, we parameterized the original model also in random fashion except that we ensured each conditional probability distribution have one component with mass no smaller than 0.6. Everything else was the same as in the first experiment. The performance of our algorithm, with BIC or CS, was better here than in the first experiment. It recovered the correct model structure from all four training sets. Cardinalities of X_2 and X_3 were estimated correctly in all cases. The cardinality of X_3 was estimated correctly in the 100k training set, while it was underestimated by 1 in all other training sets.

When AIC and LS was used, however, the algorithm performed worse in the second experiment than in the first one. It was not able to recover the correct model structure even from the 50k and 100k training sets.

Empirical Results on Real-World Data

We have also evaluated our algorithm on four real-world data sets taken from the LCA literature. The first data set is the Hannover Rheumatoid Arthritis data. It involves five binary manifest variables and consists of 7,162 records. Kohlmann and Formann (1997) conclude that the best model for this data set is a four class LC model. Using scoring metrics BIC, CS, and AIC, our algorithm discovered exactly the same model. When LS was used, however, it computed a very different model which does not fit the data well.

The second data set is known as the Coleman Data (Coleman 1964). It involves four binary manifest variables named A, B, C, and D. There are 3,398 records. This data set has been previously analyzed by Goodman (1974) and Hagenaars (1988). Goodman started with a 2-class LC model and found that it does not fit the data well ($L = 249.50$, $df = 6$, $p < 0.001$). He went on to consider the loglinear model that is represented by the path diagram M1 in Figure 7. In the model, both X_1 and X_2 are binary variables. This model fits data well ($L = 1.27$, $df = 4$, $p = 0.87$). Hagenaars examined several possible models and reached the conclusion that the loglinear model M2, where X is a binary variable, best explains the data. This model fits the data very well ($L = 1.43$, $df = 5$, $p = 0.92$).

Using scoring metric BIC, CS, and AIC, our algorithm found the model M3, where both X_1 and X_2 are binary variables. It's obvious that M3 is equivalent to M1 and hence fit data equally well. Our algorithm does not examine model M2 because it is not an HLC model. Fortunately, M2 is

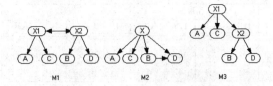

Figure 7: Models for the Coleman data.

Figure 8: Model for the HIV data.

quite close to M3. Using LS, our algorithm found a model that is the same as M3 except the number of states of X_1 is 3. This model does not fit data well ($L = 1.27$, $df = 0$, $p = 0.0$).

The third data set is known as the HIV data (Alvord *et al.* 1988). It also involves four binary manifest variables named A, B, C, and D. There are 428 records. Alvord *et al.* (1988) reasoned that there should be two latent classes, corresponding to the presence and absence of the HIV virus. However, the two-class LC model does not fit data well ($L = 16.23$, $df = 6$, $p = 0.01$). This indicates the presence of local dependence.

The performance of our algorithm on this data set is similar to that on the Coleman data set. Using BIC, CS, and AIC, it found the model in Figure 8, where both latent variables are binary variables. The model is the same as one of the equivalent models Uebersax (2000) reached using some heuristic techniques. The model fit data well ($L = 3.056$, $df = 4$, $p = 0.548$). With LS score, our algorithm produced the same model structure. However the cardinalities of both latent variables are overestimated by 2. The model fits data poorly.

The final data set we used is the housing building data (Hagenaars 1988). It involves four binary manifest variables and has 283 records. Hagenaars derived several loglinear models that fit the data well. None of those models are close to any HLC models, indicating that the data probably was not generated by an HLC model or a model that can be approximated closely by an HLC model. As such we expect our algorithm to perform poorly. This turns out to be the case. All the models produced by our algorithm fit data poorly.

Concluding Remarks

We have introduced a new class of models for cluster analysis, namely HLC models. HLC models are significantly more general than LC models and can accommodate local dependence. At the same time, the simplicity in their structures makes computation feasible. A search-based algorithm has been developed for learning HLC models from

data. Both synthetic and real-world data have been used to evaluate the performance of the algorithm with four different scoring metrics, namely AIC, BIC, CS, and LS. The results indicate that the algorithm works well with the BIC and CS scores.

The focus of this paper has been on developing a principled search-based method for learning HLC models. Not much consideration was given to computational complexity. While not prohibitive, our algorithm is quite expensive computationally. To reduce complexity one can employ various heuristics to construct initial models for search that hopefully are close to the optimal. One can also replace hill-climbing that generates and evaluates a large number of candidate models at each step with heuristic search that inspects aspects of the current model that need improvement and constructs a model for the next step heuristically.

Acknowledgement

Research was partially supported Hong Kong Research Grants Council under grant HKUST6093/99E.

I thank Tomas Kocka for insightful discussions on parsimonious and regular HLC models. I am also grateful to Finn V. Jensen, Thomas Nielsen, Kristian G. Olesen, Olav Bangso, Jose Pena, Jiri Vomlel, and Marta Vomlelova for valuable feedbacks on earlier versions of this paper.

References

Akaike, H. (1974). A new look at the statistical model identification. *IEEE Trans. Autom. Contr.*, 19, 716-723.

Alvord, W. G., Drummond, J. E., Arthur. L.O., Biggar, R. J., Goedert, J. J., Levine, P. H., Murphy, E. L. Jr, Weiss, S. H., Blattner, W. A. (1988). A method for predicting individual HIV infection status in the absence of clinical information. *AIDS Res Hum Retroviruses*, 4(4):295-304.

Bartholomew, D. J. and Knott, M. (1999). *Latent variable models and factor analysis*, 2nd edition. Kendall's Library of Statistics 7. London: Arnold.

Bohrnstedt, G. W. and Knoke D. (1994). *Statistics for social data analysis (3rd Edition)*. F. E. Peacock Publishers Inc., Itasca, Illinois.

Cheeseman, P. and Stutz, J. (1995). Bayesian classification (AutoClass): Theory and results. In Fayyad, U., Piatesky-Shaoiro, G., Smyth, P., and Uthurusamy, R. (eds.), *Advancesin Knowledge Discovery and Data Mining*, AAAI Press, Menlo Park, CA.

Chickering, D. M. and Heckerman, D. (1997). Efficient approximations for the marginal likelihood of Bayesian networks with hidden variables. *Machine Learning* 29(2-3): 181-212.

Chow, C. K. and Liu, C. N. (1968). Approximating discrete probability distributions with dependence trees. *IEEE Transactions on Information Theory*, IT-14(3): 462-467.

Coleman, J. S. (1964). *Introduction to Mathematical Sociology*. London: Free Press.

Connolly, D. (1993). Constructing hidden variables in Bayesian networks via conceptual learning. *ICML-93*, 65-72.

Cover, T. M., Thomas, J. A. (1991). *Elements of Information Theory*, John Wiley & Sons.

Cowell, R. G., Dawid, A. P., Lauritzen, S. L., and Spiegelhalter, D. J. (1999). *Probabilistic networks and expert systems*, Springer.

Dempster, A. P., Laird, N. M., and Rubin, D. B. (1977). Maximum likelihood from incomplete data via the EM algorithm. *J. Roy. Statist. Soc. B*, 39:1–38.

Durbin, R., Eddy, S., Krogh, A., and Mitchison, G. (1998). *Biological sequence analysis: probabilistic models of proteins and nucleic acids*. Cambridge University Press.

Eaton, W. W., Dryman, A., Sorenson, A., and McCutcheon, A. (1989). DSM-III Major depressive disorder in the community: A latent class analysis of data from the NIMH epidemiologic catchment area programme. *British Journal of Psychiatry*, 155, 48-54.

Elidan, G., Lotner, N., Friedman, N. and Koller, D. (2000). Discovering hidden variables: A structure-based approach. *NIPS-01*.

Elidan, G. and N. Friedman (2001). Learning the dimensionality of hidden variables. *UAI-01*.

Espeland, M. A. and Handelman, S. L. (1989). Using latent class models to characterize and assess relative error in discrete measurements. *Biometrics*, 45, 587-599.

Everitt, B. S. (1993). *Cluster Analysis*. London: Edward Arnold.

Fraley, C. (1998). Algorithms for model-based Gaussian hierarchical clustering. *SIAM J. Sci. Comput.*, 20 (1), 270-281.

Friedman, N., Ninio, M., Pe'er, I., and Pupko, T. (2002). A structural EM algorithm for phylogenetic inference. *Journal of Computational Biology*, to appear.

Garrett, E. S. and Zeger, S. L. (2000). Latent class model diagnosis. *Biometrics*, 56, 1055-1067.

Geiger, D., Heckerman, D., King, H., and Meek, C. (1998). Stratified exponential families: Graphical models and model selection. Technical Report MSR-TR-98-31, Microsoft Research.

Gibson, W. A. (1959). Three multivariate models: Factor analysis, latent structure analysis, and latent profile analysis. *Psychometrika*, 24: 229-252.

Goodman, L. A. (1974a). The analysis of systems of qualitative variables when some of the variables are unobservable. Part I-A Modified latent structure approach. *American Journal of Sociology*, 7(5), 1179-1259.

Green, P. (1998). Penalized likelihood. In *Encyclopedia of Statistical Sciences*, Update Volume 2. John Wiley & Sons.

Goodman, L. A. (1974b). Exploratory latent structure analysis using both identifiable and unidentifiable models. *Biometrika*, 61, 215-231.

Hagenaars, J. A. (1988). Latent structure models with direct effects between indicators: local dependence models. *Sociological Methods and Research*, 16, 379-405.

Hanson, R., Stutz, J., and Cheeseman, P. (1991). Bayesian classification with correlation and inheritance. In *Proc.*

12th. International Joint Conference on A.I. (IJCAI-91), 2, 692-698, Morgan Kaufmann.

Kaufman, L. and Rousseeuw, P. J. (1990). *Finding groups in data: An introduction to cluster analysis.* New York: John Wiley and Sons, Inc..

Kishino, H., Miyata, T., and Hasegawa, M. (1990). Maximum likelihood inference of protein phylogeny and the origin of the chloroplasts. J. Mol. Evol. 31, 151-160.

Kocha, T. and Zhang, N. L. (2002). Dimension correction for hierarchical latent class models. UAI-02, submitted.

Kohlmann, T., and Formann, A. K. (1997). Using latent class models to analyze response patterns in epidemiologic mail surveys. Rost, J. and Langeheine, R. (eds.). *Applications of latent trait and latent class models in the social sciences*. Muenster: Waxman Verlag.

Lanterman, A. D. (2001). Schwarz, Wallace, and Rissanen: Intertwining themes in theories of model order estimation. *International Statistical Review*, 69(2), 185-212.

Lazarsfeld, P. F., and Henry, N.W. (1968). *Latent structure analysis*. Boston: Houghton Mifflin.

Martin, J. and VanLehn, K. (1994). Discrete factor analysis: learning hidden variables in Bayesian networks. Technical Report LRGC_ONR-94-1, Department of Computer Science, University of Pittsburgh.

Meila-Predoviciu, M. (1999). *Learning with mixtures of trees*, Ph.D. Dissertation, Department of Electrical Engineering and Computer Science, MIT.

Schwarz, G. (1978). Estimating the dimension of a model. *Annals of Statistics*, 6(2), 461-464.

Swofford, D. L. (1998). *PAUP* 4.0 - Phylogenetic Analysis Using Parsimony (*and Other Methods)..* Sinauer Assoc., Sunderland, MA.

Uebersax, J. (2000). A practical guide to local dependence in latent class models. http://ourworld.compuserve.com/homepages/jsuebersax/condep.htm.

Vermunt, J.K. and Magidson, J. (2000). *Latent GOLD User's Guide*. Belmont, Mass.: Statistical Innovations, Inc..

Vermunt, J.K. and Magidson, J. (2002). Latent class cluster analysis. in Hagenaars, J. A. and McCutcheon A. L. (eds.), *Advances in latent class analysis*. Cambridge University Press.

Wasmus, A., Kindel, P., Mattussek, S. and Raspe, H. H. (1989). Activity and severity of rheumatoid arthritis in Hannover/FRG and in one regional referral center. *Scandinavian Journal of Rheumatology*, Suppl. 79, 33-44.

Zhang, N. L. (2002). Hierarchical latent class models for cluster analysis. Technical Report HKUST-CS02-02, Department of Computer Science, Hong Kong University of Science & Technology, Hong Kong, China.

Markov Decision Processes

A POMDP Formulation of Preference Elicitation Problems

Craig Boutilier
Department of Computer Science
University of Toronto
Toronto, ON, M5S 3H5, CANADA
cebly@cs.toronto.edu

Abstract

Preference elicitation is a key problem facing the deployment of intelligent systems that make or recommend decisions on the behalf of users. Since not all aspects of a utility function have the same impact on object-level decision quality, determining which information to extract from a user is itself a sequential decision problem, balancing the amount of elicitation effort and time with decision quality. We formulate this problem as a partially-observable Markov decision process (POMDP). Because of the continuous nature of the state and action spaces of this POMDP, standard techniques cannot be used to solve it. We describe methods that exploit the special structure of preference elicitation to deal with parameterized belief states over the continuous state space, and gradient techniques for optimizing parameterized actions. These methods can be used with a number of different belief state representations, including mixture models.

1 Introduction

Preference elicitation (PE) is a fundamental problem in the development of intelligent decision tools and autonomous agents. Software and agents of this type are often charged with the task of making decisions, or recommending courses of action, for a specific user. Making optimal decisions on behalf of a user requires knowing some information about her preferences or utility function. It is important to keep in mind that utility functions can vary widely from user to user (even while the other ingredients of a decision scenario, such as system dynamics, remain fixed across users). For this reason, preference elicitation—the process of extracting the necessary preference or utility information from a user—is arguably one of the more important problems facing AI. Applications of elicitation processes are pervasive, ranging from low-stakes decision processes (e.g., the control of user interaction with a product Web site) to critical decision assessment systems (e.g., clinical decision making [5; 6]).

The elicitation of preference and utility functions is complicated by the fact that utility functions are very difficult for

users to assess [8; 11]. The burden of elicitation can be lessened considerably in a given *specific* decision scenario (or a restricted set of scenarios). An optimal decision can usually be made without full knowledge of a user's preferences. For example, if some outcomes (or attribute values) simply aren't possible in a specific situation, the utilities for those outcomes (or values) have no bearing on the decision problem. Furthermore, even "relevant" utility information may have only marginal impact on decision quality. If the cost of obtaining that information exceeds the benefit it provides, then this information too can be safely ignored.

The development of optimal *elicitation strategies*, that address the tradeoff between effort expended in elicitation and the impact on object-level decision quality, has been explored very little. The chief exception is the work of Chajewska, Koller, and Parr [6], who model this problem by assuming a distribution over utility functions, and refining uncertainty over a user's utility as queries are answered. Their myopically optimal elicitation strategy involves asking the (single) query with greatest *expected value of information* with respect to the current distribution.

In this paper, we extend this point of view in several ways, the most important of which is viewing elicitation as a *sequential* decision problem to be solved (approximately) optimally rather than myopically. Intuitively, a myopic approach can fail to ask the correct questions because it neglects the value of *future* questions when determining the value of the *current* question. As is well known (and as we demonstrate), greedy approaches to computing value of information can underestimate the value of information if value can only be obtained from a sequence of queries. Specifically, if no single question can cause a change in the optimal decision, a myopic approach will never try to reduce its uncertainty. The model of [6] can easily be extended to do multistage lookahead, overcoming this difficulty. However, since the required computations in this model are online, we instead pose the elicitation problem as a partially-observable Markov decision process (POMDP). The POMDP perspective also allows for more suitable termination criteria, noisy response models, and permits policies to be constructed for arbitrary belief states (rather than solving the problem online for a fixed prior). In addition, optimal value functions (and implicitly, optimal policies) can be computed offline, allowing for fast online response during the elicitation process itself.

Conceptually, the POMDP formulation is straightforward; but practically, difficulties emerge because of the continuous nature of the underlying state (utility function) and action (query) spaces. We propose several methods for dealing with these problems that exploit the structure of the elicitation problem. In particular, we propose an approach to approximating the optimal value function that handles the continuous action and state spaces of the POMDP effectively, and allows for the concise representation of value functions for belief states represented using mixture models.

2 The Underlying Decision Problem

We assume that we have a system charged with making a decision on behalf of a user in a specific *decision scenario*. By a decision scenario, we refer to a setting in which a fixed set of choices (e.g., actions, policies, recommendations) are available to the system, and the (possibly stochastic) effects of these choices are known. The system's task is to take the decision with maximum expected utility with respect to the user's utility function over outcomes, or some approximation thereof. The system may have little information about the user's utility function, so to achieve this aim it must find out enough information to enable a good decision to be made. We assume that the system has available to it a set of queries it can ask of the user that provide such information.[1]

Formally, assume a *decision scenario* consists of a finite set of possible *decisions* D, a finite set of n possible outcomes (or states) S, and a distribution function $\Pr_d \in \Delta(S)$, for each $d \in D$.[2] The term $\Pr_d(s)$ denotes the probability of outcome s being realized if the system takes decision d. A utility function $u : S \to [0, 1]$ associates utility $u(s)$ with each outcome s. We often view u as a n-dimensional vector $\boldsymbol{u}$ whose ith component u_i is simply $u(s_i)$. We assume that utilities are normalized in the range $[0, 1]$ for convenience. The *expected utility* of decision d with respect to utility function $\boldsymbol{u}$ is:

$$EU(d, \boldsymbol{u}) = \boldsymbol{p}_d \boldsymbol{u} = \sum_{i \in S} \Pr_d(s_i) u_i$$

Note that $EU(d, \boldsymbol{u})$ is linear in $\boldsymbol{u}$. The optimal decision d^* w.r.t. $\boldsymbol{u}$ is that with *maximum expected utility (MEU)*.[3]

In general, the utility function $\boldsymbol{u}$ will not be known with certainty at the start of the elicitation process (nor at its end). Following [6], we model this uncertainty using a density P over the set of possibly utility functions

$$U = \{\boldsymbol{u} : 0 \leq \boldsymbol{u} \leq 1\} = [0, 1]^n$$

If a system makes a decision d under such conditions of uncertainty, the expected utility of d must reflect this. We define the expected utility of d given density P over U as follows:

$$EU(d, P) = \int \boldsymbol{p}_d \boldsymbol{u} P(\boldsymbol{u}) d\boldsymbol{u}$$

---

[1] We use the term "queries" for concreteness; any interaction with a user can provide (noisy) information about her utility function.

[2] The extension of our elicitation methods to a set of possible decision scenarios is straightforward.

[3] If u is represented using some more concise model, such as a linear utility model [11] or a graphical model [4], $\boldsymbol{u}$ is simply the vector of parameters required for that model. All results below apply.

Since EU is linear is $\boldsymbol{u}$, $EU(d, P)$ can be computed easily if the expectation of $\boldsymbol{u}$ w.r.t. P is known. In such a state of uncertainty, the optimal decision is that d^* with maximum expected utility $EU(d^*, P)$. We denote by $MEU(P)$ the value of being in state of P, assuming one is forced to make a decision: $MEU(P) = EU(d^*, P)$.[4]

In order to reduce its uncertainty about the user's utility function, the system has available to it a set of *queries* Q. With each query q is associated a finite set of possible *responses* $R_q = \{r_q^1, \cdots, r_q^m\}$. A common type of query is the *standard gamble w.r.t. outcome* s_i, where the user is asked if she prefers s_i to a gamble in which the best outcome $s_\top$ occurs with probability l and the worst $s_\perp$ occurs with probability $1 - l$ [11]. Note that $u(s_\top) = 1$ and $u(s_\perp) = 0$ given our normalization assumptions. We designate this query $q_i(l)$ and focus our attention on standard gamble queries. Of course, many other query types can be captured within our generic model.

For standard gamble queries we have a binary response space: $R(q) = \{yes, no\}$. The responses to a query may be noisy: we assume a *response model* of the form $\Pr(r_q^i | q, \boldsymbol{u})$ which denotes the probability of any response $r_q^i \in R_q$ to question q by a user with true utility $\boldsymbol{u}$. To keep the presentation simple, we assume fixed false positive and false negative probabilities for each query type q_i: so $\Pr(yes | q_i(l), u_i < l) = p_{fp}^i$, while $\Pr(no | q_i(l), u_i \geq l) = p_{fn}^i$. We let $p_{tp}^i = 1 - p_{fn}^i$ and $p_{tn}^i = 1 - p_{fp}^i$ be the probabilities of "correct" positive and negative responses.

Finally, each question q has a cost $c(q)$. This reflects the difficulty the user is expected to have in answering the question due to the mental burden in imposes on the user, the computational costs associated with computing an answer, the time required to process the question, or many other factors.[5]

Given a response r to a question q, the updated conditional density P_r can be determined by application of Bayes rule:

$$P_r(\boldsymbol{u}) = P(\boldsymbol{u} | r) = \frac{\Pr(r | q, \boldsymbol{u}) P(\boldsymbol{u})}{\int \Pr(r | q, \boldsymbol{u}) P(\boldsymbol{u}) d\boldsymbol{u}} \quad (1)$$

The (myopic) *expected value of information (EVOI)* of a query can be defined by considering the difference between $MEU(P)$ and the expectation (w.r.t. r) of $MEU(P_r)$. A query can be deemed worthwhile if its EVOI outweighs its cost, and a myopically optimal elicitation strategy involves asking queries with maximal EVOI at each point [6].

3 Preference Elicitation as a POMDP

Value of information plays an important role in good elicitation strategies, as proposed in [6]. We take a different, though similarly motivated, approach by formulating the elicitation problem as a POMDP. This view makes the sequential nature of the elicitation problem clear and avoids problems facing myopic EVOI. Furthermore, by posing the problem as a

---

[4] Taking the expectation w.r.t. $P(U)$ is not unproblematic: certain "calibration assumptions" of the elements of U is necessary to ensure that this expectation makes sense [3]. We do not discuss this subtlety further, but the disquieted reader can treat U as expected monetary value or some other surrogate.

[5] To keep the model simple, we assume questions have a constant cost, though costs depending on $\boldsymbol{u}$ are often reasonable.

POMDP we have access to solution techniques for constructing a policy that covers all possible initial belief states (as opposed to one policy designed for a fixed prior as in [6]). Of course, many computational difficulties must be overcome (see the next section); but if these can be surmounted, the advantages of a full POMDP formulation are clear.

3.1 A POMDP Formulation

The POMDP formulation is quite direct. The set of system states is U, the set of possibly utility functions. The set of belief states of the POMDP is simply the set of densities over U. Since our state space is a n-dimensional continuous space, we will require some parameterized representation of belief states. The system dynamics are trivial: the underlying utility function u never changes, so at each time t, u is exactly as it was at time $t - 1$. The actions available to the system are queries Q and decisions D; we let $A = Q \cup D$. Queries induce no change in the underlying system state u, but do provide information about it. Each decision d is a terminal action. The cost $c(q)$ of question q is state-independent; but the terminal reward associated with a decision d does depend on the state: $Rew(d, u) = EU(d, u)$. The sensor model for the POMDP is the response model $\Pr(r_q|q, u)$. Assuming standard gamble queries, we have a continuous action space: for each outcome s_i, we have queries of the form $q_i(l)$ for any $l \in [0, 1]$. We assume an infinite horizon model (since the process terminates at an unspecified time) with discount factor γ.

We can formulate the optimal value function and policy using the standard Bellman equations over the fully-observable *belief state MDP* [14]. We define the optimal value function V^*, ranging over belief states P, as:

$$V^*(P) = \max_{a \in A} Q_a^*(P)$$

where the Q-functions Q_a^* are defined for each query and decision. For decisions d, we have $Q_d^*(P) = EU(d, P)$. For queries $q_i(l)$ we parameterize Q_i^* by the lottery probability l:

$$Q_i^*(l, P) = c(q_i(l)) + \gamma \sum_{r \in R} \Pr(r|q_i(l), P) V^*(P_r)$$

Finally, the optimal (stationary) policy π^* is given by the action, decision or query, maximizing the value function.

3.2 Belief State Representation

Because the underlying state space is a multidimensional continuous space, solving a POMDP of this type, as well as performing belief state maintenance for policy implementation, requires a reasonable belief state representation. In such circumstances, some parametric form is often used; for instance, an n-dimensional Gaussian might be used to represent belief states (perhaps truncated at the utility boundaries). Particle filter models can also be used to solve continuous state POMDPs [15].

One difficulty with parametric models is their inflexibility. A mixture of Gaussians offers considerably more flexibility in this regard—this representation is adopted in [6]. A difficulty with Gaussian mixtures is that they are not closed under

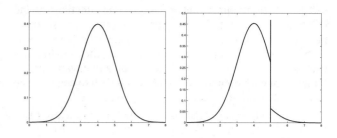

Figure 1: Update of Gaussian after query $q_i(0.5)$.

belief state update using standard gamble queries.[6] Specifically, under our model, if P is Gaussian, then P_r is a mixture of two *truncated* Gaussians, as shown in Figure 1. For instance, given the answer *yes* to query $q_i(l)$, we have $P_r(u) = \alpha^- P(u)$ if $u_i < l$ and $P_r(u) = \alpha^+ P(u)$ if $u_i \geq l$, where $\alpha = p_{tp}^i \int_{u_i < l} P(u) + p_{fp}^i \int_{u_i \geq l} P(u)$ is a normalizing constant, $\alpha^- = p_{tp}^i/\alpha$ and $\alpha^+ = p_{fp}^i/\alpha$. The relative weights of the two components is given by, $w^- = \alpha^- \int_{u_i < l} P(u)$ and $w^+ = \alpha^+ \int_{u_i \geq l} P(u)$.

While Gaussian mixtures aren't closed under update, after conditioning on a response, this "truncated" mixture model can be sampled and refit using a standard method such as EM [2]. This technique is adopted in [6]. An alternative we consider here is to use mixtures of truncated Gaussians directly as a belief state representation. This has two advantages. First, one needn't refit the belief state using computationally expensive procedures like EM—given an initial mixture, we simply retain the truncated mixtures that result from updating after a series of queries. Second, because the truncated mixture is exact with respect to the initial belief state, no belief state approximation is needed. A drawback is that the number of truncated components doubles with each update. A suitable compromise involves maintaining a truncated mixture until the number of components becomes unwieldy, then refitting this model to a new mixture using EM.

We also consider the use of uniform distributions, a parametric form that meshes well with the queries at hand. We use a prior consisting of a mixture of k uniform distributions. Updating a uniform after query $q_i(l)$ results in a mixture of two uniforms identical to the original except with the upper and lower bounds in dimension i revised. Again, EM can be used to reduce the number of components periodically.

3.3 Difficulties Facing the Formulation

Even with good belief representation, standard methods for solving a POMDP cannot be used. Methods for finite spaces rely on the fact that the optimal value function is (approximately) piecewise linear and convex (PWLC) [14]. Continuous state problems require some form of special structure

---

[6]For certain forms of queries, Kalman filter-like techniques can be used for updating Gaussians however.

(such as Gaussian belief states, linear dynamics, etc.) or the use of function approximation. The value function for the elicitation POMDP has no convenient closed form, so function approximation is needed. Let our belief state have a parametric form with parameter vector $\boldsymbol{\theta}$ (e.g., the weights of a Gaussian mixture together with the mean and covariance parameters of each component). Our goal is then to construct an estimate $\widetilde{V}(\boldsymbol{\theta})$ of the optimal value function.

Several general approaches to value function approximation for POMDPs have been proposed. Those motivated by the PWLC nature of the value function [7; 13] are not appropriate here. More general approximators, such as feedforward neural networks, seem more promising [12]. Grid-based models [10] can also used, but require computationally demanding projections (refitting) of updated belief states for each DP update. Policy search methods [9] and clustering to discretize utility space [5] might also be used.

We'll also require a method for dealing with the continuous action space. Again, unless there is some special structure, special techniques will be required to handle the large action space. Fortunately, our action space is well-parameterized; specifically, we have a finite number of query types q_i, with each type parameterized by a lottery probability l.

4 An Approximation Technique for PE

To deal with the difficulties described above we propose a technique for solving the PE POMDP using a suitable function approximation architecture. We assume our belief state is captured by a mixture model with an unspecified number of components (recall that generally the number of components increases over time). Our aim will be to compute the value function only for a single parametric component rather than for the entire mixture. Online policy implementation will require that we use this "single component" value function to determine the value of a mixture density.

4.1 Approximating the Value Function

We use $\boldsymbol{\theta}$ to denote the parameter vector for a single belief state component. Rather than approximating the value function directly, we will compute Q-functions, one for each query type q_i. The approximator $Q_i(l, \boldsymbol{\theta})$ is parameterized by the lottery probability l. We don't approximate Q_d for decisions d, since their exact computation is straightforward. We assume an approximation architecture with parameters or *weights* $\mathbf{w}$, that can be trained in some standard fashion. We also assume that the Q_i are differentiable with respect to l.[7]

We solve the PE POMDP using a form of asynchronous approximate value iteration [1]. At each iteration we sample a (non-mixture) belief state $\boldsymbol{\theta}$ and a query $q_i(l)$ according to some sampling schedule. We compute the backed up Q-value of query $q_i(l)$ at state $\boldsymbol{\theta}$ using the current approximations:

$$Q_i(\boldsymbol{\theta}, l) = c(q_i) + \gamma[\Pr(yes|q_i(l), \boldsymbol{\theta})V(\boldsymbol{\theta}_{yes}) + \\ \Pr(no|q_i(l), \boldsymbol{\theta})V(\boldsymbol{\theta}_{no})] \quad (2)$$

(here $\boldsymbol{\theta}_{yes}$ denotes the updated belief state given response yes, and similarly for no). Letting q_{new} denote the backed up

---
[7]We discuss approximation architectures below.

value, we then train our approximator Q_i with inputs l and $\boldsymbol{\theta}$ and output q_{new}.

Unfortunately, the computation of Eq. 2 is not straightforward. First, the resulting densities are mixtures of the underlying components. For instance, if $\boldsymbol{\theta}$ is a truncated Gaussian, then $\boldsymbol{\theta}_{yes}$ is a mixture of two truncated Gaussians $\boldsymbol{\theta}_{yes}^1$ and $\boldsymbol{\theta}_{yes}^2$, with mixing weights α_1 and α_2. Unfortunately, the value function (via the Q-functions) is only defined for single components. Furthermore, determining $V(\boldsymbol{\theta}_{yes})$ from the Q-function approximators requires the solution of:

$$V(\boldsymbol{\theta}_{yes}) = \max[\max_d Q_d(\boldsymbol{\theta}_{yes}), \max_i \max_l Q_i(\boldsymbol{\theta}_{yes}, l)] \quad (3)$$

Maximization over decisions d and query types q_i is straightforward, but maximizing over the continuous input l is less so. (Similar remarks obviously apply to $V(\boldsymbol{\theta}_{no})$.)

We deal with the first problem by taking advantage of the fact that we construct Q-functions—rather than the value function directly—to determine Q-values of the necessary mixtures. Specifically, suppose we have belief state $\boldsymbol{\theta} = \alpha_1\boldsymbol{\theta}_1 + \alpha_2\boldsymbol{\theta}_2$ that is the mixture of two components. Then the expected value of a decision d for the mixture is:

$$\begin{aligned} Q_d(\boldsymbol{\theta}) &= Q_d(\alpha_1\boldsymbol{\theta}_1 + \alpha_2\boldsymbol{\theta}_2) \\ &= \alpha_1 Q_d(\boldsymbol{\theta}_1) + \alpha_2 Q_d(\boldsymbol{\theta}_2) \end{aligned} \quad (4)$$

A similar fact holds for queries:

Proposition 1 $Q_i(\alpha_1\boldsymbol{\theta}_1 + \alpha_2\boldsymbol{\theta}_2, l) = \alpha_1 Q_i(\boldsymbol{\theta}_1, l) + \alpha_2 Q_i(\boldsymbol{\theta}_2, l)$

Proof: Let $\boldsymbol{\theta}$ denote the mixture $\alpha_1\boldsymbol{\theta}_1 + \alpha_2\boldsymbol{\theta}_2$. We observe that the update of $\boldsymbol{\theta}$ given response yes to query $q_i(l)$ is a mixture $\boldsymbol{\theta}^{yes} = \alpha_1^{yes}\boldsymbol{\theta}_1^{yes} + \alpha_2^{yes}\boldsymbol{\theta}_2^{yes}$, where

$$\alpha_1^{yes} = \frac{\alpha_1 \Pr(yes|\boldsymbol{\theta}_1)}{\Pr(yes|\boldsymbol{\theta})}, \quad \alpha_2^{yes} = \frac{\alpha_2 \Pr(yes|\boldsymbol{\theta}_2)}{\Pr(yes|\boldsymbol{\theta})} \quad (5)$$

and $\boldsymbol{\theta}_i^{yes}$ is the update of the component $\boldsymbol{\theta}_i$ given a yes response. Similar expressions hold for $\boldsymbol{\theta}^{no}$.

Letting c denote the query cost and suppressing the query $q_i(l)$ on the righthand side of the conditioning bars, we have:

$$\begin{aligned} Q_i(\boldsymbol{\theta}, l) &= c + \gamma[\Pr(yes|\boldsymbol{\theta})V(\boldsymbol{\theta}^{yes}) + \Pr(no|\boldsymbol{\theta})V(\boldsymbol{\theta}^{no})] \\ &= c + \gamma[\alpha_1^{yes}\Pr(yes|\boldsymbol{\theta})V(\boldsymbol{\theta}_1^{yes}) + \alpha_2^{yes}\Pr(yes|\boldsymbol{\theta})V(\boldsymbol{\theta}_2^{yes}) \\ &\quad + \alpha_1^{no}\Pr(no|\boldsymbol{\theta})V(\boldsymbol{\theta}_1^{no}) + \alpha_2^{no}\Pr(no|\boldsymbol{\theta})V(\boldsymbol{\theta}_2^{no})] \\ &= c + \gamma[\alpha_1\Pr(yes|\boldsymbol{\theta}_1)V(\boldsymbol{\theta}_1^{yes}) + \alpha_2\Pr(yes|\boldsymbol{\theta}_2)V(\boldsymbol{\theta}_2^{yes}) \\ &\quad + \alpha_1\Pr(no|\boldsymbol{\theta}_1)V(\boldsymbol{\theta}_1^{no}) + \alpha_2\Pr(no|\boldsymbol{\theta}_2)V(\boldsymbol{\theta}_2^{no})] \\ &= c + \gamma[\alpha_1(\Pr(yes|\boldsymbol{\theta}_1)V(\boldsymbol{\theta}_1^{yes}) + \Pr(no|\boldsymbol{\theta}_1)V(\boldsymbol{\theta}_1^{no})) \\ &\quad + \alpha_2(\Pr(yes|\boldsymbol{\theta}_2)V(\boldsymbol{\theta}_2^{yes}) + \Pr(no|\boldsymbol{\theta}_2)V(\boldsymbol{\theta}_2^{no}))] \\ &= \alpha_1 Q_i(\boldsymbol{\theta}_1, l) + \alpha_2 Q_i(\boldsymbol{\theta}_2, l) \end{aligned}$$

The third equality is obtained using the expressions in Eq. 5 (and analogous expressions for the no response). ◄

We deal with the second issue, maximization, as follows. Maximization over the decisions $d \in D$ is straightforward. For a given query q_i, the maximization over lottery probabilities l is achieved using some suitable optimization technique. For certain function approximators, this optimization may be computed analytically. Otherwise, since the approximator is differentiable with respect to input l (which is true for most common approximators), we can—given a fixed single component belief state—approximate the value of $\max_l Q_i(\boldsymbol{\theta}, l)$ using gradient ascent. Specifically, since $\frac{\partial Q_i(\boldsymbol{\theta}, l)}{\partial l}$ is defined, we can find a local maximum readily.[8] Of course, $\boldsymbol{\theta}_{yes}$ is a mixture of two truncated Gaussians. But we can still use gradient ascent by noting that:

$$\frac{\partial Q_i(\boldsymbol{\theta}_{yes}, l)}{\partial l} = \alpha_1 \frac{\partial Q_i(\boldsymbol{\theta}_{yes}^1, l)}{\partial l} + \alpha_2 \frac{\partial Q_i(\boldsymbol{\theta}_{yes}^2, l)}{\partial l} \quad (6)$$

Consequently, $V(\boldsymbol{\theta}_{yes})$ can be determined by computing the value of each decision d, using Eq. 6 to determine the maximum value of a query of the form q_i for each i, and then maximizing over these $|S \cup D|$ values. The value given a *no* response is determined analogously. These are combined using Eq. 2 to get an backed up estimate of $Q_i(\boldsymbol{\theta}, l)$.

4.2 Online Policy Execution

The procedure above produces a collection of Q-functions, one for each query type q_i. With this in hand, we can determine the optimal action for a single component belief state $\boldsymbol{\theta}$ as follows: compute $Q_d(\boldsymbol{\theta})$ for each d, compute $\max_l Q_i(\boldsymbol{\theta}, l)$ for each q_i using gradient ascent, then choose the action, d or $q_i(l)$, with maximum value. The resulting belief state is, however, a mixture. But even though we have computed Q-functions explicitly only for single components, we can use these to directly determine the optimal action for a mixture using the ideas described above. Optimizing over l for a mixture of k components can be accomplished using the same technique as optimizing for a 2-mixture (using the obvious extension of Eq. 6). We describe practical enhancements to this scheme in the next section.

Online policy implementation then consists of two basic steps per stage: (a) if belief state $b^t = \{\boldsymbol{\theta}^t[i], w^t[i]\}$ denotes the mixture belief state at stage t, we choose the optimal action for b, and execute it (either asking a query or recommending a decision); (b) if the action is a query, we update our belief state w.r.t. the response to produce b^{t+1}, and continue.

One difficulty with this online policy implementation technique lies in the fact that the number of mixture components may quickly become unmanageable. If the prior is a single component mixture, we will have (up to) 2^t components after t queries. Note that this fragmentation is purely a function of belief state update, and not due to policy implementation *per se*. But belief state maintenance is much more tractable if the number of components is reduced periodically. One way to do this is to prune components with low weight. This is computationally feasible, but must be done with some care to ensure that important parts of "total belief space" are not ignored. An alternative is to simply fit the current belief state to a smaller mixture model using EM. This is more computationally demanding, but will provide more accurate results if dramatic reduction in model size is desired. Computation is a critical consideration since refitting needs to be done online; but periodic refitting can be managed intelligently.

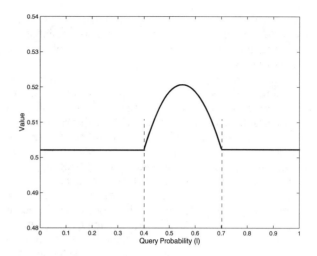

Figure 2: A 1-D View of a 2-stage Q-function.

5 Practical Tricks and Empirical Results

In this section we describe some preliminary empirical results using the elicitation method described. In our experiments we use mixtures of uniform distributions as our belief state model since updating and computing the required expectations is quite simple (as the model fits very well with the form of the queries we use).

5.1 Practical Enhancements

Each Q-function approximator has as input the parameters of an n-dimensional uniform (i.e., upper and lower bounds in each dimension) as well as a query point l. All of our results use a quadratic function approximator. We have experimented with linear approximators and feedforward neural networks as well. Linear approximators clearly do quite poorly, as the Q-functions are obviously nonlinear. Figure 2 illustrates a 1-D slice of the optimal two-stage-to-go Q-function at a fixed belief state, which is uniform (in the dimension shown) on interval $[0.4, 0.7]$. The Q-function is concave in l and quadratic in the difference of l and the mean (over the region of positive density).[9] Quadratic approximators seem to provide good quality solutions over the range of the belief state. Given an n-dimensional belief space, the quadratic approximator has $2n + 1$ inputs, and $O(n^2)$ weights to be tuned. Tuning was accomplished using simple gradient descent in weight space with momentum. Optimization over lottery probabilities l (when computing Bellman backups) was accomplished using no specific gradient information (instead Matlab's FMNBND function was used). The training schedule we used was as follows: we first trained the approximators with 2-stage-to-go Q-functions. The reason for this was that these backups require no "bootstrapping" since the one-stage function can be computed exactly (since it involves only decisions not queries). This helped quickly capture the quadratic dependence of Q-functions on the difference between the input l and the mean

---

[8]We can show that the optimal Q-function for query i is concave in l, thus if our approximator reflects this fact, we can be reasonably confident that a global maximum will be found.

[9]In general, the optimal t-stage Q-function is a degree $2t$ polynomial for a uniform distribution.

vector. After a fixed number of 2-stage backups at systematically chosen belief points, we generated random belief states and queries and applied the backup procedure described in the previous section.[10]

We exploit certain properties of value of information to restrict training and overcome approximator deficiencies. For example, given a density with upper and lower bounds u_i and l_i in dimension i, a query $q_i(c)$ with c outside that range has no value (i.e., will not alter the belief state). We restrict training to queries that lie within the range of the belief state. Since approximators generalize, they tend to assign value to queries outside the range that are *lower* than their true value, due to the nature of VOI (see Figure 2). For this reason, we restrict the value of a query outside the range of the belief state to be equal to the value at its boundary. Although asking queries outside the range of a single mixture component needn't be considered in unmixed models, assigning values to such queries is necessary when computing VOI w.r.t. a *mixture*.

Online policy implementation reflects the considerations described above. Our current implementation uses some simple pruning strategies to keep the number of mixture components manageable (pruning components of low weight), but no sophisticated refitting of mixtures. Because of the crudeness of the Q-function approximators, some heuristics are also used to ensure progress is made. For example, we only ask queries such that the mass of the belief state on either side of the query point is greater than some threshold δ.

5.2 Empirical Results

Our first example is reasonably small, involving a decision problem with four outcomes, with six decisions. For each outcome, there is one decision that achieves that outcome with probability 0.7 (and each other outcome with probability 0.1). The other two decisions achieve two of the outcomes with moderate probability 0.4, and the remaining two decision with low probability (0.1). Each query has a cost of 0.08 and noise parameter (i.e., false positive and false negative rates) 0.03. Recall that utilities lie in the range $[0, 1]$.

Figure 3 shows a plot of the sampled Bellman error as a function of the number of random backups, starting immediately after the initial systematic sweep of belief space (64000 backups). Bellman error is determined by sampling 2000 random belief-state query pairs and evaluating Bellman error at each. Results are averaged over 10 runs (error bars show standard deviation w.r.t. these runs). Average error is on the order of 2.5 per cent. Computation time for the initial backups is minimal, since 2-stage backups require no bootstrapping (hence no optimization over query points): on average these 64000 these took 83s. For the other backups, computation time is more intensive: the 160000 backups shown take on average 11899s (about 3.3 hours), or .074s per backup. The 70-fold increase in time per backup is almost exclusively due to the optimization of the query probabilities when assessing the max Q-value of a query type. This is largely due to the fact that our preliminary implementation relies on a generic optimization procedure. We expect much better performance

---

[10]All experiments were implemented in Matlab, under Linux, using a PIII 933MHz, 512Mb PC.

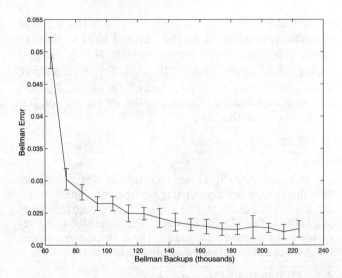

Figure 3: Bellman Error (over 10 runs): Four outcomes.

when gradient information is used to do optimization. We note, however, that: (a) the expense of this computation is borne offline; and (b) this level of Bellman error is approached long before all backups are completed.

The value of offline value function construction is borne out: determining the optimal action online takes minimal time (several hundredths of a second) and scales linearly with the number of mixture components. We report on a systematic evaluation of the number of queries in a longer version of the paper, including a comparison to the greedy query strategy . Generally, the implementation asks few queries; but we do notice that frequently the procedure will become stuck in loops or ask nonsensical queries due to the looseness of the approximate Q-functions. We are currently exploring more refined approximators, including feedforward NNs, and piecewise linear approximators.

We also ran an example with 20 outcomes and 30 decisions. Computation time per Bellman backup increases substantially because of the need to optimize over 20 queries at each backup (and the increase in the number of approximator parameters). Average backup time for 139000 2-stage backups is 0.002s, while for the 240000 full backups shown is 0.57s. The quadratic approximator does a reasonable job of capturing the value function: average Bellman error for one sample run is illustrated in Figure 4.

To illustrate the difficulty with the myopic approach, we compare the myopic strategy of [6] to the sequential model developed here on the following simple example. We have seven outcomes $s_1, \ldots, s_7$, and seven decisions $d_1, \cdots, d_7$. The decisions d_i ($i \leq 5$) each have a 0.5 chance of causing outcome s_i and s_{i+1}, while d_6 causes either s_6 or s_1. Decision d_7, in contrast, is guaranteed to realize outcome s_7.

Suppose our prior over utility functions is given by the mixture of uniforms with the fol-

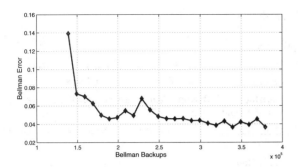

Figure 4: Bellman Error: 20 outcomes, 30 decisions.

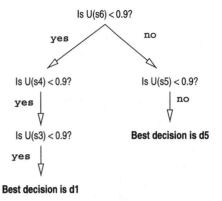

Figure 5: Example Query Paths: Myopic Problem.

lowing six components (each weighted equally):

	s_1	s_2	s_3	s_4	s_5	s_6	s_7
b_1	[.9 1]	[.9 1]	[0 .1]	[0 .1]	[0 .1]	[0 .1]	[.7 .8]
b_2	[0 .1]	[.9 1]	[.9 1]	[0 .1]	[0 .1]	[0 .1]	[.7 .8]
b_3	[0 .1]	[0 .1]	[.9 1]	[.9 1]	[0 .1]	[0 .1]	[.7 .8]
b_4	[0 .1]	[0 .1]	[0 .1]	[.9 1]	[.9 1]	[0 .1]	[.7 .8]
b_5	[0 .1]	[0 .1]	[0 .1]	[0 .1]	[.9 1]	[.9 1]	[.7 .8]
b_6	[.9 1]	[0 .1]	[0 .1]	[0 .1]	[0 .1]	[.9 1]	[.7 .8]

For each belief component b_i and state s_j, this table shows the range for which b_i assigns positive (uniform) density to $u(s_j)$. Intuitively, this prior reflects the fact that the user prefers some pair of (adjacent) outcomes from the set $\{s_1, \ldots, s_6\}$, but which exact pair is unknown. s_7 is considered to be a safe alternative. With this prior, myopic VOI associates no value to any query: a (noise-free) query can restrict the belief state to fewer than two components; but that will not be enough to change the optimal decision w.r.t. the prior (which is d_7). In contrast, the POMDP approach recognizes that the answers to a sequence of (properly chosen) queries can ensure that a better decision is made.

This problem was run using a similar training regime to those described above, with 98000 2-stage backups followed by 160000 full backups. Bellman error quickly falls to the 0.025 range (i.e., about 2.5%) after the two stage backups and hovers in that range for the remainder of the training run.[11] Backup up times for the 2-stage backups is 0.0014s per backup, while for full backups the time is 0.173s per backup. Two sample query paths for the specific prior above are shown in Figure 5. It should be noted that function approximation error can cause the value of queries to be overestimated on occasion. On a number of runs, the policy executed asks several questions about a specific utility dimension even though the current belief state contains enough information to recommend the optimal decision. We expect better function approximation strategies will help alleviate this problem. Again we point out that the myopic approach on this problem asks no questions for this prior and simply recommends the alternative, decision d_7.

As a final example, we consider a combinatorial bidding scenario, in which a bidding agent must offer bids for four different goods auctioned simultaneously in four different markets. To discretize the decision space, we assume that the

agent can offer three distinct bids—low, medium, and high—for each good. Each of these bid levels corresponds to a precise cost: should the bid win, the user pays the price associated with each bid (with, of course, higher prices associated with higher bid levels). To suppress the need for strategic reasoning, the agent has a fixed, known probability of winning a good associated with each of the three bid levels. The probabilities of winning each good are independent, and increasing in the bid level.

With four goods and three bid levels, there are 81 possible decisions (mappings from markets to bids) and 16 outcomes (subsets of goods the user might obtain). The user's utility function need not be additive with respect to the goods obtained. For instance, the user might value goods g_1 and g_2 in conjunction, but may value neither individually. Thus utility is associated with each of the 16 outcomes. We assume that the overall utility function (accounting for the price paid for each good) is quasi-linear; so the price paid is subtracted from the utility of the subset of goods obtained.[12]

A plot of the Bellman error as a function of the backups for the bidding problem is shown in Figure 6 for a single run of the problem.

Our results are certainly preliminary, but do suggest that this approach to elicitation is feasible; since the model pushes almost all of the computational burden offline, computational concerns are mitigated to a large extent. However, our results also suggest the need for further study of suitable approximation architectures, and integration with parametric *utility models*. With parametric utility, large outcome spaces can be dealt with using low dimensional belief states, which will certainly enhance the feasibility of the model.

6 Concluding Remarks

We have described an abstract model of preference elicitation that allows for a system to optimally trade off the cost of elic-

---

[11]Query cost is 0.02 and noise probabilities are 0.03.

[12]The specific parameter settings used are as follows. The prices associated with low, medium, and high bids are 0.02, 0.05 and 0.1, respectively (these are normalized on the utility scale $[0, 1]$). The probabilities of winning given a low, medium, and high bid, are 0.2, 0.4 and 0.85, respectively. These parameters are the same for all four markets. Query cost is 0.01 and responses have a 0.03 probability of being incorrect. The discount rate is 0.95.

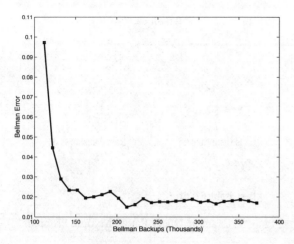

Figure 6: Bellman Error: Bidding Problem.

itation with the gain provided by elicited utility information. By casting the problem as a POMDP, the sequential and noisy nature of the process is addressed, as is the need to construct policies for arbitrary priors. Our function approximation techniques allow for optimization over continuous state and action spaces, and permit one to determine appropriate actions for mixture belief states despite the fact that we only compute value functions for single components.

We have described very preliminary experiments using specific utility, belief state, and approximation representations, but it should be clear that the general ideas apply much more broadly. Investigation of other instantiations of this model is ongoing. Of particular importance is the use of this approach with more compact utility functions representations (such as decomposed additive models), and exploiting independence in the belief state representation as well (which in turn enhances computation by reducing the inherent dimensionality of the Q-functions). Allowing more general queries is of obvious importance.

Maximizing "system utility" rather than "user utility" is an interesting variation of this model: in this case, knowledge of the user's utility function is useful if it enables good prediction of the user's behavior (e.g., purchasing patterns). The system then wishes to maximize its own utility (e.g., profit). One might also consider a game-theoretic extension in which a user wishes to conceal her preferences (to some extent) to foil this aim. Indeed, this form of elicitation could play an important role in automated negotiation and bargaining. Finally, effectively modeling long-term interactions (e.g., capturing utility functions that change over time), and learning suitable response and dynamics models, present interesting challenges.

Acknowledgements

Thanks to Fahiem Bacchus, Sam Roweis, Dale Schuurmans, and Rich Zemel for their helpful discussions, and to the anonymous referees for their comments. This research was supported by Communications and Information Technology Ontario, the Institute for Robotics and Intelligent Systems, and the Natural Sciences and Engineering Research Council of Canada.

References

[1] Dimitri P. Bertsekas. *Dynamic Programming: Deterministic and Stochastic Models*. Prentice-Hall, Englewood Cliffs, 1987.

[2] Christopher M. Bishop. *Neural Networks for Pattern Recognition*. Clarendon, Oxford, 1995.

[3] Craig Boutilier. On the foundations of *expected* expected utility. (manuscript), 2001.

[4] Craig Boutilier, Fahiem Bacchus, and Ronen I. Brafman. UCP-Networks: A directed graphical representation of conditional utilities. In *Proceedings of the Seventeenth Conference on Uncertainty in Artificial Intelligence*, pages 56–64, Seattle, 2001.

[5] U. Chajewska, L. Getoor, J. Norman, and Y. Shahar. Utility elicitation as a classification problem. In *Proceedings of the Fourteenth Conference on Uncertainty in Artificial Intelligence*, pages 79–88, Madison, WI, 1998.

[6] Urszula Chajewska, Daphne Koller, and Ronald Parr. Making rational decisions using adaptive utility elicitation. In *Proceedings of the Seventeenth National Conference on Artificial Intelligence*, pages 363–369, Austin, TX, 2000.

[7] Hsien-Te Cheng. *Algorithms for Partially Observable Markov Decision Processes*. PhD thesis, University of British Columbia, Vancouver, 1988.

[8] Simon French. *Decision Theory*. Halsted Press, New York, 1986.

[9] Eric A. Hansen. Solving POMDPs by searching in policy space. In *Proceedings of the Fourteenth Conference on Uncertainty in Artificial Intelligence*, pages 211–219, Madison, WI, 1998.

[10] Milos Hauskrecht. Value-function approximations for partially observable Markov decision processes. *Journal of Artificial Intelligence Research*, pages 33–94, 2000.

[11] R. L. Keeney and H. Raiffa. *Decisions with Multiple Objectives: Preferences and Value Trade-offs*. Wiley, New York, 1976.

[12] Long-Ji Lin and Tom. M. Mitchell. Memory approaches to reinforcement learning in non-Markovian domains. Technical Report CS-92-138, Carnegie Mellon University, Department of Computer Science, May 1992.

[13] Ronald Parr and Stuart Russell. Approximating optimal policies for partially observable stochastic domains. In *Proceedings of the Fourteenth International Joint Conference on Artificial Intelligence*, pages 1088–1094, Montreal, 1995.

[14] Richard D. Smallwood and Edward J. Sondik. The optimal control of partially observable Markov processes over a finite horizon. *Operations Research*, 21:1071–1088, 1973.

[15] Sebastian Thrun. Monte Carlo POMDPs. In *Proceedings of Conference on Neural Information Processing Systems*, pages 1064–1070, Denver, 1999.

Segmenting Time Series with a Hybrid Neural Networks - Hidden Markov Model

Laura Firoiu and **Paul R. Cohen**
Department of Computer Science
University of Massachusetts Amherst
lfiroiu@cs.umass.edu
cohen@cs.umass.edu

Abstract

This paper describes work on a hybrid HMM/ANN system for finding patterns in a time series, where a pattern is a function that can be approximated by a recurrent neural network embedded in the state of a hidden Markov model. The most likely path of the hidden Markov model is used both for re-training the HMM/ANN model and for segmenting the time series into pattern occurrences. The number of patterns is determined from the data by first increasing the number of networks as long as the likelihood of the segmentation increases, then reducing this number to satisfy an MDL criterion. In experiments with artificial data the algorithm correctly identified the generating functions. Preliminary results with robot data show that potentially useful patterns that can be associated with low-level concepts can be induced this way.

Motivation

An agent embodied in a robot receives information about its interactions with the environment as a time series of sensor vectors. As a first step in learning to represent the world, we want the agent to learn to identify segments of the time series that correspond to distinct parts of interactions, and create low-level concepts associated with these segments. For example, as illustrated in figure 1, we would like the agent to see the experience of passing an object as having two parts: approaching and passing it, then moving without the object in the visual field anymore. This example illustrates two characteristics of the concepts we wish to induce:

- A concept can be represented by a continuous function that predicts the next sensor values – the visual sensor variable varies smoothly until the object disappears from the visual field, and its variation is well described by a function vis-A-x$(t+1) = f($vis-A-x$(t),$ trans-vel$(t))$; we will call such a concept a function pattern.

- There are certain regularities in the sequence of patterns – for example, during an object passing experience, a "no object" pattern usually follows an "approach" pattern.

Given a time series of sensor data, the learning task is then to find an appropriate set of function patterns and to identify the times at which each pattern occurs, thus producing a

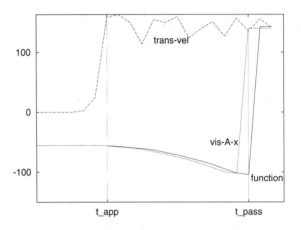

Figure 1: Sensor traces during a "pass-right" experience: while approaching the object, the evolution of the *vis-A-x* sensor (the *x*-coordinate of the object in the robot's visual field) is well predicted by the function *vis-A-x(t + 1) =* $vis\text{-}A\text{-}x(t)\left(1 - \frac{1}{1 - c*trans\text{-}vel(t)}\right)$; *trans-vel* is the robot's translational velocity. At *t_app*, the time when the approach phase begins, the parameter *c* is calculated from the observed values: *vis-A-x(t_app)*, *vis-A-x(t_app+1)*, and *trans-vel(t_app)*. At *t_pass* the robot moves past the object and sensor *vis-A-x* takes a default value.

segmentation of the time series. Intuitively, a set of function patterns and a segmentation are appropriate when:

- Every function pattern, at its assigned times, predicts well the next values in the time series.

- The segmentation is the best possible for the given pattern set, for example a data point is not assigned to a pattern when another pattern can predict it better.

Artificial neural networks (ANN) can approximate arbitrarily well any continuous function (Pinkus 1999), and we choose them to model the function patterns. Thus, we are not looking for the exact expressions of the functions that generated the observed data, but rather for functions in the class of artificial neural networks that approximate well the data generating functions. For the regularities in the sequences of function patterns we choose as models first order

Markov chains. While the first order Markov assumption may not hold in reality, it provides a simple, tractable model, which we hope is a good enough approximation at this low level of representation. The resulting model, illustrated in figure 2 and presented in more detail in the next section, is a hidden Markov model (HMM) whose states are neural networks. The learning task is defined as finding the model that produces the maximum likelihood segmentation.

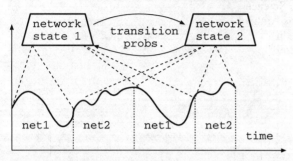

Figure 2: The hybrid HMM/ANN model: at each moment the data generating process is assumed to be in one HMM state, and the observed value is assumed to be generated by the neural network embedded in that state.

The model

While motivated by the goal of having a robot agent learn representations, the learning paradigm described here applies to time series generated by other processes as well, so it will be presented in general terms. Given a time series of observed vectors $x(1) \ldots x(t) \ldots x(T)$ of n variables, $x(t) = (x_1(t), \ldots x_i(t) \ldots x_n(t)) \in R^n$, we assume that it was generated by a set of K processes – or function patterns, each process k being described by a continuous function $f_k = R^n \rightarrow R^d$:

$$y(t) = f_k(x(t), x(t-1), \ldots)$$
$$x_{i_j}(t+1) = y_j(t) + e_k(t) \; 1 \leq j \leq d$$

with $e_k(t)$ a random normal variable representing noise. Variables $x_{i_j}(t+1)$, whose probability densities are controlled by functions f_k, are said to be the output variables; we want to identify the K processes by learning to predict the values of these variables. The remaining variables are considered input variables provided by the environment; their probability distribution will be ignored here. The partitioning into input and output variables is considered given – for example, *trans-vel*(t) and *vis-A-x*(t) sensor may be the input variables, and *vis-A-x*(t+1) the output variable. A data point at time t is the pair $\langle x(t), y(t) \rangle$, with $y \in R^d$ the vector of output variables. The pair $\langle x(t), y(t) \rangle$ will be denoted by $o(t) \in R^{n+d}$, and the resulting time series by the sequence $O = o(1) \ldots o(t) \ldots o(T)$. The likelihood of observing $o(t)$ within O, given function f_k, is the value of the multivariate normal density $N(e_k(t), 0, \Sigma^k)$:

$$\rho_k(o(t)) = \frac{1}{(2\pi|\Sigma_k|)^{d/2}} e^{-\frac{e_k(t)^t \Sigma_k^{-1} e_k(t)}{2}} \quad (1)$$

$$e_k(t) = y(t) - f_k(x(t), x(t-1), \ldots) \quad (2)$$

where $e_k(t)^t$ is the transpose of vector $e_k(t)$. The parameter Σ^k is a diagonal covariance matrix (i.e. the noise variables are assumed uncorrelated) associated with process k. The process of switching from one function pattern to another is assumed to be described by a stationary first-order Markov chain – every function pattern is a state of this process. This is a strong assumption, but for now it provides a computationally tractable model. Each function pattern k has a set $\{a_{k,l}, 1 \leq l \leq K\}$ of transition probabilities – $a_{k,l}$ is the probability that the chain will be in state l at time $t+1$ if it is in state k at t. An additional parameter $a_{0,k}$ is the probability that k is the initial state of the Markov process. The initial and transition probabilities will be denoted by vector a_k. The resulting structure

$$\lambda = \{s_k = \langle f_k, \Sigma_k, a_k \rangle, 1 \leq k \leq K\}$$

is a hidden Markov model (see Rabiner's tutorial (Rabiner 1989) for a comprehensive description of the model and its estimation algorithms) with K states $\{s_k\}$. Given a model λ, a state path $S = s(1) \ldots s(T)$ specifying the state of the process at each time, and an observed time series O, the likelihood of O being generated by λ along path S is:

$$L_\lambda(O, S \mid \lambda) = \prod_{t=1}^{T} a_{s(t-1), s(t)} * \rho_{s(t)}(o(t))$$

For time series O and model λ, the best segmentation of O is considered to be the one given by the most likely path:

$$V = arg \max_S L_\lambda(O, S \mid \lambda)$$

This path is called the Viterbi path and can be computed by the Viterbi algorithm (Rabiner 1989).

We assume that the functions f_k can be computed by recurrent neural networks. Because neural networks can approximate arbitrarily well any continuous function (see Pinkus's survey (Pinkus 1999)), and even some discontinuous functions (see (Barron 1993)), this is a weak (non-restrictive) assumption.

The learning task can now be described as finding a model $\lambda = \{\langle net_k, \Sigma_k, a_k \rangle, 1 \leq k \leq K\}$ that maximizes the likelihood $L_\lambda(O, V_\lambda)$ for a given time series O; net_k is the neural network of state k. The subscript in V_λ indicates that the segmentation depends on the model λ.

Induction algorithms

The goal is to find the model that maximizes the likelihood of the observed time series along its Viterbi path. Algorithm 1 searches heuristically for a local maximum by adding new network states as long as the likelihood keeps increasing, then reducing the number of states until a minimum description length criterion (Rissanen 1984) is satisfied.

Algorithm 1 *Main algorithm – Model induction*

1. *initialization:*
   - *available-points ← all points*

   - *create a non-content state from available-points*

2. *initial HMM/ANN induction*
   repeat while available-points $\neq \emptyset$ and $L_\lambda(O, V_\lambda)$ increases

(a) create a new network state and train the network with the "reduced support" algorithm (alg. 3) on available-points; add the network state to the model

(b) find the best model λ with the current number of states with algorithm 2, and its segmentation V_λ

(c) available-points $\leftarrow$ non-content state's points $\cup$ points poorly predicted by the networks

3. final HMM/ANN – model reduction with algorithm 4

The model is initialized with one non-content state. This state does not model the observed data with a neural network, but only with a multivariate normal density. Its goal is to collect the noisy or difficult to predict data points. Each network added to the model in step 2a has a minimal architecture and is initially trained with the "reduced support" training algorithm described later. We call the support of a network the set of points used to estimate its parameters. The algorithm 2 for finding the best model with given number of states also creates a segmentation of the observed time series, by allocating each data point to one state. The set of available points computed at step 2c contains all the points allocated to the non-content state in the previous step, and the points allocated to the content states that are poorly predicted by them. A point is poorly predicted by its network owner if the network error in that point is larger than a dynamically computed threshold.

Finding the best model with given number of states

Algorithm 2, which finds the best model with a fixed number of states, is related to the expectation maximization (EM) algorithm. It differs in that instead of trying to maximize the model's expected likelihood, it tries to maximize the model's maximum likelihood – the likelihood along the model's Viterbi path. Because it does not look at all possible paths, algorithm 2 is computationally less expensive than the Baum-Welch(Rabiner 1989) algorithm, which sums the likelihoods along all paths.

Algorithm 2 *Best model with fixed number of states:*
- *start with λ and V_λ*

- *repeat:*
  1. estimate a new model λ^* from V_λ: train the networks, calculate the variances and the transition probabilities

  2. calculate V_{λ^*}; $\lambda \leftarrow \lambda^*$, $V_\lambda \leftarrow V_{\lambda^*}$

  until the segmentation no longer changes

At step 1 each network is trained with all the points assigned to it by segmentation V. After the networks are trained to minimize the error along V, the rest of the model parameters $\{\Sigma_k, a_k\}$ can be estimated from the data by maximizing the likelihood $L_\lambda(O, V)$. The maximum can be found in this case simply by setting the partial derivatives of the likelihood to 0, and solving the resulting system of equations. The covariance matrix Σ_k is assumed diagonal, so we need to estimate only the variances σ_j^k of the y_j variables in state k. The unique solutions are the average network errors:

$$\sigma_j^k = \frac{1}{size(T_k)} \sum_{t \in T_k} (y(t) - f_k(x(t), t))^2 \quad (3)$$

where T_k is the set of (indices of) points allocated to network k in segmentation V. The solutions for the probability transitions of each state are obtained by imposing the constraint that they must sum up to 1. These solutions are:

$$a_{k,l} = \frac{\# s_k \rightarrow s_l}{\# s_k^-} \quad (4)$$

where $\# s_k \rightarrow s_l$ is the number of observed transitions from state s_k to state s_l in path V, and $\# s_k^-$ is the number of occurrences of state s_k in V (not counting the last element of sequence V). These solutions are unique, too.

At step 2 a new segmentation is computed for the new model λ^* by a dynamic programming algorithm: first the likelihood of every possible state run (contiguous repetition of the same state) $(s, t_i, t_f), 1 \le t_i \le t_f \le T$ is computed, then Dijkstra's shortest path algorithm finds the best sequence of state runs. We need to consider state runs instead of one state at a time as in the Viterbi algorithm, because the networks embedded in the HMM states are recurrent and their internal states change along state runs – the state runs, and not the state occurrences have the Markov property.

It can be easily noticed that the likelihood $L_\lambda(O, V_\lambda)$ increases at every iteration of algorithm 2:

- at step 1, $L_\lambda(O, V_\lambda) \le L_{\lambda^*}(O, V_\lambda)$ because training the networks reduces their errors along V_λ; also, the maximum likelihood estimators of the network variances and transition probabilities are easily calculated for V_λ with formulas 3 and 4;

- at step 2, $L_{\lambda^*}(O, V_\lambda) \le L_{\lambda^*}(O, V_{\lambda^*})$ because V_{λ^*} is the most likely path for model λ

We have $L_\lambda(O, V_\lambda) \le L_{\lambda^*}(O, V_\lambda) \le L_{\lambda^*}(O, V_{\lambda^*})$, meaning that the likelihood either increases or stays the same with every iteration of alg 2.

Neural networks: architecture and training

Expression 2 shows that in the general case the output value of network net_k (which computes function f_k) depends on the entire past sequence of observed variables. In order to implement this variable length memory, recurrent neural networks with the architecture depicted in figure 3 were chosen. The input and output units have identity transfer

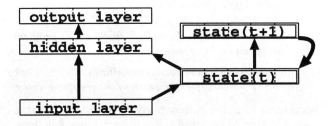

Figure 3: Recurrent network architecture: $s(t + 1) = func(s(t), x(t))$ is the network's internal state, encoded in the recurrent units.

functions, the hidden and state units have cosine activation functions. The cosine units can readily construct an approximating function – since they form the function's Fourier representation (see Barron (Barron 1993)), and unlike the more popular logistic units, they do not saturate during gradient descent. State units can also have identity transfer functions, in which case they are used as memory rather than computational units. For now, the network architecture (size, topology and transfer functions) is predetermined, not adapted during training.

Assuming an initial segmentation of the time series, each network is trained to estimate the y values within its assigned segments. The networks are trained with gradient descent on the error surface, the learning rate being adjusted automatically to follow the error surface faithfully until a local minimum is found. The error function is the normalized mean square error:

$$E = \frac{1}{2l} \sum_{t=1}^{l} \sum_{j=1}^{d} \frac{(y_j(t) - z(t))^2}{\sigma_j}$$

where $z(t) = f(x(t), t)$ is the network output, l is the number of points allocated to the network, and the first sum is taken over these points. The argument t in the function $f(x(t), t)$ computed by the recurrent network indicates that the output depends on the past inputs. The individual error of each output variable j must be normalized by the variance σ_j associated with the network's state so that one variable is not overfitted at the expense of the others. This particular error function is the one that must be minimized when maximizing the likelihood $L_\lambda(O, V)$ due to the $e^t \Sigma^{-1} e$ form in the multivariate normal density function.

Reduced support training When a new network is trained on the set "available-points" in algorithm 1, most often these points were generated by more than one function pattern. This means that a network trained to minimize the average error for the entire set is not likely to identify (approximate well on the entire domain) any of the generating functions. We try to solve this problem by allowing the network to choose its support (the set of points used to estimate its parameters) from the given training set. Algorithm 3 finds the support by iteratively excluding from the training set the points p whose errors are larger than the average network error but not smaller than a given threshold.

Algorithm 3 *Reduced support*

- *support ← available-points*
- *repeat while the support changes*
  - *train the network on the current support with gradient descent until a local minimum is reached*

  - *exclude from support the point p with:*
    error(p) > average-error, error(p) > acceptable-error

Because we do not know how many computational units are needed to approximate well any of the generating functions, and because large networks are prone to overfitting, all networks are created with a predefined minimal architecture. The price we pay for this is that several small networks may be needed to approximate well any of the generating functions, with each network covering a subdomain of the function. This means that we may have a one-to-many rather than a one-to-one correspondence between the function patterns and the network states.

Model reduction – the second HMM, the final HMM/ANN

Since a function pattern may be represented by several network states, a better – cleaner, simpler – segmentation may be obtained by partitioning the set of network states into subsets, and associate each subset with a function pattern. These subsets are not necessarily disjoint: two distinct functions can be very close on some common subdomain, so one network may approximate well both of them on that subdomain. We find these subsets by inducing a discrete hidden Markov model (Rabiner 1989), θ^*, from V_λ, the sequence of network states. The network state identifiers in V_λ are the symbols observed by the discrete HMM θ^*. We call this model's states θ^*-states, to distinguish them from the network states. Each θ^*-state is considered to represent a function pattern. Because we do not know the number of function patterns, we must estimate from V_λ the number of states in θ^*. We can do this by finding the model θ^* with m parameters that satisfies Rissanen's (Rissanen 1984) minimum description length(MDL) criterion:

$$\theta^* = arg \min_{\theta, m} \{ -\log P_\theta(V_\lambda) + \frac{1}{2} m \log T \} \qquad (5)$$

$P_\theta(V_\lambda)$ is the probability of the network state sequence V_λ under model θ, and T is the length of V_λ, the observed sequence for θ. Model θ^* is found by inducing for every k from 1 to n, the number of network states, an HMM θ with k states, and then selecting the model that minimizes the right side of expression 5. The number of parameters in a model θ with k states is $m = k * (1 + k + n)$, and $P_\theta(V_\lambda)$ is computed with the Baum-Welch algorithm. Let K be the number of states in θ^*. The segmentation of the time series is obtained by computing the Viterbi path, V_{θ^*}, of model θ^* for the sequence of network states V_λ induced by the initial HMM/ANN model . The final HMM/ANN model with K states is obtained by assuming that each θ^*-state corresponds to a function pattern – although we cannot expect a perfect correspondence –, and then applying algorithm 2 to the segmentation V_{θ^*}. The final networks are chosen larger than the initial networks, with their architecture again preselected. The pseudo-code of the model reduction algorithm is very simple:

Algorithm 4 *Model reduction*

- *induce θ^* from V_λ – determine its number of states K with the MDL criterion*
- *compute segmentation V_{θ^*}*
- *$\lambda \leftarrow$ arbitrary model with K states and given architecture; $V_\lambda \leftarrow V_{\theta^*}$*
- *estimate λ's parameters with algorithm 2*

It must be noticed that we can now address the problem of estimating the network size: assuming that each θ^*-state corresponds to a function pattern, a network can be trained with all the points allocated to a θ^*-state in V_{θ^*}, including a regularization term in the cost to be minimized. This was not possible until now (step 3 in the main algorithm), because the network's support was not considered known, and the regularization term depends on the size of the training set.

It must also be noticed that the likelihood of the observed data O under the final HMM/ANN may be smaller than the likelihood under the initial HMM/ANN. This is because the number of network states was determined with a minimum description length, not a maximum likelihood criterion, and also because there is no guarantee that the final networks have smaller approximation errors than the initial networks. For now, we prefer to eventually give up in the final step a higher likelihood model, for a simpler one that produces a less complex segmentation.

Experimental results

To understand what our induction algorithm can do, we first applied it to artificial data. We present here two such experiments. For the first experiment, a time series with 257 data points was generated by a process switching between two function patterns, f and g:

$$x(t+1) = f(\cdot) = -1.05x(t) + .05$$
$$x(t+1) = g(\cdot) = \frac{-2x+5}{.5x^2(t)+1}$$

For both patterns the self-transition probability is .9. Normally distributed noise with variance .01 was added to the output. The initial networks have two hidden and one state cosine units. The initial HMM/ANN model, λ, found at the second step of algorithm 1, has seven network states: one network gets almost all of f's points and a couple from g, five networks get most of g's points plus a few from f, and one non-content state gets several points from both f and g. Because g is a more complex function, several simple networks are needed to estimate it. The final HMM/ANN model, θ, has exactly two network states, and the resulting segmentation, as it can be seen in figure 4 where the segmentation plots show the state indices along the two best paths, identifies almost perfectly the two generating functions. The two networks of model θ were given different architectures: the one that approximates f has the same simple architecture as the initial networks; the one approximating g has nine hidden and no state units. In several runs of the model reduction algorithms, this configuration yielded the smallest approximation errors.

For the second experiment with artificial data, four functions generated a time series with 582 points:

lin1: $x(t+1) = .9 * x(t) + .1$
lin2: $x(t+1) = .9 * x(t) + .5$
quad: $x(t+1) = -1.05 * x^2(t) - 1.75 * x(t) + .25$
frac: $x(t+1) = \frac{-1.75*x^2(t)-2.5*x(t)+.5}{1.5*x^2(t)+.5*x(t)+.17}$

Again, the self-transition probability was .9, and the noise variance was .01. Table 1 shows the allocation of the four functions points to the states of the initial model λ, and final model θ. Because the linear functions "lin1" and "lin2" are similar (same slope), in each model, one network – s1 in λ, and s2 in θ – approximates most of their points. In θ, network s1 gets almost all the points generated by the quadratic function "quad", and s3 of the fractional function "frac". The algorithm was also applied to a time series collected during experiences involving a robot approaching or passing an object. There were 14 non-disjoint kinds of experiences –

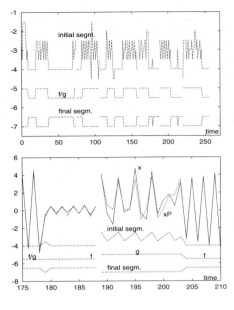

Figure 4: Top: "f/g" is the sequence of the generating functions f and g, "initial segm." is λ's best bath, "final segm." is θ's best path. Bottom: part of the generated time series, its approximation(prediction) by model θ, and the segmentations produced by the two models; "x" plots the observed data, and "xP" the predicted data.

λ	s0	s1	s2	s3	s4	s5	s6	s7	s8
lin1	0	71	0	0	0	0	2	20	0
lin2	0	133	0	79	0	0	0	0	0
quad	0	0	157	0	1	1	1	0	0
frac	16	0	2	0	24	21	5	1	48

θ	s0	s1	s2	s3	s4
lin1	5	0	88	0	0
lin2	0	0	133	0	79
quad	0	157	1	2	0
frac	8	1	0	108	0

Table 1: The allocation of the pattern points to the HMM states; s0 is the non-content state for both models.

"pass right a red object", "pass right a red object, then push a blue object", with several of each kind, totaling 1082 time steps and 42 experiences. Two thirds of the experiences were selected for the training set, and the remaining ones formed the test set. A model was induced from the training set for the task of predicting the next "vis-A-x" and "vis-A-y" sensor values from the current "trans-vel", "vis-A-x" and "vis-A-y" values. Sensors "vis-A-x" and "vis-A-y" return the coordinates of the center of an object in the robot's visual field, and "trans-vel" is the robot's translational velocity. Small networks with four hidden and two state cosine units were used. Only the initial HMM/ANN was induced (no clean-up of the resulting segmentation), with good results. In both the training and the test set the experiences of the same kind are segmented in the same way, i.e. they are represented by approximatively the same sequence of network states. During the "pass-right" experiences, one network state, network 1, is active when the robot gets close to the object and passes it, and another, network 4, is active immediately after the robot passed the object. This indicates that these two patterns can be used to describe a concept like "approaching and passing an object", and as such are potentially useful building blocks in higher level representations of the robot's environment. The segmentations of four "pass right a red object" experiences, two in the training set and two in the test set, are shown in figure 5.

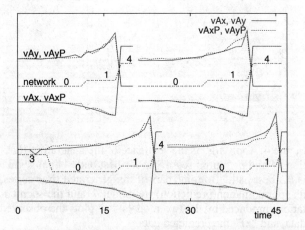

Figure 5: Induced segmentation of four "pass-right" experiences: top – from the training set, bottom – from the test set. The plots are: "vAx" is "vis-A-x", "vAy" is "vis-A-y"; "vAxP" and "vAyP" are the network outputs; "network" is the Viterbi path.

Related work

Many different hybrid HMM/ANN architectures have been developed, with the networks computing state transition probabilities or observation probability density parameters. These systems were successfully used in applications like speech recognition , or time series prediction. Among the latter, we are most interested in the work of Liehr, Kohlmorgen et. al. (Liehr *et al.* 1999) and Tani and Nolfi (Tani & Nolfi 1999). In both cases an ensemble of networks, called experts, is trained to predict the next observation, and the time series is segmented by soft competition among the experts. While their learning framework is similar with ours, there are some differences. The most important one is that their systems have a fixed number of experts, while in ours the number of networks is determined from the data. Another difference is that their systems employ a non-stationary, more complex model of the expert switching process. Liehr et. al. have a HMM whose transition probabilities are computed dynamically by a neural network, Tani et. al. have a neural network compute at every time step the expert activation probabilities. The prediction of their ensembles is a weighted sum of the individual expert predictions, with the weights depending on the dynamically calculated probabilities. It can be noticed that the non-stationary mixture of network outputs compensates for the fixed number

of experts. While the mixture can be considered a more parsimonious representation, eventually identifying more complex concepts like drifts between regimes, the fixed maximum number of low level concepts can be a drawback.

Conclusions and future work

A new hybrid HMM/ANN system for segmenting time series was presented. The main difference from other HMM/ANN approaches is that the number of networks is not fixed, but induced from the data. In experiments with artificial data the algorithm identified almost perfectly the generating functions. Preliminary results with robot data suggest that the induced patterns can be associated with low-level concepts, and are thus potentially useful representation elements. These results are preliminary not only because we need more experiments, but also because the induction algorithms and the resulting concepts are not yet part of an architecture for predicting and controlling an agent's interactions with its environment. In future work we intend to develop a hierarchical architecture for prediction and control, with the model and algorithms described in this work forming the lowest level. We also intend to employ regularization methods to estimate from the data the network architectures. This is an important problem because a network's estimation and generalizations capabilities, and thus the quality of the induced concepts, depend on its architecture.

Acknowledgements

This research is supported by DARPA under contract DARPA/USASMDCDASG60-99-C-0074. The U.S. Government is authorized to reproduce and distribute reprints for governmental purposes notwithstanding any copyright notation hereon. The views and conclusions contained herein are those of the authors and should not be interpreted as necessarily representing the official policies or endorsements either expressed or implied, of the DARPA or the U.S. Government.

References

Barron, A. R. 1993. Universal approximation bounds for superpositions of a sigmoidal function. *IEEE Transactions on Information Theory* 39(3):930–945.

Liehr, S.; Pawelzik, K.; Kohlmorgen, J.; and Muller, K. R. 1999. Hidden markov mixtures of experts with an application to EEG recordings from sleep. *Theory in Biosciences* 118(3-4):246–260.

Pinkus, A. 1999. Approximation theory of the MLP model in neural networks. *Acta Numerica* 143–195.

Rabiner, L. R. 1989. A Tutorial on Hidden Markov Models and Selected Applications in Speech Recognition. *Proceedings of the IEEE* 77(2):257–285.

Rissanen, J. 1984. Universal Coding, Information, Prediction, and Estimation. *IEEE Transactions on Information Theory* 30(4):629–636.

Tani, J., and Nolfi, S. 1999. Learning to perceive the world as articulated: an approach for hierarchical learning in sensory-motor systems. *Neural Networks* 12(7-8).

Context-Specific Multiagent Coordination and Planning with Factored MDPs

Carlos Guestrin
Computer Science Dept.
Stanford University
guestrin@cs.stanford.edu

Shobha Venkataraman
Computer Science Dept.
Stanford University
shobha@cs.stanford.edu

Daphne Koller
Computer Science Dept.
Stanford University
koller@cs.stanford.edu

Abstract

We present an algorithm for coordinated decision making in cooperative multiagent settings, where the agents' value function can be represented as a sum of context-specific *value rules*. The task of finding an optimal joint action in this setting leads to an algorithm where the coordination structure between agents depends on the current state of the system and even on the actual numerical values assigned to the value rules. We apply this framework to the task of multiagent planning in dynamic systems, showing how a joint value function of the associated Markov Decision Process can be approximated as a set of value rules using an efficient linear programming algorithm. The agents then apply the coordination graph algorithm at each iteration of the process to decide on the highest-value joint action, potentially leading to a different coordination pattern at each step of the plan.

1 Introduction

Consider a system where multiple agents must coordinate in order to achieve a common goal, maximizing their joint utility. Naively, we can consider all possible joint actions, and choose the one that gives the highest value. Unfortunately, this approach is infeasible in all but the simplest settings, as the number of joint actions grows exponentially with the number of agents. Furthermore, we want to avoid a centralized decision making process, letting the agents communicate with each other so as to reach a jointly optimal decision.

This problem was recently addressed by Guestrin, Koller, and Parr (2001a) (GKP hereafter). They propose an approach based on an approximation of the joint value function as a linear combination of local value functions, each of which relates only to the parts of the system controlled by a small number of agents. They show how factored value functions allow the agents to find a globally optimal joint action using a message passing scheme. However, their approach suffers from a significant limitation: They assume that each agent only needs to interact with a small number of other agents. In many situations, an agent can *potentially* interact with many other agents, but not at the *same* time. For example, two agents that are both part of a construction crew might need to coordinate at times when they could both be working on the same task, but not at other times. If we use the approach of GKP, we are forced to represent

value functions over large numbers of agents, rendering the approach intractable.

Our approach is based on the use of *context specificity* — a common property of real-world decision making tasks (Boutilier, Dean, & Hanks 1999). Specifically, we assume that the agents' value function can be decomposed into a set of *value rules*, each describing a context — an assignment to state variables and actions — and a value increment which gets added to the agents' total value in situations when that context applies. For example, a value rule might assert that in states where two agents are at the same house and both try to install the plumbing, they get in each other's way and the total value is decremented by 100. This representation is reminiscent of the tree-structured value functions of Boutilier and Dearden (1996), but is substantially more general, as the rules are not necessarily mutually exclusive, but can be added together to form more complex functions.

Based on this representation, we provide a significant extension to the GKP notion of a *coordination graph*. We describe a distributed decision-making algorithm that uses message passing over this graph to reach a jointly optimal action. The coordination used in the algorithm can vary significantly from one situation to another. For example, if two agents are not in the same house, they will not need to coordinate. The coordination structure can also vary based on the utilities in the model; e.g., if it is dominant for one agent to work on the plumbing (e.g., because he is an expert), the other agents will not need to coordinate with him.

We then extend this framework to the problem of sequential decision making. We view the problem as a *Markov decision process (MDP)*, where the actions are the joint actions for all of the agents, and the reward is the total reward. Once again, we use context specificity, assuming that the rewards and the transition dynamics are rule-structured. We extend the linear programming approach of GKP to construct an approximate rule-based value function for this MDP. The agents can then use the coordination graph to decide on a joint action at each time step. Interestingly, although the value function is computed once in an offline setting, the online choice of action using the coordination graph gives rise to a highly variable coordination structure.

2 Context-specific coordination

We begin by considering the simpler problem of having a group of agents select a globally optimal joint action in order to maximize their joint value. Suppose we have a collection of agents $\mathbf{A} = \{A_1, \ldots, A_g\}$, where each agent A_j must choose an action a_j from a finite set of possible actions $\text{Dom}(A_j)$. The agents are acting in a space described by a set of discrete state variables, $\mathbf{X} = \{X_1 \ldots X_n\}$, where each X_j takes on values in some finite domain $\text{Dom}(X_j)$. The agents must choose the joint action $\mathbf{a} \in \text{Dom}(\mathbf{A})$ that maximizes the total utility.

As discussed in GKP, the overall utility, or value function is often decomposed as a sum of "local" value functions, associated with the "jurisdiction" of the different agents. For example, if multiple agents are constructing a house, we can decompose the value function as a sum of the values of the tasks accomplished by each agent.

Definition 2.1 *We say that a function f is restricted to a scope* $\text{Scope}[f] = \mathbf{C} \subseteq \mathbf{X} \cup \mathbf{A}$ *if* $f : \mathbf{C} \mapsto I\!R$. ∎

Thus, we can specify the value function as a sum of agent-specific value functions Q_j, each with a restricted scope. Each Q_j is typically represented as a table, listing agent j's local values for different combinations of variables in the scope. However, this representation is often highly redundant, forcing us to represent many irrelevant interactions. For example, an agent A_1's value function might depend on the action of agent A_2 if both are trying to install the plumbing in the same house. However, there is no interaction if A_2 is currently working in another house, and there is no point in making A_1's entire value function depend on A_2's action. We represent such context specific value dependencies using *value rules*:

Definition 2.2 *Let* $\mathbf{C} \subseteq \mathbf{X} \cup \mathbf{A}$ *and* $\mathbf{c} \in \text{Dom}(\mathbf{C})$. *We say that* $\mathbf{c}$ *is* consistent *with* $\mathbf{b} \in \text{Dom}(\mathbf{B})$ *if* $\mathbf{c}$ *and* $\mathbf{b}$ *assign the same value to* $\mathbf{C} \cap \mathbf{B}$. *A value rule* $\langle \rho; \mathbf{c} : v \rangle$ *is a function* $\rho : \text{Dom}(\mathbf{X}, \mathbf{A}) \mapsto I\!R$ *such that* $\rho(\mathbf{x}, \mathbf{a}) = v$ *when* $(\mathbf{x}, \mathbf{a})$ *is consistent with* $\mathbf{c}$ *and* 0 *otherwise.* ∎

In our construction example, we might have a rule:

$\langle \rho; A_1, A_2$ in-same-house $= \textit{true} \; \wedge$

$\qquad A_1 = \textit{plumbing} \wedge A_2 = \textit{plumbing} : -100 \rangle$.

This definition of rules adapts the definition of rules for exploiting context specific independence in inference for Bayesian networks by Zhang and Poole (1999). Note that a value rule $\langle \rho; \mathbf{c} : v \rangle$ has a scope $\mathbf{C}$.

Definition 2.3 *A rule-based function* $f : \{\mathbf{X}, \mathbf{A}\} \mapsto I\!R$ *is composed of a set of rules* $\{\rho_1, \ldots, \rho_n\}$ *such that* $f(\mathbf{x}, \mathbf{a}) = \sum_{i=1}^{n} \rho_i(\mathbf{x}, \mathbf{a})$. ∎

This notion of a rule-based function is related to the tree-structure functions used by Boutilier and Dearden (1996) and by Boutilier et al. (1999), but is substantially more general. In the tree-structure value functions, the rules corresponding to the different leaves are mutually exclusive and exhaustive. Thus, the total number of different values represented in the tree is equal to the number of leaves (or rules). In the rule-based function representation, the rules are not mutually exclusive, and their values are added to form the overall function value for different settings of the variables. Different rules are added in different settings, and, in fact, with k rules, one can easily generate 2^k different possible

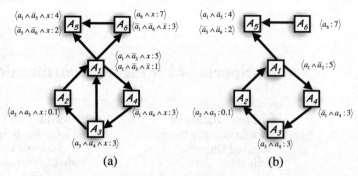

Figure 1: (a) Coordination graph for a 6-agent problem, the rules in Q_j are indicated in the figure by the rules next to A_j. (b) Graph becomes simpler after conditioning on the state $X = x$.

values. Thus, the rule-based functions can provide a compact representation for a much richer class of value functions.

We represent the local value function Q_j associated with agent j as a rule-based function:

$$Q_j = \sum_i \rho_i^j .$$

Note that if each rule ρ_i^j has scope $\mathbf{C}_i^j$, then Q_j will be a restricted scope function of $\cup_i \mathbf{C}_i^j$. The scope of Q_j can be further divided into two parts: The state variables

$$Obs[Q_j] = \{X_i \in \mathbf{X} \mid X_i \in \text{Scope}[Q_j]\}$$

are the observations agent j needs to make. The agent decision variables

$$Agents[Q_j] = \{A_i \in \mathbf{A} \mid A_i \in \text{Scope}[Q_j]\}.$$

are the agents with whom j interacts directly.

3 Cooperative action selection

Recall that the agents' task is to select a joint action $\mathbf{a}$ that maximizes $Q = \sum_j Q_j(\mathbf{x}, \mathbf{a})$. The fact that the Q_j's depend on the actions of multiple agents forces the agents to coordinate their action choices. As we now show, this process can be performed using a very natural data structure called a *coordination graph*. Intuitively, a coordination graph connects agents whose local value functions interact with each other. This definition is the directed extension of the definition proposed in GKP, and is the collaborative counterpart of the relevance graph proposed for competitive settings by Koller and Milch (2001).

Definition 3.1 *A coordination graph for a set of agents with local utilities* $Q = \{Q_1, \ldots, Q_g\}$ *is a directed graph whose nodes are* $\{A_1, \ldots, A_g\}$, *and which contains an edge* $A_i \rightarrow A_j$ *if and only if* $A_i \in Agents[Q_j]$. ∎

An example of a coordination graph with 6 agents and one state variable is shown in Fig. 1(a). See, for example, that agent A_3 has the parent A_4, because A_4's action affects Q_3.

Recall that our task is to find a coordination strategy for the agents to maximize $\sum_j Q_j$ at each state $\mathbf{x}$. First, note that the scope of the Q_j functions that comprise the value can include both action choices and state variables.

We assume that each agent j has full observability of the relevant state variables $Obs[Q_j]$. Given a particular state $\mathbf{x} = \{x_1, \ldots, x_n\}$, agent j *conditions* on the current state by discarding all rules in Q_j not consistent with the current state $\mathbf{x}$. Note that agent j only needs to observe $Obs[Q_j]$, and not the entire state of the system, substantially reducing the sensing requirements. Interestingly, after the agents observe the current state, the coordination graph may become simpler. In our example the edges $A_3 \rightarrow A_1$ and $A_1 \rightarrow A_6$ disappear after agents observe that $X = x$, as shown in Fig. 1(b). Thus, agents A_1 and A_6 will only need to coordinate directly in the context of $X = \bar{x}$.

After conditioning on the current state, each Q_j will only depend on the agents' action choices $\mathbf{A}$. Now, our task is to select a joint action $\mathbf{a}$ that maximizes $\sum_j Q_j(\mathbf{a})$. Maximization in a graph structure suggests the use of *non-serial dynamic programming* (Bertele & Brioschi 1972), or variable elimination. To exploit structure in rules, we use an algorithm similar to variable elimination in a Bayesian network with context specific independence (Zhang & Poole 1999).

Intuitively, the algorithm operates by having an individual agent "collect" value rules relevant to them from their children. The agent can then decide on its own strategy, taking all of the implications into consideration. The choice of optimal action and the ensuing payoff will, of course, depend on the actions of agents whose strategies have not yet been decided. The agent therefore communicates the value ramifications of its strategy to other agents, so that they can make informed decisions on their own strategies.

More precisely, our algorithm "eliminates" agents one by one, where the elimination process performs a maximization step over the agent's action choice. Assume that we are eliminating A_i, whose collected value rules lead to a rule function f. Assume that f involves the actions of some other set of agents $\mathbf{B}$, so that f's scope is $\{\mathbf{B}, A_i\}$. Agent A_i needs to choose its optimal action for each choice of actions $\mathbf{b}$ of $\mathbf{B}$. We use $MaxOut(f, A_i)$ to denote a procedure that takes a rule function $f(\mathbf{B}, A_i)$ and returns a rule function $g(\mathbf{B})$ such that: $g(\mathbf{b}) = \max_{a_i} f(\mathbf{b}, a_i)$. Such a procedure is a fairly straightforward extension of the variable elimination algorithm of (Zhang & Poole 1999). We omit details for lack of space. The algorithm proceeds by repeatedly selecting some undecided agent, until all agents have decided on a strategy. For a selected agent A_l:

1. A_l receives messages from its children, with all the rules $\langle \rho; \mathbf{c} : v \rangle$ such that $A_l \in \mathbf{C}$. These rules are added to Q_l. After this step, A_l has no children in the coordination graph and can be optimized independently.

2. A_l performs the local maximization step $g_l = MaxOut(Q_l, A_l)$; This local maximization corresponds to a conditional strategy decision.

3. A_l distributes the rules in g_l to its parents. At this point, A_l's strategy is fixed, and it has been "eliminated".

Once this procedure is completed, a second pass in the reverse order is performed to compute the optimal action choice for all of the agents. Note that the initial distribution of rules among agents and the procedure for distributing messages among the parent agents in step 3 do not alter the final action choice and have a limited impact on the communication required for solving the coordination problem.

The cost of this algorithm is polynomial in the number of new rules generated in the maximization operation $MaxOut(Q_l, A_l)$. The number of rules is never larger and in many cases exponentially smaller than the complexity bounds on the table-based coordination graph in GKP, which, in turn, was exponential only in the *induced width* of the graph (Dechter 1999). However, the computational costs involved in managing sets of rules usually imply that the computational advantage of the rule-based approach will only manifest in problems that possess a fair amount of context specific structure.

More importantly, the rule based coordination structure exhibits several important properties. First, as we discussed, the structure often changes when conditioning on the current state, as in Fig. 1. Thus, in different states of the world, the agents may have to coordinate their actions differently. In our example, if the situation is such that the plumbing is ready to be installed, two qualified agents that are at the same house will need to coordinate. However, they may not need to coordinate in other situations.

More surprisingly, interactions that seem to hold between agents even after the state-based simplification can disappear as agents make strategy decisions. For example, if $Q_1 = \{\langle a_1 \wedge a_2 : 5 \rangle, \langle \overline{a_1} \wedge a_2 \wedge \overline{a_3} : 1 \rangle\}$, then A_1's optimal strategy is to do a_1 regardless, at which point the added value is 5 regardless of A_3's decision. In other words, $MaxOut(Q_1, A_1) = \{\langle a_2 : 5 \rangle\}$. In this example, there is an *a priori* dependence between A_2 and A_3. However, after maximizing A_1, the dependence disappears and agents A_2 and A_3 may not need to communicate. In the construction crew example, suppose electrical wiring and plumbing can be performed simultaneously. If there is an agent A_1 that can do both tasks and another A_2 that is only a plumber, then a priori the agents need to coordinate so that they are not both working on plumbing. However, when A_1 is optimizing his strategy, he decides that electrical wiring is a dominant strategy, because either A_2 will do the plumbing and both tasks are done, or A_2 will work on another house, in which case A_1 can perform the plumbing task in the next time step, achieving the same total value.

The context-sensitivity of the rules also reduces communication between agents. In particular, agents only need to communicate relevant rules to each other, reducing unnecessary interaction. For example, in Fig. 1(b), when agent A_1 decides on its strategy, agent A_5 only needs to pass the rules that involve A_1, i.e., only $\langle a_1 \wedge \overline{a_5} : 4 \rangle$. The rule involving A_6 is not transmitted, avoiding the need for agent A_1 to consider agent A_6's decision in its strategy.

Finally, we note that the rule structure provides substantial flexibility in constructing the system. In particular, the structure of the coordination graph can easily be adapted incrementally as new value rules are added or eliminated. For example, if it turns out that two agents intensely dislike each other, we can easily introduce an additional value rule that associates a negative value with pairs of action choices that puts them in the same house at the same time.

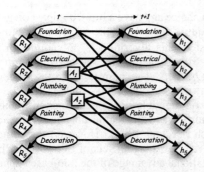

Figure 2: A DDN for a 2-agent crew and 1 house setting.

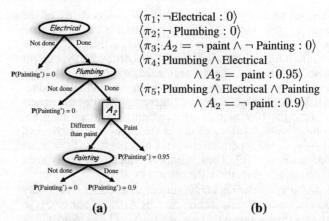

(a)   **(b)**

Figure 3: (a) Example CPD for Painting', represented as a CPD-tree. (b) Equivalent set of probability rules.

4 One-step lookahead

Now assume that the agents are trying to maximize the sum of an immediate reward and a value that they expect to receive one step in the future. We describe the dynamics of such system τ using a *dynamic decision network (DDN)* (Dean & Kanazawa 1989). Let X_i denote the ith variable at the current time and X_i' the variable at the next step. The *transition graph* of a DDN is a two-layer directed acyclic graph G whose nodes are $\{A_1, \ldots, A_g, X_1, \ldots, X_n, X_1', \ldots, X_n'\}$, and where only nodes in $\mathbf{X}'$ have parents. We denote the parents of X_i' in the graph by $Parents(X_i')$. For simplicity of exposition, we assume that $Parents(X_i') \subseteq \mathbf{X} \cup \mathbf{A}$, i.e., all of the parents of a node are in the previous time step. Each node X_i' is associated with a *conditional probability distribution (CPD)* $P(X_i' \mid Parents(X_i'))$. The transition probability $P(\mathbf{x}' \mid \mathbf{x}, \mathbf{a})$ is then defined to be $\prod_i P(x_i' \mid \mathbf{u}_i)$, where $\mathbf{u}_i$ is the value in $\mathbf{x}, \mathbf{a}$ of the variables in $Parents(X_i')$. The immediate rewards are a set of functions $r_1, \ldots, r_g$, and the next-step values are a set of functions $h_1, \ldots, h_g$.

Fig. 2 shows a DDN for a simple two-agent problem, where ovals represent the variables X_i (features of a house) and rectangles the agent actions (tasks). The arrows to the next time step variables represent dependencies, e.g., painting can only be done if both electrical wiring and plumbing are done and agent A_2 decides to paint. The diamond nodes in the first time step represent the immediate reward, while the h nodes in the second time step represent the future value associated with a subset of the state variables.

In most representations of Bayesian networks and DDNs, tables are used to represent the utility nodes r_i and h_i and the transition probabilities $P(X_i' \mid Parents(X_i'))$. However, as discussed by Boutilier *et al.* (1999), decision problems often exhibit a substantial amount of context specificity, both in the value functions and in the transition dynamics. We have already described a rule-based representation of the value function components. We now describe a rule representation (as in (Zhang & Poole 1999)) for the transition model.

Definition 4.1 *A probability rule* $\langle \pi; \mathbf{c} : p \rangle$ *is a function* $\pi : \{\mathbf{X}, \mathbf{X}', \mathbf{A}\} \mapsto [0, 1]$, *where the* context $\mathbf{c} \in \mathrm{Dom}(\mathbf{C})$ *for* $\mathbf{C} \subseteq \{\mathbf{X}, \mathbf{X}', \mathbf{A}\}$ *and* $p \in [0, 1]$, *such that* $\pi(\mathbf{x}, \mathbf{x}', \mathbf{a}) = p$ *if* $\{\mathbf{x}, \mathbf{x}', \mathbf{a}\}$ *is consistent with* $\mathbf{c}$ *and is* 1 *otherwise. A rule-based conditional probability distribution (rule CPD)* P *is a function* $P : \{X_i', \mathbf{X}, \mathbf{A}\} \mapsto [0, 1]$, *composed of a set of probability rules* $\{\pi_1, \pi_2, \ldots\}$, *such that:*

$$P(x_i' \mid \mathbf{x}, \mathbf{a}) = \prod_{i=1}^{n} \pi_i(x_i', \mathbf{x}, \mathbf{a});$$

and where every assignment $(x_i', \mathbf{x}, \mathbf{a})$ *is consistent with the context of only one rule.*

We can now define the conditional probabilities $P(X_i' \mid Parents(X_i'))$ as a rule CPD, where the context variables $\mathbf{C}$ of the rules depend on variables in $\{X_i' \cup Parents(X_i')\}$. An example of a CPD represented by a set of probability rules is shown in Fig. 3.

In the one-step lookahead case, for any setting $\mathbf{x}$ of the state variables, the agents aim to maximize:

$$Q(\mathbf{x}, \mathbf{a}) = \sum_{j=1}^{g} Q_j(\mathbf{x}, \mathbf{a})$$

$$Q_j(\mathbf{x}, \mathbf{a}) = r_j(\mathbf{x}, \mathbf{a}) + \sum_{\mathbf{x}'} P(\mathbf{x}' \mid \mathbf{x}, \mathbf{a}) h_j(\mathbf{x}').$$

In the previous section, we showed that if each Q_j is a rule-based function, it can be optimized effectively using the co-ordination graph. We now show that, when system dynamics, rewards and values are rule-based, the Q_j's are also rule based, and can be computed effectively. Our approach extends the factored backprojection of Koller and Parr (1999).

Each h_j is a rule function, which can be written as $h_j(\mathbf{x}') = \sum_i \rho_i^{(h_j)}(\mathbf{x}')$, where $\rho_i^{(h_j)}$ has the form $\left\langle \rho_i^{(h_j)}; \mathbf{c}_i^{(h_j)} : v_i^{(h_j)} \right\rangle$. Each rule is a restricted scope function; thus, we can simplify:

$$
\begin{aligned}
g_j(\mathbf{x}, \mathbf{a}) &= \sum_{\mathbf{x}'} P(\mathbf{x}' \mid \mathbf{x}, \mathbf{a}) h_j(\mathbf{x}') \\
&= \sum_i \sum_{\mathbf{x}'} P(\mathbf{x}' \mid \mathbf{x}, \mathbf{a}) \rho_i^{(h_j)}(\mathbf{x}'); \\
&= \sum_i v_i^{(h_j)} P(\mathbf{c}_i^{(h_j)} \mid \mathbf{x}, \mathbf{a});
\end{aligned}
$$

where the term $v_i^{(h_j)} P(\mathbf{c}_i^{(h_j)} \mid \mathbf{x}, \mathbf{a})$ can be written as a rule function. We denote this backprojection operation by $RuleBackproj(\rho_i^{(h_j)})$; its implementation is straightforward, and we omit details for lack of space. For example, consider the backprojection of a simple rule, $\langle \rho;$ Painting done at $t+1:10\rangle$, through the CPD in Fig. 3:

$$RuleBackproj(\rho) = \sum_{\mathbf{x}'} P(\mathbf{x}' \mid \mathbf{x}, \mathbf{a})\rho(\mathbf{x}');$$

$$= \sum_{\text{Painting}'} P(\text{Painting}' \mid \mathbf{x}, \mathbf{a})\rho(\text{Painting}');$$

$$= 10 \prod_{i=1}^{5} \pi_i(\text{Painting}', \mathbf{x}, \text{Paint}) .$$

Note that the contexts for these probability rules are mutually exclusive, and hence the product is equivalent to the CPD-tree shown in Fig. 3(a). Hence, this product is equal to 0 in most contexts, e.g., when electricity is not done at time t. The product in non-zero only in two contexts: in the context associated with rule π_4 and in the one for π_5. Thus, we can express the backprojection operation as:

$RuleBackproj(\rho) =$
$\quad \langle \text{Plumbing} \wedge \text{Electrical} \wedge A_2 = \text{paint} : 9.5\rangle +$
$\quad \langle \text{Plumbing} \wedge \text{Electrical} \wedge \text{Painting} \wedge A_2 = \neg \text{paint} : 9\rangle;$

which is a rule-based function composed of two rules.

Thus, we can now write the *backprojection* of the next step utility h_j as:

$$g_j(\mathbf{x}, \mathbf{a}) = \sum_i RuleBackproj(\rho_i^{(h_j)}); \quad (1)$$

where g_j is a sum of rule-based functions, and therefore also a rule-based function. Using this notation, we can write $Q_j(\mathbf{x}, \mathbf{a}) = r_j(\mathbf{x}, \mathbf{a}) + g_j(\mathbf{x}, \mathbf{a})$, which is again a rule-based function. This function is exactly the case we addressed in Section 3. Therefore, we can perform efficient one-step lookahead planning using the same coordination graph.

5 Multiagent sequential decision making

We now turn to the substantially more complex case where the agents are acting in a dynamic environment and are trying to jointly maximize their expected long-term return. The *Markov Decision Process (MDP)* framework formalizes this problem.

An MDP is defined as a 4-tuple $(\mathbf{X}, \mathcal{A}, \mathcal{R}, P)$ where: $\mathbf{X}$ is a finite set of $N = |\mathbf{X}|$ states; $\mathcal{A}$ is a set of actions; $\mathcal{R}$ is a *reward function* $\mathcal{R} : \mathbf{X} \times \mathcal{A} \mapsto \mathbb{R}$, such that $\mathcal{R}(\mathbf{x}, a)$ represents the reward obtained in state $\mathbf{x}$ after taking action a; and P is a *Markovian transition model* where $P(\mathbf{x}' \mid \mathbf{x}, a)$ represents the probability of going from state $\mathbf{x}$ to state $\mathbf{x}'$ with action a. We assume that the MDP has an infinite horizon and that future rewards are discounted exponentially with a discount factor $\gamma \in [0, 1)$. Given a value function $\mathcal{V}$, we define $Q_{\mathcal{V}}(\mathbf{x}, a) = R(\mathbf{x}, a) + \gamma \sum_{\mathbf{x}'} P(\mathbf{x}' \mid \mathbf{x}, a)\mathcal{V}(\mathbf{x}')$, and the *Bellman operator* T^* to be $T^*\mathcal{V}(\mathbf{x}) = \max_a Q_{\mathcal{V}}(\mathbf{x}, a)$. The optimal value function $\mathcal{V}^*$ is the fixed point of T^*: $\mathcal{V}^* = T^*\mathcal{V}^*$. For any value function $\mathcal{V}$, we can define the policy obtained by acting greedily relative to $\mathcal{V}$: $Greedy(\mathcal{V})(\mathbf{x}) = \arg\max_a Q_{\mathcal{V}}(\mathbf{x}, a)$. The greedy policy relative to the optimal value function $\mathcal{V}^*$ is the optimal policy $\pi^* = Greedy(\mathcal{V}^*)$.

There are several algorithms for computing the optimal policy. One is via linear programming. Our variables are $V_1, \ldots, V_N$, where V_i represents $\mathcal{V}(\mathbf{x}^{(i)})$ with $\mathbf{x}^{(i)}$ referring to the ith state. One simple variant of the LP is:

Minimize: $1/N \sum_i V_i$;
Subject to: $V_i \geq R(\mathbf{x}^{(i)}, a) + \gamma \sum_j P(\mathbf{x}^{(j)} \mid \mathbf{x}^{(i)}, a)V_j$
$\quad \forall i \in \{1, \ldots, N\}, a \in \mathcal{A}.$

In our setting, the state space is exponentially large, with one state for each assignment $\mathbf{x}$ to $\mathbf{X}$. We use the common approach of restricting attention to value functions that are compactly represented as a linear combination of *basis functions* $H = \{h_1, \ldots, h_k\}$. A *linear value function* over H is a function $\mathcal{V}$ that can be written as $\mathcal{V}(\mathbf{x}) = \sum_{j=1}^{k} w_j h_j(\mathbf{x})$ for some coefficients $\mathbf{w} = (w_1, \ldots, w_k)'$. The linear programming approach can be adapted to use this value function representation (Schweitzer & Seidmann 1985) by changing the objective function to $\sum_i w_i h_i$, and modifying the constraints accordingly. In this approximate formulation, the variables are $w_1, \ldots, w_k$, i.e., the weights for our basis functions. The LP is given by:

Variables: $w_1, \ldots, w_k$;
Minimize: $\sum_{\mathbf{x}} 1/N \sum_i w_i h_i(\mathbf{x})$;
Subject to: $\sum_i w_i h_i(\mathbf{x}) \geq$
$\quad R(\mathbf{x}, a) + \gamma \sum_{\mathbf{x}'} P(\mathbf{x}' \mid \mathbf{x}, a) \sum_i w_i h_i(\mathbf{x}')$
$\quad \forall \mathbf{x} \in \mathbf{X}, \forall a \in A.$

This transformation has the effect of reducing the number of free variables in the LP to k (one for each basis function coefficient), but the number of constraints remains $|\mathbf{X}| \times |\mathcal{A}|$. We address this issue by combining assumptions about the structure of the system dynamics with a particular form of approximation for the value function. First, we assume that the system dynamics of the MDP are represented using a DDN with probability rule CPDs, as described in Section 4. Second, we propose the use of value rules as basis functions, resulting in a rule-based value function. If we had a value function $\mathcal{V}$ represented in this way, then we could implement $Greedy(\mathcal{V})$ by having the agents use our message passing coordination algorithm of Section 4 at each step.

Our formulation is based on the approach of GKP, who show how to exploit the factorization of the basis functions and system dynamics in order to replace the constraints in the approximate LP by an equivalent but exponentially smaller set of constraints. First, note that the constraints can be replaced by a single, nonlinear constraint:

$$0 \geq \max_{\mathbf{x}, \mathbf{a}} \left[R(\mathbf{x}, \mathbf{a}) + \sum_i (\gamma g_i(\mathbf{x}) - h_i(\mathbf{x}))w_i \right];$$

where $g_i = RuleBackproj(h_i) = \sum_{\mathbf{x}'} P(\mathbf{x}' \mid \mathbf{x}, \mathbf{a})h_i(\mathbf{x}')$, which can be computed as described in Section 4. Although a naive approach to maximizing over the state space would require the enumeration of every state, as we have shown in Section 3, the structure in rule functions allow us to perform such maximization very efficiently. The same intuition allows us to decompose this nonlinear constraint into a set of linear constraints, whose structure is based on the intermediate results of the variable elimination process. The algorithm is directly analogous to that of GKP, except that it is based on the use of rule-based variable elimination rather than standard variable elimination. We refer the reader to (Guestrin, Koller, & Parr 2001a) for the details.

The approximate LP computes a rule-based value function, which approximates the long-term optimal value function for the MDP. These value functions can be used as the one-step lookahead value in Section 4. In our rule-based models, the overall one-step value function is also rule-based, allowing the agents to use the coordination graph in order to select an optimal joint action (optimal relative to the approximation for the long-term value function). It is important to note that, although the same value function is used at all steps in the MDP, the actual coordination structure varies substantially between steps.

Finally, we observe that the structure of the computed value rules determines the nature of the coordination. In some cases, we may be willing to introduce another approximation into our value function, in order to reduce the complexity of the coordination process. In particular, if we have a value rule $\langle \rho; \mathbf{c} : v \rangle$ where v is relatively small, then we might be willing to simply drop it from the rule set. If $\mathbf{c}$ involves the actions of several agents, dropping ρ from our rule-based function might substantially reduce the amount of coordination required.

6 Experimental results

We implemented our rule-based factored approximate linear programming and the message passing coordination algorithms in C++, using CPLEX as the LP solver. We experimented with a construction crew problem, where each house has five features {Foundation, Electric, Plumbing, Painting, Decoration}. Each agent has a set of skills and some agents may move between houses. Each feature in the house requires two time steps to complete. Thus, in addition to the variables in Fig. 2, the DDN for this problem contains "action-in-progress" variables for each house feature, for each agent, e.g., "A_1-Plumbing-in-progress-House 1". Once an agent takes an action, the respective "action-in-progress" variable becomes true with high probability. If one of the "action-in-progress" variables for some house feature is true, that feature becomes true with high probability at the next time step. At every time step, with a small probability, a feature of the house may break, in which case there is a chain reaction and features that depend on the broken feature will break with probability 1. This effect makes the problem dynamic, incorporating both house construction and house maintenance in the same model. Agents receive 100 reward for each completed feature and -10 for each "action-in-progress". The discount factor is 0.95. The basis functions used are rules over the settings of the parents of the CPDs for the house feature variables in the DDN.

Fig. 4 summarizes the results for various settings. Note that, although the number of states may grow exponentially from one setting to the other, the running times grow polynomially. Furthermore, in Problem 2, the backprojections of the basis functions had scopes with up to 11 variables, too large for the table-based representation to be tractable.

The policies generated in these problems seemed very intuitive. For example, in Problem 2, if we start with no features built, A_1 will go to House 2 and wait, as its painting skills are going to be needed there before the decoration skill are needed in House 1. In Problem 1, we get very interesting coordination strategies: If the foundation is completed, A_1 will do the electrical fitting and A_2 will do the plumbing. Furthermore, A_1 makes its decision not by coordinating with A_2, but by noting that electrical fitting is a dominant strategy. On the other hand, if the system is at the state where both foundation and electrical fitting is done, then agents coordinate to avoid doing plumbing simultaneously. Another interesting feature of the policies occurs when agents are idle; e.g., in Problem 1, if foundation, electric and plumbing are done, then agent A_1 repeatedly performs the foundation task. This avoids a chain reaction starting from the foundation of the house. Checking the rewards, there is actually a higher expected loss from the chain reaction than the cost of repeatedly checking the foundation of the house.

For small problems with one house, we can compute the optimal policy exactly. In the table in Fig. 5, we present the optimal values for two such problems. Additionally, we can compute the actual value of acting according to the policy generated by our method. As the table shows, these values are very close, indicating that the policies generated by our method are very close to optimal in these problems.

We also tested our rule-based algorithm on a variation of the multiagent SysAdmin problem of GKP. In this problem, there is a network of computers, each is associated with an administrator agent. Each machine runs processes and receives a reward if a process terminates. Processes take longer to terminate in faulty machines and dead machines can send bad packets to neighbors, causing them to become faultye. The rule-based aspect in this problem comes from a selector variable which chooses which neighboring machine to receive packets from. We tested our algorithm on a variety of network topologies and compared it to the table-based approach in GKP. For a bidirectional ring, for example, the total number of constraints generated grows *linearly* with the number of agents. Furthermore, the rule-based (CSI) approach generates considerably fewer constraints than the table-based approach (non-CSI). However, the constant overhead of managing rules causes the rule-based approach to be about two times slower than the table-based approach, as shown in Fig. 6(a).

However, note that in ring topologies the the induced width of the coordination graph is constant as the number of agents increases. For comparison, we tested on a reverse star topology, where every machine can affect the status of a central server machine, so that the number of parents of the server increases with the number of computers in the network. Here, we observe a very different behavior, as seen in Fig. 6(b). In the table-based approach, the tables grow exponentially with the number of agents, yielding an exponential running time. On the other hand, the size of the rule set only grows linearly, yielding a quadratic total running time.

Notice that in all topologies, the sizes of the state and

Prob.	♯houses	Agent skills	♯states	♯actions	Time (m)
1	1	$A_1 \in$ {Found, Elec, Plumb}; $A_2 \in$ {Plumb, Paint, Decor}	2048	36	1.6
2	2	$A_1 \in$ {Paint, Decor}, moves $A_2 \in$ {Found, Elec, Plumb, Paint}, at House 1 $A_3 \in$ {Found, Elec} and $A_4 \in$ {Plumb, Decor}, at House 2	33,554,432	1024	33.7
3	3	$A_1 \in$ {Paint, Decor}, moves $A_2 \in$ {Found, Elec, Plumb}, at House 1 $A_3 \in$ {Found, Elec, Plumb, Paint}, at House 2 $A_4 \in$ {Found, Elec, Plumb, Decor}, at House 3	34,359,738,368	6144	63.9
4	2	$A_1 \in$ {Found}, moves; $A_2 \in$ {Decor}, moves $A_3 \in$ {Found, Elec, Plumb, Paint}, at House 1 $A_4 \in$ {Elec, Plumb, Paint}, at House 2	8,388,608	768	5.7

Figure 4: Summary of results on the building crew problem.

Agent skills	*Actual* value of rule-based policy	Optimal value
$A_1 \in$ {Found, Elec}; $A_2 \in$ {Plumb, Paint, Decor}	6650	6653
$A_1 \in$ {Found, Elec, Plumb}; $A_2 \in$ {Plumb, Paint, Decor}	6653	6654

Figure 5: The actual expected value of our algorithm's rule-based policy and the value of the optimal policy for one-house problems.

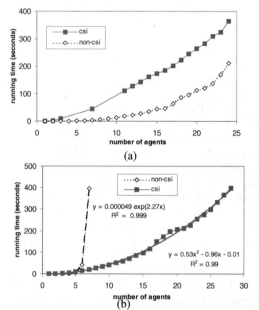

Figure 6: Running times: (a) Bidirectional ring; (b) Inverted star.

action spaces are growing exponentially with the number of machines. Nonetheless, the total running time is only growing quadratically. This exponential gain has allowed us to run very large problems, with over 10^{124} states.

7 Conclusion

We have provided a principled and efficient approach to planning in multiagent domains where the required interactions vary from one situation to another. We have shown that our results scale to very complex problems, including problems where traditional table-based representations of the value function blow up exponentially. In problems where the optimal value could be computed analytically for comparison purposes, the value of the policies generated by our approach were within 0.05% of the optimal value. From a representation perspective, our approach combines the ad-

vantages of the factored linear value function representation of (Koller & Parr 1999; Guestrin, Koller, & Parr 2001a; 2001b) with those of the tree-based value functions of (Boutilier & Dearden 1996).

We showed that the task of finding an optimal joint action in our approach leads to a very natural communication pattern, where agents send messages along a *coordination* graph determined by the structure of the value rules. The coordination structure dynamically changes according to the state of the system, and even on the actual numerical values assigned to the value rules. Furthermore, the coordination graph can be adapted incrementally as the agents learn new rules or discard unimportant ones. We believe that this graph-based coordination mechanism will provide a well-founded schema for other multiagent collaboration and communication approaches.

Acknowledgments. We are very grateful to Ronald Parr for many useful discussions. This work was supported by the DoD MURI program administered by the Office of Naval Research under Grant N00014-00-1-0637, and by Air Force contract F30602-00-2-0598 under DARPA's TASK program. C. Guestrin was also supported by a Siebel Scholarship.

References

Bertele, U., and Brioschi, F. 1972. *Nonserial Dynamic Programming*. New York: Academic Press.

Boutilier, C., and Dearden, R. 1996. Approximating value trees in structured dynamic programming. In *Proc. ICML*, 54–62.

Boutilier, C.; Dean, T.; and Hanks, S. 1999. Decision theoretic planning: Structural assumptions and computational leverage. *Journal of Artificial Intelligence Research* 11:1 – 94.

Dean, T., and Kanazawa, K. 1989. A model for reasoning about persistence and causation. *Computational Intelligence* 5(3).

Dechter, R. 1999. Bucket elimination: A unifying framework for reasoning. *Artificial Intelligence* 113(1–2):41–85.

Guestrin, C.; Koller, D.; and Parr, R. 2001a. Multiagent planning with factored MDPs. In *Proc. NIPS-14*.

Guestrin, C.; Koller, D.; and Parr, R. 2001b. Max-norm projections for factored MDPs. In *Proc. IJCAI*.

Koller, D., and Milch, B. 2001. Multi-agent influence diagrams for representing and solving games. In *Proc. IJCAI*.

Koller, D., and Parr, R. 1999. Computing factored value functions for policies in structured MDPs. In *Proc. IJCAI*.

Schweitzer, P., and Seidmann, A. 1985. Generalized polynomial approximations in Markovian decision processes. *Journal of Mathematical Analysis and Applications* 110:568 – 582.

Zhang, N., and Poole, D. 1999. On the role of context-specific independence in probabilistic reasoning. In *Proc. IJCAI*.

Nearly Deterministic Abstractions of Markov Decision Processes

Terran Lane and **Leslie Pack Kaelbling**
MIT Artificial Intelligence Laboratory
200 Technology Square
Cambridge, MA 02139
{terran,lpk}@ai.mit.edu

Abstract

We examine scaling issues for a restricted class of compactly representable Markov decision process planning problems. For one stochastic mobile robotics package delivery problem it is possible to decouple the stochastic local-navigation problem from the deterministic global-routing one and to solve each with dedicated methods. Careful construction of macro actions allows us to effectively "hide" navigational stochasticity from the global routing problem and to approximate the latter with off-the-shelf combinatorial optimization routines for the traveling salesdroid problem, yielding a net exponential speedup in planning performance. We give analytic conditions on when the macros are close enough to deterministic for the approximation to be good and demonstrate the performance of our method on small and large simulated navigation problems.

Introduction

Imagine a robot that runs errands in a large office building. At any given time, it has a set of pending requests to deliver items, pick up printer output, and so on. Perhaps it also acts as security guard, with the task of keeping certain areas under surveillance by visiting them periodically. It must also ensure that its batteries never completely run down by periodically visiting a charging station. If the robot's actions were entirely deterministic, the only uncertainty in the domain would be in the arrival of errand requests. However, there is always a certain amount of unreliability in a robot's actions.

Markov decision processes (MDP) have been popular models for uncertain planning problems, such as this one. They handle uncertainty effectively, but are computationally too complex for such large domains. While this domain can be represented quite compactly, traditional solution methods are intractable for it. If we would like to solve such large domains, we will have to give up complete optimality for a reduction in computation time. Many promising approaches to doing so, via abstraction and factorization, have been suggested in the literature. These techniques are general-purpose and it is, therefore, difficult to characterize the degree to which the behavior they generate is suboptimal. Furthermore, recent complexity results indicate

that even for compactly representable MDPs, the exact and approximate planning problems for MDPs are intractable on *general* domains (Littman 1997; Mundhenk *et al.* 2000; Lusena, Mundhenk, & Goldsmith 2001). Thus, no single algorithm can be both efficient and accurate for *all* MDPs.

In this paper we argue that it may be useful to step back from general purpose algorithms. Rather, we should seek additional special structure in our MDP domains (beyond the transition factorability that leads to compactly expressible models) and exploit it with special-purpose algorithms. For the same reason that we do not, in practice, employ a single, all-purpose graph algorithm or combinatorial optimization algorithm, we believe that we can make significant progress on MDP planning by examining restricted classes of problems.

As an example of this approach, in this work we study a particular, quite restricted, class of MDPs, and provide an approximation method with bounded error. The problem class includes a robot running errands in an office, though, in its current form, it does not extend to problems of surveillance or battery maintenance. We provide a formal description of the problem, a formulation of the domain in terms of special-purpose macro actions, and an algorithm for efficiently deriving approximately optimal solutions to the resulting semi-MDP. We give a bound on the error on the approximation as a function of properties of the domain and conclude with empirical results in small and large simulated delivery scenarios.

Formal Development

In this section, we give a brief background on Markov decision process theory, give our notation, and formally describe the package delivery domain and our planning method.

Markov Decision Processes and Options

A Markov decision process is a model of a finite, discrete, synchronous control process with noisy control actions (Puterman 1994). Formally an MDP $\mathcal{M}$ is specified by four components: a *state space*, $\mathcal{S} = \{s_1, s_2, \ldots, s_N\}$, of cardinality $|\mathcal{S}| = N$; a set of primitive (or atomic) *actions*, $\mathcal{A} = \{a_1, a_2, \ldots, a_m\}$; a *transition function*, $T : \mathcal{S} \times \mathcal{A} \times \mathcal{S} \to [0, 1]$; and a *reward function*, $R : \mathcal{S} \to \mathbb{R}$. An agent acting in an MDP is, at any time step, located at a single state $s \in \mathcal{S}$. The agent chooses an action $a \in \mathcal{A}$ and is relocated to a new state, s', determined by the transition probability distribution $T(s'|s, a)$, whereupon it receives reward $R(s')$. In this paper we are concerned with *cost to move* frameworks in which each atomic action incurs some movement cost $c < 0$ and there exists one or more zero-cost, absorbing "goal" states. We will assume here that $R(s') = c$ for all non-goal states.

In many useful domains, the state space is best expressed as a product of state variables $\mathcal{S} = \mathcal{V}_1 \times \ldots \times \mathcal{V}_m$, and the cardinality of the total state space is exponential in m. Such MDPs can often be compactly represented by exploiting structure in their transition and reward functions—writing the former as a dynamic Bayes net (DBN) and the latter as a decision tree (Boutilier, Dearden, & Goldszmidt 2000).

The output of an MDP planning algorithm is a *policy* π : $\mathcal{S} \to \mathcal{A}$ (or *plan* in this work) that specifies an action for the agent to take for any state in the state space. Our goal is to locate a plan that maximizes the expected aggregate reward received by the agent over its lifetime. In addition, because we are interested in plans for exponentially large state spaces, we will seek implicitly represented plans that specify actions only for subsets of the state space.

For our model of macro actions, we adopt the *options framework* of Sutton, Precup, and Singh (Sutton, Precup, & Singh 1999; Precup 2000). An option (or *macro* in this paper) is an abstraction that allows us to treat an entire MDP policy as a single action. In this model, an option o specifies three elements: a set $\mathcal{I} \subseteq \mathcal{S}$ from which it can be initiated, a probability mapping $\beta : \mathcal{S} \to [0, 1]$ giving the probability that the macro terminates upon reaching state s, and a policy π defining the agent's actions while the option is in force.[1] An agent acting in an MDP $\mathcal{M}$ with option set $\mu = \{o_1 \ldots o_k\}$ at each step can take any applicable option as a discrete action choice. Upon invocation of macro o_i, the agent executes actions according to π_i until the option terminates probabilistically according to β_i. The combination of such macros with an MDP yields a semi-Markov decision process (SMDP): a decision process in which actions are considered to have temporal extent with stochastic distribution.

Domain Description

This work was motivated by navigational problems arising in mobile robotics domains. We take as an example a simple package delivery problem in which an agent navigates through a building with stochastic movement commands and attempts to deliver packages to fixed locations.[2] We encode the robot's state with the state variables x and y, denoting physical location in the world, and k "indicator" bits, $b_1, \ldots, b_k$, which record the delivery status of each of k packages ($b_i = 1$ iff package i has been successfully delivered). The goal of the agent is to attain a state in which all packages have been delivered ($b_i = 1$ for all i) in the fewest steps possible. The robot has four primitive actions available, corresponding to movement in the cardinal direc-

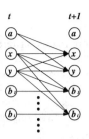

Figure 1: DBN topology for the package delivery domain. The nodes are the agent's choice of action, its x and y coordinates, and the settings of the indicator bits $b_1 \ldots b_k$.

tions. The actions are stochastic with dynamics defined by a dynamic Bayes net of the topology displayed in Figure 1.

The conditional probability table interrelating the x and y variables describes the physical geography of the world—locations of walls and doors—as well as the robot's movement dynamics. For this paper, we take a simple model in which movement in the cardinal directions succeeds with some fixed probability $p_{\text{trans}} < 1$. When movement fails, it returns the agent to its original $\langle x, y \rangle$ location or deposits it in one of the accessible adjacent grid cells with uniform probability. Walls are impenetrable except at doorways, which allow free movement. The relation between $\langle x, y \rangle$ and b_i defines the notion of package delivery—when the robot reaches the delivery location for package i, denoted $\text{loc}(i)$, the package is delivered and b_i is set to 1 with probability 1. Thereafter, b_i can never be reset to 0 (i.e., a package cannot later be wrenched away from its recipient). Importantly, the package bits are independent of each other given the robot's location—delivery of one package does not prevent delivery of another, nor does it change the dynamics of the robot's movement. This independence will later allow us to decompose the model into sub-problems corresponding to the tasks of delivering individual packages.

The reward function encodes our notion of goals for the robot. Here we consider only the simplest possible reward function: we reward the agent only for successfully completing the entire task (i.e., delivering all the packages) and we wish to minimize the total number of steps taken. This can be modeled in a infinite-horizon undiscounted model with the reward and value functions:

$$
\begin{aligned}
R(s) &= c < 0 \quad \text{iff some } b_i = 0 \text{ in state } s \\
R(s) &= 0 \quad \text{otherwise} \\
V^\pi(s) &= \mathrm{E}\left[\sum_{t=0}^{\text{final delivery}} R(s_t) \right] \quad (1)
\end{aligned}
$$

This is a negative model whose optimal value function is finite (Puterman 1994). Extension to prioritized goals is not difficult, but yields a more complex deterministic optimization problem (the minimum latency path problem (Goemans & Kleinberg 1996; Arora & Karakostas 1999)). We discuss this case fully in the extended version of this paper.

---

[1] Technically, we are using only *flat, pure Markov options* here.

[2] We may be able to address arbitrary locations by exploiting Moore et al.'s equivalent of an all-pairs shortest-paths data structure for MDPs (Moore, Baird, & Kaelbling 1999).

Optimality Criterion

While the general optimality criterion for MDPs is extremely expressive, we gain a great deal of leverage in the package delivery domain by observing that the structure of its reward function leads to a special form of optimality criterion. In particular, we can rewrite the value function of Equation 1 to reflect the underlying optimization problem:

$$
\begin{aligned}
V^\pi(s) &= \mathrm{E}\left[c(\text{\# steps to deliver all packages})\right] \\
&= c\,\mathrm{E}\left[\sum_{i=1}^{k} n(i-1,i)\right] \\
&= c\sum_{i=1}^{k}\mathrm{E}[n(i-1,i)] \\
&= c\sum_{i=1}^{k} d_{\tau(i)}(\tau(i-1)) \qquad (2)
\end{aligned}
$$

where the expectation is over trajectories through $\mathcal{M}$ under policy π and $n(i,j)$ is the random variable representing the number of steps taken between the deliveries of the ith and j^{th} *previously undelivered* packages on the trajectory (delivery of package 0 is taken to be the start state of the robot). The step from the third to fourth line removes the "previously undelivered" caveat from the distance function into an ordering variable, τ. τ is a permutation of locations: $\tau(i) = j$ indicates that package j is the ith delivered. The variable $d_i(j)$ gives the expected number of atomic steps between the location of package j and the location of package i (regardless of whether either has yet been delivered).

Thus, there are two quantities that we must address simultaneously to achieve an optimal policy: the number of steps between delivery locations and the order in which to move among locations. The independence of movement dynamics (x and y variables) from the settings of the package indicator bits ensures that we can optimize the two quantities separately. We can optimize paths between locations ($d_i(j)$) without regard to the settings of the bits, and we locate the best ordering of package deliveries (τ) without considering how to get from one location to another. We will address each of these in the next section, but the reader may observe that the first quantity can be represented with carefully constructed macros while the second (given by the sum in Equation 2) is simply the traveling salesdroid problem (TSP) optimization criterion.

Planning with Semi-Stochastic Macros

Figure 2 summarizes our decomposition and planning approach. We proceed in two phases. In the first, off-line, phase, we develop macros for achieving limited sub-goals and characterize their performance in terms of their expected accrued rewards for invocation and their transition distributions. Formally, we construct the k sub-MDPs $\mathcal{M}_i$, $i = 1\dots k$, on the state spaces $\mathcal{S}_i = \langle x, y, b_i \rangle$ by removing the extraneous variables from the transition DBN of Figure 1. In doing so, we violate no dependencies between x, y, and b_i and the resulting model is a valid MDP corresponding to the task of delivering package i in isolation. $\mathcal{S}_i$ is

1. **Preprocessing (Macro construction):**
   (a) Decompose full model $\mathcal{M}$ into sub-models $\mathcal{M}_1, \dots, \mathcal{M}_k$ corresponding to individual sub-goals
   (b) Solve sub-models using, e.g., value iteration
   (c) Construct macros $o_1, \dots, o_k$ for sub-goals
   (d) Solve for macro rewards and transition distribution

2. **Per-Episode (Macro integration):**
   (a) Construct goal graph from episode package set, s_0, and (fixed) macro characteristics
   (b) Solve deterministic graph problem (via TSP solver)
   (c) Convert graph solution to macro policy in original $\widehat{\mathcal{M}}$
   (d) Execute macro plan

Figure 2: Summary of decomposition and planning method.

exponentially smaller than $\mathcal{S}$ and, for the purposes of this paper, we will assume that it is tractable for classical MDP planning techniques.[3] This yields a policy π_i that expresses the best way to deliver package i alone from any $\langle x, y \rangle$ coordinate. We now construct the option $o_i = \langle \mathcal{I}_i, \pi'_i, \beta_i \rangle$ where $\mathcal{I}_i = \{s \in \mathcal{S} : b_i = 0\}$, $\pi'_i(s') = \pi_i(s)$ whenever $\langle x', y', b'_i \rangle = \langle x, y, b_i \rangle$, and $\beta_i(s) = 1$ whenever $\langle x, y \rangle = \mathrm{loc}(j)$ for any j such that $b_j = 0$. This option expresses the notion "whenever package i is undelivered, you can deliver it by following π_i until you reach *any* delivery location for an undelivered package." Each macro terminates with probability one at one of at most k $\langle x, y \rangle$ locations.

The set of options $\mu = \{o_1, \dots, o_k\}$ represents a set of actions for a semi-Markov decision process $\widehat{\mathcal{M}}$ over the reduced state space $\widehat{\mathcal{S}} = \{\mathrm{loc}(i)\} \times b_1 \times \dots \times b_k$. In principle, this process can be solved exactly with standard techniques, but it is still exponentially large in k. In the second, per-episode planning phase, we treat this instead as a deterministic graph and solve it with a TSP planner. To do so, we need estimates of the mean reward (cost) accrued by each macro and its distribution over next states. The first quantity, d_i, is related to the mean absorption time of the chain induced by π_i on $\mathcal{M}_i$, while the second is just the probability of absorption into each goal location (Kemeny & Snell 1976). Both can be calculated from the macros and submodels in time polynomial in $|x|$ and $|y|$. We will use the latter quantity to determine whether the macro can be reasonably approximated as deterministic.

Although $\widehat{\mathcal{M}}$ is technically a semi-MDP, it can be treated as an MDP because we are working in an undiscounted model. This means that the transit times from state to state affect the reward received on the transition, but have no effect on the future value of the resulting state. Thus, if we let the reward depend on both the start and end states of a transition, we can stay within the MDP framework. We will define $c(s, s'|a)$ to be the expected cost of making a transition from state s to s' under macro action a.

---

[3]If the remaining spatial problem is itself too large for direct solution, we can resort to further decompositions, such as hierarchical spatial partitioning, or to other scaling techniques.

On each planning episode, we are presented with a set of packages to be delivered, represented as a configuration of package delivery bits b_i, and a starting state s_0. We construct a deterministic graph G that approximates $\widehat{\mathcal{M}}$ under the assumptions that every macro reaches its nominal goal (i.e., that o_i terminates at $\langle x, y \rangle = \text{loc}(i)$) and that it takes exactly its expected duration in doing so. Formally, $G = \langle V, E \rangle$ where $V = \{\text{loc}(i) : b_i = 0$ in the episode description$\} \cup \text{loc}(0)$ and $e(i, j) = d_j(i)$ where $\text{loc}(0)$ is the location of the starting state. (We omit goals irrelevant to the current episode from the graph.) Given a starting state s_0, the minimal tour τ over G is the basis for the implicit policy for this episode.[4] Finding τ is, of course, still NP-hard, but there are very effective practical heuristic methods; good approximations for systems with hundreds of thousands of nodes can often be found in seconds (Johnson & McGeoch 2001).

Finally, we map τ back into a policy over macros in $\widehat{\mathcal{M}}$. At any $s \in \widehat{\mathcal{S}}$, the agent chooses option $o_{\tau(i)}$ for $i = \min_j \{j : b_{\tau(j)} = 0\}$ (i.e., it attempts to deliver the first as-yet-undelivered package on tour τ). This is an implicit representation of a total policy—it is defined at all states of $\widehat{\mathcal{S}}$—but it was not created to deal with circumstances such as the agent accidentally wandering into an unexpected delivery location. In the next section we will give bounds on when this willful ignorance still yields acceptable plans.

Analysis of Algorithm

In this formulation of the problem, we are making two approximation steps. The first is the move from the underlying MDP $\mathcal{M}$ to the semi-MDP $\widehat{\mathcal{M}}$, induced by the macro actions. In doing so, we are likely to introduce some error, with the macros no longer allowing us to express the true optimal policy for $\mathcal{M}$. We are currently unable to argue formally that this loss is small; however, we expect that it is, for the intuitive reason that the macros are derived expressly for the purpose of achieving subgoals that are *strictly required* in order to achieve the overall goal of the domain. However, using the macros forces the agent to choose an ordering on the subgoals (or at least, to choose a first subgoal), and does not allow it to be "agnostic"—taking a few actions to see what happens, then pursuing the subgoal that turns out to be nearer, for example. Although we cannot guarantee that such a situation does not occur in our target problems, Parr has developed a test that can discriminate whether a specific, fixed set of macros is sufficient to express a nearly optimal policy (Parr 1998a; 1998b). In practice, we could test a set of "goal-seeking" macros for near-optimality offline before proceeding to the SMDP solution phase.

The second approximation step is treating $\widehat{\mathcal{M}}$ as if it were the deterministic model G. We can provide a bound on the loss due to this approximation, given in the following theorem. The bound will depend on the degree of determinism of the original model, characterized by the parameter p.

[4]Strictly speaking, we are not seeking a full tour, as we do not require return to $\text{loc}(0)$, but we can add synthetic, zero-cost "return to start" arcs to G and find a full tour over the resulting graph.

Let p be the minimum, over all states $s \in \widehat{\mathcal{S}}$ and actions $a \in \mu$ of the maximum, over all $s' \in \widehat{\mathcal{S}}$, of $\Pr(s'|s, a)$, and let $\delta = 1 - p$. In addition, the bound depends on $\Delta_c = c_{\max} - c_{\min}$, the difference between the largest and smallest transition costs in $\widehat{\mathcal{M}}$.

Theorem 1 *For every stationary policy π defined on state space $\widehat{\mathcal{S}}$ and macro action space μ, if the non-determinism of the macro actions is bounded by*

$$\delta \leq \frac{k - \sqrt{k^2 + \frac{2\epsilon}{\Delta_c}(1 - k)}}{k^2 - k}$$

then at every state $s \in \widehat{\mathcal{S}}$, the value of state s under policy π in $\widehat{\mathcal{M}}$, $V_\pi(s)$, differs from the value of s under π in G, $D_\pi(s)$, by at most ϵ.

Proof: First note that, by construction, each macro terminates only upon delivering *some* package — its "intended package", with probability $\geq p$, or any of the other previously undelivered packages, with total probability $\leq \delta = 1 - p$. Thus, an agent started at s_0 with k packages outstanding reaches the terminal state of the episode in exactly k macro actions. A policy π on $\widehat{\mathcal{M}}$ can be coupled to G to produce some deterministic tour of cost $D_\pi(s_0) \geq kc_{\min}$ (corresponding to the path of "expected outcomes" in $\widehat{\mathcal{M}}$). We will call the trajectory of "expected outcome" states in $\widehat{\mathcal{M}}$ the *nominal path*, having *expected* cost equal to $D_\pi(s_0)$. The agent, acting according to π in $\widehat{\mathcal{M}}$, will complete the nominal path with probability p^k. If some macro terminates at an unexpected state (total probability $1 - p^k$), the agent can still complete the task with, at worst, $kc_{\max}$ cost. Thus, the true value of s_0 under π, $V_\pi(s_0)$, differs from the deterministic approximation, $D_\pi(s_0)$ by at most $\epsilon = (1 - p^k)k\Delta_c$. Rearranging and noting that, for small δ, a second-order approximation to the binomial expansion of $(1 - \delta)^k$ gives a good upper bound to p^k, yields the desired polynomial relation between ϵ and δ. $\square$

Finally, we note that every policy on $\widehat{\mathcal{M}}$ yields a nominal path (because every macro action has an expected outcome) and every nominal path has a corresponding path in G. Thus, given "reasonably deterministic" macros, the optimal policy for the approximate model G will have value within ϵ of the truly optimal policy for $\widehat{\mathcal{M}}$.

Empirical Investigation

We have implemented this planner for the package delivery domain and examined its performance in a number of synthetic floorplan scenarios: a set of small, randomly generated maps and one larger map roughly corresponding to one floor of a real office building. The random floorplans are, by design, small enough that exact solution is feasible, allowing direct comparison between hybrid and optimal solutions, while the office building simulation is large enough to be intractable to direct solution (2^{30}–2^{55} states) and serves to demonstrate the scalability of our method.

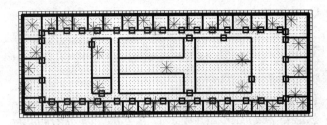

Figure 3: Office building floorplan. Asterisks mark the goal locations and small squares denote doorways.

Comparison to Exact Solution

In our first experiment, we generated a number of small delivery problems populated with randomly selected walls, doors, and goals (for an example of a similar, but non-random, floorplan, see Figure 3). The movement dynamics are those described in the "Domain Description" section, with $p_{trans} = 0.9$. We constructed floorplans varying in size between 400 and 900 locations with between 4 and 6 delivery locations, yielding MDPs with between 6400 $(400 \cdot 2^4)$ and 57,600 $(900 \cdot 2^6)$ states, the latter near the limit of our ability to solve the system directly. In these worlds we could find the optimal TSP path directly with brute-force search, so the only sources of suboptimality are from the use of macro rather than atomic actions and the deterministic approximation of $\widehat{\mathcal{M}}$.

For each of 54 such maps, we constructed both the exact atomic policy and the atomic expansion of the TSP+macro policy and evaluated both policies analytically. To strictly adhere to the terms of Theorem 1, we should evaluate a macro policy that takes the best TSP tour from *every* SMDP state (i.e., replans the TSP tour from every s in $\widehat{\mathcal{M}}$), but that code was not ready at the time of submission. We will present those results in the extended version of this work, but for this paper we evaluated the policy consisting of a *single* TSP tour—this policy does not try to replan when it falls off the tour, but simply attempts to return to the tour.

At the states corresponding to the semi-MDP states on the optimal tour, the TSP+macro planner achieved a value within 5.8% of the optimal on average. In states substantially off of the tour (e.g., non-SMDP states across the grid from $loc(0)$ with all packages undelivered), the TSP plan deviates substantially from the optimal—over 70% in some cases—but this is not unexpected, as the TSP system has explicitly neglected such states under the assumption that they are reached with very low probability. This assumption is validated by the small net influence that these states have on the values at the on-tour states. We expect replanning at off-tour SMDP states to dramatically improve these values, as will careful early termination of macros (Precup 2000).

Scaling to Large Scenarios

Our larger simulation is a set of delivery scenarios in the floorplan pictured in Figure 3, roughly modeled on one floor of a large office building. This map is quantized into 75 x and 25 y coordinates and contains 45 delivery locations in offices (and one near the elevator shafts in the center of the

map) for a total of roughly 2^{55} states. The dynamics of the world are the same as those of the floorplans of the previous section; the larger map differs only in scale and geography.

In this world, we performed thirty "delivery episodes" with different random subsets of between 20 and and all 45 of the potential delivery locations. These scenarios yield MDPs with far too many states for explicit tabular solution, but the corresponding TSP instances are trivial to approximate. In a preprocessing step, we constructed and cached 45 goal-seeking macros corresponding to the 45 potential goal locations in the world. For each episode, we generated the TSP macro solution using a minimum-spanning-tree heuristic TSP planner[5] and evaluated the plan's performance by averaging over twenty sampled trajectories from the atomic model. Over the thirty episodes, the mean deviation between the projected and sampled trajectory lengths was only 0.38% and the projected length was always within one standard deviation of the mean sampled length. Furthermore, in the tours selected by the TSP planner, $1 - p$ is on the order of 10^{-6}, so the probability of failing to correctly complete the tour is $1 - p^k \approx 10^{-5}$. Unsurprisingly, all of the the six hundred sampled trajectories successfully completed the projected TSP tour without encountering an unexpected delivery location. Together, we take these results to indicate that the deterministic graph is a good approximation of the true semi-MDP in this domain.

Related Work

Our planning method is perhaps closest in spirit to envelope methods (Dean *et al.* 1995; Baum & Nicholson 1998) which attempt to restrict the planner's attention to only a highly probable subset of the state space, either by discarding states or by suppressing dimensions. Our approach can be thought of as a two-phase envelope method: in the first phase, we use structural knowledge about the transition function to discard most dimensions and apply classical stochastic planning techniques. In the second phase, the envelope consists of only the previously discarded dimensions and we employ a deterministic planner to handle the scalability question. In general, this can be dangerous, as it explicitly assumes that the agent *won't* leave the envelope, but we provide analytic sufficient conditions (available after the first phase) on when it is reasonable to make this assumption.

A closely related class of techniques clusters groups of similar or related states together according to their behavior under the global value function (Boutilier, Dearden, & Goldszmidt 2000) or their transition distributions (Dean & Givan 1997). Planning takes place on a model constructed from the "meta states." These approaches typically begin with a coarse clustering of the state space and successively split it when necessary to maintain homogeneity within state clusters. These methods are extremely general and can converge to exact or bounded approximations of the optimal plan, but the state partitioning may, in the worst case, explode to an exponentially large set of singleton clusters. Function ap-

---

[5]Much more sophisticated TSP heuristics are available, but our interest is in the applicability of deterministic planning in general rather than in the quality of the TSP solution per se.

proximation methods (Koller & Parr 2000), on the other hand, use a bounded space representation for the MDP's value function and, thus, policy, but do not necessarily yield near-optimal plans. Both classes of methods are intended to address general compact MDPs. We instead seek to provide compact and near-optimal policies for only a restricted class of compact MDPs by exploiting additional structure in the model beyond that used to factor the transition function.

Our use of options for macros puts this method into the class of *temporal abstractions* as well (Sutton, Precup, & Singh 1999; Precup 2000). Macros have previously been used to speed up MDP planning and reinforcement learning (McGovern, Sutton, & Fagg 1997) and for knowledge reuse; our contribution is using them to "hide" stochasticity and render the semi-MDP nearly deterministic. Similar macro formulations can be used to partition state variables (rather than suppressing entire dimensions as we do), for example, to hierarchically decompose a physical space into regions such as Voronoi regions or rooms and corridors (Kaelbling 1993; Hauskrecht *et al.* 1998; Parr 1998a; 1998b; Guestrin & Ormoneit 2001). Macro integration again involves a meta-planning process which treats macros as primitive actions. The difficulty is in constructing a complete basis set of macros sufficient to respond to all possible reward scenarios—how you choose to act in one region may depend on apparent rewards in adjacent regions. In general, an exponential number of macros may be required even for a single fixed region.

Our approach, however, need not be exclusive of these other methods for scaling MDP planning. The sub-problems $\mathcal{M}_i$ resulting from the initial model decomposition (or any nondeterministic component of the original MDP in general) could still be intractably large and it may be profitable to apply one of these other techniques to them.

The analysis of our algorithm was inspired by the MDP Simulation Lemma (Kearns & Koller 1999) which demonstrates a notion of similarity between two MDPs. We develop such a similarity between stochastic and deterministic semi-MDPs (i.e., distance graphs), using the finite horizon model and bounded branching factor in place of mixing time and model parameter cardinality.

Conclusions

In this paper, we have demonstrated a method for efficient planning in a restricted class of mixed, "semi-stochastic, semi-deterministic" MDPs. By carefully selecting macros to "hide" the stochasticity of the navigational component of our package delivery problem, we are able to attack the deterministic routing problem directly with special-purpose methods. The combination of macros with the atomic MDP yields a semi-MDP corresponding to the routing problem, and we have given a tractable evaluable relation between the optimal plans for the semi-MDP and its deterministic approximation. Finally, we demonstrated that the two models are close on a large simulated domain and that the value of the optimal deterministic plan is close to that of the optimal atomic solution on some small domains.

In general, we believe that this *type* of approach holds great promise for stochastic planning. MDPs can encapsu-

late a wide variety of deterministic optimization problems for which good solutions are available; by carefully exploiting the structure of such MDPs and constructing appropriate macro actions, we could harness those solutions directly into the stochastic planning framework. While we have presented our techniques in terms of the TSP optimization problem for mobile robot navigation domains, we believe that this work will extend to related problems like shortest-path, location monitoring, battery maintenance, or vehicle routing. In the extended version of this paper, we address the prioritized packages version of package delivery which yields the more complex *prize-collecting minimum latency path* optimization problem (Goemans & Kleinberg 1996; Arora & Karakostas 1999).

We have assumed here that all macros run to termination (i.e., encountering a delivery location), but it is known that policies can be improved by terminating macros prematurely (Precup 2000). In general this requires knowing the true value of the current *full* state with respect to each available macro. We have avoided computing this term, but we can give sufficient conditions for premature termination of macros given only the *local* information of the agent's current value with respect to each macro's individual sub-goal.

In this work we have employed extensive domain knowledge to decompose the model and identify the underlying optimization problem. One of the most interesting outstanding question is how to automatically identify these quantities, especially for model-free systems. We believe these questions to be difficult, but recent advances in model structure identification and algorithm identification may provide useful insights.

Acknowledgements

The authors would like to thank Luke Zettlemoyer, Natalia H. Gardiol, and Mike Benjamin for valuable discussions on the analysis of the algorithm and comments on early drafts of this paper, and David Karger and Maria Minkoff, for insights on the underlying optimization problem. This work was supported in part by DARPA contract #DABT63-99-1-0012 and in part by NASA award #NCC2-1237.

References

Arora, S., and Karakostas, G. 1999. Approximation schemes for minimum latency problems. In *ACM Symposium on Theory of Computing*, 688–693.

Baum, J., and Nicholson, A. E. 1998. Dynamic non-uniform abstractions for approximate planning in large structured stochastic domains. In *Proceedings of the 5th Pacific Rim International Conference on Artificial Intelligence*, 587–598.

Boutilier, C.; Dearden, R.; and Goldszmidt, M. 2000. Stochastic dynamic programming with factored representations. *Artificial Intelligence* 121(1–2):49–107.

Dean, T., and Givan, R. 1997. Model minimization in Markov decision processes. In *Proceedings of the Fourteenth National Conference on Artificial Intelligence (AAAI-97)*, 106–111. Providence, RI: AAAI Press/MIT Press.

Dean, T.; Kaelbling, L. P.; Kirman, J.; and Nicholson, A. 1995. Planning under time constraints in stochastic domains. *Artificial Intelligence* 76.

Goemans, M., and Kleinberg, J. 1996. An improved approximation ratio for the minimum latency problem. In *SODA: Proceedings of the Seventh ACM-SIAM Symposium on Discrete Algorithms*.

Guestrin, C., and Ormoneit, D. 2001. Robust combination of local controllers. In Breese, J., and Koller, D., eds., *Proceedings of the Seventeenth Conference on Uncertainty in Artificial Intelligence (UAI-01)*, 178–185. Seattle, WA: Morgan Kaufmann.

Hauskrecht, M.; Meuleau, N.; Boutilier, C.; Kaelbling, L. P.; and Dean, T. 1998. Hierarchical solution of Markov decision processes using macro-actions. In Cooper, G. F., and Moral, S., eds., *Proceedings of the Fourteenth Conference on Uncertainty in Artificial Intelligence (UAI-98)*. Morgan Kaufmann.

Johnson, D. S., and McGeoch, L. A. 2001. *The Traveling Salesman Problem and its Variations*. Kluwer Academic Publishers. chapter Experimental Analysis of Heuristics for the STSP. To appear.

Kaelbling, L. P. 1993. Hierarchical learning in stochastic domains: Preliminary results. In *Proceedings of the Tenth International Conference on Machine Learning*, 167–173.

Kearns, M., and Koller, D. 1999. Efficient reinforcement learning in factored MDPs. In Dean, T., ed., *Proceedings of the Sixteenth International Joint Conference on Artificial Intelligence (IJCAI-99)*, 740–747. Stockholm, Sweden: Morgan Kaufmann.

Kemeny, J. G., and Snell, J. L. 1976. *Finite Markov Chains*. Undergraduate Texts in Mathematics. New York: Springer-Verlag.

Koller, D., and Parr, R. 2000. Policy iteration for factored MDPs. In *Uncertainty in Artificial Intelligence: Proceedings of the Sixteenth Conference (UAI 2000)*. Morgan Kaufmann.

Littman, M. 1997. Probabilisitic propositional planning: Representations and complexity. In *Proceedings of the Fourteenth National Conference on Artificial Intelligence (AAAI-97)*, 748–754. Providence, RI: AAAI Press/MIT Press.

Lusena, C.; Mundhenk, M.; and Goldsmith, J. 2001. Non-approximability results for partially observable Markov decision processes. *Journal of Artificial Intelligence Research* 14:83–103.

McGovern, A.; Sutton, R. S.; and Fagg, A. H. 1997. Roles of macro-actions in accelerating reinforcement learning. In *Proceedings of the 1997 Grace Hopper Celebration of Women in Computing*, 13–18.

Moore, A. W.; Baird, L. C.; and Kaelbling, L. 1999. Multi-value-functions: Efficient automatic action hierarchies for multiple goal MDPs. In Dean, T., ed., *Proceedings of the Sixteenth International Joint Conference on Artificial Intelligence (IJCAI-99)*. Stockholm, Sweden: Morgan Kaufmann.

Mundhenk, M.; Goldsmith, J.; Lusena, C.; and Allender, E. 2000. Complexity of finite-horizon markov decision process problems. *Journal of the ACM* 47(4):681–720.

Parr, R. 1998a. Flexible decomposition algorithms for weakly coupled Markov decision problems. In Cooper, G. F., and Moral, S., eds., *Proceedings of the Fourteenth Conference on Uncertainty in Artificial Intelligence (UAI-98)*. Morgan Kaufmann.

Parr, R. E. 1998b. *Hierarchical Control and Learning for Markov Decision Processes*. Ph.D. Dissertation, University of California at Berkeley.

Precup, D. 2000. *Temporal Abstraction in Reinforcement Learning*. Ph.D. Dissertation, University of Massachusetts, Amherst, Department of Computer Science.

Puterman, M. L. 1994. *Markov Decision Processes: Discrete Stochastic Dynamic Programming*. New York: John Wiley & Sons.

Sutton, R. S.; Precup, D.; and Singh, S. 1999. Between MDPs and semi-MDPs: A framework for temporal abstraction in reinforcement learning. *Artificial Intelligence* 112:181–211.

The Size of MDP Factored Policies

Paolo Liberatore

Dipartimento di Informatica e Sistemistica
Università di Roma "La Sapienza"
Via Salaria, 113, 00198, Roma, Italy
paolo@liberatore.org

Abstract

Policies of Markov Decision Processes (MDPs) tell the next
action to execute, given the current state and (possibly) the
history of actions executed so far. Factorization is used when
the number of states is exponentially large: both the MDP and
the policy can be then represented using a compact form, for
example employing circuits. We prove that there are MDPs
whose optimal policies require exponential space even in factored form.

Introduction

Markov Decision Processes (MDP) (Bellman 1957) have
been used in AI for planning in domains in which some
degree of uncertainty is present (Boutilier, Dean, & Hanks
1999; Littman 1997). In particular, the partially observable
extension (POMDP) formalizes scenarios in which the observations do not give a complete description of the state.
Since the result of the actions cannot be determined for sure
in advance, and/or the domain cannot be fully observed, a
plan cannot be a simple sequence of actions. Rather, it
should depend on the observations. In MDP terminology,
such conditional plans are named "policies". Finding policies of MDPs is a problem that has been deeply investigated;
algorithms have been developed, for example value iteration, policy iteration, and methods based on linear programming (Littman, Dean, & Kaebling 1995). For POMDPs,
variants of the value iteration algorithm have been developed (Cassandra, Littman, & Zhang 1997; Zhang & Zhang
2001).

MDPs can be represented explicitely, or in factored form.
In the first case, the possible states of the world are represented by the elements of a set $\{s_1, \ldots, s_n\}$, and there is
no need to specify what the elements represent, i.e., what
is true or false in the state denoted by s_i. To complete the
specification of an MDP, the set of actions, their effects in
each state, and the reward of each state are needed. The first
complexity analysis of MDPs has been done for this explicit
representation (Papadimitriou & Tsitsiklis 1987).

While the explicit representation can be sometimes useful, it is more often the case that each state is described by
the values a set of propositional variables (state variables)

assume. In such cases, the number of possible states is exponential and, therefore, the explicit representation is exponentially large as well. This is why factored representations are used instead. We assume that the states are the
possible interpretations over a set of n variables, and we
represent probability of transitions and rewards using two
circuits. Other compact representations exist, for example
using variants of BDDs, decision trees, stochastic STRIPS
operators, or two-stages Bayes networks (Boutilier, Dean,
& Hanks 1999; Littman 1997; Dean & Kanazawa 1989;
Dearden & Boutilier 1997; Hansen & Feng 2000).

While explicit representations of MDPs are always exponential in the number of state variables, factored MDPs can
be polynomially large. Factoring follows the intuition that
the formal representation of a piece of knowledge should
not be too much larger than its informal representation, e.g.,
if the description of a domain can be written in English in
a single sheet of paper, its formal representation should not
take several megabytes of storage space. While explicit representations are always exponential, an informal description
can be often turned into a formal description using circuits
that are not too large. This is exactly the aim of factorization.

Explicit and factored representations lead to very different computational properties: for example, some problems
are PSPACE-hard in the factored representations but polynomial in the explicit one (Papadimitriou & Tsitsiklis 1987;
Mundhenk *et al.* 2000). This apparent simplification is only
due to the fact that complexity is measured relative to the
size of the input, and explicit representations introduce an
artificial blow-up of the size of the input.

When the representation of the domain is factored, the
explicit representation of a policy is in general exponentially
large. Therefore, factored representations of policies are of
interest (Koller & Parr 1999).

We prove that optimal policies may take exponential
space even in factored representation. In other words, given
an MDP, even the shortest representations of the optimal policy may take exponential space. This result is new, for factored representation. In particular, the hardness of the problem of finding an optimal policy does not imply anything
about the policy size. Even in the cases in which finding
a policy is undecidable (Madani, Hanks, & Condon 1999),
the policy itself may be very short. There are many example of very hard problems, even undecidable ones, having

very short solutions: for example, the solution of the halting problem is a single bit, but finding it is undecidable. Therefore, proving that the solutions of a problem cannot be represented in polynomial space cannot be done directly from complexity results.

The result we prove affects the choice of how policies are generated and executed. There are two ways of planning in a scenario that is formalizable by an MDP: the first one is to determine all actions to execute at once (that is, determine the whole policy); the second one is to only determine the first action, execute it, check the resulting state, and then find the next action, etc. In the second solution, the process of finding the action to execute has to be done at each time step; this process is as hard as finding the optimal reward. The advantage of the first solution is that, once a polynomial sized factored representation of an optimal policy is known, finding the action to execute in a state is polynomial. This can be seen as a form of preprocessing of the problem: the policy is determined from the MDP only, and it then makes the problem of determining the action to execute in a specific state polynomial. The proof we give is actually a proof of unfeasibility of such preprocessing algorithms, and it therefore applies to any factored form that allows determining the action to execute in polynomial time.

Preliminaries

The main parts of a Markov Decision Process (MDP) are a set of operators (actions), whose effect may be stochastic, and a function that evaluates states according to a notion of goodness.

Formally, an MDP is a 5-tuple $\mathcal{M} = \langle \mathcal{S}, s_0, \mathcal{A}, t, r \rangle$, where $\mathcal{S}$ is a set of states, s_0 is a distinguished state (the initial state), and $\mathcal{A}$ is a set of actions. The functions t and r represent the effects of the actions and the reward associated to states, respectively.

We consider factored representations of MDPs: states are propositional interpretations over a given alphabet of binary variables (state variables). The set $\mathcal{S}$ is therefore implicit in the set of state variables. Thus, we do not count it in the size of an MDP. The set of state variables is assumed to be finite, and $\mathcal{S}$ is therefore finite as well.

The result of an action is not assumed to be known for sure, but only according to some probability distribution. Therefore, we cannot represent the effects of actions using a function that maps a state and an action into another state. t is instead a function from actions and pairs of states to numbers in the interval $[0, 1]$. It represents the probability of transitions: $t(s_1, s_2, a) = p$ means that the result of action a in state s_1 is the state s_2 with probability p.

The reward function is a function from states to integer numbers, formalizing how much a state matches our goals. In this paper, we assume that the functions t and r are represented by boolean circuits. This representation of MDPs subsumes other factored representations (Boutilier, Dean, & Hanks 1999; Mundhenk *et al.* 2000).

Planning in deterministic domains consists in determining a sequence of actions that allows reaching a goal state; in nondeterministic domains we have two points to take into account: first, the extent to which the goal is reached can only be probabilistically determined; second, the action to execute in a time point cannot be uniquely determined from the initial state and the actions executed so far.

Namely, the aim of planning in a nondeterministic domain is that of determining a set of actions to execute that result in the best possible states (according to the reward function). Since the result of actions is not known for sure, we can only determine an average reward. For example, if the result of applying a in the state s_0 is s_1 with probability 1/3, and s_2 with probability 2/3, then the expected reward of executing a is given by $1/3 \cdot r(s_1) + 2/3 \cdot r(s_2)$, where $r(s_1)$ and $r(s_2)$ are the rewards of s_1 and s_2, respectively. Formally, we use the average undiscounted reward, i.e., we evaluate the average reward for all states, weighted by the probability of reaching them.

The second effect of nondeterminism is that the best action to execute depends on the current state, which is not uniquely determined from the initial state and the actions executed so far, as the effect of actions are only probabilistically known. For example, executing a may result in state s_1 or in state s_2. After a is executed, we know which one is the actual result. At this point, it may be that the best action to execute in s_1 is a', while the best choice in s_2 is a''. The best action depends on the current state: in the simplest case, a policy is a function that gives the best action to execute in each state.

The reward associated to a policy is the expected average reward obtained by executing, in each state, the associated action. We assume a finite horizon, i.e., we consider only what happens up to a given number of steps. We also assume that this number is polynomial in the total size of the instance, where the size of the instance is the size of $\mathcal{M} = \langle \mathcal{S}, s_0, \mathcal{A}, t, r \rangle$ minus the size of $\mathcal{S}$ which is implicitly represented. Technically, this means that the unary representation of the horizon is part of the instance.

More complex forms of policies are possible. Indeed, we may decide what to do using not only the current state, but also the sequence of actions executed so far. Such policies can be represented as trees, in which each node is labeled with an action, and its children are associated to the possible outcoming states. These policies are called *history-dependent policies*. Policies depending only on the current state form a subclass of them, and are called *stationary policies*.

A problem of interest is whether a policy can be represented in polynomial space. The trivial representation of a policy (using a tree) may be exponentially larger than the MDP even if only one action has more than one possible outcome. However, policies may take less space in factored form. We represent policies using circuits: the input is the binary representation of the current state and of the history; the output is the next action to execute. Some policies are much smaller, in this representation: for example, the policy of executing the same action regardless of the state and the history is polynomial, even if it would require an exponentially large tree.

The question we consider in this paper is whether it is always possible to represent the optimal policy of an MDP with a polynomial circuit. We show that a positive answer would have a consequence considered unlikely in complexity theory: the polynomial hierarchy coincide with the complexity class Π_2^p. The proof is based on the fact that the existence of such circuits would allow solving the problem of determining the action to execute in each state in two steps: first, determine the whole circuit using the MDP alone; then, use the circuit and the current state to determine the next action to execute in polynomial time. This is a form of algorithm with preprocessing, in which a first step only works on part of the instance (the MDP alone, without the current state), and makes the solving of the rest of the problem easier. The unfeasibility of this schema implies the impossibility of always representing optimal policies with polynomial circuits. To this end, we use compilability classes and reductions, which we briefly present in the next section.

Complexity and Compilability

We assume the reader is familiar with the basic complexity classes such as P, NP, and the classes of the polynomial hierarchy (Stockmeyer 1976; Garey & Johnson 1979). In the sequel, C, C', etc. denote arbitrary classes of the polynomial hierarchy. We assume that the input instances of problems are strings over an alphabet Σ. The *length* of a string $x \in \Sigma^*$ is denoted by $||x||$.

We summarize some definitions and results about complexity of preprocessing (Cadoli *et al.* 2002; Gogic *et al.* 1995). We consider problems whose instances can be divided into two parts; one part is *fixed* (known in advance), and the second one is *varying* (known when the solution is needed.) The problem of determining the action to execute in a state has this structure: the MDP is the part known in advance, as it is known from the description of the domain; the state is instead only determined once the previous actions have been executed. Compilability classes and reductions formalize the complexity of such problems when the first input can be preprocessed.

A function f is called *poly-size* if there exists a polynomial p such that, for all strings x, it holds $||f(x)|| \leq p(||x||)$. When x represents a natural number we instead impose $||f(x)|| \leq p(x)$. A function g is called *poly-time* if there exists a polynomial q such that, for all x, $g(x)$ can be computed in time less than or equal to $q(||x||)$. These definitions extend to binary functions in the obvious manner.

We define a *language of pairs* S as a subset of $\Sigma^* \times \Sigma^*$. We define a hierarchy of classes of languages of pairs, the *non-uniform compilability classes*, denoted as $\|{\rightsquigarrow}C$, where C is a generic uniform complexity class, such as P, NP, coNP, or Σ_2^p.

Definition 1 ($\|{\rightsquigarrow}C$ classes) *A language of pairs $S \subseteq \Sigma^* \times \Sigma^*$ belongs to $\|{\rightsquigarrow}C$ iff there exists a binary poly-size function f and a language of pairs $S' \in C$ such that, for all $\langle x, y \rangle \in S$, it holds:*

$$\langle x, y \rangle \in S \text{ iff } \langle f(x, ||y||), y \rangle \in S'$$

$\|{\rightsquigarrow}C$ contains problems that are in C after a suitable polynomial-size preprocessing step. Clearly, any problem in C is also in $\|{\rightsquigarrow}C$. Compilation is useful if a problem

in C is in $\|{\rightsquigarrow}C'$, where C'$\subset$C, that is, preprocessing decreases the complexity of the problem. There are problems for which such reduction of complexity is possible (Cadoli *et al.* 2002).

For these classes it is possible to define the notions of *hardness* and *completeness*, based on a suitable definition of reductions.

Definition 2 (nucomp reductions) *A nucomp reduction from a problem A to a problem B is a triple $\langle f_1, f_2, g \rangle$, where f_1 and f_2 are poly-size functions, g is a polynomial function, and for every pair $\langle x, y \rangle$ it holds that $\langle x, y \rangle \in A$ if and only if $\langle f_1(x, ||y||), g(f_2(x, ||y||), y) \rangle \in B$.*

Definition 3 ($\|{\rightsquigarrow}C$-completeness) *Let S be a language of pairs and C a complexity class. S is $\|{\rightsquigarrow}C$-hard iff for all problems $A \in \|{\rightsquigarrow}C$ there exists a nucomp reduction from A to S. If S is also in $\|{\rightsquigarrow}C$, it is called $\|{\rightsquigarrow}C$-complete.*

The hierarchy formed by the compilability classes is proper if and only if the polynomial hierarchy is proper (Cadoli *et al.* 2002; Karp & Lipton 1980; Yap 1983) — a fact widely conjectured to be true.

Informally, $\|{\rightsquigarrow}$NP-hard problems are "not compilable to P". Indeed, if such compilation were possible, then it would be possible to define f as the function that takes the fixed part of the problem and gives the result of compilation (ignoring the size of the input), and S' as the language representing the on-line processing. This would implies that a $\|{\rightsquigarrow}$NP-hard problem is in $\|{\rightsquigarrow}$P, and this implies the collapse of the polynomial hierarchy.

$\|{\rightsquigarrow}$NP-hardness can be proved as follows: let us assume that $\langle r, h \rangle$ is a reduction from sat to a problem of pairs S, that is, Π is satisfiable if and only if $\langle r(\Pi), h(\Pi) \rangle \in S$. This implies that S is NP-hard, but tells nothing about hardness w.r.t. compilability classes. However, if the additional property of monotonicity holds, then S is also $\|{\rightsquigarrow}$NP-hard (Liberatore 2001). The pair $\langle r, h \rangle$ is a monotonic polynomial reduction if, for any pair of clauses Π_1 and Π_2 over the same literals, with $\Pi_1 \subseteq \Pi_2$, it holds:

$$\langle r(\Pi_1), h(\Pi_1) \rangle \in S \text{ iff } \langle r(\Pi_2), h(\Pi_1) \rangle \in S$$

Note that the second instance combines a part from Π_2 and a part from Π_1: this is not a typo. A problem is $\|{\rightsquigarrow}$NP-hard, if there exists a polynomial reduction from sat to it that can be proved to be monotonic. The definition of monotonicity will be more clear when applied to a specific problem, as we do in the next section.

Finding Policies Cannot Be Compiled

The impossibility of representing policies in polynomial space is proved using compilability classes as follows: suppose that we are able to find a circuit that: a. is of polynomial size; and b. represents an optimal policy. Such a circuit allows for deciding which action to execute in a state in polynomial time. We have therefore an algorithm for solving the problem of determining the optimal action in a state: in a first (possibly long) phase the circuit is found; a second, polynomial, phase finds the action to execute. The first phase only works on a part of the problem data, and produces a polynomial sized data structure that makes the whole problem polynomial: the problem is in $\|\leadsto$P. Polynomiality of policy size is then equivalent to the question: is the problem of determining the action to execute in a state in $\|\leadsto$P? Proving that the problem is $\|\leadsto$NP-hard gives a negative answer.

Formally, we consider the following problem: given an MDP $\mathcal{M}$, one of its states s, and one of its actions a, decide whether a is the action to execute in s according to some optimal policy. We prove this problem to be $\|\leadsto$NP-hard. This is done by first showing it NP-hard, and then proving that the employed reduction is monotonic.

Let Π be a set of clauses, each composed of three literals, over a set of variables $X = \{x_1, \ldots, x_n\}$. The reduction is as follows: given a set of clauses Π, we build the triple $\langle \mathcal{M}, s, a \rangle$, where the first element is an MDP, the second is one of its states, and the third is one of its actions.

Let L be the set of literals over X, and let $E = L \cup \{\text{sat}, \text{unsat}\}$. The MDP $\mathcal{M}$ is defined as:

$$\mathcal{M} = \langle \mathcal{S}, \epsilon, \mathcal{A}, t, r \rangle$$

The components of $\mathcal{M}$ are defined as follows.

States: $\mathcal{S}$ is the set of sequences of at most $(2n)^3 + n + 1$ elements of E;

Initial state: is the empty sequence ϵ;

Actions: $\mathcal{A}$ contains three actions A, S, and U, and one action a_i for each x_i;

Transition function: the effect of A is to randomly select (with equal probability) a literal of L and adding it to the sequence representing the current state; the effect of S and U is to add sat and unsat to the sequence, respectively (these are deterministic actions); the effect of a_i is to add either x_i or $\neg x_i$ to the sequence, with the same probability;

Reward function: This is the most involved part of the MDP. Given a sequence of $3m$ literals of L, we define a 3cnf formula as follows:

$$C(l_1^1, l_2^1, l_3^1, \ldots, l_1^m, l_2^m, l_3^m) = \{l_1^1 \vee l_2^1 \vee l_3^1, \ldots, l_1^m \vee l_2^m \vee l_3^m\}$$

Since the number of different clauses over L is less than $(2n)^3$, any set of clauses can be represented as a sequence of $3m$ literals, where $m = (2n)^3$. This is a way to encode all sets of clauses over L as sequences of literals.

The reward function is defined in terms of C: a sequence of $3m$ literals followed by unsat has reward 1; a sequence s of $3m$ literals followed by sat, further followed by a sequence $s' = l_1, \ldots, l_n$ (where l_i is either x_i or $\neg x_i$) has reward $2 \cdot 2^n$ if $C(s)$ is satisfied by s', otherwise 0; all other sequences have reward 0.

Note that most of the states have reward 0. While the total reward is an average over all reached states, r is defined in such a way all states preceeding and succeeding a nonzero reward state have reward zero. r is defined this way for the sake of making the proof simpler; however, we are still calculating the total reward over all states, including "intermediate" ones.

This MDP has a single optimal policy: execute A for $3m$ times, then execute either U or the sequence $S, a_1, \ldots, a_n$, depending on the result of the execution of A. Namely, any possible result of the execution of the first $3m$ actions corresponds to a set of clauses. The next action of the optimal policy is U if the set is unsatisfiable and S if it is satisfiable.

This is the definition of the MDP $\mathcal{M}$. The instance of the problem is composed of an MDP, a state, and an action, and the problem is to check whether the action is optimal in the state. The action is S, and the state s is the sequence of literals such that $C(s) = \Pi$. We can now prove that f is a reduction from satisfiability to the problem of the next action.

Theorem 1 *The MDP $\mathcal{M}$ has an unique optimal policy. The set of clauses Π is satisfiable if and only if S is the action to execute from s in the optimal policy of $\mathcal{M}$.*

Proof. The MDP has policies with positive reward: the sequence of actions $A^{3m}U$ has a reward equal to 1, since all its leaves have reward 1 and all internal nodes have reward 0. Note that, since the actions executed so far can be derived from the current state, stationary and history-based policies coincide.

The policies with positive reward are very similar to each other. Indeed, they all begin by executing $3m$ times the action A. Then, either U or the sequence of $S, a_1, \ldots, a_n$ is executed. Policies with positive reward can only differ on this choice of executing U or $S, a_1, \ldots, a_n$. However, a policy can take the first choice in a state, and the other one in another state: policies are not forced to make the same choice regardless of the current state.

sequence 1:	$\underbrace{A \ldots A}_{3m}\, U$
sequence 2:	$\underbrace{A \ldots A}_{3m}\, S\, a_1 \ldots a_n$

Figure 1: Sequences that can generate a reward > 0; All their fragments and extensions have reward 0.

Let us now consider the state after the execution of A for $3m$ times. Since each execution of A generates a random literal, at this point the state is a sequence of $3m$ literals. Such a sequence represents the set of clauses that is later used by the reward function. Intuitively, at this point we want the optimal policy to execute U if the set of clauses is unsatisfiable, and $S, a_1, \ldots, a_n$ if it is satisfiable. This is obtained by giving reward 1 to the subtree composed by U alone, and reward equal to double the number of models of the set of clauses to the subtree $S, a_1, \ldots, a_n$. The optimal choice will then be U if the formula is unsatisfiable (reward 1, instead of 0), and $S, a_1, \ldots, a_n$ if it is satisfiable (reward ≥ 2, instead of 1).

Summarizing, the first $3m$ actions generates a random set of clauses, while the sequence $a_1, \ldots, a_n$ generates a random interpretation. The leaves in which the interpretation satisfies the set of clauses have reward $2 \cdot 2^n$, while the other

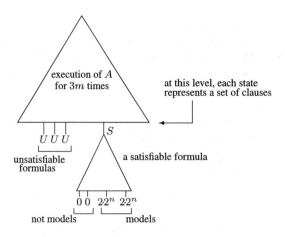

Figure 2: The optimal policy of the MDP of the proof.

ones have reward 0. If the formula is unsatisfiable then U is the best choice, as it gets a reward 1 instead of 0. □

This theorem implies that choosing the next action is an NP-hard problem, a result of really little significance by itself, in light of the PSPACE-hardness of related problems. However, the reduction can be used to prove that the problem of choosing the next action cannot be simplified to P thanks to a polynomial data structure depending only on the MDP. This, in turn, implies the nonexistence of a polynomial sized circuit representing the optimal policy.

In particular, a polynomial reduction from 3sat to a problem that satisfies the condition of monotonicity (Liberatore 2001) implies that the problem is $\Vdash$NP-hard, and therefore cannot be compiled. Since the problem instances can be divided into two parts, the reduction itself can be decomposed into two separate functions, one generating the part of the instance that can be compiled, and the other generating the rest of the instance. In our case, $\mathcal{M}$ is the part that can be compiled, while s and S are the rest of the instance. As a result, if $\langle \mathcal{M}, s, S \rangle$ is the MDP that corresponds to a set of clauses Π, the two functions are defined as:

$$r(\Pi) = \mathcal{M}$$
$$h(\Pi) = \langle s, S \rangle$$

Monotonicity holds if, for every pairs of sets of clauses Π_1 and Π_2 over the same set of literals, with $\Pi_1 \subseteq \Pi_2$ it holds that $\langle r(\Pi_1), h(\Pi_1) \rangle$ is a "yes" instance if and only if $\langle r(\Pi_2), h(\Pi_1) \rangle$ is a "yes" instance. Note that the second instance is $\langle r(\Pi_2), h(\Pi_1) \rangle$, that is, it combines a part derived from Π_2 and a part from Π_1.

Instead of trying to explain this definition better, we consider its specialization to the case of MDPs. Let $\mathcal{M}_1 = r(\Pi_1)$ and $\mathcal{M}_2 = r(\Pi_2)$ be the MDPs corresponding to the sets of clauses Π_1 and Π_2 using the construction above. Let $\langle s, S \rangle = h(\Pi_1)$. Monotonicity can be expressed as: for any two sets of clauses Π_1 and Π_2 over the same set of literals, with $\Pi_1 \subseteq \Pi_2$, it must hold that S is the optimal action to execute in the state s for the MDP $\mathcal{M}_1$ if and only if it is so in the MDP $\mathcal{M}_2$. The reduction we have defined satisfies this condition.

Theorem 2 *The reduction $\langle r, h \rangle$ is a monotonic polynomial reduction.*

Proof. Let Π_1 and Π_2 be two sets of clauses over the same set of variables, and let $\mathcal{M}_1$ and $\mathcal{M}_2$ be their corresponding MDPs. Since the MDP corresponding to a set of clauses depends—by construction—on the number of variables only, $\mathcal{M}_1$ and $\mathcal{M}_2$ are exactly the same MDP. As a result, for any state s and action S, the latter is the optimal action to execute in $\mathcal{M}_1$ if and only if it is so for $\mathcal{M}_2$, and this is the definition of monotonicity for the case of MDPs. □

This theorem implies that the problem of the next action is hard for the compilability class $\Vdash$NP. In turns, this result implies that there is no polynomial-sized representation of a policy that allows determining the next action in polynomial time.

Theorem 3 *If, for any MDP, there exists a polynomial data structure that allows determining the next action to execute according to an optimal policy in polynomial time, then $\Sigma_2^p = \Pi_2^p = \mathrm{PH}$.*

Proof. If such representation exists, the problem of the next action is in $\Vdash$P. Indeed, given the fixed part of the problem (the MDP), we can get such polynomial representation of the optimal policy. Then, determining the next action can be done in polynomial time. This implies $\Sigma_2^p = \Pi_2^p = \mathrm{PH}$ (Cadoli et al. 2002). □

The circuit representation of policies is a subcase of data structures allowing the determination of the next state in polynomial time.

Corollary 1 *If, for any MDP, there exists a polynomial circuit representing an optimal policy, then $\Sigma_2^p = \Pi_2^p = \mathrm{PH}$.*

Conclusions

Optimal policies of MDPs cannot always be represented by polynomial-sized circuits. We proved this claim using compilability classes; namely, it is implied by the fact that there is no polynomial data structure that allows determining the next action to execute in a state in polynomial time; circuits are a special case of such structures. This implies that, in a probabilistic domain, we cannot determine an optimal policy all at once, and then execute it. What we can do is either to determine only the first optimal action to execute (and then repeating once the resulting state is known), or to use a suboptimal policy that can be represented in polynomial space.

Let us now discuss how the results presented in this paper relate to similar one in the literature. As already remarked in the Introduction, complexity does not necessarily imply that policies cannot be compactly represented. Namely, even a result of undecidability does not forbid compactness of policies. As a result, such nonexistence results are not implied by complexity results.

On the other hand, a result of non-polynomiality of the size of policies of POMDPs already appeared in the literature, namely, in Papadimitriou and Tsitsiklis' paper (Papadimitriou & Tsitsiklis 1987). Their result does not imply ours, as it holds for POMDPs in the explicit representation with only nonpositive rewards; the same problem that is PSPACE-hard in their formalization is polynomial in ours (Mundhenk *et al.* 2000). To be precise, the two results cannot be derived from each other. The technique used by Papadimitriou and Tsitsiklis is also different from ours, but can be nonetheless applied in our settings, and allows for proving that the existence of a short policy implies that PSPACE is contained in NP^{PP}; technical details can be found in a technical report (Liberatore 2002).

We conclude the paper by observing that all our results holds for POMDPs, since MDPs are special cases of POMDPs in which everything is observable.

Acknowledgments

Many thanks to the anonymous referees, who helped the author to improve the quality of the paper.

References

Bellman, R. 1957. *Dynamic Programming*. Princeton University Press.

Boutilier, C.; Dean, T.; and Hanks, S. 1999. Decision-theoretic planning: Structural assumptions and computational leverage. *Journal of Artificial Intelligence Research* 11:1–94.

Cadoli, M.; Donini, F. M.; Liberatore, P.; and Schaerf, M. 2002. Preprocessing of intractable problems. *Information and Computation*. To Appear.

Cassandra, A.; Littman, M.; and Zhang, N. 1997. Incremental pruning: a simple, fast, exact method for partially observable markov decision processes. In *Proc. of UAI-97*.

Dean, T., and Kanazawa, K. 1989. A model for reasoning about persistence and causation. *Computational Intelligence* 5(3):142–150.

Dearden, R., and Boutilier, C. 1997. Abstraction and approximate decision theoretic planning. *Artificial Intelligence* 89(1):219–283.

Garey, M. R., and Johnson, D. S. 1979. *Computers and Intractability: A Guide to the Theory of NP-Completeness*. San Francisco, Ca: W.H. Freeman and Company.

Gogic, G.; Kautz, H. A.; Papadimitriou, C.; and Selman, B. 1995. The comparative linguistics of knowledge representation. In *Proceedings of the Fourteenth International Joint Conference on Artificial Intelligence (IJCAI'95)*, 862–869.

Hansen, E., and Feng, Z. 2000. Dynamic programming for POMDPs using a factored state representation. In *Proc. of AIPS-00*, 130–139.

Karp, R. M., and Lipton, R. J. 1980. Some connections between non-uniform and uniform complexity classes. In *Proceedings of the Twelfth ACM Symposium on Theory of Computing (STOC'80)*, 302–309.

Koller, D., and Parr, D. 1999. Computing factored value functions for policies in structured MDPs. In *Proceedings of the Sixteenth International Joint Conference on Artificial Intelligence (IJCAI'99)*, 1332–1339.

Liberatore, P. 2001. Monotonic reductions, representative equivalence, and compilation of intractable problems. *Journal of the ACM* 48(6):1091–1125.

Liberatore, P. 2002. On polynomial sized MDP factored policies. Technical report, Dipartimento di Informatica e Sistemistica, Università di Roma "La Sapienza".

Littman, M.; Dean, T.; and Kaebling, L. 1995. On the complexity of solving markov decision processes. In *Proc. of UAI-95*.

Littman, M. 1997. Probabilistic propositional planning: representations and complexity. In *Proceedings of the Fourteenth National Conference on Artificial Intelligence (AAAI'97)*, 748–754.

Madani, O.; Hanks, S.; and Condon, A. 1999. On the undecidability of probabilistic planning and infinite-horizon partially observable markov decision problems. In *Proceedings of the Sixteenth National Conference on Artificial Intelligence (AAAI'99)*, 541–548.

Mundhenk, M.; Goldsmith, J.; Lusena, C.; and Allender, E. 2000. Complexity of finite-horizon markov decision processes problems. *Journal of the ACM* 47(4):681–720.

Papadimitriou, C., and Tsitsiklis, J. 1987. The complexity of markov decision processes. *Mathematics of Operations Research* 12(3):441–450.

Stockmeyer, L. J. 1976. The polynomial-time hierarchy. *Theoretical Computer Science* 3:1–22.

Yap, C. K. 1983. Some consequences of non-uniform conditions on uniform classes. *Theoretical Computer Science* 26:287–300.

Zhang, N., and Zhang, W. 2001. Speeding up the convergence of value iteration in partially observable markov decision processes. *Journal of Artificial Intelligence Research* 14:29–51.

On Policy Iteration as a Newton's Method and Polynomial Policy Iteration Algorithms

Omid Madani
Department of Computing Science
University of Alberta
Edmonton, AL
Canada T6G 2E8
madani@cs.ualberta.ca

Abstract

Policy iteration is a popular technique for solving Markov decision processes (MDPs). It is easy to describe and implement, and has excellent performance in practice. But not much is known about its complexity. The best upper bound remains exponential, and the best lower bound is a trivial $\Omega(n)$ on the number of iterations, where n is the number of states.

This paper improves the upper bounds to a polynomial for policy iteration on MDP problems with special graph structure. Our analysis is based on the connection between policy iteration and Newton's method for finding the zero of a convex function. The analysis offers an explanation as to why policy iteration is fast. It also leads to polynomial bounds on several variants of policy iteration for MDPs for which the linear programming formulation requires at most two variables per inequality (MDP(2)). The MDP(2) class includes deterministic MDPs under discounted and average reward criteria. The bounds on the run times include $O(mn^2 \log m \log W)$ on MDP(2) and $O(mn^2 \log m)$ for deterministic MDPs, where m denotes the number of actions and W denotes the magnitude of the largest number in the problem description.

1 Introduction

Markov decision processes offer a clean and rich framework for problems of control and decision making under uncertainty [BDH99; RN95]. A set of central problems in this family is the fully observable Markov decision problems under infinite-horizon criteria [Ber95]. We refer to these as MDP problems in this paper. Not only are the MDP problems significant on their own, but solutions to these problems are used repeatedly in solving problem variants such as stochastic games and partially observable MDPs [Con93; HZ01]. In an MDP model, the system is in one of a finite set of states at any time point. In each state an agent has a number of actions to choose from. Execution of an action gives the agent a reward and causes a stochastic change in the system state. The problem is, given a full description of the system and actions, to find a policy, that is a mapping from states to actions, so that the expected (discounted) to-tal reward over an indefinite (or infinite) number of action executions is maximized.

Policy improvement is a key technique in solving MDPs. It is simple to describe and easy to implement, and quickly converges to optimal solutions in practice. The improvement method begins with an arbitrary policy, and improves the policy iteratively until an optimal policy is found. In each improvement step, the algorithm changes choice of action for a subset of the states, which leads to an improved policy. These algorithms differ on how the states are picked. In addition to policy improvement algorithms, other methods for solving MDPs include algorithms for linear programming, but variants of policy improvement are preferred due to speed and ease of implementation [Lit96; Han98; GKP01]. We remark that policy improvement can be viewed as a special linear programming solution method [Lit96; Ber95].

Unfortunately, the worst-case bounds on several implementations of policy improvement are exponential [MC94]. The exponential lower bounds have been shown for those policy improvement algorithms that in each iteration attempt to pick a single most promising state to improve, and are established on plausible heuristics for such a choice, such as looking ahead one or a constant number of steps. Let us call these 'selective' policy improvement. In a sense, the bounds imply that attempting to be smart about choosing which state to improve can lead to an exponentially long path to the optimal. On the other hand, the policy improvement technique is naturally implemented in a manner in which all states are examined, and any improvable state changes action. We will refer to this variation as policy iteration (PI) (see Section 2.1). It is known that PI is no worse than pseudo-polynomial[1] time [Ber95], while the exponential lower bounds on selective algorithms apply irrespective of the number representation [Lit96]. This suggests that the constraints on how PI advances may be inherently different than those for the selective policy improvement algorithms, and leaves hope for PI. But quantifying the advancement of PI has been difficult. The best upper bound on PI, besides the pseudo-polynomial bound, is also exponential $O(2^n/n)$ [MS99], where n is the number of states and each state has two actions. This upper bound is derived using certain par-

---

[1]That is, polynomial if the numbers are written in unary.

tial order and monotonicity properties of the policy space. No lower bound other than the trivial $\Omega(n)$ on the number of iterations is known.

This paper describes a measure of advancement for PI that offers an explanation of why PI is fast. While we don't derive polynomial bounds for PI on general MDPs, we give the first polynomial bounds for PI on many significant subclasses of MDPs and related problems. Fig. 1 shows the MDP problems in context. The problems get roughly harder from left to right. Our results apply to the enclosed problems. Let m be the number of actions, and W be the largest number in magnitude in the problem description[2]. We give an $O(n^2 \log nW)$ bound on the number of iterations of PI on MDP graphs that have a special structure: there exists a certain state b such that any sequence of visited states under any policy repeats state b before repeating another state. Each iteration takes $O(m)$ time or $O(m + n^2)$ time depending on the edges (Section 4.1). For the rest of the enclosed problems, we show that a variant of PI is polynomial. We discuss these problems next.

The general MDP problem can be formulated as a linear program (LP) in which the feasibility constraints have at most *three* variables per inequality [Mad02]. The subclasses of the MDPs for which we give polynomial policy improvement can be summarized as those for which the corresponding LPs require at most *two* variables per inequality (Section 4.4). We use the names MDP(2) and MDP(3) to differentiate. In the LP formulation of the MDP, finding the feasibility region under the system of inequalities is sufficient to solve the problem. We have shown that, conversely, an extension of policy iteration solves the two variable per inequality linear feasibility (TVPI) problem and have given a polynomial bound for one such type of algorithm. The way policy improvement solves the TVPI problem is different from previous algorithms, as will be described in the paper. The best bound that we give for policy improvement on MDP(2) is $O(mn^2 \log m \log W)$ and for deterministic MDPs (discounted or average reward) is $O(mn^2 \log m)$, but we expect that the bounds can be improved. In the paper, at times, we will use $\widetilde{O}()$ notation to hide extra $\log()$ factors for simplicity.

A main tool we use is the analysis of Newton's method for finding the zero of a function [Rad92; Mad00]. It was known that policy iteration was a form of Newton's method, but the well-known local quadratic convergence of Newton's method is not useful for deriving polynomial bounds. The analysis given here relates the way the process converges to attributes of the problem size. We point out that our results on deterministic MDPs do not require this analysis.

We begin with the definition of the MDP problems and policy iteration. Then we show how PI is a Newton's method on a single state problem, and describe its analysis that is used in showing polynomial bounds. We then show how this tool can be leveraged to establish polynomial bounds for various policy improvement algorithms on different problems. Complete proofs appear in [Mad02;

[2]We make the standard assumption that a fraction such as a probability is represented by the ratio of two integers.

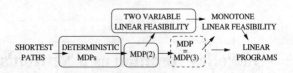

Figure 1: MDP problems in context. Problems are generalized in the direction of the arrows. Our results apply to the enclosed problems.

Mad00].

2 Preliminaries

A Markov decision process (MDP) consists of a set V of n vertices or system states, and for each vertex $v \in V$, a finite set E_v of edge choices or actions. Let m denote the total number of edges. Time is discretized and at each time point $t, t = 0, 1, \cdots$ the system occupies one vertex $v^{(t)}$, which is called the state (or vertex) of the system at time t, and $v^{(0)}$ is the initial state of the system. The means of change of vertex (system state) is edge choice. Each edge can branch out and have one or more end-vertices (Fig. 3a). By choosing edge $e \in E_u$ when the system is in state u, a *reward* of $r(e) \in R$ is obtained and the system transitions to an end-vertex v, with probability $Pr(e, v)$, where $\sum_{v \in V} Pr(e, v) = 1$. The effects of edges, *i.e.* the rewards and the transition probabilities, do not change with time, and they are completely specified as part of the problem instance. We will also use shorthand r_e to denote reward of edge e. A *policy* $\mathcal{P}$ is a mapping assigning to each vertex v a single edge choice $\mathcal{P}(v) \in E_v$. The value (vector) of a policy, denoted $\mathcal{V}_\mathcal{P}$ is a vector of n values, where $\mathcal{V}_\mathcal{P}[i]$ is the *value* of vertex v_i under policy $\mathcal{P}$, defined as the expectation of total reward $\sum_{t=0}^{\infty} r(\mathcal{P}(v^{(t)}))$, when $v^{(0)} = v_i$. We assume here that $\mathcal{V}_\mathcal{P}[i]$ is bounded and well behaved for any policy $\mathcal{P}$ and initial vertex[3].

Define the *optimal value* of a vertex v, denoted x_v^*, to be the maximum value of vertex v over all policies. A desirable and simplifying property of MDPs is that there exists an *optimal policy* which simultaneously maximizes the value of all vertices [Ber95]. Therefore the MDP problem is to find an optimal policy or compute the optimal value of all vertices.

2.1 Policy Iteration

The generic policy improvement procedure is given in Fig. 2. Evaluating a policy means finding its corresponding value vector. Policy improvement algorithms differ on how they improve the policy. In a common technique which we will refer to as (classic) policy iteration (PI), the improvement is done in 'parallel' as follows: each vertex u picks its

[3]Policy improvement algorithms can be extended to discover ill-defined problems as discussed later. Whenever a discount is used (i.e. maximize expected $\sum_{t=0}^{\infty} \beta^t r_{\mathcal{P}(v^{(t)})}$, with $\beta < 1$), the problem is well-defined, and a discount is modeled by each edge having a transition probability to an absorbing zero-reward state.

1. Begin with an arbitrary policy
2. Repeat
3.   Evaluate policy
4.   Improve policy
5. Until no improvement is possible

Figure 2: Policy improvement.

best *edge* according to:

$$\arg \max_{e \in E_u} \left(r(e) + \sum_{v \in V} Pr(e, v) x_v^{(t-1)} \right), \quad t \geq 1,$$

where $x_v^{(t-1)}$ denotes the value of vertex v from the policy computed in iteration $t-1$ or initial policy if $t-1 = 0$. Performing the policy improvement step yields a policy with a value vector that componentwise has values as high or greater than the value vector of the old policy, and as long as an optimal policy is not found, it can be shown that in at least one component the value vector improves. Therefore the algorithm takes a finite number of iterations to converge to an optimal policy. Policy evaluation can be done in polynomial time by matrix inversion in general, but is easier in the problems discussed below. The parallel improvement step also takes a polynomial $\theta(m)$ time. Therefore each iteration is polynomial.

2.2 MDP(3) and MDP(2)

Any MDP problem can be polynomially reduced to one such that for each edge the maximum number of possible end vertices is two, by introducing extra vertices and edges as necessary (see for example [Mad02]). We will refer to such a problem as MDP(3). A generic MDP(3) edge is shown in Fig. 3a. Thus each edge in MDP(3) is a branching edge, or a hyper-edge, and is parameterized by at most *three* numbers: its reward and two transition probabilities to the two end vertices. We will also be analyzing a restriction we call MDP(2), where each edge e connects two vertices, and is parameterized by two numbers[4], reward r_e, and transition probability μ_e, where $\mu_e \leq 1$. The remaining probability $1 - \mu_e$ is understood to go to an absorbing state with no reward. Therefore an MDP(2) problem is viewed as a problem on a directed graph where policies are subgraphs with one or more cycles and every vertex has a path to some cycle. The MDP(2) problem is a generalization of the discounted deterministic MDP, where in the latter all edges have equal transition probability which is equal to the $1 - \beta$, where β is the discount factor.

We call an edge of u ending in vertex v, a u-v edge. Similarly a path starting at u and ending in v is a u-v path.

---

[4]The relationship between MDP, MDP(3), and MDP(2) is similar to that among SAT, SAT(3), and SAT(2). In fact, policy iteration algorithms (and other algorithms that solve MDPs) can be seen as attempting to find the feasibility of a set of linear inequalities. In this sense, solving MDPs correspond most directly to satisfying a conjunction of horn clauses in logic. See Section 4.4.

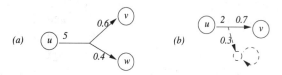

Figure 3: (a) An edge (action) with reward of 5 in an MDP (or an MDP(3)). (b) An edge in an MDP(2) has at most one (non-absorbing) end-vertex.

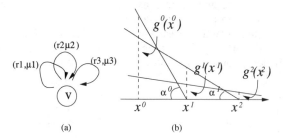

Figure 4: (a)A single-state MDP with a choice of 3 edges shown. (b) Newton's method for finding the zero of a function.

3 Policy Iteration as a Newton's Method

Consider the MDP single vertex problem (Fig. 4), where the vertex v has a finite number of self-arc edges each parameterized by the pair (r_e, μ_e) of reward and transition probability, and we assume $\mu_e < 1$. The value of each (policy) is $\frac{r_e}{1 - \mu_e}$, and the optimal value of the vertex would be $x^* = \max_e \frac{r_e}{1 - \mu_e}$ and can be discovered in a single pass over the edges. As we will see later, the edges will expand to policies and therefore there may be an exponential number of them. Now consider the behavior of policy iteration. The algorithm begins with an arbitrary edge and computes the value x of v under the edge. In selecting the next edge, it picks the edge with maximum immediate reward $r_e + \mu_e(x)$, or equivalently, the edge with maximum *gain* $r_e + \mu_e(x) - x = r_e + (\mu_e - 1)x$. We will refer to $g_e(x) = r_e + (\mu_e - 1)x$ as the the *gain function* corresponding to e. Policy iteration evaluates the new policy, and we can verify that the new value is at the zero of the gain function, i.e. x, where $g_e(x) = 0$. Policy iteration then repeats with choosing and evaluating the edge with highest gain at the new x value, until the highest gain is zero. As shown in Fig. 4 the process corresponds to finding the zero of a convex function (the upper envelope of the gain functions) using Newton's method. Therefore, the question in this case comes down to providing an effective measure of progress for the process. Note that, as discussed in [Lit96], the well-known local quadratic convergence results on Newton's method are not sufficient for proof of polynomial run time. In [Mad00] a bound is derived on the distance of each zero $(x^{(i)})$ to the zero of the optimal gain function, which is shown to geometrically decrease with each iteration, but the proof is rather long. We describe a result which has a simpler proof and a more direct geometric interpretation. It is derived in the context of the analysis of Newton's method in solving fractional linear combinatorial problems [Rad92]. From Fig. 4, it is not hard to see that both the gains $g^{(i)}(x^{(i)})$ and slopes $\mu^{(i)} - 1 = \frac{g^{(i)}(x^{(i)})}{x^{(i)} - x^{(i+1)}}$ are converging to zero. However, a stronger constraint that quantifies the convergence rates can be derived:

Lemma 3.1 *[Rad92] The values and slopes of the sequence of gain functions satisfy:* $\frac{g^{(i+1)}(x^{(i+1)})}{g^{(i)}(x^{(i)})} + \frac{\mu^{(i+1)} - 1}{\mu^{(i)} - 1} \leq 1.$

Intuitively, the geometric constraints on the process forces either the gain (height) or the angle and its tangent to decrease significantly in each iteration. The proof is simple, and works by writing the gains and slopes in terms of their definitions with substitutions and simplifications. As $\frac{g^{(i+1)}(x^{(i+1)})}{g^{(i)}(x^{(i)})} \geq 0$ and $\frac{\mu^{(i+1)} - 1}{\mu^{(i)} - 1} \geq 0$, we conclude that either $\frac{g^{(i+1)}(x^{(i+1)})}{g^{(i)}(x^{(i)})} \leq 1/2$ or $\frac{\mu^{(i+1)} - 1}{\mu^{(i)} - 1} \leq 1/2$. This result suffices for showing polynomial run-times, as we will see next.

4 Polynomial Policy Improvement

4.1 Almost Acyclic MDP Graphs

Consider the following special MDP graph, which we call *adag*, for *almost* a *directed acyclic graph*. In adags, there is an ordering on the vertices, so that edges of a vertex i can branch or end in lower numbered vertices, a special 'bottleneck' vertex b, or an absorbing zero-reward vertex, only. The edges of vertex b can branch to any vertex. Thus all interesting cycles must go through b. The analysis of policy iteration on this problem can be reduced to the above Newton analysis as follows. Consider rolling out the graph so that it becomes acyclic as follows (Fig. 5): We may think of removing the cycles in the policy by replacing vertex b by two vertices, b_s (start vertex) and b_t (target), where all branches of vertices leading to b now end in b_t, and all edges of b belong to b_s.

Now, for any policy P, we define the *value function* $f_{u,p}(x) = r_{u,p} + \mu_{u,p}x$, which is interpreted as the expected value obtained if one starts at vertex u and follows the actions prescribed by the policy, until one arrives at vertex b_t, at which time the value x of b_t is collected. $\mu_{u,p}$ and $r_{u,p}$ can be expressed in terms of the immediate neighbors of u in the policy, $\mu_{u,p} = \sum_{v \in V} Pr(e, v)\mu_{v,p}$ and $\mu_{u,p} = \sum_{v \in V} r_e + Pr(e, v)r_{v,p}$, and can be computed right to left for any policy, with $\mu_{b_t,p} = 1$ and $r_{b_t,p} = 0$. If we apply policy iteration, with any assigned value x for b_t, in at most i iterations, the value of any vertex u of order i is equal to the highest it can reach, and the policy attained is a highest valued/gain policy at value x, which we denote by P_h (x is known from the context).

Consider the original graph and policy iteration progressing on it. The functions $f_{u,p}$, for any vertex u and policy P remain well defined ($f_{b,p}(x)$ is the value vertex b_s obtains if b_t has value x and policy P is used). We just saw that if value of b remains constant for n iterations, b obtains the policy that gives it the highest value in at most n iterations. During policy iteration, values improve in general, and value

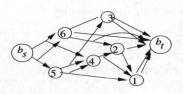

Figure 5: An MDP adag graph rolled out (b replaced by b_s and b_t). Transitions to the absorbing state, edge rewards and transition probabilities, are not shown.

of b (b_s) may increase from one iteration to the next. Nevertheless, the following lemma holds:

Lemma 4.1 *Consider policy iteration on the adag graph, and the value of b, $x^{(t_0)}$ at any iteration t_0, as policy iteration progresses, and let P_h be the highest valued policy at iteration t_0. Then for any vertex u with order i, vertex u has value equal or exceeding $f_{u,p_h}(x^{(t)})$ at all iterations $t \geq t_0 + i$.*

The lemma is proved by induction on the order of vertices, where vertex b has order n. We can now make the connection to the Newton process. Each policy P_h highest valued at a some value of b yields one such gain function, $f_{b,P_h}(x^{(t)}) - x^{(t)}$, where $x^{(t)}$ is value of b at time t. Lemma 4.1 states that such a policy or better one is obtained in at most n iterations, and as policies are evaluated, the point where its gain is zero is surpassed in at most n iterations. All we need is then to bound the maximum and the minimum of the gains and slopes corresponding to policies. Recall that W is the largest number in the input representation.

Lemma 4.2 *We have $nW^2 \geq g^{(i)}(x^{(i)}) \geq W^{-3n}$ and $1 \geq 1 - \mu^{(i)} \geq W^{-1}$.*

The number of iterations is consequently $O(n^2 \log nW)$. We expect this bound can be improved. Policy evaluation on the MDP(3) adags (when the edges' branches are constant) takes only $O(n)$ time, but on an MDP adag, when an edge can touch $\theta(n)$ vertices, it takes $O(n^2)$.

Theorem 4.3 *Policy iteration takes respectively $O(mn^2 \log nW)$ and $O((m + n^2)n^2 \log nW)$ on MDP(3) and MDP adags.*

To summarize, we showed that we may define value and gain functions for policies, and each highest gain policy correspond to a line in Fig. 4. Even though there is an exponential number of policies, policy iteration efficiently (within n iterations) surpasses the zero of the current highest gain policy.

We remark that Lemma 4.1 holds in other variations to the policy improvement step, and in particular if the policy improvement is performed sequentially rather than in parallel (such as Gauss-Siedel [Ber95]). We can also use a shortest paths algorithm to speed up finding P_h on adags: by updating the vertex values and edge choices in an increasing order, a policy P_h is discovered in $O(m)$ time rather than $O(mn)$ in an MDP(3) for example, and in $O(m + n^2)$ for MDPs. Thus the above run times reduce by a factor of n.

Figure 6: Freezing Policy Iteration.

A plausible direction to extend the analysis to general MDPs is to consider increasing the number of bottleneck vertices. However, we haven't succeeded in such an approach: it appears that a novel measure of progress or potential function is needed over two or more bottleneck vertices. Nevertheless, we can show that the Newton analysis leads to polynomial policy improvement algorithms on many problems, as shown below.

4.2 MDP(2)

We now show that a 'freezing' policy iteration algorithm has a run-time of nT where T denotes the run-time of policy iteration on an adag with MDP(2) edges, already shown polynomial above. We remark that the same algorithm works on many problem variations, including deterministic MDPs under discounted (see below) or average rewards. The freezing policy iteration works as given in Fig. 6, and has n phases. A frozen vertex does not change choice of edge during policy iteration. In each phase, one more vertex is unfrozen to select any of its edges in a policy improvement step. Each phase begins with the optimal policy found in the last phase. The basic observation is that in a single phase the source of improvements in the value of any vertex must be due to a path to the most recently unfrozen vertex b (by optimality of the policy from last phase). In particular, any new cycle created in the phase must have b in it. We now see the connection to adags. If no new cycle is created in the phase, it is not hard to see that no more than n policy iterations are needed to find a best policy for the phase. Otherwise, the above analyses apply to bound the number of cycles and iterations. A similar speed-up idea also applies, in this case using a Dijkstra style shortest path algorithm as there are cycles in the graph (but no 'negative cost' cycles in a shortest paths setting as edge probabilities are no more than 1). We omit the details.

Theorem 4.4 *The freezing policy iteration algorithm finds an optimal policy in time $O(mn^3 \log(nW))$ on MDP(2) problems. The freezing algorithm with Dijkstra style shortest paths runs in $O(mn^2 \log(m) \log(W))$.*

The best previously known run time on MDP(2), using TVPI feasibility algorithms (Sect. 4.4), is also $\widetilde{O}(mn^2)$. The polynomial bound for freezing policy iteration is independent of the order of unfreezing, and is strong evidence that plain policy iteration is also polynomial on MDP(2) problems. The freezing technique does not extend to MDP(3) problems: assume all edge rewards are zero except for the edges of the last unfrozen vertex. The problem is then equivalent to a full MDP problem where the objective is to increase the probability of reaching a certain vertex. As edges can have branches, cycles that do not include the unfrozen vertex remain significant.

4.3 Deterministic MDPs

In deterministic MDPs, all edges have equal probabilities. In the case of discounted MDPs, edge probability is $\mu = 1 - \beta$, where $\beta < 1$ is the discount factor. We do not need the analysis of the Newton's method for analyzing deterministic problems. Consider a deterministic adag graph rolled out (as in Fig. 5 but edges do not branch), and any path (policy) from any vertex v to b_t. The corresponding value function $f_{u,p}(x) = r_P + \mu_P(x)$ has slope μ^k where k is the length of the path. Thus paths of the same length correspond to value functions with equal slope, i.e. parallel increasing lines, with longer paths having smaller slope, and for each path length there is a single highest gain policy of *a fixed length* at all values of b. There are at most n such paths. We thus have,

Theorem 4.5 *Policy iteration takes $O(mn^2)$ on discounted deterministic adag graphs. Freezing policy iteration solves discounted deterministic MDPs in $O(mn^3)$, and the algorithm with the shortest path subroutine solves the problem in $O(mn^2 \log(m))$.*

Deterministic average reward problems, and minimum cost-to-time ratio cycle problems also have policy iteration algorithms, and similar arguments show that the freezing variants have similar polynomial bounds. The best known strongly polynomial[5] algorithm for deterministic average reward run in $\theta(mn)$ time [Kar78; Mad00].

4.4 Feasibility Checking

The linear programming formulation for an MDP has the constraints $x_v \geq r_e + \sum_{u \in V} Pr(e, u)$, for each pair of vertex v and edge e in E_v, and the optimal value for each vertex v is the leftmost point of the feasible interval[6] for variable x_v [Ber95]. For an MDP(2) problem, each inequality involves at most two variables. A linear feasibility problem is the problem of determining whether a system of linear inequalities is feasible, and the problem in which each inequality has at most two variables is *the two variable per inequality* problem, or TVPI (feasibility). The TVPI problem was first studied as a means of deriving polynomial time algorithms for general linear programs, but it also has applications in many network flow problems [Sho81; Meg83; Way99]. Algorithms solving TVPI, with a little modification, can report the end points of the interval of feasibility for each variable when the system is feasible. Therefore, from our comments above we observe that these algorithms also solve MDP(2) problems. We can show that the converse is true: policy improvement algorithms, appropriately extended, solve TVPI, and furthermore the techniques above show how to obtain polynomial bounds. Previous polynomial TVPI techniques (other than general linear programming) use binary search or parametric binary search to locate each endpoint of the interval of feasibility for each variable (see for example [Sho81; Meg83; HN94]). Policy improvement algorithms converge to each

---

[5]Independent of number representation.

[6]The property that the feasible region of a variable is a single contiguous interval follows from the fact that the feasible region of an LP system is convex.

endpoint of the interval of feasiblity from the infeasible side. We briefly discuss how these algorithms work.

All algorithms for TVPI feasibility represent the problem in terms of a directed graph, where each vertex corresponds to a variable and each inequality corresponds to an edge. An inequality of the form $ax - by \geq c$, can be rewritten as $x \geq \mu y + c'$, for example, and an edge is directed from v_x to v_y with parameter c' and μ, where $\mu \geq 0$. Therefore, edges have two parameters just as in MDP(2). In these graphs, cycles and paths to cycles are sources of upper and lower bounds for a variable's feasible range. Policy improvement algorithms solve the TVPI feasibility problem in two phases. Just like in the case of policy improvement on MDPs, during the algorithm, vertices have values, and vertex values converge to the left end-points of the feasibility intervals (similar to maximizing expected rewards) from the left (infeasible) side. In a second phase, right end-points are approached and discovered from their right side (similar to an MDP formulation with costs instead of rewards). Infeasibility may be detected during either phase. The complete description of algorithms, together with correctness and polynomial runtime is given in [Mad00]. A freezing version of policy iteration solves the problem in $O(mn^3 \log nW)$. The best run time for solving TVPI feasibility is currently $\tilde{O}(mn^2)$ (e.g. [HN94]).

Policy improvement algorithms described above work only on the *monotone* feasibility problem, i.e. where each inequality has at most one variable with a positive coefficient: $ax - by \geq c$, with $a, b \geq 0, c \in R$. However, an unrestricted feasibility problem can be reduced to the monotone kind for TVPI [HN94].

5 Summary and Discussion

We showed that policy iteration (PI) is polynomial on a special MDP graph and used the analysis to establish that many policy improvement algorithms are polynomial on a number of special MDPs. We also explained that the MDP linear programming formulation is a monotone linear feasibility problem and described extensions of policy improvement that solve the two variable per inequality linear feasibility (TVPI) problem in polynomial time.

The analysis of the Newton's method given was at the heart of the polynomial bounds for problems classes that are more general than deterministic MDPs in Fig. 1. We believe that the analysis provides an explanation as to why policy iteration is fast. In general, policy iteration begins with policies that give high immediate rewards but not necessarily high transition probabilities among the (good) states, and moves towards those policies with lower immediate rewards, but with higher transition probabilities resulting in higher long term accumulated rewards. The Newton analysis, and in particular geometric constraints that it has to satisfy, quantifies this progress. We conjecture that proof methods along similar lines will establish PI and variants polynomial on MDPs. We remark that there are policy improvement algorithms for two-player game versions of MDPs for which no polynomial time algorithm is known [Con93]. Again, variants of policy improvement exist (e.g. [HK66; Con93]) such that similar geometric constraints apply to

their progress. This further motivates the analysis of PI, especially along the above lines.

Acknowledgments This work was supported in part by NSF grant IIS–9523649 and was performed as a part of the PhD work of the author at the University of Washington. The author is indebted to his advisors Steve Hanks and Richard Anderson for their guidance and support throughout this research. Thanks to Nimrod Megiddo for pointing us to Radzik's analysis and to Russ Greiner for interesting discussions and useful suggestions. Many thanks to the reviewers for their valuable feedback, and especially to the reviewer who gave many suggestions for improving the presentation.

References

[BDH99] C. Boutilier, T. Dean, and S. Hanks. Decision theoretic planning: Structural assumptions and computational leverage. *JAIR*, pages 157–171, 1999.

[Ber95] D. P. Bertsekas. *Dynamic Programming and Optimal Control*. Athena Scientific, 1995.

[Con93] A. Condon. On algorithms for simple stochastic games. In *Advances in computational complexity theory*, volume 13 of *DIMACS series in discrete mathematics and theoretical computer science*. 1993.

[GKP01] C. Guestrin, D. Koller, and R. Parr. Max-norm projections for factored MDPs. In *AAAI*, pages 673–679, 2001.

[Han98] E. A. Hansen. *Finite Memory Control of Partially Observable Systems*. PhD thesis, U. of Mass., Amherst, 1998.

[HK66] A. Hoffman and R. Karp. On nonterminating stochastic games. *Management Science*, 12(5), 1966.

[HN94] D. S. Hochbaum and J. Naor. Simple and fast algorithms for linear and integer programs with two variables per inequality. *SICOMP*, 23(6):1179–1192, Dec 1994.

[HZ01] E. Hansen and S. Zilberstein. LAO*: a heuristic search algorithm that finds solutions with loops. *Artificial Intelligence*, 129:35–62, 2001.

[Kar78] R. M. Karp. A characterization of the minimum cycle mean in a digraph. *Discrete Mathematics*, 23:309–311, 1978.

[Lit96] M. Littman. *Algorithms for Sequential Decision Making*. PhD thesis, Brown, 1996.

[Mad00] O. Madani. *Complexity Results for Infinite-Horizon Markov Decision Processes*. PhD thesis, U. of Washington, 2000.

[Mad02] O. Madani. On policy iteration as a Newton's method and polynomial policy iteration algorithms. Technical report, U. of Alberta, 2002.

[MC94] M. Melekopoglou and A. Condon. On the complexity of the policy improvement algorithm for Markov decision processes. *ORSA Journal on Computing*, 6(2), 1994.

[Meg83] N. Megiddo. Towards a genuinely polynomial algorithm for linear programming. *SICOMP*, 12(2):347–353, 1983.

[MS99] Y. Mansour and S. Singh. On the complexity of policy iteration. In *Uncertainty in AI*, pages 401–408, 1999.

[Rad92] T. Radzik. Newton's method for fractional combinatorial optimization. In *33rd FOCS*, pages 659–669, 1992.

[RN95] S. Russell and P. Norvig. *Artificial Intelligence: A Modern Approach*. Prentice Hall, 1995.

[Sho81] R. Shostack. Deciding linear inequalities by computing loop residues. *J. ACM*, 28:769–779, 1981.

[Way99] K.D. Wayne. A polynomial combinatorial algorithm for generalized minimum cost flow. In *31st STOC*, 1999.

Efficient Utility Functions for Ceteris Paribus Preferences

Michael McGeachie
Laboratory for Computer Science
Massachusetts Institute of Technology
Cambridge, MA 02139
mmcgeach@mit.edu

Jon Doyle
Department of Computer Science
North Carolina State University
Raleigh, NC 27695-7535
Jon_Doyle@ncsu.edu

Abstract

Ceteris paribus (other things being equal) preference provides a convenient means for stating constraints on numeric utility functions, but direct constructions of numerical utility representations from such statements have exponential worst-case cost. This paper describes more efficient constructions that combine analysis of utility independence with constraint-based search.

Introduction

Work on qualitative decision theory (Doyle & Thomason 1999) has explored methods for logical specification of abstract and generic preference information as a way of overcoming limitations suffered by direct numerical specifications of utility, especially in supporting automated adaptation of utility functions to changes in preferences. Purely logical specifications of utility functions, however, do not support the needs of automated decision-making methods, which must typically evaluate numerical utility functions repeatedly in computing expected utilities of actions. Such computations demand methods for automatically constructing numeric utility functions that satisfy logical specifications.

McGeachie and Doyle (2002) use direct graph-theoretic methods to construct several numeric utility-function representations of sets of preference rules expressed in a language related to the *ceteris paribus* preference logic of Doyle, Shoham, and Wellman (1991). Those direct methods construct a directed graph over salient model features that represents the initial preferences, and then use standard graph-theoretic functions, such as the number of nodes reachable from a starting node, to define utility representations. Such direct constructions can prove costly because small sets of *ceteris paribus* preference rules can specify very large graphs. In particular, one can express a lexicographic (total linear) order using one rule per model feature.

The following describes provably correct heuristic methods that improve on these constructions by exploiting the notion of utility independence to reduce the problem to one of constructing and combining utility functions over smaller sets of model features. The methods described here transform *ceteris paribus* preference rules into constraints on possible combinations of these subutility functions, and then apply standard constraint-satisfaction methods to find specific combinations that yield overall utility representations of the original *ceteris paribus* preferences.

Ceteris paribus preference and utility

We employ a restricted language $\mathcal{L}$, patterned after (Doyle, Shoham, & Wellman 1991) but using only the logical operators $\neg$ and $\wedge$, over a set of atoms F corresponding to propositional features mentioned in preference statements. By $literals(F)$ we denote the atoms of F and their negations; $literals(F) = F \cup \{\neg f \mid f \in F\}$. We call a complete consistent set m of literals a *model*. That is, a set of features m is a model iff m contains, for each $f \in F$, exactly one of f and $\neg f$. We write $\mathcal{M}$ for the set of all models of $\mathcal{L}$.

A model of $\mathcal{L}$ assigns truth values to all atoms of $\mathcal{L}$, and therefore to all formulae in $\mathcal{L}$. We write $f(m)$ for the truth value assigned to feature f by model m, and say m *satisfies* a sentence p of $\mathcal{L}$, written $m \models p$, if the truth values m assigns to the atoms of p make p true. We define the *proposition* expressed by a sentence p, denoted $[p]$ by $[p] = \{m \in \mathcal{M} \mid m \models p\}$.

A *preference order* is a complete preorder (reflexive and transitive relation) $\succsim$ over $\mathcal{M}$. When $m \succsim m'$, we say that m is *weakly preferred* to m'. If $m \succsim m'$ and $m' \not\succsim m$, we write $m \succ m'$ and say that m is *strictly preferred* to m'. If $m \succsim m'$ and $m' \succsim m$, then we say m is *indifferent* to m', written $m \sim m'$. A *utility function* $u : \mathcal{M} \to \mathbb{R}$ maps each model to a real number. A utility function u represents a preference order $\succsim$ just in case $u(m) \geq u(m')$ whenever $m \succeq m'$.

We define a new language $\mathcal{L}_r$ of *preference rules* or *preference constraints* to consist of statements of the form $p \trianglerighteq q$, for $p, q \in \mathcal{L}$, meaning p is desired at least as much as q, and $p \triangleright q$, meaning p is desired more than q. Models of $\mathcal{L}_r$ consist of preference orders over models of $\mathcal{L}$. We define the meaning of preference rules in terms of the notions of $\mathcal{L}$-model equivalence and modification.

The *support* of a sentence $p \in \mathcal{L}$ is the minimal set of atoms determining the truth of p, denoted $s(p)$. The support of p is the same as the set of atoms appearing in an irredundant sum-of-products sentence logically equivalent to p.

Two models m and m' are *equivalent modulo* p if they are the same outside the support of p. Formally, $m \equiv m' \bmod p$ iff

$$m \backslash (literals(s(p))) = m' \backslash (literals(s(p)))$$

Model modification is defined as follows. A set of *model modifications of m making p true*, written $m[p]$, are those models satisfying p which assign the same truth values to atoms outside the support of p as m does. That is,

$$m[p] = \{m' \in [p] \mid m \equiv m' \bmod p\}.$$

Formally, we say that a preference order $\succsim$ *satisfies* $p \trianglerighteq q$ if and only if for all m in $\mathcal{M}$, $m' \in m[p \wedge \neg q]$ and $m'' \in m[\neg p \wedge q]$, we have $m' \succsim m''$. This means that when two models assign the same truth values to all features not in the support of either p or q, one making p true and q false is weakly preferred to one making p false and q true. The preference order satisfies a strict *ceteris paribus* preference $p \triangleright q$ iff in addition it strictly prefers some model making p true and q false to some model making p false and q true.

For a preference rule c, we write $[c]$ to denote the set of preference orders over $\mathcal{M}$ that satisfy c, that is, consistent with the constraint expressed by c. We write $[C]$ for a set of preference rules to denote the set of orders consistent with each $c \in C$, that is, $[C] = \bigcap_{c \in C}[c]$. Consistent rules and rule sets admit at least one consistent preference order. If a preference rule c implies that $m' \succ m''$, for $m', m'' \in \mathcal{M}$, we write $m' \succ_c m''$. For a set C of preference rules, we write $m' \succ_C m''$ to mean that $m' \succ_c m''$ for each $c \in C$.

We define the support of C, denoted $F(C)$, to be the set of features in $\mathcal{L}$ present in the support of statements of $\mathcal{L}$ appearing in constraints in C. Formally, $F(C)$ contains those features f such that either f or $\neg f$ appears in $\bigcup_{c \in C} s(c)$.

The following examines the problem of constructing, for a finite set C of *ceteris paribus* preference rules, a utility function u that represents some order in $[C]$ in an efficient manner.

Intermediate representation

The utility construction methods developed here employ an intermediate representation in terms of rules that relate paired patterns of specified and "don't care" feature values.

Let C be a finite set of preference rules. Because each preference rule mentions only finitely many features, $F(C)$ is also finite, and we write N to mean $|F(C)|$.

We construct utility functions representing the constraints in C in terms of model features. Features not specified in any rule in C are not relevant to compute the utility of a model, since there is no preference information about them in the set C. Accordingly, we focus our attention on $F(C)$.

We define the intermediate representation relative to an enumeration $\mathcal{V} = (f_1, \ldots, f_N)$ of $F(C)$.

We define the language $\mathcal{L}_r(\mathcal{V})$ of intermediate rules in terms of a language $\mathcal{L}(\mathcal{V})$ of intermediate propositions over the ternary alphabet $\Gamma = \{0, 1, *\}$.

A statement in $\mathcal{L}(\mathcal{V})$ consists of a sequence of N letters drawn from the alphabet Γ, so that $\mathcal{L}(\mathcal{V})$ consists of words of length N over Γ. For example, if $\mathcal{V} = (f_1, f_2, f_3)$, we have $*10 \in \mathcal{L}(\mathcal{V})$. Given a statement $p \in \mathcal{L}(\mathcal{V})$ and a feature

$f \in F(C)$, we write $f(p)$ for the value in Γ assigned to f in p. In particular, if $f = \mathcal{V}_i$, then $f(p) = p_i$.

An intermediate rule in $\mathcal{L}_r(\mathcal{V})$ consists of a triple $p \succ q$ in which $p, q \in \mathcal{L}(\mathcal{V})$ have matching $*$ values. That is, $p \succ q$ is in $\mathcal{L}_r(\mathcal{V})$ just in case $p_i = *$ if and only if $q_i = *$ for all $1 \leq i \leq N$. For example, if $\mathcal{V} = (f_1, f_2, f_3)$, $\mathcal{L}_r(\mathcal{V})$ contains the expression $*10 \succ *00$ but not the expression $*10 \succ 0*0$. We refer to the statement in $\mathcal{L}(\mathcal{V})$ left of the $\succ$ symbol in a rule r as the left-hand side of r, and denote it $LHS(r)$. We define right-hand side $RHS(r)$ analogously. Thus $p = LHS(p \succ q)$ and $q = RHS(p \succ q)$.

We regard statements of $\mathcal{L}(\mathcal{V})$ containing no $*$ letters as *models* of $\mathcal{L}(\mathcal{V})$, and write $\mathcal{M}(\mathcal{V})$ to denote the set of all such models. We say a model m *satisfies* s, written $m \models s$, just in case m assigns the same truth value to each feature as s does for each non $*$ feature in s. That is, $m \models s$ iff $f(m) = f(s)$ for each $f \in F(C)$ such that $f(s) \neq *$. For example, 0011 satisfies both $*0*1$ and $00**$.

We project models in $\mathcal{M}$ to models in $\mathcal{M}(\mathcal{V})$ by a mapping $\alpha : \mathcal{M} \to \mathcal{M}(\mathcal{V})$ defined, for each $m \in \mathcal{M}$ and $f \in F(C)$, so that $f(\alpha(m)) = 1$ if $f \in m$ and $f(\alpha(m)) = 0$ if $\neg f \in m$. This projection induces an equivalence relation on $\mathcal{M}$, and we write $[m]$ to mean the set of models in $\mathcal{M}$ mapped to the same model in $\mathcal{M}(\mathcal{V})$ as m, namely $[m] = \{m' \in \mathcal{M} \mid \alpha(m') = \alpha(m)\}$.

We say that a pair of models (m, m') of $\mathcal{L}(\mathcal{V})$ *satisfies* a rule r in $\mathcal{L}_r(\mathcal{V})$, and write $(m, m') \models r$, if m satisfies $LHS(r)$, m' satisfies $RHS(r)$, and m, m' have the same value for those features represented by $*$ in r, that is, $m_i = m'_i$ for each $1 \leq i \leq N$ such that $LHS(r)_i = *$. For example, $(100, 010) \models 10* \succ 01*$, but $(101, 010) \not\models 10* \succ 01*$.

The meaning $[r]$ of a rule r in $\mathcal{L}_r(\mathcal{V})$ is the set of all preference orders $\succ$ over $\mathcal{M}$ such that for each $m, m' \in \mathcal{M}$, if $(\alpha(m), \alpha(m')) \models r$, then $m \succ m'$. Thus a rule $**01 \succ **10$ represents the four specific preferences

$$0001 \succ 0010 \quad 0101 \succ 0110$$
$$1001 \succ 1010 \quad 1101 \succ 1110$$

Note that this says nothing at all about the preference relationship between, *e.g.*, 0101 and 1010.

Constructing subutility functions over subsets of features requires the ability to consider models restricted to these subsets. We write $\mathcal{M}[S]$ to denote the set of models over a feature set $S \subseteq F$, so that $\mathcal{M} = \mathcal{M}[F]$. If $m \in \mathcal{M}[S]$ and $S' \subseteq S$, we write $m \upharpoonright S'$ to denote the *restriction* of m to S', that is, the model $m' \in \mathcal{M}[S']$ assigning the same values as m to all features in S'. We say that a model $m \in \mathcal{M}[S]$ satisfies a model $m' \in \mathcal{M}[S']$, written $m \models m'$ just in case $S' \subseteq S$ and $m' = m \upharpoonright S'$.

The *support features* of a statement p in $\mathcal{L}(\mathcal{V})$, written $s(p)$, are exactly those features in p that are assigned value either 0 or 1, which represent the least set of features needed to determine if a model of $\mathcal{L}(\mathcal{V})$ satisfies p. The support features of a rule r in $\mathcal{L}_r(\mathcal{V})$, denoted $s(r)$, are the features in $s(LHS(r))$. The definition of $\mathcal{L}_r(\mathcal{V})$ implies that $s(LHS(r)) = s(RHS(r))$.

One can show (McGeachie 2002) that, given a set C of *ceteris paribus* rules we can convert them into a set C^* of intermediate representation rules equivalent in the sense that both sets denote the same set of preference orders $[C] = [C^*]$. Thus, we can use the language $\mathcal{L}(\mathcal{V})$ in the following and know that our conclusions hold over statements in $\mathcal{L}$.

A basic utility function

We now define one utility function, $u : \mathcal{M}(\mathcal{V}) \to \mathbb{R}$ consistent with a set C^* of rules in the intermediate representation $\mathcal{L}_r(\mathcal{V})$. Composition of this function with the projection $\alpha : \mathcal{M} \to \mathcal{M}(\mathcal{V})$ yields a utility function on $\mathcal{M}$.

To construct this utility function, we first use the rules in C^* to define a directed graph $G(C^*)$ over $\mathcal{M}(\mathcal{V})$, called a *model graph*, that represents the preferences expressed in C^*. Each node in the graph represents one of the 2^N possible models $\mathcal{M}(\mathcal{V})$. The model graph $G(C^*)$ contains an edge $e(m_1, m_2)$ from source m_1 to sink m_2 if and only if $(m_1, m_2) \models r$ for some rule $r \in C^*$. Each edge represents a preference for the source over the sink. If C^* is consistent, then $G(C^*)$ is acyclic; a cycle would indicate the inconsistency of C^*. We can determine whether m is preferred to m' by looking for a path from m to m' in $G(C^*)$. The existence of such a path means $m \succ m'$.

The utility function used here assigns to a model $m \in \mathcal{M}(\mathcal{V})$ a value $u(m)$ equal to the number of nodes on the longest path originating from m in $G(C^*)$. We call this the *minimizing* utility function and elsewhere show it consistent with the preferences expressed in C^* (McGeachie & Doyle 2002).

Utility independence

Utility independence (UI) exists when the contribution to utility of some features is independent of the values of other features. In the following subsections, we demonstrate how this expedites our calculation of utility from preferences in the intermediate representation.

The general definition for utility independence of features S_i of features S_j is

$$[(m_2 \uparrow S_i) \cup (m_1 \uparrow S_j) \succ (m_3 \uparrow S_i) \cup (m_1 \uparrow S_j)] \Rightarrow$$
$$[(m_2 \uparrow S_i) \cup (m_4 \uparrow S_j) \succ (m_3 \uparrow S_i) \cup (m_4 \uparrow S_j)] \quad (1)$$

for all m_1, m_2, m_3, m_4 (Keeney & Raiffa 1976). The idea is that values m_2 for S_i are preferred to values m_3 for S_i, no matter what values S_j happens to assume. We are interested in computing a partition $S = \{S_1, S_2, ..., S_Q\}$ of $F(C)$ such that each set S_i is utility independent of its complement, $F(C) \backslash S_i$. That is, the feature sets S_i are all *mutually utility independent* (MUI). A basic decision theory result shows that a set of MUI features has an *additive decomposition* utility function of the form

$$u(m) = \sum_{i=1}^{k} t_i u_i(m), \quad (2)$$

for *subutility* functions $u_i : \mathcal{M}(\mathcal{V}) \to \mathbb{R}$ assigning utility values to models based on the restriction of the models to S_i. Having a large number of utility independent feature sets of small cardinality therefore greatly simplifies the computation of a utility function.

Common methods for determining utility independence assume independence relations are given *a priori* or elicited directly from a human decision maker (Keeney & Raiffa 1976; Bacchus & Grove 1996). To employ this concept in automatically computing utility functions, we use a different approach. We first assume that each feature is utility independent of all other features, and then try to discover for which features this assumption is invalid by reference to the preferences in C^*. For each $f \in F(C)$, we assume that f is UI of $F(C) \backslash \{f\}$. We then look for evidence that demonstrates two feature sets are not UI of each other.

The intuitive idea is to find a pair of rules that demonstrate that preference for some features depends on the value of other features. To use a very simple example, suppose $\mathcal{V} = (f_1, f_2, f_3)$, and consider two rules in $\mathcal{L}_r(\mathcal{V})$; the rules $01* \succ 11*$ and $10* \succ 00*$. It is easy to see that the preference expressed over f_1 switches depending on the value of f_2. *I.e.*, $\{f_1\}$ is not UI of $\{f_2\}$.

Sets S_i, S_j are utility dependent if we can demonstrate models $m_1, m_2, m_3,$ and m_4 for some feature sets and a pair of rules r_1, r_2 such that the condition (1) does not hold. The correspondence is analogous to condition (1): we want all of the following

$$\begin{aligned} (m_2 \uparrow S_i) \cup (m_1 \uparrow S_j) &\models LHS(r_1), \\ (m_3 \uparrow S_i) \cup (m_1 \uparrow S_j) &\models RHS(r_1), \\ (m_2 \uparrow S_i) \cup (m_4 \uparrow S_j) &\models RHS(r_2), \\ (m_3 \uparrow S_i) \cup (m_4 \uparrow S_j) &\models LHS(r_2). \end{aligned} \quad (3)$$

A method for finding such r_1, r_2, S_i, S_j is as follows. Since S_j must be a subset of the support features of r_1, and m_1 restricted to S_j must satisfy both $LHS(r_1)$ restricted to S_j and $RHS(r_1)$ restricted to S_j, we can look for rules of this form. Lexically, these rules are easy to recognize: some of the features specified in the rule have the same value on the left- and right-hand sides of the rule. Then we look for another rule, r_2, with the same property: there is a set of features S_j' that is a subset of the support features of r_2 and there is an m_4 satisfies both $LHS(r_2)$ restricted to S_j' and $RHS(r_2)$ restricted to S_j', with the additional restriction that S_j' must be a subset of S_j. Again, we are looking for a rule that specifies the same values for the same features on the left- and right-hand sides, but these features must be a subset of those features we found for r_1. If the previous conditions hold, we have fixed $m_1, m_4,$ and S_j used in conditions (1) and (3).

We then check that r_1, r_2 are such that an S_i can be found that is disjoint with S_j and a subset of the support features of both r_1 and r_2, and an m_2 can be found that satisfies both $LHS(r_1)$ restricted to S_i and $RHS(r_2)$ restricted to S_i. Here we are looking for a preference over models restricted to S_i that switches with the values assigned to S_j. Again, this is easy to check for, by doing lexical comparisons on the left- and right-hand sides of the support feature sets of rules. If all the preceding holds for some S_i, S_j, then S_i is utility dependent on S_j. We are assured of this since the condition (1) is violated.

We require a partition $S = \{S_1, S_2, ..., S_Q\}$ of $F(C)$, into MUI feature sets. A partition can be computed by starting with a set S of singleton sets; $S_1 = \{f_1\}, S_2 = \{f_2\}$, ..., $S_N = \{f_N\}$. We consider each pair of rules (r_1, r_2) in

C^*, and check if a preference for one feature changes with the value assigned to another feature by using the preceding method. If so, we have discovered sets of utility dependent features, and we update our partition S by joining these two sets together.

After performing such overlap calculations, we have computed a partition of $F(C)$ into MUI subsets. This method clearly produces a partition by starting with one, by combining utility-dependent subsets, and by stopping when no two subsets exhibit utility dependence on each other, making the partition elements MUI.

Utility computation

We now describe how to compute one utility function consistent with the set C^* of transformed input *ceteris paribus* preferences expressed in $\mathcal{L}_r(\mathcal{V})$. Using the methods of the previous section, we find a partition of $F(C)$ into MUI feature sets $S_1, S_2, \ldots, S_Q$ and seek an additive utility function of the form given in Equation (2) consisting of a linear combination of subutilities, with each subutility function a separate function of a particular S_i.

We have two tasks: to craft the subutility functions u_i and to choose the scaling constants t_i. We accomplish these two tasks in roughly the following way. We construct subutility functions by *restricting* rules to a set S_i. This is essentially a projection of a rule onto a particular set of features, in the same manner as we have defined restriction of models to a set of features. We then apply the graph-theoretic utility function definition to these restricting rules to obtain subutility functions u_i. However, rules that do not conflict in general can conflict when restricted to different feature sets. We use a boolean constraint satisfaction solver to resolve these conflicts. To assign values to scaling parameters t_i, we define linear inequalities that constrain the variables t_i and use standard linear programming methods to solve the inequalities for suitable scaling values t_i.

Subutility functions

We first define subutility functions $u_i(m)$ that take as input the values for the features S_i, and return an integer.

We examine the structure of the rules in the intermediate representation. Since we are only concerned with the features S_i, we can ignore rules that do not have members of S_i in their support feature set. We construct a *restricted model graph*, $G_i(C^*)$, where we consider each model $m \in \mathcal{M}[S_i]$ to be a node in the graph. Each rule r and pair $(m_1, m_2) \models r$, with $m_1, m_2 \in \mathcal{M}[S_i]$, indicate a directed edge from m_1 to m_2 in $G_i(C^*)$. Note that if a rule $r \in C^*$ has $S_i \backslash s(r) \neq \emptyset$, then the rule makes more than one edge in the model graph $G_i(C^*)$. Specifically, a rule r makes

$$2^{|S_i| - |S_i \cap s(r)|}$$

edges. The construction of this graph $G_i(C^*)$ exactly parallels the construction of the general model graph G, as described earlier. We then use the minimizing utility function for u_i, wherein each node has utility equal to the length of the longest path originating at the node.

Conflicting rules Although we assume that the input preferences C^* have no conflicting rules, it is possible that a restricted model graph $G_i(C^*)$ has cycles in it even though a model graph $G(C^*)$ for $F(C)$ does not. Since our definition of graph theoretic utility functions does not handle cycles, we must fix this difficulty before we can use such a function for a subutility function.

Let R_i represent the set of rules $r \in C^*$ such that $s(r) \cap S_i \neq \emptyset$. Rules in a set R_i *conflict* if they imply a cycle in any model graph $G_i(C^*)$ of some utility independent set of features S_i. Consider now a minimal set of conflicting rules R_i, where for each r in R_i, r models $\mathcal{L}_r(\mathcal{V})$, so that for any $r \in R_i$, $R_i \backslash \{r\}$ implies no cycles or implies a different cycle in the model graph $G_i(C^*)$ of S_i. Since we assume the input preferences are not contradictory, a set of rules can only conflict when the rules are restricted to a particular subset of their support features. The restriction of a rule to a set of features S is another rule in the intermediate representation, but over fewer features:

$$r \upharpoonright S = RHS(r) \upharpoonright S \succ LHS(r) \upharpoonright S$$

Consider rules x, y in $\mathcal{L}_r(\mathcal{V})$, with $\mathcal{V} = (f_1, f_2, f_3, f_4)$, and $x = *01* \succ *10*$, $y = **01 \succ **10$. If we examine the restriction to feature three: $x \upharpoonright \{f_3\}$ and $y \upharpoonright \{f_3\}$, then we have $x \upharpoonright \{f_3\} = 1 \succ 0$ and $y \upharpoonright \{f_3\} = 0 \succ 1$. Thus, when restricted to f_3 it is inconsistent to assert both x and y. In these cases, we say that x, y conflict on f_3. If we let $S = \{f_3\}$, then we say x, y conflict on the set S.

Let $r_a, r_b, r_c \in R_i$. Suppose r_a, r_b, and r_c conflict on S_i. *E.g.* we might have $r_a \upharpoonright S_i = 001 \succ 100$, $r_b \upharpoonright S_i = 100 \succ 010$, $r_c \upharpoonright S_i = 010 \succ 001$. We resolve conflicts by choosing one of the conflicting rules and removing the rule, temporarily, from the set R_i. The following section explains how to choose which rule to remove.

Suppose there are sets of conflicting rules $Y_1, Y_2, \ldots, Y_K$, where each is composed of rules $r \in R_i$. By definition, each set Y_k represents a cycle in $G_i(C^*)$. We require that all distinct cycles in $G_i(C^*)$ are represented by (perhaps duplicate) conflicting rule sets Y_k. Since Y_k is a minimal set implying a particular cycle in $G_i(C^*)$, for any $r \in Y_k$ we know $Y_k \backslash \{r\}$ does not imply the same cycle in $G_i(C^*)$. All cycles in $G_i(C^*)$ are represented by some $Y_k \in \{Y_1, Y_2, \ldots, Y_K\}$. We will choose a rule $r \in Y_k$ for each set Y_k, and remove r from R_i (discussed below). Since we stipulate that all $r' \in Y_k$ are taken from the set R_i, when we remove r from R_i this also removes r from all sets Y_k which might contain r. After removal of r, we rebuild $G_i(C^*)$ with the remains of R_i. We now have a model graph $G_i(C^*)$ that is cycle-free. Note that, after this removal process, $|R_i| \geq 1$, since one rule cannot imply a cycle. With no cycles, we can define u_i to be the subutility function for S_i based on the minimizing utility function of $G_i(C^*)$. We say that the resulting function u_i *agrees* with rules $r \in R_i$, and that u_i *disagrees* with those rules r that were removed from R_i. When u_i agrees with r, then for all $(m_1, m_2) \models r$, $u_i(m_1) > u_i(m_2)$.

If a utility function u is consistent with a set of preferences C^*, then u represents some order in $[C^*]$. This is equivalent to having $u(m_1) > u(m_2)$ whenever $m_1 \succ_{C^*} m_2$. This translates into the following property of the subutility functions u_i relating utility contributions due to the subutility functions agreeing and disagreeing with an intermediate rule. To state the result, we define $S_a(r)$ and $S_d(r)$ to be the sets of indices of subutility functions respectively agreeing and disagreeing with r.

Theorem 1 *A utility function u is consistent with a rule r if for all $(m_1, m_2) \models r$, we have*

$$\sum_{i \in S_a(r)} t_i(u_i(m_1) - u_i(m_2)) > \sum_{j \in S_d(r)} t_j(u_j(m_2) - u_j(m_1)) \tag{4}$$

We omit the proof.

This theorem has the following important consequence.

Corollary 1 *In a utility function u of the form (2) over a partition of $F(C)$ consistent with C^*, each rule $r \in C^*$ must agree with some subutility function u_i.*

Otherwise we have $|S_a(r)| = 0$ and $|S_d(r)| \geq 1$, and Equation (4) will not be satisfied.

Choosing scaling parameters

Once we have a collection of utility independent sets S_i, we create subutility functions as described above. We can then choose scaling parameters t_i based on which rules disagree with each subutility function u_i. There are several possible strategies for choosing these parameters. Due to space constraints, we mention briefly the simplest case, then present the most general method.

If no subutility functions disagree with any rules, we have the following case. For any rule r and all i such that $r \in R_i$, u_i agrees with r. We have: $u_i(m_1) > u_i(m_2)$ for each u_i, and each pair $(m_1, m_2) \models r$. Then we are unconstrained in our choices of t_i, since $t_i u_i(m_1) > t_i u_i(m_2)$ holds for any $t_i > 0$.

Constraint satisfaction If we have several UI sets S_i with conflicts between rules, then we must use a more complicated strategy for assigning scaling parameters t_i, in which case we construct and solve a constraint satisfaction problem from the set of conflicts. Constraint solvers exist that can quickly handle problems with tens of thousands of terms (Selman, Levesque, & Mitchell 1992). Although this may be costly, this price is paid only when the utility function is constructed. The evaluation of the utility function on models of $\mathcal{L}(\mathcal{V})$ is independent of the construction cost.

Corollary 1 states that each rule r must agree with some subutility function u_i. For each utility independent feature set S_i, let $Y_{i1}, Y_{i2}, ..., Y_{iK}$ be sets of conflicting rules, where each is composed of rules $r \in R_i$. Each set Y_{ik} represents a cycle in $G_i(C^*)$; and let Y be the set of all such conflicts. Let $R_c = \cup_{i,k} Y_{ik}$ be the set of all rules involved in any conflict.

Our satisfiability problem uses a conjunction of disjunctions (conjunctive normal form) of propositional variables z_{ij}, with z_{ij} interpreted as stating that subutility function u_i agrees with rule $r_j \in R_c$. Let $X_j = \{l \mid S_l \cap s(r_j) \neq \emptyset\}$ denote the set of indices of UI sets that overlap with r_j.

Conjuncts in the formula are of one of two forms: those representing the subutility functions indicated by X_j; and those representing conflicts between rules of a particular cycle Y_{ik}. Those of the first category are of form $\vee_{i \in X_j} z_{ij}$. This represents the possible subutility functions a rule might agree with, accordingly in a solution to the formula, one of these variables must be true.

The other conjuncts represent a particular cycle on a particular UI set. If Y_{ik} is a conflict set on S_i, then the conjunct is of the form $\vee_{j:r_j \in Y_{ik}} \neg z_{ij}$. That is, u_i must disagree with at least one of the rules in Y_{ik}. Combining conjunctions of both types, we can write the entire satisfiability formula as

$$\left(\bigwedge_{j=1}^{Q} \left(\bigvee_{i \in X_j} z_{ij} \right) \right) \wedge \left(\bigwedge_{Y_{ik} \in Y} \left(\bigvee_{j:r_j \in Y_{ik}} \neg z_{ij} \right) \right)$$

Consider an example. Suppose we have sets S_1, S_2 with rule conflicts. Further suppose that $r_1, r_2 \in R_1, R_2$, and that $s(r_1) = s(r_2) = S_1 \cup S_2$. Suppose that $Y_{11} = \{r_1, r_2\}$ and $Y_{21} = \{r_1, r_2\}$, that is, r_1, r_2 conflict on both of S_1, S_2. We make a satisfiability formula as so:

$$(z_{11} \vee z_{21}) \wedge (z_{12} \vee z_{22}) \wedge (\neg z_{11} \vee \neg z_{12}) \wedge (\neg z_{22} \vee \neg z_{21})$$

Once we have this formula, we use a solver to arrive at a solution. It can be shown that the satisfiability problem is always satisfiable if the preferences C^* admit an additive decomposition utility function (McGeachie 2002). A solution to the satisfiability problem can be translated back into a construction for the subutility functions using the translation defined above, we simply look at which subutility functions disagree with which rules. We then remove those rules from the relevant sets R_i, then construct u_i according to R_i, which is now conflict-free.

Linear inequalities The satisfiability solver tells us which rules disagree with which subutility functions. However, we must then set the scaling parameters, t_i, so as to satisfy Equation (4). We can do so by building a list of constraints on the values that the scaling parameters may assume.

Suppose subutility functions for the utility-independent sets $S_d(r)$ disagreed with r, while subutility functions for the utility-independent sets $S_a(r)$ agreed with r. Then we add an inequality of the form

$$\sum_{i \in S_a(r) \cup S_d(r)} t_i u_i(m_1) > \sum_{i \in S_a(r) \cup S_d(r)} t_i u_i(m_2)$$

to a list I of inequalities for each pair $(m_1, m_2) \models r$. The inequalities I constrain the total utility function to assign higher utility to m_1 than to m_2. Note that the inequality need not contain terms for u_j for j not in $S_d(r)$ or $S_a(r)$, since, by definition of $(m_1, m_2) \models r$, we have $m_1 \uparrow S_j = m_2 \uparrow S_j$. The total number of linear inequalities is far less than $2^{F(C)}$. Specifically, each rule r contributes

$$\prod_{S_i : s(r) \cap S_i \neq \emptyset} 2^{|S_i \setminus s(r)|} \tag{5}$$

inequalities to the set I of inequalities. One obtains (5) by noticing the number of inequalities contributed by a rule is the number of different values of $u_i(m_1) - u_i(m_2)$ for $i \in (S_d(r) \cup S_a(r))$ and $(m_1, m_2) \models r$.

We solve the system of linear inequalities I using any linear inequality solver. We note that it is possible to phrase this as a linear programming problem, and use any of a number of popular linear programming techniques to find scaling parameters t_i. For example, see (Chvátal 1983).

It can be shown that if the system of linear inequalities, I, has a solution, this solution corresponds to a utility function u consistent with C^*. If the inequalities prove unsatisfiable, it may be because the preferences do not admit a linear scaling between subutility functions. We can either follow (McGeachie & Doyle 2002) and use the minimizing utility function over the degenerate partition $S = \{F(C)\}$ or, less drastically, join partition elements together to perform constraint satisfaction and linear programming on a smaller problem (a solution used in (Boutilier, Bacchus, & Brafman 2001) to solve the same problem). Work in progress addresses optimal choice of which feature sets to join together.

Conclusions

We have summarized a method for constructing numeric utility-function representations of preferences specified using the *ceteris paribus* preference logic of (Doyle, Shoham, & Wellman 1991). We sketch the complexity of our methods, then compare to similar *ceteris paribus* reasoning systems.

There are two different efficiency questions to ask. One is the time and space required to construct u, the other is the time and space required to evaluate u on a particular model m. Constructing u involves first computing the utility independent partition of features, which takes time $O(|C^*|^2)$. Then we solve a satisfiability problem, where time required depends on the number of rules involved in conflicts on each UI set. In pathological cases, the number of conflicts could be as high as $|C^*|!$, if every rule conflicts with every other set of rules. Finally we solve a system of linear inequalities, where the number of inequalities is

$$\sum_{r \in C^*} \prod_{S_i : s(r) \cap S_i \neq \emptyset} 2^{|S_i \setminus s(r)|}$$

Computing $u(m)$ involves computing $u_i(m)$, where u_i is a minimizing utility function, for all the UI feature sets. Each of the subutility functions can be exponential in the size of the UI set, $|S_i|$; in the worst case, this means exponential in $|F(C)|$.

Since we assume our input preferences $|C|$ are not inherently contradictory, we anticipate in practice there will be manageable numbers of conflicting rules. If in addition, each set S_i is of size $\log N$, our algorithm requires polynomial time and space. There are less than $|C^*| * \prod_{i=1}^{Q} 2^{\log N}$ linear inequalities, so construction of u takes polynomial time. Each model graph $G_i(C^*)$ has at most $2^{\log N}$ nodes, so evaluating $u(m)$ takes time $O(k * N)$.

Other researchers have proposed methods of computing with different representations of *ceteris paribus* preferences. The work of (Bacchus & Grove 1995) and (Mura & Shoham 1999) use quantified preference statements, in contrast to our qualitative preference statements. Our work is similar to

the work of Boutilier, Bacchus, Brafman (2001), who compute an additive decomposition utility function from quantified preferences. Their method uses subutility functions that are exponential-size lookup tables, which is similar to our exponential-size graph theoretic subutility functions. Earlier work by (Boutilier *et al.* 1999) uses qualitative conditional *ceteris paribus* preferences, and presents some strong heuristics for computing dominance queries, but uses a very different representation for *ceteris paribus* preferences.

Acknowledgements

This work was supported in part by DARPA under contract F30602-99-1-0509. Michael McGeachie is supported in part by a training grant from the National Library of Medicine, and a grant from the Pfizer corporation.

References

Bacchus, F., and Grove, A. 1995. Graphical models for preference and utility. In *Proceedings of the Eleventh Conference on Uncertainty in Artificial Intelligence*, 3–19. Morgan Kaufmann.

Bacchus, F., and Grove, A. 1996. Utility independence in a qualitative decision theory. In *Proceedings of the Fifth International Conference on Knowledge Representation and Reasoning*, 542–552. Morgan Kaufmann.

Boutilier, C.; Bacchus, F.; and Brafman, R. L. 2001. Ucp-networks: A directed graphical representation of conditional utilities. In *Proceedings of Seventeenth Conference on Uncertainty in Artificial Intelligence*. To Appear.

Boutilier, C.; Brafman, R. I.; Hoos, H. H.; and Poole, D. 1999. Reasoning with conditional ceteris paribus preference statements. In *Proceedings of Uncertainty in Artificial Intelligence 1999 (UAI-99)*.

Chvátal, V. 1983. *Linear Programming*. New York: W.H. Freeman and Company.

Doyle, J., and Thomason, R. H. 1999. Background to qualitative decision theory. *AI Magazine* 20(2):55–68.

Doyle, J.; Shoham, Y.; and Wellman, M. P. 1991. A logic of relative desire (preliminary report). In Ras, Z., ed., *Proceedings of the Sixth International Symposium on Methodologies for Intelligent Systems*, Lecture Notes in Computer Science. Berlin: Springer-Verlag.

Keeney, R., and Raiffa, H. 1976. *Decisions with Multiple Objectives: Preferences and Value Tradeoffs*. New York: Wiley and Sons.

McGeachie, M., and Doyle, J. 2002. Utility functions for ceteris paribus preferences. Submitted for publication.

McGeachie, M. 2002. Utility functions for ceteris paribus preferences. Master's thesis, Massachusetts Institute of Technology, Cambridge, Massachusetts. In preparation.

Mura, P. L., and Shoham, Y. 1999. Expected utility networks. In *Proc. of 15th conference on Uncertainty in Artificial Intelligence*, 366–373.

Selman, B.; Levesque, H. J.; and Mitchell, D. 1992. A new method for solving hard satisfiability problems. In Rosenbloom, P., and Szolovits, P., eds., *Proceedings of the Tenth National Conference on Artificial Intelligence*, 440–446. Menlo Park, California: AAAI Press.

Greedy Linear Value-approximation for Factored Markov Decision Processes

Relu Patrascu
University of Waterloo
rpatrasc@cs.uwaterloo.ca

Pascal Poupart
University of Toronto
ppoupart@cs.toronto.edu

Dale Schuurmans
University of Waterloo
dale@cs.uwaterloo.ca

Craig Boutilier
University of Toronto
cebly@cs.toronto.edu

Carlos Guestrin
Stanford University
guestrin@stanford.edu

Abstract

Significant recent work has focused on using linear representations to approximate value functions for factored Markov decision processes (MDPs). Current research has adopted linear programming as an effective means to calculate approximations for a *given* set of basis functions, tackling very large MDPs as a result. However, a number of issues remain unresolved: *How accurate are the approximations produced by linear programs? How hard is it to produce better approximations?* and *Where do the basis functions come from?* To address these questions, we first investigate the complexity of minimizing the Bellman error of a linear value function approximation—showing that this is an inherently hard problem. Nevertheless, we provide a branch and bound method for calculating Bellman error and performing approximate policy iteration for general factored MDPs. These methods are more accurate than linear programming, but more expensive. We then consider linear programming itself and investigate methods for automatically constructing sets of basis functions that allow this approach to produce good approximations. The techniques we develop are guaranteed to reduce L_1 error, but can also empirically reduce Bellman error.

1 Introduction

Markov decision processes (MDPs) pose a problem at the heart of research on optimal control and reinforcement learning in stochastic environments. This is a well studied area and classical solution methods have been known for several decades. However, the standard algorithms—value-iteration, policy-iteration and linear programming—all produce optimal control policies for MDPs that are expressed in explicit form; that is, the policy, value function and state transition model are all represented in a tabular manner that enumerates the entire state space. This renders classical methods impractical for all but toy problems. The real goal is to achieve solution methods that scale up reasonably in the size of the *state description*, not the size of the state space itself (which is usually either exponential or infinite). Justifiably, most recent work in the area has concentrated on scaling-up solution techniques to handle realistic problems.

There are two basic premises to scaling-up: (1) exploiting structure in the MDP model (i.e. structure in the reward

function and the state transition model); and (2) exploiting structure in an approximate representation of the optimal value function (or policy). Most credible attempts at scaling-up have exploited both types of structure. Even then, it is surprisingly hard to formulate an optimization method that can handle large state descriptions while reliably producing value functions or policies with small approximation errors.

Initial research on expressing MDPs compactly has considered representations such as decision trees or decision diagrams to represent the state transition model and reward function in a concise manner (Boutilier, Dearden, & Goldszmidt 2000; Boutilier, Dean, & Hanks 1999). Another recent approach has investigated using factored-table state transition and reward models, where the state variables exhibit limited dependence and have localized influence (Koller & Parr 1999). Both representational paradigms allow complex MDPs to be represented in a compact form. Unfortunately, neither ensures that the optimal value function (or policy) has a compact representation (Koller & Parr 1999). Thus, it appears that one still has to consider compact approximations to the value function (or policy) to make progress.

Numerous schemes have been investigated for representing approximate value functions and policies in a compact form, including: hierarchical decompositions (Dietterich 2000), decision trees and diagrams (Boutilier, Dearden, & Goldszmidt 2000) generalized linear functions (Koller & Parr 1999; 2000; Guestrin, Koller, & Parr 2001a), splines (Trick & Zin 1997), neural networks (Bertsekas & Tsitsiklis 1996), and products of experts (Sallans & Hinton 2000).

This paper focuses on using factored-table MDP representations in conjunction with *linear* value function approximators. Linear approximators have the advantage of providing universal approximation ability (given a sufficient basis) and allowing the widest array of computational techniques to be brought to bear. Moreover, linear approximations interact very well with factored MDP representations (Koller & Parr 1999; 2000). This combination allows approximation methods to be devised which can be feasibly applied to very large MDPs. Two recent examples of this are the approximate policy iteration technique of (Guestrin, Koller, & Parr 2001a) and the approximate linear programming approaches of (Guestrin, Koller, & Parr 2001b; Schuurmans & Patrascu 2001). Many researchers have begun to adopt linear programming as a particularly convenient method for generating value approximations for large MDPs (de Farias & Van Roy 2001). A few issues remain unclear, however. First, the extent to which linear programming sacrifices approximation accuracy for computational expedience is not well understood. Second, there is a need for a systematic method for improving approximation accuracy in cases where it is insufficient. Finally, previous research has not significantly addressed the question of where the basis functions come from in the first place. We attempt to address these three questions here.

2 Background

We will consider MDPs with finite state and action spaces and assume the goal of maximizing infinite horizon discounted reward. We assume states are represented by vectors $\mathbf{s} = s_1, ..., s_n$ of length n, where for simplicity we assume the state variables $s_1, ..., s_n$ are in $\{0, 1\}$; hence the total number of states is $N = 2^n$. We also assume that there is a small finite set of actions $A = \{a_1, ..., a_\ell\}$. An MDP is then defined by: (1) a state transition model $P(\mathbf{s}'|\mathbf{s}, a)$ which specifies the probability of the next state $\mathbf{s}'$ given the current state $\mathbf{s}$ and action a; (2) a reward function $R(\mathbf{s}, a)$ which specifies the immediate reward obtained by taking action a in state $\mathbf{s}$; and (3) a discount factor γ, $0 \leq \gamma < 1$. The problem is to determine an optimal control policy $\pi^* : \mathbf{S} \to A$ that achieves maximum expected future discounted reward in every state.

To understand the classical solution methods it is useful to define some auxiliary concepts. For any policy π, the value function $V^\pi : \mathbf{S} \to I\!R$ denotes the expected future discounted reward achieved by policy π in each state $\mathbf{s}$. This V^π satisfies a fixed point relationship $V^\pi = B^\pi V^\pi$, where B^π operates on arbitrary functions v over the state space

$$(B^\pi v)(\mathbf{s}) = R(\mathbf{s}, \pi(\mathbf{s})) + \gamma \sum_{\mathbf{s}'} P(\mathbf{s}'|\mathbf{s}, \pi(\mathbf{s}))v(\mathbf{s}')$$

Another important operator, B^a, is defined for each action

$$(B^a v)(\mathbf{s}) = R(\mathbf{s}, a) + \gamma \sum_{\mathbf{s}'} P(\mathbf{s}'|\mathbf{s}, a)v(\mathbf{s}')$$

The action-value function $Q^\pi : \mathbf{S} \times A \to I\!R$ denotes the expected future discounted reward achieved by taking action a in state $\mathbf{s}$ and following policy π thereafter; which must satisfy $Q^\pi(\mathbf{s}, a) = (B^a V^\pi)(\mathbf{s})$. Given an arbitrary function v over states, the greedy policy $\pi_{gre}(v)$ with respect to v is given by $\pi_{gre}(v)(\mathbf{s}) = \arg\max_a (B^a v)(\mathbf{s})$. Finally, if we let π^* denote the optimal policy and V^* denote its value function, we have the relationship $V^* = B^* V^*$, where $(B^* v)(\mathbf{s}) = \max_a (B^a v)(\mathbf{s})$. If, in addition, we define $Q^*(\mathbf{s}, a) = B^a V^*$ then we also have $\pi^*(\mathbf{s}) = \pi_{gre}(V^*)(\mathbf{s}) = \arg\max_a Q^*(\mathbf{s}, a)$. Given these definitions, the three fundamental methods for calculating π^* can be formulated as:

Policy iteration: Start with some $\pi^{(0)}$. Iterate $\pi^{(i+1)} \leftarrow \pi_{gre}(V^{\pi^{(i)}})$ until $\pi^{(i+1)} = \pi^{(i)}$. Return $\pi^* = \pi^{(i+1)}$.

Value iteration: Start with $v^{(0)}$. Iterate $v^{(i+1)} \leftarrow B^* v^{(i)}$ until $\|v^{(i+1)} - v^{(i)}\|_\infty < tol$. Return $\pi^* = \pi_{gre}(v^{(i+1)})$.

Linear programming: Calculate $V^* = \arg\min_v \sum_{\mathbf{s}} v(\mathbf{s})$ s.t. $v(\mathbf{s}) \geq (B^a v)(\mathbf{s})$ for all a, $\mathbf{s}$. Return $\pi^* = \pi_{gre}(V^*)$.

All three methods can be shown to produce optimal policies for the given MDP (Bertsekas 1995a; Puterman 1994) even though they do so in very different ways. However, to scale up it is necessary to exploit substantial structure in the MDP while also adopting some form of approximation for the optimal value function and policy.

2.1 Factored MDPs and linear approximators

A *factored* MDP is one that can be represented compactly by an additive reward function and a factored state transition model (Koller & Parr 1999; 2000). Specifically, we assume the reward function decomposes as $R(\mathbf{s}, a) = \sum_{r=1}^m R_{a,r}(\mathbf{s}_{a,r})$ where each local reward function $R_{a,r}$ is defined on a small set of variables $\mathbf{s}_{a,r}$. We assume the state transition model $P(\mathbf{s}'|\mathbf{s}, a)$ can be represented by a set of dynamic Bayesian networks (DBNs) on state variables—one for each action—where each DBN defines a compact transition model on a directed bipartite graph connecting state variables in consecutive time steps. Let $\mathbf{s}_{a,i}$ denote the parents of successor variable s_i' in the DBN for action a. To allow efficient optimization we assume the parent set $\mathbf{s}_{a,i}$ contains a small number of state variables from the previous time step. (It is possible to allow parents from the same time step, but we omit this possibility for simplicity.) Given this model, the probability of a successor state $\mathbf{s}'$ given a predecessor state $\mathbf{s}$ and action a is given by the product $P(\mathbf{s}'|\mathbf{s}, a) = \prod_{i=1}^n P(s_i'|\mathbf{s}_{a,i}, a)$. The main benefit of this representation is that it allows large MDPs to be encoded concisely: if the functions $R_{a,r}(\mathbf{s}_{a,r})$ and $P(s_i'|\mathbf{s}_{a,i}, a)$ depend on a small number of variables, they can be represented by small tables and efficiently combined to determine $R(\mathbf{s}, a)$ and $P(\mathbf{s}'|\mathbf{s}, a)$. It turns out that factored MDP representations interact well with linear functions.

We will approximate value functions with linear functions of the form $v_{\mathbf{w}}(\mathbf{s}) = \sum_{j=1}^k w_j b_j(\mathbf{s}_j)$, where $b_1, ..., b_k$ are a fixed set of basis functions and $\mathbf{s}_j$ denotes the variables on which basis b_j depends. For this approach to be effective the variable sets have to be small and interact well with the MDP model. Combining linear functions with factored MDPs provides many opportunities for feasible approximation. The first significant benefit of combining linear approximation with factored MDPs is that the approximate *action-value* (Q) function can also be represented concisely. Specifically, defining $q_{\mathbf{w}}(\mathbf{s}, a) = (B^a v_{\mathbf{w}})(\mathbf{s})$ we have

$$q_{\mathbf{w}}(\mathbf{s}, a) = \sum_{r=1}^m R_{a,r}(\mathbf{s}_{a,r}) + \sum_{j=1}^k w_j h_{a,j}(\mathbf{s}_{a,\mathbf{j}}) \quad (1)$$

where $h_{a,j}(\mathbf{s}_{a,\mathbf{j}}) = \gamma \sum_{\mathbf{s}_j'} P(s_j'|a, \mathbf{s}_{a,\mathbf{j}})b_j(s_j')$ and $\mathbf{s}_{a,\mathbf{j}} = \bigcup_{s_i' \in \mathbf{s}_j'} \mathbf{s}_{a,i}$. That is, $\mathbf{s}_{a,i}$ are the parent variables of s_i', and $\mathbf{s}_{a,\mathbf{j}}$ is the union of the parent variables of $s_i' \in \mathbf{s}_j'$. Thus, $h_{a,j}$ expresses the fact that in a factored MDP the expected future value of one component of the approximation depends only on the current state variables $\mathbf{s}_{a,\mathbf{j}}$ that are direct parents of the variables s_j' in b_j. If the MDP is sparsely connected then the variable sets in q will not be much larger than those in v. The ability to represent the state-action value function in a compact linear form immediately provides a feasible implementation of the greedy policy for $v_\mathbf{w}$, since $\pi_{gre}(v_\mathbf{w})(\mathbf{s}) = \arg\max_a q_\mathbf{w}(\mathbf{s}, a)$ by definition of π_{gre}, and $q_\mathbf{w}(\mathbf{s}, a)$ is efficiently determinable for each $\mathbf{s}$ and a.

2.2 Approximate linear programming

The combination of factored MDPs and linear approximators allows one to devise an efficient linear programming approach to generating value function approximations on a given basis. We refer to this as "approximate linear programming," or ALP for short.

ALP 1: Calculate $\mathbf{w} = \arg\min_\mathbf{w} \sum_\mathbf{s} v_\mathbf{w}(\mathbf{s})$ subject to $v_\mathbf{w}(\mathbf{s}) - q_\mathbf{w}(\mathbf{s}, a) \geq 0$ for all $\mathbf{s}$, a. Return $q_\mathbf{w}$.

Although this approach has been known since (Schweitzer & Seidman 1985) it has only recently been exploited with factored MDPs and linear approximators—resulting in feasible techniques that can scale up to large problems (Guestrin, Koller, & Parr 2001a; Schuurmans & Patrascu 2001). To understand how scaling-up is facilitated, first note that the LP objective can be encoded compactly

$$\sum_\mathbf{s} v_\mathbf{w}(\mathbf{s}) = \sum_{j=1}^k w_j y_j \text{ where } y_j = 2^{n-|\mathbf{s}_j|} \sum_{\mathbf{s}_j} b_j(\mathbf{s}_j) \tag{2}$$

Here the y_j components can be easily precomputed by enumerating assignments to the small sets of variables in basis functions. Second, even though there are an exponential number of constraints—one for each state-action pair—these constraints have a structured representation that allows them to be handled more efficiently than explicit enumeration. Note that the constraint $v_\mathbf{w}(\mathbf{s}) - q_\mathbf{w}(\mathbf{s}, a) \geq 0$ can be rewritten as $\mathbf{c}_{(\mathbf{s},a)} \cdot \mathbf{w} \geq r_{(\mathbf{s},a)}$ where

$$\begin{aligned} c_{(\mathbf{s},a),j} &= b_j(\mathbf{s}_j) - h_{a,j}(\mathbf{s}_{a,\mathbf{j}}) \quad \text{for } j = 1, ..., k \\ r_{(\mathbf{s},a)} &= \sum_r R_{a,r}(\mathbf{s}_{a,r}) \end{aligned} \tag{3}$$

(recall the definition of $h_{a,j}$ in (1) above). This allows one to rewrite the linear program in a more conventional form:

ALP 2: Calculate $\mathbf{w} = \arg\min_\mathbf{w} \mathbf{y} \cdot \mathbf{w}$ subject to $\mathbf{c}_{(\mathbf{s},a)} \cdot \mathbf{w} \geq r_{(\mathbf{s},a)}$ for all $\mathbf{s}$, a. Or in matrix notation: $\mathbf{w} = \arg\min_\mathbf{w} \mathbf{y}^\top \mathbf{w}$ subject to $C\mathbf{w} \geq \mathbf{r}$.

The easy part to solving this linear program is handling the objective $\mathbf{y}$. The hard part is handling the large number of constraints. However, this can be simplified by noting that one can check $\mathbf{w}$ for constraint violations by determining $\min_{\mathbf{s},a} (\mathbf{c}_{(\mathbf{s},a)} \cdot \mathbf{w} - r_{(\mathbf{s},a)})$. This can be calculated by conducting a search over state configurations, one for each action, each of which can be solved efficiently by solving a cost network. Overall, this observation allows one to either re-represent the entire set of constraints in a compact form (Guestrin, Koller, & Parr 2001a), or efficiently search for a most violated constraint in a constraint generation scheme (Schuurmans & Patrascu 2001). Either approach yields reasonable approximation methods for factored MDPs.

2.3 Approximation error

One important issue is to ascertain the approximation error of the solutions produced by linear programming. Here one can show that ALP calculates a weight vector $\mathbf{w}$ that minimizes the L_1 error between $v_\mathbf{w}$ and V^*, subject to the constraints imposed by the linear program (de Farias & Van Roy 2001): Recall that the L_1 error is given by

$$\sum_\mathbf{s} |v_\mathbf{w}(\mathbf{s}) - V^*(\mathbf{s})| \tag{4}$$

and note that the linear program constraint implies $v_\mathbf{w} \geq V^*$ (Bertsekas 1995a). Then, $\sum_\mathbf{s} |v_\mathbf{w}(\mathbf{s}) - V^*(\mathbf{s})| = \sum_\mathbf{s} v_\mathbf{w}(\mathbf{s}) - V^*(\mathbf{s}) = \sum_\mathbf{s} v_\mathbf{w}(\mathbf{s}) - C$ for $C = \sum_\mathbf{s} V^*(\mathbf{s})$.

Unfortunately, the L_1 error is not the best objective to minimize in this context. Normally we are interested in achieving a small L_∞ error, which is given by $\max_\mathbf{s} |v_\mathbf{w}(\mathbf{s}) - V^*(\mathbf{s})|$. Although minimizing L_∞ error is the ultimate goal, there are no known techniques for minimizing this objective directly. However, progress can be made by considering the closely related *Bellman error*

$$\max_\mathbf{s} |v_\mathbf{w}(\mathbf{s}) - \max_a q_\mathbf{w}(\mathbf{s}, a)| \tag{5}$$

Although Bellman error is much more convenient to work with than L_∞ error, it is still much harder minimize than the L_1 objective $\sum_\mathbf{s} v_\mathbf{w}(\mathbf{s})$. However, reducing Bellman error remains an important research question because it is directly related to the L_∞ error by the well known inequality: L_∞ *error* $\leq \frac{\gamma}{1-\gamma}$ *Bellman error* (Williams & Baird 1993).

3 Minimizing Bellman error

The first contribution of this paper is to show that some progress can be made in attacking Bellman error within the linear value function approach. However, dealing with Bellman error poses significant challenges. The first observation is that given a *fixed* weight vector $\mathbf{w}$, simply determining the Bellman error of $v_\mathbf{w}$ is a hard problem.

Theorem 1 It is *co-NP-complete* to determine whether the Bellman error of $v_\mathbf{w}$ for given $\mathbf{w}$ is less than a given δ.[1]

Proof sketch. The idea is to show that the complementary problem of deciding whether Bellman error is at least δ is NP-complete. First, it is easy to show the problem is in NP because a witness state can be used to certify a large Bellman error, and this can be verified in polynomial time using the structured computation (1). Next, to show the problem is NP-hard one can use a simple reduction from 3SAT: Given a 3CNF formula, let the state variables correspond to the propositional variables. Construct a basis function b_j for each clause, such that b_j indicates whether the clause is satisfied by the state assignment. Set the rewards to zero and the transition model to identity for each action, and set $\gamma = 0$ and $\mathbf{w} = \mathbf{1}$. The Bellman error (5) for this setup becomes $\max_\mathbf{s} \sum_{j=1}^k b_j(\mathbf{s}_j)$. If k is the number of clauses, then the Bellman error will be k if and only if the original 3CNF formula is satisfiable. ∎

Of course, the real goal is not just to evaluate Bellman error, but to *minimize* Bellman error. This, however, appears to pose an even greater computational challenge.

Theorem 2 It is *NP-hard* to determine whether there exists a weight vector $\mathbf{w}$ such that $v_\mathbf{w}$ has Bellman error less than

---

[1]Although Theorems 1 and 2 do not directly follow from the results of (Lusena, Goldsmith, & Mundhenk 2001; Mundhenk *et al.* 2000), the proofs are straightforward.

δ for a given δ. The problem, however, remains in NP^{co-NP}. (We conjecture that it is complete for this harder class.)

Proof sketch. First, to establish that the problem is in NP^{co-NP}, one can note that an acceptable $\mathbf{w}$ can be given as a certificate of small Bellman error, and this can then be verified by consulting a co-NP oracle. Second, NP-hardness follows from a trivial reduction from 3SAT: Given a 3CNF formula, let the state variables correspond to the propositional variables, and construct a local reward function r_j for each clause that is the same for each action, where r_j is set to be the indicator function for satisfaction of clause j. Choose a single trivial basis function $b_0 = 0$. Set the transition model to be identity for each action and set $\gamma = 0$. The Bellman error (5) in this setup becomes $\max_{\mathbf{s}} \sum_{j=1}^{k} r_j(\mathbf{s}_j)$. If k is the number of clauses, then $\min_{\mathbf{w}} \max_{\mathbf{s}} \sum_{j=1}^{k} r_j(\mathbf{s}_j)$ yields value k if and only if the original 3CNF formula is satisfiable. ■

Thus, dealing with Bellman error appears to involve tackling hard problems. Nevertheless, we can make some progress toward developing practical algorithms.

First, for the problem of calculating Bellman error, an effective branch and bound strategy can easily be derived. Note that the Bellman error (5) reduces to two searches

$$\min_{\mathbf{s}} \left(v_{\mathbf{w}}(\mathbf{s}) - \max_a q_{\mathbf{w}}(\mathbf{s}, a) \right)$$

$$\max_{\mathbf{s}} \left(v_{\mathbf{w}}(\mathbf{s}) - \max_a q_{\mathbf{w}}(\mathbf{s}, a) \right) \quad (6)$$

The first search is easy because it is equivalent to $\min_a \min_{\mathbf{s}} v_{\mathbf{w}}(\mathbf{s}) - q_{\mathbf{w}}(\mathbf{s}, a)$ and can be calculated by solving a cost network for each action (similar to the ALP problem above). However, the second search is much harder because it involves a maxi-min problem: $\max_{\mathbf{s}} \min_a v_{\mathbf{w}}(\mathbf{s}) - q_{\mathbf{w}}(\mathbf{s}, a)$. Nevertheless, we can calculate this value by employing a branch and bound search over states for each action. The key observation is that (6) is equivalent to

$$\max_a \max_{\mathbf{s}: \mathbf{s} \in \pi_{\mathbf{w}}^{-1}(a)} v_{\mathbf{w}}(\mathbf{s}) - q_{\mathbf{w}}(\mathbf{s}, a)$$

That is, for each state the minimum action is determined by the policy $\pi_{\mathbf{w}}(\mathbf{s}) = \arg\min_a q_{\mathbf{w}}(\mathbf{s}, a)$ defined by $\mathbf{w}$, and therefore for each action a we can restrict the search over states to regions of the space where a is the action selected by $\pi_{\mathbf{w}}$. That is, for a given action, say a_1, we search for a constrained maximum

$$\max_{\mathbf{s}} v_{\mathbf{w}}(\mathbf{s}) - q_{\mathbf{w}}(\mathbf{s}, a_1) \text{ s.t. } q_{\mathbf{w}}(\mathbf{s}, a_1) \geq q_{\mathbf{w}}(\mathbf{s}, a_2) \quad (7)$$
$$\vdots$$
$$q_{\mathbf{w}}(\mathbf{s}, a_1) \geq q_{\mathbf{w}}(\mathbf{s}, a_\ell),$$

and similarly for actions $a_2, ..., a_\ell$. An exhaustive search over the state space could determine this quantity for each action. However, we can implement a much more efficient branch and bound search by calculating upper bounds on the maximum using the Lagrangian:

$$L(\mathbf{s}, \boldsymbol{\mu}) = v_{\mathbf{w}}(\mathbf{s}) - q_{\mathbf{w}}(\mathbf{s}, a_1) + \mu_2[q_{\mathbf{w}}(\mathbf{s}, a_1) - q_{\mathbf{w}}(\mathbf{s}, a_2)]$$
$$\vdots$$
$$+ \mu_\ell[q_{\mathbf{w}}(\mathbf{s}, a_1) - q_{\mathbf{w}}(\mathbf{s}, a_\ell)]$$

Cycle problem							
$n =$	12	15	18	20	24	28	32
$N =$	4e4	3e5	3e6	1e7	2e8	3e9	4e10
Nodes	194	288	384	392	466	832	700
Time (s)	63	131	225	279	451	959	1086
B.Err.	8.1	9.6	12.3	13.8	16.7	19.5	22.4
3legs problem							
$n =$	13	16	19	22	25	28	
$N =$	8e4	7e5	5e6	4e7	3e8	3e9	
Nodes	2150	802	6950	1327	18394	3124	
Time (s)	525	291	3454	866	14639	2971	
B.Err.	8.6	12.9	12.9	17.2	17.2	21.5	

Table 1: Bellman results: singleton bases[2]

It is easy to show that $\max_{\mathbf{s}} L(\mathbf{s}, \boldsymbol{\mu})$ gives an upper bound on the constrained maximum (7) for any $\boldsymbol{\mu} \geq 0$. (The unconstrained maximum is clearly an upper bound on the constrained maximum, and if the constraints are satisfied we must again have an upper bound since $\boldsymbol{\mu}$ is nonnegative.) What is crucial about this upper bound is that it can be efficiently calculated for fixed $\boldsymbol{\mu}$ by solving a cost network over state variables (because it is just a weighted sum of functions that in principle share the same structure). By choosing good penalties $\boldsymbol{\mu}$ (and adapting them using standard subgradient optimization (Bertsekas 1995b)) we obtain an effective pruning strategy that can solve for the Bellman error in far less time than explicit enumeration. For example, Table 1 demonstrates results on two problems from (Guestrin, Koller, & Parr 2001a) where in one case the Bellman error is calculated by only expanding 700 search nodes even when the problem has 4 billion states and 33 actions.[2] Overall, this appears to be a practical algorithm, and we use it to calculate the Bellman error for all of the value approximations we produce below.

The second question—minimizing Bellman error—remains an open problem to the best of our knowledge, and we do not have an exact method. Nevertheless, a similar branch and bound search strategy can be used to implement an approximate policy iteration scheme.

API: Start with an arbitrary $\mathbf{w}^{(0)}$. Iterate $(\mathbf{w}^{(i+1)}, \delta) \leftarrow \arg\min_{(\mathbf{w}, \delta)} \delta$ subject to $-\delta \leq v_{\mathbf{w}}(\mathbf{s}) - q_{\mathbf{w}}(\mathbf{s}, \pi_{\mathbf{w}^{(i)}}(\mathbf{s})) \leq \delta$ for all $\mathbf{s}$ and $\delta \geq 0$, until $\mathbf{w}^{(i+1)} \doteq \mathbf{w}^{(i)}$.

This procedure uses a linear program to recover the weight

---

[2] We conducted most of our experiments on the computer network problems described in (Guestrin, Koller, & Parr 2001a; 2001b). For these problems there is a directed network of computer systems $s_1, ..., s_n$ where each system is either up ($s_i = 1$) or down ($s_i = 0$). Systems can spontaneously go down with some probability at each step, but this probability is increased if an immediately preceding machine in the network is down. There are $n + 1$ actions: do nothing (the default) and reboot machine i. The reward in a state is simply the sum of systems that are up, with a bonus reward of 1 if system 1 (the server) is up. The transition probabilities of the state of a computer depend only on its previous state and the state(s) of any parent computers in the network. The two network topologies reported here are "cycle" and "three legs."

	ALP		API		
n	B.Err.	time (s)	B.Err.	time (s)	Iters.
cycle problem, singleton bases					
5	2.8	2	0.9	160	10
8	4.1	8	1.8	1,600	16
10	6.7	14	2.4	5,672	22
3legs problem, singleton bases					
4	1.8	1	0.6	383	7
7	4.0	3	1.0	697	14
10	3.9	9	1.8	16,357	19

Table 2: API versus ALP results[2]

vector $\mathbf{w}^{(i+1)}$ that minimizes the one step error in approximating the value of the current policy $\pi_{\mathbf{w}^{(i)}}$ defined by $\mathbf{w}^{(i)}$. Here a branch and bound search is used to generate constraints for this linear program. The overall procedure generalizes that of (Guestrin, Koller, & Parr 2001a), and produces the same solutions in cases where both apply. However, the new technique does not require the additional assumption of a "default action" nor an explicit representation of the intermediate policies (in their case, a decision list). The drawback is that one has to perform a branch and bound search instead of solving cost networks to generate the constraints. Figure 2 shows that the new API procedure is much more expensive than ALP, but clearly produces better approximations given the same basis. However, API does not fully minimize the Bellman error of the final weight vector. Instead it achieves a bounded approximation of the Bellman error of the optimal weight vector (Guestrin, Koller, & Parr 2001a). Overall, this method appears to be too costly to justify the modest gains in accuracy it offers.

4 Minimizing L_1 error

Attacking Bellman error directly with API may yield reasonable approximations, but comes at the expense of solving many linear programs (one per policy iteration) and performing branch and bound search. Clearly the direct ALP approach is much faster, but unfortunately produces noticeably worse Bellman error than API. This raises the question of whether one can improve the approximation error of ALP without resorting to branch and bound. A related question is understanding how the basis functions might be selected in the first place. To address both questions simultaneously we investigate strategies for *automatically* constructing sets of basis functions to achieve good approximation error. We will follow the generic algorithm of Figure 1.

The three unknowns in this procedure are (1) the procedure for generating candidate domains, (2) the procedure for constructing a basis function given a candidate domain, and (3) the procedure for scoring the potential contribution of a basis function to reducing approximation error.

4.1 Scoring candidate bases

The first issue we tackle is scoring the potential merit of a basis function b_{k+1} given a current basis and weight vector. Ideally, we would like to measure the new basis function's

Greedy basis function selection Start with constant function $b_0(\emptyset)$ and initial solution w_0, and iterate:

Given a current basis $b_1(\mathbf{s}_1), ..., b_k(\mathbf{s}_k)$ and weights $\mathbf{w}$, note that each basis function b_j is defined on a subset of the state variables, $\mathbf{s}_j \subseteq \{s_1, ..., s_n\}$, which we refer to as its *domain*.
(1) Generate a set of candidate domains $\mathbf{s}'_1, ..., \mathbf{s}'_J$ from the current domains.
(2) For each candidate domain $\mathbf{s}'_j$ construct a basis function.
(3) For each basis function, score its ability to reduce approximation error. Add the best candidate to the basis, and re-solve the LP to calculate new weights on the entire basis.

Figure 1: Greedy basis function selection procedure

effect on Bellman error. However, we have seen that measuring Bellman error is a hard problem. Moreover, the ALP procedure does not minimize Bellman error, it only minimizes L_1 error. Therefore, we are really only in a position to conveniently evaluate a basis function's effect on L_1 error and hope that this leads to a reduction in Bellman error as a side effect. Our experimental results below show that this is generally the case, although it is clearly not always true. For now we focus on attacking L_1 error.

The first issue is determining whether a new basis function will allow any progress to be made in the linear program at all. To do this note that the dual of the linear program in **ALP 2** is

$$\max_{\boldsymbol{\lambda}} \boldsymbol{\lambda}^\top \mathbf{r} \text{ subject to } \boldsymbol{\lambda}^\top C \leq \mathbf{y}^\top, \boldsymbol{\lambda} \geq 0$$

(Technically we must restrict $\mathbf{w} \geq 0$, but this does not pose any insurmountable difficulties.) Imagine that we have restricted attention to some basis set $b_1, ..., b_k$ and solved the linear program with respect to this set (thus fixing $w_j = 0$ for $j > k$). Let $(\mathbf{w}, \boldsymbol{\lambda})$ be a solution pair to this linear program and let $B = \{i : \lambda_i > 0\}$ be the indices of the active primal constraints. Then by complementary slackness we must have $C_B \mathbf{w} = \mathbf{r}_B$ and hence $\mathbf{w} = C_B^{-1} \mathbf{r}_B$ where C_B is square and invertible. By a further application of complementary slackness we have $\boldsymbol{\lambda}_B^\top C_B = \mathbf{y}^\top$ and therefore $\boldsymbol{\lambda}_B^\top = \mathbf{y}^T C_B^{-1}$. Now, consider what happens if we wish to add a new basis function b_{k+1} to $\{b_1, ..., b_k\}$. This new basis function generates a new column of C which imposes a new constraint $\boldsymbol{\lambda}^\top \mathbf{c}_{:,k+1} \leq y_{k+1}$ on $\boldsymbol{\lambda}$. If the current $\boldsymbol{\lambda}$ is feasible for the new constraint, then $\boldsymbol{\lambda}$ is already a global solution to the dual problem involving this basis function, and we can make no further progress on improving the primal LP objective. This immediately yields an efficient test of whether b_{k+1} allows any progress to be made: If b_{k+1} generates a column $\mathbf{c}_{B,k+1}$ on the active constraints such that the dual constraint $\boldsymbol{\lambda}_B^\top \mathbf{c}_{B,k+1} > y_{k+1}$ is violated, then b_{k+1} allows some progress. On the other hand, if b_{k+1} satisfies the dual constraint it is useless. This provides an efficient test because the column $\mathbf{c}_{B,k+1}$ can easily be computed for b_{k+1} on the k active constraints in B.

Next to *quantify* the potential improvement of adding a basis function we consider plausible ways to score candidates. Note that any scoring function must strike a compromise between accuracy and computational cost that lies

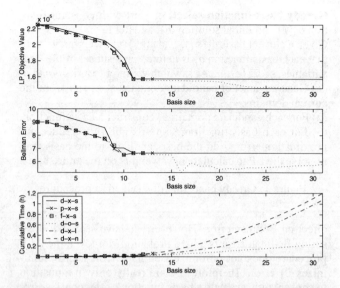

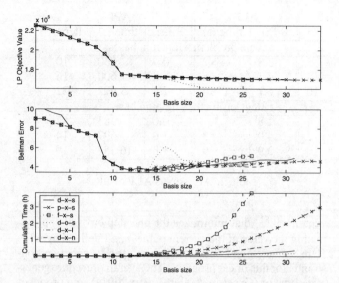

Figure 2: Basis function selection results on the cycle problem ($n = 10$).[2] Legend shows combinations of basis construction strategies. **Scores**: d = dual, p = partial, f = full. **Basis**: x = XOR, o = optimized. **Domain**: s = sequential, l = lattice, n = neighbor.

Figure 3: Basis function selection results on the 3legs problem ($n = 10$).[2] Legend shows combinations of basis construction strategies. **Scores**: d = dual, p = partial, f = full. **Basis**: x = XOR, o = optimized. **Domain**: s = sequential, l = lattice, n = neighbor.

between two extremes: The cheapest scoring function is just the degree of dual constraint violation $\lambda_B^\top c_{B,k+1} - y_{k+1}$, which we refer to as the *dual score*. In this case a larger dual constraint violation means that, to the first degree, the basis function will decrease the linear program objective faster than another basis function with a smaller degree of constraint violation. However, the dual score ignores the primal constraints and therefore may not always be predictive. Clearly, the most accurate, but most expensive scoring technique is simply to re-solve the entire linear program with the new basis function to determine its exact effect. We refer to this strategy as the *full LP score*. Our experimental results show that the full LP score does not yield noticeable improvements in approximation over the dual score and is much more expensive; see Figures 2 and 3. (We also experimented with an intermediate alternative, *partial LP score*, but it also yielded no noticeable benefit, so we omit a detailed description.) Since the dual score achieves comparable reductions to the more expensive scoring methods in our experiments, we concentrate solely on this cheap alternative below.

4.2 Constructing candidate bases

Next we turn to the problem of constructing the basis functions themselves. Assume a set of domain variables has already been selected. (Below we consider how to choose candidate domains.) Any new function we construct on the given set of variables must be nonlinear to ensure that it has a non-vacuous effect. Here one could consider a wide range of possible representations, including decision trees and decision diagrams, neural networks, etc. However, for simplicity we will just focus on table-based representations where a basis function is just represented as a lookup table over assignments to the given variables. A useful advantage of the table-

based representation, particularly in the context of ALP, is that one can *optimize* the lookup table values themselves to yield a basis function b_{k+1} that maximizes the dual score. This can be done by solving a small auxiliary linear program. (Unfortunately we have to omit the derivation in this shortened paper.) The interesting thing about this approach is that it implicitly considers an infinite space of basis functions to select the best candidate. We refer to this approach as the *optimized basis*. We compared the optimized basis approach to a simpler method that just considered a fixed basis function for each domain. In particular we considered the *XOR basis* for two-valued state variables, $s_i \in \{0, 1\}$, which is defined by $b(s_i) = (-1)^{s_i}$, $b(s_i, s_j) = (-1)^{s_i}(-1)^{s_j}$, $b(s_1, .., s_k) = (-1)^{s_1} \cdots (-1)^{s_k}$, etc. Figures 2 and 3 show that the optimized basis yields noticeable benefits in reducing the linear program objective with little additional cost to the fixed XOR basis.

4.3 Selecting candidate domains

The final issue we consider is how to select the candidate domains on which to build new basis functions. A constraint we wish to maintain is to keep the domain sizes small so that the cost networks do not become unwieldy. We consider three approaches that differ in how tightly they control the growth in domain size. The most conservative approach, which we refer to as *sequential*, only considers a domain once every smaller sized domain has been used. That is, after the trivial constant basis, it then considers only singleton domains, and then considers pairs of state variables only once the singletons are exhausted, etc. A slightly less conservative approach, which we call *lattice*, allows a candidate domain to be considered if and only if all of its proper subsets have already been added to the current basis. Finally, the least conservative approach, *neighbors*, allows a candi-

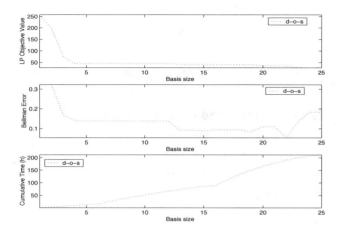

Figure 4: Basis function selection results on the resource allocation problem (2 resources, 4 tasks, 16 actions).[3]

date domain to be considered as soon as it can be constructed as the union of a current domain plus one new state variable. Figures 2 and 3 compare each of these three methods. Surprisingly, the least expensive sequential strategy matches the others in reducing the linear program objective.

4.4 Observations

Overall, the experiments exhibit interesting trends; see Figures 2–4.[3] The optimized basis approach is clearly the most effective at improving the linear program objective, although it shows a surprising "over-fitting" effect on Bellman error. Most of the remaining methods produce indistinguishable results, except in runtime. The results are somewhat promising in that the adaptive basis selection technique reduced the Bellman error of the fixed singleton basis used in the earlier experiments (6.7 to 5 for the cycle problem; 3.9 to 3.8 for the 3legs problem). Also, in every case substantial reductions were achieved in the linear programming objective; particularly using the optimized basis functions. However, these results still do not match that of the computationally much more expensive API method of Section 3. It seems apparent that for the ALP approach to achieve comparable Bellman error, one may have to add a substantial number of basis functions. Investigating the number of basis functions necessary to make ALP truly competitive with API in terms of Bellman error remains future work.

---

[3]We conducted an additional experiment in a generic resource allocation domain, where the problem is to allocate resources to a number of heterogeneous tasks. In this case, the state of the MDP is described by n *task* and m *resource* binary variables. If task T_i, $i = 1, \ldots, n$, is not active at the current time step, then it activates at the next time step with a probability that need not be the same for each task. At every stage resource variable S_j, $j = 1, \ldots, m$, is replenished or depleted (if currently applied to a task) stochastically. Applying a number of resources to an active task may fail to bring the task to completion, thus acting in a simple noisy-or fashion. Completed tasks result in rewards which are summed together. Actions assign free resources to needy tasks at a cost linear in the number of assigned resources. There are as many actions as there are ways to assign resources to tasks.

Acknowledgments

Research supported by NSERC, CITO and MITACS. Thanks to Ron Parr for his patient discussions.

References

Bertsekas, D., and Tsitsiklis, J. 1996. *Neuro-Dynamic Programming*. Athena Scientific.

Bertsekas, D. 1995a. *Dynamic Programming and Optimal Control*, volume 2. Athena Scientific.

Bertsekas, D. 1995b. *Nonlinear Optimization*. Athena Scientific.

Boutilier, C.; Dean, T.; and Hanks, S. 1999. Decision-theoretic planning: Structural assumptions and computational leverage. *JAIR* 11:1–94.

Boutilier, C.; Dearden, R.; and Goldszmidt, M. 2000. Stochastic dynamic programming with factored representations. *Artificial Intelligence*.

de Farias, D., and Van Roy, B. 2001. The linear programming approach to approximate dynamic programming.

Dietterich, T. 2000. Hierarchical reinforcement learning with the MAXQ value function decomposition. *JAIR* 13:227–303.

Guestrin, C.; Koller, D.; and Parr, R. 2001a. Max-norm projection for factored MDPs. In *Proceedings IJCAI*.

Guestrin, C.; Koller, D.; and Parr, R. 2001b. Multiagent planning with factored MDPs. In *Proceedings NIPS*.

Koller, D., and Parr, R. 1999. Computing factored value functions for policies in structured MDPs. In *Proceedings IJCAI*.

Koller, D., and Parr, R. 2000. Policy iteration for factored MDPs. In *Proceedings UAI*.

Lusena, C.; Goldsmith, J.; and Mundhenk, M. 2001. Non-approximability results for partially observable Markov decision processes. *JAIR* 14:83–103.

Mundhenk, M.; Goldsmith, J.; Lusena, C.; and Allender, E. 2000. Complexity of finite-horizon Markov decision processes. *JACM* 47(4):681–720.

Puterman, M. 1994. *Markov Decision Processes: Discrete Dynamic Programming*. Wiley.

Sallans, B., and Hinton, G. 2000. Using free energies to represent Q-values in a multiagent reinforcement learning task. In *Proceedings NIPS*.

Schuurmans, D., and Patrascu, R. 2001. Direct value-approximation for factored MDPs. In *Proceedings NIPS*.

Schweitzer, P., and Seidman, A. 1985. Generalized polynomial approximations in Markovian decision problems. *J. Math. Anal. and Appl.* 110:568–582.

Trick, M. A., and Zin, S. E. 1997. Spline approximations to value functions: A linear programming approach. *Macroeconomic Dynamics* 1:255–277.

Williams, R., and Baird, L. 1993. Tight performance bounds on greedy policies based on imperfect value functions. Technical report, Northeastern University.

Piecewise Linear Value Function Approximation for Factored MDPs

Pascal Poupart and Craig Boutilier

Dept. of Computer Science

University of Toronto

Toronto, ON, M5S 3H5

ppoupart,cebly@cs.toronto.edu

Relu Patrascu and Dale Schuurmans

Department of Computer Science

University of Waterloo

Waterloo, ON, N2L 3G1

rpatrasc,dale@cs.uwaterloo.ca

Abstract

A number of proposals have been put forth in recent years for the solution of Markov decision processes (MDPs) whose state (and sometimes action) spaces are *factored*. One recent class of methods involves linear value function approximation, where the optimal value function is assumed to be a linear combination of some set of basis functions, with the aim of finding suitable weights. While sophisticated techniques have been developed for finding the best approximation within this constrained space, few methods have been proposed for choosing a suitable basis set, or modifying it if solution quality is found wanting. We propose a general framework, and specific proposals, that address both of these questions. In particular, we examine *weakly coupled MDPs* where a number of subtasks can be viewed independently modulo resource constraints. We then describe methods for constructing a piecewise linear combination of the subtask value functions, using greedy decision tree techniques. We argue that this architecture is suitable for many types of MDPs whose combinatorics are determined largely by the existence multiple conflicting objectives.

1 Introduction

Markov decision processes (MDPs) form the foundations of most recent work in decision-theoretic planning and reinforcement learning. Classical solution techniques for MDPs, however, generally rely on explicit state and action space enumeration, and thus suffer from the "curse of dimensionality." Specifically, since realistic domains are often *factored*—that is, the state space consists of assignments of values to a set of variables—they have states spaces that grow exponentially with the number of relevant variables.

Fortunately, the factored nature of an MDP often admits compact representation [7; 3]. For example, dynamic Bayes nets (DBNs) can be used to represent the dynamics of the MDP, taking advantage of the fact that actions tend to have independent effects on state variables, and that these effects depend only on the status of a small set of other variables [6;

3]. Additive reward functions can also be used to great effect [2; 12]. Methods exist for exploiting these forms of structure when solving an MDP, obviating the need for state space enumeration, and producing compact representations of value functions (VFs) and policies. These include exact and approximate methods for piecewise constant representations [7; 3; 10; 5] and feature-based approaches [1; 18].

Among feature-based models, *linear approximations* have proven popular. In linear approximations, a small set of basis functions (over state space) is assumed, and the VF is taken to be a linear combination of these functions. Recently, several clever proposals have shown how to find the best linear approximation, given a fixed basis set, in a way that exploits the factored nature of an MDP [8; 16; 9]. These models use basis functions over a small set of variables and DBN action representations to ensure computation is effective. These approaches have the potential to scale well for certain classes of problems.

The main drawback of linear models is the need for a good basis set. While these approaches may scale, the quality of the approximation depends critically on the underlying basis. If no decent approximate VF lies in the subspace spanned by the basis, it is impossible to obtain good solutions using such techniques. Unfortunately, in the recent work on linear approximations for factored MDPs, no proposals exist for either: (a) the choice of a good basis; or (b) the modification of an existing basis to improve decision quality. Studies to date have used simple characteristic functions over (very small) subsets of state variables.

We address both of these problems in this paper. We first describe one technique for the generation of a suitable basis set, based on the notion of *subtask value functions*: these arise naturally is *weakly coupled MDPs (WCMDPs)* [12], a general class of large, factored MDPs. A WCMDP is one in which a process can be decomposed into a number of subprocesses corresponding to distinct objectives, with each of these subprocesses coupled in a weak sense. The weakly coupled nature of an MDP can be discovered through analysis of its DBN representation. Our first technique for basis function generation exploits weak coupling and can be thought of as relying on domain-specific properties. We then describe a general framework for the incremental construction of a suitable basis for linear approximation of a factored MDP. This approach relies on no special domain properties, and can be instantiated in a number of concrete ways [14]. We focus in this paper on a particular instantiation of our framework that allows for the construction of a *piecewise linear (PWL)* combination of basis functions. We argue that this model is especially suited to the solution of WCMDPs, a fact supported by our empirical results.

We begin in Section 2 with a brief overview of factored and weakly coupled MDPs and existing methods for linear approximation for factored MDPs. In Section 3, we describe our general framework for incremental basis function construction, and discuss a decision-tree approach for the construction of PWL combinations of basis functions in Section 4. We offer some preliminary experimental results in Section 5 and conclude in Section 6.

2 Linear Approximations of MDPs

We begin with an overview of MDPs, a discussion of factored and weakly-coupled MDPs, and recent techniques for linear function approximation.

2.1 Markov Decision Processes

We assume a fully-observable MDP with finite sets of states $\mathcal{S}$ and actions $\mathcal{A}$, transition function $\Pr(s, a, t)$, reward function $R(s, a)$, and a discounted infinite-horizon optimality criterion with discount factor β. $\Pr(s, a, t)$ denotes the probability with which the system transitions to state t when action a is taken at state s, while $R(s, a)$ denotes the immediate utility of taking action a at state s. A *stationary policy* $\pi : \mathcal{S} \to \mathcal{A}$ determines a particular course of action. The *value* of a policy π at state s, $V^\pi(s)$, is the expected sum of future discounted rewards over an infinite horizon:

$$E_\pi[\sum_{t=0}^{\infty} \gamma^t R^t | S^0 = s].$$

The function V^π can be computed as the solution to the following linear system:

$$V^\pi(s) = R(s, \pi(s)) + \beta \sum_{t \in \mathcal{S}} Pr(s, \pi(s), t) \cdot V^\pi(t) \quad (1)$$

The operator on the r.h.s. of Eq. 1 is referred to as the *backup operator for policy* π, denoted B^π; V^π is thus a fixed point of B^π. We denote by B^a the backup operator for the policy that applies action a at each state.

Our aim is to find a policy π^* that maximizes value at each state. The *optimal VF*, denoted V^*, is unique and is the fixed point of the following *Bellman backup operator* [11]:

$$V^*(s) = \max_{a \in \mathcal{A}} R(s, a) + \beta \sum_{t \in \mathcal{S}} Pr(s, a, t) \cdot V^*(t) \quad (2)$$

A number of algorithms exist to construct the optimal VF, including dynamic programming algorithms such as value and policy iteration. We focus here on a simple linear program (LP), whose solution is V^*:

$$Min: \sum_s V(s) \quad Subj. \ to: \ V(s) \geq (B^a V)(s), \forall a, s \quad (3)$$

Here each $V(s)$ is a variable, and the value $(B^a V)(s)$ is a linear function of these variables, as seen in Eq. 1. For many classes of MDPs, exact solution using LP methods is not as effective as using dynamic programming algorithms [15]. The value of the LP formulation, however, becomes apparent when we consider linear approximation [16; 9].

2.2 Factored and Weakly Coupled MDPs

One weakness of the classical MDP formulation is its reliance on explicit transition and reward functions. When the state space of the MDP is *factored*—i.e., when states correspond to the instantiation of state variables—an MDP can often be specified more compactly by exploiting regularities in the reward function and the dynamics [3]. We assume a set of (for simplicity, boolean) state variables $\mathbf{X} = \{X_1, \dots, X_n\}$. Each state is thus a vector $\mathbf{x}$ assigning a value to each variable.

Reward often depends only on the status of a few state variables, or additively on "local" reward functions. We assume

$$R(\mathbf{x}, a) = \sum_{j=1}^{m} R_j(\mathbf{x}_j^r, a)$$

where each R_j is a function that depends on a small subset $\mathbf{X}_j^r \subset \mathbf{X}$, and $\mathbf{x}_j^r$ denotes the restriction of $\mathbf{x}$ to the variables in $\mathbf{X}_j^r$. Similarly, dynamics can often be specified compactly. We assume the effect of each action a can be decomposed into independent effects on each variable X_i, and that its effect on X_i depends on a small subset $\mathbf{X}_i^a \subset \mathbf{X}$ of variables. A local function $\Pr(X_i | a, \mathbf{X}_i^a)$ denotes the distribution over X^i given any assignment to $\mathbf{X}_i^a$. We then have

$$\Pr(\mathbf{x}, a, \mathbf{x}') = \prod_i \Pr(x_i' | a, \mathbf{x}_i^a).$$

We refer to the local function $\Pr(X_i | a, \mathbf{X}_i^a)$ as the conditional probability table or *table* for X_i under action a. This forms the basis of DBN action representations.

This representation allows MDPs to be encoded concisely, requiring space linear in the number of variables if each table R_j or $\Pr(X_i)$ refers to a bounded number of variables. The size of the representation can be reduced even further by using specialized representations for these tables, such as decision trees [3] or ADDs [10]. Furthermore, several techniques can take advantage of this structure to avoid state space enumeration when solving the MDP. If a candidate VF depends on only a few variables, the fact that each variable depends on only a small number of parents ensures that applying a Bellman backup results in a new VF that depends only on a few variables [3].

Finally, this type of representation allows us to identify *weakly coupled MDPs (WCMDPs)*. A WCMDP is one in which the reward function is decomposable as above, and the set of variables *relevant* to the each R_j is small. The variables relevant to each R_j are determined as follows [2]: the variables $\mathbf{X}_j^r$ are relevant to R_j; and if X_i is relevant to R_j, then so are the variables $\mathbf{X}_i^a$ for all a.[1] WCMDPs arise in many guises, but most often when the combinatorics of a given problem are largely due to the existence of many competing subobjectives [2; 12]. When determining the variables relevant to one objective, other objective variables do not play a

---

[1]Note the recursive nature of this definition.

role; thus, the objectives are coupled only through the existence of a common core of relevant variables. Problems that exhibit such structure include resource allocation problems, and scheduling of tasks in multi-user domains. We elaborate on WCMDPs in Section 3.1.

2.3 Linear Approximations

A common way to approximate VFs is with linear approximators [18; 8; 16]. Given a small set of *basis functions* $\mathcal{F} = \{f_1, \cdots, f_m\}$ over state space, a *linear value function* V is defined as $V(s) = \sum_i w_i f_i(s)$, or $V = \mathbf{F}\mathbf{w}$, for some set of coefficients (or *weights*) $\mathbf{w} = \langle w_1, \ldots, w_m \rangle$. Here $\mathbf{F}$ denotes a matrix whose columns are the functions f_i. Unless $\mathbf{F}$ spans a subspace that includes V^*, any linear VF will be, at best, an approximation of V^*. The aim is then to find the best linear approximation of the true VF, using a suitable error metric.

An important challenge, the construction of good linear approximators for factored MDPs, has recently been tackled in [8; 16], resulting in techniques that can find approximately optimal linear approximators in way that exploits the structure of the MDP without enumerating state space. We assume that each basis function f_j is compact, referring only to a small set of variables $\mathbf{X}_j^f$. Linear value and policy iteration are described in [8], while a factored LP solution technique is presented in [16; 9]. We discuss the method proposed in [16].

The LP formulation of a factored MDP above can be encoded compactly when an MDP is factored. First, notice that the objective function Eq. 3 can be encoded compactly:

$$\sum_{\mathbf{x}} V(\mathbf{x}) = \sum_{\mathbf{x}} \sum_j w_j f_j(\mathbf{x}) = \sum_j w_j y_j \quad (4)$$

where $y_j = 2^{n - |\mathbf{x}_j^f|} \sum_{\mathbf{x}_j^f} f_j(\mathbf{x}_j^f)$. Intuitively, each y_j is the sum of the values assigned by function f_j, multiplied by the number of states at which they apply, and can be precomputed. Observe that the variables are the weights $\mathbf{w}$, which determine the values $V(\mathbf{x})$. Second, the set of constraints in Eq. 3 can be encoded compactly by observing that this set is equivalent to[2]

$$\max_{\mathbf{x}} V(\mathbf{x}) - (B^a V)(\mathbf{x}) \geq 0, \forall a \quad (5)$$

Since V is compactly representable as the sum of compact functions, $(B^a V)$ is similarly representable. Specifically, the construction of $(B^a f_j)$ for basis function f_j can exploit the fact that it refers only a small subset of variables; the *regression* of f_j through a produces a function that includes only those variables $\mathbf{X}_i^a$ for each $X_i \in \mathbf{X}_j^f$, and variables in $\mathbf{X}_k^r$ [3]. The maximization over $\mathbf{x}$ is nonlinear, but can encoded using the clever trick of [8]. For a fixed set of weights, a *cost network* can be solved using variable elimination to determine this max without state space enumeration. While this technique scales exponentially with the maximum number of variables in any function (i.e, the functions f_j, $(B^a f_j)$, or intermediate factors constructed during variable elimination), this "local exponential" blow up can often be avoided if more sophisticated representations like ADDs are used [10].

---

[2]When approximation is used, this LP can be viewed as approximately minimizing L_1-error.

An approach that offers even greater computational savings is the incremental constraint generation technique proposed in [16]. The LP above can be rewritten as minimizing Eq. 4, s.t.

$$\sum_j w_j C_j(\mathbf{x}, a) \geq R(\mathbf{x}, a), \forall \mathbf{x}, a \quad (6)$$

where $C_j(\cdot, a)$ is a function refers only to variables $\mathbf{X}_j^f$ and $\mathbf{X}_i^a$ for each $X_i \in \mathbf{X}_j^f$. More precisely, we have

$$C_j(\mathbf{x}, a) = f_j(\mathbf{x}_j^f) - \beta \sum_{\hat{\mathbf{x}}_j^f} \Pr(\hat{\mathbf{x}}_j^f | \mathbf{x}_{j,a}^f, a) f_j(\hat{\mathbf{x}}_j^f)$$

where $\mathbf{x}_{j,a}^f$ refers to the set instantiation of variables $\mathbf{X}_i^a$ for each $X_i \in \mathbf{X}_j^f$. This LP is solved without constraints, then using the cost network technique to compute $\min_{\mathbf{x}} \min_a \sum_j w_j C_j(\mathbf{x}, a)$, the state-action pair that maximally violates the constraints in Eq. 3 is determined. This constraint is added to the LP, which is then resolved.

In matrix form, we can rewrite this LP as

$$\min_{\mathbf{w}} \mathbf{y}^\top \mathbf{w} \ subject \ to \ \mathbf{C}\mathbf{w} \geq \mathbf{r} \quad (7)$$

where $\mathbf{C}$ is a matrix whose m columns correspond to the functions $C_j(\mathbf{x}, a)$. Thus $\mathbf{C}$ has $|\mathbf{X}||\mathcal{A}|$ rows. The advantage of constraint generation is that the rows of $\mathbf{C}$ are added incrementally, and the LPs being solved are dramatically smaller than those described above: the number of constraints ultimately added is $O(m)$ (i.e., the number of basis functions), considerably smaller than the number of constraints required by the LP generated by the cost network. Once all constraints are generated, the LP constraints are $\mathbf{C}^*\mathbf{w} \geq \mathbf{r}^*$, where $\mathbf{C}^*$ and $\mathbf{r}^*$ are restricted to the $O(m)$ active constraints.

We observe that this LP attempts to minimize L_1-error, not Bellman or L_∞-error, as is usual when solving MDPs. Furthermore, this LP model imposes a one-sided constraint on L_1-error, so it cannot strictly be viewed as minimizing L_1-error. L_∞-error can be tackled directly using algorithms like policy and value iteration [8], but at higher computational cost. The difficulties associated with minimizing different error metrics in the LP context are discussed in [14].

3 Basis Function Selection

While linear approximations scale well, determining *a priori* the solution quality one can obtain using a given basis set is difficult. Ideally, V^* would be an element of the subspace spanned by $\mathcal{F}$, in which case an exact solution could be found. If this is not the case, the quality of the best approximation could be gauged by considering the projection of V^* on this subspace. However, since we do not have access to V^*, choosing a suitable basis set is problematic. Indeed, no serious proposals for this problem exist in the recent literature on factored linear approximations. Since solution quality depends critically on the choice of basis, we must consider methods that allow selection of a good initial basis set, or intelligent revision of a basis if solution quality is unacceptable. We consider both of these problems.

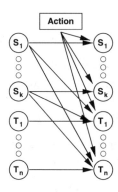

Figure 1: DBN for a generic resource allocation problem.

3.1 Subtask Value Functions

In a variety of MDPs, the combinatorial explosion in state space (and often action space) size is caused by the presence of multiple, conflicting objectives. For instance, in a manufacturing setting we might need to allocate resources (e.g., machines) to different orders placed by clients. If the process plan for a specific order is more or less fixed, then the problem is one of resource allocation. In an office environment, a robot might be charged with performing tasks of differing priorities for many users.

In problems like these, the underlying MDP is often *weakly coupled*: given a choice of action (e.g., an assignment of resources to each order) each subtask (e.g., order) has a certain small set of state variables that are relevant to determining how best to achieve it, and this subset has little or no overlap with that of other objectives. Thus, each subtask can be viewed as an independent MDP, defined over a much smaller set of variables, that can be meaningfully solved. The subtask MDPs are weakly coupled because their state and action spaces (e.g., feasible resource assignments) are linked: performing a specific action in one subtask MDP influences which actions can be concurrently executed in another (e.g., because it consumes resources).

To illustrate, consider a resource allocation problem with n potential tasks, $T_1, \ldots, T_n$, each of which may be active or inactive, and can change status stochastically (e.g., this might reflect the placement or retraction of orders). We have k resources, each of which can be applied at any point in time to the achievement of any active task. The *status* of resource j, denoted by variable S_j determines how effective that resource is in the completion of its assigned task. The status of a resource evolves stochastically, depending on its use at each time step (e.g., consider machines requiring maintenance or workers needing breaks). Multiple resources can be applied to a task, thus the size of the action space is $O(k^{n+1})$. A DBN illustrating the dependencies for such a problem is illustrated in Figure 1. Finally, we assume that a reward r_i is associated with the successful completion of an active task T_i.

This MDP can be decomposed readily into distinct subtask MDPs for each T_i. Since variables T_j ($j \neq i$) have no influence on T_i or the reward associated with T_i, the subtask MDP for T_i has as its only variables $S_1, \ldots, S_k$ and T_i. For small numbers of resources, this subtask MDP can be solved opti-

mally. Of course, the optimal solutions for the different subtask MDPs may not be compatible. The policies for different subtasks are coupled by the resources—in particular, by constraints on the feasible actions one can apply to jointly to each task. Notice that the action spaces are also considerably reduced in the subtask MDPs.

WCMDPs have been examined recently and several techniques proposed to take advantage of their structure [2; 12; 17]. Given a factored MDP with an additive reward function reflecting subtask structure, constructing a (factored) subtask MDP for each objective is straightforward (see the discussion of relevant variables in Section 2.2) [2]. In the example above, backchaining through the DBN allows us to construct the subtask MDPs for each task, starting only with the variables T_i (which are the only "reward variables").

If a subtask MDP is of manageable size, it can be solved to produce the optimal *subtask value function*, defined on the set of variables relevant to that MDP. All the techniques described in [2; 12; 17] use subtask VFs to great effect to approximate the solution of the full WCMDP. For instance, using heuristic techniques to piece together a global policy using subtask VFs, problems involving several thousand boolean variables (and similarly sized action spaces) can be solved [12].

Subtask VFs are ideal candidates for a basis set. If, for example, we have k subtasks of widely differing priorities (or having different deadlines) the optimal policy might have the form: complete the highest priority subtask (using all resources); then complete the next subtask; and so on. In this case, the optimal VF is: $V(\mathbf{x}) = V^1(\mathbf{x}^1) + \beta^{t_1} V^2(\mathbf{x}^2) + \beta^{t_1+t_2} V^2(\mathbf{x}^2) + \ldots$, where V^i is the VF for subtask i, defined over variables $\mathbf{X}^i$, and t_i is the expected time to completion of task i under the optimal policy. Thus a linear combination of subtask VFs may provide a good approximation.

Unfortunately, a linear combination of subtask VFs may not always be suitable. For instance, if subtasks become active stochastically, the allocation of resources will often depend on the status of each task. One should then focus on a high priority task i (and get value V^i) only if that task is active and suitable resources are available; otherwise one might focus on a lower priority task. Thus the optimal VF might best be approximated by a *piecewise linear* combination of subtask VFs, where different linear approximators are "used" in different regions of state space. For example, a VF might take the form: *If* $\mathbf{c}$, $V(\mathbf{x}) = V^1(\mathbf{x}^1) + \beta^{t_1} V^2(\mathbf{x}^2)$; *if* $\bar{\mathbf{c}}$, $V(\mathbf{x}) = V^3(\mathbf{x}^3) + \beta^{t_3} V^4(\mathbf{x}^4)$. Here tasks 1 and 2 should be tackled when condition $\mathbf{c}$ holds (say these two high priority tasks are active), and tasks 3 and 4 handled otherwise. We elaborate on such PWL approximators in Section 4.

3.2 Basis Function Addition

The use of subtask VFs requires that the underlying MDP exhibit a certain structure. As such, it can be viewed as a domain dependent method for boosting the performance of linear approximators. If domain dependent structure, or other heuristic information, is unavailable, domain independent methods are needed to construct a suitable basis set. For this reason, a more general framework is needed for constructing and revising basis sets. We present such a framework now. This approach is described in much more detail in [14]; but we overview the approach here, since it is relevant to our development of piecewise linear approximators in Section 4.

We assume some set of candidate basis functions $\mathcal{B}$ and an initial basis set $\mathcal{F}_0$. At each iteration k, we compute the best linear approximation w.r.t. $\mathcal{F}_k$, and estimate its error. If the error is unacceptable, and sufficient computation time is available, we then use some *scoring metric* to estimate the improvement offered by each element of $\mathcal{B}$ w.r.t. $\mathcal{F}_k$, and add the best $f \in \mathcal{B}$ to obtain $\mathcal{F}_{k+1}$.

This generic framework can be instantiated in many ways. First, we must define the set $\mathcal{B}$ suitably. We might assume a fixed *dictionary* of candidate basis functions, and score each explicitly. We will adopt this approach below. However, one might also define $\mathcal{B}$ implicitly, and use methods that *construct* a suitable candidate [14].[3]

We also require a scoring metric. An obvious, and computationally demanding, approach would involve adding each candidate function f to $\mathcal{F}_k$ and resolving, in turn, each resulting LP. This gives an exact measure of the value of adding f. Other less demanding approaches are possible. One we consider here is the *dual constraint violation* heuristic.

When we solve the LP Eq. 7, we obtain the corresponding values of the *dual variables* λ_j, one per contraint: because we use constraint generation, all constraints generally will be active, and all $\lambda_j > 0$. If we add f to our current basis set (with corresponding column $\mathbf{c}$ in the LP, and sum of values y), this is imposes a new constraint in the dual LP: $\lambda^{\top}\mathbf{c} \leq y$. If this constraint is satisfied given the current value of λ, we will make no progress (since the current solution remains optimal). The degree to which this dual constraint is *violated*—i.e., the magnitude of $\lambda^{\top}\mathbf{c} - y$, provided it is greater than 0—is a good heuristic measure of the value of adding f. Note again that the set of dual variables is $O(m)$ due to incremental constraint generation. The dual constraint violation heuristic scores each basis function in the dictionary using this measure and adds that function to the basis with maximal score.

This framework is inherently greedy: it considers the *immediate* impact of adding a candidate f to the current basis.

4 Piecewise Linear Value Functions

As suggested above, subtask VFs can often best approximate the optimal VF when combined in a piecewise linear fashion. We now describe an algorithm for constructing PWL approximations using subtask VFs as the underlying basis set. Our model uses greedy decision tree construction to determine appropriate regions of state space in which to use different combinations of basis functions. This framework can be seen as a way of incorpating both a domain dependent technique for basis function selection, and a domain independent technique for basis function addition. Indeed, nothing in this approach requires that the underlying basis set comprise the subtask VFs; but we expect WCMDPs to benefit greatly from this model.

The use of decision trees in value function approximation, both in solving MDPs and in reinforcement learning, is rather common. Examples include generalization techniques in reinforcement learing [4], dynamic discretization of continuous

state spaces [13], and their use in constructing piecewise constant value function representation for MDPs [3].

4.1 Evaluating Local Splits

We assume a small set of m basis functions $\mathcal{F}$ has been provided *a priori*, with each f_j defined over a small subset $\mathbf{X}_j^f \subset \mathbf{X}$ of our state variables. These might be, say, the optimal subtask VFs for a WCMDP, or a basis constructed using some domain-independent method. The model we adopt is one in which the linear approximation can vary in different parts of state space. These regions are determined by building a decision tree that splits on the variables $\mathbf{X}$.

Before providing details, we illustrate the intuitions by considering a single split of the VF on a fixed variable. Rather than determining the best linear approximator, suppose we allow the weight vector to take on different values, $\mathbf{w}^x$ and $\mathbf{w}^{\overline{x}}$, when variable X is true and false, respectively. So we have:

$$V(\mathbf{x}) = \sum_i w_i^x f_i(\mathbf{x}) \quad \text{for any} \quad \mathbf{x} \in [x]$$

$$V(\mathbf{x}) = \sum_i w_i^{\overline{x}} f_i(\mathbf{x}) \quad \text{for any} \quad \mathbf{x} \in [\overline{x}].$$

Letting $\mathbf{M}^x$ be a "mask" matrix that selects those states where X is true—i.e., a diagonal matrix with 1 at each x-state and 0 at each $\overline{x}$-state—and defining $\mathbf{M}^{\overline{x}}$ similarly, our approximation is

$$V = \mathbf{M}^x \mathbf{F} \mathbf{w}^x + \mathbf{M}^{\overline{x}} \mathbf{F} \mathbf{w}^{\overline{x}} \tag{8}$$

Our goal is to find the optimal *pair* of weight vectors:

Min: $\displaystyle \min_{\mathbf{w}^x, \mathbf{w}^{\overline{x}}} \sum_{\mathbf{x} \in [x]} \sum_j f_j(\mathbf{x}) w_i^x(\mathbf{x}) + \sum_{\mathbf{x} \in [\overline{x}]} \sum_j f_j(\mathbf{x}) w_j^{\overline{x}}(\mathbf{x})$

s.t.: $B^a(\mathbf{M}^x \mathbf{F} \mathbf{w}^x + \mathbf{M}^{\overline{x}} \mathbf{F} \mathbf{w}^{\overline{x}}) - (\mathbf{M}^x \mathbf{F} \mathbf{w}^x + \mathbf{M}^{\overline{x}} \mathbf{F} \mathbf{w}^{\overline{x}}) \leq 0, \forall a$

Note that unless the MDP completely decouples along variable X, we must optimize the weights $\mathbf{w}^x, \mathbf{w}^{\overline{x}}$ jointly.

This optimization can be performed in exactly the same manner as described in Section 2.3. We observe that for each function f_j, the "masked" version of this depends on the same variables as originally, with the possible addition of X. Furthermore, the dependence on X is trivial: in the positive case, the function takes the constant value 0 if X is false, and takes the value indicated by the original if X is true. An ADD representation of the masked function thus has only one more node than the original (i.e., it does *not* double the size of the function representation). Since these functions are themselves "small," the same cost network and constraint generation methods can be applied directly.

The approximation above is a *piecewise linear function* over the original basis set, but can also be viewed as *linear* approximator over a *new* basis set. We have replaced the original basis set with the masked copies: the new basis set is

$$\{\mathbf{M}^x f : f \in \mathcal{F}\} \cup \{\mathbf{M}^{\overline{x}} f : f \in \mathcal{F}\}$$

4.2 Decision Tree Construction

The intuitions above suggest an obvious greedy technique for constructing a PWL approximator. We build a decision tree,

---

[3]We explore a variety of such domain independent basis function construction techniques, and scoring metrics, in [14].

where each interior node splits the state space on some variable X, and each leaf is labeled with a suitable weight vector denoting the linear approximation to be used in that part of state space.[4] The algorithm is initialized by computing the optimal linear weight vector. The initial tree consists of a single leaf (the root). At each iteration, we extend the current tree as follows: (a) we evaluate the improvement offered by splitting each leaf using each variable, using some scoring metric; (b) the best split is applied, and the optimal PWL VF (or some approximation) for the new tree is computed. The algorithm terminates when no split offers decent improvement, or the tree reaches some size limit.

A key component of the algorithm is the choice of scoring metric. We consider three metrics in this paper:

Full LP: The full LP (FLP) metric evaluates a split of the decision tree by computing the optimal PLW approximator for the extended tree. For a tree with t leaves, evaluating a split requires solving an LP involving $m(t+1)$ weight variables: we have $t - 1$ weight vectors for the unsplit leaves, and two new weight vectors for the split leaves.

Fixed Weight LP: The fixed weight LP (FWLP) metric evaluates a split of the decision tree by computing the optimal weight vector for the two new regions created, but holds the weights for each other region fixed (to their values in the preceding solution). Evaluating a split thus requires solving an LP involving $2m$ variables.

Max Dual Constraint Violation: This metric uses the LP solution for the current tree to evaluate the degree of dual constraint violation associated with the new basis functions. A split on X at the end of a branch labeled $\mathbf{y}$ is equivalent to adding the basis functions $\mathbf{M}^{x\mathbf{y}} f_j$ (for each $f_j \in \mathcal{F}$) to the current basis. Each of these new functions is scored using the dual constraint violation heuristic, and the maximum of these scores (over each j) is taken as the score of the split.[5]

These evaluation techniques are listed from most to least expensive. The full LP method finds the myopically optimal split. It requires solving an LP (using the usual cost network method for constraint generation) for each candidate split. These LPs are larger than those for the linear approximator: since we have a larger weight set, we generally need to add more constraints, each requiring a cost network evaluation. The fixed weight LP method is similar, but since we hold all nonsplit weights fixed, there are fewer variables, fewer constraints, and fewer cost networks evaluated (at most twice the number as with the original linear method). The fixed weight technique does not necessarily find the optimal split: since values in other parts of state space are fixed, they are uninfluenced by the change in value at the split states. We can view this as analogous to asynchronous (block) dynamic programming [1]. Once a split is chosen, we can then reoptimize all weights; or if we believe the MDP is strongly decoupled, we

might use the weights computed during evaluation to label the split leaves, but not reassess other weights.

The dual constraint violation method is by far the cheapest. Each candidate split can be evaluated using with just a handful of inner product computations. No optimization is required.

Finally, with each of these scoring metrics, one heuristically choose a split by not re-evaluating the scores of previously unsplit nodes. That is, when the leaves of a tree have been scored at one iteration, they are not rescored at a subsequent tree unless they are split. This method is heuristic since the score of a split at a leaf is not local: it depends on the current basis set (viewing the union of basis functions at each leaf as the basis). However, the true score of a leaf can only go down when other leaves are split; its contribution to an extended basis set can be no greater than its contribution to a smaller set. Thus this *fixed score* method always associates with each leaf an upper bound on the true score.

There is a "hidden" cost associated with decision tree construction, since the masked basis functions $\mathbf{M}^{\mathbf{y}} f_j$ at leaf $\mathbf{y}$ refer to all variables along that branch. As the trees get deeper, table-based representations of the functions become much larger. However, as noted above, the ADD representation of these functions (nor their regressions $B^a \mathbf{M}^{\mathbf{y}} f_j$) needn't grow exponentially with the number of variables (i.e., the depth of the tree). Furthermore, the anticipated expense of cost network evaluation can be computed and combined with the scoring metric when considering a split, in an effort to induce a preference for shallower trees.

5 Empirical Results

We describe in this section some very preliminary empirical results. We demonstrate the decision quality of the tree growing technique as a function of the number of splits, using the three scoring metrics described above. We compare this to the optimal linear approximator obtained using subtask value functions, and to that obtained using bases comprising only indicator functions over one or two variables (the only method used in the literature). Naturally, since the best linear approximators are special cases of PWL approximators, decision quality can only improve as we split. What we aim to demonstrate is that quality improves significantly, and that this technique offers a *useful* way to improve a linear approximation. We use the value of the LP objective as a surrogate for quality of the resulting policy in most cases, but report on Bellman error in one example for illustration.

We consider a generic weakly coupled resource allocation problem of the type described in Section 3.1, with n periodic tasks and k indistinguishable resources. When j of the k resources are applied to an active task T_i, there is probability $1 - (q_i)^j$ of successfully *completing* that task (q_i is the probability that one unit of resource would *fail* to complete the task, a standard noisy-or model). A completed task becomes inactive. An inactive task i becomes active with probability p_i^{occ} and an active task becomes inactive (if not completed) with probability p_i^{lv}. A reward r_i is obtained if task i is completed. A resource j can be *usable* or *depleted*, indicated by status variable S_j. If usable resource j is applied to a task, it depletes with probability p_j^d, and at each stage a depleted re-

---

[4]We proceed as if all variables are binary. Binary (aggregate) and multiway splits of multivalued variables are straightforward.

[5]Other ways (e.g., conic combinations) can be used to combine the scores of these basis functions. We note that we only have to consider the scores of one masked set (e.g., X true), since $\mathbf{M}^{x\mathbf{y}} f_j, \mathbf{M}^{\mathbf{y}} f_j$ jointly span $\mathbf{M}^{\overline{x}\mathbf{y}} f_j$.

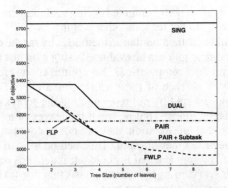

Figure 2: Resource allocation task with no dominant tasks.

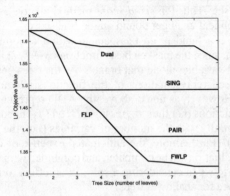

Figure 3: Resource allocation task with two dominant tasks.

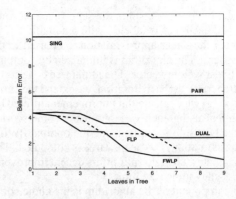

Figure 4: Bellman error for 2 resources, 5 tasks.

source has probability p_j^r of becoming usable again. assigned resources. Since this problem is weakly coupled, we use the subtask value functions for each T_i as an initial basis set.

To illustrate the benefits of PWL approximators, we first consider two small versions of this problem, with $n = 4$ tasks, and $k = 2$ resources. In the first, all tasks have roughly the same level of priority (i.e., similar rewards and probabilities). Figure 2 illustrates the value of the LP objective (which roughly minimizes L_1 error) as a function of the number of regions (i.e. number of decision tree leaves) used in the PWL approximator constructed using each of the scoring metrics described above. As we see, in all cases, decision quality improves with additional splits, which is hardly surprising. We also see that the more expensive scoring metrics are producing much better splits. FLP, since it produces optimal myopic splits, clearly dominates the other methods. FWLP, while much cheaper computationally, also finds improving splits identical to FLP except in one instance. The dual metric, unfortunately, does not fare as well. Note that each curve starts at the same spot: the value of the best linear approximator over the subtask VFs. For comparison, we include the objective value obtained by the best linear approximator over indicator functions on all single variables (SING) and all pairs of variables (PAIR). Note that after very few splits, the PWL approximators provide better VFs than these linear functions.[6] We

also include the linear approximator over the basis with PAIR indicators and the n subtasks VFs. Adding the subtasks VFs induces substantial improvement over PAIR, indicating their suitability as basis functions. Note that subtask VFs alone do not do as well as pairs, simply because the size of the pairs basis set is substantially larger and spans a larger subspace.

We show the same results in Figure 3 for a variant of the problem in which two of the four tasks have much higher priority than the others. In this case, the values of the low priority tasks have little influence on the optimal value function, since resources are often held in reserve in case a high priority task should pop up. Again we see that the same relative order emerge among the PWL approximators, and that decision quality is better than that of the linear approximators.

We also note that the PWL model can be used to produce piecewise constant VFs using a single constant basis function. In general, if the VF of an MDP has a small decision tree representation, this method will find it quickly.

We also consider some slightly larger problems. Figure 4 shows similar results for a 2-resource, 5-task problem; but Bellman error is plotted rather than LP-objective value. Notice that in this example, subtask VFs provide a better basis than either SING or PAIR even before splitting. Computation times for each iteration of the decision tree algorithm vary with the scoring metric. Averaged over the first 6 splits (7 leaves), we have (in CPU seconds) the following times: FLP – 691s; FWLP – 388s; Dual – 935s.[7] We note that the dual times are based on an unoptimized implementation and cannot be meaningfully compared to the others (but we include it for completeness).

Figure 5 shows LP-objective value for a 1-resource, 20-task problem for both DUAL and PAIR. The error for SING is not plotted as it is about 5 times as high as for PAIR. Finally, a similar plot is shown in Figure 6 for a 2-resource, 10-task problem (again SING is not shown). In the former, the dual metric offers an improved solution after only two splits, while in the latter, the subtask VFs themselves provide a better solution than the pairs. In the latter case, an improved solution is found af-

---

[6]The results for FLP are shown only up to five leaves in this and the subsequent graph.

[7]The implementation is in Matlab; calls to optimized C++ routines are used for FLP and FWLP, but not for dual. We project the same optimization applied to dual would yield 10-fold speed up. Experiments were run on a 700MHz PCs running Linux.

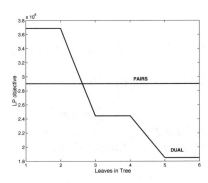

Figure 5: LP-objective value for 1 resource, 20 tasks.

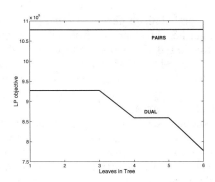

Figure 6: LP-objective value for 2 resources, 10 tasks.

ter 3 splits. Computation times for the 20-task splits average 1784s, whereas the 10-task splits average 1801s. Again we emphasize that the dual running times are based on an unoptimized implementation.

While these results should be viewed as preliminary, they are encouraging. The evidence suggests that subtask VFs provide very good basis sets for factored linear approximators. Furthermore, we see that with very few splits, the PWL approach can offer further improvement over a purely linear approximator.

6 Concluding Remarks

While linear approximators have proven to be valuable tool in the solution of factored MDPs, to date, no concrete proposals have been put forth for basis function selection and revision in the factored setting. We a described a concrete means for basis function selection using subtask VFs, and suggested a family of techniques for basis function revision. We investigated in some depth the use of decision tree techniques to produce PWL approximators. Our empirical results show that even with few splits, decision quality can be greatly improved relative to standard linear approximators.

Future research directions include the development of *hybrid* basis revision techniques, where new functions can be added directly to the basis, along with splitting of state space. Further experimentation is also needed to determine the range of problems on which this approach works well. Finally, we plan to investigate splitting criteria that tradeoff computational cost for projected improvement in decision quality.

Acknowledgements

Thanks to the referees for their comments. This research was supported by the Natural Sciences and Engineering Research Council and the Institute for Robotics and Intelligent Systems.

References

[1] D. P. Bertsekas and J.. N. Tsitsiklis. *Neuro-dynamic Programming*. Athena, Belmont, MA, 1996.

[2] C. Boutilier, R. I. Brafman, and C. Geib. Prioritized goal decomposition of Markov decision processes: Toward a synthesis of classical and decision theoretic planning. In *Proc. Fifteenth International Joint Conf. on AI*, pp.1156–1162, Nagoya, 1997.

[3] C. Boutilier, R. Dearden, and M. Goldszmidt. Exploiting structure in policy construction. In *Proc. Fourteenth International Joint Conf. on AI*, pp.1104–1111, Montreal, 1995.

[4] D. Chapman and L. P. Kaelbling. Input generalization in delayed reinforcement learning: An algorithm and performance comparisons. In *Proc. Twelfth International Joint Conf. on AI*, pp.726–731, Sydney, 1991.

[5] T. Dean, R. Givan, and S. Leach. Model reduction techniques for computing approximately optimal solutions for Markov decision processes. In *Proc. Thirteenth Conf. on Uncertainty in AI*, pp.124–131, Providence, RI, 1997.

[6] T. Dean and K. Kanazawa. A model for reasoning about persistence and causation. *Comput. Intel.*, 5(3):142–150, 1989.

[7] R. Dearden and C. Boutilier. Abstraction and approximate decision theoretic planning. *Artif. Intel.*, 89:219–283, 1997.

[8] C. Guestrin, D. Koller, and R. Parr. Max-norm projections for factored MDPs. In *Proc. Seventeenth International Joint Conf. on AI*, pp.673–680, Seattle, 2001.

[9] C. Guestrin, D. Koller, and R. Parr. Multiagent planning with factored MDPs. In *Advances in Neural Info. Processing Sys. 14 (NIPS-2001)*, Vancouver, 2001.

[10] J. Hoey, R. St-Aubin, A. Hu, and C. Boutilier. SPUDD: Stochastic planning using decision diagrams. In *Proc. Fifteenth Conf. on Uncertainty in AI*, pp.279–288, Stockholm, 1999.

[11] R. A. Howard. *Dynamic Programming and Markov Processes*. MIT Press, Cambridge, 1960.

[12] N. Meuleau, M. Hauskrecht, K. Kim, L. Peshkin, L. P. Kaelbling, T. Dean, and C. Boutilier. Solving very large weakly coupled Markov decision processes. In *Proc. Fifteenth National Conf. on AI*, pp.165–172, Madison, WI, 1998.

[13] A. W. Moore and C. G. Atkeson. The parti-game algorithm for variable resolution reinforcement learning in multidimensional state spaces. *Mach. Learn.*, 21:199–234, 1995.

[14] P. Poupart, C. Boutilier, R. Patrascu, and D. Schuurmans. Piecewise linear value function approximation for factored MDPs. In *Proc. Eighteenth National Conf. on AI*, Edmonton, 2002. to appear.

[15] M. L. Puterman. *Markov Decision Processes: Discrete Stochastic Dynamic Programming*. Wiley, New York, 1994.

[16] D. Schuurmans and R. Patrascu. Direct value approximation for factored MDPs. In *Advances in Neural Info. Processing Sys. 14 (NIPS-2001)*, Vancouver, 2001.

[17] S. P. Singh and D. Cohn. How to dynamically merge Markov decision processes. In *Advances in Neural Info. Processing Sys. 10*, pp.1057–1063. MIT Press, Cambridge, 1998.

[18] J. Tsitsiklis and B. Van Roy. Feature-based methods for large scale dynamic programming. *Mach. Learn.*, 22:59–94, 1996.

Bayesian Networks for Speech and Image Integration

Sven Wachsmuth and **Gerhard Sagerer**
Bielefeld University, Faculty of Technology, 33594 Bielefeld, Germany
swachsmu@techfak.uni-bielefeld.de

Abstract

The realization of natural human-computer interfaces suffers from a wide range of restrictions concerning noisy data, vague meanings, and context dependence. An essential aspect of everyday communication is the ability of humans to ground verbal interpretations in visual perception. Thus, the system has to be able to solve the correspondence problem of relating verbal and visual descriptions of the same object. This contribution proposes a new and innovative solution to this problem using Bayesian networks. In order to capture vague meanings of adjectives used by the speaker, psycholinguistic experiments are evaluated. Object recognition errors are taken into account by conditional probabilities estimated on test sets. The Bayesian network is dynamically built up from verbal object description and is evaluated by an inference technique combining bucket elimination and conditioning. Results show that speech and image data is interpreted more robustly in the combined case than in the case of isolated interpretations.

Introduction

Speech understanding and vision are the most important abilities in human-human communication, but also the most complex tasks for a machine. Typically, speech understanding and vision systems are realized for a dedicated application in a constrained domain. Both tasks are realized using different specialized paradigms and separated knowledge bases. They use different vocabularies to express the semantic content of an input signal. Consequently, the *correspondence problem* – namely how to correlate visual information with words, events, phrases, or entire sentences – is not easy to solve (Srihari 1994). A human speaker encodes the verbal-visual correspondences in an internal representation of the sentence he or she intends to utter. The communication partner has to decode these correspondences without knowing the mental models and internal representation of the speaker. Thus, *referential uncertainty* is inherently introduced even for perfect understanding components. Additionally, the interpretations of the signal modalities are often erroneous or incomplete such that an integrating component must consider noisy and partial interpretations. As a consequence, this contribution treats the correspondence

problem as probabilistic *decoding process*. This perspective distinguishes this approach from other approaches that propose rule-based translation schemes (Takahashi *et al.* 1998) or integrated knowledge bases (Brondsted *et al.* 1998; Srihari & Burhans 1994). These assume that a visual representation can be logically transformed into a verbal representation and vice versa.

An important issue for a system that relates erroneous and incomplete interpretations is *robustness*, i.e. how the system answer is affected by propagated errors. The proposed approach shows that even though a multi-modal system has to face multiple error sources *the combined signal can be interpreted more stably than the individual signals*. This is explicitly shown by a detailed analysis of the identification rates of an implemented system in a construction domain.

It reveals that the Bayesian network used for integration of speech and image interpretations has to combine spatial and type information. Instead of modeling these two kinds of evidence in separated Bayesian networks (Rimey & Brown 1994; Intille 1999), a novel Bayesian network scheme is developed by introducing *selection variables* and exploiting the properties of these variables during inference.

Object descriptions from vision and speech

Interpretations extracted from speech and images can only be integrated on the basis of a common notion, e.g. a visually perceived and verbally mentioned object (cf. (Jackendoff 1987)). On the speech side an object instance is verbally

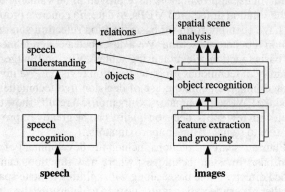

Figure 1: Object descriptions extracted from speech and images

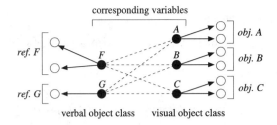

Figure 2: The correspondence problem in Bayesian networks: Two objects F, G referred by the speaker has to be related to three visually detected objects A, B, C.

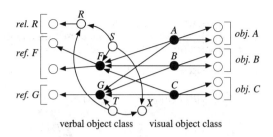

Figure 3: Modeling of the correspondence problem using selection variables S, T.

described by nouns, adjectives, and spatial relations to other object instances. On the vision side, an object instance is described by the location of grouped features, feature values, and the label provided by object recognition algorithms. Additionally, a qualitative scene description may be derived from the object locations defining relations between objects (Fig. 1). Both processes are error-prone and are typically based on separated knowledge bases. Thus, the task of establishing correspondences between vision and speech processing results should consider both processes as well as the mapping between them as probabilistic.

Bayesian networks

Bayesian networks (Pearl 1988) model a joint probability distribution over a set of random variables $\mathcal{U} = \{A_1, \ldots, A_n\}$ with discrete states. Conditional independencies between sets of variables are represented in a directed acyclic graph $\mathcal{G}$.

$$P(\mathcal{U}) = \prod_{A \in \mathcal{U}} P(A|pa(A))$$

where $pa(A)$ denotes all parents of node A in $\mathcal{G}$

In the following, upper letters denote random variables, lower letters denote states of variables. Thus, $P(A|B,C)$ is a conditional probability table (CPT) while

$$P(a_i|b_j,c) = P(A = a_i|B = b_j, C = c)$$

is the probability value after assigning the i-th state of A, the j-th state of B, and state c. Sets of variables are distinguished by raised indices, e.g. $A^{(i)} \in \{a_1^{(i)}, \ldots, a_n^{(i)}\}$.

Modeling of the correspondence problem

The correspondence problem is formulated by several subnetworks that include a set of *corresponding variables* (see Fig. 2), e.g. variables modeling the object classes for the sentence *"Take the small ring in front of the rotor"* and the scene in Fig. 6. Each variable on the speech side corresponds to another variable on the vision side, but the correct assignment is not previously known. It has to be inferred from evidences. Thus, the correspondence property has to be modeled in the language of Bayesian networks. Let F be a speech variable that corresponds to one of the vision variables A or B. This *one-to-two* mapping is represented by a

selection variable $S \in \{\tilde{a}, \tilde{b}\}$ and the conditional probability table

$$P(F|A,B,S) = [P(f_i|a_j,b_k,s); i = 1 \ldots m, j = 1 \ldots n,$$
$$k = 1 \ldots r, s \in \{\tilde{a}, \tilde{b}\}]$$

where $P(f_i|a_j, b_k, s) = \begin{cases} P(f_i|a_j) & \text{, if } s = \tilde{a} \\ P(f_i|b_k) & \text{, if } s = \tilde{c} \end{cases}$

If $S = \tilde{a}$, B is irrelevant to F. If $S = \tilde{b}$, A is irrelevant to F. A *one-to-N* mapping between variable F and variables $A^{(1)} \ldots A^{(N)}$ can be modeled by extending the possible states of $S \in \{\tilde{a}_1, \ldots, \tilde{a}_N\}$:

$$P(f|a^{(1)}, \ldots, a^{(N)}, s) = P(f|a^{(i)}), \text{if } s = \tilde{a}_i$$

Exclusive *M-to-N* mappings between variables $F^{(1)} \ldots F^{(M)}$ and $A^{(1)} \ldots A^{(N)}$ are modeled by introducing M selection variables with N states each, $S^{(1)}, \ldots, S^{(M)} \in \{\tilde{a}_1, \ldots, \tilde{a}_N\}$:

$$P(f^{(i)}|a^{(1)}, \ldots, a^{(N)}, s^{(i)}) = P(f^{(i)}|a^{(j)}), \text{if } s^{(i)} = \tilde{a}_j$$
$$\text{where } 1 \leq i \leq M, 1 \leq j \leq N$$

and an exclusive relation R with

$$P(X = 1|s^{(1)}, \ldots, s^{(M)})$$
$$= \begin{cases} 1.0, & \text{if } s^{(i)} \neq s^{(k)}, 1 \leq i,k \leq M, i \neq k \\ 0.0, & \text{otherwise} \end{cases}$$

Spatial or structural information about verbally mentioned objects can be coded by constraining possible values of selection variables. These constraints are extracted from visual information that is represented in $P(R|S,T)$ (see subsection about **Spatial modeling**). The resulting network is presented in Fig. 3.

Inference in Bayesian networks

The solution of the correspondence problem in a Bayesian network including M selection variables is a *maximum a posteriori hypothesis* (map) task. We are searching for the most probable states of the selection variables $S_1, \ldots, S_M$ with regard to the marginal distribution arising out of the observed evidences $\mathbf{e}_F^-, \mathbf{e}_G^-, \mathbf{e}_A^-, \mathbf{e}_B^-, \mathbf{e}_C^-, \mathbf{e}_R^-$. The inference algorithm used in the system presented in this paper is based on the *bucket elimination* algorithm proposed by Rina Dechter

(Dechter 1998). It can be formulated in the algebra of conditional probability tables (CPTs) as a summation and maximization over a product of CPTs:

$$s^*, t^* = \underset{s,t}{\mathrm{argmax}}\; P(X = 1|S, T)$$

$$\sum_R P(\mathbf{e}_R^-|R)\, P(R|S, T) \sum_A P(\mathbf{e}_A^-|A)\, P(A)$$

$$\sum_B P(\mathbf{e}_B^-|B)\, P(B) \sum_C P(\mathbf{e}_C^-|C)\, P(C) \sum_F P(\mathbf{e}_F^-|F)$$

$$P(F|A, B, C, S) \sum_G P(\mathbf{e}_G^-|G)\, P(G|A, B, C, T)$$

where each summation or maximization over a variable defines a bucket. Thus, the result of a summation can be interpreted as a message from one bucket to another. A straight forward evaluation of a Bayesian network that includes M selection variables with N states each results in messages to be propagated which sizes are exponential in M. However, The CPTs $P(F|A, B, C, S)$ and $P(G|A, B, C, T)$ define a context-specific independence (CSI) as discussed in (Boutilier *et al.* 1996). Instead of introducing numerous additional nodes to the Bayesian network in order to cover the CSI in the structure of the network, here, we propose an algorithmic solution by combining conditioning and bucket elimination techniques. This approach has the advantage of being better suited for extension towards approximate inference. Using conditioning over the selection variables S, T, the inference algorithm can be formulated as a conditioned sum:

$$s^*, t^* = \underset{s,t}{\mathrm{argmax}}\; P(X = 1|S, T)$$

$$\sum_R P(\mathbf{e}_R^-|R)\, P(R|S, T) \sum_A P(\mathbf{e}_A^-|A)\, P(A)$$

$$\sum_B P(\mathbf{e}_B^-|B)\, P(B) \sum_C P(\mathbf{e}_C^-|C)\, P(C)$$

$$\sum_F P(\mathbf{e}_F^-|F) \begin{cases} P(F|A, S = \tilde{a}) \\ P(F|B, S = \tilde{b}) \\ P(F|C, S = \tilde{c}) \end{cases}$$

$$\sum_G P(\mathbf{e}_G^-|G) \begin{cases} P(G|A, T = \tilde{a}) \\ P(G|B, T = \tilde{b}) \\ P(G|C, T = \tilde{c}) \end{cases}$$

After evaluation of the last two buckets, i.e. summations over G, F, and propagation of the resulting messages $\lambda_F(\dots)$ and $\lambda_G(\dots)$ we get:

$$s^*, t^* = \underset{s,t}{\mathrm{argmax}}\; P(X = 1|S, T)$$

$$\sum_R P(\mathbf{e}_R^-|R)\, P(R|S, T)$$

$$\sum_A P(\mathbf{e}_A^-|A)\, P(A) \begin{cases} \lambda_F(A, S = \tilde{a}) \begin{cases} \lambda_G(A, T = \tilde{a}) \\ \lambda_G(A, T \neq \tilde{a}) \end{cases} \\ \lambda_F(A, S \neq \tilde{a}) \begin{cases} \lambda_G(A, T = \tilde{a}) \\ \lambda_G(A, T \neq \tilde{a}) \end{cases} \end{cases}$$

$$\sum_B P(\mathbf{e}_B^-|B)\, P(B) \begin{cases} \lambda_F(B, S = \tilde{b}) \{\dots \\ \lambda_F(B, S \neq \tilde{b}) \{\dots \end{cases}$$

$$\sum_C P(\mathbf{e}_C^-|C)\, P(C) \{\dots$$

Evaluating buckets A, B, C, R, then, yields:

$$s^*, t^* = \underset{s,t}{\mathrm{argmax}}\; P(X = 1|S, T)\, \lambda_R(S, T)\, \lambda_{A,B,C}(S, T)$$

where $\lambda_{A,B,C}(S, T)$

$$= \begin{bmatrix} \lambda_A(S = \tilde{a}, T = \tilde{a}) & \lambda_A(S \neq \tilde{a}, T = \tilde{a}) \\ \lambda_A(S \neq \tilde{a}, T = \tilde{a}) & \lambda_A(S \neq \tilde{a}, T \neq \tilde{a}) \end{bmatrix}$$

$$\cdot \begin{bmatrix} \lambda_B(S = \tilde{b}, T = \tilde{b}) & \lambda_B(S \neq \tilde{b}, T = \tilde{b}) \\ \lambda_B(S \neq \tilde{b}, T = \tilde{b}) & \lambda_B(S \neq \tilde{b}, T \neq \tilde{b}) \end{bmatrix}$$

$$\cdot \begin{bmatrix} \lambda_C(S = \tilde{c}, T = \tilde{c}) & \lambda_C(S \neq \tilde{c}, T = \tilde{c}) \\ \lambda_C(S \neq \tilde{c}, T = \tilde{c}) & \lambda_C(S \neq \tilde{c}, T \neq \tilde{c}) \end{bmatrix}$$

In general, the evaluation scheme still holds if the different corresponding sub-networks are not d-separated by the variable $A, B, C, F,$ or G, respectively. In this case the conditioning structure of each bucket is more complex and the final message $\lambda_{A,B,C}$ cannot be defined by three independent factors. In practice, this causes no problem as long as the problem size is small or the subnets can be d-separated by instantiating evidential variables. As an additional step, the properties of the CPT $P(X = 1|S, T)$ are exploited during evaluation such that not all conditional summations have to be computed.

Application to a construction scenario

The Bayesian network approach for integrating speech and images has been applied to a *situated artificial communicator* in a construction scenario. The project aims at the development of a robot constructor which can be instructed by speech and gestures in the most natural way (Bauckhage *et al.* 2001).

While the communication between the human instructor and the system is constrained as little as possible, the domain setting is rather restricted. A partial collection of 23 different elementary components of a wooden toy construction kit is placed on a table. The elementary objects have characteristic colors. However, the colors do not uniquely determine the class of an object. The table scene is perceived by a calibrated stereo camera head that is used for object recognition and localization. For speech recording a wireless microphone system is employed. The robot constructor consists of two robot arms that act on the table. It can grasp objects, screw or plug them together, and can put them down again. The human instructor is assumed to be naive, i.e. he or she has not been trained on the domain. Therefore, speakers tend to use qualitative, vague descriptions of object properties instead of precise technical terms.

Speech recognition and shallow understanding is realized by a statistical speech recognizer (Fink 1999) that tightly interacts with the understanding component by means of a partial parsing component (Brandt-Pook *et al.* 1999). Verbal object descriptions may consist of type (bolt, cube, disc, etc.), color (red, blue, dark, etc.), size (small, long, etc.), and shape (round, angular, elongated, etc.) attributes. Out-of-domain nouns (e.g rotor) are mapped onto an unspecific *Object* label that refers to aggregated objects

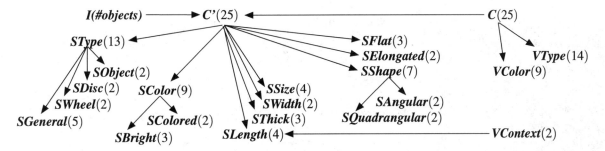

Figure 4: A Bayesian network modeling object classes. The number of states for each node is denoted in brackets.

with a higher probability. Additionally, the user can specify projective spatial relations (left-to, in-front-of, ...), locations (in-the-middle, ...), and structural relations (e.g. *the cube with the bolt*).

The object recognition component   is based on a segmentation of homogeneous color regions. Clusters of elementary objects are parsed into aggregate structures using a semantic network (Bauckhage *et al.* 1999). The visual features used in the Bayesian network are the recognized color and type attributes of an object. Regions that do not match any object class are labeled as *unknown*.

Domain modeling

In order to capture the language use of unexperienced human instructors, a series of experiments were conducted (Socher, Sagerer, & Perona 2000). From the first three experiments frequently named color, shape, and size adjectives were extracted that are presented in Fig. 5.

gelb *(yellow)*	rund *(round)*	lang *(long)*
rot *(red)*	sechseckig *(hexagonal)*	groß *(big)*
blau *(blue)*	flach *(flat)*	klein *(small)*
weiß *(white)*	rechteckig *(rectangular)*	kurz *(short)*
grün *(green)*	dünn *(thin)*	breit *(large, wide)*
hell *(light)*	länglich *(elongated)*	hoch *(high)*
orange *(orange)*	dick *(thick)*	eckig *(angular)*
lila *(violet)*	schmal *(narrow)*	

holzfarben *(wooden)*	mittellang *(medium-long)*
rautenförmig *(diamond-shaped)*	mittelgroß *(medium-sized)*

Figure 5: Frequently named color, shape, and size adjectives.

A forth experiment explored the semantics of shape and size adjectives:

- *Exp. WWW*: 426 subjects participated in a multiple choice questionnaire (274 German version, 152 English version) that was presented in the World Wide Web (WWW). Each questionnaire consisted of 20 WWW pages, one page for each elementary object type of the domain. In one version the objects were shown isolated, in another version the objects were shown together with other context objects. Below the image of the object 18 shape and size adjectives were presented that have been extracted in the previously

mentioned experiments. The subject was asked to tick each adjective that is a valid description of the object type.

The evaluation of this experiment provides frequencies of use for the different adjectives with regard to the object class and the object context. A qualitative evaluation from a psycholinguistic perspective has been performed by Constanze Vorwerg (Vorwerg 2001). She extracted the following results:

1. All attributes except 'rund' *(round)* depend on context. But the context only partially determines the selection of it. In the construction kit, there exist three different types of bars with different lengths: a three-holed, a five-holed, and a seven-holed bar. The frequency of the selection of 'kurz' *(short)* and 'lang' *(long)* decreases/increases with the length of the bar as expected. This can be observed independent of the context. However, the isolated naming of a three-holed bar yields a higher frequency of 'mittellang' *(medium-long)* than that of a five-holed bar. In the context with all three types of bars present this ordering is switched. The average selection from the context version rates similar to the isolated selection.

2. The attribute selection in the corresponding dimensions, e.g. 'long' in the dimension *size*, is very specific to the object classes. Context objects have only a small influence. For example, the longest bolt is called 'long' although it has a smaller length then the shortest bar. This is not affected by the fact that there is a bar in the context or not.

3. 'dick' *(thick)* is negatively correlated with the length of an object. The bolts have all the same width, but the shortest bolt is called 'thick' with a much higher frequency.

4. 'eckig' *(angular)* is neither a super-concept of 'rechteckig' *(rectangular)* nor 'viereckig' *(quadrangular)*. It is partially used as an alternative naming.

5. 'rechteckig' *(rectangular)* is negatively correlated with 'lang' *(long)*, 'länglich' *(elongated)* is positively correlated with it.

6. Even the selection of qualitative attributes, like 'eckig' *(angular)*, depends on the context. For example, the less objects with typical angular shape are present, the more frequent 'angular' is selected.

Altogether, it reveals that the meaning of shape and size attributes is difficult to capture. It is particularly difficult to di-

"Nimm den kleinen Ring vor dem Rotor."
[Take the small ring in front of the rotor.]

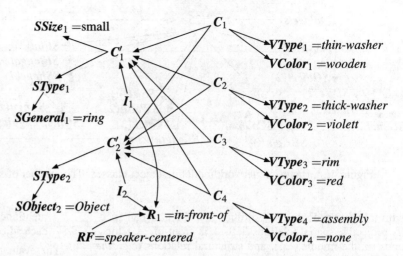

Figure 6: Bayesian network for integrating speech and image interpretations

rectly extract the applicability of such attributes from image features. The solution that has been applied in this system is to use object class statistics. A first approach was proposed in previous work of Gudrun Socher (Socher, Sagerer, & Perona 2000). However she did not consider the mentioned qualitative results in the structure of the Bayesian network nor the naming of assembled objects.

The model for naming of object classes is shown in Fig. 4. *VType, VColor* represent evidential nodes containing the visual classification results of an object in the scene. *VContext* distinguishes two different contexts as discussed in item (1.) of subsection **Domain modeling**: all three different bars present or not present. We abstract from other context dependencies because this is the only one which qualitatively changes frequency orderings. The arc from C to C' depends on the value of the corresponding selection variable I. Besides the elementary object classes, the states of the variables C, C' include one state for assembled objects and an additional state 'unknown' for inconsistent object descriptions.

The evidential variables in this network are not only leaves because some nouns and adjectives are more precise than others. The meaning of *angular* and *quadrangular* were split into a super-concept modeled by the variables *SAngular* and *SQuadrangular* and *other-angular* and *other-quadrangular* states in the variable *SShape*. Object names that are not known to denote an elementary object are instantiated in the variable *SObject*. It is an abstraction of the variable *SType* and denotes an assembled object with a higher probability than an elementary object type.

The conditional probability tables (CPTs) of the object-class model are partially set by hand and partially estimated from data:

- The CPTs $P(VType|C), P(VColor|C)$ are estimated using labeled test sets consisting of 11 images with 156 objects in the first case and a pixel-based evaluation of 27 images from 9 different scenes in the second case.

- The CPTs for named object types and colors were set by hand.

- The CPTs for named shape and size adjectives have been estimated using data from *Exp. WWW*.

Spatial modeling

Besides the object class descriptions discussed in the previous subsection, spatial relations can be exploited to constrain the selection of an intended object:

"Take the X-object in front of the Y-object."

The spatial model is treated as a black box function. It provides a *degree of application* for each object pair specifying if the named relation holds or not. Currently, the six different projective relations *in-front-of, behind, left-of, right-of, above, below* are distinguished. Instead of a complex 3-d spatial model, a 2-d spatial model was developed that considers each projective relation as a 2-d vector that has been projected onto the image plane (Wachsmuth 2001). The treatment of 3-d relations in two dimensions has the advantage that an error-prone 3-d reconstruction of the scene objects is not needed and complex 3-d shapes can be considered as more simple polygon areas. Additionally, a 2-d model accounts to the fact that nearly all objects are placed on the same table plane. The applicability of a relation depends on the positions of the objects relative to each other as well on the selected reference frame of the speaker. This may be either set by default, known from the context, known with a certain probability, or may remain unconstrained. All four cases can be modeled by introducing a random variable *RF* denoting different possible reference frames. The presented system distinguishes between a *speaker-centered* and a *hearer-centered* reference frame that are defined oppositely. In order to compute $P(R = \textit{in-front-of}|RF, I_1, I_2)$ from visual data, the degree of applicability of the spatial relation has to be transformed to a pseudo-probability. This is performed by calculating the degree of applicability of the inverse 2-d direction, the two orthogonal directions, and normalizing the computed degrees.

An example instantiation of the whole Bayesian network including four detected visual objects and a verbal instruction mentioning two objects related by *in-front-of* is shown

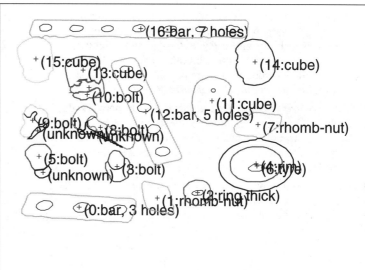

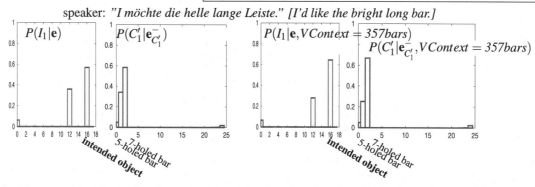

speaker: *"I möchte die helle lange Leiste."* *[I'd like the bright long bar.]*

Figure 7: Performance example: The speaker intends object 16. It is correctly recognized: $\mathbf{e}_{C_{16}}^- = \{wooden,\ 7\text{-}holed\text{-}bar\}$. The evidences extracted from speech are $\mathbf{e}_{C_1'}^- = \{bright,\ long,\ bar\}$. $\mathbf{e} = \bigcup_{i=0\ldots18} \mathbf{e}_{C_i}^- \cup \mathbf{e}_{C_1'}^-$. The first two plausibility vectors have been calculated without considering the context that all three different bar types are present in the scene. The system selects objects 12 and 16. The next two plausibility vectors have been calculated considering this context. Only the correct object 16 is selected.

in Fig. 6. Evidential variables that are not instantiated are not shown due to readability reasons. Note that the object name *ring* is an abstraction of different elementary object types and that the system has no specific semantics for the object name *rotor*. Therefore, the unspecific variable *SObject* is instantiated that indicates the denotation of an assembled object. Although the instruction is very unspecific the system is able to determine the correct intended object *2:thick-washer*.

Results

Results have been computed on a test set of 447 utterances from 10 different speakers. 10 different scenes including between 5 and 30 objects were captured by a camera and presented to them on a computer monitor. One object was marked and the speakers were asked to name it. The word error rate (WER) of speech recognition is 32%. Nevertheless the features describing an object achieve an error rate of only 15%. This is mainly an effect of the partial parser that is integrated into the speech recognition process (Wachsmuth,

Fink, & Sagerer 1998; Brandt-Pook *et al.* 1999). The object recognition results include an error rate of 25% (false positive + false negative object detection + false type/color classifications). In detail, the correctly detected but misclassified objects include 18% false type classifications and 5% false color classifications.

The task of the system is to determine the marked object given the speech and object recognition results. Many speakers describe the object class instead of the individual marked object. Thus, the system is allowed to select additional objects of the same object class besides the marked one. The criterion for selecting more than one object is based on the belief vector of variable I_1. If the difference between the highest belief component and the next highest component is greater than that to the third one, a single object is selected. Otherwise additional objects are selected.

In Fig. 7 an **example of the test set** is shown that includes a relevant context switch consisting of the presence of all three different kind of bars:

1. If this context is not considered the verbal description *"the bright long bar"* denotes a *seven-holed-bar* with highest probability and a *five-holed-bar* with significant probability. As a consequence both scene objects 16+12 have significant support and are considered in the system answer, i.e. *one additional object is selected.*

2. If the context is considered in the Bayesian network the attribute *long* supports the hypothesis of a *seven-holed-bar* more strongly. Thus, the *five-holed-bar* object in the scene is supported less and is not considered in the system answer, i.e. *no additional objects are selected.*

Besides the qualitative analysis of exemplary system results, a **quantitative evaluation** was performed. From the experimental setting the following general system behavior will be expected:

- If all objects in the scene and the spoken instruction are correctly recognized, *the identification rate of the system should be high.* Nevertheless, some system answers may fail because the speaker gave a too unspecific instruction, or selected an unusual wording (e.g. some bolts were called nuts).

- If some features that were mentioned by the speaker are misrecognized or not recognized at all, *the identification rate will decrease by a similar rate as the feature error rate.*

- If some of the marked objects have been misrecognized, *the identification rate will decrease by a similar rate as the recognition error rate.*

The system results are presented in table 1. A feature error rate of 15% decreased the identification rate by only 5%. An object recognition error rate of 20% on the marked objects affected the identification rate only by a 7% decrease. The combined noisy input results in a decrease of the identification rate by 11%. Thus, the integration scheme is able to exploit redundancy coded in the combined input in order to perform correctly.

	correct input	noisy speech	noisy vision	noisy input
error rates	-	15%	20%	15%+20%
ident. rates	0.85	0.81	0.79	0.76
decrease	-	5%	7%	11%

Table 1: Identification rates

Conclusion

A Bayesian network scheme for the integration of speech and images was presented that is able to correlate spatial and type information. A universal solution of the correspondence problem was developed that can be efficiently evaluated by combining bucket elimination and conditioning techniques. The approach was applied to a construction scenario. The network structure considers qualitative results from psycholinguistic experiments. The conditional probabilities were partially estimated from experimental data. Results show that spoken instructions can robustly be grounded into perceived visual data despite noisy data, erroneous intermediate results, and vague descriptions.

References

Bauckhage, C.; Fritsch, J.; Kummert, F.; and Sagerer, G. 1999. Towards a Vision System for Supervising Assembly Processes. In *Proc. Symposium on Intelligent Robotic Systems*, 89–98.

Bauckhage, C.; Fink, G. A.; Fritsch, J.; Kummert, F.; Lömker, F.; Sagerer, G.; and Wachsmuth, S. 2001. An Integrated System for Cooperative Man-Machine Interaction. In *IEEE International Symposium on Computational Intelligence in Robotics and Automation*, 328–333.

Boutilier, C.; Friedman, N.; Goldszmidt, M.; and Koller, D. 1996. Context-Specific Independence in Bayesian Networks. In *Proc. of the 12th Annual Conf. on Uncertainty in AI (UAI)*.

Brandt-Pook, H.; Fink, G. A.; Wachsmuth, S.; and Sagerer, G. 1999. Integrated recognition and interpretaion of speech for a construction task domain. In Bullinger, H.-J., and Ziegler, J., eds., *Proceedings 8th International Conference on Human-Computer Interaction*, volume 1, 550–554.

Brondsted, T.; Larsen, L. B.; Manthey, M.; McKevitt, P.; Moeslund, T.; and Olesen, K. G. 1998. The Intellimedia Workbench – a Generic Environment for Multimodal Systems. In *Int. Conf. on Spoken Language Processing*, 273–276.

Dechter, R. 1998. Bucket elimination: a unifying framework for probabilistic inference. In Jordan, M. I., ed., *Learning in graphical models*. Dordecht, NL: Kluwer Academic Publisher.

Fink, G. A. 1999. Developing HMM-based recognizers with ESMERALDA. In Matoušek, V.; Mautner, P.; Ocelíková, J.; and Sojka, P., eds., *Lecture Notes in Artificial Intelligence*, volume 1692, 229–234. Berlin: Springer.

Intille, S. S. 1999. *Visual Recognition of Multi-Agent Action.* Ph.D. Dissertation, Massachusetts Institute of Technology.

Jackendoff, R. 1987. On Beyond Zebra: The relation of linguistic and visual information. *Cognition* 26:89–114.

Pearl, J. 1988. *Probabilistic Reasoning in Intelligent Systems.* San Francisco, California: Morgan Kaufmann.

Rimey, R. D., and Brown, C. M. 1994. Control of Selective Perception Using Bayes Nets and Decision Theory. *International Journal of Computer Vision* 12(2/3):173–207.

Socher, G.; Sagerer, G.; and Perona, P. 2000. Bayesian reasoning on qualitative descriptions from images and speech. *Image and Vision Computing* 18:155–172.

Srihari, R., and Burhans, D. 1994. Visual Semantics: Extracting Visual Information from Text Accompanying Pictures. In *Proc. of the Nat. Conf. on Artificial Intelligence (AAAI)*, 793–798.

Srihari, R. K. 1994. Computational Models for Integrating Linguistic and Visual Information: A Survey. *Artificial Intelligence Review* 8:349–369.

Takahashi, T.; Nakanishi, S.; Kuno, Y.; and Shirai, Y. 1998. Helping Computer Vision by Verbal and Nonverbal Communication. In *Int. Conf. on Pattern Recognition*, 1216–1218.

Vorwerg, C. 2001. Kategorisierung von Grössen- und Formatributen. In *Posterbeitrag auf der 43. Tagung experimentell arbeitender Psychologen.*

Wachsmuth, S.; Fink, G. A.; and Sagerer, G. 1998. Integration of parsing and incremental speech recognition. In *Proceedings of the European Signal Processing Conference (EUSIPCO-98)*, volume 1, 371–375.

Wachsmuth, S. 2001. *Multi-modal Scene Understanding Using Probabilistic Models.* Ph.D. Dissertation, Bielefeld University. http://www.UB.Uni-Bielefeld.DE/index/abisz.htm.

Value Iteration Working With Belief Subset

Weixiong Zhang
Computational Intelligence Center and
Department of Computer Science
Washington University
St. Louis, MO 63130

Nevin L. Zhang
Department of Computer Science
Hong Kong University of Science and Technology
Clear Water Bay, Kowloon, Hong Kong

Abstract

Value iteration is a popular algorithm for solving POMDPs. However, it is inefficient in practice. The primary reason is that it needs to conduct value updates for all the belief states in the (continuous) belief space. In this paper, we study value iteration working with a subset of the belief space, i.e., it conducts value updates only for belief states in the subset. We present a way to select belief subset and describe an algorithm to conduct value iteration over the selected subset. The algorithm is attractive in that it works with belief subset but also retains the quality of the generated values. Given a POMDP, we show how to *a priori* determine whether the selected subset is a *proper* subset of belief space. If this is the case, the algorithm carries the advantages of representation in space and efficiency in time.

Introduction

Partially Observable Markov Decision Processes (POMDPs) serve as plausible models for planning under uncertainty. However, solving POMDPs is computationally difficult. There is growing interest in developing more efficient algorithms for finding solutions to POMDPs. Among the many algorithms, value iteration and its variations have been extensively studied in the literature.

Value iteration algorithm proceeds in an iterative fashion. Each iteration computes a new *value function* (which specifies a value for each belief state in the belief space) from the current one. In other words, value iteration considers the entire belief space at each iteration. Due to the continuum of the belief space, the algorithm is very inefficient. A nature way to accelerate it is to restrict it to a subset of the belief space, i.e., each iteration considers belief states in the subset. The key problem is how to deliberately select the belief subset. Certainly, if the subset is arbitrarily chosen, the quality of value functions computed can be arbitrarily poor. There is a tradeoff between the size of selected subset and the quality of value functions generated.

The algorithm we developed in this paper strikes a balance between the size of the subset and the quality of value functions. The subset is chosen to contain any belief states encountered by the modeled agent no matter which belief

state it starts from, no matter which action it performs and no matter which observation it receives. Value iteration working with this subset is called *subset value iteration*. We show how to *a priori* determine if the subset is a *proper* one. If this is the case, subset value iteration carries the space and time advantages: space advantage is because representing a value function over a subset needs fewer vectors, and time advantage is because computing sets of fewer vectors needs less computational effort. The subset value iteration is attractive in that it also retains the quality of value functions. In addition, the selected belief subset is the *minimal* subset in the sense that value iteration must work at least with the subset in order to retain the quality of value functions.

In the rest of the paper, we first introduce POMDP model and value iteration. Next, we discuss belief subset selection, representation and its relation to the entire space. Then, we develop the subset value iteration algorithm and show that it retains the quality of value functions. Before reporting experiments, we also show how the subset value functions generated can be extended to the entire space and the selected subset is minimal for value iteration to retain the quality of value functions. We conclude the paper with a brief survey of related work and some future directions.

POMDPs and Value Iteration

A POMDP $\mathcal{M}$ is a sequential decision-making model where the agent executes actions to change world states and the world provides the agent feedback reflecting the state transitions. Three sets are essential in a POMDP: the set $\mathcal{S}$ of world states, the set $\mathcal{A}$ of actions and the set $\mathcal{Z}$ of observations. The dependency between these sets is specified by two models: given a state s and an action a executed, the *action model* specifies the probability $P(s'|s, a)$ for any next state s'; given a state s and an action a, the *observation model* specifies the probability $P(z|s, a)$ for any observation z. The *reward model* specifies the reward at one step: if the agent executes action a in state s, it receives reward $r(s, a)$. Of interest is to maximize the expected discounted total rewards $E[\sum_{n=0}^{\infty} \lambda^n r_n]$ where λ is the *discount factor* less than 1 and r_n is the expected reward received at step n.

In the partially observable case, it is known that a probability distribution over the states(*belief state*) serves as a sufficient statistic for the agent's action selection (Aström 1965). The *belief space* is the set of all the possible belief states. It is often denoted by $\mathcal{B}$. If the agent starts with b, executes a and observes z, the next belief state b' is updated as follows: for any s', $b'(s') = 1/k \sum_s P(s', z|s, a)b(s)$ where $k (= P(z|b, a))$is a normalizer and the joint probability $P(s', z|s, a)$ equals to $P(s'|s, a)P(z|s', a)$. The belief state b' is sometimes denoted by $\tau(b, a, z)$.

A policy π prescribes an action for any belief state in $\mathcal{B}$. Associated with a policy π is its value function V^π which is a mapping from the belief space to the real line. For any b, $V^\pi(b)$ is the expected total discounted reward the agent receives if it starts with belief state b and follows policy π. Policy π *dominates* π_2 if $V^{\pi_1}(b) \geq V^{\pi_2}(b)$ for any b. The *optimal policy* dominates any other policies. Its value function is the *optimal value function*. An ϵ-*optimal value function* differs the optimal by at most ϵ. An ϵ-*optimal policy* is a policy whose value function is ϵ-optimal.

Value iteration starts with an initial value function V_0 and iterates using the formula:

$$V_{n+1}(b) = \max_a [r(b, a) + \lambda \sum_z P(z|b, a)V_n(\tau(b, a, z))].$$

The notation V_n is referred to as *value function at step* n. The step of computing V_{n+1} from V_n is referred to as *Dynamic-Programming* (DP) update. In practice, since value functions are representable by finite sets of vectors (Sondik 1971), DP update often refers to the process of obtaining the (minimal) representing set $\mathcal{V}_{n+1}$ of V_{n+1} from that of V_n. Value iteration terminates when the *Bellman residual*, $\max_b |V_n(b) - V_{n-1}(b)|$, falls below $\epsilon(1 - \lambda)/2\lambda$.

Belief Subset Selection

This section defines the subset, discusses its relation to the belief space and finally shows its linear representation.

Subset Selection

The expression $\tau(b, a, z)$ denotes the next belief state if the agent starts with b, executes a and observes z. The set $\{\tau(b, a, z)|b \in \mathcal{B}\}$ contains all the next belief states if the agent executes a and observes z, no matter which belief states it starts with. We denote this set by $\tau(\mathcal{B}, a, z)$. The union $\cup_{a,z}\tau(\mathcal{B}, a, z)$ consists of all belief states the agent can encounter, regardless of the initial belief states, actions executed and observations collected. For simplicity, we denote it by $\tau(\mathcal{B})$.

The set $\tau(\mathcal{B})$ is the subset we choose for value iteration to work with. Its definition is an application of reachability analysis (Boutilier, Brafman, & Geib 1998; Dean *et al.* 1993).

Relation Between Belief Subset and Belief Space

Given a pair $[a, z]$, it turns out that the following matrix plays an important role in determining the set $\tau(\mathcal{B}, a, z)$ where n is the number of states. We denote the matrix by P_{az}.

$$\begin{pmatrix} P(s'_1, z|s_1, a) & P(s'_2, z|s_1, a) & \cdots & P(s'_n, z|s_1, a) \\ P(s'_1, z|s_2, a) & P(s'_2, z|s_2, a) & \cdots & P(s'_n, z|s_2, a) \\ \cdots & \cdots & \cdots & \cdots \\ P(s'_1, z|s_n, a) & P(s'_2, z|s_n, a) & \cdots & P(s'_n, z|s_n, a) \end{pmatrix}$$

To see why, if a belief state is viewed as a row vector, $\tau(b, a, z)$ can be written as $\frac{1}{k_b}bP_{az}$ where k_b is the constant $P(z|b, a)$, and bP_{az} means matrix multiplication. The relationship between $\tau(\mathcal{B}, a, z)$ and $\mathcal{B}$ is characterized in the following lemma.

Lemma 1 *For any* $[a, z]$*, there exists a bijection between the simplex* $\tau(\mathcal{B}, a, z)$ *and the space* $\mathcal{B}$ *if and only if the matrix* P_{az} *is invertible(i.e. the determinant* $|P_{az}|$ *is non-zero).*

Due to this lemma, if the matrix P_{az} is degenerate(i.e., $|P_{az}|$ is zero), $\tau(\mathcal{B}, a, z)$ is a *proper* subset of $\mathcal{B}$. [1] The subset $\tau(\mathcal{B})$ is proper only if any $\tau(\mathcal{B}, a, z)$ is proper. Note that the these conditions can be verified *a priori*.

Theorem 1 *The set* $\tau(\mathcal{B})$ *is a proper subset of belief space* $\mathcal{B}$ *only if each matrix* P_{az} *is degenerate.*

Representation

Subset representation addresses how to represent the subsets $\tau(\mathcal{B}, a, z)$ and $\tau(\mathcal{B})$. Suppose that b_i is a unit vector ($b_i(s)$ equals 1.0 for $s = i$ and 0 otherwise). The set $\{b_1, b_2, \cdots, b_n\}$ is a *basis* of $\mathcal{B}$ in the sense that any b in $\mathcal{B}$ can be represented as a linear combination of vectors in the set. For each such b_i, $\tau(b_i, a, z)$ belongs to $\tau(\mathcal{B}, a, z)$ if $P(z|b_i, a) > 0$. It has been proven that $\{\tau(b_i, a, z)|P(z|b_i, a) > 0\}$ is a basis of the set $\tau(\mathcal{B}, a, z)$(Zhang 2001). This set is denoted by $B_{\tau(\mathcal{B},a,z)}$. For this reason, the set $\tau(\mathcal{B}, a, z)$ is said to be a *belief simplex* which is specified by the *extreme belief states* in the basis $B_{\tau(\mathcal{B},a,z)}$.

Theorem 2 *For any pair* $[a, z]$*, the subset* $\tau(\mathcal{B}, a, z)$ *is a simplex. Therefore, the subset* $\tau(\mathcal{B})$ *is a union of simplexes.*

Subset Value Iteration

This section defines an MDP whose state space is $\tau(\mathcal{B})$. Value iteration for the MDP works with a subset of the belief space. Two versions of value iteration are presented.

Subset MDP

The set $\tau(\mathcal{B})$ is a *closed* set in the sense that if the agent starts with a belief state in the set, no action can lead it to belief states outside the set. This property of $\tau(\mathcal{B})$ allows one to define a *subset MDP* as follows. Note that it differs from the belief space MDP transformed from the original POMDP only in the state space (e.g. (Zhang & Liu 1997)).

- The state space is $\tau(\mathcal{B})$ and action space is $\mathcal{A}$.
- Transition model: given a belief b in $\tau(\mathcal{B})$ and an a, if $b'=\tau(b, a, z)$ for some z, then $P(b'|b, a)$ is $P(z|b, a)$.
- Reward model: given a b in $\tau(\mathcal{B})$ and a, it specifies immediate reward $r(b, a)$ as $r(b, a) = \sum_{s \in \mathcal{S}} b(s)r(s, a)$.

The DP equation for the above MDP follows. In the equation below, $V_n^{\tau(\mathcal{B})}$ denotes its value function at step n.

For any b in $\tau(\mathcal{B})$,

$$V_{n+1}^{\tau(\mathcal{B})}(b) = \max_a \{r(b, a) + \lambda \sum_z P(z|b, a)V_n^{\tau(\mathcal{B})}(\tau(b, a, z))\}$$

---

[1]It is proper if there is one b in $\mathcal{B}$ such that $b \notin \tau(\mathcal{B}, a, z)$.

DP Updates

Similarly to value functions over the belief space, value functions over simplex and subset possess the same property. They can be represented by finite sets of vectors. A DP update computes the (minimal) set representing $V_{n+1}^{\tau(\mathcal{B})}$ from that representing $V_n^{\tau(\mathcal{B})}$. The rest of this subsection shows how to implicitly carry out DP update. Two issues must be addressed: how to compute a set representing $V_{n+1}^{\tau(\mathcal{B})}$, and how to compute the minimal set w.r.t. the subset $\tau(\mathcal{B})$.

The first issue can be settled by a similar procedure as in standard DP update. We enumerate all the possible vectors in the set representing $V_{n+1}^{\tau(\mathcal{B})}$. Each such vector can be defined by an action a and a mapping δ from $\mathcal{Z}$ to the set $\mathcal{V}_n^{\tau(\mathcal{B})}$ (It is known that the pair $[a, \delta]$ defines a policy tree in standard DP update (e.g., (Cassandra 1998)).) Given a pair $[a, \delta]$, the vector can be defined as follows and is denoted by $\beta_{a,\delta}$.

$$\beta_{a,\delta}(s) = r(s,a) + \lambda \sum_z \sum_{s'} P(s', z|s, a)\delta_z(s'). \quad (1)$$

where δ_z is the mapped vector for observation z.

The following set is obtained by altering the actions and mappings in the above definition.

$$\{\beta_{a,\delta}|a \in \mathcal{A}, \delta : \mathcal{Z} \to \mathcal{V}_n^{\tau(\mathcal{B})} \ \& \ \forall z, \delta_z \in \mathcal{V}_n^{\tau(\mathcal{B})}\}. \quad (2)$$

The set is denoted by $\mathcal{V}_{n+1}^{\tau(\mathcal{B})}$. It can be proved that the set $\mathcal{V}_{n+1}^{\tau(\mathcal{B})}$ represents value function $V_{n+1}^{\tau(\mathcal{B})}$. Furthermore, the set induces the same value function as V_{n+1} in $\tau(\mathcal{B})$.

Theorem 3 *If $\mathcal{V}_n^{\tau(\mathcal{B})}$ represents value function V_n in $\tau(\mathcal{B})$, $\mathcal{V}_{n+1}^{\tau(\mathcal{B})}$ represents V_{n+1} in the same subset.*

We now address the second issue: given a set of vectors, how to compute its minimal representation w.r.t. $\tau(\mathcal{B})$. We first explore the case for a simplex $\tau(\mathcal{B}, a, z)$. As in the standard *prune* operator, we need to prune useless vectors w.r.t. $\tau(\mathcal{B})$. Let the set be $\mathcal{V}$ and β is a vector in the set. It is useful if and only if there exists a belief state b in $\tau(\mathcal{B}, a, z)$ such that $\beta \cdot b \geq \alpha \cdot b + x$ where x is some positive number, α is a vector in the set $\mathcal{V} - \{\beta\}$ and $\cdot$ means inner product. On the other hand, b can be represented as $\sum_i \lambda_i \tau(b_i, a, z)$. If we replace b with $\sum_i \lambda_i \tau(b_i, a, z)$, the condition of determining β's usefulness is equivalent to: whether there exists a series of nonnegative numbers λ_is such that for any vector α, $\beta \cdot \sum_i \lambda_i \tau(b_i, a, z) \geq \alpha \cdot \sum_i \lambda_i \tau(b_i, a, z) + x$.

To determine β's usefulness in the set $\mathcal{V}$ w.r.t. $\tau(\mathcal{B}, a, z)$, the linear program `simplexLP` in Table 1 is used. When its optimality is reached, one checks its objective x. If it is positive, there exists a belief state in $\tau(\mathcal{B}, a, z)$ at which β dominates other vectors. The belief state is represented as $\sum_i \lambda_i \tau(b_i, a, z)$ where λ_is are the solutions (values of variables). In this case, β is useful. Otherwise, it is useless.

To determine a vector's usefulness in a set w.r.t. the subset $\tau(\mathcal{B})$, one need to consider its usefulness w.r.t. each simplex. Again, let the set be $\mathcal{V}$ and the vector be β. If β is useful

`simplexLP`$(\beta, \mathcal{V}, B_{\tau(\mathcal{B},a,z)})$:
 // Note: $B_{\tau(\mathcal{B},a,z)}$ is the basis of $\tau(\mathcal{B}, a, z)$
 Variables: x, λ_i for each i
 Maximize: x
 Constraints:
  $\beta \cdot \sum_i \lambda_i \tau(b_i, a, z) \geq \alpha \cdot \sum_i \lambda_i \tau(b_i, a, z) + x$
  for $\alpha \in \mathcal{V}$ and for each i, $\tau(b_i, a, z) \in B_{\tau(\mathcal{B},a,z)}$
  $\sum_i \lambda_i = 1, \lambda_i \geq 0$ for i.

Table 1: determining a vector's usefulness w.r.t. a simplex

w.r.t. a simplex, it must be useful w.r.t. the subset. However, if it is useless w.r.t. a simplex, it may be useful w.r.t. another simplex. Hence, for a simplex, if β has been identified as useful, there is no need to check it again for subsequent simplexes. After all the simplexes have been examined, if β is useless w.r.t. all simplexes, it is useless w.r.t. the subset.

Stopping Criterion

By MDP theory, as value iteration continues, the Bellman residual, $\max_{b \in \tau(\mathcal{B})} |\mathcal{V}_n^{\tau(\mathcal{B})} - \mathcal{V}_{n-1}^{\tau(\mathcal{B})}|$, becomes smaller. If it is smaller than $\epsilon(1 - \lambda)/2\lambda$, the algorithm terminates. The output set $\mathcal{V}_{n-1}^{\tau(\mathcal{B})}$ is ϵ-optimal for the subset MDP.

Complexity Analysis

The performance of subset value iteration heavily depends on the "largeness" of the subset $\tau(\mathcal{B})$. If it is a proper subset of $\mathcal{B}$, this leads to computational benefits. First, the algorithm is expected to be more efficient than the standard one. This is because each DP update accounts for a smaller space than $\mathcal{B}$. Second, the complexity of value functions is reduced when the domain is restricted to the subset. This means that subset value iteration generates fewer vectors.

Simplex-By-Simplex Value Iteration

The above value iteration works in a collective fashion in the sense that it directly computes value functions over $\tau(\mathcal{B})$. This subsection proposes value iteration in a simplex-by-simplex fashion. At each iteration, it computes value functions for individual simplexes. The rationale is, by letting value iteration work with the finer-grained belief subsets, it could be more efficient than its collective version.

The DP update is formulated as follows: given a collection $\{\mathcal{V}_n^{\tau(\mathcal{B},a,z)}|a \in \mathcal{A}, z \in \mathcal{Z}\}$ where each $\mathcal{V}_n^{\tau(\mathcal{B},a,z)}$ represents $V_n^{\tau(\mathcal{B})}$ only in the simplex $\tau(\mathcal{B}, a, z)$, how to construct a set $\mathcal{V}_{n+1}^{\tau(\mathcal{B},a,z)}$ for each simplex $\tau(\mathcal{B}, a, z)$.

Likewise, a vector $\beta_{a,\delta}$ in $\mathcal{V}_{n+1}^{\tau(\mathcal{B},a,z)}$ can be defined by an action a and a mapping δ. The fact that $\tau(b, a, z)$ must be in $\tau(\mathcal{B}, a, z)$ for any b implies that for any z, δ_z can be restricted to a vector in the set $\mathcal{V}_n^{\tau(\mathcal{B},a,z)}$. By altering the actions and mappings, one obtains the following set:

$$\{\beta_{a,\delta}|a \in \mathcal{A}, \quad \delta : \mathcal{Z} \to \cup_{a,z}\mathcal{V}_n^{\tau(\mathcal{B},a,z)}, \ \& \ \forall z, \delta_z \in \mathcal{V}_n^{\tau(\mathcal{B},a,z)}\}.$$

It differs from (2) in the mapping δ. The above set is denoted by $\mathcal{V}_{n+1}^{\tau(\mathcal{B},a,z)}$. The value function it induces possesses the ideal property as expected. To obtain the minimal representation, one prunes the set w.r.t. $\tau(\mathcal{B}, a, z)$.

Theorem 4 *For any a and z, the set $\mathcal{V}_{n+1}^{\tau(\mathcal{B},a,z)}$ represents value function $V_{n+1}^{\tau(\mathcal{B})}$ and V_{n+1} over $\tau(\mathcal{B}, a, z)$ if each $\mathcal{V}_n^{\tau(\mathcal{B},a,z)}$ represents $V_n^{\tau(\mathcal{B})}$ in the individual simplex.*

Though subset value iteration can be conducted in either collective or individual fashion, they are essentially the same in terms of value functions induced. This is stated in the following theorem.

Theorem 5 *Let $\mathcal{U} = \cup_{a,z} \mathcal{V}_{n+1}^{\tau(\mathcal{B},a,z)}$. For any $b \in \tau(\mathcal{B})$, $\mathcal{U}(b) = \mathcal{V}_{n+1}^{\tau(\mathcal{B})}(b)$.*

It is worthwhile of noting that for two action/observation pairs, the simplexes $\tau(\mathcal{B}, a_1, z_1)$ and $\tau(\mathcal{B}, a_2, z_2)$ might not be disjoint. Couple of remarks are in order for this case. First, the representing sets $\mathcal{V}_{n+1}^{\tau(\mathcal{B},a_1,z_1)}$ and $\mathcal{V}_{n+1}^{\tau(\mathcal{B},a_2,z_2)}$ might contain duplicates. Therefore the size $\sum_{az} |\mathcal{V}_{n+1}^{\tau(\mathcal{B},a,z)}|$ (the total number of vectors generated) could be greater than $|\mathcal{V}_{n+1}^{\tau(\mathcal{B})}|$. Second, by Theorem 4, for any b in the intersection of the simplexes, $\mathcal{V}_{n+1}^{\tau(\mathcal{B},a_1,z_1)}(b) = \mathcal{V}_{n+1}^{\tau(\mathcal{B},a_2,z_2)}(b)$. This is true because both sets of vectors represent V_{n+1} in $\tau(\mathcal{B})$.

Subset, Decision-Making and Value Iteration

This section shows that value functions generated by subset value iteration can be used for decision-making in the entire belief space. It also studies an interesting relationship between subset selection and value iteration.

Decision-making for the Entire Belief Space

When the algorithm terminates, the output set $\mathcal{V}_{n-1}^{\tau(\mathcal{B})}$ is ϵ-optimal w.r.t. the subset MDP. The agent can choose the ϵ-optimal action for belief states in $\tau(\mathcal{B})$. However, for the original POMDP, the agent can start from any belief state in $\mathcal{B}$. What action should it choose for its initial belief state if it is not in $\tau(\mathcal{B})$? It turns out that with a slightly stricter stopping criterion, the output value function generated by subset value iteration can be used for any belief states.

First, a value function over $\tau(\mathcal{B})$ can be used to define a value function over $\mathcal{B}$. In fact, given a $V^{\tau(\mathcal{B})}$, a value function V over $\mathcal{B}$ can be defined as follows: for any b in $\mathcal{B}$,

$$V(b) = \max_a \{ r(b,a) + \lambda \sum_z P(z|b,a) V^{\tau(\mathcal{B})}(\tau(b,a,z)) \}.$$

The function V is said to be $V^{\tau(\mathcal{B})}$-greedy.

Second, if $\mathcal{V}_n^{\tau(\mathcal{B})}$ represents the same value function as V_n in the subset $\tau(\mathcal{B})$, the $\mathcal{V}_n^{\tau(\mathcal{B})}$-greedy value function is actually V_{n+1}. In this sense, the set $\tau(\mathcal{B})$ is said to be *sufficient* in terms of value function representation. If subset value iteration starts with the same value function as standard value iteration, inductively, they generate the same series of value functions in terms of the subset $\tau(\mathcal{B})$. Moreover, the step value functions in standard value iteration can always be derived from those in subset value iteration.

Third, if one slightly changes the stopping criterion in subset value iteration as in Theorem 6, its output value function can directly be used for ϵ-optimal decision-making over the belief space (Zhang 2001). Note that to achieve the ϵ-optimality, subset value iteration uses a stricter criterion and therefore takes more iterations than the standard algorithm. Meanwhile, stricter criterion means that value function returned by subset value iteration is closer to the optimality.

Theorem 6 *If subset value iteration terminates when $\max_{b \in \tau(\mathcal{B})} |\mathcal{V}_n^{\tau(\mathcal{B})}(b) - \mathcal{V}_{n-1}^{\tau(\mathcal{B})}(b)| \leq \epsilon(1 - \lambda)/(2\lambda^2 |\mathcal{Z}|)$ and it outputs $\mathcal{V}_{n-1}^{\tau(\mathcal{B})}$, then $V_{n-1}^{\tau(\mathcal{B})}$-greedy value function is ϵ-optimal over the belief space.*

Belief Subset and Value Iteration

Since subset value iteration retains the quality of value functions, it can be regarded as an *exact* algorithm. One interesting problem is, if value iteration intends to retain quality, can it work with a proper subset of $\tau(\mathcal{B})$?

In general, the answer is no. The reason follows. To compute V_{n+1}, one needs to keep values $V_n^{\tau(\mathcal{B})}$ for belief states in $\tau(\mathcal{B})$. Otherwise, if one accounts for a smaller set $\mathcal{B}'$, it can be proved that there exists a belief state b in $\mathcal{B}$, an action a and an observation z such that $\tau(b, a, z)$ does not belong to $\mathcal{B}'$. It's known that the value update of $\mathcal{V}_{n+1}(b)$ depends on the values for all possible next belief states. Due to the unavailability of $V_n^{\tau(\mathcal{B})}(\tau(b, a, z))$, the value $V_{n+1}(b)$ can not be calculated exactly. Consequently, if subset value iteration works with a subset of $\tau(\mathcal{B})$, it can not be exact. In other words, it should be an *approximate* algorithm. To make it be exact, value iteration needs consider at least $\tau(\mathcal{B})$. In this sense, the subset is said to be a *minimal* sufficient set.

Empirical Studies

We implemented subset value iteration in the simplex-by-simplex version using incremental pruning (Zhang & Liu 1997; Cassandra 1998). For convenience, it is denoted by ssVI and standard algorithm by VI. Here we focus on a simple maze problem because firstly we would compare the performance for both algorithms to run to completion, and secondly it eases the analysis of performance differences. We compare VI and ssVI along two dimensions: the sizes of representing sets and time costs of DP update. For ssVI and VI, the sizes are $\sum_{a,z} |\mathcal{V}_n^{\tau(\mathcal{B},a,z)}|$ and $|\mathcal{V}_n|$ respectively.

Figure 1 presents the layout of the maze problem. There are 10 locations (states) and the goal is location 9. The agent can execute one of five actions: four "move" actions along four directions and a declare-goal action. The "move" actions can achieve intended effect with probability 0.8. The declare-goal action does not change the agent's position. In the figure thick lines stand for walls and thin lines for nothing(open). At each time point, the robot reads four sensors which inform it of whether there is a wall or nothing along a direction. So an observation is a string of four letters. For example, at location 2, the observation is owow where o means nothing and w means wall. In the following, we present two versions of the maze problem: in one version, ssVI is superior; in the other version, ssVI is inferior.

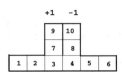

Figure 1: A maze problem

Case I: $\tau(\mathcal{B}) \subset \mathcal{B}$

In this version, the observations(strings of letters) are collected deterministically. The reward model is defined as follows: when the agent declares goal at location 9, it receives a reward of 1 unit; if it does so at location 10, it receives a penalty of -1.

The statistics are presented in Figure 2. The first chart depicts the time cost of each DP update in log-scale for `VI` and `ssVI` with the strict stopping criterion. To compute a 0.01-optimal value function, `VI` terminates within 20,000 seconds after 162 iterations while `ssVI` terminates within 1,000 seconds after 197 iterations. We note that `ssVI` needs more iterations but it still takes much less time. The performance difference is big. Moreover, more iterations means that the value function generated by `ssVI` is closer to the optimality. This is not a surprising result if we take a look at

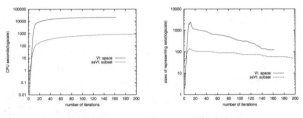

Figure 2: Performances for VI and ssVI on maze problem. Note that y-axis is in log-scale.

the matrix P_{az} for an action a and observation z. Let us assume that the observation is `owow` and hence the possible locations might be 2 or 5. Regardless of actions executed, only entries in column 2 and 5 in P_{az} can be non-zero. Therefore the matrix is highly sparse and degenerate and the simplex $\tau(\mathcal{B}, a, z)$ is much smaller than $\mathcal{B}$. This analysis holds similarly for other combinations of actions and observations. This means `ssVI` accounts for only a small portion of the belief space and thus explains why `ssVI` is more efficient. In addition, we expect that the size of the sets representing value functions over subset is much smaller.

This is confirmed in the second chart. We see that at the same iteration `VI` always generates much more vectors than `ssVI`. The sizes at both curves increase sharply at first iterations and then stabilize. The size for `VI` reaches its peak of 2466 at iteration 11 and the maximum size for `ssVI` is 139 at iteration 10. This size in `VI` is about 20 times many as that in `ssVI`. This is a magnitude consistent with the performance difference. After the sizes stabilize, they are 130 in `VI` and around 50 in `ssVI`.

Case II: $\tau(\mathcal{B}) = \mathcal{B}$

In this version, the actions set is enlarged to include a new one `stay`. If it is executed, it receives either a `null` observation with a probability 0.9 or a string with 0.1. The revised problem has more complications on the observation model. At most locations the agent receives a string as before. But due to hardware limitations, with a probability of 0.1, it wrongly reports the string `owow` as `owww` and `woww` as `wowo`. The reward model is changed to reflect new design considerations: the agent needs to pay for its information about states. For this purpose, `stay` yields no cost. In contrast, the "move" actions always cause a cost of 2.

The results are collected and presented in Figure 3. First we note both `VI` and `ssVI` are able to run only 11 iterations within a reasonable time limit (8 hours). The first chart presents the time costs along iterations. To run 11 iterations, `ssVI` takes 53,000 seconds while `VI` takes around 30,900 seconds. Therefore `ssVI` is slower than `VI` for this problem. However, the magnitude of performance difference is not big. To explain this, let us consider the matrix P_{az} de-

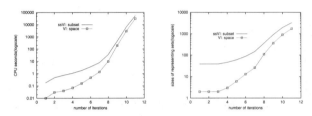

Figure 3: Performances for VI and ssVI on noisy maze.

termined by the action `stay` and observation `null`. The transition matrix is an identity and each state can lead to the `null` observation with probability of 0.9 if `stay` is executed. Therefore, the matrix P_{az} is invertible and the simplex $\tau(\mathcal{B}, a, z)$ is actually $\mathcal{B}$. Because `ssVI` needs to account for additional simplexes for other combinations of actions and observations, `ssVI` must be less efficient than `VI`. This explains the performance difference in time between `ssVI` and `VI`. For the same reason, `ssVI` should produce more vectors than `VI` due to the intersection of simplexes. This is verified and demonstrated in the second chart of Figure 3. The curve for `ssVI` is always on the upper side of that for `VI`. For the 11th iteration, `ssVI` generates 3,300 vectors and `VI` generates around 1,700 vectors.

Related Work

Two basic ideas behind subset value iteration in this paper are (1) reducing the complexity of DP updates and (2) reducing the complexity of value functions.

In a broad sense, most value iteration algorithms and their variations are common in that the efforts are devoted to reducing DP complexity. However, different algorithms and approaches take different forms for the similar purpose. These algorithms include grid-based algorithms where only belief states in the grid are considered at each iteration (Lovejoy 1991), state-space decomposition algorithms where the solution to the original MDP is constructed from the solutions of a collection of smaller state-space MDPs (e.g. (Dean & Lin 1995)), model minimization technique where states are grouped together if they lead to similar behaviors via stochastic bisimulation equivalence (Dean & Givan 1997), algorithms using reachability analysis where new states are added to the subset being considered so far (Boutilier, Brafman, & Geib 1998; Dean *et al.* 1993), and real time dynamic programming where only belief states which have been explored are added into the set for value updates (Geffner & Bonet 1998).

The second idea behind subset value iteration is concerned with the representational complexity of value functions. Intuitively, the representing set of a value function over a belief subset contains fewer vectors than that of the same function over a belief set. This fact has been observed in (Hauskrecht & Fraser 1998). In their medical treatment example, a problem state is specified by several variables. They noted that the inconsistence between the assignments of different variables can be exploited to reduce the complexity of value functions.

Conclusions and Extensions

In this paper, we study value iterations working with belief subset. We use reachability analysis to select a particular subset. The subset is (1)*closed* in that no actions can lead the agent to belief states outside it; (2) *sufficient* in that value function defined over it can be extended into the belief space; and (3) *minimal* in that value iteration needs to consider at least the subset if it intends to achieve the quality of value functions. The closedness enables one to formulate a subset MDP. We address the issues of representing the subset and pruning a set of vectors w.r.t. the subset. We then describe the subset value iteration algorithm. For a given POMDP, whether the subset is proper can be determined *a priori*. If this is the case, subset value iteration carries the advantages of representation in space and efficiency in time.

As for future directions, it would be interesting to ask the question, which POMDP classes in practice have the property whose belief subset is smaller than or the same as the belief space? (Zhang 2001) presents two POMDP classes where in one class the subset is proper while in the other class the subset is the same as the belief space. Different algorithms exploiting the subset structures have been proposed to solve different POMDP classes.

Another interesting direction is to exploit some asynchronous scheme for DP updates. At each iteration, one can conduct DP update over only a few simplexes other than their union. The residuals of consecutive value functions over individual simplexes can be used to select which simplexes to work with. One popular choice is to select those regions whose value functions have larger residuals.

Finally, the subset value iteration algorithm implemented in this paper works with POMDPs represented flatly. To achieve economy of representation from the model side (e.g. (Hansen & Feng 2000)), one promising direction is to implement a "structured" version of the algorithm for structured POMDPs. If this is feasible, one expects that the algorithm would be able to solve larger POMDPs.

Acknowledgment This work was supported in part by Hong Kong Research Grants Council under grant HKUST 6088 /01. The first author would like to thank Eric Hansen for insightful discussions, and Judy Goldsmith for valuable comments on an earlier writeup of the ideas in this paper.

References

Aström, K. J. 1965. Optimal control of Markov decision processes with incomplete state estimation. *Journal of Mathematical Analysis and Applications* 10:403–406.

Boutilier, C.; Brafman, R. I.; and Geib, C. 1998. Structured reachability analysis for Markov decision processes. In *Proceedings of the 14th Conference on Uncertainty in Artificial Intelligence (UAI)*.

Cassandra, A. R. 1998. *Exact and approximate algorithms for partially observable Markov decision processes*. Ph.D. Dissertation, Department of Computer science, Brown university.

Dean, T., and Givan, R. 1997. Model minimization in Markov decision processes. In *Proceedings of National Conference on Artificial Intelligence (AAAI)*, 106–111.

Dean, T. L., and Lin, S. H. 1995. Decomposition techniques for planning in stochastic domains. In *Proceedings of the 14th International Joint Conference on Artificial Intelligence (IJCAI)*, 1121–1127.

Dean, T. L.; Kaelbling, L. P.; Kirman, J.; and Nicholson, A. 1993. Planning with deadlines in stochastic domains. In *Proceedings of the 9th National Conference on Artificial Intelligence (AAAI)*, 574–579.

Geffner, H., and Bonet, B. 1998. Solving large POMDPs using real time dynamic programming. In *Working Notes Fall AAAI Symposium on POMDPs*, 61–68.

Hansen, E., and Feng, Z. 2000. Dynamic programming for POMDPs using a factored state representation. In *Proceedings of the 5th International Conference on Artificial Intelligence Planning and Scheduling (AIPS)*. Breckenridge, Colorado.

Hauskrecht, M., and Fraser, H. 1998. Modeling treatment of ischemic heart disease with partially observable Markov decision processes. In *American Medical Informatics Association annual symposium on Computer Applications in Health Care*, 538–542. Orlando, Florida.

Lovejoy, W. S. 1991. Computationally feasible bounds for partially observed Markov decision processes. *Operations Research* 39(1):162–175.

Sondik, E. J. 1971. *The optimal control of partially observable decision processes*. Ph.D. Dissertation, Stanford University, Stanford, California, USA.

Zhang, N. L., and Liu, W. 1997. A model approximation scheme for planning in partially observable stochastic domains. *Journal of Artificial Intelligence Research* 7:199–230.

Zhang, W. 2001. *Algorithms for partially observable Markov decision processes*. Ph.D. Dissertation, Department of Computer science, the Hong Kong University of Science and Technology.

Multiagent Systems

Complexity of Manipulating Elections with Few Candidates

Vincent Conitzer and **Tuomas Sandholm**

Computer Science Department
Carnegie Mellon University
5000 Forbes Avenue
Pittsburgh, PA 15213
{conitzer, sandholm}@cs.cmu.edu

Abstract

In multiagent settings where the agents have different preferences, preference aggregation is a central issue. Voting is a general method for preference aggregation, but seminal results have shown that all general voting protocols are manipulable. One could try to avoid manipulation by using protocols where determining a beneficial manipulation is hard. Especially among computational agents, it is reasonable to measure this hardness by computational complexity. Some earlier work has been done in this area, but it was assumed that the number of voters and candidates is unbounded. We derive hardness results for the more common setting where the number of candidates is small but the number of voters can be large. We show that with complete information about the others' votes, individual manipulation is easy, and coalitional manipulation is easy with unweighted voters. However, constructive coalitional manipulation with weighted voters is intractable for all of the voting protocols under study, except in the *Cup* protocol. Destructive manipulation tends to be easier, except in the *Single Transferable Vote* protocol. Randomizing over instantiations of the protocols (such as schedules of a Cup) can be used to make manipulation hard. Finally, we show that under weak assumptions, if weighted coalitional manipulation with complete information about the others' votes is hard in some voting protocol, then individual and unweighted manipulation is hard when there is uncertainty about the others' votes.

1. Introduction

In multiagent settings, agents generally have different preferences, and it is of central importance to be able to aggregate these, i.e. to pick a socially desirable *candidate* from a set of candidates. Candidates could be potential presidents, joint plans, allocations of goods or resources, etc. Voting is the most general preference aggregation scheme, and voting mechanisms have been applied to software agents (e.g. (Ephrati & Rosenschein 1991; 1993)).

One key problem voting schemes are confronted with is that of *manipulation* by the voters. An agent is said to vote strategically when it does not rank the alternatives according to its true preferences, but rather so as to make the eventual outcome most favorable to itself. For example, if an agent prefers Nader to Gore to Bush, but knows that Nader has

too few other supporters to win, while Gore and Bush are close to each other, the agent would be better off by declaring Gore as its top candidate. Manipulation is an undesirable phenomenon because social choice schemes are tailored to aggregate preferences in a socially desirable way, and if the agents reveal their preferences insincerely, a socially undesirable candidate may be chosen.

The issue of strategic voting has been studied extensively. A seminal negative result, the *Gibbard-Satterthwaite theorem*, shows that if there are three or more candidates, then in any nondictatorial voting scheme, there are preferences under which an agent is better off voting strategically (Gibbard 1973; Satterthwaite 1975). (A voting scheme is called dictatorial if one of the voters dictates the social choice no matter how the others vote.)

When the voters are software agents, the algorithms they use to decide how to vote must be coded explicitly. Given that the voting algorithm needs to be designed only once (by an expert), and can be copied to large numbers of agents (even ones representing unsophisticated human voters), it is likely that rational strategic voting will increasingly become an issue, unmuddied by irrationality, emotions, etc.

Especially in the context of software agents, it makes sense to ask how complex it is to compute a beneficial manipulation. *Such complexity can be used as a desirable property* because it can make manipulation infeasible to the voters. *Designing voting protocols where manipulation is complex promises to be an avenue for circumventing the fundamental impossibility results regarding the existence of nonmanipulable voting protocols.*

The computational complexity of manipulation has already received some attention (Bartholdi, Tovey, & Trick 1989a; Bartholdi & Orlin 1991). However, the results to date that do show high complexity rely on both the number of candidates and the number of voters being unbounded.

In sharp contrast to those results, in this paper we show high complexity results for the more common setting where the number of candidates is a small constant (the number of voters may be large). Furthermore, we show low complexity in certain settings where both the number of candidates and voters are unbounded.

Restricting the number of candidates to a constant reduces the number of possible votes for a single voter to a constant. If the voters all have equal weight in the election, the number of *de facto* possible combinations of votes that even a coalition can submit is polynomial in the number of voters in the coalition (since the voters have equal weight, it does not matter which agent in the coalition submitted which vote; only the multiplicities of the votes from the coalition matter). We get the following straightforward result.

Proposition 1 *Let there be a constant number of candidates, and suppose that evaluating the result of a particular combination of votes by a coalition is in $\mathcal{P}$. If there is only one voter in the coalition, or if the voters are unweighted, the manipulation problem is in $\mathcal{P}$. (This holds for all the different variants of the manipulation problem, discussed later.)*

Proof. The manipulators (an individual agent or a coalition) can simply enumerate and evaluate all possibilities (there is a polynomial number of them). ∎

In particular, in the complete-information manipulation problem in which the votes of the non-colluders are known, evaluating the result of a (coalitional) vote is as easy as determining the winner of an election, which must be in $\mathcal{P}$ for practical voting mechanisms.[1] This leaves open two avenues for deriving high complexity results with few candidates. First, we may investigate the complete-information coalitional manipulation problem when voters have *different weights*. While many human elections are unweighted, the introduction of weights generalizes the usability of voting schemes, and can be particularly important in multiagent systems settings with very heterogenous agents. We study this with deterministic voting protocols in Section 3, and in Section 4 we show that using randomization in the voting protocols can further increase manipulation complexity. Second, we may ask whether there are reasonable settings where *evaluating* a manipulation is $\mathcal{N}P$-hard. For instance, if we merely have probability distributions on the non-colluders' votes, how does the complexity of determining the probability that a given candidate wins change? We study this in Section 5, and show how to convert the results from Section 3 into stronger claims in this setting. In particular, we remove the assumptions of multiple manipulators and weighted votes.

2. Review of common voting protocols

In this section we define an election and the common voting protocols that we analyze.

Definition 1 *An* election *consists of a set of m candidates; a set of n voters (possibly weighted), who are each to provide a total order on the candidates; and a function from the set of all possible combinations of votes to the set of candidates, which determines the winner.*

Different voting protocols are distinguished by their winner determination functions. We now review the most common protocols in use, all of which will be discussed in this paper. (We define them in the case of unweighted votes; the winner determination functions for weighted votes are

defined by re-interpreting a vote of weight k as k identical unweighted votes[2]. Whenever points are defined, the candidate with the most points wins.)

- *Borda.* For each voter, a candidate receives $m-1$ points if it is the voter's top choice, $m-2$ if it is the second choice, ..., 0 if it is the last.

- *Copeland (aka. Tournament).* Simulate a pairwise election for each pair of candidates in turn (in a pairwise election, a candidate wins if it is preferred over the other candidate by more than half of the voters). A candidate gets 1 point if it defeats an opponent, 0 points if it draws, and -1 points if it loses.

- *Maximin.* A candidate's score in a pairwise election is the number of voters that prefer it over the opponent. A candidate's number of points is the lowest score it gets in any pairwise election.

- *Single Transferable Vote (STV).* Winner determination proceeds in rounds. In each round, a candidate's score is the number of voters that rank it highest among the remaining candidates; the candidate with the lowest score drops out. The last remaining candidate wins. (A vote "transfers" from its top remaining candidate to the next highest remaining candidate when the former drops out.)

- *Cup (aka. Binary Protocol).* There is a balanced binary tree with one leaf per candidate. Then, each non-leaf node is assigned the candidate that is the winner of the pairwise election of the node's children. The candidate assigned to the root wins.

The Cup protocol requires a method for assigning (*scheduling*) candidates to leaf nodes. For instance, this assignment can be given *ex ante* (the "regular" Cup protocol), or we can randomize uniformly over the assignment after the votes have been submitted (*Randomized Cup*).

The winner determination function is not defined on all possible combinations of votes in these protocols since the tie-breaking methods are not specified. For simplicity, we assume tie-breaking mechanisms are adversarial to the manipulator(s), but this assumption is easy to relax without affecting the results of this paper.

3. Complexity of coalitional manipulation with weighted voters

In this section we discuss the complexity of constructive manipulation (causing a candidate to win) and destructive manipulation (causing a candidate to not win). We represent the order of candidates in a vote as follows: $(a_1, a_2, ..., a_m)$. If a vote's weight is not specified, it is 1. All our $\mathcal{N}P$-hardness reductions, directly or indirectly, will be from the PARTITION problem.

Definition 2 PARTITION. *We are given a set of integers $\{k_i\}_{1 \le i \le t}$ (possibly with multiplicities) summing to $2K$, and are asked whether a subset of these integers sum to K.*

---

[1]Theoretical voting mechanisms exist where determining the winner is $\mathcal{N}P$-hard (Bartholdi, Tovey, & Trick 1989b).

[2]We thus assume that weights are integers. The results also apply to all rational weights because they can be converted to integers by multiplying all the weights by all the weights' denominators.

3.1. Constructive manipulation

Definition 3 CONSTRUCTIVE-COALITIONAL-WEIGHTED-MANIPULATION (CCWM). *We are given a set of weighted votes S, the weights for a set of votes T which are still open, and a preferred candidate p. We are asked whether there is a way to cast the votes in T so that p wins the election.*[3]

Theorem 1 *In the Borda protocol, CCWM is $\mathcal{NP}$-complete even with 3 candidates.*[4]

Proof. We reduce an arbitrary PARTITION instance to the following CCWM instance. There are 3 candidates, a, b and p. In S there are $6K - 1$ voters voting (a, b, p) and another $6K - 1$ voting (b, a, p). In T, for every k_i there is a vote of weight $6k_i$. We show the instances are equivalent. Suppose there is a partition. Let the votes in T corresponding to the k_i in one half of the partition vote (p, a, b), and let the other ones vote (p, b, a). Then a and b each have $24K - 3$ points, and p has $24K$ points. So there is a manipulation. Conversely, suppose there is a manipulation. Then, since moving p to the top of each vote in T will never hurt p in this protocol, there must exist a manipulation in which the only votes made in T are (p, a, b) and (p, b, a). In this manipulation, since p has $24K$ points in total and a and b each have $18K - 3$ points from the votes in S, it follows that a and b each can gain at most $6K + 2$ points from the votes in T. It follows that the voters voting (p, a, b) can have combined total weight at most $6K + 2$; hence the corresponding k_i can sum to at most $K + \frac{1}{3}$, or (equivalently) to at most K since the k_i are all integers. The same holds for the k_i corresponding to the (p, b, a) votes. Hence, in both cases, they must sum to exactly K. But then, this is a partition. ∎

Theorem 2 *In the Copeland protocol, CCWM is $\mathcal{NP}$-complete even with 4 candidates.*

Proof. We reduce an arbitrary PARTITION instance to the following CCWM instance. There are 4 candidates, a, b, c and p. In S there are $2K + 2$ voters voting (p, a, b, c), $2K + 2$ voting (c, p, b, a), $K + 1$ voting (a, b, c, p), and $K + 1$ voting (b, a, c, p). In T, for every k_i there is a vote of weight k_i. We show the instances are equivalent. First, every pairwise election is already determined without T, except for the one between a and b. p defeats a and b; a and b each defeat c; c defeats p. If there is a winner in the pairwise election between a and b, that winner will tie with p. So p wins the Copeland election if and only if a and b tie in their pairwise election. But, after the votes in S alone, a and b are tied. Thus, the votes in T maintain this tie if and only if the combined weight of the votes in T preferring a to b is the same as the combined weight of the votes in T preferring b to a. This can happen if and only if there is a partition. ∎

---

[3]To an economist, it would be more natural to define a successful manipulation as one that increases the voter's (expected) utility. It is easy to see that our definitions are special cases of this utility-based definition, so our hardness results apply to that as well.

[4]In all $\mathcal{NP}$-completeness proofs, we only prove $\mathcal{NP}$-hardness because proving that the problem is in $\mathcal{NP}$ is trivial.

Theorem 3 *In the Maximin protocol, CCWM is $\mathcal{NP}$-complete even with 4 candidates.*

Proof. We reduce an arbitrary PARTITION instance to the following CCWM instance. There are 4 candidates, a, b, c and p. In S there are $7K - 1$ voters voting (a, b, c, p), $7K - 1$ voting (b, c, a, p), $4K - 1$ voting (c, a, b, p), and $5K$ voting (p, c, a, b). In T, for every k_i there is a vote of weight $2k_i$. We show the instances are equivalent. Suppose there is a partition. Then, let the votes in T corresponding to the k_i in one half of the partition vote (p, a, b, c), and let the other ones vote (p, b, c, a). Then, p does equally well in each pairwise election: it always gets $9K$ pairwise points. a's worst pairwise election is against c, getting $9K - 1$. b's worst is against a, getting $9K - 1$. Finally c's worst is against b, getting $9K - 1$. Hence, p wins the election. So there is a manipulation. Conversely, suppose there is a manipulation. Then, since moving p to the top of each vote in T will never hurt p in this protocol, there must exist a manipulation in which all the votes in T put p at the top, and p thus gets $9K$ as its worst pairwise score. Also, the votes in T cannot change which each other candidate's worst pairwise election is: a's worst is against c, b's worst is against a, and c's worst is against b. Since c already has $9K - 1$ points in its pairwise election against b, no vote in T can put c ahead of b. Additionally, if any vote in T puts a right above c, swapping their positions has no effect other than to decrease a's final score, so we may also assume this does not occur. Similarly we can show it safe to also assume no vote in T puts b right above a. Combining all of this, we may assume that all the votes in T vote either (p, a, b, c) or (p, b, c, a). Since a already has $7K - 1$ points in the pairwise election against c, the votes in T of the first kind can have a total weight of at most $2K$; hence the corresponding k_i can sum to at most K. The same holds for the k_i corresponding to the second kind of vote on the basis of b's score. Hence, in both cases, they must sum to exactly K. But then, this is a partition. ∎

Theorem 4 *In the STV protocol, CCWM is $\mathcal{NP}$-complete even with 3 candidates.*

Proof. We reduce an arbitrary PARTITION instance to the following CCWM instance. There are 3 candidates, a, b and p. In S there are $6K - 1$ voters voting (b, p, a), $4K$ voting (a, b, p), and $4K$ voting (p, a, b). In T, for every k_i there is a vote of weight $2k_i$. We show the instances are equivalent. Suppose there is a partition. Then, let the votes in T corresponding to the k_i in one half of the partition vote (a, p, b), and let the other ones vote (p, a, b). Then in the first round, b has $6K - 1$ points, a has $6K$, and p has $6K$. So b drops out; all its votes transfer to p, so that p wins the final round. So there is a manipulation. Conversely, suppose there is a manipulation. Clearly, p cannot drop out in the first round; but also, a cannot drop out in the first round, since all its votes in S would transfer to b, and b would have at least $10K - 1$ points in the final round, enough to guarantee it victory. So, b must drop out in the first round. Hence, from the votes in T, both a and c must get at least $2K$ weight that puts them in the top spot. The corresponding k_i in either case must thus sum to at least K. Hence, in both cases, they must sum to exactly K. But then, this is a partition. ∎

3.2. Destructive manipulation

In the *destructive* version of the CCWM problem (which we call DCWM), instead of being asked whether there is a coaalitional vote that makes p win, we are asked whether there is a coalitional vote that makes h not win. It is easy to see that DCWM can never be harder than CCWM (except by a factor m) because in order to solve DCWM we may simply solve CCWM once for each candidate besides h.

Interestingly, in these protocols (except STV), destructive manipulation turns out to be drastically easier than constructive manipulation!

Theorem 5 *Consider any voting protocol where each candidate receives a numerical score based on the votes, and the candidate with the highest score wins. Suppose that the score function is monotone, that is, if voter i changes its vote so that $\{b : a >_i^{old} b\} \subseteq \{b : a >_i^{new} b\}$, a's score will not decrease. Finally, assume that the winner can be determined in polynomial time. Then for this protocol, DCWM is in $\mathcal{P}$.*

Proof. Consider the following algorithm: for each candidate a besides h, we determine what the outcome of the election would be for the following coalitional vote. All the colluders place a at the top of their votes, h at the bottom, and order the other candidates in whichever way. We claim there is a vote for the colluders with which h does not win if and only if h does not win in one of these $m - 1$ elections. The *if* part is trivial. For the *only if* part, suppose there is a coalitional vote that makes $a \neq h$ win the election. Then, in the coalitional vote we examine where a is always placed on top and h always at the bottom, by monotonicity, a's score cannot be lower and h's cannot be higher than in the successful coalitional vote. It follows that here, too, a's score is higher than h's, and hence h does not win the election. The algorithm is clearly in $\mathcal{P}$ since we do $m - 1$ winner determinations, and winner determination is in $\mathcal{P}$. ∎

Corollary 1 *DCWM is in $\mathcal{P}$ for the Borda, Copeland, and Maximin protocols.*

The theorem does not apply to STV, however. We show that in fact, in STV, DCWM is $\mathcal{N}P$-complete.

Theorem 6 *In the STV protocol, DCWM is $\mathcal{N}P$-complete even with 4 candidates.*

Proof. We reduce an arbitrary instance of CCWM for STV with 3 candidates to the following DCWM instance. Let the candidates in the original instance be a, b, and p; and let the voters (including the colluders) here have a combined weight of W. In the DCWM instance we construct, we have the same candidates plus an additional candidate h. T (the number of colluders and their weights) remains exactly the same. S includes all the votes (with weights) from the CCWM's instance's S (h is added to the bottom of these votes); additionally, there are the following 6 votes: (a, b, p, h), (a, p, b, h), (b, a, p, h), (b, p, a, h), and two times (p, h, a, b). Finally, there are $W + 5$ votes voting (h, a, b, p).

We observe the following facts. First, h will not be eliminated before the last round as it has close to half the vote weight at the start. Second, h will lose this last round if and only if it faces p in it, and all colluders have ranked p above h. (If even one more vote transfers to h, it is certain to win the election as it has more than half the vote weight; and if p drops out, the (p, h, a, b) votes will transfer to h. On the other hand, p is ranked above h in all votes in S that do not have h at the top, so while p remains none of these transfer to h.) Third, since the transfer of any additional vote to h leads to its victory, all colluders may as well place h at the bottom of their votes. Fourth, as long as p has not dropped out, the relative scores of (the remaining candidates among) a, b, and p in each round before the last will be exactly the same as in the CCWM instance if the coalition votes the same (disregarding h) in both instances. (The 6 additional votes in S are carefully chosen to always be distributed equally among them while p remains.) Thus, there is a coalitional vote that leads p to the last round if and only if the CCWM instance has a constructive manipulation. Hence, by our second observation, the instances are equivalent. ∎

4. Increasing complexity via randomization

In this section, we investigate the effect of randomizing over different instantiations of a protocol on manipulation complexity. While most protocols only have one instantiation, the Cup protocol requires a schedule to be instantiated. We show that randomization over these schedules (after the votes have been cast) is sufficient to make manipulation $\mathcal{N}P$-complete. We first show that the Cup protocol is easy to manipulate if the schedule is known in advance.

Theorem 7 *In the Cup protocol (given the assignment of candidates to leaves), CCWM is in $\mathcal{P}$.*

Proof. We demonstrate a method for finding all the potential winners of the election. In the binary tree representing the schedule, we can consider each node to be a subelection, and compute the set of potential winners for each subelection. (In such a subelection, we may say that the voters only order the candidates in that subelection since the place of the other candidates in the order is irrelevant.) Say a candidate *can* obtain a particular result in the election if it does so for some coalitional vote. The key claim to the proof, then, is the following: a candidate can win a subelection if and only if it can win one of its children, *and* it can defeat one of the potential winners of the sibling child in a pairwise election. It is easy to see that the condition is necessary. To show that it is sufficient, let p be a candidate satisfying the condition by being able to defeat h, a potential winner of the other child (or *half*). Consider a coalitional vote that makes p win its half, and another one that makes h win its half. We now let each coalitional voter vote as follows: it ranks all the candidates in p's half above all those in h's half; the rest of the order is the same as in the votes that make p and h win their halves. Clearly, this will make p and h the finalists. Also, p will win the pairwise election against h since it is always ranked above h with the colluders; and as we know that there is some coalitional vote that makes p defeat

h pairwise, this one must have the same result. The obvious recursive algorithm has running time $O(m^3 n)$ according to the Master Theorem (Cormen, Leiserson, & Rivest 1990). ∎

It turns out that randomizing over cup schedules makes manipulation hard even with few candidates, as the following definition and theorem show.

Definition 4 UNCERTAIN-INSTANTIATION-CONSTRUCTIVE-COALITIONAL-WEIGHTED-MANIPULATION (UICCWM). *We are given a set of weighted votes S, the weights for a set of votes T which are still open, a preferred candidate p, a distribution over instantiations of the voting protocol, and a number r, where $0 \le r \le 1$. We are asked whether there is a way to cast the votes in T so that p wins with probability greater than r.*

Theorem 8 *In the Randomized Cup protocol, UICCWM is $\mathcal{N}P$-complete with 7 candidates.*

Because of limited space, we only sketch the proof.

Proof sketch. Given weights for the colluders (corresponding to the k_i of a PARTITION instance), it is possible to define votes in S over the 7 candidates (a through f, and p) with the following properties. First, the colluders can only affect the outcomes of the pairwise elections between a, b, and c. Second, they can achieve the result that a defeats b (in their pairwise election), b defeats c, and c defeats a if and only if their weights can be partitioned. Third, d defeats e, e defeats f, and f defeats d. Fourth, a defeats d, b defeats e, and c defeats f; otherwise, all of d, e, and f defeat all of a, b, and c. Fifth, p defeats all of a, b, and c, but loses to all of d, e, and f. Then it can be shown that if the colluders could decide each of the pairwise elections between a, b, and c independently, letting a defeat b, b defeat c, and c defeat a strictly maximizes the probability that p wins. (This is done by drawing the Cup tree (which has one bye round) and analyzing cases.) It follows that there exists a number r ($0 \le r \le 1$) such that the colluders can make p win with probability greater than r if and only if there is a partition. ∎

5. Effect of uncertainty about others' votes

So far we discussed the complexity of coalitional manipulation when the others' votes are known. We now show how those results can be related to the complexity of manipulation by an individual voter when only a *distribution* over the others' votes is known. If we allow for arbitrary distributions, we need to specify a probability for each combination of votes by the others, that is, exponentially many probabilities (even with just two candidates). It is impractical to specify so many probabilities.[5] Therefore, it is reasonable to presume that the language used for specifying these probabilities would not be fully expressive. We derive the complexity results of this section for extremely restricted probability distributions, which any reasonable language should allow for. Thus our results apply to any reasonable language.

---

[5]Furthermore, if the input is exponential in the number of voters, an algorithm that is exponential in the number of voters is not necessarily complex in the usual sense of input complexity.

Due to limited space, we only present results on constructive manipulations, but all results apply to the destructive cases as well and the proofs are analogous.

5.1. Weighted voters

First we show that with weighted voters, in protocols where coalitional manipulation is hard in the complete-information case, even evaluating a candidate's winning probability is hard when there is uncertainty about the votes (even when there is no manipulator).

Definition 5 UNCERTAIN-VOTES-CONSTRUCTIVE-WEIGHTED-EVALUATION (UVCWE). *We are given a weight for each voter, a distribution over all the votes, a candidate p, and a number r ($0 \le r \le 1$). We are asked whether the probability of p winning is greater than r.*

Theorem 9 *If CCWM is $\mathcal{N}P$-hard for a protocol (even with k candidates), then UVCWE is also $\mathcal{N}P$-hard for it (even with k candidates), even if the votes are drawn independently and only the following types of (marginal) distributions are allowed: 1) the vote's distribution is uniform over all possible votes, and 2) the vote's distribution puts all of the probability mass on a single vote.*

Proof. For the reduction from CCWM to UVCWE, we use exactly the same voters, and p remains the same as well. If a voter was not a colluder in the CCWM instance and we were thus given its vote, in the UVCWE instance its distribution is degenerate at that vote. If the voter was in the collusion, its distribution is now uniform. We set $r = 0$. Now, clearly, in the PCWE instance there is a chance of p winning if and only if there exists some way for the latter votes to be cast so as to make p win - that is, if and only if there is an effective collusion in the CCWM problem. ∎

Next we show that if evaluating the winning probability is hard, individual manipulation is also hard.

Definition 6 UNCERTAIN-VOTES-CONSTRUCTIVE-INDIVIDUAL-WEIGHTED-MANIPULATION (UVCIWM). *We are given a single manipulative voter with a weight, weights for all the other voters, a distribution over all the others' votes, a candidate p, and a number r, where $0 \le r \le 1$. We are asked whether the manipulator can cast its vote so that p wins with probability greater than r.*

Theorem 10 *If UVCWE is $\mathcal{N}P$-hard for a protocol (even with k candidates and restrictions on the distribution), then UVCIWM is also $\mathcal{N}P$-hard for it (even with k candidates and the same restrictions).*

Proof. For the reduction from UVCWE to UVCIWM, simply add a manipulator with weight 0. ∎

Combining Theorems 9 and 10, we get that with weighted voters, if in some protocol coalitional manipulation is hard in the complete-information setting, then even individual manipulation is hard if others' votes are uncertain. Applying this to the hardness results from Section 3, this means that all of the protocols of this paper other than Cup are hard to manipulate by individuals in the weighted case when the manipulator is uncertain about the others' votes.

5.2. Unweighted voters

Finally, we show that in protocols where coalitional manipulation is hard in the weighted complete-information case, evaluating a candidate's winning probability is hard even in the unweighted case when there is uncertainty about the votes (even when there is no manipulator). This assumes that the language for specifying the probability distribution is rich enough to allow for perfect correlations among the votes of the nonmanipulators (that is, some votes are identical with probability one[6]).

Theorem 11 *If UVCWE is $\mathcal{N}P$-hard for a protocol (even with k candidates and restrictions on the distribution), then the unweighted version of UVCWE is also $\mathcal{N}P$-hard for it if we allow for perfect correlations (even with k candidates and the same restrictions—except those conflicting with perfect correlations).*

Proof. For the reduction from UVCWE to its unweighted version, we replace each vote of weight k with k unweighted votes; we then make these k votes perfectly correlated. Subsequently we pick a representative vote from each perfectly correlated group, and we impose a joint distribution on these votes identical to the one on the corresponding votes in the UVCWE problem. This determines a joint distribution over all votes. It is easy to see that the distribution over outcomes is the same as in the instance we reduced from; hence, the decision questions are equivalent. ■

6. Conclusions and future research

In multiagent settings where the agents have different preferences, preference aggregation is a central issue. Voting is a general method for preference aggregation, but seminal results have shown that all general voting protocols are manipulable. One could try to avoid manipulation by using protocols where determining a beneficial manipulation is hard. Especially among computational agents, it is reasonable to measure this hardness by computational complexity. Some earlier work has been done in this area, but it was assumed that the number of voters and candidates is unbounded.

In this paper we derived hardness results even in the practical case where the number of candidates is a small constant (but the number of voters may be large). We showed that with complete information about the others' votes, individual manipulation is easy, and coalitional manipulation is easy with unweighted voters. However, constructive coalitional manipulation with weighted voters turned out to be intractable for all of the voting protocols under study, except for the Cup protocol (which is easy to manipulate even if the number of candidates is unbounded). Destructive manipulation tends to be easier, except in the Single Transferable Vote (STV) protocol. Randomizing over instantiations of the protocols (such as schedules of a Cup) can be used to make manipulation hard. Finally, we showed that under weak assumptions, if weighted coalitional manipulation with complete information about the others' votes is hard in some voting protocol, then individual and unweighted manipulation is hard when there is uncertainty about the others' votes.

---

[6]Representation of such distributions can still be concise.

In summary, our results suggest 1) using some of the protocols studied in this paper rather than usual *plurality (majority) voting* (where constructive/destructive unweighted/weighted individual/coalitional manipulation is trivial), 2) preferring STV over the other protocols on the basis of the difficulty of destructive manipulation, and 3) randomizing over instantiations of a protocol. Our results may also lead one to be generally less concerned about the possibility of manipulation as it is hard in the common case where not too much is known about how others will vote.

All of the results on complexity of manipulation to date (including ours) use $\mathcal{N}P$-hardness as the complexity measure. This is only a weak guarantee of hardness of manipulation. It means that there are infinitely many hard instances, but many (or even most) instances may be easy to manipulate. Future work includes studying other notions of hardness in the manipulation context, such as average case completeness (Gurevich 1991) and instance complexity (Orponen *et al.* 1994). Another interesting avenue is to try to embed a practically hard problem (e.g., factoring) in the manipulation problem. Future work also includes proving hardness of manipulation in more restricted protocols such as auctions, and with more restricted preferences.

Acknowledgment

This work was supported by the National Science Foundation under CAREER Award IRI-9703122, Grant IIS-9800994, ITR IIS-0081246, and ITR IIS-0121678.

References

Bartholdi, III, J. J., and Orlin, J. B. 1991. Single transferable vote resists strategic voting. *Social Choice and Welfare* 8(4):341–354.

Bartholdi, III, J. J.; Tovey, C. A.; and Trick, M. A. 1989a. The computational difficulty of manipulating an election. *Social Choice and Welfare* 6(3):227–241.

Bartholdi, III, J. J.; Tovey, C. A.; and Trick, M. A. 1989b. Voting schemes for which it can be difficult to tell who won the election. *Social Choice and Welfare* 6:157–165.

Cormen, T. H.; Leiserson, C. E.; and Rivest, R. L. 1990. *Introduction to Algorithms.* MIT Press.

Ephrati, E.; Rosenschein, J. The Clarke tax as a consensus mechanism among automated agents. AAAI-91, 173-178.

Ephrati, E.; Rosenschein, J. Multi-agent planning as a dynamic search for social consensus. IJCAI-93, 423-429.

Gibbard, A. 1973. Manipulation of voting schemes. *Econometrica* 41:587–602.

Gurevich, Y. 1991. Average case completeness. *Journal of Computer and System Sciences* 42:346–398.

Orponen, P.; Ko, K.-I.; Schöning, U.; and Watanabe, O. 1994. Instance complexity. *J. of the ACM* 41(1):96–121.

Satterthwaite, M. A. 1975. Strategy-proofness and Arrow's conditions: existence and correspondence theorems for voting procedures and social welfare functions. *Journal of Economic Theory* 10:187–217.

A Logic-Based Model of Intentions for Multi-Agent Subcontracting[*]

John Grant
Dept. of Computer and Information Sciences
and Department of Mathematics
Towson Univ.
Towson, MD 21252 USA
jgrant@towson.edu

Sarit Kraus
Dept. of Computer Science
Bar-Ilan Univ., Ramat-Gan, 52900 Israel
and Institute for Advanced Computer Studies
Univ. of Maryland, College Park, MD 20742
sarit@umiacs.umd.edu

Donald Perlis
Dept. of Computer Science
Univ. of Maryland,
College Park 20742, USA
perlis@cs.umd.edu

Abstract

We present a formalism for representing the intentions of agents engaged in cooperative planning and acting. We focus on cases where one agent alone cannot accomplish a complex task and must subcontract with other agents. Evolving intentions over time during the planning and acting, and the conditions under which an agent can adopt and maintain an intention, are central. In particular, the time taken to plan and to subcontract are modeled explicitly in the logic. This explicit time-representation is used to account for the time it takes an agent to adopt an intention. We use a syntactic approach presenting a formal logical calculus that can be regarded as a meta-logic that describes the reasoning and activities of the agents. We write some of the axioms of this metalanguage and explain the minimal model semantics, in which one model, the intended model, represents the actual beliefs, intentions, and actions of the agents. We also prove several results showing that under the appropriate conditions the agents will act as expected.

Introduction

In this paper we argue that to properly understand computational models of intentions, especially in the context of multi-agent cooperative behavior, it is very useful to have a formal meta-theory of that behavior; and we present such a theory as well.

Logic plays at least two roles here. First, since much of what an agent must do is use its existing information to help it decide what to do, then the agent itself is employing processes for drawing conclusions, and is then using its own internal logic. Second, our own analysis of an agent's behavior can be made precise by a meta-logic in which we describe – and prove theorems about – the agent. For instance, an agent may know that another agent can perform action a, and that if a is performed then B will be true. The first agent may then conclude that, in order to make B true, it should ask the second agent to do a. This conclusion is in effect a use of modus ponens on the part of the first agent. If we have designed the agent so that it will always use Modus Ponens in such situations, then we can formulate that behavior as a meta-axiom and use it to prove general results about the

agent. Whether B will become true in the above depends, in part, on whether the second agent cooperates with the first. In this paper we assume all agents to be cooperative; giving this requirement a formal characterization involves the notion of intention. We require an agent to adopt a potential intention to perform an action if it is asked to do so. This then becomes a (real) intention if other conditions, to be described below, are met as well.

Our work differs from others in its use of a meta-theory of intentions and of an evolving notion of time that allows agents to reason about genuinely-approaching deadlines. Thus we view the reasoning of agents as ongoing processes rather than as fixed sets of conclusions. This reasoning involves rapidly evolving sets of beliefs and intentions, and is governed in part by formal rules of inference. We model beliefs and intentions in a formal logical calculus that can be regarded as a meta-logic describing an actual onboard agent logic that evolves in (and takes account of) that same passage of time. This is a style of formal representation that departs from traditional temporal logics in that there is an internally evolving notion of time that the logic must keep track of.

Our approach utilizes a strongly sorted calculus, distinguishing the application language, time, and various syntactic sorts. This allows for useful and intuitively natural characterizations of such agents' reasoning abilities. We provide formal tools for representing agent intentions and methods for reasoning with and about such intentions, especially in the context of cooperative actions. We focus on cases where one agent alone cannot accomplish a complex task and must subcontract with other agents.

One of the scenarios that we have considered for an example is that of a software agent personal assistant. Suppose that you need plans to get to the airport to catch your flight later today but are busy with other things. So you ask this assistant, named PAT, to make arrangements to get you to the airport on time. PAT may not be fully expert in web searches, for instance, but it knows what to do: contact whatever expert agents are needed to assist it in the details, so that you can catch your flight. PAT breaks down this assignment into several parts: determine likely means of transport, how to arrange them, etc. Among PAT's concerns are temporal ones: it needs to find out information and arrange for the transportation within a reasonable period of time. This

[*]This research was supported by NSF under grant IIS-9907482.

means not only knowing how soon you need to be at the airport, but also how quickly the various subtasks can be done, including ones done by auxiliary agents such as specialized web search agents and telephone agents. In the next sections we will use this example for illustration purposes.

Languages for Reasoning By and About Agents

In our framework we find it useful to introduce three related languages. The first language, L_S, is the language of the subject matter, that is, the subject that the agents reason about: e.g. web searches. The second language, L_A, is the "agent" language. This includes the subject matter language, but also has additional symbols allowing assertions about what some particular agent may believe at a given moment; this allows an agent to reason about another agent, for instance in deciding whether to ask another agent to perform some subtask based on what that other agent believes. (We assume that there is a public database with – possibly fallible – information about agent abilities.) The third language, L_M, is the meta-language used by us – as observers – to reason about the agents.

The meta-language, L_M, must be powerful enough to characterize agent behavior quite generally. For instance, in our meta-language we can write the statement that an agent always applies Modus Ponens, when that is possible. This, taken as an axiom, would assert that the agents are programmed to apply Modus Ponens; that is an aspect of their behavior. Thus, while the agent language, L_A, must allow for the expression of the formulas A, A implies B, and B, still an agent does not in general have the meta-rule such as "I apply Modus Ponens whenever I can," even if that happens to be true (and expressed in the meta-language).

In other approaches to the issue of agent reasoning, often logical omniscience is assumed. We think that our approach, where rules are applied over time is a more realistic way to model agent beliefs.

Agent Beliefs and Intentions

Because of our emphasis on changing knowledge over time, agents need to know the present time. Also, in our framework agents have introspection capabilities. By this we mean that one of the agent's beliefs may be that it believed or did not believe something at a different time. There are two types of introspection: positive and negative. An example of positive introspection is if an agent believed some fact (represented by a formula) at time t, it will then believe at time $t + 1$ that it believed that fact at time t. This way an agent can reason about its own or another agent's beliefs over time. Suppose now that at time t the agent is considering but does not believe a particular possible fact A (that is, A is not in its database). Then at the next time value, $t + 1$, it will believe (know) by negative introspection that it did not believe A at time t.

Another important capability of an agent is the inheritance of beliefs. The idea is that if an agent believes some fact A and does not believe something contradictory to it (that is, $not A$), it will continue to believe A. There are exceptions to inheritance. Things that are changing, such as the location

of a moving object, should not be inherited. A fact involving the *Now* predicate is not inherited, because if the agent believes that the time now is t, it should not continue this belief at time $t + 1$.

We have found it useful also to add axioms concerning the cooperation of agents. So for example if an agent "tells" another agent a fact, the second agent will add that fact to its database of beliefs. This assumes that agents are trustworthy. Agents may also be helpful to other agents by answering each other's questions. Note that of course there can be non-trustworthy agents, and that this is a major topic of research (see a survey in (Kraus 2001)). But here we focus on fully cooperative (and nonforgetful) agents.

The exact definition of intentions may be necessary for cooperation. For example, an agent needs to know how to interpret a belief that its partner has adopted an intention to do the given action: does this mean the action will indeed be performed by that partner if the partner is able? Thus, it is important to formally define (a) what are the minimal requirements that are needed for an agent to adopt an intention; (b) how an agent's intentions change over time (and what are the occasions when an agent will drop an intention); (c) what are the reasoning processes that the agent will perform when it adopts an intention; and (d) what are the actions that an agent will perform when it adopts an intention.

We define a notion of "potential" intention that means roughly that the agent has been given a task and is determining whether it can do it (perhaps with help). We reserve "intention" for the situation in which the agent has determined that it can do the task (perhaps with help) and in that case it will indeed attempt to carry out the task, unless in the meantime it has dropped that intention because (a) it is told to drop it; or (b) it is given another task that conflicts with the first one and which is assigned higher preference; or (c) the world changes and it finds that it can no longer do the task (perhaps because a subcontracting agent cannot do its part).

In the context of collaboration, it is also important to decide whether an agent can have intentions that another agent will perform an action. In our model, an agent can't intend directly that another agent will do an action; however, its plan for doing a, that is motivated by the intention to do a, may include the intentions of other agents.

We use the term "*recipe* for action a" (Pollack 1990) to refer to a specification of a set of actions, the doing of which constitutes performance of a. The subsidiary actions $b1, b2, ..$ in the recipe for action a, which are also referred to as subacts or subactions of a, may either be *basic actions* or complex actions. Basic actions are done by primitive acts by agents that can do them. Thus, the general situation is illustrated in the tree of Figure 1. Here an agent is given task $a1$, which has a recipe shown in the tree, i.e. to do $a1$, it is sufficient to do $b1, b2, b3$ (in that order) and $b1$ can be done by doing $c1$ and $c2$, etc. The leaves are the "basic" actions If an agent cannot do all the actions for a recipe, it then may subcontract some of them to other agents.

Sorted Language for Agent Intention

In this section we introduce the main predicates that we use in our work in the meta-language to characterize agent inten-

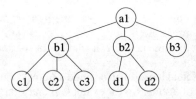

Figure 1: An example of a recipe tree.

tions. For each predicate we explain the use of the different attributes. We use a sorted language for comprehensibility and convenience so that, for example, agent names and times (for both of which we use positive integers) cannot be confused. Since the language is sorted, we use a convention for variables of different sort, namely t,i,j,k for time; m,n for agent names, a,b,c for actions, and r for recipes. As needed, e is used for the null element.

We start with the two predicates for intention: $PotInt$ and Int, as well as AskedToDo (ATD). Basically, $PotInt$ represents a potential intention for an agent asked to perform an action. Under certain conditions $PotInt$ will become Int.

The context keeps track of the tree structure of the recipe used so that when an agent has a potential intention or an intention for an action, the context of the action, if there is one, is the parent node in the tree. For instance, in the example given in the Introduction, the context for $c2$ would be $b1$ assuming that the potential intention or intention is for the same agent. For the root node, $a1$, the context is the null action e. Also, if $c2$ is the potential intention or intention of an agent requested to do $c2$ by another agent, the context is also the null action, but the requesting agent is also indicated.

$ATD(t,n,m,a,t')$ - At time t agent n asks agent m to do action a at time t'.

This predicate is used both by the agent's owner who asks an agent to do a task, as well as by other agents as they request one another to do various tasks for them: this is subcontracting. There are two times involved, the time of the asking and the time that the action needs to be done. This will also be the case for several other predicates. In the example given above, writing aat for "arrange airport transportation", we could write $ATD(14 : 30 : 00, e, PAT, aat, 17 : 00 : 00)$ to indicate that the owner (null agent) asked PAT (in the axioms we will assume for convenience that each agent is referred to by a number) at 2:30PM to arrange for airport transportation at 5PM.

$PotInt(t,m,n,b,a,t')$ -At time t agent m directly assisting agent n has the potential intention to do action b in the context of action a at time t'.

When PAT is asked to arrange the airport transportation, it adopts a potential intention to do this task at the next time period. Assuming that a time period is one second, we will have $PotInt(14 : 30 : 01, PAT, e, aat, e, 17 : 00 : 00)$ indicating that PAT will have a potential intention to arrange for airport transportation at 5PM. The task is done for the owner (hence the first e) and the arrange action is not a subaction in the context of another action (hence the second e).

$Int(t,m,n,b,a,t')$ - At time t agent m directly assisting agent n has the intention to do action b in the context of action

a at time t'.

In our example, if PAT or its assistants will adopt all the needed intentions to arrange for airport transportation, say at time 14:35:00, then in the next time period it will have $Int(14 : 35 : 01, PAT, e, aat, e, 17 : 00 : 00)$.

We distinguish between basic level actions that can be performed without planning and complex actions that consist of several actions. These actions are specified in a recipe. The actions in a recipe may themselves be complex. $BL(a)$ indicates that action a is basic level. $Rec(a, r)$ means that for action a, r is the chosen recipe (not dealing with multiple recipes at this time). $Mem(r, b, i, j, k)$ means that in recipe r, b is the i'th subaction starting at relative time j and ending at relative time k (i.e. relative to the time at the beginning of the action). These predicates do not involve time in the sense of the previous predicates, because they refer to facts that are considered true for every time period.

In the next group we deal with other relevant concepts about agents: their beliefs, abilities to do actions, and means of communication with other agents. $Bel(t, n, f)$ means that at time t agent n believes the statement expressed by formula f. $CanDo(t, n, a)$ indicates that at time t agent n can do (or at least start) action a. $Tell(t, n, m, f)$ means that at time t agent n tells agent m the statement expressed by the formula f. The formulas are the formulas of the agent language, L_A. These are the formulas that are meaningful to the agents. Each such formula has a name (its quoted version) in the meta-language L_M.

Finally we write the predicates that deal with the agents actually doing the actions, the initialization and completions of an action. $Ini(t, m, n, a)$ means that at time t agent m assisting agent n initiates action a. $Done(t, a)$ means that at time t action a has just been done.

Axioms of the Metalanguage

We present a theory T over L_M which consists of the axiom schemas that describe the desired intentions and behaviour of a team of cooperative agents and how their intentions change over time. We do not present any of the basic axioms of beliefs, time etc. that are given in (Grant, Kraus, & Perlis 2000). We also do not present the entire set of 17 axioms for intentions, but rather only about half of them to illustrate important concepts. First we sketch the general scenario for the agent potential intentions, intentions, subcontracting and doing actions.

When an agent is asked to do an action a at a particular time, in the next time period it adopts a potential-intention to do it. If the agent believes that it can do the action a, then in the basic level case, in the next time period it will adopt an intention to do it. In the case of a complex action, it will look for a recipe and in the next time period will adopt potential intentions for all the first-level subactions of the recipe. If after adopting a potential intention the agent comes to believe that it can't do the action a, in the next time period it will ask another agent, that it believes can do a, to do a

If at a particular time period an agent has a potential intention to do a complex action, it will adopt in the next time period an intention to do the action if for each subaction in the recipe it either adopted an intention to do it or it has found another agent with an intention to do it. This process of checking the needed intentions and beliefs and the adopting of an intention will be repeated while the agent still has the potential intention. Each request to perform an action has a time associated with it. If all the needed intentions have been adopted for an action, then at the associated time the agent will initiate it. The initiations will lead to the performance of all the basic actions in the recipe tree of the action at the appropriate times, assuming that the agents can actually do the actions.

We start with a group of axioms that involves the adoption of intentions by the agents. Then we will discuss the axioms involving the agents doing the actual actions. We will conclude by discussing axioms of inheritance. All the variables that are not written with existential quantification are assumed to be universal quantified. All the axioms have the same form of $\alpha \rightarrow \beta$ and typically the time of α is t and the time of β is $t+1$. This is because the axioms characterize the way the mental state of the agent and the state of the world change over time. This way we capture the property that agent reasoning, planning, and actions take time.

We present here three of the axioms of the adoption of intentions group. The first axiom deals with subcontracting an action to one of the agents that can do it. This happens when an agent has a potential intention to do an action, but does not believe that it can do it. Unless it will ask another agent, this potential intention will not become an intention. The antecedents of this axiom are that the agent has a potential intention to do an action and does not believe that it can do it and believes that agent m is the "first" agent that can do it and it has not previously asked m to do it. The consequence is that the agent will ask m to do the action.

$$PotInt(t,n,n',b,a,t') \ \& \ \neg Bel(t,n,"CanDo(t',n,b)") \ \& $$
$$Bel(t,n,"CanDo(t',m,b)") \ \& $$
$$(Bel(t,n,"CanDo(t',m',b)") \ \rightarrow \ m \leq m') \ \& $$
$$(t" < t \ \rightarrow \ \neg ATD(t",n,m,b,t')) \ \& \ t+1 < t' $$
$$\rightarrow \ ATD(t+1,n,m,b,t')$$

The second axiom states that when an agent gets an intention to do an action for another agent, it instantaneously tells this to the other agent.

$$Int(t,m,n,b,a,t') \ \rightarrow \ Tell(t,m,n,"Int(t,m,n,b,a,t')")$$

The third axiom shows how potential intention becomes intention. If an agent has a potential intention to do an action and believes that it can do the action (possibly with help) and if each subaction in the recipe is either intended by the agent or an assisting agent, then in the next time period the agent will have the intention to do the action. This means that if an agent adopts an intention for a complex action, all the basic level actions in the recipe tree must already have been intended by this or some assisting agents. We take into account the time it takes to go down (adopting potential intentions) and up (adopting intentions) in the recipe tree. Additional

time is needed for communication between agents.

$$PotInt(t,n,n',b,a,t') \ \& \ Bel(t,n,"CanDo(t',n,b)") \ \& $$
$$Rec(b,r) \ \& \ t+1 < t' \ \& $$
$$Mem(c,r,i,j,k)\&(Int(t,n,n',c,b,t'+j) \ \lor $$
$$\exists m Tell(t,m,n,"Int(t,m,n,c,e,t'+j)")) $$
$$\rightarrow \ Int(t+1,n,n',b,a,t')$$

Next we present three axioms involving agents doing actions. The first shows how the root of the recipe tree is initiated. When a basic level action is initiated by an agent, it gets done in one time period if the agent can do it. For a complex action, the agent must start by initiating the root of the recipe tree. Each node will have to be initiated in turn. Several agents may be involved in doing various subactions. We use the initiation of complex actions as a bookkeeping device to make sure that all the subactions get done at the proper time and in the right order.

The first axiom of this group is the initiation of the root action. If an agent has the intention for the root action starting at the next time step, it will initiate it.

$$Int(t,n,e,a,e,t+1) \ \rightarrow \ Ini(t+1,n,e,a)$$

If an action is the first subaction of a complex (sub)action, the agent doing the action will initiate it. A later subaction will be initiated by the agent or an assisting agent after all the previous subactions have been done. The second axiom shows that if the previous subaction was done at the right time and the agent doing the action has an assisting second agent intending to do the subaction, then this second agent will initiate the next subaction.

$$Ini(t,m,n,a) \ \& \ Rec(a,r) \ \& \ Mem(r,b,i+1,j',k') \ \& $$
$$Mem(r,c,i,j,k) \ \& \ Done(t+k,c) \ \& $$
$$Int(t+j-1,m',m,c,e,t+j) $$
$$\rightarrow \ Ini(t+j,m',m,c)$$

The third axiom of this group considers the performance of a basic level action. If an agent initiates a basic level action at time t and can do it, then it will get done at time t+1.

$$BL(a) \ \& \ Ini(t,m,n,a) \ \& \ CanDo(t,m,a) $$
$$\rightarrow \ Done(t+1,a)$$

A complex action is done when all its subactions are done.

The third group of axioms involves the inheritance of various mental states and activity formulas. We need inheritance because of our explicit representation of time. Each formula is associated with a specific time. Being true at a given time does not necessarily mean that the formula will continue to be true in the next time period. That is accomplished by the inheritance axioms that specify explicitly which formulas and under which conditions will be inherited from one time period to the other. Intentions are not inherited. Before continuing to hold an intention, an agent must check that all the conditions of having an intention are still valid, as specified in one of the axioms above. In addition to inheriting the potential intentions of a complex action, an agent also adopts potential intentions of the action's subactions (given below). Initiation of a given action is not inherited by itself, but rather by the initiation of its subactions in the proper order and the proper time.

$$PotInt(t,m,n,b,a,t') \ \& \ Bel(t,m,"CanDo(t',m,b)") \ \& $$
$$Rec(b,r) \ \& \ Mem(r,c,i,j,k) \ \& \ t+1 < t' $$
$$\rightarrow \ PotInt(t+1,m,e,c,b,t'+j)$$

Minimal Model Semantics

The axioms of the meta-theory can be shown to be consistent by constructing a model for them. In general, there will be many models for such a first-order theory that have only a tenuous relationship to the application of our interest. In fact, we are interested only in one model, the intended model that represents as its true formulas the actual beliefs, intentions, and actions of the agents as these change over time. The first restriction is to consider only Herbrand models, i.e. models that contain only elements that are ground terms of L_M. The second restriction is to consider only minimal models where we minimize each predicate for one time period at a time starting with 0 and then proceeding by induction on time. Because of the structure of the axioms, there will be only one such model. This construction is based on the construction of the unique perfect model of a locally stratified theory in logic programming. See (Grant, Kraus, & Perlis 2000) for details.

In order to have a sharp sense of how our agents behave, we simply define them to be processes that behave as in this unique minimal model. This has the desired effect of providing certain converses of the axioms as true statements in this model. In effect we are making a an assumption of complete information (akin to a closed-world assumption) about agent behavior; for example an agent comes to have a particular potential intention at time t, if and only if our axioms require that agent to have that potential intention at that time. This is a restriction of sorts; after all, much of commonsense reasoning involves situations that are usually taken to be too complex to fully axiomatize. But our view is to suppose that the complexities primarily arise from the external world and that the agent behaviors are completely characterized by the axioms, once the external inputs are given.

By studying the minimal model under certain initial conditions and known facts about agent beliefs and abilities and the structure of recipes, we can prove various results. The proofs consist of tracing the steps of the agents over time in the model. We include three results here: two positive, one negative. The two theorems show that if there is "enough" time allowed for planning a complex action all of whose subactions a single agent can do (Theorem 1) or subcontract some to other agents (Theorem 2), then the agent will do it. The Proposition shows that if one basic level action in the recipe of a complex action cannot be done by any agent, then no agent will get the intention to do the complex action. There are some models of the meta-theory where this result fails, but it is true in the intended model.

Theorem 1 *Suppose an agent is asked at time t to do an action a starting at time $t + s$, and suppose that the recipe tree for a has v levels and takes k units of time, where $s > 2v + 2$. Further suppose the agent believes that it can do each subaction (at the needed time) itself, and that it in fact can do them. Then the agent will complete the task at time $t + s + k$.*

Proof Sketch:

We show the key formulas (abbreviated leaving out agent names and time) that become true as time changes. We do not show the inherited formulas but add some comments about

them at the end. We also do not show other true formulas, such as $BL(z1)$, that are assumed to hold for all times.

t $ATD(a)$

t+1 $PotInt(a)$

t+2 $PotInt(b1), PotInt(b2), ...$ the children node of a

...

t+v+1 $PotInt(z1), PotInt(z2), ...$ the nodes at the bottom level

t+v+2 $Int(z1), Int(z2), ...$

...

t+2v+1 $Int(b1), Int(b2), ...$

t+2v+2 $Int(a)$

...

t+s $Ini(a)$

t+s+1 $Ini(b1)$

... The times for the Ini and Done of the nodes depend on the tree structure

t+s+k $Done(a)$

We note that $PotInt(a)$ will actually hold starting at time t and ending at time $t + s - 1$. In fact, in this case all the potential intentions and intentions will hold from their earliest time as indicated above (e.g. $t + 2$ for $PotInt(b1)$, $t + v + 2$ for $Int(z1)$) until $t + s' - 1$, where the subaction is supposed to be done at time $t + s'$. The theorem below generalizes the earlier one to the case of multiple agents.

Theorem 2 *Suppose an agent is asked at time t to do an action a starting at time $t + s$, and suppose that the recipe tree for a has v levels and takes k units of time, where $s > 4v + 4$. Further suppose the agent for each subaction either believes that it can do it or can successfully subcontract it to another agent that believes that it can do it (at the needed time), and in fact the intending agent can do the action or subaction. Then the agent, with the assistance of the subcontracting agents will complete the task at time $t + s + k$.*

In this case two time periods must be added at each level for possibly asking another agent to do a task and waiting for the agent to get a potential intention for it.

Proposition 1 *If there is a basic level action b in the recipe for a that no agent believes that it can do, then no agent will get an intention to do a.*

Related Work

Intentions in the context of SharedPlans were studied in (Grosz & Kraus 1996), but no formal semantics were given. Our starting point in this paper was the axioms presented by Grosz and Kraus but our requirements for an agent having an intention is much stronger than those presented in (Grosz & Kraus 1996). There, an agent may have an intention also when having a partial plan. For example, the agent may have only partial knowledge about a recipe, but a plan how to complete it; it may have only potential intentions toward subactions. In order for the agent to have an intention, we require that it have a full detailed plan to do the action and that it has adopted the appropriate intentions and beliefs. These requirements enable us to formally prove various properties about agent intentions and actions.

Since the definition of *Int* in our model is much stronger than the *Int.To* of SharedPlans, the *PotInt* predicate of our model plays a more important role in the agent's reasoning than the *Pot.Int.To* does in (Grosz & Kraus 1996). In (Grosz & Kraus 1996) *Pot.Int.To* is used only as an intermediate operator until *Int.To* is adopted. In our model the *PotInt* is kept for the duration of the agent's need for the associated intention and is used during the planning and for continuous verification of the minimal requirements for having the intention.

The SharedPlan model of collaborative planning uses the mental state model of plans (Pollack 1990). Bratman (Bratman 1987) also argues for a mental-state view of plans, emphasizing the importance of intentions to plans. He argues that intentions to do an action play three roles in rational action: having an intention to do an action constrains the other intentions an agent may adopt, focuses means-ends reasoning, and guides replanning. These roles are even more important for collaborative activity than for individual activity. In our model *Int* and *PotInt* play these roles.

(Castelfranchi 1995) studies the notion of intention for describing and understanding the activities of groups and organizations in the context of improving the exchange between AI and social and management approaches to cooperative work. His motivation is different from our aim of developing a formal logic of beliefs and intentions.

There were several attempts to develop possible worlds semantics for intentions (Konolige & Pollack 1993; Cohen & Levesque 1990; Kraus, Sycara, & Evenchik 1998; Kumar *et al.* 2000; Wooldridge 2000). Some problems arise with these attempts such as that in most of them intentions are closed under Modus Ponens or under logical equivalence and that the relations between the action's recipe and the intention are not well defined. Using a syntactic approach provides more freedom in modeling the way agents' intentions change over time. See (Wooldridge 2000) for an excellent survey. An interesting dual treatment of agents that, like ours, has both an agent language ("first-person account") (Giacomo *et al.* 2002) and a meta language ("third-person account") (Lesperance 2001), uses the Golog family of languages based on the situation-calculus. Those papers (unlike our own) are more focussed on knowledge conditions than on intentions, and also do not take time-taken-to-plan into account.

Summary and Future Work

We presented a formal logical calculus that can be regarded as a meta-logic that describes the reasoning and activities of agents. The explicit representation of evolving time is an important feature of this approach. We dealt with the case where agents are assigned tasks for which a recipe is known. Recipes have a tree structure. An agent may subcontract some of the actions/subactions to other agents. Our emphasis is on developing a framework that models the beliefs, intentions, and actions of agents as they change over time. We present a syntactic approach and propose a minimal model semantics. Using this semantics, rather than possible world semantics, allows us to model agents activity more realistically and to prove several results to show that under the appropriate conditions the agents will act as desired.

We plan to extend this work in several ways. At present we have results only for strongly positive (agents always successfully subcontract actions/subactions and their beliefs about their activities are correct) and strongly negative (there is a subaction that no agent can do) cases. We will consider more complex situations. Also we have assumed that each task has only one recipe and so will deal with the case of multiple recipes. Additionally we will deal with agents doing subactions in parallel and situations where agents have SharedPlans (and not only subcontract actions).

References

Bratman, M. E. 1987. *Intention, Plans, and Practical Reason.* Cambridge, MA: Harvard University Press.

Castelfranchi, C. 1995. Commitments: From individual intentions to groups and organizations. In *ICMAS 95.*

Cohen, P., and Levesque, H. 1990. Intention is choice with commitment. *Artificial Intelligence* 42:263–310.

Giacomo, G. D.; Lesperance, Y.; Levesque, H.; and Sardina, S. 2002. On the semantics of deliberation in indigolog—from theory to implementation. In *KR'02.*

Grant, J.; Kraus, S.; and Perlis, D. 2000. A logic for characterizing multiple bounded agents. *Autonomous Agents and Multi-Agent Systems Journal* 3(4):351–387.

Grosz, B. J., and Kraus, S. 1996. Collaborative plans for complex group activities. *AIJ* 86(2):269–357.

Konolige, K., and Pollack, M. E. 1993. A representationalist theory of intention. In *Proc. of IJCAI-93*, 390–395.

Kraus, S.; Sycara, K.; and Evenchik, A. 1998. Reaching agreements through argumentation: a logical model and implementation. *Artificial Intelligence* 104(1-2):1–69.

Kraus, S. 2001. *Strategic Negotiation in Multiagent Environments.* Cambridge, USA: MIT Press.

Kumar, S.; Huber, P.; McGee, D.; Cohen, P.; and Levesque, H. 2000. Semantics of agent communication languages for group interaction. In *AAAI 2000*, 42–47.

Lesperance, Y. 2001. On the epistemic feasibility of plans in multiagent systems specifications. In *ATAL'01.*

Pollack, M. E. 1990. Plans as complex mental attitudes. In Cohen, P.; Morgan, J.; and Pollack, M., eds., *Intentions in Communication.* Bradford Books, MIT Press.

Wooldridge, M. 2000. *Reasoning about Rational Agents.* The MIT Press.

Reinforcement Learning of Coordination in Cooperative Multi-agent Systems

Spiros Kapetanakis and **Daniel Kudenko**

{spiros, kudenko}@cs.york.ac.uk

Department of Computer Science
University of York, Heslington, York
YO10 5DD, U.K.

Abstract

We report on an investigation of reinforcement learning techniques for the learning of coordination in cooperative multi-agent systems. Specifically, we focus on a novel action selection strategy for Q-learning (Watkins 1989). The new technique is applicable to scenarios where mutual observation of actions is not possible.

To date, reinforcement learning approaches for such *independent* agents did not guarantee convergence to the optimal joint action in scenarios with high miscoordination costs. We improve on previous results (Claus & Boutilier 1998) by demonstrating empirically that our extension causes the agents to converge almost always to the optimal joint action even in these difficult cases.

Introduction

Learning to coordinate in cooperative multi-agent systems is a central and widely studied problem, see, for example (Lauer & Riedmiller 2000), (Boutilier 1999), (Claus & Boutilier 1998), (Sen & Sekaran 1998), (Sen, Sekaran, & Hale 1994), (Weiss 1993). In this context, coordination is defined as *the ability of two or more agents to jointly reach a consensus over which actions to perform in an environment*. We investigate the case of *independent* agents that cannot observe one another's actions, which often is a more realistic assumption.

In this investigation, we focus on reinforcement learning, where the agents must learn to coordinate their actions through environmental feedback. To date, reinforcement learning methods for independent agents (Tan 1993), (Sen, Sekaran, & Hale 1994) did not guarantee convergence to the *optimal* joint action in scenarios where miscoordination is associated with high penalties. Even approaches using agents that are able to build predictive models of each other (so-called *joint-action learners*) have failed to show convergence to the optimal joint action in such difficult cases (Claus & Boutilier 1998). We investigate variants of Q-learning (Watkins 1989) in search of improved convergence to the optimal joint action in the case of independent agents. More specifically, we investigate the effect of the estimated value function in the Boltzmann action selection strategy for Q-learning. We introduce a novel estimated value function and evaluate it experimentally on two especially difficult coordination problems that were first introduced by Claus & Boutilier in 1998: the *climbing game* and the *penalty game*. The empirical results show that the convergence probability to the optimal joint action is greatly improved over other approaches, in fact reaching almost 100%.

Our paper is structured as follows: we first introduce the aforementioned common testbed for the study of learning coordination in cooperative multi-agent systems. We then introduce a novel action selection strategy and discuss the experimental results. We finish with an outlook on future work.

Single-stage coordination games

A common testbed for studying the problem of multi-agent coordination is that of repeated cooperative single-stage games (Fudenberg & Levine 1998). In these games, the agents have common interests i.e. they are rewarded based on their joint action and all agents receive the same reward. In each round of the game, every agent chooses an action. These actions are executed simultaneously and the reward that corresponds to the joint action is broadcast to all agents.

A more formal account of this type of problem was given by Claus & Boutilier in 1998. In brief, we assume a group of n agents $\alpha_1, \alpha_2, \ldots, \alpha_n$ each of which have a finite set of *individual actions* A_i which is known as the agent's *action space*. In this game, each agent α_i chooses an individual action from its action space to perform. The action choices make up a *joint action*. Upon execution of their actions all agents receive the reward that corresponds to the joint action. For example, Table 1 describes the reward function for a simple cooperative single-stage game. If agent 1 executes action b and agent 2 executes action a, the reward they receive is 5. Obviously, the optimal joint-action in this simple game is (b, b) as it is associated with the highest reward of 10.

Our goal is to enable the agents to learn optimal coordination from repeated trials. To achieve this goal, one can use either *independent* or *joint-action* learners. The difference between the two types lies in the amount of information they can perceive in the game. Although both types of learners can perceive the reward that is associated with each joint action, the former are unaware of the existence of other agents

		Agent 1	
		a	b
Agent 2	a	3	5
	b	0	10

Table 1: A simple cooperative game reward function.

		Agent 1		
		a	b	c
	a	10	0	k
Agent 2	b	0	2	0
	c	k	0	10

Table 3: The penalty game table.

whereas the latter can also perceive the actions of others. In this way, joint-action learners can maintain a model of the strategy of other agents and choose their actions based on the other participants' perceived strategy. In contrast, independent learners must estimate the value of their individual actions based solely on the rewards that they receive for their actions. In this paper, we focus on individual learners, these being more universally applicable.

In our study, we focus on two particularly difficult coordination problems, the climbing game and the penalty game. These games were introduced by Claus & Boutilier in 1998. This focus is without loss of generality since the climbing game is representative of problems with high miscoordination penalty and a single optimal joint action whereas the penalty game is representative of problems with high miscoordination penalty and multiple optimal joint actions. Both games are played between two agents. The reward functions for the two games are included in Tables 2 and 3:

		Agent 1		
		a	b	c
	a	11	-30	0
Agent 2	b	-30	7	6
	c	0	0	5

Table 2: The climbing game table.

In the climbing game, it is difficult for the agents to converge to the optimal joint action (a, a) because of the negative reward in the case of miscoordination. For example, if agent 1 plays a and agent 2 plays b, then both will receive a negative reward of -30. Incorporating this reward into the learning process can be so detrimental that both agents tend to avoid playing the same action again. In contrast, when choosing action c, miscoordination is not punished so severely. Therefore, in most cases, both agents are easily tempted by action c. The reason is as follows: if agent 1 plays c, then agent 2 can play either b or c to get a positive reward (6 and 5 respectively). Even if agent 2 plays a, the result is not catastrophic since the reward is 0. Similarly, if agent 2 plays c, whatever agent 1 plays, the resulting reward will be at least 0. From this analysis, we can see that the climbing game is a challenging problem for the study of learning coordination. It includes heavy miscoordination penalties and "safe" actions that are likely to tempt the agents away from the optimal joint action.

Another way to make coordination more elusive is by including multiple optimal joint actions. This is precisely what happens in the penalty game of Table 3.

In the penalty game, it is not only important to avoid the miscoordination penalties associated with actions (c, a) and

(a, c). It is equally important to agree on which optimal joint action to choose out of (a, a) and (c, c). If agent 1 plays a expecting agent 2 to also play a so they can receive the maximum reward of 10 but agent 2 plays c (perhaps expecting agent 1 to play c so that, again, they receive the maximum reward of 10) then the resulting penalty can be very detrimental to both agents' learning process. In this game, b is the "safe" action for both agents since playing b is guaranteed to result in a reward of 0 or 2, regardless of what the other agent plays. Similarly with the climbing game, it is clear that the penalty game is a challenging testbed for the study of learning coordination in multi-agent systems.

Reinforcement learning

A popular technique for learning coordination in cooperative single-stage games is one-step Q-learning, a reinforcement learning technique. Since the agents in a single-stage game are stateless, we need a simple reformulation of the general Q-learning algorithm such as the one used by Claus & Boutilier. Each agent maintains a Q value for each of its actions. The value $Q(\text{action})$ provides an estimate of the usefulness of performing this action in the next iteration of the game and these values are updated after each step of the game according to the reward received for the action. We apply Q-learning with the following update function:

$$Q(\text{action}) \leftarrow Q(\text{action}) + \lambda(r - Q(\text{action}))$$

where λ is the learning rate ($0 < \lambda < 1$) and r is the reward that corresponds to choosing this action.

In a single-agent learning scenario, Q-learning is guaranteed to converge to the optimal action independent of the action selection strategy. In other words, given the assumption of a stationary reward function, single-agent Q-learning will converge to the optimal policy for the problem. However, in a multi-agent setting, the action selection strategy becomes crucial for convergence to *any* joint action. A major challenge in defining a suitable strategy for the selection of actions is to strike a balance between exploring the usefulness of moves that have been attempted only a few times and exploiting those in which the agent's confidence in getting a high reward is relatively strong. This is known as the *exploration/exploitation problem*.

The action selection strategy that we have chosen for our research is the Boltzmann strategy (Kaelbling, Littman, & Moore 1996) which states that agent α_i chooses an action to perform in the next iteration of the game with a probability that is based on its current estimate of the usefulness of that action, denoted by $EV(\text{action})^{1}$:

$$P(\text{action}) = \frac{e^{\frac{EV(\text{action})}{T}}}{\sum_{\text{action}' \in A_i} e^{\frac{EV(\text{action}')}{T}}}$$

In the case of Q-learning, the agent's estimate of the usefulness of an action may be given by the Q values themselves, an approach that has been usually taken to date.

We have concentrated on a proper choice for the two parameters of the Boltzmann function: the estimated value and the temperature. The importance of the temperature lies in that it provides an element of controlled randomness in the action selection: high values in temperature encourage exploration since variations in Q values become less important. In contrast, low temperature values encourage exploitation. The value of the temperature is typically decreased over time from an initial value as exploitation takes over from exploration until it reaches some designated lower limit. The three important settings for the temperature are the initial value, the rate of decrease and the number of steps until it reaches its lowest limit. The lower limit of the temperature needs to be set to a value that is close enough to 0 to allow the learners to converge by stopping their exploration. Variations in these three parameters can provide significant difference in the performance of the learners. For example, starting with a very high value for the temperature forces the agents to make random moves until the temperature reaches a low enough value to play a part in the learning. This may be beneficial if the agents are gathering statistical information about the environment or the other agents. However, this may also dramatically slow down the learning process.

It has been shown (Singh *et al.* 2000) that convergence to a joint action can be ensured if the temperature function adheres to certain properties. However, we have found that there is more that can be done to ensure not just convergence to *some* joint action but convergence to the *optimal* joint action, even in the case of independent learners. This is not just in terms of the temperature function but, more importantly, in terms of the action selection strategy. More specifically, it turns out that a proper choice for the estimated value function in the Boltzmann strategy can significantly increase the likelihood of convergence to the optimal joint action.

FMQ heuristic

In difficult coordination problems, such as the climbing game and the penalty game, the way to achieve convergence to the optimal joint action is by influencing the learners towards their individual components of the optimal joint action(s). To this effect, there exist two strategies: altering the Q-update function and altering the action selection strategy.

Lauer & Riedmiller (2000) describe an algorithm for multi-agent reinforcement learning which is based on the *optimistic* assumption. In the context of reinforcement learning, this assumption implies that an agent chooses any action it finds suitable expecting the other agent to choose the

---

[1]In (Kaelbling, Littman, & Moore 1996), the estimated value is introduced as *expected reward* (ER).

best match accordingly. More specifically, the optimistic assumption affects the way Q values are updated. Under this assumption, the update rule for playing action α defines that $Q(\alpha)$ is only updated if the new value is greater than the current one.

Incorporating the optimistic assumption into Q-learning solves both the climbing game and penalty game every time. This fact is not surprising since the penalties for miscoordination, which make learning optimal actions difficult, are neglected as their incorporation into the learning tends to lower the Q values of the corresponding actions. Such lowering of Q values is not allowed under the optimistic assumption so that all the Q values eventually converge to the maximum reward corresponding to that action for each agent. However, the optimistic assumption fails to converge to the optimal joint action in cases where the maximum reward is misleading, e.g., in stochastic games (see experiments below). We therefore consider an alternative: the *Frequency Maximum Q Value* (FMQ) heuristic.

Unlike the optimistic assumption, that applies to the Q update function, the FMQ heuristic applies to the action selection strategy, specifically the choice of $EV(\alpha)$, i.e. the function that computes the estimated value of action α. As mentioned before, the standard approach is to set $EV(\alpha) = Q(\alpha)$. Instead, we propose the following modification:

$$EV(\alpha) = Q(\alpha) + c * \text{freq}(\text{maxR}(\alpha)) * \text{maxR}(\alpha)$$

where:

① $\text{maxR}(\alpha)$ denotes the maximum reward encountered *so far* for choosing action α.

② $\text{freq}(\text{maxR}(\alpha))$ is the fraction of times that $\text{maxR}(\alpha)$ has been received as a reward for action α over the times that action α has been executed.

③ c is a weight that controls the importance of the FMQ heuristic in the action selection.

Informally, the FMQ heuristic carries the information of how frequently an action produces its maximum corresponding reward. Note that, for an agent to receive the maximum reward corresponding to one of its actions, the other agent must be playing the game accordingly. For example, in the climbing game, if agent 1 plays action a which is agent 1's component of the optimal joint-action (a, a) but agent 2 doesn't, then they both receive a reward that is less than the maximum. If agent 2 plays c then the two agents receive 0 and, provided they have already encountered the maximum rewards for their actions, both agents' FMQ estimates for their actions are lowered. This is due to the fact that the frequency of occurrence of maximum reward is lowered. Note that setting the FMQ weight c to zero reduces the estimated value function to: $EV(\alpha) = Q(\alpha)$.

In the case of independent learners, there is nothing other than action choices and rewards that an agent can use to learn coordination. By ensuring that enough exploration is permitted in the beginning of the experiment, the agents have a good chance of visiting the optimal joint action so that the FMQ heuristic can influence them towards their appropriate individual action components. In a sense, the FMQ heuristic defines a model of the environment that the agent operates in, the other agent being part of that environment.

Experimental results

This section contains our experimental results. We compare the performance of Q-learning using the FMQ heuristic against the baseline experiments i.e. experiments where the Q values are used as the estimated value of an action in the Boltzmann action selection strategy. In both cases, we use only independent learners. The comparison is done by keeping all other parameters of the experiment the same, i.e. using the same temperature function and experiment length. The evaluation of the two approaches is performed on both the climbing game and the penalty game.

Temperature settings

Exponential decay in the value of the temperature is a popular choice in reinforcement learning. This way, the agents perform all their learning until the temperature reaches some lower limit. The experiment then finishes and results are collected. The temperature limit is normally set to zero which may cause complications when calculating the action selection probabilities with the Boltzmann function. To avoid such problems, we have set the temperature limit to 1 in our experiments[2].

In our analysis, we use the following temperature function:

$$T(x) = e^{-sx} * \text{max\_temp} + 1$$

where x is the number of iterations of the game so far, s is the parameter that controls the rate of exponential decay and max_temp is the value of the temperature at the beginning of the experiment. For a given length of the experiment (max_moves) and initial temperature (max_temp) the appropriate rate of decay (s) is automatically derived. Varying the parameters of the temperature function allows a detailed specification of the temperature. For a given max_moves, we experimented with a variety of $s, \text{max\_temp}$ combinations and found that they didn't have a significant impact on the learning in the baseline experiments. Their impact is more significant when using the FMQ heuristic. This is because setting max_temp at a very high value means that the agent makes random moves in the initial part of the experiment. It then starts making more knowledgeable moves (i.e. moves based on the estimated value of its actions) when the temperature has become low enough to allow variations in the estimated value of an action to have an impact on the probability of selecting that action.

Evaluation on the climbing game

The climbing game has one optimal joint action (a, a) and two heavily penalised actions (a, b) and (b, a). We use the settings $\text{max\_temp} = 500$ and vary max_moves from 500 to 2000. The learning rate λ is set to 0.9. Figure 1 depicts the likelihood of convergence to the optimal joint action in the baseline experiments and using the FMQ heuristic with $c = 1$ and $c = 10$. The FMQ heuristic outperforms the

---

[2]This is done without loss of generality.

---

baseline experiments for both settings of c. For $c = 10$, the FMQ heuristic converges to the optimal joint action almost always even for short experiments.

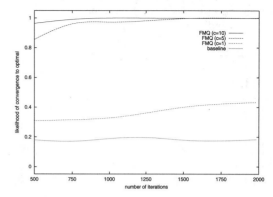

Figure 1: Likelihood of convergence to the optimal joint action in the climbing game (averaged over 1000 trials).

Evaluation on the penalty game

The penalty game is harder to analyse than the climbing game. This is because it has two optimal joint actions (a, a) and (c, c) for all values of $k \leq 0$. The extent to which the optimal joint actions are reached by the agents is affected severely by the size of the penalty. However, the performance of the agents depends not only on the size of the penalty k but also on whether the agents manage to agree on which optimal joint action to choose. Table 2 depicts the performance of the learners for $k = 0$ for the baseline experiments and with the FMQ heuristic for $c = 1$.

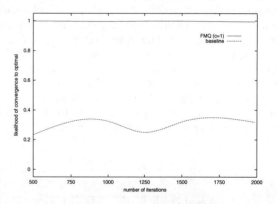

Figure 2: Likelihood of convergence to the optimal joint action in the penalty game $k = 0$ (averaged over 1000 trials).

As shown in Figure 2, the performance of the FMQ heuristic is much better than the baseline experiment. When $k = 0$, the reason for the baseline experiment's failure is not the existence of a miscoordination penalty. Instead, it is the existence of multiple optimal joint actions that causes the agents to converge to the optimal joint action so infrequently. Of course, the penalty game becomes much harder for greater penalty. To analyse the impact of the penalty on the convergence to optimal, Figure 3 depicts the likelihood that convergence to optimal occurs as a function of the penalty. The four plots correspond to the baseline experiments and using Q-learning with the FMQ heuristic for $c = 1$, $c = 5$ and $c = 10$.

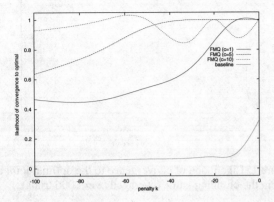

Figure 3: Likelihood of convergence to the optimal joint action as a function of the penalty (averaged over 1000 trials).

From Figure 3, it is obvious that higher values of the FMQ weight c perform better for higher penalty. This is because there is a greater need to influence the learners towards the optimal joint action when the penalty is more severe.

Further experiments

We have described two approaches that perform very well on the climbing game and the penalty game: FMQ and the optimistic assumption. However, the two approaches are different and this difference can be highlighted by looking at alternative versions of the climbing game. In order to compare the FMQ heuristic to the optimistic assumption (Lauer & Riedmiller 2000), we introduce a variant of the climbing game which we term *the partially stochastic climbing game*. This version of the climbing game differs from the original in that one of the joint actions is now associated with a stochastic reward. The reward function for the partially stochastic climbing game is included in Table 4.

		Agent 1		
		a	b	c
	a	11	-30	0
Agent 2	b	-30	14/0	6
	c	0	0	5

Table 4: The partially stochastic climbing game table.

Joint action (b, b) yields a reward of 14 or 0 with probability 50%. The partially stochastic climbing game is functionally equivalent to the original version. This is because, if the two agents consistently choose their b action, they receive the same overall value of 7 over time as in the original game.

Using the optimistic assumption on the partially stochastic climbing game consistently converges to the suboptimal joint action (b, b). This because the frequency of occurrence of a high reward is not taken into consideration at all. In contrast, the FMQ heuristic shows much more promise in convergence to the optimal joint action. It also compares favourably with the baseline experimental results. Tables 5, 6 and 7 contain the results obtained with the baseline experiments, the optimistic assumption and the FMQ heuristic for 1000 experiments respectively. In all cases, the parameters are: $s = 0.006$, $max\_moves = 1000$, $max\_temp = 500$ and, in the case of FMQ, $c = 10$.

	a	b	c
a	212	0	3
b	0	12	289
c	0	0	381

Table 5: Baseline experimental results.

	a	b	c
a	0	0	0
b	0	1000	0
c	0	0	0

Table 6: Results with optimistic assumption.

	a	b	c
a	988	0	0
b	0	4	0
c	0	7	1

Table 7: Results with the FMQ heuristic.

The final topic for evaluation of the FMQ heuristic is to analyse the influence of the weight (c) on the learning. Informally, the more difficult the problem, the greater the need for a high FMQ weight. However, setting the FMQ weight at too high a value can be detrimental to the learning. Figure 4 contains a plot of the likelihood of convergence to optimal in the climbing game as a function of the FMQ weight.

From Figure 4, we can see that setting the value of the FMQ weight above 15 lowers the probability that the agents will converge to the optimal joint action. This is because, by setting the FMQ weight too high, the probabilities for action selection are influenced too much towards the action with the highest FMQ value which may not be the optimal joint action early in the experiment. In other words, the agents become too narrow-minded and follow the heuristic blindly since the FMQ part of the estimated value function overwhelms the Q values. This property is also reflected in the experimental results on the penalty game (see Figure 3) where setting the FMQ weight to 10 performs very well in difficult experiments with $-100 < k < -50$ but there is a drop in performance for easier experiments. In contrast, for $c = 1$ the likelihood of convergence to the optimal joint action in easier experiments is significantly higher than in more difficult ones.

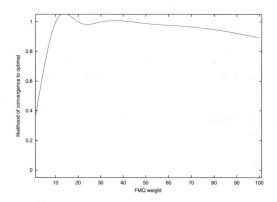

Figure 4: Likelihood of convergence to optimal in the climbing game as a function of the FMQ weight (averaged over 1000 trials).

Limitations

The FMQ heuristic performs equally well in the partially stochastic climbing game and the original deterministic climbing game. In contrast, the optimistic assumption only succeeds in solving the deterministic climbing game. However, we have found a variant of the climbing game in which both heuristics perform poorly: *the fully stochastic climbing game*. This game has the characteristic that *all* joint actions are probabilistically linked with two rewards. The average of the two rewards for each action is the same as the original reward from the deterministic version of the climbing game so the two games are functionally equivalent. For the rest of this discussion, we assume a 50% probability. The reward function for the stochastic climbing game is included in Table 8.

		Agent 1		
		a	b	c
	a	10/12	5/-65	8/-8
Agent 2	b	5/-65	14/0	12/0
	c	5/-5	5/-5	10/0

Table 8: The stochastic climbing game table (50%).

It is obvious why the optimistic assumption fails to solve the fully stochastic climbing game. It is for the same reason that it fails with the partially stochastic climbing game. The maximum reward is associated with joint action (b, b) which is a suboptimal action. The FMQ heuristic, although it performs marginally better than normal Q-learning still doesn't provide any substantial success ratios. However, we are working on an extension that may overcome this limitation.

Outlook

We have presented an investigation of techniques that allows two independent agents that are unable to sense each other's actions to learn coordination in cooperative single-stage games, even in difficult cases with high miscoordina-tion penalties. However, there is still much to be done towards understanding exactly how the action selection strategy can influence the learning of optimal joint actions in this type of repeated games. In the future, we plan to investigate this issue in more detail.

Furthermore, since agents typically have a state component associated with them, we plan to investigate how to incorporate such coordination learning mechanisms in multi-stage games. We intend to further analyse the applicability of various reinforcement learning techniques to agents with a substantially greater action space. Finally, we intend to perform a similar systematic examination of the applicability of such techniques to partially observable environments where the rewards are perceived stochastically.

References

Boutilier, C. 1999. Sequential optimality and coordination in multiagent systems. In *Proceedings of the Sixteenth International Joint Conference on Articial Intelligence (IJCAI-99)*, 478–485.

Claus, C., and Boutilier, C. 1998. The dynamics of reinforcement learning in cooperative multiagent systems. In *Proceedings of the Fifteenth National Conference on Articial Intelligence*, 746–752.

Fudenberg, D., and Levine, D. K. 1998. *The Theory of Learning in Games*. Cambridge, MA: MIT Press.

Kaelbling, L. P.; Littman, M.; and Moore, A. W. 1996. Reinforcement learning: A survey. *Journal of Artificial Intelligence Research* 4.

Lauer, M., and Riedmiller, M. 2000. An algorithm for distributed reinforcement learning in cooperative multi-agent systems. In *Proceedings of the Seventeenth International Conference in Machine Learning*.

Sen, S., and Sekaran, M. 1998. Individual learning of coordination knowledge. *JETAI* 10(3):333–356.

Sen, S.; Sekaran, M.; and Hale, J. 1994. Learning to coordinate without sharing information. In *Proceedings of the Twelfth National Conference on Artificial Intelligence*, 426–431.

Singh, S.; Jaakkola, T.; Littman, M. L.; and Szpesvari, C. 2000. Convergence results for single-step on-policy reinforcement-learning algorithms. *Machine Learning Journal* 38(3):287–308.

Tan, M. 1993. Multi-agent reinforcement learning: Independent vs. cooperative agents. In *Proceedings of the Tenth International Conference on Machine Learning*, 330–337.

Watkins, C. J. C. H. 1989. *Learning from Delayed Rewards*. Ph.D. Dissertation, Cambridge University, Cambridge, England.

Weiss, G. 1993. Learning to coordinate actions in multi-agent systems. In *Proceedings of the Thirteenth International Joint Conference on Artificial Intelligence*, volume 1, 311–316. Morgan Kaufmann Publ.

The Design of Collectives of Agents to Control Non-Markovian Systems

John W. Lawson and David H. Wolpert
NASA Ames Research Center
MS 269-2
Moffett Field, CA 94035
{lawson,dhw}@ptolemy.arc.nasa.gov

Abstract

The "Collective Intelligence" (COIN) framework concerns the design of collectives of reinforcement-learning agents such that their interaction causes a provided "world" utility function concerning the entire collective to be maximized. Previously, we applied that framework to scenarios involving Markovian dynamics where no re-evolution of the system from counter-factual initial conditions (an often expensive calculation) is permitted. This approach sets the individual utility function of each agent to be both aligned with the world utility, and at the same time, easy for the associated agents to optimize. Here we extend that approach to systems involving non-Markovian dynamics. In computer simulations, we compare our techniques with each other and with conventional "team games" We show whereas in team games performance often degrades badly with time, it steadily improves when our techniques are used. We also investigate situations where the system's dimensionality is effectively reduced. We show that this leads to difficulties in the agents' ability to learn. The implication is that "learning" is a property only of high-enough dimensional systems.

Introduction

In this paper we are concerned with large distributed collectives of interacting goal-driven computational processes, where there is a provided 'world utility' function that rates the possible behaviors of that collective (Wolpert, Tumer, & Frank 1999; Wolpert & Tumer 1999). We are particularly concerned with such collectives where the individual computational processes use machine learning techniques (e.g., Reinforcement Learning (RL) (Kaelbing, Littman, & Moore 1996; Sutton & Barto 1998; Sutton 1988; Watkins & Dayan 1992)) to try to achieve their individual goals. We represent those goals of the individual processes as maximizing an associated 'payoff' utility function, one that in general can differ from the world utility.

In such a system, we are confronted with the following inverse problem: *How should one initialize/update the payoff utility functions of the individual processes so that the ensuing behavior of the entire collective achieves large values of the provided world utility?* In particular, since in truly large

systems detailed modeling of the system is usually impossible, how can we avoid such modeling? Can we instead leverage the simple assumption that our learnering algorithms are individually fairly good at what they do to achieve a large world utility value?

We are concerned with payoff utility functions that are "aligned" with the world utility, in that modifications a player might make that would improve its payoff utility also must improve world utility.[1] Fortunately the equivalence class of such payoff utilities extends well beyond team-game utilities. In particular, in previous work we used the COllective INtelligence (COIN) framework to derive the 'Wonderful Life Utility' (WLU) payoff function (Wolpert & Tumer 1999) as an alternative to a team-game payoff utility. The WLU is aligned with world utility, as desired. In addition though, WLU overcomes much of the signal-to-noise problem of team game utilities (Tumer & Wolpert 2000; Wolpert, Tumer, & Frank 1999; Wolpert & Tumer 1999; Wolpert, Wheeler, & Tumer 2000).

In a recent paper, we extended the COIN framework with an approach based on Transforming Arguments Utility functions (TAU) before the evaluation of those functions (Wolpert & Lawson 2002). The TAU process was originally designed to be applied to the individual utility functions of the agents in systems in which the world utility depends on the final state in an episode of variables outside the collective that undergo Markovian dynamics, with the update rule of those variables reflecting the state of the agents at the beginning of the episode. This is a very common scenario, obtaining whenever the agents in the collective act as control signals perturbing the evolution of a Markovian system.

In the pre-TAU version of the COIN framework, to achieve good signal-to-noise for such scenarios requires knowing the evolution operator. However it also might require re-evolving the system from counter-factual initial states of the agents to evaluate each agent's reward for a particular episode. This can be computationally expensive. With TAU utility functions no such re-evolving is needed; the observed history of the system in the episode is transformed in a relatively cheap calculation, and then the util-

---

[1] Such alignment can be viewed as an extension of the concept of incentive compatibility in mechanism design (Fudenberg & Tirole 1991) to non-human agents, off-equilibrium behavior, etc.

ity function is evaluated with that transformed history rather than the actual one.

The TAU process has other advantages that apply even in scenarios not involving Markovian dynamics. In particular it allows us to employ the COIN framework even when not all arguments of the original utility function are observable, due for example to communication limitations. In addition, certain types of TAU transformations result in utility functions that are not exactly aligned with the world utility, but have so much better signal-to-noise that the collective performs better when agents use those transformed utility functions than it does with exactly aligned utility functions.

Here we investigate the extension of the TAU process to systems with non-Markovian dynamics where the world utility is the same function of the state of the system at every moment in time. To do this we have the agents operate on very fast time-scales compared to that dynamics, i.e., have the time-steps at which they make their successive moves be very closely packed. We also have the moves of the agents consist of very small perturbations to the underlying variables of the system rather than the direct setting of those variables. Now since the world utility is defined for every moment in time, there is a surface taking the values of those underlying variables at any time-step to the associated value of the world utility. So the problem for the agents is one of traversing that surface to try to get to values of the underlying variables to have a good associated world utility.

Since the time-scales are so small though, we can approximate the effects of the agents' moves at any time-step of the value of the world utility at the next time-step as though the intervening evolution were linear (Markovian). Now, as in the original TAU work, assume for simplicity that that linear dynamics is known for each such time-step. Then at each time-step the problem is reduced to the exact same one that was addressed in that original TAU work.

Unlike in that original work though, here the linear relation between the moves of the agents and the resultant value of the world utility at the next time-step changes from one time-step to the next, as both the underlying variables of the system change as does the associated gradient. Accordingly, the mapping the agents are trying to learn from their moves to the resultant rewards changes in time.

Here we do not confront this nonstationarity. We use a set of computer experiments to compare use of the TAU process to set the utility functions of agents to the alternative conventional approach of "team games" in this non-Markovian domain. We verify that the TAU process outperforms this alternative. In particular, in many experiments the team game resulted in world utility values that *decrease* with time, i.e., the agents steer the underlying variables to worse and worse values. In contrast, the TAU process steer the underlying variables in such a way that improved world utility with time.

We also investigate what happens as the underlying system is modified so that the moves of the individual agents become less and less consequential to the dynamics. Intuitively, one would expect in such a case that the system's effective dimensionality gets reduced, while the agents also have a harder time learning. We present tentative evidence

corroborating this prediction. The implication is that "learning" is a property only of high-enough dimensional systems.

The Mathematics of Collective Intelligence

We view the individual agents in the collective as players involved in a repeated game.[2] Let Z with elements ζ be the space of possible joint moves of all players in the collective in some stage. We wish to search for the ζ that maximizes a provided **world utility** $G(\zeta)$. In addition to G we are concerned with utility functions $\{g_\eta\}$, one such function for each variable/player η. We use the notation $\hat\eta$ to refer to all players other than η.

Intelligence and the central equation

We wish to "standardize" utility functions so that the numeric value they assign to a ζ only reflects their ranking of ζ relative to certain other elements of Z. We call such a standardization of an arbitrary utility U for player η the "**intelligence** for η at ζ with respect to U". Here we will use intelligences that are equivalent to percentiles:

$$\epsilon_U(\zeta : \eta) \equiv \int d\mu_{\zeta_{\hat\eta}}(\zeta')\Theta[U(\zeta) - U(\zeta')] , \qquad (1)$$

where the Heaviside function Θ is defined to equal 1 when its argument is greater than or equal to 0, and to equal 0 otherwise, and where the subscript on the (normalized) measure $d\mu$ indicates it is restricted to ζ' sharing the same non-η components as ζ. In general, the measure must reflect the type of system at hand, e.g., whether Z is countable or not, and if not, what coordinate system is being used. Other than that, any convenient choice of measure may be used and the theorems will still hold. Intelligence value are always between 0 and 1.

Our uncertainty concerning the behavior of the system is reflected in a probability distribution over Z. Our ability to control the system consists of setting the value of some characteristic of the collective, e.g., setting the functions of the players. Indicating that value by s, our analysis revolves around the following central equation for $P(G \mid s)$, which follows from Bayes' theorem:

$$P(G \mid s) = \int d\vec\epsilon_G P(G \mid \vec\epsilon_G, s)$$

$$\int d\vec\epsilon_g P(\vec\epsilon_G \mid \vec\epsilon_g, s) P(\vec\epsilon_g \mid s) , \qquad (2)$$

where $\vec\epsilon_g \equiv (\epsilon_{g_{\eta_1}}(\zeta : \eta_1), \epsilon_{g_{\eta_2}}(\zeta : \eta_2), \cdots)$ is the vector of the intelligences of the players with respect to their associated functions, and $\vec\epsilon_G \equiv (\epsilon_G(\zeta : \eta_1), \epsilon_G(\zeta : \eta_2), \cdots)$ is the vector of the intelligences of the players with respect to G.

Note that $\epsilon_{g_\eta}(\zeta : \eta) = 1$ means that player η is fully rational at ζ, in that its move maximizes its utility, given the moves of the players. In other words, a point ζ where

---

[2]The full mathematics of the COIN framework, however, extends significantly beyond what is needed to address such games. See (Wolpert & Tumer 2001).

$\epsilon_{g_\eta}(\zeta : \eta) = 1$ for all players η is one that meets the definition of a game-theory Nash equilibrium (Fudenberg & Tirole 1991). Note that consideration of points ζ at which not all intelligences equal 1 provides the basis for a model-independent formalization of bounded rationality game theory, a formalization that contains variants of many of the theorems of conventional full-rationality game theory (Wolpert 2001a). On the other hand, a ζ at which all components of $\vec{\epsilon}_G = 1$ is a local maximum of G (or more precisely, a critical point of the $G(\zeta)$ surface).

If we can choose s so that the third conditional probability in the integrand is peaked around vectors $\vec{\epsilon}_g$ all of whose components are close to 1, then we have likely induced large intelligences. If in addition the second term is peaked about $\vec{\epsilon}_G$ equal to $\vec{\epsilon}_g$, then $\vec{\epsilon}_G$ will also be large. Finally, if the first term is peaked about high G when $\vec{\epsilon}_G$ is large, then our choice of s will likely result in high G, as desired.

Intuitively, the requirement that the utility functions have high "signal-to-noise" (an issue not considered in conventional work in mechanism design) arises in the third term. It is in the second term that the requirement that the utility functions be "aligned with G" arises. In this work we concentrate on these two terms, and show how to simultaneously set them to have the desired form.

Details of the stochastic environment in which the collective operates, together with details of the learning algorithms of the players, are reflected in the distribution $P(\zeta)$ which underlies the distributions appearing in Equation 2. Note though that *independent of these considerations*, our desired form for the second term in Equation 2 is assured if we have chosen utility utilities such that $\vec{\epsilon}_g$ equals $\vec{\epsilon}_G$ exactly *for all* ζ. We call such a system *factored*. In game-theory language, the Nash equilibria of a factored collective are local maxima of G. In addition to this desirable equilibrium behavior, factored collectives automatically provide appropriate off-equilibrium incentives to the players (an issue rarely considered in game theory / mechanism design).

Opacity

We now focus on algorithms based on utility functions $\{g_\eta\}$ that optimize the signal/noise ratio reflected in the third term, subject to the requirement that the system be factored. To understand how these algorithms work, given a measure $d\mu(\zeta_\eta)$, define the **opacity** at ζ of utility U as:

$$\Omega_U(\zeta : \eta, s) \equiv \int d\zeta' J(\zeta' \mid \zeta) \frac{|U(\zeta) - U(\zeta'_\eta, \zeta_\eta)|}{|U(\zeta) - U(\zeta_\eta, \zeta'_\eta)|}, \quad (3)$$

where J is defined in terms of the underlying probability distributions,[3] and $(\zeta'_\eta, \zeta_\eta)$ is defined as the worldline whose $\hat{\eta}$

---

[3] Writing it out in full, $J(\zeta' \mid \zeta) \equiv J(\zeta_\eta, \zeta' \mid \zeta_\eta, s)/P(\zeta_\eta \mid \zeta_\eta, s)$, with:

$$J(\zeta_\eta, \zeta' \mid \zeta_\eta, s) \equiv \frac{P(\zeta_\eta \mid \zeta_\eta, s)P(\zeta'_\eta \mid \zeta_\eta, s)\mu(\zeta'_\eta)}{2} + \qquad (4)$$
$$\frac{P(\zeta'_\eta \mid \zeta'_\eta, s)P(\zeta_\eta \mid \zeta'_\eta, s)\mu(\zeta_\eta)}{2}.$$

components are the same as those of ζ' while its η components are the same as those of ζ ((Wolpert & Tumer 2001)).

The denominator absolute value in the integrand in Equation 3 reflects how sensitive $U(\zeta)$ is to changing ζ_η. In contrast, the numerator absolute value reflects how sensitive $U(\zeta)$ is to changing ζ_η. So the smaller the opacity of a utility function g_η, the more $g_\eta(\zeta)$ depends only on the move of player η, i.e., the better the associated signal-to-noise ratio for η. Intuitively then, lower opacity should mean it is easier for η to achieve a large value of its intelligence.

To formally establish this, we use the same measure $d\mu$ to define opacity as the one that defined intelligence. Under this choice expected opacity bounds how close to 1 expected intelligence can be (Wolpert & Tumer 2001):

$$E(\epsilon_U(\zeta : \eta) \mid s) \leq 1 - K, \text{where}$$
$$K \leq E(\Omega_U(\zeta : \eta, s) \mid s). \qquad (5)$$

So low expected opacity of utility g_η ensure that a necessary condition is met for the third term in Equation 2 to have the desired form for player η. While low opacity is not, formally speaking, also sufficient for $E(\epsilon_U(\zeta : \eta) \mid s)$ to be close to 1, in practice the bounds in Equation 5 are usually tight.

Difference Utilities

It is possible to solve for the set of all utilities that are factored with respect to a particular world utility. Unfortunately, in general it is not possible for a collective both to be factored and to have zero opacity for all of its players. However consider **difference** utilities, which are of the form

$$U(\zeta) = G(\zeta) - \Gamma(f(\zeta)) \qquad (6)$$

where $\Gamma(f)$ is independent of ζ_η. Any difference utility is factored (Wolpert 2001b), and under benign approximations, $E(\Omega_u \mid s)$ is minimized over the set of such utilities by choosing

$$\Gamma(f(\zeta)) = E(G \mid \zeta_\eta, s), \qquad (7)$$

up to an overall additive constant. We call the resultant difference utility the **Aristocrat** utility (AU), loosely reflecting the fact that it measures the difference between a player's actual action and the average action.

The COIN Framework for Systems with Markovian Evolution

We consider games which consist of multi-step "episodes". Within each episode the entire system evolves in a Markovian manner from the initial moves of the players. We are interested in such games where some of the players η are not agents whose initial state is under control of a learning algorithm that we control, but rather constitute an "environment" for those controllable agents (i.e., where some of the players correspond to the state of nature).

Let A be the Markovian single step evolution operator of the entire system through an episode,

$$\vec{\zeta}_t = A(\vec{\zeta}_{t-1}) \qquad (8)$$

Each component ζ_t^η, for example, could be a one-dimensional real number. The row vector A^η would then be η's update rule. Alternatively, each agent could be represented by one of N symbolic values. In that case, $\vec{\zeta}_t$ would be given in a unary representation as a vector in $\mathcal{R}^{N^{|\eta|}}$ (i.e. a Haar basis). Considering such large spaces are necessary to describe arbitrary, nonlinear dynamics as Markovian evolution. Here we will concentrate on the former case, where the moves of the players are all real numbers.

The full multiple time step evolution of an episode is given by single step operator in the usual way: Let

$$C = \begin{bmatrix} A \\ A^2 \\ A^3 \\ \cdot \\ \cdot \\ A^T \end{bmatrix}$$

where T is the number of time steps per episode. This operator applied to our initial state $\vec{\zeta}_0$ yields the entire "worldline" $\vec{\zeta}$, or time history, of the system.

$$\vec{\zeta} = C\vec{\zeta}_0. \tag{9}$$

We consider difference utility functions of the form

$$g_\eta(\vec{\zeta}) = G(C\vec{\zeta}_0) - \Gamma_\eta(F_\eta C\vec{\zeta}_0) \tag{10}$$

where G is the world utility function to be optimized. We will choose F_η so that the product $F_\eta C\vec{\zeta}_0$ is independent of agent η's actions. This is a necessary and sufficient condition for the associated difference utility $g_\eta(\vec{\zeta})$ to be factored with respect to the world utility G for any and all choices of Γ_η. In general, Γ_η can be chosen in such a way to optimize learnability. Here though, for simplicity, we choose $\Gamma_\eta = G$. Accordingly, application of the F_η operator is an instance of transforming the argument of the (second term of the) utility functions of the agents, i.e., it is a TAU process.

Observability restrictions

In practice, the full worldline of the system may not be fully observable to each agent. Such limited observability of a particular component may be determined by the problem. In other cases, due to communication constraints each agent is only allowed to observe a certain number of components, and must select which such components to observe, for example to optimize some auxiliary quantity like opacity. Similarly, the dynamics may not be known exactly to the agent; some rows of C may be uncertain to an agent, or simply cannot be determined. In these kinds of situations the g_η described above cannot be evaluated at the end of an episode by agent η, even if the value $G(\vec{\zeta}_t)$ is globally broadcast to all agents.

The TAU approach outlined above is well-suited to address such situations. Formally, a decimated identity operator L can be defined whose diagonal elements are $\{0, 1\}$ depending on whether or not they are observable. The corresponding factored utility for agent η is

$$g_\eta(\vec{\zeta}_t) = G(\vec{\zeta}_t) - G(LF_\eta\vec{\zeta}_t), \tag{11}$$

where in general L may vary with η. Given global broadcast to all agents of the value of $G(\vec{\zeta}_t)$, for each agent to evaluate this type of g_η only requires that those components of $F_\eta\vec{\zeta}_t$ that are non-zero (and therefore can vary) after application of the L operator be observed.

This difference utility has two main sources of noise, one from potentially poor choice of the clamping operator, and the other from the use of L in the second (subtracted) term but not in the first. To address that latter source of noise we can impose limited observability on the first term in addition to the second one, getting

$$g_\eta(\vec{\zeta}_t) = G(L\vec{\zeta}_t) - G(LF_\eta\vec{\zeta}_t). \tag{12}$$

The new utility is not factored with respect to G. According to the central equation however, it may still result in better performance than when we don't have L in the first term, if the improvement in opacity more than offsets the loss of exact factoredness. In addition to the potential for such far superior opacity, this utility has the added advantage that now we don't even need to rely on global broadcast of $G(L\vec{\zeta}_t)$ to evaluate g_η.

The non-Markovian case

To address the general nonlinear problem, we assign each agent a real-valued number r_η which is analogous to a position. The state of the system at time t is the Cartesian product of each agent's position $\vec{r}_t$. Each agent can choose among three actions which add one of the values $\{\pm\Delta, 0\}$ to r_η. If the vector $\vec{\zeta}_t$ represents the agents' action choices, then, at the end of each episode, the system is updated according to the rule $\vec{r}_{t+1} = \vec{r}_t + \Delta\vec{\zeta}_t$. Notice that this has the form of a control problem. Nonlinear evolution then occurs to $\vec{r}_t$, to produce the value at the end of the episode, $\vec{c}(\vec{r}_t)$. That value then serves as the argument of G.

Construction of factored utilities

$$g_\eta(\vec{\zeta}_t) = G(\vec{c}(\vec{r}_t)) - G(\vec{c}(\hat{C}L\vec{r}_t)) \tag{13}$$

requires that $\vec{c}(\vec{r}_t)$ be independent of η's choice of action. One way to accomplish this is to clamp (apply $\hat{C}L$) to $\vec{r}_t$ and re-evolve the system. To avoid re-evolving the system, we approximate $\vec{c}(\hat{C}L\vec{r}_t)$ with a Taylor Series expansion about the unclamped $\vec{r}_t$ starting state:

$$\vec{c}(\hat{C}L\vec{r}_t) = \vec{c}(\vec{r}_t) + \Delta(\vec{\zeta} - \hat{C}L\vec{\zeta}_t) \cdot \vec{\nabla}\vec{c}(\vec{r}_t). \tag{14}$$

Assuming not all components of $\vec{\zeta}_t$ equal 0, we can recast this as as the multiplication of a matrix $\vec{\nabla}\vec{c}(\vec{r}_t)$ times $\vec{\zeta}_t$, where that matrix is indexed by time. In doing this we reduce the system to the linear case, only with a time-dependent update matrix.

Note that varying Δ provides us a small parameter to control the expansion. It should also be noted that while this method requires that $\vec{c}(\vec{r}_t)$ be differentiable, the world utility G need not be.

Experiments

Numerical simulations were performed with 50 agents. After an initial 100-episode training period, agents selected initial actions in each subsequent episode with the same reinforcement learning algorithm used in our previous work. All players experienced a quadratic/nonlinear update rule $\vec{c}(\vec{r_t}) = \sum_{i,j} a_{i,j} r_t^i r_t^j$ that depends are agents "position" $\{r_t^i\}$. The coefficients are randomly generated. The world utility function was a spin glass,

$$G(\vec{\zeta_t}) = \sum_{i<j} J_{ij} c_i c_j. \qquad (15)$$

The agents are given a random initial starting point with $-1 < r_\eta < 1$. Because $\vec{c}$ is quadratic, $G(\vec{\zeta_t})$ is a quartic polynomial in N dimensions. Since the coefficients $\{a_{i,j}\}$ have random signs, the function G has as many increasing directions as it decreasing directions. The goal of the system is to traverse this high dimensional surface, find an increasing direction, and then follow that direction out to infinity.

We collected statistics by averaging runs over many randomly set coefficients $a_{i,j}$ and coupling constants J_{ij}. These runs were for systems whose first 25% and 75% components at the end of the episode are observable, given some canonical ordering of agents. We examined (Figure 1) world utility value vs. episode number for six utility functions:

1) TAU g for a fully observable system;

2) TAU g for 75 % observability, $g^{75\%}$;

3) The modification $g_{nf}^{75\%}$ giving a non-factored system, again with 75 % observability;

4) $g^{25\%}$ for a factored system with 25 % observability;

5) $g_{nf}^{25\%}$ for a non-factored system with 25 % observability;

6) The team game, where every $g_\eta = G$.

Even the results for limited observability clearly outperform the corresponding team game in which there is full observability. Furthermore, for 75% observability, the nonfactored utilities (L in both terms) consistently outperform their factored counterpart. In these runs factoredness fell to approximately 90%. The improvement in performance due to better signal-to-noise more than outweighs the degradation due to loss in factoredness.

It is interesting to adjust the ratio of $\pm$ signs in the coefficients of the polynomials. If we introduce, for example, more negative coefficients than positive, we expect the surface to preferentially turn down. The task for the agents becomes more challenging. We find (Figure 2), in fact, that three of the limited observability utilities perform worse over time (i.e. their world utility decreases). The team game also performs worse over time. In fact, not only does the team game give poor performance, but it fails altogether. The lowest noise TAU utilities g and $g_{nf}^{75\%}$ still give robust performance.

In this case, the team game gives worse performance than a random walk i.e. no learning is happening. In fact, the system executes essentially determistic, nonlinear behavior (Figure 3). Remarkably, as we increase the data aging parmeter (weighting more heavily data that appeared further

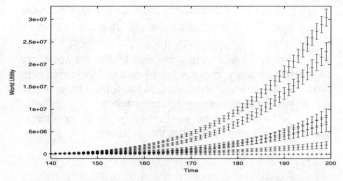

Figure 1: System performance for $N = 50$ agents using the Taylor Series method. The dynamics is governed by a quadratic function of the agents' "positions". The world utility G is a quartic in N dimensions. (upper two graphs are g and $g_{nf}^{75\%}$; middle two are $g_{nf}^{25\%}$ and $g^{75\%}$; lower two are $g^{25\%}$ and a team game G.) The initial training period is not shown.

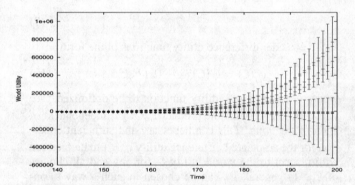

Figure 2: Taylor Series method where the quadratic coefficients have more $-$ than $+$ signs. (graphs: upper pair are g and $g_{nf}^{75\%}$; middle three are $g^{75\%}$, $g^{25\%}$, and the team game; lower is $g_{nf}^{25\%}$.) In this case, three of the limited observability utilities and the team game perform worse over time (i.e. their world utilities decrease).

in the past), the system becomes even more exotic, closely resembling a low-dimensional nonlinear system. By aging the data more severely, we effectively damp out a large portion of the degrees of freedom stored in the agents' training sets, hence the lower dimensionality. Learning, it would seem, is possible only in higher-dimensional systems.

Conclusion

We present a detailed extension of the $COIN$ framework to systems that undergo non-Markovian evolution. This builds on previous work where the Markovian case (Wolpert & Lawson 2002) was considered. The approach is applied to systems with nonlinear update rules using a perturbative technique. Results from numerical simulations find consistent, robust improvement of performance as compared to the conventional team game.

This framework naturally includes the case of limited ob-

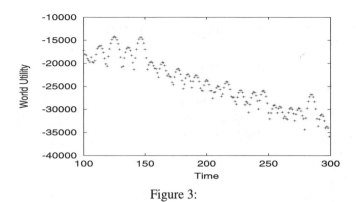

Figure 3:

servability. We found that even COIN-based utility functions constrained by limited observability often outperformed team game utilities having full observability. We also found a new class of nonfactored utilities that consistently outperformed their factored counterpart, due to improved signal-to-noise characteristics.

We find that the system's performance can depend on the characteristics of the surface being optimized. We show that in some situations a team game will fail altogether (i.e. its performance will degrade over time) while the corresponding TAU utility continues to perform well. In this "non-learning regime", the system executes interesting deterministic, nonlinear behavior, indicative of low-dimensional systems.

References

Boutilier, C.; Shoham, Y.; and Wellman, M. P. 1997. Editorial: Economic principles of multi-agent systems. *Artificial Intelligence Journal* 94:1–6.

Bradshaw, J. M., ed. 1997. *Software Agents*. MIT Press.

Caldarelli, G.; Marsili, M.; and Zhang, Y. C. 1997. A prototype model of stock exchange. *Europhysics Letters* 40:479–484.

Fudenberg, D., and Tirole, J. 1991. *Game Theory*. Cambridge, MA: MIT Press.

Hu, J., and Wellman, M. P. 1998. Multiagent reinforcement learning: Theoretical framework and an algorithm. In *Proceedings of the Fifteenth International Conference on Machine Learning*, 242–250.

Huberman, B. A., and Hogg, T. 1988. The behavior of computational ecologies. In *The Ecology of Computation*. North-Holland. 77–115.

Jennings, N. R.; Sycara, K.; and Wooldridge, M. 1998. A roadmap of agent research and development. *Autonomous Agents and Multi-Agent Systems* 1:7–38.

Johnson, N. F.; Jarvis, S.; Jonson, R.; Cheung, P.; Kwong, Y. R.; and Hui, P. M. 1998. Volatility and agent adaptability in a self-organizing market. preprint cond-mat/9802177.

Kaelbling, L. P.; Littman, M. L.; and Moore, A. W. 1996. Reinforcement learning: A survey. *Journal of Artificial Intelligence Research* 4:237–285.

Sandholm, T.; Larson, K.; Anderson, M.; Shehory, O.; and Tohme, F. 1998. Anytime coalition structure generation with worst case guarantees. In *Proceedings of the Fifteenth National Conference on Artificial Intelligence*, 46–53.

Sen, S. 1997. *Multi-Agent Learning: Papers from the 1997 AAAI Workshop (Technical Report WS-97-03*. Menlo Park, CA: AAAI Press.

Sutton, R. S., and Barto, A. G. 1998. *Reinforcement Learning: An Introduction*. Cambridge, MA: MIT Press.

Sutton, R. S. 1988. Learning to predict by the methods of temporal differences. *Machine Learning* 3:9–44.

Sycara, K. 1998. Multiagent systems. *AI Magazine* 19(2):79–92.

Tumer, K., and Wolpert, D. H. 2000. Collective intelligence and Braess' paradox. In *Proceedings of the Seventeenth National Conference on Artificial Intelligence*, 104–109.

Watkins, C., and Dayan, P. 1992. Q-learning. *Machine Learning* 8(3/4):279–292.

Wellman, M. P. 1993. A market-oriented programming environment and its application to distributed multicommodity flow problems. In *Journal of Artificial Intelligence Research*.

Wolpert, D., and Lawson, J. 2002. Designing agent collectives for systems with markovian dynamics. In *Proceedings of Autonomous Agents and MultiAgent Systems (AAMAS 2002)*. In press.

Wolpert, D. H., and Tumer, K. 1999. An Introduction to Collective Intelligence. Technical Report NASA-ARC-IC-99-63, NASA Ames Research Center. URL:http://ic.arc.nasa.gov/ic/projects/coin_pubs.html. To appear in Handbook of Agent Technology, Ed. J. M. Bradshaw, AAAI/MIT Press.

Wolpert, D. H., and Tumer, K. 2001. Optimal payoff functions for members of collectives. *Advances in Complex Systems* 4(2/3):265–279.

Wolpert, D. H.; Tumer, K.; and Frank, J. 1999. Using collective intelligence to route internet traffic. In *Advances in Neural Information Processing Systems - 11*, 952–958. MIT Press.

Wolpert, D. H.; Wheeler, K.; and Tumer, K. 2000. Collective intelligence for control of distributed dynamical systems. *Europhysics Letters* 49(6).

Wolpert, D. H. 2001a. Bounded-rationality game theory. pre-print.

Wolpert, D. H. 2001b. The mathematics of collective intelligence. pre-print.

Zhang, Y. C. 1998. Modeling market mechanism with evolutionary games. *Europhysics Letters*.

(Im)possibility of Safe Exchange Mechanism Design

Tuomas Sandholm

Computer Science Department
Carnegie Mellon University
5000 Forbes Avenue
Pittsburgh, PA 15213
sandholm@cs.cmu.edu

XiaoFeng Wang

Department of Electrical and Computer Engineering
Carnegie Mellon University
5000 Forbes Avenue
Pittsburgh, PA 15213
xiaofeng@andrew.cmu.edu

Abstract

Safe exchange is a key issue in multiagent systems, especially in electronic transactions where nondelivery is a major problem. In this paper we present a unified framework for modeling safe exchange mechanisms. It captures the disparate earlier approaches as well as new safe exchange mechanisms (e.g., reputation locking). Being an overarching framework, it also allows us to study what is *inherently possible and impossible in safe exchange*. We study this under different game-theoretic solution concepts, with and without a trusted third party, and with an offline third party that only gets involved if the exchange fails. The results vary based on the generality of the exchange setting, the existence (or creative construction) of special types of items to be exchanged, and the magnitude of transfer costs, defection costs, and escrow fees. Finally, we present an incentive-compatible negotiation protocol for selecting the best safe exchange mechanism when the agents do not know each others' costs for the different alternatives.

1. Introduction

Safe exchange is a key issue in multiagent systems, especially in electronic transactions. The rapid growth of Internet commerce has intensified this due to anonymous exchange parties, cheap pseudonyms, globality (different laws in different countries), etc. A recent study showed that 6% of people with online buying experience have reported nondelivery (NCL 1999). Software agents further exacerbate the problem due to the ability to vanish by killing their own processes. Without effective solutions, the safe exchange problem is one of the greatest obstacles to the further development of electronic commerce.

AI research has studied the problem using game-theoretic mechanism design. A safe exchange mechanism proposed in (Sandholm and Lesser 1995, Sandholm 1996) splits the exchange into small portions so that each agent benefits more by continuing the exchange than by vanishing. This idea has been operationalized in a safe exchange planner (Sandholm and Ferrandon 2000). The problem of cheap pseudonyms has been tackled by forcing new traders to pay an entry fee (Friedman and Resnick 1998), and schemes have been proposed for minimizing the needed entry fee (Matsubara and Yokoo 2000). Safe exchange was recently modeled as a dynamic game (Buttyan and Hubaux 2001).

Safe exchange has also been studied in computer security. These techniques include the coin ripping protocol (Jakobsson 1995) and zero knowledge proofs for exchanging signatures (Bao et al. 1998), which we will discuss later in this paper. Some of the techniques rely on a trusted third party (Deng et al. 1996).

This paper presents a unified exchange model that captures the previous disparate approaches (Section 2). We also present new safe exchange protocols. Most importantly, our model allows us to study *what is inherently possible and impossible to achieve in safe exchange*. We study this in the context of no trusted third party (Section 3), with a trusted third party (Section 4), and with an offline trusted third party that only gets involved if the exchange fails (Section 5). We ask whether safe exchange is possible under different game-theoretic solution concepts. We study this in the general case, with special types of items to be exchanged, and with various transfer costs, defection costs, and escrow fees. Finally, we present a negotiation mechanism for selecting among multiple safe exchange mechanisms (Section 6). To our knowledge, this is the first work to systematically investigate general exchange problems from the perspective of mechanism design.

2. Our exchange model

Our exchange setting has three parties: two strategic *agents*, $N=\{1,2\}$, that exchange *items* (for example, goods and payment), and a *trusted third party* (TTP) which facilitates the exchange. The TTP is not a strategic agent, and faithfully follows the exchange protocol. At any stage of the exchange, each party is in some *state*. The space of states of party i is denoted by S_i. $S=S_1 \times S_2 \times S_{TTP}$ is the space of *exchange states*.

The state $s_i^t = \langle P_i^t, A_i^t, \alpha_i^t, c_i^t \rangle \in S_i$ of agent i includes the following components:

- A *possession set* P_i^t which is the set of the items that the agent possesses. These items count toward the agent's utility. Intuitively, the agent can allocate these items to others.[1]

  However, we make the following key generalization which allows us to capture safe exchange mechanisms

---

[1] The model also captures duplicable items such as software. The duplication is considered to occur before the exchange, so at the start all copies are in the possession sets.

from the literature and new ones that would not fit a model based solely on possession sets. Specifically, sometimes a party may have the right to allocate an item even if it does not possess the item. For example, one can rip a $100 bill into two halves and give one of the halves to another party. Hence, neither party owns the money but can give it to the other. In order to describe an agent's control of such items that do not contribute to the agent's utility, we introduce the notion of an allocation set.

- An *allocation set* A_i^t which is the set of items that an agent does not possess, but can allocate to others (not to itself).

- An *activity* flag $\alpha_i \in \{$ ACTIVE, INACTIVE $\}$ which defines whether the party is still *active*. This technicality is needed in order to have a well-defined setting (which requires that an *outcome state* is defined). An outcome state is an exchange state where no party is active anymore (it does not necessarily mean that the exchange is complete). An active party can take actions while an inactive one cannot. For example, an agent that vanishes in the middle of an exchange becomes inactive. Once an agent becomes inactive, it cannot become active again.

- A cost $c_i^t \geq 0$ which is the cumulative cost that the agent has incurred in the exchange so far (cost of sending items, defection penalties, etc).

Because the TTP can control some items during the exchange, it has an allocation set, but because it is not a strategic player and thus does not have a utility function, it has no possession set. The TTP itself does not have a cost, but again, in order to have well-defined outcomes, the TTP does have an activity flag. Put together, the state of the TTP is $s_i^t = \langle A_i^t, \alpha_i^t \rangle \in S_{TTP}$.

The set of outcome states is O. We say that in any outcome state, all allocation sets become empty because the parties are inactive and cannot allocate items anymore. An exchange starts from an *initial state* s^0, where the possession sets P_i^0 contain the items that are to be exchanged, and the allocation sets A_i^0 are empty. In any *complete state* $s^{complete} \in O$, the exchange is successfully completed: each agent possesses the items it was supposed to receive and lost only the items it was supposed to lose.

Each party can take *actions*. $M = M_1 \times M_2 \times M_{TTP}$ is the action space of the exchange. All three exchange parties have the following types of actions:

1. **Wait**: A party can wait for others to take actions.
2. **Transfer**: A party can transfer items from a *source* set (possession set or allocation set) to a set of *destination* sets. Each party i has a Boolean function $T_i(src, item, DES)$ to determine whether the agent can transfer *item* from set *src* to *all* sets in *DES* (this does not imply the possibility of transferring it to a subset of sets in *DES*). For example, if *item* $\in P_1$, then $T_1(P_1, item, \{P_1\})=1$. Some items (e.g., $100 bill) can be moved into allocation sets.
3. **Exit**: Agent i can deactivate itself by exiting at any state.

Both agents and the TTP automatically exit if any complete state $s^{complete}$ is reached.[2]

Each action taken by an agent may incur a cost for that agent. The TTP also has an extra action type: it can *punish* an agent by adding to the agent's cumulative cost.

We assume that each agent $i \in N$ has quasi-linear preferences over states, so its utility function can be written as $u_i(s_i^t) = v_i(\lambda_1, \lambda_2, ..., \lambda_k) - c_i$, where v_i is agent *i's* valuation, λ_j is the quantity of item j the i possesses, and c_i is the cumulative cost defined above.

The tuple $E = \langle N, TTP, S, M, u_1, u_2 \rangle$ is called an *exchange environment*. An instance of the environment is an exchange. The mechanism designer operates in E to design an *exchange mechanism* $EM = \langle S', \rho, M', F, o \rangle$, where $S' \subseteq S$ and $M' \subseteq M$. The *player function* $\rho: S' \backslash O' \to N \cup \{TTP\}$ determines which party takes actions in a state. The space of *strategy profiles* is $F = F_1 \times F_2 \times F_{TTP}$. Agent i's strategy $f_i: S' \backslash O' \to M_i'$ specifies the action agent i will take in a state. The *outcome function* $o(s, f_1, f_2, f_{TTP}) \in O$ denotes the resulting outcome if parties follow strategies f_1, f_2, f_{TTP} starting from state s. Since the TTP is not a strategic player, we omit its static strategy from this function.

We denote an agent by i, and the other agent by $-i$. An exchange mechanism EM has a *dominant strategy equilibrium (DSE)* if and only if each agent $i \in N$ has a strategy f_i^* that is its best strategy no matter what strategy the other agent chooses. Formally, $u_i(o(s, f_i^*, f_{-i})) \geq u_i(o(s, f_i, f_{-i}))$ for all $f_i \in F_i$, $f_{-i} \in F_{-i}$ (the other agent's strategy) and $s \in S'$. The mechanism has a *subgame perfect Nash equilibrium* (SPNE) if and only if $u_i(o(s, f_i^*, f_{-i}^*)) \geq u_{-i}(o(s, f_i, f_{-i}^*))$ for all $f_i \in F_i$ and $s \in S'$. In either equilibrium concept, if the inequality is strict, the equilibrium is *strict*. Otherwise, it is *weak*.

An exchange can be represented as an *exchange graph* (Sandholm and Ferrandon 2000), where states are represented as vertices and actions as directed edges between states. Each edge has a *weight* indicating the cost of the move. An exchange mechanism is presented as a subgraph (see all figures[3]). A *path* from s^0 to any $s^{complete}$ is called a *completion path*. An exchange mechanism is a *safe exchange mechanism* (SEM) for an exchange in environment E if the mechanism has at least one equilibrium (f_1^*, f_2^*) in which the path of play is a completion path, that is, $o(s^0, f_1^*, f_2^*) = s^{complete}$. Such a path is called a *safe exchange path*. If the equilibrium is a (strict/weak) DSE, we say the *safe exchange is implemented in (strict/weak) DSE*. If the equilibrium is a (strict/weak) SPNE, we say the *safe exchange is implemented in (strict/weak) SPNE*.

We make the following assumptions:

---

[2] One concern is that an agent could postpone (indefinitely) without declaring exit. However, since we study exchanges for which we design well-defined exchange *protocols*, the parties can treat others' out-of-protocol actions as exit actions.

[3] When we illustrate mechanisms in this paper, for simplicity of drawing, we draw one vertex to represent all the states that have the same item allocation (but which may have different cumulated costs).

1. **Sequentiality.** *For any given state of the exchange, the SEM specifies exactly one agent that is supposed to make transfers. We make this sequentiality assumption for convenience only. Allowing for parallel actions does not affect safety because if an agent is safe in a parallel action, it would have to be safe even if the other party did not complete its portion of the parallel action.*

2. **Possessions close.** *If an agent possesses an item, the other agent has no possession of that item. There is no exogenous subsidy to the exchange. Formally, item* $\in P_i^t$ *at state* s^t *only if* $(item \in P_i^0 \cup P_{-i}^0) \wedge (item \notin P_{-i}^t)$.

3. **Exit rules.** *Both agents can exit at any state. Exiting is costless in any complete state* $s^{complete}$. *Exiting in any other state may subject the exiting agent to a cost (reputation loss, some chance of getting caught and financially penalized, etc.).*

4. **Nondecreasing utility.** *An agent's utility will not decrease from possessing additional items. Formally, if* $P_i^{t'} \subseteq P_i^t$, $u_i(s_i^{t'}) \leq u_i(s_i^t)$ *given the same costs.*

An immediate result, which we will use in several places, is that during any exchange, no agent can take action to improve its own immediate utility:

Lemma 2.1. *It is impossible to have two states* s^t, s^{t+1} *of the exchange such that* $(i \in N) \wedge ((s^t s^{t+1}) \in M_i) \wedge (u_i(s^t) < u_i(s^{t+1}))$.

3. SEM design without a TTP

In this section, we study the possibility of SEM design in an exchange environment with no TTP.

3.1. Results for unrestricted items and costs

Here we derive *general* results for safe exchange without a TTP.[4] The results are *general* in that the exchange may contain any types of items and exit costs can be arbitrary.

Proposition 3.1. *Without a TTP, there exist exchanges that cannot be implemented safely in (even weak) DSE.*

Proof. Consider an exchange of an item k. Without loss of generality, let agent i make the first move from the initial state s^0. Denote the resulting state by s^1. Let (1) $v_i(\lambda_k) < v_i(\lambda_k')$ if $\lambda_k < \lambda_k'$, and (2) say item k cannot be transferred to any allocation set. The only possible move is to transfer some amount of item k to the other agent's possession set. Thus, from (1) above and Assumption 2, we get $u_i(s^0) > u_i(s^1)$. Let f_i^* be any strategy containing the above first move. Let there be free exit at the initial state s^0, and let f_i and f_i be strategies that prescribe exit at s^0. Without a TTP, agent i becomes the only player once the other agent exits. According to Lemma 2.1, $u_i(o(s^0, f_i^*, f_{-i})) \leq u_i(s^1) < u_i(s^0) = u_i(o(s^0, f_i, f_{-i}))$. Thus, f_i^* is not a dominant strategy. Since any safe exchange path should contain the first move, we have that it is impossible to implement the safe exchange in DSE. □

In fact, we can prove a stronger claim which would imply Proposition 3.1 (we nevertheless presented the proof of 3.1 because it is based on a different principle):

Proposition 3.2. *Without a TTP, there exist exchanges that cannot be implemented safely in (even weak) SPNE.*

Proof. Consider an exchange where properties (1) and (2) from the previous proof hold (at least for the last item to be delivered), and exit costs are zero. Consider any particular state s^t that precedes a complete state $s^{complete}$. Without loss of generality, let $i \in N$ make the last action to get to $s^{complete}$. By properties (1) and (2), $u_i(s^t) > u_i(s^{complete})$. Let $f_i^* \in F_i, f_{-i}^* \in F_{-i}$ be any strategy profile which forms a path from s^0 to s^t and includes the last move. Let f_i be a strategy identical to f_i^* except that "exit" is played at s^t. Since there is no defection cost, $u_i(o(s^t, f_i, f_{-i}^*)) = u_i(s^{complete}) < u_i(s^t) \leq u_i(o(s^t, f_i, f_{-i}^*))$. Thus any strategy profile containing the last move is not a SPNE. However, a completion path has to include the last move. Therefore, it is impossible to implement the safe exchange in SPNE.[5] □

3.2. Results for exchanges including one-way items

The results above show that there are exchange settings where safe exchange is impossible without a TTP. In this section we study in more detail the conditions under which the impossibility holds. It turns out that the existence of *one-way items* to be exchanged plays a key role. A one-way item is an item the can be moved into allocation set(s). Recall that an agent that has an item in its allocation set cannot transfer the item to its own possession set. The following results highlight the importance of our introduction of allocation sets into the exchange model.

Definition 3.1. *An item k is a **one-way item** if there exists an agent i such that* $(i, j \in N) \wedge (A_j \in Y) \wedge (T_i(P_i, \lambda_k, Y) = 1)$.[5] *An item is a **one-way item** also if it is worthless to some agent (this is because the possession of such an item does not bring its owner any value while allocating it to others may increase their utility).*

The next two protocols enable safe exchange without a TTP by constructing one-way items in different ways.

Protocol 3.1. Coin ripping (Jakobsson 1995). This protocol uses a cryptographic digital coin which can be ripped into two halves. A single half has no value and once a half coin has been spent, it cannot be spent again.[6] The exchange proceeds as follows: 1) agent 1 rips a coin p and gives the first half coin to agent 2; 2) agent 2 deliveries the good g to agent 1; 3) agent 1 gives the other half of the coin to agent 2. In this protocol, the coin serves as a one-way item. In the figure, "*" denotes an inactive agent.

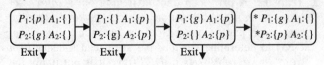

---

[5] An item may be in several agents' allocations sets simultaneously, and in some other agent's possession set.

[6] (Jakobsson 1995) proposed a scheme which allows a buyer to give a seller the hash value of a digital coin verifiable to a bank. The original coin cannot be spent (again) after the seller has given the hash value to the bank.

---

[4] The impossibility of a similar notion, *fair exchange*, has been studied in a non-game-theoretic framework (Pagnia and Gaertner 1999).

A weakness here is that agent 1 is indifferent between delivering the second half of the coin and not. Hence, the safe exchange is only a *weak* SPNE.

The coin ripping protocol requires a special cryptographic digital coin. Here, we introduce a new protocol which is applicable more broadly because it enables safe exchange even if money is not one of the items to be exchanged.

Protocol 3.2. Reputation locking. This protocol uses *reputation* as a one-way item! Suppose there is a public online reputation database. In our protocol, an agent's reputation record can be encrypted by other agents with the agent's permission, and only the agents that encrypted it can read/decrypt it. We call this *reputation locking* because the agent does not have an observable reputation while it is encrypted. The protocol proceeds as follows: 1) agent 2 permits agent 1 to lock its reputation R; 2) agent 1 gives agent 2 payment $p \leq v_2(R)$; 3) agent 2 sends good g to agent 1; 4) agent 1 unlocks the reputation. The reputation R is a one-way item which can be moved into agent 1's allocation set. This protocol implements the safe exchange in SPNE. However, as in coin ripping, it is only a weak implementation because agent 1 is indifferent between cooperation and exit at step 4.

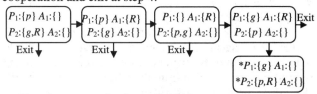

The two protocols above show that one can enable safe exchange by creatively constructing one-way items. (This is not always the case, for example, if the one-way items are too minor compared to the other items). Interestingly, creation of one-way items is the *only* approach that works in anonymous commerce where there is no trusted third party and no costs to premature exit from the exchange!

Proposition 3.3. *With zero exit costs and no TTP, an exchange can be implemented in weak SPNE only if there exists a one-way item.*

Proof. Suppose there exists an SEM for an exchange including no one-way items. By the definition of a one-way item, if an item is not a one-way item, it satisfies properties (1) and (2) from the proof of Proposition 3.1. Therefore, the proof of Proposition 3.2 applies. □

It turns out that the weakness of the coin ripping and reputation locking protocols is inevitable:

Proposition 3.4. *With zero exit costs and no TTP, no exchange can be implemented in strict SPNE (even with one-way items).*

Proof. If agent i exits at state s^t, (any particular state before a complete state) without a TTP, the other agent (say j) becomes the only player. According to Lemma 2.1, j cannot improve its own utility, so exiting becomes one of j's best response actions. In that case, agent i obtains its final utility already at s^t. Therefore, exiting at s^t becomes one of i's best response actions. Therefore, there exists a continuation equilibrium at s^t where both exit, and the exchange does not complete. □

3.3. Defection cost (cost of premature exit)

Proposition 3.4 showed that with free exit and no TTP, weak SPNE is the best one can achieve. Proposition 3.3 showed that even weak implementation requires the existence of one-way items. However, if there are costs to premature exit (defection cost) – such as loss of reputation, chance of getting caught and punished, loss of future business, etc. – then safe exchange can be achieved more broadly (Sandholm and Lesser 1995) (Sandholm 1996) (Sandholm and Ferrandon 2000). We model this by an exit cost $d_i(s^j)$ that may depend on the agent i and the exchange state s^j. We allow for the possibility that the exit cost is zero in some states (for example in the initial state in cases where participation in the exchange is voluntary).

Proposition 3.5. *Without a TTP, an exchange can be implemented safely in SPNE if and only if there exists a path $s^0...s^t s^T$ (where s^T is a complete state) such that $u_i(s^j) - u_i(s^T) \leq d_i(s^j)$ for all $j \in [0,t]$. The exchange can be implemented safely in DSE if and only if $u_i(s^j) - \min_{q=j, j+1,...,T} u_i(s^q) \leq d_i(s^j)$ for all $j \in [0,t]$ on such a path. In either case, if each inequality is strict, the equilibrium is strict. Otherwise the equilibrium is weak.*

Proof. *If part for SPNE:* Construct an exchange mechanism as follows. The players should follow the completion path. If either agent deviates from the path, both agents exit, and the deviator has to pay the exit cost $d_i(s^j)$. For any agent i, let f_i^* be a strategy that follows the path and f_i be a strategy that defects at s^j. So, $u_i(o(s^j, f_i^*, f_{-i}^*)) = u_i(s^{complete}) \geq u_i(s^j) - d_i(s^j) = u_i(o(s^j, f_i, f_{-i}^*))$. Thus (f_i^*, f_{-i}^*) is a SPNE.

Only if part for SPNE: Let $s^0 s^1 ... s^t s^{complete}$ be any particular safe exchange path for an SPNE. Thus, $u_i(s^{complete}) = u_i(o(s^j, f_i^*, f_{-i}^*)) \geq u_i(o(s^j, f_i, f_{-i}^*)) = u_i(s^j) - d_i(s^j)$ for all states on the path and for both agents.

If part for DSE: If $u_i(s^j) - \min_{q=j, j+1,...,T} u_i(s^q) \leq d_i(s^j)$ for all $j \in [0,t]$, then agent i is better off by following the exchange no matter what the other agent does.

Only if part for DSE: If there exists a state s^j where the inequality does not hold for agent i, then if the other agent's strategy is to defect at state s^m satisfying $u_i(s^j) - d_i(s^j) > u_i(s^m)$, agent i is better off by exiting at s^j. Thus following the completion path is not a dominant strategy for i. □

4. SEM design with an online TTP

A simple way of achieving safe exchange is to use a TTP. A TTP facilitates exchange by helping agents allocate items and by punishing a defector. We assume that any item from either agent's possession set can be moved to the TTP's allocation set and vice versa. We also assume that the TTP can observe the state of the exchange.

TTP-based safe exchange mechanisms have been explored in computer security (Buttyan and Hubaux 2001). Two types of TTPs have been proposed: *online TTPs* (Deng et al. 1996) and *offline TTPs* (Ba et al. 2000) (Bao et al. 1998) (Asokan et al. 1997). An online TTP is always involved in the exchange while an offline TTP only gets involved if a defection has occurred. We discuss online TTPs first.[7]

The existence of online TTP makes the safe exchange implementable in DSE:

Protocol 4.1. Online TTP-based SE. Each agent gives its items to be exchanged to the TTP. If both agents do this, the TTP swaps the items. Else the TTP returns the items.

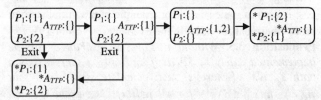

If the online TTP requires an escrow fee (as most of the current ones do), we say that the escrow fee is paid before the exchange begins. With this understanding we have:

Proposition 4.1. *With an online TTP, if (1) each agent's utility of the complete state is greater than that of the initial state, and (2) for each state on the exchange path and for each agent, the agent's sum of action costs (for transfer actions and wait actions) from that state to the complete state is less than the agent's exit cost at that state, then Protocol 4.1 implements the exchange safely in strict DSE.* The proof is not hard, and we omit it due to limited space.

5. SEM design with an offline TTP

With no TTP, the safety of the exchange can usually be assured only in weak SPNE. With an online TTP, dominant strategy implementation is achievable, but the TTP is closely involved, incurs operating expenses, and thus usually charges an escrow fee even if the exchange completes without problems. A tradeoff between these two extremes is to use an *offline TTP* which does not participate in the exchange as long as it executes correctly, but gets involved if either agent exits prematurely. Offline TTPs have been practically implemented (such as ebay's feedback system) and theoretically investigated (Matsubara and Yokoo 2000) (Asokan et al. 1997).

5.1. General results

Here we investigate what can be achieved with an offline TTP when there are no limits on item types and exit costs. If the TTP does not have (and cannot obtain) allocation rights on the defector's items after defection, the TTP can do no more than punish the defector. This is equivalent to imposing an exit cost, so Proposition 3.5 suffices to characterize what is (im)possible in this case.

So, what can be achieved with an offline TTP depends on how much penalty the TTP can impose on a defector. Punishing under different forms of information asymmetry is difficult (Friedman and Resnick 1998) (Matsubara and Yokoo 2000), for example due to cheap pseudonyms on the Internet, different laws in different countries, etc. Therefore, it is important to study what can be achieved when the TTP has too little power to punish defectors. That is what we address in the rest of this section.

5.2. Revocable and relinquishable items

When there is no reliable penalty for premature exit (defection cost is difficult to estimate or the TTP has inadequate power to punish), a TTP that has the ability to reallocate the defectors' possessions could facilitate safe exchange. Unfortunately, an offline TTP *only gets involved after the defection* at which time it has no control on any items (its allocation set is *empty*). In this case, the *active* agent (the defector is inactive) is the only one that can *give the TTP such reallocation rights on (some of) the defector's items*. This further requires that the active agent have control of the items. In the language of our exchange model, such items are in one agent's allocation set and the other agent's possession/allocation set at the same time. We now analyze such special items that an offline TTP can use to facilitate safe exchange.

We call an item *revocable* if its possessor can transfer it to the other agent's allocation or possession set while transferring it into its own allocation set (thus keeping the right to transfer the item from the other agent to the TTP). We call an item *relinquishable* if its possessor can keep it in the possession set while transferring it into the other agent's allocation set (thus giving the other agent the right to transfer the item from the former agent to the TTP).[8] Similar concepts have been discussed in the context of a particular exchange protocol for exchanging two items (Asokan et al. 1997).

Definition 5.1. *Denote by x_i the possession set or allocation set of agent i, and denote the other agent by $-i$. An item k is **revocable** to agent i if $T_i(P_i, \lambda_k, \{A_i, x_{-i}\}) = 1$.*[9] (To handle the trivial case where an item is not of strictly positive value to its original possessor, we also call such items revocable.) *An item k is **relinquishable** if there exists an agent i such that $T_i(P_i, \lambda_k, \{x_i, A_{-i}\}) = 1$.*

The following protocols use these types of special items.

Protocol 5.1. Credit card payment. A credit card payment can be viewed as a revocable item. Agent 1 pays agent 2 a payment p for good g with a credit card. At that point, $p \in A_1 \cap P_2$. If agent 2 does not deliver g, agent 1 sends a request to the offline TTP (credit card company). This corresponds to transferring p from A_1 to A_{TTP}. The company then revokes the payment (transfers p from A_{TTP}

---

[7] (Ketchpel and Garcia-Molina 1996) studied, in a non-game-theoretic way, how different parts of an exchange should be sequenced when there are several online TTPs, but each TTP is only trusted by some subset of the parties.

[8] Recall that by the definition of allocation set, the other agent can transfer the item to the TTP's allocation set or the former agent's allocation set, but not into its own possession set.

[9] Recall that agent i cannot give items that are in its allocation set into its possession set, and that agent i can give items in its allocation set to other parties, particularly the TTP's allocation set. Then the TTP can transfer the item to agent i's possession set.

and from P_2 to P_1). With zero action costs, the safe exchange path is followed in DSE.

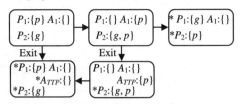

Protocol 5.2. Escrowed signature (Bao et al. 1998). The protocol is for exchanging signatures on a contract. A digital signature can be converted into a relinquishable item. The protocol proceeds as follows: 1) agent 1 encrypts its digital signature (σ_1) with the public key of an offline TTP and then sends it along with a zero knowledge proof (Bao et al. 1998) to agent 2; 2) agent 2 checks that the data is an encrypted version of agent 1's signature, and gives its signature (σ_2) to agent 1; 3) agent 1 sends agent 2 σ_1. If agent 1 instead exits at step 3, agent 2 sends the data from step 2 to the TTP for decryption, and the TTP will give the decrypted signature of agent 1 to agent 2. With zero action costs, the safe exchange path is followed in DSE. [10]

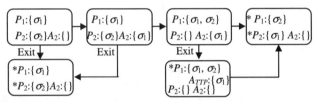

It turns out that revocable or relinquishable items are in a sense *necessary* for safe exchange!

Proposition 5.1. *Let there be only an offline TTP and zero action costs (for transfer, wait, and exit actions). Let the items to be exchanged include no revocable or relinquishable items. Now, the exchange cannot be implemented in strict SPNE or even in weak DSE.[11]*

Proof. *Strict SPNE:* After a defection, the defector is inactive, and the offline TTP's allocation set is empty. So, the only way the TTP can affect a defector's possession set is if the active agent can put items that are in the defector's possession set into the TTP's allocation set (this requires the items to be in the active agent's allocation set).[12] By the definitions of revocable/relinquishable items, such a state can be reached only if revocable or relinquishable items exist. If, on the other hand, the TTP cannot affect the defector's possession set, then Proposition 3.4 applies.

Weak DSE: Suppose there exists a completion path implemented in weak DSE. By the assumption of

---

[10] Recall we assume that the TTP can observe states so that an agent cannot get the signature decrypted without giving its own signature to the other. The protocol works even if the TTP does not observe states: in this case, each agent needs to give its own signature to the TTP (which will pass it to the other agent) to get the other's signature decrypted.

[11] As shown earlier in the paper, a weak SPNE can exist if there exists a one-way item.

[12] Recall that possessions close, so the items in the defector's possession set cannot be in the active agent's possession set. Also, by the definition of an allocation set, the active agent cannot move items from its allocation set to its own possession set.

sequential actions and the fact that eventually all items are exchanged, there has to be some state where one agent (say A) has transferred an item I into the other agent's (say B) possession set before receiving any items into its own possession set. At that state, because there are no revocable or relinquishable items, I cannot be in anyone's allocation set. If B now defects, A will have received nothing, and will have lost I which is of value to A. Therefore, A would have been strictly better off exiting in the initial state. Thus A's strategy of following the safe exchange is not a weak dominant strategy. Contradiction. □

5.3. Transfer costs and offline TTP's escrow fee

In many settings, especially when exchanging physical goods, there is a cost associated with each transfer action. Another type of cost that is associated with a transfer action is the fee that an agent has to pay an offline TTP when the agent asks the offline TTP to carry out a transfer action against a defector. (In the case of online TTPs, the escrow fee had no strategic effects because it had to be paid anyway, but in the offline TTP case it has strategic effects because it has to be paid only if the TTP's help is used).

Proposition 5.2. *With an offline TTP and **no** relinquishable items, no exchange can be safely implemented in weak DSE if the completion path contains any positive transfer cost.*

Proof. Suppose there exists a completion path implemented in weak DSE. By the assumption of sequential actions and the fact that eventually all items are exchanged, there has to be some state where one agent (say A) has transferred an item i into the other agent's (say B) possession set before receiving any items into its own possession set. At that state (say s^*), because there are no relinquishable items, A cannot control any of B's original items, but may be able to take back some of the items it gave to B. However, because there was a positive transfer cost, A would have been strictly better off exiting in the initial state. Thus A's strategy of following the safe exchange is not a weak dominant strategy. Contradiction. □

Proposition 5.3. *With a positive offline TTP fee and **no** relinquishable items, no exchange can be safely implemented in weak DSE.*

Proof. The proof is analogous to that of Proposition 5.2. □

Proposition 5.4. *With **no** revocable items, an exchange can be safely implemented in weak DSE only if for each agent i, the offline TTP's escrow fee plus i's sum of transfer costs on the completion path is at most* $u_i(s^{complete}) - u_i(s^0)$. *The proof is not hard, and we omit it due to limited space.*

6. Selecting a safe exchange mechanism

In the real world, different types of SEMs co-exist. For example, on the Internet, online TTPs such as TradeSafe exist, offline TTPs such as the Better Business Bureau exist, and obviously direct exchange is possible (and safe exchange planners for that exist (Sandholm and Ferrandon 2000)). Now, which SEM should the agents select? For a given exchange, different SEMs have different costs. Online TTPs have an escrow fee. Direct exchange and offline TTPs may have various costs: some require agents to expose their fixed entities (e.g., credit based exchange) thus incurring privacy cost; some need intensive computation (e.g., escrowed signature); almost all of them expose the agents to risks (irrational play by the other party, accidents, etc.). Furthermore, agents may have different costs for a given SEM, and the agents' costs are generally only privately known by the agent.

We present a mechanism that will select the best SEM and motivates the agents to truthfully report their costs. We present it as choosing between an online TTP based SEM (TSEM) and another SEM (ASEM). We assume that 1) the online TTP's escrow fee c is commonly known and the agents have an agreement to share it in proportions d_1 and d_2 (where $d_1+d_2=1$), and 2) agents prefer exchange through either SEM to no exchange at all.

Protocol 6.1. SEM selection. Each agent reveals to the other which SEM it prefers. If both agents prefer the same SEM, that SEM is chosen. Otherwise, the agents resolve the conflict as follows: 1) each agent i transfers a payment c (the total amount of the escrow fee) and reveals its ASEM cost $\hat{c}_i$ to the online TTP. (If the other agent does not submit its payment and cost information, the TTP returns the former agent's payment.); 2a) If $\hat{c}_1+\hat{c}_2 < c$, ASEM is chosen, the TTP returns a payment $c - \hat{c}_{-i} + d_{-i}c$ to the agent i who preferred ASEM, and returns the entire amount c to the other agent (who preferred TSEM). So, the TTP ends up keeping a nonnegative amount, which we consider its fee for resolving the SEM selection conflict. 2b) If $\hat{c}_1+\hat{c}_2 \geq c$, TSEM is chosen, the TTP returns a payment $\hat{c}_{-i}$ to the agent i that preferred TSEM, and returns d_ic to the other agent $-i$. At this point, the TTP has gotten paid the escrow fee plus a nonnegative conflict resolution fee.

Proposition 6.1. *Protocol 6.1 is ex post individually rational, weak DSE incentive compatible, and efficient (that is, the cheapest SEM is chosen).*

Proof. *Sketch.* The mechanism is an application of the Clarke tax voting scheme (Clark 1971), which has these properties. □

7. Conclusions and future research

Safe exchange is a key problem in multiagent systems, especially in electronic transactions. A large number of different approaches have been proposed for safe exchange. In this paper we presented a unified framework for modeling safe exchange mechanisms. Our framework captures the disparate earlier approaches, as well as new SEMs (e.g., reputation locking). Being an overarching framework, it also allowed us to study what is *inherently* possible and impossible in safe exchange. We showed what role special types of items play, and derived quantitative conditions on defection costs. The following table summarizes the qualitative results at a high level.

	General results	Special items	With costs
No TTP	No weak SPNE.	No strict SPNE. One-way item ← weak SPNE	Sufficient exit costs → weak/strict SPNE/DSE.
Offline TTP	Sufficient punishment → weak/strict SPNE/DSE.	(Revocable or relinquishable item) ← strict SPNE.	No relinquishable item: (transfer cost or escrow fee) → no weak DSE
			No revocable item: weak DSE → (low escrow fee & low transfer cost)
Online TTP	(Sufficient exit costs & low transfer costs) → strict DSE		

Finally, we presented an incentive-compatible mechanism for selecting the best SEM when the agents do not know each others' costs for the different SEMs.

Future work includes extending the results to exchanges with more than 2 agents, and to settings where the agents and/or the TTP are uncertain about the exchange state.

Acknowledgements

We thank Kartik Hosanagar for illuminating discussions at the early stage of this work. We also thank Ramayya Krishnan and Pradeep Khosla for their encouragement. Sandholm is supported by NSF CAREER Award IRI-9703122, and NSF grants IIS-9800994, ITR IIS-0081246, and ITR IIS-0121678. Wang is supported by NSF grant IIS-0118767, the DARPA OASIS program, and the PASIS project at CMU.

References

Asokan, N; Schunter, M; and Waidner, M.1997. Optimistic protocols for fair exchange. *ACM Computer & Communication Security Conerence*. p. 7-17.

Ba, S; Whinston, A. B.; Zhang, H. 2000. The dynamics of the electronic market: an evolutionary game approach. *Information System Frontiers* 2:1, 31-40.

Clarke, E. 1971. Multi-part pricing of public goods. *Public Choice*, 11:17-33.

Bao, F; Deng, R; and Mao, W; 1998. Efficient and practical fair exchange protocols with off-line TTP. *IEEE symposium S&P.* p. 77-85.

Buttyan, L; Hubaux, J.P. 2000. Toward a formal model of fair exchange-a game theoretic approach. *Internaional workshop on ecommerce*.

Deng, R; Gong, L; Lazar, A; and Wang, W. 1996. Practical protocols for certified electronic mail. *Journal of Network & Systems Management* 4(3), 279-297.

Friedman, E; Resnick, P. 1998. The social cost of cheap pseudonyms. *Journal of Economics and Management Strategy* 10(2): 173-199.

Jakobsson, M. 1995. Ripping coins for a fair exchange. *EUROCRYPT*, p. 220-230.

Ketchpel, S. P; Garcia-Molina, H. 1996. Making Trust Explicit in Distributed Commerce Transactions. *International Conference on Distributed Computing Systems*, p. 270-281.

Matsubara, S; Yokoo, M. 2000. Defection-free exchange mechanism for information goods. *ICMAS*, p.183-190

National Consumers League. 1999. New NCL survey shows consumers are both excited and confused about shopping online, www.natconsumersleague.org/BeEWisepr.html.

Pagnia, H; Gaertner. F. 1999. On the impossibility of fair exchange without a trusted third party. Darmstadt University of Technology, Department of Computer Science technical report TUD-1999-02.

Sandholm, T. 1996. Negotiation among Self-Interested Computationally Limited Agents. PhD Thesis. UMass Amherst, Computer Science Dept.

Sandholm, T; Lesser, V. 1995. Equilibrium analysis of the possibilities of unenforced exchange in multiagent systems. *IJCAI*, p.694-701.

Sandholm,T; Ferrandon. V. 2000. Safe exchange planner. *ICMAS*. p.255-262.

Multi-Agent Algorithms for Solving Graphical Games

David Vickrey
Computer Science Department
Stanford University
Stanford, CA 94305-9010
dvickrey@cs.stanford.edu

Daphne Koller
Computer Science Department
Stanford University
Stanford, CA 94305-9010
koller@cs.stanford.edu

Abstract

Consider the problem of a group of agents trying to find a stable strategy profile for a joint interaction. A standard approach is to describe the situation as a single multi-player game and find an equilibrium strategy profile of that game. However, most algorithms for finding equilibria are computationally expensive; they are also centralized, requiring that all relevant payoff information be available to a single agent (or computer) who must determine the entire equilibrium profile. In this paper, we exploit two ideas to address these problems. We consider structured game representations, where the interaction between the agents is sparse, an assumption that holds in many real-world situations. We also consider the slightly relaxed task of finding an approximate equilibrium. We present two algorithms for finding approximate equilibria in these games, one based on a hill-climbing approach and one on constraint satisfaction. We show that these algorithms exploit the game structure to achieve faster computation. They are also inherently local, requiring only limited communication between directly interacting agents. They can thus be scaled to games involving large numbers of agents, provided the interaction between the agents is not too dense.

1 Introduction

Consider a system consisting of multiple interacting agents, collaborating to perform a task. The agents have to interact with each other to make sure that the task is completed, but each might still have slightly different preferences, e.g., relating to the amount of resources each expends in completing its part of the task.

The framework of game theory (von Neumann & Morgenstern 1944; Fudenberg & Tirole 1991) tells us that we should represent a multi-agent interaction as a game, and find a strategy profile that forms a *Nash equilibrium* (Nash 1950). We can do so using one of several algorithms for finding equilibria in games. (See (McKelvey & McLennan 1996) for a survey.) Unfortunately, this approach is severely limited in its ability to handle complex multi-agent interactions. First, in most cases, the size of the standard game representations grows exponentially in n. Second, for games involving more than two players, existing solution algorithms scale extremely poorly even in the size of the game representation. Finally, all of the standard algorithms are based on a

centralized computation paradigm making them unsuitable for our distributed setting.

We propose an approach that modifies both the representation of the game and the notion of a solution. Following the work of LaMura (2000), Koller and Milch (2001), and Kearns, Littman, and Singh (2001a), we use a structured representations of games, that exploits the locality of interaction that almost always exists in complex multi-agent interactions, and allows games with large numbers of agents to be described compactly. Our representation is based on the *graphical game* framework of Kearns, Littman, and Singh (KLS hereafter), which applies to simultaneous-move games. We wish to find algorithms that can take advantage of this structure to find good strategy profiles effectively, and in a decentralized way.

It turns out that this goal is much easier to achieve when solving a relaxed problem. While philosophically satisfying, the Nash equilibrium requirement is often overly stringent. Although agents arguably strive to maximize their expected utility, in practice inertia or a sense of commitment will cause an agent to abide by an agreed equilibrium even if it is slightly suboptimal for him. Thus, it often suffices to require that the strategy profile form an *approximate equilibrium*, one where each agent's incentive to deviate is no more than some small ϵ.

We present two techniques for finding approximate equilibria in structured games. The first uses a greedy hill-climbing approach to optimize a global score function, whose global optima are precisely equilibria. The second uses a constraint satisfaction approach over a discretized space of agent strategies; somewhat surprisingly, the algorithm of KLS turns out to be a special case of this algorithm. We show that these algorithms allow the agents to determine a joint strategy profile using local communication between agents. We present some preliminary experimental results over randomly generated single-stage games, where we vary the number of agents and the density of the interaction. Our results show that our algorithms can find high-quality approximate equilibria in much larger games than have been previously solved.

2 Graphical games

In this section, we introduce some basic notation and terminology for game theory, and describe the framework of graphical games.

The conceptually simplest and perhaps best-studied representation of game is the *normal form*. In a normal form game, each player (agent) p_i chooses an action a_i from its action set $\{a_{i1}, a_{i2}, ..., a_{ik_i}\}$. For simplicity of notation, we assume that $k_1 = k_2 = ... = k_n = k$. The players are also allowed to play *mixed strategies* $\theta_i = \langle \theta_{i1}, \theta_{i2}, ...\theta_{ik} \rangle$ where θ_{ij} is the probability that p_i plays a_{ij}. If the player assigns probability 1 to one action — $\theta_{ij} = 1$ — and zero to the others, it is said to be playing a *pure strategy*, which we denote as r_{ij}. We use θ to denote a strategy profile for the set of players, and define (θ_{-i}, θ_i') to be the same as θ except that p_i plays θ_i' instead of θ_i.

Each player also has an associated payoff matrix M_i that specifies the payoff, or utility, for player i under each of the k^n possible combinations of strategies: $M_i(a_1, a_2, ..., a_n)$ is the reward for p_i when for all j, p_j plays a_j. Given a profile θ, we define the *expected utility* (or payoff) for p_i as

$$U_i(\theta) = \sum_{i_1, i_2, ..., i_n} \theta_{1i_1} \ldots \theta_{ni_n} M_i(a_{1i_1}, a_{2i_2}, \ldots, a_{ni_n}).$$

Given a set of mixed strategies θ, one strategy per player, we define the *regret of p_i with respect to θ* to be the most p_i can gain (on expectation) by diverging from the strategy profile θ:

$$Reg_i(\theta) = \max_{\theta_i'}(U_i((\theta_{-i}, \theta_i')) - U_i(\theta)).$$

A *Nash equilibrium* is a set of mixed strategies θ where each player's regret is 0. The Nash equilibrium condition means that no player can increase his expected reward by unilaterally changing his strategy. The seminal result of game theory is that any game has at least one Nash equilibrium (Nash 1950) *in mixed strategies*. An *ϵ-approximate Nash equilibrium* is a strategy profile θ such that each player's regret is at most ϵ.

A *graphical game* (Kearns, Littman, & Singh 2001a) assumes that each player's reward function depends on the actions of a subset of the players rather than on all other players' actions. Specifically, p_i's utility depends on the actions of some subset $\mathcal{P}_i$ of the other players, as well as on its own action. Thus, each player's payoff matrix M_i depends only on $|\mathcal{P}_i| + 1$ different decision variables, and therefore has $k^{|\mathcal{P}_i|+1}$ entries instead of k^n. We can describe this type of game using a directed graph (V, E). The nodes in V correspond to the n players, and we have a directed edge $e = (p_i, p_j) \in E$ from p_i to p_j if $p_i \in \mathcal{P}_j$, i.e., if j's utility depends on p_i's strategy. Thus, the parents of p_i in the graph are the players on whose action p_i's value depends. We note that our definition is a slight extension of the definition of KLS, as they assumed that the dependency relationship between players was symmetric, so that their graph was undirected.

Example 1: Consider the following example, based on a similar example in (Koller & Milch 2001). Suppose a road is being built from north to south through undeveloped land, and $2n$ agents have purchased plots of land along the road — the agents $w_1, ..., w_n$ on the west side and the agents $e_1, ..., e_n$ on the east side. Each agent needs to choose what

to build on his land — a factory, a shopping mall, or a residential complex. His utility depends on what he builds and on what is built north, south, and across the road from his land. All of the decisions are made simultaneously. In this case, agent w_i's parents are e_i, w_{i-1} and w_{i+1}. Note that the normal form representation consists of $2n$ matrices each of size 3^{2n}, whereas in the graphical game, each matrix has size at most $3^4 = 81$ (agents at the beginning and end of the road have smaller matrices).

If we modify the problem slightly and assume that the prevailing wind is from east to west, so that agents on the east side are not concerned with what is built across the street, then we have an asymmetric graphical game, where agent w_i's parents are e_i, w_{i-1}, w_{i+1}, whereas agent e_i's parents are e_{i-1}, e_{i+1}. ■

3 Function Minimization

Our first algorithm uses a hill-climbing approach to find an approximate equilibrium. We define a score function that measures the distance of a given strategy profile away from an equilibrium. We then use a greedy local search algorithm that starts from a random initial strategy profile and gradually improves the profile until a local maximum of the score function is reached.

More precisely, for a strategy profile θ, we define $S(\theta)$ to be the sum of the regrets of the players:

$$S(\theta) = \sum_i Reg_i(\theta).$$

This function is nonnegative and is equal to 0 exactly when θ is a Nash equilibrium. It is continuous in each of the separate probabilities θ_{ij} but nondifferentiable.

We can minimize $S(\theta)$ using a variety of function minimization techniques that apply to continuous but nondifferentiable functions. In the context of unstructured games, this approach has been explored by (McKelvey 1992). More recently, LaMura and Pearson (2001) have applied simulated annealing to this task. We chose to explore greedy hill climbing, as it lends itself particularly well to exploiting the special structure of the graphical game.

Our algorithm repeatedly chooses a player and changes that player's strategy so as to maximally improve the global score. More precisely, we define the *gain* for a player p_i as the amount that global score function would decrease if p_i changed its strategy so as to minimize the score function:

$$G_i(\theta) = \max_{\theta_i'}[S(\theta) - S((\theta_{-i}, \theta_i'))].$$

Note that this is very different from having the player change its strategy to the one that most improves its own utility. Here, the player takes into consideration the effects of its strategy change on the other players.

Our algorithm first chooses an initial random strategy θ and calculates $G_i(\theta)$ for each i. It then iterates over the following steps:

1. Choose the player p_i for which $G_i(\theta)$ is largest.
2. If $G_i(\theta)$ is positive, update $\theta_i := \text{argmax}_{\theta_i'}[S(\theta) - S((\theta_{-i}, \theta_i'))]$; otherwise, stop.

3. For each player p_j such that $G_j(\boldsymbol{\theta})$ may have changed, recalculate $G_j(\boldsymbol{\theta})$.

Notice that $Reg_i(\boldsymbol{\theta})$ depends only on the strategies of p_i and its parents in $\boldsymbol{\theta}$. Thus changing a player's strategy only affects the terms of the score function corresponding to that player and its children. We can use this to implement steps (2) and (3) efficiently. A somewhat laborious yet straightforward algebraic analysis shows that:

Proposition 2: *The following optimization problem is equivalent to finding $G_i(\boldsymbol{\theta})$ and the maximizing θ_i':*

$$
\begin{aligned}
\textit{Maximize:} \quad & U_i((\boldsymbol{\theta}_{-i}, \theta_i')) - \sum_{j:i\in\mathcal{P}_j} (y_j - U_j((\boldsymbol{\theta}_{-i}, \theta_i'))) \\
\textit{Subject to:} \quad & \theta_{im}' \geq 0 \quad \forall m \\
& \sum_m \theta_{im}' = 1 \\
& y_j \geq U_j(((\boldsymbol{\theta}_{-i}, \theta_i')_{-j}, r_{jl})) \quad \forall j, l
\end{aligned}
$$

As the expected utility functions U_j are linear in the θ_{im}', this optimization problem is simply a linear program whose parameters are the strategy probabilities of player p_i, and whose coefficients involve the utilities only of p_i and its children. Thus, the player p_i can optimize its strategy efficiently, based only on its own utility function and that of its children in the graph. We can therefore execute the optimization in step (2) efficiently. In our asymmetric **Road** example, an agent w_i could optimize its strategy based only on its children — w_{i-1} and w_{i+1}; similarly, an agent e_i needs to consider its children — e_{i-1}, e_{i+1} and w_i.

To execute step (3), we note that when p_i changes its strategy, the regrets of p_i and its children change; and when the regret of p_j changes, the gains of p_j and its parents change. More formally, when we change the strategy of p_i, the linear program for some other player p_j changes only if one of the expected utility terms changes. Since we only have such terms over p_j and its children, and the payoff of a player is affected only if the strategy at one of its parents changes, then $G_j(\boldsymbol{\theta})$ will change only if the strategy of p_j, or one of its parents, its children, or its spouses (other parents of its children) is changed. (Note the intriguing similarity to the definition of a Markov blanket in Bayesian networks (Pearl 1988).) Thus, in step (3), we only need to update the gain of a limited number of players. In our **Road** example, if we change the strategy for w_i, we need to update the gain of: w_{i-1} and w_{i+1} (both parents and children); e_i (only a parent); and w_{i-2}, w_{i+2}, e_{i-1}, and e_{i+1} (spouses).

We note that our hill climbing algorithm is not guaranteed to find a global minimum of $S(\boldsymbol{\theta})$. However, we can use a variety of techniques such as random restarts in order to have a better chance of finding a good local minimum. Also, local minima that we find are often fairly good approximate equilibria (since the score function corresponds quite closely to the quality of an approximate equilibrium).

4 CSP algorithms

Our second approach to solving graphical games uses a very different approach, motivated by the recent work of Kearns, Littman, and Singh (2001a; 2001b). They propose a dynamic programming style algorithm for the special case when the graphical game is a symmetric undirected tree.

Their algorithm has several variants. For our purposes, the most relevant (KLS 2001a) discretizes each player's set of mixed strategies, so that the tables represent a discrete grid of the players' strategy profiles. Since this variant does not explore the entire strategy space, it is limited to finding approximate equilibria. (Two other variants (KLS 2001a; 2001b) compute exact equilibria, but only apply in the very limited case of two actions per player.)

It turns out that the KLS algorithm can be viewed as applying *nonserial dynamic programming* or *variable elimination* (Bertele & Brioschi 1972) to a constraint satisfaction problem (CSP) generated by the graphical game. In this section, we present a CSP formulation of the problem of finding Nash equilibria in a general graphical game, and show how variable elimination can be applied to solve it. Unlike the KLS algorithm, our algorithm also applies to asymmetric and non-tree-structured games. We can also solve the problem as a constrained optimization rather than a constraint satisfaction problem, potentially improving the computational performance of the KLS approach.

Constraint Satisfaction There are many ways of formulating the ϵ-equilibrium problem as a CSP. Most simply, each variable V_i corresponds to the player p_i and takes values in the strategy space of p_i. The constraints C_i ensure that each player has regret at most ϵ in response to the strategies of its parents. (Recall that the each player's regret depends only its strategy and those of its parents.) Specifically, the "legal" set for C_i is

$$
\{\langle \theta_i, (\theta_j)_{j\in\mathcal{P}_i} \rangle \mid Reg_i(\theta_i, \theta_{\mathcal{P}_i}) \leq \epsilon\}.
$$

This constraint is over all of the variables in $\mathcal{P}_i \cup \{i\}$.

The variables in this CSP have continuous domains, which means that standard techniques for solving CSPs do not directly apply. We adopt the gridding technique proposed by KLS, which defines a discrete value space for each variable. Thus, the size of these constraints is exponential in the maximum family size (number of neighbors of a node), with the base of the exponent growing with the discretization density.

Variable elimination is a general-purpose nonserial dynamic programming algorithm that has been applied to several frameworks, including CSPs. Roughly speaking, we eliminate variables one at a time, combining the constraints relating to that variable into a single constraint, that describes the constraints induced over its neighboring variables. We briefly review the algorithm in the context of the constraints described above.

Example 3: Consider the three-player graphical game shown in Fig. 1(a), where we have discretized the strategy space of V into three strategies and those of U and W into two strategies. Suppose we have chosen an ϵ such that the constraints for V and W are given by Fig. 1(b),(c) (the constraint for U is not shown). The constraint for V, for example, is indexed by the strategies of U and V; a 'Y' in the table denotes that V's strategy has at most ϵ regret with respect to U's strategy. Eliminating V produces a constraint over U and W as shown in Fig. 1(d). Consider the (u_2, w_1) entry of the resulting constraint. We check each possible strategy for V. If V were playing v_1, then V would not have acceptable regret with respect to u_2, and W's strategy, w_1, would not have acceptable regret with respect to v_1. If V

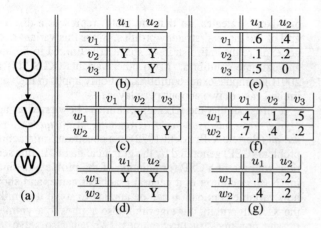

	u_1	u_2
v_1		
v_2	Y	Y
v_3		Y

(b)

	v_1	v_2	v_3
w_1		Y	
w_2			Y

(c)

	u_1	u_2
w_1	Y	Y
w_2		Y

(d)

	u_1	u_2
v_1	.6	.4
v_2	.1	.2
v_3	.5	0

(e)

	v_1	v_2	v_3
w_1	.4	.1	.5
w_2	.7	.4	.2

(f)

	u_1	u_2
w_1	.1	.2
w_2	.4	.2

(g)

(a)

Figure 1: (a) A simple 3-player graphical game. (b) Constraint table for V. (c) Constraint table for W. (d) Constraint table after elimination of V. (e) Regret table for V. (f) Regret table for W. (g) Regret table after elimination of V.

were playing v_3, V's strategy would be acceptable with respect to U's, but W's would not be acceptable with respect to V's. However, if V were playing v_2, then both V and W would be playing acceptable strategies. As there is a value of V which will produce an acceptable completion, the entry in the corresponding table is 'Y'. The (u_1, w_1) entry is not 'Y' since there is no strategy of V which will ensure that both V and W are playing acceptably. ∎

In general, we can eliminate variables one by one, until we are left with a constraint over a single variable. If the domain of this variable is empty, the CSP is unsatisfiable. Otherwise, we can pick one of its legal values, and execute this process in reverse to gradually extend each partial assignment to a partial assignment involving one additional variable. Note that we can also use this algorithm to find all solutions to the CSP: at every place where we have several legal assignments to a variable, we pursue all of them rather than picking one.

For undirected trees, using an "outside-in" elimination order, variable elimination ends up being very similar to the KLS algorithm. We omit details for lack of space. However, the variable elimination algorithm also applies as is to graphical games that are not trees, and to asymmetric games. Furthermore, the realization that our algorithms are simply solving a CSP opens the door to the application of alternative CSP algorithms, some of which might perform better in certain types of games.

Note that the value of ϵ is used in the CSP algorithm to define the constraints; if we run the algorithm with too coarse a grid, it might return an answer that says that no such equilibrium exists. Thus to be sure of obtaining an ϵ-optimal equilibrium, we must choose the grid according to the bound provided by KLS. Fortunately, the proof given is not specific to undirected trees, and thus we are provided with a gridding density (which is exponential only in the maximum family size) which will guarantee we find a solution. Unfortunately, the bound is usually very pessimistic and leads to unreasonably fine grids. For example, in a 2-

action Road game (which is discussed in Section 6), to guarantee a 0.2-approximate equilibrium, the KLS discretization would need to be approximately .0008, which means we would need about 1250 grid points per strategy.

Cost Minimization

An alternative to viewing the regret bounds as hard constraints is to try to directly reduce the worst-case regret over the players. This approach, which is a variant of a *cost-minimization problem (CMP)*, allows us to choose an arbitrary grid density and find the best equilibrium for that density. In our CMP algorithm, we replace the constraints with tables which have the same structure but instead of containing 'Y' or being blank, they simply contain the regret of the player under that set of strategies. More precisely, we have one initial factor for each player p_i, which contains one entry for each possible strategy profile $(\theta_i, \theta_{\mathcal{P}_i})$ for p_i and its parents $\mathcal{P}_i$. The value of this entry is simply $Reg_i(\theta_i, \theta_{\mathcal{P}_i})$. (As we discussed, regret only depends on the strategies of the player and his parents.)

Example 4: Consider again the three-player graphical game of Fig. 1(a). The regret tables for V, W are shown in Fig. 1(e),(f). Eliminating V produces a table over U and W, shown in Fig. 1(g). Consider the (u_2, w_1) entry of the resulting table. We check each possible strategy for V. If V plays v_1, then V would have regret .4 with respect to u_2, and W's strategy, w_1, would have regret .4 with respect to v_1; thus, we can only obtain a minimal regret of .4 when V plays v_1. If V plays v_3, V would have regret 0, but W would have regret .5, so the minimum regret over all players is .5. Finally, if V plays v_2, then V would have regret .2 and W would have regret .1, for a minimum regret of .2. Thus, the minimum value over all strategies of V of the lowest achievable regret is .2. ∎

More generally, our elimination step in the CMP algorithm is similar to the CSP algorithm, except that now the entry in the table is the minimum achievable value (over strategies of the eliminated player) of the maximum over all tables involving the eliminated player. More precisely, let $F_1, F_2, \ldots, F_k$ be a set of factors each containing p_i, and let N_j be the set of nodes contained in F_j. When we eliminate p_i, we generate a new factor F over the variables $N = \cup_{j=1}^{k} N_j - \{p_i\}$ as follows: For a given set of policies θ_N, the corresponding entry in F is $\min_{\theta_i} \max_j F_j[(\theta_F, \theta_i)_{N_j}]$. Each entry in a factor F_j corresponds to some strategy profile for the players in N_j. Intuitively, it represents an upper bound on the regret of some of these players, assuming this strategy profile is played. To eliminate p_i, we consider all of his strategies, and choose the one that guarantees us the lowest regret.

After eliminating all of the players, the result is the best achievable worst-case regret — the one that achieves the minimal regret for the player whose regret is largest. The associated completion is precisely the approximate equilibrium that achieves the best possible ϵ. We note that the CSP algorithm essentially corresponds to first rounding the entries in the CMP tables to either 0 or 1, using ϵ as the rounding cutoff, and then running CMP; an assignment is a solution to the CSP iff it has value 0 in the CMP.

Finally, note that all of the variable elimination algorithms naturally use local message passing between players in the game. In the tree-structured games, the communication directly follows the structure of the graphical game. In more complex games, the variable elimination process might lead to interactions between players that are not a priori directly related to each other. In general, the communication will be along edges in the *triangulated graph* of the graphical game (Lauritzen & Spiegelhalter 1988). However, the communication tends to stay localized to "regions" in the graph, except for graphs with many direct interactions between "remote" players.

5 Hybrid algorithms

We now present two algorithms that combine ideas from the two techniques presented above, and which have some of the advantages of both.

Approximate equilibrium refinement

One problem with the CSP algorithm is the rapid growth of the tables as the grid resolution increases. One solution is to find an approximate equilibrium using some method, construct a fine grid around the region of the approximate equilibrium strategy profile, and use the CMP or CSP algorithms to find a better equilibrium over that grid. If we find a better equilibrium in this finer grid, we recenter our grid around this point, shifting our search to a slightly different part of the space. If we do not find a better equilibrium with the specified grid granularity, we restrict our search to a smaller part of the space but use a finer grid. This process is repeated until some threshold is reached.

Note that this strategy does not guarantee that we will eventually get to an exact equilibrium. In some cases, our first equilibrium might be at a region where there is a local minimum of the cost function, but no equilibrium. In this case, the more refined search may improve the quality of the approximate equilibrium, but will not lead to finding an exact equilibrium.

Subgame decomposition

A second approach is based on the idea that we can decompose a single large game into several subgames, solve each separately, and then combine the results to get an equilibrium for the entire game. We can implement this general scheme using an approach that is motivated by the clique tree algorithm for Bayesian network inference (Lauritzen & Spiegelhalter 1988).

To understand the intuition, consider a game that is composed of two almost independent subgames. Specifically, we can divide the players into two groups C_1 and C_2 whose only overlap is the single player p_i. We assume that the games are independent given p_i, in other words, for any $j \neq i$, if $p_j \in C_k$, then $\mathcal{P}_j \subseteq C_k$. If we fix a strategy θ_i of p_i, then the two halves of the game no longer interact. Specifically, we can find an equilibrium for the players in C_k, ensuring that the players' strategies are a best response both to each other's strategies and to θ_i, without considering the strategies of players in the other cluster. However, we must make sure that these strategy profiles will combine to form an equilibrium for the entire game. In particular,

all of the players' strategies must be a best response to the strategy profiles of their parents. Our decomposition guarantees this property for all the players besides p_i. To satisfy the best-response requirement for p_i we must address two issues. First, it may be the case that for a particular strategy choice of p_i, there is no total equilibrium, and thus we may have to try several (or all) of his strategies in order to find an equilibrium. Second, if p_i has parents in both subgames, we must consider both subgames when reasoning about p_i, eliminating our ability to decouple them. Our algorithm below addresses both of these difficulties.

We decompose the graph into a set of overlapping clusters $C_1, \dots, C_\ell$, where each $C_l \subseteq \{p_1, \dots, p_n\}$. These clusters are organized into a tree $\mathcal{T}$. If C_l and C_m are two neighboring clusters, we define S_{lm} to be the intersection $C_l \cap C_m$. If $p_i \in C_m$ is such that $\mathcal{P}_i \subseteq C_m$, then we say that p_i is *associated* with C_m. If all of a node's parents are contained in two clusters (and are therefore in the separator between them), we associate it arbitrarily with one cluster or the other.

Definition 5: We say that $\mathcal{T}$ is a *cluster tree* for a graphical game if the following conditions hold:

- **Running intersection:** If $p_i \in C_l$ and $p_i \in C_m$ then p_i is also in every C_o that is on the (unique) path in $\mathcal{T}$ between C_l and C_m.
- **No interaction:** All p_i are associated with a cluster.

The *no interaction* condition implies that the best response criterion for players in the separator involves at most one of the two neighboring clusters, thereby eliminating the interaction with both subgames.

We now use a CSP to find an assignment to the separators that is consistent with some global equilibrium. We have one CSP variable for each separator S_{lm}, whose value space are joint strategies $\theta_{S_{lm}}$ for the players in the separator. We have a binary constraint for every pair of neighboring separators S_{lm} and S_{mo} that is satisfied iff there exists a strategy profile θ for C_m for which the following conditions hold:

1. θ is consistent with the separators $\theta_{S_{lm}}$ and $\theta_{S_{mo}}$.
2. For each p_i associated with C_m, the strategy θ_i is an ϵ-best response to $\theta_{\mathcal{P}_i}$; note that all of p_i's parents are in C_m, so their strategies are specified.

It is not hard to show that an assignment $\theta_{S_{lm}}$ for the separators that satisfies all these constraints is consistent with an approximate global equilibrium. First, the constraints assert that there is a way of completing the partial strategy profile with a strategy profile for the players in the clusters. Second, the running intersection property implies that if a player appears in two clusters, it appears in every separator along the way; condition (1) then implies that the same strategy is assigned to that player in all the clusters where it appears. Finally, according to the *no interaction* condition, each player is associated with some cluster, and that cluster specifies the strategies of its parents. Condition (2) then tells us that this player's strategy is an ϵ-best response to its parents. As all players are playing ϵ-best responses, the overall strategy profile is an equilibrium.

There remains the question of how we determine the existence of an approximate equilibrium within a cluster given strategy profiles for the separators. If we use the CSP algorithm, we have gained nothing: using variable elimination within each cluster is equivalent to using variable elimination (using some particular ordering) over the entire CSP. However, we can solve each subgame using our hill climbing approach, giving us yet another hybrid algorithm — one where a CSP approach is used to combine the answers obtained by the hill-climbing algorithm in different clusters.

6   Experimental Results

We tested hill climbing, cost minimization, and the approximate equilibrium refinement hybrid on two types of games.

The first was the Road game described earlier. We tested two different types of payoffs. One set of payoffs corresponded to a situation where each developer can choose to build a park, a store, or a housing complex; stores want to be next to houses but next to few other stores; parks want to be next to houses; and houses want to be next to exactly one store and as many parks as possible. This game has pure strategy equilibria for all road lengths; thus, it is quite easy to solve using cost minimization where only the pure strategies of each developer are considered. A 200 player game can be solved in about 1 second. For the same 200 player game, hill climbing took between 10 and 15 seconds to find an approximate equilibrium with ϵ between .01 and .04 (the payoffs range from 0 to 2).

In the other payoff structure, each land developer plays a game of paper, rock, scissors against each of his neighbors; his total payoff is the sum of the payoffs in these separate games, so that the maximum payoff per player is 3. This game has no pure strategy equilibria; thus, we need to choose a finer discretization in order to achieve reasonable results. Fig. 2(a),(b) shows the running times and equilibria quality for each of the three algorithms. Cost minimization was run with a grid density of 0.2 (i.e., the allowable strategies all have components that are multiples of 0.2). Since each player has three possible actions, the resulting grid has 21 strategies per player. The hybrid algorithm was run starting from the strategy computed by hill-climbing. The nearby area was then discretized so as to have 6 strategies per player within a region of size roughly .05 around the current equilibrium. We ran the hybrid as described above until the total size is less than .00001.

Each algorithm appears to scale approximately linearly with the number of nodes, as expected. Given that the number of strategies used for the hybrid is less than that used for the actual variable elimination, it is not surprising that cost minimization takes considerably longer than the hybrid. The equilibrium error is uniformly low for cost minimization; this is not surprising as, in this game, the uniform strategy $(1/3, 1/3, 1/3)$ is always an equilibrium. The quality of the equilibria produced by all three algorithms is fairly good, with a worst ϵ value of about 10% of the maximum payoffs in the game. The error of the equilibria produced by hill climbing grows with the game size, a consequence of the fact that the hill-climbing search is over a higher-dimensional space. Somewhat surprising is the extent to which the hybrid approach improves the quality of the equilibria, at least for this type of game.

We also tested the algorithms on symmetric 3-action games structured as a ring of rings, with payoffs chosen at random from $[0, 1]$. The results are shown in Fig. 2(c),(d). For the graph shown, we varied the number of nodes on the internal ring; each node on the inner ring is also part of an outer ring of size 20. Thus, the games contain as many as 400 nodes. For this set of results, we set the gridding density for cost minimization to 0.5, so there were 6 strategies per node. The reduced strategy space explains why the algorithm is so much faster than the refinement hybrid: each step of the hybrid is similar to an entire run of cost minimization (for these graphs, the hybrid is run approximately 40 times).

The errors obtained by the different algorithms are somewhat different in the case of rings of rings. Here, refinement only improves accuracy by about a factor of 2, while cost minimization is quite accurate. In order to explain this, we tested simple rings, using cost minimization over only pure strategies. Based on 1000 trial runs, for 20 player rings, the best pure strategy equilibria has $\epsilon = 0$ 23.9% of the time; between $\epsilon \in [0, .05]$ 45.8% of the time; $\epsilon \in [.05, .1]$ 25.7%; and $\epsilon > .1$ 4.6%. We also tested (but did not include results for) undirected trees with random payoffs. Again, using a low gridding density for variable elimination, we obtained results similar to those for rings of rings. Thus, it appears that, with random payoffs, fairly good equilibria often exist in pure strategies.

Clearly the discretization density of cost minimization has a huge effect on the speed of the algorithm. Fig. 2(e)&(f) shows the results for CMP using different discretization levels as well as for hill climbing, over simple rings of various sizes with random payoffs in $[0,1]$. The level of discretization impacts performance a great deal, and also noticeably affects solution quality. Somewhat surprisingly, even the lowest level of discretization performs better than hill climbing. This is not in general the case, as variable elimination may be intractable for games with high graph width.

In order to get an idea of the extent of the improvement relative to standard, unstructured approaches, we converted each graphical game into a corresponding strategic form game (by duplicating entries), which expands the size of the game exponentially. We then attempted to find equilibria using the available game solving package Gambit[1] specifically using the QRE algorithm with default settings. (QRE seems to be the fastest among the algorithms implemented in Gambit). For a road length of 1 (a 2-player game) QRE finds an equilibrium in 20 seconds; for a road of length 2, QRE takes 7min56sec; and for a road of length 3, about 2h30min.

Overall, the results indicate that these algorithms can find good approximate equilibria in a reasonable amount of time. Cost minimization has a much lower variance in running time, but can get expensive when the grid size is large. The quality of the answers obtained even with coarse grids are often surprisingly good, particularly when random payoffs are used so that there are pure strategy profiles that are almost equilibria. Our algorithms provide us with a criterion for evaluating the error of a candidate solution, allowing us to refine our answer when the error is too large. In such cases, the hybrid algorithm is often a good approach.

_____

[1] http://www.hss.caltech.edu/gambit/Gambit.html.

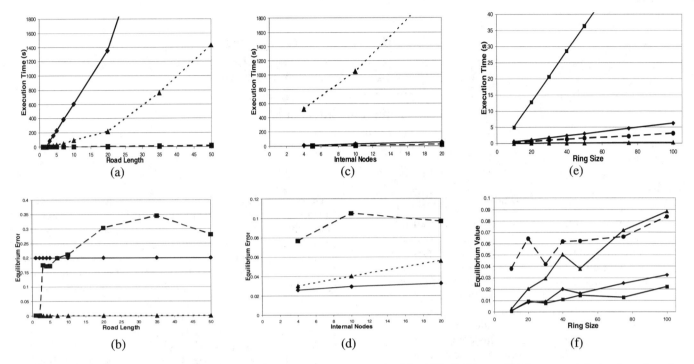

Figure 2: Comparison of Algorithms as number of players varies: Dashed for hill climbing, solid for cost minimization, dotted for refinement. Road games: (a) running time; (b) equilibrium error. Ring of rings: (c) running time; (d) equilibrium error. CMP on single ring with different grid density and hill climbing in simple ring. Dashed line indicates hill climbing, solid lines with squares, diamonds, triangles correspond to grid densities of 1.0 (3 strategies), 0.5 (6 strategies), and 0.333 (10 strategies) respectively. (e) running time; (f) equilibrium error.

7 Conclusions

In this paper, we considered the problem of collaboratively finding approximate equilibria in a situation involving multiple interacting agents. We focused on the idea of exploiting the locality of interaction between agents, using graphical games as an explicit representation of this structure. We provided two algorithms that exploit this structure to support solution algorithms that are both computationally efficient and utilize distributed collaborative computation that respects the "lines of communication" between the agents. Both strongly use the locality of regret: hill climbing in the score function, and CSP in the formulation of the constraints. We showed that our techniques provide good solutions for games with a very large number of agents.

We believe that our techniques can be applied much more broadly; in particular, we plan to apply them in the much richer *multi-agent influence diagram* framework of (Koller & Milch 2001), which provides a structured representation, similar to graphical games, but for substantially more complex situations involving time and information.

Acknowledgments. We are very grateful to Ronald Parr for many useful discussions. This work was supported by the DoD MURI program administered by the Office of Naval Research under Grant N00014-00-1-0637, and by Air Force contract F30602-00-2-0598 under DARPA's TASK program.

References

Bertele, U., and Brioschi, F. 1972. *Nonserial Dynamic Programming*. New York: Academic Press.

Fudenberg, D., and Tirole, J. 1991. *Game Theory*. MIT Press.

Kearns, M.; Littman, M.; and Singh, S. 2001a. Graphical models for game theory. In *Proc. UAI*.

Kearns, M.; Littman, M.; and Singh, S. 2001b. An efficient exact algorithm for singly connected graphical games. In *Proc. 14th NIPS*.

Koller, D., and Milch, B. 2001. Multi-agent influence diagrams for representing and solving games. In *Proc. IJCAI*.

LaMura, P. 2000. Game networks. In *Proc. UAI*, 335–342.

Lauritzen, S. L., and Spiegelhalter, D. J. 1988. Local computations with probabilities on graphical structures and their application to expert systems. *J. Royal Stat. Soc. B* 50(2):157–224.

McKelvey, R., and McLennan, A. 1996. Computation of equilibria in finite games. In *Handbook of Computational Economics*, volume 1. Elsevier Science. 87–142.

McKelvey, R. 1992. A Liapunov function for Nash equilibria. unpublished.

Nash, J. 1950. Equilibrium points in n-person games. *PNAS* 36:48–49.

Pearl, J. 1988. *Probabilistic Reasoning in Intelligent Systems*. Morgan Kaufmann.

Pearson, M., and La Mura, P. 2001. Simulated annealing of game equilibria: A simple adaptive procedure leading to nash equilibrium. Unpublished manuscript.

von Neumann, J., and Morgenstern, O. 1944. *Theory of games and economic behavior*. Princeton Univ. Press.

Distributed Breakout Revisited

Weixiong Zhang and **Lars Wittenburg**

Computer Science Department

Washington University

St. Louis, MO 63130

Email: {zhang,larsw}@cs.wustl.edu

Abstract

Distributed breakout algorithm (DBA) is an efficient method for solving distributed constraint satisfaction problems (CSP). Inspired by its potential of being an efficient, low-overhead agent coordination method for problems in distributed sensor networks, we study DBA's properties in this paper. We specifically show that on an acyclic graph of n nodes, DBA can find a solution in $O(n^2)$ synchronized distributed steps. This completeness result reveals DBA's superiority over conventional local search on acyclic graphs and implies its potential as a simple self-stabilization method for tree-structured distributed systems. We also show a worst case of DBA in a cyclic graph where it never terminates. To overcome this problem on cyclic graphs, we propose two stochastic variations to DBA. Our experimental analysis shows that stochastic DBAs are able to avoid DBA's worst-case scenarios and has similar performance as that of DBA.

1 Introduction and Overview

Our primary motivation of studying distributed breakout algorithm (DBA) [9; 11] is to apply it as a simple, low-overhead method for coordinating agents in distributed sensor networks [13]. One important class of problems among distributed agents is the coordination of their distributed actions in such a way that overall inter-agent constraints are not violated. Such a problem can be captured as a distributed constraint satisfaction problem (CSP) [9].

DBA is a remarkable extension of breakout algorithm for centralized CSP [6]. Centralized breakout algorithm is a local search method with an innovative method for escaping local minima. This is realized by introducing weights to constraints and dynamically increasing some of the weights so as to force agents to dynamically adjust their values. It has been shown experimentally that on certain constraint problems, it is more efficient than local search algorithms with multiple restarts and asynchronous weak-commitment search [9; 11].

Despite their unique features and early success, breakout and distributed breakout algorithms have not been studied thoroughly. For example, their completeness is not fully understood and their complexity remains unknown. It is also not clear what constraint graph structures will render worst cases for these algorithms. To our best knowledge, the work on these two algorithms is limited to the original publications on the subject, specifically [6; 9; 11].

Motivated by our real-world applications of distributed sensor networks in which DBA can apply [13] and inspired by its possible great potential in solving large distributed CSP, we study DBA in this paper. After a brief overview of breakout and distributed breakout algorithms (Section 2), we analyze the completeness and computational complexity of DBA (Section 3). We prove that on acyclic constraint graphs, DBA is complete, in the sense that it is guaranteed to find a solution if one exists. We also show that its complexity, the number of synchronized distributed steps, is $O(n^2)$ on an acyclic graph with n nodes. These analytical results reveal the superiority of DBA over conventional centralized and distributed local search, which is not complete on acyclic graph. In addition, we identify the best and worst arrangements for variable identifiers on acyclic graphs, which are critical elements of the algorithm. These results indicate that DBA is an efficient, low-overhead method for self-stabilization [8] in tree-structured distributed systems. Furthermore, on cyclic graphs, we construct a case in which DBA is unable to terminate, leading to its incompleteness in this case. To avoid DBA's worst-case behavior on cyclic graphs, we introduce stochastic features to DBA (Section 4). We propose two stochastic variations to DBA and experimentally demonstrate that they are able to increase DBA's completeness on cyclic graphs and have similar anytime performance as the original algorithm.

Finally, we discuss previous related work in Section 5 and conclude in Section 6.

2 Breakout and Distributed Breakout

The breakout algorithm [6] is a local search method equipped with an innovative scheme of escaping local minima for CSP. Given a CSP, the algorithm first assigns a weight of one to all constraints. It then picks a value for every variable. If no constraint is violated, the algorithm terminates. Otherwise, it chooses a variable that can reduce the total weight

Algorithm 1 Sketch of DBA

```
set the local weights of constraints to one
value ← a random value from domain
while (no termination condition met) do
    exchange value with neighbors
    WR ← BestPossibleWeightReduction()
    send WR to neighbors and collect their WRs
    if (WR > 0) then
        if (it has the biggest improvement among neighbors)
        then
            value ← the value that gives WR
        end if
    else
        if (no neighbor can improve) then
            increase violated constraints' weights by one
        end if
    end if
end while
```

of the unsatisfied constraints if its value is changed. If such a weight-reducing variable-value pair exists, the algorithm changes the value of a chosen variable. The algorithm continues the process of variable selection and value change until no weight-reducing variable can be found. At that point, it reaches a local minimum if a constraint violation still exists. Instead of restarting from another random initial assignment, the algorithm tries to escape from the local minimum by increasing the weights of all violated constraints by one and proceeds as before. This weight change will force the algorithm to alter the values of some variables to satisfy the violated constraints.

Centralized breakout can be extended to distributed breakout algorithm (DBA) [9; 11]. Without loss of generality, we assign an agent to a variable, and assume that all agents have unique identifiers. Two agents are *neighbors* if they share a common constraint. An agent communicates only with its neighbors. At each step of DBA, an agent exchanges its current variable value with its neighbors, computes the possible weight reduction if it changes its current value, and decides if it should do so. To avoid simultaneous variable changes at neighboring agents, only the agent having the maximal weight reduction has the right to alter its current value. If ties occur, the agents break the ties based on their identifiers. The above process of DBA is sketched in Algorithm 1. For simplicity, we assume each step is synchronized among the agents. This assumption can be lifted by a synchronization mechanism [8].

In the description of [9; 11], each agent also maintains a variable, called *my-termination-counter* (MTC), to help detect a possible termination condition. At each step, an agent's MTC records the diameter of a subgraph centered around the agent within which all the agents' constraints are satisfied. For instances, an agent's MTC is zero if one of its neighbors has a violated constraint; it is equal to one when its immediate neighbors have no violation. Therefore, if the diameter of the constraint graph is known to each agent, when an agent's MTC is equal to the known diameter, DBA can terminate with

the current agent values as a satisfying solution. However, MTCs may never become equal to the diameter even if a solution exists. There are cases in which the algorithm is not complete in that it cannot guarantee to find a solution even if one exists. Such a worst case depends on the structure of a problem, a topic of the next section. We do not include the MTC here to keep our description simple.

It is worth pointing out that the node, or agent, identifiers are not essential to the algorithm. They are only used to set up a priority between two competing agents for tie breaking. As long as such priorities exists, node identifiers are not needed.

3 Completeness and Complexity

In this section, we study the completeness and computational complexity of DBA on binary constraint problems in which no constraint involves more than two variables. This is not a restriction as a non-binary constraint problem can be converted to a binary one with cycles [1; 7]. One advantage of using binary problems is that we can focus on the main features of DBA rather than pay attention to the degree of constraints of the underlying problem. In the rest of the paper, we use constraint problems to refer to binary problems if not explicitly stated. In addition, the complexity is defined as DBA's number of synchronized distributed steps. In one step, value changes at different nodes are allowed while one variable can change its value at most once. We also use variables, nodes and agents interchangeably in our discussion.

3.1 Acyclic graphs

First notice that acyclic graphs are 2-colorable. Thus, any acyclic constraint problem must have a satisfying solution if the domain size of a variable is at least two. In addition, larger domains make a problem less constrained. Therefore, it is sufficient to consider acyclic constraint problems with variable domains no more than two.

To simplify our discussion and for pedagogical reasons, we first consider chains, which are special acyclic graphs. The results on chains will also serve as a basis for trees.

Chains

We will refer to the combination of variable values and constraint weights as a *problem state*, or *state* for short. A *solution* of a constraint problem is a state with no violated constraint. We say two states are *adjacent* if DBA can move from one state to the other within one step.

Lemma 1 *On a chain, DBA will not visit the same problem state more than once.*

Proof: Assume the opposite, i.e., DBA can visit a state twice in a process as follows, $S_x \rightarrow S_y \rightarrow \cdots \rightarrow S_z \rightarrow S_x$. Obviously no constraint weight is allowed to increase at any state on this cycle. Suppose that node x changes its value at state S_x to resolve a conflict C involving x. In the worst case a new conflict at the other side of the node will be created. C is thus "pushed" to the neighbor of x, say y. Two possibilities exist. First, C is resolved at y or another node along the chain, so that no state cycle will form. Second, C returns to x, causing x to change its value back to its previous value. Since nodes are ordered, i.e., they have prioritized identifiers, violations may only move in one direction and C cannot return to x from y without changing a constraint weight. This means that C must move back to x from another path, which contradicts the fact that the structure is a chain. □

Lemma 2 *On a chain of n variables, each of which has a domain size at least two, DBA can increase a constraint weight to at most $\lfloor n/2 \rfloor$.*

Proof: The weight of the first constraint on the left of the chain will never change and thus remain at one, since the left end node can always change its value to satisfy its only constraint. The weight of the second constraint on the left can increase to two at the most. When the weight of the second constraint is two and the second constraint on the left is violated, the second node will always change its value to satisfy the second constraint because it has a higher weight than the first constraint. This will push the violation to the left end node and force it to change its value and thus resolve the conflict. This argument can be inductively applied to the other internal nodes and constraints along the chain. In fact, it can be applied to both ends of the chain. So the maximal constraint weight on the chain will be $\lfloor n/2 \rfloor$. □

Immediate corollaries of this lemma are the best and worst arrangements of variable identifiers. In the best case, the end nodes of the chain should be most active, always trying to satisfy the only constraint, and resolving any conflict. Therefore, the end nodes should have the highest priority, followed by their neighbors, and so on to the middle of the chain. The worst case is simply the opposite of the best case; the end nodes are most inactive and have the lowest priority, followed by their neighbors, and so on.

Theorem 1 *On a chain of n nodes, DBA terminates in at most n^2 steps with a solution, if it exists, or with an answer of no solution, if it does not exist.*

Proof: As a chain is always 2-colorable, the combination of the above lemmas gives the result for a chain with nodes of domain sizes at least two. It is possible, however, that no solution exists if some variables have domain sizes less than two. In this case, it is easy to create a conflict between two nodes with domain size one, which will never be resolved. As a result, the weights of the constraints between these two nodes will be raised to n. If each agent knows the chain length n, DBA can be terminated when a constraint weight is more than n. (In fact, the chain length can be computed in $O(n)$ steps as follows. An end node first sends number 1 to its only neighbor. The neighboring node adds one to the number received and then passes the new number to the other neighbor. The number reached at the other end of the chain is the chain length, which can be subsequently disseminated to the rest of the chain. The whole process takes $2n$ steps.) Furthermore, a node needs at most $n-1$ steps to increase a constraint weight. This worst case occurs when a chain contains two variables at two ends of the chain which have the lowest priorities and unity domain sizes so neither of them can change its value. On such a chain, a conflict can be pushed around between the two end nodes many time. Every time a conflict reaches an end node, the node increases the constraint weight to push the

conflict back. Since a constraint weight will be no more than n, the result follows. □

A significant implication of these results is a termination condition for DBA on a chain. If DBA does not find a solution in n^2 steps, it can terminate with an answer of no solution. This new termination condition and DBA's original termination condition of my-termination-counter guarantee DBA to terminate on a chain.

Trees

The key to the proof for the chain and tree structures is that no cycle exists in an acyclic graph, so that the same conflict cannot return to a node without increasing a constraint weight.

The arguments on the maximal constraint weight for chains hold for general acyclic graphs or trees. First consider the case that each variable has a domain size at least two. In an acyclic graph, an arbitrary constraint (link) C connects two disjoint acyclic graphs, G_1 and G_2. Assume G_1 and G_2 have n_1 and n_2 nodes, respectively, and $n_1 \leq n_2$. Then the maximal possible weight W on C cannot be more than n_1, which is proven inductively as follows. If the node v associated with C is the only node of G_1, then the claim is true since v can always accommodate C. If G_1 is a chain, then the arguments for Lemma 2 apply directly and the maximal possible weight of a constraint is the number of links the constraint is away from the end variable of G_1. If v is the only node in G_1 that connects to more than one constraint in G_1, which we call a branching node, then a conflict at C may be pushed into G_1 when the weight of C is greater than the sum of the weights of all constraints in G_1 linked to v, which is at most equal to the number of nodes of G_1. The same arguments equally apply when v is not the only branching node of G_1. Therefore, the maximal constraint weight is bounded by n.

The worst-case complexity can be derived similarly. A worst case occurs when all end variables of an acyclic graph have fixed values, so that a conflict may never be pushed out of the graph. A constraint weight can be bumped up by one after a conflict has traveled from an end node to other end nodes and back, within at most n steps.

Based on these arguments, we have the following result.

Theorem 2 *On an acyclic graph with n nodes, DBA terminates in at most n^2 steps with either an optimal solution, if it exists, or an answer of no solution, if it does not exist.*

The above completeness result can be directly translated to centralized breakout algorithm, leading to its completeness on acyclic graphs as well. Moreover, since each step in DBA is equivalent to n steps in the centralized algorithm, each of which examines a distinct variable, the complexity result on DBA also means that the worst-case complexity of the centralized algorithm is $O(n^3)$. These analytical results reveal the superiority of centralized breakout algorithm and DBA over conventional local search methods on acyclic graphs, which are not complete even on a chain.

Our experimental results also show that the number of steps taken by DBA is much smaller than the n^2 upper bound, as shown in Figure 1. In our experiments, we used different size chains and trees and averaged the results over 100 random trials. We considered the best- and worst-case identi-

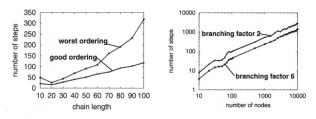

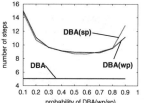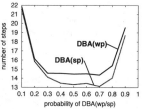

Figure 1: The number of steps taken by DBA on chains with the best and worst variable identifier arrangements (left) and on trees with worst identifier arrangements (right).

Figure 3: Steps taken by DBA and variants on the example of Figure 2 with random initial assignments (left) and the specific assignment of Figure 2 (right).

fier arrangements for chains (Figure 1 left) and worst-case arrangement for trees (where more active nodes are closer to the centers of the trees) with different branching factors. As the figure shows, the average number of steps taken by DBA is near linear for the worst-case identifier arrangement, and the number of steps is linear on trees with a worst-case identifier arrangement (Figure 1 right). Furthermore, for a fixed number of nodes the number of steps decreases inversely when branching factors of the trees increase. In short, DBA is efficient on acyclic graphs.

3.2 Cyclic graphs

Unfortunately, DBA is not complete on cyclic constraint graphs. This will include non-binary problems as they can be converted to binary problems with cycles. This is also the reason that breakout algorithm is not complete on Boolean satisfiability with three variables per clause [6], which is equivalent to a constraint with three variables.

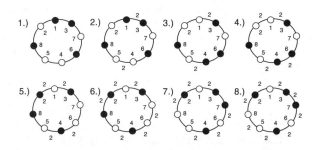

Figure 2: A worst case for DBA on a ring.

When there are cycles in a graph, conflicts may walk on these cycles forever. To see this, consider a problem of coloring a ring with an even number of nodes using two colors (black and white), as shown in Figure 2, where the node identifiers and constraint weights are respectively next to nodes and edges. Figure 2(1) shows a case where two conflicts appear at locations between nodes 1 and 3 and between nodes 4 and 5, that are not adjacent to each other. The weights of the corresponding edges are increased accordingly in Figure 2(2). As node 1 (node 4) has a higher priority than node 3 (node 5), it changes its value and pushes the conflict one step counterclockwise in Figure 2(3). The rest of Figure 2 depicts the subsequent steps until all constraint weights have been increased

to 2. This process can continue forever with the two conflicts moving in the same direction on the chain at the same speed, chasing each other endlessly and making DBA incomplete.

4 Stochastic Variations

A lesson that can be learned from the above worst-case scenario is that conflicts should not move at the same speed. We thus introduce randomness to alter the speeds of possible conflict movements on cycles of a graph. This stochastic feature may increase DBA's chances of finding a solution possibly with a penalty on convergence to solution for some cases.

4.1 DBA(wp) and DBA(sp)

We can add randomness to DBA in two ways. In the first, we use a probability for tie breaking. The algorithm will proceed as before, except that when two neighboring variables have the same improvement for the next step, they will change their values probabilistically. This means that both variables may change or not change, or just one of them. We call this variation weak probabilistic DBA, denoted as DBA(wp).

In the second method, which was inspired by the distributed stochastic algorithm [3; 4; 12], a variable will change if it has the best improvement among its neighbors. However, when it can improve but the improvement is not the best among its neighbors, it will change based on a probability. This variation is more active than DBA and the weak probabilistic variation. We thus call it strong probabilistic DBA, DBA(sp) for short.

One favorable feature of these variants is that no variable identifiers are needed, which may be important for some applications where node identifiers across the whole network is expensive to compute. Moreover, these variants give two families of variations to DBA, depending on the probabilities used. It will be interesting to see how they vary under different parameters, the topic that we consider next.

4.2 DBA(wp) versus DBA(sp)

We first study the two variants on the example of coloring an 8-node ring of Figure 2. In the first set of tests, node identifiers and initial colors are randomly generated and 10,000 trials are tested. DBA is unable to terminate on 15% of the total trials after more than 100,000 steps[1], while on the other 85%

---

[1] Our additional tests also show that DBA's failure rate decreases as the ring size increases.

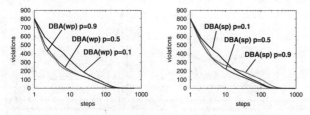
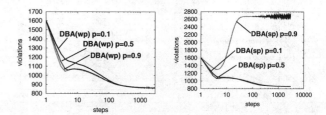

Figure 4: DBA(wp) and DBA(sp) on grid 20×20 and $k = 4$.

Figure 5: DBA(wp) (left) and DBA(sp) (right) on graph with 400 nodes and k=8.

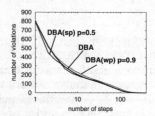

of the trials DBA finds a solution after 5 steps on average as shown in Figure 3(left). In contrast, DBA(wp) and DBA(sp) always find solutions but require almost twice as many steps on average with the best probability around 0.6.

In the second set of tests, we use the exact worst-case initial assignment as shown in Figure 2. As expected, DBA failed to terminate. DBA(wp) and DBA(sp) find all solutions on 1,000 trials. Since they are stochastic, each trial may run a different number of steps. The average number of steps under different probability is shown in Figure 3(right).

Next we study these two families of variants on grids, graphs and trees. We consider coloring these structures using 2 colors. For grids, we consider 20×20, 40×40, and 60×60 grids with connectivities equal to $k = 4$ and $k = 8$. To simulate infinitely large grids in our experiments, we remove the grid boundaries by connecting the nodes on the top to those on the bottom as well as the nodes on the left to those on the right of the grids to create $k = 4$ grid. For $k = 8$ grid, we further link a node to four more neighbors, one each to the top left, top right, bottom left and bottom right. This renders the problem overconstrained for two-coloring. Hence, the algorithms may only try to improve the solution quality by minimizing the number of violated constraints.

The results of 20×20 grids with $k = 4$ are shown in Figure 4, averaged over 2,000 trials. As the figures show, the higher the probability the better DBA(wp)'s performance. For DBA(sp) $p = 0.5$ is the best probability.

We generate 2,000 graphs with 400 nodes with an average connectivity per node equal to $k = 4$ and $k = 8$ by adding, respectively, 1,600 and 3,200 edges to randomly picked pairs of unconnected nodes. These two graphs are generated to make a correspondence to the grid structures of $k = 4$ and $k = 8$ considered previously, except that both random graphs are not two-colorable. All algorithms are applied to the same set of graphs for a meaningful comparison. Figure 5 shows the results on graphs with $k = 8$. There is no significant difference within the DBA(wp) family. However, DBA(sp) with large probabilities can significantly degrade to very poor performance, exhibiting a phenomenon similar to phase transitions. Since DBA(sp) with high probability is close to distributed stochastic algorithm [3; 4; 12], the results here are in line with those of [12].

We also consider DBA(wp) and DBA(sp) on random trees with various depths and branching factors. Due to space limitations, we do not include detailed experimental results here, but give a brief summary. As expected, they all find optimal solutions for all 10,000 2-coloring instances. Within DBA(wp) family, there is no significant difference. However,

Figure 6: DBA and random DBAs on grid 20×20 and $k = 4$.

DBA(sp) with a high probability has a poor anytime performance.

Combining all the results on the constraint structures we considered, DBA(sp) appears to be a poor algorithm in some cases, especially when its probability is very high.

4.3 DBA(wp) and DBA(sp) versus DBA

The remaining issue is how DBA(wp) and DBA(sp) compare with DBA. Here we use the best parameters for these two variants from the previous tests and compare them directly with DBA. We average the results over the same sets of problem instances we used in Section 4.2. Figures 6, 7 and 8 show the experimental results on grids, random graphs and trees, respectively. With their best parameters, DBA(wp) and DBA(sp) appear to be compatible with DBA. Furthermore, as discussed earlier, DBA(wp) and DBA(sp) increase the probability of convergence to optimal solutions. DBA(wp), in particular, is a better alternative in many cases if its probability is chosen carefully. Stochastic features do not seem to impair DBA's anytime performance on many problem structures and help overcome the problem of incompleteness of DBA on graphs with cycles.

5 Related Work and Discussions

It is well known that acyclic constraint problems can be solved in linear time by an arc consistency algorithm followed by a backtrack-free value assignment [5]. However, on acyclic graphs there exists no uniform distributed algorithm that is self-stabilizable in the sense that it is guaranteed to reach a solution from an arbitrary initial state [2]. In a uniform distributed algorithm [8], all nodes execute the same procedure and two nodes do not differentiate themselves. Therefore, DBA is not a uniform algorithm as two adjacent nodes can differ from each other by their different priorities. It has also been shown that by introducing only one unique node to a constraint graph, an exponential-complexity

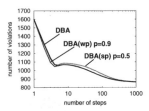

Figure 7: DBA and random DBAs on graph with 400 nodes and k=8.

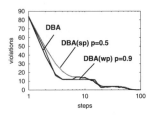

Figure 8: DBA and random DBAs on tree with depth $d = 4$ and branching factor $k = 4$.

self-stabilization algorithm exists [2]. In that regard, our results of DBA on acyclic graph indicate that node priorities are merely a tool for reducing complexity.

One related algorithm for distributed CSP is asynchronous weak-commitment (AWC) search algorithm [9; 10]. One major difference between AWC and DBA is that node priorities in AWC may change dynamically while node priorities in DBA are stationary. In contrast, constraint weights may increase dynamically in DBA while they are static in AWC. With a sufficient amount of memory to record the states (agent views) that an agent has visited, AWC is guaranteed to converge to a solution if it exists. In the worst case, the amount of memory required is exponential of the problem size. In contrast, DBA converges to a solution on acyclic graphs without any additional memory. It may be also the case that AWC does not require an exponential amount of memory to reach a solution on acyclic graph, an interesting future research topic.

Another related algorithm for distributed CSP is distributed stochastic algorithm (DSA) [3; 4; 12]. DSA is a family of stochastic search algorithms with two members being different from each other on the degrees of parallelism of agent actions. Contrasting to DBA, DSA does not require priorities among agents and is not guaranteed to find a solution either, even if one exists. Our limited experimental results showed that DBA is more efficient than DSA on acyclic graphs, which is supported by our analytical results in this paper, and on many underconstrained cyclic constraint problems. Our complete results comparing these two algorithms will be included in our final report of this research.

6 Conclusions

We closely examined the completeness and computational complexity of distributed breakout algorithm (DBA) in this paper. We showed that DBA is complete and has low polynomial complexity on acyclic graphs. This result is important as it shows the superiority of DBA over conventional local search, which does not guarantee the completeness even on a chain. The result also implies that DBA can be used as a method for self stabilization in tree-structured distributed systems. We also identified a simple worst-case node identifier arrangement on a ring in which DBA may not terminate. This helps to understand the behavior of DBA on graphs and non-binary constraint problems. We further proposed and experimentally demonstrated that randomization can overcome such worst-case situations without a significant penalty to DBA's anytime performance.

Acknowledgment

This research was funded in part by NSF Grants IIS-0196057 and IET-0111386, and in part by DARPA Cooperative Agreements F30602-00-2-0531 and F33615-01-C-1897. Thanks to Stephen Fitzpatrick, Guandong Wang and Zhao Xing for discussions and to the anonymous referees for comments.

References

[1] F. Bacchus and P. van Beek. On the conversion between non-binary and binary constraint satisfaction problems. In *Proc. AAAI-98*, pages 310–318, 1998.

[2] Z. Collin, R. Dechter, and S. Katz. Self-stabilizing distributed constraint satisfaction. *Chicago Journal of Theoretical Computer Science*, 3(4), 2000.

[3] M. Fabiunke. Parallel distributed constraint satisfaction. In *Proc. Intern. Conf. on Parallel and Distributed Processing Techniques and Applications (PDPTA-99)*, pages 1585–1591, 1999.

[4] S. Fitzpatrick and L. Meertens. An experimental assessment of a stochastic, anytime, decentralized, soft colourer for sparse graphs. In *Proc. 1st Symp. on Stochastic Algorithms: Foundations and Applications*, pages 49–64, 2001.

[5] A. K. Mackworth and E. C. Freuder. The complexity of some polynomial network consistency algorithms for constraint satisfaction problems. *Artificial Intelligence*, 25:65–74, 1985.

[6] P. Morris. The breakout method for escaping from local minima. In *Proc. AAAI-93*, pages 40–45.

[7] F. Rossi, C. Petrie, and V. Dhar. On the equivalence of constraint satisfaction problems. In *Proc. ECAI-90*, pages 550–556, 1990.

[8] G. Tel. *Introduction to Distributed Algorithms*. Cambridge University Press, 2000.

[9] M. Yokoo. *Distributed Constraint Satisfaction: Foundations of Cooperation in Multi-Agent Systems*. Springer Verlag, 2001.

[10] M. Yokoo, E. H. Durfee, T. Ishida, and K. Kuwabara. The distributed constraint satisfaction problem: formalization and algorithms. *IEEE Trans. PAMI*, 10(5):673–685, 1998.

[11] M. Yokoo and K. Hirayama. Distributed breakout algorithm for solving distributed constraint satisfaction problems. In *Proc. ICMAS-96*.

[12] W. Zhang, G. Wang, and L. Wittenburg. Distributed stochastic search for implicit distributed coordination: Parallelism, phase transitions and performance. In *submitted to AAAI-02 Workshop on Probabilistic Approaches in Search*.

[13] W. Zhang and L. Wittenburg. Implicit distributed coordination in sensor networks. In *Proc. AAMAS-02, to appear*.

Multiagent Systems
Auctions

Solving Concisely Expressed Combinatorial Auction Problems

Craig Boutilier
Department of Computer Science
University of Toronto
Toronto, ON, M5S 3H5, CANADA
cebly@cs.toronto.edu

Abstract

Combinatorial auctions provide a valuable mechanism for the allocation of goods in settings where buyer valuations exhibit complex structure with respect to substitutability and complementarity. Most algorithms are designed to work with explicit "flat" bids for concrete bundles of goods. However, logical bidding languages allow the expression of complex utility functions in a natural and concise way, and have recently attracted considerable attention.

Despite the power of logical languages, no current winner determination algorithms exploit the specific structure of logically specified bids to solve problems more effectively. In this paper, we describe techniques to do just this. Specifically, we propose a direct integer program (IP) formulation of the winner determination problem for bids in the $\mathcal{L}_{GB}$ logical language. This formulation is linear in the size of the problem and can be solved effectively using standard optimization packages. We compare this formulation and its solution time to those of the corresponding set of flat bids, demonstrating the immense utility of exploiting the structure of logically expressed bids. We also consider an extension of $\mathcal{L}_{GB}$ and show that these can also be solved using linear constraints.

1 Introduction

Combinatorial auctions (CAs) generalize traditional market mechanisms to allow the direct specification of bids over *bundles* of items [10; 11; 16]. When a bidder's preferences exhibit complex structure with respect to complementarity and substitutability, such combinatorial (or bundle) bids allow bidders to avoid the risk of obtaining incomplete bundles. Given a set of combinatorial bids, the seller then decides how best to allocate individual goods to those bundles for which bids were placed, with the aim of maximizing revenue. Because bundles generally overlap, this is—conceptually—a straightforward optimization problem, equivalent to weighted set packing. As a result, *winner determination* for CAs is NP-complete [11].

By expressing her preferences, or prices, directly over bundles, a potential buyer can, in principle, very accurately reflect her utility function, regardless of its structure. In practice, however, specifying explicit "flat" bids over all relevant bundles may be difficult: many utility functions will require the specification of a number of bundle bids that is exponential in the number of goods of interest to the bidder. This is especially true for utility functions involving the complementarities and substitutability for which CAs are best-suited. To circumvent this, several researchers have proposed *logical bidding languages* that allow might allow complex utility functions to be expressed relatively concisely in a suitable language [12; 13; 5; 8; 2]. The recent $\mathcal{L}_{GB}$ language of Boutilier and Hoos [2], for example, allows goods to be "joined" using logical connectives, and prices to be attached to arbitrary subformulae. Despite their attractiveness, the computational aspects of logical bidding languages have received little attention. Indeed, no studies of which we are aware exploit the structure of logically specified bids in winner determination. Instead, a set of logical bids is usually converted to an equivalent set of flat bids and solved using methods designed for flat bids.

In this paper, we solve the winner determination problem for $\mathcal{L}_{GB}$ problems without conversion to flat bids. Rather we directly formulate the optimization problem in a way that exploits the structure of underlying bids. More precisely, we describe a very concise integer program (IP) formulation of the winner determination problem for $\mathcal{L}_{GB}$ that makes the logical structure explicit. The well-documented fact that the number of flat bids required to capture a particular problem may be exponentially larger than the set of logical bids suggests that this strategy could be useful. However, it could be that standard optimization techniques can discover the "lost" structure in a set of flat bids (and hence solve the flat problem effectively) or that the structure cannot be exploited (and hence the structured problem cannot be solved effectively). Our results show that neither is the case: the direct solution of structured problems offers immense computational savings in winner determination. Since logical languages generally, and $\mathcal{L}_{GB}$ specifically, offer advantages both in terms of the expression of bids and in winner determination, we expect that this approach will prove vital for handling large CAs.

The paper is organized as follows. We describe relevant background on CAs, winner determination, and bidding languages in Section 2. We focus on the $\mathcal{L}_{GB}$ language since it is fully expressive, and strictly more compact than any other language in the literature. In Section 3 we describe the IP formulation of the winner determination problem for $\mathcal{L}_{GB}$. Through the introduction of several auxiliary variables, this formulation can be made very compact, linear in the size of the set of logical bids. We describe an extension of $\mathcal{L}_{GB}$ and how it also can be modeled using a concise set of constraints. We also show how an equivalent set of flat bids can be constructed and solved using the "standard" IP formulation. We present empirical results in Section 4 showing that conversion to flat bids cannot be competitive for problems of even moderate size.

2 CAs and Bidding Languages

In this section, we briefly review CAs and logical bidding languages.

2.1 Combinatorial Auctions

We suppose a seller has a set of goods $G = \{g_1, \ldots, g_n\}$ to be auctioned. Potential buyers value different subsets or *bundles* of goods, $b \subseteq G$, and offer bids of the form $\langle b, p \rangle$ where p is the amount the buyer is willing to pay for bundle b. We often use the term "flat bid" for such a bundle bid, to distinguish it from the structured bids we consider below. Given a collection of bids $B = \{\langle b_i, p_i \rangle : i \leq m\}$, the seller must find an allocation of goods to bids that maximizes revenue. We define an *allocation* to be any $L = \{\langle b_i, p_i \rangle\} \subseteq B$ such that the bundles b_i making up L are disjoint. The *value* of an allocation $v(L)$ is given by $\sum \{p_i : \langle b_i, p_i \rangle \in L\}$. An *optimal allocation* is any allocation L with maximal value (taken over the space of allocations). The *winner determination* problem is that of finding an optimal allocation given a bid set B. We sometimes consider *assignments* $A : G \to B$ of goods to bids. Assignment A induces allocation L_A whose bids are those that have been assigned all required goods (i.e., $b_i \subseteq A^{-1}(\langle b_i, p_i \rangle)$).

The winner determination problem is a straightforward combinatorial optimization problem, and can be formulated quite directly as an IP. Let x_i be a boolean variable indicating whether bid b_i is satisfied. Then we wish to solve the IP:

$$\text{Maximize:} \quad \sum_i p_i x_i \qquad (1)$$

$$\text{Subject to:} \quad \sum \{x_i : g_k \in b_i\} \leq 1, \forall k \leq n \qquad (2)$$

This formulation has m variables (one per bid) and n constraints (one per good), with constraints having z terms on average, where z is the average number of bids in which a good occurs. Winner determination is equivalent to the weighted set packing problem [11] and as such is NP-complete. Despite this, generic combinatorial optimization techniques seem to work quite well in practice. For example, results reported in [1; 15] suggest that using generic CPLEX IP solution techniques is reasonably competitive with recent algorithms designed specifically for CAs. Recent search algorithms—both complete methods [4; 12; 14] as well as stochastic techniques [5]—have been proposed in the AI literature and have also proven quite successful solving problems of reasonable size, often running faster than CPLEX.

2.2 Logical Bidding Languages

Most work on combinatorial auctions assumes that a bid is expressed using a simple bundle of goods associated with a price for that bundle. However, a buyer with a complex utility function will generally need to express multiple flat bids in order to accurately reflect her utility function. Logical bidding languages overcome this by allowing a bidder to express a single bid in which the logical structure of the utility function is captured. A number of different types of bidding languages have been proposed in the literature, among these languages that allow flat bids to be combined logically [12; 13; 8], and that allow goods to be combined logically [5].

The recent $\mathcal{L}_{GB}$ language of Boutilier and Hoos [2] generalizes these languages by allowing goods to be "joined" using logical connectives, and prices to be attached to arbitrary subformulae. $\mathcal{L}_{GB}$ is fully expressive (i.e., can express any utility function over goods) and is strictly more compact than existing languages (i.e., any bid expressible in these languages can be expressed at least as concisely in $\mathcal{L}_{GB}$). Indeed, for certain natural classes of utility functions, $\mathcal{L}_{GB}$ can express bids exponentially more compactly than any proposed languages [2]. For this reason, we focus on $\mathcal{L}_{GB}$.

Let G denote the set of goods, forming the atomic elements of the language. The syntax of $\mathcal{L}_{GB}$ is defined as follows:

- $\langle g, p \rangle \in \mathcal{L}_{GB}$, for any good $g \in G$ and any non-negative price $p \in \mathbf{R}_0^+$.
- If $b_1, b_2 \in \mathcal{L}_{GB}$, then $\langle b_1 \wedge b_2, p \rangle$, $\langle b_1 \vee b_2, p \rangle$, and $\langle b_1 \oplus b_2, p \rangle$ are all in $\mathcal{L}_{GB}$ for any non-negative price p.

Bids so-defined correspond to arbitrary propositional formulae over the goods, using connectives $\wedge$ (conjunction), $\vee$ (disjunction) and $\oplus$ (XOR), where each subformula is annotated with a price. We often don't mention the price for a subformula if $p = 0$, and loosely say that no price is associated with such a subformula. Examples of sentences include

$$(a : 1 \wedge b : 2) : 5 \quad \text{and} \quad (a \vee b) : 2 \oplus c : 3.$$

A sentence $b \in \mathcal{L}_{GB}$ is a *generalized logical bid (GLB)*. The *formula associated with b*, denoted $\Phi(b)$, is the logical formula obtained by removing all prices from subformulae.

The semantics of GLBs defines the price to be paid by a bidder given a particular assignment of goods to her GLB. Roughly, the underlying idea is that the *value* of a GLB b is given by summing the prices associated with all satisfied subformulae (with one exception). We first define what it means for an assignment to satisfy a (priceless) formula.

Let A be an assignment $A : G \to B$ of goods to GLBs. Let $\Phi(b)$ be the formula associated with b. We write $\sigma(\Phi(b), A) = 1$ to denote that A *satisfies* b, and $\sigma(b, A) = 0$ to denote that A does not satisfy b. The relation is defined as follows:

- If $\Phi(b) = g$ for some $g \in G$ then $\sigma(\Phi(b), A) = 1$ iff $A(g) = b$.
- If $\Phi(b) = \Phi_1 \vee \Phi_2$ or $\Phi(b) = \Phi_1 \oplus \Phi_2$ then $\sigma(\Phi(b), A) = \max(\sigma(\Phi_1, A), \sigma(\Phi_2, A))$
- If $\Phi(b) = \Phi_1 \wedge \Phi_2$ then $\sigma(\Phi(b), A) = \min(\sigma(\Phi_1, A), \sigma(\Phi_2, A))$

Given a bid b and assignment A of goods to bids, we define the *value of b under A*, denoted $\Psi(b, A)$, recursively. If g is a good, b_1, b_2 are bids, and p is a price:

$$\Psi(\langle g, p \rangle, A) = p \cdot \sigma(g, A)$$
$$\Psi(\langle b_1 \wedge b_2, p \rangle, A) =$$
$$\Psi(b_1, A) + \Psi(b_2, A) + p \cdot \sigma(\Phi(b_1) \wedge \Phi(b_2), A)$$
$$\Psi(\langle b_1 \vee b_2, p \rangle, A) =$$
$$\Psi(b_1, A) + \Psi(b_2, A) + p \cdot \sigma(\Phi(b_1) \vee \Phi(b_2), A)$$
$$\Psi(\langle b_1 \oplus b_2, p \rangle, A) =$$
$$\max\{\Psi(b_1, A), \Psi(b_2, A)\} + p \cdot \sigma(\Phi(b_1) \vee \Phi(b_2), A)$$

Intuitively, the value of a bid is the value of its components, together with the additional price p if certain logical conditions are met. $\langle b_1 \wedge b_2, p \rangle$ pays price p if the formulae associated with both b_1 and b_2 are both satisfied; $\langle b_1 \vee b_2, p \rangle$ and $\langle b_1 \oplus b_2, p \rangle$ both pay price p if either (or both) of b_1 or b_2 are satisfied. The semantics of $\vee$ and $\oplus$ differ in how subformula value is used. Specifically, the value of a disjunctive bid given an assignment is the sum of the values of the subformulae: in this sense, both subformulae are of value to the bidder. In contrast, a "valuative XOR" bid allows only the maximum value of its subformulae to be paid: thus the subformulae are viewed as substitutes.[1] It is important to realize that the valuative XOR connective does not have a logical XOR interpretation; rather it refers to the valuation of the formula, stating that the bidder is willing to pay for the satisfaction of at most one subformula. Notice that an assumption of free disposal is built in to the semantics.

We refer to [2] for further details of the language and examples of its expressive power. We give three examples here to illustrate the intuitions. Consider the bid

$$\langle \langle a, 1 \rangle \wedge \langle b, 1 \rangle \wedge \langle c, 3 \rangle \wedge \langle d, 5 \rangle, 50 \rangle.$$

This might reflect that a, b, c, and d are complementary goods with joint value 50, and that the individual goods have some intrinsic (e.g., salvage) value over and above that of their role within the group. As a second example, consider

$$\langle \langle a, 1 \rangle \vee \langle b, 1 \rangle \vee \langle 3, c \rangle \vee \langle d, 5 \rangle, 50 \rangle.$$

Here the individual goods are substitutes: they provide a basic functionality of value 50, but perhaps do so with differing quality (or each has different intrinsic value) reflected in the "bonus" associated with each good.

As a final example, consider a scenario in which we have a number of goods $\{r_1, \cdots, r_k\}$ whose utilities/prices p_i are conditionally *dependent* on the presence of another good m but are (conditionally) additive *independent* of each other [2]. For instance, think of the r_i as resources or raw materials, and of m as a machine used for processing those resources. This situation can be captured using a single GLB of the form:

$$\langle m \wedge r_1, p_1 \rangle \vee \langle m \wedge r_2, p_2 \rangle \vee \cdots \vee \langle m \wedge r_k, p_k \rangle$$

To express the same utility function using other languages would require a number of bids exponential in k (essentially

---

requiring the enumeration of all subsets of resources). For example, with one machine m and four resources r_1, r_2, r_3, r_4 (worth 1, 2, 3, and 4, respectively), we'd need the following bid:

$$\langle mr_1, 1 \rangle \vee \langle mr_2, 2 \rangle \vee \langle mr_3, 3 \rangle \vee \langle mr_4, 4 \rangle$$
$$\vee \langle mr_1 r_2, 3 \rangle \vee \langle mr_1 r_3, 4 \rangle \vee \langle mr_1 r_4, 5 \rangle \vee \langle mr_2 r_3, 5 \rangle$$
$$\vee \langle mr_2 r_4, 6 \rangle \vee \langle mr_3 r_4, 7 \rangle \vee \langle mr_1 r_2 r_3, 6 \rangle \vee \langle mr_1 r_2 r_4, 7 \rangle$$
$$\vee \langle mr_1 r_3 r_4, 8 \rangle \vee \langle mr_2 r_3 r_4, 9 \rangle \vee \langle mr_1 r_2 r_3 r_4, 10 \rangle$$

We note that each of the connectives is commutative and associative, so we can safely treat them as having more than two operands (e.g., it is legitimate to refer to the conjunction of $k > 2$ bids).

The notion of a *k-of* bid, explored in the context of logical bids without priced subformulae [5], can be extended to $\mathcal{L}_{GB}$ quite readily. Let $\mathcal{L}_{GB}^{k\text{-}of}$ denote the extension of $\mathcal{L}_{GB}$ with the *k-of* operator. Intuitively, $\langle k\text{-}of(b_1, b_2, \ldots, b_d), p \rangle$ is satisfied if any k of the d bids $b_1, \ldots, b_d$ is satisfied (and a price of p is associated with its satisfaction). As in the semantics above, the value of a *k-of* bid is determined by the price p as well as the values of any satisfied subformulae.[2]

Since combinatorial auctions are still relatively rare in practice, it is difficult to say whether $\mathcal{L}_{GB}$ can naturally and concisely express utility functions that are likely to arise in practice. However, the examples above suggest that it does capture a lot of the natural structure in utility functions. In addition, since it can directly "emulate" any existing bidding language, it should be considered state of the art at this point.

3 Winner Determination for LGB

The expressive advantages of logical bidding languages are readily apparent. One might also hope that such languages permit CAs to be solved more effectively as well. If one can express bids concisely, there must be structure in the underlying utility function. If this is so, we should be able to exploit this structure computationally in winner determination. Unfortunately, to date there has been no serious investigation of this possibility.

There are several ways to exploit logical structure computationally. First, one might convert the logical bids to a set of flat bids and hope that existing algorithms discover the "hidden" structure. Evidence that this might work was described in [5], but we will show that for realistic sized problems this approach is doomed. Second, one might devise special purpose procedures for winner determination that exploit the logical structure, such as the stochastic local search procedure suggested in [2].

Finally, one could simply formulate the optimization problem directly in terms of $\mathcal{L}_{GB}$ bids and use generic IP solvers to solve the problem. It is this final approach that we now consider. Expressing logical relationships among goods directly in an IP is reminiscent of the use of optimization techniques to solve problems in logical inference, as proposed by Chandru and Hooker [3].

---

[1]This semantics of XOR is just one of several natural interpretations. The practical use of XOR may determine other semantics.

[2]This extends the treatment of *k-of* bids in [5], which allowed choosing any k of n *goods* rather than *bids*.

3.1 A Direct IP Formulation for LGB

Our aim is to formulate an IP that directly expresses the winner determination problem for a set of $\mathcal{L}_{GB}$ bids. We first consider the objective function and then the constraints. We assume a set of n goods $\{g_i : i \leq n\}$ and m bids $\{b_i : i \leq m\}$ expressed in $\mathcal{L}_{GB}$. We use the following variables:

- $x_{ij} \in \{0, 1\}$ for each good g_i that occurs in bid b_j: true (1) if g_i is assigned to b_j.

- $s_\beta \in \{0, 1\}$ for each subformula β of any bid: true (1) if β is satisfied by the optimal assignment.

- v_β for each subformula β of any bid: this denotes the value of β under the optimal assignment.[3]

- $t_\beta \in \{0, 1\}$ for each subformula β of any bid that is an *immediate* subformula of an XOR: true (1) if β is the (unique) formula that contributes value to the encompassing XOR.

As a trivial example, consider two bids:

$$b_1 = \langle\langle\langle a, 1\rangle \vee \langle b, 2\rangle, 3\rangle \oplus \langle c, 3\rangle, 7\rangle \tag{3}$$

$$b_2 = \langle\langle\langle a, 1\rangle \wedge \langle b, 2\rangle \wedge \langle d, 1\rangle, 3\rangle \vee \langle c, 4\rangle, 8\rangle \tag{4}$$

There are seven variables x_{ij} corresponding to the assignment of (relevant) goods to each bid. b_1 has five s-variables, one per subformula (a, b, $a \vee b$, c, $(a \vee b) \oplus c$), while b_2 also has five s-variables (note that we view $\wedge$ as a ternary connective in this example). There is also a corresponding v-variable for each subformula of each bid. Finally, b_1 has two t-variables, one for subformula $a \vee b$ and one for c, since these are the immediate subformulae of an XOR. The number of variables in linear in the size of the logical formulation of the bids.

The objective function is straightforward:

Maximize: $\sum\{v_\beta : \beta$ *corresponds to a top-level bid*$\}$

In our example, the objective function is $v_{\beta_1} + v_{\beta_2}$, where v_{β_1} is the v-variable for b_1's formula, $(a \vee b) \oplus c$, and similarly for b_2. There is one term in the objective for each bid.

A set of constraints is imposed for each subformula of each bid. The constraints will vary with the main connective. The constraints place upper bounds on the values of all variables, since the objective value can only increase with increasing variable values. For each atomic subformula β of the form $\langle g_i, p\rangle$ in bid b_j, we impose two constraints:

$$s_\beta \leq x_{ij}; \qquad v_\beta \leq p \cdot s_\beta$$

Thus the formula is satisfied only if g_i is assigned to b_j (and value is determined correspondingly).

For each subformula $\beta = \langle\beta_1 \vee \cdots \vee \beta_d, p\rangle$, we impose two constraints:

$$s_\beta \leq \sum_{i \leq d} s_{\beta_i}; \qquad v_\beta \leq p \cdot s_\beta + \sum_{i \leq d} v_{\beta_i}$$

This ensures β is considered satisfied if any subformula is, and assigns value as dictated by our semantics.

For each subformula $\beta = \langle\beta_1 \wedge \cdots \wedge \beta_d, p\rangle$, we impose two constraints:

$$d \cdot s_\beta \leq \sum_{i \leq d} s_{\beta_i}; \qquad v_\beta \leq p \cdot s_\beta + \sum_{i \leq d} v_{\beta_i}$$

This ensures β is considered satisfied if all subformula are.

Finally, for each subformula $\beta = \langle\beta_1 \oplus \cdots \oplus \beta_d, p\rangle$, we impose four constraints:

$$s_\beta \leq \sum_{i \leq d} s_{\beta_i}; \qquad v_\beta \leq p \cdot s_\beta + \sum_{i \leq d} v_{\beta_i}$$

$$\sum_{i \leq d} t_{\beta_i} \leq 1; \qquad v_{\beta_i} \leq maxval \cdot t_{\beta_i}, \ \forall i \leq d$$

The penultimate constraint ensures that only one subformula of the XOR is *selected* for contribution of value to the XOR as a whole, while the final constraint ensures that only the selected subformula has positive value. *maxval* is a large constant assured to be larger than the value of any formula.[4]

The number of constraints is linear in the number of subformulae (hence in the size of the bid specification), and the size of each constraint is bounded by the "actual" arity of the connective involved. Thus, the IP formulation is very compact.

The IP formulation also extends naturally to $\mathcal{L}_{GB}^{k\text{-}of}$. Let β be a subformula of the form $\langle k\text{-}of(\beta_1, \beta_2, \ldots, \beta_d), p\rangle$. We introduce a new variable n_β for each $k\text{-}of$ bid denoting the number of satisfied subformulae. We then impose the following three linear constraints:

$$n_\beta \leq \sum_{i \leq d} s_{\beta_i}; \qquad s_\beta \cdot k \leq n_\beta$$

$$v_\beta \leq p \cdot s_\beta + \sum_{i \leq d} v_{\beta_i}$$

The first constraint ensures that number n_β of subbids counted as satisfied is legitimate, while the second ensures the $k\text{-}of$ bid is satisfied only if at least k of the subbids are satisfied.

3.2 Converting LGB to Flat Bids

The utility function represented by a GLB b can be captured using an equivalent set of flat bids. Let $G(b)$ denote the set of goods occurring in b. The required set of flat bids $f(b)$ can be generated using a very simple strategy: since each good mentioned in b may contribute to value, every subset $s \subseteq G(b)$ can be viewed as a potential flat bid having some utility to the customer, and this utility can be determined by calculating the value of the assignment s to b. Of course, only one such subset is of interest, so we insert a single dummy good into each flat bid (subset) to ensure that only one such bid can be satisfied. More precisely:

$$f(b) = \{\langle s \cup \{d_b\}, \Psi(b, s)\rangle : s \subseteq G(b)\}$$

where d_b is a dummy good associated with GLB b. The winner determination problem for $\mathcal{L}_{GB}$ can be solved by converting each GLB b into a set of flat bids, and solving the corresponding "flat" problem using these.

---

[3]For simplicity, we treat this as an integer, which is valid if all prices are integral. Allowing a mixed formulation is not problematic.

[4]This constraint can be formulated without such a constant through the introduction of additional variables.

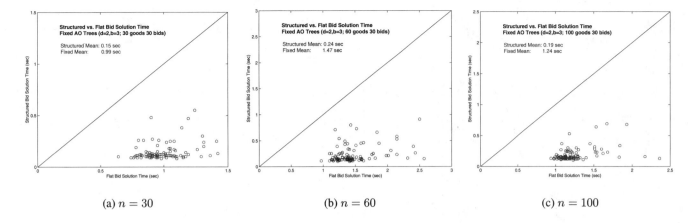

| (a) $n = 30$ | (b) $n = 60$ | (c) $n = 100$ |

Figure 1: Flat vs. structured solution times with varying number of goods

4 Empirical Results

In this section we report on experiments run to compare the relative effectiveness of solving the direct IP formulation of an $\mathcal{L}_{GB}$ problem with the IP formulation for the corresponding set of flat bids. In all experiments, the CPLEX optimization package (Version 7.1.0) was used to solve the IP. CPLEX has a number of strategies for solving IPs, and algorithm choice was left to the software. Running times reported include pre-solve times, but do not include read times (which would put the large flat bid formulations at a disadvantage). All experiments were run under Linux with a 933MHz, PIII, 512Mb PC.

A number of researchers have proposed candidate problem distributions for CAs in order to facilitate the comparison of different evaluation techniques. Many of these problems are very abstract and it is unclear how these might arise in practice. In an effort to alleviate this problem, a suite of test problems—or more precisely a suite of schemes for generating random test problems—has been proposed that draws on somewhat more realistic intuitions [7]. This collection of problems, CATS, arguably reflects structure that is more likely to arise in practical problems. Unfortunately, the problems in this suite are largely designed to generate structured "subsets" of goods, and hence reflect little of the natural structure suited to a logical language such as $\mathcal{L}_{GB}$. For this reason, we consider the generation of logical bids directly. We first consider some abstract problems, and then consider a class of problems that exhibit the same type of "natural" structure that motivated the development of CATS. The development of a suite of realistic "logical" test problems is an important future goal.

Our first set of experiments focus on randomly generated

GLBs with conjunction and disjunction.[5] Bids are generated using randomly constructed parse trees of a given depth and branching factor. One parameterized distribution we consider is RandAO-d-b-m-n-p: these problems have m bids over n goods, with each bid having a parse tree of depth d and branching factor b. At each interior node a connective $\wedge$ or $\vee$ is inserted (with equal probability), while at each leaf a random good is inserted (drawn uniformly). At each node (interior or leaf), a price is included, drawn uniformly from the range $[0, p]$. For example, the bid

$$\langle\langle\langle a, 2\rangle \wedge \langle b, 3\rangle, 0\rangle \wedge \langle\langle a, 2\rangle \wedge \langle c, 0\rangle, 1\rangle, 20\rangle$$

is a bid with depth $d = 2$ and branching factor $b = 2$. We also consider variants AltAO-d-b-m-n-p and AltOA-d-b-m-n-p, where the connectives $\wedge$ and $\vee$ strictly alternate at each level of the tree (starting with $\wedge$ at the root of AO-trees, and $\vee$ at the root of OA-trees).

We start with the RandAO distributions with $m = n = 30$.[6] On very small GLBs, with $b = 2$ and $d = 2$ (thus inducing a tree with four leaves, and at most 15 flat bids), the IP solution of the flat bids dominates that of the structured bids, with mean times of 0.02s and 0.06s, respectively. However, if we increase the branching factor to 3 (thus each GLB corresponds to as many as 511 flat bids), structured solutions dominate flat solutions, with mean times of 0.15s and 0.99s, respectively. The scatterplot of solution times shown in Figure 1(a) shows that the the structured solution time is less than the flat time on each problem instance. Figures 1(b) and (c) show the relative solution times with larger numbers of goods: with $n = 60$, the average solution times are 0.24s and 1.47s, respectively, while with $n = 100$, average times are 0.19s and 1.24s, respectively.

The advantages of solving structured CAs directly is even more apparent with only slightly larger problems.

---

[5]We report on XOR and *k-of* bids in the longer version of the paper. Results are similar.

[6]In all experiments, $p = 50$. All results are averages over 100 random instances except where noted.

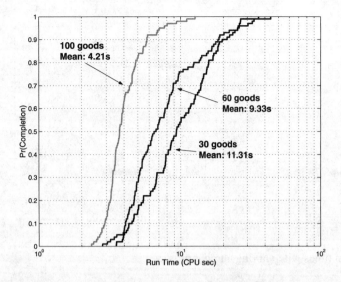

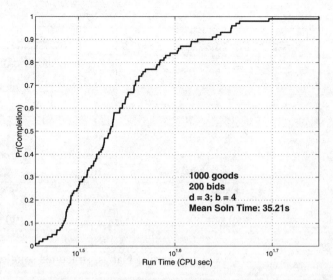

Figure 2: Cumulative runtime distributions for different numbers of goods. RandAO distributions, with $d = 3, b = 4$ and 30 bids. Number of goods: 30, 60, 100. Each distribution generated from 100 problem instances.

Figure 3: Cumulative runtime distribution for large problems ($d = 3, b = 4, n = 1000, m = 200$). Generated from 100 problem instances.

The following table shows the solution times (in seconds) for five random instances with $d = 2, b = 4$ (each GLB corresponds to 65535 flat bids), 20 goods and 40 bids:

Instance	I1	I2	I3	I4	I5	Mean
Structured	0.14	0.10	0.12	0.22	0.14	**0.14**
Flat	364.9	172.2	218.3	184.8	169.4	**221.9**

Even though these structured bids are of fairly small size (with only 16 leaves in the parse tree), solving the flat version of the problem takes at least three orders of magnitude longer.

The next results illustrate run times on larger problems, for which solving flat versions of the problem proved infeasible. Figure 2 shows the change in runtime distributions as the good:bid ratio varies. In these problems $d = 3, b = 4$ (each GLB thus corresponds to as many as 2^{64} flat bids). In each instance, 30 bids are present. Each line shows the cumulative runtime distribution for a different number of goods (hence the x-axis shows the run time, while the y-axis shows the probability that an instance will be solved by that time). Note that as the number of goods increases, random problems become less constrained and hence somewhat easier to solve. Figure 3 shows the runtime distribution for similar problems but with a much larger number of bids (200) and goods (1000). The mean solution time of 35.21s is very encouraging for such large problems, where the corresponding flat bids sets could scarcely be enumerated.

Finally, Figure 4 shows the runtime distribution for 10 problem instances for GLBs with $d = 4$ and $b = 4$: the set of flat bids for each such GLB could be as large as 2^{256} (if we have at least 256 goods from which to draw). Each problem has 30 GLBs over 100 goods. The mean solution time is 472.9 seconds. It scarcely needs to be mentioned that using flat bids can't even be contemplated for problems of this magnitude.

Further empirical study is needed of different structured bid distributions. While for problems involving GLBs of more than depth 2 and branching factor 3, flat solution methods will unlikely be feasible for any distribution, for "small" GLBs, the specific problem distributions may prove more or less advantageous for flat formulations. Studies of AltAO and AltOA distributions, for instance, with $d = 2$ and $b = 3$ (these bids are the same "size" as those evaluated in Figure 1), reveal that the flat IP is competitive with the structured IP for AltOA: over 100 instances, the flat mean solution time is 1.08s, while the structured mean is 1.07s; furthermore the flat solution time has much lower variance. In contrast, the advantage of the structured over the flat IP is even greater in AltAO problems than for RandAO: the structured technique takes on average 0.15s, while flat takes 1.07s.

We have not reported on XOR or *k-of* bids. The structured IP retains its extreme advantage over the flat IP, naturally; but it is worth pointing out that different semantics for XOR have fairly dramatic impact on the structured solution times, while seeming to have less impact on the flat technique. We have done only preliminary experimentation with *k-of* bids, but these suggest that the structured IP can handle problems of the same order of magnitude reported above.

Other variants of these problem distributions need to be considered as well. The abstract distributions above assign prices randomly to subformulae, without regard to the number of items required to satisfy them. We plan to study more biased (and realistic) price distributions in the future.

The second set of problems we consider are motivated by more realistic considerations. The parameterized distribution Mach-n-m-r-b-p captures the resource allocation problems discussed in Section 2.2. This distribution assumes a set of m machines and r resources available for auction. Each of the b bidders wants one (specific) machine from this collection and n of the r resources. The form of the bid is exactly as

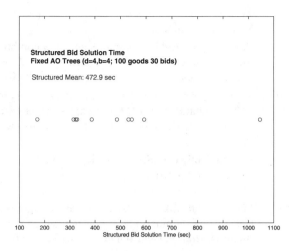

Figure 4: Runtimes for very large problems ($d = 4, b = 4, n = 100, m = 30$), over 10 instances.

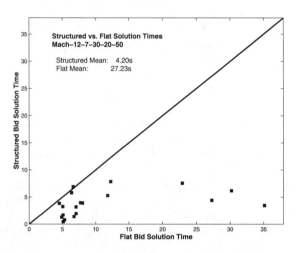

Figure 5: Flat vs. structured solution times for small Mach problems ($n = 12, m = 7, r = 30, b = 20$).

specified in Section 2.2: a bidder is willing to pay some price p_i for the conjunction $m \wedge r_i$ for each of its requested resources r_i. The price p_i is drawn uniformly from the range $[0, p]$. The machine and resources needed by each bidder are also drawn uniformly from the set of machines and resources.

We first compare the structured and flat solution methods on the Mach distribution with $m = 7, r = 30$, each bidder requesting $n = 12$ distinct resources, and $b = 20$ bidders.[7] The scatterplot of solution times shown in Figure 5 shows that the structured solution time is considerably less than the flat time on each of 20 problem instances, even for such small problems.[8] The mean solution times are 4.2s and 27.2s for the structured and flat methods, respectively.

For even slightly larger problems, solving the set of flat in-

---

[7]In all Mach-distribution experiments, $p = 50$.

[8]One outlying point is removed: for this problem, the structured solution time was 10.9s, while the flat solution time was 325.4s.

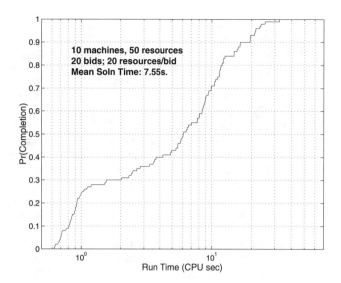

Figure 6: Cumulative runtime distribution for medium sized Mach problems ($n = 20, m = 10, r = 50, b = 20$). Generated from 100 problem instances.

stances becomes infeasible. A systematic test of the Mach-15-8-50-20-50 distribution on flat bids is impractical. For one typical instance, the solution time was 1933.14s (approximately half an hour). By contrast, the runtime distribution based on 100 random problem instances for the harder problem distribution Mach-20-10-50-20-50 is shown in Figure 6. The mean solution time over these instances is 7.55s. Note that in each instance, 20 bidders are competing for 10 machines. Furthermore, since each bidder requests 20 resources from the set of 50, each of the 20 GLBs in these instances would correspond to 2^{20} flat bids.

Finally, the following table shows the structured solution times (in seconds) for five random instances with drawn from Mach-30-10-200-100-50:

Instance	I1	I2	I3	I4	I5	Mean
Time	114.0	25.3	85.9	148.6	157.2	**106.2**

Again we see that the structured formulation offers considerable advantages, allowing very large resource allocation problems to be solved effectively.

5 Concluding Remarks

We have described a technique for producing a compact IP reflecting the winner determination problem for CAs involving the generalized logical bidding language $\mathcal{L}_{GB}$ and its extension $\mathcal{L}_{GB}^{k\text{-}of}$. Apart from the expressive advantages of $\mathcal{L}_{GB}$, our empirical results demonstrate the unequivocal superiority of computational methods that directly exploit the logical structure of these bids in winner determination. We have provided evidence for several representative problem distributions, though the combinatorics alone imply that these advantages will obtain for any distribution over GLBs of moderate size.

A number of extensions of this work are being pursued. One is the extension of $\mathcal{L}_{GB}$ and the IP formulation to multi-unit CAs. This extension is straightforward; we expect the same computational advantages to persist. We are also currently exploring the use of stochastic local search techniques for solving CAs expressed using $\mathcal{L}_{GB}$. Specifically, the procedure proposed in [2] seems to provide a useful anytime method for solving bids expressed in $\mathcal{L}_{GB}$ in a way that exploits their logical structure.

The development of realistic problem distributions for logically structured utility functions remains an important task. The Mach distributions proposed here seem to reflect natural intuitions about certain types of resource allocation problems, but additional problem classes are needed to fully verify the usefulness of our technique. A test suite for logically specified CAs, similar to CATS [7], would be a great step in this direction.

Finally, the problem of sharing partial solutions across related CAs might be one that can readily exploit logical structure. Related CAs arise, for instance, in the implementation of generalized Vickrey-Clarke-Groves mechanisms [9; 6], where multiple CAs are solved with different bidders removed. Logical structure in utility functions could be used to facilitate the "transfer" of partial solutions.

Acknowledgements

Thanks to Holger Hoos and Tuomas Sandholm for their helpful discussions and the anonymous referees for their suggestions. This research was supported by CombineNet, Inc.

References

[1] Arne Andersson, Mattias Tenhunen, and Fredrik Ygge. Integer programming for combinatorial auction winner determination. In *Proceedings of the Fourth International Conference on Multiagent Systems*, pages 39–46, Boston, 2000.

[2] Craig Boutilier and Holger H. Hoos. Bidding languages for combinatorial auctions. In *Proceedings of the Seventeenth International Joint Conference on Artificial Intelligence*, pages 1211–1217, Seattle, 2001.

[3] Vijay Chandru and John N. Hooker. *Optimization Methods for Logical Inference*. Wiley, New York, 1999.

[4] Yuzo Fujisima, Kevin Leyton-Brown, and Yoav Shoham. Taming the computational complexity of combinatorial auctions. In *Proceedings of the Sixteenth International Joint Conference on Artificial Intelligence*, pages 548–553, Stockholm, 1999.

[5] Holger H. Hoos and Craig Boutilier. Solving combinatorial auctions using stochastic local search. In *Proceedings of the Seventeenth National Conference on Artificial Intelligence*, pages 22–29, Austin, TX, 2000.

[6] Noa E. Kfir-Dahav, Dov Monderer, and Moshe Tennenholtz. Mechanism design for resource bounded agents. In *Proceedings of the Fourth International Conference on Multiagent Systems*, Boston, 2000.

[7] Kevin Leyton-Brown, Mark Pearson, and Yoav Shoham. Towards a universal test suite for combinatorial auction algorithms. In *ACM Conference on Electronic Commerce (EC-2000)*, pages 66–76, Minneapolis, MI, 2000.

[8] Noam Nisan. Bidding and allocations in combinatorial auctions. In *ACM Conference on Electronic Commerce (EC-2000)*, pages 1–12, Minneapolis, MI, 2000.

[9] Noam Nisan and Amir Ronen. Computationally feasible VCG mechanisms. In *ACM Conference on Electronic Commerce (EC-2000)*, pages 242–252, Minneapolis, MI, 2000.

[10] S. J. Rassenti, V. L. Smith, and R. L. Bulfin. A combinatorial auction mechanism for airport time slot allocation. *Bell Journal of Economics*, 13:402–417, 1982.

[11] Michael H. Rothkopf, Aleksander Pekeč, and Ronald M. Harstad. Computationally manageable combinatorial auctions. *Management Science*, 44(8):1131–1147, 1998.

[12] Tuomas Sandholm. An algorithm for optimal winner determination in combinatorial auctions. In *Proceedings of the Sixteenth International Joint Conference on Artificial Intelligence*, pages 542–547, Stockholm, 1999. Extended version, Washington Univ. Report WUCS-99-01.

[13] Tuomas Sandholm. eMediator: a next generation electronic commerce server. In *Proceedings of the Fourth International Conference on Autonomous Agents*, pages 341–348, Barcelona, 2000.

[14] Tuomas Sandholm, Subash Suri, Andrew Gilpin, and David Levine. CABOB: A fast optimal algorithm for combinatorial auctions. In *Proceedings of the Seventeenth International Joint Conference on Artificial Intelligence*, pages 1102–1108, Seattle, 2001.

[15] Dale Schuurmans, Finnegan Southey, and Robert C. Holte. The exponentiated subgradient algorithm for heuristic boolean programming. In *Proceedings of the Seventeenth International Joint Conference on Artificial Intelligence*, pages 334–341, Seattle, 2001.

[16] Michael P. Wellman, William E. Walsh, Peter R. Wurman, and Jeffrey K. MacKie-Mason. Auction protocols for decentralized scheduling. *Games and Economic Behavior*, 35:271–303, 2001.

Partial-revelation VCG Mechanism for Combinatorial Auctions

Wolfram Conen
XONAR GmbH
Wodanstr. 7
42555 Velbert, Germany
conen@gmx.de

Tuomas Sandholm
Carnegie Mellon University
Computer Science Department
5000 Forbes Avenue
Pittsburgh, PA 15213
sandholm@cs.cmu.edu

Abstract

Winner determination in combinatorial auctions has received significant interest in the AI community in the last 3 years. Another difficult problem in combinatorial auctions is that of eliciting the bidders' preferences. We introduce a progressive, partial-revelation mechanism that determines an efficient allocation and the Vickrey payments. The mechanism is based on a family of algorithms that explore the natural lattice structure of the bidders' combined preferences. The mechanism elicits utilities in a natural sequence, and aims at keeping the amount of elicited information and the effort to compute the information minimal. We present analytical results on the amount of elicitation. We show that no value-querying algorithm that is constrained to querying feasible bundles can save more elicitation than one of our algorithms. We also show that one of our algorithms can determine the Vickrey payments as a costless by-product of determining an optimal allocation.

Introduction

Combinatorial auctions, where agents can submit bids on *bundles* of items, are economically efficient mechanisms for selling m items to bidders, and are attractive when the bidders' valuations on bundles exhibit *complementarity* (a bundle of items is worth more than the sum of its parts) and/or *substitutability* (a bundle is worth less than the sum of its parts). Determining the winners in such auctions is a complex optimization problem that has recently received considerable attention (e.g., (Rothkopf, Pekeč, & Harstad 1998; Sandholm 2002; Fujishima, Leyton-Brown, & Shoham 1999; Sandholm & Suri 2000; Nisan 2000; Andersson, Tenhunen, & Ygge 2000; Sandholm *et al.* 2001)).

An equally important problem, which has received much less attention, is that of bidding. There are $2^m - 1$ bundles, and each agent may need to bid on all of them to fully express its preferences. This can be undesirable for any of several reasons: (1a) determining one's valuation for any given bundle can be computationally intractable (Sandholm 1993; 2000b; Parkes 1999; Larson & Sandholm 2001); (1b) there is a huge number of bundles to evaluate; (2) communicating the bids can incur prohibitive overhead (e.g., network traffic); and (3) agents may prefer not to reveal all of their val-

uation information due to reasons of privacy or long-term competitiveness. Appropriate bidding languages (Sandholm 2002; Fujishima, Leyton-Brown, & Shoham 1999; Sandholm 2000a; Nisan 2000; Hoos & Boutilier 2001) can potentially solve the communication overhead in some cases (when the bidder's utility function is compressible). However, they still require the agents to completely determine and transmit their valuation functions and as such do not solve all the issues. So in practice, when the number of items for sale is even moderate, the bidders will not bid on all bundles.

We study the situation in which a benevolent auctioneer (or arbitrator) wants to implement an efficient allocation of a set of heterogeneous, indivisible goods. The preferences of the participating agents (or consumers) are private information. The auctioneer tries to design a mechanism that gives no incentive for the bidders to misreport preferences.

It is well known that a Generalized Vickrey Auction (GVA), that is based on the elicitation of all utilities, is such an incentive-compatible mechanism. However, in that mechanism, each bidder evaluates each of the exponentially many bundles, and communicates a value for each one.[1] This is clearly impractical even for auctions with moderate numbers of goods.

Another important thread tries to identify iterative or progressive auction protocols that try to limit the space of preferences that are to be revealed in comparison to the fully revealing, naive GVA. Recently, auctions that follow certain solution procedures for primal/dual linear programs have been studied extensively and with respect to incentive-compatibility (see (Bikhchandani *et al.* 2001) for an overview and new suggestions). Another approach (A*k*BA) has been suggested (Wurman & Wellman 2000), though a detailed analysis of incentive-compatibility properties has yet to be performed. Iterative auctions are price-based, which requires that to guarantee that Vickrey payments are determined by the auction, prices must be computable that coincide with the Vickrey payments. Depending on the allowed price structures[2], equilibrium prices (that solve an underlying dual model) may or may not exist. The

---

[1] In general, preference communication in combinatorial auctions is provably exponential (even to find an approximately optimal solution) in the theoretical worst case (Nisan & Segal 2002).

[2] Price for a bundle additive in the prices of the contained goods,

existence depends on properties of preferences which will be considered either individually (e.g. submodularity) or, more general, with respect to the combination of agent types ("agents are substitutes", (Bikhchandani & Ostroy 2001)). The allowed price structure will also influence the applicability of the suggested mechanisms. For example, the unconstrained anonymous prices used in A*k*BA, see (Wurman & Wellman 2000), may require an enforcement of the condition that each agent is only allowed to purchase one bundle in one transaction (at the price quoted for that bundle and not, for example, in two transactions as may seem attractive if the sum of prices for sub-bundles is below the quoted price). Similar considerations are necessary for the unconstrained non-linear (and non-anonymous) prices used in auctions based on and extending the work of Bikhchandani et. al (see, for example, (Bikhchandani & Ostroy 2001; Parkes & Ungar 2000a; 2000b; Bikhchandani *et al.* 2001)).

We develop a partially-revealing, direct mechanism that does not exhibit the disadvantages of a GVA. It may save bidders from specifying or considering valuations for every bundle and, with respect to the existence of a protocol that establishes an incentive-compatible outcome and with respect to the burden put on necessary communication between consumers and auctioneer and computation of valuations on the side of the consumers, it exhibits certain limit properties that may allow to compare its attractiveness to those of iterative auctions in the general setting.

The basic idea is as follows: preferences can be elicited in a natural sequence, from most preferred towards least preferred. Combinations of individual preferences determine collections of preferred bundles. The individual preferences induce a partial *dominance* order on these collections. This relation can be exploited to guide a search for the best feasible collection through the space of infeasible collections with higher aggregated valuation.

We will present two algorithms to compute efficient allocations and an extension to determine Vickrey payments without requiring additional information. An efficient, incentive-compatible mechanism based on these algorithms will be described. We will consider aspects of the optimality of the algorithms and derive two results that bound the informational requirements for a certain class of algorithms.

The model

Our basic setting extends the concepts introduced in (Conen & Sandholm 2001). We consider a combinational economy consisting of n consumers, $N = \{1, \ldots, n\}$, a seller 0, and m goods, $\Omega = \{1, \ldots, m\}$. Each consumer $i \in N$ has utility over bundles, given by a function $u_i : 2^\Omega \to \mathbb{Q}_0^+$, where $u_i(\emptyset) = 0$. (For now, we will neither assume quasi-linearity nor monotony, because our first result does not rely on such assumptions.) The seller has all the goods; the consumers

own none of them. We will neglect the seller for now. If the seller has reservation values (for bundles), he can be modeled as an additional consumer.

It is well known that an agent's preferences can be represented by a utility function only if the preference order is *rational*, that is, the preference order over alternatives is transitive and defined on all pairs of alternatives (equal preference between alternatives is fine). This preference order induces a rank function as follows.

Definition 1 (Rank function, Inverted Rank function). *Let R be the set of the first 2^m natural numbers, $\{1, \ldots, 2^m\}$. Let, for every agent i, the rational preference order $\succsim_i$ be defined over 2^Ω. A bijective function $R_i : 2^\Omega \to R$ will be called the* rank function *for agent i if it assigns a unique value (rank) to each bundle, such that, for every pair $x, y \subseteq \Omega$ of bundles with $x \succ_i y$, $R_i(x) < R_i(y)$ holds. The inverse R_i^{-1} of R_i gives the bundle that corresponds to a rank.*

Proposition 2. *A rank function and its inverse exist for every rational preference relation.*

A rank function is not necessarily unique. Indifferences in the preference order are arbitrarily resolved in the above definition, as the following example demonstrates.

Example 1. *Let the set of goods be $\Omega = \{A, B\}$ and let the preference order of agent i be*

$$\succsim_i: \{AB\} \succ \{A\} \sim \{B\} \succ \{\emptyset\}.$$

Only the following bijective functions are rank functions:

$$R_i^1 : \{AB\} \to 1, \{A\} \to 2, \{B\} \to 3, \{\emptyset\} \to 4$$
$$R_i^2 : \{AB\} \to 1, \{B\} \to 2, \{A\} \to 3, \{\emptyset\} \to 4$$

Now, a combination of ranks of the agents can be viewed as representing a potential solution to the allocation problem at hand. Some of these potential solutions are invalid, though. The others determine *allocations*.

Definition 3 (Combination of Ranks). *Let C be the set of all possible n-ary tuples over R, that is $C = R \times \cdots \times R$. An element $c \in C$, $c = (r_1, \ldots, r_n)$ will be called* combination of ranks. *(If, for every position i of c, the corresponding function R_i^{-1} is applied, a* collection of bundles, b^c, *will be obtained.)*

Definition 4 (Feasible Combination). *A combination c of ranks is* feasible *if no item is allocated more than once. Formally, a combination c of ranks is feasible if the corresponding collection b^c of bundles is a partition of a (not necessarily proper) subset of Ω. A feasible combination determines an allocation X^c with $X_i = b^c[i]$, $i = 1, \ldots, n$ and the seller keeps the item set $X_0 = \Omega / \bigcup_i b^c[i]$. Here, $[i]$ denotes the i'th element of a tuple.*

Definition 5 (Dominance of Rank Combinations). *A binary relation $\succeq \subseteq C \times C$ will be called a* dominance *relation if, for all $x, y \in C$, $(x, y) \in \succeq$ if and only if $x[i] <= y[i]$ for all $i \in N$.*

Proposition 6 (Rank Lattice). *$\succeq$ is a partial order and C forms a complete lattice with respect to $\succeq$ with $lub(C) = (n, \ldots, n)$ and $glb(C) = (1, \ldots, 1)$.*

---

unconstrained, non-linear prices for every bundle, coherent prices for bundles (the price for a bundle may not exceed the sum of prices of the bundles in any partition of the bundle, the prices for super bundles of the bundles in the supported allocation are additive); anonymous prices, different prices for the set of buyers and the set of sellers, different prices for each individual.

The observation exploited by the following algorithms is that a combination that is feasible and not dominated by any other feasible combination will be Pareto-efficient. In addition, if the context is that of transferable utility, the welfare-maximizing allocation will be among these feasible Pareto-efficient combinations. The following algorithms will search the space of combinations (including infeasible ones) to determine the efficient allocations.

Efficient allocations

The first algorithm finds all Pareto-efficient allocations. We proposed it in (Conen & Sandholm 2001); we restate it here because we will use it to prove a bound on the number of valuations of combinations that are necessary to determine a welfare-maximizing allocation.

Algorithm **PAR (Pareto optimal)**:
(1) OPEN = [(1, . . . , 1)]
(3) **while** OPEN $\neq$ [] **do**
(4)   *Remove*$(c, OPEN)$; SUC = suc$(c)^3$
(5)   **if** *Feasible(c)* **then**
(6) $PAR = PAR \cup \{c\}$; *Remove*$(SUC, OPEN)$
(7)   **else foreach** $n \in$ SUC **do**
(8)   **if** $n \notin$ OPEN and *Undominated*(n, PAR)
(9)   **then** *Append*$(n, OPEN)$

Proposition 7. *The algorithm* **PAR** *determines the set of all Pareto-efficient allocations if the utility functions are injective (that is, no agent is indifferent between any two bundles).*[4]

The second algorithm (family) determines a welfare-maximizing allocation (with respect to reported utilities). It assumes a setting with transferable utility (and makes the usual assumption that utility functions are quasi-linear in money). The algorithm is an improved version of an algorithm that we developed earlier (Conen & Sandholm 2001). Unlike the earlier version, this algorithm does not assume unique utilities.

Algorithm **EBF (Efficient Best First)**:
(1) OPEN = $\{(1, \ldots, 1)\}$;
(2) **loop**
(3)   **if** $|OPEN| = 1$ **then** c = combination in OPEN
        else Determine
        $M = \{k \in OPEN | v(k) = \max_{d \in OPEN} v(d)\}$.
        if $|M| \geq 1 \wedge \exists d \in M$ with *Feasible(d)* **then return** d
        else Choose $c \in M$ such that
            no $d \in M$ exists with $d \succ c$;
        OPEN = OPEN $\setminus \{c\}$.
(4)   **if** *Feasible(c)* **then return** c
(5)   SUC = suc(c)
(6)   **foreach** $n \in$ SUC **do**
        if $n \notin$ OPEN **then** OPEN = OPEN $\cup \{n\}$

---

[3]suc(c) determines the immediate successors of c, $\{d \in C \mid \exists j$ with $d[j] = c[j] + 1$ and $d[i] = c[i] \ \forall i \neq j\}$.

[4]If the utility functions are not injective, the algorithm determines a subset of the Pareto-efficient allocations. Furthermore, (even in the non-injective case), the set of solutions found includes a welfare-maximizing allocation (whenever " welfare-maximizing" is defined in a transferable utility context).

Proposition 8. *Any* **EBF** *algorithm determines an efficient (that is, welfare-maximizing) allocation.*

Optimality considerations

The problem is to chose an allocation $X = (X_1, \ldots, X_n)$ with $\bigcup_{i \in N} X_i \subseteq \Omega$ and $\bigcap_{i \in N} X_i = \emptyset$ so as to maximize social welfare, $\sum u_i(X_i)$. Problem instances will be called *economies* $(\Omega; u_1, \ldots, u_n)$.

Definition 9. *An algorithm is* admissible, *if it determines an efficient (that is, welfare-maximizing), feasible combination for every problem instance. This combination is called a* solution combination.

As we have already seen, **EBF** is admissible. Also, **PAR** can easily be turned into an admissible algorithm by comparing the value of all the determined Pareto-optimal allocations and picking a maximizing one. We will refer to this variant of **PAR** as **MPAR** (maximizing PAR). Both algorithms make use of bundle information ("What is your k'th ranked bundle?") and value information ("What is your valuation for bundle X?"). We will now study questions related to optimal use of this information. Roughly, an algorithm (or a family of algorithms) will be considered (weakly) optimal with respect to certain kind of information, if no admissible and "similarly informed" algorithm requires less information for every problem instance. We will show that **EBF** (resp. **MPAR**) are limiting cases for the use of bundle (resp. value) information.

We assume that a valuation function $v : C \to \mathbb{Q}$ is available that can be used to determine the aggregated utility of every possible combination (note that for all a, b with $(a, b) \in \succeq$, $v(a) \geq v(b)$ holds). There is also a feasibility function $f : C \to \{T, F\}$, which allows one to check for every combination in the lattice, whether the combination is feasible (T) or infeasible (F). Further information is not available. Additionally, a successor function is available to determine the next unvisited direct successors of a combination. All of these functions will be considered elementary (with unit costs).

In addition, every algorithm will have to determine a set of combinations to start with; inserting a combination into this set is considered to be an elementary operation. Combinations that are an element of the initial set or that have been "created" as successor by applying (possibly iteratively) the successor function, will be called *visited* combinations. Only visited combinations can be valued or checked for feasibility.

Definition 10. *An algorithm is* admissibly equipped *if only the above mentioned elementary operations are used to obtain lattice-related information.*

EBF is admissibly equipped. However, as given above, **EBF** is not deterministic–it chooses a combination among a set of equally valued combinations arbitrarily in step (3). In effect, **EBF** determines a family of **EBF** algorithms differing in the choice (or *tie breaking*) rule. It is clear that different tie breaking rules may lead to differently efficient (with respect to utilization of information) solution paths.

Now, can some deterministic algorithm search the lattice more efficiently than **EBF** algorithms?

Costs of feasibility checking

Theorem 11 (Efficiency of Feasibility Checking). *There is no admissible, admissibly equipped and deterministic algorithm* **A** *which requires fewer feasibility checks for every problem instance than every algorithm of the* **EBF** *family.*

The proof uses the following propositions (whose proofs we omit due to limited space).

Proposition 12. *Let l be a solution combination that has been determined by an arbitrary* **EBF** *algorithm. Let k be a combination with $v(k) > v(l)$. Then, any admissible, admissibly equipped and deterministic algorithms* **A** *must check the feasibility of k.*

Proposition 13. *No* **EBF** *algorithm* **B** *checks a combination k for feasibility which has a lower value than the solution combination l that* **B** *will determine.*

Proposition 14.

(a) Every **EBF** *algorithm checks precisely one feasible combination for feasibility.*
(b) Every admissible, admissibly equipped and deterministic algorithm checks at least one feasible combination for feasibility.

Now, let l be a solution combination that has been found by an **EBF** algorithm. The theorem holds for every problem instance that does not imply the existence of an infeasible combination with the same value as l. If no such combination exists, **A** has to check *at least* all infeasible combinations with a value larger then $v(l)$ (which is precisely the number of checks that any **EBF** algorithm will perform). ∎

Note that from the non-injectivity of the valuations of the combinations, it follows that **EBF** algorithms may check infeasible combinations (for feasibility) that have the same value as the solution combination. There are even problem instances where *all* **EBF** algorithms will have to perform such checks. One such instance is shown in Fig. 1.

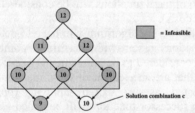

Figure 1: *Part of a lattice that will give any* **EBF** *instance reason to check at least one combination for feasibility that has a value that equals the value of the solution (these are the combinations in the emphasized region).*

In this case, it might be possible that an algorithm **A** performs fewer feasibility checks than any **EBF** algorithm – therefore, the above theorem cannot be formulated more tightly.[5]

---

[5]It is, however, straightforward to give a version of the algorithm that works with equivalence classes of ranks instead of "linearizing" the partial order of the preferences. This allows one to consider all equally valuable combinations at the same time in the selection step. It would, however, make the presentation more awkward.

We will now turn our attention to the **MPAR** algorithm that allows us to formulate some results with respect to the costs of valuating combinations.

Theorem 15. *No admissible, admissibly equipped and deterministic algorithm that calls the valuation function for feasible combinations only will require fewer calls than the* **MPAR** *algorithm.*

The worst case for the **MPAR** algorithm will occur if all feasible allocations that distribute all goods to the consumers are Pareto-optimal. This is the case if all utilities for goods are equal and utilities for bundles are additive, that is $u_i(\{x\}) = c$ for some $c \in \mathbb{Q}_0^+$ and all $x \in \Omega$, $u_i(\emptyset) = 0$, and $u_i(z) = \sum_{x \in z} u_i(\{x\}) = |z| * c$ for all $z \subseteq \Omega$, $z \neq \emptyset$, $i \in N$. It is immediate that every fully distributive allocation leads to the same welfare $W = |\Omega| * c = m * c$. Now, the number of combinations to be valued is the number of allocations that distribute all goods to the customers[6] which is equal to counting the possibilities to distribute m objects to n buckets without further restriction, that is n^m. So:

Proposition 16. MPAR *requires at most n^m calls to the valuation function. By the above theorem, this extends to all admissible and admissibly equipped algorithms that are restricted to call the valuation function for feasible combinations only.*

The version of **PAR** that we gave above will determine the set of all Pareto-optimal allocations that are undominated with respect to the chosen ranking. Assume that we have 2 goods, 2 agents and the following utilities $u_x(A) = u_x(B) = 3$, $u_x(AB) = 6$, $x \in \{1, 2\}$ and the ranks $r_1(A) = 1, r_1(B) = 2, r_1(AB) = 3, r_1(\emptyset) = 4$, $r_2(B) = 1, r_2(A) = 2, r_2(AB) = 3, r_2(\emptyset) = 4$. Then, **PAR** only generates the feasible rank combination $(1, 1)$ representing an efficient allocation $(\{A\}, \{B\})$. However, with an unfortunate ordering, more work would have to be done: $r_1(AB) = 1, r_1(A) = 2, r_1(B) = 3, r_1(\emptyset) = 4$ $r_2(AB) = 1, r_2(A) = 2, r_2(B) = 3, r_2(\emptyset) = 4$ would generate $(1, 4), (4, 1), (2, 3)$ and $(3, 2)$.[7] So, the above bound is not sharp but depends on the chosen order of ranks that may vary within each class of individual ranks that map to bundles with equal valuations. The worst case corresponds to the number of combinations in the middle layer of the lattice, see Fig. 2.

With respect to the **EBF** family of algorithms, intuitively a worst case with respect to the number of required valuations would occur if all infeasible combinations would have a higher value than the best feasible combination. This, of course, cannot happen in the considered setting. Instead we have to consider the maximal amount of infeasible combinations that are at least as valuable as the best allocation and are undominated by feasible allocations. This number is $(2^{mn} - n^m)/2$ in the above example and generally.[8]

---

[6]We could extend this to all allocations that include the arbitrator as well and set c to 0. However, with monotonous preferences, the arbitrator can be excluded from consideration.

[7]Requiring agents to rank bundles with equal value from small to large can be beneficial.

[8]In the particular example, all valuation information is elicited.

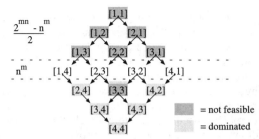

Figure 2: *A worst case: All feasible, Pareto-optimal combinations have the same value. The number of undominated Pareto-optimal combinations cannot be larger than in the example. If in the upper part of the lattice such a combination could be found, at least two of the combinations in the middle layer would be dominated. By symmetry, moving undominated combinations into the lower part will lead to fewer undominated combinations as well.*

Proposition 17. *Any* **EBF** *algorithm requires at most* $\frac{2^{mn}-n^m}{2}+1$ *calls to the valuation function.*

Vickrey payments

Recall that the Vickrey payment of an agent i reflects the effect of her participation in an economy E: a consumer i will pay an amount equal to the utility that the other consumers will loose due to the participation of i, that is

$$t(i) \; = \; V(E_{-i}) \; - \sum_{j \in N, j \neq i} u_j(X_j)$$

where E_{-i} is the economy E without i and $V(E_{-i})$ is the utility that can be realized implementing a welfare-maximizing allocation for E_{-i}.

We will now assume that an execution of an **EBF** algorithm has determined an efficient allocation X for an economy E.

Theorem 18. *No valuation information in addition to the information already obtained by* **EBF** *is necessary to determine the Vickrey payments.*

Proof. We assume that n is the solution combination that was found by the algorithm and that it represents X. (a) First, note that valuation information for all combinations with higher value than n have been obtained already. (b) Now assume that consumer i will be removed from the allocation $X = (X_1, \ldots, X_i, \ldots, X_n)$. The value $V(X^{-X_i})$ of the reduced allocation X^{-X_i} is a lower bound for the maximal value that can be obtained from allocating the goods in Ω to the agents in the remaining set of consumers, N^{-i} (and determines the second term in the equation for the Vickrey payment of i without requiring any additional information). Now assume that a reduced $(n-1)$-ary allocation $Y^{-i} = (Y_1, \ldots, Y_n)$ (leaving out the agent i resp. its index) can be found with a value that exceeds $V(X^{-X_i})$. Further assume that additional valuation information would be required. Then a combination $c = (Y_1, \ldots, X_i, \ldots, Y_n)$ could

be constructed that would have a higher value than X and that would have required additional valuation information to determine its value, thus contradicting (a). □

It is now clear that all required valuation information has already been determined.[9] A consequence of the arguments for (b) is that the partial combinations which solve the restricted allocation problem optimally are part of the already visited combinations. This allows one to extend **EBF** straightforwardly to keep track of the best allocation for each subset of N with $n-1$ elements visited so far (an implementation is straightforward). After the execution of such an extended **EBF** algorithm, Vickrey payments can be determined immediately from the collected maximum valuations and the efficient allocation. From the argumentation above, it follows immediately that

Proposition 19. *An* **EBF** *algorithm, extended as described above, determines an efficient allocation and corresponding Vickrey payments.*

The results obtained on the costs can be carried over to extended **EBF** algorithms. The result above shows that, in the context of admissibly equipped algorithms, the complexity of the determination of Vickrey payments is directly tied to the complexity of the determination of an efficient allocation. In other words: If it is possible to determine (with an **EBF** algorithm) an efficient allocation with a tractable amount of computation (implying also that only a tractable amount of information is required if latency is neglected), it is also possible to tractably compute the Vickrey payments.

The mechanism

To outline a mechanism that is based on the extended **EBF** algorithm, a set of allowed questions, a data structure to store retrieved information and a policy to generate questions are fixed. To fulfill the informational needs of the underlying algorithm, the following two questions will be allowed: (1) *give me the bundle with the next higher rank number* (that is the next weakly less preferred bundle), (2) give me your valuation for bundle x. We assume that all participants know the underlying set of goods. The consumers will consider the first rank question as the start of the mechanism and will answer it with their most preferred bundle (with rank 1). The arbitrator is considered to be trustworthy[10]. In the end, the arbitrator will announce the computed pair $(X_i, t(i))$ to each agent i. Note that the questions allow only for a rather natural sequence of bundle questions–from most preferred towards less preferred.[11]

If we assume a trivial, binary encoding of the $n * 2^m$ values from $\mathbb{Q}_0^+$ and restrict their size to a reasonable constant k, $n * 2^m \log_2 k$ bits of information are required in the worst case.

[9]If the initial combination is feasible and, consequently, no valuation information is available, the Vickrey payments are 0 (every agent receives her most preferred bundle)–therefore no valuation information is necessary to determine Vickrey payments.

[10]An independent institution may assess the trustworthiness of the arbitrator by sampling the sent messages

[11]If the potentially exponential space requirement of the algorithm does not allow one to keep track of all received bundle and value information, polynomial space versions of the algorithm can be used (adapted to, e.g., iterative deepening, see (Zhang & Korf 1995)), requiring that sequences of questions are repeated.

The received information can, for example, be stored in a data structure similar to the augmented order graph of (Conen & Sandholm 2001). Each node represents a quadruple consisting of agent, rank, bundle and value information. Nodes will be created as preferences are explored and information will be added to the nodes upon becoming available. The elicitation of information will be tied into the execution of the algorithm in step (3). To determine the set of value-maximizing combinations in OPEN, all missing bundle/value pairs of combinations in OPEN have to be requested. With one exception, the algorithm immediately implies that valuation requests can be done with the "next worse bundle" question.[12] Together with choosing a tie breaking rule (deciding which value-maximizing combination to expand next), this fixes and implements a straightforward elicitation policy. Implementing the complete mechanism would be straightforward. The resulting mechanism is a member of the family of **RANK** mechanisms that differ only with respect to the tie breaking rule. The following propositions follow immediately from the results above.

Proposition 20. *A* **RANK** *Mechanism is incentive compatible and economically efficient.*

Proposition 21. *Let* **B** *be the* **EBF** *algorithm that is used in a specific* **RANK** *mechanism. Then there does not exists any other mechanism based on an admissible, admissibly equipped and deterministic algorithm that requires fewer checks of the feasibility of combinations for all instances of the allocation problem.*

Conclusions and future research

We presented a partial-revelation mechanism for combinatorial auctions that explores the natural lattice structure of the bidders' preference combinations. This mechanism gives a possibility to analyze computational and informational requirements of a class of mechanisms from first principles. Analytical results on the amount of elicitation were derived. Two categories of costs were studied. The results carry over to (direct or indirect) mechanisms that do not explore the rank lattice and use valuation questions only (possibly iterative).

Theorem 15 shows that it is impossible to improve upon the number of combinations to be valued without allowing the elicitation algorithm to query the value of infeasible combinations. If this is allowed, the comparison to **EBF** algorithms with respect to required feasibility checks becomes relevant (due to Theorem 11)–in this sense, **EBF** and **MPAR** are, in spite of their simplicity, limit cases (**EBF** algorithms with respect to feasibility checking and **MPAR** with respect to valuation if only feasible combinations are valued.) The mechanism is also of interest because it ties the computational effort required for Vickrey payments directly to the effort required for computing an efficient allocation.

As future work we plan to study the effect of preference restrictions on the performance of **EBF** algorithms. We have already started conducting experiments on how effective preference elicitation in combinatorial auctions is in practice (Hudson & Sandholm 2002). Future work also includes analyzing the efficiency of elicitation in the sense of the ratio of utility information elicited to the amount of information that is required, *at a minimum* to determine an efficient allocation and corresponding Vickrey payments. We expect that, for a given problem instance, an optimally chosen tie-breaking rule will not leave much room for improvement—however, optimally choosing the tie-breaking rule will generally not be possible *a priori*.

References

Andersson, A.; Tenhunen, M.; and Ygge, F. 2000. Integer programming for combinatorial auction winner determination. *ICMAS*, 39–46.

Bikhchandani, S., and Ostroy, J. 2001. The package assignment model. UCLA Working Paper Series, mimeo.

Bikhchandani, S.; de Vries, S.; Schummer, J.; and Vohra, R. V. 2001. Linear programming and Vickrey auctions.

Conen, W., and Sandholm, T. 2001. Preference elicitation in combinatorial auctions: Extended abstract. *ACM Conference on Electronic Commerce*, 256–259. A more detailed description of the algorithms appeared in the IJCAI-2001 Workshop on Economic Agents, Models, and Mechanisms, pp. 71–80.

Fujishima, Y.; Leyton-Brown, K.; and Shoham, Y. 1999. Taming the computational complexity of combinatorial auctions: Optimal and approximate approaches. *IJCAI*, 548–553.

Hoos, H., and Boutilier, C. 2001. Bidding languages for combinatorial auctions. *IJCAI*, 1211–1217.

Hudson, B., and Sandholm, T. 2002. Effectiveness of preference elicitation in combinatorial auctions. Technical report, Carnegie Mellon University, Computer Science Department, CMU-CS-02-124, March.

Larson, K., and Sandholm, T. 2001. Costly valuation computation in auctions. *Theoretical Aspects of Rationality and Knowledge (TARK VIII)*, 169–182.

Nisan, N., and Segal, I. 2002. The communication complexity of efficient allocation problems. Draft. Second version March 5th.

Nisan, N. 2000. Bidding and allocation in combinatorial auctions. *ACM Conference on Electronic Commerce*, 1–12.

Parkes, D. C., and Ungar, L. 2000a. Iterative combinatorial auctions: Theory and practice. *AAAI*, 74–81.

Parkes, D. C., and Ungar, L. 2000b. Preventing strategic manipulation in iterative auctions: Proxy-agents and price-adjustment. *AAAI*, 82–89.

Parkes, D. C. 1999. Optimal auction design for agents with hard valuation problems. *Agent-Mediated Electronic Commerce Workshop at IJCAI*.

Rothkopf, M. H.; Pekeč, A.; and Harstad, R. M. 1998. Computationally manageable combinatorial auctions. *Management Science* 44(8):1131–1147.

Sandholm, T., and Suri, S. 2000. Improved algorithms for optimal winner determination in combinatorial auctions and generalizations. *AAAI*, 90–97.

Sandholm, T.; Suri, S.; Gilpin, A.; and Levine, D. 2001. CABOB: A fast optimal algorithm for combinatorial auctions. *IJCAI*, 1102–1108.

Sandholm, T. 1993. An implementation of the contract net protocol based on marginal cost calculations. *AAAI*, 256–262.

Sandholm, T. 2000a. eMediator: A next generation electronic commerce server. In *International Conference on Autonomous Agents (AGENTS)*, 73–96. Early version: AAAI-99 Workshop on AI in Electronic Commerce, Orlando, FL, pp. 46–55, July 1999, and as Washington University, St. Louis, Computer Science WU-CS-99-02, Jan. 1999.

Sandholm, T. 2000b. Issues in computational Vickrey auctions. *International Journal of Electronic Commerce* 4(3):107–129. Special Issue on Applying Intelligent Agents for Electronic Commerce. Early version: ICMAS, pages 299–306, 1996.

Sandholm, T. 2002. Algorithm for optimal winner determination in combinatorial auctions. *Artificial Intelligence* 135:1–54. First appeared as an invited talk at the International Conference on Information and Computation Economies, Charleston, SC, Oct. 25–28, 1998. Also: Washington Univ. Computer Science, WUCS-99-01, Jan 28th, 1999. Conference version: IJCAI, pp. 542–547, 1999.

Wurman, P. R., and Wellman, M. P. 2000. AkBA: A progressive, anonymous-price combinatorial auction. *ACM Conference on Electronic Commerce*, 21–29.

Zhang, W., and Korf, R. E. 1995. Performance of linear-space search algorithms. *Artificial Intelligence* 79(2):241–292.

---

[12]The exception occurs if $(1, \ldots, 1)$ is not feasible which leads to a comparison with its successors, where the implementation has to make sure that the first received value information elicited from each agent is attached to the node representing rank 1.

Bidding Clubs in First-Price Auctions
Extended Abstract

Kevin Leyton-Brown, Yoav Shoham and Moshe Tennenholtz

Department of Computer Science
Stanford University, Stanford, CA 94305
Email: {kevinlb;shoham;moshe}@cs.stanford.edu
Full version: http://robotics.stanford.edu/~kevinlb/recent_work.htm

Abstract

We introduce a class of mechanisms, called *bidding clubs*, that allow agents to coordinate their bidding in auctions. Bidding clubs invite a set of agents to join, and each invited agent freely chooses whether to accept the invitation or whether to participate independently in the auction. Clubs first conduct a "pre-auction"; depending on the outcome of the pre-auction some subset of the members of the club bid in the primary auction in a prescribed way. We model this setting as a Bayesian game, including agents' choices of whether or not to accept a bidding club's invitation. We examine the specific case of bidding clubs for first-price auctions, showing the existence of a Bayes-Nash equilibrium where agents choose to participate in bidding clubs when invited and truthfully declare their valuations to the coordinator. Furthermore, we show that the existence of bidding clubs benefits all agents, including those who do not belong to a bidding club.

Introduction

Economic and game-theoretic models have had significant impact on recent work in AI. Of particular interest has been work on economic mechanism design dealing with protocols for non-cooperative environments, which has not only applied the existing theory to computational settings, but has also extended it in various ways (Boutilier, Shoham, & Wellman 1997; Tennenholtz 1999). Work in AI has revisited the assumptions underlying optimal mechanism design (e.g. (Monderer & Tennenholtz 2000)), and considered computational issues in the design of such mechanisms (e.g. (Sandholm *et al.* 2001)). Much of the game-theoretic multiagent work in AI differs from related work in economics by approaching problems from agents' perspectives rather than from the perspective of the seller or mechanism designer. There is a body of work in AI that concerns agent behavior in various economic settings where the choice of mechanism is out of the agents' control, but where the mechanism is sufficiently elaborate to permit some form of strategic manipulation. Greenwald introduced the use of shopbots (Greenwald 1999) as a (relatively non-strategic) way for buyers to profit from competition between sellers on the internet; Parkes and Ungar studied proxy bidding (Parkes & Ungar 2000). In the recent Trading Agent Competition (see, e.g., (Stone &

Greenwald 2000)) many AI researchers constructed competitive agents to operate in a rich economic setting; although strategic considerations were essential in this competition, the complexity of the setting defied theoretical analysis and forced agent behavior to rely on heuristics.

In this work we continue in the AI tradition of taking an agent's perspective, but tackle a fundamental economic mechanism which is simple enough to permit a theoretical approach. Auctions are the most well-studied and basic economic mechanisms, and have received a great deal of attention as a general approach for resource allocation in non-cooperative environments. We present a class of systems to assist sets of bidders, *bidding clubs*. The idea is similar to the idea behind "buyer clubs" on the internet (e.g., www.mobshop.com): to aggregate the market power of individual bidders. Buyer clubs work when buyers' interests are perfectly aligned; the more buyers join in a purchase the lower the price for everyone. In auctions held on the internet it is relatively easy for multiple agents to cooperate, hiding behind a single auction participant. Intuitively, these bidders should be able to gain by causing others to lower their bids in the case of a first-price auction or by possibly removing the second-highest bidder in the case of a second-price auction. However, the situation in auctions is not as simple as in buyer clubs, because while bidders can gain by sharing information, the competitive nature of auctions means that bidders' interests are not aligned. Thus there is a complex strategic relationship among bidders in a bidding club, and bidding club rules must be designed accordingly. This work comes under the umbrella of *collusion* in auctions, a negative term reflecting a seller-oriented perspective. We adopt a more neutral stance towards such bidder activities and thus use the term *bidding clubs* rather than the terms *bidding rings* and *cartels* that have been used in the past. Of course, the technical development is not impacted by such subtle differences in moral attitude.

There are four classical auction types: first-price, second-price, Dutch and English. Since first-price and Dutch are strategically equivalent, the latter may be omitted for our purposes without loss of generality. Agents cooperation in second-price auctions (and in English auctions, which are equivalent under standard economic assumptions) is well studied, most notably in (Graham & Marshall 1987). Cooperation among agents in the framework of first-price auctions has received much less attention. This is possibly explained by the fact that since second-price auctions give rise to dominant strategies, it is possible to study collusion in many settings related to these auctions without performing strategic equilibrium analysis. The key exception to the scarcity of formal work on first-price auctions is a very influential paper by McAfee and McMillan (McAfee & McMillan 1992). Several sections of their paper are directly applicable to our work, including the discussion of enforcement and the argument for independent private values as a model of agents' valuations as well as parts of their model. However, the setting introduced in their work assumes that a fixed number of agents participate in the auction and that all agents are part of a single cartel that coordinates its behavior in the auction. The authors show optimal collusion protocols for "weak" cartels (in which transfers between agents are not permitted: all bidders bid the reserve price, using the auctioneer's random tie-breaking rule to select a winner) and for "strong" cartels (the cartel holds a pre-auction, the winner of which bids the reserve price in the main auction while all other bidders sit out; the winner distributes some of his gains to other cartel members through side payments). A small part of the paper deals with the case where in addition to the single cartel there are also additional agents. However, results are shown only for two cases: (1) when non-cartel members bid without taking the existence of a cartel into account and (2) when each agent i has valuation $v_i \in \{0, 1\}$.

An earlier paper (Leyton-Brown, Shoham, & Tennenholtz 2000) anticipated some of our results, considering bidding clubs for five different economic mechanisms. This earlier paper considered bidding clubs for first-price auctions, second-price auctions, parallel second-price auctions with substitutable goods, second-price auctions with complementary goods, and general mechanisms where agents' valuations are drawn from a finite set. However, this earlier paper was not developed in the context of a general game-theoretic model. For example, it relied upon the assumption that only a single bidding club exists and that bidders who were not invited to join the club behave as though they are not aware of the possibility that a bidding club might exist. This makes the analysis carried out in that earlier work restrictive and limited from a game-theoretic perspective. Our current paper is a substantial extension and generalization of that earlier work, concentrating on the case of first-price auctions.

Distinguishing Features of our Model

Our goal in this work is to study cooperation between self-interested bidders in a rich model that captures many of the characteristics of auctions on the internet. This leads to many differences between our model and models proposed in (McAfee & McMillan 1992) and (Graham & Marshall 1987). We argue that a model of internet auctions with bidding clubs should include the following features:

1. The number of bidders is stochastic.
2. A bidding club may contain any subset of the bidders in the auction (e.g., it is not restricted to contain all bidders)
3. No limit to the number of bidding clubs in any auction.
4. All agents behave strategically, taking into account the possibility that other agents may collude.

The first feature above is crucial. In many real-world internet auctions, bidders are not aware of the number of other agents in the economic environment. A bidding club that drops one or more bidders is thus undetectable to other bidders in such an auction. An economic environment with a fixed number of bidders would not model this uncertainty, as the number of involved bidders would be common knowledge among all bidders regardless of the number of bids received in the auction. For this reason, we consider economic environments where the number of bidders is chosen at random, drawing on a model of auctions with stochastic numbers of participants from a second paper by McAfee and McMillan which is unrelated to collusion (McAfee & McMillan 1987); we also refer to equilibrium analysis of this model from (Harstad, Kagel, & Levin 1990).

To make bidding clubs a reasonable model of collusion in internet auctions, we restrict our protocols as follows:

1. Bidders must be free to decline an invitation to join a bidding club without (direct) penalty. In this way we include the choice to collude as one of agents' strategic decisions, rather than assuming that agents will collude.
2. Bidding club coordinators must make money on expectation, and must never lose money. This ensures that third-parties have incentive to run bidding club coordinators.
3. The bidding club protocol must give rise to an equilibrium where all invited agents choose to participate, even when the bidding club operates in a single auction as opposed to a sequence of auctions. Thus agents can not be induced to collude in a given auction by the threat of being denied future opportunities to collude. This restriction is necessary for modelling internet auction settings in which the pool of participants varies substantially from one auction to the next, and where many bidders are interested in participating only in single auctions.

Overview

The first part of our paper does not directly concern bidding clubs. First, we consider different variations on the first-price auction mechanism. We begin with classical first-price auctions, in which the number of bidders is common knowledge, and then consider first-price auctions where the number of bidders is drawn from a known distribution. Combining results from both auction types, we present first-price auctions with participation revelation: auctions in which the number of bidders is stochastic, but the auctioneer announces the number of participants before taking bids. This is the auction mechanism upon which we will base our bidding club protocol for first-price auctions.

The second part of our paper is concerned explicitly with bidding clubs, using material from the first part to present a general model of bidding clubs and then a bidding club protocol for first-price auctions. First, we describe an economic environment with the following novel features:

- A finite set of bidding clubs is selected from an infinite set of potential bidding clubs.

- A finite set of agents is selected to participate in the auction, from an infinite set of potential agents. Some agents are associated with bidding clubs, and the whole procedure is carried out in such a way that no agent can gain information about the total number of agents in the economic environment from the fact of his own selection.

- The space of agent types is expanded to include both an agent's valuation, and the number of agents present in that agent's bidding club (equal to one if the agent does not belong to a bidding club).

We introduce notation to describe each agent's beliefs about the number of agents in the economic environment, conditioned on that agent's private information. Next, we examine bidding club protocols for first-price auctions. We begin with two assumptions about the distribution of agent valuations: the first related to continuity of the distribution, and the second to monotonicity of equilibrium bids. We then give a bidding club protocol for first-price auctions with participation revelation, and present our main technical results:

- It is an equilibrium for agents to accept invitations to join bidding clubs when invited and disclose their true valuations to their coordinator, and for singleton agents to bid as they would in an auction with a stochastic number of participants in an economic environment without bidding clubs, in which the distribution over the number of participants is the same as in the bidding clubs setting.

- In equilibrium each agent is better off as a result of his own club (that is, his expected payoff is higher than would have been the case if his club never existed, but other clubs—if any—still did exist).

- In equilibrium each club increases all non-members' expected payoffs, as compared to equilibrium in the case where all club members participated in the auction as singleton bidders, but all other clubs—if any—still existed.

- In equilibrium each agent's expected payoff is identical to the case in which no clubs exist. If clubs are willing to make money (or break even) only on expectation, they could distribute some of their *ex ante* expected profits among the club members, ensuring that all bidders gain.

First-Price Auctions

Let $\mathcal{T}$ be the set of possible agent types. The type $\tau_i \in \mathcal{T}$ of agent i is the tuple $(v_i, s_i) \in V \times \mathcal{S}$. v_i denotes an agent's valuation: his maximal willingness to pay for the good offered by the center. We assume that v_i represents a purely private valuation for the good, and that v_i is selected independently from the other v_j's of other agents from a known distribution, F, having density function f. By s_i we denote agent i's signal: his private information about the number of agents in the auction. In this section we will consider the simple case where $\mathcal{S} = \{\varnothing\}$: it is common knowledge that all agents receive the null signal, and hence gain no additional information about the number of agents. Recall that the economic environment itself is always common knowledge, and so agents always have some information about the number of agents even when they receive the null signal.

Classical first-price auctions

In a classical first-price auction, the economic environment consists of n agents. Each participant submits a bid in a sealed envelope; the agent with the highest bid wins the good and pays the amount of his bid, and all other participants pay nothing. In the case of a tie, the winner of the auction is selected uniformly at random from the bidders who tied for the highest bid. The equilibrium analysis of first-price auctions is quite standard:

Proposition 1 *If valuations are selected independently and uniformly from* $[0, 1]$ *then it is a symmetric equilibrium for each agent i to follow the strategy* $b(v_i) = \frac{n-1}{n} v_i$.

Using classical equilibrium analysis it is possible to show how classical first-price auctions can be generalized to an arbitrary continuous distribution F.

Proposition 2 *If valuations are selected from a continuous distribution F then it is a symmetric equilibrium for each agent i to follow the strategy* $b(v_i) = v_i - F(v_i)^{-(n-1)} \int_0^{v_i} F(u)^{n-1} du$.

In both cases, observe that although n is a free variable, n is not a parameter of the strategy; the same is true of the distribution F. Agents deduce this information from their full knowledge of the economic environment. It is useful, however, to have notation specifying the amount of the equilibrium bid as a function of both v and n. We write $b^e(v_i, n) = v_i - F(v_i)^{-(n-1)} \int_0^{v_i} F(u)^{n-1} du$.

First-price auctions with a stochastic number of bidders

It is also possible to model an economic environment in which the number of agents is not a constant, but is instead chosen stochastically from a known probability distribution P; by p_j we denote the probability that there are exactly j agents. An equilibrium for this setting was demonstrated in (Harstad, Kagel, & Levin 1990):

Proposition 3 *If valuations are selected from a continuous distribution F and the number of bidders is selected from the distribution P then it is a symmetric equilibrium for each agent i to follow the strategy* $b(v_i) = \sum_{j=2}^{\infty} p_j b^e(v_i, j)$.

Observe that $b^e(v_i, j)$ is the amount of the equilibrium bid for a bidder with valuation v_i in a setting with j bidders as described above. P is deduced from the economic environment. We overload our previous notation for the equilibrium bid, this time as a function of the agent's valuation and the probability distribution P. Thus we write $b^e(v_i, P) = \sum_{j=2}^{\infty} p_j b^e(v_i, j)$.

First-price auctions with participation revelation

In an economic environment with a stochastic number of bidders, the auctioneer may choose to reveal the number of participants to all bidders, for example by introducing a two-phase mechanism with revelation of the number of participants between the stages. Specifically, we define a first-price auction with participation revelation as follows:

1. Agents indicate their intention to bid in the auction.

2. The auctioneer announces n, the number of agents who registered in the first phase.
3. Agents submit bids to the auctioneer. The auctioneer only accepts bids from agents who registered in the first phase.
4. The agent who submitted the highest bid is awarded the good for the amount of his bid; all other agents pay 0.

Unsurprisingly, it is an equilibrium for bidders to bid as in a classical first-price auction:

Proposition 4 *There exists an equilibrium of the first-price auction with participation revelation where every agent i indicates the intention to participate and bids $b^e(v_i, n)$.*

In our discussion of bidding clubs we will be concerned with first-price auctions with information revelation, but we will show an equilibrium in which the number of agents registering in the first phase is smaller than the total number of agents participating in the auction, because some bidders with low valuations drop out as part of a collusive agreement. The auctioneer's declaration acts as a signal about the total number of bidders, but individual agents will still be uncertain about the total number of opponents they face.

Auction Model for Bidding Clubs

We now give a formal description of the economic environment in which bidding clubs operate, define the bidding club mechanism for bidding club members, and define symmetric Bayes-Nash equilibria. Because our aim is not to model a situation where agents' *decision* to collude is exogenous—as this would gloss over the question of whether the collusion is stable—we include the collusive protocol as part of the model and show that it is individually rational *ex post* (i.e., after agents have observed their valuations) for agents to choose to collude. However, we do consider exogenous the selection of the sets of agents who are *invited* to collude.

The Economic Environment

We construct an economic environment E consisting of a set of agents who have non-negative valuations for a good at auction, the distinguished agent 0 and a set of bidding club coordinators who may invite agents to participate in a bidding club. Intuitively, the number of agents in each bidding club is independent of the number of agents in every other bidding club, because we construct an environment where an agent's belief update after observing the number of agents in his bidding club does not result in any change in the distribution over the number of *other* agents in the auction.

Coordinators Coordinators are not free to choose their own strategies; rather, they act as part of the mechanism for a subset of the agents in the economic environment. We denote the probability that an auction will involve n_c potential coordinators as $\gamma_C(n_c)$. γ_C may be any distribution satisfying $\gamma_C(0) = \gamma_C(1) = 0$: at least two potential coordinators will be associated with each auction. We assume that the name of each potential coordinator is selected from the uniform distribution on $[0, 1]$.

Agents The probability that n agents will be associated with a potential coordinator is denoted $\gamma_A(n)$. γ_A may be any distribution satisfying $\gamma_A(0) = 0$ and $\gamma_A(1) < 1$. If only one (actual) agent is associated with a potential coordinator, the potential coordinator will not be actualized and hence the agent will not belong to a bidding club. In this way we model agents who participate directly in the auction without being associated with a coordinator. If more than one agent is associated with a potential coordinator, the coordinator *is* actualized and all the agents receive an invitation to participate in the bidding club. As before, we assume that the name of each agent associated with a potential coordinator is selected from the uniform distribution on $[0, 1]$. The key consequence of our technical construction of coordinator and agent names is that an agent's knowledge of the coordinator with whom he is associated does not give him additional information about what other agents have been selected. Any other technique for providing this property may also be used; e.g., other constructions draw coordinator and agent names from finite sets.

Signals Each agent receives a signal informing him of the number of agents in his bidding club; we denote this signal s_i. Of course, if this number is 1 then there is no coordinator for the agent to deal with, and he will simply participate in the main auction. Note also that agents are neither aware of the number of potential coordinators for their auction nor the number of actualized potential coordinators, though they are aware of both distributions.

Beliefs Each agent has beliefs about the number of agents in the economic environment. Not all agents have the same beliefs—agents who have been signaled that they belong to a bidding club will expect a larger number of agents than singleton agents. We denote by $p_m^{n,k}$ the (true) probability that there will be a total of m agents in the auction, given that n potential coordinators were selected and that there are k agents associated with one of the potential coordinators; we denote the whole distribution $P^{n,k}$. Because the numbers of agents in each bidding club are independent, every agent in the whole auction has the same beliefs about the number of other agents in the economic environment discounting those agents in his own bidding club. Hence agent i's beliefs are described by the distribution P^{n,s_i}.

The Auction Mechanism

Bidding clubs, in combination with a main auction (along the lines of (Monderer & Tennenholtz 2000)), induce this auction mechanism for their members:

1. A set of bidders is invited to join the bidding club.
2. Each agent i sends a message μ_i to the bidding club coordinator. This may be the null message, which indicates that the agent will not participate in the coordination and will instead participate freely in the main auction. Otherwise, agent i agrees to be bound by the bidding club rules, and μ_i is agent i's declared valuation for the good. Of course, i can lie about his valuation.
3. Based on commonly-known rules, and on the information all the members supply, the coordinator selects a subset

of the agents to bid in the main auction. The coordinator may bid on behalf of these agents (e.g., using their ID's on the auction web site) or it may instruct agents on how to bid. In either case we assume that the coordinator can force agents to bid as desired, for example by imposing a charge on agents who do not behave as directed.

4. If a bidder represented by the coordinator wins the main auction, he is made to pay the amount required by the auction mechanism to the auctioneer, and may be required to make an additional payment to the coordinator.

Any number of coordinators may participate in an auction. However, we assume that all coordinators follow the same protocol, which is common knowledge. Singleton bidders submit messages directly to the auctioneer in the main auction, pay the amount of their message if they win.

The Bayesian Game

Given our economic environment and auction mechanism, a well-defined Bayesian game will be specified by every tuple of primary auction type, bidding club rules and distributions over agent types, numbers of agents and numbers of bidding clubs. A strategy $b_i : \mathcal{T} \to \mathcal{M}$ for agent i is a mapping from his type τ_i to a message μ_i. This may be the null message, which indicates non-participation in the auction. Σ denotes the set of possible strategies, i.e., the set of functions from types to messages in $\mathcal{M}$. Each agent's type is that agent's private information, but the whole setting is common knowledge. For notational simplicity we only define symmetric equilibria, where all agents bid the same function of their type, as this is sufficient for our purposes in this paper. By $L_i(\tau_i, b_i, b^{j-1})$ we denote agent i's *ex post* expected utility given that his type is τ_i, he follows the strategy b_i, all other agents use the strategy b, and there are a total of j agents. Let A be the set of participants in the auction, where $|A| = n$. The strategy profile $b^n \in \Sigma^n$ is a symmetric Bayes-Nash equilibrium if and only if $\forall i \in A, \forall \tau_i \in \mathcal{T}, b \in \text{argmax}_{b_i \in \Sigma} \sum_{j=2}^{\infty} p_j^{\tau_i} L_i(\tau_i, b_i, b^{j-1})$.

Bidding Clubs for First-Price Auctions

Assumptions

Our results hold for a broad class of distributions of agent valuations—all those for which the following two assumptions are true. First, we assume that F is continuous and atomless. Before giving our second assumption, we define $P_{x \geq i} = \sum_{x=i}^{\infty} p_x$, and define the relation "$<$", corresponding to a notion of stochastic dominance: $P < P'$ iff $\exists l (\forall i < l, P_{x \geq i} = P'_{x \geq i}$ and $\forall i \geq l, P_{x \geq i} < P'_{x \geq i})$. Our second assumption is that $(P < P')$ implies that $\forall v, b^e(v, P) < b^e(v, P')$. Intuitively, we assume that every agent's symmetric equilibrium bid in a setting with a stochastic number of participants drawn from P' is strictly greater than that agent's symmetric equilibrium bid in a setting with a stochastic number of participants drawn from P, whenever P' stochastically dominates P.

First-Price Auction Bidding Club Protocol

What follows is the first-price auction bidding club protocol for a coordinator who has invited k agents:

1. Each agent i sends a message μ_i to the coordinator.
2. If at least one agent declines participation then the coordinator registers in the main auction for every agent who accepted the invitation to the bidding club. For each bidder i, the coordinator submits a bid of $b^e(\mu_i, P^{n,k})$, where n is the number of bidders announced by the auctioneer.
3. If all agents accepted the invitation, the coordinator drops all bidders except the bidder with the highest reported valuation, who we will denote as bidder h. For h the coordinator will place a bid of $b^e(\mu_h, P^{n,1})$ in the main auction.
4. If bidder h wins in the main auction, he is made to pay $b^e(\mu_h, P^{n,1})$ to the center and $b^e(\mu_h, P^{n,k}) - b^e(\mu_h, P^{n,1})$ to the coordinator.

Theorem 1 *It is an equilibrium for all bidding club members to choose to participate and to truthfully declare their valuations to their respective bidding club coordinators, and for all non-bidding club members to participate in the main auction with a bid of $b^e(v, P^{n,1})$.*

Remark. Despite the fact that this is the central theorem of this paper, it is difficult to summarize here as it makes use of two general lemmas and consists of a lengthy case analysis. In particular, in one of these lemmas we identify a particular class of auction mechanisms that are asymmetric in the sense that every agent is subject to the same allocation rule but to a potentially different payment rule, and furthermore that agents may receive different signals. We show that truthful bidding is an equilibrium for this class of mechanisms. Under the equilibrium demonstrated in the theorem the coordinator makes money on expectation and never loses money. The equilibrium also gives rise to an economically efficient allocation: i.e., the good is allocated to the agent with the globally highest valuation.

Do bidding clubs cause agents to gain?

We can show that bidders are better off being invited to a bidding club than being sent to the auction as singleton bidders. Intuitively, an agent gains by not having to consider the possibility that other bidders who would otherwise have belonged to his club might themselves be bidding clubs.

Theorem 2 *An agent i has higher expected utility in a bidding club of size k bidding as described in theorem 1 than he does if the bidding club does not exist and k additional agents (including i) participate directly in the main auction as singleton bidders, again bidding as in theorem 1.*

We can also show that singleton bidders and members of other bidding clubs benefit from the existence of each bidding club in the same sense. Intuitively, other bidders gain from not having to consider the possibility that additional bidders might represent bidding clubs. Paradoxically, other bidders' gain from the existence of a given bidding club is greater than the gain of that club's members.

Corollary 1 *In the equilibrium described in theorem 1, singleton bidders and members of other bidding clubs have higher expected utility when other agents participate in a given bidding club of size $k \geq 2$, as compared to a case where k additional agents participate directly in the main auction as singleton bidders.*

Finally, we can show that agents are indifferent between participating in the equilibrium from theorem 1 in a bidding club of size k (thus, where the number of agents is distributed according to $P^{n,k}$) and participating in an economic environment with a stochastic number of bidders distributed according to $P^{n,k}$, but with no coordinators.

Theorem 3 *For all $\tau_i \in \mathcal{T}$, for all $k \geq 1$, for all $n \geq 2$, agent i obtains the same expected utility by:*

1. *participating in a bidding club of size k in the bidding club economic environment and following the equilibrium from theorem 1;*
2. *participating in a first-price auction with participation revelation in an economic environment with a stochastic number of bidders distributed according to $P^{n,k}$ where all bidders receive the null signal and no coordinators exist.*

This theorem shows that an agent would be as happy in a world without bidding clubs as he is in our economic environment. The difference between the two worlds is that in the latter bidding club coordinators make a positive profit on expectation, and indeed never lose money. That is, in the bidding club economic environment some expected profit is shifted from the auctioneer to the bidding club coordinator(s) without affecting the bidders' expected utility. We observe that it would be easy for coordinators to redistribute some of these gains to bidders along the lines of the second-price auction protocol proposed by (Graham & Marshall 1987): coordinators make a payment to every bidder who accepts the invitation to join, where the amount of this payment is less than or equal to the *ex ante* expected difference that the bidder makes to the coordinator's profit. With this modification coordinators would be budget balanced only on expectation (violating our earlier requirement that coordinators *never* lose money), but agents would strictly prefer the bidding club economic environment to the economic environment in which coordinators do not exist.

Disrupting Bidding Clubs

There are two things an auctioneer can do to disrupt bidding clubs in a first-price auction. First, she can permit "false-name bidding" (see, e.g., (Yokoo, Sakurai, & Matsubara 2000)). Our auction model has assumed that each agent may place only a single bid in the auction, and that the center has a way of uniquely identifying agents. (For example, the auctioneer might make it impossible for bidders to place bids claiming to originate from different agents by keying user accounts to credit card billing addresses in combination with a reputation ranking.) Second, she can refrain from publicly disclosing the winner of the auction. If the auctioneer does either of these things, a given bidder i has incentive to deviate from the equilibrium in theorem 1 by accepting the invitation to join the bidding club but placing a very low bid with the coordinator and at the same time directly submitting a competitive bid in the main auction. Agent i will gain when all other agents bid truthfully because the bidding club will drop all but one of its members (lowering the number of participants announced by the auctioneer) and will also require its high bidder to bid less than he would if he were not bound to the coordination protocol. If false-name bidding is impossible and the winner of the auction is publicly disclosed then the bidding club coordinator can detect an agent who has deviated in this way and impose a punitive fine, making the deviation unprofitable.

Conclusion

We have presented a formal model of bidding clubs which departs in many ways from models traditionally used in the study of collusion; most importantly, all agents behave strategically based on correct information about the economic environment, including the possibility that other agents will collude. Other features of our setting include a stochastic number of agents and a stochastic number of bidding clubs in each auction. Agents' strategy space is expanded so that the decision of whether or not to join a bidding club is part of an agent's choice of strategy. Bidding clubs never lose money, and gain on expectation. We have showed a bidding club protocol for first-price auctions that leads to a (globally) efficient allocation in equilibrium, and which does not make use of side-payments; we also showed that this protocol can benefit agents in three different senses.

References

Boutilier, C.; Shoham, Y.; and Wellman, M. 1997. Economic principles of multi-agent systems (editorial). *Artificial Intelligence* 94.

Graham, D., and Marshall, R. 1987. Collusive bidder behavior at single-object second-price and english auctions. *Journal of Political Economy* 95:579–599.

Greenwald, A. 1999. Shopbots and Pricebots. In *IJCAI-99*, 506–511.

Harstad, R.; Kagel, J.; and Levin, D. 1990. Equilibrium bid functions for auctions with an uncertain number of bidders. *Economic Letters* 33(1):35–40.

Leyton-Brown, K.; Shoham, Y.; and Tennenholtz, M. 2000. Bidding clubs: institutionalized collusion in auctions. In *ACM Conference on Electronic Commerce*.

McAfee, R., and McMillan, J. 1987. Auctions with a stochastic number of bidders. *Journal of Economic Theory* 43:1–19.

McAfee, R., and McMillan, J. 1992. Bidding rings. *The American Economic Theory* 82:579–599.

Monderer, D., and Tennenholtz, M. 2000. Optimal Auctions Revisited. *Artificial Intelligence* 120(1):29–42.

Parkes, D., and Ungar, L. 2000. Preventing Strategic Manipulation in Iterative Auctions: Proxy-Agents and Price-Adjustment. In *AAAI-00*, 82–89.

Sandholm, T.; Suri, S.; Gilpin, A.; and Levine, D. 2001. Cabob: A fast optimal algorithm for combinatorial auctions. In *IJCAI-01*, 1102–1108.

Stone, P., and Greenwald, A. 2000. The first international trading agent competition: autonomous bidding agents. *Journal of Electronic Commerce Research* 1–36.

Tennenholtz, M. 1999. Electronic commerce: From game-theoretic and economic models to working protocols. In *IJCAI-99*.

Yokoo, M.; Sakurai, Y.; and Matsubara, S. 2000. Robsut combinatorial auction protocol against false-name bids. In *Proceedings of the 17th national conference on Artificial Intelligence*, 110–115.

Truthful Approximation Mechanisms for Restricted Combinatorial Auctions
Extended Abstract

Ahuva Mu'alem and **Noam Nisan**

School of Computer Science and Engineering
The Hebrew University of Jerusalem
{ahumu, noam}@cs.huji.ac.il

Abstract

When attempting to design a truthful mechanism for a computationally hard problem such as combinatorial auctions, one is faced with the problem that most efficiently computable heuristics can not be embedded in any truthful mechanism (e.g. VCG-like payment rules will not ensure truthfulness).

We develop a set of techniques that allow constructing efficiently computable truthful mechanisms for combinatorial auctions in the special case where only the valuation is unknown by the mechanism (the single parameter case). For this case we extend the work of Lehmann O'Callaghan, and Shoham, who presented greedy heuristics, and show how to use IF-THEN-ELSE constructs, perform a partial search, and use the LP relaxation. We apply these techniques for several types of combinatorial auctions, obtaining truthful mechanisms with provable approximation ratios.

Introduction

Recent years have seen a surge of interest in combinatorial (also called combinational) auctions, in which a number of non-identical items are sold concurrently and bidders express preferences about combinations of items and not just about single items. Such combinatorial auctions have been suggested for a host of auction situations such as those for spectrum licenses, pollution permits, landing slots, computational resources, online procurement and others. See (Vohra & de Vries 2000) for a survey.

Beyond their direct applications, combinatorial auctions are emerging as the central representative problem for a whole new field of research that is sometimes called algorithmic mechanism design. This field deals with the interplay of algorithmic considerations and game-theoretic considerations that stem from computing systems that involve participants (players, agents) with differing goals. Many leading examples are motivated by Internet applications, e.g., various networking protocols, electronic commerce, and non-cooperative software agents. See e.g. (Rosenschein & Zlotkin 1994) for an early treatment, and (Nisan 1999; Papadimitriou 2001) for more recent surveys. The combinatorial auction problem is attaining this central status due to two elements: First, the problem is very expressive

(e.g. a competition for network resources needed for routing can be modeled as a combinatorial auction of bandwidth on the various communication links). Second, dealing with combinatorial auctions requires treating a very wide spectrum of issues.

Indeed implementation of combinatorial auctions faces many challenges ranging from purely representational questions of succinctly specifying the various bids, to purely algorithmic challenges of efficiently solving the resulting, NP-hard, allocation problems, to pure game-theoretic questions of bidders' strategies and equilibria. Much work has recently been done on these topics, see e.g., (Vohra & de Vries 2000; Sandholm *et al.* 2001; Nisan 2000; Lehmann, O'Callaghan, & Shoham 1999) and many references therein.

Perhaps the most interesting questions are those that intimately combine computational considerations and game theoretic ones. Possibly the most central problem of this form is the difficulty of getting algorithmically efficient truthful mechanisms. The basic game-theoretic requirement in mechanism design is that of "truthfulness" (incentive compatibility), i.e. that the participating agents are motivated to cooperate with the protocol [1]. The basic algorithmic requirement is computational efficiency. Each of these requirements can be addressed separately: "VCG mechanisms" (Vickrey 1961; Clarke 1971; Groves 1973) – the basic possibility result of mechanism design – ensure truthfulness, and a host of algorithmic techniques (e.g. (Sandholm *et al.* 2001; Vohra & de Vries 2000; Zurel & Nisan 2001)) can achieve reasonably good allocations for most practical purposes (despite the general NP-hardness of the allocation problem). Unfortunately, these two requirements do conflict with each other! It has been noticed (Lehmann, O'Callaghan, & Shoham 1999; Nisan & Ronen 1999) that when VCG mechanisms are applied to non-optimal allocation algorithms (as any computationally efficient algorithm must be), truthfulness is not obtained. This problem was studied further in (Nisan & Ronen 2000; Monderer *et al.* 2001).

The key positive result known so far is due to Lehmann,

---

[1] We defer the exact game theoretic definitions to section 2. In general one only needs equilibria, but the revelation principle allows concentration on truthful mechanisms.

O'Callaghan, & Shoham. They restrict the set of preferences that agents may have to be what they call "single minded", i.e. agents that are only interested in a single bundle of items. For this class of bidders they present a family of simple greedy mechanisms that are both algorithmically efficient and truthful! They also show that one mechanism in this family has provable approximation properties. In this paper we continue this line of research. We slightly further restrict the agents, but we obtain a much richer class of algorithmically efficient truthful mechanisms. In fact we present a set of general tools that allow the creation of such mechanisms. Many of our results, but not all of them, apply also to the general class of single-minded bidders.

In our model, termed "*known* single minded bidders", we not only assume that each agent is only interested in a single bundle of goods, but also that the identity of this bundle can be verified by the mechanism (in fact it suffices that the cardinality of the bundle can be verified). This assumption is reasonable in a wide variety of situations where the required set of goods can be inferred from context, e.g. messages that needs to be routed over a set of network links, or bundles of a given cardinality. Our model captures the general case where only a single parameter (a one-dimensional valuation) is unknown to the mechanism and must be handled in a truthful way. (The single parameter case has also been studied from a computational point of view in a different context in (Archer & Tardos 2001).) We first present an array of general algorithmic techniques that can be used to obtain truthful algorithms:

- Generalizations of the greedy family of algorithms suggested by Lehmann, O'Callaghan, & Shoham.

- A technique based on linear programming.

- Finitely bounded exhaustive search.

- A "MAX" construct: this construction combines different truthful algorithms and takes the best solution.

- An If-Then-Else construct: this construction allows branching, according to a condition, to one of many truthful algorithms.

The combination of these techniques provides enough flexibility to allow construction of many types of truthful algorithms. In particular it allows many types of partial search algorithms – the basic heuristic approach in many applications. We demonstrate the generality and power of our techniques by constructing polynomial-time truthful algorithms for several important cases of combinatorial auctions for which we prove approximation guarantees:

- An $\epsilon\sqrt{m}$-approximation for the general case for any fixed $\epsilon > 0$. This improves over the $\sqrt{m}$ ratio proved in (Lehmann, O'Callaghan, & Shoham 1999), where m is number of items. This is, in fact, the best algorithm (due to (Halldórsson 2000)) known for combinatorial auctions even without requiring truthfulness!

- A very simple 2-approximation for the homogeneous (multi-unit) case. Despite the extensive literature on multi unit auctions (starting with the seminal paper (Vickrey 1961)) this is the first polynomial time truthful mechanism with valuations that are not downward sloping!

- An $m+1$-approximation for multi-unit combinatorial auctions with m types of goods.

The rest of this paper is structured as follows. In section 2 we formally present our model and notations. In section 3 we also provide a simple algorithmic characterization of truthful mechanisms. In section 4 we present our basic techniques and prove their correctness, and in section 5 we present our operators for combining truthful mechanisms. In section 6 we present our applications and prove their approximation properties. Finally, in section 7, we shortly mention which of our results generalize to the single-minded case.

The Model

Combinatorial Auctions

We consider an auction of a set U of m distinct items to a set N of n bidders. We assume that bidders value combinations of items: i.e., items may be complements or substitutes of each other. Formally, each bidder j has a *valuation function* $v_j()$ that describes his valuation for each subset $S \subseteq U$ of items, i.e. $v_j(S) \geq 0$ is the maximal amount of money $j \in N$ is willing to pay for S.

An *allocation* $S_1, ..., S_n$ is a partition of the items U among the bidders. We consider here auctions that aim to maximize the total *social welfare*, $w = \sum_j v_j(S_j)$, of the allocation. The auction rules describe a *payment* p_j for each bidder j. We assume the bidders have *quasi linear utilities*, so bidder j's overall utility for winning the set S_j and paying p_j is $u_j = v_j(S_j) - p_j$.

Known Single Minded Bidders

In this paper we only discuss a limited class of bidders, single minded bidders, that were introduced by Lehmann, O'Callaghan, & Shoham.

Definition 1 *(Lehmann, O'Callaghan, & Shoham 1999) Bidder j is single minded if there is a set of goods $S_j \subseteq U$ and a value $v_j^* \geq 0$ such that* $v_j(S) = \begin{cases} v_j^* & S \supseteq S_j \\ 0 & otherwise. \end{cases}$

I.e., the bidder is willing to pay v_j^* as long as he is allocated S_j. We assume that each v_j^* is privately known to bidder j. We deviate from Lehmann, O'Callaghan, & Shoham and assume that the subsets S_j's are known to the mechanism (or alternatively can be independently deduced or authenticated by the mechanism). We call this case, *known single minded bidders*. It is easy to verify that all our results apply even if only the cardinality of S_j is known. Some of our results hold even if the S_j's are only privately known (as in Lehmann, O'Callaghan, & Shoham). We shortly describe this case in the last section.

The Mechanism

We consider only closed bid auctions where each bidder $j \in N$ sends his bid v_j to the mechanism, and then the mechanism computes an allocation and determines the payments for each bidder. The allocation and payments depend on the bidders' declarations $v = (v_1, ..., v_n)$. Thus the auction mechanism is composed of an *allocation algorithm* $A(v)$, and a *payment rule* $p(v)$.

Treated as an algorithm, the allocation algorithm A is given as input not only the bids $v_1...v_n$, but also the sets $S_1...S_n$ that are desired by the bidders. Its output specifies a subset $A(v) \subseteq N$ of *winning bids* that are pair-wise disjoint, $S_i \cap S_j = \emptyset$ for each $i \neq j \in A(v)$. Thus bidder j wins the set S_j if $j \in A(v)$ and wins nothing otherwise.

Let v_{-j} be the partial declaration vector $(v_1,...,v_{j-1},v_{j+1},...,v_n)$, and let $v = (v_j, v_{-j})$. For given valuations v_{-j} and allocation algorithm A, we say that v_j is a *winning declaration* if $j \in A(v_j, v_{-j})$. Otherwise we say that v_j is a *losing declaration*. Sometimes we shall simply say that j wins S_j if $j \in A(v)$.

The *(revealed) social welfare* obtained by the algorithm is thus $w_A(v) = \Sigma_{j \in A(v)} v_j$. While our allocation algorithms attempt maximizing this social welfare, they of course can not find optimal allocations since that it is NP-hard ("weighted set packing") and we are interested in computationally efficient allocation algorithms.

Bidders' strategies

Bidder's j utility in a mechanism (A, p) is thus $u_j(v) = v_j - p_j$ if $j \in A(v)$, and $u_j(v) = -p_j$ otherwise. A mechanism is *normalized* if non-winners pay zero, i.e. $p_j = 0$ for all $j \notin A(v)$. In this case $u_j = 0$ for all $j \notin A(v)$.

Bidder j may strategically prefers to declare a value $v_j \neq v_j^*$ in order to increase his utility. We are interested in truthful mechanisms where this does not happen.

Definition 2 *A mechanism is called truthful (equivalently, incentive compatible) if truthfully declaring $v_j = v_j^*$ is a dominant strategy for each bidder. I.e. for any declarations of the other bidders v_{-j}, and any declaration v_j of bidder j, $u_j(v_j^*, v_{-j}) \geq u_j(v_j, v_{-j})$.*

Multi unit Auctions

In a *Multi Unit Combinatorial Auction* we have many types of items and many identical items of each type. We consider a multiset U with m different types of items, where m_i is the number of identical items of type $i = 1, \ldots, m$. Let M be the total number of goods, that is $M = \Sigma_{i=1}^m m_i = |U|$.

The special case $m = 1$ where all items are identical, is called a *Multi Unit Auction*. The knapsack problem is a special case of the allocation problem of Multi Unit Auction.

All our results apply also to multi-unit combinatorial auctions, and so we assume that a bidder is interested in a fixed number of goods of each type. I.e. instead of having a single set S_j, each bidder has a tuple $q_1...q_m$, specifying that he desires (has value v_j) a multiset of items that contains at least q_i items of type i, for all i.

Characterization of Truthful Mechanisms

It is well known that truthful mechanisms are strongly related to certain monotonicity conditions on the allocation algorithm. This was formalized axiomatically in the context of combinatorial auctions with single minded bidders in Lehmann, O'Callaghan, & Shoham. We present here a simple characterization for the case of known single minded bidders. The problem of designing truthful mechanisms then reduces to that of designing monotone algorithms.

Monotone Allocation Algorithms

An allocation algorithm is monotone if, whenever S_j is allocated and the declared valuation of j increases, then S_j remains allocated to j. Formally:

Definition 3 *An allocation algorithm A is monotone if, for any bidder j and any v_{-j}, if v_j is a winning declaration then any higher declaration $v_j' \geq v_j$ also wins.*

Lemma 1 *Let A be a monotone allocation algorithm. Then, for any v_{-j} there exists a single critical value $\theta_j(A, v_{-j}) \in (R_+ \cup \infty)$ such that $\forall v_j > \theta_j(A, v_{-j})$, v_j is a winning declaration, and $\forall v_j < \theta_j(A, v_{-j})$, v_j is a losing declaration.*

Fix an algorithm A and bids of the other bidders, v_{-j}. Note that $\theta_j = \theta_j(A, v_{-j})$ is the infimum value that j should declare in order to win S_j. In particular, note that θ_j is independent of v_j. Consider an auction of a single item. It is easy to see that the winner's critical value is the value of the 2nd highest bid. Note that the 2nd price (Vickerey) auction fixes this value as the payment scheme. This can be generalized.

Definition 4 *The payment scheme p_A associated with the monotone allocation algorithm A that is based on the critical value is defined by: $p_j = \theta_j(A, v_{-j})$ if j wins S_j, and $p_j = 0$ otherwise.*

The Characterization

It turns out that monotone allocation algorithms with critical value payment schemes capture essentially all truthful mechanisms. Formally they capture exactly truthful normalized mechanisms, but any truthful mechanism can be easily converted to be normalized.

Theorem 1 *A normalized mechanism is truthful if and only if its allocation algorithm is monotone and its payment scheme is based on critical value.*

The theorem also implies the following (using binary search).

Lemma 2 *If the allocation algorithm of a truthful normalized mechanism is computable in polynomial time, then so is the payment scheme.*

Bitonic Allocation Algorithms

We use a special case of monotone allocation algorithms, called *bitonic*. Given a monotone algorithm A, the property of bitonicity involves the connection between v_j and the social welfare of the allocation $A(v_j, v_{-j})$. What it requires is that the welfare does not increase with v_j when v_j loses, $v_j < \theta_j$, and does increase with v_j when v_j wins, $v_j > \theta_j$.

Definition 5 *A monotone allocation algorithm A is bitonic if for every bidder j and any v_{-j}, one of the following conditions holds: (i) The welfare $w_A(v_{-j}, v_j)$ is a non-increasing function of v_j for $v_j < \theta_j$ and a non-decreasing function of v_j for $v_j \geq \theta_j$; or, (ii) The welfare $w_A(v_{-j}, v_j)$ is a non-increasing function of v_j for $v_j \leq \theta_j$ and a non-decreasing function of v_j for $v_j > \theta_j$.*

One would indeed expect that a given bid does not affect the allocation between the other bids, and thus for $v_j < \theta_j$

we would expect w_A to be constant, and for $v_j > \theta_j$ we would expect w_A to grow linearly with v_j. Most of our examples, as well as the optimal allocation algorithm, indeed follow this pattern. This need not hold in general though and there do exist non-bitonic monotone algorithms.

Example 1 *A non-bitonic monotone allocation algorithm*

XOR-algorithm(Y, i, j, k)

Input: $Y \in R^+$ and $i, j, k \in N$.

If the valuation v_i of bidder i is below Y then bidder j wins. Else if v_i is below $2Y$ then bidder k wins. Else bidder i wins.

The XOR-algorithm is monotone (the critical value for any bidder other than i is either zero or infinity, and the critical value for bidder i is $2Y$). Focusing on bidder i, observe that the welfare in the interval $[0, 2Y)$ may be increasing, and so the XOR-algorithm is not bitonic in general.

Some Basic Truthful Mechanisms

In this section we present several monotone allocation algorithms. Each of them may be used as a basis for a truthful mechanism. They can also be combined between themselves using the operators described later on.

Greedy

The main algorithmic result of Lehmann, O'Callaghan, & Shoham was the identification of the following scheme of greedy algorithms as truthful. First the bids are reordered according to a certain "monotone" ranking criteria. Then, considering the bids in the new order, bids are allocated greedily. We start with a slight generalization of their result.

Definition 6 *A ranking r is a collection of n real valued functions $(r_1(), r_2(), \ldots, r_n())$, where $r_j() = r_j(v_j, S_j), j \in N$. A ranking r is monotone if each $r_j()$ is non-decreasing in v_j.*

We will use the following monotone rankings.

1. The **value ranking**: $r_j(.) = v_j$, $j = 1..n$.

2. The **density ranking**: $r_j(.) = \frac{v_j}{|S_j|}$, $j = 1..n$.

3. The **compact ranking by k**: $r_j(.) = \begin{cases} v_j & |S_j| \leq \sqrt{\frac{M}{k}} \\ 0 & \text{otherwise} \end{cases}$

   where $k > 0$ is fixed, $j = 1..n$.

Greedy Algorithm G_r based on ranking r

1. Reorder the bids by decreasing value of $r_j(.)$.

2. *WinningBids* $\leftarrow \emptyset$, *NonAllocItems* $\leftarrow U$.

3. For $j = 1..n$ (in the new order) if $(S_j \subseteq NonAllocItems)$
   - *WinningBids* $\leftarrow$ *WinningBids* $\cup \{j\}$.
   - *NonAllocItems* $\leftarrow$ *NonAllocItems* $- S_j$.

4. Return *WinningBids*.

Lemma 3 *(essentially due to Lehmann, O'Callaghan, & Shoham) Any greedy allocation scheme G_r that is based on a monotone ranking r is monotone.*

It turns out that a greedy algorithm is in fact bitonic.

Lemma 4 *Any greedy allocation scheme G_r that is based on a monotone ranking r is bitonic.*

Partial Exhaustive Search

The second algorithm we present, performs an exhaustive search over all combinations of at most k bids. The running time is polynomial for every fixed k.

Exst-k Search Algorithm

1. *WinningBids* $\leftarrow \emptyset$, *Max* $\leftarrow 0$.

2. For each (subset $J \subseteq \{1, \ldots, n\}$ such that $|J| \leq k$):
   if $(\forall i, j \in J, i \neq j : S_i \cap S_j = \emptyset)$ then
   - if $(\Sigma_J v_i > Max)$ then
     $Max \leftarrow \Sigma_J v_i$ and *WinningBids* $\leftarrow J$.

3. Return *WinningBids*.

The extreme cases are of interest: Exst-1 simply returns the bid with the highest valuation; and Exst-n is the naive optimal algorithm which searches the entire solution space. We shall use Exst-1, and hence give it an additional name.

Largest Algorithm Return the bid with the highest valuation $v_h = max_{j \in N} v_j$.

Lemma 5 *For every k, Exst-k is monotone and bitonic.*

LP based

Since the combinatorial auction problem is an integer programming problem, many authors have tried heuristics that follow the standard approach of using the linear programming relaxation (Nisan 2000; Zurel & Nisan 2001; Vohra & de Vries 2000). In general such heuristics are not truthful (i.e., not monotone). In this section we present a very simple heuristic based on the LP relaxation that is truthful.

In this subsection we use general notation of multi unit combinatorial auctions. The multiset S_j can be regarded as the m-tuple $(q_{1j}, \ldots, q_{mj})$, where q_{ij} it the number of items of type i in S_j. The optimal allocation problem can be formulated as the following integer program, denoted $IP(v)$.

$$\text{maximize} \quad \Sigma_{j=1}^n z_j v_j$$
$$\text{subject to:} \quad \begin{array}{ll} \Sigma_{j=1}^n z_j q_{ij} \leq m_i & i = 1, \ldots, m \\ z_j \in \{0, 1\} & j = 1, \ldots, n \end{array}$$

Removing the integrality constraint we get the following linear program relaxation, denoted $LP(v)$:

$$\text{maximize} \quad \Sigma_{j=1}^n x_j v_j$$
$$\text{subject to:} \quad \begin{array}{ll} \Sigma_{j=1}^n x_j q_{ij} \leq m_i & i = 1, \ldots, m \\ x_j \in [0, 1] & j = 1, \ldots, n \end{array}$$

Natural heuristics for solving the integer program would attempt using the values of x_j in order to decide on the integral allocation. We show that the following simple rule does indeed provide a monotone allocation rule.

LP-Based Algorithm

1. Compute an optimal basic solution x for $LP(v)$.

2. Satisfy all bids j for which $x_j = 1$.

Theorem 2 *Algorithm LP-Based is monotone.*

The proof is based on the following lemma.

Lemma 6 $\forall v_{-j}$, x_j *is a non-decreasing function of v_j.*

Combining Truthful Mechanisms

In this section we present two techniques for combining monotone allocation algorithms as to obtain an improved monotone allocation algorithm. These combination operators together with the previously presented algorithms provide a general algorithmic toolbox for constructing monotone allocation algorithms and thus also truthful mechanisms. This toolbox will be used in order to construct truthful approximation mechanisms for various special cases of combinatorial auctions.

The MAX Operator

Perhaps the most natural way to combine two allocations algorithms is to try both and pick the best one – the one providing the maximal social welfare.

MAX (A_1, A_2) Operator

1. Run the algorithms A_1 and A_2.
2. if $w_{A_1}(v) \geq w_{A_2}(v)$ return $A_1(v)$, else return $A_2(v)$.

Unfortunately this algorithm is not in general guaranteed to be monotone. For example the maximum of two XOR-algorithms, with parameters Y, i, j, k and Y', i, j', k', is not monotone in general for bidder i. We are able to identify a condition that ensures monotonicity.

Theorem 3 *Let A_1 and A_2 be two monotone bitonic allocation algorithms. Then, $M = MAX(A_1, A_2)$ is a monotone bitonic allocation algorithm.*

Since the maximum of two bitonic algorithms is also bitonic, then inductively the maximum of any number of bitonic algorithms is monotone.

The If-Then-Else Operator

The max operator had to run both algorithms. In many cases we wish to have conditional execution and only run one of the given algorithms, where the choice depends on some condition. This is the usual If-The-Else construct of programming languages.

If cond() Then $A1$ Else A_2 Operator

If *cond(v)* holds
    return the allocation $A_1(v)$.
Else
    return the allocation $A_2(v)$.

The monotonicity of the two algorithms does not by itself guarantee that the combination is monotone. As a simple example consider the following algorithm: If $\Sigma_{i=1}^n v_i$ is even then the bid with largest valuation wins, otherwise bidder 1 wins. For a fixed v_{-j}, observe that if v_j is a winning declaration (j wins) then $v_j + 1$ is a losing declaration (1 wins instead), and so the algorithm is not monotone for bidder j. We require a certain "alignment" between the condition and the algorithms in order to ensure monotonicity of the result.

Definition 7 *The boolean function cond() is aligned with the allocation algorithm A if for any v_{-j} and any two values $v_j \leq v'_j$ the following hold:*

1. *If $cond(v_{-j}, v_j)$ holds and $v_j \geq \theta_j(A, v_{-j})$ then $cond(v_{-j}, v'_j)$ holds.*
2. *If $cond(v_{-j}, v'_j)$ holds and $v'_j \leq \theta_j(A, v_{-j})$ then $cond(v_{-j}, v_j)$ holds.*

Theorem 4 *If A_1 and A_2 are monotone allocation algorithms and cond() is aligned with A_1 then the operator If-Then-Else (cond, A_1, A_2) is monotone.*

Applications: Approximation Mechanisms

In this section we use the toolbox previously developed to construct truthful approximation mechanisms for several interesting cases of combinatorial auctions (all with known single minded bidders). These mechanisms all run in polynomial time and obtain allocations that are within a provable gap from the optimum.

Multi Unit Auctions

In multi-unit auctions we have a certain number of identical items, and each known single-minded bidder is willing to offer the price v_j for the quantity q_j. In fact we are required to solve the NP-complete knapsack problem. Indeed, despite the vast economic literature, starting with Vickrey's seminal paper (Vickrey 1961), that deals with multi-unit auctions, this case was never studied, and attention was always restricted to "downward sloping bids" that can always be partially fulfilled. While the knapsack problem has fully polynomial approximation schemes, these are not monotone and thus do not yield truthful mechanisms. We provide a truthful 2-approximation mechanism.

Let G_v be the algorithm Greedy based on a value ranking. Let G_d be the algorithm Greedy based on a density ranking.

Apx-MUA Algorithm

Return the allocation determined by MAX(G_v, G_d).

Theorem 5 *The mechanism with Apx-MUA as the allocation algorithm and the associated critical value payment scheme is 2-approximation truthful mechanism for multi unit auctions.*

General Combinatorial Auctions

The general combinatorial auction allocation problem is NP-hard to approximate to within a factor of $m^{\frac{1}{2}-\epsilon}$ (for any fixed $\epsilon > 0$) (Hastad 1999; Sandholm 1999; Lehmann, O'Callaghan, & Shoham 1999). A $\sqrt{m}$-approximation truthful mechanism is given in Lehmann, O'Callaghan, & Shoham for the case of single minded bidders. We narrow the gap between the upper bound and lower bound even further and present truthful mechanisms with performance guarantee of $\epsilon\sqrt{m}$, for every fixed $\epsilon > 0$.

Let G_k be the Greedy algorithm Greedy based on the compact ranking by k.

k-Apx-CA Algorithm

Return the allocation determined by MAX(Exst-k, G_k).

Theorem 6 *The mechanism with $\lfloor \frac{4}{\epsilon^2} \rfloor$-Apx-CA as the allocation algorithm and the associated critical value payment scheme is an ($\epsilon\sqrt{m}$)-approximation truthful mechanism.*

Multi unit Combinatorial Auctions

Here we consider the general case of multi-unit combinatorial auctions. We provide a monotone allocation algorithm that provides good approximations in the case that the number of types of goods, m, is small.

$(m+1)$-Apx-MUCA Algorithm

1. Compute an optimal basic solution x to $LP(v)$.

2. Let $v_h = max_j v_j$.

3. If $\Sigma_{l=1}^{n} x_l v_l < (m+1) v_h$ Then return Largest(v); Else return LP-Based(v).

Theorem 7 *The mechanism with $(m+1)$-Apx-MUCA as the allocation algorithm and the associated critical value payment scheme is $(m+1)$-approximation truthful mechanism for multi unit combinatorial auctions with m types of goods.*

Single Minded Bidders

Some of our techniques apply to the more general model of Single Minded Bidders of Lehmann, O'Callaghan, & Shoham. In this section we shortly mention which techniques do generalize and how. A single minded bidder j has a privately known (S_j, v_j^*), and it then submits to the mechanism a single bid of the form (T_j, v_j), where $T_j \subseteq U$. The definition of truthfulness of a mechanism, for single minded bidders, is that bidding the truth $(T_j, v_j) = (S_j, v_j^*)$ is a dominant strategy for all bidders j. An allocation algorithm A is *monotone* if for any bidder j and declarations of the other bidders (T_{-j}, v_{-j}), whenever (T_j, v_j) is a winning declaration for j so is any bid (T_j', v_j') where $T_j' \subseteq Tj$ and $v_j' \geq v_j$. We mention whether and how each of our results generalizes.

- **Characterization:** The characterization of truthful mechanisms is now modified to include algorithmic monotonicity in T_j.

- **Basic algorithms**: All 3 basic algorithms (Exst-k, LP-based, and Greedy) generalize. Greedy is due to Lehmann, O'Callaghan, & Shoham and requires the ranking r to be also monotone in T_j.

- **Operators:** If-Then-Else is monotone. The proof goes through once the definition of alignment is modified to take into account the declared sets. MAX is not monotone in general, as can be witnessed by example 2.

- **Applications:** The approximation mechanisms presented previously are not necessarily truthful for single minded bidders. However, we provide an alternative 2-approximation mechanism for multi-unit auctions with single minded bidders.

Example 2 *MAX is not monotone for single minded bidders. Applying $MAX(G_v, G_d)$ on the bids: $B_1 = (\{a\}, 6)$, $B_2 = (\{b, c\}, 5)$, $B_3 = (\{c, d, e\}, 7)$, $B_4 = (\{a, b, c, d, e\}, 12)$, where $B_i = (T_i, v_i)$. Then B_1 loses. If player 1 increases his set and bids $B_1' = (\{a, b\}, 2)$ he wins!*

Acknowledgments

We thank Daniel Lehmann, Ron Lavi and Liad Blumrosen for helpful comments and Gil Kalai for an early discussion.

References

Archer, A., and Tardos, E. 2001. Truthful mechanisms for one-parameter agents. In *to appear in the 42nd Annual Symposium on Foundations of Computer Science*.

Caprara, A.; Kellerer, H.; Pferschy, U.; and Pisinger, D. 2000. Approximation algorithms for knapsack problems with cardinality constraints. *European Journal of Operational Research* 123:333–345.

Clarke, E. H. 1971. Multipart pricing of public goods. *Public Choice* 17–33.

Groves, T. 1973. Incentives in teams. *Econometrica* 617–631.

Halldórsson, M. M. 2000. Approximations of weighted independent set and hereditary subset problems. *J. Graph Algorithms Appl.* 4:no. 1, 16 pp.

Hastad, J. 1999. Clique is hard to approximate to within $n^{1-\epsilon}$. *Acta Mathematica* 182.

Lehmann, D.; O'Callaghan, L. I.; and Shoham, Y. 1999. Truth revelation in rapid, approximately efficient combinatorial auctions. In *1st ACM conference on electronic commerce*.

Martello, S., and Toth, P. 1990. *Knapsack Problems*. Wiley.

Monderer, D.; Holzman, R.; Kfir-Dahav, N.; and Tennenholtz, M. 2001. Bundling equilibrium in combinatorial auctions. Technical report, Faculty of Industrial Engineering and Management, Technion.

Nisan, N., and Ronen, A. 1999. Algorithmic mechanism design. In *STOC*.

Nisan, N., and Ronen, A. 2000. Computationally feasible VCG mechanisms. In *ACM Conference on Electronic Commerce*, 242–252.

Nisan, N. 1999. Algorithms for selfish agents. In *STACS*.

Nisan, N. 2000. Bidding and allocation in combinatorial auctions. In *ACM Conference on Electronic Commerce*.

Papadimitriou, C. H. 2001. Algorithms, games, and the internet. In *STOC*.

Rosenschein, J. S., and Zlotkin, G. 1994. *Rules of Encounter: Designing Conventions for Automated Negotiation Among Computers*. MIT Press.

Sandholm, T.; Suri, S.; Gilpin, A.; and D., L. 2001. Cabob: A fast optimal algorithm for combinatorial auctions. In *IJCAI*.

Sandholm, T. 1999. An algorithm for optimal winner determination in combinatorial auctions. In *IJCAI-99*.

Vickrey, W. 1961. Counterspeculation, auctions and competitive sealed tenders. *Journal of Finance* 8–37.

Vohra, R., and de Vries, S. 2000. Combinatorial auctions: A survey. Available from http://www.kellogg.nwu.edu/faculty/vohra/htm/res.htm.

Zurel, E., and Nisan, N. 2001. An efficient approximate allocation algorithm for combinatorial auctions. In *To appear in ACM conference on electronic commerce*. Available from http://www.cs.huji.ac.il/~noam/mkts.html.

Structural Leverage and Fictitious Play in Sequential Auctions

Weili Zhu & Peter R. Wurman

Computer Science
North Carolina State University
Raleigh, NC 27695-7535 USA
wzhu@unity.ncsu.edu, wurman@csc.ncsu.edu

Abstract

We model sequential, sealed-bid auctions as a sequential game with imperfect and incomplete information. We develop an agent that, through fictitious play, constructs a policy for the auctions that takes advantage of information learned in the early stages of the game, and is flexible with respect to assumptions about the other bidders' valuations. Because the straightforward expansion of the incomplete information game is intractable, we develop more concise representations that take advantage of the sequential auctions' natural structure. We examine the performance of our agent versus agents that play perfectly, agents that also create policies using Monte-Carlo, and agents that play myopically. The technique performs quite well in these empirical studies, though the tractable problem size is still quite small.

Introduction

Trading agents are software programs that participate in electronic markets on behalf of a user. Simple bidding tools, like eSnipe[1], have begun to appear that enable bidders to automate their last second bids on eBay. However, bidders often have a plethora of auctions in which they could participate, and need agents which can manage bidding across several auctions possibly hosted at multiple auction sites. In addition, it is apparently common on eBay for a small community of expert collectors to recognize each other, which creates the opportunity to directly model one's competitors.

We model this common scenario as a sequence of single-unit auctions with a small set of identified, risk-neutral participants, each of whom wants one unit of the item and has an independent, private value for the item. We assume that our agent knows the distribution of the other agents' valuations, but not their actual values.

The premise of this work is that information we gain about the other bidders can be used to improve play in later stages of the game. In particular, our observations of a bidder's actions in previous auctions should affect our belief about her valuation. For example, if we notice that Sue has placed bids at high values in previous auctions but not yet won anything, we are more likely to believe that Sue has a high valuation, which may influence how we should bid in future auctions.

[1]http://www.esnipe.com

We cast the problem as an incomplete, imperfect information game. However, the straightforward expansion of the game is intractable even for very small problems, and it is beyond the capability of the current algorithms to solve for the Bayes-Nash equilibria. Thus, we examine the construction of a bidding policy through fictitious play. In particular, we sample the opponents' valuations, assume they play perfectly, and solve the resulting imperfect information game. We accumulate the results of the sampling into a heuristic strategy for the incomplete information game. The resulting strategy implicitly captures the belief updating associated with observing the opponents' bids in earlier auctions.

We also find that the straightforward expansion of the imperfect information game cannot be solved directly by current game solvers (e.g., GAMBIT). Thus, we develop methods to take advantage of the sequential structure that greatly reduces the space required to represent the game and enables us to solve much larger games with GAMBIT.

Model

Consider an agent, i, that has the task of purchasing one item from a set of items, K, which are being auctioned sequentially. Let q be the number of items in K, and c_k be the auction for the kth item. Let J denote the other bidders in the market. The total number of bidders, including i, is $n = |J| + 1$.

Our agent has a value $v_i(k)$ for item k, and bidder $j \in J$, has valuation $v_j(k)$. In this study, we assume that the items in K are identical and that all participants are interested in only a single unit. We believe that the techniques we develop can be extended to auctions of heterogeneous items if an agent's valuations for the items are correlated.

Agent i does not know bidder j's true value for the items, but knows that it is drawn from a distribution, D_j. In this model, we assume that valuations are independent and private, but we do not make any particular assumptions about the functional form of the distributions, nor do we assume that the distributions are identical for all of the bidders. We will make various assumptions about whether the bidders in J know each other's valuations or agent i's valuation.

Naturally, the rules of the auctions will affect the bidders' choices of actions. Although the examples we study assume first-price, sealed-bid auctions, the techniques are generalizable to other auction formats.

Given a sequence of first-price, sealed-bid auctions, the agent must select a bid to place in each auction. Let B^k be the set of bid choices that are acceptable in auction k. Typically, we assume that B^k is the set of integers in some range, $[0, R^k]$, and is identical across all of the auctions. However, the techniques we develop admit different bid choices in each auction. Let $m = |B^k|$. Denote agent j's bid in auction c_k as b_j^k.

A buyer that does not win in auction c_k will participate in auction c_{k+1}. We assume that the auctioneer makes public a list of all of the bids once the auction is complete. This is consistent, for instance, with eBay's policy. Let h_j^k be the sequence of bids that agent j placed in the auctions up to, but not including, c_k. That is, $h_j^k = \{b_j^1, \ldots, b_j^{k-1}\}$. We call h_j^k bidder j's *history* up to auction k. The history of all J bidders is denoted H_J^k.

We model the sequential auction scenario as an extensive form game, $\Gamma(\mathcal{A}, V_{\mathcal{A}}, B^K, K)$, where $\mathcal{A} = J \cup i$ and B^K denotes the bid choices for all of the auctions. A *subgame* has the same structure, except that part of the game has already been played. For example the subgame that results when bidder j wins the first item is $\Gamma(\mathcal{A}, V_{\mathcal{A}}, B^\kappa, \kappa)$ where $\mathcal{A} = J \setminus j \cup i$ and $\kappa = K \setminus \{1\}$.

It is also useful to identify the game structure of individual auctions. Denote a *component* auction game $\gamma(\mathcal{A}, V_{\mathcal{A}}^k, B^k)$, in which agents $\mathcal{A}$, with valuations $V_{\mathcal{A}}^k$ for item k, choose bids from the set B^k. Note that a game (or subgame) is a sequence of component games. In game theoretic terms, γ is the game in which $\mathcal{A}$ is the set of players, B^k are the actions, and the payoff is $v_j(k) - b_j^k$ for the bidder with the highest bid, and zero for everyone else. Because the auction is sealed bid, all of the bidders' actions are simultaneous, and the game involves imperfect information.

A simple example with three agents, two items, and two bid levels is shown in Figure 1. The circles are labeled with the ID of the agent, and the arcs with the bid value ($\{1, 2\}$). The game consists of two stages, the first of which corresponds to the first auction involving all three agents. The second stage involves the two agents who did not win the first item. The individual subgames are labeled A–H. The small squares at the leaves of the tree represent terminal states, and for the purpose of illustration, one of these is labeled with payoffs corresponding to initial valuations of 3 for each bidder. Finally, the dotted lines connect decision nodes in the same information set.

For this example, and those used in our tests, ties were broken in favor of the agent with the lowest index. Admittedly, this creates a bias in the experimental results that we intend to address in future work. The technique we develop could be extended to allow other tie breaking policies by branching the nodes where the tie occurred with a move by nature for each of the possible outcomes. This type of move by nature can be handled relatively easily because it does not introduce any asymmetric information. Moreover, it is amenable to the decompositions we introduce in the next section.

Note that a particular component game, γ, can appear many times in the overall game Γ. For instance, in Figure 1,

the component game in which the second item is auctioned to bidders 2 and 3 appears five times. When necessary, we will distinguish these component games by their histories, $\gamma_{H_J^k}$. The history information is sufficient to uniquely identify each component game.

In addition to the imperfect information generated by the sealed bids, the agent also faces incomplete information because it does not know the other bidders' true values, and therefore does not know the other bidders' payoffs. Harsanyi (1967) demonstrated that incomplete information games can be modeled by introducing an unobservable move by nature at the beginning of the game which establishes the unknown values. This approach transforms the incomplete information game into a game with imperfect information.

Unfortunately, the move-by-nature approach is computationally problematic. First, the number of possible moves available to nature is m^n, where m is the size of the domain of $v_j(k)$, and n is the number of agents. Our model defines a continuous range for valuation functions, so the number of choices is not enumerable. In some special cases, analytical solutions can be found to auction games with continuous types (Fudenberg & Tirole 1996). However this analysis is complex and typically requires restrictive assumptions about the distributions of values. Second, even if we restrict the valuation functions to a countable set, the standard algorithms for solving the incomplete information game cannot solve even very small problems in a reasonable amount of time on current computing hardware.

For these reasons, we investigate the use of fictitious play to generate heuristic bidding policies for the incomplete information game. Our approach to the problem can be summarized as follows:

1. Create a sample complete-information game by drawing a set of valuations for other bidders.

2. Solve for a Nash equilibrium of the sample game.

3. Update the agent's bidding policy.

The first step is straightforward Monte Carlo sampling. The second and third steps are the subject of the next two sections.

Leveraging Substructure

We built our agent on top of the GAMBIT Toolset.[2] Although GAMBIT includes algorithms that can solve multiplayer games with incomplete, imperfect information, it cannot solve the straightforward expansion of even very small instances of the complete-information, sequential auction game in a reasonable amount of time.

To see why, consider the size of the extensive form of the complete information game. The assumption that bidders want only one item means that the winner of the first auction will not participate in the next auction. Thus, each auction has one fewer participant than the previous. The number of

---

[2]The GAMBIT toolset is a software program and set of libraries that support the construction and analysis of finite and extensive form multi-player games. See http://www.hss.caltech.edu/gambit/Gambit.html.

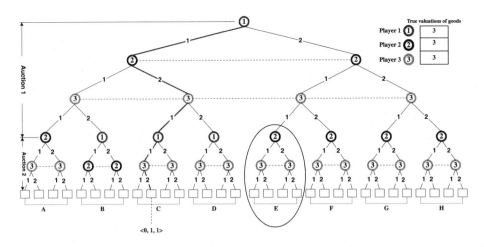

Figure 1: A sealed-bid auction with three agents, two items and two bid levels.

nodes in the extensive form representation of the game with q auctions is $\frac{m^e - 1}{m - 1}$ where $e = q(n - (q-1)/2)$. A five agent, four item sequential auction with five bid choices has 1.5 billion decision nodes. Thus, to use GAMBIT to compute solutions to our sampled games, we need to improve its performance.

The computational aspects of game theory have been studied by economists and computer scientists in the past few years (Koller & Megiddo 1992; Koller, Megiddo, & von Stengel 1994; 1996; McLennan & McKelvey 1996) A very promising thread of work is focused on representations of games that capture their inherent structure and facilitate solution computation. Koller and Pfeffer's GALA language (1997) can be used to represent games in *sequence* form, and the authors have developed solution techniques for two-player, zero-sum games represented in this format.

The success of GALA is based on the intuition that significant computational savings can be achieved by taking advantage of a game's substructure. This intuition holds for the sequential auction model, and we have employed it to improve upon GAMBIT's default solution method.

The default representation of this game in GAMBIT is to expand each of the leaves with an appropriate subgame. Given that the bidders have complete information, all subgames with the same players remaining have the same solution(s). Thus, a single sealed-bid auction with n agents has at most n *unique* subgames—one for each possible set of non-winners. Figure 2 illustrates the four unique component games for the sequential auction shown in Figure 1.

Our agent's approach is to create all possible component games and solve them using GAMBIT's C++ libraries. The process is equivalent to standard backward induction, enhanced with caching. The expected payoffs from the solution to a component game γ involving bidders $\mathcal{J}$ are used as the payoffs for the respective agents on the leaves of any component games which lead to γ in Γ. The agent solves all possible smallest component games (i.e. games of size $z = n - q + 1$). Then, using the results of the lower order solutions, the agent solves all possible component games of size $z + 1$, until it solves the root game.

The number of decision nodes required to express a game in its component form is

$$\sum_{t=1}^{q} \binom{n}{t-1} \frac{m^{n-t+1} - 1}{m - 1}.$$

The component form representation is exponential in the number of agents and the number of bidding choices. However, the total number of nodes required to express the game is exponentially less than in the full expansion. For example, the five agent, four item sequential auction with five bid choices requires only 1931 nodes to encode, compared to the 1.5 billion required for the naive expansion.

It should be noted that the solutions that we are using in the above analysis are Nash equilibria found by GAMBIT for each particular subgame. These solutions may involve either pure or mixed strategies. It is well known (Nash 1950), that at least one mixed strategy equilibrium always exists, however it is also often true that more than one Nash equilibria exist. In this study, we simply take the first equilibria found by GAMBIT, and leave the question of how, and even whether, to incorporate multiple equilibria to future research.

While the decomposition provides an exponential improvement in the number of nodes needed to represent (and hence solve) the game, the computational cost of finding equilibria for the subgames remains a bottleneck.

Fictitious Play

In order to participate in this environment, the agent must construct a *policy*, Π, that specifies what action it should take in any state of the game that it might reach. One simple strategy that our agent could implement is to compute the equilibrium strategy in each component game, and to bid accordingly. For example, the equilibrium strategy of a single first-price, sealed-bid auction in which the other bidders' valuations are drawn uniformly from $[0, 1]$ is to bid $b_i^k = (1 - 1/n)v_i(k)$, where n is the number of bidders (McAfee & McMillan 1987). We define Π_{myopic} to be the strategy in which the agent bids according the the

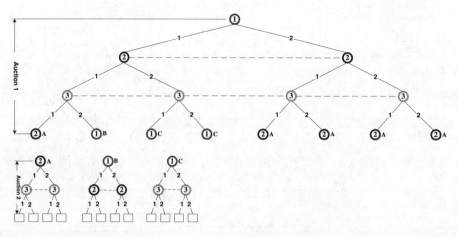

Figure 2: The decomposition of the three bidder, two item game into unique component games.

equilibrium of each individual sealed-bid auction. Thus, the strategy has one element for each potential game size, $\Pi_{\text{myopic}} = \{\pi_z\}$ where z is the size, in number of bidders, of the component game.

If the distributions from which the bidders draw values are not identical, then it would behoove our agent to have a policy that accounted for which other bidders were in the subgame. Thus, $\Pi_{\text{not-id}} = \{\pi_{\mathcal{J} \subseteq J}\}$. That is, the actions in the policy depend upon which subset, $\mathcal{J}$, of agents remain.

$\Pi_{\text{not-id}}$ is memoryless; it ignores the bids the remaining opponents made in previous auctions. On the other extreme is a policy that uses all possible history information. $\Pi_{\text{history}} = \{\pi_{\mathcal{J}, H^k_j}\}$ encodes the entire tree because the decision at each decision node is a function of the entire history.

The policy that our agent learned in this study is $\Pi_{\text{agg-hist}} = \{\pi_{\mathcal{J}, H^k_{\mathcal{J}}}\}$ where $H^k_{\mathcal{J}} = \{h^k_{j \in \mathcal{J}}\}$, the histories of all agents still in the game. It is based on the assumption that bidders who are no longer active in the sequential auction (because they have won an item) are irrelevant. Therefore, all component games that have the same agents and identical previous actions by those agents, are aggregated into a class of component games, $\gamma_{\mathcal{J}, H^k_{\mathcal{J}}}$. This differs from Π_{history} because policies are classified by the histories of only those bidders that remain active ($\mathcal{J}$), rather than by J.

In the example in Figure 1 suppose player 3 is our agent. Subgame B can be ignored because player 3 won the item in the first auction. Of the remaining subgames, the set {A, E, F} have identical histories—bidder 2 bids \$1 in both of them—as does the set {G, H}. Thus, our agent will construct a policy for each of the following decision sets: {A, E, F}, {C}, {D}, and {G, H}.

The agent constructs the policy by sampling the distributions of the other bidders and solving the resulting complete information game. Let L be the collection of sample games constructed, and l a single instance. Denote the solution to instance l as Ω^l. Ω^l is a (possibly mixed) strategy that the agent would play in equilibrium for this game instance. Thus, Ω^l specifies a probability function over all bid choices at each component game, and ω^l_γ is the policy for subgame

γ. Note that some decision nodes may not be reachable if the actions that lead to them are played with zero probability. To simplify the notation, we include these unreachable nodes even though they have no effect on the solution.

We now compute the policy, $\pi_{\mathcal{J}, H^k_{\mathcal{J}}}$, for a decision node $\gamma_{\mathcal{J}, H^k_{\mathcal{J}}}$ by taking the weighted sum of the equilibrium solutions across all sample games. Let

$$w(b^k_i | \pi_{\mathcal{J}, H^k_{\mathcal{J}}}) = \sum_{l \in L} \sum_{\gamma \in \gamma_{H^k_{\mathcal{J}}}} \Pr(\gamma | \Omega^l) U(\gamma, \Omega^l) \Pr(b^k_i | \omega^l_\gamma)$$

be the weight assigned to action b^k_i in the class of games identified by $\gamma_{H^k_{\mathcal{J}}}$. Here, $\Pr(\gamma | \Omega^l)$ is the probability that i would reach γ given that it is playing Ω^l (i.e. the product of the probabilities on the path leading to γ), $U(\gamma, \Omega^l)$ is the expected utility the subgame rooted at γ, and $\Pr(b^k_i | \omega^l_\gamma)$ is the probability associated with bid b^k_i in solution ω^l_γ. The first two terms in the summation represent the amount to weight this sample in comparison with other observations of this decision node. The inclusion of utility in the equation biases the agent toward maximizing its expected utility—a useful heuristic, but one that is not necessarily consistent with equilibrium behavior.

Finally, we normalize the computed weights to derive the probabilities.

$$Pr(b^k_i | \pi_{\mathcal{J}, H^k_{\mathcal{J}}}) = \frac{w(b^k_i | \pi_{\mathcal{J}, H^k_{\mathcal{J}}})}{\sum_{b \in B^k} w(b | \pi_{\mathcal{J}, H^k_{\mathcal{J}}})}$$

The result of this process is a policy that specifies a (possibly mixed) strategy for each unique class of component games.

There are obvious connections between our scheme and *belief revision*. Space does not permit a full discussion, but we point out that the policy at a node implicitly captures the agent's beliefs about which opponent valuations would explain the fact that the agent arrived at a particular decision point in the game tree.

Empirical Results

To evaluate the agent's ability to perform effectively in this environment, we experimented with a scenario involving

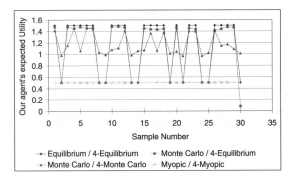

Figure 3: Our agent's expected utility when the other bidders' valuation are drawn from a uniform distribution.

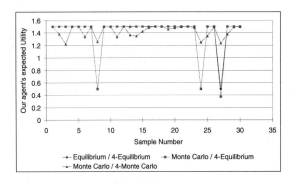

Figure 4: Our agent's expected utility when other bidders' valuation are drawn from a left-skewed Beta distribution.

four other bidders with valuations drawn from [1, 5], and a sequence of four first-price, sealed-bid auctions. The bidders actions were restricted to four bid options. Our agent's valuation always remains in the middle of the valuation interval, and we varied the distribution of the other bidders' valuations. The agent trained with 100 samples of the opponent valuations. We then compared our agent's performance in various combinations of its strategy and the strategies of the other bidders.

Equilibrium / 4-Equilibrium - represents the combination in which all participants play the Nash equilibrium strategy. It assumes all participants have complete information. We use it as a perfect benchmark because we can't play better than our agent's Nash equilibrium strategy with other players all playing their Nash equilibrium strategies.

Monte Carlo / 4-Equilibrium - shows the performance of our agent using the heuristic strategy when the four other bidders play their Nash equilibrium strategy. This is a *best defense* scenario, in which we assume that the other players know our agent's valuation and will play the game perfectly even though our agent does not know their valuations.

Monte Carlo / 4-Monte Carlo - all five participants learn and then play a heuristic strategy generated by Monte Carlo simulation.

Myopic / 4-Myopic - represents the case where all agents use a simple myopic strategy. The myopic strategy is to play the equilibrium strategy for each auction individually.[3]

Figure 3 shows our agent's expected utility in each of 30 different problem instances where the other bidders' valuations were drawn from a uniform distribution. For each problem instance we tested the four combinations of strategies listed above.

The experimental results show that our learned strategy performs better than the myopic strategy and quite close to the optimal equilibrium strategy. On average, the heuristic strategy performs better against other bidders also playing the heuristic strategy than against bidders playing Nash equilibrium strategies. However, we suspect that this may

---

[3]An anonymous reviewer correctly pointed out that a better strawman would be the sequential auction equilibrium strategy: bid the expected price of the $(q - k + 2)$th item under the assumption the agent wins (Weber 1983).

be an effect of the tie-breaking rule, which favors our agent because it has the lowest index.

Figure 4 shows the corresponding results when the other bidders' valuations are drawn from a left-skewed Beta distribution in the range [1,5]. The graph shows the same features as the Figure 3, including the fact that the agent's performance is quite close to the optimal play. Our agent's averaged utility is higher against the left-skewed bidders than against the uniform bidders. This is consistent with our expectation that with left-skewed valuations, our agent is more likely to be among the highest valuers and thus will have a better chance of winning with greater surplus. Symmetric results were produced with a right-skewed distribution.

We also measured the effect of the heuristic behavior on the social welfare. Figure 5 illustrates the social welfare of this sequential auction. In all of the experiments, the Nash equilibrium always supported an optimal allocation. The heuristic strategy will (on expectation) result in an allocation very close to the perfect one. On this measure, the myopic strategy performs better than our heuristic strategy because it ensures the best allocation in each individual auction, which will result in an optimal allocation for the overall game.

Related Work

A great deal of research has addressed auctions for multiple units of homogeneous objects. See Klemperer (1999) for a broad review of auction literature, including a discussion of sequential auctions for homogeneous objects. Weber (1983) shows that the equilibrium strategies for the bidders when the objects are sold in sequential first-price, sealed-bid auctions is to bid the expected price of the object in each auction. This result is developed under the assumption that only the clearing price is revealed in previous auctions. In many current online auction environments, the actual bids and their associated bidders are revealed. As far as we know, none of the theoretical results have addressed the model with complete bid revelation.

Anthony, et al. (2001) investigate agents that can participate in multiple online auctions. The authors posit a set of "tactics" and then empirically compare the performance of these tactics in a simulated market that consists of simultaneous and sequential English, Dutch, and Vickrey auctions. Boutilier et al. (1999) develop a sequential auction model

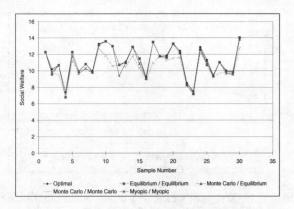

Figure 5: Social welfare averaged over the 30 sample games with valuations drawn from the uniform distribution.

in which the agent values combinations of resources while all other participants value only a single item. Unlike our model, the Boutilier formulation does not explicitly model the opponents.

Monte Carlo sampling has been previously used in conjunction with games of incomplete information. Frank et al. (1997) describes an empirical study of the use of Monte Carlo sampling method on a simple complete binary game tree. They draw the discouraging conclusion that the error rate quickly approaches 100% as the depth of the game increases. However, perhaps because Frank et al. consider only pure strategy equilibrium in a two-person, zero-sum game, these negative results did not evidence themselves in our study.

Howard James Bampton (1994) investigated the use of Monte Carlo sampling to create a heuristic policy for the (imperfect information) game of Bridge. In Bampton's paper, he simply collected the player's decision in every sampled game and accumulated the chance-minimax values for each alternative at each decision node. Our method of accumulating sampled data is quite different from Bampton's approach, again because our game is not a two-player zero-sum game.

Conclusion

This study represents a first step in exploring the implementation of computational game theory in a simple trading agent. By using fictitious play, the agent is able to learn a sophisticated strategy whose performance is comparable to optimal play in our tests. This strategy takes advantage of information revealed in prior auctions in the sequence to improve play in later auctions. Importantly, the architecture is flexible, in that it can handle a variety of simple auction types, and different types of other bidders.

We plan to continue this work and integrate more auction types, and to explore scenarios in which the agent's and other bidders' preferences are more complex. We would also like to add an aggregate buyer to the model to represent the large number of unmodeled opponents often found in these markets. Finally, we plan to explore auction sequences in which the bidders' valuations are correlated across the items, but not necessarily identical.

Acknowledgments

This project was funded by NSF CAREER award 0092591-0029728000 to the second author. We wish to thank William Walsh, the members of the Intelligent Commerce Research Group at NCSU, and the anonymous reviewers for their insightful comments. Although not all of the reviewers' comments could be addressed in this paper, we look forward to doing so in future work.

References

Anthony, P.; Hall, W.; Dang, V.; and Jennings, N. R. 2001. Autonomous agents for participating in multiple on-line auctions. In *IJCAI Workshop on E-Business and the Intelligent Web*, 54–64.

Bampton, H. J. 1994. Solving imperfect information games using the monte carlo heuristic. Technical report, University of Tennessee, Knoxville.

Boutilier, C.; Goldszmidt, M.; and Sabata, B. 1999. Sequential auctions for the allocation of resources with complementarities. In *Sixteenth International Joint Conference on Artificial Intelligence*, 527–534.

Frank, I.; Basin, D.; and Matsubara, H. 1997. Monte-carlo sampling in games with imperfect information: Empirical investigation and analysis. In *Game Tree Search Workshop*.

Fudenberg, D., and Tirole, J. 1996. *Game Theory*. MIT Press.

Harsanyi, J. C. 1967-8. Games with incomplete information played by bayesian players. *Management Science* 14:159–182,320–334,486–502.

Koller, D., and Megiddo, N. 1992. The complexity of two-person zero-sum games in extensive form. *Games and Economic Behavior* 4:528–552.

Koller, D., and Pfeffer, A. 1997. Representations and solutions for game-theoretic problems. *Artificial Intelligence* 94(1):167–251.

Koller, D.; Megiddo, N.; and von Stengel, B. 1994. Fast algorithms for finding randomized strategies in game trees. In *26th ACM Symposium on the Theory of Computing*, 750–759.

Koller, D.; Megiddo, N.; and von Stengel, B. 1996. Efficient computation of equilibria for extensive two-person games. *Games and Economic Behavior* 14(2):247–259.

McAfee, R. P., and McMillan, J. 1987. Auctions and bidding. *Journal of Economic Literature* 25:699–738.

McLennan, A., and McKelvey, R. 1996. Computation of equilibria in finite games. In Amman, H.; Kendrick, D. A.; and Rust, J., eds., *The Handbook of Computational Economics*, volume I. Elsevier Science B.V. 87–142.

Nash, J. 1950. Two-person cooperative games. *Proceedings of the National Academy of Sciences* 21:128–140.

Weber, R. J. 1983. Multiple-object auctions. In Engelbrecht-Wiggans, R.; Shubik, M.; and Stark, R. M., eds., *Auctions, Bidding and Contracting: Uses and Theory*. New York University Press. 165–91.

AAAI-02
Edmonton/Alberta
IAAI-02

Multiagent Systems
Game Theory

Vote Elicitation: Complexity and Strategy-Proofness

Vincent Conitzer and **Tuomas Sandholm**

Computer Science Department
Carnegie Mellon University
5000 Forbes Avenue
Pittsburgh, PA 15213
{conitzer, sandholm}@cs.cmu.edu

Abstract

Preference elicitation is a central problem in AI, and has received significant attention in single-agent settings. It is also a key problem in multiagent systems, but has received little attention here so far. In this setting, the agents may have different preferences that often must be aggregated using voting. This leads to interesting issues because what, if any, information should be elicited from an agent depends on what other agents have revealed about their preferences so far. In this paper we study effective elicitation, and its impediments, for the most common voting protocols. It turns out that in the Single Transferable Vote protocol, even knowing when to terminate elicitation is $\mathcal{N}P$-complete, while this is easy for all the other protocols under study. Even for these protocols, determining how to elicit effectively is $\mathcal{N}P$-complete, even with perfect suspicions about how the agents will vote. The exception is the Plurality protocol where such effective elicitation is easy. We also show that elicitation introduces additional opportunities for strategic manipulation by the voters. We demonstrate how to curtail the space of elicitation schemes so that no such additional strategic issues arise.

1. Introduction

Preference elicitation is a central problem in AI. To build a bot that acts intelligently on behalf of any type of agent (a human, a corporation, a software agent, etc.), the bot needs to know about the agent's preferences. However, the bot should only elicit pertinent preference information from the agent because determining and expressing preferences can be arduous. Significant work has been done on selective preference elicitation (e.g., (Boutilier *et al.* 1997; Vu & Haddawy 1998; Chajewwska, Koller, & Parr 2000)).

Preference elicitation is also a key problem in multiagent systems, but has received little attention so far.[1] The agents may have different preferences over the set of *candidates* that the agents must collectively choose among (e.g., potential presidents, joint plans, resource allocations, task allocations, etc.). The most general method for aggregating preferences is voting.[2] In traditional voting, each voter is asked for its complete preferences. We observe that intelligently eliciting preferences from the voters can allow the voting protocol to determine the outcome well before all of the preferences have been elicited. This is desirable for any of several reasons: 1) it can be costly for an agent to determine

its own preferences (e.g., computationally (Sandholm 1993; Larson & Sandholm 2001)), 2) communicating the preferences introduces overhead (network traffic, traveling to the voting booth to vote, traveling door to door to collect votes, etc.), and 3) less preference revelation is desirable due to privacy reasons.

Attempting to efficiently elicit preferences leads to interesting issues in the voting context because what, if any, information should be elicited from an agent depends on what other agents have revealed about their preferences so far. The goal here is to determine the right outcome while eliciting a minimal amount of preference information from the voters. The most effective elicitation schemes make use of *suspicions* about the agents' preferences. Such suspicions can be the result of votes in previous elections, an understanding of the candidates in the election, an understanding of how each agent relates to each candidate, etc. To see how suspicions may help the elicitation process, consider a simple election with two candidates. If the elicitor knew beforehand which agents would vote for the eventual winner, simply querying enough of those voters would suffice.

In this paper we analyze the possibility of effective vote elicitation, and demonstrate two categories of impediments. First, optimal elicitation can be computationally complex. In Section 4 we show that even determining whether enough information has been elicited is $\mathcal{N}P$-complete for some voting protocols. In Section 5 we show that for most of the voting protocols, determining an efficient elicitation policy is $\mathcal{N}P$-complete (even with perfect suspicions). Second, in Section 6 we show that in various ways, elicitation can introduce additional opportunities for strategically manipulating the election. We then show how to avoid such problems by curtailing the space of elicitation schemes.

2. Common voting protocols

We consider elections with m candidates and n voters (agents). A voting protocol defines a function from the set of all possible combinations of votes to the set of candidates, the *winner determination function*. We now review the most common protocols in use. We will study all of them.

- *Plurality.* Each candidate receives one point for each voter that ranked it first. The candidate with the most points wins.

- *Borda.* For each voter, a candidate receives $m-1$ points if it is the voter's first choice, $m-2$ if it is the second, ..., 0 if it is the last. The candidate with the most points wins.

- *Copeland (aka. Tournament).* The protocol simulates a pairwise election for each pair of candidates in turn (in a pairwise election, a candidate wins if it is preferred over

[1] A notable exception is bid elicitation in combinatorial auctions (Conen & Sandholm 2001).

[2] Voting mechanisms have been used also for computational agents (e.g. (Ephrati & Rosenschein 1991; 1993)).

the other candidate by more than half of the voters). A candidate gets 1 point if it defeats an opponent, 0 points if it draws, and -1 points if it loses. The candidate with the most points wins.

- *Maximin*. A candidate's *score* in a pairwise election is the number of voters that prefer it over the opponent. A candidate's number of points is its lowest score in any pairwise election. The candidate with the most points wins.

- *Single Transferable Vote (STV)*. The winner determination process proceeds in rounds. In each round, a candidate's score is the number of voters that rank it highest among the remaining candidates, and the candidate with the lowest score drops out. The last remaining candidate wins. (The name comes from the fact that a vote *transfers* from its top remaining candidate to the next highest remaining candidate when the former drops out.)

- *Approval*. Each voter labels each candidate as either approved or disapproved. The candidate that is approved by the largest number of voters wins.

3. Definition of elicitation

We now formally define elicitation. We distinguish between *full elicitation*, where the entire vote is elicited from every agent; *coarse elicitation*, where upon querying an agent the elicitor always asks for the agent's entire vote; and *fine elicitation* where this need not be the case (for example, an agent may be asked only what its most preferred candidate is). We formalize elicitation policies as trees.

Definition 1 *A coarse elicitation tree is a tree with the following properties:*

- *Each nonleaf node v is labeled with an agent a_v to be queried.*

- *Each nonleaf node v has a child for each of the possible votes of agent a_v.*

- *On each path from the root to a leaf, each agent occurs at most once.*

This tree determines how the elicitation will proceed for any combination of votes by the agents. The elicitor starts at the root. At each node, it queries the corresponding agent, and subsequently moves to the child corresponding to the obtained vote. We say the tree is *valid* for a protocol when for each leaf, given the votes corresponding to the path from the root to that leaf, the election's outcome is determined.

Definition 2 *A fine elicitation tree is a tree with the following properties:*

- *Each nonleaf node v is labeled with an agent a_v to be queried, a subset of that agent's possible votes S_v (the ones consistent with a_v's responses so far), and a query to be asked at that node. The query is given by a partition T_v of S_v; once the query is answered, one element of T_v is the set of remaining consistent votes.*

- *Each nonleaf node v has a child for each element of T_v.*

- *Given a nonleaf v, if a_v does not occur anywhere else on the path from the root to v, then S_v is the set of all possible votes by a_v; otherwise, consider the node w closest to*

v on that path with $a_v = a_w$. *The element of T_w corresponding to w's child on the way to v must equal S_v.*

- *Each partition T_x has at least 2 elements.*

The interpretation is as follows. Each node still corresponds to a query to the corresponding agent. A subset at a node is the set of the agent's possible votes that are consistent with its responses so far. The partition indicates the various ways in which this set may be reduced through the query.

We say the tree is *valid* for a protocol if for each leaf, the outcome of the election is determined by the responses to the queries on the path to that leaf. From now on, we only consider valid trees.

Our model of elicitation is very general. It can be used to represent intuitively reasonable queries as well as baroque ones such as *"Is it true that a is your most preferred candidate or that you prefer b to c?"* (which could impose a computational burden on the voter disproportionate to the fact that it is only one query). Reasonable fine elicitation policies will have some restriction on the types of T_v allowed. Also, elicitation trees can be extremely large. Therefore, it can be unreasonable to expect the elicitor to use this explicit representation for its elicitation policy, much less to do an exhaustive search over these trees to find one that minimizes the number of queries (for example, in the average case). Nevertheless, each well-defined elicitation policy corresponds to an elicitation tree, and hence elicitation trees are useful tools for analysis.

4. Hardness of terminating elicitation

Any sensible elicitation policy would need to be able to determine when it can safely terminate. Otherwise, there would be no benefit from elicitation. In this section, we first show that for the STV protocol, it can be hard to determine when the elicitation process can terminate. Then we show that this is easy for the other voting protocols.

Definition 3 (ELICITATION-NOT-DONE) *We are given a set of votes S, a number t of votes that are still unknown, and a candidate h. We are asked whether there is a way to cast the t votes so that h will not win.*[3]

In order to prove our hardness result, we make use of the following result from the literature on the difficulty of manipulating an election.

Definition 4 (EFFECTIVE-PREFERENCE) *We are given a set of votes S and a candidate c. One vote is not yet known. Is there a way to cast the last vote that makes c win?*

Theorem 1 (Known) *For the STV protocol, EFFECTIVE-PREFERENCE is $\mathcal{N}P$-complete, even under the restriction that at least one of the votes in S puts c in the top spot.*

Proof: This was proven in (Bartholdi & Orlin 1991). ∎

---

[3]The problem of determining whether elicitation is done is actually the same problem as that of determining whether a coalition of voters can make a candidate lose (Conitzer & Sandholm 2002). This suggests a deep connection between the complexity of elicitation and that of manipulation.

Theorem 2 *For the STV protocol, ELICITATION-NOT-DONE is $\mathcal{N}P$-complete, even when $t = 1$.*[4]

Proof: We reduce an arbitrary instance of EFFECTIVE-PREFERENCE (with the restriction that at least one of the votes in S puts c at the top) to an instance of ELICITATION-NOT-DONE as follows. In the EFFECTIVE-PREFERENCE instance, let the candidate set be C_{EP} and the set of given votes S_{EP}. Then, in our ELICITATION-NOT-DONE instance, the candidate set is $C_{EP} \cup \{h\}$. The known (elicited) set of votes S includes all the votes from S_{EP}, where h is appended to these votes at the bottom – with the exception that one of the votes with c at the top inserts h into the second place (right behind c). Additionally, S includes $|S_{EP}|$ additional votes which place h in the top spot and rank the other candidates in whichever order. Finally, we set $t = 1$. We prove the instances are equivalent by making the following observations. First, h will always survive until the last round as it has almost half the votes at the start. Second, if there exists a way for the last vote to be cast such that h does not win the election, we may assume that this vote places h at the bottom, since if this vote ever transferred to h, h would win the election as it would hold more than half the votes. Third, h will not win the election if and only if it faces c in the last round (if c gets eliminated, the vote that ranks h right below c would transfer to h and h would win the election; on the other hand, c is ranked above h in all the votes that do not put h at the top, so c would win the last round). Fourth, as long as c remains in the election, the score of each candidate (besides h) in each round before the last will be exactly the same as the corresponding score in the EFFECTIVE-PREFERENCE instance (if we give the same value to the unknown vote in both instances). This follows from the fact that in this case, no vote will ever transfer to or from h and the relevant votes are identical otherwise. It follows that the remaining vote can be cast in such a way as to lead c to the final round if and only if the remaining vote in the EFFECTIVE-PREFERENCE instance can make c win the election. But then, by our third observation, the instances are equivalent. ∎

Theorem 2 applies to both fine and coarse elicitation because in both the elicitor might end up in a situation where it has elicited some votes completely and others not at all.

For the other protocols studied in this paper, determining whether elicitation can be terminated is easy. We have constructed a polynomial-time algorithm for accomplishing this, which applies to each of the other protocols. This greedy algorithm (omitted due to limited space) is guaranteed to find t votes that make h not win if such t votes exist.

5. Hardness of deciding which votes to elicit

The elicitor could use its suspicions about how the agents will vote to try to design the elicitation policy so that few queries are needed. The suspicions could be represented by a joint prior distribution over the agents' votes. It is not too

surprising that in this general setting, computational complexity issues arise with regard to optimal elicitation, because the number of probabilities in a general joint prior distribution is $(m!)^n$. Given that this is an impractically large amount of information to generate (and to input into an elicitor bot), it is reasonable to presume that the language the elicitor uses to express its suspicions is not fully expressive. With such a restricted language, one might hope that the optimal elicitation problem is tractable. However, this turns out not to be the case! We show that if this language even accomodates as little as degenerate distributions (all the probability mass on a single vote), determining an optimal coarse elicitation policy is hard. In other words, it is hard even with perfect suspicions. We define the effective elicitation problem with perfect suspicions as follows:

Definition 5 (EFFECTIVE-ELICITATION) *We are given a set of votes S and a number k. We are asked whether there is a subset of S of size $\leq k$ that decides the election constituted by the votes in S.*

All the reductions in this section will be from 3-COVER.

Definition 6 (3-COVER) *We are given a set U of size $3q$ and a collection of subsets $\{S_i\}_{1 \leq i \leq r}$ of U (where $r > q$), each of size 3. We are asked if there is a cover of U consisting of q of the subsets.*

Theorem 3 *For the Approval protocol, EFFECTIVE-ELICITATION is NP-complete.*

Proof: We reduce an arbitrary 3-COVER instance to the following EFFECTIVE-ELICITATION instance. The candidate set is $U \cup \{w\}$. The votes are as follows. For every S_i there is a vote approving $S_i \cup \{w\}$. Additionally, we have $r - 2q + 2$ votes approving only $\{w\}$, for a total of $2r - 2q + 2$ votes. Finally, we set $k = r - q + 2$. We claim the problem instances are equivalent. First suppose there is a 3-cover. Then we elicit all the votes that approve only w, and the votes that correspond to sets in the cover, for a total of k votes. Then w is $r - q + 1$ points ahead of all other candidates, with only $r - q$ votes remaining. Hence there is an effective elicitation. On the other hand, suppose there is no 3-cover. Then eliciting k votes will always give one of the candidates in U at least 2 votes, so that w can be at most $r - q$ points ahead of this candidate. Hence, with $r - q$ votes remaining, the election cannot possibly be decided. So there is no effective elicitation. ∎

Theorem 4 *For the Borda protocol, EFFECTIVE-ELICITATION is NP-complete.*

Proof: We reduce an arbitrary 3-COVER instance to the following EFFECTIVE-ELICITATION instance. The candidate set is $U \cup \{w\} \cup B$ where $B = \{b_1, b_2, \ldots, b_{64r^2}\}$. The votes are as follows. For each S_i there is a vote ranking the candidates $(B/2, U - S_i, B/2, S_i, w)$, where the occurrence of a set in the ranking signifies all of its elements in whichever order, and $B/2$ signifies some subset of B containing half its elements. Finally, there are $4r - 2q - 2$ votes that rank the candidates $(w, b_1, \ldots, b_{8r^2}, u_1, \ldots, u_{3q}, b_{8r^2+1}, \ldots, b_{64r^2})$,

---

[4] In all $\mathcal{N}P$-completeness proofs, we only prove $\mathcal{N}P$-hardness because proving that the problem is in $\mathcal{N}P$ is trivial.

and another $4r - 2q - 2$ that rank them $(w, b_{64r^2}, \ldots, b_{56r^2+1}, u_{3q}, \ldots, u_1, b_{56r^2}, \ldots, b_1)$. Let $g = 8r - 4q - 4$, so that we have a total of $g + r$ votes. Also, let $l = 64r^2 + 3q$, which is the number of points a candidate gets for being in first place. Finally, we set $k = g + q$. We claim the problem instances are equivalent. First suppose there is a 3-cover. We elicit all the votes that put w on top, and the votes that correspond to sets in the cover, for a total of k votes. Even after eliciting just the ones that put w on top, w is more than $\frac{gl}{2} \geq 2rl$ (since $g \geq 4r$) points ahead of all the elements of B, and with only r votes remaining it is impossible to catch up with w for anyone in B. For a given element u of U, the votes that put w on top result in a net difference of $g(8r^2 + \frac{3}{2}q + \frac{1}{2})$ points between w and u. Of the q remaining elicited votes, precisely $q - 1$ placed u ahead of half the elements of B, so the net difference in points between w and u most favorable to u arising from these would be $-(q-1)(32r^2 + 3q)$. Finally, the vote that put u below all the elements of b might contribute another -3. Adding up all these net differences, we find that w is ahead by at least $64r^3 - 64qr^2 + 12qr - 9q^2 + 4r - 5q - 5$ points. On the other hand, the maximum number of points u could gain on w with the remaining number of votes is $(r - q)(64r^2 + 3q) = 64r^3 - 64qr^2 + 3qr - 3q^2$. It is easily seen that the second expression is always smaller, and hence w is guaranteed to win the election. So there is an effective elicitation. On the other hand, suppose there is no 3-cover. First, we observe that w will always win the election - we have already shown that the votes that put w on top guarantee it does better than any element of B. For any element u of U, even if u is always placed above all the other votes in U in the r votes corresponding to the S_i, it will still only gain $r(32r^2 + 3q)$ points on w here, which is fewer than the $g(8r^2 + \frac{3}{2}q + \frac{1}{2})$ votes it loses on w with the other votes (since $g \geq 4r$). So we can only hope to guarantee that w wins. Now, if there is an elicitation that guarantees this, there is also one that elicits all the g votes that put w on top, since replacing one of the other votes with such a vote in the elicitation never hurts w's relative performance to another candidate. But in such an elicitation, there is at least one candidate u in U that is never ranked below all the elements of B in the q votes elicited that put w at the bottom, since there is no 3-cover. Let us investigate how many points w may be ahead of u after eliciting these votes. Again, the votes that put w on top result in a net difference of $g(8r^2 + \frac{3}{2}q + \frac{1}{2})$ points. In the scenario most favorable to w, u would only gain $q(32r^2 + 4)$ points with the other q votes. Adding this up, w is ahead by at most $64r^3 - 64qr^2 - 32r^2 + 12qr - 6q^2 + 4r - 6q - 2$ after the elicitation. The maximum number of points u could gain on w with the remaining number of votes is still $64r^3 - 64qr^2 + 3qr - 3q^2$. It is easily seen that the second expression is always larger, so we cannot guarantee that w wins. So there is no effective elicitation. ∎

Theorem 5 *For the Copeland protocol, EFFECTIVE-ELICITATION is NP-complete.*

Theorem 6 *For the Maximin protocol, EFFECTIVE-ELICITATION is NP-complete.*

The proofs are omitted due to limited space – the ideas are similar to those used for the Approval and Borda protocols.

So far we have shown that determining an effective elicitation policy is hard for most of the voting protocols, and that for the STV protocol even knowing when to terminate is hard. The remaining protocol is Plurality, where it is easy to elicit effectively given perfect suspicions (start eliciting the winner's votes first; if all of them have been elicited and termination is still not possible, elicit votes in a round-robin manner, one for each non-winning candidate (as long as it has votes left), until the elicitation can terminate).

6. Strategy-proofness of elicitation

We now turn to strategic issues that may be introduced into a voting protocol by an elicitation process. Elicitation may reveal information about other agents' votes to an agent, which the agent may use to change its vote strategically. This is undesirable for two reasons. First, it gives agents that are elicited later an unfair advantage, causing the protocol to put undue weight on their preferences. Second, it leads to less truthful voting by the agents. This is undesirable because, while voting protocols are designed to select a socially desirable candidate if agents vote truthfully, untruthful voting can lead to a reduction in the social desirability of the outcome. We demonstrate how such strategic issues may arise, and then suggest avenues to circumvent them. However, these avenues entail restricting the space of possible elicitations, causing a reduction in the potential savings from elicitation.

To analyze strategic interactions, we need some tools from game theory. To bring the voting setting into the framework of noncooperative game theory, we assume that agent i's preferences are defined by its *type* θ_i; the agent gets utility $u_i(\theta_i, c)$ if candidate c wins. We first define a game:

Definition 7 *In a (normal form) game, we are given a set of agents A; a set of types Θ_i for each agent i; a commonly known prior distribution ϕ over $\Theta_1 \times \Theta_2 \times \ldots \times \Theta_{|A|}$; a set of strategies Σ_i for each agent $i \in A$; a set of outcomes O (candidates in the case of voting); an outcome function $o : \Sigma_1 \times \Sigma_2 \times \ldots \times \Sigma_{|A|} \to O$; and a utility function $u_i : \Theta_i \times O \to \Re$ for each agent $i \in A$.*

An agent knows its own type and can thus let its strategy depend on its type according to a function $f_i : \Theta_i \to \Sigma_i$. We also need a notion of how an agent would play a game strategically. This may depend on how others play.

Definition 8 *A strategy function profile $(f_1, f_2, \ldots, f_{|A|})$ is a Bayes-Nash equilibrium (BNE), if for each agent $i \in A$, each $\theta_i \in \Theta_i$, and each strategy $\sigma_i \in \Sigma_i$, $E_\phi(u_i(\theta_i, o(f_1(\theta_1), f_2(\theta_2), \ldots, f_i(\theta_i), \ldots, f_{|A|}(\theta_{|A|})))|\theta_i) \geq E_\phi(u_i(\theta_i, o(f_1(\theta_1), f_2(\theta_2), \ldots, \sigma_i, \ldots, f_{|A|}(\theta_{|A|})))|\theta_i)$ (that is, each f_i chooses, for each θ_i, a strategy that maximizes i's expected utility given the other players' $f_j s$).*

We are now ready to state our results.

6.1. Coarse elicitation

First we show that coarse elicitation may lead to strategic manipulations when it reveals even slightly more than just the fact that the agent is being elicited. Suppose that an agent can infer (e.g., from the time its type is elicited) how many other agents have had their types elicited before it.

Theorem 7 *In a coarse elicitation protocol, the following properties can hold simultaneously:*

- *the protocol reveals no information to any agent except that the agent's type is elicited, and how many other agents have had their types elicited before,*
- *the elicitation policy is optimized to finish as quickly as possible on average given the distribution over the agents' types (presuming the agents vote truthfully), and*
- *truthful voting is a BNE with full elicitation,*
- *truthful voting is not a BNE here. In particular, an agent may have an incentive to vote differently depending on how the other agents vote.*

Proof: Consider an Approval election[5] with 3 voters, i, j and k, and 3 candidates, a, b, and c. Ties are broken randomly. Define truth-telling to mean approving all candidates that give you utility $\geq \frac{1}{2}$. Ties are broken randomly. Agents' types are independent and the distributions are as follows. With probability $\frac{1}{2}$, i has utility 1 for c, and utility 0 for a and b; with probability $\frac{1}{2}$, it has utility 1 for a, and utility 0 for b and c. With probability $\frac{1}{2}$, j has utility 1 for c, and utility 0 for a and b; with probability $\frac{1}{2}$, it has utility 1 for b and c, and utility 0 for a. It is easy to see that truth-telling is always an optimal strategy for i and j. With probability 1, k has utility 1 for a, $\frac{1}{4}$ for b, and 0 for c. For k not to approve c, and to approve a, is always optimal. In the full elicitation case, should k approve b? If j has its first type, it makes no difference. What if j has its second type? If i has its first type, approving b leads to a tie between b and c, and (expected) utility $\frac{1}{8}$; not approving b leads to a victory for c and utility 0. If i has its second type, approving b leads to a tie between a and b and utility $\frac{5}{8}$; not approving b leads to a victory for a and utility 1. Hence, in the full elicitation case, given that we are in a case where it matters whether k approves b, approving b gives utility $\frac{3}{8}$, and not approving b gives utility $\frac{1}{2}$; so not approving b is optimal. Thus, truth-telling is a BNE here.

For the coarse elicitation case, we first design a policy that is optimal with respect to the agents' type distributions. Query $Q(l)$ asks voter l which candidates it approves. Then an optimal elicitation protocol is: *1*: first ask $Q(i)$; *2a*: if the answer was $\{c\}$, ask $Q(j)$; *2b*: otherwise, ask $Q(k)$; *3*: if do not know the winner yet, query the last voter.

To show optimality, assume the agents reply truthfully. If i has its first type, and j its first, we finish after *2a*, in 2 steps. If i has its second type, we finish after *2b*, in 2 steps. But these are the only cases in which we can hope to finish in only two steps, so the protocol is optimal.

Now, if k is queried second, this implies to it that i is of its second type, and it is motivated to answer truthfully. But if i

---

[5]We use the Approval protocol to demonstrate the negative results (Theorems 7 and 9) because 1) this demonstrates that these strategic issues can occur even in a very simple protocol, and 2) the protocol has a natural query type also for fine elicitation. However, similar strategic issues arise in any reasonable protocol.

is queried third, this implies to it that i is of its first type, and j of its second type; and k is motivated to lie and approve b. So truth-telling is not a BNE here. ∎

However, if the elicitation reveals no information to the agent being elicited (beyond the fact that the agent is being elicited), then elicitation does not introduce strategic issues:

Theorem 8 *Consider a coarse elicitation protocol which manages to reveal nothing more to the agent than whether or not his type is elicited. Then, the set of BNEs is the same as in the corresponding full elicitation voting game.[6]*

Proof: We claim that the normal form of the game is identical to that in the full elicitation setting; this implies the theorem. Obviously, the Θ_i, the u_i, and ϕ remain the same. Now consider the Σ_i. Because no information is revealed upon elicitation, the voter cannot condition its response on anything but its type, as in the full elicitation case. That is, each agent need only decide on the one vote that it will always cast if it is elicited. Hence, the strategy set of an agent is simply the space of votes, as it is in the full elicitation case. Finally, by our requirement that this elicitation produces the same outcome as full elicitation, o is the same. ∎

Future work includes designing an elicitation protocol that reveals no information about how many agents have had their types elicited so far. This seems difficult: most protocols at least betray the real time at which an agent is queried.

6.2. Fine elicitation

We now show that, unlike coarse elicitation, fine elicitation can lead to additional strategic issues even if no unnecessary information is revealed to the agents.

Theorem 9 *In a fine elicitation protocol, the following properties can hold simultaneously:*

- *the protocol reveals no information to any agent except the queries to the agent and the order of those queries,*
- *the elicitation policy is optimized to finish as quickly as possible on average given the distribution over the agents' types (presuming the agents vote truthfully), and*
- *truthful voting is a BNE with full elicitation,*
- *truthful voting is not a BNE here. In particular, an agent may have an incentive to vote differently depending on how the other agents vote.*

Proof: Consider an Approval election with 2 voters, i and j, and 3 candidates, a, b, and c. Define truth-telling to mean approving all candidates that give you utility $\geq \frac{1}{2}$. Ties are broken randomly. Agents' types are independent and the distributions are as follows. With probability $\frac{1}{2}$, i has utility 1 for b and c, and utility 0 for a; with probability $\frac{1}{2}$, it has utility 1 for a and b, and utility 0 for c. It is easy to see that truth-telling is always an optimal strategy for i. With probability 1, j has utility 1 for a, $\frac{3}{4}$ for b, and 0 for c. For j not to approve c, and to approve a, is always optimal. In

---

[6]For the game-theoretically inclined, we observe that some of the BNEs in the coarse elicitation case are not subgame perfect. These equilibria are unstable in the full elicitation case as well.

the full elicitation case, should j approve b? If i has its first type, approving b leads to victory for b and a utility of $\frac{3}{4}$; not approving b leads to a 3-way tie and utility of $\frac{7}{12}$. If i has its second type, approving b leads to a 2-way tie between a and b and utility $\frac{7}{8}$; not approving b leads to a victory for a and utility 1. Hence, in the full elicitation case, approving b gives utility $\frac{13}{16}$, and not approving b gives utility $\frac{19}{24}$; so approving b is optimal. Thus, truth-telling is a BNE here.

For the fine elicitation case, we first design a policy that is optimal with respect to the agents' type distributions. The natural restriction here is to allow only the following type of query: query $Q(k, d)$ asks voter k if it approves candidate d. Then an optimal elicitation protocol is: *1*: first ask $Q(i, a)$; *2a*: if the answer was 'no', ask $Q(i, b)$; $Q(j, b)$; $Q(j, c)$; *2b*: otherwise, ask $Q(j, a)$; $Q(i, b)$; $Q(j, b)$; $Q(i, c)$. *3*: if we do not know the winner yet, ask the remaining queries.

To show optimality, assume the agents reply truthfully. If i has its first type, we finish after *2a*, in 4 steps; if i has its second type, we finish after *2b*, in 5 steps. This is optimal.

Now, if the first query to j is $Q(j, b)$, this implies to it that i is of its first type and it is motivated to answer truthfully. But if the first query to j is $Q(j, a)$, this implies to it that i is of its second type; and i is motivated to lie and not approve b. So truth-telling is not a BNE here. ∎

Finally, we show that with a certain restriction on elicitation policies, we can guarantee that fine elicitation does not introduce any strategic effects.

Definition 9 *A fine elicitation policy is* nondivulging *if the next query to an agent (if it comes) depends only on that agent's own responses to previous queries. (Whether or not the next query is asked can depend on the agent's and the other agents' responses to queries so far.)*

Theorem 10 *Consider a fine elicitation protocol which manages to reveal nothing more to the agent than the queries to the agent and the order of those queries. If the elicitation policy is nondivulging, then the set of BNEs is the same as in the full elicitation voting game.*

Proof: We claim that the normal form of the game is identical to that in the full elicitation setting; this implies the theorem. Obviously, the Θ_i, the u_i, and ϕ remain the same. Now consider the Σ_i. Because the agent knows the first query to it (if it comes), it can determine its response up front. The next query (if it comes) can only depend on this response, so the agent knows it, and can prepare a response to it up front as well; and so on. So, in this setting, we can define the agent's strategy to be this entire sequence of responses. But this sequence correponds to exactly one vote in the full elicitation case.[7] Hence, the strategy set of an agent is simply the space of votes, as it is in the full elicitation case. Finally, by our requirement that this elicitation produces the same outcome as full elicitation, o is the same. ∎

While a restriction to nondivulging elicitation policies avoids introducing additional strategic effects, it can reduce the efficiency of elicitation.

---

[7] By our definition of fine elicitation, no queries are asked that enable an agent to express inconsistent (e.g., cyclical) preferences.

7. Conclusion and future research

Preference elicitation is a central problem in AI, and has received significant attention in single-agent settings. Preference elicitation is also a key problem in multiagent systems, but has received little attention. The agents may have different preferences that often must be aggregated using voting. This leads to interesting issues because what, if any, information should be elicited from an agent depends on what other agents have revealed about their preferences so far.

In this paper we studied effective elicitation for the most common voting protocols. It turned out that for the STV protocol, even knowing when to terminate elicitation is $\mathcal{N}P$-complete, while this is easy for all the other protocols. Even for these protocols, determining how to elicit effectively is $\mathcal{N}P$-complete, even with perfect suspicions about how the agents will vote. The exception is the Plurality protocol where such effective elicitation is easy.

Our results on strategy-proofness showed that in general settings, elicitation introduces additional opportunities for strategic manipulation of the election by the voters. We demonstrated how to curtail the space of elicitation schemes so that no such additional strategic issues arise.

Future research includes studying elicitation policies that choose the right outcome with high *probability* rather than with certainty. It also includes designing new voting protocols that combine the computational ease of elicitation in the Plurality protocol with the expressiveness of the other protocols. Finally, it would be interesting to study specific fine elicitation schemes in more detail.

Acknowledgments
This work was supported by the National Science Foundation under CAREER Award IRI-9703122, Grant IIS-9800994, ITR IIS-0081246, and ITR IIS-0121678.

References

Bartholdi, III, J. J., and Orlin, J. B. 1991. Single transferable vote resists strategic voting. *Social Choice and Welfare* 8(4):341–354.

Boutilier, C.; Brafman, R.; Geib, C.; and Poole, D. 1997. A constraint-based approach to preference elicitation and decision making. *AAAI Spring Symposium: Qualitative Decision Theory*.

Chajewwska, U.; Koller, D.; and Parr, R. 2000. Making rational decisions using adaptive utility elicitation. *AAAI*, 363–369.

Conen, W., and Sandholm, T. 2001. Preference elicitation in combinatorial auctions: Extended abstract. *ACM Conference on Electronic Commerce (ACM-EC)*, 256–259. More detailed description of the algorithms appeared in the IJCAI-2001 Workshop on Economic Agents, Models, and Mechanisms, pp. 71–80.

Conitzer, V., and Sandholm, T. 2002. Complexity of manipulating elections with few candidates. *AAAI*.

Ephrati, E., and Rosenschein, J. 1991. The Clarke tax as a consensus mechanism among automated agents. *AAAI*, 173–178.

Ephrati, E., and Rosenschein, J. S. 1993. Multi-agent planning as a dynamic search for social consensus. *IJCAI*, 423–429.

Larson, K.; Sandholm, T. 2001. Bargaining with limited computation: Deliberation equilibrium. *Artificial Intelligence* 132:183-217.

Sandholm, T. 1993. An implementation of the contract net protocol based on marginal cost calculations. *AAAI*, 256–262.

Vu, H.; Haddawy, P. 1998. Towards case-based preference elicitation: Similarity measures on preference structures. *UAI*, 193-201.

Dispersion Games: General Definitions and Some Specific Learning Results[*]

Trond Grenager and **Rob Powers** and **Yoav Shoham**

Computer Science Department
Stanford University
Stanford, CA 94305
{grenager, powers, shoham}@cs.stanford.edu

Abstract

Dispersion games are the generalization of the *anti-coordination game* to arbitrary numbers of agents and actions. In these games agents prefer outcomes in which the agents are maximally dispersed over the set of possible actions. This class of games models a large number of natural problems, including load balancing in computer science, niche selection in economics, and division of roles within a team in robotics. Our work consists of two main contributions. First, we formally define and characterize some interesting classes of dispersion games. Second, we present several learning strategies that agents can use in these games, including traditional learning rules from game theory and artificial intelligence, as well as some special purpose strategies. We then evaluate analytically and empirically the performance of each of these strategies.

Introduction

A natural and much studied class of games is the set of so-called *coordination games*, one-shot games in which both agents win positive payoffs only when they choose the same action (Schelling 1960).[1] A complementary class that has received relatively little attention is the set of games in which agents win positive payoffs only when they choose distinct actions; these games have sometimes been called the *anti-coordination games*. Most discussion of these games has focused only on the two-agent case (see Figure 1), where the coordination game and the anti-coordination game differ by only the renaming of one player's actions. However, with arbitrary numbers of agents and actions, the two games diverge; while the generalization of the coordination game is quite straightforward, that of the anti-coordination game is more complex. In this paper we study the latter, which we call *dispersion games* (DGs), since these are games in which agents prefer to be more dispersed over actions.[2] Although one can transform a dispersion game into a coordi-

[*]This work is supported in part by DARPA Grant F30602-00-2-0598 and by a Benchmark Stanford Graduate Fellowship.

[1]In this paper, we assume familiarity with basic game theory; our formulations are in the style of (Osborne & Rubinstein 1994).

[2]We chose this name after (Alpern 2001) who studies a subclass of these games which he calls *spatial dispersion problems*.

	A	B
A	1	0
B	0	1

	A	B
A	0	1
B	1	0

Figure 1: Two-agent coordination game (left) and anti-coordination game (right).

nation game in which agents coordinate on a maximally dispersed assignment of actions to agents, the number of such assignments grows exponentially with the number of agents.

DGs model natural problems in a number of different domains. Perhaps the most natural application is presented by the much studied *load balancing* problem (see, e.g., Azar *et al.* 2000). This problem can be modeled as a DG in which the agents are the users, the possible actions are the resources, and the equilibria of the game are the outcomes in which agents are maximally dispersed. Another natural application of DGs is presented by the *niche selection* problem studied in economics and evolutionary biology. In a general niche selection problem, each of n oligopoly producers wishes to occupy one of k different market niches, and producers wish to occupy niches with fewer competitors. Other niche selection problems include the *Santa Fe bar problem* proposed by Arthur (1994), and the class of *minority games* (Challet & Zhang 1997). These niche selection problems can all be modeled in a straightforward manner by DGs. Finally, we note that DGs can also serve as a model of the process of role formation within teams of robots. In fact, the initial motivation for this research came from empirical work on reinforcement learning in RoboCup (Balch 1998).

This paper makes two types of contributions. First, we formally define and characterize some classes of DGs that possess special and interesting properties. Second, we analyze and experimentally evaluate the performance of different learning strategies in these classes of games, including two standard learning rules from game theory and artificial intelligence, as well as two novel strategies. The remainder of this article is organized as follows. In the first section we present the game definitions. In the second and third sections we present the learning strategies and the results and analysis of their performance. Finally, in the last section we discuss these findings and present ideas for future research.

Dispersion Game Definitions

In this section we begin by discussing some simple dispersion games, and work our way gradually to the most general definitions. All of the DGs we define in this section are subclasses of the set of *normal form games*, which we define as follows.

Definition 1 (CA, CP, CACP games) *A normal form game G is a tuple $\langle N, (A_i)_{i \in N}, (\succeq_i)_{i \in N} \rangle$, where*

- *N is a finite set of n agents,*
- *A_i is a finite set of actions available to agent $i \in N$, and*
- *$\succeq_i$ is the preference relation of agent $i \in N$, defined on the set of outcomes $O = A^n$, that satisfies the von Neumann-Morgenstern axioms.*

A game G is a common action (CA) game if there exists a set of actions A such that for all $i \in N$, $A_i = A$; we represent a CA game as $\langle N, A, (\succeq_i)_{i \in N} \rangle$. Similarly, a game is a common preference (CP) game if there exists a relation $\succeq$ such that for all $i \in N$, $\succeq_i = \succeq$; we represent a CP game as $\langle N, (A_i)_{i \in N}, \succeq \rangle$. We denote a game that is both CA and CP as CACP. We represent a CACP game as $\langle N, A, \succeq \rangle$

Note that we use the notation $\langle a_1, \ldots, a_n \rangle$ to denote the outcome in which agent 1 chooses action a_1, agent 2 chooses action a_2, and so on. In a CA game where $|A| = k$, there are k^n total outcomes.

Common Preference Dispersion Games

Perhaps the simplest DG is that in which n agents independently and simultaneously choose from among n actions, and the agents prefer only the outcomes in which they all choose distinct actions. (This game was defined independently in (Alpern 2001).) We call these outcomes the *maximal dispersion outcomes* (MDOs).

This simple DG is highly constrained. It assumes that the number of agents n is equal to the number of actions k available to each agent. However, there are many problems in which $k \neq n$ that we may wish to model with DGs. When $k > n$ the game is similar to the $k = n$ game but easier: there is a larger proportion of MDOs. When $k < n$ however, the situation is more complex: there are no outcomes in which all agents choose distinct actions. For this reason, we will need a more general definition of an MDO. In the definitions that follow, we use the notation n_a^o to be the number of agents selecting action a in outcome o.

Definition 2 (MDO) *Given a CA game G, an outcome $o = \langle a_1, \ldots, a_i, \ldots, a_n \rangle$ of G is a maximal dispersion outcome iff for all agents $i \in N$ and for all outcomes $o' = \langle a_1, \ldots, a_i', \ldots, a_n \rangle$ such that $a_i' \neq a_i$, it is the case that $n_{a_i}^o \leq n_{a_i'}^{o'}$.*

In other words, an MDO is an outcome in which no agent can move to an action with fewer other agents. Note that when the number of agents is less than or equal to the number of actions, an MDO allocates exactly one agent to each action, as above.

Under this definition, the number of MDOs in a general CA game with k actions is given by

$$MDO(n, k) = n! \frac{\binom{k}{n \bmod k}}{\lceil n/k \rceil^{n \bmod k} \lfloor n/k \rfloor!^k}.$$

When $k = n$ this expression simplifies to $n!$, since there are $n!$ ways to allocate n agents to n actions.

The simple DG presented above also makes another strong assumption. It assumes that an agent's preference over outcomes depends only on the overall configuration of agents and actions in the outcome (such as the number of agents that choose distinct actions), but not on the particular identities of the agents or actions (such as the identities of the actions that are chosen). We call these the assumptions of *agent symmetry* and *action symmetry*. However, many situations we might like to model are not agent and action symmetric. For example, role formation on soccer teams is not action symmetric. The identity of a particular field position in an outcome can affect the performance of the team: a team with a goalie but no halfback would probably perform better than one with a halfback but no goalie, all else being equal. Robot soccer is also not necessarily agent symmetric. If agent 1 is a better offensive than defensive player, then a team may perform better if agent 1 is a forward instead of a fullback, all else being equal. We use the following formal definitions of symmetry.

Definition 3 (Agent Symmetry) *A CA game $G = \langle N, A, (\succeq_i)_{i \in N} \rangle$ is agent symmetric iff for all outcomes $o = \langle a_1, \ldots, a_i, \ldots, a_n \rangle$, and for all permutations $o' = \langle a_1', \ldots, a_i', \ldots, a_n' \rangle$ of o, for all $i \in N$, $o \succeq_i o'$ and $o' \succeq_i o$.*

Definition 4 (Action Symmetry) *A CA game $G = \langle N, A, (\succeq_i)_{i \in N} \rangle$ is action symmetric iff for all outcomes $o = \langle a_1, \ldots, a_i, \ldots, a_n \rangle$ and $o' = \langle a_1', \ldots, a_i', \ldots, a_n' \rangle$, if there exists a one-to-one mapping $f : A \to A$ such that for all $i \in N$, $f(a_i) = a_i'$, then for all $i \in N$, $o \succeq_i o'$ and $o' \succeq_i o$.*

In fully symmetric games, agents cannot distinguish between outcomes with the same configuration of numbers of agents choosing actions. Thus we use the abbreviated notation $\{n_1, \ldots, n_k\}$ to refer to the set of outcomes in which n_1 agents choose some action, n_2 agents choose a different action, and so on. By convention, we order the actions from most to least populated.

We are now ready to state the formal definition of a weak DG that is well defined over the set of all CACP games, including asymmetric games and games with arbitrary n, k.

Definition 5 (Weak DG) *A CACP game $G = \langle N, A, \succeq \rangle$ is a weak dispersion game iff the set of $\succeq$-maximal outcomes of G is a subset of the set of MDOs of G.*

This definition requires only that at least one of the MDOs is a preferred outcome, and that none of the non-MDOs is a preferred outcome. This definition is weak because it places no constraints on the preference ordering for the non-maximally-preferred outcomes.[3] For this reason, we also

---

[3] The reader may wonder why our definitions don't require that

state a strong definition. Before we can state the definition, however, we will need the following *dispersion relation*.

Definition 6 ($\sqsupseteq$) *Given two outcomes $o = \langle a_1, \ldots, a_i, \ldots, a_n \rangle$ and $o' = \langle a'_1, \ldots, a'_i, \ldots, a'_n \rangle$, we have that $o \mathbf{D} o'$ iff there exists a agent $i \in N$ such that $a'_i \neq a_i$, and $n^o_{a_i} < n^{o'}_{a'_i}$, and for all other agents $j \in N, j \neq i, a_j = a'_j$. We let the dispersion relation $\sqsupseteq$ be the reflexive and transitive closure of $\mathbf{D}$.*

In other words, o is more dispersed than o' if it is possible to transform o' into o by a sequence of steps, each of which is a change of action by exactly one agent to an action with fewer other agents. It is important to note that the dispersion ordering is a structural property of any CACP game. The dispersion relation over the set of outcomes forms a partially ordered set (poset). Note that the set of MDOs is just the set of $\sqsupseteq$-maximal elements of O.

There are many other measures that we could use instead of the qualitative dispersion relation. Entropy is consistent with, but stronger than our dispersion relation: if $o \sqsupseteq o'$ then the entropy of o is higher than that of o', but the converse is not necessarily true. We have chosen to base our definitions on the weaker dispersion relation because it is the most general, and because it corresponds directly to a single agent's change of actions.

Using this dispersion relation, we can state the formal definition of strong DGs.

Definition 7 (Strong DG) *A CACP game $G = \langle N, A, \succeq \rangle$ is a strong dispersion game iff for all outcomes $o, o' \in O$, it is the case that if $o \sqsupseteq o'$ but not $o' \sqsupseteq o$, then $o \succeq o'$ but not $o' \succeq o$.*

Recall that the preference relation $\succeq$ forms a total ordering while the dispersion relation $\sqsupseteq$ forms a partial ordering. Thus this definition requires that o is strictly preferred to o' when o is strictly more dispersed than o'.

If the strong definition has such nice properties, why bother to state the weak definition at all? There are many situations which have a dispersion quality but which cannot be modeled by games in the stronger class. Consider the situation faced by Alice, Bob, and Charlie who are each choosing among three possible roles in the founding of a company: CEO, COO, and CFO. Because they will be compensated as a group, the situation can be modeled as a CP game. However, suppose that Bob would be a terrible CEO. Clearly, the agents would most prefer an outcome in which each role is filled and Bob is not CEO; thus the game satisfies the weak definition. However, rather than have all roles filled and Bob alone be CEO, they would prefer an outcome in which Bob shares the CEO position with one of the other agents (i.e., both Bob and another agent select the "CEO" action), even though it leaves one of the other roles empty. In other words, the preference relation conflicts with the dispersion ordering, and the game does not satisfy the strong definition.

___
all MDOs are maximal outcomes. In fact, it is easy to verify that this must be the case in a fully symmetric DG.

Non-Common-Preference Dispersion Games

There are also several interesting classes of non-CP dispersion games we might like to model. Due to space considerations we will not define these classes formally, but instead present a few motivating examples.

Consider again the load balancing application in which each of n users simultaneously wishes to use one of k different resources. If the users all belong to a single organization, the interest of the organization can be well modeled by a CP DG, since the productivity of the organization will be highest if the users are as dispersed as possible among the servers. However, the users' preferences may be more *selfish*: a user may prefer individually to use a resource with the fewest possible other users, regardless of the welfare of the rest of the group. Additionally, users' preferences may reflect some combination of individual and group welfare. These problems may be modeled with the class of *selfish dispersion games*.

Consider again the niche selection problem, in which each of n oligopoly producers wishes to occupy one of k different market niches. It may be the case that in addition to a general preference for dispersal (presumably to avoid competition) each producer has an *exogenous* preference for one of the niches; these preferences may or may not be aligned. For example, it may be that one of the market niches is larger and thus preferred by all producers. Alternatively, a producer may have competencies that suit it well for a particular niche. Note that the two agent case can be modeled by what one might call the *anti-battle-of-the-sexes game* in which a man and his ex-wife both wish to attend one of two parties, one of which is more desirable, but both prefer not to encounter each other (the reader familiar with the original BoS game will appreciate the humor). These problems can be modeled with the class of *partial dispersion games*, in which agents' preferences may align with either the dispersion ordering or with a set of exogenous preferences.

Learning Strategy Definitions

Now that we have defined a few interesting classes of dispersion games, let us consider the task of playing them in a repeated game setting. There are two perspectives we may adopt: that of the individual agent wishing to maximize his individual welfare, and that of a system designer wishing to implement a distributed algorithm for maximizing the group welfare. In the present research, we adopt the latter.

Let us begin with the problem of finding an MDO as quickly as possible in a weak CACP DG.[4] Note that this problem is trivial if implemented as a centralized algorithm. The problem is also trivial if implemented as a distributed algorithm in which agents are allowed unlimited communication. Thus we seek distributed algorithms that require no explicit communication between agents. Each algorithm takes the form of a set of identical learning rules for each

___
[4]Note that any mixed strategy equilibrium outcome is necessarily preference dominated by the pure strategy MDOs. For this reason, we henceforth disregard mixed strategy equilibria, and focus on the problem of finding one of the MDOs.

agent, each of which is a function mapping observed histories to distributions over actions.

Consider the most naive distributed algorithm. In each round, each agent selects an action randomly from the uniform distribution, stopping only when the outcome is an MDO. Note that this naive learning rule imposes very minimal information requirements on the agents: each agent must be informed only whether the outcome is an MDO. Unfortunately, the expected number of rounds until convergence to an MDO is

$$\frac{k^n}{MDO(n, k)}.$$

It is easy to see that for $k = n$ the expected time is $n^n/n!$, which is exponential in n.

We began by evaluating traditional learning rules from game theory and artificial intelligence. Game theory offers a plethora of options; we looked for simplicity and intuitive appropriateness. We considered both fictitious play (Brown 1951; Robinson 1951) and rational learning (Kalai & Lehrer 1993). Rational learning did not seem promising because of its dependence on the strategy space and initial beliefs of the agents. Thus we focused our attention on fictitious play.

In evaluating learning rules from artificial intelligence the decision was more straightforward. Recently there has been significant interest in the application of reinforcement learning to the problem of multi-agent system learning (Littman 1994; Claus & Boutilier 1998; Brafman & Tennenholtz 2000). We chose to implement and test the most common reinforcement learning algorithm: *Q-learning*.

Finally, we developed a few special purpose strategies to take advantage of the special structure of DGs.

Note that the different strategies we describe require agents to have access to different amounts of information about the outcome of each round as they play the game. At one extreme, agents might need only a Boolean value signifying whether or not the group has reached an MDO (this is all that is required for the naive strategy). At the other extreme, agents might need complete information about the outcome, including the action choices of each of the other agents.

Fictitious Play Learning

Fictitious play is a learning rule in which an agent assumes that each other agent is playing a fixed mixed strategy. The fictitious play agent uses counts of the actions selected by the other agents to estimate their mixed strategies and then at each round selects the action that has the highest expected value given these beliefs. Note that the fictitious play rule places very high information requirements on the agents. In order to update their beliefs, agents must have full knowledge of the outcome. Our implementation of fictitious play includes a few minor modifications to the basic rule.

One modification stems from the well known fact that agents using fictitious play may never converge to equilibrium play. Indeed our experiments show that fictitious play agents in CP DGs often generate play that oscillates within sets of outcomes, never reaching an MDO. This results from the agents' erroneous belief in the others' use of a fixed

mixed strategy. To avoid this oscillation, we modify the fictitious play rule with stochastic perturbations of agents' beliefs as suggested by (Fudenberg & Levine 1998). In particular, we apply a uniform random variation of -1% to 1% on the expected reward of each action before selecting the agent's best response.

The other modifications were necessary to make the agents' computation within each round tractable for large numbers of agents. Calculating the expected value of each possible action at each round requires time that is exponential in n. To avoid this, we store the history of play as counts of observed outcomes rather than counts of each agents' actions. Also, instead of maintaining the entire history of play, we use a bounded memory of observed outcomes. The predicted joint mixed strategy of the other agents is then calculated by assuming the observed outcomes within memory are an unbiased sample. [5]

Reinforcement Learning

Reinforcement learning is a learning rule in which agents learn a mapping from states to actions (Kaelbling, Littman, & Moore 1996). We implemented the *Q-learning* algorithm with a Boltzman exploration policy. In Q-learning, agents learn the expected reward of performing an action in a given state. Our implementation of Q-learning includes a few minor modifications to the basic algorithm.

It is well known that the performance of Q-learning is extremely sensitive to a number of implementation details. First, the choice of a state space for the agent's Q-function is critical. We chose to use only a single state, so that in effect agents learn Q-values over actions only. Second, the selection of initial Q-values and temperature is critical. We found it best to set the initial Q-values to lie strictly within the range of the highest possible payoff (i.e., being alone) and the next highest (i.e., being with one other agent). We chose to parameterize the Boltzman learning function with an initial low temperature. These choices allow agents that initially choose a non-conflicting action to have high probability of continuing to play this action, and allow those that have collided with other agents to learn eventually the true value of the action and successively choose other actions until they find an action that does not conflict.

In our implementation we chose to give the agents a selfish reward instead of the global common-preference reward. The reward is a function of the number of other agents that choose the same action, not of the degree of dispersion of the group as a whole. This selfish reward has the advantage of giving the agents a signal that is more closely tied to the effects of their actions, while still being maximal for each agent when the agents have reached an MDO.

Specialized Strategies

The first specialized strategy that we propose is the *freeze strategy*. In the freeze strategy, an agent chooses actions

---

[5]The reader might be concerned that this approximation changes the convergence properties of the rule. Although this may be the case in some settings, in our experiments with small n no difference was observed from those using the full history.

randomly until the first time she is alone, at which point she continues to replay that action indefinitely, regardless of whether other agents choose the same action. It is easy to see that this strategy is guaranteed to converge in the limit, and that if it converges it will converge to an MDO. The freeze strategy also has the benefit of imposing very minimal information requirements: it requires an agent to know only how many agents chose the same action as she did in the previous round.

An improvement on the freeze strategy is the *basic simple strategy*, which was originally suggested by Alpern (2001). In this strategy, each agent begins by randomly choosing an action. Then, if no other agent chose the same action, she chooses the same action in the next round. Otherwise, she randomizes over the set of actions that were either unoccupied or selected by two or more agents. Note that the basic simple strategy requires that agents know only which actions had a single agent in them after each round.

Definition 8 (Basic Simple Strategy) *Given an outcome $o \in O$, an agent using the* basic simple strategy *will*

- *If $n_a^o = 1$, select action a with probability 1,*
- *Otherwise, select an action from the uniform distribution over actions $a' \in A$ for which $n_{a'}^o \neq 1$.*

We have extended the basic simple strategy to work in the broader class of games for which $n \neq k$.

Definition 9 (Extended Simple Strategy) *Given an outcome $o \in O$, an agent using the* extended simple strategy *will*

- *If $n_a^o \leq \lfloor n/k \rfloor$, select action a with probability 1,*
- *Otherwise, select action a with probability $\frac{n/k}{n_a^o}$ and with probability $(1 - \frac{n/k}{n_a^o})$ randomize over the actions a' for which $n_{a'}^o < \lceil n/k \rceil$.*

Unlike the basic strategy, the extended strategy does not assign uniform probabilities to all actions that were not chosen by the correct number of agents. Consider agents reacting to the outcome $\{2, 2, 0, 0\}$. In this case each agent is better off staying with probability 0.5 and jumping to each of the empty slots with probability 0.25, than randomizing uniformly over all four slots. The extended simple strategy can actually be further improved by assigning non-uniform probabilities to the actions a' for which $n_{a'}^o < \lceil n/k \rceil$. We have found empirically that the learning rule converges more rapidly when agents place more probability on the actions that have fewer other agents in them. Note that the extended simple strategy requires that agents know the number of agents selecting each action in the round; the identity of these agents is not required, however.

Experimental Results

The learning rules and strategies described above differ significantly in the empirical time to converge. In Figure 2 we plot as a function of n the convergence time of the learning rules in repeated symmetric weak DGs, averaged over 1000 trials. Table 1 summarizes the observed performance of each strategy (as well as the information requirements of

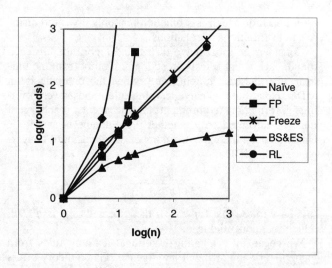

Figure 2: Log-log plot of the empirical performance of different strategies in symmetric CACP dispersion games.

Learning Rule	Information Requirements	Avg. Rounds to Converge ($f(n)$)
Naive	Whether MDO	EXP
FP	Full Information	EXP
RL	Num. in Own Action	POLY
Freeze	Num. in Own Action	LINEAR
BS & ES	Num. in All Actions	LOG

Table 1: Applicability of strategies to various classes of games with information requirements and estimated complexity class.

each strategy). We discuss the performance of each of the strategies in turn.

We begin with the learning rules. In our empirical tests we found that stochastic fictitious play always converged to an MDO. However, the number of rounds to converge was on average exponential in n. In our empirical tests of the reinforcement learning strategy we found that on average play converges to an MDO in a number of rounds that is linear in n. An interesting result is that for $n \neq k$, the algorithm didn't converge to a unique selection of actions for each agent, but rapidly adopted a set of mixed strategies for the agents resulting in average payoffs close to the optimal deterministic policy.

The specialized strategies generally exhibited better performance than the learning rules. Our empirical observations show that the number of rounds it takes for the freeze strategy to converge to an MDO is linear in n. Our empirical tests of both basic and extended simple strategies show that on average, play converges to an MDO in a number of steps that is logarithmic in the number of agents.[6]

---

[6]For $n > k$ certain ratios of n/k led consistently to superlogarithmic performance; slight modifications of the extended simple strategy were able to achieve logarithmic performance.

Discussion

In this paper we have introduced the class of DGs and defined several important subclasses that display interesting properties. We then investigated certain representative learning rules and tested their empirical behavior in DGs. In the future, we intend to continue this research in two primary directions.

First, we would like to further investigate some new types of DGs. We gave examples above of two classes of non-CP dispersion games that model common problems, but due to space limitations we were not able to define and characterize them in this paper. On a different note, we are also interested in a possible generalization of DGs which models the allocation of some quantity associated with the agents, such as skill or usage, to the different actions. We would like to define these classes of games formally, and explore learning rules that can solve them efficiently.

Second, we would like to continue the research on learning in DGs that we have begun in this paper. The learning rules we evaluated above are an initial exploration, and clearly many other learning techniques also deserve consideration. Additionally, we would like to complement the empirical work presented here with some analytical results. As a preliminary result, we can prove the following loose upper bound on the expected convergence time of the basic simple strategy.

Proposition 1 *In a repeated fully symmetric weak dispersion game with n agents and actions, in which all agents use the basic simple strategy, the expected number of rounds until convergence to an MDO is in $O(n)$.*

Informally, the proof is as follows. The probability that a particular agent chooses an action alone is $((n-1)/n)^{n-1}$, and so the expected number of rounds until she is alone is just $(n/(n-1))^{n-1}$. Because of the linearity of expectation, the expected number of rounds for all agents to find themselves alone must be no more than $n^n/(n-1)^{n-1}$, which is less than ne for all $n > 1$. Using similar techniques it is possible to show a quadratic bound on the expected convergence time of the freeze strategy.

Unfortunately, our empirical results show that the basic simple strategy converges in time that is logarithmic in n, and that the freeze strategy converges in linear time. This gap between our preliminary analysis and our empirical results begs future analytical work. Is it possible to show a tighter upper bound, for these learning rules or for others? Can we show a lower bound?

We would also like to better understand the optimality of learning rules. It is possible in principal to derive the optimal reactive learning rule for any finite number of agents using dynamic programming. Note that the optimal strategies obtained using this method are arbitrarily complex, however. For example, even upon reaching the simple outcome $\{2, 2, 0, 0\}$, an optimal reactive strategy for each agent chooses the same action with probability 0.5118 (not 0.5, as the extended simple strategy would dictate).

Dispersion games clearly play an important role in cooperative multiagent systems, and deserve much more discussion and scrutiny. We view the results of this paper as opening the door to substantial additional work on this exciting class of games.

References

Alpern, S. 2001. Spatial dispersion as a dynamic coordination problem. Technical report, The London School of Economics.

Arthur, B. 1994. Inductive reasoning and bounded rationality. *American Economic Association Papers* 84:406–411.

Azar, Y.; Broder, A. Z.; Karlin, A. R.; and Upfal, E. 2000. Balanced allocations. *SIAM Journal on Computing* 29(1):180–200.

Balch, T. 1998. Behavioral diversity in learning robot teams.

Brafman, R. I., and Tennenholtz, M. 2000. A near-optimal polynomial time algorithm for learning in certain classes of stochastic games. *Artificial Intelligence* 121(1-2):31–47.

Brown, G. 1951. Iterative solution of games by fictitious play. In *Activity Analysis of Production and Allocation*. New York: John Wiley and Sons.

Challet, D., and Zhang, Y. 1997. Emergence of cooperation and organization in an evolutionary game. *Physica A* 246:407.

Claus, C., and Boutilier, C. 1998. The dynamics of reinforcement learning in cooperative multiagent systems. In *AAAI/IAAI*, 746–752.

Fudenberg, D., and Levine, D. K. 1998. *The Theory of Learning in Games*. Cambridge, MA: MIT Press.

Kaelbling, L. P.; Littman, M. L.; and Moore, A. P. 1996. Reinforcement learning: A survey. *Journal of Artificial Intelligence Research* 4:237–285.

Kalai, E., and Lehrer, E. 1993. Rational learning leads to nash equilibrium. *Econometrica* 61(5):1019–1045.

Littman, M. L. 1994. Markov games as a framework for multi-agent reinforcement learning. In *Proceedings of the 11th International Conference on Machine Learning (ML-94)*, 157–163. New Brunswick, NJ: Morgan Kaufmann.

Osborne, M., and Rubinstein, A. 1994. *A Course in Game Theory*. Cambridge, Massachusetts: MIT Press.

Robinson, J. 1951. An iterative method of solving a game. *Annals of Mathematics* 54:298–301.

Schelling, T. 1960. *The Strategy of Conflict*. Cambridge, Massachusetts: Harvard University Press.

Competitive Safety Analysis

Moshe Tennenholtz

Computer Science Department
Stanford University
Stanford, CA 94305 *

Abstract

Much work in AI deals with the selection of proper actions in a given (known or unknown) environment. However, the way to select a proper action when facing other agents is quite unclear. Most work in AI adopts classical game-theoretic equilibrium analysis to predict agent behavior in such settings. Needless to say, this approach does not provide us with any guarantee for the agent. In this paper we introduce competitive safety analysis. This approach bridges the gap between the desired normative AI approach, where a strategy should be selected in order to guarantee a desired payoff, and equilibrium analysis. We show that a safety level strategy is able to guarantee the value obtained in a Nash equilibrium, in several classical computer science settings. Then, we discuss the concept of competitive safety strategies, and illustrate its use in a decentralized load balancing setting, typical to network problems. In particular, we show that when we have many agents, it is possible to guarantee an expected payoff which is a factor of 8/9 of the payoff obtained in a Nash equilibrium. Finally, we discuss the extension of the above concepts to Bayesian games, and illustrate their use in a basic auctions setup.

Introduction

Deriving solution concepts for multi-agent encounters is a major challenge for researchers in various disciplines. The most famous and popular solution concept in the economics literature is the Nash equilibrium. Although Nash equilibrium and its extensions and modifications are powerful descriptive tools, and have been widely used in the AI literature (see e.g. (Rosenschein & Zlotkin 1994; Kraus 1997; Sandholm & Lesser 1995)), their appeal from a normative AI perspective is somewhat less satisfactory.[1] We wish to equip an agent with an action that guarantees some desired outcome, or expected utility, without relying on other agents' rationality.

This paper shows that, surprisingly, the desire for obtaining a guaranteed expected payoff, where this payoff is of the order of the value obtained in a Nash equilibrium, is achievable in various classical computer science settings. Our results are inspired by several interesting examples for counter-intuitive behaviors obtained by following Nash equilibria and other solution concepts (Roth 1980; Aumann 1985). One of the most interesting and challenging examples has been introduced by Aumann (Aumann 1985). Aumann presented a 2-person 2-choice (2×2) game g, where the safety-level (probabilistic maximin) strategy of the game is not a Nash equilibrium of it, but it does yield the expected payoff of a Nash equilibrium of g. This observation may have significant positive ramifications from an agent's design perspective. If a safety-level strategy of an agent guarantees an expected payoff that equals its expected payoff in a Nash equilibrium, then it can serve as a desirable robust protocol for the agent!

Given the above, we are interested in whether an optimal safety level strategy leads to an expected payoff similar to the one obtained in a Nash equilibrium of simple games that represent basic variants of classical computer science problems. As we show, this is indeed the case for 2×2 games capturing simple variants of the classical load balancing and leader election problems.

A more general question refers to more general 2×2 games. We show that if the safety-level strategy is a (strictly) mixed one, then its expected payoff is identical to the expected payoff obtained in a Nash equilibrium in any generic non-reducible 2×2 game. We also show that this is no longer necessarily the case if we have a pure safety-level strategy. In addition, we consider general 2-person set-theoretic games (which naturally extend 2×2 leader election games) and show that if a set-theoretic game g possesses a strictly mixed strategy equilibrium then the safety level value for a player in that game equals the expected payoff it obtains in that equilibrium.

Following this, we define the concept of C-competitive safety strategies. Roughly speaking, a strategy will be called

---

*Permanent address: Faculty of Industrial Engineering and Management, Technion, Haifa 32000, Israel

[1] If we restrict ourselves to cases where there exists an equilibrium in dominant strategies (as is done in some of the CS literature; see e.g. (Nisan & Ronen 1999)) then the corresponding equilibrium is appealing from a normative perspective. However, such cases rarely exist.

a C-competitive safety strategy, if it guarantees an expected payoff that is $\frac{1}{C}$ of the expected payoff obtained in a Nash equilibrium. We show that in an extended decentralized load balancing setting a 9/8-competitive strategy exists, when the number of players is large. We also discuss extensions of this result to more general settings. Then, we discuss C-competitive strategies in the context of Bayesian games. In particular we show the existence of an e-competitive safety strategy for a classical first-price auctions setup.

Previous work has been concerned with comparing the payoffs that can be obtained by an optimal centralized (and Pareto-efficient) controller to the expected payoffs obtained in the Nash-equilibria of the corresponding game (Koutsoupias & Papadimitriou 1999). That work is in the spirit of competitive analysis, a central topic in theoretical computer science (Borodin & El-Yaniv 1998). Our work can be considered as suggesting a complementary approach, comparing the safety-level value to the agent's expected payoff in a Nash equilibrium. Needless to say that in computational settings, where failures are possible, and rationality assumptions about participants' behavior should be minimized, a safety-level strategy has a special appeal, especially when it yields a value that is close to the expected payoff obtained in a Nash equilibrium.

Basic definitions and notations

A *game* is a tuple $G = \langle N = \{1, \ldots, n\}, \{S_i\}_{i=1}^n, \{U_i\}_{i=1}^n \rangle$, where N is a set of n players, S_i is a finite set of pure strategies available to player i, and $U_i : \Pi_{i=1}^n S_i \to \Re$ is the payoff function of player i.

Given S_i, we denote the set of probability distributions over the elements of S_i by $\Delta(S_i)$. An element $t \in \Delta(S_i)$ is called a *mixed strategy* of player i. It is called a pure strategy if is assigns probability 1 to an element of S_i, and it is called a strictly mixed strategy if it assigns a positive probability to each element in S_i. A tuple $t = (t_1, \ldots, t_n) \in \Pi_{i=1}^n \Delta(S_i)$ is called a *strategy profile*. We denote by $U_i(t)$ the expected payoff of player i given the strategy profile t.

A strategy profile $t = (t_1, \ldots, t_n)$ is a *Nash equilibrium* if $\forall i \in N$, $U_i(t) \geq U_i(t_1, t_2, \ldots, t_{i-1}, t_i', t_{i+1}, \ldots, t_n)$ for every $t_i' \in S_i$. The Nash equilibrium $t = (t_1, \ldots, t_n)$ is called a *pure strategy Nash equilibrium* if t_i is a pure strategy for every $i \in N$. The Nash equilibrium $t = (t_1, \ldots, t_n)$ is called a *strictly mixed strategy Nash equilibrium* if for every $i \in N$ we have that t_i is a strictly mixed strategy.

Given a game g and a mixed strategy of player i, $t \in \Delta(S_i)$, the safety level value obtained by i when choosing t in the game g, denoted by $val(t, i, g)$, is the minimal expected payoff that player i may obtain when employing t against arbitrary strategy profiles of the other players. A strategy t' of player i for which $val(., i, g)$ is maximal is called a *safely-level strategy* (or a *probabilistic maximin strategy*) of player i.

A strategy $e \in S_i$ *dominates* a strategy $f \in S_i$ if for every $(s_1, s_2, \ldots, s_{i-1}, s_{i+1}, \ldots, s_n) \in \Pi_{j \neq i} \Delta(S_j)$ we have

$U_i(s_1, \ldots, s_{j-1}, e, s_{j+1}, \ldots, s_n) \geq$
$U_i(s_1, \ldots, s_{j-1}, f, s_{j+1}, \ldots, s_n)$, with a strict inequality for at least one such tuple.

A game is called *non-reducible* if there do not exist $e, f \in S_i$, for some $i \in N$, such that e dominates f. A game is called *generic* if for every $i \in N$, and pair of strategies $e, f \in \Pi_{j=1}^n S_j$, we have that $U_i(e) = U_i(f)$ only if player i's strategies in e and f coincide.

A game is called a 2×2 game if $n = 2$ and $|S_1| = |S_2| = 2$.

Decentralized load balancing

In this section we consider decentralized load balancing, where two rational players need to submit messages in a simple communication network: a network of two parallel communication lines e_1, e_2 connecting nodes s and t. Each player has a message that he needs to deliver from s to t, and he needs to decide on the route to be taken. The communication line e_1 is a faster one, and therefore the value of transmitting a single message along e_1 is $X > 0$ while the value of transmitting a single message along e_2 is αX for some $0.5 < \alpha < 1$. Each player needs to decide on the communication line to be used for sending its message from s to t. If both players choose the same communication line then the value for each one of them drops in a factor of two (a player will obtain $\frac{X}{2}$ if both players choose e_1, and a player will obtain $\frac{\alpha X}{2}$ if both players choose e_2). In a matrix form, this game can be presented as follows:

$$M = \begin{pmatrix} X/2, \; X/2 & X, \quad \alpha X \\ \alpha X, \quad X & \alpha X/2, \; \alpha X/2 \end{pmatrix}$$

Proposition 1 *The optimal safety-level value for a player in the decentralized load balancing game equals its expected payoff in the strictly mixed strategy equilibrium of that game.*

The proof of the above proposition appears in the full paper. The above proposition shows that an agent can *guarantee* itself an expected payoff that equals its payoff in a Nash equilibrium of the decentralized load balancing game. This is obtained using a strategy that differs from the agent's strategies in the Nash equilibria of that game (which do not provide that guarantee).

Leader election: decentralized voting

In a leader election setting, the players vote about the identity of the player who will take the lead on a particular task. A failure to obtain agreement about the leader is a bad output, and can be modelled as leading to a 0 payoff. Assume that the players' strategies are either "vote for 1" or "vote for 2", denoted by a_1, a_2 respectively, then $U_i(a_j, a_k) > 0$, where $i, j, k \in \{1, 2\}$, and $j \neq k$. Notice that this setting captures various forms of leader election, e.g. when a player prefers to be selected, when it prefers the other player to be selected, etc. In a matrix form, this game can be presented as follows (where $a, b, c, d > 0$):

$$M = \begin{pmatrix} a, b & 0, 0 \\ 0, 0 & c, d \end{pmatrix}$$

Proposition 2 *The optimal safety-level value for a player in the leader election game equals its expected payoff in the strictly mixed strategy equilibrium of that game.*

The proof of the above proposition appears in the full paper. The above proposition shows that a agent can *guarantee* itself an expected payoff that equals its payoff in a Nash equilibrium of the leader election game. As in the decentralized load balancing game, this is obtained using a strategy that differs from the agent's strategies in the Nash equilibria of that game (which do not provide that guarantee).

Safety level in general 2×2 games

The results presented in the previous sections refer to 2-person 2-choice variants of central problems occurring in computational contexts. However, it is of interest to see whether these can be extended to other forms of 2×2 games. It is easy to observe that both the load balancing and the leader election settings can be represented as non-reducible generic 2×2 games. The same is true with regard to the game presented by Aumann:

$$M = \begin{pmatrix} 2, 6 & 4, 2 \\ 6, 0 & 0, 4 \end{pmatrix}$$

We can now show:

Theorem 1 *Let G be a 2×2 non-reducible generic game. Assume that the optimal safety level value of a player is obtained by a strictly mixed strategy, then this value coincides with the expected payoff of that player in a Nash equilibrium of G.*

Sketch of proof: Denote the strategies available to the players by a_1, a_2. Use the following notation: $a = U_1(a_1, a_1), b = U_1(a_1, a_2), c = U_1(a_2, a_1), d = U_1(a_2, a_2), e = U_2(a_1, a_1), f = U_2(a_1, a_2), g = U_2(a_2, a_1), h = U_2(a_2, a_2)$

If a strictly mixed strategy Nash equilibrium exists then it should satisfy that:

$$qa + (1-q)b = qc + (1-q)d$$

and

$$pe + (1-p)g = pf + (1-p)h$$

where p and q are the probabilities for choosing a_1 by players 1 and 2, respectively.

We get that we should have $qa + b - qb = qc + d - qd$, which implies that $q(a - b - c + d) = d - b$. Similarly, we get that we should have $pe + g - pg = pf + h - ph$, which implies that $p(e - g - f + h) = h - g$.

Hence, in a strictly mixed strategy Nash equilibrium we should have:

$$q = \frac{d - b}{a - b - c + d}$$

and

$$p = \frac{h - g}{e - g - f + h}$$

Notice that since the game is generic then $d \neq b$. If $d > b$ then if q is not in between 0 and 1 then $c > a$ which will contradict non-reducibility. If $d < b$ then in if q is not in between 0 and 1 then $a > c$, which also contradicts non-reducibility. Similarly, since the game is generic then $h \neq g$. If $h > g$ then if p is not in between 0 and 1 then $f > e$ which will contradict non-reducibility. If $h < g$ then in if p is not in between 0 and 1 then $e < f$, which also contradicts non-reducibility.

Given the above we get that p and q define a strictly mixed strategy equilibrium of G.

Consider now the safety level strategy of player 1. If player 1 chooses a_1 with probability p' then it satisfies that:

$$p'a + (1-p')c = p'b + (1-p')d$$

This implies that we need to have $p'a + c - p'c = p'b + d - p'd$, which implies $p'(a - c - b + d) = d - c$. Hence, we have

$$p' = \frac{d - c}{a - c - b + d}$$

and

$$1 - p' = \frac{a - b}{a - c - b + d}$$

Compute now the expected payoff for player 1 in the strictly mixed Nash equilibrium, given that $1 - q = \frac{a - c}{a - b - c + d}$, we have that:

$$qa + (1-q)b = \frac{(d - b)a + (a - c)b}{a - b - c + d} = \frac{da - cb}{a - b - c + d}$$

The expected payoff of the safety level strategy for player 1 will be:

$$p'a + (1-p')c = \frac{(d - c)a + (a - b)c}{a - b - c + d} = \frac{da - cb}{a - b - c + d}$$

Hence, we get that the expected payoffs of the Nash equilibrium and the safety level strategies for player 1 coincide. The computation for player 2 is similar. ∎

The case of pure safety-level strategies

The reader may wonder whether the previous result can be also proved for the case where there are no restrictions on the structure of the safety-level strategy of the game g. As we now show, there exists a generic non-reducible 2×2 game g, where the optimal safety level strategy for a player is pure, and the expected payoff for that player is lower than the expected payoff for that player in all Nash equilibria of g.

Consider a game g, where $U_1(1,1) = 100, U_1(1,2) = 40, U_1(2,1) = 60, U_1(2,2) = 50$, and $U_2(1,1) = 100, U_2(1,2) = 210, U_2(2,1) = 200, U_2(2,2) = 90$. In a matrix form this game looks as follows:

$$M = \begin{pmatrix} 100, 100 & 40, 210 \\ 60, 200 & 50, 90 \end{pmatrix}$$

It is easy to check that g is generic and non-reducible. The game has no pure Nash equilibria. In a strictly mixed strategy equilibrium the probability q of choosing a_1 by player 2 should satisfy $100q + 40(1-q) = 60q + 50(1-q)$, i.e. that $60q + 40 = 10q + 50$, $q = 0.2$. In that equilibrium the probability that player 1 will choose a_1 is $p = 0.5$, and the expected payoff of player 1 is $100q + 40(1-q) = 52$. The safety-level strategy for player 1 is to perform a_2, guaranteeing a payoff of 50, given that (a_2, a_2) is a saddle point in a zero-sum game where the payoffs of player 2 are taken to be the complement to 0 of player 1's original payoffs. Hence, the value of the safety level strategy for player 1 is $50 < 52$.

∎

Beyond 2×2 games

The leader election game is an instance of a more general set of games: *set-theoretic games*. In a set theoretic game the sets of strategies available to the players are identical, and the payoff of each player is uniquely determined by the *set* of strategies selected by each player. For example, in a 2-person set-theoretic game we will have that $U_1(s,t) = U_1(t,s), U_2(s,t) = U_2(t,s)$ for every $s, t \in S_1 = S_2$. Notice that set-theoretic games are very typical to voting contexts.

We can prove the following:

Proposition 3 *Given a 2-person set theoretic game g with a strictly mixed strategy Nash equilibrium, then the value of an optimal safety level strategy of a player equals its expected payoff in that equilibrium.*

The proof of the above proposition appears in the full paper. Notice that the proposition considers games with a strictly mixed strategy Nash equilibrium. The proposition does not hold without this restriction.

Competitive safety strategies

Let S be a set of strategies. Consider a sequence of games $(g_1, g_2, \ldots, g_j, \ldots)$ where i is a player at each of them, its set of strategies at each of these games is S, and there are j players, in addition to i, in g_j. As an example, consider a sequence of decentralized load balancing settings. The $(n-1)$-th game in this extended load-balancing setting will consist of n players, one of them is i. The players submit their messages along e_1 and e_2. The payoff for player i when participating in an n-person decentralized load balancing game is $\frac{X}{k}$ (resp. $\frac{\alpha X}{k}$) if he has chosen e_1 (resp. e_2) and additional $k-1$ participants have chosen that communication line.

A mixed strategy $t \in \Delta(S)$ will be called a *C-competitive safety strategy* if there exists some constant $C > 0$, such that

$$\lim_{j \to \infty} \frac{nash(i, g_j)}{val(t, i, g_j)} \leq C$$

where $nash(i, g_j)$ is the lowest expected payoff player i might obtain in some equilibrium of g_j, and $val(t, i, g_j)$ is the expected payoff guaranteed for i by choosing t is the game g_j.

The extended decentralized load balancing setting is a typical and basic network problem. If C is small, a C-competitive safety strategy for that context will provide a useful protocol of behavior.

We can show:

Theorem 2 *There exists a $9/8$-competitive safety strategy for the extended decentralized load-balancing setting.*

Sketch of proof: Consider the following strategy profile for the players in an n-person decentralized load balancing game: players $\{1, 2, \ldots, \lceil \frac{1}{1+\alpha} n \rceil\}$ will choose e_1, and the rest will choose e_2. W.l.o.g we assume that $i = 1$ is the player for which we will make the computation of expected payoffs. It is easy to verify that the above strategy profile is an equilibrium of the game, with an expected payoff for player i that is bounded above by

$$\frac{X(1+\alpha)}{n} \quad (*)$$

Consider now the following strategy t for player i: select e_1 with probability $\frac{\alpha}{1+\alpha}$ and select e_2 with probability $\frac{1}{1+\alpha}$. It is easy to see that t (if adopted by all participants) is not a Nash equilibrium. However, we will show that it is a competitive safety strategy for small $C > 0$. Consider an arbitrary number of participants n, where $\beta(n-1)$ of the other (i.e. excluding player i) $n-1$ participants use e_2 while the rest use e_1, for some arbitrary $0 \leq \beta \leq 1$. The expected payoff obtained using t will be:

$$\frac{1}{1+\alpha} \frac{\alpha X}{\beta(n-1)+1} + \frac{\alpha}{1+\alpha} \frac{X}{(1-\beta)(n-1)+1}$$

This value is greater or equal to:

$$\frac{1}{1+\alpha}\frac{\alpha X}{\beta n + 1} + \frac{\alpha}{1+\alpha}\frac{X}{(1-\beta)n + 1}$$

The above equals

$$\frac{X\alpha}{1+\alpha}\left[\frac{1}{\beta n + 1} + \frac{1}{(1-\beta)n + 1}\right]$$

Simplifying the above we get:

$$\frac{X\alpha}{1+\alpha}\frac{n+2}{(1+\beta n)(n - \beta n + 1)} = (**)$$

Dividing (*) by (**) we get that the ratio is:

$$\frac{(1+\alpha)^2}{\alpha}\frac{(\beta - \beta^2)n^2 + n + 1}{n(n+2)}$$

When n approaches infinity the above ratio approaches

$$\frac{(1+\alpha)^2}{\alpha}(\beta - \beta^2)$$

Given that $0.5 \le \alpha < 1$ and $0 \le \beta \le 1$ we get that the above ratio is bounded by $9/8$ as desired. ∎

Extensions: Arbitrary speeds and m links

In this section we generalize the result obtained in the context of decentralized load balancing to the case where we have m parallel communication lines leading from source to target. The value obtained by the agent (w.l.o.g. agent 1) when submitting its message along line i, where n_i agents have decided to submit their messages through that line is given by $\frac{X \cdot \alpha_i}{n_i}$, where $1 = \alpha_1 \ge \alpha_2 \ge \cdots \ge \alpha_m > 0$.

Our extension will enable to handle the general binary case where $0 < \alpha < 1$, as well as to discuss cases where a safety level strategy can be very effective in the general m-lines situation.

Using the ideas developed for the case $m = 2$, we can now show:

Theorem 3 *There exists a $\frac{\sum_{i=1}^{m}\alpha_i \sum_{i=1}^{m}\Pi_{j\neq i}\alpha_j}{m^2\Pi_{i=1}^{m}\alpha_j}$-competitive safety strategy for the extended decentralized load-balancing setting, when we allow m (rather than only 2) parallel communication lines, and arbitrary α_i's.*

The proof of Theorem 3, as well as of the following corollaries appear in the full paper.

In the general binary case, where $\alpha_1 = 1$, and $\alpha_2 = \alpha$, where $0 < \alpha \le 1$, the above implies the existence of an

$$\frac{(1+\alpha)^2}{4\alpha}$$

competitive strategy.

Corollary 1 *Given an extended load balancing setting, where $m = 2$, with arbitrary speeds of the communication lines ($0 < \alpha \le 1$), there exists a $\frac{4}{3}$-competitive strategy.*

Consider now the general m-links (i.e. m parallel communication lines) case. The average network quality (or speed), Q, can be defined as $\frac{\sum_{i=1}^{m}\alpha_i}{m}$. A network will be called k-regular if $\frac{Q}{\alpha_m} \le k$. Many networks are k-regular for small k. For example, if $\alpha_m \ge 0.5$ as before, then the network is 2-regular regardless of the number of edges.

Corollary 2 *Given a k-regular network, there exists a k-competitive safety strategy for the extended decentralized load-balancing setting, when we allow m (rather than only 2) parallel edges.*

Together, Theorem 3 and corollaries 1 and 2 extend the results on decentralized load balancing to the general case of m parallel communication lines.

Competitive safety analysis in Bayesian games

The results presented in the previous sections refer to games with complete information. Similar ideas however can be applied to games with incomplete information. We now show the use of competitive safety strategies in games with incomplete information. We have chosen to consider a very basic mechanism, the first-price auction. The selection of first-price auction is not an accident. Auctions are fundamental to the theory of economic mechanism design, and among the auctions that do no possesses a dominant strategy, assuming the independent private value model, first-price auctions are probably the most common ones.

We consider a setting where a good g is put for sale, and there are n potential buyers. Each such buyer has a valuation (i.e. maximal willingness to pay) for g that is drawn from a uniform distribution on the interval of real numbers $[0, 1]$. The valuations are assumed to be independent from one another. In a first price auction, each potential buyer is asked to submit a bid for the good g. We assume that the bids of a buyer with valuation v is a number in the interval $[0, v]$.[2] The good will be allocated to the bidder who submitted the highest bid (with a lottery to determine the winner in a case of a tie).

The auction setup can be defined using a Bayesian game.[3] In this game the players are the potential bidders, and the payoff of a player with valuation v is $v - p$ if he wins the good and pays p, and 0 if he does not get the good. The equilibrium concept can be also extended to the context of Bayesian games. In particular, in equilibrium of the above

---

[2]In general, buyers may submit bids that are higher than their valuations, but these strategies are dominated by other strategies, and their existence will not effect the equilibrium discussed in this paper.

[3]A formal definition and exposition of Bayesian games in our context will be presented in the full paper

game the bid of a player with valuation v is $(1 - \frac{1}{n})v$. Following the revelation principle, discussed in the economic mechanism design literature, one can replace the above-mentioned first-price auction with the following auction: each bidder will be asked to reveal his valuation, and the good will be sold to the bidder who reported the highest valuation; if agent i who reported valuation v' will turn out to be the winner then he will be asked to pay $(1 - \frac{1}{n})v'$. It turns out that reporting the true valuation is an equilibrium of that auction, and that it will yield (in equilibrium) the same allocation and payments as the original auction. It is convenient to consider the above *revelation mechanism*, since when facing *any* number of participants, a bidder's strategy in equilibrium will always be the same.

A first-price auction setup will be identified with a sequence of (Bayesian) games $(g_1, g_2, \dots)$ where g_j is the Bayesian game associated with (the revelation mechanism of) first-price auction with $j + 1$ potential buyers. The definition of C-competitive strategies can now be applied to the above context as well.

The proof of the following appears in the full paper:

Theorem 4 *There exists an e-competitive strategy for the first-price auction setup.*

Our result can be obtained also if we consider standard first-price auctions, rather than the revelation mechanisms associated with them; nevertheless, this will require to allow a player to choose its action knowing the number of potential bidders.

Discussion

Some previous work in AI has attempted to show the potential power of decision-theoretic approaches that do not rely on classical game-theoretic analysis. In particular, work in theoretical computer science on competitive analysis has been extended to deal with rationality constraints (Tennenholtz 2001), in order to become applicable to multi-agent systems. We introduced competitive safety analysis, bridging the gap between the normative AI/CS approach and classical equilibrium analysis. We have shown that an observation, which is of great interest from a descriptive perspective to economists, can be extended and generalized to provide a powerful normative tool for computer scientists and AI researchers interested in protocols for non-cooperative environments. We have illustrated the use and power of competitive safety analysis in various contexts. We have shown general results about 2×2 games, as well as about games with many participants, and introduced the use of competitive safety analysis in the context of decentralized load balancing, leader election, and auctions. Notice that our work is concerned with a normative approach to decision making in multi-agent systems. We make no claims as for the applicability of this approach for descriptive purposes. Although there exists much literature on the failure of Nash equilibrium, it is still the most powerful concept for action prediction in multi-agent systems.

References

Aumann, R. 1985. On the non-transferable utility value: A comment on the Roth-Shaper examples. *Econometrica* 53(3):667–677.

Borodin, A., and El-Yaniv, R. 1998. *On-Line Computation and Competitive Analysis*. Cambridge University Press.

Koutsoupias, E., and Papadimitriou, C. 1999. Worst-Case Equilibria. In *STACS*.

Kraus, S. 1997. Negotiation and cooperation in multi-agent environments. *Artificial Intelligence* 94:79–97.

Nisan, N., and Ronen, A. 1999. Algorithmic mechanism design. Proceedings of STOC-99.

Rosenschein, J. S., and Zlotkin, G. 1994. *Rules of Encounter*. MIT Press.

Roth, A. E. 1980. Values for games without side payments: Some difficulties with current concepts. *Econometrica* 48(2):457–465.

Sandholm, T. W., and Lesser, V. 1995. Equilibrium Analysis of the Possibilities of Unenforced Exchange in Multiagent Syustems. In *Proc. 14th International Joint Conference on Artificial Intelligence*, 694–701.

Tennenholtz, M. 2001. Rational Competitive Analysis. In *Proc. of the 17th International Joint Conference on Artificial Intelligence*, 1067–1072.

Natural Language Processing

Learning Pattern Rules for Chinese Named Entity Extraction

Tat-Seng Chua and Jimin Liu

School of Computing,
National University of Singapore,
3 Science Drive 2, Singapore 117543
{chuats, liujm}@comp.nus.edu.sg

Abstract

Named entity (NE) extraction in Chinese is very difficult task because of the flexibility in the language structure and uncertainty in word segmentation. It is equivalent to relation and information extraction problems in English. This paper presents a hybrid rule induction approach to extract NEs in Chinese. The method induces rules and names and their context, and generalizes these rules using linguistic lexical chaining. In order to handle the ambiguities and other contextual problems peculiar to Chinese, we supplement the basic method with other approaches such as the default-exception tree and decision tree. We tested our method on the MET2 test set and the method has been found to out-perform all reported methods with an overall F_1 measure of over 91%.

1. Introduction

Named entity (NE) recognition is a task in which meaningful entities in a document are detected and classified into categories such as person, organization, location, time and date. NE recognition is one of the most important tasks in information extraction. Many approaches have been proposed to tackle this problem. Earlier approaches used mostly handcrafted heuristic rules (Appelt et al. 1995, Weischedel 1995), while recent methods focused on using machine learning approaches, such as the hidden Markov model (Cucerzan & Yarowsky 1999, Bikel et al. 1999), decision tree (Sekine et al. 1998) and maximum entropy (Borthwick 1999, Isozaki 2001) etc. Most of these methods utilize some form of syntactic and semantic knowledge of text in detecting NEs.

NE extraction is not a serious problem in English, in which recent methods have reported high accuracy of over 97% (Marsh & Perzanowski 1998). However, there are four fundamental problems that are either unique to Chinese or are not serious in English.

One of the most serious problems is the word segmentation problem (Sproat et al. 1996, Palmer 1997, Yu et al 1998). In Chinese, there is no implicit blank between words, where a word is defined as consisting of one or more characters representing a linguistic token. Word is a vague concept in Chinese, and linguists often do not have generally accepted guidelines on what constitutes a word. Without well-defined word boundaries, most syntactical and semantic analysis methods that assume words as basic entities cannot be performed effectively.

Second, there are three main types of names – the person, place and organization names. Each type of names has its own structure and cue-words. Although the presence of specific context or cue-words is needed to induce a name, there are many ambiguous cases that this is not true, especially when word segmentation is also uncertain. Also a proper name in Chinese may contain commonly used names, which further complicates NE recognition using probabilistic approaches.

Third, there are two types of names in Chinese. The first is called the S-Name, which is constructed according to Chinese semantics. The second is termed P-Name, which is a translated foreign name based on its phonetics such as the name"贝克利" (Ber-ke-ley). Each type of name includes all categories of proper names. The rules for the construction of S-Names and P-Names are different and need to be handled differently.

Fourth, there are few openly available language resources that can be used to build and evaluate Chinese language systems. Examples of such resources include: Chinese Treebank (Xia et al. 2000), MET2 (Marsh & Perzanowski 1998), PKU-Corpus (Yu 1999) and Hownet (Dong & Dong 2000), These resources are relatively small and are in less widespread use as compared to those in English. Thus one major issue is how to make the best use of existing limited resources with minimum labor cost.

Because of these problems, the usual techniques that require proper word segmentation and utilize syntactic and semantic knowledge of words cannot be applied effectively to Chinese. Also, because of the flexibility in the language in which common words often appear as part of the names, the method developed must be able to handle ambiguities and exceptions well. In fact, the problem of NE recognition should not be isolated from the word segmentation and part-of-speech tagging (Yu et al. 1998).

In many aspects, the problems of Chinese NE recognition are similar to that of relation and information extraction (IE) in English, which is a much harder problem than English NE extraction. In English, the template-based rule induction approach has been popular in extracting structured data from the input documents such as the newswire articles or web pages (Muslea 1999). For free text, most such methods use syntactic and semantic constructs as the basis to identify and extract items of interests (Riloff 1993, Soderland et al. 1995). For on-line and web-based documents, the current methods rely on a combination of domain knowledge and known structure of documents. All these techniques cannot be applied directly to Chinese free-text as explained earlier.

In this paper, we propose a template-based rule induction approach that incorporates other machine learning techniques. The method first adopts a greedy method to extract word tokens and possible names that may be overlapping. It then uses the generalized rules induced together with other techniques, such as the DE-(default exception) trees and decision tree, to resolve the ambiguities in the extracted names. The rules are induced from the training corpus and generalized using linguistic techniques such as the semantic clustering. Our initial results demonstrate that the approach is very effective in Chinese NE extraction.

The rest of the paper discusses the use of template for Chinese NE extraction, describes the details of the induction and generalization of rules, and discusses the results of applying the system to a standard test corpus.

2. The Structures and Problems in Chinese NE Extraction

Different types of names have different structures and require different context and cue words (CWs) for their recognition. The simplest type of name is the Chinese person S-name, which has a very regular structure of:

$$\text{S-Person-Name} := <\text{surname}> <\text{first name}> \qquad (1)$$

Most surnames (several hundreds) have only one character, with only very few (about 8) having two characters. The first name is usually composed of one or two words, and the number of characters in each word is less than or equal to 2. The surnames come from a small list of names such as "张" (Zhang), "刘" (Liu), and can be used as CWs to induce a name. We can also use the person titles such as "主席" (chair-person), "经理" (manager), as the context to confirm the presence and boundary of person names.

A typical full Chinese place name is more complicated and takes the form of:

$$\text{Place-Name} := <p_1><p_2>\ldots<p_n> \qquad (2)$$

where $n \geq 1$; and $p_i := <\text{pl-name}_i>\{<\text{pl-suffix}_i>\}$. Each p_i is itself a place name, and from left to right, p_{i-1} represents a bigger place than p_i. This is in reverse order to that in English. Each name p_i has an optional <pl-suffix> such as the province (省), river (河) and road ("路") etc. <pl-suffix> provides the CW to trigger the extraction of a place name.

A typical full Chinese organization name is even more complicated and typically takes the form of:

$$\text{Org-Name} := \{ [<\text{Place-Name}>]^* [<\text{person-name}> | \\ <\text{org-name}>] \}^{\times} [<\text{org-generic-name}>] \\ <\text{org-suffix}> \qquad (3)$$

where []* means repeat zero or more times, and {}× means select at least one of the enclosed items. An example of a full organization name is "山东大成农药股份有限公司", where [山东] is a place name [大成] is the organization name, [农药] is a generic name for drug which indicates that this is a drug company, and [股份有限公司] (limited company) is the organization suffix. These suffices can be used as CWs to induce the names.

To facilitate the detection of different types of names, respective lists of CWs can be extracted from the training corpus and from known lists. Although in most cases, the presence of context or CWs at the beginning or end of the string helps to induce a name, there are many cases that are ambiguous. Examples of CW ambiguity include "该公司" (that company) that does not introduce a company name, or "爬山" (climb mountain) that does not introduce a mountain name, etc. These problems are aggravated by the uncertainty in word segmentation.

Finally, a name can be an S-Name or a P-Name. As with S-Names, a P-Name may includes any character and in any combination, and can often be confused with other common names. Fortunately, the combination of characters is often unique to P-Names and can thus be recognized using a probabilistic approach. Here we used a quasi-probabilistic model to locate all possible P-Names. The method uses bigram statistics obtained from both the training corpus and the name list. The details of P-Name finder can be found in Xiao, Liu & Chua (2002).

3. Template-based Rule Induction Approach

The above discussions suggest that a Chinese NE extraction system must meet at least three major requirements. First, it must be able to work with uncertain word segmentation and has the ability to deal with different and conflicting word combinations. Second, it must be able to handle different types of names, often with radically different format, and triggered by the presence of different CWs. Third it must consider the context of possible names in order to resolve ambiguities in NE extraction. Employing a purely probabilistic approach will not be adequate as the system will likely confuse a name from common words or vice versa, and thus either miss the name completely or segment the name wrongly. To tackle this problem, we adopt the template-based rule induction approach commonly employed in IE tasks in English (Muslea 1999). We combine rule induction with other machine learning techniques to tackle the ambiguity problems.

We employ the template similar to that used in Riloff (1996) for Chinese NE extraction. The template composes of four parts (see Figure 1): trigger, pattern list, constraint, and output. The trigger pattern <p> can be a CW or a P-Name. As CW for different types of names are different, it also provides indication on the type of possible names to be extracted.

Trigger: <p>
Pattern Rules: R_{name}, $R_{context}$
Constraint set: D
Output: $<t_1, b_1, e_1> .... <t_m, b_m, e_m>$

Figure 1: Template for NE extraction

At the triggering position, we fire the appropriate rules to induce the name and its context. As the key to NE extraction is the detection of the name and its boundaries, we utilize the CWs and context to derive generalized pattern rules for name (R_{name}) and context ($R_{context}$) as:

$$R_{name} := \text{S-Person-Name} \mid \text{Place-Name} \mid \quad (4)$$
$$\text{Organization-Name}$$

$$R_{context} := [\text{left context}] [\text{left CW}] \quad (5)$$
$$<\text{possible name}> [\text{right CW}] [\text{right context}]$$

We use the appropriate name pattern rules to identify all possible names, and then employ the context pattern rules to narrow down the list of possible names with more precise boundaries. The application of rules must satisfy the corresponding constraints given in the set D.

The output is a list of possibly overlapping names of the form $<t_i, b_i, e_i>$, where i=1, .. m, the number of names in the output list. Here t_i indicates the category (of type person, location or organization) of the ith name that starts at atomic pattern p_{bi} and ends at p_{ei}. When m>1, we employ a decision tree to select the best possible names.

One main design consideration of our approach is that the system is able to tolerate uncertainty in word segmentation and possible name extractions at all stages of NE processing. Thus a greedy approach is employed at the initial stages to identify all possible names.

4. The induction of Generalized Pattern Rules

This Section discusses the induction of pattern rules for NE extraction. Given a training corpus with proper tagging of names and common words, we apply the rule templates given in Equations (4-5) to extract all instances of names together with their context. Although it is easy to extract all instances of rules from the corpus, the key, however, is how to generalize the context to handle more general cases.

An example of a specific name instance is the tagged name segment "[经理]<张实>[在][接见][记者][时][表示]" or translated as [Manager] <张实> [when] [meeting] [the reporters] [indicates]). Although by applying template (5) to this example, we can extract a context pattern rule of the form: "[经理] <X>[在>][接见]" that will introduce a person name X. However, this rule is too specific, since its left and right contexts are words. To generalize the rules, we need to replace the words in the rules with more general patterns.

One possible approach to generalize the context is to use the syntactic and semantic tags of words (Riloff 1993, 1996, & Soderland et al. 1995). Unfortunately, for Chinese language, before the words are correctly segmented, it is difficult to obtain such tagging information. Comparatively, by using synsets to replace specific words seems to be a more feasible approach. In the example above, we can generalize the [接见] by its synset {[接见, 会见....]}. However, in some cases, simply considering the synset is still too specific.

Based on these observations, we adopt a lexical chaining approach to generate the semantic grouping for the context words, and use these semantic groups to replace specific words in the rule patterns to generalize rules.

4.1 Lexical Semantic Clustering

Lexical chaining is a commonly used approach to cluster semantically related words (Green 1999, Liu & Chua 2001). Here we utilize Hownet (Dong & Dong 2000) to find lexical chains. Hownet is an important lexical semantic dictionary in Chinese NLP and can be used as the counterpart to WordNet. Each word w_j in Hownet has a set of definitions, defining different "points of view" of this word. Examples of different "points" include the definitions of its basic meaning $D_B(w_j)$ and its parent $D_P(w_j)$ etc. In this research, we consider only these two "points" of view. That is, if $D_B(w_j) = w_k$, then w_k has the same meaning as w_j, and if $D_P(w_j) = w_P$, then w_P is the parent of w_j.

By treating words related to by D_B and D_P as semantically related, we develop an algorithm to generate semantic groups in a specific domain via lexical chaining.

1) Initialize:

a) $\underline{W}_S \leftarrow \{(w_1,f_1), (w_2,f_2), \ldots,(w_n,f_n)\}$,

where f_i is the frequency of occurrences of word w_i in a given domain containing n unique words.

b) Set the output group as empty: $\underline{G}_{out} \leftarrow \Phi$

2) Generate all possible semantic groups:

a) For each word w_i in $\underline{W}_S$, use Hownet to find out its two selected "points" of view, ie $D_B(w_i)$ and $D_P(w_i)$.

b) Generate all possible groupings of words as:

$\underline{G}_{all} \leftarrow \{(\underline{G}_1, c_1), (\underline{G}_2, c_2), \ldots, (\underline{G}_n, c_n)\}$

where $\underline{G}_i$ contains words that have the same meanings as that of w_i in the sense of $D_B(w_i)$ and $D_P(w_i)$, i.e.:

$\underline{G}_i = \{w_k \mid D_B(w_k)=\{D_B(w_i), D_P(w_i)\}$ or $D_P(w_k)=\{D_B(w_i), D_P(w_i)\} \}$

and c_i is the prominence measure of $\underline{G}_i$, which is simply the aggregate frequency of all words in $\underline{G}_i$:

$$ci = \sum_{w_k \in \underline{G}_i} f_k$$

3) Select the prominent groups as the semantic groups:

a) From $\underline{G}_{all}$, select the group with maximum c_i as:

$$(\underline{G}_{max}, c_{max}) \leftarrow \arg\max_{\underline{G}_i \in \underline{G}_{all}} \{c_i\} ;$$

Terminate the process if $c_{max} < \sigma$

b) Move $\underline{G}_{max}$ to $\underline{G}_{out}$, ie

$\underline{G}_{out} \leftarrow \underline{G}_{out} \cup (\underline{G}_{max}, c_{max})$, $\underline{G}_{all} \leftarrow \underline{G}_{all} - \underline{G}_{max}$

c) For each remaining group $\underline{G}_j$ in $\underline{G}_{all}$, do the followings:

$\forall \underline{G}_j \in \underline{G}_{all}$,

set $\underline{G}_j \leftarrow \underline{G}_j - \underline{G}_{max}$, $c_j \leftarrow c_j - \sum_{w \in \underline{G}_j \cap \underline{G}_{max}} c$,

and if $\underline{G}_j = \Phi$, then $\underline{G}_{all} \leftarrow \underline{G}_{all} - \underline{G}_j$

d) Repeat the process from step (3a) if $\underline{G}_{all} \neq$ null.

At the end of applying the above lexical chaining algorithm, we obtain a set of semantic groups, each containing a cluster of related words. These semantic groups can be used as the basis to generalize both the name and context pattern rules.

4.2 The Generalization of Name Pattern Rules

The rules for person and place names are relatively simple and can be easily generalized by replacing the surnames in S-person-names by the general pattern

<surname>, and the place suffices in the place names by a general pattern <pl-suffix>.

The structure of the organization names as defined in Equation (3) is more complex and there exists many possible rule combinations. We first generalize the organization suffices using CWs for organization, and names of person and location using Equations (1) and (2) respectively. For the remaining characters within the organization instances, we identify high frequency words as possible generic name of the organization. We then use lexical chaining to generalize these likely generic names into semantic group representations, which are used as generalized <org-generic-name>. Finally, we extract the set of generalized organization rule patterns from the training examples.

4.3 The Generalization of Context Pattern Rules

Given the training corpus, we extract all instances of names together with their context as:

$\underline{RS} = \{R^{(r)} \mid R^{(r)} = <w_{-2}><w_{-1}><name><w_1><w_2>\}$ (6)

where $r = 1, ..$ number of name instances.

Here we consider the preceding and succeeding two words as the context to <name>. We consider only two-word context because we want to capture context information of the form: <verb>+<CW>, <CW>+<verb>, and <adverb>+<verb> etc. While one-word context is insufficient, more than two-word context would be too costly.

Given n different words $\{w_1, w_2, \ldots w_n\}$ appear in the context of the rules, together with their occurrence frequencies as the context words. We can apply the proposed lexical chaining algorithm to generate m semantic groups from these context words as: $\{(\underline{G}_1, c_1)\ldots(\underline{G}_m, c_m)\}$, where m<<n. We generalize each rule $R^{(k)}$ by replacing each context word w_c in $R^{(k)}$ by its corresponding semantic word group $\underline{G}_c$.

4.4. Selection of Best Rules using Decision Tree

When more than one pattern rule can be applied at a certain situation, it will result in multiple overlapping possible names being detected. Thus there is a need to select the best rule or the best possible name in a given context. What we want is to train a decision function, $f(\underline{RS} \otimes \underline{RS} \rightarrow \{-1,1\})$, so that given two conflicting rules $R^{(i)}$ and $R^{(j)}$, we are able to resolve which rule is better. To learn such a decision function, we need to compare the support and length of both rules by capturing the difference vector D_{ij} containing 6 discrete features:

$D_{ij}((R^{(i)}, R^{(j)}) = \{f_1, f_2, f_3, f_4, f_5, f_6\}$ (7)

where f_1 and f_2 respectively measure the differences between the length of the name part and the whole rule pattern between $R^{(i)}$ and $R^{(j)}$; f_3 and f_4 respectively compute the differences in length of their left and right context; f_5 measures their relative name occurrence frequency; and f_6 gives the relative support of the CW in both rules.

From the training corpus, we identify all positions with conflicting name resolutions. At each position, if there are u+v rules $\{R^{(p1)},...R^{(pu)}, R^{(n1)},...R^{(nv)}\}$ that are applicable, in which, u rules $R^{(p1)},...R^{(pu)}$ give the correct names, and v rules $\{R^{(n1)},...R^{(nv)}\}$ give the wrong names. We generate u*v positive training examples by using the name differences $D_{(pi)(nj)}(R^{(pi)}, R^{(nj)})$, for i=1,..u, j=1..v. Similarly, we can generate u*v negative training examples by using the name differences -- $D_{(pi)(nj)}(R^{(pi)}, R^{(nj)})$. After we have setup the D_{ij} values for all conflicting cases, we employ the C5.0 algorithm to learn the decision function f.

5. The Overall NE Recognition Process

Given an input document, the overall process of extracting NEs is as follows (see Figure 2).

a. The first essential step is to perform word segmentation, including p-name recognition. As with all other approaches (Yu et al. 98, Chen et al. 98), we make extensive use of corpus statistics, word dictionary, and known name lists to perform the preliminary segmentation by: (i) extracting the numbers, dates and times using reliable techniques; (ii) segmenting words by using the simple dictionary-based forward longest matching technique; (iii) identifying possible P-Names; (iv) locating typical S-Names, again, using dictionary look-up. The result is a list of possibly overlapping words and P-Names, and positions of all CWs that indicate the presence of possible names and their types.

b. We next employ the DE (Default exception)-trees to identify possible exceptions on the use of CWs to induce a name. The DE-tree is derived from the training corpus and it enumerates all exceptions found in the usage of a particular CW and its context. For example, while in most cases the pattern "*山" (or * Mountain) induces the name of a mountain, such as "黄山", "昆仑山", there are cases such as "千山万水" (meaning vast territory), "爬山" (meaning climb mountain) etc that the CW "山" does not introduce a mountain name. Thus the DE-tree for "山" would contain all exceptions together with their context. Although it is impossible to enumerate all possible usage of "山" to induce a name, it is possible to find all its exceptions from the training corpus. The details of the generation of DE-tree for each CW can be found in (Liu & Chua 02). As a result of this step,

some segmented words many be removed or new word segments are introduced.

c. At each CW or P-Name position, we employ the appropriate name pattern rules (4) to extract the possible names, and refine these names using the context pattern rules (5). The result is a list of possibly overlapping or conflicting names.

d. In case of ambiguities in the list of NEs recognized, we employ the decision tree to find the best possible name in that specific context. The final result is a list of non-overlapping names.

e. When a name occurs for the first time, it is usually expressed in full with the necessary context. However, subsequent occurrences of the same name will have less context and may be abbreviated. To handle such names, we use a separate sub-string matching technique to locate other occurrences of a new name in all likely name positions. In addition, we also employ heuristic rules to detect names that appear in an enumerated list.

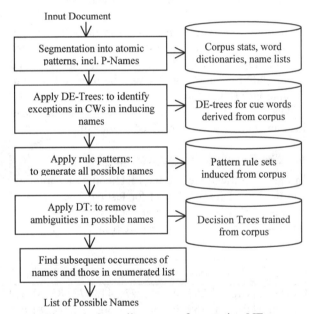

Figure 2: Overall process of extracting NEs

6. Experimental Results and Discussions

6.1 The Datasets used in the Experiments

One serious problem in Chinese NLP is the lack of openly available datasets, making it difficult to evaluate and compare systems. Bearing this in mind, we use only openly available datasets for our training and testing. Here, we use a combination of PKU-corpus, Hownet, MET2 Chinese resources, and two name lists (for foreign and organization names) collected from the web by a bootstrap approach. The PKU corpus (Yu 1999) contains one-month of news report from China's People Daily. The corpus is manually segmented into words with appropriate POS tags. It contains 1,121,787 words. We use the PKU corpus and other resources to build the following dictionaries and name lists:

a) We use the PKU corpus to build a common word dictionary by removing all words that are tagged as number, time, and name. The resulting common word dictionary contains 37,025 words.

b) We use the PKU corpus to extract a list of CWs for names. First we select all words tagged as <surname> in a surname list. If a noun occurs before or after a person name, and it has a high occurrence frequency (of over 50), then it is selected as a person context CW. If an organization name or place name composes of more than one word, and the last word is a noun, then the last word is selected as a place or organization suffix. In addition, we supplement this list by using the Chinese name designators derived from the MET2 resource.

c) We obtain a list of Chinese location names from MET2.

d) In order to learn the rules for organization names and the bigram model for P-Name detection, we also collected about 8,000 organization names, and 100,000 P-Names from the web by using a bootstrap approach (Xiao, Liu & Chua 2002).

The resources we derived are available for down loading at http://www.pris.nus.edu.sg/ie.html.

6.2 The Experiment and Results

In our experiment, we use the PKU corpus for training, and the MET2 formal dataset for testing. The results of the experiment are presented in Table 1. For comparison purpose, we also list results reported in Yu et al. (1998) and Chen et al. (1998).

	Type	N_C	N_P	N_W	N_M	N_S	Rc	Pr	F_1
NTU's Results (Chen et al. 98)	Org^n	293	0	7	77	44	78	85	81.3
	Person	159	0	0	15	56	91	74	81.6
	Place	583	0	65	102	194	78	69	73.2
KDRL's results (Yu et al 98)	Org^n	331	0	14	32	25	88	89	88.5
	Person	160	0	7	7	74	92	66	76.7
	Place	682	0	1	67	83	91	89	90.0
NUS-PRIS	Org^n	347	2	14	14	20	92	91	91.5
	Person	171	1	0	2	17	98	91	94.4
	Place	691	0	17	42	61	92	90	91.0

Table 1: The results of MET2 test

The Table tabulates the results in terms of precision (Pr), recall (Rc) and F_1 measures. The definitions of these measures are:

$$Pr = (N_C + 0.5*N_P)/(N_C + N_W + N_P + N_M)$$
$$Rc = (N_C + 0.5*N_P)/(N_C + N_W + N_P + N_S)$$
$$F_1 = 2*Pr*Rc/(Pr+Rc)$$

where N_C, N_P, N_W and N_M respectively give the number of NEs in the test corpus that are correctly recognized, partially recognized, incorrectly recognized, and missed. N_S gives the number of NEs found by the system but not in the tagged list.

The results show that our system significantly outperforms other existing systems in the extraction of all name types, especially for person and organization names. The results demonstrate that our approach in using rule induction learning that is tolerant to word segmentation and name extraction errors is very effective. In particular, our strategy of adopting a greedy approach to locate all likely and overlapping names enables us to find most names together with many false detections. Fortunately, our generalized rule and decision tree approaches are sufficiently robust to remove most false detections. One further point to note is that although we collected large name dictionaries for testing, the base line performance of using these dictionaries directly for name look-up is only less than 30%.

The main sources of errors in our system are:

a) We miss out many Japanese names as our system is not tuned for recognizing Japanese names, which is neither a Chinese name nor P-Name.

b) We miss some person names because of the unexpected format (like the presence of a blank between the surname and the first name) and missing surname in the CW list (like the surname "义")

c) Some place and organization names are wrongly or inconsistently tagged within and between the training sets.

d) Some common nouns, such as 月球 (moon), 太阳 (sun) and 土星 (Saturn), are tagged as names in the test corpus, they are thus missed out in our results.

e) The Hownet we used is not very complete, and the semantic sets we extracted contain some missing concepts.

Some of these errors are also reported in Chen et al. (1998). We are now in the process of acquiring and testing our system using the 6-month PKU-Corpus. We expect similar results to be achieved on this large-scale corpus.

7. Review of Related Research

Since named entity recognition is almost the first step in Chinese NLP, there have been many researches on this topic. Most approaches used handcrafted rules, supplemented by word or character frequency statistics. These methods require a lot of resources to model the internal features of each name. Luo & Song (2001) collected large dictionaries for place, person, foreign person, foreign place and organization names. They tested their system on one-month of data from the people's daily and reported high accuracy. However, their resources are not openly available so it is hard to assess the performance of their system. Chen et al. (1998) used 1-billion person name dictionary in their system participated in MET2 test. They used mainly internal word statistics with no generalization. Yu et al. (1998) also collected large person, location and organization name lists. They employed a single framework to model both the context and information residing within the entities, and performed rule generalization using POS and some semantic tags.

In contrast to these systems, we induce rules directly from both the name lists and tagged corpus, and thus require less training resources. We also use lexical chaining to perform rule generalization, instead of POS tags. Finally, we incorporate various approaches to resolve uncertainty and ambiguity in NE recognition.

In many aspects, our system is also similar to those reported in Riloff (1993, 1996), and Soderland et at. (1995) for free text information extraction. However, our system differs from theirs on the main points discussed above.

8. Conclusion

Chinese NE is a difficult problem because of uncertainty in word segmentation and ambiguities in NE location. Many existing techniques that require knowledge on word segmentation, and syntactic or semantic tagging of text cannot be applied. In this paper, we extend the template-based rule induction method popularly used in information and relation extraction tasks. The main contributions of our approach are two-fold. First we induce rules for names and their context, and generalize these rules using lexical chaining. Second, we adopt a greedy approach in generating multiple overlapping word tokens and possible names, and employ a combination of generalized induction rules, DE-trees and decision tree to resolve the ambiguities. We tested the system on the MET2 test set and the results have been found to be superior to all reported systems.

We plan to further test our system on a large-scale test corpus. We will refine our techniques on a wide variety of text corpuses, and in overcoming the problem of data sparseness. Finally, we will extend our work to perform relation and information extraction in Chinese.

Acknowledgments
The authors would like to acknowledge the support of A*STAR, and the Ministry of Education of Singapore for the provision of a research grant RP3989903 under which this research is carried out.

References

Appelt, D.E., et al. 1995. SRI International FASTUS System MUC-6 Test Results and Analysis. *Proc. of the Sixth Message Understanding Conference.* 237–248. Morgan Kaufmann Publishers.

Bikel, D.M., Schwartz, R. and Weischedel, R.M. 1999. An Algorithm that Learns What's in a Name. *Machine Learning* 34(1-3), 211-231

Borthwick, A. 1999. A Maximum Entropy Approach to Named Entity Recognition. Ph.D. Thesis, New York Univ.

Chen, H.H., Ding, Y.W. Tsai, S.C. and Bian, G.W. 1998. Description of the NTU System used for MET-2. *Proc. of the Seventh Message Understanding Conference*

Cucerzan, S. and Yarowsky, D. 1999. Language Independent Named Entity Recognition Combining Morphological and Contextual Evidence. *Proc. of Joint SIGDAT Conference on Empirical Methods in NLP and Very Large Corpora*, 90-99

Dong, Z.D. and Dong, Q. 2000. HowNet, available at http://www.keenage.com/zhiwang/e_zhiwang.html

Green, S.J. 1999, Lexical Semantics and Automatic Hypertext Construction. *ACM Computing Surveys* 31(4), Dec.

Isozaki, H. 2001. Japanese Named Entity Recognition Based on a Simple Rule Generator and Decision Tree Learning, *Proc. of Association for Computational Linguistics*, 306-313

Liu, J.-M. and Chua, T.S. 2001. Building Semantic Perceptron Net for Topic Spotting, *Proc. of the Association for Computational Linguistics*, 306-313

Liu, J.-M. and Chua, T.S. 2002. A Hybrid Rule Induction Model for Chinese Name-Entity Recognition. Technical Report, School of Computing, National University of Singapore.

Luo, Z.-Y. and Song, R. 2001. An Integrated and Fast Approach to Chinese Proper Name Recognition in Chinese Word Segmentation, *Proc. of the Int'l Chinese Computing Conference*, Singapore, 323-328.

Marsh, E. & Perzanowski, D. 1998. MUC-7 Evaluation of IE Technology: Overview of Results, *Proc. of the*

Seventh Message Understanding Conference, at: http://www.itl.nist.gov/iaui/894.02/related_projects/ muc/proceedings/muc_7_toc.html.

Muslea, I. 1999. Extraction Patterns for Information Extraction Tasks: A Survey. *Proc. of AAAI Workshop.*

Palmer, D.D. 1997. A Trainable Rule-based Algorithm for Word Segmentation. *Proc. of the Association for Computational Linguistic, and Eighth Conference of the European Chapter of the Association for Computational Linguistics.*

Riloff, E. 1993. Automatically Constructing a Dictionary for Information Extraction Tasks. *Proc. of AAAI-93,* 811-816

Riloff, E. 1996. Automatically Generating Extraction Patterns from Untagged Text. *Proc. of AAAI'96,* 1044-1049

Sekine, S., Grishman, R. and Shinnou, H. 1998. A Decision Tree Method for Finding and Classifying Names in Japanese Texts. *Proc. of the 6th Workshop on Very Large Corpora,* Montreal, Canada

Soderland, S., Fisher, D. Aseltine, J. and Lehnert, W. 1995. Crystal: Inducing a Concept Dictionary, *IJCAI'95*

Sproat, R., Shih, C., Gail, W. and Chang, N. 1996. A Stochastic Finite-state Word Segmentation Algorithm for Chinese. *Computational Linguistics,* 22(3), 377-404

Weischedel, R. 1995. BBN: Description of the PLUM System as Used for MUC-6. *Proc. of the 6th Message Understanding Conference,* 55–69.

Xiao, J., Liu, J.-M. and Chua, T.S. 2002. Extracting Pronunciation-translated Named Entities from Chinese Texts using Bootstrapping Approach. Submitted to *2002 Conference on Empirical Methods in Natural Language Processing (EMNLP'2002).*

Xia, F., Palmer, M., Xue N.W., Okurowski, M.E., Kovarik, J., Chiou, F.D., Huang, S-Z., Kroch, T. and Marcus, M. 2000. Developing Guidelines and Ensuring Consistency for Chinese Text Annotation. *Proc of the 2nd International Conference on Language Resources and Evaluation (LREC-2000),* Athens, Greece, 2000

Yu, S.H., Bai, S.H. and Wu, P. 1998. Description of the Kent Ridge Digital Labs System used For MUC-7, *Proc. of the 7th Message Understanding Conference*

Yu, S.W. 1999. The Specification and Manual of Chinese Word Segmentation and Part of Speech Tagging. At: http://www.icl.pku.edu.cn/Introduction/ corpustagging.htm

Language Modeling for Soft Keyboards

Joshua Goodman
Microsoft Research
Redmond, WA 98052
joshuago@microsoft.com
www.research.microsoft
.com/~joshuago

Gina Venolia
Microsoft Research
Redmond, WA 98052
ginav@microsoft.com

Keith Steury
Microsoft Corp.
Redmond, WA 98052
keithste@microsoft.com

Chauncey Parker
Univ. of Washington
Seattle, WA 98195
chaunce@
u.washington.edu

Abstract

We describe how language models, combined with models of pen placement, can be used to significantly reduce the error rate of soft keyboard usage, by allowing for cases in which a key press is outside of a key boundary. Language models predict the probabilities of words or letters. Soft keyboards are images of keyboards on a touch screen used for input on Personal Digital Assistants. When a soft keyboard user hits a key near the boundary of a key position, we can use the language model and key press model to select the most probable key sequence, rather than the sequence dictated by strict key boundaries. This leads to an overall error rate reduction by a factor of 1.67 to 1.87.

Introduction

A *language model* is a probability distribution over strings. Their most common use is in speech recognition, for distinguishing phrases such as "recognize speech" and "wreck a nice beach." While the two phrases sound almost identical, the likelihood of the former is much higher than that of the latter. Language models allow the speech recognizer to select the correct one. Besides speech recognition, language models are also used in many other areas, including handwriting recognition (Srihari and Baltus, 1992), machine translation (Brown et al. 1990), and spelling correction (Golding and Schabes, 1996).

A soft keyboard is an image of a keyboard, displayed on a touch sensitive screen. The screens are used with a stylus, or less frequently with a finger or a mouse. Soft keyboards represent perhaps the fastest commonly available technique for inputting information into Personal Digital Assistants (PDAs) such as Windows CE devices and Palm Pilots.

Soft keyboard displays tend to be small, and as PDA/cellular phone combinations become more popular, will probably become smaller still. Because of this, and because speed and accuracy tend to be inversely related, a corollary of Fitts' (1954) law, errors are fairly common.

We propose a novel use for language models, reducing errors for soft keyboard input. We call such keyboards *corrective keyboards*. Imagine that a user taps the center of the "q" key, and then taps the boundary of the "u" and "i" keys. It is a much better bet that the user intended the "u" than the "i". Similarly, imagine that the user taps the boundary between the "q" and "w" keys, and then taps the center of the "u" key. The most likely intended key sequence was "qu." Thus, in ambiguous situations like these, knowing the relative probabilities of letter sequences can help resolve the intended key sequences. We can extend this reasoning to cases when the tap is not on a boundary, or even near one. When the user attempts to hit a given key, there is some probability that he will hit inside some other key. By combining the probability of the intended key with the probability of the actual pen down location, we can find the most likely key sequence.

In this paper, we first examine the mathematical models needed for using language modeling with soft keyboards. Next, we compare our research to previous work. Then we describe experiments we have done with soft keyboards. In the following section, we analyze the experimental results. Finally, in the last section, we conclude by examining the usefulness of these techniques in practice, and their applicability to other input techniques.

Mathematical Models

In this section, we first describe the typical use of language models – for speech recognition – and then show that simple modifications can be made to apply language models to soft keyboards. Next, we describe in more detail how to build language models. Finally, we describe the models of position sequences that are needed.

Relationship to Speech Recognition

The canonical equation of speech recognition is

$$\underset{\text{word sequences}}{\arg\max} \; P(\text{word sequence} \mid \text{acoustic sequence})$$

Applying Bayes' rule, this is equivalent to

$$\underset{\text{word sequences}}{\arg\max} \; \frac{P(\text{word sequence}) \times P(\text{acoustic sequence} \mid \text{word sequence})}{P(\text{acoustic sequence})}$$

The acoustic sequence will be constant for all possible word sequences and can thus be removed from the argmax:

$$\underset{\text{word sequences}}{\arg\max} \quad P(\text{word sequence}) \times P(\text{acoustic sequence} \mid \text{word sequence})$$

which is the formula that most speech recognizers attempt to maximize. The probability $P(\text{word sequence})$ is the probability according to the language model.

We can apply the same type of reasoning to soft keyboard input. In this case, it is convenient to use language models over letter sequences instead of over word sequences. The input to such a system is not acoustic input, but instead a sequence of observed pen down positions. We can then follow the same reasoning to achieve:

$$\underset{\text{letter sequences}}{\arg\max} \quad P(\text{letter sequence} \mid \text{pen down positions}) =$$

$$\underset{\text{letter sequences}}{\arg\max} \quad \frac{P(\text{letter sequence}) \times P(\text{pen down positions} \mid \text{letter sequence})}{P(\text{pen down positions})} =$$

$$\underset{\text{letter sequences}}{\arg\max} \quad P(\text{letter sequence}) \times P(\text{pen down positions} \mid \text{letter sequence})$$

Letter Sequence Language Model

Standard language modeling can be used to compute the probability of letter sequences. To compute the probability of a letter sequence $L_1, L_2, ..., L_n$, first, note that

$$P(L_1, L_2, ..., L_n) = P(L_1) \times P(L_2 \mid L_1) \times ... \times P(L_n \mid L_1...L_{n-1})$$

Now, to compute $P(L_i/L_1...L_{i-1})$ we make an approximation, such as the *trigram* approximation:

$$P(L_i \mid L_1...L_{i-1}) \approx P(L_i \mid L_{i-2}L_{i-1})$$

In other words, we assume that the probability of letter L_i is independent of letters that are more than two back. We are therefore predicting letters based on triples: the current letter, plus the previous two; thus the name trigram. The trigram approximation tends to be a reasonable one in typical language modeling applications where it is assumed that the probability of a word depends on the previous two words, but for smaller units, namely letters, it is too simplistic. For our experiments, we used 7-grams, as a reasonable compromise between memory and performance, but give our examples using trigrams, since these are easier to explain. A realistic product might primarily use word-based models, since these tend to be more accurate, although letter-based models would still be needed for entering words not in the system's dictionary.

To compute $P(L_i/L_{i-2}L_{i-1})$ we obtain some training data, say newspaper text, and count, for each letter sequence $L_{i-2}L_{i-1}L_i$ how many times it occurs, which we denote by $C(L_{i-2}L_{i-1}L_i)$; also, we count occurrences of $L_{i-2}L_{i-1}$. Then

$$P(L_i \mid L_{i-2}, L_{i-1}) \approx \frac{C(L_{i-2}L_{i-1}L_i)}{\sum_L C(L_{i-2}L_{i-1}L)} = \frac{C(L_{i-2}L_{i-1}L_i)}{C(L_{i-2}L_{i-1})}$$

The problem with this approximation is that it will predict that 0 probability is assigned to sequences that do not occur in the training data, making it impossible to type such sequences; this is likely to lead to irritated to users. When considering trigram letter sequences, such unseen sequences are likely to be rare, but for the 7-grams we used, they are very common. Thus, it is necessary to *smooth* these approximations, combining more specific approximations with less exact, but smoother approximations. Let λ and μ be constants that are determined empirically; then in practice we might use:

$$P(L_i \mid L_{i-2}L_{i-1}) \approx$$

$$\lambda \frac{C(L_{i-2}L_{i-1}L_i)}{C(L_{i-2}L_{i-1})} + (1-\lambda)\left(\mu \frac{C(L_{i-1}L_i)}{C(L_{i-1})} + (1-\mu) \frac{C(L_i)}{\sum_L C(L)} \right)$$

By smoothing, we ensure that any letter sequence can be entered, even words that have never been seen before. In the experiments we performed, we intentionally picked test data unrelated to our training data (Wall Street Journal sentences) to check that our improvements would not be limited to cases where the user entered phrases familiar to the system, but was likely to generalize broadly.

Chen and Goodman (1999) give a short introduction to language modeling with a detailed exploration of smoothing. Goodman (2000) describes the state of the art.

Pen Down Position Model

The model above has two components: the language model, and a probability distribution over pen down positions given the letter sequences. While language modeling is well-studied, we are not aware of previous work on modeling pen positions, especially in two dimensions. Previous research, such as Fitts' law, describes the relationship between accuracy, speed, and distance but does not give a probabilistic model for observed pen positions given target pen positions. Thus, one of the most interesting areas of research was in determining what these probability distributions looked like.

Corrective keyboard data collection is a bit of a chicken-and-egg problem: users typing on a normal keyboard will aim strictly within key boundaries, leading to user models that are almost strictly within key boundaries; etc. We performed pilot experiments in which we gathered data using a "cheating" version of the corrective keyboard in which whenever users were "close" to the correct key (as judged from the prompts), the correct letter appeared. We built models with this data for a round of non-cheating data collection, which was used to build models for the experiments reported here. We analyzed various dependencies in the second round to make the best models for the final round. By assuming user behavior was roughly independent of the exact models used, we could perform simulations with different models of pen down position, to determine the best model to use for the final round of experiments.

We considered a fairly wide variety of models, during our pilot experiments. Several of these did not improve accuracy. These included a model that examined the correlation between position at one time and the previous time, and another that considered relative position from the center at one time and the previous time. We also considered whether pen up position might give additional information. Finally, we examined whether when the user was typing faster, there was higher variance or different means in the observed positions. In the pilot experiments, none of these models led to significant improvements over the simple model we describe below.

We did find four results which were a bit surprising, three of which we used to form better models. All of these results can be seen in Figure 2, which illustrates the distribution of key presses. First, and most important, the average position for each key was not the center of the key. Instead, the average position was slightly shifted down and towards the center of the keyboard, both vertically and horizontally. This could have been a user attempt to minimize stylus movement, or perhaps due to misregistration or parallax effects. From a modeling viewpoint it does not matter: the model was able to learn about and correct for the discrepancy. Second, the variances in the x and y position are typically different. Third, some of the distributions are rotated slightly, rather than being symmetric or perpendicular to the axes of the keyboard; in other words, there is noticeable covariance between the x and y coordinates. We used these three observations in our final model. Our last observation, which we did not implement, was that the variance, especially on wide keys, such as "enter" or "space", appeared to be different for the left sides and the right sides, an observation that could be exploited in future work.

Based on these observations, we use the following model of pen down positions. We computed the mean, variance, and covariance of the x and y positions for each key, and then used a standard bi-variate Gaussian to model the probability of the observed pen down positions. The probability of a sequence of pen positions is modeled as the product of their individual probabilities.

Comparison to Previous Work

In this section, we survey related previous work. While we are not aware of any similar work that is directly applicable, there are a number of related approaches.

One completely different approach to optimizing soft keyboards is redesign of the layout of the keyboard, as exemplified by the work of MacKenzie et al. (1999). In this approach, letter co-occurrence statistics are used to rearrange the layout of the soft keyboard to minimize the distance between the most common key pairs. Our approach is orthogonal to that one, and could easily be combined with it.

Historically, there has of course been much research on typing. Unfortunately, much of the work on conventional keyboards is not relevant to the work on soft keyboards,

since the actual mechanics of entry are so different: all fingers working together, versus a few fingers typing indirectly with a single stylus. Furthermore, with a hard keyboard, position information is not available. On the other hand, even with a hard keyboard, language models can be used to correct some errors. This approach has been used for spelling correction (Golding and Schabes, 1996). In spelling correction, the model used is typically of the form

$$\underset{\text{intended letter sequence}}{\arg\max} P(\text{intended letter sequence}) \times P(\text{observed letter sequence}|\text{intended letter sequence})$$

This maximization is very similar to the one we use for the corrective keyboard. The difference is that the corrective keyboard formulation takes into account the actual position hit by the user, rather than just the key identity, a factor that spelling correctors do not use. It would be reasonable to think of the corrective keyboard as a spelling corrector that has been extended to use this additional information.

Language models have previously been used with keyboard input when trying to disambiguate truly ambiguous input sequences (Goldstein et al., 1999). In that work, a ten key keypad is used, with each key corresponding to several letters. This means that each input sequence is ambiguous, and a language model is essential for choosing among the possible letter sequences. The results of the experiments showed that while the device was inferior to a full-size keyboard, it was superior to several other portable-sized input techniques. Similarly, language models can be used for text entry using the numeric keypad of a cellular phone (MacKenzie et al. 2001). Note, however, that commonly deployed systems, such as T9 (www.tegic.com) use a dictionary sorted by word frequency, rather than a language model.

Salvucci (1999) applied a simple language model to decoding eye-traces for use in an eye-typing input method. He showed that better language models resulted in more accurate results. Unlike our approach, his model did not contain an explicit model of the observed positions given the intended letter. It would be easy to apply our approach to an eye-typing system, including our explicit position model, although, of course, the parameters would be different. The best language model used by Salvucci was a hierarchical grammar, instead of a simple n-gram model. This meant that it took up to 9 seconds to compute the results. Even their letter bigram model (called a digram or digraph model in some communities) required up to three seconds to evaluate results. Our implementation used straightforward beam thresholding techniques well known in speech recognition, and allowed us to always run with no noticeable delays, and minimal effort spent on optimization.

Experimental Methods

In this section, we describe our experimental methods. Additional details on the subjects and the task are given in the extended technical report version of this paper.

Subjects Eight subjects participated in the study. They were screened for the following: not a regular user of PDAs (personal digital assistants); at least moderate computer use; normal or normal corrected vision; and right handed. The study was balanced for gender.

Task We wanted a task in which the subjects would be encouraged to type both accurately and quickly, and in which they could intuit the tradeoff between these. We assumed most subjects would attempt to finish the tasks as quickly as possible, so we wanted a task where there would be a temporal penalty for excessive inaccuracy. Thus, users were asked to type 1000 "net" characters, from a set of short prompts, where a net character is the number of correct characters, minus the number of wrong characters. This task had the property that to finish as quickly as possible, users needed to type both reasonably accurately and quickly. Each insertion, deletion, or substitution error was counted as one error. Somewhat unrealistically, users were not allowed to use the backspace key, and were instructed to not correct errors. This simplified measurement of error rates. It would be interesting to perform studies without this restriction.

We also wanted to determine how significant learning effects would be. Furthermore, we wanted to give the users some minimal experience with both corrective and non-corrective keyboards, because in pilot experiments we had found that users liked to "play" a bit with the keyboard, complicating data analysis with spurious errors. We therefore ran three sets of pairs of conditions per user. The first set, Set 0, consisted of 5 prompts for each of corrective and non-corrective. The following sets, Set 1 and Set 2, consisted of enough prompts for the users to complete 1000 net characters in each condition. Corrective and non-corrective conditions were presented alternately. We balanced for order and counterbalanced by gender – that is, letting C stand for "corrective" and N for "non-corrective", two men used the order NCNCNC and two used the order CNCNCN. Similarly, two women used each order. The subjects were told for each set whether they were using the corrective or non-corrective keyboard, so that they would know they could type outside of key boundaries with the corrective version. To prevent learning effects, 6 different prompt sets were used. The prompt sets were always used in the same order, so that a given group of prompts was used with 4 subjects in the corrective condition, and with 4 subjects in the non-corrective condition. The prompts were designed to be homogeneous in terms of word length and reading ease. All prompts contained only lowercase alphabetic words.

Figure 1 shows a sample screen from the data collection task. In the sample screen, the top line shows the prompt,

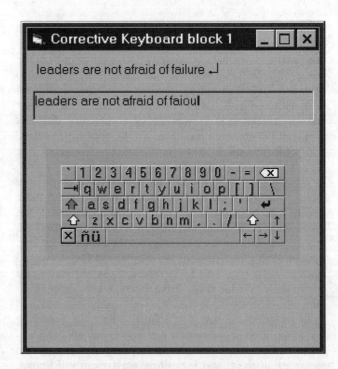

Figure 1: Corrective keyboard sample screen

the second line shows what the user has typed so far, and the keyboard is where the user presses with the stylus. One can see that an error has been made where the "l" in "failure" should be, and an "o" has been substituted. In this particular case, the user had actually pressed the letter "l", but the corrective keyboard had "corrected" it to an "o", which can occasionally happen. Notice that the letter "o" is a slightly different shade than the other letters. This indicates that the system considers this letter to still be ambiguous, and, depending on the following keystrokes, may actually change its interpretation. Indeed, upon hitting "re", the system did change the "o" to an "l".

The corrective keyboard experiments were implemented using a Wacom PL 400 touch screen connected to a PC, using only a fraction of the full display, so that it's size was the same as it would be in a typical PDA.

Experimental Results

In this section, we analyze our experimental results. There are two main results we can examine: throughput, and error rate. While on average, throughput was marginally faster with the corrective keyboard (19.8 words per minute for the corrective keyboard, versus 20 words per minute non-corrective), the differences were not statistically significant. For error rate results, there are many different ways to examine the error rates; we begin by justifying the technique we chose.

One issue is how to compare results. One can either analyze the data using arithmetic means, or geometric means[1]. Arithmetic means tend to heavily weight users with high error rates, who swamp the results, while geometric means tends to be fairer. Because some users made significantly more errors than others, we decided to use the geometric mean. Another issue is how to examine the two sets that users did. One way is to measure each of the two sets separately; another way is to measure the two sets together. This gives three different results: Set 1; Set 2; or both blocks combined. The final issue is how to determine the size of the block. One way is to use all of the data from a given user for a given block. This assumes that the "correct" way to determine a block is by the task. The other way is to take only the first 1000 characters typed by each user; since different users typed different numbers of characters, this method ensures that the same amount of data is analyzed from each user.

Altogether, we have 6 different results we can report, as given in Table 1, which shows each of the different ways of analyzing the data. The first column is labeled "set." It is "1" if we are analyzing the first set of data, "2" for analyzing the second set, and "both" if analyzing both sets of data pooled together. The ratio column gives the ratio between the geometric mean of the error rate using the non-corrective keyboard, and the geometric mean of the error rate using the corrective keyboard The "p" column shows the significance of the differences between the means, according to a one-tailed paired t-test assuming unequal variances. The test was performed by comparing the distributions of the logarithms of the error rates, which is the appropriate way to perform the test when using geometric means. The prompts column tells whether or not we used only the first *1000* characters that the user was prompted for in each set, or used *all* characters that the user was prompted for, enough to finish the task of entering 1000 net characters.

An examination of Table 1 shows that there were always significantly fewer errors with the corrective keyboard than with the non-corrective keyboard: between a factor of 1.67 and a factor of 1.87. Table 2 shows the times to enter each part of each set. Time was measured by summing the time from the first pen down on a prompt, to the enter key, giving users time to rest and read the prompts before typing.

A quick examination of Table 2 shows that users were fairly consistent in the time it took them to complete each part of each set, and there do not appear to be any important trends, other than a slight tendency to be faster on the second set than the first, as users become more experienced.

---

[1] The geometric mean is a multiplicative average:

$$\sqrt[n]{\prod_{i=1}^{n} x_i} \text{ or equivalently, } \exp\left(\frac{1}{n}\sum_{i=1}^{n}\log x_i\right).$$ The

arithmetic mean is the usual average.

Set	prompts	ratio	p<
1	1000	1.81	0.015
2	1000	1.82	0.032
Both	1000	1.67	0.007
1	all	1.87	0.014
2	all	1.87	0.028
Both	all	1.72	0.005

Table 1: Error ratios and significance

	Set 1, N	Set 1, C	Set 2, N	Set 2, C
mean	564.4	548.6	516.2	515.9
stdev	98.2	102.6	78.8	98.4

Table 2: Time to complete condition, in seconds

In Figure 2 we show the distribution of points hit by users. The chart is shown as a bubble chart, with points hit more often represented by larger bubbles. Whitish circles are shown on the physical center points of each key. It is clear that for many keys, there is a significant difference between the physical center, and the actual mean. This is particularly striking for the space bar. It was for this reason that in the models of key position, it was important to use the actual observed mean positions rather than the mean physical center of the keys. On some keys, such as "ZXCVB" the correlation between x and y position (leading to a slightly diagonal ellipse) can be seen, which is why we specifically modeled covariance.

Notice that different keys exhibit different shifting patterns. This implies that the shifting is less likely to be an artifact of some misalignment in the display, and more likely to be due to actual user preferences, such as for reducing pen movement.

Users were also given a short questionnaire to answer after completing each set. The questionnaire and its results are described in the extended, technical report version of this paper. Briefly, users consistently preferred the corrective keyboard; consistently thought it helped them make fewer errors; and consistently were not bothered by the automatic correction of errors.

Conclusion

The corrective keyboard results are very promising. They show that the use of language models can significantly reduce error rates in a soft keyboard task, by a factor of 1.67 to 1.87. Some newer soft keyboards we have seen, such as on Japanese i-Mode phones, are even smaller than those found on currently shipping PDAs. We expect that error rate improvements will be even higher on these smaller form factors. In addition, it seems that the techniques described here could be applied to a variety of other input methodologies. For instance, pie menus,

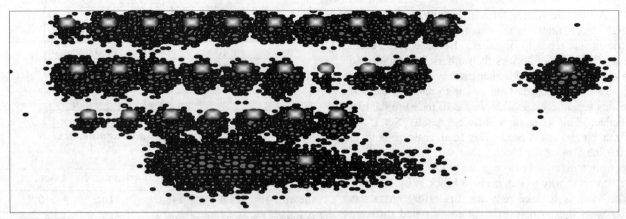

Figure 2: Distribution of points hit by subjects

especially when used for text input, could use analogous techniques. The language model could be combined with a model of mouse/stylus movement to handle cases where a user's selection was ambiguous. Similarly, our model could be easily used with eye-tracking systems (Salvucci 1999).

Further research in a number of areas does remain. It would be interesting to try longer tests, in order to get a more thorough view of learning effects. It would also be interesting to try more realistic experiments along a number of axes, including composition instead of transcription; allowing correction; and tasks with all keys, not just alphabetic keys. It would also be interesting to try making user-specific models, a technique which has been very helpful in speech recognition. Finally, it would be interesting to try more complex language models; the 7-gram letter models reported here are relatively simple by speech recognition standards.

Overall, we are very pleased with the large error rate reductions we have found, and look forward to further progress applying language models to soft keyboards, as well as applying these techniques in other areas.

Acknowledgments

We would like to thank Xuedong Huang, Derek Jacoby, and Mary Czerwinski for useful discussions.

References

Brown, P.F., Cocke J., Della Pietra, S.A., Della Pietra, V.J., Jelinek. F., Lafferty, J.D., Mercer, R.L. and Roosin, P.S. A statistical approach to machine translation. *Computational Linguistics 16*.2 (June 1990), pp. 79-85.

Chen, S.F. and Goodman, J. An Empirical study of smoothing techniques for language modeling. *Computer Speech and Language, 13* (October 1999), pp. 359-394.

Darragh, J.J.; Witten, I. H.; and James, M. L. 1990. The reactive keyboard: A predictive typing aid. *IEEE Computer 23(11)*:41-49.

Fitts, P.M. The information capacity of the human motor system in controlling the amplitude of movement, *Journal of Experimental Psychology 47* (1954), pp. 381-391.

Golding, A.R. and Schabes. Y. Combining trigram-based and feature-based methods for context-sensitive spelling correction, in *Proceedings of the 34th Annual Meeting of the Association for Computational Linguistics*, Santa Cruz, CA, 1996, pp. 71-78.

Goldstein, M., Book, R. Alsiö, G., Tessa, S. Non-keyboard touch typing: a portable input interface for the mobile user. *Proceedings of CHI '99*, Pittsburgh, pp. 32-39.

Goodman, J. Putting it all together: language model combination, in *ICASSP-2000*, Istanbul, June 2000.

MacKenzie, I.S., Kober, H., Smith, D., Jones, T., Skepner, E. LetterWise: Prefix-based disambiguation for mobile text input. *Proceedings of the ACM Symposium on User Interface Software and Technology - UIST 2001*. New York.

MacKenzie, I.S. and Zhang, X.S. The Design and Evaluation of a High-Performance Soft Keyboard, *Proceeding of CHI '99*, Pittsburgh, pp. 25-31.

Salvucci, D.D. Inferring intent in eye-based interfaces: tracing eye movements with process models. *Proceedings of CHI '99*, Pittsburgh, pp. 254-261.

Srihari, R. and Baltus, C. Combining statistical and syntactic methods in recognizing handwritten sentences, in AAAI Symposium: Probabilistic Approaches to Natural Language, (1992), pp. 121-127

CobotDS: A Spoken Dialogue System for Chat

Michael Kearns†, Charles Isbell‡, Satinder Singh§, Diane Litman¶, Jessica Howe♠

†Department of Computer and Information Science, University of Pennsylvania, mkearns@cis.upenn.edu
‡College of Computing, Georgia Institute of Technology, isbell@cc.gatech.edu
§Syntek Capital, baveja@cs.colorado.edu
¶Computer Science Department and LRDC, University of Pittsburgh, litman@cs.pitt.edu
♠ Laboratory for Artificial Intelligence, Massachussetts Institute of Technology, howej@ai.mit.edu

Abstract

We describe CobotDS, a spoken dialogue system providing access to a well-known internet chat server called LambdaMOO. CobotDS provides real-time, two-way, natural language communication between a phone user and the multiple users in the text environment. We describe a number of the challenging design issues we faced, and our use of summarization, social filtering and personalized grammars in tackling them. We report a number of empirical findings from a small user study.

Introduction

We describe the design, implementation and empirical experiences of CobotDS (for *Cobot Dialogue System*). CobotDS extends our ongoing work on Cobot (Isbell *et al.* 2000; 2001), a software agent that resides in a well-known, text-based internet chat environment called LambdaMOO. Founded in 1990, LambdaMOO (Cherny 1999; Foner 1997) is frequented by hundreds of users who converse with each other using both natural language text and *verbs* for expressing (in text) common real-world gestures (such as laughing, hugging, nodding and many others).[1] Cobot is one of the most popular LambdaMOO residents, and both chats with human users, and provides them with "social statistics" summarizing their usage of verbs and interactions with other users (such as who they interact with, who are the most "popular" users, and so on).

CobotDS provides LambdaMOO users with spoken telephony access to Cobot, and is an experiment in providing a rich social connection between a telephone user and the text-based LambdaMOO users. To support conversation, CobotDS passes messages and verbs from the phone user to LambdaMOO users (via automatic speech recognition, or ASR), and from LambdaMOO to the phone user (via text-to-speech, or TTS). CobotDS also provides "listening" (allowing phone users to hear a description of all LambdaMOO activity), chat summarization and filtering, personalized grammars, and many other features.

[1]Lines L1 and L14 in Table 1 illustrate the use of chat and verbs in LambdaMOO, respectively, and will be explained in detail below.

Our goal in building CobotDS was twofold. First, many LambdaMOO users log on as a form of regular social activity with a collection of friends and acquaintances. As a practical matter, we hope that CobotDS may provide an alternate means of access to LambdaMOO—either out of necessity (such as when a user is unable to access the internet), out of a desire to use a different input modality (speech instead of typing), or as an entertaining accompaniment to logging on directly. Second, we find it interesting to build a system that deliberately forms a connection, and blurs the distinction, between a world typically thought of as "real" (the world of telephones) and one typically thought of as "virtual". We also believe our experiences may hold lessons for future attempts to provide spoken access to text systems (such as instant messaging), and more generally for multimodal systems.

Traditional dialogue systems are designed to provide access to a relatively structured and static back-end database (such as airline reservation information), where users have well-defined, task-oriented goals (DARPA 2001; Sidner 2000). Compared to such systems, CobotDS is novel in a number of ways, and raises interesting challenges for dialogue system design.

First, CobotDS is one of the first dialogue systems to provide speech access to a complex social environment, where users participate primarily for entertainment or a sense of community. As such, it is difficult to anticipate user expectations or desires for CobotDS. For example, it was unclear whether users would prefer to use CobotDS for interaction with their LambdaMOO friends, or more as a passive listening mechanism. It was also unclear whether users would use the system primarily for LambdaMOO access when they were unable to log in to the text environment directly, or as an accompaniment to online access. Our approach to these questions is to try to provide enough functionality to shed some light on user needs, rather than fixing a model of them in advance. Thus, CobotDS should be viewed as an exploratory and evolving system.

Second, the "database" accessed by CobotDS is a dynamic and unstructured stream of natural language text, verb exchanges, and other actions. Conversational topics are interleaved, and users enter and exit at will. Providing the phone user with a useful view of this activity, as well as sufficiently rich means of participating in it, is a demanding

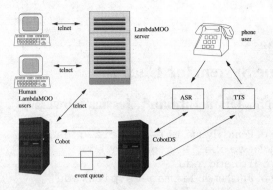

Figure 1: Architectural sketch of CobotDS, Cobot, and LambdaMOO, providing two-way communication between phone and chat users.

design problem. Some of the methods we applied and will discuss include summarization and filtering (to reduce the load on the phone user during busy times), and the use of "personal" grammars (to provide phone users with a rich set of personalized utterances within the current limitations of ASR).

Third, there are many issues of imbalance and asynchrony between the CobotDS phone user and the LambdaMOO text users. The phone user has a limited channel *to* LambdaMOO (due to the imperfections of ASR), and a potentially rich and cognitively challenging channel *from* LambdaMOO (as the phone user must absorb the action in real time via TTS, and does not have text-based scroll back capabilities). We have taken first steps in bridging this gap, and dealing with its consequences—such as time lag—but clearly more research is needed.

In the remainder of this paper, we sketch some salient points about the system architecture, provide an overview of the functionality provided by CobotDS to both phone and LambdaMOO users, and report on a number of interesting empirical findings derived from a small user study.

CobotDS Architecture

Cobot connects to the LambdaMOO server as a client, just as any human user would, and maintains information about LambdaMOO that he uses for his chat interactions and social statistics services. Although CobotDS and Cobot appear to users as a single system, in reality CobotDS is implemented as a separate set of processes handling ASR, TTS, telephony, dialogue management, and semantic processing, built using a general purpose platform for spoken dialogue systems (Levin *et al.* 1999). Thus, Cobot interacts with LambdaMOO and its users, while CobotDS interacts with the phone user. Figure 1 provides a sketch of the overall architecture.

LambdaMOO events or messages to be communicated from Cobot to CobotDS (and thus to the phone user) are handled by an *event queue* lying between Cobot and CobotDS. As such events occur, Cobot places them in the event queue, which CobotDS flushes at each dialogue turn. The event queue is a buffering mechanism designed to address the fact that the rate at which events can be pushed to the phone user

may sometimes lag considerably behind the rate at which they are being generated in LambdaMOO. The desire to minimize this lag led to our implementation of some interesting queue *filtering* mechanisms (discussed later).

In the other direction, events to be passed from the phone user to LambdaMOO are immediately passed from CobotDS to Cobot. No explicit queuing mechanism is necessary. As Cobot notices messages from the phone user he processes them, just as he processes events from LambdaMOO as they occur.

CobotDS Functionality Overview

Table 1 is a sample dialogue illustrating all of the commands provided by CobotDS to both the phone and LambdaMOO users, and will be used extensively for expository purposes. Although hypothetical, the dialogue is representative of the actual dialogues discussed in the section on empirical findings, and all of the functionality shown is implemented.

After a brief login procedure (turns C1 and C2 of Table 1)[2], the phone user is placed in the *main command loop*, where he is repeatedly prompted for a CobotDS command (as in line C3S). User response is interpreted through ASR, and the resulting command executed. For example, after C3U, on the phone side, CobotDS tells the phone user what was heard, executes the command, and passes any messages or verbs directed towards them (via Cobot) from LambdaMOO users (line C4S). In LambdaMOO, completion of the CobotDS user login causes Cobot to announce the call in LambdaMOO (lines L3-L4).

Communicating with the Phone User

LambdaMOO users can pass messages to the phone user by directing a text message beginning with **phone:** to Cobot, as on line L7. If the text following **phone:** can be interpreted as a common LambdaMOO verb (line L11), it is passed on as such to the phone user via TTS (line C9S); otherwise, it is treated as an act of directed speech (lines L7 and C6S). In either case, the LambdaMOO user invoking **phone:** on Cobot is credited with the action.

Basic LambdaMOO Verbs

We now move on to discuss the commands provided to the phone user that can be invoked after prompting in the main command loop. The most basic functionality is the replication of the most common LambdaMOO verbs, such as waving and hugging (currently CobotDS supports 38 such verbs). These verbs can be invoked either without or with a user name (lines C4U and C6U, respectively), generating different behaviors by Cobot in LambdaMOO (lines L5 and L9-L10, respectively). Note that LambdaMOO users are already accustomed to using the same simple syntax for these verbs.

Conversation and Grammars

Despite the importance of verb use, LambdaMOO remains primarily a chat environment. To the extent possible, we felt

---

[2]To control system access and load, only a limited set of users have been granted CobotDS passwords. There are currently 33, including the authors.

CobotDS Transcript *(spoken; phone user and CobotDS alternate)*	**LambdaMOO Transcript** *(text, joined in progress; multiple users and Cobot in ongoing, interleaved dialogues)*
C1S. **Hello, who is this?** *(CobotDS prompt)*	L1. HFh [to Betwixt]: And thanks to TiVo, I was able to see the game when I got home.
C1U. *Buster. (phone user response)*	L2. Betwixt [to HFh]: I missed the first half because I was busy shoveling our record snowfall. But the second half was pretty spectacular.
C2S. **Secret password?**	L3. Cobot turns to pick up the phone. [C(a)]
C2U. *Eight three two two.* [C(a), successful login]	L4. Cobot begins talking to Buster! [C(a)]
C3S. **Hi, Buster. What do you want to do?**	L5. Cobot holds up a sign: Buster passes on a wave from the phone. [C(b)]
C3U. *Who.*	L6. HFh pats Cobot on the head.
C4S. **You who. I am with Cocobot, Betwixt, and HFh.**	L7. HFh [to Cobot]: phone: How was the movie? [L(a)]
C4U. *Wave.* [C(b)]	L8. Betwixt [to HFh]: Overall, it's one of their better stretches this year.
C5S. **You wave.**	L9. Cobot smiles at Betwixt. [C(c)]
C5U. *Where.*	L10. Cobot [to Betwixt]: That was from Buster. [C(c)]
C6S. **You where. I am in The Cobotatory. HFh says How was the movie?, to you.** [L(a)]	L11. Betwixt [to Cobot]: phone: wave [L(b)]
C6U. *Smile Betwixt.* [C(c)]	L12. Cobot [to HFh]: Fantastic [C(d)]
C7S. **You smile to Betwixt.**	L13. Cobot [to HFh]: That was from Buster. [C(d)]
C7U. *Say HFh.*	L14. HFh nods to Betwixt.
C8S. **What message would you like to pass?**	L15. Cobot [to Betwixt]: But it can't last. The soap opera always takes over at some point. Drama over basketball.
C8U. *Fantastic.* [C(d), smalltalk ASR grammar]	L16. Cobot holds up a sign: Buster says, 'What's going on in the MOO' from the phone. [C(e)]
C9S. **You say Fantastic, to HFh. Betwixt waves to you.** [L(b)]	L17. HFh [to Cobot]: phone: I am providing hoops wisdom to Betwixt. [L(c)]
C9U. *Say.*	L18. Betwixt [to Cobot]: phone: HFh is pontificating on the Knicks again. Where are you? [L(d)]
C10S. **What message would you like to pass?**	L19. Betwixt [to HFh]: Your problem is you have no faith.
C10U. *What's going on in the MOO?.* [C(e), smalltalk ASR grammar]	L20. HFh [to Betwixt]: Yours is that you have too much in the wrong team.
C11S. **You say What's going on in the MOO, to everyone.**	L21. HFh cackles madly at Betwixt!
C11U. *Summarize.*	L22. Cobot holds up a sign: Buster says, 'I am in Hoboken' from the phone. [C(f)]
C12S. **You summarize. Recently, HFh and Betwixt chatted. Betwixt and GreenBean bickered. HFh and Natto had a friendly conversation. I added to the noise. HFh made the most noise.**	L23. Betwixt [to Cobot]: phone: nod [L(e)]
C12U. *Grammar (ASR rejects the utterance, and returns nothing).*	L24. Cobot holds up a sign: Buster passes on a listen from the phone. [C(g)]
C13S. **Next. HFh says I am providing hoops wisdom to Betwixt, to you, and then, Betwixt says, HFh is pontificating on the Knicks again. Where are you?, to you.** [L(c),L(d)]	L25. HFh [to Betwixt]: Sprewell can always be counted on to go straight to the rim, but Houston settles for jumpers from the parking lot. [L(f)]
C13U. *Grammar.*	L26. Cobot [to HFh]: This is from Buster: [C(h),L(g)]
C14S. **Which grammar would you like to use? The choices are smalltalk, personal, and cliche.**	L27. Cobot grins at HFh. [C(h),L(g)]
C14U. *Personal.*	L28. Betwixt [to HFh]: With Camby's rebounding they have a chance to at least win the East. [L(h)]
C15S. **The grammar is now set to Buster.**	L29. HFh [to Betwixt]: Ummm, as long as he doesn't send his coach to intensive care first. [L(i)]
C15U. *Say Betwixt.*	L30. Natto teleports in from the Living Room. [L(j)]
C16S. **What message would you like to pass?**	L31. Betwixt [to HFh]: Good point [L(k)].
C16U. *I am in Hoboken.* [C(f), Buster personal grammar]	
c17S. **You say I am in Hoboken, to Betwixt.**	
C17U. *Listen.* [C(g), listen mode turned on]	
C18S. **You listen. Betwixt gives you a nod. HFh to Betwixt, Sprewell can always be counted on to go straight to the rim, but Houston settles for jumpers from the parking lot, and then, I grin to HFh.** [L(e),L(f),L(g)]	
C18U. *Grin HFh.* [C(h)]	
C19S. **You grin to HFh. Betwixt to HFh, With Camby's rebounding they have a chance to at least win the East, and then, HFh to Betwixt, Ummm, as long as he doesn't send his coach to intensive care first, and then, Natto teleports in from the Living Room, and then, Betwixt to HFh, Good point.** [L(h),L(i),L(j),L(k)]	

Table 1: Parallel CobotDS-LambdaMOO transcripts for a sample dialogue. The left-hand column shows a dialogue with CobotDS, with the *i*th dialogue turn numbered C*i*S (system) and C*i*U (user). The right-hand side shows the activity taking place in LambdaMOO during this call, with the *i*th event numbered L*i*. Events in CobotDS that cause announcements in LambdaMOO are labeled as [C(x)] on the left-hand side, with the same label marking the resulting announcements on the right-hand side. Similarly, events in LambdaMOO that cause announcements in CobotDS are labeled as [L(x)] on the right-hand side, with the same label marking the resulting announcements on the left-hand side.

it important to provide some reasonably expressive mechanisms for conversational exchange. It is rather easy to provide unconstrained message-passing from LambdaMOO to the phone user; however, communication from the phone user to LambdaMOO is severely hampered by the limitations of ASR. Nonetheless, CobotDS provides a **say** command (that takes an optional user name argument). Upon invoking the **say** command (as in line C7U), the phone user enters a one-step sub dialogue where he is prompted for the utterance he wishes to pass (turn C8). This utterance is then given to ASR, along with the recognition *grammar* that is currently in effect. Before passing the output of ASR on to LambdaMOO, CobotDS performs a *backmatching* step: the ASR output phrase is matched against each of the phrases in the current recognition grammar, and the phrase most similar to the ASR phrase is then passed on to LambdaMOO (lines L12-L13).[3]

CobotDS has two built-in grammars, the *smalltalk* and *cliche* grammars, and a *personal* grammar that differs for each phone user. The smalltalk grammar consists of 228 hand-constructed phrases providing basic conversational queries, responses, and remarks. (Examples include variants of "yes" and "no"; locational assertions such as "I am at home"; exclamations like "fantastic" or "terrible"; LambdaMOO-specific phrases such as "What's going on in the MOO?" and "My connection is down"; and conversational staples such as "How are you" and "I am fine".) The cliche grammar consists of 2950 common English sayings (such as "It takes one to know one" and "A rose by any other name would smell as sweet"). The personal grammar consists of a list of phrases provided by each phone user. The smalltalk grammar is initially in effect. The phone user can change the grammar by using the **grammar** command (line C13U), initiating a one-step sub dialogue where the phone user is prompted for a grammar name (turn C14).[4]

The hope is that the smalltalk grammar provides the rudiments of conversation, the cliche grammar contains common witticisms allowing the phone user to occasionally make an appropriate remark on LambdaMOO action, and the personal grammar can be used for the favorite phrases of the user. The use of multiple grammars for the **say** command, and allowing users to construct grammars, are potentially interesting experiments in placing users in more direct control of technology.

Listening and Social Filtering

In addition to allowing the phone user to send and receive messages, we anticipate that phone users may sometimes wish to hear *all* the action in LambdaMOO. Indeed, it is possible that some phone users may primarily use CobotDS as a passive source of entertainment (somewhat like listening to a radio talk show), interacting only minimally. The **listen**

---

[3]Here, the similarity of two phrases is determined by treating each as a vector of word counts and computing the normalized inner product between them. This is a common and well-understood technique from information retrieval.

[4]The user only has to say "personal", because his identity, and thus the grammar to load, is known from the login process.

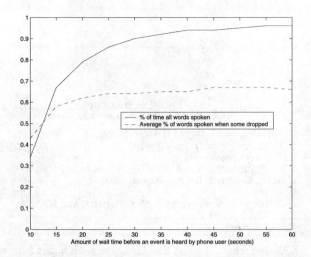

Figure 2: Information loss due to filtering, computed from LambdaMOO event logs. The x-axis shows the maximum number of seconds allotted between the time an event occurs in LambdaMOO and the time its filtered version is read to the phone user. (This interval includes the overhead time required to record the phone user's command, about 7 seconds.) For the solid line, the y-axis shows the fraction of turns for which no filtering of events was necessary (because in the allotted time, it was possible to read out completely the events generated in the last dialogue turn). For the dashed line, the y-axis shows the ratio of the length of the filtered text to the length of the original whenever filtering had to be used. This graph was computed from several days of LambdaMOO activity; nearly identical plots were obtained for other time periods. Note that increasing the allowed lag beyond 20-25 seconds (corresponding to about 59 words) does not significantly increase the overall information reaching the phone user.

command (line C17U) puts CobotDS into a special mode where every system prompt in the main command loop includes a *filtered* version of all the activity taking place in LambdaMOO during the last dialogue turn (lines C18S and C19S). This mode is turned off by invoking the **mute** command.

One difficulty that arises in implementing **listen** is the empirical fact that the rate at which TTS can read text can lag considerably behind the rate at which text is being generated in LambdaMOO. Our solution is to *fix* the length of the text that will be read with each prompt (independent of how much activity took place), but to use this text to summarize *all* activity since the last turn; hence the need for a filtering mechanism.

A trade-off arises in choosing the length of the text to be read: a shorter length results in lower maximum time lag for the phone user, but forces more severe filtering. We empirically determined that a length of 59 words strikes a good balance (see Figure 2). We also decided to *personalize* the filtering for each user based on their past *social* interactions in the text environment, as observed by Cobot. There is an ordered set of filtering rules, and each rule is applied in turn until the desired length is met. While the earliest of these rules is not personalized, eventually all the activity generated by users with whom the phone user has little or no past interaction may be dropped from the summary.

Special Informational Commands

Finally, CobotDS provides commands giving information on the current state of the text environment (which generate responses to phone users but not to LambdaMOO users). The **where** and **who** commands (lines C5U and C3U) tell the phone user which room of LambdaMOO Cobot currently occupies[5] (line C6S), and which LambdaMOO users are present there (line C4S), respectively.

More interesting is the **summarize** command (line C11U), which presents the phone user with a coarse summary of the last 10 minutes of activity in LambdaMOO (or the last n minutes, if the phone user utters an integer argument). Cobot uses his social statistics to compute which users have generated the most activity (in terms of number of verb invocations), which pairs of users have interacted the most, and which players have entered and exited (as in line C12S). The pairwise interactions may be characterized as "friendly" (if the fraction of verbs such as **smile** exceeds a certain threshold), or "nasty" (if the fraction of verbs such as **kick** exceeds a threshold).

The motivation behind **summarize** is to allow the phone user, either upon login or later in the dialogue, to get a brief synopsis of who is present and the nature of their interactions, if any. We view the command as a "batch" operation crudely summarizing a long time period. By contrast, the filtering mechanism used by the **listen** command gives a "play by play" synopsis of the action, and is designed for real-time summarization.

Empirical Findings

As of this writing, over 300 calls have been placed to CobotDS. Excluding the authors, 18 users have placed at least one call to the system. CobotDS is thus an active service provided to select LambdaMOO users, and a wide variety of experiences and usage patterns have been reported to and observed by us.

To quantify the empirical use of CobotDS in a more controlled manner, we conducted a small and informal user study during a recent two-week period. We restricted our attention to five (non-author) users who made at least 5 calls each to CobotDS during the study period (two females, three males, all native speakers). This section describes a number of quantitative and anecdotal findings derived from our complete logs (on both the CobotDS and LambdaMOO sides) of the calls made by this restricted user group, as well as from the personal grammars submitted by the users. Note, however, that the logs represent CobotDS's (post-ASR) interpretation of the user's utterances, and are thus only an approximation of the phone user's true intent.

Some of our findings are given in Table 2. Each column represents a user, and the rows show CobotDS or LambdaMOO usage statistics for that user. Note that there are

---

[5]LambdaMOO actually consists of multiple distinct chat rooms, connected by virtual exits and entrances that are navigable by standard system commands. Cobot divides his time between two different LambdaMOO rooms.

many differences between users. For example, the average number of dialogue turns per call (row 2) varies from 31.6 for Benny to 106.6 for Nisa. This latter figure corresponds to an average call duration of over 20 minutes, suggesting that CobotDS is being used for extended social interaction by some users.

This view is supported by other figures in the table. Consider turns where (CobotDS believes that) the phone user executed an *interaction* command (either **say** or any LambdaMOO verb), affecting both the phone and LambdaMOO users. The fraction of interaction commands (row 4) across all users is 0.50 (ranging from Etoile's 0.33 to Huey's 0.59). Among the interaction turns, users vary in their use of **say** versus other verbs (row 5). Etoile is relatively verbal (at 0.83), while Huey is relatively gestural (at 0.38).

Users often provided username arguments for interaction commands (*directed* interaction, rows 6 and 7), and tended to interact with multiple LambdaMOO users (rows 8 and 9). Interestingly, the LambdaMOO users communicating with the phone user tended to use **say** more frequently (about 79 percent of the time) than the verbs (row 11). This is in contrast with the usage of **say** between LambdaMOO users (roughly 43 percent).

The **listen** command was also reasonably popular, with an average of 0.61 invocations per dialogue across all users (row 12). Some users enter **listen** mode and stay there for considerable periods of time (row 14, particularly Huey), but users also tend to turn listen mode on only later in the dialogue (row 15, where we see that listen mode is first invoked after 38 turns on average). This is consistent with our informal observation that there is typically a flurry of interaction between the phone and LambdaMOO users when Cobot first announces that a user is on the phone, thus providing the phone user with a sense of participation, but that as this initial exchange dies down, they switch to listen mode. There is also some evidence for the use of **listen** in "radio" mode, in which the phone user simply listens to LambdaMOO without giving any CobotDS commands. For example, rows 16 and 17 demonstrate that user Nisa is silent (empty string returned from ASR) a much greater fraction of time in listen mode than in non-listen mode.

Recall that if the phone user is listening during a busy time, he may receive a filtered version of LambdaMOO activity (personalized by past social interaction). We note that our filtering mechanism performed reasonably well: the average real-time lag in hearing the filtered version of LambdaMOO events was only about 10 seconds (which includes the "overhead" time for recording the phone user's command). When filtering was necessary at all (that is, the filtered version of LambdaMOO events differed from the original), the filtered text length was on average 0.70 times the unfiltered length. This is quite consistent with Figure 2.

We also see that users took advantage of the **grammar** command: it was invoked an average of 1.4 times per dialogue across all users (row 18), and used to set the grammar to personal 69 percent of the time (row 19). The first change of grammar occurred relatively early (row 20), confirming our observation that users would often change to personal grammars quickly, and remain there for entire dialogue.

		Jethromeo	Etoile	Nisa	Huey	Benny	*Average*
1	number of dialogues	5	7	9	5	5	6.2
2	mean number of turns per dialogue	36.2	39.3	106.6	92.2	31.6	65.3
3	mean interactions to the MOO	8.2	6.85	29.1	27.2	5.8	16.0
4	fraction of interaction commands	0.43	0.33	0.55	0.59	0.36	0.50
5	fraction of say interactions	0.68	0.83	0.54	0.38	0.59	0.54
6	fraction of directed says	0.42	0.86	0.41	0.62	0.47	0.52
7	fraction of directed interactions	0.41	0.86	0.48	0.65	0.55	0.56
8	mean MOO recipients	2.6	3.0	5	5	2	3.7
9	mean MOO pushers	2	2.43	3.2	2.8	0.8	2.4
10	mean interactions from MOO	5.2	5.1	11.3	12.4	1.2	7.4
11	fraction of MOO say interactions	0.85	0.83	0.73	0.85	0.66	0.79
12	mean number of listens	0.6	0.57	0.44	1.2	0.4	0.61
13	mean number of mutes	0	0.43	0.71	0.8	0.2	0.42
14	mean turns taken for a listen	15	4.6	22.5	32.8	21	18.7
15	mean turn number to begin listen	63	30.5	43	39.7	15.5	38.4
16	fraction of silent turns in listen	0.53	0.5	0.73	0.46	0.19	0.52
17	fraction of silent turns in mute	0.46	0.48	0.48	0.52	0.59	0.49
18	mean grammar changes	0.8	1.5	1.5	1.6	1.0	1.4
19	fraction of grammar changes to personal	1.0	0.55	0.57	0.75	1.0	0.69
20	mean turn number of grammar change	8.5	17	6.2	9.75	7.2	9.8

Table 2: CobotDS usage statistics. Here we list statistics summarizing how CobotDS was used by our most active phone users during the recent two-week study. A *command* is any completed transaction with the system, from the (post-ASR) perspective of CobotDS. An *interaction* is a command that results in some kind of verbal or gestural communication with a LambdaMOO user (either the **say** command or a LambdaMOO verb). A **say** or other interaction is called *directed* if it addresses a specific LamdbaMOO user. A user is always considered to be in either *listen* or *mute* mode. Finally, a *silent turn* happens when a user decides not to issue any kind of command (or when ASR misrecognizes a command as silence). See the text for a more complete discussion.

Personal grammars had an average length of 29.6 phrases (ranging from 6 to 60). Typically a personal grammar included set phrases commonly invoked by the user in LambdaMOO itself. Thus Huey's personal grammar contained "Can I get an amen", while Nisa included "Chillin' like a villain". Interestingly, some personal grammars evolved to include phrases compensating for ASR errors and the limitations of the grammars themselves.[6] Thus, users added phrases such as "I can't answer that question given my limited vocabulary", "I don't have the words to convey my feeling towards the issue at hand", "I didn't mean to say that", and "Cobot misunderstood that's not what I meant". Some users added sentences containing acoustically distinct keywords to increase the chances of recognition, sometimes pronouncing just those keywords (taking advantage of our use of backmatching). Users also included phrases along the lines of the smalltalk grammar, but that were missing, such as "Going to lunch." By contrast, users made minimal use of the cliche grammar.

Users in the study also completed a brief survey that queried their experiences with CobotDS and solicited suggestions for improvements to the system. Overall, users seemed to find CobotDS interesting, fun, and useful. However, common themes in the responses included frustration with poor ASR performance (particularly for the **say** command), and the difficulty of sustaining conversation with the restrictive grammars. Interesting suggestions included providing the ability to update the personal grammar instanta-

neously (which is unfortunately precluded by our internal development environment, but is available on some commercial platforms), and providing confirmation for the utterance in the **say** command. Initially, we believed that confirming long utterances would prove irritating, but are now contemplating allowing users the ability to turn it on and off for the **say** command. There were also comments suggesting that users be able to selectively **listen** to the activity generated by some, but not all, LambdaMOO users. This confirms our suspicion that the amount of LambdaMOO activity at busy times overwhelms the TTS-bound phone user, and that filtering activity by prior social interaction is an avenue worth exploring even further.

References

Cherny, L. 1999. *Conversation and Community: Discourse in a Social MUD*. CLFI Publications.

DARPA. 2001. Communicator web page, http://www.darpa.mil/ito/research/com/index.html.

Foner, L. 1997. Entertaining Agents: a Sociological Case Study. In *Proc. of Autonomous Agents*.

Isbell, C. L.; Kearns, M.; Kormann, D.; Singh, S.; and Stone, P. 2000. Cobot in LambdaMOO: A Social Statistics Agent. *Proc. of AAAI 2000*.

Isbell, C. L.; Shelton, C. R.; Kearns, M.; Singh, S.; and Stone, P. 2001. A Social Reinforcement Learning Agent. *Proc. of Autonomous Agents 2001*.

Levin, E.; Pieraccini, R.; Eckert, W.; Fabbrizio, G. D.; and Narayanan, S. 1999. Spoken language dialogue: From theory to practice. In *Proc. IEEE ASRU99 Workshop*.

Sidner, C., ed. 2000. *ANLP/NAACL Workshop on Conversational Systems*.

---

[6]During the trial, we gave our users the opportunity to occasionally update their personal grammars.

Exploiting Auditory Fovea in Humanoid-Human Interaction

Kazuhiro Nakadai[†], Hiroshi G. Okuno[†*], and Hiroaki Kitano[†‡]

†Kitano Symbiotic Systems Project, ERATO, Japan Science and Technology Corp.

Mansion 31 Suite 6A, 6-31-15 Jingumae, Shibuya-ku, Tokyo 150-0001, Japan

Tel: +81-3-5468-1661, Fax: +81-3-5468-1664

* Department of Intelligence Sciece and Technology, Graduate School of Informatics, Kyoto University

‡Sony Computer Science Laboratories, Inc.

nakadai@symbio.jst.go.jp, okuno@nue.org, kitano@csl.sony.co.jp

Abstract

A robot's auditory perception of the real world should be able to cope with motor and other noises caused by the robot's own movements in addition to environment noises and reverberation. This paper presents the *active direction-pass filter* (ADPF) that separates sounds originating from a specified direction detected by a pair of microphones. Thus the ADPF is based on directional processing – a process used in visual processing. The ADPF is implemented by hierarchical integration of visual and auditory processing with hypothetical reasoning of interaural phase difference (IPD) and interaural intensity difference (IID) for each sub-band. The ADPF gives differences in resolution in sound localization and separation depending on where the sound comes from: the resolving power is much higher for sounds coming directly from the front of the humanoid than for sounds coming from the periphery. This directional resolving property is similar to that of the eye whereby the visual fovea at the center of the retina is capable of much higher resolution than is the periphery of the retina. To exploit the corresponding "auditory fovea", the ADPF controls the direction of the head. The human tracking and sound source separation based on the ADPF is implemented on the upper-torso of the humanoid and runs in real-time using distributed processing by 5 PCs networked via a gigabit ethernet. The signal-to-noise ratio (SNR) and noise reduction ratio of each sound separated by the ADPF from a mixture of two or three speeches of the same volume were increased by about 2.2 dB and 9 dB, respectively.

Introduction

Robots are often used as a real-world test-beds in the research fields of AI and cognition. Robots can serve as remote communication agents with a real body. Such a robot can provide remote conferencing of high quality than conventional TV conferencing by enabling listeners to hear several things simultaneously or to keep attention on a specific speaker. The robot achieves this by providing sound with a high signal-to-noise ratio (SNR) obtained by suppressing unwanted sounds from other speakers and by suppression of the noises from the robot's own motors.

Therefore, a remote robot should be able to cope with a general sound, i.e. a mixture of sounds. To localize and separate sound sources accurately, the robot needs to be equipped with two or more microphones and the difference in resolution, according to the direction of the sound, needs to be taken into account.

When a robot has a pair of microphones in ear positions, the sensitivity of sound source localization in the azimuth is the highest to the front of the head, and degrades towards the periphery. In humans, this phenomenon has been known for over a century (Blauert 1999). Neurons of horseshoe bats are narrowly tuned in a specialized region inside the cochlea to detect frequency shifts in the echo signal that are caused by Doppler-effects. In neuroethology, then this is termed an "auditory fovea" corresponding to the visual fovea in the primate retina (Schuller & Pollak). The concepts of the phenomena in sound source localization by the robot and the cochlea in horseshoe bats are similar to visual fovea in the primate retina in a point of selective attention. So, we can say that the phenomenon in sound source localization by the robot is a kind of auditory fovea. In this paper, we use an auditory fovea in a sense of higher sensitivity in front direction of the robot's head.

In the retina, the resolution of images is high in the fovea, which is located at the center of the retina, and much poorer towards the periphery which serves to capture information from a much larger area. Because the visual fovea gives a good compromise between the resolution and field-of-view without the cost of processing a large amount of data, it is useful for robots (Klarquist & Bovik 1998; Rougeaux & Kuniyoshi 1997). The visual fovea must face the target object to obtain good resolution, so it is a kind of *active vision* (Aloimonos, Weiss, & Bandyopadhyay. 1987). Akin to the visual fovea, the auditory fovea also needs to be directed at the target object, such as a speaker. Therefore, it too relies on active motion. Such integration of sound and active motion, termed *active audition* (Nakadai et al. 2000b), can be used to attain improved auditory perception. The active motion is essential in audition and vision not only for friendly humanoid-human interaction, but also for better perception.

Active audition has been integrated with multiple face recognition and visual localization. A real-time multiple human tracking system has been developed (Nakadai et al.

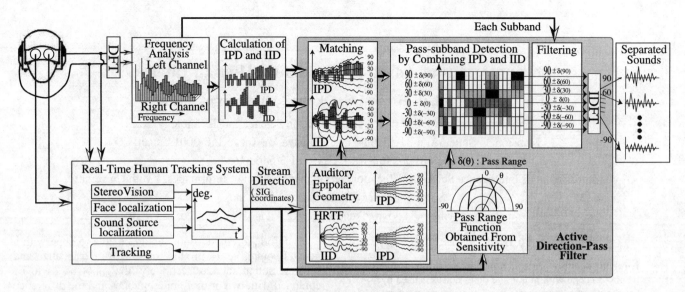

Figure 1: Active Direction-Pass Filter

2001). The system can even simultaneously track more than one voice, owing to robust auditory processing of harmonic structures of sound and time-streamed audio-visual integration.

However, the system has drawbacks:

1. Localization is attained but without sound source separation or enhancement.
2. Multiple sound sources are localized by a simple grouping strategy using harmonic structure of sounds.
3. The accuracy of sound source localization is not high enough for sound source separation.
4. No visual information is used when a face is not in sight.
5. The system network is difficult to scale-up.

To cope with the first and second issues, we propose a new sound source separation method called the *active direction-pass filter (ADPF)*. It is a kind of direction pass filter (DPF) that extracts a sound from a specific direction with hypothetical reasoning about the interaural phase difference (IPD) and interaural intensity difference (IID) of each sub-band (Okuno *et al.* 2001). It enables more accurate sound source extraction by auditory fovea based separation, active motion, and accurate localization by audio-visual integration. Other common techniques of sound source separation are a beam forming with a microphone array (Asano, Asoh, & Matsui 1999), ICA as blind source separation (Okuno, Ikeda, & Nakatani 1999), and computational auditory scene analysis (CASA) techniques for understanding general sounds. However, these techniques assume that assumes that the microphone setting is fixed. Some techniques assume that the number of microphones is more than or equal to the number of sound sources – an assumption that may not hold in a real-world environment. Asano *et al.* also reported a robot which separates and localizes sound sources by using a 8 ch circle microphone array in an ordinary office room (Asano *et al.* Sep 2001). However, their system requires a lot of measurement for separation and localization in ad-

vance, and has difficulty in sound source separation during motion, while human can hear during motion. It is not enough for robot audition to be deployed in the real world yet. A sound source separation method based on audio-visual integration has been reported (Nakagawa, Okuno, & Kitano 1999). However, it uses only simple visual clues for integration and works only in off-line and simulated environments because the data was created by convolution of a *head related transfer function (HRTF)* measured in an anechoic room.

For the third and fourth issues, stereo vision is introduced for accurate and robust localization even when a person looks away. In addition, a Kalman filter is implemented for reducing measurement and process noises in localization.

For the last issue, because a PC is added to the system for stereo vision, a more scalable network is required. In our network, gigabit and fast ether were combined to improve scalability. In addition, accurate synchronization between PCs is given by using a network time protocol (NTP) and an original synchronization protocol. To summarize, in this paper, we describe the following achievements:

1. sound source separation by using an auditory fovea
2. accurate stream formation by a Kalman filter
3. accurate localization by stereo vision
4. scalable network communication by the NTP and the synchronization protocol.

The rest of this paper is organized as follows: Section 2 describes the active direction-pass filter. Section 3 explains the real-time human tracking system refined by the Kalman filter and stereo vision. Section 4 evaluates the performance of the ADPF. The last sections provide a discussion and a conclusion.

Active Direction Pass Filter

The architecture of the ADPF is shown in Figure 1. The ADPF separates sound sources from four inputs – a spec-

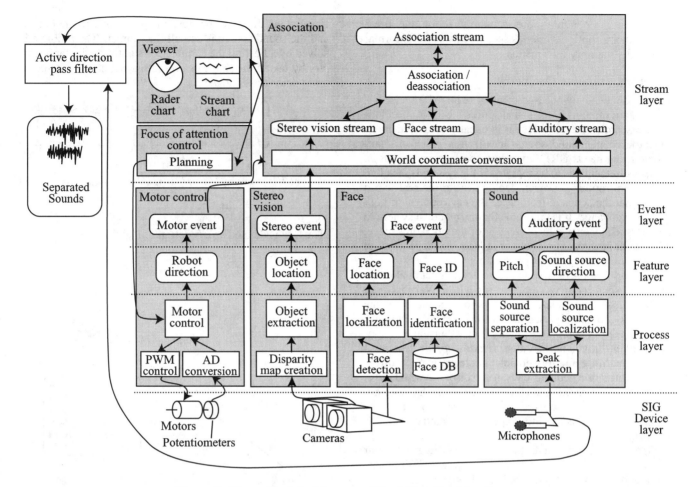

Figure 2: Hierarchical Architecture of Real-Time Tracking System

trum of input sound, interaural intensity difference (IID), interaural phase difference (IPD) and sound source directions. The spectrum is obtained from sound captured by the robot's microphone. The IPD and IID are calculated from spectra of the left and right channels. Sound source directions are obtained from streams generated in the real-time human tracking system as described in a later section.

The APDF uses two key techniques, auditory epipolar geometry and auditory fovea. The auditory epipolar geometry is a localization method by IPD without using HRTFs. The auditory epipolar geometry is described in the next section in detail. In this paper, the ADPF is implemented to use both HRTFs and auditory epipolar geometry for evaluation. The auditory fovea is used to control the pass range of the ADPF: the pass range is narrow in the front direction and wider in the periphery. The detailed algorithm of the ADPF is described below:

1. IPD $\Delta\varphi'$ and IID $\Delta\rho'$ in each sub-band are obtained by the difference between the left and right channels.
2. Let θ_s be the azimuth of a stream with current attention in the robot coordinate system in the real-time human tracking system. θ_s is sent to the ADPF through the gigabit ether network with consideration of the latency of the pro-

cessing.
3. The pass range $\delta(\theta_s)$ of the ADPF is selected according to θ_s. The pass range function δ has a minimum value in the *SIG* front direction, because then it has maximum sensitivity. δ has a larger value at the peripheral because of the lower sensitivity. Let us $\theta_l = \theta_s - \delta(\theta_s)$ and $\theta_h = \theta_s + \delta(\theta_s)$.
4. From a stream direction, the IPD $\Delta\varphi_E(\theta)$ and IID $\Delta\rho_E(\theta)$ are estimated for each sub-band by the auditory epipolar geometry. Likewise, the IPD $\Delta\varphi_H(\theta)$ and IID $\Delta\rho_H(\theta)$ are obtained from HRTFs.
5. The sub-bands are collected if the IPD and IID satisfy the specified condition. Three conditions are applied:

   A: $f < f_{th}$: $\Delta\varphi_E(\theta_l) \leq \Delta\varphi' \leq \Delta\varphi_E(\theta_h)$,
   B: $f < f_{th}$: $\Delta\varphi_H(\theta_l) \leq \Delta\varphi' \leq \Delta\varphi_H(\theta_h)$, and
   $f \geq f_{th}$: $\Delta\rho_H(\theta_l) \leq \Delta\rho' \leq \Delta\varphi_H(\theta_h)$,
   C: $f < f_{th}$: $\Delta\varphi_E(\theta_l) \leq \Delta\varphi' \leq \Delta\varphi_E(\theta_h)$, and
   $f \geq f_{th}$: $\Delta\rho_H(\theta_l) \leq \Delta\rho' \leq \Delta\varphi_H(\theta_h)$.

   f_{th} is the upper boundary of frequency which is efficient for localization by IPD. It depends on the baseline of the ears. In *SIG*'s case, the f_{th} is 1500 Hz.
6. A wave consisting of collected sub-bands is constructed.

Note, that to obtain a more accurate direction, the direction of an association stream is specified by visual information not by auditory information.

Auditory Epipolar Geometry

HRTFs obtained by measurement of a lot of impulse responses are often used for sound source localization in binaural research. Because HRTF is usually measured in an anechoic room, sound source localization in an ordinary echoic room needs HRTF including room acoustic, that is, the measurement has to be repeated if the system is installed at different room. However, deployment to the real world means that the acoustic features of the environment are not known in advance. It is infeasible for any practical system to require such extensive measurement of the operating space. Thus, audition system without or at least less dependent on HRTF is essential for practical systems.

Auditory Epipolar Geometry can extract directional information of sound sources without using HRTF (Nakadai *et al.* 2000a). In stereo vision research, epipolar geometry is one of the most commonly used localization methods (Faugeras 1993). Auditory epipolar geometry is an extension of epipolar geometry in vision (hereafter, *visual epipolar geometry*) to audition. Since auditory epipolar geometry extracts directional information geometrically, it can dispense with HRTF. However, the reported auditory epipolar geometry does not take the effect of the cover into account and so it must be refined. The refined auditory epipolar geometry works as follows:

First, for each sub-band, it calculates the IPD from a pair of spectra obtained by *fast fourier transform* (FFT). Then, the sound source direction is estimated by

$$\theta = D^{-1}\left(v/(2\pi f)\Delta\varphi\right), \quad (1)$$

where D represents the difference between the distances of the left and right ears from a sound source, v is the velocity of sound, f is the frequency of sound and $\Delta\varphi$ is *IPD*. In this paper, the velocity of sound is fixed at 340m/sec, irrespective of temperature and humidity.

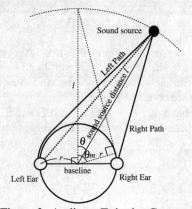

Figure 3: Auditory Epipolar Geometry

On defining D, the influence of the cover of *SIG* should be considered. The cover prevents sound from reaching the ears directly. The sound in Figure 3, for example, has to

travel along the cover because the path between the left ear and the sound source is actually not direct. The problem is solved by adjusting the formula for auditory epipolar geometry by taking the shape of *SIG* into account. The formulae are specified as follows:

$$D(\theta, l) = \begin{cases} r(\pi - \theta - \theta_m) + \delta(\theta, l) & \left(0 \leq \theta < \frac{\pi}{2} - \theta_m\right) \\ r(\pi - 2\theta) & \left(|\theta - \frac{\pi}{2}| \leq \theta_m\right) \\ r(\theta - \theta_m) + \delta(\pi - \theta, l) & \left(\frac{\pi}{2} + \theta_m < \theta \leq \pi\right) \end{cases}$$
$$(2)$$

$$\delta(\theta, l) = \sqrt{l^2 - r^2} - \sqrt{l^2 + r^2 - 2rl\cos\theta}, \quad (3)$$

$$\theta_m = \arcsin\frac{r}{l}. \quad (4)$$

Thus, D is defined as a function of θ and l. Figure 4 shows

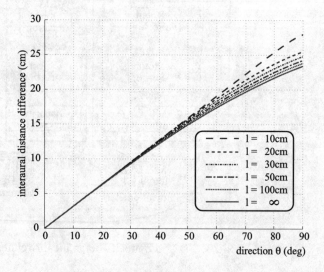

Figure 4: IPD and distance from sound source

the relationship of D, θ and l obtained by simulation. The larger the θ, the bigger the influence of l. However, when l is more than 50 cm, the influence of l can be ignored. In such a case, we can take l to be infinite and define D as a function of only θ as follows:

$$D(\theta) = \lim_{l\to\infty} D(\theta, l)$$
$$= r(\theta + \sin\theta). \quad (5)$$

Since the baselines for vision and audition are in parallel in *SIG*, whenever a sound source is localized by visual epipolar geometry, it can be easily converted into the angle θ. This means that a symbolic representation of direction is used as a clue for the integration of the visual and auditory information. We have reported the feasibility of such an integration based on epipolar geometry (Nakadai *et al.* 2000a).

Real-Time Human Tracking System

The following sections describe other components associated with the ADPF – the humanoid *SIG* and the real-time human tracking system. They provide input to the ADPF.

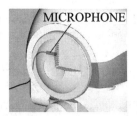

Figure 6: *SIG* microphone

Figure 5: Humanoid *SIG*

Compared with the reported system (Nakadai *et al.* 2001), the real-time tracking system has been improved by tracking based on a Kalman filter which gives a stronger directional property.

Platform: SIG

The upper torso humanoid *SIG*, shown in Figure 5, is a testbed for humanoid-human interaction . *SIG* has a fiber reinforced plastic (FRP) cover designed to acoustically separate the *SIG* inner and external worlds. A pair of CCD cameras (Sony EVI-G20) is used for stereo vision. Two pairs of microphones are used for auditory processing. One pair is located in the left and right ear positions for sound source localization (Figure 6). The other pair is installed inside the cover, mainly for canceling noise from the robot's motors. *SIG* has 4 DC motors (4 DOFs), the position and velocity of which are controlled through potentiometers.

The Real-Time Human Tracking System

The architecture of the real-time human tracking system is shown in Figure 2. It consists of seven modules, Sound, Face, Stereo Vision, Association, Focus-of-Attention, Motor Control and Viewer.

Sound localizes sound sources. Face detects multiple faces by combining skin-color detection, correlation based matching, and multiple scale image generation (Hidai *et al.* 2000). It identifies each face by Linear Discriminant Analysis (LDA), which creates an optimal subspace to distinguish classes and continuously updates the subspace on demand with a little of computation (Hiraoka *et al.* 2000). In addition, the faces are localized in 3-D world coordinates by assuming an average face size. Stereo Vision is a new module to localize precisely lengthwise objects such as people precisely by using fast disparity map generation (Kagami *et al.* 1999). It improves the robustness of the system by being able to track a person who looks away and does not talk. Association forms *streams* and associates them into a higher level representation, that is, an *association* stream according to proximity. The directions of the streams are sent to the ADPF with captured sounds. Focus-of-Attention plans *SIG*'s movement based on the status of streams. Motor Control is activated by the Focus-of-Attention module and generates pulse width modulation (PWM) signals to the DC motors. Viewer shows the status of auditory, visual and association

streams in the radar and scrolling windows. The whole system works in real-time with a small latency of 500 ms by distributed processing with 5 PCs, networked through gigabit and fast ethernet.

Stream Formation and Association: Streams are formed in Association by connecting events from Sound, Face and Stereo Vision to a time course.

First, since location information about sound, face and stereo vision events is observed in a *SIG* coordinate system, the coordinates are converted into world coordinates by comparing a motor event observed at the same time.

The converted events are connected to a stream through a Kalman filter based algorithm. The Kalman filter efficiently reduces the influence of process and measurement noises in localization, especially in auditory processing with bigger ambiguities.

In Kalman filter based stream formation, position p with a dimension N is approximated by a recursive equation defined by

$$
\begin{aligned}
p_{k+1} &= p_k + v_k \Delta T \\
&= p_k + (p_k - p_{k-l})/l,
\end{aligned} \tag{6}
$$

where l is a parameter for average velocity.

When x_k is a state vector represented as $(p_k, p_{k-1}, \cdots, p_{k-l})$ and y_k is a measurement represented as a position vector, and functions to estimate the state and measurement of the process are defined by

$$
\begin{aligned}
x_{k+1} &= F x_k + G w_k, \\
y_k &= H x_k + v_k,
\end{aligned} \tag{7}
$$

where w_k and v_k represent the process and measurement noise, respectively. F, G and H are defined as follows:

$$
F = \begin{pmatrix} \frac{l+1}{l}I_N & 0 & \cdots & 0 & -\frac{1}{l}I_N \\ I_N & & & 0 & \\ & \ddots & & & 0 \\ 0 & & & I_N & \end{pmatrix}, \tag{8}
$$

$$
\begin{aligned}
G &= \begin{pmatrix} I_N & 0 & \cdots & 0 \end{pmatrix}^T, \\
H &= \begin{pmatrix} I_N & 0 & \cdots & 0 \end{pmatrix},
\end{aligned} \tag{9}
$$

where I_N is the identity matrix of $N \times N$ dimensions.

Then, the Kalman filter is defined as follows:

$$
\begin{aligned}
\hat{x}_{k|k} &= \hat{x}_{k|k-1} + K_k(y_k - H\hat{x}_{k|k-1}), \\
\hat{x}_{k+1|k} &= F x_{k|k}, \tag{10}
\end{aligned}
$$

$$
K_k = \hat{P}_{k|k-1}H^T(I_N + H\hat{P}_{k|k-1}H^T)^{-1}, \tag{11}
$$

$$
\begin{aligned}
\hat{P}_{k|k} &= \hat{P}_{k|k-1} - K_k H \hat{P}_{k|k-1}, \\
\hat{P}_{k+1|k} &= F \hat{P}_{k|k} F^T + \sigma_w^2/\sigma_v^2 G G^T, \\
\hat{x}_{0|-1} &= \bar{x}_0, \quad \hat{P}_{0|-1} = \sum x_0/\sigma_v^2, \tag{12}
\end{aligned}
$$

where $\hat{x}$ is an estimation of x, K_k is the Kalman gain, $\hat{P}$ is an error covariance matrix. σ_w^2 and σ_v^2 are variance-covariance matrixes of w_k and v_k.

An current position vector is estimated by

$$
\hat{y}_k = H\hat{x}_{k|k}. \tag{13}
$$

In sound stream formation, when a sound stream and an event have a harmonic relationship, and the difference in azimuth between $\hat{y}_k$ of the stream and a sound event is less than $\pm 10°$, they are connected.

In face and stereo vision stream formation, a face or a stereo stream event is connected to a face or a stereo vision stream when the difference in distance between $\hat{y}_k$ of the stream and the event is within $40\,cm$, and when they have the same event ID. An event ID is a face name or an object ID generated in face or stereo vision module.

When the system judges that multiple streams originate from the same person, they are associated into an association stream, a higher level stream representation. When one of the streams forming an association stream is terminated, the terminated stream is removed from the association stream, and the association stream is de-associated into one or more separated streams.

Control of Tracking: The tracking is controlled by Focus-of-Attention to keep the direction of a stream with attention and sends motor events to Motor. By selecting a stream with attention and tracking it, the ADPF can continue to make the best use of foveal processing The streams are separated, according to the surrounding situations, that is, the Focus-of-Attention control is programmable. In this paper, for the ADPF, the precedence of Focus-of-Attention control for an associated stream, including a sound stream, has the highest priority, a sound stream has the second priority and other visual streams have the third priority.

Performance Evaluation

The performance of the ADPF was evaluated by two kinds of experiments. In these experiments, *SIG* and loudspeakers of B&W Nautilus 805 were located in a room of 10 square meters. The *SIG* and loudspeakers were set at exactly the same height, 1 m apart shown in Figure 7. The number of loudspeakers depends on each experiment. The direction of the loudspeaker was represented as 0° when facing towards the *SIG*.

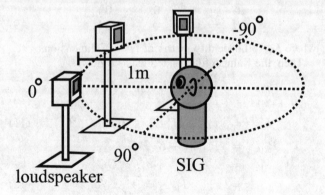

Figure 7: Conditions in the evaluation

For speech data, 20 sentences were read by men and women from the Mainichi Newspaper articles in ASJ Continuous Speech Corpus. Four kinds of metrics were used in the evaluation:

1. a difference in SNR in the frequency domain between the input and separated speech defined by

$$R_1 = 10 \log_{10} \frac{\sum_{j=1}^{n} \sum_{i=1}^{m} (|sp(i,j)| - \beta |sp_o(i,j)|)^2}{\sum_{j=1}^{n} \sum_{i=1}^{m} (|sp(i,j)| - \beta |sp_s(i,j)|)^2}, \quad (14)$$

where $sp(i,j)$, $sp_o(i,j)$ and $sp_s(i,j)$ are the spectra of the original signal, the signal picked-up by the robot's microphones and the signal separated by the ADPF, respectively. m and n are the number of sub-bands and samples, respectively. β is the attenuation ratio of amplitude between the original and observed signals.

2. signal loss between the input and separated speech is defined by

$$R_2 = 10 \log_{10} \frac{\sum_{n \in S} (s(n) - \beta s_o(n))^2}{\sum_{n \in S} (s(n) - \beta s_s(n))^2}, \quad (15)$$

where $s(n)$, $s_o(n)$ and $s_s(n)$ are the original signal, the signal picked by the robot's microphones and the signal separated by the ADPF, respectively. S is a set of samples with signals, that is, a set of i satisfying $s(i) - \beta s_o(i) \geq 0$.

3. effect of noise suppression is defined by

$$R_3 = 10 \log_{10} \frac{\sum_{n \in N} (s(n) - \beta s_o(n))^2}{\sum_{n \in N} (s(n) - \beta s_s(n))^2}, \quad (16)$$

where $s(n)$, $s_o(n)$ and $s_s(n)$ are the same as Eq. (15). N is a set of samples with noises, that is, a set of i satisfying $s(i) - \beta s_o(i) < 0$.

4. evaluation by experts in audio signal processing.

Experiment 1: The errors of sound source localization of Sound, Face and Stereo Vision were measured with the sound source direction varied between 0° and 90°.

Experiment 2: The efficiency of the Kalman filter was measured. Two loudspeakers were used. One was fixed in the direction of 60°. The other was repeatedly moved from left to right within $\pm 30°$. Voices from the second loudspeaker were extracted by the ADPF. Two kinds of sound streams – with and without the Kalman filter – were used as inputs to the ADPF. The extracted sounds were compared by R_1.

Experiment 3: The efficiency of the ADPF by each filtering condition **A** to **C** described in the section "Active Direction Pass Filter" were measured by using the metrics R_1, R_2 and R_3. The separation of two or three simultaneous voices were assessed. The first loudspeaker was fixed at 0°. In the separation of two simultaneous voices, the second one was facing in a direction of 30°, 60° and 90° with respect to the *SIG*. In the separation of three simultaneous voices, the second and third speakers were in a direction of $\pm 30°$, $\pm 60°$ and $\pm 90°$ with respect to the *SIG*. The loudspeakers simultaneously emitted voices of the same volume. The filter pass range $\delta(\theta)$ was $\pm 20°$ when the loudspeaker was in the direction of 0° and 30°,

Metrics for evaluation		$R_1(dB)$				$R_2(dB)$				$R_3(dB)$			
Direction of a speaker		0°	30°	60°	90°	0°	30°	60°	90°	0°	30°	60°	90°
Condition of ADPF	A	2.0	1.3	2.2	0.5	-2.8	-3.1	-3.3	-7.7	10.4	4.7	2.6	-3.5
	B	2.2	1.4	1.6	0.8	-2.1	-3.4	-3.8	-7.3	9.1	4.6	3.4	-2.8
	C	2.2	1.1	2.1	0.6	-2.5	-4.0	-3.3	-7.7	10.3	6.8	2.6	-3.5

Table 1: Evaluation by R_1, R_2 and R_3 for separation of two simultaneous speeches

Interval of speakers		30°			60°			90°		
Direction of each speaker		−30°	0°	30°	−60°	0°	60°	−90°	0°	−90°
Condition of ADPF	A	4.9	8.1	5.1	3.2	9.6	3.1	-1.9	10.5	-1.7
	B	4.8	9.1	4.7	3.7	9.2	3.8	-1.7	9.1	-1.3
	C	5.7	7.4	5.9	3.5	9.6	3.1	-2.0	9.8	-2.0

Table 2: Evaluation by $R_3(dB)$ for separation of three simultaneous speeches

and was $\pm30°$ when the loudspeaker was in the direction of 60° and 90°. These values were defined according to the performance of the auditory fovea for a single sound source.

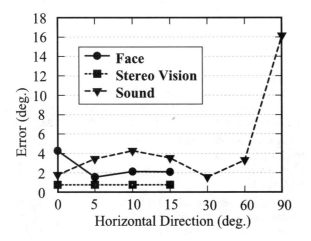

Figure 8: Error of localization by Face, Stereo Vision and Sound

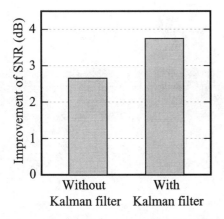

Figure 9: Moving speaker extraction

Sound source localization by Stereo Vision was the most

accurate, as shown in Figure 8. The error was within 1°. Generally, localization by vision is more accurate than by audition. However, Sound has the advantage of an omni-directional sensor. That is, Sound can estimate the direction of sound from more than $\pm15°$ of azimuth. The sensitivity of localization by Sound depends on the sound source direction. It was the best in the front direction. The error was within $\pm5°$ from 0° to 30° and became worse at more than 30°. This proves that the correctness of using the auditory fovea and the efficiency of active motion, such as turning to face a sound source.

Figure 9 shows that the performance of the ADPF was increased by about 1 dB by the Kalman filter based stream formation. This indicates that the Kalman filter provides improved stream formation and accurate sound source direction.

Tables 1 and 2 show the results of sound source separation of two and three simultaneous voices, respectively. The similar tendencies of the performance were found in all filtering conditions. The difference between filtering condition **A**, which uses frequencies of below than 1500 Hz, and the other conditions is small, because sub-bands with frequencies higher than 1500 Hz collected by IID have lower power. This proves that auditory epipolar geometry is enough to separate sound sources by the ADPF even in real-world environments. R_1 and R_3 were the optimum in the front direction of *SIG*, and became worse towards the periphery. In the front direction, the efficiency of noise suppression was about 9 dB even with three simultaneous voices. But separation of two speakers closer together than 30° would be more difficult.

The loss of signal is 2–4 dB by R_2 in Table 1. According to two experts in audio signal processing, the filtering condition with the best clarity is **C**. The quality of the separated sounds is as good as the separation by 14 ch linear or 16 ch circle microphone arrays. On evaluation by listening, the ADPF is good at sound source separation. Our method of sound source separation currently does not have a function to cope with overlap in the frequency sub-bands of the different sources. This means that the system deals with sound mixture with a small amount of overlap such as voices properly. The system should have a function to solve overlap problems for more precise separation and separation of sounds with a lot of overlap such as music.

Conclusion

This paper reports sound source separation by an ADPF connected to a real-time multiple speaker tracking system. The ADPF with adaptive sensitivity control is shown to be effective in improving sound source separation. The sensitivity of the ADPF has not been reported so far in the literature and the idea of the ADPF lies in active motion to face a sound source to make the best use of the sensitivity. The ADPF would be efficient for front-end processing for Automatic Speech Recognition (ASR). The combination of the most up-to-date robust automatic speech recognition with the ADPF filter is one exciting research project now being planned.

Acknowledgements

We thank Prof. Tatsuya Kawahara of Kyoto University and Prof. Seiichi Nakagawa of Toyohashi University of Technology for their invaluable advice. We also thank Ken-ichi Hidai of Sony Corporation for his contribution which was made when he was in our laboratory and our colleagues of Symbiotic Intelligence Group, Kitano Symbiotic Systems Project for their discussions.

References

Aloimonos, Y.; Weiss, I.; and Bandyopadhyay., A. 1987. Active vision. *International Journal of Computer Vision.*

Asano, F.; Asoh, H.; and Matsui, T. 1999. Sound source localization and signal separation for office robot "jijo-2". In *Proc. of IEEE Int. Conf. on Multisensor Fusion and Integration for Intelligent Systems (MFI-99)*, 243–248.

Asano, F.; Goto, M.; Itou, K.; and Asoh, H. Sep. 2001. Real-time sound source localization and separation system and its application to automatic speech recognition. In *Proceedings of International Conference on Speech Processing (Eurospeech 2001)*, 1013–1016. ESCA.

Blauert, J. 1999. *Spatial Hearing.* The MIT Press.

Faugeras, O. D. 1993. *Three Dimensional Computer Vision: A Geometric Viewpoint.* MA.: The MIT Press.

Hidai, K.; Mizoguchi, H.; Hiraoka, K.; Tanaka, M.; Shigehara, T.; and Mishima, T. 2000. Robust face detection against brightness fluctuation and size variation. In *Proc. of IEEE/RAS Int. Conf. on Intelligent Robots and Systems (IROS-2000)*, 1397–1384. IEEE.

Hiraoka, K.; Yoshizawa, S.; Hidai, K.; Hamahira, M.; Mizoguchi, H.; and Mishima, T. 2000. Convergence analysis of online linear discriminant analysis. In *Proc. of IEEE/INNS/ENNS Int. Joint Conference on Neural Networks*, III–387–391. IEEE.

Kagami, S.; Okada, K.; Inaba, M.; and Inoue, H. 1999. Real-time 3d optical flow generation system. In *Proc. of Int. Conf. on Multisensor Fusion and Integration for Intelligent Systems (MFI'99)*, 237–242.

Klarquist, W., and Bovik, A. 1998. Fovea: A foveated vergent active stereo vision system for dynamic 3-dimensional scene recovery. *RA* 14(5):755–770.

Nakadai, K.; Lourens, T.; Okuno, H. G.; and Kitano, H. 2000a. Active audition for humanoid. In *Proc. of 17th National Conference on Artificial Intelligence (AAAI-2000)*, 832–839. AAAI.

Nakadai, K.; Matsui, T.; Okuno, H. G.; and Kitano, H. 2000b. Active audition system and humanoid exterior design. In *Proc. of IEEE/RAS Int. Conf. on Intelligent Robots and Systems (IROS-2000)*, 1453–1461. IEEE.

Nakadai, K. Hidai, K.; Mizoguchi, H.; Okuno, H. G.; and Kitano, H. 2001. Real-time auditory and visual multiple-object tracking for robots. In *Proc. of the 17th Int. Joint Conf. on Atificial Intelligence (IJCAI-01)*, 1424–1432.

Nakagawa, Y.; Okuno, H. G.; and Kitano, H. 1999. Using vision to improve sound source separation. In *Proc. of 16th National Conference on Artificial Intelligence (AAAI-99)*, 768–775. AAAI.

Okuno, H.; Nakadai, K.; Lourens, T.; and Kitano, H. 2001. Separating three simultaneous speeches with two microphones by integrating auditory and visual processing. In *Proc. of European Conf. on Speech Processing(Eurospeech 2001)*. ESCA.

Okuno, H.; Ikeda, S.; and Nakatani, T. 1999. Combining independent component analysis and sound stream segregation. In *Proc. of IJCAI-99 Workshop on Computational Auditory Scene Analysis (CASA'99)*, 92–98. IJCAI.

Rougeaux, S., and Kuniyoshi, Y. 1997. Robust real-time tracking on an active vision head. In *Proc. of IEEE/RAS Int. Conf. on Intelligent Robots and Systems (IROS-97)*, 873–879. IEEE.

Schuller, G., and Pollak, G. Disproportionate frequency representation in the inferior colliculus of horsehoe bats: evidence for an "acoustic fovea". In *J. Comp. Physiol. A.*

Towards CST-Enhanced Summarization

Zhu Zhang
School of Information
University of Michigan
Ann Arbor, MI 48109
zhuzhang@umich.edu

Sasha Blair-Goldensohn
School of Information
University of Michigan
Ann Arbor, MI 48109
sashabg@umich.edu

Dragomir R. Radev
School of Information and
Department of EECS
University of Michigan
Ann Arbor, MI 48109
radev@umich.edu

Abstract

In this paper, we propose to enhance the process of automatic extractive multi-document text summarization by taking into account cross-document structural relationships as posited in Cross-document Structure Theory (CST). An arbitrary multi-document extract can be CST-enhanced by replacing low-salience sentences with other sentences that increase the total number of CST relationships included in the summary. We show that CST-enhanced summaries outperform their unmodified counterparts using the relative utility evaluation metric. We also show that the effect of a CST relationship on an extract depends on its type.

Introduction

Text summarization

Text summarization is "... the process of distilling the most important information from one a source (or sources) to produce an abridged version for a particular user (or users) and task (or tasks)" (Mani & Maybury 1999).

One distinguishes single-document summarization (SDS) and multi-document summarization (MDS). MDS, which our approach will be focusing on, is much more complicated than SDS in nature. Besides the obvious difference in input size, several other factors account for the complication, e.g.:

- Multiple documents might come from different sources, be written by different authors, and therefore have different styles, although they are topically related. This means that a summarizer cannot make the same coherence assumption that it can for a single article.

- Multiple documents might come out of different time frames. Therefore an intelligent summarizer has to take care of the temporal information and try to maximize the overall temporal cohesiveness of the summary.

- Descriptions of the same event may differ in perspective, or even conflict with one another. The summarizer should provide a mechanism to deal with issues of this kind.

We make the distinction between information-extraction-vs. sentence-extraction-based summarizers. The former, such as SUMMONS (Radev & McKeown 1998), rely on

an information extraction system to extract very specific aspects of some events and generate abstracts thereof. This approach can produce good summaries but is usually knowledge intensive and domain dependent. Sentence extraction techniques (Luhn 1958; Radev, Jing, & Budzikowska 2000), on the other hand, compute a score for each sentence based on certain features and output the most highly ranked sentences. This approach is conceptually straightforward and usually domain independent, but the summaries produced by it often need further revision to be more smooth and coherent.

Centroid-based summarization and MEAD

Centroid-based summarization is a method of multi-document summarization. It operates on a cluster of documents with a common subject (the cluster may be produced by a Topic Detection and Tracking, or TDT, system). A cluster centroid, a collection of the most important words from the whole cluster, is built. The centroid is then used to determine which sentences from individual documents are most representative of the entire cluster.

MEAD is a publicly available toolkit for multi-document summarization (Radev, Jing, & Budzikowska 2000; MEAD 2002). It is based on sentence extraction. For each sentence in a cluster of related documents, MEAD computes a number of features and uses a linear combination of them to determine what sentences are most salient.

In this paper, we will investigate the effect of inter-document rhetorical relationships on summary extraction. Two potential summaries for the same cluster are illustrated in Figure 1. As we can see, there is an obvious contradiction between sentences 2 of both summaries (which are obviously from different sources). The eventual summary is well justified to either include both of them (to provide an all-sided view of the event, e.g.) or to include only one of them (to accommodate readers' bias over sources, e.g.).

The structure of the paper will be the following. First we highlight some related work; second we introduce the CST theory (Radev 2000) that we developed and formalize our framework; third, we present a CST identification user study; then we propose the idea of enhancing summarization using CST relationships and present corresponding experimental results; we conclude the paper with some discussion of future work.

| S1: A Gulf Air Airbus A320 carrying 143 people from Cairo, Egypt, to Bahrain crashed today in the Persian Gulf. |
| S2: A320 has a good accident record; the crash in the Persian Gulf today that killed 143 people was the aircraft's *fourth* air disaster. |
| S3: ... |

| S1: A Gulf Air Airbus A320 carrying 143 people from Cairo, Egypt, to Bahrain crashed today in the Persian Gulf. |
| S2: A320 has been involved in *six* accidents, including Wednesday's. |
| S3: ... |

Figure 1: Two sample summaries

Related work

Our work bears a strong connection to Rhetorical Structure Theory (RST) (Mann & Thompson 1988), which is a comprehensive functional theory of text organization. RST offers an explanation of the coherence of texts by positing the existence of coherent relations among text spans. Most relations consist of one or more *nuclei* (the more central components of a rhetorical relation) and zero or more *satellites* (the supporting component of the relation). An example of a RST relation is "evidence", which is decomposed into a nucleus (a claim) and a satellite (text that supports the claim).

RST is intentionally limited to single documents as it is based on the notion of deliberate writing. In contrast, Cross-document Structure Theory (CST), the theory that we propose, will attempt to discover rhetorical structure in sets of related textual documents. Unlike RST, we cannot rely on the deliberateness of writing. We can, however, make use of some observations of structure across documents that, while clearly not deliberate in the RST sense, can be quite predictable and useful.

A recent representative work on RST and its applications is (Marcu 1997). He proposes a first-order formalization of the high-level, rhetorical structure of text, and provides theoretical analysis and empirical comparison of four algorithms for automatic derivation of text structures. A set of empirically motivated algorithms are designed for rhetorical parsing, i.e., determining the elementary textual units of a text, hypothesizing rhetorical relations that hold among these units, and eventually deriving the discourse structure of the text. Most relevant to our work, Marcu explores using RST for summarization. The basic idea of the discourse-based summarization algorithm is to induce a partial ordering on the importance of the units in a text based on the text structure, and output the most important units according to a certain threshold.

Another significant piece of work that inspired ours is (Salton *et al.* 1997). The authors generate intra-document semantic hyperlinks (between passages of a document which are related by a lexical similarity higher than a certain threshold) and characterize the structure of the text based on the intra-document linkage pattern. They represent each single document in the form of text relationship maps. A text summary is generated by selectively extracting important paragraphs from the text, more specifically, by automatically identifying the important paragraphs in a text relationship map and traversing the selected nodes in text order or along a certain path. The assumption underlying their technique is that highly "bushy" nodes are more likely to contain information central to the topic of the article.

All summarization techniques described above are limited to one single document. What we present in this paper is a more general framework for multi-document summarization using cross-document rhetorical relationships. We get better summaries by taking these relationships into account.

Cross-document Structure Theory

We propose Cross-document Structure Theory (CST), which enables multi-document summarization through identification of cross-document rhetorical relationships within a cluster of related documents. The proposed taxonomy for CST relationships can be found in Table 1. Notice that some CST relationships, such as *identity*, are symmetric (*multinuclear*, in RST terms), while some other ones, such as *subsumption*, do have directionality, i.e., they have *nucleus* and *satellite*. Some of the relationships are direct descendents of those used in (Radev & McKeown 1998). However, in CST, the relationships are domain-independent.

Whereas Marcu relied on "cue phrases" in implementing algorithms to discover the valid RST "trees" for a single document, such a technique is not very plausible for discovering CST "links" between documents. For instance, the "cue phrase" "*although statement X, statement Y*" might indicate the RST relationship "concession" in some circumstances. Marcu is able to use these phrases for guidance because of the conventions of writing and the valid assumption that authors tend to write documents using certain rhetorical techniques. However, in the case of multiple documents and CST inter-document relationships (links), we cannot expect to encounter a reliable analog to the cue phrase. This is because separate documents, even when they are related to a common topic, are generally not written with an overarching structure in mind. Particularly in the case of news, we are most often looking at articles which are written by different authors working from partially overlapping information as it becomes available. So, except in cases of explicit citation, we cannot expect to find a static phrase in one document which reliably indicates a particular relationship to some phrase in another document.

How, then, to approach the problem of discovering CST relationships in a set of documents? We present in a later section an exploratory experiment, in which human subjects were asked to find these relationships over a multi-document news cluster.

Formalization of the problem
Extractive summarizer

Suppose we have a document cluster C, which contains documents d_1 through d_l; each document d_i entails a list of sentences s_1 through s_{n_i}. The set of all sentences in the cluster is defined as S.

An extractive summarizer E produces an extract S', such that $S' \subset S$. Technically, an extract is simply a condensed representation of a summary, i.e., there is a one-to-one map-

Relationship	Description	Text span 1 (S1)	Text span 2 (S2)
Identity	The same text appears in more than one location	Tony Blair was elected for a second term today.	Tony Blair was elected for a second term today.
Equivalence (Paraphrase)	Two text spans have the same information content	Derek Bell is experiencing a resurgence in his career.	Derek Bell is having a "comeback year."
Translation	Same information content in different languages	Shouts of "Viva la revolucion!" echoed through the night.	The rebels could be heard shouting, "Long live the revolution".
Subsumption	S1 contains all information in S2, plus additional information not in S2	With 3 wins this year, Green Bay has the best record in the NFL.	Green Bay has 3 wins this year.
Contradiction	Conflicting information	There were 122 people on the downed plane.	126 people were aboard the plane.
Historical Background	S1 gives historical context to information in S2	This was the fourth time a member of the Royal Family has gotten divorced.	The Duke of Windsor was divorced from the Duchess of Windsor yesterday.
Citation	S2 explicitly cites document S1	Prince Albert then went on to say, "I never gamble."	An earlier article quoted Prince Albert as saying "I never gamble."
Modality	S1 presents a qualified version of the information in S2, e.g., using "allegedly"	Sean "Puffy" Combs is reported to own several multimillion dollar estates.	Puffy owns four multimillion dollar homes in the New York area.
Attribution	S1 presents an attributed version of information in S2, e.g. using "According to CNN,"	According to a top Bush advisor, the President was alarmed at the news.	The President was alarmed to hear of his daughter's low grades.
Summary	S1 summarizes S2.	The Mets won the Title in seven games.	After a grueling first six games, the Mets came from behind tonight to take the Title.
Follow-up	S1 presents additional information which has happened since S2	102 casualties have been reported in the earthquake region.	So far, no casualties from the quake have been confirmed.
Indirect speech	S1 indirectly quotes something which was directly quoted in S2	Mr. Cuban then gave the crowd his personal guarantee of free Chalupas.	"I'll personally guarantee free Chalupas," Mr. Cuban announced to the crowd.
Elaboration / Refinement	S1 elaborates or provides details of some information given more generally in S2	50% of students are under 25; 20% are between 26 and 30; the rest are over 30.	Most students at the University are under 30.
Fulfillment	S1 asserts the occurrence of an event predicted in S2	After traveling to Austria Thursday, Mr. Green returned home to New York.	Mr. Green will go to Austria Thursday.
Description	S1 describes an entity mentioned in S2	Greenfield, a retired general and father of two, has declined to comment.	Mr. Greenfield appeared in court yesterday.
Reader Profile	S1 and S2 provide similar information written for a different audience.	The Durian, a fruit used in Asian cuisine, has a strong smell.	The dish is usually made with Durian.
Change of perspective	The same entity presents a differing opinion or presents a fact in a different light.	Giuliani criticized the Officer's Union as "too demanding" in contract talks.	Giuliani praised the Officer's Union, which provides legal aid and advice to members.

Table 1: CST relationships and examples

ping between extracts and summaries. We will not distinguish these two terms from now on.

The summarizer E can be characterized by the following components:

1. A scoring algorithm A_S that computes a numeric score, which is a function of a number of features, for each sentence. Specifically, $score(s_i) = A_S(f_{1i}, f_{2i}, \ldots f_{ki})$, where f_1 through f_k are the features of each sentence.

2. A re-ranker R that adjusts sentence scores by looking at some other (usually global) information, such as lexical similarity or CST relationships between pair of sentences. Specifically, $score(s_i) = score(s_i) + \Delta(S)$, where the adjustment is determined is by certain global information with regard to S. Notice that Δ can be negative.

3. A compression ratio r, such that $0 \le r \le 1$.

4. A ranking algorithm A_R that selects the highest-score sentences, such that $N_{S'} = \lceil N_S \cdot r \rceil$ where N_S is the number of sentences in the original text and $N_{S'}$ is the number of sentences in the extract.

CST connectivity

For any extract S', we can define a connectivity matrix M, the elements of which are defined as:

$$m_{ij} = \begin{cases} 1 & : \quad \text{connectivity condition holds} \\ 0 & : \quad \text{otherwise} \end{cases}$$

The CST connectivity of the extract S' is defined as

$$\chi = \sum_{i=1}^{N_{S'}} \sum_{j=1}^{N_{S'}} m_{ij}$$

Depending on our purposes, we could define different connectivity conditions for the elements in the connectivity matrix to be equal to 1. In our study, we define the condition as existence of a certain relationship with agreement strength higher than a certain threshold.

CST identification

In this section, we present an experiment in which subjects were asked to analyze a set of documents using the set of proposed relationships in Table 1. We then present the experimental results and consider the implications for further work in CST.

Experiment 1: establishing CST relationships

The experiment which we conducted required subjects to read a set of news articles and write down the inter-document relationships which they observed. Specifically, the 11 articles were on the subject of an airplane crash of a flight from Egypt to Bahrain in August 2000. They were written by several different news organizations and retrieved from online news web sites in the days following the accident.

The subjects were eight graduate students and one professor. The instructions specified five article pairs comprised of random pairings from within the eleven articles mentioned

above. No article was included in more than two pairs. For each pair, the subjects were instructed to first read the articles carefully. They were then instructed to look for and note down any occurrences of relationships like those in Figure 1. (Subjects were also provided with the examples shown in Figure 1 to illustrate each relationship type.) It was stated in the instructions that the relationships comprised only a "proposed" list, and were not to be considered exhaustive. Subjects were invited to make up new relationship types if they observed cross-document relationships which did not correspond to those in Table 1.

Although subjects were given examples of the proposed relationships at the sentence level, the instructions also explicitly stated that it was possible for a relationship to hold with one or both text spans being more than one sentence long. There was no provision for subjects to mark text spans shorter than a full sentence. Subjects were instructed not to pay attention to possible *intra*-document rhetorical relationships. Also, subjects were instructed that it was possible for more than one relationship to exist across the same pair of text spans, and to note down as many relationships as they observed for each pair of text spans.

Results

A summary of the raw results of the experiment is shown in Table 2. The relationships are presented in descending order of observed frequency. On average, each subject identified approximately 45 occurrences of the proposed relationships. The relationships "Elaboration/Refinement," "Equivalence," and "Description" were identified most frequently. Other relationships, such as "Translation," "Citation," and "Summary," were observed either never or only by one subject. Although subjects were encouraged in the study instructions to name new relationships, none did so.

Relationship Type	Sum	Average
Elaboration / Refinement	85	9.44
Equivalence	70	7.78
Description	64	7.11
Historical Background	44	4.89
Follow-up	42	4.67
Subsumption	39	4.22
Contradiction	31	3.22
Attribution	15	1.67
Identity	7	0.78
Indirect speech	6	0.67
Fulfillment	4	0.44
Modality	2	0.22
Summary	1	0.11
Reader Profile	1	0.11
Change of Perspective	1	0.11
Translation	0	0.00
Citation	0	0.00
Total	415	45.44

Table 2: Identifications of CST relationships by type

Table 3 describes the sentence pairs for which judges noted relationships. The total number of sentence pairs for all five article pairs assigned was 4579, which is $\sum_{i=1}^{5} n_i \times m_i$, where i is the number of the article pair, n is the number of sentences in the first article in the pair, and m is the number of sentences in the second article in the pair.

Judges Finding a Relationship	Number of Sentence Pairs
No Judges	4,291
One Judge	200
Multiple Judges	88

Table 3: Sentence pairs by number of judges marking a CST relationship

As can be seen in Table 3, there are 88 sentence pairs for which multiple judges identify at least one CST relationship. Table 4 describes the breakdown of these 88 pairs in terms of inter-judge agreement. Although subjects were permitted to mark more than one relationship per sentence pair, they are counted as "in agreement" here if at least one of the relations they marked agrees with one of the relations marked by another judge.

Discrete Relationship Types Observed	Judges in Agreement	Sentences
Only one	All	16
More than one	At least two	35
More than one	None	37

Table 4: Judge agreement on relationship types among sentence pairs marked by multiple judges

Observations

Because our data comes from observations about a subset of document pairs from a single news cluster, it would clearly be premature to make conclusions about the natural frequencies of these relationships based on the data in Table 2. Nonetheless, we can at least speculate that human subjects are capable of identifying some subset of these relationships when reading news articles.

We obviously need more data before we can say if the lack of identifications for those unobserved / rarely observed relationships is because of a true lack of frequency or some other factor. For instance, some of the proposed relationship names, like "modality," may not be intuitive enough for judges to feel comfortable identifying them, even when examples are given.

However, the most encouraging data concerns the relatively high level of overlap when multiple judges made an observation for a sentence. In 51 of 88 cases where more than one judge marked a sentence pair, at least two judges concurred about at least one relationship holding for the pair. Although approximately two-thirds of the marked pairs were marked by only one judge, the overall data sparseness makes this ratio less discouraging. Apparently, before we can attempt to build automated means of detecting CST links, we must have a better understanding of what (if any) empirical properties reliably indicate CST relationships.

Another key step is to gather further data. In order to do so, an automated markup tool in the style of Alembic Workbench (Day *et al.* 1997) or SEE (Lin 2001) would be

extremely helpful. Not only is there a great deal of transcription (and associated possibilities for error) involved in running this experiment on paper, but a number of subjects expressed the belief that an automated tool would allow them to provide better and more consistent data.

CST-enhanced summarization
Motivation

In our experiments with CST-enhanced summarization, we try to explore the effects of different CST relationships on the quality of output summary. A motivating example is illustrated in Figure 2. As the first step, a 10-sentence extract (denoted by the bold circles) is generated by MEAD from a 3-article cluster. The original CST connectivity is 1, as is denoted by the relationship arc between sentence 44 in article 81 and sentence 10 in article 87. Now we try to increase the CST connectivity of the summary to 2 by including sentence 46 in article 81 (which has a CST relationship with sentence 26 in article 41) and drop sentence 22 in article 87 (the lowest ranked sentence in the original extract). Based on linguistic intuition, we postulate the following hypotheses:

Hypothesis 1 Enhancing the CST connectivity of a summary will significantly affect its quality as measured by relative utility.

Hypothesis 2 The effect of the enhancement will be dependent on the type of CST relationship added into the summary.

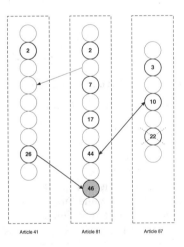

Figure 2: Graph representation of a sample cluster

Experiment 2: utility-based evaluation

The setup We produce summaries using MEAD and CST-enhanced version of it and compare the quality of the summaries. A significant difference in terms of summary quality will indicate the effect of CST enhancement.

First we need to measure the quality of summaries. We don't want to have human judges look at a number of summaries and determine how good they are, which is too tedious and too expensive. Therefore we decided to resort to sentence utility judgement. More specifically, we had 9 judges read the 11 articles in the same cluster used in the CST identification user study and assign utility scores (0 to 10) to each sentence. We then average the utility score for each sentence respectively and use the total utility of a summary as a proxy of its quality measure. This way we can control the amount of the work human judges have to do and reuse the utility judgement through a large number of experiments.

To run the experiments, we used the re-ranker module in MEAD to adjust the content of a summary. In the default version of MEAD, the re-ranker only looks at the lexical similarity between the sentence under consideration and the sentences already in the summary and drop the current sentence if it is too similar to those already in the summary. To enhance the summary using CST relationship, we ended up implementing a new re-ranker which includes new sentences into the summary according to the notion of increasing CST connectivity and dropping the lowest-ranked sentences correspondingly.

The evaluation metrics we use are the same as those used in (Radev, Jing, & Budzikowska 2000). All the summary performance numbers calculated in the experiments are relative utility scores.

The algorithm The algorithm is described in Algorithm 1. With this rather naive algorithm, we expect to show the feasibility of CST-enhancement, instead of claiming that this is "the" best way to do it.

In the actual experiments, we used the following parameters:

- Total number of clusters: 10
- Compression ratio: 10% through 30%,
- Total number of CST relationships: 17
- Threshold to hypothesize a CST relationship: 1

Experiments, results and analysis We also consider the distinction between incoming and outgoing relationships, in the sense of the directionality of the added relationship according to user judgement (e.g., in Figure 2, incorporating sentence 46 in article 81 is enhancement by outgoing relationship). The intuition behind this is obviously that some CST relationships do have directionality and the directionality could potentially make some difference on the resultant summary.

First we look at the overall effect of CST enhancement by comparing the average utility of all CST-enhanced summaries and the utility of baseline summaries (Table 5). As we can see, overall, CST enhancement significantly improves the utility of resultant summary in both incoming and outgoing scenarios. This justifies our first hypothesis.

	p-value	Sign
Incoming	0.008	+
Outgoing	0.026	+

Table 5: Average effect of CST enhancement (The p-values are for two-tailed pairwise T-tests), *average* case.

Algorithm 1 Experiment algorithm for CST-enhanced summarization

for all clusters c **do**
  for all compression ratios r **do**
    Produce baseline summary S for cluster c at compression ratio r using MEAD
    Compute relative utility measure for S
    for all possible CST relationship R **do**
      S_E=CST_Enhance(S,R,c)
      Compute relative utility measure for S_E
    end for
  end for
end for

Function CST_Enhance(S,R,c)
$S_E = S$
Initialize list L to null
for all sentences s in c but not in S **do**
  if s has CST relationship R with any sentence in S **then**
    Add s into L
  end if
end for
if L not null **then**
  if $NumberOfElements(L) > 1$ **then**
    Randomly choose a sentence s from L
  else
    Use the only sentence s in L
  end if
  s_0 = lowest ranked sentence in S_E with no CST relationship to other sentences
  Add sentence s into summary S_E
  Drop s_0 from S_E
end if
Return S_E

Does the compression ratio matter? Although we didn't experiment with long summaries ($r > 0.3$) since we believe those wouldn't make much practical sense, we still expect to observe some preliminary patterns in the data. Table 6 gives the comparison of pre-enhancement and post-enhancement summary performance by compression ratio. There is a tendency that, although not strong enough to be conclusive, CST-enhancement is relatively more helpful for shorter summaries.

		10%	20%	30%
Incoming	pre-enhancement	0.242	0.287	0.322
	post-enhancement	0.246	0.293	0.325
	difference	0.004	0.006	0.003
Outgoing	pre-enhancement	0.242	0.287	0.322
	post-enhancement	0.247	0.292	0.323
	difference	0.005	0.005	0.001

Table 6: Effects of CST enhancement at different compression ratios

To show how we tested our second hypothesis, we present the results by different CST relationship types in Table 7. The observations are the following:

- It appears that some CST relationships have no effect on the quality of enhanced summaries. This is not necessarily true, though, because all the unchanged utility numbers are due to the sparseness of user judgement data, in other words, the enhancement algorithm couldn't find any occurrence of these relationships to enhance the baseline summary.

- Most relationships that do affect the enhanced summary are "positive" ones, in the sense that incorporating them into the baseline summary significantly increases relative utility.

- Two CST relationships, *historical background* and *description*, stand out as potential "negative" ones, in that incorporaing them reduces the utility of post-enhancement summary to some extent.

CST relationship	Incoming		Outgoing	
	p-value	Sign	*p*-value	Sign
Identity	1.000	N	1.000	N
Equivalence	0.007	+	0.032	+
Translation	1.000	N	1.000	N
Subsumption	0.011	+	0.006	+
Contradiction	0.044	+	0.002	+
Historical	0.131	-	0.491	-
Citation	1.000	N	1.000	N
Modality	1.000	N	1.000	N
Attribution	0.049	+	0.255	+
Summary	1.000	N	1.000	N
Follow-up	0.002	+	0.055	+
Indirect speech	0.057	+	0.172	+
Elaboration	0.004	+	0.006	+
Fulfillment	1.000	N	1.000	N
Description	0.008	-	0.102	-
Reader Profile	1.000	N	1.000	N
Change of Perspective	1.000	N	1.000	N

Table 7: Effects of different CST relationships (The *p*-values are for two-tailed pairwise T-tests), *breakdown-by-type* case.

In both the "average" case and "break-down-by-type" case, the importance of directionality doesn't emerge. As can be again explained by the sparseness of user judgement data, this is disappointing but not surprising.

Conclusions and future work

In this paper, we showed that taking CST relationships into account affects the quality of extractive summaries. Moreover, enhancement by adding different types of CST relationships has different effects on resulting summaries.

In the long run, we foresee the following directions in future work:

- The proposed CST relationships (as shown in Table 1) need more refinement. A reasonably standardized taxonomy should be in place and act as ground for future research along this line.

- Currently, all CST relationships are based on human judgement. To automatically enhance summaries in the light of CST, we need to be able to automatically parse CST relationships. The first step is to build a CST-annotated corpus.

- It seems both theoretically and empirically interesting to find more about the connection between RST and CST.

Maybe first identifying the intra-document RST relationships can help CST parsing?

- Having showed that a relatively naive CST-enhancement algorithm does help in improving the quality of extractive summarization, we need to find a more intelligent version of it and to incorporate it into the MEAD summarizer.

- At this moment, either sentence utility scores by user judgement or sentence ranking scores by MEAD are really "inherent utility", in the sense that $score(s_i)$ doesn't depend on $score(s_j)$. It might be interesting and useful, however, to pursue the notion of "conditional utility" of sentences (thus acknowledging that the utility of one sentence depends on the utilities of other sentences), which could potentially influence the output of the summarizer.

Acknowledgements

This work was partially supported by the National Science Foundation's Information Technology Research program (ITR) under grant IIS-0082884. Our thanks go to Jahna Otterbacher, Adam Winkel, and all the anonymous reviewers for their very helpful comments.

References

Day, D.; Aberdeen, J.; Hirschman, L.; Kozierok, R.; Robinson, P.; and Vilain, M. 1997. Mixed-initiative development of language processing systems.

Lin, C.-Y. 2001. See - summary evaluation environment. WWW site, URL: http://www.isi.edu/ cyl/SEE/.

Luhn, H. 1958. The Automatic Creation of Literature Abstracts. *IBM Journal of Research Development* 2(2):159–165.

Mani, I., and Maybury, M., eds. 1999. *Advances in automatic text summarization*. Cambridge, MA: MIT Press.

Mann, W. C., and Thompson, S. A. 1988. Rhetorical Structure Theory: towards a functional theory of text organization. *Text* 8(3):243–281.

Marcu, D. 1997. *The Rhetorical Parsing, Summarization, and Generation of Natural Language Texts*. Ph.D. Dissertation, Department of Computer Science, University of Toronto.

MEAD. 2002. Mead documentation. WWW site, URL: http://www.clsp.jhu.edu/ws2001/groups/asmd/meaddoc.ps.

Radev, D. R., and McKeown, K. R. 1998. Generating natural language summaries from multiple on-line sources. *Computational Linguistics* 24(3):469–500.

Radev, D. R.; Jing, H.; and Budzikowska, M. 2000. Centroid-based summarization of multiple documents: sentence extraction, utility-based evaluation, and user studies. In *ANLP/NAACL Workshop on Summarization*.

Radev, D. 2000. A common theory of information fusion from multiple text sources, step one: Cross-document structure. In *Proceedings, 1st ACL SIGDIAL Workshop on Discourse and Dialogue*.

Salton, G.; Singhal, A.; Mitra, M.; and Buckley, C. 1997. Automatic text structuring and summarization. *Information Processing & Management* 33:193–207.

Planning

Planning with a Language for Extended Goals

Ugo Dal Lago and **Marco Pistore** and **Paolo Traverso**

ITC-IRST
Via Sommarive 18, 38050 Povo (Trento), Italy
{dallago,pistore,traverso}@irst.itc.it

Abstract

Planning for extended goals in non-deterministic domains is one of the most significant and challenging planning problems. In spite of the recent results in this field, no work has proposed a language designed specifically for planning. As a consequence, it is still impossible to specify and plan for several classes of goals that are typical of real world applications, like for instance "try to achieve a goal whenever possible", or "if you fail to achieve a goal, recover by trying to achieve something else".

We propose a new goal language that allows for capturing the intended meaning of these goals. We give a semantics to this language that is radically different from the usual semantics for extended goals, e.g., the semantics for LTL or CTL. Finally, we implement an algorithm for planning for extended goals expressed in this language, and experiment with it on a parametric domain.

Introduction

Several applications (e.g., space and robotics) often require planning in non-deterministic domains and for extended goals: actions are modeled with different outcomes that cannot be predicted at planning time, and goals are not simply states to be reached ("reachability goals"), but also conditions on the whole plan execution paths ("extended goals"). This planning problem is challenging. It requires planning algorithms that take into account the possibly different action outcomes, and that deal in practice with the explosion of the search space. Moreover, goals should take into account non-determinism and express behaviors that should hold for all paths and behaviors that should hold only for some paths.

The work described in (Pistore & Traverso 2001) and (Pistore, Bettin, & Traverso 2001) proposes an approach to this problem, and shows that the approach is theoretically founded (a formal notion of when a plan satisfies an extended goal is provided) and practical (an implementation of the planning algorithm is experimentally evaluated on a parametric domain). In those papers, CTL is used as the language for expressing goals. CTL (Emerson 1990) is a well-known and widely used language for the formal verification of properties by model checking. It provides the ability to express temporal behaviors that take into account

the non-determinism of the domain. In CTL, this is done by means of a universal quantifier (A) and of an existential quantifier (E). The former requires a property to hold in all the execution paths, the latter in at least one. However, in many practical cases, we found CTL inadequate for planning, since it cannot express different kinds of goals that are relevant for applications in non-deterministic domains. Consider, for instance, the classical goal of reaching a state that satisfies a given condition p. If the goal should be reached in spite of non-determinism ("strong reachability"), we can use the CTL formula $\mathrm{AF}\, p$, intuitively meaning that for all its execution paths (A), the plan will finally (F) reach a state where p holds. As an example, we could strongly require that a mobile robot reaches a given room. However, in many applications, strong reachability cannot be satisfied. In this case, a reasonable requirement for a plan is that *"it should do everything that is possible to achieve a given condition"*. For instance, the robot should actually try – "do its best" – to reach the room. Unfortunately, in CTL it is impossible to express such goal: the weaker condition imposed by the existential path quantifier $\mathrm{EF}\, p$ only requires that the plan has one of the many possible executions that reach a state where p holds. Moreover, if we have plans that actually try to achieve given goals, their executions should raise a failure on the paths in which the goals are not reachable anymore. Goals should be able to express conditions for controlling and recovering from failure. For instance, a reasonable goal for a robot can be "try to reach a room and, in case of failure, do reach a different room". Again, CTL offers the possibility to compose goals with disjunctions, like $\mathrm{EF}\, p \vee \mathrm{AF}\, q$. However, this formula does not capture the idea of failure recovery: there is no preference in which is the main goal to be achieved (e.g., $\mathrm{EF}\, p$), and which is the recovery goal (e.g., $\mathrm{AF}\, q$) to be achieved just in case of failure.

In this paper we define a new goal language designed to express extended goals for planning in non-deterministic domains. The language has been motivated from a set of applications we have been involved in (see, e.g., (Aiello *et al.* 2001)). The language provides basic goals for expressing conditions that the system should *guarantee* to reach or maintain, and conditions that the system should *try* to reach or maintain. Basic goals can be concatenated by taking into account possible failures. For instance, it is possible to specify goals that we should achieve as a reaction to failure, and

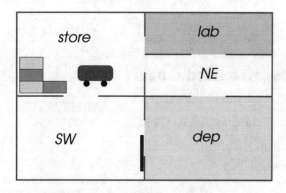

Figure 1: A simple navigation domain

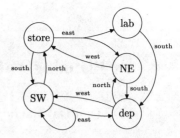

Figure 2: The transition graph of the navigation domain

goals that we should repeat to achieve until a failure occurs.

We extend the planning algorithm described in (Pistore & Traverso 2001; Pistore, Bettin, & Traverso 2001) to deal with the new language and implement it in the planner MBP (Bertoli *et al.* 2001). We evaluate the algorithm on the domain described in (Pistore, Bettin, & Traverso 2001). Given the new goal language, the algorithm generates better plans than those generated for CTL goals, maintaining a comparable performance.

A full version of this paper, with the details of the planning algorithm and of the experimental evaluation, is available at URL http://sra.itc.it/tools/mbp.

Background on Planning for Extended Goals

We review some basic definitions presented in (Pistore & Traverso 2001; Pistore, Bettin, & Traverso 2001).

Definition 1 *A (non-deterministic) planning domain $\mathcal{D}$ is a tuple $(\mathcal{B}, \mathcal{Q}, \mathcal{A}, \rightarrow)$, where $\mathcal{B}$ is the finite set of (basic) propositions, $\mathcal{Q} \subseteq 2^{\mathcal{B}}$ is the set of states, $\mathcal{A}$ is the finite set of actions, and $\rightarrow \subseteq \mathcal{Q} \times \mathcal{A} \times \mathcal{Q}$ is the transition relation, that describes how an action leads from one state to possibly many different states. We write $q \xrightarrow{a} q'$ for $(q, a, q') \in \rightarrow$.*

We require that relation $\rightarrow$ is total, i.e., for every $q \in \mathcal{Q}$ there is some $a \in \mathcal{A}$ and $q' \in \mathcal{Q}$ such that $q \xrightarrow{a} q'$. We denote with $\text{Act}(q) \triangleq \{a : \exists q'. q \xrightarrow{a} q'\}$ the set of the actions that can be performed in state q, and with $\text{Exec}(q, a) \triangleq \{q' : q \xrightarrow{a} q'\}$ the set of the states that can be reached from q performing action $a \in \text{Act}(q)$.

A simple domain is shown in Fig. 1. It consists of a building of five rooms, namely a *store*, a department *dep*, a laboratory *lab*, and two passage rooms *SW* and *NE*. A robot can move between the rooms. The intended task of the robot is to deliver objects from the store to the department, avoiding the laboratory, that is a dangerous room. For the sake of simplicity, we do not model explicitly the objects, but only the movements of the robot. Between rooms *SW* and *dep*, there is a door that the robot cannot control. Therefore, an *east* action from room *SW* successfully leads to room *dep* only if the door is open. Another non-deterministic outcome occurs when the robot tries to move *east* from the *store*: in this case, the robot may end non-deterministically either in

room *NE* or in room *lab*. The transition graph for the domain is represented in Fig. 2. For all states in the domain, we assume to have an action *wait* (not represented in the figure) that leaves the state unchanged.

In order to deal with extended goals, plans allow for specifying actions to be executed that depend not only on the current state of the domain, but also on the *execution context*, i.e., on an "internal state" of the executor, which can take into account, e.g., previous execution steps.

Definition 2 *A plan for a domain $\mathcal{D}$ is a tuple $\pi = (C, c_0, act, ctxt)$, where C is a set of contexts, $c_0 \in C$ is the initial context, $act : \mathcal{Q} \times C \rightharpoonup \mathcal{A}$ is the action function, and $ctxt : \mathcal{Q} \times C \times \mathcal{Q} \rightharpoonup C$ is the context function.*

If we are in state q and in execution context c, then $act(q, c)$ returns the action to be executed by the plan, while $ctxt(q, c, q')$ associates to each reached state q' the new execution context. Functions *act* and *ctxt* may be partial, since some state-context pairs are never reached in the execution of the plan. For instance, consider the plan π_1:

$act(store, c_0) = south$	$ctxt(store, c_0, SW) = c_0$
$act(SW, c_0) = east$	$ctxt(SW, c_0, dep) = c_0$
	$ctxt(SW, c_0, SW) = c_1$
$act(dep, c_0) = wait$	$ctxt(dep, c_0, dep) = c_0$
$act(SW, c_1) = north$	$ctxt(SW, c_1, store) = c_1$
$act(store, c_1) = south$	$ctxt(store, c_1, SW) = c_1$

According to this plan, the robot moves south, then it moves east; if *dep* is reached, it waits there forever; otherwise it continues to move north and south forever.

The executions of a plan can be represented by an *execution structure*, i.e, a Kripke Structure (Emerson 1990) that describes all the possible transitions from (q, c) to (q', c') that can be triggered by executing the plan.

Definition 3 *The execution structure of plan π in a domain $\mathcal{D}$ from state q_0 is the structure $K = \langle S, R, L \rangle$, where:*

- $S = \{(q, c) : act(q, c) \text{ is defined}\}$,
- $R = \{((q, c), (q', c')) \in S \times S : q \xrightarrow{a} q \text{ with } a = act(q, c) \text{ and } c' = ctxt(q, c, q')\}$
- $L(q, c) = \{b : b \in q\}$.

The execution structure K_{π_1} of plan π_1 is shown in Fig. 3.

Extended goals in (Pistore & Traverso 2001; Pistore, Bettin, & Traverso 2001) are expressed with CTL formulas, and the standard semantics for CTL (Emerson 1990) is used to define when a goal g is true in a state (q, c) of the execution structure K (written $(q, c) \models g$).

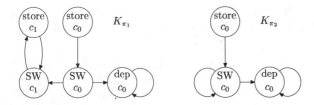

Figure 3: Two examples of execution structures

Definition 4 *Let π be a plan for domain $\mathcal{D}$ and K be the corresponding execution structure. Plan π satisfies goal g from initial state q_0, written $\pi, q_0 \models g$, if $(q_0, c_0) \models g$. Plan π satisfies goal g from the set of initial states Q_0 if $\pi, q_0 \models g$ for each $q_0 \in Q_0$.*

For instance, goal $AG \neg lab \wedge EF\, dep$ ("the robot should never enter the *lab* and should have a possibility of reaching the *dep*") is satisfied by plan π_1 from the initial state *store*.

The Goal Language

We propose the following language that overcomes some main limitations of CTL as a goal language. Let $\mathcal{B}$ be the set of *basic propositions*. The *propositional formulas* $p \in \mathcal{P}rop$ and the *extended goals* $g \in \mathcal{G}$ over $\mathcal{B}$ are defined as follows:

$$p := \top \mid \bot \mid b \mid \neg p \mid p \wedge p \mid p \vee p$$

$$g := p \mid g \textbf{ And } g \mid g \textbf{ Then } g \mid g \textbf{ Fail } g \mid \textbf{Repeat } g \mid$$
$$\textbf{DoReach } p \mid \textbf{TryReach } p \mid \textbf{DoMaint } p \mid \textbf{TryMaint } p$$

We now provide some intuitions and motivations for this language (and illustrate the intended meaning of the constructs on the example in Fig. 2). We often need a plan that is guaranteed to achieve a given goal. This can be done with operators **DoReach** (that specifies a property that should be reached) and **DoMaint** (that specifies a property that should be maintained true). However, in several domains, no plans exist that satisfy these strong goals. This is the case, for instance, for the goal **DoMaint** $\neg lab$ **And DoReach** dep, if the robot is initially in *store*. We need therefore to weaken the goal, but at the same time we want to capture its *intentional aspects*, i.e., we require that the plan *"does everything that is possible"* to achieve it. This is the intended meaning of **TryReach** and **TryMaint**. These operators are very different from operators EF and EG in CTL, which require plans that have just a possibility to achieve the goal. In the example, consider the goal **DoMaint** $\neg lab$ **And TryReach** dep. According to our intended meaning, this goal is not satisfied by plan π_1 (see previous section), that just tries one time to go east. Instead, the goal is satisfied by a plan π_2 that first moves the robot *south* to room SW, and then keeps trying to go *east*, until this action succeeds and the *dep* is reached. CTL goal $AG \neg lab \wedge EF\, dep$ is satisfied by both plans π_1 and π_2: indeed, the execution structures corresponding to these plans (see Fig. 3) have a path that reaches *dep*. Plan π_1 is not valid if we specify CTL goal $AG \neg lab \wedge AG\, EF\, dep$, that requires that there is always a path that leads to *dep* (this is a "strong

cyclic" reachability goal). Also in this case, however, the intentional aspect is lost; an acceptable plan for the CTL goal (but not for the original goal) is the one that tries one time to go *east* and, if this move fails, goes back to the *store* before trying again.

In several applications, goals should specify reactions to failures. For instance, a main goal for a mobile robot might be to continue to deliver objects to a given room, but when this is impossible, the robot should not give up, but recover from failure by delivering the current object to a next room. Consider, for instance, the goal (**TryMaint** $\neg lab$ **Fail DoReach** *store*) **And DoReach** *dep*. In order to satisfy it from the *store*, the robot should first go *east*. If room *lab* is entered after this move, then goal **TryMaint** $\neg lab$ fails, and the robot has to go back to the *store* to satisfy recovery goal **DoReach** *store*. This is very different from CTL goal $AG\,(lab \rightarrow AF\, store)$ that requires that if the robot ends in the lab it goes to the store. Indeed, this goal does not specify the fact that the *lab* should be avoided and that going back to the *store* is only a recovery goal. The CTL goal is satisfied as well by a plan that "intentionally" leads the robot into the *lab*, and then takes it back to the *store*.

Construct **Fail** is used to model recovery from failure. Despite its simplicity, this construct is rather flexible. In combination with the other operators of the language, it allows for representing both failures that can be detected at planning time and failures that occurs at execution time. Consider, for instance, goal **DoReach** *dep* **Fail DoReach** *store*. Sub-goal **DoReach** *dep* requires to find a plan that is guaranteed to reach room *dep*. If such a plan exists from a given state, then sub-goal **DoReach** *dep* cannot fail, and the recovery goal **DoReach** *store* is never considered. If there is no such plan, then sub-goal **DoReach** *dep* cannot be satisfied from the given state and the recovery goal **DoReach** *store* is tried instead. In this case, the failure of the primary goal **DoReach** *dep* in a given state can be decided *at planning time*. Consider now goal **TryReach** *dep* **Fail DoReach** *store*. In this case, sub-goal **TryReach** *dep* requires to find a plan that *tries* to reach room *dep*. During the execution of the plan, a state may be reached from which it is not possible to reach the *dep*. When such a state is reached, goal **TryReach** *dep* fails and the recovery goal **DoReach** *store* is considered. That is, in this case, the failure of the primary goal **TryReach** *dep* is decided *at execution time*.

We remark that the goal language does not allow for arbitrary nesting of temporal operators, e.g., it is not possible to express goals like **DoReach** (**TryMaint** p). However, it provides goal **Repeat** g, that specifies that sub-goal g should be achieved cyclically, until it fails. In our experience, the **Repeat** construct replaces most of the usages of nesting.

We now provide a formal semantics for the new goal language that captures the desired intended meaning. Due to the features of the new language, the semantics of goals cannot be defined following the approach used for CTL (Emerson 1990), that associates to each formula the set of states that satisfy it. Instead, for each goal g, we associate to each state s of the execution structure two sets $\mathcal{S}_g(s)$ and $\mathcal{F}_g(s)$ of finite paths in the execution structure. They represent the paths that lead to a success or to a failure in the achievement of goal g from state s. We say that an execution structure satisfies a goal g from state s_0 if $\mathcal{F}_g(s_0) = \emptyset$, that is, if no failure path exists for the goal. Let us consider, for instance, the case of goal $g = \textbf{TryReach}\ dep$. Set $\mathcal{S}_g(s)$ contains the paths that lead from s to states where dep holds, while set $\mathcal{F}_g(s)$ contains the paths that lead from s to states where dep is not reachable anymore. In the case of execution structure K_{π_1} of Fig. 3, we have $\mathcal{S}_g(store, c_0) = \{((store, c_0), (SW, c_0), (dep, c_0))\}$ and $\mathcal{F}_g(store, c_0) = \{((store, c_0), (SW, c_0), (SW, c_1))\}$. We remark that we do not consider $((store, c_0), (SW, c_0), (dep, c_0), (dep, c_0))$ as a success path, since its prefix $((store, c_0), (SW, c_0), (dep, c_0))$ is already a success path. In the case of execution structure K_{π_2} of Fig. 3, $\mathcal{F}_g(store, c_0) = \emptyset$, while $\mathcal{S}_g(store, c_0)$ contains all paths $((store, c_0), (SW, c_0), \ldots, (SW, c_0), (dep, c_0))$; that is, we take into account that a success path may stay in (SW, c_0) for an arbitrarily number of steps before the dep is eventually reached. Paths $((store, c_0), (SW, c_0), \ldots, (SW, c_0))$ are neither success paths nor failure paths: indeed, condition dep is never satisfied along these paths, but they can be extended to success paths. According to this semantics, goal $\textbf{TryReach}\ dep$ is not satisfied by execution structure K_{π_1}, while it is satisfied by execution structure K_{π_2}.

Some notations on paths are now in order. We use ρ to denote infinite paths and σ to denote finite paths in the execution structure. We represent with $\mathrm{first}(\sigma)$ the first state of path σ and with $\mathrm{last}(\sigma)$ the last state of the path. We write $s \in \sigma$ if state s appears in σ. We represent with $\sigma; \sigma'$ the path obtained by the concatenation of σ and σ'; concatenation is defined only if $\mathrm{last}(\sigma) = \mathrm{first}(\sigma')$. We write $\sigma \le \sigma'$ if σ is a prefix of σ', i.e., if there is some path σ'' such that $\sigma; \sigma'' = \sigma'$. As usual, we write $\sigma < \sigma'$ if $\sigma \le \sigma'$ and $\sigma \ne \sigma'$. Finally, given a set Σ of finite paths, we define the set of minimal paths in Σ as follows: $\min(\Sigma) \equiv \{\sigma \in \Sigma : \forall \sigma'.\sigma' < \sigma \implies \sigma' \notin \Sigma\}$.

We now define sets $\mathcal{S}_g(s)$ and $\mathcal{F}_g(s)$. The definition is by induction on the structure of g.

Goal $g = p$ is satisfied if condition p holds in the current state, while it fails if condition p does not hold. Formally, if $s \models p$, then $\mathcal{S}_g(s) = \{(s)\}$ and $\mathcal{F}_g(s) = \emptyset$. Otherwise, $\mathcal{S}_g(s) = \emptyset$ and $\mathcal{F}_g(s) = \{(s)\}$.

Goal $g = \textbf{TryReach}\ p$ has success when a state is reached that satisfies p. It fails if condition p cannot be satisfied in any of the future states. Formally, $\mathcal{S}_g(s) = \min\{\sigma : \mathrm{first}(\sigma) = s \wedge \mathrm{last}(\sigma) \models p\}$ and $\mathcal{F}_g(s) = \min\{\sigma : \mathrm{first}(\sigma) = s \wedge \forall s' \in \sigma.s' \not\models p \wedge \forall \sigma' \ge \sigma.\mathrm{last}(\sigma') \not\models p\}$.

Goal $g = \textbf{DoReach}\ p$ requires that condition p is eventually achieved despite non-determinism. If this is the case, then the successful paths are those that end in a state satisfying p. If there is some possible future computation from a state s along which p is never achieved, then goal g fails immediately in s. Formally, if there is some infinite path ρ from

s such that $s' \not\models p$ for each $s' \in \rho$, then $\mathcal{S}_g(s) = \emptyset$ and $\mathcal{F}_g(s) = \{(s)\}$. Otherwise, $\mathcal{S}_g(s) = \min\{\sigma : \mathrm{first}(\sigma) = s \wedge \mathrm{last}(\sigma) \models p\}$ and $\mathcal{F}_g(s) = \emptyset$.

Goal $g = \textbf{TryMaint}\ p$. Maintainability goals express conditions that should hold forever. No finite success path can thus be associated to maintainability goals. On the other hand, these goals may have failure paths. Goal $g = \textbf{TryMaint}\ p$ fails in all those states where condition p does not hold. Formally, $\mathcal{S}_g(s) = \emptyset$ and $\mathcal{F}_g(s) = \min\{\sigma : \mathrm{first}(\sigma) = s \wedge \mathrm{last}(\sigma) \not\models p\}$.

Goal $g = \textbf{DoMaint}\ p$ fails immediately in all those states that do not guarantee that condition p can be maintained forever. Formally, if $s' \models p$ holds for all states s' reachable from s, then $\mathcal{F}_g(s) = \emptyset$. Otherwise $\mathcal{F}_g(s) = \{(s)\}$. In both cases, $\mathcal{S}_g(s) = \emptyset$.

Goal $g = g_1\ \textbf{Then}\ g_2$ requires to satisfy sub-goal g_1 first and, once g_1 succeeds, to satisfy sub-goal g_2. Goal $g_1\ \textbf{Then}\ g_2$ succeeds when also goal g_2 succeeds. It fails when either goal g_1 or goal g_2 fail. Formally, $\mathcal{S}_g(s) = \{\sigma_1; \sigma_2 : \sigma_1 \in \mathcal{S}_{g_1}(s) \wedge \sigma_2 \in \mathcal{S}_{g_2}(\mathrm{last}(\sigma_1))\}$ and $\mathcal{F}_g(s) = \{\sigma_1 : \sigma_1 \in \mathcal{F}_{g_1}(s)\} \cup \{\sigma_1; \sigma_2 : \sigma_1 \in \mathcal{S}_{g_1}(s) \wedge \sigma_2 \in \mathcal{F}_{g_2}(\mathrm{last}(\sigma_1))\}$.

Goal $g = g_1\ \textbf{Fail}\ g_2$ permits to recover from failure. Sub-goal g_1 is tried first. If it succeeds, then the whole goal $g_1\ \textbf{Fail}\ g_2$ succeeds. If sub-goal g_1 fails, then g_2 is taken into account. Formally, $\mathcal{S}_g(s) = \{\sigma_1 : \sigma_1 \in \mathcal{S}_{g_1}(s)\} \cup \{\sigma_1; \sigma_2 : \sigma_1 \in \mathcal{F}_{g_1}(s) \wedge \sigma_2 \in \mathcal{S}_{g_2}(\mathrm{last}(\sigma_1))\}$ and $\mathcal{F}_g(s) = \{\sigma_1; \sigma_2 : \sigma_1 \in \mathcal{F}_{g_1}(s) \wedge \sigma_2 \in \mathcal{F}_{g_2}(\mathrm{last}(\sigma_1))\}$.

Goal $g = g_1\ \textbf{And}\ g_2$ succeeds if both sub-goals succeed, and fails if one of the sub-goals fails. Formally, $\mathcal{S}_g(s) = \min\{\sigma : \exists \sigma_1 \le \sigma.\sigma_1 \in \mathcal{S}_{g_1}(s) \wedge \exists \sigma_2 \le \sigma.\sigma_2 \in \mathcal{S}_{g_2}(s)\}$ and $\mathcal{F}_g(s) = \min(\mathcal{F}_{g_1}(s) \cup \mathcal{F}_{g_2}(s))$.

Goal $g = \textbf{Repeat}\ g'$ requires to achieve goal g in a cyclic way. That is, as soon as goal g' has success, a new instance of goal g' is activated. Goal $\textbf{Repeat}\ g'$ fails as soon as one of the instances of goal g' fails. Formally, $\mathcal{S}_g(s) = \emptyset$ and $\mathcal{F}_g(s) = \{\sigma_0; \sigma_1; \ldots; \sigma_n; \sigma' : \sigma' \in \mathcal{F}_{g'}(\mathrm{first}(\sigma')) \wedge \exists \sigma_i' \in \mathcal{S}_{g'}(\mathrm{first}(\sigma_i')). \sigma_i = \sigma_i'; (\mathrm{last}(\sigma_i'), \mathrm{last}(\sigma_i))\}$.

We can now define the notion of a plan that satisfies a goal expressed in the new language.

Definition 5 *Let π be a plan for domain $\mathcal{D}$ and K be the corresponding execution structure. Plan π satisfies goal $g \in \mathcal{G}$ from initial state q_0, written $\pi, q_0 \models g$, if $\mathcal{F}_g(q_0, c_0) = \emptyset$ for execution structure K. Plan π satisfies goal g from the set of initial states Q_0 if $\pi, q_0 \models g$ for each $q_0 \in Q_0$.*

Outline of the algorithm

In this section we extend to the new goal language the symbolic planning algorithm defined in (Pistore, Bettin, & Traverso 2001) for CTL. The algorithm is based on control automata. They are used to encode the requirements expressed by the goal, and are then exploited to guide the search of the plan. The states of a control automaton define the different goals that the plan intends to achieve in different instants; they correspond to the contexts of the plan under construction. The transitions of the control automaton define constraints on the behaviors that the states of the domain should exhibit in order to be *compatible* with the control states, i.e., to satisfy the corresponding goals. In this section, we first define a mapping from the new goal language into (an enriched version of) control automata. The mapping we propose departs substantially from the construction defined in (Pistore, Bettin, & Traverso 2001). Then we show how control automata can be used to guide the search of the plan. In the search phase, the algorithms of (Pistore, Bettin, & Traverso 2001) can be re-used with minor changes.

Construction of the control automaton

Definition 6 *A control automaton is a tuple* (C, c_0, T, RB), *where:*

- C *is the set of* control states*;*
- $c_0 \in C$ *is the* initial control state*;*
- $T(c) = \langle t_1, t_2, \ldots, t_m \rangle$ *is the list of* transitions *for control state c; each transition t_i is either* normal*, in which case $t_i \in \mathcal{P}rop \times (C \times \{\circ, \bullet\})^*$; or* immediate*, in which case $t_i \in \mathcal{P}rop \times (C \cup \{\text{succ}, \text{fail}\})$.*
- $RB = \{rb_1, \ldots, rb_n\}$, *with $rb_i \subseteq C$, is the set of* red blocks*.*

A list of transitions $T(c)$ is associated to each control state c: each transition is a possible behavior that a state can satisfy in order to be compatible with the control state c. The order of the list represents the preference among these transitions. The transitions of a control automaton are either *normal* or *immediate*. The former transitions correspond to the execution of an action in the plan. The latter ones describe updates in the control state that do not correspond to the execution of an action; they resemble ϵ-transitions of classical automata theory. The *normal transitions* are defined by a condition (that is, a formula in $\mathcal{P}rop$) and by a list of target control states. Each target control state is marked either by a $\circ$ or by a $\bullet$. State s satisfies a normal transition $(p, \langle (c_1', k_1'), \ldots, (c_n', k_n') \rangle)$ (with $k_i' \in \{\circ, \bullet\}$) if it satisfies condition p and if there is some action a from s such that: (i) all the next states reachable from s doing action a are compatible with some of the target control states; and (ii) some next state is compatible with each target state marked as $\bullet$. The *immediate transitions* are defined by a condition and by a target control state. A state satisfies an immediate transition (p, c') if it satisfies condition p and if it is compatible with the target control state c'. Special target control states succ and fail are used to represent success and failure: all states are compatible with success, while no state is compatible with failure. The *red blocks* of a control automaton represent sets of control states where the execution cannot stay forever. Typically, a red block consists of the set of control states in which the execution is trying to achieve a given condition, as in the case of a reachability goal. If an execution persists inside such a set of control states, then the condition is never reached, which is not acceptable for a reachability goal. In the control automaton, a red block is used to represent the fact that any valid execution should eventually leave these control states.

We now describe the control automata corresponding to the goal language. Rather than providing the formal definition of the control automata, we represent them using a graphical notation. We start with goal **DoReach** p:

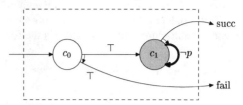

The control automaton has two control states: c_0 (the initial control state) and c_1. There are two transitions leaving control state c_1. The first one, guarded by condition p, is a success transition that corresponds to the cases where p holds in the current domain state. The second transition, guarded by condition $\neg p$, represents the case where p does not hold in the current state, and therefore, in order to achieve goal **DoReach** p, we have to assure that the goal can be achieved in *all the next* states. We remark that the second transition is a normal transition since it requires the execution of an action in the plan; the first transition, instead, is immediate. In the diagrams, we distinguish the two kinds of transitions by using thin arrows for the immediate ones and thick arrows for the normal ones. A domain state is compatible with control state c_1 only if it satisfies goal **DoReach** p, that is, if condition p holds in the current state (first transition from c_1), or if goal **DoReach** p holds in all the next states (second transition from c_1). According to the semantics of **DoReach** p, it is not possible for an execution to stay in state c_1 forever, as this corresponds to the case where condition p is never reached. That is, set $\{c_1\}$ is a red block of the control automaton. In the diagrams, states that are in a red block are marked in gray. Control state c_0 takes into account that it is not always possible to assure that condition p will be eventually reached, and that if this is not the case, then goal **DoReach** p fails. The precedence order among the two transitions from control state c_0, represented by the small circular arrow between them, guarantees that the transition leading to a failure is followed only if it is not possible to satisfy the constraints of control state c_1.

The control automaton for **TryReach** p is the following:

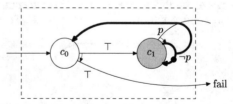

The difference with respect to the control automaton for **DoReach** p is in the transition from c_1 guarded by condition $\neg p$. In this case we do not require that goal **TryReach** p holds for *all* the next states, but only for *some* of them. Therefore, the transition has two possible targets, namely control states c_1 (corresponding to the next states were we expect to achieve **TryReach** p) and c_0 (for the other next states). The semantics of goal **TryReach** p requires that there should be always *at least one* next state that satisfies

TryReach p; that is, target c_1 of the transition is marked by •
in the control automaton. This "non-emptiness" requirement
is represented in the diagram with the • on the arrow leading
back to c_1. The preferred transition from control state c_0 is
the one that leads to c_1. This ensures that the algorithm will
try to achieve goal **TryReach** p whenever possible.

The control automaton for **DoMaint** q is the following:

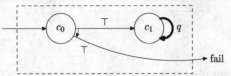

The transition from control state c_1 guarantees that a state s
is compatible with control state c_1 only if s satisfies condition q and all the next states of s are also compatible with
c_1. Control state c_1 is not gray. Indeed, a valid computation
that satisfies **DoMaint** q remains in control state c_1 forever.

The control automaton for the remaining basic goals
TryMaint q and p are, respectively:

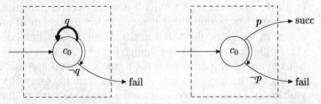

The control automata for the compound goals are defined
compositionally, by combining the control automata of their
sub-goal. The control automaton for goal g_1 **Then** g_2 is the
following:

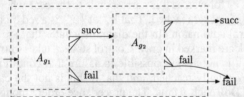

The initial state of the compound automaton coincides with
the initial state of automaton A_{g_1}, and the transitions that
leave the A_{g_1} with success are redirected to the initial state
of A_{g_2}. The control automaton for goal g_1 **Fail** g_2 is defined
similarly. The difference is that in this case the transitions
that leave A_{g_1} with *failure* are redirected to the initial state of
A_{g_2}. The control automaton for goal **Repeat** g is as follows:

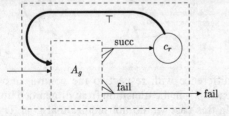

A new control state c_r is added to the automaton. This guarantees that, if goal g has been successfully fulfilled in state
s, then the achievement of a new instance of goal g starts
from the next states, not directly in s.

The control automaton for goal g_1 **And** g_2 has to perform a parallel simulation of the control automata for the
two sub-goals, and to accept only those behaviors that are
accepted separately by A_{g_1} and by A_{g_2}. Technically, this
corresponds to take the *synchronous product* $A_{g_1} \otimes A_{g_2}$ of
the control automata for the sub-goals. We skip the formal
definition of synchronous product for lack of space. It can
be found in the full version of this paper. It is simple, but
is long and rather technical, since it has to take into account
several special cases. Here, we present a simple example
of synchronous product. The control automaton for goal
DoMaint q **And TryReach** p (i.e., the synchronous product
of the control automata A_g for goal **DoMaint** q and $A_{g'}$ for
TryReach p) is as follows:

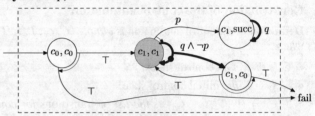

The control states of the product automaton are couples
(c, c'), where c is a control state of A_g and c' is a control
state of $A_{g'}$. The extra control state $(c_1, succ)$ is added to
take into account the case where goal **TryReach** p has been
successfully fulfilled, but goal **DoMaint** q is still active. The
transitions from control states (c, c') are obtained by combining in a suitable way the transitions of A_g from c and
the transitions of $A_{g'}$ from c'. For instance, in our example,
the normal transition with condition $q \wedge \neg p$ from control
state (c_1, c_1) corresponds to the combination of the two normal transitions of the control automata for **DoMaint** q and
TryReach p.

Plan search

Once the control automaton corresponding to a goal has
been built, the planning algorithm performs a search in the
domain, guided by the strategy encoded in the control automaton. During this search, a set of domain states is associated to each state of the control automaton. Intuitively, these
are the states that are compatible with the control state, i.e.,
for which a plan exists for the goal encoded in the control
state. Initially, all the domain states are considered compatible with all the control states, and this initial assignment
is then iteratively refined by discarding those domain states
that are recognized incompatible with a given control state.
Once a fix-point is reached, the information gathered during
the search is exploited in order to extract a plan. We remark
that iterative refinement and plan extraction are independent
from the goal language. In fact, for them we have been able
to re-use the algorithms of (Pistore, Bettin, & Traverso 2001)
with minor changes.

In the iterative refinement algorithm, the following conditions are enforced: **(C1)** a domain state s is associated to a
control state c only if s can satisfy the behavior described by
some transition of c; and **(C2)** executions from a given state
s are not acceptable if they stay forever inside a red block.
In each step of the iterative refinement, either a control state
is selected and the corresponding set of domain states is refined according to **(C1)**; or a red block is selected and all

the sets of domain states associated to its control states are refined according to **(C2)**. The refinement algorithm terminates when no further refinement step is possible, that is, when a fix-point is reached.

The core of the refinement step resides is function $ctxt\text{-}assoc_A(c, \gamma)$. It takes as input the control automaton $A = (C, c_0, T, RB)$, a control state $c \in C$, and the current association $\gamma : C \to 2^{\mathcal{Q}}$, and returns the new set of domain states to be associated to c. It is defined as follows:

$$ctxt\text{-}assoc_A(c, \gamma) \triangleq$$
$$\{q \in \mathcal{Q} : \exists t \in T(c). \ q \in trans\text{-}assoc_A(t, \gamma)\}.$$

According to this definition, a state q is compatible with a control state c if it satisfies the conditions of some transition t from that control state. If $t = (p, c')$ is an immediate transition, then:

$$trans\text{-}assoc_A(t, \gamma) \triangleq \{q \in \mathcal{Q} : \ q \models p \ \land \ q \in \gamma(c')\}.$$

where we assume that $\gamma(\text{fail}) = \emptyset$ and $\gamma(\text{succ}) = \mathcal{Q}$. That is, in the case of an immediate transition, we require that q satisfies property p and that it is compatible with the new control state c' according to the current association γ. If $t = (p, \langle (c'_1, k'_1), \ldots, (c'_n, k'_n) \rangle)$ is a normal transition, then:

$$trans\text{-}assoc_A(t, \gamma) \triangleq \{q \in \mathcal{Q} : \ q \models p \ \land \ \exists a \in \text{Act}(q).$$
$$(q, a) \in gen\text{-}pre\text{-}image\big((\gamma(c'_1), k'_1), \ldots, (\gamma(c'_n), k'_n)\big)\}$$

where:

$$gen\text{-}pre\text{-}image\big((Q_1, k_1), \ldots (Q_n, k'_n)\big) \triangleq$$
$$\{(q, a) : \exists Q'_1 \subseteq Q_1 \ldots Q'_k \subseteq Q_k.$$
$$\text{Exec}(q, a) = Q'_1 \cup \cdots \cup Q'_k \ \land$$
$$Q'_i \cap Q'_j \text{ if } i \neq j \ \land \ Q'_i \neq \emptyset \text{ if } k_i = \bullet\}.$$

Also in the case of normal transitions, $trans\text{-}assoc_A$ requires that q satisfies property p. Moreover, it requires that there is some action a such that the next states $\text{Exec}(q, a)$ satisfy the following conditions: (i) all the next states are compatible with some of the target control states, according to association γ; and (ii) some next state is compatible with each target control state marked as $\bullet$. These two conditions are enforced by requiring that the state-action pair (q, a) appears in the *generalized pre-image* of the sets of states $\gamma(c'_i)$ associated by γ to the target control states c'_i. The generalized pre-image, that is computed by function $gen\text{-}pre\text{-}image$, can be seen as a combination and generalization of the *strong-pre-image* and *multi-weak-pre-image* used in (Pistore, Bettin, & Traverso 2001).

Function $ctxt\text{-}assoc$ is used in the refinement steps corresponding to **(C1)** as well as in the refinement steps corresponding to **(C2)**. In the former case, the refinement step simply updates $\gamma(c)$ to the value of $ctxt\text{-}assoc_A(c, \gamma)$. In the latter case, the refinement should guarantee that any valid execution eventually leaves the control states in the selected red block rb. To this purpose, the empty set of domain states is initially associated to the control states in the red block; then, iteratively, one of the control states $c \in rb$ is chosen, and its association $\gamma(c)$ is updated to $ctxt\text{-}assoc_A(c, \gamma)$;

these updates terminate when a fix-point is reached, that is, when $\gamma(c) = ctxt\text{-}assoc_A(c, \gamma)$ for each $c \in rb$. In this way, a least fix-point is computed, which guarantees that a domain state is associated to a control state in the red block only if there is a plan from that domain state that leaves the red block in a finite number of actions.

Once a stable association γ from control states to sets of domain states is built for a control automaton, a plan can be easily obtained. The contexts for the plan correspond to the states of the control automaton. The information necessary to define functions act and $ctxt$ is implicitly computed during the execution of the refinement steps. Indeed, function $trans\text{-}assoc$ defines the possible actions $a = act(q, c)$ to be executed in the state-context pair (q, c), namely the actions that satisfy the constraints of one of the normal transitions of the control automaton. Moreover, function $gen\text{-}pre\text{-}image$ defines the next execution context $ctxt(q, c, q')$ for any possible next state $q' \in \text{Exec}(q, a)$. The preference order among the transitions associated to each control state is exploited in this phase, in order to guarantee that the extracted plan satisfies the goal in the best possible way. A detailed description of the plan extraction phase appears in the full version of this paper.

Implementation and experimental evaluation

We have implemented the algorithm in the MBP planner (Bertoli *et al.* 2001). In the plan search phase, we exploit the BDD-based symbolic techniques (Burch *et al.* 1992) provided by MBP, thus allowing for a very efficient exploration of large domains. We have done some preliminary experiments for testing the expressiveness of the new goal language and for comparing the performance of the new algorithm w.r.t. the one presented in (Pistore, Bettin, & Traverso 2001) for CTL goals. For the experiments, we have used the test suite for extended goals made available in the MBP package (see http://sra.itc.it/tools/mbp). The tests are based on the robot navigation domain proposed by (Kabanza, Barbeau, & St-Denis 1997). The small domain described in Fig. 1 is a very trivial instance of this class of domains. Some of the tests in the suite correspond to domains with more than 10^8 states.

The results of the tests (reported in the full version of this paper) are very positive. We have been able to express all the CTL goals in the test suite using the new goal language. Moreover, in spite of the fact that the domain was proposed for CTL goals, the quality of the generated plans is much higher in the case of the new goal language. For instance, in the case of **TryReach** goals, the plans generated by the new algorithm lead the robot to the goal room avoiding the useless moves that are present in the plans generated from the corresponding CTL goals. The new algorithm compares well with the CTL planning algorithm also in terms of performance: despite the more difficult task, in all the experiments the time required by the new algorithm for building the plan is comparable with the time required for CTL goals. In the worst cases, the new algorithm requires about twice the time of the algorithm for CTL, while in other cases the new algorithm behaves slightly better than the old one. The experiments show that the overhead for building a more complex control automaton is irrelevant w.r.t. the symbolic search phase. The slight differences in performances are mainly due to the use of different sequences of BDD operations in the search phase.

Concluding remarks

We have described a new language for extended goals for planning in non-deterministic domains. This language builds on and overcomes the limits of the work presented in (Pistore & Traverso 2001), where extended goals are expressed in CTL. The main new features w.r.t. CTL are the capability of representing the "intentional" aspects of goals and the possibility of dealing with failure. We have defined a formal semantics for the new language that is very different from the standard CTL semantics. We have extended the planning algorithm described in (Pistore, Bettin, & Traverso 2001) to the new goal language. Our experimental evaluation shows that the new algorithm generates better plans than those generated from CTL goals, maintaining a comparable performance.

As far as we know, this language has never been proposed before, neither in the AI planning literature, nor in the field of automatic synthesis (see, e.g., (Vardi 1995)). The language is somehow related to languages for tactics in theorem proving. In deductive planning, tactics have been used to express plans, rather than extended goals (see (Stephan & Biundo 1993; Spalazzi & Traverso 2000)). The aim of these works is significantly different from ours. Besides (Pistore & Traverso 2001), other works in planning have dealt with the problem of extended goals. Most of these works are based on extensions of LTL, see, e.g., (Kabanza, Barbeau, & St-Denis 1997). Similarly to CTL, LTL cannot capture the goals defined in our language. Several other works only consider the case of deterministic domains (see, e.g., (de Giacomo & Vardi 1999; Bacchus & Kabanza 2000)). In (Bacchus, Boutilier, & Grove 1996) a past version of LTL is used to define temporally extended rewarding functions that can be used to provide "preferences" among temporally extended goals for MDP planning. This work shares with us the motivations for dealing with the problem of generating acceptable plans when it is impossible to satisfy a "most preferred" goal. In the framework of (Bacchus, Boutilier, & Grove 1996), preferences are expressed with "quantitative measures", like utility functions. We propose a complementary approach where the goal language is enriched with logical operators (e.g., **TryReach** and **Fail**) that can be used to specify sort of "qualitative preferences". The comparison of the expressive power and of the practical applicability of the two approaches is an interesting topic for future evaluation. Moreover, the combination of the two approaches is a compelling topic for future research.

Further possible directions for future work are the extension of the language with arbitrary nesting of temporal operators (in the style of CTL or LTL), an extension to planning under partial observability (Bertoli *et al.* 2002) and to adversarial planning (Jensen, Veloso, & Bowling 2001). More important, we plan to evaluate in depth the proposed approach in the real applications that originally motivated our work.

References

Aiello, L. C.; Cesta, A.; Giunchiglia, E.; Pistore, M.; and Traverso, P. 2001. Planning and verification techniques for the high level programming and monitoring of autonomous robotic devices. In *Proceedings of the ESA Workshop on On Board Autonoy*. ESA Press.

Bacchus, F., and Kabanza, F. 2000. Using temporal logic to express search control knowledge for planning. *Artificial Intelligence* 116(1-2):123–191.

Bacchus, F.; Boutilier, C.; and Grove, A. 1996. Rewarding Behaviors. In *Proc. of AAAI'96*. AAAI-Press.

Bertoli, P.; Cimatti, A.; Pistore, M.; Roveri, M.; and Traverso, P. 2001. MBP: a Model Based Planner. In *Proc. of IJCAI'01 workshop on Planning under Uncertainty and Incomplete Information*.

Bertoli, P.; Cimatti, A.; Pistore, M.; and Traverso., P. 2002. Plan validation for extended goals under partial observability (preliminary report). In *Proc. of the AIPS'02 Workshop on Planning via Model Checking*.

Burch, J. R.; Clarke, E. M.; McMillan, K. L.; Dill, D. L.; and Hwang, L. J. 1992. Symbolic Model Checking: 10^{20} States and Beyond. *Information and Computation* 98(2):142–170.

de Giacomo, G., and Vardi, M. 1999. Automata-theoretic approach to planning with temporally extended goals. In *Proc. of ECP'99*.

Emerson, E. A. 1990. Temporal and modal logic. In van Leeuwen, J., ed., *Handbook of Theoretical Computer Science, Volume B: Formal Models and Semantics*. Elsevier.

Jensen, R. M.; Veloso, M. M.; and Bowling, M. H. 2001. OBDD-based optimistic and strong cyclic adversarial planning. In *Proc. of ECP'01*.

Kabanza, F.; Barbeau, M.; and St-Denis, R. 1997. Planning control rules for reactive agents. *Artificial Intelligence* 95(1):67–113.

Pistore, M., and Traverso, P. 2001. Planning as Model Checking for Extended Goals in Non-deterministic Domains. In *Proc. of IJCAI'01*. AAAI Press.

Pistore, M.; Bettin, R.; and Traverso, P. 2001. Symbolic techniques for planning with extended goals in non-deterministic domains. In *Proc. of ECP'01*.

Spalazzi, L., and Traverso, P. 2000. A Dynamic Logic for Acting, Sensing and Planning. *Journal of Logic and Computation* 10(6):787–821.

Stephan, W., and Biundo, S. 1993. A New Logical Framework for Deductive Planning. In *Proc. of IJCAI'93*.

Vardi, M. Y. 1995. An automata-theoretic approach to fair realizability and synthesis. In *Proc. of CAV'95*.

Symbolic Heuristic Search for Factored Markov Decision Processes

Zhengzhu Feng
Computer Science Department
University of Massachusetts
Amherst, MA 01003
fengzz@cs.umass.edu

Eric A. Hansen
Computer Science Department
Mississippi State University
Mississippi State, MS 39762
hansen@cs.msstate.edu

Abstract

We describe a planning algorithm that integrates two approaches to solving Markov decision processes with large state spaces. State abstraction is used to avoid evaluating states individually. Forward search from a start state, guided by an admissible heuristic, is used to avoid evaluating all states. We combine these two approaches in a novel way that exploits symbolic model-checking techniques and demonstrates their usefulness for decision-theoretic planning.

Introduction

Markov decision processes (MDPs) have been adopted as a framework for research in decision-theoretic planning. Classic dynamic programming algorithms solve MDPs in time polynomial in the size of the state space. However, the size of the state space grows exponentially with the number of features describing the problem. This "state explosion" problem limits use of the MDP framework, and overcoming it has become an important topic of research.

Over the past several years, approaches to solving MDPs that do not rely on complete state enumeration have been developed. One approach exploits a feature-based (or factored) representation of an MDP to create state abstractions that allow the problem to be represented and solved more efficiently (Dearden & Boutilier 1997; Hoey et al. 1999; and many others). Another approach limits computation to states that are reachable from the starting state(s) of the MDP (Barto, Bradtke, & Singh 1995; Dean *et al.* 1995; Hansen & Zilberstein 2001). In this paper, we show how to combine these two approaches. Moreover, we do so in a way that demonstrates the usefulness of symbolic model-checking techniques for decision-theoretic planning.

There is currently great interest in using symbolic model-checking to solve artificial intelligence planning problems with large state spaces. This interest is based on recognition that the problem of finding a plan (i.e., a sequence of actions and states leading from an initial state to a goal state) can be treated as a reachability problem in model checking. The planning problem is solved symbolically in the sense that reachability analysis is performed by manipulating sets of states, rather than individual states, alleviating the state

explosion problem. Recent work has shown that symbolic model checking provides a very effective approach to non-deterministic planning (Cimatti, Roveri, & Traverso 1998). Nondeterministic planning is similar to decision-theoretic planning in that it considers actions with multiple outcomes, allows plan execution to include conditional and iterative behavior, and represents a plan as a mapping from states to actions. However, decision-theoretic planning is more complex than nondeterminsitic planning because it associates probabilities and rewards with state transitions. The problem is not simply to construct a plan that reaches the goal, but to find a plan that maximizes expected value.

The first use of symbolic model checking for decision-theoretic planning is the SPUDD planner (Hoey *et al.* 1999), which solves factored MDPs using dynamic programming. Although it does not use reachability analysis, it uses symbolic model-checking techniques to perform dynamic programming efficiently on sets of states. Our paper builds heavily on this work, but extends it in an important way. Whereas dynamic programming solves an MDP for all possible starting states, we use knowledge of the starting state(s) to limit planning to reachable states. In essence, we show how to improve the efficiency of the SPUDD framework by using symbolic reachability analysis together with dynamic programming. Our algorithm can also be viewed as a generalization of heuristic-search planners for MDPs, in which our contribution is to show how to perform heuristic search symbolically for factored MDPs. The advantage of heuristic search over dynamic programming is that it focuses planning resources on the relevant parts of the state space.

Factored MDPs and decision diagrams

A Markov decision process (MDP) is defined as a tuple (S, A, P, R) where: S is a set of states; A is a set of actions; P is a set of transition models $P^a : S \times S \to [0, 1]$, one for each action, specifying the transition probabilities of the process; and R is a set of reward models $R^a : S \to \Re$, one for each action, specifying the expected reward for taking action a in each state. We consider MDPs for which the objective is to find a policy $\pi : S \to A$ that maximizes total discounted reward over an infinite (or indefinite) horizon, where $\gamma \in [0, 1]$ is the discount factor. (We allow a discount factor of 1 for indefinite-horizon problems only, that is, for MDPs that terminate after a goal state is reached.)

In a factored MDP, the set of states is described by a set of random variables $\mathbf{X} = \{X_1, \ldots, X_n\}$. Without loss of generality, we assume these are Boolean variables. A particular instantiation of the variables corresponds to a unique state. Because the set of states $S = 2^{\mathbf{X}}$ grows exponentially with the number of variables, it is impractical to represent the transition and reward models explicitly as matrices when the number of states variables is large. Instead we follow Hoey *et al.*(1999) in using algebraic decision diagrams to achieve a more compact representation.

Algebraic decision diagrams (ADDs) are a generalization of binary decision diagrams (BDDs), a compact data structure for Boolean functions used in symbolic model checking. A decision diagram is a data structure (corresponding to an acyclic directed graph) that compactly represents a mapping from a set of Boolean state variables to a set of values. A BDD represents a mapping to the values 0 or 1. An ADD represents a mapping to any finite set of values. To represent these mappings compactly, decision diagrams exploit the fact that many instantiations of the state variables map to the same value. In other words, decision diagrams exploit state abstraction. BDDs are typically used to represent the characteristic functions of sets of states and the transition functions of finite-state automata. ADDs can represent weighted finite-state automata, where the weights correspond to transition probabilities or rewards, and thus are an ideal representation for MDPs.

Hoey *et al.* (1999) describe how to represent the transition and reward models of a factored MDP compactly using ADDs. We adopt their notation and refer to their paper for details of this representation. Let $\mathbf{X} = \{X_1, \ldots, X_n\}$ represent the state variables at the current time and let $\mathbf{X}' = \{X_1', \ldots, X_n'\}$ represent the state variables at the next step. For each action, an ADD $P^a(\mathbf{X}, \mathbf{X}')$ represents the transition probabilities for the action. Similarly, the reward model $R^a(\mathbf{X})$ for each action a is represented by an ADD. The advantage of using ADDs to represent mappings from states (and state transitions) to values is that the complexity of operators on ADDs depends on the number of nodes in the diagrams, not the size of the state space. If there is sufficient regularity in the model, ADDs can be very compact, allowing problems with large state spaces to be represented and solved efficiently.

Symbolic LAO* algorithm

To solve factored MDPs, we describe a symbolic generalization of the LAO* algorithm (Hansen & Zilberstein 2001). LAO* is an extension of the classic search algorithm AO* that can find solutions with loops. This makes it possible for LAO* to solve MDPs, since a policy for an infinite-horizon MDP allows both conditional and cyclic behavior. Like AO*, LAO* has two alternating phases. First, it expands the best partial solution (or policy) and evaluates the states on its fringe using an admissible heuristic function. Then it performs dynamic programming on the states visited by the best partial solution, to update their values and possibly revise the currently best partial solution. The two phases alternate until a complete solution is found, which is guaranteed to be optimal.

AO* and LAO* differ in the algorithms they use in the dynamic programming step. Because AO* assumes an acyclic solution, it can perform dynamic programming in a single backward pass from the states on the fringe of the solution to the start state. Because LAO* allows solutions with cycles, it relies on an iterative dynamic programming algorithm (such as value iteration or policy iteration). In organization, the LAO* algorithm is similar to the "envelope" dynamic programming approach to solving MDPs (Dean *et al.* 1995). It is also closely related to RTDP (Barto, Bradtke, & Singh 1995), which is an on-line (or "real time") search algorithm for MDPs, in contrast to LAO*, which is an off-line search algorithm.

We call our generalization of LAO* a symbolic search algorithm because it manipulates sets of states, instead of individual states. In keeping with the symbolic model-checking approach, we represent a set of states S by its characteristic function χ_S, so that $s \in S \iff \chi_S(s) = 1$. We represent the characteristic function of a set of states by an ADD. (Because its values are 0 or 1, we can also represent a characteristic function by a BDD.) From now on, whenever we refer to a set of states, S, we implicitly refer to its characteristic function, as represented by a decision diagram.

In addition to representing sets of states as ADDs, we represent every element manipulated by the LAO* algorithm as an ADD, including: the transition and reward models; the policy $\pi : S \to A$; the state evaluation function $V : S \to \Re$ that is computed in the course of finding a policy; and an admissible heuristic evaluation function $h : S \to \Re$ that guides the search for the best policy. Even the discount factor γ is represented by a simple ADD that maps every input to a constant value. This allows us to perform all computations of the LAO* algorithm using ADDs.

Besides exploiting state abstraction, we want to limit computation to the set of states that are reachable from the start state by following the best policy. Although an ADD effectively assigns a value to every state, these values are only relevant for the set of reachable states. To focus computation on the relevant states, we introduce the notion of *masking* an ADD. Given an ADD D and a set of relevant states U, masking is performed by multiplying D by χ_U. This has the effect of mapping all irrelevant states to the value zero. We let D_U denote the resulting *masked ADD*. (Note that we need to have U in order to correctly interpret D_U). Mapping all irrelevant states to zero can simplify the ADD considerably. If the set of reachable states is small, the masked ADD often has dramatically fewer nodes. This in turn can dramatically improve the efficiency of computation using ADDs.[1]

Our symbolic implementation of LAO* does not maintain an explicit search graph. It is sufficient to keep track of the set of states that have been "expanded" so far, denoted G, the *partial value function*, denoted V_G, and a *partial policy*,

---

[1] Although we map the values of irrelevant states to zero, it does not matter what value they have. This suggests a way to simplify a masked ADD further. After mapping irrelevant states to zero, we can change the value of a irrelevant state to any other non-zero value whenever doing so further simplifies the ADD.

```
policyExpansion(π, S⁰, G)
1.    E = F = ∅
2.    from = S⁰
3.    REPEAT
4.        to = ⋃ₐ Image(from ∩ Sₐπ, Pᵃ)
5.        F = F ∪ (to − G)
6.        E = E ∪ from
7.        from = to ∩ G − E
8.    UNTIL (from = ∅)
9.    E = E ∪ F
10.   G = G ∪ F
11.   RETURN (E, F, G)

valueIteration(E, V)
12.   saveV = V
13.   E' = ⋃ₐ Image(E, Pᵃ)
14.   REPEAT
15.       V' = V
16.       FOR each action a
17.           Vᵃ = Rₑᵃ + γ ∑ₑ' Pₑ∪ₑ'ᵃ V'ₑ'
18.       M = maxₐ Vᵃ
19.       V = Mₑ + saveV_Ē
20.       residual = ‖Vₑ − V'ₑ‖
21.   UNTIL stopping criterion met
22.   π = extractPolicy(M, {Vᵃ})
23.   RETURN (V, π, residual)

LAO*({Pᵃ}, {Rᵃ}, γ, S⁰, h, threshold )
24.   V = h
25.   G = ∅
26.   π = 0
27.   REPEAT
28.       (E, F, G) = policyExpansion(π, S⁰, G)
29.       (V, π, residual) = valueIteration(E, V)
30.   UNTIL (F = ∅) AND (residual ≤ threshold)
31.   RETURN (π, V, E, G).
```

Table 1: Symbolic LAO* algorithm.

denoted π_G. For any state in G, we can "query" the policy to determine its associated action, and compute its successor states. Thus, the graph structure is implicit in this representation. Note that throughout the whole LAO* algorithm, we only maintain one value function V and one policy π. V_G and π_G are implicitly defined by G and the masking operation.

Symbolic LAO* is summarized in Table 1. In the following, we give a more detailed explanation.

Policy expansion In the policy expansion step of the algorithm, we perform reachability analysis to find the set of states F that are not in G (i.e., have not been "expanded" yet), but are reachable from the set of start states, S^0, by following the partial policy π_G. These states are on the "fringe" of the states visited by the best policy. We add them to G and to the set of states $E \subseteq G$ that are visited by the current partial policy. This is analogous to "expanding" states on the frontier of a search graph in heuristic search. Expanding a

partial policy means that it will be defined for a larger set of states in the dynamic-programming step.

Symbolic reachability analysis using decision diagrams is widely used in VLSI design and verification. Our policy-expansion algorithm is similar to the traversal algorithms used for sequential verification, but is adapted to handle the more complex system dynamics of an MDP. The key operation in reachability analysis is computation of the *image* of a set of states, given a transition function. The image is the set of all possible successor states. To perform this operation, it is convenient to convert the ADD $P^a(\mathbf{X}, X')$ to a BDD $T^a(\mathbf{X}, X')$ that maps state transitions to a value of one if the transition has a non-zero probability, and otherwise zero. The image computation is faster using BDDs than ADDs. Mathematically, the image is computed using the relational-product operator, defined as follows:

$$Image_{\mathbf{X}'}(S, T^a) = \exists \mathbf{x} \left[T^a(\mathbf{X}, X') \wedge \chi_S(\mathbf{X}) \right].$$

The conjunction $T^a(\mathbf{X}, X') \wedge \chi_S(\mathbf{X})$ selects the set of valid transitions and the existential quantification extracts and unions the successor states together. Both the relational-product operator and symbolic traversal algorithms are well studied in the symbolic model checking literature, and we refer to that literature for details about how this is computed, for example, (Somenzi 1999).

The *image* operator returns a characteristic function over $\mathbf{X}'$ that represents the set of reachable states *after* an action is taken. The assignment in line 4 implicitly converts this characteristic function so that it is defined over $\mathbf{X}$, and represents the current set of states ready for the next expansion.

Because a policy is associated with a set of transition functions, one for each action, we need to invoke the appropriate transition function for each action when computing successor states under a policy. For this, it is useful to represent the partial policy π_G in another way. We associate with each action a the set of states for which the action to take is a under the current policy, and call this set of states S_π^a. Note that $S_\pi^a \cap S_\pi^{a'} = \emptyset$ for $a \neq a'$, and $\cup_a S_\pi^a = G$. Given this alternative representation of the policy, line 4 computes the set of successor states following the current policy using the *image* operator.

Dynamic programming The dynamic-programming step of LAO* is performed using a modified version of the SPUDD algorithm. The original SPUDD algorithm performs dynamic programming over the entire state space. We modify it to focus computation on reachable states, using the idea of masking. Masking lets us perform dynamic programming on a subset of the state space instead of the entire state space. The pseudocode in Table 1 assumes that dynamic programming is performed on E, the states visited by the currently best (partial) policy. This has been shown to lead to the best performance of LAO*, although a larger or smaller set of states can also be updated (Hansen & Zilberstein 2001). Note that all ADDs used in the dynamic-programming computation are masked to improve efficiency.

Because π_G is a partial policy, there can be states in E with successor states that are not in G, denoted E'. This is true until LAO* converges. In line 13, we identify these states so that we can do appropriate masking. To perform dynamic programming on the states in E, we assign admissible values to the "fringe" states in E', where these values come from the current value function. Note that the value function is initialized to an admissible heuristic evaluation function at the beginning of the algorithm.

With all components properly masked, we can perform dynamic programming using the SPUDD algorithm. This is summarized in line 17. The full equation is

$$V^a(\mathbf{X}) = R_E^a(\mathbf{X}) + \gamma \sum_{E'} P_{E \cup E'}^a(\mathbf{X}, X') \cdot V_{E'}'(\mathbf{X}').$$

The masked ADDs R_E^a and $P_{E \cup E'}^a$ need to be computed only once for each call to $valueIteration()$ since they don't change between iterations. Note that the product $P_{E \cup E'}^a \cdot V_{E'}'$ is effectively defined over $E \cup E'$. After the summation over E', which is accomplished by existentially abstracting away all post-action variables, the resulting ADD is effectively defined over E only. As a result, V^a is effectively a masked ADD over E, and the maximum M at line 18 is also a masked ADD over E. In line 19, we use the notation M_E to emphasize that V is set equal to the newly computed values for E and the saved values for the rest of the state space. There is no masking computation performed.

The residual in line 20 can be computed by finding the largest absolute value of the ADD $(V_E - V_E')$. We use the masking subscript here to emphasize that the residual is computed only for states in the set E. The masking operation can actually be avoided here since at this step, $V_E = M$, which is computed in line 18, and V_E' is the M from the previous iteration.

Dynamic programming is the most expensive step of LAO*, and it is usually not efficient to run it until convergence each time this step is performed. Often a single iteration gives the best performance. After performing value iteration, we extract a policy in line 22 by comparing M against the action value function V^a (breaking ties arbitrarily):

$$\forall s \in E \ \ \pi(s) = a \ \text{if} \ M(s) = V^a(s).$$

The symbolic LAO* algorithm returns a value function V and a policy π, together with the set of states E that are visited by the policy, and the set of states G that have been "expanded" by LAO*.

Convergence test At the beginning of LAO*, the value function V is initialized to the admissible heuristic h that overestimates the optimal value function. Each time value iteration is performed, it starts with the current values of V. Hansen and Zilberstein (2001) show that these values decrease monotonically in the course of the algorithm; are always admissible; and converge arbitrarily close to optimal. LAO* converges to an optimal or ϵ-optimal policy when two conditions are met: (1) its current policy does not have any unexpanded states, and (2) the error bound of the policy is less than some predetermined threshold. Like other heuristic search algorithms, LAO* can find an optimal solution without visiting the entire state space. The convergence proofs for the original LAO* algorithm carry over in a straightforward way to symbolic LAO*.

Admissible heuristics LAO* uses an admissible heuristic to guide the search. Because a heuristic is typically defined for all states, a simple way to create an admissible heuristic is to use dynamic programming to create an approximate value function. Given an error bound on the approximation, the value function can be converted to an admissible heuristic. (Another way to ensure admissibility is to perform value iteration on an initial value function that is admissible, since each step of value iteration preserves admissibility.) Symbolic dynamic programming can be used to compute an approximate value function efficiently. St. Aubin et al. (2000) describe an approximate dynamic programming algorithm for factored MDPs, called APRICODD, that is based on SPUDD. It simplifies the value function ADD by aggregating states with similar values. Another approach to approximate dynamic programming for factored MDPs described by Dearden and Boutilier (1997) can also be used to compute admissible heuristics.

Use of dynamic programming to compute an admissible heuristic points to a two-fold approach to solving factored MDPs. First, dynamic programming is used to compute an approximate solution for all states that serves as a heuristic. Then heuristic search is used to find an exact solution for a subset of reachable states.

Experimental results

Table 2 compares the performance of LAO* and SPUDD on the factory examples (f to f6) used by Hoey *et al.*(1999) to test the performance of SPUDD, as well as some additional examples (a1 to a4). We use additional test examples because many of the state variables in the factory examples represent resources that cannot be affected by any action. As a result, we found that only a small number of states are reachable from a given start state in these examples. Examples a1 to a4 (which are artificial examples) are structured so that every state variable can be changed by some action, and thus, most or all of the state space can be reached from any start state. Such examples present a greater challenge to a heuristic-search approach.

Because the performance of LAO* depends on the start state, the experimental results reported for LAO* in Table 2 are averages for 50 random starting states. To create an admissible heuristic, we performed several iterations (ten for the factory examples and twenty for the others) of an approximate value iteration algorithm similar to APRICODD (St-Aubin, Hoey, & Boutilier 2000). The algorithm was started with an admissible value function created by assuming the maximum reward is received each step. The time used to compute the heuristic for these examples is between 2% and 8% of the running time of SPUDD on the same examples. Experiments were performed on a Sun UltraSPARC II with a 300MHz processor and 2 gigabytes of memory.

LAO* achieves its efficiency by focusing computation on a subset of reachable states. The column labelled $|E|$ shows the average number of states visited by an optimal policy, beginning from a random start state. Clearly, the factory examples have an unusual structure, since an optimal policy for these examples visits very few states. The numbers are

Example			Reachability Results Symb-LAO*			Size Results				Timing Results				
						Symb-LAO*		SPUDD		Symb-LAO*			LAO*	SPUDD
	$|S|$	$|A|$	$|E|$	$|G|$	reach	N	L	N	L	exp.	DP	total	total	total
f	2^{17}	14	5	105	190	55	5	1220	246	0.3	6.4	6.7	3.8	34.5
f0	2^{19}	14	5	62	132	61	5	1597	246	0.2	3.5	3.7	3.7	46.2
f1	2^{21}	14	4	54	107	54	4	3101	327	0.1	3.6	3.7	3.7	101.6
f2	2^{22}	14	4	66	125	53	4	3101	327	0.2	4.1	4.4	4.1	105.0
f3	2^{25}	15	4	59	136	74	4	9215	357	0.2	4.7	4.9	3.7	289.1
f4	2^{28}	15	4	49	125	78	4	22170	527	0.1	5.0	5.2	3.7	645.3
f5	2^{31}	18	5	218	509	83	4	44869	1515	1.2	35.9	37.3	4.4	1524.2
f6	2^{35}	23	9	1419	2386	106	5	169207	3992	13.5	771.5	792.6	9.3	7479.5
a1	2^{20}	25	3.0×10^3	3.3×10^3	1.0×10^6	181	19	15758	4056	0.5	53.6	54.0	39.01	12774.3
a2	2^{20}	30	1.0×10^4	3.3×10^4	1.0×10^6	6240	2190	9902	4594	57.7	1678.5	1738.1	4581.9	10891.7
a3	2^{30}	10	1.8×10^6	1.9×10^6	6.7×10^7	3522	439	25839	6434	7.3	344.8	352.1	NA	11169.9
a4	2^{40}	10	9.6×10^4	2.8×10^6	1.7×10^{10}	99	4	NA	NA	0.7	75.5	76.3	NA	NA

Table 2: Performance comparison of LAO* (both symbolic and non-symbolic) and SPUDD.

much larger for examples a1 through a4. The column labeled *reach* shows the average number of states that can be reached from the start state, by following *any* policy. The column labelled $|G|$ is important because it shows the number of states "expanded" by LAO*. These are states for which a backup is performed at some point in the algorithm, and this number depends on the quality of the heuristic. The better the heuristic, the fewer states need to be expanded to find an optimal policy. The gap between $|E|$ and *reach* reflects the potential for increased efficiency using heuristic search, instead of simple reachability analysis. The gap between $|G|$ and *reach* reflects the actual increased efficiency.

The columns labeled N and L, under LAO* and SPUDD respectively, compare the size of the final value function returned by symbolic LAO* and SPUDD. The columns under N give the number of nodes in the respective value function ADDs, and the columns under L give the number of leaves. Because LAO* focuses computation on a subset of the state space, it finds a much more compact solution (which translates into increased efficiency).

The last five columns compare the average running times of symbolic LAO* to the running times of non-symbolic LAO* and SPUDD. Times are given in CPU seconds. For many of these examples, the MDP model is too large to represent explicitly. Therefore, our implementation of non-symbolic LAO* uses the same ADD representation of the MDP model as symbolic LAO* and SPUDD. However, non-symbolic LAO* performs heuristic search in the conventional way by creating a search graph in which the nodes correspond to "flat" states that are enumerated individually.

The total running time of symbolic LAO* is broken down into two parts; the column "exp." shows the average time for policy expansion and the column "DP" shows the average time for dynamic programming. These results show that dynamic programming consumes most of the running time. This is in keeping with a similar observation about the original (non-symbolic) LAO* algorithm. The time reported for dynamic programming includes the time for masking. For this set of examples, masking takes between 0.5% and 2.1% of the running time of the dynamic programming step.

The last three columns compare the average time it takes symbolic LAO* to solve each problem, for 50 random starting states, to the running times of non-symbolic LAO* and SPUDD. This comparison leads to several observations.

First, we note that the running time of non-symbolic LAO* is correlated with $|G|$, the number of states evaluated (i.e., expanded) during the search, which in turn is affected by the starting state, the reachability structure of the problem, and the accuracy of the heuristic function. As $|G|$ increases, the running time of non-symbolic LAO* increases. The search graphs for examples a3 and a4 are so large that these problems cannot be solved using non-symbolic LAO*. (NA indicates that the problem could not be solved.)

The running time of symbolic LAO* depends not only on $|G|$, but on the degree of state abstraction the symbolic approach achieves in representing the states in G. For the factory examples and example a1, the number of states evaluated by LAO* is small enough that the overhead of symbolic search outweighs the improved efficiency from state abstraction. For these examples, symbolic LAO* is somewhat slower than non-symbolic LAO*. But for examples a2 to a4, the symbolic approach significantly – and sometimes dramatically – improves the performance of LAO*. Symbolic LAO* also outperforms SPUDD for all examples. This is to be expected since LAO* solves the problem for only part of the state space. Nevertheless, it demonstrates the power of using heuristic search to focus computation on relevant states.

We conclude by noting that examples a3 and a4 are beyond the range of both SPUDD and non-symbolic LAO*, or can only be solved with great difficulty. Yet symbolic LAO* solves both examples efficiently. This illustrates the advantage of combining heuristic search and state abstraction, rather than relying on either approach alone.

Related work

As noted in the introduction, symbolic model checking techniques have been used previously for nondeterministic planning. In both nondeterministic and decision-theoretic planning, plans may contain cycles that represent iterative, or "trial-and-error," strategies. In nondeterministic planning, the concept of a *strong cyclic plan* plays a central role (Cimatti, Roveri, & Traverso 1998; Daniele, Traverso, & Vardi 1999). It refers to a plan that contains an iterative strategy and is guaranteed to eventually achieve the goal. The concept of a strong cyclic plan has an interesting analogy in decision-theoretic planning. LAO* was originally developed for the framework of stochastic shortest-path problems. A stochastic shortest-path problem is an MDP with a goal state, where the objective is to find an optimal policy (usually containing cycles) among policies that reach the goal state with probability one. A policy that reaches the goal with probability one, also called a *proper policy*, can be viewed as a probabilistic generalization of the concept of a strong cyclic plan. In this respect and others, the symbolic LAO* algorithm presented in this paper can be viewed as a decision-theoretic generalization of symbolic algorithms for nondeterministic planning.

One difference is that the algorithm presented in this paper uses heuristic search to limit the number of states for which a policy is computed. An integration of symbolic model checking with heuristic search has not yet been explored for nondeterministic planning. However, Edelkamp & Reffel(1998) describe a symbolic generalization of A* that combines symbolic model checking and heuristic search in solving deterministic planning problems. A combined approach has also been explored for conformant planning (Bertoli, Cimatti, & Roveri 2001).

In motivation, our work is closely related to the framework of *structured reachability analysis*, which exploits reachability analysis in solving factored MDPs (Boutilier, Brafman, & Geib 1998). However, there are important differences. The symbolic model-checking techniques we use differ from the approach to state abstraction used in that work, which is derived from GRAPHPLAN. More importantly, their concept of reachability analysis is weaker than the approach adopted here. In their framework, states are considered irrelevant if they cannot be reached from the start state by following *any policy*. By contrast, our approach considers states irrelevant if it can be proved (by gradually expanding a partial policy guided by an admissible heuristic) that these states cannot be reached from the start state by following *an optimal policy*. Use of an admissible heuristic to limit the search space is characteristic of heuristic search, in contrast to simple reachability analysis. As Table 2 shows, LAO* evaluates much less of the state space than simple reachability analysis. The better the heuristic, the smaller the number of states it examines.

Conclusion

We have described a symbolic generalization of LAO* that solves factored MDPs using heuristic search. Given a start state, LAO* uses an admissible heuristic to focus computation on the parts of the state space that are reachable from the start state. The stronger the heuristic, the greater the focus and the more efficient a planner based on this approach. Symbolic LAO* also exploits state abstraction using symbolic model checking techniques. It can be viewed as a decision-theoretic generalization of symbolic approaches to nondeterministic planning.

To solve very large MDPs, we believe that decision-theoretic planners will need to employ a collection of complementary strategies that exploit different forms of problem structure. Showing how to combine heuristic search with symbolic techniques for state abstraction is a step in this direction. Integrating additional strategies into a decision-theoretic planner is a topic for future research.

Acknowledgments This work was supported, in part, by NSF grant IIS-9984952 and by NASA grants NAG-2-1463 and NAG-2-1394.

References

Barto, A.; Bradtke, S.; and Singh, S. 1995. Learning to act using real-time dynamic programming. *Artificial Intelligence* 72:81–138.

Bertoli, P.; Cimatti, A.; and Roveri, M. 2001. Heuristic search + symbolic model checking = efficient conformant planning. In *Proceedings of the 17th International Joint Conference on Artificial Intelligence*, 467–472.

Boutilier, C.; Brafman, R. I.; and Geib, C. 1998. Structured reachability analysis for Markov decision processes. In *Proceedings of the 14th International Conference on Uncertainty in Artificial Intelligence*, 24–32.

Cimatti, M.; Roveri, M.; and Traverso, P. 1998. Automatic OBDD-based generation of universal plans in nondeterministic domains. In *Proceedings of the 15th National Conference on Artificial Intelligence*, 875 – 881.

Daniele, M.; Traverso, P.; and Vardi, M. 1999. Strong cyclic planning revisited. In *Proceedings of the 5th European Conference on Planning*.

Dean, T.; Kaelbling, L.; Kirman, J.; and Nicholson, A. 1995. Planning under time constraints in stochastic domains. *Artificial Intelligence* 76:35–74.

Dearden, R., and Boutilier, C. 1997. Abstraction and approximate decision-theoretic planning. *Artificial Intelligence* 89:219–283.

Edelkamp, S., and Reffel, F. 1998. OBDDs in heuristic search. In *German Conference on Artificial Intelligence (KI)*, 81–92.

Hansen, E., and Zilberstein, S. 2001. LAO*: A heuristic search algorithm that finds solutions with loops. *Artificial Intelligence* 129:35–62.

Hoey, J.; St-Aubin, R.; Hu, A.; and Boutilier, C. 1999. SPUDD: Stochastic planning using decision diagrams. In *Proceedings of the 15th Conference on Uncertainty in Articial Intelligence*, 279–288.

Somenzi, F. 1999. Binary decision diagrams. In Broy, M., and Steinbruggen, R., eds., *Calculational System Design*, volume 173 of *NATO Science Series F: Computer and Systems Sciences*. IOS Press. 303–366.

St-Aubin, R.; Hoey, J.; and Boutilier, C. 2000. APRICODD: Approximate policy construction using decision diagrams. In *Proceedings of NIPS-2000*.

Plan Evaluation with Incomplete Action Descriptions

Andrew Garland and Neal Lesh
Cambridge Research Laboratory, MERL
201 Broadway, Cambridge, MA 02139
{garland,lesh}@merl.com

Abstract

This paper presents a framework that justifies an agent's goal-directed behavior, even in the absence of a provably correct plan. Most prior planning systems rely on a complete causal model and circumvent the *frame problem* by implicitly assuming that no unspecified relationships exist between actions and the world. In our approach, a domain modeler provides explicit statements about which actions have been incompletely specified. Thus, an agent can minimize its dependence on implicit assumptions when selecting an action sequence to achieve its goals.

Introduction

Traditional work on planning makes the simplifying assumption that the planner is given a complete and correct description of the current state of the world, and a complete and correct model of actions it can perform. Past research on dealing with incomplete information has developed two kinds of approaches: *acquire* better information or *minimize* dependence on incomplete information.

Both approaches have been used to overcome incomplete state information. The acquisition approach involves plans with sensing actions (Etzioni *et al.*, 1992), while the minimization approach typically involves constructing plans that will succeed in all states of the world consistent with the known information (Smith & Weld, 1998). To date, however, only the acquisition approach has been used to overcome incompleteness in action models. In particular, machine learning techniques have been applied to the results of executing actions in order to acquire more accurate action descriptions (Gil, 1994; Wang, 1995; Oates & Cohen, 1996).

We describe novel techniques for minimizing dependence on incomplete information in a given action model. We present a tractable algorithm for identifying the *risks* of a plan, each of which represents a potential source of execution failure due to incompleteness of the action model. Our work is motivated by the observation that producing complete action descriptions is an exceedingly difficult and time-consuming task. In our approach, the domain experts who generate the action descriptions can provide additional information about the completeness of the model, similar to statements used to reason about incomplete states (Levesque,

1996; Golden, 1998; Babaian & Schmolze, 2000). For example, the experts can indicate which actions have been completely described, or that executing an action will not change the truth value of a predicate. This information can be used to eliminate risks of candidate plans.

Essentially, we are revisiting the infamous *frame problem* (McCarthy & Hayes, 1969), which motivated the traditional completeness assumptions (Reiter, 1991). Without the completeness assumptions, it is necessary for the effects of an action description to include all facts whose truth value does *not* change as a result of executing it. The conceptual shift we make is to a willingness to execute plans with some risk of failure if the action model is incomplete. Our methods simply prefer to execute plans with fewer risks.

The advantage of our approach is to execute plans that achieve their goal more often. As a simple example, a plan composed of completely-modeled actions is more likely to succeed than one with incompletely-modeled actions. Additionally, our techniques will sometimes prefer a plan because of certain orderings of actions, the inclusion of "extra" steps that reestablish conditions that could have been clobbered, or the substitution of an action by one with similar effects. We show that even in the case where the domain expert provides no information about the completeness of the model, our techniques can select plans that are more likely to succeed than if the incompleteness of the model is ignored.

In this paper, we present a linear-time algorithm for identifying risks and a flexible framework for evaluating plans based on risks. We prove that plans with certain *critical* risks cannot be guaranteed to succeed. Finally, we describe two experimental case studies that measure the impact of our techniques on plan success.

Formulation

We assume a traditional planning representation. We also assume that for any planning domain, there exists a set of complete and correct action descriptions, which we will refer to as D_{true}. The set of action descriptions D available to a planner (or plan evaluator) will be a subset of the information in D_{true}.

Each action description consists of a specification of its preconditions and effects as sets of fluent literals. Thus, each action description a in D may include only a subset of a's preconditions and effects in D_{true}. In future work, we will look to extend the representations and techniques in this work to accommodate action descriptions that include conditional effects.

A plan is a sequence of actions that is intended to achieve a goal when executed in an initial state. Executing an action in a state in which all of its preconditions are true will produce a new state in which all of its effects are true and all other fluents remain unchanged. Executing an action with any false preconditions has no effect on the state.

In order to focus on issues related to incomplete action models, we do not address uncertainty about the state in this paper. Instead, we assume that the planner is given a complete state of the world, s_0. However, this does not sidestep any fundamental issues because executing actions with incompletely modeled effects creates uncertainty about the state of the world.

In our discussion, we will often need to reason about whether a plan will be successful given the information contained in D. We define $achieves(D, s_0, g, p)$ as returning true iff the goal g is true in the state that results from simulating the execution of plan p from state s_0 assuming that D is correct and complete.

Representing incomplete action descriptions

We now present a language for supplementing D with statements about the completeness of action descriptions. Our approach follows the use of locally closed-world (LCW) statements that are used to overcome incomplete state information. In that setting, an LCW statement expresses limited knowledge of the state, such as that all the files that exist in a particular directory are known by a software agent (Golden, 1998; Babaian & Schmolze, 2000).

In our work, an LCW statement expresses limited completeness of action descriptions. These statements are defined in terms of three predicates: $DoesNotRelyOn$, $DoesNotMakeTrue$, and $DoesNotMakeFalse$. The truth value of these predicates is directly specified by the user; no inference is performed.

The statement $DoesNotRelyOn(a, x)$ asserts that action a does not have precondition x or $\neg x$ in D_{true}, where x is an atom. We define $CompletePreconditions(a)$ as a shorthand for the formula:

$$\forall x . x \notin preconditions(a) \supset DoesNotRelyOn(a, x)$$

which is equivalent to explicitly stating that the completeness of preconditions assumption is valid for a.

The statement $DoesNotMakeTrue(a, x)$ asserts that a does not have effect x in D_{true}, where x is a literal. The statement $DoesNotMakeFalse(a, x)$ asserts that a does not have effect $\neg x$ in D_{true}. We define $CompleteEffects(a)$ as a shorthand for the formula:

$$\forall x . x \notin effects(a) \supset DoesNotMakeTrue(a, x) \wedge \\ DoesNotMakeFalse(a, x)$$

which is equivalent to explicitly stating that the completeness of effects assumption is valid for a.

There is a set of potential LCW statements that warrant special consideration. If an action a maintains (i.e., does not clobber) a listed precondition x, it is possible that x will not

be listed as an effect (since it is implied by the completeness of effects assumption). However, in most domains, $DoesNotMakeFalse(a, x)$ can safely be assumed to be true. Thus, our implementation can, optionally, automatically add such frame axioms to the user-specified LCW statements.[1]

Plan selection

A *plan selection problem* is a 5-tuple (g, C, s_0, D, L), where g is a goal, C is a set of candidate plans, s_0 describes the initial state, D is a potentially incomplete action model, and L is a set of locally closed world statements. The ideal solution to this problem is to find the plan that will achieve its goal given the actual action descriptions. More precisely, the objective is to find $c_i \in C$ so that $achieves(D_{true}, s_0, g, c_i)$. The quality of a plan selection algorithm can be measured by how frequently it chooses a plan that actually achieves g. Another measure is how often the plan selection algorithm indicates that no plan should be executed if, in fact, no plan in C will achieve g given D_{true}.

Algorithm and Analysis

We consider the following four types of risks, each of which is a potential source of execution failure, for a plan composed of actions $a_1, ..., a_n$. Without loss of generality, we encode the initial state as an action a_0 with no preconditions and effects s_0 and encode the goal g as action a_{n+1} which has preconditions g and no effects.

- POSSCLOB(a_i, x) :: action a_i might have the effect $\neg x$, and there exists action a_j, for $i < j$ that has precondition x in D and no action between a_i and a_j has effect x in D.

- PRECOPEN(a_i) :: action a_i might have an unlisted precondition that will not be true when a_i is executed in $a_0, .., a_n$.

- PRECFALSE(a_i, x) :: a_i has a precondition x in D which will be false when executed in $a_0, .., a_n$, according to D.

- HYPOTHESIZEDEFFECT(a_i, x) :: the correctness of the plan relies on an effect x of a_i that is not listed in D, but might be part of D_{true}. This means that x is consistent with the description of a_i in D, but there is no evidence to support the hypothesis that x is part of the description of a_i in D_{true}.

The first two types of risks correspond to relying on knowledge implied by completeness assumptions, i.e., that D is a good approximation to D_{true}. In contrast, the latter two risks rely on the incompleteness of the model in order to justify plans that would fail if $D = D_{true}$. For example, an action with a PRECFALSE(a_i, x) risk cannot successfully execute unless a previous action has an effect x that is not in D, or the action that negates x has an unlisted precondition.

If no plan justified by the action descriptions in D can achieve goal g then it is worth considering plans with other possible risks. For example, it seems preferable to execute a plan with one hypothesized effect than one with five such

---

[1]This can be done trivially by a pre-processor.

```
FINDRISKS (<a_1, ..., a_n>, g, L) ≡
  RiskSet ← ∅
  Unsupported ← g
  for i = n to 1
    Supported ← Unsupported ∩ EFFECTS(a_i)
    Supported ← Supported \ PRECONDITIONS(a_i)
    Unsupported ← Unsupported \ Supported
    forall literals x in Unsupported
      if DoesNotMakeFalse(a_i, x) ∉ L
        RiskSet ← RiskSet ∪ { POSSCLOB(a_i, x) }
    if CompletePreconditions(a_i) ∉ L
      RiskSet ← RiskSet ∪ { PRECOPEN(a_i) }
    Unsupported ← Unsupported ∪ PRECONDITIONS(a_i)
  return RiskSet
```

Figure 1: Finding risks in a provably correct plan.

effects.[2] However, these plans must be weighed against the alternative of doing nothing, which can be the best option if the chance of achieving a goal is small. Assessing these options would be more practical within a probabilistic framework.

The function FINDRISKS, shown in Figure 1, produces the set of risks of a plan $c = a_1, ..., a_n$, a goal g, and a set of locally closed world statements L. The algorithm requires $O(nm)$ time, where n is the length of the plan, and m is the number of literals in D. The pseudo-code is streamlined by assuming that c is a provably-correct plan in D; therefore, there is no need to check for hypothesized effects, false preconditions, or that g is achieved.[3]

FINDRISKS requires one pass over the plan, working backwards from the last action. During processing, it keeps track of the set of literals that must eventually be achieved by an earlier action or be true in the initial state of the world. Each action a_i may provide support for some of these literals, namely the literals that are made true by the action. For each remaining unsupported literal x, the set of LCW statements L is checked to see if a_i might clobber x; if so, POSSCLOB(a_i, x) is added to the result. Also, L is checked to see if a_i's preconditions are completely modeled; if not, PRECOPEN(a_i) is added to the result. It might seem strange that PRECONDITIONS(a_i) is not checked to be true; however, this is not needed since we assume that the input plan is provably correct in D.

Analysis

We now discuss the implications of risks. We show that a plan without risks cannot fail. We then describe a tractable method for identifying a subset of risks which imply the possibility of plan failure.

Roughly speaking, we say that it is possible for a plan to fail if there exists a possible world that is consistent with the

---

[2]How and why a planner would hypothesize such effects are beyond the scope of this paper.

[3]A more general version of this algorithm exists that efficiently finds these risks as well. When simulating the execution of the plan using D, if an action's preconditions are false, we treat it as having no effects and add a PRECFALSE risk to RiskSet.

information given the planner in which p does not achieve its goals. More precisely, we mean there exists some D' such that $D \subseteq D'$, D' is consistent with the locally-closed world statements L, and $\neg achieves(D', s_0, g, c)$.

Determining if a plan will succeed involves reasoning over all possible states that might occur in the execution of the plan, which is exponential in the length of the the plan if there is uncertainty in the outcome of the actions. Under our assumption of a correct but incomplete model, any plan that can fail in D_{true} will have at least one risk. The following theorem states that a plan that has no risks and will succeed given action model D will also succeed given any action model that is a superset of D (and a subset of D_{true}). As a corollary, the plan will succeed given D_{true}.

Theorem: if $D \subseteq D' \subseteq D_{true}$ and FINDRISKS(c, g, L) contains no risks and $achieves(D, s_0, g, c)$ then $achieves(D', s_0, g, c)$.

Proof sketch: Consider the first action a_1 in c. Given that there are no PRECFALSE risks, all of a_1's preconditions in D must be true in s_0. Since there are no PRECOPEN risks, all of a_1's preconditions in D' must be true in s_0 and thus a_1 will execute successfully in s_0. A similar argument says that a_2 will execute successfully as long as no effect of action a_1 clobbered a precondition x of a_2 that was true in s_0. However, if such a clobbering existed and x were in D then there would be a POSSCLOB(a_1, x) risk. If x were not in D then there would have to be an PRECOPEN(a_2) risk. Thus a_2 will execute successfully. By induction, the entire plan will execute successfully, including the last action which can encode the goal, as described above.

A plan with risks may also succeed when executed in the world because the actions are, in fact, completely modeled or the omissions in the model do not adversely effect the plan or because the plan succeeds with all possible action descriptions that are consistent with D. We can, however, define a subset of risks which are *critical*. A *critical* risk is not guaranteed to cause plan failure, but it does guarantee the possibility of failure.

In order to identify the critical risks, we first identify a set of *vulnerable* conditions in p. Intuitively, a condition is vulnerable if has only one source of support in a plan. Formally, we define vulnerability recursively as follows. A conjunct of the goal is vulnerable in a plan iff it is established exactly once by an action in the plan or the initial state s_0. A precondition x of an action in a plan is vulnerable iff the action has an effect which establishes a vulnerable condition and x is established exactly once by either a prior action in the plan or by the initial state. The set of vulnerable conditions in a plan can be quickly computed in a simple pass backwards through the plan.

We can now define critical risks for the actions in a plan $p = a_1, ..., a_n$. A PRECOPEN(a_i) risk is critical if a_i establishes a vulnerable condition. A HYPOTHESIZEDEFFECT(a_i, x) condition is critical if x is vulnerable. A POSSCLOB(a_i, x) is critical if x is vulnerable and a_i would execute successfully under the assumption that D is complete. A PRECFALSE(a_i, x) risk is critical if action

a_i establishes a vulnerable condition. The critical risks can also be easily computed in a single pass through the plan.

The following theorem states that critical risks guarantee possible plan failure.

Theorem: If FINDRISKS(c, g, L) contains a critical risk, then there exists some D' such that $D \subset D'$, D' is consistent with the LCW in L, and $\neg achieves(D', s', g, c)$.

Proof sketch: We briefly consider each type of risk. In each case, we show there exists a D' such that a vulnerable condition of the plan will not be established or will be clobbered, which causes plan failure. An action a_i with a critical PREC-OPEN risk can fail because there exists an x (or $\neg x$) that is a precondition of a_i in D' such that x will be false after a_{i-1} is executed. If a plan has a critical POSSCLOB(a_i, x) risk then it can fail if D' is identical to D except that action a_i has effect x, which will clobber a vulnerable condition. If $D' = D$, then a plan with a critical HYPOTHESIZEDEFFECT or PRECFALSE action will fail.

Plan selection algorithm

We now present our solution to the plan selection problem. Below we list a variety of policies for preferring one plan to another. Each policy takes two candidate plans, c_1 and c_2, and returns true if c_1 is preferred to c_2. We use $risks(c)$ as a shorthand for FINDRISKS(c, g, L). We assume that a plan that achieves its goal with the given action descriptions is preferable to any plan that does not. Thus we assume that either both c_1 and c_2 achieve the goal given D or neither do.

- $RP_\emptyset(c_1, c_2) :: risks(c_1) = \emptyset$, and $risks(c_2)$ contains a critical risk.

- $RP_\subset(c_1, c_2) :: risks(c_1) \subset risks(c_2)$.

- $RP_<(c_1, c_2)$ :: the number of each type of risk in $risks(c_1)$ is less than that the number of that type of risk in $risks(c_2)$.

- $RP_w(c_1, c_2) :: weighted(c_1) < weighted(c_2)$ where $weighted(c)$ returns a real number by adding together the number of each type of risk multiplied by a pre-defined weight for that risk type.

Risks assessment can be incorporated with other methods for preferring plans. For example, most planners have an implicit preference for selecting the shortest plan that achieves the goal. These preference rules can either dominate the pre-existing preference method or be used only to break ties. Let $TieBreak(RP, c_1, c_2)$ return true if either the pre-existing preference method prefers c_1 to c_2 or it ranks them equal and $RP(c_1, c_2)$ is true.

The $TieBreak(RP_\emptyset, c_1, c_2)$ policy is the most conservative use of the techniques discussed in this paper. It only uses our techniques in the case where two candidate plans are considered equal (ignoring the incompleteness issues) and one has no risks and the other has at least one critical risk. We present it as an extreme case in which reasoning about incompleteness clearly (if infrequently) improves plan selection. As shown above, if the action descriptions in D are correct but incomplete then a plan with critical risks might fail, while a plan without risks cannot fail. If there

is no other basis for preferring one plan to another, it seems obviously beneficial to prefer the plan that cannot fail.

The other policies are more widely applicable but can prefer a plan that happens to fail to one that happens to succeed given D_{true}. This can happen with $RP_<$ and RP_w if plan c_1 has fewer risks than c_2, but all risks in c_1 happen to correspond to real discrepancies between D and D_{true} while all the risks in c_2 happen not to.

Somewhat surprisingly, however, even if c_1 has a subset of the risks of c_2, it is possible that c_1 will fail and c_2 will succeed. One reason for this is that a POSSCLOB(a_i, x) risk can be *realized*, i.e., a_i does have effect x in D_{true}, but then *corrected* by another action which has a $\neg x$ effect which is also missing from D. Further, it is possible that the risk will be corrected in c_2 but not in c_1 if only c_2 has the correcting action. If c_2 has some other risks which are not realized, then it will succeed while c_1 fails, even though c_1 has a subset of c_2's risks.

While the policies other than $TieBreak(RP_\emptyset)$ can choose the inferior plan in certain cases, they are likely to improve plan selection, on average, under a reasonable set of assumptions about the distribution of planning problems. For example, for any given POSSCLOB risk, it seems much more likely that it will be realized than that it will be both realized and then corrected. If one plan has more POSS-CLOB risks than another, then it is more likely to have a realized but uncorrected risk than the other, and therefore is more likely to fail.

Examples

We now describe three classes of planning problems for which it is beneficial to reason about the incompleteness of the action descriptions.

The first class of problems concerns the order of actions in a plan. Figure 2 shows a simple example designed to illustrate how our risk analysis can prefer one ordering of plan actions over another. In this figure, actions are drawn as links, from the action's preconditions on the left to the action's effects on the right.

Figure 2 shows a goal that can be achieved by executing two actions, a_1 and a_2, in either order. If the action model is complete then both plans will achieve their goal.

Either plan can fail, however, if the model is incomplete. Candidate plan $C_1 = [a_1, a_2]$ could fail if a_2 has an effect $\neg r$ which clobbers a_1's effect. Similarly, plan $C_2 = [a_2, a_1]$ could fail if a_1 clobbers a_2's effect. However, C_2 could also

init	plan C_1	goal		init	plan C_2	goal
$\{p\}$	$p \xrightarrow{a_1} r \quad \xrightarrow{a_2} q$	$\{r,q\}$		$\{p\}$	$\xrightarrow{a_2} q \quad p \xrightarrow{a_1} r$	$\{r,q\}$

Risks	Risks
PRECOPEN(a_1)	PRECOPEN(a_1)
PRECOPEN(a_2)	PRECOPEN(a_2)
POSSCLOB(a_2, r)	POSSCLOB(a_1, q)
	POSSCLOB(a_2, p)

Figure 2: **Action order.** These two plans differ only in the order of the actions, but they have different numbers of risks.

init	plan C_1	goal
$\{p\}$	$\overrightarrow{a_1}q$ $q\overrightarrow{a_2}r$ $r\overrightarrow{a_3}s$ $s,p\overrightarrow{a_4}t$	$\{t\}$

Risks

PRECOPEN(a_1)	POSSCLOB(a_1, p)
PRECOPEN(a_2)	POSSCLOB(a_2, p)
PRECOPEN(a_3)	POSSCLOB(a_3, p)
PRECOPEN(a_4)	

init	plan C_2	goal
$\{p\}$	$\overrightarrow{a_1}q$ $q\overrightarrow{a_2}r$ $r\overrightarrow{a_3}s$ $\overrightarrow{a_5}p$ $s,p\overrightarrow{a_4}t$	$\{t\}$

Risks

PRECOPEN(a_1)	POSSCLOB(a_5, s)
PRECOPEN(a_2)	
PRECOPEN(a_3)	
PRECOPEN(a_4)	
PRECOPEN(a_5)	

Figure 3: **Additional steps.** The extra step a_5 in plan C_2 reduces the number of possible clobberings of action a_4.

fail if a_2 has effect $\neg p$ which would clobber a_1's known precondition. Thus, C_2 has more POSSCLOB risks than C_1 and both the $RP_<$ and RP_w policies would prefer C_1 to C_2.

The preference for C_1 over C_2 is justified by imagining what we could add to D in order to create a D_{true} in which the plans would fail. For any combination of additional conditions and effects that would cause C_2 to fail, there is a corresponding modification that would cause C_1 to fail. However, in order to "match" the risk introduced by adding $\neg p$ as an effect of C_2, we have to add both a precondition and an effect to C_1. Thus, in the absence of any LCW information, C_1 seems the safer choice. On the other hand, if the given LCW eliminates the risks of plan C_2, then it becomes the better plan to execute.

The second class of problems we consider are ones in which our plan selection policies will sometimes prefer plans with what seem like extra steps, i.e., steps that are not required to make the plan execute successfully given D. Figure 3 shows a simple example of how this could happen. If a precondition x of an action a_i is established by the initial state or by an early action then it has many chances to be clobbered. By adding in a "cleanup" step just before a_i to reestablish x, these potential clobberings risks are removed. However, the added step may also introduce risks, such as the PRECOPEN risk in Figure 3. If POSSCLOB risks are

init	plan C_1	goal		init	plan C_2	goal
$\{w\}$	$\overrightarrow{a_1}r,q$ $w,q\overrightarrow{a_2}s$	$\{r,s\}$		$\{w\}$	$w\overrightarrow{a_3}p$ $p\overrightarrow{a_4}r,s$	$\{r,s\}$

Risks		Risks
PRECOPEN(a_1)		PRECOPEN(a_3)
PRECOPEN(a_2)		PRECOPEN(a_4)
POSSCLOB(a_1, w)		
POSSCLOB(a_2, r)		

Figure 4: **Operator choice.** The second plan is preferred because there are possible clobberings in the first.

weighted more than half the weight of PRECOPEN risks, then the RP_w will prefer plan C_2 in this example. Additionally, C_2 can be preferred to C_1 by any of the other selection policies if LCW excludes enough risks in C_2.

The third and final class of problems arises when there are alternative actions with similar effects. The issues that arise in the ordering of actions and in adding additional steps also come up in the choice of actions to achieve the same goal or subgoal of a plan. The most obvious role of our techniques would be to prefer to use operators that are completely modeled over ones that are not. Additionally, Figure 4 shows two plans that look equally correct if the prospect of missing effects and preconditions is ignored, but one plan has more risks than the other.

Experiments

We conducted two experiment to measure how useful risk assessment is for plan selection. First, we implemented a modified version of the Fast Forward (FF) planning system (Hoffmann & Nebel, 2001) that exploits augmented domain descriptions to find the risks in each generated plan. The domain descriptions allow some preconditions and effects to be marked as "hidden", i.e. knowledge that is in D_{true} but not in D. Thus, our version of FF can generate plans using D, and then evaluate them using D_{true}.

Our first attempt to evaluate our plan-selection framework was to slightly modify the domain descriptions for the planning domains that FF comes with. However, because the planning domains were highly crafted, we found that even small differences between D and D_{true} often meant that almost none of the plans generated using D would be successful in D_{true}. This did not seem to represent a realistic situation in which a domain model would be incomplete and yet still usable.

Each of our two experiments are based on a suite of pseudo-randomly generated triples $< g, D, D_{true} >$, where g is a planning goal that can be solved in D but the solution may not achieve g when executed in D_{true}. There are precondition / effect dependencies in both D and D_{true} that reduce the number of plans produced by FF. Some additional dependencies are added to D_{true} but not to D so that between 65% and 85% of the solutions in D will achieve their goal in D_{true}. For these experiments, add effects in D_{true} were never hidden in D because if a hidden add-effect is needed to achieve goal g, then FF will not generate any successful plans when given D. Preconditions and delete effects were hidden at random. Also, each action was given, on average, the same number of preconditions to avoid introducing a bias.

In the first experiment, we measured the impact of risk assessment in action ordering decisions. The triples $< g, D, D_{true} >$ were generated such that D (and D_{true}) contained exactly seven actions, all of which had to be executed exactly once to achieve g. Our risk-assessment techniques were used to select which ordering of these seven actions should be executed.

In the second experiment, we measured the impact of risk assessment in operator selection decisions. The triples $< g, D, D_{true} >$ were generated so that g is always achieved

	Percentiles of the number of risks distribution										Avg # of risks	Dev. of risks	Min # of risks	Max # of risks	Number of plans
Run	t_{10}	t_{20}	t_{30}	t_{40}	t_{50}	t_{60}	t_{70}	t_{80}	t_{90}	t_{100}					
AO	87.6	86.2	84.7	84.0	83.1	82.3	81.4	80.3	78.9	76.7	49.4	4.3	42.0	74.0	195254
OC	85.4	83.0	81.4	80.9	79.8	79.0	77.9	77.1	76.3	74.7	72.0	7.8	55.0	115.0	341469

Table 1: Impact of risk assessment on likelihood of successfully executing plans.

by a sequence of length 10. For each position i in the plan, there are two possible choices $a_{i,0}$ and $a_{i,1}$. These two actions share a common effect and a common precondition (which is the common effect of both $a_{(i-1),0}$ and $a_{(i-1),1}$). Our risk-assessment techniques were used to decide which combination of operators should be executed.

Table 1 gives statistics showing how risks and success percentages are related for the two experiments. The first row presents results for the action ordering (abbreviated "AO") and the second presents results for operator choice ("OC"). Within each row, there are 10 columns that show the likelihood of successfully executing a plan drawn at random from different subsets of the set of generated plans. The final five columns show general statistics about the distribution of risks in the set of generated plans.

Within each row, the success percentages in the columns labelled $t_{10}, \ldots, t_{100}$ are derived from different subsets of the set of generated plans. For t_k, the subset contains all plans whose number of risks are in the lowest kth percentile of distribution. For example, t_{50} includes all plans with fewer risks than the median number of risks, and t_{100} includes all plans.

The results show what a significant impact risk assessment can have. For both runs, generating two plans and preferring the one with fewer risks will, on average, increase the chance of success for roughly 75% to 80%. Generating more candidates continues to provide benefits, as selecting a plan from t_{10} increase the likelihood of success to over 85%.

Related Work

Much previous work has addressed the problem of planning with incomplete state information and non-deterministic or conditional effects (e.g, Kushmerick, Hanks, & Weld (1995); Smith & Weld (1998)). This is similar to the problem of planning with incomplete action models in the sense that both problems are concerned with uncertainty about the effects of actions. One important difference, however, is that non-deterministic planning systems demand even more elaborate action descriptions than traditional planners. For example, the action descriptions are required to describe all the different possible sets of effects that an action might have. In contrast, our techniques can improve planning even without any additional information, and we provide a framework in which any additional effort to produce LCW statements can be factored into the planning process. Further, our techniques are designed to exploit various types of information, even statements about which fluents an action does *not* effect.

Additionally, the objective of work on non-deterministic planning is usually to generate plans that are guaranteed to succeed, or are guaranteed to succeed with some probability.

As a result, even assessing a probabilistic or conditional plan to determine if it will succeed requires exponential computation win the length of the plan. In contrast, our methods simply prefer to execute plans with fewer risks. Further, our techniques are linear in the length of the plan and the size of the state, though we do require the planner to generate multiple plans to choose from.

Prior work has addressed the complementary problem of improving action models between planning episodes. One approach has been to develop knowledge acquisition systems that help domain experts convey their knowledge to a computer. For example, Tecuci et. al. (Tecuci et al., 1999) present techniques for producing hierarchical if-then task reduction rules by demonstration and discussion from a human expert. A second approach is to develop techniques for improving action descriptions based on the observed results of executing actions (Gil, 1994; Wang, 1995; Oates & Cohen, 1996). Our techniques are complementary since our methods are designed to improve planning when there are incomplete action descriptions. One possible synergy between these two lines of research would be to develop techniques for automatically learning LCW or helping to elicit it from the domain experts.

Conclusions and Future Work

This work is motivated by our belief that the primary obstacle to the practical application of planning technology is the difficulty of obtaining task models. This problem should be addressed both by developing better techniques for eliciting models, and by adapting planning algorithms to use models that are less difficult to elicit. In this paper, we pursue the latter approach.

Our future work includes incorporating other types of knowledge about how to do things into a planning process that reasons about incomplete action models. As mentioned above, if an important effect or precondition is missing from the action descriptions given to a planner, it can have little chance of achieving its goal. Indeed, once we forgo the completeness assumption, the set of valid plans can no longer be deduced from the action descriptions. Thus, it becomes especially useful for human experts to provide additional information about how to accomplish goals and subgoals by, for example, providing a library of pre-defined goal-decomposition rules (also called recipes and hierarchical task networks). We are particularly interested in using LCW information to allow more flexible use of goal-decomposition knowledge.

Another line of future research is to integrate the techniques presented here into a system that integrates (re)planning and execution. The planning system will keep track of what actions it has executed and what state information it has sensed at different time points. Our techniques for assessing risks can be applied to the execution history in order to determine which fluents it should most rely on. If the preconditions of an executed action had many risks associated with it, then the planner should be wary of using that action's presumed effects to support the preconditions of future actions.

Acknowledgements

We gratefully thank Charles Rich, Candace Sidner, and the anonymous reviewers for their insightful comments.

References

Babaian, T., and Schmolze, J. G. 2000. PSIPlan: Open World Planning with ψ-forms. In *Proc. 5th Int. Conf. on AI Planning Systems*, 292–307.

Etzioni, O.; Hanks, S.; Weld, D.; Draper, D.; Lesh, N.; and Williamson, M. 1992. An approach to planning with incomplete information. In *Proc. 3rd Int. Conf. on Principles of Knowledge Representation and Reasoning*, 115–125.

Gil, Y. 1994. Learning by Experimentation: Incremental Refinement of Incomplete Planning Domains. In *Eleventh Intl Conf on Machine Learning*, 87–95.

Golden, K. 1998. Leap before you Look: Information Gathering in the PUCCINI planner. In *Proc. 4th Int. Conf. on AI Planning Systems*, 70–77.

Hoffmann, J., and Nebel, B. 2001. The FF planning system: Fast plan generation through heuristic search. *Journal of Artificial Intelligence Research* 14:253–302.

Kushmerick, N.; Hanks, S.; and Weld, D. 1995. An Algorithm for Probabilistic Planning. *Artificial Intelligence* 76:239–286.

Levesque, H. J. 1996. What is planning in the presence of sensing. In *Proc. 13th Nat. Conf. AI*, 1139–1146.

McCarthy, J., and Hayes, P. J. 1969. Some philosophical problems from the standpoint of Artificial Intelligence. In Meltzer, B., and Michie, D., eds., *Machine Intelligence 4*. Edinburgh University Press. 463–502.

Oates, T., and Cohen, P. 1996. Searching for planning operators with context-dependent and probabilistic effects. In *Proc. 13th Nat. Conf. AI*, 863–868.

Reiter, R. 1991. The Frame Problem in the Situation Calculus: A Simple Solution (Sometimes) and a Completeness Result for Goal Regression. In Lifschitz, V., ed., *Artificial Intelligence and Mathematical Theory of Computation: Papers in Honor of John McCarthy*. Academic Press. 359–380.

Smith, D., and Weld, D. 1998. Conformant Graphplan. In *Proc. 15th Nat. Conf. AI*, 889–896.

Tecuci, G.; Boicu, M.; Wright, K.; Lee, S.; Marcu, D.; and Bowman, M. 1999. An integrated shell and methodology for rapid development of knowledge-based agents. In *Proc. 16th Nat. Conf. AI*, 250–257.

Wang, X. 1995. Learning by observation and practice: an incremental approach for planning operator acquisition. In *Proc. 12th Int. Conf. on Machine Learning*, 549–557.

Algorithms for a Temporal Decoupling Problem in Multi-Agent Planning

Luke Hunsberger
Department of Engineering and Applied Sciences
Harvard University
Cambridge, MA 02138
luke@eecs.harvard.edu

Abstract

The Temporal Decoupling Problem (TDP) arises when a group of agents collaborating on a set of temporally-dependent tasks seek to coordinate their execution of those tasks by applying additional temporal constraints sufficient to ensure that agents working on different tasks may operate independently. This paper: (1) formally defines the TDP, (2) presents theorems that give necessary and sufficient conditions for solutions to the TDP, (3) presents a family of sound and complete algorithms for solving the TDP, and (4) compares the performance of several variations of the basic algorithm. Although this work was motivated by a problem in collaborative multi-agent planning, it represents a contribution to the theory of Simple Temporal Networks that is independent of the motivating application.

Introduction

In prior work on collaborative, multi-agent systems, Hunsberger and Grosz (2000) presented a group decision-making mechanism based on a combinatorial auction in which agents bid on sets of tasks in a proposed group activity. That work focused on the *winner-determination* problem in which the auctioneer seeks to determine whether there is a consistent set of bids covering all the tasks in the proposed activity. Later work (Hunsberger 2002) focused on the *bidding* phase in which bidders protect their private schedules of pre-existing commitments by including temporal constraints in their bids. This paper addresses a third problem, one that agents face after the awarding of bids, namely, how agents can ensure that the network of temporal constraints among their tasks will *remain* consistent until all of the tasks have been completed.

The following scenario illustrates some of the issues involved. Bill and Sue have committed to doing tasks β_1 and β_2 subject to the temporal constraints

$$3:00 \leq \beta_1 \leq \beta_2 \leq 5:00,$$

with Bill doing β_1 and Sue doing β_2. For simplicity, assume that these tasks have zero duration. The above constraints are satisfied by infinitely many pairs of execution times for β_1 and β_2; however, should Bill decide to execute β_1 at 4:15 (which is consistent with the above constraints) while Sue

independently decides to execute β_2 at 3:45 (also consistent with the original constraints), they will end up violating the constraint $\beta_1 \leq \beta_2$. To avoid doing so, they could agree to one of the following:

- Add further constraints (e.g., $\beta_1 \leq 4:25 \leq \beta_2$) that would effectively decouple their tasks; or
- Have Sue wait until Bill announces a fixed time for β_1 before she decides to fix a time for β_2.

The first approach imposes additional constraints on the constituent tasks, but ensures that Bill and Sue may henceforth operate independently (without any further communication). The second approach gives Bill greater flexibility in that he may operate independently, but makes Sue dependent on Bill and requires him to communicate his choice of execution time for β_1 to her. This paper focuses on generalizing the first approach: providing algorithms to generate additional constraints to temporally decouple the subproblems being worked on by different agents. We leave to future work finding algorithms that follow the second approach (i.e., asymmetrically distributing authority for adding new constraints).

Simple Temporal Networks

The algorithms in this paper manipulate Simple Temporal Networks (Dechter, Meiri, & Pearl 1991). In this section, we briefly review STNs, highlighting their relevant properties.

Definition 1 (Simple Temporal Network) *(Dechter, Meiri, & Pearl 1991) A* Simple Temporal Network $\mathcal{S}$ *is a pair* $(\mathcal{T}, \mathcal{C})$, *where* $\mathcal{T}$ *is a set* $\{t_0, t_1, \ldots, t_N\}$ *of time-point variables and* $\mathcal{C}$ *is a finite set of binary constraints on those variables, each constraint having the form* $t_j - t_i \leq \delta$ *for some real number* δ. *The "variable"* t_0 *represents an arbitrary, fixed reference point on the time-line. (In this paper, we fix* t_0 *to the value 0 and refer to it as the* zero *time-point variable, or z.)*

A solution *to the STN* $\mathcal{S}$ *is a set of variable assignments*

$$\{z = 0, t_1 = v_1, \ldots, t_N = v_N\}$$

satisfying all the constraints in $\mathcal{C}$. *An STN* $\mathcal{S}$ *that has at least one solution is called* consistent.

Constraints involving z are equivalent to unary constraints. For example:

$$L_i \leq t_i \quad \Leftrightarrow \quad 0 - t_i \leq -L_i \quad \Leftrightarrow \quad z - t_i \leq -L_i.$$

Definition 2 (Distance Graph) *(Dechter, Meiri, & Pearl 1991) The* distance graph *for an STN* $S = (\mathcal{T}, \mathcal{C})$ *is a weighted, directed graph* $G_S = (\mathcal{V}_S, \mathcal{E}_S)$, *whose vertices correspond to the time points of* S *and whose edges correspond to the temporal constraints of* S, *as follows:*

$$\mathcal{V}_S = \mathcal{T} \quad \text{and} \quad \mathcal{E}_S = \{(t_i, \delta, t_j) : (t_j - t_i \leq \delta) \in \mathcal{C}\}.$$

Thus, each constraint $t_j - t_i \leq \delta$ in S is represented in G_S by a directed edge from t_i to t_j with weight (or length) δ.

In an STN, the *explicit* constraints in $\mathcal{C}$ may give rise to additional *implicit* constraints. For example, the explicit constraints $t_j - t_i \leq 100$ and $t_k - t_j \leq 200$ combine to entail the implicit constraint $t_k - t_i \leq 300$, as follows:

$$t_k - t_i = (t_k - t_j) + (t_j - t_i) \leq 200 + 100 = 300.$$

In graphical terms, the edges from t_i to t_j to t_k form a *path* of length 300 from t_i to t_k, as illustrated below.

Theorem 1 *(Dechter, Meiri, & Pearl 1991) An STN* S *is* consistent *(i.e., has a solution) if and only if its distance graph* G_S *has no negative cycles (i.e., the path length around any loop is non-negative).*

Definition 3 (Temporal Distance) *(Dechter, Meiri, & Pearl 1991)[1] The* temporal distance *from* t_i *to* t_j *in an STN* S *is the length of the* shortest path *from* t_i *to* t_j *in the corresponding distance graph* G_S.

Equivalently, the temporal distance from t_i to t_j specifies the *strongest implicit constraint* from t_i to t_j in S (where "implicit constraints" is taken to subsume "explicit constraints").

If no path exists from t_i to t_j in G_S, then the temporal distance is infinite, representing that the temporal *difference*, $t_j - t_i$, is unconstrained. On the other hand, if there is a negative cycle in the distance graph, then some temporal distance is negative infinity, representing a constraint that cannot be satisfied.

Definition 4 (Distance Matrix) *(Dechter, Meiri, & Pearl 1991)[2] The* distance matrix *for an STN* $S = (\mathcal{T}, \mathcal{C})$ *is a matrix* $\mathcal{D}$ *such that:*

$$\mathcal{D}(i,j) = \text{Temporal Distance from } t_i \text{ to } t_j \text{ in } S.$$

Abusing notation slightly, we may write $\mathcal{D}(t_i, t_j)$ where t_i and t_j are time-point variables rather than indices.

Fact 2 *(Dechter, Meiri, & Pearl 1991) The distance matrix may be computed in* $O(N^3)$ *time using, for example, Floyd-Warshall's all-pairs shortest-path algorithm (Cormen, Leiserson, & Rivest 1990).*

Fact 3 *From Definitions 3 and 4, we get that the following inequalities hold for any time-points* t_i *and* t_j *in an STN:*

$$-\mathcal{D}(t_j, t_i) \leq t_j - t_i \leq \mathcal{D}(t_i, t_j).$$

---

[1]The concept of temporal distance, implicit in Dechter et al., is made explicit in Tsamardinos (2000).

[2]The concept of the distance matrix is implicit in Dechter et al. Tsamardinos (2000) uses the term *distance array*.

Typically, adding a constraint to an STN causes some entries in the distance matrix to change. The following theorem specifies which constraints can be added without threatening the consistency of the STN.

Theorem 4 *(Dechter, Meiri, & Pearl 1991) For any time-points* t_i *and* t_j *in an STN* S, *the new constraint* $t_j - t_i \leq \delta$ *will not threaten the consistency of* S *if and only if* δ *satisfies* $-\mathcal{D}(t_j, t_i) \leq \delta$. *Furthermore, the consistent STN* S *has a solution in which* $t_j - t_i = \sigma$ *if and only if* $\sigma \in [-\mathcal{D}(t_j, t_i), \mathcal{D}(t_i, t_j)]$.

Corollary 5 *The quantity* $\mathcal{D}(t_i, t_j) + \mathcal{D}(t_j, t_i)$, *which specifies the length of the interval* $[-\mathcal{D}(t_j, t_i), \mathcal{D}(t_i, t_j)]$, *also specifies the maximum amount by which the strongest implicit constraint from* t_i *to* t_j *may be* tightened.

Fact 6 *Given Theorem 1, the following inequality holds for any time-points* t_i *and* t_j *in a consistent STN:*

$$\mathcal{D}(t_i, t_j) + \mathcal{D}(t_j, t_i) \geq 0.$$

Fact 6 says that the length of the shortest path from t_i to t_j and back to t_i is always non-negative. Corollary 5 and Fact 6 together motivate the following new definition.

Definition 5 (Flexibility) *Given time-points* t_i *and* t_j *in a consistent STN, the relative* flexibility *of* t_i *and* t_j *is the (non-negative) quantity:*

$$Flex(t_i, t_j) = \mathcal{D}(t_i, t_j) + \mathcal{D}(t_j, t_i).$$

Rigid Components. Adding a constraint $t_j - t_i \leq \delta$ in the extreme case where $\delta = -\mathcal{D}(t_j, t_i)$ (recall Theorem 4), causes the *updated* distance matrix entries to satisfy:

$$-\mathcal{D}(t_j, t_i) = t_j - t_i = \mathcal{D}(t_i, t_j).$$

In such a case, the temporal difference $t_j - t_i$ is fixed (equivalently, $Flex(t_i, t_j) = 0$), and t_i and t_j are said to be *rigidly connected* (Tsamardinos, Muscettola, & Morris 1998).

The following measure of rigidity will be used in the experimental evaluation section.[3]

Definition 6 (Rigidity) *The relative* rigidity *of the pair of time-points* t_i *and* t_j *in a consistent STN is the quantity:*

$$Rig(t_i, t_j) = \frac{1}{1 + Flex(t_i, t_j)} = \frac{1}{1 + \mathcal{D}(t_i, t_j) + \mathcal{D}(t_j, t_i)}.$$

The RMS rigidity *of a consistent STN* S *is the quantity:*

$$Rig(S) = \sqrt{\frac{2}{N(N+1)} \sum_{i<j} [Rig(t_i, t_j)]^2}.$$

Since $Flex(t_i, t_j) \geq 0$, we have both that $Rig(t_i, t_j) \in [0, 1]$ and that $Rig(S) \in [0, 1]$. If t_i and t_j are part of a rigid component, then $Rig(t_i, t_j) = 1$. Similarly, if S is completely rigid, then $Rig(S) = 1$. At the opposite extreme, if S has absolutely no constraints, then $Rig(S) = 0$.

Fact 7 (Triangle Inequality) *(Tsamardinos 2000) From Definitions 3 and 4, we get that the following holds among each triple of time-points* t_i, t_j *and* t_k *in an STN:*

$$\mathcal{D}(t_i, t_k) \leq \mathcal{D}(t_i, t_j) + \mathcal{D}(t_j, t_k).$$

Definition 7 (Tight Edge/Constraint) *(Morris & Muscettola 2000) A* tight *constraint (or edge) is an explicit constraint* $(t_j - t_i \leq \delta)$ *for which* $\delta = \mathcal{D}(t_i, t_j)$.

---

[3]An earlier paper (Hunsberger 2002) defines a similar measure of rigidity.

The Temporal Decoupling Problem

This section formally defines the Temporal Decoupling Problem and presents theorems characterizing its solutions. To simplify the presentation, we restrict attention to the case of partitioning an STN S into two independent subnetworks S_X and S_Y. The case of an arbitrary number of decoupled subnetworks is analogous.

Definition 8 (z-Partition) *If T, T_X and T_Y are sets of time-point variables such that:*

$$\mathcal{T}_X \cap \mathcal{T}_Y = \{z\} \quad and \quad \mathcal{T}_X \cup \mathcal{T}_Y = \mathcal{T},$$

then we say that $\mathcal{T}_X$ and $\mathcal{T}_Y$ z-partition $\mathcal{T}$.

Definition 9 (Temporal Decoupling) *We say that the STNs $S_X = (\mathcal{T}_X, \mathcal{C}_X)$ and $S_Y = (\mathcal{T}_Y, \mathcal{C}_Y)$ are a temporal decoupling of the STN $S = (\mathcal{T}, \mathcal{C})$ if:*

- *S_X and S_Y are consistent STNs;*
- *$\mathcal{T}_X$ and $\mathcal{T}_Y$ z-partition $\mathcal{T}$; and*
- *(Mergeable Solutions Property) Merging any solutions for S_X and S_Y necessarily yields a solution for S.*

(We may also say that S_X and S_Y partition S into temporally independent subnetworks.)

Result 8 *If S_X and S_Y are a temporal decoupling of S, then S is consistent.*

Proof Since S_X and S_Y are required to be consistent, each has at least one solution; the merging of any such solutions yields a solution for S. ∎

Definition 10 (The Temporal Decoupling Problem) *Given an STN S whose time-points $\mathcal{T}$ are z-partitioned by $\mathcal{T}_X$ and $\mathcal{T}_Y$, find sets of constraints $\mathcal{C}_X$ and $\mathcal{C}_Y$ such that $(\mathcal{T}_X, \mathcal{C}_X)$ and $(\mathcal{T}_Y, \mathcal{C}_Y)$ temporally decouple S.*

Result 9 *Any instance of the TDP in which S is consistent has a solution.*

Proof Let S be a consistent STN whose time-points $\mathcal{T}$ are z-partitioned by $\mathcal{T}_X = \{z, x_1, \ldots, x_m\}$ and $\mathcal{T}_Y = \{z, y_1, \ldots, y_n\}$. Let

$$\{z = 0, x_1 = v_1, \ldots, x_m = v_m; y_1 = w_1, \ldots, y_n = w_n\}$$

be an arbitrary solution for S. Then the following specifies a temporal decoupling of S:

$$\begin{aligned}
\mathcal{C}_X &= \{x_1 = v_1, \ldots, x_m = v_m\} \\
\mathcal{C}_Y &= \{y_1 = w_1, \ldots, y_n = w_n\}. \blacksquare
\end{aligned}$$

We call such decouplings *rigid decouplings*. One problem with rigid decouplings is that the subnetworks S_X and S_Y are completely rigid (i.e., completely inflexible). Below, we provide necessary and sufficient characterizations of solutions to the TDP that will point the way to TDP algorithms that yield more flexible decoupled subnetworks.

Theorem 10 (Necessary Conditions) *If the STNs S_X and S_Y are a temporal decoupling of the STN S, then the following four properties must hold:*

(1) $\mathcal{D}_X(x_i, x_j) \leq \mathcal{D}(x_i, x_j)$ for each $x_i, x_j \in \mathcal{T}_X$;

(2) $\mathcal{D}_Y(y_i, y_j) \leq \mathcal{D}(y_i, y_j)$ for each $y_i, y_j \in \mathcal{T}_Y$;

(3) $\mathcal{D}_X(x, z) + \mathcal{D}_Y(z, y) \leq \mathcal{D}(x, y)$ for each $x \in \mathcal{T}_X$ and $y \in \mathcal{T}_Y$; and

(4) $\mathcal{D}_Y(y, z) + \mathcal{D}_X(z, x) \leq \mathcal{D}(y, x)$ for each $x \in \mathcal{T}_X$ and $y \in \mathcal{T}_Y$,

where $\mathcal{D}_X$, $\mathcal{D}_Y$, and $\mathcal{D}$ are the distance matrices for S_X, S_Y and S, respectively.

Proof Let $S_X = (\mathcal{T}_X, \mathcal{C}_X)$ and $S_Y = (\mathcal{T}_Y, \mathcal{C}_Y)$ be an arbitrary temporal decoupling of the STN $S = (\mathcal{T}, \mathcal{C})$. From Definition 9, both S_X and S_Y must be consistent.

Property 1: Let $x_i, x_j \in \mathcal{T}_X$ be arbitrary. By Theorem 4, there is a solution $\mathcal{X}$ for S_X in which $x_j - x_i = \mathcal{D}_X(x_i, x_j)$. Let $\mathcal{Y}$ be an arbitrary solution for S_Y. Since S_X and S_Y are a temporal decoupling of S, merging the solutions $\mathcal{X}$ and $\mathcal{Y}$ must yield a solution for S. In that solution (for S) we have that $x_j - x_i = \mathcal{D}_X(x_i, x_j)$. However, being a solution for S also implies that: $x_j - x_i \leq \mathcal{D}(x_i, x_j)$.

Property 3: Let $x \in \mathcal{T}_X$ and $y \in \mathcal{T}_Y$ be arbitrary. Let $\mathcal{X}$ be a solution for S_X in which $z - x = \mathcal{D}_X(x, z)$. Similarly, let $\mathcal{Y}$ be a solution for S_Y in which $y - z = \mathcal{D}_Y(z, y)$. Merging the solutions $\mathcal{X}$ and $\mathcal{Y}$ must yield a solution for S. In that solution, we have that: $y - x = (y - z) + (z - x) = \mathcal{D}_Y(z, y) + \mathcal{D}_X(x, z)$. However, being a solution for S also implies that: $y - x \leq \mathcal{D}(x, y)$.

Properties 2 and 4 are handled analogously. ∎

Theorem 11 (Sufficient Conditions) *Let $S = (\mathcal{T}, \mathcal{C})$, $S_X = (\mathcal{T}_X, \mathcal{C}_X)$ and $S_Y = (\mathcal{T}_Y, \mathcal{C}_Y)$ be consistent STNs such that $\mathcal{T}_X$ and $\mathcal{T}_Y$ z-partition $\mathcal{T}$. If Properties 1–4 of Theorem 10 hold, then S_X and S_Y are a temporal decoupling of S.*

Proof Suppose S, S_X and S_Y satisfy the above conditions. The only part of the definition of a temporal decoupling (Definition 9) that is non-trivial to verify in this setting is the Mergeable Solutions Property. Let

$$\begin{aligned}
\mathcal{X} &= \{z = 0, x_1 = v_1, \ldots, x_m = v_m\} \text{ and} \\
\mathcal{Y} &= \{z = 0, y_1 = w_1, \ldots, y_n = v_n\}
\end{aligned}$$

be arbitrary solutions for S_X and S_Y, respectively. We need to show that $\mathcal{X} \cup \mathcal{Y}$ is a solution for S. Let $E: t_j - t_i \leq \delta$ be an arbitrary constraint in $\mathcal{C}$. We need to show that the constraint E is satisfied by the values in $\mathcal{X} \cup \mathcal{Y}$.

Case 1: $t_i = x_p$ and $t_j = x_q$ are both elements of $\mathcal{T}_X$. Since $\mathcal{X}$ is a solution for S_X, we have that: $v_q - v_p \leq \mathcal{D}_X(x_p, x_q)$. Since Property 1 holds, we have that: $\mathcal{D}_X(x_p, x_q) \leq \mathcal{D}(x_p, x_q)$. Finally, since E is a constraint in $\mathcal{C}$, we have that: $\mathcal{D}(x_p, x_q) \leq \delta$. Thus, $v_q - v_p \leq \delta$ (i.e., E is satisfied by $x_p = v_p$ and $x_q = v_q$).

Case 2: $t_i = y_p$ and $t_j = y_q$ are both elements of $\mathcal{T}_Y$. Handled analogously to Case 1.

Case 3: $t_i = x_p \in \mathcal{T}_X$ and $t_j = y_q \in \mathcal{T}_Y$. Since $x_p = v_p$ is part of a solution for S_X, we have that: $0 - v_p \leq \mathcal{D}_X(x_p, z)$. Similarly, $w_q - 0 \leq \mathcal{D}_Y(z, y_q)$. Thus $w_q - v_p \leq \mathcal{D}_X(x_p, z) + \mathcal{D}_Y(z, y_q)$. Since Property 3 holds, we get that: $\mathcal{D}_X(x_p, z) + \mathcal{D}_Y(z, y_q) \leq \mathcal{D}(x_p, y_q)$.

Finally, since E is a constraint in $\mathcal{C}$, we have that: $\mathcal{D}(x_p, y_q) \leq \delta$. Thus, $w_q - v_p \leq \delta$ (i.e., the constraint E is satisfied by $x_p = v_p$ and $y_q = w_q$).

Case 4: $t_i = y_q \in \mathcal{T}_Y$ and $t_j = x_p \in \mathcal{T}_X$.

Handled analogously to Case 3.

Since the constraint E was chosen arbitrarily from $\mathcal{C}$, we have that $\mathcal{X} \cup \mathcal{Y}$ is a solution for $\mathcal{S}$. $\blacksquare$

Toward a TDP Algorithm

Definition 11 (xy-Pairs, xy-Edges) *Let $\mathcal{T}_X$, $\mathcal{T}_Y$ and $\mathcal{T}$ be sets of time-points such that $\mathcal{T}_X$ and $\mathcal{T}_Y$ z-partition $\mathcal{T}$. Let t_i and t_j be arbitrary time-points in $\mathcal{T}$. The pair (t_i, t_j) is called an* xy-pair *if:*

$$(t_i \in \mathcal{T}_X \text{ and } t_j \in \mathcal{T}_Y) \quad \text{or} \quad (t_i \in \mathcal{T}_Y \text{ and } t_j \in \mathcal{T}_X).$$

If, in addition, neither t_i nor t_j is the zero time-point variable z, then (t_i, t_j) is called a proper xy-pair. *A constraint (or edge), $(t_j - t_i \leq \delta)$, is called an* xy-edge *if (t_i, t_j) is an xy-pair. An xy-edge is called a* proper xy-edge *if the corresponding pair is a proper xy-pair.*

Definition 12 (Zero-Path-Shortfall) *Let E be a tight, proper xy-edge $(t_j - t_i \leq \delta)$. The* zero-path shortfall *(ZPS) associated with E is the quantity:*

$$\text{ZPS}(E) = [\mathcal{D}(t_i, z) + \mathcal{D}(z, t_j)] - \delta.$$

Result 12 *For any tight, proper xy-edge E, $ZPS(E) \geq 0$.*

Proof Let E be a tight, proper xy-edge $(t_j - t_i \leq \delta)$. Since E is tight, we have: $\mathcal{D}(t_i, t_j) = \delta$; hence, from the Triangle Inequality: $\delta = \mathcal{D}(t_i, t_j) \leq \mathcal{D}(t_i, z) + \mathcal{D}(z, t_j)$. $\blacksquare$

Definition 13 (Dominated by a Path through Zero) *If the ZPS value for a tight, proper xy-edge is zero, we say that that edge is* dominated by a path through zero.

Result 13 *If adding a set of constraints to a consistent STN $\mathcal{S}$ does not make $\mathcal{S}$ inconsistent, then the ZPS values for any pre-existing tight, proper xy-edges in $\mathcal{S}$ cannot increase.*

Proof Adding constraints to an STN causes its shortest paths to become shorter or stay the same, and hence its distance matrix entries to decrease or stay the same. Given that δ is a constant, this implies that $[\mathcal{D}(t_i, z) + \mathcal{D}(z, t_j)] - \delta$ can only decrease or stay the same. $\blacksquare$

The following lemma shows that we can restrict attention to tight, proper xy-edges when seeking a solution to an instance of the TDP.

Lemma 14 *If $\mathcal{D}(t_p, z) + \mathcal{D}(z, t_q) \leq \delta$ holds for every tight, proper xy-edge $(t_q - t_p \leq \delta)$ in a consistent STN, then $\mathcal{D}(t_i, z) + \mathcal{D}(z, t_j) \leq \mathcal{D}(t_i, t_j)$ holds for every xy-pair (t_i, t_j) in that STN.*

Proof Suppose that $\mathcal{D}(t_p, z) + \mathcal{D}(z, t_q) \leq \delta$ holds for every tight, proper xy-*edge* $(t_q - t_p \leq \delta)$. Let (t_i, t_j) be an arbitrary xy-*pair* in $\mathcal{S}$. We must show that $\mathcal{D}(t_i, z) + \mathcal{D}(z, t_j) \leq \mathcal{D}(t_i, t_j)$ holds.

If t_i or t_j is the zero time-point z, then the inequality holds trivially (since $\mathcal{D}(z, z) = 0$ in a consistent STN). Thus, suppose that (t_i, t_j) is a *proper* xy-pair. Without loss of generality, suppose $t_i \in \mathcal{T}_X$ and $t_j \in \mathcal{T}_Y$. Let P be an arbitrary

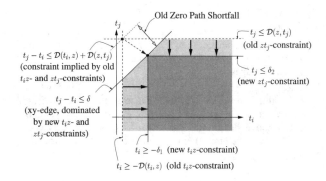

Figure 1: Reducing the zero-path shortfall for an xy-edge

shortest path from t_i to t_j in $\mathcal{S}$. If z is on the path P, then the inequality holds (since the subpaths from t_i to z and from z to t_j must also be shortest paths).

Now suppose z is not on P. Then P must contain at least one proper xy-edge E_{xy} of the form $(y - x \leq \delta_{xy})$, where $x \in \mathcal{T}_X$ and $y \in \mathcal{T}_Y$. Since E_{xy} is on a shortest path, it must be tight; hence $\delta_{xy} = \mathcal{D}(x, y)$. Thus, using the Triangle Inequality: $\delta_{xy} = \mathcal{D}(x, y) \leq \mathcal{D}(x, z) + \mathcal{D}(z, y)$ holds. But the Lemma's premise, applied to the tight, proper xy-edge E_{xy}, gives us that: $\mathcal{D}(x, z) + \mathcal{D}(z, y) \leq \delta_{xy}$. Thus, $\delta_{xy} = \mathcal{D}(x, z) + \mathcal{D}(z, y)$. Thus, we may replace E_{xy} in P by a pair of shortest paths, one from x to z, one from z to y, without changing the length of P. But then this version of P is a shortest path from t_i to t_j that contains z. As argued earlier, this implies that the desired inequality holds. $\blacksquare$

Algorithms for Solving the TDP

This section presents a family of sound and complete algorithms for solving the Temporal Decoupling Problem. We begin by presenting a preliminary TDP algorithm, directly motivated by Theorem 11, above. The preliminary algorithm is sound, but not complete: because it is not guaranteed to terminate. In Theorems 21 and 22, below, we specify ways of strengthening the preliminary algorithm to ensure that it terminates and, hence, that it is complete.

The Preliminary TDP Algorithm

The main tool of the TDP algorithm is to reduce the zero-path shortfall for each tight, proper xy-edge, $t_j - t_i \leq \delta$, by strengthening the corresponding $t_i z$- and/or $z t_j$-edges. Figure 1 illustrates the case of an xy-edge's ZPS value being reduced to zero through the addition of edges $z - t_i \leq \delta_1$ (i.e., $t_i \geq -\delta_1$) and $t_j - z \leq \delta_2$ (i.e., $t_j \leq \delta_2$). Adding weaker constraints may reduce the zero-path shortfall but not eliminate it entirely.

The preliminary algorithm is given in pseudo-code in Figure 2. It takes as input an STN $\mathcal{S}$ whose time-points are z-partitioned by the sets $\mathcal{T}_X$ and $\mathcal{T}_Y$.

At Step 1, the algorithm checks whether $\mathcal{S}$ is consistent. If $\mathcal{S}$ is inconsistent, the algorithm returns NIL and halts because, by Result 8, only consistent STNs can be decoupled. Otherwise, the algorithm initializes the set $\mathcal{E}$ to the set of

Given: An STN $\mathcal{S}$ whose time-points $\mathcal{T}$ are z-partitioned by the sets $\mathcal{T}_X$ and $\mathcal{T}_Y$.

(1) Compute the distance matrix $\mathcal{D}$ for $\mathcal{S}$. If $\mathcal{S}$ is inconsistent, return NIL and halt; otherwise, initialize $\mathcal{E}$ to the set of tight, proper xy-edges in $\mathcal{S}$, and continue.

(2) Select a tight, proper xy-edge $E = (t_j - t_i \leq \delta)$ in $\mathcal{E}$ whose ZPS value is positive. (If, in the process, any edges in $\mathcal{E}$ are discovered that are no longer tight or that have a ZPS value of zero, remove those edges from $\mathcal{E}$.) If no such edges exist (i.e., if $\mathcal{E}$ has become empty), go to Step 6; otherwise, continue.

(3) Pick values δ_1 and δ_2 such that:
$$
\begin{aligned}
-\mathcal{D}(z, t_i) &\leq & \delta_1 & \leq & \mathcal{D}(t_i, z), \\
-\mathcal{D}(t_j, z) &\leq & \delta_2 & \leq & \mathcal{D}(z, t_j), \text{ and} \\
\delta &\leq & \delta_1 + \delta_2 & < & \mathcal{D}(t_i, z) + \mathcal{D}(z, t_j).
\end{aligned}
$$

(4) Add the constraints, $E_1\colon z - t_i \leq \delta_1$ and $E_2\colon t_j - z \leq \delta_2$, to $\mathcal{S}$, updating $\mathcal{D}$ to reflect the new constraints.

(5) Go to Step 2.

(6) Return: $\mathcal{C}_X = \{(t_j - t_i \leq \mathcal{D}(t_i, t_j)) : t_i, t_j \in \mathcal{T}_X\}$;
$\mathcal{C}_Y = \{(t_j - t_i \leq \mathcal{D}(t_i, t_j)) : t_i, t_j \in \mathcal{T}_Y\}$.

Figure 2: Pseudo-code for the Preliminary TDP Algorithm

tight, proper xy-edges in $\mathcal{S}$, an $O(N^2)$ computation that requires checking each edge against the corresponding entries in the distance matrix. The algorithm then iteratively operates on edges drawn from $\mathcal{E}$ until each such edge is dominated by a path through zero (recall Definition 13).

For each iteration, the algorithm does the following. In Step 2, a tight, proper xy-edge $E\colon (t_j - t_i \leq \delta)$ with a positive zero-path shortfall is selected from the set $\mathcal{E}$. In Steps 3 and 4, new constraints involving the zero time-point variable z are added to $\mathcal{S}$. After propagating these constraints (i.e., after updating the distance matrix to reflect the new constraints), the new values of $\mathcal{D}(t_i, z)$ and $\mathcal{D}(z, t_j)$ will be δ_1 and δ_2, respectively, where δ_1 and δ_2 are the values from Step 3. Thus, the *updated* ZPS value for E, which we denote ζ^*, will be: $\zeta^* = \delta_1 + \delta_2 - \delta$.

Upon adding the Step 4 edges to $\mathcal{S}$, it may be that some of the edges in $\mathcal{E}$ are no longer tight or no longer have positive ZPS values. However, the algorithm need not check for that in Step 4. Instead, if any such edges are ever encountered during the selection process in Step 2, they are simply removed from $\mathcal{E}$ at that time.

If it ever happens that every tight, proper xy-edge is dominated by a path through zero, as evidenced by the set $\mathcal{E}$ becoming empty, then the algorithm terminates (see Steps 2 and 6). The sets $\mathcal{C}_X$ and $\mathcal{C}_Y$ returned by the algorithm are derived from the distance matrix $\mathcal{D}$ which has been updated to include all of the constraints added during passes of Step 4.

Soundness of the Preliminary TDP Algorithm

The values δ_1 and δ_2 chosen in Step 3 of the algorithm specify the strengths of the constraints E_1 and E_2 added in Step 4. It is also useful to think in terms of the amount by which the ZPS value for the edge under consideration is thereby reduced (call it R), as well as the fractions of

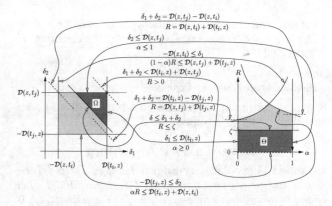

Figure 3: The regions Ω and Θ from Lemma 16

this ZPS reduction due to the tightening of the $t_i z$- and $z t_j$-edges, respectively (specified by α and $1 - \alpha$). Lemma 16 below gives the precise relationship between the pairs of values (δ_1, δ_2) and (R, α). We subsequently use the results of Lemma 16 to prove that the preliminary TDP algorithm is sound. Result 15 is used in Lemma 16.

Result 15 *For an edge E of the form $t_j - t_i \leq \delta$, if that edge is tight, then the following inequalities necessarily hold:*
$$\mathcal{D}(t_i, z) - \mathcal{D}(t_j, z) \leq \delta \text{ and } \mathcal{D}(z, t_j) - \mathcal{D}(z, t_i) \leq \delta.$$

Proof The first inequality may be proven as follows:
$$
\begin{aligned}
\mathcal{D}(t_i, z) &\leq \mathcal{D}(t_i, t_j) + \mathcal{D}(t_j, z) &&\text{(Triangle Inequality)} \\
\mathcal{D}(t_i, z) &\leq \delta + \mathcal{D}(t_j, z) &&\text{(Since } E \text{ is a tight edge)} \\
\mathcal{D}(t_i, z) - \mathcal{D}(t_j, z) &\leq \delta &&\text{(Rearrange terms)}
\end{aligned}
$$
The second inequality follows similarly. ∎

Lemma 16 *Let E be some tight, proper xy-edge $t_j - t_i \leq \delta$ whose ZPS value $\zeta = ZPS(E)$ is positive. Let Ω be the set of ordered pairs (δ_1, δ_2) satisfying the Step 3 requirements of the preliminary algorithm (recall Figure 2). Let Θ be the set of ordered pairs (R, α) such that $R \in (0, \zeta)$ and $\alpha \in [0, 1]$. Let T_1 and T_2 be the following 2-by-2 transformations:*

$$T_1\colon \begin{cases} \delta_1 = f(R, \alpha) = \mathcal{D}(t_i, z) - \alpha R \\ \delta_2 = g(R, \alpha) = \mathcal{D}(z, t_j) - (1 - \alpha)R \end{cases}$$

$$T_2\colon \begin{cases} R = u(\delta_1, \delta_2) = \mathcal{D}(t_i, z) + \mathcal{D}(z, t_j) - (\delta_1 + \delta_2) \\ \alpha = v(\delta_1, \delta_2) = \dfrac{\mathcal{D}(t_i, z) - \delta_1}{\mathcal{D}(t_i, z) + \mathcal{D}(z, t_j) - (\delta_1 + \delta_2)} \end{cases}$$

Then T_1 and T_2 are invertible transformations between Ω and Θ (with $T_1^{-1} = T_2$) such that for any pair $(\delta_1, \delta_2) \in \Omega$, the corresponding pair $(R, \alpha) \in \Theta$ satisfies that:

- *R is the amount by which the pair of corresponding Step 4 constraints, $E_1\colon z - t_i \leq \delta_1$ and $E_2\colon t_j - z \leq \delta_2$, reduce the ZPS value for the edge E, and*

- *α and $(1 - \alpha)$ represent the fractions of this ZPS reduction due to the tightening of the $t_i z$- and $z t_j$-edges, respectively.*

Proof The Step 3 requirements (from Figure 2) correspond to the boundaries of the region Ω in Figure 3. Note that the point $(\mathcal{D}(t_i, z), \mathcal{D}(z, t_j))$ is *not* part of Ω due to the strict inequality: $\delta_1 + \delta_2 < \mathcal{D}(t_i, z) + \mathcal{D}(z, t_j)$. Also, by Result 15,

$\mathcal{D}(t_i, z) - \mathcal{D}(t_j, z) \leq \delta$ and $\mathcal{D}(z, t_j) - \mathcal{D}(z, t_i) \leq \delta$.
These inequalities ensure that the diagonal boundary of Ω, which corresponds to the constraint $\delta \leq \delta_1 + \delta_2$, lies above and to the right of the lines $\mathcal{D}(t_i, z) - \mathcal{D}(t_j, z) = \delta_1 + \delta_2$ and $\mathcal{D}(z, t_j) - \mathcal{D}(z, t_i) = \delta_1 + \delta_2$ (shown as dashed lines in the $\delta_1\delta_2$-plane in Figure 3).

The amount of reduction in the ZPS value ζ that results from adding the corresponding Step 4 constraints, E_1: $z - t_i \leq \delta_1$ and E_2: $t_j - z \leq \delta_2$, is given by:

(old ZPS value) - (new ZPS value) $= \zeta - \zeta^*$
$= [\mathcal{D}(t_i, z) + \mathcal{D}(z, t_j) - \delta] - [\delta_1 + \delta_2 - \delta]$
$= \mathcal{D}(t_i, z) + \mathcal{D}(z, t_j) - (\delta_1 + \delta_2)$

which is precisely the value $R = u(\delta_1, \delta_2)$. The amount by which the $t_i z$-edge is strengthened is given by:

(old value) - (new value) $= \mathcal{D}(t_i, z) - \delta_1$.

Hence, the fraction of the total ZPS reduction produced by strengthening the $t_i z$-edge is precisely $\alpha = v(\delta_1, \delta_2)$, from which it also follows that $\delta_1 = f(R, \alpha) = \mathcal{D}(t_i, z) - \alpha R$. Similarly, the fraction of the total ZPS reduction produced by strengthening the $z t_j$-edge is precisely $(1 - \alpha)$, and $\delta_2 = g(R, \alpha) = \mathcal{D}(z, t_j) - (1 - \alpha)R$.

It is easy to verify that the transformations T_1 and T_2 are inverses of one another. The arrows in Figure 3 show how the boundaries of the regions Ω and Θ correspond.

Finally, from Theorem 4, the quantity $\mathcal{D}(z, t_j) + \mathcal{D}(t_j, z)$ specifies the maximum amount that the $z t_j$-edge can be tightened without threatening the consistency of the STN. The following establishes that ζ (i.e., the ZPS value for the edge E) is no more than this amount:

$\mathcal{D}(t_i, z) - \mathcal{D}(t_j, z) \leq \delta$ (Established earlier)
$\Rightarrow \mathcal{D}(t_i, z) + \mathcal{D}(z, t_j) - \delta \leq \mathcal{D}(z, t_j) + \mathcal{D}(t_j, z)$
$\Rightarrow \zeta \leq \mathcal{D}(z, t_j) + \mathcal{D}(t_j, z)$ (Defn. of ζ)

Thus, the entire zero-path-shortfall for E may be eliminated by tightening only the $z t_j$-constraint. Similarly, the entire zero-path-shortfall may be eliminated by instead tightening only the $t_i z$-constraint. In Figure 3, these constraints on ζ ensure that the top horizontal boundary of the region Θ lies below the curves $\alpha R = \mathcal{D}(t_i, z) + \mathcal{D}(z, t_i)$ and $(1 - \alpha)R = \mathcal{D}(z, t_j) + \mathcal{D}(t_j, z)$. Thus, the values for R and α may be independently chosen. ∎

Corollary 17 *Let E: $t_j - t_i \leq \delta$ be a tight, proper xy-edge with ZPS value $\zeta > 0$. Let $R \in (0, \zeta]$ and $\alpha \in [0, 1]$ be arbitrary. It is always possible to choose δ_1 and δ_2 satisfying the Step 3 requirements such that the ZPS value for E will be reduced by R and such that the $t_i z$- and $z t_j$-edges will be tightened by the amounts αR and $(1 - \alpha)R$, respectively.*

Theorem 18 *Suppose S is a consistent STN and that E: $t_j - t_i \leq \delta$ is a tight, proper xy-edge whose ZPS value is positive. Let δ_1 and δ_2 be arbitrary values chosen according to the requirements of Step 3. Then adding the pair of corresponding Step 4 constraints (i.e., E_1 and E_2 in Figure 2) will not threaten the consistency of S.*

Proof Let $\zeta > 0$ be the ZPS value for edge E. Suppose that adding the corresponding Step 4 constraints E_1 and E_2 caused S to become inconsistent. Then, by Theorem 1, there

must be a loop in G_S with negative path-length. By Theorem 4, the first two Step 3 requirements (from Figure 2) imply that E_1 and E_2 are individually consistent with S. Thus, any loop with negative path length in G_S must contain *both* E_1 and E_2. Of all such loops, let L be one that has the minimum number of edges.

Now consider the subpath from z (at the end of E_1) to z (at the beginning of E_2). This is itself a loop. Since that loop has fewer edges than L, it must, by the choice of L, have non-negative path-length. But then extracting this subpath from L would result in a loop L' still having negative path-length. Since the choice of L precludes L' having fewer edges than L, it must be that the subpath from z to z is empty. However, part of the third Step 3 requirement (from Figure 2) says that $\delta \leq \delta_1 + \delta_2$, which implies that the edges E_1 and E_2 in L could be replaced by the edge, $t_j - t_i \leq \delta$, resulting in a loop having negative path-length but with fewer edges than L, contradicting the choice of L. Thus, no such L exists. Thus, adding both E_1 and E_2 to S leaves S consistent. ∎

Theorem 19 (Soundness) *If the temporal decoupling algorithm terminates at Step 6, then the constraint sets $\mathcal{C}_X$ and $\mathcal{C}_Y$ returned by the TDP algorithm are such that $(\mathcal{T}_X, \mathcal{C}_X)$ and $(\mathcal{T}_Y, \mathcal{C}_Y)$ are a temporal decoupling of the input STN S.*

Proof During each pass of Step 4, the TDP algorithm modifies the input STN by adding new constraints. To distinguish the input STN S from the modified STN existing at the end of the algorithm's execution (i.e., at Step 6), we shall refer to the latter as S'. If $\mathcal{C}'$ is the set of all Step 4 constraints added during the execution of the algorithm, then $S' = (\mathcal{T}, \mathcal{C} \cup \mathcal{C}')$. Let $\mathcal{D}'$ be the distance matrix for S'. (Thus, using this notation, it is $\mathcal{D}'$ that is used to construct the constraint sets $\mathcal{C}_X$ and $\mathcal{C}_Y$ in Step 6.) Since every constraint in S is present in S', $\mathcal{D}'(t_i, t_j) \leq \mathcal{D}(t_i, t_j)$ for all $t_i, t_j \in \mathcal{T}$.

To show that S_X and S_Y are a temporal decoupling of S, it suffices (by Theorem 11) to show that S_X and S_Y are each consistent and that Properties 1–4 from Theorem 10 hold. (It is given that the sets $\mathcal{T}_X$ and $\mathcal{T}_Y$ z-partition $\mathcal{T}$.)

Theorem 18 guarantees that S' is consistent. Furthermore, since any solution for S' must satisfy the constraints represented in $\mathcal{D}'$, which cover all the constraints in $\mathcal{C}_X$ and $\mathcal{C}_Y$, both S_X and S_Y must also be consistent.

By construction, $\mathcal{D}_X(x_p, x_q) = \mathcal{D}'(x_p, x_q)$ for every x_p and x_q in $\mathcal{T}_X$. Since $\mathcal{D}'(x_p, x_q) \leq \mathcal{D}(x_p, x_q)$, Property 1 of Theorem 10 holds. Similarly, Property 2 also holds.

To prove that Property 3 holds, first notice that the premise of Lemma 14 is equivalent to saying that ZPS ≤ 0 for each tight, proper xy-*edge*, which is precisely what the exit clause of Step 2 requires. Thus, the algorithm will not terminate at Step 6 unless the premise of Lemma 14 holds—with respect to S'. Hence, from the conclusion of Lemma 14, we have that for any xy-*pair* in S': $\mathcal{D}'(t_i, z) + \mathcal{D}'(z, t_j) \leq \mathcal{D}'(t_i, t_j)$. In the case where $t_i \in \mathcal{T}_X$ and $t_j \in \mathcal{T}_Y$, we have that $\mathcal{D}'(t_i, z) = \mathcal{D}_X(t_i, z)$

and $\mathcal{D}'(z, t_j) = \mathcal{D}_Y(z, t_j)$. Since $\mathcal{D}'(t_i, t_j) \leq \mathcal{D}(t_i, t_j)$, we get that $\mathcal{D}_X(t_i, z) + \mathcal{D}_Y(z, t_j) \leq \mathcal{D}(t_i, t_j)$, which is Property 3. Similarly, Property 4 holds. ∎

Ensuring Completeness for the TDP Algorithm

The Step 3 requirement that $\delta_1 + \delta_2 < \mathcal{D}(t_i, z) + \mathcal{D}(z, t_j)$ ensures that the ZPS value for the edge under consideration will decrease. However, it does not ensure that *substantial* progress will be made. As a result, the preliminary algorithm, as shown in Figure 2, is not guaranteed to terminate. Theorems 21 and 22, below, specify two ways of strengthening the Step 3 requirements, each sufficient to ensure that the TDP algorithm will terminate and, hence, that it is complete. Each strategy involves a method for choosing R, the amount by which the ZPS value for the edge currently under consideration is to be reduced (recall Lemma 16). Each strategy leaves the distribution of additional constrainedness among the $t_i z$ and $z t_j$ edges (i.e., the choice of α) unrestricted.

Fact 20 will be used in the proofs of the theorems.

Fact 20 *If an xy-edge ever loses its tightness, it cannot ever regain it. Thus, since the algorithm never adds any proper xy-edges, the pool of tight, proper xy-edges relevant to Step 2 can never grow. Furthermore, by Result 13, the ZPS values cannot ever increase. Thus, any progress made by the algorithm is never lost.*

Theorem 21 (Greedy Strategy) *If at each pass of Step 3, the entire zero-path-shortfall for the edge under consideration is eliminated—which is always possible by Corollary 17—then the TDP algorithm will terminate after at most $2|\mathcal{T}_X||\mathcal{T}_Y|$ iterations.*

Proof By Fact 20, the algorithm needs to do Step 3 processing of each tight, proper xy-edge at most once. There are at most $2|\mathcal{T}_X||\mathcal{T}_Y|$ such edges. ∎

Barring some extravagant selection process in Step 2, the computation in each iteration of the algorithm is dominated by the propagation of the temporal constraints added in Step 4. This is no worse than $O(N^3)$, where $N + 1$ is the number of time-points in $\mathcal{S}$ (recall Fact 2).

The following theorem specifies a less-greedy approach which, although more computationally expensive than the greedy approach, is shown in the experimental evaluation section to result in decoupled networks that are more flexible. In this strategy, the ZPS value of the edge under consideration in Step 3 is reduced by a fractional amount (unless it is already below some threshold). Unlike the Greedy strategy, this strategy requires all of the initial ZPS values to be finite—which is always the case in practice.

Theorem 22 (Less-Greedy Strategy) *Let Z be the maximum of the initial ZPS values among all the tight, proper xy-edges in $\mathcal{S}$. Let $\epsilon > 0$ and $r \in (0, 1)$ be arbitrary constants. Suppose that at each pass of Step 3 in the TDP algorithm, R (the amount by which the ZPS value ζ for the edge currently under consideration is reduced) is given by:*

$$R = \begin{cases} r\zeta, & \text{if } \zeta > \epsilon \\ \zeta, & \text{otherwise} \end{cases}$$

Step 2 Choice	R	Randomly choose an edge from $\mathcal{E}$.
	K	Randomly select a K-item subset of $\mathcal{E}$, where K is one of $\{2, 4, 8\}$; choose edge from that subset whose processing in Step 3 will result in minimal change to STN's rigidity.
Choice of R	G	Greedy strategy
	L	Less-Greedy strategy where $r = 0.5$ and the computation-multiplier is either 6 or 18.
Choice of α	B	Randomly choose α from $\{0, 1\}$.
	U	Randomly choose α from $[0, 1]$ (uniform distribution).
	F	Randomly choose α from $[0, 1]$ with distribution weighted by flexibility of $t_i z$- and $z t_j$-edges.

Figure 4: Variations of the TDP Algorithm Tested

(Corollary 17 ensures that this is always possible.) If Z is finite, then this strategy ensures that the algorithm will terminate after at most $2|\mathcal{T}_X||\mathcal{T}_Y| \left[\frac{\log(Z/\epsilon)}{\log(1/(1-r))} + 1 \right]$ iterations.

Proof Let $\mathcal{E}_0$ be the initial set of tight, proper xy-edges having positive ZPS values. Let $E \in \mathcal{E}_0$ be arbitrary. Let ζ be E's initial ZPS value. Suppose E has been processed by the algorithm (in Step 3) n times so far. Given the above strategy for choosing R, E's current ZPS value ζ is necessarily bounded above by $\zeta_0(1 - r)^n$ and hence also by $Z(1 - r)^n$. If $n > \frac{\log(Z/\epsilon)}{\log(1/(1-r))}$, we get that $Z(1 - r)^n < \epsilon$. Thus, after at most $\left[\frac{\log(Z/\epsilon)}{\log(1/(1-r))} + 1 \right]$ appearances of E in Step 3, its ZPS value ζ will be zero. Since E was arbitrary and $|\mathcal{E}_0| \leq 2|\mathcal{T}_X||\mathcal{T}_Y|$, the result is proven. ∎

The factor $\left[\frac{\log(Z/\epsilon)}{\log(1/(1-r))} + 1 \right]$ specifies an upper bound on the run-time using the Less Greedy strategy as compared to the Greedy strategy. In practice, this factor may be kept small by choosing ϵ appropriately. For example, if $r = 0.5$ and $Z/\epsilon = 1000$, this factor is less than 11.

Corollary 23 (Completeness) *Using either the Greedy or Less-Greedy strategy, the TDP algorithm is complete.*

Proof Suppose a solution exists for an instance of the TDP for an STN $\mathcal{S}$. By Result 8, $\mathcal{S}$ must be consistent. Thus, the TDP algorithm will not halt at Step 1. Using either of the strategies in Theorems 21 or 22, the algorithm will eventually terminate at Step 6. By Theorem 19, this only happens when the algorithm has found a solution to the TDP. ∎

Experimental Evaluation

In this section, we compare the performance of the TDP algorithm across the following dimensions: (1) the function used in Step 2 to select the next edge to work on; (2) the function used in Step 3 to determine R (i.e., the amount of ZPS reduction); and (3) the function used in Step 3 to determine α, which governs the distribution of additional constrainedness among the $t_i z$- and $z t_j$-edges. The chart in Figure 4 shows the algorithm variations tested in the experiments. Each variation is identified by its parameter settings using the abbreviations in the chart.

Option K for the Step 2 choice function is expected to be computationally expensive since for each edge in the K-item subset, constraints must be propagated (and reset) and

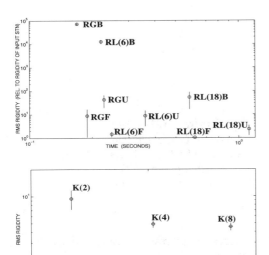

Figure 5: Experimental Results

the rigidity of the STN must be computed. However, it is hypothesized that this method will result in more flexible decouplings. Similarly, the Less-Greedy strategy, which is computationally more expensive than the Greedy strategy, is hypothesized to result in decouplings that are more flexible. Regarding the choice of α, it is hypothesized that one of the pseudo-continuous strategies (i.e., U or F) will result decouplings that are more flexible than when using the discrete strategy (i.e., B).

The first experiment tested the random Step 2 function (R). It consisted of 500 trials, each restricted to the time-interval $[0, 100]$. For each trial, the STN contained start and finish time-points for 30 actions (i.e., 60 time-points). Half of the actions/time-points were allocated to $\mathcal{T}_X$, half to $\mathcal{T}_Y$. Constraints were generated randomly, as follows. For each action, a lower bound d was drawn uniformly from the interval $[0, 1]$; an upper bound was drawn from $[d, d + 1]$. Also, 400 constraints among time-points in $\mathcal{T}_X$, 400 among time-points in $\mathcal{T}_Y$, and 800 xy-edges were generated, the strength of each determined by selecting a random value from $[0, F]$, where F was 30% of the maximum amount the constraint could be tightened.

The results of the first experiment are shown in the top half of Figure 5. The horizontal axis measures time in seconds. The vertical axis measures the rigidity of the STN after the decoupling (as a multiple of the rigidity of the STN before the decoupling). 95% confidence intervals are shown for both time and rigidity, but the intervals for time are barely visible. Both scales are logarithmic.

As hypothesized, the Greedy approach (G) is faster, but the Less-Greedy approach (L) results in decouplings that are substantially more flexible (i.e., less rigid). Similarly, using a larger computation-multiplier in the Less-Greedy approach (18 vs. 6), which corresponds to a smaller value of ϵ, results in decouplings that are more flexible. The most

surprising result is the dramatic benefit from using either of the two pseudo-continuous methods, U or F, for choosing α. Biasing the distribution according to the flexibility in the t_iz- and zt_j-edges (as is done in the F method) gives consistently more flexible decouplings, while taking less time to do so. The RL(18)F variation produced decouplings that were scarcely more rigid than the input STN.

The second experiment used only the K-item-set function (K) for the Step 2 selection function, varying the size of the subset (2, 4 or 8). The other dimensions were fixed: Less-Greedy approach with a computation-multiplier of 6, together with the F method of selecting α. The experiment consisted of 200 trials. For each trial the STN contained 40 actions (80 time-points), as well as 1600 constraints among time-points in $\mathcal{T}_X$, 1600 among time-points in $\mathcal{T}_Y$ and 3200 xy-edges. The results are shown in the bottom of Figure 5. As hypothesized, using the K-item-subset Step 2 function can generate decoupled networks that are substantially more flexible. However, using this method is not immune from the Law of Diminishing Returns. In this case, using an 8-item subset was not worth the extra computational effort.

Conclusions

In this paper, we formally defined the Temporal Decoupling Problem, presented theorems giving necessary and sufficient characterizations of solutions to the TDP, and gave a parameterized family of sound and complete algorithms for solving it. Although the algorithms were presented only in the case of decoupling an STN into two subnetworks, they are easily extended to the case of multiple subnetworks.

Acknowledgments

This research was supported by NSF grants IIS-9978343 and IRI-9618848. The author thanks Barbara J. Grosz and David C. Parkes for their helpful suggestions.

References

Cormen, T. H.; Leiserson, C. E.; and Rivest, R. L. 1990. *Introduction to Algorithms*. Cambridge, MA: The MIT Press.

Dechter, R.; Meiri, I.; and Pearl, J. 1991. Temporal constraint networks. *Artificial Intelligence* 49:61–95.

Hunsberger, L., and Grosz, B. J. 2000. A combinatorial auction for collaborative planning. In *Fourth International Conference on MultiAgent Systems (ICMAS-2000)*, 151–158. IEEE Computer Society.

Hunsberger, L. 2002. Generating bids for group-related actions in the context of prior commitments. In *Intelligent Agents VIII*, volume 2333 of *LNAI*. Springer-Verlag.

Morris, P., and Muscettola, N. 2000. Execution of temporal plans with uncertainty. In *Proc. of the 17th National Conference on Artificial Intelligence (AAAI-2000)*, 491–496.

Tsamardinos, I.; Muscettola, N.; and Morris, P. 1998. Fast transformation of temporal plans for efficient execution. In *Proc. of the 15th Nat'l. Conf. on AI (AAAI-98)*. 254–261.

Tsamardinos, I. 2000. Reformulating temporal plans for efficient execution. Master's thesis, Univ. of Pittsburgh.

D* Lite

Sven Koenig
College of Computing
Georgia Institute of Technology
Atlanta, GA 30312-0280
skoenig@cc.gatech.edu

Maxim Likhachev
School of Computer Science
Carnegie Mellon University
Pittsburgh, PA 15213
maxim+@cs.cmu.edu

Abstract

Incremental heuristic search methods use heuristics to focus their search and reuse information from previous searches to find solutions to series of similar search tasks much faster than is possible by solving each search task from scratch. In this paper, we apply Lifelong Planning A* to robot navigation in unknown terrain, including goal-directed navigation in unknown terrain and mapping of unknown terrain. The resulting D* Lite algorithm is easy to understand and analyze. It implements the same behavior as Stentz' Focussed Dynamic A* but is algorithmically different. We prove properties about D* Lite and demonstrate experimentally the advantages of combining incremental and heuristic search for the applications studied. We believe that these results provide a strong foundation for further research on fast replanning methods in artificial intelligence and robotics.

Introduction

Incremental search methods, such as DynamicSWSF-FP (Ramalingam & Reps 1996), are currently not much used in artificial intelligence. They reuse information from previous searches to find solutions to series of similar search tasks much faster than is possible by solving each search task from scratch. An overview is given in (Frigioni, Marchetti-Spaccamela, & Nanni 2000). Heuristic search methods, such as A* (Nilsson 1971), on the other hand, use heuristic knowledge in form of approximations of the goal distances to focus the search and solve search problems much faster than uninformed search methods. An overview is given in (Pearl 1985). We recently introduced LPA* (Lifelong Planning A*), that generalizes both DynamicSWSF-FP and A* and thus uses two different techniques to reduce its planning time (Koenig & Likhachev 2001). In this paper, we apply LPA* to robot navigation in unknown terrain. The robot could use conventional graph-search methods when replanning its paths after discovering previously unknown obstacles. However, the resulting planning times can be on the order of minutes for the large terrains that are often used, which adds up to substantial idle times (Stentz 1994). Focussed Dynamic A* (D*) (Stentz 1995) is a clever heuristic search method that achieves a speedup of one to two orders of magnitudes(!) over repeated A* searches by mod-

ifying previous search results locally. D* has been extensively used on real robots, including outdoor HMMWVs (Stentz & Hebert 1995). It is currently also being integrated into Mars Rover prototypes and tactical mobile robot prototypes for urban reconnaissance (Matthies *et al.* 2000; Thayer *et al.* 2000). However, it has not been extended by other researchers. Building on LPA*, we therefore present D* Lite, a novel replanning method that implements the same navigation strategy as D* but is algorithmically different. D* Lite is substantially shorter than D*, uses only one tie-breaking criterion when comparing priorities, which simplifies the maintenance of the priorities, and does not need nested if-statements with complex conditions that occupy up to three lines each, which simplifies the analysis of the program flow. These properties also allow one to extend it easily, for example, to use inadmissible heuristics and different tie-breaking criteria to gain efficiency. To gain insight into its behavior, we present various theoretical properties of LPA* that also apply to D* Lite. Our theoretical properties show that LPA* is efficient and similar to A*, a well known and well understood search algorithm. Our experimental properties show that D* Lite is at least as efficient as D*. We also present an experimental evaluation of the benefits of combining incremental and heuristic search across different navigation tasks in unknown terrain, including goal-directed navigation and mapping. We believe that our theoretical and empirical analysis of D* Lite will provide a strong foundation for further research on fast replanning methods in artificial intelligence and robotics.

Motivation

Consider a goal-directed robot-navigation task in unknown terrain, where the robot always observes which of its eight adjacent cells are traversable and then moves with cost one to one of them. The robot starts at the start cell and has to move to the goal cell. It always computes a shortest path from its current cell to the goal cell under the assumption that cells with unknown blockage status are traversable. It then follows this path until it reaches the goal cell, in which case it stops successfully, or it observes an untraversable cell, in which case it recomputes a shortest path from its current cell to the goal cell. Figure 1 shows the goal distances of all traversable cells and the shortest paths from its current cell to the goal cell both before and after the robot has moved

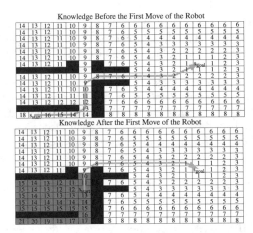

Knowledge Before the First Move of the Robot

Knowledge After the First Move of the Robot

Figure 1: Simple Example.

along the path and discovered the first blocked cell it did not know about. Cells whose goal distances have changed are shaded gray. The goal distances are important because one can easily determine a shortest path from its current cell of the robot to the goal cell by greedily decreasing the goal distances once the goal distances have been computed. Notice that the number of cells with changed goal distances is small and most of the changed goal distances are irrelevant for recalculating a shortest path from its current cell to the goal cell. Thus, one can efficiently recalculate a shortest path from its current cell to the goal cell by recalculating only those goal distances that have changed (or have not been calculated before) *and* are relevant for recalculating the shortest path. This is what D* Lite does. The challenge is to identify these cells efficiently.

Lifelong Planning A*

Lifelong Planning A* (LPA*) is shown in Figure 2. LPA* is an incremental version of A*. It applies to finite graph search problems on known graphs whose edge costs increase or decrease over time (which can also be used to model edges or vertices that are added or deleted). S denotes the finite set of vertices of the graph. $Succ(s) \subseteq S$ denotes the set of successors of vertex $s \in S$. Similarly, $Pred(s) \subseteq S$ denotes the set of predecessors of vertex $s \in S$. $0 < c(s, s') \leq \infty$ denotes the cost of moving from vertex s to vertex $s' \in Succ(s)$. LPA* always determines a shortest path from a given start vertex $s_{start} \in S$ to a given goal vertex $s_{goal} \in S$, knowing both the topology of the graph and the current edge costs. We use $g^*(s)$ to denote the start distance of vertex $s \in S$, that is, the length of a shortest path from s_{start} to s. Like A*, LPA* uses heuristics $h(s, s_{goal})$ that approximate the goal distances of the vertices s. The heuristics need to be nonnegative and consistent (Pearl 1985), that is, obey the triangle inequality $h(s_{goal}, s_{goal}) = 0$ and $h(s, s_{goal}) \leq c(s, s') + h(s', s_{goal})$ for all vertices $s \in S$ and $s' \in Succ(s)$ with $s \neq s_{goal}$.

The pseudocode uses the following functions to manage the priority queue: U.Top() returns a vertex with the smallest priority of all vertices in priority queue U. U.TopKey() returns the smallest priority of all vertices in priority queue U. (If U is empty, then U.TopKey() returns $[\infty; \infty]$.) U.Pop() deletes the vertex with the smallest priority in priority queue U and returns the vertex. U.Insert(s, k) inserts vertex s into priority queue U with priority k. U.Update(s, k) changes the priority of vertex s in priority queue U to k. (It does nothing if the current priority of vertex s already equals k.) Finally, U.Remove(s) removes vertex s from priority queue U.

procedure CalculateKey(s)
{01} return $[\min(g(s), rhs(s)) + h(s, s_{goal}); \min(g(s), rhs(s))]$;

procedure Initialize()
{02} $U = \emptyset$;
{03} for all $s \in S$ $rhs(s) = g(s) = \infty$;
{04} $rhs(s_{start}) = 0$;
{05} U.Insert(s_{start}, CalculateKey(s_{start}));

procedure UpdateVertex(u)
{06} if ($u \neq s_{start}$) $rhs(u) = \min_{s' \in Pred(u)}(g(s') + c(s', u))$;
{07} if ($u \in U$) U.Remove(u);
{08} if ($g(u) \neq rhs(u)$) U.Insert(u, CalculateKey(u));

procedure ComputeShortestPath()
{09} while (U.TopKey() $\dot{<}$ CalculateKey(s_{goal}) OR $rhs(s_{goal}) \neq g(s_{goal})$)
{10} u = U.Pop();
{11}   if ($g(u) > rhs(u)$)
{12} $g(u) = rhs(u)$;
{13}   for all $s \in Succ(u)$ UpdateVertex(s);
{14}   else
{15} $g(u) = \infty$;
{16}   for all $s \in Succ(u) \cup \{u\}$ UpdateVertex(s);

procedure Main()
{17} Initialize();
{18} forever
{19}   ComputeShortestPath();
{20}   Wait for changes in edge costs;
{21}   for all directed edges (u, v) with changed edge costs
{22}   Update the edge cost $c(u, v)$;
{23}   UpdateVertex(v);

Figure 2: Lifelong Planning A*.

Lifelong Planning A*: The Variables

LPA* maintains an estimate $g(s)$ of the start distance $g^*(s)$ of each vertex s. These values directly correspond to the g-values of an A* search. LPA* carries them forward from search to search. LPA* also maintains a second kind of estimate of the start distances. The rhs-values are one-step lookahead values based on the g-values and thus potentially better informed than the g-values. They always satisfy the following relationship (*Invariant 1*):

$$rhs(s) = \begin{cases} 0 & \text{if } s = s_{start} \\ \min_{s' \in Pred(s)}(g(s') + c(s', s)) & \text{otherwise.} \end{cases} \quad (1)$$

A vertex is called locally consistent iff its g-value equals its rhs-value, otherwise it is called locally inconsistent. Iff all vertices are locally consistent, then the g-values of all vertices equal their respective start distances. In this case one can trace back a shortest path from s_{start} to any vertex u by always transitioning from the current vertex s, starting at u, to any predecessor s' that minimizes $g(s') + c(s', s)$ (ties can be broken arbitrarily) until s_{start} is reached. (This is different from Figure 1, where the goal distances instead of the start distances are used to determine a shortest path and one can follow a shortest path from s_{start} to s_{goal} by always moving from the current vertex s, starting at s_{start}, to any successor s' that minimizes $c(s, s') + g(s')$, until s_{goal} is reached.) However, LPA* does not make all vertices locally consistent after some edge costs have changed. Instead, it uses the heuristics to focus the search and updates only the g-values that are relevant for computing a shortest path. To this end, LPA* maintains a priority queue. The priority queue always contains exactly the locally inconsistent vertices *(Invariant 2)*. These are the vertices whose g-values LPA* potentially needs to update to make them locally consistent. The priority of a vertex in the priority queue is always the same as its key *(Invariant 3)*, which is a vector with two components: $k(s) = [k_1(s); k_2(s)]$, where $k_1(s) = \min(g(s), rhs(s)) + h(s, s_{goal})$ and $k_2(s) = \min(g(s), rhs(s))$ {01} (numbers in brackets refer to line numbers in Figure 2). The first component of the keys $k_1(s)$ corresponds directly to the f-values $f(s) := g^*(s) + h(s, s_{goal})$ used by A* because both the g-values and rhs-values of LPA* correspond to the g-values of A* and the h-values of LPA* correspond to the h-values of A*. The second component of the keys $k_2(s)$ corresponds to the g-values of A*. Keys are compared according to a lexicographic ordering. For example, a key $k(s)$ is less than or equal to a key $k'(s)$, denoted by $k(s) \dot{\le} k'(s)$, iff either $k_1(s) < k_1'(s)$ or $(k_1(s) = k_1'(s)$ and $k_2(s) \le k_2'(s))$. LPA* always expands the vertex in the priority queue with the smallest key (by expanding a vertex, we mean executing {10-16}). This is similar to A* that always expands the vertex in the priority queue with the smallest f-value if it breaks ties towards the smallest g-value. The resulting behavior of LPA* and A* is also similar. The keys of the vertices expanded by LPA* are nondecreasing over time just like the f-values of the vertices expanded by A* (since the heuristics are consistent).

Lifelong Planning A*: The Algorithm

The main function Main() of LPA* first calls Initialize() to initialize the search problem {17}. Initialize() sets the g-values of all vertices to infinity and sets their rhs-values according to Equation 1 {03-04}. Thus, initially s_{start} is the only locally inconsistent vertex and is inserted into the otherwise empty priority queue {05}. This initialization guarantees that the first call to ComputeShortestPath() performs exactly an A* search, that is, expands exactly the same vertices as A* in exactly the same order. Note that, in an actual implementation, Initialize() only needs to initialize a vertex when it encounters it during the search and thus does not need to initialize all vertices up front. This is important because the number of vertices can be large and only a few of them might be reached during the search. LPA* then waits for changes in edge costs {20}. To maintain Invariants 1-3 if some edge costs have changed, it calls UpdateVertex() {23} to update the rhs-values and keys of the vertices potentially affected by the changed edge costs as well as their membership in the priority queue if they become locally consistent or inconsistent, and finally recalculates a shortest path {19} by calling ComputeShortestPath(), that repeatedly expands locally inconsistent vertices in the order of their priorities.

A locally inconsistent vertex s is called locally overconsistent iff $g(s) > rhs(s)$. When ComputeShortestPath() expands a locally overconsistent vertex {12-13}, then it sets the g-value of the vertex to its rhs-value {12}, which makes the vertex locally consistent. A locally inconsistent vertex s is called locally underconsistent iff $g(s) < rhs(s)$. When ComputeShortestPath() expands a locally underconsistent vertex {15-16}, then it simply sets the g-value of the vertex to infinity {15}. This makes the vertex either locally

consistent or overconsistent. If the expanded vertex was locally overconsistent, then the change of its g-value can affect the local consistency of its successors {13}. Similarly, if the expanded vertex was locally underconsistent, then it and its successors can be affected {16}. To maintain Invariants 1-3, ComputeShortestPath() therefore updates rhs-values of these vertices, checks their local consistency, and adds them to or removes them from the priority queue accordingly {06-08}. ComputeShortestPath() expands vertices until s_{goal} is locally consistent and the key of the vertex to expand next is no less than the key of s_{goal}. This is similar to A* that expands vertices until it expands s_{goal} at which point in time the g-value of s_{goal} equals its start distance and the f-value of the vertex to expand next is no less than the f-value of s_{goal}. If $g(s_{goal}) = \infty$ after the search, then there is no finite-cost path from s_{start} to s_{goal}. Otherwise, one can trace back a shortest path from s_{start} to s_{goal} by always transitioning from the current vertex s, starting at s_{goal}, to any predecessor s' that minimizes $g(s') + c(s', s)$ (ties can be broken arbitrarily) until s_{start} is reached. This is similar to what A* can do if it does not use backpointers.

Analytical Results

We now present some properties of LPA* to show that it terminates, is correct, similar to A*, and efficient. All proofs can be found in (Likhachev & Koenig 2001).

Termination and Correctness

Our first theorem shows that LPA* terminates and is correct:

Theorem 1 *ComputeShortestPath() expands each vertex at most twice, namely at most once when it is locally underconsistent and at most once when it is locally overconsistent, and thus terminates. After ComputeShortestPath() terminates, one can trace back a shortest path from s_{start} to s_{goal} by always transitioning from the current vertex s, starting at s_{goal}, to any predecessor s' that minimizes $g(s') + c(s', s)$ until s_{start} is reached (ties can be broken arbitrarily).*

Similarity to A*

When we described LPA*, we already pointed out strong algorithmic similarities between LPA* and A*. We now show additional similarities between LPA* and A*. Theorem 1 already showed that ComputeShortestPath() expands each vertex at most twice. This is similar to A*, that expands each vertex at most once. Moreover, the next theorem states that the keys of the vertices expanded by ComputeShortestPath() are monotonically nondecreasing over time. This is similar to the nondecreasing order of f-values of the vertices expanded by A*.

Theorem 2 *The keys of the vertices that ComputeShortestPath() selects for expansion on line {10} are monotonically nondecreasing over time until ComputeShortestPath() terminates.*

The next three theorems show that ComputeShortestPath() expands locally overconsistent vertices in a way very similar to how A* expands vertices. The next theorem, for example, shows that the first component of the key of a locally overconsistent vertex at the time ComputeShortestPath() expands it is the same as the f-value of the vertex. The second component of its key is its start distance.

Theorem 3 *Whenever ComputeShortestPath() selects a locally overconsistent vertex s for expansion on line $\{10\}$, then its key is $k(s) \doteq [f(s); g^*(s)]$.*

Theorems 2 and 3 imply that ComputeShortestPath() expands locally overconsistent vertices in the order of monotonically nondecreasing f-values and vertices with the same f-values in the order of monotonically nondecreasing start distances. A* has the same property provided that it breaks ties in favor of vertices with smaller start distances.

Theorem 4 *ComputeShortestPath() expands locally overconsistent vertices with finite f-values in the same order as A*, provided that A* always breaks ties among vertices with the same f-values in favor of vertices with the smallest start distances and breaks remaining ties suitably.*

The next theorem shows that ComputeShortestPath() expands at most those locally overconsistent vertices whose f-values are less than the f-value of the goal vertex and those vertices whose f-values are equal to the f-value of the goal vertex and whose start distances are less than or equal to the start distances of the goal vertex. A* has the same property provided that it breaks ties in favor of vertices with smaller start distances.

Theorem 5 *ComputeShortestPath() expands at most those locally overconsistent vertices s with $[f(s); g^*(s)] \dot{\leq} [f(s_{goal}); g^*(s_{goal})]$.*

Efficiency

We now show that LPA* expands many fewer vertices than suggested by Theorem 1. The next theorem shows that LPA* is efficient because it performs incremental searches and thus calculates only those g-values that have been affected by cost changes or have not been calculated yet in previous searches.

Theorem 6 *ComputeShortestPath() does not expand any vertices whose g-values were equal to their respective start distances before ComputeShortestPath() was called.*

Our final theorem shows that LPA* is efficient because it performs heuristic searches and thus calculates only the g-values of those vertices that are important to determine a shortest path. Theorem 5 has already shown how heuristics limit the number of locally overconsistent vertices expanded by ComputeShortestPath(). The next theorem generalizes this result to all locally inconsistent vertices expanded by ComputeShortestPath().

Theorem 7 *The keys of the vertices that ComputeShortestPath() selects for expansion on line $\{10\}$ never exceed $[f(s_{goal}); g^*(s_{goal})]$.*

To understand the implications of this theorem on the efficiency of LPA* remember that the key $k(s)$ of a vertex s is $k(s) \doteq [\min(g(s), rhs(s)) + h(s, s_{goal}); \min(g(s), rhs(s))]$. Thus, the more informed the heuristics are and thus the larger they are, the fewer vertices satisfy $k(s) \dot{\leq} [f(s_{goal}); g^*(s_{goal})]$ and thus are expanded.

---

procedure CalculateKey(s)
{01'} return $[\min(g(s), rhs(s)) + h(s_{start}, s) + k_m; \min(g(s), rhs(s))]$;

procedure Initialize()
{02'} $U = \emptyset$;
{03'} $k_m = 0$;
{04'} for all $s \in S$ $rhs(s) = g(s) = \infty$;
{05'} $rhs(s_{goal}) = 0$;
{06'} U.Insert(s_{goal}, CalculateKey(s_{goal}));

procedure UpdateVertex(u)
{07'} if $(u \neq s_{goal})$ $rhs(u) = \min_{s' \in Succ(u)}(c(u, s') + g(s'))$;
{08'} if $(u \in U)$ U.Remove(u);
{09'} if $(g(u) \neq rhs(u))$ U.Insert(u, CalculateKey(u));

procedure ComputeShortestPath()
{10'} while (U.TopKey()$\dot{<}$CalculateKey(s_{start}) OR $rhs(s_{start}) \neq g(s_{start})$)
{11'} $k_{old} = $ U.TopKey();
{12'} $u = $ U.Pop();
{13'} if ($k_{old}\dot{<}$CalculateKey(u))
{14'} U.Insert(u, CalculateKey(u));
{15'} else if $(g(u) > rhs(u))$
{16'} $g(u) = rhs(u)$;
{17'} for all $s \in Pred(u)$ UpdateVertex(s);
{18'} else
{19'} $g(u) = \infty$;
{20'} for all $s \in Pred(u) \cup \{u\}$ UpdateVertex(s);

procedure Main()
{21'} $s_{last} = s_{start}$;
{22'} Initialize();
{23'} ComputeShortestPath();
{24'} while $(s_{start} \neq s_{goal})$
{25'} /* if $(g(s_{start}) = \infty)$ then there is no known path */
{26'} $s_{start} = \arg\min_{s' \in Succ(s_{start})}(c(s_{start}, s') + g(s'))$;
{27'} Move to s_{start};
{28'} Scan graph for changed edge costs;
{29'} if any edge costs changed
{30'} $k_m = k_m + h(s_{last}, s_{start})$;
{31'} $s_{last} = s_{start}$;
{32'} for all directed edges (u, v) with changed edge costs
{33'} Update the edge cost $c(u, v)$;
{34'} UpdateVertex(u);
{35'} ComputeShortestPath();

Figure 3: D* Lite.

D* Lite

So far, we have described LPA*, that repeatedly determines shortest paths between the start vertex and the goal vertex as the edge costs of a graph change. We now use LPA* to develop D* Lite, that repeatedly determines shortest paths between the current vertex of the robot and the goal vertex as the edge costs of a graph change while the robot moves towards the goal vertex. D* Lite is shown in Figure 3. It does not make any assumptions about how the edge costs change, whether they go up or down, whether they change close to the current vertex of the robot or far away from it, or whether they change in the world or only because the robot revised its initial estimates. D* Lite can be used to solve the goal-directed navigation problem in unknown terrain (as described in the section on "Motivation"). The terrain is modeled as an eight-connected graph. The costs of its edges are initially one. They change to infinity when the robot discovers that they cannot be traversed. One can implement the robot-navigation strategy by applying D* Lite to this graph with s_{start} being the current vertex of the robot and s_{goal} being the goal vertex.

Search Direction

We first need to switch the search direction of LPA*. The version of LPA* presented in Figure 2 searches from the start vertex to the goal vertex and thus its g-values are estimates of the start distances. D* Lite searches from the goal vertex to the start vertex and thus its g-values are estimates of the goal distances. It is derived from LPA* by exchanging the start and goal vertex and reversing all edges in the pseudo code. Thus, D* Lite operates on the original graph and there are no restrictions on the graph except that it needs to be able to determine the successors *and* predecessors of the vertices, just like LPA*. After ComputeShortestPath() returns, one can then follow a shortest path from s_{start} to s_{goal} by always moving from the current vertex s, starting at s_{start}, to any successor s' that minimizes $c(s, s') + g(s')$ until s_{goal} is reached (ties can be broken arbitrarily).

Heap Reordering

To solve robot navigation problems in unknown terrain, Main() now needs to move the robot along the path determined by CalculatePath(). Main() could recalculate the priorities of the vertices in the priority queue every time the robot notices a change in edge costs after it has moved. Unless the priorities are recalculated, they do not satisfy Invariant 3 since they are based on heuristics that were computed with respect to the old vertex of the robot. However, the repeated reordering of the priority queue can be expensive since the priority queue often contains a large number of vertices. D* Lite therefore uses a method derived from D* (Stentz 1995) to avoid having to reorder the priority queue, namely priorities that are lower bounds on the priorities that LPA* uses for the corresponding vertices. The heuristics $h(s, s')$ now need to be nonnegative and satisfy $h(s, s') \leq c^*(s, s')$ and $h(s, s'') \leq h(s, s') + h(s', s'')$ for all vertices $s, s', s'' \in S$, where $c^*(s, s')$ denotes the cost of a shortest path from vertex $s \in S$ to vertex $s' \in S$. This requirement is not restrictive since both properties are guaranteed to hold if the heuristics are derived by relaxing the search problem, which will almost always be the case and holds for the heuristics used in this paper. After the robot has moved from vertex s to some vertex s' where it detects changes in edge costs, the first element of the priorities can have decreased by at most $h(s, s')$. (The second component does not depend on the heuristics and thus remains unchanged.) Thus, in order to maintain lower bounds, D* Lite needs to subtract $h(s, s')$ from the first element of the priorities of all vertices in the priority queue. However, since $h(s, s')$ is the same for all vertices in the priority queue, the order of the vertices in the priority queue does not change if the subtraction is not performed. Then, when new priorities are computed, their first components are by $h(s, s')$ too small relative to the priorities in the priority queue. Thus, $h(s, s')$ has to be added to their first components every time some edge costs change. If the robot moves again and then detects cost changes again, then the constants need to get added up. We do this in the variable k_m {30'}. Thus, whenever new priorities are computed, the variable k_m has to be added to their first components, as done in {01'}. Then, the order of the vertices in the priority queue does not change after the robot moves and the priority queue does not need to get reordered. The priorities, on the other hand, are always lower bounds on the corresponding priorities of LPA* after the first component of the priorities of LPA* has been increased by the current value of k_m. We exploit this property by changing ComputeShortestPath() as follows. Af-

```
procedure CalculateKey(s)
{01"} return [min(g(s), rhs(s)) + h(s_start, s) + k_m; min(g(s), rhs(s))];
procedure Initialize()
{02"} U = ∅;
{03"} k_m = 0;
{04"} for all s ∈ S rhs(s) = g(s) = ∞;
{05"} rhs(s_goal) = 0;
{06"} U.Insert(s_goal, [h(s_start, s_goal); 0]);
procedure UpdateVertex(u)
{07"} if (g(u) ≠ rhs(u) AND u ∈ U) U.Update(u, CalculateKey(u));
{08"} else if (g(u) ≠ rhs(u) AND u ∉ U) U.Insert(u, CalculateKey(u));
{09"} else if (g(u) = rhs(u) AND u ∈ U) U.Remove(u);
procedure ComputeShortestPath()
{10"} while (U.TopKey()<CalculateKey(s_start) OR rhs(s_start) > g(s_start))
{11"}    u = U.Top();
{12"}    k_old = U.TopKey();
{13"}    k_new = CalculateKey(u));
{14"}    if(k_old<k_new)
{15"}       U.Update(u, k_new);
{16"}    else if (g(u) > rhs(u))
{17"}       g(u) = rhs(u);
{18"}       U.Remove(u);
{19"}       for all s ∈ Pred(u)
{20"}          if (s ≠ s_goal) rhs(s) = min(rhs(s), c(s, u) + g(u));
{21"}          UpdateVertex(s);
{22"}    else
{23"}       g_old = g(u);
{24"}       g(u) = ∞;
{25"}       for all s ∈ Pred(u) ∪ {u}
{26"}          if (rhs(s) = c(s, u) + g_old)
{27"}             if (s ≠ s_goal) rhs(s) = min_{s'∈Succ(s)}(c(s, s') + g(s'));
{28"}          UpdateVertex(s);
procedure Main()
{29"} s_last = s_start;
{30"} Initialize();
{31"} ComputeShortestPath();
{32"} while (s_start ≠ s_goal)
{33"}    /* if (g(s_start) = ∞) then there is no known path */
{34"}    s_start = arg min_{s'∈Succ(s_start)}(c(s_start, s') + g(s'));
{35"}    Move to s_start;
{36"}    Scan graph for changed edge costs;
{37"}    if any edge costs changed
{38"}       k_m = k_m + h(s_last, s_start);
{39"}       s_last = s_start;
{40"}       for all directed edges (u, v) with changed edge costs
{41"}          c_old = c(u, v);
{42"}          Update the edge cost c(u, v);
{43"}          if (c_old > c(u, v))
{44"}             if (u ≠ s_goal) rhs(u) = min(rhs(u), c(u, v) + g(v));
{45"}          else if (rhs(u) = c_old + g(v))
{46"}             if (u ≠ s_goal) rhs(u) = min_{s'∈Succ(u)}(c(u, s') + g(s'));
{47"}          UpdateVertex(u);
{48"}       ComputeShortestPath();
```

Figure 4: D* Lite (optimized version).

ter ComputeShortestPath() has removed a vertex u with the smallest priority $k_{old} =$ U.TopKey() from the priority queue {12'}, it now uses CalculateKey() to compute the priority that it should have had. If $k_{old}<$CalculateKey(u) then it reinserts the removed vertex with the priority calculated by CalculateKey() into the priority queue {13'-14'}. Thus, it remains true that the priorities of all vertices in the priority queue are lower bounds on the corresponding priorities of LPA* after the first components of the priorities of LPA* have been increased by the current value of k_m. If $k_{old}\geq$CalculateKey(u), then it holds that $k_{old}=$CalculateKey(u) since k_{old} was a lower bound of the value returned by CalculateKey(). In this case, ComputeShortestPath() expands vertex u (by expanding a vertex, we mean executing {15'-20'}) in the same way as LPA*.

Optimizations

Figure 4 shows D* Lite with several optimizations. An example is the termination condition of ComputeShortestPath() that can be changed to make ComputeShortestPath() more efficient. As stated, ComputeShortestPath() terminates when the start vertex is locally consistent and its key is less than or equal to U.TopKey() {10'}. However, ComputeShortestPath() can already terminate when the start vertex is not locally underconsistent and its key is less than or equal to U.TopKey(). To understand why this is so, assume that the start vertex is locally overconsistent and its key is less than or equal to U.TopKey(). Then, its key must be equal to U.TopKey() since U.TopKey() is the smallest key of any locally inconsistent vertex. Thus, ComputeShortestPath() could expand the start vertex next, in which case it would set its g-value to its rhs-value. The start vertex then becomes locally consistent, its key is less than or equal to U.TopKey(), and ComputeShortestPath() thus terminates. At this point in time, the g-value of the start vertex equals its goal distance. Thus, ComputeShortestPath() can already terminate when the start vertex is not locally underconsistent and its key is less than or equal to U.TopKey() {10}. In this case, the start vertex can remain locally inconsistent after ComputeShortestPath() terminates and its g-value thus may not be equal to its goal distance. This is not a problem since the g-value is not used to determine how the robot should move.

Analytical Results

ComputeShortestPath() of D* Lite is similar to ComputeShortestPath() of LPA* and thus shares many properties with it. For example, ComputeShortestPath() of D* Lite expands each vertex at most twice until it returns. The following theorem shows that ComputeShortestPath() of D* Lite terminates and is correct.

Theorem 8 *ComputeShortestPath*() *of D* Lite always terminates and one can then follow a shortest path from s_{start} to s_{goal} by always moving from the current vertex s, starting at s_{start}, to any successor s' that minimizes $c(s, s') + g(s')$ until s_{goal} is reached (ties can be broken arbitrarily).*

Experimental Results

We now compare D* and various versions of the optimized version of D* Lite. We implemented all methods using standard binary heaps as priority queues (although using more complex data structures, such as Fibonacci heaps, as priority queues could possibly make U.Update() more efficient). The robot always observed which of its eight adjacent cells were traversable and then moved to one of them. We used the maximum of the absolute differences of the x and y coordinates of any two cells as approximations of their distance. Since all methods move the robot in the same way and D* has already been demonstrated with great success on real robots, we only need to perform a simulation study. We need to compare the total planning time of the methods. Since the actual planning times are implementation and machine dependent, they make it difficult for others to reproduce the results of our performance comparison. We there-

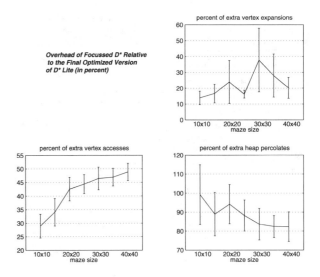

Figure 5: Comparison of D* Lite and D*.

fore used three measures that all correspond to common operations performed by the methods and thus heavily influence their planning times, yet are implementation and machine independent: the total number of vertex expansions, the total number of heap percolates (exchanges of a parent and child in the heap), and the total number of vertex accesses (for example, to read or change their values). Figure 5 compares D* Lite and D* for goal-directed navigation in unknown terrain (as described in the section on "Motivation") of seven different sizes, averaged over 50 randomly generated terrains of each size whose obstacle density varies from 10 to 40 percent. The terrain is discretized into cells with uniform resolution. The figure graphs the three performance measures of D* as percent difference relative to D* Lite. Thus, D* Lite always scores zero and methods that score above zero perform worse than D* Lite. D* Lite performs better than D* with respect to all three measures, justifying our claim that it is at least as efficient as D*. The figure also shows the corresponding 95 percent confidence intervals to demonstrate that our conclusions are statistically significant. In the following, we study to which degree the combination of incremental and heuristic search that D* Lite implements outperforms incremental or heuristic searches individually. We do this for two different but related tasks, namely goal-directed navigation in unknown terrain and mapping of unknown terrain, using similar setups as in the previous experiment.

Goal-Directed Navigation in Unknown Terrain

Figure 6 compares D* Lite, D* Lite without heuristic search, and D* Lite without incremental search (that is, A*) for goal-directed navigation in unknown terrain, using the same setup as in the previous experiment. We decided not to include D* Lite without both heuristic and incremental search in the comparison because it performs so poorly that graphing its performance becomes a problem. D* Lite outper-

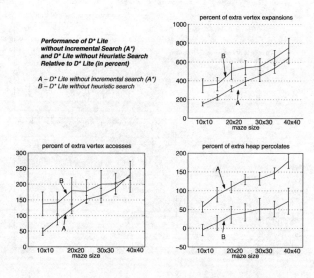

Figure 6: Goal-Directed Navigation (Uniform).

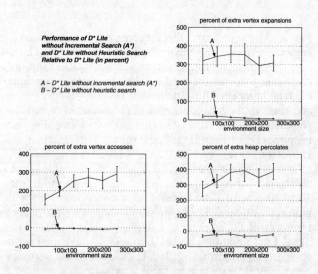

Figure 7: Goal-Directed Navigation (Adaptive).

forms the other two search methods according to all three performance measures, even by more than a factor of seven for the vertex expansions. Moreover, its advantage seems to increase as the terrain gets larger. Only for the number of heap percolates for terrain of size 10 by 10 and 15 by 15 is the difference between D* Lite and D* Lite without heuristic search statistically not significant. These results also confirm earlier experimental results that D* can outperform A* for goal-directed navigation in unknown terrain by one order of magnitude or more (Stentz 1995).

The terrain can also be discretized with nonuniform resolution. Uniform discretizations can prevent one from finding a path if they are too coarse-grained (for example, because the resolution prevents one from noticing small gaps between obstacles) and result in large graphs that cannot be searched efficiently if they are too fine-grained. Researchers have therefore developed adaptive resolution

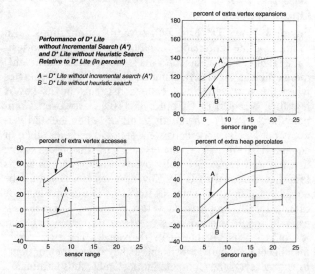

Figure 8: Mapping (Uniform).

schemes (Moore & Atkeson 1995; Yahja *et al.* 1998). We therefore used D* Lite to implement a deterministic version of the parti-game algorithm (Moore & Atkeson 1995) with adaptive discretization that discretizes terrain into cells with nonuniform resolution. In this context, Figure 7 compares D* Lite, D* Lite without heuristic search, and D* Lite without incremental search (that is, A*) for goal-directed navigation in unknown terrain terrains of six different sizes, averaged over 25 randomly generated terrains of each size with an obstacle density of 30 percent each. D* Lite outperforms D* Lite without incremental search (that is, A*) according to all three performance measures, even more than a factor of four for the vertex expansions. On the other hand, different from goal-directed navigation in unknown terrain with uniform discretization, D* Lite and D* Lite without heuristic search perform about equally well.

Mapping of Unknown Terrain

D* Lite can also be used to implement greedy mapping (Koenig, Tovey, & Halliburton 2001), a simple but powerful mapping strategy that has repeatedly been used on mobile robots by different research groups (Thrun *et al.* 1998; Koenig, Tovey, & Halliburton 2001; Romero, Morales, & Sucar 2001). Greedy mapping discretizes the terrain into cells with uniform resolution and then always moves the robot from its current cell to the closest cell with unknown traversability, until the terrain is mapped. In this case, the graph is an eight-connected grid. The costs of its edges are initially one. They change to infinity when the robot discovers that they cannot be traversed. There is one additional vertex that is connected to all grid vertices. The costs of these edges are initially one. They change to infinity once the corresponding grid vertex has been visited. One can implement greedy mapping by applying D* Lite to this graph with s_{start} being the current vertex of the robot and s_{goal} being the additional vertex.

Figure 8 compares D* Lite, D* Lite without heuristic search, and D* Lite without incremental search (that is, A*) for greedy mapping with different sensor ranges, averaging over 50 randomly generated grids of size 64 by 25. The terrain is discretized into cells with uniform resolution. We varied the sensor range of the robot to simulate both short-range and long-range sensors. For example, if the sensor range is four, then the robot can sense all untraversable cells that are up to four cells in any direction away from the robot as long as they are not blocked from view by other untraversable cells. The number of vertex expansions of D* Lite is always far less than that of the other two methods. This also holds for the number of heap percolates and vertex accesses, with the exception of sensor range four for the heap percolates and the number of vertex accesses of D* Lite without incremental search.

Conclusions

In this paper, we have presented D* Lite, a novel fast replanning method for robot navigation in unknown terrain that implements the same navigation strategies as Focussed Dynamic A* (D*). Both algorithms search from the goal vertex towards the current vertex of the robot, use heuristics to focus the search, and use similar ways to minimize having to reorder the priority queue. D* Lite builds on our LPA*, that has a solid theoretical foundation, a strong similarity to A*, is efficient (since it does not expand any vertices whose g-values were already equal to their respective goal distances) and has been extended in a number of ways. Thus, D* Lite is algorithmically different from D*. It is easy to understand and extend, yet at least as efficient as D*. We believe that our experimental and analytical results about D* Lite provide a strong algorithmic foundation for further research on fast replanning methods in artificial intelligence and robotics and complement the research on symbolic replanning methods in artificial intelligence (Hanks & Weld 1995) as well as the research on incremental search methods in both algorithm theory (Frigioni, Marchetti-Spaccamela, & Nanni 2000) and artificial intelligence (Edelkamp 1998).

Acknowledgments

We thank Anthony Stentz for his support of this work. The Intelligent Decision-Making Group is partly supported by NSF awards under contracts IIS-9984827, IIS-0098807, and ITR/AP-0113881 as well as an IBM faculty fellowship award. The views and conclusions contained in this document are those of the authors and should not be interpreted as representing the official policies, either expressed or implied, of the sponsoring organizations and agencies or the U.S. government.

References

Edelkamp, S. 1998. Updating shortest paths. In *Proceedings of the European Conference on Artificial Intelligence*, 655–659.

Frigioni, D.; Marchetti-Spaccamela, A.; and Nanni, U. 2000. Fully dynamic algorithms for maintaining shortest paths trees. *Journal of Algorithms* 34(2):251–281.

Hanks, S., and Weld, D. 1995. A domain-independent algorithm for plan adaptation. *Journal of Artificial Intelligence Research* 2:319–360.

Koenig, S., and Likhachev, M. 2001. Incremental A*. In *Proceedings of the Neural Information Processing Systems*.

Koenig, S.; Tovey, C.; and Halliburton, W. 2001. Greedy mapping of terrain. In *Proceedings of the International Conference on Robotics and Automation*, 3594–3599.

Likhachev, M., and Koenig, S. 2001. Lifelong Planning A* and Dynamic A* Lite: The proofs. Technical report, College of Computing, Georgia Institute of Technology, Atlanta (Georgia).

Matthies, L.; Xiong, Y.; Hogg, R.; Zhu, D.; Rankin, A.; Kennedy, B.; Hebert, M.; Maclachlan, R.; Won, C.; Frost, T.; Sukhatme, G.; McHenry, M.; and Goldberg, S. 2000. A portable, autonomous, urban reconnaissance robot. In *Proceedings of the International Conference on Intelligent Autonomous Systems*.

Moore, A., and Atkeson, C. 1995. The parti-game algorithm for variable resolution reinforcement learning in multidimensional state-spaces. *Machine Learning* 21(3):199–233.

Nilsson, N. 1971. *Problem-Solving Methods in Artificial Intelligence*. McGraw-Hill.

Pearl, J. 1985. *Heuristics: Intelligent Search Strategies for Computer Problem Solving*. Addison-Wesley.

Ramalingam, G., and Reps, T. 1996. An incremental algorithm for a generalization of the shortest-path problem. *Journal of Algorithms* 21:267–305.

Romero, L.; Morales, E.; and Sucar, E. 2001. An exploration and navigation approach for indoor mobile robots considering sensor's perceptual limitations. In *Proceedings of the International Conference on Robotics and Automation*, 3092–3097.

Stentz, A., and Hebert, M. 1995. A complete navigation system for goal acquisition in unknown environments. *Autonomous Robots* 2(2):127–145.

Stentz, A. 1994. Optimal and efficient path planning for partially-known environments. In *Proceedings of the International Conference on Robotics and Automation*, 3310–3317.

Stentz, A. 1995. The focussed D* algorithm for real-time replanning. In *Proceedings of the International Joint Conference on Artificial Intelligence*, 1652–1659.

Thayer, S.; Digney, B.; Diaz, M.; Stentz, A.; Nabbe, B.; and Hebert, M. 2000. Distributed robotic mapping of extreme environments. In *Proceedings of the SPIE: Mobile Robots XV and Telemanipulator and Telepresence Technologies VII*, volume 4195.

Thrun, S.; Bücken, A.; Burgard, W.; Fox, D.; Fröhlinghaus, T.; Hennig, D.; Hofmann, T.; Krell, M.; and Schmidt, T. 1998. Map learning and high-speed navigation in RHINO. In Kortenkamp, D.; Bonasso, R.; and Murphy, R., eds., *Artificial Intelligence Based Mobile Robotics: Case Studies of Successful Robot Systems*. MIT Press. 21–52.

Yahja, A.; Stentz, A.; Brumitt, B.; and Singh, S. 1998. Framed-quadtree path planning for mobile robots operating in sparse environments. In *International Conference on Robotics and Automation*.

Speeding Up the Calculation of Heuristics
for Heuristic Search-Based Planning

Yaxin Liu, Sven Koenig and **David Furcy**
College of Computing
Georgia Institute of Technology
Atlanta, GA 30312-0280
{yxliu,skoenig,dfurcy}@cc.gatech.edu

Abstract

Heuristic search-based planners, such as HSP 2.0, solve
STRIPS-style planning problems efficiently but spend about
eighty percent of their planning time on calculating the
heuristic values. In this paper, we systematically evaluate alternative methods for calculating the heuristic values for HSP
2.0 and demonstrate that the resulting planning times differ
substantially. HSP 2.0 calculates each heuristic value by solving a relaxed planning problem with a dynamic programming
method similar to value iteration. We identify two different
approaches for speeding up the calculation of heuristic values, namely to order the value updates and to reuse information from the calculation of previous heuristic values. We
then show how these two approaches can be combined, resulting in our PINCH method. PINCH outperforms both of
the other approaches individually as well as the methods used
by HSP 1.0 and HSP 2.0 for most of the large planning problems tested. In fact, it speeds up the planning time of HSP 2.0
by up to eighty percent in several domains and, in general, the
amount of savings grows with the size of the domains, allowing HSP 2.0 to solve larger planning problems than was possible before in the same amount of time and without changing
its overall operation.

Introduction

Heuristic search-based planners were introduced by (Mc-
Dermott 1996) and (Bonet, Loerincs, & Geffner 1997) and
are now very popular. Several of them entered the second planning competition at AIPS-2000, including HSP 2.0
(Bonet & Geffner 2001a), FF (Hoffmann & Nebel 2001a),
GRT (Refanidis & Vlahavas 2001), and AltAlt (Nguyen,
Kambhampati, & Nigenda 2002). Heuristic search-based
planners perform a heuristic forward or backward search
in the space of world states to find a path from the start
state to a goal state. In this paper, we study HSP 2.0,
a prominent heuristic search-based planner that won one
of four honorable mentions for overall exceptional performance at the AIPS-2000 planning competition. It was one
of the first planners that demonstrated how one can obtain
informed heuristic values for STRIPS-style planning problems to make planning tractable. In its default configuration, it uses weighted A* searches with inadmissible heuristic values to perform forward searches in the space of world

states. However, the calculation of heuristic values is time-
consuming since HSP 2.0 calculates the heuristic value of
each state that it encounters during the search by solving
a relaxed planning problem. Consequently, its calculation
of heuristic values comprises about 80 percent of its planning time (Bonet & Geffner 2001b). This suggests that
one might be able to speed up its planning time by speeding up its calculation of heuristic values. Some heuristic
search-based planners, for example, remove irrelevant operators before calculating the heuristic values (Hoffmann
& Nebel 2001b) and other planners cache information obtained in a preprocessing phase to simplify the calculation
of all heuristic values for a given planning problem (Bonet &
Geffner 1999; Refanidis & Vlahavas 2001; Edelkamp 2001;
Nguyen, Kambhampati, & Nigenda 2002).

Different from these approaches, we speed up HSP 2.0
without changing its heuristic values or overall operation. In
this paper, we study whether different methods for calculating the heuristic values for HSP 2.0 result in different planning times. We systematically evaluate a large number of
different methods and demonstrate that, indeed, the resulting planning times differ substantially. HSP 2.0 calculates
each heuristic value by solving a relaxed planning problem
with a dynamic programming method similar to value iteration. We identify two different approaches for speeding up
the calculation of heuristic values, namely to order the
value updates and to reuse information from the calculation
of previous heuristic values by performing incremental calculations. Each of these approaches can be implemented
individually in rather straightforward ways. The question
arises, then, how to combine them and whether this is beneficial. Since the approaches cannot be combined easily,
we develop a new method. The PINCH (Prioritized, IN-
Cremental Heuristics calculation) method exploits the fact
that the relaxed planning problems that are used to determine the heuristic values for two different states are similar
if the states are similar. Thus, we use a method from algorithm theory to avoid the parts of the plan-construction
process that are identical to the previous ones and order the
remaining value updates in an efficient way. We demonstrate
that PINCH outperforms both of the other approaches individually as well as the methods used by HSP 1.0 and HSP
2.0 for most of the large planning problems tested. In fact,
it speeds up the planning time of HSP 2.0 by up to eighty

	Non-Incremental Computations	Incremental Computations
Unordered Updates	VI, HSP2	IVI
Ordered Updates	GBF, HSP1, GD	PINCH

Table 1: Classification of Heuristic-Calculation Methods

percent in several domains and, in general, the amount of savings grows with the size of the domains, allowing HSP 2.0 to solve larger planning problems in the same amount of time than was possible before and without changing its overall operation.

Heuristic Search-Based Planning: HSP 2.0

In this section, we describe how HSP 2.0 operates. We first describe the planning problems that it solves and then how it calculates its heuristic values. We follow the notation and description from (Bonet & Geffner 2001b).

The Problem

HSP 2.0 solves STRIPS-style planning problems with ground operators. Such STRIPS-style planning problems consist of a set of propositions P that are used to describe the states and operators, a set of ground operators O, the start state $I \subseteq P$, and the partially specified goal $G \subseteq P$. Each operator $o \in O$ has a precondition list $Prec(o) \subseteq P$, an add list $Add(o) \subseteq P$, and a delete list $Delete(o) \subseteq P$. The STRIPS planning problem induces a graph search problem that consists of a set of states (vertices) 2^P, a start state I, a set of goal states $\{X \subseteq P | G \subseteq X\}$, a set of actions (directed edges) $\{o \in O | Prec(o) \subseteq s\}$ for each state $s \subseteq P$ where action o transitions from state $s \subseteq P$ to state $s - Delete(o) + Add(o) \subseteq P$ with cost one. All operator sequences (paths) from the start state to any goal state in the graph (plans) are solutions of the STRIPS-style planning problem. The shorter the path, the higher the quality of the solution.

The Method and its Heuristics

In its default configuration, HSP 2.0 performs a forward search in the space of world states using weighted A* (Pearl 1985) with inadmissible heuristic values. It calculates the heuristic value of a given state by solving a relaxed version of the planning problem, where it recursively approximates (by ignoring all delete lists) the cost of achieving each goal proposition individually from the given state and then combines the estimates to obtain the heuristic value of the given state. In the following, we explain the calculation of heuristic values in detail. We use $g_s(p)$ to denote the approximate cost of achieving proposition $p \in P$ from state $s \subseteq P$, and $g_s(o)$ to denote the approximate cost of achieving the preconditions of operator $o \in O$ from state $s \subseteq P$. HSP 2.0 defines these quantities recursively. It defines for all $s \subseteq P$, $p \in P$, and $o \in O$ (the minimum of an empty set is defined to be infinity and an empty sum is defined to be zero):

$$g_s(p) = \begin{cases} 0 & \text{if } p \in s \\ \min_{o \in O | p \in Add(o)}[1 + g_s(o)] & \text{otherwise} \end{cases} \quad (1)$$

$$g_s(o) = \sum_{p \in Prec(o)} g_s(p). \quad (2)$$

```
procedure Main()
   forever do
      set s to the state whose heuristic value needs to get computed next
      for each q ∈ P ∪ O \ s do set x_q := ∞
      for each p ∈ s do set x_p := 0
      repeat
         for each o ∈ O do set x_o := ∑_{p∈Prec(o)} x_p
         for each p ∈ P \ s do set x_p := min_{o∈O|p∈Add(o)}[1 + x_o]
      until the values of all x_q remain unchanged during an iteration
      /* use h_add(s) = ∑_{p∈G} x_p */
```

Figure 1: VI

Then, the heuristic value $h_{add}(s)$ of state $s \in S$ can be calculated as $h_{add}(s) = \sum_{p \in G} g_s(p)$. This allows HSP 2.0 to solve large planning problems, although it is not guaranteed to find shortest paths.

Calculation of Heuristics

In the next sections, we describe different methods that solve Equations 1 and 2. These methods are summarized in Table 1. To describe them, we use a variable p if its values are guaranteed to be propositions, a variable o if its values are guaranteed to be operators, and a variable q if its values can be either propositions or operators. We also use variables x_p (a proposition variable) for $p \in P$ and x_o (an operator variable) for $o \in O$. In principle, the value of variable x_p satisfies $x_p = g_s(p)$ after termination and the value of variable x_o satisfies $x_o = g_s(o)$ after termination, except for some methods that terminate immediately after the variables x_p for $p \in G$ have their correct values because this already allows them to calculate the heuristic value.

VI and HSP2: Simple Calculation of Heuristics

Figure 1 shows a simple dynamic programming method that solves the equations using a form of value iteration. This VI (Value Iteration) method initializes the variables x_p to zero if $p \in s$, and initializes all other variables to infinity. It then repeatedly sweeps over all variables and updates them according to Equations 1 and 2, until no value changes any longer.

HSP 2.0 uses a variant of VI that eliminates the variables x_o by combining Equations 1 and 2. Thus, this HSP2 method performs only the following operation as part of its repeat-until loop:

for each $p \in P \setminus s$ do set $x_p := \min_{o \in O | p \in Add(o)}[1 + \sum_{p' \in Prec(o)} x_{p'}]$.

HSP2 needs more time than VI for each sweep but reduces the number of sweeps. For example, it needs only 5.0 sweeps on average in the Logistics domain, while VI needs 7.9 sweeps.

Speeding Up the Calculation of Heuristics

We investigate two orthogonal approaches for speeding up HSP 2.0's calculation of heuristic values, namely to order the value updates (ordered updates) and to reuse information from the calculation of previous heuristic values (incremental computations), as shown in Table 1. We then describe how to combine them.

```
procedure Main()
    forever do
        set s to the state whose heuristic value needs to get computed next
        for each q ∈ P ∪ O \ s do set x_q := ∞
        for each p ∈ s do set x_p := 0
        repeat
            for each o ∈ O do
                set x_o^new := ∑_{p∈Prec(o)} x_p
                if x_o^new ≠ x_o then
                    set x_o := x_o^new
                    for each p ∈ Add(o) do
                        set x_p := min(x_p, 1 + x_o)
        until the values of all x_q remain unchanged during an iteration
        /* use h_add(s) = ∑_{p∈G} x_p */
```

Figure 2: GBF

IVI: Reusing Results from Previous Searches

When HSP 2.0 calculates a heuristic value $h_{add}(s)$, it solves equations in $g_s(p)$ and $g_s(o)$. When HSP 2.0 then calculates the heuristic value $h_{add}(s')$ of some other state s', it solves equations in $g_{s'}(p)$ and $g_{s'}(o)$. If $g_s(p) = g_{s'}(p)$ for some $p \in P$ and $g_s(o) = g_{s'}(o)$ for some $o \in O$, one could just cache these values during the calculation of $h_{add}(s)$ and then reuse them during the calculation of $h_{add}(s')$. Unfortunately, it is nontrivial to determine which values remain unchanged. We explain later, in the context of our PINCH method, how this can be done. For now, we exploit the fact that the values $g_s(p)$ and $g_{s'}(p)$ for the same $p \in P$ and the values $g_s(o)$ and $g_{s'}(o)$ for the same $o \in O$ are often similar if s and s' are similar. Since HSP 2.0 calculates the heuristic values of all children of a state in a row when it expands the state, it often calculates the heuristic values of similar states in succession. This fact can be exploited by changing VI so that it initializes x_p to zero if $p \in s$ but does not re-initialize the other variables, resulting in the IVI (Incremental Value Iteration) method. IVI repeatedly sweeps over all variables until no value changes any longer. If the number of sweeps becomes larger than a given threshold then IVI terminates the sweeps and simply calls VI to determine the values. IVI needs fewer sweeps than VI if HSP 2.0 calculates the heuristics of similar states in succession because then the values of the corresponding variables x_q tend to be similar as well. For example, IVI needs only 6.2 sweeps on average in the Logistics domain, while VI needs 7.9 sweeps.

GBF, HSP1 and GD: Ordering the Value Updates

VI and IVI sweep over all variables in an arbitrary order. Their number of sweeps can be reduced by ordering the variables appropriately, similarly to the way values are ordered in the Prioritized Sweeping method used for reinforcement learning (Moore & Atkeson 1993).

Figure 2 shows the GBF (Generalized Bellman-Ford) method, that is similar to the variant of the Bellman-Ford method in (Cormen, Leiserson, & Rivest 1990). It orders the value updates of the variables x_p. It sweeps over all variables x_o and updates their values according to Equation 2. If the update changes the value of variable x_o, GBF iterates over the variables x_p for the propositions p in the add list of operator o and updates their values according to Equation 1. Thus, GBF updates the values of the variables x_p only if their values might have changed.

```
procedure Main()
    forever do
        set s to the state whose heuristic value needs to get computed next
        for each q ∈ P ∪ O \ s do set x_q := ∞
        for each p ∈ s do set x_p := 0
        set L_p := s
        while L_p ≠ ∅
            set L_o := the set of operators with no preconditions
            for each p ∈ L_p do set L_o := L_o ∪ {o|p ∈ Prec(o)}
            set L_p := ∅
            for each p ∈ P do set x_p^new := x_p
            for each o ∈ L_o do
                set x_o := ∑_{p∈Prec(o)} x_p
                for each p ∈ Add(o)
                    if x_p^new > 1 + x_o
                        set x_p^new := 1 + x_o
                        set L_p := L_p ∪ {p}
            for each p ∈ P do set x_p := x_p^new
        /* use h_add(s) = ∑_{p∈G} x_p */
```

Figure 3: HSP1

Figure 3 shows the method used by HSP 1.0. The HSP1 method orders the value updates of the variables x_o and x_p, similar to the variant of the Bellman-Ford method in (Bertsekas 2001). It uses an unordered list to remember the propositions whose variables changed their values. It sweeps over all variables x_o that have these propositions as preconditions and updates their values according to Equation 2. After each update of the value of a variable x_o, GBF iterates over the variables x_p for the propositions p in the add list of operator o and updates their values according to Equation 1. The unordered list is then updated to contain all propositions whose variables changed their values in this step. Thus, HSP1 updates the values of the variables x_o and x_p only if their values might have changed.

Finally, the GD (Generalized Dijkstra) method (Knuth 1977) is a generalization of Dijkstra's graph search method (Dijkstra 1959) and uses a priority queue to sweep over the variables x_o and x_p in the order of increasing values. Similar to HSP1, its priority queue contains only those variables x_o and x_p whose values might have changed. To make it even more efficient, we terminate it immediately once the values of all $g_s(p)$ for $p \in G$ are known to be correct. We do not give pseudocode for GD because it is a special case of the PINCH method, that we discuss next.[1]

PINCH: The Best of Both Worlds

The two approaches for speeding up the calculation of heuristic values discussed above are orthogonal. We now describe our main contribution in this paper, namely how to combine them. This is complicated by the fact that the approaches themselves cannot be combined easily because the methods that order the value updates exploit the property that the values of the variables cannot increase during each computation of a heuristic value. Unfortunately, this property no longer holds when reusing the values of the variables from the calculation of previous heuristic values. We

---

[1]PINCH from Figure 5 reduces to GD if one empties its priority queue and reinitializes the variables x_q and rhs_q before SolveEquations() is called again as well as modifies the while loop of SolveEquations() to terminate immediately once the values of all $g_s(p)$ for $p \in G$ are known to be correct.

thus need to develop a new method based on a method from algorithm theory. The resulting PINCH (Prioritized, INCremental Heuristics calculation) method solves Equations 1 and 2 by calculating only those values $g_{s'}(p)$ and $g_{s'}(o)$ that are different from the corresponding values $g_s(p)$ and $g_s(o)$ from the calculation of previous heuristic values. PINCH also orders the variables so that it updates the value of each variable at most twice. We will demonstrate in the experimental section that PINCH outperforms the other methods in many large planning domains and is not worse in most other large planning domains.

DynamicSWSF-FP

In this section, we describe DynamicSWSF-FP (Ramalingam & Reps 1996), the method from algorithm theory that we extend to speed up the calculation of the heuristic values for HSP 2.0. We follow the presentation in (Ramalingam & Reps 1996). A function $g(x_1, \ldots, x_j, \ldots, x_k)$: $\mathbb{R}_+^k \rightarrow \mathbb{R}_+$ is called a strict weakly superior function (in short: swsf) if, for every $j \in 1 \ldots k$, it is monotone non-decreasing in variable x_j and satisfies: $g(x_1, \ldots, x_j, \ldots, x_k) \leq x_j \Rightarrow g(x_1, \ldots, x_j, \ldots, x_k) = g(x_1, \ldots, \infty, \ldots, x_k)$. The swsf fixed point (in short: swsf-fp) problem is to compute the unique fixed point of k equations, namely the equations $x_i = g_i(x_1, \ldots, x_k)$, in the k variables $x_1, \ldots, x_k$, where the g_i are swsf for $i = 1 \ldots k$. The dynamic swsf-fp problem is to maintain the unique fixed point of the swsf equations after some or all of the functions g_i have been replaced by other swsf's. DynamicSWSF-FP solves the dynamic swsf-fp problem efficiently by recalculating only the values of variables that change, rather than the values of all variables. The authors of DynamicSWSF-FP have proved its correctness, completeness, and other properties and applied it to grammar problems and shortest path problems (Ramalingam & Reps 1996).

Terminology and Variables

We use the following terminology to explain how to use DynamicSWSF-FP to calculate the heuristic values for HSP 2.0. If $x_i = g_i(x_1, \ldots, x_k)$ then x_i is called consistent. Otherwise it is called inconsistent. If x_i is inconsistent then either $x_i < g_i(x_1, \ldots, x_k)$, in which case we call x_i underconsistent, or $x_i > g_i(x_1, \ldots, x_k)$, in which case we call x_i overconsistent. We use the variables rhs_i to keep track of the current values of $g_i(x_1, \ldots, x_k)$. It always holds that $rhs_i = g_i(x_1, \ldots, x_k)$ (Invariant 1). We can therefore compare x_i and rhs_i to check whether x_i is overconsistent or underconsistent. We maintain a priority queue that always contains exactly the inconsistent x_i (to be precise: it stores i rather than x_i) with priorities $\min(x_i, rhs_i)$ (Invariant 2).

Transforming the Equations

We transform Equations 1 and 2 as follows to ensure that they specify a swsf-fp problem, for all $s \subseteq P$, $p \in P$ and $o \in O$:

$$g'_s(p) = \begin{cases} 0 & \text{if } p \in s \\ \min_{o \in O | p \in Add(o)} [1 + g'_s(o)] & \text{otherwise} \end{cases} \quad (3)$$

$$g'_s(o) = 1 + \sum_{p \in Prec(o)} g'_s(p). \quad (4)$$

```
procedure AdjustVariable(q)
    if q ∈ P then
        if q ∈ s then set rhs_q := 0
        else set rhs_q := 1 + min_{o∈O|q∈Add(o)} x_o
    else /* q ∈ O */ set rhs_q := 1 + ∑_{p∈Prec(q)} x_p
    if q is in the priority queue then delete it
    if x_q ≠ rhs_q then insert q into the priority queue with priority min(x_q, rhs_q)

procedure SolveEquations()
    while the priority queue is not empty do
        delete the element with the smallest priority from the priority queue and assign it to q
        if rhs_q < x_q then
            set x_q := rhs_q
            if q ∈ P then for each o ∈ O such that q ∈ Prec(o) do AdjustVariable(o)
            else if q ∈ O then for each p ∈ Add(q) with p ∉ s do AdjustVariable(p)
        else
            set x_q := ∞
            AdjustVariable(q)
            if q ∈ P then for each o ∈ O such that q ∈ Prec(o) do AdjustVariable(o)
            else if q ∈ O then for each p ∈ Add(q) with p ∉ s do AdjustVariable(p)

procedure Main()
    empty the priority queue
    set s to the state whose heuristic value needs to get computed
    for each q ∈ P ∪ O do set x_q := ∞
    for each q ∈ P ∪ O do AdjustVariable(q)
    forever do
        SolveEquations()
        /* use h_add(s) = 1/2 ∑_{p∈G} x_p */
        set s' := s and s to the state whose heuristic value needs to get computed next
        for each p ∈ (s \ s') ∪ (s' \ s) do AdjustVariable(p)
```

Figure 4: PINCH

The only difference is in the calculation of $g'_s(o)$. The transformed equations specify a swsf-fp problem since 0, $\min_{o \in O | p \in Add(o)} [1 + g'_s(o)]$, and $1 + \sum_{p \in C} g'_s(p)$ are all swsf in $g'_s(p)$ and $g'_s(o)$ for all $p \in P$ and all $o \in O$. This means that the transformed equations can be solved with DynamicSWSF-FP. They can be used to calculate $h_{add}(s)$ since it is easy to show that $g_s(p) = 1/2 g'_s(p)$ and thus $h_{add}(s) = \sum_{p \in G} g_s(p) = 1/2 \sum_{p \in G} g'_s(p)$.

Calculation of Heuristics with DynamicSWSF-FP

We apply DynamicSWSF-FP to the problem of calculating the heuristic values of HSP 2.0, which reduces to solving the swsf fixed point problem defined by Equations 3 and 4. The solution is obtained by SolveEquations() shown in Figure 4. In the algorithm, each x_p is a variable that contains the corresponding $g'_s(p)$ value, and each x_o is a variable that contains the corresponding $g'_s(o)$ value.

PINCH calls AdjustVariable() for each x_q to ensure that Invariants 1 and 2 hold before it calls SolveEquations() for the first time. It needs to call AdjustVariable() only for those x_q whose function g_q has changed before it calls SolveEquations() again. The invariants will automatically continue to hold for all other x_q. If the state whose heuristic value needs to get computed changes from s' to s, then this changes only those functions g_q that correspond to the right-hand side of Equation 3 for which $p \in (s \setminus s') \cup (s' \setminus s)$, in other words, where p is no longer part of s (and the corresponding variable thus is no longer clamped to zero) or just became part of s (and the corresponding variable thus just became clamped to zero). SolveEquations() then operates as follows. The x_q solve Equations 3 and 4 if they are all consistent. Thus, SolveEquations() adjusts the values of the inconsistent x_q. It always removes the x_q with the smallest priority from the priority queue. If x_q is overconsistent then SolveEqua-

```
procedure AdjustVariable(q)
    if x_q ≠ rhs_q then
        if q is not in the priority queue then insert it with priority min(x_q, rhs_q)
        else change the priority of q in the priority queue to min(x_q, rhs_q)
    else if q is in the priority queue then delete it

procedure SolveEquations()
    while the priority queue is not empty do
        assign the element with the smallest priority in the priority queue to q
        if q ∈ P then
            if rhs_q < x_q then
                delete q from the priority queue
                set x_old := x_q
                set x_q := rhs_q
                for each o ∈ O such that q ∈ Prec(o) do
                    if rhs_o = ∞ then
                        set rhs_o := 1 + Σ_{p∈Prec(o)} x_p
                    else set rhs_o := - x_old + x_q
                    AdjustVariable(o)
            else
                set x_q := ∞
                if q ∉ s then
                    set rhs_q := 1 + min_{o∈O|q∈Add(o)} x_o
                    AdjustVariable(q)
                for each o ∈ O such that q ∈ Prec(o) do
                    set rhs_o := ∞
                    AdjustVariable(o)
        else /* q ∈ O */
            if rhs_q < x_q then
                delete q from the priority queue
                set x_q := rhs_q
                for each p ∈ Add(q) with p ∉ s do
                    rhs_p = min(rhs_p, 1 + x_q)
                    AdjustVariable(p)
            else
                set x_old := x_q
                set x_q := ∞
                set rhs_q := 1 + Σ_{p∈Prec(q)} x_p
                AdjustVariable(q)
                for each p ∈ Add(q) with p ∉ s do
                    if rhs_p = 1 + x_old then
                        set rhs_p := 1 + min_{o∈O|p∈Add(o)} x_o
                        AdjustVariable(p)

procedure Main()
    empty the priority queue
    set s to the state whose heuristic value needs to get computed
    for each q ∈ P ∪ O do set rhs_q := x_q := ∞
    for each o ∈ O with Prec(o) = ∅ do set rhs_o := x_o := 1
    for each p ∈ s do
        rhs_p := 0
        AdjustVariable(p)
    forever do
        SolveEquations()
        /* use h_add(s) = 1/2 Σ_{p∈G} x_p */
        set s' := s and s to the state whose heuristic value needs to get computed next
        for each p ∈ s \ s' do
            rhs_p := 0
            AdjustVariable(p)
        for each p ∈ s' \ s do
            rhs_p := 1 + min_{o∈O|p∈Add(o)} x_o
            AdjustVariable(p)
```

Figure 5: Optimized PINCH

tions() sets it to the value of rhs_q. This makes x_q consistent. Otherwise x_q is underconsistent and SolveEquations() sets it to infinity. This makes x_q either consistent or overconsistent. In the latter case, it remains in the priority queue. Whether x_q was underconsistent or overconsistent, its value got changed. SolveEquations() then calls AdjustVariable() to maintain the Invariants 1 and 2. Once the priority queue is empty, SolveEquations() terminates since all x_q are consistent and thus solve Equations 3 and 4. One can prove that it changes the value of each x_q at most twice, namely at most once when it is underconsistent and at most once when it is overconsistent, and thus terminates in finite time (Ramalingam & Reps 1996).

Algorithmic Optimizations

PINCH can be optimized further. Its main inefficiency is that it often iterates over a large number of propositions or operators. Consider, for example, the case where $q \in O$ has the smallest priority during an iteration of the while-loop in SolveEquations() and $rhs_q < x_q$. At some point in time, SolveEquations() then executes the following loop

$$\text{for each } p \in Add(q) \text{ with } p \notin s \text{ do AdjustVariable}(p)$$

The for-loop iterates over all propositions that satisfy its condition. For each of them, the call AdjustVariable(p) executes

$$\text{set } rhs_p := 1 + \min_{o \in O | p \in Add(o)} x_o$$

The calculation of rhs_p therefore iterates over all operators that contain p in their add list. However, this iteration can be avoided. Since $rhs_q < x_q$ according to our assumption, SolveEquations() sets the value of x_q to rhs_q and thus decreases it. All other values remain the same. Thus, rhs_p cannot increase and one can recalculate it faster as follows

$$\text{set } rhs_p := \min(rhs_p, 1 + x_q)$$

Figure 5 shows PINCH after this and other optimizations. In the experimental section, we use this method rather than the unoptimized one to reduce the planning time. This reduces the planning time, for example, by 20 percent in the Logistics domain and up to 90 percent in the Freecell domain.

Summary of Methods

Table 1 summarizes the methods that we have discussed and classifies them according to whether they order the value updates (ordered updates) and whether they reuse information from the calculation of previous heuristic values (incremental computations).

Both VI and IVI perform full sweeps over all variables and thus perform unordered updates. IVI reuses the values of variables from the computation of the previous heuristic value and is an incremental version of VI. We included HSP2 although it is very similar to VI and belongs to the same class because it is the method used by HSP 2.0. Its only difference from VI is that it eliminates all operator variables, which simplifies the code.

GBF, HSP1, and GD order the value updates. They are listed from left to right in order of increasing number of binary ordering constraints between value updates. GBF performs full sweeps over all operator variables interleaved with partial sweeps over those proposition variables whose values might have changed because they depend on operator variables whose values have just changed. HSP1, the method used by HSP 1.0, alternates partial sweeps over operator variables and partial sweeps over proposition variables. Finally, both GD and PINCH order the value updates completely and thus do not perform any sweeps. This enables GD to update the value of each variable only once and PINCH to update the value of each variable only twice. PINCH reuses the values of variables from the computation of the previous heuristic value and is an incremental version of GD.

Problem Size	#P	#O	Length	#CV	#CV/#P	HSP2	VI	IVI	GBF	HSP1	GD	PINCH
LOGISTICS-4-0	48	78	26	15.10	11.98%	0.07	0.09 (-29%)	0.09 (-29%)	0.06 (14%)	0.06 (14%)	0.09 (-29%)	0.05 (29%)
LOGISTICS-7-0	99	174	52	29.43	10.78%	0.82	1.13 (-38%)	0.97 (-18%)	0.58 (29%)	0.60 (27%)	1.13 (-38%)	0.49 (40%)
LOGISTICS-10-0	168	308	59	39.73	8.35%	1.06	1.54 (-45%)	1.32 (-25%)	0.69 (35%)	0.76 (28%)	1.51 (-42%)	0.52 (51%)
LOGISTICS-13-0	275	650	102	52.48	5.67%	5.25	8.08 (-54%)	6.54 (-23%)	3.52 (33%)	3.77 (28%)	13.75 (-162%)	2.05 (61%)
LOGISTICS-16-0	384	936	121	63.33	4.80%	12.01	18.27 (-52%)	15.03 (-25%)	7.86 (35%)	8.13 (32%)	19.69 (-64%)	4.11 (66%)
LOGISTICS-19-0	511	1274	144	84.26	4.72%	30.93	43.12 (-39%)	34.36 (-11%)	18.25 (41%)	18.55 (40%)	45.45 (-47%)	9.16 (70%)
LOGISTICS-22-0	656	1664	160	108.65	4.68%	101.72	165.72 (-63%)	137.86 (-36%)	69.67 (32%)	71.64 (30%)	178.57 (-76%)	34.98 (66%)
LOGISTICS-25-0	855	2664	206	104.28	2.96%	104.12	168.14 (-61%)	128.58 (-23%)	73.15 (30%)	87.08 (16%)	188.62 (-81%)	27.99 (73%)
LOGISTICS-28-0	1040	3290	243	124.14	2.86%	201.38	316.96 (-57%)	249.55 (-24%)	140.38 (30%)	151.34 (25%)	362.90 (-80%)	51.09 (75%)
LOGISTICS-31-0	1243	3982	269	148.05	2.83%	315.95	491.25 (-55%)	382.49 (-21%)	201.35 (36%)	220.12 (30%)	546.57 (-73%)	72.86 (77%)
LOGISTICS-34-0	1464	4740	291	161.16	2.60%	434.81	688.98 (-58%)	518.06 (-19%)	296.51 (32%)	307.26 (29%)	801.60 (-84%)	105.07 (76%)
LOGISTICS-37-0	1755	6734	316	165.82	1.95%	1043.80	1663.30 (-59%)	1333.00 (-28%)	759.29 (27%)	824.53 (21%)	2132.00 (-104%)	219.82 (79%)
LOGISTICS-40-0	2016	7812	337	186.08	1.89%	1314.80	2112.70 (-61%)	1464.30 (-11%)	900.32 (32%)	936.42 (29%)	2488.30 (-89%)	275.39 (79%)

Table 2: Experimental Results in the Logistics Domain

Experimental Evaluation

After describing our experimental setup and the collected data, we discuss the results and draw conclusions.

Experimental Setup

To compare the various methods for calculating the heuristic values, we integrated them into the publicly available code for HSP 2.0.[2] We used the default configuration of HSP 2.0 for all experiments, namely forward weighted A* searches with a weight of 2.0.

HSP2 is already part of the publicly available code for HSP 2.0. We therefore used it as the baseline method against which we compared the other methods. To make this baseline as efficient as possible, we deleted all code from the existing implementation of HSP2 whose results are not used when planning with the default configuration, which reduces the planning time of HSP2, for example, by over 20 percent in the Logistics domain.

Most of our test problems came from the publicly available AIPS-98 and AIPS-00 competition problem sets. We used all instances of the Gripper, Mprime and Mystery domains from AIPS-98. In addition, we generated random problems in the Gripper domain that are larger than those from AIPS-98. We used all domains from AIPS-00: all instances of the Blocks World, Elevator, Freecell, and Logistics domains and small instances (with two to nine parts) from the Schedule domain. Finally, we generated additional problems in the Blocks World domain that are larger than those from AIPS-00. These problems, randomly drawn from a uniform distribution of problems, allow us to reliably identify a trend for large problems (these results appear in a separate graph).

We performed the experiments on a cluster of 32 Sun Sparc Ultra 10 workstations with 256 MBytes of memory each. We limited the planning time to 10 minutes for each problem.

Reported Data

Table 2 contains detailed data for the Logistics domain. These results are not directly comparable to the results from

the AIPS-00 competition since HSP 2.0 solved most Logistics problems in the competition with backward search (Bonet & Geffner 2001a). The rows corresponds to problems of increasing size. The first column contains the problem name. The next two columns contain the number #P of propositions that are contained in at least one add or delete list of the applicable ground operators and the number #O of applicable ground operators, respectively. The sum of #O and #P is the size of the graph used to compute the heuristic values. The fourth column contains the length of the plan found by HSP 2.0. The fifth column contains the average number #CV of proposition variables whose values changed from the calculation of one heuristic value to the next. The sixth column contains the ratio of #CV and #P. The seventh column contains the planning time for HSP2, our baseline. Finally, the next six columns contain both the planning times of the other methods and their relative speedup over HSP2. None of the planning times include the time required for generating the propositions and ground operators because it is the same for each method.

Figure 6 contains less detailed data for all planning domains. It plots, for each domain, the relative speedup in planning time of all methods over HSP2 as a function of the size of the graph used to compute the heuristic values. (Thus, the horizontal line at y=0 corresponds to HSP2.) Each data point corresponds to a single problem. Lines average over all problems of the same size. When a problem could not be solved within 10 minutes, we approximated the relative speedup in planning time with the relative speedup in node generation rate and indicated this with a dashed line. This approximation is justified because we checked empirically that the node generation rate remains roughly constant over time.

Results and Discussion

The relative speedups of the methods in planning time over HSP2 vary substantially, both across different methods in the same domain and across different domains for the same method. However, we can draw two conclusions.

First, PINCH and GBF are the best and second best methods for large domains, respectively. Indeed, PINCH is significantly faster than GBF in five domains, about as fast as GBF in two other domains, and only significantly slower than GBF in the Freecell domain. (GBF, in turn, is significantly faster than all methods other than PINCH in all but three domains.) Furthermore, the relative speedup in plan-

---

[2]We followed the publicly available code for HSP 1.0 when reimplementing HSP1. All priority queues were implemented as binary heaps. The threshold on the number of sweeps for the IVI method was set to 10.

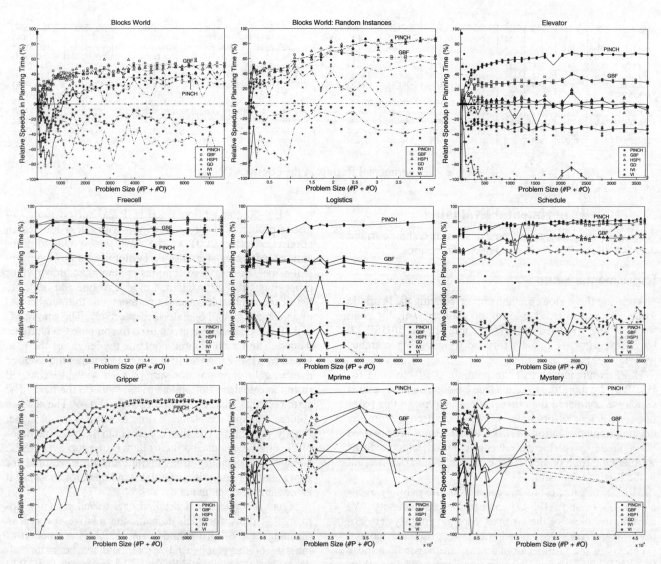

Figure 6: Relative Speedup in Planning Time over HSP2

ning time of PINCH over HSP2 tends to increase with the problem size. For example, PINCH outperforms HSP2 by over 80 percent for large problems in several domains. According to theoretical results given in (Ramalingam & Reps 1996), the complexity of PINCH depends on the number of operator and proposition variables whose values change from the calculation of one heuristic value to the next. Since some methods do not use operator variables, we only counted the number of proposition variables whose values changed. Table 2 lists the resulting dissimilarity measure for the Logistics domain. In this domain, #CV/#P is a good predictor of the relative speedup in planning time of PINCH over HSP2, with a negative correlation coefficient of -0.96. More generally, the dissimilarity measure is a good predictor of the relative speedup in planning time of PINCH over HSP2 in all domains, with negative correlation coefficients ranging from -0.96 to -0.36. This insight can be used to explain the relatively poor scaling behavior of PINCH in the

Freecell domain. In all other domains, the dissimilarity measure is negatively correlated with the problem size, with negative correlation coefficients ranging from -0.92 to -0.57. In the Freecell domain, however, the dissimilarity measure is positively correlated with the problem size, with a positive correlation coefficient of 0.68. The Freecell domain represents a solitaire game. As the problem size increases, the number of cards increases while the numbers of columns and free cells remain constant. This results in additional constraints on the values of both proposition and operator variables and thus in a larger number of value changes from one calculation of the heuristic value to the next. This increases the dissimilarity measure and thus decreases the relative speedup of PINCH over HSP2. Finally, there are problems that HSP 2.0 with PINCH could solve in the 10-minute time limit that neither the standard HSP 2.0 distribution, nor HSP 2.0 with GBF, could solve. The Logistics domain is such a domain.

Second, GBF is at least as fast as HSP1 and HSP1 is at least as fast as GD. Thus, the stricter the ordering of the variable updates among the three methods with ordered updates and nonincremental computations, the smaller their relative speedup over HSP2. This can be explained with the increasing overhead that results from the need to maintain the ordering constraints with increasingly complex data structures. GBF does not use any additional data structures, HSP1 uses an unordered list, and GD uses a priority queue. (We implemented the priority queue in turn as a binary heap, Fibonacci heap, and a multi-level bucket to ensure that this conclusion is independent of its implementation.) Since PINCH without value reuse reduces to GD, our experiments demonstrate that it is value reuse that allows PINCH to counteract the overhead associated with the priority queue, and makes the planning time of PINCH so competitive.

Conclusions

In this paper, we systematically evaluated methods for calculating the heuristic values for HSP 2.0 with the h_{add} heuristics and demonstrated that the resulting planning times differ substantially. We identified two different approaches for speeding up the calculation of the heuristic values, namely to order the value updates and to reuse information from the calculation of previous heuristic values. We then showed how these two approaches can be combined, resulting in our PINCH (Prioritized, INCremental Heuristics calculation) method. PINCH outperforms both of the other approaches individually as well as the methods used by HSP 1.0 and HSP 2.0 for most of the large planning problems tested. In fact, it speeds up the planning time of HSP 2.0 by up to eighty percent in several domains and, in general, the amount of savings grows with the size of the domains. This is an important property since, if a method has a high relative speedup for small problems, it wins by fractions of a second which is insignificant in practice. However, if a method has a high relative speedup for large problems, it wins by minutes. Thus, PINCH allows HSP 2.0 to solve larger planning problems than was possible before in the same amount of time and without changing its operation. We also have preliminary results that show that PINCH speeds up HSP 2.0 with the h_{max} heuristics (Bonet & Geffner 2001b) by over 20 percent and HSP 2.0 with the h_{max}^2 (Haslum & Geffner 2000) heuristic by over 80 percent for small blocks world instances. We are currently working on demonstrating similar savings for other heuristic search-based planners. For example, PINCH also applies in principle to the first stage of FF (Hoffmann & Nebel 2001a), where FF builds the planning graph.

Acknowledgments

We thank Blai Bonet and Hector Geffner for making the code of HSP 1.0 and HSP 2.0 available to us and for answering our questions. We also thank Sylvie Thiébaux and John Slaney for making their blocksworld planning task generator available to us. The Intelligent Decision-Making Group is partly supported by NSF awards to Sven Koenig under contracts IIS-9984827, IIS-0098807, and ITR/AP-0113881 as well as an IBM faculty partnership award. The views and conclusions contained in this document are those of the authors and should not be interpreted as representing the official policies, either expressed or implied, of the sponsoring organizations, agencies, companies or the U.S. government.

References

Bertsekas, D. 2001. *Dynamic Programming and Optimal Control.* Athena Scientific, 2nd edition.

Bonet, B., and Geffner, H. 1999. Planning as heuristic search: New results. In *Proceedings of the 5th European Conference on Planning*, 360–372.

Bonet, B., and Geffner, H. 2001a. Heuristic search planner 2.0. *Artificial Intelligence Magazine* 22(3):77–80.

Bonet, B., and Geffner, H. 2001b. Planning as heuristic search. *Artificial Intelligence – Special Issue on Heuristic Search* 129(1):5–33.

Bonet, B.; Loerincs, G.; and Geffner, H. 1997. A robust and fast action selection mechanism. In *Proceedings of the National Conference on Artificial Intelligence*, 714–719.

Cormen, T.; Leiserson, C.; and Rivest, R. 1990. *Introduction to Algorithms.* MIT Press.

Dijkstra, E. 1959. A note on two problems in connection with graphs. *Numerical Mathematics* 1:269–271.

Edelkamp, S. 2001. Planning with pattern databases. In *Proceedings of the 6th European Conference on Planning*, 13–24.

Haslum, P., and Geffner, H. 2000. Admissible heuristics for optimal planning. In *Proceedings of the International Conference on Artificial Intelligence Planning and Scheduling*, 70–82.

Hoffmann, J., and Nebel, B. 2001a. The FF planning system: Fast plan generation through heuristic search. *Journal of Artificial Intelligence Research* 14:253–302.

Hoffmann, J., and Nebel, B. 2001b. RIFO revisited: Detecting relaxed irrelevance. In *Proceedings of the 6th European Conference on Planning*, 325–336.

Knuth, D. 1977. A generalization of Dijkstra's algorithm. *Information Processing Letters* 6(1):1–5.

McDermott, D. 1996. A heuristic estimator for means-ends analysis in planning. In *Proceedings of the International Conference on Artificial Intelligence Planning and Scheduling*, 142–149.

Moore, A., and Atkeson, C. 1993. Prioritized sweeping: Reinforcement learning with less data and less time. *Machine Learning* 13(1):103–130.

Nguyen, X.; Kambhampati, S.; and Nigenda, R. S. 2002. Planning graph as the basis for deriving heuristics for plan synthesis by state space and csp search. *Artificial Intelligence* 135(1–2):73–123.

Pearl, J. 1985. *Heuristics: Intelligent Search Strategies for Computer Problem Solving.* Addison-Wesley.

Ramalingam, G., and Reps, T. 1996. An incremental algorithm for a generalization of the shortest-path problem. *Journal of Algorithms* 21:267–305.

Refanidis, I., and Vlahavas, I. 2001. The GRT planning system: Backward heuristic construction in forward state-space planning. *Journal of Artificial Intelligence Research* 15:115–161.

Iterative-Refinement for Action Timing Discretization

Todd W. Neller

Department of Computer Science
Gettysburg College
Gettysburg, PA 17325, USA
tneller@gettysburg.edu

Abstract

Artificial Intelligence search algorithms search discrete systems. To apply such algorithms to continuous systems, such systems must first be discretized, i.e. approximated as discrete systems. Action-based discretization requires that both action parameters and action timing be discretized. We focus on the problem of action timing discretization.

After describing an ϵ-admissible variant of Korf's recursive best-first search (ϵ-RBFS), we introduce iterative-refinement ϵ-admissible recursive best-first search (IR ϵ-RBFS) which offers significantly better performance for initial time delays between search states over several orders of magnitude. Lack of knowledge of a good time discretization is compensated for by knowledge of a suitable solution cost upper bound.

Introduction

Artificial Intelligence search algorithms search discrete systems, yet we live and reason in a continuous world. Continuous systems must first be discretized, i.e. approximated as discrete systems, to apply such algorithms. There are two common ways that continuous search problems are discretized: state-based discretization and action-based discretization. State-based discretization (Latombe 1991) becomes infeasible when the state space is highly dimensional. Action-based discretization becomes infeasible when there are too many degrees of freedom. Interestingly, biological high-degree-of-freedom systems are often governed by a much smaller collection of motor primitives (Mataric 2000). We focus here on action-based discretization.

Action-based discretization consists of two parts: (1) action parameter discretization and (2) action timing discretization, i.e. *how* and *when* to act. See Figure 1. For example, consider robot soccer. Search can only sample action parameter continua such as kick force and angle. Similarly, search can only sample infinite possible action timings such as when to kick. The most popular form of discretization is uniform discretization. It is common to sample possible actions and action timings at fixed intervals.

In this paper, we focus on action timing discretization. Experimental evidence of this paper and previous studies (Neller 2000) suggests that a fixed uniform discretization of time is not advisable for search if one has a desired

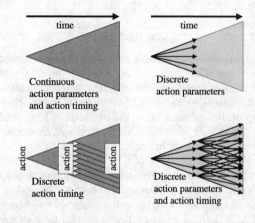

Figure 1: Action-based discretization.

solution cost upper bound. Rather, a new class of algorithms that dynamically adjust action timing discretization can yield significant performance improvements over static action timing discretization.

Iterative-refinement algorithms use a simple means of dynamically adjusting the time interval between search states. This paper presents the results of an empirical study of the performance of different search algorithms as one varies the initial time interval between search states. We formalize our generalization of search, present our chosen class of problems, describe the algorithms compared, and present the experimental results.

The key contributions of this work are experimental insight into the importance of searching with dynamic time discretization, and two new iterative-refinement algorithms, one of which exceeds the performance of ϵ-RBFS across more than four orders of magnitude of the initial time delay between states.

Search Problem Generalization

Henceforth, we will assume that the action discretization, i.e. which action parameters are sampled, is already given. From the perspective of the search algorithm, the action discretization is static, i.e. cannot be varied by the algorithm. However, action timing discretization is dynamic, i.e. the search algorithm can vary the action timing discretization. For this reason, we will call such searches "SADAT searches" as they have Static Action and Dynamic Action Timing discretization.

We formalize the SADAT search problem as the quadruple:

$$\{S, s_0, A, G\}$$

where

- S is the state space,

- $s_0 \in S$ is the initial state,

- $A = \{a_1, \ldots, a_n\}$ is a finite set of action functions $a_i : S \times \Re^+ \to S \times \Re$, mapping a state and a positive time duration to a successor state and a transition cost, and

- $G \subset S$ is the set of goal states.

The important difference between this and classical search formulations is the generalization of actions (i.e. operators). Rather than mapping a state to a new state and the associated cost of the action, we additionally take a time duration parameter specifying how much time passes between the state and its successor.

A goal path can be specified as a sequence of action-duration pairs that evolve the initial state to a goal state. The cost of a path is the sum of all transition costs. Given this generalization, the state space is generally infinite, and the optimal path is generally only approximable through a sampling of possible paths through the state space.

Sphere Navigation Problem

Since SADAT search algorithms will generally only be able to approximate optimal solutions, it is helpful to test them on problems with known optimal solutions. Richard Korf proposed the problem of navigation between two points on the surface of a sphere as a simple benchmark with a known optimal solution.[1] Our version of the problem is given here.

The shortest path between two points on a sphere is along the great-circle path. Consider the circle formed by the intersection of a sphere and a plane through two points on the surface of the sphere and the center of the sphere. The *great-circle path* between the two points is the shorter part of this circle between the two points. The *great-circle distance* is the length of this path.

The state space S is the set of all positions and headings on the surface of a unit sphere along with all nonnegative time durations for travel. Essentially, we encode path cost (i.e. time) in the state to facilitate definition of G. The initial state s_0 is arbitrarily chosen to have position (1,0,0) and velocity (0,1,0) in spherical coordinates, with no time elapsed initially.

The action $a_i \in A$, $0 \le i \le 7$ takes a state and time duration, and returns a new state and the same time duration (i.e. cost = time). The new state is the result of changing the heading $i * \pi/4$ radians and traveling with unit velocity at that heading for the given time duration on the surface of the

[1] Personal communication, 23 May 2001.

unit sphere. If the position reaches a goal state, the system stops evolving (and incurring cost).

The set of goal states G includes all states that are both (1) within ϵ_d great-circle distance from a given position p_g, and (2) within ϵ_t time units of the optimal great-circle duration to reach such positions. Put differently, the first requirement defines the size and location of the destination, and the second requirement defines how directly the destination must be reached. Position p_g is chosen at random from all possible positions on the unit sphere with all positions being equiprobable.

If d is the great-circle distance between (1,0,0) and p_g, then the optimal time to reach a goal position at unit velocity is $d - \epsilon_d$. Then the solution cost upper bound is $d - \epsilon_d + \epsilon_t$. For any position, the great-circle distance between that position and p_g minus ϵ_d is the optimal time to goal at unit velocity. This is used as the admissible heuristic function h for all heuristic search.

Algorithms

In this section we describe the four algorithms used in our experiments. The first pair use fixed time intervals between states. The second pair dynamically refine time intervals between states. The first algorithm, ϵ-admissible iterative-deepening A*, features an improvement over the standard description. Following that we describe an ϵ-admissible variant of recursive best-first search and two novel iterative-refinement algorithms.

ϵ-Admissible Iterative-Deepening A*

ϵ-admissible iterative-deepening A* search, here called ϵ-IDA*, is a version of IDA* (Korf 1985) where the f-cost limit is increased "by a fixed amount ϵ on each iteration, so that the total number of iterations is proportional to $1/\epsilon$. This can reduce the search cost, at the expense of returning solutions that can be worse than optimal by at most ϵ." (Russell & Norvig 1995).

Actually, our implementation is an improvement on ϵ-IDA* as described above. If Δf is the difference between (1) the minimum f-value of all nodes beyond the current search contour, and (2) the current f-cost limit, then the f-cost limit is increased by $\Delta f + \epsilon$. (Δf is the increase that would occur in IDA*.) This improvement is significant in cases where f-cost limit changes between iterations can significantly exceed ϵ.

To make this point concrete, suppose the current iteration of ϵ-IDA* has an f-cost limit of 1.0 and returns no solution and a new f-cost limit of 2.0. The new f-cost limit is the minimum heuristic f-value of all nodes beyond the current search contour. Let us further assume that ϵ is 0.1. Then increasing the f-cost limit by this fixed ϵ will result in the useless search of the same contour for 9 more iterations before the new node(s) beyond the contour are searched.

It is important to note that when we commit to an action timing discretization, the ϵ-admissibility of search is relative to the optimal solution of this discretization rather than the optimal solution of the original continuous-time SADAT search problem.

Much work has been done in discrete search to tradeoff solution optimality for speed. Weighted evaluation functions (e.g. $f(n) = (1 - \omega)g(n) + \omega h(n), 0 \leq \omega \leq 1$ or $f(n) = g(n) + Wh(n), W = \omega/(1 - \omega)$) (Pohl 1970; Korf 1993) provide a simple means to find solutions that are suboptimal by no more than a multiplicative factor of ω. For a good comparison of IDA*-styles searches, see (Wah & Shang 1995). For approximation of search trees to exploit phase transitions with a constant relative solution error, see (Pemberton & Zhang 1996).

ϵ-Admissible Recursive Best-First Search

ϵ-admissible recursive best-first search, here called ϵ-RBFS, is an ϵ-admissible variant of recursive best-first search that follows the description of (Korf 1993, §7.3) without further search after a solution is found. As with our implementation of ϵ-IDA*, local search bounds increase by at least ϵ (when not limited by B) to reduce redundant search.

In Korf's style of pseudocode, ϵ-RBFS is as follows:

```
eRBFS (node: N, value: F(N), bound: B)
IF f(N)>B, RETURN f(N)
IF N is a goal, EXIT algorithm
IF N has no children, RETURN infinity
FOR each child Ni of N,
  IF f(N)<F(N), F[i] := MAX(F(N),f(Ni))
  ELSE F[i] := f(Ni)
sort Ni and F[i] in increasing order of F[i]
IF only one child, F[2] := infinity
WHILE (F[1] <= B and F[1] < infinity)
  F[1] := eRBFS(N1, F[1],
                MIN(B, F[2] + epsilon))
  insert Ni and F[1] in sorted order
RETURN F[1]
```

The difference between RBFS and ϵ-RBFS is in the computation of the bound for the recursive call. In RBFS, this is computed as MIN(B, F[2]) whereas in ϵ-RBFS, this is computed as MIN(B, F[2] + epsilon). F[1] and F[2] are the lowest and second-lowest stored costs of the children, respectively. A correctness proof of ϵ-RBFS is described in the Appendix.

The algorithm's initial call parameters are the root node r, $f(r)$, and ∞. Actually, both RBFS and ϵ-RBFS can be given a finite bound b if one wishes to restrict search for solutions with a cost of no greater than b and uses an admissible heuristic function. If no solution is found, the algorithm will return the f-value of the minimum open search node beyond the search contour of b.

In the context of SADAT search problems, both ϵ-IDA* and ϵ-RBFS assume a fixed time interval between a node and its child. The following two algorithms do not.

Iterative-Refinement ϵ-RBFS

Iterative-refinement (Neller 2000) is perhaps best described in comparison to iterative-deepening. Iterative-deepening depth-first search (Figure 2(a)) provides both the linear memory complexity benefit of depth-first search and the minimum-length solution-path benefit of breadth-first search at the cost of node re-expansion. Such re-expansion

costs are generally dominated by the cost of the final iteration because of the exponential nature of search time complexity.

Iterative-refinement depth-first search (Figure 2(b)) can be likened to an iterative-deepening search to a fixed time-horizon. In classical search problems, time is not an issue. Actions lead from states to other states. When we generalize such problems to include time, we then have the choice of how much time passes between search states. Assuming that the vertical time interval in Figure 2(b) is Δt, we perform successive searches with delays Δt, $\Delta t/2$, $\Delta t/3$, ... until a goal path is found.

Iterative-deepening addresses our lack of knowledge concerning the proper depth of search. Similarly, iterative-refinement addresses our lack of knowledge concerning the proper time discretization of search. Iterative-deepening performs successive searches that grow exponentially in time complexity. The complexity of previous unsuccessful iterations is generally dominated by that of the final successful iteration. The same is true for iterative-refinement.

However, the concept of iterative-refinement is not limited to the use of depth-first search. Other algorithms such as ϵ-RBFS may be used as well. In general, for each iteration of an iterative-refinement search, a level of (perhaps adaptive) time-discretization granularity is chosen for search and an upper bound on the solution cost is given. If the iteration finds a solution within this cost bound, the algorithm terminates with success. Otherwise, a finer level of time-discretization granularity is chosen, and search is repeated. Search is successively refined with respect to time granularity until a solution is found.

Iterative-Refinement ϵ-RBFS is one instance of such search. The algorithm can be simply described as follows:

```
IReRBFS (node: N, bound: B, initDelay: DT)
FOR I = 1 to infinity
  Fix the time delay between states at DT/I
  eRBFS(N, f(N), B)
  IF eRBFS exited with success,
    EXIT algorithm
```

Iterative-Refinement ϵ-RBFS does not search to a fixed time-horizon. Rather, each iteration searches within a search contour bounded by B. Successive iterations search to the same bound, but with finer temporal detail. DT/I is assigned to a global variable governing the time interval between successive states in search.

Iterative-Refinement DFS

The algorithm for Iterative-Refinement DFS is given as follows:

```
IRDFS (node: N, bound: B, initDelay: DT)
FOR I = 1 to infinity
  Fix the time delay between states at DT/I
  DFS-NOUB(N, f(N), B)
  IF DFS-NOUB exited with success,
    EXIT algorithm
```

Our depth-first search implementation DFS-NOUB uses a node ordering (NO) heuristic and has a path cost upper-bound (UB). The node-ordering heuristic is as usual: Nodes

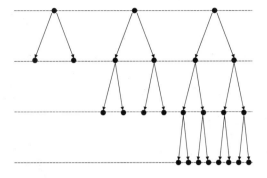

(a) Iterative-deepening DFS.

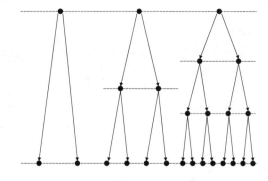

(b) Iterative-refinement DFS.

Figure 2: Iterative search methods.

are expanded in increasing order of f-value. Nodes are not expanded that exceed a given cost upper bound. Assuming admissibility of the heuristic function h, no solutions within the cost upper-bound will be pruned from search.

Experimental Results

In these experiments, we vary only the initial time delay Δt between search states and observe the performance of the algorithms we have described. For ϵ-IDA* and ϵ-RBFS, the initial Δt is the only Δt for search. The iterative-refinement algorithms search using the harmonic refinement sequence Δt, $\Delta t/2$, $\Delta t/3$, ..., and are limited to 1000 refinement iterations. ϵ-admissible searches were performed with $\epsilon = .1$.

Experimental results for success rates of search are summarized in Figure 3. Each point represents 500 trials over a fixed, random set of sphere navigation problems with $\epsilon_d = .0001$ and ϵ_t computed as 10% of the optimal time. Thus, the target size for each problem is the same, but the varying requirement for solution quality means that different delays will be appropriate for different search problems. Search was terminated after 10 seconds, so the success rate is the fraction of time a solution was found within the allotted time and refinement iterations.

In this empirical study, means and 90% confidence intervals for the means were computed with 10000 bootstrap resamples.

Let us first compare the performance of iterative-refinement (IR) ϵ-RBFS and ϵ-RBFS. To the left of the graph, where the initial Δt_0 is small, the two algorithms have identical behavior. This region of the graph indicates conditions under which a solution is found within 10 seconds on the first iteration or not at all. There is no iterative-refinement in this region; the time complexity of the first

iteration leaves no time for another.

At about $\Delta t_0 = .1$, we observe that IR ϵ-RBFS begins to have a significantly greater success rate than ϵ-RBFS. At this point, the time complexity of search allows for multiple iterations, and thus we begin to see the benefits of iterative-refinement.

Continuing to the right with greater initial Δt_0, IR ϵ-RBFS nears a 100% success rate. At this point, the distribution of Δt's over different iterations allows IR ϵ-RBFS to reliably find a solution within the time constraints. We can see the distribution of Δt's that most likely yield solutions from the behavior of ϵ-RBFS.

Where the success rate of IR ϵ-RBFS begins to fall, the distribution of first 1000 Δt's begins to fall outside of the region where solutions can be found. With our refinement limit of 1000, the last iteration uses a minimal $\Delta t = \Delta t_0/1000$. The highest Δt_0 trials fail not because time runs out. Rather, the iteration limit is reached. However, even with a greater refinement limit, we would eventually reach a Δt_0 where the iterative search cost incurred on the way to the good Δt range would exceed 10 seconds.

Comparing IR ϵ-RBFS with IR DFS, we first note that there is little difference between the two for large Δt_0. For $3.16 \leq \Delta t_0 \leq 100$, the two algorithms are almost always able to perform complete searches of the same search contours through all iterations up to the first iteration with a solution path. The largest statistical difference occurs at $\Delta t_0 = 316$ where IR DFS's success rate is 3.8% higher. We note that our implementation of IR DFS has a faster node-expansion rate, and that ϵ-RBFS's ϵ-admissibility necessitates significant node re-expansion. For these Δt_0's, the use of IR DFS trades off ϵ-optimality for speed and a slightly higher success rate.

For mid-to-low-range Δt_0 values, however, we begin to see the efficiency of ϵ-RBFS over DFS with node ordering

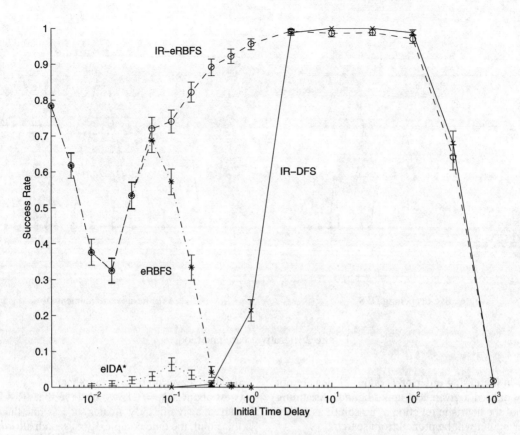

Figure 3: Effect of varying initial Δt.

as the first iteration with a solution path presents a more computationally costly search. Since the target destination is so small, the route that actually leads through the target destination is not necessarily the most direct route. Without a perfect heuristic where complex search is necessary, ϵ-RBFS shows its strength relative to DFS. Rarely will problems be so unconstrained and offer such an easy heuristic as this benchmark problem, so IR ϵ-RBFS will be generally be better suited for all but the simplest search problems.

Comparing IR ϵ-RBFS with ϵ-IDA*, we note that ϵ-IDA* performs relatively poorly over all Δt_0. What is particularly interesting is the performance of ϵ-IDA* over the range where IR ϵ-RBFS behaves as ϵ-RBFS, i.e. where no iterative-refinement takes place. Here we have empirical confirmation of the significant efficiency of ϵ-RBFS over ϵ-IDA*.

In summary, iterative-refinement algorithms are statistically the same as or superior to the other searches over the range of Δt_0 values tested. IR ϵ-RBFS offers the greatest average success rate across all Δt_0. With respect to ϵ-RBFS, IR ϵ-RBFS offers significantly better performance for Δt_0 spanning more than four orders of magnitude. These findings are in agreement with previous empirical studies concerning a submarine detection avoidance problem (Neller 2000).

This is significant for search problems where reasonable values for Δt are unknown. This is also significant for

search problems where reasonable values for Δt are known and one wishes to find a solution more quickly and reliably. This performance comes at a reasonable price for many applications. Lack of knowledge of a good time discretization is compensated for by knowledge of a suitable solution cost upper bound.

Conclusions

This empirical study concerning sphere navigation provides insight into the importance of searching with dynamic time discretization. Iterative-refinement algorithms are given an initial time delay Δt_0 between search states and a solution cost upper bound. Such algorithms iteratively search to this bound with successively smaller Δt until a solution is found.

Iterative-refinement ϵ-admissible recursive best-first search (IR ϵ-RBFS) was shown to be similar to or superior to all other searches studied for Δt_0 spanning over five orders of magnitude. With respect to ϵ-RBFS (without iterative-refinement), a new ϵ-admissible variant of Korf's recursive best-first search, IR ϵ-RBFS offers significantly better performance for Δt_0 spanning over four orders of magnitude.

Iterative-refinement algorithms are important for search problems where reasonable values for Δt are (1) unknown or (2) known and one wishes to find a solution more quickly and reliably. The key tradeoff is that of knowledge. Lack of knowledge of a good time discretization is compensated for by knowledge of a suitable solution cost upper bound. If one knows a suitable solution cost upper bound for a problem where continuous time is relevant, an iterative-refinement algorithm such as IR ϵ-RBFS is recommended.

Future Work

The reason that our iterative-refinement algorithms made use of a harmonic Δt refinement sequence (i.e. Δt, $\Delta t/2$, $\Delta t/3$, ...) was to facilitate comparison to iterative-deepening. It would be interesting to see the performance of different Δt refinement sequences. For example, a geometric refinement sequence Δt, $c\Delta t$, $c^2\Delta t$, ... with $0 < c < 1$ would yield a uniform distribution of Δt's on the logarithmic scale.

Even more interesting would be a machine learning approach to the problem in which a mapping was learned between problem initial conditions and Δt refinement sequences expected to maximize the utility of search. The process could be viewed as an optimization of searches over Δt. Assuming that both time and the success of search have known utilities, one would want to choose the next Δt so as to maximize expected success in minimal time across future iterations.

Acknowledgements

The author is grateful to Richard Korf for suggesting the sphere navigation problem, and to the anonymous reviewers for good insight and suggestions. This research was done both at the Stanford Knowledge Systems Laboratory with support by NASA Grant NAG2-1337, and at Gettysburg College.

Appendix: ϵ-RBFS Proof of Correctness

Proof of the correctness of ϵ-RBFS is very similar to the proof of the correctness of RBFS in (Korf 1993, pp. 52–57). For brevity, we here include the changes necessary to make the correctness proof of (Korf 1993) applicable to ϵ-RBFS. It will be necessary for the reader to have the proof available to follow these changes.

Lemma 4.1 *All calls to ϵ-RBFS are of the form $\epsilon RBFS(n, F(n), b)$, where $F(n) \leq b$.*

Substitute "$\epsilon RBFS$" for "RBFS" through all proofs. For the second to last sentence of this lemma proof, substitute: "Thus, $F[1] < F[2] + \epsilon$. Thus, $F[1] \leq \min(b, F[2] + \epsilon)$."

Lemma 4.2 *If b is finite, and $T(n, b)$ does not contain an interior goal node, then $\epsilon RBFS(n, F(n), b)$ explores $T(n, b)$ and returns $MF(n, b)$.*

In the induction step's first and fourth paragraphs, substitute "$\min(b, F[2] + \epsilon)$" for "$\min(b, F[2])$". In the last sentence of induction step paragraph two, the assumption of "no infinitely increasing cost sequences" is not necessary because the $F[2] + \epsilon$ term forces a minimum increment of ϵ while less than b.

Lemma 4.3 *For all calls $\epsilon RBFS(n, F(n), b)$, $F(n) \leq OD(n)$ and $b \leq ON(n) + \epsilon$.*

Note the addition of "$+ \epsilon$" to the lemma and make a similar addition everywhere a bound is compared to an ON term. For the third sentence of the second to last paragraph, substitute "Since $b' = \min(b, F[2] + \epsilon)$, then $b' \leq F[2] + \epsilon$. Because $F[2] \leq OD(n2)$ and nodes are sorted by F value, $b' \leq OD(m') + \epsilon$ for all siblings m' of n'."

Lemma 4.4 *When a node is expanded by ϵ-RBFS, its f value does not exceed the f values of all open nodes at the time by more than ϵ.*

Note the lemma change. "v" in the second paragraph is the "value" parameter. Wherever "$ON(n)$" occurs, substitute "$ON(n) + \epsilon$". In the last sentence, substitute "...$f(n)$ does not exceed the f values of all open nodes in the tree when n is expanded by more than ϵ."

Theorem 4.5 *$\epsilon RBFS(r, f(r), \infty)$ will perform a complete ϵ-admissible search of the tree rooted at node r, exiting after finding the first goal node chosen for expansion.*

For the first sentence, substitute "Lemma 4.4 shows that ϵ-RBFS performs an ϵ-admissible search." In the second to last sentence, substitute "Since the upper bound on each of these calls is the next lowest F value plus ϵ, the upper bounds must also increase continually, ...".

References

Korf, R. E. 1985. Depth-first iterative-deepening: an optimal admissible tree search. *Artificial Intelligence* 27(1):97–109.

Korf, R. E. 1993. Linear-space best-first search. *Artificial Intelligence* 62:41–78.

Latombe, J.-C. 1991. *Robot Motion Planning*. Boston, MA, USA: Kluwer Academic Publishers.

Mataric, M. J. 2000. Sensory-motor primitives as a basis for imitation: Linking perception to action and biology to robotics. In Nehaniv, C., and Dautenhahn, K., eds., *Imitation in Animals and Artifacts*. Cambridge, MA, USA: MIT Press. See also USC technical report IRIS-99-377.

Neller, T. W. 2000. *Simulation-Based Search for Hybrid System Control and Analysis*. Ph.D. Dissertation, Stanford University, Palo Alto, California, USA. Available as Stanford Knowledge Systems Laboratory technical report KSL-00-15 at www.ksl.stanford.edu.

Pemberton, J. C., and Zhang, W. 1996. Epsilon-transformation: Exploiting phase transitions to solve combinatorial optimization problems. *Artificial Intelligence* 81(1–2):297–325.

Pohl, I. 1970. Heuristic search viewed as path finding in a graph. *Artificial Intelligence* 1:193–204.

Russell, S., and Norvig, P. 1995. *Artificial Intelligence: a modern approach*. Upper Saddle River, NJ, USA: Prentice Hall.

Wah, B. W., and Shang, Y. 1995. Comparison and evaluation of a class of IDA* algorithms. *Int'l Journal of Tools with Artificial Intelligence* 3(4):493–523.

A Logical Measure of Progress for Planning

Aarati Parmar

Department of Computer Science
Stanford University
Gates Building, 2A Wing
Stanford, CA 94305-9020
aarati@cs.stanford.edu

Abstract

Heuristic search planners are so far the most successful. Almost all use as their heuristic an estimate of the distance to a goal state. We formalize a *logical measure of progress*, defined as a predicate $P(\bar{x}, s)$ true of objects $\bar{x}$ at a situation s. Actions which increase P's extension are guaranteed to move closer to a goal situation, so that P enables us to form plans without search. One example of a measure of progress is the concept of final position used in BlocksWorld. It is not clear how to find a P for an arbitrary domain, so instead we identify three different classes of domains and conditions which allow us to construct a measure of progress.

An *obvious* P will not deliver optimal plans, but it should encode plans which are "good enough." Our paradigm is entirely within first-order logic, allowing us to extend our results to concurrent domains and those containing non-trivial state constraints. It turns out P not only encodes goal orderings, but subgoal orderings. P also gives rise to a strategy function $a(s)$ which can be used to create a universal (complete) teleo-reactive (TR) program. Given the fact that P-increasing actions will never require backtracking, this TR program can be a powerful on-line planner.

1   Introduction

Planners that use *heuristic search* have been the most successful to date, garnering four out of the top six spots in the recent AIPS 2000 planning competition (Bacchus 2000). These planners reduce planning to heuristic search, where the heuristic estimates the distance to the goal state. Most use ADL operators, which not only express what STRIPS can, but also disjunctive preconditions, conditional effects, and quantification.

The planners mentioned above all use some estimate of distance to the goal, derived from a relaxed version of the plan, where operators' delete lists are ignored. However, they use slightly different heuristics, in different ways. HSP2 (Bonet & Geffner 2001) employs a strategy of different heuristic functions, simultaneously. MIPS (Edelkamp & Helmert 2001) uses a symbolic heuristic search, where an estimate of the goal distance is associated with each proposition, and combined accordingly. If a domain looks like a route-planning or resource allocation problem, STAN4 (Fox

& Long 2001) cleverly estimates a distance heuristic that takes advantage of the domain structure. FF (Hoffmann 2001a), the top heuristic planner in the competition, uses GraphPlan to compute its estimate, which automatically takes into account positive interactions between goals.

Heuristic search planners are extremely effective. However, the heuristics used are not very elucidating; they only estimate a distance to a goal, without giving any motivation in terms of the structure of the domain. In this paper we define *a logical measure of progress*, that not only produces an action leading *directly* towards the goal, but also explains *why* it works, in terms of properties of the domain. Our avenue of research is orthogonal to the current state of the art in planning; we are more interested in understanding what properties of domains lead to efficient planning rather than finding faster and better algorithms.[1]

We follow the epistemological approach proposed by (McCarthy 1959) regarding the Advice Taker: "behavior will be improvable merely by making statements to it, telling it about its symbolic environment." Intelligent robots operating in the world will need to identify and take advantage of regularities in the world in order to reason efficiently. This research is one step towards this goal.

This work can also be viewed as a bridge between domain independent and dependent planning. We share the motivation of the creators of TIM (Long & Fox 2000), in that discovering domain-specific heuristics from a domain's structure, is an important task for planning, and AI. While TIM identifies generic types, we find a logical measure of progress within the domain.

Before continuing we discuss some related research. The other top planner in AIPS 2000 is TALplanner (Doherty & Kvarnström 2001), a forward chaining planner guided by first order temporal formulas. This approach retains a high level of expressivity and control, without damaging performance. Our logical measure of progress could be used as control formulas for TALplanner, avoiding the need for a user to define them.[2] (Sierra-Santibañez 2001)

---

[1] (Hoffmann 2001b) finds properties leading to efficiency based on the *topology* of the search space (in terms of local minima, plateaus, etc.); we want to find properties based upon the structure of the domain (in terms of local predicates).

[2] One of the reviewers points out that finding a measure of progress could be just as much work as writing a proper control

uses a declarative formalization of strategies for action selection. The approach utilizes user-defined *action selection rules* of the form $\phi(\bar{x}, a, b, s) \implies \psi(a, b, s)$, where $\psi(a, b, s) = Good(a, s) \mid Bad(a, s) \mid Better(a, b, s)$. The planner then uses these categorizations to search. Our approach will give reasons why a particular action is *Good* or *Bad*.

More details, including full proofs, may be found in the technical report (Parmar 2002).

2 Preliminaries

The language of a planning domain traditionally includes some finite set of objects *Objects* and predicates $\{p(\bar{x})\}$. A planning problem consists of predicates true of the initial state I, a goal formula G, and a set of STRIPS or ADL operator schema O. We translate this specification into a theory T of first-order logic, using the situation calculus.[3] We use first-order logic, instead of STRIPS or ADL, for the greater expressivity and because logic provides a more generalizable framework, addressed more in the Conclusions. The language of T has three sorts, *Situations*, *Actions*, and *Objects*:

1. *Objects*: One of the crucial assumptions made throughout this paper is that *our domain has finitely many objects.* Hence T has a domain closure axiom (DCA) of the form: $(\forall x)[x = x_1 \vee ... \vee x = x_n]$, along with a unique names axiom over these objects: $UNA[x_1, ..., x_n]$.

2. Predicates: Only one fluent relation $\Phi(\bar{y}, s)$ is used in T, assuming each original predicate can be coded by defining $\Phi(code(p), \bar{x}, s)$ for each $p(\bar{x})$, where $code(p)$ is a tuple of object constants.[4] $\Phi(\bar{y}, s)$ which do not code a particular fluent, are defined to be $\top$. Φ provides a single handle to talk about any fluent. In this way Φ is similar to the well-known situation calculus predicate $Holds(f, s)$ which asserts that fluent f is true in situation s.

3. Initial state: I, the initial state, is mapped to S_0, the initial situation. All facts true in the initial state are true of S_0.

4. Goal formula: $goal(s)$ abbreviates the goal formula G.

5. Operators: An action $a(\bar{y})$ corresponds to each operator schema $o(\bar{y})$. Any ADL operator can be translated to a successor state axiom of the form:

$$\Phi(\bar{x}, res(a(\bar{y}), s)) \iff \gamma_\Phi^+(\bar{x}, a(\bar{y}), s) \vee$$
$$(\Phi(\bar{x}, s) \wedge \neg\gamma_\Phi^-(\bar{x}, a(\bar{y}), s)),$$

where $\gamma_\Phi^+(\bar{x}, a(\bar{y}), s)$ is a fluent formula abbreviating the conditions under which $\Phi(\bar{x}, \cdot)$ is true after $a(\bar{y})$, while $\gamma_\Phi^-(\bar{x}, a(\bar{y}), s)$ are those where $\Phi(\bar{x}, \cdot)$ becomes false. Successor state axioms are written such that the truth of $\Phi(\bar{x}, res(a(\bar{y}), s))$ is only a function of the fluents true at s and are thus Markovian. While we assume the number of

Objects is finite, we make no such restriction on the numbers of action schema (which can even be uncountable).

$Poss(a, s)$, used to abbreviate *action preconditions*, is omitted. Instead the γ_Φs are written such that when $\neg Poss(a, s)$ holds, $\Phi(\bar{x}, res(a(\bar{y}), s)) \iff \Phi(\bar{x}, s)$. Indeterminacy of inapplicable actions is replaced with inertia, so that the entire tree of situations is utilized, minimizing technical complications.

For the rest of this paper assume T is a domain theory satisfying the constraints given above.

3 A Strong Measure of Progress

We are motivated by the well-known idea of final position used in BlocksWorld planning. A block is in *final position* if the object it is on is the object it is on in the goal state, and that object is in final position. The table is always in final position. This strategy avoids the Sussman anomaly by building towers from the bottom up.

Final position is a good measure of progress, because putting something into final position will lead us closer to the goal. It also identifies objects so that putting something into final position will not prevent the completion of the other goals. We will *never* have to backtrack on any action that increases the extension of final position. Final position is a sort of Dynamic Programming for AI – it identifies optimal substructure to promote tractable solutions to a problem.

Our *logical measure of progress* is generalized as a similar predicate over objects in the domain. Increasing its extension will lead us closer to the goal, without undoing any subgoals. Note that it is a predicate over *objects* in the domain, and *not* some property relating situations to their [estimated] distance to the goal. The purpose of our construction is to force our measure of progress to be a function of the properties of the domain:

Definition 1 (*A Strong Measure of Progress*)
Let s be a situation variable, $x_1, ..., x_n$ object variables, and $P(x_1, ..., x_n, s)$ a fluent formula. Call P a strong, n-ary measure of progress with respect to *goal(s)* if:

$$T \models (\forall s)[\neg goal(s) \implies (\exists a)[ext(P, s) \subset ext(P, res(a, s))]] \tag{1}$$

$ext(P, s) =_{def} \{\bar{x} \mid P(\bar{x}, s)\}$. *Hence $ext(P, s) \subset ext(P, s')$ abbreviates* $(\forall \bar{x})(P(\bar{x}, s) \implies P(\bar{x}, s')) \wedge (\exists \bar{y})(\neg P(\bar{y}, s) \wedge P(\bar{y}, s'))$.

P captures a very strong notion of progress. If $\neg goal(s)$, the definition guarantees that there is an action a that strictly increases the extension of P. Furthermore, when $P(\bar{x}, s)$ is true for all tuples in the domain, $goal(s)$ holds. An action which increases the extension of P not only necessarily gets us closer to the goal, but does so without undoing any other goals along the way.

Equation (1) assures us that in a domain with finitely many objects, we can reach the goal situation from any situation; if T has a strong measure of progress P, then T is

---

formula. If this is the case, our approach will at least provide some foundations for how to construct the control formula in the first place.

[3] We abbreviate *res* for *result*.

[4] We assume our domain includes at least two object constants. The reason why fluents are coded using object constants will be apparent when we define our measure of progress.

deadlock-free. Intuitively this is obvious as the predicate P above is strictly extendible in *any* situation, and if there are finitely many objects to cover, eventually they must all be covered, which means by definition the goal is achieved:

Theorem 1
Let P be a strong, n-ary measure of progress. Then, from any non-goal situation s we can reach a situation satisfying goal, *within* $|Objects|^n - |ext(P, s)|$ *steps.*

Proof: Clearly, at s there are $|Objects|^n - |ext(P, s)|$ object tuples not in P. We need to apply at most that many P-increasing actions to have P be true for all object tuples, at which point we are at the goal. ∎

We can replace the existentially quantified variable a in Equation (1) with the skolem function $a(s)$.[5] This $a(s)$ becomes our *strategy function*, mapping situations to actions. With P, planning is straightforward – we find an action a strictly increasing the extension of P and apply it. This will guarantee that we move closer to the goal. By requiring a *strict* extension of P with every action, P leads directly to the goal – no local minima or plateaus clutter our path.

If a domain has a strong measure of progress then it is deadlock-free. The converse also holds:

Theorem 2
*Let T be a planning domain such that, from every non-*goal *situation s, there is a finite sequence of actions which will lead to a* goal *situation. Then there exists an n and P such that P is a strong n-ary measure of progress.*

Proof Sketch: Let $\ell(s)$ be the shortest distance from the situation s to a goal situation. The idea is to construct, for each n, a fluent formula $G(n, s)$ true of exactly those s for which $\ell(s) = n$. Since $\ell(s)$ is bounded, we can bijectively code each object tuple to each value of $\ell(s)$. Then we define $P(\bar{x}, s)$ to be true of all tuples whose code is greater than $\ell(s)$. The proof relies on the fact that we have finitely many fluents and objects (so that $\ell(s)$ is bounded), and that the progression from s to $res(a, s)$ is only a function of the fluents at s (so that $G(n, s)$ is well-defined). ∎

One can see from the details of the construction that the strong measure of progress defined in this way will generate optimal plans.

Theorems 1 and 2 indicate that the planning domains which have a strong measure of progress with respect to *goal* are precisely those which are deadlock free (with respect to *goal*). This is why P is termed as *strong* – it is equivalent to the universal reachability of a goal situation and thus will not exist in domains with deadlocks.

Another problem is that any domain that is deadlock free will have a strong measure of progress P, but it does not necessarily have to be *obvious* in the sense of (McAllester 1991).[6] That is, it may not be immediately evident from

P's definition that it is a strong measure of progress with respect to the structure of the domain. A P that is obvious will be concise, clearly expressed, and meaningful, such as final position is in BlocksWorld. But unfortunately, un-obvious strong measures of progress exist, such as obscure encodings of the distance to the goal. For example, Rubik's cube is a deadlock-free domain. By Theorem 2, strong measures of progress must exist for solving the cube, but if any were obvious, Rubik's cube would not be the intriguing puzzle it is.

We believe however that most domains in the real world do exhibit an obvious strong measure of progress, as humans plan in them with little search. These domains are easy because they contain enough structure that the measure of progress is clear. In the following sections we formalize what sorts of domain structures give rise to such P. If we cannot automatically construct an adequate P for a domain, perhaps we can at least identify these structures, and from that construct a P.

4 Constructing Strong Measures of Progress
It is not clear how to automatically obtain a strong measure of progress P for a given theory T and *goal*. One could use inductive logic programming or genetic algorithms to look for definitions of P, and promote obvious solutions by using the *local rule sets* of (McAllester 1991) to generate hypotheses for P. Or, one could analyze the state-space graph of small domains for a P which satisfies the constraints, and try to generalize from there, as pointed out by (Lin 2002). We note that finding a P will be at least PSPACE-hard, since finding plans is at least that hard. But the good news is that once we find a P for a given *goal*, we can reuse it to construct any plan with the same (or logically weaker – see (Parmar 2002)) goal, so the cost of finding P is amortized over the times it is used.

Automatic construction of P is an avenue for future work which is beyond the scope of this paper. Instead we study planning domains which admit obvious strong measures of progress, and distill what properties are fundamental. The hope is that we can automatically discover these fundamental properties and perhaps combine them to construct more complicated, strong measures of progress for arbitrary domains.

4.1 Kitchen Cleaning Domain
In the Kitchen Cleaning Domain posed in (Nilsson 1998), cleaning any object makes it clean. However, cleaning the stove or fridge dirties the floor, and cleaning the fridge generates garbage and messes up the counters. Cleaning either the counters or floor dirties the sink. The goal is for all the appliances to be clean and the garbage emptied.

Regardless of the initial state, there is a natural order to cleaning the kitchen. One should clean the sink last, as we may dirty it while cleaning other objects. Cleaning the stove and fridge can safely be done first, as they cannot get dirtied by any subsequent actions. The successor state axioms of T_{KC} and *goal* are shown in Equation (2). $\Phi(x, s)$ represents "x is clean," except when $x = garbage$, in which case it means the garbage is not empty.

---

[5]The Axiom of Choice will be required in case we have uncountably many actions.

[6]It is *obvious* that a king can traverse all squares on a chessboard; but not that a knight can.

$$goal(s) \equiv_{abbrev} \Phi(fridge, s) \wedge \Phi(stove, s) \wedge$$
$$\Phi(floor, s) \wedge \Phi(counters, s) \wedge$$
$$\Phi(sink, s) \wedge \neg\Phi(garbage, s)$$

$$\Phi(fridge, res(a, s)) \iff a = c(fridge) \vee \Phi(fridge, s)$$
$$\Phi(stove, res(a, s)) \iff a = c(stove) \vee \Phi(stove, s)$$
$$\Phi(floor, res(a, s)) \iff a = c(floor) \vee$$
$$\Phi(floor, s) \wedge \neg(a = c(stove) \vee a = c(fridge))$$
$$\Phi(counters, res(a, s)) \iff a = c(counters) \vee$$
$$\Phi(counters, s) \wedge \neg(a = c(fridge))$$
$$\Phi(sink, res(a, s)) \iff a = c(sink) \vee$$
$$\Phi(sink, s) \wedge \neg(a = c(counters) \vee a = c(floor))$$
$$\Phi(garbage, res(a, s)) \iff a = c(fridge) \vee$$
$$\Phi(garbage, s) \wedge \neg(a = empty\text{-}garbage)$$

$$(2)$$

An obvious notion of progress $P_{\mathcal{KC}}$ would clean appliances in the order suggested above. But how do we come up with such a notion automatically? Here is one approach:

4.2 A Measure of Progress for Kitchen Cleaning

Assume $goal(s) \equiv_{abbrev} \Psi(x_1, s) \wedge ... \wedge \Psi(x_n, s)$, where Ψ appears positively. The successor state axioms are rewritten in terms of Ψ, and the positive and negative causes for $\Psi(x, \cdot)$ under a are denoted by $\gamma_\Psi^+(x, a, s)$ and $\gamma_\Psi^-(x, a, s)$. For the Kitchen Cleaning Domain, $\Psi(x, s) \equiv \Phi(x, s)$, except that $\Psi(garbage, s) \equiv \neg\Phi(garbage, s)$.

Definition 2 ($<_P$ ordering)

$$x <_P y \equiv_{def} (\exists a\ s)[\gamma_\Psi^+(x, a, s) \wedge \gamma_\Psi^-(y, a, s)]$$

This ordering suggests we should make $\Psi(x, s)$ true before $\Psi(y, s)$, since in accomplishing $\Psi(x, s)$ it is possible that we could make $\Psi(y, s)$ false. $<_P$ is a shortsighted, weakened version of the *reasonable* ordering relation $\leq_r$ presented in (Koehler & Hoffmann 2000).

Definition 3 (P_{simple})
P_{simple} *is one of the simplest constructions we can produce:*

$$P_{simple}(x, s) \iff \Psi(x, s) \wedge \bigwedge_{y <_P x} P_{simple}(y, s)$$

Definition 4 (Well-founded Relation)
A relation $\prec$ *is well-founded on a set S if every nonempty subset $A \subseteq S$ contains a $\prec$-minimal element:*

$$(\forall A \subseteq S)[A \neq \emptyset \implies (\exists x \in A)(\forall y \in A)[\neg y \prec x]]$$

With these definitions, we can prove when P_{simple} is a strong measure of progress:

Theorem 3 (P_{simple} is a Strong Measure of Progress.)
Assume that T entails that $<_P$ is well-founded over Objects, and for any situation s, every $<_P$ minimal element v has an action a_v such that $\gamma_\Psi^+(v, a_v, s)$. Then P_{simple} is a strong measure of progress.

Proof Sketch: If $\neg goal(s)$, $(\exists x)\neg P_{simple}(x, s)$. The $<_P$-minimal element v over the non-empty set $\{x \mid \neg P_{simple}(x, s)\}$ is the extra object moved into P_{simple} using action a_v. All other objects are guaranteed to stay in P_{simple} due to how P_{simple} is defined, with the help of the well-founded rule of induction. ∎

In practice the above requirements are not too restrictive. The well-foundedness of $<_P$ is the same as requiring that every set A of objects contains one "protected" object v, such that we can make $\Psi(y, res(a, s))$ hold for any $y \in A$ without causing $\Psi(v, res(a, s))$ to be false. The well-foundedness hints at the ordering of putting objects into P so that they won't ever have to be taken out.

The additional requirement that $\Psi(v, res(a_v, s))$ be achievable is also not too restrictive. Usually we plan in spaces where actions "chain," that is, for every action a there is another action b which enables a and doesn't do much else. When actions have no prerequisites this is immediately satisfied.

From Theorem 2 we know the Kitchen Cleaning Domain has a strong measure of progress. We include it here, constructed by means of Definition 3 and Theorem 3, for the reader's benefit:

$$P_{\mathcal{KC}}(fridge, s) \iff \Psi(fridge, s)$$
$$P_{\mathcal{KC}}(stove, s) \iff \Psi(stove, s)$$
$$P_{\mathcal{KC}}(counters, s) \iff \Psi(counters, s) \wedge P_{\mathcal{KC}}(fridge, s)$$
$$P_{\mathcal{KC}}(floor, s) \iff \Psi(floor, s) \wedge P_{\mathcal{KC}}(fridge, s) \wedge$$
$$P_{\mathcal{KC}}(stove, s)$$
$$P_{\mathcal{KC}}(garbage, s) \iff \Psi(garbage, s) \wedge P_{\mathcal{KC}}(fridge, s)$$
$$P_{\mathcal{KC}}(sink, s) \iff \Psi(sink, s) \wedge P_{\mathcal{KC}}(floor, s) \wedge$$
$$P_{\mathcal{KC}}(counters, s)$$

We have shown how to generate a strong 1-ary measure of progress, and we can generalize this for any n by replacing single variables above with tuples of variables. Note that the assumptions for Theorem 3 must be proven within T, which means extra facts (static constraints, for example) can be used to verify the assumptions.

$T_{\mathcal{KC}}$ is extremely basic. There are no preconditions for any action – each is immediately achievable. Hence none of the goals need to be regressed through their preconditions. This lack of regression is demonstrated by the fact that the measure of progress, $P_{\mathcal{KC}}$, has the same arity as Ψ – the $<_P$ relation encodes dependencies between each goal, so the only state left for $P_{\mathcal{KC}}$ to record is whether it has achieved its part of the goal or not.

5 A Tiered Measure of Progress

In this section we present another template for domains where goals need to be regressed, but the goals are all uniform. By uniform, we mean that there is one sequence $\bar{a}(\bar{x})$ of action schema, such that each goal conjunct can be made true by applying some subsequence of $\bar{a}$, with the proper instantiation. We also assume that we can achieve some goal conjunct without negatively interfering with the rest. A domain that fits this description is the Logistics World (Veloso 1992), where packages are transported between cities by airplanes and around cities by trucks. Any sub-sequence of sending a truck to a package's location, picking it up, driving it to the airport, putting it on a plane, flying it to its destination city, loading it onto a truck, and then delivering it will put any package in its goal location. If we ignore goal locations for the trucks and planes we do have uniformity.

We formalize the properties described above in logic:

Definition 5 (Tiered Uniformity)

A planning domain T has the tiered uniformity *characteristic if there exists a collection of fluent formulas $\Theta_1(x,s), ..., \Theta_n(x,s)$ such that:*

1. *$goal(s) \equiv_{def} \bigwedge_x \Theta_n(x,s)$*
2. *The $\Theta_i(x,s)$ are a partition, in particular, $(\exists k)\Theta_k(x,s)$, and $\Theta_i(x,s) \implies (\forall j \neq i)\neg\Theta_j(x,s)$.*
3. *If there is an object z such that $\neg\Theta_n(z,s)$ (goal incomplete), then $(\exists a)[(\exists x\, i\, j)[\Theta_i(x,s) \wedge \Theta_j(x, res(a,s)) \wedge j > i] \wedge (\forall y\, k\, l)[\Theta_k(y,s) \wedge \Theta_l(y, res(a,s)) \implies k \leq l]]$.*

Θ_n defines the fluent formula by which the goal may be expressed. The second requirement formalizes the notion that the sequence $\Theta_1(x,s), ..., \Theta_n(x,s)$ represents the stages through which x may traverse on its way to its goal $\Theta_n(x,s)$. The final requirement says that if not all objects have reached Θ_n, then we can find a object x at state i, and we can move it up to a higher state Θ_j, without hurting the positions of other objects, and possibly making them better.

Definition 6 (P_{tiered})

Assume T has the tiered uniformity characteristic. Then define for each $i \in [1, n-1]$,

$$P_{tiered}(x,i,s) \equiv_{def} \Theta_i(x,s) \vee P_{tiered}(x, i+1, s)$$
$$and \quad P_{tiered}(x,n,s) \equiv_{def} \Theta_n(x,s)$$

Each number is just a code for some of tuple of objects, thereby staying within our finite domain restrictions.

Each tier $P_{tiered}(x,i,s)$ corresponds to achieving the ith goal on each object x's path. If $\Theta_j(x,s)$ holds, that is, the object is already at level j, then $P_{tiered}(x,i,s)$ holds for all $i \leq j$. This encoding will obey the definition in Equation (1):

Theorem 4 (P_{tiered} is a strong measure of progress.)

If T has the tiered uniformity characteristic, then P_{tiered}, defined above, is a strong measure of progress.

Proof Sketch: The proof is just a straightforward application of Definitions 5 and 6 to Equation (1). ■

The problem of constructing a strong measure of progress for domains with tiered uniformity is pushed back to finding such tiers obeying the requirements of Definition 5. This is still a difficult problem, which will require the use of powerful domain analysis techniques. Note that the tiers constitute a partition which is mutually exclusive to the extent that advancing one object forward through stages will at worst leave other objects alone and at best push them forward as

well. Perhaps we can take advantage of the mutual exclusion information used in planners such as GraphPlan to extract the tiers we require. Or, if we suspect a domain has the tiered uniformity property, we could run a known planner to solve $\Theta_n(x,s)$ for an arbitrary object x, and then test if the stages x proceeds through in the plan satisfy Definition 5.[7]

Theorem 5

Consider a planning problem in the Logistics World (Veloso 1992), with goal $\bigwedge_{p_i} At(p_i, l_i, s)$, where p_i are packages and l_i goal locations. Then we can find a strong measure of progress $P_{\mathcal{LW}}$ of the form in Definition 6.

Proof Sketch: We can define our Θ_is as the stages of moving an arbitrary package to its goal location (being at a non-goal location, no truck nearby; at the non-goal location, with truck nearby; in the truck; ...). Clearly these Θ_is will form a partition, and one can show that they obey requirement 3 in Definition 5 by reasoning by cases. ■

It turns out many other domains have the tiered uniformity characteristic, including the Gripper, AI-office, Ferry, and Briefcase domains.

Before proceeding, we introduce a useful method for combining two different strong measures of progress. This will ameliorate the constraint that the goals be uniform, since we can construct strong measures of progress for different kinds of goals, and then combine them:

Theorem 6 (Combining strong measures of progress)

Let P be a strong measure of progress with respect to $goal_P(s)$, and Q with respect to $goal_Q(s)$. Further assume that P-increasing actions do not affect Q's extension negatively and vice versa. Then the predicate defined as:

$$R(0,x,s) \equiv_{def} P(x,s) \quad and \quad R(1,x,s) \equiv_{def} Q(x,s),$$

with $R(i,x,s) \equiv \top$ for i different from 0 and 1, is a strong measure of progress with respect to $goal_P(s) \wedge goal_Q(s)$.

Proof Sketch: The proof is a direct application of the definitions of P and Q to Equation (1). ■

If goals for two different types of objects are noninteracting, then we can formulate measures of progress for each independently, and then combine them.

6 Orthogonal Measures of Progress

In this section we show how we can construct a measure of progress based on orthogonal measures of progress. By "orthogonal" we mean we have predicates $P(x,s)$ and $C(x,s)$, and while we prefer to increase P, sometimes it is not possible and our only option is to work on C. Thankfully, continually increasing C will lead to a point where we can again

---

[7]There are much more complicated versions of Logistics World where the tiered uniformity is not clear, or does not exist. If we limit a truck's capacity, we still have a strong measure of progress because we can drop off packages when necessary. If we add a fuel component, we simply refine our P to fuel up when the tank gets low. But if we only provide a finite amount of fuel, we could have deadlocks in the space (Helmert 2001).

increase P. Intuitively, P-increasing actions are meant to move directly to the goal, while C-increasing ones do not, instead sidestepping or removing obstacles to the goal.

BlocksWorld exhibits this characteristic. P defined as final position cannot by itself be a strong measure of progress, because its extension cannot always be increased (blocks could be in the way). But we can always move these offending blocks out of the way, onto the table, (in C) until we can put a block into final position P. Any instance of BlocksWorld can be solved using these two kinds of actions.

We can also visualize this phenomenon as traversing a contour map on P and C. When possible, we choose actions which move directly up the P-gradient to increase its extension. However at some situations it is not possible to move "up", and instead we move "sideways" increasing C.[8] A graphical depiction of this with respect to BlocksWorld is given in the left side of Figure 1, and defined below:

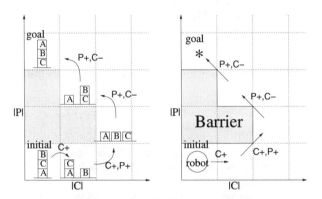

Figure 1: The left graph shows how the orthogonal measures of progress lead us to the solution. Note how they also avoid the Sussman anomaly. The right graph shows how the exact same ideas can be used to do robot motion planning.

Definition 7 (Orthogonal Measures of Progress)
P and C are orthogonal measures of progress if they satisfy:

$$\neg goal(s) \implies$$
$$(\exists a_P)[ext(P,s) \subset ext(P, res(a_P, s)) \land$$
$$(\forall \mathbf{w})[\mathbf{C(w,s)} \land \neg \mathbf{C(w, res(a_P, s))} \implies$$
$$\mathbf{P(w, res(a_P, s))}]] \lor$$
$$(\exists a_C)[ext(P,s) = ext(P, res(a_C, s)) \land$$
$$ext(C,s) \subset ext(C, res(a_C, s)) \land$$
$$(\forall \mathbf{w})[\neg \mathbf{C(w,s)} \land \mathbf{C(w, res(a_C, s))} \implies$$
$$\neg \mathbf{P(w,s)}]]$$

The definition is a lexicographic ordering over P and C, except for the parts in bold, which stipulate that any loss in C due to a P-increasing action must be made up by an increase

---

[8]It is possible to have available at a situation both a P-increasing action a_P and a C-increasing action a_C. If we stubbornly prefer a_C over a_P we will still reach a (less efficient) solution; eventually we will get to a point where C's extension is full and cannot be increased, in which case a_P will be the only action available.

in P, and the only objects which can be moved into C in a C-increasing action must not be in P.

We can encode P and C as a binary predicate, which does in fact satisfy Equation (1):

Theorem 7
Let P and C be orthogonal measures of progress. Define:

$$R(0, x, s) \equiv_{def} C(x, s) \lor R(1, x, s)$$
$$and \; R(1, x, s) \equiv_{def} P(x, s),$$

with $R(n, x, s) \equiv_{def} \top$ for all other possible values for n.

Then $R(x, y, s)$ is a strong measure of progress with respect to goal.

Proof Sketch: The proof is a straightforward application of Definition 7 and Equation (1). ∎

The *deadlocked sets of blocks* defined in (Gupta & Nau 1991) correspond to the situation where we cannot increase P, but can increase C, thus resolving the deadlock. The form of R and Theorem 1 reassures us of the well-known result that any plan following our strategy will take at most $2m$ steps, where m is the number of misplaced blocks in our domain.[9]

This orthogonal notion can be generalized to multiple predicates. It applies to other domains as well. For example, in robot motion planning, P represents the greedy act of moving directly towards a goal. If there were no obstacles, this would be a strong measure of progress. In the presence of obstacles, C, which directs the robot to move around an obstacle, will be required as shown in the right side of Figure 1.[10]

7 Conclusions and Discussion

In this paper not only have we demonstrated a new paradigm for expressing a logical (as opposed to numeric) measure of progress for planning, but have shown how to actually construct one for certain kinds of domains. The intuitions behind our measure of progress reflects those of a human's, and by the construction proving Theorem 2, we know strong measures of progress can express optimal plans. We prefer obvious strong measures of progress however because they are more likely to elucidate the structure of domain. But for non-trivial domains, obvious measures of progress cannot be optimal. This is for the same reason an NP-complete problem is so difficult; if it were obvious how to exploit its structure to generate efficient solutions, the problem would be easy to solve. Nevertheless, we believe obvious measures of progress will generate "good enough" plans, for two reasons. First, by definition they divide up the domain to promote efficiency; subgoals are never undone. Secondly, they

---

[9]Remember that $R(\cdot, s)$ can only be false on the tuples $\langle 0, x \rangle$ and $\langle 1, x \rangle$.

[10]Technically, Figure 1 is incorrect for the robot example; the P-gradient instead of pointing up should always point towards the goal, while the C-gradient will be orthogonal to it. Pictorially, the P-gradient will be rays pointing toward the goal location, while the C-gradient is a set of concentric circles centered around the goal. Clearly P and C in BlocksWorld play analogous roles in the robot motion planning domain.

are concisely represented and therefore not too complicated. This generally means that P has a low arity, so that by Theorem 1 the plans will not get too long. In short, obvious measures of progress will take advantage of enough salient structural features to remain efficient, without getting too complicated. They will give rise to self-explanatory strategies.

Furthermore, it should be easy to improve measures of progress, to make them "good enough," when they do generate inefficient plans. In general the reason why a plan is terribly inefficient (such as moving only one ball at a time in Gripper), is easily articulated, as are the immediate improvements. Since our measure of progress is declaratively specified, encoding these improvements as a more efficient P is straightforward.

There are a number of restrictions which apply to our paradigm. The most pressing is the fact that a strong measure of progress exists only in those domains without deadlocks. Clearly, some measure of progress exists in domains with deadlocks; if anything humans discover a measure of "regress" that is used to avoid deadlock-causing actions. Equation (1) must be weakened if we want a measure of progress for such domains. One way is to find a formula $R(s)$ true only of those states reachable from the goal, and apply Equation (1) over those situations:

$$(R(s) \wedge \neg goal(s)) \implies (\exists a)[ext(P, s) \subset ext(P, res(a, s))].$$

However we must be careful because this essentially expresses a tautology and may lack any structural content.

Another issue is the apparent lack of concurrency in situation calculus. The situation calculus can be extended to handle multiple actions in parallel using the techniques in (Reiter 1996), while still staying within our framework. Then we can define progress in terms of groups of parallel actions, leading to even more efficient plans.

Another minor extension would handle domains with more expressive ramifications. The current ADL formalizations of domains can handle some ramifications, either by artifice of the language, or by constructs such as conditional effects. (McIlraith 2000) provides successor state axioms that include the effects of ramifications, if essentially no circularities exist between the ramification fluents. These successor state axioms are syntactically adaptable to our paradigm.

The insightful reader will recognize that the strong measure of progress encodes a goal ordering. Our work is parallel to (Koehler & Hoffmann 2000), in that we both want to steadily increase the truth of our set of goals. (Koehler & Hoffmann 2000) derives a partition $G_1, ..., G_k$ over the set of goals, and then achieves G_1, and then from that state achieves $G_1 \cup G_2$, etc. In practice this works well. (Korf 1985)'s approach is similar. Korf learns efficient strategies for solving problems such as Rubik's Cube by searching for *macro-operators*, a sequence of primitive operators, and an ordering of the goal conjuncts $g_1, ..., g_n$ such that every goal conjunct g_i has a macro m_i which accomplishes g_i, without changing the truth of conjuncts $g_1, ..., g_{i-1}$ (although they may change during the course of the macro).

However, in these above approaches, intermediate subgoals are hidden away in the intermediate plans/macros. On the other hand, (Porteous, Sebastia, & Hoffmann 2001) extracts *landmarks* (subgoals true on every path to the goal) which can be used to break down a planning task into many smaller ones. (Porteous, Sebastia, & Hoffmann 2001) also approximates orderings which are *natural* (necessary orderings of landmarks) and *weakly reasonable* (orderings on subgoals which prevent unnecessary actions). Our P encodes similar information. For example, the typical final position heuristic for BlocksWorld will avoid the Sussman anomaly by noting that B is not really in its goal position until C is, as depicted in the left side of Figure 1. In fact, we can interpret each instance of $P(\bar{x}, s)$ as a fluent formula encoding a subgoal and the degree it has been achieved. For Logistics World, it encodes the package's progress through the various transports. For BlocksWorld it encodes whether a block is in clear or in final position.

The strategy function $a(s)$ briefly referred to has important uses. (Bryson 2001) points out that $a(s)$ is a teleoreactive (TR) program (Nilsson 1994). In the examples we have encountered, proving that a predicate P is a strong measure of progress leads to construction of rules of the form:

$$\neg goal(s) \wedge \phi_i(s) \implies a(s) := a,$$

where ϕ_i is some fluent condition on the situation, $\bigvee_i \phi_i(s) \equiv \top$, and a is the action that increases $ext(P, s)$. Therefore from $a(s)$ we can construct a *universal* TR program that will achieve *goal*.

Finally, we have shown how to construct measures of progress for some simple domains, and even how to combine them (Theorem 6). Interesting future work would extend this arsenal of measures, and create an algebra to combine them. We should also look into refining the measures themselves – clearly an action that moves multiple objects into P is better than one which moves only one, especially for domains such as Logistics World or Gripper. We can construct more elaborate versions of Equation (1) which will select these better actions and avoid inefficient plans.

8   Acknowledgments

The author would like to thank John McCarthy and Tom Costello for first pointing out this problem, and members of the Formal Reasoning Group and the Logic Group for intriguing observations, comments, and feedback. We also thank the anonymous referees for their valuable suggestions and directions for improvement. This research has been partly supported by SNWSC contract N66001-00-C-8018.

References

Bacchus, F. 2000. AIPS 2000 Planning Competition Webpage[11].

Bonet, B., and Geffner, H. 2001. Heuristic Search Planner 2.0[12]. *AI Magazine*.

[11]http://www.cs.toronto.edu/aips2000/
[12]http://www.ai.ldc.usb.ve/~hector/software/hsp2.ps

Bryson, J. 2001. Personal communication.

Doherty, P., and Kvarnström, J. 2001. TALplanner: A Temporal Logic Based Planner[13]. *AI Magazine*.

Edelkamp, S., and Helmert, M. 2001. The Model Checking Integrated Planning System (MIPS)[14]. *AI Magazine* 67–71.

Fox, M., and Long, D. 2001. Hybrid STAN: Identifying and managing combinatorial optimisation sub-problems in planning[15]. In *IJCAI-01*.

Gupta, N., and Nau, D. S. 1991. Complexity results for blocks world planning. In *AAAI-91*.

Helmert, M. 2001. On the Complexity of Planning in Transportation Domains[16]. In *ECP'01*, Lecture Notes in Artificial Intelligence. New York: Springer-Verlag.

Hoffmann, J. 2001a. FF: The fast-forward planning system. *AI Magazine*.

Hoffmann, J. 2001b. Local Search Topology in Planning Benchmarks: An Empirical Analysis[17]. In *IJCAI*, 453–458.

Koehler, J., and Hoffmann, J. 2000. On Reasonable and Forced Goal Orderings and their Use in an Agenda-Driven Planning Algorithm[18]. *Journal of Artificial Intelligence Research* 12:338–386.

Korf, R. 1985. *Learning to Solve Problems by Searching for Macro Operators*. Ph.D. Dissertation, Carnegie Mellon University.

Lin, F. 2002. Personal communication.

Long, D., and Fox, M. 2000. Automatic synthesis and use of generic types in planning. In *AIPS-00*, 196–205.

McAllester, D. 1991. Some Observations on Cognitive Judgements[19]. In *AAAI-91*, 910–915. Morgan Kaufmann Publishers.

McCarthy, J. 1959. Programs with Common Sense[20]. In *Mechanisation of Thought Processes, Proceedings of the Symposium of the National Physics Laboratory*, 77–84. London, U.K.: Her Majesty's Stationery Office.

McIlraith, S. 2000. An axiomatic solution to the ramification problem. *Artificial Intelligence* 116:87–121.

Nilsson, N. J. 1994. Teleo-Reactive Programs for Agent Control[21]. *Journal of Artificial Intelligence Research* 1:139–158.

Nilsson, N. 1998. *Artificial Intelligence: A New Synthesis*. Morgan-Kaufman.

Parmar, A. 2002. A Logical Measure of Progress for Planning (Technical Report)[22]. Technical report, FRG.

Porteous, J.; Sebastia, L.; and Hoffmann, J. 2001. On the Extraction, Ordering and Usage of Landmarks in Planning[23]. In *Proceedings of ECP'01*.

Reiter, R. 1996. Natural Actions, Concurrency and Continuous Time in the Situation Calculus[24]. In Aiello, L.; Doyle, J.; and Shapiro, S., eds., *Proceedings KR96*, 2–13.

Sierra-Santibañez, J. 2001. Heuristic planning: a declarative forward chaining approach. In *Working Notes of Common Sense 2001*, 228–234. Fifth Symposium on Logical Formalizations of Commonsense Reasoning.

Veloso, M. 1992. *Planning and Learning by Analogical Reasoning*. Ph.D. Dissertation, School of Computer Science, Carnegie Mellon University.

---

[13] ftp://ftp.ida.liu.se/pub/labs/kplab/people/patdo/www-aimag.ps.gz

[14] http://citeseer.nj.nec.com/edelkamp00model.html

[15] http://www.dur.ac.uk/~dcs0www/research/stanstuff/Papers/sigpaper.ps

[16] http://www.informatik.uni-freiburg.de/~helmert/publications/ECP01_Complexity.pdf

[17] http://www.informatik.uni-freiburg.de/~hoffmann/papers/ijcai01.ps.gz

[18] http://www.informatik.uni-freiburg.de/~hoffmann/papers/jair00.ps.gz

[19] http://www.autoreason.com/aaai91a.ps

[20] http://www-formal.stanford.edu/jmc/mcc59.html

[21] http://www.cs.cmu.edu/afs/cs/project/jair/pub/volume1/nilsson94a.ps

---

[22] http://www-formal.Stanford.edu/aarati/techreports/aaai-2002-tr.ps

[23] http://www.dur.ac.uk/~dcs0www/research/stanstuff/Papers/PorteousSebastiaHoffmann_ecp_01.ps.gz

[24] http://www.cs.toronto.edu/cogrobo/natural.ps.Z

AAAI-02
Edmonton/Alberta
IAAI-02

Planning
Actions and Temporal Reasoning

Reasoning about Actions in a Probabilistic Setting

Chitta Baral, Nam Tran and Le-Chi Tuan
Department of Computer Science and Engineering
Arizona State University
Tempe, Arizona 85287
{*chitta,namtran,lctuan*}*@asu.edu*

Abstract

In this paper we present a language to reason about actions in a probabilistic setting and compare our work with earlier work by Pearl. The main feature of our language is its use of static and dynamic causal laws, and use of unknown (or background) variables – whose values are determined by factors beyond our model – in incorporating probabilities. We use two kind of unknown variables: inertial and non-inertial. Inertial unknown variables are helpful in assimilating observations and modeling counterfactuals and causality; while non-inertial unknown variables help characterize stochastic behavior, such as the outcome of tossing a coin, that are not impacted by observations. Finally, we give a glimpse of incorporating probabilities into reasoning with narratives.

Introduction and Motivation

One of the main goals of 'reasoning about actions' is to have a compact and elaboration tolerant (McCarthy 1998) representation of the state transition due to actions. Many such representations – (Sandewall 1998) has several survey papers on these – have been developed in the recent literature. *But most of these elaboration tolerant representations do not consider probabilistic effect of actions.* When actions have probabilistic effects, the state transition due to actions is an MDP (Markov decision process). In an MDP we have the probabilities $p_a(s'|s)$ for all actions a, and states s' and s, which express the probability of the world reaching the state s' after the action a is executed in the state s. *One of our main goals in this paper is to develop an elaboration tolerant representation for MDPs.*

There has been several studies and attempts of compact representation of MDPs in the decision theoretic planning community. Some of the representations that are suggested are probabilistic state-space operators (PSOs) (Kushmerick, Hanks, & Weld 1995), 2 stage temporal Bayesian networks (2TBNs) (Boutilier, Dean, & Hanks 1995; Boutilier & Goldszmidt 1996), sequential effect trees (STs) (Littman 1997), and independent choice logic (ICL) (Poole 1997). All these except ICL focus on only planning. Qualitatively, the two drawbacks of these representations are: (i) Although compact they do not aim at being elaboration tolerant. I.e., it is

not easy in these formalisms to add a new causal relation between fluents or a new executability condition for an action, without making wholesale changes. (ii) They are not appropriate for reasoning about actions issues other than planning, such as: reasoning about values of fluents at a time point based on observations about later time points, and counterfactual reasoning about fluent values after a hypothetical sequence of actions taking into account observations. Pearl in (Pearl 1999; 2000) discusses the later inadequacy at great length.

Besides developing an elaboration tolerant representation, *the other main goal of our paper* is to show how the other reasoning about action aspects of observation assimilation and counter-factual reasoning can be done in a probabilistic setting using our representation.

Our approach in this paper is partly influenced by (Pearl 1999; 2000). Pearl proposes moving away from (Causal) Bayes nets to *functional causal models* where causal relationships are expressed in the form of deterministic, *functional* equations, and probabilities are introduced through the assumption that certain variables in the equations are unobserved. As in the case of the functional causal models, *in this paper* we follow the Laplacian model in introducing probabilities through the assumption that certain variables are unobserved. (We call them 'unknown'[1] variables.) *We differ from the functional causal models in the following ways:* (i) We allow actions as first class citizens in our language, which allows us to deal with sequence of actions. (ii) In our formulation the relationship between fluents is given in terms of static causal laws, instead of structural equations. The static causal laws are more general, and more elaboration tolerant and can be compiled into structural equations. (iii) We have two different kind of unknown variables which we refer to as inertial and non-inertial unknown variables. While the inertial unknown variables are similar to Pearl's unknown variables, the non-inertial ones are not. The non-inertial ones are used to characterize actions such as tossing a coin whose outcome is probabilistic, but after observing the outcome of a coin toss to be head we do not expect the outcome of the next coin toss to be head. This is modeled

---

[1]They are also referred to as (Pearl 1999) 'background variables' and 'exogenous variables'. *They are variables whose values are determined by factors external to our model.*

by making the cause of the coin toss outcome a non-inertial unknown variable. *Overall, our formulation can be considered as a generalization of Pearl's formulation of causality to a dynamic setting with a more elaboration tolerant representation and with two kinds of unknown variables.*

We now start with the syntax and the semantics our language *PAL*, which stands for *probabilistic action language*.

The Language PAL

The alphabet of the language PAL (denoting probabilistic action language) – based on the language $\mathcal{A}$ (Gelfond & Lifschitz 1993) – consists of four non-empty disjoint sets of symbols $\mathbf{F}$, $\mathbf{U}_I$, $\mathbf{U}_N$ and $\mathbf{A}$. They are called the set of fluents, the set of inertial unknown variables, the set of non-inertial unknown variables and the set of actions. A *fluent literal* is a fluent or a fluent preceded by $\neg$. An unknown variable literal is an unknown variable or an unknown variable preceded by $\neg$. A *literal* is either a fluent literal or an unknown variable literal. A *formula* is a propositional formula constructed from literals.

Unknown variables represent unobservable characteristics of environment. As noted earlier, there are two types of unknown variables: *inertial* and *non-inertial*. *Inertial* unknown variables are not affected by agent's actions and are independent of fluents and other unknown variables. *Non-inertial* unknown variables may change their value respecting a given probability distribution, but the pattern of their change due to actions is neither known nor modeled in our language.

A state s is an interpretation of fluents and unknown variables that satisfy certain conditions (to be mentioned while discussing semantics); For a state s, we denote the sub-interpretations of s restricted to fluents, inertial unknown variables, and non-inertial unknown variables by s_F, s_I, and s_N respectively. We also use the shorthand such as $s_{F,I} = s_F \cup s_I$. An n-state is an interpretation of only the fluents. That is, if s is a state, then $s = s_F$ is an n-state. A u-state (s_u) is an interpretation of the unknown variables. For any state s, by s_u we denote the interpretation of the unknown variables of s. For any u-state s_u, $I(s_u)$ denotes the set of states s, such that $s_u = s_u$. We say $s \models s$, if the interpretation of fluents in s is same as in s.

PAL has four components: a domain description language PAL_D, a language to express unconditional probabilities about the unknown variables PAL_P, a language to specify observations PAL_O, and a query language.

PAL_D: The domain description language

Syntax Propositions in PAL_D are of the following forms:

$$a \textbf{ causes } \psi \textbf{ if } \varphi \qquad (0.1)$$

$$\theta \textbf{ causes } \psi \qquad (0.2)$$

$$\textbf{impossible } a \textbf{ if } \varphi \qquad (0.3)$$

where a is an action, ψ is a *fluent* formula, θ is a formula of fluents and *inertial* unknown variables, and φ is a formula of fluents and *unknown* variables. Note that the above propositions guarantee that values of unknown variables are not affected by actions and are not dependent on the fluents. But the effect of an action on a fluent may be dependent

on unknown variables; also only inertial unknown variables may have direct effects on values of fluents.

Propositions of the form (0.1) describe the direct effects of actions on the world and are called *dynamic causal laws*. Propositions of the form (0.2), called *static causal laws*, describe causal relation between fluents and unknown variables in a world. Propositions of the form (0.3), called *executability conditions*, state when actions are not executable. A *domain description* $\mathcal{D}$ is a collection of propositions in PAL_D.

Semantics of PAL_D: Characterizing the transition function A domain description given in the language of PAL_D defines a transition function from actions and states to a set of states. Intuitively, given an action (a), and a state (s), the transition function (Φ) defines the set of states ($\Phi(a,\text{s})$) that may be reached after executing the action a in state s. If $\Phi(a,\text{s})$ is an empty set it means that a is not executable in s. We now formally define this transition function.

Let $\mathcal{D}$ be a domain description in the language of PAL_D. An *interpretation* I of the fluents and unknown variables in PAL_D is a maximal consistent set of literals of PAL_D. A literal l is said to be true (resp. false) in I iff $l \in I$ (resp. $\neg l \in I$). The truth value of a formula in I is defined recursively over the propositional connective in the usual way. For example, $f \wedge q$ is true in I iff f is true in I and q is true in I. We say that ψ holds in I (or I satisfies ψ), denoted by $I \models \psi$, if ψ is true in I.

A set of formulas from PAL_D is *logically closed* if it is closed under propositional logic (w.r.t. PAL_D).

Let V be a set of formulas and K be a set of static causal laws of the form θ **causes** ψ. We say that V is closed under K if for every rule θ **causes** ψ in K, if θ belongs to V then so does ψ. By $Cn_K(V)$ we denote the least logically closed set of formulas from PAL_D that contains V and is also closed under K.

A *state* s of $\mathcal{D}$ is an interpretation that is closed under the set of static causal laws of $\mathcal{D}$.

An action a is *prohibited (not executable)* in a state s if there exists in $\mathcal{D}$ an executability condition of the form **impossible** a **if** φ such that φ holds in s.

The *effect of an action a* in a state s is the set of formulas $E_a(\text{s}) = \{\psi \mid \mathcal{D} \text{ contains a law } a \textbf{ causes } \psi \textbf{ if } \varphi \text{ and } \varphi \text{ holds in s}\}$.

Given a domain description $\mathcal{D}$ containing a set of static causal laws R, we follow (McCain & Turner 1995) to formally define $\Phi(a,\text{s})$, the set of states that may be reached by executing a in s as follows.

If a is not prohibited (i.e., executable) in s, then

$$\Phi(a,\text{s}) = \{\text{ s}' \mid \text{s}'_{F,I} = Cn_R((\text{s}_{F,I} \cap \text{s}'_{F,I}) \cup E_a(\text{s}))\}; \quad (0.4)$$

If a is prohibited (i.e., not executable) in s, then $\Phi(a,\text{s})$ is $\emptyset$. We now state some simple properties of our transition function.

Proposition 1 *Let $U_N \subseteq U$ be the set of non-inertial variables in U.*

1. *If $\text{s}' \in \Phi(a,\text{s})$ then $\text{s}'_I = \text{s}_I$. That is, the inertial unknown variables are unchanged through state transitions.*

2. *For every* $s' \in \Phi(a, s)$ *and for every interpretation* w *of* U_N, *we have that* $(s'_{F,I} \cup w) \in \Phi(a, s)$.

Every domain description $\mathcal{D}$ in a language PAL_D has a unique transition function Φ, and we say Φ is the transition function of $\mathcal{D}$.

We now define an extended transition function (with a slight abuse of notation) that expresses the state transition due to a sequence of actions.

Definition 1 $\Phi([a], s) = \Phi(a, s)$;
$\Phi([a_1, \ldots, a_n], s) = \bigcup_{s' \in \Phi(a_1, s)} \Phi([a_2, \ldots, a_n], s')$

Definition 2 Given a domain description $\mathcal{D}$, and a state s, we write $s \models_{\mathcal{D}} \varphi$ **after** $a_1, \ldots, a_n$,
if φ is true in all states in $\Phi([a_1, \ldots, a_n], s)$.

(Often when it is clear from the context we may simply write $\models$ instead of $\models_{\mathcal{D}}$.)

PAL_P: **Probabilities of unknown variables**

Syntax A probability description $\mathcal{P}$ of the unknown variables is a collection of propositions of the following form:

$$\textbf{probability of } u \textbf{ is } n \quad (0.5)$$

where u is an unknown variable, and n is a real number between 0 and 1.

Semantics Each proposition above directly gives us the probability distribution of the corresponding unknown variable as: $P(u) = n$.

Since we assume (as does Pearl (Pearl 2000)) that the values of the unknown variables are independent of each other defining the joint probability distribution of the unknown variables is straight forward.

$$P(u_1, \ldots, u_n) = P(u_1) \times \ldots \times P(u_n) \quad (0.6)$$

Note: $P(u_1)$ is a short hand for $P(U_1 = true)$. If we have multi-valued unknown variables then $P(u_1)$ will be a short hand for $P(U_1 = u_1)$.

Since several states may have the same interpretation of the unknown variables and we do not have any unconditional preference of one state over another, the unconditional probability of the various states can now be defined as:

$$P(s) = \frac{P(s_u)}{|I(s_u)|} \quad (0.7)$$

PAL_Q: **The Query language**
Syntax A query is of the form:

$$\textbf{probability of } [\varphi \textbf{ after } a_1, \ldots, a_n] \textbf{ is } n \quad (0.8)$$

where φ is a formula of fluents and unknown variables, a_i's are actions, and n is a real number between 0 and 1. When $n = 1$, we may simply write: φ **after** $a_1, \ldots, a_n$, and when $n = 0$, we may simply write $\neg \varphi$ **after** $a_1, \ldots, a_n$.

Semantics: Entailment of Queries in PAL_Q We define the entailment in several steps. First we define the transitional probability between states due to a single action.

$$P_{[a]}(s'|s) = P_a(s'|s) = \frac{|\Phi(a,s)|}{2^{|U_N|}} P(s'_N) \text{ if } s' \in \Phi(a, s);$$
$$= 0, \text{ otherwise }. \quad (0.9)$$

The intuition behind (0.9) is as follows: Since inertial variables do not change their value from one state to the next,

$P_a(s'|s)$ will depend only on the conditioning of fluents and non-inertial variables: $P_a(s'|s) = P_a(s'_{F,N}|s)$. Since non-inertial variables are independent from the transition, we have $P_a(s'_{F,N}|s) = P_a(s'_F|s) * P(s'_N)$. Since there is no distribution associated with fluents, we assume that $P_a(s'_F|s)$ is uniformly distributed. Then $P_a(s'_F|s) = \frac{|\Phi(a,s)|}{2^{|U_N|}}$, because there are $\frac{|\Phi(a,s)|}{2^{|U_N|}}$ possible next states that share the same interpretation of unknown variables.

We now define the (probabilistic) correctness of a single action plan given that we are in a particular state s.

$$P(\varphi \textbf{ after } a|s) = \sum_{s' \in \Phi(a,s) \wedge s' \models \varphi} P_a(s'|s) \quad (0.10)$$

Next we recursively define the transitional probability due to a sequence of actions, starting with the base case.

$$P_{[\,]}(s'|s) = 1 \text{ if } s = s'; \text{ otherwise it is } 0. \quad (0.11)$$
$$P_{[a_1, \ldots a_n]}(s'|s) = \sum_{s''} P_{[a_1, \ldots, a_{n-1}]}(s''|s) P_{a_n}(s'|s'') \quad (0.12)$$

We now define the (probabilistic) correctness of a (multi-action) plan given that we are in a particular state s.

$$P(\varphi \textbf{ after } \alpha|s) = \sum_{s' \in \Phi([\alpha],s) \wedge s' \models \varphi} P_{[\alpha]}(s'|s) \quad (0.13)$$

PAL_O: **The observation language**
Syntax An observations description $\mathcal{O}$ is a collection of proposition of the following form:

$$\psi \textbf{ obs\_after } a_1, \ldots, a_n \quad (0.14)$$

where ψ is a fluent formula, and a_i's are actions. When, $n = 0$, we simply write **initially** ψ. *Intuitively, the above observation means that ψ is true after a particular – because actions may be non-deterministic – hypothetical execution of $a_1, \ldots, a_n$ in the initial state.* The probability $P(\varphi \textbf{ obs\_after } \alpha|s)$ is computed by the right hand side of (0.13). Note that observations in $\mathcal{A}$ and hence in PAL_O are hypothetical in the sense that they did not really happen. In a later section when discussing narratives we consider real observations.

Semantics: assimilating observations in PAL_O We now use Bayes' rule to define the conditional probability of a state given that we have some observations.

$$P(s_i|\mathcal{O}) = \frac{P(\mathcal{O}|s_i)P(s_i)}{\sum_{s_j} P(\mathcal{O}|s_j)P(s_j)} \text{ if } \sum_{s_j} P(\mathcal{O}|s_j)P(s_j) \neq 0$$
$$= 0, \text{ otherwise }. \quad (0.15)$$

Queries with observation assimilation

Finally, we define the (probabilistic) correctness of a (multi-action) plan given only some observations. This corresponds to counter-factual queries of Pearl (Pearl 2000) when the observations are about a different sequence of actions than the one in the hypothetical plan.

$$P(\varphi \textbf{ after } \alpha|\mathcal{O}) = \sum_s P(s|\mathcal{O}) \times P(\varphi \textbf{ after } \alpha|s) \quad (0.16)$$

Using the above formula, we now define the entailment between a theory (consisting of a domain description, a probability description of the unknown variables, and an observation description) and queries:

Definition 3 $\mathcal{D} \quad \cup \quad \mathcal{P} \quad \cup \quad \mathcal{O} \quad \models$ **probability of** $[\varphi \text{ after } a_1, \ldots, a_n]$ **is** n iff $P(\varphi \text{ after } a_1, \ldots, a_n | \mathcal{O}) = n$

Since our observations are hypothetical and are about a particular hypothetical execution, it is possible that[2] $P(\varphi \text{ after } \alpha | \varphi \text{ obs\_after } \alpha) < 1$, when α has non-deterministic actions. Although it may appear unintuitive in the first glance, it is reasonable as just because a particular run of α makes φ true does not imply that *all* run of α would make φ true.

Examples

In this section we give several small examples illustrating the reasoning formalized in PAL.

Ball drawing

We draw a ball from an infinitely large "black box". Let *draw* be the action, *red* be the fluent describing the outcome and u be an unknown variable that affects the outcome. The domain description is as follow:

draw **causes** *red* **if** u.   *draw* **causes** $\neg red$ **if** $\neg u$. **probability of** u **is** 0.5.

Let $\mathcal{O} = red$ **obs_after** *draw* and $Q = red$ **after** *draw, draw*. Different assumptions about the variable u will lead to different values of $p = P(Q|\mathcal{O})$.

Let $\mathsf{s}_1 = \{red, u\}$, $\mathsf{s}_2 = \{red, \neg u\}$, $\mathsf{s}_3 = \{\neg red, u\}$ and $\mathsf{s}_4 = \{\neg red, \neg u\}$.

1. Assume that the balls in the box are of the same color, and there are 2 possibilities: the box contains either all red or all blue balls. Then u is an inertial unknown variable. We can now show that $P(Q|\mathcal{O}) = 1$. Here, the initial observation tells us all about the future outcomes.

2. Assume that half of the balls in the box are red and the other half are blue. Then u is a non-inertial unknown variable. We can show that $P(\mathsf{s}_1|\mathcal{O}) = P(\mathsf{s}_3|\mathcal{O}) = 0.5$ and $P(\mathsf{s}_2|\mathcal{O}) = P(\mathsf{s}_4|\mathcal{O}) = 0$. By (0.13), $P(Q|\mathsf{s}_j) = 0.5$ for $1 \leq j \leq 4$. By (0.16), $P(Q|\mathcal{O}) = 0.5 * \sum_{\mathsf{s}_j} P(\mathsf{s}_j|\mathcal{O}) = 0.5$. Here, the observation $\mathcal{O}$ does not help in predicting the future.

The Yale shooting

We start with a simple example of the Yale shooting problem with probabilities. We have two actions *load* and *shoot*, and two fluents *loaded* and *alive*. To account for the probabilistic effect of the actions, we have two inertial unknown variables u_1 and u_2. The effect of the actions *shoot* and *load* can now be described by $\mathcal{D}_1$ consisting of the following:

shoot **causes** $\neg alive$ **if** *loaded*, u_1
load **causes** *loaded* **if** u_2

The probabilistic effects of the action *shoot* and *load* can now be expressed by $\mathcal{P}_1$, that gives probability distributions of the unknown variables.

probability of u_1 **is** p_1.   **probability of** u_2 **is** p_2.

Now suppose we have the following observations $\mathcal{O}_1$.

initially *alive*;   **initially** $\neg loaded$

We can now show that $\mathcal{D}_1 \cup \mathcal{P}_1 \cup \mathcal{O}_1 \models$ **probability of** $[alive \text{ after } load, shoot]$ **is** $1 - p_1 \times p_2$.

[2]We thank an anonymous reviewer for pointing this out.

Pearl's example of effects of treatment on patients

In (Pearl 2000), Pearl gives an example of a joint probability distribution which can be expressed by at least two different causal models, each of which have a different answer to a particular counter-factual question. We now show how both models can be modeled in our framework. In his example, the data obtained on a particular medical test where half the patients were treated and the other half were left untreated shows the following:

treated	true	true	false	false
alive	true	false	true	false
fraction	.25	.25	.25	.25

The above data can be supported by two different domain descriptions in PAL, each resulting in different answers to the following question involving counter-factuals. *"Joe was treated and he died. Did Joe's death occur due to the treatment. I.e., Would Joe have lived if he was not treated."*

Causal Model 1: The domain description $\mathcal{D}_2$ of the causal model 1 can be expressed as follows, where the actions in our language are, *treatment* and *no_treatment*.

treatment **causes** *action_occurred*
no_treatment **causes** *action_occurred*
$u_2 \wedge action\_occurred$ **causes** $\neg alive$
$\neg u_2 \wedge action\_occurred$ **causes** *alive*

The probability of the inertial unknown variable u_2 can be expressed by $\mathcal{P}_2$ given as follows:
probability of u_2 **is** 0.5

The probability of the *occurrence* of *treatment* and *no_treatment* is 0.5 each. (Our current language does not allow expression of such information. Although, it can be easily augmented, to accommodate such expressions, we do not do it here as it does not play a role in the analysis we are making.)

Assuming u_2 is independent of the occurrence of *treatment* it is easy to see that the above modeling agrees with data table given earlier.

The observations $\mathcal{O}_2$ can be expressed as follows:
initially $\neg action\_occurred$ **initially** *alive*
$\neg alive$ **obs_after** *treatment*

We can now show that $\mathcal{D}_2 \cup \mathcal{P}_2 \cup \mathcal{O}_2 \not\models Q_2$, where Q_2 is the query: *alive* **after** *no_treatment*; and $\mathcal{D}_2 \cup \mathcal{P}_2 \cup \mathcal{O}_2 \models \neg alive$ **after** *no_treatment*

Causal Model 2: The domain description $\mathcal{D}_3$ of the causal model 2 can be expressed as follows:
treatment **causes** $\neg alive$ **if** u_2
no_treatment **causes** $\neg alive$ **if** $\neg u_2$

The probabilities of unknown variables ($\mathcal{P}_3$) is same as given in $\mathcal{P}_2$. The probability of occurrence of *treatment* and *no_treatment* remains 0.5 each. Assuming u_2 is independent of the occurrence of *treatment* it is easy to see that the above modeling agrees with data table given earlier.

The observations $\mathcal{O}_3$ can be expressed as follows:
initially *alive* $\neg alive$ **obs_after** *treatment*

Unlike in case of the causal model 1, we can now show that $\mathcal{D}_3 \cup \mathcal{P}_3 \cup \mathcal{O}_3 \models Q_2$.

The state transition vs the n-state transition

Normally an MDP representation of probabilistic effect of actions is about the n-states. In this section we analyze the transition between n-states due to actions and the impact of observations on these transitions.

The transition function between n-states

As defined in (0.9) the transition probability $P_a(\mathsf{s}'|\mathsf{s})$ has either the value zero or is uniform among the s' where it is non-zero. This is counter to our intuition where we expect the transition function to be more stochastic. This can be explained by considering n-states and defining transition functions with respect to them.

Let s be a n-state. We can then define $\Phi_n(a, s)$ as:

$$\Phi_n(a, s) = \{\ s'\ |\ \exists \mathsf{s}, \mathsf{s}' : (\mathsf{s} \models s) \wedge (\mathsf{s}' \models s') \wedge \mathsf{s}' \in \Phi(a, \mathsf{s})\ \}.$$

We can then define a more stochastic transition probability $P_a(s'|s)$ where s and s' are n-states as follows:

$$P_a(s'|s) = \sum_{\mathsf{s}_i \models s} \left(\frac{P(\mathsf{s}_i)}{P(s)} \sum_{\mathsf{s}'_j \models s'} P_a(\mathsf{s}'_j|\mathsf{s}_i) \right) \qquad (0.17)$$

The above also follows from (0.16) by having φ describing s', $\alpha = a$ and $\mathcal{O}$ expressing that the initial state satisfies s.

Impact of observations on the transition function

Observations have no impact on the transition function $\Phi(a, \mathsf{s})$ or on $P_a(\mathsf{s}'|\mathsf{s})$. But they do affect $\Phi(a, s)$ and $P_a(s'|s)$. Let us analyze why.

Intuitively, observations may tell us about the unknown variables. This additional information is monotonic in the sense that since actions do not affect the unknown variables their value remains unchanged. Thus, in presence of observations $\mathcal{O}$, we can define $\Phi_{\mathcal{O}}(a, s)$ as follows:

$\Phi_{\mathcal{O}}(a, s) = \{s' : s'$ is the interpretation of the fluents of a state in $\bigcup_{\mathsf{s} \models s \& \mathsf{s} \models \mathcal{O}} \Phi(a, \mathsf{s})\}$

As evident from the above definition, as we have more and more observations the transition function $\Phi_{\mathcal{O}}(a, s)$ becomes more deterministic. On the other hand, as we mentioned earlier the function $\Phi(a, \mathsf{s})$ is not affected by observations. Thus, we can accurately represent two different kind of non-deterministic effects of actions: the effect on states, and the effect on n-states.

Extending PAL to reason with narratives

We now discuss ways to extend PAL to allow actual observations instead of hypothetical ones. For this we extend PAL to incorporate narratives (Miller & Shanahan 1994), where we have time points as first class citizens and we can observe fluent values and action occurrences at these time points and do tasks such as reason about missing action occurrences, make diagnosis, plan from the current time point, and counter-factual reasoning about fluent values if a different sequence of actions had happened in a past (not just initial situation) time point. Here, we give a quick overview of this extension of PAL which we will refer to as $PALN$.

$PALN$ has a richer observation language $PALN_O$ consisting of propositions of the following forms:

$$\varphi \ \textbf{at} \ t \qquad (0.18)$$

$$\alpha \ \textbf{between} \ \ t_1, t_2 \qquad (0.19)$$
$$\alpha \ \textbf{occur\_at} \ \ t \qquad (0.20)$$
$$t_1 \ \textbf{precedes} \ \ t_2 \qquad (0.21)$$

where φ is a fluent formula, α is a (possibly empty) sequence of actions, and t, t_1, t_2 are time points (also called situation constants) which differ from the current time point t_C.

A narrative is a pair $(\mathcal{D}, \mathcal{O}')$, where $\mathcal{D}$ is a domain description and $\mathcal{O}'$ is a set of observations of the form (0.18-0.21). Observations are interpreted with respect to a domain description. While a domain description defines a transition function that characterize what states may be reached when an action is executed in a state, a narrative consisting of a domain description together with a set of observations defines the possible histories of the system. This characterization is done by a function Σ that maps time points to action sequences, and a sequence Ψ, which is a finite trajectory of the form $\mathsf{s}_0, a_1, \mathsf{s}_1, a_2, \ldots, a_n, \mathsf{s}_n$ in which $\mathsf{s}_0, \ldots, \mathsf{s}_n$ are states, $a_1, \ldots, a_n$ are actions and $\mathsf{s}_i \in \Phi(a_i, \mathsf{s}_{i-1})$ for $i = 1, \ldots, n$. Models of a narrative $(\mathcal{D}, \mathcal{O}')$ are interpretations $\mathcal{M} = (\Psi, \Sigma)$ that satisfy all the facts in $\mathcal{O}'$ and minimize unobserved action occurrences. (A more formal definition is given in (Baral, Gelfond, & Provetti 1997).) A narrative is *consistent* if it has a model. Otherwise, it is *inconsistent*. When $\mathcal{M}$ is a model of a narrative $(\mathcal{D}, \mathcal{O}')$ we write $(\mathcal{D}, \mathcal{O}') \models \mathcal{M}$.

Next we define the conditional probability that a particular pair $\mathcal{M} = (\Psi, \Sigma) = ([\mathsf{s}_0, a_1, \mathsf{s}_1, a_2, \ldots, a_n, \mathsf{s}_n], \Sigma)$ of trajectories and time point assignments is a model of a given domain description $\mathcal{D}$, and a set of observations. For that we first define the weight of a $\mathcal{M}$ (with respect to $\mathcal{D}$ which is understood from the context) denoted by $Weight(\mathcal{M})$ as:

$$
\begin{aligned}
Weight(\mathcal{M}) \quad & = 0 \text{ if } \Sigma(t_C) \neq [a_1, \ldots, a_n]; \text{ and} \\
& = P(\mathsf{s}_0) \times P_{a_1}(\mathsf{s}_1|\mathsf{s}_0) \times \ldots \times P_{a_n}(\mathsf{s}_n|\mathsf{s}_{n-1}) \\
& \quad \text{otherwise.}
\end{aligned}
$$

Given a set of observation $\mathcal{O}'$, we then define

$$
\begin{aligned}
P(\mathcal{M}|\mathcal{O}') \quad & = 0 \text{ if } \mathcal{M} \text{ is not a model of } (\mathcal{D}, \mathcal{O}'); \\
& = \frac{Weight(\mathcal{M})}{\sum_{(\mathcal{D}, \mathcal{O}') \models \mathcal{M}'} Weight(\mathcal{M}')} \text{ otherwise.}
\end{aligned}
$$

The probabilistic correctness of a plan from a time point t with respect to a model $\mathcal{M}$ can then be defined as

$$
\begin{aligned}
P(\varphi \ \textbf{after} \ \alpha \ \textbf{at} \ t|\mathcal{M}) \quad & = \sum_{s' \in \Phi([\beta], \mathsf{s}_0) \wedge s' \models \varphi} P_{[\beta]}(s'|\mathsf{s}_0) \\
& \text{where } \beta = \Sigma(t) \circ \alpha
\end{aligned}
$$

Finally, we define the (probabilistic) correctness of a (multi-action) plan from a time point t given a set of observations. This corresponds to counter-factual queries of Pearl (Pearl 2000) when the observations are about a different sequence of actions than the one in the hypothetical plan.

$$
\begin{aligned}
P(\varphi \ \textbf{after} \ \alpha \ \textbf{at} \ t|\mathcal{O}') \quad & = \sum_{(\mathcal{D}, \mathcal{O}') \models \mathcal{M}} P(\mathcal{M}|\mathcal{O}') \\
& \times P(\varphi \ \textbf{after} \ \alpha \ \textbf{at} \ t|\mathcal{M})
\end{aligned}
$$

One major application of the last equation is that it can be used for action based diagnosis (Baral, McIlraith, & Son 2000), by having φ as $ab(c)$, where c is a component. Due to lack of space we do not further elaborate here.

Related work, Conclusion and Future work

In this paper we showed how to integrate probabilistic reasoning into 'reasoning about actions'. the key idea behind our formulation is the use of two kinds of unknown variables: inertial and non-inertial. The inertial unknown variables are similar to the unknown variables used by Pearl. The non-inertial unknown variables plays a similar role as the role of nature's action in Reiter's formulation (Chapter 12 of (Reiter 2001)) and are also similar to Lin's magic predicate in (Lin 1996). In Reiter's formulation a stochastic action is composed of a set of deterministic actions, and when an agent executes the stochastic action nature steps in and picks one of the component actions respecting certain probabilities. So if the same stochastic action is executed multiple times in a row an observation after the first execution does not add information about what the nature will pick the next time the stochastic action is executed. In a sense the nature's pick in our formulation is driven by a non-inertial unknown variable. We are still investigating if Reiter's formulation has a counterpart to our inertial unknown variables.

Earlier we mentioned the representation languages for probabilistic planning and the fact that their focus is not from the point of view of elaboration tolerance. We would like to add that even if we consider the Dynamic Bayes net representations as suggested by Boutilier and Goldszmidt, our approach is more general as we allow cycles in the causal laws, and by definition they are prohibited in Bayes nets.

Among the future directions, we believe that our formulation can be used in adding probabilistic concepts to other action based formulations (such as, diagnosis, and agent control), and execution languages. Earlier we gave the basic definitions for extending PAL to allow narratives. This is a first step in formulating action-based diagnosis with probabilities. Since our work was inspired by Pearl's work we now present a more detailed comparison between the two.

Comparison with Pearls' notion of causality

Among the differences betweens his and our approaches are:

(1) Pearl represents causal relationships in the form of deterministic, functional equations of the form $v_i = f_i(pa_i, u_i)$, with $pa_i \subset U \cup V \setminus \{v_i\}$, and $u_i \in U$, where U is the set of unknown variables and V is the set of fluents. Such equations are only defined for v_i's from V.

In our formulation instead of using such equations we use static causal laws of the form (0.2), and restrict ψ to fluent formulas. I.e., it does not contain unknown variables. A set of such static causal laws define functional equations which are embedded inside the semantics. The advantage of using such causal laws over the equations used by Pearl is the ease with which we can add new static causal laws. We just add them and let the semantics take care of the rest. (This is one manifestation of the notion of 'elaboration tolerance'.) On the other hand Pearl would have to replace his older equation by a new equation. Moreover, if we did not restrict ψ to be a formula of only fluents, we could have written $v_i = f_i(pa_i, u_i)$ as the static causal law $true$ **causes** $v_i = f_i(pa_i, u_i)$.

(2) We see one major problem with the way Pearl reasons about actions (which he calls 'interventions') in his formulation. To reason about the intervention which assigns a particular value v to a fluent f, he proposes to modify the original causal model by removing the link between f and its parents (i.e., just assigning v to f by completely forgetting the structural equation for f), and then reasoning with the modified model. This is fine in itself, except that if we need to reason about a sequence of actions, one of which may change values of the predecessors of f (in the original model) that may affect the value of f. Pearl's formulation will not allow us to do that, as the link between f and its predecessors has been removed when reasoning about the first action.

Since actions are first class citizens in our language we do not have such a problem. In addition, we are able to reason about executability of actions, and formulate indirect qualification, where static causal laws force an action to be inexecutable in certain states. In Pearl's formulation, all interventions are always possible.

Acknowledgment This research was supported by the grants NSF 0070463 and NASA NCC2-1232.

References

Baral, C.; Gelfond, M.; and Provetti, A. 1997. Representing Actions: Laws, Observations and Hypothesis. *Journal of Logic Programming* 31(1-3):201–243.

Baral, C.; McIlraith, S.; and Son, T. 2000. Formulating diagnostic problem solving using an action language with narratives and sensing. In *KR 2000*, 311–322.

Boutilier, C., and Goldszmidt, M. 1996. The frame problem and bayesian network action representations. In *Proc. of CSCSI-96*.

Boutilier, C.; Dean, T.; and Hanks, S. 1995. Planning under uncertainty: Structural assumptions and computational leverage. In *Proc. 3rd European Workshop on Planning (EWSP'95)*.

Gelfond, M., and Lifschitz, V. 1993. Representing actions and change by logic programs. *Journal of Logic Programming* 17(2,3,4):301–323.

Kushmerick, N.; Hanks, S.; and Weld, D. 1995. An algorithm for probabilistic planning. *Artificial Intelligence* 76(1-2):239–286.

Lin, F. 1996. Embracing causality in specifying the indeterminate effects of actions. In AAAI 96.

Littman, M. 1997. Probabilistic propositional planning: representations and complexity. In *AAAI 97*, 748–754.

McCain, N., and Turner, H. 1995. A causal theory of ramifications and qualifications. In *Proc. of IJCAI 95*, 1978–1984.

McCarthy, J. 1998. Elaboration tolerance. In *Common Sense 98*.

Miller, R., and Shanahan, M. 1994. Narratives in the situation calculus. *Journal of Logic and Computation* 4(5):513–530.

Pearl, J. 1999. Reasoning with cause and effect. In *IJCAI 99*, 1437–1449.

Pearl, J. 2000. *Causality*. Cambridge University Press.

Poole, D. 1997. The independent choice logic for modelling multiple agents under uncertainty. *Artificial Intelligence* 94(1-2):7–56.

Reiter, R. 2001. *Knowledge in action: logical foundation for describing and implementing dynamical systems*. MIT press.

Sandewall, E. 1998. Special issue. *Electronic Transactions on Artificial Intelligence* 2(3-4):159–330. http://www.ep.liu.se/ej/etai/.

A Method for Metric Temporal Reasoning

Mathias Broxvall [*]

Department of Computer and Information Science
Linköpings Universitet
S-581 83 Linköping, Sweden
matbr@ida.liu.se

Abstract

Several methods for temporal reasoning with metric time have been suggested—for instance, Horn Disjunctive Linear Relations (Horn DLRs). However, it has been noted that implementing this algorithm is non-trivial since it builds on fairly complicated polynomial-time algorithms for linear programming. Instead, an alternative approach which augments Allen's interval algebra with a Simple Temporal Problem (STP) has been suggested (Condotta, 2000). In this paper, we present a new point-based approach STP* for reasoning about metric temporal constraints. STP* subsumes the tractable preconvex fragment of the augmented interval algebra and can be viewed as a slightly restricted version of Horn DLRs. We give an easily implementable algorithm for deciding satisfiability of STP* and demonstrate experimentally its efficiency. We also give a method for finding solutions to consistent STP* problem instances.

Introduction

Temporal reasoning in various forms has long been an important task in many areas of AI. Examples of tasks that have been studied is that of deciding consistency or finding a solution of a set of constraints over temporal variables. Typically these variables represents time points or time intervals over a linear time domain. The constraints imposed on these variables can either be of a purely qualitative nature, stating relations such as precedence or equality, or of a more quantitative nature. Examples of the later case would be to state that a certain time point occurs at least a given amount of time units before another or that an interval is of a certain length.

The time complexity for qualitative reasoning is fairly well understood. Reasoning about intervals is commonly done using Allen's interval algebra (Allen 1983) for which the satisfiability problem is NP-complete in the general case but for which several tractable fragments have been identified. One of the more useful tractable fragments is the ORD-Horn fragment (Nebel & Bürckert 1995) which consists of the 868 interval relations which can be expressed by conjunctions of constraints of the form $x \; R \; y \lor z \neq$

---

[*]This research has been supported by the ECSEL graduate student program.

w where x, y, z, w denotes endpoints of the intervals and $R \in \{\leq, \neq\}$. Note that x, y or z, w may denote the same endpoints for non-disjunctive constraints such as the interval constraint "before or meets" which can be written as $x^+ \leq y^- \lor x^+ \neq x^+$. The ORD-Horn fragment is also known as the set of preconvex interval algebra relations. Qualitative reasoning on time points is done using the point algebra and satisfiability can easily be decided using path consistency.

A number of methods has been proposed for reasoning about metric time. One of these is *Horn Disjunctive Linear Relations* (Jonsson & Bckstrm 1998; Koubarakis 2001), Horn DLRs for short. This is a temporal constraint formalism for which satisfiability can be checked in polynomial time. The expressibility of Horn DLRs subsumes the ORD-Horn algebra and most of the other tractable formalisms for temporal reasoning and satisfiability is decided using a linear programming approach. As a consequence, the algorithm for deciding satisfiability is not trivial to implement and special considerations need to be taken to the numerical precision during calculations. These problems have been pointed out in a number of papers, cf. (Condotta 2000; Pujari & Sattar 1999). For a good presentation of the polynomial time algorithms for linear programming and the numerical issues involved see eg. (Papadimitriou & Steiglitz 1982). Another slightly more efficient algorithm solving the linear programming problem has been presented by Vaidya (1987).

A method proposed by Condotta (2000) handles metric time by augmenting Allen's interval algebra and the rectangle algebra (Güsgen 1989) with quantitative STP constraints on the endpoints. Although this method yields an algorithm which is simpler to implement than the Horn DLR approach it lacks the expressibility of Horn DLRs and has the rather high time complexity of $O(n^5)$.

In this paper we present yet another approach for handling metric time called STP* which has an expressibility subsuming that of the tractable ORD-Horn fragment of the augmented interval (and rectangle) algebra but slightly more restricted than Horn DLRs. By restricting ourselves to using this method we get a very simple algorithm for deciding satisfiability that has a low practical time complexity and a good expressibility. We recall that the Simple Temporal Problem (STP) allows metric constraints of the form

```
1   Algorithm: STP-1
2   Input: A set $C$ of $STP^*$ clauses over the set of variables $1 \ldots n$.
3   Let $M$ be the $n \times n$ matrix such that $M[k][l] = 0$ if $k = l$ and $\infty$ otherwise .
4   repeat
5       $changed \leftarrow false$
6       update $M$ to contain the shortest path between every pair of variables.
7       if $\exists x : M[x][x] < 0$ then reject
8       for every clause $c = x_1 + r_1 \leq y_1 \vee x_2 + r_2 \neq y_2 \vee \cdots \vee x_m + r_m \neq y_m$ in $C$ do
9           if $r_1 < M[x_1][y_1] \wedge \neg \exists i > 1 : M[x_i][y_i] \neq r_i \vee M[y_i][x_i] \neq r_i$ then
10              $M[x_1][y_1] \leftarrow r_1$
11              $changed \leftarrow true$
12              remove $c$ from $C$
13          end
14      until $changed = false$
15  accept
```

Figure 1: The algorithm for solving STP* problem instances

$x + r \leq y$ where x, y represents point variables and r is a real constant. The satisfiability problem for STPs and STPs augmented with disequality constraints (STP$^{\neq}$) relations has been well investigated previously (Dechter, Meiri, & Pearl 1991; Gerevini & Cristani 1997) and efficient algorithms has been identified for deciding satisfiability. By basing our approach on STPs and allowing disjunctions of disequality we get an expressive formalism that retain most of the simplicity and efficiency of the satisfiability algorithms for STP and STP$^{\neq}$. As we will see later in this paper the practical cost of adding metric information is relatively small when we use this method.

We continue this paper by recalling the definitions of STP$^{\neq}$, presenting STP* and an algorithm for solving the satisfiability problem in the next section. In the following section we investigate the expressibility of STP* and show that the tractable preconvex fragment of the augmented interval algebra can be expressed in terms of STP* constraints and that certain rectangle algebra relations also can be expressed in STP*. After this we continue with some studies and comparisons of an actual implementation of this algorithm to other approaches. Finally, in the last section we have some concluding remarks and open questions.

Simple Temporal Problem

We begin this section by giving the definition of STP$^{\neq}$ introduced by Gerevini and Cristani (1997) and recall some of their previous results. This is in turn followed by the necessary definitions for extending STP$^{\neq}$ with disjunctions of disequality, yielding STP*, and an algorithm for deciding satisfiability of STP* problem instances.

Definition 1 An STP$^{\neq}$ problem instance is a tuple $\langle V, C \rangle$ of a set of variables V and constraints C such that all constraints in C is of the form $x + r \leq y$ or $x + r \neq y$ for $x, y \in V$ and $r \in \mathrm{R}$. The satisfiability problem for STP$^{\neq}$ is that of finding a mapping from the variables onto R satisfying all the constraints C.

We say that an STP$^{\neq}$ problem instance $\mathcal{T}$ entails $x + d = y$ iff there exists no solution for $\mathcal{T}$ such that $x + d \neq y$. An STP$^{\neq}$ problem instance can also be considered as a labeled

graph over its variables with an edge labeled r between x, y for each constraint $x - r \leq y$. This graph is called the distance graph of the instance. For STP$^{\neq}$ we have the following result proven by Gerevini and Cristani (1997) which is helpful for deciding satisfiability of STP$^{\neq}$ problem instances. This will later be used in the proofs for the algorithm deciding satisfiability of STP* instances.

Lemma 2 An STP$^{\neq}$ problem instance $\mathcal{T}$ is consistent iff $\mathcal{T}$ does not have negative cycles in its distance graph, and it does not entail $w + d = v$ for any inequation $w + d \neq v$ in $\mathcal{T}$.

We are now ready to define the STP* point algebra and the satisfiability problem for it. As we will see, STP* and STP$^{\neq}$ are closely related and the algorithm for deciding satisfiability of STP* problem instances resembles that for deciding satisfiability of STP$^{\neq}$ instances given by Gerevini and Cristani (1997).

Definition 3 An STP* problem instance is a tuple $\langle V, C \rangle$ of a set of variables V and constraints C such that all constraints in C is of the form $x_1 + r_1 \leq y_1 \vee x_2 + r_2 \neq y_2 \vee \cdots \vee x_n + r_n \neq y_n$ for $x, y \in V, r \in \mathrm{R}$ and $n \geq 1$. The satisfiability problem for STP* is that of finding a mapping from the variables onto R satisfying all the constraints C.

The maximum clause size of a problem instance is the largest n for all the constraints in it. Note that the definition allows simple $x + r \leq y$ constraints by having $n = 1$. Since STP* is a restriction of the Horn-DLR framework satisfiability could in principle be decided using the independence algorithm (Cohen *et al.* 2000) and a solver for STP$^{\neq}$. Indeed, the algorithm we present here is largely based on the independence algorithm but by using Lemma 2 we have enhanced the algorithm so that a solution is created incrementally and a complete call to an underlying STP$^{\neq}$ solver can be avoided in each iteration which makes the algorithm more efficient when a shortest path algorithm which handles incremental changes is used in step 6 of the algorithm. In our implementation a modified Floyd-Warshall (Cormen, Leiserson, & Rivest 1997) that keep tracks of modified variables is used for this purpose. We can now prove that the algorithm given in Figure 1 only accepts satisfiable problem instances.

Theorem 4 Algorithm STP-1 accepts only satisfiable STP* problem instances

Proof: Let Π be an STP* problem instance that is accepted by STP-1 and let M, C be the adjacency matrix and the set of clauses left when the algorithm accepts. We construct an STP$^{\neq}$ problem instance Π' from Π by having the constraints $x - M[x][y] \leq y$ for all x, y such that $M[x][y] < \infty$. For each clause $c = x_1 + r_1 \leq y_1 \vee x_2 + r_2 \neq y_2 \vee \cdots \vee x_m + r_m \neq y_m$ in C we add the constraint $x_i + r_i \neq y_i$ for some i such that $M[x_i][y_i] \neq r_i$ or $M[y_i][x_i] \neq r_i$.

Obviously, Π is satisfiable if Π' is satisfiable. We note that Π' contains no negative cycles and that for each constraint $x + r \neq y$ we have that Π does not entail $x + r = y$. By lemma 2 we have that Π' is satisfiable and thus Π is also satisfiable. $\square$

We continue by proving that the algorithm only rejects unsatisfiable STP* problem instances.

Theorem 5 Algorithm STP-1 rejects only unsatisfiable STP* problem instances.

Proof: Let Π be an STP* problem instance that is rejected by the algorithm and let M, C be the adjacency matrix and the set of clauses left when the algorithm rejects. Assume that Π is satisfiable. It is then possible to construct an STP$^{\neq}$ problem instance Π' by selecting one term of each clause in Π such that Π' is satisfiable. From lemma 2 we know that Π' contains no negative cycles and that for each $x + r \neq y$ constraint we have that Π' does not entail $x + r = y$.

We say that M contain a constraint $x - r \leq y$ if $M[x][y] = r$ and $r < \infty$ and we show that M only contains constraints that are present in Π' by induction on the number of constraints in M. The base case of zero constraints is trivially true. For the inductive case assume that this holds for the first n constraints added to M by the algorithm and let $c = x_1 + r_1 \leq y_1 \vee x_2 + r_2 \neq y_2 \vee \cdots \vee x_m + r_m \neq y_m$ be the clause containing the $(n+1)$'th constraint $x_1 + r_1 \leq y_1$ added. Since we have $\neg \exists i > 2 : M[x_i][y_i] \neq r_i \vee M[y_i][x_i] \neq r_i$ and all constraints in M are also present in Π' we see that $x_i + r_i = y_i$ is entailed by Π' for all $i > 2$. Thus, Π' must also contain the constraint $x_1 + r_1 \leq y_1$ added by the algorithm to M.

Now, since M only contains constraints in Π' and the algorithm rejects we see that M and Π' has a negative cycle. Which contradicts lemma 2. Thus, Π is unsatisfiable. $\square$

Next, we note that the algorithm runs in $O(|C|(|V|^3 + |C|t))$ time for problem instances $\langle V, C \rangle$ with maximum clause size t since the shortest path problem can be solved in $O(n^3)$ using eg. the Floyd-Warshall algorithm (Cormen, Leiserson, & Rivest 1997). For converted interval and rectangle problem instances our algorithm thus takes $O(n^5)$ time where n is the number of variables in the original problem instance. Thus, our algorithm has the same asymptotical time complexity as Condottas algorithm for the preconvex fragment of the augmented interval algebra but with with a greater expressibility.

For some applications it is not sufficient to show that a problem instance is satisfiable but an actual solution is also sought for. Finding the solution to a given consistent STP* problem instance can be done by constructing the equivalent STP$^{\neq}$ problem instance implied by the algorithm STP-1 and using for instance the approach found in (Gerevini & Cristani 1997) to find the solution to the STP$^{\neq}$ problem instance. The conversion to STP$^{\neq}$ is done by converting each disjunctive clause $c = x_1 + r_1 \leq y_1 \vee x_2 + r_2 \neq y_2 \vee \cdots \vee x_n + r_n \neq y_n$ that is removed at step 12 of the algorithm to the STP$^{\neq}$ constraints $x_1 + r_1 \leq y_1$ and for each clause remaining in C when the algorithm accepts convert it to the STP$^{\neq}$ constraint $x_i + r_i \neq y_i$ where $i > 2$ and $M[x_i][y_i] \neq r_i \vee M[y_i][x_i] \neq r_i$.

Expressing Interval and Rectangle Algebra Problems in STP*

In this section we discuss how interval and rectangle algebra problems can be expressed in terms of STP* problems. We demonstrate that the full set of preconvex interval algebra relations (ie. the ORD-Horn algebra) can be expressed using STP* and that the expressibility of STP* subsumes that of the preconvex fragment of the augmented interval algebra (Condotta 2000).

The interval algebra was introduced by Allen (1983) and is a relational algebra consisting of 13 atomic relations and their disjunctions. The relations of the interval algebra operate over intervals in a real valued domain are the following: *before (b), after (a), meets (m), met-by (mi), overlaps (o), overlapped-by (oi), during (d), includes (di), starts (s), started-by (si), finishes (f), finished-by (fi)* and *equals (eq)*. An interval algebra network is a set of variables and a set of binary constraints over the variables where each constraint is a disjunction of the atomic relations.

In the rectangle algebra the variables represents rectangles and the constraints disjunctions of tuples of interval constraints over the rectangles projected onto two orthogonal axes. For instance, the constraint $x(b, m)y$ signifies that the rectangle x should come strictly before y on the first axis and should meet y along the second axis.

In order to be able to compare the STP* formalism with the augmented interval algebra we need the definition of it as well. The following definition come from Condotta (2000).

Definition 6 An augmented interval network $\mathcal{M}$ is a pair $\langle \mathcal{N}, \mathcal{S} \rangle$ where $\mathcal{N} = \langle V, C \rangle$ is an interval network which represents the qualitative constraints on the intervals in V and $\mathcal{S} = \langle Points(V), C' \rangle$ is an STP instance representing the quantitative constraints on the distances between the bounds of the intervals in V.

Condotta (2000) has proven that deciding satisfiability for augmented interval networks containing only preconvex relations in its qualitative part can be done in $O(n^5)$ time.

Theorem 7 The satisfiability problem for the augmented interval algebra restricted to problem instances containing only preconvex relations can be reduced to the satisfiability problem for STP* in linear time.

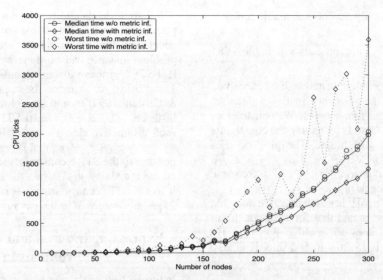

Figure 2: Running time of the STP* solver for converted interval algebra problem instances with and without constraints imposed on the lengths of intervals. For each sample 500 problem instances was generated and solved.

Proof: Let $\mathcal{M} = \langle \mathcal{N}, \mathcal{S} \rangle$ be an augmented interval network such that $\mathcal{N}$ contains only preconvex (ORD-Horn) relations. By definition we know that there exists a constant number of equivalent STP* constraints for each preconvex relation. We construct an STP* problem instance by introducing two STP* variables x^+ and x^- and the constraint $x^- \leq x^+$ for each interval x in $\mathcal{N}$ and translate each qualitative $\mathcal{IA}$ constraint in $\mathcal{N}$ into a constant number of STP* constraints. By also including the STP constraints $\mathcal{S}$ we have an an STP* problem instance which is satisfiable iff $\mathcal{M}$ is satisfiable. $\square$

Furthermore, STP* is able to express constraints which cannot be expressed with only the preconvex relations of the interval algebra. For instance, let $x \; R \; y$ be an interval algebra constraint with a preconvex relation R and C the corresponding set of STP* constraints. If we let C' be C with the term $z^+ \neq w^+$ added to each clause and C'' be C with the term $z^- \neq w^-$ added we can express for instance the non binary constraints $x \; R \; y \vee z \; neq \; w$ as $C' \cup C''$ and $x \; R \; y \vee z \neg (f \vee fi)w$ as C'. We continue by recalling the definition of the augmented rectangle algebra as given by Condotta (2000) and will see that STP* manages to express some of the constraints in this algebra too.

Definition 8 An augmented rectangle network $\mathcal{M}$ is a triple $\langle \mathcal{N}, \mathcal{S}_1, \mathcal{S}_2 \rangle$ where $\mathcal{N} = \langle V, C \rangle$ is a rectangle network which represents the qualitative constraints on the rectangles in V. $\mathcal{S}_1 = \langle Points(V'), C' \rangle$ and $\mathcal{S}_2 = \langle Points(V''), C'' \rangle$ are two STPs representing the quantitative constraints on the distances between the bounds of the interval of V' and V'' respectively, where V', V'' represents the set of the projections of the rectangles in V onto the first and second axis respectively.

In this case, we represent each rectangle with four STP* variables representing the endpoints of the rectangles projected onto each axis. For instance, the rectangle algebra constraint $x(b, mi)y$ representing the fact that x lies left of

and meets y from above can be expressed by the STP* constraints $x_1^+ \leq y_1^-$, $x_1^+ \neq y_1^-$, $x_2^- \leq y_2^+$ and $y_2^+ \leq x_2^-$. Obviously, since deciding satisfiability for the full rectangle algebra is an NP-complete problem STP* cannot express all the relations in the full rectangle algebra. Note however that there exists large tractable fragments of the rectangle algebra such as the set of strongly preconvex rectangle algebra relations (Balbiani, Condotta, & Fariñas del Cerro 1999). The full extent of which rectangle algebra relations that can be expressed in terms of STP* constraints remains an open question. Note that all the basic relations in the rectangle algebra can be expressed using STP* constraints.

Evaluating STP*

As was shown in the previous section the expressibility of STP* subsumes that of the preconvex fragment of the augmented interval algebra while still retaining a fairly simple algorithm for deciding satisfiability. In this section we investigate the actual runtime properties of this algorithm. We note that algorithm STP-1 is both simple to implement and gives a practical and efficient method for reasoning about points and intervals with metric information. Although the theoretical time complexity of the algorithm is $O(|C|(|V|^3 + |C|t))$ for problem instances $\langle V, C \rangle$ with maximum clause size t (for most applications t is a fixed constant and can be disregarded) it runs in almost cubic time with regard to the number of variables in practice.

In order to test the running time of the algorithm we have first generated random sets of problem instances (without metric information) of the interval algebra. We choose a random graph structure for these problems and with a constant factor chosen from the phase transition region (Cheeseman, Kanefsky, & Taylor 1991) as the average constraintedness. We tested the algorithm on these data and noted that it ran in approximately $O(n^{3.35})$ time for this specific problem ensemble. A reasonable guess considering the behavior of the algorithm would be that adding metric information (in this

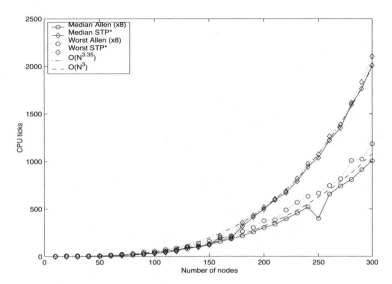

Figure 3: Measured running times for the solvers varying number of nodes in problem instances. For each sample 100 problem instances was generated and solved. Note that the cpu time for the Allen algebra based solver has been exaggerated a factor of eight to better illustrate the asymptotical behavior of the solvers.

case, constraints on the lengths of intervals) will not affect the practical time complexity of the algorithm considerably. As can be seen in Figure 2 adding metric information to our problem instances gives a slight performance increase in the median case, since more problem instances can be found unsatisfiable at an earlier stage, and a small constant performance decrease in the worst case for each problem instance ensemble.

We continue by comparing the running time of this algorithm by that of another solver working directly on the intervals of a problem instance that was used for evaluating the efficiency of using the ORD-Horn fragment (Nebel 1997). For this we generate a number of instances having only qualitative preconvex interval constraints from Allen's interval algebra and solve these instances using both an efficient solver (Nebel 1997) deciding path consistency on the interval constraints directly and using our solver. The conversion of the interval algebra constraints is done by a simple translation procedure containing a case for each possible interval relation, the cost of translating the constraints is thus linear with the number of interval constraints which is quadric with respect to the number of variables. In the graphs we have omitted the cost of translating the constraints since it is assumed that in a real world application the translation should either be done in the modeling of the problem or with a more efficient in-memory approach.

As can be seen the cost of using our solver is relatively low. Since the size of problem instances are doubled when working on point relations, using STP* takes a constant factor of eight times longer. In order to easier compare the asymptotic behavior of the two different approaches this constant factor has been removed in the figures but it is important to remember this extra constant cost induced by the extended expressibility of STP* compared to the interval algebra when solving real world problems. Furthermore, the addition of metric constraints gives a higher time com-

plexity, but in practice not as high as the theoretical $O(n^5)$. Overall, the cost of allowing metric information in problem instances seems to be small and is mostly dominated by the constant factor eight for problem instances of reasonable size. The running times for the two different approaches using the same problem instances can be found in Figure 3. It would here also have been interesting with a comparison of the STP* solver and a solver for Horn DLRs. However, as far as we know there exists no publicly available implementation of such a solver.

Of further interest is also to study the two different approaches with respect to the probability of satisfiability for the problem instances. This is done in Figure 4 by varying the average degree of problem instances. Again, the running times of the approach based on Allen's interval algebra has been scaled by a factor eight to ease comparisons. As we can see the effect of varying the constraintedness of the problem instances is much larger for the $\mathcal{IA}$ approach than for STP* where the running time has very little correlation with the constraintedness of problem instances. This can perhaps best be explained by noting that information is lost in the conversion from interval algebra problems to the point algebra approach used in STP*.

Concluding Remarks

In this paper we have introduced a new extension STP* of the Simple Temporal Problem (STP) which allows disjunctions of disequalities in the constraints and demonstrate how this algebra can be used efficiently for temporal reasoning with metric time. We have given a simple and efficient algorithm for deciding satisfiability of STP* and shown how a solution to a given STP* instance can be found by means of a reduction to STP$^{\neq}$.

The expressibility of STP* extends that of the set of preconvex relations for the augmented interval algebra, which is the only tractable set of relations for this algebra which con-

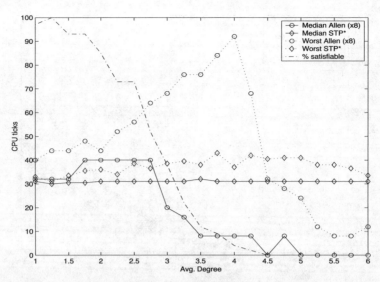

Figure 4: Measured running times for the solvers using 100 problem instances of 100 nodes each and varying the average degree. Note that the cpu time for the Allen algebra based solver has been exaggerated a factor of eight to simplify comparisons.

tains all the basic relations. Furthermore, this algebra can be used not only for temporal reasoning but can also handle for instance fractions of the rectangle algebra.

For future work, it would be interesting to enhance the algorithm so that intervals involving only purely qualitative constraints would be handled as they are, without being converted into two STP* points. This would remove some of the efficiency loss induced by having twice as large problem instances for converted $\mathcal{IA}$ instances. Another open question is that of which rectangle algebra relations can be expressed in terms of STP* constraints. Is it possible to express the full set of strongly-preconvex $\mathcal{RA}$ relations using only the point constraints allowed in STP*?

References

Allen, J. F. 1983. Maintaining knowledge about temporal intervals. *Communications of the ACM* 26(11):832–843.

Balbiani, P.; Condotta, J.-F.; and Fariñas del Cerro, L. 1999. A new tractable subclass of the rectangle algebra. In *Proceedings of the 16th International Joint Conference on Artificial Intelligence (IJCAI-99)*, 442–447. Stockholm, Sweden: Morgan Kaufmann Publishers.

Cheeseman, P.; Kanefsky, B.; and Taylor, W. M. 1991. Where the really hard problems are. In *Proceedings of the 12th International Joint Conference on Artificial INtelligence (IJCAI-91)*, 331–337. Morgan Kaufmann.

Cohen, D.; Jeavons, P.; Jonsson, P.; and Koubarakis, M. 2000. Building tractable disjunctive constraints. *Journal of the ACM* 47(5):826–853.

Condotta, J.-F. 2000. The augmented interval and rectangle networks. In *Proceedings of the Seventh International Conference on Principles of Knowledge Representation and Reasoning (KR2000)*, 571–579. Trento, Italy: Morgan Kaufmann Publishers.

Cormen, T. H.; Leiserson, C. E.; and Rivest, R. L. 1997. *Introduction to Algorithms*. MIT press.

Dechter, R.; Meiri, I.; and Pearl, J. 1991. Temporal constraint networks. *Artificial Intelligence* 49(1-3):61–95.

Gerevini, A., and Cristani, M. 1997. On finding a solution in temporal constraint satisfaction problems. In *Proceedings of the Fifteenth International Joint Conference on Artificial Intelligence (IJCAI 97)*, 1460–1465.

Güsgen, H. 1989. Spatial reasoning based on allen's temporal logic. Technical Report ICSI TR89-049, International Computer Science Institute.

Jonsson, P., and Bckstrm, C. 1998. A unifying approach to temporal constraint reasoning. *Artificial Intelligence* 102(1):143–155.

Koubarakis, M. 2001. Tractable disjunctions of linear constraints: basic results and applications to temporal reasoning. *Theoretical Computer Science* 266(1-2):311–339.

Nebel, B., and Bürckert, H.-J. 1995. Reasoning about temporal relations: A maximal tractable subclass of Allen's interval algebra. *Journal of the ACM* 42(1):43–66.

Nebel, B. 1997. Solving hard qualitative temporal reasoning problems: Evaluating the efficiency of using the ord-horn class. *Constraints* 1(3):175–190. Archive of C-programs: **ftp://ftp.informatik.uni-freiburg.de/ documents/papers/ki/allen-csp-solving.programs.tar.gz**.

Papadimitriou, C. H., and Steiglitz, K. 1982. *Combinatorial Optimization: Algorithms and Complexity*. New Jersey: Prentice-Hall.

Pujari, A. K., and Sattar, A. 1999. A new framework for reasoning about points, intervals and durations. In *Proceedings of the Sixteenth International Joint Conference on Artificial Intelligence (IJCAI 99)*, 1259–1267.

Vaidya, P. M. 1987. An algorithm for linear programming which requires $O(((m+n)n^2+(m+n)^{1.5}n)L)$ arithmetic operations. In *Proceedings of the Nineteenth Annual ACM Symposium on Theory of Computing*, 29–38.

Non-Markovian Control in the Situation Calculus

Alfredo Gabaldon

Department of Computer Science
University of Toronto
Toronto, Canada M5S 3G4
alfredo@cs.toronto.edu

Abstract

The property that the executability and the effects of an action are determined entirely by the current state or situation is known as the Markov property and is assumed in most formalizations of action. It is not difficult, however, to run into scenarios when the Markov property is not present. We consider removing this assumption from the situation calculus based formalization of actions of Reiter, which forms the basis of the programming language Golog, and define an operator for regressing formulas that quantify over past situations, with respect to such nonMarkovian basic action theories.

Introduction and Motivation

Reasoning about the effects of actions is one of the most important problems in AI and has been devoted a great deal of effort. This work has resulted in several powerful formalisms. There are the Situation Calculus (McCarthy 1963; McCarthy & Hayes 1969), the Event Calculus (Kowalski & Sergot 1986), the action language $\mathcal{A}$ (Gelfond & Lifschitz 1993) and its extensions, the Features and Fluents approach (Sandewall 1994) and the Fluent calculus (Thielscher 1998) among others.

A common assumption made in these formalisms is the so called *Markov property*: whether an action can be executed and what its effects are is determined entirely by the current state or situation. The fact is, however, that it is not difficult to run into scenarios when the Markov property is not present and the executability and effects of an action depend not only on what holds in the current situation, but also on whether some conditions were satisfied at some point in the past.

For example, imagine a robot that works in a biological research facility with different safety-level areas. The dynamics are such that a material will be considered polluted after the robot touches it if the robot has been to a low safety area or directly touched a hazardous material and has not been to the disinfection station since then. So the effect of touching the material depends on the recent history of robot activities. We could also imagine that the robot cannot execute the action $open(Entrance, Lab1)$ if $temp(Lab1) >$

30 was true at any point since $closed(Entrance, Lab1)$. This would be an example of an action with nonMarkovian preconditions. Although this can be formalized with a Markovian theory by introducing more variables (e.g. more fluents) and axioms describing their dynamics, the resulting theory can be considerably larger and it will often be more natural and convenient simply not to assume the Markov property.

Furthermore, this work is motivated by a variety of research problems which involve the formalization of dynamic properties.

1. There has been work in database theory concerned with the semantics of dynamic integrity constraints (Saake & Lipeck 1988; Chomicki 1995). These constraints are typically expressed in terms of Past Temporal Logic, a logic with temporal connectives *Previous*, *Sometime* (in the past), *Always* (in the past), and *Since*. In a formalization of a database system in the situation calculus, such temporal connectives amount to references to past situations, and the constraints to restrictions on when a sequence of actions can be considered a "legal" database system evolution. As we will see, these past temporal logic connectives have an encoding as formulas in the nonMarkovian situation calculus and hence this can be used as a logical framework for the study, specification and modeling of databases with dynamic integrity constraints.

2. Also in the area of databases, more specifically in work on database transaction systems, the *rollback* operation clearly has a nonMarkovian flavour: its effects depend not on what is true in the current state, but on the state right before the transaction being reversed started. Indeed, (Kiringa 2001) presents a logical specification of database transactions in the nonMarkovian situation calculus.

3. In planning, the use of domain dependent knowledge to control search as suggested by Bacchus and Kabanza (1996; 2000) led to impressive computational improvements. Bacchus and Kabanza's TLPlan system, a forward chaining planner based on STRIPS, uses search control knowledge in the form of temporal logic constraints. Reiter (2001) applied the same idea in his Golog planners. These planners perform an iterative deepening forward search, eliminating partial plans if they lead to a "bad situation." Search control knowledge is encoded in a pred-

icate $badSituation(s)$ but this is limited to properties of the current situation s. The nonMarkovian situation calculus allows the definition of this predicate to refer to any situation that precedes s, i.e. to the full past of the current situation. As we mentioned above, past temporal logic expressions can be encoded in the nonMarkovian situation calculus and be used in the definition of $badSituation(s)$. This means that we can use search control knowledge of a similar form and expressivity as the one used in TLPlan.

4. The Markovian property may also be absent if the system specification includes stochastic actions and reward functions. The need to accommodate nonMarkovian dynamics and reward functions has been recognized in the work (Bacchus, Boutilier, & Grove 1996; 1997) who have developed techniques for solving nonMarkovian Decision Processes for decision-theoretic planning.

5. Finally, some time ago John McCarthy (1992) described a programming language called "Elephant 2000" which, among other features, does not forget. In other words, it is a language that allows the programmer to explicitly refer to past states of the programming environment in the program itself. The nonMarkovian situation calculus and the regression operator we present here can form the foundation for an non-forgetting version of Golog. Such a dialect of Golog would allow test conditions in terms of Past temporal logic and so one could write, for instance, a statement **if** $(P$ **since** $Q)$ **then** $exec(\delta)$**endIf** in programs.

In this paper, we generalize the situation calculus based formalization of actions of Reiter (1991) to the nonMarkovian case. We modify the regression operator to work with nonMarkovian basic action theories and formulas that quantify over past situations and prove the new regression operator to be correct.

The language of the Situation Calculus

In this section we briefly review the language of the situation calculus. For a complete description see (Pirri & Reiter 1999).

The language $\mathcal{L}_{sitcalc}$ is a second order language with equality and with three disjoint sorts: *action*, *situation* and *object*. In addition to $\wedge, \neg, \exists$ and definitions in terms of these for the other standard logical symbols, the alphabet of $\mathcal{L}_{sitcalc}$ includes a countably infinite number of variable symbols of each sort and predicate variables of all arities. A constant symbol S_0 and a function do of sort : *action* $\times$ *situation* $\to$ *situation*, a binary predicate symbol $\sqsubset$ used to define an ordering relation on situations, a binary predicate symbol $Poss : action \times situation$, and for each $n \geq 0$ a countably infinite number of function symbols of sort[1] $(action \cup object)^n \to action$ called *actions*, a countably infinite number of predicate symbols of sort $(action \cup object)^n \times situation$ called *relational fluents*, and a countably infinite number of function symbols of sort $(action \cup object)^n \times situation \to action \cup object$ called *functional fluents*. The language includes also a countably

---

[1]We use $(s_1 \cup s_2)^n$ as a shorthand for $s_{v_1} \times \ldots \times s_{v_n}$, $v_i \in \{1, 2\}$.

---

infinite number of predicates and functions without a situation argument. We will refer to these as *situation independent* predicates and functions.

Intuitively, situations are finite sequences of actions (sometimes referred to as *histories*) and this intuition is captured by a set of four *Foundational Axioms* (Pirri & Reiter 1999) (denoted by Σ)[2]:

$$do(a_1, s_1) = do(a_2, s_2) \supset a_1 = a_2 \wedge s_1 = s_2,$$
$$(\forall P).P(S_0) \wedge (\forall a, s)[P(s) \supset P(do(a, s))] \supset (\forall s)P(s),$$
$$\neg s \sqsubset S_0,$$
$$s \sqsubset do(a, s') \equiv s \sqsubset s' \vee s = s'.$$

The initial situation or empty history is denoted by constant S_0. Non-empty histories are built by means of the function do.

Basic nonMarkovian Theories of Action

In this section we introduce the basic nonMarkovian theories of action. In the Markovian action theories, the Markov assumption is realized by requiring that the formulas in the Action Precondition Axioms and Successor State Axioms refer only to one situation, a variable s, which is prenex universally quantified in the axioms. In nonMarkovian action theories, situation terms other than s will be allowed under the restriction that they refer to the past or to an explicitly bounded future relative to s. To make this formal, we need to introduce the notion of situation-bounded formulas. Intuitively, an $\mathcal{L}_{sitcalc}$ formula is bounded by situation term σ if all the situation variables it mentions are restricted, through equality or the $\sqsubset$ predicate, to range over subsequences of σ. This notion is useful because in order to apply regression on a formula, one needs to know how many actions there are in each situation, i.e. how many regression steps to apply. A formula that mentions a situation variable can be regressed provided that the variable is restricted to be a subsequence of some situation term with a known number of actions in it.

The following notation is used through out: for $n \geq 0$, we write $do([\alpha_1, \ldots, \alpha_n], \lambda)$ to denote the term of sort *situation* $do(\alpha_n, do(\alpha_{n-1}, \ldots, do(\alpha_1, \lambda) \ldots))$ where $\alpha_1, \ldots, \alpha_n$ are terms of sort *action* and λ stands for a variable s of sort *situation* or the constant S_0.

Definition 1 For $n \geq 0$, define the *length* of the situation term $do([\alpha_1, \ldots, \alpha_n], \lambda)$ to be n.

Definition 2 (Rooted Terms) For $n \geq 0$, let $\alpha_1, \ldots, \alpha_n$ be terms of sort *action*. A term $do([\alpha_1, \ldots, \alpha_n], s)$ is *rooted at* s iff s is the only variable of sort *situation* mentioned by $\alpha_1, \ldots, \alpha_n$ or no variable of that sort is mentioned. A term $do([\alpha_1, \ldots, \alpha_n], S_0)$ is *rooted at* S_0 iff $\alpha_1, \ldots, \alpha_n$ mention no variables of sort *situation*.

In writing bounded formulas, we will use the following abbreviations:

---

[2]Lower case Roman characters denote variables. Free variables are implicitly universally prenex quantified.

$$(\exists s : \sigma' \sqsubset \sigma)W \stackrel{\text{def}}{=} (\exists s)[\sigma' \sqsubset \sigma \wedge W]$$
$$(\exists s : \sigma' = \sigma)W \stackrel{\text{def}}{=} (\exists s)[\sigma' = \sigma \wedge W]$$
$$(\forall s : \sigma' \sqsubset \sigma)W \stackrel{\text{def}}{=} \neg(\exists s)[\sigma' \sqsubset \sigma \wedge \neg W] \quad (1)$$
$$(\forall s : \sigma' = \sigma)W \stackrel{\text{def}}{=} \neg(\exists s)[\sigma' = \sigma \wedge \neg W]$$

Definition 3 (Bounded Formulas) For $n \geq 0$, let σ be a term $do([\alpha_1, \ldots, \alpha_n], \lambda)$ rooted at λ. The formulas of $\mathcal{L}_{sitcalc}$ *bounded* by σ are the smallest set of formulas such that:

1. If t_1, t_2 are terms of the same sort whose subterms of sort *situation* (if any) are all rooted at λ, then $t_1 = t_2$ is a formula bounded by σ.

2. If σ' is a term of sort *situation* rooted at some situation variable or constant S_0, then $\sigma' \sqsubset \sigma$ is a formula bounded by σ.

3. For each $n \geq 0$, each n-ary situation independent predicate P, each $(n+1)$-ary fluent F and each n-ary action A, if $t_1, \ldots, t_n$ are terms of sort *action* or *object* whose subterms of sort *situation* are all rooted at λ, then $P(t_1, \ldots, t_n)$, $F(t_1, \ldots, t_n, \sigma)$ and $Poss(A(t_1, \ldots, t_n), \sigma)$ are formulas bounded by σ.

4. If σ' is a term of sort *situation* rooted at s and W is a formula bounded by a possibly different term of sort *situation* also rooted at s, then $(\exists s : \sigma' \sqsubset \sigma)W$, $(\exists s : \sigma' = \sigma)W$, $(\forall s : \sigma' \sqsubset \sigma)W$ and $(\forall s : \sigma' = \sigma)W$ are formulas bounded by σ.

5. If W_1, W_2 are formulas bounded by situation terms rooted at λ, then $\neg W_1$, $W_1 \wedge W_2$ and $(\exists v)W_1$, where v is of sort *action* or *object*, are formulas bounded by σ.

Example 1 For the purpose of illustrating the above definitions, consider the following sentence

$$(\exists a).(\exists s' : do(a, s') \sqsubset$$
$$do([get\_coffee, deliver\_coffee, gotoMailRm], s))$$
$$batteryCharged(do(chargeBatt, s')).$$

Intuitively it says that there is a situation in the past of $do([get\_coffee, deliver\_coffee, gotoMailRm], s))$ when executing *chargeBatt* would have (successfully) resulted in charged battery. This sentence is bounded by $do([get\_coffee, deliver\_coffee, gotoMailRm], s)$, with subformula $batteryCharged(do(chargeBatt, s'))$ bounded by $do(chargeBatt, s')$. Here, variable s' ranges over the subsequences of $do(get\_coffee, s)$. Note that this formula actually refers to a situation which is not in the past relative to the bounding situation $do([get\_coffee, deliver\_coffee, gotoMailRm], s)$.

We also need a strict version of boundedness.

Definition 4 (Strictly Bounded Formulas) Strictly bounded formulas are defined by replacing conditions 1, 4, and 5 in the definition of bounded formulas with the following:

$1'$ If t_1, t_2 are terms of the same sort whose subterms of sort *situation* (if any) are all subterms of σ, then $t_1 = t_2$ is a formula strictly bounded by σ.

$4'$. If σ' is a term of sort *situation* rooted at s and W is a formula strictly bounded by a subterm of σ', then $(\exists s : \sigma' \sqsubset \sigma)W$, $(\exists s : \sigma' = \sigma)W$, $(\forall s : \sigma' \sqsubset \sigma)W$ and $(\forall s : \sigma' = \sigma)W$ are formulas strictly bounded by σ.

$5'$. If W_1, W_2 are formulas strictly bounded by a subterm of σ, then $\neg W_1$, $W_1 \wedge W_2$ and $(\exists v)W_1$, where v is of sort *action* or *object*, are formulas strictly bounded by σ.

So we require that the situation term that binds W not only have the same root, but be one of the subterms of σ'. Intuitively, a formula W that is strictly bounded by σ has its situation terms restricted to the past relative to σ. Reference to hypothetical "alternative futures" as in Example 1, which is allowed in bounded formulas, is disallowed.

Example 2 In the situation calculus, to refer to the past means to refer to past situations. In this sense, one can write expressions that capture the intuitive meaning of the past temporal logic connectives *previous, since, sometime,* and *always*:[3]

$$prev(\varphi, s) \stackrel{\text{def}}{=} (\exists a).(\exists s' : do(a, s') = s) \, \varphi[s'].$$
$$since(\varphi_1, \varphi_2, s) \stackrel{\text{def}}{=} (\exists s' : s' \sqsubset s).\varphi_2[s'] \wedge$$
$$(\forall s'' : s'' \sqsubseteq s).s' \sqsubset s'' \supset \varphi_1[s''].$$
$$sometime(\varphi, s) \stackrel{\text{def}}{=} (\exists s' : s' \sqsubset s) \, \varphi[s'].$$
$$always(\varphi, s) \stackrel{\text{def}}{=} (\forall s' : s' \sqsubset s) \, \varphi[s'].$$

It is easy to see that these formulas are strictly bounded by s.

We are now ready to define nonMarkovian Action Precondition Axioms and Successor State Axioms.

Definition 5 An *action precondition axiom* is a sentence of the form:
$$Poss(A(x_1, \ldots, x_n), s) \equiv \Pi_A(x_1, \ldots, x_n, s),$$
where A is an n-ary action function symbol and $\Pi_A(x_1, \ldots, x_n, s)$ is a first order formula with free variables among $x_1, \ldots, x_n, s$ that is bounded by a situation term rooted at s and does not mention the predicate symbol $Poss$.

Example 3 Suppose that there is a lab where the robot works whose door should not be opened if the temperature inside reached some dangerous level d since it was closed. The robot's theory would include a precondition axiom:
$$Poss(open(Lab1), s) \equiv (\exists s' : do(close(Lab1), s') \sqsubseteq s).$$
$$(\forall s'' : s'' \sqsubset s)\neg(s' \sqsubset do(open(Lab1), s'')) \wedge$$
$$(\forall s'' : s'' \sqsubset s).s' \sqsubset s'' \supset temp(Lab1, s'') < d.$$

Definition 6 A *successor state axiom* for an $(n+1)$-ary relational fluent F is a sentence of the form:
$$F(x_1, \ldots, x_n, do(a, s)) \equiv \Phi_F(x_1, \ldots, x_n, a, s),$$
where $\Phi_F(x_1, \ldots, x_n, a, s)$ is a first order formula with free variables among $x_1, \ldots, x_n, a, s$ that is strictly bounded by s and does not mention constant S_0 nor the predicate symbol $Poss$.

A *successor state axiom* for an $(n+1)$-ary functional fluent f is a sentence of the form:
$$f(x_1, \ldots, x_n, do(a, s)) = y \equiv \phi_f(x_1, \ldots, x_n, y, a, s),$$

---

[3] We use $\sigma \sqsubseteq \sigma'$ as an abbreviation for $\sigma = \sigma' \vee \sigma \sqsubset \sigma'$.

where $\phi_f(x_1, \ldots, x_n, y, a, s)$ is a first order formula with free variables among $x_1, \ldots, x_n, y, a, s$ that is strictly bounded by s and does not mention constant S_0 nor the predicate symbol $Poss$.

Example 4 Consider again the robot that works at a biore-search lab. One of the successor state axioms in its theory could be (using the past temporal logic abbreviations from Example 2):

$polluted(mat, do(a, s)) \equiv polluted(mat, s) \lor$
$a = touch(mat) \land (\exists loc).safetyLevel(loc, Low) \land$
$since(\neg atLoc(DisinfSt), atLoc(loc), s)$.

Relaxing the strict boundedness condition in successor state axioms to simply boundedness, complicates regression. Consider the following successor state axioms:

$P(do(a, s)) \equiv (\exists s' : s' \sqsubset s) \, Q(do([B_1, B_2, B_3], s'))$.
$Q(do(a, s)) \equiv (\exists s' : s' \sqsubset s) \, P(do([C_1, C_2, C_3], s'))$.

Intuitively, "regressing" $P(do[A_1, A_2], S_0)$ with respect to the above axioms would result in $Q(do([B_1, B_2, B_3], S_0))$ and this in turn in $P([C_1, C_2, C_3], S_0) \lor P([B_1, C_1, C_2, C_3], S_0)$. Clearly, regression is not working here since the situation terms are growing. This is not a problem in action precondition axioms because the predicate $Poss$ is not allowed in formula Π, so this kind of "loop" as the above cannot occur.

A *nonMarkovian Basic Action Theory* $\mathcal{D}$ consists of: the foundational axioms Σ; a set of successor state axioms $\mathcal{D}_{ss}$, one for each relational fluent and functional fluent; a set of action precondition axioms $\mathcal{D}_{ap}$, one for each action; a set of unique name axioms for actions $\mathcal{D}_{una}$; and a set of first order sentences $\mathcal{D}_{S_0}$ that mention no situation terms other than S_0 and represent the initial theory of the world. NonMarkovian basic action theories, as the Markovian ones, are assumed to satisfy the *functional fluent consistency property* which intuitively says that for each fluent f, the rhs of its successor state axiom, ϕ_f, defines one and only one value for f in situation $do(a, s)$.

The following theorem formalizes the intuition that the truth value of a formula that is strictly bounded by some history, depends only on the truth value of fluents throughout such history and on situation independent predicates and functions.

Theorem 1 Let S, S' be structures of $\mathcal{L}_{sitcalc}$ with the same domain Act for sort *action*, Obj for sort *object* and Sit for sort *situation*. Let $\mathfrak{s} \in Sit$ and $\mathfrak{S} = \{\mathfrak{s}\} \cup \{\mathfrak{s}' \in Sit | \mathfrak{s}' \sqsubset^S \mathfrak{s}\}$. Further, let $\phi(\vec{x}, \sigma)$ be an $\mathcal{L}_{sitcalc}$ formula strictly bounded by σ that does not mention $Poss$[4] and whose only free variable of sort *situation*, if any, is the root of σ. If,

1. S and S' satisfy Σ and $\mathcal{D}_{una}$, and interpret all situation independent functions and predicates the same way;

2. for each relational fluent $F(\vec{x}, s)$ and valuation v such that $v(s) \in \mathfrak{S}$,
$S, v \models F(\vec{x}, s)$ iff $S', v \models F(\vec{x}, s)$

---

[4] $Poss$ can be allowed to appear in $\phi(\vec{x}, \sigma)$ by adding a condition similar to (2) on this predicate.

3. for each functional fluent $f(\vec{x}, s)$ and valuation v such that $v(s) \in \mathfrak{S}$,[5]
$f^S(\vec{x}[v], v(s)) = f^{S'}(\vec{x}[v], v(s))$

then, for every valuation v such that for some situation variable s, $v(s) \in \mathfrak{S}$, $S, v \models (s = \sigma)$ and $S', v \models (s = \sigma)$, $S, v \models \phi(\vec{x}, \sigma)$ iff $S', v \models \phi(\vec{x}, \sigma)$.

For Markovian basic action theories, Pirri and Reiter (1999) proved that a satisfiable initial database and unique names axioms for actions remains satisfiable after adding the action precondition and successor state axioms. NonMarkovian basic action theories satisfy this property as well.

Theorem 2 A nonMarkovian basic action theory $\mathcal{D}$ is satisfiable iff $\mathcal{D}_{una} \cup \mathcal{D}_{S_0}$ is.

Regression

In this section we define a *regression operator* $\mathcal{R}$, based on the operator for Markovian theories, for regressing bounded formulas of $\mathcal{L}_{sitcalc}$ with respect to a nonMarkovian basic action theory.

Definition 7 A formula W of $\mathcal{L}_{sitcalc}$ is *regressable* iff

1. W is first order.
2. W is bounded by a term of sort *situation* rooted at S_0 and has no free variables of this sort.
3. For every atom of the form $Poss(\alpha, \sigma)$ mentioned by W, α has the form $A(t_1, \ldots, t_n)$ for some n-ary action function symbol A of $\mathcal{L}_{sitcalc}$.

In the following definitions and proofs, we assume that quantified variables have been renamed and are all different.

Definition 8 *(Regression)* Let W be a regressable formula of $\mathcal{L}_{sitcalc}$.

1. If W is a regressable atom[6] of one of the following forms:
   - an equality atom of the form: $do([\alpha'_1, \ldots, \alpha'_m], S_0) = do([\alpha_1, \ldots, \alpha_n], S_0)$,
   - a $\sqsubset$-atom of the form: $do([\alpha'_1, \ldots, \alpha'_m], S_0) \sqsubset do([\alpha_1, \ldots, \alpha_n], S_0)$, • an atom $Poss(A(\vec{t}), \sigma)$,
   - an atom whose only situation term is S_0,
   - an atom that mentions a functional fluent term of the form $g(\vec{t}, do(\alpha, \sigma))$,
   - a relational fluent atom $F(\vec{t}, do(\alpha, \sigma))$,
   then $\mathcal{R}[W]$ is defined exactly as for theories with the Markov property so we will not reproduce it here.

2. Suppose W is a regressable formula of the form $(\exists s : do([\alpha_1, \ldots, \alpha_m], s) \sqsubset do([\alpha'_1, \ldots, \alpha'_n], S_0)) \, W'$. If $m \geq n$, then $\mathcal{R}[W] = false$. If $m < n$, then $\mathcal{R}[W] =$

$$\mathcal{R}[(\exists s : do([\alpha_1, \ldots, \alpha_m], s) = do([\alpha'_1, \ldots, \alpha'_{n-1}], S_0)) \, W'] \lor$$
$$\mathcal{R}[(\exists s : do([\alpha_1, \ldots, \alpha_m], s) \sqsubset do([\alpha'_1, \ldots, \alpha'_{n-1}], S_0)) \, W'].$$

---

[5] We use $\vec{x}[v]$ to denote $v(x_1), \ldots, v(x_n)$ where the x_i's are the variables in $\vec{x}$.

[6] Notice that situation variables may not appear in a regressable atom.

3. Suppose W is a regressable formula of the form:
$(\exists s : do([\alpha_1, \ldots, \alpha_m], s) = do([\alpha'_1, \ldots, \alpha'_n], S_0))\, W'$.
where $m \geq 1$.
If $m > n$, then $\mathcal{R}[W] = false$.
If $m \leq n$, then $\mathcal{R}[W] =$

$$\mathcal{R}[(\exists s : s = do([\alpha'_1, \ldots, \alpha'_{n-m}], S_0)) \\ \alpha_1 = \alpha'_{n-m+1} \wedge \ldots \wedge \alpha_m = \alpha'_n \wedge W'].$$

4. Suppose W is a regressable formula of the form:
$(\exists s : s = do([\alpha_1, \ldots, \alpha_n], S_0))\, W'$.
Then $\mathcal{R}[W] = \mathcal{R}[W'|^s_{do([\alpha_1, \ldots, \alpha_n], S_0)}]$.

5. For the remaining possibilities, regression is defined as follows:
$\mathcal{R}[\neg W] = \neg \mathcal{R}[W]$,
$\mathcal{R}[W_1 \wedge W_2] = \mathcal{R}[W_1] \wedge \mathcal{R}[W_2]$.
$\mathcal{R}[(\exists v)W] = (\exists v)\mathcal{R}[W]$.

Theorem 3 Suppose W is a regressable formula of $\mathcal{L}_{sitcalc}$ and $\mathcal{D}$ is a basic nonMarkovian action theory. Then,

1. $\mathcal{R}[W]$ is a formula uniform in S_0.[7]

2. $\mathcal{D} \models (\forall)W \equiv \mathcal{R}[W]$.

Proof 1 This proof is similar to the proof of soundness and completeness of regression for Markovian theories of action from (Pirri & Reiter 1999). We use induction based on a binary relation $\prec$ that is an ordering on tuples of integers that represent the number of connectives, quantifiers, the length of certain situation terms, etc., in formulas. We will not give a precise definition of $\prec$ here. Let us define the tuples $\prec$ is defined on.

Given a bounded regressable formula W, let $L(W)$ be the sum of the lengths of all maximal situation terms σ rooted at a variable s in W such that σ does not appear in W through one of the abbreviations (1) with s being quantified.

Define $index(W)$ as follows:

$$index(W) \stackrel{\text{def}}{=} ((C, E, I, \lambda_1, \lambda_2, \ldots), P).$$

where C is the number of connectives and quantifiers in W, E is the number of equality atoms on situation terms in W, I is the number of $\sqsubset$-atoms on situation terms in W, for $m \geq 1$, λ_m is the number of occurrences in W of maximal situation terms of length $m - L(W)$ rooted at S_0, and P the number of $Poss$ atoms mentioned by W.

Our definition of $index(W)$ differs from the one used by Pirri and Reiter in two ways. Parameters E and I appear now before the λs because regressing a fluent may introduce new equality and $\sqsubset$-atoms. More noticeably, the λs here are "shifted" right by $L(W)$, e.g. if there is one term of length k then $\lambda_{k+L(W)} = 1$. Notice that a regression step on a formula with a situation variable may result in a situation term being replaced by a longer one. For instance, the formula $(\exists s : s = do(A, S_0))\, P(do(B, s))$ would be regressed to $P(do([A, B], S_0))$. The λs are shifted to discount this increase in length when substituting variables with ground terms.

---

[7]A formula is uniform in σ iff it is first order, does not mention $Poss$, $\sqsubset$, situation variables, equality on situations, and σ is the only situation term mentioned by fluents in their situation argument. For the formal definition see (Pirri & Reiter 1999).

Consider a regressable formula W. Assume the theorem for all regressable formulas with index $\prec index(W)$. Due to space limitations, we prove here only the following case: Suppose W is a regressable formula of the form $(\exists s : s = do([\alpha_1, \ldots, \alpha_n], S_0))W'$. $\mathcal{R}[W]$ is defined as the regression of the formula $W'' = W'|^s_{do([\alpha_1, \ldots, \alpha_n], S_0)}$. If W' is empty ($True$), the result follows immediately. Otherwise, it must be a formula bounded by a situation term rooted at s. Hence W'' is clearly regressable.

It remains to show that $index(W'') \prec index(W)$. The value of P is clearly the same for both formulas. Let us show that the λ's are the same as well. Consider a maximal term $do(\vec{\alpha}_1, s)$ from W' and let m be its length. Let $do(\vec{\alpha}_2, S_0)$ stand for $do([\alpha_1, \ldots, \alpha_n], S_0)$ and W^* for $W'|^{do(\vec{\alpha}_1, s)}_{do(\vec{\alpha}_1, do(\vec{\alpha}_2, S_0))}$. Note that $n + L(W)$ is the index of the value λ that accounts for term $do(\vec{\alpha}_2, S_0)$ in $index(W)$ and $n + m + L(W^*)$ the index of the value λ that accounts for $do(\vec{\alpha}_1, do(\vec{\alpha}_2, S_0))$. Also, since $L(W^*) = L(W) - m$, $n + L(W) = n + m + L(W^*)$. This implies that after the substitution that results in W^* the λ's are the same. Since this is true after the substitution of any term rooted at s, $index(W)$ and $index(W'')$ have the same λ's. Hence that $index(W'')$ differs from $index(W)$ only in the values of C and E which are both smaller in $index(W'')$. Therefore, $index(W'') \prec index(W)$ and the induction hypothesis applies. Finally, the formulas W and W'' are clearly equivalent. $\qquad\square$

Soundness and completeness of the regression operator $\mathcal{R}$ follow from Theorems 2 and 3. This is established in the following theorem:

Theorem 4 Suppose W is a regressable sentence of $\mathcal{L}_{sitcalc}$ and $\mathcal{D}$ is a basic nonMarkovian theory of actions. Then, $\mathcal{D} \models W$ iff $\mathcal{D}_{S_0} \cup \mathcal{D}_{una} \models \mathcal{R}[W]$.

Conclusion

We have generalized Reiter's situation calculus based formalization of actions (Reiter 1991; Pirri & Reiter 1999) to allow nonMarkovian action theories, i.e. theories where action precondition and successor state axioms may refer to past situations. We revised the class of formulas that can be regressed and modified the regression operator to work with this class of formulas and action theories. Finally, we prove the soundness and completeness of this regression operator.

As we mentioned in the introduction, most of the proposals that have been introduced for reasoning about actions assume the Markov Property. Removing this assumption from Reiter's basic action theories without major complications was possible because histories are first order objects in these theories. Removing this assumption from other formalizations where this is not the case would require considerably more effort. For example, the action languages based on $\mathcal{A}$ (Gelfond & Lifschitz 1993) have semantics based on state-to-state transitions. So removing the Markovian assumption seems to require a different kind of semantics. An exeption are the languages in (Giunchiglia & Lifschitz 1995; Mendez et al. 1996). The former does not allow one to specify in the language that the value of a fluent depends on the history. The latter does. Both of these languages have semantics based on mappings from sequences of actions to states. This type of semantics was abandoned in more recent $\mathcal{A}$-type action languages in favor of state-to-state mappings.

Although it may be possible to transform a nonMarkovian action theory into a Markovian one by introducing new fluents, the resulting theory can be considerably more complex, having more predicates and successor state axioms. Moreover, it may not necessarily be computationally better. For instance, regressing the atom $sometimeP(do(\alpha, S_0))$ with respect to a Markovian theory that has a successor state axiom $sometimeP(do(a, s)) \equiv P(s) \vee sometimeP(s)$ results in a disjunction of the same size as regressing the bounded formula $(\exists s' : s' \sqsubset do(\alpha, S_0))P(s')$. A thorough analysis of the computational tradeoffs is among our plans for future work along with a proof of the correctness of a Prolog implementation of our interpreter for non-Markovian basic action theories. We also plan to explore extensions of Golog/ConGolog (Levesque *et al.* 1997; Giacomo, Lesperance, & Levesque 1997) with nonMarkovian features. These languages are used to program complex behaviours in terms of the primitive actions of a basic action theory. In order to execute Golog/ConGolog programs with respect to a nonMarkovian basic action theory, one simply needs to append the interpreter for such action theories to the Golog/ConGolog interpreter. Such an interpreter is used by Kiringa (Kiringa 2001) in his database transaction systems simulations. Moreover, as mentioned in the introduction, they can be extended with temporal test conditions.

Acknowledgments

We are thankful to Ray Reiter and the members of the Cognitive Robotics group at the U. of Toronto. We also thank the anonymous referees for their useful comments.

References

Bacchus, F., and Kabanza, F. 1996. Using temporal logic to control search in a forward chaining planner. In Ghallab, M., and Milani, A., eds., *New Directions in Planning*. IOS Press. 141–153.

Bacchus, F., and Kabanza, F. 2000. Using temporal logics to express search control knowledge for planning. *Artificial Intelligence* 16:123–191.

Bacchus, F.; Boutilier, C.; and Grove, A. 1996. Rewarding behaviors. In *Procs. of 13th National Conference on Artificial Intelligence (AAAI-96)*, 1160–1167.

Bacchus, F.; Boutilier, C.; and Grove, A. 1997. Structured solution methods for non-markovian decision processes. In *Procs. 14th National Conference on Artpificial Intelligence (AAAI-97)*, 112–117.

Chomicki, J. 1995. Efficient checking of temporal integrity constraints using bounded history encoding. *ACM Transactions on Database Systems* 20(2):148–186.

Gelfond, M., and Lifschitz, V. 1993. Representing Actions and Change by Logic Programs. *Journal of Logic Programming* 17:301–322.

Giacomo, G. D.; Lesperance, Y.; and Levesque, H. J. 1997. Reasoning about concurrent execution, prioritized interrupts, and exogenous actions in the situation calculus. In Pollack, M., ed., *Proceedings of the 15th International Joint Conference on Artificial Intelligence (IJCAI-97)*, 1221–1226. Morgan Kaufmann.

Giunchiglia, E., and Lifschitz, V. 1995. Dependent fluents. In *Proceedings of IJCAI-95*, 1964–1969.

Kiringa, I. 2001. Simulation of advanced transaction models using Golog. In *Procs. 8th Biennial Workshop on Data Bases and Programming Languages (DBPL'01)*.

Kowalski, R., and Sergot, M. 1986. A logic-based calculus of events. *New Generation Computing* 4(1):67–95.

Levesque, H. J.; Reiter, R.; Lespérance, Y.; Lin, F.; and Scherl, R. B. 1997. Golog: A logic programming language for dynamic domains. *Journal of Logic Programming* 31(1–3):59–83.

McCarthy, J., and Hayes, P. 1969. Some philosophical problems from the standpoint of artificial intelligence. In Meltzer, B., and Michie, D., eds., *Machine Intelligence 4*. Edinburgh University Press. 463–502. Also appears in N. Nilsson and B. Webber (editors), Readings in Artificial Intelligence, Morgan-Kaufmann.

McCarthy, J. 1963. Situations, actions and causal laws. Technical report, Stanford University. Reprinted in Semantic Information Processing (M. Minsky ed.), MIT Press, Cambridge, Mass., 1968, pp. 410–417.

McCarthy, J. 1992. Elephant 2000: A programming language based on speech acts. Available at http://www-formal.stanford.edu/jmc/.

Mendez, G.; Lobo, J.; Llopis, J.; and Baral, C. 1996. Temporal logic and reasoning about actions. In *Third Symposium on Logical Formalizations of Commonsense Reasoning Commonsense 96*.

Pirri, F., and Reiter, R. 1999. Some contributions to the metatheory of the Situation Calculus. *Journal of the ACM* 46(3):325–364.

Reiter, R. 1991. The frame problem in the situation calculus: A simple solution (sometimes) and a completeness result for goal regression. In Lifschitz, V., ed., *Artificial Intelligence and Mathematical Theory of Computation*. Academic Press. 359–380.

Reiter, R. 2001. *Knowledge in Action: Logical Foundations for Describing and Implementing Dynamical Systems*. Cambridge, MA: MIT Press.

Saake, G., and Lipeck, U. W. 1988. Foundations of Temporal Integrity Monitoring. In Rolland, C.; Bodart, F.; and Leonard, M., eds., *Proc. of the IFIP Working Conf. on Temporal Aspects in Information Systems*, 235–249. Amsterdam: North-Holland.

Sandewall, E. 1994. *Features and Fluents: The Representation of Knowledge about Dynamical Systems*. Oxford University Press.

Thielscher, M. 1998. Introduction to the fluent calculus. *Linköping Electronic Articles in Computer and Information Science* 3(14). http://www.ep.liu.se/ea/cis/1998/'1'/.

Probabilistic and Causal Reasoning

Visual Exploration and Incremental Utility Elicitation

Jim Blythe

USC Information Sciences Institute
4676 Admiralty Way, Marina del Rey, CA 90292
blythe@isi.edu

Abstract

Incremental utility elicitation (IUE) is a decision-theoretic framework in which tools simultaneously make suggestions to a human decision maker based on an incomplete model of the decision maker's utility function, and update the model based on feedback from the user. Most systems that perform IUE construct and ask questions about a small number of alternatives in order to build a model of the user's preferences. We describe a system called VEIL that is based on visual exploration of the available alternatives and provides visual cues about their estimated utility based on IUE. VEIL uses a linear programming formulation to make fast updates to the utility estimate based on the user's expressed preferences between pairs of alternatives. In experiments, VEIL's update method converges quickly to make good suggestions and help the user form an overall impression of the space of alternatives.

Introduction

Decision theory is a well-tested approach to helping a user choose from a set of alternatives when the user's preference structure is known. The preferences are usually represented as a utility function on the set of alternatives such that the user prefers an alternative exactly when it has higher utility. In cases where the utility function is unknown or partially known, it must be elicited from the user in order for decision theory to be applicable, and this can often be a time-consuming process that has unknown payoff for the user.

Systems based on incremental utility elicitation (IUE) interleave utility elicitation with applying the current utility model to the set of alternatives in order to make suggestions (Chajewska, Koller, & Parr 2000; Linden *et al.* 1997; Ha & Haddawy 1997). With this approach, the system can make suggestions to users from the start, often based on a default utility, and can improve its suggestions over time as new information is gathered about the utility. Incremental utility elicitation can also be more focused than elicitation made prior to decision making, because users may recognize that an optimal or near-optimal solution has been found even though the system does not have the full, potentially complex utility model.

Most existing systems using IUE follow an approach where only a small number of alternatives is shown to the user at one time. Some of these approaches are based on the standard gamble elicitation technique (von Neumann & Morgenstern 1967), in which the utility of one outcome is ascertained by comparing it to a lottery involving two others. Others are inspired by instances of decision making involving human agents, for example a travel agent, where only a few options are explicitly discussed because of the limitations of the telephone or email. Decision makers often benefit from an information-rich environment that shows a considerable range of alternatives, or from more detailed information about the space of alternatives than is used in these techniques. A visualization of the alternatives can be employed to help users make choices when there are many multi-variate alternatives (Ahlberg & Shneiderman 1994; Pu & Faltings 2000). However, these techniques are typically based on incremental query construction, and most do not provide feedback on the utility of the alternatives.

We present an implemented system, VEIL[1], that provides a visualization of many alternatives that emphasizes some of their important features, and uses incremental utility elicitation to build a model of the user's preferences and make suggestions. This work has three main contributions. First is the use of a visual exploration tool to display alternatives combined with incremental utility elicitation. The user can view alternatives through either custom or user-generated two-dimensional projections and can drill down on the information about a particular alternative. At the same time visual feedback is presented on the system's current utility estimates for all the displayed alternatives. The user can provide utility information either by changing weights or by indicating a preference between two alternatives directly in the interface. We show by example that the richer information environment can help users make better decisions more quickly.

Second, we describe a novel scheme for utility updates based on the set of preferences from the user. The system represents a utility function as a linear combination of constraint features. The update scheme maintains the utility weights as the vector solution of a linear programming problem whose constraints correspond to the user's prefer-

---

[1] Visual Exploration and Incremental eLicitation

ence vectors. This leads to an efficient update scheme that maintains an incremental utility estimate that is relatively stable, and provides a efficient test for violation of the linear utility assumption.

Third, the system uses a more expressive language than many systems performing incremental utility elicitation. The utility model is a linear combination of attributes that are themselves open to modification and creation by the user. For example, while preferring low cost alternatives in a travel planning system, the user can easily incorporate a discount on certain airlines in the computation of flight cost, essentially linking the two attributes. Tools provided in Constable (Blythe *et al.* 2001) allow the attributes to be modified or new attributes to be defined through an English paraphrase. The system will also suggest modifications to the attributes when the assumption of a linearly additive utility is violated.

In the next section we discuss existing systems for interactive utility elicitation and describe the flight planning domain, used for examples in this paper. Next we describe the VEIL tool that integrates visual exploration and IUE and show an example of a user's interaction with the system. The next section describes the utility vector update scheme used in VEIL, followed by empirical results with different update algorithms and different measures of convergence. Next we show how users can edit the attributes used in the utility vector and how changes are suggested by the tool. Finally we discuss the relation to existing approaches and describe possible future work.

Incremental utility elicitation

In the general multi-attribute decision problem (Keeney & Raiffa 1993) we have a set O of outcomes and a set S of strategies, each of which has an associated probability distribution over the outcomes. Our aim is to find a strategy that is preferred by the user based on her preference structure over outcomes. We assume the user is rational, so the preferences can be expressed by a utility function $u^*()$ that maps O to the real numbers, such that outcome o_1 is preferred to o_2 if and only if $u^*(o_1) > u^*(o_2)$. The outcomes are described by a set of attributes A where each $a_i \in A$ is a function $a_i : O \to \text{domain}(a_i)$. The utility $u^*()$ is assumed to be a function of the attributes. We do not have access to the user's true utility $u^*()$ but instead create a model $u'()$ based on information from the user. We refer to $u'(o)$ as the *estimated utility* of o. In the rest of this paper, we assume a correspondence between strategies and outcomes, so the user task is to choose an outcome. We refer to the outcomes as alternatives.

Choosing a round-trip flight between two locations is an example of this problem. The set O of alternatives is the set of available flights, described by attributes like cost, time of departure and airline. Many tools exist on the web that can retrieve flights and allow the user to browse them through a fixed scheme, for example for browsing by price, airline, or time of departure or arrival. However these sites can easily generate thousands of flights for a query and a fixed browsing scheme can be cumbersome if it does not match the user's requirements (Pu & Faltings 2000).

Visual exploration of alternatives

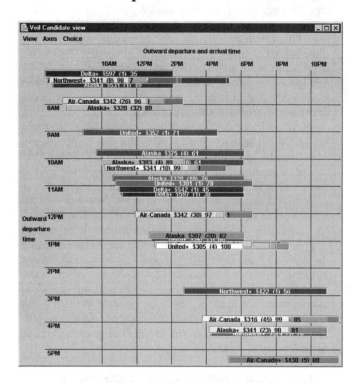

Figure 1: A projection of the alternative flights by outbound departure time, with width showing outbound duration and with grey-scale coloring according to the initial estimated utility.

In the VEIL system, users interact with a two-dimensional projection of the alternatives corresponding to two attributes used for the x and y coordinates, and optionally others depicted with shape, width, height and a textual label. For example, Figure 1 shows a projection of alternatives for a round-trip flight from Los Angeles to Victoria, British Columbia. In this projection, both x and y coordinates are based on the outbound departure time, while the width of each bar shows the duration of the outbound flight. Users can change the projection at any time by choosing the attributes to use for each axis, and the projection is automatically scaled — this layout was chosen because no rectangle is likely to completely obscure another. The flight data were retrieved from the web using wrappers, and represent 500 alternatives. However, since many round-trip flights share the same outbound leg, only 91 distinct alternatives are visible and each visible rectangle accounts for a group of 5 flights on average. The label on each rectangle first shows the airline and cost of the represented flight that has the maximum estimated utility for the group. Next to the cost is shown the number of separate alternatives in the group, and finally the maximum estimated utility, re-scaled to range from 0 to 100. Users can select a rectangle to bring it to the front of the display or to see more information about that choice in a separate window.

This display broadly follows the Star field approach (Ahlberg & Shneiderman 1994), which is a popular technique for displaying large sets of multi-attribute data. We chose to organize alternatives spatially by two attributes because the attributes in travel planning carry intuitive meaning. Other display methods use techniques such as multidimensional scaling that project the alternatives onto two dimensions in a more flexible way (Marks *et al.* 1997). While these approaches can place items more efficiently and avoid occlusion, it is harder to draw conclusions about the attributes of items from their positions.

Two features of the layout are chosen to help the user find high-utility alternatives easily. First, the grey-scale shading of each rectangle is chosen to represent its rank in the ordering based on utility, with the best alternative in white and the worst in black. Second, because the layout of alternatives is directly proportional to two attributes, the rectangles for alternatives may overlap as in Figure 1. When this happens, the alternative with higher estimated utility is placed on top.

Figure 1 shows a default utility that minimizes cost and the outbound and return flight durations, with equal weight after the attributes are normalized. The display provides the user with summary information despite the large number of alternatives. For instance, there are good flights leaving at regular intervals through the day until about 4pm. The preferred option according to the default utility is the United flight leaving at 1pm.

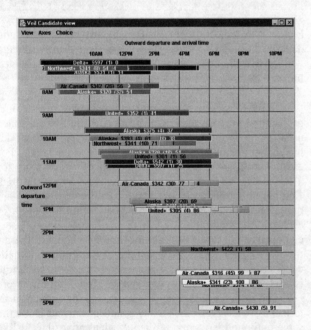

Figure 2: Choices with grey-scale shading according to the adjusted utility

For the purpose of finding an optimal solution, the value of this tool is limited by how well the utility estimate matches the user's true utility. The user can update the utility estimate directly, through a window where each attribute and its weight is shown and can be changed. The utility can also be updated indirectly by stating a direct preference on the alternatives displayed on the screen. In this example, the user prefers to depart as late as possible, and expresses this

as a preference for the Air Canada flight departing at 1pm over the flight departing at 12pm. Figure 2 shows the resulting utility estimate that has been adjusted to take this preference into account. Preferred flights are now mostly found in the lower right corner of the screen, and the new preferred alternative is the Alaska flight leaving after 4pm. The next section describes how the utility function is updated based on the preference.

Using estimated utilities to both order and highlight good flights significantly helps users in the task of searching for good flights. As an illustration, we inspected a version of the display in Figure 1 but with uniform colors and a random ordering of overlapping rectangles. Since some flights were obscured, we found either a Northwest flight leaving at 4pm or a United flight leaving at 1pm. The option suggested by the tool is significantly better than these.

Interaction style

Can the graphical system support the same kind of interactions that decision makers are used to? We analyzed an email conversation with a travel planner to pick a flight, fragments of which are shown below, and compared the activities it contained with the types of interaction supported by our tool. The activities can all be classified as seeking or providing information, either about available alternatives or about the utility function.

The first passage suggests an option, explains why it cannot be improved on one dimension but suggests an alternative that improves on this feature by making other compromises. This suggestion also elicits utility information.

Here is a tentative itinerary. Leaving Victoria on the 22nd, can't get much later due to the time change and flight times from Seattle - DC. There is a red-eye that leaves at 10.30pm out of Seattle if you are interested in leaving later?

VEIL suggests options with high estimated utility but does not offer explanatory information. The reply both provides utility information about specific domain attributes and seeks information about alternatives.

Thanks. Is there anything later leaving on the 20th? [outbound leg]. The flight from Victoria to Dulles is ok, I don't want a red-eye.

VEIL allows preferences between options to change utility weights, providing this information as we showed with the example above. The information sought could be found from a projection of the alternatives.

Updating the utility model

As well as directly changing weights an alternatives, the user can update the utility by expressing a direct preference on alternatives in the display, as described above. This is sometimes preferable because the user does not need an explicit understanding of the relative weights of different features in the utility function. It can also provide more information because in addition to indicating attributes whose weights should change, it also gives a lower bound on the amount of change required in order to accomodate the new preference.

VEIL uses a linear estimate for utility, so

$$u'(o) = \sum_{i=1}^{n} w_i u_i(o)$$

where the utility function has n components $u_i()$, and w_i is the weight attached to the ith component. For example, one component might be the cost of a flight, another might be its duration and a third might encode a preference over the airline used. The components are normalized so that each ranges from 0 to 1 in value over all outcomes under consideration.

For convenience we identify the outcome o with the vector of component utility functions $\mathbf{o} = (u_i(o), 1 \le i \le n)$, and write the summation as a dot product, so $u'(o) = \mathbf{w'}.\mathbf{o}$, the dot product of the weight and utility vectors. When a new pairwise preference is introduced to the system, say $\mathbf{a} > \mathbf{b}$ for alternatives $\mathbf{a}$ and $\mathbf{b}$, this is interpreted as a linear constraint on $\mathbf{w'}$:

$$\mathbf{w'}.\mathbf{a} > \mathbf{w'}.\mathbf{b}$$

so

$$\mathbf{w'}.(\mathbf{a} - \mathbf{b}) > 0$$

We refer to $\mathbf{a} - \mathbf{b}$ as the *preference vector*. Each preference vector therefore induces a linear constraint on the weight vector $\mathbf{w'}$, a half-space in which $\mathbf{w'}$ must lie. There is a solution for $\mathbf{w'}$ if and only if the polytope defined by the intersection of the half-spaces orthogonal to each preference vector is non-empty. Any vector lying in the polytope will constitute a solution. However it is computationally expensive to enumerate the faces of the convex hull in more than a few dimensions, so instead we solve a linear programming (LP) problem whose constraints include the preference vectors:

Maximize $\mathbf{c}.\mathbf{w}$
Subject to: $\mathbf{Aw} > \mathbf{0}$,
$\quad -1 \le w_i \le 1$ for $1 \le i \le n$

where the vector $\mathbf{w}$ has n dimensions and the preference matrix $\mathbf{A}$ has rows corresponding to the preference vectors. The final conditions on the w_i ensure that the solution is bounded. If this LP problem is infeasible, then the original assumption of linearity in the utility model is violated. Otherwise, any solution will correspond to a utility function that respects the user's preferences, regardless of the choice of the objective function, specified by the vector $\mathbf{c}$. We adopt the solution $\mathbf{w'}$ as the new utility estimate.

There are several choices for $\mathbf{c}$ that lead to interesting properties for $\mathbf{w'}$. If we choose $\mathbf{c} = \mathbf{w'_o}$, the previous utility estimate, the LP makes the new estimate as close as possible to the old one, leading to a conservative update algorithm. If we choose $\mathbf{c} = \sum_i a_i$, the sum of the preference vectors, the new estimate will be as close as possible to an average of the user's stated preferences. In practice we solve for a small number of different values of $\mathbf{c}$ in order to sample the space of feasible utilities.

Our utility update algorithm adds a new row to the preference matrix $\mathbf{A}$ and solves the new LP problem whenever the user adds a preference. We skip this step if the previous utility is feasible and the objective function would choose it. In VEIL, the LP problems are solved using the Simplex algorithm. Although this is known to have exponential worst-case behavior, the algorithm is often competitive with the polynomial-time interior-point method in practice (Spielman & Teng 2001). We have not found the running time of the LP solver to be a problem, but a potential improvement is to maintain a set of extremal preference vectors, so that the rank of $\mathbf{A}$ is as low as possible while still representing the same polytope.

In most domains we would like the tool to begin with a default utility that captures common preferences, for instance to minimize duration and cost of both outbound and return parts of the roundtrip flight. These are captured by preference vectors that are unioned with the set of user-specified preference vectors. The size of the convex space defined by the vectors can be adjusted to control the latitude that the user has to deviate from the default utility.

Choosing the features to update

The basic update scheme above might produce unexpected utility weights when only a small number of preferences is given in a high-dimensional space. In addition, decision makers can often point to a reason why one alternative is preferred over another, in terms of a subset of the features of the alternatives, although they may find it hard to describe an explicit utility function. To exploit of this information, the user can also nominate a subset of the features whose weights are to be altered when a preference is given. We first attempt to update the utility estimate while modifying only these weights, by solving the linear programming problem created from the original by setting the remaining variables to their values in the current utility estimate. If there is no feasible solution for this more constrained LP we relax the conditions and seek a solution with the original set of non-zero weights.

The nominated subset of attributes is chosen when the user expresses the preference in the alternatives display, through a menu that shows the attributes of the alternatives that could be used as components of the utility function. Attributes that have the same value for the two alternatives are not selectable and are shown greyed out in the menu. Using a subset of features allows a more natural interaction with the decision maker, including expressions like 'I prefer this flight because it arrives later'.

Experiments

VEIL includes two different ways that a decision maker can modify the utility estimate: either by altering the weights directly or by expressing pairwise preferences on the alternatives that are displayed in the visualization. The decision maker must have a good idea of how to interpret her preferences in terms of global weights in order to use the direct approach effectively. Since updates based on pairwise preferences do not require this knowledge, one can ask how much more interaction is generally required for the tool to converge on a utility estimate that well represents the decision maker's preferences. Perhaps surprisingly, our experiments indicate that, in some cases, little extra interaction is required.

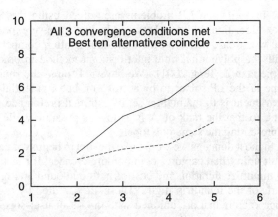

Figure 3: Rates of convergence for utility update based on pairwise preferences, as a function of the number of linear components in the 'true' utility.

Before describing experiments that support this, we discuss notions of convergence for utility estimates. The strictest form of convergence is to ask that the estimated utility and the decision maker's true utility function be identical up to a scale factor (which will not affect preferences). However, a less precise match will generally be adequate for the decision-making task and might require less work from the user. One might measure the utility loss, in terms of the decision maker's true utility, of accepting the suggested alternative based on the estimated utility. However in a visual tool like VEIL, the user will also inspect a number of alternatives apart from the best under the estimated utility.

Therefore we include two other measures of convergence. First, the Kendall rank correlation coefficient τ measures how close are the rankings on the alternatives induced by the two utility functions on the set of available alternatives (Noether 1986). This is the difference of the proportion of pairs of alternatives in the same order in each ranking and the proportion of pairs in the opposite order. The value of τ ranges from 1 for identical rankings to -1 for precisely opposite rankings. For the second measure, we take into account the limited cognitive effort that the decision maker is likely to spend examining alternatives. We assume that the user will check only the best ten items according to the estimated utility, and test whether this coincides with the best ten items in the true utility measure, although perhaps in a different order. There are clearly many variations of these measures that might be appropriate in certain situations, but these are sufficient to compare the rates of convergence of the two utility update schemes in VEIL.

For our experiments, we assumed that the decision maker's true utility is a linear combination of between 2 and 5 features. The features are known to the system, but not their correct weights. The tool begins with a uniform weighting of features and selects a pair of alternatives such that the preference in the true utility is the reverse of the preference in the estimated utility. This preference is used to update the estimated utility using the linear programming technique described above. We considered three convergence measures: the Kendall rank correlation > 0.95, the utility loss zero (*i.e.* a maximally preferred item is selected by the estimated utility), and finally the condition that the best ten alternatives in the true utility are also the best ten under the utility estimate.

For each value of n we ran at least 30 trials with randomly generated utility functions on 500 real flights generated in response to a travel request. The upper line in Figure 3 shows the average number of pairwise preferences that have to be specified for all three convergence measures to be met. It can be seen that the average number of preferences required is one or two more than the number of features involved for this range of values. A direct update to the utility function would require up to $n - 1$ weights to be set, so the amount of interaction required for VEIL to estimate the utility function based on pairwise preferences is comparable. The lower line on the graph shows the average number of preferences required for convergence according to the 'best ten' measure.

In the experiment, knowledge of the true utility was used to select a pair of alternatives whose utilities do not reflect the true preference, a task we expect the user to perform in real use. Global knowledge of the true weights is not necessary for the algorithm to converge, however in order to achieve the convergence rates shown in Figure 3, the pairs were selected so that their utility difference was above a threshold. When random pairs of alternatives were selected, convergence was considerably slower. It seems plausible that users will provide information about preferences that are clearly different from those of the current estimate rather than preferences with only a slight difference, but user experiments are needed to test this hypothesis.

Editing the features for expressivity

The tool makes the assumption that the utility can be modelled as the weighted sum of attribute values. When this assumption is violated, the violation is detected in our utility update scheme when the linear program has no feasible solutions. In this case the tool can suggest ways to change the attributes that are used in the linear sum. First we describe how the features themselves can be changed, with some examples of typical changes.

The attributes that form the linear components of the utility estimate in VEIL are represented as declarative functions written in the EXPECT language (Blythe *et al.* 2001). This system includes tools that allow users to form expressions based on the domain features that include iteration and conditional tests, as well as arithmetic and set theoretic operations. A flight cost utility component can be modified to model a 15% discount on United, for example, or a departure time component can model 'departure time close to 9am or close to 5pm'.

Rather than store the preference vectors directly, VEIL stores the pairs of outcomes for which the user expressed a preference. Thus when the component utility features are changed, the preference vectors corresponding to the outcome pairs can easily be recomputed. The set of preferences nominated by the user is likely to be fairly small, making this approach feasible.

Recovering from a violated linearity assumption

We note that a piecewise linear utility function can be defined to capture at least the ordering of a finite set of alternatives in any utility. The boundaries of the piecewise linear utilities can be represented within each feature computation, preserving the summation form of the overall utility model. When a new preference vector leads to the linearity assumption being violated, we find a minimal set of preference vectors that violate the assumption (ie, are linearly dependent). This must include the most recently added preference vector. Next we look at the features nominated in the preferences, if any, and suggest modifying one of these. For each one, a break-point is suggested with alternative weights on either side, which are chosen so that the corresponding LP is feasible.

Although we treat the violation of the linearity assumption as evidence that the component utility features are inadequate to represent the user's utility, users often enter inconsistent preferences in practice for a variety of reasons. While indicating a minimal set of inconsistent preferences and showing how the utility functions may be adjusted to accomodate them, VEIL may also allow the user to modify the preferences in case they were in error or the user's utility function is changing.

Discussion

VEIL is a decision-making aid that integrates incremental utility elicitation with visual exploration of alternatives. VEIL provides an information-rich environment for the decision maker, while using an incremental utility estimate to help guide the search for a good alternative. The utility estimate can be updated based on preferences that are expressed directly in the exploration tool, or by modifying the weights. The resulting system can make a suggestion at any time, and the user can terminate the session at any time.

VEIL can detect when the linearity assumption is violated and offer suggestions to recover. The recovery strategy may be either to enrich the utility measure or to modify the user's preferences. In this respect, the combination of a visual environment with immediate feedback on changes in the utility model may allow users more quickly to catch mistaken preferences, or those with unexpected consequences.

Although we gave examples and described experiments in the domain of air travel planning, the principles and techniques used are domain independent. VEIL is also being applied to a special operations forces planning domain, but we omit details for reasons of space.

Ha and Haddawy (1997) motivate incremental utility elicitation and describe a system that constructs queries for the user. They propose a heuristic based on rank correlation for choosing the question to ask. Chajewska et al. (2000) describe an approach to incremental utility elicitation that makes use of a prior probability distribution on possible utility models. At each step, their algorithm constructs a question for the user with optimal value of information, stopping when the expected utility loss is below a threshold. Our approach does not assume a prior distribution on utilities, and follows a principle of providing more information and

more control for the decision maker. Thus, we allow users to supply preference information rather than answer queries constructed by the system. Although the system can be terminated at any time, we use stopping criteria that consider the ordering of some or all of the alternatives to show empirical rates of convergence. Hanks et al. (1997) describe the Automated Travel Assistant that presents a shortlist of examples to the user and allows direct updates to the utility weights. Like us, Pu and Faltings (2000) use a visual approach to help a user choose a flight, but they do not make use of utility estimates.

Work in mixed-initiative problem solving also emphasizes shared control between the user and the computer program and has typically been applied to planning or scheduling problems (Ferguson, Allen, & Miller 1996; Anderson *et al.* 2000; Myers 1996). The problem addressed by VEIL is less complex than these, but because of its mixed-initiative strategy it may be an appropriate component in more sophisticated mixed-initiative systems, helping to present results and giving users an opportunity to influence the problem-solving behaviour of the system.

The application of VEIL within more complicated planning and scheduling tasks is something we intend to study in the future. Other areas to explore are how the existence of a population of users or tasks can be exploited within this framework. Intuitively, the utility functions of a decision maker for two different flights are likely to be quite similar, perhaps depending on the destination and purpose of travel. Chajewska et al. (1998) have used clustering techniques that might be applicable in VEIL through the objective functions or constraints used in its linear program formulations. There are also many directions to explore with both the utility update and the visualization portions of VEIL. Our initial work shows this to be a promising approach in an increasingly important research area.

Acknowledgments

Discussions with Yolanda Gil, Jihie Kim and Fred Bobbit were very helpful, as were the comments of the anonymous reviewers. I gratefully acknowledge support from DARPA contracts F30602-00-2-0513 as part of the Active Templates program, and N66001-00-C-8018, with subcontract number 34-000-145 to SRI International, as part of the Rapid Knowledge Formation program.

References

Ahlberg, C., and Shneiderman, B. 1994. Visual information seeking: Tight coupling of dynamic query filters with starfield displays. In *Human Factors in Computing Systems. Conference Proceedings CHI'94*, 313–317.

Anderson, D.; Anderson, E.; Lesh, N.; Marks, J.; Mirtich, B.; Ratajczak, D.; and Ryall, K. 2000. Human-guided simple search. In *Proc. Seventeenth National Conference on Artificial Intelligence.* AAAI Press.

Blythe, J.; Kim, J.; Ramachandran, S.; and Gil, Y. 2001. An integrated environment for knowledge acquisition. In *Proc. Conference on Intelligent User Interfaces.*

Chajewska, U.; Getoor, L.; Norman, J.; and Shahar, Y. 1998. Utility elicitation as a classification problem. In *Proc. Fourtheenth Conference on Uncertainty in Artificial Intelligence*, 79–88. Madison, Wisconsin: Morgan Kaufmann.

Chajewska, U.; Koller, D.; and Parr, R. 2000. Making rational decisions using adaptive utility elicitation. In *Proc. Seventeenth National Conference on Artificial Intelligence*, 363–369. AAAI Press.

Ferguson, G.; Allen, J.; and Miller, B. 1996. Trains-95: Towards a mixed-initiative planning assistant. In Drabble, B., ed., *Proc. Third International Conference on Artificial Intelligence Planning Systems*. University of Edinburgh: AAAI Press.

Ha, V., and Haddawy, P. 1997. Problem-focused incremental elicitation of multi-attribute utility models. In Besnard, P., and Hanks, S., eds., *Proc. Thirteenth Conference on Uncertainty in Artificial Intelligence*, 215–222. Providence, Rhode Island: Morgan Kaufmann.

Keeney, R., and Raiffa, H. 1993. *Decisions With Multiple Objectives*. The Pitt Building, Trumpington Street, Cambridge, UK: Cambridge University Press.

Linden, G.; Hanks, S.; ; and Lesh, N. 1997. Interactive assessment of user preference models: The automated travel assistant. Sixth International Conference on User Modelling.

Marks, J.; Andalman, B.; Beardsley, P.; Freeman, W.; Gibson, S.; Hodgins, J.; and T.Kang. 1997. Design galleries: A general approach to setting parameters for computer graphics and animation. In *Proc. of SIGGRAPH*, 389–400.

Myers, K. 1996. Strategic advice for hierarchical planners. In *Proceedings of the International Conference on Knowledge Representation*.

Noether, G. E. 1986. Why kendall tau? In *Best of Teaching Statistics*. Teaching Statistics. available at http://science.ntu.ac.uk/rsscse/TS/bts/noether/text.html.

Pu, P., and Faltings, B. 2000. Enriching buyers' experiences: the smartclient approach. In *ACM CHI Conference on Human Factors in Computing Systems*, 289–296.

Spielman, D., and Teng, S.-H. 2001. Smoothed analysis: Why the simplex algorithm usually takes polynomial time. In *The Thirty-Third Annual ACM Symposium on Theory of Computing*, 296–305.

von Neumann, J., and Morgenstern, O. 1967. *Theory of Games and Economic Behaviour*. Princeton University Press, 3rd edition.

A Graphical Criterion for the Identification of Causal Effects in Linear Models

Carlos Brito and Judea Pearl
Cognitive Systems Laboratory
Computer Science Department
University of California, Los Angeles, CA 90024
fisch@cs.ucla.edu judea@cs.ucla.edu

Abstract

This paper concerns the assessment of direct causal effects from a combination of: (i) non-experimental data, and (ii) qualitative domain knowledge. Domain knowledge is encoded in the form of a directed acyclic graph (DAG), in which all interactions are assumed linear, and some variables are presumed to be unobserved. The paper establishes a sufficient criterion for the identifiability of all causal effects in such models as well as a procedure for estimating the causal effects from the observed covariance matrix.

Introduction

This paper explores the feasibility of inferring linear cause-effect relationships from various combinations of data and theoretical assumptions. The assumptions considered will be represented in the form of an acyclic causal diagram which contains both arrows and bi-directed arcs (Pearl 1995; 2000). The arrows represent the potential existence of direct causal relationships between the corresponding variables, and the bi-directed arcs represent spurious correlations due to unmeasured common causes. All interactions among variables are assumed to be linear. Our task will be to decide whether the assumptions represented in the diagram are sufficient for assessing the strength of causal effects from non-experimental data and, if sufficiency is proven, to express the target causal effect in terms of estimable quantities.

This decision problem has been tackled in the past half century, primarily by econometricians and social scientists, under the rubric "The Identification Problem" (Fisher 1966) – it is still unsolved. Certain restricted classes of models are nevertheless known to be identifiable, and these are often assumed by social scientists as a matter of convenience or convention [Wright, 1960; Duncan, 1975]. McDonald [1997] characterizes a hierarchy of three such classes: (1) no bidirected arcs, (2) bidirected arcs restricted to root variables, and (3) bidirected arcs restricted to variables that are not connected through directed paths. The structural equations in all three classes are regressional, and the parameters can therefore be estimated uniquely using OLS techniques (Bollen [1989, pp.104]).

Figure 1: (a) a "bow-pattern", and (b) a bow-free model

Recently, (Brito & Pearl 2002) have shown that the identification of the entire model is ensured if variables standing in direct causal relationship (i.e., variables connected by arrows in the diagram) do not have correlated errors; no restrictions need to be imposed on errors associated with indirect causes. This class of models was called "bow-free", since their associated causal diagrams are free of any "bow pattern" (Pearl 2000) (see Figure 1).

In this work, we provide a new sufficient graphical criterion for the identification of general linear models. The distinctive characteristic of our criterion is the fact that it does not rely on the conditional independences implied by the model. As a consequence, it can be successfully applied to prove the identification of models with few conditional independences, while most existing methods would fail.

The remainder of the paper is organized as follows. We begin with a brief introduction to linear models and the identification problem, and review some useful definitions. Then, we describe our approach and define the fundamental concept of Auxiliary Variable. Next, we give a complete characterization of the Auxiliary variables and present a sufficient graphical criterion for identification. Finally, we provide an algorithm to find a suitable set of auxiliary variables in the model.

Linear Models and Identification

An equation $Y = \beta X + e$ encodes two distinct assumptions: (1) the possible existence of (direct) causal influence of X on Y; and, (2) the absence of causal influence on Y of any variable that does not appear on the right-hand side of the equation. The parameter β quantifies the (direct) causal effect of X on Y. That is, the equation claims that a unit increase in X would result in β units increase of Y. The variable e is called an "error" or "disturbance"; it represents unobserved background factors that the modeler decides to keep unexplained.

A linear model for a set of random variables $\mathbf{Y} =$

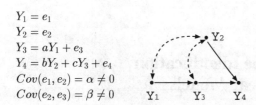

$$Y_1 = e_1$$
$$Y_2 = e_2$$
$$Y_3 = aY_1 + e_3$$
$$Y_4 = bY_2 + cY_3 + e_4$$
$$Cov(e_1, e_2) = \alpha \neq 0$$
$$Cov(e_2, e_3) = \beta \neq 0$$

Figure 2: A simple linear model and its causal diagram

$\{Y_1, \ldots, Y_n\}$ is defined by a set of equations of the form

$$Y_j = \sum_i c_{ji} Y_i + e_j \qquad , j = 1, \ldots, n \qquad (1)$$

where the error terms e_j are assumed to have normal distribution with zero mean, and variance/covariance matrix Ψ, $[\Psi_{ij}] = Cov(e_i, e_j)$.

The equations and the pairs of error-terms (e_i, e_j) with non-zero correlation define the structure of the model. The model structure can be represented by a directed graph, called causal diagram, in which the set of nodes is defined by the variables $Y_1, \ldots, Y_n$, and there is a directed edge from Y_i to Y_j if the coefficient of Y_i in the equation for Y_j is distinct from zero. Additionally, if error-terms e_i and e_j have non-zero correlation, we add a (dashed) bidirected edge between Y_i and Y_j. Figure 2 shows a simple model and the respective causal diagram.

The structural parameters of the model, denoted by θ, are the coefficients c_{ij}, and the values of the non-zero entries of the error covariance matrix Ψ. The models considered in this work are assumed to be recursive, that is, $c_{ji} = 0$ for $i \geq j$.

Fixing the model structure and assigning values to the parameters θ, the model determines a unique covariance matrix Σ over the observed variables $\{Y_1, \ldots, Y_n\}$, given by (see (Bollen 1989), page 85)

$$\Sigma(\theta) = (I - C)^{-1} \Psi \left[(I - C)^{-1} \right]' \qquad (2)$$

where C is the matrix of coefficients c_{ji}.

Conversely, in the Identification problem, after fixing the structure of the model, one attempts to solve for θ in terms of the observed covariance Σ. This is not always possible. In some cases, no parametrization of the model could be compatible with a given Σ. In other cases, the structure of the model may permit several distinct solutions for the parameters. In these cases, the model is called *nonidentifiable*.

A convenient way of relating parameter identification to the structure of the model is to write Eq.(2) for each term σ_{ij} of Σ using Wright's method of path coefficients (Wright 1960). Wright's method consists of equating the (standardized) covariance σ_{ij} with the sum of products of parameters (or path coefficients) along unblocked paths between Y_i and Y_j (examples are given later). If the resulting equations give a unique solution to some path coefficient c_{ij}, independent of (unobserved) error correlations, that coefficient is identifiable.

Background

Definition 1 *A* path *in a graph is a sequence of edges (directed or bidirected) such that each edge starts in the node ending the preceding edge. A* directed path *is a path composed only by directed edges, all oriented in the same direction. We say that node X is an* ancestor *of node Y if there is a directed path from X to Y. A path is said to be* blocked *if there is a node Z and a pair of consecutive edges in the path such that both edges are oriented toward Z (e.g., $\ldots \to Z \leftarrow \ldots$).*

Let p be a path between nodes X and Y. We say that path p points to X (Y) if the edge of p incident to X (Y) is oriented toward it. Let Z be an intermediate variable of path p. We denote the subpath of p consisting of the edges between X and Z by $p[X \sim Z]$.

Definition 2 *Define the* depth *of a node in a DAG as the length (in number of edges) of the longest directed path between the node and any of its ancestors. Nodes with no ancestors have depth 0.*

Definition 3 *Define the* distance *between two nodes X and Y, denote by $dist(X, Y)$, as the length (in number of edges) of the shortest path (blocked or unblocked) between variables X and Y, and for $\mathbf{Y} = \{Y_1, \ldots, Y_k\}$, we define $dist(X, \mathbf{Y}) = min_j\{dist(X, Y_j)\}$.*

Lemma 1 *Let X, Y be nodes in the causal diagram of a recursive model, such that $depth(X) \geq depth(Y)$. Then, every path between X and Y which includes a node Z with $depth(Z) \geq depth(X)$ must be blocked.*

Basic Approach

Our strategy for the identification problem is as follows. For a fixed variable Y, we assume that the parameters of edges connecting variables at depth smaller than Y are already identified. Then, we establish graphical conditions on the causal diagram such that the parameters of the edges incoming Y are identifiable. Once we have such a criterion, it is easy to implement an iterative procedure to verify the identifiability of the entire model by examining the variables in increasing depths.

Fix a variable Y in the model and let $depth(Y) = k$. Assume that the parameters of all edges connecting variables at depth smaller than k are identified. Let $\mathbf{X} = \{X_1, \ldots, X_m\}$ [1] be the set of variables at depth smaller than k which are connected to Y by an edge.

We further divide the variables in $\mathbf{X}$ into subsets $\overline{\mathbf{X}}$, $\widehat{\mathbf{X}}$ and $\widehat{\overline{\mathbf{X}}}$. A variable X_i belongs to $\overline{\mathbf{X}}$ if it is connected to Y only by a directed edge; $X_i \in \widehat{\mathbf{X}}$ if it is connected to Y only by a bidirected edge; and $X_i \in \widehat{\overline{\mathbf{X}}}$ if there is a directed and a bidirected edge between X_i and Y.

Define the following set of edges incoming Y:

$$Inc(Y) = \{(X_i, Y) : X_i \in \mathbf{X}\}$$

---

[1] In the following, we will also use letters X, Z, W to refer to variables in the model to avoid overloading the subscripts.

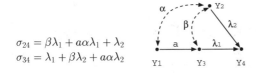

$$\sigma_{24} = \beta\lambda_1 + a\alpha\lambda_1 + \lambda_2$$
$$\sigma_{34} = \lambda_1 + \beta\lambda_2 + a\alpha\lambda_2$$

Figure 3: Wright's equations

Note that if $X_i \in \widehat{\widehat{\mathbf{X}}}$, then there are two edges denoted by (X_i, Y) (one directed and one bidirected) and both of them are in $Inc(Y)$. So, if $|\widehat{\widehat{\mathbf{X}}}| = n$, then

$$|Inc(Y)| = |\mathbf{X}| + |\widehat{\widehat{\mathbf{X}}}| = m + n$$

For each $X_i \in \mathbf{X}$, we apply Wright's method to the pair $\{X_i, Y\}$, and obtain the following equations:

$$\sigma_{X_i,Y} = \sum_{\text{paths } p_l} T(p_l) \qquad , i = 1, \ldots, m \qquad (3)$$

where term $T(p_l)$ is the product of the parameters of edges along the path p_l, and the summation is over all unblocked paths between X_i and Y. Figure 3 shows Eq. (3) for Y_4 as the fixed variable in a simple model.

In the following, we refer to the equation obtained by applying Wright's method to the pair $\{X_i, Y\}$ as the Wright's equation for X_i and Y.

Let $\lambda_1, \ldots, \lambda_{m+n}$, denote the parameters of the edges in $Inc(Y)$. Then, Eq. (3) can be rewritten as:

$$\sigma_{X_i,Y} = \sum_{j=1}^{m+n} a_{ij} \cdot \lambda_j \qquad , i = 1, \ldots, m \qquad (4)$$

where terms in coefficient a_{ij} correspond to unblocked paths between X_i and Y including edge (X_j, Y).

Nonlinear terms (e.g., $\lambda_j\lambda_i$) do not appear in these equations, because each unblocked path from X_i to Y contains exactly one edge from $Inc(Y)$. Moreover, it follows from Lemma 1 and our assumptions, that all the factors appearing in a_{ij} are identified parameters.

Let Φ denote the system of linear equations (4). The following result was proved in (Brito & Pearl 2002):

Theorem 1 *The equations in Φ are linearly independent.*

If $\widehat{\widehat{\mathbf{X}}} = \emptyset$, then Φ has m equations for m unknowns. Hence, theorem 1 guarantees that Φ has unique solution, and so the parameters $\lambda_1, \ldots, \lambda_m$ are identifiable

If $|\widehat{\widehat{\mathbf{X}}}| = n > 0$, then we have to find n variables providing additional independent equations to obtain the identification of parameters λ_i's. This motivates the following definition:

Definition 4 *A variable Z at depth smaller than k is said to be an Auxiliary Variable if and only if the Wright's equation for Z and Y is linearly independent from the equations in Φ.*

We restrict ourselves to variables at depth smaller than k so that we maintain the desirable property that every factor appearing in the coefficients of the equation is an identified parameter.

The AV Criterion

Our definition of Auxiliary Variable is closely related to the well-known concept of Instrumental Variable, in the sense that both enable the identification of causal-effects. The traditional definition qualifies a variable Z as instrumental, relative to a cause X and effect Y if (Pearl 2000):

1. Z is independent of all error terms that have an influence on Y that is not mediated by X;

2. Z is not independent of X.

The intuition behind this definition is that all correlation between Z and Y must be intermediated by X. If we can find Z with these properties, then the causal effect of X on Y, denoted by c, is identified and given by $c = \sigma_{ZY}/\sigma_{ZX}$. In the following, we provide a weaker set of conditions that completely characterize the Auxiliary variables. The conditions are based on the existence of a path (or sequence of paths) between Z and X in the path diagram, with a few restrictions. No condition is imposed on the existence of alternative paths between Z and Y which do not go through X, except that Z cannot be connected to Y by an edge.

AV Criterion:

Variable Z satisfies the AV criterion if we can find $X_{i_1} \in \widehat{\widehat{\mathbf{X}}}$ and $X_{i_2}, \ldots, X_{i_k} \in \overline{\mathbf{X}}$ such that:

(i) for $j = 1, \ldots, k-1$, there is an unblocked path p_j between X_{i_j} and $X_{i_{j+1}}$ pointing to both variables;

(ii) there is an unblocked path p_k between Z and X_{i_k} pointing to X_{i_k};

(iii) for $1 \leq j \leq k$, if some $X_l \in \mathbf{X}$ is an intermediate variable of path p_j, then we must have that $X_l \in \widehat{\mathbf{X}}$ and subpath $p_j[X_l \sim X_{i_{j+1}}]$ points to X_l (or subpath $p_k[X_l \sim Z]$, if $j = k$).

We call the sequence of paths $\langle p_1, \ldots, p_k \rangle$ an auxiliary chain C. The variables $Z, X_{i_1}, \ldots, X_{i_k}$ are the terminal variables of C, and any other variable appearing in some path p_j is called an intermediate variable of C.

Figure 4 shows some models in which the variable Z satisfies the AV criterion. For example, in model (a) we have a chain consisting of the edge $Z \to X_1$. In model (d), we have the chain with paths: $Z \to W_2 \to X_2$ and $X_2 \leftrightarrow W_2 \leftarrow W_1 \to X_1$. Figure 5 shows some models in which the variable Z does not satisfy the AV criterion. In each of those models, at least one condition of the AV criterion is not satisfied.

Theorem 2 *Let Z be such that $depth(Z) < depth(Y)$ and $Z \notin \mathbf{X}$. Then Z is an Auxiliary Variable if and only if Z satisfies the AV criterion.*

The GAV Criterion

As mentioned in section 3, if $|\widehat{\widehat{\mathbf{X}}}| = n$, then we need n auxiliary variables to obtain the identification of the parameters λ_i's. Here, we provide a sufficient condition on a set of auxiliary variables $\mathbf{Z} = \{Z_1, \ldots, Z_n\}$ for the system consisting of Wright's equations for each variable in $\mathbf{X} \cup \mathbf{Z}$ and Y to be linearly independent.

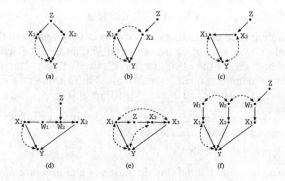

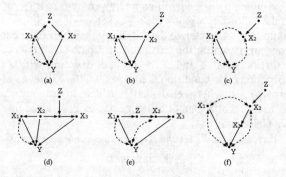

Figure 4: Variable Z satisfying AV criterion

Figure 5: Variable Z not satisfying AV criterion

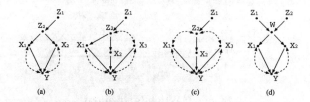

Figure 6: Models requiring 2 or more auxiliary variables

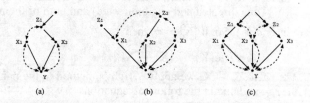

Figure 7: Variables satisfying the GAV criterion

Intuitively, for each $X_i \in \widehat{\mathbf{X}}$ we should have a unique $Z_i \in \mathbf{Z}$ such that there is an auxiliary chain between Z_i and X_i. That is, two variables $X_i, X_j \in \widehat{\mathbf{X}}$ could not share the same auxiliary variable in $\mathbf{Z}$.

However, although necessary, this is not a sufficient condition. Next, we use the models in Figure 6 to illustrate the aspects in the structure of the model that allow to obtain independent equations.

In model (a), we have the chains $C_1 : \langle Z_1 \rightarrow Z_2 \rightarrow X_1 \rangle$, and $C_2 : \langle Z_2 \rightarrow X_2 \rangle$, but the system of equations provided by $\{X_1, X_2, Z_1, Z_2\}$ is not linearly independent. The problem seems to be that Z_2 appears in every chain between Z_1 and some $X_h \in \widehat{\mathbf{X}}$.

However, this is still not complete, since in model (b) Z_2 also appears in every chain between Z_1 and some $X_h \in \widehat{\mathbf{X}}$, and the equations provided by $\{X_1, X_2, X_3, Z_1, Z_2\}$ are linearly independent. Moreover, in model (d), neither Z_1 appears in any chain between Z_2 and some $X_h \in \widehat{\mathbf{X}}$, nor vice-versa, but a common variable W appears in every such chains, and as a result the equations provided by $\{X_1, X_2, Z_1, Z_2\}$ are not linearly independent.

Finally, observe that the orientation of the edges in the chains is an important issue. Note that the only difference between models (b) and (c) is the orientation of the edge (Z_2, X_1), but while the variables $\{X_1, X_2, X_3, Z_1, Z_2\}$ provide independent equations in model (b), this is not the case in model (c).

The GAV criterion presented below formalizes those ideas and provides a sufficient condition to obtain linearly independent equations.

The GAV Criterion:

Let $\widehat{\mathbf{X}} = \{X_1, \ldots, X_n\}$, and let $\mathbf{Z} = \{Z_1, \ldots, Z_n\}$ be a set of auxiliary variables. Then, $\mathbf{Z}$ satisfies the GAV criterion if and only if we can find auxiliary chains $C_1, \ldots, C_n$, such that

(i) C_i is a chain between Z_i and X_i;

(ii) no $X_j \in \mathbf{X}$ appears as a terminal variable in more than one chain;

(iii) if p_i and p_j are paths of distinct chains, then they do not have any intermediate variable in common;

(iv) if p is a path in chain C_j connecting the terminal variables X_l and X_{l+1}, and Z_i appears as intermediate variable in p, then both the subpath $p[Z_i \sim X_{l+1}]$ and the last path of chain C_i must point to variable Z_i.

Figure 7 shows some examples in which the variables Z_i marked in the model satisfy the GAV criterion. In model (a), we have chains $C_1 : \langle Z_1 \leftrightarrow X_1 \rangle$ and $C_2 \langle Z_2 \rightarrow Z_1 \rightarrow X_2 \rangle$, which clearly satisfy conditions $(i) - (iii)$ above. To see that condition (iv) also holds, note that both path $Z_1 \leftrightarrow X_1$ and subpath $Z_2 \rightarrow Z_1$ point to Z_1. We have a similar situation in model (b).

In model (c), we have more than one choice for the chains C_1, C_2 and C_3. If we take, for instance, $C_1 : \langle Z_1 \leftrightarrow X_2 \rangle$, $C_2 : \langle Z_2 \rightarrow X_3 \rangle$ and $C_3 : \langle Z_3 \rightarrow Z_1 \rightarrow X_1 \rangle$, then we see that they satisfy all the conditions $(i) - (iv)$.

Theorem 3 *If a set of Auxiliary variables $\mathbf{Z} = \{Z_1, \ldots, Z_n\}$ satisfies the GAV criterion, then the system consisting of Wright's equations for each variable in $\mathbf{X} \cup \mathbf{Z}$ and Y is linearly independent.*

The GAV criterion may appear somewhat restrictive at first. In fact, it is easy to find examples of sets of auxiliary variables which do not satisfy the GAV criterion, but still provide independent equations. However, in all such examples we could always find another set of auxiliary variables satisfying the GAV criterion. So, we conjecture that the GAV criterion is also a necessary condition to obtain independent equations from auxiliary variables.

Algorithm

In more elaborate models, it may not be an easy task to check if a set of auxiliary variables satisfies the GAV criterion. In this section we present an algorithm to find a set of auxiliary variables satisfying the GAV criterion, if such set exists. The basic idea is to reduce the problem to that of solving an instance of the maximum flow problem.

(Cormen, C.Leiserson, & Rivest 1990) define the maximum flow problem as follows. A flow network $G = (V, E)$ is a directed graph in which each edge $(u, v) \in E$ has a non-negative capacity $c(u, v) \geq 0$. Two vertices are distinguished in the flow network: a source s and a sink t. A flow in G is a real-valued function $F : V \times V \to R$, satisfying:

- $F(u, v) \leq c(u, v)$, for all $u, v \in V$;
- $F(u, v) = -F(v, u)$, for all $u, v \in V$;
- $\sum_{v \in V} F(u, v) = 0$, for all $u \in V - \{s, t\}$.

The value of a flow F is defined as $|F| = \sum_{v \in V} F(s, v)$. In the maximum flow problem, we have to find a flow from s to t with maximum value.

Before describing the construction of the flow network G, we present an important result which allows to considerably reduce the number of candidates to compose the set of auxiliary variables.

Lemma 2 *If there is any set of auxiliary variables $\mathbf{Z}'$ satisfying the GAV criterion, then we can always find another set $\mathbf{Z} = \{Z_1, \ldots, Z_n\}$ which also satisfies the GAV criterion, such that:*

$$dist(Z_j, \mathbf{X}) \leq \lfloor log|\widehat{\overline{\mathbf{X}}}| \rfloor + 1 \quad , j = 1, \ldots, n$$

According to Lemma 2, we only need to consider variables with distance at most $\lfloor log|\widehat{\overline{\mathbf{X}}}| \rfloor + 1$ from $\mathbf{X}$, to find a set of auxiliary variables satisfying the GAV criterion.

Now, the set of vertices of flow network G consists of:

- a vertex V_i for each variable $X_i \in \mathbf{X}$;
- vertices $V_{\widehat{Z}}$ and $V_{\overline{Z}}$, for each variable $Z \notin \mathbf{X}$, with
  $depth(Z) < depth(Y)$ and $dist(Z, \mathbf{X}) \leq \lfloor log|\widehat{\overline{\mathbf{X}}}| \rfloor + 1$;
- a source vertex s, and a sink vertex t.

We have two vertices representing each variable $Z \notin \mathbf{X}$ because such variables may appear in more than one auxiliary chain (in fact, at most two).

The set E of edges in G is defined as follows. The goal is to have a correspondence between auxiliary chains in the model and directed paths from s to t in the flow network G. To obtain such correspondence, we include $V_i \to V_j$ in E if and only if the variables corresponding to V_i and V_j in the model, say X_i and X_j, are connected by an edge, and such edge can be traversed by a path in an auxiliary chain in the direction from X_i to X_j.

Let us analyze the situation for $X_i \in \overline{\mathbf{X}}$ and $X_j \in \widehat{\mathbf{X}}$. Assume that X_i and X_j are represented by vertices V_i and V_j, respectively, in G. If $X_i \to X_j$ is the only edge between

X_i and X_j in the model, then we do not include any edge between V_i and V_j in E, because edge $X_i \to X_j$ cannot appear in a path of an auxiliary chain. If edge $X_j \to X_i$ is present in the model, then we include edge $V_j \to V_i$ in E but do not include $V_i \to V_j$, because edge $X_j \to X_i$ can only be traversed from X_j to X_i in a path of an auxiliary chain. Similarly, if edge $X_i \leftrightarrow X_j$ exists in the model, then we include edge $V_i \to V_j$ in the model but do not include $V_j \to V_i$.

In some cases, one edge in the model corresponds to two edges in E. For example, if $X_i, X_j \in \overline{\mathbf{X}}$ and we have edge $X_i \leftrightarrow X_j$ in the model, then we include edges $V_i \to V_j$ and $V_j \to V_i$ in E.

For edges incident to some $Z \notin \mathbf{X}$ we have a more complex procedure, because such variables are represented by two vertices in G, and we have to ensure that condition (iv) of the GAV criterion is satisfied. We omit the technical details here, and give a table with all types of edges in the model and the corresponding edges in G in the appendix.

The following edges are also required:

- for each $X_h \in \widehat{\overline{\mathbf{X}}}$, we include $V_h \to t$;
- for each $Z \notin \mathbf{X}$, we include $s \to V_{\widehat{Z}}$;

Figure 9 shows an example of a model and the corresponding flow network.

In order to solve the maximum flow problem on G, we assign capacity 1 to every edge in E, and impose the additional constraint of maximum flow capacity of 1 to the vertices of G (this can be implemented by splitting each vertex into two and connecting them by an edge with capacity 1), except for vertices s and t.

We solve the maximum flow problem on G using the Ford-Fulkerson method and obtain a flow F. From the integrality theorem (see Cormen et al, p.603) we get that F allocates a non-negative integer amount of flow to each edge. Since we assign capacity 1 to every edge, we can interpret the solution F as a selection of directed paths $p_1, \ldots, p_{|F|}$, from s to t. Moreover, it follows from the additional constraint that these paths do not share any common vertex other than s and t.

Finally, note that vertex s is connected only to vertices $V_{\widehat{Z_i}}$, representing some $Z_i \notin \mathbf{X}$, and such vertices can appear only once in a directed path from s to t. Thus, each path p_i can be associated with a unique variable $Z_i \notin \mathbf{X}$. Hence, if $|F| = |\widehat{\overline{\mathbf{X}}}|$, the algorithm returns the set of variables associated with paths $p_1, \ldots, p_{|F|}$. Figure 8 summarizes the steps of the algorithm.

Theorem 4 *The algorithm is sound, that is, the returned set of variables satisfies the GAV criterion.*

Theorem 5 *The algorithm is complete, that is, it always find a set of variables satisfying the GAV criterion if such set exists.*

Conclusion and Discussion

In this paper we have introduced a new graphical criterion for parameter identification in linear models. Most exist-

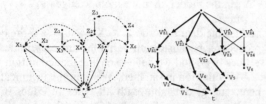

Algorithm:
1. Construct a flow network based on the model structure;
2. Solve the maximum flow problem on G using the Ford-Fulkerson method to obtain a flow F.
3. If $|F| = |\widehat{\overline{\mathbf{X}}}|$, return the set of variables associated with paths p_i. Otherwise, return the empty set.

Figure 8: Algorithm to find auxiliary variables.

Figure 9: A model and the corresponding flow network

$X_i \leftrightarrow X_j$	:	$V_i \to V_j$ and $V_j \to V_j$
$X_i \leftrightarrow X_l$	:	$V_i \to V_l$
$X_l \to X_i$	:	$V_l \to V_i$
$X_l \to X_k$	:	$V_l \to V_k$
$X_i \leftrightarrow X_h$	:	$V_i \to V_h$
$X_l \to X_h$	:	$V_l \to V_h$
$Z \to X_h$	:	$V_{\overline{Z}} \to V_h$
$Z \leftrightarrow X_h$	:	$V_{\widehat{Z}} \to V_h$
$Z \to X_l$	:	$V_{\overline{Z}} \to V_l$
$Z \leftrightarrow X_l$	:	$V_{\widehat{Z}} \to V_l$
$X_l \to Z$	:	$V_l \to V_{\overline{Z}}$
$Z \to X_i$	:	$V_{\overline{Z}} \to V_i$
$Z \leftrightarrow X_i$	:	$V_{\widehat{Z}} \to V_i$ and $V_i \to V_{\overline{Z}}$
$Z_1 \to Z_2$	:	$V_{\overline{Z}_1} \to V_{\overline{Z}_2}$
$Z_1 \leftrightarrow Z_2$	:	$V_{\widehat{Z}_1} \to V_{\overline{Z}_2}$ and $V_{\widehat{Z}_2} \to V_{\overline{Z}_1}$
$\forall Z \notin \mathbf{X}$	:	$V_{\widehat{Z}} \to V_{\overline{Z}}$

ing methods for this problem take advantage of the conditional independence relations implied by the model. Since our method does not make any use of this feature, it is appropriate even for models which are not rich in conditional independences.

Although our criterion can prove the identifiability of a large class of models, it is not complete. Figure 10 shows an example of a completely identifiable model for which our criterion fails. Manipulating the set of Wright's equations for each pair of variables in this model, one can prove the identification of every parameter.

Our criterion, fails because there is no variable at depth smaller than $depth(Y)$ satisfying the conditions of an Auxiliary variable. However, we note that variable Z has all properties to be an auxiliary variable, except that $depth(Z) > depth(Y)$. Thus, relaxing the definition of Auxiliary Variable to include such cases could be a natural extension of this work.

Appendix

Let $X_i, X_j \in \overline{\mathbf{X}}$, $X_l, X_k \in \overline{\mathbf{X}}$, $X_g, X_h \in \widehat{\overline{\mathbf{X}}}$, $Z, Z_1, Z_2 \notin \mathbf{X}$. Then, the correspondence of edges in the model and in the flow network is given by:

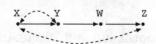

Figure 10: An identifiable model

References

Bollen, K. 1989. *Structural Equations with Latent Variables.* John Wiley, New York.

Brito, C., and Pearl, J. 2002. A new identification condition for recursive models with correlated errors. *To appear in Structural Equation Modelling.*

Cormen, T.; C.Leiserson; and Rivest, R. 1990. *Introduction to Algorithms.* The MIT Press.

Duncan, O. 1975. *Introduction to Structural Equation Models.* Academic Press, New York.

Fisher, F. 1966. *The Identification Problem in Econometrics.* McGraw-Hill, New York.

McDonald, R. 1997. Haldane's lungs: A case study in path analysis. *Multiv. Behav. Res.* 1–38.

Pearl, J. 1995. Causal diagrams for empirical research. *Biometrika* 82(4):669–710.

Pearl, J. 2000. *Causality: Models, Reasoning, and Inference.* Cambridge University Press, New York.

Wright, S. 1960. Path coefficients and path regressions: alternative or complementary concepts? *Biometrics* 189–202.

A Distance Measure for Bounding Probabilistic Belief Change

Hei Chan and **Adnan Darwiche**
Computer Science Department
University of California, Los Angeles
Los Angeles, CA 90095
{*hei,darwiche*}@*cs.ucla.edu*

Abstract

We propose a distance measure between two probability distributions, which allows one to bound the amount of belief change that occurs when moving from one distribution to another. We contrast the proposed measure with some well known measures, including KL-divergence, showing how they fail to be the basis for bounding belief change as is done using the proposed measure. We then present two practical applications of the proposed distance measure: sensitivity analysis in belief networks and probabilistic belief revision. We show how the distance measure can be easily computed in these applications, and then use it to bound global belief changes that result from either the perturbation of local conditional beliefs or the accommodation of soft evidence. Finally, we show that two well known techniques in sensitivity analysis and belief revision correspond to the minimization of our proposed distance measure and, hence, can be shown to be optimal from that viewpoint.

Introduction

We propose in this paper a distance measure which allows one to bound the amount of belief change that results from transforming one probabilistic state of belief into another. Specifically, given a probability distribution Pr representing an initial state of belief, and a distribution Pr' representing a new state of belief, we define a distance measure which allows us to tightly bound belief change as follows: $1/k \leq O'(\alpha \mid \beta)/O(\alpha \mid \beta) \leq k$. Here, k is a constant that depends on the proposed distance, α and β are arbitrary events, $O(\alpha \mid \beta)$ is the odds of event α given β with respect to Pr, and $O'(\alpha \mid \beta)$ is the odds of event α given β with respect to Pr'. We show a number of theoretical results about the proposed measure and then present two of its key applications.

On the theoretical side, we prove that our proposed measure satisfies the three properties of distance. We also contrast our distance measure with classical measures, such as KL-divergence (Kullback & Leibler 1951), and show how the classical measures fail to be the basis for bounding belief change in the sense given above. Specifically, we show that belief change between two states of belief can be unbounded, even when their KL-divergence tends to zero.

On the practical side, we present two main applications of our proposed distance measure. The first application is sensitivity analysis in belief networks, an area which concerns itself with bounding global belief change that results from applying a local perturbation to a belief network (Laskey 1995; Castillo, Gutiérrez, & Hadi 1997; Kjaerulff & van der Gaag 2000; Darwiche 2000; Chan & Darwiche 2001). We show three key results here. First, we show that if Pr is the distribution induced by a belief network N, and if Pr' is the distribution induced by a belief network N' that results from changing some conditional probability table (CPT) in N, then the distance between Pr and Pr' can be computed locally by only examining the changed CPT. Second, we use our distance measure to provide a bound on global belief change that results from a local CPT change, and show that our bound generalizes and provides more insights into the bound given by Chan and Darwiche recently (Chan & Darwiche 2001). Finally, we use our proposed distance measure to prove the optimality of a prevalent, but formally unjustified, technique in the literature on sensitivity analysis relating to changing the CPTs of multivalued variables (Laskey 1995; Kjaerulff & van der Gaag 2000; Darwiche 2000).

The second application we consider for our distance measure is in belief revision (Gärdenfors 1988). Here, we show how our distance measure can be used to bound belief change that results from incorporating uncertain evidence according to both Jeffrey's rule (Jeffrey 1965) and Pearl's method of virtual evidence (Pearl 1988). We actually prove the optimality of Jeffrey's rule with regards to minimizing belief change and, finally, consider the application of our distance measure to quantifying the strength of evidence, as measured by the amount of belief change it induces.

Proofs of theorems are omitted for space limitations and are available in the full paper (Chan & Darwiche 2002).

A probabilistic distance measure

Our proposed measure is defined between two probability distributions.

Definition 1 *Let Pr and Pr' be two probability distributions over the same set of worlds w. We define a measure $D(Pr, Pr')$ as follows:*

$$D(Pr, Pr') \stackrel{def}{=} \ln \max_w \frac{Pr'(w)}{Pr(w)} - \ln \min_w \frac{Pr'(w)}{Pr(w)},$$

where 0/0 is defined as 1.

We will say that two probability distributions Pr and Pr' *have the same support*, if for every world w, $Pr(w) = 0$ iff $Pr'(w) = 0$. Note that if two distributions Pr and Pr' do not have the same support, $D(Pr, Pr') = \infty$.

Our first result on the defined measure is that it satisfies the three properties of distance, hence, it is a *distance measure*.

Theorem 1 *Let Pr, Pr' and Pr'' be three probability distributions over the same set of worlds. The distance measure given in Definition 1 satisfies these three properties:*

Positiveness: $D(Pr, Pr') \geq 0$, *and* $D(Pr, Pr') = 0$ *iff* $Pr = Pr'$;

Symmetry: $D(Pr, Pr') = D(Pr', Pr)$;

Triangle Inequality: $D(Pr, Pr') + D(Pr', Pr'') \geq D(Pr, Pr'')$.

The interest in the defined distance measure stems from two reasons. First, it can be easily computed in a number of practical situations which we discuss in later sections. Second, it allows us to bound the difference in beliefs captured by two probability distributions.

Theorem 2 *Let Pr and Pr' be two probability distributions over the same set of worlds. Let α and β be two events. We then have:*

$$e^{-D(Pr, Pr')} \leq \frac{O'(\alpha \mid \beta)}{O(\alpha \mid \beta)} \leq e^{D(Pr, Pr')},$$

where $O(\alpha \mid \beta) = Pr(\alpha \mid \beta)/Pr(\overline{\alpha} \mid \beta)$ is the odds of event α given β with respect to Pr, and $O'(\alpha \mid \beta) = Pr'(\alpha \mid \beta)/Pr'(\overline{\alpha} \mid \beta)$ is the odds of event α given β with respect to Pr'.[1] The bound is tight in the sense that for every pair of distributions Pr and Pr', there are events α and β such that:

$$\frac{O'(\alpha \mid \beta)}{O(\alpha \mid \beta)} = e^{D(Pr, Pr')}, \quad \frac{O'(\overline{\alpha} \mid \beta)}{O(\overline{\alpha} \mid \beta)} = e^{-D(Pr, Pr')}.$$

We can express the bound of Theorem 2 in two other useful forms. First, we can use logarithms:

$$|\ln O'(\alpha \mid \beta) - \ln O(\alpha \mid \beta)| \leq D(Pr, Pr'). \quad (1)$$

Second, we can use probabilities instead of odds:

$$\frac{p\, e^{-d}}{p\,(e^{-d} - 1) + 1} \leq Pr'(\alpha \mid \beta) \leq \frac{p\, e^d}{p\,(e^d - 1) + 1}, \quad (2)$$

where $p = Pr(\alpha \mid \beta)$ is the initial belief in α given β, and $d = D(Pr, Pr')$ is the distance. The bounds of $Pr'(\alpha \mid \beta)$ are plotted against p for several different values of d in Figure 1.

---

[1] Of course, we must have $Pr(\beta) \neq 0$ and $Pr'(\beta) \neq 0$ for the odds to be defined.

In the applications we shall discuss next, Pr is a distribution which represents some initial state of belief, and Pr' is a distribution which represents a new state of belief. The new state of belief results form applying some kind of (usually local) change to the initial state. Examples include the change in some conditional belief or the incorporation of new evidence. Our goal is then to assess the global impact of such local belief changes. According to Theorem 2, if we are able to compute the distance measure $D(Pr, Pr')$, then we can bound global belief change in a very precise sense. For example, we can use Equation 2 to compute the bound on any query $Pr'(\alpha \mid \beta)$. We will later show two applications from sensitivity analysis and belief revision where the distance measure can be computed efficiently.

But first, we need to settle a major question: Can we bound belief change in the sense given above using one of the classical probabilistic measures? We show next that this is not possible using at least two of the most commonly used measures.

Kullback-Leibler (KL) divergence One of the most common measures for comparing probability distributions is the KL-divergence (Kullback & Leibler 1951).

Definition 2 *Let Pr and Pr' be two probability distributions over the same set of worlds w. The KL-divergence between Pr and Pr' is defined as:*

$$KL(Pr, Pr') \stackrel{def}{=} -\sum_w Pr(w) \ln \frac{Pr'(w)}{Pr(w)}.\,[2]$$

The first thing to note about KL-divergence is that it is incomparable with our distance measure.

Example 1 *Consider the following distributions, Pr, Pr' and Pr'', over worlds w_1, w_2 and w_3:*

$Pr(w_1) = .50,\quad Pr(w_2) = .25,\quad Pr(w_3) = .25;$
$Pr'(w_1) = .50,\quad Pr'(w_2) = .30,\quad Pr'(w_3) = .20;$
$Pr''(w_1) = .43,\quad Pr''(w_2) = .32,\quad Pr''(w_3) = .25.$

Computing the KL-divergence gives us: $KL(Pr, Pr') = .0102$ and $KL(Pr, Pr'') = .0137$. Computing our distance measure gives us: $D(Pr, Pr') = .405$ and $D(Pr, Pr'') = .398$. Therefore, according to KL-divergence, Pr' is closer to Pr than Pr'', while according to our distance measure, Pr'' is closer to Pr than Pr'.

We are now faced with two questions:

1. Can we use KL-divergence to bound belief change as we did using our distance measure? The answer is no as we show next.

2. Given that our goal is to minimize belief change, should we try to minimize our distance measure or some other measure, such as KL-divergence? We answer this question only partially in the following sections, by showing that two proposals that come from the literatures on sensitivity analysis and belief revision do correspond to the minimization of our distance measure.

---

[2] Note that KL-divergence is asymmetric, and is thus technically not a distance measure.

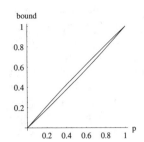 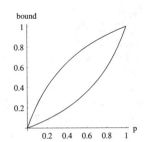 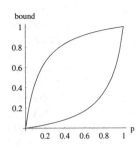 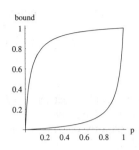

Figure 1: The bounds of $Pr'(\alpha \mid \beta)$, as given by Equation 2, plotted against the initial belief $p = Pr(\alpha \mid \beta)$ for several different values of distance $d = D(Pr, Pr')$: (from left to right) $d = .1$, $d = 1$, $d = 2$ and $d = 3$.

The following example addresses the first question.

Example 2 *Consider the following distributions, Pr and Pr', over worlds w_1, w_2 and w_3:*

$$Pr(w_1) = p, \qquad Pr(w_2) = q - p, \qquad Pr(w_3) = 1 - q;$$
$$Pr'(w_1) = kp, \quad Pr'(w_2) = q - kp, \quad Pr'(w_3) = 1 - q;$$

where p, q and k are constants, with $0 \le p \le q \le 1$ and $0 \le k \le q/p$. The KL-divergence between Pr and Pr' is:

$$KL(Pr, Pr') = -p \ln k - (q - p) \ln \frac{q - kp}{q - p}.$$

Assume we have events $\alpha = w_1$ and $\beta = w_1, w_2$. The odds ratio of α given β between Pr and Pr' is:

$$\frac{O'(\alpha \mid \beta)}{O(\alpha \mid \beta)} = \frac{k(q - p)}{q - kp}.$$

We can see that as p approaches 0, the KL-divergence also approaches 0, while the odds ratio $O'(\alpha \mid \beta)/O(\alpha \mid \beta)$ approaches k.

This example shows that we can make the KL-divergence arbitrarily close to 0, while keeping some odds ratio arbitrarily close to some constant k. In this example, we condition on event β, which has a probability of q that can be arbitrarily large. However, the probability of α, which is p according to Pr and kp according to Pr', is very small. Hence, although we have $Pr'(\alpha)/Pr(\alpha) = k$, this ratio is ignored by KL-divergence because the term $-p \ln k$ is very small as p approaches 0. More generally, the "contribution" of a world w to KL-divergence is equal to $-Pr(w) \ln(Pr'(w)/Pr(w))$. Therefore for a fixed ratio $Pr'(w)/Pr(w)$, this "contribution" becomes closer to 0 as $Pr(w)$ decreases, and becomes infinitesimal when $Pr(w)$ approaches 0.

Euclidean distance Another popular measure to compare two probability distributions is the Euclidean distance.

Definition 3 *Let Pr and Pr' be two probability distributions over the same set of worlds w. The Euclidean distance between Pr and Pr' is defined as:*

$$ED(Pr, Pr') \stackrel{def}{=} \sum_w \sqrt{(Pr'(w) - Pr(w))^2}.$$

That is, when computing the Euclidean distance, we add up the squared differences between pairs of probability values. Therefore, this measure has the same problem as KL-divergence: even if there is a large relative difference for the probability of a world with respect to Pr and Pr', it will be ignored if this probability is very small. Consequently, we cannot provide any guarantee on the ratio $O'(\alpha \mid \beta)/O(\alpha \mid \beta)$, no matter how small the Euclidean distance is (unless it is zero).

To summarize, neither KL-divergence nor Euclidean distance can be used to provide guarantees on the ratio $O'(\alpha \mid \beta)/O(\alpha \mid \beta)$, as we did in Theorem 2 using our distance measure.

Applications to sensitivity analysis

We now consider a major application of our distance measure to sensitivity analysis in belief networks (Laskey 1995; Castillo, Gutiérrez, & Hadi 1997; Kjaerulff & van der Gaag 2000; Darwiche 2000; Chan & Darwiche 2001). A belief network is a graphical probabilistic model, composed of two parts: a directed acyclic graph where nodes represent variables, and a set of conditional probability tables (CPTs), one for each variable (Pearl 1988; Jensen 2001). The CPT for variable X with parents $\mathbf{U}$ defines a set of conditional beliefs of the form $\theta_{x|\mathbf{u}} = Pr(x \mid \mathbf{u})$, where x is a value of variable X, $\mathbf{u}$ is an instantiation of parents $\mathbf{U}$, and $\theta_{x|\mathbf{u}}$ is the probability value of x given $\mathbf{u}$, and is called a network parameter.

One of the key questions with respect to belief networks is this: what can we say about the global effect of changing some parameter $\theta_{x|\mathbf{u}}$ to a new value $\theta'_{x|\mathbf{u}}$? That is, what is the effect of such a local parameter change on the value of some arbitrary query $Pr(\alpha \mid \beta)$?

Chan and Darwiche (2001) have provided a partial answer to this question, for the case where: variable X is binary (it has only two values, x and $\bar{x}$); α is the value y of some variable Y; β is the instantiation $\mathbf{e}$ of some variables $\mathbf{E}$, and neither $\theta_{x|\mathbf{u}}$ nor $\theta'_{x|\mathbf{u}}$ is extreme (equal to 0 or 1). Specifically under these conditions, they have shown that:

$$\left| \ln O'(y \mid \mathbf{e}) - \ln O(y \mid \mathbf{e}) \right| \le \left| \ln \frac{\theta'_{x|\mathbf{u}}}{\theta'_{\bar{x}|\mathbf{u}}} - \ln \frac{\theta_{x|\mathbf{u}}}{\theta_{\bar{x}|\mathbf{u}}} \right|.$$

Using the above bound, Chan and Darwiche have provided

a formalization of a number of intuitions relating to the sensitivity of probabilistic queries to changes in network parameters. We will now show how our distance measure can be used to derive a generalization of the above bound, which applies without any of the previously mentioned restrictions.

Suppose that our initial belief network is N and it induces a probability distribution Pr. By changing the CPT for variable X, we produce a new belief network N' that induces a probability distribution Pr'. If we are able to compute the distance between Pr and Pr', $D(Pr, Pr')$, we can then use Theorem 2 to provide a guarantee on the global effect of the local CPT change. As it turns out, the distance can be computed locally as given by the following theorem.

Theorem 3 *Let N and N' be belief networks which induce distributions Pr and Pr' respectively, and let X be a variable with parents $\mathbf{U}$ in network N. Suppose that N' is obtained from N by changing the conditional probability distribution of variable X given parent instantiation $\mathbf{u}$ from $\Theta_{X|\mathbf{u}}$ to $\Theta'_{X|\mathbf{u}}$, i.e. we change parameter $\theta_{x|\mathbf{u}}$ to $\theta'_{x|\mathbf{u}}$ for every value x. If $Pr(\mathbf{u}) > 0$, then:*

$$D(Pr, Pr') = D(\Theta_{X|\mathbf{u}}, \Theta'_{X|\mathbf{u}}).$$

The above theorem shows that the distance between the global probability distributions induced by networks N and N' is exactly the distance between the local distributions of X given $\mathbf{u}$, assuming that all other local distributions in N and N' are the same.

Theorem 3 is of great practical importance as it allows us to invoke Theorem 2 to provide a generalized sensitivity analysis formula for belief networks.

Corollary 1 *Let N and N' be belief networks which induce distributions Pr and Pr' respectively, and let X be a variable with parents $\mathbf{U}$ in network N. Suppose that N' is obtained from N by changing the conditional probability distribution of variable X given parent instantiation $\mathbf{u}$ from $\Theta_{X|\mathbf{u}}$ to $\Theta'_{X|\mathbf{u}}$, i.e. we change parameter $\theta_{x|\mathbf{u}}$ to $\theta'_{x|\mathbf{u}}$ for every value x. If $Pr(\mathbf{u}) > 0$, then:*

$$e^{-D(\Theta_{X|\mathbf{u}}, \Theta'_{X|\mathbf{u}})} \leq \frac{O'(\alpha \mid \beta)}{O(\alpha \mid \beta)} \leq e^{D(\Theta_{X|\mathbf{u}}, \Theta'_{X|\mathbf{u}})}.$$

The bound of Chan and Darwiche is a special case of Corollary 1, when X has only two values x and $\bar{x}$. In this case, the distance $D(\Theta_{X|\mathbf{u}}, \Theta'_{X|\mathbf{u}})$ is equal to:

$$D(\Theta_{X|\mathbf{u}}, \Theta'_{X|\mathbf{u}}) = \left| \ln \frac{\theta'_{x|\mathbf{u}}}{\theta_{x|\mathbf{u}}} - \ln \frac{\theta'_{\bar{x}|\mathbf{u}}}{\theta_{\bar{x}|\mathbf{u}}} \right|$$

$$= \left| \ln \frac{\theta'_{x|\mathbf{u}}}{\theta'_{\bar{x}|\mathbf{u}}} - \ln \frac{\theta_{x|\mathbf{u}}}{\theta_{\bar{x}|\mathbf{u}}} \right|.$$

We have therefore generalized their results on sensitivity analysis to arbitrary events and belief networks. We have also relaxed the condition that neither $\theta_{x|\mathbf{u}}$ nor $\theta'_{x|\mathbf{u}}$ can be extreme.

We now close this section with a final application of our distance measure. Suppose X is a variable with parents $\mathbf{U}$, values x_1, x_2 and x_3, and parameters $\theta_{x_1|\mathbf{u}} = .6$,

$\theta_{x_2|\mathbf{u}} = .3$ and $\theta_{x_3|\mathbf{u}} = .1$. Suppose further that we want to change the parameter $\theta_{x_1|\mathbf{u}} = .6$ to $\theta'_{x_1|\mathbf{u}} = .8$. As a result, we will need to change the other parameters $\theta_{x_2|\mathbf{u}}$ and $\theta_{x_3|\mathbf{u}}$ so that the sum of all three parameters remains to be 1. Because X is multivalued, there are infinitely many ways to change the other two parameters and the question is: which one of them should we choose? One popular scheme, which we will call the *proportional scheme*, distributes the mass $1 - \theta'_{x_1|\mathbf{u}} = 1 - .8 = .2$ among the other two parameters proportionally to their initial values. That is, the new parameters will be $\theta'_{x_2|\mathbf{u}} = .2(.3/.4) = .15$ and $\theta'_{x_3|\mathbf{u}} = .2(.1/.4) = .05$. This scheme has been used in all approaches to sensitivity analysis we are familiar with (Laskey 1995; Kjaerulff & van der Gaag 2000; Darwiche 2000), yet without justification. As it turns out, we can use our distance measure to prove the optimality of this scheme in a very precise sense.

Theorem 4 *When changing a parameter $\theta_{x|\mathbf{u}}$ to $\theta'_{x|\mathbf{u}}$ for a multivalued variable X, the proportional scheme, i.e. the one that sets $\theta'_{x_i|\mathbf{u}} = (1 - \theta'_{x|\mathbf{u}})(\theta_{x_i|\mathbf{u}}/(1 - \theta_{x|\mathbf{u}}))$ for all $x_i \neq x$, leads to the smallest distance between the original and new distributions of X, which is given by:*

$$D(\Theta_{X|\mathbf{u}}, \Theta'_{X|\mathbf{u}}) = \left| \ln \frac{\theta'_{x|\mathbf{u}}}{\theta_{x|\mathbf{u}}} - \ln \frac{\theta'_{\bar{x}|\mathbf{u}}}{\theta_{\bar{x}|\mathbf{u}}} \right|$$

$$= \left| \ln \frac{\theta'_{x|\mathbf{u}}}{\theta'_{\bar{x}|\mathbf{u}}} - \ln \frac{\theta_{x|\mathbf{u}}}{\theta_{\bar{x}|\mathbf{u}}} \right|,$$

where we define $\theta'_{\bar{x}|\mathbf{u}} = 1 - \theta'_{x|\mathbf{u}}$ and $\theta_{\bar{x}|\mathbf{u}} = 1 - \theta_{x|\mathbf{u}}$.

Theorem 4 thus justifies the use of the proportional scheme on the grounds that it leads to the tightest bound on the amount of associated belief change.

Applications to belief revision

The problem of probabilistic belief revision can be defined as follows. We are given a probability distribution Pr, which captures a state of belief and assigns a probability p to some event γ. We then obtain evidence suggesting a probability of $q \neq p$ for γ. Our goal is to change the distribution Pr to a new distribution Pr' such that $Pr'(\gamma) = q$. The are two problems here. First, usually there are many choices for Pr'. Which one should we adopt? Second, if we decide to choose the new state of belief Pr' according to some specific method, can we provide any guarantee on the amount of belief change that will be undergone as a result of moving from Pr to Pr'?

As for the first question, we will consider two methods for updating a probability distribution in the face of new evidence: Jeffrey's rule (Jeffrey 1965) and Pearl's method of virtual evidence (Pearl 1988). As for the second question, we will show next that we can indeed provide interesting guarantees on the amount of belief change induced by both methods. We present the guarantees first and then some of their applications.

Jeffrey's rule We start with Jeffrey's rule for accommodating uncertain evidence.

Definition 4 *Let Pr be a probability distribution over worlds w, and let $\gamma_1, \ldots, \gamma_n$ be a set of mutually exclusive and exhaustive events that are assigned probabilities $p_1, \ldots, p_n$, respectively, by Pr. Suppose we want to change Pr to a new distribution Pr' such that the probabilities of $\gamma_1, \ldots, \gamma_n$ become $q_1, \ldots, q_n$, respectively. Jeffrey's rule defines the new distribution Pr' as follows:*

$$Pr'(w) \stackrel{def}{=} Pr(w)\frac{q_i}{p_i}, \quad if\ w \models \gamma_i.$$

The main result we have about Jeffrey's rule is that the distance between probability distributions Pr and Pr' can be computed directly from the old and new probabilities of $\gamma_1, \ldots, \gamma_n$. This immediately allows us to invoke Theorem 2 as we show next.

Theorem 5 *Let Pr and Pr' be two distributions, where Pr' is obtained by applying Jeffrey's rule to Pr as given in Definition 4. We then have:*

$$D(Pr, Pr') = \ln \max_i \frac{q_i}{p_i} - \ln \min_i \frac{q_i}{p_i}.$$

We immediately get the following bound.

Corollary 2 *If O and O' are the odds functions before and after applying Jeffrey's rule as given in Definition 4, then:*

$$e^{-d} \leq \frac{O'(\alpha \mid \beta)}{O(\alpha \mid \beta)} \leq e^d,$$

where $d = \ln \max_i (q_i/p_i) - \ln \min_i (q_i/p_i)$.

To consider an example application of Corollary 2, we use a simple example from Jeffrey (1965).

Example 3 *Assume that we are given a piece of cloth, where its color can be one of: green (c_g), blue (c_b), or violet (c_v). We also want to know whether in the next day, the cloth will be sold (s), or remain unsold ($\bar{s}$). Our original state of belief is given by the probability distribution of the worlds Pr:*

$$Pr(s, c_g) = .12, \quad Pr(s, c_b) = .12, \quad Pr(s, c_v) = .32,$$
$$Pr(\bar{s}, c_g) = .18, \quad Pr(\bar{s}, c_b) = .18, \quad Pr(\bar{s}, c_v) = .08.$$

Therefore, our original state of belief on the color of the cloth (c_g, c_b, c_v) is given by the distribution $(.3, .3, .4)$. Assume that we now inspect the cloth by candlelight, and we want to revise our state of belief on the color of the cloth to the new distribution $(.7, .25, .05)$ using Jeffrey's rule. The distance between the original and new distributions of the worlds can be computed by simply examining the original and new distributions on the color variable as given by Theorem 5. Specifically, the distance between the two distributions is $\ln(.7/.3) - \ln(.05/.4) = 2.93$. We can now use this distance to provide a bound on the change in any of our beliefs. Consider for example our belief that the cloth is green given that it is sold tomorrow, $Pr(c_g|s)$, which is initially $.214$. Suppose we want to find the bound on the change in this belief induced by the new evidence. Given Corollary 2 and Equation 2, we have:

$$.0144 \leq Pr'(c_g|s) \leq .836,$$

which suggests that a dramatic change in belief is possible in this case. If we actually apply Jeffrey's rule, we get the new distribution Pr':

$$Pr'(s, c_g) = .28, \quad Pr'(s, c_b) = .10, \quad Pr'(s, c_v) = .04,$$
$$Pr'(\bar{s}, c_g) = .42, \quad Pr'(\bar{s}, c_b) = .15, \quad Pr'(\bar{s}, c_v) = .01,$$

according to which $Pr'(c_g|s) = .667$, which does suggest a dramatic change. On the other hand, if the new evidence on the color of the cloth is given by the distribution $(.25, .25, .50)$ instead, the distance between the old and new distributions will be $.406$, and our bound will be: $.153 \leq Pr'(c_g|s) \leq .290$, which is obviously much tighter as this evidence is much weaker.

We close this section by showing that Jeffrey's rule commits to a probability distribution which minimizes our distance measure. Hence, Jeffrey's rule leads to the strongest bound on the amount of belief change.

Theorem 6 *The new distribution Pr' obtained by applying Jeffrey's rule to an initial distribution Pr is optimal in the following sense. Among all possible distributions that assign probabilities $q_1, \ldots, q_n$ to events $\gamma_1, \ldots, \gamma_n$, Pr' is the closest to Pr, according to the distance measure defined in Definition 1.*

Pearl's method We now consider Pearl's method of virtual evidence. According to this method, we also have a new evidence η that bears on a set of mutually exclusive and exhaustive events $\gamma_1, \ldots, \gamma_n$, but the evidence is not specified as a set of new probabilities for these events. Instead, for each γ_i, $i \neq 1$, we are given a number λ_i which is interpreted as the ratio $Pr(\eta \mid \gamma_i)/Pr(\eta \mid \gamma_1)$. That is, λ_i represents the likelihood ratio that we would obtain evidence η given γ_i, compared with given γ_1. Note that under this interpretation, we must have $\lambda_1 = 1$.

Definition 5 *Let Pr be a probability distribution over worlds w, and let $\gamma_1, \ldots, \gamma_n$ be a set of mutually exclusive and exhaustive events that are assigned probabilities $p_1, \ldots, p_n$, respectively, by Pr. Suppose we want to change Pr to a new distribution Pr' to incorporate virtual evidence η, specified by $\lambda_1, \ldots, \lambda_n$, with $\lambda_1 = 1$ and $\lambda_i = Pr(\eta \mid \gamma_i)/Pr(\eta \mid \gamma_1)$ if $i \neq 1$. Pearl's method of virtual evidence defines the new distribution Pr' as follows:*

$$Pr'(w) \stackrel{def}{=} Pr(w)\frac{\lambda_i}{\sum_j p_j \lambda_j}, \quad if\ w \models \gamma_i.$$

Again, we can easily compute the distance between distributions Pr and Pr' using only local information.

Theorem 7 *Let Pr and Pr' be two distributions, where Pr' is obtained from Pr by accommodating virtual evidence as given by Definition 5. We then have:*

$$D(Pr, Pr') = \ln \max_i \lambda_i - \ln \min_i \lambda_i.$$

This immediately gives us the following bound.

Corollary 3 *If O and O' are the odds functions before and after applying Pearl's method as given in Definition 5, then:*

$$e^{-d} \leq \frac{O'(\alpha \mid \beta)}{O(\alpha \mid \beta)} \leq e^d,$$

where $d = \ln \max_i \lambda_i - \ln \min_i \lambda_i$.

For the special case where our evidence η bears only on $\neg\gamma$ versus γ, with $\lambda = Pr(\eta \mid \gamma)/Pr(\eta \mid \neg\gamma)$, the above bound reduces to $|\ln O'(\alpha \mid \beta) - \ln O(\alpha \mid \beta)| \leq |\ln \lambda|$. Therefore, the bound is tighter when λ is closer to 1. Clearly, when $\lambda = 1$, the evidence is trivial and the two distributions are the same.

Consider the following example from Pearl (1988).

Example 4 *On any given day, there is a burglary on any given house with probability $Pr(b) = 10^{-4}$, while the alarm of Mr. Holmes' house will go off if there is a burglary with probability $Pr(a \mid b) = .95$, and go off if there is no burglary with probability $Pr(a \mid \bar{b}) = .01$. One day, Mr. Holmes' receives a call from his neighbor, Mrs. Gibbons, saying she may have heard the alarm of his house going off. Mr. Holmes concludes that there is an 80% chance that Mrs. Gibbons did hear the alarm going off. According to Pearl's method, this evidence can be interpreted as: $\lambda = Pr(\eta \mid a)/Pr(\eta \mid \bar{a}) = 4$. Therefore, the distance between the original distribution Pr, and the new distribution Pr' which results from incorporating the virtual evidence, is $|\ln \lambda| = |\ln 4| = 1.386$. We can use this distance to bound the change in any of our beliefs. In particular, we may want to bound the new probability that there was a burglary at Mr. Holmes' house. Equation 2 gives us:*

$$2.50 \times 10^{-5} \leq Pr'(b) \leq 4.00 \times 10^{-4}.$$

If we actually apply Pearl's method, we get $Pr'(b) = 3.85 \times 10^{-4}$.

Our distance measure is then useful for approximate reasoning given *soft evidence*, as we can use the bound to approximate the probability of any event after the accommodation of such evidence. The approximation itself takes constant time to compute since we only need to compute the distance measure and apply Equation 2. We stress, however, that the bound becomes trivial in the case of *hard evidence* since the initial and new distributions no longer have the same support in this case, making the distance between them infinitely large.

We close this section by a final application of our distance measure, relating to the notion of *evidence strength*.

Example 5 *Going back to Example 3, we ask: What kind of evidence will assure us that our belief in the cloth being green given that it is sold tomorrow, which is now at .214, would not exceed .3? Equation 2 can be used in this case to obtain a sufficient condition on the strength of evidence which will ensure this. Specifically, Equation 2 gives us:*

$$\frac{.214\, e^{-d}}{.214\, (e^{-d} - 1) + 1} \leq Pr'(c_g|s) \leq \frac{.214\, e^d}{.214\, (e^d - 1) + 1}.$$

To ensure that $Pr'(c_g|s) \leq .3$, we must find a distance d that equates the above upper bound to .3. A value of $d = .454$

has this property. Hence, any piece of evidence which has a distance of no more than .454 from the current distribution on color, $(.3, .3, .4)$, would guarantee that $Pr'(c_g|s)$ does not exceed .3. Following are some pieces of evidence which satisfy this condition: $(.25, .25, .5)$, $(.25, .3, .45)$ and $(.35, .3, .35)$.

Conclusion

We proposed a distance measure between two probability distributions, which allows one to bound the amount of belief change that occurs when moving from one distribution to the other. We also contrasted the proposed measure with some well known measures, including KL-divergence, showing how they fail to be the basis for bounding belief change as is done using the proposed measure. We then presented two practical applications of the proposed distance measure: sensitivity analysis in belief networks and probabilistic belief revision. We showed how the distance measure can be easily computed in these applications, and then used it to bound global belief changes that result from either the perturbation of local conditional beliefs or the accommodation of soft evidence. Finally, we showed that two well known techniques in sensitivity analysis and belief revision correspond to the minimization of our proposed distance measure and, hence, can be shown to be optimal from that viewpoint.

Acknowledgments

This work has been partially supported by NSF grant IIS-9988543, MURI grant N00014-00-1-0617, and by DiMI grant 00-10065.

References

Castillo, E.; Gutiérrez, J. M.; and Hadi, A. S. 1997. Sensitivity analysis in discrete Bayesian networks. *IEEE Transactions on Systems, Man, and Cybernetics, Part A (Systems and Humans)* 27:412–423.

Chan, H., and Darwiche, A. 2001. When do numbers really matter? In *Proceedings of the 17th Conference on Uncertainty in Artificial Intelligence (UAI)*, 65–74. San Francisco, California: Morgan Kaufmann Publishers.

Chan, H., and Darwiche, A. 2002. A distance measure for bounding probabilistic belief change. Technical Report D–124, Computer Science Department, UCLA.

Darwiche, A. 2000. A differential approach to inference in Bayesian networks. In *Proceedings of the 16th Conference on Uncertainty in Artificial Intelligence (UAI)*, 123–132. San Francisco, California: Morgan Kaufmann Publishers.

Gärdenfors, P. 1988. *Knowledge in Flux: Modeling the Dynamics of Epistemic States*. Cambridge, Massachusetts: MIT press.

Jeffrey, R. 1965. *The Logic of Decisions*. New York: McGraw-Hill.

Jensen, F. V. 2001. *Bayesian Networks and Decision Graphs*. New York: Springer-Verglag.

Kjaerulff, U., and van der Gaag, L. C. 2000. Making sensitivity analysis computationally efficient. In *Proceedings of the 16th Conference on Uncertainty in Artificial Intelligence (UAI)*, 317–325. San Francisco, California: Morgan Kaufmann Publishers.

Kullback, S., and Leibler, R. A. 1951. On information and sufficiency. *Annals of Mathematical Statistics* 22:79–86.

Laskey, K. B. 1995. Sensitivity analysis for probability assessments in Bayesian networks. *IEEE Transactions on Systems, Man, and Cybernetics* 25:901–909.

Pearl, J. 1988. *Probabilistic Reasoning in Intelligent Systems: Networks of Plausible Inference*. San Mateo, California: Morgan Kaufmann Publishers.

Strategies for Determining Causes of Events

Mark Hopkins

Department of Computer Science
University of California, Los Angeles
Los Angeles, CA 90095
mhopkins@cs.ucla.edu

Abstract

In this paper, we study the problem of determining actual causes of events in specific scenarios, based on a definition of actual cause proposed by Halpern and Pearl. To this end, we explore two different search-based approaches, enrich them with admissible pruning techniques and compare them experimentally. We also consider the task of designing algorithms for restricted forms of the problem.

Introduction

Recently, there has been a renewed interest in establishing a precise definition of event-to-event causation, also referred to as "actual cause." Although a definitive answer has been elusive, many proposals have shown promise. This paper focuses on a definition proposed by (Halpern & Pearl 2001), and seeks to find an efficient algorithm to determine whether one event causes another event under this definition.

Complexity results by (Eiter & Lukasiewicz 2001) have shown that in general, the problem of determining actual cause under this definition is Σ_2^P-complete. Therefore, this paper proposes and evaluates search-based strategies, for both the complete and restricted forms of the problem. We are not aware of any other attempts made to address this problem from an algorithmic perspective.

Due to limited space, we provide only proof sketches for some results. Full proofs are available in (Hopkins 2002b).

Formal Description of the Problem

This paper addresses the issue of how to detect whether some event A caused another event B, based on a causal model-based definition proposed in (Halpern & Pearl 2001). Intuitively, the overarching goal is to answer causal queries regarding a fully specified story, and more ambitiously, to generate explanations automatically, in response to "why" questions. An example that illustrates some of the complexities of such a task is called The Desert Traveler, a story inspired by Patrick Suppes and featured in (Pearl 2000).

Example A desert traveler T has two enemies. Enemy 1 poisons T's canteen, and Enemy 2, unaware of Enemy 1's action, shoots and empties the canteen before T drinks. A

week later, T is found dead and the two enemies confess to action and intention. A jury must decide whose action was the actual cause of T's death.

Here, the task is to determine whether Enemy 1's action or Enemy 2's action was the actual cause of T's death. (Pearl 2000) phrases the general question in the language of structural causal models.

Before proceeding to formalizations, let us establish some preliminaries. We will generally use upper-case letters (e.g. X, Y) to represent random variables, and the lower-case correspondent (e.g. x, y) to represent a particular value of that variable. $Dom(X)$ will denote the domain of a random variable X. We will use bold-face upper-case letters to represent a set of random variables (e.g. $\mathbf{X}, \mathbf{Y}$). The lower-case correspondent (e.g. $\mathbf{x}, \mathbf{y}$) will represent a value for the corresponding set. Specifically, for $\mathbf{X} = \{X_1, ..., X_n\}$, a value $\mathbf{x}$ would be a mapping $\mathbf{x} : \mathbf{X} \to Dom(X_1) \cup ... \cup Dom(X_n)$, such that $\mathbf{x}(X_i) \in Dom(X_i)$. $Dom(\mathbf{X})$ is the set of all possible values for $\mathbf{X}$.

Formally, a *causal model* is a triple $(\mathbf{U}, \mathbf{V}, \mathbf{F})$, in which $\mathbf{U}$ is a finite set of exogenous random variables, $\mathbf{V}$ is a finite set of endogenous random variables (disjoint from $\mathbf{U}$), and $\mathbf{F} = \{F_X | X \in \mathbf{V}\}$ where F_X is a function $Dom(\mathbf{R}) \to Dom(X)$ that assigns a value to X for each setting of the remaining variables in the model $\mathbf{R} = \mathbf{U} \cup \mathbf{V} \backslash \{X\}$. For each X, we can define $\mathbf{PA}_X$, the *parent set* of X, to be the set of variables in $\mathbf{R}$ that can affect the value of X (i.e. are non-trivial arguments of F_X).

Causal models can be depicted as a *causal network*, a graph whose nodes correspond to the variables in $\mathbf{U} \cup \mathbf{V}$ with an edge from Y to $X \in \mathbf{V}$ if and only if $Y \in \mathbf{PA}_X$. The *endogenous causal network* is defined similarly, but over only the variables in $\mathbf{V}$. *Recursive causal models* are causal models whose causal networks are directed acyclic graphs. In this paper, we restrict our analysis to recursive causal models (following the analysis of (Halpern & Pearl 2001) and (Eiter & Lukasiewicz 2001)).

We will further assume that the domain of each random variable is finite and explicit, that each F_X is computable in polynomial time, and that the number of parents for any particular variable is bounded by a constant.

Example In Fig. 1, we see the Desert Traveler scenario expressed as a recursive causal model. Here, $\mathbf{U} = \{U_X, U_P\}$

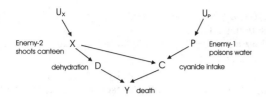

Figure 1: Causal model for the Desert Traveler scenario. All variables are propositional. $X = U_X$; $P = U_P$; $D = X$; $C = P \wedge \neg X$; $Y = C \vee D$.

and $\mathbf{V} = \{X, P, D, C, Y\}$. All variables are propositional, with value 1 indicating a true proposition, and value 0 indicating that the proposition is false.

An important aspect of causal models is their ability to store counterfactual information. We can express counterfactual contingencies through the use of submodels. Intuitively, a submodel fixes the values of a set of endogenous variables $\mathbf{X}$ at $\mathbf{x}$. Consequently, the values of the remaining variables represent what values they *would have had* if $\mathbf{X}$ had been $\mathbf{x}$ in the original model. Formally, given a causal model $M = (\mathbf{U}, \mathbf{V}, \mathbf{F})$, $\mathbf{X} \subseteq \mathbf{V}$, $\mathbf{x} \in Dom(\mathbf{X})$, the *submodel* of M under *intervention* $\mathbf{X} = \mathbf{x}$ is $M_{\mathbf{X}=\mathbf{x}} = (\mathbf{U}, \mathbf{V}, \mathbf{F}_{\mathbf{X}=\mathbf{x}})$, where $\mathbf{F}_{\mathbf{X}=\mathbf{x}} = \{F_R | R \in \mathbf{V} \backslash \mathbf{X}\} \cup \{F_{X'} = \mathbf{x}(X')|X' \in \mathbf{X}\}$. $M_{\mathbf{X}=\mathbf{x}}$ and $\mathbf{F}_{\mathbf{X}=\mathbf{x}}$ are typically abbreviated $M_{\mathbf{x}}$ and $\mathbf{F}_{\mathbf{x}}$.

In a recursive causal model, the values of the exogenous variables uniquely determine the values of the endogenous variables. Hence for a causal model $M = (\mathbf{U}, \mathbf{V}, \mathbf{F})$ and a set of endogenous variables $\mathbf{Y} \in \mathbf{V}$ we can refer to the unique value of $\mathbf{Y}$ under $\mathbf{u} \in Dom(\mathbf{U})$ as $\mathbf{Y}_M(\mathbf{u})$ (or simply $\mathbf{Y}(\mathbf{u})$). We can define $\mathbf{Y}_{M_{\mathbf{x}}}(\mathbf{u})$ analogously for a submodel $M_{\mathbf{x}}$ (and abbreviate it $\mathbf{Y}_{\mathbf{x}}(\mathbf{u})$). Since we are dealing with the issue of determining actual cause in a fully-specified scenario, this amounts to asking causal questions in a causal model for which the values of the exogenous variables are given. For causal model $M = (\mathbf{U}, \mathbf{V}, \mathbf{F})$ and $\mathbf{u} \in Dom(\mathbf{U})$, we refer to the pair $(M, \mathbf{u})$ as a *causal world*.

The following properties of recursive causal models, established in (Pearl 2000), will be useful:

Proposition 1 *Let* $M = (\mathbf{U}, \mathbf{V}, \mathbf{F})$ *be a recursive causal model. Let* $\mathbf{u} \in Dom(\mathbf{U})$, $\mathbf{X} \subseteq \mathbf{V}$, $\mathbf{W} \subseteq \mathbf{V}$, $\mathbf{w} \in Dom(\mathbf{W})$, $Y \in \mathbf{V}$. *Then the following properties hold:*

(a) $Y_{\mathbf{w}}(\mathbf{u}) = Y_{\mathbf{wx}}(\mathbf{u})$ *for any* $\mathbf{x} \in Dom(\mathbf{X})$ *if all directed paths from* $\mathbf{X}$ *to* Y *in the causal network of* M *are intercepted by* $\mathbf{W}$.

(b) $Y_{\mathbf{w}}(\mathbf{u}) = Y_{\mathbf{wx}}(\mathbf{u})$ *if* $\mathbf{X}_{\mathbf{w}}(\mathbf{u}) = \mathbf{x}$.

Equipped with this background, we can now proceed to define actual cause:

Definition 2 *Let* $M = (\mathbf{U}, \mathbf{V}, \mathbf{F})$ *be a causal model. Let* $\mathbf{X} \subseteq \mathbf{V}$, $\mathbf{Y} \subseteq \mathbf{V}$. $\mathbf{X} = \mathbf{x}$ *is an* actual cause *of* $\mathbf{Y} = \mathbf{y}$ *(denoted* $\mathbf{x} \propto \mathbf{y}$*) in a causal world* $(M, \mathbf{u})$ *if the following three conditions hold:*

(AC1) $\mathbf{X}(\mathbf{u}) = \mathbf{x}$ *and* $\mathbf{Y}(\mathbf{u}) = \mathbf{y}$.

(AC2) There exists $\mathbf{W} \subseteq \mathbf{V} \backslash \mathbf{X}$ *and values* $\mathbf{x}' \in Dom(\mathbf{X})$ *and* $\mathbf{w} \in Dom(\mathbf{W})$ *such that:*

(a) $\mathbf{Y}_{\mathbf{x}'\mathbf{w}}(\mathbf{u}) \neq \mathbf{y}$.

(b) $\mathbf{Y}_{\mathbf{xw}}(\mathbf{u}) = \mathbf{y}$.

(c) $\mathbf{Y}_{\mathbf{xwz}}(\mathbf{u}) = \mathbf{y}$, *for all* $\mathbf{Z} \subseteq \mathbf{V} \backslash (\mathbf{X} \cup \mathbf{W})$ *such that* $\mathbf{z} = \mathbf{Z}(\mathbf{u})$.

(AC3) $\mathbf{X}$ *is minimal; no subset of* $\mathbf{X}$ *satisfies conditions AC1 and AC2.*

Intuitively, $\mathbf{x}$ is an actual cause of $\mathbf{y}$ if (AC1) $\mathbf{x}$ and $\mathbf{y}$ are the "actual values" of $\mathbf{X}$ and $\mathbf{Y}$ (i.e. the values of $\mathbf{X}$ and $\mathbf{Y}$ under no intervention), and (AC2) under some counterfactual contingency $\mathbf{w}$, the value of $\mathbf{Y}$ is dependent on $\mathbf{X}$, such that setting $\mathbf{X}$ to its actual value will ensure that $\mathbf{Y}$ maintains its "actual value," even if we force all other variables in the model back to their "actual values." (AC3) is a simple minimality condition.

Example In the Desert Traveler example, we see that $X = 1$ (shooting the canteen) is indeed an actual cause of $Y = 1$ (death), since $X(\mathbf{u}) = 1$, $Y(\mathbf{u}) = 1$, $Y_{X=0,C=0}(\mathbf{u}) = 0$, and $Y_{X=1,C=0}(\mathbf{u}) = 1$. Here, our $\mathbf{w}$ is $C = 0$. Notice also that $P = 1$ is *not* an actual cause of $Y = 1$ under this definition.

The question that this paper addresses is: given a causal world $(M, \mathbf{u})$, how can we efficiently determine whether $\mathbf{x}$ is an actual cause of $\mathbf{y}$? Unfortunately, it turns out that this problem is Σ_2^P-complete (Eiter & Lukasiewicz 2001).

Because of this, we focus on search strategies for determining actual cause. For simplicity, we will be restricting our examination to single variable causation, i.e. whether $X = x$ causes $Y = y$, for $X, Y \in \mathbf{V}$. This restriction is partially justified by the following theorem, proven in (Eiter & Lukasiewicz 2001), and independently in (Hopkins 2002a):

Theorem 3 *Let* $M = (\mathbf{U}, \mathbf{V}, \mathbf{F})$ *be a causal model. Let* $\mathbf{X}, \mathbf{Y} \subseteq \mathbf{V}$ *and* $\mathbf{x} \in Dom(\mathbf{X})$, $\mathbf{y} \in Dom(\mathbf{Y})$. *If* $\mathbf{x} \propto \mathbf{y}$ *under* $\mathbf{u}$, *then* $\mathbf{X}$ *is a singleton.*

This theorem establishes that any candidate cause that contains multiple variables will inevitably violate the minimality requirement of the actual cause definition. Thus we may restrict our focus to singleton causes.

We also do not consider our effect to be a Boolean conjunction of primitive events $\mathbf{Y} = \mathbf{y}$, since $X = x$ is an actual cause of $(\mathbf{Y} = \mathbf{y} \wedge \mathbf{Z} = \mathbf{z})$ iff $X = x$ is an actual cause of $\mathbf{Y} = \mathbf{y}$ and $X = x$ is an actual cause of $\mathbf{Z} = \mathbf{z}$. Thus any algorithm that determines actual cause between primitive events can immediately be applied in the more general case through repeated applications of the algorithm.

Thus, let us consider the task of determining whether $x \propto y$ holds in a given causal world. The first thing to notice is that checking AC1 and AC3 are easy tasks. To check AC1, we merely need to check the value of two different random variables under a single intervention (specifically, the null intervention). We can compute the value of every random variable in a causal world under a single intervention in polynomial time, by the following simple procedure: choose a variable for whom the values of the parents are determined, then compute the value for that variable; continue until values for all variables are computed. Clearly, this procedure is always executable in a recursive causal world. AC3 is trivial, in light of Thm. 3.

The difficulty lies in checking whether or not AC2 holds. The remainder of this paper deals with strategies for deciding this. We should point out that the task of determining whether AC2 holds boils down to searches through two different search spaces:

1. A search through possible $\mathbf{w}$. The top-level task is to find a set of variables $\mathbf{W}$, and a particular value $\mathbf{w} \in Dom(\mathbf{W})$ that satisfies all three constraints of AC2.

2. A search through possible $\mathbf{Z}$. Notice that for a given $\mathbf{w}$, AC2(a) and AC2(b) can be checked in polynomial time (since each merely requires us to compute the value of a variable under a single intervention). However, AC2(c) is more involved. It requires us to check that there is no set $\mathbf{Z}$ such that $Y_{\mathbf{xwz}}(\mathbf{u}) \neq y$, where $\mathbf{z} = \mathbf{Z}(\mathbf{u})$. Here we are searching for a set of variables, rather than for a particular value for a set of variables, as in the search for $\mathbf{w}$.

Algorithm-Independent Optimizations

Naturally we would like to reduce the size of these search spaces as much as possible. To this end, we define the notion of the *projection* of a causal world.

Definition 4 *Let* $M = (\mathbf{U}, \mathbf{V}, \mathbf{F})$ *be a recursive causal model. Suppose we have a causal world* $(M, \mathbf{u})$ *such that* $\mathbf{V} = \{V_1, ..., V_n\}$. *To* delete *a variable* V_i *from* $(M, \mathbf{u})$, V_i *is removed from* $\mathbf{V}$, *and the structural equation* F_X *of each child* X *of* V_i *is replaced with* $F_X|_{v_i}$, *where* $v_i = V_i(\mathbf{u})$. *The* projection *of* $(M, \mathbf{u})$ *over variables* $V_1, V_2, ..., V_k$ *is a new causal model in which* $V_{k+1}, V_{k+2}, ..., V_n$ *are deleted from* $(M, \mathbf{u})$. *The* W-projection *of* $(M, \mathbf{u})$ *with respect to* $x \propto y$ *is the projection of* $(M, \mathbf{u})$ *over* X, Y, *the variables* $\mathbf{V}^{XY}$ *on a path from* X *to* Y *in the causal network of* M, *and the parents of* $\mathbf{V}^{XY}$ *and* Y *in the causal network of* M.

Intuitively, *deleting* a variable gives us the same result as permanently fixing it at its actual value. Now we can prove that the question of whether x is an actual cause of y in $(M, \mathbf{u})$ depends only on the paths that connect X to Y in the causal network of M, and the nodes which influence nodes on these paths (i.e. the W-projection). All other nodes either do not influence Y, or do so through a parent of a node on a path, and can be safely ignored.

Theorem 5 *Let* $M = (\mathbf{U}, \mathbf{V}, \mathbf{F})$ *be a recursive causal model and suppose we have a causal world* $(M, \mathbf{u})$. *Then* $x \propto y$ *in* $(M, \mathbf{u})$ *iff* $x \propto y$ *in* $(M', \mathbf{u})$, *where* M' *is the W-projection of* $(M, \mathbf{u})$.

Proof Suppose $x \propto y$ in $(M, \mathbf{u})$. Then we must have $\mathbf{W} \subseteq \mathbf{V} \backslash X$, $\mathbf{w} \in Dom(\mathbf{W})$, and $x' \in Dom(X)$ such that AC2 is satisfied. Now consider the set $\mathbf{P}$ of variables which are parents to variables on a path from X to Y (except parents of X), but are not themselves on a path from X to Y. Suppose $\mathbf{P}_{\mathbf{w}}(\mathbf{u}) = \mathbf{p}$. Define $\mathbf{W}'$ as the union of $\mathbf{P}$ with the subset of $\mathbf{W}$ on a directed path from X to Y, and define $\mathbf{w}'$ such that $\mathbf{w}'(V) = \mathbf{w}(V)$ for $V \in \mathbf{W}$ and $\mathbf{w}'(V) = V_{\mathbf{w}}(\mathbf{u})$ for $V \in \mathbf{P}$.

We will show that this $\mathbf{w}' \in Dom(\mathbf{W}')$ also satisfies AC2. By Prop. 1(a), $Y_{x'\mathbf{w}'}(\mathbf{u}) = Y_{x'\mathbf{pw}}(\mathbf{u})$. Then, since $P_{\mathbf{w}}(\mathbf{u}) = P_{x'\mathbf{w}}(\mathbf{u})$ by Prop. 1(a), therefore $Y_{x'\mathbf{pw}}(\mathbf{u}) =$

$Y_{x'\mathbf{w}}(\mathbf{u})$ by Prop. 1(b). Hence $Y_{x'\mathbf{w}'}(\mathbf{u}) = Y_{x'\mathbf{w}}(\mathbf{u}) \neq y$, so $\mathbf{w}'$ satisfies AC2(a).

Now we show that it satisfies AC2(b) and (c). Take any $\mathbf{Z} \subseteq \mathbf{V} \backslash (X \cup \mathbf{W})$ and let $\mathbf{z} = \mathbf{Z}(\mathbf{u})$. By Prop. 1(a), $Y_{x\mathbf{w}'\mathbf{z}}(\mathbf{u}) = Y_{x\mathbf{pwz}}(\mathbf{u})$. Also by Prop. 1(a), $Y_{x\mathbf{pwz}}(\mathbf{u}) = Y_{x\mathbf{pwz}'}(\mathbf{u})$, where $\mathbf{Z}'$ is the subset of $\mathbf{Z}$ on a directed path from X to Y, and $\mathbf{z}' = \mathbf{Z}'(\mathbf{u})$. Since $P_{\mathbf{w}}(\mathbf{u}) = P_{x\mathbf{wz}'}(\mathbf{u})$ by Prop. 1(a), therefore $Y_{x\mathbf{pwz}'}(\mathbf{u}) = Y_{x\mathbf{wz}'}(\mathbf{u})$ by Prop. 1(b). Hence $Y_{x\mathbf{w}'\mathbf{z}}(\mathbf{u}) = Y_{x\mathbf{wz}'}(\mathbf{u}) = y$, so $\mathbf{w}'$ satisfies AC2(b) and AC2(c).

Hence we can always devise an intervention consisting only of variables on a path from X to Y and variables in $\mathbf{P}$ that satisfies AC2. Clearly, AC1 and AC3 are also satisfied in $(M', \mathbf{u})$. Hence, $X = x$ is an actual cause of $Y = y$ in $(M', \mathbf{u})$. The converse of this theorem is trivial. ∎

Looking at Fig. 2, we see how this can substantially reduce the number of nodes in the causal network (while not increasing the connectivity). Notice that such projection can be done before attempting *any algorithm* for determining whether x is an actual cause of y. Henceforth, unless stated otherwise, we will implicitly assume that our algorithms are operating on the W-projection with respect to the query.

Brute-Force Approach

Recall that the task of determining whether AC2 holds can be divided into two stages: a search through possible $\mathbf{w}$, and a search through possible $\mathbf{Z}$. For the next two sections, we will focus on the first stage, and assume that we have a black box to check AC2(c).

There is a rather obvious brute-force search algorithm through the space of possible $\mathbf{w}$. For some ordering of the variables of our causal world (excluding Y), we simply assign a value (including a possible "non-assignment" value $\emptyset$, indicating that the variable is not part of $\mathbf{W}$) to each variable, one at a time, until all variables have been assigned values. Then we check to see whether AC2 is satisfied by this $\mathbf{w}$. Here, we are lumping X into $\mathbf{W}$, thus to check AC2(a) and (b), we simply check that $Y_{\mathbf{w}}(\mathbf{u}) \neq y$ and $Y_{\mathbf{w}'x}(\mathbf{u}) = y$, where $\mathbf{w}'$ is merely $\mathbf{w}$ with the setting for X removed. If AC2(a) and (b) hold, then we check AC2(c) with our black box. If this also holds, then $x \propto y$. If not, we try another setting of the variables, until we find one that satisfies AC2 or until all possibilities are exhausted.

The obvious drawback of this approach is that it amounts to a brute-force search of a tree with depth $N-1$ and branching factor $c + 1$, where N is the number of variables in the causal network (minus one, for Y), and c is the size of each variable domain in the network (plus one, for $\emptyset$) Here, we assume for simplicity that each variable domain has the same

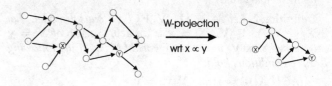

Figure 2: Demonstration of W-Projection

size. Thus this search tree has $O((c+1)^N)$ leaf nodes.

To check whether any given leaf in the search tree satisfies AC2(a) and (b), we potentially need to calculate the value of each node in our network under two different interventions – as we have discussed, this task is polynomial in the number of endogenous variables. Supposing now that $O(\lambda)$ is the worst-case complexity of the algorithm to check AC2(c), we can say that the worst-case running time of this brute-force algorithm is $O(\lambda N^p (c+1)^N)$, for some constant p.

One approach to pruning the brute-force search tree is based on the following theorem:

Theorem 6 *Let N be the causal network of recursive causal model $M = (\mathbf{U}, \mathbf{V}, \mathbf{F})$. Let $\mathbf{u} \in Dom(\mathbf{U})$, $X, Y \in \mathbf{V}$, $x, x' \in Dom(X)$, $y \in Dom(Y)$. Suppose $\mathbf{W} \subseteq \mathbf{V} \backslash X$ and that every path from X to Y in N is blocked by some variable in $\mathbf{W}$. Then for any $\mathbf{w} \in Dom(\mathbf{W})$, $Y_{x'\mathbf{w}}(\mathbf{u}) = Y_{x\mathbf{w}}(\mathbf{u})$. In other words, either AC2(a) or AC2(b) must fail. Furthermore, any $\mathbf{W}' \supseteq \mathbf{W}$ also has this property.*

Proof By Prop. 1(a), $Y_{x'\mathbf{w}'}(\mathbf{u}) = Y_{\mathbf{w}'}(\mathbf{u}) = Y_{x\mathbf{w}'}(\mathbf{u})$, for any $\mathbf{W}' \supseteq \mathbf{W}$, $\mathbf{w}' \in Dom(\mathbf{W}')$. ∎

Theorem 6 implies that we can prune any subtree rooted at node S from our search tree, where S is any node representing a partial variable setting I for which every path from X to Y in the causal network contains some variable set by I to a non- $\emptyset$ value.

The cost per node of determining whether all paths from X to Y are blocked is simply the cost of a depth-first search of the graph, which is linear in the number of network nodes. Thus adding this pruning to our brute-force algorithm does not add any complexity to our asymptotic running time.

The benefit of this pruning will depend on the order in which we assign values to variables, and this paper does not address this issue.

Intervention-Proving Approach

Let us continue to treat AC2(c) as a black box, and examine a different approach to searching through the space of possible $\mathbf{w}$. To determine whether AC2(a) and (b) are satisfied for query $x \propto y$, we are looking for some $\mathbf{w}$, such that $Y_{x\mathbf{w}}(\mathbf{u}) = y$ and $Y_{x'\mathbf{w}}(\mathbf{u}) \neq y$ for some $x' \neq x$. We can actually encode part of this goal into the search space itself. For example, we could choose to only search the space of interventions $\mathbf{w}'$ such that $Y_{\mathbf{w}'}(\mathbf{u}) \neq y$. Then for each intervention of the form $\mathbf{w}' = x'\mathbf{w}$, we would need only to check that $Y_{x\mathbf{w}} = y$.

We can think of this as "proving" interventions $\mathbf{w}'$ such that $Y_{\mathbf{w}'}(\mathbf{u}) \neq y$ in the causal model. We begin by supposing that $Y \neq y$, and work backwards to prove which interventions would be consistent with $Y \neq y$. Take, for instance, the Desert Traveler formulation. Suppose we want to determine whether $X = 1$ is an actual cause of $Y = 1$. Suppose that $Y \neq 1$. What are the possible instantiations of Y's parents in that case? In fact, the only possibility is $\{D = 0, C = 0\}$. It is easy to see that under every intervention $\mathbf{w}'$ such that $Y_{\mathbf{w}'}(\mathbf{u}) \neq 1$, it must be the case that $D_{\mathbf{w}'}(\mathbf{u}) = 0$ and $C_{\mathbf{w}'}(\mathbf{u}) = 0$. More importantly, our claim is that $Y_{D=0,C=0}(\mathbf{u}) \neq 1$. Now let us take this new intervention we have produced, and attempt to eliminate C from

it in the same way. Notice that the intervention requires that condition $C = 0$ will materialize. There are three full instantiations of the parents of C that force C's value to be 0: $\{X = 0, P = 0\}$, $\{X = 1, P = 0\}$, $\{X = 1, P = 1\}$. Thus, we can replace $C = 0$ with these three instantiations to create three new interventions. Furthermore, if we continue this process (eliminating the variables in a reverse topological order), as shown in Fig. 3, then for every intervention $\mathbf{w}'$ we produce, $Y_{\mathbf{w}'}(\mathbf{u}) \neq 1$.

A few observations are in order. At certain points, it is possible to derive inconsistent interventions. These are immediately thrown out (marked by X's in the figure). Also, each level of the tree can be thought of as "eliminating" a single variable in the manner described above. However, at each level, we may also choose *not* to eliminate the variable (indicated by the rightmost child of each node).

Once we have derived a number of interventions $\mathbf{w}'$ such that $Y_{\mathbf{w}'}(\mathbf{u}) \neq y$, we simply take the ones of the form $\mathbf{w}' = x'\mathbf{w}$, and check to see if $Y_{x\mathbf{w}} = y$ and AC2(c) are satisfied. The relevant interventions are circled in the figure. Notice that the intervention $\{X = 0, C = 0\}$ is discovered.

The pseudocode for the general intervention-proving algorithm is presented in Fig. 4. Notice that Fig. 3 does not correspond exactly to the tree searched by Fig. 4, in the sense that if we choose to keep the setting for variable $I(k)$ at depth k of the tree, we do not actually generate a duplicate intervention at depth $k + 1$. Instead, we merely keep track of our "virtual depth" in the tree that ensures that we only eliminate variables in reverse topological order.

It is clear that if the intervention-proving search tree generates every intervention $\mathbf{w}'$ such that $Y_{\mathbf{w}'}(\mathbf{u}) \neq y$, and no intervention $\mathbf{w}'$ such that $Y_{\mathbf{w}'}(\mathbf{u}) = y$, then this algorithm will work correctly. Indeed, we can prove half of this.

Lemma 7 *For every intervention $\mathbf{w}'$ found by $IP((M, \mathbf{u}), x, y)$, $Y_{\mathbf{w}'}(\mathbf{u}) \neq y$.*

Proof sketch For a node N in the IP search tree, define $\mathbf{w}(N)$ as the intervention that N represents. It can be proven by induction that if $\mathbf{w}(N)$ sets variable V to v, then for any descendant D of N in the IP search tree, we have $V_{\mathbf{w}(D)} = v$. Thus, since the root of the IP search tree generates only nodes corresponding to interventions of the form $Y = y'$ such that $y' \neq y$, Lem. 7 follows as a simple corollary. ∎

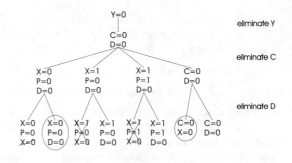

Figure 3: Intervention-Proving Search Tree for the Desert Traveler Scenario (query: $(X = 1) \propto (Y = 1)$)

Algorithm IP(CausalWorld (M,**u**), Cause X=x, Effect Y=y):
1. Let M' be the W-projection of (M,**u**) wrt x   y.
2. Let I(n) be a reverse topological order of the
   endogenous variables of M' such that Y=I(0).
3. For all interventions y' such that y'   y:
   - if(IPTreeWalk(y', 0) == true) then return true.
4. Return false.

bool IPTreeWalk(Intervention **w'**, int treedepth):
1. If **w'** is of the form x'**w**, then check that $Y_{x\mathbf{w}}(\mathbf{u})$ = y.
   If so, then check that **w** satisfies AC2(c). If so, then
   return true.
2. For every (single) variable assignment V=v in **w'**
   such that V   X, V=I(k) for k >= treedepth:
   3. For every full instantiation **p** of V's parents such
      that $F_V(\mathbf{p})$ = v:
      4. **w₂**   (**w'** \ v)   **p**.
      5. If **w₂** is internally consistent, then return true
         if IPTreeWalk(**w₂**, k) returns true
6. Return false.

Figure 4: Pseudocode for the IP Algorithm

Although it is not the case that IP generates *every* intervention $\mathbf{w'}$ such that $Y_{\mathbf{w'}}(\mathbf{u}) \neq y$, we can nevertheless characterize the interventions that it produces.

Lemma 8 $IP((M, \mathbf{u}), x, y)$ *finds only interventions* $\mathbf{w'}$ *subject to the following two conditions:*
(a) $\mathbf{W'}$ *contains a node on every path from a root node to* Y *in the endogenous causal network of* M
(b) If $\mathbf{W'}\backslash\{V\}$ *contains a node on every path from variable* V *to* Y, *then* $V \notin \mathbf{W'}$.

Proof sketch The proof is a straightforward induction on the depth of the IP search tree. ∎

Lemma 9 $IP((M, \mathbf{u}), x, y)$ *finds every intervention* $\mathbf{w'}$ *such that* $Y_{\mathbf{w'}}(\mathbf{u}) \neq y$, *subject to conditions (a) and (b) of Lem. 8.*

Proof sketch For node N in the IP search tree, define $\mathbf{w}(N)$ as the intervention that N represents. Define $\mathbf{W}(N)$ as the set of endogenous variables fixed by $\mathbf{w}(N)$. Let $\mathbf{w'}$ be an intervention satisfying the conditions of the lemma.

Let $Q(k)$ be the following proposition: "At depth k of the IP search tree, there exists a node N such that for all $V \in \{I(j)|j <= k-1\}$, we have: (i) $V \notin \mathbf{W'} \Leftrightarrow V \notin \mathbf{W}(N)$, (ii) $V \in \mathbf{W'} \Leftrightarrow V \in \mathbf{W}(N)$, (iii) $\forall V \in \mathbf{W}(N), V_{\mathbf{w'}}(\mathbf{u}) \in \mathbf{w}(N)$." $Q(k)$ can be proven by induction on k. From this result, the lemma immediately follows, since it implies that at depth $n + 1$ of the IP search tree, IP will find a node N such that $\mathbf{w}(N) = \mathbf{w'}$. ∎

From these lemmas, we can prove the correctness of IP.

Theorem 10 IP *returns as output* "$x \propto y$" *iff* $x \propto y$.

Proof From Lem. 7, it is clear that IP returns "$x \propto y$" only if $x \propto y$, since IP only finds interventions that satisfy AC2(a), then checks to see if they satisfy AC2(b) and (c).

Now suppose that $x \propto y$. Then there is some intervention $x'\mathbf{w}$ that satisfies AC2. Now consider the set of root nodes $\mathbf{R} = \{R_i | R_i \notin \mathbf{W} \cup \{X\}\}$ in the endogenous causal network. Create a new intervention $x'\mathbf{wr}$, where $\mathbf{r} = \mathbf{R}(\mathbf{u})$.

Notice that since $\mathbf{R}$ are root nodes, $\mathbf{R}(\mathbf{u}) = \mathbf{R}_{x'\mathbf{w}}(\mathbf{u})$, thus this new intervention must also satisfy AC2. Now consider any node $S \in \mathbf{W} \cup \mathbf{A}$ for which every path from S to Y contains some node in $\mathbf{W}\backslash\{S\}$. Notice that the value of Y is therefore independent of the value of S, and hence we can remove S from our intervention and this new intervention will still satisfy AC2. Thus we can always create a new intervention that satisfies AC2 and also satisfies the two conditions specified in Lem. 8. Hence by Lem. 9, IP will find this intervention, and return "$x \propto y$". ∎

The running time of this algorithm will vary substantially, depending on the topology and quantification of the causal network, but we can say with certainty that in the worst-case, IP generates no more nodes than the brute-force search tree of the previous section.

Theorem 11 *The search tree generated by* IP *contains no duplicate nodes, i.e. no two nodes that represent the same intervention.*

Proof sketch Proof by contradiction. Assume that there are two distinct nodes D and E in the IP search tree that represent the same intervention. Let A be the common ancestor of D and E, and let B and C be the children of A on the path to D and E, respectively. Then it can be shown that B and C must differ on the value of at least one variable set in their respective interventions, and that this difference propagates down to D and E. Hence D and E must represent different interventions. ∎

Since the tree generated by IP contains no duplicate nodes, IP generates asympototically no more nodes than the brute-force search tree, since that tree contains nodes representing every possible intervention, and the IP search tree contains only a subset of possible interventions (note that in addition, IP generates a certain number of inconsistent nodes, then immediately throws them away; this adds only a constant amount of work per node, and thus does not impact asymptotic running time). We can characterize the worst-case number of nodes that IP will generate in terms of the size of the subset of interventions that it generates. Define S as the subset of interventions $\mathbf{w'}$ such that $Y_{\mathbf{w'}}(\mathbf{u}) \neq y$ and $\mathbf{w'}$ satisfies the conditions specified in Lem. 8. Then from Lem. 8, IP generates $|S|$ nodes in the worst-case.

For each node, we need to check that AC2(b) holds, which as we have seen, is polynomial in the number of nodes N in the causal network. We also need to examine every table entry for the variable we are eliminating, in order to generate the children of the node. This takes $O(c^k)$ time, where c is the maximum size of the domain of the network variables and k is the maximum number of parents per node. We will assume that the number of parents per node is bounded by a constant, as is the maximum size of the domain of the network variables. Hence c^k becomes a constant. Once again supposing that checking AC2(c) takes $O(\lambda)$ time, we can say that the worst-case asymptotic running time of IP is $O(c^k \lambda N^p |S|) = O(\lambda N^p |S|)$ Borrowing from the results we derived in the previous section, we can say that $O(\lambda N^p |S|) = O(\lambda N^p (c + 1)^N)$. It is not clear how much tighter a bound $O(\lambda N^p |S|)$ is, compared with

$O(\lambda N^p (c+1)^N)$. Experimental results, however, suggest that the difference is quite significant.

Checking AC2(c)

Once we find an intervention $\mathbf{w}$ that satisfies AC2(a) and AC2(b), we then face the challenge of checking whether AC2(c) is also satisfied by $\mathbf{w}$. To do this, we need to search through the space of possible $\mathbf{Z}$. For each $\mathbf{Z}$, we need to check that $Y_{x\mathbf{w}\mathbf{z}} = y$, where $\mathbf{z} = \mathbf{Z}(\mathbf{u})$.

For a particular $\mathbf{Z}$, it is not difficult to check this. We merely need to compute the value of Y under an intervention, which can be done in polynomial time. The problem is that if $\mathbf{Z}^C$ represents the set of variables that are candidates for inclusion in $\mathbf{Z}$, then there are $2^{|\mathbf{Z}^C|}$ possible $\mathbf{Z}$.

Thus, one critical issue is to limit the size of $\mathbf{Z}^C$, the candidate set for $\mathbf{Z}$. Unfortunately, the definition itself specifies that $\mathbf{Z}^C$ contains every variable in the causal world that is not X, Y, or a member of $\mathbf{W}$. Fortunately, we can do better.

Theorem 12 *Define $x \propto' y$ similarly to $x \propto y$, except with AC2(c) replaced by the following:*

AC2(c)': $Y_{xwz}(\mathbf{u}) = y$, for all $\mathbf{Z} \subseteq \mathbf{Z}^C$ such that $\mathbf{z} = \mathbf{Z}(\mathbf{u})$ and $\mathbf{Z}^C = \{V \in \mathbf{V} \backslash (X \cup \mathbf{W}) | V$ appears on one or more directed paths from X to Y in the causal network of M that do not contain a member of $\mathbf{W}\}$.

Then $x \propto' y$ iff $x \propto y$.

Proof Suppose $x \propto' y$. Then there exists some intervention $x'\mathbf{w}$ that satisfies the modified version of AC2. Consider the set $\mathbf{Z}^A = (\mathbf{V} \backslash (\{X\} \cup \mathbf{W})) \backslash \mathbf{Z}^C$. For all $Z \in \mathbf{Z}^A$, either $\mathbf{W}$ intercepts all paths from Z to Y in the endogenous causal network of M, or $\mathbf{W}$ intercepts all paths from X to Z (otherwise $Z \in \mathbf{Z}^C$). Thus define $\mathbf{Z}^{XZ}$ as $\{Z \in \mathbf{Z}^A | \mathbf{W}$ intercepts all paths from X to $Z\}$, and $\mathbf{Z}^{ZY}$ as $\mathbf{Z}^A \backslash \mathbf{Z}^{XZ}$. Create a new intervention $x'\mathbf{w}\mathbf{Z}^{XZ}_{x'\mathbf{w}}(\mathbf{u})$. We want to show that this new intervention satisfies the original version of AC2.

Since by Prop. 1(b) $Y_{x'\mathbf{w}\mathbf{Z}^{XZ}_{x'\mathbf{w}}(\mathbf{u})}(\mathbf{u}) = Y_{x'\mathbf{w}}(\mathbf{u}) \neq y$, clearly AC2(a) is satisfied. Using Prop. 1(a) and (b), $Y_{x\mathbf{w}\mathbf{Z}^{XZ}_{x'\mathbf{w}}(\mathbf{u})}(\mathbf{u}) = Y_{x\mathbf{w}\mathbf{Z}^{XZ}_{x\mathbf{w}}(\mathbf{u})}(\mathbf{u}) = Y_{x\mathbf{w}}(\mathbf{u}) = y$, so AC2(b) is also satisfied. Finally, take any $\mathbf{Z} \subseteq (\mathbf{V} \backslash (\{X\} \cup \mathbf{W} \cup \mathbf{Z}^{XZ}))$. $Y_{x\mathbf{w}\mathbf{Z}^{XZ}_{x'\mathbf{w}}(\mathbf{u})\mathbf{Z}(\mathbf{u})}(\mathbf{u}) = Y_{x\mathbf{w}\mathbf{Z}^{XZ}_{x'\mathbf{w}}(\mathbf{u})\mathbf{Z}'(\mathbf{u})}(\mathbf{u})$, where $\mathbf{Z}'$ is $\mathbf{Z}$ with all members of $\mathbf{Z}^{ZY}$ removed (by Prop. 1(a), since $\mathbf{W}$ intercepts all paths from these variables to Y). Furthermore, using Prop. 1(a) and (b), $Y_{x\mathbf{w}\mathbf{Z}^{XZ}_{x'\mathbf{w}}(\mathbf{u})\mathbf{Z}'(\mathbf{u})}(\mathbf{u}) = Y_{x\mathbf{w}\mathbf{Z}^{XZ}_{x\mathbf{w}}(\mathbf{u})\mathbf{Z}'(\mathbf{u})}(\mathbf{u}) = Y_{x\mathbf{w}\mathbf{Z}'(\mathbf{u})}(\mathbf{u}) = y$, so AC2(c) is satisfied.

Hence $x \propto' y \rightarrow x \propto y$. The converse is trivial. ∎

Given this result, we can construct a binary search tree to check AC2(c) in the following manner: for a given ordering of the variables in $\mathbf{Z}^C$, assign each variable to either be included in $\mathbf{Z}$ or to not be included in $\mathbf{Z}$. The leaves of such a tree will then be the possible $\mathbf{Z}$ we need to check. Hence, we can apply a simple dfs, and whenever we hit a leaf, check that the $\mathbf{Z}$ represented by the leaf is consistent with AC2(c). If not, then AC2(c) fails. If all leaves are consistent with AC2(c), then AC2(c) holds.

We can define the *value* of this search tree as 1 if all leaves are consistent with AC2(c), and 0 otherwise. The search tree can be pruned, by use of the following theorem:

Theorem 13 *Let N be a node of this search tree. N represents the choice of a certain subset $\mathbf{Z}(N)$ of $\mathbf{Z}^C$ for inclusion in $\mathbf{Z}$. If there exists a variable $V \in \mathbf{Z}^*$ such that every path from V to Y in the causal network is blocked by some other variable in $\mathbf{Z}(N)$, then the subtree rooted at this node can be pruned from the search tree with no change to the value of the tree.*

Proof Suppose that there is some $\mathbf{Z}$ such that $\mathbf{Z}(N) \subseteq \mathbf{Z}$ and such that $Y_{x\mathbf{w}\mathbf{Z}(\mathbf{u})}(\mathbf{u}) \neq y$. If we have variable $V \in \mathbf{Z}(N)$ for which every path from V to Y is blocked by some other variable in $\mathbf{Z}(N)$, then by Prop. 1(a), $Y_{x\mathbf{w}\mathbf{Z}(\mathbf{u})}(\mathbf{u}) = Y_{x\mathbf{w}(\mathbf{Z} \backslash \{V\})(\mathbf{u})}(\mathbf{u})$. Hence there exists a $\mathbf{Z}'$ in another subtree of the search tree that also violates AC2(c). Thus we can prune the subtree rooted at N with no change to the overall value of the tree. ∎

This paper does not address which variable ordering heuristics can help to maximize the impact of such pruning.

Restricted Forms

So far, we have outlined only complete strategies for handling the general problem of determining $x \propto y$. In this section, we consider whether we can develop better algorithms for restricted forms of the problem.

Intuitively speaking, a problem in Σ_2^P suggests two sources of complexity. We have identified these sources as the search for $\mathbf{w}$ and the search for $\mathbf{Z}$. In order to achieve a polynomial-time algorithm for actual cause, we would need to eliminate both sources of complexity. Unfortunately, to do so, we would likely be restricting the problem to such an extent as to render the solution useless in practice. Nevertheless, we can try to eliminate one of the sources of complexity to improve the speed of our algorithm (although the algorithm will still be exponential-time).

One method of doing so takes advantage of the following result from (Eiter & Lukasiewicz 2001):

Theorem 14 *Let M be a causal world for which all variables are binary. Suppose for a given $\mathbf{x}, \mathbf{y}, \mathbf{w}$, AC1, AC2(a), and AC2(b) hold. Then AC2(c) holds iff $\mathbf{Y}_{\mathbf{xwz}}(\mathbf{u}) = \mathbf{y}$, where $\mathbf{z} = \mathbf{Z}(\mathbf{u})$ and $\mathbf{Z} = \mathbf{V} \backslash (\mathbf{X} \cup \mathbf{W})$.*

In other words, under a binary causal world, there is no need to search through the space of possible $\mathbf{Z}$. It is sufficient to simply check the set $\mathbf{V} \backslash (\{X\} \cup \mathbf{W})$. This amounts to checking the value of Y under a single intervention, which as we have noted, takes polynomial time. Thus we can replace our exponential-time AC2(c) check with a simple polynomial-time check. Hence the asymptotic running time of IP becomes $O(N^p|S|)$, whereas the more general procedure requires $O(2^{|\mathbf{Z}^C|}N^p|S|)$.

Experimental Results

To test the algorithms outlined in this paper, we generated random causal worlds through the following process:

1. We generated a random DAG over n variables by adding an edge from variable k to variable l, $k < l$ with probability P_E. We also limited the number of parents allowed per node at L.

2. We quantified the table for variable V by randomly choosing the value of each table entry from a uniform distribution over the domain (of size D) of V.

Let V_1 be variable 1, and let $v_1 = V_1(\mathbf{u})$. Let V_n be variable n, and let $v_n = V_n(\mathbf{u})$. The query to our algorithms was $v_1 \propto v_n$. Note that V_1 is a root of the endogenous causal network, and V_n is a leaf.

We first tested the average size of the W-projection of a randomly generated causal world. We generated 2000 random networks by the process described above (with $L = 3$, $D = 2$), then pruned each with regard to $v_1 \propto v_n$. The averaged results are presented in Table 1. Such pruning can provide dramatic results for lower values of P_E.

We then implemented three algorithms: the brute-force algorithm, the same algorithm with the tree pruning described by Thm. 6, and the IP algorithm. Each used the CheckAC2c procedure with the pruning described by Thm. 13. For the brute-force algorithm with pruning, we used an arbitrary topological order of the causal network variables as our variable ordering. To compare these algorithms, we generated 5000 random causal worlds over 25 variables by the process described above with $P_E = .15$, $L = 3$, and $D = 3$. Then we computed the W-projection of each world with respect to query $x \propto y$. Finally, we ran each algorithm on the W-projections (on a Sun Ultra 10 workstation). The results are presented in Table 2, where N is the number of variables in the W-projection (hence $N \leq 25$). We display only values of N from 2 to 18. Clearly, IP enjoys a considerable advantage over the brute-force approach with pruning. Observe that the average time to generate each node seems to be larger for IP than for the brute-force algorithms (by a factor of about 2 or 3). Still, the savings that IP provides in terms of the total number of generated nodes easily makes up for this cost. Moreover, the performance of IP on binary worlds shows an even greater contrast, with mean execution time of 40 seconds and 20000 generated nodes on 18-node W-projections.

Conclusions

In this paper, we have presented basic algorithms for determining actual cause according to the definition presented in (Halpern & Pearl 2001). First, we presented a method of

P_E	Nodes in original network	Avg nodes in W-projection
.1	10	2.27
	20	3.32
	30	5.29
.3	10	5.14
	20	13.16
	30	22.76

Table 1: W-Projection Size (avg of 2000 nets)

N	Brute Force		BF w/ Pruning		IP	
	Avg nodes	Avg Δt(s)	Avg nodes	Avg Δt(s)	Avg nodes	Avg Δt(s)
2	1	<1	1	<1	1	<1
3	4	<1	4	<1	3	<1
4	22	<1	15	<1	7	<1
5	91	<1	53	<1	18	<1
6	304	<1	127	<1	24	<1
7	1416	<1	484	<1	51	<1
8	5413	1	1253	<1	106	<1
9	19692	4	3963	<1	199	<1
10	81490	18	15283	3	406	<1
11	-	-	52142	14	851	<1
12	-	-	-	-	1767	1
13	-	-	-	-	3453	2
14	-	-	-	-	7539	5
15	-	-	-	-	19119	16
16	-	-	-	-	40924	38
17	-	-	-	-	76207	81
18	-	-	-	-	248152	272

Table 2: Algorithm Performance Comparison

reducing the problem size by projecting a causal world onto a reduced set of (query-dependent) variables. Then, we explored two approaches to solving the problem and devised proven methods of pruning the search space. The second attempt, the intervention-proving approach, achieved superior experimental results. Finally, we considered the task of deriving algorithms for restricted forms of the problem, and showed how the IP algorithm could be adapted to run more efficiently for binary causal worlds.

Acknowledgments

The author would like to thank Judea Pearl, Richard Korf, and the anonymous reviewers for their helpful advice. This research was supported in part by grants from NSF, ONR, AFOSR, and the DoD MURI program.

References

Eiter, T., and Lukasiewicz, T. 2001. Complexity results for structure-based causality. In *In Proceedings of the International Joint Conference on Artificial Intelligence*, 35–40. San Francisco, CA: Morgan Kaufmann.

Halpern, J., and Pearl, J. 2001. Causes and explanations: A structural-model approach – part i: Causes. In *Proceedings of the Seventeenth Conference on Uncertainty in Artificial Intelligence*, 194–202. San Francisco, CA: Morgan Kaufmann.

Hopkins, M. 2002a. A proof of the conjunctive cause conjecture in 'causes and explanations: A structural-model approach'. Technical Report R–306, UCLA Cognitive Systems Laboratory.

Hopkins, M. 2002b. Strategies for determining causes of events. Technical Report R–302–L, UCLA Cognitive Systems Laboratory.

Pearl, J. 2000. *Causality: Models, Reasoning, and Inference*. Cambridge University Press.

Tree Approximation for Belief Updating

Robert Mateescu, Rina Dechter and Kalev Kask

Department of Information and Computer Science
University of California, Irvine, CA 92697-3425
{mateescu,dechter,kkask}@ics.uci.edu

Abstract

The paper presents a parameterized approximation scheme for probabilistic inference. The scheme, called *Mini-Clustering (MC)*, extends the partition-based approximation offered by mini-bucket elimination, to tree decompositions. The benefit of this extension is that all single-variable beliefs are computed (approximately) at once, using a two-phase message-passing process along the cluster tree. The resulting approximation scheme allows adjustable levels of accuracy and efficiency, in anytime style. Empirical evaluation against competing algorithms such as iterative belief propagation and Gibbs sampling demonstrates the potential of the MC approximation scheme for several classes of problems.

Introduction and related work

Probabilistic reasoning using Belief networks, computing the probability of one or more events given some evidence, is known to be NP-hard (Cooper 1990). However most commonly used exact algorithms for probabilistic inference such as join-tree clustering (Lauritzen & Spiegelhalter 1988; Jensen, Lauritzen, & Olesen 1990) or variable-elimination (Dechter 1996; Zhang & Poole 1994), exploit the network structure. These algorithms are time and space exponential in a graph parameter capturing the density of the network called tree-width. Yet, for large belief networks, the tree-width is often large, making exact inference impractical and therefore approximation methods must be pursued. Although approximation within given error bounds is also NP-hard (Dagum & Luby 1993; Roth 1996), some approximation strategies work well in practice.

The paper presents an anytime approximation scheme for probabilistic inference called mini-clustering (MC), which allows a flexible tradeoff between accuracy and efficiency. MC extends the partition-based approximation offered by mini-bucket elimination (Dechter & Rish 1997) to tree decompositions. The benefit of this extension is that all single-variable beliefs are computed (approximately) at once, using a two-phase message-passing process along the cluster tree. We present new empirical evaluation against competing algorithms such as iterative belief propagation and Gibbs sampling. The experiments demonstrate the anytime behavior of this methodology and its overall potential: On several

classes of problems (e.g. random noisy-or, grid networks and CPCS networks) mini-clustering exhibited superior performance.

Related work. Approximation algorithms proposed for belief updating fall into two main categories: 1. Monte Carlo sampling algorithms. Those algorithms sample the probability distribution and compute the probability required based on the obtained sample. Algorithms in this class are logic sampling (Henrion 1986), Gibbs sampling (Pearl 1988), likelihood weighting (Shachter & Peot 1989) and importance sampling (Cheng & Druzdzel 2000). 2. Algorithms that weaken or ignore some of the network's dependencies, forcing the generated dependencies of the network to be bounded. The mini-bucket scheme and the currently presented mini-cluster scheme fall into this second category.

Another algorithm in this class is *Iterative belief propagation (IBP)*, also called loopy belief propagation, that applies Pearl's belief propagation algorithm for singly connected networks to loopy-networks (Pearl 1988). It was recently observed that this algorithm works extremely well for coding applications (McEliece, MacKay, & Cheng 1997; Weiss 1997; Welling & Teh 2001). A related algorithm that removes *weak dependencies* in a join-tree clustering is given in (Kjæaerulff 1994) and another, for stochastic processes is in (Boyen & Koller 1998).

Hybrid methods exploiting both structure and Monte Carlo sampling were also introduced (Koller, Lerner, & Angelov 1998). Finally, an orthogonal collection of approximation algorithms using variational methods (Jaakkola & Jordan 1996) does not fall exactly in these two categories.

Preliminaries

Belief networks provide a formalism for reasoning about partial beliefs under conditions of uncertainty. A belief network is defined by a directed acyclic graph over nodes representing random variables of interest.

Belief networks. A *belief network* is a quadruple $BN =< X, D, G, P >^1$ where $X = \{X_1, \ldots, X_n\}$ is a set of random variables, $D = \{D_1, ..., D_n\}$ is the set of the corresponding domains, G is a directed acyclic graph over X and $P = \{p_1, ..., p_n\}$, where $p_i = P(X_i|pa_i)$ (pa_i are

---

[1] Also abbreviated $< G, P >$ when X and D are clear.

the parents of X_i in G) denote conditional probability tables (CPTs). Given a function f, we denote by $scope(f)$ the set of arguments of function f. The *moral graph* of a directed graph is the undirected graph obtained by connecting the parent nodes of each variable and eliminating direction.

Belief updating. The *belief updating* problem defined over a belief network (also referred to as *probabilistic inference*) is the task of computing the posterior probability $P(Y|e)$ of *query* nodes $Y \subseteq X$ given evidence e. We will focus on the basic case when Y consists of a single variable X_i. Namely, computing $Bel(X_i) = P(X_i = x|e)$, $\forall X_i \in X$, $\forall x \in D_i$.

Tree-decomposition schemes

We will describe our algorithms relative to a unifying tree-decomposition framework based on (Gottlob, Leone, & Scarello 1999). It generalizes tree-decompositions to include join-trees, bucket-trees and other variants applicable to both constraint processing and probabilistic inference.

DEFINITION 1 (tree-decomposition, cluster tree) *Let $BN =< X, D, G, P >$ be a belief network. A tree-decomposition for BN is a triple $< T, \chi, \psi >$, where $T = (V, E)$ is a tree, and χ and ψ are labeling functions which associate with each vertex $v \in V$ two sets, $\chi(v) \subseteq X$ and $\psi(v) \subseteq P$ satisfying:*
1. For each function $p_i \in P$, there is exactly one vertex $v \in V$ such that $p_i \in \psi(v)$, and $scope(p_i) \subseteq \chi(v)$.
2. For each variable $X_i \in X$, the set $\{v \in V | X_i \in \chi(v)\}$ induces a connected subtree of T. This is also called the running intersection property.
We will often refer to a node and its functions as a cluster *and use the term* tree-decomposition *and* cluster tree *interchangeably.*

DEFINITION 2 (tree-width, separator, eliminator)
The tree-width *(Arnborg 1985) of a tree-decomposition $< T, \chi, \psi >$ is $max_{v \in V} |\chi(v)|$. Given two adjacent vertices u and v of a tree-decomposition, the* separator *of u and v is defined as $sep(u, v) = \chi(u) \cap \chi(v)$, and the* eliminator *of u with respect to v is $elim(u, v) = \chi(u) - \chi(v)$.*

Join-trees and cluster-tree-elimination

The most used tree decomposition method is called join-tree decomposition (Lauritzen & Spiegelhalter 1988). Such decompositions can be generated by embedding the network's moral graph, G, in a chordal graph, often using a triangulation algorithm and using its maximal cliques as nodes in the join-tree. Such a join-tree satisfies the properties of tree-decomposition.

There are a few variants for processing join-trees for belief updating (Jensen, Lauritzen, & Olesen 1990; Shafer & Shenoy 1990). The variant which we use here, called cluster-tree-elimination (CTE) is applicable to tree-decompositions in general and is geared toward space savings. It is a message passing algorithm (either two-phase message passing, or in asynchronous mode). Algorithm CTE for belief updating denoted CTE-BU is given in Figure 1. The algorithm pays a special attention to the processing of observed variables since the presence of evidence is a central component in belief updating. When a cluster sends

---

Algorithm CTE for Belief-Updating (CTE-BU)
Input: A tree decomposition $< T, \chi, \psi >$, $T = (V, E)$ for $BN =< X, D, G, P >$. Evidence variables $var(e)$.
Output: An augmented tree whose nodes are clusters containing the original CPTs and the messages received from neighbors. $P(X_i, e)$, $\forall X_i \in X$.

Denote by $H_{(u,v)}$ the message from vertex u to v, $ne_v(u)$ the neighbors of u in T excluding v.
$cluster(u) = \psi(u) \cup \{H_{(v,u)} | (v, u) \in E\}$.
$cluster_v(u) = cluster(u)$ excluding message from v to u.

- **Compute messages:**
For every node u in T, once u has received messages from all $ne_v(u)$, compute message to node v:

1. **process observed variables**
   Assign relevant evidence to all $p_i \in \psi(u)$

2. **Compute the combined function:**

$$h_{(u,v)} = \sum_{elim(u,v)} \prod_{f \in A} f.$$

   where A is the set of functions in $cluster_v(u)$ whose scope intersects $elim(u, v)$.
   Add $h_{(u,v)}$ to $H_{(u,v)}$ and add all the individual functions in $cluster_v(u) - A$
   Send $H_{(u,v)}$ to node v.

- **Compute $P(X_i, e)$:**
For every $X_i \in X$ let u be a vertex in T such that $X_i \in \chi(u)$.
Compute $P(X_i, e) = \sum_{\chi(u) - \{X_i\}} (\prod_{f \in cluster(u)} f)$

Figure 1: Algorithm Cluster-Tree-Elimination for Belief Updating (CTE-BU)

a message to a neighbor, the algorithm operates on all the functions in the cluster except the message from that particular neighbor. The message contains a single *combined* function and *individual* functions that do not share variables with the relevant eliminator. All the non-individual functions are *combined* in a product and summed over the eliminator.

Example 1 *Figure 2 describes a belief network and a join-tree decomposition for it. Figure 3 shows the trace of running CTE-BU. In this case no individual functions appear between any of the clusters. To keep the figure simple, we only show the combined functions $h_{(u,v)}$ (each of them being in fact the only element of the set $H_{(u,v)}$ that represents the corresponding message between clusters u and v).*

Similar to (Dechter, Kask, & Larossa 2001) we can show that:

THEOREM 1 (Complexity of CTE-BU) *The time complexity of CTE-BU is $O(deg \cdot (n + N) \cdot d^{w^*+1})$ and the space complexity is $O(N \cdot d^{sep})$, where deg is the maximum degree of a node in the tree, n is the number of variables, N is the number of nodes in the tree decomposition, d is the maximum domain size of a variable, w^* is the tree-width and sep is the maximum separator size.*

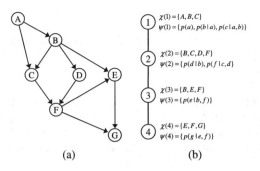

$\chi(1) = \{A, B, C\}$
$\psi(1) = \{p(a), p(b|a), p(c|a, b)\}$

$\chi(2) = \{B, C, D, F\}$
$\psi(2) = \{p(d|b), p(f|c, d)\}$

$\chi(3) = \{B, E, F\}$
$\psi(3) = \{p(e|b, f)\}$

$\chi(4) = \{E, F, G\}$
$\psi(4) = \{p(g|e, f)\}$

(a)　　　　(b)

Figure 2: *a*) A belief network; *b*) A join-tree decomposition;

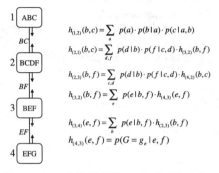

$h_{(1,2)}(b, c) = \sum_a p(a) \cdot p(b|a) \cdot p(c|a, b)$

$h_{(2,1)}(b, c) = \sum_{d, f} p(d|b) \cdot p(f|c, d) \cdot h_{(3,2)}(b, f)$

$h_{(2,3)}(b, f) = \sum_{c, d} p(d|b) \cdot p(f|c, d) \cdot h_{(4,2)}(b, c)$

$h_{(3,2)}(b, f) = \sum_e p(e|b, f) \cdot h_{(4,3)}(e, f)$

$h_{(3,4)}(e, f) = \sum_b p(e|b, f) \cdot h_{(2,3)}(b, f)$

$h_{(4,3)}(e, f) = p(G = g_e | e, f)$

Figure 3: Execution of CTE-BU; no individual functions appear in this case.

Mini-Clustering for belief updating

The time, and especially the space complexity of CTE-BU renders the algorithm infeasible for problems with high tree-width. In this section we introduce the mini-clustering, a partition-based anytime algorithm which computes approximate values or bounds on $P(X_i, e)$ for every variable X_i in the network. It is a natural extension of the mini-bucket idea to tree-decompositions. Rather than computing the mini-bucket approximation n times, one for each variable as would be required by the mini-bucket approach, the algorithm performs an equivalent computation with just two message passings along each arc of the cluster tree. The idea is to partition each cluster into mini-clusters having at most i variables, where i is an accuracy parameter. Node u partitions its cluster into p mini-clusters $mc(1), \ldots, mc(p)$. Instead of computing $h_{(u,v)} = \sum_{elim(u,v)} \prod_{k=1}^p \prod_{f \in mc(k)} f$ as in CTE-BU, we can compute an upper bound by migrating the summation operator into each mini-cluster. However, this would give $\prod_{k=1}^p \sum_{elim(u,v)} \prod_{f \in mc(k)} f$ which is an unnecessarily large upper bound on $h_{(u,v)}$ in which each $\prod_{f \in mc(k)} f$ is bounded by its sum over $elim(u, v)$. Instead, we rewrite $h_{(u,v)} = \sum_{elim(u,v)} (\prod_{f \in mc(1)} f) \cdot (\prod_{i=2}^p \prod_{f \in mc(i)} f)$. Subsequently, instead of bounding $\prod_{f \in mc(i)} f, (i \geq 2)$ by summation over the eliminator, we bound it by its maximum over the eliminator, which yields $(\sum_{elim(u,v)} \prod_{f \in mc(1)} f) \cdot \prod_{k=2}^p (\max_{elim(u,v)} \prod_{f \in mc(k)} f)$. Therefore, if we are interested in an upper bound, we marginalize one mini-cluster by summation and the others by maximization. Note that the

---

Procedure MC for Belief Updating (MC-BU(i))

2. **Compute the combined mini-functions:**
   Make an (i)-size mini-clusters partitioning of $cluster_v(u)$, $\{mc(1), \ldots, mc(p)\}$;
   $h_{(u,v)}^1 = \sum_{elim(u,v)} \prod_{f \in mc(1)} f$
   $h_{(u,v)}^i = \max_{elim(u,v)} \prod_{f \in mc(i)} f \quad i = 2, \ldots, p$
   add $\{h_{(u,v)}^i | i = 1, \ldots, p\}$ to $H_{(u,v)}$. Send $H_{(u,v)}$ to v.

Compute upper bounds on $P(X_i, e)$:
For every $X_i \in X$ let $u \in V$ be a cluster such that $X_i \in \chi(u)$. Make (i) mini-clusters from $cluster(u), \{mc(1), \ldots, mc(p)\}$; Compute
$(\sum_{\chi(u) - X_i} \prod_{f \in mc(1)} f) \cdot (\prod_{k=2}^p \max_{\chi(u) - X_i} \prod_{f \in mc(k)} f)$.

Figure 4: Procedure Mini-Clustering for Belief Updating (MC-BU)

summation in the first mini-cluster must be over *all* variables in the eliminator, even if some of them might not appear in the scope of functions in $mc(1)$.

Consequently, the combined functions are approximated via mini-clusters, as follows. Suppose $u \in V$ has received messages from all its neighbors other than v (the message from v is ignored even if received). The functions in $cluster_v(u)$ that are to be combined are partitioned into mini-clusters $\{mc(1), \ldots, mc(p)\}$, each one containing at most i variables. One of the mini-clusters is processed by summation and the others by maximization over the eliminator, and the resulting combined functions as well as all the individual functions are sent to v.

Lower-bounds and mean approximations. We can also derive a lower-bound on beliefs by replacing the max operator with min operator (see above derivation for rationale). This allows, in principle, computing both an upper bound and a lower bound on the joint beliefs. Alternatively, if we yield the idea of deriving a bound (and indeed the empirical evaluation encourages that) we can replace max by a *mean* operator (taking the sum and dividing by the number of elements in the sum), deriving an approximation of the joint belief.

Algorithm MC-BU for upper bounds can be obtained from CTE-BU by replacing step 2 of the main loop and the final part of computing the upper bounds on the joint belief by the procedure given in Figure 4.

Partitioning strategies. In our current implementation, the partitioning is done in an arbitrary brute-force manner and the choice of the first mini-cluster for upper bound computation is random. Clearly, a more informed approach may improve the accuracy significantly but this exploration is outside the scope of the current paper.

Example 2 *Figure 5 shows the trace of running MC-BU(3) on the problem in Figure 2. First, evidence $G = g_e$ is assigned in all CPTs. There are no individual functions to be sent from cluster 1 to cluster 2. Cluster 1 contains only 3 variables, $\chi(1) = \{A, B, C\}$, therefore it is not partitioned. The combined function $h_{(1,2)}^1(b, c) = \sum_a p(a) \cdot$*

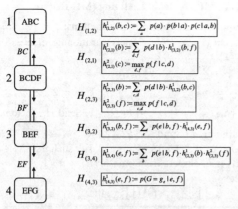

Figure 5: Execution of MC-BU for $i = 3$

$p(b|a) \cdot p(c|a,b)$ *is computed and the message* $H_{(1,2)} = \{h^1_{(1,2)}(b,c)\}$ *is sent to node* 2. *Now, node* 2 *can send its message to node* 3. *Again, there are no individual functions. Cluster* 2 *contains* 4 *variables,* $\chi(2) = \{B, C, D, F\}$, *and a partitioning is necessary: MC-BU(3) can choose* $mc(1) = \{p(d|b), h_{(1,2)}(b,c)\}$ *and* $mc(2) = \{p(f|c,d)\}$. *The combined functions* $h^1_{(2,3)}(b) = \sum_{c,d} p(d|b) \cdot h_{(1,2)}(b,c)$ *and* $h^2_{(2,3)}(f) = \max_{c,d} p(f|c,d)$ *are computed and the message* $H_{(4,3)} = \{h^1_{(2,3)}(b), h^2_{(2,3)}(f)\}$ *is sent to node* 3. *The algorithm continues until every node has received messages from all its neighbors. An upper bound on* $p(a, G = g_e)$ *can now be computed by choosing cluster* 1, *which contains variable* A. *It doesn't need partitioning, so the algorithm just computes* $\sum_{b,c} p(a) \cdot p(b|a) \cdot p(c|a,b) \cdot h^1_{(2,1)}(b) \cdot h^2_{(2,1)}(c)$. *Notice that unlike CTE-BU which processes* 4 *variables in cluster* 2, *MC-BU(3) never processes more than* 3 *variables at a time.*

Properties of Mini-Clustering

THEOREM 2 *Algorithm MC-BU(i) with* max *(respectively* min*) computes an upper (respectively lower) bound on the joint probability* $P(X, e)$ *of each variable and each of its values.*

A similar mini-clustering scheme for combinatorial optimization was developed in (Dechter, Kask, & Larossa 2001) having similar performance properties as MC-BU.

THEOREM 3 (Complexity of MC-BU(i)) *(Dechter, Kask, & Larossa 2001) The time and space complexity of MC-BU(i) is* $O(n \cdot hw^* \cdot d^i)$ *where* n *is the number of variables,* d *is the maximum domain size of a variable and* $hw^* = max_u|\{f|scope(f) \cap \chi(u) \neq \phi\}|$, *which bounds the number of functions that may travel to a neighboring cluster via message-passing.*

Accuracy. For a given i, the accuracy of MC-BU(i) can be shown to be not worse than that of executing the mini-bucket algorithm MB(i) n times, once for each variable (an algorithm that we call nMB(i)). Given a specific execution of MC-BU(i), we can show that for every variable X_i, there exists an ordering of the variables and a corresponding partitioning such that MB(i) computes the same approximation

value for $P(X_i, e)$ as does $MC - BU(i)$. In empirical analysis (Kask 2001) it is shown that MC-BU has an up to linear speed-up over nMB(i).

Normalization

The MC-BU algorithm using max operator computes an upper bound $\overline{P}(X_i, e)$ on the joint probability $P(X_i, e)$. However, deriving a bound on the conditional probability $P(X_i|e)$ is not easy when the exact value of $P(e)$ is not available. If we just try to divide (multiply) $\overline{P}(X_i, e)$ by a constant, the result is not necessarily an upper bound on $P(X_i|e)$. In principle, if we can derive a lower bound $\underline{P}(e)$ on $P(e)$, then we can compute $\overline{P}(X_i, e)/\underline{P}(e)$ as an upper bound on $P(X_i|e)$. However, due to compound error, it is likely to be ineffective. In our empirical evaluation we experimented with normalizing the upper bound as $\overline{P}(X_i, e)/\sum_{X_i} \overline{P}(X_i, e)$ over the values of X_i. The result is not necessarily an upper bound on P($X_i|e$). Similarly, we can also normalize the values when using $mean$ or min operators. It is easy to show that normalization with the $mean$ operator is identical to normalization of MC-BU output when applying the summation operator in all the mini-clusters.

Empirical evaluation

We tested the performance of our scheme on random noisy-or networks, random coding networks, general random networks, grid networks, and three benchmark CPCS files with 54, 360 and 422 variables respectively (these are belief networks for medicine, derived from the Computer based Patient Case Simulation system, known to be hard for belief updating). On each type of network we ran Iterative Belief Propagation (IBP) - set to run at most 30 iterations, Gibbs Sampling (GS) and MC-BU(i), with i from 2 to the tree-width w^* to capture the anytime behavior of MC-BU.

We immediately observed that the quality of MC-BU in providing upper or lower bounds on the joint $P(X_i, e)$ was ineffective. Although the upper bound decreases as the accuracy parameter i increases, it still is in most cases greater than 1. Therefore, following the ideas explained in the previous section we report the results with normalizing the upper bounds (called max) and normalizing the mean (called $mean$). We notice that MC-BU using the $mean$ operator is doing consistently better.

For noisy-or networks, general random networks, grid networks and for the CPCS networks we computed the exact solution and used three different measures of accuracy: 1. Normalized Hamming Distance (NHD) - We picked the most likely value for each variable for the approximate and for the exact, took the ratio between the number of disagreements and the total number of variables, and averaged over the number of problems that we ran for each class. 2. Absolute Error (Abs. Error) - is the absolute value of the difference between the approximate and the exact, averaged over all values (for each variable), all variables and all problems. 3. Relative Error (Rel. Error) - is the absolute value of the difference between the approximate and the exact, divided by the exact, averaged over all values (for each variable),

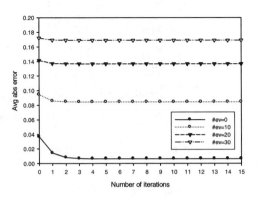

Random Bayesian N=50 K=2 P=2 C=48

Figure 6: Convergence of IBP

N=50, P=3, 25 instances										
10 |e| 20 30	NHD		Abs. Error		Rel. Error		Time			
	max	mean	max	mean	max	mean	max	mean		
IBP		0		1.3E-04		7.9E-01		0.242		
		0		3.6E-04		2.2E+00		0.184		
		0		6.8E-04		4.2E+00		0.121		
MC-BU(2)	0	0	1.3E-03	9.6E-04	8.2E+00	5.8E+00	0.107	0.108		
	0	0	5.3E-04	4.0E-04	3.1E+00	2.4E+00	0.077	0.077		
	0	0	2.3E-04	1.9E-04	1.4E+00	1.2E+00	0.064	0.064		
MC-BU(5)	0	0	1.0E-03	8.3E-04	6.4E+00	5.1E+00	0.133	0.133		
	0	0	4.6E-04	4.1E-04	2.7E+00	2.4E+00	0.104	0.105		
	0	0	2.0E-04	1.9E-04	1.2E+00	1.2E+00	0.098	0.095		
MC-BU(8)	0	0	6.6E-04	5.7E-04	4.0E+00	3.5E+00	0.498	0.509		
	0	0	1.8E-04	1.8E-04	1.1E+00	1.0E+00	0.394	0.406		
	0	0	3.4E-05	3.4E-05	2.1E-01	2.1E-01	0.300	0.308		
MC-BU(11)	0	0	2.6E-04	2.4E-04	1.6E+00	1.5E+00	2.339	2.378		
	0	0	3.8E-05	3.8E-05	2.3E-01	2.3E-01	1.421	1.439		
	0	0	6.4E-07	6.4E-07	4.0E-03	4.0E-03	0.613	0.624		
MC-BU(14)	0	0	4.2E-05	4.1E-05	2.5E-01	2.4E-01	7.805	7.875		
	0	0	0	0	0	0	2.075	2.093		
	0	0	0	0	0	0	0.630	0.638		

Table 1: Performance on noisy-or networks, w*=16

N=50, P=2, 50 instances								
0 |e| 10 20	NHD		Abs. Error		Rel. Error		Time	
	max	mean	max	mean	max	mean	max	mean
IBP		0.01840		0.00696		0.01505		0.100
		0.19550		0.09022		0.34608		0.080
		0.27467		0.13588		3.13327		0.062
GS		0.50400		0.10715		0.26621		13.023
		0.51400		0.15216		0.57262		12.978
		0.51267		0.18066		4.71805		13.321
MC-BU(2)	0.11400	0.08080	0.03598	0.02564	0.07950	0.05628	0.055	0.055
	0.10600	0.08800	0.04897	0.03957	0.12919	0.10579	0.047	0.048
	0.08667	0.07333	0.04443	0.03639	0.13096	0.10694	0.041	0.042
MC-BU(5)	0.10120	0.06480	0.03392	0.02242	0.07493	0.04937	0.071	0.072
	0.06950	0.05850	0.03254	0.02723	0.08613	0.07313	0.063	0.065
	0.03933	0.03400	0.02022	0.01831	0.05533	0.04984	0.059	0.060
MC-BU(8)	0.05080	0.02680	0.01872	0.01030	0.04103	0.02262	0.216	0.221
	0.01550	0.01450	0.00743	0.00587	0.01945	0.01547	0.178	0.180
	0.00600	0.00400	0.00228	0.00200	0.00597	0.00542	0.129	0.134

Table 2: Performance on random networks, w*=10

BER	σ = .22		σ = .26		σ = .32		σ = .40		σ = .51		Time
	max	mean	max	mean	max	mean	max	mean	max	mean	
N=100, P=3, 50 instances, w*=7											
IBP	0.000	0.000	0.000	0.000	0.002	0.002	0.022	0.022	0.088	0.088	0.00
GS	0.483	0.483	0.483	0.483	0.483	0.483	0.483	0.483	0.483	0.483	31.36
MC-BU(2)	0.002	0.002	0.004	0.004	0.024	0.024	0.068	0.068	0.132	0.131	0.08
MC-BU(4)	0.001	0.001	0.002	0.002	0.018	0.018	0.046	0.045	0.110	0.110	0.08
MC-BU(6)	0.000	0.000	0.000	0.000	0.004	0.004	0.038	0.038	0.106	0.106	0.12
MC-BU(8)	0.000	0.000	0.000	0.000	0.002	0.002	0.023	0.023	0.091	0.091	0.19
N=100, P=4, 50 instances, w*=11											
IBP	0.000	0.000	0.000	0.000	0.002	0.002	0.013	0.013	0.075	0.075	0.00
GS	0.506	0.506	0.506	0.506	0.506	0.506	0.506	0.506	0.506	0.506	39.85
MC-BU(2)	0.006	0.006	0.015	0.015	0.043	0.043	0.093	0.094	0.157	0.157	0.19
MC-BU(4)	0.006	0.006	0.017	0.017	0.049	0.049	0.104	0.102	0.158	0.158	0.19
MC-BU(6)	0.005	0.005	0.011	0.011	0.035	0.034	0.071	0.074	0.151	0.150	0.29
MC-BU(8)	0.002	0.002	0.004	0.004	0.022	0.022	0.059	0.059	0.121	0.122	0.71
MC-BU(10)	0.001	0.001	0.001	0.001	0.008	0.008	0.033	0.032	0.101	0.102	1.87

Table 3: BER for coding networks

all variables and all problems. For coding networks, we report only one measure, Bit Error Rate (BER). In terms of the measures defined above, BER is the normalized Hamming distance between the approximate (computed by an algorithm) and the actual input (which in the case of coding networks may be different from the solution given by exact algorithms), so we denote them differently to make this semantic distinction. We also show the time taken by each algorithm.

In Figure 6 we show that IBP converges after about 5 iterations. So, while in our experiments we report its time for 30 iterations, its time is even better when sophisticated termination is used. These results are typical of all runs.

The random noisy-or networks and the random networks were generated using parameters (N,K,C,P), where N is the number of variables (a square integer for grid networks), K is their domain size (we used only K=2), C is the number of conditional probability matrices and P is the number of parents in each conditional probability matrix. The grid networks have the structure of a square, with edges directed to form a diagonal flow (all parallel edges have the same direction). They were generated by specifying N (a square integer) and K (we used K=2). We also varied the number of evidence nodes, denoted by |e| in the tables. The parameter

values are reported in each table.

Comment: Note that since our evaluation measures are based on comparing against exact figures, we had to restrict the instances to be relatively small or sparse enough to be managed by exact algorithms.

For all the problems, Gibbs sampling performed consistently poorly so we only include part of the results in the following tables.

Random noisy-or networks results are summarized in Table 1. For NHD, both IBP and MC-BU gave perfect results. For the other measures, we noticed that IBP is more accurate for no evidence by about an order of magnitude. However, as evidence is added, IBP's accuracy decreases, while MC-BU's increases and they give similar results. We also notice that MC-BU gets better as the accuracy parameter i increases, which shows its anytime behavior. We also observed a similar pattern of behavior when experimenting with smaller noisy-or networks, generated with P=2 (w*=10).

General random networks results are summarized in Table 2. They are in general similar to those for random noisy-or networks. NHD is non-zero in this case. Again, IBP has the best result only for few evidence variables. It is remarkable how quickly MC-BU surpasses the performance of IBP as evidence is added. We also experimented with larger networks generated with P=3 (w*=16) and observed a similar behavior.

N=225, 10 instances, *mean* operator				
|e| = 0, 10, 20, 30	NHD	Abs. Error	Rel. Error	Time
IBP	0.0094	0.0037	0.0080	0.071
	0.0665	0.0665	0.0761	0.070
	0.1205	0.0463	0.1894	0.068
	0.1462	0.0632	0.1976	0.062
GS	0.5178	0.1096	0.2688	9.339
	0.5047	0.5047	0.3200	9.392
	0.4849	0.1232	0.4009	9.524
	0.4692	0.1335	0.4156	9.220
MC-BU(2)	0.1256	0.0474	0.1071	0.049
	0.1312	0.1312	0.1070	0.041
	0.1371	0.0523	0.1205	0.042
	0.1287	0.0512	0.1201	0.053
MC-BU(6)	0.1050	0.0356	0.0775	0.217
	0.0944	0.0944	0.0720	0.064
	0.0844	0.0313	0.0701	0.059
	0.0759	0.0286	0.0652	0.120
MC-BU(10)	0.0406	0.0146	0.0313	0.500
	0.0358	0.0358	0.0288	0.368
	0.0337	0.0122	0.0272	0.484
	0.0256	0.0116	0.0265	0.468
MC-BU(14)	0.0233	0.0081	0.0173	2.315
	0.0209	0.0209	0.0152	2.342
	0.0146	0.0055	0.0126	2.225
	0.0118	0.0046	0.0105	2.350
MC-BU(17)	0.0089	0.0031	0.0065	10.990
	0.0116	0.0116	0.0069	10.105
	0.0063	0.0022	0.0048	9.381
	0.0036	0.0017	0.0038	9.573

Table 4: Performance on 15x15 grid, w*=22

N=54, 50 instances								
0 |e| 10 20	NHD		Abs. Error		Rel. Error		Time	
	max	mean	max	mean	max	mean	max	mean
IBP		0.01852		0.00032		0.00064		2.450
		0.15727		0.03307		0.07349		2.191
		0.20765		0.05934		0.14202		1.561
GS		0.49444		0.07797		0.18034		17.247
		0.51409		0.09002		0.21298		17.208
		0.48706		0.10608		0.26853		17.335
MC-BU(2)	0.16667	0.07407	0.02722	0.01221	0.05648	0.02520	0.154	0.153
	0.11636	0.07636	0.02623	0.01843	0.05581	0.03943	0.096	0.095
	0.10529	0.07941	0.02876	0.02196	0.06357	0.04878	0.067	0.067
MC-BU(5)	0.18519	0.09259	0.02488	0.01183	0.05128	0.02454	0.157	0.155
	0.10727	0.07682	0.02464	0.01703	0.05239	0.03628	0.112	0.112
	0.08059	0.05941	0.02174	0.01705	0.04790	0.03778	0.090	0.087
MC-BU(8)	0.12963	0.07407	0.01487	0.00619	0.03047	0.01273	0.438	0.446
	0.06591	0.05000	0.01590	0.01040	0.03394	0.02227	0.369	0.370
	0.03235	0.02588	0.00977	0.00770	0.02165	0.01707	0.292	0.294
MC-BU(11)	0.11111	0.07407	0.01133	0.00688	0.02369	0.01434	2.038	2.032
	0.02818	0.01500	0.00600	0.00398	0.01295	0.00869	1.567	1.571
	0.00353	0.00353	0.00124	0.00101	0.00285	0.00236	0.867	0.869

Table 5: Performance on cpcs54.erg, w*=15

N=360, 5 instances, *mean* operator				
|e| = 0, 20, 40	NHD	Abs. Error	Rel. Error	Time
IBP	0.0000	0.0027	0.0054	82
	0.0112	0.0256	3.4427	76
	0.0363	0.0629	736.1080	60
MC-BU(8)	0.0056	0.0125	0.0861	16
	0.0041	0.0079	0.0785	14
	0.0113	0.0109	0.2997	9
MC-BU(12)	0.0000	0.0072	0.0562	71
	0.0000	0.0052	0.0525	71
	0.0063	0.0067	0.0796	60
MC-BU(16)	0.0000	0.0015	0.0123	775
	0.0000	0.0023	0.0155	784
	0.0000	0.0009	0.0080	548

Table 6: Performance on cpcs360.erg, w*=20

N=422, 1 instance, *mean* operator				
|e| = 0, 20, 40	NHD	Abs. Error	Rel. Error	Time
IBP	0.0024	0.0062	0.0150	2838
	0.0721	0.0562	7.5626	2367
	0.0654	0.0744	37.5096	2150
MC-BU(3)	0.0687	0.0455	1.4341	161
	0.0373	0.0379	0.9792	85
	0.0366	0.0233	2.8384	48
MC-BU(7)	0.0545	0.0354	0.1531	146
	0.0249	0.0253	0.3112	77
	0.0262	0.0164	0.5781	45
MC-BU(11)	0.0166	0.0175	0.0738	152
	0.0448	0.0352	0.6113	95
	0.0340	0.0237	0.6978	63
MC-BU(15)	0.0024	0.0039	0.0145	526
	0.0398	0.0278	0.5338	564
	0.0183	0.0113	0.5248	547

Table 7: Performance on cpcs422.erg, w*=23

Random coding networks results are given in Tables 3. The instances fall within the class of linear block codes, (σ is the channel noise level). It is known that IBP is very accurate for this class. Indeed, these are the only problems that we experimented with where IBP outperformed MC-BU throughout. The anytime behavior of MC-BU can again be seen in the variation of numbers in each column.

Grid networks results are given in Table 4. We only report results with *mean* operator for a 15x15 grid for which the induced width is w*=22. We notice that IBP is more accurate for no evidence and MC is better as more evidence is added. The same behavior was consistently manifested for smaller grid networks that we experimented with (from 7x7 up to 14x14).

CPCS networks results. We also tested on three CPCS benchmark files. The results are given in Tables 5, 6 and 7. It is interesting to notice that the MC scheme scales up even to fairly large networks, like the real life example of CPCS422 (induced width 23). IBP is again slightly better for no evidence, but is quickly surpassed by MC when evidence is added.

Discussion and conclusion

The paper presents an approximation scheme for probabilistic inference, the single most important task over belief networks. The scheme, called mini-clustering, is governed by a controlling parameter that allows adjustable levels of accuracy and efficiency in an anytime style.

We presented empirical evaluation of mini-cluster approximation on several classes of networks, comparing its anytime performance with competing algorithms such as Gibbs Sampling and Iterative Belief Propagation, over benchmarks of noisy-or random networks, general random networks, grid networks, coding networks and CPCS type networks. Our results show that, as expected, IBP is superior to all other approximations for coding networks. However, for random noisy-or, general random networks, grid networks and the CPCS networks, in the presence of evidence, the mini-clustering scheme is often superior even in its weakest form. Gibbs sampling was particularly bad and we believe that enhanced variants of Monte Carlo approach, such as likelihood weighting and importance sampling, should be compared with (Cheng & Druzdzel 2000). The empirical results are particularly encouraging as we use an unoptimized scheme that exploits a universal principle applicable to many reasoning tasks.

The contribution of the current paper beyond recent works

in this area (Dechter & Rish 1997; Dechter, Kask, & Larossa 2001) is in: 1. Extending the partition-based approximation for belief updating from mini-buckets to general tree-decompositions, thus allowing the computation of the updated beliefs for all the variables at once. This extension is similar to the one proposed in (Dechter, Kask, & Larossa 2001) but replaces optimization with probabilistic inference. 2. Providing for the first time empirical evaluation demonstrating the effectiveness of the partition-based idea for belief updating.

There are many potential ways for improving the MC scheme. Among the most important, the partitioning step can be further elaborated. In our present work we used only a brute-force approach for partitioning. It remains to be seen if more refined schemes can make the upper/lower bounds on the joint belief tighter, and if normalizing such results gives a better estimate of exact belief.

One extension we recently pursued (Dechter, Kask, & Mateescu 2002) is an iterative version of MC called Iterative Join-Graph Propagation (IJGP), which is both anytime and iterative and belongs to the class of generalized belief propagation methods (Yedidia, Freeman, & Weiss 2001). Rather than assuming an underlying join-tree, IJGP works on a join-graph that may contain loops. IJGP is related to MC in a similar way as IBP is related to BP (Pearl's belief propagation). Experimental work shows that in most cases iterating improves the quality of the MC approximation even further, especially for low i-bounds.

Acknowledgments

This work was supported in part by NSF grant IIS-0086529 and by MURI ONR award N00014-00-1-0617.

References

Arnborg, S. A. 1985. Efficient algorithms for combinatorial problems on graphs with bounded decomposability - a survey. *BIT* 25:2–23.

Boyen, X., and Koller, D. 1998. Tractable inference in complex stochastic processes. In *Artificial Intelligence (UAI'98)*, 33–42.

Cheng, J., and Druzdzel, M. 2000. AIS-BN: An adaptive importance sampling algorithm for evidential reasoning in large bayesian networks. *Journal of Artificial Intelligence Research* 13:155–188.

Cooper, G. 1990. The computational complexity of probabistic inferences. *Artificial Intelligence* 393–405.

Dagum, P., and Luby, M. 1993. Approximating probabilistic inference in bayesian belief networks is np-hard. In *National Conference on Artificial Intelligence (AAAI-93)*.

Dechter, R., and Rish, I. 1997. A scheme for approximating probabilistic inference. In *Artificial Intelligence (UAI'97)*, 132–141.

Dechter, R.; Kask, K.; and Larossa, J. 2001. A general scheme for multiple lower bound computation in constraint optimization. In *Constraint Programming*.

Dechter, R.; Kask, K.; and Mateescu, R. 2002. Iterative join-graph propagation. Technical report, UCI.

Dechter, R. 1996. Bucket elimination: A unifying framework for probabilistic inference algorithms. In *Uncertainty in Artificial Intelligence (UAI'96)*, 211–219.

Gottlob, G.; Leone, N.; and Scarello, F. 1999. A comparison of structural CSP decomposition methods. *IJCAI-99*.

Henrion, M. 1986. Propagating uncertainty by logic sampling. In *Technical report, Department of Engineering and Public Policy, Carnegie Melon University*.

Jaakkola, T. S., and Jordan, M. I. 1996. Recursive algorithms for approximating probabilities in graphical models. *Advances in Neural Information Processing Systems* 9.

Jensen, F.; Lauritzen, S.; and Olesen, K. 1990. Bayesian updating in causal probabilistic networks by local computation. *Computational Statistics Quarterly* 4:269–282.

Kask, K. 2001. Approximation algorithms for graphical models. Technical report, Ph.D. thesis, Information and Computer Science, University of California, Irvine.

Kjæaerulff, U. 1994. Reduction of computational complexity in bayesian networks through removal of weak dependencies. In *Uncertainty in Artificial Intelligence (UAI'94)*.

Koller, D.; Lerner, U.; and Angelov, D. 1998. A general algorithm for approximate inference and its applciation to hybrid bayes nets. In *Uncertainty in Artificial Intelligence (UAI'98)*, 324–333.

Lauritzen, S., and Spiegelhalter, D. 1988. Local computation with probabilities on graphical structures and their application to expert systems. *Journal of the Royal Statistical Society, Series B* 50(2):157–224.

McEliece, R.; MacKay, D.; and Cheng, J.-F. 1997. Turbo decoding as an instance of pearl's belief propagation algorithm. *IEEE J. Selected Areas in Communication*.

Pearl, J. 1988. *Probabilistic Reasoning in Intelligent Systems*. Morgan Kaufmann.

Roth, D. 1996. On the hardness of approximate reasoning. *AI* 82(1-2):273–302.

Shachter, R. D., and Peot, M. A. 1989. Simulation approaches to general probabilistic inference on belief networks. In *Uncertainty in Artificial Intelligene (UAI'89)*.

Shafer, G. R., and Shenoy, P. 1990. Probability propagation. *Anals of Mathematics and Artificial Intelligence* 2:327–352.

Weiss, Y. 1997. Belief propagation and revision in networks with loops. In *NIPS*.

Welling, M., and Teh, Y. 2001. Belief optimization for binary networks: A stable alternative to loopy belief propagation. In *UAI'01*, 554–561.

Yedidia, J. S.; Freeman, W.; and Weiss, Y. 2001. Generalized belief propagation. In *Advances in Neural Information Processing Systems 13*.

Zhang, N., and Poole, D. 1994. A simple algorithm for bayesian network computations. In *Proc of the tenth Canadian Conference on Artificial Intelligence*, 171–178.

Accuracy vs. Efficiency Trade-offs in Probabilistic Diagnosis

Irina Rish and **Mark Brodie** and **Sheng Ma**

IBM T.J. Watson Research Center
30 Saw Mill River Road
Hawthorne, NY 10532
{*rish,brodie,shengma*}*@us.ibm.com*

Abstract

This paper studies the accuracy/efficiency trade-off in probabilistic diagnosis formulated as finding the *most-likely explanation (MPE)* in a Bayesian network. Our work is motivated
by a practical problem of efficient real-time fault diagnosis
in computer networks using test transactions, or *probes*, sent
through the network. The key efficiency issues include both
the cost of probing (e.g., the number of probes), and the computational complexity of diagnosis, while the diagnostic accuracy is crucial for maintaining high levels of network performance. Herein, we derive a lower bound on the diagnostic
accuracy that provides necessary conditions for the number
of probes needed to achieve an asymptotically error-free diagnosis as the network size increases, given prior fault probabilities and a certain level of noise in probe outcomes. Since
the exact MPE diagnosis is generally intractable in large networks, we investigate next the accuracy/efficiency trade-offs
for very simple and efficient *local* approximation techniques,
based on variable-elimination (the mini-bucket scheme). Our
empirical studies show that these approximations "degrade
gracefully" with noise and often yield an optimal solution
when noise is low enough, and our initial theoretical analysis
explains this behavior for the simplest (greedy) approximation. These encouraging results suggest the applicability of
such approximations to certain almost-deterministic diagnostic problems that often arise in practical applications.

Introduction

Accurate diagnosis of some unobserved states of the world
from the outcomes of some measurements, or tests, is one
of the most common problems occurring in practice. Numerous examples include medical diagnosis, computer troubleshooting, airplane failure isolation, noisy channel coding,
and speech recognition, just to name a few. However, an accurate diagnosis often comes at a cost of large number of
tests or a computationally expensive inference. Thus, our
objective is to develop cost-efficient approaches to diagnosis that yield a good trade-off between the solution accuracy
and the computational efficiency.

A practical motivation for our work is the problem of
fault diagnosis in distributed computer systems by using a
selected set of *probes*, or test transactions, that can be sent
through the network in order to provide information about

its components (e.g., a probe can be *ping* or *traceroute* command, test email message, or web-page access request). A
set of probe outcomes (e.g., response times or return codes)
can be used to diagnose the states of system components.
The rapid growth of distributed computer systems and networks in size and complexity makes fault diagnosis an increasingly challenging task, and requires extremely efficient
inference techniques. The key efficiency issues include minimizing both the number of probes (tests) and the computational complexity of diagnosis while maximizing its accuracy. From a theoretical prospective, we wish to investigate
the achievable limits of diagnostic accuracy for given levels
of noise and fault probabilities.

We approach the problem from a probabilistic prospective and use the graphical probabilistic framework called
Bayesian (belief) networks (Pearl 1988) that provides a compact representation for multivariate probabilistic distributions and allows for efficient inference techniques. Given
a set of observations (e.g., probe outcomes), the diagnosis
problem can be formulated as finding the most-likely vector of states of all unobserved nodes (e.g., network components), called the *most-likely explanation (MPE)*. Clearly,
there are alternative formulations of the diagnosis problem,
such as, for example, finding the posterior probability distribution for each node and selecting the k most-likely faults.
However, in this paper, we focus on the MPE formulation,
which is in our view a more general approach that does not
make any additional assumptions (e.g., about the number
of faults). This approach is sometimes criticized as being
too complex and computationally intractable; note, however,
that updating the probability of a single node is also an NP-
hard problem (Cooper 1990) that can be (in the worst case)
as time consuming as finding an MPE. This is exactly why
the main focus of this paper is on *approximation* techniques
and their accuracy/efficiency trade-offs.

The complexity of inference is usually associated with
large probabilistic dependencies recorded during inference
(clique size, or *induced width*)(Dechter 1996). Thus, a popular approximation approach is to restrict the complexity by
focusing only on local interactions. We investigated the performance of two *local inference* techniques, *greedy-mpe* and
approx-mpe(1), which are the simplest members of the parametric family of variable-elimination algorithms known as
mini-bucket approximations (Dechter & Rish 1997; 2002).

The mini-bucket scheme is closely related to other local approximations, such as *iterative belief propagation (IBP)* and *generalized belief propagation (GBP)* algorithms (Yedidia, Freeman, & Weiss 2001), that recently became the state-of-the-art approximation techniques successfully used in practical applications such as probabilistic error-correcting coding (Frey & MacKay 1998). The mini-bucket algorithms can be viewed as simplified, non-iterative versions of those approaches. The reason for focusing on the mini-bucket scheme instead of those more popular techniques was our desire to gain a theoretical understanding of the empirical success of the mini-bucket scheme on problems with low-noise (nearly-deterministic) dependencies, reported both in this paper and in the existing literature (Dechter & Rish 1997; 2002). Also, we hope that a theoretical understanding of very simple local approximations can later provide us with insights for the analysis of more complicated iterative approximations[1].

In this paper, we (1) propose a Bayesian network formulation for the problem of fault diagnosis in distributed systems using probes; (2) derive a bound on the diagnosis accuracy and analyze it with respect to the problem parameters such as noise level and the number of tests, suggesting feasible regions when an asymptotic (with problem size) error-free diagnosis can be achieved; (3) evaluate empirically the performance of two efficient local approximation schemes with respect to network parameters, such as the level of noise; and (4) provide some theoretical explanation of the accuracy vs. noise relation. In summary, the accuracy of diagnosis is affected both by the quality of a model (diagnosis error based on the exact MPE solution) and by the accuracy of approximation to MPE. Our results suggest that the quality of approximation is higher for higher-quality (i.e., higher-MPE) models, and that it "degrades gracefully" with increasing noise. On the other hand, the computational complexity of the approximation used here is linear in the number of nodes, instead of exponential for exact inference. We conclude that simple local inference algorithms provide a promising approach to handling large-scale diagnosis, especially for low-noise problems often encountered in various practical application areas.

The rest of the paper is structured as follows. The next section provides background information on Bayesian networks and defines the fault diagnosis problem. Then, in the subsequent section, a theoretical bound on the diagnosis accuracy is derived. Next, we analyze the complexity of diagnosis and study the approximation schemes. The paper concludes with a summary and discussion of related work.

Background and problem formulation

As a motivating application, we consider a particular problem of network fault diagnosis using probes, although most of our results can be applied in a more general setting. Let us assume simplified model of a computer network where

---

[1]To the best of our knowledge, existing theoretical analysis of IBP and GBP properties is mostly focused on their convergence but does not address directly their behavior on low-noise problems (Weiss 2000; Yedidia, Freeman, & Weiss 2001).

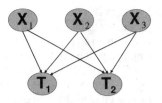

Figure 1: A two-layer Bayesian network structure for a set $\mathbf{X} = (X_1, X_2, X_3)$ of network elements and a set of probes $\mathbf{T} = (T_1, T_2)$.

each node (router, server, or workstation) can be in one of two states, 0 (fault) or 1 (no fault). The states of n network elements are denoted by a vector $\mathbf{X} = (X_1, ..., X_n)$ of *unobserved* Boolean variables. Each probe, or test, T_j, originates at a particular node (probing workstation) and goes to some destination node (server or router). We also make an assumption that source routing is supported, i.e. we can specify the probe path in advance. A vector $\mathbf{T} = (T_1, ..., T_m)$ of *observed* Boolean variables denoting the outcomes (0 - failure, 1 - OK) of m probes. Lower-case letters, such as x_i and t_j, denote the values of the corresponding variables, i.e. $\mathbf{x} = (x_1, ..., x_n)$ denotes a particular assignment of node states, and $\mathbf{t} = (t_1, .., t_m)$ denotes a particular outcome of m probes. We assume that the probe outcome is affected by *all nodes on its path*, and that node failures are marginally independent. These assumptions yield a causal structure depicted by a two-layer Bayesian network, such as one shown in Figure 1. The network represent a joint probability $P(\mathbf{x}, \mathbf{t})$:

$$P(\mathbf{x}, \mathbf{t}) = \prod_{i=1}^{n} P(x_i) \prod_{j=1}^{m} P(t_j | \mathbf{pa}(t_j)), \qquad (1)$$

where $P(t_j | \mathbf{pa}(t_j))$ is the *conditional probability distribution (CPD)* of node T_i given the set of its *parents* $\mathbf{Pa_i}$, i.e. the nodes pointing to T_i in the directed graph, and $P(x_i)$ is the prior probability that $X_i = x_i$. Formally, a Bayesian network BN over a set of variables $X_1, ..., X_k$ is a tuple (G,P) where G is the directed acyclic graph encoding the independence assumptions of the joint distribution $P(\mathbf{X})$, and where $P = \{P(x_i | \mathbf{pa}(\mathbf{x_i}))\}$ is the set of all CPDs.

We now specify the quantitative part of those network, i.e. the CPDs $P(t_j | \mathbf{pa}(t_j))$. In general, a CPD defined on binary variables is represented as a k-dimensional table where $k = |Pa(t_j)|$. Thus, just the specification complexity is $O(2^k)$ which is very inefficient, if not intractable, in large networks with long probe path (i.e. large parent set). It seems reasonable to assume that each element on the probe's path affects the probe's outcome independently, so that there is no need to specify the probability of T_i for all possible value combinations of $X_{i_1}, ..., X_{i_k}$ (the assumption known as *causal independence* (Pearl 1988; Heckerman & Breese 1995)). For example, in the absence of uncertainty, a probe fails if and only if at least one node on its path fails, i.e. $T_i = X_{i_1} \wedge ... \wedge X_{i_k}$, where $\wedge$ denotes logical AND, and $X_{i_1}, ..., X_{i_k}$ are all the nodes probe T_i goes through; therefore, once it is known that some $X_{i_j} = 0$, the probe fails independently of the values of other components. In practice, however, this relationship may be disturbed by "noise". For example, a probe can fail even though all nodes it goes through are OK (e.g., if network performance degradation leads to high response times interpreted as a failure). Vice versa, there is a chance the probe succeeds even if a node on its path is failed, e.g. due to routing change. Such uncertainties yield a *noisy-AND* model which implies that several causes (e.g., node failures) contribute independently to a common effect (probe failure)and is formally defined as follows:

$$P(t = 1 | x_1, \ldots, x_k) = (1 - l) \prod_{x_i=0}^{n} q_i, \text{ and} \quad (2)$$

$$P(t = 1 | x_1 = 1, \ldots, x_k = 1) = 1 - l, \quad (3)$$

where l is the *leak probability* which accounts for the cases of probe failing even when all the nodes on its path are OK, and the *link probabilities*, q_i, account for the second kind of "noise" in the noisy-AND relationship, namely, for cases when probe succeeds with a small probability q_i even if node X_i on its path fails[2].

Once a Bayesian network is specified, the diagnosis task can be formulated as finding the *maximum probable explanation (MPE)*, i.e. a most-likely assignment to all X_i nodes given the probe outcomes, i.e. $\mathbf{x}^* = \arg\max_{\mathbf{x}} P(\mathbf{x}|\mathbf{t})$. Since $P(\mathbf{x}|\mathbf{t}) = \frac{P(\mathbf{x},\mathbf{t})}{P(\mathbf{t})}$, where $P(\mathbf{t})$ does not depend on $\mathbf{x}$, we get $\mathbf{x}^* = \arg\max_{\mathbf{x}} P(\mathbf{x}, \mathbf{t})$.

Accuracy of diagnostis

In this section, we will derive a lower bound on the diagnosis error. Note that the bound is not tight in many cases, and defines only necessary conditions for the asymptotically error-free diagnosis. Identifying tighter error bounds and thus more accurate conditions for error-free MPE diagnosis appears to be a much harder problem and remains a direction for future work [3]

The error of the MPE diagnosis, denoted Err_{MPE}, is defined (similarly to 0/1 classification error) as the probability of making a mistake, i.e. the probability $P(\mathbf{X} \neq \mathbf{X}^*(\mathbf{T}))$ that the diagnosis vector $\mathbf{X}^*(\mathbf{T})$ differs from the true state of unknown variables, a random vector $\mathbf{X}$ (by its definition

---

[2]Note that this noisy-AND definition is equivalent to the *noisy-OR* definition in (Pearl 1988; Henrion *et al.* 1996) if we replace every value by its logical negation (all 0's will be replaced by 1's and vice versa). We also note that instead of considering the leak probability separately, we may assume there is an additional "leak node" always set to 0 that affects an outcome of a probe T_i according to its link probability $(1 - l_i)$.

[3]This problem can be viewed as an asymptotic error analysis of a *constrained code*, where the probe outcomes "encode" the node-state vector, but the encoding is restricted by the nature of probes (logical-AND functions of node states) and by the network topology constraints on the possible set of probes. Note that well-known information-theoretic result, the Shannon's limit (Shannon 1948; Cover & Thomas 1991)), provides the asymptotic error for MAP decoding in case of unconstrained codes; extending this result to a particular type of a constrained code may not be straightforward.

as the most-likely explanation, $\mathbf{X}^*(\mathbf{T})$ is the deterministic function of the random probe vector $\mathbf{T}$, assuming a deterministic tie-breaking rule given multiple MPEs). Then, by the rule of total probability, we get

$$Err_{MPE} = P(\mathbf{X} \neq \mathbf{X}^*(\mathbf{T})) = \sum_{\mathbf{x},\mathbf{t}} P(\mathbf{x} \neq \mathbf{x}^*(\mathbf{t}), \mathbf{x}, \mathbf{t}) =$$

$$\sum_{\mathbf{x},\mathbf{t}} P(\mathbf{x}, \mathbf{t}) P(\mathbf{x} \neq \mathbf{x}^*(\mathbf{t}) | \mathbf{t}).$$

Since $P(\mathbf{x} \neq \mathbf{x}^*(\mathbf{t}) | \mathbf{t}) = I_{\mathbf{x} \neq \mathbf{x}*(\mathbf{t})}$, where I_s is the *indicator function* ($I_s = 1$ if $s = true$ and $I_s = 0$ otherwise), we obtain

$$Err_{MPE} = \sum_{\mathbf{x},\mathbf{t}} P(\mathbf{x}, \mathbf{t}) I_{\mathbf{x} \neq \mathbf{x}^*(\mathbf{t})} = \quad (4)$$

$$\sum_{\mathbf{t}} (1 - P(\mathbf{x}^*(\mathbf{t}) | \mathbf{t})) = 1 - \sum_{\mathbf{t}} P(\mathbf{x}^*(\mathbf{t}), \mathbf{t}). \quad (5)$$

From now on, we will use $\mathbf{x}^*$ as a shorthand for $\mathbf{x}^*(\mathbf{t})$.
Assumptions. In order to simplify our further analysis, we will use the following notation. We denote as p the maximum prior probability over all nodes and their possible states, i.e. $p = \max_i \max\{P(X_i = 0), 1 - P(X_i = 0)\}$. For example, we may assume that all nodes have same prior probabilities, and that $p > 0.5$ is the probability of being in the OK state ($p = P(X_i = 1)$). Also, we denote as α_0 the maximum conditional probability value (over all test variables and their corresponding parent assignments) attained when a test outcome is 0, namely, $\alpha_0 = \max_i \max_{\mathbf{pa}(t_i)} P(t_i = 0 | \mathbf{pa}(t_i))$. Similarly, we define $\alpha_1 = \max_i \max_{\mathbf{pa}(t_i)} P(t_i = 1 | \mathbf{pa}(t_i))$. Then we get $P(\mathbf{x}^*, \mathbf{t}) = \max_{\mathbf{x}} \prod_{j=1}^{n} P(x_j) \prod_{i=1}^{m} P(t_i | \mathbf{pa}(t_i)) \leq$ $\leq p^n \prod_{t_i=0} \alpha_0 \prod_{t_i=1} \alpha_1 = p^n \alpha_0^r \alpha_1^{m-r}$, where r is the number of $t_i = 0$ in $\mathbf{t}$. Since there are $\binom{m}{r}$ vectors $\mathbf{t}$ having exactly r variables T_i assigned $t_i = 0$, we obtain

$$\sum_{\mathbf{t}} P(\mathbf{x}^*, \mathbf{t}) \leq p^n \sum_{r=0}^{m} \binom{m}{r} \alpha_0^r \alpha_1^{m-r} = p^n (\alpha_0 + \alpha_1)^m \quad (6)$$

and therefore, we get $Err_{MPE} = 1 - \sum_{\mathbf{t}} P(\mathbf{x}^*, \mathbf{t}) \geq L_{MPE}$, where L_{MPE} is the *lower bound* on the MPE diagnosis error. Thus, we just proved the following

Lemma 1 *Given Bayesian network BN=(G,P) defining a joint distribution $P(\mathbf{x}, \mathbf{t})$ as specified by the equation 1, the MPE diagnosis error is given by $Err_{MPE} = 1 - \sum_{\mathbf{t}} P(\mathbf{x}^*, \mathbf{t}) \geq L_{MPE}$, and*

$$L_{MPE} = 1 - p^n (\alpha_0 + \alpha_1)^m = 1 - [p(\alpha_0 + \alpha_1)^{m/n}]^n, \quad (7)$$

where $p = \max_i \max\{P(X_i = 0), 1 - P(X_i = 0)\}$, and $\alpha_k = \max_i \max_{\mathbf{pa}(t_i)} P(t_i = k | \mathbf{pa}(t_i))$.

Our next question is *whether an error-free diagnosis is achievable asymptotically with $n \to \infty$.* We will assume a constant *test rate* $k = m/n$ (inspired by similar notion of code rate measuring the redundancy added to the input signal in order to decrease the decoding error in noisy channel coding). From the lower bound on the diagnosis error (expression 7), we get the following *necessary condition* of (asymptotic) error-free diagnosis:

$$\lim_{n \to \infty} [p(\alpha_0 + \alpha_1)^k]^n \to z, \qquad (8)$$

where the limit z must satisfy $z \geq 1$. This is equivalent to

$$p(\alpha_0 + \alpha_1)^k \geq 1 \Leftrightarrow (\alpha_0 + \alpha_1)^k \geq 1/p. \qquad (9)$$

Note that $1 \leq 1/p \leq 2$ and $1 \leq \alpha_0 + \alpha_1 \leq 2$. The largest $1/p = 2$ (the "worst case" in terms of diagnostic error) corresponds to uniform priors $P(X_i)$. Then, in order to achieve an error-free diagnosis, it is necessary to have $k \geq 1$, i.e. $m \geq n$. In general, from 9 we get the following condition on the "amount of redundancy", or "code rate" $k = m/n$, necessary for the error-free diagnosis (note that the condition may not be sufficient for actually *achieving* zero error since we still have to investigate when the lower bound L_{MPE} is achievable):

$$L_{MPE} = 0 \Leftrightarrow k = m/n \geq \frac{\log(1/p)}{\log(\alpha_0 + \alpha_1)} \qquad (10)$$

Applying the lemma 1 to the particular case of noisy-AND diagnosis with probing, we get the following

Corollary 2 *Given Bayesian network BN=(G,P) defining a joint distribution $P(\mathbf{x}, \mathbf{t})$ as specified by the equation 1, where all nodes X_i have same prior probability $p = P(X_i = 0) \leq 0.5$, and where all $P(t_j | \mathbf{pa}(\mathbf{t_j}))$ are noisy-AND CPDs having same link probability q, leak probability l, and the number of parents r, the MPE diagnosis error is at least*

$$L_M = 1 - (1 - p)^n ((1 - l)(1 - q^r) + 1)^m. \qquad (11)$$

Note that in the absence of noise ($l=0$ and $q=0$) we get $L_M = 1 - (1 - p)^n 2^m$, thus, for uniform fault priors, $p = 0.5$, an error-free MPE diagnosis is only possible if $n = m$, as we noted before; however, for smaller p, zero-error can be achieved with smaller number of probes. Namely, solving $L_M \leq 0$ for m yields the necessary condition for zero lower bound, $m \geq -n \frac{log(1-p)}{log(1+(1-l)(1-q^r))}$, plotted in Figure 2 as a function of p. Generally, solving $L_M \leq 0$ for m provides a way of specifying the minimum necessary number of probes that yield zero lower bound for a specified values of other parameters[4]. Also, the expression 11 error (bound) increases with increasing number of nodes n, fault probability p, leak probability l, and link probability q, but decreases with increasing number of probes m and probe route length r, which agrees with ones intuition that having more nodes on probe's path, as well as a larger number of probes, provides more information about the true node states.

Diagnosis complexity and approximations

We focus first on the MPE diagnosis in the absence of noise (i.e., for deterministic test outcomes). The deterministic

---

[4]Clearly, finding a set of probes that may actually *achieve* the bound, if such set of probes exists, is a much harder task.

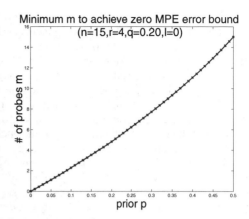

Figure 2: Minimum number of probes m to guarantee zero error bound, versus fault prior p: low prior yields lower than $n = 15$ number of probes.

CPDs reduce to a set of constraints imposed by the test outcomes on the values of $X_1, ..., X_n$. For example, in the fault diagnosis domain, each probe outcome $T_i = t_i$ imposes a logical-AND constraint $t_i = x_{i_1} \wedge ... \wedge x_{i_k}$ on the values of its parent nodes $X_{i_1}, ..., X_{i_k}$. The MPE diagnosis becomes a constrained optimization problem of finding $\mathbf{x}^* = \arg\max_{x_1,...,x_n} \prod_{j=1}^n P(x_j)$ subject to those constraints. In a particular case of uniform priors $P(x_j)$, diagnosis is reduced to solving a constraint satisfaction problem. The problem can also be cast as a constraint satisfaction rather than optimization if there exist a unique solution satisfying the constraints (see (Brodie, Rish, & Ma 2001) for more details on how to construct such probe sets).

Although constrained optimization and constraint satisfaction problems (CSPs) are generally NP-hard, it is interesting to note that the probing domain yields a tractable set of constraints.

Proposition 3 *A set of constraints $t_j = x_{j_1} \wedge ... \wedge x_{j_k}$, $j = 1, ..., m$ over a set of variables $X_1, ..., X_n$, where $x_i \in \{0, 1\}, t_j \in \{0, 1\}$ for $i = 1, ..., n$ and $j = 1, ..., m$, defines a propositional Horn theory, and can be, therefore, solved in $O(n)$ time by the unit-propagation algorithm*

Indeed, each successful probe yields a constraint $x_{i_1} \wedge ... \wedge x_{i_k} = 1$ which implies $x_i = 1$ for any node X_i on its path; the rest of the nodes are only included in constraints of the form $x_{i_1} \wedge ... \wedge x_{i_k} = 0$, or equivalently, $\neg x_{i_1} \wedge ... \wedge \neg x_{i_k} = 1$ imposed by failed probes which yields a *Horn theory* (i.e. a conjunction of clauses, or disjuncts, where each disjunct includes no more than one positive literal). Thus, a $O(n)$-time algorithm assigns 1 to every node appearing on the path of a successful probe, and 0 to the rest of nodes. This is equivalent to applying *unit propagation* to our Horn theory.

In the presence of noise, the MPE diagnosis task can be written as finding $\mathbf{x}^* = \arg\max_{x_1} ... \max_{x_n} \prod_i P(x_i | pa_i) =$

$$= \arg\max_{x_1} F_1(x_1) ... \max_{x_n} F_n(x_n, S_n), \qquad (12)$$

where each $F_i(x_i, \mathbf{S_i}) = \prod_{\mathbf{x_k}} \mathbf{P}(\mathbf{x_k} | \mathbf{pa}(\mathbf{x_k}))$ is the product of all probabilistic components involving X_i and a subset of lower-index variables $\mathbf{S_i} \subseteq \{\mathbf{X_1}, ..., \mathbf{X_{i-1}}\}$, but *not* involving any X_j for $j > i$. The set of all such components is also called the *bucket* of X_i (Dechter 1996). An exact algorithm for finding MPE solution, called *elim-mpe* (Dechter 1996), uses *variable-elimination* (also called *bucket-elimination*) as a preprocessing: it computes the product of functions in the bucket of each variable X_i, from $i = n$ to $i = 1$ (i.e., from right to left in the equation 12), maximizes it over X_i, and *propagates* the resulting function $f(\cdot)$ to the bucket of its highest-order variable. Once variable-elimination is completed, the algorithm finds an optimal solution by a backtrack-free greedy procedure that, going from $i = 1$ to $i = n$ (i.e., in the opposite direction to elimination), assigns $X_i = \arg\max_{x_i} F_i(x_i, \mathbf{S_i} = \mathbf{s_i})$ where $\mathbf{S_i} = \mathbf{s_i}$ is the current assignment to $\mathbf{S_i}$. It is shown that *elim-mpe* is guaranteed to find an optimal solution and that the complexity of the variable-elimination step is $O(n \cdot exp(w^*))$ where w^*, called the *induced width*, is the largest number of arguments among the functions (old and newly recorded) in all buckets (Dechter 1996). For the probing domain, it is easy to show that $w^* \geq k$ where k is the maximum number parents of a probe node, and $w^* = n$ in the worst case.

Since the exact MPE diagnosis is intractable for large-scale networks, we focused on *local* approximation techniques. Particularly, we used a simple (O(n) time) backtrack-free greedy algorithm, called here *greedy-mpe*, which performs no variable-elimination preprocessing, and the simplest and fastest member of the *mini-bucket* approximation family, algorithm *approx-mpe(1)* (Dechter & Rish 1997; 2002), that performs a very limited preprocessing similar to *relational arc-consistency* (Dechter & Rish 2002) in constraint networks.

The greedy algorithm *greedy-mpe* does no preprocessing (except for replacing observed variables with their values in all related function prior to algorithm's execution). It computes a suboptimal solution

$$\mathbf{x'} = (\arg\max_{x_1} F_1(x_1), ..., ..., \arg\max_{x_n} F_n(x_n, S_n = \mathbf{s_n})),$$
(13)

where $S_i = \mathbf{s_i}$, as before, denotes the current assignment to the variables in S_j computed during the previous $i - 1$ maximization steps.

Generally, the mini-bucket algorithms *approx-mpe(i)* perform a limited level of variable-elimination, similar to enforcing directional i-consistency, prior to the greedy assignment. The preprocessing allows to find an upper bound U on $M = \max_{\mathbf{x}} P(\mathbf{x}, \mathbf{t})$, where $\mathbf{t}$ is the evidence (clearly, $MPE = M/P(\mathbf{t})$), while the probability $L = P(\mathbf{x'}, \mathbf{e})$ of their suboptimal solution provides a lower bound on M. Generally, L increases with the level of preprocessing controlled by i, thus allowing a flexible accuracy vs. efficiency trade-off. The algorithm returns the suboptimal solution $\mathbf{x'}$ and the upper and lower bounds, U and L, on M; ratio U/L is a measure of the approximation error.

We tested *greedy-mpe* and *approx-mpe(1)* on the networks constructed in a way that guarantees the unique diagnosis in the absence of noise. Particularly, besides m tests each having r randomly selected parents, we also generated n *direct* tests $\hat{T}_i$, $i = 1, ..., n$, each having exactly one parent node

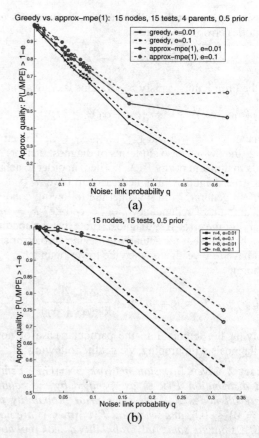

Figure 3: (a) Graceful degradation of the approximation quality of both greedy solution and an *approx-mpe(1)* solution with noise, where the approximation quality is measured as $P(L/M) > 1 - e$ for $e = 0.01$ and $e = 0.1$; the quality of *approx-mpe(1)* approximation degrades much slower than the quality of the greedy solution for larger noise (especially, for $q > 0.3$; (b) "zooming-in" on the quality of *approx-mpe(1)* for lower noise, $q \leq 0.32$; the accuracy gets higher for longer (more informative) probes (i.e., $r = 8$ vs. $r = 4$).

X_i. It is easy to see that, for such networks, both *greedy-mpe* and *approx-mpe(1)* find an exact diagnosis in the absence of noise: *approx-mpe(1)* reduces to unit-propagation, an equivalent of relational-arc-consistency, while *greedy-mpe*, applied along a *topological* order of variables in the network's directed acyclic graph (DAG)[5], immediately finds the correct assignment which simply equals the outcomes of the direct tests.

Adding noise in a form of link probability q caused graceful degradation of the approximation quality, as shown in Figure 3. The figure summarizes the results for 50 randomly generated networks with $n = 15$ unobserved nodes (having uniform fault priors $p = P(x_i = 0) = 0.5$), $n = 15$ direct probes, one for each node, and $n = 15$ noisy-AND probes, each with $r = 4$ randomly selected parents among

---

[5] A *topological* (or ancestral) ordering of a DAG is an ordering where a child node never appears before its parent.

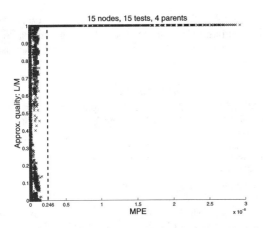

Figure 4: The accuracy of the solution $\mathbf{x}'$ found by algorithm *greedy-mpe*, measured by L/M, where $L = P(\mathbf{x}', \mathbf{t})$ and $M = P(\mathbf{x}^*, \mathbf{t})$, versus M. The results obtained for

the unobserved nodes, zero leak $l = 0$ probability. The link probability (noise level) q varied from 0.01 to 0.64, taking 15 different values; the results are shown for all noise levels together. For each network, 100 instances of evidence (probe outcomes) were generated by Monte-Carlo simulation of $\mathbf{x}$ and $\mathbf{t}$ according to their conditional distributions. Thus, we get 50x100=5000 samples for each value of noise q.

Figure 3a plots both for *greedy-mpe* and for *approx-mpe(1)* the fraction of cases when the ratio L/MPE (where L is the solution probability) was within the interval $[1-e, 1]$ for small values of e. As expected, *approx-mpe(1)* yields a slower accuracy degradation with noise, especially for higher noise levels (i.e. even the simplest preprocessing pays off). Also, we observed that longer probes ($r = 8$ vs. $r = 4$) yield higher diagnosis accuracy, i.e. are more informative (Figure 3b).

Also, as demonstrated in Figure 4 for the same set of experiments as above (i.e., $n = 14$ and $r = 4$), the approximation accuracy of *greedy-mpe*, measured as L/M where $L = P(\mathbf{x}', \mathbf{t})$ and $M = P(\mathbf{x}^*, \mathbf{t})$, clearly increases with increasing value M, and therefore with the probability of the exact diagnosis, which also depends on the "diagnostic ability" of a probe set (for same probe set size, a better probe set yields a higher MPE diagnosis, and therefore, a better approximation quality). There is an interesting threshold phenomenon, observed both for *greedy-mpe* and for *approx-mpe(1)* solutions (the results for *approx-mpe(1)* are omitted due to space restrictions), and for various problem sizes n: the suboptimal solution $\mathbf{x}'$ found by algorithm *greedy-mpe* suddenly becomes (almost always) an exact solution $\mathbf{x}^*$ (i.e., $L/M = 1$, where $L = P(\mathbf{x}', \mathbf{t})$ and $M = P(\mathbf{x}^*, \mathbf{t})$) when $M > \theta$ where θ is some threshold value. For $n = 15$, the threshold is observed between $2e - 6$ and $3e - 6$. A theoretical analysis in the next section yields a quite accurate prediction of $\theta \approx 2.46e - 6$.

The effect of noise on approximation error

We will prove this claim formally for the simplest approximation algorithm *greedy-mpe*.

Let $BN = (G, P)$ be a Bayesian network, where $\mathbf{T} = \mathbf{t}$ is evidence, i.e. a value assignment $\mathbf{t}$ to a subset of variables $\mathbf{T} \subset \mathbf{X}$. We will also make an important assumption that the all observed variables are replaced by their values in all CPD functions. Also, recall that $F_i(x_i, \mathbf{s_i})$ is the product of functions in the bucket of X_i along the ordering o, given the assignment $\mathbf{s_i}$ of some variables in the previous buckets. Then

Lemma 4 [*greedy-mpe* optimality.] *Given a Bayesian network $BN = (G, P)$, an evidence assignment $\mathbf{T} = \mathbf{t}$ applied to all relevant probability functions, and a topological ordering o of unobserved nodes in the graph G, the algorithm* greedy-mpe *applied along o is guaranteed to find an optimal MPE solution if $P(\mathbf{x}', \mathbf{t}) \geq F_i(x_i, \mathbf{s'_i})$ for every $i = 1, ..., n$ and for every $x_i \neq x'_i$, where $\mathbf{S_i} = \mathbf{s'_i}$ is a partial assignment already found by* greedy-mpe.

Proof. Clearly, the solution $\mathbf{x}'$ found by *greedy-mpe* is optimal, i.e. $\mathbf{x}' = \mathbf{x}^* = \arg\max_{\mathbf{x}} P(\mathbf{x}, \mathbf{t})$ if $P(\mathbf{x}', \mathbf{t}) \geq P(\mathbf{x}, \mathbf{t})$ for every $\mathbf{x} \neq \mathbf{x}'$. Since $\mathbf{x} \neq \mathbf{x}'$ implies $x_i \neq x'_i$ for some i (let us choose the smallest of such i's), by the condition of lemma we get $P(\mathbf{x}', \mathbf{t}) \geq F_i(x_i, \mathbf{s'_i})$, and, therefore, $P(\mathbf{x}', \mathbf{t}) \geq \prod_{j=1}^{n} F_j(x_j, \mathbf{s_j})$ since each $F_j(x_j, s_j)$ is a product of probabilities, and therefore, $0 \geq F_j(x_j, s_j) \geq 1$. But $\prod_{j=1}^{n} F_j(x_j, \mathbf{s_j}) = P(\mathbf{x}, \mathbf{t})$ by equation 12, which concludes the proof. ∎

We now discuss some particular classes of Bayesian networks that satisfy the conditions of lemma 4.

Lemma 5 (nearly-deterministic CPDs, no observations.) *Given a Bayesian network $BN = (G, P)$ having no observed variables, and all conditional (and prior) probabilities being nearly-deterministic, i.e. satisfying the condition* $\max_{x_i} P(x_i|pa(X_i)) > 1 - \delta$, *where* $0 \leq \delta \leq 0.5$, *algorithm* greedy-mpe *applied along a topological ordering o of G is guaranteed to find an optimal MPE assignment if* $(1 - \delta)^n \geq \delta$.

Proof. Given a topological ordering and no evidence variables, the bucket of every node X_i contains a single function $P(x_i|pa(X_i))$. Thus, the greedy solution $\mathbf{x}'$ yields $P(\mathbf{x}') = \prod_{i=1}^{n} \max_{x_i} P(x_i|pa(X_i)) = (1 - \delta)^n$, while any other $\mathbf{x}$ has the probability $P(\mathbf{x}) = \prod_{i=1}^{n} P(x_i|pa(X_i)) < \delta$ since for the very first i such that $x_i \neq x'_i$ we get $P(x_i|pa(X_i)) < \delta$ and this value can only decrease when multiplied by other probabilities $0 \leq P(x_j|pa(X_j)) \leq 1$. ∎

Let us consider a simulation that happened to select only the most-likely values for $\hat{T}_i$ and T_i, i.e. $t'_i = \arg\max_{t_i} P(t_i|pa(T_i))$, which can be viewed as an error-free "transmission over a noisy channel". From 3 we get $\max_{t_i} P(t_i|pa(T_i)) \geq (1 - q)$; also, for any $t''_i \neq \arg\max_{t_i} P(t_i|pa(T_i))$, $P(t''_i|pa(T_i)) < q$. It is easy to show (similarly to lemma 4) that algorithm *greedy-mpe* will find an assignment that produced this most-likely evidence, thus yielding $P(\mathbf{x}', \hat{\mathbf{t}}, \mathbf{t}) = \prod_{i=1}^{n} P(x_i) \prod_{i=1}^{n} P(\hat{t}_i) \prod_{i=1}^{n} P(t_i) > \frac{1}{2^n}(1 - q)^{n+m}$. On the other hand, for any other $\mathbf{x}$ there exists $T_j = t_j$ where

t_j is not the most-likely choice for T_j given $\mathbf{x}$, and thus $P(t_i|pa(t_i)) < q$ as can be seen from the noisy-AND definition. Thus, the greedy solution $\mathbf{x}'$ is guaranteed to be optimal once for any $\mathbf{x} \neq \mathbf{x}'$, $P(\mathbf{x}', \hat{\mathbf{t}}, \mathbf{t}) > P(\mathbf{x}, \hat{\mathbf{t}}, \mathbf{t})$, i.e. once $(1-q)^{n+m} > q$ (the constant $\frac{1}{2^n}$ on both sides of the inequality was cancelled). Note that simulating an unlikely evidence yields a low joint probability $M = P(\mathbf{x}^*, \hat{\mathbf{t}}, \mathbf{t}) < q$ for the optimal diagnosis $\mathbf{x}^*$.

In our experiments, $n = m = 15$, thus resolving $(1-q)^{30} = q$ gives a threshold value $q \approx 0.0806$, and therefore $M = P(\mathbf{x}', \hat{\mathbf{t}}, \mathbf{t}) = \frac{1}{2^{15}}(1-q)^{30} > \frac{1}{2^{15}}q \approx 2.46e-6$, which is surprisingly close to the empirical threshold observed in Figure 4 which separates suboptimal from the optimal behavior of algorithm *greedy-mpe*.

Discussion and conclusions

In this paper, we address both theoretically and empirically the problem of the most-likely diagnosis given the observations (MPE diagnosis), studying as an example the fault diagnosis in computer networks using probing technology. The key efficiency issues include minimizing both the number of tests and the computational complexity of diagnosis while maximizing its accuracy. Herein, we derive a lower bound on the diagnostic accuracy that provides necessary conditions for the number of probes needed to achieve an asymptotically error-free diagnosis as the network size increases, given a certain level of noise in probe outcomes and prior fault probabilities. Since the exact MPE diagnosis is generally intractable in large networks, we investigate next the accuracy/efficiency trade-offs for very simple and efficient approximation techniques, based on variable-elimination (the mini-bucket scheme), and provide both an empirical study on randomly generated networks and an initial theoretical explanation of the results. We show that even the most simple and inexpensive members of the mini-bucket algorithmic family (e.g., the greedy approximation) often provide an exact solution given sufficiently low levels of noise; as the noise increases, a "graceful degradation" of the accuracy is observed. Our results suggest the applicability of such approximations to nearly-deterministic diagnosis problems that are often encountered in practical applications.

Although there exists an extensive literature on fault diagnosis in computer networks (Kliger *et al.* 1997; Huard & Lazar 1996; I.Katzela & M.Schwartz 1995), we are not aware of any previous work that would both consider the problem of "active" diagnosis using probes, and provide theoretical and empirical analysis of diagnostic error, as well as a study of efficient approximation algorithms as presented in this paper. A closely related recent work in (Brodie, Rish, & Ma 2001) proposes efficient algorithms for the optimal probe set construction, although only in deterministic setting. Extending this approach to noisy environments is an interesting direction for future work. Further investigation, both theoretical and empirical, should focus on more accurate, but also more expensive local approximation techniques such as *approx-mpe(i)* and the related family of recently proposed *generalized belief propagation* techniques

(Yedidia, Freeman, & Weiss 2001), as well as on the variational approximation techniques that has been successfully used in two-layer noisy-OR networks for medical diagnosis (Jaakkola & Jordan 1999).

References

Brodie, M.; Rish, I.; and Ma, S. 2001. Optimizing probe selection for fault localization. In *Distributed Systems Operation and Management*.

Cooper, G. 1990. The computational complexity of probabilistic inference using Bayesian belief networks. *Artificial Intelligence* 42(2–3):393–405.

Cover, T., and Thomas, J. 1991. *Elements of information theory*. New York:John Wiley & Sons.

Dechter, R., and Rish, I. 1997. A scheme for approximating probabilistic inference. In *Proc. Thirteenth Conf. on Uncertainty in Artificial Intelligence (UAI97)*.

Dechter, R., and Rish, I. 2002. Mini-buckets: A General Scheme for Approximating Inference. *To appear in J. of ACM*.

Dechter, R. 1996. Bucket elimination: A unifying framework for probabilistic inference. In *Proc. Twelfth Conf. on Uncertainty in Artificial Intelligence*, 211–219.

Frey, B., and MacKay, D. 1998. A revolution: Belief propagation in graphs with cycles. *Advances in Neural Information Processing Systems* 10.

Heckerman, D., and Breese, J. 1995. Causal independence for probability assessment and inference using Bayesian networks. Technical Report MSR-TR-94-08, Microsoft Research.

Henrion, M.; Pradhan, M.; Favero, B. D.; Huang, K.; Provan, G.; and O'Rorke, P. 1996. Why is diagnosis using belief networks insensitive to imprecision in probabilities? In *Proc. Twelfth Conf. on Uncertainty in Artificial Intelligence*.

Huard, J., and Lazar, A. 1996. Fault isolation based on decision-theoretic troubleshooting. Technical Report 442-96-08, Center for Telecommunications Research, Columbia University, New York, NY.

I.Katzela, and M.Schwartz. 1995. Fault identification schemes in communication networks. In *IEEE/ACM Transactions on Networking*.

Jaakkola, T. S., and Jordan, M. I. 1999. Variational probabilistic inference and the qmr-dt network. *Journal of Artificial Intelligence Research* 10:291–322.

Kliger, S.; Yemini, S.; Yemini, Y.; Ohsie, D.; and Stolfo, S. 1997. A coding approach to event correlation. In *Intelligent Network Management (IM)*.

Pearl, J. 1988. *Probabilistic Reasoning in Intelligent Systems*. Morgan Kaufmann.

Shannon, C. 1948. A mathematical theory of communication. *Bell System Technical Journal* 27:379–423,623–656.

Weiss, Y. 2000. Correctness of local probability propagation in graphical models with loops. *Neural Computation* 12:1–41.

Yedidia, J.; Freeman, W. T.; and Weiss, Y. 2001. Generalized belief propagation. In *NIPS 13*, 689–695. MIT Press.

A General Identification Condition for Causal Effects

Jin Tian and Judea Pearl
Cognitive Systems Laboratory
Computer Science Department
University of California, Los Angeles, CA 90024
{jtian, judea}@cs.ucla.edu

Abstract

This paper concerns the assessment of the effects of actions or policy interventions from a combination of: (i) nonexperimental data, and (ii) substantive assumptions. The assumptions are encoded in the form of a directed acyclic graph, also called "causal graph", in which some variables are presumed to be unobserved. The paper establishes a necessary and sufficient criterion for the identifiability of the causal effects of a singleton variable on all other variables in the model, and a powerful sufficient criterion for the effects of a singleton variable on any set of variables.

Introduction

This paper explores the feasibility of inferring cause effect relationships from various combinations of data and theoretical assumptions. The assumptions considered will be represented in the form of an acyclic causal diagram which contains both arrows and bi-directed arcs (Pearl 1995; 2000). The arrows represent the potential existence of direct causal relationships between the corresponding variables, and the bi-directed arcs represent spurious dependencies due to unmeasured confounders. Our main task will be to decide whether the assumptions represented in any given diagram are sufficient for assessing the strength of causal effects from nonexperimental data and, if sufficiency is proven, to express the target causal effect in terms of estimable quantities.

It is well known that, in the absence of unmeasured confounders, all causal effects are *identifiable*, that is, the joint response of any set Y of variables to intervention on a set T of treatment variables, denoted $P_t(y)$,[1] can be estimated consistently from nonexperimental data (Robins 1987; Spirtes, Glymour, & Scheines 1993; Pearl 1993). If some confounders are not measured, then the question of identifiability arises, and whether the desired quantity can be estimated depends critically on the precise locations (in the diagram) of those confounders vis a vis the sets T and Y. Sufficient graphical conditions for ensuring the identification of $P_t(y)$ were established by several

authors (Spirtes, Glymour, & Scheines 1993; Pearl 1993; 1995) and are summarized in (Pearl 2000, Chapters 3 and 4). For example, a criterion called "back-door" permits one to determine whether a given causal effect $P_t(y)$ can be obtained by "adjustment", that is, whether a set C of covariates exists such that

$$P_t(y) = \sum_c P(y|c,t)P(c) \qquad (1)$$

When there exists no set of covariates that is sufficient for adjustment, causal effects can sometimes be estimated by invoking multi-stage adjustments, through a criterion called "front-door" (Pearl 1995). More generally, identifiability can be decided using *do*-calculus derivations (Pearl 1995), that is, a sequence of syntactic transformations capable of reducing expressions of the type $P_t(y)$ to subscript-free expressions. Using *do*-calculus as a guide, (Galles & Pearl 1995) devised a graphical criterion for identifying $P_x(y)$ (where X and Y are singletons) that combines and expands the "front-door" and "back-door" criteria (see (Pearl 2000, pp. 114-8)).

This paper develops new graphical identification criteria that generalize and simplify existing criteria in several ways. We show that $P_x(v)$, where X is a singleton and V is the set of all variables excluding X, is identifiable if and only if there is no consecutive sequence of confounding arcs between X and X's immediate successors in the diagram.[2] When interest lies in the effect of X on a subset S of outcome variables, not on the entire set V, it is possible that $P_x(s)$ would be identifiable even though $P_x(v)$ is not. To this end, the paper gives a sufficient criterion for identifying $P_x(s)$, which is an extension of the criterion for identifying $P_x(v)$. It says that $P_x(s)$ is identifiable if there is no consecutive sequence of confounding arcs between X and X's children in the subgraph composed of the ancestors of S. Other than this requirement, the diagram may have an arbitrary structure, including any number of confounding arcs between X and S. This simple criterion is shown to cover all criteria reported in the literature (with X singleton), including the "back-door", "front-door", and those developed by (Galles & Pearl 1995).

---

[1](Pearl 1995; 2000) used the notation $P(y|set(t))$, $P(y|do(t))$, or $P(y|\hat{t})$ for the post-intervention distribution, while (Lauritzen 2000) used $P(y||t)$.

[2]A variable Z is an "immediate successor" (or a "child") of X if there exists an arrow $X \rightarrow Z$ in the diagram.

Notation, Definitions, and Problem Formulation

The use of causal models for encoding distributional and causal assumptions is now fairly standard (see, for example, (Pearl 1988; Spirtes, Glymour, & Scheines 1993; Greenland, Pearl, & Robins 1999; Lauritzen 2000; Pearl 2000)). The simplest such model, called *Markovian*, consists of a directed acyclic graph (DAG) over a set $V = \{V_1, \ldots, V_n\}$ of vertices, representing variables of interest, and a set E of directed edges, or arrows, that connect these vertices. The interpretation of such a graph has two components, probabilistic and causal. The probabilistic interpretation views the arrows as representing probabilistic dependencies among the corresponding variables, and the missing arrows as representing conditional independence assertions: Each variable is independent of all its nondescendants given its direct parents in the graph.[3] These assumptions amount to asserting that the joint probability function $P(v) = P(v_1, \ldots, v_n)$ factorizes according to the product

$$P(v) = \prod_i P(v_i | pa_i) \qquad (2)$$

where pa_i are (values of) the parents of variable V_i in the graph.[4]

The causal interpretation views the arrows as representing causal influences between the corresponding variables. In this interpretation, the factorization of (2) still holds, but the factors are further assumed to represent autonomous data-generation processes, that is, each conditional probability $P(v_i | pa_i)$ represents a stochastic process by which the values of V_i are chosen in response to the values pa_i (previously chosen for V_i's parents), and the stochastic variation of this assignment is assumed independent of the variations in all other assignments. Moreover, each assignment process remains invariant to possible changes in the assignment processes that govern other variables in the system. This modularity assumption enables us to predict the effects of interventions, whenever interventions are described as specific modifications of some factors in the product of (2). The simplest such intervention involves fixing a set T of variables to some constants $T = t$, which yields the post-intervention distribution

$$P_t(v) = \begin{cases} \prod_{\{i | V_i \notin T\}} P(v_i | pa_i) & v \text{ consistent with } t. \\ 0 & v \text{ inconsistent with } t. \end{cases} \qquad (3)$$

Eq. (3) represents a truncated factorization of (2), with factors corresponding to the manipulated variables removed. This truncation follows immediately from (2) since, assuming modularity, the post-intervention probabilities $P(v_i | pa_i)$

corresponding to variables in T are either 1 or 0, while those corresponding to unmanipulated variables remain unaltered.[5] If T stands for a set of treatment variables and Y for an outcome variable in $V \setminus T$, then Eq. (3) permits us to calculate the probability $P_t(y)$ that event $Y = y$ would occur if treatment condition $T = t$ were enforced uniformly over the population. This quantity, often called the *causal effect* of T on Y, is what we normally assess in a controlled experiment with T randomized, in which the distribution of Y is estimated for each level t of T.

We see from Eq. (3) that the model needed for predicting the effect of interventions requires the specification of three elements

$$M = \langle V, G, P(v_i | pa_i) \rangle$$

where (i) $V = \{V_1, \ldots, V_n\}$ is a set of variables, (ii) G is a directed acyclic graph with nodes corresponding to the elements of V, and (iii) $P(v_i | pa_i), i = 1, \ldots, n$, is the conditional probability of variable V_i given its parents in G. Since $P(v_i | pa_i)$ is estimable from nonexperimental data whenever V is observed, we see that, given the causal graph G, all causal effects are estimable from the data as well.[6]

Our ability to estimate $P_t(v)$ from nonexperimental data is severely curtailed when some variables in a Markovian model are unobserved, or, equivalently, if two or more variables in V are affected by unobserved confounders; the presence of such confounders would not permit the decomposition in (2). Let V and U stand for the sets of observed and unobserved variables, respectively. Assuming that no U variable is a descendant of any V variable (called a *semi-Markovian* model), the observed probability distribution, $P(v)$, becomes a mixture of products:

$$P(v) = \sum_u \prod_i P(v_i | pa_i, u^i) P(u) \qquad (4)$$

where pa_i and u^i stand for the sets of the observed and unobserved parents of V_i, and the summation ranges over all the U variables. The post-intervention distribution, likewise, will be given as a mixture of truncated products

$$P_t(v)$$
$$= \begin{cases} \sum_u \prod_{\{i | V_i \notin T\}} P(v_i | pa_i, u^i) P(u) & v \text{ consistent with } t. \\ 0 & v \text{ inconsistent with } t. \end{cases} \qquad (5)$$

and, the question of identifiability arises, i.e., whether it is possible to express $P_t(v)$ as a function of the observed distribution $P(v)$.

Formally, our semi-Markovian model consists of five elements

$$M = \langle V, U, G_{VU}, P(v_i | pa_i, u^i), P(u) \rangle$$

---

[3] We use family relationships such as "parents," "children," "ancestors," and "descendants," to describe the obvious graphical relationships. For example, the parents PA_i of node V_i are the set of nodes that are directly connected to V_i via arrows pointing to V_i.

[4] We use uppercase letters to represent variables or sets of variables, and use corresponding lowercase letters to represent their values (instantiations).

[5] Eq. (3) was named "Manipulation Theorem" in (Spirtes, Glymour, & Scheines 1993), and is also implicit in Robins' (1987) *G*-computation formula.

[6] It is in fact enough that the parents of each variable in T be observed (Pearl 2000, p. 78).

where G_{VU} is a causal graph consisting of variables in $V \times U$. Clearly, given M and any two sets T and S in V, $P_t(s)$ can be determined unambiguously using (5). The question of identifiability is whether a given causal effect $P_t(s)$ can be determined uniquely from the distribution $P(v)$ of the observed variables, and is thus independent of the unknown quantities, $P(u)$ and $P(v_i|pa_i, u^i)$, that involve elements of U.

In order to analyze questions of identifiability, it is convenient to represent our modeling assumptions in the form of a graph G that does not show the elements of U explicitly but, instead, represents the confounding effects of U using bidirected edges. A bidirected edge between nodes V_i and V_j represents the presence (in G_{VU}) of a divergent path $V_i \leftarrow -- U_k --\rightarrow V_j$ going strictly through elements of U. The presence of such bidirected edges in G represents unmeasured factors (or confounders) that may influence two variables in V; we assume that substantive knowledge permits us to decide if such confounders can be ruled out from the model. See Figure 1 for an example graph with bidirected edges.

Definition 1 (Causal-Effect Identifiability) *The* causal effect *of a set of variables T on a disjoint set of variables S is said to be* identifiable *from a graph G if the quantity $P_t(s)$ can be computed uniquely from any positive probability of the observed variables—that is, if $P_t^{M_1}(s) = P_t^{M_2}(s)$ for every pair of models M_1 and M_2 with $P^{M_1}(v) = P^{M_2}(v) > 0$ and $G(M_1) = G(M_2) = G$.*

In other words, the quantity $P_t(s)$ can be determined from the observed distribution $P(v)$ alone; the details of M are irrelevant.

The Identification of $P_x(v)$

Let X be a singleton variable. In this section we study the problem of identifying the causal effect of X on $V' = V \setminus \{X\}$, (namely, on all other variables in V), a quantity denoted by $P_x(v)$.

The easiest case

Theorem 1 *If there is no bidirected edge connected to X, then $P_x(v)$ is identifiable and is given by*

$$P_x(v) = P(v|x, pa_x)P(pa_x) \qquad (6)$$

Proof: Since there is no bidirected edge connected to X, then the term $P(x|pa_x, u^x) = P(x|pa_x)$ in Eq. (4) can be moved ahead of the summation, giving

$$
\begin{aligned}
P(v) &= P(x|pa_x) \sum_u \prod_{\{i|V_i \neq X\}} P(v_i|pa_i, u^i) P(u) \\
&= P(x|pa_x) P_x(v). \qquad (7)
\end{aligned}
$$

Hence,

$$P_x(v) = P(v)/P(x|pa_x) = P(v|x, pa_x)P(pa_x). \qquad (8)$$

$\square$

Theorem 1 also follows from Theorem 3.2.5 of (Pearl 2000) which states that for any disjoint sets S and T in a Markovian model M, if the parents of T are measured, then $P_t(s)$ is identifiable.

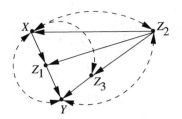

Figure 1:

A more interesting case

The case where there is no bidirected edge connected to any child of X is also easy to handle. Letting Ch_x denote the set of X's children, we have the following theorem.

Theorem 2 *If there is no bidirected edge connected to any child of X, then $P_x(v)$ is identifiable and is given by*

$$P_x(v) = \Big(\prod_{\{i|V_i \in Ch_x\}} P(v_i|pa_i) \Big) \sum_x \frac{P(v)}{\prod_{\{i|V_i \in Ch_x\}} P(v_i|pa_i)} \qquad (9)$$

Proof: Let $S = V \setminus (Ch_x \cup \{X\})$ and $A = \prod_{\{i|V_i \in S\}} P(v_i|pa_i, u^i)$. Since there is no bidirected edge connected to any child of X, the factors corresponding to the variables in Ch_x can be moved ahead of the summation in Eqs. (4) and (5). We have

$$P(v) = \Big(\prod_{\{i|V_i \in Ch_x\}} P(v_i|pa_i) \Big) \sum_u P(x|pa_x, u^x) \cdot A \cdot P(u), \qquad (10)$$

and

$$P_x(v) = \Big(\prod_{\{i|V_i \in Ch_x\}} P(v_i|pa_i) \Big) \sum_u A \cdot P(u). \qquad (11)$$

The variable X does not appear in the factors of A, hence we augment A with the term $\sum_x P(x|pa_x, u^x) = 1$, and write

$$
\begin{aligned}
\sum_u A \cdot P(u) &= \sum_x \sum_u P(x|pa_x, u^x) \cdot A \cdot P(u) \\
&= \sum_x \frac{P(v)}{\prod_{\{i|V_i \in Ch_x\}} P(v_i|pa_i)}. \quad \text{(by (10))} \qquad (12)
\end{aligned}
$$

Substituting this expression into Eq. (11) leads to Eq. (9). $\square$

The usefulness of Theorem 2 can be demonstrated in the model of Figure 1. Although the diagram is quite complicated, Theorem 2 is applicable, and readily gives

$$
\begin{aligned}
P_x(z_1, z_2, z_3, y) &= P(z_1|x, z_2) \sum_{x'} \frac{P(x', z_1, z_2, z_3, y)}{P(z_1|x', z_2)} \\
&= P(z_1|x, z_2) \sum_{x'} P(y, z_3|x', z_1, z_2) P(x', z_2). \qquad (13)
\end{aligned}
$$

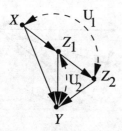

Figure 2:

The general case

When there are bidirected edges connected to the children of X, it may still be possible to identify $P_x(v)$. To illustrate, consider the graph in Figure 2, for which we have

$$P(v) = \sum_{u_1} P(x|u_1)P(z_2|z_1,u_1)P(u_1)$$
$$\cdot \sum_{u_2} P(z_1|x,u_2)P(y|x,z_1,z_2,u_2)P(u_2), \quad (14)$$

and

$$P_x(v) = \sum_{u_1} P(z_2|z_1,u_1)P(u_1)$$
$$\cdot \sum_{u_2} P(z_1|x,u_2)P(y|x,z_1,z_2,u_2)P(u_2). \quad (15)$$

Let

$$Q_1 = \sum_{u_1} P(x|u_1)P(z_2|z_1,u_1)P(u_1), \quad (16)$$

and

$$Q_2 = \sum_{u_2} P(z_1|x,u_2)P(y|x,z_1,z_2,u_2)P(u_2). \quad (17)$$

Eq. (14) can then be written as

$$P(v) = Q_1 \cdot Q_2, \quad (18)$$

and Eq. (15) as

$$P_x(v) = Q_2 \sum_x Q_1. \quad (19)$$

Thus, if Q_1 and Q_2 can be computed from $P(v)$, then $P_x(v)$ is identifiable and given by Eq. (19). In fact, it is enough to show that Q_1 can be computed from $P(v)$ (i.e., identifiable); Q_2 would then be given by $P(v)/Q_1$. To show that Q_1 can indeed be obtained from $P(v)$, we sum both sides of Eq. (14) over y, and get

$$P(x,z_1,z_2) = Q_1 \cdot \sum_{u_2} P(z_1|x,u_2)P(u_2). \quad (20)$$

Summing both sides of (20) over z_2, we get

$$P(x,z_1) = P(x) \sum_{u_2} P(z_1|x,u_2)P(u_2), \quad (21)$$

hence,

$$\sum_{u_2} P(z_1|x,u_2)P(u_2) = P(z_1|x). \quad (22)$$

From Eqs. (22) and (20),

$$Q_1 = P(x,z_1,z_2)/P(z_1|x) = P(z_2|x,z_1)P(x), \quad (23)$$

and from Eq. (18),

$$Q_2 = P(v)/Q_1 = P(y|x,z_1,z_2)P(z_1|x). \quad (24)$$

Finally, from Eq. (19), we obtain

$$P_x(v) = P(y|x,z_1,z_2)P(z_1|x) \sum_{x'} P(z_2|x',z_1)P(x'). \quad (25)$$

From the preceding example, we see that because the two bidirected arcs in Figure 2 do not share a common node, the set of factors (of $P(v)$) containing U_1 is disjoint of those containing U_2, and $P(v)$ can be decomposed into a product of two terms, each being a summation of products. This decomposition, to be treated next, plays an important role in the general identifiability problem.

C-components Let a path composed entirely of bidirected edges be called a *bidirected path*. The set of variables V can be partitioned into disjoint groups by assigning two variables to the same group if and only if they are connected by a bidirected path. Assume that V is thus partitioned into k groups $S_1,\ldots,S_k$, and denote by N_j the set of U variables that are parents of those variables in S_j. Clearly, the sets $N_1,\ldots,N_k$ form a partition of U. Define

$$Q_j = \sum_{n_j} \prod_{\{i|V_i \in S_j\}} P(v_i|pa_i,u^i)P(n_j), \; j=1,\ldots,k. \quad (26)$$

The disjointness of $N_1,\ldots,N_k$ implies that $P(v)$ can be decomposed into a product of Q_j's:

$$P(v) = \prod_{j=1}^{k} Q_j. \quad (27)$$

We will call each S_j a *c-component* (abbreviating "confounded component") of V in G or a c-component of G, and Q_j the *c-factor* corresponding to the c-component S_j. For example, in the model of Figure 2, V is partitioned into the c-components $S_1 = \{X,Z_2\}$ and $S_2 = \{Z_1,Y\}$, the corresponding c-factors are given in equations (16) and (17), and $P(v)$ is decomposed into a product of c-factors as in (18).

Let $Pa(S)$ denote the union of a set S and the set of parents of S, that is, $Pa(S) = S \cup (\cup_{V_i \in S} PA_i)$. We see that Q_j is a function of $Pa(S_j)$. Moreover, each Q_j can be interpreted as the post-intervention distribution of the variables in S_j, under an intervention that sets all other variables to constants, or

$$Q_j = P_{v \setminus s_j}(s_j) \quad (28)$$

The importance of the c-factors stems from that all c-factors are identifiable, as shown in the following lemma.

Lemma 1 *Let a topological order over V be $V_1 < \ldots < V_n$, and let $V^{(i)} = \{V_1, \ldots, V_i\}$, $i = 1, \ldots, n$, and $V^{(0)} = \emptyset$. For any set C, let G_C denote the subgraph of G composed only of variables in C. Then*

(i) Each c-factor Q_j, $j = 1, \ldots, k$, is identifiable and is given by

$$Q_j = \prod_{\{i | V_i \in S_j\}} P(v_i | v^{(i-1)}). \tag{29}$$

(ii) Each factor $P(v_i | v^{(i-1)})$ can be expressed as

$$P(v_i | v^{(i-1)}) = P(v_i | pa(T_i) \setminus \{v_i\}), \tag{30}$$

where T_i is the c-component of $G_{V^{(i)}}$ that contains V_i.

Proof: We prove (i) and (ii) simultaneously by induction on the number of variables n.

Base: $n = 1$; we have one c-component $Q_1 = P(v_1)$, which is identifiable and is given by Eq. (29), and Eq. (30) is satisfied.

Hypothesis: When there are n variables, all c-factors are identifiable and are given by Eq. (29), and Eq. (30) holds for all $V_i \in V$.

Induction step: When there are $n + 1$ variables in V, assuming that V is partitioned into c-components $S_1, \ldots, S_l, S'$, with corresponding c-factors $Q_1, \ldots, Q_l, Q'$, and that $V_{n+1} \in S'$, we have

$$P(v) = Q' \prod_i Q_i. \tag{31}$$

Summing both sides of (31) over v_{n+1} leads to

$$P(v^{(n)}) = (\sum_{v_{n+1}} Q') \prod_i Q_i. \tag{32}$$

It is clear that each S_i, $i = 1, \ldots, l$, is a c-component of $G_{V^{(n)}}$. By the induction hypothesis, each Q_i, $i = 1, \ldots, l$, is identifiable and is given by Eq. (29). From Eq. (31), Q' is identifiable as well, and is given by

$$Q' = \frac{P(v)}{\prod_i Q_i} = \prod_{\{i | V_i \in S'\}} P(v_i | v^{(i-1)}), \tag{33}$$

which is clear from Eq. (29) and the chain decomposition $P(v) = \prod_i P(v_i | v^{(i-1)})$.

By the induction hypothesis, Eq. (30) holds for i from 1 to n. Next we prove that it holds for V_{n+1}. In Eq. (33), Q' is a function of $Pa(S')$, and each term $P(v_i | v^{(i-1)})$, $V_i \in S'$ and $V_i \neq V_{n+1}$, is a function of $Pa(T_i)$ by Eq. (30), where T_i is a c-component of the graph $G_{V^{(i)}}$ and therefore is a subset of S'. Hence we obtain that $P(v_{n+1} | v^{(n)})$ is a function only of $Pa(S')$ and is independent of $C = V \setminus Pa(S')$, which leads to

$$P(v_{n+1} | pa(S') \setminus \{v_{n+1}\})$$
$$= \sum_c P(v_{n+1} | v^{(n)}) P(c | pa(S') \setminus \{v_{n+1}\})$$
$$= P(v_{n+1} | v^{(n)}) \sum_c P(c | pa(S') \setminus \{v_{n+1}\})$$
$$= P(v_{n+1} | v^{(n)}) \tag{34}$$

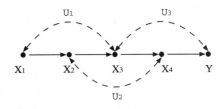

Figure 3:

$\square$

The proposition (ii) in Lemma 1 can also be proved by using d-separation criterion (Pearl 1988) to show that V_i is independent of $V^{(i)} \setminus Pa(T_i)$ given $Pa(T_i) \setminus \{V_i\}$.

We show the use of Lemma 1 by an example shown in Figure 3, which has two c-components $S_1 = \{X_2, X_4\}$ and $S_2 = \{X_1, X_3, Y\}$. $P(v)$ decomposes into

$$P(x_1, x_2, x_3, x_4, y) = Q_1 Q_2, \tag{35}$$

where

$$Q_1 = \sum_{u_2} P(x_2 | x_1, u_2) P(x_4 | x_3, u_2) P(u_2), \tag{36}$$

$$Q_2 = \sum_{u_1, u_3} P(x_1 | u_1) P(x_3 | x_2, u_1, u_3) P(y | x_4, u_3)$$
$$\cdot P(u_1) P(u_3). \tag{37}$$

By Lemma 1, both Q_1 and Q_2 are identifiable. The only admissible order of variables is $X_1 < X_2 < X_3 < X_4 < Y$, and Eq. (29) gives

$$Q_1 = P(x_4 | x_1, x_2, x_3) P(x_2 | x_1), \tag{38}$$
$$Q_2 = P(y | x_1, x_2, x_3, x_4) P(x_3 | x_1, x_2) P(x_1). \tag{39}$$

We can also check that the expressions obtained in Eq.s (23) and (24) for Figure 2 satisfy Lemma 1.

The identification criterion for $P_x(v)$ Let X belong to the c-component S^X with corresponding c-factor Q^X. Let Q_x^X denote the c-factor Q^X with the term $P(x | pa_x, u^x)$ removed, that is,

$$Q_x^X = \sum_{n^X} \prod_{\{i | V_i \neq X, V_i \in S^X\}} P(v_i | pa_i, u^i) P(n^X). \tag{40}$$

We have

$$P(v) = Q^X \prod_i Q_i, \tag{41}$$

$$P_x(v) = Q_x^X \prod_i Q_i. \tag{42}$$

Since all Q_i's are identifiable, $P_x(v)$ is identifiable if and only if Q_x^X is identifiable, and we have the following theorem.

Theorem 3 *$P_x(v)$ is identifiable if and only if there is no bidirected path connecting X to any of its children. When*

$P_x(v)$ is identifiable, it is given by

$$P_x(v) = \frac{P(v)}{Q^X} \sum_x Q^X, \qquad (43)$$

where Q^X is the c-factor corresponding to the c-component S^X that contains X.

Proof: (**if**) If there is no bidirected path connecting X to any of its children, then none of X's children is in S^X. Under this condition, removing the term $P(x|pa_x, u^x)$ from Q^X is equivalent to summing Q^X over X, and we can write

$$Q_x^X = \sum_x Q^X. \qquad (44)$$

Hence from Eq.s (42) and (41), we obtain

$$P_x(v) = (\sum_x Q^X) \prod_i Q_i = (\sum_x Q^X)\frac{P(v)}{Q^X}, \qquad (45)$$

which proves the identifiability of $P_x(v)$.

(**only if**) Sketch: Assuming that there is a bidirected path connecting X to a child of X, one can construct two models (by specifying all conditional probabilities) such that $P(v)$ has the same values in both models while $P_x(v)$ takes different values. The proof is lengthy and is given in (Tian & Pearl 2002). □

We demonstrate the use of Theorem 3 by identifying $P_{x_1}(x_2, x_3, x_4, y)$ in Figure 3. The graph has two c-components $S_1 = \{X_2, X_4\}$ and $S_2 = \{X_1, X_3, Y\}$, with corresponding c-factors given in (38) and (39). Since X_1 is in S_2 and its child X_2 is not in S_2, Theorem 3 ensures that $P_{x_1}(x_2, x_3, x_4, y)$ is identifiable and is given by

$$P_{x_1}(x_2, x_3, x_4, y) = Q_1 \sum_{x_1} Q_2$$

$$= P(x_4|x_1, x_2, x_3)P(x_2|x_1)$$

$$\sum_{x_1'} P(y|x_1', x_2, x_3, x_4)P(x_3|x_1', x_2)P(x_1'). \qquad (46)$$

A Criterion for Identifying $P_x(s)$

Let X be a singleton variable and $S \subseteq V$ be any set of variables. Clearly, whenever $P_x(v)$ is identifiable, so is $P_x(s)$. However, there are obvious cases where $P_x(v)$ is not identifiable and still $P_x(s)$ is identifiable for some subsets S of V. In this section we give a criterion for identifying $P_x(s)$.

Let $An(S)$ denote the union of a set S and the set of ancestors of the variables in S, and let $G_{An(S)}$ denote the subgraph of G composed only of variables in $An(S)$. Summing both sides of Eq. (4) over $V \setminus An(S)$, we have that the marginal distribution $P(an(S))$ decomposes exactly according to the graph $G_{An(S)}$. Therefore, if $P_x(s)$ is identifiable in $G_{An(S)}$, then it is computable from $P(an(S))$, and thus is computable from $P(v)$. A direct extension of Theorem 3 then leads to the following sufficient criterion for identifying $P_x(s)$.

Theorem 4 $P_x(s)$ *is identifiable if there is no bidirected path connecting X to any of its children in $G_{An(S)}$.*

When the condition in Theorem 4 is satisfied, we can compute $P_x(an(S))$ by applying Theorem 3 in $G_{An(S)}$, and $P_x(s)$ can be obtained by marginalizing over $P_x(an(S))$.

This simple criterion can classify correctly all the examples treated in the literature with X singleton, including those contrived by (Galles & Pearl 1995). In fact, for X and S being singletons, it is shown in the Appendix that if there is a bidirected path connecting X to one of its children such that every node on the path is in $An(S)$, then none of the "back-door", "front-door", and (Galles & Pearl 1995) criteria is applicable. However, this criterion is *not necessary* for identifying $P_x(s)$. Examples exist in which $P_x(s)$ is identifiable but Theorem 4 is not applicable.[7] An improved criterion that covers those cases is described in (Tian & Pearl 2002).

Conclusion

We developed new graphical criteria for identifying the causal effects of a singleton variable on a set of variables. Theorem 4 has important ramifications to the theory and practice of observational studies. It implies that the key to identifiability lies not in blocking back-door paths between X and S but, rather, in blocking back-door paths between X and its immediate successors on the pathways to S. The potential of finding and measuring intermediate variables that satisfy this condition opens new vistas in experimental design.

Acknowledgements

This research was supported in parts by grants from NSF, ONR, AFOSR, and DoD MURI program.

Appendix

In this appendix we show that Theorem 4 covers the criterion in (Galles & Pearl 1995) (which will be called the G-P criterion). The G-P criterion is for identifying $P_x(y)$ with X and Y being singletons, and it includes the "front-door" and "back-door" criteria as special cases (see (Pearl 2000, pp. 114-8)). We will prove that if there is a bidirected path connecting X to one of its children such that every node on the path is an ancestor of Y, then the G-P criterion is not applicable. There are four conditions in the G-P criterion, among which Condition 1 is a special case of Condition 3, and Condition 2 is trivial. Therefore we only need to consider Condition 3 and 4.

Proof: Assume that there is a bidirected path p from X to its child Y_1 such that every node on p is an ancestor of Y, and that there is a directed path q from Y_1 to Y. We will show by contradiction that neither Condition 3 nor Condition 4 is applicable for identifying $P_x(y)$. For any set Z, a node will be called Z-*active* if it is in Z or any of its descendants is in Z, otherwise it will be called Z-*inactive*.

(**Condition 3**) Assume that there exists a set Z that blocks all back-door paths from X to Y so that $P_x(z)$ is identifi-

---

[7]This implies that, contrary to claims, the criterion developed in (Galles & Pearl 1995) is *not* complete.

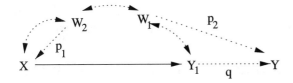

Figure 4:

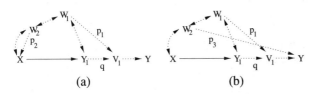

(a)   (b)

Figure 5:

able.[8] If every internal node on p is an ancestor of X, or if every nonancestor of X on p is Z-active, then let $W_1 = Y_1$, otherwise let W_1 be the Z-inactive non-ancestor of X that is closest to X on p (see Figure 4). If every internal node on the subpath $p(W_1, X)$ [9] is Z-active, then let $W_2 = X$, otherwise let W_2 be the Z-inactive node that is closest to W_1 on $p(W_1, X)$. From the definition of W_1 and W_2, W_2 must be an ancestor of X (or be X itself), and let p_1 be any directed path from W_2 to X. (i) If $W_1 \neq Y_1$, letting p_2 be any directed path from W_1 to Y, then from the definition of W_1 and W_2 the path $p' = (p_1(X, W_2), p(W_2, W_1), p_2(W_1, Y))$ is a back-door path from X to Y that is not blocked by Z (see Figure 4) since W_2 is Z-inactive, all internal nodes on $p(W_2, W_1)$ is Z-active, and W_1 is Z-inactive. (ii) If $W_1 = Y_1$, there are two situations:

(a) Z consists entirely of nondescendants of X. Then the path $p'' = (p_1(X, W_2), p(W_2, Y_1), q(Y_1, Y))$ is a back-door path from X to Y that is not blocked by Z.

(b) Z contains a variable Y' on $q(Y_1, Y)$ so that $P_x(z)$ is identifiable. By the definition of W_1, every node on p is an ancestor of Z. $P_x(z)$ can not be identified by Theorem 4, and the G-P criterion is not applicable for identifying $P_x(z)$ if Z contains more than one variable. If Z contains only one variable Y', then every node on p is an ancestor of Y'. If $P_x(y')$ is identifiable by Condition 3 of the G-P criterion (Condition 4 is not applicable as proved later), then from the preceding analysis there is a Y'' on the path $q(Y_1, Y')$ such that every node on p is an ancestor of Y'' and $P_x(y'')$ is identifiable. By induction, in the end we have every node on p is an ancestor of Y_1 and $P_x(y_1)$ is identifiable, which does not hold from the preceding analysis.

(**Condition 4**) Assume that there exist sets Z_1 and Z_2 that satisfy all (i)–(iv) conditions in Condition 4. Since Z_1 has to block the path $((X, Y_1), q(Y_1, Y))$, let V_1 be the variable in Z_1 that is closest to Y_1 on the path q (see Figure 5(a)). If none of the internal node on p is in $An(V_1) \setminus An(X)$ (the set of ancestors of V_1 that are not ancestors of X) or if every

variable in $An(V_1) \setminus An(X)$ on p is Z_2-active, then let $W_1 = Y_1$, otherwise let W_1 be the Z_2-inactive variable in $An(V_1) \setminus An(X)$ that is closest to X on p. Let p_1 be any directed path from W_1 to V_1. If every internal node on the subpath $p(W_1, X)$ is Z_2-active, then let $W_2 = X$, otherwise let W_2 be the Z_2-inactive node that is closest to W_1 on $p(W_1, X)$. Since W_2 must be an ancestor of Y, from the definition of W_1 and W_2, there are two possible situations:

(a) W_2 is an ancestor of X or $W_2 = X$. Let p_2 be any directed path from W_2 to X (see Figure 5(a)). From the definition of W_1 and W_2, the path $p' = (p_2(X, W_2), p(W_2, W_1), p_1(W_1, V_1))$ is a back-door path from X to $V_1 \in Z_1$ that is not blocked by Z_2 that does not contain any descendant of X (see Figure 5(a)).

(b) W_2 is an ancestor of Y but not ancestor of V_1 ($W_2 \in An(Y) \setminus An(V_1)$). Let p_3 be any directed path from W_2 to Y (see Figure 5(b)). From the definition of W_1 and W_2, the path $p'' = (p_1(V_1, W_1), p(W_1, W_2), p_3(W_2, Y))$ is a back-door path from $V_1 \in Z_1$ to Y that is not blocked by Z_2 (see Figure 5(b)). □

References

Galles, D., and Pearl, J. 1995. Testing identifiability of causal effects. In Besnard, P., and Hanks, S., eds., *Uncertainty in Artificial Intelligence 11*. San Francisco: Morgan Kaufmann. 185–195.

Greenland, S.; Pearl, J.; and Robins, J. 1999. Causal diagrams for epidemiologic research. *Epidemiology* 10:37–48.

Lauritzen, S. 2000. Graphical models for causal inference. In Barndorff-Nielsen, O.; Cox, D.; and Kluppelberg, C., eds., *Complex Stochastic Systems*. London/Boca Raton: Chapman and Hall/CRC Press. chapter 2, 67–112.

Pearl, J. 1988. *Probabilistic Reasoning in Intelligence Systems*. San Mateo, CA: Morgan Kaufmann.

Pearl, J. 1993. Comment: Graphical models, causality, and intervention. *Statistical Science* 8:266–269.

Pearl, J. 1995. Causal diagrams for experimental research. *Biometrika* 82:669–710.

Pearl, J. 2000. *Causality: Models, Reasoning, and Inference*. NY: Cambridge University Press.

Robins, J. 1987. A graphical approach to the identification and estimation of causal parameters in mortality studies with sustained exposure periods. *Journal of Chronic Diseases* 40(Suppl 2):139S–161S.

Spirtes, P.; Glymour, C.; and Scheines, R. 1993. *Causation, Prediction, and Search*. New York: Springer-Verlag.

Tian, J., and Pearl, J. 2002. On the identification of causal effects. Technical Report R-290-L, Department of Computer Science, University of California, Los Angeles.

---

[8]A path from X to Y is said to be a *back-door* path if it contains an arrow into X.

[9]We use $p(W_1, X)$ to represent the subpath of p from W_1 to X.

A New Characterization of the Experimental Implications of Causal Bayesian Networks

Jin Tian and Judea Pearl

Cognitive Systems Laboratory
Computer Science Department
University of California, Los Angeles, CA 90024
{jtian, judea }@cs.ucla.edu

Abstract

We offer a complete characterization of the set of distributions that could be induced by local interventions on variables governed by a causal Bayesian network. We show that such distributions must adhere to three norms of coherence, and we demonstrate the use of these norms as inferential tools in tasks of learning and identification. Testable coherence norms are subsequently derived for networks containing unmeasured variables.

Introduction

The use of graphical models for encoding distributional and causal information is now fairly standard (Pearl 1988; Spirtes, Glymour, & Scheines 1993; Heckerman & Shachter 1995; Lauritzen 2000; Pearl 2000; Dawid 2001). The most common such representation involves a *causal Bayesian network*, namely, a directed acyclic graph (DAG) G which, in addition to the usual conditional independence interpretation, is also given a causal interpretation. This additional feature permits one to infer the effects of interventions, such as policy decisions and ordinary actions. Specifically, if an external intervention fixes any set T of variables to some constants t, the DAG permits us to infer the resulting post-intervention distribution, denoted by $P_t(v)$,[1] from the pre-intervention distribution $P(v)$.

In this paper, we seek a characterization for the set of interventional distributions, $P_t(v)$, that could be induced by some causal Bayesian network. Whereas (Pearl 2000, pp.23-4) has given such characterization relative to a given network, we assume that the underlying network, if such exists, is unknown. Given a collection of distribution functions, $P_t(s)$, each obtained by observing a set S of variables under experimental conditions $T = t$, we ask whether the collection is compatible with the predictions of some underlying causal Bayesian network, and we identify three properties (of the collection) that are both necessary and sufficient for the existence of such an underlying network. We subsequently identify necessary properties of distributions

induced by causal Bayesian networks in which some of the variables are unmeasured. We further show how these properties can be used as symbolic inferential tools for predicting the effects of actions from nonexperimental data in the presence of unmeasured variables. The Conclusion Section outlines the use of these properties in learning tasks which aim at uncovering the structure of the network.

Causal Bayesian Networks and Interventions

A causal Bayesian network (also known as a *Markovian model*) consists of two mathematical objects: (i) a DAG G, called a *causal graph*, over a set $V = \{V_1, \ldots, V_n\}$ of vertices, and (ii) a probability distribution $P(v)$, over the set V of discrete variables that correspond to the vertices in G. The interpretation of such a graph has two components, probabilistic and causal.[2] The probabilistic interpretation views G as representing conditional independence restrictions on P: Each variable is independent of all its non-descendants given its direct parents in the graph. These restrictions imply that the joint probability function $P(v) = P(v_1, \ldots, v_n)$ factorizes according to the product

$$P(v) = \prod_i P(v_i | pa_i) \qquad (1)$$

where pa_i are (values of) the parents of variable V_i in G.

The causal interpretation views the arrows in G as representing causal influences between the corresponding variables. In this interpretation, the factorization of (1) still holds, but the factors are further assumed to represent autonomous data-generation processes, that is, each conditional probability $P(v_i | pa_i)$ represents a stochastic process by which the values of V_i are assigned[3] in response to

---

[1](Pearl 1995; 2000) used the notation $P(v|set(t))$, $P(v|do(t))$, or $P(v|\hat{t})$ for the post-intervention distribution, while (Lauritzen 2000) used $P(v||t)$.

[2]A more refined interpretation, called *functional*, is also common (Pearl 2000, chapter 1), which, in addition to interventions, supports counterfactual readings. The functional interpretation assumes strictly deterministic, functional relationships between variables in the model, some of which may be unobserved. Complete axiomatizations of deterministic counterfactual relations are given in (Galles & Pearl 1998; Halpern 1998). We are not aware of an axiomatization of the probabilistic predictions of functional models.

[3]In contrast with functional models, here the probability of each V_i, not its precise value, is determined by the other variables in the model.

the values pa_i (previously chosen for V_i's parents), and the stochastic variation of this assignment is assumed independent of the variations in all other assignments in the model. Moreover, each assignment process remains invariant to possible changes in the assignment processes that govern other variables in the system. This modularity assumption enables us to predict the effects of interventions, whenever interventions are described as specific modifications of some factors in the product of (1). The simplest such intervention, called *atomic*, involves fixing a set T of variables to some constants $T = t$, which yields the post-intervention distribution

$$P_t(v) = \begin{cases} \prod_{\{i|V_i \notin T\}} P(v_i|pa_i) & v \text{ consistent with } t. \\ 0 & v \text{ inconsistent with } t. \end{cases} \tag{2}$$

Eq. (2) represents a truncated factorization of (1), with factors corresponding to the manipulated variables removed. This truncation follows immediately from (1) since, assuming modularity, the post-intervention probabilities $P(v_i|pa_i)$ corresponding to variables in T are either 1 or 0, while those corresponding to unmanipulated variables remain unaltered.[4] If T stands for a set of treatment variables and Y for an outcome variable in $V \setminus T$, then Eq. (2) permits us to calculate the probability $P_t(y)$ that event $Y = y$ would occur if treatment condition $T = t$ were enforced uniformly over the population. This quantity, often called the "causal effect" of T on Y, is what we normally assess in a controlled experiment with T randomized, in which the distribution of Y is estimated for each level t of T.

Let $\mathbf{P}_*$ denote the set of all interventional distributions

$$\mathbf{P}_* = \{P_t(v)|T \subseteq V, t \in Dm(T)\} \tag{3}$$

where $Dm(T)$ represents the domain of T. In the next section, we will give a set of properties that fully characterize the $\mathbf{P}_*$ set.

Interventional Distributions in Markovian Models

The $\mathbf{P}_*$ set induced from a Markovian model must satisfy three properties: effectiveness, Markov, and recursiveness.

Property 1 (Effectiveness) *For any set of variables T,*

$$P_t(t) = 1. \tag{4}$$

Effectiveness states that, if we force a set of variables T to have the value t, then the probability of T taking that value t is one.

For any set of variables S disjoint with T, an immediate corollary of effectiveness reads:

$$P_{t,s}(t) = 1, \tag{5}$$

which follows from

$$P_{t,s}(t) \geq P_{t,s}(t,s) = 1. \tag{6}$$

---

[4] Eq. (2) was named "Manipulation Theorem" in (Spirtes, Glymour, & Scheines 1993), and is also implicit in Robins' (1987) G-computation formula.

Equivalently, if $T_1 \subseteq T$, then

$$P_t(t_1) = \begin{cases} 1 & \text{if } t_1 \text{ is consistent with } t. \\ 0 & \text{if } t_1 \text{ is inconsistent with } t. \end{cases} \tag{7}$$

We further have that, for $T_1 \subseteq T$ and S disjoint of T,

$$P_t(s, t_1) = \begin{cases} P_t(s) & \text{if } t_1 \text{ is consistent with } t. \\ 0 & \text{if } t_1 \text{ is inconsistent with } t. \end{cases} \tag{8}$$

Property 2 (Markov) *For any two disjoint sets of variables S_1 and S_2,*

$$P_{v \setminus (s_1 \cup s_2)}(s_1, s_2) = P_{v \setminus s_1}(s_1)P_{v \setminus s_2}(s_2). \tag{9}$$

An equivalent form of the Markov property is: For any set of variables $T \subseteq V$,

$$P_t(v \setminus t) = \prod_{\{i|V_i \in V \setminus T\}} P_{v \setminus \{v_i\}}(v_i). \tag{10}$$

Eq. (10) can be obtained by repeatedly applying Eq. (9), and Eq. (9) follows from Eq. (10) as follows:

$$\begin{aligned} P_{v \setminus (s_1 \cup s_2)}(s_1, s_2) &= \prod_{V_i \in S_1 \cup S_2} P_{v \setminus \{v_i\}}(v_i) \\ &= \prod_{V_i \in S_1} P_{v \setminus \{v_i\}}(v_i) \prod_{V_i \in S_2} P_{v \setminus \{v_i\}}(v_i) \\ &= P_{v \setminus s_1}(s_1)P_{v \setminus s_2}(s_2). \end{aligned} \tag{11}$$

Definition 1 *For two single variables X and Y, define "X affects Y", denoted by $X \rightsquigarrow Y$, as $\exists W \subset V, w, x, y$, such that $P_{x,w}(y) \neq P_w(y)$. That is, X affects Y if, under some setting w, intervening on X changes the distribution of Y.*

Property 3 (Recursiveness) *For any set of variables $\{X_0, \ldots, X_k\} \subseteq V$,*

$$(X_0 \rightsquigarrow X_1) \wedge \ldots \wedge (X_{k-1} \rightsquigarrow X_k) \Rightarrow \neg(X_k \rightsquigarrow X_0). \tag{12}$$

Property 3 is a stochastic version of the (deterministic) recursiveness axiom given in (Halpern 1998). It comes from restricting the causal models under study to those having acyclic causal graphs. For $k = 1$, for example, we have $X \rightsquigarrow Y \Rightarrow \neg(Y \rightsquigarrow X)$, saying that for any two variables X and Y, either X does not affect Y or Y does not affect X. (Halpern 1998) pointed out that, recursiveness can be viewed as a collection of axioms, one for each k, and that the case of $k = 1$ alone is not enough to characterize a recursive model.

Theorem 1 (Soundness) *Effectiveness, Markov, and recursiveness hold in all Markovian models.*

Proof: All three properties follow from the factorization of Eq. (2).

Effectiveness From Eq. (2), we have

$$P_t(T = t') = 0 \quad \text{for } t' \neq t, \tag{13}$$

and since

$$\sum_{t' \in Dm(T)} P_t(t') = 1, \tag{14}$$

we obtain the effectiveness property of Eq. (4).

Markov From Eq. (2), we have

$$P_t(v \setminus t) = P_t(t, v \setminus t) = \prod_{V_i \in V \setminus T} P(v_i | pa_i). \quad (15)$$

Letting $T = V \setminus \{V_i\}$ in Eq. (15) yields

$$P_{v \setminus \{v_i\}}(v_i) = P(v_i | pa_i). \quad (16)$$

Substituting Eq. (16) back into Eq. (15), we get the Markov property (10), which is equivalent to (9).

Recursiveness Assume that a total order over V that is consistent with the causal graph is $V_1 < \cdots < V_n$, such that V_i is a nondescendant of V_j if $V_i < V_j$. Consider a variable V_j and a set of variables $S \subseteq V$ which does not contain V_j. Let $B_j = \{V_i | V_i < V_j, V_i \in V \setminus S\}$ be the set of variables not in S and ordered before V_j, and let $A_j = \{V_i | V_j < V_i, V_i \in V \setminus S\}$ be the set of variables not in S and ordered after V_j. First we show that

$$P_{v_j, s}(b_j) = P_s(b_j). \quad (17)$$

We have

$$P_{v_j, s}(b_j) = \sum_{a_j} P_{v_j, s}(a_j, b_j)$$

$$= \sum_{a_j} P_{v_j, s, a_j}(b_j) P_{v_j, s, b_j}(a_j), \quad \text{(by Eq. (9))} \quad (18)$$

where $P_{v_j, s, a_j}(b_j) = \prod_{\{i | V_i \in B_j\}} P(v_i | pa_i)$ is a function of b_j and its parents. Since all variables in A_j are ordered after the variables in B_j, $P_{v_j, s, a_j}(b_j)$ is not a function of a_j. Hence Eq. (18) becomes

$$P_{v_j, s}(b_j) = P_{v_j, s, a_j}(b_j) \sum_{a_j} P_{v_j, s, b_j}(a_j)$$

$$= P_{v_j, s, a_j}(b_j) \quad (19)$$

Similarly,

$$P_s(b_j) = \sum_{v_j, a_j} P_s(v_j, a_j, b_j)$$

$$= \sum_{v_j, a_j} P_{v_j, s, a_j}(b_j) P_{s, b_j}(v_j, a_j)$$

$$= P_{v_j, s, a_j}(b_j) \sum_{v_j, a_j} P_{s, b_j}(v_j, a_j) = P_{v_j, s, a_j}(b_j) \quad (20)$$

Eq. (17) follows from (19) and (20).

From Eq. (17), we have that, for any two variables $V_i < V_j$ and any set of variables S,

$$P_{v_j, s}(v_i) = P_s(v_i), \quad (21)$$

which states that if X is ordered before Y then Y does not affect X, based on our definition of "X affects Y". Therefore, we have that if X affects Y then X is ordered before Y, or

$$X \rightsquigarrow Y \Rightarrow X < Y. \quad (22)$$

Recursive property (12) then follows from (22) because the relation "$<$" is a total order.

To facilitate the proof of the completeness theorem, we give the following lemma.

Lemma 1 *(Pearl 1988, p.124) Given a DAG over V, if a set of functions $f_i(v_i, pa_i)$ satisfy*

$$\sum_{v_i \in Dm(V_i)} f_i(v_i, pa_i) = 1, \text{ and } 0 \le f_i(v_i, pa_i) \le 1, \quad (23)$$

and $P(v)$ can be decomposed as

$$P(v) = \prod_i f_i(v_i, pa_i), \quad (24)$$

then we have

$$f_i(v_i, pa_i) = P(v_i | pa_i), \quad i = 1, \ldots, n. \quad (25)$$

Theorem 2 (Completeness) *If a $\mathbf{P}_*$ set satisfies effectiveness, Markov, and recursiveness, then there exists a Markovian model with a unique causal graph that can generate this $\mathbf{P}_*$ set.*

Proof: Define a relation "$\prec$" as: $X \prec Y$ if $X \rightsquigarrow Y$. Then the transitive closure of $\prec$, $\prec^*$, is a partial order over the set of variables V from the recursiveness property as shown in (Halpern 1998). Let "$<$" be a total order on V consistent with $\prec^*$. We have that

$$\text{if } X < Y \text{ then } P_{y, s}(x) = P_s(x) \quad (26)$$

for any set of variables S. This is because if $P_{y, s}(x) \ne P_s(x)$, then $Y \rightsquigarrow X$, and therefore $Y \prec X$, which contradicts the fact that $X < Y$ is consistent with $\prec^*$.

Define a set PA_i as a minimal set of variables that satisfies

$$P_{pa_i}(v_i) = P_{v \setminus \{v_i\}}(v_i). \quad (27)$$

We have that

$$\text{if } V_i < V_j, \text{ then } V_j \notin PA_i. \quad (28)$$

Otherwise, assuming $V_j \in PA_i$ and letting $PA'_i = PA_i \setminus \{V_j\}$, from Eqs. (26) and (27) we have

$$P_{pa'_i}(v_i) = P_{pa'_i, v_j}(v_i) = P_{v \setminus \{v_i\}}(v_i), \quad (29)$$

which contradicts the fact that PA_i is minimal. From Eq. (28), drawing an arrow from each member of PA_i toward V_i, the resulting graph G is a DAG.

Substituting Eq. (27) into the Markov property (10), we obtain, for any set of variables T,

$$P_t(v \setminus t) = \prod_{\{i | V_i \notin T\}} P_{pa_i}(v_i). \quad (30)$$

By Lemma 1, we get

$$P_{pa_i}(v_i) = P(v_i | pa_i). \quad (31)$$

From Eqs. (30), (31), and the effectiveness property (8), Eq. (2) follows. Therefore, a Markovian model with a causal graph G can generate this $\mathbf{P}_*$ set.

Next, we show that the set PA_i is unique. Assuming that there are two minimal sets PA_i and PA'_i both satisfying Eq. (27), we will show that their intersection also satisfies Eq. (27). Let $A = PA_i \cap PA'_i$, $B = PA_i \setminus A$, $B' = PA'_i \setminus A$, and $S = V \setminus (PA_i \cup PA'_i \cup \{V_i\})$. From the Markov property Eq. (9), we have

$$
\begin{aligned}
P_a(b, b', s, v_i) &= P_{a,v_i}(b, b', s) P_{v \setminus \{v_i\}}(v_i) \\
&= P_{a,v_i}(b, b', s) P_{a,b}(v_i) \quad (32)
\end{aligned}
$$

Summing both sides of (32) over B' and S, we get

$$
P_a(b, v_i) = P_{a,v_i}(b) P_{a,b}(v_i). \quad (33)
$$

Substituting $P_{pa_i}(v_i)$ with $P_{pa'_i}(v_i)$ in (33), we get

$$
P_a(b, v_i) = P_{a,v_i}(b) P_{a,b'}(v_i). \quad (34)
$$

Summing both sides of (34) over B, we obtain

$$
P_a(v_i) = P_{a,b'}(v_i) = P_{pa'_i}(v_i), \quad (35)
$$

which says that the set $A = PA_i \cap PA'_i$ also satisfies Eq. (27). This contradicts the assumption that both PA_i and PA'_i are minimal. Thus PA_i is unique. $\square$

A Markovian model also satisfies the following properties.

Property 4 *If a set B is composed of nondescendants of a variable V_j, then for any set of variables S,*

$$
P_{v_j,s}(b) = P_s(b). \quad (36)
$$

Proof: If B is disjoint of S, Eq. (36) follows from Eq. (17) since $B \subseteq B_j$. If B is not disjoint of S, Eq. (36) follows from the Effectiveness property and Eq. (17). $\square$

Property 5 *For any set of variables $S \subseteq V \setminus (PA_i \cup \{V_i\})$,*

$$
P_{pa_i,s}(v_i) = P_{pa_i}(v_i). \quad (37)
$$

Proof: Let $S' = V \setminus (PA_i \cup \{V_i\} \cup S)$.

$$
\begin{aligned}
P_{pa_i,s}(v_i) &= \sum_{s'} P_{pa_i,s}(s', v_i) \\
&= \sum_{s'} P_{v \setminus \{v_i\}}(v_i) P_{pa_i,s,v_i}(s') \quad \text{(by Eq. (9))} \\
&= P_{pa_i}(v_i) \sum_{s'} P_{pa_i,s,v_i}(s') \quad \text{(by Eq. (27))} \\
&= P_{pa_i}(v_i) \quad (38)
\end{aligned}
$$

$\square$

Property 6

$$
P_{pa_i}(v_i) = P(v_i | pa_i). \quad (39)
$$

Property 6 has been given in Eq. (31).

Property 7 *For any set of variables $S \subseteq V$, and $V_i \notin S$,*

$$
P_s(v_i | pa_{\bar{i}}) = P(v_i | pa_i), \quad \text{for } pa_i \text{ consistent with } s. \quad (40)
$$

Proof: Let $S' = V \setminus (PA_i \cup \{V_i\} \cup S)$. Assuming that pa_i is consistent with s, we have

$$
\begin{aligned}
P_s(v_i, pa_i) &= \sum_{s'} P_s(v_i, pa_i, s') \\
&= \sum_{s'} P_{v \setminus \{v_i\}}(v_i) P_{s,v_i}(pa_i, s') \quad \text{(by Eq. (9))} \\
&= P(v_i | pa_i) \sum_{s'} P_{s,v_i}(pa_i, s') \quad \text{(by Eq. (16))} \\
&= P(v_i | pa_i) P_{s,v_i}(pa_i) \\
&= P(v_i | pa_i) P_s(pa_i) \quad \text{(by Property 4)} \quad (41)
\end{aligned}
$$

which leads to Eq. (40). $\square$

Interventional Distributions in Semi-Markovian Models

When some variables in a Markovian model are unobserved, the probability distribution over the observed variables may no longer be decomposed as in Eq. (1). Let $V = \{V_1, \ldots, V_n\}$ and $U = \{U_1, \ldots, U_{n'}\}$ stand for the sets of observed and unobserved variables respectively. If no U variable is a descendant of any V variable, then the corresponding model is called a *semi-Markovian* model. In a semi-Markovian model, the observed probability distribution, $P(v)$, becomes a mixture of products:

$$
P(v) = \sum_u \prod_i P(v_i | pa_i, u^i) P(u) \quad (42)
$$

where PA_i and U^i stand for the sets of the observed and unobserved parents of V_i, and the summation ranges over all the U variables. The post-intervention distribution, likewise, will be given as a mixture of truncated products

$$
P_t(v) = \begin{cases} \sum_u \prod_{\{i | V_i \notin T\}} P(v_i | pa_i, u^i) P(u) & v \text{ consistent with } t. \\ 0 & v \text{ inconsistent with } t. \end{cases} \quad (43)
$$

If, in a semi-Markovian model, no U variable is an ancestor of more than one V variable, then $P_t(v)$ in Eq. (43) factorizes into a product as in Eq. (2), regardless of the parameters $\{P(v_i | pa_i, u^i)\}$ and $\{P(u)\}$. Therefore, for such a model, the causal Markov condition holds relative to G_V (the subgraph of G composed only of V variables), that is, each variable V_i is independent on all its non-descendants given its parents PA_i in G_V. And by convention, the U variables are usually not shown explicitly, and G_V is called the causal graph of the model.

The causal Markov condition is often assumed as an inherent feature of causal models (see e.g. (Kiiveri, Speed, & Carlin 1984; Spirtes, Glymour, & Scheines 1993)). It reflects our two basic causal assumptions: (i) include in the model every variable that is a cause of two or more other variables in the model; and (ii) Reichenbach's (1956) common-cause assumption, also known as "no correlation without causation," stating that, if any two variables are dependent, then one is a cause of the other *or* there is a third variable causing both.

If two or more variables in V are affected by unobserved confounders, the presence of such confounders would not permit the decomposition in Eq. (1), and, in general, $P(v)$ generated by a semi-Markovian model is a mixture of products given in (42). However, the conditional distribution $P(v|u)$ factorizes into a product

$$P(v|u) = \prod_i P(v_i|pa_i, u^i), \qquad (44)$$

and we also have

$$P_t(v|u) = \begin{cases} \prod_{\{i|V_i \notin T\}} P(v_i|pa_i, u^i) & v \text{ consistent with } t. \\ 0 & v \text{ inconsistent with } t. \end{cases}$$
$$(45)$$

Therefore all Properties 1–7 hold when we condition on u. For example, the Markov property can be written as

$$P_{v\setminus(s_1 \cup s_2)}(s_1, s_2|u) = P_{v\setminus s_1}(s_1|u)P_{v\setminus s_2}(s_2|u). \qquad (46)$$

Let $\mathbf{P}_*(u)$ denote the set of all conditional interventional distributions

$$\mathbf{P}_*(u) = \{P_t(v|u)|T \subseteq V, t \in Dm(T)\} \qquad (47)$$

Then $\mathbf{P}_*(u)$ is fully characterized by the three properties effectiveness, Markov, and recursiveness, conditioning on u.

Let $\mathbf{P}_*$ denote the set of all interventional distributions over observed variables V as in (3). From the properties of the $\mathbf{P}_*(u)$ set, we can immediately conclude that the $\mathbf{P}_*$ set satisfies the following properties: effectiveness (Property 1), recursiveness (Property 3), Property 4, and Property 5, while Markov (Property 2), Property 6, and Property 7 do not hold. For example, Property 5 can be proved from its conditional version,

$$P_{pa_i,s}(v_i|u) = P_{pa_i}(v_i|u), \qquad (48)$$

as follows

$$P_{pa_i,s}(v_i) = \sum_u P_{pa_i,s}(v_i|u)P(u)$$
$$= \sum_u P_{pa_i}(v_i|u)P(u) = P_{pa_i}(v_i). \qquad (49)$$

Significantly, the $\mathbf{P}_*$ set must satisfy inequalities that are unique to semi-Markovian models, as opposed, for example, to models containing feedback loops. For example, from Eq. (43), and using

$$P(v_i|pa_i, u^i) \le 1, \qquad (50)$$

we obtain the following property.

Property 8 *For any three sets of variables, T, S, and R, we have*

$$P_{tr}(s) \ge P_t(r, s) + P_r(t, s) - P(t, r, s) \qquad (51)$$

Additional inequalities, involving four or more subsets, can likewise be derived by this method. However, finding a set of properties that can completely characterize the $\mathbf{P}_*$ set of a semi-Markovian causal model remains an open challenge.

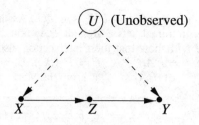

Figure 1:

Applications in the Identification of Causal Effects

Given two disjoint sets T and S, the quantity $P_t(s)$ is called the *causal effect* of T on S. $P_t(s)$ is said to be *identifiable* if, given a causal graph, it can be determined uniquely from the distribution $P(v)$ of the observed variables, and is thus independent of the unknown quantities, $P(u)$ and $P(v_i|pa_i, u^i)$, that involve elements of U. Identification means that we can learn the effect of the action $T = t$ (on the variables in S) from sampled data taken prior to actually performing that action. In Markovian models, all causal effects are identifiable and are given in Eq. (2). When some confounders are unobserved, the question of identifiability arises. Sufficient graphical conditions for ensuring the identification of $P_t(s)$ in semi-Markovian models were established by several authors (Spirtes, Glymour, & Scheines 1993; Pearl 1993; 1995) and are summarized in (Pearl 2000, Chapters 3 and 4). Since

$$P_t(s) = \sum_u P_t(s|u)P(u), \qquad (52)$$

and since we have a complete characterization over the set of conditional interventional distributions ($\mathbf{P}_*(u)$), we can use Properties 1–3 (conditioning on u) for identifying causal effects in semi-Markovian models.

The assumptions embodied in the causal graph can be translated into the language of conditional interventional distributions as follows:

For each variable V_i,

$$P_{v\setminus\{v_i\}}(v_i|u) = P_{pa_i}(v_i|u^i). \qquad (53)$$

The Markov property (10) conditioning on u then becomes

$$P_t(v \setminus t|u) = \prod_{\{i|V_i \in V\setminus T\}} P_{pa_i}(v_i|u^i). \qquad (54)$$

The significance of Eq. (54) rests in simplifying the derivation of elaborate causal effects in semi-Markov models. To illustrate this derivation, consider the model in Figure 1, and assume we need to derive the causal effect of X on $\{Z, Y\}$, a task analyzed in (Pearl 2000, pp.86-8) using do-calculus. Applying (54) to $P_x(y, z|u)$, (with x replacing t), we obtain:

$$P_x(y, z) = \sum_u P_x(y, z|u)P(u)$$
$$= \sum_u P_z(y|u)P_x(z)P(u)$$
$$= P_x(z)P_z(y) \qquad (55)$$

Each of these two factors can be derived by simple means; $P_x(z) = P(z|x)$ because Z has no unobserved parent, and $P_z(y) = \sum_{x'} P(y|x', z)P(x')$ because X blocks all backdoor paths from Z to Y (they can also be derived by applying (54) to $P(x, y, z|u)$). As a result, we immediately obtain the desired quantity:

$$P_x(y, z) = P(z|x) \sum_{x'} P(y|x', z)P(x'), \quad (56)$$

a result that required many steps in do-calculus.

In general, from (54), we have

$$P_t(v \setminus t) = \sum_u \prod_{\{i | V_i \in V \setminus T\}} P_{pa_i}(v_i|u^i)P(u). \quad (57)$$

Depending on the causal graph, the right hand side of (57) may sometimes be decomposed into a product of summations as

$$P_t(v \setminus t) = \prod_j \sum_{n_j} \prod_{V_i \in S_j} P_{pa_i}(v_i|u^i)P(n_j)$$

$$= \prod_j P_{v \setminus s_j}(s_j), \quad (58)$$

where N_j's form a partition of U and S_j's form a partition of $V \setminus T$. Eq. (55) is an example of such a decomposition. Therefore the problem of identifying $P_t(v \setminus t)$ is reduced to identifying some $P_{v \setminus s_j}(s_j)$'s. Based on this decomposition, a method for systematically identifying causal effects is given in (Tian & Pearl 2002). This method provides an alternative inference tool for identifying causal effects. At this stage of research it is not clear how the power of this method compares to that of do-calculus.

Conclusion

We have shown that all experimental results obtained from an underlying Markovian causal model are fully characterized by three norms of coherence: Effectiveness, Markov, and Recursiveness. We have further demonstrated the use of these norms as inferential tools for identifying causal effects in semi-Markovian models. This permits one to predict the effects of actions and policies, in the presence of unmeasured variables, from data obtained prior to performing those actions and policies.

The key element in our characterization of experimental distributions is the generic formulation of the Markov property (9) as a relationship among three experimental distributions, instead of the usual formulation as a relationship between a distribution and a graph (as in (1)). The practical implication of this formulation is that violations of the Markov property can be detected without knowledge of the underlying causal graph; comparing distributions from just three experiments, $P_{v \setminus (s_1 \cup s_2)}(s_1, s_2)$, $P_{v \setminus s_1}(s_1)$, and $P_{v \setminus s_2}(s_2)$, may reveal such violations, and should allow us to conclude, prior to knowing the structure of G, that the underlying data-generation process is non-Markovian. Alternatively, if our confidence in the Markovian nature of the data-generation process is unassailable, such a violation would imply that the three experiments were not conducted on the same population, under the same conditions, or that the experimental

interventions involved had side effects and were not properly confined to the specified sets S_1, S_2, and $S_1 \cup S_2$.

This feature is useful in efforts designed to infer the structure of G from a combination of observational and experimental data; a single violation of (9) suffices to reveal that unmeasured confounders exist between variables in S_1 and those in S_2. Likewise, a violation of any inequality in (51) would imply that the underlying model is not semi-Markovian; this means that feedback loops may operate in data generating process, or that the interventions in the experiments are not "atomic".

Acknowledgements

This research was supported in parts by grants from NSF, ONR, AFOSR, and DoD MURI program.

References

Dawid, A. 2001. Influence diagrams for causal modelling and inference. *International Statistical Review*. Forthcoming.

Galles, D., and Pearl, J. 1998. An axiomatic characterization of causal counterfactuals. *Foundations of Science* 3(1):151–182.

Halpern, J. 1998. Axiomatizing causal reasoning. In Cooper, G., and Moral, S., eds., *Uncertainty in Artificial Intelligence*. San Francisco, CA: Morgan Kaufmann. 202–210.

Heckerman, D., and Shachter, R. 1995. Decision-theoretic foundations for causal reasoning. *Journal of Artificial Intelligence Research* 3:405–430.

Kiiveri, H.; Speed, T.; and Carlin, J. 1984. Recursive causal models. *Journal of Australian Math Society* 36:30–52.

Lauritzen, S. 2000. Graphical models for causal inference. In Barndorff-Nielsen, O.; Cox, D.; and Kluppelberg, C., eds., *Complex Stochastic Systems*. London/Boca Raton: Chapman and Hall/CRC Press. chapter 2, 67–112.

Pearl, J. 1988. *Probabilistic Reasoning in Intelligence Systems*. San Mateo, CA: Morgan Kaufmann.

Pearl, J. 1993. Comment: Graphical models, causality, and intervention. *Statistical Science* 8:266–269.

Pearl, J. 1995. Causal diagrams for experimental research. *Biometrika* 82:669–710.

Pearl, J. 2000. *Causality: Models, Reasoning, and Inference*. NY: Cambridge University Press.

Reichenbach, H. 1956. *The Direction of Time*. Berkeley: University of California Press.

Robins, J. 1987. A graphical approach to the identification and estimation of causal parameters in mortality studies with sustained exposure periods. *Journal of Chronic Diseases* 40(Suppl 2):139S–161S.

Spirtes, P.; Glymour, C.; and Scheines, R. 1993. *Causation, Prediction, and Search*. New York: Springer-Verlag.

Tian, J., and Pearl, J. 2002. On the identification of causal effects. Technical Report R-290-L, Department of Computer Science, University of California, Los Angeles.

Robotics

Robust Global Localization Using Clustered Particle Filtering

Adam Milstein, Javier Nicolás Sánchez, Evan Tang Williamson

Computer Science Department
Stanford University
Stanford, CA
{ahpmilst, jsanchez, etang} @cs.stanford.edu

Abstract

Global mobile robot localization is the problem of determining a robot's pose in an environment, using sensor data, when the starting position is unknown. A family of probabilistic algorithms known as Monte Carlo Localization (MCL) is currently among the most popular methods for solving this problem. MCL algorithms represent a robot's belief by a set of weighted samples, which approximate the posterior probability of where the robot is located by using a Bayesian formulation of the localization problem. This article presents an extension to the MCL algorithm, which addresses its problems when localizing in highly symmetrical environments; a situation where MCL is often unable to correctly track equally probable poses for the robot. The problem arises from the fact that sample sets in MCL often become impoverished, when samples are generated according to their posterior likelihood. Our approach incorporates the idea of clusters of samples and modifies the proposal distribution considering the probability mass of those clusters. Experimental results are presented that show that this new extension to the MCL algorithm successfully localizes in symmetric environments where ordinary MCL often fails.

1. Introduction

In mobile robotics, the task of navigation requires the ability for robots to identify where they are. Given a map of the environment and a starting pose (x-y position, orientation) in relation to the map, the task of localization is a tracking task. With unknown initial location, the task is known as global localization, in which a robot has to recover its pose from scratch [9,10]. The problem of localization is to compensate for sensor noise and errors in odometry readings.

One popular approach to robot localization is to use Kalman filters. Kalman filters are computationally efficient, but they require that the initial localization error be bounded---which makes them inapplicable to global localization problems. Additionally, Kalman filters assume linear-Gaussian measurement and motion dynamics. To overcome these limitations, a class of solutions was recently proposed that uses particle filters to represent the probability that the robot is in a particular location. This approach is commonly known as Monte Carlo Localization (MCL) [1].

In global localization, the robot starts off with no idea of where it is relative to its map. With a reasonably accurate map of the environment, MCL has been shown to be effective in many situations. However, MCL suffers an important limitation: When samples are generated according to their posterior probability (as is the case in MCL), they often too quickly converge to a single, high-likelihood pose. This might be undesirable in symmetric environments, where multiple distinct hypotheses have to be tracked for extended periods of time. MCL often converges to one single location too quickly, ignoring the possibility that the robot might be somewhere else. This problem leads to suboptimal behavior if there are two or more similarly likely poses. In symmetric environments, it is desirable to maintain a higher diversity of the samples, despite the fact that likelihood-weighted sampling will favor a single robot pose.

The approach we present in this article introduces the idea of clusters of particles and modifies the proposal distribution to take into account the probability of a cluster of similar poses. Each cluster is considered to be a hypothesis of where the robot might be located and is independently developed using the MCL algorithm. The update of the probability of each cluster is done using the same Bayesian formulation used in MCL, thus effectively leading to a particle filter that works at two levels, the particle level and the cluster level. While each cluster possesses a probability that represents the belief of the robot being at that location, the cluster with the highest probability would be used to determine the robot's location at that instant in time.

Experiments have been conducted with both simulated data as well as data obtained from a robot, using laser range finder data collected at multiple sites. The environments are highly symmetric and the corresponding datasets possess only a very small number of distinguishing features that allow for global localization. Thus, they are good testbeds for our proposed algorithm. Results show that the Cluster-MCL algorithm is able to successfully determine the position of the robot in these datasets, while ordinary MCL often fails.

2. Background

Monte Carlo Localization and Bayes filter

MCL is a recursive Bayes filter that estimates the posterior distribution of robot poses conditioned on sensor data. Central to the idea of Bayes filters is the assumption that the environment is Markovian, that is, past and future are conditionally independent given knowledge of the current state.

The key idea of Bayes filtering is to estimate a probability density over the state space conditioned on the data. This posterior is typically called the *belief* and is denoted by

$$Bel(x_t) = p(x_t \mid z_t, u_{t-1}, z_{t-1}, u_{t-2}, ..., z_0) \quad (1)$$

Here x_t denotes the state at time t, z_t is the *perceptual data* (such as laser range finder or sonar measurements) at time t, and u_t is the *odometry data* (i.e. the information about the robot's motion) between time t-1 and time t.

Bayes filters estimate the belief *recursively*. The *initial* belief characterizes the *initial* knowledge about the system state, which in the case of global localization, corresponds to a *uniform distribution* over the state space as the initial pose is unknown.

To derive a recursive update equation, we observe that Expression (1) can be transformed by Bayes rule:

$$Bel(x_t) = \frac{p(z_t \mid x_t, u_{t-1}, ..., z_0) p(x_t \mid u_{t-1}, ..., z_0)}{p(z_t \mid u_{t-1}, ..., z_0)} \quad (2)$$

Because the denominator is a normalizer constant relative to the variable x_t we can write equation (2) as

$$Bel(x_t) = \eta p(z_t \mid x_t, u_{t-1}, ..., z_0) p(x_t \mid u_{t-1}, ..., z_0) \quad (3)$$

where $\eta = p(z_t \mid u_{t-1}, ..., z_0)^{-1}$ \quad (4)

As stated previously, Bayes filters make the Markov independence assumption. This assumption simplifies equation (3) to the following expression

$$Bel(x_t) = \eta p(z_t \mid x_t) p(x_t \mid u_{t-1}, ..., z_0) \quad (5)$$

The rightmost term in the previous equation can be expanded by integrating over the state at time t-1:

$$Bel(x_t) = \eta p(z_t \mid x_t)$$
$$\int p(x_t \mid u_t, x_{t-1}, ..., z_0) p(x_{t-1} \mid u_{t-1}, ..., z_0) dx_{t-1} \quad (6)$$

And by application of the Markov assumption it can be simplified to

$$Bel(x_t) = \eta p(z_t \mid x_t)$$
$$\int p(x_t \mid u_t, x_{t-1}) p(x_{t-1} \mid u_{t-1}, ..., z_0) dx_{t-1} \quad (7)$$

Defining $z^{t-1} = \{z_0, ..., z_{t-1}\}$ and $u^{t-1} = \{u_0, ..., u_{t-1}\}$ equation (7) can then be expressed as:

$$Bel(x_t) = \eta p(z_t \mid x_t) \int p(x_t \mid u_t, x_{t-1}) p(x_{t-1} \mid z^{t-1}, u^{t-1}) dx_{t-1} \quad (8)$$

It can be seen from equation (8) that the rightmost term is $Bel(x_{t-1})$. Therefore, this equation is recursive and is the update equation for Bayes filters. To calculate (8) one needs to know two conditional densities: the probability $p(x_t \mid u_t, x_{t-1})$, which is called the *motion model*, and the density $p(z_t \mid x_t)$, which is called the *sensor model*. The motion model is a probabilistic generalization of robot dynamics. The sensor model depends on the type of sensor being used and considers the noise that can appear in the sensor readings.

Particle approximation

If the state space is continuous, as is the case in mobile robot localization, implementing (8) is not trivial, particularly if one is concerned with efficiency. The idea of MCL is to represent the belief $Bel(x_t)$ by a set of N weighted samples distributed according to $Bel(x_t)$:

$$Bel(x_t) \approx \left\{ x_t^{[i]}, w_t^{[i]} \right\}_{i=1,...,N}$$

Here each $x_t^{[n]}$ is a *sample* of the random variable x, that is, a hypothesized state (pose). The non-negative numerical parameters, $w_t^{[n]}$, are called importance factors and they determine the importance of each sample. The set of samples thus define a discrete probability function that approximates the continuous belief $Bel(x_t)$.

In the case of global localization, the initial pose is unknown, thus the prior is uniform over the space of possible poses, and therefore each weight $w_t^{[n]} = 1/N$. Let X_{t-1} be a set of particles representing the estimate $p(x_{t-1} \mid z^{t-1}, u^{t-1})$ at time $t-1$. The t-th particle set, X_t, is then obtained via the following sampling routine:

1. First, draw a random particle $x_{t-1}^{[n]}$ from X_{t-1}. By assumption, this particle is distributed according to $p(x_{t-1} \mid z^{t-1}, u^{t-1})$. Strictly speaking, this is only true as N goes to infinity, but we ignore the bias in the finite case.
2. Next, draw a state $x_{t-1}^{[n]} \sim p(x_t \mid u_t, x_{t-1}^{[n]})$.
3. Finally, calculate the importance factor $w_t^{[n]} = p(z_t \mid x_t^{[n]})$ for this particle, and memorize the particle and its importance factor.

This routine is repeated N times. The final set of particles, X_t is obtained by randomly drawing (with replacement) N memorized particles $x_t^{[n]}$ with probability proportional to the respective importance factor, $w_t^{[n]}$. The resulting set of particles is then an approximate representation for $Bel(x_t) = p(x_t \mid z^t, u^t)$. For a more detailed discussion on the implementation of MCL and examples see [6].

3. Global Localization using clustered particle filtering

We will now analyze how particle filters work and from that we will motivate our approach. To understand particle filters, it is worthwhile to analyze the specific choice of the importance factor. In general, the importance factor accounts for the "difference" between the target distribution and the proposal distribution. The target distribution is $p(x_t | z^t, u^t)$. The proposal distribution is given by $p(x_t | u_t, x_{t-1}) p(x_{t-1} | z^{t-1}, u^{t-1})$. This is the distribution of the samples values $x_t^{[n]}$ before the re-sampling step. The importance factor is calculated as follows:

$$w_t^{[n]} = \frac{\text{target distribution}}{\text{proposal distribution}}$$

$$w_t^{[n]} = \frac{p(x_t^{[n]} | z^t, u^t)}{p(x_t^{[n]} | u_t, x_{t-1}) p(x_{t-1} | z^{t-1}, u^{t-1})}$$

$$w_t^{[n]} = \frac{\eta p(z^t | x_t^{[n]}) p(x_t^{[n]} | u_t, x_{t-1}) p(x_{t-1} | z^{t-1}, u^{t-1})}{p(x_t^{[n]} | u_t, x_{t-1}) p(x_{t-1} | z^{t-1}, u^{t-1})}$$

$$w_t^{[n]} = \eta p(z_t | x_t^{[n]}) \tag{9}$$

The constant η can easily be ignored, since the importance weights are normalized in the re-sampling step. This leaves the term $p(z_t | x_t^{[n]})$, which is the importance factor used in MCL.

Our analysis above suggests that a much broader range of functions may be used as proposal distributions. In particular, let $f_t(x_t)$ be a positive function over the state space. Then the following particle filter algorithm generates samples from a distribution $\propto f_t(x_t) p(x_t | z^t, u^t)$. Initially, samples are drawn from $f_0(x_0)$.

New sample sets are then calculated via the following procedure:

1. First, draw a random particle $x_{t-1}^{[n]}$ from X_{t-1}. By assumption, this particle is (asymptotically) distributed according to $f_{t-1}(x_{t-1}) p(x_{t-1} | z^{t-1}, u^{t-1})$ for very large N.
2. Next, draw a state $x_t^{[n]} \sim p(x_t | u_t, x_t^{[n]})$.

In this case the resulting importance factor is easily computed as:

$$w_t^{[n]} = \frac{\text{target distribution}}{\text{proposal distribution}}$$

$$w_t^{[n]} = \frac{f_t(x_t^{[n]}) p(x_t^{[n]} | z^t, u^t)}{f_{t-1}(x_{t-1}^{[n]}) p(x_t^{[n]} | u_t, x_{t-1}) p(x_{t-1} | z^{t-1}, u^{t-1})}$$

$$w_t^{[n]} = \frac{f_t(x_t^{[n]}) \eta p(z^t | x_t^{[n]}) p(x_t^{[n]} | u_t, x_{t-1}) p(x_{t-1} | z^{t-1}, u^{t-1})}{f_{t-1}(x_{t-1}^{[n]}) p(x_t^{[n]} | u_t, x_{t-1}) p(x_{t-1} | z^{t-1}, u^{t-1})}$$

$$w_t^{[n]} \propto p(z_t | x_t^{[n]}) \frac{f_t(x_t^{[n]})}{f_{t-1}(x_{t-1}^{[n]})} \tag{10}$$

The clustering particle filter proposed employs such a modified proposal distribution. In particular, each particle is associated with one out of K clusters. We will use the function $c(x_t)$ to denote the cluster number. The function f_t assigns to each particle in the same cluster the same value; but this value may differ among different clusters. Moreover, f_t is such that the cumulative weight over all the particles in each cluster is the same for each cluster.

$$\sum_{x_t^{[n]} \in X_t : c(x_t^{[n]}) = k} f(x_t^{[n]}) p(x_t^{[n]} | z^t, u^t)$$
$$= \sum_{x_t^{[n]} \in X_t : c(x_t^{[n]}) = k'} f(x_t^{[n]}) p(x_t^{[n]} | z^t, u^t) \tag{11}$$

for $k \neq k'$.

From above we see that this is valid, however, we need to define $f(x_t^{[n]})$. Since these are equal for all x such that $c(x) = k$, it is sufficient to define $f(x_t^{[n]}) = \frac{1}{B_{k,t}}$ where $k = c(x_t^{[n]})$ and $B_{k,t}$ is the probability, at time t, that cluster k contains the actual robot position. We can estimate the $B_{k,t}$ values using standard Bayes filters. Here, we use k to represent the probability distribution over the clusters:

$$B_{k,t} = p(k_t | z^t, u^t)$$
$$= \eta \int p(z_t | k_t) p(k_t | u_t, k_{t-1}) p(k_{t-1} | z^{t-1}, u^{t-1}) dk_{t-1} \tag{12}$$

Since we use a finite number of samples to approximate the distribution, this becomes:

$$B_{k,t} = \eta \frac{\sum p(z_t | k_t) p(k_t | u_t, k_{t-1}) p(k_{t-1} | z^{t-1}, u^{t-1})}{n} \tag{13}$$

Now we note that, although the robot can move from one point to another, particles cannot change clusters. That is, each particle starts in one cluster and remains in that cluster. This being the case,

$$p(k_t | u_t, k_{t-1}) = \begin{cases} 0 & \text{if } k_t \neq k_{t-1} \\ 1 & \text{if } k_t = k_{t-1} \end{cases} \tag{14}$$

Therefore, $B_{k,t} \propto p(z_t | k_t) p(k_{t-1} | z^{t-1}, u^{t-1})$ (15)

We also note that a cluster is composed of a set of points. Therefore, $p(z_t | k_t)$ is related to $p(z_t | x_t)$. In fact, the distribution of sensor readings for a cluster must be the sum of the distributions of sensor readings for all points in the cluster. That is:

$$p(z_t | k_t) \propto p(k_{t-1} | z^{t-1}, u^{t-1}) \sum_{x_t^{[n]} \in X_t : c(x_t^{[n]}) = k} p(z_t | x_t^{[n]}) \tag{16}$$

Given equations (12) and (16) we can write

$$B_{k,t} = \gamma B_{k,t-1}^2 \sum_{x_t^{[n]} \in X_t : c(x_t^{[n]}) = k} p(z_t | x_t^{[n]}) \tag{17}$$

where γ is a normalization factor.

Having defined $f(x_t^{[n]}) = \frac{1}{B_{k,t}}$, we maintain the condition stated in equation (11) by normalizing after each iteration. Therefore, we have shown that our modified proposal distribution is sound.

4. Cluster-MCL

Algorithm:

Based on the mathematical derivation above, we have implemented an extension to MCL, called Cluster-MCL. Cluster-MCL tracks multiple hypotheses organized in clusters. The first task is to identify probable clusters. By iterating several steps through ordinary MCL, with an initial uniform distribution of a large number of points, clusters develop in several locations. We then use a simple clustering algorithm to separate the points into different clusters. We match each point with a cluster based on the distance, in all three dimensions, between that point and the source point of the cluster. The initial probability of a cluster is based on the number of points it contains. There are more robust clustering algorithms, based on the EM algorithm; however, these methods rely on knowing the number of clusters a priori. Our method generates sets of clusters of arbitrary size. The drawback is that several clusters may be created in almost the same location. We solve this problem by occasionally checking for overlapping clusters and combining them. Once clusters are generated, we select the most probable ones and discard the others.

Each cluster is then independently evolved using ordinary MCL, thus points selected for a particular cluster can only be drawn from that cluster. The probability of each cluster is tracked by multiplying the prior probability of the cluster by the average of the likelihood of the points in that cluster. These probabilities are kept normalized and correspond to the $B_{k,t}$ values as defined above.

There is the problem that, if there is an error in the map in the initial location, there may be no cluster generated at the correct location. We solve this problem, and also the kidnapped robot problem, by taking advantage of the independence of our clusters. The kidnapped robot problem is where the robot is moved by an outside force after being localized. Since clusters do not interfere with each other, we can add a cluster in a new location without affecting our existing clusters. After a predetermined number of steps, we restart a new instance of global MCL with a higher convergence rate, with the purpose of finding the most likely cluster based on the current sensor data. Once global MCL has converged to a location, we check whether this new location overlaps an existing cluster. If it does not, we initialize it to have a small probability and begin tracking it. Otherwise, we discard it and repeat the process. By doing this, we remain open to consideration of a completely new location for the robot based on the current sensor data.

To limit the number of clusters from growing out of bounds and to remain computationally efficient, we limit the number of clusters to a maximum pre-defined value. Additionally, by keeping the number of clusters fixed at all points in time, we prevent a cluster from gaining a high probability by competing with only few other clusters, which would tend to prevent that cluster from being overtaken when there are many other clusters. When adding a new cluster, the least probable cluster is removed, in order to keep the size fixed.

The robot's estimate of its own location is based on the most likely cluster, and obtained by fitting a Gaussian through the corresponding particles.

5. Experimental Results

Experimentation:

The Cluster-MCL algorithm was implemented and tested in both simulated and real environments. In these tests, we compare the performance of our Cluster-MCL algorithm with that of ordinary MCL. In all cases, we found that Cluster-MCL performed as well as ordinary MCL, and in several cases where ordinary MCL failed, Cluster-MCL succeeded.

Simulated Data. For simulated environments, we generated two highly symmetrical maps to test on. Testing MCL and Cluster-MCL using these maps, we observed that Cluster-MCL correctly maintains all equally probable clusters, while ordinary MCL incorrectly and prematurely converges to a single cluster. In Figure 2, we display the results of Cluster-MCL using one of the maps, and we can clearly see that there are multiple distinct clusters. Notice that Cluster-MCL maintains a posterior belief comprised of four distinctive poses, in contrast to conventional MCL, whose outcome is shown in Figure 1. Moreover, the clusters in Figure 2 are all just about equally probable, as demonstrated by our observation of the constant trading off of which cluster is most probable. We obtained similar results on the second map, which was a simple rectangle.

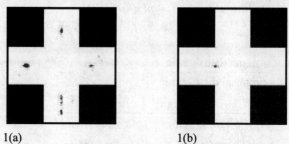

1(a)   1(b)

Figure 1: Global localization using ordinary MCL.

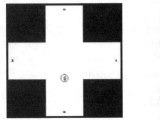 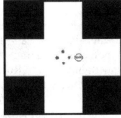

2(a)   2(b)

Figure 2: Global localization using Cluster-MCL. The extra cluster (circled) is a randomly drawn cluster, used to make Cluster-MCL robust to the kidnapped robot problem.

Real Data. To elucidate the workings of our algorithm in practice, additional tests were performed using data collected from two real world environments. Our first environment consisted of a long corridor in Wean Hall at Carnegie Mellon University, with equally spaced doors and few distinguishing features, thus providing an environment with some symmetry. Our second environment consists of a room in the Gates Building at Stanford University, with two entrances opposite each other, two benches symmetrically placed and a file cabinet in each corner of the room. The datasets in both locations were collected using a robot equipped with a laser range finder.

From these environments we collected nine datasets. From Wean Hall, we collected four datasets. In each dataset, the robot was given a different path with different features of the environment observed. Of the four cases, MCL was only able to correctly localize in three of them, while Cluster-MCL correctly identified the robot's position in all cases. In Figure 3, a comparison is given between MCL and Cluster-MCL on a particular dataset, number 3, from Wean Hall. On multiple executions over that particular dataset, ordinary MCL failed 100% of the time while Cluster-MCL had a 100% success rate. We show that ordinary MCL converges to the wrong location, while Cluster-MCL correctly identifies the robot's position.

In the Gates Building environment, five datasets on two different maps were collected. In all cases, Cluster-MCL performs at least as well as ordinary MCL. In four of the datasets, MCL and Cluster-MCL both correctly identify the robot's location. However, in the final dataset, MCL failed to consistently identify the correct location of the robot, while Cluster-MCL was able to localize to the correct position. The difference between the Wean Hall and Gates datasets is in the level of symmetry. To demonstrate the benefits of Cluster-MCL, we chose a more highly symmetrical environment in Gates and attempted to collect datasets, which had two possible localizations until the final segment of them. We ran MCL and Cluster-MCL several times on those datasets and the results show that MCL had 50% accuracy in determining the correct position, while Cluster-MCL had 100% accuracy.

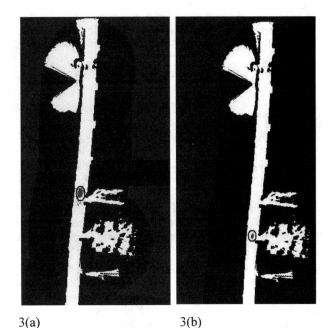

3(a)   3(b)

Figure 3: Results of MCL and Cluster-MCL on Wean Hall dataset 3. MCL converges to an incorrect cluster in 3(a), while Cluster-MCL converges to the correct location in 3(b).

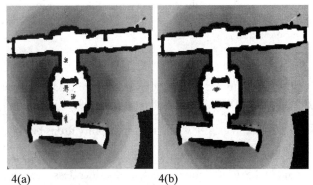

4(a)   4(b)

Figure 4: Results of MCL and Cluster-MCL on Gates data. Cluster-MCL tracks multiple possible clusters in 4(a) while ordinary MCL converges to a single, incorrect, cluster in 4(b).

6. Related Work

Related work in this area involves the use of multi-hypothesis Kalman filters to represent multiple beliefs. This however inherits Kalman filters limitations in that it requires noise to be Gaussian. A common solution to this problem is to perform low-dimension feature extraction, which ignores much of the information acquired by the robot's sensors [4,5]. Most of the work involving multi-hypothesis Kalman filters surrounds the tracking of multiple targets and feature detection, whereas we apply the concept of multiple hypotheses to represent our belief of the position of the robot.

Other improvements to MCL like, dual-MCL and Mixture MCL [6,11,12] attempt to improve the proposal distribution. Likewise, we attempt to improve the proposal distribution by way of tracking multiple hypotheses.

7. Conclusions and Future Work

Conclusion

In this paper we introduced a cluster-based extension to MCL localization. Ordinary MCL can fail if the map is symmetrical, however, we proposed a method that retains multiple hypotheses for where the robot is located, consistent with our sensor data. Our method involves clustering the points, and then tracking the clusters independently, so as to avoid discarding other possible locations in favor of the most probable cluster at the current time step. By considering the probability of multiple clusters over a longer time, we are able to get a more accurate idea of their likelihood. We have shown that this method is valid and that the additional information we take into account allows us to eliminate some of the bias from MCL and better approximate the true posterior. Our experiments show that Cluster-MCL performs at least as well as ordinary MCL on several real datasets, and in cases where MCL fails, Cluster-MCL still finds the correct location. Finally, we have shown that Cluster-MCL maintains all of the correct possible locations in symmetrical environments, while MCL converges to a single cluster.

Future Work

Future work might involve dynamically re-clustering the points on every time step in order to provide a true second-order MCL algorithm. We might also consider dropping clusters automatically when their probability drops below a certain threshold, instead of keeping a constant number of them. Since our algorithm retains less probable locations, it might be useful for a robot to consider less probable clusters when planning a motion. It might not be desirable for a robot to take an action that would be dangerous even if the corresponding cluster's likelihood is low. See [13] for an attempt to achieve this in the context of particle filtering.

References

1. Thrun, S. 2000. Probabilistic Algorithms in Robotics. School of Computer Science, Carnegie Mellon University. Pittsburgh, PA.
2. Thrun, S.; Montemerlo, M.; and Whittaker, W. 2002. Conditional Particle filters for Simultaneous Mobile Robot Localization and People-Tracking. Forthcoming.
3. Schulz D.; Burgard W.; Fox D.; and Cremers A. 2001. Tracking Multiple Moving Targets with a Mobile Robot Using Particles Filters and Statistical Data Association. In Proceedings of the IEEE International Conference on Robotics and Automation, Seoul, Korea.
4. Jensfelt, P., and Kristensen, S. 1999. Active Global Localisation for a Mobile Robot Using Multiple Hypothesis Tracking. Workshop on Reasoning with Uncertainty in Robot Navigation. (IJCAI'99). Stockholm, Sweden.
5. Austin, D., and Jensfelt, P. 2000. Using Multiple Gaussian Hypotheses to Represent Probability Distributions for Mobile Robot Localization. In Proceedings of IEEE International Conference on Robotics and Automation, San Francisco, CA.
6. Thrun, S.; Fox, D.; Burgard, W.; and Dellaert, F. 2001. Robust Monte Carlo Localization for Mobile Robots. *Artificial Intelligence Magazine*.
7. Doucet, A. 1998. On Sequential simulation-based methods for Bayesian filtering. Technical Report CUED/F-INFENG/TR 310, Cambridge University, Department of Engineering, Cambridge, UK.
8. J.Liu and R. Chen. 1998. Sequential monte carlo methods for dynamic systems. *Journal of the American Statistical Association* 93:1032-1044.
9. Borenstein, J.; Everett, B.; and Feng, L. 1996. *Navigating Mobile Robots: Systems and Techniques*. A.K. Peters, Ltd. Wellesley, MA.
10. Weib, G.; Wetzler, C.; and von Puttkamer, E. 1994. Keeping Track of Position and Orientation of Moving Indoor Systems by Correlation of Range-finder Scans. In Proceedings of the International Conference on Intelligent Robots and Systems, 595-601.
11. Lenser, S.; and Veloso, M. 2000. Sensor Resetting Localization for Poorly Modeled Mobile Robots. In Proceedings of the International Conference on Robotics and Automation, San Francisco, CA.
12. Thrun, S.; Fox, D.; and Burgard, W. 2000. Monte Carlo Localization with Mixture Proposal Distribution. In Proceedings of the AAAI National Conference on Artificial Intelligence, Austin, TX.
13. Thrun, S.; Langford, L.; and Verma, V. 2002. Risk-sensitive particle filters. In Proceedings of the Neural Information Processing Systems Conference, Vancouver, CA.

Experiences with a Mobile Robotic Guide for the Elderly

Michael Montemerlo, Joelle Pineau, Nicholas Roy, Sebastian Thrun and Vandi Verma

Robotics Institute, Carnegie Mellon University
5000 Forbes Ave
Pittsburgh, PA 15213
{mmde,jpineau,nickr,thrun,vandi}@cs.cmu.edu

Abstract

This paper describes an implemented robot system, which relies heavily on probabilistic AI techniques for acting under uncertainty. The robot *Pearl* and its predecessor *Flo* have been developed by a multi-disciplinary team of researchers over the past three years. The goal of this research is to investigate the feasibility of assisting elderly people with cognitive and physical activity limitations through interactive robotic devices, thereby improving their quality of life. The robot's task involves escorting people in an assisted living facility—a time-consuming task currently carried out by nurses. Its software architecture employs probabilistic techniques at virtually all levels of perception and decision making. During the course of experiments conducted in an assisted living facility, the robot successfully demonstrated that it could autonomously provide guidance for elderly residents. While previous experiments with fielded robot systems have provided evidence that probabilistic techniques work well in the context of navigation, we found the same to be true of human robot interaction with elderly people.

Introduction

The US population is aging at an alarming rate. At present, 12.5% of the US population is of age 65 or older. The Administration of Aging predicts a 100% increase of this ratio by the year 2050 [26]. By 2040, the number of people of age of 65 or older per 100 working-age people will have increased from 19 to 39. At the same time, the nation faces a significant shortage of nursing professionals. The Federation of Nurses and Health Care Professionals has projected a need for 450,000 additional nurses by the year 2008. It is widely recognized that the situation will worsen as the baby-boomer generation moves into retirement age, with no clear solution in sight. These developments provide significant opportunities for researchers in AI, to develop assistive technology that can improve the quality of life of our aging population, while helping nurses to become more effective in their everyday activities.

To respond to these challenges, the *Nursebot Project* was conceived in 1998 by a multi-disciplinary team of investigators from four universities, consisting of four health-care faculty, one HCI/psychology expert, and four AI researchers. The goal of this project is to develop mobile robotic assistants for nurses and elderly people in various settings. Over the course of 36 months, the team has developed two prototype autonomous mobile robots, shown in Figure 1.

From the many services such a robot could provide (see [11, 16]), the work reported here has focused on the task

of reminding people of events (e.g., appointments) and guiding them through their environments. At present, nursing staff in assisted living facilities spends significant amounts of time escorting elderly people walking from one location to another. The number of activities requiring navigation is large, ranging from regular daily events (e.g., meals), appointments (e.g., doctor appointments, physiotherapy, hair cuts), social events (e.g., visiting friends, cinema), to simply walking for the purpose of exercising. Many elderly people move at extremely slow speeds (e.g., 5 cm/sec), making the task of helping people around one of the most labor-intensive in assisted living facilities. Furthermore, the help provided is often not of a physical nature, as elderly people usually select walking aids over physical assistance by nurses, thus preserving some independence. Instead, nurses often provide important cognitive help, in the form of reminders, guidance and motivation, in addition to valuable social interaction.

In two day-long experiments, our robot has demonstrated the ability to guide elderly people, without the assistance of a nurse. This involves moving to a person's room, alerting them, informing them of an upcoming event or appointment, and inquiring about their willingness to be assisted. It then involves a lengthy phase where the robot guides a person, carefully monitoring the person's progress and adjusting the robot's velocity and path accordingly. Finally, the robot also serves the secondary purpose of providing information to the person upon request, such as information about upcoming community events, weather reports, TV schedules, etc.

From an AI point of view, several factors make this task a challenging one. In addition to the well-developed topic of robot navigation [15], the task involves significant interaction with people. Our present robot Pearl interacts through speech and visual displays. When it comes to speech, many elderly have difficulty understanding even simple sentences, and more importantly, articulating an appropriate response in a computer-understandable way. Those difficulties arise from perceptual and cognitive deficiencies, often involving a multitude of factors such as articulation, comprehension, and mental agility. In addition, people's walking abilities vary drastically from person to person. People with walking aids are usually an order of magnitude slower than people without, and people often stop to chat or catch breath along the way. It is therefore imperative that the robot adapts to individual people—an aspect of people interaction that has been poorly explored in AI and robotics. Finally, safety concerns are much higher when dealing with the elderly population, especially in crowded situations (e.g., dining areas).

The software system presented here seeks to address these challenges. All software components use probabilistic techniques to accommodate various sorts of uncertainty. The robot's navigation system is mostly adopted from [5], and therefore will not be described in this paper. On top of

Figure 1: Nursebots Flo (left) and Pearl (center and right) interacting with elderly people during one of our field trips.

this, our software possesses a collection of probabilistic modules concerned with people sensing, interaction, and control. In particular, Pearl uses efficient particle filter techniques to detect and track people. A POMDP algorithm performs high-level control, arbitrating information gathering and performance-related actions. And finally, safety considerations are incorporated even into simple perceptual modules through a risk-sensitive robot localization algorithm. In systematic experiments, we found the combination of techniques to be highly effective in dealing with the elderly test subjects.

Hardware, Software, And Environment

Figure 1 shows images of the robots Flo (first prototype, now retired) and Pearl (the present robot). Both robots possess differential drive systems. They are equipped with two on-board Pentium PCs, wireless Ethernet, SICK laser range finders, sonar sensors, microphones for speech recognition, speakers for speech synthesis, touch-sensitive graphical displays, actuated head units, and stereo camera systems. Pearl differs from its predecessor Flo in many respects, including its visual appearance, two sturdy handle-bars added to provide support for elderly people, a more compact design that allows for cargo space and a removable tray, doubled battery capacity, a second laser range finder, and a significantly more sophisticated head unit. Many of those changes were the result of feedback from nurses and medical experts following deployment of the first robot, Flo. Pearl was largely designed and built by the Standard Robot Company in Pittsburgh, PA.

On the software side, both robots feature off-the-shelf autonomous mobile robot navigation system [5, 24], speech recognition software [20], speech synthesis software [3], fast image capture and compression software for online video streaming, face detection tracking software [21], and various new software modules described in this paper. A final software component is a prototype of a flexible reminder system using advanced planning and scheduling techniques [18].

The robot's environment is a retirement resort located in Oakmont, PA. Like most retirement homes in the nation, this facility suffers from immense staffing shortages. All experiments so far primarily involved people with relatively mild cognitive, perceptual, or physical inabilities, though in need of professional assistance. In addition, groups of elderly in similar conditions were brought into research laboratories for testing interaction patterns.

Navigating with People

Pearl's navigation system builds on the one described in [5, 24]. In this section, we describe three major new modules, all concerned with people interaction and control. These modules overcome an important deficiency of the work described by [5, 24], which had a rudimentary ability to interact with people.

Locating People

The problem of locating people is the problem of determining their x-y-location relative to the robot. Previous approaches to people tracking in robotics were feature-based: they analyze sensor measurements (images, range scans) for the presence of features [13, 22] as the basis of tracking. In our case, the diversity of the environment mandated a different approach. Pearl detects people using map differencing: the robot learns a map, and people are detected by significant deviations from the map. Figure 3a shows an example map acquired using preexisting software [24].

Mathematically, the problem of people tracking is a combined posterior estimation problem and model selection problem. Let N be the number of people near the robot. The posterior over the people's positions is given by

$$p(y_{1,t}, \ldots, y_{N,t} | z^t, u^t, m) \qquad (1)$$

where $y_{n,t}$ with $1 \leq n \leq N$ is the location of a person at time t, z^t the sequence of all sensor measurements, u^t the sequence of all robot controls, and m is the environment map. However, to use map differencing, the robot has to know its own location. The location and total number of nearby people detected by the robot is clearly dependent on the robot's estimate of its own location and heading direction. Hence, Pearl estimates a posterior of the type:

$$p(y_{1,t}, \ldots, y_{N,t}, x^t | z^t, u^t, m) \qquad (2)$$

where x^t denotes the sequence of robot poses (the path) up to time t. If N was known, estimating this posterior would be a high-dimensional estimation problem, with complexity cubic in N for Kalman filters [2], or exponential in N with particle filters [9]. Neither of these approaches is, thus, applicable: Kalman filters cannot globally localize the robot, and particle filters would be computationally prohibitive.

Luckily, under mild conditions (discussed below) the posterior (2) can be factored into $N + 1$ conditionally independent estimates:

$$p(x^t | z^t, u^t, m) \prod_n p(y_{n,t} | z^t, u^t, m) \qquad (3)$$

This factorization opens the door for a particle filter that scales linearly in N. Our approach is similar (but not identical) to the Rao-Blackwellized particle filter described in [10]. First, the robot path x^t is estimated using a particle filter, as in the Monte Carlo localization (MCL) algorithm [7] for mobile robot localization. However, each particle in this filter is associated with a set of N particle filters, each representing one of the people position estimates $p(y_{n,t} | z^t, u^t, m)$. These *conditional* particle filters represent people position estimates *conditioned* on robot path estimates—hence capturing the inherent dependence of people and robot location estimates. The data association between measurements and people is done using maximum likelihood, as in [2]. Under the (false) assumption that this maximum likelihood estimator is always correct, our approach can be shown to converge to the correct posterior, and it does so with update time linear in N. In practice, we found that the data association is correct in the vast majority of situations. The nested particle filter formulation

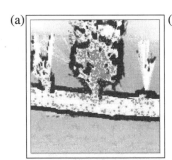 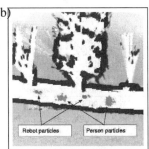 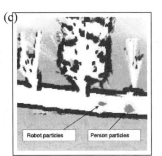 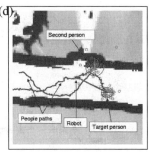

Figure 2: (a)-(d) Evolution of the conditional particle filter from global uncertainty to successful localization and tracking. (d) The tracker continues to track a person even as that person is occluded repeatedly by a second individual.

has a secondary advantage that the number of people N can be made dependent on individual robot path particles. Our approach for estimating N uses the classical AIC criterion for model selection, with a prior that imposes a complexity penalty exponential in N.

Figure 2 shows results of the filter in action. In Figure 2a, the robot is globally uncertain, and the number and location of the corresponding people estimates varies drastically. As the robot reduces its uncertainty, the number of modes in the robot pose posterior quickly becomes finite, and each such mode has a distinct set of people estimates, as shown in Figure 2b. Finally, as the robot is localized, so is the person (Figure 2c). Figure 2d illustrates the robustness of the filter to interfering people. Here another person steps between the robot and its target subject. The filter obtains its robustness to occlusion from a carefully crafted probabilistic model of people's motion $p(y_{n,t+1}|y_{n,t})$. This enables the conditional particle filters to maintain tight estimates while the occlusion takes place, as shown in Figure 2d. In a systematic analysis involving 31 tracking instances with up to five people at a time, the error in determining the number of people was 9.6%. The error in the robot position was 2.5 ± 5.7 cm, and the people position error was as low as 1.5 ± 4.2 cm, when compared to measurements obtained with a carefully calibrated static sensor with ± 1 cm error.

When guiding people, the estimate of the person that is being guided is used to determine the velocity of the robot, so that the robot maintains roughly a constant distance to the person. In our experiments in the target facility, we found the adaptive velocity control to be absolutely essential for the robot's ability to cope with the huge range of walking paces found in the elderly population. Initial experiments with fixed velocity led almost always to frustration on the people's side, in that the robot was either too slow or too fast.

Safer Navigation

When navigating in the presence of elderly people, the risks of harming them through unintended physical contact is enormous. As noted in [5], the robot's sensors are inadequate to detect people reliably. In particular, the laser range system measures obstacles 18 cm above ground, but is unable to detect any obstacles below or above this level. In the assisted living facilities, we found that people are easy to detect when standing or walking, but hard when on chairs (e.g., they might be stretching their legs). Thus, the risk of accidentally hitting a person's foot due to poor localization is particularly high in densely populated regions such as the dining areas.

Following an idea in [5], we restricted the robot's operation area to avoid densely populated regions, using a manually augmented map of the environment (black lines in Figure 3a

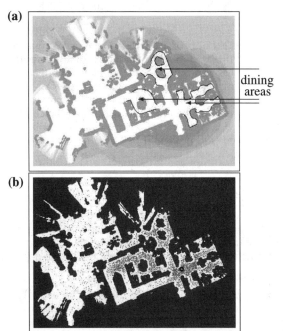

Figure 3: (a) Map of the dining area in the facility, with dining areas marked by arrows. (b) Samples at the beginning of global localization, weighted expected cumulative risk function.

– the white space corresponds to unrestricted free space). To stay within its operating area, the robot needs accurate localization, especially at the boundaries of this area. While our approach yields sufficiently accurate results on average, it is important to realize that probabilistic techniques never provide hard guarantees that the robot obeys a safety constraint. To address this concern, we augmented the robot localization particle filter by a sampling strategy that is sensitive to the increased risk in the dining areas (see also [19, 25]). By generating samples in high-risk regions, we minimize the likelihood of being mislocalized in such regions, or worse, the likelihood of entering prohibited regions undetected. Conventional particle filters generate samples in proportion to the posterior likelihood $p(x^t|z^t, u^t, m)$. Our new particle filter generates robot pose samples in proportion to

$$l(x_t)\, p(x^t|z^t, u^t, m) \prod_n p(y_{n,t}|z^t, u^t, m) \qquad (4)$$

where l is a *risk* function that specifies how desirable it is to sample robot pose x_t. The risk function is calculated by considering an immediate cost function $c(x, u)$, which assigns costs to actions a and robot states x (in our case: high costs

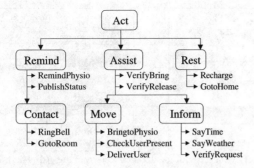

Figure 4: Dialog Problem Action Hierarchy

Observation	True State	Action	Reward
pearl hello	request_begun	say_hello	100
pearl what is like	start_meds	**ask_repeat**	-100
pearl what time is it for will the	want_time	say_time	100
pearl was on abc	want_tv	ask_which_station	-1
pearl was on abc	want_abc	say_abc	100
pearl what is on nbc	want_nbc	**confirm_channel_nbc**	-1
pearl yes	want_nbc	say_nbc	100
pearl go to the that pretty good what	send_robot	ask_robot_where	-1
pearl that that hello be	send_robot_bedroom	**confirm_robot_place**	-1
pearl the bedroom any i	send_robot_bedroom	go_to_bedroom	100
pearl go it eight a hello	send_robot	ask_robot_where	-1
pearl the kitchen hello	send_robot_kitchen	go_to_kitchen	100

Table 1: An example dialog with an elderly person. Actions in bold font are clarification actions, generated by the POMDP because of high uncertainty in the speech signal.

for violating an area constraints, low costs elsewhere). To analyze the effect of poor localization on this cost function, our approach utilizes an augmented model that incorporates the localizer itself as a state variable. In particular, the state consists of the robot pose x_t, and the state of the localizer, b_t. The latter is defined as accurate ($b_t = 1$) or inaccurate ($b_t = 0$). The state transition function is composed of the conventional robot motion model $p(x_t|u_{t-1}, x_{t-1})$, and a simplistic model that assumes with probability α, that the tracker remains in the same state (good or bad). Put mathematically:

$$p(x_t, b_t|u_{t-1}, x_{t-1}, b_{t-1}) =$$
$$p(x_t|u_{t-1}, x_{t-1}) \cdot \left[\alpha I_{b_t=b_{t-1}} + (1-\alpha)I_{b_t \neq b_{t-1}} \right] \quad (5)$$

Our approach calculates an MDP-style value function, $V(x, b)$, under the assumption that good tracking assumes good control whereas poor tracking implies random control. This is achieved by the following value iteration approach:

$$V(x, b) \longleftarrow$$
$$\begin{cases} \min_u c(x, u) + \gamma \sum_{x'b'} p(x', b'|x, b, u)V(x', b') \\ \qquad \text{if } b = 1 \text{ (good localization)} \\ \\ \sum_u c(x, u) + \gamma \sum_{x'b'} p(x', b'|x, b, u)V(x', b') \\ \qquad \text{if } b = 0 \text{ (poor localization)} \end{cases} \quad (6)$$

where γ is the discount factor. This gives a well-defined MDP that can be solved via value iteration. The risk function is them simply the difference between good and bad tracking: $l(x) = V(x, 1) - V(x, 0)$. When applied to the Nursebot navigation problem, this approach leads to a localization algorithm that preferentially generates samples in the vicinity of the dining areas. A sample set representing a uniform uncertainty is shown in Figure 3b—notice the increased sample density near the dining area. Extensive tests involving real-world data collected during robot operation show not only that the robot was well-localized in high-risk regions, but that our approach also reduced costs after (artificially induced) catastrophic localization failure by 40.1%, when compared to the plain particle filter localization algorithm.

High Level Robot Control and Dialog Management

The most central new module in Pearl's software is a probabilistic algorithm for high-level control and dialog management. High-level robot control has been a popular topic in AI, and decades of research has led to a reputable collection of architectures (e.g., [1, 4, 12]). However, existing architectures rarely take uncertainty into account during planning.

Pearl's high-level control architecture is a hierarchical variant of a partially observable Markov decision process

(POMDP) [14]. POMDPs are techniques for calculating optimal control actions under uncertainty. The control decision is based on the full probability distribution generated by the state estimator, such as in Equation (2). In Pearl's case, this distribution includes a multitude of multi-valued probabilistic state and goal variables:
- robot location (discrete approximation)
- person's location (discrete approximation)
- person's status (as inferred from speech recognizer)
- motion goal (where to move)
- reminder goal (what to inform the user of)
- user initiated goal (e.g., an information request)

Overall, there are 288 plausible states. The input to the POMDP is a factored probability distribution over these states, with uncertainty arising predominantly from the localization modules and the speech recognition system. We conjecture that the consideration of uncertainty is important in this domain, as the costs of mistaking a reply can be large.

Unfortunately, POMDPs of the size encountered here are an order of magnitude larger than today's best exact POMDP algorithms can tackle [14]. However, Pearl's POMDP is a highly structured POMDP, where certain actions are only applicable in certain situations. To exploit this structure, we developed a *hierarchical* version of POMDPs, which breaks down the decision making problem into a collection of smaller problems that can be solved more efficiently. Our approach is similar to the MAX-Q decomposition for MDPs [8], but defined over POMDPs (where states are unobserved).

The basic idea of the hierarchical POMDP is to partition the action space—not the state space, since the state is not fully observable—into smaller chunks. For Pearl's guidance task the action hierarchy is shown in Figure 4, where *abstract actions* (shown in circles) are introduced to subsume logical subgroups of lower-level actions. This action hierarchy induces a decomposition of the control problem, where at each node all lower-level actions, if any, are considered in the context of a local sub-controller. At the lowest level, the control problem is a regular POMDP, with a reduced action space. At higher levels, the control problem is also a POMDP, yet involves a mixture of physical and abstract actions (where abstract actions correspond to lower level POMDPs.)

Let $\bar{u}$ be such an abstract action, and $\pi_{\bar{u}}$ the control policy associated with the respective POMDP. The "abstract" POMDP is then parameterized (in terms of states x, observations z) by assuming that whenever $\bar{u}$ is chosen, Pearl uses

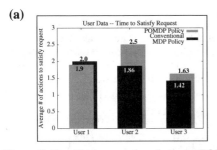
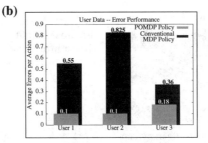
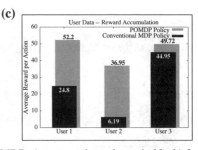

Figure 5: Empirical comparison between POMDPs (with uncertainty, shown in gray) and MDPs (no uncertainty, shown in black) for high-level robot control, evaluated on data collected in the assisted living facility. Shown are the average time to task completion (a), the average number of errors (b), and the average user-assigned (*not* model assigned) reward (c), for the MDP and POMDP. The data is shown for three users, with good, average and poor speech recognition.

lower-level control policy $\pi_{\bar{u}}$:

$$
\begin{aligned}
p(x'|x, \bar{u}) &= p(x'|x, \pi_{\bar{u}}(x)) \\
p(z|x, \bar{u}) &= p(z|x, \pi_{\bar{u}}(x)) \\
R(x, \bar{u}) &= R(x, \pi_{\bar{u}}(x))
\end{aligned}
\tag{7}
$$

Here R denotes the reward function. It is important to notice that such a decomposition may only be valid if reward is received at the leaf nodes of the hierarchy, and is especially appropriate when the optimal control transgresses down along a single path in the hierarchy to receive its reward. This is approximately the case in the Pearl domain, where reward is received upon successfully delivering a person, or successfully gathering information through communication.

Using the hierarchical POMDP, the high-level decision making problem in Pearl is tractable, and a near-optimal control policy can be computed off-line. Thus, during execution time the controller simply monitors the state (calculates the posterior) and looks up the appropriate control. Table 1 shows an example dialog between the robot and a test subject. Because of the uncertainty management in POMDPs, the robot chooses to ask a clarification question at three occasions. The number of such questions depends on the clarity of a person's speech, as detected by the Sphinx speech recognition system.

An important question in our research concerns the importance of handling uncertainty in high-level control. To investigate this, we ran a series of comparative experiments, all involving real data collected in our lab. In one series of experiments, we investigated the importance of considering the uncertainty arising from the speech interface. In particular, we compared Pearl's performance to a system that ignores that uncertainty, but is otherwise identical. The resulting approach is an MDP, similar to the one described in [23]. Figure 5 shows results for three different performance measures, and three different users (in decreasing order of speech recognition performance). For poor speakers, the MDP requires less time to "satisfy" a request due to the lack of clarification questions (Figure 5a). However, its error rate is much higher (Figure 5b), which negatively affects the overall reward received by the robot (Figure 5c). These results clearly demonstrate the importance of considering uncertainty at the highest robot control level, specifically with poor speech recognition.

In a second series of experiments, we investigated the importance of uncertainty management in the context of highly imbalanced costs and rewards. In Pearl's case, such costs are indeed highly imbalanced: asking a clarification question is much cheaper than accidentally delivering a person to a wrong location, or guiding a person who does not want to be walked. In this experiment we compared performance using

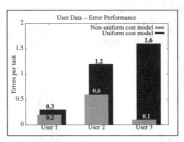

Figure 6: Empirical comparison between uniform and non-uniform cost models. Results are an average over 10 tasks. Depicted are 3 example users, with varying levels of speech recognition accuracy. Users 2 & 3 had the lowest recognition accuracy, and consequently more errors when using the uniform cost model.

two POMDP models which differed only in their cost models. One model assumed uniform costs for all actions, whereas the second model assumed a more discriminative cost model in which the cost of verbal questions was lower than the cost of performing the wrong motion actions. A POMDP policy was learned for each of these models, and then tested experimentally in our laboratory. The results presented in figure 6 show that the non-uniform model makes more judicious use of confirmation actions, thus leading to a significantly lower error rate, especially for users with low recognition accuracy.

Results

We tested the robot in five separate experiments, each lasting one full day. The first three days focused on open-ended interactions with a large number of elderly users, during which the robot interacted verbally and spatially with elderly people with the specific task of delivered sweets. This allowed us to gauge people's initial reactions to the robot.

Following this, we performed two days of formal experiments during which the robot autonomously led 12 full guidances, involving 6 different elderly people. Figure 7 shows an example guidance experiment, involving an elderly person who uses a walking aid. The sequence of images illustrates the major stages of a successful delivery: from contacting the person, explaining to her the reason for the visit, walking her through the facility, and providing information after the successful delivery—in this case on the weather.

In all guidance experiments, the task was performed to completion. Post-experimental debriefings illustrated a uniform high level of excitement on the side of the elderly. Overall, only a few problems were detected during the operation. None of the test subjects showed difficulties understanding the major functions of the robot. They all were able to operate the robot after less than five minutes of introduction. However, initial flaws with a poorly adjusted speech recognition

(a) Pearl approaching elderly	(b) Reminding of appointment

(c) Guidance through corridor	(d) Entering physiotherapy dept.

(e) Asking for weather forecast	(f) Pearl leaves

Figure 7: Example of a successful guidance experiment. Pearl picks up the patient outside her room, reminds her of a physiotherapy appointment, walks the person to the department, and responds to a request of the weather report. In this interaction, the interaction took place through speech and the touch-sensitive display.

system led to occasional confusion, which was fixed during the course of this project. An additional problem arose from the robot's initial inability to adapt its velocity to people's walking pace, which was found to be crucial for the robot's effectiveness.

Discussion

This paper described a mobile robotic assistant for nurses and elderly in assisted living facilities. Building on a robot navigation system described in [5, 24], new software modules specifically aimed at interaction with elderly people were developed. The system has been tested successfully in experiments in an assisted living facility. Our experiments were successful in two main dimensions. First, they demonstrated the robustness of the various probabilistic techniques in a challenging real-world task. Second, they provided some evidence towards the feasibility of using autonomous mobile robots as assistants to nurses and institutionalized elderly. One of the key lessons learned while developing this robot is that the elderly population requires techniques that can cope with their degradation (e.g., speaking abilities) and also pays special attention to safety issues. We view the area of assistive technology as a prime source for great AI problems in the future.

Possibly the most significant contribution of this research to AI is the fact that the robot's high-level control system is entirely realized by a *partially observable Markov decision process* (POMDP) [14]. This demonstrates that POMDPs have matured to a level that makes them applicable to real-world robot control tasks. Furthermore, our experimental results suggest that uncertainty matters in high-level decision

making. These findings challenge a long term view in mainstream AI that uncertainty is irrelevant, or at best can be handled uniformly at the higher levels of robot control[6, 17]. We conjecture instead that when robots interact with people, uncertainty is pervasive and has to be considered at all levels of decision making, not solely in low-level perceptual routines.

References

[1] R. Arkin. *Behavior-Based Robotics*. MIT Press, 1998.

[2] Y. Bar-Shalom and T. E. Fortmann. *Tracking and Data Association*. Academic Press, 1998.

[3] A.W. Black, P. Taylor, and R. Caley. *The Festival Speech Synthesis System*. University of Edinburgh, 1999.

[4] R.A. Brooks. A robust layered control system for a mobile robot. TR AI memo 864, MIT, 1985.

[5] W. Burgard, A.B., Cremers, D. Fox, D. Hähnel, G. Lakemeyer, D. Schulz, W. Steiner, and S. Thrun. The interactive museum tour-guide robot. *AAAI-98*

[6] G. De Giacomo, editor. Notes *AAAI Fall Symposium on Cognitive Robotics*, 1998.

[7] F. Dellaert, D. Fox, W. Burgard, and S. Thrun. Monte Carlo localization for mobile robots. *ICRA-99*

[8] T. Dietterich. The MAXQ method for hierarchical reinforcement learning. *ICML-98*.

[9] A. Doucet, N. de Freitas, and N.J. Gordon, editors. *Sequential Monte Carlo Methods In Practice*. Springer, 2001.

[10] A Doucet, N. de Freitas, K. Murphy, and S. Russell. Rao-Blackwellised particle filtering for dynamic bayesian networks. *UAI-2000*.

[11] G. Engelberger. Services. In *Handbook of Industrial Robotics*, John Wiley and Sons, 1999.

[12] E. Gat. Esl: A language for supporting robust plan execution in embedded autonomous agents. Noted *AAAI Fall Symposium on Plan Execution*, 1996.

[13] D. M. Gavrila. The visual analysis of human movement: A survey. *Computer Vision and Image Understanding*, 73(1), 1999.

[14] L.P. Kaelbling, M.L. Littman, and A.R. Cassandra. Planning and acting in partially observable stochastic domains. *Artificial Intelligence*, 101, 1998.

[15] D. Kortenkamp, R.P. Bonasso, and R. Murphy, editors. *AI-based Mobile Robots: Case studies of successful robot systems*, MIT Press, 1998.

[16] G. Lacey and K.M. Dawson-Howe. The application of robotics to a mobility aid for the elderly blind. *Robotics and Autonomous Systems*, 23, 1998.

[17] G. Lakemeyer, editor. Notes *Second International Workshop on Cognitive Robotics*, Berlin, 2000

[18] C.E. McCarthy, and M. Pollack. A Plan-Based Personalized Cognitive Orthotic. *AIPS-2002*.

[19] P. Poupart, L.E. Ortiz, and C. Boutilier. Value-directed sampling methods for monitoring POMDPs. *UAI-2001*.

[20] M. Ravishankar. Efficient algorithms for speech recognition, 1996. Internal Report.

[21] H.A. Rowley, S. Baluja, and T. Kanade. Neural network-based face detection. *IEEE Transactions on Pattern Analysis and Machine Intelligence*, 20(1), 1998.

[22] D. Schulz, W. Burgard, D. Fox, and A. Cremers. Tracking multiple moving targets with a mobile robot using particles filters and statistical data association. *ICRA-2001*.

[23] S. Singh, M. Kearns, D. Litman, and M. Walker. Reinforcement learning for spoken dialogue systems. *NIPS-2000*.

[24] S. Thrun, M. Beetz, M. Bennewitz, W. Burgard, A.B. Cremers, F. Dellaert, D. Fox, D. Hähnel, C. Rosenberg, N. Roy, J. Schulte, and D. Schulz. Probabilistic algorithms and the interactive museum tour-guide robot Minerva. *International Journal of Robotics Research*, 19(11), 2000.

[25] S. Thrun, Langford. J., and V. Verma. Risk sensitive particle filters. *NIPS-2002*.

[26] US Department of Health and Human Services. Health, United states, 1999. Health and aging chartbook, 1999.

FastSLAM: A Factored Solution to the Simultaneous Localization and Mapping Problem

Michael Montemerlo and **Sebastian Thrun**
School of Computer Science
Carnegie Mellon University
Pittsburgh, PA 15213
mmde@cs.cmu.edu, thrun@cs.cmu.edu

Daphne Koller and **Ben Wegbreit**
Computer Science Department
Stanford University
Stanford, CA 94305-9010
koller@cs.stanford.edu, ben@wegbreit.com

Abstract

The ability to simultaneously localize a robot and accurately map its surroundings is considered by many to be a key prerequisite of truly autonomous robots. However, few approaches to this problem scale up to handle the very large number of landmarks present in real environments. Kalman filter-based algorithms, for example, require time quadratic in the number of landmarks to incorporate each sensor observation. This paper presents FastSLAM, an algorithm that recursively estimates the full posterior distribution over robot pose and landmark locations, yet scales logarithmically with the number of landmarks in the map. This algorithm is based on an exact factorization of the posterior into a product of conditional landmark distributions and a distribution over robot paths. The algorithm has been run successfully on as many as 50,000 landmarks, environments far beyond the reach of previous approaches. Experimental results demonstrate the advantages and limitations of the FastSLAM algorithm on both simulated and real-world data.

Introduction

The problem of *simultaneous localization and mapping*, also known as SLAM, has attracted immense attention in the mobile robotics literature. SLAM addresses the problem of building a map of an environment from a sequence of landmark measurements obtained from a moving robot. Since robot motion is subject to error, the mapping problem necessarily induces a robot localization problem—hence the name SLAM. The ability to simultaneously localize a robot and accurately map its environment is considered by many to be a key prerequisite of truly autonomous robots [3, 7, 17].

The dominant approach to the SLAM problem was introduced in a seminal paper by Smith, Self, and Cheeseman [16]. This paper proposed the use of the extended Kalman filter (EKF) for incrementally estimating the posterior distribution over robot pose along with the positions of the landmarks. In the last decade, this approach has found widespread acceptance in field robotics, as a recent tutorial paper [2] documents. Recent research has focused on scaling this approach to larger environments with more than a

few hundred landmarks [6, 8, 9] and to algorithms for handling data association problems [18].

A key limitation of EKF-based approaches is their computational complexity. Sensor updates require time quadratic in the number of landmarks K to compute. This complexity stems from the fact that the covariance matrix maintained by the Kalman filters has $O(K^2)$ elements, all of which must be updated even if just a single landmark is observed. The quadratic complexity limits the number of landmarks that can be handled by this approach to only a few hundred—whereas natural environment models frequently contain millions of features. This shortcoming has long been recognized by the research community [6, 8, 15].

In this paper we approach the SLAM problem from a Bayesian point of view. Figure 1 illustrates a generative probabilistic model (dynamic Bayes network) that underlies the rich corpus of SLAM literature. In particular, the robot poses, denoted $s_1, s_2, \ldots, s_t$, evolve over time as a function of the robot controls, denoted $u_1, \ldots, u_t$. Each of the landmark measurements, denoted $z_1, \ldots, z_t$, is a function of the position θ_k of the landmark measured and of the robot pose at the time the measurement was taken. From this diagram it is evident that the SLAM problem exhibits important conditional independences. In particular, knowledge of the robot's path $s_1, s_2, \ldots, s_t$ renders the individual landmark measurements *independent*. So for example, if an oracle provided us with the exact path of the robot, the problem of determining the landmark locations could be decoupled into K independent estimation problems, one for each landmark. This observation was made previously by Murphy [13], who developed an efficient particle filtering algorithm for learning grid maps.

Based on this observation, this paper describes an efficient SLAM algorithm called *FastSLAM*. FastSLAM decomposes the SLAM problem into a robot localization problem, and a collection of landmark estimation problems that are conditioned on the robot pose estimate. As remarked in [13], this factored representation is exact, due to the natural conditional independences in the SLAM problem. FastSLAM uses a modified particle filter for estimating the posterior over robot paths. Each particle possesses K Kalman filters that estimate the K landmark locations conditioned on the path estimate. The resulting algorithm is an instance of the Rao-Blackwellized particle filter [5, 14]. A naive implementation of this idea leads to an algorithm that requires

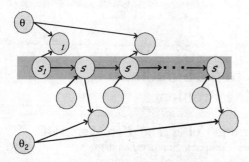

Figure 1: The SLAM problem: The robot moves from pose s_1 through a sequence of controls, $u_1, u_2, \ldots, u_t$. As it moves, it observes nearby landmarks. At time $t = 1$, it observes landmark θ_1 out of two landmarks, $\{\theta_1, \theta_2\}$. The measurement is denoted z_1 (range and bearing). At time $t = 1$, it observes the other landmark, θ_2, and at time $t = 3$, it observes θ_1 again. The SLAM problem is concerned with estimating the locations of the landmarks and the robot's path from the controls u and the measurements z. The gray shading illustrates a conditional independence relation.

$O(MK)$ time, where M is the number of particles in the particle filter and K is the number of landmarks. We develop a tree-based data structure that reduces the running time of FastSLAM to $O(M \log K)$, making it significantly faster than existing EKF-based SLAM algorithms. We also extend the FastSLAM algorithm to situations with unknown data association and unknown number of landmarks, showing that our approach can be extended to the full range of SLAM problems discussed in the literature.

Experimental results using a physical robot and a robot simulator illustrate that the FastSLAM algorithm can handle orders of magnitude more landmarks than present day approaches. We also find that in certain situations, an increased number of landmarks K leads to a mild *reduction* of the number of particles M needed to generate accurate maps—whereas in others the number of particles required for accurate mapping may be prohibitively large.

SLAM Problem Definition

The SLAM problem, as defined in the rich body of literature on SLAM, is best described as a probabilistic Markov chain. The robot's pose at time t will be denoted s_t. For robots operating in the plane—which is the case in all of our experiments—poses are comprised of a robot's x-y coordinate in the plane and its heading direction.

Poses evolve according to a probabilistic law, often referred to as the *motion model*:

$$p(s_t \mid u_t, s_{t-1}) \tag{1}$$

Thus, s_t is a probabilistic function of the robot control u_t and the previous pose s_{t-1}. In mobile robotics, the motion model is usually a time-invariant probabilistic generalization of robot kinematics [1].

The robot's environment possesses K immobile landmarks. Each landmark is characterized by its location in space, denoted θ_k for $k = 1, \ldots, K$. Without loss of generality, we will think of landmarks as points in the plane, so that locations are specified by two numerical values.

To map its environment, the robot can sense landmarks. For example, it may be able to measure range and bearing to

a landmark, relative to its local coordinate frame. The measurement at time t will be denoted z_t. While robots can often sense more than one landmark at a time, we follow commonplace notation by assuming that sensor measurements correspond to exactly one landmark [2]. This convention is adopted solely for mathematical convenience. It poses no restriction, as multiple landmark sightings at a single time step can be processed sequentially.

Sensor measurements are governed by a probabilistic law, often referred to as the *measurement model*:

$$p(z_t \mid s_t, \theta, n_t) \tag{2}$$

Here $\theta = \{\theta_1, \ldots, \theta_k\}$ is the set of all landmarks, and $n_t \in \{1, \ldots, K\}$ is the index of the landmark perceived at time t. For example, in Figure 1, we have $n_1 = 1, n_2 = 2$, and $n_3 = 1$, since the robot first observes landmark θ_1, then landmark θ_2, and finally landmark θ_1 for a second time. Many measurement models in the literature assume that the robot can measure range and bearing to landmarks, confounded by measurement noise. The variable n_t is often referred to as *correspondence*. Most theoretical work in the literature assumes knowledge of the correspondence or, put differently, that landmarks are uniquely identifiable. Practical implementations use maximum likelihood estimators for estimating the correspondence on-the-fly, which work well if landmarks are spaced sufficiently far apart. In large parts of this paper we will simply assume that landmarks are identifiable, but we will also discuss an extension that estimates the correspondences from data.

We are now ready to formulate the SLAM problem. Most generally, SLAM is the problem of determining the location of all landmarks θ and robot poses s_t from measurements $z^t = z_1, \ldots, z_t$ and controls $u^t = u_1, \ldots, u_t$. In probabilistic terms, this is expressed by the posterior $p(s^t, \theta \mid z^t, u^t)$, where we use the superscript ^{t} to refer to a set of variables from time 1 to time t. If the correspondences are known, the SLAM problem is simpler:

$$p(s^t, \theta \mid z^t, u^t, n^t) \tag{3}$$

As discussed in the introduction, all individual landmark estimation problems are independent if one knew the robot's path s^t and the correspondence variables n^t. This conditional independence is the basis of the FastSLAM algorithm described in the next section.

FastSLAM with Known Correspondences

We begin our consideration with the important case where the correspondences $n^t = n_1, \ldots, n_t$ are known, and so is the number of landmarks K observed thus far.

Factored Representation

The conditional independence property of the SLAM problem implies that the posterior (3) can be factored as follows:

$$p(s^t, \theta \mid z^t, u^t, n^t)$$
$$= p(s^t \mid z^t, u^t, n^t) \prod_k p(\theta_k \mid s^t, z^t, u^t, n^t) \tag{4}$$

Put verbally, the problem can be decomposed into $K+1$ estimation problems, one problem of estimating a posterior over robot paths s^t, and K problems of estimating the locations of the K landmarks conditioned on the path estimate. This factorization is exact and always applicable in the SLAM problem, as previously argued in [13].

The FastSLAM algorithm implements the path estimator $p(s^t \mid z^t, u^t, n^t)$ using a modified particle filter [4]. As we argue further below, this filter can sample efficiently from this space, providing a good approximation of the posterior even under non-linear motion kinematics. The landmark pose estimators $p(\theta_k \mid s^t, z^t, u^t, n^t)$ are realized by Kalman filters, using separate filters for different landmarks. Because the landmark estimates are conditioned on the path estimate, each particle in the particle filter has its own, local landmark estimates. Thus, for M particles and K landmarks, there will be a total of KM Kalman filters, each of dimension 2 (for the two landmark coordinates). This representation will now be discussed in detail.

Particle Filter Path Estimation

FastSLAM employs a particle filter for estimating the path posterior $p(s^t \mid z^t, u^t, n^t)$ in (4), using a filter that is similar (but not identical) to the *Monte Carlo localization (MCL)* algorithm [1]. MCL is an application of particle filter to the problem of robot pose estimation (localization). At each point in time, both algorithms maintain a set of particles representing the posterior $p(s^t \mid z^t, u^t, n^t)$, denoted S_t. Each particle $s^{t,[m]} \in S_t$ represents a "guess" of the robot's path:

$$S_t = \{s^{t,[m]}\}_m = \{s_1^{[m]}, s_2^{[m]}, \ldots, s_t^{[m]}\}_m \quad (5)$$

We use the superscript notation $[m]$ to refer to the m-th particle in the set.

The particle set S_t is calculated incrementally, from the set S_{t-1} at time $t-1$, a robot control u_t, and a measurement z_t. First, each particle $s^{t,[m]}$ in S_{t-1} is used to generate a probabilistic guess of the robot's pose at time t

$$s_t^{[m]} \sim p(s_t \mid u_t, s_{t-1}^{[m]}), \quad (6)$$

obtained by sampling from the probabilistic motion model. This estimate is then added to a temporary set of particles, along with the path $s^{t-1,[m]}$. Under the assumption that the set of particles in S_{t-1} is distributed according to $p(s^{t-1} \mid z^{t-1}, u^{t-1}, n^{t-1})$ (which is an asymptotically correct approximation), the new particle is distributed according to $p(s^t \mid z^{t-1}, u^t, n^{t-1})$. This distribution is commonly referred to as the *proposal distribution* of particle filtering.

After generating M particles in this way, the new set S_t is obtained by sampling from the temporary particle set. Each particle $s^{t,[m]}$ is drawn (with replacement) with a probability proportional to a so-called *importance factor* $w_t^{[m]}$, which is calculated as follows [10]:

$$w_t^{[m]} = \frac{\text{target distribution}}{\text{proposal distribution}} = \frac{p(s^{t,[m]} \mid z^t, u^t, n^t)}{p(s^{t,[m]} \mid z^{t-1}, u^t, n^{t-1})} \quad (7)$$

The exact calculation of (7) will be discussed further below. The resulting sample set S_t is distributed according to an approximation to the desired pose posterior $p(s^t \mid z^t, u^t, n^t)$, an approximation which is correct as the number of particles M goes to infinity. We also notice that only the most recent robot pose estimate $s_{t-1}^{[m]}$ is used when generating the particle set S_t. This will allows us to silently "forget" all other

pose estimates, rendering the size of each particle independent of the time index t.

Landmark Location Estimation

FastSLAM represents the conditional landmark estimates $p(\theta_k \mid s^t, z^t, u^t, n^t)$ in (4) by Kalman filters. Since this estimate is conditioned on the robot pose, the Kalman filters are attached to individual pose particles in S_t. More specifically, the full posterior over paths and landmark positions in the FastSLAM algorithm is represented by the sample set

$$\mathcal{S}_t = \{s^{t,[m]}, \mu_1^{[m]}, \Sigma_1^{[m]}, \ldots, \mu_K^{[m]}, \Sigma_K^{[m]}\}_m \quad (8)$$

Here $\mu_k^{[m]}$ and $\Sigma_k^{[m]}$ are mean and covariance of the Gaussian representing the k-th landmark θ_k, attached to the m-th particle. In the planar robot navigation scenario, each mean $\mu_k^{[m]}$ is a two-element vector, and $\Sigma_k^{[m]}$ is a 2 by 2 matrix.

The posterior over the k-th landmark pose θ_k is easily obtained. Its computation depends on whether or not $n_t = k$, that is, whether or not θ_k was observed at time t. For $n_t = k$, we obtain

$$p(\theta_k \mid s^t, z^t, u^t, n^t) \quad (9)$$
$$\overset{\text{Bayes}}{\propto} p(z_t \mid \theta_k, s^t, z^{t-1}, u^t, n^t) \, p(\theta_k \mid s^t, z^{t-1}, u^t, n^t)$$
$$\overset{\text{Markov}}{=} p(z_t \mid \theta_k, s_t, n_t) \, p(\theta_k \mid s^{t-1}, z^{t-1}, u^{t-1}, n^{t-1})$$

For $n_t \neq k$, we simply leave the Gaussian unchanged:

$$p(\theta_k \mid s^t, z^t, u^t, n^t) = p(\theta_k \mid s^{t-1}, z^{t-1}, u^{t-1}, n^{t-1}) \quad (10)$$

The FastSLAM algorithm implements the update equation (9) using the extended Kalman filter (EKF). As in existing EKF approaches to SLAM, this filter uses a linearized version of the perceptual model $p(z_t \mid s_t, \theta, n_t)$ [2]. Thus, FastSLAM's EKF is similar to the traditional EKF for SLAM [16] in that it approximates the measurement model using a linear Gaussian function. We note that, with a linear Gaussian observation model, the resulting distribution $p(\theta_k \mid s^t, z^t, u^t, n^t)$ is exactly a Gaussian, even if the motion model is not linear. This is a consequence of the use of sampling to approximate the distribution over the robot's pose.

One significant difference between the FastSLAM algorithm's use of Kalman filters and that of the traditional SLAM algorithm is that the updates in the FastSLAM algorithm involve only a Gaussian of dimension two (for the two landmark location parameters), whereas in the EKF-based SLAM approach a Gaussian of size $2K+3$ has to be updated (with K landmarks and 3 robot pose parameters). This calculation can be done in constant time in FastSLAM, whereas it requires time quadratic in K in standard SLAM.

Calculating the Importance Weights

Let us now return to the problem of calculating the importance weights $w_t^{[m]}$ needed for particle filter resampling, as defined in (7):

$$w_t^{[m]} \propto \frac{p(s^{t,[m]} \mid z^t, u^t, n^t)}{p(s^{t,[m]} \mid z^{t-1}, u^t, n^{t-1})}$$
$$\overset{\text{Bayes}}{=} \frac{p(z_t, n_t \mid s^{t,[m]}, z^{t-1}, u^t, n^{t-1})}{p(z_t, n_t \mid z^{t-1}, u^t, n^{t-1})}$$

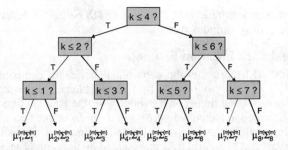

Figure 2: A tree representing $K = 8$ landmark estimates within a single particle.

$$\frac{p(s^{t,[m]} \mid z^{t-1}, u^t, n^t)}{p(s^{t,[m]} \mid z^{t-1}, u^t, n^t)}$$

$$= \quad \frac{p(z_t, n_t \mid s^{t,[m]}, z^{t-1}, u^t, n^{t-1})}{p(z_t, n_t \mid z^{t-1}, u^t, n^{t-1})}$$

$$\propto \quad p(z_t, n_t \mid s^{t,[m]}, z^{t-1}, u^t, n^{t-1})$$

$$= \quad \int p(z_t, n_t \mid \theta, s^{t,[m]}, z^{t-1}, u^t, n^{t-1})$$

$$p(\theta \mid s^{t,[m]}, z^{t-1}, u^t, n^t) \, d\theta$$

$$\overset{\text{Markov}}{=} \int p(z_t, n_t \mid \theta, s_t^{[m]})$$

$$p(\theta \mid s^{t-1,[m]}, z^{t-1}, u^{t-1}, n^{t-1}) \, d\theta$$

$$= \quad \int p(z_t \mid \theta, s_t^{[m]}, n_t) \, p(n_t \mid \theta, s_t^{[m]})$$

$$p(\theta \mid s^{t-1,[m]}, z^{t-1}, u^{t-1}, n^{t-1}) \, d\theta$$

$$\propto \quad \int p(z_t \mid \theta, s_t^{[m]}, n_t)$$

$$p(\theta \mid s^{t-1,[m]}, z^{t-1}, u^{t-1}, n^{t-1}) \, d\theta$$

$$\overset{\text{EKF}}{\approx} \int p(z_t \mid \theta_{n_t}^{[m]}, s_t^{[m]}, n_t) \, p(\theta_{n_t}^{[m]}) \, d\theta_{n_t} \quad (11)$$

Here we assume that the distribution $p(n_t \mid \theta, s_t^{[m]})$ is uniform—a common assumption in SLAM. In the last line, "EKF" makes explicit the use of a linearized model as an approximation to the observation model $p(z_t \mid \theta_{n_t}^{[m]}, s_t^{[m]})$, and the resulting Gaussian posterior $p(\theta_{n_t}^{[m]})$. The final integration is easily calculated in closed form for a linear Gaussian.

Efficient Implementation

The FastSLAM algorithm, as described thus far, may require time linear in the number of landmarks K for each update iteration if implemented naively. This is because of the resampling step; every time a particle is added to $\mathcal{S}_t$, its has to be copied. Since each particle contains K landmark estimates, this copying procedure requires $O(MK)$ time. However, most of this copying can be avoided.

Our approach makes it possible to execute a FastSLAM iteration in $O(M \log K)$ time. The basic idea is that the set of Gaussians in each particle is represented by a balanced binary tree. Figure 2 shows such a tree for a single particle, in the case of 8 landmarks. The Gaussian parameters $\mu_k^{[m]}$ and $\Sigma_k^{[m]}$ are located at the leaves of the tree. Clearly, accessing

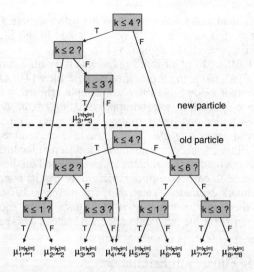

Figure 3: Generating a new particle from an old one, while modifying only a single Gaussian. The new particle receives only a partial tree, consisting of a path to the modified Gaussian. All other pointers are copied from the generating tree.

each Gaussian requires time logarithmic in K.

Suppose FastSLAM incorporates a new control u_t and a new measurement z_t. Each new particle in $\mathcal{S}_t$ will differ from the corresponding one in $\mathcal{S}_{t-1}$ in two ways: First, it will possess a different path estimate obtained via (6), and second, the Gaussian with index n_t will be different in accordance with (9). All other Gaussians will be equivalent to the generating particle.

When copying the particle, thus, only a single path has to be modified in the tree representing all Gaussians. An example is shown in Figure 3: Here we assume $n_t = 3$, that is, only the Gaussian parameters $\mu_3^{[m]}$ and $\Sigma_3^{[m]}$ are updated. Instead of generating an entirely new tree, only a single path is created, leading to the Gaussian $n_t = 3$. This path is an incomplete tree. To complete the tree, for all branches that leave this path the corresponding pointers are copied from the tree of the generating particle. Thus, branches that leave the path will point to the same (unmodified) subtree as that of the generating tree. Clearly, generating such an incomplete tree takes only time logarithmic in K. Moreover, accessing a Gaussian also takes time logarithmic in K, since the number of steps required to navigate to a leaf of the tree is equivalent to the length of the path (which is by definition logarithmic). Thus, both generating and accessing a partial tree can be done in time $O(\log K)$. Since in each updating step M new particles are created, an entire update requires time in $O(M \log K)$.

Data Association

In many real-world problems, landmarks are not identifiable, and the total number of landmarks K cannot be obtained trivially—as was the case above. In such situations, the robot has to solve a data association problem between momentary landmarks sightings z_t and the set of landmarks in the map θ. It also has to determine if a measurement corresponds to a new, previously unseen landmark, in which case the map should be augmented accordingly.

(a)  (b)  (c)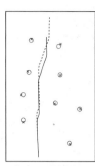

Figure 4: (a) Physical robot mapping rocks, in a testbed developed for Mars Rover research. (b) Raw range and path data. (c) Map generated using FastSLAM (dots), and locations of rocks determined manually (circles).

In most existing SLAM solutions based on EKFs, these problems are solved via maximum likelihood. More specifically, the probability of a data association n_t is given by

$$
\begin{aligned}
& p(n_t \mid z^t, u^t) \\
& = \int p(n_t \mid s^t, z^t, u^t) \, p(s^t \mid z^t, u^t) \, ds^t \\
& \stackrel{\text{PF}}{\approx} \sum_m p(n_t \mid s^{t,[m]}, z^t, u^t) \\
& \stackrel{\text{Markov}}{=} \sum_m p(n_t \mid s_t^{[m]}, z_t) \\
& \stackrel{\text{Bayes}}{\propto} \sum_m p(z_t \mid s_t^{[m]}, n_t) \qquad (12)
\end{aligned}
$$

The step labeled "PF" uses the particle filter approximation to the posterior $p(s^t \mid z^t, u^t)$. The final step assumes a uniform prior $p(n_t \mid s_t)$, which is commonly used [2]. The maximum likelihood data association is simply the index n_t that maximizes (12). If the maximum value of $p(n_t \mid z^t, u^t)$—with careful consideration of all constants in (12)—is below a threshold α, the landmark is considered previously unseen and the map is augmented accordingly.

In FastSLAM, the data association is estimated on a per-particle basis: $n_t^{[m]} = \operatorname{argmax}_{n_t} p(z_t \mid s_t^{[m]}, n_t)$. As a result, different particles may rely on different values of $n_t^{[m]}$. They might even possess different numbers of landmarks in their respective maps. This constitutes a primary difference to EKF approaches, which determine the data association only once for each sensor measurement. It has been observed frequently that false data association will make the conventional EKF approach fail catastrophically [2]. FastSLAM is more likely to recover, thanks to its ability to pursue multiple data associations simultaneously. Particles with wrong data association are (in expectation) more likely to disappear in the resampling process than those that guess the data association correctly.

We believe that, under mild assumptions (e.g., minimum spacing between landmarks and bounded sensor error), the data association search can be implemented in time logarithmic in N. One possibility is the use of kd-trees as an indexing scheme in the tree structures above, instead of the landmark number, as proposed in [11].

Experimental Results

The FastSLAM algorithm was tested extensively under various conditions. Real-world experiments were complimented by systematic simulation experiments, to investigate the scaling abilities of the approach. Overall, the results indicate favorably scaling to large number of landmarks and small particle sets. A fixed number of particles (e.g., $M = 100$) appears to work well across a large number of situations.

Figure 4a shows the physical robot testbed, which consists of a small arena set up under NASA funding for Mars Rover research. A Pioneer robot equipped with a SICK laser range finder was driven along an approximate straight line, generating the raw data shown in Figure 4b. The resulting map generated with $M = 10$ samples is depicted in Figure 4c, with manually determined landmark locations marked by circles. The robot's estimates are indicated by x's, illustrating the high accuracy of the resulting maps. FastSLAM resulted in an average residual map error of 8.3 centimeters, when compared to the manually generated map.

Unfortunately, the physical testbed does not allow for systematic experiments regarding the scaling properties of the approach. In extensive simulations, the number of landmarks was increased up to a total of 50,000, which FastSLAM successfully mapped with as few as 100 particles. Here, the number of parameters in FastSLAM is approximately 0.3% of that in the conventional EKF. Maps with 50,000 landmarks are out of range for conventional SLAM techniques, due to their enormous computational complexity. Figure 5 shows example maps with smaller numbers of landmarks, for different maximum sensor ranges as indicated. The ellipses in Figure 5 visualize the residual uncertainty when integrated over all particles and Gaussians.

In a set of experiments specifically aimed to elucidate the scaling properties of the approach, we evaluated the map and robot pose errors as a function of the number of landmarks K, and the number of particles M, respectively. The results are graphically depicted in Figure 6. Figure 6a illustrates that an increase in the number of landmarks K mildly reduces the error in the map and the robot pose. This is because the larger the number of landmarks, the smaller the robot pose error at any point in time. Increasing the number of particles M also bears a positive effect on the map and pose errors, as illustrated in Figure 6b. In both diagrams, the bars correspond to 95% confidence intervals.

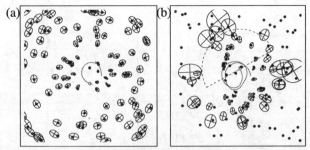

Figure 5: Maps and estimated robot path, generated using sensors with (a) large and (b) small perceptual fields. The correct landmark locations are shown as dots, and the estimates as ellipses, whose sizes correspond to the residual uncertainty.

Conclusion

We presented the FastSLAM algorithm, an efficient new solution to the concurrent mapping and localization problem. This algorithm utilizes a Rao-Blackwellized representation of the posterior, integrating particle filter and Kalman filter representations. Similar to Murphy's work [13], FastSLAM is based on an inherent conditional independence property of the SLAM problem, using Rao-Blackwellized particle filters in the estimation. However, Murphy's approach maintains grid maps with discrete values similar to occupancy grid maps [12], hence does not address the common SLAM problem of estimating continuous landmark locations.

In FastSLAM, landmark estimates are efficiently represented using tree structures. Updating the posterior requires $O(M \log K)$ time, where M is the number of particles and K the number of landmarks. This is in contrast to the $O(K^2)$ complexity of the common Kalman-filter based approach to SLAM. Experimental results illustrate that FastSLAM can build maps with orders of magnitude more landmarks than previous methods. They also demonstrate that under certain conditions, a small number of particles works well regardless of the number of landmarks.

Acknowledgments We thank Kevin Murphy and Nando de Freitas for insightful discussions on this topic. This research was sponsored by DARPA's MARS Program (Contract number N66001-01-C-6018) and the National Science Foundation (CAREER grant number IIS-9876136 and regular grant number IIS-9877033). We thank the Hertz Foundation for their support of Michael Montemerlo's graduate research. Daphne Koller was supported by the Office of Naval Research, Young Investigator (PECASE) grant N00014-99-1-0464. This work was done while Sebastian Thrun was visiting Stanford University.

References

[1] F. Dellaert, D. Fox, W. Burgard, and S. Thrun. Monte Carlo localization for mobile robots. *ICRA-99*.

[2] G. Dissanayake, P. Newman, S. Clark, H.F. Durrant-Whyte, and M. Csorba. An experimental and theoretical investigation into simultaneous localisation and map building (SLAM). *Lecture Notes in Control and Information Sciences: Experimental Robotics VI*, Springer, 2000.

[3] G. Dissanayake, P. Newman, S. Clark, H.F. Durrant-Whyte, and M. Csorba. A solution to the simultaneous localisation and map building (SLAM) problem. *IEEE Transactions of Robotics and Automation*, 2001.

[4] A. Doucet, J.F.G. de Freitas, and N.J. Gordon, editors. *Sequential Monte Carlo Methods In Practice*. Springer, 2001.

[5] A Doucet, N. de Freitas, K. Murphy, and S. Russell. Rao-Blackwellised particle filtering for dynamic Bayesian networks. *UAI-2000*.

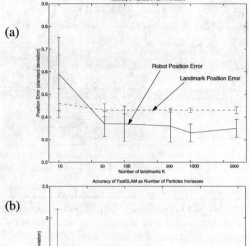

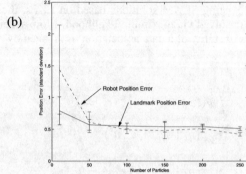

Figure 6: Accuracy of the FastSLAM algorithm as a function of (a) the number of landmarks N, and (b) the number of particles M. Large number of landmarks reduce the robot localization error, with little effect on the map error. Good results can be achieved with as few as 100 particles.

[6] J. Guivant and E. Nebot. Optimization of the simultaneous localization and map building algorithm for real time implementation. *IEEE Transaction of Robotic and Automation*, May 2001.

[7] D. Kortenkamp, R.P. Bonasso, and R. Murphy, editors. *AI-based Mobile Robots: Case studies of successful robot systems*, MIT Press, 1998.

[8] J.J. Leonard and H.J.S. Feder. A computationally efficient method for large-scale concurrent mapping and localization. *ISRR-99*.

[9] F. Lu and E. Milios. Globally consistent range scan alignment for environment mapping. *Autonomous Robots*, 4, 1997.

[10] N. Metropolis, A.W. Rosenbluth, M.N. Rosenbluth, A.H. Teller, and E. Teller. Equations of state calculations by fast computing machine. *Journal of Chemical Physics*, 21, 1953.

[11] A.W. Moore. Very fast EM-based mixture model clustering using multiresolution kd-trees. *NIPS-98*.

[12] H. P. Moravec. Sensor fusion in certainty grids for mobile robots. *AI Magazine*, 9(2):61–74, 1988.

[13] K. Murphy. Bayesian map learning in dynamic environments. *NIPS-99*.

[14] K. Murphy and S. Russell. Rao-blackwellized particle filtering for dynamic bayesian networks. In *Sequential Monte Carlo Methods in Practice*, Springer, 2001.

[15] P. Newman. *On the Structure and Solution of the Simultaneous Localisation and Map Building Problem*. PhD thesis, Univ. of Sydney, 2000.

[16] R. Smith, M. Self, and P. Cheeseman. Estimating uncertain spatial relationships in robotics. In *Autonomous Robot Vehnicles*, Springer, 1990.

[17] C. Thorpe and H. Durrant-Whyte. Field robots. *ISRR-2001*.

[18] S. Thrun, D. Fox, and W. Burgard. A probabilistic approach to concurrent mapping and localization for mobile robots. *Machine Learning*, 31, 1998.

Watch their Moves:
Applying Probabilistic Multiple Object Tracking to Autonomous Robot Soccer

Thorsten Schmitt, Michael Beetz, Robert Hanek, and Sebastian Buck
Munich University of Technology,
Department of Computer Science,
D-80290 Muenchen
{schmittt,beetzm,hanek,buck}@in.tum.de

Abstract

In many autonomous robot applications robots must be capable of estimating the positions and motions of moving objects in their environments. In this paper, we apply probabilistic multiple object tracking to estimating the positions of opponent players in autonomous robot soccer. We extend an existing tracking algorithm to handle multiple mobile sensors with uncertain positions, discuss the specification of probabilistic models needed by the algorithm, and describe the required vision-interpretation algorithms. The multiple object tracking has been successfully applied throughout the RoboCup 2001 world championship.

Introduction

In many autonomous robot applications robots must be capable of estimating the positions and motions of moving objects in their environments. Autonomous cars driving on a highway, for example, must know where the other cars are and what they do (Dickmanns 1997). Robots navigating through crowded regions must keep track of the individual persons (Thrun *et al.* 2000). Autonomous robots playing soccer must know where their opponents are in order to make the right moves and plays (Beetz *et al.* 2002).

In most cases, the robots employ specific state estimation algorithms for keeping track of the moving objects in their environments. For various reasons, these kinds of tracking systems are difficult to realize. Observations of the robots are inaccurate and incomplete. Sometimes the sensors hallucinate objects. Often the robots cannot perceptually distinguish the individual objects in their environments. To reliably estimate the positions and motions of the objects despite these perturbations, researchers have proposed multi object tracking algorithms. Tracking algorithms use motion models of the objects and sequences of observation to distinguish real object observations from clutter and can thereby keep track of object positions both more reliably and more accurately.

Some of the most successful approaches to the multi object tracking problem are probabilistic tracking algorithms, such as Multiple Hypothesis Tracking (MHT) (Reid 1979; Cox & Hingorani 1996) and Joint Probabilistic Data Association Filter (JPDAF) (Bar-Shalom & Fortmann 1988;

Schulz *et al.* 2001). Using probabilistic motion and sensing models these algorithms maintain probabilistic estimates of the objects' positions and update these estimates with each new observation. Probabilistic tracking algorithms are attractive because they are concise, elegant, well understood, and remarkably robust.

In this paper, we apply MHT, one of the probabilistic tracking algorithms introduced above, to estimating the positions of opponent players in autonomous robot soccer based on image data. In robot soccer (middle-size league) two teams of four autonomous robots play soccer against each other. The tracking problem in autonomous robot soccer confronts probabilistic tracking methods with a unique combination of difficult challenges. The state is to be estimated by multiple mobile sensors with uncertain positions, the soccer field is only partly visible for each sensor, occlusion of robots is a problem, the robots change their direction and speed very abruptly, and the models of the dynamic states of the robots of the other team are very crude and uncertain.

In this paper we show how the MHT algorithm can be applied to opponent tracking in autonomous robot soccer. This application requires programmers to equip the robots with sophisticated mechanisms for observing the required information, and to provide probabilistic domain descriptions that the algorithm needs for successful operation. These probabilistic descriptions include motion models and sensing models, such as the probability of the robot detecting an object within sensor range. We show that such mechanisms enable the MHT to reliably and accurately estimate the positions of opponent robots using passive vision-based perception where the cameras have a very restricted field of view. In addition, we will show that the cooperation between robots provides the robots with a more complete estimate of the world state, a substantial speed up in the detection of motions, and more accurate position estimates.

In the remainder of the paper we proceed as follows. The next section describes the MHT algorithm. In the subsequent section we provide a detailed account of how to apply the MHT to autonomous robot soccer. Then we discuss how good parameter settings for autonomous robot soccer can be found and how cooperation between the robots can be exploited to obtain better performance. We conclude with a discussion of these findings and a discussion of related work.

Multiple Hypothesis Tracking

Multiple hypothesis tracking considers the following state estimation problem. The world is populated with a set of stationary and moving objects. The number of objects may vary and they might be occluded and out of sensor range. Robots are equipped with sensing routines that are capable of detecting objects within sensor range, of estimating the positions of the detected objects, and of assessing the accuracy of their estimate.

The objective of the MHT algorithm is to keep a set of object hypotheses, each describing a unique real object and its position, to maintain the set of hypotheses over time, and to estimate the likelihood of the individual hypotheses.

The basic data structure used by the MHT algorithm is the object hypothesis. An object hypothesis consists of an estimated position, orientation, and velocity of an object, a measure of uncertainty associated with the estimation, and a second measure that represents the degree of belief that this hypothesis accurately reflects an existing object. Because the number of objects might vary new hypotheses might have to be added and old ones might have to be deleted.

Before we dive into the details of the MHT algorithm let us first get an intuition of how it works. The MHT algorithm maintains a forest of object hypotheses, that is a set of trees. The nodes in the forest are object hypotheses and represent the association of an observed object with an existing object hypothesis. Each hypothesis has an association probability, which indicates the likelihood that observed object and object hypothesis refer to the same object. In order to determine this probability the motion model is applied to the object hypothesis of the previous iteration, in order to predict where the object will be now. Then the association probability is computed by weighing the distance between the predicted and the observed object position. Thus in every iteration of the algorithm each observation is associated with each existing object hypothesis.

The MHT Algorithm

Our MHT algorithm is an extension of Reid's algorithm (Reid 1979). It extends Reid's version in that it can handle multiple mobile sensors with uncertain positions. The computational structure of the algorithm is shown in Fig. 1.

An iteration begins with the set of hypotheses of object states $H^k = \{h_1^k, \ldots, h_m^k\}$ from the previous iteration k. Each h_i^k is a random variable ranging over the state space of a single object and represents a different assignment of measurements to objects, which was performed in the past. The algorithm maintains a Kalman filter for each hypothesis.

With the arrival of new sensor data (6), $Z(k+1) = \{z_1(k+1), \ldots, z_{n_{k+1}}(k+1)\}$, the motion model (7) is applied to each hypothesis and intermediate hypotheses $\widehat{h}_i^{k+1}$ are predicted. Assignments of measurements to objects (10) are accomplished on the basis of a statistical distance measurement, such as the Mahalanobis distance. Each subsequent child hypothesis represents one possible interpretation of the set of observed objects and, together with its parent hypothesis, represents one possible interpretation of all past observations. With every iteration of the MHT probabilities

---

algorithm MULTIPLEHYPOTHESISTRACKING()

```
1    let Ĥᵏ = {ĥ₁ᵏ,...,ĥ_{mₖ}ᵏ}   % pred.hypos.
2        Z(k) = {z₁(k),...,z_{nₖ}(k)}   % ob.feat.
3        Hᵏ = {h₁ᵏ,...,h_{oₖ}ᵏ}   % new hypos.
4        Xᵏ⁻ᴺ   % world state at time k-N.
5    do for k ← 1 to ∞
6        do Z(k) ← INTERPRETSENSORDATA();
7           Ĥᵏ ← APPLYMOTIONMODEL(Hᵏ⁻¹, M);
8           for i ← 1 to nₖ
9           do for j ← 1 to mₖ
10             do hᵢⱼᵏ ← ASSOCIATE(ĥⱼᵏ, zᵢ(k));
11                COMPUTE(P(hᵢⱼᵏ|Z(k)))
12          for j ← 1 to nₖ
13          do Hᵏ ← Hᵏ ∪ {GENERNEWHYP(zⱼ(k))};
14          PRUNEHYPOTHESIS(Hᵏ);
15          Xᵏ⁻ᴺ ← {x₁ᵏ⁻ᴺ,...,x_{o_{k-N}}ᵏ⁻ᴺ}
```

Figure 1: The multiple hypothesis tracking algorithm.

---

(11) describing the validity of an hypothesis are calculated. Furthermore for every observed object an new hypothesis with associated probability is created (13).

In order to constrain the growth of the hypothesis trees the algorithm prunes improbable branches (14). Pruning is based on a combination of ratio pruning, i.e. a simple lower limit on the ratio of the probabilities of the current and best hypotheses, and the N-scan-back algorithm (Reid 1979). This algorithm assumes that any ambiguity at time k is resolved by time $k + N$. Consequently if at time k hypothesis h_i^{k-1} has m children, the sum of the probabilities of the leaf notes of each branch is calculated. The branch with the greatest probability is retained and the others are discarded. After pruning the world state of X^{k-N} can be extracted (15). Please note that this world state is always N steps delayed behind the latest observations. However, in the Application section we will demonstrate that this delay can be overcome by N observers performing observations in parallel.

Computing the Likelihood of Hypotheses

Obviously, the heart of the MHT algorithm is the computation of the likelihood of the different hypothesis-observation associations, $P(h_{ij}^{k+1}|Z(k))$, in line 11 of the algorithm in figure 1. In this section we derive the formula that is used in order to compute this probability. The derivation of this formula is critical because it tells us which probabilities must be specified by programmers in order to apply the algorithm to specific applications.

Let Z^k be the sequence of all measurements up to time k. A new hypothesis of an object at time k is made up of the current set of assignments (also called an event), $\theta(k)$, and a previous state of this hypothesis, h_j^{k-1}, based on observed features up to time step $k - 1$ inclusively.

We can transform the probability of an object's hypothesis $P(h_i^t|Z^k)$ using Bayes' rule and the Markov assumption in

---

order to obtain an easier expression.

$$P(h_i^k|Z^k) = P(\theta(k), h_i^{k-1}|Z(k), Z^{k-1}) \qquad (1)$$
$$= P(\theta(k), h_i^{k-1}|Z(k), H^k) \qquad (2)$$
$$= \alpha * p(Z(k)|\theta(k), h_j^{k-1}, Z^{k-1}) \qquad (3)$$
$$P(\theta(k)|h_j^{k-1}, Z^{k-1})P(h_j^{k-1}|Z^{k-1})$$

Here α is a normalization factor ensuring that $P(h_i^k|Z^k)$ sums up to one over all h_i^k. The last term of this equation is probability of the parent global hypothesis that has been computed in the previous iteration. The second factor can be evaluated as follows (Bar-Shalom & Fortmann 1988):

$$P(\theta(k)|h_j^{k-1}, Z^{k-1}) = \frac{\phi!\nu!}{m_k!}\mu_F(\phi)\mu_N(\nu) \qquad (4)$$
$$\prod_t (P_D^t)^{\delta_t}(1-P_D^t)^{1-\delta_t}(P_T^t)^{\tau_t}(1-P_T^t)^{1-\tau_t}$$

where $\mu_F(\phi)$ and $\mu_N(\nu)$ are prior probability mass functions of the number of spurious measurements and new geometric features. P_D^t and P_T^t are the probabilities of detection and termination of track t (originating from hypothesis h_t^{k-1}) and δ_t and τ_t are indicator variables. δ_t (τ_t) is 1, if track t is detected (deleted) at time k and 0 otherwise. The indicator variable δ_t depends on the observing robots camera orientation. It is 1, if the track t is within the sensors field of perception and track t is not occluded by another team mate. $P_T^{\tau_t}$ is used to model the declination of an unobserved hypothesis probability over time. It is defined as $P_T^{\tau_t} = 1 - e^{-\frac{\Delta k}{\lambda_T}}$. Δk is the number of consecutive time steps an hypothesis was not observed. λ_T determines the speed of the declination process. Larger λ_T result in a slower declination of the hypothesis probability.

The first term on the right hand side of equation 3 denotes the association probability of a measurement and an hypothesis. In order to determine this term is is assumed that a measurement z_i^k has a Gaussian probability density function if it is associated with object t_i.

$$N_{t_i}(z_i(k)) = N_{t_i}(z_i(k), \widehat{h}_i^k, S_{t_i}^k) = \qquad (5)$$
$$|2\pi S_{t_i}^k|^{-\frac{1}{2}}e^{-\frac{1}{2}\{(z(k)-\widehat{h}_i^k)^T\{S_{t_i}^k\}^{-1}(z(k)-\widehat{h}_i^k))\}}$$

Here $\widehat{h}_i^k$ denotes the predicted measurement for hypothesis t_i and $S_{t_i}^k$ is the associated innovation covariance. The probability of a new object and a spurious measurement are taken to be uniformly distributed over the observation volume V. In our implementation the observation volume V is the intersection of the field of view (neglecting occlusions) and the soccer field. Thus V is a function of the robot's pose estimate and the camera's field of view.

$$p(Z(k)|\theta(k), h_j^{k-1}, Z^{k-1}) = \prod_i^{m_k}[N_{t_i}(z_i(k))]^{\kappa_i}V^{-(1-\kappa_i)} \qquad (6)$$

ϕ and ν are the total numbers of false alarms and new geometric features, respectively and κ_i is another indicator variable which is 1, if $z_i(k)$ came from a known track and 0 otherwise.

Applying MHT to Autonomous Robot Soccer

Robotic soccer has become a standard "real-world" testbed for autonomous multi robot control. In robot soccer (mid-size league) two teams of four autonomous robots — one goal keeper and three field players — play soccer against each other. The soccer field is four by nine meters big surrounded by walls. The key characteristics of mid-size robot soccer is that the robots are completely autonomous. Consequently, all sensing and all action selection is done on board of the individual robots. Skillful play requires our robots to recognize objects, such as other robots, field lines, and goals, and even entire game situations.

The AGILO RoboCup team consists of four Pioneer I robots; one of them is depicted in Fig. 1(a). The robot is equipped with a single on board linux computer (2), a wireless Ethernet (1) for communication, and several sonar sensors (4) for collision avoidance. A color CCD camera with an opening angle of 90° (3) is mounted fix on the robot. The robot also has a dribbling (5) and a kicking device (6) that enable the robot to dribble and shoot the ball. Autonomous robot soccer confronts object tracking mecha-

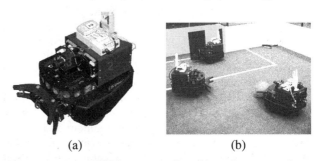

    (a)   (b)

Figure 2: An AGILO soccer robot (a) and a game situation (b).

nisms with challenging research problems. The camera system with an opening angle of 90° and pointed to the front gives an individual robot only a very restricted view of the game situation. Therefore, the robot needs to cooperate to get a more complete picture of the game situation. Vibrations of the camera, spot light effects, and poor lighting conditions cause substantial inaccuracies. Even small vibrations that cause jumps of only two or three pixel lines cause deviations of more than half a meter in the depth estimation, if the objects are several meters away. The opponent robots change their speed and moving directions very quickly and therefore an iteration of the tracking algorithm has to be very fast such that the inaccuracies of the motion model does not have such a huge effect.

Sensor Data Interpretation for Robot Soccer

Let us first look at the sensor data interpretation process for tracking in robot soccer. The information needed for object tracking is provided by the perception system and includes the following kinds of information: (1) partial state estimates broadcasted by other robots, (2) feature maps extracted from captured images, and (3) odometric information. The estimates broadcasted by the team mates comprise the respective robot's location and the locations of the oppo-

Figure 3: The figure shows an image captured by the robot and the feature map that is computed for self, ball, and opponent localization.

nents. From the captured camera images the feature detectors extract problem-specific feature maps that correspond to (1) static objects in the environment including the goal, the borders of the field, and the lines on the field, (2) a color blob corresponding to the ball, and (3) the visual features of the opponents. The working horse of the perception component are a color classification and segmentation algorithm that is used to segment a captured image into colored regions and blobs (see Fig. 3). The color classifier is learned in a training session before tournaments in order to adapt the vision system to specific lighting conditions and effects. We are currently working on the next version of the classifier, which will be capable of automatically adjusting itself to changing lighting conditions during the game.

The color segmented image is then processed by a feature extraction algorithm that estimates the 3D positions Ψ and the covariances C_ψ of the objects of interest. At present it is assumed that the objects are colored black, constructed in the same way and have approximately circular shape. Object detection is performed on the basis of blob analysis. The position of an object is estimated on the basis of a pinhole camera model. Due to rotations and radial distortions of the lenses this model is highly non-linear. The uncertainty estimation process is based on the unscented transformation (Julier & Uhlmann 1997). This allows the use of non-linear measurement equations, the incorporation of parameters describing the measurement uncertainty of the sensor at hand as well as an efficient way of propagating the uncertainty of the observing robots pose. A detailed description of the feature extraction algorithm and uncertainty estimation process can be found in (Schmitt *et al.* 2001).

Implementation and Parameter Selection

Every robot of the soccer team is equipped with its own computer (Pentium III 500 MHz). On this computer several processes are running in order to perform the image processing, path planning, action selection and object tracking. Currently every robot processes approx. 15 frames per second. From every frame a set of opponent observations is

extracted and sent via a wireless Ethernet to all other robots of the team. Every robot iterates the MHT algorithm once for every set of opponent observations (own and team mates) and generates a new world state. This state serves as input for action selection and path planning.

In the following we will discuss the remaining parameters of the MHT algorithm. The probability of detection P_D represents the probability that a track is detected by an observing robot, if it is within it's field of view. Special image interpretation routines handle the case of partially occluded objects by detecting and analyzing cascaded object blobs. Later in section "Predictive Models" we will look at the issue of providing a more informative probabilistic model for P_D. During the experiments in section "Results from the RoboCup" we have set P_D to 0.9.

By default we set the termination likelihood λ_T to 40. This allows an unconfirmed hypothesis to survive for approx. 2 seconds. Remembering objects that are currently not visible is important to avoid collisions and thereby reduce the risks of being charged for fouls. The mean rates of false observations λ_F and new tracks λ_N are 0.0002 and 0.04 respectively. This means that no observations are ignored. The depth N of the tracking tree is set to four. This is the minimal depth that allows each team mate to contribute an observation to the hypothesis fusion process. The empirical investigations will show that the update-times of the MHT within our application domain are fast enough to handle the observations of all four robots. Thus the first set of global hypotheses, after the initialization of the MHT, is already created after every robot has performed only one local opponent observation. Since these observations are performed in parallel and integrated through the MHT in real time (before the next opponent observations are performed) a depth of four contributes sustainable to the quality of the global opponent hypotheses. The maximum number of hypothesis was limited to 50 and the value for ratio pruning was set to 0.001.

Empirical Investigation

The multiple object tracking algorithm described in this paper has been employed by our AGILO robot soccer team in the fifth robot soccer world championship in Seattle (2001). The team has played six games for a total of about 120 minutes. The team advanced to the quarter finals. Unfortunately, in middle size robot soccer there is no external sensing device which records a global view of the game and can be used as the ground truth for experiments. Thus for the experimental results in this section we can only use the subjective information of our robots and argue for the plausibility of their behavior and belief states. To do so, we have written log files and recorded the games using video cameras in order to evaluate our algorithm.

Results from the RoboCup

The analysis of the log files from RoboCup 2001, revealed that an average MHT update takes between 6 to 7 msecs. This allows our implementation to process all observations of all robots (max. frame rate: 25Hz) in real time. The minimum and maximum iteration times were measured to be

1.1 msecs and 86 msecs respectively. On average the MHT tracked 3.2 opponents. This is a reasonable number since there are maximal 4 opponent players and players can be send off or have to be rebooted off field. In breaks of the games (when people get on to the field) or when there are crowds of robots the MHT successfully tracked up to 11 objects. A typical result of the AGILO game state estimator is

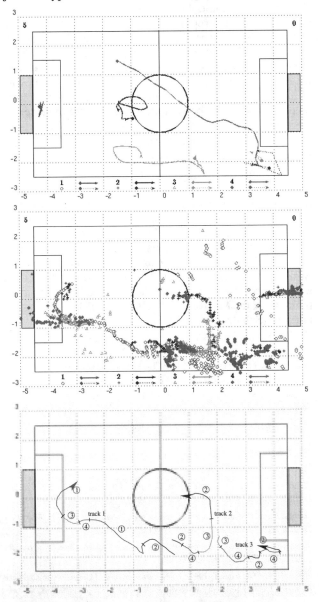

Figure 4: Opponent observations and resolved tracks.

shown in Fig. 4. The upper picture shows the positions of the AGILO players of the own team, computed through vision-based self localization (Hanek & Schmitt 2000). The middle picture shows the individual observations of the opponent robots. The tokens indicate which AGILO robot made the observations. It is good visible how the individual observations of the different robots are merged into a consistent track. In the lower picture the tracks as they were resolved by the MHT are displayed. They are divided into subsec-

tions. The number of the robot that contributed the most observations to this part of the track is denoted next to the track.

Qualitatively, we can estimate the accuracy of the game state estimation by looking for the jumps in the tracked lines. The tracks of the opponents look very reasonable. They are less accurate and sometimes only partial. This is due to the high inaccuracy and incompleteness of the sensory data. However, it is observable that several tracks resulted from merging the observations of different robots. In addition, the merging of the different observations results in fewer hallucinated obstacles and therefore allows for more efficient navigation paths. Several wrong opponent observations made by the goal keeper (1) were correctly omitted by the MHT and not assigned to a track. We have cross checked the tracks computed by the algorithm using video sequences recorded during the matches. The tracks are qualitatively correct and seem to be accurate. A more thorough evaluation is only possibly based on the ground truth for the situations. We are currently implementing tracking software for a camera mounted above the field that allows us to compute the ground truth for the next RoboCup championship.

The cooperation of the different robots increases both, the completeness and the accuracy of state estimation. Accuracy can be substantially increased by fusing the observations of different robots because the depth estimate of positions are much more inaccurate than the lateral positions in the image. This can be accomplished through the Kalman filter's property to optimally fuse observations from different robots into global hypotheses with smaller covariances.

The completeness of state estimation can be increased because all the robots can see only parts of the field and can be complemented with observations of the team mates. The other effect we observed was that cooperation allowed to maintain the identity of opponent players over an extended period of time, even though the field of view of the observing robots is limited. This point is well illustrated in Fig. 4. The three opponent field players were tracked successfully over a period of 30 seconds.

A Predictive Model for the Use of Observations

In section "Applying MHT to Robot Soccer" we have assumed that the probabilities needed as parameters by the MHT can be simply supplied by the programmer. In this section we want to take a more thorough look at this issue. The first characteristic of our parameterization is that we have provided the different parameters as a priori probabilities. This does not match our intuitions because we would expect, for example, that observations of the robots are much more inaccurate and unreliable in situations where the robot turns quickly, mainly because of time delays between capturing the camera image and taking odometric readings.

To test this hypothesis we first defined a set of features which we expected to influence the quality of observations, and then learned a decision tree[1] in order to predict whether

---

[1]Given a feature language and a set of examples Quinlan's C4.5 is capable of devising a set of rules of the form if $f_1 \wedge \ldots \wedge f_2$ then $class$.

an observation made in a given context can be expected to be reliable and accurate. Again the lack of ground truth is hampering a thorough investigation of this issue. Therefore we used a much weaker notion than reliability and accuracy. We take as the concept to be learned whether the observation can be expected to contribute to a long track or not. We chose this concept under the assumption that, if an observation can be assigned to a long and well established track, then it must have features identifying it as a good observation.

In order to describe an observation the following feature language $F = \{R, T, V, W, O, D, U\}$ was used. R specifies the number of the observing robot. The observation type, T, describes whether an observation is an unknown robot, an opponent robot and a cascaded robot. V and W are continuous features representing the translational and rotational velocities of the observing robot. The observational angle O, and the distance D describe the relative polar coordinates of an observation within the field of view. The continuous feature U represented the area of the covariance ellipse of an observation. These features were computed for every observation and an off-line run of the MHT filter with hypothesis trees of depth $N = 20$ generated positive and negative training examples. We then applied C4.5 to this set, which derived the following rules:

if $W \leq 41$ **then** *use observation for* MHT
if $W > 41 \wedge D > 2.4$ **then** *use observation for* MHT
if $W > 41 \wedge D < 2.4$ **then** *discard observation*

The rules state that an observation of an object closer than 2.4 meters performed by an robot rotating with more than 41 degrees per second should be discarded. This rule is reasonable as the image processing routines are computational expensive and observations of close objects with high rotational velocities are errors-prone. All other features, except D and W, were omitted by C4.5 and were not included in the decision rules.

This is a strong indication that the only features influencing the quality of an observation are D and W. One rationale for this is, that all robots are equipped with identical sensors. Furthermore, these results indicate that the performance of the algorithm can be greatly improved by substituting the a priori probabilities through probabilities conditioned on the context of observations. To obtain these probabilities we need more accurate sensing models. These can be learned by using the camera providing the ground truth and computing the probability distributions over observations based on experiences acquired in the soccer games.

Related Work

Related work comprises work done on object tracking in the robot soccer domain and probabilistic and vision-based tracking of moving targets. To the best of our knowledge no probabilistic state estimation method has been proposed for tracking the opponent robots in robot soccer or similar application domains. Dietl, Guttmann and Nebel 2001 estimate the positions of the opponents and store them in the team world model but they do not probabilistically integrate the different pieces of information. Probabilistic tracking of multiple moving objects has been proposed by(Schulz *et al.*

2001). They apply sample-based JPDAF estimation to the tracking of moving people with a moving robot using laser range data. The required computational power for the particle filters is opposed by the heuristic based pruning strategies of the MHT algorithm. Hue et al. 2000 are also tracking multiple objects with particle filters. In their work data association is performed on the basis of the Gibbs sampler. Our approach to multiple hypothesis tracking is most closely related to the one proposed by Cox and Hingorani (Cox & Hingorani 1996). Indeed our algorithm is based on their implementation. We extend their work on multiple hypothesis tracking in that we apply the method to a much more challenging application domain where we have multiple moving observers with uncertain positions. In addition, we perform object tracking at an object rather than on a feature level.

Conclusions

In this paper, we have extended and analyzed a probabilistic object tracking algorithm for a team of vision-based autonomously moving robots. Our results suggest that purely image-based probabilistic estimation of complex game states is feasible in real time even in complex and fast changing environments. Finally, we have seen how the state estimation modules of individual robots can cooperate in order to produce more accurate and reliable state estimation. Besides an empirical analysis of the parameter settings and learning accurate sensing models, we intend to compare in future work the MHT algorithm with the JPDAF implementation of (Schulz *et al.* 2001).

References

Bar-Shalom, Y., and Fortmann, T. 1988. Tracking and data association. Ac. Press.

Beetz, M.; Buck, S.; Hanek, R.; Schmitt, T.; and Radig, B. 2002. The AGILO autonomous robot soccer team: Computational principles, experiences, and perspectives. In *AAMAS*

Cox, I., and Hingorani, S. 1996. An Efficient Implementation of Reid's Multiple Hypothesis Tracking Algorithm and Its Evaluation for the Purpose of Visual Tracking. *IEEE PAMI* 18(2):138–150.

Dickmanns, E. D. 1997. Vehicles capable of dynamic vision. In *IJCAI*, 1577–1592.

Dietl, M.; Gutmann, J.-S.; and Nebel, B. 2001. Cooperative sensing in dynamic environments. In *IROS*, 1706–1713.

Hanek, R., and Schmitt, T. 2000. Vision-based localization and data fusion in a system of cooperating mobile robots. In *IROS*, 1199–1204.

Hue, C.; Le Cadre, J.-P.; and Perez, P. 2000. Tracking multiple objects with particle filtering. Technical Report 1361, IRISA.

Julier, S., and Uhlmann, J. 1997. A new extension of the kalman filter to nonlinear systems. The 11th Int. Symp. on Aerospace/Defence Sensing, Simulation

Reid, D. 1979. An algorithm for tracking multiple targets. IEEE Trans. on Automatic Control, 24(6):843–854.

Schmitt, T.; Hanek, R.; Buck, S.; and Beetz, M. 2001. Cooperative probabilistic state estimation for vision-based autonomous mobile robots. In *IROS*, 1630–1638.

Schulz, D.; Burgard, W.; Fox, D.; and Cremers, A. 2001. Multiple object tracking with a mobile robot. In *CVPR*, 371–377.

Thrun, S.; Beetz, M.; Bennewitz, M.; Cremers, A.; Dellaert, F.; Fox, D.; Hähnel, D.; Rosenberg, C.; Roy, N.; Schulte, J.; and Schulz, D. 2000. Probabilistic algorithms and the interactive museum tour-guide robot minerva. *International Journal of Robotics Research* 19(11):972–999.

CD*: A Real-time Resolution Optimal Re-planner for Globally Constrained Problems

Anthony Stentz

Robotics Institute, Carnegie Mellon University
Pittsburgh, PA 15213
tony@cmu.edu

Abstract

Many problems in robotics and AI, such as the find-path problem, call for optimal solutions that satisfy global constraints. The problem is complicated when the cost information is unknown, uncertain, or changing during execution of the solution. Such problems call for efficient re-planning during execution to account for the new information acquired. This paper presents a novel real-time algorithm, Constrained D* (CD*), that re-plans resolution optimal solutions subject to a global constraint. CD* performs a binary search on a weight parameter that sets the balance between the optimality and feasibility cost metrics. In each stage of the search, CD* uses Dynamic A* (D*) to update the weight selection for that stage. On average, CD* updates a feasible and resolution optimal plan in less than a second, enabling it to be used in a real-time robot controller. Results are presented for simulated problems. To the author's knowledge, CD* is the fastest algorithm to solve this class of problems.

Introduction

Many problems in robotics and AI call for optimal solutions, for instance, the find-path problem for manipulators and mobile robots, automated component assembly, job shop scheduling, reinforcement learning, and others. The optimization problem can be cast as minimizing or maximizing some objective function, such as distance travelled, time elapsed, energy consumed, jobs processed, information gained, and error between predicted and observed data. Often, the set of feasible solutions is limited by one or more constraints, which can be local or global. A local constraint can be evaluated at a single step in the solution, such as the constraint that a mobile robot must avoid all obstacles in the find-path problem. A global constraint applies to the entire solution, or at least a large portion of it, such as the constraint that a mobile robot must reach its goal before exhausting its battery.

For example, consider a variant of the find-path problem. A mobile robot is tasked with finding the stealthiest obstacle-free path to the goal. A "stealthy path" is one that moves along the perimeter of obstacles to minimize visibility. Additionally, the robot must reach the goal before exhausting its battery. To optimize its objective function,

the robot favors paths that hop from obstacle to obstacle and avoid cutting across open areas. But these longer paths are precisely the ones that are likely to violate the global energy constraint.

Assuming a feasible and optimal solution can be produced, it may need to be modified as the "plan" is executed. In the example given, the mobile robot may detect unknown obstacles enroute, requiring it to re-plan part or all of the remaining path to the goal. Re-planning from scratch for each such occurrence can be impractical if the planning time is long.

Exhaustive search can be used to find an optimal solution by enumerating and evaluating the possibilities. Local constraints are trivial to handle, but global constraints are more problematic. Another variable or dimension can be added to the search space that tracks each global constraint and prunes the search when one is violated, but this approach can dramatically increase the complexity of the search. While exhaustive search may be acceptable for the initial, off-line plan, it is generally unacceptable for re-planning during execution, since ideally the robot waits for the re-planner to complete before proceeding.

The most comprehensive and formal treatment of the problem in the AI literature is Logan's ABC algorithm (Logan 1998). ABC is a generalized A* search capable of handling multiple global constraints of a variety of forms. For a limited class of these constraints, the algorithm is both optimal and complete. Given that constraints are tracked in each state and non-dominated paths are retained, we expect ABC to exhibit the same complexity problems as the exhaustive search described above, since the problem is NP-complete (Garey and Johnson 1979). The results presented are for a small planning space with two constraints and no run times are provided.

A similar problem, called Quality of Service (QoS), is addressed in the communications and network literature. QoS addresses the problem of shortest-path routing through a data network subject to constraints like bandwidth, delay, and jitter. In most cases, the costs are additive and the constraints are inequalities. The A*Prune algorithm (Liu and Ramakrishnan 2001) solves the QoS problem and is optimal and complete, but it also exhibits exponential growth. To circumvent the complexity of exact solutions, the QoS literature is replete with polynomial algorithms for producing approximate solutions (Jaffe 1984) (Hassin 1992) (Korkmaz et al. 2000) (Korkmaz and Krunz 2001).

Noticeably absent from the literature is a computationally efficient *re-planner* for globally constrained problems with unknown, uncertain, or changing cost data. The problem of real-time, optimal re-planning was first addressed by Stentz (Stentz 1994) (Stentz 1995) with the D* (Dynamic A*) algorithm. D* produces an initial plan using known, assumed, and/or estimated cost data, commences execution of the plan, and then rapidly re-plans enroute each time new cost information arrives. By itself, D* optimizes a single cost metric and does not offer an efficient way to optimize globally constrained problems.

This paper introduces the CD* (Constrained D*) algorithm, which produces a resolution-optimal solution for problems with a global constraint. We begin by developing CA* (Constrained A*), an efficient, resolution optimal planner similar to Korkmaz's work in QoS (Korkmaz et al. 2000). We then transform CA* into CD* to make an efficient re-planner, prove its correctness, and measure its speed through experiments in simulation.

Algorithm Descriptions

The Constrained D* (CD*) algorithm is a computationally efficient planning and re-planning algorithm. CD* realizes this efficiency by avoiding the addition of dimensions to the search space to handle a global constraint; instead, the algorithm incorporates the constraint in the objective function itself. The constraint is multiplied by a weight, which the algorithm adjusts using a binary search algorithm. The search problem is solved end to end multiple times, with CD* adjusting the weight from one iteration to the next to converge to an optimal solution that satisfies the global constraint.

To plan in real time, CD* saves each stage of the binary search process. When new information arrives during execution, CD* repairs the first stage. If the weight selection for the second stage is unchanged, CD* repairs the stage and continues. CD* re-plans from scratch at stage i only when stage $i-1$ selects a different weight. In practice, this occurs infrequently and is the basis for CD*'s speed. We start by introducing CA*, an efficient algorithm capable of finding a resolution optimal solution that satisfies the global constraint, then we show how this algorithm can be modified to efficiently re-plan (CD*).

The Constrained A* Algorithm

Let $f_0(°)$ be the objective function to optimize, and let $f_1(°)$ be the global constraint to satisfy. Without a loss of generality, assume that $f_0(°)$ is optimized when it is minimized. Assume that $f_1(°)$ is satisfied when its value is less than or equal to some constant K. Both functions are defined across candidate solutions to the problem, X. For the example given in the introduction, X is a path (sequence of grid cells) leading from the goal state to the start state in a two-dimensional grid, $f_0(°)$ is the sum of the visibility costs along X, and $f_1(°)$ is the required energy to reach the goal along X.

The objective for CA* is to find the X that minimizes $f_0(°)$ such that $f_1(X) \leq K$. To do this, CA* minimizes a composite function $f(°)$ with the following form:

Equation 1: $f(X, w) = f_0(X) + wf_1(X)$

where w is a non-negative weight that sets the balance between minimizing the objective function and satisfying the global constraint. CA* picks an initial value for w and minimizes $f(°)$. If the global constraint is violated (i.e., $f_1(X) > K$) then CA* increases w to steer the solution away from those states that violate the constraint, and re-starts the search to minimize $f(°)$ again. If the global constraint is satisfied (i.e., $f_1(X) \leq K$), then CA* reduces w to find a lower value for $f_0(°)$ that still satisfies the constraint. The algorithm repeats until it finds a value for w that is just large enough to avoid violating the global constraint. The corresponding X and $f_0(°)$ are the optimal solution and optimal cost, respectively, that satisfy the constraint.

To minimize the number of iterations required to find the appropriate w, CA* uses binary search. If $f(°)$ is a dynamic programming function (see next section), then A* can be used to find the optimal X. The notation $X = A^*(f(°), w, G)$ means that A* is called on a graph G and returns the optimal X for a given objective function $f(°)$ and weight value w (*NOPATH* is returned if no solution exists). N is the number of stages in the binary search, and (w_{min}, w_{max}) is a pair of weights that bracket the optimal, constrained solution. The complete algorithm is given below:

L1 $X \leftarrow CA^*(f(°), K, w_{min}, w_{max}, N, G)$:
L2 $\quad X_{min} \leftarrow \varnothing$; $X_{max} \leftarrow \varnothing$
L3 $\quad$ for $i \leftarrow 1$ to $N-1$
L4 $\quad\quad w \leftarrow (w_{max} + w_{min})/2$
L5 $\quad\quad X \leftarrow A^*(f(°), w, G)$
L6 $\quad\quad$ if $X = NOPATH$ then return $NOPATH$
L7 $\quad\quad$ if $f_1(X) \leq K$ then
L8 $\quad\quad\quad w_{max} \leftarrow w$; $X_{max} \leftarrow X$
L9 $\quad\quad$ else
L10 $\quad\quad\quad w_{min} \leftarrow w$; $X_{min} \leftarrow X$
L11 $\quad$ if $X_{min} = \varnothing$ then
L12 $\quad\quad X_{min} \leftarrow A^*(f(°), w_{min}, G)$
L13 $\quad$ if $X_{min} = NOPATH$ then return $NOPATH$
L14 $\quad$ if $f_1(X_{min}) \leq K$ then return $HIGHRANGE$
L15 $\quad$ if $X_{max} = \varnothing$ then
L16 $\quad\quad X_{max} \leftarrow A^*(f(°), w_{max}, G)$
L17 $\quad$ if $f_1(X_{max}) > K$ then return $LOWRANGE$
L18 $\quad$ return X_{max}
L19 end

The CA* algorithm finds the optimal solution for objective function that satisfies the global constraint to within a weight error of $(w_{max} - w_{min})/2^{N-1}$. If w_{max} is too small, CA* returns *LOWRANGE*. If w_{min} is too large, CA* returns

HIGHRANGE. For such cases, the algorithm can be run again with an adjusted weight range.

The Constrained D* Algorithm

The problem with CA* is that it must re-plan from scratch whenever a new piece of cost information arrives (i.e., G changes). For example, a robot may discover that a door is unexpectedly closed, thereby requiring the robot to re-plan the remaining path to the goal. The algorithm D* is very efficient at re-planning whenever new information arrives (Stentz 1995). The notation $(X, G) = D^*(f(\circ), w, G, \Delta)$ means that D* is called on a graph G and returns the optimal X for a given function $f(\circ)$ and weight value w (*NOPATH* is returned if no solution exists). At first invocation, D* runs in time comparable to A*, as it produces the initial, optimal solution. The parameter Δ represents changes to G (e.g., costs or connectivity). Initially, G is set to $\varnothing$ and Δ is set to the entire graph itself. Subsequent calls to D* on G with changes Δ produce a new optimal solution X and an updated graph G which incorporates the changes. This updated solution can be calculated very quickly--it is much faster than calling A* on the modified graph. The difference, however, is in run time only. Both approaches produce the same solution, barring ties. If D* is called with a new weight w, it is equivalent to changing every edge cost in G. Thus, the algorithm must re-plan from scratch, and the run time for that stage is comparable to A*.

The complete algorithm for CD* is given below. CD* is similar to CA*, except that it uses D* instead of A*, and it maintains an array of N graphs $G[1...N]$, one for each weight value w explored by the algorithm. Only the weights differ; the cost and connectivity information for each graph are identical.

L1 $(X, G[1...N]) \leftarrow CD^*(f(\circ), K, w_{min}, w_{max}, N, G[1...N], \Delta)$:
L2 $X_{min} \leftarrow \varnothing$; $X_{max} \leftarrow \varnothing$
L3   for $i \leftarrow 1$ to $N - 1$
L4 $w \leftarrow (w_{max} + w_{min})/2$
L5 $(X, G[i]) \leftarrow D^*(f(\circ), w, G[i], \Delta)$
L6   if $X = NOPATH$ then return *NOPATH*
L7   if $f_1(X) \leq K$ then
L8 $w_{max} \leftarrow w$; $X_{max} \leftarrow X$
L9   else
L10 $w_{min} \leftarrow w$; $X_{min} \leftarrow X$
L11   if $X_{min} = \varnothing$ then
L12 $(X_{min}, G[N]) \leftarrow D^*(f(\circ), w_{min}, G[N], \Delta)$
L13   if $X_{min} = NOPATH$ then return *NOPATH*
L14   if $f_1(X_{min}) \leq K$ then return *HIGHRANGE*
L15   if $X_{max} = \varnothing$ then
L16 $(X_{max}, G[N]) \leftarrow D^*(f(\circ), w_{max}, G[N], \Delta)$
L17   if $f_1(X_{max}) > K$ then return *LOWRANGE*
L18   return $(X_{max}, G[1...N])$
L19 end

Since D* produces equivalent solutions to A*, CD* produces equivalent results to CA*. But is it significantly faster for re-planning? At the first invocation of CD*, the algorithm constructs N graphs, one for each weight investigated. If the graph is to be modified with Δ changes, a subsequent call to CD* will again perform a binary search, incrementally updating each of the N graphs. Provided none of the *weights* change, all N of these incremental updates will be very fast. If the *i-th* weight changes, then D* essentially plans from scratch for graphs i through N. The worst case occurs when the weight changes at position $i = 2$ (it cannot change at $i = 1$). In that case, D* re-plans from scratch for $N - 1$ graphs. This worst case is comparable to calling CA* on the modified graph. As shown in the experimental results section, CD* re-plans its subproblems from scratch infrequently, so that CD* is a significantly faster algorithm than CA* for re-planning.

Proofs of Correctness

Like D*, CD* also operates on a graph, $G = (V, E)$, consisting of vertices V and edges E. We can think of the vertices as states and the edges as *actions* that transition from one state to another. For vertices (states) we use lower case letters, such as x and y. For edges (actions) we use the function $c(Y, X)$, which returns the action costs of moving across the edge from x to y. Capital letters refer to sequences of states $X = \{x_0, x_1, x_2, ..., x\}$. X_i refers to the subsequence $\{x_0, x_1, ..., x_i\}$.

A *path function* $f(\circ)$ is defined to be a function of a sequence X. The function can be specified recursively as $f(X_i) = f(c(X_i, X_{i-1}), f(X_{i-1}))$ and $f(X_0) = 0$. Consider two sequences, X and Y, that share the first state. A path function $f(\circ)$ is defined to be a *dynamic programming (DP) function* if $f^*(X_i) = f(c(X_i, X_{i-1}), f^*(X_{i-1}))$ and if $f(X_i) \geq f(X_{i-1})$ for all X and i. The first condition states the the optimal path for sequence X_i is strictly a function of the optimal sequence to X_{i-1} and the connecting action. The second condition states that $f(\circ)$ is monotonic. In Equation 1, we define $f(\circ)$, $f_0(\circ)$, and $f_1(\circ)$ to be path functions; $f(\circ)$ to be a DP function; and w to be a non-negative weight.

Consider the following definitions that will be used in the theorems below:

Definition 1: Let X_w be the sequence that minimizes $f(X, w)$ in Equation 1. If multiple minimizing sequences exist, X_w is defined to be a sequence that minimizes $f_1(X)$.

Definition 2: Let X_u be the sequence that minimizes $f(X, u)$ in Equation 1. If multiple minimizing sequences exist, X_u is defined to be a sequence that minimizes $f_1(X)$.

The following theorem proves the necessary condition for the binary search to operate, namely that increasing the weight w in Equation 1 drives down the constraint value and drives up the objective function value.

Theorem 1: If $u > w$, then $f_0(X_u) \geq f_0(X_w)$ and $f_1(X_u) \leq f_1(X_w)$.

Proof: we prove the above pair of relationals by disproving the other three possible cases. Case 1: $f_0(X_u) \geq f_0(X_w)$ and $f_1(X_u) > f_1(X_w)$. Then $f_0(X_w) + uf_1(X_w) < f_0(X_u) + uf_1(X_u)$ and Definition 2 is violated. Case 2: $f_0(X_u) < f_0(X_w)$ and $f_1(X_u) \leq f_1(X_w)$. Then $f_0(X_u) + wf_1(X_u) < f_0(X_w) + wf_1(X_w)$ and Definition 1 is violated. Case 3: $f_0(X_u) < f_0(X_w)$ and $f_1(X_u) > f_1(X_w)$. For X_u to be the optimal sequence for $f(X, u)$, then $f_0(X_u) + uf_1(X_u) \leq f_0(X_w) + uf_1(X_w)$. This equation can be rewritten as $f_0(X_w) - f_0(X_u) \geq u(f_1(X_u) - f_1(X_w))$. Since $u > w$, then $u(f_1(X_u) - f_1(X_w)) > w(f_1(X_u) - f_1(X_w))$. Substituting the latter equation into the former, we have $f_0(X_w) - f_0(X_u) > w(f_1(X_u) - f_1(X_w))$. This equation can be rewritten as $f_0(X_u) + wf_1(X_u) < f_0(X_w) + wf_1(X_w)$, which violates Definition 1. The remaining case is $f_0(X_u) \geq f_0(X_w)$ and $f_1(X_u) \leq f_1(X_w)$. QED.

We now prove the correctness of CA*.

Theorem 2: Let W be the set of weights w_i that evenly divides the range $[w_{min}, w_{max}]$ into $2^{N-1} + 1$ weights inclusive (provided $N > 0$ and $w_{min} < w_{max}$). Let X_{wo} be a sequence with the smallest weight w_o such that X_{wo} minimizes $f_0(°)$ and X_{wo} satisfies $f_1(°)$. CA* returns either 1) a sequence X, such that $f_0(X) \leq f_0(X_{wi})$ for all w_i for which $f_1(X_{wi}) \leq K$, if $w_{min} < w_o \leq w_{max}$, 2) *LOWRANGE*, if $w_o > w_{max}$ or X_{wo} does not exist, 3) *HIGHRANGE*, if $w_o \leq w_{min}$, or 4) *NOPATH*, if no path of any measure to the goal exists.

Proof: Let w_k be the smallest threshold weight such that $f_1(X_{wk}) \leq K$. From Theorem 1, increasing the weight w non-decreases $f_0(°)$ and non-increases $f_1(°)$. Therefore, all weights $w < w_k$ are infeasible. Again from Theorem 1, all weights $w \geq w_k$ are feasible, and the smallest such weight has the minimal $f_0(°)$; therefore, $w_k = w_o$ and $X_{wk} = X_{wo}$. CA* evaluates a discrete set of weights. From Theorem 1, it follows directly that the smallest w_i such that $w_i \geq w_k$ minimizes $f_0(°)$ and satisfies $f_1(°)$ across all w_i in W. CA* performs a binary search on w to find the smallest such w_i.

The search converges on w_k and then selects the smallest w_i greater than or equal to w_k after exiting the loop. At each iteration through the loop (L3 through L10), CA* divides the interval between the upper and lower bounds on w_k in half and establishes a new upper or lower bound. The sequences and the weights for both bounds are recorded. The proper lower bound (w_{min}) on w_k must be infeasible, since by Theorem 1 the corresponding sequence must have a larger $f_1(°)$ value than $f_1(X_{wk}) = K$. Similarly, the proper upper bound (w_{max}) on w_k must be feasible. Thus, the appropriate bound is adjusted by examining the feasibility of w at line L7.

After exiting the loop, the proper weight is selected. If the original input weights bound w_k (case 1), then the updated weights preserve this property: $w_{min} < w_k \leq w_{max}$. Furthermore, w_{min} and w_{max} represent consecutive weights in the sequence w_i for $i = 1$ to $2^{N-1} + 1$. Therefore, the smallest w_i such that $w_i \geq w_k$ is w_{max} (L18). If the original weight range is below w_k (i.e., case 2: $w_k > w_{max}$), then all weights in the range yield infeasible sequences (Theorem 1). Only w_{min} is updated (L10) in each iteration of the loop, and w_{max} retains its original value yielding an infeasible sequence. This condition is detected at line L17 and *LOWRANGE* is returned. Similarly, if the original weight range is above w_k (i.e., case 3: $w_k \leq w_{min}$), then all weights in the range yield feasible sequences (Theorem 1). In this case, w_{min} retains its original value, and *HIGHRANGE* is reported at line L14.

Finally, there is no path of any measure, inside or outside of the weight range, if the first call to A*() returns no path (L13 if $N = 1$ and L6 if $N > 1$). This is case 4. Changing the weight on a term in the objective function $f(°)$ does not affect whether or not a path through the graph exists. QED.

We now prove the correctness of CD*.

Theorem 3: If $G' = G + \Delta$, $X = CA^*(f(°), w_{min}, w_{max}, N, G')$, and $(Y, G[1...N]) = CD^*(f(°), w_{min}, w_{max}, N, G[1...N], \Delta)$, then $f_0(X) = f_0(Y)$ and $f_1(X) = f_1(Y)$.

Proof: There are two differences between CA* and CD*: 1) CA* calls A* and CD* calls D*, and 2) CA* operates on a single input graph and CD* operates on an array of graphs. Since all elements of the array are initialized to G, D* operates on G in every stage of the binary search. Since $A^*(f(°), w, G')$ and $D^*(f(°), w, G, \Delta)$ produce equivalent results (i.e., $f(°)$ values are the same), CA* and CD* produce equivalent results. QED.

Discussion

CA* is computationally efficient because it performs a binary search on the constraint dimension. Its complexity is $NO(A^*)$, rather than $2^N O(A^*)$ for the equivalent exhaustive search. CD* is even more efficient provided it avoids changing the weights often. Let p be the fraction of cases where a D* graph is re-planned from scratch (e.g., due to a weight change) rather than updated. Then the complexity of CD* is approximately $N(pO(A^*) + (1-p)O(D^*))$. If p is small, then CD* is much faster at re-planning than CA*, since D* is much faster at re-planning than A*. The parameter p is typically problem dependent.

We can easily modify both CA* and CD* to terminate when the difference between the computed optimal solution $f_0(X)$ and the exact optimal solution is less than some value, ε, rather than terminate after a fixed number of iterations, N. This is done by evaluating $f_0(X_{max}) - f_0(X_{min})$ at each iteration and stopping when the difference is less than ε, or when the difference ceases to shrink (no solution).

To properly bound the optimal, constrained solution, the initial weights should be selected so that w_{min} yields an infeasible solution, if one exists, and w_{max} yields a feasible solution, if one exists. We do not have a rigorous rule for this selection; otherwise, we would incorporate it in the algorithm itself. Instead, we advocate a heuristic approach. We recommend $w_{min} = 0$, since zero is the lower bound for w in Equation 1. For w_{max}, it is important that the $f_1(°)$ term of Equation 1 dominate the $f_0(°)$ term, so that $f_1(°)$ is minimized. The selection $w_{max} = \infty$ guarantees the proper solution if one exists, but large values of w require a commensurate increase in N (and corresponding increase in runtime and memory usage) in order to find a solution with the same weight resolution. So we recommend using the largest w_{max} possible that still yields required runtime performance. For the case where $f_0(°)$ and $f_1(°)$ are additive functions of positive costs, we recommend $w_{max} = 10c_0/c_1$, where c_0 is the average additive weight for $f_0(°)$ and c_1 is the average additive weight for $f_1(°)$. If the optimal, constrained solution is improperly bounded, this condition is reported by both CA* and CD* at lines L14 and L17, and a new pair of bounds can be chosen.

Although we require $f(°)$ to be a DP function so that we can use both A* and D*, note that there is no requirement that $f_0(°)$ and $f_1(°)$ be DP functions. This means that our formulation is broader than that used in QoS, where path functions are strictly additive and the edges of the graph non-negative. For example, assume we would like to compute the lowest cost path through a network of both positive and negative weights, such that the path has no more than M segments. Therefore, we would like to minimize

$$Equation\ 2:\ f_0(X_M) = \sum_{i=1}^{M} c_i(X_i, X_{i-1})$$

where $c_i(°)$ are the edge costs. Assuming there is at least one negative $c_i(°)$ in the graph, define C to be the absolute value of the most negative edge in the graph. The constraint can be defined as $f_1(X_M) = MC$ with the threshold $K = MC$. Therefore,

$$Equation\ 3:\ f(X_M) = \sum_{i=1}^{M} c_i + wMC = \sum_{i=1}^{M} (c_i + wC).$$

If $w \geq 1$, then each term in the summation is non-negative. Thus, $f(°)$ is monotonically non-decreasing and is a DP function, even though $f_0(°)$ is not. Both CA* and CD* can be used to solve this problem by setting $w_{min} = 1$.

Route Planning Example

Consider the route planning example described in the introduction, where the robot plans a path to a goal that minimizes visibility (maximizes stealth) without exhausting its battery. To make the problem more realistic, the robot knows about some of the obstacles in its environment (shown in light gray) but not about others (shown in dark gray). The robot is equipped with a contact sensor to detect the unknown obstacles. Whenever it detects an obstacle, it updates its map and re-plans the remainder of the path to the goal.

Since the environment is not completely known, the robot cannot guarantee that its traverse will not deplete the battery. Therefore, we establish the additional constraint that if the robot determines, based on known information, that it cannot reach the goal without exhausting its battery, it must return to the start. Under no circumstances may it be "caught in the middle" with a dead battery. This is a realistic scenario since there could charging stations at both the start and goal but not in between. Assume that E is the energy in the battery at any point in time and E_{max} is battery capacity. The worst case occurs when the robot travels all of the way to the goal and then discovers the goal is completely obstructed. Since the only paths with guaranteed energy costs are those previously traversed, the robot must then backtrack to the start along its approach path. To allow for this contingency, we first call CD* with energy constraint $K = E_{max}/2$ and begin traversing the planned route.

When the robot's sensor detects an obstacle, we update the map (i.e., edge costs in graphs) and invoke CD* again. But we must also update the constraint, to account for the energy expended during execution. Let E_{trav} be the amount of energy expended on the traverse so far. The constraint is updated to be $K = (E_{max} - 2E_{trav})/2 = E_{max}/2 - E_{trav}$, meaning that the maximum energy available is the battery capacity minus twice the traversal cost so far (to permit a return), all divided by two (to account for worst case of goal blockage). A new plan is produced, and the process repeats until the goal is reached. At every point in a traverse, the robot follows a path that is optimal with respect to stealth and that satisfies the energy constraint, taking into account all information known and detected in aggregate to that point. If the robot determines it cannot reach the goal without exhausting its battery, it retreats to the start and recharges. It then ventures out again for another attempt, capitalizing on the new information it acquired from the previous traverse.

Figure 1 shows the first traverse taken by the robot. The traverse was aborted (at point P) and the robot retreated, since it determined at P that it could not travel to the goal G and then retreat to S without violating the energy constraint, given the field of known obstacles. Figure 2 shows a subsequent traverse, using the information acquired from previous traverses, exploring to the left of the center cluster of obstacles. Again, this traverse was aborted at point P. Figure 3 shows a later traverse, exploring to the opposite side, since the left side was found to be cluttered. This traverse was also aborted. Figure 4 shows the final attempt by the robot that ended in success. With each attempt, the robot discovered more of the obstacle clutter and progressively traded away stealth (i.e., perimeter following) for more direct paths to meet the energy constraint.

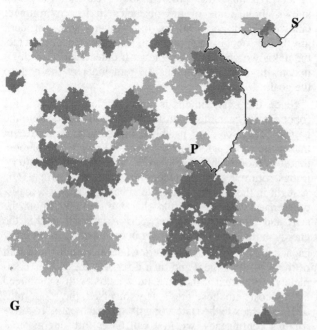

Figure 1: Robot traverse on first aborted attempt

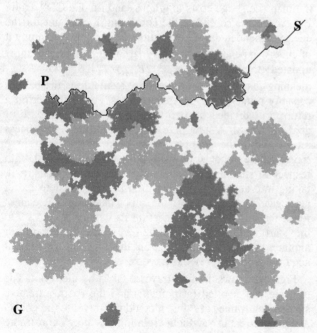

Figure 2: Robot traverse exploring to the left side

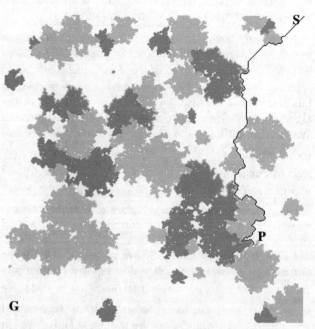

Figure 3: Robot traverse exploring to the right side

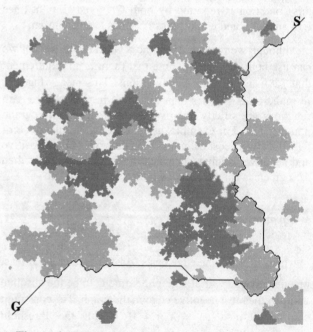

Figure 4: Robot traverse on final, successful attempt

Constraint	Attempts	No. of Steps	No. of Re-plans	CA* re-plan time (sec)	CD* re-plan time (sec)	CD* re-plan %
Tight	4.4	2654	372	3.51	0.35	7.7%
Loose	1.0	1290	367	3.27	0.045	0.7%

Table 1: Experimental results from simulation

Experimental Results

Given the lack of other real-time re-planning algorithms available for this problem, we evaluated CD* against CA*. CA* is not a re-planning algorithm, but it is an efficient *planning* algorithm. The optimal alternative to incremental re-planning is to plan from scratch each time new information arrives. This comparison is analogous to the earlier comparison of D* to A* (Stentz 1994). We generated environments of size 400 x 400 like the one in the previous section. Each environment consisted of 80 obstacles of maximum radial size 40 and randomly distributed. The visibility cost of traversing open space was set to 10 times the cost of traversing an obstacle perimeter. Half the obstacles were unknown. The degree of the binary search (N) was set to 8. The energy constraint was set both *tight* (4X diagonal distance) and *loose* (8X diagonal). The performance was measured by running five experiments for each constraint and averaging the results. The algorithms were compared on a 600 MHz Pentium III, and the results are given in Table 1.

The first data column lists the average number of attempts the robot made to reach the goal, with all but the last ending in retreat. An attempt was aborted when the robot determined that further progress could not be made while still guaranteeing a successful retreat in the event the goal was blocked. The second column lists the total number of steps (grid cells) in all attempts taken together. The third column lists the number of times the robot detected new information, causing a reformulation of the constraint and a re-plan of the remaining path to the goal. The fourth column lists the average CPU time CA* required to re-plan a path (once) during execution. The fifth column lists the average re-planning time for CD*. The sixth column lists the percentage of times CD* re-planned a graph from scratch rather than just updating it. Re-planning from scratch was required whenever one of the weights in the binary search changed.

From the experiments, CD* is one to two orders of magnitude faster than CA* for re-planning, even though CA* by itself is a fairly fast algorithm. With a tight constraint, the robot has less visibility "slack" to trade away to meet the constraint, and the detection of an unknown obstacle is more likely to abort an attempt. Furthermore, near the constraint boundary, the weights are more likely to change, causing CD* to re-plan more of its graphs from scratch, thus slowing it down. With a loose constraint, the robot has more visibility slack to trade away, enabling it to avoid unknown obstacles without risking energy depletion. For the experiments conducted, all first attempts were successful. Furthermore, the robot operates closer to the true unconstrained optimum with a loose constraint, and re-planning operations need only to incrementally update the optimal stealthly path.

Summary and Future Work

This paper presents a novel algorithm, CD*, for real-time re-planning of optimal paths that satisfy a global constraint.

The algorithm is fast enough to compute new paths for every new piece of sensor information detected by a robot, and can be integrated directly into a robot's controller. Although the examples and experiments in this paper were motivated by robot route planning problems, the formulation is very general, and we expect CD* to be useful for a wide variety of AI applications, in the same way that both A* and D* are. We are presently working to extend CD* to handle multiple constraints and expect that each new constraint will add a factor of N in run-time complexity, rather than 2^N for the exhaustive search case.

Acknowledgments

This work was sponsored in part by the U.S. Army Research Laboratory, under contract "Robotics Collaborative Technology Alliance" (contract number DAAD19-01-2-0012). The views and conclusions contained in this document are those of the author and should not be interpreted as representing the official policies or endorsements of the U.S. Government.

References

Garey, M. R., and Johnson, D. S. 1979. Computers and Intractability, A Guide to the Theory of NP-Completeness. San Francisco, California: Freeman.

Hassin, R. 1992. Approximation schemes for restricted shortest path problem. Mathematics of Operations Research 17(1):36-42.

Jaffe, J. M. 1984. Algorithms for Finding Paths with Multiple Constraints. Networks 14:95-116.

Korkmaz, T., Krunz, M., and Tragoudas, S. 2000. An Efficient Algorithm for Finding a Path Subject to Two Additive Constraints. In Proceedings of the ACM SIGMETRICS 2000 Conference, 318-327, Santa Clara, CA.

Korkmaz, T., and Krunz, M. 2001. Multi-Constrained Optimal Path Selection. In Proceedings of the IEEE INFOCOM 2001 Conference, 834-843, Anchorage, Alaska.

Logan, B., and Alechina, N. 1998. A* with Bounded Costs. In Proceedings of the 15th National Conference on Artificial Intelligence, 444-449. AAAI Press.

Lui, G., and Ramakrishnan, K. G. 2001. A* Prune: An Algorithm for Finding K Shortest Paths Subject to Multiple Constraints. In Proceedings of the IEEE INFOCOM 2001 Conference, Anchorage, Alaska.

Stentz, A. 1994. Optimal and Efficient Path Planning for Partially-Known Environments. In Proceedings of the IEEE International Conference on Robotics and Automation, San Diego, California.

Stentz, A. 1995. The Focussed D* Algorithm for Real-Time Replanning. In Proceedings of the 14th International Joint Conference on Artificial Intelligence, 1652-1659, Montreal, Canada.

AAAI-02
Edmonton/Alberta
IAAI-02

Satisfiability

Enhancing Davis Putnam with Extended Binary Clause Reasoning

Fahiem Bacchus
Dept. Of Computer Science
University Of Toronto
Toronto, Ontario
Canada, M5S 1A4
fbacchus@cs.toronto.edu

Abstract

The backtracking based Davis Putnam (DPLL) procedure remains the dominant method for deciding the satisfiability of a CNF formula. In recent years there has been much work on improving the basic procedure by adding features like improved heuristics and data structures, intelligent backtracking, clause learning, etc. Reasoning with binary clauses in DPLL has been a much discussed possibility for achieving improved performance, but to date solvers based on this idea have not been competitive with the best unit propagation based DPLL solvers. In this paper we experiment with a DPLL solver called 2CLS+EQ that makes more extensive use of binary clause reasoning than has been tried before. The results are very encouraging—2CLS+EQ is competitive with the very best DPLL solvers. The techniques it uses also open up a number of other possibilities for increasing our ability to solve SAT problems.

Introduction

Many interesting problems can be encoded as satisfiability problems, e.g., planning problems (Kautz & Selman 1992), probabilistic planning problems (Majercik & Littman 1998), verification problems (Biere *et al.* 1999), etc. For many of these problems a decision procedure is required, e.g., in many verification problems one wants to prove that no model of a buggy configuration exists.

In the realm of decision procedures, the backtracking based Davis Putnam (DPLL) procedure dominates.[1] Over the past ten years the basic procedure has been significantly improved with better heuristics (Li & Anbulagan 1997), data structures (Zhang 1997), intelligent backtracking (Bayardo & Schrag 1997), clause learning (Moskewicz *et al.* 2001), equality reasoning (Li 2000), etc. These improvements have had such an impact on performance, that converting a problem to SAT and using DPLL can often be the fastest solution technique. For example, in the verification community it has been shown that for many problems DPLL can be faster than

[1]The original Davis Putnam procedure used directed resolution not backtracking. The backtracking version was developed by Davis, Logemann and Loveland (Cook & Mitchell 1997). Hence our use of "DPLL" instead of "DP".

other techniques (or at least just as fast and much easier to use) (Copty *et al.* 2001).

With one notable exception (Van Gelder 2001) current DPLL solvers utilize unit clause reasoning, i.e., unit propagation (UP). The advantage of using UP is that it can be implemented very efficiently, while the disadvantage is that it has limited pruning power and thus DPLL might explore a large number of nodes during its search for a solution. It is also possible to use binary clause reasoning in DPLL. This yields the dual: it is significantly less efficient to implement, but it can also cause DPLL to explore many fewer nodes due to its greater pruning power. This tradeoff between more reasoning at each node of a backtracking tree and the exploration of fewer nodes is well known. And, as we shall see, on some problems this tradeoff does not favor binary clause reasoning. However, we will also see that an extremely competitive DPLL solver based on binary clause reasoning can be built.

In the sequel we first introduce DPLL, UP and the various types of binary clause reasoning that we employ, then a number of formal properties concerning the relative power of these various forms of reasoning are presented and related previous work is discussed. This leads to the 2CLS+EQ sat solver that employs binary clause reasoning. The system uses two additional features to improve its performance—intelligent backtracking and a technique called pruneback. These are discussed next. A number of empirical results are presented to give a picture of the performance that 2CLS+EQ achieves, and finally, we close with some concluding remarks.

UP and Binary Clause reasoning in DPLL

DPLL takes as input a CNF formula which is a conjunctive set of clauses, with each clause being a disjunctive set of literals, and each literal being either a propositional variable v or its negation $\bar{v}$. DPLL decides whether or not there exists a truth assignment that satisfies the formula.

DPLL is most easily presented as a recursive algorithm, in which case we can view its inputs as being a pair (F, A), where F is a CNF formula, and A is a set of literals that have already been assigned TRUE by previous invocations. Initially DPLL is called with the input formula $\mathcal{F}$ and $A = \emptyset$, i.e., with $(\mathcal{F}, \emptyset)$.

There are 2 basic transformations that DPLL can perform on its input prior to invoking itself recursively. First, it can compute the reduction of its input by a literal ℓ (also called *forcing* ℓ), denoted by $(F, A)[\ell]$. $(F, A)[\ell] = (F', A')$ where F' is generated from F by removing from F all clauses containing ℓ and then removing $\bar{\ell}$ from all the remaining clauses, and A' is simply $A \cup \{\ell\}$. For example, $(\{(a, b, \bar{c}), (\bar{a}, d), (e, f)\}, [g, \bar{h}])[a] = (\{(d), (e, f)\}, [a, g, \bar{h}])$

Second, it can perform various modifications on the formula component of its input. The most important of these is unit clause reduction. Unit clause reduction simply selects a clause from the input formula that has length 1 (a unit clause) and performs a reduction of the input by the literal in that clause. For example, reduction of the unit clause (a) converts the input $(\{(a), (\bar{a}, b), (a, c)\}, [d])$ to $(\{(b)\}, [a, d])$. A unit clause reduction can generate new unit clauses. *Unit Propagation* (UP) is the iterative process of doing unit clause reductions until either (a) a contradiction is achieved, or (b) there are no more unit clauses in the input. The order in which the unit clause reductions occur is not important to the correctness of the algorithm. An *contradiction* is achieved when the set of assigned literals, A, contains both ℓ and $\bar{\ell}$ for some literal ℓ. For example, $\text{UP}(\{(a), (\bar{a}), (b, c, d), (b)\}, [d]) = (\{(b, c, d), (b)\}, [d, a, \bar{a}])$ where a contradiction has been discovered.

With these two components, the basic implementation of DPLL is to first perform unit propagation on the input formula. If the resulting formula is empty, i.e., all clauses have been satisfied, then A is a satisfying truth assignment (any variable not assigned a value in A is free to take any value) and we return TRUE to the calling invocation. Otherwise, if A contains a contradiction then this particular collection of assigned literals cannot be extended to a solution, and we backtrack by returning FALSE. Otherwise, DPLL recursively searches for a satisfying truth assignment containing ℓ and if none exist, for one that contains $\bar{\ell}$. If neither extension succeeds DPLL backtracks by returning false to the calling invocation. Note that DPLL is doing a depth-first search of a tree with each DPLL invocation being a new node visited in the tree, and each return being a backtrack in the tree search.

DPLL(T,A)
```
1.  (T',A')=UP(T,A)
2.  if A' contains a contradiction
3.      return(FALSE)
4.  elseif T' is empty
5.      return(TRUE)
6.  l := selectVarNotInA(T,A)
7.  if(DPLL((T,A)[l])
8.      return(TRUE)
9.  else
10.     return(DPL((T,A)[l̄]))
```

Except for the 2clsVER system of (Van Gelder 2001), current DPLL solvers use this basic algorithm (along with other orthogonal improvements). In particular, unit propagation is all that is used in the formula reduction phase.

The input formula might also contain many binary clauses, and it is possible to do various kinds of reductions of the input formula by reasoning with these clauses as well, as is done by the system we describe in this paper. All of these reductions are done in conjunction with UP.

The first is to perform all possible resolutions of pairs of binary clauses. Such resolutions yield only new binary clauses or new unit clauses. We denote by BinRes the transformation of the input that consists of repeatedly (a) adding to the formula all new binary or unit clauses producible by resolving pairs of binary clauses, and (b) performing UP on any new unit clauses that appear (which in turn might produce more binary clauses causing another iteration of (a)), until either (1) a contradiction is achieved, or (2) nothing new can be added by a step of (a) or (b). For example, $\text{BinRes}(\{(a, b), (\bar{a}, c), (\bar{b}, c)\}, []) = (\{(a, b)\}, [c])$: resolving the binary clauses produces the new binary clauses (b, c), (a, c), and $(c, c) = (c)$. Then unit propagation yields the final reduction.

This example shows that BinRes can produce more literal assignments than can UP, as UP applied to this input formula yields no changes. This also means that BinRes can produce a contradiction in situations where UP cannot: e.g., if we enhance the above example so that BinRes also produces the clause $(\bar{c})$ we will get a contradiction. BinRes gives us the obvious algorithm DPLL-BinRes in which we substitute BinRes for UP in line 1.

OBSERVATION 1 *DPLL-BinRes has the potential to explore exponentially fewer nodes than DPLL-UP.*

At a particular node DPLL-BinRes might detect a contradiction while DPLL-UP might descend trying other literals and exploring an exponentially sized subtree. However, this is only a potential savings: the subtrees that DPLL-BinRes avoids may turn out to be easy for DPLL-UP to refute.

Another common technique used in DPLL solvers is failed literal detection (Freeman 1995). Failed literal detection is a one-step lookahead with UP. Say we force literal ℓ and then perform UP. If this process yields a contradiction then we know that $\bar{\ell}$ is in fact entailed by the current input and we can force it (and then perform UP). DPLL solvers often perform failed literal detection on a set of likely literals at each node. The SATZ system (Li & Anbulagan 1997) was the first to show that very aggressive failed literal detection can pay off. Failed literal detection and binary resolution are related.

OBSERVATION 2 *If BinRes forces the literal ℓ, then failed literal detection on $\bar{\ell}$ would also detect that ℓ is entailed.*

For example, BinRes forces c in the formula $(\{(a, b), (\bar{a}, c), (\bar{b}, c)\}, [])$. On the other hand if $\bar{c}$ is forced UP will generate a contradiction: i.e., that c is entailed will be detected by the failed literal test. This observation can be proved by examining the implication graph representation of binary clauses.

OBSERVATION 3 *Failed literal detection is able to detect entailed literals that cannot be detected by BinRes.*

For example, if we test c with failed literal detection in the formula $(\{(\bar{c}, a), (\bar{c}, b), (\bar{c}, d), (\bar{a}, \bar{b}, \bar{d})\}, [])$, we will detect a contradiction and thus that $\bar{c}$ is entailed. BinRes on the other hand, does not force $\bar{c}$. So we see that failed literal detection is strictly stronger than BinRes.

This example indicates that a weakness of BinRes is that it does not consider the non-binary clauses. This weakness can be addressed by hyper-resolution.

Hyper-resolution is a resolution step that involves more than two clauses. Here we define a hyper-resolution step to take as input *one* n-ary clause ($n \geq 2$) $(l_1, l_2, ..., l_n)$ and $n - 1$ binary clauses each of the form $(\bar{l_i}, \ell)$ ($i = 1, ..., n - 1$). It produces as output the new binary clause (ℓ, l_n). For example, using hyper-resolution on the inputs (a, b, c, d), $(h, \bar{a})$, $(h, \bar{c})$, and $(h, \bar{d})$, produces the new binary clause (h, b). Note that the standard resolution of two binary clauses is covered by this definition (with $n = 2$).

With this hyper-resolution step we define a more powerful form of formula reduction. We denote by HypBinRes the transformation of the input that is exactly like BinRes except that it performs the above hyper-resolution instead of simply resolving binary clauses. DPLL-HypBinRes is then defined to be DPLL with HypBinRes substituted for UP.

OBSERVATION 4 *HypBinRes detects the same set of forced literals as repeatedly (a) doing a failed literal test on **all** literals, and (b) performing UP on all detected entailed literals, until either (1) a contradiction is achieved, or (2) no more entailed literals are detected.*

This observation can be proved by showing that HypBinRes forces a literal if and only if it can be detected by the failed literal test. The requirement for repeating the failed literal test follows from fact that HypBinRes is run to closure. Note that simply performing the failed literal test on every literal is not as powerful as HypBinRes. One would have to retest every literal every time an entailed literal is unit propagated until no new entailed literals are detected. As a result it is much more efficient to perform HypBinRes rather than repeated failed literal tests—HypBinRes does not need to repeat work in the same way.

OBSERVATION 5 *DPLL-HypBinRes has the potential to explore exponentially fewer nodes than DPLL-BinRes.*

This follows from the fact that DPLL-HypBinRes can detect contradictions that DPLL-BinRes cannot.

HypBinRes is also very useful when it comes to computing heuristics. A very useful heuristic is to rank literals by the number of new literals they would force under UP. The idea is to split next on the literal that along with its negation will cause the largest reduction in the formula under UP—thus the two recursions will both have to deal with a smaller formula. This is the heuristic used by the SATZ (Li & Anbulagan 1997). However, this heuristic is costly to compute, and can usually only be estimated. SATZ for example evaluates this heuristic on some set of candidate literals by unit propagating each one and then counting the number of newly forced literals. (Failed literal detection is an important side effect of this process). HypBinRes has the following property:

OBSERVATION 6 *A literal ℓ will force a literal ℓ' under UP if and only if the binary clause $(\bar{\ell}, \ell')$ is in the formula after performing HypBinRes.*

Thus after performing HypBinRes a simple count of the

number of binary clauses a literal's negation participates in yields the precise number of literals that would be forced by unit propagating that literal. This observation is a direct corollary of Observation 4.

Finally, there is one more type of binary clause reasoning that is useful, equality reduction. If a formula F contains $(\bar{a}, b)$ as well as $(a, \bar{b})$ (i.e., $a \Rightarrow b$ as well as $b \Rightarrow a$), then we can form a new formula EqReduce(F) by equality reduction. Equality reduction involves (a) replacing all instances of b in F by a (or vice versa), (b) removing all clauses which now contain both a and $\bar{a}$, (c) removing all duplicate instances of a (or $\bar{a}$) from all clauses. This process might generate new binary clauses.

For example, EqReduce$\big(\{(a, \bar{b}), (\bar{a}, b), (a, \bar{b}, c), (b, \bar{d}), (a, b, d)\}, [e]\big) = \big(\{(a, d), (a, \bar{d})\}, [e]\big)$. Clearly EqReduce($F$) will have a satisfying truth assignment if and only if F does. Furthermore, any truth assignment for EqReduce(F) can be extended to one for F by assigning b the same value as a.

EqReduce can be added to HypBinRes (HypBinRes+eq) by repeatedly doing (a) equality reduction, (b) hyper-resolution, and (c) unit propagation, until nothing new is added or a contradiction is found. DPLL-HypBinRes+eq is then defined to be DPLL using HypBinRes+eq instead of UP

OBSERVATION 7 *HypBinRes+eq detects the same set of forced literals as HypBinRes.*

The two binary clauses $(a, \bar{b})$ and $(\bar{a}, b)$ allow HypBinRes to deduce everything that HypBinRes+eq can.

This means that modulo changes in the heuristic choices it might make, DPLL-HypBinRes+eq does not have the potential to produce exponential savings over DPLL-HypBinRes. The benefit of using equality reduction is that for many problems equality reduction significantly simplifies the formula. This can have a dramatic effect on the time it takes to compute HypBinRes.

We have implemented DPLL-HypBinRes+eq along with two key extra improvements, which we describe in the next section. But first we relate DPLL-HypBinRes+eq to the closest previous work.

EQSAT (Li 2000) is a system specialized for equality reasoning. It does much more with equalities than the simple equality reduction described above. In particular, it represents ternary equalities with a special non-causal formula and does more extensive reasoning with these higher order equalities. As a result it is the only sat solver capable of solving the parity-32 family of problems which involve large numbers of equalities. However, it is not particularly successful at solving other types of theories. See (Simon & Chatalic 2001) for detailed empirical results on EQSAT and other solvers.

2clsVER (Van Gelder 2001) is a DPLL solver that does binary clause reasoning. However, it does only BinRes not HypBinRes. On the other hand, it does extensive subsumption checking which our system does not do. Nevertheless, its performance lags significantly behind our system.

2-simplify (Brafman 2001) is a preprocessor that uses binary clause reasoning to simplify the formula. It does a limited version of HypBinRes+eq. In particular, it does

BinRes as well as EqReduce but only a limited form of hyper-resolution (a step called "derive shared implications" in (Brafman 2001)). In addition it does not repeat these reductions until closure is achieved, but rather only performs these reductions once. Achieving closure can make a tremendous difference in practice.

DCDR (Rish & Dechter 2000) is a solver that can choose to resolve away a variable during search rather than split on it (the more recent 2clsVER system also does this). The resolution steps are restricted so that they never generate a resolvant larger than k literals, for some small k. Although it worked well on some problems, the system was not competitive with UP based solvers. Interestingly, we can unroll the hyper-resolution step we have defined here into a sequence of ordinary resolution steps. However, these steps would produce intermediary resolvants of arbitrary size. Hyper-resolution allows us to avoid generating these large intermediate resolvants, moving instead directly to the small final resolvant. In one sense, hyper-resolution acts as macro that allows us to capture specific useful sequences of resolution steps.

The Sat Solver 2CLS+EQ

We have implemented DPLL-HypBinRes+eq in a system called 2CLS+EQ. 2CLS+EQ also contains two key extra improvements, intelligent backtracking and a simplified form of clause learning that is closely related to the pruneback techniques described in (Bacchus 2000). In this section we discuss these two improvements. The implementation itself has a number of interesting features, but space precludes discussing them.

Intelligent backtracking has been found to be essential for solving the more realistic structured problems that arise in, e.g., AI planning problems and hardware verification problems. Intelligent backtracking in DPLL was first implemented in (Bayardo & Schrag 1997) and it is an essential component of what is probably the most powerful current DPLL solver ZCHAFF (Moskewicz *et al.* 2001).

The set of assigned literals A can be divided into two subsets. The set of choice literals (those literals that were assigned as a result of being split on by DPLL), and the other literals that were forced by whatever reduction process is being used. When a contradiction is found A will contain a literal ℓ and its negation $\bar{\ell}$. Intelligent backtracking is based on identifying a subset of the choice literals that was responsible for forcing ℓ and a subset responsible for forcing $\bar{\ell}$. The union of these two sets $\bar{C} = \{l_1, \ldots, l_k\}$ is a set of choice literals that cannot be simultaneously made true. That is, $\mathcal{F} \models \neg(l_1 \wedge \cdots \wedge l_k)$, or in clausal form $\mathcal{F} \models C = (\bar{l}_1, \cdots, \bar{l}_k)$. This new clause allows DPLL to backtrack to the deepest level where one of these literals was assigned (i.e., the shallowest level they were all assigned), say literal l_k at level i, perhaps skipping many intermediate levels, to try the alternate branch ($\bar{l}_k$) at that level—the clause gives a proof that no solutions exist in the subtree under the assignment l_k. If after trying $\bar{l}_k$ in the alternate branch DPLL again backtracks to level i, it would in a similar manner have discovered another new clause $C' = (\bar{l}'_1, \ldots, \bar{l}'_h, l_k)$ this time containing l_k (the negation of

the current assignment at level i). C and C' can thus be resolved to yield a new clause $C_1 = (\bar{l}_1, \ldots, \bar{l}_{k-1}, \bar{l}'_1, \ldots, \bar{l}'_h)$ that allows DPLL to now backtrack to the deepest assignment in C_1. This backtrack might also skip a number of levels.

Notice that the kind of reasoning used to infer ℓ and $\bar{\ell}$ from the set of choice literals is irrelevant to this process. As long as we can identify a subset of choice literals responsible for forcing a literal, we can then compute a valid new clause by unioning the subset that forced ℓ with that which forced $\bar{\ell}$. Intelligent backtracking can then be performed. In DPLL-UP this identification process is relatively simple. A literal ℓ can only be forced by an original clause that has became unit. Hence the choice literals that forced ℓ is simply the union of the choice literals that forced the negations of the other literals in clause, and this set can be computed by simply backtracing through the clauses that forced each literal. In other words, all the bookkeeping that is required is to associate a clause with each forced literal.

With HypBinRes+eq the bookkeeping required is considerably more complex. Since a literal could be forced by the resolution of two binary clauses, we must also keep track of the (potentially complex) reasons the binary clauses came into existence. Nevertheless, it is possible to implement the necessary record structures to support backtracing from a literal to a set of choice literals that entailed it. An initial implementation had been completed when we discovered the approach described in (Van Gelder 2001) which presented a much cleaner record structure supporting greater structure sharing. 2CLS+EQ implements Van Gelder's method.[2]

The other technique we implemented is related to the backpruning techniques described in (Bacchus 2000). It is best described by a example. Say that a contradiction is discovered at level 30 in the search tree, and we compute that new clause $C = (\bar{a}, \bar{b}, \bar{c}, \bar{d})$ with a having been assigned at level 1, b at level 5, c at level 10, and d at level 25. This clause allows us to backtrack to level 25 and there try $\bar{d}$. Suppose we subsequently backtrack from the subtree rooted by $\bar{d}$ to level 23 to try an alternate branch. It is quite possible that in this new branch we could again try to assign d. But we know from the clause C that d cannot hold while a, b and c are still true—which they are since we have not as yet backtracked that far. Assigning d would violate the newly discovered clause C. In fact, $\bar{d}$ must be forced at all levels until we backtrack to level 10 to unassign c.

We have not as yet implemented clause learning, and if we had the forcing of $\bar{d}$ would be taken care of by the presence of the new clause C. Instead, we use a simpler approach of "backpruning" d to the next highest level in C at the time we discover C. We then discard C. Backpruning has the effect of disallowing d (i.e., forcing $\bar{d}$) at every level until we backtrack to level 10. A related backprune is that we also know from C that the binary clause $(\bar{c}, \bar{d})$ must hold between levels 5 (while b and a are still assigned) and 10

---

[2]We also had to solve the problem of garbage collecting these record structures on backtrack. This problem was mentioned as open in (Van Gelder 2001). We were able to allocate off a stack and reduce garbage collection to a single move of the stack pointer.

(below level 10 $\bar{d}$ will be forced and this binary clause will be subsumed). Using a similar approach we force this binary clause at these levels. In this way we get significant use out of the clause C without having to record it.[3]

Empirical Results

In our empirical tests we made use of the wonderful Sat-Ex resource. We ran 2CLS+EQ on a variety of local machines and then normalized all of our timings to the Sat-Ex machine standard (71.62 using the Dimacs machine scale program). As a check that this normalization was reasonable we also ran ZCHAFF on our local machines on a number of problems and compared its normalized times to those reported in Sat-Ex, the timings were accurate to 5%. Hence, the reader can reasonably compare the timings we report here to those available on-line at the Sat-Ex site.[4]

2CLS+EQ is intended to be a general purpose sat solver capable of solving a wide variety of sat problems. Hence, the first experiment we ran was to try to solve a large collection of problems that the best general purpose sat solvers find easy. We used the following benchmark families (named as in the Sat-Ex site): aim-100, aim-200, aim-50, ais, bf, blockworld, dubois, hole, ii-16, ii-8, jnh, morphed-8-0, morphed-8-1, parity-8, ssa, ucsc-bf, and ucsc-ssa. These families contained a total of 722 problems. 2CLS+EQ was able to solve all of these problems in 16m 39s (999.52 sec). The fastest solver for these problems was ZCHAFF which completed in 4m 13s (253 sec) Second was SATO (v.3.00) which took 8m 43s (523 sec). Then RELSAT-2000 which took 31m 36s, and RELSAT (v.1.12) 34m 37s. The next fastest solver SATZ failed to solve 2 problems from the dubois family and one of the blocksworld problems within a 10,000 sec. timebound, EQSAT failed to solve 9 problems from the ucsc-bf family, and SATO-v.3.21 failed to solve three problems from the ii-16 family. Thus we see that 2CLS+EQ was third fastest on this suite of problems, was only 4 times as slow as ZCHAFF, and was one of only 4 solvers able to solve all problems.

In all of our experiments we used the same heuristic for variable selection. This heuristic first performs a restricted amount of lookahead to see if it can detect any binary clauses that are entailed by both a literal and its negation.[5] If any such clauses are found, they are added to the theory and HypBinRes+eq performed. Then to choose the next variable it simply counts the number of binary clauses each literal participates in. As pointed out in the previous section, under HypBinRes this is equivalent to the number of literals that it would forced under UP. These counts, for the literal (p) and its negation (n), are combined with a Freeman like function: $n+p+1+1024*n*p$. Ties are broken randomly.[6]

[3]In our context the complexity of hyper-resolution is heavily dependent on the number of clauses, so clause learning must be carefully implemented.

[4]The Sat-Ex data is quite accurate, and since it represents over 1 year of CPU time, difficult to reproduce locally.

[5]In particular, the procedure check if there are any pairs of 3-clauses of the form (ℓ, a, b) and $(\bar{\ell}, a, b)$ from which it can conclude the new binary clause (a, b).

[6]The random tie breaking turns out to be essential—it causes

However, there are a few families for which this heuristic fails badly: par-16, ii-32, pret-60, and pret-150. For these families we found that replacing the final scoring stage with one that estimates the number of new binary clauses that would be forced by a literal under UP to be vastly superior (i.e., we estimate the number of new binary clauses rather count than the number of new unit clauses). With the standard heuristic, 2CLS+EQ required 30930.75 sec. to solve the 10 par-16 problems (ranking 20th fastest among the 24 sat solvers tested by Sat-Ex), 2229.66 sec. to solve the 17 ii-32 problems (ranking 10th), 48.97 sec. to solve the 4 pret-60 problems (ranking 15th), and *cannot solve* any of the pret-150 problems within a 10,000 sec. timebound (tied for 13th with 12 other solvers, including POSIT and SATZ). However, with scores based on estimating the number of binary clauses it required only 45.32 sec. to solve the par-16 family (ranking 4th), 495.73 sec. to solve ii-32 (ranking 7th), 0.82 sec. to solve pret-60 (ranking 10th), and 56.34 sec. to solve pret-150 (ranking 11th).

The first experiment indicates that the competitive solvers in the general purpose category are ZCHAFF, RELSAT-2000, and SATO-v3.00. (this is also confirmed by the solver ranking given on the Sat-Ex site). The next experiment examines 2CLS+EQ's performance on a collection of families that these three solvers find most difficult. We excluded the families parity-32, g, and f, as none of the general purpose solvers can solve these problems and neither can 2CLS+EQ. The results on the families we experimented with are shown in Table 1. (We used the standard heuristic of counting the number of new unit clauses and doing our simple lookahead, in all of these tests. In some cases our experiments were limited by our ability to locate the problem suites.) Included in the table are the results obtained by ZCHAFF, RELSAT-2000, and SATO-v3.00 as well as where 2CLS+EQ ranks (timewise) among all 23 solvers for which Sat-Ex has data. The table shows the total cpu time (in seconds) required to solve all members of the family. The number of problems in the family are indicated in brackets after the family name, and the number of problems that a solver failed on (with a 10,000 sec. timebound) are also indicated in brackets before the total time. We follow the Sat-Ex convention and count 10,000 as the increment in time for an unsolvable problem.[7]

The miters family is where 2CLS+EQ has its best performance. It is the only solver among the 23 cited on Sat-Ex that is able to solve all of these problems (all other solvers fail on 2 or more problems). ZCHAFF fails on the two problems c6288-s and c6288, and is unable to solve them even when given 172,800 sec. (48hrs) of CPU time. Interesting, 2CLS+EQ solves both of these problems without any search; i.e., an initial application of HypBinRes+eq suffices to show these problems unsatisfiable. Thus 2CLS+EQ has some potential as a preprocessor. In contrast, the 2Simplify (Brafman 2001) system does not reduce the difficulty of these

the search to cover different possibilities rather than get stuck repeatedly trying the same best scoring variable.

[7]There are many problems with this convention, but following it does allow our results to be more readily compared with those presented at the Sat-Ex site.

Family (#problems)	2CLS+EQ	2CLS+EQ ranking	RELSAT-2000	SATO-v3.00	ZCHAFF
hfo4(40)	2,622.95	13th	**569.51**	33,785.92	6,506.10
eq-checking(34)	32.53	3rd	13.88	(1) 10,007.25	**2.45**
facts(15)	95.24	5th	75.46	**12.78**	13.45
quasigroup(22)	6,760.12	8th	2,347.83	1,087.70	**845.89**
queueinvar(10)	273.93	5th	236.04	(2) 20,400.45	**15.39**
des-encryption(32)	(8) 80,258.05	3rd	(8) 80,729.42	(8) 80,402.84	**(2) 22,726.43**
fvp-unsat.1.0(4)	(2) 27,672.40	2nd	(3) 30,006.79	(3) 30,006.35	**1,224.86**
Beijing(16)	(2) 30,435.00	8th	(2) 24024.57	(4) 44078.88	**(2) 20268.12**
barrel(8)	4,793.61	3rd	(1) 11,872.80	(1) 10,417.70	**912.22**
longmult(16)	4,993.56	2nd	41,243.77	(1) 22,270.98	**4,502.49**
miters(25)	**419.80**	1st	(7) 86,670.25	(20) 209,123.33	(2) 21,289.77

Table 1: Results of the best general purpose Sat Solvers. Bracketed numbers indicate number of failures for that family. Ranking is with respect to all 23 solvers on Sat-Ex. The best times are in **bold**.

problems: the 2Simplified versions remain unsolvable by ZCHAFF (within 48hrs of CPU time).

The results demonstrate that the extended reasoning performed by 2CLS+EQ can be a competitive way of solving sat problems. In fact, the system is in many respects superior to all previous general purpose SAT solvers, except for ZCHAFF. The fvp-unsat.1.0 problems,[8] des-encryption, and some other tests we ran, show that ZCHAFF remains in a class of its own on many types of problems. Examining 2CLS+EQ's behavior on these problems indicates that 2CLS+EQ makes good progress in the search, but then becomes stuck in a part of the tree that is very difficult to exit from. A similar phenomenon occurs when using the wrong heuristic for the pret150 family. It is clear that restarts and clause learning are essential for improved performance on these types of problems, and that these features have to be implemented in 2CLS+EQ. We suspect that with these features 2CLS+EQ will be able to outperform ZCHAFF on many other problems.

The Beijing family indicates that 2CLS+EQ will, however, never be uniformly superior to UP based DPLL solvers. In this family of problems 2CLS+EQ actually performs quite well on the first 8 problems, and like the other 3 solvers is unable to solve 3bitadd_31 or 3bitadd_32. However, it takes a total of 8943.58 sec. to solve the 6 e?ddr2-10-by-5-? problems. Many other solvers find these problems very easy. 2CLS+EQ only needs to examine a total of 764 nodes during its search to solve all six problems. However, it requires an average of 11.7 seconds to examine each node. In these problems 90,058,925 binary clauses are added and retracted as we move up and down the search trees examining these 764 nodes. It seems that for these problems massive numbers of binary clauses can be generated with little or no pruning effect. In contrast, ZCHAFF solves all 6 of these problems in 18.14 sec, searching 37,690 nodes at the rate of 0.0005 seconds per node.

Finally, 2CLS+EQ utilizes a number of different features and a legitimate question is the relative impact of these features. We do not have the space to present a proper ablative study, but we can make the following general remarks. Hyper-resolution turns out to be essential in almost every case. Without it the binary sub-formula tends not to interact much with the rest of the formula and hence it forces relatively few literals.[9] Intelligent backtracking is also essential for most problems, e.g., without it 2CLS+EQ fails on 5 of the miters problems. Backpruning is less important, but without it, e.g., 2 of the miters problems cannot be solved. In some cases, however, intelligent backtracking can be a waste of time. For example, without it 2CLS+EQ can solve the barrel family in 1527.58 sec. For these problems intelligent backtracking does not decrease the number of nodes searched. Normally, however, the overhead for the record keeping intelligent backtracking requires is more like 25% rather than the 300% of this extreme example.

Conclusions

We have presented a DPLL solver that is based on doing much more extensive reasoning in order to reduce the formula at each node. We have shown that with this can in fact pay off. The result is a very robust solver that is competitive with the best general purpose solvers. More interesting is that the solver is by no means as fast as it could be. More engineering effort could be put into making it faster, and most importantly restarts and clause learning could be added. The solver also has the potential of being used as a powerful preprocessor. The overall message is that for building faster SAT solvers we do not have to be confined by the recent trends of investigating faster ways of doing simple things, but rather we can continue to investigate more interesting and powerful reasoning techniques.

References

Bacchus, F. 2000. Extending forward checking. In *Principles and Practice of Constraint Programming—CP2000,*

---

[8]A range of interesting hardware verification problems, including the fvp-unsat.1.0 problem suite, have been generated by M.N. Velev and are available from http://www.ece.cmu.edu/-mvelev.

[9]This is one of the reasons van Gelder's 2clsVER system is not competitive with the best solvers.

number 1894 in Lecture Notes in Computer Science, 35–51. Springer-Verlag, New York.

Bayardo, R. J., and Schrag, R. C. 1997. Using csp lookback techniques to solve real-world sat instances. In *Proceedings of the AAAI National Conference (AAAI)*, 203–208.

Biere, A.; Cimatti, A.; Clarke, E.; Fujita, M.; and Zhu, Y. 1999. Symbolic model checking using sat procedures instead of bdds. In *Proc. 36th Design Automation Conference*, 317–320. IEEE Computer Society.

Brafman, R. I. 2001. A simplifier for propositional formulas with many binary clauses. In *Proceedings of the International Joint Conference on Artifical Intelligence (IJCAI)*, 515–522.

Cook, S. A., and Mitchell, D. G. 1997. Finding hard instances of the satisfiability problem: A survey. In Du, D.; Gu, J.; and Pardalos, P. M., eds., *Satisfiability Problem: Theory and Applications*, volume 35 of *DIMACS Series in Discrete Mathematics and Theoretical Computer Science*. American Mathematical Society. 1–18.

Copty, F.; Fix, L.; Fraer, R.; Giunchiglia, E.; Kamhi, G.; Tacchella, A.; and Vardi, M. Y. 2001. Benefits of bounded model checking at an industrial setting. In *Computer Aided Verification (CAV)*, 436–453.

Freeman, J. W. 1995. *Improvements to Propositional Satisfiability Search Algorithms*. Ph.D. Dissertation, University of Pennsylvania.

Kautz, H., and Selman, B. 1992. Planning as satisfiability. In *Proceedings of the European Conference on Artificial Intelligence (ECAI)*, 359–363.

Li, C. M., and Anbulagan. 1997. Heuristics based on unit propagation for satisfiability problems. In *Proceedings of the International Joint Conference on Artifical Intelligence (IJCAI)*, 366–371.

Li, C. M. 2000. Integrating equivalence reasoning into davis-putnam procedure. In *Proceedings of the AAAI National Conference (AAAI)*, 291–296.

Majercik, S. M., and Littman, M. L. 1998. Maxplan: A new approach to probabilistic planning. In *Proceedings of the International Conference on Artificial Intelligence Planning and Scheduling (AIPS)*, 86–93.

Moskewicz, M.; Madigan, C.; Zhao, Y.; Zhang, L.; and Malik, S. 2001. Chaff: Engineering an efficient sat solver. In *Proc. of the Design Automation Conference (DAC)*.

Rish, I., and Dechter, R. 2000. Resolution versus search: Two strategies for SAT. *Journal of Automated Reasoning* 24(1):225–275.

Simon, L., and Chatalic, P. 2001. Satex: A web-based framework for SAT experimentation (http://www.lri.fr/~simon/satex/satex.php3). In Kautz, H., and Selman, B., eds., *LICS 2001 Workshop on Theory and Applications of Satisfiability Testing (SAT 2001)*, volume 9 of *Electronic Notes in Discrete Mathematics*. Elsevier.

Van Gelder, A. 2001. Combining preorder and postorder resolution in a satisfiability solver. In Kautz, H., and Selman, B., eds., *LICS 2001 Workshop on Theory and Applications of Satisfiability Testing (SAT 2001)*, volume 9 of *Electronic Notes in Discrete Mathematics*. Elsevier.

Zhang, H. 1997. Sato: An efficient propositional prover. In *Proceedings of the Fourteenth International Conference on Automated Deduction (CADE)*, volume 1249 of *LNCS*, 272–275. Springer-Verlag.

Comparing Phase Transitions and Peak Cost in PP-Complete Satisfiability Problems[*]

Delbert D. Bailey, Víctor Dalmau[†], Phokion G. Kolaitis

Computer Science Department
University of California, Santa Cruz
Santa Cruz, CA 95064, U.S.A
{dbailey,dalmau,kolaitis}@cs.ucsc.edu

Abstract

The study of phase transitions in algorithmic problems has revealed that usually the critical value of the constrainedness parameter at which the phase transition occurs coincides with the value at which the average cost of natural solvers for the problem peaks. In particular, this confluence of phase transition and peak cost has been observed for the Boolean satisfiability problem and its variants, where the solver used is a Davis-Putnam-type procedure or a suitable modification of it. Here, we investigate the relationship between phase transitions and peak cost for a family of PP-complete satisfiability problems, where the solver used is a symmetric Threshold Counting Davis-Putnam (TCDP) procedure, i.e., a modification of the Counting Davis-Putnam procedure for computing the number of satisfying assignments of a Boolean formula. Our main experimental finding is that, for each of the PP-complete problems considered, the asymptotic probability of solvability undergoes a phase transition at some critical ratio of clauses to variables, but this critical ratio does *not* always coincide with the ratio at which the average search cost of the symmetric TCDP procedure peaks. Actually, for some of these problems the peak cost occurs at the boundary or even outside of the interval in which the probability of solvability drops from 0.9 to 0.1, and we analyze why this happens.

Introduction and Summary of Results

During the past decade, there has been an in-depth study of phase transitions in NP-complete problems; more recently, this study has been extended to decision problems that are complete for complexity classes higher than NP. There are both intrinsic and pragmatic goals in pursuing this line of investigation. The main intrinsic goal is to analyze the "structure" of presumably intractable problems from an angle that had not been explored earlier in computer science (note that phase transition phenomena in graph theory have been extensively studied by combinatorialists for several decades). A more pragmatic goal is to relate phase transitions in a decision problem to the average-case performance of solvers

[*]Research of the authors was partially supported by NSF Grants No. CCR-9732041, and IIS-9907419.

[†]Current Address: Departament de Tecnologia, Universitat Pompeu Fabra, Barcelona, Spain.

for that problem and, ultimately, make progress in understanding the average-case complexity of the problem itself.

The study of phase transitions in decision problems entails the identification of a "constrainedness" parameter that is used to partition the space of problem instances. With each parameter value one associates the asymptotic probability of solvability (i.e., the probability of a random instance being a "yes" instance) in the subspace determined by that parameter value. A phase transition occurs at a critical value of the parameter if the asymptotic probability of solvability abruptly changes from 1 to 0 in the vicinity of that critical value. Starting with the influential paper (Mitchell, Selman, & Levesque 1992) on 3SAT, numerous investigations revealed that for several different NP-complete problems the critical value at which a phase transition occurs is also the place where the average cost of solvers for the problem peaks. For instance, this correlation between phase transition and peak cost has been observed for kSAT in (Kirkpatrick & Selman 1994), for the Traveling Salesman Problem in (Gent & Walsh 1996b), and for the Number Partitioning problem in (Gent & Walsh 1996a). Moreover, it has been observed for problems that are complete for certain higher complexity classes, including the second level of polynomial hierarchy PH (Gent & Walsh 1999) and PP (Bailey, Dalmau, & Kolaitis 2001).

This confluence of phase transition and peak cost raised the intriguing possibility that the average cost of every reasonable solver for a combinatorial problem peaks in the vicinity of the phase transition. Recent investigations, however, have revealed a more subtle state of affairs to the effect that the peak cost may very well be solver-dependent and, therefore, may occur at a value different from the critical value for the phase transition of the asymptotic probability. In particular, this was found by (Coarfa et al. 2000) and (Aguirre & Vardi 2001), when they experimented with 3SAT solvers whose underlying algorithms are fundamentally different from the Davis-Putnam-Logemann-Loveland procedure (DPLL) used in the original experiments for random 3SAT by (Mitchell, Selman, & Levesque 1992). Thus far, however, it has remained the case that, for decision problems solved using the DPLL-procedure or certain DPLL extensions, the peak average cost occurs at the critical value at which the asymptotic probability of solvability undergoes a phase transition. For instance, this has been the case for kSAT, $k \geq 3$ (Kirkpatrick & Selman 1994), and for 3SAT(B) (Zhang 2001), a family of NP-complete decision problems extracted from the optimization problem MAX 3SAT. Beyond NP, this has also been the case for 2QSAT, a complete problem for the second level Σ_2^P of the polynomial hierarchy PH (Gent & Walsh 1999), as well as for #3SAT($\geq 2^{n/2}$), a complete problem for the class PP of all decision problems solvable using a polynomial-time probabilistic Turing machine (Bailey, Dalmau, & Kolaitis 2001).

In this paper we report on a detailed experimental investigation of a family of PP-complete satisfiability problems, aiming to compare phase transitions in these problems with average peak cost of a DPLL extension for solving them. Before describing our main findings, we discuss briefly the class PP and also present an overview of related work. A *probabilistic Turing machine* is a nondeterministic polynomial time Turing machine M with the following accepting condition: a string x is accepted by M if and only if at least half of the computations of M on input x are accepting. As mentioned above, PP is the class of all decision problems solvable using such machines. It is known that PP contains both NP and coNP, and is contained in PSPACE; moreover, PP-complete problems are considered to be substantially harder than NP-complete problems (see (Papadimitriou 1994)). This is so because PP is tightly connected to the class #P of all functions that count the number of accepting paths of nondeterministic polynomial time Turing machines. As shown by (Valiant 1979), the prototypical #P-complete problems are #SAT and #3SAT, i.e., the problems of counting the number of satisfying assignments of CNF-formulas and 3CNF-formulas. Since that time, natural #P-complete problems have been encountered in logic, algebra, graph theory, and artificial intelligence. In particular, #P-complete problems arising in AI include computing Dempster's rule for combining evidence (Orponen 1990) and computing probabilities in Bayesian belief networks (Roth 1996). The aforementioned tight connection between #P and PP was unveiled by (Angluin 1980), who showed that $P^{\#P} = P^{PP}$; this means that the class of decision problems computable in polynomial time using #P oracles coincides with the class of decision problems computable in polynomial time using PP oracles. Thus, PP-complete problems are decision problems that capture the inherent computational complexity of #P-complete problems.

The class PP was first studied by (Simon 1975) and (Gill 1977), who showed that the following satisfiability problem, often called MAJ SAT, is PP-complete: given a CNF-formula φ and a positive integer i, does φ have at least i satisfying assignments? In (Littman 1999) and also in (Littman, Majercik, & Pitassi 2001), initial experiments are reported on the performance of a DPLL extension on instances (φ, i) of MAJ SAT, where φ is a 3CNF-formula in the space of random 3CNF-formulas under the fixed-clauses-to-variables model. Note that an instance of MAJ SAT consists of both a Boolean formula and an arbitrary integer that serves as a threshold for the count of satisfying assignments. It turns out, however, that PP-complete problems can also be obtained by taking certain concrete functions as thresholds for the count. In particular, (Bailey, Dalmau, & Kolaitis 2001) showed that for every rational number α with $0 < \alpha < 1$, the following problem #3SAT($\geq 2^{\alpha n}$) is PP-complete: given a 3CNF-formula φ with n variables, does φ have at least $2^{\alpha n}$ satisfying assignments? Intuitively, each of these problems can be thought of as a question about the occurrence of 1 in a prefix part of the binary representation of the total number of satisfying assignments. For instance, #3SAT($\geq 2^{n/2}$) asks whether at least one of the first $n/2$ bits of the number of satisfying assignments is equal to 1.

(Bailey, Dalmau, & Kolaitis 2001) embarked on a study of phase transitions for the family #3SAT($\geq 2^{\alpha n}$), $0 < \alpha < 1$, of PP-complete problems under the fixed clauses-to-variables ratio model. Specifically, for each of these problems, they obtained analytical upper and lower bounds for the value of the critical ratio $r^*(\alpha)$ of clauses to variables at which a phase transition in the asymptotic probability of solvability may occur. Moreover, they carried out a set of experiments for the problem #3SAT($\geq 2^{n/2}$) using a modification of the Counting Davis-Putnam procedure (CDP), which was designed by (Birnbaum & Lozinskii 1999) for solving #SAT. These experiments suggested that the critical ratio $r^*(1/2)$ for #3SAT($\geq 2^{n/2}$) is approximately equal to 2.5; in addition, the average search cost of the modified CDP procedure peaks around 2.5 as well.

We can now describe the results of the present paper. We carried out a detailed experimental investigation of the PP-complete problems #3SAT($\geq 2^{\alpha n}$) with α varying from 0.1 to 0.9 in 0.1 steps (i.e., nine PP-complete problems in total). For this, we implemented a modified CDP procedure, called *symmetric Threshold Counting Davis-Putnam* (TCDP) procedure, in which both an upper and a lower bound on the count of satisfying assignments is maintained. Our main finding is that, for each of these PP-complete problems, the asymptotic probability of solvability undergoes a phase transition at some critical ratio $r^*(\alpha)$ of clauses to variables, but this critical ratio does *not* always coincide with the ratio at which the average search cost of the symmetric TCDP procedure peaks. Actually, for $\alpha = 0.8$ and $\alpha = 0.9$, the peak cost occurs at the boundary or even outside of the interval in which the probability of solvability drops from 0.9 to 0.1. To the best of our knowledge, these findings represent the first case of a satisfiability problem under the fixed clauses-to-variables ratio model for which the phase transition of the probability does not coincide with the peak cost of a natural modification of the Davis-Putnam procedure for solving this problem. It should be noted that, although our findings are about the peak of the average (mean) cost for solving #3SAT($\geq 2^{\alpha n}$), they are also applicable to the peak of the median cost for solving these problems, since in our experiments median behaves very similarly to the average. This should be contrasted with the findings of (Hogg & Williams 1994; Baker 1995) concerning differences between the average cost and the median cost for solving GRAPH COLORING, and similar findings of (Gent & Walsh 1994) for 3SAT under the constant probability model.

Another experimental finding is that the average search

cost of the symmetric TCDP for solving each of the problems #3SAT($\geq 2^{\alpha n}$) increases with α. This is consistent with the initial experimental results of (Littman 1999) and (Littman, Majercik, & Pitassi 2001) for MAJ SAT. Thus, the symmetric TCDP procedure uncovers differences between the problems #3SAT($\geq 2^{\alpha n}$) with $\alpha = 0.1$ to $\alpha = 0.9$, even though these problems are indistinguishable from the viewpoint of PP-completeness. Furthermore, the highest peak cost of the symmetric TCDP procedure occurs when the ratio of clauses-to-variables is equal to 1.2; interestingly enough, this is the ratio at which the CDP procedure for #SAT peaks (Birnbaum & Lozinskii 1999). Later on, we provide an explanation for this tight relationship between the peak costs of solvers for PP-complete and #P-complete satisfiability problems.

Finally, as a byproduct of our experimental results, there is a surprising finding concerning the tightness of the analytical techniques used to prove upper bounds for critical ratios at which phase transitions may occur. In (Bailey, Dalmau, & Kolaitis 2001), an upper bound for the value of $r^*(\alpha)$ was obtained using a standard application of Markov's inequality. This technique was originally used to derive an upper bound for the critical ratio of 3SAT, but that bound turned out to be rather loose. Specifically, when applied to 3SAT, Markov's inequality yields an upper bound of 5.19, while experimentally the critical ratio for 3SAT has been estimated to be around 4.3. In contrast, it turns out that, for the PP-complete problems #3SAT($\geq 2^{\alpha n}$), Markov's inequality gives progressively tighter upper bounds for $r^*(\alpha)$ as α increases from 0.1 to 0.9. In particular, for $\alpha = 0.9$ Markov's inequality gives 0.5195 as an upper bound for $r^*(0.9)$, while the experimental estimate for $r^*(0.9)$ is 0.51.

Phase Transitions for #3SAT($\geq 2^{\alpha n}$)

If n is a positive integer and r is a rational number such that rn is a positive integer, then $F_3(n, r)$ denotes the space of random 3CNF-formulas with n variables and rn clauses generated by selecting three variables without replacement and then negating each variable with probability $1/2$. Let $X_3^{n,r}$ be the random variable on $F_3(n, r)$ such that $X_3^{n,r}(\varphi)$ is the number of truth assignments on $x_1, \ldots, x_n$ that satisfy φ, where φ is a random 3CNF-formula in $F_3(n, r)$. Thus, φ is a "yes" instance of #3SAT($\geq 2^{\alpha n}$) if and only if $X_3^{n,r}(\varphi) \geq 2^{\alpha n}$. The following conjecture concerning phase transitions for the family #3SAT($\geq 2^{\alpha n}$), $0 < \alpha < 1$, was formulated in (Bailey, Dalmau, & Kolaitis 2001).

Conjecture 1: For every rational number α between 0 and 1, there is a positive real number $r^*(\alpha)$ such that:

- If $r < r^*(\alpha)$, then $\lim_{n \to \infty} \Pr[X_3^{n,r} \geq 2^{\alpha n}] = 1$.
- If $r > r^*(\alpha)$, then $\lim_{n \to \infty} \Pr[X_3^{n,r} \geq 2^{\alpha n}] = 0$.

Note that each decision problem #3SAT($\geq 2^{\alpha n}$) is a *monotone* property of 3CNF-formulas, i.e., if a 3CNF-formula φ has fewer than $2^{\alpha n}$ satisfying assignments, then adding clauses to φ gives rise to a formula with fewer than $2^{\alpha n}$ satisfying assignments. (Bollobas & Thomason 1987) have shown that every monotone property has a *threshold* function. The existence of a threshold function, however,

is a much weaker condition than possessing a phase transition of the type described in Conjecture 1. More recently, (Friedgut 1999) has established that if a monotone property is "non-locally-approximable" in a certain technical sense, then it has a *sharp threshold* function. This condition is more stringent than having a threshold function, but, in general, is weaker than having a phase transition, since the latter is equivalent to having a sharp threshold function of the form r^*n, i.e., a linear function in which the constant coefficient r^* is the critical value in the phase transition. It should also be noted that (Friedgut 1999) proved that 3SAT is "non-locally-approximable" and, consequently, it possesses a sharp threshold function. This, however, does not settle the existence of a phase transition for 3SAT. Going back to the family #3SAT($\geq 2^{\alpha n}$), $0 < \alpha < 1$, it is not known whether the problems in this family are "non-locally-approximable" in Friedgut's sense; in fact, determining whether or not this is the case appears to be a rather difficult problem. Consequently, it is not known whether these problems have a sharp threshold function, let alone whether they exhibit a phase transition as described in Conjecture 1.

Although settling the above conjecture remains an open problem, (Bailey, Dalmau, & Kolaitis 2001) established the following analytical upper and lower bounds for the possible values of $r^*(\alpha)$.

Proposition 2: *Let α be a rational between 0 and 1.*

- *If* $r > (1 - \alpha)\frac{1}{(3 - \lg(7))}$, *then*

$$\lim_{n \to \infty} \Pr[X_3^{n,r} \geq 2^{\alpha n}] = 0.$$

Hence, if $r^*(a)$ exists, then $r^*(\alpha) \leq (1 - \alpha)\frac{1}{(3 - \lg(7))}$.

- *If* $0 < r < 1 - \alpha$, *then*

$$\lim_{n \to \infty} \Pr[X_3^{n,r} \geq 2^{\alpha n}] = 1.$$

Hence, if $r^*(\alpha)$ exists, then $r^*(\alpha) \geq 1 - \alpha$.

Algorithms

We modified the basic CDP (Counting Davis-Putnam Procedure) in (Birnbaum & Lozinskii 1999) to make a symmetric TCDP (Threshold Counting Davis-Putnam Procedure). The basic CDP is a recursive function CDP(φ, n) where φ is a CNF-formula that contains no clause which is a tautology and n is the number of variables in the space considered. It is similar to the DPLL-procedure and actually simpler.

- if φ is empty, return 2^n;
- if φ contains an empty clause, return 0;
- if φ contains a unit clause $\{u\}$

    return CDP($\varphi|_{u \leftarrow 1}$, $n - 1$)

- otherwise, choose any variable v in φ

    return CDP($\varphi|_{v \leftarrow 1}$, $n - 1$) + CDP($\varphi|_{v \leftarrow 0}$, $n - 1$).

The symmetric TCDP is the CDP with a modification to maintain upper and lower bounds on the count. Initially, the upper bound is set to 2^n and the lower bound to 0. The lower bound at any time is the accumulated count so far. Termination occurs whenever the lower bound (i.e. the accumulated count) equals or exceeds the counting threshold or whenever the upper bound becomes lower than the counting threshold in which case we know that additional counting cannot result in the counting threshold being met.

The symmetric TCDP is a recursive function $sTCDP(\varphi, n, t, LB, UB)$, where φ is a CNF-formula that contains no clause which is a tautology, n is the number of variables, t is the counting threshold value being tested, LB is the current lower bound on the count, and UB is the current upper bound on the count. sTCDP returns 1 if it detects that the count will equal or exceed t; it returns 0 if the count is completed and is less than t; and returns -1 if it detects that the count will not be able to reach t or more. Initially, LB and UB are respectively set to 0 and 2^n.

- if φ is empty,

    $LB \leftarrow LB + 2^n$

    if $LB \geq t$, then return 1, else return 0;

- if φ contains an empty clause,

    $UB \leftarrow UB - 2^n$

    if $UB < t$, then return -1, else return 0;

- if φ contains a unit clause $\{u\}$,

    $UB \leftarrow UB - 2^{n-1}$

    if $UB < t$, then return -1,

        else return $sTCDP(\varphi|_{u \leftarrow 1}, n - 1, t, LB, UB)$

- otherwise, choose any variable v in φ

    $temp = sTCDP(\varphi|_{v \leftarrow 1}, n - 1, t, LB, UB)$

    if $temp = 1$ or -1, return $temp$,

        else return $sTCDP(\varphi|_{v \leftarrow 0}, n - 1, t, LB, UB)$.

The performance measure used in our experiments was the number of recursive calls. To reduce linkage overhead, t, LB, and UB were implemented as globals.

Experimental Results

Experiments were run for random 3CNF-formulas with 10, 20, 30 and 40 variables, by implementing the symmetric TCDP algorithm on a dual 1GHz i686s/4GB memory/Linux 2.4.2-2smp workstation with C and the GNU Multiple Precision package. For each space, individual runs were made for thresholds of $2^{\alpha n}$ with α varying from 0.1 to 0.9 in 0.1 steps.

The results are depicted in Figures 1, 2 and 3. In these figures the horizontal axis is the ratio of the number of clauses to the number of variables in the space. The ranges of formula sizes represented in the graphs are 1 to 50, 1 to 100, 1 to 150, and 1 to 200 for the 10, 20, 30 and 40 variable spaces respectively.

The probability phase transition graphs in Figure 3 show for each test point the fraction of 1200 newly generated random formulas that had a number of satisfying truth assignments greater than or equal to the $2^{\alpha n}$ threshold. For each α, the window in which the probability drops from 1 to 0 becomes narrower and steeper as the number of variables increases. We used finite-size scaling, assuming a power law of the form $\frac{(r - r^*(\alpha))n^\nu}{r^*(\alpha)}$, to obtain estimates for the critical ratio $r^*(\alpha)$ and for the exponent ν. The estimates for

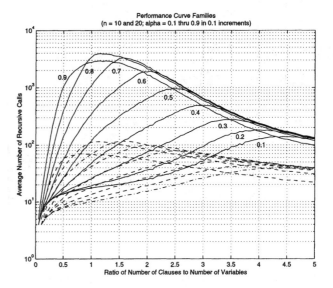

Figure 1: Average Search Cost Graphs for 10 and 20 Variables

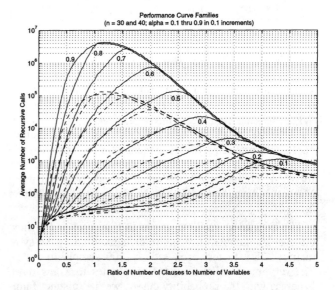

Figure 2: Average Search Cost Graphs for 30 and 40 Variables

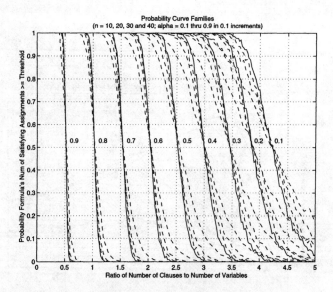

Figure 3: Probabilty Phase Transition Graphs

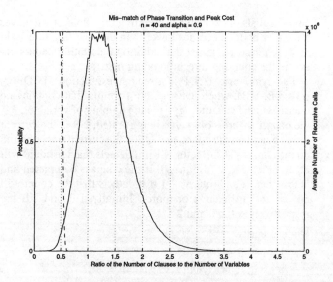

Figure 4: Peak Cost Outside Transition Window

Table 1: Markov Upper Bound vs. Estimate for r^*

α	MUB $r^*(\alpha)$	Estimate $r^*(\alpha)$	Transition Window	Peak Cost $(n = 40)$
0.1	4.6718	4.19	[3.775, 4.725]	4.5-
0.2	4.1527	3.84	[3.475, 4.300]	4.0-
0.3	3.6336	3.45	[3.150, 3.800]	3.4
0.4	3.1145	3.00	[2.775, 3.275]	3.0-
0.5	2.5954	2.50	[2.325, 2.750]	2.5-
0.6	2.0764	2.02	[1.875, 2.175]	2.0
0.7	1.5573	1.53	[1.425, 1.675]	1.6-
0.8	1.0382	1.02	[0.950, 1.200]	1.2
0.9	0.5191	0.51	[0.475, 0.575]	1.2

the values of $r^*(\alpha)$ are given in the second column of Table 1; the respective estimates for the values of ν, as α varies from 0.1 to 0.9 in 0.1 steps are: 0.4968, 0.5112, 0.5899, 0.5849, 0.5800, 0.5021, 0.5021, 0.4931, and 0.6598. When the data were accordingly rescaled, the four curves ($n = 10, 20, 30, 40$) for each α-family collapsed to a single curve, thus providing further evidence for the existence of a phase transition at $r^*(\alpha)$. Table 1 shows how the estimates for $r^*(\alpha)$ compare with the upper bounds obtained using Markov's inequality (MUB) in the first part of Proposition 2.

The average search cost graphs in Figures 1 and 2 show the average number of recursive calls required by the symmetric TCDP to test each set of 1200 sample formulas. The run-times varied from a few minutes to a few days. Whereas with the probability curves we had distinct families for each value of α, here we have distinct families corresponding to each value of n. Figure 1 depicts the families for $n = 10$ and $n = 20$, while Figure 2 depicst the families for $n = 20$ and $n = 40$. Obviously, the number of recursive calls increases with increasing values of n. The interesting outcome is that for any particular value of n

the difficulty varies with both α and r. For a fixed n and fixed α, there is the characteristic "easy-hard-easier" pattern of difficulty for increasing values of r. Moreover, as α increases from 0.1 to 0.9, the peaks move to the left, for example in the 40 variable family, they appear to occur at $4.5-, 4.0-, 3.4, 3.0-, 2.5-, 2.0, 1.6-, 1.2, 1.2$.

For every α, we define the *transition window* for #3SAT$(\geq 2^{\alpha n})$ to be the interval of ratios r in which the 40 variable curve drops from a probability of 0.9 to 0.1. Note that when $\alpha \leq 0.7$, the ratio r at which the peak cost occurs is well inside the transition window; in fact, it either coincides with or is close to the experimental estimate for $r^*(\alpha)$, as would be expected from the conventional conjecture that the peak cost occurs at or near the phase transition point (see Table 1). The state of affairs, however, changes for $\alpha = 0.8$ and $\alpha = 0.9$. Indeed, the $\alpha = 0.8$ curve peaks at 1.2, which is the boundary of the transition window. Even more dramatically, the $\alpha = 0.9$ curve also peaks at 1.2, which is well to the right of the transition window $[0.475, 0.575]$. See Figure 4.

Also noteworthy is the fact that the peak cost for $\alpha = 0.8$ and $\alpha = 0.9$ occurs at $r = 1.2$, which is the ratio at which the CDP procedure for #SAT peaks (Birnbaum & Lozinskii 1999). We now provide an analysis of the relationship between the peak cost of CDP and that of the symmetric TCDP or other variants of it.

A naive algorithm to solve threshold counting satisfiability problems, such as #3SAT$(\geq 2^{\alpha n})$, is to simply run CDP to find the exact number of satisfying assignments and then compare the result with the threshold count. The most obvious and direct improvement to this naive algorithm is to consider a threshold variant of CDP in which a lower bound on the count is maintained; we will refer to this variant as the *basic* TCDP. The symmetric TCDP considered here is a further refinement of the basic TCDP in which both a lower bound and an upper bound are maintained. In other words, the basic TCDP can be obtained from the symmetric TCDP by disabling the upper bound check.

Threshold variants of CDP, such as the basic TCDP and the symmetric TCDP, only allow for speeding it up. They terminate earlier than CDP does, i.e., before a full count is completed, only when they determine that the threshold is exceeded or cannot be exceeded. They will make full count, however, if this early termination does not occur. Consequently, for every CNF-formula φ, the number of recursive calls of the basic TCDP or of the symmetric TCDP on φ, required to determine if the number of satisfying assignments is greater than or equal to a threshold value t, cannot exceed the number of CDP recursive calls required to count all of the satisfying assignments. Moreover, if the number of satisfying assignments is less than the threshold value t, then the number of recursive calls required by the symmetric TCDP and the CDP will be equal except for cases in which the upper bound check is able to cause early termination. By the same token, if the number of satisfying assignments is less than the threshold value t, then the number if recursive calls of the basic TCDP will be equal to those of the CDP.

Now, from the preceding comments and the definition of the critical ratio $r^*(\alpha)$, it follows that as n becomes arbitrarily large, for every $r > r^*(\alpha)$ the difference between the cost curves of the basic TCDP and the CDP will essentially diminish. Moreover, for every $r < r^*(\alpha)$ the cost curves for the basic and the symmetric TCDP will be lower than the cost curve for the CDP. (Even though the existence of the critical ratios $r^*(\alpha)$ has not been established analytically, the above remains true, when r is taken to be respectively bigger or smaller than the upper and lower bounds for $r^*(\alpha)$ given in Proposition 2.) Finally, suppose that the cost curve of the CDP for n variables has a peak at some ratio r_c and consider an α such that the critical value $r^*(\alpha)$ for the phase transition is less than r_c. In this case, the peak cost of the basic TCDP *cannot* occur at $r^*(\alpha)$.

These remarks suggest a qualitative way that we can predict and describe the peak formation in the average cost curves of the basic TCDP. When the critical $r^*(\alpha)$ for a particular α is greater than the ratio r_c value at which CDP peaks, then the average cost curves of the basic TCDP for that α will nearly match the CDP curve for all r values to the right of the phase transition region because the formulas concerned have a very low probability of having enough satisfying assignments to cause the basic TCDP to terminate doing a complete count. As r values move into the phase transition region, formulas will begin to have enough satisfying assignments to terminate the algorithm early and cause the performance curve to start to break away from the CDP curve. To the left of the phase transition region nearly every formula will have enough satisfying assignments to cause the early termination (also note that there are greater and greater numbers of satisfying assignments as r gets smaller and smaller since smaller r's correspond to fewer constraints). On the other hand, when the critical $r^*(\alpha)$ for a particular α is less than the r_c value for the peak difficulty of the CDP, then the peak difficulty of the basic TCDP for that α must match the peak for the CDP, since, coming from the right, the break will not occur until $r < r^*(\alpha)$, which means r's to the left of the CDP peak.

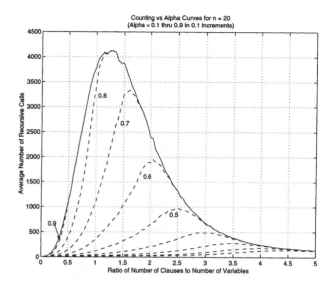

Figure 5: CDP vs. Basic TCDP Search Costs

Strictly speaking, the above analysis applies to the basic TCDP algorithm. Our experiments with the symmetric TCDP depicted in Figures 1 and 2 reveal that the symmetric TCDP basically exhibits a similar behavior except that the curves appear to drop for higher α values. To further corroborate these findings, we ran experiments with the CDP and the basic TCDP. Figure 5 shows the results for 20 variable runs; it also includes the curve for CDP, which is an envelope for the curves of the basic TCDP. We note that at its peak the symmetric TCDP requires about 4,000 recursive calls for $\alpha = 0.8$ and about 3,000 recursive calls for $\alpha = 0.9$, while at its peak the basic TCDP requires about 4,200 recursive calls for $\alpha = 0.8$ and also for $\alpha = 0.9$. We also note that, for $\alpha = 0.9$, the region $r < 0.5$ is the only region of ratios in which the difference in performance between CDP and the basic TCDP is apparent.

(Bayardo & Pehoushek 2000) designed and implemented a different DPLL extension for solving #SAT, called Decomposing Davis-Putnam (DDP), which utilizes connected components in the constraint graph associated with a CNF-formula. Their experiments showed that the DDP performs better than the CDP and that its average peak cost occurs when $r \approx 1.5$. The analysis presented earlier is also applicable to the DDP and its threshold variants, as regards the qualitative relationship between the location of phase transitions for #3SAT($\geq 2^{\alpha n}$), $0 < \alpha < 1$, and search cost of threshold variants of DDP on this family. We plan to carry out an experimental investigation to complement this analysis with quantitative findings.

As mentioned in the introduction, other researchers have considered both median performance and average (mean) performance in phase transition experiments for certain NP-complete problems, and have discovered differences in the behavior of these quantities. Here, we reported the average because of its intrinsic relationship to expectation; moreover, in our experiments median behaves very similarly to the average, as can be seen in Figure 6.

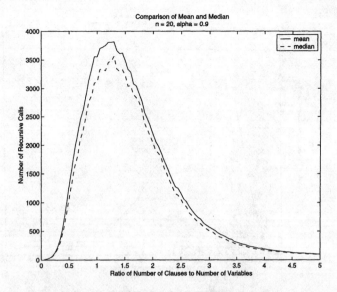

Figure 6: Alpha = 0.9

Concluding Remarks

In this paper, we studied the family #3SAT($\geq 2^{\alpha n}$), $0 < \alpha < 1$, of PP-complete satisfiability problems each of which exhibits a phase transition at a different ratio $r^*(\alpha)$ that depends on the parameter α. We also investigated the average peak cost of the symmetric TCDP, a natural threshold counting algorithm for solving instances of these problems. Since the occurrence of the phase transition differs from problem to problem in the family, we have been able to see how the phase transition affects the performance of the algorithm and, in the process, have discovered that peak cost does not always occur at the location of the phase transition.

Acknowledgments We thank the anonymous reviewers for their constructive comments and pointers to the literature.

References

Aguirre, A. S. M., and Vardi, M. Y. 2001. Random 3-SAT and BDDs: the plot thickens further. *Proc. 7th Int'l. Conf. on Principles and Practice of Constraint Programming, CP 2001* 121–136.

Angluin, D. 1980. On counting problems and the polynomial-time hierarchy. *Theoretical Computer Science* 12:161–173.

Bailey, D. D.; Dalmau, V.; and Kolaitis, P. G. 2001. Phase transitions of PP-complete satisfiability problems. *Proc. of the 17th International Joint Conference on Artificial Intelligence (IJCAI 2001)* 183–189.

Baker, A. 1995. Intelligent backtracking on the hardest constraint problems. Technical report, CIRL, University of Oregon.

Bayardo, R., and Pehoushek, J. 2000. Counting models using connected components. In *17th Nat'l Conf. on Artificial Intelligence*, 157–162.

Birnbaum, E., and Lozinskii, E. 1999. The good old Davis-Putnam procedure helps counting models. *Journal of Artificial Intelligence Research* 10:457–477.

Bollobas, B., and Thomason, A. 1987. Threshold functions. *Combinatorica* 7:35–38.

Coarfa, C.; Demopoulos, D. D.; Aguirre, A. S. M.; Subramanian, D.; and Vardi, M. Y. 2000. Random 3-SAT: the plot thickens. *Proc. 6th Int'l. Conf. on Principles and Practice of Constraint Programming, CP 2000* 143–159.

Friedgut, E. 1999. Sharp threshold of graph properties and the k-SAT problem. *J. Amer. Math. Soc.* 12:1917–1054.

Gent, I., and Walsh, T. 1994. Easy problems are sometimes hard. *Artificial Intelligence* 70:335–345.

Gent, I., and Walsh, T. 1996a. Phase transitions and annealed theories: number partitioning. *Proc. of 12th European Conf. on Artificial Intelligence, ECAI-96* 170–174.

Gent, I., and Walsh, T. 1996b. The TSP phase transition. *Artificial Intelligence* 88(1–2):349–358.

Gent, I., and Walsh, T. 1999. Beyond NP: the QSAT phase transition. In *Proc. 16th National Conference on Artificial Intelligence*, 653–658.

Gill, J. 1977. Computational complexity of probabilistic Turing machines. *SIAM J. Comput.* 6(4):675–695.

Hogg, T., and Williams, C. P. 1994. The hardest constraint problems: A double phase transition. *Artificial Intelligence* 69(1-2):359–377.

Kirkpatrick, S., and Selman, B. 1994. Critical behavior in the satisfiability of random formulas. *Science* 264:1297–1301.

Littman, M.; Majercik, S.; and Pitassi, T. 2001. Stochastic Boolean satisfiability. *Journal of Automated Reasoning* 27(3):251–296.

Littman, M. 1999. Initial experiments in stochastic satisfiability. In *Proc. of the 16th National Conference on Artificial Intelligence*, 667–672.

Mitchell, D. G.; Selman, B.; and Levesque, H. 1992. Hard and easy distributions of SAT problems. *Proc. 10th Nat'l. Conf. on Artificial Intelligence* 459–465.

Orponen, P. 1990. Dempster's rule of combination is #-P-complete. *Artificial Intelligence* 44:245–253.

Papadimitriou, C. H. 1994. *Computational complexity.* Addison-Wesley.

Roth, D. 1996. On the hardness of approximate reasoning. *Artificial Intelligence* 82(1-2):273–302.

Simon, J. 1975. *On some central problems in computational complexity.* Ph.D. Dissertation, Cornell University, Computer Science Department.

Valiant, L. G. 1979. The complexity of computing the permanent. *Theoretical Computer Science* 8(2):189–201.

Zhang, W. 2001. Phase transitions and backbones of 3-SAT and Maximum 3-SAT. *Proc. 7th Int'l. Conf. on Principles and Practice of Constraint Programming, CP2001* 153–167.

A Compiler for Deterministic, Decomposable Negation Normal Form

Adnan Darwiche

Computer Science Department
University of California
Los Angeles, CA 90095
darwiche@cs.ucla.edu

Abstract

We present a compiler for converting CNF formulas into deterministic, decomposable negation normal form (d-DNNF). This is a logical form that has been identified recently and shown to support a number of operations in polynomial time, including clausal entailment; model counting, minimization and enumeration; and probabilistic equivalence testing. d-DNNFs are also known to be a superset of, and more succinct than, OBDDs. The polytime logical operations supported by d-DNNFs are a subset of those supported by OBDDs, yet are sufficient for model-based diagnosis and planning applications. We present experimental results on compiling a variety of CNF formulas, some generated randomly and others corresponding to digital circuits. A number of the formulas we were able to compile efficiently could not be similarly handled by some state-of-the-art model counters, nor by some state-of-the-art OBDD compilers.

Introduction

A tractable logical form known as *Deterministic, Decomposable Negation Normal Form,* d-DNNF, has been proposed recently (Darwiche 2001c), which permits some generally intractable logical queries to be computed in time polynomial in the form size (Darwiche 2001c; Darwiche & Marquis 2001). These queries include clausal entailment; counting, minimizing, and enumerating models; and testing equivalence probabilistically (Darwiche & Huang 2002). Most notably, d-DNNF has been shown to be more succinct than OBDDs (Bryant 1986), which are now quite popular in supporting various AI applications, including diagnosis and planning. Moreover, although OBDDs are more tractable than d-DNNFs (support more polytime queries), the extra tractability does not appear to be relevant to some of these applications.

An algorithm has been presented in (Darwiche 2001a; 2001c) for compiling Conjunctive Normal Form (CNF) into d-DNNF. The algorithm is structure-based in two senses. First, its complexity is dictated by the connectivity of given CNF formula, with the complexity increasing exponentially with increased connectivity. Second, it is insensitive to non-structural properties of the given CNF: two formulas with the same connectivity are equally difficult to compile by the

given algorithm. However, most CNF formulas of interest—including random formulas and those that arise in diagnosis, formal verification and planning domains—tend to have very high connectivity and are therefore outside the scope of this structure-based algorithm. Morever, some of these formulas can be efficiently compiled into OBDDs using state-of-the-art compilers such as CUDD. Given that d-DNNF is more succinct than OBDDs (in fact, d-DNNF is a strict superset of OBDD), such formulas should be efficiently compilable into d-DNNF too.

We present in this paper a CNF to d-DNNF compiler which is structure-based, yet is sensitive to the non-structural properties of a CNF formulas. The compiler is based on the one presented in (Darwiche 2001a) but incorporates a combination of additional techniques, some are novel, and others are well known in the satisfiability and OBDD literatures. Using the presented compiler, we show that we can successfully compile a wide range of CNF formulas, most of which have very high connectivity and, hence, are inaccessible to purely structure-based methods. Moreover, most of these formulas could not be compiled into OBDDs using a state-of-the-art OBDD compiler. The significance of the presented compiler is two fold. First, it represents the first CNF to d-DNNF compiler that practically matches the expectations set by theoretical results on the comparative succinctness between d-DNNFs and OBDDs. Second, it allows us to answer queries about certain CNF formulas that could not be answered before, including certain probabilistic queries about digital circuits.

Tractable forms: d-DNNF and OBDD

A negation normal form (NNF) is a rooted directed acyclic graph in which each leaf node is labeled with a literal, *true* or *false*, and each internal node is labeled with a conjunction $\wedge$ or disjunction $\vee$. Figure 1 depicts an example. For any node n in an NNF graph, $Vars(n)$ denotes all propositional variables that appear in the subgraph rooted at n, and $\Delta(n)$ denotes the formula represented by n and its descendants. A number of properties can be stated on NNF graphs:

- Decomposability holds when $Vars(n_i) \cap Vars(n_j) = \emptyset$ for any two children n_i and n_j of an and-node n. The NNF in Figure 1 is decomposable.

- Determinism holds when $\Delta(n_i) \wedge \Delta(n_j)$ is logically in-

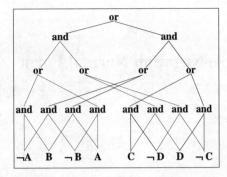

Figure 1: A negation normal form graph.

consistent for any two children n_i and n_j of an or-node n. The NNF in Figure 1 is deterministic.

- <u>Decision</u> holds when the root node of the NNF graph is a decision node. A *decision node* is a node labeled with *true*, *false*, or is an or-node having the form

  or
  and   and
  X α ¬X β

  where X is a variable, α and β are decision nodes. Here, X is called the *decision variable* of the node. The NNF in Figure 1 does not satisfy the decision property since its root is not a decision node.

- <u>Ordering</u> is defined only for NNFs that satisfy the decision property. Ordering holds when decision variables appear in the same order along any path from the root to any leaf.

Satisfiability and clausal entailment can be decided in linear time for decomposable negation normal form (DNNF) (Darwiche 2001a). Moreover, its models can be enumerated in output polynomial time, and any subset of its variables can be forgotten (existentially quantified) in linear time. Deterministic, decomposable negation normal form (d-DNNF) is even more tractable as we can count its models given any variable instantiation in polytime (Darwiche 2001c; Darwiche & Marquis 2001). Decision implies determinism. The subset of NNF that satisfies decomposability and decision (hence, determinism) corresponds to Free Binary Decision Diagrams (FBDDs) (Gergov & Meinel 1994). The subset of NNF that satisfies decomposability, decision (hence, determinism) and ordering corresponds to Ordered Binary Decision Diagrams (OBDDs) (Bryant 1986; Darwiche & Marquis 2001). In OBDD notation, however,

or
and   and
X α ¬X β

the NNF fragment is drawn more compactly as

(X)
α   β

. Hence, each non-leaf OBDD node generates three NNF nodes and six NNF edges.

Immediate from the above definitions, we have the following strict subset inclusions OBDD $\subset$ FBDD $\subset$ d-DNNF $\subset$ DNNF. Moreover, we have OBDD $>$ FBDD $>$ d-DNNF

$>$ DNNF, where $>$ stands for "less succinct than."[1] OBDDs are more tractable than DNNF, d-DNNF and FBDD. General entailment among OBDDs can be decided in polytime. Hence, the equivalence of two OBDDs can be decided in polytime. The equivalence of two DNNFs cannot be decided in polytime (unless P=NP). The equivalence question is still open for d-DNNF and FBDD, although both support polynomial probabilistic equivalence tests (Blum, Chandra, & Wegman 1980; Darwiche & Huang 2002). For a comprehensive analysis of these forms, the reader is referred to (Darwiche & Marquis 2001).

We close this section by noting that the polytime operations supported by DNNF are sufficient to implement model-based diagnosers whose complexity is linear in the size of compiled device, assuming the device is expressed as a DNNF (Darwiche 2001a). Moreover, for planning and formal verification applications, there is no need for a polytime test for general entailment as long as the goal (or property to be verified) can be expressed as a CNF (clausal entailment can be used here). Finally, polytime equivalence testing is not needed here as it is only used to check for fixed points: whether the models of some theory Δ^t (reachable states at time t) equal the models of some theory Δ^{t+1} (reachable states at time $t+1$), where $\Delta^t \models \Delta^{t+1}$ (the states reachable at t are included in those reachable at $t+1$). The two theories are equivalent in this case iff they have the same number of models. Hence, counting models is sufficient to detect fixed points in these applications.

Compiling CNF into d-DNNF

Figure 2 depicts the pseudocode of an algorithm for compiling a CNF into a d-DNNF. The presented algorithm uses a

CNF2DDNNF(n, Ω)
1. if n is a leaf node, return CLAUSE2DDNNF$(Clauses(n) \mid \Omega)$
2. $\psi \leftarrow$ CNF2KEY$(Clauses(n) \mid \Omega)$
3. if CACHE$_n(\psi) \neq$ NIL, return CACHE$_n(\psi)$
4. $\Gamma \leftarrow$ CASE_ANALYSIS(n, Ω)
5. CACHE$_n(\psi) \leftarrow \Gamma$
6. return Γ

CASE_ANALYSIS(n, Ω)
7. $\Sigma \leftarrow Sep(n, \Omega)$
8. if $\Sigma = \emptyset$, return CONJOIN(CNF2DDNNF(n_l, Ω),CNF2DDNNF(n_r, Ω))
9. $X \leftarrow$ choose a variable in Σ
10. WHILE_CASE$(X, true, \Pi)$:
11.   if $\Pi = \emptyset$, $\alpha^+ \leftarrow false$
12.   else $\alpha^+ \leftarrow$ CONJOIN$(\Pi,$ CASE_ANALYSIS$(n, \Pi \cup \Omega))$
13. WHILE_CASE$(X, false, \Pi)$:
14.   if $\Pi = \emptyset$, $\alpha^- \leftarrow false$
15.   else $\alpha^- \leftarrow$ CONJOIN$(\Pi,$ CASE_ANALYSIS$(n, \Pi \cup \Omega))$
16. return DISJOIN(α^+, α^-)

Figure 2: Compiling a CNF into d-DNNF.

---

[1]That DNNF is strictly more succinct than d-DNNF assumes the non-collapse of the polynomial heirarchy (Darwiche & Marquis 2001).

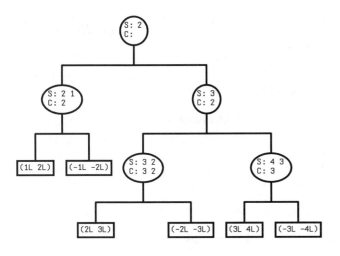

Figure 3: A decomposition tree for a CNF. Each leaf node is labeled with a clause (a set of literals). Each internal node is labeled with a separator (S) and a context (C).

data structure, known as a *decomposition tree (dtree)*, which is a full binary tree with its leaves corresponding to clauses in the given CNF (Darwiche 2001a). Figure 3 shows an example dtree, where each leaf node is labeled with a clause and each internal node is labeled with two sets of variables to be explained later. The algorithm works as follows. Each node n in the dtree corresponds to the set of clauses, $Clauses(n)$, appearing in the subtree rooted at n. Let n_l and n_r denote the left and right children of node n. If $Clauses(n_l)$ and $Clauses(n_r)$ do not share variables, then we can convert $Clauses(n_l)$ into a d-DNNF α_l and $Clauses(n_r)$ into a d-DNNF α_r and simply return $\alpha_l \wedge \alpha_r$ as the d-DNNF of $Clauses(n)$. In general, $Clauses(n_l)$ and $Clauses(n_r)$ do share variables, called a *separator* for dtree node node n. In that case, we choose one of these variables, call it X, and then perform a case analysis on it.

Case analysis. To perform case analysis on a variable X is to consider two cases, one under which X is set to true and another under which it is set to false. Under each case, X is eliminated from the given set of clauses. If α^+ is the result of converting $Clauses(n)$ into d-DNNF under $X = true$, and if α^- is the result of converting $Clauses(n)$ into d-DNNF under $X = false$, then $(X \wedge \alpha^+) \vee (\neg X \wedge \alpha^-)$ is a d-DNNF equivalent to $Clauses(n)$.[2] Case analysis is implemented using the macro WHILE_CASE(X,v,Π) on Lines 10 & 13, which replaces every occurrence of the variable X by v, performs unit resolution, and then collects all derived literals (including $X = v$) in Π. Note here that Π not only contains the literal $X = v$ as suggested above, but also all other literals derived by unit resolution (this leads to better results in general). If unit resolution derives a contradiction, Π is then the empty set.

---

[2]This is known as the Shannon expansion of $Clauses(n)$ in the literature on Boolean logic. It was initially proposed by Boole, however (Boole 1848).

Separators. We may have to perform case analysis on more than one variable before we can decompose $Clauses(n_l)$ and $Clauses(n_r)$; that is, before we eliminate every common variable between them. In general though, we do not need to perform case analysis on every variable common between $Clauses(n_l)$ and $Clauses(n_r)$. By setting a variable X to some value, some clauses under n_l or n_r may become subsumed, hence, eliminating some more variables that are common between them. This is why the separator for node n is defined with respect to a set of literals Ω on Line 7. That is, $Sep(n, \Omega)$ is defined as the variables common between $Clauses(n_l) \mid \Omega$ and $Clauses(n_r) \mid \Omega$, where $Clauses(.) \mid \Omega$ is the result of *conditioning* the clauses . on the literals Ω. That is, $Clauses(.) \mid \Omega$ is the set of clauses which results from eliminating the variables in Ω from . and replacing them by either true or false according to their signs in Ω.[3] Figure 3 depicts the separator for each node the given dtree, assuming $\Omega = \emptyset$.

The choice of which variable to set next from the separator $Sep(n, \Omega)$ on Line 9 has an effect on the overall time to compile into d-DNNF and also on the size of resulting d-DNNF. In our current implementation, we choose the variable that appears in the largest number of binary clauses. Finally, the base case in the recursive procedure of Figure 2 is when we reach a leaf node n in the dtree (Line 1), which means that $Clauses(n)$ contains a single clause. In this case, CLAUSE2DDNNF(.) is a constant time procedure which converts a clause into a d-DNNF.[4]

Unique nodes. Another technique we employ comes from the literature on OBDDs and is aimed at avoiding the construction of redundant NNF nodes. Two nodes are redundant if they share the same label (disjunction or conjunction) and have the same children. To avoid redundancy, we cache every constructed NNF node, indexed by its children and label. Before we construct a new NNF node, we first check the cache and construct the node only if no equivalent node is found in the cache. This technique is implicit in the implementation of CONJOIN and DISJOIN.[5]

Caching. Probably the most important technique we employ comes from the literature on dynamic programming. Specifically, each time we compile $Clauses(n) \mid \Omega$ into a d-DNNF α, we store (the root of) d-DNNF α in a cache associated with dtree node n; see Line 5. When the algorithm tries to compile $Clauses(n) \mid \Omega$ again, the cache associated with node node n is first checked (Lines 2&3). The *cache key* we use to store the d-DNNF α is a string generated from $Clauses(n) \mid \Omega$: each non-subsumed clause in $Clauses(n) \mid \Omega$ has two characters, one capturing its identity and the other capturing its literals. The generation of such a key is expensive, but the savings introduced by this

---

[3]This process is also known as *restriction* in the literature on Boolean logic.

[4]A clause $l_1, \ldots, l_m$ can be converted into a d-DNNF as follows: $\bigvee_{i=1}^{m} l_i \bigwedge_{j=1}^{i-1} \neg l_j$.

[5]CONJOIN and DISJOIN will construct nodes with multiple children when possible. For example, when conjoining two conjunctions, CONJOIN will generate one node labeled with $\wedge$ and have it point to the children of nodes being conjoined.

caching scheme are critical. This caching scheme is a major improvement on the one proposed in (Darwiche 2001a; 2001c). In the cited work, a *context* for node n, $Context(n)$, is defined as the set of variables that appear in the separator of some ancestor of n and also in the subtree rooted at n; see Figure 3. It is then suggested that d-DNNF α of $Clauses(n) \mid \Omega$ be cached under a key, which corresponds to the subset of literals Ω pertaining to the variables in $Context(n)$. That is, if $Clauses(n) = \{A \vee \neg B, C \vee D\}$, then $Clauses(n) \mid \{A\}$ could be cached under key A, and $Clauses(n) \mid \{\neg B\}$ could be cached under key $\neg B$, hence, generating two different subproblems. Using our caching approach, both $Clauses(n) \mid \{A\}$ and $Clauses(n) \mid \{\neg B\}$ will generate the same key, and will be treated as instances of the same subproblem, since both are equivalent to $\{C \vee D\}$.

Constructing dtrees. Another major factor that affects the behavior of our algorithm is the choice of a dtree. At first, one may think that we need to choose a dtree where the sizes of separators are minimized. As it turns out, however, this is only one important factor which needs to be balanced by minimizing the size of contexts as defined above. The smaller the separators, the fewer case analyses we have to consider. The smaller the contexts, the higher the cache hit rate. Unfortunately, these two objectives are conflicting: dtrees with small separator tend to have large contexts and the other way around. A better paramater to optimize is the size of clusters. The cluster of node n is the union of its separator and context. The size of the maximum cluster -1 is known as the *dtree width* (Darwiche 2001a). In our current implementation, we construct dtrees using the method described in (Darwiche & Hopkins 2001), which is based on recursive hypergraph decomposition. Specifically, the given CNF Δ is converted into a hypergraph G, where each clause in Δ is represented as a *hypernode* in G. Each variable X in CNF Δ is then represented as a *hyperedge* in G, which connects all hypernodes (clauses) of G in which X appears. Once the hypergraph G is constructed, we partition it into two pieces G_l and G_r, hence, partitioning the set of clauses in Δ into two corresponding sets Δ_l and Δ_r. This decomposition corresponds to the root of our dtree, and the process can be repeated recursively until the set of clauses in Δ are decomposed into singletons. Hypergraph decomposition algorithms try to attain two objectives: minimize the number of hyperedges that cross between G_l and G_r, and balance the sizes of G_l and G_r. These two objectives lead to generating dtrees with small widths as has been shown in (Darwiche & Hopkins 2001). The construction of a dtree according to the above method is quite fast and predictable, so we don't include the time for converting a CNF into a dtree in the experimental results to follow. We have to mention two facts though about the method described above. First, the hypergraph partitioning algorithm we use is randomized, hence, it is hard to generate the same dtree again for a given CNF. This also means that there is no guarantee that one would obtain the same d-DNNF for a given CNF, unless the same dtree is used across different runs. Second, the hypergraph partitioning algorithm requires a balance factor, which is used to enforce the balance constraint. We have found that a balance factor of 3/1 seems to generate good results in general. Therefore, if one does not have time to search across different balance factors, a balance factor of 3/1 is our recommended setting.

We close this section by noting that to compile a CNF Δ into a d-DNNF, we have to first construct a dtree with root n for Δ and then call CNF2DDNNF$(n, \emptyset)$.

Experimental results

We will now apply the presented CNF2DDNNF compiler to a number of CNFs. The experiment were run on a Windows platform, with a 1GHz processor. Our implementation is in LISP! We expect a C implementation to be an order of magnitude faster. The compiler is available through a web interface—please contact the author for details.

Random CNF formulas

Our first set of CNFs comes from SATLIB[6] and includes satisfiable, random 3CNF formulas in the crossover region, in addition to formulas corresponding to graph coloring problems; see Table 1.[7] Random 3CNF formulas (uf50–uf200) could be easily compiled with less than a minute on average for the largest ones (200 vars). Compiling such CNFs into OBDDs using the state-of-the-art CUDD[8] compiler was not feasible in general.[9] For example, we could not compile the first instance of uf100 within four hours. Moreover, the first instance in uf50 takes about 20 minutes to compile. More than 2 million nodes are constructed in the process, with more than 500 thousand nodes present in memory at some point (the final OBDD has only 82 nodes though). We have to point out here that we used CUDD in a straightforward manner. That is, we simply constructed an OBDD for each clause and then conjoined these clauses according to their order in the CNF. There are more sophisticated approaches for converting CNFs into OBDDs that have been reported recently (Aloul, Markov, & Sakallah 2001; December 2001). No experimental results are available at this stage, however, on compiling random CNFs into OBDDs using these approaches. We will report on these approaches with respect to other datasets later on though.

We also report on the compilation of graph coloring problems in Table 1 (flat100 and flat200). As is clear from the table, these CNFs can be easily compiled into small d-DNNFs that have a large number of models. Each one of these models is a graph coloring solution. Not only can we count these solutions, but we can also answer a variety of queries about these solutions in linear time. Examples: How many solutions set the color of node n to c? Is it true that when node n_1 is assigned color c_1, then node n_2 must be assigned color c_2? And so on? Although compiling a flat200 CNF takes 11 minutes on average, answering any of the previous queries can be done by simply traversing the compiled d-DNNF only once (Darwiche 2001c), which takes less than a

---

[6]*http://www.intellektik.informatik.tu-darmstadt.de/SATLIB/*

[7]Sets uf50 and uf100 contain 1000 instances each. We only use the first 100 instances.

[8]*http://vlsi.colorado.edu/ fabio/CUDD/*

[9]We used the sift-converge dynamic ordering heuristic in our experiments.

Name	Vars/Clause	d-DNNF nodes	d-DNNF edges	Model count	Time (sec)
uf50	50/218	111	258.4	362.2	1
uf100	100/430	1333.3	4765.3	1590706.1	2
uf150	150/645	3799.8	15018.5	68403010	8
uf200	200/860	4761.8	19273.3	1567696500	37
flat100	300/1117	1347.2	8565.2	8936035	4
flat200	600/2237	4794.9	46951.3	2.2202334e+13	636

Table 1: CNF benchmarks from SATLIB. Each set contains a 100 instances. We report the average over all instances.

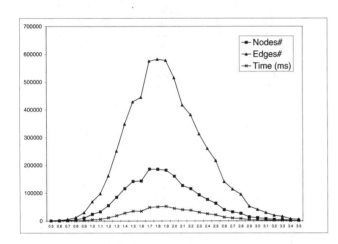

Figure 4: Difficulty of compilation according to clauses/vars ratio. Each point is the average over 100 instances.

second in this case. Hence, the compilation time is amortized over all queries which makes the time-to-compile a worthy investment in this case. We note here that the first instance of flat100 could not be compiled into an OBDD using CUDD within a cutoff time of 1 hour. One can count the models of flat100 efficiently however using the RELSAT[10] model counter, but we report in the following section on other CNFs which could not be handled efficiently using RELSAT.

We also experimented with planning CNFs from SATLIB. We could compile blocks-world CNFs anomaly, medium, huge, and large.a within a few minutes each. But we could not compile large.b, nor the logistics CNFs within a few hours.

We close this section by noting that random 3CNF formulas in the crossover region, those with clauses/vars ratio of about 4.3, are easier to compile than formulas with lower ratios. The same has been observed for counting models, where the greatest difficulty is reported for ratios around 1.2 by (Birnbaum & Lozinskii 1999) and around 1.5 by (Ba-

yardo & Pehoushek 2000). Figure 4 plots information about compilations of random 3CNFs with 50 variables each, for clauses/vars ratio ranging from .5 to 3.5 at increments of .1. As is clear from this plot, the peak for the number of nodes, number of edges, and time is around a ratio of 1.8.

Boolean Circuits

We now consider CNFs which correspond to digital circuits. Suppose we have a circuit with inputs I, outputs O and let W stand for all wires in the circuit that are neither inputs nor outputs. We will distinguish between three types of representations for the circuit:

Type I representation: A theory Δ over variables I, O, W where the models of Δ correspond to instantiations of I, O, W that are compatible with circuit behavior. A CNF corresponding to Type I representation can be easily constructed and in a modular way by generating a set of clauses for each gate in the circuit.[11]

Type II representation: A theory Δ over input/output variables I, O, where the models of Δ correspond to input/output vectors compatible with circuit behavior. If Δ is a Type I representation, then $\exists W \Delta$ is a Type II representation.[12]

Type III representation for circuit output o: A theory over inputs I, where the models correspond to input vectors that generate a 1 at output o. If Δ is a Type II representation, then $\exists o.\Delta \wedge o$ is a Type III representation for output o.

Clearly, Type I is more expressive than Type II, which is more expressive than Type III. The reason we draw this distinction is to clarify that in the formal verification literature, one usually constructs Type III representations for circuits since this is all one needs to check the equivalence of two circuits. In AI applications, however, such as diagnosis, one is mostly interested in Type I representations, which are much harder to obtain.

We compute Type II representations by simply replacing Lines 12 & 15 in CNF2DDNNF by

$$\alpha^+ \leftarrow \text{CONJOIN}(\Pi', \text{CASE\_ANALYSIS}(n, \Pi \cup \Omega)),$$

---

[11]Type I representations are called *Circuit Consistency Functions* in (Aloul, Markov, & Sakallah 2001; December 2001).

[12]Recall: $\exists w \Delta$, where w is a single variable, is defined as $\Delta^+ \vee \Delta^-$, where Δ^+ (Δ^-) is the result of replacing w with *true* (*false*) in Δ. $\exists W \Delta$ is the result of quantifying over variables in W, one at a time (Darwiche & Marquis 2001).

---

[10]*http://www.almaden.ibm.com/cs/people/bayardo/vinci/index.html*

and

$$\alpha^- \leftarrow \text{CONJOIN}(\Pi', \text{CASE\_ANALYSIS}(n, \Pi \cup \Omega)),$$

respectively, where Π' is obtained from Π by removing all literals corresponding to variables in W. We also have to modify the boundary condition handled by CLAUSE2DDNNF, so that CLAUSE2DDNNF(.) returns *true* if the clause . contains a literal pertaining to W, and behaves as usual otherwise. Given the above changes—which implement the proposal given in (Darwiche 2001a) for existential quantification—CNF2DDNNF$(n, \emptyset)$ is then guaranteed to return $\exists W \Delta$ in d-DNNF, where n is the root of a dtree for CNF Δ.[13]

To compute efficient Type III representations, one needs to use multi-rooted NNFs, where each root corresponds to the compilation of one circuit output. This is how it is done in the formal verification literature, where multi-rooted OBDDs are known as *shared OBDDs*. Our compiler does not handle multi-rooted d-DNNFs yet, so we do not report on Type III representations.

Tables 2 and 3 contain results on the first five circuits in the ISCAS85 benchmark circuits.[14] We were able to obtain Type I and Type II representations for all these circuits expressed as d-DNNFs. The most difficult was c1908, which took around 1.5 hrs, followed by c880 which took around 30 minutes. We are not aware of any other compilations of these circuits of Types I and II, although the formal verification literature contains successful compilations of Type III, represented as multi-rooted OBDDs. We could not compile c499, c880, c1355, nor c1908 into Type I OBDDs using CUDD, nor could we count their models using RELSAT, within cutoff times of 1hr, 1hr, 1hr and 3hrs, respectively (we actually tried CUDD on c499 for more than a day). For c432, we tried several OBDD ordering heuristics. The best OBDD we could obtain for this circuit had 15811 nodes.

We note here that although d-DNNF does not support a deterministic test of equivalence, one can easily test the equivalence of a d-DNNF Δ, and a CNF $\Gamma = \gamma_1 \wedge \ldots \wedge \gamma_m$, which corresponds to a Type I representation of a circuit. By construction, the number of models for Γ is 2^k, where k is the number of primary inputs for the circuit. Therefore, Δ and Γ are equivalent iff (1) the number of models for Δ is 2^k and (2) $\Delta \models \Gamma$. The first condition can be checked in time linear in the size of Δ since d-DNNF supports model counting in linear time. The second condition can be checked by verifying that $\Delta \models \gamma_i$ for each i, a test which can also be performed in time linear in the size of Δ since d-DNNF supports a linear test for clausal entailment. We actually use the above technique for checking the correctness of our d-DNNF compilations.

Table 4 contains further results from ISCAS89.[15] These are sequential circuits, which have been converted into com-

Name	Vars/Clause	d-DNNF nodes	d-DNNF edges	Clique size	Time (sec)
c432	196/514	2899	19779	28	6
c499	243/714	691803	2919960	23	448
c880	443/1112	3975728	7949684	24	1893
c1355	587/1610	338959	3295293	23	809
c1908	913/2378	6183489	12363322	45	5712

Table 2: Type I compilations of ISCAS85 circuits.

Name	I/O vars	d-DNNF nodes	d-DNNF edges	Time (sec)
c432	36/7	952	3993	1
c499	41/32	68243	214712	127
c880	60/26	718856	2456827	1774
c1355	41/32	65017	201576	483
c1908	33/25	326166	1490315	4653

Table 3: Type II compilations of ISCAS85 circuits.

binational circuits by cutting feedback loops into flip-flops, treating a flip-flop's input as a circuit output and its output as a circuit input. Most of these circuits are easy to compile and have relatively small d-DNNFs. Type I OBDD representations for some ISCAS89 circuits are reported in (Aloul, Markov, & Sakallah 2001; December 2001), which is probably the most sophisticated approach for converting CNFs into OBDDs. In addition to proposing a new method for ordering OBDD variables based on the connectivity of given CNF, a proposal is made for ordering the clauses during the OBDD construction process. (Aloul, Markov, & Sakallah 2001; December 2001) report on the maximum number of OBDD nodes during the construction process, not on the size of final OBDDs constructed. Yet, their experiments appear to confirm the theoretical results reported in (Darwiche & Marquis 2001) on the relative succinctness of d-DNNF and OBDD representations. For example, circuits s832, s953, s1196 and s1238 were among the more difficult ones in these experiments, leading to constructing 115×10^3, 1.8×10^6, 2×10^6, and 2×10^6 nodes, respectively—s1238 is the largest circuit they report on. These numbers are orders of magnitude larger than what we report in Table 4.[16] We note here that the total number of nodes constructed by our d-DNNF compiler is rarely more than twice the number of nodes in the final d-DNNF.[17] We finally note that no experimental results are provided in (Aloul, Markov, & Sakallah 2001;

---

[13] In general, this only guarantees that the result is in DNNF (Darwiche 2001a). For CNFs corresponding to digital circuits, however, determinism is also guaranteed due to the following property: for every instantiation α of I, O, there is a unique instantiation β of W such that $\Delta \wedge \alpha \models \beta$.

[14] *http://www.cbl.ncsu.edu/www/CBL_Docs/iscas85.html*

[15] *http://www.cbl.ncsu.edu/www/CBL_Docs/iscas89.html*

[16] One has to admit though that it is hard to tell exactly how much of this difference is due to relative succinctness of OBDD vs d-DNNF, and how much of it is due to the effectiveness of different compilation techniques, since none of the compilers discussed are guaranteed to generate optimal OBDDs or d-DNNFs.

[17] This is in contrast to OBDD compilers, where the number of intermediate OBDD nodes can be much larger than the size of final OBDD returned. We believe this is due to the top-down construction method used by our compiler, as opposed to the bottom-up methods traditionally used by OBDD compilers.

Name	Vars/Clause	d-DNNF nodes	d-DNNF edges	Clique size	Time (sec)
s298	136/363	830	4657	12	1
s344	184/429	962	4973	9	1
s349	185/434	1017	5374	10	1
s382	182/464	1034	5081	17	1
s386	172/506	1401	10130	21	2
s400	186/482	1021	5137	18	1
s444	205/533	1091	5872	16	1
s499	175/491	1090	5565	20	2
s510	236/635	967	5755	38	2
s526	217/638	2621	19605	22	1
s526n	218/639	2611	20115	22	1
s635	320/762	1360	4845	9	1
s641	433/918	7062	84596	21	1
s713	447/984	7128	90901	21	10
s820	312/1046	2774	21365	29	2
s832	310/1056	2757	21224	28	2
s938	512/1233	2207	12342	14	2
s953	440/1138	11542	110266	64	14
s967	439/1157	20645	443233	60	117
s991	603/1337	2382	13107	8	2
s1196	561/1538	12554	261402	51	60
s1238	540/1549	14512	288143	53	58
s1423	748/1821	112701	1132322	24	162
s1488	667/2040	6338	62175	49	11
s1494	661/2040	6827	64888	51	12
s1512	866/2044	12560	140384	21	27
s3330	1961/4605	358093	8889410	43	5853
s3384	1911/4440	44487	392223	17	45

Table 4: Type I compilations of ISCAS89 circuits.

December 2001) for Type I OBDD representations of IS-CAS85 circuits, which are much harder to compile than IS-CAS89 circuits.

One implication of our ability to compile these circuits is that we can now perform a variety of reasoning tasks about these circuits in time linear in the size of given d-DNNF. Some example queries: Given a distribution over the circuit inputs, what is the probability that Wire 45 is high? How may circuit inputs will generate a high on the first circuit output and a low on the fifth output? Is it true that whenever Wires 33 and 87 are high, then Wire 19 must be low? How may input vectors will generate a particular output vector? Each one of these queries can be answered by a single traversal of the d-DNNF circuit representation (Darwiche 2001b; 2001a; 2001c).

We also report in Tables 2–4 on the best clique sizes obtained for these circuits when converting their structures into jointrees (Jensen, Lauritzen, & Olesen 1990). This is needed for reasoning about these circuits probabilistically using state-of-the-art algorithms for Bayesian networks. These algorithms have exponential complexity in the clique size. Hence, most of these circuits are outside the scope of such algorithms. We are not aware of any algorithm for probabilistic reasoning which can handle these circuits, except the one we report on in (Darwiche 2001b) which is based on these d-DNNF compilations. We close this section

by noting that the algorithm reported in (Darwiche 2001a; 2001c) also has a time complexity which is exponential in the clique size. Hence, most of the CNFs we considered in this paper are outside the scope of the mentioned algorithm.

Relationship to Davis-Putnam

One cannot but observe the similarity between our proposed algorithm and the Davis-Putnam (DP) algorithm for propositional satisfiability (Davis, Logemann, & Loveland 1962), and its recent extensions for counting propositional models: the CDP algorithm in (Birnbaum & Lozinskii 1999) and the DDP algorithm in (Bayardo & Pehoushek 2000).

The DP algorithm solves propositional satisfiability by performing case analysis until a solution is found or an inconsistency is established. When performing case analysis on variable X, the second value for X is considered only if the first value does not lead to a solution. The CDP algorithm in (Birnbaum & Lozinskii 1999) observed that by always considering both values, we can extend the DP algorithm to count models since $ModelCount(\Delta) = ModelCount(\Delta^+) + ModelCount(\Delta^-)$, where Δ^+ and Δ^- are the result of setting X to $true$ and to $false$, respectively, in Δ. The DDP algorithm in (Bayardo & Pehoushek 2000) incorporated yet another idea: If Δ can be decomposed into two disconnected subsets Δ^1 and Δ^2, then $ModelCount(\Delta) = ModelCount(\Delta^1)ModelCount(\Delta^2)$. Hence, DDP will apply case analysis until the CNF is disconnected into pieces, in which case each piece is attempted independently.

The CDP algorithm can in fact be easily adapted to compile a CNF into a d-DNNF, by simply constructing the NNF fragment $X \wedge \mathrm{CDP}(\Delta^+) \vee \neg X \wedge \mathrm{CDP}(\Delta^-)$ each time a case analysis is performed on variable X. Here, $\mathrm{CDP}(.)$ is the result of compiling . into d-DNNF using the same algorithm recursively. This extension of CDP will generate a strict subset of d-DNNF: the one which satisfies the decision and decomposability properties (hence, an FBDD) and that also has a tree structure (FBDDs have a graph structure in general). FBDDs are known to be less succinct than d-DNNFs, even in their graph form (Darwiche & Marquis 2001). The tree-structured form is even more restrictive.

The DDP algorithm can also be easily adapted to compile a CNF into a d-DNNF, by constructing the NNF fragment $X \wedge \mathrm{DDP}(\Delta^+) \vee \neg X \wedge \mathrm{DDP}(\Delta^-)$ each time a case analysis is performed on X, and by constructing the fragment $\mathrm{DDP}(\Delta^1) \wedge \mathrm{DDP}(\Delta^2)$ each time a decomposition is performed as given above. This extension of DDP will actually generate d-DNNFs which are not FBDDs, yet are still tree-structured which is a major limitation. The important point to stress here is that any CNF which can be processed successfully using the DDP algorithm, can also be compiled successfully into a d-DNNF.

The algorithm we present can be viewed as a further generalization of the discussed DDP extension in the sense that it generates graph NNFs as opposed to tree NNFs. The graph structure is due to two features of CNF2DDNNF: the caching and unique-node schemes. Each time a node is looked up from a cache, its number of parents will potentially increase by one. Moreover, the CONJOIN and DISJOIN operations will often return a pointer to an existing NNF node instead of constructing a new one, again, increasing the number of parents per node.[18] Another major difference with the above proposed extension of DDP is the use of dtrees to guide the decomposition process as they restrict the set of variables considered for case analysis at any given time. The use of dtrees can then be viewed as a variable splitting heuristic which is geared towards decomposition as opposed to solution finding.

Conclusion

We presented a compiler for converting CNF formulas into deterministic, decomposable negation normal form (d-DNNF). This is a logical form that has been identified recently and shown to support a number of operations in polynomial time, including clausal entailment; model counting, minimization and enumeration; and probabilistic equivalence testing. d-DNNFs are also known to be a superset of, and more succinct than, OBDDs. The logical operations supported by d-DNNFs are a subset of those supported by OBDDs, yet are sufficient for model-based diagnosis and planning applications. We presented experimental results on compiling a variety of CNF formulas, some generated randomly and others corresponding to digital circuits. A number of the formulas we were able to compile efficiently could not be similarly handled by some state-of-the-art model counters, nor by some state-of-the-art OBDD compilers. Moreover, our ability to successfully compile some of these CNFs allowed us to answer some queries for the very first time.

Acknowledgments

The author would like to thank Fadi Aloul, Roberto Bayardo, Rolf Haenni and Pierre Marquis for helpful comments and suggestions regarding earlier drafts of this paper. This work has been partially supported by NSF grant IIS-9988543 and MURI grant N00014-00-1-0617.

References

Aloul, F. A.; Markov, I. L.; and Sakallah, K. A. 2001. Faster SAT and smaller BDDs via common function structure. In *International Conference on Computer Aided Design (ICCAD)*, 443–448.

Aloul, F. A.; Markov, I. L.; and Sakallah, K. A. December, 2001. Faster SAT and smaller BDDs via common function structure. Technical Report CSE-TR-445-01, Computer Science and Engineering Division, University of Michigan.

Bayardo, R., and Pehoushek, J. 2000. Counting models using connected components. In *AAAI*, 157–162.

Birnbaum, E., and Lozinskii, E. 1999. The good old Davis-Putnam procedure helps counting models. *Journal of Artificial Intelligence Research* 10:457–477.

Blum, M.; Chandra, A. K.; and Wegman, M. N. 1980. Equivalence of free Boolean graphs can be decided probabilistically in polynomial time. *Information Processing Letters* 10(2):80–82.

Boole, G. 1848. The calculus of logic. *The Cambridge and Dublin Mathematical Journal* 3:183–198.

Bryant, R. E. 1986. Graph-based algorithms for Boolean function manipulation. *IEEE Transactions on Computers* C-35:677–691.

Darwiche, A., and Hopkins, M. 2001. Using recursive decomposition to construct elimination orders, jointrees and dtrees. In *Trends in Artificial Intelligence, Lecture notes in AI, 2143*. Springer-Verlag. 180–191.

Darwiche, A., and Huang, J. 2002. Testing equivalence probabilistically. Technical Report D–123, Computer Science Department, UCLA, Los Angeles, Ca 90095.

Darwiche, A., and Marquis, P. 2001. A perspective on knowledge compilation. In *Proc. International Joint Conference on Artificial Intelligence (IJCAI)*, 175–182.

Darwiche, A. 2001a. Decomposable negation normal form. *Journal of the ACM* 48(4):1–42.

Darwiche, A. 2001b. A logical approach to factoring belief networks. Technical Report D–121, Computer Science Department, UCLA, Los Angeles, Ca 90095. To appear in KR-02.

Darwiche, A. 2001c. On the tractability of counting theory models and its application to belief revision and truth maintenance. *Journal of Applied Non-Classical Logics* 11(1-2):11–34.

Davis, M.; Logemann, G.; and Loveland, D. 1962. A machine program for theorem proving. *CACM* 5:394–397.

Gergov, J., and Meinel, C. 1994. Efficient analysis and manipulation of OBDDs can be extended to FBDDs. *IEEE Transactions on Computers* 43(10):1197–1209.

Jensen, F. V.; Lauritzen, S.; and Olesen, K. 1990. Bayesian updating in recursive graphical models by local computation. *Computational Statistics Quarterly* 4:269–282.

---

[18] (Bayardo & Pehoushek 2000) rightfully suggest that "learning goods," which corresponds to caching non-zero counts, is essential for efficient counting of models, but do not pursue the technique citing technical difficulties.

Inference Methods for a Pseudo-Boolean Satisfiability Solver

Heidi E. Dixon and Matthew L. Ginsberg

CIRL
1269 University of Oregon
Eugene, OR 97403-1269
{dixon, ginsberg}@cirl.uoregon.edu

Abstract

We describe two methods of doing inference during search for a pseudo-Boolean version of the RELSAT method. One inference method is the pseudo-Boolean equivalent of learning. A new constraint is learned in response to a contradiction with the purpose of eliminating the set of assignments that caused the contradiction. We show that the obvious way of extending learning to pseudo-Boolean is inadequate and describe a better solution. We also describe a second inference method used by the Operations Research community. The method cannot be applied to the standard resolution-based AI algorithms, but is useful for pseudo-Boolean versions of the same AI algorithms. We give experimental results showing that the pseudo-Boolean version of RELSAT outperforms its clausal counterpart on problems from the planning domain.

Introduction

Building boolean satisfiability solvers that implement strong proof systems is an important goal for the field of AI. This goal is motivated by results from the field of proof complexity showing that some proof systems are more limited than others. An inference system is limited if it is impossible to construct short proofs of unsatisfiability for certain families of problems. These results have significant consequences for systematic satisfiability solvers. Because systematic solvers can be viewed primarily as constructing proofs of unsatisfiability, it follows that these solvers are subject to the limitations of the proof systems they implement.

Throughout the AI community, satisfiability problems are typically represented as a set of constraints in conjunctive normal form (CNF) with resolution as the primary inference step. We believe that resolution-based methods are prevalent because of their simplicity. Unfortunately, many unsatisfiable problems have no short resolution proofs of unsatisfiability. An example is the pigeonhole problem which states that $n + 1$ pigeons cannot be placed in n holes. The shortest resolution proof of unsatisfiability for the pigeonhole problem is exponential in the number of pigeons (Haken 1985). Because resolution is a weak proof system, resolution-based methods have poor performance on a variety of easy problems like the pigeonhole problem. They may also be unnecessarily slow on structured problems from areas like plan-

ning and scheduling where embedded pigeonhole problems are common. Refining current algorithms may yield improvements, but can never provide polynomial time scaling on these problems unless the underlying representation and inference used by the solver is changed.

One approach to addressing the problem of representation is to adapt a successful resolution-based method to use a stronger representation. The work done on resolution-based methods has yielded successful strategies and produced significant improvements in performance. The hope is that the progress made will carry over into new representations. The growing number of solvers taking this approach show that such implementations are possible. This is the approach used in FDPLL (Baumgartner 2000); a version of the Davis-Putnam-Logeman-Loveland (DPLL) procedure lifted to solve first-order logic problems. This is also the approach used in OPBDP (Barth 1995), PRS (Dixon & Ginsberg 2000) and SATIRE (Whittemore, Kim, & Sakallah 2001). These solvers borrow from the Operations Research using pseudo-Boolean (PB) representation.

This paper discusses some of the challenges and benefits of lifting the RELSAT style of learning to use pseudo-Boolean representation. The algorithm RELSAT is an extension of the DPLL method. Both algorithms work by taking a valid partial assignment and attempting to extend it to a valid full assignment by incrementally assigning values to variables. An important difference between the algorithms is that RELSAT infers new constraints during search by using resolution. It uses the technique of relevance-bounded learning to keep the size of the constraint set manageable (Bayardo & Schrag 1997; Ginsberg 1993). Learned constraints are removed from the constraint set when they are less likely to be needed. These added abilities give RELSAT a dramatic advantage over DPLL on structured problems.

Our primary focus will be on the way inference is used during search and how this role changes when we move from CNF to pseudo-Boolean representation. RELSAT will infer a new clause every time a contradiction is encountered. The purpose of the new clause is to eliminate the set of assignments that caused the contradiction. The resolution inference rule happens to be perfect for this purpose.

A comparable pseudo-Boolean version of this method should achieve the same goals. In the pseudo-Boolean case we have more options to consider when generating a new constraint in response to a contradiction. The correct way to infer new constraints is less clear. Pseudo-Boolean inference has added benefits that result directly from the more expressive nature of pseudo-Boolean constraints. In some cases, a new constraint may eliminate assignments corresponding to parts of the search space not yet explored, in addition to eliminating the set of assignments that caused a contradiction. This, in a sense, eliminates mistakes before they are made. In other cases, care must be taken to ensure that the generated constraint actually eliminates the set of assignments that led to the contradiction. We will give explicit examples showing each of these cases, and we will describe a learning method for the pseudo-Boolean case that meets the requirement of eliminating a specific set of assignments in response to a contradiction. We present experimental results comparing the performance of the clausal version of RELSAT to the pseudo-Boolean version PRS.

Another benefit of using pseudo-Boolean representation is that new kinds of inferences are possible that are not possible in a resolution system. A more expressive constraint can be inferred from a set of simple disjunctive constraints. Automating these inferences present a new challenge because they have no precedents in resolution-based methods. We describe a technique from the field of Operations Research that can be used to automate this kind of inference and show how it can be used in an AI style solver.

Preliminaries

Representation and Inference

Conjunctive normal form and resolution Within the AI community, satisfiability problems are typically represented as a set of constraints in conjunctive normal form (CNF). A constraint or clause is a disjunction of literals and a problem instance is the conjunction over a list of clauses. The primary inference step is resolution.

$$\frac{\begin{array}{c} a_1 \vee \cdots \vee a_k \vee l \\ b_1 \vee \cdots \vee b_m \vee \bar{l} \end{array}}{a_1 \vee \cdots \vee a_k \vee b_1 \vee \cdots \vee b_m}$$

Two clauses resolve if there is exactly one literal l that appears positively in one clause and negatively in the other. A new clause is derived by disjoining the two clauses and removing both l and $\neg l$. If a literal appears twice in the resulting clause, the clause can be rewritten with the literal appearing only once. This is known as factoring.

Linear inequalities and cutting planes Pseudo-Boolean representation comes from the Operations Research community and is a subset of their general representation in which constraints are expressed as linear inequalities

$$\sum a_j x_j \geq k$$

Here, the x_i are non-negative integer variables and the a_i and k are integers. The corresponding inference system is called the cutting plane system (CP). There are two rules of inference: (i) derive a new inequality by taking a linear combination of a set of inequalities, (ii) given an inequality

$\sum a_j x_j \geq k$ derive $\sum \lceil \frac{a_j}{d} \rceil x_j \geq \lceil \frac{k}{d} \rceil$, where d is a positive integer. The notation $\lceil q \rceil$ denotes the least integer greater than or equal to q. If the inequality $0 \geq 1$ is derived then the original set of inequalities is inconsistent. If the integer variables are restricted to the domain $\{0, 1\}$, then the inequality is called *pseudo-Boolean*. The expression $\bar{x}$ refers to the negation of the variable x, so that for all literals x, $\bar{x} = 1 - x$.

The CP inference system is properly stronger than resolution. The existence of a polynomial-length resolution proof implies the existence of a polynomial-length cutting plane proof, but the reverse does not hold (Cook, Coullard, & Turán 1987). The pigeonhole problem which has only exponential-length proofs in resolution has polynomial-length proofs in CP (Cook, Coullard, & Turán 1987).

Translating between representations A disjunction of literals $x_0 \vee x_1 \vee \cdots \vee x_n$, can be equivalently written as a linear pseudo-Boolean inequality.

$$x_0 + x_1 + \cdots + x_n \geq 1$$

Pseudo-Boolean inequalities with a right hand side that is equal to 1 are called clausal inequalities.

We can translate a pseudo-Boolean constraint into a set of clauses in CNF as follows. Given a constraint

$$\sum_{i=1}^{n} a_i x_i \geq k \qquad (1)$$

Let $L = \{x_1, x_2, \ldots, x_n\}$ be the set of literals in (1). For any set $S = \{y_1, y_2, \ldots, y_j\}$ such that $S \subseteq L$, if

$$\sum_{x_i \notin S} a_i \leq k - 1$$

then the disjunction $y_1 \vee y_2 \vee \cdots \vee y_j$ is implied by the constraint (1). In other words, if the sum over the coefficients of the remaining literals cannot satisfy the constraint, then at least one of the literals in S must be true. For example, given the constraint

$$2a + b + c \geq 2$$

we can derive the clause $a \vee b$, since c alone is not enough to satisfy the constraint. The constraint (1) is logically equivalent to the conjunction over the set of all disjunctions generated this way (Benhamou, Sais, & Siegel 1994).

Understanding RELSAT

The algorithm RELSAT (Bayardo & Schrag 1997) is a version of the classic Davis-Putnam-Logeman-Loveland method (Davis & Putnam 1960; Loveland 1978) with the addition of relevance-bounded learning. If the relevance-bounded learning feature is disabled during execution, then RELSAT becomes a DPLL implementation.

Davis-Putnam-Logeman-Loveland DPLL takes a valid partial assignment and attempts to extend it to a valid full assignment by incrementally assigning values to variables. This creates a binary tree where each node corresponds to a set of assignments. DPLL explores the tree using depth first search with backtracking. A backtrack occurs when a contradiction is encountered. The algorithm terminates when a solution is found or when the entire space has been explored.

Procedure 0.1 Davis-Putnam-Logeman-Loveland *Given a SAT problem S and a partial assignment of values to variables P, to compute* `solve(C, P)`:

if `unit-propagate(P)` fails, **then** return failure
else set $P :=$ `unit-propagate(P)`
if all clauses are satisfied by P, **then** return P
$v :=$ an atom not assigned a value by P
if `solve(C, P ∪ (v := true))` succeeds,
   then return $P \cup (v := \texttt{true})$
else return `solve(C, P ∪ (v := false))`

Variables are assigned values in two ways. In the first way, unit propagation, clauses are identified that have no satisfied literals and exactly one unvalued literal. In each such clause, the unvalued literal is valued favorably. This process is repeated until a contradiction is encountered, a solution is found, or no more clauses meet the necessary conditions. If the unit propagation function terminates without reaching a contradiction or finding a solution, then a variable is selected and assigned a value by a branching heuristic.

Procedure 0.2 Unit propagation
to compute `unit-propagate(P)`:

while there is a currently unsatisfied clause $c \in C$
           that contains at most one literal
           unassigned a value by P **do**
   if every atom in c is assigned a value by P,
   then return failure
   else $a :=$ the atom in c unassigned by P
       augment P by valuing a so that c is satisfied
   end if
end while
return P

Learning and relevance-bounded learning One way that solvers use inference is through learning (Stallman & Sussman 1977). A drawback to simple backtracking algorithms like DPLL is that they may end up solving the same subproblems repeatedly. Learning new valid constraints can prevent this from happening. When a contradiction is encountered, the set of assignments that caused the contradiction are identified. We will call this set the *conflict set*. A new constraint is constructed that excludes the assignments in the conflict set. The constraint is added to the constraint database to ensure that the faulty set of assignments will be avoided in the future. An example might look like this. Given the partial assignment $\{a = \texttt{true}, b = \texttt{false}, d = \texttt{true}, e = \texttt{false}\}$ (which we write somewhat more compactly as $\{a, \bar{b}, d, \bar{e}\}$), together with the two clauses

$$\bar{a} \vee b \vee c \vee e$$

$$\bar{c} \vee \bar{d}$$

We encounter a contradiction for variable c. The first clause requires c, while the second requires $\bar{c}$. The conflict set $\{a, \bar{b}, d, \bar{e}\}$ is the union of the unfavorable assignments for

each clause. Before we backtrack, we construct a new clause that is the resolvent of the preceding two clauses.

$$\bar{a} \vee b \vee e \vee \bar{d} \tag{2}$$

This clause has the property of being unsatisfied by the current partial assignment. It disallows the assignments that caused the contradiction, and we can use (2) to determine how far we must backtrack before we can safely move forward again. The derived clause "fixes" the mistake that was made in that we are protected from repeating the mistake as long as we keep the new clause in our constraint database.

Learning new constraints reduces the size of the search space by eliminating parts of the space that cannot contain solutions. Unfortunately, reducing the size of the search space does not always correspond to a reduction is execution time. The number of constraints learned can be exponential in the size of the problem. This can exhaust memory resources. The algorithm spends more time managing its large database of constraints and performance degrades. The learning process must be restricted in some way to prevent an unmanageable number of constraints from accumulating.

Relevance-bounded learning is a restricted version of learning. Our focus is not relevance-bounded learning, so we give only a high level description of it. Relevance-bounded learning defines an integer measure of how relevant a learned constraint is in relation to the current position in the search space. The relevance of a constraint estimates the likelihood that the constraint can be used to prune the search space. Constraints with low values are more relevant then those with higher values. As the position in the search space changes the relevance of the clause will change in response. A *relevance bound* is established, and constraints are discarded when their relevance exceeds the bound.

Learning with pseudo-Boolean constraints

The pseudo-Boolean case is similar to the clausal case in that a contradiction occurs when a partial assignment together with two constraints causes a variable to be labelled both 1 and 0. A good solution should generate a constraint that disallows the set of assignments that caused the contradiction. We will describe two ways of generating a new constraint in response to a contradiction. The first way generates a complex constraint that may eliminate extra sets of assignments in addition to those in the conflict set. Unfortunately, in certain cases it may not eliminate the exact set of assignments in the conflict set. The second way eliminates exactly the set of assignments in the conflict set. A good learning strategy can be built by combining the two methods.

One way of generating a new constraint is to do a pseudo-Boolean version of resolution, taking a linear combination of the two constraints in a way that causes the contradiction variable to be canceled out of the resulting constraint. Consider the following example. Suppose we have a partial assignment $\{c = 1, e = 1, b = 0, d = 0\}$, and constraints

$$a + d + \bar{e} \;\geq\; 1 \tag{3}$$
$$\bar{a} + b + c \;\geq\; 2 \tag{4}$$

These cause the variable a to be simultaneously 1 and 0. We generate a new constraint by adding (3) and (4) to get $d + \overline{e} + b + c \geq 2$.

By inspection, we can see that the conflict set is $\{b = 0, d = 0, e = 1\}$, and that the derived constraint excludes this assignment. This constraint also eliminates some additional bad assignments. For example, it also eliminates the assignment $\{c = 0, d = 0, e = 1\}$. In addition to fixing the current assignment error, we've learned something new about a different part of the search space. In the clausal version, learned constraints prevent us from repeating a mistake. Here we have the potential to prevent mistakes before they happen.

Unfortunately it is possible to construct cases where the constraint derived does not exclude the set of assignments causing the contradiction. Given the partial assignment $\{c = 1, e = 1, b = 0, d = 0\}$ and constraints

$$2a + d + e \geq 2$$
$$2\overline{a} + b + c \geq 2$$

Adding gives $d + e + b + c \geq 2$, which still allows the set of assignments in the conflict set $\{b = 0, d = 0\}$. We may make the same bad assignment again later in the search. Also this constraint does not give any direction to the backtrack since it is satisfied under the current partial assignment.

We define a second method of generating a constraint in response to a contradiction that is guaranteed to eliminate the necessary set of assignments. We begin by constructing a weakening of each parent constraint into a clausal inequality using the method described earlier for generating valid CNF clauses from a pseudo-Boolean constraint. Each constraint will satisfy two properties: it contains the contradiction variable in the same form as it appears in the parent constraint, and all other literals are unsatisfied under the current partial assignment. When choosing literals to add to the constraint, priority is given to literals whose assignments occur earliest in the partial assignment. The two constraints generated can be resolved together to create a new valid constraint that is unsatisfied under the current partial assignment. The size of the resulting backjump will be maximized because the learned constraint contains the failed literals valued earliest in the partial assignment. In the previous example the two weakened constraints would be $a + d \geq 1$ and $\overline{a} + b \geq 1$, which we could then resolve together to get $d + b \geq 1$. This constraint correctly eliminates the assignments in the conflict set and gives direction to the backtrack.

It can be determined before hand by inspecting the parent constraints if a constraint generated with the linear combination method will eliminate the conflict set. We consider the coefficients of the contradiction variable in each constraint. If either of these coefficients is equal to 1 then the constraint generated by the first method will subsume the constraint generated by the second method and therefore eliminate the conflict set. If neither coefficient is equal to 1, then it is undetermined whether the conflict set will be eliminated. In our implementation we use the first method when it is guaranteed to eliminate the conflict set. In all other cases we generate a constraint with both methods and choose the constraint that causes the larger backtrack.

Constraint strengthening

An advantage of using pseudo-Boolean representation is that some interesting new inference techniques become possible. The following method is from the Operations Research field and is used to preprocess mixed integer programming problems (Savelsbergh 1994; Guignard & Spielberg 1981).

Suppose we make the assumption $\{x_0 = 1\}$ and, applying some form of propagation to our constraint set, we discover that under this assumption a constraint $\sum a_i x_i \geq r$ becomes oversatisfied by an amount s in that the sum of the left hand side is greater (by s) than the amount required by the right hand side of the inequality. The oversatisfied constraint can be replaced by the following:

$$s\overline{x}_0 + \sum a_i x_i \geq r + s \qquad (5)$$

If $x_0 = 1$, we know that $\sum a_i x_i \geq r + s$, so (5) holds. If $x_0 = 0$, then $s\overline{x}_0 = s$ and we still must satisfy the original constraint $\sum a_i x_i \geq r$, so (5) still holds. The new constraint implies the original one, so no information is lost in the replacement. The OR community uses this technique during preprocessing. A literal is fixed, propagation is applied, and any oversatisfied constraint is strengthened. Consider the following set of clauses:

$$a + b \geq 1$$
$$a + c \geq 1$$
$$b + c \geq 1$$

If we set $\{a = 0\}$, we must then value $\{b = 1, c = 1\}$ or the first two constraints will become unsatisfied. The third constraint is oversatisfied and can thus be replaced by

$$a + b + c \geq 2.$$

The power of this method is that it allows us to build more complex statements from a set of simple statements. The strengthened constraint will often subsume some or all of the constraints involved in generating it. In this case the new constraint subsumes all three of the generating constraints.

This rule can be generalized as follows. Given any set of assumptions $A = \{x_0, x_1, \ldots, x_k\}$, if we apply some form of propagation and discover that under these assumptions the constraint $\sum a_i x_i \geq r$ becomes oversatisfied by an amount s, we can add to our constraint set the constraint

$$s \sum_{i=1}^{k} \overline{x}_i + \sum a_i x_i \geq r + s \qquad (6)$$

In the case where all the assumptions hold, we know that $\sum a_i x_i \geq r + s$, so (6) holds. If any assumption x_j fails, then $s\overline{x}_j \geq s$ and $\sum a_i x_i \geq r$, so (6) still holds.

In addition to use during preprocessing, this method can be applied during search as well. When a constraint becomes oversatisfied under the current partial assignment, the set of assignments that caused the constraint to be oversatisfied can be determined in time $O(n^2)$. The constraint is strengthened or a new constraint is learned. We have implemented this method both as a preprocessor and as an inference method during search. We have not yet run extensive

Instance	RELSAT sec	RELSAT nodes	Pre. sec	PRS sec	PRS nodes
hole8.cnf	2	26670	0	0	11
hole9.cnf	29	270726	0	0	12
hole10.cnf	393	3049835	0	0	17
hole11.cnf	7488	37573080	0	0	15
hole12.cnf			0	0	20
hole20.cnf			0	0	34
hole30.cnf			4	0	52
hole40.cnf			25	0	75
hole50.cnf			95	0	95

Table 1: Run time (seconds) and no. of node expansions

experiments, but we suspect that for most problems attempting a strengthening for every occurrence of an oversatisfied constraint will be far too expensive. It is unclear whether an efficient implementation will provide benefits beyond those gained by preprocessing alone. However, excessive preprocessing can be expensive, so it may be valuable to let the search direct the strengthening process. This would also allow the possibility of strengthening constraints learned in response to contradictions.

Experimental Results

We have implemented the described learning methods in the algorithm PRS (Pseudo-boolean RelSat) and we compare its performance to its clausal counterpart RELSAT. Using pseudo-Boolean constraints has computational cost, although in theory this cost is linear. In practice we find an increase in the run time of unit propagation of a factor of 2 to 5. A discussion of these costs and other implementation details can be found elsewhere (Dixon & Ginsberg 2000).

The pigeonhole problem is an important benchmark for evaluating pseudo-Boolean solvers because short cutting plane proofs of unsatisfiability exist for the problem. Excellent performance on these problems should be a base requirement for a systematic pseudo-Boolean solver. We present some results comparing performance of RELSAT and PRS on the pigeonhole problem. Both algorithms used the same CNF descriptions of the problems. PRS inputs files in CNF and represents each clause as a clausal inequality. The pseudo-Boolean version used the preprocessing method described above before solving the problems. All experiments were run on a 900 Mhz AMD Athlon processor. The times shown are for optimal choices of relevance bounds. For RELSAT this is a bound of 0, and for PRS this is a bound of 1. The times are an average over 10 trials. The first two columns give time in seconds and number of nodes explored for RELSAT. The next three columns show preprocessing time in seconds, solution time in seconds, and the number of nodes explored for PRS.

PRS with preprocessing dramatically outperformed RELSAT on the pigeonhole problem. This result is not surprising. There are two things to note here: first, that PRS fulfills the basic requirement of efficiently solving pigeonhole problems, and second that the constraint strengthening inference is required to build the pseudo-Boolean constraints that are needed to improve performance. Without the preprocessing

phase the performance of PRS on the same problems is similar to the performance for RELSAT.

A more interesting experiment considers logistics planning problems (Kautz & Selman 1996). The original problems are too easy for current solvers and are only available in CNF. The problem domain involves using a set of planes to move a collection of packages from their initial locations to final locations during a given time period. These problems contain a number of constraints that are easy to encode in pseudo-Boolean. For instance, the constraint that says a plane can be in only one location at a time can be written as

$$\overline{p}_{i1k} + \overline{p}_{i2k} + \cdots + \overline{p}_{ink} \geq n - 1 \tag{7}$$

The variable p_{ijk} represents plane i being in location j at time k, and n is the number of locations. The equivalent expression in CNF requires $\binom{n}{2}$ binary clauses. The problems were randomly generated with a variety of parameter values. We discarded problems that were trivial for both solvers or were satisfiable. Because these problems were generated by hand, it is difficult to know how hard these problems are relative to an easy/hard phase transition.

A design goal was to focus the comparison on the effect of learning methods. Ideally we'd like to eliminate differences in performance due to branching heuristics. Branching heuristics play an important role in reducing the size of the search space for the clausal versions of DPLL and RELSAT. We believe that they will also be important for pseudo-Boolean versions as well. We chose to use the $PROP_{31}$ heuristic (Li & Anbulagan 1997) for both algorithms. More recent heuristics have shown better results for some problem domains, but $PROP_{31}$ is a good heuristic and the implementations for each algorithm were similar. It is unclear whether this heuristic is equally good when used on pseudo-Boolean constraints. We still felt that this choice would bias our results less than abandoning branching heuristics altogether, because branching heuristics are so important for successful solvers.

For each instance we generated a CNF version and two pseudo-Boolean versions. The first pseudo-Boolean version was generated by using cardinality constraints like (7) to express sets of constraints more concisely. The rest of the constraints were written as clausal inequalities. The second pseudo-Boolean version was generated by running the strengthening preprocessor directly on the clausal version.

We report the average execution time over ten trials for each instance. Removing the highest and lowest times (to test for outliers) did not significantly affect the results.

Although PRS needs to manage a more complex representation, the benefit on these instances of using pseudo-Boolean representation outweighs the cost. Both pseudo-Boolean formulations provided better overall performance. In most cases the cost of preprocessing was made up for by reduced solution time.

Conclusion and future work

As we begin to experiment with more complex representations in our solvers, we deepen our understanding of the relationship between search and inference. The familiar learning technique used by DPLL style algorithms can be

Instance	V	clausal		PB formulation 1		PB formulation 2		
		C	RELSAT	C	PRS	C	Pre.	PRS
log8.15.6.5.2	1418	21452	6	13612	2	12772	6	1
log8.15.6.5.4	1418	21452	9	13612	1	12772	6	1
log8.15.6.5.6	1418	21452	11	13612	3	12772	6	2
log8.15.6.5.3	1418	21452	115	13612	15	12772	6	30
log10.13.7.5.5	1625	24687	52	17142	16	16142	7	17
log14.8.4.6.42	1424	15096	30	11760	19	10752	2	26
log14.8.4.6.4	1424	15096	86	11760	36	10752	2	45
log8.16.7.5.1	1616	26351	46	16626	10	15706	10	7
log9.15.7.5.2	1668	26830	139	17610	15	16602	9	16

Table 2: Number of variables (V), clauses (C), and run time (seconds)

adapted to use pseudo-Boolean representation. However, the role played by learning in response to a contradiction has changed. A learned pseudo-Boolean constraint may eliminate assignments in parts of the search space not yet explored in addition to eliminating the set of assignments that caused the contradiction. Further work on learning methods is needed if we are to understand this new role. Branching heuristics and relevance policies will also need to be revisited with respect to pseudo-Boolean representation. Lazy data structures such as the watched literal implementation (M.Moskewicz *et al.* 2001) also need to be investigated. It is encouraging that our preliminary implementation of pseudo-Boolean RELSAT outperformed its clausal counterpart in the planning domain despite the large number of unanswered questions. The constraint strengthening technique is an important missing link to the puzzle. It provides a way to construct the more expressive constraints that are needed to improve performance. Further work is needed to understand how this form of inference can be incorporated into the search process.

Acknowledgments This work was sponsored in part by grants from Defense Advanced Research Projects Agency (DARPA), number F30602-98-2-0181, and DARPA and Air Force Research Laboratory, Rome, NY, under agreement numbered F30602-00-2-0534. The U.S. Government is authorized to reproduce and distribute reprints for Government purposes notwithstanding any copyright annotation thereon. The views and conclusions contained herein are those of the authors and should not be interpreted as necessarily representing the official policies or endorsements, either expressed or implied, of DARPA, Rome Laboratory, or the U.S. Government.

References

Barth, P. 1995. A Davis-Putnam based enumeration algorithm for linear pseudo-boolean optimization. Technical Report MPI-I-95-2-003, Max Planck Institut für Informatik, Saarbrücken, Germany.

Baumgartner, P. 2000. FDPLL - a first-order Davis-Putnam-Logeman-Loveland procedure. In P. Baumgartner, C. Fermuller, N. P., and Zhang, H., eds., *CADE 2000*.

Bayardo, R. J., and Schrag, R. C. 1997. Using CSP lookback techniques to solve real-world SAT instances. In *Proc. AAAI-97*.

Benhamou, B.; Sais, L.; and Siegel, P. 1994. Two proof procedures for a cardinality based language in propositional calculus. In *Proceedings of STACS94, volume 775 de Lecture Notes in Computer Science*.

Cook, W.; Coullard, C.; and Turán, G. 1987. On the complexity of cutting plane proofs. *Journal of Discrete Applied Math* 18:25–38.

Davis, M., and Putnam, H. 1960. A computing procedure for quantification theory. *Journal of the Association for Computing Machinery* 7:201–215.

Dixon, H. E., and Ginsberg, M. L. 2000. Combining satisfiability techniques from AI and OR. *The Knowledge Engineering Review* 15(1).

Ginsberg, M. L. 1993. Dynamic backtracking. *Journal of Artificial Intelligence Research* 1:25–46.

Guignard, M., and Spielberg, K. 1981. Logical reduction methods in zero-one programming. *Operations Research* 29.

Haken, A. 1985. The intractability of resolution. *Theoretical Computer Science* 39:297–308.

Kautz, H., and Selman, B. 1996. Pushing the envelope: Planning, propositional logic, and stochastic search. In *Proc. AAAI-96*.

Li, C. M., and Anbulagan. 1997. Heuristics based on unit propagation for satisfiability problems. In *Proc. IJCAI-97*.

Loveland, D. W. 1978. *Automated Theorem Proving: A Logical Basis*. North Holland.

M.Moskewicz; C.Madigan; Zhao, Y.; Zhang, L.; and Malik, S. 2001. Chaff: Engineering an efficient SAT solver. In *Proc. of the Design Automation Conference*.

Savelsbergh, M. W. P. 1994. Preprocessing and probing for mixed integer programming problems. *ORSA Journal on Computing* 6:445–454.

Stallman, R. M., and Sussman, G. J. 1977. Forward reasoning and dependency directed backtracking in a system for computer aided circuit analysis. *Artificial Intelligence* 9(2):135–196.

Whittemore, J.; Kim, J.; and Sakallah, K. 2001. SATIRE: A new incremental satisfiability engine. In *Proc. of the Design Automation Conference*.

Automated Discovery of Composite SAT Variable-Selection Heuristics

Alex Fukunaga

Computer Science Department
University of California, Los Angeles
fukunaga@cs.ucla.edu

Abstract

Variants of GSAT and Walksat are among the most successful SAT local search algorithms. We show that several well-known SAT local search algorithms are the result of novel combininations of a set of variable selection primitives. We describe CLASS, an automated heuristic discovery system which generates new, effective variable selection heuristic functions using a simple composition operator. New heuristics discovered by CLASS are shown to be competitive with the best Walksat variants, including Novelty+ and R-Novelty+. We also analyze the local search behavior of the learned heuristics using the depth, mobility, and coverage metrics recently proposed by Schuurmans and Southey.

1 Introduction

Local search procedures for satisfiability testing (SAT) have been widely studied since the introduction of GSAT (Selman, Levesque, & Mitchell 1992). It has been shown that for many problem classes, incomplete local search procedures can quickly find solutions (satisfying assignments) to satisfiable CNF formula. Local search heuristics have improved dramatically since the original GSAT algorithm. Some of the most significant improvements have been the result of developing a new variable selection heuristic for the standard GSAT local search framework. These include: GSAT with Random Walk (Selman & Kautz 1993), Walksat (Selman, Kautz, & Cohen 1994), Novelty/R-Novelty (McAllester, Selman, & Kautz 1997), and Novelty+/R-Novelty+ (Hoos & Stutzle 2000).

In this paper, we consider how new, effective variable selection heuristics could be automatically discovered. First, we review the known variable selection heuristics, and identify some common structural elements. We then formulate the problem of designing a variable selection heuristic as a meta-level optimization problem, where the task is to combine various "interesting" variable-selection primitives into an effective composite heuristic function. We describe CLASS, a system that searches for good SAT variable selection heuristics. CLASS is shown to successfully generate a new variable selections heuristic which are competitive with the best known GSAT/Walksat-based algorithms.

```
T:= randomly generated truth assignment
For j:= 1 to cutoff
 If T satisfies formula then return T
 V:= Choose a variable using some
   variable selection heuristic
 T':=T with value of V reversed
Return failure (no satisfying
 assignment found)
```

Figure 1: SAT local search algorithm template

2 Common Structures in Composite Variable Selection Heuristics

Many of the standard SAT local search procedures can be succinctly described as the template of Figure 1 with a particular variable selection heuristic.

We now introduce some terminology to facilitate the discussion of the common structural elements of Walksat-family SAT variable selection heuristics throughout this paper.

Definition 1 (Positive/Negative/Net Gain) *Given a candidate variable assignment T for a CNF formula F, let B_0 be the total number of clauses that are currently unsatisfied in F. Let T' be the state of F if variable V is flipped.*

Let B_1 be the total number of clauses which would be unsatisfied in T'. The net gain *of V is $B_1 - B_0$. The* negative gain *of V is the number of clauses which are currently satisfied in T, but will become unsatisfied in T' if V is flipped. The positive gain of V is the number of clauses which are currently unsatisfied in T, but will become unsatisfied in T' if V is flipped.*

Definition 2 (Variable Age) *The* age *of a variable is the number of flips since it was last flipped.*

The standard heuristics we refer to in the rest of this paper are the following:

GSAT (Selman, Levesque, & Mitchell 1992): Select variable with highest net gain.

HSAT (Gent & Walsh 1993b) Same GSAT, break ties in favor of maximum age variable.

GWSAT (Selman & Kautz 1993): With probability p, select a variable in a randomly unsatisfied (broken) clause; otherwise same as GSAT.

Walksat (Selman, Kautz, & Cohen 1994): Pick random broken clause BC from F. If any variable in BC has a negative gain of 0, then randomly select one of these to flip. Otherwise, with probability p, select a random variable from BC to flip, and with probability $(1-p)$, select the variable in BC with minimal negative gain (breaking ties randomly).

Novelty (McAllester, Selman, & Kautz 1997): Pick random unsatisfied clause BC. Select the variable v in BC with maximal net gain, unless v has the minimal age in BC. In the latter case, select v with probability $(1-p)$; otherwise, flip v_2 with second highest net gain.

Novelty+ (Hoos & Stutzle 2000): Same as Novelty, but after BC is selected, with probability p_w, select random variable in BC; otherwise continue with Novelty.

R-Novelty (McAllester, Selman, & Kautz 1997) and **R-Novelty+** (Hoos & Stutzle 2000) are similar to Novelty and Novelty+, but more complicated (we omit their description due to space constraints).

Based on the descriptions above, it is clear that these heuristics share some significant structural (syntactic) features:

2.1 Common Primitives

All of the above heuristics combine a number of "selection heuristic primitives" into a single decision procedure. These conceptual primitives are the following:

Scoring of variables with respect to a gain metric: Variables are scored with respect to net gain or negative gain. Walksat uses negative gain, while GSAT and the Novelty variants use net gain. Restricting the domain of variables: Whereas GSAT allows the selection of any variable in the formula, Walksat and Novelty variants restrict the variable selection to a single, randomly selected unsatisfied clause.

Ranking of variables and greediness: The variables in the domain are ranked with respect to the scoring metric. Of particular significance is the best (greedy) variable, which is considered by all of the heuristics. Novelty also considers the second best variable.

Variable age: The age of a variable is the number of flips since a variable was last flipped. This historical information seems to be useful for avoiding cycles and forcing exploration of the search space. Age used by the Novelty variants, as well as HSAT. Walksat with a tabu list was also evaluated in (McAllester, Selman, & Kautz 1997).

Conditional branching: In most of the heuristics, some simple Boolean condition (either a random coin toss or a function of one or more of the primitives listed above) is evaluated as the basis for a branch in the decision process.

Compact, nonobvious combinatorial structure: All of the heuristics can be implemented as relatively simple functions built by composing the various primitives discussed above. Even R-Novelty, which is the most complex of the above heuristics, can be represented as a 3-level decision diagram (Hoos & Stutzle 2000).

For all except possibly the simplest GSAT variants, it is difficult to determine a priori how effective any given heuris-

tic is. Empirical evaluation is necessary to evaluate complex heuristics. For example, although there are many possible heuristics that combine the elements of Walksat (random walk, some greediness, localization of the variable domain to a single randomly selected broken clause), the performance of Walksat-variants varies significantly depending on the particular choice and structural organization of these "Walksat elements". Furthermore, significant performance differences between superficially similar local search heuristics can not be eliminated by merely tuning control parameters. See, for example, the comparison of Walksat/G, Walksat/B, and Walksat/SKC in (McAllester, Selman, & Kautz 1997).

3 CLASS: A System for Discovering Composite Variable Selection Heuristics

How can we discover new, effective variable selection heuristics? Some existing heuristics were a result of a focused design process, which specifically addressed a weakness in an existing heuristic. GWSAT and Novelty+ added random walk to GSAT and Novelty after observing behavioral deficiencies of the predecessors (Selman & Kautz 1993; Hoos & Stutzle 2000). However, some major structural innovations involve considerable exploratory empirical effort. For example, (McAllester, Selman, & Kautz 1997) notes that over 50 variants of Walksat were evaluated in their study (which introduced Novelty and R-Novelty).

It appears that although human researchers can readily identify interesting primitives (Section 2) that are relevant to variable selection the task of combining of these primitives into composite variable selection heuristics may benefit from automation. We therefore developed a system for automatically discovering new SAT heuristics, **CLASS** (**C**omposite heuristic **L**earning **A**lgorithm for **S**AT **S**earch). The main components of CLASS are:

- A minimal language for expressing variable selection heuristics s-expressions, and

- A population-based search algorithm that searches the space of possible selection heuristics by repeated application of a composition operator.

CLASS represents variable selection heuristics in a Lisp-like s-expressions language. In each iteration of the local search (Figure 1), the s-expression is evaluated in place of a hand-coded variable selection heuristic. To illustrate the primitives built into CLASS, Figure 2 shows some standard heuristics represented as CLASS s-expressions (See Appendix and Section 3.1 for language primitive definitions).

The space of possible s-expressions expressible in our language is obviously enormous, even if we bound the size of the expressions. Furthermore, we currently lack principled, analytical meta-heuristics that can be used to guide a systematic meta-level search algorithm. Therefore, CLASS uses a population-based search algorithm to search for good variable selection heuristics (Figure 3).

The `Initialize` function creates a population of randomly generated s-expressions. The expressions are generated using a context-free grammar as a constraint, so that

```
GSAT with Random Walk (GWSAT):
(If (rand 0.5)
 RandomVarBC0
 VarBestNetGainWFF)

Walksat:
(IfVarCond == NegGain 0
 VarBestNegativeGainBC0
 (If (rand 0.5)
  VarBestNegativeGainBC0
 RandomVarBC0))
Novelty:
(IfNotMinAge BC0
 VarBestNetGainBC0
 (If (rand 0.5)
  VarBestNetGainBC0
  VarSecondBestNetGainBC0))
```

Figure 2: Walksat, GSAT with Random Walk, and Novelty represented in the CLASS language.

```
Initialize(population,populationsize)
For I = 1 to MaxIterations
Pick parent1 and parent2 from population
 Children = Composition(parent1,parent2)
 Evaluate(Children)
 Insert(Children,Population)
```

Figure 3: CLASS Meta-Search Algorithm

each s-expression is guaranteed to be a syntactically valid heuristic that returns a variable index when evaluated. The Pick function picks two s-expressions from the population, where the probability of selecting a particular s-expression is a function of its rank in the population according to its objective function score (the higher an expression is ranked, the more likely it is to be selected). The composition operator (detailed below) is applied to the parents to generate a set of children, which are then inserted into the population. Each child replaces a randomly selected member of the population, so that the population remains constant in size (the lower the ranking, the more likely it is that an s-expression will be replaced by a child). The best heuristic found during the course of the search is returned.

3.1 The composition operator

Recall that GWSAT and Novelty+ were derived by adding random walk to GSAT and Novelty. This can be generalized into a general meta-heuristic for creating new variable selection strategies: Given two heuristics H_1 and H_2, combine the two into a new heuristic that chooses between H_1 and H_2 using the schema:

If Condition H_1 else H_2

where Condition is a Boolean expression.

We call this the *composition* operator. Intuitively, this is a reasonable meta-heuristic because it "blends" (switches between) the behavior of H_1 and H_2 according to some

boolean condition. The special case where Condition is a randomization function (i.e., If (rnd<p) then ...) is a *probabilistic composition*.

Probabilistic composition has a desirable theoretical property. Hoos (Hoos 1998) defines a SAT local search procedure to be PAC (approximately correct) if with increasing run-time the probability of finding a solution for a satisfiable instance approaches one. An algorithm that is not PAC is called essentially incomplete. GSAT, Novelty, and R-Novelty were shown to be essentially incomplete; however, their performance is significantly improved by adding random walk, which was proven to make these algorithms PAC (Hoos 1998). That is, the historical process by which GWSAT and Novelty+ were generated can be modeled as an application of probabilistic composition. The composition operator has the generalization of this formal property:

Property 1 *Let H_1 and H_2 be two variable selection heuristics. If (without loss of generality) H_1 is PAC, then the composite heuristic (If (rnd p) then H_1 else H_2), which is the result of applying the probabilistic composition operator is also PAC for all $p > 0$. [Proof: follows from the fact that as long as $p > 0$, there is a sequence of coin flips which continues to choose H_1]*

Thus, during the discovery process, if we have a heuristic whose major deficiency is essential incompleteness, then probabilistic composition with any PAC heuristic in the population theoretically removes that deficiency.

The full composition operator used by CLASS takes two heuristics s-expressions H_1 and H_2 as input and outputs the 10 new heuristics to be inserted into the population:

- Five probabilistic compositions of the form (If (rnd p) H_1 H_2), for p=0.1, p=0.25, p=0.5, p=0.75, and p=0.9

- (OlderVar H_1 H_2) - evaluates H_1 and H_2, and returns the variable with maximal age.

- (IfTabu 5 H_1 H_2) - Let variable v be the result of H_1. If $age(v)$ is tabu (i.e., less than 5), then evaluate H_2.

- (IfVarCond == NegativeGain 0 H_1 H_2) - Let v_1 be the result of H_1. if $NegativeGain(v_1) = 0$ return v_1, else return v_2, the result of H_2.

- (IfVarCompare <= NegGain H_1 H_2) - Let v_1 be the results of H_1, v_2 the result of H_2. If $NegativeGain(v_1)$ is less than or equal to $NegativeGain(v_2)$, then return v_1, else v_2.

- (IfVarCompare <= NetGain H_1 H_2) - same as above, but uses net gain as the comparator.

3.2 Evaluating the utility of a candidate heuristic

The Evaluate function in Figure 3 evaluates the utility of a candidate s-expression on a set of training instances. We selected the class of hard, randomly generated 3-SAT problem instances (Mitchell, Selman, & Levesque 1992) as our training set. First, the heuristic was run on 200 satisfiable, 50 variable, 215-clause random 3-SAT instances, with a cutoff of 500 flips. If more than 130 of these descents

```
(If (rand 0.5)
 (If (rand 0.25)
  (IfVarCompare > NetGain
   VarBestNetGainBC0
   (OlderVar VarBestNegativeGainBC1
    VarBestNegativeGainBC0))
  (OlderVar (OlderVar
   VarBestNegativeGainBC0
   (IfVarCond == NegativeGain 0
    VarBestNegativeGainBC0
    RandVarBC0))
   VarBestNegativeGainBC1))
 (If (rand 0.1)
  (If (rand 0.5) VarBestNetGainWFF
   VarRandomWFF)
  (OlderVar VarBestNegativeGainBC1
   VarBestNegativeGainBC0)))
```

Figure 4: CH1, a heuristic learned by CLASS

was successful, then the heuristic was run for 2000 satisfiable, 100-variable, 430-clause random 3-SAT instances with a 4000 flip cutoff. The score of an individual is: (# of 50-var successes) + (5 * (# of 100-var successes)) + ($1/MeanFlipsInSuccessfulRuns$)

Although the purpose of this scoring function design is to train heuristics on 100-variable problems, the 50-variable problems serve as a filter that quickly identifies very poor individuals and saves us from evaluating the large set of 100-variable problems. Nevertheless, this is a relatively expensive objective function, which can require up to a minute of computation for some individuals on a 500-Mhz Pentium III machine (largely due to inefficiencies in our implementation). We have experimented with using only smaller problem instances in the objective function, but in preliminary studies, we found that heuristics generated using only 25 and 50-variable instance training sets did not scale when executed on 100-variable problem instances (this is because on extremely small problems, it is difficult to distinguish the performance between mediocre heuristics and good heuristics, so the discovery algorithm receives insufficient bias).

The heuristic CH1 (Figure 4) was the best heuristic discovered in a CLASS run using a population of 300, after 3000 candidate expressions were generated and evaluated. Another heuristic, CH2 (not shown due to space constraints) was discovered in a run with population 400 and 5000 evaluations. Both CH1 and CH2 will be empirically evaluated below. Heuristics of similar quality can be reliably generated in a 5000 evaluation run. However, since each run of CLASS currently takes several days on a Pentium III-500MHz machine, we have not yet had the resources to perform a statistically meaningful study of learning algorithm performance.

3.3 CLASS-L: Extensions to the algorithm

In order to improve the quality of the heuristics discovered by CLASS, we introduced two enhancements, resulting in the CLASS-L system. Rather than relying on a completely random initial population to serve as the building blocks of

```
(If (rand 0.10)
 (NovSchema BC1 NegativeGain 0.50)
 (OlderVar
  (If (rand 0.10)
   (IfVarCond == NegativeGain 0
    (If (rand 0.25)
     VarBestNetGainBC0
     (RNovschema BC1
      NetGain 0.60))
    (If (rand 0.10)
     VarSecondBestNegativeGainWFF
     (Select2Rank PositiveGain
      NetGain)))
   (IfTabu age5
    (RNovSchema BC1 NetGain 0.40)
    (If (rand 025)
     VarRandomBC0
     VarBestNegGainBC1)))
  (IfTabu age5
   (RNovSchema BC1 Net 0.40)
   (If (rand 0.25)
    (NovSchema BC0 Negative 0.45)
    (If (rand 0.25)
     VarBestNegativeGainBC1
     VarBestNetGainBC0)))))
```

Figure 5: CLH1, a heuristic discovered by CLASS-L

the composed heuristics, it is intuitive to attempt to help the learning system by providing "good" building blocks. We therefore added a library of hand-selected s-expressions. The library is used as follows. CLASS-L still generates a random population, but in addition, it loads the library into a separate array. The new CLASS-L selection function, with probability p_L, picks an individual from the library, instead of the population; otherwise, it picks an individual from the population. Currently, the library consists of 50 s-expressions, including encodings of all of the standard heuristics (GSAT, GWSAT, all the Walksat variants in (McAllester, Selman, & Kautz 1997), Novelty, and R-Novelty), as well as s-expressions which perform poorly by themselves but were believed to be possibly useful as building blocks. In addition, we added two new primitives so that we could compactly represent variants of Novelty and R-Novelty:

(NovSchema clause gaintype P_{noise}) - executes the Novelty decision procedure on the given clause as defined in (McAllester, Selman, & Kautz 1997), using P_{noise} as the noise parameter. Instead of using only net gain (as done by the version presented in (McAllester, Selman, & Kautz 1997), any gain metric can be used depending on gaintype. For example, the standard Novelty heuristic is (NovSchema BC0 netgain 0.5).

(RNovSchema clause gaintype P_{noise}) - similar to NovSchema, but executes the R-Novelty decision process schema. Using CLASS-L, we generated a new variable selection heuristic, CLH1 (Figure 5) after a 400-population run which generated 6000 candidate heuristcs.

4 Experimental Results

We empirically evaluated the automatically discovered heuristics CH1, CH2, and CLH1, using a set of standard SAT local search benchmark instances. The experimental design is similar to that of (Schuurmans & Southey 2001). For comparison, the results of Walksat with noise parameter 0.5, Novelty with a noise parameter of 0.5, and Novelty+ with noise parameter 0.5 and random walk probability 0.01) taken from (Schuurmans & Southey 2001) are shown in Table 1

All of the benchmark instances in this paper were obtained from SATLIB (www.satlib.org). Failure % is the percentage of runs which terminated without finding a solution; flips is the mean number of flips used by the runs which succeeded.

4.1 Evaluation of Learned Heuristic vs. Standard Local Search Heuristics

Performance vs. Test instances from Target Distribution
Recall that CLASS uses a training set of 50 and 100 variable random 3-SAT instances as the training instances during the learning process. We first evaluated the performance of the learned heuristics on test instances from the same problem problem class as the training instances (the 1000 instances in the uf100-430 benchmark set). To evaluate how the learned heuristics performed relative to the best hand-coded heuristics on the target distribution, we first needed to find the best control parameter values for the best standard heuristics. We tuned R-Novelty by varying the noise parameter at 0.01 increments, and we also tuned R-Novelty+ by varying both the noise parameter and the random walk parameter at 0.01 increments, and measuring their performance on 100 independent runs on the 1000 uf100-430 benchmark instances. We found that R-Novelty with a noise setting of 0.68 had the best performance (with a cutoff of 500,000 flips; mean of 100 runs per instance). As shown on Table 1, the performance of CH1 and CH2, which were generated by CLASS, is competitive with all but the highly tuned R-Novelty(0.68). CLH1, which was generated by CLASS-L, actually outperforms R-Novelty(0.68).

Generalization and Scaling We have already shown that the learned heuristics are capable of some generalization, since they performed well on the uf100-430 instances, which are different problem instances than the problems in the training set (although they are from the same abstract class of 100 variable, 430 clause random generate 3-SAT problems).

Next, we evaluated the learned heuristics (and also the tuned R-Novelty(0.68)) on benchmarks from different problem classes to see how well the heuristics generalized and scaled beyond the test distribution for which they were specifically trained. As shown in Table 1, CH1 CH2, and CLH1 scaled and generalized well on larger hard 3-SAT instances from the phase-transition region (uf150, uf200, and uf250, which are 150-250 variable instances). They generalized fairly well to the graph-coloring and All-Interval-Series instances (flat125, ais6, 8, 10). CLH1 also generalized well on the planning instances (medium, huge, bw_large(a-c),

	successes	flips	depth	mobility	coverage
GWSAT	285	4471	7.998	11.6829	0.00007854
Walksat	902	2151	6.965	14.5036	0.0004819
R-Novelty	987	1101	8.232	23.237	0.001183
CLH1	989	1045	7.892	22.468	0.001249
CH1	958	1624	7.30	18.42	0.000789
CH2	952	1771	7.08	20.505	0.000882

Table 2: Local search characteristics of learned and standard heuristics (100 instances, 10 runs, cutoff=10000)

and logistics.c), but CH1 and CH2 significantly degraded on the larger planning instances.

It is important to keep in mind that none of the heuristics (hand-coded or learned) were tuned for these other instances; we present this data in order to show how well the learned heuristic generalizes relative to the generalization of the tuned, hand-coded heuristics.

In order to discover heursitics which perform very well on structured problem instances, it is likely that the training instances need to be tailored to the target class of structured instances. Research in the related area of variable selection heuristics for systematic, Davis-Putnam-Loveland based SAT algorithms has shown that variable selection heuristics have various utilities depending on the class of problems to which they are obtained.[1] Nevertheless, the data shows that traning based on hard random 3-SAT instances is sufficient to generate heuristics with respectable performance on structured problems.

4.2 Local search characteristics of learned heuristics

Schuurmans and Southey (Schuurmans & Southey 2001) recently identified several metrics of local search behavior that were shown to predict the problem solving efficiency of standard SAT heuristics. Depth measures how many clauses remain unsatisfied over the course of a run, Mobility measures how rapidly a search moves in the search space, and Coverage measures how systematically the search explores the search space (see (Schuurmans & Southey 2001) for detailed definitions of the metrics). We measured these characteristics for CH1, CH2, and CLH1 on 100 instances from the uf100-430 benchmarks (uf100-0001 through uf100-0100, 10 runs per instance, 10,000 flips). As shown in Table 2, the depth, mobility, and coverage characteristics of the learned heuristics relative to the standard algorithms are consistent with their performance.

Next, we conducted a large-scale experiment to test the predictive power of the depth, mobility, and coverage metrics on a large sample of heuristics generated by CLASS. 1200 heuristics were chosen as follows: 400 from the population at the end of the CLASS run which produced CH2, 400 from the initial (random) population of the same run, and 400 from the population at the end of the CLASS-L run

---

[1]Unit propagation-based heuristics have been found to be highly effective for random 3-SAT instances (Li & Anbulagan 1997), while simpler strategies have been found effective for structured instances (Moskewicz et al. 2001).

Instance Set*	Walksat(0.5)		Novelty(0.5)		Novelty+(.5,.01)		R-Novelty(0.68)		CLH-1		CH-1		CH-2	
	fail %	flips	fail %	flips	fail %	flips	fail %	flips	fail %	flips	fail %	flips	fail %	flips
uf100(1000)	0	3655	0	3801	0	2298	0	1258	0	1124	0	2112	0	2205
uf150(100)	0.3	14331	0.15	9573	0.03	8331	0	5102	0	4317	0.09	8176	0.02	8777
uf200(100)	2.9	41377	2.5	31794	2.3	28529	2.03	19946	1.67	14533	2.08	19162	2.66	22358
uf250(100)	1.6	41049	2.1	32864	2.2	31560	2.82	23849	1.47	16541	0.96	23578	1.67	28457
medium(1)	0	1167	0	392	0	537	0	332	0	316	0	510	0	525
huge(1)	0	20211	0	11382	0	12419	0	12167	0	6454	0	10901	0	9805
logistics.c(1)	42	332822	2	135382	1	163622	7	152218	0	81306	83	221030	23	203460
bw_large.a(1)	0	20336	0	9695	0	10788	0	10151	0	6656	0	10126	0	11803
bw_large.b(1)	58	377348	48	343078	53	373001	79	245243	24	186508	72	223377	46	192420
ais6(1)	0	1377	92	460007	0	12031	0	7279	0	1413	0	1001	0	660.96
ais8(1)	0	36499	99	495003	8	169626	16	139036	0	43050	0	24952	0	21559
ais10(1)	37	317323	100	n/a	84	451222	73	259861	60	216420	34	203709.8	31	184884.6
flat125(100)	1.5	74517	3.2	91004	0.8	37408	18.21	125946	4.63	71125	0.94	60219	0.97	41220

Table 1: Performance on SATLIB benchmarks. Each entry is the mean of 100 runs on each instance; cutoff=500,000 flips per run.
* Number in parentheses are the # of instances in each instance set; values for Walksat, Novelty, and Novelty+ are from (Schuurmans & Southey 2001)

which generated CH2, and. This way, we sought to sample a wide range of heuristics, ranging from very poor (random) to good (the population with CH2) to very good (the population containing CLH1). Each of these heuristics was executed on 100 instances from the uf50-215 (50 variable, 215 clause) benchmarks from SATLIB (100 runs per instance with cutoff of 1000 flips). Figures 5 shows the depth, mobility, and coverage metrics versus the heuristic's performance (number of successful runs). There is a very high correlation between performance and coverage (r=0.89), and weaker correlations with depth (r= -0.31) and mobility (r=0.138). The weak correlations between performance and the mobility metric is caused by the large number of very bad heuristics in the randomly generated subset of heuristics which exhibit extreme reckless mobility. Without the random heuristics, the correlation increased to r=0.30. On the other hand, the correlation between depth and performance without the random heuristics was 0.22 (note the change in the sign of the coefficient). Figure 6 indicates that high coverage seems to be both a necessary and sufficient characteristic for local search success on these random 3-SAT instances. Similarly, for mobility and depth, there is apparently a "correct" range of values which are necessary, although not sufficient, for good performance.

5 Related work

Several previous systems have learned to improve the performance of constraint satisfaction systems by modifying heuristics using what is essentially a heuristically guided generate-and-test procedure like CLASS. MULTI-TAC (Minton 1996) adapts generalized constraint-satisfaction heuristics for specific problem classes. COMPOSER was used to configure an antenna-network scheduling algorithm (Gratch & Chien 1996). STAGE (Boyan & Moore 2000) is a learning algorithm applied to SAT local search. STAGE uses an on-line learning to adapt its heuristic by predicting objective function values based on features seen during the search; in contrast, CLASS is an off-line learning system. CLASS strongly resembles a genetic programming

(GP) system (Koza 1992). In fact, we can view the CLASS as a heavily modified GP - specifically, a strongly-typed (Montana 1993), steady-state GP using only a novel composition operator. Note that unlike our composition operator, standard GP operators recombine and modify arbitrary subcomponents of the parents, and do not propagate the PAC property. Our experiments with implementation of various GP mutation and crossover operators in CLASS have not been successful yet.

6 Discussion and Future Work

We have described and evaluated an automated discovery system for finding SAT local search variable selection heuristics. It is interesting that repeated brute-force application of a single operator, composition, to randomly generated heuristics is sufficient to generate CH1 and CH2, which are competitive with Walksat and Novelty variants. CLASS-L, an extension that uses the Novelty schema as primitives, generated CLH1, which is competitive with the best, tuned version of the standard local search heuristics on the target problem class (100-variable random 3-SAT). All three learned heuristics were shown to scale and generalize well on larger random instances; generalization to other problem classes varied.

Despite of the good performance on the benchmarks, there is a concern that the automatically generated heuristics might be "getting lucky", or exploiting some bizarre, hidden structure of the benchmarks. Measurements of the depth, mobility, and coverage metrics show that CH1, CH2, and CLH1 exhibit the characteristics of successful local search algorithms as identified in (Schuurmans & Southey 2001). The best learned heuristics seems to descend to promising regions and explore near the bottom of the objective as rapidly (low depth), broadly (high mobility), and systematically (high coverage) as possible, compared to the standard algorithms. In other words, there is convincing evidence that the best learned heuristics perform well because they behave in the way that good local search algorithms are expected to behave (according to our current scientific understanding of local search), and not because of some unexplainable exploitation of the benchmark instances. Furthermore, note that with a little effort, one can study Figures 4-5 and observe that the learned heuristics encode "reasonable" behavior.

Recent algorithms such as DLM (Wu & Wah 1999) and SDF (Schuurmans & Southey 2001) are significantly different from the GSAT and Walksat family considered in this paper, due to 1) clause-weightinsg and 2) objective function metrics that go beyond the simple gain metrics identified in Section 2. For example, SDF uses a scoring metric based on the number of variables that satisfy each clause. Such advances in the building blocks of SAT local search algorithms are orthogonal to the issue addressed by CLASS, which is the problem of combining these building blocks into effective decision procedures. Future work will extend CLASS with a clause-weighting mecshanism, as well new objective function metrics (such as the SDF scoring function).

In our current implementation, the learned heuristic functions are slower (execute fewer flips per second) than the standard heuristics. In principle, learned heuristics based on primitives which only select variables from a particular clause should not be much more expensive than Walksat, and learned heuristics which require maintaining globally optimal variables should not be much more expensive than GSAT. This is because in an efficient implementation, the complexity of a variable flip is dosminated by the incremental computation of gain values, which scales linearly with the size of the problem (average # of clauses per variable), while repeatedly accessing these values repeatedly in a complex selection heuristic is a constant overhead, which should become asymptotically insignificant. In addition, although there is currently no mechanism in CLASS to bias the system for the discovery of faster, simpler heuristics, there is much that can be done to speed up the learned heuristics. For example, runtime, size, and complexity could be used as part of the scoring function for the discovery algorithm. Also, post-processing optimizations of the heuristics is possible. For example, in CH1, the single occurrence of the VarBest-NetGainWFF primitive requires instantiation of the GSAT-equivalent data structures to identify the globally optimal variable with respect to net gain, causing significant slowdown; without this symbol, CH1 would only need Walksat-equivalent data structures. However, since that primtive is only called 2.5% of the time (it is called only after 3 layers of randomization), an optimizing postprocessor could try to eliminate this kind of bottleneck from the heuristic while maintaining search efficiency.

Evaluation of 1200 new heuristics generated by CLASS with respect to depth, mobility, and coverage metrics (Schuurmans & Southey 2001) supported the conjecture that these metrics are widely applicable for analyzing SAT local search heuristics. In particular, the coverage rate seems to be the most highly correlated with performance on random 3-SAT instances. Furthermore, this result indicates that CLASS could possibly use the metrics (particularly coverage) as a partial proxy for actual algorithm runs in order to evaluate candidate heuristics much faster is currently possible.

Local search algorithms are very sensitive to control parameters (McAllester, Selman, & Kautz 1997; Hoos & Stutzle 2000). CLASS currently does not explicitly perform parameter tuning, although nested probabilistic compositions yields the equivalent in some cases (CH1 obviously exploits this trick). While we have implemented parameter tuning, it is currently turned off because in our current implementation, local optimization via control parameter tuning takes just as much computational resources as evaluating an entirely new heuristic; so far, the tradeoff has favored broader exploration of the space of structures. However, using metrics such as those in (Schuurmans & Southey 2001; McAllester, Selman, & Kautz 1997) as a proxy for complete runs might enable fast parameter tuning.

While the surprisingly good performance of heuristics learned by CLASS is interesting, the primary motivation of this work is to explore an automated approach to the process of designing composite search heuristics. Humans excel at finding and classifying the relevant features/components that can be used to solve problems, such the primitives identified in Section 2. Note that all of these primitives were proposed in the literature by 1993, shortly after the introduction of GSAT - variants that used variable age, negative gain, random walk can be found in (Gent & Walsh 1993a; Selman & Kautz 1993). However, the task of combining these features into effective composite heuristics appears to be a combinatorial problem that is difficult for humans. As evidence for this, note that Novelty was not introduced until 1997 (McAllester, Selman, & Kautz 1997). We have shown that this task can be effectively formulated and solved as a meta-level search problem. SAT local search algorithms have been intensely studied by many researchers for 10 years. The demonstration that a simple mechanical procedure which composes previously proposed primitives can compete with some of the best human-designed heuristics suggests that the problem of designing composite search heuristics, in general, might benefit from an automated discovery system (especially for problem domains which have not been as intensely studied as SAT).

Acknowledgments

Thanks to Rich Korf and Jason Fama for helpful discussions. Finnegan Southey provided valuable clarifications regarding the implementation of the coverage metric measurements.

References

Boyan, J., and Moore, A. 2000. Learning evaluation functions to improve optimization by local search. *Journal of Machine Learning Research* 1(2).

Gent, I., and Walsh, T. 1993a. An empirical analysis of search in gsat. *Journal of Artificial Intelligence Research* 1:47–59.

Gent, I., and Walsh, T. 1993b. Towards an understainding of hill-climbing procedures for sat. In *Proceedings of National Conf. on Artificial Intelligence (AAAI)*, 28–33.

Gratch, J., and Chien, S. 1996. Adaptive problem-solving for large-scale scheduling problems: A case study. *Journal of Artificial Intelligence Research* 4:365–396.

Hoos, H., and Stutzle, T. 2000. Local search algorithms for sat: An empirical evaluation. *Journal of Automated Reasoning* 24:421–481.

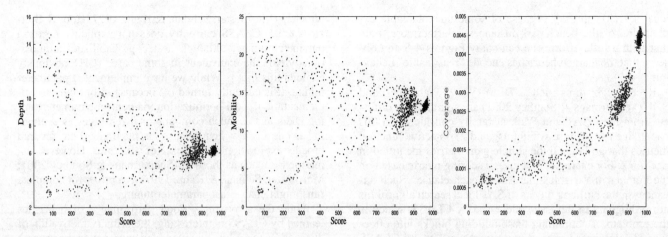

Figure 6: Average depth, mobility, and coverage rates vs. Score (# of successful runs) for 1200 automatically genserated heuristics

Hoos, H. 1998. *Stochastic local search - methods, models, applications*. Ph.D. Dissertation, TU Darmstadt.

Koza, J. 1992. *Genetic Programming: On the Programming of Computers By the Means of Natural Selection*. MIT Press.

Li, C. M., and Anbulagan. 1997. Heuristics based on unit propagation for satisfiability problems. In *Proc. Intl. Joint Conf. Artificial Intelligence (IJCAI)*, 366–371.

McAllester, D.; Selman, B.; and Kautz, H. 1997. Evidence for invariants in local search. In *Proceedings of National Conf. on Artificial Intelligence (AAAI)*, 459–465.

Minton, S. 1996. Automatically configuring constraint satisfaction problems: a case study. *Constraints* 1(1).

Mitchell, D.; Selman, B.; and Levesque, H. 1992. Hard and easy distributions of sat problems. In *Proceedings of National Conf. on Artificial Intelligence (AAAI)*, 459–65.

Montana, D. 1993. Strongly typed genetic programming. Technical report, Bolt, Beranek and Neuman (BBN).

Moskewicz, M. W.; Madigan, C. F.; Zhao, Y.; Zhang, L.; and Malik, S. 2001. Chaff: Engineering an efficient SAT solver. In *Design Automation Conference*, 530–535.

Schuurmans, D., and Southey, F. 2001. Local search characteristics of incomplete sat procedures. *Artificial Intelligence* 132:121–150.

Selman, B., and Kautz, H. 1993. Domain-independent extensions to gsat: Solving large structured satisfiability problems. In *Proc. Intl. Joint Conf. Artificial Intelligence (IJCAI)*.

Selman, B.; Kautz, H.; and Cohen, B. 1994. Noise strategies for improving local search. In *Proceedings of National Conf. on Artificial Intelligence (AAAI)*.

Selman, B.; Levesque, H.; and Mitchell, D. 1992. A new method for solving hard satisfiability problems. In *Proceedings of National Conf. on Artificial Intelligence (AAAI)*, 440–446.

Wu, Z., and Wah, B. 1999. Trap escaping strategies in discrete lagrangian methods for solving hard satisfiability and maximum satisfiability problems. In *Proceedings of National Conf. on Artificial Intelligence (AAAI)*, 673–678.

Appendix: Additional CLASS Language Primitives

List of some CLASS language primitives that appear in Fig. 2,4,5. The actual syntax of the CLASS s-expressions differs slightly, but we present a simplified version for brevity and clarity (see Section 3.1 and 3.3 for definitions of some other primitives).

(rnd num) - true if random number $r < num$, else returns false.

BC0 - randomly selected broken clauses. Note that BC0 refers to the same broken clause throughout an s-expression. Also, note that the symbol BC1 refers to a different randomly selected clause.

(NegativeGain v) and (NetGain v) returns the negative gain and net gain of variable v.

VarRandomBC0 - a random variable from broken clause *BC0*

VarRandomWFF - random variable in the formula

VarBestNetGainBC0 - variable with the best net gain in *BC0*.

VarBestNegativeGainBC1 - var. with best negative gain in *BC1*.

VarBestNetGainWFF - the var. with best net gain in the formula

(OlderVar v_1 v_2) - picks the var with the max age from v_1 and v_2.

(IfNotMinAge varset v_1 v_2) - if v_1 does not have minimal age among variables in a set of vars then return v_1, else v_2.

(Select2RankWFF gaintype1 gaintype2) - select best variable from formula according to *gaintype1*, breaking ties using *gaintype2*.

Learning for Quantified Boolean Logic Satisfiability

Enrico Giunchiglia and **Massimo Narizzano** and **Armando Tacchella**

DIST - Università di Genova
Viale Causa 13, 16145 Genova, Italy
{enrico,mox,tac}@mrg.dist.unige.it

Abstract

Learning, i.e., the ability to record and exploit some information which is unveiled during the search, proved to be a very effective AI technique for problem solving and, in particular, for constraint satisfaction. We introduce learning as a general purpose technique to improve the performances of decision procedures for Quantified Boolean Formulas (QBFs). Since many of the recently proposed decision procedures for QBFs solve the formula using search methods, the addition of learning to such procedures has the potential of reducing useless explorations of the search space. To show the applicability of learning for QBF satisfiability we have implemented it in QUBE, a state-of-the-art QBF solver. While the backjumping engine embedded in QUBE provides a good starting point for our task, the addition of learning required us to devise new data structures and led to the definition and implementation of new pruning strategies. We report some experimental results that witness the effectiveness of learning. Noticeably, QUBE augmented with learning is able to solve instances that were previously out if its reach. To the extent of our knowledge, this is the first time that learning is proposed, implemented and tested for QBFs satisfiability.

Introduction

The goal of learning in problem solving is to record in a useful way some information which is unveiled during the search, so that it can be reused later to avoid useless explorations of the search space. Learning leads to substantial speed-ups when solving constraint satisfaction problems (see, e.g., (Dechter 1990)) and, more specifically, propositional satisfiability problems (see, e.g., (Bayardo, Jr. & Schrag 1997)).

We introduce learning to improve the performances of decision procedures for Quantified Boolean Formulas (QBFs). Due to the particular nature of the satisfiability problem for QBFs, there are both unsuccessful and successful terminal nodes. The former correspond to assignments violating some constraint, while the latter correspond to assignments satisfying all the constraints. With our procedure, we are able to learn from both types of terminal nodes. Learning from constraint violations —best known in the literature as *nogood* learning— has been implemented and tested in other

contexts, but never for QBFs. Learning from the satisfaction of all constraints —called *good* learning in (Bayardo Jr. & Pehoushek 2000)— is formally introduced, implemented and tested here for the first time. Furthermore, learning goods enables to extend Boolean Constraint Propagation (BCP) (see, e.g., (Freeman 1995)) to universally quantified literals. Such an extension, which does not make sense in standard QBF reasoning, is obtained as a side effect of our learning schema.

To show the effectiveness of learning for the QBFs satisfiability problem, we have implemented it in QUBE, a state-of-the-art QBF solver. Since learning exploits information collected during backtracking, the presence of a backjumping engine in QUBE provides a good starting point for our task. Nevertheless, the dual nature of learned data, i.e., nogoods as well as goods, and the interactions with standard QBFs pruning techniques, require the development of ad hoc data structures and algorithms. Using QUBE, we have done some experimental tests on several real-world QBFs, corresponding to planning (Rintanen 1999a) and circuit verification (Abdelwaheb & Basin 2000) problems. The results witness the effectiveness of learning. Noticeably, QUBE augmented with learning is able to solve in a few seconds instances that previously were out of its reach.

Finally, we believe that the learning techniques that we propose enjoy a wide applicability. Indeed, in the last few years we have witnessed the presentation of several implemented decision procedures for QBFs, like QKN (Kleine-Büning, Karpinski, & Flögel 1995), EVALUATE (Cadoli, Giovanardi, & Schaerf 1998), DECIDE (Rintanen 1999b), QSOLVE (Feldmann, Monien, & Schamberger 2000), and QUBE (Giunchiglia, Narizzano, & Tacchella 2001b). Most of the above decision procedures are based on search methods and thus the exploitation of learning techniques has the potential of improving their performances as well. Furthermore, we believe that the ideas behind the good learning mechanism can be exploited also to effectively deal with other related problems, as the one considered in (Bayardo Jr. & Pehoushek 2000).

The paper is structured as follows. We first review the logic of QBFs, and the ideas behind DLL-based decision procedures for QBFs. Then, we introduce learning, presenting the formal background, the implementation and the experimental analysis. We end with some final remarks.

Quantified Boolean Logic

Logic

Consider a set P of propositional letters. An *atom* is an element of P. A *literal* is an atom or the negation of an atom. In the following, for any literal l,

- $|l|$ is the atom occurring in l; and

- $\bar{l}$ is $\neg l$ if l is an atom, and is $|l|$ otherwise.

A *propositional formula* is a combination of atoms using the k-ary ($k \geq 0$) connectives $\wedge, \vee$ and the unary connective $\neg$. In the following, we use TRUE and FALSE as abbreviations for the empty conjunction and the empty disjunction respectively.

A *QBF* is an expression of the form

$$\varphi = Q_1 x_1 Q_2 x_2 \ldots Q_n x_n \Phi \qquad (n \geq 0) \qquad (1)$$

where

- every Q_i ($1 \leq i \leq n$) is a quantifier, either existential $\exists$ or universal $\forall$,

- $x_1, \ldots, x_n$ are pairwise distinct atoms in P, and

- Φ is a propositional formula in the atoms $x_1, \ldots, x_n$.

$Q_1 x_1 \ldots Q_n x_n$ is the *prefix* and Φ is the *matrix* of (1). We also say that a literal l is *existential* if $\exists |l|$ belongs to the prefix of (1), and is *universal* otherwise. Finally, in (1), we define

- the *level of an atom* x_i, to be 1 + the number of expressions $Q_j x_j Q_{j+1} x_{j+1}$ in the prefix with $j \geq i$ and $Q_j \neq Q_{j+1}$;

- the *level of a literal* l, to be the level of $|l|$;

- the *level of the formula*, to be the level of x_1.

The semantics of a QBF φ can be defined recursively as follows. If the prefix is empty, then φ's satisfiability is defined according to the truth tables of propositional logic. If φ is $\exists x \psi$ (respectively $\forall x \psi$), φ is satisfiable if and only if φ_x or (respectively and) $\varphi_{\neg x}$ are satisfiable. If $\varphi = Qx\psi$ is a QBF and l is a literal, φ_l is the QBF obtained from ψ by substituting l with TRUE and $\bar{l}$ with FALSE. It is easy to see that if φ is a QBF without universal quantifiers, the problem of deciding the satisfiability of φ reduces to SAT.

Two QBFs are *equivalent* if they are either both satisfiable or both unsatisfiable.

DLL Based Decision Procedures

Consider a QBF (1). From here on, we assume that Φ is in conjunctive normal form (CNF), i.e., that it is a conjunction of disjunctions of literals. Using common clause form transformations, it is possible to convert any QBF into an equivalent one meeting the CNF requirement, see, e.g., (Plaisted & Greenbaum 1986). As standard in propositional satisfiability, we represent Φ as a set of clauses, and assume that for any two elements l, l' in a clause, it is not the case that $l = \bar{l'}$. With this notation,

- The empty clause $\{\}$ stands for FALSE,

- The empty set of clauses $\{\}$ stands for TRUE,

- The propositional formula $\{\{\}\}$ is equivalent to FALSE.

Thus, for example, a typical QBF is the following:

$$\exists x \forall y \exists z \exists s \{\{\neg x, \neg y, z\}, \{x, \neg y, \neg s\}, \\ \{\neg y, \neg z\}, \{y, z, \neg s\}, \{z, s\}\}. \qquad (2)$$

In (Cadoli, Giovanardi, & Schaerf 1998), the authors showed how it is possible to extend DLL in order to decide satisfiability of φ. As in DLL, variables are selected and are assigned values. The difference wrt DLL is that variables need to be selected taking into account the order in which they occur in the prefix. More precisely, a variable can be selected only if all the variables at higher levels have been already selected and assigned. The other difference is that backtracking to the last universal variable whose values have not been both explored occurs when the formula simplifies to TRUE. In the same paper, the authors also showed how the familiar concepts of "unit" and "monotone" literal from the SAT literature can be extended to QBFs and used to prune the search. In details, a literal l is

- *unit* in (1) if l is existential, and, for some $m \geq 0$,

  - a clause $\{l, l_1, \ldots, l_m\}$ belongs to Φ, and

  - each expression $\forall |l_i|$ ($1 \leq i \leq m$) occurs at the right of $\exists |l|$ in the prefix of (1).

- *monotone* if either l is existential [resp. universal], l belongs to some [resp. does not belong to any] clause in Φ, and $\bar{l}$ does not belong to any [resp. belongs to some] clause in Φ.

If a literal l is unit or monotone in Φ, then φ is satisfiable iff φ_l is satisfiable. Early detection and assignment of unit and monotone literals are fundamental for the effectiveness of QBF solvers. See (Cadoli, Giovanardi, & Schaerf 1998) for more details.

A typical computation tree for deciding the satisfiability of a QBF is represented in Figure 1.

Learning

CBJ and SBJ

The procedure presented in (Cadoli, Giovanardi, & Schaerf 1998) uses a standard backtracking schema. In (Giunchiglia, Narizzano, & Tacchella 2001b), the authors show how Conflict-directed Backjumping (CBJ) (Prosser 1993b) can be extended to QBFs, and introduce the concept of Solution-directed Backjumping (SBJ). The idea behind both forms of backjumping is to dynamically compute a subset ν of the current assignment which is "responsible" for the current result. Intuitively, "responsible" means that flipping the literals not in ν would not change the result. In the following, we formally introduce these notions to put the discussion on firm grounds.

Consider a QBF φ. A sequence $\mu = l_1; \ldots; l_m$ ($m \geq 0$) of literals is an *assignment for* φ if for each literal l_i in μ

- l_i is unit, or monotone in $\varphi_{l_1; \ldots; l_{i-1}}$; or

- for each atom x at a higher level of l_i, there is an l_j in μ with $j < i$ and $|l_j| = x$.

For any sequence of literals $\mu = l_1; \ldots; l_m$, φ_μ is the QBF obtained from φ by

$$\varphi_1 : \exists x \forall y \exists z \exists s \{\{\neg x, \neg y, z\}, \{x, \neg y, \neg s\}, \{\neg y, \neg z\}, \{y, z, \neg s\}, \{z, s\}\}$$

$\langle \neg x, \mathrm{L} \rangle \qquad\qquad\qquad\qquad \langle x, \mathrm{R} \rangle$

$$\varphi_2 : \forall y \exists z \exists s \{\{\neg y, \neg s\}, \{\neg y, \neg z\}, \{y, z, \neg s\}, \{z, s\}\} \qquad \varphi_5 : \forall y \exists z \exists s \{\{\neg y, z\}, \{\neg y, \neg z\}, \{y, z, \neg s\}, \{z, s\}\}$$

$\langle \neg y, \mathrm{L} \rangle, \langle z, \mathrm{P} \rangle \quad \langle y, \mathrm{R} \rangle, \langle \neg s, \mathrm{U} \rangle, \langle \neg z, \mathrm{U} \rangle \qquad \langle \neg y, \mathrm{L} \rangle, \langle z, \mathrm{P} \rangle \quad \langle y, \mathrm{R} \rangle, \langle z, \mathrm{U} \rangle$

$\varphi_3 : \{\} \qquad\qquad \varphi_4 : \{\{\}\} \qquad\qquad\qquad \varphi_6 : \{\} \qquad\qquad \varphi_7 : \{\{\}\}$

Figure 1: A typical computation tree for (2). U, P, L, R stand for UNIT, PURE, L-SPLIT, R-SPLIT respectively, and have the obvious meaning.

- deleting the clauses in which at least one of the literals in μ occurs;

- removing $\bar{l}_i$ $(1 \leq i \leq m)$ from the clauses in the matrix; and

- deleting $|l_i|$ $(1 \leq i \leq m)$ and its binding quantifier from the prefix.

For instance, if φ is (2) and μ is $\neg x$, then φ_μ is the formula φ_2 in Figure 1.

Consider an assignment $\mu = l_1; \ldots; l_m$ for φ.
A set of literals ν is a *reason for φ_μ result* if

- $\nu \subseteq \{l_1, \ldots, l_m\}$, and

- for any sequence μ' such that
  - $\nu \subseteq \{l : l \text{ is in } \mu'\}$,
  - $\{|l| : l \text{ is in } \mu'\} = \{|l| : l \text{ is in } \mu\}$,

  $\varphi_{\mu'}$ is satisfiable iff φ_μ is satisfiable.

According to previous definitions, e.g., if φ is (1) and μ is $\neg x; \neg y; z$ then $\varphi_\mu = \varphi_3 = \{\}$ and $\{\neg y, z\}$ is a reason for φ_μ result (see Figure 1).

Reasons can be dynamically computed while backtracking, and are used to skip the exploration of useless branches. In the previous example, the reason $\{\neg y, z\}$ is computed while backtracking from φ_3.

Let ν be a reason for φ_μ result. We say that

- ν is a *reason for φ_μ satisfiability* if φ_μ is satisfiable, and

- ν is a *reason for φ_μ unsatisfiability*, otherwise.

See (Giunchiglia, Narizzano, & Tacchella 2001b) for more details.

Learning

The idea behind learning is simple: reasons computed during the search are stored in order to avoid discovering the same reasons in different branches. In SAT, the learnt reasons are "nogoods" and can be simply added to the set of input clauses. In the case of QBFs, the situation is different. Indeed, we have two types of reasons ("good" and "nogood"), and they need different treatments. Further, even restricting to nogoods, a reason can be added to the set of input clauses only under certain conditions, as sanctioned by the following proposition.

Consider a QBF φ. We say that an assignment $\mu = l_1; \ldots; l_m$ for φ is *prefix-closed* if for each literal l_i in μ, all the variables at higher levels occur in μ.

Proposition 1 *Let φ be a QBF. Let $\mu = l_1; \ldots; l_m$ $(m \geq 0)$ be a prefix-closed assignment for φ. If ν is a reason for φ_μ unsatisfiability then φ is equivalent to*

$$Q_1 x_1 \ldots Q_n x_n (\Phi \wedge (\vee_{l \in \nu} \bar{l})).$$

As an application of the above proposition, consider the QBF φ

$$\exists x \forall y \exists z \exists s \{\{y, z\}, \{\neg y, \neg z, s\}, \{\neg x, z\}, \{\neg y, \neg s\}, \{y, \neg s\}\}$$

We have that φ is satisfiable, and

- the sequences $x; y; z$ and $x; z; y$ are prefix-closed assignments for φ,

- $\varphi_{x;y;z} = \varphi_{x;z;y} = \exists s \{\{s\}, \{\neg s\}\}$ is unsatisfiable, and $\{y, z\}$ is a reason for both $\varphi_{x;y;z}$ and $\varphi_{x;z;y}$ unsatisfiability,

- we can add $\{\neg y, \neg z\}$ to the matrix of φ and obtain an equivalent formula.

On the other hand, using the same example, we can show that the requirement that μ be prefix-closed in Proposition 1 cannot be relaxed. In fact, we have that

- the sequence $x; z$ is an assignment for φ, but it is not prefix-closed,

- $\varphi_{x;z} = \forall y \exists s \{\{\neg y, s\}, \{\neg y, \neg s\}, \{y, \neg s\}\}$ is unsatisfiable, and $\{z\}$ is a reason for $\varphi_{x;z}$ unsatisfiability,

- if we add $\{\neg z\}$ to the matrix of φ, we obtain an unsatisfiable formula.

Notice that the sequence $x; z$ is a prefix-closed assignment if we exchange the y with the z quantifiers, i.e.,

$$\exists x \exists z \forall y \exists s \{\{y, z\}, \{\neg y, \neg z, s\}, \{\neg x, z\}, \{\neg y, \neg s\}, \{y, \neg s\}\}.$$

In the above QBF φ, $\{z\}$ is a reason for $\varphi_{x;z}$ unsatisfiability; we can add $\{\neg z\}$ to the matrix of φ; and we can immediately conclude that φ is unsatisfiable.

In the hypotheses of Proposition 1, we say that the clause $(\vee_{l \in \nu} \bar{l})$ is a *nogood*. Notice, that if we have only existential quantifiers —as in SAT— any assignment is prefix-closed, each reason corresponds to a nogood ν, and ν can be safely added to (the matrix of) the input formula.

A proposition "symmetric" to Proposition 1 can be stated for good learning.

Proposition 2 *Let φ be a QBF. Let $\mu = l_1; \ldots; l_m$ $(m \geq 0)$ be a prefix-closed assignment for φ. If ν is a reason for φ_μ satisfiability then φ is equivalent to*

$$Q_1 x_1 \ldots Q_n x_n (\neg (\vee_{l \in \nu} \bar{l}) \vee \Phi).$$

As before, in the hypotheses of Proposition 2, we say that the clause $(\vee_{l \in \nu} \bar{l})$ is a *good*. For example, with reference to the formula φ at the top of Figure 1,

- the assignment $\neg x; \neg y; z$ is prefix-closed,

- $\varphi_{\neg x; \neg y; z} = \varphi_3 = \{\}$ is satisfiable, and $\{\neg y; z\}$ is a reason for $\varphi_{\neg x; \neg y; z}$ satisfiability,

- the clause $(y \vee \neg z)$ is a good, and its negation can be put in disjunction with the matrix of φ.

An effective implementation of learning requires an efficient handling of goods and nogoods. The situation is more complicated than in SAT because goods have to be added as disjunctions to the matrix. However, once we group all the goods together, we obtain the negation of a formula in CNF, and ultimately the negation of a set of clauses. The treatment of nogoods is not different from SAT: we could simply add them to the matrix. However, since exponentially many reasons can be computed, some form of space bounding is required. In SAT, the two most popular space bounded learning schemes are

- *size learning of order n* (Dechter 1990): a nogood is stored only if its cardinality is less or equal to n,

- *relevance learning of order n* (Ginsberg 1993): given a current assignment μ, a nogood ν is stored as long as the number of literals in ν and not in μ is less or equal to n.

(See (Bayardo, Jr. & Miranker 1996) for their complexity analysis). Thus, in size learning, once a nogood is stored, it is never deleted. In relevance learning, stored nogoods are dynamically added and deleted depending on the current assignment.

The above notions of size and relevance learning trivially extend to QBFs for both goods and nogoods, and we can take advantage of the fast mechanisms developed in SAT to efficiently deal with learnt reasons. In practice, we handle three sets of clauses:

- the set of clauses Ψ corresponding to the goods learnt during the search;

- the set of clauses Φ corresponding to the input QBF; and

- the set of clauses Θ corresponding to the nogoods learnt during the search.

From a logical point of view, we consider Extended QBFs. An *Extended QBF* (EQBF) is an expression of the form

$$Q_1 x_1 \ldots Q_n x_n \langle \Psi, \Phi, \Theta \rangle \qquad (n \geq 0) \qquad (3)$$

where

- $Q_1 x_1 \ldots Q_n x_n$ is the prefix and is defined as above, and

- Ψ, Φ and Θ are sets of clauses in the atoms $x_1, \ldots, x_n$ such that both

$$Q_1 x_1 \ldots Q_n x_n (\neg \Psi \vee \Phi) \qquad (4)$$

and

$$Q_1 x_1 \ldots Q_n x_n (\Phi \wedge \Theta) \qquad (5)$$

are logically equivalent to (1).

Initially Ψ and Θ are the empty set of clauses, and Φ is the input set of clauses. As the search proceeds,

- Nogoods are determined while performing CBJ and are added to Θ; and

- Goods are determined while performing SBJ and are added to Ψ.

In both cases, the added clauses will be eventually deleted when performing relevance learning (this is why the clauses in Θ are kept separated from the clauses in Φ). Notice that in a nogood C (and in the input clauses as well) the universal literals that occur to the right of all the existential literals in C can be removed (Kleine-Büning, Karpinski, & Flögel 1995). Analogously, in a good C, the existential literals that occur to the right of the universal literals in C can be removed.

Notice that the clauses in Ψ have to be interpreted — because of the negation symbol in front of Ψ in (4)— in the dual way wrt the clauses in Φ or Θ. For example, an empty clause in Ψ allows us to conclude that Ψ is equivalent to FALSE and thus that (1) is equivalent to TRUE. On the other hand, if Ψ is the empty set of clauses, this does not give us any information about the satisfiability of Φ.

Because of the clauses in Ψ and Θ the search can be pruned considerably. Indeed, a terminal node can be anticipated because of the clauses in Ψ or Θ. Further, we can extend the notion of unit to take into account the clauses in Ψ and/or Θ. Consider an EQBF (3). A literal l is

- *unit* in (3) if

  - either l is existential, and, for some $m \geq 0$,

    * a clause $\{l, l_1, \ldots, l_m\}$ belongs to Φ or Θ, and
    * each expression $\forall |l_i|$ ($1 \leq i \leq m$) occurs at the right of $\exists |l|$ in the prefix of (3).

  - or l is universal, and, for some $m \geq 0$,

    * a clause $\{l, l_1, \ldots, l_m\}$ belongs to Ψ, and
    * each expression $\exists |l_i|$ ($1 \leq i \leq m$) occurs at the right of $\forall |l|$ in the prefix of (3).

Thus, existential and universal literals can be assigned by "unit propagation" because of the nogoods and goods stored. The assignment of universal literals by unit propagation is a side effect of the good leaning mechanism, and there is no counterpart in standard QBF reasoning.

To understand the benefits of learning, consider the QBF (2). The corresponding EQBF is

$$\exists x \forall y \exists z \exists s \langle \{\}, \{\{\neg x, \neg y, z\}, \{x, \neg y, \neg s\}, \\ \{\neg y, \neg z\}, \{y, z, \neg s\}, \{z, s\}\}, \{\} \rangle. \qquad (6)$$

With reference to Figure 1, the search proceeds as in the Figure, with the first branch leading to φ_3. Then, given what we said in the paragraph below Proposition 2, the good $\{y, \neg z\}$ (or $\{y\}$) is added to the initial EQBF while backtracking from φ_3. As soon as x is flipped,

- y is detected to be unit and consequently assigned; and

- the branch leading to φ_6 is not explored.

As this example shows, (good) learning can avoid the useless exploration of some branches.

Test File	T/F	LV.	$\#\exists x$	$\#\forall x$	# CL.	TIME-BT	NODES-BT	TIME-BJ	NODES-BJ	TIME-LN	NODES-LN
Adder.2-S	T	4	35	16	109	0.03	1707	0.04	1643	0.10	1715
Adder.2-U	F	3	44	9	110	2.28	150969	0.49	20256	0.20	1236
B*3i.4.4	F	3	284	4	2928	> 1200	–	> 1200	–	0.07	903
B*3ii.4.3	F	3	243	4	2533	> 1200	–	2.28	59390	0.04	868
B*3ii.5.2	F	3	278	4	2707	> 1200	–	52.47	525490	1.59	3462
B*3ii.5.3	T	3	300	4	3402	> 1200	–	> 1200	–	203.25	39920
B*3iii.4	F	3	198	4	1433	> 1200	–	0.56	18952	0.04	807
B*3iii.5	T	3	252	4	1835	> 1200	–	> 1200	–	1.83	11743
B*4ii.6.3	F	3	831	7	15061	> 1200	–	> 1200	–	176.21	53319
B*4iii.6	F	3	720	7	9661	> 1200	–	> 1200	–	65.63	156896
Impl08	T	17	26	8	66	0.08	12509	0.03	3998	0.00	65
Impl10	T	21	32	10	82	0.60	93854	0.20	22626	0.01	96
Impl12	T	25	38	12	98	4.49	698411	1.15	127770	0.00	133
Impl14	T	29	44	14	114	33.22	5174804	6.72	721338	0.00	176
Impl16	T	33	50	16	130	245.52	38253737	39.03	4072402	0.00	225
Impl18	T	37	56	18	146	> 1200	–	227.45	22991578	0.01	280
Impl20	T	41	62	20	162	> 1200	–	> 1200	–	0.01	341
L*BWL*A1	F	3	1098	1	62820	> 1200	–	224.57	265610	21.63	20000
L*BWL*B1	F	3	1870	1	178750	> 1200	–	> 1200	–	57.44	34355
C*12v.13	T	3	913	12	4582	0.20	4119	0.23	4119	8.11	4383

Table 1: QUBE results on 20 structured problems. Names have been abbreviated to fit into the table.

Implementation and Experimental Analysis

In implementing the above ideas, the main difficulty that has to be faced is caused by the unit and monotone pruning rules. Because of them, many assignments are not prefix-closed and thus the corresponding reasons, according to Propositions 1 and 2, cannot be stored in form of goods or nogoods. One obvious solution is to enable the storing only when the current assignment is prefix-closed. Unfortunately, it may be the case that the assignment is not prefix-closed because of a literal at its beginning. In these cases, learning would give no or little benefits. The other obvious solution is to allow the generation of prefix-closed assignments only. This implies that unit and monotone literals get no longer propagated as soon as they are detected, but only when the atoms at higher levels are assigned. This solution may cause a dramatic worsening of the performances of the QBF solver.

A closer analysis to the problem, reveals that troubles arise when backtrack occurs on a literal l, and in the reason for the current result there is a "problematic" literal l' whose level is minor than the level of l. Indeed, if this is the case, the assignment resulting after the backtracking will not be prefix-closed. To get rid of each of these literals l', we substitute l' with the already computed reason for rejecting $\overline{l'}$. The result may still contain "problematic" literals (these literals may have been introduced in the reason during the substitution process), and we go on substituting them till no one is left. Intuitively, in each branch we are computing the reasons corresponding to the assignment in which the "problematic" literals are moved to the end of the assignment.

We have implemented the above ideas in QUBE, together with a relevance learning scheme. QUBE is a state-of-the-art QBF solver (Giunchiglia, Narizzano, & Tacchella 2001b; 2001a). To test the effectiveness of learning, we considered the structured examples available at www.mrg.dist.

unige.it/qbflib. This test-set consists of structured QBFs corresponding to planning problems (Rintanen 1999a) and formal verification problems (Abdelwaheb & Basin 2000). The results on 20 instances are summarized in Table 1. In the Table:

- T/F indicates whether the QBF is satisfiable (T) or not (F),
- LV. indicates the level of the formula,
- $\#\exists x$ (resp. $\#\forall x$) shows the number of existentially (resp. universally) bounded variables,
- #CL. is the number of clauses in the matrix,
- TIME-BT/NODES-BT (resp. TIME-BJ/NODES-BJ, resp. TIME-LN/NODES-LN) is the CPU time in seconds and number of branches of QUBE-BT (resp. QUBE-BJ, resp. QUBE-LN). QUBE-BT, QUBE-BJ, QUBE-LN are QUBE with standard backtracking; with SBJ and CBJ enabled; with SBJ, CBJ and learning of order 4 enabled, respectively.

The tests have been run on a network of identical Pentium III, 600MHz, 128MB RAM, running SUSE Linux ver. 6.2. The time-limit is fixed to 1200s. The heuristic used for literal selection is the one described in (Feldmann, Monien, & Schamberger 2000).

The first observation is that QUBE-LN, on average, produces a dramatic reduction in the number of branching nodes. In some cases, QUBE-LN does less than 0.1% of the branching nodes of QUBE-BJ and QUBE-BT. However, in general, QUBE-LN is not ensured to perform less branching nodes than QUBE-BJ. Early termination or pruning may prevent the computation along a branch whose reason can enable a "long backjump" in the search stack, see (Prosser 1993a). For the same reason, there is no guarantee that by increasing the learning order, we get a reduction in the number of branching nodes. For example, on L*BWL*B1,

QuBE-LN branching nodes are 45595, 34355 and 55509 if run with learning order 2, 4 and 6 respectively. In terms of speed, learning may lead to very substantial improvements. The first observation is that QuBE-LN is able to solve 7 more examples than QuBE-BJ, and 12 more than QuBE-BT. Even more, some examples which are not solved in the time-limit by QuBE-BJ and QuBE-BT, are solved in less than 1s by QuBE-LN. However, learning does not always pay-off. To have an idea of the learning overhead, consider the results on the C*12v.13 example, shown last in the table. This benchmark is peculiar because backjumping plays no role, i.e., QuBE-BT and QuBE-BJ perform the same number of branching nodes.[1] On this example, QuBE-LN performs more branching node than QuBE-BJ. These extra branching nodes of QuBE-LN are not due to a missed "long backjump". Instead, they are due to the fact that QuBE-BT and QuBE-BJ skip the branch on a variable when it does not occur in the matrix of the current QBF, while QuBE-LN takes into account also the databases of the learnt clauses.

The table above shows QuBE-LN performances with relevance learning of order 4. Indeed, by changing the learning order we may get completely different figures. For example, on L*BWL*B1, QuBE-LN running times are 95.54, 57.44 and 112.73s with learning order 2, 4 and 6 respectively. We do not have a general rule for choosing the best learning order. According to the experiments we have done, 4 seems to be a good choice.

Conclusions

In the paper we have shown that it is possible to generalize nogood learning to deal with QBFs. We have introduced and implemented good learning. As we have seen, the interactions between nogood/good learning and the unit/monotone pruning heuristic is not trivial. We have implemented both nogood and good learning in QuBE, together with a relevance learning scheme for limiting the size of the learned clauses database. The experimental evaluation shows that very substantial speed-ups can be obtained. It also shows that learning has some overhead. However, we believe that such overhead can be greatly reduced extending ideas presented in (Moskewicz *et al.* 2001) for SAT. In particular, the extension of the "two literal watching" idea, originally due to (Zhang & Stickel 1996), seems a promising direction. This will be the subject of future research. Finally, we believe that the learning techniques that we propose can be successfully integrated in other QBFs solvers, and that similar ideas can be exploited to effectively deal with other related problems, such as the one considered in (Bayardo Jr. & Pehoushek 2000).

We have also tested QuBE-LN on more than 120000 randomly generated problems for checking the correctness and robustness of the implementation. These tests have been generated according to the "model A" described in (Gent & Walsh 1999). The results will be the subject of a future paper. QuBE-LN is publicly available on the web.

---

[1]In SAT, this happens for randomly generated problems.

References

Abdelwaheb, A., and Basin, D. 2000. Bounded model construction for monadic second-order logics. In *Proc. CAV*, 99–113.

Bayardo, Jr., R. J., and Miranker, D. P. 1996. A complexity analysis of space-bounded learning algorithms for the constraint satisfaction problem. In *Proc. AAAI*, 298–304.

Bayardo Jr., R. J., and Pehoushek, J. D. 2000. Counting models using connected components. In *Proc. AAAI*.

Bayardo, Jr., R. J., and Schrag, R. C. 1997. Using CSP look-back techniques to solve real-world SAT instances. In *Proc. AAAI*, 203–208.

Cadoli, M.; Giovanardi, A.; and Schaerf, M. 1998. An algorithm to evaluate QBFs. In *Proc. AAAI*.

Dechter, R. 1990. Enhancement schemes for constraint processing: Backjumping, learning, and cutset decomposition. *Artificial Intelligence* 41(3):273–312.

Feldmann, R.; Monien, B.; and Schamberger, S. 2000. A distributed algorithm to evaluate quantified boolean formulae. In *Proc. AAAI*.

Freeman, J. W. 1995. *Improvements to propositional satisfiability search algorithms*. Ph.D. Dissertation, University of Pennsylvania.

Gent, I., and Walsh, T. 1999. Beyond NP: the QSAT phase transition. In *Proc. AAAI*, 648–653.

Ginsberg, M. L. 1993. Dynamic backtracking. *Journal of Artificial Intelligence Research* 1:25–46.

Giunchiglia, E.; Narizzano, M.; and Tacchella, A. 2001a. An analysis of backjumping and trivial truth in quantified boolean formulas satisfiability. In *Proc. AI*IA, LNAI 2175*.

Giunchiglia, E.; Narizzano, M.; and Tacchella, A. 2001b. Backjumping for quantified boolean logic satisfiability. In *Proc. IJCAI*, 275–281.

Kleine-Büning, H.; Karpinski, M.; and Flögel, A. 1995. Resolution for quantified boolean formulas. *Information and computation* 117(1):12–18.

Moskewicz, M. W.; Madigan, C. F.; Zhao, Y.; Zhang, L.; and Malik, S. 2001. Chaff: Engineering an Efficient SAT Solver. In *Proc. DAC*.

Plaisted, D., and Greenbaum, S. 1986. A Structure-preserving Clause Form Translation. *Journal of Symbolic Computation* 2:293–304.

Prosser, P. 1993a. Domain filtering can degrade intelligent backjumping search. In *Proc. IJCAI*, 262–267.

Prosser, P. 1993b. Hybrid algorithms for the constraint satisfaction problem. *Computational Intelligence* 9(3):268–299.

Rintanen, J. 1999a. Constructing conditional plans by a theorem prover. *Journal of Artificial Intelligence Research* 10:323–352.

Rintanen, J. 1999b. Improvements to the evaluation of quantified boolean formulae. In *Proc. IJCAI*, 1192–1197.

Zhang, H., and Stickel, M. E. 1996. An efficient algorithm for unit propagation. In *Proc. of the 4th International Symposium on Artificial Intelligence and Mathematics*.

An Adaptive Noise Mechanism for WalkSAT

Holger H. Hoos

University of British Columbia
Computer Science Department
2366 Main Mall
Vancouver, BC, V6T 1Z4, Canada
hoos@cs.ubc.ca

Abstract

Stochastic local search algorithms based on the WalkSAT architecture are among the best known methods for solving hard and large instances of the propositional satisfiability problem (SAT). The performance and behaviour of these algorithms critically depends on the setting of the noise parameter, which controls the greediness of the search process. The optimal setting for the noise parameter varies considerably between different types and sizes of problem instances; consequently, considerable manual tuning is typically required to obtain peak performance. In this paper, we characterise the impact of the noise setting on the behaviour of WalkSAT and introduce a simple adaptive noise mechanism for WalkSAT that does not require manual adjustment for different problem instances. We present experimental results indicating that by using this self-tuning noise mechanism, various WalkSAT variants (including WalkSAT/SKC and Novelty$^+$) achieve performance levels close to their peak performance for instance-specific, manually tuned noise settings.

Introduction and Background

The WalkSAT family of algorithms (Selman, Kautz, & Cohen 1994; McAllester, Selman, & Kautz 1997) comprises some of the most widely studied and best-performing stochastic local search (SLS) algorithms for the propositional satisfiability problem (SAT). WalkSAT algorithms are based on an iterative search process that in each step selects a currently unsatisfied clause of the given SAT instance at random (according to a uniform probability distribution), selects a variable appearing in that clause and flips it, *i.e.*, changes its truth value from true to false or vice versa. Different methods are used for the variable selection within unsatisfied clauses, giving rise to various WalkSAT algorithms (McAllester, Selman, & Kautz 1997; Hoos 1999; Hoos & Stützle 2000a). All of these use a parameter called the *noise parameter* to control the degree of greediness in the variable selection process, *i.e.*, the degree to which variables are likely to be selected that, when flipped, lead to a maximal decrease in the number of unsatisfied clauses.

The noise parameter, which for all WalkSAT algorithms except for WalkSAT/TABU represents a probability and hence takes values between zero and one, has a major impact on the performance of the respective algorithm, as measured by the probability of finding a solution, *i.e.*, a model of the given formula, within a fixed number of steps, or by

the expected number of steps required for finding a solution. Not only is there a significant quantitative impact of the noise parameter setting on performance, but the qualitative behaviour of the algorithm can be different depending on the noise setting. In particular, it has been shown that for sufficiently high noise settings, the other important parameter common to all WalkSAT algorithms, the number of steps after which the search process is restarted from a randomly selected variable assignment (also called *cutoff parameter*) has little or no impact on the behaviour of the algorithm (Parkes & Walser 1996; Hoos & Stützle 1999). For low noise settings, however, finding an appropriate cutoff setting is typically crucial for obtaining good performance (Hoos & Stützle 2000a). Fortunately, for many of the most prominent and best-performing WalkSAT algorithms, including WalkSAT/SKC, WalkSAT/TABU, Novelty$^+$, and R-Novelty$^+$, peak performance is obtained for noise settings high enough that the cutoff parameter does not affect performance unless it is chosen too low, in which case, performance is degraded. This leaves the noise setting to be optimised in order to achieve maximal performance of these WalkSAT algorithms.[1]

Unfortunately, finding the optimal noise setting is typically a difficult task. Because optimal noise settings appear to differ considerably depending on the given problem instance, this task often requires experience and substantial experimentation with various noise values (Hoos & Stützle 2000a). We will see later that even relatively minor deviations from the optimal noise setting can lead to a substantial increase in the expected time for solving a given instance; and to make matters worse, the sensitivity of WalkSAT's performance *w.r.t.* the noise setting seems to increase with the size and hardness of the problem instance to be solved. This complicates the use of WalkSAT for solving SAT instances as well as their evaluation, and hence the development, of new WalkSAT algorithms.

One obvious approach for developing a self-tuning mechanism for the noise parameter in WalkSAT is to build on McAllester *et al.*'s "invariants" that relate optimal noise parameter settings to certain statistics of the number of unsatisfied clauses over a (partial) WalkSAT trajectory (McAllester,

---

[1] It may be noted that Novelty$^+$ and R-Novelty$^+$ have an additional secondary noise parameter, which, however, seems to have less impact on performance than the primary noise parameter. Furthermore, one uniform setting of this parameter seems to achieve excellent performance for a broad range of SAT instances and instance types (Hoos 1999; Hoos & Stützle 2000a).

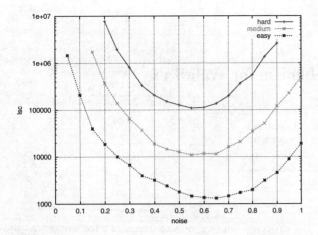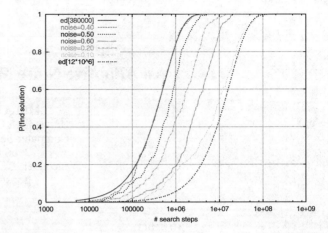

Figure 1: *Left:* Noise response for Novelty[+] on easy, medium, and hard instances from test-set `flat100-239-100`. *Right:* RTDs for for WalkSAT/SKC on SAT-encoded block world planning instance `bw_large.b` for approx. optimal, lower and higher noise settings.

Selman, & Kautz 1997). Recently, it has been demonstrated that these invariants can be used as the basis for automatically tuning the noise parameter in WalkSAT/SKC (Patterson & Kautz 2001). It should be noted, however, that these relationships are of an approximate nature and that thus far, they have only be established for WalkSAT algorithms.

The approach followed in this paper is based on a more general principle that can easily be generalised to SLS algorithms other than the WalkSAT architecture and to hard combinatorial problems different from SAT. It substantially differs from the method proposed in (Patterson & Kautz 2001), which optimises the noise setting for a given problem instance prior to the actual (unmodified) search process, during which the noise parameter setting is held fixed. The key idea behind our noise mechanism is to use high noise values only when they are needed to escape from stagnation situations in which the search procedure appears to make no further progress towards finding a solution. This idea is closely related to the motivation behind Reactive Tabu Search (Battiti & Tecchiolli 1994) and Iterated Local Search (Lourenço, Martin, & Stützle 2000), two high-performing SLS algorithms for combinatorial optimisation. Applied to WalkSAT algorithms such as Novelty[+], this approach not only achieves a remarkably robust and high performance, in some cases it also improves over the peak performance of the best previously known WalkSAT variant for the respective problem instance.

The Noise Response

We use the term *noise response* to refer to the functional dependency of the local search cost on the setting of the noise parameter. The noise response captures the characteristic impact of the noise setting on the performance of a given algorithm for a specific problem instance. *Local search cost* (abbreviated *lsc*) is defined as the expected time required by a given algorithm (for specific parameter settings) to solve a given problem instance. We estimate *lsc* by taking the average of an empirical run-time distribution (RTD). Since the variance of WalkSAT RTD is typically very high, stable estimates of *lsc* require empirical RTDs based on a large number

of successful runs. Unless specifically stated otherwise, the *lsc* measurements reported in this paper are based on at least 250 successful runs. Furthermore, random restart within runs was generally disabled by setting WalkSAT's cutoff parameter effectively to infinity. As we will see later, this does not affect the peak performance of the algorithms studied here.

Measuring the noise response for more than 300 SAT instances (most of which were taken from the SATLIB Benchmark Collection), including SAT-encoded planning and graph colouring problems, we found that the noise response for WalkSAT/SKC, Novelty[+], and R-Novelty[+] always has the same characteristic, concave shape: There exists a unique optimal noise setting minimising *lsc*; for noise higher than this optimal value, *lsc* increases monotonically; likewise, *lsc* increases monontonically as noise is decreased below the optimum value (typical examples are shown in Figure 1). The response curve is asymmetric, with a steeper increase in *lsc* for lower-than-optimal than for higher-than-optimal noise values, and there is no evidence for discontinuities in any of its derivatives.

As a consequence of this shape of the noise response curve, there is a certain robustness *w.r.t.* minor variations in the noise setting around the optimal value. Furthermore, lower-than-optimal noise values tend to cause significantly more difficulty in solving a problem instance than higher-than-optimal noise values. (This is particularly the case for some of the best-performing WalkSAT variants, such as Novelty[+] and R-Novelty[+].)

It has been previously observed that for optimal and higher-than-optimal noise settings, WalkSAT and other SLS algorithms for SAT show exponential RTDs (Hoos & Stützle 1999). For lower-than-optimal noise settings, RTDs indicate stagnation behaviour reflected in an increase in the variation coefficient (mean/stddev) with decreasing noise (Hoos & Stützle 2000a). (Typical RTDs are shown in Figure 1.) Because of the effect of the initial search phase that is most pronounced for relatively easy problem instances (relative to their size) around the optimal noise value, the variation coefficient can also slightly increase as the noise is increased beyond its optimal value.

There has also been some evidence in the literature that for

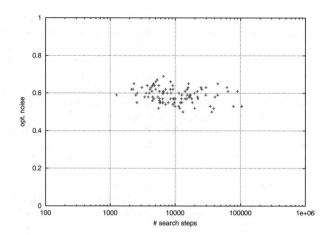

Figure 2: Approx. optimal noise values *vs. lsc* for Novelty[+] on test-set `flat100-239-100`.

sets of syntactically very similar problem instances, in particular for test-sets sampled from Uniform Random-3-SAT distributions (Cheeseman, Kanefsky, & Taylor 1991), the optimal noise values for WalkSAT/SKC are very similar (Hoos & Stützle 1999). This observation appears to hold for other sets of syntactically similar problem instances as well as for other WalkSAT variants. A typical example is shown in Figure 2; note that despite the syntactical similarity of the instances there are substantial differences in local search cost, which, however, are not significantly correlated with optimal noise settings. It may be noted that even at 250 tries per instance the *lsc* estimates, and hence our estimates for optimal noise settings, are often not very stable. For the test-set used in Figure 2, differences in search cost between the extreme optimal noise values obtained were smaller than a factor of 1.5.

However, optimal noise settings vary considerably with instance type and size (McAllester, Selman, & Kautz 1997; Hoos & Stützle 2000a). This is particularly noticable for the widely used SAT-encoded blocksworld planning instances (Kautz & Selman 1996; Hoos & Stützle 2000b), where the optimal noise values appear to decrease monotonically with problem size. For other instance types, including Uniform Random-3-SAT instances and SAT-encoded Flat Graph Colouring instances, the optimal noise value is apparently not affected by instance size. Overall, it appears that for those types of SAT instances where optimal noise changes with instance size, larger instances tend to have smaller optimal noise values (*cf.* Table 1).

Finally, there are significant differences in optimal noise levels between different WalkSAT variants. This is not surprising, considering the differences in how the noise parameter is used within these variants; but it is relevant in this context because it means that when comparing the performance of the variance for a given set of problem instances, the noise parameter setting needs to be optimised for each variant individually. This observation is particularly relevant in the context of recent findings that no single WalkSAT variant generally outperforms all others (Hoos & Stützle 2000a).

These observations suggest the following approach to manually tuning the noise parameter: For two initial guesses for the optimal noise value, empirical RTDs are measured and

lsc values are calculated from these. These two initial noise values are guessed in such a way that they are likely to be slightly higher than the optimal noise value. Assuming that the *lsc* measurements are reasonably accurate, and exploiting the typical concave shape of the noise response curve, a simple iterative method can be used to narrow down the optimal noise value by measuring additional *lsc* values for appropriately chosen noise settings. Typically, RTDs for no more than four noise values need to be evaluated in order to obtain a noise setting for which the *lsc* value is no more than 20% above the minimum. The initial guesses are often based on obvious structural properties of the problem instances, such as the ratio of clauses to variables, or background knowledge about the origin of the problem instances, including the transformations used for encoding them into SAT.

The drawback of this method is that it requires solving the problem instance under consideration hundreds, maybe thousands of times. This only makes sense when tuning an algorithm for a whole class of problem instances in a scenario where a large number of similar problem instances have to be solved subsequently. According to our observation that for several widely studied classes of SAT instances the optimal noise settings seem to be very similar or identical over whole distributions of problem instances, this situation is not unrealistic (especially in the context of comparative studies of SLS algorithms over a wide range of problem instances).

WalkSAT with Dynamic Noise

Given the observations made in the previous section, it appears very desirable to have a mechanism that automatically adjusts the noise parameter in such a way that manual parameter tuning is no longer necessary for obtaining optimal performance.

There are at least four types of information that can potentially be used by such a mechanism:

(a) background knowledge provided by the algorithm designer; this knowledge might reflect extensive experience with the algorithm on various types of instances or theoretical insights into the algorithm's behaviour;

(b) syntactic information about the problem instance; for SAT instances, this may include the number of clauses and variables as well as information about clause lengths, *etc.*;

(c) information collected over the run of the algorithm so far; in particular, this includes information about the search space positions and objective function values encountered over the (incomplete) search trajectory;

(d) information collected by specific mechanisms (or agents) that perform certain types of "semantic" analyses on the given problem instances; this can include active measurements of properties of the underlying search space, such as autocorrelation lengths for random walks (Weinberger 1990) or density of local optima (Frank, Cheeseman, & Stutz 1997).

Obviously, a self-tuning noise mechanism can integrate various types of information. In the following, we study a technique that is based on information of type (a), (b), and (c). Ultimately, we believe that information of type (d) should also be integrated, leading to a more robust and even better performing algorithm. However, from a scientific perspective as well as from an engineering point of view, it seems preferable to start with rather simple self-tuning algorithms before studying complex combinations of techniques.

Our approach is based on a simple and fairly general idea: Based on the effect of the noise setting on the search process, as described previously, and consistent with earlier observations by McAllester *et al.* (1997), it appears that optimal noise settings are those that achieve a good balance between an algorithms ability to greedily find solutions by following local gradients, and its ability to escape from local minima and other regions of the search space that attract the greedy component of the algorithm, yet contain no solutions. From this point of view, the standard static noise mechanism that performs non-greedy (or not-so greedy) search steps required to escape from situations in which the search would otherwise stagnate with a constant probability, seems to be a rather crude and wasteful solution. Instead, it appears much more reasonable to use this escape mechanism only when it is really needed.

This leads to our adaptive noise approach, in which the probability for performing greedy steps (or noise setting) is dynamically adjusted based on search progress, as reflected in the time elapsed since the last improvement in the objective function has been achieved. At the beginning of the search process, we use greedy search exclusively (noise=0). This will typically lead to a series of rapid improvements in the objective function value, followed by stagnation (unless a solution to the given problem instance is found). In this situation, the noise value is increased. If this increase is not sufficient to escape from the stagnation situation, *i.e.*, if it does not lead to an improvement in objective function value within a certain number of steps, the noise value is further increased. Eventually, the noise value should be high enough that the search process overcomes the stagnation, at which point, the noise can be gradually decreased, until the next stagnation situation is detected or a solution to the given problem instance is found.

Our first implementation of the adaptive noise mechanism uses very simple techniques for the basic components of stagnation detection, noise increase, and noise decrease. As an indicator for search stagnation we use a predicate that is true iff no improvement in objective function value has been observed over the last $\theta \cdot m$ search steps, where m is the number of clauses of the given problem instance and $\theta = 1/6$. Every incremental increase in the noise value is realised as $wp := wp + (1 - wp) \cdot \phi$. the decrements are defined as $wp := wp - wp \cdot 2\phi$, where wp is the noise level and $\phi = 0.2$.

The asymmetry between increases and decreases in the noise setting is motivated by the fact that detecting search stagnation is computationally more expensive than detecting search progress and by the earlier observation that it is advantageous to approximate optimal noise levels from above rather than from below. After the noise setting has been increased or decreased, the current objective function value is stored and becomes the basis for measuring improvement, and hence for detecting search stagnation. As a consequence, between increases in noise level there is always a phase during which the trajectory is monitored for search progress without further increasing the noise. No such delay is enforced between successive decreases in noise level.

It may be noted that this adaptive noise mechanism uses two internal parameters, θ and ϕ, that control its behaviour.

While it appears that this merely replaced the problem of tuning one parameter, wp, by the potentially more difficult problem of tuning these new parameters, the values of θ and ϕ used in this study were determined in preliminary experiments and then kept fixed throughout the rest of this study. In particular, the same values for θ and ϕ were used for all problem instances used in our performance evaluation. As we will see in the next section, various WalkSAT algorithms, when using the adaptive noise mechanism introduced here, achieve very impressive performance for the same fixed values of θ and ϕ, while the same algorithms, for the same fixed value of wp perform substantially worse. This indicates that, while our adaptive mechanism has some possible internal adjustments, these adjustments do not have to be tuned for each problem instance or instance type to achieve good performance.

Experimental Results and Discussion

The adaptive noise mechanism described in the previous section can be easily integrated into existing implementations of WalkSAT. In order to evaluate its performance against peak performance as obtained for manually tuned static noise, we conducted extensive computational experiments on widely used benchmark instances for SAT obtained from SATLIB (Hoos & Stützle 2000b). The benchmark set used for our evaluation comprises SAT-encoded blocksworld and logistics planning instances, two types of SAT-encoded graph colouring problems, critically constrained Uniform Random-3-SAT instances, and SAT-encoded all-interval-series problems. In addition, primarily to assess scaling behaviour, we generated a new test-set of 100 critically constrained, satisfiable Uniform Random-3-SAT instances with 400 variables and 1700 clauses each. The instances labelled uf*-hard are those instances from the respective critically constrained Uniform Random-3-SAT test-sets with the highest *lsc* for WalkSAT using manually tuned static noise.

As can be seen from Table 1, Novelty$^+$ with dynamic noise performs very well, considering the fact that it used no instance-specific parameter tuning, and keeping in mind that when using the standard static noise mechanism, especially for hard and large instances, even relatively small deviations from the optimal noise setting can easily lead to increases in *lsc* of more than an order of magnitude. It may be noted that the weakest performance is observed for the large DIMACS graph colouring instances, g125_17 and g125_18. Additional experiments (not shown here) indicated that by using a different stagnation criterion, performance on these instances can be significantly improved; this stagnation criterion, however, does not perform as well on the other instances tested here. Similarly, we observed that for different parameter settings θ and ϕ of the dynamic noise mechanism, the performance on almost all instances can be further improved. These observations suggest that more sophisticated mechanisms for adjusting the noise should be able to achieve overall performance improvements and in some cases are likely to exceed the performance of the best known SLS algorithms for SAT.

It is worth noting that in three cases, dynamic noise achieves better performance than approx. optimal static noise. At first glance, this might appear surprising; however, it should be noted that the adaptive noise mechanism does not merely attempt to find the optimal static noise level, but is rather based on the idea of using noise only when it is

instance	nov+opt		nov+dyn		dyn / opt
	lsc	noise	*lsc*	noise	*lsc* ratio
bw_large.a	9,388	0.40	12,156	0.47 ± 0.07	1.29
bw_large.b	197,649	0.35	212,671	0.30 ± 0.05	1.08
bw_large.c	$7.57 \cdot 10^6$	0.20	$8.77 \cdot 10^6$	0.19 ± 0.02	1.16
log.c	123,984	0.40	141,580	0.34 ± 0.03	1.14
flat100-hard	139,355	0.60	111,772	0.44 ± 0.07	0.80
g125_18	8,634	0.45	32,498	0.55 ± 0.04	3.76
g125_17	$0.84 \cdot 10^6$	0.25	$1.41 \cdot 10^6$	0.26 ± 0.03	1.68
uf100-hard	38,473	0.55	41,733	0.46 ± 0.07	1.08
uf250-hard	$3.71 \cdot 10^6$	0.55	$2.92 \cdot 10^6$	0.37 ± 0.02	0.79
uf400-hard	$22.9 \cdot 10^6$	0.55	$22.8 \cdot 10^6$	0.32 ± 0.01	1.00
ais10	$1.96 \cdot 10^6$	0.40	$1.72 \cdot 10^6$	0.33 ± 0.04	0.88

Table 1: Novelty$^+$ with approx. optimal static noise *vs.* dynamic noise mechanism on individual benchmark instances. *lsc* estimates are based on at least 250 runs for all instances except for uf400-hard, for which only 100 runs have been conducted. For Novelty$^+$ with dynamic noise, the mean and standard deviation of the noise over all runs are reported.

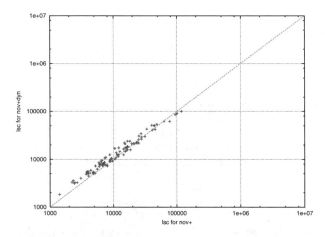

Figure 3: Correlation between *lsc* for Novelty$^+$ with optimal static noise *vs.* dynamic noise mechanism on test-set flat100-239-100.

actually needed. Nevertheless, as can be seen from comparing the approx. optimal static noise levels and the statistics over the noise levels used by the dynamic variants, there is a correlation between the noise levels used in both cases. An interesting exception can be observed for the hard Random-3-SAT instances, for which the adaptive noise mechanism uses noise levels that are significantly lower than the optimal static noise setting. Generally, the low variation in noise level for the dynamic mechanism indicates that the noise levels used within runs on an individual instance are very consistent.

Table 2 shows the relative performance obtained by Novelty$^+$ with dynamic *vs.* approx. optimal static noise across four of the test-sets of instances used in our evaluation. Interestingly, the dynamic noise variant achieves a significantly lower variation in *lsc* across all test-sets, as can be seen by comparing the respective variation coefficients (vc). Furthermore, as illustrated in Figure 3, there is a very strong correlation between the performance of both variants, with a small but significant tendency for dynamic noise to achieve lower *lsc* than static noise on hard instances. This is consistent with the intuition that the adaptive noise mechanism requires a certain amount of time before reaching good noise

levels. (This "homing in" phenomenon can be observed from traces of the actual noise level over search trajectories of the algorithm, not shown here.)

As noted earlier, a significant advantage for conventional WalkSAT algorithms including WalkSAT/SKC, Novelty$^+$, R-Novelty$^+$ with static noise lies in the fact that they show memory-less behaviour for optimal noise levels. This makes their performance robust *w.r.t.* the cutoff parameter and provides the basis for achieving optimal speedup using a straight-forward multiple independent tries parallelisation. It turns out that the WalkSAT variants with dynamic noise also have this property. In all cases, the respective RTDs can be approximated well with exponential distributions, which is indicative of the same memory-less behaviour as observed for approx. optimal static noise.

So far, we have only compared run-times in terms of individual variable flips. But obviously, the time-complexity of these search steps also needs to be taken into account when assessing the performance of the new WalkSAT variants with dynamic noise. The time-complexity of search steps was measured on a PC with dual Pentium III 733MHz CPUs, 256MB CPU cache, and 1GB RAM running Redhat Linux Version 2.4.9-6smp. It was found that for Novelty$^+$, R-Novelty$^+$, and WalkSAT/SLK on a broad set of benchmark instances, the CPU-time per variable flip was typically about 5–10% higher for the dynamic noise variant compared to the respective versions with standard static noise. This confirms that even when using a straight-forward implementation, the dynamic noise mechanism causes only a minimal overhead *w.r.t.* the time-complexity of search steps. It may be noted that in some cases, such as for WalkSAT/SKC when running on bw_large.c, search steps were up to 20% faster for dynamic than for static noise. This is caused by the fact that the time-complexity of WalkSAT search steps depends on the number of unsatisfied clauses, which in these cases drops more rapidly in the initial search phase when using the adaptive noise mechanism.

Due to space constraints, in this paper we report performance results for Novelty$^+$ with dynamic noise only. We obtained, however, empirical evidence indicating that the same adaptive noise mechanism appears to work well for WalkSAT/SKC and R-Novelty$^+$. Using the same values for θ and ϕ as in the present study, the performance (*lsc*) achieved by

test-set	lsc for nov+opt			lsc for nov+dyn		
	mean	cv	median	mean	cv	median
flat100-239	17,205	1.18	10,497	21,102	1.07	13,231
flat200-479	495,018	1.70	241,981	573,176	1.47	317,787
uf100-430*	2512.8	2.98	898.5	2550.9	2.16	1121.8
uf250-1065	53,938	5.26	8,755	64,542	4.72	13,015

Table 2: Novelty$^+$ with dynamic *vs.* approx. optimal static noise on various sets of benchmark instances. (∗) The data for test-set uf100-430 was computed for 100 randomly selected instances from that set. 'cv' denotes the coefficient of variation, *i.e.*, stddev/mean, of the distribution of *lsc* across the respective test-sets.

R-Novelty$^+$ with dynamic noise is within a factor of 1.5 of the performance obtained using approx. optimal static noise settings for 8 of the 11 instances listed in Table 1; in four of these cases, using dynamic noise results in substantially better performane than using approx. optimal static noise. Even better performance can be achieved for slightly different θ and ϕ settings. Similar results were obtained for WalkSAT/SKC; full reports on these experiments will be included in an extended version of this paper (currently available as a technical report).

Conclusions

We have characterised the noise response of WalkSAT algorithms and introduced an adaptive noise mechanism that achieve very good performance on a broad range of widely used benchmark problems when compared to the peak performance of traditional variants of WalkSAT with static noise.

In principle, this adaptive noise mechanism is easily applicable to a much wider range of stochastic local search algorithms for SAT and other combinatorial problems. This is particularly attractive for other high-performance algorithms, such as WalkSAT/TABU (McAllester, Selman, & Kautz 1997) and GSAT with tabu lists (Selman, Kautz, & Cohen 1994), DLM (Wu & Wah 1999), or ESG (Schuurmans, Southy, & Holte 2001), which all have parameters that are in many ways analogous to the noise parameter in the WalkSAT variants studied here. While the implementation of our adaptive noise strategy for these algorithms is rather straightforward, its effectivity in terms of achieving good and robust performance remains to be shown.

Another avenue for further investigation is the development and analysis of different and improved criteria for search stagnation which can be used within our generic adaptive mechanism. We strongly believe that the simple stagnation criteria studied here can be substantially improved, *e.g.*, by including measures such as search mobility (Schuurmans & Southy 2000) or the ones used in McAllester *et al.*'s invariants (McAllester, Selman, & Kautz 1997). Further improvements of the noise adaption mechanism and of adaptive SLS algorithms in general could possibly be achieved by integrating simple search space analysis techniques into the search control. Another promising avenue for further investigation is to study the use of machine learning techniques for identifying features that are effective for detecting search stagnation or for predicting optimal noise values.

Finally, it should be noted that the deeper reasons underlying the characteristic shape of the noise response curve for WalkSAT algorithms and the shape of the corresponding run-time distributions are unknown. Since these are intimitely connected to crucial aspects of SLS behaviour, further investigation in this direction could lead to improvements in our understanding of current SLS algorithms and in the design of future methods.

References

Battiti, R., and Tecchiolli, G. 1994. The reactive tabu search. *ORSA J. on Computing* 60(2):126–140.

Cheeseman, P.; Kanefsky, B.; and Taylor, W. M. 1991. Where the Really Hard Problems Are. In *Proc. IJCAI-91*, 331–337.

Frank, J.; Cheeseman, P.; and Stutz, J. 1997. When Gravity Fails: Local Search Topology. *(Electronic) Journal of Artificial Intelligence Research* 7:249–281.

Hoos, H., and Stützle, T. 1999. Towards a Characterisation of the Behaviour of Stochastic Local Search Algorithms for SAT. *Artificial Intelligence* 112:213–232.

Hoos, H., and Stützle, T. 2000a. Local search algorithms for SAT: An empirical evaluation. *J. Automated Reasoning* 24:421–481.

Hoos, H., and Stützle, T. 2000b. SATLIB: An Online Resource for Research on SAT. In I.P. Gent, H. M., and Walsh, T., eds., *SAT 2000*, 283–292. IOS Press.

Hoos, H. 1999. On the run-time behaviour of stochastic local search algorithms for SAT. In *Proc. AAAI-99*, 661–666.

Kautz, H., and Selman, B. 1996. Pushing the envelope: Planning, propositional logic, and stochastic search. In *Proc. AAAI-96*, 1194–1201.

Lourenço, H.; Martin, O.; and Stützle, T. 2000. Iterated Local Search. Technical Report AIDA–00–06, Technische Universität Darmstadt. (To appear in F. Glover and G. Kochenberger, editors, Handbook of Metaheuristics, Kluwer, 2002).

McAllester, D.; Selman, B.; and Kautz, H. 1997. Evidence for invariants in local search. In *Proc. IJCAI-97*, 321–326.

Parkes, A. J., and Walser, J. P. 1996. Tuning Local Search for Satisfiability Testing. In *Proc. AAAI-96*, 356–362.

Patterson, D. J., and Kautz, H. 2001. A Self-Tuning Implementation of Walksat. *Electronic Notes on Discrete Mathematics* 9. (Presented at the LICS 2001 Workshop on Theory and Applications of Satisfiability Testing).

Schuurmans, D., and Southy, F. 2000. Local search characteristics of incomplete SAT procedures. In *Proc. AAAI-2000*, 297–302.

Schuurmans, D.; Southy, F.; and Holte, R. 2001. The exponentiated subgradient algorithm for heuristic boolean programming. In *Proc. IJCAI-01*, 334–341.

Selman, B.; Kautz, H. A.; and Cohen, B. 1994. Noise strategies for improving local search. In *Proc. AAAI-94*, 337–343.

Weinberger, E. 1990. Correlated and uncorrelated fitness landscapes and how to tell the difference. *Biological Cybernetics* 63:325–336.

Wu, Z., and Wah, B. 1999. Trap Escaping Strategies in Discrete Lagrangian Methods for Solving Hard Satisfiability and Maximum Satisfiability Problems. In *Proc. AAAI-99*, 673–678.

A Mixture-Model for the Behaviour of SLS Algorithms for SAT

Holger H. Hoos

University of British Columbia
Computer Science Department
2366 Main Mall
Vancouver, BC, V6T 1Z4, Canada
hoos@cs.ubc.ca

Abstract

Stochastic Local Search (SLS) algorithms are amongst the most effective approaches for solving hard and large propositional satisfiability (SAT) problems. Prominent and successful SLS algorithms for SAT, including many members of the WalkSAT and GSAT families of algorithms, tend to show highly regular behaviour when applied to hard SAT instances: The run-time distributions (RTDs) of these algorithms are closely approximated by exponential distributions. The deeper reasons for this regular behaviour are, however, essentially unknown. In this study we show that there are hard problem instances, *e.g.*, from the phase transition region of the widely studied class of Uniform Random 3-SAT instances, for which the RTDs for well-known SLS algorithms such as GWSAT or WalkSAT/SKC deviate substantially from exponential distributions. We investigate these irregular instances and show that the respective RTDs can be modelled using mixtures of exponential distributions. We present evidence that such mixture distributions reflect stagnation behaviour in the search process caused by "traps" in the underlying search spaces. This leads to the formulation of a new model of SLS behaviour as a simple Markov process. This model subsumes and extends earlier characterisations of SLS behaviour and provides plausible explanations for many empirical observations.

Introduction and Background

The propositional satisfiability problem (SAT) is a model combinatorial problem whose conceptual simplicity facilitates the design and analysis of algorithms for other hard combinatorial problems. For the past decade, various types of stochastic local search (SLS) methods have been applied very successfully to SAT. These include the GSAT and WalkSAT families of algorithms (Selman, Kautz, & Cohen 1994; Gent & Walsh 1993; McAllester, Selman, & Kautz 1997), as well as several other algorithms based on similar ideas (Gu 1992; Wah & Shang 1997; Wu & Wah 2000; Schuurmans & Southy 2000; Schuurmans, Southy, & Holte 2001). GSAT and WalkSAT algorithms have been extensively studied in the literature, and include some of the best-performing SAT algorithms known to date (Hoos & Stützle 2000a; Schuurmans, Southy, & Holte 2001). Compared to other state-of-the-art SAT algorithms, such as Satz (Li &

Anbulagan 1997), these methods are rather simplistic and it is not well understood how they can solve many classes of large and difficult SAT instances surprisingly efficiently. It is also largely unclear under which conditions (*i.e.*, on which types of instances, and for which parameter settings) these SLS algorithms work well.

The run-time behaviour of GSAT and WalkSAT algorithms when applied to hard SAT instances and when using sufficiently high noise parameter settings, is typically characterised by exponential run-time distributions (RTDs) (Hoos 1998; Hoos & Stützle 1999). Here, "sufficiently high" includes the range in which optimal performance, as reflected in minimal mean run-time, is achieved. These RTD characterisation can be extended to easier SAT instances by using a generalised class of exponential distributions that supports modelling the initial search phase (as reflected in the left tail of a run-time distribution), during which the success probability increases faster than for a memory-less search process characterised by an exponential RTD (Hoos 1998).

As we will show in this study, for a small but significant number of hard instances, *e.g.*, from the widely studied "phase transition region" of the Uniform Random-3-SAT instance distribution (Cheeseman, Kanefsky, & Taylor 1991), SLS algorithms such as GWSAT or WalkSAT/SKC show a behaviour that cannot be captured by these models. This irregular behaviour is interesting for at least two reasons: Firstly, as will become clear later, it can be seen as a type of stagnation behaviour that, if present, appears to severely degrade SLS performance as the search progresses beyond a certain point. Clearly, a sufficient understanding of this phenomenon is likely to be the key towards eliminating the undesirable behaviour. Secondly, the irregularities provide a basis for refining previous models of SLS behaviour; such models are valuable for purely scientific as well as for practical reasons, as they improve our ability to understand, to predict, and to improve the performance and behaviour of SLS algorithms for SAT.

In the following, we investigate this irregular SLS behaviour in detail, focussing on GWSAT and WalkSAT/SKC, two of the most widely studied SLS algorithms for SAT, and the prominent class of Uniform Random-3-SAT "phase tran-

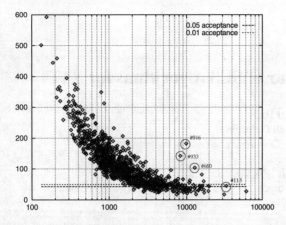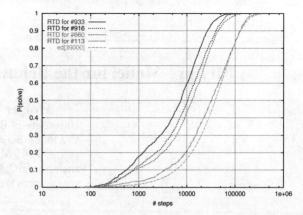

Figure 1: *Left:* Correlation between instance hardness (mean run-time for WalkSAT with approx. optimal noise measured in variable flips over 100 successful runs/instance; horizontal) and χ^2 values (vertical) from testing the RTDs of individual instances versus a best-fit exponential distribution for SATLIB test-set uf100-430; the horizontal lines indicate the acceptance thresholds for the 0.01 and 0.05 acceptance levels of the χ^2 test. *Right:* Irregular WalkSAT RTDs for outlier instances; note the deviation from a typical exponential distribution, indicated by the right-most curve.

sition" instances.[1] We show that the corresponding RTDs can be characterised by simple mixtures of exponential distributions, and provide evidence that this characterisation appears to apply to all hard problem instances for which irregular SLS behaviour is observed. Empirical evidence is presented for an explanation of this phenomenon based on search stagnation caused by "traps" in the underlying search spaces. Based on the insights from our analysis of irregular instances and search stagnation, we developed a conceptually simple Markov chain model which shows exactly the same behaviour as observed for GWSAT and WalkSAT/SKC on the irregular SAT instances studied here. This model provides simple and straight-forward explanations for our empirical results. Furthermore, it suggests several intuitive and testable connections between SLS behaviour and the structure of SAT instances.

Irregular Instances and Mixture Models

Our investigation starts with the observation that when studying the RTDs for WalkSAT (using approx. optimal noise settings) on sets of critically constrained Uniform Random-3-SAT instances, there are hard instances (as indicated by a high expected number of search steps for finding a solution) for which the search behaviour appears to deviate substantially from the typical memory-less behaviour reflected in exponential RTDs. Figure 1 shows the correlation between instance hardness for WalkSAT/SKC and the deviation of the corresponding RTD from a best-fit exponential distribution for test-set uf100-430, a set of critically constrained Uniform Random-3-SAT instances obtained from SATLIB[2] (Hoos & Stützle 2000b). This data was obtained using the same method as described in (Hoos & Stützle

---

[1]Algorithm outlines for GWSAT and WalkSAT/SKC, as well as a detailed description of the Uniform Random-3-SAT instances used in this study can be found in (Hoos & Stützle 2000a).

[2]www.satlib.org

1999). All RTDs reported in this study are based on at least 100 runs of the algorithm using cutoff parameter settings high enough to guarantee that a solution was found in each run without using any kind of restart mechanism. As noted by Hoos & Stützle (2000a), the high χ^2 values consistently observed for easy instances are due to effects of the initial search phase. In the present study, we largely ignore the effect of the initial search phase, which has been previously discussed and characterised in the literature (Hoos & Stützle 2000a).

The deviations reflected by high χ^2 values for hard instances, some of which are highlighted in Figure 1, are of a different nature. Closer inspection reveals that these irregular RTDs have an untypically high coefficient of variation (stddev/mean); all of them can be well aproximated by mixtures of exponential distributions of the form

$$\sum_{i=1}^{k-1} w_i \cdot ed[m_i] + \left(1 - \sum_{i=1}^{k-1} w_i\right) ed[m_k],$$

where $ed[m](x) = 1 - 2^{-x/m}$ is the cumulative distribution of an exponential distribution with median m and the w_i are the mixture weights. It should be noted that while for large k such mixtures can approximate any cumulative distribution function arbitrarily well, all approximations presented in this study use two components only and are hence significantly more restricted. Since the approximated empirical RTDs are generally based on at least 1,000 runs each, good approximations with this restricted mixture model reflect a rather surprising regularity of the underlying SLS behaviour rather than an overfitting effect due to an overly flexible model.

Additional experiments showed the same type of "outlier instances" for SATLIB test-sets uf50-218 and uf20-91; in all cases, WalkSAT and GWSAT showed RTDs that could be well approximated by 2-component mixtures of exponential distributions. (See, *e.g.*, Figure 2; these results are reported in more detail in the extended version of this

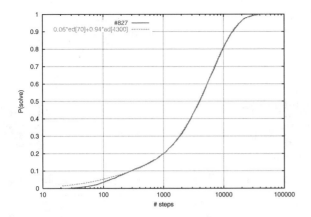

Figure 2: RTD for WalkSAT(noise=0.55) on hard irregular instance from test-set `uf50-218` and approximation by 2-component mixture of exponential distributions.

paper.) Overall, using 2-component mixtures of the previously mentioned generalised exponential distributions, all observed RTDs could be perfectly approximated to the degree supported by the sample size underlying the empirical RTD data. (The quality of these approximations can be seen, in a slightly different context, in Figure 5.) Interestingly, the extreme tails of all irregular RTDs are extremely well approximated by a model fitted to the whole distribution. In particular, there is no indication for so-called "heavy tails", as have been reported for the RTDs of certain high-performing randomised complete SAT algorithms (Gomes, Selman, & Kautz 1998).

Multiple Competing Solutions?

Perhaps the most obvious explanation for the observed mixture RTDs is based on the following idea: For instances with multiple solutions, one could assume that each solution (or cluster of solutions) has its own "basin of attraction", and that the attractivity of these basins might sometimes differ widely between various solutions. If conditional of being pulled into one given basin, the RTD of GWSAT or Walk-SAT were an exponential distribution, then a biased random selection of the respective basin at the beginning of the search process would lead to the observed exponential mixture RTDs. Such a selection could be the result of the fact that GWSAT and WalkSAT both start the search at a randomly chosen assignment.

There are two ways of investigating the validity of this explanation: The first is based on a modification of the algorithms such that the search process is no longer initialised randomly, but at a specific variable assignment. If the proposed explanation of the irregular search behaviour were correct, using the fixed initialisation for the irregular instances from above should result in regular RTDs which, depending on the fixed initial assignment chosen, correspond to the components of the mixture obtained for random initialisation. A second validation experiment uses the unmodified algorithms (with random initialisation) and studies their RTDs on single-solution instances. If the attractivity of different solutions were the sole cause of mixture RTDs, these should not be observed on single solution instances.

For the first approach, we measured RTDs for a modified version of WalkSAT that always starts at a specific assignment applied to one of the irregular instances from test-set `uf50-218-1000`. Figure 3 (left) shows the RTD for WalkSAT/SKC with the standard, randomised initialisation as well as RTDs for a WalkSAT/SKC variant that always starts the search from the same given initial assignment. The specific initial assignments used here were the following: one at Hamming distance 10 from one of the instance's 48 solutions, one setting all variables to false, and one at Hamming distance 50 to a specific solution. With the exception of this last case, the resulting RTDs are mixture distributions rather than pure (generalised) exponentials, an observation that does not support the explanation proposed above. It is interesting to note that for this instance, the maximal Hamming distance between any two solutions is only 16, while the mean Hamming distance between solutions is 7. Hence, it appears that only when the search is initialised Hamming distant from the loosely clustered solutions, WalkSAT shows a simple exponential RTD. (This result is further confirmed by the RTDs for additional initial starting assignments, not shown here.)

For our investigation of the second approach, we generated sets of single-solution Uniform Random-3-SAT phase transition instances. This was done by generating Uniform Random-3-SAT instances in the usual (unbiased) way and subsequently checking for each instance whether it has exactly one solution.[3] For the three test-sets thus obtained, WalkSAT/SKC RTDs were measured (using approx. optimal noise) and fitted with exponential distributions, as described in the previous section. As can be seen in Figure 3 (right), the same kind of outlier instances as for the standard Uniform Random-3-SAT test-sets can be detected. The RTDs for these outlier instances are very similar to those shown in Fig. 1 and can be equally well approximated by mixtures of exponential distributions. These results indicate that single solution instances can exhibit the same irregular SLS behaviour, characterised by mixture RTDs, as instances with multiple solutions. Furthermore, it may be noted that test-sets of single-solution instances show a variability in search cost between the instances similar to the respective unrestricted test-sets. This clearly indicates that factors other than solution density have an important impact on the performance of SLS algorithms like WalkSAT. (Similar results were obtained for test-sets of critically constrained single-solution instances with 50 and 20 variables.)

It may be noted that the observations from the first of the two experiments described above still allow for an explanation in which the attraction areas of several or all solutions (or solution clusters) overlap at most or all locations in the given search space. While consistent with the nature of the randomised iterative improvement search process underlying WalkSAT/SKC and GWSAT, this modified hypothesis would still not explain the occurrence of mixture RTDs on

---

[3]This test was performed using REL_SAT, version 2.00 (Bayardo & Pehoushek 2000).

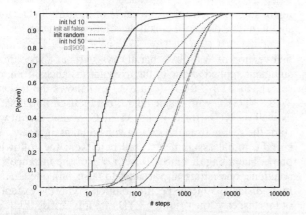 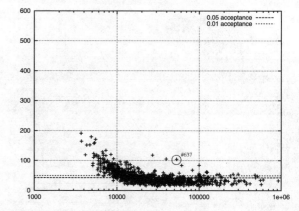

Figure 3: *Left:* RTDs for WalkSAT with fixed initialisation for irregular instance #168 from test-set uf50-218-1000. *Right:* Correlation between mean run-time for WalkSAT (horizontal) and χ^2 values (vertical) from testing the RTDs of individual instances versus a best-fit exponential distribution for test-set uf100-430-1000-s1; the horizontal lines indicate the acceptance thresholds for the 0.01 and 0.05 acceptance levels of the χ^2 test.

single-solution instances.

Overall, the evidence from the two experiments does not support our initial hypothesis that mixture RTDs are simply caused by the presence of multiple solutions and respective basins of attraction.

Traps and Search Stagnation

An alternate explanation of the observed irregular behaviour is based on the assumption that for the respective problem instances, the local search process somehow gets trapped in regions of the search space that are attractive yet do not contain solutions. Intuitively, once trapped in such a region, it might take quite long before an SLS algorithm manages to escape from this region and find a route that finally leads to a solution. In this case, the mixture RTDs observed for the previously identified irregular instances reflect a stagnation of the search process caused by such traps. If this explanation were correct, we should be able to observe mixture RTDs and high search cost for SAT instances containing such traps.

To investigate this hypothesis, we first devised a way of combining two single-solution instances into a new SAT instance that contains one solution and a trap: For a single-solution instance F over n variables, $x_1, \ldots, x_n$, let $M(F) = (m_1, \ldots, m_n)$ denote the unique model of F, *i.e.*, F is true under the variable assignment $x_1 := m_1, \ldots, x_n := m_n$. Then for given single-solution instances F, G, we define the *plugged combination instances* $CP1[F, G]$ and $CP2[F, G]$ as follows:

$$CP1[F, G] = \bigwedge_{i=1}^{l} (\neg \hat{x} \vee \bigvee_{j=1}^{k} p_{ij}) \wedge \bigwedge_{i=1}^{m} (\hat{x} \vee \bigvee_{j=1}^{k} q_{ij}) \wedge \bigvee_{j=1}^{n} \neg m_j$$

where $M(F) = (m_1, \ldots, m_n)$ is the unique model of F; and

$$CP2[F, G] = CP1[G, F].$$

This construction uses a discriminator variable $\hat{x}$ to "switch" between the two component instances. Furthermore, the

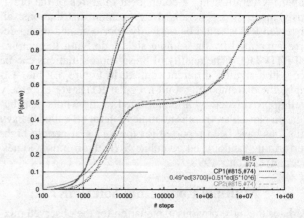

Figure 4: RTDs for GWSAT (noise=0.55) on easy instances from test-set uf100-430-1000-s1 and plugged combinations and approximation with 2-component mixtures of exponential distributions. (The RTD for CP2(#815, #74) can be equally well approximated with a 2-component mixture of exponentials.)

solution corresponding to one of the component instances is plugged by adding a single clause of length n. Note that adding this clause does not affect the objective function value (number of unsatisfied clauses) of any assignment other than the plugged solution; this implies that the difference between $C[F, G]$ and $CP1[F, G]$ is only visible to GWSAT or WalkSAT when the respective search process has reached the immediate neighbourhood of $M(F)$.

We now assume that single-solution instances that are extremely easy for a given SLS algorithm are made easy by the fact that their single solution is very attractive for the algorithm. Based on this assumption, plugged combinations of easy single-solution instances would contain a very attractive trap, which should render them substantially more difficult to solve than the respective component instances.

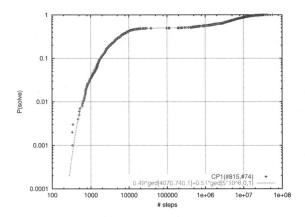

Figure 5: Approximation of GWSAT RTD for plugged combination of easy instances from test-set uf100-430-1000-s1 with a mixture of two generalised exponential distributions; the empirical RTD data is the same as shown in Figure 4. The fit is equally good in both tails of the empirical distribution.

This conjecture was confirmed experimentally. Figure 4 shows a typical result, illustrating the hardness of plugged combinations of easy single-solution instances as well as the irregular RTDs obtained by solving these instances with GWSAT, which can be very well approximated by two-component mixtures of exponential distributions. When using mixtures of generalised exponential distributions[4] to model the initial search phase, we obtain perfect approximations (see Figure 5). Analogous results were obtained in numerous similar experiments using other component instances and test-sets. Overall, this confirms our hypothesis that traps, *i.e.*, attractive areas of the search space that do not contain solutions, can lead to search stagnation and the same type of irregular behaviour as previously observed for "outlier" Random-3-SAT instances.[5]

Based on this explanation, we now present a simpe abstract model for the observed SLS behaviour. Note that the behaviour of an SLS algorithm for SAT, such as GWSAT or WalkSAT, applied to a given SAT instance can be modelled as a Markov chain. Intuitively, the states of this chain represent areas of the search space, *i.e.*, sets of variable assignments that are considered equivalent in a certain sense. Simple examples for such sets of equivalent states are all assignments at a certain Hamming distance from the

---

[4]This class of distribution is characterised by the cumulative distribution function

$$ged[m, \gamma, \delta](x) = 1 - 2^{-(x/m)^{1+(\gamma/x)^{\delta}}};$$

in most cases, empirical RTDs can be excellently approximated with a special case of this distribution for which $\delta = 1$.

[5]It should be noted that WalkSAT's behaviour on the plugged combination instances is slightly different from GWSAT's. This difference is due to the variable selection mechanism in WalkSAT and the occurrence of the discriminator variable in all clauses of a plugged combination instance; a detailed discussion can be found in the extended version of this paper.

nearest solution, all assignments that satisfy a certain number of clauses, or all assignments that belong to a specific certain plateau region (Frank, Cheeseman, & Stutz 1997; Yokoo 1997; Hoos 1998). The transitions between the states thus defined correspond to the conditional probabilities of reaching a specific state from a given current state. Note that these transition probabilities depend on the problem instance as well on the SLS algorithm applied to it.

Here, we will consider a simplified version of such a model of SLS behaviour. Our model consists of a Markov chain with k states $s_1, \ldots, s_k$ (see Figure 6a). Let $p_{i,j}$ be the probability for a transition from state i to state j. We make the following assumptions:

$$p_{1,1} = 1 \tag{1}$$
$$p_{k,k-1} = 1 \tag{2}$$
$$\forall i; 1 < i < k : p_{i,i+1} = p^+ > 0 \tag{3}$$
$$\forall i; 1 < i < k : p_{i,i-i} = p^- > 0 \tag{4}$$
$$p^- = 1 - p^+ \tag{5}$$

The first assumption reflects the fact that state s_1 is an absorbing state representing the solution(s) of the given problem instance; SLS algorithms for SAT typically terminate as soon as a solution is found. Assumption (2) states that s_k is a reflecting boundary; it captures the intuition that any measure of distance to a solution modelled by this Markov chain will have a finite upper bound. The primary purpose of assumptions (3), (4), and (5) is to keep the model as simple as possible while allowing it to represent differences in problem size (reflected by k) and the attractivity of solutions (reflected by p^+ and p^-).

Interestingly, this simple Markov chain model shows precisely the same type of behaviour as GWSAT or WalkSAT applied to typical SAT instances for sufficiently high noise parameter settings. This can be seen empirically by comparing the respective RTDs, where an RTD for the model is defined as the distribution of the number of transitions needed to reach the solution state s_1 for the first time, starting from s_k (see Figure 6). It is worth noting that the same family of generalised exponential distributions introduced in (Hoos 1998; Hoos & Stützle 2000a) for accurately modelling the full RTDs of GWSAT and various WalkSAT variants can also be used to perfectly approximate the RTDs for the Markov chain model presented here. Unfortunately, so far it could not be formally proven that the RTDs for the model are always approximable by this family of distributions.

This Markov chain model can be easily extended to cases where the problem instances contain the kind of trap described in the previous section. In particular, the plugged combinations instances defined above can be modelled in a straight-forward way: We just combine the two models corresponding to the component instances into a branched chain model, as illustrated in Figure 6, where one of the two solution states is transformed into a reflecting boundary of the model (this state corresponds to the plugged solution), while the other becomes the single solution state of the branched model.

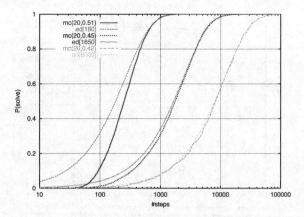

Figure 6: *Left:* Structure of simple Markov chain model (a) and branched model with trap (b); *right:* RTD for unbranched model (a) with $k = 20$, $p^+ = 0.52$, and $p^- = 0.48$.

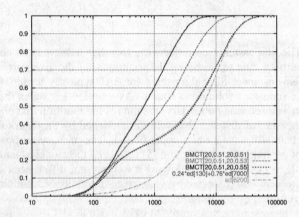

Figure 7: RTDs for branched Markov model with trap using different parameter settings can be approximated by mixtures of exponential distributions.

The RTDs for these branched Markov chain models are remarkably similar to those observed for the irregular SAT instances and for the plugged combination instances studied before. Depending on the length of the trap and solution branches and their respective transition probabilities p_t^- and p_s^-, we get the same type of mixture distribution as previously observed for GWSAT and WalkSAT/SKC. Consistent with the intuition behind the model and previous results for plugged combination instances, the two exponential components of the mixture RTD for the branched Markov chain model are more prominent for longer and more attractive trap branches (see Figure 7).

In the light of this model, the mixture distributions that are characteristic for the irregular instances reported earlier in this study are likely caused by prominent traps in the underlying search spaces. This hypothesis is consistent with the fact that many of the irregular instances are relatively hard, while none were detected amongst the easiest 10–15% of the instances within each of the respective test-sets. The model is also consistent with our observations on the be-

haviour of WalkSAT when using fixed initialisation from various points in the search space. When modelling an irregular instance by a branched Markov chain with a trap, it is clear that depending on the state at which the Markov process is initialised, we will observe the same qualitative differences in the resulting RTDs as observed for WalkSAT with fixed initialisation. In particular, when initialising at or near the trap state, the resulting RTD will show little or no irregular behaviour, but an increased search cost for all but the right tail of the distribution. Note that having the search space regions corresponding to the trap and solution states at high Hamming distance will maximise the area in which the attraction of either one dominates the behaviour of the search process and will thus lead to more prominent irregular SLS behaviour. Hence, it is reasonable to assume that for a prominently irregular instance, initialising Hamming distant from the solutions should be equivalent to initialising close to a prominent trap.

Conclusions and Future Work

Our study has shown that the run-time behaviour of two well-known SLS algorithms, GWSAT and WalkSAT/SKC, can be empirically characterised by mixtures of exponential distributions with a small number of mixture components. This extends previous empirical results to instances on which deviations from the typical, memory-less behaviour characterised by exponential distributions are observed; these "irregular" instances are not uncommon in the phase transition region of Uniform-Random-3-SAT and tend to be hard when compared to other instances from the same problem distribution.

As we have seen, the occurence of mixture RTDs can be explained based on a trap-based model of search stagnation. Somewhat surprisingly, we found that the empirically observed behaviour of the search process can generally be modelled by a very simple abstract model based on branched Markov chains. The model is based on the intuition that the search process implemented by procedures such as GWSAT or WalkSAT/SKC progresses through discrete stages, each of which has a characteristic "distance" to the nearest solution. It is not entirely clear if and how these stages are explicitly manifested in the form of easily identifiable search space features; our current understanding of SLS behaviour suggests that the search stages might correspond to extensive plateau regions (Frank, Cheeseman, & Stutz 1997; Yokoo 1997; Hoos 1999). Furthermore, it is likely that at least one type of trap corresponds to the "failed clusters" observed by Parkes (1997). We currently investigate this hypothesis using advanced search space analysis techniques as well as the RTD characterisations and abstract search model developed in this study. Furthermore, it appears to be interesting to explore potential connections between traps and the factors underlying the hardness of Random-3-SAT instances studied by Singer *et al.* (2000), in particular backbone robustness.

Obviously, the simple Markov model is only an approximation of the behaviour of SLS algorithms such as GWSAT or WalkSAT in the multi-dimensional, complex search spaces corresponding to the SAT instances studied here. This approximation, however, seems to capture the essential features for the observed behaviour; therefore, it appears that by establishing the relation between it and identifiable features of the respective instances, considerable progress can be made towards a characterisation of the factors underlying the hardness of problem instances *w.r.t.* SLS algorithms. (It is worth noting that a slightly modified Markov chain model, where the probabilities of staying within the same state are not zero, *i.e.*, $p^- + p^+ < 1$, shows exactly the same type of RTDs as the simpler model studied here.)

There is some preliminary experimental evidence suggesting that the RTD characterisations and the abstract Markov model presented here might be rather broadly applicable. Apparently, the stagnation behaviour typically observed for GWSAT and WalkSAT when using lower-than-optimal settings of the noise parameter can be characterised and modelled analogous to the behaviour observed on irregular instances. It appears also likely that our characterisation generalises to other SLS algorithms for SAT (such as Walk-SAT/TABU, Novelty$^+$, and R-Novelty$^+$), to randomised systematic search algorithms for SAT (such as Satz_RAND), and to SLS algorithms for other hard combinatorial problems (such as Iterated Local Search for MaxSAT or the Travelling Salesperson Problem). These observations and hypothesis are currently under further investigation.

Another direction for future research is of a more theoretical nature: It appears that relatively simple probabilistic models such as the branched Markov chain model for SLS behaviour presented here, should be amenable to theoretical analysis, such that the full RTDs for these models can be characterised analytically rather than experimentally, as was done in this study. Unfortunately, for the model proposed here, so far we have not been able to find in the literature or to derive analytic characterisations of the corresponding RTDs. Further questions of theoretical interest, such as under which conditions the RTDs of a Markov process can be characterised by mixtures of exponentials, appear to be also currently unanswered.

Acknowledgements

This research is supported by NSERC Individual Research Grant #238788. We gratefully acknowledge helpful comments and suggestions by Ian P. Gent, Henry Kautz, and Bart Selman as well as by the anonymous reviewers.

References

Bayardo, R., and Pehoushek, J. D. 2000. Counting Models using Connected Components. In *Proc. AAAI-2000*, 157–162.

Cheeseman, P.; Kanefsky, B.; and Taylor, W. M. 1991. Where the Really Hard Problems Are. In *Proc. IJCAI-91*, 331–337.

Frank, J.; Cheeseman, P.; and Stutz, J. 1997. When Gravity Fails: Local Search Topology. *(Electronic) J. of Artificial Intelligence Research* 7:249–281.

Gent, I. P., and Walsh, T. 1993. Towards an understanding of hill–climbing procedures for SAT. In *Proc. AAAI-93*, 28–33.

Gomes, C. P.; Selman, B.; and Kautz, H. 1998. Boosting Combinatorial Search Through Randomization. In *Proc. AAAI-98*, 431–437.

Gu, J. 1992. Efficient local search for very large-scale satisfiability problems. *ACM SIGART Bulletin* 3(1):8–12.

Hoos, H., and Stützle, T. 1999. Towards a Characterisation of the Behaviour of Stochastic Local Search Algorithms for SAT. *Artif. Intelligence* 112:213–232.

Hoos, H., and Stützle, T. 2000a. Local search algorithms for SAT: An empirical evaluation. *J. Automated Reasoning* 24:421–481.

Hoos, H., and Stützle, T. 2000b. SATLIB: An Online Resource for Research on SAT. In I.P. Gent, H. M., and Walsh, T., eds., *SAT 2000*, 283–292. IOS Press.

Hoos, H. 1998. *Stochastic Local Search - Methods, Models, Applications*. Ph.D. Dissertation, TU Darmstadt, Germany.

Hoos, H. 1999. SAT-encodings, search space structure, and local search performance. In *Proc. IJCAI-99*, 296–302.

Li, C. M., and Anbulagan. 1997. Look-ahead versus look-back for satisfiability problems. In *Proc. CP'97*, 341–355. Springer Verlag.

McAllester, D.; Selman, B.; and Kautz, H. 1997. Evidence for invariants in local search. In *Proc. IJCAI-97*, 321–326.

Parkes, A. J. 1997. Clustering at the Phase Transition. In *Proc. AAAI-97*, 340–345.

Schuurmans, D., and Southy, F. 2000. Local search characteristics of incomplete SAT procedures. *Artif. Intelligence* 132:121–150.

Schuurmans, D.; Southy, F.; and Holte, R. 2001. The exponentiated subgradient algorithm for heuristic boolean programming. In *Proc. IJCAI-01*.

Selman, B.; Kautz, H. A.; and Cohen, B. 1994. Noise strategies for improving local search. In *Proc. AAAI-94*, 337–343.

Singer, J.; Gent, I. P.; and Smaill, A. 2000. Backbone fragility and the local search cost peak. *J. of Artificial Intelligence Research* 12:235–270.

Wah, B., and Shang, Y. 1997. Discrete Lagrangian-Based Search for Solving MAX-SAT Problems. In *Proc. IJCAI-97*, 378–393.

Wu, Z., and Wah, B. 2000. An Efficient Global-Search Strategy in Discrete Lagrangian Methods for Solving Hard Satisfiability Problems. In *Proc. AAAI-2000*, 310–315.

Yokoo, M. 1997. Why Adding More Constraints Makes a Problem Easier for Hill-Climbing Algorithms: Analyzing Landscapes of CSPs. In *Proc. CP-97*, number 1330 in LNCS, 357–370. Springer Verlag.

SetA*: An Efficient BDD-Based Heuristic Search Algorithm

Rune M. Jensen, Randal E. Bryant, and **Manuela M. Veloso**

Computer Science Department, Carnegie Mellon University,
5000 Forbes Ave, Pittsburgh, PA 15213-3891, USA
{runej,bryant,mmv}@cs.cmu.edu

Abstract

In this paper we combine the goal directed search of A* with the ability of BDDs to traverse an exponential number of states in polynomial time. We introduce a new algorithm, SetA*, that generalizes A* to expand sets of states in each iteration. SetA* has substantial advantages over BDDA*, the only previous BDD-based A* implementation we are aware of. Our experimental evaluation proves SetA* to be a powerful search paradigm. For some of the studied problems it outperforms BDDA*, A*, and BDD-based breadth-first search by several orders of magnitude. We believe exploring sets of states to be essential when the heuristic function is weak. For problems with strong heuristics, SetA* efficiently specializes to single-state search and consequently challenges single-state heuristic search in general.

Introduction

During the last decade, powerful search techniques using an implicit state representation based on the *reduced ordered binary decision diagram* (BDD, Bryant 1986) have been developed in the area of *symbolic model checking* (McMillan 1993). Using blind exploration strategies these techniques have been successfully applied to verify systems with very large state spaces. Similar results have been obtained in well-structured AI search domains (Cimatti *et al.* 1997). However for hard combinatorial problems the search fringe often grows exponentially with the search depth.

A classical AI approach for avoiding the state explosion problem is to use heuristics to guide the search toward the goal states. The question is whether heuristics can be applied to BDD-based search such that their ability to efficiently expand a large set of states in each iteration is preserved. The answer is non-trivial since heuristic search algorithms require values to be associated with each state and manipulated during search a task for which BDDs often have proven less efficient.

In this paper, we present a new search algorithm called SetA*. The main idea is to avoid the above problem by generalizing A* (Hart, Nilsson, & Raphael 1968) from single states to sets of states in the search queue. Recall that A*

associates two values g and h with each state in the search queue. g is the cost of reaching the state and h is an estimate of the remaining cost of reaching the goal given by a *heuristic function*. In SetA* states with similar g and h values are merged such that we can represent them implicitly by a BDD without having to store any numerical information. In each iteration, SetA*: 1) pops the set with highest priority, 2) computes its next states, and 3) partitions the next states into child sets with unique g and h values, which are reinserted into the queue. A straightforward implementation of the three phases has disappointing performance (see PreSetA*, Table 2). A key idea of our work is therefore to combine phase 2 and 3. The technique fits nicely with the so called disjunctive partitioning of BDD-based search (Clarke, Grumberg, & Peled 1999). In addition it can be applied to any heuristic function. Our experimental evaluation of SetA* proves it a powerful search paradigm. For some problems it dominates both A* and BDD-based breadth-first search (see Table 2). In addition, it outperforms the only previous BDD-based implementation of A* (Edelkamp & Reffel 1998), we are aware of, by up to two orders of magnitude (see Table 3).

Directed BDD-based search has received little attention in symbolic model checking. The reason is that the main application of BDDs in this field is verification where all reachable states must be explored. For Computation Tree Logic (CTL) checking, guiding techniques have been proposed to avoid a blow-up of intermediate BDDs (Bloem, Ravi, & Somenzi 2000). However these techniques are not applicable to search since they are based on defining lower and upper bounds on the fixed-point. Directed search techniques are relevant for *falsification* where the goal is to find a state not satisfying an invariant. As far as we know, BDD-based directed search was first considered for this application (Yang & Dill 1998). The proposed algorithm is a simple best-first search where the search fringe is partitioned with a specialized BDD-operator according to the *Hamming distance* to the goal state (number of different bits). Even though this operation is fairly efficient for the Hamming distance, it is not obvious how to define it in general. The only previous BDD-based implementation of A* that we are aware of, is BDDA* (Edelkamp & Reffel 1998). BDDA* can use a general heuristic function and has been applied to planning as well as model checking. However, BDDA* re-

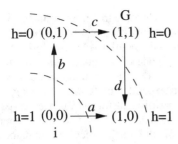

Figure 1: An example search problem consisting of four states and four transitions a,b,c, and d. The dashed lines indicate the two search fringes of a BDD-based breadth-first search from the initial state $i = (0,0)$ to the goal states $G = \{(1,1)\}$. The h-values is a heuristic function equal to the vertical goal distance.

quires arithmetic operations at the BDD level during search and includes no tools to control the growth of the search fringe or for cycle detection. In practice this often leads to substantial performance penalties (see Table 3). Another limitation of BDDA* is that the generalization to weighted A* is non-trivial.

The remainder of the paper is organized as follows. First we briefly describe BDDs and BDD-based search techniques. We then define the SetA* algorithm and evaluate it experimentally in a range of search and planning domains. Finally we draw conclusions and discuss directions for future work.

BDD-based Search

A BDD is a directed acyclic graph representing a Boolean function on a set of ordered variables. Due to two reduction rules the BDD is a canonical and compact representation. Another advantage is that a large set of BDDs can share structure in a multi-rooted BDD and be efficiently manipulated by a general function for applying Boolean operators. Due to the space limitations of this paper we will treat BDDs as a black-box. Readers interested in a thorough introduction are referred to (Bryant 1986).

A search problem is a 4-tuple (S, T, i, G). S is a set of states. $T : S \times S$ is a *transition relation* defining the search graph. $(s, s') \in T$ iff there exists a transition leading from s to s'. i is the initial state of the search while G is the set of goal states. A solution to a search problem is a path $\pi = s_0, \cdots, s_n$ where $s_0 = i$ and $s_n \in G$ and $\bigwedge_{j=0}^{n-1}(s_j, s_{j+1}) \in T$. Assuming that states can be encoded as bit vectors, BDDs can be used to represent the *characteristic function* of a set of states and the transition relation. To make this clear, consider the simple search problem shown in Figure 1. A state s is represented by a bit vector with two elements $\vec{s} = (s_0, s_1)$. Thus the initial state is represented by a BDD for the expression $\neg s_0 \wedge \neg s_1$. Similarly we have $G = s_0 \wedge s_1$. To encode the transition relation, we need to refer to current state variables and next state variables. We adopt the usual notation in BDD literature of primed vari-

ables for the next state

$$
\begin{aligned}
T(s_0, s_1, s_0', s_1') \;=\; & \neg s_0 \wedge \neg s_1 \;\wedge\; s_0' \wedge \neg s_1' \\
\vee\; & \neg s_0 \wedge \neg s_1 \;\wedge\; \neg s_0' \wedge s_1' \\
\vee\; & \neg s_0 \wedge s_1 \;\wedge\; s_0' \wedge s_1' \\
\vee\; & s_0 \wedge s_1 \;\wedge\; s_0' \wedge \neg s_1'.
\end{aligned}
$$

The main idea in BDD-based search is to stay at the BDD level when finding the next states of a set of states. This can be done by computing the image of a set of states V encoded in current state variables

$$
\text{Img} = \big(\exists \vec{s}.\, V(\vec{s}) \wedge T(\vec{s}, \vec{s}')\big)[\vec{s}/\vec{s}'].
$$

Consider the first step of the search from i in the example domain. We have $V(s_0, s_1) = \neg s_0 \wedge \neg s_1$. Thus,

$$
\begin{aligned}
\text{Img} \;=\; & \big(\exists \vec{s}.\, \neg s_0 \wedge \neg s_1 \wedge T(s_0, s_1, s_0', s_1')\big)[\vec{s}/\vec{s}'] \\
=\; & \big(s_0' \wedge \neg s_1' \;\vee\; \neg s_0' \wedge s_1'\big)[\vec{s}/\vec{s}'] \\
=\; & s_0 \wedge \neg s_1 \;\vee\; \neg s_0 \wedge s_1.
\end{aligned}
$$

A common problem in BDD-based search is that intermediate BDDs in the image computation tend to be large compared to the BDD representing the result. In symbolic model checking, a range of techniques has been proposed to avoid this problem. Among the most successful of these are *transition relation partitioning*. For search problems, where each transition normally only modifies a small subset of the state variables, the suitable partitioning technique is *disjunctive partitioning* (Clarke, Grumberg, & Peled 1999). To make a disjunctive partitioning, the part of the individual transition expressions keeping the unmodified variables unchanged is removed. The transition expressions are then partitioned according to what variables they modify. For our example we get two partitions

$$
\begin{aligned}
P_1 \;=\; & \neg s_0 \wedge \neg s_1 \wedge s_0' \;\vee\; \neg s_0 \wedge s_1 \wedge s_0' \\
m_1 \;=\; & (s_0) \\
P_2 \;=\; & \neg s_0 \wedge \neg s_1 \wedge s_1' \;\vee\; s_0 \wedge s_1 \wedge \neg s_1' \\
m_2 \;=\; & (s_1).
\end{aligned}
$$

In addition to large space savings, disjunctive partitioning often lowers the complexity of the image computation which now can skip the quantifications on unchanged variables and operate on smaller expressions

$$
\text{Img} = \bigvee_{j=1}^{|P|} \big(\exists m_j.\, V(\vec{s}) \wedge P_j(\vec{s}, m_j')\big)[m_j/m_j'].
$$

SetA*

SetA* is a generalization of weighted A* where the definition of f is changed from $f = g + h$ to $f = (1 - w)g + wh$, $w \in [0, 1]$ (Pohl 1970). Similar to BDDA*, SetA* assumes a finite search domain and unit-cost transitions. SetA* expands a set of states instead of just a single state. The main input is what we will call, an *improvement partitioning*. That is, a disjunctive partitioning where the transitions of a partition reduce the h-value by the same amount. The improvement partitioning is non-trivial to compute. The reason is that it may be intractable to calculate

```
function SetA*(IP, init, goal, u, w)
1    Q.initialize(u, w, goal)
2    g ← 0
3    h ← h(init)
4    Q.insert(init, g, h)
5    R.update(init, g)
6    while ¬Q.empty() and ¬Q.topAtGoal()
7        top ← Q.pop()
8        for j = 0 to |IP|
9            next ← image(top, IP_j)
10           R.prune(next)
11           g ← top.g + 1
12           h ← top.h − impr(IP_j)
13           Q.insert(next, g, h)
14           R.update(next, g)
15   if Q.empty() then NoPathExists
16   else R.extractPath()
```

Figure 2: The SetA* algorithm.

each transition expression in turn. Fortunately large sets of transitions are often described in more abstract terms (e.g., by *actions* or *guarded commands*) that can be directly translated into BDDs. This allows for an implicit way to partition a set of transitions according to their improvement. Assume that a set of transitions are represented by a BDD $T(\vec{s}, \vec{s}')$. Given a BDD $h(\vec{s}, \vec{v})$ encoding the heuristic function, such that $\vec{v}$ is a bit vector representation of the h-value associated with state s, the set of transitions with improvement equal to k is

$$T(\vec{s}, \vec{s}') \wedge h(\vec{s}, \vec{v}) \wedge h(\vec{s}', \vec{v}') \wedge \vec{v} - \vec{v}' = \vec{k}.$$

The improvement partitioning is computed only once prior to the search, and in practice it turns out that it often can be produced directly from the description of transitions or by splitting the disjunctive partitioning. In fact, for the heuristics we have studied so far, no BDD encoding of the heuristic function has been necessary.

SetA* uses two main data structures: a prioritized queue Q and a reach structure R. Each node in Q contains a BDD representing a set of states with particular g and h values. The node with lowest f-value has highest priority. Ties are solved by giving highest priority to the entry with lowest h-value. An important parameter of Q is an upper bound u on the BDD sizes. When inserting a new node it is unioned with an existing node in Q with the same g and h value if the sum of the size of their two BDDs is less than u. Otherwise a new entry is created for the node. The reach structure is for loop detection. R keeps track of the lowest g-value of every reached state and is used to prune states from a set of next states already reached with a lower g-value. The algorithm is shown in Figure 2. All sets and set operations are carried out with BDDs. SetA* takes five arguments. **IP** is the improvement partitioning described above. *init* and *goal* are the initial and goal states of the search. u is the upper bound parameter of Q and w is the usual weight parameter of weighted A*. Initially the algorithm inserts the

initial state in Q. Observe that the h-value of the initial state has to be found. However since *init* is a single state this is trivial. Similar to the regular A* algorithm, SetA* continues popping the top node of the queue until the queue is either empty or the states of the top node overlaps with the goal. The top node is expanded by finding the image of it for each improvement partition in turn (l.9). Before being inserted in Q, the new nodes are pruned for states seen at a lower search depth, and the reach structure is updated (l.10-14). If the loop was aborted due to Q being empty no solution path exists. Otherwise the path is extracted by applying transitions backwards on the states in R from one of the reached goal states.

SetA* is *sound* due to the soundness of the image computation. Since no states reached by the search are pruned, SetA* is also *complete*. Given an *admissible heuristic* and $w = 0.5$, SetA* further finds *optimal length paths*. As for A*, the reason is that a state on the optimal path eventually will reach the top of Q because states on finalized but suboptimal paths have higher f-value (Pearl 1984).

The upper bound u can be used to adjust how many states SetA* expands. If each partition in **IP** contains a single transition and $u = 0$ then SetA* specializes to A*. For problems with many shortest length solution paths like the DVM and Logistics described in the next section, it may be an advantage to focus on a subset of them by choosing a low u-value. A similar approach is used by A_ϵ^* described in (Pearl 1984)

The weight w has the usual effect. For $w = 0.5$ Set A* behaves like A*. For $w = 1.0$ it performs best-first search, and for $w = 0.0$ it carries out a regular breadth-first search. The fact that w can take any value in the range $[0, 1]$ is important in practice, since it can be used to increase an underestimating heuristic or decrease an overestimating heuristic.

We end this section by demonstrating SetA* on our example problem. For this demonstration we assume $w = 0.5$ and $u = \infty$. The heuristic function is the vertical distance to the goal state. In Figure 1 the states have been labeled with h-values. We see that **IP** must contain at least three partitions: one containing transition d that improves by minus one, one containing a and c that improve by zero, and one containing b that improves by one. Initially we have

$$Q_0 = \ <(f = 0.5, g = 0, h = 1, \{(0,0)\}) >$$
$$R_0 = \ <(g = 0, \{(0,0)\}) > .$$

In the first iteration, state $(0,0)$ is expanded to one child containing state $(1,0)$ and one child containing $(0,1)$. According to the improvements of the partitions, we get

$$Q_1 = \ <(f = 0.5, g = 1, h = 0, \{(0,1)\}),$$
$$(f = 1.0, g = 1, h = 1, \{(1,0)\}) >$$
$$R_1 = \ <(g = 0, \{(0,0)\}), (g = 1, \{(0,1), (1,0)\}) > .$$

In the second iteration, only the c transition can fire resulting in

$$Q_2 = \ <(f = 1.0, g = 2, h = 0, \{(0,1)\}),$$
$$(f = 1.0, g = 1, h = 1, \{(1,0)\}) >$$
$$R_2 = \ <(g = 0, \{(0,0)\}), (g = 1, \{(0,1), (1,0)\}),$$
$$(g = 2, \{(1,1)\}) > .$$

The tie breaking rule causes the goal state to be at the top of Q at the beginning of the third iteration. Thus the while loop is aborted and the solution path $(0,0), (0,1), (1,1)$ is extracted from R_2.

Experimental Evaluation

SetA* has been implemented in the UMOP multi-agent planning framework (Jensen & Veloso 2000) to study its performance characteristics relative to blind bidirectional BDD-based breadth-first search (also implemented in UMOP) and an A* implementation with explicit state representation and cycle detection. In a second evaluation round we developed a domain independent STRIPS planning system called DOP. The state encoding and heuristic function used by the MIPS planner (Edelkamp & Helmert 2001) was reproduced in order to conduct a fair comparison with BDDA* implemented in MIPS. In addition to SetA*, two blind BDD-based breadth-first search algorithms were implemented in DOP, one searching forward and one searching backward.

All experiments were carried out on a Linux 5.2 PC with a 500 MHz Pentium 3 CPU, 512 KB L2 cache and 512 MB RAM. The time limit (TIME) was 600 seconds and the memory limit (MEM) was 450 MB. For UMOP and DOP the number allocated BDD nodes of the BDD-package and the number of partitions in the disjunctive partitioning were hand-tuned for best performance.

Artificial Problems

Two problems IG^k and $D^xV^yM^z$ were defined and studied using the minimum Hamming distance to a goal state as heuristic function. In these experiments the improvement partitioning was computed by splitting a disjunctive partitioning using a specialized BDD-function. Given an improvement k, this function traverses the BDD of an action and picks transitions of the action improving k. The complexity of the function is linear in the size of the action BDD when the goal is a conjunction and the variable ordering interleaves current and next state variables.

IG^k This problem is simplest to define using the STRIPS language (Fikes & Nilsson 1971). A state is a set of facts and an action is a triple of sets of facts. In a given state S, an action (pre, add, del) is applicable if $pre \subseteq S$, and the resulting state is $S' = (S \cup add) \setminus del$. The actions are

$$
\begin{array}{lll}
\mathbf{A}_1^1 & \mathbf{A}_j^1 \, j = 2, \cdots, n & \mathbf{A}_j^2 \, j = 1, \cdots, n \\
pre : \{I^*\} & pre : \{I^*, G_{j-1}\} & pre : \{\} \\
add : \{G_1\} & add : \{G_j\} & add : \{I_j\} \\
del : \{\} & del : \{\} & del : \{I^*\}.
\end{array}
$$

The initial state is $\{I^*\}$ and the goal state is $\{G_j | k < j \leq n\}$. Only $\mathbf{A}_j^1$ actions should be applied to reach the goal. Applying an $\mathbf{A}_j^2$ action in any state leads to a wild path since I^* is deleted. The only solution is $\mathbf{A}_1^1, \cdots, \mathbf{A}_n^1$ which is non-trivial to find, since the heuristic gives no information to guide the search on the first k steps. The purpose of the experiment is to investigate how well SetA* copes with this situation compared to A*. For SetA* $w = 0.5$ and $u = \infty$. n of IG^k is 16. The results are shown in Table 1. The experiment shows a

	SetA*		A*	
k	Time	#it	Time	#it
0	0.2	16	0.1	16
2	0.2	16	0.4	145
4	0.2	16	7.4	2861
6	0.2	16	80.1	24931
8	0.2	16	344.0	90080
10	0.2	16	TIME	-
12	0.2	16	TIME	-
14	0.2	16	TIME	-

Table 1: Results for the IG^k problem. Time is in seconds. #it is the number of iterations.

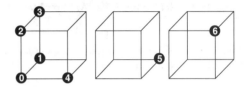

Figure 3: The initial state of $D^5V^3M^7$.

fast degradation of A*'s performance with the number of unguided steps. A* gets lost expanding an exponentially growing set of states on wild paths. SetA* is hardly affected by the lack of guidance. The reason is that all transitions on the unguided part improve by zero. Thus on this part, SetA* performs a regular BDD-based breadth-first search, which scales well due to the structure of the problem.

$D^xV^yM^z$ In this domain a set of sliders are moved between the corner positions of hypercubes. In any state, a corner position can be occupied by at most one slider. The dimension of the hypercubes is y. There are z sliders of which x are moving on the same cube. The remaining $z - x$ sliders are moving on individual cubes. Figure 3 shows the initial state of $D^5V^3M^7$. The purpose of $D^xV^yM^z$ is to investigate the performance of SetA* for hard combinatorial problems relative to A* and BDD-based breadth-first search. In this experiment we study the $D^xV^4M^{15}$ problem. We also show the results of PreSetA*, an earlier version of SetA* finding the next states and splitting them in two separate phases. Both versions of SetA* were run with $w = 0.5$ and $u = 200$. The results are shown in Table 2. For this problem disjunctive partitioning of the transition relation is crucial for large values of x. Despite applying this technique, BDD-based bidirectional search does not scale due to a blow-up of the search fringe in both directions. A* works well when x is small since f is a perfect or near perfect discriminator. However when the quality of the heuristic degrades A* gets lost tracking equally promising paths. The good performance of SetA* is due to the upper bound setting that focuses the search on a reasonable subset of the paths. Interestingly the search time is very low even for the hardest problems. Time and memory are spent on building and splitting the transition relation. Separating the next state

x	SetA*	PreSetA*	A*	BiDir
1	0.6	0.8	1.1	0.7
2	0.7	0.9	1.1	0.7
3	0.6	1.4	1.1	1.6
4	0.6	1.5	1.1	8.1
5	0.6	3.5	1.0	334.0
6	0.8	14.4	TIME	TIME
7	1.3	39.8	TIME	TIME
8	2.1	50.7	TIME	TIME
9	6.8	202.6	TIME	TIME
10	16.3	297.2	TIME	TIME
11	39.3	TIME	TIME	TIME
12	MEM	TIME	TIME	TIME

Table 2: Results for the $D^x V^4 M^{15}$ problem.

Planning Problems

Like MIPS, the DOP planning system uses an approximation to the HSPr heuristic (Bonet & Geffner 1999) for STRIPS domains. In addition, it performs similar analysis to minimize the state encoding length. HSPr is an efficient but non-admissible heuristic. We approximate it by summing the depth $d(f)$ of each fact in a state given by a relaxed forward breadth-first search. The heuristic is applied in a backward search from the goal states to the initial state. For any action (pre, add, del) leading from S to S' (when applied in forward direction), we assume

$$del \subseteq pre \text{ and } add \not\subseteq pre.$$

Since the search is backward the improvement of the action is

$$
\begin{aligned}
impr &= h(S') - h(S) \\
&= h(S' \cap (pre \cup add)) - h(S \cap (pre \cup add)) \\
&= \sum_{f \in add \setminus S} d(f) - \sum_{f \in del} d(f).
\end{aligned}
$$

Thus the improvement of an action can be computed without any BDD-based encoding of the heuristic function. Each action is partitioned in up to $2^{|add|}$ sets of transitions with different improvement.

The problems, we consider, are *Gripper* from the STRIPS track of the AIPS-98 planning competition (Long 2000) and *Logistics* from the first round of the STRIPS track of the AIPS-00 planning competition (Bacchus 2001). The purpose of these experiments is to compare the performance of SetA* and BDDA*, not to solve the problems particularly fast. In that case, a more informative heuristic like the FF heuristic (Hoffmann 2001) should be applied.

Gripper This domain considers a robot with two grippers moving an increasing number of balls between two connected rooms. The first experiment compares forward BDD-based breadth-first search, SetA* with $w = 1.0$ and $u = \infty$, backward BDD-based breadth-first search, pure

#p	For-ward	SetA*	Back-ward	Pure BDDA*	BDDA*
2	0.1	0.1	0.1	3.97	3.89
4	0.2	0.3	0.6	8.01	7.13
6	0.4	0.6	1.4	22.37	15.36
8	0.9	1.0	2.9	72.54	47.08
10	1.2	1.4	5.3	317.15	TIME
12	1.7	2.0	9.1	TIME	TIME
14	2.2	2.7	17.2	TIME	TIME
16	3.5	3.5	19.7	TIME	TIME
18	3.9	4.9	27.5	TIME	TIME
20	5.0	5.8	37.2	TIME	TIME

Table 3: Results of the first gripper experiment. #p is the problem number and time is in seconds.

w	$|p|$	#it	Time
0.0	125	360	7.6
0.2	125	354	7.9
0.4	125	338	8.0
0.6	125	204	6.1
0.8	125	204	6.2
1.0	125	204	5.9

Table 4: Results of the second gripper experiment for problem 20. w is the weight, $|p|$ is the solution length and #it is the number of iterations. Time is in seconds.

BDDA* and BDDA*. Pure BDDA* performs best-first search. The results are shown in Table 3. All algorithms find optimal length solutions. BDDA* spends up to 10% of the time computing BDD formulas for the arithmetic operations. During the search even the moderate growth of the search fringe impairs the efficiency considerably. The problem turns out to be most efficiently solved with BDD-based breadth-first search. However it is challenged by SetA* even though this algorithm relies on the slower backward expansion.

The second experiment shows the impact of the weight setting in problem 20. The results are shown in Table 4. Even though SetA* can solve the problem performing breadth-first search the heuristic improves its performance.

Logistics This domain considers moving packages with trucks between sub-cities and with airplanes between cities. In the first experiment SetA* was run with $w = 1.0$ and $u = 200$. The results are shown in Table 5. The HSPr heuristic is very efficient in this domain. The solutions of BDDA* are a couple of steps shorter than the solutions of SetA*. SetA* and pure BDDA* produce plans of similar quality. Again the construction of arithmetic formulas takes up considerable time for BDDA*. The upper bound of 200 speeds up SetA* on the last five problems where the fringe BDDs otherwise grow considerably.

The second experiment was carried out on problem 7 of the Logistics domain. In this experiment SetA* was run with $u = \infty$. The results are shown in Table 6. As depicted HSPr

#p	SetA*	Pure BDDA*	For- ward	BDDA*	Back- ward
4	0.2	6.5	0.3	7.7	0.38
5	0.3	6.7	0.5	9.5	0.81
6	0.3	6.7	0.4	8.4	0.94
7	0.9	13.9	99.0	TIME	396.93
8	1.0	14.1	59.5	138.5	TIME
9	0.9	14.0	100.0	132.6	TIME
10	2.5	25.1	MEM	TIME	TIME
11	2.2	25.2	MEM	TIME	TIME
12	2.0	24.9	MEM	TIME	TIME
13	8.5	57.5	MEM	TIME	TIME
14	7.7	56.7	MEM	TIME	TIME
15	7.3	53.9	MEM	TIME	TIME

Table 5: Results of the first logistics experiment. #p is the problem number and time is in seconds.

w	$|p|$	#it	Time
0.0	25	279	8.6
0.2	25	203	8.9
0.4	25	102	4.7
0.6	29	49	0.9
0.8	31	31	0.8
1.0	31	31	0.9

Table 6: Results of the second logistics experiment. w is the weight, $|p|$ is the solution length and #it is the number of iterations. Time is in seconds.

is a good heuristic for this domain increasing the speed significantly while preserving a relative high solution quality.

Conclusion and Outlook

In this paper, we have successfully combined BDD-based search and heuristic search into a new search paradigm. The experimental evaluation of SetA* proves it a powerful algorithm often several orders of magnitude faster than BDD-based breadth-first search and A*. Today planning problems are efficiently solved by heuristic single-state search algorithms. However as recently noticed, the success may be due to an inherent simplicity of the benchmark domains when using the right heuristics (Hoffmann 2001). For less domain-tuned heuristics, we believe that the ability of SetA* to explore an exponentially growing set of paths in polynomial time is essential. Our ongoing research includes identifying such problems and comparing the performance of SetA* and single-state search algorithms.

Acknowledgments

This research is sponsored in part by the Danish Research Agency and the United States Air Force under Grants Nos F30602-00-2-0549 and F30602-98-2-0135. The views and conclusions contained in this document are those of the authors and should not be interpreted as necessarily representing the official policies or endorsements, either expressed or implied, of the Defense Advanced Research Projects Agency, the Air Force, or the US Government.

References

Bacchus, F. 2001. AIPS'00 planning competition : The fifth international conference on artificial intelligence planning and scheduling systems. *AI Magazine* 22(3):47–56.

Bloem, R.; Ravi, K.; and Somenzi, F. 2000. Symbolic guided search for CTL model checking. In *Proceedings of the 37th Design Automation Conference (DAC'00)*, 29–34. ACM.

Bonet, B., and Geffner, H. 1999. Planning as heuristic search: New results. In *Proceedings of the European Conference on Planning (ECP-99)*. Springer.

Bryant, R. E. 1986. Graph-based algorithms for boolean function manipulation. *IEEE Transactions on Computers* 8:677–691.

Cimatti, A.; Giunchiglia, E.; Giunchiglia, F.; and Traverso, P. 1997. Planning via model checking: A decision procedure for $\mathcal{AR}$. In *Proceedings of the 4th European Conference on Planning (ECP'97)*, 130–142. Springer.

Clarke, E.; Grumberg, O.; and Peled, D. 1999. *Model Checking*. MIT Press.

Edelkamp, S., and Helmert, M. 2001. MIPS the model-checking integrated planning system. *AI Magazine* 22(3):67–71.

Edelkamp, S., and Reffel, F. 1998. OBDDs in heuristic search. In *Proceedings of the 22nd Annual German Conference on Advances in Artificial Intelligence (KI-98)*, 81–92. Springer.

Fikes, R. E., and Nilsson, N. J. 1971. STRIPS: A new approach to the application of theorem proving to problem solving. *Artificial Intelligence* 2:189–208.

Hart, P. E.; Nilsson, N. J.; and Raphael, B. 1968. A formal basis for heuristic determination of minimum path cost. *IEEE Transactions on SSC* 100(4).

Hoffmann, J. 2001. Local search topology in planning benchmarks: An empirical analysis. In *Proceedings of the 17th International Joint Conference on Artificial Intelligence (IJCAI-01)*, 453–458. Morgan Kaufmann.

Jensen, R., and Veloso, M. M. 2000. OBDD-based universal planning for synchronized agents in non-deterministic domains. *Journal of Artificial Intelligence Research* 13:189–226.

Long, D. 2000. The AIPS-98 planning competition. *AI Magazine* 21(2):13–34.

McMillan, K. L. 1993. *Symbolic Model Checking*. Kluwer Academic Publ.

Pearl, J. 1984. *Heuristics : Intelligent Search Strategies for Computer Problem Solving*. Addison-Wesley.

Pohl, I. 1970. First results on the effect of error in heuristic search. *Machine Intelligence* 5:127–140.

Yang, C. H., and Dill, D. L. 1998. Validation with guided search of the state space. In *Proceedings of the 35th Design Automation Conference (DAC'98)*, 599–604. ACM.

Dynamic Restart Policies

Henry Kautz
University of Washington
kautz@cs.washington.edu

Eric Horvitz
Microsoft Research
horvitz@microsoft.com

Yongshao Ruan
University of Washington
ruan@cs.washington.edu

Carla Gomes
Cornell University
gomes@cs.cornell.edu

Bart Selman
Cornell University
selman@cs.cornell.edu

Abstract

We describe theoretical results and empirical study of context-sensitive restart policies for randomized search procedures. The methods generalize previous results on optimal restart policies by exploiting dynamically updated beliefs about the probability distribution for run time. Rather than assuming complete knowledge or zero knowledge about the run-time distribution, we formulate restart policies that consider real-time observations about properties of instances and the solver's activity. We describe background work on the application of Bayesian methods to build predictive models for run time, introduce an optimal policy for dynamic restarts that considers predictions about run time, and perform a comparative study of traditional fixed versus dynamic restart policies.

Introduction

The possibility of developing tractable approaches to combinatorial search has been a long-held goal in AI. We describe theoretical results on *dynamic restarts*, restart policies for randomized search procedures that take real-time observations about attributes of instances and about solver behavior into consideration. The results show promise for speeding up backtracking search—and thus, move us one step closer to tractable methods for solving combinatorial search problems.

Researchers have noted that combinatorial search algorithms in many domains exhibit a high degree of unpredictability in running time over any given set of problems (Selman, Kautz, & Cohen 1993; Gent & Walsh 1993; Kirkpatrick & Selman 1994; Hogg, Huberman, & Williams 1996; Gomes & Selman 1997; Walsh 1999). In the most extreme case, the running time of a search algorithm over a problem set is best modeled by a *heavy-tailed* (powerlaw) distribution, having *infinite* mean and/or variance (Gomes, Selman, & Crato 1997; Gomes, Selman, & Kautz 1998a; Gomes *et al.* 2000).[1] Investigators have sought to understand the basis for such great variation by modeling search as a process that generates self-similar or *fractal* trees (Smythe & Mahmound 1995). Research on *algorithm portfolios* and

[1]Technically, because real-world search spaces are large but finite, there must always be some upper bound on the running time. However, it is common practice to refer to such truncated heavy-tailed distributions simply as "heavy tailed," in the case where a heavy-tailed distribution fits the data over several orders of magnitude.

on *randomized restarts* has shown that it is possible to develop more predictable and efficient procedures (Gomes & Hoos 2000) by minimizing the risk associated with committing large amounts of computation to instances that are likely to have long run times. In the first approach, a portfolio of search algorithms is executed in parallel. Experiments have shown that such portfolios may exhibit a low mean and low variance in run time, even if each member of the portfolio has high mean and variance (Gomes & Selman 2001). In the second method, randomness is added to the branching heuristic of a systematic search algorithm. If the search algorithm does not find a solution within a given number of backtracks, known as the *cutoff*, the run is terminated and the algorithm is restarted with a new random seed. Randomized restarts have been demonstrated to be effective for reducing total execution time on a wide variety of problems in scheduling, theorem proving, circuit synthesis, planning, and hardware verification (Luby, Sinclair, & Zuckerman 1993; Huberman, Lukose, & Hogg 1997; Gomes, Selman, & Kautz 1998b; Moskewicz *et al.* 2001).

In this paper, we extend prior results on *fixed* restart policies to more efficient *dynamic restarts* by harnessing predictive models to provide solvers with a real-time ability to *update beliefs* about run time. We first review previous work on restart policies. Then we review recent work on constructing Bayesian models that can be used to infer probability distributions over the run time of backtracking search procedures based on observational evidence. We introduce new results on optimal restart policies that consider observations about solver behavior. Finally, we demonstrate the efficacy of the restart policies with empirical studies of backtracking search for solving quasigroup, graph-coloring, and logistics-planning problems.

Research on Restart Policies

The basis for the value of randomized restarts is straightforward: the longer a backtracking search algorithm runs without finding a solution, the more likely it is that the algorithm is exploring a barren part of the search space, rather than branching early on states of critical variables necessary for a solution. But when should the algorithm give up on a particular run and restart the execution after some randomization? The designers of restart policies must grapple with minimization of total run time given a tradeoff: As the cutoff time is reduced, the probability that any particular run will reach a solution is diminished, so runs become shorter but more numerous.

Previous theoretical work on the problem of determining an ideal cutoff has made two assumptions: first, that the only feasible observation is the *length* of a run; and second, that the system has either *complete* knowledge or *no* knowledge of the run-time distribution of the solver on the given instance. Under these conditions Luby *et al.* (1993) described provably optimal restart policies. In the case of complete knowledge, the optimal policy is the fixed cutoff that minimizes $E(T_c)$, the expected time to solution restarting every c backtracks. In the case of no knowledge, Luby further showed that a universal schedule of cutoff values of the form

$$1, 1, 2, 1, 1, 2, 4, \dots$$

gives an expected time to solution that is within a log factor of that given by the best fixed cutoff, and that no other universal schedule is better by more than a constant factor.

Although these results were taken by many in the research community to have settled all open issues on restart strategies, real-life scenarios typically violate both assumptions. For one, we often have *partial* knowledge of the run-time distribution of a problem solver. For example, consider the case of a satisfiability (SAT) solver running on a mix of satisfiable and unsatisfiable problem instances. In general, run-time distributions over satisfiable and unsatisfiable instances are quite different (Frost, Rish, & Vila 1997). We might know that a new given instance was drawn from one of several different distributions of satisfiable and unsatisfiable problems, but not know *which* distribution. We cannot calculate a fixed optimal cutoff value, but still wish to take advantage of the knowledge that we do have; the "log factor" of the simple universal schedule can be quite large in practice (two or more orders of magnitude including the constant factors).

The assumption that only the running time of the solver can be observed may also be violated. Beyond run time, other evidence about the behavior of a solver may be valuable for updating beliefs about the run-time distribution. Indeed, watching a trace or visualization of a backtracking search engine in action can be quite enlightening. Observers can watch the algorithm make a few bad variable assignments and then thrash for millions of steps in the "wrong" area of the search space. A person watching the system often has intuitions about when it might be best to restart the search.[2] Can a program also make such judgments? Can it recognize dynamically changing *patterns of activity* that indicate that the search is lost and would best be restarted?

Recently Horvitz *et al.* (2001), motivated by such questions—and the associated promise of developing sound dynamic restart policies—introduced a framework for constructing Bayesian models that can predict the run time of problem solvers. They showed that observations of various features over time capturing the trajectory of states of the solver during the first few seconds of a run could be fused to predict the length of a run with a useful degree of accuracy. They also sketched an approach to using learned predictive models to control the restart policy of the solver.

Our paper builds upon the framework of Horvitz *et al.* (2001) and presents theoretical and empirical results on optimal restart policies in the presence of observations about the state of a solver and partial knowledge of the run-time distribution. Our specific contributions include:

- Characterization of the knowledge conditions under which the runs of a solver are dependent or independent, and the impact this has on the nature of optimal restart policies;

- Specification of a class of provably optimal dynamic restart policies in the presence of solver-state observations;

- Empirical evaluation of these dynamic policies against the best fixed-cutoff policies; and

- An empirical study of the sensitivity of the predictive models to diminishing periods of observation, that shows that a surprisingly short period of observation is necessary to create accurate models.

Dependent and Independent Runs

Most work on restart strategies for backtracking search assume explicitly or implicitly that runs are *probabilistically independent* from one another; in the analyses, no information is considered to be carried over from one run to the next.[3] However, a careful analysis of informational relationships among multiple runs reveals that runs may be *dependent* in some scenarios: observing run i influences the probability distribution we assign to run $i + 1$.

Knowledge conditions under which the runs are independent include: (i) a new instance is drawn from a static ensemble of instances for each run, and the full run-time distribution for the ensemble is known; or (ii) some feature of each run can be observed that classifies the particular run as a random sample from a known run-time distribution D_i, regardless of whether the problem instance is fixed or changes with each run. By contrast, an example of dependent runs is when we know the run-time distributions of several different problem ensembles, a problem instance is drawn randomly from one of the ensembles, and each run is performed on that same instance. In this case, the failure of each run to find a solution within some cutoff changes our beliefs about which ensemble was selected.

The families of restart policies that are appropriate for the independent and dependent situations are distinct. Consider the simple case of identifying the best fixed cutoff policies where D_1 and D_2 are point probabilities. Suppose in the independent case a run always ends in 10 or 100 steps with equal probability: the optimal policy is to always restart after 10 steps if the problem is not solved. On the other hand, consider the dependent case where in D_1 all runs take 10 steps and in D_2 all runs take 100 steps, and an instance is chosen from one of the distributions. Then the best fixed-cutoff policy is to run with no cutoff, because a fixed cutoff of less than 100 gives a finite probability of never solving the problem.[4]

Independent Runs in Mixed Distributions

The restart policy for the case of independent runs in light of a single known probability distribution over run time is covered by Luby *et al.* (1993)'s results, as described above.

---

[2]Research in AI on restart strategies began with just such informal observations.

[3]An exception to this is recent work by di Silva on combining clause learning with restarts, where clauses learned in one run are carried over to the next run (Baptista & Marques-Silva 2000).

[4]In the general dependent case, optimal policies actually use a series of different cutoffs, as discussed in Ruan *et al.* (2002).

We consider, therefore, the case where each run is a random sample from one of a number of known run-time distributions, $D_1, D_2, \cdots, D_n$, where the choice of D_i is an independent event made according to some prior probability distribution.

If the system has no knowledge of which D_i is selected and makes no observations other than the length of the run, then this case also collapses to that handled by Luby *et al.* (1993):

Proposition 1 *The optimal restart policy for a mixed run-time distribution with independent runs and no additional observations is the optimal fixed cutoff restart policy for the combined distribution.*

It is more interesting, therefore, to consider situations where the system can make observations that update beliefs about the current D_i. Horvitz *et al.* (2001) segment observations into *static* and *dynamic* classes of evidence. Static observations are directly measurable features of a problem instance. As an example, one could measure the clause to variable ratio in a SAT instance, as has been long considered in work on random k-SAT (Mitchell *et al.* 1992; Selman & Kirkpatrick 1996). Dynamic features are measurements obtained via the process of problem solving; they are observations of a search algorithm's state while it is in the process of trying to solve a particular instance. Both kinds of evidence are useful for identifying the source distribution of an instance.

We shall simplify our analysis without loss of generality by considering a single evidential feature F that summarizes all observations made of the current instance/run pair. In the experiments described below F is a function of a decision tree over a set of variables that summarize the trace of the solver for the initial 1,000 steps of a run. The variables include the initial, final, average, and first derivatives of such quantities as the number of unassigned variables in the current subproblem, the number of unsatisfied constraints, the depth of the backtracking stack, and so on (see Horvitz *et al.* 2001 for a more detailed discussion for features and their use in probabilistic models of run time). The decision trees are created by labeling a set of test run traces as "long" or "short" relative to the median time to solution, and then employing a Bayesian learning procedure (Chickering, Heckerman, & Meek 1997) to build probabilistic dependency models that link observations to probability distributions over run time. Note that because the summary variables include some quantities that refer to the initial, unreduced problem (such as the initial number of unbound variables), the feature F combines static and dynamic observations.

The feature F may be binary-valued, such as whether the decision tree predicts that the current run will be longer than the median run time. In other experiments, described below, we define a multivalued F, where its value indicates the *particular leaf* of the decision tree that is reached when trace of a partial run is classified. In an ideal situation, F would indicate the D_i for which the current run is a random sample with perfect accuracy. Such an ideal F simplifies the analysis of optimal restart strategies, because we do not have to consider error terms. We can in fact achieve such perfect accuracy by a *resampling* technique, described below, whereby the F is used to *define* a set of distributions D_i (which in general are different from the distributions used to

create the original decision tree). Therefore, without loss of generality, we will assume that F always indicates the actual D_i for the run.

Let us assume first that F is binary valued, so there are two distributions D_1 and D_2, and we wish to find the optimal restart policy. First we must decide what we mean by "optimal:" do we wish to minimize expected run time, minimize variance in run time, or some combination of both? In this paper, we pursue the minimization of expected run time, although in some applications one may be willing to trade off an increase in expected run time for a decrease in variance; such tradeoffs are discussed in work on algorithm portfolios (Huberman, Lukose, & Hogg 1997; Gomes, Selman, & Kautz 1998b).

Next, let us consider the *form* of the policy. Is the policy the same for every run, or can it evolve over time; that is, is the policy stationary? The assumption that the runs are independent immediately entails that the policy is indeed stationary as we do not learn anything new about the D_i over time. This is the key distinction between policies for independent and dependent restart situations. Therefore we can conclude that the policy must be a function of F alone:

Theorem 1 *In the case of independent runs, where the (only) observation F is made after T_0 steps during each run, and where F indicates whether a run is a member of D_1 or D_2, the optimal restart policy is either of the form:*

Set the cutoff to T_1 for a fixed $T_1 < T_0$.

or of the form:

Observe for T_0 steps and measure F;
If F is true then set the cutoff to T_1, else set the cutoff to T_2

for appropriate constants T_1, T_2.

The first case is the degenerate one where waiting to observe F is never helpful. In the second situation, we are able to take advantage of our prediction of how "lucky" the current run will be. In general, this kind of dynamic policy outperforms the optimal static policy where the observation is ignored. In fact, the dynamic policy can outperform the optimal static policy even if the optimal static cutoff is *less* than the time T_0 required to make an observation, if predictions are sufficiently accurate.

Optimal Dynamic Policies

What values should be chosen for T_1 and T_2? They are *not*, in general, the same as the optimal static cutoffs for the individual distributions. The optimal dynamic cutoff values are found by deriving an expression for the expected time to solution for any T_1 and T_2, and then selecting values that minimize the expression given the data available for D_1 and D_2.

Let us begin by reviewing the formula for the expected time to solution of a fixed cutoff policy for a single distribution. Let $p(t)$ be the probability distribution over a run stopping exactly at t, and $q(t) = \sum_{t' \le t} p(t')$ be the cumulative probability distribution function of $p(t)$. For a given cutoff T, the expected number of runs required to find a solution is the mean of the Bernoulli distribution for independent trials with probability $q(T)$, $1/q(T)$. The expected length of each run is $(1 - q(T))T + \sum_{t \le T} tp(t) = T - \sum_{t < T} q(t)$

(Luby, Sinclair, & Zuckerman 1993). Multiplying the expected time per run and the expected number of runs gives an expected time to solution of

$$E(T) = \frac{T - \sum_{t<T} q(t)}{q(T)} \qquad (1)$$

We can extend this result to the case of multiple distributions by considering the probability of different distributions and computing a new expectation. Taking d_i as the prior probability of a run being chosen from distribution D_i, $p_i(t)$ as the probability that a run selected from D_i will stop exactly at t, and $q_i(t)$ as the cumulative function of $p_i(t)$, the expected number of runs to find a solution using cutoff T_i, whenever a sample comes from D_i, is now $1/(\sum_i d_i q_i(T_i))$. The expected length of each run is $\sum_i d_i(T_i - \sum_{t<T_i} q_i(t))$ The product of these quantities yields the expected run time for a particular choice of T_i, and thus the optimal cutoff values are those that minimize this expectation.

Theorem 2 *For independent runs where each run is selected with probability d_i from known distribution D_i, the optimal dynamic restart policy uses cutoffs*

$$(T_1^*, \quad ..., \quad T_n^*) = \arg \min_{T_1,...,T_n} E(T_1,...T_n) \qquad (2)$$

$$= \arg \min_{T_1,...,T_n} \frac{\sum_i d_i(T_i - \sum_{t<T_i} q_i(t))}{\sum_i d_i q_i(T_i)} \qquad (3)$$

If the search algorithm runs for at least T_0 steps to identify the relevant distribution D_i, then the optimal cutoffs are either uniformly some $T < T_0$, or are bounded below by T_0:

$$(T_1^*,...,T_n^*) = \arg \min_{T_i \geq T_0} E(T_1,...T_n) \qquad (4)$$

In the most general case, the set of T_i^* that minimizes the expected overall time to solution can be determined by a brute-force search over the empirical data. Beyond brute-force minimization, there is opportunity to use parameterized probability distributions to model the empirical data and to derive closed-form expressions for the T_i^*.

Optimal Pruning of Runs after Observation

An interesting special case of the optimal dynamic policy is the situation where the best action for one or more of the distributions is to restart immediately after observation. We wish to identify conditions where it is best to simply remove from consideration runs we determine to be "unlucky," following analysis of static features of the instance or some initial observation of the solver's behavior. We shall consider here the pruning conditions for the case of two distributions, based on properties of the distributions.

For a given cutoff T_1, we seek to identify the conditions under which $E(T_1, T_0 + \Delta)$ is never less than $E(T_1, T_0)$. By substituting in the formula for the expected time to solution (Equation 3) and performing some simplification, one can show that runs from D_2 should be pruned if, for all $\Delta > 0$, it is the case that:

$$\frac{\Delta - \sum_{T_0 \leq t < T_0 + \Delta} q_2(t)}{q_2(T_0 + \Delta) - q_2(T_0)} > E(T_1, T_0) \qquad (5)$$

The left-hand side of the inequality is the cost–benefit ratio for extending runs in D_2 following observation, and the

right-hand side, representing the expected run time of the pruned policy, can be computed from the empirical data. An interesting feature of this formula is that d_1 and d_2 *disappear* from the left-hand side: the prior probabilities assigned to the two distributions are irrelevant.

Empirical Studies

We performed a set of empirical studies to explore the dynamic restart policies given evidence gathered about solver behavior. Our first benchmark domain was a version of the Quasigroup Completion Problem (QCP) (Gomes & Selman 1997). The basic QCP problem is to complete a partially-filled Latin square, where the "order" of the instance is the length of a side of the square. We used a version called *Quasigroup with Holes* (QWH), where problem instances are generated by erasing values from a completed Latin square. QWH problems are "balanced" if the same number of missing values appear in each row and column. QWH is NP-complete, and balanced QWH is the hardest known subset of QWH (Achlioptas *et al.* 2000; Kautz *et al.* 2001). Note that QWH problems are satisfiable by definition.

For the QWH domain, we experimented with both CSP and SAT (Boolean) problem encodings. The CSP solver was designed specifically for QWH and built using the ILOG constraint programming library. The CSP problems were (non-balanced) random QWH problems of order 34 with 380 unassigned holes (the hardest hole/order ratio for random problems). The SAT-encoded problems were solved with Satz-Rand (Gomes, Selman, & Kautz 1998b), a randomized version of the Satz system of Li and Anbulagan (Li & Anbulagan 1997). Satz implements the Davis-Putnam-Longemann-Loveland (DPLL) procedure with look-ahead and a powerful variable-choice heuristic. The SAT-encoded problems were balanced QWH problems of order 34 with 410 unassigned holes (the hardest hole/order ratio for balanced problems).

Following the cycle of experiments with QCP, we applied the methods to the propositional satisfiability (SAT) encodings of the Graph Coloring Problem (GCP) and Logistics Planning (LPlan) problems.

For the GCP domain, we experimented with the randomized SAT algorithm running on Boolean encodings. The instances used in our studies are generated using Culberson's flat graph generator (Culberson & Luo 1996). Each instance contains 450 vertices and 1,045 randomly generated edges. The challenge is to decide whether the instances are 3-colorable. The instances are generated in such a way that all 3-colorable instances are 2-uncolorable and all 3-uncolorable instances are 4-colorable. Half of the problems were 3-colorable (satisfiable in the Boolean encoding) and half were not (unsatisfiable).

For the LPlan domain, we again experimented with Satz-Rand algorithm running on Boolean encodings. Kautz and Selman (Kautz & Selman 1996) showed that propositional SAT encodings of STRIPS-style planning problems could be efficiently solved by SAT engines. The logistics domain involves moving packages on trucks and airplanes between different locations in different cities. In the logistics domain, a state is a particular configuration of packages and vehicles. We generated instances with 5 cities, 15 packages, 2 planes, and 1 truck per city, where the initial and goal placements of packages was randomly determined. The parallel-plan length was fixed at 12 steps. To decrease the variance among instances, we filtered the output of the problem generator so that the satisfiable instances could be solved with 12 parallel steps but not 11 steps, and the unsatisfiable instances could not be solved with 12 steps but could be solved in 13 steps. As before, we selected half satisfiable and half unsatisfiable instances.

We implemented the methods described by Horvitz *et al.* (2001) to learn predictive models for run time for a problem solving scenario Horvitz *et al.* (2001) refer to as the *multiple-instance* problem. In multiple-instance problems, we draw instances from a distribution of instances and seek to solve *any* instance as soon as possible, or as many instances as possible for any amount of time allocated. For each case, we consider the states of multiple evidential variables observed during the observation horizon. In our experiments, observational variables were collected over an observational horizon of up to 1,000 solver choice points. *Choice points* are the states in search procedures where the algorithm assigns a value to variables where that assignment is not forced via propagation of previous set values. Such a situation occurs with unit propagation, backtracking, look-ahead, and forward-checking. At these points in problem solving a variable assignment is chosen according the solver's particular heuristics.

For the studies described, we represented run time as a probability distribution over a binary variable with discrete states "short" versus "long." We defined short runs as cases completed before the median run time for the problem domain (see Table 1 for the median run times for each benchmark). As described in Horvitz *et al.* (2001), we employed Bayesian learning methods (Chickering, Heckerman, & Meek 1997) to generate graphical probabilistic models for solver run time. The resulting probabilistic graphical models, and associated decision trees that represent a compact encoding of the learned conditional probability distributions, are thus formulated to predict the likelihood of a run completing in the less than the median time, on the basis of observations of the beginning of the run.

Each of the training sets contained 2,500 runs (where each run is on a different instance), except for the QWH Boolean encoded problems, where the training set was of size 5,000. A separate test set of the same size as the training set for each domain was also created for the final evaluation of the different policies we considered.

Generating Distributions via Resampling

Using the inferred run-time distributions directly in our studies would imply an assumption that the model's inferences are accurate, gold-standard distributions. However, we know that the models are imperfect classifiers. The assumption of perfect model accuracy can be appropriately relaxed by overlaying additional error modeling. Such error modeling introduces terms that represent classification accuracy. To bypass the use of more cumbersome analyses that include a layer of error analysis, we instead performed resampling of the training data: we used the inferred decision trees to *define* different classes (representing specific sets of values of observed states of solver behavior), and relabeled the training data according to these classes. In other words, we use the branching structure of the decision trees—the leafs indicated by different sets of observations—to *define*

each sub-distribution $D_1, D_2, ...D_n$ and obtain statistics on each of these distributions by running the training data back through the decision tree, and computing the different run-time distributions for each value of F. Resampling the data to generate distributions lets us create distributions that encode predictive errors in an implicit manner.

Experiments with Dynamic Restarts

We performed experiments to compare dynamic restart policies with the fixed optimal restart policy of Luby *et al.* (1993). We considered two basic formulations of the dynamic restart policies, that we refer to as *binary* and *n-ary* policies. For the binary policy, runs are classified as either having *short* or *long* run-time distributions, based on the values of features observed during the observation phase. Runs from the training data are first bucketed into the different leafs of the decision tree based on the observed values of run-time observations. We define long and short distributions in terms of the decision-tree path indicated by the set of observations, asserting that all cases at a leaf of the decision tree that contains more than 60% of short runs are classified as a member of the short distribution, and otherwise as a member of the long distribution[5] For the *n-ary* policy, each leaf in the decision tree is considered as defining a *distinct* distribution.

For identifying the optimal set of cutoff–observation pairs in a dynamic restart policy, we used Eqn. 3 to search for the combination of cutoffs associated with minimum expected run time. We also considered a range of different observation periods, ranging from 10 to 1,000 choice points. The shortest window turned out to yield policies with the lowest expected run times; below we discuss specific results on the sensitivity of the policies to the length of the window.

For the binary dynamic restart case, the cutoff for the long distribution was found to be optimal, in both Satz and CSP experiments, when it is equal to the ideal observation horizon; thus, the optimization indicated that runs falling into the long distribution should be pruned in both of these cases. We confirmed the optimality of the pruning of the long distributions with the pruning condition specified by the inequality described in Eqn. 5.

For the *n-ary* restart case, we could not directly optimize the cutoffs with brute-force optimization, given the size of the decision trees. For example, in the Boolean-encoded QWH domain, the decision tree has 20 leafs, and in principle we would need to simultaneously vary 20 parameters. Therefore we simplified the search problem by pruning all runs that fell into leafs that contained less than 60% short runs, and then performing brute-force search to find the set of optimal cutoffs for the "short" leafs. Finally, we confirmed that pruning runs from the long leafs was indeed optimal by checking the pruning condition (Eqn. 5).

Beyond the dynamic policies and the fixed-optimal policy, we investigated for comparative purposes the time to solution with Luby's universal restart policy, and a *binary–naive* restart policy, composed by selecting distinct, separately optimal fixed cutoffs for the long and for the short distributions in the binary setting.

---

[5]Intuitively any threshold greater than 50% could be used. We empirically found for the benchmark domains studied that using a threshold of 60% gave the best performance for the restart policies that were ultimately formulated.

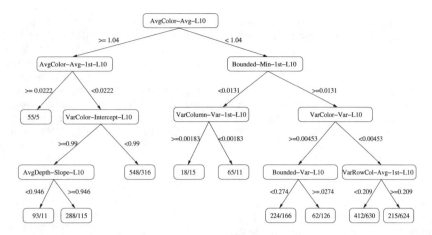

Figure 1: A predictive decision tree for a CSP QWH multiple-instance problem learned using an observation horizon of 10 choice points. Nodes represent observed features and arcs show the branching values. The number of cases of short versus long runs associated with the path are indicated at the leaves.

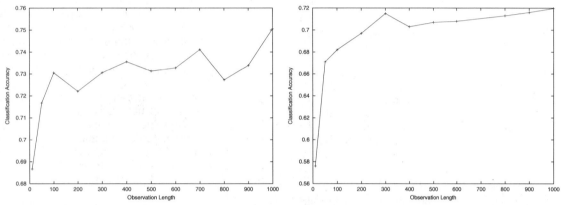

Figure 2: Analysis of the sensitivity of classification accuracy to the length of the observation horizon for CSP (left) and SATZ (right) on QWH multiple instances.

Sensitivity of Predictions to the Observation Horizon

As we highlighted in our earlier discussion of the pruning condition (Eqn. 5), the length of the observation window T_0 influences the optimal restart strategy. Long observation periods can limit the value of the dynamic methods by imposing a high constant tax whether or not an instance should be pruned immediately following the observation. Shorter horizons shift relationships and allow for a more efficient overall restart analysis; for example, a shorter horizon allows for the earlier pruning of runs following observations. Explicit knowledge of the relationship between observation horizon and accuracy thus provides another parameter for an optimization procedure to consider. Therefore, we studied the sensitivity of the predictive power of models to reduction of the observational horizon.

For the QWH domain, for both CSP and SATZ solvers, we collected run-time data for each instance over different observational horizons, varying from 10 to 1,000 choice points and constructed and tested the predictive power of distinct models. Fig. 1 displays an example of a learned decision trees for the CSP solver with observation horizon of 10 choice points. The internal nodes are labeled with the

name of the low-level solver-trace variable branched on. For example, along the left-hand branch we encounter the first two decision variables are:

- AvgColor-Avg-L10 — the average number of available colors for each empty square, averaged over the 10 choice points.

- AvgColor-Avg-1st-L10 — the first derivative of the average number of available colors for each empty square, measured at choice point 10.

The leaves are labeled with the number of short and long runs that appear there in the training data. For example, 93 short runs and 11 long runs reached the left-most leaf.

The learned predictive models for run time were found to overall show increasing classification accuracy with the use of longer observation horizons. Fig. 2 shows the sensitivity of the classification accuracy of the two solvers on the QWH multiple-instance problem to changes in the observation horizon. We found a steep increase in classification accuracy when the observation horizon is extended from the first 10 choice points to 100 choice points. Then the curve rises only slightly when the observation horizon is extended from 100 to 1,000 choice points. The sensitivity analysis demonstrates that evidence collected in the first 100 choice yields the most discriminatory information. We believe that this finding makes intuitive sense; it is commonly believed that the first few choice points in the search of backtrack solvers have the most influence on the overall run time.

Despite the fact that predictive power was significantly better after 100 choice points than following 10 choice points, our optimization search over all possibly restart policies at different window sizes determined that the smallest window actually had the best cost/benefit ratio.[6] Thus, we used a window of 10 steps for the final experiments.

Results

After all the policies were constructed as described in the previous section, a fresh set of test data was used to evaluate each. The results, summarized in Table 1, were consistent across all of the problem domains: the dynamic n-ary policy is best, followed by the dynamic binary policy. We believe that the dominance of the n-ary dynamic restart policy over the binary dynamic policy is founded on the finer-grained, higher-fidelity optimization made possible with use of multiple branches of the decision trees. Improvements in solution times with the use of the dynamic policies range from about 40% to 65% over the use of Luby's fixed optimal restart policy.

The "naive" policy of using observations to predict the distribution for each run, and then using the optimal fixed cutoff for that distribution alone, performed poorly. This shows the importance of pruning long runs, and the value of the compute-intensive optimization of key parameters of the restart policy. Finally, the knowledge-free universal policy is about a factor of six slower than the best dynamic policy.

Summary and Directions

We introduced *dynamic restarts*, optimal randomized restart policies that take into consideration observations with relevance to run-time distributions. Our analysis included a consideration of key relationships among variables underlying decisions about pruning runs from consideration. To investigate the value of the methods, we performed several experiments that compare the new policies with static optimal restart procedures. To highlight the general applicability of the methods, studies were performed for quasigroup, graph coloring, and logistics planning problems.

We are pursuing several extensions to the results on dynamic restarts presented here. In one vein of work, we are exploring optimal randomized restart policies for the case of probabilistically *dependent* runs. As we noted above, with dependent runs, observations made in previously observed runs may influence the distribution over future runs. Dependent runs capture the situation where a solver performs restarts on the same instance. In this setting, observations about the time exhibited until a restart of one or more prior runs of the same instance can shift the probability distribution distribution over run time of current and future runs. Beyond dependent and independent runs, we are interested in policies for new kinds of challenges, representing mixes

of dependent and independent runs. For example, we are interested in the scenario where a solution can be generated either by continuing to restart a current instance until it is solved or by drawing a new instance from an ensemble. In another direction on generalization, we are exploring ensembles of instances containing satisfiable as well as unsatisfiable problems. In this work, we consider the likelihood of satisfiability in the analysis, given prior statistics and the updated posterior probabilities of satisfiability based on observations within and between runs. We are also exploring the use of richer observational models. Rather than rely on a single observational window, coupled with offline optimization, we are exploring the real-time adaptive control of when, how long, and which evidence is observed. As an example, our efforts on characterizing the sensitivity of predictive power of run-time predictions to the duration of the observation window suggest that the window might be controlled dynamically. In another thread of research, we are interested in leveraging inferences about run-time distributions to control search at a finer microstructure of problem solving. That is, we can move beyond the implicit restriction of being limited to the control of a parameter that dictates a cutoff time. We believe that reasoning about partial randomized restarts, using inferences about run time to guide decisions about backing up a solver to an intermediate state (rather than a complete restart) may lead to more flexible, efficient solvers.

We are excited about dynamic restart policies as representing a new class of procedures that tackle difficult combinatorial search problems via increased awareness of critical uncertainties and informational relationships. We hope that this work will stimulate additional efforts to integrate and harness explicit representations of uncertainty in methods for tackling difficult reasoning problems.

References

Achlioptas, D.; Gomes, C. P.; Kautz, H. A.; and Selman, B. 2000. Generating satisfiable problem instances. In *AAAI/IAAI*, 256–261.

Baptista, L., and Marques-Silva, J. P. 2000. The interplay of randomization and learning on real-world instances of satisfiability. In Gomes, C., and Hoos, H., eds., *Working notes of the AAAI-2000 Workshop on Leveraging Probability and Uncertatinty in Computation.* AAAI.

Chickering, D. M.; Heckerman, D.; and Meek, C. 1997. A Bayesian approach to learning Bayesian networks with local structure. In *Proceedings of the Thirteenth Conference On Uncertainty in Artificial Intelligence (UAI-97)*, 80–89. Providence, RI: Morgan Kaufman Publishers.

Culberson, J. C., and Luo, F. 1996. Exploring the k-colorable landscape with iterated greedy. In Johnson, D. S., and Trick, M. A., eds., *Cliques, Coloring and Satisfiability*, volume 26 of *DIMACS Series*. AMS. 245–284.

Frost, D.; Rish, I.; and Vila, L. 1997. Summarizing CSP hardness with continuous probability distributions. In *Proceedings of the Fourteenth National Conference on Artificial Intelligence (AAAI-97)*, 327–334. New Providence, RI: AAAI Press.

Gent, I., and Walsh, T. 1993. Easy Problems are Sometimes Hard. *Artificial Intelligence* 70:335–345.

---

[6]We also experimented with a window of 0 steps—that is, using only static observations—but results were inconclusive. We are investigating the extent to which a carefully-chosen set of static features for a problem domain can match the performance of dynamic features for the multiple-instance case.

Restart Policy	Expected Runtime (Choice Points)			
	QCP (CSP)	QCP (Satz)	Graph Coloring (Satz)	Planning (Satz)
Dynamic n-ary (pruned)	3,295	8,962	9,499	5,099
Dynamic binary	5,220	11,959	10,157	5,366
Fixed optimal	6,534	12,551	13,894	6,402
Binary naive	17,617	12,055	14,669	6,962
Universal	12,804	29,320	38,623	17,359
Median (no cutoff)	69,046	48,244	39,598	25,255

Table 1: Comparative results of restart policies. Units are in choice points, which scales linearly with run time. The dynamic-binary policies pruned all runs classified as long. The fixed-optimal policy is that of Luby et al. (1993), based only on the complete run-time distribution without observations. The universal policy is Luby's log-optimal policy for unknown distributions. The binary-naive policy uses the decision tree to predict the distribution for the run, and then uses Luby's fixed optimal cutoff for that distribution.

Gomes, C., and Hoos, H. 2000. Aaai-2000 workshop on leveraging probability and uncertainty in computation.

Gomes, C. P., and Selman, B. 1997. Problem Structure in the Presence of Perturbations. In *Proceedings of the Fourteenth National Conference on Artificial Intelligence (AAAI-97)*, 221–227. New Providence, RI: AAAI Press.

Gomes, C. P., and Selman, B. 2001. Algorithm portfolios. *Artificial Intelligence* 126(1-2):43–62.

Gomes, C. P.; Selman, B.; Crato, N.; and Kautz, H. 2000. Heavy-tailed phenomena in satisfiability and constraint satisfaction problems. *J. of Automated Reasoning* 24(1–2):67–100.

Gomes, C. P.; Selman, B.; and Crato, N. 1997. Heavy-tailed Distributions in Combinatorial Search. In Smolka, G., ed., *Principles and practice of Constraint Programming (CP97) Lecture Notes in Computer Science*, 121–135. Linz, Austria.: Springer-Verlag.

Gomes, C. P.; Selman, B.; and Kautz, H. 1998a. Boosting Combinatorial Search Through Randomization. In *Proceedings of the Fifteenth National Conference on Artificial Intelligence (AAAI-98)*, 431–438. New Providence, RI: AAAI Press.

Gomes, C. P.; Selman, B.; and Kautz, H. A. 1998b. Boosting combinatorial search through randomization. In *AAAI/IAAI*, 431–437.

Hogg, T.; Huberman, B.; and Williams, C. 1996. Phase Transitions and Complexity (Special Issue). *Artificial Intelligence* 81(1–2).

Horvitz, E.; Ruan, Y.; Gomes, C.; Kautz, H.; Selman, B.; and Chickering, M. 2001. A Bayesian approach to tackling hard computational problems. In *Proceedings of the 17th Conference on Uncertainty in Artificial Intelligence (UAI-2001)*, 235–244. Morgan Kaufmann Publishers.

Huberman, B. A.; Lukose, R. M.; and Hogg, T. 1997. An economics approach to hard computational problems. *Science* 275(51).

Kautz, H., and Selman, B. 1996. Pushing the envelope: planning, propositional logic, and stochastic search. In *Proceedings of the Thirteenth National Conference on Artificial Intelligence (AAAI-96)*, 1188–1194. Portland, OR: AAAI Press.

Kautz, H.; Ruan, Y.; Achlioptas, D.; Gomes, C. P.; Selman, B.; and Stickel, M. 2001. Balance and filtering in

structured satisfiable problems. In *Proceedings of the Sixteenth International Joint Conference on Artificial Intelligence (IJCAI-01)*.

Kirkpatrick, S., and Selman, B. 1994. Critical behavior in the satisfiability of random Boolean expressions. *Science* 264:1297–1301.

Li, C. M., and Anbulagan. 1997. Heuristics based on unit propagation for satisfiability problems. In *Proceedings of the International Joint Conference on Artificial Intelligence*, 366–371. AAAI Pess.

Luby, M.; Sinclair, A.; and Zuckerman, D. 1993. Optimal speedup of las vegas algorithms. *Information Process. Letters* 173–180.

Mitchell, D.; Selman, B.; ; and Levesque, H. 1992. Hard and easy distributions of sat problems. In *Proceedings of the Tenth National Conference on Artificial Intelligence (AAAI-92)*, 459–465. AAAI Press.

Moskewicz, M. W.; Madigan, C. F.; Zhao, Y.; Zhang, L.; and Malik, S. 2001. Chaff: Engineering an efficient SAT solver. In *Design Automation Conference*, 530–535.

Ruan, Y.; Horvitz, E.; and Kautz, H. 2002. Restart policies that consider dependence among runs: A dynamic programming approach. Submitted for publication.

Selman, B., and Kirkpatrick, S. 1996. Finite-Size Scaling of the Computational Cost of Systematic Search. *Artificial Intelligence* 81(1–2):273–295.

Selman, B.; Kautz, H.; and Cohen, B. 1993. Local search strategies for satisfiability testing. In Johnson, D., and Trick, M., eds., *Dimacs Series in Discrete Mathematics and Theoretical Computer Science, Vol. 26*. AMS. 521–532.

Smythe, R., and Mahmound, H. 1995. A survey of recursive trees. *Theoretical Probability and Mathematical Statistics* 51:1–27.

Walsh, T. 1999. Search in a Small World. In *Proceedings of the International Joint Conference on Artificial Intelligence*.

Using Weighted MAX-SAT Engines to Solve MPE

James D. Park

Computer Science Department
University of California
Los Angeles, CA 90095
jd@cs.ucla.edu

Abstract

Logical and probabilistic reasoning are closely related. Many examples in each group have natural analogs in the other. One example is the strong relationship between weighted MAX-SAT and MPE. This paper presents a simple reduction of MPE to weighted MAX-SAT. It also investigates approximating MPE by converting it to a weighted MAX-SAT problem, then using the incomplete methods for solving weighted MAX-SAT to generate a solution. We show that converting MPE problems to MAX-SAT problems and using a method designed for MAX-SAT to solve them often produces solutions that are vastly superior to the previous local search methods designed directly for the MPE problem.

Introduction

Probabilistic reasoning has a strong relation to logical reasoning. Many problems from one class have natural analogs in the other. The similarities between the problems from probabilistic reasoning and logical reasoning sometimes allows solution techniques to be transfered from one domain to the other. For example, previous results for the Most Probable Explanation (MPE) (Kask & Dechter 1999) have been obtained by noticing the similarity between MPE and satisfiability, and leveraging incomplete methods designed for satisfiability in order to approximately solve the MPE problem. In the other direction, methods used in probabilistic problems have been applied in order to improve the theoretical analysis of logical problems (Rish & Dechter 2000).

The *Most Probable Explanation* (MPE) is the problem of finding the variable instantiation of a Bayesian network that has the highest probability given some evidence. Essentially it provides the most likely state of the system given what has been observed. MPE has a number of applications including diagnosis and explanation. Unfortunately, MPE is an NP-complete problem (Littman 1999), so approximation techniques are necessary. As mentioned above, local search techniques for MPE have been inspired by the relation between satisfiability and MPE. MPE enjoys even closer ties with weighted maximum satisfiability (weighted MAX-SAT), another problem from logic which shares MPE's optimization characteristics. *Weighted MAX-*

SAT is the problem of taking a set of clauses with associated weights, and finding the instantiation that produces the largest sum of the weights of satisfied clauses. Weighted MAX-SAT is used for example to resolve conflicts in a knowledge base. Finding approximate solutions to weighted MAX-SAT has received significant research attention, and novel algorithms have been developed that have proved to be very successful.

This paper investigates using local search algorithms developed for weighted MAX-SAT and applying them to approximately solve MPE. Local search is a general optimization technique which can be used alone or as a method for improving solutions found by other approximation methods. We compare two successful local search algorithms in the MAX-SAT domain (Discrete Lagrangian Multipliers (Wah & Shang 1997), and Guided Local Search (Mills & Tsang 2000)) to the local search method proposed for MPE (Kask & Dechter 1999). For large problems, the MAX-SAT algorithms proved to be significantly more powerful, typically providing instantiations that are orders of magnitude more probable.

The paper is organized as follows: First, we formally introduce the MPE and MAX-SAT problems. Then we present the reduction of MPE to MAX-SAT. We then introduce the MAX-SAT algorithms that will be evaluated. Finally, we provide experimental results comparing the solution quality of MPE approximations using the MAX-SAT methods to the previously proposed local search method developed for MPE.

MPE and MAX-SAT

The variables that appear in the Bayesian networks we will consider are over a finite domain of possible values. Each variable can take on a single value from a finite set of mutually exclusive possibilities.

Definition 1 *An <u>instantiation</u> of a set of variables is a function that assigns a value to each variable in the set. Two instantiations are <u>compatible</u> if they agree on the assignment of all of the variables that they have in common.*

We denote instantiations by the values of each variable to simplify the notation since the variable it is associated with will be clear from the context. Consider, for example, a variable A that can take on values in $\{a_1, a_2, a_3\}$, and variable

A	$Pr(A)$
a_1	.3
a_2	.5
a_3	.2

A	B	$Pr(B\|A)$
a_1	b_1	.2
a_1	b_2	.8
a_2	b_1	1
a_2	b_2	0
a_3	b_1	.6
a_3	b_2	.4

Figure 1: CPTs for a Bayesian network $A \to B$.

B that can take on values in $\{b_1, b_2\}$. Then instantiation (a_1) is compatible with instantiations (a_1, b_2) and (b_3), but not with (a_2, b_2). For boolean variables, we denote the values by the lowercase variable name or the negated variable name. For example for boolean variables C and D, the instantiation $(c, \overline{d})$ represents the assignment of C to true and D to false.

Definition 2 *A conditional probability table (CPT) T for a variable V with a set of parent variables $\mathbf{P}$ is a function that maps each instantiation of $V \cup \mathbf{P}$ to a real value in $[0, 1]$ such that for any instantiation $\mathbf{p}$ of $\mathbf{P}$, $\sum_v T(\{v\} \cup \mathbf{p}) = 1$ where v ranges over the values of V.*

A CPT provides the probability for each possible value of V given a particular instantiation of the parents. It is called a table since it is often represented in tabular form, enumerating the conditional probability associated with each instantiation. Figure 1 contains example CPTs corresponding to $Pr(A)$ and $Pr(B|A)$

Bayesian networks represent a probability distribution over a set of variables, factored into a specific form. It consists of a directed graph which specifies specific independence relationships between the variables, together with a conditional probability table for each variable. Formally,

Definition 3 *A Bayesian network is a pair $(\mathcal{G}, \mathcal{P})$ where $\mathcal{G}$ is a directed acyclic graph whose nodes are variables, and $\mathcal{P}$ is a set which consists of the CPT of each variable in $\mathcal{G}$, where the parents of each CPT correspond to the parents of the corresponding variable in the graph.*

Because of the way Bayesian networks are factored, computing the probability of a complete instantiation of its variables is very simple. The probability of a complete instantiation is the product of the entry of each CPT that is compatible with the instantiation. For example, in the network in Figure 1 the instantiation (a_3, b_1) has probability $.2 * .6 = .12$

The *MPE* problem is defined as follows: Given a Bayesian Network and an instantiation of a subset of the variables (the *evidence*), find the (not necessarily unique) complete instantiation with the highest probability that is compatible with the evidence.

Now we will consider some related concepts in logical reasoning. Unlike in probabilistic reasoning, logical reasoning deals with propositional variables. We will use the following standard terminology:

Definition 4 *A literal is a variable or its negation. A clause is a disjunction of literals and a weighted clause is a clause, together with a non-negative weight. A weighted CNF formula is a set of weighted clauses.*

We denote clauses using standard CNF formula conventions. Weights are denoted as superscripts. We denote a weighted CNF formula by the weighted clauses conjoined together. For example, the following formula consists of three weighted clauses : $(x \vee \overline{y} \vee \overline{z})^3 \wedge (\overline{x})^{10.1} \wedge (y)^{.5}$. The weight of a complete instantiation of a weighted CNF formula is the sum of the weight of the satisfied clauses. So, for the previous example, the instantiation $(x, y, \overline{z})$ has weight $3 + .5 = 3.5$ since it satisfies the first and third clauses, but not the second.

The *MAX-SAT* problem is defined as follows: Given a weighted CNF formula, find the (not necessarily unique) instantiation which has the highest weight.

Reducing MPE to MAX-SAT

An MPE problem can be converted into a weighted CNF expression whose MAX-SAT solution immediately produces the solution to the corresponding MPE problem. We begin by showing how to reduce a Bayesian network with only binary variables and positive CPT entries, and later show how to extend it to handle zeros, non-binary variables, and evidence.

The basic idea is that each CPT entry induces a weighted clause in the induced MAX-SAT problem. The only instantiations that do not satisfy the clause $l_1 \vee l_2 \vee ... \vee l_n$ are the instantiations in which each literal in the clause evaluates to false. We use this fact as the basis of the conversion. Each row in the CPT generates a weighted clause which contains the negation of each of the variables in the row and is weighted with the negative log of the conditional probability. For example, the network $C \to D$ with CPTs :

C	$Pr(C)$
c	.3
$\overline{c}$	.7

C	D	$Pr(D\|C)$
c	d	.2
c	$\overline{d}$	.8
$\overline{c}$	d	.1
$\overline{c}$	$\overline{d}$	.9

induces the weighted CNF expression

$$(\overline{c})^{-\log .3} \wedge (c)^{-\log .7} \wedge (\overline{c} \vee \overline{d})^{-\log .2}$$

$$\wedge (\overline{c} \vee d)^{-\log .8} \wedge (c \vee \overline{d})^{-\log .1} \wedge (c \vee d)^{-\log .9}$$

Consider, for example, the instantiation $c, \overline{d}$. It satisfies all of the clauses except $(\overline{c})^{-\log .3}$ and $(\overline{c} \vee d)^{-\log .8}$. So the sum of weights of the unsatisfied clauses is $-\log .24$ which is the negative log of the probability of that instantiation. Notice that for any instantiation of the variables, the sum of the weights of the unsatisfied clauses equals the negative log of the probability of the instantiation in the Bayesian network. This is true in general and forms the basis for the reduction.

Theorem 1 *For any instantiation I of a positive Bayesian Network which contains only binary variables, the sum of the weights of the clauses that I leaves unsatisfied in the induced weighted CNF expression equals $-\log \Pr(I)$.*

Proof: The unsatisfied clauses are those in which every literal evaluates to false. A clause is not satisfied if and only if the corresponding CPT entry is compatible with the instantiation. Thus the sum of the weights of the unsatisfied clauses is the sum of the negative logs of the compatible CPT entries. Since the probability of a complete instantiation I is the product of the CPT entries compatible with I, the sum of the weights of the unsatisfied clauses is $-\log \Pr(I)$.

Maximizing the weight of the satisfied clauses minimizes the sum of the excluded clauses which is equivalent to maximizing the probability in the original network. Thus solving the MAX-SAT problem also solves the MPE problem.

Handling Zeros

A CPT entry which has zero probability can not be transformed by the previous transformation because the log of zero is undefined. This problem can be circumvented by replacing the clause weight $-\log 0$ with a sufficiently large value w_0. The value must be large enough that it preserves the ordering of the solution qualities. In other words, if one instantiation of the Bayesian network has a higher probability than another, the corresponding MAX-SAT instantiations should be ordered in the same way. Letting w_0 be larger than the sum of all of the weights of the clauses associated with non-zero CPT entries is sufficient.

Theorem 2 *Let w_0 be a greater than the sum of the negative logs of the non-zero CPT entries of a Bayesian network with binary variables. Let the weight of the clauses whose associated CPT entries are zero have weight w_0, with the other weights as before. Then, any positive probability instantiation I has a higher score for the weighted CNF expression than any zero probability instantiation. Additionally, the sum of the weights of the unsatisfied clauses for I remains $-\log \Pr(I)$.*

Proof: Because w_0 is larger than the sum of all of the non w_0 weights, any instantiation that satisfies the w_0 clauses (corresponding to a positive Bayesian network instantiation) has a higher score than any instantiation that does not satisfy one of them (corresponding to a zero probability network instantiation). For those that satisfy the w_0 clauses, the sum of the unsatisfied clauses remains $-\log \Pr(I)$, so the solution ordering is preserved.

Replacing $-\log 0$ with a constant has the added benefit that hill climbing can be performed in the MAX-SAT space, even when in the MPE space all neighbors of the state have zero probability.

Beyond Binary Variables

When there are more than 2 possible values for a variable, we can not interpret it as a single boolean variable. Instead, we introduce a variable (the *indicator variable*) for

each value the network variable can take on, with additional clauses to enforce the constraint that exactly one of them must be true. The clauses for the CPT entries are created as before except the indicator variables appear in the clause instead. An additional weighted clause of the form $(v_1 \vee .... \vee v_n)$ with a large weight is introduced to force one of the values to be true. By choosing a large enough weight, any locally maximal MAX-SAT instantiation will include at least one positive assignment of an indicator corresponding to each network variable. One possible choice for the weight of a constraint clause for a variable is double the sum of the weights of the other clauses that contain the corresponding indicators.

We must also ensure that only one indicator corresponding to a particular network variable is set in the resulting solution. An obvious way to ensure that is to add clauses with large weight of the form $\overline{v_i} \vee \overline{v_j}$ for each pair of indicators associated with a network variable. The problem with this scheme is that it adds a lot of clauses, which complicates the problem. There is a simpler alternative. Note that all of the indicators appear negatively except in the constraint clause. Thus having multiple indicators instantiated can not improve the score. In fact, setting more than one indicator for a particular network variable will decrease the score unless all of the non-constraint clauses that contain the extra variable have weight zero. All we need to ensure is that each clause contributes some positive weight. This is satisfied automatically for sensible networks since a sufficient condition is that the network variable does not necessarily attain a particular value. In other words, for at least one parent instantiation, it has a probability of less than one of achieving that value. Still, for completeness such a perverse network can be handled by adding a small constant to each of the weights associated with the CPT entry clauses before computing the weights for the constraint clauses, or by treating that variable as if it were set to the necessary value by some evidence. Thus we have

Theorem 3 *Any locally maximal instantiation of the induced weighted CNF expression satisfies the constraint that exactly one of the indicator variables is true for each variable. Additionally, the weight of the unsatisfied clauses for positive probability instantiation I remains $-\log \Pr(I)$.*

To illustrate, we return to our original example. The network from Figure 1 induces the weighted CNF formula

$$(\overline{a_1})^{-\log(.3)} \wedge (\overline{a_2})^{-\log(.5)} \wedge (\overline{a_3})^{-\log(.2)} \wedge$$
$$(a_1 \vee a_2 \vee a_3)^{\omega_a} \wedge (\overline{a_1} \vee \overline{b_1})^{-\log(.2)} \wedge (\overline{a_1} \vee \overline{b_2})^{-\log(.8)} \wedge$$
$$(\overline{a_2} \vee \overline{b_1})^{-\log(1)} \wedge (a_2 \vee b_2)^{w_0} \wedge (\overline{a_3} \vee \overline{b_1})^{-\log(.6)} \wedge$$
$$(\overline{a_3} \vee \overline{b_2})^{-\log(.4)} \wedge (b_1 \vee b_2)^{\omega_b}$$

where w_0, ω_a, and ω_b are chosen as described above.

Entering Evidence

Evidence for a Bayesian network is an instantiation of a subset of its variables. Evidence is entered simply by replacing the propositional variables that correspond to the evidence to their appropriate values then simplifying by dropping any clause that contains true, and removing false from all clauses. Any clause that would not be satisfied by an instantiation compatible with the evidence would still not be satisfied for a compatible instantiation over the new problem. Thus the sum of the unsatisfied clauses remains the same. Continuing with the example, entering evidence (a_1) replaces a_1 with true, and a_2 and a_3 with false, resulting in the weighted CNF formula

$$()^{-\log(.3)} \wedge (\overline{b_1})^{-\log(.2)} \wedge (\overline{b_2})^{-\log(.8)}$$

.

MAX-SAT Algorithms

There are a variety of algorithms in the literature for approximating MAX-SAT. We consider two methods that have been shown to be particularly effective in solving MAX-SAT problems. They are the method of Discrete Lagrangian Multipliers (DLM) and Guided Local Search (GLS).

Both of the algorithms that we consider are local search techniques. Local search is a general optimization technique. The most basic local search method is hill climbing. Hill climbing works by repeatedly improving the current solution by moving to a better neighboring solution. This continues until no neighbor is a better solution. For our purposes, we define the neighbors of an instantiation to be those instantiations produced by changing which indicator corresponding to a particular network variable is set. For example, for the MAX-SAT problem induced by the network in Figure 1, the neighbors of the instantiation $(a_1, \overline{a_2}, \overline{a_3}, b_1, \overline{b_2})$ are $(\overline{a_1}, a_2, \overline{a_3}, b_1, \overline{b_2})$, $(\overline{a_1}, \overline{a_2}, a_3, b_1, \overline{b_2})$, and $(a_1, \overline{a_2}, \overline{a_3}, \overline{b_1}, b_2)$.

Both DLM and GLS use hill climbing as a subroutine. They work by modifying the cost function used to search each time a local optimum is found. Instead of simply using the sum of the weights of the unsatisfied clauses as the cost function, another criteria, which changes throughout execution is chosen. This allows the algorithms to naturally explore the search space even after a local minimum has been obtained. Empirically this has been shown to be much better than randomly choosing a new instantiation each time a local minimum is encountered. At a high level they both work as follows:

do
    current=hillClimb(p,current)
    augmentCostFunction(p,current)
while(termination condition not met)

Here p is the problem instance. The hillClimb routine iterates through the variables, selecting the best change for each (as measured by the current cost function) until a local minimum is reached. It also computes the true score (as opposed to the score for the modified cost function) at each step and remembers the best state encountered.

The MAX-SAT algorithms we consider differ only in the way in which they generate the objective function.

Discrete Lagrangian Multipliers

Discrete Lagrangian Multipliers (Wah & Shang 1997) is a framework for combinatorial optimization subject to constraints. It has a solid theoretical foundation which is based on an extension of constrained optimization using Lagrange multipliers for continuous variables. In the weighted MAX-SAT domain, the clauses are the constraints, and the sum of the weights of the unsatisfied clauses is the cost function. In addition to the weight w_C, a Lagrangian multiplier λ_C is associated with each clause C. The cost function function for DLM is of the form

$$\sum_C w_C + \sum_C \lambda_C$$

where C ranges over the unsatisfied clauses. Initially, each λ_C is zero. Each time a local minimum is encountered, the λs corresponding to the unsatisfied clauses are increased by adding a constant.

Guided Local Search

As opposed to the theoretically based DLM, Guided Local Search (Mills & Tsang 2000) is a heuristically developed method for solving combinatorial optimization problems. It has been shown to be extremely successful in solving general weighted MAX-SAT problems. The initial cost function is the number of unsatisfied clauses. Like DLM, GLS associates an additional weight with each clause. Since the number of unsatisfied clauses is constant for MPE based formulas with the neighbor definition we use, the objective function essentially becomes $\sum_C \lambda_C$ where C ranges over the unsatisfied clauses. When a local minimum is reached, the weights of some of the unsatisfied clauses are increased. Specifically, the λs of the unsatisfied clauses with the maximum utility are incremented by 1 where the utility of a clause C is given by $w_C/(1 + \lambda_C)$. Notice that unlike DLM which increments the λs of all of the unsatisfied clauses, GLS modifies only a few (often just one) of them.

Additionally, the authors of both algorithms note that it is advantageous to periodically scale the weights of the the the λs when augmenting the objective function. This prevents the search space from becoming too rugged. We implemented the rescaling by multiplying each λ by .8 every 200 times a local minimum is found.

Experimental Results

We implemented DLM, GLS as well as a previous stochastic local search (SLS) based MPE approximation (Kask & Dechter 1999) that performed well when compared to other MPE approximation schemes. SLS is a local search algorithm that at each step performs either a hill climbing or a stochastic variable change. Periodically the search is restarted in order to escape local maxima.

For SLS, we used the parameters specified in (Kask & Dechter 1999). We found no mention of the preferred probability for taking a stochastic flip, so tuned it experimentally. We used networks drawn from the same distribution as those in the first data set. The value that worked best was 0.2. For DLM, the increment used to modify the weights was chosen in the same manner. The value chosen was 0.02. GLS had no parameters to tune.

We experimented with three synthetic sets of 100 Bayesian networks consisting of binary variables, and ten

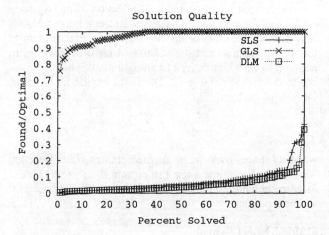

Figure 2: A plot of the ratios of the approximate solution to the exact MPE probability. The values are sorted, so that for a particular point on the X axis it means that X percentage of the instances had solutions that were at least as far off as the Y value for that point.

	SLS	GLS	DLM
exact	0	100	0
non-zero	0	100	7

Table 1: Only GLS was able to perform well on the deterministic data sets.

real world networks. In the first and second data sets, we generated networks with 100 variables, and widths[1] around 16 in order to be large enough to be difficult for the local search methods, but small enough to be able to use an exact algorithm for comparison. We used the method described in (Darwiche 2001) to generate the network topology. In the third set each network had 500 variables. We generated the network topology so that the probability of having an edge between any two nodes was a constant. This has the effect of producing very connected networks that are beyond the reach of structure based methods (they typically have widths of over 100). The CPTs for the first and third sets were instantiated randomly. In the second, each non-root CPT was instantiated as a deterministic function of its parents, while the root CPTs were instantiated randomly. For the first and second sets, we computed the exact MPE probability in order to be able to compare solutions. We then gave each algorithm 30 seconds per network to generate the best solution it could. Each algorithm was initialized to start at the same location.

In all three synthetic experiments, GLS clearly dominated the other methods. GLS was able to produce the exact an-

[1]The width of a Bayesian network is a property of the network topology that is related to how connected the network is. The state of the art algorithms that perform inference on Bayesian networks typically have complexity that is linear in the number of variables and exponential in the width.

	Worst	Median	Best
SLS/GLS	7×10^{-14}	1×10^{-10}	2×10^{-7}
DLM/GLS	3×10^{-11}	6×10^{-7}	1×10^{-3}

Table 2: GLS dominated the other methods. We show some statistics of the ratio of the other methods to GLS. The GLS solution was several orders of magnitude more probable, even for the closest solution.

swer for most of the problems in the first two data sets. In the third set, we were unable to compute the exact MPE values so we can not tell how close to the exact value each algorithm achieved, but GLS produced significantly better solutions than the other methods.

Figure 2 shows the results for the first data set. The ratio of the probability of the found solution to the probability of the true solution is plotted for each algorithm. The ratio values are sorted from worst to best solution quality for each method. Only GLS was able to compute the exact value of any problem, and it did so in 65 of the 100 instances. The lowest score it produced was 0.76 of the optimal value. SLS and DLM had very similar performance on this data set.

Table 1 shows the result for the second data set. For the deterministic problems, the vast majority of the instantiations have probability 0. The table shows how many of the 100 problems that each method was able to solve exactly, as well as how many were able to find a solution with a non-zero probability. In the deterministic set GLS again dominated, solving all problems exactly. DLM performed slightly better than SLS in that it was able to find non zero solutions for seven of the networks.

In the third set, we again gave each algorithm 30 seconds per network to produce a solution. These networks were too connected to produce exact solutions, so we compare only the relative performance between the algorithms.

GLS significantly outperformed the other methods on the third data set as well. Table 2 provides some statistics on the solution quality produced by SLS and DLM relative to GLS. The worst median, and best columns show the worst median, and best ratios of the found value to the GLS for the 100 networks. So for example, even at its best, SLS produced a solution that was only 2×10^{-7} as large as the GLS solution for that network.

In each MPE problem in all three synthetic sets, GLS produced a better solution than the other two methods, and in many cases, produced solutions that were many times better.

We also experimented with 10 real world networks obtained from the Bayesian network repository(Bayesian network repository). For each network, we ran 20 test cases. Each test case had 10 randomly selected evidence variables. Care was taken to ensure that the probability of evidence was positive. The parameters and time limit were the same as the ones used for the synthetic network experiments.

The results on the real world networks showed significant differences in the performance characteristics of the algorithms. Table 3 summarizes the results. For each network we list the number of variables and the average and maximum number of possible values for its variables. We also

Network	# vars	var insts		SLS/GLS			DLM/GLS			SLS		DLM		GLS	
		avg	max	min	med	max	mid	med	max	best	> 0	best	> 0	best	> 0
Barley	48	8	67	9e-2	1e2	9e9	7e-2	1e2	3e10	11	20	6	20	3	20
Diabetes	413	11	21	1	1	1	1	1	∞	14	0	20	6	14	0
Link	724	2	4	0	0	0	0	0	0	0	0	0	0	20	20
Mildew	35	17	100	0	1.4	3e1	0	1.2	2e1	15	19	4	19	7	20
Munin1	189	5	21	0	0	0	0	0	5e3	0	0	1	7	19	20
Munin2	1003	5	21	0	0	0	0	0	3e76	0	0	9	9	11	20
Munin3	1044	5	21	0	0	0	0	0	1e101	0	0	8	8	12	20
Munin4	1041	5	21	0	0	1	0	0	5e111	2	0	8	6	14	18
Pigs	441	3	3	0	0	1	1e-19	1e-2	1	1	1	6	20	20	20
Water	32	3	4	1	1	1	1	1	1	20	20	20	20	20	20

Table 3: Statistics for experiments on 10 real world networks.

provide minimum, median and maximum statistics for the ratio of SLS and DLM to GLS over the 20 runs. We also count the number of times the solution was the best of the three algorithms, as well as the number of positive probability solutions found.

No method dominated the others for all networks. For networks with a relatively small number of variables with many values per variable (ex. Barley, Mildew), SLS slightly outperformed DLM, and significantly outperformed GLS. For the networks with many variables, GLS and DLM performed significantly better. GLS excelled at finding positive instantiations, finding a positive instantiation in nearly every case for every network except Diabetes. It also produced the best solutions most often for the large networks. DLM was not able to find as many positive solutions, but for some of the large networks (ex. Munin2, Munin3, Munin4) generated solutions vastly superior to GLS on those in which it was able to find a positive solution. We thought that this may be a result of too little search time for such large problems, but we found increasing the time limit from 30 seconds to 2 minutes did not qualitatively alter this relationship. It appears from the data we generated, that DLM performance relative to GLS increases as the number of states per variable increases, although more study would be needed to verify this.

All of the methods have their merits. SLS seems to do well for networks with few variables and many values per variable, though it performs poorly on problems in which the vast majority of instantiations have 0 probability. DLM performs better than SLS when the number of variables is increased, and can sometimes outperform GLS. GLS provided the best overall performance, providing the best answer of the three algorithms in the majority of cases. Still, in a significant minority of the cases for the large networks, DLM was able to outperform GLS.

Conclusion

MPE and MAX-SAT problems are strongly related. The reduction from MPE to MAX-SAT is easy to perform. Using this conversion, methods for approximating weighted MAX-SAT can be leveraged to approximate MPE. Both DLM and GLS can often provides answers that are far superior to those produced by the local search method designed directly for MPE.

References

Bayesian network repository. www.cs.huji.ac.il/labs/compbio/Repository.

Darwiche, A. 2001. Recursive conditioning. *Artifical Intelligence Journal* 125(1-2):5–41.

Kask, K., and Dechter, R. 1999. Stochastic local search for Bayesian networks. In *Workshop on AI and Statistics 99*, 113–122.

Littman, M. 1999. Initial experiments in stochastic satisfiability. In *Proceedings of the Sixteenth National Conference on Artificial Intelligence*, 667–672.

Mills, P., and Tsang, E. 2000. Guided local search for solving SAT and weighted MAX-SAT problems. *Journal of Automated Reasoning* 24:205–233.

Rish, I., and Dechter, R. 2000. Resolution versus search: Two strategies for SAT. *Journal of Automated Reasoning* 24(1/2):225–275.

Wah, B., and Shang, Y. 1997. Discrete Lagrangian-based search for solving MAX-SAT problems. In *Proceedings of the 15th International Joint Conference on Artificial Intelligence*, 378–383.

Easy Predictions for the Easy-Hard-Easy Transition

Andrew J. Parkes

CIRL

1269 University of Oregon

Eugene OR 97403, USA

http://www.cirl.uoregon.edu/parkes

Abstract

We study the scaling properties of sequential and parallel versions of a local search algorithm, WalkSAT, in the easy regions of the easy-hard-easy phase transition (PT) in Random 3-SAT.

In the underconstrained region, we study scaling of the sequential version of WalkSAT. We find linear scaling at fixed clause/variable ratio. We also study the case in which a parameter inspired by "finite-size scaling" is held constant. The scaling then also appears to be a simple power law. Combining these results gives a simple prediction for the performance of WalkSAT over most of the easy region. The experimental results suggest that WalkSAT is acting as a threshold algorithm, but with threshold below the satisfiability threshold.

Performance of a parallel version of WalkSAT is studied in the over-constrained region. This is more difficult because it is an optimization rather than decision problem. We use the solution quality, the number of unsatisfied clauses, obtained by the sequential algorithm to set a target for its parallel version. We find that qualities obtained by the sequential search with $O(n)$ steps, are achievable by the parallel version in $O(log(n))$ steps. Thus, the parallelization is efficient for these "easy MAXSAT" problems.

Introduction

Many systems, both physical and combinatorial, exhibit a phase transition (PT): the probability of a large instance having some property, Q, changes rapidly from zero to one as an "order parameter" passes through some critical value. If the decision problem for the property Q is NP-hard then one might also observe what has been dubbed (somewhat inaccurately) an "easy-hard-easy" transition in the average search cost to solve an instance, i.e to determine whether Q holds (Cheeseman, Kanefsky, & Taylor 1991). Solving instances is hardest when they are taken from the phase transition region, but becomes much easier as we move away.

An extensively studied example of an easy-hard-easy phase transition is that occurring in Random 3-SAT (see, for example, (Kirkpatrick & Selman 1994; Crawford & Auton 1996; Friedgut & Kalai 1996)). If instances are characterized by the number of variables n, and clauses c, then the relevant order parameter is $\alpha = c/n$. It is believed that, in

the large n limit, the probability, $P[\alpha, n]$, of an instance being satisfiable exhibits a PT. that is, for some critical value α_C then $\alpha < \alpha_C$ gives $\lim_{n \to \infty} P(\alpha, n) = 1$, and $\alpha > \alpha_C$ gives $\lim_{n \to \infty} P(\alpha, n) = 0$. Empirical estimates are that $\alpha \approx 4.26$ (Crawford & Auton 1996).

In this paper, we will avoid the computationally hard region near α_C and instead focus on properties in the easy regions. The essential question we ask is "How is easy is easy". A theoretical motivation is that current theoretical lower-bounds on α_C are obtained by analysis of polynomial algorithms. For example, analysis of a simple iterated greedy algorithm shows $\alpha_C \geq 3.003$ (Frieze & Suen 1996). A better understanding of the easy region might lead to better lower bounds, and maybe even shed light on the PT itself. Practical motivation comes from the broad correspondence between optimization and decision problems; finding optimal solutions corresponds to solving problems at the PT. However, the associated exponential scaling is often unacceptable, instead scaling must be polynomial, and so sub-optimal solutions accepted, corresponding to solving problems in the easier satisfiable region.

We are also motivated by the common use of iterative repair algorithms for large realistic problems. Hence, we study the iterative repair algorithm "WalkSAT" (WSAT) (Selman, Kautz, & Cohen 1996). Although it is incomplete, and so can never prove unsatisfiability, it is usually very effective on satisfiable instances.

The main portion of the paper presents results on the scaling of WSAT in the easy satisfiable region. Previous work (Parkes 2001) showed that scaling of the number of flips is $O(n)$ if α is held constant. We improve upon that work by finding a simple expression for the median flips needed to solve instances. The expression gives a good prediction of performance over a large portion of the easy region.

"Easy" is usually taken to mean polytime. However, this is specific to sequential algorithms. It is also natural to ask how easy the underconstrained regions are for parallel algorithms. The question is non-trivial because it is generally believed not all polytime algorithms can be done efficiently in parallel. "Easy" in the parallel world corresponds to solving in polylog time, $O(log(n)^k)$, i.e "Nicks class", **NC** (see (Papadimitriou 1994)). Problems that are **P**-complete, such as HORNSAT, are easy for sequential algorithms but still hard for parallel algorithms. Earlier work studied a parallel version of WSAT and found it to be an efficient parallelization on underconstrained problems (Parkes 2001). Here, we consider the over-constrained region, (the other "easy"), treating the problem as MAXSAT. We find that solution qualities achievable in $O(n)$ time by the sequential version are achievable by the parallel version in polylog time; again suggesting that, on average, this form of "easy" is also "easy parallel."

Scaling of WSAT

The version of WSAT that we use is:

```
for i := 1 to MAX-TRIES
    P := a randomly generated truth assignment
    for j := 1 to MAX-FLIPS
        if P is a solution, then return P
        else c := a randomly selected unsatisfied clause
            foreach literal l ∈ c
                B(l) = number of clauses that would
                        break if were to flip l
            m = minimum value of B(l)
            L = { l | B(l) = m }
            if m = 0 then flip a random literal from L
            else
                with probability p flip a random literal in c
                else flip a random literal from L
return failure
```

At each iteration an unsatisfied clause is selected randomly and one of its literals is flipped. The heuristic for selection of the literal is to avoid breaking of other clauses. Though sometimes, controlled by a "noise parameter," p, a random choice is made.

To study scaling requires making a choice for α as we increase n, that is, a "slice" through (c, n) space. We first consider the simplest choice: a "fixed-α slice". Previous work (Parkes 2001) showed that the average number of flips increased linearly along such a slice. For completeness, we first repeat the fixed-α experiments of (Parkes 2001). Studying scaling not only requires a selection of problem instances, but also requires decisions about how algorithm parameters, such as p, should be varied. Here we make the simplifying assumption that parameters are constant. In (Parkes 2001), the noise parameter, p was set to 0.3, and although this is close to optimal in the under-constrained region, we will see later that it is significantly sub-optimal as we move closer to the PT. Here, we use $p = 0.5$ which gives better performance.

To obtain the mean, Maxflips was set large enough, 5×10^7, that problems are generally solved on the first try. Unlike (Parkes 2001), we determined not only the mean but also the median numbers of flips. Figure 1 gives the results along fixed-α slices for a representative set of α values. When we are well below the PT then median and mean values essentially coincide and scaling is clearly a simple linear. As α increases then, for smaller values of n the mean is significantly below the mean, but as n increases the two averages converge again.

Since the mean and median are so close, we decided to focus on the median because it requires much less CPU time. To find medians we set MAX-FLIPS large enough to solve

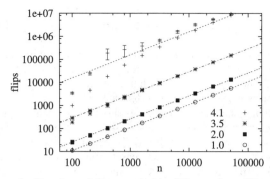

Figure 1: Number of flips needed by WSAT along "fixed-α slices." For each indicated value of α both the mean and median points are plotted; when not overlapping they can be distinguished because the mean is higher and is also given error-bars (corresponding to the usual 95% confidence interval, not the standard deviation).

over 50% of the instances on the first try. In this case, it is sufficient to set MAX-TRIES=1, keep MAX-FLIPS small and leave many instances unsolved. Also the median tends to be less susceptible to outliers. For small values of n we filter out unsatisfiable instances using a complete solver. For larger n this was impractical, but for the easy regions studied here, this turned out not to be important (very few instances are expected to be unsatisfiable).

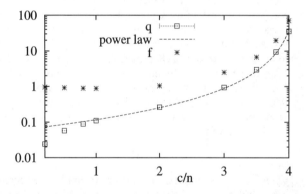

Figure 2: Empirical values for the $q(\alpha)$ of (1), and the flip inefficiency measure $f(\alpha)$ of (2). The "power law" fitted to the $q(\alpha)$ is $1.27/(4.19 - x)^{2.055}$.

The (asymptotic) linearity in Figure 1 suggests the median number of flips F is given by

$$F = q(\alpha)n \qquad (1)$$

Note, F is the number of flips that will solve 50% of the (satisfiable) instances. In WSAT the initial truth assignment is random and so, for Random 3-SAT, can be expected to leave $c/8$ of the clauses unsatisfied. At fixed α this is also linear in n, and so it is useful to define

$$f(\alpha) = \frac{F}{c/8} = \frac{8q(\alpha)}{\alpha} \qquad (2)$$

which can be regarded as an "inefficiency measure". Fits to the data gave values for the $q(\alpha)$ and $\hat{f}(\alpha)$ as plotted in Figure 2. We will return to the "power law" later. Observe that for small α the repairs are efficient, approximately one flip is needed per initial unsatisfied clause. This is consistent with the expectation that clauses are loosely coupled and so repairs will show little interference.

The results at fixed-α slices show linear scaling but have two drawbacks. They give no insight into the nature of $q(\alpha)$. Also, the phase transition (PT) region covers an ever narrower region of α as n increases, and so there is a reasonable sense in which a fixed α moves away from the PT as n increases. This movement could make the fixed-α slice artificially easy. Both deficiencies are overcome if we also study slices that cause α to increase as n increases. A natural candidate would be a slice at a fixed value of "probability an instance is unsatisfiable." However, in the underconstrained region such probabilities are too small to measure directly; to sidestep this difficulty we use methods inspired by "finite-size rescaling".

For any finite value of n the transition is not a step function, but instead become sharper as n is increased. The behavior of the satisfiability probability, $P[\alpha, n]$, was illuminated by ideas from physics (Kirkpatrick & Selman 1994) which suggested defining a new parameter

$$u(\alpha, n) = (\alpha - \alpha_C)n^{1/\nu} \qquad (3)$$

The expectation was that for well-chosen ν the probability would be close to some function $P(u)$ depending on u only. Keeping u constant as n increases drives $\alpha \to \alpha_C$ in such a way that the "probability of satisfiability" stays constant, just as desired for our slice. Experimentally, this was found to happen for $\nu = 3/2$ (Kirkpatrick & Selman 1994). However, these early results had $\alpha_C = 4.17$ whereas more extensive studies later suggested $\alpha_C = 4.24$ or $\alpha_C = 4.26$ depending on exactly how the data was analyzed (Crawford & Auton 1996). Given this uncertainty we decided to relax the definition for u to

$$u_{\alpha_0}(\alpha, n) = (\alpha_0 - \alpha)n^{2/3} \qquad (4)$$

where α_0 was another parameter, (initially) expected to come out to be the same as α_C. (Also, for convenience, we have flipped signs so that $u > 0$ corresponds to the satisfiable side of the PT).

Hence, we define a "fixed-u slice" as a sequence of problems with

$$\alpha(n) = \alpha_0 - u_{\alpha_0} n^{-2/3} \qquad (5)$$

Note that $\alpha \to \alpha_0$ as n increases.

Firstly, we took slices took slices at $u = 100$ and with $\alpha_0 = 4.24$ and $\alpha_0 = 4.17$. Results are shown in Figure 3. In all cases, "flips" refers to median number of flips over a set of (satisfiable) instances. (Usually 1000 instances were used per point, except for the vary largest slowest ones. However, away from the PT, the variances are often small and so not many instances are needed to obtain a reliable estimate.) Both cases are close to straight lines on the log-log scale and so close to power laws, however the slopes change

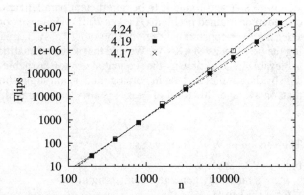

Figure 3: Scaling at $u = 100$, but with different values of α_0. The lines are best-fits of (6).

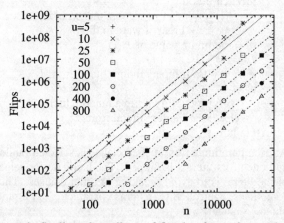

Figure 4: Scaling along lines of fixed u for various values of u with $\alpha_0 = 4.19$. Associated lines are fits to (7) with $p_b = 2.37$ and only p_a allowed to vary with u.

slowly with n. This suggested considering a modified power law:

$$v_3(n) = p_a n^{(p_b + p_c \log(n))} \qquad (6)$$

where p_a, p_b, and p_c are adjustable constants, and a positive value of p_c corresponds to a power-law with a slowly increasing exponent. This gave gave reasonable fits to both the $\alpha_0 = 4.24$ and $\alpha_0 = 4.17$ lines. However, as is clear from the trends in the slopes, $p_c > 0$ for $\alpha_0 = 4.24$ but $p_c < 0$ for $\alpha_0 = 4.17$. Given these opposing trends it was natural to ask whether some intermediate value of α_0 was closer to a power law. Trial and error suggested $\alpha_0 = 4.19$, and the associated data is also shown in Figure 3. (In this section our aim is to find a simple functional approximation to the data and so the informal use "trial and error" is adequate.) Fitting to (6) gave a value for p_c that was consistent with zero, that is, within the confidence limits reported by the fit facility in gnuplot that we used for all function fitting.

Having identified $\alpha_0 = 4.19$ as giving a simple power law along the $u = 100$ slice we then moved to try other values of u. Results are shown in Figure 4. Except for deviations at the end of the range that we will discuss later, each value of u also seems to be a straight-line. More surprisingly the

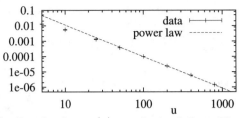

Figure 5: Results for $p_a(u)$ as obtained from Figure 4 and (7) with $p_b = 2.37$. The associated "power law" is $1.27/u^{2.055}$.

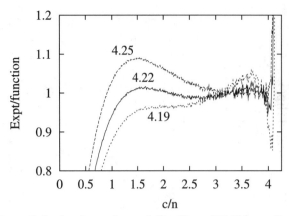

Figure 6: Ratio of experimental F to "best-fit" G for various α_0. (At $n = 51200$ with $p = 0.5$)

lines are parallel on the log-log plot suggesting that they all corresponds to power law scaling with the same exponent. This suggested fitting the data to a 2-parameter restriction of (6)

$$F = p_a(u)n^{p_b} \tag{7}$$

Trial and error gave $p_b = 2.37$. The coefficients $p_a(u)$ were then extracted using each slice; the results are plotted in Figure 5.

We now have two descriptions of the scaling. For constant α, F is O(n), and given by (1). For constant $u_{4.19}$, it is O(n^{p_b}), and given by (7). Consistency requires

$$q(\alpha)n \equiv p_a(u)n^{2.37} \tag{8}$$

Eliminating n using (4) gives

$$q(\alpha)(\alpha_0 - \alpha)^{2.055} = p(u)u^{2.055} \tag{9}$$

The sides of this equation then depend on independent variables and so by "separation of variables" must both be some constant, g_0, whence

$$q(\alpha) = \frac{g_0}{(\alpha_0 - \alpha)^{2.055}} \tag{10}$$

$$p(u) = \frac{g_0}{u^{2.055}} \tag{11}$$

We find that $g_0 = 1.27$ gives a good fit to both $q(\alpha)$ and $p(u)$. The corresponding "power laws" are illustrated along with the empirical coefficients in Figure 2 and Figure 5.

Hence, we find $F \approx G$ where

$$G = \frac{g_0 n}{(\alpha_0 - \alpha)^{g_1}} \tag{12}$$

with $g_0 \approx 1.27$, $\alpha_0 \approx 4.19$, and $g_1 \approx 2.055$.

Refinements of the Scaling Results

The functional form of G suggests that we can generalize the definition of u and a fixed-u slice to

$$\alpha(n) = \alpha_0 - u_{\alpha_0}n^{-\beta} \tag{13}$$

for which

$$G = \frac{g_0}{u}n^{1+\beta g_1} \tag{14}$$

That is, for any value $\beta > 0$, we obtain a slice for which $\alpha \to \alpha_0$ as $n \to \infty$, and for which G is a simple power-law.

Conversely, it suggests imposing polynomial growth on F also forces us below α_0, that is, α_0 would be a threshold between polynomial and super polynomial (though not necessarily exponential) growth. It is important to note that the finite-size scaling value, $\beta = 2/3$, turns out not to be preferred in any way. Hence, although the results were inspired by finite-size scaling, they are ultimately independent. This also answers objections to using finite-size scaling parameters far outside the PT region.

The value $\alpha_0 \approx 4.19$ is somewhat surprising since the PT itself is believed to be at $\alpha_C \approx 4.24$ which is distinctly above this value. Since previous experiments to determine α_C were limited to $n \leq 400$ whereas we have worked up to $n = 51,200$, it is possible that the PT has shifted slightly for these values of n. However, we do not know any reason to disbelieve $\alpha_C \approx 4.24$. Also, Figure 4 show the data deviates from the fitted lines for both small and large α. Hence, in this section, we make a closer investigation of the scaling.

Experiments are performed at fixed values of n and at intervals of $\Delta\alpha = 0.01$ and with 101 instances per point, and with a single run of WSAT per instance. This small sample size leaves some noise in the data, as will be evident from the graphs, but was essential in order to keep the total cpu time practical for the large values of n used.

Firstly, Figure 6 gives the ratio of experimental F to various "best fits" for G. The differences are systematic rather than just random. Over most of the range the difference is less than 10%, and so the function G still provides an good predictor of F within the easy region. However, the systematic discrepancies do mean that fitting G to the data will give slightly different values for the parameters α_0, g_0 and g_1 depending on the range used for the fit. Furthermore, the tendencies in the deviations are such as to favor the small value of α_0 obtained in the experiments along constant-u slices.

The failure of G for small values of α is not unreasonable. For typical instances many variables will not occur at all, and the clauses are highly likely to be very decoupled. They could easily have a qualitatively different behavior. Hopefully, the small deviations of the flip inefficiency from 1.0 could be derivable analytically, and G modified accordingly.

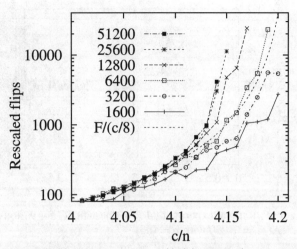

Figure 7: Rescaled flips, $f = F/(c/8)$. For noise $p = 0.5$. G is selected by fitting to $n = 25600$ over the range [3.0,4.1] giving $\alpha_0 = 4.21$, $g_1 = 2.10$, and $g_0 = 1.43$.

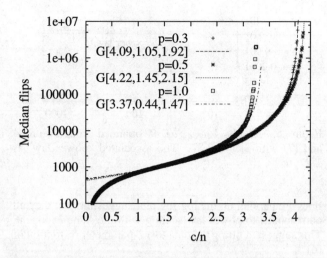

Figure 8: Median flips for indicated values of the noise parameter p. The lines are those of G, using the indicated "best-fit-values" for the parameter lists $[\alpha_0, g_0, g_1]$.

Generally, instances close to the PT are more important, and so the discrepancies at large values of α are more of a concern. Hence, consider Figure 7 where we show empirical values for, f, "flips/(c/8)," close the the PT. On reading Figure 7 it helps to consider the case that flips were a simple power law, $F = an^b$, and so $f(n) = (8a/\alpha)n^{b-1}$. With fixed α, this gives $log(f(2n)) - log(f(n)) = b - 1$. Each doubling of n leads to the same increment on the y-axis, and linear scaling corresponds to zero increment between lines.

For $\alpha < 4.1$ and large n the points on Figure 7 indicate that the scaling approaches linear scaling, though after initially being super-linear for $n < 3200$. However, at $\alpha = 4.15$ the increment on doubling n seems to be increasing each time, suggesting that growth is faster than a simple power-law. Also, observe that the formula for G, even with $\alpha_0 = 4.21$, gives a line that severely underestimates F for large n once we are in the region $\alpha > 4.15$, and again the underestimation seems to increase with n.

Hence, the data indicates a transition at $\alpha \approx 4.15$ from power-law to super-polynomial scaling. Note that the transition is not associated with unsatisfiable instances (for these values of α and n we are well outside the PT).

Assuming the threshold is real, then it is natural to ask whether it is sensitive to the exact algorithm used, or is possibly tied to some (unknown) change in properties of the instances. Hence, in Figure 8 we give medians flips for $p = 0.3$ and 1.0 as well as the $p = 0.5$ used until this point. Again, G gives good fits to the data over the middle range of α values, but we see that the obtained values for the parameters do change significantly. This suggests the thresholds are as driven more by failings of the algorithm, rather directly by semantic properties of instances.

Interestingly, performance at smaller values of α is insensitive to p, presumably reflecting the lesser need for escape from local minima on such easy instances.

Lastly we look at Figure 9 which is the same type of plot as Figure 7 but for $p = 1.0$ instead of $p = 0.5$. In the region

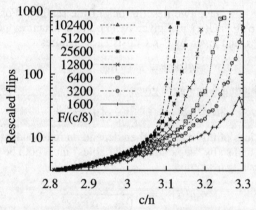

Figure 9: Rescaled flips, $f = F/(c/8)$. For noise $p = 1.0$. G is selected by fitting to $n = 25600$ over the range [2.0,3.0] giving $\alpha_0 = 3.27$, $g_1 = 1.30$, and $g_0 = 0.39$.

$n \approx 10^5$, then for $\alpha_T < 3.0$ scaling approaches linear for the largest n values used. Whereas for $\alpha > 3.1$ it seems to be growing faster than a power law. This time there appears to emerge a transition at $\alpha_T \approx 3.1$ from linear to super-linear (and apparently super-polynomial). At $p = 1.0$, WSAT is particularly simple: a "no-breaks" move is taken if possible, otherwise a literal is flipped at random. Hopefully, the extra simplicity will eventually allow an analytic derivation the non-trivial asymptotic behavior observed.

We should note that in all these apparent thresholds it is hard to eliminate the possibility that the threshold moves slowly as n increases. For example, a slow decrease in the threshold, would correspond to scaling, at fixed-α, being linear until some large value of n and then changing to super-linear or super-polynomial at very large n. We see no evidence for such behavior, but cannot eliminate it.

We also remark that the thresholds only become apparent for large n. Although a few hundred variables are sufficient to show a clear satisfiability threshold, it seems that the algorithmic thresholds here needs tens of thousands in order to become clear. The ability of WSAT to escape local minima effectively might only diminish when faced with the (presumably) much deeper local minima occurring in large theories. Also the results often only show linear growth once reaching large n. In practice, this means that scaling results obtained at small n (meaning $n < 1000$) might be misleading. Unfortunately, experiments with such large values of n are currently impractical except in the easy region.

Previous studies of the scaling of WSAT have generally focussed on the PT region. The behavior of WSAT along the phase transition line was studied in (Singer, Gent, & Smaill 2000)).(Gent *et al.* 1997) study scaling across the PT region; Although they only study much smaller values on n it might well be valuable to relate their results at the edge of the PT region to ours at the edge of the easy region. Also, see (Coarfa *et al.* 2000) for recent studies of scaling of systematic algorithms in the underconstrained region, and a useful overview of other scaling results.

Parallel WSAT and Empirical Scaling Results

A direct parallelization of WSAT is simply to repair all the unsatisfied clauses in parallel, rather than a randomly selected one (Parkes 2001). For WSAT(PAR) the central loop of WSAT(SEQ) is replaced with a "parallel flip" or "parflip":

parallel: foreach clause c
  if c is unsatisfied
    foreach literal $l \in c$
      $B(l)$ = number of clauses that would
             break if were to flip l
    m = minimum value of $B(l)$
    $L = \{ l \mid B(l) = m \}$
    if $m = 0$ **then** flip a random literal from L
    else
      with probability p flip a random literal in c
      else flip a random literal from L

Note that $O(n)$ flips are done simultaneously, and so it is reasonable to hope for a linear speedup. If the sequential version takes $O(n)$ then it is also reasonable to hope that the parallel version would run in (poly-)logarithmic number of flips. Observing that constant-α slices are $O(n)$ for sequential WSAT, Previous studies (Parkes 2001) of the above parallel version found that the hoped for speedup did indeed occur. Empirically, constant-α slices were $O(\log(n)^2)$.

One might study the behavior of WSAT(PAR) along constant-u slices however this would probably not be interesting. The sequential is polynomial, $O(n^{2.37})$ rather than linear, and so (presumably) the most one can hope for is to reduce this to $O(n^{1.37})$.

Instead, we are motivated from the fact that many problems are over-constrained and are treated as optimization rather than decision problems. We take this to correspond to taking $\alpha > \alpha_C$ and treating the problems as MAXSAT rather than SAT. In this case one goal might be to satisfy as many clauses as possible; however, this is NP-hard and

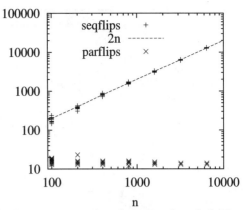

Figure 10: Instances are taken from Random 3-SAT with $\alpha = 6$, and an associated target quality is fixed to that achieved by WSAT(SEQ) in $2n$ flips. For each instance, we then plot both the average sequential flips and parallel flips needed to achieve the target quality.

can be expected to take exponential time. In practice, suboptimal solutions are sought, and local repair methods such as WSAT are still effective.

Hence, we ask whether the WSAT(PAR) gives an effective parallelization on over-constrained optimization problems. Unfortunately, doing optimization rather than simple satisfiability means that there is no natural meaning of "success" for a search attempt. To overcome this we took a simple method to evaluate WSAT(PAR) with respect to WSAT(SEQ).

1. select a value of Maxflips m(n)

2. for each instance we determine a target quality T by

  (a) for each instance we run WSAT(SEQ) for m(n) flips and determine the smallest number of unsatisfied clauses that occurred

  (b) this is averaged over multiple runs of WSAT(SEQ)

3. this target quality is then used as "success criterion." That is, WSAT is considered to succeed as soon as the number of unsatisfied clauses is reduced to T or better.

4. both WSAT(SEQ) and WSAT(PAR) are then evaluated by this success criterion.

Not surprisingly, WSAT(SEQ) then takes $O(m(n))$ flips. If $m(n)$ is selected to be linear then it is reasonable to hope that WSAT(PAR) will reduce this to polylog flips. This appears to be confirmed by experiments, of which we report just a typical representative in Figure 10: Qualities achievable by WSAT(SEQ) in $2n$ flips, are, on average, achievable in $O(\log(n))$ flips by WSAT(PAR).

More challenging for WSAT(PAR) is to give $O(n \log(n))$ flips to WSAT(SEQ). A typical result is given in Figure 11. In this case WSAT(PAR) fails to achieve a linear speedup. However, we noted that WSAT(PAR) can make sets of flips that are likely to be too drastic. In particular, it can cause clauses that satisfied by two or more literals to become unsatisfied. Hence, we implemented a second

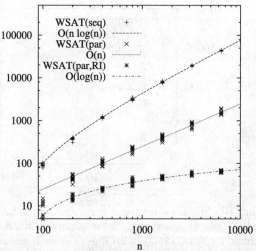

Figure 11: Points are determined as for Figure 10 except that the target quality is determined using $n(1 + \log_2(n/100))$ flips of WSAT(SEQ). We also plot points giving the performance of the modified parallel WSAT.

version WSAT(par,NI), that only allows one of the literals to be flipped in such cases. In this case, Figure 11 a linear speedup, from $O(n \log(n))$ to $O(\log(n))$ was again observed.

We take this as evidence that the "easy MAXSAT" problems we have defined using the over-constrained region of Random 3-SAT are also easy for parallel algorithms.

Closing Comments and Future Work

We have found a remarkably simple expression, (12), that is a good predictor of the median number of flips used by WSAT over a large portion of the easy region below the phase transition in Random 3-SAT.

The expression (12) along with other results presented, suggest that WSAT has a threshold value of α beyond which the median flips scaling is super-polynomial, but below which scaling is linear. The position of the threshold depends on the noise parameter. It would be interesting to see whether other versions of local repair show similar behavior.

The greatest deficiency of this work is that it is purely empirical, and so cannot prove anything about true asymptotic behavior. Hopefully, some of the results can eventually be supported by analytic studies, if only for small values of α, or for simpler versions of WSAT such as with the noise parameter $p = 1$.

Acknowledgments

This work was sponsored in part by grants from Defense Advanced Research Projects Agency (DARPA), number F30602-98-2-0181, and DARPA and Air Force Research Laboratory, Rome, NY, under agreement numbered F30602-00-2-0534. The U.S. Government is authorized to reproduce and distribute reprints for Government purposes notwithstanding any copyright annotation thereon. The views and conclusions contained herein are those of the authors and should not be interpreted as necessarily representing the official policies or endorsements, either expressed or implied, of DARPA, Rome Laboratory, or the U.S. Government.

References

Cheeseman, P.; Kanefsky, B.; and Taylor, W. M. 1991. Where the really hard problems are. In *Proceedings of the Ninth National Conference on Artificial Intelligence (AAAI–91)*, 331–337.

Coarfa, C.; Demopoulos, D. D.; Aguirre, A. S. M.; Subramanian, D.; and Vardi, M. Y. 2000. Random 3-SAT: The plot thickens. In *Principles and Practice of Constraint Programming*, 143–159.

Crawford, J. M., and Auton, L. D. 1996. Experimental results on the crossover point in random 3-SAT. *Artificial Intelligence* 81:31–57.

Friedgut, E., and Kalai, G. 1996. Every monotone graph property has a sharp threshold. *Proc. Amer. Mathl. Soc.* 124:2993–3002.

Frieze, A., and Suen, S. 1996. Analysis of two simple heuristics on a random instance of k-SAT. *Journal of Algorithms* 20:312–355.

Gent, I.; MacIntyre, E.; Prosser, P.; and Walsh, T. 1997. The scaling of search cost. In *Proceedings of the Fourteenth National Conference on Artificial Intelligence (AAAI–97)*, 315–320.

Kirkpatrick, S., and Selman, B. 1994. Critical behavior in the satisfiability of random boolean expressions. *Science* 264:1297–1301.

Papadimitriou, C. 1994. *Computational Complexity*. Addison-Wesley.

Parkes, A. J. 2001. Distributed local search, phase transitions, and polylog time. In *Proceedings of the workshop on "Stochastic Search Algorithms", held at "Seventeenth International Joint Conference on Artificial Intelligence (IJCAI-01)"*.

Selman, B.; Kautz, H.; and Cohen, B. 1996. Local search strategies for satisfiability testing. In Johnson, D. S., and Trick, M. A., eds., *Cliques, Coloring and Satisfiability*, 521–531. American Mathematical Society. Proceedings of the second DIMACS Implementation Challenge, October 1993.

Singer, J.; Gent, I. P.; and Smaill, A. 2000. Local search on random 2+p-sat. In *Proceedings of ECAI-2000*, 113–117.

The Interface between P and NP: COL, XOR, NAE, 1-in-k, and Horn SAT

Toby Walsh

Cork Constraint Computation Center
University College Cork
Cork
Ireland
`tw@4c.ucc.ie`

Abstract

We study in detail the interface between P and NP by means of five new problem classes. Like the well known 2+p-SAT problem, these new problems smoothly interpolate between P and NP by mixing together a polynomial and a NP-complete problem. In many cases, the polynomial subproblem can dominate the problem's satisfiability and the search complexity. However, this is not always the case, and understanding why remains a very interesting open question. We identify phase transition behavior in each of these problem classes. Surprisingly we observe transitions with both smooth and sharp regions. Finally we show how these problem classes can help to understand algorithm behavior by considering search trajectories through the phase space.

Introduction

Where makes NP-complete problems hard to solve? Research into phase transition behavior has given much insight into this question. See, for example, (Cheeseman, Kanefsky, & Taylor 1991; Mitchell, Selman, & Levesque 1992; Gomes & Selman 1997; Walsh 1999). Propositional satisfiability (SAT) is the canonical NP-complete problem and one in which we have perhaps the most insight into phase transition behavior and problem hardness. For random SAT problems with few clauses, problems are almost surely satisfiable and it is easy to guess one of the many satisfying assignments. For random SAT problems with many clauses, problems are almost surely unsatisfiable and it is easy to prove that there can be no satisfying assignments. The hardest random SAT problems tend to be inbetween, when problems are neither obviously satisfiable or unsatisfiable. If we look more closely, especially within a search algorithm like the Davis Logemann Loveland (DLL) procedure, we see both polynomial subproblems (for example, clauses of length 2) and subproblems which are NP-complete (clauses of length 3 or more). As we explain in the next section, there may be interesting and unexpected interactions between them. To study this in more detail, Monasson et al. introduced the 2+p-SAT problem class (Monasson *et al.* 1999) which mixes together polynomial and NP-complete SAT problems and lets us explore in detail the interface between P and NP. We continue this research programme by introducing five new problems at the interface between P and NP.

2+p-SAT

A random k-SAT problem in n variables has l clauses of length k drawn uniformly at random. A sharp transition in satisfiability has been proved for random 2-SAT at $l/n = 1$ (Chvatal & Reed 1992; Goerdt 1992), and conjectured for random 3-SAT at $l/n \approx 4.3$ (Mitchell, Selman, & Levesque 1992). Associated with this transition is a rapid increase in problem difficulty. The random 2-SAT transition is continuous as the backbone (the fraction of variables taking fixed values) increases smoothly. On the other hand, the random 3-SAT transition is discontinuous as the backbone jumps in size at the phase boundary (Monasson *et al.* 1998).

To study this in more detail, Monasson et al. introduced the 2+p-SAT problem class (Monasson *et al.* 1999). This interpolates smoothly from the polynomial 2-SAT problem to the NP-complete 3-SAT problem. A random 2+p-SAT problem in n variables has l clauses, a fraction $(1 - p)$ of which are 2-SAT clauses, and a fraction p of which are 3-SAT clauses. This gives pure 2-SAT problems for $p = 0$, and pure 3-SAT problems for $p = 1$. For any fixed $p > 0$, the 2+p-SAT problem class is NP-complete since the embedded 3-SAT subproblem can be made sufficiently large to encode other NP-complete problems within it.

By considering the satisfiability of the embedded 2-SAT subproblem and by assuming that the random 3-SAT transition is at $l/n \approx 4.3$, we can bound the location the random 2+p-SAT transition to:

$$1 \le \frac{l}{n} \le \min(\frac{1}{1 - p}, 4.3)$$

Surprisingly, the upper bound is tight for $p \le 2/5$ (Achlioptas *et al.* 2001b). That is, the 2-SAT subproblem *alone* determines satisfiability up to $p = 2/5$. Asymptotically, the 3-SAT clauses do not determine if problems are satisfiable, even though they determine the worst-case complexity. Several other phenomena occur at $p = 2/5$ reflecting this change from a 2-SAT like transition to a 3-SAT like transition. For example, the transition shifts from continuous to discontinuous as the backbone jumps in size (Monasson *et al.* 1998). In addition, the average cost to solve problems appears to increase from polynomial to exponential both for complete and local search algorithms (Monasson *et al.* 1998; Singer, Gent, & Smaill 2000). Random 2+p-SAT problem thus look like polynomial 2-SAT problems up to $p = 2/5$ and NP-complete 3-SAT problems for $p > 2/5$.

The 2+p-SAT problem class helps us understand the performance of the DLL algorithm for solving 3-SAT (Cocco & Monasson 2001). At each branch point in its backtracking search tree, the DLL algorithm has a mixture of 2-SAT and 3-SAT clauses. We can thus view each branch as a trajectory in the 2+p-SAT phase space. For satisfiable problems solved without backtracking (i.e. $l/n < 3$), trajectories stay within the satisfiable part of the phase space. For satisfiable problems that require backtracking (i.e. $3 < l/n < 4.3$), trajectories cross the phase boundary separating the satisfiable from the unsatisfiable phase. The length of the trajectory in the unsatisfiable phase gives a good estimate of the amount of backtracking needed to solve the problem. Finally, for unsatisfiable problems, trajectories stay within the unsatisfiable part of the phase space. The length of the trajectory again gives a good estimate of the amount of backtracking needed to solve the problem.

2+p-COL

Given the insight that 2+p-SAT has provided into computational complexity and algorithm performance, we decided to look more deeply into the interface between P and NP by means of some new problem classes. The first problem is 2+p-COL, a mix of 2-coloring and 3-coloring. A random k-COL problem consists of n vertices, each with k possible colors, and e edges drawn uniformly and at random. Like k-SAT, k-COL is NP-complete for $k \geq 3$ but polynomial for $k = 2$. To interpolate smoothly from P to NP, a random 2+p-COL problem has a fraction $(1 - p)$ of its vertices with 2 colors, and a fraction p with 3 colors. Note that the vertices with 2 colors are fixed at the start and cannot be chosen freely. We obtained similar results if the 2-colorable vertices have 2 colors chosen at random from the 3 possible or (as here) the same 2 fixed colors. Like 2+p-SAT, the 2+p-COL problem class is NP-complete for any fixed $p > 0$.

2+p-COL has one major difference to 2+p-SAT. Whilst 2-SAT, 3-SAT and 3-COL all have sharp transitions, 2-COL has a smooth transition (Achlioptas 1999). The probability that a random graph is 2-colorable is bounded away from 1 as soon as the average degree is bounded away from 0, and drops gradually as the average degree is increased, only hitting 0 with the emergence of the giant component (and an odd length cycle). Hence 2-colorability does not drop sharply around a particular average degree (as in 3-colorability) but over an interval that is approximately $0 < e/n < 1/2$.

In Figure 1, we see how the random 2+p-COL transition varies as we increase p and n. At $p \approx 0.8$, the 2+p-COL transition appears to sharpen significantly. In Figure 2, we look more closely at $p = 0.8$. For $p = 0.8$, there is a region up to around $e/n \approx 1.8$ in which the transition appears smooth and like that of 2-COL. The nature of the transition then appears to change to a sharp 3-COL like transition, with the probability of colorability dropping rapidly from around 90% to 0%. We thus appear to have both smooth and sharp regions.

We define δ_{2+p} as the largest ratio e/n at which 100% of problems are colorable:

$$\delta_{2+p} = \sup\{\frac{e}{n} \mid \lim_{n \mapsto \infty} \text{prob}(2+p\text{-colorable}) = 1\}$$

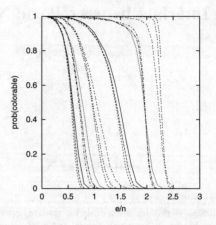

Figure 1: Probability that 2+p-COL problem is colorable (y-axis) against e/n (x-axis). Plots are for $p=0$ (leftmost), 0.2, 0.4, 0.6, 0.8 and 1.0 (rightmost) for 100, 200 and 300 vertex graphs (increasing sharpness).

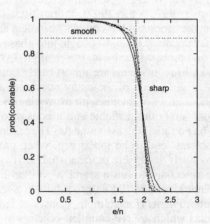

Figure 2: Probability that 2+p-COL problem is colorable (y-axis) against e/n (x-axis) for $p = 0.8$. Plots are for n=50, 100, 150, 200 and 250 vertex graphs.

From (Achlioptas 1999), $\delta_2 = 0$ and $1.923 < \delta_3 < 2.522$. For any fixed $p < 1$, a random 2+p-COL problem contains a 2-COL subproblem that grows in size with n and has average degree bounded away from 0. This subproblem has a probability of being 2-colorable that asymptotically is less than 1. Hence, the random 2+p-COL problem has a probability of being 2+p-colorable that asymptotically is also less than 1, and $\delta_{2+p} = 0$ for all $p < 1$.

We can define a dual parameter γ_{2+p}, which is the smallest ratio e/n at which 0% of problems are colorable:

$$\gamma_{2+p} = \inf\{\frac{e}{n} \mid \lim_{n \mapsto \infty} \mathrm{prob}(2+p\text{-colorable}) = 0\}$$

Since colorability is a monotonic property (adding edges can only ever turn a colorable graph into an uncolorable graph), $\gamma_{2+p} \geq \delta_{2+p}$. Note that δ_{2+p} marks the start of the phase transition whilst γ_{2+p} marks its end. The start stays fixed at $\delta_{2+p} = 0$ for all $p < 1$ and jumps discontinuously to γ_3 at $p = 1$. The end appears to behave more smoothly, increasing smoothly as we increase p. From (Achlioptas 1999), $\gamma_2 \approx \frac{1}{2}$, and $1.923 < \gamma_3 < 2.522$. For a sharp transition like 3-coloring, $\gamma_3 = \delta_3$. As with 2+p-SAT:

$$\gamma_2 \leq \gamma_{2+p} \leq \min(\gamma_3, \frac{\gamma_2}{1-p})$$

In Figure 3, we have estimated experimentally the location of γ_{2+p} by analysing data for graphs with up to 300 vertices and compared the observed location of the (end of the) phase transition with the upper and lower bounds. As with 2+p-SAT, the upper bound (which looks just at the 2-COL subproblem) appears to be tight for $p < 0.8$.

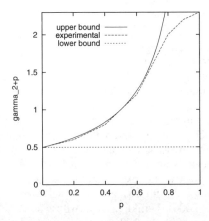

Figure 3: The location of the end of the 2+p-COL phase transition, γ_{2+p} (y-axis) against p (x-axis) for $p = 0$ to 1 in steps of 1/10.

The cost of 2+p-coloring also increases around $p \approx 0.8$. To solve 2+p-COL problems, we encode them into SAT and use zchaff, which is currently the fastest DLL procedure. Our results are thus algorithm dependent and should be repeated with other solvers. Note that the encodings of 2+p-COL problems into SAT give 2+p-SAT problems (but does not sample uniformly). In Figure 4, we see that there is a

change in the search cost around $p \approx 0.8$ where we appear to move from polynomial to exponential search cost. This is despite 2+p-COL being NP-complete for all fixed and nonzero p. However, this is perhaps not so surprisng as up to $p \approx 0.8$, the polynomial 2-COL subproblem *alone* appears to determine asymptotically if the problem is colorable. Beyond this point, the NP-complete 3-COL subproblem contributes to whether the problem is colorable or not.

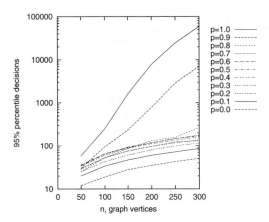

Figure 4: 95% percentile in the search cost to solve 2+p-COL problems at the phase boundary (y-axis logscale) against number of vertices (x-axis). Plots are for $p = 0$ to 1 in steps of 1/10 (increasing hardness)

2+p-COL can be used in a similar way to 2+p-SAT to study 3-coloring algorithms. At each branching decision in a coloring algorithm, some vertices have three colors available, whilst others only have two. If any vertex has only a single color available, we are not at a branching point as we can commit to this color and simplify the problem. The algorithm thus has a sequence of 2+p-COL problems to solve, and we can view each branch in the algorithm's search tree as a trajectory in the 2+p-COL phase space. In Figure 5, we plot a number of trajectories for 3-coloring graphs with Brelaz's algorithm (Brelaz 1979). The trajectories are qualitatively very similar to those of the DLL algorithm in the 2+p-SAT phase space (Cocco & Monasson 2001). For $e/n \leq 1.5$, problems are solved without backtracking. Trajectories trace an arc that stays within the 'colorable' part of the phase space. On the other hand, the algorithm backtracks for problems with $e/n \geq 2$. For graphs with $e/n = 2$, the trajectory starts in the 'colorable' part of the phase space and crosses over into the 'uncolorable' part of the phase space. The algorithm then backtracks till we return to the 'colorable' part of the phase space. This sort of knowledge might be used both to model algorithms and to improve them. For example, we could develop a randomization and restart strategy which restarts when we estimate to have branched into an insoluble part of the phase space.

XOR SAT

We now turn to some other tractable satisfiability problems. Schaeffer's famous dichotomy result (Schaeffer 1978)

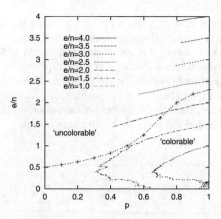

Figure 5: Trajectories in the 2+p-COL phase space for Brelaz's graph coloring algorithm on 3-COL problems with $n = 300$ and e/n from 1 to 4. The crossed line gives the experimental observed values of γ_{2+p}. The region marked 'uncolorable' is where graphs are asymptotically not 2+p-colorable, whilst the region marked 'colorable' is where graphs are asymptotically sometimes 2+p-colorable.

identifies the four non-trivial tractable and maximal restrictions of propositional satisfiability: 2-SAT, HORN SAT, dual HORN SAT, and XOR SAT. The later class is where clauses have the usual "or" replaced with an "exclusive or" (or its negation). This reduces the complexity from NP to P.

In a XOR k-SAT problem, we have l clauses defined over n variables, and each clause is an "exclusive or" of k literals (which ensures that an odd number of the literals are true) or its negation. Random XOR 3-SAT has a sharp threshold in the interval $0.8894 \leq l/n \leq 0.9278$ (Creognou, Daude, & Dubois 2001). Experiments put the transition at $l/n \approx 0.92$, whilst statistical mechanical calculations place it at $l/n = 0.918$ (Franz *et al.* 2001). To interpolate smoothly from P to NP, we introduce the random XOR2SAT problem, with a fraction $(1 - p)$ of XOR 3-SAT clauses and a fraction p of 3-SAT clauses. Like 2+p-SAT, XOR2SAT is NP-complete for any fixed $p > 0$. Like 2+p-SAT but unlike 2+p-COL, the XOR2SAT threshold is always sharp.

In Figure 6, we have estimated experimentally the location of the phase boundary and compared it with the bounds:

$$0.92 \leq \frac{l}{n} \leq \min(\frac{0.92}{1 - p}, 4.3)$$

The upper bound (which looks just at the polynomial XOR 3-SAT subproblem) appears to be loose for all $p > 0$. The NP-complete 3-SAT subproblem thus contributes to satisfiability for all $p > 0$. This contrasts with 2+p-SAT and 2+p-COL where the polynomial subproblem alone determines satisfiability for $0 < p \leq p_c$. It remains a very interesting open question why XOR2SAT is so different to 2+p-SAT in this respect. We expected the polynomial XOR 3-SAT subproblem in XOR2SAT to be even more dominate than the polynomial 2-SAT subproblem in 2+p-SAT. Each XOR 3-SAT clause rules out twice as many assignments as a 2-SAT clause, and

the XOR 3-SAT phase transition occurs at a smaller clause to variable ratio than the 2-SAT transition. It is therefore very surprising that the XOR 3-SAT subproblem does not dominate the XOR2SAT phase transition like the 2-SAT subproblem dominates the 2+p-SAT phase transition.

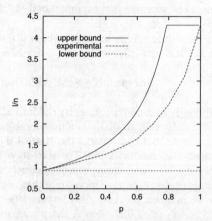

Figure 6: The location of the phase boundary for random XOR2SAT problems (y-axis) against p (x-axis) for $p = 0$ to 1 in steps of 1/10.

We encoded XOR2SAT problems into 3-SAT and solved them with zchaff. The search cost at the phase boundary appears to grow exponentially with n for all p. Given that the NP-complete 3-SAT subproblem contributes to satisfiability for all $p > 0$, it should perhaps not be surprising that we observe exponential growth in search cost for all $p > 0$.

Horn SAT

To complete the coverage of Schaeffer's dichotomy result, we turn to HORN SAT. Horn clauses of a fixed size $k > 1$ are trivially always satisfiable; every clause contains at least one negative literal and is satisfied by assigning all variables to false. We therefore consider a less trivial problem class in which we sample Horn clauses uniformly up to some fixed size. Such problems can contain (positive) unit clauses and so are not always satisfiable. In a k-HORN SAT problem, each clause is up to length k and Horn (i.e. contains at most one positive literal). Random k-HORN SAT has a smooth threshold whose shape is known analytically for $k = 2$ (Istrate 2000). Unlike 2-COL (whose smooth threshold starts at $e/n > 0$), the 2-HORN SAT threshold only starts at $l/n = 3/2$.

To interpolate smoothly from P to NP, we introduce the HORN2SAT problem, which has a fraction $(1 - p)$ of 2-HORN SAT clauses and a fraction p of 3-SAT clauses. Like 2+p-SAT, HORN2SAT is NP-complete for any fixed $p > 0$. Although the HORN2SAT transition appears to sharpen immediately $p > 0$, there again appears to be a change around $p \approx 0.6$. The location of the transition starts to increase rapidly for $p > 0.6$. At the same time, search cost (especially in the higher percentiles) appears to go from polynomial to exponential

1-in-k-SAT

To finish our study of the interface between P and NP, we look at two more satisfiability problems in which phase transition behavior has been observed: 1-in-k-SAT and NAE SAT. In a 1-in-k-SAT problem, each clause specifies that exactly one out of k literals is true. For $k \geq 3$, the phase transition is sharp, occurs at $l/n = 2/k(k-1)$ and is continuous (Achlioptas *et al.* 2001a). Like k-SAT, 1-in-k-SAT is NP-complete for $k \geq 3$ and polynomial for $k = 2$. A 1-in-2-SAT problem can be readily mapped into a 2-COL problem and vice versa. Each 1-in-2-SAT clause fixes two variables either to opposite truth values (which is equivalent to an edge fixing two vertices to different colors) or to the same truth value (which is equivalent to merging two vertices so that they have the same color). We therefore expect the 1-in-2-SAT phase boundary to be smooth like that for 2-COL. To interpolate smoothly from P to NP, we introduce the 1-in-2+p-SAT problem, with a fraction $(1 - p)$ of 1-in-2-SAT clauses and a fraction p of 1-in-3-SAT clauses. Like 2+p-SAT, this problem class is NP-complete for all fixed $p > 0$.

Although 1-in-3-SAT is NP-complete, random 1-in-3-SAT problems are much easier to solve than random 3-SAT problems of a similar size. This may be related to the fact that we can prove the exact location of the 1-in-3-SAT phase transition. The proof bounds the location of the phase transition from the satisfiable side by showing that a simple unit clause heuristic will almost surely decide all satisfiable problems. On the unsatisfiable side, the proof uses the fact that the backbone is of size $O(n)$ to show that adding a single clause is likely to cause unsatisfiability with constant probability. As satisfying assignments are easy to guess and proofs of unsatisfiability are likely to be short, random 1-in-3-SAT problems are unlikely to be hard to solve. Since there is no rapid jump in problem hardness, it is hard to be sure where the 1-in-2+p-SAT transition shifts from a smooth 1-in-2-SAT like transition to a sharp 1-in-3-SAT like transition. Our results suggest that this occurs in the interval $0.3 < p < 0.6$. As with 2+p-COL, the transition appears to have both smooth and sharp regions when p is small.

NAE SAT

Our final problem class is NAE SAT. In a NAE k-SAT problem, each clause specifies that k literals cannot all take the same truth value (i.e. they are Not All Equal). Like k-SAT, this problem class is NP-complete for $k \geq 3$ but is polynomial for k=2. Random NAE 3-SAT has a sharp threshold in the interval $1.514 \leq l/n \leq 2.215$ (Achlioptas *et al.* 2001a). Experimental results put the transition at $l/n \approx 2.1$.

To interpolate smoothly from P to NP, we introduce the random NAE 2+p-SAT problem, with a fraction $(1 - p)$ of NAE 2-SAT clauses and a fraction p of NAE 3-SAT clauses. For any fixed $p > 0$, NAE 2+p-SAT is NP-complete. As with 2+p-COL, the transition appears to go from smooth (at $p = 0$) to sharp (at $p = 1$) and has both smooth and sharp regions for intermediate values of p. We again define a parameter γ_{2+p} identifying the end of the phase transition; this is the smallest clause to variable ratio at which 0% of problems are

satisfiable. Like 2+p-COL,

$$\gamma_2 \leq \gamma_{2+p} \leq \min(\gamma_3, \frac{\gamma_2}{1 - p})$$

In Figure 7, we have estimated experimentally the location of γ_{2+p}. The upper bound (which looks just at the NAE 2-SAT subproblem) appears to be tight for a large range of p. The polynomial NAE 2-SAT subproblem appears to determine satisfiability for p up to around 0.8. Not surprisingly, the search cost only appears to go from polynomial to exponential for $p \geq 0.8$.

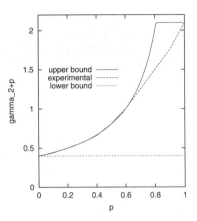

Figure 7: The location of the end of the NAE 2+p-SAT phase transition, γ_{2+p} (y-axis) against p (x-axis) for $p = 0$ to 1 in steps of 1/10.

A NAE 3-SAT clause on the literals a, b and c can be represented by the 3-SAT clauses $a \vee b \vee c$ and $\neg a \vee \neg b \vee \neg c$. We can therefore encode a NAE 3-SAT problem into 3-SAT by doubling the number of clauses (but keeping the number of variables constant). Achlioptas et al. observe that it would be *"truly remarkable"* if the random NAE 3-SAT phase transition occured at a clause to variable ratio half that of random 3-SAT since this encoding introduces significant correlations between the clauses (Achlioptas *et al.* 2001a). However, their experimental results put the random NAE 3-SAT phase transition at $l/n \approx 2.1$, which is tantalisingly close to half the 4.3 value believed to hold for random 3-SAT. To look at this issue in more detail, we introduce the NAE2SAT problem, with a fraction $(1 - p)$ of NAE 3-SAT clauses and a fraction p of 3-SAT clauses.

If we ignore correlations between clauses, each NAE 3-SAT clause is twice as constraining as a 3-SAT clause. Hence $(1 - p)l$ NAE 3-SAT clauses and pl 3-SAT clauses should behave like $2(1 - p)l + pl$ 3-SAT clauses. That is, $(2 - p)l$ 3-SAT clauses. The "effective" clause to variable ratio (in terms of 3-SAT clauses) is thus $(2 - p)l/n$. To test this idea, Figure 8 plots the probability of satisfiability against $(2 - p)l/n$. Very surprisingly, the phase transition occurs around an "effective" 3-SAT clause to variable ratio of 4.3. It appears that correlations between the NAE 3-SAT clauses can be almost completely ignored. To steal Achlioptas et al.'s words, this is "truly remarkable". NAE 3-SAT behaves like 3-SAT at twice the clause to variable ratio.

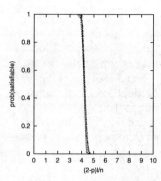 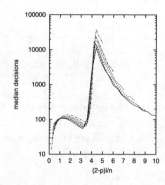

Figure 8: Probability that a NAE2SAT problem is satisfiable (left graph y-axis) and median search cost to solve a NAE2SAT problem (right graph, y-axis) against $(2-p)l/n$ (x-axes) for $n = 200$ and $p = 0, 0.2, 0.4, 0.6, 0.8$ and 1.

Conclusions

We have studied in detail the interface between P and NP by means of five new problem classes: 2+p-COL, XOR2SAT, HORN2SAT, NAE 2+p-SAT and 1-in-2+p-SAT. These problems smoothly interpolate between P and NP. In many cases, the polynomial subproblem dominates the problem's satisfiability and the search complexity up to some $p_c > 0$. For example, 2+p-COL behaves like the embedded polynomial 2-COL subproblem up to $p \approx 0.8$. Similarly, NAE 2+p-SAT behaves like the embedded polynomial NAE 2-SAT subproblem also up to $p \approx 0.8$. However, this is not always the case. In particular, in the XOR2SAT problem, both the 3-SAT clauses and the polynomial XOR 3-SAT clauses appear to contribute to the problem's satisfiability for all $p > 0$.

What important lessons can be learnt from this study? First, we can have transitions with both smooth and sharp regions. Problems like 2+p-COL and NAE 2+p-SAT let us study in detail how transitions sharpen and the large impact this has on search cost. Second, whilst the polynomial 2-SAT subproblem dominates 2+p-SAT up to $p = 2/5$, there are problems like XOR2SAT in which the polynomial subproblem does not dominate even though it is more tightly constraining than 2-SAT. Understanding this phenomenon is likely to bring fresh insight into problem hardness. Third, problem classes like these can help us understand algorithm behavior. For instance, we can view Brelaz's 3-coloring algorithm as searching trajectories in the 2+p-COL phase space. And finally, given the insights gained from studying the interface between P and NP, it is may be worth looking at the interface between other complexities classes. For example, we might study the interface between NP and PSpace.

Acknowledgements

This research was supported in full by an EPSRC advanced research fellowship. The author wishes to thank the members of the APES research group, as well as Carla Gomes, Bart Selman, and Christian Bessiere.

References

Achlioptas, D.; Chtcherba, A.; Istrate, G.; and Moore, C. 2001a. The phase transition in 1-in-k SAT and NAE SAT. In *Proc. of 12th Annual ACM-SIAM Symp. on Discrete Algorithms (SODA'01)*, 719–720.

Achlioptas, D.; Kirousis, L.; Kranakis, E.; and Krizanc, D. 2001b. Rigorous results for (2+p)-SAT. *Theoretical Computer Science* 265(1-2):109–129.

Achlioptas, D. 1999. *Threshold phenomena in random graph colouring and satisfiability*. Ph.D. Dissertation, Dept. of CS, University of Toronto.

Brelaz, D. 1979. New methods to color the vertices of a graph. *Communications of ACM* 22:251–256.

Cheeseman, P.; Kanefsky, B.; and Taylor, W. 1991. Where the really hard problems are. In *Proc. of 12th IJCAI*, 331–337.

Chvatal, V., and Reed, B. 1992. Mick gets some (the odds are on his side). In *Proc. of 33rd Annual Symp. on Foundations of Computer Science*, 620–627. IEEE.

Cocco, S., and Monasson, R. 2001. Trajectories in phase diagrams, growth processes and computational complexity: how search algorithms solve the 3-satisfiability problem. *Phys. Rev. Letters* 86(8):1654–1657.

Creognou, N.; Daude, H.; and Dubois, O. 2001. Approximating the satisfiability threshold for random k-XOR-formulas. Tech. Report LATP/UMR6632 01-17, Lab. d'Informatique Fondamentale de Marseille.

Franz, S.; Leone, M.; Ricci-Tersenghi, F.; and Zecchina, R. 2001. Exact solutions for diluted spin glasses and optimization problems. *Phys. Rev. Letters* 87(12):127209.

Goerdt, A. 1992. A theshold for unsatisfiability. In Havel, I., and Koubek, V., eds., *Mathematical Foundations of Computer Science*, LNCS. 264–274.

Gomes, C., and Selman, B. 1997. Problem structure in the presence of perturbations. In *Proc. of 14th National Conference on AI*, 221–226.

Istrate, G. 2000. Dimension-dependent behavior in the satisfability of random k-Horn formulae. Tech. report, Center for Nonlinear Studies, Los Alamos National Lab. Available from http://xxx.lanl.gov/ as cs.DS/0007029.

Mitchell, D.; Selman, B.; and Levesque, H. 1992. Hard and Easy Distributions of SAT Problems. In *Proc. of 10th National Conference on AI*, 459–465.

Monasson, R.; Zecchina, R.; Kirkpatrick, S.; Selman, B.; and Troyansky, L. 1998. Determining computational complexity for characteristic 'phase transitions'. *Nature* 400:133–137.

Monasson, R.; Zecchina, R.; Kirkpatrick, S.; Selman, B.; and Troyansky, L. 1999. 2+p SAT: Relation of typical-case complexity to the nature of the phase transition. *Random Structures and Algorithms* 15(3-4):414–435.

Schaeffer, T. 1978. The complexity of satisfiability problems. In *Proc. of 10th ACM Symp. on Theory of Computation*, 216–226.

Singer, J.; Gent, I.; and Smaill, A. 2000. Local search on random 2+p-SAT. In *Proc. of 14th ECAI*.

Walsh, T. 1999. Search in a small world. In *Proc. of 16th IJCAI*.

AAAI-02
Edmonton/Alberta
IAAI-02

Search

Scheduling Contract Algorithms on Multiple Processors

Daniel S. Bernstein, Theodore J. Perkins,
Shlomo Zilberstein
Department of Computer Science
University of Massachusetts
Amherst, MA 01003
{bern,perkins,shlomo}@cs.umass.edu

Lev Finkelstein
Computer Science Department
Technion—Israel Institute of Technology
Haifa 32000, Israel
lev@cs.technion.ac.il

Abstract

Anytime algorithms offer a tradeoff between computation time and the quality of the result returned. They can be divided into two classes: contract algorithms, for which the total run time must be specified in advance, and interruptible algorithms, which can be queried at any time for a solution. An interruptible algorithm can be constructed from a contract algorithm by repeatedly activating the contract algorithm with increasing run times. The acceleration ratio of a run-time schedule is a worst-case measure of how inefficient the constructed interruptible algorithm is compared to the contract algorithm. The smallest acceleration ratio achievable on a single processor is known. Using multiple processors, smaller acceleration ratios are possible. In this paper, we provide a schedule for m processors and prove that it is optimal for all m. Our results provide general guidelines for the use of parallel processors in the design of real-time systems.

Introduction

The complex reasoning problems faced by both natural and artificial agents can rarely be solved exactly in time for the solution to be useful. Game-playing programs, trading/e-commerce agents, information retrieval systems, and medical diagnosis systems must all act under time pressure from their environments, from other agents, or from users with limited patience. A successful AI system must be able to use whatever time is available for deliberation to maximum advantage, and not miss opportunities or incur costs or disfavor through slow action.

Algorithms that produce solutions of different qualities depending on available computation time are called *anytime* algorithms (Horvitz 1987; Dean & Boddy 1988; Russell & Wefald 1991). A distinction can be made between two types of anytime algorithms. *Interruptible* algorithms, once started, can be interrupted at any time and queried for a solution. For example, local search approaches to optimization such as hill climbing and simulated annealing are interruptible algorithms. *Contract* algorithms need to be given the query time as input. These algorithms set internal parameters so that they produce a solution before the query time.

A contract algorithm need not produce any solution before the query time arrives, and may have trouble utilizing spare time if it finds a solution quickly or if the query time is delayed. All other things being equal, interruptible algorithms are more convenient to use and more widely applicable than contract algorithms. But contract algorithms are often more intuitive to design, and typically use simpler data structures and control structures, making them easier to implement and maintain.

An interruptible algorithm can be formed from a contract algorithm by running a sequence of contracts of increasing lengths, returning the last solution produced when an interruption occurs. This sequencing problem has been solved informally in various domains. For example, Dechter and Rish (1998) develop the mini-bucket algorithm for approximate automated reasoning tasks, such as Bayesian inference. Their algorithm allows the user to specify bounds on the number of variables in any dependency that arises during execution (larger bounds lead to better solutions, at the expense of computation time), and they propose a method for scheduling a sequence of bounds so that solutions of improving quality are produced over time. In a similar vein, Munos and Moore (1999) propose various heuristics for incrementally refining discretizations of continuous-state optimal control problems. The incremental refinements produce a sequence of finite-state approximations which are increasingly complex to solve, but which provide solutions of increasing quality for the original, continuous-state problem.

We are interested in developing general contract schedules and providing formal justification for their use. In the case of serial execution of contracts, Russell and Zilberstein (1991) suggest the following sequence of contract lengths: $1, 2, 4, 8, \ldots$ They show that for any interruption time $t > 1$, the last contract completed is always of length at least $t/4$. This factor of four is the *acceleration ratio* of the schedule, a worst-case measure of the loss due to the transformation from contract algorithm to interruptible algorithm. Zilberstein, Charpillet, and Chassaing (1999) show that no sequence of contracts on a single processor has an acceleration ratio of less than four. Only with multiple processors can a more efficient transformation be made.

In this paper, we propose a simple strategy for producing an interruptible algorithm by scheduling a contract algorithm on m processors in parallel. We analyze the strategy, deriving an explicit formula for its acceleration ratio as a function of m. Furthermore, we show that no schedule yields a better acceleration ratio for any m, thus the strategy is optimal. These results provide general guidelines for the use of parallel processors in the design of real-time systems. Finally, we discuss extensions to this work and a connection to a formally similar problem involving multiple robots searching multiple rays for a goal.

Scheduling a Contract Algorithm

An anytime algorithm A, when applied to an optimization problem instance for time t, produces a solution of some real-valued quality $Q_A(t)$. Q_A is called A's *performance profile* on the instance. Performance profiles are defined for both interruptible and contract algorithms. If A is interruptible, then $Q_A(t)$ is the quality of the solution returned by A upon interruption at time t. If A is contract, then $Q_A(t)$ is the quality of the solution returned by A after time t, given that t was specified *in advance*. In general, one does not know an algorithm's performance profile on a problem instance. Nevertheless the concept of a performance profile is useful in reasoning about anytime algorithms. We assume that the performance profile of an anytime algorithm on any problem instance is defined for all $t \geq 0$ and is a nondecreasing function of t.

An interruptible algorithm can be constructed from a contract algorithm by scheduling a sequence of contracts on m processors in parallel. A schedule is a function $X : \{1, \ldots, m\} \times \mathbb{N} \to \mathbb{R}$, where $X(i, j)$ is the length of the jth contract run on processor i. We assume, without loss of generality, that $X(1,1) = 1$ and that $X(i,j) \geq 1$ for all i and j.

We use B to denote the interruptible algorithm formed from the contract algorithm A and schedule X. When B is interrupted, it returns the best solution found by any of the contracts that have completed. Since we assume performance profiles are nondecreasing, this is equivalent to returning the solution of the longest contract that has completed. This is illustrated in Figure 1.

The interruptible algorithm's performance profile, Q_B, depends on A's profile and the schedule X. When B is interrupted, it has spent some time running contracts that are superseded by later results. Also, when contracts are interrupted, the time spent on them does not contribute to the final solution. In general, $Q_B(t) \leq Q_A(t)$, and often the inequality is strict.

We wish to find the schedule that is optimal for any given number of processors, with no assumptions about the query time or the contract algorithm's performance profile. The metric that we use to compare schedules is the *acceleration ratio*, which is a measure similar to the competitive ratio for on-line algorithms (Sleator & Tarjan 1985). The acceleration ratio tells us how much faster the interruptible algorithm would need to run in order to ensure the same quality as the contract algorithm for any interruption time.

Before formally defining acceleration ratio, we establish a formula for B's performance profile in terms of A's performance profile and the schedule X. We define the total time

spent by processor i executing its first j contracts as

$$G_X(i, j) = \sum_{k=1}^{j} X(i, k).$$

For all times t, we define a function that specifies which contracts finish before t by

$$\Phi_X(t) = \{(i, j) | G_X(i, j) < t\}.$$

We take the view that when a contract completes at time t, its solution is available to be returned upon interruption at any time $\tau > t$. The length of the longest contract to complete before time t is

$$L_X(t) = \begin{cases} \max_{(i,j) \in \Phi_X(t)} X(i, j) & \text{if } \Phi_X(t) \neq \emptyset \\ 0 & \text{if } \Phi_X(t) = \emptyset \end{cases}.$$

Thus the performance profile for the interruptible algorithm B is

$$Q_B(t) = Q_A(L_X(t)).$$

We can now give a precise definition of acceleration ratio.

Definition 1 *The* acceleration ratio, $R(X)$, *for a given schedule X on m processors is the smallest constant r for which $Q_B(t) \geq Q_A(t/r)$ for all $t > 1$ and any contract algorithm A.*

Although acceleration ratio is defined in terms of a property of solution quality, the following lemma allows us to formulate it without reference to Q.

Lemma 1 *For all X, $R(X) = \sup_{t>1} t/L_X(t)$.*

Proof: From the definitions given above, we have $Q_B(t) = Q_A(L_X(t)) \geq Q_A(t/R(X))$ for all $t > 1$. Since this holds for any algorithm A, we can suppose an algorithm A with performance profile $Q_A(t) = t$. Thus $L_X(t) \geq t/R(X) \Rightarrow R(X) \geq t/L_X(t)$ for all $t > 1$. This implies $R(X) \geq \sup_{t>1} t/L_X(t)$. To show that equality holds, assume the contrary and derive a contradiction with the fact that $R(X)$ is defined as the smallest constant enforcing the inequality between Q_B and Q_A. $\square$

Intuitively, the worst time to interrupt a schedule is just before a contract ends, because the contract time has been spent, but the solution is not yet available. The following lemma formalizes this notion and consequently enables us to consider only finishing times from here on.

Lemma 2 *For all X,*

$$\sup_{t>1} \frac{t}{L_X(t)} = \sup_{(i,j) \neq (1,1)} \frac{G_X(i, j)}{L_X(G_X(i, j))}.$$

Proof: $L_X(t)$ is left-continuous everywhere and piecewise constant, with the pieces delimited by the time points $G_X(i, j)$. For $t > 1$, $t/L_X(t)$ is left-continuous and piecewise linear and increasing. Thus, the local maxima of $t/L_X(t)$ occur at the points $G_X(i, j)$, $(i, j) \neq (1, 1)$; no other times may play a role in the supremum. $\square$

We define the minimal acceleration ratio for m processors to be

$$R_m^* = \inf_X R(X).$$

Zilberstein, Charpillet, and Chassaing (1999) prove that $R_1^* = 4$. In the following sections, we derive an expression for R_m^* for general m and provide a schedule that achieves this ratio.

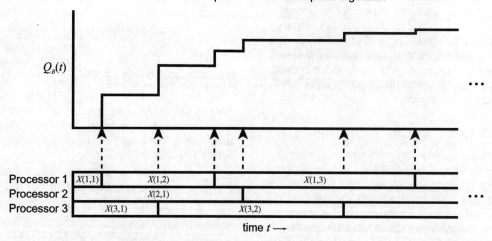

Figure 1: Constructing an interruptible algorithm by scheduling a contract algorithm on three processors.

An Exponential Schedule

A simple approach to scheduling a contract algorithm is to have the contract lengths increase exponentially. Russell and Zilberstein (1991) study the one-processor schedule $X(1, j) = 2^{j-1}$. We consider a generalization of this schedule to m processors in which contracts are assigned to processors in a round-robin fashion, with each contract being $(m + 1)^{1/m}$ times longer than the previous one. Formally, the schedule is expressed as $E(i, j) = (m + 1)^{(i-1+m(j-1))/m}$.

Theorem 1 $R(E) = \frac{(m+1)^{\frac{m+1}{m}}}{m}$.

Proof: It is straightforward to show that for $(i, j) \neq (1, 1)$

$$L_E(G_E(i, j)) = \begin{cases} E(i-1, j) & \text{if } i \neq 1 \\ E(m, j-1) & \text{if } i = 1 \end{cases}.$$

Also, the following is true for all $(i, j) \neq (1, 1)$:

$$
\begin{aligned}
G_E(i, j) &= \sum_{k=1}^{j} E(i, k) \\
&= \sum_{k=1}^{j} (m + 1)^{\frac{i-1+m(k-1)}{m}} \\
&= (m + 1)^{\frac{i-1-m}{m}} \sum_{k=1}^{j} (m + 1)^{k} \\
&= (m + 1)^{\frac{i-1-m}{m}} \left(\frac{(m+1)^{j+1} - (m+1)}{m} \right).
\end{aligned}
$$

So, for all i, j such that $i \neq 1$,

$$
\begin{aligned}
\frac{G_E(i, j)}{L_E(G_E(i, j))} &= \frac{G_E(i, j)}{E(i-1, j)} \\
&= \frac{(m+1)^{\frac{i-1+mj}{m}}}{m(m+1)^{\frac{i-2+mj-m}{m}}} - \frac{(m+1)^{\frac{i-1}{m}}}{m(m+1)^{\frac{i-2+mj-m}{m}}} \\
&= \frac{(m+1)^{\frac{m+1}{m}}}{m} - \frac{(m+1)^{\frac{m-mj+1}{m}}}{m},
\end{aligned}
$$

and for all i, j such that $i = 1$ and $j \neq 1$,

$$
\begin{aligned}
\frac{G_E(i, j)}{L_E(G_E(i, j))} &= \frac{G_E(i, j)}{E(m, j-1)} \\
&= \frac{(m+1)^{j}}{m(m+1)^{\frac{mj-m-1}{m}}} - \frac{1}{m(m+1)^{\frac{mj-m-1}{m}}} \\
&= \frac{(m+1)^{\frac{m+1}{m}}}{m} - \frac{(m+1)^{\frac{m-mj+1}{m}}}{m}.
\end{aligned}
$$

We see that the same expression is derived in each case. Note also that the expression is independent of i and increases with j. Thus,

$$
\begin{aligned}
R(E) &= \sup_{(i,j) \neq (1,1)} \frac{G_E(i, j)}{L_E(G_E(i, j))} \\
&= \lim_{j \to \infty} \frac{(m+1)^{\frac{m+1}{m}}}{m} - \frac{(m+1)^{\frac{m-mj+1}{m}}}{m} \\
&= \frac{(m+1)^{\frac{m+1}{m}}}{m}.
\end{aligned}
$$

$\square$

Optimality of the Exponential Schedule

In this section, we show that the exponential schedule is optimal by proving that no schedule can achieve a smaller acceleration ratio. It is convenient to index contracts by their relative finishing times. The following function counts how many contracts finish no later than the jth contract on the ith processor finishes. For a schedule X, let

$$\Psi_X(i, j) = |\{(i', j')|G_X(i', j') \leq G_X(i, j)\}|.$$

We assume without loss of generality that no two contracts finish at exactly the same time. It is straightforward to show that any schedule that doesn't satisfy this condition is dominated by a schedule that does. This assumption guarantees that Ψ_X is one-to-one; it is also onto and thus a bijection. We refer to $\Psi_X(i, j)$ as the *global index* of the jth contract run on processor i.

We introduce a contract length function that takes as input a global index. For all i, j, let

$$Y_X(\Psi_X(i,j)) = X(i,j).$$

We further define a finishing-time function that takes as input a global index:

$$H_X(\Psi_X(i,j)) = G_X(i,j).$$

Without loss of generality, we can assume that $Y_X(k) < Y_X(k+1)$ for all $k \geq 1$. Any schedule that doesn't have this property is dominated by one that does.

Lemma 3 *For all X and all $k \geq 1$,*

$$H_X(k+1) \leq R(X)Y_X(k).$$

Proof: This follows directly from the assumption above and the definition of acceleration ratio. $\square$

Finally, we define a function to represent the sum of the lengths of all the contracts finishing no later than contract k finishes:

$$H_X'(k) = \sum_{l=1}^{k} Y_X(l).$$

The following lemma expresses a property of this function.

Lemma 4 *For all X and all $k \geq 1$,*

$$H_X'(k+m+1) \leq R(X)(H_X'(k+m) - H_X'(k)).$$

Proof: Consider the contract with global index $k+m+1$. We define the set S such that $s \in S$ if and only if s is the global index of the last contract on some processor to finish no later than contract $k+m+1$ finishes. It follows that $H_X'(k+m+1) = \sum_{s \in S} H_X(s)$. Note that S contains at most m distinct integers, each between 1 and $k+m+1$. Since H_X is increasing,

$$\sum_{s \in S} H_X(s) \leq \sum_{l=1}^{m} H_X(k+l+1).$$

Using Lemma 3, we get

$$
\begin{aligned}
\sum_{l=1}^{m} H_X(k+l+1) &\leq R(X) \sum_{l=1}^{m} Y_X(k+l) \\
&= R(X)\left(H_X'(k+m) - H_X'(k)\right).
\end{aligned}
$$

$\square$

Theorem 2 $R_m^* = \frac{(m+1)^{\frac{m+1}{m}}}{m}$.

Proof: Let us define $P(k) = H_X'(k+1)/H_X'(k)$ for all $k \geq 1$. From Lemma 4, we have

$$H_X'(k+m+1) \leq R(X)(H_X'(k+m) - H_X'(k)),$$

and thus

$$R(X)\left(1 - \frac{H_X'(k)}{H_X'(k+m)}\right) \geq \frac{H_X'(k+m+1)}{H_X'(k+m)},$$

so

$$R(X)\left(1 - \frac{1}{P(k)\cdots P(k+m-1)}\right) \geq P(k+m). \quad (1)$$

We let

$$P^*(k) = \max\{P(k), \ldots, P(k+m)\}.$$

There are two cases to consider. In the first case, there exists some $k' \geq 1$ such that $P^*(k') = P(k'+m)$. Then we have $P(k')\cdots P(k'+m-1) \leq P(k'+m)^m$, and

$$R(X)\left(1 - \frac{1}{P(k'+m)^m}\right) \geq P(k'+m).$$

Thus

$$R(X) \geq \frac{P(k'+m)^{m+1}}{P(k'+m)^m - 1}. \quad (2)$$

We are interested in how small $R(X)$ can be. Let $c = P(k'+m)$. Suppose we minimize the right-hand side with respect to the only free variable, c, over the region $c > 1$. Setting the derivative to zero, we find

$$
\begin{aligned}
\frac{d}{dc}\frac{c^{m+1}}{c^m - 1} &= \frac{(m+1)c^m}{c^m - 1} - \frac{c^{m+1}mc^{m-1}}{(c^m - 1)^2} = 0 \\
\Rightarrow \quad & (m+1)c^m(c^m - 1) - mc^{2m} = 0 \\
\Rightarrow \quad & c^{2m} - (m+1)c^m = 0.
\end{aligned}
$$

The only solution is $c = (m+1)^{1/m}$. At the boundaries $c = 1$ and $c = \infty$, the value goes to infinity, so this solution is the one and only minimum. Substituting into inequality (2), we find

$$R(X) \geq \frac{(m+1)^{\frac{m+1}{m}}}{(m+1)^{\frac{m}{m}} - 1} = \frac{(m+1)^{\frac{m+1}{m}}}{m}.$$

In the second case, we have $P^*(k) \neq P(k+m)$ for all $k \geq 1$. Thus

$$
\begin{aligned}
P^*&(k+1) \\
&= \max\{P(k+1), \ldots, P(k+m), P(k+m+1)\} \\
&= \max\{P(k+1), \ldots, P(k+m)\} \\
&\leq P^*(k),
\end{aligned}
$$

which means that the $P^*(k)$ form a nonincreasing sequence. Since $P^*(k) \geq 1$ for all k, the sequence must have a limit. We use d to denote this limit. By the definition of $P^*(k)$, it follows that $\limsup_{k\to\infty} P(k) = d$. Applying $\limsup_{k\to\infty}$ to both sides of inequality (1), we get

$$R(X)\left(1 - \frac{1}{\limsup_{k\to\infty} P(k)\cdots P(k+m-1)}\right)$$
$$\geq \limsup_{k\to\infty} P(k+m).$$

Thus

$$R(X)\left(1 - \frac{1}{d^m}\right) \geq d.$$

Using the same analysis as in the previous case, we have that

$$R(X) \geq \frac{(m+1)^{\frac{m+1}{m}}}{m}.$$

Combining this with Theorem 1, we get the desired result. $\square$

Discussion

We studied the problem of constructing an interruptible algorithm by scheduling a contract algorithm to run on multiple processors. Our proposed schedule was shown to be optimal for any number of processors. As the number of processors increases, the optimal acceleration ratio approaches one and thus the distinction between contract and interruptible algorithms becomes less important. These results provide insight into the role of parallelism in the design of real-time systems.

In this work, we assumed no knowledge of the deadline or of the contract algorithm's performance profile. With problem-specific knowledge, more sophisticated scheduling strategies become appropriate. Zilberstein, Charpillet, and Chassaing (1999) consider the case where the performance profile is known and the deadline is drawn from a known distribution. In this case, the problem of scheduling a contract algorithm on a single processor to maximize the expected quality of results at the deadline can be framed as a Markov decision process. It remains to extend this work to the multiple processor case.

Another avenue for future research is to extend the contract algorithm model to include a broader class of algorithms. A number of algorithms have time complexity that scales with the values of input parameters, but in a fairly unpredictable way. For example, the worst-case time complexity of depth-bounded search scales with the depth bound and the maximum branching factor. However, the actual search time can be much less than the upper bound. Also, some contract-like algorithms are able to save information from one instantiation and use the information to accelerate the next instantiation. Finally, it may be interesting to consider contract algorithms that are themselves parallelizable, rather than just scheduling inherently sequential contracts on different processors. One challenge is to produce a contract algorithm model that takes these characteristics into account while still allowing for insightful analysis.

Finally, we note that the results presented in this paper may shed light on an abstract robotics problem involving multiple robots searching for a goal. In this problem, m robots start at the intersection of $m + 1$ rays and move along the rays until the goal is found. An optimal search strategy is defined to be one that minimizes the *competitive ratio*, which is the worst-case ratio of the time spent searching to the time that would have been spent if the goal location was known initially. The problem with $m = 1$ is considered in (Baeza-Yates, Culberson, & Rawlins 1993), where it is shown that the optimal competitive ratio is 9. It turns out that this problem is nearly identical to that of scheduling contracts on a single processor (Zilberstein, Charpillet, & Chassaing 1999). A contract schedule corresponds to a sequence of search extents for the robot, where a search extent is the distance the robot goes out on a ray before returning to the origin. If we let r denote the acceleration ratio for a schedule, then $1 + 2r$ is the competitive ratio for the corresponding sequence of search extents. In the multiprocessor case, each processor corresponds to a different robot. We conjecture that the same relationship between acceleration ratio and competitive ratio holds in this case.

Acknowledgments

We thank François Charpillet and Philippe Chassaing for fruitful discussions of this work. Support was provided in part by the National Science Foundation under grants ECS-0070102, ECS-9980062, INT-9612092, and IIS-9907331, and by NASA under grants NAG-2-1394 and NAG-2-1463. Daniel Bernstein was supported by a NASA GSRP Fellowship. Any opinions, findings, and conclusions or recommendations expressed in this material are those of the authors and do not reflect the views of the NSF or NASA.

References

Baeza-Yates, R.; Culberson, J.; and Rawlins, G. 1993. Searching in the plane. *Information and Computation* 106:234–252.

Dean, T., and Boddy, M. 1988. An analysis of time-dependent planning. In *Proceedings of the Seventh National Conference on Artificial Intelligence*.

Dechter, R., and Rish, I. 1998. Mini-buckets: a general scheme for approximating inference. Technical report, Department of Information and Computer Science, University of California, Irvine.

Horvitz, E. 1987. Reasoning about beliefs and actions under computational resource constraints. In *Workshop on Uncertainty in Artificial Intelligence*.

Munos, R., and Moore, A. 1999. Variable resolution discretization for high-accuracy solutions of optimal control problems. In *Proceedings of the Sixteenth International Joint Conference on Artificial Intelligence*.

Russell, S., and Wefald, E. H. 1991. *Do the Right Thing: Studies in Limited Rationality*. Cambridge, MA: MIT Press.

Russell, S. J., and Zilberstein, S. 1991. Composing real-time systems. In *Proceedings of the Twelfth International Joint Conference on Artificial Intelligence*.

Sleator, D. D., and Tarjan, R. E. 1985. Amortized efficiency of list update and paging rules. *Communications of the ACM* 28:202–208.

Zilberstein, S.; Charpillet, F.; and Chassaing, P. 1999. Real-time problem-solving with contract algorithms. In *Proceedings of the Sixteenth International Joint Conference on Artificial Intelligence*.

Searching for Backbones and Fat:
A Limit-Crossing Approach with Applications

Sharlee Climer and Weixiong Zhang

Computer Science Department
Washington University
St. Louis, MO 63130
Email: {sclimer,zhang}@cs.wustl.edu

Abstract

Backbone variables are the elements that are common to all optimal solutions of a problem instance. We call variables that are absent from every optimal solution *fat* variables. Identification of backbone and fat variables is a valuable asset when attempting to solve complex problems. In this paper, we demonstrate a method for identifying backbones and fat. Our method is based on an intuitive concept, which we refer to as *limit crossing*. Limit crossing occurs when we force the lower bound of a graph problem to exceed the upper bound by applying the lower-bound function to a constrained version of the graph. A desirable feature of this procedure is that it uses approximation functions to derive exact information about optimal solutions. In this paper, we prove the validity of the limit-crossing concept as well as other related properties. Then we exploit limit crossing and devise a pre-processing tool for discovering backbone and fat arcs for various instances of the Asymmetric Traveling Salesman Problem (ATSP). Our experimental results demonstrate the power of the limit-crossing method. We compare our pre-processor with the Carpaneto, Dell'Amico, and Toth pre-processor for several different classes of ATSP instances and reveal dramatic performance improvements.

Introduction

The *backbone* of a problem instance is referred to as the set of variables that are common to all optimal solutions for the given instance. These variables are critically constrained as the elimination of any one of them will negate any possibility of finding any optimal solution. Currently, there is a significant amount of research activity in finding backbone variables (Schneider *et al.* 1996) and correlating the size of the backbone with problem hardness and phase transitions (Monasson *et al.* 1999; Slaney & Walsh 2001; Zhang 2001; 2002).

In this paper, we develop and demonstrate a method for searching backbone variables as well as variables of the opposite type - those that are not part of any optimal solution. We will call this set of variables the *fat* of the problem instance, as we would like to trim away these variables and derive a sparser problem instance that still retains all of the variables that are part of any optimal solution. When fat

variables are found, we permanently delete them so as to reduce the size of the problem to be solved.

Our technique for discovering backbones and fat is a product of a general graph reduction technique which we call *limit crossing*. In this paper, we formulate the concept of limit crossing formally and prove its validity along with other related properties. Then we exploit limit crossing and devise a mechanism for discovering backbone and fat arcs for various instances of the Asymmetric Traveling Salesman Problem (ATSP). (The ATSP is the NP-hard problem of finding a minimum-cost complete tour for a set of cities in which the cost from city i to city j may not be the same as the cost from city j to city i.)

Limit crossing is a general procedure that is based on the concept of inclusion and exclusion principle from the field of combinatorics. It can be used on graph problems that have lower-bound and upper-bound functions. The essence of the concept is to make the lower-bound value exceed the upper-bound value by applying the lower-bound function to a constrained version of the graph. The branch-and-bound method was built on top of this concept.

To use limit crossing, we first find an upper bound for a problem instance by finding a feasible, though not necessarily optimal, solution. Then we exclude a set of variables from the graph and apply a lower-bound function to the new graph. If this lower bound is greater than the original upper bound, we realize that all optimal solutions for this problem instance must include at least one of the variables from the excluded set. A benefit of limit crossing is that we can use approximation techniques to extract exact information about optimal solutions.

We use limit crossing to identify backbone and fat variables. These identifications allow us to reduce the problem graph and solve the instance more quickly. Reducing the problem size is of great value for problems with high complexities, such as the ATSP. The next section describes examples of some existing graph reduction techniques. Then we formalize limit crossing, prove its validity, and present its properties. In the following section, we use limit crossing to reduce ATSP instances. The results of our experiment are then presented. Finally, in the last section, we conclude and plan for the future.

Previous and Related Work

The limit-crossing method is based on an intuitive idea, and as such, has appeared in a variety of forms in previous work. In this section we briefly describe several examples of related work in the realm of the Traveling Salesman Problem (TSP).

Our first example is a hypothetical algorithm described by Papadimitriou in (Papadimitriou 1995), where multiple decision problems are solved in order to construct an optimal solution. In this algorithm, the cost C of an optimal tour is found for a TSP instance by solving a series of decision problems in a binary search of the possible tour cost values. Then the arcs that comprise this optimal tour are discovered by considering each arc (i, j) in the entire graph one at a time. The cost of (i, j) is set to $C + 1$ and it is determined if the modified graph has a tour with a cost of C or less. If so, then this arc is not a necessary part of the optimal solution and its cost may be left equal to $C+1$. If there is no tour with a cost less than or equal to C, then (i, j) is part of the optimal tour and its cost must be returned to the original value. After all of the arcs are considered, the ones with values less than $C + 1$ comprise the optimal tour. In this case, the graph is completely reduced. The only arcs that remain are part of the optimal solution. (This algorithm assumes that there is only one optimal solution.) It is an example of the limit-crossing concept in which the excluded set of arcs contains only one element and the upper- and lower-bound functions are exact. However, the implementation of this hypothetical algorithm would not be practical.

Following is a brief description of three examples of pre-processing tools for graph reduction, or *sparsification*, techniques that have been developed to aid the solution of ATSP problem instances.

In (Miller & Pekny 1991), Miller and Pekny present a modified version of a popular branch-and-bound method for solving large ATSP instances. In a pre-processing step, all of the arcs with cost greater than a specified threshold are eliminated from the graph. After an optimal solution is found for the sparse graph, it is checked for optimality for the original dense graph. If it is not optimal, the threshold is increased and the entire process is repeated. This procedure continues until an optimal solution for the original graph is found. Although the entire process may have to be repeated a number of times, the total time for searching several sparse graphs for optimal solutions may be less than the time required to search a dense graph only once.

Both of the other sparsification examples are due to Carpaneto, Dell'Amico, and Toth (Carpaneto, Dell'Amico, & Toth 1995). In their paper, two variations of a reduction procedure are presented as pre-processing tools for the previously mentioned branch-and-bound method for optimally solving large ATSP instances. The reduction procedure is essentially a limit-crossing technique, however, only one of the variants yields exact information. This variant first finds an upper bound for the problem instance. We use this variant for comparisons with our pre-processor in the Experimental Results section. The other variant calculates an "artificial" upper bound by multiplying the lower-bound value by a predetermined value α. For both variants, the lower bound is found by applying the Assignment Problem (AP) method to the graph (Martello & Toth 1987). (The AP method involves finding a minimum-cost matching on a bipartite graph constructed by including all of the arcs and two nodes for each city where one node is used for the tail of all its outgoing arcs, and one is used for the head of all its incoming arcs.)

In both variations of the algorithm a *reduced cost* is calculated for each arc (i, j) by subtracting the value of its *dual variables* (derived from the AP) from the original cost of the arc. From sensitivity analysis in linear programming, the reduced cost is a lower bound on the increase of the value of the AP solution if the arc were forced to be included in the solution. Thus if the reduced cost of (i, j) is greater than or equal to the difference between the upper and lower bounds, inclusion of (i, j) in a solution will necessarily lead to a tour cost that is at least as large as the upper bound that is already derived. Therefore, the arc is eliminated from the graph.

This algorithm searches for limit crossing when a single arc (i, j) is forced to be included. It is important to observe that forcing the inclusion of an arc (i, j) is the same as forcing the exclusion of all other arcs with tail i or head j. Therefore, this algorithm is an example of limit crossing.

If there is only one optimal solution for the problem instance, this sparsification is exact for the first variant. (If there is more than one optimal solution, some arcs from optimal solutions may be excluded.) When an artificial upper bound is used, the procedure may need to be repeated a number of times, as in the Miller and Pekny algorithm. After the branch-and-bound search is completed, the solution is compared with the artificial upper bound. If it is greater than the artificial upper bound, then α is increased and the entire procedure is repeated. The program terminates when the solution for the sparse graph is less than or equal to the artificial upper bound.

The essential idea of limit crossing is very general and appears in a great number of loosely related methods. Following is an example of a technique that differs from our use of limit crossing, yet it embodies the fundamental limit crossing concept.

Our example is the previously mentioned depth-first branch-and-bound search method used to find optimal or approximate solutions for the ATSP (Carpaneto, Dell'Amico, & Toth 1995; Miller & Pekny 1991; Zhang 1993). We use this algorithm to optimally solve ATSP instances in the Experimental Results section. The AP method is used for the lower-bound function and a current upper bound is maintained throughout the search. For each node in the search tree, there are two corresponding sets of arcs. One set of arcs is forced to be included in a constrained AP solution, the other set is forced to be excluded. The sets are empty for the root node. Furthermore, the sets for each child node are supersets of their parent's sets. Whenever the value of the AP solution is greater than or equal to the upper bound, it is clear that the given sets of included / excluded arcs cannot lead to a solution that is better than the current upper bound. Since the descendents of this node will have supersets of these sets, they cannot yield better solutions either. Therefore, the node is pruned. This depth-first search uses limit crossing on the search space, as opposed to our use on the problem graph, and it eliminates nodes in the search tree, rather than arcs in the original problem graph.

Limit Crossing Formalized

In this section, we prove the validity of limit crossing and present two related properties. Let us consider a directed graph $G = (V, A)$ with vertex set $V = \{1, \ldots, n\}$, arc set $A = \{(i, j) \mid i, j = 1, \ldots, n\}$, and cost matrix $c_{n \times n}$ such that, for all $i, j \in V$, c_{ij} is the cost associated with arc (i, j) and $c_{ij} \geq 0$. Assume that we can exclude an arc (i, j) from G by setting c_{ij} to ∞, and that this exclusion has no effect on other values in the cost matrix.

Many graph problems can be defined as minimizing (or maximizing) functions subject to specific constraints. Without loss of generality, let us consider a minimizing function F operating on graph G as follows:

$$F(G) = min \left(\sum_{i \in V} \sum_{j \in V} c_{ij} x_{ij} \right) \qquad (1)$$

$$x_{ij} \in \{0, 1\}, \; i, j \in V$$

subject to constraints $\{C_1, \ldots, C_m\}$.

Let O_G be a set of arcs representing an optimal solution of G i.e., $O_G = \{(i, j) \mid x_{ij} = 1\}$. Note that if $F(G)$ exists (if the constraints are satisfiable) then there exists at least one set of arcs O_G for graph G and $\sum_{(i,j) \in O_G} c_{ij} = F(G)$.

Theorem 1 *Let LB and UB, respectively, be any lower-bound and upper-bound functions, such that $LB(G) \leq F(G) \leq UB(G)$ for all directed graphs G for which $F(G)$ exists. If $S \subset A$, and $LB(G \setminus S) > UB(G)$, then every optimal solution O_G associated with $F(G)$ contains at least one arc s, such that $s \in S$.*

Proof By definition $F(G \setminus S) \geq LB(G \setminus S)$, by assumption $LB(G \setminus S) > UB(G)$, and by definition $UB(G) \geq F(G)$. Therefore,

$$F(G \setminus S) > F(G). \qquad (2)$$

Assume there exists a set of arcs O_G associated with $F(G)$ such that $O_G \cap S = \emptyset$. Since O_G and S are disjoint, O_G is a feasible solution for $G \setminus S$ and its associated cost is $\sum_{(i,j) \in O_G} c_{ij} = F(G)$. Now, since O_G is a feasible solution for $G \setminus S$ and $F(G \setminus S)$ is a minimizing function of $G \setminus S$, $F(G \setminus S) \leq F(G)$.

This results in a contradiction, as from (2), we have $F(G \setminus S) > F(G)$. Therefore, every optimal solution O_G associated with $F(G)$ contains at least one arc that is an element of S. $\square$

If S is composed of only one arc, then that arc is essential for all optimal solutions. This gives us the following corollary:

Corollary 2 *If $a \in A$ and $LB(G \setminus \{a\}) > UB(G)$, then a is part of the backbone of $F(G)$.*

Assume our lower-bound function LB is the same minimizing function as (1), with one or more of the constraints $C_1, \ldots, C_m$ relaxed. (A minimizing function with one or more constraints relaxed will necessarily yield values less than or equal to the values computed by the same minimizing function with all the constraints enforced.)

Let L_G be the set of arcs associated with this lower-bound function acting on G. Therefore, $LB(G) = \sum_{(i,j) \in L_G} c_{ij}$.

Theorem 3 *If $LB(G \setminus S) > UB(G)$, then there exists an $s \in S$ such that $s \in L_G$.*

The proof of this theorem is similar to the proof of theorem 1. This theorem provides information that is useful when selecting arcs to be included in set S. In order to make it possible for limits to cross, S must include at least one arc from the set associated with the lower-bound function acting on G.

Pushing Traveling Salesmen Across the Limits

In this section we apply the limit-crossing method to the ATSP. First we develop the mathematical tools we will use. Then our algorithm will be summarized and its complexity considered.

Given directed graph $G = (V, A)$ with vertex set $V = \{1, \ldots, n\}$, arc set $A = \{(i, j) \mid i, j = 1, \ldots, n\}$, and cost matrix $c_{n \times n}$ such that $c_{ij} \geq 0$ and $c_{ii} = \infty$, the ATSP can be defined as a constrained minimizing function TS as follows:

$$TS(G) = min \left(\sum_{i \in V} \sum_{j \in V} c_{ij} x_{ij} \right) \qquad (3)$$

subject to the following constraints:

$$x_{ij} \in \{0, 1\}, \; i, j \in V \qquad (4)$$

$$\sum_{i \in V} x_{ij} = 1, \; j \in V \qquad (5)$$

$$\sum_{j \in V} x_{ij} = 1, \; i \in V \qquad (6)$$

$$\sum_{i \in W} \sum_{j \in W} x_{ij} \leq |W| - 1, \; \forall \, W \subset V, \, W \neq \emptyset \qquad (7)$$

Let T_G be the set of arcs representing an optimal tour of G: $T_G = \{(i, j) \mid x_{ij} = 1\}$.

Assume there exists a lower-bound function LTS, such that $LTS(G) \leq TS(G)$ and an upper-bound function UTS, such that $UTS(G) \geq TS(G)$ for all directed graphs G.

Assume $i \in V$, $V_s \subset V$, and $S = \{(i, k) \mid k \in V_s, k \neq i\}$. That is, S is a subset of the arcs for which i is the tail.

Theorem 4 *If $LTS(G \setminus S) > UTS(G)$, then no arc (i, j) such that $j \notin V_s$ can be part of any optimal solution for graph G.*

Proof Since $LTS(G \setminus S) > UTS(G)$, it follows from theorem 1 that every optimal solution for graph G contains at least one arc $s \in S$. However, constraint (6) dictates that there is precisely one arc with tail i in every optimal solution. Therefore, arcs (i, j) such that $j \notin V_s$ cannot be a part of any optimal solution. $\square$

Similarly, for $j \in V$, $V_s \subset V$, and $S = \{(k, j) \mid k \in V_s, k \neq j\}$; $LTS(G \setminus S) > UTS(G)$ entails that there is no arc $(k, j) \mid k \notin V_s$ that can be part of any optimal solution for graph G.

These theorems provide us with tools for finding backbone and fat arcs and allow us to reduce the size of ATSP graphs. We directly apply these tools in our algorithm as described below.

Our algorithm is comprised of two steps: finding an upper bound for the original graph, then eliminating sets of arcs with common tail vertices. We are currently using the Assignment Problem method for finding the lower bound for our problem instances. Let $|AP|$ equal the cost of the Assignment Problem solution, and AP equal the set of arcs corresponding to this solution.

First, we find an upper bound value using the Zhang algorithm (Zhang 1993). This algorithm provides a good approximation very quickly (Johnson *et al.* in print). Next, we consider each vertex i and attempt to eliminate a set of arcs with i as their tail. We use theorem 4 to accomplish this. From theorem 3 we know that an arc from the AP solution must be in S for there to be any possibility of the limits crossing, so the first arc selected is $(i, j) \in AP$. Note there is precisely one arc that is in AP with tail i. We exclude this arc from G and find $|AP|$ for $G - (i, j)$. If this value is greater than the original upper bound, we have found an arc that is part of the backbone for the problem instance. If not, we add another arc to S and try again. The next arc to be excluded is the arc (i, k) that is in the AP solution for $G - (i, j)$. If the $|AP|$ for this graph exceeds the upper bound, then we know that no other arc with tail i can be in any optimal solution, so we exclude those arcs permanently, keeping only (i, j) and (i, k). If the limits do not cross, we continue to exclude arcs returned by the AP solutions and checking for crossings. Whenever the crossing occurs, we retain the arcs in S and permanently eliminate the arcs that have tail i and are not in S. The eliminated arcs are part of the fat of the problem instance.

The time complexity of finding the upper bound using the Zhang algorithm is $O(n^4)$, where n is the number of cities (Zhang 1993). In the second step, an AP solution is derived for each arc in set S. The first of the AP calls requires $O(n^3)$ time, but this call is made during the Zhang procedure in the previous step. The rest require $O(n^2)$ time (Martello & Toth 1987). Therefore, the overall time complexity for the second step is $O(kn^2)$, where k is the number of arcs kept in the graph after applying limit crossing.

In the next section, we compare our limit-crossing pre-processor with the pre-processor that was developed by Carpaneto, Dell'Amico, and Toth (CDT) and described previously. Although the CDT pre-processor identifies backbone and fat arcs using a limit-crossing procedure, it is fundamentally different from our method. First of all, the CDT technique is tied to the AP lower bound, whereas the limit-crossing technique can be used with any lower-bound function. This is advantageous as the AP lower bound is not very tight for many classes of ATSP graphs (Johnson *et al.* in print). Second, the CDT algorithm considers each arc, one at a time. Our procedure is more powerful as we are free to choose clusters of arcs. Finally, the CDT pre-processor can only identify backbone arcs by the process of elimina-

tion. Only fat arcs can be directly discovered. If all but one of the arcs with a common head or tail are identified as fat arcs, then a backbone arc is found. Our method works in the opposite direction. We consider a set of arcs with a common tail and check to see if we can identify a backbone arc immediately. If we can't identify a backbone arc in the set, we search for the minimum subset of these arcs that we can identify as containing all of the arcs from the original set that are not fat arcs. Although these pre-processors possess some similarities, our method derives more power by fully exploiting the limit-crossing concept.

Experimental Results

In this section, we first compare the limit-crossing pre-processor with the CDT pre-processor that was described previously for a variety of ATSP classes. Then we compare the two pre-processors for various sizes of random problem instances. In our tests, we used a general AP algorithm. The time requirement for pre-processed graphs could be reduced by substituting an AP algorithm that is particularly suited for sparse graphs (Carpaneto, Dell'Amico, & Toth 1995), instead of this general method. Therefore, the CPU times shown in our tables could be reduced.

We use the Zhang algorithm to compute the upper bound for the CDT pre-processor so that both pre-processors employ the same upper-bound function. Furthermore, since we are searching for backbones and fat, we adjusted the CDT pre-processor to only exclude arcs in which the lower bound exceeded the upper bound; thus retaining arcs for which the limits are equal.

In our tests, the backbone and fat arcs that were identified using the CDT pre-processor were a subset of those found using limit crossing. This is not surprising as both methods use the same upper-bound function and variations of the AP solution for the lower-bound function.

In our first set of tests, we compare the numbers of backbone and fat arcs found by both pre-processors for ten different classes of problem instances. These classes are described in detail in (Cirasella *et al.* 2001; Johnson *et al.* in print) and correspond to real-world applications of the ATSP.

For our tests, we used 300 cities with a generator parameter of 300. (Larger values for the generator parameter generally correspond to a larger range of values for the arc costs, however, the classes super and coins are not dependent on the generator parameter). We computed the average values for 100 trials for each class.

Table 1 shows the effectiveness of each of the pre-processors. The table also shows the relative error, or *duality gap*, for the upper- and lower-bound functions. This error is equal to the difference of the two bounds divided by the lower-bound value. The relative errors for the classes fall into two well-defined clusters. The classes amat, tmat, disk, super, and crane have relative errors that are less than 3%. All of the other classes have relative errors in the range of 22% to 46%.

For the amat, tmat, and disk classes, the limit-crossing pre-processor found more than twice as many backbone arcs as the CDT pre-processor. An interesting result

class	% rel. error	CDT pre-processor		Limit crossing		% more bb found	% more fat found
		backbone arcs found	fat arcs found	backbone arcs found	fat arcs found		
tmat	0.06	46.20	78,326	93.02	82,538	101	5.4
amat	0.47	39.26	88,562	104.88	88,959	167	0.4
disk	0.85	5.33	85,140	14.49	86,032	172	1.0
super	1.25	0.00	37	0.00	144	-	289
crane	2.78	0.00	56,762	0.00	60,999	-	7.5
coins	22.53	0.00	0	0.00	0	-	-
tsmat	27.25	0.00	0	0.00	0	-	-
stilt	32.72	0.00	0	0.00	0	-	-
rtilt	35.55	0.00	0	0.00	0	-	-
smat	45.81	0.00	41,978	0.00	42,474	-	1.2

Table 1: Comparisons of the pre-processors for various classes of ATSP instances ($n = 300$).

is that the super class has a small relative error, however, pre-processing is not nearly as effective for this class as it is for the other classes with small relative errors. We observed that super problem instances tend to have a large number of optimal solutions. (We found an average of 58.4 solutions for 100-city instances.)

The other five classes form a cluster with large relative errors. Four of these classes have poor results, as can be expected. Surprisingly, a large number of fat arcs were found for the smat instances despite a relative error of 45.81%. These graphs contain 89,700 arcs and nearly half of these arcs were identified as fat. It is interesting to note that for tsmat - the variant of smat that obeys the triangle inequality - not one fat arc was discovered.

In our second set of tests, we pre-processed random ATSP graphs and then found all the optimal solutions using each of the two methods. We used a depth-first branch-and-bound method (similar to the method discussed previously) to find all of the optimal solutions for the reduced graphs. We varied the number of cities n and ran 100 trials for each value of n. Furthermore, the arc cost values range uniformly from zero to n for each case. These values result in a large number of solutions, and finding all of these solutions is a computationally expensive task (Zhang 2002).

Table 2 presents the results of these tests. Note that the relative errors are extremely small as our upper- and lower-bound functions are exceptionally tight for these random instances. Furthermore, the relative error decreases with increasing n because the AP function becomes more accurate as n increases.

As shown in table 2, the limit-crossing method finds two to three times more backbone arcs than the AP-based method. Furthermore, roughly half of the fat arcs that are overlooked by the CDT pre-processor are found using limit crossing. Although the limit-crossing method requires more AP calls for the pre-processing step, the total number of AP calls is still less, due to the increased sparsification. Note that the average time divided by the number of AP calls tends to be larger for the CDT method than for the limit-crossing method. This is probably due to the fact that a number of AP calls are made in the pre-processing stage for the limit-crossing method, and other computational costs in this

stage are very small.

In these tests, the time to find all of the optimal solutions is less when the limit-crossing pre-processor is used. Furthermore, the time savings tend to increase with larger problem sizes. For the cases with $n \geq 500$, the limit-crossing method required less than one-third the time required by the CDT method. After more than five days of running, the CDT tests with $n = 700$ have not finished. For the first 50 trials, the median time was 559 seconds (yielding a median time ratio of about 3.8).

Conclusions and Future Directions

In this paper, we developed a technique for identifying backbone and fat variables. We also formalized limit crossing, an intuitive concept that uses approximation techniques to derive exact information about backbone and fat variables and, consequently, about optimal solutions. Although limit crossing has been previously utilized in a variety of forms, we exploit this concept and demonstrate its utility and power for discovering backbone and fat variables. The identification of backbone and fat variables allows us to reduce the problem graph and optimally solve the instance in less time. Our experimental results comparing the limit-crossing pre-processor with the Carpaneto, Dell'Amico, and Toth (CDT) pre-processor attest the power of limit crossing. Whenever either method identified backbone or fat arcs, limit crossing consistently found more fat arcs than CDT and it consistently found two to three times as many backbone arcs. In many cases, instances that were pre-processed with limit crossing required less than one-third the time to solve than the same instances that were pre-processed using the CDT method. Furthermore, the benefits of limit crossing appear to increase with increasing problem size for the class of random asymmetric matrices.

For the immediate future, we plan to experiment with approximation functions for the ATSP and study interesting structural properties of ATSP graphs. These properties include number of cities, range of cost values, degree of symmetry, degree of obeyance of the triangle inequality, number of solutions, size of backbone, size of fat, and accuracy of approximation functions. We are interested in the interplay

n	% rel. error	CDT pre-processor					Limit-crossing pre-processor					median time ratio
		% bb found	% fat found	# AP calls	mean time	median time	% bb found	% fat found	# AP calls	mean time	median time	
100	1.55	16.32	97.28	1737	0.15	0.10	42.34	98.61	1516	0.12	0.08	1.3
200	0.74	16.11	98.68	9188	2.44	1.37	43.67	99.35	6828	1.38	0.76	1.8
300	0.47	17.02	99.16	33,604	18.5	10.0	45.46	99.60	24,070	8.99	3.56	2.8
400	0.37	17.22	99.33	138,105	130	31.7	46.91	99.67	99,337	50.5	15.9	2.0
500	0.28	16.94	99.48	431,377	625	95.6	47.21	99.75	259,152	199	31.8	3.0
600	0.21	19.17	99.60	640,220	1266	398	51.58	99.81	442,695	609	119	3.3
700	0.19	-	-	-	-	-	48.98	99.83	1,293,702	2541	148	-

Table 2: Comparisons of the pre-processors when finding all optimal solutions for random ATSP instances.

of these properties and the effectiveness of limit crossing.

Our long-term plans include studying other graph problems with high complexities and attempting to derive limit-crossing tools that may be useful to identify backbone and fat variables within their domains.

Acknowledgments

This research was funded in part by NSF Grants IIS-0196057 and IET-0111386, NDSEG and Olin Fellowships, and in part by DARPA Cooperative Agreements F30602-00-2-0531 and F33615-01-C-1897. We are grateful for useful suggestions provided by the anonymous referees.

References

Carpaneto, G.; Dell'Amico, M.; and Toth, P. 1995. Exact solution of large-scale, asymmetric Traveling Salesman Problems. *ACM Trans. on Mathematical Software* 21:394–409.

Cirasella, J.; Johnson, D.; McGeoch, L.; and Zhang, W. 2001. The asymmetric traveling salesman problem: Algorithms, instance generators, and tests. In *Proc. of the 3rd Workshop on Algorithm Engineering and Experiments*.

Johnson, D. S.; Gutin, G.; McGeoch, L. A.; Yeo, A.; Zhang, W.; and Zverovich, A. in print. Experimental analysis of heuristics for the ATSP. To appear in The Traveling Salesman Problem and its Variations, G. Gutin and A. Punnen, Editors, Kluwer Academic Publishers.

Martello, S., and Toth, P. 1987. Linear assignment problems. *Annals of Discrete Math.* 31:259–282.

Miller, D. L., and Pekny, J. F. 1991. Exact solution of large asymmetric traveling salesman problems. *Science* 251:754–761.

Monasson, R.; Zecchina, R.; Kirkpatrick, S.; Selman, B.; and Troyansky, L. 1999. Determining computational complexity from characteristic 'phase transitions'. *Nature* 400:133–137.

Papadimitriou, C. H. 1995. *Computational Complexity*. New York, NY: Addison-Wesley.

Schneider, J.; Froschhammer, C.; Morgenstern, I.; Husslein, T.; and Singer, J. M. 1996. Searching for backbones - an efficient parallel algorithm for the traveling salesman problem. *Comput. Phys. Commun.* 96:173–188.

Slaney, J., and Walsh, T. 2001. Backbones in optimization and approximation. In *IJCAI-01*.

Zhang, W. 1993. Truncated branch-and-bound: A case study on the Asymmetric Traveling Salesman Problem. In *Proc. of AAAI 1993 Spring Symp. on AI and NP-Hard Problems*, 160–166.

Zhang, W. 2001. Phase transitions and backbones of 3-sat and maximum 3-sat. In *7th Intern. Conf. on Principles and Practice of Constraint Programming (CP-2001)*, 153–167.

Zhang, W. 2002. Phase transitions, backbones, measurement accuracy, and phase-aware approximation: The ATSP as a case study. *Proc. of CP-AI-OR 02* 345–357.

Multiple-goal Search Algorithms and their Application to Web Crawling

Dmitry Davidov and **Shaul Markovitch**

Computer Science Department
Technion, Haifa 32000,Israel
email:dmitry,shaulm@cs.technion.ac.il

Abstract

The work described in this paper presents a new framework for heuristic search where the task is to collect as many goals as possible within the allocated resources. We show the inadequacy of traditional distance heuristics for this type of tasks and present alternative types of heuristics that are more appropriate for multiple-goal search. In particular we introduce the yield heuristic that estimates the cost and the benefit of exploring a subtree below a search node. We present a learning algorithm for inferring the yield based on search experience. We apply our adaptive and non-adaptive multiple-goal search algorithms to the web crawling problem and show their efficiency.

Introduction

WWW search engines build their indices using brute-force crawlers that attempt to scan large portions of the web. Due to the size of the web, these crawlers require several weeks to complete one scan, even when using very high computational power and bandwidth (Brin & Page 1998). Many times, however, there is a need to retrieve only a small portion of the web of pages dealing with a specific topic or satisfying some user criteria. Using brute-force crawlers for such a task would require enormous resources with most being wasted on non-relevant pages. Is it possible to design a smart crawler that would scan only relevant parts of the web and would retrieve the desired pages using much less resources than the exhaustive crawlers?

Since the web can be viewed as a large graph (Kumar *et al.* 2000), where pages are nodes and links are arcs, we may look for a solution to the problem of selective crawling in the field of heuristic graph-search algorithms. A quick analysis, however, reveals that the problem definition assumed by the designers of heuristic search algorithms is different than the setup for selective crawling which makes them inappropriate for the given task. The crucial difference between the two setups is the success criteria. In both setups there is a *set* of goal states. In the heuristic search setup, however, the search is completed as soon as a single goal state is found, while in the selective crawling setup, the search continues to collect as many goal states as possible within the given resources.

One of the reasons why common search techniques are not applicable to multiple-goal search is that most are based on a heuristic function that estimates the distance from a node to the nearest goal node. Such heuristics are not useful for multiple-goal search. To understand why, consider the search graph described in Figure 1.

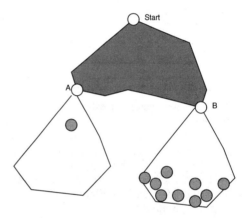

Figure 1: Using distance heuristic for a multiple-goal problem.

The grey area is the expanded graph. Assume that we evaluate nodes A and B using a distance-based heuristic. Obviously node A has a better heuristic value and will therefore be selected for pursuing. This is indeed a right decision for traditional search where the task is to find *one* goal. For multiple-goal search, however, B looks a much more promising direction since it leads to an area with a high density of goal nodes.

In this research we define a new class of graph-search problems called *multiple-goal search* and develop algorithms to deal with such problems. We define a new class of heuristic functions, called *yield* heuristics, and show that they are more appropriate for multiple-goal search than the traditional distance-estimation heuristics. We show search algorithms that use such heuristics and present learning mechanisms for acquiring such heuristic functions from experience. Finally, we show the application of the framework to the selective crawling and present results of an experimental study in the web domain.

The multiple-goal search problem

The multiple-goal search problem is similar to the single-goal search problem in several aspects. We assume that we are given a finite set of start states, an expand function that gives the successors of every state and a goal predicate. We assume that we search for goals by repeatedly expanding states. The main difference between our framework and the traditional one is the stopping criteria. In the traditional single-goal search framework the search algorithm stops as soon as it encounters a goal state (or, in the case of optimizing search, as soon as a lowest-cost path to a goal state is found). In our multiple-goal search framework we define two alternative stopping criteria for the algorithm:

- When it spends a given allocation of resources.

- When it finds a given portion of the total goals.

The performance of multiple-goal search algorithm is evaluated using two alternative methods corresponding to the above stopping criteria. In the first case, we evaluate the performance by the number of goal states found using the given resources. In the second case we evaluate the performance by the resources spent for finding the required portion. An alternative approach would be to treat the search algorithm as *anytime algorithm*. In such a case we evaluate the algorithm by its performance profile.

Heuristics for multiple-goal problems

In the introduction we have shown an example that illustrates the problem of using traditional distance-estimation heuristic for multiple-goal search. One of the main problems with using such a distance heuristic is that it does not take into account goal concentration but only the distance to the nearest goal. This can lead the search into a relatively futile branch such as the left branch in Figure 1 instead of the much more fruitful right branch.

There are several possible alternatives for this approach. If the set of goal states, S_G, is given explicitly, we can use the distance heuristic to estimate the sum of distances to S_G. Such heuristic will prefer the right branch of the search graph in Figure 1 since moving in that direction reduces the sum of distances significantly. If S_G is not given we can try to build an estimator for the sum-of-heuristic distances function. Sometimes, instead of getting S_G, we may be supplied with a set of heuristic functions that estimate the distances to individual members or subsets of S_G. In such a case we can sum the values returned by the given set of heuristics. One problem with the *sum* heuristic is its tendency to try to progress towards all the goals simultaneously. Thus, if there are groups of goals scattered around the search front, all the states around the front will have similar heuristic values. Each step reduces some of the distances and increases some of them leading to a more-or-less constant sum.

One possible remedy to this problem is giving higher weight to progress. As before, we assume that we have either the explicit goal list S_G or, more likely, a set of distance heuristics to goals or goal groups (categories). Instead of measuring the global progress towards the whole goal set, we measure the global progress towards each of the

goals or goal groups and prefer steps that lead to progress towards more goals. More formally, we use the heuristic $H(n) = |\{g \in S_G | h(n, g) < \min_{c \in Closed} h(c, g)\}|$ where $Closed$ is the list of already expanded nodes. We call this strategy *front advancement*.

Another approach for multiple-goal heuristic is to deal explicitly with the expected cost and expected benefit of searching from the given node. Obviously, we prefer subgraphs where the cost is low and the benefit is high. In other words, we would like high return for our resource investment. We call a heuristic that tries to estimate this return a *yield* heuristic.

For a finite graph, we can estimate the yield by the following pessimistic estimation $Y(n, S_G) = |N \cap S_G| / |N|$ where N is set of all nodes which can be reached from n. This estimation assumes that the whole subgraph is traversed in order to collect its goals. Alternatively we can estimate the yield by the optimistic estimation $Y(n, S_G) = |N \cap S_G| / |g(n, N, S_G)|$ where N is defined as above and $g(n, N, S_G)$ are the nodes of a directed graph with minimal number of edges such that it contains a directed path from n to each node in $N \cap S_G$. This estimation assumes that we do not waste resources unnecessarily when collecting $N \cap S_G$. The above two definitions can be modified to include a depth limit d. Then, instead of looking at the graph N of all nodes reachable from n we restrict the definition to nodes that are at depth of at most d from n.

Naturally, it is very difficult to build yield estimation heuristics. In the following sections we will show how such heuristics can be adapted.

Heuristic search for multiple-goal problems

Assuming that we have a heuristic function suitable for multiple goal search as described above, we can now use this heuristic in traditional heuristic search algorithms such as best-first search. The main difference, in addition to the different type of heuristic, is that when a goal is encountered, the algorithm collects it and continues (unlike the single-goal best-first search which would stop as soon as a goal is found). Figure 2 shows the multiple-goal version of best-first search.

```
procedure MGBestFirst(StartNodes,RLimit)
    Open ← StartNodes Closed ← {}
    Goals ← {} RCount ← 0
    loop while Open ≠ {} AND RCount < RLimit
        let n be a node with minimal h(n) in Open
        Open ← Open \{n} ; Closed ← Closed ∪{n}
        RCount ← RCount + 1
        For each n' ∈ Succ(n)
            If n' ∉ Closed ∪ Open
                If G(n') then Goals ← Goals ∪ {n'}
                Open ← Open ∪ {n'}
    Return Goals
```

Figure 2: The multiple-goal best-first search algorithm

One possible side-effect of not stopping when discovering

goals is the continuous influence of the already-discovered goals on the search process. The found goals continue to attract the search front while we would have preferred that the search would progress towards undiscovered goals. The problem is intensified when the paths leading to undiscovered goals pass through or nearby discovered goals.

One possible solution to this problem is to eliminate the effect or reduce the weight of discovered goals in the heuristic calculation. Thus, for example, if the set of goals (or a set of distance-heuristic functions to goals) is given, the discovered goals can be removed from the heuristic calculation. If a set of heuristics to subsets of S_G is given, then we can reduce the weight of the subset (which may be defined by a category) of the discovered goal.

Learning yield heuristics

While it is quite possible that yield heuristics will be supplied by the user, in many domains such heuristics are very difficult to design. We can use learning approach to acquire such yield heuristics online during the search. We present here two alternative approaches for inferring yield:

1. Accumulate partial yield information for every node in the search graph. Assume that the yield of the explored part of a subtree is a good predictor for the yield of the unexplored part.

2. Accumulate yield statistics for explored nodes. Create a set of examples of nodes with high yield and nodes with low yield. Apply an induction algorithm to infer a classifier for identifying nodes with high yield.

Inferring yield from partial yield

The *partial* yield of a node n at step t of executing multiple-goal search algorithm is the number of goals found so far in the subtree below n divided by the number of nodes generated so far in this subtree. We use the partial yield of a node to estimate the expected yield of its brothers and their descendants. For each expanded node n we maintain D partial

```
procedure UpdateNewNode(n,G)
  ; AN(n, d) – Actual number of nodes to depth d
  ; AG(n, d) – Actual number of goals to depth d
  For d from 1 to D
    AN(n, d) = 1
    If G(n) then AG(n, d) = 1
    else AG(n, d) = 0
  UpdateParents(n, 1, G(n))

procedure UpdateParents(n,Depth,GoalFlag)
  if Depth < D
    For d from Depth to D
      AN(p, d) ← AN(p, d) + 1
      if GoalFlag then GN(p, d) ← GN(p, d) + 1
    For p ∈ parents(n)
      UpdateParents(p, Depth + 1, GoalFlag)
```

Figure 3: An algorithm for updating the partial yield

yield values for depth from 1 to D where D is a predefined depth limit. For computing the partial yield we keep in the node, for each depth, the number of nodes generated and the number of goals discovered so far to this depth. When generating a new node we initialize the counters for the node and recursively update its ancestors up to D levels above. The algorithm is described in Figure 3. To avoid updating an ancestor twice due to multiple paths, one must mark already updated ancestors. For simplicity we listed the algorithm without this mechanism. The estimated yield of a node is

```
procedure Yield(n,d)
  C ← {s ∈ Childs(n)|AN(s, d − 1) > Threshold}
  if |C| > 0 then
    Return Avg({ GN(c,d−1)/AN(c,d−1) |c ∈ C})
  else Return
    Avg({Yield(p, Min(d + 1, D))|p ∈ Parents(n)})
```

Figure 4: An algorithm for yield estimation

the average yields of its supported children – those are children with sufficiently large expanded subtrees. If there are no such children, the yield is estimated (recursively) by the average yield of the node parents. The depth values are adjusted appropriately. The algorithm is listed in Figure 4. For simplicity we avoided listing the handling of special cases. When calling the yield estimation algorithm, we can adjust the depth parameter according to the resource limit or to the number of goals required. For example, we can use similar algorithm to estimate the tree sizes and require depth for which the estimated tree size is below the resource limit.

The algorithms described above assume that each goal node has the same value. The scheme can be easily generalized to the case where each goal node carries different value. In such a case, the node weight should be added to the counter instead of 1.

Generalizing yield

One problem with the above approach is that partial yield information allows us to predict yield only to nodes that are near-by in the graph structure. If we can extract a vector of domain-dependent features for each state (node), we can use induction algorithms to infer yield based on states that are near-by in the feature space. Examples will be supported nodes (with sufficiently large subtrees). The examples will be tagged by their partial yield. We can then apply common induction algorithms to distinguish between states with low and high yield, or, more generally, to infer the yield function. Since learning is performed online, we are interested in reducing both learning cost and classification (prediction) cost. For reducing learning costs we can use *lazy* learners such as KNN. These algorithms, however, carry high prediction cost which can be somewhat reduced by indexing. Decision tree algorithms have the advantage of low-cost prediction but high learning cost. This can be somehow reduced by enlarging the time gap between learning sessions.

Applying our framework to the WWW domain

One of the main motivations for this research is the problem of *focused crawling* in the web (Chakrabarti, van den Berg, & Dom 1999; Cho & Garcia-Molina 2000; Menczer *et al.* 2001). The task is to find as many goal pages as possible using limited resources where the basic resource unit is usually retrieving a page from a link. Previous work on focused crawling concentrated on web-specific techniques for directing the search. We believe that our generalization of single-goal heuristic search to multiple-goal search can contribute to the task of focused crawling. In this section we discuss various issues related to implementing the above framework to the web domain.

- There are several ways to define goal web pages.
  - Boolean keywords query – this can be extended to word in a specific tag environment such as titles or meta-tags.
  - Parametric query – request pages that satisfy some parameter specifications. A known example for such a parameter is the page-rank (Najork & Wiener 2001).
  - Query by example – a set of pages tagged as goals or none-goals. These pages can be used to build a classifier for recognizing goals.

- When using a keyword-based goal predicate, we can use the keywords also for the multiple-goal heuristics for indicating distance to goals. The vector of keywords can also serve to produce a vector of heuristic distances needed for the *sum* and similar accumulating heuristics. In addition, one can use specific domain-independent keywords such as "index" or "collection" to indicate good hubs (Kleinberg 1999; Borodin *et al.* 2001; Cohen & Fan 1999).

- When describing the web as a search graph, web pages are considered as states and links can be considered as operators. Thus, in addition to using page-heuristics to evaluate a particular page (state), we can also use link-heuristics to evaluate the application of a specific operator in the given state. Such heuristics can use, for example, the text around the link and the link itself.

- When generalizing over web pages for estimating yield, we can use any of the known schemes for extracting features of web pages. For example, we can use words with high information content measured by various methods such as TFIDF (Joachims 1997).

Empirical evaluation

In this section we show an empirical evaluation of the multiple-goal search methods described above.

Experimental methodology

We test our algorithm by running it until it searches the whole graph and counting the number of goals it collects. This gives us the performance profile of the algorithm which is a general indicator for its expected performance. Our experiments are conducted in the context of two domains. Most of our experiments are in the web domain. Performing rigorous empirical research on the web is problematic. First, the web is dynamic and therefore may be changed between

different runs of the algorithms. Second, crawling in the web require enormous time which disallow parametric experimentation. To solve the above problems we downloaded a small section of the web to local storage and performed the experiments using the local copy (Hirai *et al.* 2000). Specifically, we downloaded the domain `stanford.edu` which contains, after some cleanup, approximately 350000 valid and accessible HTML pages.

To show the generality of our approach we also run our algorithms on the task of planing object collection in a simulated grid environment of 50×50 with random "walls" inserted as obstacles. There are parameters controlling the maximal length of walls and desired density of the grid. Walls are inserted randomly making sure that the resulting graph remains connected.

Basic experiment in the Grid domain

Our basic experiment involves running the multiple-goal best-first algorithm with the *sum* heuristic with and without front-advancement. We compared their performance to a multiple-goal version of BFS and multiple-goal best-first with traditional Manhattan distance heuristic. Figure 5

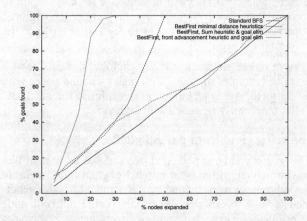

Figure 5: Working with several algorithms on grid domain.

shows the results obtained. Each point in the graphs is an average of 100 runs. For each run a new random grid was generated and a random set of goal states was selected. As expected the regular heuristic method is better than BFS and the front-advancement method is much better than the others. If we are limited, for example, to generate 20% of the total nodes, this method finds 3.5 times as many goals as the other methods. It is a bit surprising that the *sum* heuristic performed miserably. This is probably due to its attempt to progress towards all goals simultaneously.

Experiments in the WWW domain

We defined 8 goal predicates relevant to the Stanford domain and tagged the pages according to the defined predicates. Those goal sets included the set of all personal home pages, the set of pages about robotics and others. For each of the goal predicate, we run BFS and multiple-goal best-first search with goal-specific heuristic based on the goal keywords and general "hub" keywords as described in the previous section. Figure 6 shows the results obtained for

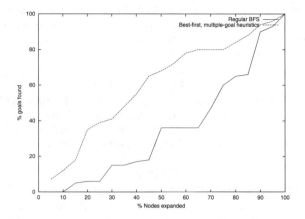

Figure 6: Multiple-goal best-first applied to the web domain

the "robotics" goal predicates. We can see that the heuristic method shows much better performance than the blind method. For example, if allocated a number of page retrievals which is 30% of the total pages, the heuristic method retrieves 3 times the goals retrieved by the blind method. Similar results were obtained for the other goal predicates.

Using front advancement in the WWW domain

We tested the front advancement method in the web domain for the "home pages" goal predicate restricted for a specific set of 100 people. We obtained a set of distance heuristics, one for each person. The functions are based on a summary table, found in the domain, which contains a short information about each person. We used these 100 heuristics for multiple-goal heuristic implementing the front-advancement method. Figure 7 shows the results obtained compared to

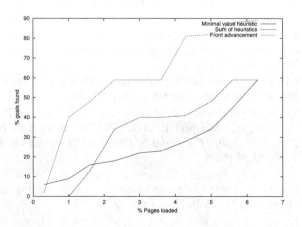

Figure 7: The effect of front advancement

the *sum* and minimal-value heuristics. We can see that indeed the *sum* heuristic is better than the simple minimizing heuristic but the front advancement is superior to both.

Learning yield during search progress

We tested both of our learning methods in the web domain. For generalizing yield we have used nearest-neighbor classification. Figure 8 shows the results obtained. We can see that

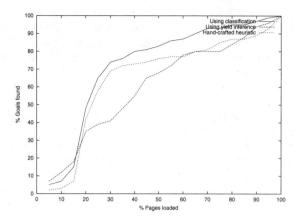

Figure 8: Learning yield in the web domain

using yield inference leads to better performance than using a hand-crafted heuristic. Using the generalizing method produced even better results.

Combining heuristic and yield methods

If we look carefully at the graphs of Figure 8 we can see that at the initial stages of the search the heuristic method performs better than the adaptive methods. The reason is that the adaptive methods require sufficient examples to generate predictions. We decided to try a combined method which uses a linear combination of the yield prediction and the heuristic estimation. Figure 9 shows the results obtained for the yield-inference method, the heuristic method

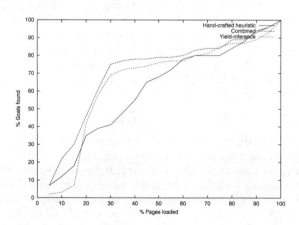

Figure 9: Combining yield-inference with heuristic search

tained for the yield-inference method, the heuristic method and the combined algorithm. We can see that indeed the combined method is better than both algorithms. An interesting phenomenon is that the combined method improves over *both* methods (rather than combining the maximum of both). The reason is that very early in the search process the hand-crafted heuristic leads to enough goals to jump-start the learning process much earlier.

Contract algorithm versus anytime algorithm

In the previous subsections we have shown results for multiple-goal search behaving as an anytime algorithm. In practice we expect to use the search methods as *contract* algorithms (Russell & Zilberstein 1991) where the allocation of resources (or the requirement for the number of goals) are given as input to the algorithm. Contract algorithms can use the resource allocation input to improve their performance versus anytime algorithms. To obtain such improvement we can use the ability of the yield estimation algorithm to take into account the resource allocation or the number of goals requirement. In Table 1 we show the performance of our yield-inference algorithm when given a resource allocation (given by the percentage of page retrievals out of the total number of pages) for the two versions: the version that takes into account the limit and the version that does not. We can

Resource allocation	%goals found	
	Contract	Anytime
5%	7%	19%
10%	22%	33%
20%	46%	59%
50%	79%	83%

Table 1: Contract vs. anytime performance.

see that indeed using the allocation as input improves the performance of the algorithm by up to 250%. Similar results were obtained when the algorithm is limited by the number of goals instead of the number of page retrievals.

The results reported in this section are based on the assumption that the dominant resource is page retrieval over the net. There is a small overhead associated with maintaining the statistics for each node. The cost of learning can be high, but can be reduced by evoking the induction process less frequently. The space complexity is linear in the number of visited pages. If this number becomes too high, we can use one of the methods developed for memory-bounded heuristic search.

Conclusions

The work described in this paper presents a new framework for heuristic search. In this framework the task is to collect as many goals as possible within the allocated resources. We showed the inadequacy of traditional heuristics to this type of tasks and present heuristics that are more appropriate for multiple-goal search. In particular we introduced the *yield* heuristic that attempts to estimate the cost and the benefit of exploring a subtree below a search node. We also introduced two methods for online learning of the yield heuristic. One which is based on the partial yield of brother nodes and another which generalizes over the state feature space. We applied our methodology to the task of selective web crawling and showed its merit under various conditions. Our framework is not limited to the web domain. We showed an example of applying it to the task of planing object collection in

a simulated grid environment. Our framework is applicable for a wide variety of problems where we are interested in finding many goals states instead of only one. For example, in the context of constraint satisfaction it may be useful to find many solutions and apply another algorithm for selecting between the found set.

Acknowledgments

We would like to thank Adam Darlo, Irena Koifman and Yaron Goren who helped us in programming. This research was supported by the fund for the promotion of research at the Technion and by the Israeli Ministry of Science.

References

Borodin, A.; Roberts, G. O.; Rosenthal, J. S.; and Tsaparas, P. 2001. Finding authorities and hubs from link structures on the world wide web. In *The 10th international WWW conference*, 415–429. ACM Press.

Brin, S., and Page, L. 1998. The anatomy of a large-scale hypertextual Web search engine. *Computer Networks and ISDN Systems* 30(1–7):107–117.

Chakrabarti, S.; van den Berg, M.; and Dom, B. 1999. Focused crawling: a new approach to topic-specific Web resource discovery. *Computer Networks* 31(11–16):1623–1640.

Cho, J., and Garcia-Molina, H. 2000. The evolution of the Web and implications for an incremental crawler. In El Abbadi, A.; Brodie, M. L.; Chakravarthy, S.; Dayal, U.; Kamel, N.; Schlageter, G.; and Whang, K.-Y., eds., *VLDB 2000*, 200–209. Los Altos, CA 94022, USA: Morgan Kaufmann Publishers.

Cohen, W. W., and Fan, W. 1999. Learning page-independent heuristics for extracting data from Web pages. *Computer Networks* 31(11–16):1641–1652.

Hirai, J.; Raghavan, S.; Garcia-Molina, H.; and Paepcke, A. 2000. Webbase: A repository of web pages. In *Proceedings of the 9th International WWW Conference*, 277–293.

Joachims, T. 1997. A probabilistic analysis of the Rocchio algorithm with TFIDF for text categorization. In *Proc. 14th International Conference on Machine Learning*, 143–151. Morgan Kaufmann.

Kleinberg, J. M. 1999. Authoritative sources in a hyper-linked environment. *Journal of the ACM* 46(5):604–632.

Kumar, R.; Raghavan, P.; Rajagopalan, S.; Sivakumar, D.; Tomkins, A.; and Upfal, E. 2000. The Web as a graph. In *Proc. 19th Symp. Principles of Database Systems, PODS*, 1–10. ACM Press.

Menczer, F.; Pant, G.; Srinivasan, P.; and Ruiz, M. 2001. Evaluating Topic-Driven web crawlers. In *Proceedings of SIGIR-01)*, 241–249. New York: ACM Press.

Najork, M., and Wiener, J. L. 2001. Breadth-first crawling yields high-quality pages. In *Proceedings of the 10th International World-Wide Web Conference*, 114–118.

Russell, S. J., and Zilberstein, S. 1991. Composing real-time systems. In *Proceedings of IJCAI-91*. Sydney: Morgan Kaufmann.

Optimal Schedules for Parallelizing Anytime Algorithms: The Case of Independent Processes

Lev Finkelstein and Shaul Markovitch and Ehud Rivlin

Computer Science Department
Technion, Haifa 32000
Israel
{lev,shaulm,ehudr}@cs.technion.ac.il

Abstract

The performance of anytime algorithms having a non-deterministic nature can be improved by solving simultaneously several instances of the algorithm-problem pairs. These pairs may include different instances of a problem (like starting from a different initial state), different algorithms (if several alternatives exist), or several instances of the same algorithm (for non-deterministic algorithms).

In this paper we present a general framework for optimal parallelization of independent processes. We show a mathematical model for this framework, present algorithms for optimal scheduling, and demonstrate its usefulness on a real problem.

Introduction

Assume that we try to train an expert system for identifying paintings with a good potential. Assume that we possess a set of example paintings and that we have an access to two human experts in this field for tagging examples. The tagged examples are passed to an inductive algorithm for generating a classifier. Our goal is to obtain a classifier of a given quality (judged, for example, using a validation set). Since we do not assume that the two experts have necessarily similar views of what is considered to be a good painting, we want to train a classifier based on examples tagged by the same expert. On one hand, we would like to finish the task as fast as possible, which could be achieved by parallel training. On the other hand, we would like to minimize the total number of examples sent to tagging, which can be achieved by choosing only one expert. We can also design a more elaborated schedule where we switch between the above modes. Assuming that there is a known cost function that specifies the tradeoff between learning time and tagging cost, what should be the optimal schedule for minimizing this cost?

Another example is a Mars mission which is out of water. There are two known sources of water in two opposite directions. Two robots are sent to the two sources. Our goal is to get water as fast as possible using minimal amount of fuel. Again, given the tradeoff between the cost of fuel and

the cost of waiting for water, what should be the optimal schedule for the robots?

What is common to the above examples?

- There are potential benefits to be gained from the uncertainty in solving more than one instance of the algorithm-problem pair. In the first example, the probabilistic characteristics of the learning process are determined by the learning algorithm. Learning from the two experts can be considered as two instances of the same problem. In the second example, the probabilistic characteristics of each of the robot processes are determined by the terrain and are different for the two directions.

- Each process is executed with the purpose of satisfying a given goal predicate. The task is considered accomplished when one of the instances is solved.

- If the goal predicate is satisfied at time t^*, then it is also satisfied at any time $t > t^*$. This property is equivalent to quality monotonicity of *anytime algorithms* (Dean & Boddy 1988; Horvitz 1987), while solution quality is restricted to Boolean values.

- Our objective is to provide a schedule that minimizes the expected cost, maybe under some constraints. Such problem definition is typical for *rational-bounded* reasoning (Simon 1982; Russell & Wefald 1991).

This problem resembles those faced by *contract algorithms* (Russell & Zilberstein 1991; Zilberstein 1993). There, the task is, given resource allocation, to construct an algorithm providing a solution of the highest quality. In our case, the task is, given quality requirement, to construct an algorithm providing a solution using minimal resources.

There are several research works that are related to the above framework. Simple parallelization, with no information exchange between the processes, may speedup the process due to high diversity in solution times. For example, Knight (1993) showed that using many reactive instances of RTA* search (Korf 1990) is more beneficial than using a single deliberative RTA* instance. Yokoo & Kitamura (1996) used several search agents in parallel, with agent rearrangement after pregiven periods of time. Janakiram, Agrawal, & Mehrotra (1988) showed that for many common distributions of solution time, simple parallelization leads to at most linear speedup. One exception is the family of *heavy-tailed* distributions (Gomes, Selman, & Kautz 1998) for which it is possible to obtain super-linear speedup by simple parallelization.

A superlinear speedup can also be obtained when we have access to the internal structure of the processes involved. For example, Clearwater, Hogg, & Huberman (1992) reported superlinear speedup for cryptarithmetic problems as a result of information exchange between the processes. Another example is the works of Kumar and Rao (1987; 1987; 1993) devoted to parallelizing standard search algorithms where superlinear speedup is obtained by dividing the search space.

The case of non-deterministic algorithms that can be restarted an arbitrary number of times, was analyzed in details by Luby, Sinclair, & Zuckerman (1993) for the case of single processor and by Luby & Ertel (1994) for the multiprocessor case. In particular, it was proven that for a single processor, the optimal strategy is to periodically restart the algorithm after a constant amount of time until the solution is found. This strategy was successfully applied to combinatorial search problems (Gomes, Selman, & Kautz 1998). Restart strategy, however, cannot be applied to our settings, since we consider a finite number of heterogeneous processes and do not assume the availability of infinite number of instances of the same process.

An interesting approach in a domain-independent direction is based on "portfolio" construction (Huberman, Lukose, & Hogg 1997; Gomes & Selman 1997). This approach provides the processes (agents) with a different amount of resources, which enabled to reduce both the expected resource usage and its variance. The experiments showed the applicability of this approach to many hard computational problems. In the field of anytime algorithms, similar works were mostly concentrated on scheduling different anytime algorithms or decision procedures in order to maximize overall utility (like in the work of Boddy & Dean (1994)). Their settings, however, are different from those presented above.

The goal of this research is to develop algorithms that design an optimal scheduling policy based on the statistical characteristics of the process(es). We present a formal framework for scheduling parallel anytime algorithms. Finkelstein, Markovitch, & Rivlin (2001) present such framework for the case where the processes share resources (a single processor model). In this work we present similar framework for the case where the processes are *independent* in the sense that usage of resources by one process does not imply constraints on usage of resources of the others. The framework assumes that we know the probability of the goal condition to be satisfied as a function of time (a *performance profile* (Simon 1955; Boddy & Dean 1994) restricted to Boolean quality values). We analyze the properties of optimal schedules for suspend-resume model and present an algorithm for building optimal schedules. Finally, we present experimental results.

Motivation: a simple example

Before starting the formal discussion, we would like to give a simple example. Assume that two instances of DFS with random tie-breaking are applied to a simple search space

shown in Figure 1. We assume that each process uses a separate processor. There is a very large number of paths to the goal, half of them of length 10, and the other half of length 40. When one of the instances finds a solution, the task is considered accomplished. We have two utility

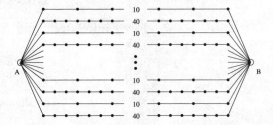

Figure 1: A simple search task: two instances of DFS search for a path from A to B. Scheduling the processes may reduce cost.

components – the *time*, which is the elapsed time required for the system to find a solution, and the *resources*, which is total CPU time consumed by both processes. If the two search processes start together, the expected time usage will be $10 \times 3/4 + 40 \times 1/4 = 17.5$ units, while the expected resource usage will be $20 \times 3/4 + 80 \times 1/4 = 35$ units. If we apply only one instance, both time and resource usage will be $10 \times 1/2 + 40 \times 1/2 = 25$ units. Assume now that the first process is active for the first 10 time units, then it stops and the second process is active for the next 10 time units, and then the second process stops and the first process continues the execution. Both the expected time and resource usage will be $10 \times 1/2 + 20 \times 1/4 + 50 \times 1/4 = 22.5$ units. Finally, if we consider a schedule, where the processes start together and work in a simultaneous manner for 10 time units, and only one continues the execution in the case of failure, the expected time will be $10 \times 3/4 + 40 \times 1/4 = 17.5$ units, while the expected resource usage will be $20 \times 3/4 + 50 \times 1/4 = 27.5$ units. It is easy to see, that the results for the last two scenarios, with interleaved execution, are better than the other results. The tradeoff between time and resource cost determines the best model between the two – if time and resource cost are equal, the last two models are equivalent.

A framework for parallelization scheduling

In this section we formalize the intuitive description of parallelization scheduling. This framework is similar to the frameworks presented in (Finkelstein & Markovitch 2001; Finkelstein, Markovitch, & Rivlin 2001).

Let S be a set of states, t be a time variable with non-negative real values, and A be a random process such that each realization (trajectory) $A(t)$ of A represents a mapping from $\mathcal{R}^+$ to S. Let $G : S \to \{0, 1\}$ be a *goal predicate*. Let A be *monotonic* over G, i.e. for each trajectory $A(t)$ of A the function $\widehat{G_A}(t) = G(A(t))$ is a non-decreasing function. Under the above assumptions, $\widehat{G_A}(t)$ is a step function with at most one discontinuity point, which we denote by $\widehat{t}_{A,G}$ (this is the first point after which the goal predicate is true). If $\widehat{G_A}(t)$ is always 0, we say that $\widehat{t}_{A,G}$ is not defined. Therefore, we can define a random variable, which for each trajectory $A(t)$ of $\mathcal{A}$ with $\widehat{t}_{A,G}$ defined, corresponds to $\widehat{t}_{A,G}$. The behavior of this variable can be described by its distribution function $F(t)$. At the points where $F(t)$ is differentiable, we use the probability density $f(t) = F'(t)$.

This scheme resembles the one used in anytime algorithms. The goal predicate can be viewed as a special case of the quality measurement used in anytime algorithms, and the requirement for its non-decreasing value is a standard requirement of these algorithms. The trajectories of $\mathcal{A}$ correspond to conditional performance profiles (Zilberstein & Russell 1992; Zilberstein 1993).

In practice, not every trajectory of $\mathcal{A}$ leads to goal predicate satisfaction even after infinitely large time. That is why we define the *probability of success* p as the probability of selecting a trajectory $A(t)$ that leads to satisfaction of G within finite time (i.e. with $\widehat{t}_{A,G}$ defined) [1].

Assume now that we have a system of n random processes $\mathcal{A}_1, \ldots \mathcal{A}_n$ with corresponding distribution functions $F_1, \ldots, F_n$ and goal predicates $G_1, \ldots, G_n$. We define a *schedule* of the system as a set of binary functions $\{\theta_i\}$, where at each moment t, the i-th process is active if $\theta_i(t) = 1$ and idle otherwise. We refer to this scheme as *suspend-resume* scheduling.

A possible generalization of this framework is to extend the suspend/resume control to a more refined mechanism allowing us to determine the *intensity* with which each process acts. For software processes that means to vary the fraction of CPU usage; for tasks like robot navigation this implies changing the speed of the robots. Mathematically, using intensity control is equivalent to replacing the binary functions θ_i with continuous functions with a range between 0 and 1.

Note that scheduling makes the term *time* ambiguous. On one hand, we have the *subjective* time for each process which is consumed only when the process is active. This kind of time corresponds to some resource consumed by the process. On the other hand, we have an *objective* time measured from the point of view of an external observer. The performance profile of each algorithm is defined over its subjective time, while the cost function (see below) may use both kinds of times. Since we are using several processes, all the formulas in this paper are based on the objective time.

Let us denote by $\sigma_i(t)$ the total time that process i has been active before t. By definition,

$$\sigma_i(t) = \int_0^t \theta_i(x)\,dx. \qquad (1)$$

In practice $\sigma_i(t)$ provides the mapping from the objective time t to the subjective time of the i-th process, and we refer to them as *subjective schedule functions*. Since θ_i can be obtained from σ_i by differentiation, we often describe schedules by $\{\sigma_i\}$ instead of $\{\theta_i\}$.

The processes $\{\mathcal{A}_i\}$ with goal predicates $\{G_i\}$ running under schedules $\{\sigma_i\}$ result in a new process $\mathcal{A}$, with a goal predicate G. G is the disjunction of G_i ($G(t) = \bigvee_i G_i(t)$),

and therefore $\mathcal{A}$ is monotonic over G. We denote the distribution function of the corresponding random variable by $F_n(t, \sigma_1, \ldots, \sigma_n)$, and the corresponding distribution density by $f_n(t, \sigma_1, \ldots, \sigma_n)$.

Assume that we are given a monotonic non-decreasing *cost* function $u(t, t_1, \ldots, t_n)$, which depends on the objective time t and the subjective times per process t_i. Since the subjective times can be represented as $\sigma_i(t)$, we actually have $u = u(t, \sigma_1(t), \ldots, \sigma_n(t))$.

The *expected* cost of schedule $\{\sigma_i\}$ can be, therefore, expressed as [2]

$$E_u(\sigma_1, \ldots, \sigma_n) = \int_0^{+\infty} u(t, \sigma_1, \ldots, \sigma_n) f_n(t, \sigma_1, \ldots, \sigma_n)\,dt \qquad (2)$$

(for the sake of readability, we omit t in $\sigma_i(t)$). Under the suspend-resume model assumptions, σ_i must be differentiable (except a countable set of rescheduling points), and have derivatives of 0 or 1 that would ensure correct values for θ_i. Under intensity control assumptions, the derivatives of σ_i must lie between 0 and 1.

We consider two alternative setups regarding resource sharing between the processes:

1. The processes share resources on a mutual exclusion basis. An example for such framework are several algorithms running on a single processor.

2. The processes are fully independent. An example for such framework are n algorithms running on n processors.

The difference between these two alternatives is the additional constraints on σ_i: in the case of shared resources the sum of derivatives of σ_i cannot exceed 1, while in the case of independent processes this constraint does not exist. Our goal is to find a schedule that minimizes the expected cost (2) under the corresponding constraints.

The current paper is devoted to the case of independent processes. The case of shared resources was studied in (Finkelstein, Markovitch, & Rivlin 2001).

Suspend-resume based scheduling

In this section we consider the case of suspend-resume based control (σ_i are continuous functions with derivatives 0 or 1).

Claim 1 *The expressions for the goal-time distribution $F_n(t, \sigma_1, \ldots, \sigma_n)$ and the expected cost $E_u(\sigma_1, \ldots, \sigma_n)$ are as follows* [3]:

$$F_n(t, \sigma_1, \ldots, \sigma_n) = 1 - \prod_{i=1}^n (1 - F_i(\sigma_i)), \qquad (3)$$

$$E_u(\sigma_1, \ldots, \sigma_n) = \int_0^{+\infty} \left(u_t' + \sum_{i=1}^n \sigma_i' u_{\sigma_i}' \right) \prod_{i=1}^n (1 - F_i(\sigma_i))\,dt. \qquad (4)$$

---

[1]Another way to express the possibility that the process will not stop at all is to use profiles that approach $1 - p$ when $t \to \infty$. We prefer to use p explicitly because the distribution function must meet the requirement $\lim_{t \to \infty} F(t) = 1$.

[2]It is possible to show that the generalization to the case where the probabilities of success p_i are not 1 is equivalent to replacing $F_i(t)$ and $f_i(t)$ by $p_i F_i(t)$ and $p_i f_i(t)$ respectively.

[3]u_t' and u_{σ_i}' stand for partial derivatives of u by t and by σ_i respectively.

The proofs in this paper are omitted due to the lack of space, and can be found in (Finkelstein, Markovitch, & Rivlin 2002).

In this section we assume that the total cost is a linear combination of the objective time cost and the resource cost, and that the resource cost is proportional to the subjective time spent:

$$u(t, \sigma_1, \ldots, \sigma_n) = at + b \sum_{i=1}^{n} \sigma_i(t). \quad (5)$$

Without loss of generality we can assume $a + b = 1$, which leads to the following minimization problem:

$$E_u(\sigma_1, \ldots, \sigma_n) =$$
$$\int_0^\infty \left((1-c) + c \sum_{i=1}^{n} \sigma_i' \right) \prod_{j=1}^{n} (1 - F_j(\sigma_j)) dt \to \min, \quad (6)$$

where $c = b/(a+b)$ can be viewed as a normalized resource weight. For the case of suspend-resume scheduling we have the constraints following from the nature of the problem:

$$\sigma_i' \in \{0, 1\}. \quad (7)$$

Necessary conditions for optimal solution for two processes

Let A_1 and A_2 be two independent processes. For suspend-resume model, only three states of the system are possible: A_1 is active and A_2 is idle (S^{01}); A_1 is idle and A_2 is active (S^{10}); and both A_1 and A_2 are active (S^{11}). We ignore the case where both processes are idle, since removing such state from the schedule will not increase the cost.

Assume that the system continuously alternates between the three states: $S^{01} \to S^{10} \to S^{11} \to S^{01} \to \ldots$. This scheme is general if the time spent at each state is allowed to be zero. We call each triplet $\langle S^{01}, S^{10}, S^{11} \rangle$ a *phase* and denote phase k by Φ_k. We denote the time when state S^x of Φ_k ends by t_k^x ($x \in \{01, 10, 11\}$). For illustration see Figure 2. Let us denote by ζ_k^x the total cumulative time spent in state

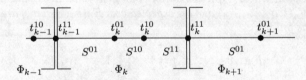

Figure 2: Notations for times, states and phases.

S^x in phases 1 to k. There is a one-to-one correspondence between the sequence $\{\zeta_k^x\}$ and the sequence $\{t_k^x\}$, and

$$\zeta_{k-1}^{10} + \zeta_{k-1}^{11} + \zeta_k^{01} = t_k^{01},$$
$$\zeta_{k-1}^{11} + \zeta_k^{01} + \zeta_k^{10} = t_k^{10},$$
$$\zeta_k^{01} + \zeta_k^{10} + \zeta_k^{11} = t_k^{11}.$$

By definition of t_k^x, the subjective schedule functions σ_1 and σ_2 in time intervals $[t_{k-1}^{11}, t_k^{01})$ (state S^{01}) have the form

$$\sigma_1(t) = t - t_{k-1}^{11} + \zeta_{k-1}^{01} + \zeta_{k-1}^{11} = t - \zeta_{k-1}^{10},$$
$$\sigma_2(t) = \zeta_{k-1}^{10} + \zeta_{k-1}^{11}. \quad (8)$$

Similarly, in the intervals $[t_k^{01}, t_k^{10})$ (state S^{10}) the subjective schedule functions are defined as

$$\sigma_1(t) = \zeta_{k-1}^{11} + \zeta_k^{01},$$
$$\sigma_2(t) = t - t_k^{01} + \zeta_{k-1}^{10} + \zeta_{k-1}^{11} = t - \zeta_k^{01}. \quad (9)$$

Finally, in the intervals $[t_k^{10}, t_k^{11})$ (state S^{11}) the subjective schedule functions can be represented as

$$\sigma_1(t) = t - t_k^{10} + \zeta_{k-1}^{11} + \zeta_k^{01} = t - \zeta_k^{10},$$
$$\sigma_2(t) = t - t_k^{10} + \zeta_{k-1}^{11} + \zeta_k^{10} = t - \zeta_k^{01}. \quad (10)$$

Substituting the expressions for σ_i into (6) and using the constraints for suspend-resume scheduling (7), we obtain the following function to minimize:

$$E_u(\zeta_1^{01}, \zeta_1^{10}, \zeta_1^{11}, \ldots) =$$
$$\sum_{k=0}^{\infty} \left[(1 - F_2(\zeta_{k-1}^{10} + \zeta_{k-1}^{11})) \int_{\zeta_{k-1}^{01}}^{\zeta_k^{01}} (1 - F_1(x + \zeta_{k-1}^{11})) dx \right.$$
$$+ (1 - F_1(\zeta_{k-1}^{11} + \zeta_k^{01})) \int_{\zeta_{k-1}^{10}}^{\zeta_k^{10}} (1 - F_2(x + \zeta_{k-1}^{11})) dx$$
$$\left. + (1 + c) \int_{\zeta_{k-1}^{11}}^{\zeta_k^{11}} (1 - F_1(x + \zeta_k^{01}))(1 - F_2(x + \zeta_k^{10})) dx \right]. \quad (11)$$

The minimization problem (11) is equivalent to the original problem (6), and the dependency between their solutions is described by (8), (9) and (10). The only constraints are the monotonicity of the sequence $\{\zeta_k^x\}$ for a fixed x, and therefore we obtain

$$\zeta_0^x = 0 \leq \zeta_1^x \leq \zeta_2^x \leq \ldots \leq \zeta_k^x \leq \ldots. \quad (12)$$

Since (11) reaches its optimal values either when

$$\frac{du}{d\zeta_k^x} = 0 \text{ for } k = 1, \ldots, n, \ldots, \quad (13)$$

or on the border described by (12), we can prove the following theorem:

Theorem 1 (The chain theorem for two processes)

1. *The value for ζ_{k+1}^{01} may either be ζ_k^{01}, or can be computed given ζ_{k-1}^{11}, ζ_k^{01}, ζ_k^{10} and ζ_k^{11} using the formula*

$$- f_2(\zeta_k^{10} + \zeta_k^{11}) \int_{\zeta_k^{01}}^{\zeta_{k+1}^{01}} (1 - F_1(x + \zeta_k^{11})) dx -$$
$$(1 + c) \int_{\zeta_{k-1}^{11}}^{\zeta_k^{11}} (1 - F_1(x + \zeta_k^{01})) f_2(x + \zeta_k^{10}) dx + \quad (14)$$
$$(1 - F_1(\zeta_{k-1}^{11} + \zeta_k^{01}))(1 - F_2(\zeta_{k-1}^{11} + \zeta_k^{10})) -$$
$$(1 - F_1(\zeta_k^{11} + \zeta_{k+1}^{01}))(1 - F_2(\zeta_k^{10} + \zeta_k^{11})) = 0.$$

2. *The value for ζ_{k+1}^{10} may either be ζ_k^{10}, or can be computed given ζ_k^{01}, ζ_k^{10}, ζ_k^{11} and ζ_{k+1}^{01} using the formula*

$$- f_2(\zeta_k^{10} + \zeta_k^{11}) \int_{\zeta_k^{01}}^{\zeta_{k+1}^{01}} (1 - F_1(x + \zeta_k^{11})) dx -$$

$$f_1(\zeta_k^{11} + \zeta_{k+1}^{01}) \int_{\zeta_k^{10}}^{\zeta_{k+1}^{10}} (1 - F_2(x + \zeta_k^{11})) dx +$$

$$c(1 - F_1(\zeta_k^{01} + \zeta_k^{11}))(1 - F_2(\zeta_k^{10} + \zeta_k^{11})) -$$

$$c(1 - F_1(\zeta_k^{11} + \zeta_{k+1}^{01}))(1 - F_2(\zeta_{k+1}^{11} + \zeta_{k+1}^{10})) = 0.$$

(15)

3. *The value for ζ_{k+1}^{11} may either be ζ_k^{11}, or can be computed given ζ_k^{10}, ζ_k^{11}, ζ_{k+1}^{01} and ζ_{k+1}^{10} using the formula*

$$- f_1(\zeta_k^{11} + \zeta_{k+1}^{01}) \int_{\zeta_k^{10}}^{\zeta_{k+1}^{10}} (1 - F_2(x + \zeta_k^{11})) dx -$$

$$(1 + c) \int_{\zeta_k^{11}}^{\zeta_{k+1}^{11}} f_1(x + \zeta_{k+1}^{01})(1 - F_2(x + \zeta_{k+1}^{10})) dx +$$

$$(1 - F_1(\zeta_k^{11} + \zeta_{k+1}^{01}))(1 - F_2(\zeta_k^{10} + \zeta_k^{11})) -$$

$$(1 - F_1(\zeta_{k+1}^{01} + \zeta_{k+1}^{11}))(1 - F_2(\zeta_{k+1}^{10} + \zeta_{k+1}^{11})) = 0.$$

(16)

This theorem shows a way to compute the values for ζ_k^x in a sequential manner, each time using four previously computed values. This leads to the following algorithm for building an optimal schedule.

Optimal solution for two processes: an algorithm[4]

Assume that S^{01} is the first state which takes a non-zero time ($\zeta_1^{11} > 0$). By Theorem 1, given the values of $\zeta_0^{11} = 0$, ζ_1^{01}, ζ_1^{10} and ζ_1^{11} we can determine all the possible values for ζ_2^{01} (either ζ_1^{01} or one of the roots of (14)). Given the values up to ζ_2^{01}, we can determine the values for ζ_2^{10}, and so on.

Therefore, the first three values of ζ (given $\zeta_1^{01} \neq 0$) provide us with a tree of possible values of ζ_k^x. The branching factor of this tree is determined by the number of roots of (14), (15) and (16). Each possible sequence $\zeta_1^{01}, \zeta_1^{10}, \zeta_1^{11}, \ldots$ can be evaluated using (11). The series in that expression must converge, so we stop after a finite number of points. For each triplet $Z_1 = \langle \zeta_1^{01}, \zeta_1^{10}, \zeta_1^{11} \rangle$ we can find the best sequence using one of the standard search algorithms, such as Branch-and-Bound. Let us denote the value of the best sequence for Z_1 by $E_u(Z_1)$. Performing global optimization of $E_u(Z_1)$ by $\zeta_1^{01}, \zeta_1^{10}$ and ζ_1^{11} provides us with an optimal solution for the case where S^{01} is the first state of non-zero time.

Note, that the value of ζ_1^{01} may also be 0 (if S^{10} or S^{11} happen first), so we need to compare the value obtained by optimization of the triplet $\zeta_1^{01}, \zeta_1^{10}$ and ζ_1^{11} with the value obtained by optimization of the triplet $\zeta_1^{10}, \zeta_1^{11}$ and ζ_2^{01} given $\zeta_1^{01} = 0$, and with the value obtained by optimization of the triplet $\zeta_1^{11}, \zeta_2^{01}$ and ζ_2^{10} given $\zeta_1^{01} = \zeta_1^{10} = 0$.

---

[4]Due to the lack of space we present only the main idea of the algorithm.

Using optimal scheduling for parallelizing the Latin Square problem

We tested our algorithm for optimal scheduling of independent processes solving the partial Latin Square problem. The task is to use N colors to color a $N \times N$ square such that each color appears only once at each row and each column. Some of the tiles may be already colored.

We assume that we are allocated two processors and that we attempt to accelerate the time of finding a solution by starting from two different initial configurations in parallel. Each of the processes employs heuristic DFS with the First-Fail heuristic (Gomes & Selman 1997). We also assume that there is a cost associated with the actual CPU time consumed by each of the processors. Note that our goal is not to build the best algorithm for solving this problem but rather to find the best schedule for the two instances of the given algorithms.

Our experiments were performed with $N = 20$ and 10% of the square pre-colored. The performance profile was induced based on a run of $50,000$ instances. We compare the optimal schedule produced by our algorithm to the schedule which runs both processes in parallel.

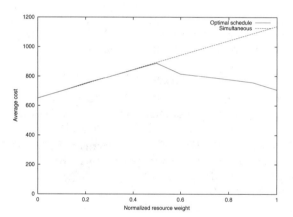

Figure 3: Average cost as a function of normalized resource weight c.

Figure 3 shows how the tradeoff between time and CPU cost influences the resulting cost of the schedules. Each point represents an average over $25,000$ pairs of problems. The x axis corresponds to the normalized weight c of the CPU cost. Thus, $c = 0$ means that we consider elapsed time only; $c = 1$ means that we consider CPU time only; and $c = 0.5$ means that the costs of elapsed and CPU time are equal. The y axis stands for the average cost measured by the number of generated nodes.

We can see that when the weight of CPU time is high enough, the optimal schedules found by our algorithm outperform the simple parallelization scheme.

Conclusions

In this work we present a theoretical framework for optimal scheduling of parallel anytime algorithms for the case of independent processes. We analyze the properties of optimal schedules for the suspend-resume model, and provide an algorithm for designing such schedules. Initial experimentation demonstrates the merit of our scheduling algorithm. The advantage of optimal scheduling over simple parallelization becomes more significant when the weight of the resource cost increases.

One potential weakness of the presented algorithm is its high complexity. This complexity can be represented as a multiplication of three factors: 3-variable function minimization, Branch-and-Bound search and solving Equations (14), (15) and (16). The only exponential component is the Branch-and-Bound search. We found, however, that in practice the branching factor, which is roughly the number of roots of the equations above, is rather small, while the depth of the search tree can be controlled by iterative-deepening strategies. The presented framework can be generalized for an arbitrary number of processes although a straightforward generalization will lead to complexity exponential by this number.

Our algorithm assumes the availability of the performance profiles of the involved processes. Such performance profiles can be derived analytically using theoretical models of the processes or empirically from previous experience with solving similar problems. Online learning of performance profiles, which could expand the applicability of the proposed framework, is a subject of ongoing research.

References

Boddy, M., and Dean, T. 1994. Decision-theoretic deliberation scheduling for problem solving in time-constrained environments. *Artificial Intelligence* 67(2):245–286.

Clearwater, S. H.; Hogg, T.; and Huberman, B. A. 1992. Cooperative problem solving. In Huberman, B., ed., *Computation: The Micro and Macro View*. Singapore: World Scientific. 33–70.

Dean, T., and Boddy, M. 1988. An analysis of time-dependent planning. In *Proceedings of the Seventh National Conference on Artificial Intelligence (AAAI-88)*, 49–54. Saint Paul, Minnesota, USA: AAAI Press/MIT Press.

Finkelstein, L., and Markovitch, S. 2001. Optimal schedules for monitoring anytime algorithms. *Artificial Intelligence* 126:63–108.

Finkelstein, L.; Markovitch, S.; and Rivlin, E. 2001. Optimal schedules for parallelizing anytime algorithms. In *Papers from the 2001 AAAI Fall Symposium*, 49–56.

Finkelstein, L.; Markovitch, S.; and Rivlin, E. 2002. Optimal schedules for parallelizing anytime algorithms: The case of independent processes. Technical Report CIS-2002-04, CS department,Technion, Haifa, Israel.

Gomes, C. P., and Selman, B. 1997. Algorithm portfolio design: Theory vs. practice. In *Proceedings of UAI-97*, 190–197. San Francisco: Morgan Kaufmann.

Gomes, C. P.; Selman, B.; and Kautz, H. 1998. Boosting combinatorial search through randomization. In *Proceedings of the 15th National Conference on Artificial Intelligence (AAAI-98)*, 431–437. Menlo Park: AAAI Press.

Horvitz, E. J. 1987. Reasoning about beliefs and actions under computational resource constraints. In *Proceedings of UAI-87*.

Huberman, B. A.; Lukose, R. M.; and Hogg, T. 1997. An economic approach to hard computational problems. *Science* 275:51–54.

Janakiram, V. K.; Agrawal, D. P.; and Mehrotra, R. 1988. A randomized parallel backtracking algorithm. *IEEE Transactions on Computers* 37(12):1665–1676.

Knight, K. 1993. Are many reactive agents better than a few deliberative ones. In *Proceedings of the Thirteenth International Joint Conference on Artificial Intelligence*, 432–437. Chambéry, France: Morgan Kaufmann.

Korf, R. E. 1990. Real-time heuristic search. *Artificial Intelligence* 42:189–211.

Kumar, V., and Rao, V. N. 1987. Parallel depth-first search on multiprocessors part II: Analysis. *International Journal of Parallel Programming* 16(6):501–519.

Luby, M., and Ertel, W. 1994. Optimal parallelization of Las Vegas algorithms. In *Proceedings of the Annual Symposium on the Theoretical Aspects of Computer Science (STACS '94)*, 463–474. Berlin, Germany: Springer.

Luby, M.; Sinclair, A.; and Zuckerman, D. 1993. Optimal speedup of las vegas algorithms. *Information Processing Letters* 47:173–180.

Rao, V. N., and Kumar, V. 1987. Parallel depth-first search on multiprocessors part I: Implementation. *International Journal of Parallel Programming* 16(6):479–499.

Rao, V. N., and Kumar, V. 1993. On the efficiency of parallel backtracking. *IEEE Transactions on Parallel and Distributed Systems* 4(4):427–437.

Russell, S., and Wefald, E. 1991. *Do the Right Thing: Studies in Limited Rationality*. Cambridge, Massachusetts: The MIT Press.

Russell, S. J., and Zilberstein, S. 1991. Composing real-time systems. In *Proceedings of the Twelfth National Joint Conference on Artificial Intelligence (IJCAI-91)*, 212–217. Sydney: Morgan Kaufmann.

Simon, H. A. 1955. A behavioral model of rational choice. *Quarterly Journal of Economics* 69:99–118.

Simon, H. A. 1982. *Models of Bounded Rationality*. MIT Press.

Yokoo, M., and Kitamura, Y. 1996. Multiagent real-time-A* with selection: Introducing competition in cooperative search. In *Proceedings of the Second International Conference on Multiagent Systems (ICMAS-96)*, 409–416.

Zilberstein, S., and Russell, S. J. 1992. Efficient resource-bounded reasoning in AT-RALPH. In *Proceedings of the First International Conference on AI Planning Systems*, 260–266.

Zilberstein, S. 1993. *Operational Rationality Through Compilation of Anytime Algorithms*. Ph.D. Dissertation, Computer Science Division, University of California, Berkeley.

Optimal Depth-First Strategies for And-Or Trees

Russell Greiner   **Ryan Hayward**
Dept of Computing Science
University of Alberta
{greiner, hayward}@cs.ualberta.ca

Michael Molloy
Dept of Computer Science
University of Toronto
molloy@cs.toronto.edu

Abstract

Many tasks require evaluating a specified boolean expression φ over a set of probabilistic tests where we know the probability that each test will succeed, and also the cost of performing each test. A strategy specifies when to perform which test, towards determining the overall outcome of φ. This paper investigates the challenge of finding the strategy with the minimum expected cost.

We observe first that this task is typically NP-hard — e.g., when tests can occur many times within φ, or when there are probabilistic correlations between the test outcomes. We therefore focus on the situation where the tests are probabilistically independent and each appears only once in φ. Here, φ can be written as an and-or *tree, where each internal node corresponds to either the "And" or "Or" of its children, and each leaf node is a probabilistic test.*

There is an obvious depth-first approach to evaluating such and-or *trees: First evaluate each penultimate subtree in isolation; then reduce this subtree to a single "mega-test" with an appropriate cost and probability, and recur on the resulting reduced tree. After formally defining this approach, we prove first that it produces the optimal strategy for shallow (depth 1 or 2)* and-or *trees, then show it can be arbitrarily bad for deeper trees. We next consider a larger, natural subclass of strategies — those that can be expressed as a linear sequence of tests — and show that the best such "linear strategy" can also be very much worse than the optimal strategy in general. Finally, we show that our results hold in a more general model, where* internal *nodes can also be probabilistic tests.*

Keywords: Satisficing search, Diagnosis, Computational complexity

1 Introduction

Baby J is a fussy eater, who only likes foods that are sweet, or contain milk and fruit, or contain milk and cereal; see Figure 1. Suppose that you want to determine whether J will like some new food, and that you can test whether the food satisfies J's basic food-properties (Sweet, Milk, Fruit, Cereal), where each test has a known cost (say unit cost for this example). Notice that the outcome of one test may render other test(s) unnecessary (if the food has Fruit, it

does not matter whether it has Cereal), so the cost of determining whether J finds a food yummy depends on the order in which tests are performed as well as their outcomes.

A strategy[1] describes the order in which tests are to be performed. For example, the strategy $\xi_{\langle SMCF \rangle}$ first performs the Sweet test, returning true (aka Yummy) if it succeeds; if it fails, $\xi_{\langle SMCF \rangle}$ will perform the Milk test, returning false if it fails. Otherwise (if Sweet fails and Milk succeeds), $\xi_{\langle SMCF \rangle}$ will perform the Cereal test, returning false if it fails; if it succeeds, $\xi_{\langle SMCF \rangle}$ will perform the Fruit test, returning true/false if it succeeds/fails. See Figure 2(a). Notice that $\xi_{\langle SMCF \rangle}$ will typically perform only a subset of the 4 tests; e.g., it will skip all of the remaining tests if Sweet succeeds.

Of course, there are other strategies for this situation, including $\xi_{\langle SMFC \rangle}$, which differs from $\xi_{\langle SMCF \rangle}$ only by testing Fruit before Cereal, and $\xi_{\langle SCFM \rangle}$, which tests the Cereal-Fruit component before Milk. Each strategy is correct, in that it correctly determines whether J will like a food or not. However, for a given food, different strategies will perform different subsets of the tests. (E.g., while $\xi_{\langle SMCF \rangle}$ will perform all of the tests for a non-sweet, milky non-cereal with fruit, $\xi_{\langle SMFC \rangle}$ will not need to perform the final Cereal test.) Hence, different strategies can have different costs. If we also know the likelihood that each test will succeed, we can then compute the *expected cost* of a strategy, over the distribution of foods considered.

In general, there can be an exponential number of strategies, each of which returns the correct answer, but which vary in terms of their expected costs. This paper discusses the task of computing the best — that is, minimum cost and correct — strategy, for various classes of problems.

1.1 Framework

Each of the strategies discussed so far is *depth-first* in that, for each and-or subtree, the tests on the leaves of the subtree appear together in the strategy. We will also consider strategies that are not depth-first; e.g., $\xi_{\langle CSMF \rangle}$ is not depth-first, since it starts with Cereal and then moves on to Sweet before completing the evaluation of the i#2-rooted subtree.

This strategy, like the depth-first ones, is *linear*, as it can be described in a *linear* fashion: proceed through the tests in

---

[1] Formal definitions are presented in §2.

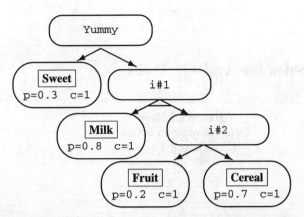

Figure 1: An and-or tree, T_1. Here and-nodes are indicated with a horizontal bar through the descending arcs; i#1 is an and-node while Yummy and i#2 are or-nodes.

the given order, omitting tests only if logically unnecessary.

There are also non-linear strategies. For example, the ξ_{nl} strategy, Figure 2(b), first tests Cereal and if positive, tests Milk then (if necessary) Sweet. However, if the Cereal test is negative, it then tests Sweet then (if necessary) Fruit then Milk. Notice no linear sequence can describe this strategy as, for some instances, it tests Milk before Sweet, but for others, it tests Sweet before Milk.

We consider only *correct* strategies, namely those that return the correct value for any assignment. We can measure the performance of a strategy by the expected cost of returning the answer. A standard simplifying assumption is to require that these tests be independent of each other — *e.g.*, Figure 1 indicates that 30% of the foods sampled are Sweet, 80% are with Milk, etc. While each strategy returns the correct boolean value, they have different expected costs. For example, the expected cost of $\xi_{\langle SMCF \rangle}$ is

$$C[\xi_{\langle SMCF \rangle}] = c(S) + Pr(-S) \times [c(M) + Pr(+M) \times [c(C) + Pr(-C)\, c(F)]]$$

where $Pr(+T)$ (resp., $Pr(-T)$) is the probability that test T succeeds (resp., fails), and $c(T)$ is the cost of T.

Suppose that we are given a particular *probabilistic boolean expression* (PBE), which is a boolean formula, together with the success probabilities and costs for its variables. A strategy is *optimal* if it (always returns the correct value and) has minimum expected cost, over all such strategies. This paper considers the so-called minimum cost resolution strategy problem (MRSP): given such a formula, probabilities and costs, determine an optimal strategy.

§2 describes these and related notions more formally. §3 describes an algorithm, DFA [Nat86], that produces a depth-first strategy, then proves several theorems about this algorithm; in particular, that DFA produces the optimal *depth-first* strategy, that this DFA strategy is optimal for and-or trees with depth 1 or 2 (Theorem 4), but it can be quite far from optimal in general (Theorem 6). §4 then formally defines *linear strategies*, shows they are strict generalizations of depth-first strategies, and proves (Theorem 8) that the best linear strategy can be far from optimal. §5 motivates and defines an extension to the PBE model, called "Precondition

PBE", where each test can only performed in some context (*i.e.*, if some boolean condition is satisfied), and shows that the same results apply. The extended paper [GHM02] provides the proofs for the theorems.

1.2 Related Work

We close this section by framing our problem, and providing a brief literature survey (see also §5.1). The notion of MRSP appears in Simon and Kadane [SK75], who use the term *satisficing search* in place of *strategy*. Application instances include screening employment candidates for a position [Gar73], competing for prizes at a quiz show [Gar73], mining for gold buried in Spanish treasure chests [SK75], and performing inference in a simple expert system [Smi89; GO91].

We motivate our particular approach by considering the complexity of the MRSProblem for various classes of probabilistic boolean expressions. First, in the case of arbitrary boolean formulae, MRSP is NP-hard. (Reduction from SAT [GJ79]: if there are no satisfying assignments to a formula, then there is no need to perform any tests, and so a 0-cost strategy is optimal.)

We can try to avoid this degeneracy by considering only "positive formulae", where every variable occurs only positively. However, the MRSP remains NP-hard here. (Proof: reduction from ExactCoverBy3Set, using the same construction that [HR76] used to show the hardness of finding the smallest decision tree.)

A further restriction is to consider "read-once" formulae, where each variable appears only one time. As noted above, we can view each such formula as an "and-or tree". The MRSP complexity here is not known.

This paper considers some special cases. Barnett [Bar84] discusses how the choice of optimal strategy depends on the probability values in a special case when there are two independent tests (and so only two alternative search strategies). Geiger and Barnett [GB91] note that the optimal strategies for and-or trees cannot be represented by a linear order of the nodes. Natarajan [Nat86] introduced the efficient algorithm we call DFA for dealing with and-or trees, but did not investigate the question of when it is optimal. Our paper proves that this simple algorithm in fact solves the MRSP for very shallow-trees, of depth 1 or 2, but can do very poorly in general.

We consider the tests to be statistically independent of each other; this is why it suffices to use simply $Pr(+X)$, as test X does not depend on the results of the other experiments that had been performed earlier. If we allow statistical dependencies, then the read-once restriction is not helpful, as we can convert any non-read-once but independent PBE to a read-once but correlated PBE by changing the i-th occurrence of the test "X" to a new "X_i", but then insist that X_1 is equal to X_2, etc. We will therefore continue to consider the tests to be independent.

2 Definitions

We focus on read-once formulae, which correspond to and-or trees — *i.e.*, a tree structure whose leaf nodes are each

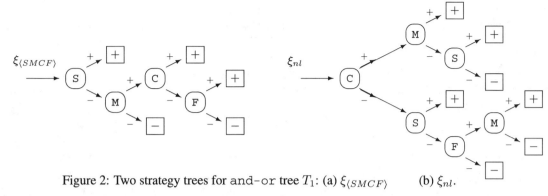

Figure 2: Two strategy trees for and-or tree T_1: (a) $\xi_{\langle SMCF \rangle}$ (b) ξ_{nl}.

labeled with a probabilistic test (with a known positive cost[2] and success probability) and whose internal nodes are each labeled as an or-node or an and-node, with the understanding that the subtree rooted at an and-node (or-node) is satisfied if and only if all (at least one) of the subtrees are satisfied.

Given any assignment of the probabilistic tests, for example $\{-S, +M, -F, +C\}$, we can propagate the assignment from the leaf nodes up the tree, combining them appropriately at each internal node, until reaching the root node; the *value* is the tree's overall evaluation of the assignment.

A *strategy* ξ for an and-or tree T is a procedure for evaluating the tree, with respect to any assignment. In general, we present a strategy itself as a tree, whose internal nodes are labeled with probabilistic tests and whose leaf nodes are labeled either true + or false -, and whose arcs are labeled with the values of the parent's test (+ or -). By convention, we will draw these strategy trees sideways, from left-to-right, to avoid confusing them with top-to-bottom and-or trees. Figure 2 shows two such strategy trees for the T_1 and-or tree. Different nodes of a strategy tree may be labeled with the same test. Recall that the strategy need not corresponds to a simple linear sequence of experiments; see discussion of ξ_{nl}.

For any and-or tree T, we will only consider the set of *correct* strategies $\Xi(T)$, namely those that return the correct value for all test assignments. For T_1 in Figure 1, each of the strategies in $\Xi(T_1)$ returns the value $S \vee (M \wedge [F \vee C])$.

For any test assignment γ, we let $k(\xi, \gamma)$ be the cost of using the strategy ξ to determine the (correct) value. For example, for $\gamma = \{-S, +M, -F, +C\}$, $k(\xi_{\langle SMFC \rangle}, \gamma) = c(S) + c(M) + c(F) + c(C)$ while $k(\xi_{\langle CMSF \rangle}, \gamma) = c(C) + c(M)$.

The *expected cost* of a strategy ξ is the average cost of evaluating an assignment, over all assignments, namely

$$C[\xi] = \sum_{\gamma: \text{Assignment}} \Pr(\gamma) \times k(\xi, \gamma). \quad (1)$$

Given the independence of the tests, there is a more efficient way to evaluate a strategy than the algorithm implied

<hr/>

[2] We can also allow 0-cost tests, in which case we simply assume that a strategy will perform all such tests first, leaving us with the challenge of evaluating the reduced MRSP whose tests all have strictly-positive costs.

by Equation 1. Extending the notation $C[\cdot]$ to apply to any strategy sub-tree, the expected cost of a leaf node is $C[\boxed{+}] = C[\boxed{-}] = 0$, and of a (sub)tree φ_χ rooted at a node labeled χ is just

$$C[\varphi_\chi] = c(\chi) + \Pr(+\chi) \times C[\varphi_{+\chi}] + \Pr(-\chi) \times C[\varphi_{-\chi}] \quad (2)$$

where $\varphi_{+\chi}$ ($\varphi_{-\chi}$) is the subtree rooted at χ's + branch (− branch).

To define our goal:

Definition 1 *A correct strategy* $\xi^* \in \Xi(T)$ *is optimal for an* and-or *tree* T *if and only if its cost is minimal, namely*
$$\forall \xi \in \Xi(T), \quad C[\xi_T] \leq C[\xi].$$

Depth, "Strictly Alternating": We define the *depth* of a tree to be the maximum number of internal nodes in any leaf-to-root path. (Hence depth 1 corresponds to simple conjunctions or disjunctions, and depth 2 corresponds to CNF or DNF.)

For now (until §5), we will assume that an and-or tree is *strictly alternating*, namely that the parent of each internal and-node is an or-node, and vice versa. If not, we can obtain an equivalent tree by collapsing any or-node (and-node) child of an or-node (and-node). Any strategy of the original tree is a strategy of the collapsed one, with identical expected cost.

3 The depth-first algorithm DFA

To help define our DFA algorithm, we first consider depth 1 trees.

Observation 1 *[SK75] Let* T_O *be a depth 1 tree whose root is an* or *node, whose children correspond to tests* $A_1, \ldots, A_r$, *with success probabilities* $\Pr(+A_i)$ *and costs* $c(A_i)$. *Then the optimal strategy for* T_O *is the one-path strategy* $A_{\pi_1}, \ldots, A_{\pi_r}$, *(Figure 3(c)) where* π *is defined so that* $\Pr(+A_{\pi_j})/c(A_{\pi_j}) \geq \Pr(+A_{\pi_{j+1}})/c(A_{\pi_{j+1}})$ *for* $1 \leq j < r$.

Proof: As we can stop as soon as any test succeeds, we need only consider what action to perform after each initial sequence of tests has failed; hence we need only consider strategy trees with "one-path" structures. Towards a contradiction, suppose the optimal strategy ξ_{AB} did not satisfy this ordering, in that there was (at least one) pair of tests, A and B such that A came before B but $\Pr(+A)/c(A) <$

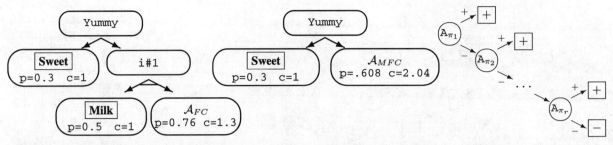

Figure 3: Intermediate results of DFA on T_1 (a) after 1 iteration (b) after 2 iterations. (c) A one-path strategy tree.

$\Pr(+B)/c(B)$. Now consider the strategy ξ_{BA} that reordered these tests; and observe that ξ_{BA}'s expected cost is strictly less than ξ_{AB}'s, contradicting the claim that ξ_{AB} was optimal. □

An isomorphic proof shows ...

Observation 2 *Let T_A be a depth 1 tree whose root is an* and *node, defined analogously to T_O in Observation 1. Then the optimal strategy for T_A is the one-path strategy $A_{\phi_1}, \ldots, A_{\phi_r}$, where ϕ is defined so that $\Pr(-A_{\phi_j})/c(A_{\phi_j}) \geq \Pr(-A_{\phi_{j+1}})/c(A_{\phi_{j+1}})$ for $1 \leq j < r$.*

Now consider a depth-s alternating tree. The DFA algorithm will first deal with the bottom tree layer, and order the children of each final internal node as suggested here: in order of $\Pr(+A_i)/c(A_i)$ if the node is an or-node. (Here we focus on the or-node case; the and-node case is analogous.) For example, if dealing with Figure 1's T_1, DFA would compare $\Pr(+F)/c(F) = 0.2/1$ with $\Pr(+C)/c(C) = 0.7/1$, and order C first, as $0.7 > 0.2$.

DFA then replaces this penultimate node and its children with a single mega-node; call it $\mathcal{A}$, whose success probability is

$$\Pr(+\mathcal{A}) = 1 - \prod_i \Pr(-A_i)$$

and whose cost is the expected cost of dealing with this subtree:

$$c(\mathcal{A}) = c(A_{\pi_1}) + \Pr(-A_{\pi_1}) \times [c(A_{\pi_2}) + \Pr(-A_{\pi_2}) \times (\ldots c(A_{\pi_{r-1}}) + \Pr(-A_{\pi_{r-1}}) \times c(A_{\pi_r}))]$$

Returning to T_1, DFA would replace the $i\#2$-rooted subtree with the single $\mathcal{A}_{FC}$-labeled node, with success probability $\Pr(+\mathcal{A}_{FC}) = 1 - (\Pr(-F) \times \Pr(-C)) = 1 - 0.8 \times 0.3 = 0.76$, and cost $c(\mathcal{A}_{FC}) = c(C) + \Pr(-C) \times c(F) = 1 + 0.3 \times 1 = 1.3$; see Figure 2(a).

Now recur: consider the and-node that is the parent to this mega-node $\mathcal{A}$ and its siblings. DFA inserts this $\mathcal{A}$ test among these siblings based on its $\Pr(-\mathcal{A})/c(\mathcal{A})$ value, and so forth.

On T_1, DFA would then compare $\Pr(-M)/c(M) = 0.2/1$ with $\Pr(-\mathcal{A}_{FC})/c(\mathcal{A}_{FC}) = 0.24/1.3$ and so select the M-labeled node to go first. Hence, the substrategy associated with the $i\#1$ subtree will first perform M, and return $-$ if unsuccessful. Otherwise, it will then perform the $\mathcal{A}_{FC}$ megatest: Here, it first performs C, and returns $+$ if C succeeds. Otherwise this substrategy will perform F, and return $+$ if it succeeds or $-$ otherwise.

DFA then creates a bigger mega-node, $\mathcal{A}_{MFC}$, with success probability $\Pr(+\mathcal{A}_{MFC}) = \Pr(+M) \times \Pr(+\mathcal{A}_{FC}) = 0.8 \times 0.76 = 0.608$, and cost $c(\mathcal{A}_{MFC}) = c(M) + \Pr(+M) \times c(\mathcal{A}_{FC}) = 1 + 0.8 \times 1.3 = 2.04$; see Figure 2(b).

Finally, DFA compares S with $\mathcal{A}_{MFC}$, and selects S to go first as $\Pr(+S)/c(S) = 0.3/1 > 0.608/2.04 = \Pr(+\mathcal{A}_{MFC})/c(\mathcal{A}_{MFC})$. This produces the $\xi_{\langle SMCF \rangle}$ strategy, shown in Figure 2.

This DFA algorithm is very efficient: As it examines each node only in the context of computing its position under its immediate parent (which requires sorting that node and its siblings), DFA requires only $O(\sum_v d^+(v) \log d^+(v)) = O(n \ln r)$ time, where n is the total number of nodes in the and-or tree, and $d^+(v)$ is the out-degree of the node v, which is bounded above by r, the largest out-degree of any internal node.

Notice also that DFA keeps together all of the tests under each internal node, which means it is producing a *depth-first strategy*. To state this more precisely, we first identify each (sub)tree S of a given and-or tree T with an associated boolean expression $\phi(S)$. (E.g., the boolean expression associated with $S_{i\#1}$, the subtree of Figure 1's T_1 rooted in $i\#1$, is $\phi(S_{i\#1}) \equiv M\&(F \vee C)$.) During the evaluation of a strategy for T, an and-or subtree S is "determined" once we know the value of $\phi(S)$.

Definition 2 *A strategy ξ for T is depth-first if, for each subtree S, whenever a leaf of S is tested, ξ will determine the boolean value of $\phi(S)$ before performing any test outside of S.*

To see that $\xi_{\langle SMCF \rangle}$ (Figure 2(a)) is depth-first, notice that every time C appears, it is followed (when necessary) by F; notice this $C - F$ block will determine the value of the $S_{i\#2}$ subtree. Similarly, the $M - C - F$ block in $\xi_{\langle SMCF \rangle}$ will always determine the value of the $S_{i\#1}$ subtree. By contrast, the $\xi_{\langle CMSF \rangle}$ strategy is not depth-first, as there is a path where C is performed but, before the $S_{i\#2}$ subtree is determined (by testing F) another test (here M) is performed. Similarly ξ_{nl} is not depth-first.

3.1 DFA Results

First observe that DFA is optimal over a particular subclass of strategies:

Observation 3 DFA *produces a strategy that has the lowest cost among all depth-first strategies.*

Proof: By induction on the depth of the tree. Observations 1 and 2 establish the base case, for depth-1 trees. Given the depth-first constraint, the only decision to make when considering depth-$s+1$ trees is how to order the strategy subtree blocks associated with the depth-s `and-or` subtrees; here we just re-use Observations 1 and 2 on the mega-blocks. □

Observations 1 and 2 show that DFA produces the best possible strategy, for the class of depth-1 trees. Moreover, an inductive proof shows ...

Theorem 4 DFA *produces the optimal strategies for depth-2* `and-or` *trees, i.e., read-once DNF or CNF formulae.*

Theorem 4 holds for arbitrary costs — *i.e.*, the proof does not require unit costs for the tests. It is tempting to believe that DFA works in all situations. However ...

Observation 5 DFA *does not always produce the optimal strategy for depth* 3 `and-or` *trees, even in the unit cost case.*

We prove this by just considering T_1 from Figure 1. As noted above, DFA will produce the $\xi_{\langle SMCF \rangle}$ strategy, whose expected cost (using Equation 2 with earlier results) is $C[\xi_{\langle SMCF \rangle}] = c(\text{S}) + \Pr(-\text{S}) \times c(\mathcal{A}_{MCF}) = 1 + 0.7 \times 2.04 = 2.428$. However, the ξ_{nl} strategy, which is *not* depth-first, has lower expected cost $C[\xi_{nl}] = 1 + 0.7[1 + 0.2 \times 1] + 0.3[1 + 0.7 \times (1 + 0.2 \times 1)] = 2.392$.

Still, as this difference in cost is relatively small, and as ξ_{nl} is not linear, one might suspect that DFA returns a reasonably good strategy, or at least the best *linear* strategy. However, we show below that this claim is far from being true.

In the unit-cost situation, the minimum cost for any nontrivial n-node tree is 1, and the maximum possible is n; hence a ratio of $n/1 = n$ over the optimal score is the worst possible — *i.e.*, no algorithm can be off by a factor of more than n over the optimum.

Theorem 6 *For every* $\epsilon > 0$*, there is a unit-cost* `and-or` *tree* T *for which the best depth-first strategy costs* $n^{1-\epsilon}$ *times as much as the best strategy.*

4 Linear Strategies

As noted above (Definition 2) we can write down each of these DFA-produced strategies in a linear fashion; *e.g.*, $\xi_{\langle SMCF \rangle}$ can be viewed as test S, then if necessary test M, then if necessary test C and if necessary test F. In general...

Definition 3 *A strategy is* linear *if it performs the tests in fixed linear order, with the understanding that the strategy will skip any test that will not help determine the value of the tree, given what is already known.*

Hence, $\xi_{\langle SMCF \rangle}$ will skip all of M, C, F if the S test succeeds; and it will skip the C and F tests if M fails, and will skip F if C succeeds.

As any permutation of the tests corresponds to a linear strategy, there are of course $n!$ such strategies. One natural question is whether there are simple ways to produce "good" strategies from this class. The answer here is "yes":

Observation 7 DFA *algorithm produces linear strategies.*

Proof: Argue by induction on the depth k. For $k = 1$, the result holds by Observations 1 and 2. For $k \geq 2$, use the inductive hypothesis to see that DFA will produce a linear ordering for each subtree (as each subtree is of depth $\leq k-1$). DFA will then form a linear strategy by simply sequencing the linear strategies of the subtrees. □

Observation 3 implies there is always a linear strategy (perhaps that one produced by DFA) that is at least as good as any depth-first strategy. Unfortunately the converse is not true — the class of strategies considered in Theorem 6 are in fact linear, which means the best depth-first strategy can cost $n^{1-\epsilon}$ times as much as the best *linear* strategy, for any $\epsilon > 0$.

Is there always a linear strategy whose expected cost is near-optimal? Unfortunately, ...

Theorem 8 *For every* $\epsilon > 0$*, there is an* `and-or` *tree* T *for which the best linear strategy costs* $n^{1/3-\epsilon}$ *times as much as an optimal strategy.*

5 Precondition BPE Model

Some previous researchers have considered a generalization of our PBE model that identifies a precondition with each test — *e.g.*, test T can only be performed after test S has been performed and returned $+$. We show below that we get identical results even in this situation.

To motivate this model, suppose there is an external lab that can determine the constituent components of some unknown food, and in particular detect whether it contains milk, fruit or cereal. As the post office will, with probability $1 - \Pr(\text{i\#1})$, lose packages sent to the labs, we therefore view i#1 as a probabilistic test. There is also a cost for mailing a food sample to this lab $c(\text{i\#1})$, which is in addition to the cost associated with each of the specific tests (for Milk, or for Fruit, etc.). Hence if the first test performed in some strategy is Milk, then its cost will be $c(\text{i\#1}) + c(\text{M})$. If we later perform, say, Fruit, the cost of this test is only $c(\text{F})$ (and not $c(\text{i\#1}) + c(\text{F})$), as the sample is already at the lab.

This motivates the notion of a "preconditioned probabilistic boolean expression" (P-PBE) which, in the context of `and-or` trees, allows each internal node to have both a cost and a probability. Notice this cost structure means that a pure or-tree will not collapse to a single level, but can be of arbitrary depth. (In particular, we cannot simply incorporate the cost $c(\text{i\#2})$ into both F and C, as only the first of these tests, within any evaluation process, will have to pay this cost. And we cannot simply associate this cost with one of these tests as it will only be required by the first test, and we do not know which it will be; indeed, this first test could, conceivably, be different for different situations.)

We define the *alternation number* of an `and-or` tree to be the maximum number of alternations, between and-nodes and or-nodes, in any path from the root. Notice that the alternation number of a strictly alternating `and-or` tree is one less than its depth. For example, T_1 in Figure 1 has depth 3 and alternation number 2.

5.1 Previous P-PBE Results

There are a number of prior results within this P-PBE framework. Garey [Gar73] gives an efficient algorithm for finding optimal resolution strategies when the precedence constraints can be represented as an or tree (that is, a tree with no conjunctive subgoals); Simon and Kadane [SK75] extend this to certain classes of or DAGs (directed-acyclic-graphs whose internal nodes are all or). Below we will use the Smith [Smi89] result that, if the P-PBE is read-once and involves only or connections, then there is an efficient algorithm for finding the optimal strategy — essentially linear in the number of nodes [Smi89]. However, without the read-once property, the task becomes NP-hard; see [Gre91]. (Sahni [Sah74] similarly shows that the problem is NP-hard if there can be more than a single path connecting a test to the top level goal, even when all success probabilities are 1.)

One obvious concern with this P-PBE model is the source of these probability values. In the standard PBE framework, it is fairly easy to estimate the success probability of any test, by just performing that test as often as it was needed. This task is more complicated in the P-PBE situation, as some tests can only be performed when others (their preconditions) had succeeded, which may make it difficult to collect sufficient instances to estimate the success probabilities of these "blockable" tests. However, [GO96] shows that it is always possible to collect the relevant information, for any P-PBE structure.

5.2 P-PBE Results

Note first that every standard PBE instance corresponds to a P-PBE where each internal node has cost 0 and success probability 1. This means every negative result about PBE (Theorems 6 and 8) applies to P-PBE.

Our only positive result above is Theorem 4, which proved that an optimal strategy $\xi^*(T)$ for a depth-2 ($\approx$ 1-alternation) and-or tree T is depth-first; i.e., it should explore each sub-tree to completion before considering any other sub-tree. In the DNF case $T \equiv (X_1^1 \& \ldots \& X_{k_1}^1) \lor \cdots \lor (X_1^m \& \ldots \& X_{k_m}^m)$, once we evaluate any term — say $(X_1^i \& \ldots \& X_{k_i}^i)$ — $\xi^*(T)$ will sequentially consider each of these X_j^i until one fails, or until they all succeed, but it will never intersperse any X_ℓ^j ($j \neq i$) within this sequence.

This basic idea also applies to the P-PBE model, but using the [Smi89] algorithm to deal with each "pure" subtree, rather than simply using the $\Pr(\pm X)/c(X)$ ordering. To state this precisely: A subtree is "pure" if all of its internal nodes all have the same label — either all "Or" or all "And"; hence the i#2-rooted subtree in Figure 1 is a pure subtree (in fact, every penultimate node roots a pure subtree), but the subtree rooted in i#1 is not. A pure subtree is "maximal" if it is the entire tree, or if the subtree associated with the parent of its root is not pure; e.g., the i#2-rooted subtree is maximal. Now let DFA* be the variant of DFA that forms a strategy from the bottom up: use [Smi89] to find a substrategy for each maximal pure subtree of the given and-or tree, compute the success probability p and expected cost c of this substrategy, then replace that pure subtree with a single mega-node with probability p and cost c, and recur on the new reduced and-or tree. On the Figure 1 tree, this would produce the reduced trees shown in Figure 2. DFA* terminates when it produces a single node; it is then easy to join the substrategies into a single strategy.

As a corollary to Theorem 4 (using the obvious corollary to Observation 3),

Corollary 9 *In the P-PBE setting,* DFA* *produces the optimal strategies for* 1-*alternation* and-or *trees.*

6 Conclusions

This paper addresses the challenge of computing the optimal strategy for and-or trees. As such strategies can be exponentially larger than the original tree in general, we investigate the subclass of strategies produced by the DFA algorithm, which are guaranteed to be of reasonable size — in fact, linear in the number of tests. After observing that these DFA-produced strategies are the optimal **depth-first** strategies, we then prove that these strategies are in fact the optimal possible strategies for trees with depth 1 or 2. However, for deeper trees, we prove that these depth-first strategies can be arbitrarily worse than the best linear strategies. Moreover, we show that these best linear strategies can be considerably worse than the best possible strategy. We also show that these results also apply to the more general model where intermediate nodes are also probabilistic tests.

Acknowledgements

All authors gratefully acknowledge NSERC. RH also acknowledges a University of Alberta Research Excellence Award; and MM also acknowledges a Sloan Research Fellowship. We also gratefully acknowledge receiving helpful comments from Adnan Darwiche, Rob Holte, Omid Madani and the anonymous reviewers.

References

[Bar84] J. Barnett. How much is control knowledge worth?: A primitive example. *Artificial Intelligence*, 22:77–89, 1984.

[Gar73] M. Garey. Optimal task sequencing with precedence constraints. *Discrete Mathematics*, 4, 1973.

[GB91] D. Geiger and J. Barnett. Optimal satisficing tree searches. In *Proc, AAAI-91*, pages 441–43, 1991.

[GHM02] R. Greiner, R. Hayward, and M. Malloy. Optimal depth-first strategies for And-Or trees. Tech. rep, U. Alberta, 2002.

[GJ79] M. Garey and D. Johnson. *Computers and Intractability: A Guide to the Theory of NP-Completeness.* 1979.

[GO91] R. Greiner and P. Orponen. Probably approximately optimal derivation strategies. In *Proc, KR-91*, 1991.

[GO96] R. Greiner and P. Orponen. Probably approximately optimal satisficing strategies. *Artificial Intelligence*, 82, 1996.

[Gre91] R. Greiner. Finding the optimal derivation strategy in a redundant knowledge base. *Artificial Intelligence*, 50, 1991.

[HR76] L. Hyafil and R. Rivest. Constructing optimal binary decision trees is NP-complete. *Information Processing Letters*, 35(1):15–17, 1976.

[Nat86] K. Natarajan. Optimizing depth-first search of AND-OR trees. Report RC-11842, IBM Watson Research Center, 1986.

[Sah74] S. Sahni. Computationally related problems. *SIAM Journal on Computing*, 3(4):262–279, 1974.

[SK75] H. Simon and J. Kadane. Optimal problem-solving search: All-or-none solutions. *Artificial Intelligence*, 6:235–247, 1975.

[Smi89] D. Smith. Controlling backward inference. *Artificial Intelligence*, 39(2):145–208, June 1989.

A New Algorithm for Optimal Bin Packing

Richard E. Korf
Computer Science Department
University of California, Los Angeles
Los Angeles, CA 90095
korf@cs.ucla.edu

Abstract

We consider the NP-complete problem of bin packing. Given a set of numbers, and a set of bins of fixed capacity, find the minimum number of bins needed to contain all the numbers, such that the sum of the numbers assigned to each bin does not exceed the bin capacity. We present a new algorithm for optimal bin packing. Rather than considering the different bins that each number can be placed into, we consider the different ways in which each bin can be packed. Our algorithm appears to be asymptotically faster than the best existing optimal algorithm, and runs more that a thousand times faster on problems with 60 numbers.

Introduction and Overview

Given a set of numbers, and a fixed bin capacity, the bin-packing problem is to assign each number to a bin so that the sum of all numbers assigned to each bin does not exceed the bin capacity. An optimal solution to a bin-packing problem uses the fewest number of bins possible. For example, given the set of elements 6, 12, 15, 40, 43, 82, and a bin capacity of 100, we can assign 6, 12, and 82 to one bin, and 15, 40, and 43 to another, for a total of two bins. This is an optimal solution to this problem instance, since the sum of all the elements (198) is greater than 100, and hence at least two bins are required.

Optimal bin packing one of the classic NP-complete problems (Garey & Johnson 1979). The vast majority of the literature on this problem concerns polynomial-time approximation algorithms, such as first-fit and best-fit decreasing, and the quality of the solutions they compute, rather than optimal solutions. We discuss these approximation algorithms in the next section.

The best existing algorithm for optimal bin packing is due to Martello and Toth (Martello & Toth 1990a; 1990b). We present a new algorithm for optimal bin packing, which we call *bin completion*, that explores a different problem space, and appears to be asymptotically faster than the Martello and Toth algorithm. On problems of size 60, bin completion runs more than a thousand times faster than Martello and Toth's algorithm. We are able to optimally solve problems with 90 elements in an average of 2.5 seconds per problem.

Approximation Algorithms

A simple approximation algorithm is called first-fit decreasing (FFD). The elements are sorted in decreasing order of size, and the bins are kept in a fixed order. Each element is placed into the first bin that it fits into, without exceeding the bin capacity. For example, given the elements 82, 43, 40, 15, 12, 6, and a bin capacity of 100, first-fit decreasing will place 82 in the first bin, 43 in a second bin, 40 in the second bin, 15 in the first bin, 12 in the second bin, and 6 in a third bin, for a total of three bins, which is one more than optimal.

A slightly better approximation algorithm is known as best-fit decreasing (BFD). It also sorts the elements in decreasing order of size, but puts each element into the *fullest* bin in which is fits. It can be implemented by keeping the bins sorted in increasing order of their remaining capacity, and placing each element into the first bin in which it fits. For example, given the set of elements 82, 43, 40, 15, 12, 6, best-fit decreasing will place 82 in bin a, 43 in bin b, 40 in bin b, 15 in bin b, because it is fuller than bin a, 12 in bin a, and 6 in bin a, for a total of two bins, which is optimal.

Both FFD and BFD can be implemented in $O(n \log n)$ time, but are not guaranteed to return optimal solutions. However, either algorithm is guaranteed to return a solution that uses no more than 11/9 of the optimal number of bins (Johnson 1973). On average, BFD performs slightly better than FFD. For example, on problems of 90 elements, where the elements are uniformly distributed from zero to one million, and the bin capacity is one million, BFD uses an average of 47.732 bins, while FFD uses an average of 47.733 bins. On these same problem instances, the optimal solution averages 47.680 bins. The FFD solution is optimal 94.694% of the time, and the BFD solution is optimal 94.832% of the time on these problem instances.

Optimal Solutions

Given the high quality solutions returned by these approximation algorithms, why bother trying to find optimal solutions? There are at least four reasons. In some applications, it may be important to have optimal solutions. In particular, with small numbers of bins, even a single extra bin is relatively expensive. In addition, being able to determine the optimal solutions to problem instances allows us to more accurately gauge the quality of approximate solutions. For example, the above comparisons of FFD and BFD solutions to optimal solutions were only possible because we could compute the optimal solutions. Another reason is that an anytime algorithm for finding optimal solutions, such as those presented in this paper, can make use of any additional time available to find better solutions than those returned by BFD or FFD, which run very fast in practice. Finally, optimal bin packing is an interesting computational challenge, and may lead to insights applicable to other problems.

Estimated Wasted Space or L2 Lower Bound

A lower bound function for bin packing takes a problem instance, and efficiently computes a lower bound on the minimum number of bins needed. If we find a solution that uses the same number of bins as a lower bound, then we know that solution is optimal, and we can terminate the search.

An obvious lower bound is to sum all the elements, divide by the bin capacity, and round up to the next larger integer. A better bound starts with the sum of the elements, and adds an estimate of the total bin capacity that must be wasted in any solution, before dividing by the bin capacity. This is the L2 bound of Martello and Toth (Martello & Toth 1990a; 1990b), but we give a simpler and more intuitive algorithm for computing it below.

For example, consider the set of elements 99, 97, 94, 93, 8, 5, 4, 2, with a bin capacity of 100. There is no element small enough to go in the same bin as the 99, so that bin will have one unit of wasted space in any solution. The only element small enough to go in the same bin as the 97 is the 2, so the 2 can be placed with the 97 without sacrificing optimality, leaving a second unit of wasted space.

There are two remaining elements that could be placed with the 94, the 5 or the 4. In reality, only one of these elements could be placed with the 94, but to make our lower-bound calculation efficient and avoid any branching, we assume that we can place as much of their sum (9) as will fit in the bin with the 94, or 6 units. Thus, we assume there is no wasted space in this bin, and 3 units are carried over to the next bin, which contains the 93. The sum of all elements less than or equal to the residual capacity of this bin (7) is just the 3 units carried over from the previous bin. Therefore, at least $7 - 3 = 4$ additional units will be wasted between this bin and the previous one. Finally, there are no remaining elements to be placed with the 8, so 92 units must be wasted in this bin. Thus, the total wasted space will be at least $1 + 1 + 4 + 92 = 98$ units, which is added to the sum of all the elements before dividing by the bin capacity.

This estimated wasted-space calculation proceeds as follows. We consider the elements in decreasing order of size. Given an element x, the residual capacity r of the bin containing x is $r = c - x$, where c is the bin capacity. We then consider the sum s of all elements less than or equal to r, which have not already been assigned to a previous bin. There are three possible cases. The first is that r equals s. In that case, there is no estimated waste, and no carry over to the next bin. If $s < r$, then $r - s$ is added to the estimated waste, and again there is no carryover to the next bin. Finally, if $r < s$, then there is no waste added, and $s - r$ is carried over to the next bin. Once the estimated waste is

computed, it is added to the sum of the elements, which is divided by the bin capacity, and then rounded up.

This estimated wasted space adds significantly to the sum of the elements. For example, on problems with 90 elements, uniformly distributed from zero to one million, with a bin capacity of one million, the estimated wasted-space lower bound averages 47.428 bins, while the simple sum lower bound averages only 45.497. For comparison, the average optimal solution for these problem instances is 47.680.

Martello and Toth Algorithm

The best existing algorithm for finding optimal solutions to bin-packing problems is due to Martello and Toth (Martello & Toth 1990a; 1990b). Their branch-and-bound algorithm is complex, and we describe here only the main features. Their basic problem space takes the elements in decreasing order of size, and places each element in turn into each partially-filled bin that it fits in, and into a new bin, branching on these different alternatives. This results in a problem space bounded by $n!$, where n is the number of elements, but this is a very pessimistic upper bound, since many elements won't fit in the same bins as other elements.

At each node of the search tree, Martello and Toth compute the first-fit, best-fit, and worst-fit decreasing completion of the corresponding partial solution. A partial solution to a bin-packing problem is one where some but not all elements have already been assigned to bins. A completion of a partial solution takes the current partially-filled bins, and assigns the remaining unassigned elements to bins. The worst-fit decreasing algorithm places each successive element in the partially-filled bin with the largest residual capacity that will accommodate that value.

Each of these approximate solutions is compared to a lower bound on the remaining solution that they call L3. The L3 bound is computed by successively relaxing the remaining subproblem by removing the smallest element, and then applying the L2 bound to each of the relaxed instances, returning the largest such lower bound. Martello and Toth's L2 bound equals the estimated wasted-space bound described above, but they use a more complex algorithm to compute it. If the number of bins used by any of the approximate completions equals the lower bound for completing the corresponding partial solution, no further search is performed below that node. If the number of bins in any approximate solution equals the lower bound on the original problem, the algorithm terminates, returning that solution as optimal.

The main source of efficiency of the Martello and Toth algorithm is a method to reduce the size of the remaining subproblems, which we will discuss below under "Dominance Relations". First, however, we very briefly discuss another optimal bin-packing program due to Fekete and Schepers.

Fekete and Schepers Lower Bound

Fekete and Schepers (Fekete & Schepers 1998) use the same algorithm as Martello and Toth, but with a more accurate lower-bound function. They claim that the resulting algorithm outperforms Martello and Toth's algorithm, based on solving more problems with the same number of node generations, but didn't report running times. We implemented both algorithms, but found that the Fekete and Schepers algorithm was slower than that of Martello and Toth, because their lower bound function took longer to compute, and this wasn't compensated for by the reduced node generations.

Dominance Relations

Some sets of elements assigned to a bin are guaranteed to lead to solutions that are at least as good as those achievable by assigning other sets of elements to the same bin. We begin with some simple examples of these dominance relations, and then consider the general formulation.

First, consider two elements x and y, such that $x + y = c$, where c is the bin capacity. Assume that in an optimal solution, x and y are in different bins. In that case, we can swap y with all other elements in the bin containing x, without increasing the number of bins. This gives us a new optimal solution with x and y in the same bin. Thus, given a problem with two values x and y such that $x + y = c$, we can always put x and y in the same bin, resulting in a smaller problem (Gent 1998). Unfortunately, this does not extend to three or more elements that sum to exactly the bin capacity.

As another example, consider an element x such that the smallest two remaining elements added to x will exceed c. In other words, at most one additional element can be added to the bin containing x. Let y be the largest remaining element such that $x + y \leq c$. Then, we can place y in the same bin as x without sacrificing solution quality. The reason is that if we placed any other single element z with x, then we could swap y with z, since $z \leq y$ and $x + y \leq c$.

As a final example, assume that y is the largest remaining element that can be added to x such that $x + y \leq c$, and that y equals or exceeds the sum of *any* set of remaining elements that can be added to x without exceeding c. In that case, we can again put x and y in the same bin, without sacrificing solution quality. The reason is that any other set of elements that were placed in the same bin as x could be swapped with y without increasing the number of bins.

The general form of this dominance relation is due to Martello and Toth (Martello & Toth 1990a; 1990b). Define a *feasible* set as any set of elements whose sum doesn't exceed the bin capacity. Let A and B be two feasible sets. If all the elements of B can be packed into a set of bins whose capacities are the elements of A, then set A *dominates* set B. Given all the feasible sets that contain a common element x, only the undominated sets need be considered for assignment to the bin containing x.

Martello and Toth use this dominance relation to reduce the size of subproblems generated by their search. Given a partially-solved problem where some elements have already been assigned to bins, Martello and Toth first convert the partially-solved problem to an equivalent initial problem, where no elements have been assigned to bins, in two steps. First, any element that is unassigned, or assigned to a bin with no other elements, is left unchanged. Second, for each bin that contains more than one element, all the elements assigned to that bin are replaced with a single element equal to their sum, guaranteeing that any elements assigned to the same bin will stay together.

To reduce the size of such a problem, Martello and Toth take each element x in turn, starting with the largest element, and check to see if there is a *single* set of three or fewer elements, including x, that dominates all feasible sets containing x. If so, they place x with those elements in the same bin, and recursively apply the same reduction algorithm to the resulting reduced problem. They also use dominance relations to prune some placements of elements into bins.

Bin-Completion Algorithm

Our optimal bin-packing algorithm, which we call *bin completion*, makes more effective use of these dominance relations. Like the Martello and Toth algorithm, bin completion is also a branch-and-bound algorithm, but searches a different problem space. Rather than considering each element in turn, and deciding which bin to place it in, we consider each bin in turn, and consider the undominated feasible sets of elements that could be used to complete that bin. We sort the elements in decreasing order of size, and consider the bins containing each element in turn, enumerating all the undominated completions of that bin, and branching if there are more than one. In other words, we first complete the bin containing the largest element, then complete the bin containing the second largest element, etc.

Example Problem

To illustrate our algorithm, consider an example problem consisting of the elements {100, 98, 96, 93, 91, 87, 81, 59, 58, 55, 50, 43, 22, 21, 20, 15, 14, 10, 8, 6, 5, 4, 3, 1, 0}, with a bin capacity of 100. The 100 completely occupies a bin, and the 0 takes no space, resulting in the problem {98, 96, 93, 91, 87, 81, 59, 58, 55, 50, 43, 22, 21, 20, 15, 14, 10, 8, 6, 5, 4, 3, 1}. The only element that can go with 98 is 1, so we put them together, leaving {96, 93, 91, 87, 81, 59, 58, 55, 50, 43, 22, 21, 20, 15, 14, 10, 8, 6, 5, 4, 3}. We place 96 and 4 together, since they sum to exactly the bin capacity, leaving {93, 91, 87, 81, 59, 58, 55, 50, 43, 22, 21, 20, 15, 14, 10, 8, 6, 5, 3}. Since the sum of the two smallest remaining elements, 5 and 3, exceeds the residual capacity of the bin containing 93, we can't place more than one element in that bin, and choose the largest such element 6 to go with 93,, leaving {91, 87, 81, 59, 58, 55, 50, 43, 22, 21, 20, 15, 14, 10, 8, 5, 3}. We can complete the bin containing 91 with 8, 5, 3, or 5 + 3. Since the 8 dominates the other single elements, and also the set 5 + 3, we place 8 with 91, leaving {87, 81, 59, 58, 55, 50, 43, 22, 21, 20, 15, 14, 10, 5, 3}. The bin containing 87 can be completed with 10, 5, 3, 10 + 3 or 5 + 3. All of these are dominated by 10 + 3, so we place 10 + 3 with 87, resulting in {81, 59, 58, 55, 50, 43, 22, 21, 20, 15, 14, 5}. Up to this point, no branching is needed, since there is only one undominated choice for completing each of the bins considered so far.

The bin containing 81 can be completed with 15, 14, 5, or 14 + 5. Both 15 and 14 + 5 dominate both 14 and 5 individually. However, neither 15 nor 14 + 5 dominate each other, so both must be considered, producing a two-way branch in the search. Heuristically, we choose to explore the completion with the largest sum first, adding $14 + 5$ to the bin with 81, leaving $\{59, 58, 55, 50, 43, 22, 21, 20, 15\}$. We can complete the bin containing 59 with 22, 21, 20, 15, $22 + 15$, $21 + 20$, $21 + 15$, or $20 + 15$. Of these, only $22 + 15$ and $21 + 20$ are undominated by any of the others. This produces another two-way branch in the search, and we choose the alternative with the greater sum, $21 + 20$, to place first with 59, leaving $\{58, 55, 50, 43, 22, 15\}$. To complete the bin with 58, there is only one undominated choice, $22 + 15$, so we put these three elements together, leaving $\{55, 50, 43\}$.

Note that the only elements which could possibly be placed in the same bin with an element of size 58 or larger are those of size 42 or smaller. At this point, all elements of size 42 or smaller have already been placed in a bin with an element of size 58 or larger. While we could rearrange some of the smaller elements in those bins, no such rearrangement could possibly reduce the number of such bins, because each element of size 58 or larger requires its own bin. Thus, there is no need to backtrack to either of the branch points we encountered, and we can continue the search as if all the previous decisions were forced. The general form of this rule is the following: If $x > c/2$, where c is the bin capacity, and all elements $\leq c - x$ have been placed in bins containing elements $\geq x$, then any branch points generated in filling bins with elements $\geq x$ can be ignored.

The remaining problem of $\{55, 50, 43\}$ requires two more bins, yielding an optimal solution of eleven bins, as follows: $\{100\}$, $\{98, 1\}$, $\{96, 4\}$, $\{93, 6\}$, $\{91, 8\}$, $\{87, 10, 3\}$, $\{81, 14, 5\}$, $\{59, 21, 20\}$, $\{58, 22, 15\}$, $\{55, 43\}$, $\{50\}$.

General Algorithm

Our overall bin-completion algorithm is as follows. First we compute the best-fit decreasing (BFD) solution. Next, we compute a lower bound on the entire problem using the wasted-space bound described above. If the lower bound equals the number of bins in the BFD solution, it is returned as the optimal solution. Otherwise we initialize the best solution so far to the BFD solution, and start a branch-and-bound search for strictly better solutions. Once a partial solution uses as many bins as the best complete solution found so far, we prune that branch of the search. Experimentally, it was not worthwhile to also compute the first-fit decreasing (FFD) solution, since the FFD solution very rarely uses fewer bins than the BFD solution.

We consider the elements in decreasing order of size, and generate all the undominated completions of the bin containing the current element. If there are no completions or only one undominated completion, we complete the bin in that way and go on to the bin containing the next largest element. If there is more than one undominated completion, we order them in decreasing order of total sum, and consider the largest first, leaving the others as potential future branch points. Whenever we find a complete solution that is better than the best so far, we update the best solution found so far.

For a lower bound on a partial solution, we use the sum of all the elements, plus the actual space remaining in the bins completed so far, divided by the bin capacity and rounded up to the next larger integer. Equivalently, we can add the

number of bins completed to the sum of the remaining elements, divided by the bin capacity and rounded up. This lower bound is more effective than the estimated wasted-space bound described above, because it includes the actual wasted space in the completed bins. Furthermore, it is computed in constant time, by just accumulating the amounts of wasted space in the completed bins. Surprisingly, given this computation, it doesn't help to additionally compute the estimated wasted space in the remaining bins, for reasons we don't have sufficient space to describe here. Thus, we replace a linear-time lower-bound function with a more accurate constant-time function, with no loss in pruning power. If the lower bound on a partial solution equals or exceeds the number of bins in the best solution so far, we prune consideration of that partial solution.

Most of the time in our algorithm is spent computing the undominated completions of a bin. Our current implementation generates a subset of the feasible completions, then tests these for dominance. Given a particular element x, we first find the largest element y for which $x + y \leq c$.

We then compute all feasible pairs w and z, such that $x + w + z \leq c$, which are undominated by the single element y, i.e. $w + z > y$, and such that no pair dominates any other pair. Given two pairs of elements, $d + e$ and $f + g$, all four elements must be distinct, or the pair with the larger sum will dominate the other. Assume without loss of generality that $d > f$. In that case, g must be greater than e, or $d + e$ will dominate $f + g$. Thus, given any two pairs of elements, neither of which dominates the other, one must be completely "nested" inside the other in sorted order. We can generate all such undominated pairs in linear time by keeping the remaining elements sorted, and maintaining two pointers into the list, a pointer to a larger element and a pointer to a smaller element. If the sum of the two elements pointed to exceeds the bin capacity, we bump the larger pointer down to the next smaller element. If the sum of the two elements pointed to is less than or equal to y, we bump the smaller pointer up to the next larger element. If neither of these cases occur, we have an undominated pair, and we bump the larger pointer down and the smaller pointer up. We stop when the pointers reach each other.

After computing all undominated completion pairs, we then compute all triples d, e, and f, such that $x + d + e + f \leq c$ and $d + e + f > y$, then all quadruples, etc. To compute all triples, we choose each feasible first element, and then use our undominated pairs algorithm for the remaining two elements. For all quadruples, we choose all possible feasible pairs, then use our undominated pairs algorithm for the remaining two elements, etc. These larger feasible sets will in general include dominated sets.

Given two feasible sets, determining if the one with the larger sum dominates the other is another bin-packing problem. This problem is typically so small that we solve it directly with brute-force search. We believe that we can significantly improve our implementation, by directly generating all and only undominated completions, eliminating the need to test for dominance.

N	Optimal	L2 bound	% Optimal		Martello + Toth		Bin Completion		Ratio
			FFD	BFD	Nodes	Time	Nodes	Time	Time
5	3.215	3.208	100.000%	100.000%	0.000	7	.013	6	1.17
10	5.966	5.937	99.515%	99.541%	.034	15	.158	13	1.15
15	8.659	8.609	99.004%	99.051%	.120	25	.440	19	1.32
20	11.321	11.252	98.570%	98.626%	.304	37	.869	27	1.37
25	13.966	13.878	98.157%	98.227%	.741	55	1.500	36	1.53
30	16.593	16.489	97.790%	97.867%	2.146	87	2.501	44	1.98
35	19.212	19.092	97.478%	97.561%	7.456	185	4.349	55	3.36
40	21.823	21.689	97.153%	97.241%	39.837	927	8.576	73	12.70
45	24.427	24.278	96.848%	96.946%	272.418	6821	20.183	103	66.22
50	27.026	26.864	96.553%	96.653%	852.956	20799	57.678	189	110.05
55	29.620	29.445	96.304%	96.414%	6963.377	200998	210.520	609	330.05
60	32.210	32.023	96.036%	96.184%	58359.543	2153256	765.398	2059	1045.78
65	34.796	34.598	95.780%	95.893%			11758.522	28216	
70	37.378	37.167	95.556%	95.684%			16228.245	41560	
75	39.957	39.736	95.322%	95.447%			90200.736	194851	
80	42.534	42.302	95.112%	95.248%			188121.626	408580	
85	45.108	44.866	94.854%	94.985%			206777.680	412576	
90	47.680	47.428	94.694%	94.832%			1111759.333	2522993	

Table 1: Experimental Results

Experimental Results

Martello and Toth tested their algorithm on only twenty instances each of sizes 50, 100, 200, 500, and 1000 elements. They ran each problem instance for up to 100 seconds, and reported how many were optimally solved in that time, and the average times for those problems. Fekete and Schepers ran 1000 problem instances each, of size 100, 500, and 1000. They ran each instance for 100,000 search nodes, and reported the number of instances solved optimally. Both sets of authors used a bin capacity of 100, and chose their values from three distributions: uniform from 1 to 100, uniform from 20 to 100, and uniform from 35 to 100.

We found these experiment unsatisfactory for several reasons. The first is that we observed over eleven orders of magnitude variation in the difficulty of individual problem instances. For most problems, the number of bins in the BFD solution equals the lower bound, requiring no search at all. The hardest problems we solved required over 100 billion node generations, however. Performance on a large set of problems is determined primarily by these hard problems. A problem set of only 20 or even 1000 problems is unlikely to include really hard problems, and furthermore, they terminated the processing of their hard problems when a certain computational budget was exhausted.

Another difficulty with this approach is the use of integer values no larger than 100. Problems with such low precision values are significantly easier than problems with high precision values. For example, the simple preprocessing step of removing all pairs of elements that sum to exactly the bin capacity will eliminate most elements from a problem with 500 or 1000 elements up to 100. In contrast, with real numbers, we would expect no such reduction in problem size.

Finally, two of the distributions used by Martello and Toth and Fekete and Schepers eliminate small values, namely 20 to 100 and 35 to 100. As their data show, these problems are significantly easier than problems in which the values are chosen uniformly from one to the bin capacity. The reason is that all elements greater than one-half the bin capacity get their own bins, and no bins can contain very many elements.

For these reasons, we performed a different set of experiments. To include hard problems, we completed the optimal solution of all problem instances. Given the enormous variation in individual problem difficulty, one must address considerably larger problem sets in order to get meaningful averages. We solved ten million problem instances of each size from 5 to 50, and one million problem instances of each larger size. To avoid easy problems resulting from low precision values, we chose our values uniformly from zero to one million, with a bin capacity of one million. This simulates real numbers, but allows integer arithmetic for efficiency. This also avoids the easier truncated distributions described above. Table 1 above shows our results.

The first column is the problem size, or the number of elements. The second column is the average number of bins used in the optimal solution. As expected, it is slightly more than half the number of elements, with the difference due to wasted space in the bins. The third column is the average value of the L2 or wasted-space lower bound. The next two columns show the percentage of problem instances in which the first-fit decreasing (FFD) and best-fit decreasing (BFD) heuristics return the optimal solution. Note that these are not all easy problems, since verifying that the heuristic solution is optimal can be very expensive. For example, in 94.832% of problems of size 90 the BFD solution was optimal, but in only 69.733% of problems of this size was the L2 lower bound equal to the number of bins in the BFD solution, meaning that the BFD solution could be returned as the optimal solution with no search. All these percentages decrease monotonically with increasing problem size.

The sixth column is the average number of nodes generated by the Martello and Toth algorithm, and the seventh column is the average running time in microseconds per problem. The eighth column is the average number of nodes generated by our bin-completion algorithm, and the ninth column is the average running time in microseconds per problem on the same problem instances. The last column gives the running time of the Martello and Toth algorithm divided by the running time of our bin-completion algorithm. Both programs were implemented in C, and run on a 440 megahertz Sun Ultra 10 workstation.

It is clear that our bin-completion algorithm dramatically outperforms the Martello and Toth algorithm on the larger problems. The ratio of the running times of the two algorithms appears to increase without bound, strongly suggesting that our algorithm is asymptotically faster. On problems of size 60, which were the largest for which we could solve a million instances using the Martello and Toth algorithm, their algorithm took almost 25 days, while our algorithm took less than 35 minutes, which is over a thousand times faster. We were able to run the Martello and Toth algorithm on 10,000 problem instances of size 65, in a total of 614,857 seconds, which is over a week. Our bin completion algorithm took 19 seconds to solve the same instances, which is 32,360 times faster. Another view of this data is that we were able to increase the size of problems for which we could solve a million instances from 60 elements with the Martello and Toth algorithm, to 90 elements with our bin completion algorithm, an increase of 50% in problem size.

Some problems were hard for both algorithms, and others were hard for one algorithm were easy for the other. In general, the difficult problems required significantly fewer bins than average problems of the same size, or equivalently, packed more elements per bin. For example, on 60 problems of size 90, the bin-completion algorithm generated more than a billion nodes. The average number of bins used by the optimal solutions to these problems was 38.4, compared to 47.68 bins for an average problem of this size.

Conclusions and Discussion

We have presented a new algorithm for optimal bin packing. Rather than branching on the number of different possible bins that an element can be assigned to, we branch on the number of undominated ways in which a bin can be completed. Our bin-completion algorithm appears to be asymptotically faster than the best existing algorithm, and runs more than a thousand times faster on problems of 60 elements. We also presented a simpler derivation of Martello and Toth's L2 lower bound, and an efficient algorithm for computing it. An additional advantage of our bin-completion algorithm is that it is much simpler and easier to implement than the Martello and Toth algorithm.

Since both algorithms use depth-first branch-and-bound, they are anytime algorithms, meaning that they can be run for as long as time allows, and then return the best solution found at that point. For large problems where solution quality is important, it may be worthwhile to spend more time than is required to run an $O(n \log n)$ approximation algorithm such as best-fit or first-fit decreasing. In that case, either the Martello and Toth or bin completion algorithms could be run as an anytime algorithm, but the above data suggest that bin completion will find better solutions faster.

Many hard combinatorial problems involve packing elements of one set into another. For example, floor planning, cutting stock, and VLSI layout problems involve packing elements of various shapes and sizes into a single region of minimum size. The usual approach to optimally solve these problems involves considering the elements one at time, in decreasing order of size, and deciding where to place them in the overall region. The analog of our bin-completion algorithm would be to consider the most constrained regions of the space, and determine which elements can be placed in those regions. A clear example of the virtue of this approach is solving a jigsaw puzzle. Rather than individually considering each piece and where it might go, it's much more efficient to consider the most constraining regions of a partial solution, and find the pieces that can go into that region.

This duality between pieces and spaces has been exploited by Knuth in exact covering problems, such as polyominoe puzzles (Knuth 2000). We have shown that this alternative problem space can also be very useful in non-exact covering problems such as bin packing. Since many other packing problems have similar features, we believe that our general approach will be applicable to other problems as well.

Acknowledgements

Thanks to Russell Knight for helpful discussions concerning this research, and to Victoria Cortessis for a careful reading of the manuscript. This research was supported by NSF under grant No. IIS-9619447, and by NASA and JPL under contract No. 1229784.

References

Fekete, S., and Schepers, J. 1998. New classes of lower bounds for bin packing problems. In Bixby, R.; Boyd, E.; and Rios-Mercado, R., eds., *Integer Programming and Combinatorial Optimization: Proceedings of the 6th International IPCO Conference*, 257–270. Houston, TX: Springer.

Garey, M., and Johnson, D. 1979. *Computers and Intractability: A Guide to the Theory of NP-Completeness*. San Francisco: W.H. Freeman.

Gent, I. 1998. Heuristic solution of open bin packing problems. *Journal of Heuristics* 3:299–304.

Johnson, D. 1973. *Near-Optimal Bin Packing Algorithms*. Ph.D. Dissertation, Dept. of Mathematics, M.I.T., Cambridge, MA.

Knuth, D. 2000. Dancing links. In Davies, J.; Roscoe, B.; and Woodcock, J., eds., *Millenial Perspectives in Computer Science*. Palgrave: Houndmills, Bashingstake, Hampshire. 187–214.

Martello, S., and Toth, P. 1990a. Bin-packing problem. In *Knapsack Problems: Algorithms and Computer Implementations*. Wiley. chapter 8, 221–245.

Martello, S., and Toth, P. 1990b. Lower bounds and reduction procedures for the bin packing problem. *Discrete Applied Mathematics* 28:59–70.

Memory-Efficient A* Heuristics for Multiple Sequence Alignment

Matthew McNaughton and **Paul Lu** and **Jonathan Schaeffer** and **Duane Szafron**

Department of Computing Science
University of Alberta
Edmonton, Alberta
Canada T6G 2E8
{mcnaught,paullu,jonathan,duane}@cs.ualberta.ca

Abstract

The time and space needs of an A* search are strongly influenced by the quality of the heuristic evaluation function. Usually there is a trade-off since better heuristics may require more time and/or space to evaluate. Multiple sequence alignment is an important application for single-agent search. The traditional heuristic uses multiple pairwise alignments that require relatively little space. Three-way alignments produce better heuristics, but they are not used in practice due to the large space requirements. This paper presents a memory-efficient way to represent three-way heuristics as an octree. The required portions of the octree are computed on demand. The octree-supported three-way heuristics result in such a substantial reduction to the size of the A* open list that they offset the additional space and time requirements for the three-way alignments. The resulting multiple sequence alignments are both faster and use less memory than using A* with traditional pairwise heuristics.

Introduction

The problem of aligning s DNA/protein sequences of (average) length t is one of the most important problems in computational biology today. Obtaining the optimal alignment can be expressed as a dynamic programming problem over a lattice. However, a naïve solution to this problem has time and space complexities of $O(t^s)$, which are prohibitively large for real-world alignments. There are several algorithms in the literature that can reduce the space needs to $O(t^{s-1})$ but this is still unacceptably large. The space issue has received attention from both the computing science (Hirschberg 1975; Korf 1999; Korf & Zhang 2000; Yoshizumi, Miura, & Ishida 2000) and the biology communities (Spouge 1989; Myers & Miller 1988; Chao, Hardison, & Miller 1994).

A* (and its variants) have been used for this problem. The exponential time concerns are dampened by the elimination of irrelevant portions of the search space. The need for space is determined by the size of the open list, and it varies considerably with the quality of the heuristic function (h) used by A*. Nevertheless, it is not unusual for A* to rapidly consume all available memory.

Most space-related single-agent-search research concentrates on the search algorithm. This is appealing since it can generally be done in an application-independent way. In contrast, evaluation function discussions tend to be either too general to be useful, or too specific so that it is application dependent. However, a better h results in a more focused A* search and, hence, a smaller open list. Using space to improve the heuristic evaluation function quality in exchange for a (presumably) smaller open list is an important issue. For example, the pattern database work applied to the sliding-tile puzzles used large tables of heuristic values to reduce the search tree sizes by many orders of magnitude (Culberson & Schaeffer 1998; Korf 2000).

This paper shows how the dynamic (re-)computation of heuristic information can reduce the space requirements for A*-based search. Specifically, multiple sequence alignment (MSA) is used to illustrate these ideas. The standard heuristic used is the sum of pairwise alignments (see Section 2). Using three-way alignments can improve the quality of the evaluation function, but this is usually not feasible because of the space requirements. In this paper we show how an octree can be used to dynamically calculate relevant portions of three-way (or more) alignments. By saving this information in a storage-efficient way and recomputing parts as needed, the overall space requirements for large multiple alignment problems are dramatically reduced.

Note that the memory technique presented in this paper provides space/time tradeoffs for computing A* bounds. The search algorithm—A* or one of its variants—is orthogonal. Hence, one could use one of the recent AI algorithms for solving these types of problems, such as Divide-and-Conquer Frontier Search (Korf & Zhang 2000) or Partial-Expansion A* (Yoshizumi, Miura, & Ishida 2000), to further enhance performance.

This research makes the following contributions:

1. a new, memory-efficient algorithm for computing and recomputing heuristics for lattice computations on an as-needed basis,

2. application of this algorithm to the optimal MSA problem, reducing both the time and memory requirements needed for large alignments, and

3. a case study showing that for heuristic functions which require a significant amount of space, a better evaluation

function can lead to *both* a time and space improvement.

Although this paper uses the MSA problem as a sample application, the ideas are not restricted to this problem. The message of this paper, that the investment of time and space for the generation of better quality heuristics can result in a win/win situation, has received little attention in the literature.

Section 2 motivates the multiple sequence alignment problem and the need for better quality heuristics. Section 3 introduces the octree and an algorithm for selecting a set of heuristics for the search. Section 4 analyzes the performance of our algorithm. Finally, Section 5 presents future work.

Multiple Sequence Alignment

Each DNA or protein sequence is represented by a sequence of letters over a restricted alphabet. For example, DNA uses A, T, G, and C to represent the four nucleic acids. During sequence alignment, gaps (denoted by -) can be inserted into the sequences to make more letters in the sequences align with each other. An optimal alignment is one that minimizes a scoring function that assigns scores to corresponding letters and/or gaps in the sequences. A simple scoring function assigns -2 for an exact match, +1 for a mismatch and +2 for each gap. For example, the optimal alignment of the sequences s_1 = GATAGTC and s_3 = AGGTGCA is:

```
-GATAGTC
AGGT-GCA
```

since this alignment has a score of +1(3 matches, 3 mismatches, and 2 gaps) (Table 1(c)) and all other alignments have a higher score.

There are efficient dynamic programming (DP) solutions to this problem. Given two sequences of length j and k, the naïve DP algorithms require an array of size $O(j \times k)$. They require time $O(j \times k)$, to compute the array score entries, and then time $O(j+k)$ to identify the minimum-score path in the matrix. Unfortunately, $O(j \times k)$ space can be limiting, especially given that a DNA sequence can be millions of characters long. Even aligning two (small) sequences of 10,000 requires a prohibitive amount of storage (i.e., 100,000,000 entries).

Hirschberg was first to report a way of aligning two sequences using linear space (Hirschberg 1975), by recomputing some values in a classic space-time tradeoff.

In multiple sequence alignment, three or more sequences must be aligned, so even with Hirschberg-style one-dimensional space reductions, DP algorithms still require too much storage. There are two approaches to solving the multiple-alignment problem. The most popular algorithms used by biologists are based on a series of progressive pairwise alignments to generate non-optimal multiple alignments (e.g., DCA (Reinert, Stoye, & Will 2000) and CLUSTAL W (Thompson, Higgins, & Gibson 1994)). In contrast, the large space requirement of the optimal multiple alignment problem is viewed as a research challenge by AI researchers interested in heuristic search (Korf 1999; Korf & Zhang 2000; Yoshizumi, Miura, & Ishida 2000).

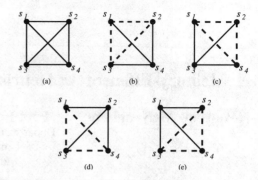

Figure 1: Covering a 4-way MSA with 2-way (solid line) and 3-way (dashed line) Alignments.

	s_1, s_2, s_3, s_4	s_1, s_2	s_1, s_3	$\overline{s_1, s_2, s_3}$
s_1	GATAGT-C-	GATAGTC	-GATAGTC	GATAG-TC-
s_2	-ATAG-GC-	-ATAGGC		-ATAG-GC-
s_3	-A-GGTGCA		AGGT-GCA	-A-GGTGCA
s_4	-A-ATTGCA			
	(a)	(b)	(c)	(d)

Table 1: Optimal 4-way MSA, Example 2-way Alignments, and an Example 3-way MSA.

In A*, we want the lowest score for a goal node, where $f(n) = g(n)+h(n)$ of node n, $g(n)$ is the known score from the root node to n, and $h(n)$ is a heuristic score from n to the goal node. For the heuristic $h(n)$ to be admissible, for all nodes n, it must never be more than the actual value $h^*(n)$. As the search approaches a goal node, $f(n)$ approaches the actual score from below. For search efficiency, $h(n)$ should be a tight bound on $h^*(n)$.

Assuming there are s sequences to align, one technique for computing $h(n)$ is to align strict subsets of the original s sequences and combine the scores of the subsets. We call the s-way MSA the *full-sized alignment* and k-way alignments, where $k < s$, *lower-dimensional optimal alignments* (Reinert & Lermen 2000).

It is a theorem that the (locally) optimal alignment of any lower-dimensional k-way alignment of the sequences, where $k < s$, has a score that is no worse than the score attributed to the same k sequences in the full-sized s-way MSA (Carrillo & Lipman 1988). In particular, one way to construct $h(n)$ is to sum the optimal alignment scores of each pair of sequences. By the preceding, this sum is guaranteed to be an admissible value. To improve the quality of $h(n)$ and still be admissible, we may incorporate a larger, 3-way MSA.

Consider a 4-way MSA where s_1 = GATAGTC, s_2 = ATAGGC, s_3 = AGGTGCA, and s_4 = AATTGCA. We can represent the four sequences as the nodes of a graph, where the arcs are alignments between specific sequences (Figure 1). We denote the 3-way MSA of s_1, s_2, and s_3 as $\overline{s_1, s_2, s_3}$ and similarly for 2-way alignments. The standard definition for the score of a 4-way MSA is the sum of the constituent pairwise alignments. In other words, the scoring function for a 4-way MSA is composed of only 2-way alignments and does not include any 3-way alignment scoring functions. Therefore, the optimal 4-way MSA is the alignment with the lowest score when all possible pairwise alignments are considered. In particular, for a 4-way MSA, there are $\binom{4}{2} = 6$ different pairwise alignments that cover the four sequences (Figure 1(a), solid lines).

In our example, the optimal MSA $\overline{s_1, s_2, s_3, s_4}$ has a score of -12 and the alignment is shown in Table 1(a). Note how, in the context of a 4-way MSA, the alignment between s_1 and s_3 (in Table 1(a)) is different than $\overline{s_1, s_3}$ (Table 1(c)). The locally optimal $\overline{s_1, s_3}$ is not necessarily globally optimal for the 4-way MSA.

Now, suppose we want to compute the heuristic value $h(n)$ for the root node of the search tree (i.e., $g(root) = 0$) by summing the optimal alignment scores of each pair of sequences. $\overline{s_1, s_2}$ (Table 1(b)) has a score of -7, and $\overline{s_1, s_3}$ (Table 1(c)) has a score of 1. $\overline{s_1, s_4}$, $\overline{s_2, s_3}$, $\overline{s_2, s_4}$, and $\overline{s_3, s_4}$ have scores of -2, -1, -1, and -8, respectively (not shown). The sum of all the optimal pairwise alignments is -18 (Figure 1(a)): $h(n) = \sum_{1 \le i < j \le 4} \overline{s_i, s_j} = -18$. As discussed earlier, the optimal 4-way MSA has an actual score of -12, but $h(n) = -18$ is still an admissible heuristic value.

To improve the quality of $h(n)$ and still be admissible, we can incorporate a larger, 3-way MSA into our example. Therefore, instead of requiring six 2-way alignments to cover our 4-way problem (Figure 1(a)), we only need one 3-way and three 2-way alignments (Figure 1(b)). In fact, for a 4-way MSA, there are $\binom{4}{3} = 4$ possible 3-way MSAs and their corresponding 2-way alignments that cover the graph (Figure 1(b), (c), (d), (e)). Intuitively, a 3-way MSA better captures global trade-offs when aligning multiple pairs of sequences, and therefore 3-way MSAs should provide better $h(n)$ values than 2-way alignments.

Consider the optimal 3-way MSA $\overline{s_1, s_2, s_3}$ (Table 1(d)), which has has a score of -4. Using this 3-way MSA, we estimate $h(n)$ to be -15: $h(n) = \overline{s_1, s_2, s_3} + \overline{s_1, s_4} + \overline{s_2, s_4} + \overline{s_3, s_4} = -15$ (Figure 1(b)). Although -15 with a single 3-way MSA is still not ideal, it is a better $h(n)$ than the score of -18 obtained using only 2-way alignments. The closer $h(n)$ comes to the optimal value, the smaller the A* search tree becomes.

Since different choices of 3-way MSAs can result in different values of $h(n)$, the quality of the heuristic can depend on the specific choice of the 3-way MSA. For example, if we had used $\overline{s_1, s_2, s_4} = -10$, we would have obtained $h(n) = -18$ (Figure 1(c)). For $\overline{s_1, s_3, s_4} = -6$, $h(n) = -15$ (Figure 1(d)). Finally, for $\overline{s_2, s_3, s_4} = -6$, $h(n) = -18$ (Figure 1(e)). Therefore, for our example, using either $\overline{s_1, s_2, s_3}$ or $\overline{s_1, s_3, s_4}$ would give us the best $h(n) = -15$. However, choosing either of the two remaining possible 3-way MSAs results in a $h(n)$ estimate that is no better than using only 2-way alignments.

We know of only one work that attempts to use a 3-way alignment heuristic (Reinert & Lermen 2000). However, they only use part of a single 3-way alignment (due to storage constraints).

Representing Heuristics as an Octree

A sequence alignment heuristic that uses 3-way alignments is desirable but requires too much storage (t^3 for strings of length t). We use an octree to efficiently represent the three-dimensional (3D) dynamic programming tables of 3-way alignments. An octree stores only those portions of the table that are needed by the search, and efficiently regenerates omitted portions as they are needed. Octrees have been used traditionally in CAD, GIS, fluid dynamics simulations, and other 3D image processing applications to compress grid representations of space containing large uniform volumes.

An octree is a tree data structure that represents a 3D space using rectangular blocks (Figure 2). Each node in the octree represents a rectangular portion of the full dynamic programming table for three sequences. An internal node has eight children, each of which represents one octant (corner) of its parent's space in more detail. A leaf node is either 'empty' or 'full'. A 'full' leaf node contains all of the values of the dynamic programming matrix for the portion of the space it represents. An 'empty' leaf node contains only the values over the surface of the volume, so that the contents may be regenerated as needed. Obviously, the root node represents the entire table. The pseudo-code for octree construction is in Figure 3.

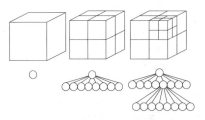

Figure 2: Octree Data Structure.

At the start of the A* search, the octree contains only internal nodes and 'empty' leaf nodes. As table values are requested by the search, 'empty' leaves containing the queried position are converted to internal nodes with new children. Children for areas beneath a threshold volume τ are created as 'full' nodes, and those above, as 'empty' nodes. 'Full' children can answer queries without further computation.

Our implementation uses $10,000$ for the leaf type threshold τ. Experiments indicate that this is a good trade-off between the fixed memory overhead for each node, the storage of unneeded table cells in excessively large 'full' nodes, and the time to traverse deep trees.

As Figure 1 shows, many 3-way alignments may be used. The program must decide which 2- and 3-way alignments to use for its heuristic function. To maintain admissibility, optimal 3-way alignments used in the heuristic are not permitted to have a pair of sequences in common, because each pair of sequences must contribute a score to the heuristic at most once (eg., in a set of five sequences, only two optimal 3-way alignments may be used). We determine which combination is best by evaluating each candidate heuristic at the root node and picking the one with the highest score. This heuristic is

```
Lookup(node,x,y,z):
  if node is Internal then
    octant o = octantFor(node.bounds,x,y,z)
    return Lookup(node.child[o],x,y,z)
  else if node is Full Leaf then
    return node.table[x][y][z]
  else if node is Empty Leaf then
    Node n = allocateInternal(node.bounds)
    addChildren(n)
    // regenerate table from node.surface
    node = n
    return Lookup(node,x,y,z)
  endif
end Lookup

addChildren(node):
  for each octant o of node.bounds
    if volume(o) > tau then
      node.child[o] = allocateEmptyLeaf(o)
    else
      node.child[o] = allocateFullLeaf(o)
    endif
  endfor
end addChildren
```

Figure 3: Pseudo-code for Octree Construction.

used for the rest of the search. Experiments indicate that for two such heuristics h_1 and h_2, there is a good correlation between the fact $h_1(r) > h_2(r)$ and $h_1(n) > h_2(n)$ for the root node r and any node n. That is, the heuristic which is best at the root node tends to be better at other nodes in the search space.

The octree conserves memory by storing a leaf as 'full' only once a table cell from that leaf's volume is demanded by the A* search. In the worst case that the search demands table values from every region of the space, the octree would be forced to store the entire table, and if carefully implemented to take advantage of the A* search's access pattern, would recompute the table once.

The octree may be made to use $O(t^2)$-bounded storage by fixing the number of 'full' leaves available and recycling them in LRU-order. For our experiments we allowed unbounded storage for the octree and never freed 'full' leaves once constructed.

Note that the octree structure can be generalized to any number of dimensions, with the two-dimensional case known as a quadtree.

The idea of doing dynamic computations to improve heuristic evaluation quality is not new. Examples include hierarchical A* (Holte 1996) and pattern search (Junghanns & Schaeffer 2001).

Experiments

Experiments were done using the Needleman-Wunsch global optimal alignment algorithm (Needleman & Wunsch 1970) using the well-known Dayhoff PAM250 (Dayhoff, Schwartz, & Orcutt 1979) scoring matrix with a linear gap cost of 8. For simplicity (and comparison with the other computing-science related work), leading/trailing

blanks and affine gaps are not included in our implementation. The program uses A* without any enhancements. The program is coded in C++ and was compiled with GNU CC version 2.95.2. The experiments were run on a Sun E/420 with 4 GB of RAM and 4 CPUs running at 450 MHz. Runs were stopped if they used more than 2 GB of RAM. The octree used a parameter setting of $\tau = 10,000$.

The experiments tested the following heuristic evaluation functions: Pairwise (uses the conventional sum of all pairs of sequences heuristic score), 1 Full (uses a single 3-way alignment, storing the entire matrix in memory), 2 Full (uses two 3-way alignments, storing both matrices in memory), 1 Octree (uses a single 3-way alignment stored as an octree), and 2 Octree (uses two 3-way alignments, each stored as an octree).

A data set of 74 real biological sequences was used (Gallin 2001) with an average sequence length of 300. Random combinations of five sequences were selected to see which MSAs could be completed with the given space constraint. There were 161 5-way alignments attempted, of which 41 were solved by both pairwise and octree versions, 27 were solved only by the octree version, and 93 were not solved by any version. Note that there was no instance where a pairwise heuristic solved an alignment but the octree did not.

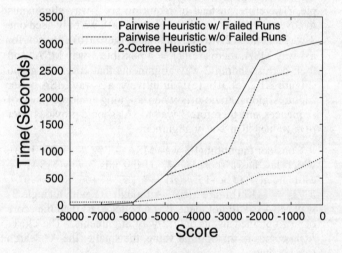

Figure 4: 5-way MSA Time.

Figure 4 shows the time used by the various A* searches as a function of the alignment score; Figure 5 shows the memory usage. The more negative the score is, the better the alignment. The data has been grouped into buckets of 1,000. For example, all multiple alignments with a score between -8000 and -7000 were averaged into a single data point at -8000.

Figure 4 shows a positive correlation between the optimal alignment score and the ease of computation. For sequences with good optimal alignments (low scores), the pairwise heuristic does a reasonable job of estimating the score and the searches are small. For these easy alignments, the pairwise time may be marginally faster than the octree because the cost of doing the 3-way alignment is not offset by the

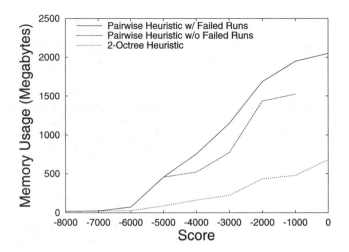

Figure 5: 5-way MSA Memory.

savings in the A* search. As the quality of the score decreases (ie., the score increases), it becomes harder to find the optimal solution. Beyond scores of -6000, the octree dominates the pairwise results, with the performance gap widening as the difficulty of the alignment increases. For the -3000 bucket, the run time is roughly three times faster for the data points where the pairwise heuristic completed. The figure also shows an estimate of the pairwise time that includes the cases where the octree finished but the pairwise did not. Here the pairwise was conservatively assumed to take exactly 2 GB and 3500 seconds (roughly the time it took to exhaust memory). Clearly this is a lower bound, and the performance gap is larger than what is portrayed in the figure.

Even though the octree has the additional preprocessing overhead of the 3-way alignments and the cost of re-computing values, it still runs faster. For large problems, the cost of the more expensive heuristic is more than offset by the much smaller A* search.

The total memory used by the octree program is significantly smaller than the memory used by the pairwise program (see Figure 5). Although the two 3-way octrees require more memory than the pairwise heuristic tables, this is offset by the substantially smaller A* open list that it produces.

As Figures 4 and 5 show, the time and memory for a 5-way sequence alignment grows with the difficulty of the alignment. Extrapolating these curves indicates that there is an exponential growth. This is expected, since the A* search grows exponentially in the length of the solution path. The octrees's better-informed heuristics dampen the exponential growth.

A more detailed study can be seen of the (-3000,-2000) bucket (the bucket with the most data points). Figure 6 shows a breakdown of the alignment times for this bucket. Figure 7 shows the number of A* nodes considered, broken down by number of open and closed nodes stored at the end of the search. The first bar expresses only open nodes because failed program runs did not report this information, and the total number of nodes given here is an estimate based

on the running time. Figure 8 shows the total memory requirements (heuristics and open list). There are some interesting points to notice in these graphs:

1. The 2 octree implementation is almost 4 times faster than the pairwise, and more than 6-fold faster if one includes the pairwise data points that did not complete. These numbers are similar for the memory usage. This is a clear win/win situation for the octree. The program runs substantially faster and uses substantially less memory.

2. A full matrix is slightly faster than the octree. Computationally, the matrix should be faster since it has no re-computations. However, the more compact octree gets more favorable cache performance, almost completely offsetting the re-computation costs.

3. Predictably, the octree uses less memory than the full matrix. It is interesting to note that the total memory usage for a search employing two full matrices or two octrees is *less* than that of one of either! Clearly, they use more memory to store the heuristics, but the better quality evaluation function reduces the size of the open list, resulting in an overall reduction in space.

4. Compared to the pairwise scoring function, two 3-way alignments reduce the open list size by at least a factor of 4.

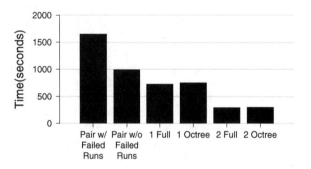

Figure 6: Time (-3000 bucket).

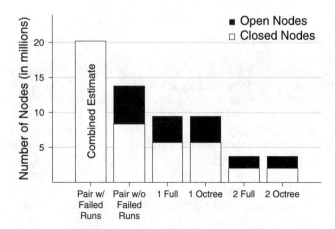

Figure 7: Search Space (-3000 bucket).

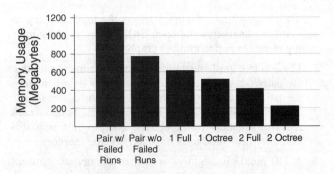

Figure 8: Memory (-3000 bucket).

The octree's space savings come from a two-fold time investment: computing the set of heuristics to use at the start of the search, and dynamically computing octree values throughout the search. For the data sets used, our implementation requires approximately 45 seconds to initially compute the two dynamic programming matrices required by the 2 octree heuristic set. It initially caches three levels of the tree, that is, down to empty leaves of side length one-quarter that of the root node.

Over 10 runs, an average of 20% of the table is recomputed by the octree, at an estimated time cost of 9 seconds. Accurate measurement is confounded by the favorable cache effects resulting from smaller dynamic programming tables that hold spatially close table values closer together in memory, and the unfavorable slowdown from the several recursive calls required to reach the table.

It is interesting to note that our implementation requires 70 seconds to compute and store the full matrix, 30% longer than the $O(t^2)$-space initial generation of the table for the octree. We posit that poor cache behavior accounts for this slower speed.

We have solved a few difficult 6-way alignments. The results are not reported here since the (predictably) large pairwise runs could not complete. For one data set, the pairwise alignment heuristic gave an average score that was 558 from the optimal score. Enhancing the heuristic evaluation to include a single 3-way alignment reduced this to 437, and two 3-way alignments lowered it to 320. For a 6-way alignment (but not a 5-way), it is possible to use three 3-way alignments in the evaluation function. Here the average score is off by only 265. In effect, the use of three 3-way alignments decreases the error in the evaluation function by more than a factor of 2. Korf's analysis of IDA* shows that halving the error in h results in halving the exponent of the search growth (Korf & Reid 1998). IDA*'s search growth is asymptotically the same as A*. Hence, the improvements in h roughly correspond to reducing the search effort to the square root in size.

Search effort is strongly tied to the sequences' degree of similarity (Figure 4) and the final alignment score: similar sequences yield alignments with low scores, few gaps and mismatches, and the search space examined is smaller than for dissimilar sequences that have optimal alignments with higher scores and many gaps and mismatches. Conse-

quently, performance numbers for any MSA algorithm need to be qualified by the quality of the alignment. For example, this paper reports 5- and 6-way alignments. It would be easy to dismiss these results, citing previous work that reports 7- and 8-way alignments (Yoshizumi, Miura, & Ishida 2000). However, the sequences aligned by (Yoshizumi, Miura, & Ishida 2000) are in the "easy" category where the octrees are of relatively little value since the search using the pairwise heuristic can be completed before a 3-way heuristic table can be computed (we have done the experiments).

Future Work

This paper does not use the cited work of partial-expansion A* (Yoshizumi, Miura, & Ishida 2000) because it would have complicated measuring the benefits of the octree heuristic. Partial-expansion A* works by delaying putting child nodes with poor scores onto the priority queue, with the hope that the goal node will be found before they need to be re-examined. Its efficacy is dependent upon the ability of the heuristic to discriminate between nodes on the optimal path and irrelevant nodes. We implemented PEA*, and found that the space savings and time costs realized varied with the difficulty of the search and with the quality of the heuristic. On a difficult problem instance with optimal score -669, the 2-octree heuristic saved 62% of the search space when using a cutoff of 0 instead of a cutoff at infinity(normal A*), but on an easier instance with score -7605, it saved 87%. In the latter case the search took nearly 10 times as long to perform when using the cutoff at 0. In addition, we found that the 2-octree heuristic realized proportionally more savings than the pairwise heuristic – where the 2-octree heuristic saved 62% of the search space on the difficult instance and took ten times as long, the pairwise heuristic saved only 39%, and took twenty times as long. This pattern was repeated on the easy instance. This makes sense because using two three-way alignments in the heuristic should allow better discrimination between nodes. Note that both instances had 5 sequences, meaning they each had a branching factor of 31. The lesson seems to be that PEA* can realize substantial benefits with a strong heuristic, but suffers when the problem becomes difficult. However, more work is required to conclusively characterize the situations where PEA* provides a benefit. Regardless, its use would have complicated our analysis, though it seems likely that it would have portrayed the octree in an even more favourable light compared to the pairwise heuristic.

It has been difficult to compare the performance of search techniques for sequence alignment that have come out of the AI community because researchers have made up their own data sets rather than using a standard benchmark of sequences. Future results will be published against BAl-iBASE (Thompson, Plewniak, & Poch 1999), a benchmark set of alignments that covers a broad range of lengths and degrees of similarity of interest to biologists, with hand-verified reference alignments. Initial results indicate that the linear gap cost function used in this paper and in others from the AI community (Yoshizumi, Miura, & Ishida 2000; Korf & Zhang 2000) does not typically produce high-quality optimal alignments. Our future work will use the quasi-natural affine gap model (Altschul 1989) which requires a larger search space but produces better-quality alignments according to initial tests on BAliBASE.

Conclusions

This paper illustrates that single-problem instances can benefit from computing (large) heuristic tables. The cost in time and space for the heuristics can be subsumed by the time and space savings from a smaller open list. Many single-agent search applications use generic heuristics that cover a wide range of problem instances. Generic heuristics seem best, since the cost of computing the heuristic can be amortized over multiple problems. However, as the MSA problem shows, a time and space investment in a problem-instance-specific heuristic can provide a more focused, faster, and space-efficient solution. This happens because there are two ways to use memory in an A* search: the open/closed lists, and heuristic evaluation function tables. This is not a zero-sum game. Storage can be used (and reused) to improve evaluation function quality. For the MSA application, the octree provides a nice framework for increasing the quality of a heuristic evaluation using a reasonable amount of space.

Acknowledgments

Financial support was provided by the Natural Sciences and Engineering Research Council of Canada (NSERC), Alberta's Informatics Circle of Research Excellence (iCORE) and the Canadian Protein Engineering Network of Centres of Excellence (PENCE). The authors would like to thank Dr. Robert Holte for his comments.

References

Altschul, S. F. 1989. Gap costs for multiple sequence alignment. *J. of Theoretical Biology* 138:297–309.

Carrillo, H., and Lipman, D. 1988. The multiple sequence alignment problem in biology. *SIAM J. on Applied Mathematics* 48(5):1073–1082.

Chao, K.; Hardison, R.; and Miller, W. 1994. Recent developments in linear-space alignment methods: A survey. *J. of Computational Biology* 1(4):271–291.

Culberson, J., and Schaeffer, J. 1998. Pattern databases. *Computational Intelligence* 14(3):318–334.

Dayhoff, M. O.; Schwartz, R. M.; and Orcutt, B. C. 1979. A model of evolutionary change in proteins. In Dayhoff, M. O., ed., *Atlas of Protein Structure*, volume 5(Suppl. 3). Silver Spring, Md.: National Biomedical Reasearch Foundataion. 345–352.

Gallin, W. 2001. A selection of potassium channel protein sequences. http://www.cs.ualberta.ca/ bioinfo/sequences/pchannel/.

Hirschberg, D. 1975. A linear space algorithm for computing maximal common subexpressions. *CACM* 18(6):341–343.

Holte, R. 1996. Hierarchical A*: Searching abstraction hierarchies efficiently. *AAAI* 530–535.

Junghanns, A., and Schaeffer, J. 2001. Enhancing single-agent search using domain knowledge. *Artificial Intelligence* 129(1-2):219–251.

Korf, R., and Reid, M. 1998. Complexity analysis of admissible heuristic search. *AAAI* 305–310.

Korf, R., and Zhang, W. 2000. Divide-and-conquer frontier search applied to optimal sequence alignment. *AAAI* 910–916.

Korf, R. 1999. Divide-and-conquer bidirectional search: First results. *IJCAI* 1184–1189.

Korf, R. 2000. Recent progress in the design and analysis of admissible heuristic functions. *AAAI* 1165–1170.

Myers, E., and Miller, W. 1988. Optimal alignments in linear space. *CABIOS* 4(1):11–17.

Needleman, S., and Wunsch, C. 1970. A general method applicable to the search for similarities in the amino acid sequences of two proteins. *J. of Molecular Biology* 48:443–453.

Reinert, K., and Lermen, M. 2000. The practical use of the A* algorithm for exact multiple sequence alignment. *J. of Computational Biology* 7(5):655–671.

Reinert, K.; Stoye, J.; and Will, T. 2000. An iterative method for faster sum-of-pairs multiple sequence alignment. *Bioinformatics* 16(9):808–814.

Spouge, J. 1989. Speeding up dynamic programming algorithms for finding optimal lattice paths. *SIAM J. of Applied Mathematics* 49(5):1552–1566.

Thompson, J.; Higgins, D.; and Gibson, T. 1994. CLUSTAL W: Improving the sensitivity of progressive multiple sequence alignment through sequence weighting, position-specific gap penalties and weight matrix choice. *Nucleic Acids Research* 22:4673–4680.

Thompson, J.; Plewniak, F.; and Poch, O. 1999. BAliBASE: a benchmark alignment database for the evaluation of multiple alignment programs. *Bioinformatics* 15(1):87–88.

Yoshizumi, T.; Miura, T.; and Ishida, T. 2000. A* with partial expansion for large branching factor problems. *AAAI* 923–929.

PROMPTDIFF: A Fixed-Point Algorithm for Comparing Ontology Versions

Natalya F. Noy and **Mark A. Musen**
Stanford Medical Informatics, Stanford University, 251 Campus Drive, Stanford, CA 94305, USA
{noy, musen}@smi.stanford.edu

Abstract

As ontology development becomes a more ubiquitous and collaborative process, the developers face the problem of maintaining versions of ontologies akin to maintaining versions of software code in large software projects. Versioning systems for software code provide mechanisms for tracking versions, checking out versions for editing, comparing different versions, and so on. We can directly reuse many of these mechanisms for ontology versioning. However, version comparison for code is based on comparing text files—an approach that does not work for comparing ontologies. Two ontologies can be identical but have different text representation. We have developed the PROMPTDIFF algorithm, which integrates different heuristic matchers for comparing ontology versions. We combine these matchers in a fixed-point manner, using the results of one matcher as an input for others until the matchers produce no more changes. The current implementation includes ten matchers but the approach is easily extendable to an arbitrary number of matchers. Our evaluation showed that PROMPTDIFF correctly identified 96% of the matches in ontology versions from large projects.

Structural Diffs Between Ontologies

Several recent developments have made ontologies—explicit formal specifications of concepts and relations in a domain—almost ubiquitous. Examples include the emergence of the Semantic Web with formal ontologies as its backbone and the development of easy-to-use tools, which significantly lowered the barrier for ontology development. With tools such as Protégé-2000 (2002) for example, ontology development is no longer an enterprise available only to researchers with graduate degrees in AI. In a sense, ontology development in the worlds of e-commerce and the Semantic Web is becoming a counterpart to conventional software engineering.

As a result, ontology developers now face the same problem that software engineers began to encounter long ago: **versioning and evolution**. Tools for managing versions of software code, such as CVS (Fogel & Bar 2001), have become indispensable for software engineers participating in dynamic collaborative projects. These tools provide a uniform storage mechanism for versions, the ability to check out a particular piece of code for editing, an archive of earlier versions, and mechanisms for comparing versions and merging changes and updates.

Ontologies change just as the software code does. These changes are caused by changes in the domain itself (our knowledge about the domain changes or the domain itself changes) or in the conceptualization of the domain (we may introduce new distinctions or eliminate old ones). Furthermore, ontology development in large projects is a dynamic process in which multiple developers participate, releasing subsequent versions of an ontology. Naturally, collaborative development of dynamic ontologies requires tools that are similar to software-versioning tools. In fact, ontology developers can use the storage, archival, and check-out mechanisms of tools like CVS with very little change. There are two areas, however, that require new techniques to manage versions of ontologies: (1) representation formalisms to store ontologies and (2) version comparison based on *structure* of the data. To address the first issue, researchers are actively developing representation formalisms, such as RDF and RDF Schema (W3C 2000), OIL (Fensel *et al.* 2000), DAML+OIL (Hendler & McGuinness 2000), and so on. The work we are presenting in this paper addresses the second issue: structure-based comparison of ontologies.

Comparison of versions of software code entails a comparison of text files. Code is a set of text documents and the result of comparing the documents—the process is called a **diff**—is a list of lines that differ in the two versions. This approach does not work for comparing ontologies: two ontologies can be exactly the same conceptually but have very different text representations. For example, their storage syntax may be different. The order in which definitions are introduced in the text file may be different. A representation language may have several mechanisms to express the same thing. Therefore, text-file comparison is largely useless in comparing versions of ontologies. The PROMPTDIFF algorithm, which we describe in this paper, compares the *structure* of ontology versions and not their text serialization.

We use a knowledge model compatible with the Open Knowledge Base Connectivity (OKBC) protocol (Chaudhri *et al.* 1998): an ontology has classes, class hierarchy, instances of classes, slots as first-class objects, slot attachments to class to specify class properties, and facets to specify constraints on slot values.[1] All these elements are also present in other representation formalisms such as RDFS and DAML+OIL (sometimes in a slightly different form). Therefore, our results apply to ontologies defined in these languages as well.

Suppose that we are developing an ontology of wines. In the first version (Figure 1a), there is a class *Wine* with three subclasses, *Red wine*, *White wine*, and *Blush wine*. The

---

[1] OKBC also allows procedural attachments and specialized axioms, which we do not consider.

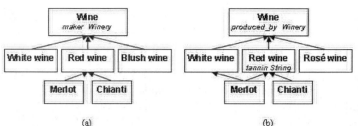

f1	f2	renamed	operation	map level
	S tannin level	No	Add	
C Blush wine	C Rosé wine	Yes	Map	Isomorphic
S maker	S produced_by	Yes	Map	Isomorphic
C Chianti	C Chianti	No	Map	Isomorphic
C Merlot	C Merlot	No	Map	Changed
C Red wine	C Red wine	No	Map	Changed
C White wine	C White wine	No	Map	Changed
C Wine	C Wine	No	Map	Isomorphic
C Winery	C Winery	No	Map	Unchanged

(a)   (b)   (c)

Figure 1: Two versions of a wine ontology (a and b) and the PROMPTDIFF table showing the difference between the versions

class $Wine$ has a slot $maker$ whose values are instances of class $Winery$. The class $Red\ wine$ has two subclasses, $Chianti$ and $Merlot$. Figure 1b shows a later version of the same ontology fragment. Note the changes: we changed the name of the $maker$ slot to $produced\_by$ and the name of the $Blush\ wine$ class to $Rosé\ wine$; we added a $tannin\ level$ slot to the $Red\ wine$ class; and we discovered that $Merlot$ can be white and added another superclass to the $Merlot$ class. Figure 1c shows the differences between the two versions in a table produced automatically by PROMPTDIFF. The first two columns are pairs of matching frames from the two ontologies. Informally, given two versions of an ontology O, V_1 and V_2, two frames F_1 from V_1 and F_2 from V_2 **match** if F_1 became F_2. Other columns in the table provide more information about the match. The third column identifies whether or not the frame has been renamed. The last two columns specify how much the frame has changed, if at all (see the next section). Similar to the diff between text files, the table in Figure 1c presents an **ontology diff**. We give a formal definition of the ontology diff in the next section.

The PROMPTDIFF algorithm consists of two parts: (1) an extensible set of heuristic matchers and (2) a fixed-point algorithm to combine the results of the matchers to produce a structural diff between two versions. Each matcher employs a small number of structural properties of the ontologies to produce matches. The fixed-point step invokes the matchers repeatedly, feeding the results of one matcher into the others, until they produce no more changes in the diff.

Our approach to automating the comparison is based on two observations: (1) When we compare two versions of the same ontology, a large fraction of frames remains unchanged (in fact, in our experiments, 97.9% of frames remained unchanged) and (2) If two frames have the same type (i.e., they are both classes, both slots, etc.) and have the same or very similar name, one is almost certainly an image of the other. Both of these observations are not true if we are comparing two *different* ontologies that came from different sources rather than two versions of the *same* ontology. Consider a class $University$ for example. In two different ontologies, the class may represent either a university campus, or a university as an organization, with its departments, faculty, and so on. If we encounter a class $University$ in two versions of the same ontology, we can be almost certain that it represents exactly the same concept (and because we have a human looking at the results in the end, we can tolerate the "almost" adverb in that sentence).

At the same time, the tasks of comparing different ontologies (for example, for the purposes of ontology merging or

integration) and comparing versions of the same ontology are closely related. In both cases, we have two overlapping ontologies and we need to determine a mapping between their elements. When we compare ontologies from different sources, we concentrate on *similarities*, whereas in version comparison we need to highlight the *differences*, which can be a complementary process. We used heuristics that are similar to the ones we present in this paper to provide suggestions in interactive ontology merging (Noy & Musen 2000). However, because in PROMPTDIFF we are dealing with two versions of the same ontology, we can be much more certain about the results the heuristics produce and require significantly less input and verification from the user.

The process of comparing versions of ontologies would have been greatly simplified if we had logs of changes between versions. However, given the de-centralized environment of ontology development today, it is unrealistic to expect that such logs will be available. Many ontology-development tools do not provide any logging capability. Ontology libraries are set up to publish versions of ontologies but not the logs of changes. Representation formats address representation of the ontologies themselves but not changes in ontologies. Therefore, we can expect that the need for comparing versions when a log of changes between them is not available will continue to grow.

In the rest of this paper we describe different heuristic matchers that we used, and the way we combined them in the PROMPTDIFF algorithm. Specifically, this paper makes the following contributions:

- We define the notion of a structural diff between ontology versions.
- We present a set of heuristic matchers for finding a structural diff automatically.
- We present an efficient and extendable fixed-point algorithm that combines the matchers to produce the diff.
- We evaluate the algorithm's performance using versions of large real-world ontologies.

Structural Diff and PROMPTDIFF Table

We define a **structural diff** between two ontology versions.
Definition 1 (Structural diff) *Given two versions of an ontology O, V_1 and V_2, a* **structural diff** *between V_1 and V_2, $D(V_1, V_2)$, is a set of frame pairs $\langle F_1, F_2 \rangle$ where:*

- $F_1 \in V_1$ *or* $F_1 = null$; $F_2 \in V_2$ *or* $F_2 = null$
- F_2 *is an* **image** *of* F_1 (**matches** F_1), *that is, F_1 became F_2. If F_1 or F_2 is null, then we say that F_2 or F_1 respectively does not have a match.*
- *Each frame from V_1 and V_2 appears in at least one pair.*

- *For any frame F_1, if there is at least one pair containing F_1, where $F_2 \neq null$, then there is no pair containing F_1 where $F_2 = null$ (if we found at least one match for F_1, we do not have a pair that says that F_1 is unmatched). The same is true for F_2.*

Note that the definition implies that for any pair of frames F_1 and F_2, there is at most one entry $\langle F_1, F_2 \rangle$.

The structural diff describes which frames have changed from one version to another. However, for a diff to be more useful to the user, it should include not only *what* has changed but also some information on *how* the frames have changed. A PROMPTDIFF table, which results from the PROMPTDIFF algorithm, provides this more detailed information (Figure 1c).

Definition 2 (PROMPTDIFF **table**) *Given two versions of an ontology O, V_1 and V_2, the PROMPTDIFF **table** is a set of tuples $\langle F_1, F_2, rename\_value, operation\_value, mapping\_level \rangle$ where:*

- *There is a tuple $\langle F_1, F_2, rename\_value, operation\_value, mapping\_level \rangle$ in the table iff there is a pair $\langle F_1, F_2 \rangle$ in the structural diff $D(V_1, V_2)$.*
- *rename_value is true if frame names for F_1 and F_2 are the same; rename_value is false otherwise.*
- *operation_value $\in OpS$, where $OpS = \{add, delete, split, merge, map\}$*
- *mapping_level $\in MapS$, where $MapS = \{unchanged, isomorphic, changed\}$*

The operations in the operation set OpS indicate to the user how a frame has changed from one version to the other: whether it was added or deleted, whether it was split in two frames, or whether two frames were merged. We assign a *map* operation to a pair of frames if none of the other operations applies. The *mapping_level* indicates whether the matching frames are different enough from each other to warrant the user's attention. If the *mapping_level* is *unchanged*, then the user can safely ignore the frames—nothing has changed in their definitions. If two frames are *isomorphic*, then their corresponding slots and facet values are images of each other, but not necessarily identical images. The *mapping_level* is *changed* if the frames have slots or facet values that are not images of each other. In Figure 1c, the *Red wine* class has changed: It got a new slot. The pair of the *Chianti* classes is marked as *isomorphic*: Even though the frames themselves have not changed, the frames that they directly reference (*Red wine*) have. Our implementation of PROMPTDIFF also provides the information to the user explaining why the table row contains a particular operation or mapping level (not shown in Figure 1c).

PROMPTDIFF **Heuristic Matchers**

The PROMPTDIFF algorithm combines an arbitrary number of heuristic matchers, each of which looks for a particular property in the unmatched frames. Before describing some of the matchers that we used, we define a **monotonicity principle**, a principle to which all the matchers in PROMPTDIFF must conform.

Definition 3 (Monotonicity principle) *Let M be a matching algorithm and T_1 and T_2 be the PROMPTDIFF tables before and after execution of M. Then for every two frames F_1 and F_2, such that $F_1 \in V_1$ and $F_2 \in V_2$, if the pair $\langle F_1, F_2 \rangle$ is present in T_1, then $\langle F_1, F_2 \rangle$ is present in T_2.*

A matcher conforms to the monotonicity principle iff it does not retract any matches already in the table. It may delete the rows where one of the frames is *null* by creating new matches. But it must keep all the existing matches.

We now describe some of the heuristic matchers that we used. Note that each of the matchers is fairly simple and the strength of our approach lies in the combination of these matchers. Also, each of the matchers looks at a particular part of the ontology structure: *is−a* hierarchy, slots attached to a class, and so on.

Each of the matchers in the list is a *heuristic* matcher. Therefore, there can always be an example when the result produced by the matcher is wrong. However, we have examined ontology versions in several large projects, and we have not come across such examples. Therefore, we believe that most of the time the matchers would produce correct results. Furthermore, PROMPTDIFF presents the matching results to a human expert for analysis, highlighting the frames that have changed. The expert can examine the matches for these changed frames to see if they are correct. These frames usually constitute only a small fraction of all the frames in an ontology. Therefore, even for very large ontologies, human experts need to examine only a small number of frames.

In the following descriptions of matchers, F_n denotes a frame of any type, class, slot, facet, or instance; C_n denotes a class; S_n denotes a slot. The heuristic matchers compare two ontology versions looking for the following situations:

1. **Frames of the same type with the same name.** In Figure 1, both ontology versions, V_1 and V_2, have a frame *Wine*, and in both versions this frame is a class. In this situation, the matcher declares that the two frames match. In general, if $F_1 \in V_1$ and $F_2 \in V_2$ and F_1 and F_2 have the same name and type, then F_1 and F_2 match. Frames can be of type class, slot, facet, or instance. In our experiments, this matcher produced an average of 97.9% of all the matches since ontologies usually do not change a lot from one version to the next.

2. **Single unmatched sibling.** In the example in Figure 1, suppose we matched the classes *Wine*, *Red wine*, and *White wine* from V_1 to their counterparts with the same names in V_2. Then the *Wine* class in both versions has exactly one unmatched subclass: *Blush wine* in V_1 and *Rosé wine* in V_2. In this situation, we conclude that the *Rosé wine* class is the image of the *Blush wine* class. In general, if $C_1 \in V_1$ and $C_2 \in V_2$, C_1 and C_2 match, and each of the classes has exactly one unmatched subclass, $subC_1$ and $subC_2$, respectively, then $subC_1$ and $subC_2$ match. We have a similar matcher for multiple unmatched siblings that can be distinguished by their sets of slots.

3. **Siblings with the same suffixes or prefixes.** Taking the example in 1 further, suppose we remove "wine" from the class name for subclasses of the *Wine* class (Figure 2a). Therefore, all the names for those subclasses have changed. However, if we observe that they have all changed in the same way—the same suffix has been removed—we can create the corresponding matches any-

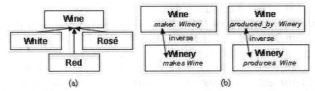

Figure 2: (a) Class names for subclasses of $Wine$ are the same as in Figure 1b except for the "wine" suffix; (b) slots $maker$ and $makes$ are inverse slots in one version; slots $produced\_by$ and $produces$ are inverse slots in another version.

way. In general, if $C_1 \in V_1$ and $C_2 \in V_2$, C_1 and C_2 match, and the names of all subclasses of C_1 are the same as the names of all subclasses of C_2 except for a constant suffix or prefix, then the subclasses match.

4. **Single unmatched slot.** In the example in Figure 1, suppose we matched the class $Wine$ from the first version to its counterpart in the second version. Each of the two classes has a single slot that is so far unmatched: $maker$ and $produced\_by$, respectively. Not only is each of these slots the only unmatched slot attached to its respective class, but also the range restriction for the slot is the same: the class $Winery$. Therefore, we can match the slots $maker$ and $produced\_by$. In general, if $C_1 \in V_1$ and $C_2 \in V_2$, C_1 and C_2 match, and each of the classes has exactly one unmatched slot, S_1 and S_2 respectively, and S_1 and S_2 have the same facets, then S_1 and S_2 match.

5. **Unmatched inverse slots.** If a knowledge model allows definition of inverse relationships, we can take advantage of such relationships to create matches as well. Suppose we have a slot $maker$ in V_1 (at the $Wine$ class in Figure 1), which has an inverse slot $makes$ at the $Winery$ class (Figure 2b); and a slot $produced\_by$ in V_2, which has an inverse slot $produces$. Once we match the slots $maker$ and $produced\_by$, we can match the slots $makes$ and $produces$ because they are inverses of the slots that match. In general, if $S_1 \in V_1$ and $S_2 \in V_2$, S_1 and S_2 match, $invS_1$ and $invS_2$ are inverse slots for S_1 and S_2 respectively, and $invS_1$ and $invS_2$ are unmatched, then $invS_1$ and $invS_2$ match.

6. **Split classes.** Suppose that an early definition of our wine ontology included only white and red wines and we simply defined all rosé wines as instances of $White\ wine$. In the next version, we introduced a $Rosé\ wine$ class and moved all instances corresponding to rosé wines to this new class. In other words, the class $White\ wine$ was split into two classes: $White\ wine$ and $Rosé\ wine$. In general, if $C_0 \in V_1$ and $C_1 \in V_2$ and $C_2 \in V_2$, and for each instance of C_0, its image is an instance of either C_1 or C_2, then C_0 was split into C_1 and C_2. A similar matcher identifies classes that were merged.

Note that each of the matchers in the list considers only the frames that have not yet been matched. Thus, even though potentially each of the matchers will need to examine every tuple in the current PROMPTDIFF table, in practice, each matcher, except for the first one, examines only a very small number of tuples (the ones that have null values either for F_1 or F_2).

The PROMPTDIFF Algorithm

We combine all the available heuristic matchers (such as the ones we described in the previous section as well as any other available matchers) in the PROMPTDIFF algorithm, a fixed-point algorithm that produces the complete PROMPTDIFF table for two ontology versions. PROMPTDIFF runs all the matchers until they produce no new changes in the table. Because no matcher retracts the results of previous matchers or its own results from previous runs (the monotonicity principle), the algorithm always converges.

Dependency Among Matchers

A simple-minded implementation of such a fixed-point algorithm will run a set of all matchers in sequence until the whole set produces no more changes. However, we can greatly improve the efficiency of the algorithm using the following observations. First, not all matchers use all the information available in the table. For instance, the **single unmatched siblings** matcher never considers matches between slots. The **inverse slots** matcher does not care about the class-matching information. Second, the type of information in the table that each matcher can modify is limited. The **single unmatched sibling** matcher can create new matches between classes but never between slots. The **inverse slot** matcher can create new matches between slots but never between classes. Therefore, if each matcher declares what type of matching information it uses and what type of matching information it modifies, we can create a dependency table among the matchers and use this table to make the implementation more efficient.

Table 1 shows a dependency table for the matchers we described. For each matcher, we specify what type of information—matches between classes or slots—it uses and modifies (we omit facets and instances due to lack of space). Based on this specification, we determine dependency among the matchers (the last column in Table 1). Notice that none of the matchers affects the first matcher, which compares names and types of frames. After we run it once, we do not need to run it again: the results of other matchers will not change its results. Conversely, the **single unmatched slots** matcher uses existing matches between classes and slots and therefore all the matchers that modify this information affect this matcher (in our example, this list includes all matchers). Thus, if any of the matchers changes the PROMPTDIFF table, we need to run this matcher again.

PROMPTDIFF uses the dependency table to determine the order in which it executes the matchers. It keeps a stack of matchers it still needs to run. It starts by putting the matchers that do not affect any other matchers at the bottom of the stack and matchers that are not affected by other matchers at the top. Then it executes matcher M at the top of the stack. If M produced changes in the PROMPTDIFF table, the algorithm adds to the stack all the matchers that depend on M, removing duplicates. It runs until the stack is empty.

Performance Analysis

Given two versions of an ontology, V_1 and V_2, with n and m frames, respectively, we show that PROMPTDIFF converges after a linear number of steps and its running time

Matcher	Uses info about		Modifies info about		Affects matchers
	classes	slots	classes	slots	
1. Same type same name	−	−	+	+	2, 3, 4, 5
2. Single unmatched sibling	+	−	+	−	2, 3, 4
3. Siblings with same suffixes	+	−	+	−	2, 3, 4
4. Single unmatched slot	+	+	−	+	4, 5
5. Unmatched inverse slot	−	+	−	+	4, 5
6. Split classes	+	−	+	−	2, 3, 4

Table 1: Dependency table for the matchers in the paper

is $T_{max}O(max(n, m))$, where T_{max} is the running time for the least efficient of the matchers.

We first estimate the size of the PROMPTDIFF table. Without the split and merge operations, there is at most one tuple for each frame in V_1 and V_2. Thus, the number of tuples is $O(n + m) = O(M)$, where $M = max(n, m)$. We allow splits only of one class into two classes and merges of only two classes into one class. Therefore, even if every frame in V_1 were split into two frames in V_2, the size of the table is still $O(n)$. Similarly, even if every frame in V_2 resulted from a merge of two frames in V_1, the size of the table is $O(m)$. Thus, the table size is $O(M)$ and is linear in the size of the ontologies. When PROMPTDIFF runs, it starts with the table where all the frames from V_1 and V_2 are unmatched. The table contains $n + m$ rows. Performing a similar analysis, we can show that the maximum number of possible monotonic changes to the table is finite and it is limited by $O(M)$. If a matcher produced a change in the table, we will have to run at most c more matchers where c is the total number of matchers in the system, a constant. Therefore, the running time of PROMPTDIFF is $T_{max}O(M)$, where T_{max} is the running time for the least efficient algorithm.

All the matchers that we presented in the previous section, except the first one, are linear in the size of the ontologies. The first matcher runs in $O(M)log(M)$ time but it is executed only once. Therefore, given this set of matchers, the running time is $O(M)log(M) + O(M)O(M) = O(M^2)$.

Evaluation

Empirical evaluation is particularly important for heuristic algorithms, because there is no provable way to verify their correctness. We implemented PROMPTDIFF as a plugin for the Protégé-2000 ontology-editing environment (2002). We then evaluated PROMPTDIFF using ontology versions in two large projects at our department: the EON project,[2] and the PharmGKB project.[3] Both projects rely heavily on ontologies, both use Protégé-2000 for ontology development, and both keep records of different versions of their ontologies. We compared consecutive versions of the ontologies, as well as versions that were farther apart. For each pair of versions, we created the PROMPTDIFF table manually (given that the ontologies contained between 300 and 1900 concepts, it was a onerous process) and compared this manually generated table with the one that PROMPTDIFF produced.

Table 2 presents characteristics of the source ontologies

[2]http://www.smi.stanford.edu/projects/eon

[3]http://www.pharmgkb.org

and the results of our evaluation. Experiments 1, 2 and 3 used the ontologies form the EON project, which had between 314 and 320 frames in each version. Experiments 1 and 2 compared consecutive versions, whereas experiment 3 compared non-consecutive versions: the first version from experiment 1 and the second version from experiment 2. Experiments 4, 5 and 6 used the ontologies from the PharmGKB project, which had between 1886 and 1895 frames in each version. We compared consecutive versions and then the versions that were farther apart. On average, 97.9% of frames in each version remained unchanged. To evaluate the accuracy of our algorithm, we considered the frames that had changed (the remaining 2.1%)—exactly the frames that a user would need to look at. On average, PROMPTDIFF identified 96% of matches between those frames (this measure is similar to *recall* in information retrieval). 93% of the matches that PROMPTDIFF identified were correct (*precision* in information-retrieval terms).[4] More important, *all* the discrepancies between the manual and the automatic results were confined to the rows that had *null* in one of the first two columns. In other words, when PROMPTDIFF did find a match for a frame, it was always correct. Sometimes, the algorithm failed to find a match when a human expert could find one. A human expert can determine that two frames are similar even if a rule that he applied in a specific case is not sufficiently general to apply in all cases. It can be a significant overlap in a class name (e.g., $Finding$ versus $Physical\_Finding$), similarity in the slot range (e.g., two slots at matching frames that have the same range), and so on. At the same time, the matchers have to use rules that are sufficiently general to apply them to any ontology.

Let us interpret these numbers from the user's point of view. In the last experiment, for example (row 6 in Table 2), 83 frames from V_1 have changed (in fact, names of 67 of those frames were replaced with system-generated names by accident). The PROMPTDIFF result contained 19 unmatched frames. Given that we can trust the matches that PROMPTDIFF generated, we need to examine only these 19 unmatched frames instead of examining all 1886 in V_1, a significantly simpler task (it turned out that 14 of those frames did not have any matches). As a result, even for very large ontologies, users need to examine manually only a tiny fraction of frames—the ones for which PROMPTDIFF did not find any matches. And PROMPTDIFF conveniently shows these frames first in the PROMPTDIFF table.

Note that the performance of the algorithm did not deteriorate when we considered versions that were farther apart. In fact, both recall and precision were better than in the worst of the two cases for consecutive versions: because there were more changed frames, PROMPTDIFF identified a larger fraction of the frames correctly.

We used ten matchers in the experiments. On average, each matcher was executed 2.3 times in each experiment. Each matcher produced a new result at least once.

We have also experimented with executing matches in different order (still subject to the constraints that the dependency table imposes). We could not find cases where the

[4]We use the terms *precision* and *recall* in Table 2

	Ontologies	# frames in V_1	# frames in V_2	% frames changed from V_1	# frames unchanged from V_1	# of matches for changed frames that PROMPTDIFF identified	# of **correct** matches for changed frames that PROMPTDIFF identified	Recall	Precision
1	EON1 and EON2	314	320	5	98.4%	15	13	93%	87%
2	EON2 and EON3	320	319	1	99.7%	1	1	100%	100%
3	EON1 and EON3	314	319	6	98.1%	16	14	93%	87%
4	Pharm1 and Pharm2	1886	1891	11	99.4%	18	16	94%	89%
5	Pharm2 and Pharm3	1891	1895	71	96.2%	382	372	99%	97%
6	Pharm1 and Pharm3	1886	1895	83	95.6%	400	389	98%	97%
average					**97.9%**			**96%**	**93%**

Table 2: PROMPTDIFF evaluation results

final set of matches would be different depending on the order in which the matchers were executed. A particular match may be identified by a different matcher, but the final set of matches itself remained unchanged. It is likely that as we extend the set of matchers, we will find cases where the execution order of matchers indeed makes a difference.

Related Work

Current research in *ontology versioning* has addressed two issues: (1) identifying ontology versions in a distributed environments such as the Semantic Web (Klein & Fensel 2001) and (2) specifying explicitly logs of changes between versions (Oliver *et al.* 1999; Heflin & Hendler 2000). However, given the de-centralized nature of ontology development, logs of changes may not always be available. Our research complements these efforts by providing an automatic way to compare different versions based on the semantics encoded in their structure when logs of changes are not available.

The main thrust of research in *database-schema versioning* also uses the assumption that a record of changes between versions is readily available (Roddick 1995). Usually, researchers identify a canonical set of schema-change operations and consider effects of these operations on instance data as it migrates from one version to another (Banerjee *et al.* 1987). Lerner (2000) addresses automatic methods for comparing schema versions. She identifies complex operations such as grouping slots of a class into a different class, which is referenced by the original class and so on. As we try to perform more fine-grained comparison between ontology versions, we will no doubt draw upon her work.

Unlike in the schema-evolution research where the assumption that we have a log of changes is almost universal, the research in *database-schema integration* automates comparison between schemas that originated from different sources. Rahm and Bernstein (2001) survey the approaches that use linguistic techniques to look for synonyms, machine-learning techniques to propose matches based on instance data, information-retrieval techniques to compare information about attributes, and so on. Cupid (Madhavan, Bernstein, & Rahm 2001), for example, integrates many of these approaches in an algorithm that starts by matching leaf concepts in the hierarchy and then proceeding up the hierarchy trees to generate new matches based on matches of the subtrees. In fact, this field can potentially supply many heuristic matchers to integrate in the PROMPTDIFF algorithm. However, none of these algorithms was designed to

compare versions of the same schema, but rather different schemas. It would be interesting to see how well they perform in our case. There is one schema-integration algorithm that does rely on source schemas being similar. In designing the TranScm system for data translation, Milo and Zohar (1998) observe that when we need to translate data from an XML document to an object-oriented database, for example, the underlying schemas are often very similar since they describe the same type of data. Therefore, a small number of explicit rules can account for a large number of transformations. TranScm could benefit from many of the simple heuristics we described in this paper, whereas PROMPTDIFF could use some of the TranScm rules as its matchers.

There is a number of large *taxonomies for natural-language processing*, and researchers in that field developed semi-automated techniques for creating mappings between these resources. O'Hara and colleagues (1998) present a heuristic-based approach for finding correspondences between synsets in WordNet (Miller 1995) and concepts in the Mikrokosmos ontology (Mahesh & Nirenburg 1995). The heuristics compare the English representation of terms in both hierarchies, similarity of this representation for ancestors in the hierarchy, overlap in the definition of siblings and children. Daudé and colleagues (2001) used relaxation labeling to map between two versions of WordNet. The authors mainly use the hypernym–hyponym relationships, increasing the weight for a connection if it includes nodes whose hypernym or hyponyms are also connected. They experimented with using both direct and indirect hypernyms and hyponyms. Unlike these approaches, PROMPTDIFF examines not only hierarchical relations but also other relations, such as slot attachment, inverse slots, and instances.

Even though researchers on *semi-automated ontology mapping* also compare disparate ontologies rather than versions of the same ontology, the tools may provide another set of useful extensions for PROMPTDIFF. Ontology-merging tools, such as PROMPT (Noy & Musen 2000), use semantics of links between frames and user's action to produce hypotheses on matching frames. FCA-Merge (Stumme & Mädche 2001) uses a set of shared instances between two ontologies to find candidate matching classes and hierarchical links between them. AnchorPROMPT (Noy & Musen 2001), the articulation engine of the SKAT tool (Mitra, Wiederhold, & Kersten 2000), and Similarity-Flooding algorithm (Melnik, Garcia-Molina, & Rahm 2002) use similarities in the ontology graph structure to suggest candidate matches. Because they use different ontologies, all these algorithms have to be much more "conservative" in their comparisons requiring much more than a simple name and type match between frames to declare that they are similar. However, because the PROMPTDIFF framework is so easily extensible, we can incorporate these algorithms as new matchers in the fixed-point stage and integrate the results. Furthermore, most of the algorithms that we have mentioned either do not use the semantics of links at all or treat only is-a links in a special way. In the matchers that we described in this paper, we have used the semantics of *is-a* links, *instance-of*, slot attachment, slot range, and facet attachment links.

Future Work

In addition to incorporating other comparison algorithms to improve further the accuracy of PROMPTDIFF there are other possible directions to explore.

We can use features present in other formalisms, such as DAML+OIL, in the matchers. For example, we can consider if definitions of disjointness, necessary and sufficient conditions, subproperties, and so on can provide useful clues in the mappings.

We can use the information in the PROMPTDIFF table to generate transformation scripts from one version to another. Computer programs can then use these scripts to migrate instance data (as in schema versioning) or to query one version using another version. Minimizing the number of lossy transformations, which cause values to be lost at intermediate steps, is the main challenge in this task.

In our implementation, we used Java to define matchers. We could use a declarative language like the one described by Abiteboul and colleagues (2001) instead. Declarative specification could enable logic-based inference on rule definitions and their properties.

Another promising extension is assigning an uncertainty factor to the results of different matchers (i.e., a probability that the result is correct) and integrating the results taking into account these probabilities. Doan and colleagues (2001) use a similar approach to integrate results of machine learners for mapping between ontologies.

Acknowledgments

AnHai Doan provided very useful feedback on the paper. We also thank anonymous reviews for their comments, which greatly improved the paper. This work was supported in part by a contract from the U.S. National Cancer Institute.

References

Abiteboul, S.; Cluet, S.; and Milo, T. 2001. Correspondence and translation for heterogeneous data. *Theoretical Comp. Science*.

Banerjee, J.; Kim, W.; Kim, H.-J.; and Korth, H. F. 1987. Semantics and implementation of schema evolution in object-oriented databases. In *SIGMOD Conference*, 311–322.

Chaudhri, V. K.; Farquhar, A.; Fikes, R.; Karp, P. D.; and Rice, J. P. 1998. OKBC: A programmatic foundation for knowledge base interoperability. In *15th Nat. Conf. on Artificial Intelligence (AAAI-98)*, 600–607.

Daudé, J.; Padró, L.; and Rigau, G. 2001. A complete WN1.5 to WN1.6 mapping. In *NAACL-2001 Workshop on WordNet and Other Lexical Resources*.

Doan, A.; Madhavan, J.; Domingos, P.; and Halevy, A. 2001. Learning to map between ontologies on the semantic web. In *The 11th International WWW Conference*.

Fensel, D.; Horrocks, I.; van Harmelen, F.; Decker, S.; Erdmann, M.; and Klein, M. 2000. OIL in a nutshell. In *12th Conf. on Knowledge Engineering and Management (EKAW-2000)*.

Fogel, K., and Bar, M. 2001. *Open Source Development with CVS*. The Coriolis Group, 2nd edition.

Heflin, J., and Hendler, J. 2000. Dynamic ontologies on the web. In *17th Nat. Conf. on Artificial Intelligence (AAAI-2000)*.

Hendler, J., and McGuinness, D. L. 2000. The DARPA agent markup language. *IEEE Intelligent Systems* 16(6):67–73.

Klein, M., and Fensel, D. 2001. Ontology versioning on the Semantic Web. In *The First Semantic Web Working Symposium*.

Lerner, B. S. 2000. A model for compound type changes encountered in schema evolution. *ACM Transactions on Database Systems* 25(1):83–127.

Madhavan, J.; Bernstein, P. A.; and Rahm, E. 2001. Generic schema matching using Cupid. In *27th Int. Conf. on Very Large Data Bases (VLDB '01)*.

Mahesh, K., and Nirenburg, S. 1995. A situated ontology for practical NLP. In *Workshop on Basic Ontological Issues In Knowledge Sharing*.

Melnik, S.; Garcia-Molina, H.; and Rahm, E. 2002. Similarity flooding: A versatile graph matching algorithm and its application to schema matching. In *18th Int. Conf. on Data Engineering (ICDE-2002)*. San Jose, CA: IEEE Computing Society.

Miller, G. A. 1995. WordNet: A lexical database for english. *Communications of ACM* 38(11):39–41.

Milo, T., and Zohar, S. 1998. Using schema matching to simplify heterogeneous data translation. In *24th Int. Conf. on Very Large Data Bases (VLDB'98)*, 122–133. New York: Morgan Kaufmann.

Mitra, P.; Wiederhold, G.; and Kersten, M. 2000. A graph-oriented model for articulation of ontology interdependencies. In *Conf. on Extending Database Technology 2000 (EDBT'2000)*.

Noy, N. F., and Musen, M. 2000. PROMPT: Algorithm and tool for automated ontology merging and alignment. In *17th Nat. Conf. on Artificial Intelligence (AAAI-2000)*.

Noy, N. F., and Musen, M. A. 2001. Anchor-PROMPT: Using non-local context for semantic matching. In *Workshop on Ontologies and Information Sharing at IJCAI-2001*.

O'Hara, T.; Mahesh, K.; and Nirenburg, S. 1998. Lexical acquisition with WordNet and the Mikrokosmos ontology. In *COLING/ACL Wordkshop on Usage of WordNet in NLP Systems*. ACL.

Oliver, D. E.; Shahar, Y.; Shortliffe, E. H.; and Musen, M. A. 1999. Representation of change in controlled medical terminologies. *Artificial Intelligence in Medicine* 15:53–76.

Protege. 2002. The Protege project. *http://protege.stanford.edu*.

Rahm, E., and Bernstein, P. A. 2001. A survey of approaches to automatic schema matching. *VLDB Journal* 10(4).

Roddick, J. F. 1995. A survey of schema versioning issues for database systems. *Information and Software Technology* 37(7).

Stumme, G., and Mädche, A. 2001. FCA-Merge: Bottom-up merging of ontologies. In *7th Intl. Conf. on Artificial Intelligence (IJCAI '01)*, 225–230.

W3C. 2000. Resource description framework (RDF).

On Preference-based Search in State Space Graphs

Patrice Perny
LIP6 - University of Paris VI
4 Place Jussieu
75252 Paris Cedex 05, France
patrice.perny@lip6.fr

Olivier Spanjaard
LAMSADE - University of Paris IX
Place du Maréchal de Lattre de Tassigny
75775 Paris Cedex 16, France
spanjaar@lamsade.dauphine.fr

Abstract

The aim of this paper is to introduce a general framework for preference-based search in state space graphs with a focus on the search of the preferred solutions. After introducing a formal definition of preference-based search problems, we introduce the PBA* algorithm, a generalization of the A* algorithm, designed to process quasi-transitive preference relations defined over the set of solutions. Then, considering a particular subclass of preference structures characterized by two axioms called *Weak Preadditivity* and *Monotonicity*, we establish termination, completeness and admissibility results for PBA*. We also show that previous generalizations of A* are particular instances of PBA*. The interest of our algorithm is illustrated on a preference-based web access problem.

Introduction

In heuristic search, the quality of a potential solution is often represented by a scalar-valued cost function to be minimized. This is the case in classical state space graphs problems, where the value of a path between two nodes is defined as the sum of the costs of its arcs. This particular feature makes it possible to resort to constructive search algorithms like A* and A*$_\epsilon$ (Hart, Nilsson, and Raphael 1968; Pearl 1984), performing the implicit enumeration of feasible solutions, directed by a numerical evaluation function.

However, in practical situations, preferences over solutions are not always representable by such a numerical cost function and the traditional search algorithms do not fit. As an illustrative example, consider the following problem derived from (Etzioni *et al.* 1996; Papadimitriou and Yannakakis 2000):

The Web Access Problem. Suppose that you want to retrieve a list of documents from the world-wide web, requesting an "information marketplace" supported by automatic billing protocols. In order to gather the desired information, you have the possibility to query n information sources (web sites) simultaneously, each being accessible with charges. The following data are available for each site: the access cost

c_i to site i (expressed in USD), the reliability r_i of the site (qualitative evaluation on a finite ordered scale), the probability p_i that a given information will be found on site i (this probability represents the richness of the site) and the access time t_i to site i. The problem is to determine which subset $S \subseteq \{1, \ldots, n\}$ of sites should we choose for launching a multiple query?

Assuming that your resources are bounded in time and money by $\bar{t}$ and $\bar{c}$ respectively, the search is restricted to subsets S verifying the following constraints:

$$\max_{i \in S}\{t_i\} \leq \bar{t} \text{ and } \sum_{i \in S} c_i \leq \bar{c} \qquad (1)$$

Let us assume that, for any pair of feasible solutions S, S', the preferences in terms of reliability and richness are respectively represented by relations $\succ_1$, $\succ_2$. We introduce first the preferences in terms of reliability:

$$S \succ_1 S' \iff \begin{cases} \exists j \leq k, \ \forall i < j, \ L_i^S = L_i^{S'} \\ \text{and } L_j^S > L_j^{S'} \end{cases} \qquad (2)$$

where $k = \min\{|S|, |S'|\}$ and L^S is the sublist of $(r_i)_{i \in S}$ containing the k greatest values sorted by decreasing order. The definition of $\succ_1$ aims at favoring subsets including at least one site of high reliability. This principle could be represented by a maximum operation, but the lexicographic comparison rule used here is a refinement, known as *LexiMax* (for more details, see (Dubois, Fargier, and Prade 1996)). We introduce now the preferences in terms of richness:

$$S \succ_2 S' \iff \prod_{i \in S}(1 - p_i) < \prod_{i \in S'}(1 - p_i) \qquad (3)$$

The quantity $\prod_{i \in S}(1 - p_i)$ represents the probability of failure of the multiple query characterized by S, under the assumption that the success of one source is independent of the success or failure of the other sources.

It can easily be checked that relations $\succ_1$ and $\succ_2$ are transitive. From these relations, we derive the following dominance relation:

$$S \succ S' \iff S \succ_1 S' \text{ and } S \succ_2 S' \qquad (4)$$

The question under consideration is now to determine the subset of non-dominated solutions with respect to $\succ$, in other words the set of feasible solutions which are not dominated by any other feasible solution.

One can imagine various reformulations of this problem as a preferred-path problem in a state space graph. For example, consider a graph where the nodes represent all possible decisions concerning subsets of type $S_i = \{1, \ldots, i\}$ for $i = 1, \ldots, n$. Formally, each node is characterized by a vector $(s, b_1, \ldots, b_i)$ representing a state in which the decision concerning the i first sites has been made. The component b_k is a boolean which is true if and only if site k is selected, for every $k \in S_i$, and the starting node is (s) and corresponds to the initial state where no decision has been made. In this graph, each node of type $(s, b_1, \ldots, b_i)$ has two successors, $(s, b_1, \ldots, b_i, 0)$ and $(s, b_1, \ldots, b_i, 1)$ or less if some of them fail to satisfy the constraints (1). The goals are all feasible nodes of type $(s, b_1, \ldots, b_n)$. Clearly, we have to find the preferred paths from (s) to these nodes.

In this problem, we have to deal with a partial preference relation $\succ$ that cannot be represented by an additive scalar cost function to be minimized, and thus A* algorithm does not apply. Remark that none of the common preference-based extensions of A* applies to such a problem. The U* algorithm (White, Stewart, and Carraway 1992) which is a variation of A* designed to deal with utility-based preferences cannot be used because $\succ$ is not necessarily complete and thus, cannot be represented by a single utility function. The MOA* which is specially designed to process multiple objective does not apply either. Indeed, a preference relation like $\succ_1$ is not representable by a criterion function (note that, on that dimension, the value of a subset S may vary depending on the other subset it is compared to). Moreover, $\succ_1$ as many other partial preference orders cannot easily be represented using several criteria. Indeed, even if any partial order can be represented by an arbitrary large number of criteria (using a dominance relation), the computation of this representation is prohibitive due to the combinatorial number of elements to be compared. The same arguments apply to the ABC algorithm proposed in (Logan and Alechina 1998) for the search under flexible constraints.

For these reasons, we need a general framework to cope with partial preference relations in state space graphs. A similar statement has been discussed and clearly illustrated in (Dasgupta, Chakrabarti, and DeSarkar 1996; Müller 2001), in the context of game tree search. More generally, a systematic approach admitting any preference relation to direct the search is worth studying. In particular, this would make it possible to resort to useful qualitative preference models as those recently developed in the AI community, see e.g. (Boutilier 1994; Dubois, Fargier, and Prade 1996; Brafman and Tennenholtz 1997; 2000).

This idea is already present in the framework of constraint satisfaction problems. For example, the algebraic generalization of CSP algorithms proposed in (Schiex, Fargier, and Verfaillie 1995; Bistarelli, Montanari, and Rossi 1997) significantly increases the range of potential application of the algorithms by considering all ordered semiring structures on valuations. Our aim in this paper is to follow a similar line for search algorithms in state space graphs.

We are going to generalize and factorize various extensions of the A* algorithm at once, keeping only the key properties of preferences structures used to direct the search. The basic idea is to define a general framework where evaluation functions (like f, g and h in A*) are replaced by multi-sets of valuations, partially ordered by the preference $\succ$. In this framework, we will introduce the PBA* algorithm, a general preference-based extension of A*. Then, we will characterize a wide class of preferences structures for which our algorithm is admissible and show how this algorithm should be modified to cope with preference structures out of this class.

Preliminary Definitions

Let us first recall the following definitions about binary relations.

Definition 1 *For any binary relation $\succsim$ on a set X, the asymmetric and symmetric part of $\succsim$ are defined by:*
$$\forall x, x' \in X, \quad (x \succ x') \iff ((x \succsim x') \text{ and } not(x' \succsim x))$$
$$\forall x, x' \in X, \quad (x \sim x') \iff ((x \succsim x') \text{ and } (x' \succsim x))$$

Definition 2 *For any binary relation $\succsim$ defined on a set X, the set of maximal elements is defined by:*
$$M(X, \succsim) = \{x \in X \mid \forall x' \in X \quad not(x' \succ x)\}$$

In this paper, $\succsim$ represents a weak-preference relation and therefore $\succ$ is the associated strict preference relation. The proposition $x \succsim x'$ means x is at least as good as x' whereas $x \succ x'$ means x is strictly preferred to x'.

Definition 3 *A binary relation $\succsim$ defined on a set X is said to be:*

- *complete iff $\forall x, x' \in X, x \succsim x'$ or $x' \succsim x$*

- *quasi-transitive iff $\succ$ is transitive*

We have to introduce the notion of *multi-set*, which is an unordered collection of values which may have duplicates. More formally:

Definition 4 *For any set E, the set $\mathcal{M}(E)$ of multi-sets of E is the set of functions $x : E \to \mathbb{N}$, representing the number of occurrences of each element. We call support of a multi-set x the set $E_x = \{e \in E \mid x(e) \neq 0\}$. The empty multi-set is denoted $\mathbb{1}_\emptyset$.*

We also have to define the sum of two multi-sets:

Definition 5 *Let x and y be two multi-sets in $\mathcal{M}(E)$. The addition and the difference of x and y are defined as follows:*
$$\forall e \in E, (x + y)(e) = x(e) + y(e)$$
$$\forall e \in E, (x - y)(e) = \max(0, x(e) - y(e))$$

The inclusion of a multi-set x in a multi-set y is defined as follows:
$$x \subseteq y \iff \forall e \in E_x, \ x(e) \leq y(e)$$

The cardinality of a multi-set x is defined as follows:
$$|x| = \sum_{e \in E_x} x(e)$$

Problem Formulation

A*-like search algorithms look for best paths in a state space graph. Let N be a finite set of nodes, $A \subseteq N \times N$ be a set of directed valued arcs, $N(P)$ be the set of all nodes on a path P and $S(n)$ be the set of all successors of a node n. We denote $\mathcal{P}(n, X)$ the set of all paths linking n to a node in X. Let $s \in N$ be the source of the graph and $\Gamma \subseteq N$ be the subset of goal nodes. Then, $\mathcal{P}(s, \Gamma)$ denotes the set of all paths from s to a goal node $\gamma \in \Gamma$, and $\mathcal{P}(n, n')$ the set of all paths linking n to n'. We call solution-path a path from s to a goal node $\gamma \in \Gamma$. Moreover, we assume we get a valuation function $v : A \to E$. Let $P \cap \mathcal{P}(n, n')$ be the segment of P linking n to n'. Let x_P be the multi-set of valuations of arcs on P. We assume a reflexive and quasi-transitive preference relation $\succsim$ is defined on $\mathcal{M}(E)$ (set of multi-sets of valuations). Notice that we will always consider finite multi-sets (*i.e.* with finite supports).

Concerning the definition of the preference relation, we can distinguish two main cases:

1. Most of the time, the preference relation $\succsim$ on $\mathcal{M}(E)$ is constructed from a commutative and associative internal composition operator $\otimes$ on the valuation space E, and a preference relation $\succsim_E$ on E. We denote $e^k = e \otimes \ldots \otimes e$ (k times). Then, $v(x)$ denotes the image of a multi-set x of elements in E, *i.e.*: $v(x) = \bigotimes_{e \in E_x} e^{x(e)}$. It leads to the following preference relation on $\mathcal{M}(E)$:

$$\forall x \in \mathcal{M}(E), \ x \succsim y \iff v(x) \succsim_E v(y)$$

For instance, for the usual A* algorithm, E is $\mathbb{R}$, $\otimes$ is the sum operator $+$ and $\succsim_E = \leq$. In such a case, we can work directly in the valuation space E.

2. Sometimes, it is not possible to represent the preference relation $\succsim$ by resorting to an internal composition operator on E. For example, in the web acces problem, no composition operator on the reliability scale E could induce a convenient representation of the *LexiMax* preference relation (see Equation (2)), which writes:

$$x \succ_1 y \iff L^x \neq L^y \text{ and } \max_{e \in E_{L^x - L^y}} e > \max_{e \in E_{L^y - L^x}} e$$

in terms of multi-sets. In such a case, we have to work in $\mathcal{M}(E)$ and therefore to design an algorithm able to operate in such a framework.

We denote $M(\mathcal{P}, \succsim)$ the set of maximal paths in a set $\mathcal{P}$:

$$M(\mathcal{P}, \succsim) = \{P \in \mathcal{P} \mid \forall P' \in \mathcal{P} \ \text{not}(x_{P'} \succ x_P)\}$$

We call *multi-valuation* a multi-set of valuations. We introduce now the main issue of this paper:

The Preference-Based Search Problem. Consider a finite state space graph G, *i.e.* a graph containing a finite number of arcs and therefore a finite number of non-isolated vertices, and assume there exists at least one path P_0 with a finite length (number of arcs, denoted $|P_0|$) between s and a goal node $\gamma \in \Gamma$. The goal is to determine the entire set $M(\{x_P \mid P \in \mathcal{P}(s, \Gamma)\}, \succsim)$.

From now on, unless otherwise stated, we work in $\mathcal{M}(E)$ for the sake of generality. For example, coming back to the web access problem mentioned in the introduction, the multi-valuation of any path from (s) to a node $(s, b_1, \ldots, b_k)$ is the multi-set of pairs (r_i, p_i), $i \leq k$ such that $b_i = \text{true}$.

The PBA* Algorithm

We propose here a variation of the A* search algorithm specifically designed to work with a preference relation on $\mathcal{M}(E)$. It is more general than an algebraic approach of the problem (Rote 1998; Bistarelli, Montanari, and Rossi 1997), that would consist in assuming there is a partially ordered semigroup on an evaluation space E. Indeed, we do not assume the transitivity of the symmetric part of the preference relation, neither the existence of an internal composition operator on E (which permits to consider the *LexiMax* preference relation). We call our algorithm PBA* for *Preference-Based A**. At any node n, we consider: $G^*(n)$ the set of maximal multi-valuations of paths P in $\mathcal{P}(s, n)$, $H^*(n)$ the set of maximal multi-valuations of paths P in $\mathcal{P}(n, \Gamma)$ and $F^*(n)$ the set of maximal multi-valuations of paths P in $\mathcal{P}(s, \Gamma)$ such that $n \in N(P)$. As soon as the Bellman principle is verified, this last set derives from the two other ones as follows:

$$F^*(n) = M(G^*(n) \odot H^*(n), \succsim)$$

where $\odot$ is an internal composition operator defined, for any sets X, Y of multi-valuations, by:

$$X \odot Y = \bigcup_{x \in X, y \in Y} (x + y)$$

As in the A* algorithm, $G^*(n)$, $H^*(n)$ and $F^*(n)$ are unknown during the search. Consequently, the evaluation of a node n is based on the following approximations: $G(n)$ the set of maximal multi-valuations of generated paths, $H(n)$ the set of multi-valuations resulting from a heuristic estimation of $H^*(n)$ and $F(n) = M(G(n) \odot H(n), \succsim)$. $H(n)$ is assumed to be *coincident*, in other words, the following property holds: $\forall \gamma \in \Gamma, H(\gamma) = \mathbb{1}_\emptyset$.

As in A*, the PBA* algorithm divides the set of generated nodes into a set O of open nodes (labeled but not yet developed) and a set C of closed nodes (labeled and already developed). At any iteration, we develop a node $n \in O$ such that $F(n)$ contains at least one maximal multi-valuation among labels. Formally, one chooses n in the set MAX of most promising nodes, defined as a subset of nodes $n \in O$ such that:

$$\exists f \in F(n), \begin{cases} \forall n' \in O, \forall f' \in F(n'), \ \text{not}(f' \succ f) \\ \forall c \in CHOICE, \ c \neq f \text{ and not}(c \succ f) \end{cases}$$
$$(5)$$

where $CHOICE$ denotes the current set of maximal labels at the goal nodes. The goal nodes which have already been selected for development are stored in a set denoted $GOALS$. More precisely, we propose Algorithm 1 given below:

Algorithm 1 PBA^*

> Initialization: $O \leftarrow \{s\}$; $C \leftarrow \emptyset$; $G(s) \leftarrow \emptyset$; $MAX \leftarrow \{s\}$;
> $GOALS \leftarrow \emptyset$; $CHOICE \leftarrow \emptyset$; $n \leftarrow s$;
> While $[MAX \neq \emptyset]$
>> Move n from O to C
>> If $[n \notin \Gamma]$ then for $n' \in S(n)$ do
>>> If $[n' \notin O \cup C]$ then:
>>>> $G(n') \leftarrow M(G(n) \odot x_{(n,n')}, \succsim)$
>>>> $F(n') \leftarrow M(G(n') \odot H(n'), \succsim)$
>>>> Put n' in O
>>> end
>>> else n' is already labelled, then:
>>>> $G(n') \leftarrow M(G(n') \cup (G(n) \odot x_{(n,n')}), \succsim)$
>>>> $F(n') \leftarrow M(G(n') \odot H(n'), \succsim)$
>>>> If $G(n')$ is modified, put n' in O
>>> end
>> end
>> If $[O \neq \emptyset]$ then
>>> compute MAX according to Equation (5)
>> end
>> Else $MAX = \emptyset$
>> If $[MAX \neq \emptyset]$ choose $n \in MAX$ with respect to an
>> heuristic specific to the application, with priority to $n \in \Gamma$.
>> If $[MAX \neq \emptyset]$ and $[n \in \Gamma]$ then:
>>> $GOALS \leftarrow GOALS \cup \{n\}$
>>> $CHOICE \leftarrow M(CHOICE \cup G(n), \succsim)$
>> end
> end
> If $[GOALS = \emptyset]$ then exit with failure;
> Exit with all the efficient paths obtained by backtracking from
> the labels in $CHOICE$;

end

Remark 1 *If a commutative and associative internal operator has been used to define the preference relation, then the entire search can be done in the valuation space (i.e. the labels are in E instead of $\mathcal{M}(E)$).*

Remark 2 *For the sake of simplicity, we have omitted the management of pointers allowing the preferred paths to be recovered. This can be easily implemented, as shown in (Stewart and White III 1991). This additional functionality is assumed to exist in the sequel.*

Axioms

As the preference relation used is not specified in our algorithm, we introduce here some axioms on preference which will be necessary to establish the termination, completeness and admissibility of the algorithm.

Weak Preadditivity (WP)

$$\forall x, y, z \in \mathcal{M}(E), \ x \succ y \Longrightarrow x + z \succ y + z$$

This axiom is a weak version of De Finetti's qualitative additivity (De Finetti 1974) and can also be seen as a qualitative counterpart of the monotonicity property considered in dynamic programming (Mitten 1964; Morin 1982). Moreover, if an internal composition operator $\otimes$ on E has been used to define the preference relation $\succsim$,

this axiom translates into distributivity of $\otimes$ over the selection operation represented by $M(., \succsim)$ (Zimmermann 1981; Rote 1998). Note that WP holds within the framework of A* and its direct extensions mentioned above. Moreover, concerning the web access problem, this axiom is also satisfied by the preference relations defined in Equations (2), (3), and therefore (4).

Proposition 1 *When $\succsim$ satisfies WP, the Bellman principle is verified: any subpath of a maximal path is maximal.*

Proof. Let P be a path from a node n_1 to a node n_4. Let n_2, n_3 be two nodes along this path, $P' = P \cap \mathcal{P}(n_1, n_2)$, $P'' = P \cap \mathcal{P}(n_2, n_3)$ and $P''' = P \cap \mathcal{P}(n_3, n_4)$. Assume that P'' is not maximal, then there exists $Q \in \mathcal{P}(n_2, n_3)$ such that $x_Q \succ x_{P''}$ and by WP we get $x_{P' \cup Q \cup P'''} = x_Q + x_{P' \cup P'''} \succ x_{P''} + x_{P' \cup P'''} = x_P$. $\square$

Remark 3 *Whenever $\succsim$ is transitive, $\sim$ is an equivalence relation defining indifference classes. Hence, one might be interested in determining only one maximal path by indifference class. For that purpose, the key property would be:*

$$\forall x, y, z \in \mathcal{M}(E), \ x \succ y \Longrightarrow x + z \succsim y + z \ (\text{WP}')$$

instead of Weak Preaditivity, thus opening new possibilities. For example, the preference relation defined by $x \succsim y$ iff $\max_{e \in E_x} e \geq \max_{e \in E_y} e$ satisfies WP$'$ but not WP.

In the classical A* algorithm, the hypothesis of a strictly positive inferior bound on the valuations of the arcs insures that a cyclic path cannot be maximal. Therefore, as the graph is finite and each reopening of a node corresponds to the detection of a new acyclic path, the algorithm is guaranteed to terminate in finite time. However, in our algorithm, we have to reopen a node as soon as we detect a new path that is not worse than any other label at this node. Therefore, we need the following axiom to insure the termination of the algorithm:

Monotonicity (M)

$$\forall x, y \in \mathcal{M}(E), \ x \subset y \Longrightarrow x \succ y$$

This monotonicity axiom guarantees that a subpath is always preferred to the path it is extracted from. In other words, a path including a cycle cannot be maximal. Remark that in acyclic graphs (as in the web access problem), that axiom can be omitted.

Termination and Completeness

Termination and completeness are both algorithmic properties of main interest. As usual, an algorithm is said to *terminate* if it necessarily stops after a finite number of iterations. It is said to be *complete* if it outputs at least one solution-path as soon as a solution-path exists. The following lemma, valid for A*, still holds for PBA*, since its proof does not depend on the preference relation used.

Lemma 1 *Let $n \in N$ and $P \in \mathcal{P}(s, n)$. At any step of the algorithm, either at least one node on P is in O, or every node on P is in C.*

The following termination result holds thanks to the monotonicity axiom entailing the cancellation of any cyclic path during the search.

Theorem 1 *If $\succsim$ satisfies M, PBA* terminates for any problem such that at least one solution-path exists.*

Proof. Consider a yet developed node n. For this node to be redeveloped, it is necessary to find another path which is maximal with respect to $G(n)$. Such a path is necessarily acyclic due to axiom M. Since there exists only a finite number of acyclic paths in a finite graph, n can only be developed a finite number of times. Therefore PBA* terminates after a finite number of iterations. □

The following result holds also for any best-first strategy (see (Pearl 1984) for the definition of a best-first strategy):

Theorem 2 *If $\succsim$ is quasi-transitive and satisfies M, PBA* is complete.*

Proof. While no solution-path is detected, there is necessarily a node $n \in N(P_0)$ which is in O (by Lemma 1). As $O \neq \emptyset$ and $CHOICE = \emptyset$, $MAX = M(\bigcup_{n \in O} F(n), \succsim)$. Hence, MAX cannot be empty due to the quasi-transitivity of $\succsim$. However, thanks to M and Theorem 1, we know that the algorithm terminates after a finite number of iterations. Therefore, as the termination rule is $MAX = \emptyset$, a solution-path is necessarily found. This establishes the completeness of the algorithm. □

It can be shown that PBA* is complete even for infinite (but locally finite) graphs as soon as $\succsim$ is quasi-transitive and the following archimedean axiom is verified: If x is a finite multi-set of $\mathcal{M}(E)$, then there exists $k \in \mathbb{N}^*$, $\forall y \in \mathcal{M}(E)$, $|y| \geq k \implies x \succ y$. Unfortunately, such a result is rather theoretical since the archimedean axiom is not satisfied by several natural preference relations. For instance, Equation (2) in our example fails to satisfy this axiom.

Admissibility

We now define the notion of *optimistic* heuristic in our framework, in order to establish the admissibility of PBA*. In this framework, an algorithm is said to be *admissible* if it guarantees to terminate with the whole set $M(\{x_P \mid P \in \mathcal{P}(s, \Gamma)\}, \succsim)$ for any problem such that at least one solution path exists.

Definition 6 *An optimistic heuristic is a set H of multi-valuations fulfilling the following conditions: $\forall n \in N$, $\forall h^* \in M(H^*(n), \succsim)$, $\exists h \in H(n)$ s.t. $h \succ h^*$ or $h = h^*$.*

For example, in the web access problem, we can choose as heuristic, at node $(s, b_1, \ldots, b_k)$, the multi-set of pairs (r_i, p_i) for $i > k$. Let us now introduce two intermediary results:

Lemma 2 *Let P be a maximal path from s to a node n (possibly outside Γ) in the graph, and n' be the first open node on this path. If $\succsim$ satisfies WP, then there exists $g \in G(n')$ such that $g = x_{P \cap \mathcal{P}(s, n')}$.*

Proof. The path $P' = P \cap \mathcal{P}(s, n')$ has been detected since all the predecessors of n' on P are closed. Moreover,

by the Bellman principle which holds thanks to WP, $P \in M(\mathcal{P}(s, n), \succsim)$ implies $P' \in M(\mathcal{P}(s, n'), \succsim)$. Consequently: $\exists g \in G(n')$ such that $g = x_{P \cap \mathcal{P}(s, n')}$ □

Lemma 3 *Let $\succsim$ be a preference relation which satisfies WP. At every step of the algorithm, if $P \in M(\mathcal{P}(s, \Gamma), \succsim)$ and P is not yet detected, there exists in O a node n' of P and $f \in F(n')$ such that $f \succ x_P$ or $f = x_P$.*

Proof. Let n' be the first open node on P. Let $P' = P \cap \mathcal{P}(s, n')$ and $P'' = P \setminus P'$. By Lemma 2, $\exists g \in G(n')$ such that $g = x_{P'}$. On the other hand, $\exists h \in H(n')$ such that $h \succ x_{P''}$ or $h = x_{P''}$ since h is optimistic. Therefore $\exists f \in F(n')$ such that $f = g + h = x_{P'} + h \succ x_{P'} + x_{P''} = x_P$ by WP or $f = g + h = x_{P'} + h = x_{P'} + x_{P''} = x_P$. □

We now present the main result of this section:

Theorem 3 *If $\succsim$ is quasi-transitive and satisfies WP and M, then PBA* is admissible.*

Proof. Thanks to M and Theorem 1, the algorithm terminates after a finite number of iterations. Assume that there exists x_P in $M(\{x_P \mid P \in \mathcal{P}(s, \Gamma)\}, \succsim)$ that is not in $CHOICE$ when PBA* stops. As P is not detected, $O \neq \emptyset$ (by Lemma 1). When PBA* stops, $MAX = \emptyset$ and therefore all the nodes in O satisfy: $\forall f \in F(n)$, $\exists c \in CHOICE$, $c = f$ or $c \succ f$. However, by Lemma 3, there exists a node n' of P in O and $f \in F(n')$ such that $f \succ x_P$ or $f = x_P$. Therefore $c \succ x_P$ or $c = x_P$, but $c \succ x_P$ contradicts the maximality of P and $c = x_P$ contradicts $x_P \notin CHOICE$. Hence, $M(\{x_P \mid P \in \mathcal{P}(s, \Gamma)\}, \succsim) \subseteq CHOICE$. Moreover, by construction, $\succ$ is empty on $CHOICE$, which completes the proof. □

Considering the web access problem mentioned in the introduction, since the state space graph is acyclic and the preference relation $\succ$ defined by (4) is transitive and satisfies WP, Theorem 3 shows that PBA* can be used to determine the preferred solutions.

Approximation of the Preference Relation

It should be noticed that the previous results, despite their generality, do not cover the entire class of "rational" preference relations. For example, for bi-criteria optimization problems characterized by two valuations v_1 and v_2, the egalitarian preference: $x_P \succsim x_Q \Leftrightarrow \max\{v_1(x_P), v_2(x_P)\} \leq \max\{v_1(x_Q), v_2(x_Q)\}$ (where $v_j(x_P) = \sum_{a \in P} v_j(a)$) fails to satisfy the WP axiom. Nevertheless, PBA* might be properly used with an approximation $\succsim'$ of $\succsim$ which satisfies the WP axiom (e.g. $x_P \succsim' x_Q \Leftrightarrow v_j(x_P) \leq v_j(x_Q)$ for $j = 1, 2$). For this reason, we introduce the following definition, which makes sense only in acyclic graphs (to escape the monotonicity problem):

Definition 7 *A preference relation $\succsim'$ is an approximation of $\succsim$ if and only if: $\forall X \subseteq \mathcal{M}(E)$, $M(X, \succsim) \subseteq M(X, \succsim')$*

Then, we have:

Proposition 2 *Let $\succsim$ be a preference relation and $\succsim'$ an approximation of $\succsim$ which is quasi-transitive and satisfies WP,* applying PBA* with $\succsim'$ yields a superset of $M(\{x_P \mid P \in \mathcal{P}(s, \Gamma)\}, \succsim)$.

Moreover, during the search with respect to $\succsim'$, we can remove labels f for which there exists a detected solution-path P such that $x_P \succ f$. By this way, we reduce computational efforts and we get exactly the set $M(\{x_P | P \in \mathcal{P}(s, \Gamma)\}, \succsim)$.

Comparison with Other A* Algorithms

In this section, we show that various well-known variations of the A* algorithm can be seen as particular instances of PBA*. Each variation is characterized by the choice of the valuation set E, the valuation space (E or $\mathcal{M}(E)$) and the preference relation (which mostly satisfies WP and M). This is also the case for the A* algorithm itself. Indeed, we can instantiate our model as follows: $E = \mathbb{R}$, the valuation space is E, $\otimes = +$ and $x_P \succsim x_Q \Leftrightarrow \sum_{a \in P} v(a) \leq \sum_{a \in Q} v(a)$, and the goal is to find one maximal path.

The multi-criteria variation of A* algorithm, namely MOA* (Stewart and White III 1991), gives the following instance: $E = \mathbb{R}^n$, the valuation space is E, $x_P \succsim x_Q \Leftrightarrow \forall i = 1, \ldots, n, \sum_{a \in P} v_i(a) \leq \sum_{a \in Q} v_i(a)$, and the goal is to determine $M(\mathcal{P}(s, \Gamma), \succsim)$.

The multiattribute utility variation of A* algorithm, namely U* (White, Stewart, and Carraway 1992), gives the following instance (here, $v(x)$ denotes a multiattribute reward vector): $E = \mathbb{R}^n$, the valuation space is E, $x_P \succsim x_Q \Leftrightarrow u(v(x_P)) \geq u(v(x_Q))$, approximated by: $x_P \succsim' x_Q \Leftrightarrow \forall i = 1, \ldots, n, \sum_{a \in P} v_i(a) \leq \sum_{a \in Q} v_i(a)$, and we are looking for one maximal path.

The ABC algorithm (Logan and Alechina 1998) is a variation of U* designed for multicriteria problems where the overall objective is expressed by n soft constraints on criteria. E is the criteria space and the preference relation is $x \succsim y \Leftrightarrow (x_1, \ldots, x_n) \sqsubseteq (y_1, \ldots, y_n)$ where x_j (resp. y_j) is a boolean representing the satisfaction index of constraint C_j and $\sqsubseteq$ is any reflexive and transitive extension of the dominance order on boolean vectors (induced by $1 \sqsubseteq 0$).

Conclusion

We have proposed a new algorithm for preference-based search which extends previous A*-like algorithms in a very natural way. The termination, completeness and admissibility results established in the paper prove its practical interest for a wide class of preference relations characterized by axioms WP and M. When preferences escape this class, we still have the possibility to determine the preferred paths, provided a convenient approximation of the preference relation is found. A more elaborate study on the construction of efficient approximations seems to be of main interest.

References

Bistarelli, S.; Montanari, U.; and Rossi, F. 1997. Semiring-based constraint satisfaction and optimization. *Journal of the Association for Computing Machinery* 44(2).

Boutilier, C. 1994. Toward a logic for qualitative decision theory. In *Proceedings of the Fourth International Conference on Principles of Knowledge Representation and Reasoning, KR-94,* 75–86.

Brafman, R., and Tennenholtz, M. 1997. On the axiomatization of qualitative decision theory. In *Proceedings of the Fourteenth National Conference on Artificial Intelligence, AAAI-97,* 76–81. AAAI Press/MIT Press.

Brafman, R., and Tennenholtz, M. 2000. An axiomatic treatment of three qualitative decision criteria. *Journal of the ACM* 47(3):452–482.

Dasgupta, P.; Chakrabarti, P.; and DeSarkar, S. 1996. Searching game trees under a partial order. *Artificial Intelligence* 82:237–257.

De Finetti, B. 1974. *Probability Theory Vol. I.* London: Wiley.

Dubois, D.; Fargier, H.; and Prade, H. 1996. Refinements of the maximin approach to decision-making in fuzzy environment. *Fuzzy Sets and Systems* 81:103–122.

Etzioni, O.; Hanks, S.; Jiang, T.; Karp, R. M.; Madari, O.; and Waarts, O. 1996. Efficient information gathering on the internet. In *Proceedings of the 37th IEEE Symposium on Foundation of Computer Science,* 234–243.

Hart, P. E.; Nilsson, N. J.; and Raphael, B. 1968. A formal basis for the heuristic determination of minimum cost paths. *IEEE Trans. Syst. and Cyb.* SSC-4 (2):100–107.

Logan, B., and Alechina, N. 1998. A* with bounded costs. In *Proceedings of the Fifteenth National Conference on Artificial Intelligence, AAAI-98.* AAAI Press/MIT Press.

Mitten, L. 1964. Composition principles for the synthesis of optimal multi-stage processes. *Operations Research* 12.

Morin, T. 1982. Monotonicity and the principle of optimality. *J. of Math. Analysis and Applications* 86:665–674.

Müller, M. 2001. Partial order bouding: a new approach to evaluation in game tree search. *Artificial Intelligence* 129:279–231.

Papadimitriou, C. H., and Yannakakis, M. 2000. On the approximability of trade-offs and optimal access of web sources. In *Proc. of the 41th IEEE Symp. on FOCS,* 86–92.

Pearl, J. 1984. Intelligent search strategies for computer problem solving.

Rote, G. 1998. Paths problems in graphs. Technical report, Institute of mathematics, technical university of Graz.

Schiex, T.; Fargier, H.; and Verfaillie, G. 1995. Valued constraint satisfaction problems: Hard and easy problems. In Mellish, C., ed., *Proceedings of the International Joint Conference on Artificial Intelligence, IJCAI-95.*

Stewart, B., and White III, C. 1991. Multiobjective A*. *Journal of the Association for Computing Machinery* 38(4):775–814.

White, C.; Stewart, B.; and Carraway, R. 1992. Multiobjective, preference-based search in acyclic OR-graphs. *European Journal of Operational Research* 56:357–363.

Zimmermann, U. 1981. *Linear and combinatorial optimization in ordered algebraic structures.* Number 10 in Annals of discrete mathematics. North holland publishing company.

An Average-case Analysis of Graph Search

Anup K. Sen

Indian Institute of Management Calcutta
Joka, D. H. Road, Post Box 16757
Calcutta 700 027, INDIA
sen@iimcal.ac.in

Amitava Bagchi ♣

School of Management
University of Texas at Dallas
Richardson, Texas 75083
abagchi@utdallas.edu

Weixiong Zhang ♠

Computer Science Department
Washington University
St. Louis, Missouri 63130
zhang@cs.wustl.edu

Abstract

Many problems in real-world applications require searching graphs. Understanding the performance of search algorithms has been one of the eminent tasks of heuristic search research. Despite the importance of graph search algorithms, the research of analyzing their performance is limited, and most work on search algorithm analysis has been focused on tree search algorithms. One of the major obstacles to analyzing graph search is that no single graph is an appropriate representative of graph search problems. In this paper, we propose one possible approach to analyzing graph search: Analyzing the performance of graph search algorithms on a representative graph of a cluster of problems. We specifically consider job-sequencing problems in which a set of jobs must be sequenced on a machine such that a penalty function is minimized. We analyze the performance of A* graph search algorithm on an abstract model that closely represents job sequencing problems. It is an extension to a model widely used previously for analyzing tree search. One of the main results of our analysis is the existence of a gap of computational cost between two classes of job sequencing problems, one with exponential and the other with polynomial complexity. We provide experimental results showing that real job sequencing problems indeed have a huge difference on computational costs under different conditions.

Introduction and Overview

Graph search has been shown in many cases to be more effective and efficient than tree search. There are real-world applications where tree search is simply not feasible. For example, sequence alignment, an important problem in computational biology that can be formulated as a shortest-path problem in a grid, is only amenable to graph search algorithms [Korf and Zhang 2000]. There are also real problems that can be solved more efficiently by graph search algorithms. For instance, it was shown in [Sen and Bagchi 1996] that when the evaluation function is non-order-preserving ([Pearl 1984], pp. 100-102), graph search for job sequencing problems significantly outperforms tree search in terms of running time. Moreover, a graph search usually uses much less memory than a tree search [Sen, Bagchi and Ramaswamy 1996], making many large problems solvable on our current machines.

Despite its importance in understanding, characterizing and solving difficult problems, the performance analysis of graph search algorithms is almost an untouched topic. This sharply contrasts to a large amount of effort and literature devoted to the topic of performance analysis of tree search algorithms [Huyn, Dechter and Pearl 1980, Pearl 1984, Bagchi and Sen 1988, Davis 1990, Chenoweth and Davis 1991, Zhang and Korf 1995, Korf, Reid and Edelkamp 2001]. To further advance the state-of-the-art on heuristic search, especially on performance analysis, it is desirable to extend our current research to the performance analysis of graph search.

One major difficulty that has crippled the research on the performance analysis of graph search algorithms is perhaps that no single graph is an authenticated representative of various real search problems. Therefore, general results on the performance of graph search seem to be out of reach, which to some extent explains and reflects the state-of-the-art on performance analysis of graph search. On the other end of the spectrum of possibilities to performance analysis, we may consider each individual problem that we encounter. There are numerous important graph search problems. To solve many of them and try to generalize the results may be a tedious and difficult task.

In this research, we consider an alternative to the performance analysis of graph search. We take a middle ground between a "general" graph search problem and a single problem, i.e., we consider a representative model of a set of related problems. We hope that the results will not only shed lights on individual class of problems, but also can be combined relatively easily to provide a deep understanding of graph search problems and algorithms.

In this paper, we are particularly interested in a class of job sequencing problem, an important topic in Computer Science and Operations Research. Job sequencing and scheduling problems appear in many real applications in manufacturing and production systems as well as in information-processing environments [Pinedo 1995]. We consider the class of problems in which N jobs must be so sequenced on a machine that a penalty function on job completion time is minimized. The penalty function may be

♣ On leave from Indian Institute of Management Calcutta.

♠ Funded in part by NSF Grants IIS-0196057 and IET-0111386, and in part by DARPA Cooperative Agreements F30602-00-2-0531 and F33615-01-C-1897.

in various other different forms, such as to minimize the mean job lateness and/or earliness, weighted sum of non-linear functions of completion times, etc.

Our analytic model of job sequencing problems is a graph that defines a partial ordering of subsets of a set of N elements under the set inclusion property. In this graph, there are 2^N nodes; the set of N elements is the root node at level 0 and the empty set is the goal node at level N. Thus it is a directed acyclic graph (DAG) with one goal node and allows multiple solution paths.

To make analysis feasible, following [Pearl 1984] it is assumed that the normalized errors of heuristic estimates of non-goal nodes are independent, identically distributed (i.i.d.) random variables. Using this abstract model, we analyze the expected complexity of A* graph search algorithm, measured by the number of node expansions [Pearl 1984]. We choose A* because it is optimal in terms of the number of node expansions among all algorithms that use the same heuristic information [Dechter and Pearl 1985]. Therefore, the results reflect the expected complexity of searching the abstract model as well as the underlying problems represented by the model.

We present two main theoretical results in this paper. First, we show that under certain weak conditions the expected number of distinct nodes expanded by A* increases exponentially with the number of jobs N for large N. This result matches the previous experimental results on the single machine job sequencing applications [Sen, Bagchi and Ramaswamy 1996]. Second, we identify cases of interest where the expected number of node expansions of A* is polynomial in N for large N. These two classes of complexity indicate that the expected complexity of A* graph algorithm on job sequencing problems has two phases, one exponential and the other polynomial, showing a huge gap similar to a phenomenon of phase transitions. Indeed, our experimental results on single machine job sequencing problems support our theoretical analysis. Specifically, we summarize the previous results for the exponential case, and provide new test results on the polynomial case.

The paper is organized as follows. The basic concepts and the analytic graph model are introduced in the next section. We then analyze the expected complexity of A* using the model. The proofs to the theorems are included in the Appendix. Then we present our experimental results. Concluding remarks are given at the end.

Basic Concepts

A *search graph* (or *network*) G is a finite directed graph with nodes n, n', n_1, n_2, ... The search always begins at the *start* (or *root*) node s, and ends at the *goal* node r. Each directed arc (n_1, n_2) in G has a finite *arc cost* $c(n_1, n_2) > 0$. A path is a sequence of directed arcs. A *solution path* is a path that begins at the start node s and ends at the goal node r. The cost c(P) of a path P is the sum of the costs of the arcs that make up the path. The objective of a search algorithm like A* is to find a solution path of minimum cost in G. To find such a solution path, A* uses a nonnegative *heuristic estimate* h(n) associated with each nongoal node n in G; h(n) can be viewed as an estimate of h*(n), which is the cost of a path of least cost from n to the goal node.

Let g*(n) be the cost of a path of least cost from the start node to node n, and let f*(n) = g*(n)+h*(n). Then f*(n) can be viewed as the cost of a solution path of least cost constrained to pass through node n. During an execution of A*, we use g(n) to represent the cost of the path of least cost currently known from s to n. So g(n) can be viewed as the current estimate of g*(n), and f(n) = g(n)+h(n) as the current estimate of f*(n). As is customary, f*(r) denotes the cost of a minimum cost solution path in G.

Our networks are directed acyclic graphs. In such graphs, introducing more than one goal node adds no extra generality because there are many paths from the root to the goal node. When A* is run on such a network, a node may reenter OPEN from CLOSED; as a result, a node may get expanded more than once. Let Z_d and Z_t denote, respectively, the number of distinct nodes expanded by A* and the total number of node expansions made by A* when run on a given network G. Our primary goal is to determine the expected values $E(Z_d)$ and $E(Z_t)$.

In order to assign a probability distribution on the heuristic estimates of nongoal nodes in G in a meaningful way, we adopt the notion of a *normalizing function* [Pearl 1984, pp. 184]. A normalizing function Φ(.) is a total function with the set of nonnegative real numbers as domain and the set of real numbers ≥ 1 as range. It has the following properties:

(i) $\Phi(0) = 1$;
(ii) $\Phi(x)$ is nondecreasing in x;
(iii) $\Phi(x)$ is unbounded, i.e. the range of Φ has no finite upper bound.

We allow Φ to take one of three functional forms, viz. identity, less-than-linear and logarithmic:

$\Phi(x) = \max\{1, x\}$ identity
$\Phi(x) = \max\{1, x^\delta\}$ for some δ, $0 < \delta < 1$,   less-than-linear
$\Phi(x) = \max\{1, \ln x\}$ logarithmic

The *normalized error* at a nongoal node n is $X(n) = (h(n)-h^*(n))/\Phi(h^*(n))$. We assume that for all nongoal nodes in G, the normalized errors X(n) are i.i.d. random variables. The normalizing function Φ determines the accuracy of the heuristic estimate function. When Φ is the identity function, the magnitude of the error h(n)-h*(n) is proportional to h*(n). The purpose of allowing other functions, such as logarithmic ones for example, is to enable us to study the consequences of limiting the error h(n)-h*(n) to lower order values, implying greater accuracy of heuristic estimates. We use X in place of X(n), as the X(n)'s are identically distributed. Let $F_X(x) = \text{Prob}\{X \leq x\}$ be the cumulative probability distribution function of X, which is nondecreasing in x. We allow $F_X(x)$ to have discontinuities; these must be left-discontinuities, since $F_X(x)$ by definition is right-continuous. We do not assume any specific functional form for $F_X(x)$.

A heuristic function h is *admissible* if for every nongoal node n in the network G, $h(n) \leq h^*(n)$. Otherwise h is *inadmissible*. If $F_X(x) = 1$ for $x \geq 0$, then all nongoal nodes have admissible heuristic estimates with probability 1. Let $a_1 = \text{lub }\{x \mid F_X(x) = 0\}$ and $a_2 = \text{glb }\{x \mid F_X(x) = 1\}$. For $x < a_1$,

$F_X(x)$ is identically 0, while for $x \geq a_2$, $F_X(x)$ is identically 1. The heuristic estimate function is admissible if $a_2 \leq 0$; it is *purely inadmissible* if $a_1 > 0$. Note that when $\Phi(x)$ is the identity function, we must have $a_1 \geq -1$. From now onwards, whenever a normalizing function is under discussion, we assume that the corresponding a_1 and a_2 are finite.

Minimum Penalty Job Sequencing

Let S_N be the set $\{1, 2, ..., N\}$. The subsets of S_N under the partial ordering relation induced by set inclusion form a directed acyclic graph G_{js} of 2^N nodes. In this graph S_N is the root node at level 0; and the empty set $\{\}$ is the goal node at level N. The immediate successors of a node n are the various subsets of S_N obtained from n by removing one element. Thus a node corresponding to a subset of k elements has k immediate successors. G_{js} for N = 4 is shown in Figure 1. Such a graph has the following characteristics:

i) A node with i elements is at level N-i.
ii) There are i! distinct paths to a node at level i.
iii) There are ^NC_i nodes at level i.
iv) The total number of paths starting at the root and going up to level i is $^NC_i.(i!)$.

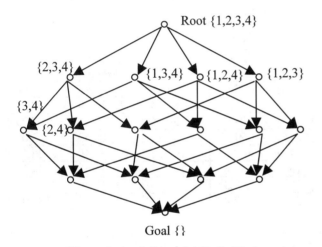

Root $\{1,2,3,4\}$

$\{2,3,4\}$ $\{1,3,4\}$ $\{1,2,4\}$ $\{1,2,3\}$

$\{3,4\}$ $\{2,4\}$

Goal $\{\}$

Figure 1: Analytic model G_{js} for N=4

G_{js} is representative of the type of search graphs that arise in certain single machine job-sequencing problems. These search graphs were searched using A* or TCBB [Kaindl et al 1995]. In the analysis below, we restrict ourselves to the A* algorithm due to its optimality in terms of node expansions.

Suppose that jobs J_i with processing times $A_i > 0$, $1 \leq i \leq N$, have been submitted to a one-machine job shop at time 0. The jobs are to be processed on the given machine one at a time. In this analysis we assume that jobs have no setup times. Let the processing of job J_i be completed at time T_i.

Penalty functions $H_i(.)$ are supplied such that the penalty associated with completing job J_i at time T_i is $H_i(T_i) > 0$. H_i is nondecreasing, and in general nonlinear. The jobs must be sequenced on the machine in such a way that the total penalty $F = \Sigma\{H_i(T_i)| 1 \leq i \leq N\}$ is minimized. Nodes in G_{js} correspond to (unordered) subsets of jobs that remain to be processed; the root node corresponds to the set of all N

jobs, and the goal node to the empty set of jobs. Arc costs are assigned as follows. Suppose there is an arc from node n_1 to node n_2, and suppose job J_i is present in the subset of jobs associated with n_1 but absent from the subset of jobs at n_2; then $c(n_1,n_2) = H_i(T_i)$. Here T_i is the time at which the processing of job J_i is completed; its value does not depend on the order in which jobs prior to job J_i are processed. Since setup times are ignored in this model, arc costs are *order preserving* [Pearl 1984].

We now assign a probability distribution on the heuristic estimates of nodes. To compute the number of nodes expanded, we impose some restrictions on the job processing times and the penalty functions. We first suppose that $1 \leq A_i \leq k$, $1 \leq i \leq N$, for some constant $k > 1$. Thus we do not permit jobs to have arbitrarily large processing times. We then assume that there is a positive integer constant β such that $H_i(x)$ is $o(x^\beta)$, $1 \leq i \leq N$. This means that each penalty function is polynomial in its argument, with the highest power in the polynomial being less than β. These are both reasonable assumptions to make about the processing of jobs in single machine job sequencing problems. Similar assumptions were made in [Sen, Bagchi and Ramaswamy 1996]. Under these circumstances, when the normalizing function is the identity function and the heuristic is not purely inadmissible, the expected number of distinct nodes expanded turns out to be exponential in N for large N.

Theorem 1: Suppose that for $1 \leq i \leq N$, $H_i(x)$ is $o(x^\beta)$ where β is a positive integer constant, and $1 \leq A_i \leq k$ for some constant $k > 1$. If $\Phi(x)$ is the identity function and $a_1 < 0$, then $E(Z_d)$, the expected number of distinct nodes of G_{js} that get expanded, is exponential in N for large N.

Proof: See Appendix. ◆

This theorem is quite general and covers a wide variety of situations that arise in minimum-penalty sequencing (see quadratic penalty problems and other forms in [Sen and Bagchi 1996]). For example:

i) There is really no need to assume a constant upper bound on the job processing times. In the proof, we may assume that there exists a (small) positive integer constant ϵ such that A_i is $o(N^\epsilon)$, $1 \leq i \leq N$.

ii) The proof also applies to normalizing functions that are less-than-linear i.e. to $\Phi(x) = x^\delta$, $0 < \delta < 1$.

Experimental results for the above case have been described in Section 4.

What happens if the normalizing function is logarithmic? Nothing specific can be said in general as described in the following example.

Example 1: Let all arcs in G_{js} have unit cost.

i) Suppose the heuristic estimate function h is perfect. Then $E(Z_t)$ can be linear to exponential in N depending on how ties are resolved.

ii) Suppose that the heuristic estimates are not perfect. Suppose $a_1 < 0$, i.e. heuristic estimates of nodes have a nonzero probability of being admissible. Then for any nongoal node n, $f(n) < N$ with probability $p > 0$, so that $E(Z_d) = E(Z_t) \geq 1 + p\,^NC_1 + p^2\,^NC_2 + ... + p^N\,^NC_N$ which is exponential in N for large N. This holds even when the normalizing function is logarithmic. ◆

There exist cases of polynomial complexity when the normalization function is logarithmic in nature. In such cases, we don't need the restriction of the constant upper bound on arc costs; instead, we put restrictions on the number of outgoing arcs emanating from a node with arc costs lying within a give upper bound. This assumption covers the cases where the arcs below a node may have varying cost structure. Our assumptions are as follows:

- We restrict ourselves to graphs G_{js} with a cost function defined on its arcs. In such graphs, not too many outgoing arcs at a node have arc costs lying within a given upper bound. Thus, we may assume that for each nongoal node in G_{js}, and for each y, y > 0 and integer, there are at most min(N-i, $\lfloor\theta(y)\rfloor$) outgoing arcs from node n with arc cost ≤ y, where i is the level of node n in G_{js} and θ: { 1,2,…,N } → R be a given non-decreasing (total) function with the positive real numbers as domain as well as range. Further, for every nongoal node, there is at least one outgoing arc of arc cost ≤ k for some given constant k ≥ 1 independent of N. Let's call such job sequencing search graphs as *θ-restricted*.

- In addition, we assume that the processing times of jobs are distinct. Then S_N represents the set of jobs with distinct processing times and therefore the jobs in S_N can be viewed as ordered in increasing order of processing times. The costs of the outgoing arcs would then have the same relative order as the processing times of jobs that have been scheduled from the subset. The outgoing arc corresponding to the scheduling of the job with the smallest processing time from a node n would have the lowest cost, and so on. We call such job sequencing graphs *C-ordered*. Thus, for the penalty functions considered in ([Kaindl et al 1995, Sen, Bagchi and Ramaswamy 1996]), the graphs are C-ordered so long as the processing times of jobs are distinct.

Theorem 2: Let $\theta(y) = y^\beta$ for integer y > 0 and 0 < β ≤ 1, and let (G_{js}, C) be θ-restricted and C-ordered. If $\Phi(x)$ is the logarithmic function and $a_1 < 0$, then $E(Z_t)$ is polynomial in N for large N.
Proof: See Appendix. ◆

The following theorem specifies the sufficient condition to be imposed on θ-restricted graphs for which the total number of nodes expanded by A* will always be polynomial in N for large N.

Theorem 3: Let y_0 be a given positive integer independent of N. Let

$$\theta(y) = y^\beta \quad \text{for } y \leq y_0, \ \beta > 0$$
$$= y_0^\beta \quad \text{for } y > y_0.$$

Let (G_{js}, C) be θ-restricted and the graph be C-ordered. Then regardless what $\Phi(x)$ is, $E(Z_t)$ is polynomial in N for large N.
Proof: See Appendix. ◆

We now present our experimental findings in the next section.

Experimental results

We carried out a number of experiments on a single machine job sequencing problem in which the penalty function for a job is proportional to the square of its completion time. Jobs have processing times but no setup times. All jobs are submitted at time t=0. The objective is to find a sequence of jobs so that the sum of the penalties is minimized [Townsend 1978]. Penalty coefficients (proportionality constants) were taken as integers and were generated randomly in the range 1 to 9 from a uniform distribution. Processing times were also integers and were generated randomly in the range 1 to 99 from a uniform distribution. For a given number of jobs, 100 random instances were generated and each of these instances were solved using A*. The results averaged over these 100 runs are presented in the tables.

Exponential Complexity

We first solved the random instances using A*. The heuristic estimate at a node was computed as suggested in [Townsend 1978], which is known to be consistent [Pearl 1984]. Table 1 below presents the average number of nodes generated and expanded by A* on problems of different sizes. No node is expanded more than once since heuristic is consistent. These results[1] were also presented in [Sen, Bagchi and Ramaswamy 1996]. The nodes generated and expanded are exponential in job size.

Table 1: Performance of A* using consistent heuristic

Job	Nodes Generated		Nodes Expanded	
	Mean	Std Dev	Mean	Std Dev
6	23.99	4.18	5.96	1.54
8	53.06	17.54	10.88	4.52
10	104.05	38.56	17.38	7.25
12	191.78	82.12	26.63	13.06
14	372.51	198.53	44.49	26.28
16	688.61	399.27	71.53	46.30
18	1299.37	837.37	119.70	86.13
20	2327.02	1523.12	191.52	137.97

Next, we experimented assuming that normalizing function is the identity function (Theorem 1). For each of the problem instance,
i) we used the quadratic penalty job sequencing problem where $H_i(T_i)=C_i T_i^2$, that is, β=3 in Theorem 1;
ii) processing times $A_i <= 99$ for all i.
iii) $\Phi(x)$ is the identity function.
iv) heuristic estimates (h) are admissible.
v) h = h* - ℘ h* since $\Phi(x)$ is identity function, and ℘ is a random number satisfying uniform distribution

The results are given in Table 2. Since heuristic estimate became inconsistent, same node was repeatedly expanded along different paths to a node. As a result, the number of nodes expanded may be more than the number of nodes generated. The results clearly indicate that the performance

---

[1] Relatively, a little less number of generated and expanded nodes was reported in [Sen, Bagchi and Ramaswamy 1996] since a pruning rule was applied.

of A* with admissible heuristic deteriorates very fast with N when normalizing function is an identity function.

Table 2: A* performance with linear error

Job	Nodes Generated		Nodes Expanded	
	Mean	Std Dev	Mean	Std Dev
6	61.22	4.69	60.55	18.31
8	249.24	22.27	317.28	87.12
10	1001.67	96.65	1606.49	443.89
12	4029.92	400.12	7906.96	1886.63
14	16156.33	1623.79	39349.97	10288.72
16	64752.36	6529.43	185991.06	40743.79

Polynomial Complexity

Next we assumed that the normalizing function is logarithmic in nature (Theorem 2). For each problem instance of the quadratic penalty problem,

i)   we generated C-ordered graphs (distinct processing times) which by the nature of the problem are also θ-restricted;

ii) below every node, there are at most N arcs with arc costs $< 10 \times (100 \ N)^2$;

iii) heuristic estimates (h) are admissible;

iv) $h = h^* - \wp \log(h^*)$ since $\Phi(x)$ is logarithmic function and $\wp$ is a random number satisfying uniform distribution.

Table 3: A* performance with logarithmic error

Job	Nodes Generated		Nodes Expanded	
	Mean	Std Dev	Mean	Std Dev
6	21.00	0.00	5.00	0.00
8	36.00	0.00	7.00	0.00
10	55.00	0.00	9.00	0.00
12	78.00	0.00	11.00	0.00
14	105.62	2.49	13.06	0.24
16	136.51	2.52	15.12	0.91

We also experimented with $h = h^* - \log(\kappa h^*)$ where κ is a large constant, the objective being to have a relatively larger logarithmic error. The result obtained is similar, as shown for $\kappa = 10^6$ in Table 4.

Table 4: A* performance with logarithmic error, $\kappa = 10^6$

Job	Nodes Generated		Nodes Expanded	
	Mean	Std Dev	Mean	Std Dev
6	21.04	0.40	5.01	0.10
8	36.12	0.84	7.02	0.14
10	55.16	1.13	9.02	0.14
12	78.09	0.90	11.01	0.10
14	105.84	2.89	13.08	0.27
16	136.92	3.89	15.15	0.94

With logarithmic error, the node generations and node expansions reduce drastically, and appear polynomial in problem size. Since the error is assumed to be logarithmic, the heuristic estimates are close to perfect heuristic and

hence, with distinct arc costs below a node, the performance of algorithm A* becomes polynomial in problem size.

Conclusion and Future Directions

In this paper, we proposed a method to extend the analysis of the average-case performance of A* from tree search problems to graph search problems. The topic has importance because many practical problems can be solved more efficiently using graph search algorithms and a better understanding of their performance may help to characterize the features of real graph search problems. Our main contribution consists of a set of average-case complexity results of A* graph search algorithm on an analytic model that captures the main features of various job sequencing problems. Both our analytical and experimental results show that the expected complexity of job sequencing problems may change from exponential to polynomial with the accuracy of heuristic functions used. In other words, the expected complexity exhibits an exponential to polynomial transition when the heuristic function becomes accurate.

We expect that the approach we proposed and the results we obtained here can be generalized in a number of directions. The first direction is to use a model similar to the incremental random trees [Karp and Pearl 1983, Zhang and Korf 1995]. The second possibility is to directly compare the expected complexity of graph and tree search algorithm on graph problems. The questions to be answered along this direction include the expected savings on the number of nodes explored that a graph search algorithm, such as A*, can provide. Such analysis will help decide which algorithm to use for real applications in practice.

Appendix

Proof of Theorem 1: We renumber jobs if needed and assume that there is a minimal cost solution path in G of cost $M \geq N$, such that if we move along it from root to goal, jobs get scheduled from the set $\{1,2, ...,N\}$ in the sequence $1\ 2\ ...\ N$. Choose $0 < \delta < 1/(\beta+1)$, and consider the nongoal nodes in G_{js} for which all the missing jobs, corresponding to the jobs already completed, belong to the set $\{1,2,...,V\}$, where $V = N^\delta$. There are $2^V - 1$ such nodes excluding the root, and for any such node n, $g(n) < V(Vk)^\beta$ and $h^*(n) > M - V(Vk)^\beta$.

Let n' be the node for which the missing elements are exactly $1,2,...,V$. Then $h^*(n') < M$, since n' lies on the minimum cost solution path, and the cost of the path to n' from any predecessor n of n' cannot exceed $V(Vk)^\beta$. It follows that $M - V(Vk)^\beta < h^*(n) < M + V(Vk)^\beta$. Let $a' = a_1/2 < 0$, so that $p = F_X(a') > 0$. Then $h(n) \leq h^*(n)+a'\Phi(h^*(n))$ with probability p, so that $f(n) < M$ with probability p, provided $g(n)+h^*(n) < M - a'\Phi(h^*(n))$ with probability p. As $a' < 0$ and Φ is the identity function, it suffices to show $M + 2V(Vk)^\beta < M - a'M + a'V(Vk)^\beta$, which always holds for large N because V is of smaller order than N. The above conditions are true for n' or any ancestor of n'. Thus if node n is at level i, it gets expanded with probability p^i. Therefore, $E(Z_d) \geq 1+pV+p^2 \ {}^VC_2+...+p^V = (1+p)^V$ which is exponential in N for large N. ♦

Proof of Theorem 2: We first show that $E(Z_d)$ is polynomial in N. To do this, we need to find out the total number of nodes n with $g^*(n) + h(n) \leq f^*(r) + a_2 \ln (f^*(r))$. If node n is at level i, expressing $h(n)$ in terms of $h^*(n)$ as $h(n) \geq h^*(n) + a_1\ln(h^*(n))$, the condition becomes $g^*(n) \leq h^*(r) - h^*(n) + a_2 \ln (h^*(r)) - a_1\ln(h^*(n))$ or $g^*(n) < k\,i + k_0 \ln (kN)$ where k and k_0 are constants, k_0 given by

$$k_0 = \begin{cases} a_2 + |a_1| & \text{if } a_1 < 0 \\ a_2 & \text{if } a_1 \geq 0. \end{cases}$$

Since G is θ-restricted, outgoing arcs at a node have costs bounded below by 1, $2^{1/\beta}$, $3^{1/\beta}$, ..., respectively. In computing upper bounds on the number of expanded nodes, these lower bounds can be viewed as the exact costs of the outgoing arcs. We have to find out, for a node n at level i, how many paths from the root to node n of length i have arc costs summing up to at most $k\,i + k_0 \ln (kN)$.

Assuming G_{js} is C-ordered. Consider the subset of jobs corresponding to a node n at level i. Let $J_1, J_2, ..., J_i$ be the jobs of the subset which are in S_N but are missing from node n. Suppose $J_1 < J_2 < ... < J_i$. There are i! ways of scheduling the i jobs leading to i! paths to node n from the root. The scheduling of the jobs in the sequence $J_1, J_2, ..., J_i$ will determine the path of least cost from the root to node n. The arc costs in such a path from the root to node n will form a nondecreasing sequence. Thus, to find an upper bound on $E(Z_d)$, we have to count the number of nondecreasing sequences of length i which sum up to at most $k\,i + k_0 \ln (kN)$ such that each element in the sequence has values 1, $2^{1/\beta}$, $3^{1/\beta}$, ..., since $1/\beta \geq 1$, $k^{1/\beta} \geq k'$ for any integer $k' > 1$. So to get an upper bound, it is enough to find out the total number of partitions of a positive integer k'' and then sum over all $k'' \leq k_0 \ln(kN)$ and over all levels i. Using the Hardy-Ramanujan asymptotic formula [Andrews 1976, pp. 70, 97] for the number of partitions of an integer, we get

$$E(Z_d) \leq [k\,N\,(k_0 \ln (kN))\,A_1\,e^{A2\sqrt{(ko\ln(kN))}}]/[\,k_0 \ln (kN)\,]$$

where A_1, A_2 are positive real constants. Thus $E(Z_d) \leq A_1\,N\,e^{A2\sqrt{(ko\,(\ln kN))}}$ which is polynomial in N for large N.

To get an upper bound on $E(Z_t)$, we have to find out the number of paths from the root to a node n of distinct cost, since n can get expanded along each of these paths in the worst case. Since the outgoing arc costs at a node may be taken as 1, $2^{1/\beta}$, $3^{1/\beta}$, ..., the total number of paths of distinct cost to a node at a level $i \leq N$ will be polynomial in N. Hence $E(Z_t)$ is also polynomial in N for large N. ◆

Proof of Theorem 3: Let $k_0 = y_0^\beta$, a constant. Every node at level i, $1 \leq i \leq N$, will have at most $\min(k_0, N\text{-}i)$ outgoing arcs having arc costs $\leq y$ for any $y \geq y_0$; other outgoing arcs can be viewed as having infinite cost. The number of nodes at level i with finite g^*-value is $\leq {}^{ko+i-1}C_i$ since the job sequencing graph is C-ordered. So the total number of nodes in the graph with finite g^*-value is $\leq \Sigma\{\,{}^{ko+i-1}C_i \,|\, 1 \leq i \leq N\,\} + 1 \leq {}^{ko+N}C_N$ which is polynomial in N for large N. As the total number of paths of distinct cost to a node at a level $i \leq N$ will be polynomial in N, $E(Z_t)$ is polynomial in N as well. ◆

References

Andrews, George E. 1976. The Theory of Partitions, *Encyclopedia of Mathematics and Its Applications*, vol. 2, Ed. Gian Galo Rota.: Addison –Wesley.

Bagchi, A., and Sen, Anup K. 1988. Average-case analysis of heuristic search in tree-like networks. *Search in Artificial Intelligence* (Ed L N Kanal and V Kumar), Springer-Verlag, pp. 131-165.

Chenoweth, Stephen V., and Davis, H W. 1991. High performance A* search using rapidly growing heuristics. In *Proc* International Joint Conference on Artificial Intelligence (*IJCAI-91*), Sydney, Australia: Morgan Kaufman Publishers, pp. 198-203.

Davis, H. W. 1990. Cost-error relationships in A* tree-searching. *JACM* **37**(2):195-199.

Dechter, R. and Pearl, J. 1985. Generalized best-first search strategies and the optimality of A*. *JACM* **32**: 505-536.

Huyn, N.; Dechter, R.; and Pearl, J. 1980. Probabilistic analysis of the complexity of A*. *Artificial Intelligence* **15**: 241-254.

Kaindl, H.; Kainz, G.; Leeb, A.; and Smetana, H. 1995. How to Use Limited Memory in Heuristic Search. In *Proc. Fourteenth International Joint Conference on Artficial Intelligence (IJCAI-95)*. San Francisco, CA: Morgan Kaufman Publishers, pp. 236—242.

Karp, R. and Pearl J. 1983, Searching for an optimal path in a tree with random costs. *Artificial Intelligence* **21**:99-117.

Korf, R. E.; Reid, M.; and Edelkamp, S. 2001. Time complexity of iterative-deepening-A*. *Artificial Intelligence* **129**:199-218.

Korf, R. E., and Zhang W. 2000. Divide-and-Conquer Frontier Search Applied to Optimal Sequence Alignment, In *Proc AAAI-2000*, Austin, TX: Morgan Kaufman Publishers, pp. 910-916.

Pearl, J. 1984. Heuristics: Intelligent Search Strategies for Computer Problem Solving.: Addison- Wesley

Pinedo, M. 1995, *Scheduling: Theory, Algorithms and Systems*. Prentice Hall.

Sen, Anup K., Bagchi, A.; and Ramaswamy, R. 1996. Searching graphs with A*: applications to job sequencing. *IEEE Trans. Syst., Man Cybern. Part A Syst, Humans* **26**:168-173.

Sen, Anup K. and Bagchi, A. 1996. Graph search methods for non-order-preserving evaluation functions: Applications to job sequencing problems. *Artificial Intelligence* **86**(1):43-73.

Townsend, W. 1978. The single machine problem with quadratic penalty function of completion times: A branch and bound solution. *Management Science* **24**(5):530-534.

Zhang, W. and Korf, R. E. 1995. Performance of linear-space search algorithms. *Artificial Intelligence* **79**:241-292.

Vision

Detection and Classification of Motion Boundaries

Richard Mann
School of Computer Science
University of Waterloo
Waterloo, ON N2L 3G1 CANADA

Allan D. Jepson
Dept. of Computer Science
Univerity of Toronto
Toronto, ON M5S 3H5 CANADA

Abstract

We segment the trajectory of a moving object into piece-wise smooth motion intervals separated by *motion boundaries*. Motion boundaries are classified into various types, including starts, stops, pauses, and discontinuous changes of motion due to force impulses. We localize and classify motion boundaries by fitting a mixture of two polynomials near the boundary. Given a classification of motion boundaries, we use naive physical rules to infer a set of changing contact relationships which explain the observed motion. We show segmentation and classification results for several image sequences of a basketball undergoing gravitational and nongravitational motion.

Introduction

Given the trajectory of a moving object, what physically meaningful aspects of the motion can be recovered? Here we segment the trajectory of a moving object into piece-wise smooth motion intervals separated by *motion boundaries*. We consider the motion of a single passive object, such as a basketball, undergoing gravitational and nongravitational motion. (See Fig. 1.) The ball may roll on a surface, fall, or bounce off the floor or walls. In addition an active object, such as a hand, may act on the object by carrying, lifting, hitting, etc. A sample sequence is shown in the first row of Fig. 2. Here a hand pushes a ball along a table top. The ball rolls on the table, falls, and bounces several times on the ground.

Our eventual goal is to characterize events based on *qualitative scene dynamics*. For example, given the sequence in Fig. 3 we should infer that an "active" hand is moving a "passive" ball by applying a force. Once released, the ball is undergoing passive motion as it rolls and falls off the table. In (Mann, Jepson, & Siskind 1997) a system was presented that infers scene dynamics based on the Newtonian mechanics of a simplified scene model. However, that system was limited to the instantaneous analysis of continuous motion. Sequences were processed on a frame by frame basis, and discontinuous motions (due to contact changes, collisions, or starts and stops of motion) were explicitly removed.

To apply dynamics analysis to extended sequences, we require a way to identify the motion boundaries, and to de-

Figure 1: A composite of the tracking results for a sequence where a subject throws a basketball.

termine the allowable motion at such boundaries. Here we present a simplified system that considers the trajectory of a single object (the ball) and extracts motion boundaries corresponding to contact changes, application or removal of forces, starts and stops of motion, etc. In particular, we show that from the trajectory of the ball, and possibly the proximity of the hand, we can infer motion boundaries, as well as changes in hand and surface contact. This information should provide suitable input for event description and recognition (Siskind 2000).

This paper makes three contributions. First, we present a characterization of motion boundaries, based on the velocity and acceleration changes around a discontinuity. Second, given an initial segmentation into piecewise quadratic segments, we present an algorithm that classifies the motion boundaries into various categories. Our classification is based on a novel fitting process that fits a mixture of two polynomials within the neighborhood of the discontinuity. Finally, we show how physical knowledge of plausible motion boundaries can be used to infer surface contact, even though this is not directly observed in the input. We show segmentation and fitting results for several image sequences of a basketball undergoing gravitational and nongravitational motion.

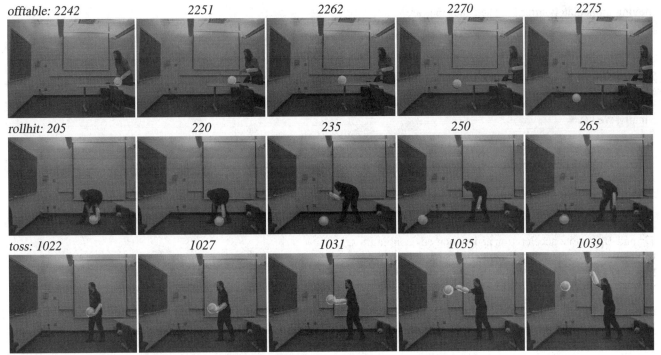

Figure 2: Video sequences used for tracking and segmentation experiments. The ball and forearm are modeled by an circle and an (elongated) octagon, respectively. See text for details.

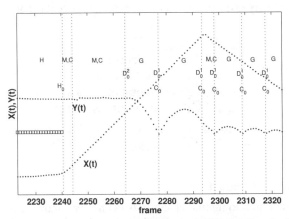

Figure 3: Segmentation of the basketball's motion in the "offtable" sequence (first row of Fig. 2) into piecewise smooth motion intervals separated by motion boundaries. The bar shows frames where the hand and ball overlap in the image. Intervals are labeled, H: hand contact, G: gravitational motion, M: nongravitational motion. D_0^1 and D_0^2 denote velocity and acceleration discontinuities. C denotes contact interval, C_0 denotes instantaneous contact.

Characterizing motion boundaries

We characterize motion by piecewise smooth intervals separated by boundaries (motion "transitions") where there are changes in velocity, acceleration, or contact relations with other objects.

Motion boundaries are defined by two consecutive open time intervals separated by an instant t_0. We describe motion boundaries using a set of *fluents* (time varying propositions) $P(t)$. Let $P_-(t_0)$ be the truth value of $P(t)$ on an open interval immediately preceding t_0 and $P_+(t_0)$ be the value of P immediately following t_0. P_0 is the value of P at the transition t_0 (if it is defined).

The motion transition is an idealized model. For example, during a collision a large force is exerted over a nonvanishing temporal duration while the colliding objects are in contact. In our model, this will be represented as an instantaneous event, due to limits on the temporal resolution. A related issue is that, since we measure position only at discrete times, we can never say conclusively whether a motion discontinuity has occurred. For any sequence of n sample points, we can always fit the data exactly with a continuous polynomial of order $n - 1$. In practice, however, velocity and acceleration changes can be inferred by fitting low order polynomials to both sides of a discontinuity and looking for large changes in the slope and/or curvature of the data fit.

We now provide event definitions based on changes of motion and/or contact fluents at motion boundaries.

Motion transitions

Let $p(t)$ denote the position of the object along a trajectory, which we assume to be continuous and piecewise differentiable. Let $M(t)$ indicate that the object is moving at time t. We have $M(t) \equiv v(t) = dp(t)/dt \neq 0$.[1] Let $M_-(t_0)$ denote that the object is moving on an open interval immediately preceding t_0 and $M_+(t_0)$ indicate that the object is

---

[1] Here we consider only the *speed* of the object. A similar representation may be constructed to describe direction discontinuities.

moving immediately after t_0. The conditions are:

$$M_-(t_0) \equiv \exists \epsilon > 0, s.t. \ \forall t, t_0 - \epsilon < t < t_0, v(t) \neq 0 \quad (1)$$

$$M_+(t_0) \equiv \exists \epsilon > 0, s.t. \ \forall t, t_0 < t < t_0 + \epsilon, v(t) \neq 0 \quad (2)$$

Note that if the velocity $v(t)$ has a zero crossing at $t = t_0$ we still have $M_-(t_0)$ and $M_+(t_0)$, but no motion at time t_0. This corresponds to an (instantaneous) *pause* at time t_0.[2] Finally, we have

$$M_0(t_0) \equiv v(t_0) \neq 0 \quad (3)$$

Let $D_0^n(t_0)$, $n > 0$ denote a discontinuity of order n at $t = t_0$. We have:

$$D_0^n(t_0) \equiv \lim_{t \uparrow t_0} \frac{d^n p(t)}{dt^n} \neq \lim_{t \downarrow t_0} \frac{d^n p(t)}{dt^n} \quad (4)$$

D_0^2 and D_0^1 denote acceleration and velocity discontinuities, respectively. Acceleration discontinuities result from the application or removal of forces (eg., due to contact changes or starts and stops of motion) while velocity discontinuities result from force impulses (eg., collisions). We use D_0 to represent a general discontinuity, either in velocity or acceleration. In general, we may have a motion discontinuity of any order. For example, D_0^3 indicates a discontinuity in the *rate of change* of acceleration. Furthermore, several orders of discontinuity may occur simultaneously, such as when a force and an impulse are applied to an object simultaneously. For the purpose of distinguishing collisions and gravitational and nongravitational motion, however, it is sufficient to consider only first (D_0^1) and second (D_0^2) order discontinuities.[3] In the next section we will use Eqn. (4) to classify motion boundaries based on the derivatives of low-order polynomials fit to either side of the transition.

Fig. 4 shows the eight possible motion transitions (Jepson & Feldman 1996). The transitions are determined by combining the motion fluents subject to the following constraints: 1) the trajectory is continuous (but the velocity may not be); 2) the velocity at a discontinuity is not defined. Note that of the eight possible transitions, only six of them correspond to motion changes. The remaining two are "nonevents" corresponding to smooth motion and no motion, respectively. We specify the above constraints as follows:

Axiom 1 (Disjoint motion labels) *Exactly one of the labels in each of the sets $\{M_-, \overline{M}_-\}$, $\{M_0, \overline{M}_0, D_0\}$, $\{M_+, \overline{M}_+\}$ must hold for the motion before, at, and after the transition.*

Axiom 2 (Motion value (zeros)) $(\overline{M}_- \vee \overline{M}_+) \wedge \overline{D}_0 \supset \overline{M}_0$. *If there is zero motion on the open interval $t < t_0$ or $t > t_0$, and there is no discontinuity at t_0 there must be zero motion at the boundary t_0.*

Axiom 3 (Motion discontinuities) $D_0 \supset \neg(\overline{M}_- \wedge \overline{M}_+)$. *Discontinuities change the motion value (from non-motion to motion).*

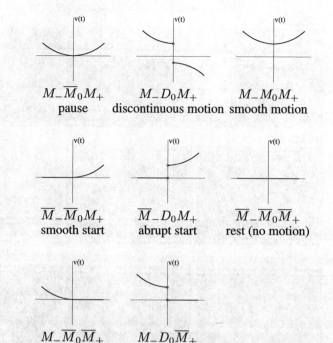

Figure 4: The eight possible motion transitions. M_-, M_0, M_+ denote motion before, at, and after the transition, respectively. $\overline{M}$ denotes rest (absence of motion). D_0 denotes a velocity discontinuity at the transition. See text for details.

Transition	Event
$C_- C_0 C_+$	continuous contact
$\overline{C}_- C_0 C_+$	onset of contact
$C_- C_0 \overline{C}_+$	removal of contact
$\overline{C}_- C_0 \overline{C}_+$	instantaneous contact

Table 1: Consistent contact transitions. C denotes surface contact. Similar conditions apply for H (hand contact).

Contact transitions

In addition to motion changes, we consider contact with an active object, such as a hand, and contact with a surface, such as a ground plane, a table, or a wall. Let $t = t_0$ be a place where motion and/or contact changes. H_-, H_0, H_+ and C_-, C_0, C_+ denote hand and surface contact, respectively.

Table 1 shows the allowable motion transitions for contact. These are the same as that in Fig. 4 except that since contact is a spatial variable, it must be piecewise continuous:

Axiom 4 (Continuity of spatial fluents) $C_- \vee C_+ \supset C_0$. *Contact in the preceding or following interval implies contact at the transition.[4]*

Note that hand and surface contact are not directly observed; they must be inferred from the image information, and from the motion discontinuities. Hand contact can be

---

[2] Another type of pause will occur over a nonzero interval. Such a pause can be decomposed into a "stop" transition at t_1 followed by a "start" at $t_2 > t_1$.

[3] (Rubin 1986) observes that humans typically perceive only the lowest order discontinuity, and that we have trouble distinguishing second order from higher order discontinuities.

[4] C and $\overline{M}$ correspond to special values (zeros) of fluents. (Galton 1990) refers to these as *fluents of position*.

inferred from the overlap of the hand and the ball in the image. Surface contact must be inferred from support information and motion changes, such as collisions, and starts and stops of motion.

Plausible motion boundaries

Using motion boundaries we may describe a wide variety of natural events. Table 2 shows a partial list of transitions, along with their typical physical events.

We begin by distinguishing gravitational and nongravitational motions. This gives four possible transitions: $G_- \to G_+$, $G_- \to \overline{G}_+$, $\overline{G}_- \to G_+$, $\overline{G}_- \to \overline{G}_+$. Transitions of gravitational motion must satisfy:

Axiom 5 (Motion value (gravity)) $\overline{G}_- \wedge G_+ \supset D_0^2$, $G_- \wedge \overline{G}_+ \supset D_0^2$, $G_- \wedge G_+ \supset \overline{D}_0^2$. *Gravitational motion corresponds to a specific value of acceleration. Acceleration changes occur iff D_0^2.*

Within each transition we consider the onset and/or removal of hand and surface contact. We arrive at the events in Table 2 by considering a few simple constraints based on our naive physical knowledge of the scene:

Constraint 1 (Support) $\overline{G} \supset H \vee C$. *An object that is not falling must be "supported", either by hand or surface contact.*

A full determination of support requires an analysis of dynamics (the forces among objects) (Mann, Jepson, & Siskind 1997) and/or the kinematics (allowable motion of objects under a gravitational field) (Siskind 2000). Here we simply allow support whenever there is hand or surface contact.

Constraint 2 (Gravitational motion implies no contact) $G \supset \overline{C} \wedge \overline{H}$.

This is the converse of Constraint 1. While it is possible for falling objects to have contact, eg., against a wall, we consider such motions unlikely.[5]

Constraint 3 (Discontinuities require contact) $D_0 \supset C_0 \vee H_0$. *Velocity and acceleration discontinuities can only result from surface or hand contact (eg. hitting, bouncing, etc).*

Note that these constraints are very weak. In particular, they allow arbitrary events, such as launching, starting, stopping, etc. as long as there is a corresponding contact. Nonetheless, we can infer surface contact over intervals of nongravitational motion (ie., support by a surface), and at instants where there are velocity discontinuities (ie., collisions with a surface). Note that these inferences are only valid when there is no hand contact. In the case of hand contact we are indifferent about surface contact. We return to this issue in the Conclusion.

---

[5]See (Jepson, Richards, & Knill 1996) for a discussion of how to specify possible motion states using *qualitative probabilities*.

Transition	Event
$G_- \to G_+$	
$G_- D_0 C_0 G_+$	bounce
$G_- D_0 H_0 G_+$	hit
$G_- \to \overline{G}_+$	
$G_- D_0 C_0 \overline{G}_+ C_+$	splat
$G_- D_0 H_0 \overline{G}_+ H_+$	catch
$\overline{G}_- \to G_+$	
$\overline{G}_- C_- D_0 C_0 G_+$	launch
$\overline{G}_- H_- D_0 H_0 G_+$	drop/throw
$\overline{G}_- \to \overline{G}_+$	
$\overline{G}_- C_- D_0 C_0 \overline{G}_+ C_+$	bounce (on surface)
$\overline{G}_- C_- D_0 C_0 H_0 \overline{G}_+ C_+$	hit (on surface)
$\overline{G}_- C_- H_- D_0 C_0 H_0 \overline{G}_+ C_+$	release (on surface)
$\overline{G}_- C_- D_0 C_0 H_0 \overline{G}_+ C_+ H_+$	catch (on surface)

Table 2: Some natural events expressed as transitions between gravitational (G) and nongravitational ($\overline{G}$) motion. See text for details.

Temporal consistency

Given two adjacent motion boundaries at time t_n and t_{n+1} we require that: 1) the fluents after t_n are consistent with the fluents before t_{n+1}; 2) there are no intervening times where the fluents change value.

Preference 1 (Consistency of adjacent boundaries) $\forall n, P_+(t_n) \equiv P_-(t_{n+1})$

Preference 2 (No unobserved changes within intervals) $\forall n, \forall t, t', s.t.\ t_n < t, t' < t_{n+1}. P(t) \equiv P(t')$

We write these conditions as preferences, since it is possible that our segmentation algorithm missed some transitions, or that our boundary classification algorithm misclassified some of the motion boundaries. Assuming a segmentation algorithm that finds all motion boundaries, we can enforce consistency by fitting intervals between adjacent breakpoints. (See Experiments section.)

Classification of motion boundaries

Suppose we are given a trajectory $\mathbf{X}(t) = [X(t), Y(t)]^T$ and a potential transition point t_0. We classify the motion transition by fitting polynomials to the trajectory immediately before and immediately after t_0. In practice, however, we may have: 1) poor localization of transitions, 2) trajectory noise, eg., due to tracker error, 3) false breakpoints, where there is no discontinuity.

We address these problems by fitting a mixture of two low-order polynomials within a narrow window surrounding the discontinuity. This approach was first used in (Mann 1998) to estimate instantaneous velocity and acceleration from trajectory data. However, no attempt was made to detect whether a discontinuity was present. Furthermore, since there was no constraint on assignments of data points to the two competing polynomials, polynomials sometimes fit non-contiguous parts of the trajectory.

Here we extend the mixture model by adding a temporal support window to each component. The data likelihood is given by:

$$P(\mathcal{X}|\theta_1, \mu_{t_1}, \sigma_{t_1}, \theta_2, \mu_{t_2}, \sigma_{t_2}, \sigma) = \prod_{t=t_0-\frac{W}{2}+1}^{t_0+\frac{W}{2}}$$
$$\left[\pi_1 \mathcal{N}(t; \mu_{t_1}, \sigma_{t_1}) \mathcal{N}(\mathbf{X}(t); \hat{\mathbf{X}}_1(t; \theta_1), \sigma) \right.$$
$$\left. + \pi_2 \mathcal{N}(t; \mu_{t_2}, \sigma_{t_2}) \mathcal{N}(\mathbf{X}(t); \hat{\mathbf{X}}_2(t; \theta_2), \sigma) + \pi_0 p_0 \right] \tag{5}$$

$\hat{\mathbf{X}}_1(t; \theta_1)$ and $\hat{\mathbf{X}}_2(t; \theta_2)$ are the polynomials intended to fit the left and right portion of the boundary. $\mathcal{N}(t; \mu_{t_1}, \sigma_{t_1})$ and $\mathcal{N}(t; \mu_{t_2}, \sigma_{t_2})$ are (Gaussian) windows that weight the data fit on either side of the transition. π_1 and π_2 are the mixing proportions for the two polynomials ($\pi_1 + \pi_2 + \pi_0 = 1.$). p_0 is a (uniform) "outlier" process. σ is the standard deviation of the tracker noise.

Fig. 5 shows the data fit using quadratic polynomials. The model was initialized using temporal windows centered at the left and right side of the proposed boundary. The polynomial coefficients and the temporal support windows were updated using an *EM* algorithm. σ began at 16 and was gradually reduced to 1. A last step was performed to estimate σ from the data. Both $X(t)$ and $Y(t)$ were fit independently, but shared the same mixing proportions and temporal weighting. To determine whether a discontinuity is present, we compare the log likelihood of the data with a model that has only one mixture component. We use a *penalized likelihood* criterion (a penalty of -10 in log likelihood for the two component mixture) to decide if a discontinuity is present.[6] Penalized likelihood correctly chooses a two component model when there is a discontinuity (Fig. 5) and a one component model when there is no discontinuity (Fig. 6).

Experiments

We consider the segmentation of the motion trajectory of an object, such as a basketball, undergoing gravitational and nongravitational motion (see Fig. 2). In each sequence the forearm and the ball were tracked by an adaptive view-based tracker described in (El-Maraghi In Preparation).

In general, we should apply the model fitting at every possible breakpoint. Instead, we use a heuristic procedure, based on dynamic programming, to identify possible breakpoints (Mann, Jepson, & El-Maraghi 2002). The algorithm separates the trajectory into hand segments (whenever the hand overlaps the ball in the image), in which the ball may have arbitrary motion, and piecewise quadratic segments, in which the ball is under free motion. At each breakpoint we apply the fitting algorithm described in the previous section to determine if a motion discontinuity is present, and if so, to classify the boundary.

Our eventual goal is to find a consistent labeling into motion, hand, and contact fluents. In general this may require

[6]We could apply a Bayesian criterion (MacKay 1992), but this was not necessary here due to the large difference in log likelihood between the two models.

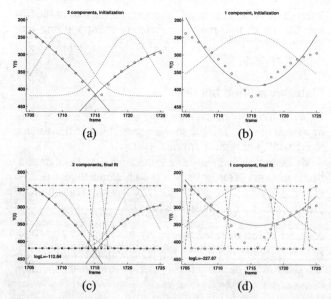

(a)   (b)

(c)   (d)

Figure 5: Robust mixture model fit at a motion discontinuity. Dotted lines show the temporal support window(s). (a,b) Initialization for the one and two component models. (c,d) Final fit for the one and two component models. $+$ and $\times$ show the ownership for the first and second model, respectively. The squares show the ownership for the outlier process. Note the rejection of noisy track points at frames 1715, 1716 in (c). In (d) many points are rejected as outliers.

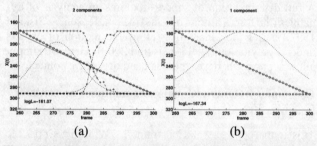

(a)   (b)

Figure 6: Robust mixture model fit where there is no discontinuity. (a) Fit with two component model. (b) Fit with one component model.

top-down information and filling in of undetected or missing breakpoints (DeCoste 1990). Here we assume that the segmentation algorithm has provided all breakpoints (or a superset of the breakpoints) for places where the ball is under free motion. We begin with the initial set of breakpoints and perform a local fit using the mixture model.[7] This allows us to reject spurious breakpoints and to localize the motion boundaries. Motion boundaries were detected and classified by using the boundary conditions (velocity and acceleration) at each interval.[8] For intervals that had inconsistent motion

[7]We used a classification window of nine samples on either side of the discontinuity, or the distance to the neighboring transition, whichever was smaller. To avoid brief contact intervals, we merged intervals shorter than five samples before processing.

[8]The thresholds for discontinuities were $\Delta V = 5.0$ pixels/frame and $\Delta A = 1.0$ pixels/frame^2. An acceleration was con-

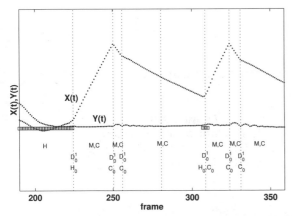

Figure 7: Segmentation and motion labeling for "rollhit".

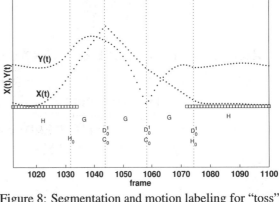

Figure 8: Segmentation and motion labeling for "toss".

labels (eg. M_- and G_+), we fit a global (quadratic) polynomial to determine the motion type. Surface contact was inferred whenever there was nongravitational motion on an interval. Surface contact at transitions was inferred whenever there was either: 1) surface contact at a neighboring interval, or 2) a velocity discontinuity without the presence of hand contact.

The classification results for *offtable* were shown in Fig. 3. Once the hand segment is removed, we are left with rolling motion (frames 2241–2263), falling (frames 2264–2276), and bouncing (frames 2277, etc.). Note the bounce off the wall (frame 2294). The system correctly infers discontinuities (D_0^2 when falling begins, and D_0^1 at bounces). Note that, due to tracker errors, there is an extra discontinuity at frame 2246 and that the segment after frame 2293 is mis-classified (M, C instead of G).

Fig. 7 shows the results for *rollhit*. Here a hand rolls the ball against the wall. The ball hits the wall (frame 250), bounces upwards briefly (due to spin), hits the ground (frame 256), and continues to roll. The hand hits the ball at frames 307–310. The spurious breakpoint at frame 280 was removed by the classifier. Note that the small bounces after frames 250 and 324 are not large enough to be detected as gravitational motion, therefore the system incorrectly infers surface contact during these intervals.

Fig 8 shows the results for *toss*. Here the hand throws the ball against the wall, and catches it after one bounce on the floor. Discontinuities are detected at both bounces, and at the catch.

Conclusion

We showed how to detect and classify motion boundaries for an object undergoing gravitational and nongravitational motion.

While successful, there are a number of outstanding issues. First, rather than processing in a bottom-up fashion, multiple event models should be incorporated into the tracking process (Isard & Blake 1998). Second, since hand contact alone is sufficient to explain nongravitational motion, we require a more elaborate model of hand motion if we are

sidered to be gravitational if $A \in [1, 2]$ pixels/frame^2

to infer surface contact in intervals containing hand contact. Finally, we require additional physical constraints on events, such as forces among objects (Mann, Jepson, & Siskind 1997), energy conservation at collisions, transfer of angular momentum (eg., spin), etc.

References

DeCoste, D. 1990. Dynamic across-time measurement interpretation. In *Proceedings of AAAI-90*.

El-Maraghi, T. F. In Preparation. *Robust Online Appearance Models for Visual Tracking*. Ph.D. Diss., Dept. of Computer Science, Univ. of Toronto.

Galton, A. 1990. A critical examination of allen's theory of action and time. *Artificial Intelligence* 42:159–188.

Isard, M., and Blake, A. 1998. A mixed-state condensation tracker with automatic model-switching. In *International Conference on Computer Vision (ICCV-98)*.

Jepson, A. D., and Feldman, J. 1996. A biased view of perceivers. In Knill, D., and Richards, W., eds., *Perception as Bayesian Inference*. Cambridge University Press.

Jepson, A. D., Richards, W., and Knill, D. 1996. Modal structure and reliable inference. In *Perception as Bayesian Inference*.

MacKay, D. J. C. 1992. Bayesian interpolation. *Neural Computation* 4:415–447.

Mann, R., Jepson, A., and El-Maraghi, T. 2002. Trajectory segmentation by dynamic programming. In *International Conference on Pattern Recognition (ICPR-02)*.

Mann, R., Jepson, A., and Siskind, J. M. 1997. The computational perception of scene dynamics. *Computer Vision and Image Understanding* 65(2):113–128.

Mann, R. 1998. *Computational Perception of Scene Dynamics*. Ph.D. Diss., Dept. of Computer Science, Univ. of Toronto.

Rubin, J. 1986. *Categories of Visual Motion*. Ph.D. Diss., M.I.T. Dept. Brain and Cognitive Sciences.

Siskind, J. M. 2000. Grounding the lexical semantics of verbs in visual perception using force dynamics and event logic. *Journal of Artificial Intelligence Research* 15:31–90.

Recognizing Multitasked Activities from Video using Stochastic Context-Free Grammar

Darnell Moore
Texas Instruments
Video & Imaging Processing / DSP R&D Center
Dallas, TX 75243, USA

Irfan Essa
Georgia Institute of Technology
GVU Center / College of Computing
Atlanta, GA 30332-0280, USA

Abstract

In this paper, we present techniques for recognizing complex, multitasked activities from video. Visual information like image features and motion appearances, combined with domain-specific information, like object context is used initially to label events. Each action event is represented with a unique symbol, allowing for a sequence of interactions to be described as an ordered symbolic string. Then, a model of stochastic context-free grammar (SCFG), which is developed using underlying rules of an activity, is used to provide the structure for recognizing semantically meaningful behavior over extended periods. Symbolic strings are parsed using the Earley-Stolcke algorithm to determine the most likely semantic derivation for recognition. Parsing substrings allows us to recognize patterns that describe high-level, complex events taking place over segments of the video sequence. We introduce new parsing strategies to enable error detection and recovery in stochastic context-free grammar and methods of quantifying group and individual behavior in activities with separable roles. We show through experiments, with a popular card game, the recognition of high-level narratives of multi-player games and the identification of player strategies and behavior using computer vision.

Introduction & Related Work

Computer vision research has made significant progress in recent years at recognizing what people are doing. Most of the work in recognition of human activity has relied on recognizing a sequence of states using stochastic model-based approaches. For example, hidden Markov models (HMMs) have become very popular for recognizing gestures (Bobick & Wilson 1997; Schlenzig, Hunter, & Jain 1994), sign-language (Vogler & Metaxas 2001; Starner, Weaver, & Pentland 1998), and actions (Moore, Essa, & Hayes 1999a; Yamato, Ohya, & Ishii 1994; Brand, Oliver, & Pentland 1997).

However, when it comes to recognizing activities with some predefined context or inherent semantics, purely probabilistic methods can be limiting unless they are augmented by additional structure. These activities include parking cars or dropping off people at the curb, (Ivanov and Bobick (2000) recognized using stochastic parsing), longer term office and cooking activities (Moore and Essa (1999b),

recognized using contextual information), airborne surveillance tasks (Bremond and Medioni (1998), recognized using deterministic structure), observing simple repair tasks (Brand (1997), recognized using interactions as a metric), and American sign language recognition (Starner and Pentland (1998), recognized using a grammar).

Our goal in this paper is to recognize separable, multitasked activities. We define multitasked activities as *the intermittent co-occurrence of events involving multiple people, objects, and actions, typically over an extended period of time.* By definition, a multitasked activity is composed of several single-tasked activities. To exploit syntax present in many interactions that are based on rules or well-defined context, we concentrate on a class of multitasked activities that possesses group separability. Grammar is then used to explain dependencies between interactions occurring within separable groups. By using syntactic models, we can more easily deal with variation in the occurrence, distribution and transition between events.

As an example, we highlight our approach using a casino card game that has multiple participants who interact with each other both independently and dependently over the duration of the game. Although the rules of play are well-defined, a great deal of variation is permitted. To recognize these and other such activities, we leverage stochastic models based on grammar to interpret syntactic structure and use computer vision to image-, detect visual primitives.

Ivanov and Bobick have accomplished complex activity recognition by combining syntactic pattern recognition with statistical approaches to recognize activity taking place over extended sequences (Ivanov & Bobick 2000). In their work, HMMs are used to propose candidates of low-level temporal features. These outputs provide the input stream for a Stochastic Context-Free Grammar (SCFG) parsing mechanism that enforces longer range temporal constraints, corrects uncertain or mislabelled low-level detections, and allows the inclusion of prior knowledge about the structure of temporal events in a given domain.

The application of syntactic information is not new to AI and computer vision and having been employed for natural language processing and for pattern/object recognition in still images for many years now. The use of SCFG instead of CFG is motivated by the fact that the stochastic-based approach provides a representation to attach a probability to a particular sequence of events. We extend the work of Ivanov and Bobick by introducing new techniques for error detection and recovery as well as strategies for quantifying participant behavior over time. We also experiment with a very challenging domain of card playing to validate our approach for complex multitasked activities.

Representation using SCFG

To characterize multitasked activities, we need models that can identify the regularities associated with complex tasks while also tolerating the dynamics associated with multiple participants and interactions scattered through time. Grammar is a mechanism that uses a system of rules to generate semantically meaningful *expressions*. Its ability to accommodate variation makes it a compelling choice for modeling complex activities, particularly those that are *rule-based, event-driven*.

Grammar is not susceptible to some of the limitations of probabilistic finite state machine representations, like the HMMs. Finite state machines are appropriate for modeling a single hypothesis or a series of them in parallel. However, as variation becomes more pronounced, it becomes exceedingly difficult to collapse additional hypotheses into a single finite state model. In contrast, the generative process associated with grammar is non-deterministic, allowing the derivation of a much longer and elaborate sequence of events (Taylor 1998). Grammar allows us to use a single, compact representation for well-understood interactive events that also accommodates the natural generalizations that occur during their performance. However, because grammar is very domain dependent and very difficult to learn without supervision, we consider manually specified grammar.

Stochastic context-free grammar (SCFG) is an extension of context-free grammar (CFG) where a probability p is added to every production rule, *i.e.*, $X \rightarrow \lambda$ We can also express the rule probability p as $P(X \rightarrow \lambda)$, which essentially gives the conditional likelihood of the production $X \rightarrow \lambda$. We estimate rule probabilities by calculating the average production likelihood. The average simply divides the *count*, the number of times a rule is applied, denoted $c(X \rightarrow \lambda)$ for production $X \rightarrow \lambda$, by the count of all rules with X on the left hand side, *i.e.*,

$$P(X \rightarrow \lambda) = \frac{c(X \rightarrow \lambda)}{\sum_{\mu} c(X \rightarrow \mu)}, \quad (1)$$

where μ represents all nonterminals generated by nonterminal X.

SCFGs are superior to non-stochastic context-free grammar because the probability attached to each rule provides a quantitative basis for ranking and pruning parses as well as for exploiting dependencies in a language model. While SCFGs are computationally more demanding than simpler language models that employ finite-state and n-gram approaches, they typically perform well using a modest amount of training data and can also be extended in a straightforward fashion by adding production rules and their associated probabilities for each new primitive event (Stolcke & Segal 1994). Rule-based activities, in particular, make good candidates for use with a SCFG because they can be described using a relatively small lexicon of primitive events.

In a SCFG, the probability of the complete derivation of a string is determined by the product of the rule probabilities in the derivation. The notion of context-freeness is extended to include probabilistic conditional independence of the expansion of a nonterminal from its surrounding context (Stolcke 1994). Our motivation for using stochastic context-free grammar is to aggregate low-level events detected so that we can construct higher-level models of interaction.

Symbol Generation (Event Detection): To facilitate event detection, we need to manage prior and newly discovered information about people objects, and their interactions. Such information in the form of image-, object-, or action-based evidence that is collected into object-oriented "containers" (Moore, Essa, & Hayes 1999a). In the specific example of BlackJack, a simple vision system is used which allows for object segmentation and tracking as well as template matching so that hands can be followed or newly dealt cards can be detected. Hands are also tracked making it easy to associate the new card with the person that placed it (Figure 1). By adding domain-specific heuristics, we construct detectors for determining when betting chips are added or removed from the scene. Where applicable, we also consider an articles's location relative to the entire scene as well as in respect to other objects or people.

When a particular event is observed, its corresponding symbolic terminal is appended to the end of the activity string x, which is parsed by the Earley-Stolcke algorithm. Again, in general terms, for some domain $\mathcal{C}$, we let $\mathbf{D}_{\mathcal{C}} = \{D_1, D_2, \ldots\}$ represent the set of detectors for generating the set of terminal symbols V_T. For convenience, the likelihood of a detected event, *i.e.*, the likelihood of generating the terminal symbol x_i corresponding to detector D_i, is given by $P_{\mathbf{D}}(x_i) = P(D_i)$, where $P(D_i)$ is defined on a case by case basis. By processing an activity sequence in domain $\mathcal{C}$, we use $\mathbf{D}_{\mathcal{C}}$ to generate symbolic string $x = x_1 x_2, \ldots, x_l$, with length, $l = |x|$.

When parsing is discussed in the next section, we will show that it is possible to compute the syntactical likelihood of a sequence of events $P(x)$. Such a likelihood offers a measure of how much semantic merit a sequence has. Using the independence assumption guaranteed by the use of context-free grammar, we can also describe the likelihood of string formation based on detection alone, *i.e.*,

$$P_{\mathbf{D}}(x) = \prod_{i=1}^{l} P_{\mathbf{D}}(x_i). \quad (2)$$

Unfortunately, as the length l increases, the overall likelihood of the string decreases from repeated multiplication of values less than unity. A better measure of confidence normalizes the likelihood according to l, which we describe by simply calculating the sample mean likelihood of the string, *i.e.*,

$$\tilde{P}_{\mathbf{D}}(x) = \frac{1}{l} \sum_{i=1}^{l} P_{\mathbf{D}}(x_i). \quad (3)$$

The Earley-Stolcke Parsing

For parsing input strings, we employ the Earley-Stolcke algorithm (Stolcke 1994; Earley 1968). The Earley-Stolcke algorithm uses a top-down parsing approach and context-free productions to build strings that are derivable from left to right. It maintains multiple hypotheses of all possible derivations that are consistent with the input string up to a certain point. Scanning input from left to right, the number of hypotheses increases as new options become available or decrease as ambiguities are resolved.

A set of states, determined by the length of the string, is created for each symbol in the input. Each state describes all candidate derivations. The entire set of states forms the *Earley chart*. We preserve notation[1] introduced by Earley to represent a state, which is given by

$$i : {}_kX \to \lambda.\mu , \qquad (4)$$

where i is the index of the current position in the input stream and k is the *starting* index of the substring given by nonterminal X. Nonterminal X contains substring $x_k \ldots x_i \ldots x_l$, where x_l is the last terminal of the substring μ. When we are in position i, the substring $x_0 \ldots x_{i-1}$ has already been processed by the parser. *State set i* represents all of the states that describe the parsing at this position. There is always one more state set than input symbols, *i.e.*, set 0 describes the parser before any input is processed while set l depicts the parser after all processing.

Parsing Stages: Parsing proceeds iteratively through three steps: *prediction, scanning,* and *completion*. The prediction step is used to hypothesize the possible continuation of the input based on the current position in the derived string. We expand one branch of the derivation tree down to the set of its leftmost term to predict the next possible input terminal.

During prediction, we create a list of all the states that are syntactically possible based on prior input. These states provide the candidate terminal symbols that we can anticipate at the next position in the input string. The scanning step is where we read the next input symbol and match it against all states under consideration. Scanning ensures that the terminal symbols produced in a derivation match the input string. The scanning step promotes the states for the next iteration.

Given a set of states which have just been confirmed by scanning, the completion step updates the positions in all pending derivations throughout the derivation tree. Each completion corresponds to the end of a particular nonterminal expansion which was initiated by an earlier prediction step.

States produced by each of these steps are called *predicted, scanned,* and *completed,* respectively. A state is called *complete* (not to be confused with *completed*) if the substring $x_j \ldots x_i$ has been fully expanded and is syntactically correct (which is written with the dot located in the rightmost position of the state, *i.e.*, $i : {}_jY \to \nu.$). To determine the likelihood of a string at the current index i, the *forward probability* α gives the likelihood of selecting the next state at step i, along with probability of selecting previous states, *i.e.*, $x_1 \ldots x_{i-1}$. The *inner probability* γ measures the likelihood of generating a substring of the input from a given nonterminal using a particular production. Unlike the forward probability, which starts from the beginning of the string, the inner probability starts at position k in the string.

---

[1]Earley notation uses **only one** "." (index point) when defining states. The reader is encouraged to pay close attention to the location of the index, which is easily confused with a period.

Parsing in Uncertainty: Human error, *i.e.*, violating rules of the activity, and mistakes made during symbol generation can produce activity sentences that are semantically meaningless. Recall $P_\mathbf{D}(x_i)$, which is the probability of the detectors producing symbol x_i. We factor in the likelihood of the input into the parsing mechanism by multiplying $P_\mathbf{D}(x_i)$ by the forward and inner probabilities during the scanning step, *i.e.*,

$$\begin{aligned} \alpha' &= \alpha(i : {}_kX \to \lambda.a\mu)P_\mathbf{D}(a), \\ \gamma' &= \gamma(i : {}_kX \to \lambda.a\mu)P_\mathbf{D}(a), \end{aligned} \qquad (5)$$

where a is the terminal sampled from the input in state set i. The revised values for α' and γ' reflect the weight of the likelihood of competing derivations as well as the certainty associated with the scanned input symbol.

Selecting the ML Parse: With uncertainty present in the input, we are not guaranteed to recover a unique parse. Motivated by the use of the Viterbi parsing in the HMM, we apply a generalization of the Viterbi method for parsing a string x to retrieve the most likely probability among all possible derivations for x (in a manner similar to the one proposed by Ivanov & Bobick (2000)). In our case, this will give the most likely interactive summary of events over the duration of the sequence. To compute the Viterbi parse, each state set must maintain the maximal path probability leading to it as well as the predecessor states associated with that maximum likelihood path. Path probabilities are recursively multiplied during completion steps using the inner probabilities as accumulators (Stolcke 1994). By familiar backtracking along the maximal predecessor states, the maximum probability parse can be recovered.

To implement this Viterbi computation, we modify the parser such that each state computes its *Viterbi probability* v. Note that v is propagated similarly to γ, except that during completion the summation is replaced by maximization, such that $v_i({}_kX \to \lambda Y.\mu)$ is the maximum of all products $v_i({}_jY \to \nu.)v_j({}_kX \to \lambda.Y\mu)$ along paths that lead to the completed state ${}_kX \to \lambda Y.\mu$, *i.e.*,

$$v_i({}_kX \to \lambda Y.\mu) = \max_{\lambda,\mu}\{v_i({}_jY \to \nu.)v_j({}_kX \to \lambda.Y\mu)\}.$$

The state associated with the maximum is listed as the Viterbi path predecessor of ${}_kX \to \lambda Y.\mu$, *i.e.*,

$${}_kX \to \lambda.Y\mu = \arg\max_{\lambda,\mu}\{v_i({}_jY \to \nu.)v_j({}_kX \to \lambda.Y\mu)\}.$$

A familiar recursive procedure is required to recover the maximum likelihood (ML) derivation tree associated with the Viterbi parse. During the normal parsing operation described earlier, state ${}_kX \to \lambda.Y\mu$ maintains a pointer to the state ${}_jY \to \nu.$ that completes it, providing a path for backtracking. After arriving in the final state, the ML tree is reproduced by visiting predecessor states as identified by pointers.

Parsing Separable Activities

We recognize that individuals can have roles that influence how they interact with objects and other people in a process. Activities with *separable groups* are characterized by wholly independent interactive relationships between two or

	Production Rules			Description			
S	$\rightarrow$	AB	[1.0]	Blackjack $\rightarrow$ "play game" "determine winner"			
A	$\rightarrow$	CD	[1.0]	play game $\rightarrow$ "setup game" "implement strategy"			
B	$\rightarrow$	EF	[1.0]	determine winner $\rightarrow$ "eval. strategy" "cleanup"			
C	$\rightarrow$	HI	[1.0]	setup game $\rightarrow$ "place bets" "deal card pairs"			
D	$\rightarrow$	GK	[1.0]	implement strategy $\rightarrow$ "player strategy"			
E	$\rightarrow$	LKM	[0.6]	eval. strategy $\rightarrow$ "dealer down-card" "dealer hits" "player down-card"			
	$\rightarrow$	LM	[0.4]	eval. strategy $\rightarrow$ "dealer down-card" "player down-card"			
F	$\rightarrow$	NO	[0.5]	cleanup $\rightarrow$ "settle bet" "recover card"			
	$\rightarrow$	ON	[0.5]	$\rightarrow$ "recover card" "settle bet"			
G	$\rightarrow$	J	[0.8]	player strategy $\rightarrow$ "Basic Strategy"			
	$\rightarrow$	Hf	[0.1]	$\rightarrow$ "Splitting Pair"			
	$\rightarrow$	$bfffH$	[0.1]	$\rightarrow$ "Doubling Down"			
H	$\rightarrow$	l	[0.5]	place bets	**Symbol**	**Domain-Specific Events (Terminals)**
	$\rightarrow$	lH	[0.5]		a	dealer removed card from house
I	$\rightarrow$	ffI	[0.5]	deal card pairs	b	dealer removed card from player
	$\rightarrow$	ee	[0.5]		c	player removed card from house
J	$\rightarrow$	f	[0.8]	Basic strategy	d	player removed card from player
	$\rightarrow$	fJ	[0.2]		e	dealer added card to house
K	$\rightarrow$	e	[0.6]	house hits	f	dealer dealt card to player
	$\rightarrow$	eK	[0.4]		g	player added card to house
L	$\rightarrow$	ae	[1.0]	Dealer downcard	h	player added card to player
M	$\rightarrow$	dh	[1.0]	Player downcard	i	dealer removed chip
N	$\rightarrow$	k	[0.16]	settle bet	j	player removed chip
	$\rightarrow$	kN	[0.16]		k	dealer pays player chip
	$\rightarrow$	j	[0.16]		l	player bets chip
	$\rightarrow$	jN	[0.16]			
	$\rightarrow$	i	[0.18]			
	$\rightarrow$	iN	[0.18]			
O	$\rightarrow$	a	[0.25]	recover card		
	$\rightarrow$	aO	[0.25]			
	$\rightarrow$	b	[0.25]			
	$\rightarrow$	bO	[0.25]			

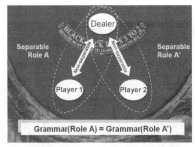

Seperable, Independent roles

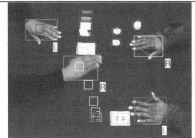

Vision system tracking the game.

Figure 1: (left) Table showing SCFG V_{BJ} for Blackjack card game: Production rules, probabilities, and descriptions. Detectable domain-specific events make up the terminal alphabet V_T of V_{BJ}. This grammar generates a language that can describe the role between any deal-player couple. (right-top) Each dealer-player group represents separable (*independent*) roles. Within each group, individual roles are non-separable (*dependent*) and share the same grammar. (right-bottom) Cards and betting chips recognized using image feature templates. The minimum square distance between hand and object centroid is calculated to determine the last person to touch an object. The location of the object can also be used as valuable context information. This heuristic enables us to label events like, "Dealer dealt car to player."

more agents, *i.e.,* multiple speakers, but separate, independent conversations. Conversely, *non-separable roles* occur when multiple agents take on collaborative, inter-dependent behavior, *i.e.,* an argument between speakers that talk at the same time concerning the same topic.

To assess overall task interactions while preserving individual behaviors, our approach divides activities into separable groups, then develops grammars that describe the non-separable interactions in each. In the card game of Blackjack, for example, a player's conduct is motivated by how the dealer is expected to behave. While there can be many players in a single game, each bets against the dealer, independent of any other player. Since there is rarely any correlation between player interactions, each player-dealer pair represents a separable group. Interactions between player and dealer are non-separable. Consequently, we only need one simple grammar to describe interactions in a game with multiple players. The production rules for this grammar are listed in Figure 1. Terminal symbols used in alphabet V_{BJ} are based on primitive events detected.

While monitoring interactions in the game, we maintain a separate symbolic string for each person m, where $\mathbf{p} = \{p_1, p_2, ... p_m\}$ represents all participating players including the dealer. In our case, the relation between any event and person is established by two measures: (a) the person in contact with an article, and (b) the "owner" of the article. These tags are important in Blackjack because they help us associate an article with a respective player. Moreover, the tags remove potential ambiguity that can confuse the parser. In practice, the first measure is easily established when we detect an overlap between the image regions bounding the hand and the object. The second measure is largely determined by

a proximity zone, $\mathbf{z}_m = [x_l \; y_t \; x_r \; y_b]^T$, for each person which is defined manually when the scene is initialized, then labeled with the same ID as the respective person. These tags are attached during the scanning stage when the next state is added, such that

$$i + 1: \; {_k}X \rightarrow \lambda a.\mu \, [\alpha, \gamma, p_j, o(\mathbf{z}_m)],$$

where $o(\mathbf{z}_m)$ returns the ID p_j corresponding to the zone defined by $o(\mathbf{z}_m)$. During play, we track hand position to establish ownership of objects (see Figure 1).

By tagging interactions and leveraging separability, we provide an elegant treatment for evaluating concurrency using context from both exemplars and models when multiple participants and objects are involved. Ivanov and Bobick (2000) uses a much more complicated alternative that performs interleaved consistency checks on serialized event during parsing. Since we do not have to modify grammar or tag labels during parsing, much less complexity is required by our parser.

Exploiting separability also allows us to assess the probabilistic behavior of individuals in the scene by isolating certain production rules that occur within a non-separable relationship. To model a particular behavior, we manually select a subset of the production rules, *i.e.,* $\mathcal{P}_\varsigma \in \mathcal{P}$, that provides a basis for characterizing interactions. We define $\mathbf{b}_\varsigma$ to be a vector that represents all n production probabilities in subset $\mathcal{P}_\varsigma$. We determine $\mathbf{b}_\varsigma$ from training data taken over several trials, allowing us to establish baseline models of particular behavior. For example in Blackjack, certain strategies designed to improve the odds of winning are more likely to be used by a more experienced player versus a novice. In this case, we identify $P(G \rightarrow J), P(G \rightarrow bfffH)$ and

$P(G \to Hf)$ as listed in Figure 1 as some of the metrics for determining player skill.

Each person maintains a subset of the production likelihoods $\hat{\mathbf{b}}_\varsigma$ (to reflect his/her probability of using certain rules), which is reset initially to reflect a uniform distribution. In other words, for a nonterminal X that generates n other strings of terminals and nonterminals, *i.e.*, $X \to \mu_1 | \mu_2 | \ldots | \mu_n$, all respective likelihoods $\mathbf{b}_X = \beta_1, \beta_2, \ldots, \beta_n$ are set identically to $\frac{1}{n}$. During separable role characterization, each individual shares the same initial set of rule likelihoods $\mathbf{b}_X$ over $\mathcal{P}_\varsigma$. Using Equation (1), rule probabilities for each individual are "tuned" *via running mean* based on observations of selected productions over the course of several trials. Comparisons between individually tuned rule probabilities $\hat{\mathbf{b}}_\varsigma$ and pre-trained models $\mathbf{b}_\varsigma$ can be made using the mean sum of the square differences or mean square error (MSE),*i.e.*,

$$err(\mathbf{b}_\varsigma - \hat{\mathbf{b}}_\varsigma) = \frac{1}{n} \sum_{i=1}^{n} (\beta_i - \hat{\beta}_i)^2. \quad (6)$$

The MSE is used to measure the pairwise distance so that the likelihood of a behavior given a model for it can be established by

$$P(\hat{\mathbf{b}}_\varsigma | \mathbf{b}_\varsigma) = 1 - \sqrt{err(\mathbf{b}_\varsigma - \hat{\mathbf{b}}_\varsigma)}. \quad (7)$$

Tuning grammars based on an individual's performance, we can assess player behavior by evaluating production probabilities. This characterization of behavior naturally improves as the number of trials is increased.

Error Detection & Recovery

Errors in the input can generate ungrammatical strings, causing the parsing algorithm to fail. We provide techniques for detecting and recovering from failures caused by certain types of errors. A *substitution error* occurs when the wrong terminal symbol is generated because the actual event is not detected as the most likely. *Insertion errors* take place when spurious symbols that do not correspond to actual events are added to the input. Finally, *deletion errors* represent failures to detect events that actually occurred.

Because we use domain-specific heuristics to detect low-level events, substitution and insertion errors are rare. However, deletion errors are more frequent because our domain-specific detectors are less robust at identifying events that deviate significantly from our heuristic models. Ivanov and Bobick handle substitution and insertion errors by modifying the grammar so that the parser accepts input that would, otherwise, generate a fatal syntax error (Ivanov & Bobick 2000). For rule-based activities, like card games, any attempt at correcting an error in this way will compromise the benefit of being able to detect rule violations. We have a vested interest in determining how, when, where, and by whom errors occur. At the same time, we wish to make parsing robust enough to tolerate erroneous input.

We attempt to recover from parsing failures by taking advantage of grammatical structure. Although the arrangement of terminals in the input is non-deterministic, it is constrained by *a priori* known rules that we leverage to anticipate future input. Parsing errors occur in the scanning stage when the symbol sampled from the input does not match any of the terminals from the prediction stage. This invariably happens during a nonterminal expansion. We revisit the prediction stage during the expansion of nonterminal X, which creates a list of productions $Y \to \nu$ that are syntactically consistent with the expansion, *i.e.*,

$$i : {}_k X \to \lambda . Y \mu \, [\alpha, \gamma] \Rightarrow i : {}_i Y \to .\nu \, [\alpha', \gamma'].$$

Every nonterminal Y is also expanded until the next terminal is predicted, *i.e.*, $i : {}_i Y \to .a\xi$. Solutions to a parsing failure are motivated by the nature of the error. We consider the following three scenarios:

If the failure is caused by an insertion error, we simply ignore the scanned terminal, and return the state of the parser to the point prior to scanning. The same pending expansions for prediction are maintained.

If the failure is caused by a substitution error, we promote each pending prediction state as if it were actually scanned, creating a new path for each hypothetical terminal. (At this point, these become hypothetical paths). We proceed with normal parsing, but instead of maintaining paths that spawn from a single, legitimately scanned terminal, we accommodate all paths from each hypothetical terminal appearing as a result of a simulated scan. A hypothetical path is terminated if another failure occurs in the next real scanning step. The actual likelihood of the event associated with the hypothetical terminal $P_\mathbf{D}(a)$ is recovered, then multiplied to prediction values of α and γ such that we get,

$$\begin{aligned} \alpha' &= \alpha(i : {}_i Y \to .a\xi) P_\mathbf{D}(a) \\ \gamma' &= \gamma(i : {}_i Y \to .a\xi) P_\mathbf{D}(a), \end{aligned} \quad (8)$$

If the failure is caused by a deletion error, again we promote each pending prediction state and create a separate path for each hypothetical symbol. We proceed through the completion stage, then to prediction to generate the next state terminal. During a simulated scan, hypothetical paths that are inconsistent with the symbol that caused the first failure are terminated. When a deletion error is assumed, there is no detection likelihood to recover for the missing symbol. We approximate this likelihood, denoted as $\widetilde{P}_\mathbf{D}(a)$, using empirical values that we select by hand, which are influenced by historical probability values for the detection of symbol a. Modified forward and inner probabilities in the first scanning step are given as

$$\begin{aligned} \alpha' &= \alpha(i : {}_i Y \to .a\xi) \widetilde{P}_\mathbf{D}(a) \\ \gamma' &= \gamma(i : {}_i Y \to .a\xi) \widetilde{P}_\mathbf{D}(a), \end{aligned} \quad (9)$$

while those of the second simulated scanning step can be recovered from the original scan likelihood, *i.e.*,

$$\begin{aligned} \alpha' &= \alpha(i + 1 : {}_{i+1} Y \to .b\xi) P_\mathbf{D}(b) \\ \gamma' &= \gamma(i + 1 : {}_{i+1} Y \to .b\xi) P_\mathbf{D}(b). \end{aligned} \quad (10)$$

Using these methods, the parser is guaranteed to generate a syntactically legal interpretation but provides no warranty of its semantic legitimacy. The parser supplies the framework with the erroneous symbol and its corresponding likelihood so that records of potential failures can be attached to the appropriate person. In this way, substrings with bad

(A) Grammar	(B) Earley Chart	(C) Insertion	(C) Substitution	(C) Deletion
$S \rightarrow AB$	*predicted*	*scanned "b"*	*scanned "b"*	*scanned "b"*
$A \rightarrow aa$	$0 : {}_0 \rightarrow .S$	failed, expecting "a"	failed, expecting "a"	failed, expecting "a"
$A \rightarrow aaA$	$0 : {}_0S \rightarrow .AB$	ignore "b"	*scanned "a"	*scanned "a"
$B \rightarrow bc$	$0 : {}_0A \rightarrow .aa$	*predicted*	$2 : {}_1A \rightarrow aa.$	$2 : {}_1A \rightarrow aa.$
$B \rightarrow bcB$	$0 : {}_0A \rightarrow .aaA$	$1 : {}_1A \rightarrow a.a$	$2 : {}_1A \rightarrow aa.A$	$2 : {}_1A \rightarrow aa.A$
	scanned "a"	$1 : {}_1A \rightarrow a.aA$	*completed*	*completed*
	$1 : {}_0A \rightarrow a.a$	*scanned "c"*	$2 : {}_1A \rightarrow aa.$	$2 : {}_1A \rightarrow aa.$
	$1 : {}_0A \rightarrow a.aA$	failed, expecting "a"	$2 : {}_0S \rightarrow A.B$	$2 : {}_0S \rightarrow A.B$
	none completed	TERMINATED	*predict*	*predict*
	predicted		$2 : {}_2A \rightarrow .aa$	$2 : {}_2A \rightarrow .aa$
	$1 : {}_1A \rightarrow a.a$		$2 : {}_2A \rightarrow .aaA$	$2 : {}_2A \rightarrow .aaA$
	$1 : {}_1A \rightarrow a.aA$		$2 : {}_2B \rightarrow .bc$	$2 : {}_2A \rightarrow .bc$
			$2 : {}_2B \rightarrow .bcB$	$2 : {}_2A \rightarrow .bcB$
			scanned "c"	*scanned "b" (retry)
			failed, expecting "b"	$3 : {}_2A \rightarrow b.c$
			TERMINATED	$3 : {}_2A \rightarrow b.cB$
				none completed
				predicted
				$3 : {}_3A \rightarrow b.c$
				$3 : {}_3A \rightarrow b.cB$
				scanned "c"
				$3 : {}_2A \rightarrow b.c$
				$3 : {}_2A \rightarrow b.cB$
				$3 : {}_2A \rightarrow b.cB$

Figure 2: (A) Consider this simple context-free grammar, which we will use to construct the input sequence $aabc\ldots$. A *deletion error* occurs in the detection of events such that the input only contains $abc\ldots$ (B) Shows the Earley chart after the first symbol a, is predicted and successfully scanned. The next scanned symbol, b, will cause parsing to fail under normal conditions since a was the only symbol anticipated during prediction. (C) Continuation of the Earley Chart shows parser recovery attempts under different error assumptions. Under the *insertion* assumption, we ignore b and repeat the last prediction state. Under *substitution*, we replace b with a and attempt to continue, but eventually fail when c is scanned (for both assumptions). Under *deletion*, we assume that we missed the detection of a, so we simulate its scan. This not only allows us to complete the parse, but suggests the kind of error that may have taken place. *Scan of hypothetical symbol is simulated to promote parsing step. Associated rule probabilities are ignored here for simplicity.

syntax can be more closely scrutinized to determine when an illegal action takes place.

Figure 2 illustrates how the parser attempts to recover from failures using the three error scenarios mentioned above. We maintain every recovered path, even if multiple tracks (each representing one of the three error scenarios) are formed from a single failure. For each of the error scenarios, we elect to tolerate only two consecutive failures before terminating the parse of that path. However, our approach can be applied iteratively so that more consecutive failures can be tolerated. A consequence of accepting more failures must be reflected by increasing the uncertainty in our approximation of $P_{\mathbf{D}}(a)$, denoted as $\widehat{P}_{\mathbf{D}}(a)$. We rely on the exponential to serve as a penalty function that is applied by multiplication to the historical mean likelihood $\widetilde{P}_{\mathbf{D}}(a)$, i.e.,

$$\widehat{P}_{\mathbf{D}}(a) = e^{\frac{-n}{\rho}}\, \widetilde{P}_{\mathbf{D}}(a), \qquad (11)$$

where n is the number of consecutive failures and ρ is empirically derived.

The algorithmic complexity of tracking multiple paths, which is a function of the production rules involved, tends to grow linearly for grammars with small terminal and non-terminal alphabets but can expand exponentially for larger grammars or for very long terminal strings. When computation and memory resources must be delicately managed, we prune recovered paths that have low overall likelihoods. Unlike the example provided in Figure 2, we can also entertain hybrid error scenarios in order to generate the most likely parse, i.e., instead of treating each consecutive error by the same type of scenario, all three alternatives can be consider for each bad input symbol.

Experimental Results

We provide real examples of our approach in the domain of the card game, Blackjack. Every rule of the game was used as a production rule in the grammar with full coverage (recall Table 1). A vision system, that ran in real-time, was used for tracking activities in a controlled environment.

Experiment I: Event Detection Accuracy: Twenty-eight sequences were used to generate 700 example events, which were compiled to determine the detection rate of each detector. Each sequence consisted of a full game of Blackjack with at least one player. For example, a sequence might generate six examples of the event "player bet a chip," five examples of "dealer removed player card," etc. The overall detection rate for all events is 96.2%. The error rates for insertion, substitution, and deletion errors were 0.4%, 0.1%, and 3.4%, respectively (assessed manually). Table 1 shows the results of this examination.

Experiment II: Error Detection & Recovery: A semantically legitimate sequence was then tried with no insertion, substitution, or deletion errors, and we are able to parse the activity with 100% accuracy. To provide a more diverse sample of sequences, two testing corpa were compiled from several minutes of video where Blackjack was played, primarily with two people (one dealer and one player). Corpus A contained 28 legitimate sequences with at least one detection error per sequence (either a deletion, substitution, or insertion error). Corpus B represents a family of 10 illegitimate sequences with various errors. Sequences in Corpus B often contained illegal moves, dealer mistakes, cheating, etc. **Error recovery disabled**, only 12 of the 28 sequences (42.9%) in Corpus A could be entirely parsed without terminating in failure. Of those that could be parsed, the mean detection rate for 320 events was 70.1%. The error rates for insertion, substitution, and deletion errors were 5.8%, 14.5%, and 9.6%, respectively. None of the sequences in Corpus B could be entirely parsed.

Error recovery enabled (accepting up to 2 consecutive failures), 25 of the 28 sequences (85.7%) from Corpus A could be parsed with 93.8% of all 625 events detected accurately. Insertion, substitution, and deletion errors were *reduced* by 70.5%, 87.3%, 71.9%, respectively. Parsing im-

S	Domain-Specific Events	Detect Rate	Error Rate (%) Ins	Sub	Del
a	dlr removed house card	100.0	0.0	0.0	0.0
b	dlr removed plyr card	100.0	0.0	0.0	0.0
c	plyr removed house card[†]	100.0	0.0	0.0	0.0
d	plyr removed plyr card	100.0	0.0	0.0	0.0
e	dlr add card to house	94.6	0.0	0.0	5.4
f	dlr dealt card to plyr	92.2	0.0	0.0	7.8
g	plyr add card to house[†]	100.0	0.0	0.0	0.0
h	plyr add card to plyr	89.3	3.6	0.0	7.1
i	dlr removed chip	93.7	0.0	0.0	6.3
j	plyr removed chip	96.9	0.0	0.0	3.1
k	dlr pays plyr chip	96.9	0.0	0.0	3.1
l	plyr bet chip	90.5	1.1	1.1	7.4

Table 1: *Experiment I*: Detection rate of events which make up the terminal alphabet V_T of V_{BJ}. Errors are categorized as insertion, substitution, and deletion, respectively. [†] Denotes events with no significance to legitimate Blackjack play, but can be used to detect illegal occurrences.

S	Detect % on	off	Ins Err on	off	Sub Err on	off	Del Err on	off
a	98.8	92.5	0.0	0.0	0.0	0.0	1.2	7.5
b	97.8	90.8	0.0	0.0	0.0	0.0	2.2	9.2
c	100.0	80.0	0.0	0.0	0.0	20.0	0.0	0.0
d	100.0	91.7	0.0	0.0	0.0	0.0	0.0	8.3
e	94.0	74.9	1.2	5.0	1.2	7.5	3.6	12.5
f	95.6	70.3	0.0	2.3	0.0	9.2	4.4	18.3
g	100.0	50.0	0.0	0.0	0.0	50.0	0.0	0.0
h	80.0	41.7	4.0	8.3	8.0	33.3	8.0	16.7
i	92.9	88.9	0.0	0.0	0.0	0.0	7.1	11.1
j	96.5	92.7	0.0	0.0	0.0	0.0	3.5	7.3
k	79.0	12.5	10.5	36.5	10.5	43.8	0.0	7.3
l	90.6	55.8	4.7	17.2	2.4	9.8	2.4	17.2

Table 2: *Experiment II*: Detection and error rates for Corpus A with error recovery turned on and off. Error recovery improves overall detection rate by 33.8%.

proved by 40% for Corpus B sequences with error recovery turned on, with an average 85.4% of high-level events recognized accurately. This improvement in the parsing rate is attributed to recovering from insertion errors, which simply skipped over rule violations encountered during the sequence. We assessed that 22.5%, 17.5%, and 60.0% of errors were caused by insertion, substitution, and deletion errors, respectively.

To measure the performance of the parser under a variety of conditions, including consecutive error burst, Corpus C was developed from 113 simulated terminal strings representing legal plays with various errors. Using this data, the probability of detection for each event $P_D(a)$ is estimated using the average determined in Table 1. Homogeneous error types present the worst-case system complexity due to contiguous blocks of substitution and deletion errors. Heterogeneous error scenarios benefit from the treatment used for insertion errors, which only need to maintain the same set of pending states, effectively lowering overall system complexity. We also learn empirically that to recover from an error burst of length n, we must accept at least n consecutive failures to recover.

Experiment III: High-level Behavior Assessment: We examined non-separable roles between a player and the dealer to assess patterns of behavior. The conduct of the dealer is strictly regulated by the rules of Blackjack, but the player is permitted to execute a range of different strategies to improve his/her chance of winning. We define a *novice* as a player whose moves are limited to *basic strategy*[2] where *experts* employ more advanced strategies, such as "splitting pairs" and "doubling down." The profile for these two behaviors is shown in Figure 3.

---

[2]When no extra cards are dealt to the player after the initial card pair, basic strategy is assumed.

Figure 3: *Experiment III*: (left) Trained behavior profiles of player strategy for novice and expert. (right) Table of Classification of behaviors.

We can also assess other behaviors, such as whether a player is a low-risk or high-risk player by evaluating betting amounts. After tuning several behaviors with actual and synthetic training data, roughly 10 trials per individual were conducted to assess behavior. Results are shown in Figure 3.

Summary

We show that SCFG is a powerful method for extracting high-level behaviors from sequences that have multiple people, objects, and tasks taking place over an extended period of time. By monitoring how frequently some production rules are used, we demonstrate a quantitative technique for assessing behaviors in non-separable roles. Using a strategy that proposes multiple hypotheses for recovering from errors in the input, our results show that parsing improves by over 40% and reduces some errors by as much as 87%. By closely examining multitasked, collaborative tasks such as card games, we develop methods that are appropriate for treating other highly complicated human activities.

References

Bobick, A. F., and Wilson, A. D. 1997. A state based approach to the representation and recognition of gesture. *PAMI* 19(12):1325–1337.

Brand, M.; Oliver, N.; and Pentland, A. 1997. Coupled hidden markov models for complex action recognition. In *CVPR*.

Brand, M. 1997. Understanding manipulation in video. In *Proceedings of Second International Conference on Face and Gesture Recognition*, 94–99.

Bremond, F., and Medioni, G. 1998. Scenario recognition in airborne video imagery. In *DARPA Image Understanding Workshop 1998*, 211–216.

Earley, J. C. 1968. *An Efficient Context-Free Parsing Algorithm*. Ph.D. Dissertation, Carnegie-Mellon University.

Ivanov, Y., and Bobick, A. 2000. Recognition of visual activities and interactions by stochastic parsing. *PAMI* 22(8):852–872.

Moore, D.; Essa, I.; and Hayes, M. 1999a. Context management for human activity recognition. In *Proceedings of Audio and Vision-based Person Authentication 1999*.

Moore, D.; Essa, I.; and Hayes, M. 1999b. Exploiting human actions and object context for recognition tasks. In *ICCV'99*, 80–86.

Schlenzig, J.; Hunter, E.; and Jain, R. 1994. Recursive identification of gesture inputs using hidden markov models. In *WACV94*, 187–194.

Starner, T.; Weaver, J.; and Pentland, A. 1998. Real-time american sign language recognition using desk and wearable computer based video. *PAMI* 20(12):1371–1375.

Stolcke, A., and Segal, J. 1994. Precise n-gram probabilities from stochastic context-free grammars. In *Proceedings of the 32nd Annual Meeting of the Association for Computational Linguistics*, 74–79. Las Cruces, NM.

Stolcke, A. 1994. *Bayesian Learning of Probabilistic Language Models*. Ph.d., University of California at Berkeley.

Taylor, R. G. 1998. *Models of Computation and Formal Languages*. Oxford University Press.

Vogler, C., and Metaxas, D. 2001. A framework for recognizing the simultaneous aspects of american sign language. *CVIU* 81(3):358–384.

Yamato, J.; Ohya, J.; and Ishii, K. 1994. Recognizing human action in time-sequential images using a hidden Markov model. In *CVPR1992*, 379–385.

The OD Theory of TOD:
The Use and Limits of Temporal Information for Object Discovery

Brandon C. S. Sanders and **Randal C. Nelson**
Department of Computer Science
University of Rochester
Rochester, NY 14627
[sanders,nelson]@cs.rochester.edu

Rahul Sukthankar
Compaq Research (CRL)
One Cambridge Center
Cambridge, MA 02142
rahul.sukthankar@compaq.com

Abstract

We present the theory behind TOD (the Temporal Object Discoverer), a novel unsupervised system that uses only temporal information to discover objects across image sequences acquired by any number of uncalibrated cameras. The process is divided into three phases: (1) Extraction of each pixel's *temporal signature*, a partition of the pixel's observations into sets that stem from different objects; (2) Construction of a global schedule that explains the signatures in terms of the lifetimes of a set of quasi-static objects; (3) Mapping of each pixel's observations to objects in the schedule according to the pixel's temporal signature. Our Global Scheduling (GSched) algorithm provably constructs a valid and complete global schedule when certain observability criteria are met. Our Quasi-Static Labeling (QSL) algorithm uses the schedule created by GSched to produce the maximally-informative mapping of each pixel's observations onto the objects they stem from. Using GSched and QSL, TOD ignores distracting motion, correctly deals with complicated occlusions, and naturally groups observations across cameras. The sets of 2D masks recovered are suitable for unsupervised training and initialization of object recognition and tracking systems.

Introduction

Computers capable of intelligent interaction with physical objects must first be able to discover and recognize them. "Object Discovery" (OD) is the problem of grouping all observations springing from a single object without including any observations generated by other objects (for an example see Figure 1). Because robust OD is a prerequisite for reasoning about physical objects, relationships, actions and activities, OD is of fundamental importance to AI systems seeking to interact with the physical world. A number of different approaches have been considered that make different assumptions about the world.

Static OD systems seek to discover objects in single images without using temporal information. Object recognizers may be used to discover known objects in static images (Papageorgiou & Poggio 2000; Schiele & Crowley 2000). The primary limitation of object recognizers is the often extensive training they require to discover objects. Static OD approaches that do not require an *a priori* model of each

Figure 1: Sample OD results for TOD, a direct implementation of the theory presented in this paper. (*top*) Examples from sequences acquired by three different uncalibrated cameras. (*bottom*) The objects discovered. The complete remote is recovered even though it is partially occluded by either the bowl or the rabbit in every image in which cameras 0 and 1 observe it. Notably, temporal information alone is sufficient to group the pixels in and across the cameras.

object of interest typically rely upon local homogeneity of color (Liu & Yang 1994), texture (Mao & Jain 1992), or a combination of these cues (Belongie *et al.* 1998). Because real objects are not visually homogeneous through space, traditional segmentation often returns pieces of objects or incorrectly groups parts stemming from multiple objects.

Dynamic OD systems find objects that move independently in the world and so introduce temporal information into the mix. The discovery of moving objects typically depends upon spatial homogeneity of motion flow vectors

(Wang & Adelson 1994); sometimes this data is also combined with texture or color (Altunbasak, Eren, & Tekalp 1998). Dynamic OD systems often rely upon background subtraction (Toyama *et al.* 1999) to initially separate moving objects from a static background. Dynamic OD systems typically require high frame rates and cannot separate objects from the person manipulating them.

In this paper we present the theory behind *TOD*, the Temporal Object Discover. TOD is a system that uses temporal rather than spatial information to discover objects across multiple uncalibrated cameras. We decompose the problem of object discovery into three phases: (1) Generation of a temporal signature for each pixel; (2) Construction of a global schedule that satisfies the constraints encoded in the temporal signatures; (3) Explanation of each individual pixel's temporal signature in terms of a mapping from its observations to objects in the global schedule.

Because we do not use spatial information, our approach complements the existing body of segmentation work, most of which relies upon local spatial homogeneity of color, texture or optical flow. Despite ignoring spatial information, TOD achieves good results even on sequences having complex object occlusion relationships (see Figure 1). The advantages of our method include: (1) Human supervision is not required; (2) Low frame rates (*i.e.,* 1-5Hz) suffice; (3) Entire objects are discovered even in some cases where they are always partially occluded; (4) The approach scales naturally to and benefits from multiple uncalibrated cameras. The recovered multi-view 2D masks are suitable for unsupervised training and initialization of object recognition and tracking systems.

The remainder of the paper is structured as follows. First we introduce the quasi-static world assumed by TOD. Then we describe how each pixel's *temporal signature* is constructed. Following the section on signature construction, we introduce GSched, an algorithm that creates a valid and complete schedule of object lifetimes when certain observability criteria are met. We then present the QSL algorithm that solves the labeling problem using each pixel's temporal signature and the global schedule created by GSched. We conclude with a discussion of some limitations of temporal information and a short look at promising directions for future work.

TOD and the Quasi-static Model

In this section we define the quasi-static world model used throughout the remainder of the paper. This model is attractive because it imposes enough restrictions on the world to be theoretically treatable while maintaining practical application to real systems. The quasi-static model assumes that the only objects of interest are those that undergo motion on some time interval and are stationary on some other time interval (*i.e.,* objects that stay still for a while). Thus the quasi-static world model targets objects that are picked up and set down while ignoring the person manipulating them.[1]

---

[1]Of course, according to the quasi-static world model when a person is completely stationary he/she becomes an object of interest.

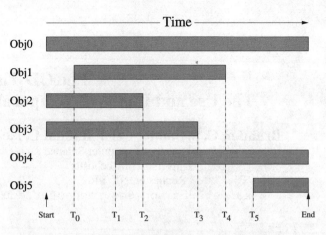

Figure 2: A global schedule consists of the lifetimes of a set of quasi-static objects and a special static background object (Obj0). The ordering of the object lifetimes in this figure is arbitrary and should not be interpreted as a layered representation containing occlusion information.

The following definitions will be used throughout the paper in connection with the quasi-static model:

Physical object: A chunk of matter that leads to consistent observations through space and time. Physical objects are objects in the intuitive sense. We define physical objects in order to contrast them with *quasi-static objects*. In the quasi-static world, a single physical object may be interpreted as any number of quasi-static objects. A physical object is *mobile* if it is observed to move in the scene.

Quasi-static object: The quasi-static world interpretation of a mobile physical object that is stationary over a particular time interval. For every interval on which a mobile physical object is observed to be stationary, the quasi-static world model interprets the physical object as a unique quasi-static object that arrives at the beginning of the stationary interval and departs at the end of the stationary interval. A single quasi-static object can only arrive once and depart once. We use the term *object* variously throughout the paper to refer to a physical object, a quasi-static object, and to a quasi-static object's entry in the global schedule. Where the usage of the word object is not clear from the context, we use a fully descriptive phrase instead.

Quasi-static object lifetime: The time interval over which a mobile physical object is stationary at a single location. When a mobile physical object m moves around the scene and is stationary at multiple physical locations, each stationary location i is interpreted as a separate quasi-static object o_i.

Global schedule: A set of quasi-static objects and their lifetimes (Figure 2).

Pixel visage: A set of observations at a given pixel that are interpreted as stemming from a particular quasi-static object. Each of a pixel's visages is disjoint with its other visages and forms a history of a particular quasi-static object's visual appearance through time according to the pixel. The pixel visage v is said to be *observed by* pixel p at time t if the observation made by p at t is in v. A pixel visage is *valid* if each of its observations stems from a single quasi-static object.

The quasi-static world model assumes that each pixel can reliably group observations that stem from a single quasi-static object. In other words, the observations belonging to one visage for a particular pixel are discriminable from the observations belonging to any other visage for that pixel. The next section presents the method we use to perform this grouping into visages. The following scheduling and labeling sections then describe how to determine the identity of the quasi-static object responsible for each visage.

Computing Temporal Signatures

In the first phase of object discovery, *signature extraction*, we start with a pixel's sequence of observations and partition them into pixel visages, sets of observations that all stem from a single object. A pixel's visages directly encode the temporal structure in the pixel's observation history in the form of a *temporal signature*. The set of temporal signatures gathered across all views will later be used in the *schedule generation* phase to hypothesize the existence of a small set of objects whose arrivals and departures explain the signatures. The hypothesized set of objects, or global schedule (Figure 2), is in turn used during the *labeling* phase to determine the mapping from observations to objects. Before describing our temporal signature generation algorithm, we first take a moment to define what we mean by *temporal signature* and several other related terms.

Stationary interval: A period of time during which every observation made by a given pixel stems from a single quasi-static object. A stationary interval is said to *belong to* the pixel visage that contains its observations. In Figure 3, the stationary intervals are labeled A through G.

Interruption: A non-stationary interval that comes between two stationary intervals belonging to the *same* pixel visage. In Figure 3, the gap between stationary intervals B and C and the gap between C and D and the gap between F and G are all interruptions.

Transition: An non-stationary interval that comes between two stationary intervals belonging to *different* pixel visages. Every transition contains either the arrival of an object or the departure of a different object. In Figure 3, the gaps between stationary intervals A and B, between D and E and between E and F are transitions.

Unambiguous transition: A transition in a signature that admits only one interpretation. If the object that supposedly arrived at a particular transition was previously observed at some time prior to the transition, then the object cannot have arrived during the transition. Similarly, if the object that supposedly departed at a particular transition is again observed at some time after the transition, then the object cannot have departed during the transition. In Figure 3 the first and third transitions are unambiguous because they cannot involve 0. The second transition is

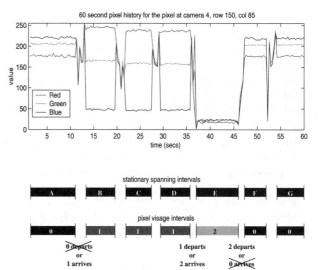

Figure 3: A pictorial walk-through of the constituents of a pixel's temporal signature starting from the pixel's sequence of observations and working down to through an unambiguous labeling of several transitions observed by the pixel.

ambiguous because it could contain the arrival of 2 or the departure of 1.

Temporal signature: A pixel's temporal signature (Figure 3) encodes the temporal structure found in its observation history. This representation includes the transitions the pixel has witnessed as well as a pixel visage for each unique quasi-static object the pixel observes. In Figure 3, the stationary intervals for the three pixel visages are labeled 0 through 2 according to the visage observed on the interval.

Because we are interested in determining the utility of temporal information for OD, we ignore spatial information in every phase of the algorithm. This means that during the temporal signature generation phase, we assume that knowing the visual appearance of an object in one pixel provides zero information about the object's visual appearance in every other pixel. Our method for signature extraction depends upon the following definition of an atomic interval and involves several steps:

Atomic interval: An atomic interval A is any sequence of at least two observations $A = \langle x_i, x_{i+1}, \ldots, x_{i+n} \rangle$ such that the difference between the first observation's time-stamp and the last observation's time-stamp exceeds the minimum time for stability t_{min} and A does not contain a proper subsequence that also spans t_{min}.

Temporal signature construction

1. Check every *atomic interval* A for stationarity by verifying that every observation[2] $x_i \in A$ is close to every other observation $x_j \in A$ in visual appearance space (in

---

[2]The observations used to compute the temporal signatures are spatially averaged over a 3x3 region to remove high frequency spatial artifacts. This step is essential for real image sequences.

our current implementation we measure distance in RGB color space).

2. Group temporally overlapping atomic stationary intervals into *spanning stationary intervals*. Because we consider stationarity on atomic intervals rather than on spanning intervals, the visual appearance of an object in a pixel is allowed to change as long as the change is gradual (*e.g.,* movement of the sun across an outdoor scene).

3. Construct a pixel visage by collecting the observations from spanning stationary intervals that share the same visual appearance. To evaluate whether two spanning stationary intervals share the same visual appearance, we evaluate whether the temporally nearest ends of the two spanning intervals are close in RGB color space (using the means of the nearest atomic intervals).

Establishing a Global Schedule

In the second phase of object discovery, *schedule construction*, we use the set of temporal signatures gathered across all pixels in all views to hypothesize the existence of a small set of objects whose arrivals and departures satisfy the constraints of the signatures and thus explain them. This hypothesized set of objects and object lifetimes constitutes a global schedule (Figure 2). For a global schedule to be *valid*, the lifetime of each quasi-static object it contains must exactly match an interval on which some mobile physical object was stationary in the scene. To be *complete*, a global schedule must explain every transition observed by some pixel. A valid and complete global schedule is a correct schedule in the intuitive sense.

Each pixel's temporal signature places constraints upon the global schedule (see Figure 4). In order to be valid and complete, a global schedule must all of these constraints. In general, the constraints from temporal information alone are not enough to completely determine the schedule. Specifically, temporal information cannot determine whether an object o has arrived or departed unless o has both arrived and departed during the period of observation. Even though temporal information cannot, in general, completely determine a global schedule, many cases exist where temporal information does suffice. In fact, if the following observability criteria are met, the Global Scheduling (GSched) algorithm we present later in this section is guaranteed to find a complete and valid global schedule using only temporal information.

GSched Observability Criteria: Temporal information alone is sufficient to construct a valid and complete global schedule if the following observability criteria are met:

1. **Valid visages criterion:** Every pixel visage is valid. In other words, within each pixel, observations of each object are correctly grouped. In our implementation this generally implies that all of a stationary pixel's observations of a stationary object lie in a small region of RGB space.

2. **Temporally discriminability criterion:** Across all pixels, every arrival and departure event is temporally discriminable from every other event. Essentially,

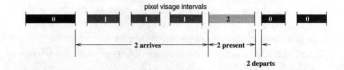

Figure 4: The arrival and departure times for a visage v are constrained by observation of another visage that bounds v. In this example, 0 bounds both 1 and 2. The constraints for 2 are shown. To explain 2, the global schedule must contain an object that arrives during 2's arrival interval and departs during 2's departure interval.

when the transition intervals from all the signatures are considered together, each event must clearly stand out as separate from the others.

3. **Clean world criterion:** Every quasi-stationary object both arrives and departs.[3]

4. **Observability criterion:** For every object o, some pixel p observes both the arrival and departure of o (neither event is hidden by some other object) and furthermore p is able to unambiguously identify either o's arrival or o's departure (Figure 3). This criterion becomes more likely to be met as the number of different viewpoints of each object increases.

The criteria listed above lead directly to the straightforward *global scheduling algorithm* presented below.

Global Scheduling (GSched) algorithm Given that the GSched observability criteria listed above are met, the following algorithm establishes a valid and complete global schedule:

1. Build a global list E of unambiguous events by creating a set of events that explains each unambiguous transition. The unambiguous transitions are processed in order from shortest transition to longest. If no event in E explains an unambiguous transition when the transition is processed, a new event is added to E that does explain the transition. If the *observability criterion* is met, E will contain at least one unambiguous event (arrival or departure) for every quasi-static object in the scene.

2. For each event e in E:

 (a) Remove e from E.

 (b) If e is the *arrival* of an object o, find the corresponding *departure* of o by determining the latest time t at which o is observed by some pixel that observes e. If some event $e' \in E$ matches t, then e' must be the departure of o according to the *temporal discriminability criterion*. If e' exists, remove it from E so that it is not processed twice. Create a global object hypothesis g_i with lifetime spanning from the time of arrival (determined from e) to the time of departure t. Enter g_i into the the global schedule S.

---

[3]The background is treated specially and is the union of all objects that never arrive nor depart.

(c) If e is the *departure* of an object o, find the corresponding *arrival* of o by determining the earliest time t at which o is observed by some pixel that observes e. If some event $e' \in E$ matches t, then e' must be the arrival of o according to the *temporal discriminability criterion*. If e' exists, remove it from E so that it is not processed twice. Create a global object hypothesis g_i with lifetime spanning from the time of arrival t to the time of departure (determined from e). Enter g_i into the the global schedule S.

Steps a and b are valid because some pixel p' has observed both the arrival and departure of o (according to the *observability criterion*). Thus p' is guaranteed to have observed e regardless of whether e is an arrival or departure, and p' has observed o at least as early and at least as late as any other pixel.

Mapping Observations to Objects

During the labeling phase of object discovery, we use the schedule generated by the GSched algorithm and the temporal signature computed during the first phase to map the observations in each pixel visage to the objects in the schedule that those observations could have stemmed from. This labeling of observations is the ultimate goal of object discovery. Once each observation has been mapped to the objects that could have given rise to it, we can easily assemble multi-view 2D masks of each object from the observations attributed to the object. In this section we describe our Quasi-Static Labeling (QSL) algorithm for solving the mapping problem, and argue that (1) Given a valid and complete global event schedule such as that returned by GSched, each pixel's observation labeling problem is independent of every other pixel's observations; (2) The QSL algorithm produces the maximally-informative mapping of a pixel's observations onto the objects they stem from. We begin this section by defining the observation labeling problem.

Observation labeling problem Given a pixel p and a valid and complete global schedule, determine for each of p's visages v_i the smallest set of quasi-static objects in the schedule guaranteed to contain the actual quasi-static object that generated p's observations of v_i.

Because we do not assume an object is visually homogeneous through space, we cannot link observations across pixels based on similarity of color and/or texture. Rather, to conclude that two pixels have observed the same object o, both pixels must have made observations that are temporally consistent with the arrival and departure of o. The only information salient to this decision are the times at which o arrives and departs. For every object, these arrival and departure times are contained in the global schedule. Thus, given the complete global schedule, each pixel's labeling problem is independent of every other pixels' observations.

The independence of labeling problems has several important consequences. First, any labeling algorithm that only uses temporal information may be easily parallelized simply by running multiple copies of a single labeler on subsets of the pixels. Second, since each pixel's labeling problem is independent of the pixel's spatial location, we may treat every

pixel identically regardless of its physical location. In other words, it doesn't matter what camera, row, and column a pixel comes from. Finally, this independence property allows us to show that QSL generates the globally maximally-informative mapping from observations to objects simply by showing that QSL correctly solves the pixel labeling problem for any given pixel taken in isolation.

The remainder of this section is written from the perspective of a single pixel's labeling problem and assumes the existence of a valid and complete global schedule containing all known objects. We begin by defining several terms used to describe the QSL algorithm. We then introduce the inference rules that drive QSL and show that each inference rule leads to a valid mapping according to the constraints of the quasi-static world model. Finally, we introduce the QSL algorithm and argue that it recovers the maximally informative mapping from observations to objects. To describe the inference rules and the labeling algorithm we need the following definitions:

Contemporaneous object set: A contemporaneous object set X is a set of objects such that each object $o \in X$ is present in the scene at some time t. A *maximal* contemporaneous object set X_t^* is the set of *all* objects present in the scene at time t.

$$X_t^* = \{o : o \text{ is present at time } t\}$$

Intersection set: For a pixel visage v, v's intersection set I_v is the set of all objects such that each object is present at *every* time at which v is observed.

$$I_v = \bigcap_t X_t^* \qquad t : v \text{ is observed at time } t$$

Union set: For a pixel visage v, v's union set U_v is the set of all objects such that each object is present at *some* time at which v is observed.

$$U_v = \bigcup_t X_t^* \qquad t : v \text{ is observed at time } t$$

Bounding visage: For pixel visages v and b, b is a bounding visage of v if the following hold:

1. b is observed sometime *prior to* every observation of v;
2. b is observed sometime *after* every observation of v.

Bounded set For a pixel visage v, v's bounded set B_v is the set of all objects such that each object is present at *every* time that v is observed, and no object is present at *any* time at which a bounding visage of v is observed. In other words, a visage's bounded set contains every object whose lifetime is consistent with the visage's constrained arrival and departure intervals (see Figure 4).

$$B_v = I_v - \bigcup_b U_b \qquad b : b \text{ is a bounding visage of } v$$

Given the quasi-static assumptions, the object bounded set B_v for a visage v contains the actual object observed by v.

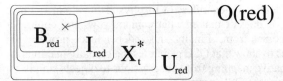

$$O(red)$$

For all X_t^* such that red is observed at t

Figure 5: The relationship between the sets for a visage *red*. Because $O(red)$ is in B_{red}, $O(red)$ is also in each of the other sets. Similarly, since $O(red)$ is in front of every object in U_{red}, $O(red)$ is also in front of every object in each of the other sets.

Object function: The object function $O(v) = o$ maps a visage v onto an object o. This function represents abstractly the true state of the world. The goal of the labeling process is to find the smallest set of candidate objects C such that $O(v) \in C$ is true given that the model assumptions hold. In some cases it is not physically possible to narrow C down to a singleton.

Front function: The front function $F(C) = o$ for a pixel p maps a set of candidate objects C onto the object $o \in C$ that is in front of the other objects. The front object o is said to *occlude* the other objects in C. $F(C) = o$ is unique for all sets C such that for every other $o' \in C$, at some time t, both o and o' are simultaneously present and p observes o at time t. Any subset of the union set for a visage v that contains $O(v)$ meets this condition. Like the object function $O()$, $F()$ represents abstractly the true state of the world, not what we know about it.

The following lemmas and theorems provide the foundation for the labeling algorithm. To make the discussion easier to follow, we use color names to refer to particular pixel visages.

Lemma 1 *For any pixel visage red, and any candidate object set C such that every object in C is present at some time when red is observed and $O(red) \in C$, $O(red) = F(C)$ (i.e., $O(red)$ is in front of every other object in C).*

This follows directly from the physics of the quasi-static world.

Lemma 2 *According to lemma 1, the following four statements are all true:*

1. $O(red) = F(B_{red})$;
2. $O(red) = F(I_{red})$;
3. $O(red) = F(X_t^*)$, $\quad \forall t:$ *red is observed at t;*
4. $O(red) = F(U_{red})$.

These four statements follow directly from lemma 1 and the relations: $O(red) \in B_{red} \subseteq I_{red} \subseteq X_t^* \subseteq U_{red}$, for all t such that red is observed at t. The relationships between the sets and the object and front functions is illustrated in figure 5. These relationships follow directly from the definitions of the sets and the object and front functions.

The following QSL Theorem is central to the QSL algorithm. In essence, the QSL Theorem provides a general rule

that allows us to use one pixel visage's union set (*e.g.*, U_{blue}) to rule out candidates for $O(red)$ for some other visage *red*. Iterative invocation of this theorem forms the heart of QSL and allows us to find the most informative mapping from visages to objects.

Theorem 3 *QSL Theorem Given distinct visages red, blue and contemporaneous subsets X_{red}, X_{blue} such that $O(red) = F(X_{red})$ and $O(blue) = F(X_{blue})$:*

$$X_{blue} \subset U_{red} \;\Rightarrow\; O(red) \text{ occludes } O(blue)$$
$$\Rightarrow\; O(red) = F(X_{red} - U_{blue})$$

Proof The gist of the proof hangs upon determining when the front object of one set of objects occludes the front object of another set of objects.

1. $\mathbf{X_{blue} \subset U_{red} \Rightarrow O(red) \notin X_{blue}}$. The front object in U_{red} is $O(red)$. Whenever a subset of U_{red} contains $O(red)$, the front object of the subset is $O(red)$. Since X_{blue} is a subset of U_{red} and the front object of X_{blue} is $O(blue)$ not $O(red)$, X_{blue} cannot contain $O(red)$.

2. $\mathbf{O(red) \notin X_{blue} \Rightarrow O(red)}$ **occludes o for every object o** $\in \mathbf{X_{blue}}$. According to the definition of the union set, every object in U_{red} is present at some time when *red* is observed. Thus $X_{blue} \subset U_{red}$ guarantees that *red* is observed at some time t when o is present. Since $O(red)$ is the object visible whenever *red* is observed, $O(red)$ is in front of o at time t.

3. $\mathbf{O(red)}$ **occludes o for every object o** $\in \mathbf{X_{blue}}$ $\Rightarrow \mathbf{O(red)}$ **occludes** $\mathbf{O(blue)}$. $O(blue) \in X_{blue}$ satisfies the previous step.

4. $\mathbf{O(red)}$ **occludes** $\mathbf{O(blue) \Rightarrow O(red) \notin U_{blue}}$. Since $O(red)$ is in front of $O(blue)$, $O(red)$ cannot be any object that is ever present when *blue* is observed. Since every object in U_{blue} is present at some time when *blue* is observed, no object in U_{blue} can be $O(red)$.

5. $\mathbf{O(red) \notin U_{blue} \wedge O(red) = F(X_{red})}$ $\Rightarrow \mathbf{O(red) = F(X_{red} - U_{blue})}$. ∎

The definitions and results presented above allow us to state the Quasi Static Labeling (QSL) algorithm succinctly. The algorithm maintains a collection **R** of statements of the form $O(v_i) = F(C_i)$, one for each visage v_i, where the elements of a set C_i essentially encode a set of candidates for the object that maps to visage v_i, as determined by QSL at some point in the algorithm. We start with an initial set of true statements and attempt to produce new, smaller true statements by applying the QSL Theorem. The ultimate goal is to obtain for each visage the true statement with the smallest possible front function subset argument.

Quasi-Static Labeling (QSL) algorithm Given a complete global schedule, for each pixel p and its set of pixel visages V_p:

1. For each pixel visage $v \in V_p$ find v's union set U_v.
2. For each pixel visage $v \in V_p$ find v's bounded set B_v, and add the statement $O(v) = F(B_v)$ to the collection **R**. By Lemma 2 these are all true statements.

3. Repeatedly apply the QSL Theorem to appropriate pairs of statements in **R** to shrink the subset argument of one of the statements. Repeat until no further applications are possible.

If the QSL Theorem applies to a pair of statements, it equally applies to the pair of statements if either statement's subset argument shrinks. Thus the result is independent of the order in which the transformations are applied. Because the size of an argument subset is always smaller than one of the parent statements and the size of these subsets must remain positive, the algorithm is guaranteed to terminate. The final candidate label set C_v^* for each pixel visage v can be read from the subset argument for v's statement $O(v) = F(C_v)$ in **R**.

If there are m visages in the temporal signature and n objects in the global schedule ($m \leq n$), the number of times the QSL Theorem can be invoked to remove objects from subset arguments is bounded by mn, the maximum number of objects in all subset arguments in **R**. The number of comparisons between subset arguments and union sets required to find a match for the QSL Theorem is m^2 in the worst case. Each set comparison involves at most n element comparisons. This gives QSL a worst-case runtime complexity of $m^3 n^2$.

Given a complete and valid global schedule S and a pixel p having only valid visages, the labeling the QSL algorithm returns is maximally-informative in the sense that it fully preserves and utilizes the following observable properties of the quasi-static world. Out of space considerations, we refer you to (Sanders, Nelson, & Sukthankar 2002) for the proofs of these theorems.

Theorem 4 *For any object $o \in S$ and any two distinct visages v, v' observed by p, the QSL algorithm never assigns $O(v) = O(v') = o$.*

Theorem 5 *For any visage v observed by p and any two distinct objects $o, o' \in S$, the QSL algorithm never assigns $O(v) = o = o'$.*

Theorem 6 *For any object $o \in S$, if p observes o's arrival, the QSL algorithm correctly assigns $O(v) = o$ to the visage v observed by p immediately after the arrival. Likewise if p observes o's departure, the QSL algorithm correctly assigns $O(v) = o$ to the visage v observed by p immediately before the departure.*

Theorem 7 *For any visage v observed by p and object $o \in S$, the QSL algorithm determines $O(v) \neq o$ if there exists outside of o's lifetime a time t at which p observes v.*

Theorem 8 *For each of p's visages v_i, the QSL algorithm determines $O(v_i) \neq o$ for every object $o \in S$ that is in front of $O(v_i)$ in every world configuration that is consistent with S and each of p's visages.*

Conjecture 9 *For each of p's visages v_i, the QSL algorithm determines $O(v_i) \neq o$ for every object $o \in S$ that is behind $O(v_i)$ in every world configuration that is consistent with S and each of p's visages.*

The QSL algorithm uses the QSL theorem to implicitly generate a directed acyclical graph encoding all occlusion

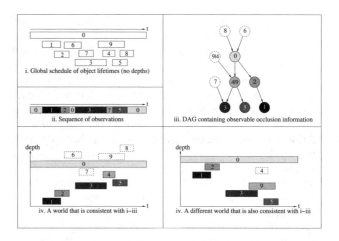

i. Global schedule of object lifetimes (no depths)

ii. Sequence of observations

iii. DAG containing observable occlusion information

iv. A world that is consistent with i–iii

iv. A different world that is also consistent with i–iii

Figure 6: Given a global schedule (*i*), observation of a pixel's visages (*ii*) determines a partial depth ordering of the objects that map to the visages. This partial ordering can be represented as a directed acyclical graph (*iii*). The objects with the dashed boundaries are not directly observed by the pixel and so may be occluded or may simply not be present in the part of the scene observed this pixel. When a directed path between two objects exists, the object at the end of the path is said to be *in front* of the object at the start of the path while the object at the start of the path is said to be *behind* the object at the end of the path. If two such objects are present in the scene simultaneously, the in-front object is said to *occlude* the behind object. Often (as in this case) it is possible to determine the occlusion order of two pixel visages without necessarily being able to uniquely determine the global object that one or the other visage maps to.

relationships between schedule objects that are observable given the schedule and a particular pixel's signature (Figure 6). Once the observations in the sequence have been mapped to the objects they stem from, it is trivial to assemble multi-view 2D masks of the objects from the observations attributed to them. Since the observations used to construct the masks may come from any time during the sequence, a complete object mask of an object that is never entirely visible at at any one time can be created from observations made at various times when different parts of the object were visible.

Limitations of Temporal Information

The quasi-static world model assumes that a given stationary physical object looks the same through time from each vantage point that observes it. In practice, when other objects arrive or depart from the scene, the lighting conditions for a stationary object (*e.g.*, a toy rabbit) may be affected. Even if the objects arriving and leaving do not occlude the part of the rabbit a pixel observes, shadows and reflections from the other objects can significantly alter the rabbit's visual appearance in the pixel. However, not all representations of visual appearance are equally susceptible to shadows and reflections. For example, an HSI color space may allow easier rejection of appearance changes due to shadows than the corresponding RGB color space.

While temporal information alone is often enough to both construct a global schedule and map observations to objects using that schedule, there are situations for each of these tasks in which the problem cannot be completely solved using temporal information alone. Consider the scheduling problem. In many real world situations, the *clean world* criterion is not satisfied by some objects that either only arrive or only depart. As was mentioned earlier, temporal information by itself cannot determine whether an event is the arrival or departure of an object *o*, unless *o* has also respectively departed or arrived. While temporal information cannot resolve these tricky events, several straightforward and robust spatial methods based upon edge features may be used in concert with the temporal information to finish the job.

As with construction of a global schedule, mapping observations to objects cannot always be completely solved using temporal information alone. Certain world configurations are inherently ambiguous with respect to temporal information alone. Instead of a single candidate quasi-static object per visage, some visages have a set of possible objects they could map to. Even in these difficult situations, QSL determines the smallest set of candidates that fully covers all possible world configurations. These sets, as provided by QSL, could be combined with spatial techniques, such as connected components, to finish constraining the assignment of observations to objects.

Conclusion

TOD, as described by the theory in this paper, ignores distracting motion, correctly deals with complex occlusions, and recovers entire objects even in cases where the objects are partially occluded in every frame (see Figure 1 for example results). Because we do not use spatial information to perform our clustering, our approach is significantly different from and complements traditional spatially based segmentation algorithms. The advantages of our method include: (1) Human supervision is not required; (2) Low frame rates (*i.e.*, 1-5Hz) suffice; (3) Entire objects are discovered even in some cases where they are always partially occluded; (4) The approach scales naturally to and benefits from multiple uncalibrated cameras. Since our approach is well suited to train and initialize object recognition and tracking systems without requiring human supervision, our method represents significant progress toward solving the object discovery problem.

A few promising directions for future work include: (1) Using the 2D masks generated by TOD to train an object recognizer automatically; (2) Integrating TOD with a spoken language system where TOD is used to perceptually ground the nouns; (3) Evaluating a variety of techniques for generating temporal signatures that allow the *distinct visages* and *temporal discriminability* observability criteria to be weakened; (4) Combining temporal and spatial information in a unified framework that removes the requirement of *temporal discriminability* altogether; (5) Extending TOD to run online by causing GSched and QSL to periodically commit to their interpretations of the sequences; (6) Converting the deterministic scheduling and labeling phases into probabilistic versions; (7) Integrating the currently separate scheduling and labeling phases into a single phase. More details are in (Sanders, Nelson, & Sukthankar 2002) available from `http://www.cs.rochester.edu/~sanders`.

Acknowledgments

This work funded in part by NSF Grant EIA-0080124, NSF Grant IIS-9977206, Department of Education GAANN Grant P200A000306 and a Compaq Research Internship.

References

Altunbasak, Y.; Eren, P. E.; and Tekalp, A. M. 1998. Region-based parametric motion segmentation using color information. *GMIP* 60(1).

Belongie, S.; Carson, C.; Greenspan, H.; and Malik, J. 1998. Color- and texture-based image seg. using EM and its app. to content-based image retrieval. In *Proc. ICCV*.

Liu, J., and Yang, Y. 1994. Multiresolution color image segmentation. *IEEE PAMI* 16(7).

Mao, J., and Jain, A. K. 1992. Texture classification and segmentation using multiresolution simultaneous autoregressive models. *PR* 25(2).

Papageorgiou, C., and Poggio, T. 2000. A trainable system for object detection. *IJCV* 38(1).

Sanders, B. C. S.; Nelson, R. C.; and Sukthankar, R. 2002. Discovering objects using temporal information. Technical Report 772, U. of Rochester CS Dept, Rochester, NY 14627.

Schiele, B., and Crowley, J. L. 2000. Recognition without correspondence using multidimensional receptive field histograms. *IJCV* 36(1).

Toyama, K.; Krumm, J.; Brumitt, B.; and Meyers, B. 1999. Wallflower: Principles and practice of background maintenance. In *Proc. ICCV*.

Wang, J. Y. A., and Adelson, E. H. 1994. Representing moving images with layers. *IEEE Trans. on Image Proc. Special Issue: Image Sequence Compression* 3(5).

Web and Information Extraction

A Maximum Entropy Approach to
Information Extraction from Semi-Structured and Free Text

Hai Leong Chieu
DSO National Laboratories
20 Science Park Drive
Singapore 118230
chaileon@dso.org.sg

Hwee Tou Ng
Department of Computer Science
School of Computing
National University of Singapore
3 Science Drive 2, Singapore 117543
nght@comp.nus.edu.sg

Abstract

In this paper, we present a classification-based approach towards single-slot as well as multi-slot information extraction (IE). For single-slot IE, we worked on the domain of Seminar Announcements, where each document contains information on only one seminar. For multi-slot IE, we worked on the domain of Management Succession. For this domain, we restrict ourselves to extracting information sentence by sentence, in the same way as (Soderland 1999). Each sentence can contain information on several management succession events. By using a classification approach based on a maximum entropy framework, our system achieves higher accuracy than the best previously published results in both domains.

Introduction

Information Extraction (IE) can be defined as the task of automatically extracting fragments of text to fill slots in a database. Examples include extracting speaker and start-time of seminars from seminar announcements, or extracting persons moving in and out of corporate positions in a news article. Single-slot IE means that at most one template (or database record) is found in each document. Multi-slot IE means that zero or more templates can be found in one document. Recent research on machine learning IE focused mainly on single-slot, semi-structured domains (Califf 1998; Freitag and McCallum 1999; Ciravegna 2001). Work on IE on free text was mostly based on pattern-learning approaches (Soderland 1999; Yangarber et al. 2000). Both Soderland and Yangarber et al. have worked on the domain of Management Succession, where IE was rendered more difficult not only by the style of writing used in news articles, but also because one document might contain information on several distinct events (multi-slot IE).

Taira and Soderland (Soderland 2001; Taira and Soderland 2000) have also developed another system to do IE in the domain of medical reports. This system aims to extract templates from whole reports instead of individual sentences. They reported excellent results in the domain of thoracic radiology reports, but stated that human intervention is required before a rule is finally accepted during learning. McCallum, Freitag and Pereira (2000) used Maximum Entropy Markov Models for extracting question-answer pairs in lists of Frequently Asked Questions (FAQs). Although they made use of the maximum entropy framework, their method is still based on Markov Models. We show how IE can be addressed as a classification problem.

In this paper, we present our work on a single-slot, semi-structured domain (Seminar Announcements) as well as a multi-slot, free text domain (Management Succession). Both IE systems presented in this paper are built on maximum entropy classifiers. We have used the Java-based opennlp maximum entropy package[1].

Maximum Entropy Classifier

The maximum entropy framework estimates probabilities based on the principle of making as few assumptions as possible, other than the constraints imposed. Such constraints are usually derived from training data, expressing some relationship between features and outcome. The probability distribution that satisfies the above property is the one with the highest entropy. It is unique, agrees with the maximum-likelihood distribution, and has the exponential form (Della Pietra, Della Pietra, and Lafferty 1997):

$$p(o|h) = \frac{1}{Z(h)} \prod_{j=1}^{k} \alpha_j^{f_j(h,o)},$$

where o refers to the outcome and h the history (or context). $Z(h)$ is a normalization function. Each feature function $f_j(h,o)$ is a binary function. For example, in predicting if a word belongs to a word class, o is either true or false, and h refers to the surrounding context:

$$f_j(h,o) = \begin{cases} 1 & \textit{if } o = true \textit{ and previous word} = the \\ 0 & \textit{otherwise} \end{cases}$$

---

1 http://maxent.sourceforge.net

The parameters α_j are estimated by a procedure called Generalized Iterative Scaling (GIS) (Darroch and Ratcliff 1972). This is an iterative method that improves the estimation of the parameters at each iteration. We have run all our experiments with 300 iterations.

Due to sparse data, certain contexts are not seen with all outcomes. For example, in the seminar announcements domain, the context of "*previous word = at*" might never have been seen with the outcome *speaker*. Smoothing is implemented by simply adding a training instance for each context with each outcome.

The ability of the maximum entropy framework to take into account features that are not independent makes it suitable for the two tasks we are working on.

Seminar Announcements

For the single-slot task, we have chosen to work in the domain of seminar announcements. Previous work in this domain includes (Ciravegna 2001; Freitag and Kushmerick 2000; Freitag and McCallum 1999). Our approach is similar to that of (Borthwick 1999), where the task attempted was that of identifying named entities, such as person names. The features we used are however different from those used by Borthwick. From each seminar announcement, 4 slots are to be extracted: *speaker, start time, end time,* and *location*. We further divide each slot into 4 sub-classes, e.g. s*peaker-begin, speaker-continue, speaker-end,* and *speaker-unique*. A word that does not fill any slot belongs to another class called *not-a-slot*. During training, each word is used to generate one training example, and during testing, the trained classifier will classify each word into one of the 17 classes.

Features for Seminar Announcement

We define below several groups of features. For each group, a training or test instance would typically have one feature set to 1, and the rest of the features in that group will be set to 0. The groups are:

(i) Unigrams. The string of each word w is used as a feature. So is that of the previous word w_{-1} and the next word w_{+1}. Each example has three features w, w_{-1} and w_{+1} set to 1 for this group.

(ii) Bigrams. The pair of word strings (w_{-2}, w_{-1}) of the previous two words is used as a feature. So is that of the next two words (w_{+1}, w_{+2}).

(iii) Zone and InitCaps. Some announcements contain sentence tags. The system will process each document sentence by sentence. Texts within the pair of tags *<sentence>* and *</sentence>* are taken to be one sentence. Texts that are outside of sentence tags are processed as one continuous sentence. Words within sentence tags are taken to be in *TXT* zone. Words outside such tags are taken to be in a *FRAG* zone. This group of features consists of 2 features *(InitCaps, TXT)* and *(InitCaps, FRAG)*. For words starting with a capital letter *(InitCaps)*, one of the 2

Who: Dr. Koji Ikuta
        Center for Robotics in Microelectronics
        University of California, Santa Barbara
Topic: Shape Memory Alloy Servo Actuator

Figure 1: Part of a seminar announcement

features *(InitCaps, TXT)* or *(InitCaps, FRAG)* will be set to 1, depending on the zone the word appears in. If a word does not start with a capital letter, then both features are set to 0.

(iv) Zone and InitCaps of w_{-1} and w_{+1}. If the previous word has *InitCaps*, another feature *(InitCaps, TXT)$_{PREV}$* or *(InitCaps, FRAG)$_{PREV}$* will be set to 1. Same for the next word.

(v) Heading. Heading is defined to be the word before the last colon ":". For example, in Figure 1, the heading of the words "*Dr. Koji Ikuta*" and "*Center for Robotics in Microelectronics*" is "*Who*". The system will distinguish between words on the first line of the heading (e.g. *Who-first-line*) from words on other lines (*Who-other-lines)*. There is at most one feature set to 1 for this group.

(vi) First Word. This group contains only one feature *FIRSTWORD*, which is set to 1 if the word is the first word of a sentence.

(vii) Time Expressions. If the word string of w matches the regular expression: *[digit]+:[digit]+*, then this feature will be set to 1.

(viii) Names. We used lists of first names and last names downloaded from the U.S. Census Bureau website[2]. If w has *InitCaps* and is found in the list of first names, the feature *FIRSTNAME* will be set to 1. If w_{-1} (or w_{+1}) has *InitCaps* and is found in the list of first names then *FIRSTNAME$_{PREV}$* (*FIRSTNAME$_{NEXT}$*) will be set to 1. Similarly for *LASTNAME*.

(ix) New Word. If w is not found in /usr/dict/words on Linux, then a feature *NEW* will be set to 1.

Testing

During testing, it is possible that the classifier produces a sequence of inadmissible classes (e.g. *speaker-begin* followed by *location-unique*). To eliminate such sequences, we define the transition probability between word classes $P(c_i|c_j)$ to be equal to 1 if the sequence is admissible, and 0 otherwise. The Viterbi algorithm is then used to select the sequence of word classes with the highest probability. The probability of a sequence s of words is defined as follows:

$$P(c_1, c_2, ..., c_n | s) = \prod_{i=1}^{n} P(c_i | s) * P(c_i | c_{i-1}),$$

where $P(c_i|s)$ is determined by the maximum entropy classifier. It is possible that for certain slots (e.g. *speaker*), more than one instance is found within the same seminar

2 http://www.census.gov/genealogy/names

	SP	LOC	ST	ET	All
ME$_2$	72.6	82.6	99.6	94.2	86.9
(LP)^2	77.6	75.0	99.0	95.5	86.0
SNoW	73.8	75.2	99.6	96.3	85.3
ME$_1$	65.3	82.3	99.6	94.5	85.0
BWI	67.7	76.7	99.6	93.9	83.9
HMM	76.6	78.6	98.5	62.1	81.8
Rapier	53.0	72.7	93.4	96.2	77.3
SRV	56.3	72.3	98.5	77.9	77.0
Whisk	18.3	66.4	92.6	86.0	64.8

Table 1: F-measure on CMU seminar announcements. SP = speaker, LOC = location, ST = start time, and ET = end time. "All" is the weighted average of the 4 slots.

announcement. In that case, only the best instance (with the highest probability) is used.

Experimental Results

The data consists of 485 seminar announcements[3] (895 KB, 102K words). We did a 5-fold experiment. In each trial, we partition the data into two halves, using one half for training and the other half for testing. Our results in Table 1 are the average of these 5 trials. Other than our own and SNoW's (Roth and Yih 2001) results, accuracy on the 4 slots of all other systems are taken from (Ciravegna 2001).

We used the MUC7-scorer to score each slot. The all-slots score is the weighted average of the four slots, where each slot is weighted by the total number of possible slots in the whole data set (485 seminar announcements have *start times*, 464 have *locations*, 409 have *speakers*, and 228 have *end times*). We compare our two systems ME$_1$ and ME$_2$ with other published systems. ME$_1$ uses only feature groups (i) to (vii) (i.e. no external knowledge). ME$_2$ uses all the 9 feature groups. Comparing the all-slots scores, ME$_2$ outperforms (LP)^2 (Ciravegna 2001), SNoW (Roth and Yih 2001), BWI (Freitag and Kushmerick 2000), HMM (Freitag and McCallum 1999), Rapier (Califf 1998), SRV (Freitag 1998), and Whisk (Soderland 1999).

Both (LP)^2 and SNoW use shallow natural language processing: (LP)^2 uses a morphological analyzer, a part-of-speech tagger, and a user defined dictionary (e.g. *pm* is of semantic category *timeid*). SNoW also uses part-of-speech tagging. Without any external knowledge, ME$_1$ outperforms all systems other than (LP)^2 and SNoW. ME$_2$ used only three lists: first names, last names, and a lexicon list. BWI reported an improvement from 67.7 to 73.5 for the speaker slot when the same three lists are used. However, they did not report results of all 4 slots in this experimental setting.

We have shown that a classification-based approach like maximum entropy is able to achieve state-of-the-art accuracy when provided with informative features.

---

3 Downloaded from http://www.isi.edu/~muslea/RISE/index.html

Management Succession

In this paper, we do not attempt the full MUC-6 Scenario Template task. We present a system that attempts IE on a sentence-by-sentence basis, extracting templates of 4 slots. The 4 slots are person-in (person moving into a corporate position), person-out (person leaving a corporate position), the corporate position, and the corporate name. This task has been defined by Soderland (1999). We show that by using a series of classifiers, our system outperforms WHISK (Soderland 1999). Collins and Miller (1998) also worked on this domain, and achieved excellent results. However, their method requires the test data to be manually tagged with indicator words, making the task a lot easier (sentences with two events are tagged with two indicator words).

In this domain, multi-slot IE is required. A sentence might contain zero, one, or more templates. The approach used for single-slot IE can only give us the possible candidates that can fill each slot. Another classifier is required to decide which candidates should fill the same template, and which should fill a different template.

One can build up a list of candidates for each slot by using our approach for single-slot extraction. In this case, all candidates should fill some template. Another way is to use all entities of a certain semantic class as candidates for a particular slot. For example, all persons can be candidates for the slot of person-in and person-out in the management succession task. Using this approach, some candidates will have to be rejected and not go into any template. The determination of semantic class might require considerable domain knowledge. Riloff and Jones (1996) used an unsupervised approach to build semantic lexicons. Grishman (2001) reiterated the importance of word class discovery in IE. In this paper, we use as input sentences syntactically analyzed by BADGER (Fisher et al. 1995). In these sentences, person, organization, and position names are tagged. In each sentence, we use as candidates for corporate positions all position names tagged and candidates for corporate names all the organization names tagged. For person-in and person-out, we built two separate classifiers to produce the list of candidates for the two slots. A relation classifier is then built to classify binary relationship between each pair of candidates. In a sentence in which a total of n candidates have been found, there are $n(n-1)/2$ possible binary relations.

Figure 2 shows an example output by the relation classifier. The whole process is shown in Figure 3. This approach is new and different from other published methods on this task.

Overview of the System

The multi-slot IE system is made up of four components:

(i) Text-Filtering. During testing, a text categorization module is first used to eliminate documents that do not contain any relevant templates. For this module, we used

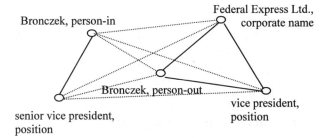

Figure 2: Result of relation classification for the sentence *"Bronczek, vice president of Federal Express Ltd., was named senior vice president, Europe, Africa and Mediterranean, at this air-express concern."* A solid line means that the relation is classified as positive, and a dashed line means it is classified as negative. The difficulty in extracting two templates from this sentence is evident. The relation classifier got this one right.

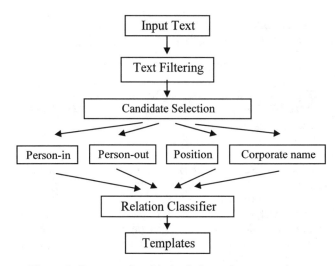

Figure 3: Process of multi-slot information extraction

svmlight (Joachims 1998), and trained it with documents containing relevant templates as positive examples and those that do not as negative examples. Each document is represented by a feature vector, which is the normalized vector of term frequencies of selected terms. The terms are selected using the correlation metric (Ng, Goh, and Low 1997):

$$C = \frac{(N_{r+}N_{n-} - N_{r-}N_{n+})\sqrt{N}}{\sqrt{(N_{r+} + N_{r-})(N_{n+} + N_{n-})(N_{r+} + N_{n+})(N_{r-} + N_{n-})}}$$

where N_{r+} (N_{n+}) is the number of relevant (non-relevant) training documents in which a term occurs, N_{r-} (N_{n-}) is the number of relevant (non-relevant) training documents in which a term does not occur, and N is the total number of documents. The top 1000 terms (with highest C), and the bottom 1000 terms (with lowest C) are used as features.

For the 100 test documents, 50 of them contain relevant templates. This module found 60 test documents to be relevant, out of which 49 are really relevant: false negative of 1 document and false positive of 11 documents.

(ii) Candidate Selection. For corporate positions and corporate names, all positions and organizations tagged in the BADGER output are used as candidates. The selection process can be considered to be the tagging of all position and organization names. For person-in and person-out, as there are usually more clues within a sentence indicating a person as in or out, we have built a classifier for each slot. Each classifier is trained using sentences from relevant documents only (out of the 498 training documents, 298 are relevant). During testing, sentences belonging to the 60 documents found to be positive in the text-filtering module will be processed, and each person appearing in these sentences can be classified as person-in, person-out, both, or neither.

(iii) Relation Classification. The relation classifier finds pair-wise relations between entities, for example *(Bronczek, person-in)* and *(senior vice president, position)*.

It is possible to have position-position where a person either moves into or leaves two different posts at once. As a result, we have allowed all $4^2=16$ relations.

(iv) Template Building. Only templates that contain at least a person-in or a person-out will be considered as valid templates to be output. Given a graph of relations between entities in a sentence (see Figure 2), an edge exists between two entities if and only if their relation is classified as positive. The system will first try to find the largest clique (complete subgraph). Among cliques of the same size, it will choose the one with the highest product of the probabilities of relations. The use of product implicitly assumes that the relations within the same template are independent, which is untrue. However, this is just used as a means of selecting between templates of the same size, and serves well for this purpose.

Once a template is formed, the entities that form that template will be removed from the graph, and the system will start anew with the new graph of remaining entities. From this new graph, if there are still persons left, then a second (and possibly a third, fourth, and so on) template can be formed. In Figure 2, two templates will be formed, one from each clique.

Features for Person-in and Person-out Classifier

These features are derived from the BADGER output format (see Figure 4). A BADGER sentence is divided into phrases, of the following 10 types: *SUBJ, VB, OBJ, PP, REL_S, REL_V, REL_O, REL_P, ADVP,* and *SAID.* Verbs are tagged with their lemma. Verbs in the *VB* phrase in the passive voice are also tagged. The feature groups are:

(i) Candidate Phrase Type and VB Phrase. Candidate phrase type refers to the type of the phrase in which the candidate is found. For the example in Figure 4, *"Alan G. Spoon"* is found in the *SUBJ* phrase. For the candidate *"Alan G. Spoon"*, the feature *(SUBJ, WILL_SUCCEED)* will be set to 1.

```
{SUBJ @PN[ ALAN G. SPOON ]PN }
{VB    WILL SUCCEED @SUCCEED }
{OBJ   MR. @PN[ GRAHAM ]PN }
{PP    AS @PS[ PRESIDENT OF THE COMPANY ]PS . }
```

Figure 4: Example of BADGER output of sentence: *"Alan G. Spoon will succeed Mr. Graham as president of the company."*

(ii) Nearest Seed Word in Sentence.

We automatically determined a list of seed words from the training data. These are words with the highest correlation metric C as defined in the last section. The seed words found are *President, Officer, Succeed, Nam (lemma of name), Vice, Chief, Executive,* and *Chairman*. Intuitively, the presence of these seed words in a sentence will improve the chance of a person name in the sentence to fill a person-in or person-out slot. In Figure 4, *"Alan G. Spoon"* will have the feature *seed_SUCCEED* set to 1.

(iii) Agent Verbs.

Verbs for which the candidate is an agent. These verbs are determined by a few rules listed in Table 2. For example, if a candidate is in the *SUBJ* phrase, all verbs of the active voice found in phrases of type *VB, REL_S,* and *REL_V* will be taken to be agent verbs. Each of these verbs will have a feature set to 1. In Figure 4, *"Alan G. Spoon"* will have only one agent verb feature set to 1: *agent_SUCCEED*.

(iv) Patient Verbs.

Verbs for which the candidate is a patient. The rules are analogous to those of Table 2. In Figure 4, *"Alan G. Spoon"* has no patient verbs, and *"Graham"* has one patient verb feature *patient_SUCCEED*.

For the example in Figure 4, *"Alan G. Spoon"* will have the following 3 features set to 1: *(SUBJ, WILL_SUCCEED), seed_SUCCEED,* and *agent_SUCCEED*. *"Graham"* will have the following 3 features set to 1: *(OBJ, WILL_SUCCEED), seed_PRESIDENT,* and *patient_SUCCEED*.

Features for Relation Classifier

The input to the relation classifier is a pair of entities *{(name1, class1), (name2, class2)}*, for example, *{(Spoon, person-in), (Graham, person-out)}*. One classifier is used to classify all such input pairs into true or false. All features used by the relation classifier are characterized by the class combination *(class1, class2)*, e.g. *(person-in, person-out)*.

The following feature groups are used:

(i) Same Phrase.

If *name1* and *name2* are identical, the feature *(class1, class2, same-phrase)* is set to 1. In this case, all other features used in the relation classifier will be set to 0. The same phrase will never fill two different slots in the same template. There are altogether $4^2=16$ features in this group, one for each class combination.

(ii) Words between *Name1* and *Name2*.

This is the feature *(class1, class2, STRING)*, where *STRING* is the exact string between *name1* and *name2*.

Candidate	Voice	Agent Verb Phrase
SUBJ	Active	*VB, REL_S, REL_V*
OBJ	Active	*REL_O*
	Passive	*VB, REL_V*
PP	Active	*REL_P*
REL_O *REL_S*	Active	Verbs after the candidate in the same phrase

Table 2: Rules for the determination of agent verbs.

System	Recall	Precision	F-measure
Soderland	46.4	68.9	55.5
Our results	49.1	74.6	59.2

Table 3: Comparison of recall, precision, and F-measure

(iii) Phrase Types.

This is the feature *(class1, class2, phrase_type1, phrase_type2)*, where *phrase_type1* and *phrase_type2* are the phrase types of the two entities.

(iv) Other Entities.

These features indicate whether there exist a person (including pronouns), position, or organization between *name1* and *name2*. If there are no person or pronoun between name1 and name2, then a feature *(class1, class2, NO_PERSON_BETWEEN)* is set to 1. Similarly for corporate names and positions.

For the input pair of entities *{(Spoon, person-in), (Graham, person-out)}*, the following 5 features are set to 1: *(person-in, person-out, WILL_SUCCEED_MR)*
(person-in, person-out, SUBJ, OBJ)
(person-in, person-out, NO_PERSON_BETWEEN)
(person-in, person-out, NO_ORG_BETWEEN)
(person-in, person-out, NO_POST_BETWEEN)

Experimental Results

We used the same training and test data, and the same scoring criteria as Soderland (1999). In order for an output template to be considered correct, all the slots of the template must match a key template in the manually annotated templates. If the output template contains an extra slot, all slots of the output template are considered as false positives. The data provided by Soderland contains 6,915 training instances and the test data are sentences extracted from 100 test documents, comprising 2,840[4] instances, with a total of 169 templates, 84 person-ins, 100 person-outs, 148 positions, and 92 organizations. In Table 3, "Soderland" refers to his best results in terms of F-measure, obtained by using all 6,900 instances for training. Our system achieves higher accuracy than Soderland's.

Conclusion

Most previous work on machine learning approaches to information extraction focused on single-slot IE for semi-structured text. Relatively less research was done on multi-

---

4 Soderland stated that he used 2,839 instances. This difference is due to a formatting error in the test data for the instance 9301060123-29.

slot IE. Past work on multi-slot IE for free text mainly used pattern-learning approaches. In this paper, we have tackled the problem using a classification approach instead, incorporating two separate steps: candidate selection and template building (by a relation classifier). On two benchmark data sets, our system achieves higher accuracy than the best previously published results on IE from semi-structured as well as free text. In order to do a statistical significance test, we need to know the detailed test results of previous systems. Since these are not available, we are unable to conduct such a significance test.

In recent years, the emphasis on IE has shifted to adaptive IE. We feel that a classification approach allows systems to adapt to a new domain simply by using a standard set of features. Besides, there are many machine learning classifier algorithms available (such as support vector machines, decision trees, and neural networks). This should offer an attractive alternative to pattern-learning methods.

Acknowledgements

Many thanks to Stephen Soderland for sharing with us his training and test data for the Management Succession task.

References

Borthwick, A. 1999. A Maximum Entropy Approach to Named Entropy Recognition. Ph.D. dissertation. Computer Science Department. New York University.

Califf, M. E. 1998. Relational Learning Techniques for Natural Language Information Extraction. Ph.D. dissertation, University of Texas at Austin.

Ciravegna, F. 2001. Adaptive Information Extraction from Text by Rule Induction and Generalisation. In *Proceedings of the Seventeenth International Joint Conference on Artificial Intelligence (IJCAI)*, 1251-1256.

Collins, M. and Miller, S. 1998. Semantic Tagging using a Probabilistic Context Free Grammar. In *Proceedings of the Sixth Workshop on Very Large Corpora*, 38-48.

Darroch, J. N. and Ratcliff, D. 1972. Generalized Iterative Scaling for Log-Linear Models. *The Annals of Mathematical Statistics, 43(5)*: 1470-1480.

Della Pietra, S., Della Pietra, V., and Lafferty J. 1997. Inducing Features of Random Fields. *IEEE Transactions on Pattern Analysis and Machine Intelligence 19(4)*, 380-393.

Fisher, D., Soderland, S., McCarthy, J., Feng, F., and Lehnert, W. 1995. Description of the UMass System as used for MUC-6. In *Proceedings of the Sixth Message Understanding Conference*, 221-236.

Freitag, D. 1998. Information Extraction from HTML: Application of a General Machine Learning Approach. In *Proceedings of the Fifteenth National Conference on Artificial Intelligence*, 517-523.

Freitag, D. and Kushmerick, N. 2000. Boosted Wrapper Induction. In *Proceedings of the Seventeenth National Conference on Artificial Intelligence (AAAI)*, 577-583.

Freitag, D. and McCallum, A. 1999. Information Extraction with HMM and Shrinkage. In *Proceedings of the Fifteenth National Conference on Artificial Intelligence (AAAI)*, 31-36.

Grishman, R. 2001. Adaptive Information Extraction and Sublanguage Analysis. In *Proceedings of IJCAI Workshop on Adaptive Text Extraction and Mining*, 77-79.

Joachims, T. 1998. Text Categorization with Support Vector Machines: Learning with Many Relevant Features. In *Proceedings of the Tenth European Conference on Machine Learning*, 137-142.

McCallum, A., Freitag, D., and Pereira, F. 2000. Maximum Entropy Markov Models for Information Extraction and Segmentation. In *Proceedings of the Seventeenth International Conference on Machine Learning*, 591-598.

Ng, H. T., Goh, W. B., and Low, K. L. 1997. Feature Selection, Perceptron Learning, and a Usability Case Study for Text Categorization. In *Proceedings of the 20th Annual International ACM SIGIR Conference on Research and Development in Information Retrieval (SIGIR)*, 67-73.

Riloff, E. and Jones, R. 1996. Learning Dictionaries for Information Extraction by Multi-level Bootstrapping. In *Proceedings of the Sixteenth National Conference on Artificial Intelligence (AAAI)*, 1044-1049.

Roth, D. and Yih, W. T. 2001. Relational Learning via Propositional Algorithms: An Information Extraction Case Study. In *Proceedings of the Seventeenth International Joint Conference on Artificial Intelligence (IJCAI)*, 1257-1263.

Soderland, S. 1999. Learning Information Extraction Rules for Semi-Structured and Free Text. *Machine Learning* 34:233-272.

Soderland, S. 2001. Building a Machine Learning Based Text Understanding System. In *Proceedings of IJCAI Workshop on Adaptive Text Extraction and Mining*, 64-70.

Taira, R. K. and Soderland, S. 2000. A Statistical Natural Language Processor for Medical Reports. In *Proceedings of the International Conference on Mathematics and Engineering Techniques in Medicine and Biological Sciences*.

Yangarber, R., Grishman, R., Tapanainen, P., and Huttunen, S. 2000. Unsupervised Discovery of Scenario-Level Patterns for Information Extraction. In *Proceedings of the Sixth Applied Natural Language Processing Conference*. 282-289.

Reviewing the Design of DAML+OIL:
An Ontology Language for the Semantic Web

Ian Horrocks
University of Manchester
Manchester, UK
horrocks@cs.man.ac.uk

Peter F. Patel-Schneider
Bell Labs Research
Murray Hill, NJ, U.S.A.
pfps@research.bell-labs.com

Frank van Harmelen
Vrije Universiteit
Amsterdam, the Netherlands
Frank.van.Harmelen@cs.vu.nl

Abstract

In the current "Syntactic Web", uninterpreted syntactic constructs are given meaning only by private off-line agreements that are inaccessible to computers. In the Semantic Web vision, this is replaced by a web where both data and its semantic definition are accessible and manipulable by computer software. DAML+OIL is an ontology language specifically designed for this use in the Web; it exploits existing Web standards (XML and RDF), adding the familiar ontological primitives of object oriented and frame based systems, and the formal rigor of a very expressive description logic. The definition of DAML+OIL is now over a year old, and the language has been in fairly widespread use. In this paper, we review DAML+OIL's relation with its key ingredients (XML, RDF, OIL, DAML-ONT, Description Logics), we discuss the design decisions and trade-offs that were the basis for the language definition, and identify a number of implementation challenges posed by the current language. These issues are important for designers of other representation languages for the Semantic Web, be they competitors or successors of DAML+OIL, such as the language currently under definition by W3C.

Introduction

In the short span of its existence, the World Wide Web has resulted in a revolution in the way information is transferred between computer applications. It is no longer necessary for humans to set up channels for inter-application information transfer; this is handled by TCP/IP and related protocols. It is also no longer necessary for humans to define the syntax and build parsers used for each kind of information transfer; this is handled by HTML, XML and related standards. However, it is still not possible for applications to interoperate with other applications without some pre-existing, human-created, and outside-of-the-web agreements as to the meaning of the information being transferred.

The next generation of the Web aims to alleviate this problem—making Web resources more readily accessible to automated processes by adding information that describes Web content in a machine-accessible and manipulable fashion. This coincides with the vision that Tim Berners-Lee calls the Semantic Web in his recent book "Weaving the Web" (Berners-Lee 1999).

If such information (often called *meta-data*) is to make resources more accessible to automated agents, it is essential that its meaning can be understood by such agents. Ontologies will play a pivotal role here by providing a source of shared and precisely defined terms that can be used in such meta-data. An ontology typically consists of a hierarchical description of important concepts in a domain, along with descriptions of the properties of each concept. The degree of formality employed in capturing these descriptions can be quite variable, ranging from natural language to logical formalisms, but increased formality and regularity clearly facilitates machine understanding.

Ontologies can be profitably used, e.g., in e-commerce sites (McGuinness 1998), where they can facilitate machine-based communication between buyer and seller, enable vertical integration of markets, and allow descriptions to be reused in different marketplaces; in search engines, where they can help searching to go beyond the current keyword-based approach, and allow pages to be found that contain syntactically different, but semantically similar words/phrases; in Web services (McIlraith, Son, & Zeng 2001), where they can provide semantically richer service descriptions that can be more flexibly interpreted by intelligent agents.

DAML+OIL: An Ontology Language for the Semantic Web

The recognition of the key role that ontologies are likely to play in the future of the Web has led to the extension of Web markup languages in order to facilitate content description and the development of Web based ontologies, e.g., XML Schema[1], RDF[2] (Resource Description Framework), and RDF Schema. (See (Decker *et al.* 2000) for the role of each of these on the Semantic Web). RDF Schema (RDFS) in particular is recognisable as an ontology language: it talks about classes and properties, range and domain constraints, and subclass and subproperty relations.

RDFS is, however, a very limited language and more expressive power is clearly both necessary and desirable in order to describe data in sufficient detail. Moreover, such descriptions should be amenable to *automated reasoning* if

---

[1] http://www.w3.org/XML/Schema/
[2] http://www.w3c.org/RDF/

they are to be used effectively by automated processes, e.g., to determine the semantic relationships between syntactically different terms.

DAML+OIL is the result of merging DAML-ONT (an early result of the DARPA Agent Markup Language (DAML) programme[3]) and OIL (the Ontology Inference Layer) (Fensel *et al.* 2001), developed by a group of (largely European) researchers, several of whom were members of the European-funded On-To-Knowledge consortium.[4]

Until recently, the development of DAML+OIL has been undertaken by a committee largely made up of members of the two language design teams (and rather grandly titled the Joint EU/US Committee on Agent Markup Languages).[5] More recently, DAML+OIL has been submitted to W3C as a proposal for the basis of the W3C Web Ontology language.[6]

As it is an ontology language, DAML+OIL is designed to describe the *structure* of a domain. DAML+OIL takes an object oriented approach, with the structure of the domain being described in terms of *classes* and *properties*. An ontology consists of a set of *axioms* that assert characteristics of these classes and properties. Asserting that resources are instances of DAML+OIL classes or that resources are related by properties is left to RDF, a task for which it is well suited.

Since the definition of DAML+OIL is available elsewhere,[7] we will not repeat it here. Instead, in the following sections, we will review a number of fundamental design choices that were made for DAML+OIL: foundations in Description Logic, XML datatypes, layering on top of RDFS, comparison with its predecessor OIL, and the role of inference for a Semantic Web ontology language.

Foundations in Description Logic

DAML+OIL is, in essence, equivalent to a very expressive Description Logic (DL), with a DAML+OIL ontology corresponding to a DL terminology. As in a DL, DAML+OIL classes can be names (URI's in the case of DAML+OIL) or *expressions*, and a variety of *constructors* are provided for building class expressions. The expressive power of the language is determined by the class (and property) constructors provided, and by the kinds of axioms allowed.

Figure 1 summarises the constructors in DAML+OIL. The standard DL syntax is used in this paper for compactness as the RDF syntax is rather verbose. In the RDF syntax, for example, Human $\sqcap$ Male would be written as

```
<daml:Class>
  <daml:intersectionOf
      rdf:parseType="daml:collection">
    <daml:Class rdf:about="#Human"/>
    <daml:Class rdf:about="#Male"/>
  </daml:intersectionOf>
</daml:Class>
```

[3] http://www.daml.org/

[4] http://www.ontoknowledge.org/oil

[5] http://www.daml.org/committee

[6] http://www.w3.org/Submission/2001/12/

[7] http://www.daml.org/2001/03/daml+oil-index.html

Constructor	DL Syntax	Example
intersectionOf	$C_1 \sqcap \ldots \sqcap C_n$	Human $\sqcap$ Male
unionOf	$C_1 \sqcup \ldots \sqcup C_n$	Doctor $\sqcup$ Lawyer
complementOf	$\neg C$	$\neg$Male
oneOf	$\{x_1 \ldots x_n\}$	$\{$john, mary$\}$
toClass	$\forall P.C$	$\forall$hasChild.Doctor
hasClass	$\exists P.C$	$\exists$hasChild.Lawyer
hasValue	$\exists P.\{x\}$	$\exists$citizenOf.$\{$USA$\}$
minCardinalityQ	$\geqslant n\, P.C$	$\geqslant 2$ hasChild.Lawyer
maxCardinalityQ	$\leqslant n\, P.C$	$\leqslant 1$ hasChild.Male
cardinalityQ	$= n\, P.C$	$= 1$ hasParent.Female

Figure 1: DAML+OIL class constructors

The meanings of the first three constructors from Figure 1 are just the standard boolean operators on classes. The oneOf constructor allows classes to be defined by enumerating their members.

The toClass and hasClass constructors correspond to slot constraints in a frame-based language. The class $\forall P.C$ is the class all of whose instances are related via the property P only to resources of type C, while the class $\exists P.C$ is the class all of whose instances are related via the property P to at least one resource of type C. The hasValue constructor is just shorthand for a combination of hasClass and oneOf.

The minCardinalityQ, maxCardinalityQ and cardinalityQ constructors (known in DLs as qualified number restrictions) are generalisations of the hasClass and hasValue constructors. The class $\geqslant n\, P.C$ ($\leqslant n\, P.C$, $= n\, P.C$) is the class all of whose instances are related via the property P to at least (at most, exactly) n *different* resources of type C. The emphasis on different is because there is no unique name assumption with respect to resource names (URIs): it is possible that many URIs could name the same resource.

Note that arbitrarily complex nesting of constructors is possible. The formal semantics of the class constructors is given by DAML+OIL's model-theoretic semantics[8] or can be derived from the specification of a suitably expressive DL (e.g., see (Horrocks & Sattler 2001)).

Figure 2 summarises the axioms allowed in DAML+OIL. These axioms make it possible to assert subsumption or equivalence with respect to classes or properties, the disjointness of classes, the equivalence or non-equivalence of individuals (resources), and various properties of properties.

A crucial feature of DAML+OIL is that subClassOf and sameClassAs axioms can be applied to arbitrary class expressions. This provides greatly increased expressive power with respect to standard frame-based languages where such axioms are invariably restricted to the form where the left hand side is a class name, there is only one such axiom per name, and there are no cycles (the class on the right hand side of an axiom cannot refer, either directly or indirectly, to the class name on the left hand side).

A consequence of this expressive power is that all of the class and individual axioms, as well as the uniqueProperty

[8] http://www.w3.org/TR/daml+oil-model

Axiom	DL Syntax	Example
subClassOf	$C_1 \sqsubseteq C_2$	Human $\sqsubseteq$ Animal $\sqcap$ Biped
sameClassAs	$C_1 \equiv C_2$	Man $\equiv$ Human $\sqcap$ Male
subPropertyOf	$P_1 \sqsubseteq P_2$	hasDaughter $\sqsubseteq$ hasChild
samePropertyAs	$P_1 \equiv P_2$	cost $\equiv$ price
disjointWith	$C_1 \sqsubseteq \neg C_2$	Male $\sqsubseteq \neg$Female
sameIndividualAs	$\{x_1\} \equiv \{x_2\}$	$\{$President_Bush$\} \equiv \{$G_W_Bush$\}$
differentIndividualFrom	$\{x_1\} \sqsubseteq \neg\{x_2\}$	$\{$john$\} \sqsubseteq \neg\{$peter$\}$
inverseOf	$P_1 \equiv P_2^-$	hasChild $\equiv$ hasParent$^-$
transitiveProperty	$P^+ \sqsubseteq P$	ancestor$^+$ $\sqsubseteq$ ancestor
uniqueProperty	$\top \sqsubseteq \,\leqslant 1\, P$	$\top \sqsubseteq \,\leqslant 1\,$hasMother
unambiguousProperty	$\top \sqsubseteq \,\leqslant 1\, P^-$	$\top \sqsubseteq \,\leqslant 1\,$isMotherOf$^-$

Figure 2: DAML+OIL axioms

and unambiguousProperty axioms, can be reduced to subClassOf and sameClassAs axioms (as can be seen from the DL syntax).

As we have seen, DAML+OIL also allows properties of properties to be asserted. It is possible to assert that a property is unique (i.e., functional) and unambiguous (i.e., its inverse is functional). It is also possible to use inverse properties and to assert that a property is transitive.

XML Datatypes in DAML+OIL

DAML+OIL supports the full range of datatypes in XML Schema: the so called primitive datatypes such as string, decimal or float, as well as more complex derived datatypes such as integer sub-ranges. This is facilitated by maintaining a clean separation between instances of "object" classes (defined using the ontology language) and instances of datatypes (defined using the XML Schema type system). In particular, the domain of interpretation of object classes is disjoint from the domain of interpretation of datatypes, so that an instance of an object class (e.g., the individual "Italy") can never have the same denotation as a value of a datatype (e.g., the integer 5), and that the set of object properties (which map individuals to individuals) is disjoint from the set of datatype properties (which map individuals to datatype values).

The disjointness of object and datatype domains was motivated by both philosophical and pragmatic considerations:

- Datatypes are considered to be already sufficiently structured by the built-in predicates, and it is, therefore, not appropriate to form new classes of datatype values using the ontology language (Hollunder & Baader 1991).

- The simplicity and compactness of the ontology language are not compromised: even enumerating all the XML Schema datatypes would add greatly to its complexity, while adding a logical theory for each datatype, even if it were possible, would lead to a language of monumental proportions.

- The semantic integrity of the language is not compromised—defining theories for all the XML Schema datatypes would be difficult or impossible without extending the language in directions whose

semantics would be difficult to capture within the existing framework.

- The "implementability" of the language is not compromised—a hybrid reasoner can easily be implemented by combining a reasoner for the "object" language with one capable of deciding satisfiability questions with respect to conjunctions of (possibly negated) datatypes (Horrocks & Sattler 2001).

From a theoretical point of view, this design means that the ontology language can specify constraints on data values, but as data values can never be instances of object classes they cannot apply additional constraints to elements of the object domain. This allows the type system to be extended without having any impact on the ontology language, and vice versa. Similarly, the formal properties of hybrid reasoners are determined by those of the two components; in particular, the combined reasoner will be sound and complete if both components are sound and complete.

From a practical point of view, DAML+OIL implementations can choose to support some or all of the XML Schema datatypes. For supported datatypes, they can either implement their own type checker/validater or rely on some external component. The job of a type checker/validater is simply to take zero or more data values and one or more datatypes, and determine if there exists any data value that is equal to every one of the specified data values and is an instance of every one of the specified data types.

Extending RDF Schema

DAML+OIL is tightly integrated with RDFS: RDFS is used to express DAML+OIL's machine readable specification,[9] and RDFS provides the only serialisation for DAML+OIL. While the dependence on RDFS has some advantages in terms of the re-use of existing RDFS infrastructure and the portability of DAML+OIL ontologies, using RDFS to completely define the structure of DAML+OIL is quite difficult as, unlike XML, RDFS is not designed for the precise specification of syntactic structure. For example, there is no way in RDFS to state that a restriction (slot constraint) should consist of exactly one property (slot) and one class.

---

[9]http://www.daml.org/2001/03/daml+oil.daml

The solution to this problem adopted by DAML+OIL is to define the semantics of the language in such a way that they give a meaning to any (parts of) ontologies that conform to the RDFS specification, including "strange" constructs such as restrictions with multiple properties and classes. The meaning given to strange constructs may, however, include strange "side effects". For example, in the case of a restriction with multiple properties and classes, the semantics interpret this in the same way as a conjunction of all the constraints that would result from taking the cross product of the specified properties and classes, but with the added (and probably unexpected) effect that all these restrictions must have the same interpretation (i.e., are equivalent).

DAML+OIL's dependence on RDFS may also have consequences for the decidability of the language. Decidability is lost when cardinality constraints can be applied to properties that are transitive, or that have transitive sub-properties. (Horrocks, Sattler, & Tobies 1999). There is no way to formally capture this constraint in RDFS, so decidability in DAML+OIL depends on an informal prohibition of cardinality constraints on non-simple properties.

DAML+OIL vs. OIL

From the point of view of language constructs, the differences between OIL and DAML+OIL are relatively trivial. Although there is some difference in "keyword" vocabulary, there is usually a one to one mapping of constructors, and in the cases where the constructors are not completely equivalent, simple translations are possible.

OIL also uses RDFS for its serialisation (although it also provides a separate XML-based syntax). Consequently, OIL's RDFS based syntax would seem to be susceptible to the same difficulties as described above for DAML+OIL. However, in the case of OIL there does not seem to be an assumption that any ontology conforming to the RDFS meta-description should be a valid OIL ontology—presumably ontologies containing unexpected usages of the meta-properties would be rejected by OIL processors as the semantics do not specify how these could be translated into $\mathcal{SHIQ}(\mathbf{D})$. Thus, OIL and DAML+OIL take rather different positions with regard to the layering of languages on the Semantic Web.

Another effect of DAML+OIL's tight integration with RDFS is that the frame structure of OIL's syntax is much less evident: a DAML+OIL ontology is more DL-like in that it consists largely of a relatively unstructured collection of subsumption and equality axioms. This can make it more difficult to use DAML+OIL with frame based tools such as Protégé (Grosso et al. 1999) or OilEd (Bechhofer et al. 2001) because the axioms may be susceptible to many different frame-like groupings. (Bechhofer, Goble, & Horrocks 2001).

The treatment of individuals in OIL is also very different from that in DAML+OIL. In the first place, DAML+OIL relies wholly on RDF for assertions involving the type (class) of an individual or a relationship between a pair of objects. In the second place, DAML+OIL treats individuals occurring in the ontology (in `oneOf` constructs or `hasValue`

restrictions) as true individuals (i.e., interpreted as single elements in the domain of discourse) and not as primitive concepts as is the case in OIL. This weak treatment of the `oneOf` construct is a well known technique for avoiding the reasoning problems that arise with existentially defined classes, and is also used, e.g., in the CLASSIC knowledge representation system (Borgida & Patel-Schneider 1994). Moreover, DAML+OIL makes no unique name assumption: it is possible to explicitly assert that two individuals are the same or different, or to leave their relationship unspecified.

This treatment of individuals is very powerful, and justifies intuitive inferences that would not be valid for OIL, e.g., that persons all of whose countries of residence are Italy are kinds of person that have at most one country of residence:

$$\text{Person} \sqcap \forall \text{residence}.\{\text{Italy}\} \sqsubseteq \leqslant 1\,\text{residence}$$

Inference in DAML+OIL

As we have seen, DAML+OIL is equivalent to a very expressive DL. More precisely, DAML+OIL is equivalent to the $\mathcal{SHIQ}$ DL (Horrocks, Sattler, & Tobies 1999) with the addition of existentially defined classes (i.e., the oneOf constructor) and *datatypes* (often called concrete domains in DLs (Baader & Hanschke 1991)). This equivalence allows DAML+OIL to exploit the considerable existing body of description logic research to define the semantics of the language and to understand its formal properties, in particular the decidability and complexity of key inference problems (Donini et al. 1997); as a source of sound and complete algorithms and optimised implementation techniques for deciding key inference problems (Horrocks, Sattler, & Tobies 1999; Horrocks & Sattler 2001); and to use implemented DL systems in order to provide (partial) reasoning support (Horrocks 1998a; Patel-Schneider 1998; Haarslev & Möller 2001).

A important consideration in the design of DAML+OIL was that key inference problems in the language, in particular class consistency/subsumption, to which most other inference problems can be reduced, should be decidable, as this facilitates the provision of reasoning services. Moreover, the correspondence with DLs facilitates the use of DL algorithms that are known to be amenable to optimised implementation and to behave well in realistic applications in spite of their high worst case complexity (Horrocks 1998b; Haarslev & Möller 2001).

Maintaining the decidability of the language requires certain constraints on its expressive power that may not be acceptable to all applications. However, the designers of the language decided that reasoning would be important if the full power of ontologies was to be realised, and that a powerful but still decidable ontology language would be a good starting point.

Reasoning can be useful at many stages during the design, maintenance and deployment of ontologies.

Reasoning can be used to support ontology design and to improve the quality of the resulting ontology. For example, class consistency and subsumption reasoning can be used to check for logically inconsistent classes and (possibly unexpected) implicit subsumption relationships (Bechhofer et al. 2001). This kind of support has been shown to be particularly important with large ontologies, which are often built and maintained over a long period by multiple authors. Other reasoning tasks, such as "matching" (Baader *et al.* 1999) and/or computing least common subsumers (Baader & Küsters 1998) could also be used to support "bottom up" ontology design, i.e., the identification and description of relevant classes from sets of example instances.

Like information integration (Calvanese *et al.* 1998), ontology integration can also be supported by reasoning. For example, integration can be performed using inter-ontology assertions specifying relationships between classes and properties, with reasoning being used to compute the integrated hierarchy and to highlight any problems/inconsistencies. Unlike some other integration techniques, this method has the advantage of being non-intrusive with respect to the original ontologies.

Reasoning with respect to deployed ontologies will enhance the power of "intelligent agents", allowing them to determine if a set of facts is consistent w.r.t. an ontology, to identify individuals that are implicitly members of a given class etc. A suitable service ontology could, for example, allow an agent seeking secure services to identify a service requiring a userid and password as a possible candidate.

Challenges

Class consistency/subsumption reasoning in DAML+OIL is known to be decidable (as it is contained in the C2 fragment of first order logic (Grädel, Otto, & Rosen 1997)), but many challenges remain for implementors of "practical" reasoning systems, i.e., systems that perform well with the kinds of reasoning problem generated by realistic applications.

Individuals Unfortunately, the combination of DAML+OIL individuals with inverse properties is so powerful that it pushes the worst case complexity of the class consistency problem from EXPTIME (for $\mathcal{SHIQ}$/OIL) to NEXPTIME. No "practical" decision procedure is currently known for this logic, and there is no implemented system that can provide sound and complete reasoning for the whole DAML+OIL language. In the absence of inverse properties, however, a tableaux algorithm has been devised (Horrocks & Sattler 2001), and in the absence of individuals (in extensionally defined classes), DAML+OIL can exploit implemented DL systems via a translation into $\mathcal{SHIQ}$ (extended with datatypes) similar to the one used by OIL. It would, of course, also be possible to translate DAML+OIL ontologies into $\mathcal{SHIQ}$ using OIL's weak treatment of individuals, but in this case reasoning with individuals would not be complete with respect to the semantics of the language. This approach is taken by some existing applications, e.g., OilEd (Bechhofer *et al.* 2001)

Scalability Even without the oneOf constructor, class consistency reasoning is still a hard problem. Moreover, Web ontologies can be expected to grow very large, and with deployed ontologies it may also be desirable to reason w.r.t. a large numbers of class/property instances.

There is good evidence of empirical tractability and scalability for implemented DL systems (Horrocks 1998b; Haarslev & Möller 2001), but this is mostly w.r.t. logics that do not include inverse properties (e.g., $\mathcal{SHF}$ (Horrocks, Sattler, & Tobies 1999)). Adding inverse properties makes practical implementations more problematical as several important optimisation techniques become much less effective. Work is required in order to develop more highly optimised implementations supporting inverse properties, and to demonstrate that they can scale as well as $\mathcal{SHF}$ implementations. It is also unclear if existing techniques will be able to cope with large numbers of class/property instances (Horrocks, Sattler, & Tobies 2000).

Finally, it is an inevitable consequence of the high worst case complexity that some problems will be intractable, even for highly optimised implementations. It is conjectured that such problems rarely arise in practice, but the evidence for this conjecture is drawn from a relatively small number of applications, and it remains to be seen if a much wider range of Web application domains will demonstrate similar characteristics.

New Reasoning Tasks So far we have mainly discussed class consistency/subsumption reasoning, but this may not be the only reasoning problem that is of interest. Other tasks could include querying, explanation, matching, computing least common subsumers, etc. Querying in particular may be important in Semantic Web applications. Some work on query languages for DLs has already been done (Calvanese, De Giacomo, & Lenzerini 1999; Horrocks & Tessaris 2000), and work is underway on the design of a DAML+OIL query language, but the computational properties of such a language, either theoretical or empirical, have yet to be determined.

Explanation may also be an important problem, e.g., to help an ontology designer to rectify problems identified by reasoning support, or to explain to a user why an application behaved in an unexpected manner. As discussed above, reasoning problems such as matching and computing least common subsumers could also be important in ontology design.

Discussion

There are other concerns with respect to the place DAML+OIL has in the Semantic Web. After DAML+OIL was developed, the W3C RDF Core Working Group devised a model theory for RDF and RDFS[10], which is incompatible with the semantics of DAML+OIL, an undesirable state of affairs. Also, in late 2001 W3C initiated the Web Ontology working group[11], a group tasked with developing an ontology language for the Semantic Web. DAML+OIL has been submitted to this working group as a starting point for a W3C recommendation on ontology languages.

A W3C ontology language needs to fit in with other W3C recommendations even more than an independent DAML+OIL would. Work is thus needed to develop a semantic web ontology language, which the Web Ontology

---

[10] http://www.w3.org/TR/rdf-mt/
[11] http://www.w3.org/2001/sw/WebOnt/

working group has tentatively name OWL, that layers better on top of RDF and RDFS.

Unfortunately, the obvious layering (that is, using the same syntax as RDF and extending its semantics, just as RDFS does) is not possible. Such an extension results in semantic paradoxes—variants of the Russell paradox. These paradoxes arise from the status of all classes (including DAML+OIL restrictions) as individuals, which requires that many restrictions be present in all models; from the status of the class membership relationship as a regular property (rdf:type); from the ability to make contradictory statements; and from the ability to create restrictions that refer to themselves. In an RDFS-compliant version of DAML+OIL, a restriction that states that its instances have no rdf:type relationships to itself is not only possible to state, but exists in all models, resulting in an ill-formed logical formalism.

The obvious way around this problem, that of using non-RDF syntax for DAML+OIL restrictions, appears to be meeting with considerable resistance so either further education or some other solution is needed.

Conclusion

We have discussed a number of fundamental design decisions underlying the design of DAML+OIL, in particular its foundation in Description Logic, its use of datatypes from XML Schema, its sometimes problematic layering on top of RDF Schema, and its deviations from its predecessor OIL. We have also described how various aspects of the language are motivated by the desire for tractable reasoning facilities.

Although a number of challenges remain, DAML+OIL has considerable merits. In particular, the basic idea of having a formally-specified web language that can represent ontology information will go a long way towards allowing computer programs to interoperate without pre-existing, outside-of-the-web agreements. If this language also has an effective reasoning mechanism, then computer programs can manipulate this interoperability information themselves, and determine whether a common meaning for the information that they pass back and forth is present.

References

Baader, F., and Hanschke, P. 1991. A schema for integrating concrete domains into concept languages. In *Proc. of IJCAI-91*, 452–457.

Baader, F., and Küsters, R. 1998. Computing the least common subsumer and the most specific concept in the presence of cyclic $\mathcal{ALN}$-concept descriptions. In *Proc. of KI'98*, 129–140. Springer-Verlag.

Baader, F.; Küsters, R.; Borgida, A.; and McGuinness, D. L. 1999. Matching in description logics. *J. of Logic and Computation* 9(3):411–447.

Bechhofer, S.; Horrocks, I.; Goble, C.; and Stevens, R. 2001. OilEd: a reason-able ontology editor for the semantic web. In *Proc. of the Joint German/Austrian Conf. on Artificial Intelligence (KI 2001)*, 396–408. Springer-Verlag.

Bechhofer, S.; Goble, C.; and Horrocks, I. 2001. DAML+OIL is not enough. In *Proc. of the First Semantic Web Working Symposium (SWWS'01)*, 151–159. CEUR Electronic Workshop Proceedings, http://ceur-ws.org/.

Berners-Lee, T. 1999. *Weaving the Web*. San Francisco: Harper.

Borgida, A., and Patel-Schneider, P. F. 1994. A semantics and complete algorithm for subsumption in the CLASSIC description logic. *J. of Artificial Intelligence Research* 1:277–308.

Calvanese, D.; De Giacomo, G.; Lenzerini, M.; Nardi, D.; and Rosati, R. 1998. Information integration: Conceptual modeling and reasoning support. In *Proc. of CoopIS'98*, 280–291.

Calvanese, D.; De Giacomo, G.; and Lenzerini, M. 1999. Answering queries using views in description logics. In *Proc. of DL'99*, 9–13. CEUR Electronic Workshop Proceedings, http://ceur-ws.org/Vol-22/.

Decker, S.; van Harmelen, F.; Broekstra, J.; Erdmann, M.; Fensel, D.; Horrocks, I.; Klein, M.; and Melnik, S. 2000. The semantic web: The roles of XML and RDF. *IEEE Internet Computing* 4(5).

Donini, F. M.; Lenzerini, M.; Nardi, D.; and Nutt, W. 1997. The complexity of concept languages. *Information and Computation* 134:1–58.

Fensel, D.; van Harmelen, F.; Horrocks, I.; McGuinness, D. L.; and Patel-Schneider, P. F. 2001. OIL: An ontology infrastructure for the semantic web. *IEEE Intelligent Systems* 16(2):38–45.

Grädel, E.; Otto, M.; and Rosen, E. 1997. Two-variable logic with counting is decidable. In *Proc. of LICS-97*, 306–317. IEEE Computer Society Press.

Grosso, W. E.; Eriksson, H.; Fergerson, R. W.; Gennari, J. H.; Tu, S. W.; and Musen, M. A. 1999. Knowledge modelling at the millenium (the design and evolution of protégé-2000). In *Proc. of Knowledge acqustion workshop (KAW-99)*.

Haarslev, V., and Möller, R. 2001. High performance reasoning with very large knowledge bases: A practical case study. In *Proc. of IJCAI-01*.

Hollunder, B., and Baader, F. 1991. Qualifying number restrictions in concept languages. In *Proc. of KR-91*, 335–346.

Horrocks, I., and Sattler, U. 2001. Ontology reasoning in the $\mathcal{SHOQ}$(D) description logic. In *Proc. of IJCAI-01*. Morgan Kaufmann.

Horrocks, I., and Tessaris, S. 2000. A conjunctive query language for description logic Aboxes. In *Proc. of AAAI 2000*, 399–404.

Horrocks, I.; Sattler, U.; and Tobies, S. 1999. Practical reasoning for expressive description logics. In Ganzinger, H.; McAllester, D.; and Voronkov, A., eds., *Proc. of LPAR'99*, 161–180. Springer-Verlag.

Horrocks, I.; Sattler, U.; and Tobies, S. 2000. Reasoning with individuals for the description logic $\mathcal{SHIQ}$. In *Proc. of CADE-17*, LNAI, 482–496.

Horrocks, I. 1998a. The FaCT system. In de Swart, H., ed., *Proc. of TABLEAUX-98*, 307–312. Springer-Verlag.

Horrocks, I. 1998b. Using an expressive description logic: FaCT or fiction? In *Proc. of KR-98*, 636–647.

McGuinness, D. L. 1998. Ontological issues for knowledge-enhanced search. In *Proc. of FOIS*, Frontiers in Artificial Intelligence and Applications. IOS-press.

McIlraith, S.; Son, T.; and Zeng, H. 2001. Semantic web services. *IEEE Intelligent Systems* 16(2):46–53.

Patel-Schneider, P. F. 1998. DLP system description. In *Proc. of DL'98*, 87–89. CEUR Electronic Workshop Proceedings, http://ceur-ws.org/Vol-11/.

Stochastic Link and Group Detection

Jeremy Kubica[*]   **Andrew Moore**   **Jeff Schneider**   **Yiming Yang**

School of Computer Science
Carnegie Mellon University
Pittsburgh, PA 15213
{jkubica,awm,schneide,yiming}@cs.cmu.edu

Abstract

Link detection and analysis has long been important in the social sciences and in the government intelligence community. A significant effort is focused on the structural and functional analysis of "known" networks. Similarly, the detection of individual links is important but is usually done with techniques that result in "known" links. More recently the internet and other sources have led to a flood of circumstantial data that provide probabilistic evidence of links. Co-occurrence in news articles and simultaneous travel to the same location are two examples.

We propose a probabilistic model of link generation based on membership in groups. The model considers both observed link evidence and demographic information about the entities. The parameters of the model are learned via a maximum likelihood search. In this paper we describe the model and then show several heuristics that make the search tractable. We test our model and optimization methods on synthetic data sets with a known ground truth and a database of news articles.

Introduction

Link detection and analysis has long been important in the social sciences (Wasserman and Faust 1994) and in the government intelligence community. Recently the internet and other sources have led to both a flood of circumstantial data and and increased interest in new link detection methods.

Consider a database that logs the international flights taken by many travelers. Most of the people on a particular flight are unrelated to each other. However, with a large amount of data we may observe that certain pairs of travelers fly together more often than would be expected by chance. Considering n-tuples (n>2) of travelers can yield even stronger evidence. Extending the idea further, we can hypothesize the existence of groups (or cells) where not all members of the group interact directly but the accumulated evidence of all their observed interactions clearly identifies the group's existence and membership.

Our system takes two types of input data: 1) a database of entities and their demographic information and 2) a database of link data. By searching for maximum likelihood parameters in our model, the system outputs a set of group memberships, which can then be used to answer queries such as:

1. List all the members of group G1.

2. List all the groups for which E1 and E2 are both members.

3. List a set of suspected aliases (entities that are in the same group(s), but never appear in the same link).

After discussing some related work, we describe our model and the methods we use to learn its parameters. We test our system on synthetic data since it allows us to compare with a known ground truth. We also show the output of running it on a large news article database to demonstrate its scalability. Finally we discuss extensions to the model and the additional queries we expect to be able to answer with them.

Related Work

Many of the social sciences use network analysis in their attempts to understand organizational structure and function (Wasserman and Faust 1994). A significant effort is focused on the structural and functional analysis of "known" networks. Similarly, the detection of individual links is important but is usually done with techniques that result in "known" links. Link analysis continues to expand into new domains including criminal intelligence (Sparrow 1991), large databases (Goldberg and Senator 1995), and the internet (Kautz *et al.* 1997). Our main distinction from these approaches is the probabilistic treatment of the data and the queries and the handling of n-ary links.

Recently the fields of computer science and statistics have also seen a significant interest in link and group detection. In (Cohn and Hofmann 2001) Cohn and Hoffman present a model for document and hypertext connectivity, where the document terms play a role similar to our demographic information. Their model explicitly assumes that documents are generated by a mixture of sources. In contrast, we assume that links are generated either randomly or by a mixture of a single group and noise. In (Taskar *et al.* 2001) Taskar et. al. propose a clustering approach based on the relational aspects of the data. Despite the additional power that may be yielded by incorporating the relational structure of the data, it is not immediately clear how to best adapt this

---

[*]Supported by the Fannie and John Hertz Foundation

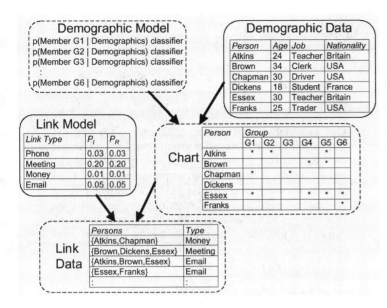

Figure 1: Probabilistic model of group membership and link generation. Dashed borders indicated hidden information and solid borders indicate observed data

problem into a well-defined and powerful relational structure. In (Gibson *et al.* 1998) Gibson et. al. discuss the use of hyperlink information to find "web communities". Their technique makes use of the inherent directionality of hyperlinks to define hubs and authorities. In contrast, we examine links without this directional property and thus do not make use of the concept of hubs and authorities. For example, the concept of a authority does not have a well defined meaning when talking about a list of people seen at lunch together.

While our approach is similar to those above, the main difference is in how we structure the generative model. We assume links a generated as noisy subsets of group members who have definite group membership. To this end, our model is designed to easily and directly capture the group membership nature of the data, including the fact that a person can be a member of many groups.

One approach we have elected to avoid is a mixture model in which each person is assumed to belong to a single hidden group that must be inferred from data. This model (which could be implemented as a simple mixture model) would allow evidence to associate a person probabilistically with any group (caused for example by a political party affiliation, for example). But as the evidence for that group membership increased it would by definition push down the probabilities for competing groups (e.g. a coffee-shop they may frequent). In the limit of infinite data everyone would each be a member of only one group. In contrast, the model presented here will allow simultaneous high confidence membership in many groups.

A Probabilistic Model of Group Membership and Link Generation

The goal of the algorithm is to find groupings of people given demographics and link data. Here, as in many clustering algorithms, the number of groups is given by the user and the groupings are then "discovered" so as to optimize some criteria. To this end, our proposed model is designed to capture a fairly diverse and noisy link generation process. Given this generative model, the algorithm attempts to find the groupings that maximize the probability of having seen the input. Figure 1 shows the model, which takes the form of a Bayesian network.

Our problem is simply stated: Given **evidence** in the form of *observed demographic data* and *observed link data*, find the most likely values of the three remaining data structures in the three remaining network nodes: the demographic model, the link model, and most importantly, the chart.

We will now proceed to describe each component of the network.

- **Demographic Data (DD).** DD contains all the people under consideration and their demographic information. The word "demographic" should not be interpreted too narrowly as it can include any information available about that person. In fact, neither the algorithm nor our software implementation assumes a pre-specification of its fields.

  DD is an observed node.

- **Demographic Model (DM).** DM is a model predicting group membership for each of N_G possible groups. Note that instead of one classifier predicting a N_G-valued output, we have N_G classifiers, the i'th of which predicts the True/False-valued output of whether the person is in Group i. This allows people to be in multiple groups. Our current model is very simple: we assume that group memberships are conditionally independent of each other given demographics. Further, our classifiers are also simple: they are merely naive Bayes classifiers. In later work both of the preceding assumptions may be relaxed if the statistics warrant.

  DM is a hidden node.

- **Chart (CH).** The Chart represents which people are in which groups. The generative model assumes that memberships of people in groups within the chart has been determined by, for each group g and each person p:

  1. Look up p's demographics in DD.
  2. Use DM to predict $P(p \in g \mid p$'s demographics$)$.
  3. Randomly choose whether $p \in g$ according to this probability.

  We can thus easily define $log\,P(CH|DM, DD)$ as:

  $$log\,P(CH|DM, DD) =$$
  $$\sum_p \sum_G \begin{cases} log\,P(p \in G|\text{DM}, p\text{'s dems}) & p \in G \\ log\,(1 - P(p \in G|\text{DM}, p\text{'s dems})) & p \notin G \end{cases}$$

  CH is a hidden node.

- **Link Model (LM).** LM consists of various parameters (introduced when we define Link Data) used to determine the probabilities of various observed links. LM is a hidden node.

- **Link Data (LD).** The second piece of input, the link database (LD), is a set of records specifying n-tuples of entities that are linked by some event. Again, the word "link" should not be interpreted too narrowly as the event may be as circumstantial as their having simultaneously traveled to the same country.

Further, our definition of a link is as an inherently noisy piece of information. We explicitly provide for two different types of noise. Specifically, links are generated assuming that it is possible to have both completely random links (Innocent Link Assumption) and group generated links that contain random non-group members (Innocent Link Member Assumption). We interchangeably use the terms "innocent" and "guilty" to mean "coincidental" and "indicative of a true linkage." These two types of innocence are captured by the probabilities P_I and P_R, which represent the probability of an innocent link and the probability of a innocent (random) link member respectively. Another important aspect of the model is the incorporation of different link types. Each link type is assumed to have a different set of properties, the values P_I and P_R which are recorded in the Link Model (LM). For example, the link that captures people being in the same city can be expected to have significantly higher P_I then a link that captures a monetary transaction.

$P(LD|LM, CH)$ is defined generatively by declaring that a link L between k people from a link type with parameters P_I and P_R is generated as:

- With probability P_I: place k random, unique people into L.
- Else with probability $(1 - P_I)$:
  * Randomly choose a group G from the set of groups that have at least k people.
  * While $|L| < k$
    · With probability P_R add a random person who is not a member of G, $p \notin G$ and $p \notin L$, to L.
    · Else with probability $(1 - P_R)$ add a random member of G, $p \in G$ and $p \notin L$, to L.

We make the simplifying assumption that the priors for each group generating a link are equal. This allows us to calculate $log\, P(LD|LM, CH)$ as:

$$log\, P(LD|LM, CH) = \sum_{LinkType} \sum_{L \in LinkType} log\, P(L|LM, CH) \quad (1)$$

where $P(L|LM, CH)$ is the probability of an individual link given the link model and the chart and, under the above generative assumptions, is:

$$P(L|LM, CH) = \left(\frac{P_I}{\binom{N_P}{|L|}} + \frac{1 - P_I}{N_G} \sum_G P(L|G, LM) \right)$$

$P(L|G, LM)$ is the probability that link L was generated given that group G generated it and is defined as below in (2). Note in the equation below, K_1 is the number of people in the link that are members of group G and K_2 is

the number of people in the link that are not members of G.

$$P(L|G, LM) = \left(\frac{(P_R)^{K_2}(1 - P_R)^{K_1}\binom{K_1 + K_2}{K_1}}{\binom{|G|}{K_1}\binom{N - |G|}{K_2}} \right) \quad (2)$$

One important possible approximation is shown in (3). This allows the concept of a group "owning" a link and can lead to significant computational speedups as discussed below. It makes the assumption that for each link L, there is usually overwhelming evidence of which group generated the link, or else overwhelming evidence that the link was generated randomly. Thus the approximation assumes that just one of the probabilities in 2 dominates all the others.

$$log\, P(L|LM, CH)$$
$$\approx log MAX \left(\frac{P_I}{\binom{N_P}{|L|}}, \frac{1 - P_I}{N_G} MAX_G(P(L|G, LM)) \right) \quad (3)$$

Fitting the hidden nodes

We wish to find

$$\underset{LM, CH, DM}{argmax} \quad P(LM, CH, DM|DD, LD) =$$

$$\underset{LM, CH, DM}{argmax} \quad \frac{P(LM, CH, DM, DD, LD)}{P(DD, LD)} =$$

$$\underset{LM, CH, DM}{argmax} \quad P(LM, CH, DM, DD, LD) =$$

$$\underset{LM, CH, DM}{argmax} \left(\begin{array}{c} P(LD|LM, CH)P(LM) \times \\ P(CH|DM, DD)P(DM)P(DD) \end{array} \right)$$

where the second step is justified by noticing that P(DD,LD) is constant within the argmax. By noting that P(DD) is also constant, and by assuming a uniform prior over LM and DM, we see we need to find

$$\underset{LM, CH, DM}{argmax} \quad P(LD|LM, CH)P(CH|DM, DD) =$$

$$\underset{CH}{argmax} \left(\underset{LM}{max}\, P(LD|LM, CH) \right)\left(\underset{DM}{max}\, P(CH|DM, DD) \right)$$

Thus the outer loop of our search is over charts, and for each new chart we quickly compute the value of LM that maximizes the likelihood of the LD the value of DM that maximizes the likelihood of CH.

At each iteration of optimization, one or more changes are made to the chart. The MLE DM is then calculated directly from the new chart and the DB—this is very fast for a naive Bayes LM. The LM can also be optimized using a simple EM update, although for the experiments described below the LM was held fixed. Finally, $log\, P(LM, CH, DM|DD, LD)$ is calculated. The difference between the two log-likelihoods represents the improvement, or lack there of, in making that change.

In future work we will evaluate the extent to which our current direct optimization approach could be accelerated by an EM algorithm.

Stochastic hill-climbing was used for optimization. In addition, the model described above was designed to be *optimization friendly*. For example, by allowing links generated by group g to probabilistically have some non-g participants, the optimization is able to fill in groups one person at a time and see incremental improvements in likelihood.

The optimization method used was a noisy hill climbing method. Specifically, at each iteration a bit (p, g) in the chart was flipped and the new score $log P(LM, CH, DM | DD, LD)$ was calculated. Moves resulting in improvement were always accepted and all other moves were accepted with some probability P_{worse}. It was found that looking at a number of neighbors before "committing" one, greatly improves performance. Looking at more neighbors per iteration allows the search to more thoroughly explore the immediate neighborhood. At the limit where the search examines all neighbors, the optimization becomes gradient descent.

It is also important to note that when using such an optimization method, the max approximation shown in (3) can lead to significant computational speedups. These speedups result from the fact that for a given (p, g, t) flip $\Delta log P(LD | LM, CH)$ can be approximated by looking at $log P(L | G, LM)$ for only a few groups instead of all of the groups. Specifically, for each link $\Delta log P(L | LM, CH)$ can be approximated as:

$$\Delta log P(L | LM, CH) \approx P(L | G_{MAX}, LM)_{OLD}$$
$$-MAX \left(P(L | G_{MAX}, LM), P(L | g, LM), \frac{P_I}{\binom{N_P}{|L|}} \right)$$

where G_{MAX} was the most probable group to have generated link L before the flip and $P(L | G_{MAX}, LM)_{OLD}$ was its score before the flip. In other words, the change in the probability of a link can be approximated by the three cases: the former G_{MAX} still "owns" the link, group g now "owns" the link, or it is more probable that the link is now "innocent". Thus, approximating $\Delta log P(LD | LM, CH)$ for multiple neighbors can be done in time independent of the number of groups, N_G. This independence can lead to an $O(N_G)$ speedup for examining neighbors. Additional speedups can also be gained by caching G_{MAX} and $P(L | G_{MAX}, LM)_{OLD}$ for each link.

Empirical results

Tubeworld

Initial tests were performed on a simulated world called Tubeworld. Tubeworld, shown in Figure 2, consists of a finite two dimensional world where people occupy randomly generated points. Each group is defined by a parallelogram and consists of all people whose location falls within this parallelogram. Groups can overlap and are assumed to contain at least two members. The small rectangles in Figure 2 represent the people and are color-coded according to the groups to which a person belongs. The real-valued (x,y)-coordinates of the people are hidden from the algorithm. Demographic information consists of breaking the X and Y world coordinates into D discrete blocks, giving a total of D^2 possible demographic labelings. Finally, the N_L links

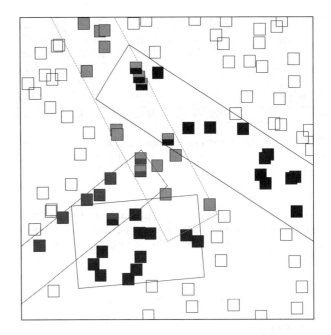

Figure 2: Example tubeworld with 100 people and 4 groups.

are generated based on the groups and according the the generating assumption given above.

Tubeworld Results

The tests consisted of 50 randomly generated tubeworlds, each containing 100 people, 4 groups, and 1000 links. Runs using the Innocent Link Assumption (ILA) and/or Innocent Link Member Assumption (ILMA) used the values $P_I = 0.1$ and $P_R = 0.1$. The charts produced are the result of set number of optimization iterations.

In order to compare the performance of the algorithm using various combinations of the ILA and the ILMA, a 4 by 4 test was used. For each tubeworld the linkbase was generated using each possible combination of ILA and ILMA, namely: ILA + ILMA, ILA, ILMA, none. In addition, for each such linkbase the chart was learned using each possible combination of ILA and ILMA. For each generating/learned pair, error in the learned chart was calculated as the difference in the log-likelihood of the learned chart and the log-likelihood of the generating chart. The average errors are shown in Table 1. The columns represent the different learning methods and the rows represent the different generation methods. Note that larger, less negative, numbers indicate better performance.

In addition, we examined a second performance metric, a paired membership error test. This test looked at all possible pairs of people and all groups. The error between two charts for each pair of people, p_1 and p_2, is defined as the absolute value of the difference between the number groups in each chart that contain both p_1 and p_2. The total error between two charts is the sum of errors for each pair of people. Thus, if two charts are identical this error would be zero, because each pair of people would belong to the same number of groups in both charts. This test has the advantages of

True World:	Model assumes ILA/ILMA	Model assumes ILA	Model assumes ILMA	Model assumes neither
ILA/ILMA	-89.0	-543.7	-159.2	-3134.0
ILA	-84.5	-338.9	-186.1	-3194.6
ILMA	-36.7	-602.9	-101.7	-3271.6
-	-169.6	-336.2	-306.1	-1505.4

Table 1: Log-likelihood error rates for charts learned. The rows and columns represent the probability assumptions for generation and learning respectively.

being simple, computationally cheap, and providing a good measure of the difference between two charts. The average error for each of the 16 probability assumptions are given in Table 2 below.

True World:	Model assumes ILA/ILMA	Model assumes ILA	Model assumes ILMA	Model assumes neither
ILA/ILMA	316.5	2102.3	930.1	7700.0
ILA	132.5	877.2	626.7	4940.1
ILMA	91.4	1576.5	165.6	5836.1
-	34.1	160.3	47.8	813.0

Table 2: Paired person error rates for charts learned. The rows and columns represent the probability assumptions for generation and learning respectively.

While the results of the 16x16 pairwise significance tests are omitted for space considerations, we do examine the significance in the success of the learners using the ILMA/ILA versus other learners. Specifically, we examine the statistical significance of the difference in mean paired person error rates between column 1 and the other columns for a given row. With two exceptions, the differences in the mean paired person errors between the models learned using the ILMA/ILA and all other assumptions were statistically significant, using $\alpha = 0.05$. The two exceptions were that when the True World was "ILMA" or "Neither" then there is no significant difference between the scores for "Learner ILMA" and Learner "ILMA/ILA".

From Table 1 and Table 2 we can see the relative performance of the different learners on linkbases generated by different methods. On average, learners using both the ILMA and ILA performed better than the other learners. This supports the belief that incorporating both forms of innocence allows the model to represent a wider range of underlying generation models while not harming performance on simpler models.

The results reveal that assuming only guilty links but innocent link members leads to superior performance over assuming innocent links and no guilty link members. One reason for this might be the fact that under the ILMA if link sizes are small, random links may still be attributed to a group to which one of the link members belongs. Thus, although the link is innocent, the ILMA can account for it as a guilty link with a few innocent members. This may

be important in cases where a search is adding members to a group. Another important trend is the poor performance of the learners that do not assume either type of innocence. Since they do not make either assumption, the link data is assumed to be noiseless. This assumption is inherently flawed when working with real world data.

It is also interesting to note the extent to which the *optimization friendly* assumption of the previous section was important. On average the learners using both the ILMA and ILA outperformed the other learners regardless to how the linkbases were generated. One example of this benefit is as follows. A pair of people might be in a group together, but initially be placed in the wrong group. Assuming they have a large number of links in common, removing one of them may result in a drastic worsening in score. Using the ILMA and the ILA might reduce this problem, because some of these links can temporarily be accounted for by innocent interactions until both people are moved.

Finally, it is interesting to note that performance of all learners on charts generated using ILMA and ILA is worse than on charts generated with other assumptions. This suggests an increased difficulty of these problems arising from the larger amount of noise in the linkbase.

News article experiments

In order to test scalability and performance on real data, we ran our algorithms on a database of news articles. The data is part of a benchmark evaluation collection named Reuters Corpus Volume I and contains over 800,000 news stories from Reuters between August 1996 and August 1997. The corpus has been used by the 2001 Text Retrieval Conference (TREC-10) for the evaluation of document filtering methods. For our tests we selected a subset of approximately 35,000 articles.

Automated extraction of named entities, such as *Person*, *Organization*, *Location*, *Date* and *Time*, has been successfully applied to many information extraction problems since its initial success in the Message Understanding Conferences (MUC) (Borthwick *et al.*). A Hidden Markov Model (HMM) approach by BBN is one of the most successful methods, which obtained a performance of 96% on the F_1 measure (the harmonic average of recall and precision) on English documents in a MUC evaluation(Bikel *et al.* 1997). We applied a pre-trained BBN HMM model to automatically extract person's proper names from the articles.

We then treated each article as a link between all of the people mentioned in the article. We preprocessed the results by excluding all articles that referred to less than two people. Following that, we also eliminated any people that were not referred to by any articles with at least two people in them. The final result was a database of 9000 entities and a set of 9913 (2-ary or higher) links relating them to each other.

Sample results. After some manual experimentation we found 30 to be a good number of groups for this data set. It turned out that most of the 9000 entities were not mentioned frequently enough to merit their inclusion in groups. After about two hours of optimization on a 1 Gigahertz Pentium, some examples of the groups found are:

```
   G2 (john major,dick spring,ernesto
zedillo,zedillo,richard alston,sabah, abdus samad
azad,stella mapenzauswa,finmin,mccurry,viktor
klima,ron woodward, alexander smith,iss price,glenn
somerville,yevgeny primakov,washington, joan
gralla,bernie fraser,stahl,danka,sally,palladium,van
der biest,fausto)
   G22 (clinton,blair,tom brown,ernesto
zedillo,leon,neumann,h.d.  deve gowda, rob davies,karmen
korbun,fran,consob,saharan blend,englander,garcia,
bruce dennis,jonathan lynn,laurence lau,h.  carl mc-
call,fraser, anne vleminckx,delphis,collin co,elaine
hardcastle,alain van der biest, david martin)
```

These groups illustrate some successes and remaining issues. The name Washington appears in group G2, but in fact was misidentified as a person's name by the named entity extraction software. Similarly, ISS price is a technical label used in quoting various financial instruments. A larger problem is the frequent occurence of single name entities. This happens when the writer uses only a first or last name to refer to a person and effectively results in numerous aliases appearing in the database. In some cases the connection is found. For example, Ernesto Zedillo appears with Zedillo in G2. However, the match is not made in G22 and Bill Clinton is also not included in G22 with Clinton.

Despite these difficulties, several interesting patterns appear in the groups. G22 contains the leaders of the US, the UK, and Mexico. It also illustrates an unintended result. Tom Brown and Jonathan Lynn are writers. Many of the groups ended up consisting of a combination of various writers and the subjects they most often wrote about. Writers ended up being linked by writing about common subjects and subjects ended up being linked even when not appearing in the same article, by being written about by the same person.

Detecting aliases. As already mentioned, the intentional or unintentional use of aliases presents a serious problem for link detection algorithms. As a first step toward identifying aliases we consider a specific type: single user, non-co-occurring aliases. These are aliases used by only one individual and have the property that they never appear together in the same link. This type of alias is a poor model for what happens in news articles, but may be a very good model for the use of fake passports for example. Provided the fake passport is not shared with others, you do not expect to see the real and the fake passport to be used for entry to the same country in a short period of time or for them both to be used to board the same commercial flight.

We propose a simple algorithm to detect these types of aliases. We search for pairs of individuals that are placed in the same group, but never appear together in any link. We rank these hypothesized aliases according to the size of the group in which they appear. In general, membership in smaller groups is a stronger indication of a link between two entities.

Ideally, we could test our algorithm by identifying some of the aliases already existing in the news article data and checking if our algorithm can find them. Since the only method we know of doing this is the manual identification

of the aliases we chose an alternative test. We automatically generated aliases for a random set of 450 of the 9000 entities in the database. In each case, we went through the link data referring to each of those 450. For each link, with probability 50%, we substituted the name of the entity with its alias. In this case, we were rarely able to detect the aliases. The problem is that most of the 9000 entities appear in very few links. Taking the small number of links and cutting them in half (by relabeling half of them to be the newly created alias) made it difficult to even get these entities into appropriate groups, much less identify which were aliases for each other. Unfortunately, this is exactly the real problem encountered when doing link detection in the face of aliases.

To simplify the task, we selected only the entities with at least 10 links in the database (there are 273) and made aliases for them. The following table shows the results of the alias detection algorithm:

```
True aliases:              273
Hypothesized aliases: 57849
Group rank  False Negatives  False Pos
    0             272             76
    1             272            190
    2             271            628
    3             269           2579
    4             268           5318
    5             263          12536
    6             263          21251
    7             260          30741
    8             258          44141
    9             256          57832
```

The i'th row specifies the number of false positives and false negatives found when considering the aliases found in only the groups which are smaller than the i'th group (ranked according to size). Using all of the groups we see that out of 273 true aliases, only 17 were found and 57832 false discoveries were made. The high number of false positives is not necessarily bad. Some of the original names in the news articles really are aliases as we observed earlier. Also, the whole purpose of the group model is to identify members of the same group even though there may be no direct link evidence between them. Many of the false positives are just the result of the algorithm doing its job. Finally we observe that a random selection of 57832 pairs would not expect to find any of the 273 aliases by chance. Usually an alias detection algorithm would be used to generate hypothetical aliases that would be checked by other means.

Research Area Groupings from Web Pages

A third source of test data came from the Carnegie Mellon University Robotics' Institute webpages. Specifically, we looked at the groupings of people within the Robotics' Institute based purely on their publicly declared research interests. Each person with an official webpage was treated as an entity. Each link was defined by a single research interest, such as machine learning, and included all people who listed that interest on their official page. Note that in this case no demographic information was used, but one could consider using such information as whether a person is a faculty member or a student.

The algorithm was run with 8 groups. We expected to find groupings that roughly matched project groups and lab groups. The results returned were largely consistent with people's declared interests, but were often noisy combinations of several related lab groups and people with similar interests. This is most likely due to the fact that the Robotics' Institute contains significantly more than 8 lab groups and a significant number of members of the Robotics' Institute did not declare any research interests.

A more illuminating example reverses the above roles of people and research interests. In this case each research interest is treated as an entity. A link is defined as all of the entities that appear together under a single person's research interests. Again, no demographic information was used. The algorithm was run with 5 groups and found results that agree with intuition. For example, two of the groups were:

```
G0 (actuators, control, field robotics, legged loco-
motion, manipulation, mechanisms, mechatronics, mobile
robots, motion planning, multi-agent systems, space
robotics)

G4 (animation, graphics, computer vision, visualiza-
tion, geometric modeling, human-computer interaction,
image compression, image processing, machine learning,
object recognition, pattern recognition, sensor fusion,
stereo vision, video systems, visual tracking)
```

Note that both of these groups agree with intuition for a grouping of research areas within the field of robotics. It is also important to note that many of the items in the groups, while intuitively similar, did not appear together on a page. In other words, while some people's webpages contain many consistent interests such as "3-D perception, computer vision, mobile robots, and range data", a large number of people's interests contained diverse topics such as "computer vision, entertainment robotics, machine learning, mobile robots, and obstacle avoidance" or only a incomplete list of what be considered related interests, such as "machine learning" without "artificial intelligence".

Discussion

The algorithm described in this paper is only the core of the link detection and analysis system currently under development. We are working on the following extensions:

Posterior probability distribution of charts. Ultimately, the discovery of the maximum likelihood instantiation of model parameters (even if it could be found), may not be the most useful result. A more desirable alternative is a posterior distribution of parameter instantiations. We will use Markov Chain Monte Carlo (MCMC) methods to generate distributions from which we will be able to answer the following additional queries:

1. What is the probability that entity E1 is a member of group G1? This is answered by counting the frequency of samples for which E1 is in G1.

2. What is the probability that E1 and E2 are in the same group? Again, simple counting is used.

Dynamic group membership. In reality, we expect entities' memberships in groups to evolve rather than being static across all time covered by the link data. A straightforward extension to the chart allows it to represent each entity's membership in groups at each discrete time step. The model is extended such that membership at time t depends probabilistically on the demographic model, the demographic data, and the membership at time $t-1$. The result is significantly more parameters in the model, thus making the optimization more difficult. By solving the computational challenge we hope to obtain more reliable answers to the queries and their time-based analogs.

Conclusion

We have proposed a generative model for group membership and link generation. The strength of this model is its ability to process probabilistic link data and reason probabilistically about links and group memberships. This approach simultaneously provides the ability to incorporate information about n-ary ($n > 2$) links.

We have developed a search method to optimize the parameters of that model given observational data. Our experimental results show the ability of the optimization to identify groups and links, as well as generating alias hypotheses. The experimental results and the computation required to generate them show that the performance of the system is still constrained by the ability of the optimizer to find the best parameter settings and our future work will focus on scalability. Finally, we have described our plans for a complete system capable of answering a broad array of probabilistic queries about links, membership in groups, and aliases.

References

D.M. Bikel, S. Miller, R. Schwartz, and R. Weischedel. Nymble: a high-performance learning named-finder. In *In Fifth Conference on Applied Natural Language Processing*, 1997.

A. Borthwick, J. Sterling, E. Agichtein, and R.Grishman. Description of the mene named entity system as used in muc-7. In *Proceedings of the Seventh Message Understanding Conference (MUC-7)*, Fairfx, Virginia.

David Cohn and Thomas Hofmann. The missing link - a probabilistic model of document content and hypertext connectivity. In *Neural Information Processing Systems 13*, 2001.

D. Gibson, J. Kleinberg, and P. Raghavan. Inferring web communities from link topology. In *Proc. 9th ACM Conference on Hypertext and Hypermedia*, 1998.

H. Goldberg and T. Senator. Restructuring databases for knowledge discovery by consolidation and link formation. In *First International Conference on Knowledge Discovery and Data Mining*, 1995.

H. Kautz, B. Selman, and M. Shah. The hidden web. *AI Magazine*, 1997.

M. Sparrow. The application of network analysis to crminal intelligence: an assessment of prospects. *Social Networks*, 13, 1991.

B. Taskar, E. Segal, and D. Koller. Probabilistic clustering in relational data. In *Seventeenth International Joint Conference on Artificial Intelligence*, pages 870–876, Seattle, Washington, August 2001.

S. Wasserman and K. Faust. *Social Network Analysis: Methods and Applications*. Cambridge University Press, 1994.

AAAI-02
Edmonton/Alberta
IAAI-02

Innovative Applications
of Artificial Intelligence

Deployed Applications

MiTAP, Text and Audio Processing for Bio-Security: A Case Study

Laurie Damianos[†], Jay Ponte[†], Steve Wohlever[†],
Florence Reeder[‡], David Day[†], George Wilson[‡], Lynette Hirschman[†]

The MITRE Corporation
[†]202 Burlington Road; Bedford, MA 01730
[‡]7798 Old Springhouse Road; McLean, VA 22101
{laurie, ponte, wohlever, freeder, day, gwilson, lynette}@mitre.org

Abstract

MiTAP (MITRE Text and Audio Processing) is a prototype system available for monitoring infectious disease outbreaks and other global events. MiTAP focuses on providing timely, multi-lingual, global information access to medical experts and individuals involved in humanitarian assistance and relief work. Multiple information sources in multiple languages are automatically captured, filtered, translated, summarized, and categorized by disease, region, information source, person, and organization. Critical information is automatically extracted and tagged to facilitate browsing, searching, and sorting. The system supports shared situational awareness through collaboration, allowing users to submit other articles for processing, annotate existing documents, post directly to the system, and flag messages for others to see. MiTAP currently stores eight hundred thousand articles and processes an additional 2000 to 10,000 daily, delivering up-to-date information to dozens of regular users.

Global Tracking of Infectious Disease Outbreaks and Emerging Biological Threats

Over the years, greatly expanded trade and travel have increased the potential economic and political impacts of major disease outbreaks, given their ability to move rapidly across national borders. These diseases can affect people (West Nile virus, HIV, Ebola, Bovine Spongiform Encephalitis), animals (foot-and-mouth disease) and plants (citrus canker in Florida). More recently, the potential of biological terrorism has become a very real threat. On September 11th, 2001, the Center for Disease Control alerted states and local public health agencies to monitor for any unusual disease patterns, including chemical and biological agents. In addition to possible disruption and loss of life, bioterrorism could foment political instability, given the panic that fast-moving plagues have historically engendered.

Appropriate response to disease outbreaks and emerging threats depends on obtaining reliable and up-to-date information, which often means monitoring many news

sources, particularly local news sources, in many languages worldwide. Analysts cannot feasibly acquire, manage, and digest the vast amount of information available 24 hours a day, seven days a week. In addition, access to foreign language documents and the local news of other countries is generally limited. Even when foreign language news is available, it is usually no longer current by the time it is translated and reaches the hands of an analyst. This is a very real problem that raises a very urgent need to develop automated support for global tracking of infectious disease outbreaks and emerging biological threats.

The MiTAP (MITRE Text and Audio Processing) system was created to explore the integration of synergistic TIDES language processing technologies: Translation, Information Detection, Extraction, and Summarization. TIDES aims to revolutionize the way that information is obtained from human language by enabling people to find and interpret needed information quickly and effectively, regardless of language or medium. MiTAP is designed to provide the end user with timely, accurate, novel information and present it in a way that allows the analyst to spend more time on analysis and less time on finding, translating, distilling and presenting information.

On September 11th, 2001, the research prototype system became available to real users for real problems.

Text and Audio Processing for Bio-Security

MiTAP focuses on providing timely, multi-lingual, global information access to analysts, medical experts and individuals involved in humanitarian assistance and relief work. Multiple information sources (epidemiological reports, newswire feeds, email, online news) in multiple languages (English, Chinese, French, German, Italian, Portuguese, Russian, and Spanish) are automatically captured, filtered, translated, summarized, and categorized into searchable newsgroups based on disease, region, information source, person, organization, and language. Critical information is automatically extracted and tagged to facilitate browsing, searching, and sorting. The system supports shared situational awareness through collaboration, allowing users to submit other articles for processing, annotate existing documents, and post directly to the system. A web-based search engine supports source-specific, full-text information retrieval. Figure 1 represents a graphical overview of the services provided by the MiTAP system.

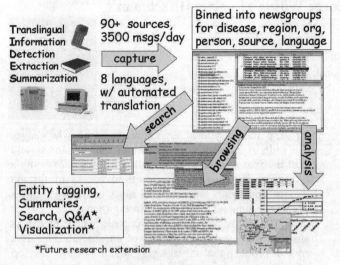

Figure 1 MiTAP Overview

Figure 2 illustrates the three phases of the underlying architecture: information capture, information processing, and user interface.

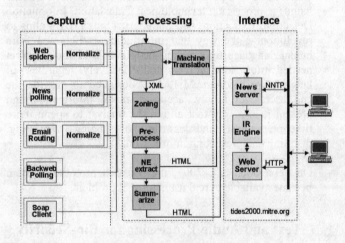

Figure 2 MiTAP Architecture

Information Capture

The capture process supports web sources, electronic mailing lists, newsgroups, news feeds, and audio/video data. The first four of these categories are automatically harvested and filtered, and the resulting information is normalized prior to processing. The ViTAP system (Merlino 2002) captures and transcribes TV news broadcasts, making the text transcriptions available to MiTAP via a SOAP-based interface (SOAP Version 1.2 Part 1 2001). The data from all of these sources are then

sent on to the processing phase, where the individual TIDES component technologies are employed.

Information Processing

Each normalized message is passed through a zoner that uses human-generated rules to identify the source, date, and other fields such as headline or title, article body, etc. The zoned messages are preprocessed to identify paragraph, sentence, and word boundaries as well as part-of-speech tags. This preprocessing is carried out by the Alembic natural language analyzer (Aberdeen et al. 1995; Aberdeen et al. 1996; Vilain and Day 1996; Vilain 1999) which is based on the Brill (1995) tagger and uses machine-learned rules. The preprocessed messages are then fed into the Alembic named entity recognizer, which identifies person, organization and location names as well as dates, diseases, and victim descriptions using human-generated rules. This extended set of named entities is critical in routing the messages to the appropriate newsgroups and is also used to color-code the text so users can quickly scan the relevant information. Finally, the document is processed by WebSumm (Mani and Bloedorn 1999), which generates modified versions of extracted sentences as a summary. WebSumm depends on the TempEx normalizing time expression tagger (Mani and Wilson 2000) to identify the time expressions and normalize them according to the TIDES Temporal Annotation Guidelines, a standard for representing time expressions in normal form (Ferro 2001; Ferro et al. 2001). For non-English sources, the CyberTrans machine translation system (Miller et al. 2001), which "wraps" commercial and research translation engines and presents a common set of interfaces, is used to translate the messages automatically into English. The translated messages are then processed as the English sources are. Despite translation errors, the translated messages have been judged by users to be useful. There is generally enough information for users to determine the relevance of a given message, and the original, foreign language documents remain available for human translation, if desired. Without the machine translation, these articles would effectively be invisible to analysts and other users.

User Interface

The final phase consists of the user interface and related processing. The processed messages are converted to HTML, with color-coded named entities, and routed to newsgroups hosted by a Network News Transport Protocol (NNTP) server, InterNetNews (INN 2001). (See figure 3.) The newsgroups are organized by category (i.e., source, disease, region, language, person, and organization) to allow analysts, with specific information needs, to locate material quickly. The article summaries are included via a web link and JavaScript code embedded in the HTML that displays a pop-up summary when the mouse is dragged over the link. Another type of summary, pop-up tables, show lists of named entities found in the document.

Machine-translated documents contain a web link to the original foreign language article. Figure 4 shows a sample message with color-coded named entities and pop-up summary.

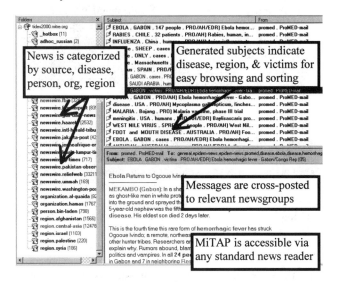

Figure 3 MiTAP viewed through standard newsreader

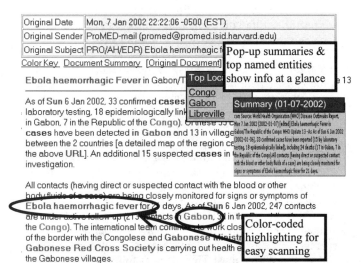

Figure 4 Sample MiTAP article

One major advantage to using the NNTP server is that users can access the information using a standard mail/news browser such as Netscape Messenger or Outlook Express. There is no need to install custom software, and the instant sense of familiarity with the interface is crucial in gaining user acceptance - little to no training is required. Mail readers also provide additional functionality such as alerting to new messages on specified topics, flagging messages of significance, and local directories that can be used as a private workspace. Other newsgroups can be created as collaborative repositories for users to share collective information.

To supplement access to the data, messages are indexed using the Lucene information retrieval system (The Jakarta Project 2001), allowing users to do full text, source-specific queries over the entire set of messages. As the relevance of messages tends to be time dependent, we have implemented an optimized query mechanism to do faster time-constrained searches.

MiTAP Development and Deployment

The initial MiTAP system was put together over a 9-month period. Our goal was to build a prototype quickly to demonstrate the results of integrating multiple natural language processing (NLP) technologies. The longer-term strategy is to upgrade the components progressively as better performing modules become available and to migrate towards our developing architecture. For the initial implementation, we chose components based on availability as well as ease of integration and modification. This meant that we used components developed at MITRE (extraction, summarization) or developed with MITRE involvement (translation support), or commercial off-the-shelf (COTS) components (translation engines, information retrieval, news server, news browser interface). In cases where no component was readily available, we developed a minimal capability for MiTAP, e.g., scripts for capture of news sources, or use of named entity extraction for headline generation and binning of messages into appropriate newsgroups.

Since July 2000, we have been working to incorporate modules from other groups (e.g., Columbia's NewsBlaster, McKeown et al. 2002), to redesign the architecture, and to specify a protocol to support service-based access to other modules, such as information extraction, summarization, or topic clustering.

As part of the long-term efforts, we have been concurrently developing a framework known as Catalyst (Mardis et al. 2001). Catalyst provides a common data model based on standoff annotation, efficient compressed data formats, distributed processing, and annotation indexing. Standoff annotation (see, for example, Bird et al. 2000) means that the linguistic annotations are kept separate from the original text or audio as opposed to e.g., inline XML markup, where the annotations are added to the underlying signal. The advantages of standoff annotation are threefold. First, the limitations of the markup language do not limit the allowable annotations. For example, with inline XML, the tags must be strictly nested. If two language processing modules do not agree on, say sentence boundary detection, there is the potential for 'crossing brackets' in the markup. This is a problem for inline XML markup but not for standoff annotation. Second, when annotations are kept separate from signal, system components receive customized views of the signal. That means that a component need not ever receive annotations that it does not explicitly require. This makes systems both more efficient and easier to test and debug. Efficiency is greater, sometimes considerably so, since annotations can account for a large proportion of the data in a complex language processing system. New modules added to the system do not affect existing modules unless explicit dependencies are also added, simplifying the testing process. Finally, standoff annotations are easy to compress and index, making further optimizations possible.

Uses of AI Technology

Artificial Intelligence (AI) technology and techniques pervade MiTAP to support its multi-faceted, multi-lingual and multi-functional requirements. From automated natural language processing techniques to information retrieval, the NLP modules utilize AI extensively. The techniques utilized fall predominantly into the data-driven camp of methods. Below we describe the components, roughly in their order of processing flow.

The CyberTrans machine translation server employs a combination of AI techniques to optimize the performance of COTS machine translation (MT) systems. Since system developers have only the most basic insight into the MT systems, we will not describe related AI techniques in depth here, and interested readers are referred to (Arnold et al. 1994; Hutchins & Somers 1992). MT systems in the last 30 or so years have been marvels of knowledge engineering, from the encoding of the lexical entries to the writing of grammatical rules. The simplest form of MT is word-for-word substitution, and all knowledge is encoded in the lexicon itself. While this type of system is easy and quick to construct given a translation dictionary, it also provides a hard-to-read translation, imposing a greater burden on the users of the system. To provide more well-formed output, systems perform increasingly sophisticated levels of analysis of the source language text using grammatical rules and lexicons. This analysis produces an intermediate structure which is then transformed by another set of rules to a format sufficient for generating the target language. The level of analysis increases in sophistication – from words to syntax to semantics to pragmatics with the "holy grail" of MT being a language-independent representation or interlingua. At this level, there is increasing overlap with traditional knowledge-base and ontology engineering, hence the increased reliance in computational linguistics on AI techniques (see Yakama and Knight 2001 for an example).

COTS MT systems are designed primarily for interactive use in situations where users have control over the language, formatting and well-formedness of the input text. In adapting CyberTrans for real users and real-world data, the necessity for supporting technologies was quickly apparent. Three of these are of particular interest: automated language identification, automated code set conversion, and automated spelling correction, particularly for the incorporation of diacritics. The resulting tools can be used individually and eventually as standalone modules, but are currently integrated into the CyberTrans processing flow.

The first, most essential, part of automated processing of language data is to determine both the language and code set representation of the input text. While it would seem obvious that users know at least what the language of a given document is, this has proven not to be the case, particularly in non-Romanized languages such as Arabic or Chinese. In these situations, documents appear as unintelligible byte streams. In addition, some of the data sources contain documents in a mix of languages, so knowledge of the source does not necessarily determine the language. This is a classical categorization problem with a search a space of N*M where N is the number of languages to be recognized and M the number of code set representations. The categories are determined by a combination of n-graph measurements using the Acquaintance algorithm (Huffman 1996) with simple heuristics whittling down the search space.

Once the code set has been determined, it is converted into a standard representation. This process is not without information loss, so spelling corrections are applied. The most straight-forward spelling correction involves the reinsertion of diacritical markers where they are missing. This is treated as a word-sense disambiguation problem (Yarowsky 1994) and relies on both language spelling rules and trained probabilities of word occurrences. Here, the solution is a hybrid system where hand-coded rules are enforced using statistical measures of likely word occurrences.

"Tagging" refers to a range of natural language processing stages that associate information with a word or multi-word phrases. The tagging used in MiTAP relies on a combination of hand-crafted and machine discovered rules. Tagging operations begin with sentence and word boundary identification ("word segmentation"), most of which is manually created and relies on narrowly defined regular expression heuristics implemented as regular expression pattern transformations. This stage is followed by part-of-speech tagging, implemented as a "transformational rule sequence" (Brill 1995). A transformational rule sequence can be viewed as set of cascaded finite state transformations. This restrictive computational model allows a range of machine learning techniques to be applied iteratively to derive the rules during training. The rules for part-of-speech tagging are heavily influenced by pre-computed word lists (lexicons), in which words are associated with parts-of-speech derived from a large corpus of annotated textual data. In Alembic, part-of-speech tagging is followed by a separate set of rule sequences, developed through a mixture of manual and machine learning methods. These rule sequences perform "named entity tagging" that identifies such things as personal names, place names and times. These have been manually extended to capture nominal expressions that refer to diseases and victims.

In addition, a specialized tagging operation occurs, that of temporal resolution. While dates such as *09 September 2000* are relatively unambiguous, many time references found in natural language are not, for instance *last Tuesday*. To get the time sequencing of events of multiple stories correct, it is necessary to resolve the possible wide range of time references accurately. In this case, the resolution algorithm also combines basic linguistic knowledge with rules learned from corpora (Mani and Wilson 2000).

Similarly, place names are often only partially specified. For example, there are a great many places in South America named La Esperanza. We are currently developing a module to apply a mix of hand-written rules and machine learning to metadata and contextual clues drawn from a large corpus to disambiguate place names.

This range of tagging procedures represents a strong shift in natural language processing research over the past fifteen years towards "corpus-based" methods. This work begins with the manual annotation of a corpus, a set of naturally occurring linguistic artifacts, by which some level of linguistic analysis (word segmentation, part-of-speech, semantic referent, syntactic phrase, etc.) is associated with the relevant portion of text. The resulting data provides a rich basis for empirically-based research and development, as well as formal evaluations of systems attempting to re-create this analysis automatically. The availability of such corpora have spurred a significant interest in machine learning and statistical methods in natural language processing research, of which those mentioned above are just a few. One of the benefits of the rule-sequence model adopted in MiTAP's Alembic component is its support for easily and effectively combining automatically derived heuristics with those developed manually. This was a key element in successfully modifying the Alembic NLP system for MiTAP in the absence of any significant annotated corpus.

Summarization is achieved through several machine learning techniques including Standard Canonical Discriminant Function (SCDF) analysis (SPSS 1997), C4.5 rules (Quinlan 1992) and AQ15c (Wnek et al. 1995). The feature set is an interesting twist on the summarization problem where the abstracts of documents are treated as queries that represent the user's information needs. In essence, the features being trained on are constructed from the criteria for successful summarization (Mani and Bloedorn 1999). Summarization features then use information retrieval metrics such as tf.idf, which measures the likelihood that a given phrase or word is relevant to the topic at hand, in combination with other more fine-grained metrics such as number of unique sentences with a synonym link to the given sentence.

Information retrieval services are provided by the Lucene information retrieval engine. Our search interface provides Boolean queries and relevance based queries. Since our users require timely access to information, we have developed an optimized search algorithm for relevance ranked searches within date ranges. The default behavior of Lucene was to produce the entire ranked list and then re-sort by date. An entire relevance ranked list can be quite large, and so the optimized algorithm for small date ranges does repeated searches by date for each date in the range and presents the results in relevance ranked order. For the small ranges of dates that our users prefer, we realize a significant savings in query latency through the optimized algorithm.

The utilization of classical AI techniques is a surface just being scratched in the computational linguistics community. Like many domains, the field has hit the wall of knowledge engineering familiar to most AI practitioners. We are therefore looking for corpus-based learning techniques akin to data mining and data modeling for gaining language knowledge quickly without pools of experts. It then follows that we are also learning some of the hard lessons from AI – that no one technique is a silver bullet for complex problems like translation or summarization. In addition, we eventually find ourselves up against the knowledge-engineering bottleneck as well as the fact that eventually all knowledge is encoded in a "language" and must be read and understood.

MiTAP Maintenance

One or two individuals are typically responsible for the daily maintenance of the MiTAP system. This includes a number of administrative tasks, such as adding new user accounts as they are requested, informing users (via an e-mail distribution list) of changes to the system (e.g., new data sources, outages for planned maintenance, etc.), and obtaining user feedback via online surveys. The other major tasks deal with adding new data sources to MiTAP and maintaining the processing elements that make up the system.

When a useful online news source (i.e., a web site) is identified, assuming there are no copyright issues, it can take as little as a half hour to build a custom capture script to start capturing data from the source. Feeding a new e-mail list into the system is even faster. Data sources that deliver content via a mechanism other than the web or e-mail may require more time to integrate (e.g., a subscription-based data feed). There is a wide range of methods by which such data may be delivered, and a general solution for feeding such data into the system is not always available. However, these types of sources are rare. Most of the sources that are currently connected to MiTAP are either web sites or e-mail lists. Of the various types of data sources, web-based sources require the most maintenance. Each web capture script is designed for a specific web site. If the format of that site changes, the web capture may not perform as expected, and the capture script has to be updated.

Perl and Unix shell scripts make up most of the "glue" that connects the various NLP components into a processing pipeline. These scripts require little maintenance although we occasionally modify them to improve the formatting of the posted messages or to fix a minor bug when a new source is added. Only general knowledge of the underlying scripting languages is needed to maintain the non-NLP portions of the system.

Infrequent updates to the various NLP components (e.g., Alembic, CyberTrans, or WebSumm) usually require the assistance of an individual with more specialized knowledge of the relevant component. For example, in order to improve our named entity tagging (e.g., to better handle Arabic names), a programmer or linguist familiar with Alembic needs to develop new tagging rules and, working with one of the general MiTAP administrators, upgrade the running system.

MiTAP Usage, Evaluation and Utility

Usage

MiTAP has been accessible to users since June 2001. Data can be accessed in two ways: via newsgroups or through a web-based search engine. No special software is needed - just a standard news reader or web browser and an account on the system. The number of users that the system can support at one time is limited only by the loads that can be handled by the web and news servers. At the time of this writing, we have close to 100 user accounts. Up to 18 people have used the system on any particular day, with a daily average of seven regular users, including weekends. Our user base includes medical analysts, doctors, government and military officials, members of non-governmental organizations, and members of humanitarian assistance/disaster relief organizations. They access the system for updates on disease outbreaks as well as to read current news from around the world.

Figure 5 illustrates averaged daily MiTAP activity from July 2001 through February 2002. The bold line, on the left axis, shows messages processed and posted to the system while the broken line, on the right axis, shows user access via newsgroups or search engine.

To support collaborative work, there is a newsgroup, called *hotbox*, to which users can submit news, messages of current interest, personal opinions, and annotations. Almost all of our subscribers read the contents of *hotbox* every time they log on to the system.

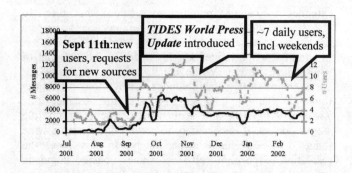

Figure 5 Daily MiTAP activity

One regular user, a consultant to an organization of medical professionals, spends one to two hours a day reading 800 to 1000 MiTAP articles from over 50 mostly foreign sources. He is able to isolate between 20 and 50 articles of significance and five to 15 articles of high importance. These selected articles are used to create the *TIDES World Press Update* (TIDES World Press Update 2001), a daily newsletter available to users of MiTAP (through *hotbox*) and distributed to an internationally-wide list of readers. The consultant considers MiTAP a "*labor-saving and intelligence gathering tool*" and credits the accurate headline extraction and color-coded highlighting of named entities for his ability to extract critical information quickly.

Evaluation

The *Disease of the Month Experiment*, a series of user-centered, task-based mini-evaluations was designed to assess utility, evaluate usability, measure progress, and provide iterative feedback to MiTAP developers. We chose a scenario familiar to analysts (i.e., research a current disease outbreak and prepare a report) to help minimize dependent variables and reduce training. Test groups were compared monthly to control groups in order to measure the utility of the system. Comparing MiTAP to the web and its vast amount of information, we hypothesized that 1) MiTAP users can produce better analytic reports in a shorter amount of time, where "better" means more up-to-date and more complete, and 2) MiTAP users spend less time reading documents and can read more in a given period of time. Test groups were also compared across iterations to measure the progress of development. Simultaneously, we performed independent usability studies.

For purposes of contrasting and comparing test versus control and test versus test across months, we defined five categories of metrics: efficiency, task success, data quality, user satisfaction, and usability. These categories were adopted and modified from those established by Walker et al. (2001) for the DARPA Communicator project.

In our experiments, MiTAP users provided more detail and more up-to-date information on disease outbreaks than just the web alone; however, they did not necessarily spend less time doing so. Our results also show that the test groups were able to find a larger number of relevant articles in fewer searches. In fact, the test groups, who were also permitted to use the web to find information, cited MiTAP articles in their reports an average of three times more than articles found on the web, and often the links to the relevant web information were found via MiTAP articles. Over the course of this experiment series, the feedback has enabled the MiTAP development team to improve the overall system performance (e.g., throughput increased by a factor of 2.5 while source integration time decreased by a factor of 4). As a result, we have been able to add a multitude of new sources, producing a significantly richer, broader, and larger data collection.

This ongoing evaluation series has proven to be an invaluable method of measuring utility, usability, and progress of MiTAP. The results of the experiments have guided development, improved the system on many levels, inspired creative thinking, and given us a more comprehensive understanding of what our real users do and how we can better help them. User surveys as well as unprovoked feedback from our users have supplemented our evaluation efforts.

Utility

The popularity of MiTAP and the *TIDES World Press Update* is growing monthly by word of mouth. Users request additional news sources, coverage of other areas, and more languages. The dynamic nature of the system has allowed it to become broader in scope and richer in detail over time. Most of our users (89%) are repeat users, with 63% logging in to the system at least once a week. We measure the success of the MiTAP system by the ever-increasing number of accounts requested, the high repeat user rate, the popularity of the *TIDES World Press Update* (read by MiTAP account-holders as well as 120+ subscribers, many of whom re-distribute the newsletter), and the overwhelmingly positive user feedback. An additional measure of success is the number of immediate complaints we receive the few times we have had temporary access or network problems.

Although MiTAP contains only open-source information, much of it is sensitive, as are its usage and the identity of our users. Below are several quotes from government users, decision makers on whom MiTAP and the *TIDES World Press Update*, a product of MiTAP, have made a major impact.

> I look it over each day and consider it a tool in the war on terrorism. - *Advisor on bioterrorism, in a White House office since September 13th, 2001*

> I use it to improve my understanding of opinions that affect our Nation's safety. - *Director of Homeland Security for the National Guard*

> Superb work and an asset to the new war in which information sometimes trumps fire and steel. My staff uses it daily. - *Vice-Admiral, Director of Warfighting Requirements (N7), the Pentagon*

MiTAP has clearly become a national asset. It is enhancing our national security and, perhaps, altering the course of the war by informing those making decisions on topics critical to our understanding of the forces arrayed against us. This is a war, like all others, decided by information, but the opposition is obscure, affecting, and affected by, voices we cannot hear unless something like MiTAP amplifies and illuminates them. - *Former Fleet Surgeon, Third Fleet, US Navy*

For more information or to apply for an account on the system, go to http://tides2000.mitre.org.

Acknowledgments

This work is supported, in part, under DARPA contract number DAAB07-01-C-C201.

References

Aberdeen, J., Burger, J., Day, D., Hirschman, L., Palmer, D., Robinson, P., Vilain, M. 1996. MITRE: Description of the Alembic System as Used in MET. In *Proceedings of the TIPSTER 24-Month Workshop*.

Aberdeen, J., Burger, J., Day, D., Hirschman, L., Robinson, P., and Vilain, M. 1995. MITRE: Description of the Alembic System as Used for MUC-6. In *Proceedings of the Sixth Message Understanding Conference (MUC-6)*.

Arnold, D., Balkan, L., Meijer, S., Humphreys, R., & Sadler, L. 1994. *Machine Translation: An Introductory Guide*. http://clwww.essex.ac.uk/~doug/book/book.html.

Bird, S., Day, D., Garofolo, J., Henderson, J., Laprun, C., and Liberman, M. 2000. ATLAS: A Flexible and Extensible Architecture for Linguistic Annotation. In *Proceedings of the Second International Language Resources and Evaluation Conference*. Paris: European Language Resources Association.

Brill, E. 1995. Transformation-based Error-driven Learning and Natural Language Processing: A Case Study in Part of Speech Tagging, Computational Linguistics.

Ferro, L. 2001. Instruction Manual for the Annotation of Temporal Expressions. MITRE Technical Report MTR 01W0000046. McLean, Virginia: The MITRE Corporation.

Ferro, L, Mani, I, Sundheim, B, and Wilson, G. 2001. TIDES Temporal Annotation Guidelines: Version 1.0.2, MITRE Technical Report MTR 01W0000041. McLean, Virginia: The MITRE Corporation.

Huffman, S. 1996. Acquaintance: Language-Independent Document Categorization by N-Grams. In The Fourth Text Retrieval Conference (TREC-4), 359 – 371. Gaithersburg, MD: National Institute of Standards and Technology.

Hutchins, H., & Somers, H. 1992. *An Introduction to Machine Translation.* Academic Press.

INN: InterNetNews, Internet Software Consortium 2001, http://www.isc.org/products/INN.

The Jakarta Project, 2001 http://jakarta.apache.org/lucene/docs/index.html.

Mani, I. and Bloedorn, E. 1999. Summarizing Similarities and Differences Among Related Documents. Information Retrieval 1(1), 35-67.

Mani, I. and Wilson, G. 2000. Robust Temporal Processing of News. In *Proceedings of the 38th Annual Meeting of the Association for Computational Linguistics (ACL'2000)*, 69-76.

Mardis, S., Burger, J., Anand, P., Anderson, D., Griffith, J., Light, M., McHenry, C., Morgan, A., and Ponte, J. 2001. Qanda and the Catalyst Architecture. In *Proceedings of the Tenth Text REtrieval Conference (TREC-10)*, Gaithersburg, MD.

McKeown, K., Barzilay, R., Evan, D., Hatzivassiloglou, V., Klavans, J., Sable, C., Schiffman, B., Sigelman, S. 2002. Tracking and Summarizing News on a Daily Basis with Columbia's Newsblaster. In *Proceedings of HLT 2002: Human Language Technology Conference.*

Merlino, A. 2002. ViTAP Demonstration. In *Proceedings of HLT2002: Human Language Technology Conference.*

Miller, K., Reeder, F., Hirschman, L., Palmer, D. 2001. Multilingual Processing for Operational Users, *NATO Workshop on Multilingual Processing at EUROSPEECH.*

MiTAP (MITRE Text and Audio Processing) System 2001, http://tides2000.mitre.org/.

Quinlan, J. 1992. C4.5: Programs for Machine Learning. Morgan-Kaufmann. San Mateo, CA.

SOAP Version 1.2 Part 1: Messaging Framework. Eds. Gudgin, M., Hadley, M., Moreau, J., Nielsen, H. 2001. http://www.w3.org/TR/soap12-part1/ (work in progress).

SPSS Base 7.5 Applications Guide 1997. SPSS Inc. Chicago.

TIDES World Press Update 2001. http://www.carebridge.org/~tides/.

Vilain, M. 1999. Inferential Information Extraction in Pazienza, M., ed., *Information Extraction*, Lecture notes of the 1999 SCIE Summer School on Information Extraction. Springer Verlag.

Vilain, M. and Day, D. 1996. Finite-state phrase parsing by rule sequences. In *Proceedings of the 1996 International Conference on Computational Linguistics (COLING-96)*, Copenhagen, Denmark.

Walker, M., Aberdeen, J., Boland, J., Bratt, E., Garofolo, J., Hirschman, L., Le, A., Lee, S., Narayanan, S., Papineni, K., Pellom, B., Polifroni, J., Potamianos, A., Prabhu, P., Rudnicky, A., Sanders, G., Seneff, S., Stallard, D., Whittaker, S. 2001. DARPA Communicator Dialog Travel Planning Systems: The June 2000 Data Collection. In *EUROSPEECH 2001.*

Wnek, K., Bloedorn, E., and Michalski, R. 1995. Selective Inductive Learning Method AQ15C: The Method and User's Guide. Machine Learning and Inference Laboratory Report ML95-4. George Mason University, Fairfax, VA.

Yakama, K and Knight, K. 2001. A Syntax-Based Statistical Translation Model. In *Proceedings of the 39th Annual Meeting of the Association of Computational Linguistics.*

Yarowsky, D. 1994. Decision Lists for Lexical Ambiguity Resolution: Application to Accent Restoration in Spanish and French. In *Proceedings of the 32nd Annual Meeting of the Association of Computational Linguistics.*

RightNow eService Center:

Internet customer service using a self-learning knowledge base

Stephen D. Durbin, Doug Warner, J. Neal Richter, and Zuzana Gedeon

RightNow Technologies, Inc., P. O. Box 9300, Bozeman, MT 59718
{sdurbin, doug, nealr, zgedeon}@rightnow.com

Abstract

Delivering effective customer service via the Internet requires attention to many aspects of knowledge management if it is to be convenient and satisfying for customers, while at the same time efficient and economical for the company or other organization. In RightNow eService Center, such management is enabled by automatically gathering meta-knowledge about the Answer documents held in the core knowledge base. A variety of AI techniques are used to facilitate the construction, maintenance, and navigation of the knowledge base. These include collaborative filtering, swarm intelligence, fuzzy logic, natural language processing, text clustering, and classification rule learning. Customers using eService Center report dramatic decreases in support costs and increases in customer satisfaction due to the ease of use provided by the "self-learning" features of the knowledge base.

Introduction

Many companies small and large, as well as various types of non-corporate organizations, now find it imperative to maintain a significant presence on the World Wide Web. One of the major organizational functions that is still in the early stages of being delivered via the Internet is customer service, i.e. remedying complaints or providing answers to a particular audience. This task involves many aspects of knowledge management, at least if it is to be convenient and satisfying for customers, while at the same time efficient and inexpensive for the company or organization. On a basic level, it is essential (but not sufficient) to handle the administrative overhead of tracking incoming questions and complaints, together with outgoing responses, over different channels such as e-mail, web forms, and live chat. Beyond this, to support customer service representatives (CSRs), and to assist customers seeking help at peak load times or after hours, it is necessary to provide both a knowledge base containing needed information and a convenient, intuitive means of accessing that knowledge base. Even were it not for the expense of maintaining a large staff of CSRs available at

all times, it is found that many users prefer to find answers to their questions directly, rather than take the time to compose a sufficiently detailed e-mail or wait in a telephone queue, possibly playing tag with a CSR for days before resolving their concerns. Furthermore, CSRs may experience boredom and burnout from constantly handling similar questions, and in any case are not using their skills most efficiently.

The most common response to this situation is to write and make available on a web page or pages a set of answers to frequently asked questions (FAQs). This provides a basic solution to the problems mentioned above, but, except in the simplest and most static cases, it requires continued expert maintenance to keep the FAQ list current and organized. In addition, especially if the number of FAQs is relatively large, it becomes difficult for users to navigate the FAQ pages to find the answers they seek.

Recently, a number of more conversational interfaces to knowledge bases have appeared, which may be personified as human or character "chatbots," or represented more soberly as simple input and response text fields. A user is expected to enter natural language questions and will receive replies, the quality of which depends on the level of natural language understanding the system has of both queries and items in the knowledge base. Although continuing progress is being made in the question-answering field [Voorhees & Harman 2001], the commercially available chatbots are based mainly on pattern recognition and pre-written scripts, which require a sizable knowledge engineering effort to create and maintain. We believe that some sort of meta-knowledge (as is represented by the patterns and scripts) is indeed an essential element in facilitating access to knowledge. However, it is also one of our goals to minimize the level of human effort necessary to construct and maintain the knowledge base.

Our approach centers around a dynamic database of FAQ documents, which we call Answers. Meta-knowledge relating to the usefulness of and relationships among Answers is acquired automatically as the knowledge base is used. This is used to spare the experts from most organizational upkeep, and also to make it easier for users to find Answers. By means of the architectural design, with its close coupling of end-user questions and CSR answers, the creators of the knowledge base are necessarily kept up to date on the information needs of end-users, closing a feedback loop that optimizes operation of the system.

In this paper, we describe how this approach is embodied in RightNow eService Center (eSC). After briefly introducing the overall system, we describe in greater detail those aspects of the application related to the knowledge base, as this is where most of the artificial intelligence (AI) techniques come into play. We also present the results obtained by customers using eService Center.

The RightNow eService Center Application

RightNow eService Center is an integrated application that combines e-mail management, web self-service, collaborative live chat, and knowledge management. Most customers choose to deploy it in a hosted environment, but it is also available for individual installation on multiple platforms. It consists of over 500,000 lines of code, primarily in C, but also in C++, Java, and PHP, as well as HTML. The first prototype was constructed 4 years ago; the most recent significant upgrade, to version 5.0, involved about 11 months of effort by approximately 16 full-time developers and 7 quality assurance testers.

The core of the application, from an AI perspective, is the publicly visible Answer knowledge base and the tools by which it is created, maintained, and accessed. This is discussed more fully in the following section. In addition, there is a roughly parallel set of private customer service Incidents which are fully tracked from initial creation, which can be via e-mail, web form, or live chat, through resolution and archiving. For many of our customers, the Answer knowledge base is quite dynamic and may

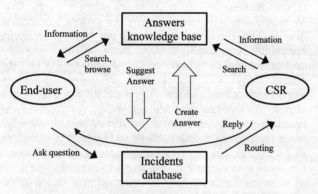

Figure 1. Principal knowledge-related transactions in RightNow Web eService Center. End-users search the Answer knowledge base for information; if they cannot find what they need, they submit a question, which is stored and tracked in an Incidents database, and replied to by a CSR. CSRs also use the knowledge base, and add to it by creating new Answers, typically suggested by frequently asked questions. Answers to questions can be suggested from the knowledge base, either to assist CSRs in forming replies or as auto-replies to end-users.

comprise 100's or 1,000's of documents; numbers of non-public Incidents are typically much larger.

Other important features of eSC, not discussed in this paper, include extensive administrative functions, customization options, and a wide variety of reports to aid in analysis of transaction statistics, CSR performance, and website usage. One AI-related feature which we allude to briefly here is an emotional index that is determined for incoming messages, as well as in real time for agents involved in live chat sessions with end-users. The emotional index places a message on a scale from negative (upset, angry) through neutral to positive (happy), and is derived using a lexicon of rated words and a set of grammatical rules applied to the part-of-speech tagged text, produced as described in a later section. This index may be used in rules for routing incoming messages, for example, sending angry messages to a veteran CSR while perhaps providing an automated response to positive ones meeting some other criteria.

Constructing an organic knowledge base

In traditional practice, knowledge bases have been constructed by domain experts, who do their best to record, in some form of document, what they know and believe to be necessary for a given task or situation. This paradigm may work reasonably well in capturing knowledge for narrow, static subject areas, but in the case where information needs are constantly changing, the burden of frequently adding new knowledge items can become significant. Although it may be easy to predict that introduction of a new product will lead to inquiries related to that product, it is not so easy to foretell what external events, such as a new law or regulation, or new products offered by competing companies, will cause a shift of end-user information needs. In the absence of human maintenance, conventional Answer lists are brittle in the sense that they break as information becomes out-of-date or irrelevant. Our aim has been to construct a more robust framework that would use AI methods to do as much as possible, and thus require minimal human resources.

The eSC knowledge base is termed organic, because of the natural way it is seeded and evolves over time. A key element of our system is that both growth and organization are responsive to end-users' shifting demands. This is a result of the way in which eSC integrates question and answer channels, and works in the following way (refer to Figure 1). The knowledge base is first seeded with a relatively small set of Answers to the most predictable or frequently asked questions. Many end-users coming to the support website will find their answers among these, but if not, they are encouraged to submit their questions via e-mail or the web-based form provided on the support home page. As CSRs respond to these, they naturally tend to become aware of trends and commonalities among incidents. At any time, a CSR reply, or an edited and extended version of one, can be proposed as a potential Answer. Depending on organizational practices, the item could be reviewed or edited by collaborators or managers before being made a publicly available Answer. The general availability of the answer should then result in a reduction of incoming queries on that topic. Even if such queries continue, there is now an item in the knowledge base available to end-users and CSRs as a Suggested Answer. Answers are suggested by treating the end-user's message as a search query, then filtering the returned set of Answers by requiring them to be in the same cluster as the query. They can be provided automatically to end-users or CSRs.

In this "just in time" paradigm, it is the end-users and their needs which drive knowledge creation, while the CSRs' or other experts' time and effort are conserved. This means that users are more likely to be satisfied, and the CSRs will have more time to focus on the usually smaller fraction of non-repetitive questions.

Navigating a self-learning knowledge base

It is widely understood that knowledge comprises not only facts or data, but also relationships among them, as

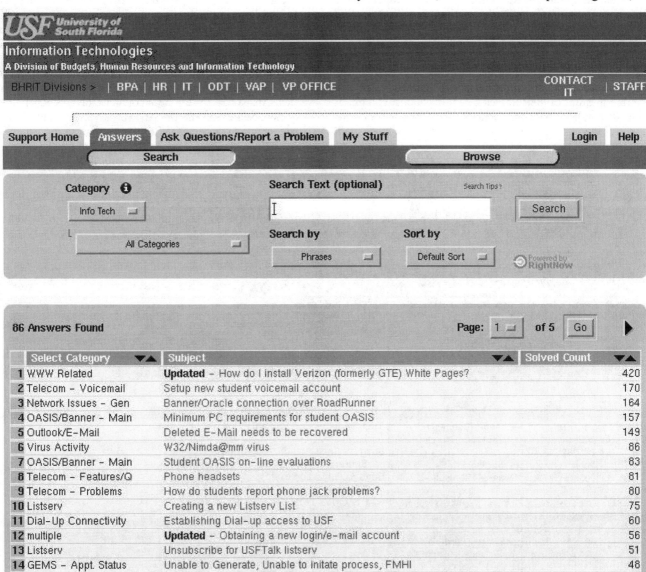

Figure 2. Portion of the web browser display from the eSC support page of the University of South Florida Information Technology division. The page is configured to list by default the historically most useful Answers (highest solved count). As a result, there is a high probability that a relevant Answer can be viewed with a single click. Users may search in various modes by entering search text, or they may view a browsable interface to the knowledge base by clicking the Browse button (see Figure 3). The Ask a Question tab provides a form via which questions can be submitted to support personnel (e.g. CSRs), and the My Stuff tab leads to a personal page with information on the status of any questions submitted. Some end-users may have access to more privileged information via the Login tab.

well as perspective on their importance, relevance, etc. A knowledge base organized to reflect such meta-knowledge forms a much better match to human user habits and expectations, and is consequently easier to use. We call the eSC knowledge base "self-learning" because it acquires this meta-knowledge through a number of AI-related techniques, rather than through human-constructed ontologies, templates, or other form of knowledge engineering. The techniques we use include natural language tools for feature selection, adaptive clustering and classification of text documents, and collaborative filtering and swarm intelligence methods to extract implicit user feedback. We will discuss these as they might come into play during an interaction with the knowledgebase.

An illustration of the first end-user view of a typical knowledge base is shown in Figure 2. By default, this page lists a configurable number of knowledge base Answers, sorted in order of their Solved Count (rightmost column of the display). The latter quantity is a measure of how helpful the answer is likely to be, based on the analysis of

previous user activity, as will be described shortly.

If the title of an Answer looks promising to an end-user, a click on it brings up the full text (along with graphics or any other additional information that can be provided on an HTML page). If the information there does not completely answer the user's question, he may return to the original list, or he may elect to follow one of a ranked set of Related Answer links attached to the Answer page. The relatedness ranking is derived from two sources: a simple document similarity measure based on word co-occurrence (with stopword removal and stemming) and accumulated implicit recommendations of previous users

To capture user perceptions of usefulness and relatedness of Answers, we use both explicit and implicit feedback in a manner inspired by collaborative filtering [Levy & Weld 2000] and swarm intelligence [Dorigo, Di Caro, & Gambardella 1999] algorithms. Associated with each Answer is a usefulness counter (solved count) which is increased each time the Answer is viewed, and can also be increased (or decreased) by an explicit rating which the

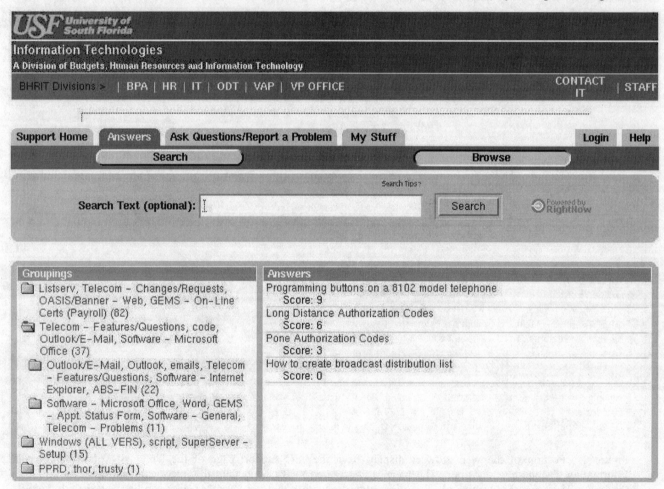

Figure 3. Web browser display from the Browse view of the eSC support page of the University of South Florida Information Technology division. This page displays a hierarchical set of folders and subfolders, where a given folder (like a typical computer file system) may contain both subfolders and Answer documents. The selected folder is the second one at the highest level of the hierarchy (leftmost in the display). Searching can be carried out within a selected browse folder.

user submits by clicking one of a set of rating buttons displayed with the Answer. In addition, a sparse link matrix structure is maintained, the corresponding element of which is incremented each time an end-user navigates from one Answer to another, presumably related one. Because a new knowledge base has no user-derived links, these are initially supplied according to statistical text similarity alone. In a way analogous to pheromone evaporation in ant navigation, both usefulness and link values are periodically reduced in strength when not reinforced. This "aging" keeps the knowledge base responsive by emphasizing recent usage patterns.

Of course, this links matrix contains noise in the sense that not every transition is necessarily made by users only on the basis of perceived relatedness. Nonetheless, when averaged over many users who each tend to be searching for information related to a specific need, we have found that the strong links indicate useful relationships. The potential tendency for highly ranked Answers to be overly reinforced due to their position in the list is mitigated by several factors. A user is unlikely to select an Answer if it does not appear related to her information need (as in any information or web page design, titles are important). If a selection turns out to be mistaken, its usefulness can be downgraded directly via the explicit rating mechanism, and indirectly relative to later Answers that satisfy the user's needs via the implicit mechanism. Also, the aging process decreases each Answer's usefulness (solved count) by a constant multiplicative factor, which reduces higher solved counts by greater amounts. For a fuller discussion of these collaborative and swarm intelligence methods, see [Warner, Richter, Durbin, & Banerjee 2001].

Users with specific information demands, especially if they are less common, may locate information most quickly by searching the knowledge base. Queries entered in the search box allow for a variety of search modes, including natural language input and similar phrase searching (which carries out spelling correction and synonym expansion). A search may be restricted to a given product and/or category, and returned Answers can be ordered by match weight or historical usefulness. The frequency with which terms are searched for constitutes one report that is useful to system managers. If some commonly entered search terms happen not to appear in the Answer documents, these terms can be added either to the synonym list, or to Answer-specific lists of keywords.

End-users may or may not come to a support web site seeking specific information, but in either case they may find it convenient to browse the knowledge base from a higher-level point of view, gaining a broad perspective on the available information. As shown in Figure 3, our system offers a browse mode of access where categories of documents are displayed as folders, which are labeled with the key terms most descriptive of their contents. Clicking on a folder opens it to display documents and sub-folders corresponding to more specific categories. Merely glancing at the labels on the folders at the highest level gives an outline summary of the contents of the knowledge base. Because the user can navigate by selecting subfolders and individual documents without needing to type search terms, this browse mode is especially helpful when the user is unfamiliar with the terminology used in the Answers and hence would have difficulty forming a productive search query. Thus we enlist the user's tacit knowledge, his or her ability to recognize more easily than articulate.

Supporting a browse function without a human-defined ontology requires clustering and categorization of the text items in the knowledge base. For this we employ a heavily modified version of the fast, hierarchical clustering algorithm BIRCH [Zhang, Ramakrishnan, & Livny 1996], which is run repeatedly while varying the threshold parameter. The best result, according to a clustering figure of merit, is used to learn RIPPER-style classification rules [Cohen 1995]. The final topic hierarchy is created by classifying knowledge base items according to the rules, allowing each item to potentially be classified in multiple places. Multiple classification recognizes the inherent multiplicity and subjectivity of similarity relationships. It makes searching via the browse interface much more convenient, as the end-user can locate an item along various paths without backtracking, and does not have to guess what rigid classification might control the listing.

The features on which the clustering is based are obtained from the document texts by shallow natural language processing involving part-of-speech tagging with a transformation-based tagger [Brill 1994]. Noun phrases are identified and receive the highest weight as features, but selected other words are also used. In addition, customer-supplied keywords and product or category names provide highly weighted features. These features are increased in weight if they are frequently searched for by users.

Extraction of the classification rules allows new knowledge base items, as they are created, to simply be inserted into the hierarchy in the same way as previous Answers. However, after a predetermined amount of change in the knowledge base, due to modification, addition, or removal of documents, a re-clustering is performed so that the browse hierarchy reflects the current state of the knowledge base, rather than a fixed hierarchy.

User Experience with eService Center

The system we describe has been used, through several versions, by a wide variety of commercial, educational, and governmental organizations. Drawing from their accumulated experience, we have gathered both aggregate statistics and numerous case studies demonstrating the dramatic reduction of time and effort for knowledge base creation and maintenance, and the increase in satisfaction of knowledge base users. This holds across the spectrum of organizations and applications, including those outside the area of conventional customer service.

The ease of installation is such that it has been accomplished in as little as a day, if initial seed Answers are available and major customization is not needed. As a demonstration that is part of our sales process, companies can set up pilot installations in 2-5 days. Once set up, the knowledge base can grow rapidly. For example, the United States Social Security Administration started with 284 items in their initial knowledge base, and over 200 new items based on user-submitted questions were added within two weeks. Now, after two years, the number has stabilized at about 600.

The ability of a web self-service system to handle dynamic fluctuations in usage can be very important. As one example, the January 2001 announcement of a rate hike by the U.S. Postal Service led to a short term increase in visitors to the support site of Pitney-Bowes, which provides mailing services, of nearly 1000% over that for the previous rate hike. Attempting to handle such volume via telephone or e-mail would have resulted in huge backlogs.

A quantitative measure of end-user success in finding information, as well as of cost reductions to a company, is the self-service index, defined as the percentage of end-users who are able to find their own answers online, rather than sending a message to a CSR. Table 1 is excerpted from a Doculabs study [Watson, Donnelly, & Shehab 2001] in which it was found that, depending on the type of organization, the self-service index using eSC ranged from 75% to almost 99%, averaging 87%. According to anecdotal statements from customers, these benefits are largely attributable to the key elements of the self-learning knowledge base as described above [Case studies]. We believe that credit is also due to the knowledge acquisition processes facilitated by eSC: the experts' time and energy is used much more effectively [Durbin, Warner, Richter, &Gedeon 2002].

In addition to standard customer service, eService Center is flexible enough to be used in other knowledge management settings. A number of organizations use it internally to provide information to their members, from general interest news to specific areas like personnel forms and procedures. Within our company, RightNow Technologies, it is also used as a shared information resource between quality assurance and development teams. In this use, quality assurance testers submit bug reports (analogous to customer questions), while developers respond to them. A single bug history may contain a number of transactions involving several people on each team. This system not only facilitates the communication between the two workgroups, but provides a valuable organizational memory for future reference.

Discussion

Despite our emphasis on the successes of eSC, there is certainly room to do better. Some improvements, such as making clustering more adaptive to differing knowledge bases, are fairly straightforward. More difficult is the problem of automatically producing good summary labels for the clusters; our current heuristics work well in some cases, and less well in others. The area of multi-document

Industry	Visits	Escalations	Self-Service Index
General Equipment	342,728	4,144	98.79%
Manufacturing	22,784	489	97.85%
Education	8,400	317	96.23%
Entertainment/Media	113,047	4,622	95.91%
Financial Services	40,574	1,972	95.14%
Contract Manufacturers	77,838	4,203	94.60%
Utility/Energy	19,035	1,122	94.11%
ISP/Hosting	147,671	8,771	94.06%
IT Solution Providers	53,804	3,277	93.91%
Computer Software	449,402	27,412	93.90%
Dot Coms	267,346	20,309	92.40%
Medical Products/Resources	17,892	1,451	91.89%
Professional Services	24,862	2,142	91.38%
Insurance	40,921	3,537	91.36%
Automotive	3,801	373	90.19%
Retail/Catalog	44,145	6,150	86.07%
Consumer Products	1,044,199	162,219	84.46%
Computer Hardware	101,209	15,759	84.43%
Government	108,955	17,347	84.08%
Travel/Hospitality	27,099	4,610	82.99%
Association/Nonprofit	14,620	2,772	81.04%
Telecommunications	809,320	202,158	75.02%
Overall Total	**3,779,652**	**495,156**	**86.90%**

Table 1. Self-service index for various types of organizations using RightNow eService Center. The self-service index is the fraction of end-users that find needed information in the Answer knowledge base, rather than initiating contact with a support person (escalating) via e-mail or online chat.

summarization is one of active current research (see e.g. Mani & Maybury 1999) and one of our priorities is to improve this aspect of eSC in future releases.

More qualitative enhancements can be obtained from applying AI techniques to a greater number of functions. Incident routing, text categorization, and natural language processing are all areas we are working on.

As knowledge bases inevitably become larger and more complex, the need for a system like eSC increases. The knowledge bases with which eSC has been used so far have not been extremely large, very seldom reaching more than a few thousands of documents (though many more items are usually in the Incidents database). Algorithmic changes may become necessary to scale some of the behavior to much larger databases, especially for processing that is done while an end-user is waiting.

Another trend affecting many Internet-based applications is that toward greater personalization of user interfaces. Care must be exercised to ensure such customization facilitates and enhances rather than constrains and obscures. In an information-finding task, one doesn't want to miss something because of an agent's faulty assumption. The extent to which significant personalization is feasible and desirable for frequent or for one-time users is still being investigated.

Conclusions

We have described the web-based customer service application RightNow eService Center, which relies on a number of AI techniques to facilitate construction, maintenance, and navigation of a knowledge base of answers to frequently asked questions. These techniques include collaborative filtering, swarm intelligence, fuzzy logic, shallow natural language processing, text clustering, and classification rule learning. Many of these individual techniques have been employed for similar purposes in other commercial applications, but we know of no other system that combines all of them. Customers using eSC report dramatic decreases in support costs and increases in customer satisfaction due to the ease of use provided by the "self-learning" features of the knowledge base.

The principles and methods embodied in eSC are also applicable in other settings. For example, the relationship between a government agency and concerned citizens is closely analogous to that between a business and its customers. In fact, organizations and associated constituencies with information needs are ubiquitous in our modern society. In the conception and development of eSC, we have emphasized the generalizable features of dynamic focus on current information needs, ease of updating and maintenance, and facilitated access to the knowledge base.

References

Brill, E. 1994. Some advances in transformation-based part of speech tagging. In Proceedings of the Twelfth National Conference on Artificial Intelligence. AAAI Press.

Case studies are available at the following web page: http://www.rightnow.com/resource/casestudies.php.

Cohen, W. H. 1995. Fast effective rule induction. In Machine Learning: Proceedings of the Twelfth International Conference. Morgan Kaufmann.

Dorigo, M., Di Caro, G. & Gambardella, L. M. 1999. Ant algorithms for discrete optimization. Artificial Life, 5(2), 137-172.

Durbin, S. D., Warner, D., Richter, J. N., & Gedeon, Z. 2002. Organic knowledge management for web-based customer service. In Nemati, H. & Barko, C, (Eds.), Organizational Data Mining: Leveraging Enterprise Data Resources for Optimal Performance, in press.

Levy, A. Y. & Weld, D. S. 2000. Intelligent Internet systems. Artificial Intelligence, 118, 1-14.
Voorhees, E. M., & Harman, D. K., (Eds.). 2001. NIST Special Publication 500-249: The Ninth Text REtrieval Conference. U. S. Department of Commerce, National Institute of Standards and Technology.

Mani, I., & Maybury, M. T. (Eds.). 1999. Advances in Automatic Text Summarization. Cambridge: MIT Press.

Warner, D., Richter, J. N., Durbin, S. D., & Banerjee, B. 2001. Mining user session data to facilitate user interaction with a customer service knowledge base in RightNow Web. In Proceedings of the Seventh ACM SIGKDD International Conference on Knowledge Discovery and Data Mining, pp. 467-472. Association for Computing Machinery.

Watson, J., Donnelly, G., & Shehab, J. 2001. The Self-Service Index Report: Why Web-Based Self-Service is the ROI Sweet-Spot of CRM. http://www.doculabs.com

Zhang, T., Ramakrishnan, R. & Livny, M. 1996. BIRCH: an efficient data clustering method for very large databases. In Proceedings of the 1996 ACM SIGMOD International Conference on Management of Data, pp. 103-114. Association for Computing Machinery

Staff Scheduling for Inbound Call Centers and Customer Contact Centers

Alex Fukunaga, Ed Hamilton, Jason Fama, David Andre, Ofer Matan, Illah Nourbakhsh

Blue Pumpkin Software
884 Hermosa Court, Suite 100
Sunnyvale, CA 94086
{afukunaga,ehamilton,jfama,dandre,ofer, illah}@blue-pumpkin.com

Abstract

The staff scheduling problem is a critical problem in the call center (or more generally, customer contact center) industry. This paper describes Director, a staff scheduling system for contact centers. Director is a constraint-based system that uses AI search techniques to generate schedules that satisfy and optimize a wide range of constraints and service quality metrics. Director has been successfully deployed at over 800 contact centers, with significant measurable benefits, some of which are documented in case studies included in this paper.

1. Introduction

Staff scheduling is the following classic, operations research problem: Given a set of employees, assign them to a schedule such that they are working when they are most needed, while ensuring that certain constraints are maintained (e.g., employees must work no more than 40 hours a week, and must have at least 12 hours between work shifts). Even the simplest variations of this problem are known to be NP-complete (Garey and Johnson, 1978).

While staff scheduling has long been an important operations research problem, scheduling has recently become an important component of an emerging class of business software applications known as *workforce management software*. The need for effective workforce management systems has been driven primarily by the recent, rapid growth of the call center / customer contact center industry, in which efficient deployment of human resources is of crucial, strategic importance. Traditionally, in this industry, staff scheduling has been performed using ad hoc methods and operations research techniques (Cleveland and Mayben, 1997). However, we found that this domain is particularly amenable to the application of constraint-based and heuristic scheduling techniques from artificial intelligence.

This paper describes Blue Pumpkin Director, a recently developed staff scheduling system, which is currently being used by hundreds of contact centers. First, we describe the staff scheduling problem for call centers and contact centers. Then, we describe the design and implementation

of Director. Finally, examples of successful deployments of the application will be given.

2. Staff Scheduling in Contact Centers

When a consumer calls a software vendor to ask for technical support, or if he calls a credit card company with a billing inquiry, the call is often routed to an *inbound call center* (or more generally, *contact center*), a large, centralized pool of trained *agents* (contact center employees) who are qualified to address the customer's inquiry.[1]

If all agents who can handle the call are busy, then the customer's call waits in a queue until an agent becomes available. Naturally, long wait times result in frustrated, dissatisfied customers, and it is therefore important for call centers to be staffed so that the wait times experienced by customers are acceptable. At the same time, businesses wish to avoid overstaffing (having idle agents when few customer calls arrive) in order to minimize the cost of operating the call center and maximize overall business profitability.

A standard goal for call center operations is to achieve a certain *service level*, i.e., answer X% of calls within Y seconds, while minimizing overstaffing.

It is well known that acquiring a new customer is several times more expensive (in terms of marketing/sales expenses) than deriving revenues from an existing customer. Therefore, maintaining customer satisfaction by achieving good service levels has a significant impact on corporate revenues. In addition, personnel costs account for 60-70% of the operational cost of a contact center. Efficient contact center staff scheduling is therefore important to a business both from the perspective of revenue ("the top line") as well as for operating margins and profitability ("the bottom line").

Internal corporate call centers are the centralized customer service organizations that serve as the foci of customer contact for businesses. There is also a large industry of outsourced call centers. Businesses regularly outsource

---

[1] Note that by "centralized" we refer to organizational centralization. Call centers are frequently geographically distributed, with calls being routed to the most appropriate resource around the world. One of the challenges in modern call center scheduling is creating a coordinated schedule that utilizes resources from distributed call centers.

some of their customer service functions to outsourcers, who are committed by the terms of a service level agreement in the contract to achieve specified service goals (e.g., Outsourcer X agrees to handle Manufacturer Y's sales inquiries, and promises that 80% of the calls will be answered within 20 seconds). Therefore, efficient staff scheduling is particularly critical for these outsourcers, so that they can deliver the contractually agreed upon service levels while operating profitably.

Although most interactive contact between customers and businesses still takes place through the telephone, customer contact through other media such as e-mail, on-line chat / instant messaging is rapidly increasing. A *contact center* is a generalization of a call center, where agents handle these other media, in addition to traditional media such as phone calls and faxes. Contact centers offer some new challenges for staff scheduling systems, as described below.

Since the call center industry is not well-known in the AI/computer science communities, it is worth noting some relevant market statistics. In the beginning of 2001, there were over 82,000 contact centers (employing over 1.5 million agents) in the U.S. alone, expected to almost double by 2004 (Frost and Sullivan, 2001; Saddletree, 2001, Datamonitor, 1998). Approximately 7% of U.S. call centers were using a workforce management system. Note that the market penetration of workforce management software is still very low, in part because modern workforce management systems with the full capabilities and ease of use required by the call center market are relatively new. However, because of the clear economic benefits, the market for workforce management software is growing rapidly (the annual revenues for the call center workforce management software market were $175 million in 2001, expected to grow to over $500 million by 2006). (Frost and Sullivan, 2001; Saddletree, 2001).

The contact center scheduling problem poses a very challenging problem. Meeting the demand profile implied by the forecasts of incoming calls/contacts is by itself a difficult combinatorial optimization problem, especially considering that the forecasts are probabilistic. At minimum, a one-week schedule with a 15-minute granularity must be generated. Typically, contact centers have hundreds of agents that need to be scheduled; some have thousands of agents. In addition to service goals, numerous hard and soft constraints reflecting the contact center's operational constraints, local labor rules, and employee preferences must be satisfied. The agents' schedules must be specified at a minimum of 15-minute granularity; in addition to specifying the start time and duration of a work shift, all of the "off-phone" activities such as breaks also need to be scheduled. Furthermore, the recent advent of multi-skilled scheduling and multi-contact scheduling (see below) has significantly complicated the problem of optimizing service goals. Traditional methods (manual scheduling and mathematical programming approaches) have been unable to keep up with the rapidly evolving, increasingly difficult scheduling requirements of the modern contact center.

3. The Director System

We now describe the Director application. After a brief discussion of the overall system architecture, we will describe the major components most relevant to the algorithmic/AI aspects of the system.

System Architecture

From a scheduling-centric point of view, Director consists of:

- The scheduling engine, which loads an input scenario and generates a schedule that satisfies hard constraints and optimizes schedule quality metrics;

- Infrastructure for persisting scheduling scenario inputs and outputs in a relational database; and

- A GUI.

In addition, there is a major software component required for integration with ACD's (automatic call distributors), which are the hardware/software routers that route incoming calls/contacts to the appropriate agent in the contact center.

Workforce management software systems for contact centers includes much more additional functionality, such as real-time monitoring of agent adherence to the published schedule and an extensive reporting facility; however these other features in Director are beyond the scope of this paper, which focuses on the scheduling functionality.

The current version of Director (3.1) is implemented as a set of Microsoft COM components, mostly implemented in C++. It is a traditional client-server system, which consists of a back-end database (Microsoft SQL Server or Oracle relational database) running on a server, and a *client*, which consists of business logic components (including the scheduling engine) and GUI components. A new version of Director Enterprise will be released in 2002 which is based on a more modern multi-tiered web-oriented architecture (a relational database, a J2EE application server running business logic and other middle-tier services, and a "thin" web-based GUI client).

In addition, there is another version of Blue Pumpkin Director, called *Director Essential*, which is designed for use by small and medium sized contact centers (typically with fewer than 100 agents). Its scheduling engine is implemented in C++, the scheduling scenarios are stored in a Microsoft Access relational database, and the GUI is implemented in Visual Basic. The emphasis of Essential is on ease of use and installation. Director Essential was actually the predecessor of Director Enterprise, and development on Essential has continued, focusing on its target user base of smaller contact centers. Many algorithmic ideas used in Enterprise originated in Essential. In the rest of this paper, we will focus on the Enterprise version, since it provides a superset of the features of Essential.

Using Director to schedule contact center agents generally involves the following workflow. First, a model of the contact center is built in the client, and is stored in the relational database. The main model elements are the characteristics of the contact center, the agents (resources), and the operational constraints. Then, rules/constraints that apply to the agents (e.g., how many hours per week she can work, which days she is available, what times he prefers to work, etc) are entered and linked. Typically, that part of the scheduling scenario is relatively static from week to week.[2] For each week, the user (contact center manager) generates a forecast of the incoming calls/contacts (the demand profile). Then, she specifies a target service goal which the schedule should satisfy, and runs the scheduling algorithm to generate the schedule. The schedule is posted and distributed to the contact center agents. Each of the major steps and components is described below.

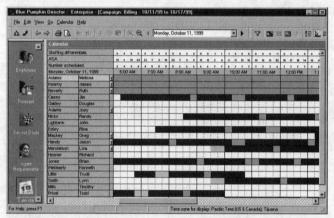

Figure 1: A screenshot of the Director GUI for manipulating schedules. Each row display's an agent's schedule (currently showing part of a day).

Forecasting

In the forecasting step, users create a prediction of the series of contacts that will arrive in the contact center during the time period to be scheduled. A basic forecast can be specified as a sequence of tuples $(t, numContacts\_t, AHT\_t)$, where $numContacts$ is the number of contacts that arrive during the time period t, and AHT is the average handling time for the contacts (e.g., the amount of time a contact center agent will spend talking on the phone, or the time it takes to write a reply to an e-mail inquiry). In Director, forecasting is done with a 15-minute granularity. For example, the user might enter a forecast which specifies that from 8:00AM-8:15AM, 10 calls arrive, with an AHT of 200 seconds, then from 8:15-8:30, 15 calls arrive with an AHT of 205 seconds, and so on.

---

[2] The standard period for which Director is used to generate schedules is one week.

Currently, Director uses a simple forecasting model, where the user can either manually enter a forecast, or create a forecast by combining (using weighted averaging) forecasts from previous scheduling periods. Although it may be possible to improve the accuracy of the forecasts by applying more sophisticated learning techniques, users report satisfaction with the current approach.

Service Goals, Computation of Agent Requirements, and Modeling Over/Understaffing

Given the forecast for a contact queue, the next step in scheduling is to specify a service goal for the queue. The following are some service goals:

- Answer 90% of the incoming calls within 20 seconds.
- Send a reply to 99% of the e-mail inquiries within 24 hours.
- Answer calls within 30 seconds on average.
- Limit abandoned calls to 5% of the incoming calls (calls are abandoned when a customer hangs up the phone before an agent becomes available to talk to the customer).
- No agent should be idle more than 25% of the time.

Combinations of the above are possible, e.g., "Answer 80% calls within 30 seconds, no more than 5% of the calls can be abandoned, and no agent should be idle more than 20% of the time."

In a scenario where there is a single queue of calls, and any agent in the contact center can answer the call, it is possible to compute an agent requirement for a time period. That is, the number of agents who must be working during that time period to satisfy the service goal, given the forecast. Agent requirements are computed by applying the well-known Erlang-C formula from operations research/queueing theory (c.f. Kleinrock, 1976) and some straightforward extensions. Given a candidate schedule, we say a time interval is understaffed if the number of agents scheduled to be working during the interval is less than the agent requirements, and overstaffed if there are fewer agents scheduled than required. By computing the over/understaffing for each time interval in the scheduling period, we have the basis for an objective function for evaluating a candidate schedule with respect to service goals.

Now, consider the following case: There are two queues, the "Widget Sales" inquiry queue, and the "Widget Tech Support" queue. There are three agents, Bob (who is qualified to answer sales inquiries), John (qualified to answer technical support inquiries), and Mary (qualified to answer either sales or support inquiries). This *multi-skilled* scenario differs from the previously described single-queue case, because it is no longer possible to straightforwardly compute how over/understaffed the schedule is for a particular time interval, due to the interaction between the queues. For example, suppose all agents are initially available, and three calls arrive in rapid succession. The first call arrives on the Sales queue, and is answered by Bob. The second call arrives on the Tech Support queue, and is immediately followed by a third call, which is a Sales call. If John answers the call, the third call will be answered by Mary. However, suppose that Mary answers the second call. Then, the third call will be put on hold (even though John is available, he is not able to respond to Sales calls).

These interactions between the agents, their skills, the order of calls arriving on the queues, and the way in which the calls are routed makes it very difficult to answer the question, "is the schedule understaffed or overstaffed"? In fact, there is currently no known, closed form formula (such as the Erlang-C formula) for computing the service level for the multi-skilled scheduling problem. It is possible to compute the service level by simulating the schedule and the call routing algorithm. However, simulations are very expensive (in the context of generating and optimizing schedule by a generate-and-test framework such as iterative repair).

Another important case where the traditional operations research approaches do not apply is when modeling queues that are significantly different from phone queues, such as e-mail contact queues (and similar types of media such as faxes). E-mail contacts differ from phone calls in several important ways. First, the service goal usually involves much longer time periods than phone calls (an e-mail reply is usually expected within a day or so, while people expect phone calls to be answered within seconds or minutes). Second, e-mail inquiries are usually partitioned into many, sparse, virtual queues. Third, while phone calls are "abandoned" and leaves a queue when the customer becomes frustrated after waiting too long on hold, e-mail contacts are never abandoned. Because of these factors, the standard Erlang formulas are not applicable when modeling scheduling agents to staff e-mail queues.

An increasing number of contact centers now handle a mixture of phone and e-mail contacts *simultaneously*. For example a contact center agent might normally answer phone calls from the set of queues for which he is skilled, and when no calls are pending, she would reply to e-mail inquiries. Therefore, a modern contact center agent can no longer be modeled as a generic staffing unit who can simply be aggregated into the input of an Erlang-C formula.

A scheduling system for the modern contact center must simultaneously solve both the multi-skilled scheduling and the non-phone-media scheduling problems described above, in addition to the traditional single, phone queue scheduling problem. This complexity makes it difficult to apply traditional operations research approaches (mathematical programming), since all known existing solutions (proprietary algorithms in commercial systems, including Director) rely on some form of simulation model. This makes constraint-based and iterative scheduling

approaches from AI particularly appealing for the contact center scheduling problem.

Constraints

Employees have various constraints that determine how/when they can be scheduled. Some constraints are a result of the policies of the contact center. Some constraints are mandated either by law or by labor union agreements. Other constraints reflect the personal preferences of the staff.

The primitive building block of a schedule is a *shift*, which represents a class of object representing a contiguous span of time for which an agent is scheduled to answer phone calls.[3] A shift may contain a number of *off-phone activities* during which she is not available to pick up calls (e.g., 1-hour meal breaks, 15-minute breaks, etc).

The basic constraints in Director specify parameters such as the duration and possible start times of shifts, the duration and possible start times of off-phone activities. For example, we can specify that an "8-hour standard shift" is 8 hours long, starts between 9AM and 1PM. Furthermore, we can specify that this class of shift contains a "lunch break", 1-hour off–phone activity, which starts between 3-4 hours after the start of the shift, as well as a 15-minute "break" that can be scheduled at any time during the shift. Director builds upon these building blocks with *shift pattern* constraints that specify constrain which shifts can be worked on which day. For example, we can say that Joe can either work an "8-hour Standard Shift" or "4-hour Special Shift" on Monday, must work a 4-hour Special Shift on Tuesday, and must not work any shifts on Sundays.

The user can also specify constraints on the number/amount of occurrence of various objects, e.g., "Bob must work between 3 and 4 weekend shifts per month", "Alice must work no more than 80 hours per 2 weeks", "John can not work more than 5 consecutive days in a row",

Most constraints involve only a single agent. However, there are constraints that can involve more than one employee. For example, we can specify that "John, Mary, and Robert must all have the same number of weekend shifts between 1/1/02 and 6/1/02".

Agents can express their *preferences* about their own schedules, and these are treated as soft constraints by Director. One type of preference is a rank-ordering on the start times of the shifts, e.g., John prefers to start between 8-9AM on Mondays, but if that's not possible, start between 9-10AM, and would really prefer not to start shifts in the evenings. Agents can also express preferences about the set of shifts they work, e.g., "I would much rather work

---

[3] For clarity, we restrict this discussion to the simple scenario when agents only answer phone calls. The definition of shifts and shift activities is slightly more complex when considering that agents can partition their time among several media types (e.g., we can specify that an agent only answers phone calls during a shift, or he can fully "blend" his phone and e-mail answering activities during a shift).

on the day shifts Monday through Friday than on the night shifts".[4]

Although most planning/scheduling systems with a highly expressive constraint system use a programming-language-like textual modeling language to specify constraints, this would make the system excessively complex for the intended users of our system, who are not engineers. The most commonly used rules are specified using various GUI elements, and the less frequently used constraints are entered using a pseudo-natural language "sentence builder" interface, similar to those used by some commercial rule-based systems such as the Versata Logic Suite and ILOG Rules. This enables most of the end users of Director to specify complete scheduling scenarios with little, if any, assistance from Blue Pumpkin consultants or technical support staff.[5]

The constraint system in Director is very expressive, and can express almost all constraints currently required by the contact center market (due to lack of space, we have limited this discussion to a basic subset that illustrates the capabilities of the system).

The Scheduling Algorithm

Once the scenario is defined, the process of schedule generation and optimization can begin.

The major design goal of the Director scheduling algorithm is to allow users to quickly generate satisfactory schedules with the absolute minimum amount of hassle. Therefore, the scheduling algorithm needs to be an extremely robust "black box" with acceptable performance.

The only user-adjustable parameter that influences the scheduling algorithm's behavior is a switch which determines whether the algorithm terminates after satisfying an internal termination criterion, or continues to search for better solutions until explicitly interrupted by the user ("Normal" scheduling mode vs., "Schedule Until Interrupted" mode).

Internally, the scheduling problem is formulated as a hybrid constraint satisfaction / global optimization problem. There is a global objective function, which is a prioritized vector of scoring terms. For each class of constraint, there is a corresponding score term that represents the degree to which that class of constraint is being violated. The score terms corresponding to "hard" constraints have higher priority than "soft" constraints and terms corresponding to service goals.

For each agent, there is a *slot* variable, which represents the shift (if any) that the agent is scheduled to work on that day. Instantiating a shift in a slot results in the instantiation of variables representing off-phone activities (thus, there is

a one-level abstraction hierarchy consisting of slot and off-phone activity variables). A *schedule* is therefore a complete assignment of variables to values. The scheduling algorithm tries to generate a schedule with a maximal score.

The Director scheduling algorithm is a hybrid algorithm, combining elements from standard iterative repair and heuristic global optimization algorithms.

The foundation of the Director scheduler is a library of search algorithms, including depth-first backtracking, beam search, and iterative sampling. A search algorithm takes a set of variables and returns a new set of value bindings for those variables that maximizes the value of the global objective function. The objective function is incrementally updated after each variable binding, which enables a flexible framework where arbitrary search pruning and backtracking control policies can be implemented in the search algorithms. We currently make heavy use of a heuristic algorithm inspired by simulated annealing.

In this framework, the simplest scheduling algorithm would be: Instantiate a search algorithm which takes as input all of the slots for all the agents, then run the search algorithm until some termination criterion is met.

While this strategy (using the annealing algorithm as the search algorithm) actually works for small, relatively unconstrained scenarios, brute-force search is insufficient to solve large problems with difficult constraints. Therefore, the Director algorithm is an iterative procedure, which repeatedly selects some set of variables and optimizes the value bindings by applying some search algorithm to that limited search space. In classical iterative repair (Minton et al 1992), the goal of each "repair" is to resolve a constraint violation, but the Director algorithm is similar in spirit to recent "repair-based optimization" scheduling systems such as OPIS (Smith 1994), DCAPS (Chien et al 1999) and ASPEN (Rabideau, et al 1999), in that rather than only repairing constraint violations, a search algorithm could be run on a set of variables either for optimization (e.g., "one by one, unbind each slot variable, and try to locally slide the start time of the shift to improve the service goal score", or because we have observed that it is a good policy to run some heuristic periodically (e.g., "once in a while, unbind all slots for an agent and reschedule him").

The time required for the scheduling algorithm to generate a satisfactory schedule depends largely on the size of the contact center (number of agents), the number and types of queues, and the complexity of the constraints. A one-week schedule for a "typical" 150-agent scenario (at a 15-minute granularity) can be scheduled in under 5 minutes on a 500Mhz Pentium-III desktop machine; a 1000-agent multi-skilled scenario takes 30-60 minutes. The complexity of the algorithm scales roughly linearly with the number of skills times the number of agents (assuming a fixed set of constraints). Interestingly, if the number of agents increases without a corresponding increases in the number of skills,

---

[4] Preferences are entered either using the call center manager's Director GUI client, or by the agents themselves using a web-based interface.

[5] The underlying, structured scenario model in Director can be manipulated as an XML document. However, it is hidden from end users.

then the scaling is better than linear. This is because there are few hard constraints that involve more than a single agent, which means that the more agents there are, the more flexibility the algorithm has with respect to meeting the service goals, which makes the problem "easier" in some sense.

Besides the scheduling algorithm itself, a great deal of effort has gone into the development of efficient data structures and algorithms that enable the incremental computation of the objective function. The major computational bottleneck in Director is incremental, on-demand recomputation of the service goal terms in the objective function. For example, when the start time of a shift is changed from 8AM to 9AM, what is the impact on the service goals? For a single phone queue scenario, this computation is relatively inexpensive (but still the major bottleneck); for multi-skilled scenarios with e-mail queues, this becomes a major bottleneck, which must be alleviated using various lazy evaluation, caching, and approximation algorithms.

As we noted already, almost all hard constraints involve only one agent. This means that in practice, satisfying hard constraints is relatively easy for the majority of the scenarios encountered by Director. Most of the search effort is spent optimizing the soft constraints such as the service goals and agent preferences. Therefore, the current scheduling algorithm does not attempt to perform much constraint propagation, focusing instead on brute-force, rapid generation and evaluation of candidate schedule states. This constrasts with constraint-directed refinement search methods (c.f., Jonsson et al 2000, Smith et al 2000) which make heavy use of constraint propagation.

In addition to the standard scheduling problem described above, there are a number of related scheduling problems that are addressed by Director. We describe some of these below.

Event Scheduling

In addition to scheduling agent work schedules, Director also schedules various *events* attended by one or more of the agents. Examples of events are: training sessions and group meetings. Traditional, manual meeting scheduling systems such as Microsoft Outlook rely on the user finding a time when all attendees are available. More advanced, "agent-based" systems (c.f. Maes, 1994) automatically schedule a meeting and notify attendees, but only consider the availability and preferences of the attendees. However, in contact centers, it is dangerous to schedule an event based only on availability or individual preferences, since it can have a direct, negative impact on the center's service goals.

When scheduling events after the agents' schedules have already been finalized, Director takes into consideration the impact on service goals. In other words, Director will schedule an event at a time where all attendees are available, and when the contact queues on which the agents are working are least understaffed.

In addition, if the agent schedules are not finalized yet, Director goes one step further and simultaneously reschedules the agent schedules and the event schedules in order to minimize the negative impact on service goals.

Workforce Planning

So far, we have assumed a version of the scheduling problem in which the task is to generate schedules for a group of existing agents.

A related scheduling problem is: Given a forecast of future contacts, a set of "employee class profiles" which represent typical subclasses of agents (and are linked to various constraints), and some additional constraints (e.g., restrictions on the number of percentage of class profile instances, budget constraints), generate a schedule consisting of "phantom agents" (instances of the employee class profiles) which optimizes the global objective function.

This *workforce planning* problem is important for users who need to plan future hiring of contact center agents, i.e., how many agents need to be hired, and what skills should they have?

In some sense, this optimization problem is more difficult than the standard staff scheduling problem, because of the combinatorial explosion. Suppose that there are 2 employee class profiles. Profile#1 represents an agent who can only answer Widget Sales calls, costs $15 per hours, and works 40 hours per week. Profile#2 represents an agent who answers both Widget Sales and Technical Support calls, works 20 hours per week, and earns $25 per hour. There are many combinations of instances of Profile#1 and Profile#2, and for each combination, there is a different optimal schedule.

Director solves this problem with a modified version of its standard scheduling algorithm, but workforce planning is a new application where there is clearly a need for further research.

Multi-week Constraints and Scheduling

Currently, Director schedules one week at a time. This is because a week is a natural unit, and weekly scheduling is standard contact center industry practice. Most contact centers create and publish schedules on a weekly basis, regardless of whether they use workforce management software.

However, there are various constraints that have a time period other than one week, e.g., "Joe must work between 2-3 weekend shifts every 4 weeks." The Director scheduling algorithm handles such multi-week constraints by assuming that the shifts can be distributed evenly among 4 weeks, but it is clear that such heuristics can fail. It might seem that if we scheduled all four weeks at a time, then this is not an issue, as long as the algorithm scales up. However, aside from any algorithmic problems related to scheduling longer time periods, there is a modeling problem in that the longer the time period being scheduled, the higher the probability that assumptions about the forecast and agent availability (due to unscheduled absences) become invalid (or the data required to make reasonable assumptions might be unavailable). Therefore, scheduling with multi-week constraints is another area where we will focus further research and development efforts in the future.

4. Application Deployment and Case Studies

Blue Pumpkin Director (including both the Enterprise version and the Essential version) is currently in use at over 800 contact centers combined in a wide range of industries; over 110,000 contact center agents are being scheduled by Director. Director Enterprise (the version of Director which is the focus of this paper) is in use by approximately 400 customers, including 3M, Apple Computer, Federal Express, GE, AT&T, Kaiser Permanente, Time-Warner Cable, Verizon, and Yahoo!. Director Enterprise is also widely used by major outsourced contact centers, which handle inbound calls for companies such as AOL and Canon. The typical Director Enterprise user is a large contact centers with 150-1000 agents. In addition, Essential (described in the "System Architecture" section) is also in use by over 400 customers, including AOL/CompuServe Europe, Peoplesoft, Airborne Express, and EDS. Director Essential users are typically small to mid-sized contact centers with fewer than 200 agents.

Like other enterprise-class business application software, deployment of Director involves a team of implementation specialists and includes some end user training. It is worth noting, that in most cases, the deployment complexity is in the integration of the software with the ACD (see System Architecture section), and setting up the server. In many cases, the end users create the scheduling scenarios and run the scheduling algorithm themselves (including all constraints) using the Director GUI. In some cases, it only requires several hours of training for a contact center manager to become proficient with Director Essential. For Director Enterprise, the training period is typically several a few days before the users become proficient with modeling and scheduling. For complex scenarios, Blue Pumpkin consultants assist the users with building the first models, but subsequent models are usually built by the customers themselves. We believe that this relative simplicity represents a significant step forward in the "popularization" of constraints and AI scheduling technology.

Below, we describe several cases studies of customers using Director Enterprise.

Borders Group

Borders Group is a leading global retailer of books, music, movies, and related items. The seasonal nature of the Borders Group business combined with a multi-skilled contact center made optimizing its workforce a formidable challenge. Borders Group plans for its staffing needs well in advance of the holiday season where customer expectation is higher than usual. Meeting these expectations is critical as Borders Group transacts a high volume of its business during the holiday season. During this period, there is a surge of over 35% in call volume, making optimizing available resources and staff essential.

After deploying Director, Borders Group evaluated various staffing scenarios to design a workforce optimization strategy that accurately reflected all of Borders' business goals. Based upon a selected schedule generated by Director, Borders Group knew how many seasonal workers to hire, covering which hours and requiring what skills – making the hiring process much easier. In addition, by focusing on the two most required skills instead of cross-training agents on multiple skills, Borders Group was able to get seasonal staff on the phones 33% faster, allowing them to be productive in one week instead of three.

Director enabled Borders Group to increase agent productivity by 53%, with a 33% reduction in expenses by allocating agent time more effectively over operating hours. Customer service levels of 88% were achieved during the holiday period with most calls answered in under 10 seconds. Borders Group claims that "[Director] enabled us to clearly drive down our costs and deliver a high level of customer service not experienced before at Borders Group" (Charlie Moore, Director of Customer Service, Borders Group). Borders was also able to reduce turnover of non-seasonal employees from 15 percent to 10 percent. These factors contributed to a 25% reduction in overall recruiting and training expenses.

SGI

SGI recently created a virtual contact center by installing a new switch that connected its four facilities located throughout the country. In the past, SGI developed schedules manually, relying on local critical needs assessment to develop a plan. Now they needed a more efficient and accurate method for accommodating the complexities of a workforce physically located in four time zones. SGI also decided to bring all customer contact in-house, increasing call volumes 50% to 2,500 to 3,000 calls per week. Budget constraints discouraged increasing the percentage of staff to accommodate the added influx of new calls. Thus, SGI needed to improve service metrics without increasing its budget.

When call volumes doubled from bringing all contacts in-house, headcount had been a concern. However, by using Director to generate schedules, the new volumes were handled with only an 8% increase in staffing. The new optimized plan resulted in a 37% increase in agent productivity. SGI was also able to improve customer service levels by 40% and avoid millions of dollars in additional agent-related expenses. In addition, SGI increased caller satisfaction ratings by 47%.

Timberline Software

Timberline Software Corporation is an international supplier of accounting and estimating software for construction and property management companies. Timberline's workforce manager for client services previously spent a full 40-hour work week creating a one-week schedule. Despite her long hours, creating the schedule manually could not accommodate last minute changes and made it difficult to predict future staffing needs. Director enabled Timberline to reduce the schedule creation time by 80%. This time savings allows Timberline management to focus on other duties such as reporting, forecasting, and analysis.

Prior to deploying Director, one of Timberline's greatest challenges was predicting future staffing needs. Using their traditional manual scheduling model, they predicted that they'd need to increase their staff to 138 full-time specialists in 2000 in order to support their call volume. However, once they performed the analysis, using Director, they discovered they only needed as few as 107 full-time specialists. That reduction in future staffing represents substantial potential savings for Timberline, totaling more than $1,000,000.

Compaq Canada Consumer Helpdesk

Compaq's Canadian Consumer Helpdesk had already been previously recognized for operational excellence by being named "Call Center of the Year" by industry media in recent years. Recently, by deploying Director, they were able to optimize their workforce processes even further and saw an immediate increase in customer service performance and, correspondingly, in financial returns. In just the first quarter after deployment, Compaq Canada experienced the following performance and productivity improvements:

- Call abandonment rate decreased 65.3%
- Average hold time decreased 57.3%
- Net service levels increased 16.3%
- Operational expenses decreased 15%
- Point of sale revenue per agent increased by 17%
- Gross margins increased 18%

Conclusions

Staff scheduling has always been a problem of great practical importance. The recent growth in the contact center industry has highlighted the need for effective staff scheduling systems.. Real-world staff scheduling problems, with their numerous complexities have proven to be a fruitful application for artificial intelligence-based techniques.

This paper described Blue Pumpkin Director, a staff scheduling system for contact centers. Director represents a significant application of AI techniques to solve a critical problem for an important industry.

Director Enterprise and its predecessor, Director Essential, have been successfully deployed at over 800 contact centers worldwide, and have provided significant, quantified benefits to their users. In addition, Director is used daily (for scenario creation, modification, and scheduling) by call center managers with less than a week of training. This demonstrates that powerful, expressive constraint-based systems can be used successfully by users without an engineering or operations research background.

Acknowledgements

Director represents the work of a large engineering and product marketing team at Blue Pumpkin Software. Thanks to Serdar Uckun, Rich Frainier, and Steve Chien for helpful comments and suggestions on this paper.

References

Chien S, Rabideau G, Willis J, Mann T, Automating Planning and Scheduling of Shuttle Payload Operations," Artificial Intelligence, 114, pp.239-255, 1999.

Cleveland B, Mayben J. Call Center Management on Fast Forward. Call Center Press, 1997.

Frost & Sullivan Research Report 6317-62, Agent Performance Optimization Software Markets, San Jose, CA, 2001.

Datamonitor Corporation Research Report, New York, 1998.

Garey M, Johnson D. *Computers and Intractability*. New York: W. H. Freeman. 1979.

Jonsson A, Morris P, Muscettola N, Rajan K, Smith B, Planning in interplanetary space: Theory and practice," Proc.5th Intl Conf Artificial Intelligence Planning Systems, CO. April, 2000.

Kleinrock, L. *Queueing Systems*, Vol 1, New York: Wiley, 1976.

Minton S, Johnston M, Philips A, Laird P. Minimizing conflicts: a heuristic repair method for constraint satisfaction and scheduling problems. Artificial Intelligence, 58:161--205, 1992.

Maes P. Agents that Reduce Work and Information Overload. Communications of the ACM. Vol. 37, No.7,pp. 31-40, 146, ACM Press, July 1994.

Rabideau G, Chien S, Willis J, Mann T. "Using Iterative Repair to Automate Planning and Scheduling of Shuttle Payload Operations," Innovative Applications of Artificial Intelligence (IAAI), Orlando, Florida, July 1999.

Rabideau G, Knight R, Chien S, Fukunaga A, Govindjee A. "*Iterative Repair Planning for Spacecraft Operations in the ASPEN System*," International Symposium on Artificial Intelligence Robotics and Automation in Space, Noordwijk, The Netherlands, June 1999.

Saddletree Research Report 0101, The U.S. Workforce Management Software Market, 2000-2004. Scottsdale, AZ, 2001

Smith D, Frank J, Jonsson A. Bridging the gap between planning and scheduling. Knowledge Engineering Review, 15(1):61--94, 2000.

Smith SF. OPIS: A Methodology and Architecture for Reactive Scheduling. In M. Fox and M. Zweben, ed., Intelligent Scheduling. Morgan Kaufmann, 1994.

A Decision-Support System for Quote Generation

Richard Goodwin, Rama Akkiraju, Fred Wu

IBM T. J. Watson Research Center
Yorktown Heights, NY
{rgoodwin, akkiraju, fywu}@us.ibm.com

Abstract

In this paper, we describe a prototype agent-based decision-support system for helping suppliers respond to requests for quote in a business-to-business supply chain. The system provides suggested ways of fulfilling requests and shows alternatives that illustrate tradeoffs in quality, cost and timelines, which allows the decision maker to consider alternatives that reduce cost and improve customer value. The system is implemented in Java and we use examples from paper manufacturing to illustrate the features of our system. In on going work, we are enhancing the prototype to include probabilistic reasoning techniques so that it can create conditional plans that maximize expected utility, subject to the risk preferences of the decision maker. We are also exploring the use of data mining techniques to infer customer preferences and to estimate the probability of winning an order, with a given quote.

Introduction

The proliferation of e-commerce Websites and the growth of business-to-business e-commerce has made it easier for sellers to reach larger numbers of potential buyers of their products, and for buyers to reach larger numbers of potential suppliers of products. These changes are affecting the market for goods and services exchanged in direct procurement, that is, goods that are used in the manufacture of the enterprise's finished products, as well as those exchanged in indirect procurement, those goods that are used in maintenance, repairs, and operations of the enterprise. Unlike retailers, most businesses in the supply chain do not generally sell at fixed prices, but instead negotiate terms with each customer, either for a one-time purchase or a long-term contract. This negotiation process can be time consuming and labor intensive.

Auctions are a long-standing mechanism by which price negotiation is sometimes conducted. In a forward auction, a seller is offering goods or services to a number of buyers, and the auction mechanism is used to determine the price. However, the concept of an auction can be broadened in several ways. First, an auction can be used not only by a seller to sell his products, but also by a buyer to procure needed products; this is commonly referred to as 'RFQ' (Request for Quote) or 'reverse auction.' Second, commodities can be exchanged between multiple sellers and buyers, as in a stock exchange; this is known as a double auction. Third, an auction can be used to negotiate more than price; such multi-parameter auctions could also determine terms of sale such as delivery date, payment terms, and product features. In this paper, although we describe a system for use in quote/bid generation for RFQs, the system and techniques are equally applicable to the analogous cases of forward, reverse, double-sided, combinatorial, and multi-parameter auctions.

As e-commerce sites make it easier to create and run auctions, the number of potential auctions open to each bidder can grow enormously. This can have the effect of overwhelming the persons responsible for bidding in auctions. The bidders need to consider each auction independently for the effect it can have on a number of business objectives, such as production efficiency, profitability, and customer satisfaction. Furthermore, they need to consider auctions collectively because winning a large percentage of them affects the business objectives as compared with winning a small percentage of them. For example, when business is strong and the rate at which auctions are offered is low, a direct procurement buyer may wish to win a large fraction of the items it bids on, and may be willing to quote higher prices to achieve those wins. On the other hand, when the volume of auctions is large, the bidder may not wish to win most of the bids because they would exceed the capacity of his enterprise to consume the product, perhaps leading to excess raw material inventory problems. Similarly, a general contractor bidding in reverse auctions to provide construction services needs to win enough auctions to employ all the tradesmen working for the contractor, but not so many that the jobs cannot be completed on time. How to bid in one auction should depend on outstanding bids in other auctions and intended bids in future auctions. Furthermore, the intention to bid in a future auction may be conditional on the outcome of a previous auction.

In this paper, we focus on the problem of quote generation for RFQs, and describe a decision-support system that aids in generating and evaluating such quotes. This agent-based system makes use of information about production schedules, inventory and availability of goods through electronic marketplaces to recommend good quotes. The current system can quickly consider large numbers of auctions in the context of the current business conditions and recommend sets of quotes in sets of auctions, to relieve the bidder of the burden of performing numerous what-if analyses. This allows the bidder to focus on pricing and non-tangibles, like customer relationship building. We are also extending the system to make use of data mining techniques to elicit buyer preferences about tradeoffs in quote attributes, such as product quality, delivery date and substitutions. We are combining this information with probabilistic reasoning techniques to suggest pricing and bidding strategies that maximize expected profit, subject to the bidders' risk preferences.

Our Approach

To address the problem of quote generation, we are building on our work in production scheduling (Murthy et al. 1999) and promotion creation (Keskinocak et al. 1999). In earlier work, we used an agent based architecture to match supply with demand to create a set of schedules that maximize a set of objectives. In the case of production scheduling, we match orders with production capacity and inventory. We allow for inventory at various stages of production and we allow for reworking of inventory to meet the requirements of an order. In our promotions system, we matched excess inventory from multiple suppliers with expected customer demand, based on salesperson's knowledge of the customer's operation. The resulting matches were presented to customers when the cost of the goods, plus a profit markup, were well below current market prices. This allowed the supplier to offer these items as special deals, tailored to the individual customer.

For quote generation, we have extended the system to pull information on demand and supply from new sources using new integration methods based on web services. In addition, we have enhanced the model to generate quotes for groups of RFQs and not to match each demand in isolation as was done in the promotion generation system. In the promotion system, promotions were offered on a first come first serve basis and if one supply item were offered to multiple customers, the first to respond would have the first option to buy it. In an RFQ setting, there are some significant differences: In some cases, quotes are binding, or withdrawing a quote can reflect negatively on the supplier. There is also a lag in time between when quotes are submitted and orders are awarded, causing uncertainty in availability of resources for making new quotes. Finally, the combination of quotes that are won affects production efficiency, and therefore the cost and the quote price needed to return a profit. The price of the quote in turn affects the likelihood of winning the order, causing a circular dependency.

In our approach to providing decision support for quote generation, we divide the problem into three stages: a demand filtering stage, a supply search stage and a matching stage. In the demand filtering stage, the system retrieves the details of RFQs that the decision maker could respond to. These RFQs are filtered to select only those RFQs for goods and services that the bidder could potentially supply. For example, a paper manufacturer would not want to consider public RFQs for printer's ink, but would entertain RFQs for paper from the same set of printers. The search stage consists of formulating search queries loosely based on the attributes of the input set of RFQs and dispatching them to various sources to obtain supply items that might potentially match the given RFQs' requirements. The search queries are formulated to retrieve not only exact matches for the requested items (finished goods), but also work-in-process or raw materials that the manufacturer can use to produce the requested items. Once the demand and supply items are obtained, the decision-support engine employs a team of agents to generate and evaluate a set of possible solutions that describe how each RFQ could be fulfilled, either in isolation or in combination with other RFQs (Rachlin et al. 1999). The decision support system evaluates the solutions based on a configurable set of evaluation criteria, such as cost, quality of match and delivery date. Finally, a non-dominated set of solutions is presented to the user along with their evaluations. A solution becomes a quote when the decision maker selects it and commits it to the RFQ/Quote system.

System Overview

Figure 1 shows our decision support system for quote generation. It consists of a user interface, a set of RFQ retriever agents, a set of search agents and a decision support engine.

User Interface: A decision maker can use the graphical user interface (GUI) to initiate the quote generation process, step 2 in figure 1. Once the decision support engine generates a set of solutions, user can then view the suggested quotes and their evaluations, together with the supply and demand items used to generate the solutions. The decision maker is then free to drill down into the details, modify the solutions and generate new ones and have these changes evaluated (step13). When the decision maker is satisfied, the chosen quotes are submitted to the RFQ system, step 14.

RFQ retriever agents: RFQ retriever agents retrieve RFQs from one or more RFQ/Quote systems, steps 4 and 5 in figure 1. These systems can include web sites run by the supplier, sites run by the buyer and sites run by a neutral third party market maker. The RFQ retrieval agents not only handle the technical aspects of communication with the RFQ/Quote system but also provide various filters that can be used to focus attention on particular types of RFQs. For instance, a decision maker might prefer to attend to urgent RFQ's first by picking only the ones that are due in a week's time or a user might want to focus on preferred customers' inquiries or on inquiries for specific product types. The filters on the retriever agents are configured by the settings in the user interface that the decision maker selects.

Search agents: The primary task of search agents is to find supply items that are 'potential matches' for the RFQs retrieved by the retriever agents, steps 6 to 10 in figure 1.

Search agents come in two types: generic search agents and domain-aware search agents.

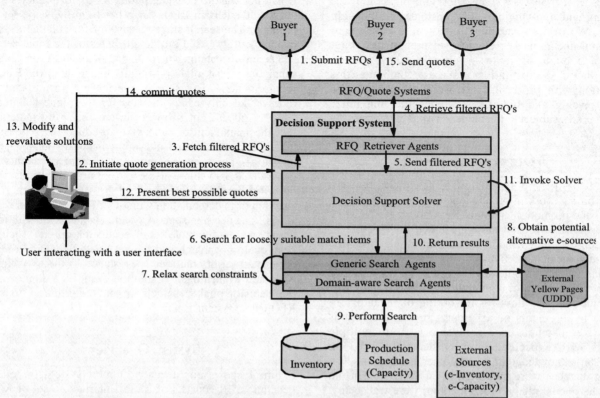

Figure 1: Steps in generating quotes for RFQs using our decision support approach.

Generic search agents: These agents are vested with general knowledge of the sources of supply items. These sources include not only the inventory management, and the production scheduling systems of the enterprise but also external electronic sources such as e-marketplaces. While the location and access details of the enterprise systems can be specified as part of initial configuration, information about external sources can be more dynamic in nature. These agents can obtain information on external sources from public yellow pages directories, such as UDDI (Universal Description, Discovery and Integration) directories. Generic search agents invoke the search services of external sources via Web Services, a set of open standards that facilitate program-to-program interaction by specifying a programmatic means to describe, publish, discover and bind application interfaces.

Domain-aware search agents: While generic search agents handle the technical aspects of communication with the sources of supply items, domain-aware agents deal primarily with reframing the search query to be dispatched to the destinations in order to obtain suitable matches for RFQs based on domain knowledge. For instance, domain-aware search agents have the knowledge of what attributes of an RFQ item can be relaxed while staying within the acceptable parameter ranges. They also have the knowledge of which attributes of a supply item can be

modified through reworking and which kinds of machines can be used to do the rework. For example, our paper manufacturing domain agents know that rolls of paper can be trimmed to reduce their width, but can not be made wider, and they know that the diameter of a roll can be decreased by cutting or increased by rolling two rolls onto one spindle. Using such domain knowledge, domain-aware search agents relax the item attribute constraints of a search query to obtain supply items that could include transformable and substitutable items as search results. This relaxed search query, set up by the search agents, results in a set of supply items that gives the decision support system greater flexibility to explore best matches by evaluating the tradeoffs among quality mismatches, price and delivery dates.

Decision support engine: Once the RFQs and the corresponding supply items are obtained, the decision support engine employs a set of agents to generate and evaluate a set of non-dominated solutions. A given supply item could be matched with more than one RFQ item. These combinations yield interesting tradeoffs in the evaluations, namely cost, delivery date, quality, and schedule disruptions. In some cases, the supply items that could be matched with each RFQ form disjoint sets. In such a case, quotes for each RFQ can be generated separately, without a need to consider combinations of quotes or how winning one quote would affect the resources available to supply another. In other cases, a supply item could be used to satisfy more than one RFQ. In such cases, the system considers combinations of quotes and the problem becomes much more interesting. Within the decision support engine, there is a set of agents that generate and improve a population of solutions. Each agent selects which problems and/or partial solutions to work on and employs an algorithm to generate new solutions. This matching problem can be approximated as instances of standard problems such as knapsack problem, bin packing, minimum cost flow etc. and the agents embody many of the standard techniques for addressing these standard problems. Depending on the size of the problem, we also employ mathematical programming techniques such as integer programming. Employing a combination of exact techniques and iterative improvement heuristics techniques results in a robust system that generates high quality solutions that illustrate tradeoffs in cost, tardiness, quality and manufacturing disruptions. More details about the algorithms were discussed in our earlier work on decision support for paper industry (Murthy et al. 1999).

Example

To illustrate how the system works and to show how the system assists the decision maker in placing quotes, we provide the following example of a paper converter creating quotes for rolls of paper. We start with some background about a fictional paper converter. Converters are value-add manufacturers that purchase large rolls of paper and cut them into smaller rolls as required by their customers' printing presses or other equipment. We simplify the problem by making a number of assumptions. Of the numerous relevant physical characteristics of paper, we consider only grade and roll width. Our sample problem deals with two grades of paper, A and B, in which grade B can be substituted for grade A, with a slight loss of quality. The converter has two machines, M1 and M2, which can cut wide rolls into narrower rolls; we assume that all rolls have the same diameter, such that each 1000 mm of roll width weighs 1 ton. Each machine has a limit on the width of the roll it can handle; M2 cannot be used on the larger rolls. The machines are committed to other orders until certain dates, after which their time is available. We consider the cost of the raw materials and the use of the machines, but ignore setup time, conversion time, shipping time and shipping costs.

Item	Grade	Width	Quantity (Rolls)	Due Date
D1	A	400	25	2002-04-012002-04-01
D2	A	600	30	

Figure 2: RFQs representing demand.

Figure 2 shows two RFQs, one for 25 rolls of 400 mm wide grade A paper to be delivered on April 1 and the other

for 30 rolls of 600 mm wide paper on the same delivery date. Figure 3 shows three types of available resources: inventory, production capacity and e-inventory available from a wholesale e-marketplace.

Supply (Inventory) Items:

Item	Grade	Width	Quantity (Rolls)	Cost per Ton
S1	A	2300	10	80
S2	A	2500	5	90
S3	B	1900	12	60

Electronic Inventory Items:

Item	Grade	Width	Quantity (Rolls)	Date Available	Cost per Ton
E1	A	600	10	03-15	100
E2	B	1500	30	03-01	80
E3	A	900	30	03-15	105

Production Capacity:

Machine	Max. Width	Date Available	Cost per Ton
M1	2500	04-06	15
M2	2000	03-15	10

Figure 3: Three types of resources: inventory, production capacity and e-inventory.

The task for the decision maker is to decide which RFQs to bid on and how much to quote for each one. To assist in this process, the decision support system generates suggestions for how to fulfill each RFQ with the available supply and evaluates each solution in terms of cost, tardiness, quality and manufacturing disruptions. Cost is a measure of the cost of acquiring the material and of machine time for any necessary conversion. Tardiness is measured in ton-days late. Since partial deliveries are generally allowed, this is a measure of the quantity that is late times the number of days that it is late. For comparing the solutions, quality is measured as the number of tons of grade B paper that is substituted for the grade A paper requested. Manufacturing disruptions are measured as the number of tons of paper production in the committed schedule that must be displaced in time in order to produce the new item before the due date. All four objectives (Tardiness, Quality exceptions, Cost, and Disruptions) are to be minimized.

In running the decision support system, the decision maker can choose to create solutions that satisfy any or all of the selected RFQs. Solutions generated to satisfy multiple RFQs are premised on winning all those RFQs; therefore those solutions do not commit any single resource to more than one RFQ. On the other hand, solutions designed to satisfy a single RFQ are created without regard for other RFQs, and are free to utilize all resources available. If the decision maker chooses to examine both types of solutions, (s)he can make contingency plans in case an auction has an unexpected result, i.e. (s)he wins more or less than expected.

Sol	Supply Item	Supply Rolls	Demand Item	Demand Rolls	Machine	Machine Date	T	Q	C	D
1	S2	5	D1	30	M1	04-06	50	0	1312	0
2	S2	5	D1	30	M1	03-30	0	0	1312	12
3	S3	7	D1	28	M2	03-15	0	10	931	0
4	S1	5	D1	25	M1	04-06	50	0	1092	0
5	E3	13	D1	26	M2	03-15	0	0	1345	0
6	S1	10	D2	30	M1	04-06	90	0	2185	0
7	S1	10	D2	30	M1	03-30	0	0	2185	23
8	S2	5	D2	20	M1	04-06	90	0	2186	0
	S1	4	D2	12	M1	04-06				
9	S3	10	D2	30	M2	03-15	0	18	1330	0
10	S2	5	D2	20	M1	04-06	60	0	2312	0
	E1	10	D2	10						
11	S2	5	D2	20	M1	04-06	60	6	2025	0
	E2	5	D2	10	M2	03-15				
12	E3	30	D2	30	M2	03-15	0	0	3105	0
13	S1	10	D2/D1	30/10	M1	04-06	140	0	2972	0
	S2	3	D1	18	M1	04-06				
14	S1	10	D2/D1	30/10	M1	04-06	110	6	2717	0
	S3	4	D1	16	M2	03-15				
15	S2	5	D2	20	M1	04-06	134	0	3040	0
	S1	4	D2/D1	4/16	M1	04-06				
	S1	3	D2/D1	6/6	M1	04-06				
	E1	3	D1	3	M2	03-15				
16	S1	10	D2/D1	30/10	M1	03-15	30	0	2972	23
	S2	3	D1	18	M1	04-06				
17	S3	10	D2	30	M2	03-15	50	18	2422	0
	S1	5	D1	25	M1	04-06				
18	E3	13	D1	26	M2	03-15	60	0	3258	0
	E1	10	D2	10		04-06				
	S2	5	D2	20	M1					
19	S3	10	D2	30	M2	03-15	0	28	2406	0
	S3	2	D1	8	M2	03-15				
	E2	6	D1	18	M2	03-15				
20	E3	13	D1	26	M2	03-15	0	0	3923	2
	E1	10	D2	10						
	E3	17	D2	17	M2	03-15				
	S1	1	D2	1	M1	03-30				
21	S1	10	D2/D1	30/10	M1	03-30	0	0	2972	30
	S2	3	D1	18	M1	03-30				
22	E1	10	D2	10			0	0	3005	24
	S2	5	D2/D1	10/15	M1	03-30				
	S1	5	D2/D1	10/10	M1	03-30				

Figure 4: Possible solutions. Solutions 1 and 8 are dominated and would not be shown to the decision maker.

In the context of our example, by using the system to generate solutions that satisfy only D1, solutions that satisfy only D2, and solutions that satisfy both D1 and D2, the user can observe the tradeoffs between the various ways to produce each item singly, and the potential benefits that accrue from winning both.

Figure 4 shows a set of 22 possible solutions for this example. The first 5 solutions produce D1 independently. For example, solution 1 prescribes consuming 5 rolls of the supply item S2 from inventory, to produce 30 rolls of D1, using time on machine M1 to cut each 2500 mm wide roll into six 400 mm wide rolls, with 100 mm of waste. The product will be scheduled for machine M1 on April 6. The evaluations of the solutions appear in the four rightmost columns. Since the RFQ quantity is 10 tons and production will be 5 days late, the tardiness is 50 ton-days. Since the product will be made from grade A paper, there are no quality exceptions. The cost is computed as the weight of the 5 rolls of S2 (12.5 tons) times the sum of the per ton material cost and the per ton conversion cost on machine M1 (90 + 15), yielding 1312.5. There are no disruptions because the production is scheduled after the machine availability date.

Among solutions 1 - 5, solution 5 avoids tardiness, quality problems, and disruptions entirely, but at a high cost. In solution 2, the schedule of M1 is modified to produce the D1 items on time. This results in zero tardiness, but 12 tons of schedule disruption. Solution 3 minimizes the cost, but sacrifices quality. Solution 4 has the same tardiness, quality, and disruption evaluations as solution 1, but lower cost; consequently it dominates solution 1. Our system would therefore not recommend (or display) solution 1 to the user.

Among solutions 6 - 12, which produce D2 independently, only solution 8 is dominated. Solutions 7 and 12 show the tradeoff between disruptions and cost.

Solutions 10 and 11, and solutions 9 and 12 show two different tradeoffs between cost and quality. Note that solutions 8, 10, and 11 each use two different supply items to produce the D2 items. Also note that in solution 10, supply item E1 can be used without any conversion to satisfy the RFQ.

Solutions 13 - 22 produce both D1 and D2. With multiple RFQ items, the number of good solutions grows rapidly; all 10 solutions shown are non-dominated. Solution 13 illustrates the possibility of combining D1 and D2 in the consumption of rolls of one supply item, S1. This reduces waste, as can be seen by comparing the evaluations of solution 13 with the combined evaluations of solutions 1 and 6.

As mentioned above, by examining solutions that make RFQ items singly and in groups, the decision maker can evaluate the risks of winning more or fewer auctions than expected. Knowing the evaluations of the contingency plans, the user can adjust the aggressiveness of his/her quotes. For example, if the solutions for making two RFQ items individually evaluate poorly compared to the solutions that make them together, the user might quote more conservatively to increase the likelihood of winning both.

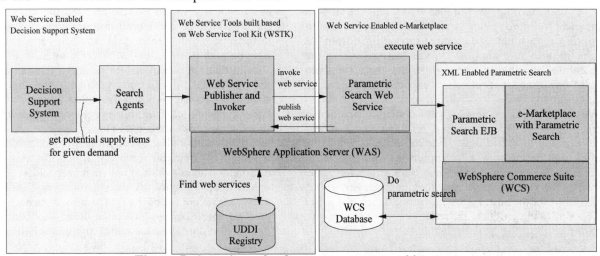

Figure 5: Overview of software component architecture.

Implementation

Our decision support system, implemented in Java, makes use of emerging standards-based technologies such as Web Services (Clement 2002), UDDI (Ariba, IBM, Microsoft 2000), WSDL (Ogbuji 2000) SOAP (Box et al. 2000) and IBM's products, including WebSphere™ Application Server (IBM 2002), and WebSphere Commerce Suite Marketplace Edition™ (IBM 2000). To simulate external supply and demand sources, we created an instance of an e-marketplace with B2B catalog based sales model, that provides RFQs, reverse auctions, forward auctions and double sided auctions. We then made the parametric catalog search facility and the RFQ facilities of the e-marketplace available as web services and published them in a UDDI registry. Using IBM Web Services Tool Kit,

WSTK 2.2, (IBM 2001) infrastructure, we web-service enabled the decision support engine. This includes setting up the infrastructure required to find service providers (e-marketplaces) that provide parametric catalog search and RFQ services, to bind to the services once found and to invoke them when required. Figure 5 summarizes the architecture of our system.

Current Status and Future Work

We currently have a working prototype of the system running in our labs at the IBM T. J. Watson Research Center in Yorktown Height, New York. The data used in this prototype was derived from data gathered from customers and used for testing our promotions system. It reflects the characteristics and distribution of attributes requested by real customers of paper manufactures. We plan to pilot deployment of the system with potential customers in the near future.

In addition, we are working to extend the system to add probabilistic reasoning and data mining techniques to enhance the functionality of the system. We have been extending our work on using Markov models to model auctions (Liu, Goodwin, Koenig 2001) and have enhanced our solution language to include probabilistic events and conditional plans. This allows us to generate probability distributions over cost and delivery dates when considering multiple RFQs with non-disjoint sources of supply. Probabilistic models are also required when generating bid to buy goods when there are multiple auctions or other sources of supply. One needs to consider the probability of acquiring a good for a particular cost in an auction versus the cost of manufacturing it or buying it under a fixed price contract.

The use of probabilistic reasoning requires probability estimates. We have already used market simulation to estimate the probability of winning an auction given a particular bid. However, the simulation models require numerous parameters. One approach we are considering is to use data mining techniques to learn the model parameters to improve estimates. Another approach is to try to directly estimate the required probabilities from the results of previous auctions. With estimates for the probabilities of winning with a given bid, the system can suggest bid prices that maximize expected utility, taking into account the bidder's risk preferences.

We are also looking at using data mining techniques to extract buyer's preferences and willingness to accept various kinds of substitutes. For example, it would be useful to determine if a customer is typically more concerned with quality, cost, substitutions or delivery date. Knowing the relative importance can help suggest which options to offer the customer to maximize their satisfaction and maximize the profits of the seller.

Related Work

The company Perfect.com (Perfect 2002) has identified the need for e-marketplace systems that assist on-line suppliers who are receiving large volumes of RFQs. The Perfect.com system offers several mechanisms to reduce the amount of manual work imposed by RFQs. The simple mechanism is a filter that discards those RFQs whose attributes are not sufficiently close to those that the supplier defines as acceptable. The attributes would likely include purchase terms and product characteristics. The filter therefore reduces the number of RFQs that the supplier must consider. The other mechanism offered by Perfect.com is an automated bidding engine that applies preferences provided by the buyer and cost information provided by the supplier to generate quotes automatically. These quotes use the specified preferences and costs to modify the attributes of the product offered from the

original RFQ, if such modifications improve the product's value to the buyer. Both mechanisms are implemented in the Perfect.com marketplace system.

The filter mechanism offered by the Perfect.com system is both useful and likely to be acceptable to both buyers and suppliers because it can function without requiring buyers and suppliers to reveal detailed private information. Filter criteria such as "we want only blue widgets" or "we make only yellow widgets" may be considered public and could therefore be used for automatic filtering by the e-marketplace. It is similar to the filter mechanism that our system offers, with the exception that our system allows the filter to be refined per session.

On the other hand, many buyers and suppliers will probably be reluctant to reveal to a Perfect.com-like e-marketplace the detailed private information needed for Perfect.com's system to generate automatic quotes. Such private information as "a blue widget is worth $40 dollars more to me than a yellow widget" or "it costs me $30 dollars more to make a blue widget than a yellow widget" may be too sensitive and dynamic for users to reveal to others. Even though Perfect.com may not permit buyers to view a supplier's cost structure directly, buyers could infer this information by submitting multiple RFQs with systematically varied parameters. Furthermore, some of the criteria to be considered in responding to an RFQ are not static, but depend on the current production environment of the supplier. Accessing such data would require that the e-marketplace have tight integration with the supplier's information systems, which may not be acceptable to the supplier from both privacy and cost standpoints. In contrast, our system can reside within the suppliers security domain, to give it easy and secure access to private data and allow suppliers to deal with multiple sources of demand and supply without revealing information about which suppliers it is considering.

Maxager Technology Inc. (Maxager 2002) offers software that computes the profitability of manufacturing a product in real-time. Maxager Precision Bidding™ is designed to communicate with a supplier's ERP and MES systems to get up-to-date data needed to compute profitability. These data can include raw material costs and the production rates on equipment. The profitability is the difference between the customer's price and the current production costs. This is helpful when deciding whether to accept an order, but is not sufficient because it may sometimes be advisable to reject an order with low profit with the expectation that a higher profit order will arrive in the near future. Maxager Precision Bidding aims to address the issue that participants are unwilling to reveal private information by providing suppliers with a system that assists them in responding to RFQs. However, it reduces all the data to profitability, ignoring other important business measures like customer satisfaction, quality, and smooth production line operation.

Yet another aspect of responding to RFQs not addressed by existing art is consideration of other RFQs that the supplier has received in the same time period. A supplier will probably use a different strategy to respond to RFQs when he has received a large number of them for the same product than if the volume of RFQs for that product is small. There is a need for a tool that considers the RFQs received in aggregate when recommending responses.

Gimenez-Funes, in their work use the history of bidding results from previous auctions to estimate the probability of winning an auction with a given bid and situation. They modify bidding strategy based on actual current auction conditions, and find the bid price that maximizes short-term expected benefit of an auction, where the value is determined by the resale price. Finally they choose the decision with the highest global utility. However, the authors do not make use of production scheduling and planning to determine the value of an item, and they do not propose strategies for participating in multiple simultaneous auctions (or RFQs). Furthermore they do not discuss adjusting the bidding strategy based on the bidder's degree of risk.

Conclusions

In this paper, we have presented a system for suggesting how to fulfill a request for quote, taking into account current inventory, production capacity, reworking of goods and purchase of goods from external sources. The solutions provided highlight ways of combining orders from multiple RFQs to improve efficiency and reduce cost. The system provides the human decision maker with the information needed to make good quotes, taking into account possible substitutions and relaxation of requirements that can improve efficiency and profitability.

In future work, we intend to extend the system to suggest quote prices that maximize expected utility and to suggest which attributes of an RFQ a buyer might be willing to compromise on or pay more to have fulfilled.

References

Ariba, IBM, Microsoft; 2002. UDDI Technical White Paper: http://www.uddi.org/pubs/Iru_UDDI_Technical_White_Paper.pdf

Box et al., 2000. Simple Object Access Protocol (SOAP)1.1, W3C Note 08 May 2000 http://www.w3.org/TR/SOA Don Box, David Ehnebuske, Gopal Kakivaya, Andrew Layman, Noah Mendelsohn, Henrik Frystyk Nielsen, Satish Thatte, Dave Winer

Clement t, 2002. Web services: Why all the buzz? . CNET News http://www.news.com

Gimenez-Funes et al 1998. Designing Bidding Strategies for Trading Agents in Electronic Auctions. E. Gimenez-Funes, L Godo, J.A. Rodriguez-Aguilar, and P. Garcia-Calves. Proceedings of the Third International Conference on Multi-Agent Systems, Paris, France 3-7 July 1998, IEEE Computer Society

IBM 2002. WebSphere Application Server: http://www-3.ibm.com/software/webservers/appserv/

IBM 2000. WebSphere Commerce Business Edition: http://www-3.ibm.com/software/webservers/commerce/wc_be/

IBM 2001. Web Services Toolkit (WSTK): http://www.alphaworks.ibm.com/tech/webservicestoolkit

Keskinocak et al. 1999. Decision-Support for Managing an Electronic Supply Chain", Pinar Keskinocak, Richard Goodwin, Frederick Wu, Rama Akkiraju, Sesh Murthy, Workshop on Electronic Commerce, 1st Asia Pacific Conference on Intelligent Agent Technology, Hong Kong.

Liu, Goodwin Koening 2001. Risk Averse Auction Planning and its integration into Supply Chain Management Systems. Yaxin Liu, Richard Goodwin, Sven Koenig, AAAI spring symposium on Game Theoretic and Decision Theoretic Agents, 2001.

Maxager Technology Inc. 2002. http://www.maxager.com

Murthy et al 1999. Cooperative Multi-Objective Decision-support for the Paper Industry. Murthy S., Akkiraju R., Goodwin R, Wu F,. Interfaces Volume 29 #5 1999.

Ogbuji, U; 2000. Using WSDL in SOAP applications: An introduction to WSDL for SOAP programmers, Fourthought, Inc. Http://www-106.ibm.com/developerworks/webservices/library/ws-soap/index.html

Perfect.com 2002. http://www.Perfect.com

Rachlin et al 1999. A-Teams: An Agent Architecture for Optimization and Decision-Support. John Rachlin, Richard Goodwin, Sesh Murthy, Rama Akkiraju, Fred Wu, Santhosh Kumaran, Raja Das. Intelligent Agents V, Springer-Verlag 1999.

UTTSExam: A Campus-Wide University Exam-Timetabling System

Andrew Lim, Juay-Chin Ang, Wee-Kit Ho, Wee-Chong Oon

School of Computing, National University of Singapore
3 Science Drive 2
Singapore 117543, Singapore
{alim, angjc, howk, oonwc}@comp.nus.edu.sg

Abstract

UTTSExam is the exam-scheduling portion of the University Timetable Scheduler (*UTTS*) software, an automated university timetabling program developed in the National University of Singapore. It was successfully used to schedule the examination timetable for the first semester of the 2001/2002 academic year in NUS, a task involving 27,235 students taking 1,350 exams. The use of the software resulted in significant time savings in the scheduling of the timetable and a shortening of the examination period. This paper explains the development and design of *UTTSExam*.

Introduction

The National University of Singapore (NUS)[1] introduced the modular academic course structure in 1993. This allowed students to choose the modules that they wished to study in order to complete their degree requirements. As a result of this added flexibility, the task of scheduling the examination timetables in NUS became much more complex, especially in view of the increasing number of cross-faculty modules (i.e. modules that can be taken by students from different faculties).

The task of scheduling examination timetables was previously done manually, an error-prone process that tends to take several weeks to complete. As a result, in 1999 the university sponsored the development of the University Timetable Scheduler (*UTTS*) software, an automated university timetable-scheduling program. When completed, the program is expected to automatically schedule both the course and examination timetables for all the faculties in the entire university that employ the modular academic course structure.

The course-scheduling portion of the program is currently still under development (Lim et al. 2000a). However, the exam-scheduling portion (Lim et al. 2000b), called *UTTSExam*, has reached the deployment stage and was used to generate the examination timetable for the first semester of the 2001/2002 academic year in NUS.

---

1 http://www.nus.edu.sg

This paper describes the steps involved in the development of *UTTSExam* from its conception to its completion, along with a breakdown of the inner workings of each portion of the software.

Problem Description

This examination-timetabling problem (ETTP) involves creating a schedule such that a set of examinations is allocated into venues with limited capacities within an examination period. ETTP is an instance of the Constraint Satisfaction Optimization Problem (CSOP) (Tsang 1993), which is a combination of two types of problems. The first is the Constraint Satisfaction Problem (CSP), which involves:

- A set of variables $X = \{x_1, \ldots x_n\}$
- For each variable x_i, a finite set D_i of possible values (its domain)
- A set of *critical* constraints restricting the values that sets of variables may take simultaneously

A solution to the CSP is an assignment of values to all variables such that every constraint is satisfied. General timetabling and scheduling problems, which are NP-Hard (Garey and Johnson 1979), may be modeled as a CSP. In particular, the ETTP can be modeled as a CSP by treating each examination as a variable, and the domain of each variable would be the available examination sessions. The ETTP has a further provision that the solution should take up as few sessions as possible. The two critical constraints for all ETTP are as follows:

- Two examinations that are taken by any particular student cannot be scheduled in the same session.
- The total number of candidates taking the papers scheduled in a particular venue must not exceed the venue's capacity.

Real-life ETTP problems also have another set of *non-critical* constraints, which may be violated while still retaining the feasibility of the solution. The *quality* of two feasible solutions may be measured by a weighted sum of its non-critical constraint violations. The best fulfillment of these non-critical constraints, as measured by a weighted sum, is an optimization problem.

In the case of the first semester of the 2001/2002 academic year in NUS, this involves 27,235 students each taking one or more of 1,350 examinations (for a total of 100,599 student-examination tuples), to be scheduled in the following venues (Table 1):

Alias	Venue	Capacity
STC	Suntec City Exhibition Hall	1600
GYM	Gymnasium	312
MPH1	Multi-Purpose Sports Hall 1	750
MPH2	Multi-Purpose Sports Hall 2	850
CH	Competition Hall	396
EH	Eusoff Hall	175
TH	Temasek Hall	136
LT8	Lecture Theatre 8	117
LT11	Lecture Theatre 11	125
LT13	Lecture Theatre 13	81
LT17	Lecture Theatre 17	112

Table 1: List of Examination Venues

The examination period was from the 12th to 26th November 2001. There were 3 sessions a day (morning, afternoon and evening) for the 12 available days in this period, equaling 36 sessions in total. Suntec City is a commercial venue that was unavailable for the last 5 sessions of the examination period.

Scheduling Strategy

In general, there are two approaches to the scheduling of university timetables, namely *centralized* or *de-centralized*. Both approaches have their own advantages and disadvantages.

Initially, we utilized the centralized approach, whereby a central authority uses the software to schedule the timetable for the entire university. In theory, this grants a global view of the problem domain, presenting all the information necessary to best create the timetable. Unfortunately, the sheer size of the problem proved to be too difficult, such that the scheduling program was unable to create a high-quality feasible timetable. Furthermore, co-ordination between the faculties and the central authority was difficult and error-prone.

Alternatively, the de-centralized approach lets each faculty schedule its own examination timetable using its own venue resources. However, this approach would rapidly become infeasible as more cross-faculty modules are introduced, since it works best if communication between faculties can be reduced to a minimum. There is also a problem in scheduling large examinations if the faculty does not have access to large venues.

We eventually adopted a hybrid centralized and de-centralized approach to scheduling (Ho, Lim and Oon 2002). Before student registration, the examinations' enrolment estimates were used to proportionally allocate a fixed number of *seats* for each faculty (called their *venue partition*). Each faculty would then schedule their exams according to their venue partitions, disregarding the actual venues and the effects of cross-faculty modules. These faculty timetables are then merged into a campus-wide tentative timetable.

The central authority would be able to obtain the finalized information for each exam after student registration. At this point, the tentative timetable is updated with the finalized information. Finally, the exams would then be allocated to their actual venues, verified by the individual faculties and published. This approach proved to create a much better timetable than the initial centralized approach.

Application Description

The structure of the *UTTSExam* program is governed by the hybrid scheduling approach. Aside from the basic functions of data entry and scheduling, facilities must be provided for venue partitioning and transfer and communication of data. Minor side-applications include the creation of a candidate seating plan and the printing of reports.

Hardware & Software

The system was coded in *Java 1.3* with *Swing™* components using the *IBM VisualAge™ for Java 3.5* software and *Microsoft Access™ 2000* databases. The central machine used was a *Pentium-800* PC with 256MB RAM.

System Design

There are two versions of *UTTSExam*. The *Registrar Version* is the full-fledged program that has access to all the features of the program. This is controlled by the Registrars' Office (the central authority). Instead, the individual faculties operate the stripped-down *Faculty Version*, which they use to enter the enrolment estimates for their faculty's examinations, as well as schedule their faculty timetables according to their venue partitions.

The *UTTSExam* system design is based on the 3-Tier architecture that is commonly used when building Client/Server applications. It keeps distinct the GUI, object oriented and data storage portions of our program. By separating the system into 3 tiers, they can be worked on independently (Reese, 1997).

UTTSExam is divided into the following 3 tiers. The *View* tier involves the graphical user interface. The *Application* tier is composed of the modules in an object-oriented paradigm that manipulate the objects in the system. This includes the scheduling engine, the printing modules and the report generator. Finally, the *Persistence* layer consists of the actual database access. Figure 1 shows the system design.

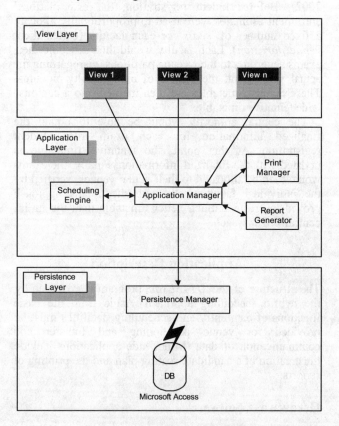

Figure 1: UTTS System Architecture

Variable Definitions

UTTSExam contains several screens that enable the user to define all the variables of the timetabling problem, including:

- Examination information
- Venue information
- Candidate information
- Exam session particulars
- Constraint definitions

The Faculty version can only make changes and assign constraints to exams pertaining to that particular faculty.

Constraint Definitions

Of particular interest are the constraint definitions. It is imperative that the program allows the users to define all the necessary constraints. *UTTSExam* allows the definition of a multitude of constraints:

- Separate all examinations with different duration.
- Spread all examinations of a student over the examination period as much as possible.

- Any 2 papers of a student should be placed minimally x sessions or y days apart.
- *Paper A* be placed x days away from *Paper B*
- *Paper A* be placed x sessions away from *Paper B*
- *Paper A* to be held before *Paper B*
- *Paper A* and *Paper B* to be held at the same time
- *Paper A* and *Paper B* are not to be held at the same time
- *Paper A* and *Paper B* to be held at the same time and same venue
- *Paper A* to be held as early/late as possible in the examination period
- *Paper A* is to be held in session s
- *Paper A* is not to be held in session s
- *Paper A* is to be held on/before/after date d
- *Paper A* is to be held within period $(d1, d2)$
- *Paper A* must not be held during period $(d1, d2)$
- *Paper A* is to be held in week n.
- *Paper A* is to be held at venue v.
- *Paper A* is to be held at a venue belonging to venue group g.

For ease of entry, *UTTSExam* also allows the definition of examination paper groups. In this way, the user can define both intra- and inter-group constraints, thereby allowing the definition of constraints between several papers at a time. In addition, the introduction of paper groups allows the following constraints:

- At most x papers from this group can be held in the same time slot
- Papers in this group must be held as far apart as possible

Figure 2 shows the Constraint Definition Screen.

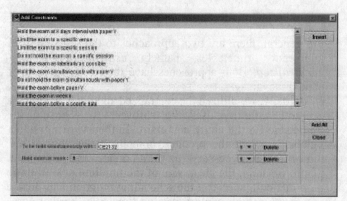

Figure 2: Constraint Definition Screen

Venue Partitioning

When the faculties'enrolment estimates have been made, this information is used to proportionally assign venue partitions to each faculty in the form of the number of seats for each session. The heuristics used are given in the next section. *UTTSExam* provides a user interface for the manipulation and assignment of venue partitions to the faculties.

Import/Export

Co-ordination between the faculties and the Registrars' Office is achieved via a central database. The Faculty Version allows the exporting of the enrolment estimates and examination information for retrieval by the Registrars' Office. With this information, the venue partitioning is done and uploaded to the database for retrieval by the faculties. The faculties then schedule their timetables and export the results. The merging of the various faculties'timetables is then done. This col lated timetable is once more uploaded to the database for verification by the individual faculties. Once the changes are finalized, the timetable can be published.

Output

Various reports can be created for reference by the program. These include the interim and finalized timetables; the constraints defined; examination, venue and candidate information; and the seating plan for each session. All of these reports are generated in html files, so that they can be displayed on the university webpages.

Figure 3 gives a section of the timetable generated for semester 1 of the 2001/2002 academic year.

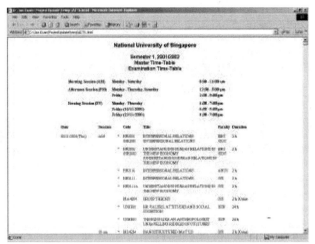

Figure 3: Scheduled timetable output

Scheduling Engine

The heart of the program is the scheduling engine, including the merging process. The system allows manual intervention both before and after the automated scheduling process. The timetabling administrator might wish to manually insert some examinations into specific slots before invoking the scheduling engine. He can also tweak the generated timetable after the scheduling is done.

The details of the scheduling algorithm are given in the next section. Figure 4 shows the Scheduling Screen.

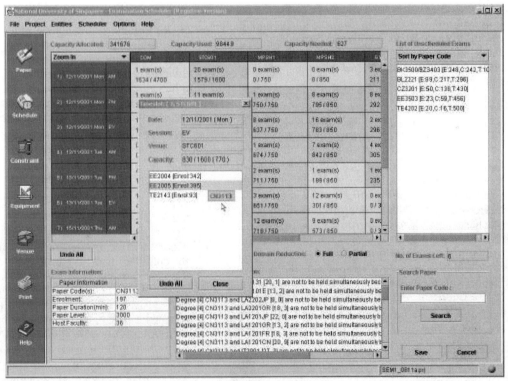

Figure 4: Scheduling Screen

Uses of AI Technology

The main aim of *UTTSExam* is to create the examination timetable for NUS, and to that end there are three separate processes to examine, namely the venue partitioning process, the scheduling of the faculty timetables and the merging of the faculty timetables into the collated whole.

Venue partitioning is a complex problem. In order to decide the size and composition of the venue partitions to be allocated to each faculty, the following criteria must be taken into account:

- Obviously, the number of seats allocated should be proportional to the total candidacy of the faculty.
- The number of large papers for that faculty determines the number of large venue partitions given.
- Each faculty should be given extra seats so that they have some room to maneuver when scheduling the papers. However, the number of extra seats should *not* be strictly proportional to the total candidacy of the faculty. If too few extra seats are given, they are superfluous. Also, faculties with large candidacies tend to not need many extra seats since they have many small papers.

Currently, the process of venue partitioning is done manually. Although an automated venue-partitioning tool implementing the above heuristics is planned, manual intervention is probably still necessary. This is because it is difficult to specify all the pertinent constraints for a program to use, but relatively easy for a human to keep track of them. For example, past experience may reveal that one faculty tends to have many heavily constrained papers, and therefore needs larger partitions. This information is hard to express to an automated program.

When the venue partitions are obtained, the faculty timetables are scheduled using the Combined Method for solving CSOP (Ho and Lim, 2001). This involves first employing a stochastic search technique to find a high-quality solution that may violate some hard constraints. This solution is then used to guide a selection algorithm with consistency checking to create a feasible timetable with minimal changes to the initial solution. *UTTSExam* uses the Genetic Algorithm (Marin 1998) with Tabu Search post-optimization (Rayward-Smith et al. 1996), which is used to guide the Variable Ordering Method with AC-3 (Mackworth 1977) consistency checking.

To merge the faculty timetables, *UTTSExam* once again makes use of the Variable Ordering Method with AC-3. As each examination is considered, the program tries to schedule it into the slot depicted by the faculty timetable. If this causes a conflict, the examination is set aside. When all the examinations have been considered, the program attempts to insert the remaining exams into the schedule by a trial and error process: the program chooses a slot, then inserts the offending examination into it by removing the conflicting exams that were originally in the slot. This process is repeated several times until no such improving exchanges can be found.

If there are examinations left that still cannot be scheduled, there is no recourse but to contact the relevant faculties to request a loosening of the constraints. For the first semester of 2001/2002, there were 12 examinations left over at the end of the process. These were eventually inserted into the schedule after discussion with the relevant faculties.

This process produced a much better timetable than making use of the Combined Method alone to schedule the entire timetable. In fact, over 1000 examinations could not be scheduled using the Combined Method alone.

Application Use and Payoff

UTTSExam was used to create the examination timetable for the recently completed semester 1 of the 2001/2002 academic year. The semester 2 examination timetable has already been scheduled based on the enrolment estimates. At the time of writing, student registration is under way. Upon its completion, the merging process could then begin.

Even though the program has only been used for one semester so far, the benefits of automating examination timetabling is obvious:

- In this initial implementation of the program, data entry and constraint specification was the most time-consuming part of the process, taking up to 2 weeks. However, subsequent semesters require much less data entry since the examination information remains largely the same. The actual scheduling, once the data entry was completed, takes less than 5 minutes.
- Assuming that the constraints entered are accurate, *UTTSExam* ensures that the produced timetable is conflict-free. This is especially important when taking into account the added complexity that cross-faculty modules bring to the task.
- Last-minute changes can be quickly catered for.
- Since each faculty is using the same system, all the output formats have been standardized.
- The speed of the system allows experimentation with different parameters and policies. Previously, the NUS examination period usually spanned a month, and there were only 2 sessions a day. It is only with the automated system that the new policy of 3-session days over 2 weeks could be implemented.
- The shortening of the examination period means that the renting of commercial venues (like Suntec City) is minimized. This translates to a substantial monetary saving.

Application Development and Deployment

The *UTTSExam* program started development in NUS in mid-1999 when it became obvious that the introduction of cross-faculty modules would make the scheduling of course and examination timetables an increasingly difficult process. The existing manual timetabling process became exceedingly time-consuming, and cases of overlooked conflicts became more and more frequent. NUS therefore provided funding for the development of the University Timetable Scheduler program. This provided for two full-time application programmers and finances for research into timetable scheduling algorithms.

To facilitate the development of the program, a timetabling committee was set up containing two representatives from the administrative sections of each of the seven involved faculties, along with representatives from the Registrars' Office. Weekly meetings were held between the committee and the development team to discuss design issues, required features and other important points. Frequent email correspondence helped to keep both parties up to date with developments.

The initial meetings were concerned largely with formulating a data representation scheme that was sufficient to handle the requirements of the problem. Once that was done, the development team began converting the existing data from the university's central database into the *UTTSExam* format, while the faculty representatives worked out their respective constraints. To facilitate the entry of these constraints into the system, the Faculty Versions of *UTTSExam* was developed. Meanwhile, research was being done on various scheduling methods.

When all the data was obtained, preliminary experiments on scheduling the timetables for the entire university produced discouraging results. Due to the enormity of the problem, the scheduling engine was unable to create a feasible timetable at all (over 1000 examinations could not be placed within the examination period). We then decided to try the distributed approach, making use of the Faculty Versions (which were originally intended for data entry purposes only) by allowing each faculty to perform their own scheduling based on venue partitions.

Interestingly, even though the Faculty Versions made use of the same scheduling algorithm, this partition-schedule-merge approach managed to produce a timetable that was able to fit in all but 12 exams. After negotiation with the individual faculties, these exams were incorporated with the minimum of hassle.

As with all initial deployments of new software, there were a few teething problems. Up until the deadline for the publication of the timetable, numerous last-minute changes had to be made as a result of occurrences like late registrations and invigilator unavailability. There were also a few data entry errors that went unnoticed until very late in the process, which is always a potential problem on initial deployments. The automated system was able to cater to all of these changes quickly while maintaining the feasibility of the entire timetable, something that would be immensely difficult to do manually.

Maintenance

Currently, the role of the Registrars' Office central authority is being played by the development team as alterations to the program are made as required. Control of the program will be handed over to Registrars' Office personnel in a few months, once some final issues are ironed out. Since the program is simple and instinctive to use, minimal training will be required (although an understanding of scheduling and constraints would aid its use). Data entry will also be minimal, as most modules will have much the same information and constraints across academic years.

UTTSExam can already unabashedly claim to be able to generate an examination timetable based on the more commonly encountered constraints. However, there are some rare special cases that need to be addressed. One such case involves an examination that had to be divided into two or more venues within the same session, since it was offered to students from different faculties who must be given different examinations (of the same module).

We are confident that the *UTTSExam* program will be able to produce examination timetables for NUS quickly and efficiently for years to come.

Conclusion

This paper takes a look at what is required in the development of the examination-scheduling portion of the *UTTS* automated university timetable-scheduling program, entitled *UTTSExam*. We described the size and complexity of the problem of scheduling the exam timetables for a large university like NUS that employs a modular course structure with several cross-faculty modules, along with the strategy employed to best overcome these difficulties. The program's design, features and scheduling approach was also described.

Even though *UTTSExam* has only been deployed for one semester, the advantages of an automated examination-scheduling program are obvious and significant. Despite the difficulties encountered in its developmental process, all agree that it has been well worth the effort. We hope that our work will inspire other universities to consider automated timetable scheduling as well.

References

Garey, M. R. and Johnson, D. S. *Computers and Intractability: A Guide to the Theory of NP-Completeness*, 1979.

Ho, W. K. and Lim, A. *A Hybrid-Based Framework for Constraint Satisfaction Optimization Problems*, in International Conference on Information Systems (ICIS) 2001, pg. 65-76.

Ho, W. K.; Lim, A.; and Oon, W. C. *UTTSExam: A University Examination Timetabling System*, submitted to IEEE Intelligent Systems 2002.

Lim, A.; Oon, W. C.; Ang, J. C.; and Ho, W. K *Development of a Campus-wide University Course Timetabling Application*, in 3rd International Conference on the Practice and Theory of Automated Timetabling (PATAT) 2000, pg. 71-77.

Lim, A.; Ang, J. C.; Ho, W. K.; and Oon, W. C. *A Campus-Wide University Examination Timetabling Application*, in Innovative Applications in Artificial Intelligence (AAAI/IAAI) 2000, pg. 1020-1025

Mackworth, A. K. *Consistency in Networks of Relations*, in Artificial Intelligence 8 (1977): 88-119

Marin, H. T. "Combinations of GA and CSP Strategies for Solving the Examination Timetabling Problem", *Ph.D. thesis, Instiuto Technologico y de Estudios Superiores de Menterrey*, 1998.

Rayward-Smith, V. J.; Osman, I. H.; Reeves, C. R.; and Smith, G. D. *Modern Heuristic Search Methods*, 1996.

Reese, G. *Database Programming with JDBC and Java*, OReilly 1997.

Tsang, E. *Foundations of Constraint Satisfaction*, 1993.

A Structure Based Configuration Tool:
Drive Solution Designer - DSD

Christoph Ranze[2], Thorsten Scholz[1], Thomas Wagner[1], Andreas Günter[3],
Otthein Herzog[1], Oliver Hollmann[2], Christoph Schlieder[1], Volker Arlt[4]

University of Bremen, TZI[1],
Universitaetsallee 21-23,
D-28359 Bremen
{cs, herzog, scholz, twagner}
@tzi.de
Tel: +49 421 218 7090
Fax: +49 421 218 7196

encoway GmbH & Co KG[2]
Universitätsalle 21-23,
D-28359 Bremen
{hollmann, ranze}
@encoway.de
Tel: +49 421 246 770
Fax: +49 421 246 7710

University of Hamburg[3],
Dept. of Computer Science and
HiTec e.V.
Vogt-Koelln-Str. 30,
D-22527 Hamburg
guenter@informatik.uni-hamburg.de

Lenze AG[4]
Hameln
Hans-Lenze-Strasse 1
D-31763 Hameln
arlt@lenze.de
Tel: +49 5154 82 2534
Fax: +49 5154 82 1920

Abstract

In this paper, we describe the configuration tool *Drive Solution Designer* (DSD). The DSD is used by sales engineers of the company *Lenze AG (www.lenze.com)* for the configuration of complex drive systems in order to make on-site offers together with the customer. The aim of this process is to generate a consistent solution which fulfills the functional requirements of the user along with optimization criteria such as price and delivery time. The preparation of a technical offer requires fundamental knowledge of complex physical and in particular technical correlations of drive components, in depth knowledge of the product catalog as well as high empirical knowledge about the order of the parameterization of the components. In order to meet these requirements knowledge-based AI-techniques are required. In the DSD we use a domain independent incremental *structure-based configuration* approach with different knowledge representation mechanisms and a sophisticated declarative control. Currently DSD is used with great success by approx. 150 sales engineers of the company *Lenze* for the design layout task. The introduction of the DSD lead to a drastic time reduction for drive solution development and reduces incorrect solutions to nearly 0 percent.

Task Description

The growing complexity of drive configurations in industrial sales and distribution scenarios makes high demands on sales engineers. This is caused by the highly dynamical product evolution in combination with constant improvement of the product features and the increasing complexity of customer-stipulated solutions as well as tighter optimality criteria.

This applies especially to products which require profound expert knowledge. The degree of complexity mainly depends on the structure of the products and the closely

connected sales scenario. In [Hollmann et.al. 2001] we distinguish three different sales scenarios:

Click & Buy: This is the most simple scenario. Only non-customizable, complete products are offered to the customer from a product catalog (e.g. www.amazon.com). The customer is able to choose a product without taking expert configuration knowledge into account. Complexity- and consistency problems need not be handled and the use of AI-technologies is not necessary.

Customize & Buy: In this scenario, products can be customized with regard to the customers desires. This scenario is found at many car manufacturers like BMW (www.bmw.com) or at computer vendors like Dell (www.dell.com). The combination of valid configurations of components is still restricted and can be represented explicitly (e.g. within the product catalog). Thus complexity and consistency still play a minor role and can be handled by standard information technologies.

Configure & Buy: This is the most complex scenario and requires the use of AI-technologies. The vast amount of possible combinations of components and the multitude of complex domain-specific restrictions lead to a serious complexity problem as it is infeasible to list the set of possible solutions. Thus the generation of a valid solution requires explicit expert knowledge and therefore cannot be done by customers on their own. Even with detailed expert knowledge the creation of valid solutions remains a difficult task which in some cases leads to faulty configurations. An example of this scenario is the *Lenze*-domain handled by the DSD.

The Drive Configuration Task

The problem of designing drives (e.g. for printing- and sorting machines, automated saw, etc.) lies in finding a consistent combination of an engine, a gear and a drive controller while starting from a very limited set of basic data like motor power and torque. The configuration has to fulfill to a high degree the imprecise requirements of the customer while being as cost-efficient as possible. The selection of the required components and their parameterization implies a high level of engineering knowledge and detailed knowledge about the product catalog. The goal was to develop a software configuration tool for the *Lenze AG (www.lenze.com)* to support sales engineers in this complex task.

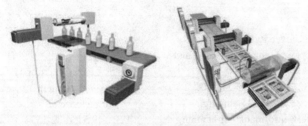

Figure 1: Sample applications: Installation (left) and printing machine (right)

The complexity of this special task is captured by the fact that there are thousands of different engines, gears, engine controller and additional components and their variants manufactured by *Lenze* (and even more off-company products). If all the combinations of all components were to be considered, this would lead to a solution space of 10^{21} of possibly consistent products. Additionally, the complexity is increased by the fact that central components like engines and gears may have hundreds of parameters and restrictions constraining possible solutions.

When parameterizing and specializing components, there is a highly complex constraint-net between the parameters within as well as the parameters of other components. These constraints reflect the complex physical correlations (both mechanical and kinetic) and result in a difficult consistency problem.

A special problem arises from the assistance aspect. In order to support sales engineers intuitively, the control mechanism of the system has to be able to represent the sequence of specifying the values for the parameters. This has a great impact on the quality of the configured solution. Additionally, the values have to be specified according to the individual requirements of each customer in order to get high quality solutions.

Because of this general set-up, it is very time-consuming to achieve a high-quality and consistent solution in direct cooperation with the customer.

In practice, the basically hand-made configuration of a drive system did not ensure that the resulting solution was complete and consistent. This resulted in a number of problems, when an error occurred, since the faulty solution was the foundation of the offer. The main problems can be summarized as follows:

1. The consistency of the generated solution, composed of a number of engines, gears, drive controllers and support components, has to be checked by engineers at the main manufacturing site of *Lenze*. This means that all solu-

tions developed at the customer's location are subject to inconsistency and therefore possibly cannot be built.

2. The validation of a solution (i.e. a detailed sketch) is a very time-consuming task. In some cases, highly qualified engineers need days to perform this work.

3. New, innovative products are often not taken into consideration by sales engineers, since it is almost impossible for them to keep up with all new developments.

4. This also may apply to more cost-efficient solutions by choosing standardized components which can be a serious drawback on the profitableness and might result in longer delivery times.

5. The sales engineers are in most cases highly qualified specialists in a certain field, who excel in finding optimal solutions for their field. There is no easy way to make this knowledge available to other non-experts in the specific domain.

System Goals

The goal of the project was the development of a software tool to support knowledge-based configuration in order to assist sales engineers in preparing an offer. The main system goals can be described as follows:

- *Domain-independent configuration engine:* Although DSD was designed to solve a specific problem, the configuration engine itself should be domain-independent, so that it can be used in different projects. This ensures the future availability of software updates and support.

- *Assisting the configuration task:* The system is supposed to assist the user in the configuration task without taking over the whole work. It should propose solutions for the given problem, but leave the key decision to the sales engineers.

- *Increasing the speed to place an offer:* Placing an offer for a drive solution could take anything from 3 to 30 hours. Assisted by the system, this time should be reduced significantly.

- *Handling the amount of variants:* The system should make it possible to handle the high amount of possible combinations. It should be possible to browse through the space of currently valid components at any given time.

- *Ensuring the consistency of the offer/solution:* As a key requirement, the final configuration should be consistent according to the physical knowledge and the product catalog.

- *Controlling the configuration process:* The system should be able to guide the user through the configuration process in an intuitive way based on empirical knowledge of other experts.

- *Building and maintaining the knowledge base:* As the domain of drive systems is a rapidly changing domain, it should be easy to build and maintain the knowledge base.

Additionally, a number of other requirements like a modern software architecture for web-integration, consideration of alternative solutions and building a case-base for successful solutions have also been made.

Application Description

The software tool "Drive Solution Designer" (DSD) has been developed by the TZI (Center for Computing Technologies) of the University of Bremen, the companies *encoway GmbH & Co KG,* and *Lenze* AG.

It provides extensive assistance for a sales engineer in the *Configure & Buy* scenario and its usage resulted in a considerable increase of the quality of the products as well as in a significant reduction of the development period. It is a software assistant used by *Lenze* sales engineers at the customer's location in order to validate technical offers for drive systems with respect to their possible construction with the aid of *structure-based configuration* (Günter/Cunis 1992, Günter 1995a.). Based on the domain-independent configuration engine EngCon, the DSD supports ETO (Engineering to Order) configuration.

Consequently, the DSD does not only calculate physical correlations with the help of various formulas, but it also computes a correct solution which can be built and delivered, containing a sensible combination of the Lenze products.

Configuration with EngCon

The central component of the DSD is, as already mentioned, the domain-independent structure-based configuration engine EngCon. EngCon is a standardized configuration platform based on long-term AI research (Hollmann et. al. 2000). The configuration engine allows the stepwise assembly of a drive system by constantly controlling the consistency of the partial solution. In contrary to the common configuration approaches which perform something similar to breadth-first search resulting in all possible solutions, structure-based configuration performs a depth-first search, resulting in only one given solution (global consistency can not be ensured for partial solutions without performing a complete look-ahead search). At the first glance, this may seem a drawback, however, this is not the case: The complexity of the domain of offer validation for technical drives is extremely high. With constraint-based configuration engines, all possible solutions would be made available to the salesman who in turn would have to choose one concrete product out of this large set.

By adding domain specific knowledge about the configuration task as well as providing sophisticated modeling techniques, the structure based configuration provides a single solution. There are three types of knowledge used in the configuration task: The product catalog, the relationships between the components from that catalog and a control structure on how to perform the configuration task.

If an offer for a drive solution is going to be configured with the DSD, the user starts with choosing a certain type of product. By specifying parameters and relations for this initial concept, it is decomposed into its parts, which in turn are decomposed again, until a solution is found. To make sure that only a consistent solution is produced the configuration engine EngCon applies various AI techniques described in the AI technology section. All the time, the user is guided by a configuration control, which helps to produce high quality solutions by applying domain expert knowledge about the order of the decomposition task.

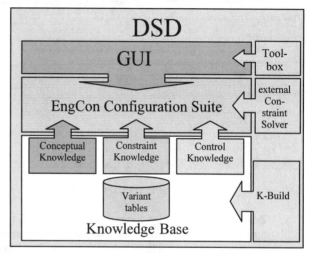

Figure 2: Architecture of the DSD

System Architecture

The DSD has been completely implemented in Java™ 1.3 technology, using the standard API as well as Java Swing. There are three major components in the DSD: The domain-independent configuration engine EngCon, the user interface, and the knowledge bases (see figure 2).

Within the central component EngCon, taxonomical inferences and constraint-propagation is performed in order to ensure a consistent solution resulting from the configuration process. EngCon utilizes interchangeable external constraint solver for propagating constraints over infinite domains and intervals. These may rank from C-libraries (CSP) to Prolog Systems (CLP) connected to EngCon via the Java Native Interface (JNI). Additionally to these constraints, EngCon uses variant tables which are stored in a database accessed through the ODBC/JDBC interface.

The second vital part of the DSD is the knowledge base, containing the product knowledge. The knowledge base contains three types of knowledge: The component knowledge, the constraint knowledge, and the control knowledge. For the maintenance of the knowledgebase, a domain-independent, Web-based service tool is available, the K-Build.

Guiding the sales engineer through the configuration process is the GUI, visualizing the technical details (see figure 3). On top of it, the so called sketch is visualizing the already chosen components, providing a rough overview about the configuration process as well as component details. The sales engineer is able to enter the data required for building a drive solution in various sheets and graphs on the bottom part of the GUI.

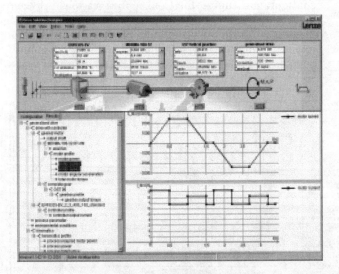

Figure 3: The DSD User Interface

Additionally to these components, a set of tools for calculating the correct parameters for components is available to the user in order to facilitate the process of configuration.

Uses of AI Technology

In other domains e.g. the telecommunications domain, classical configuration systems have been successfully deployed (e.g. (Focacci, et.al. 1997), (Chow and Perett, 1997), (Bach 2000)). Unfortunately, these constraint-based configurators proved inappropriate for the task described here. The main reasons are:

- **Knowledge acquisition** in constraint-based configuration is difficult for non constraint experts.
- **Search space size**: In the DSD, search space is far too complex to compute each and every solution from a given number of starting parameters. Nearly every concept has a number of real intervals whose values will be restricted during a step-by-step configuration process.
- **Control**: The succession of the configuration steps has a deep impact on the quality of the solution. In a constraint system it is hardly if not almost impossible to model the knowledge about the order of the configuration. The knowledge about which order leads to a high-quality solution is an important resource of an experienced sales engineer. It is necessary to describe this knowledge and make it available for other, less experienced sales engineers.
- **Assisting the configuration task:** The customer neither knows, how many components the configured solution requires nor its exact parameter values. He only knows what the solution is supposed to do. Consequently, a

system assisting the salesman in the incremental process of parameterization is needed.

For these reasons, a strict constraint-based solution did not suffice and a different solution had to be chosen.

Structure-Based Configuration

An interesting alternative to the strict constraint approach are the methods for heuristic, structure-based configuration developed in the projects TEX-K and PROKON[1] (e.g. Günter1995b) (see also: Hollmann et.al. 2000). The key requirement for the use of this approach is the component structure of the domain. Especially in technical domains like the *Lenze-drive-system* domain the component structure is commonly found.

This approach is based on three different knowledge representations:

1. Knowledge about the objects of the domain are represented in an ontology according to their taxonomic- and partonomic relations and the relevant attributes.

2. Dependencies between objects and their relations and attributes are represented with constraints by a meta-constraint modeling language.

3. Knowledge about the control process i.e. order of configuration steps, calculation methods and the priority among them as well as the use of conflict resolution methods is declaratively described by strategies.

The configuration process is started by the user (sales engineer) choosing a task object (e.g. a printing machine) from a list of predefined objects. Based on this task-object EngCon generates a first simple partial solution by instantiating the concept. Afterwards the control component calculates all configuration steps that have to be performed in order to determine terminal values for all relations and attributes and adds them to a configuration agenda. Three kinds of configuration steps are supported: a decomposition-, a specialization- and parameterization step. A decomposition configuration step restricts the values of has-part relations, which may result in the instantiation of new objects. Given a has-part relation, *has-part: engine [0 2]*, which the user or the system is able to restrict to *[1 1]* then a new instance of the concept *engine* is created and appended to the current partial solution. Similar to the decomposition step the specialization step restricts the values of the ISA- relation and the parameterization step restricts the attribute values. New or restricted values may result in new configuration agenda entries.

A key feature of the structure-based approach is that not only the value of already instantiated constraints are restricted incrementally but also new constraints may be added to the already given constraint net. Therefore the control component checks after each configuration step if new constraints have to be added, due to new components (after decomposition), or new or more restricted attributes

---

[1] These projects have been supported by the *German Ministry for Education and Science*.

(after specialization or parameterization). In this approach, constraint propagation is not handled as a calculation function but rather as a consistency-ensuring process which is invoked automatically after each of the current partial solutions.

A final solution is reached once all attributes and relations have been restricted to terminal values.

The central components, ontology, configuration control, and constraint module will be described in more detail in the following sections.

The Ontology Component

For the modeling of the conceptual knowledge (i.e. the product catalog), the proprietary knowledge representation language EngConKR has been developed. Instead of using already existing languages (e.g. OIL and Ontolingua for details see: Fensel, Horrocks, Harmele and Decker, 2000, Farquhar, Fikes and Rice 1996), a separate approach has been chosen for two reasons: First, while the functional requirements for EngCon could be described in a clear way, the requirements for the expressional power of the representation language were elusive without having modeled part of the application domain (i.e. EngConKR has been extended with discontinuous intervals, like *[[0.0 20.15], [30.42 78.85]]*). Secondly, even though existing ontology-languages like Oil support e.g. real numbers, given reasoners like FACT are not capable to perform the adequate inferences.

The domain knowledge is modeled by ISA-specialization- and has-parts relations. The specialization relation has a stringent semantics, i.e. attributes from superior concepts are inherited and maybe restricted by more special attributes. Multiple inheritance is not allowed. In addition to the standard attribute types like sets, intervals and atomic values discontinuous intervals are allowed also.

Taxonomic inferences: The fundamental assumption for the inference mechanism of EngCon is the (strong) closed world assumption (CWA). A situation, where there is no way to specialize an instance of a partial solution to a leaf concept, will be interpreted as a conflicted solution. Even though this assumption is insufficient for many domains, it is well fitted for technical domains. Products in EngCon are modeled as a leaf concept. If an instance may not be specialized to a leaf concept, there is no product for the current task. Thus it seems plausible to presume CWA for this domain.

Based on the CWA, EngCon has two fundamental taxonomical inference modules: a dynamic and a static one. Optimally, the static inference module may be applied prior to the configuration in order to propagate terminal values from the leaf concepts alongside to the specialization hierarchy. With the help of this mechanism, a wide range of conflicts resulting from improper input may possibly be prevented.

The dynamic taxonomic inference module supports primarily four types of inferences:

1. automatic specialization to n-th level

2. automatic specialization to a leaf concept
3. automatic specialization along the has-part relation
4. automatic pre-decomposition

The first inference is equal to the common classification inference of description logic (DL). If the value of an attribute of an instance allows for a classification to a more special concept, an automatic specialization is triggered. The automatic specialization to a leaf concept is implicitly performed by the first inference. It takes a conflict avoidance role by ensuring that a specialization to a leaf concept is possible, if the static taxonomic inference module is not used. The fourth inference, the automatic decomposition, is better regarded as a heuristic rule instead of as a logic inference. It is only applicable in a true top-down configuration. If it is specified in a has-part relation of an instance of the concept *engine* that the engine has at least one cooler (that is i.e. *[1 inf]*), as a result of this inference an instance of a cooler will be automatically added to the solution.

The Control Component

For the simulation of an expert's procedure, EngCon employs an agenda-based control guided by declarative control knowledge (Günter A, 1992). For this purpose, a knowledge engineer defines strategies on how the configuration process of an application is divided into phases, and additionally defines the order of the tasks and their calculation method. By this, it is possible to model different kinds of procedures for different groups of users.

Schematically, the control flow is as follows:

1. *Definition of the task*
2. *Creation of an initial partial solution*
3. *Determining the current strategy*
4. *Creation of an agenda:* The configuration focus defined in the strategy determines which entries are going to be included into the current agenda. These entries specify which attribute of which component of the current solution will be modified next. Here, strategy-specific agenda selection criteria define the order of the entries in the agenda. The agenda contains all tasks to be processed in a strategy and may be accessed at any time by the user.
5. *Selection of agenda entry:* The next step is choosing the entry with the highest priority.
6. *Selection of calculation method*: With the help of the order of the calculation methods defined in the strategy, the method to be employed will be chosen. Valid calculation methods are: Defaults, dynamic defaults, calculation function, user input. If the highest priority calculation method may not be applied, i.e. a default is not applicable the next calculation method with a lower priority is used. If there is no automatic method left to apply, the user will be asked for input. The interfaces within the EngCon configuration engine are open for the

integration of new calculation methods, i.e. simulation without much effort.

7. *Execution of calculation method:* The result of the modification method is acquired.

8. *Calculation of consequences:* The current partial solution is retrofitted with the results of the calculation method and the consequences are calculated: *(a) Taxonomic inferences, (b) Constraints:* resulting from i.e. new components perhaps new constraints have to be added to the constraint net.

9. *Updating the agenda:* First, redundant entries resulting from constraints or taxonomic inferences are removed from the agenda and it is checked whether new entries have to be added to the agenda. Finally, it is evaluated whether a change of strategy has to be performed, and the configuration cycle starts again with 5.

The Constraint Component

Constraints are used for the description of the complex dependencies between the parameters of the objects of the ontology/the product catalog. Three different concepts have been realized:

1. Complex functional and predicate constraints are used to represent equations and functions. They are propagated in an interchangeable external constraint solver[1].

2. Extensional constraints (tuple of values) explicitly list the set of possible variants and are managed within an external database.

3. Additionally, Java-Constraints provide the flexibility for the user to integrate functions and calculations into the configuration, which are impossible to realize with functional or extensional constraints (i.e. summing up attribute values of several concepts).

The constraints are represented in a declarative manner in a meta modeling language and may be modified and extended without having to recompile parts of the whole system[2].

Future Work

Although we applied a wide range of AI-techniques, some extensions seem to be reasonable. The practical use of the system by the sales engineers showed, that once the user runs into a conflict, an detailed explanation of the underlying reasons is required. There are two possible sources for conflicts: taxonomic inferences and the constraint satisfaction. While taxonomic conflicts may be handled with a kind of dependency network, constraint conflicts are much more tricky because of the dependency between several constraints in the net. How complex constraint conflicts can be presented to the user, however, remains an open question. A more abstract question is how explanations can be generated (not only in the case of conflicts) which support users with the appropriate background knowledge in order to understand the underlying reasoning processes. Plan recognition methods are in investigation in order to provide the configuration engine with useful information about the intention and the background knowledge of the user to guide the explanation generation (see (Carberry 2001) for an overview).

Although user specific defaults may be defined, it seems to be reasonable that a user model should be learned automatically. Also, even though it is already possible to re-use a partial solution for various applications (variants), it is not possible to reconfigure complete solutions in the sense of CBR.

Application Use and Payoff

The DSD was introduced in May 2001, when it was shipped to the sales engineers of the *Lenze AG.* Since then, it has been used by about 150 sales engineers, who have been trained to use the system for technical offer preparation.

Using structure-based configuration for this construction and validation process has led to a number of benefits, which result in a high competitive advantage.

Time Reduction for Offer Placement

The time for placing an offer has drastically been reduced. Before the introduction of the DSD, the sales engineers had to get to the customer, take down the requirements for the solution and make a first sketch of the drive. This process took anything from 3 hours to 30 hours working time with an average of 4 hours.

With the help of the DSD, the time it takes for a sales engineer to come to a consistent, high quality solution has been significantly reduced by a factor of 5-10. Now, in easy cases, a consistent solution without the need of asking other experts can be found in approx. 15 minutes if a lot of standard components and values (defaults) can be used. The more complex tasks now take up to 150 minutes, if a lot of things need to be adapted. In average, 30 minutes are now required.

Reduction of Errors

Prior to the introduction of the DSD, too many of the validated offers had to be revised in the course of the actual preparation. These errors caused high costs to both *Lenze* and their clients, since the sales engineer had to check back with the customers again and the delivery of the drive was delayed.

By configuring the solution with the DSD, these errors were reduced to almost 0% of the offered drive systems since the knowledge of various domain experts now assist the sales engineers in executing the offer.

Increase of Quality and Use of new Components

Due to the fact that configuring a drive solution with the DSD uses the experience of many domain experts, the overall quality of the solution was significantly improved

---

[1] The currently used constraint solver is subject to privacy.
[2] This requirement led to the disqualification of i.e. the ILOG-solver.

by providing less expensive solutions which have a better performance. Even though the domain of drive systems is a very complex one, with thousands of different components, some of these are still standardized. Also, newly developed components were rarely included into a solution, since the sales engineers could not always keep up with the new product inventions.

With the introduction of the DSD, the configuration engine now proposes these standardized components, if they are fitting into a solution and thus improving its quality and delivery time. In the same instance, the DSD takes care, that the additional components combined with the standard one are fitting to it as well as newly developed components are taken into consideration for the solution.

Reduction of Costs

Prior to the introduction of the DSD, many components chosen were individual solutions. This led to higher production and maintenance costs for the individual solutions.

With the help of the DSD, more standard components are considered for drive solutions. This helps reducing the production costs – a standard component is easier to produce in less time – as well as reducing the maintenance costs by allowing the usage of standard spare parts. Thus, a considerable competitive advantage is gained, since lower costs result in more satisfied customers.

Application Development and Deployment

The development of the EngCon configuration engine was initiated in 1998. Starting with experiences from the already mentioned research projects (TEX-K, PROKON), a project team was initially formed by *Lenze* and the TZI of the University of Bremen. At the TZI of the University of Bremen, the development staff consisted of a project manager, two research staff, a software engineer and several students.

The TZI was responsible for the development of the domain independent configuration engine EngCon as well as providing support for the knowledge engineering process. The project team at *Lenze* was responsible both for the development of the knowledge base and the DSD application. This team consisted of a project manager, a software engineer and two domain experts.

Having a modern and web-enabled application in mind, JAVA was chosen as the implementation language. During the first 18 month the core functionality of the configuration engine was designed and implemented at the TZI. With a delay of three months, In parallel, the team of domain experts at *Lenze* defined the expressional requirements and developed a prototypical knowledge base for the application DSD. In course of this, the knowledge representation had to be adapted several times.

At the beginning the EngCon configuration engine was designed with the *unified modeling language* (UML) using the Rational Rose. Since several problems arose with the round-trip engineering using Rational Rose to update and develop the software model, the usage of the tool for this purpose was given up. Instead it was only used for the review processes. In order to implement the UML-model a beta version of the Java development environment *Visual J* was chosen. But due to several update delays and compatibility problems, a change to the *Inprise JBuilder* was made.

A first milestone was reached in 1999 - a first implementation of the EngCon engine and a prototypical version of the application DSD. As a result of market surveys, the stakeholders decided to set up a separate company to continue the development of the configuration engine EngCon towards a product. As a result *encoway GmbH & Co KG* was founded early in 2000 as a spin-off of the TZI of the Bremen University. After two years, *encoway* now has a staff of 30.

Since then, the development and implementation tasks for the software (EngCon, DSD) where shifted from the TZI to *encoway* to ensure product quality (maintenance, services, documentation) for the systems. During this period the project team at the TZI enhanced the underlying methodologies e.g. for conflict handling and explanation generation and prepared them for an integration into EngCon.

After three months of field tests and several adjustments, the DSD was finally shipped in May, 2001. Since then, it has been in use by about 150 sales engineers for the technical offer preparation.

The overall investments for the project EngCon and the application DSD are summed up to approx. 30 man years.

Maintenance

The domain of technical drive systems is changing very rapidly. New developments in engineering result in specialized or completely new components, which either add to the already existing ones or completely replace them. In order to make sure, that these new drives, gearings and other related components are made available to the customers, the knowledge base has to be adapted to these changes. Therefore, maintenance of the knowledgebase is a key requirement for the success of the application.

The KBuild software tool for the configuration engine EngCon, which domain-independently allows to maintaining the knowledgebase has been developed for this purpose. KBuild is not only a tool for maintaining the knowledgebase, but is used as well for the initial knowledge acquisition and building of the knowledgebase itself.

In KBuild, validation of the newly inserted concepts is performed with the help of the same taxonomical inferences used within the EngCon configuration engine as described in chapter 'Uses of AI Technology'. Constraint knowledge is modeled with the same tool. With the help of the KBuild knowledge acquisition tool, the maintenance of the knowledge base can be performed by any domain expert.

Conclusion

As has been shown, for more simple scenarios standard methods from computer science sufficed to fulfill the task of customizing products. The configuration of drive systems, however, is a highly complex engineering task which requires profound knowledge about the whole range of products as well as an in-depth understanding of underlying physical dependencies. Therefore, the problem domain of drive construction required sophisticated AI-methods in order to become feasible. The Drive Solution Designer (DSD) which has been introduced in this paper, uses a structure-based configuration engine, EngCon to provide extensive assistance to sales engineers of the *Lenze* company for their daily work.

With the help of the DSD, their actual working time for an offer could be drastically reduced from an average of 4 hours to an average of 30 minutes.. This went along with a significant reduction of faulty offers, since the consistency of an offered solution is now ensured. By maintaining the knowledge base to keep up with the latest developments in the drive engineering domain, these innovations are now easier brought to the attention of the sales engineer who in employs them to turn build drive solutions. Regarding the benefits the DSD had for the daily work of a sales engineer as well as the fulfillment of the other requirements for the development of the software, it has to be considered as a very successful application.

The major component of the DSD, the structure based configuration engine EngCon, has been developed as a domain independent tool. This allows its wide-spread use by exchanging the knowledge bases and the GUIs with domain specific ones while keeping the configuration engine unchanged. Currently, there are applications in technical domains (industrial robots, pumps and sensors) as well as service domains (financial planning and insurances) under development. For these applications, prototypes have already build .

Acknowledgements

The authors would like to thank the *Lenze* AG who supported the development of the DSD. In special, we would like to express our appreciation for the patience and work of Olaf Götz and Torsten Hesse, the domain experts and knowledge engineering team.

Finally, we would like to thank Sven Peter for the hours of work he put into the implementation of the DSD.

References

Arlt,; Günter; Hollmann,; Hotz,; Wagner. 1999. Engineering&Configuration - A Knowledge-based Software Tool for Complex Configuration Tasks. Workshop on Configuration at AAAI-99, http://wwwold.ifi.uni-klu.ac.at/~alf/aaai99/

Artale; Franconi,; Guarino; Pazzi. 1996. Part-Whole Relations in Object-Centered Systems. An Overview. In Data and Knowledge Engineering, North Holland, Elsevier 20:337-384.

Bach. 2000. IPAS: An Integrated Application Toolsuite for the Configuration of Diesel Engines. ECAII'00 Workshop Configuration, http://www.cs.hut.fi/~pdmg/ECAI2000WS/Proceedings.pdf

Carberry. 2001. Techniques for Plan Recognition. User Modeling and User-Adapted Interaction, Volume 11, Number 1-2, pp. 31-48, 2001.

Chow; Perett. 1997. Airport Counter Allocation using Constraint Logic Programming, in: Proc. Of Practical Application of Constraint Technology (PACT98), London, UK

Cunis; Günter; Strecker. 1991. The PLAKON Book - An Expert System for Planning and Configuration Tasks in Technical Domains. Springer.

Cunis; Günter; Syska; Peters; Bode. 1999. PLAKON - An Approach to Domain-independent Construction, 866-874. Tennesse USA: ACM-Press.

Farquhar; Fikes; Rice. 1996. The Ontolingua Server: A Tool for Collaborative Ontology Construction. Technical Report, Stanford KSL 96-26

Fensel; Horrocks; Harmelen von; Decker. 2000. OIL in a Nutshell. In: Knowledge Aquisation, Modelling and Management, 1-16, citeseer.nj.nec.com/fensel00oil.html

Focacci; Lamma; Mello; Milano. 1997. Constraint Logic Programming for the Crew Rostering Problem, in Proc. Of Practical Application of Constraint Technology (PACT97), London, UK

Günter. 1995b. KONWERK - a modular configuration tool, 1-18. Richter (ed.). Kaiserslautern: INFIX Press.

Günter, A.; Cunis, R. 1992. Flexible Control in Expert Systems for Construction Tasks. International Journal Applied Intelligence, Kluwer Academic Press 2.

Günter. 1992. Flexible Control in Expert Systems for Planning and Configuration in Technical Domains, PhD-Thesis. In: PHD-Thesis in Artificial Intelligence, Volume 3, INFIX press

Hollmann; Wagner; Günter. 2000. EngCon - A Flexible Domain-Independent Configuration Engine. Workshop Configuration at ECAI-2000, http://www.cs.hut.fi/~pdmg/ECAI2000WS/Proceedings.pdf

Hollmann; Günter; Ranze; Wagner. 2001. Knowledge-based Configuration - About Complex Highly-Variant Products in Internet-based Scenarios. KI 01/01 (German AI Journal), Arendtap.

McGuiness; Wright. 1998. Conceptual Modelling for Configuration: A Description Logic-based Approach. AIEDAM 12(4): 333-344.

Development and Deployment of a Disciple Agent
for Center of Gravity Analysis

Gheorghe Tecuci[1,2], Mihai Boicu[1], Dorin Marcu[1], Bogdan Stanescu[1], Cristina Boicu[1],
Jerry Comello[2], Antonio Lopez[2], James Donlon[1,2], William Cleckner[2]

[1] Learning Agents Laboratory, Computer Science Department, MS 4A5, George Mason University, 4400 University Dr, Fairfax, VA 22030
{tecuci, mboicu, dmarcu, bstanesc, ccascava}@gmu.edu, http://lalab.gmu.edu
[2] Center for Strategic Leadership, US Army War College, 650 Wright Ave, Carlisle Barracks, PA 17013
ComelloJ@awc.carlisle.army.mil, tlopez@xula.edu, james.donlon@us.army.mil, william.cleckner@csl.carlisle.army.mil

Abstract

This paper presents new significant advances in the Disciple
approach for building knowledge-based systems by subject
matter experts. It describes the innovative application of this
approach to the development of an agent for the analysis of
strategic centers of gravity in military conflicts. This
application has been deployed in several courses at the US
Army War College, and its use has been evaluated. The
presented results are those of a multi-faceted research and
development effort that synergistically integrates research in
Artificial Intelligence, Center of Gravity analysis, and
practical deployment of an agent into Education.

1 Introduction

The Learning Agents Laboratory of George Mason
University is developing a theory, methodology and a
family of tools, called the Disciple approach, for building
instructable knowledge-based systems or agents (Tecuci
1998). This effort directly addresses the knowledge
acquisition bottleneck which we consider to be one of the
major barriers in the development and maintenance of
Artificial Intelligence applications. The Disciple approach
relies on a powerful learning agent shell that can be trained
to solve problems by a subject matter expert, requiring only
limited assistance from a knowledge engineer. As an expert
system shell (Clancey 1984), the Disciple learning agent
shell includes a general problem solving engine that can be
reused for multiple applications. In addition, it includes a
multistrategy learning engine for building the knowledge
base through a mixed-initiative interaction with the subject
matter expert.

As the Disciple approach evolved, we have developed a
series of increasingly advanced learning agent shells
forming the Disciple family. The most recent family
member, Disciple-RKF, represents a significant
advancement over its predecessors: Disciple-WA (Tecuci
et al. 1999) and Disciple-COA (Tecuci et al. 2001). All
these three systems were developed as part of the "High

Performance Knowledge Bases" and "Rapid Knowledge
Formation" programs supported by DARPA and AFOSR
(Burke 1999). Both programs emphasized the use of
innovative challenge problems to focus and evaluate the
research and development efforts.

Disciple-RKF is the result of a multi-objective
collaboration between the Learning Agent Laboratory of
George Mason University and the Center for Strategic
Leadership of the US Army War College that
synergistically integrates research in Artificial Intelligence
(AI), with research in military Center of Gravity (COG)
analysis (Clausewitz 1832), and the practical use of agents
in education. The AI research objective is to develop the
technology that will enable subject matter experts who do
not have computer science or knowledge engineering
experience to develop instructable agents that incorporate
their problem solving expertise. The COG research
objective is to clarify and formalize the process of the
identification of the centers of gravity for enemy and
friendly forces at the strategic and operational levels of
war, and to enable the development of an intelligent
assistant for solving this complex problem. Finally, the
educational objective is to enhance the educational process
of senior military officers through the use of intelligent
agent technology. Each of these three objectives is
recognized as important and difficult in its own right. Our
experience with addressing them together in a synergistic
manner has resulted in faster progress in each of them.
Moreover, it offers a new perspective on how to combine
research in AI, with research in a specialized domain, and
with the development and deployment of prototype systems
in education and practice.

The paper presents the current status of this research and
development effort. The next section presents the COG
challenge problem. This is followed by an end-user
perspective on the developed Disciple-RKF/COG agent.
Section 4 presents an overview of the Disciple-RKF shell
and its use to build the Disciple-RKF/COG agent,
emphasizing its new capabilities with respect to the
previous Disciple shells. Then section 5 discusses the
deployment and evaluation of Disciple in two courses at the
US Army War College, "Case Studies in Center of Gravity

Analysis," and "Military Applications of Artificial Intelligence." The paper concludes with a summary of the synergistic aspects of this collaborative work.

2 The Center of Gravity Problem

The military literature distinguishes between three levels of conflicts: a strategic level focusing on winning wars, an operational level focusing on winning campaigns, and a tactical level focusing on winning battles. One of the most difficult problems that senior military leaders face at the strategic level is the determination and analysis of the centers of gravity for friendly and opposing forces. Originally introduced by Clausewitz in his classical work "On War" (1832), the center of gravity is now understood as representing "those characteristics, capabilities, or localities from which a military force derives its freedom of action, physical strength, or will to fight" (Department of the Army 2001). A combatant should eliminate or influence the enemy's strategic center of gravity, while adequately protecting its own (Giles and Galvin 1996).

Correctly identifying the centers of gravity of the opposing forces is of highest importance in any conflict. Therefore, in the education of strategic leaders at all the US senior military service colleges, there is a great emphasis on the center of gravity analysis (Strange 1996). COG determination requires a wide range of background knowledge, not only from the military domain, but also from the economic, geographic, political, demographic, historic, international, and other domains. In addition, the situation, the adversaries involved, their goals, and their capabilities can vary in important ways from one scenario to another. When performing this analysis, experts rely on their own professional experience and intuitions, without following a rigorous approach. Recognizing these difficulties, the Center for Strategic Leadership of the US Army War College started in 1993 an effort to elicit and formalize the knowledge of a number of experts in center of gravity. This research resulted in a COG monograph (Giles and Galvin 1996), which provided a basis for the application of Disciple to this high value application domain, and to the development of the Disciple-RKF/COG instructable agent presented in the next section.

3 A Disciple Agent for COG Analysis

Disciple-RKF/COG is an agent used in the US Army War College course titled "Case Studies in Center of Gravity Analysis." In this course Disciple-RKF/COG supports the students to develop a center of gravity analysis report for a war scenario.

First, a personal copy of Disciple-RKF/COG guides the student to identify, study and describe the aspects of a scenario (such as the 1945 US invasion of the island of Okinawa) that are relevant for COG analysis. The student-agent interaction takes place as illustrated in Figure 1. The left part of the window is a table of contents, whose elements indicate various aspects of the scenario. When the student selects one such aspect, Disciple asks specific questions intended to acquire from the student a description

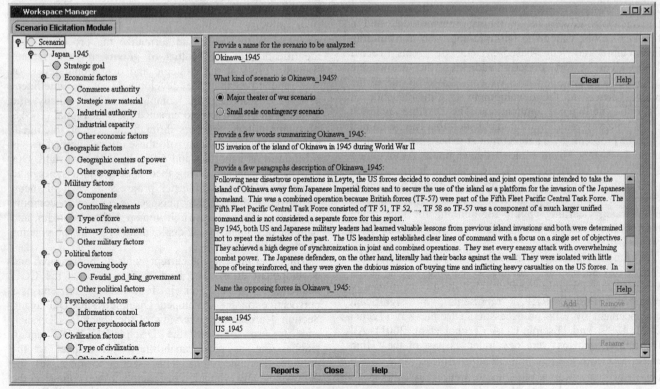

Figure 1: Scenario specification interface

of that aspect, or to update a previously specified description. All the answers are in natural language.

Taking the Okinawa_1945 scenario as our example, Disciple starts by asking for a name and a description of the scenario, and then asks for the opposing forces. Once the student indicates Japan_1945 and US_1945 as opposing forces, Disciple includes them in the table of contents, together with their characteristics that the student needs to specify (see the left hand side of Figure 1). Then, the student may click on any of these aspects (e.g. "Industrial capacity" under "Economic factors" of Japan_1945) and the agent guides the student in specifying it. The student's specification may prompt additional questions from Disciple, and a further expansion of the table of contents. An orange, yellow, or white circle marks each title in the table of contents, indicating respectively that all, some, or none of the corresponding questions of Disciple have been answered. The student is not required to answer all the questions and Disciple can be asked, at any time, to identify and test the strategic center of gravity candidates for the current specification of the scenario.

The right hand side of Figure 2 shows some of the solutions generated by Disciple for the Okinawa_1945 scenario. Each solution identifies an entity as a strategic COG candidate and then indicates whether or not it can be eliminated. In the case of Japan_1945, some of the identified strategic center of gravity candidates are Emperor Hirohito, Japanese Imperial General Staff, the industrial capacity of Japan, and the military of Japan. When a solution is selected in the right hand side of the problem solving interface, its justification, at various levels of abstractions, is displayed in the left hand side.

The left-hand side of Figure 2 shows the detailed justification for the identification and testing of Emperor Hirohito as a strategic COG candidate. Disciple uses the task reduction paradigm to perform the top level problem solving task: "Identify and test a strategic COG candidate for the Okinawa_1945 scenario." To perform this task, Disciple asks itself a series of questions. The answer of each question allows Disciple to reduce the current task to a simpler one, until Disciple has enough information to first identify a strategic COG candidate, and then to determine whether it should be eliminated or not.

Emperor Hirohito is identified as a strategic COG candidate for Japan_1945 in the Okinawa_1945 scenario because, as the feudal god-king of Japan, he is its main controlling element. After being identified as a candidate, Emperor Hirohito is analyzed based on various elimination tests, but he passes all of them. Because the people of Japan see him as divine, and his will is actually their will, Emperor Hirohito could impose them to accept the unconditional surrender of Japan, which is the main strategic goal of the US. As god-king of Japan and commander in chief of the military, he can also impose his will on the military of Japan. Also, as head of the government, he can impose the government of Japan to accept unconditional surrender. Being able to impose his will on the Clausewitz's trinity of power (people, military and government), Emperor Hirohito is very likely to be the strategic center of gravity of Japan in 1945.

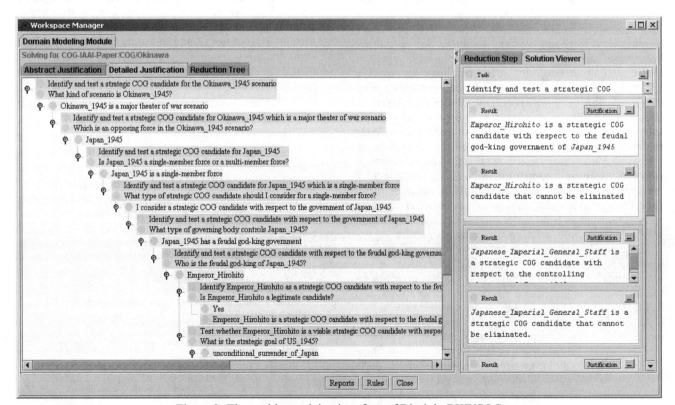

Figure 2: The problem solving interface of Disciple-RKF/COG

As another example, consider the industrial capacity of Japan_1945, which is another source of strength, power and resistance because it produces the war materiel and transports of Japan. Disciple, however, eliminates this strategic COG candidate, because the military and the people of Japan_1945 are determined to fight to death and not surrender even with diminished war materiel and transports.

In the example scenario portrayed here, Disciple eliminates all but two candidates for Japan -- Emperor Hirohito and the Japanese Imperial General Staff -- and suggests that the student should select one of them as the strategic Center of Gravity of Japan in 1945. It is important to point out that this example is only a representative approach to the analysis of Japan's center of gravity for the Okinawa campaign. We recognize that subject matter experts often differ in their judgments as to the identification and analysis of center of gravity candidates for any particular scenario. The important point for agent development is that the Disciple agent can accommodate the preferences of the expert who teaches it.

To our knowledge, this is the first time that an intelligent agent for the strategic COG identification and testing has been developed. More details about its specific use in the COG and MAAI classes are presented in section 4.

4 Agent Development with Disciple-RKF

The Disciple-RKF/COG agent presented in the previous section was developed by using the Disciple-RKF learning agent shell, as will be described in this section. Disciple-RKF consists of an integrated set of knowledge acquisition, learning and problem solving modules for a generic knowledge base having two main components: an object ontology that defines the concepts from a specific application domain, and a set of task reduction rules expressed with these concepts. Disciple-RKF represents a significant evolution compared to the previous Disciple shells. It implements more powerful knowledge representation and reasoning mechanisms, and has an improved interface that facilitates mixed-initiative reasoning. Even more significantly, Disciple-RKF incorporates new modules that allow a subject matter expert to perform additional knowledge engineering tasks, such as scenario specification, modeling of his problem solving process, and task formalization.

In general, the process of developing a specific knowledge-based agent with Disciple-RKF consists of two major stages: 1) the development of the object ontology by the knowledge engineer and the subject matter expert, and 2) the training of Disciple by the subject matter expert.

In the first development stage, a knowledge engineer works with a subject matter expert to specify the type of problems to be solved by the Disciple agent, to clarify how these problems could be solved using Disciple's task reduction paradigm, and to develop an object ontology.

A fragment of the object ontology developed for the COG domain is shown in Figure 3. The object ontology

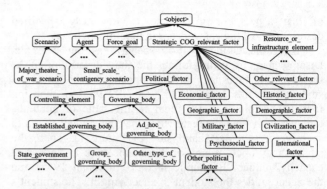

Figure 3: A fragment of the COG object ontology

consists of hierarchical descriptions of objects and features, represented as frames, according to the knowledge model of the Open Knowledge Base Connectivity (OKBC) protocol (Chaudhri et al. 1998). Disciple-RKF includes several types of ontology browsers and editors that facilitate the ontology development process. The careful design and development of the object ontology is of utmost importance because it is used by Disciple as its generalization hierarchy for learning.

A new capability of Disciple-RKF is that ontology development includes the definition of elicitation scripts for objects and features. These scripts guide the expert to define the instances that occur in a scenario (such as Okinawa_1945 or Emperor Hirohito, as illustrated in Section 3). Figure 4 shows the elicitation scripts associated with the "Scenario" object. The top script specifies the question to be asked by Disciple to elicit the name of the scenario, how the user's answer should be used to update the ontology, what other scripts should be called after updating the ontology, and even the appearance of the

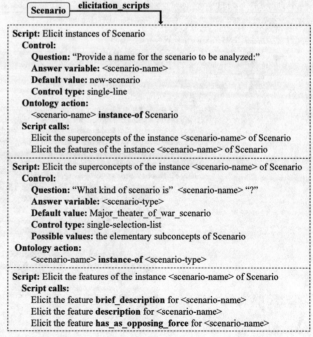

Figure 4: Sample elicitation scripts

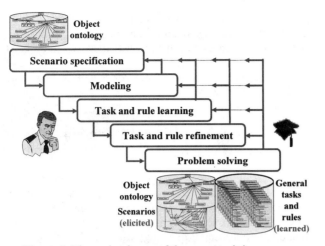

Figure 5: The main phases of the agent training process

interface. The use of the elicitation scripts allows a knowledge engineer to rapidly build customized interfaces for Disciple agents, such as the one illustrated in Figure 1, thus effectively transforming this software development task into a knowledge engineering one.

The result of the first development stage is a customized Disciple agent. This agent is trained to solve problems by a subject matter expert, with very limited assistance from a knowledge engineer, in the second major stage of agent development. Figure 5 shows the main phases of the agent training process, which starts with a knowledge base that contains only a general object ontology (but no instances, no problem solving tasks, and no task reduction rules), and ends with a knowledge base that incorporates expert problem solving knowledge.

During the **Scenario specification** phase, the Scenario Specification module (which is a new module of Disciple-RKF) guides the expert in describing the objects that define a specific strategic scenario (e.g. the US invasion of the island of Okinawa in 1945). The expert does not work directly with the object ontology in order to specify the scenario. Instead, the expert-agent interaction takes place as

presented in section 3 and illustrated in Figure 1, this all being directed by the execution of the elicitation scripts. Experimental results show that the experts can easily perform this task.

After the expert has specified the Okinawa_1945 scenario, he can start the **Modeling** of his COG reasoning for this particular scenario. The expert uses the Modeling module (which is another new module of Disciple-RKF) to express his reasoning in English as a sequence of task reduction steps like the ones illustrated in the left hand side of Figure 2. An example of one task reduction step, defined during modeling, is illustrated in the left hand side of Figure 6. The top task is the current task that needs to be reduced. The expert has to define a question that is relevant to the reduction of this task, then answer the question, and reduce the top task to a simpler one that incorporates the information from the answer. Experimental results show that this is the most challenging agent training activity for the expert.

In the **Task and rule learning** phase, Disciple learns general tasks and general rules from the task reduction steps defined in the modeling phase. For instance, consider the reduction step from the left hand side of Figure 6, consisting of a task, a question, an answer, and a subtask. Because all these expressions are in natural language, the expert and the agent collaborate to translate them into the formal logical expressions on the right hand side of Figure 6. First the natural language expression of each task is structured into an abstract phrase called the task name, which does not contain any instance, and several specific phrases representing the task's features. The formalization is proposed by the agent and may be modified by the expert. Next the expert and the agent collaborate to also formalize the question and the answer from the left hand side of Figure 6 into the explanation on the right hand side of Figure 6. This explanation represents the best approximation of the meaning of the question-answer pair that can be formed with the elements of the object ontology. In essence, the agent will use analogical

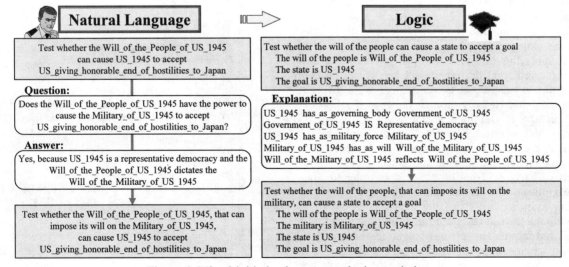

Figure 6: Mixed-initiative language to logic translation

```
Test whether the ?O1 can cause ?O2 to accept ?O3

Test whether the will of the people can cause a state to
accept a goal
        The will of the people is ?O1
        The state is ?O2
        The goal is ?O3
Plausible Upper Bound Condition
?O1   is  Strategic_cog_relevant_factor
?O2   is  Agent
      is  Strategic_cog_relevant_factor
?O3   is  Force_goal
Plausible Lower Bound Condition
?O1 is  Will_of_the_People_of_US_1945
?O2 is  US_1945
?O3 is  US_giving_honorable_end_of_hostilities_to_Japan
```

Figure 7: Task learned from the example in Figure 6

reasoning and guidance from the expert to propose a set of plausible explanation pieces from which the expert will select the most appropriate ones (Tecuci et al. 2001).

Based on the formalizations from Figure 6 and the object ontology from Figure 3, the Disciple agent learns the general task shown in Figure 7 and the general rule shown in Figure 8. Both the learned task and the learned rule have an informal structure (that preserves the natural language of the expert and is used in agent-user communication), and a formal structure (that is used in the internal formal reasoning of the agent).

Initially, when the agent has no rules and no tasks, the expert teaches Disciple how to solve problems and Disciple generates partially learned tasks and rules, as indicated above. As Disciple learns from the expert, the interaction between the expert and Disciple evolves from a teacher-student interaction, toward an interaction where both collaborate in solving a problem. During this mixed-initiative *Problem Solving* phase, Disciple learns not only from the contributions of the expert, but also from its own successful or unsuccessful problem solving attempts.

The learned formal rule in Figure 8 includes two applicability conditions, a plausible upper bound (PUB) condition, and a plausible lower bound (PLB) condition. The PUB condition allows the rule to be applicable in many analogous situations, but the result may not be correct. The PLB condition allows the rule to be applicable only in the situation from which the rule was learned. The agent will apply this rule to solve new problems and the feedback received from the expert will be used to further refine the rule. In essence, the two conditions will converge toward one another (usually through the specialization of the PUB condition and the generalization of the PLB condition), both approaching the exact applicability condition of the rule. *Rule refinement* could lead to a complex task reduction rule, with additional Except-When conditions which should not be satisfied in order for the rule to be applicable. Tasks are refined in a similar way.

It is important to stress that the expert does not deal directly with the learned tasks and rules, but only with their examples used in problem solving. Therefore, the complex knowledge engineering operations of defining and debugging problem solving rules are replaced in the

Disciple approach with the much simpler operations of defining and critiquing specific examples.

After the Disciple agent has been trained, it can be used in the autonomous problem solving mode, to identify and test the strategic COG candidates for a new scenario, as was illustrated in Section 3.

5 Deployment and Evaluation of Disciple-RKF/COG

The US Army War College regularly offers the courses "Case Studies in Center of Gravity Analysis" and "Military Applications of Artificial intelligence." In the first course (the COG course), the students use Disciple-RKF/COG as an intelligent assistant that supports them to develop a center of gravity analysis report for a war scenario, as described in section 3. In the second course (the MAAI course), the students act as subject matter experts that teach personal Disciple-RKF agents their own reasoning in

```
IF: Test whether the ?O1 can cause ?O2 to accept ?O3
Question: Does the ?O1 have the power to cause the ?O4 to
accept ?O3?
Answer: Yes, because ?O2 is a representative democracy
and the ?O1 dictates the ?O5
THEN: Test whether the ?O1, that can impose its will on the
?O4, can cause ?O2 to accept ?O3

IF: Test whether the will of the people can cause a state to
accept a goal
        The will of the people is ?O1
        The state is ?O2
        The goal is ?O3
Explanation
?O2 has_as_governing_body ?O6
?O6 IS Representative_democracy
?O2 has_as_military_force ?O4 has_as_will ?O5 reflects ?O1
Plausible Upper Bound Condition
?O1   is  Will_of_agent
?O2   is  Force
      has_as_military_force ?O4
      has_as_governing_body ?O6
?O3   is  Force_goal
?O4   is  Military_force
      has_as_will ?O5
?O5   is  Will_of_agent
      reflects ?O1
?O6   is  Representative_democracy
Plausible Lower Bound Condition
?O1   is  Will_of_the_People_of_US_1945
?O2   is  US_1945
      has_as_military_force ?O4
      has_as_governing_body ?O6
?O3   is  US_giving_honorable_end_of_hostilities_to_Japan
?O4   is  Military_of_US_1945
      has_as_will ?O5
?O5   is  Will_of_the_Military_of_US_1945
      reflects ?O1
?O6   is  Government_of_US_1945
THEN: Test whether the will of the people, that can impose
its will on the military, can cause a state to accept a goal
        The will of the people is ?O1
        The military is ?O4
        The state is ?O2
        The goal is ?O3
```

Figure 8: Rule learned from the example in Figure 6

Center of Gravity analysis, as described in section 4.

As briefly illustrated in section 3, Disciple-RKF/COG guides the student to identify, study and describe the relevant aspects of the opposing forces in a particular scenario. Then Disciple identifies and tests the strategic center of gravity candidates and generates a draft analysis report that the student needs to finalize. The student must examine Disciple's reasoning, correct or complete it, or even reject it and provide an alternative line of reasoning. This is productive for several reasons. First the given agent generates its proposed solutions by applying general reasoning rules and heuristics learned previously from the course's instructor, to a new scenario described by the student. Secondly, COG analysis is influenced by personal experiences and subjective judgments, and the student (who has unique military experience and biases) may have a different interpretation of certain facts.

This requirement for the critical analysis of the solutions generated by the agent is an important educational component of military commanders that mimics military practice. Commanders have to critically investigate several courses of actions proposed by their staff and to make the final decision on which one to use.

During the 2001 academic year, Disciple was successfully used in both the Winter and Spring sessions of the COG course. As a result of this initial success, the USAWC decided to continue and expand the integration of Disciple in this course for the next academic year and beyond. At the end of the courses the students completed detailed evaluation forms about Disciple and its modules, addressing a wide range of issues, ranging from judging its usefulness in achieving course's objectives, to judging its methodological approach to problem solving, and to judging the ease of use and other aspects of various modules. For instance, on a 5-point scale, from strongly disagree to strongly agree, 7 out of 13 students agreed and the other 6 s trongly agreed that the Scenario Specification module should be used in future versions of the course. Furthermore, 8 out of 11 students agreed, 1 strongly agreed, and 2 were neutral that subject matter experts who are not computer scientists can learn to express their reasoning process using the task reduction paradigm. As another example, 10 out of 13 students agreed, 1 strongly agreed, 1 disagreed and 1 strongly disagreed that the Scenario Specification tool is easy to use.

Several of the students that took the COG course in the Winter 2001 session, together with additional students, took the "Military Applications of Artificial Intelligence Course" in the Spring 2001 session. In this course the students were given a general overview of Artificial Intelligence, as well as an introduction to Disciple-RKF. These students used Disciple-RKF as subject matter experts. The students were organized in five two-person teams, with each team given the project to train a personal Disciple-RKF agent shell according to its own reasoning in COG identification for its historical scenario. All five teams succeeded in developing working agents, with each team addressing a unique scenario: 1) the capture of the Leyte Island by the US forces in 1944; 2) the Inchon

landing during the Korean War in 1950; 3) the Falklands war between Argentina and Britain in 1982; 4) the stabilization mission in the Grenada Island in 1983; and 5) the US invasion of Panama in December 1989.

In the last two 3-hour class sessions, all the five teams participated in a controlled agent development experiment that was videotaped in its entirety. Each team was again provided with a copy of Disciple-RKF that contained the generic object ontology from Figure 3, but no specific instances, no tasks and no rules. They received a 7-page report describing the Okinawa scenario, and were asked to train their Disciple agent to identify center of gravity candidates, based on that scenario. After each significant phase of agent training and knowledge base development (i.e. scenario specification, modeling, rule learning, and rule refinement) a knowledge engineer reviewed their work, and the team then made any necessary corrections under the supervision of the knowledge engineer. Each team succeeded in specifying the scenario and training the agent, in a very short time, as indicated in Figure 9.

The top table in Figure 9 shows the size of the initial object ontology. Each team interacted with Disciple to populate this ontology with different instances and features representing the Okinawa scenario. After that, each team taught its Disciple agent to identify COG candidates for this scenario. The bottom table in Figure 9 indicates both the time spent by each team, and the number of knowledge elements defined during this time. On average they defined 85.4 instances and 93.8 feature values in 1 hour and 6 minutes. The average number of rules per team was 18.8, and the average time interval was 4 hours and 7 minutes. Although obviously incomplete (both because of the use of a single training scenario, and because of incomplete training for that scenario), the knowledge bases were good enough for identifying correct COG candidates not only for the Okinawa (evaluation) scenario, but also for "new" scenarios whose inputs were taken from the class projects.

At the end of this final experiment, the students completed a detailed questionnaire, containing questions about the main components of Disciple. One of the most significant results was that 7 out of the 10 experts agreed, 1 expert strongly agreed and 2 experts were neutral with respect to the statement: "I think that a subject matter expert can use Disciple to build an agent, with limited assistance from a knowledge engineer." We consider this experiment to be a very significant success. Indeed, to our knowledge, this is the first time that subject matter experts

Initial KB	Generic Object Ontology	
	Concepts	Features
	144	79

Teams	Okinawa Scenario			General Tasks and Rules		
	Instances	Feat Val	Time	Tasks	Rules	Time
Team 1	94	103	1h 21min	18	17	3h 52min
Team 2	78	86	55min	23	22	4h 21min
Team 3	72	79	52min	22	19	4h 35min
Team 4	105	111	1h 23min	18	17	3h 58min
Team 5	78	90	59min	20	19	3h 46min
Average	85.4	93.8	1h 06min	20.2	18.8	4h 07min

Figure 9: Knowledge base development during the final experiment

have trained an agent their own problem solving expertise, with very limited assistance from a knowledge engineer.

The deployment and evaluation of Disciple have also revealed several limitations of this approach and have provided numerous ideas for improvement. For instance, while the subject matter expert has an increased role and independence in agent development, the knowledge engineer still has a critical role to play. He has to assure the development of a fairly complete object ontology. He also has to develop a generic modeling of the problem solving process based on the task reduction paradigm. Even guided by this generic modeling, and using natural language, the subject matter expert has difficulties in expressing his reasoning process. Therefore more work is needed to develop methods for helping the expert in this task.

Several other research groups are addressing the problem of direct knowledge acquisition from subject matter experts, as part of the DARPA's "Rapid Knowledge Formation" program (Burke 1999). These groups, however, are currently emphasizing the acquisition of textbook knowledge, relying primarily on reusing knowledge from existing knowledge repositories. In contrast, the emphasis of our research is on acquiring expert's problem solving knowledge that is not normally represented in textbooks, and relies primarily on teaching and learning.

6 Conclusions

This paper presented the current status of a multi-faceted research and development effort that synergistically integrates research in AI, research in COG analysis, and the practical application to education.

The AI research in knowledge bases and agent development by subject matter experts has benefited from the COG domain that provided a complex challenge problem. Identification and testing of strategic COG candidates exemplifies expert problem solving that relies on a wide range of domain knowledge, a significant part of which is tacit. This research has also benefited from its practical application to education. The COG and MAAI courses allowed us to perform thorough experimentation with real experts, resulting in the validation of our methods and providing ideas for future improvements.

The research in COG analysis has benefited from the AI research in that the agent development has helped clarify and formalize the COG identification and testing process. The COG reasoning models developed were validated in the COG and MAAI classes, and are leading to a significant revision and improvement of the COG monograph of Giles and Galvin (1996).

Finally, the innovative application of the AI and COG research to education through the use of the Disciple agent, has had a significant impact on improving the COG and MAAI courses. Done as a very successful experiment in 2001, it was made a regular part of the syllabi for 2002, to be continued in the following years.

Acknowledgments

This paper is dedicated to Mihai Draganescu who supported the first research projects on the Disciple approach at the Research Institute for Informatics and the Romanian Academy. The research described in this paper was sponsored by DARPA, AFRL, AFMC, USAF, under agreement number F30602-00-2-0546, by AFOSR under grant no. F49620-00-1-0072, and by the US Army War College. Michael Bowman, Catalin Balan, Marcel Barbulescu, Xianjun Hao and other members of the LALAB contributed to the development of Disciple-RKF.

References

Burke, M. 1999. Rapid Knowledge Formation Program Description, http://www.darpa.mil/ito/research/rkf/

Chaudhri, V. K.; Farquhar, A.; Fikes, R.; Park, P. D.; and Rice, J. P. 1998. OKBC. A Programmatic Foundation for Knowledge Base Interoperability. In *Proceedings of the Fifteenth National Conference on Artificial Intelligence*, 600–607. Menlo Park, California: AAAI Press.

Clancey, W. J. 1984. NEOMYCIN: Reconfiguring a rule-based system with application to teaching. In Clancey W. J. and Shortliffe, E. H. eds. *Readings in Medical Artificial Intelligence*, 361-381. Reading, MA: Addison-Wesley.

Clausewitz, C.V. 1832. *On War,* translated and edited by M. Howard and P. Paret. Princeton, NJ: Princeton University Press, 1976.

Department of the Army 2001. *Field Manual 3-0, Operations.* Washington, D.C.: U.S. Gov. Printing Office.

Giles, P.K., and Galvin, T.P. 1996. *Center of Gravity: Determination, Analysis and Application.* CSL, U.S. Army War College, PA: Carlisle Barracks.

Strange, J. 1996. Centers of Gravity & Critical Vulnerabilities: *Building on the Clausewitzian Foundation So That We Can All Speak the Same Language.* Quantico, VA: Marine Corps University Foundation.

Tecuci, G. 1998. *Building Intelligent Agents: An Apprenticeship Multistrategy Learning Theory, Methodology, Tool and Case Studies.* London, England: Academic Press.

Tecuci, G.; Boicu, M.; Wright, K.; Lee, S. W.; Marcu, D.; and Bowman, M. 1999. An Integrated Shell and Methodology for Rapid Development of Knowledge-Based Agents. In *Proceedings of the Sixteenth National Conference on Artificial Intelligence*, 250-257. Menlo Park, California: AAAI Press.

Tecuci G.; Boicu M.; Bowman M.; and Marcu D. with a commentary by Burke M. 2001. An Innovative Application from the DARPA Knowledge Bases Programs: Rapid Development of a High Performance Knowledge Base for Course of Action Critiquing. *AI Magazine* Vol. 22, No. 2: 43-61.

Emerging Applications

Getting from Here to There:
Interactive Planning and Agent Execution for Optimizing Travel

José Luis Ambite, Greg Barish,
Craig A. Knoblock, Maria Muslea, Jean Oh
Information Sciences Institute
University of Southern California
4676 Admiralty Way, Marina del Rey, CA 90292, USA
{ambite,barish,knoblock,mariam,jeanoh}@isi.edu

Steven Minton
Fetch Technologies
4676 Admiralty Way,
Marina del Rey, CA 90292, USA
steve.minton@fetch.com

Abstract

Planning and monitoring a trip is a common but complicated human activity. Creating an itinerary is nontrivial because it requires coordination with existing schedules and making a variety of interdependent choices. Once planned, there are many possible events that can affect the plan, such as schedule changes or flight cancellations, and checking for these possible events requires time and effort. In this paper, we describe how Heracles and Theseus, two information gathering and monitoring tools that we built, can be used to simplify this process. Heracles is a hierarchical constraint planner that aids in interactive itinerary development by showing how a particular choice (e.g., destination airport) affects other choices (e.g., possible modes of transportation, available airlines, etc.). Heracles builds on an information agent platform, called Theseus, that provides the technology for efficiently executing agents for information gathering and monitoring tasks. In this paper we present the technologies underlying these systems and describe how they are applied to build a state-of-the-art travel system.

Introduction

The standard approach to planning business trips is to select the flights, reserve a hotel, and possibly a car at the destination. Choices of which airports to fly into and out of, whether to park at the airport or take a taxi, and whether to rent a car at the destination are often ad hoc choices based on past experience. These choices are frequently suboptimal, but the time and effort required to make more informed choices usually outweighs the cost. Similarly, once a trip has been planned it is usually ignored until a few hours before the first flight. A traveler might check on the status of the flights or use one of the services that automatically notify a traveler of flight status information, but otherwise a traveler just copes with problems that arise as they arise. Beyond flight delays and cancellations there a variety of possible events that occur in the real world that one would ideally like to anticipate, but again the cost and effort required to monitor for these events is not usually deemed to be worth the trouble. Schedules can change, prices may go down after purchasing a ticket, flight delays can result in missed connections, and hotel rooms and rental cars are given away because travelers arrive late.

To address these issues we have developed an integrated travel planning and monitoring system. The *Travel Assistant* provides an interactive approach to making travel plans where all of the information required to make informed choices is available to the user. For example, when deciding whether to park at the airport or take a taxi, the system compares the cost of parking and the cost of a taxi given other selections, such as the airport, the specific parking lot, and the starting location of the traveler. Likewise, when the user is deciding which airport to fly into, the system provides not only the cost of the flights, but also determines the impact on the cost of the ground transportation at the destination. Once a trip is planned, the monitoring tasks are addressed by a set of information agents that can attend to details for which it would be impractical for a human assistant to monitor. For example, beyond simply notifying a traveler of flight delays, an agent will also send faxes to the hotel and car rental agencies to notify them of the delay and ensure that the room and car will be available. Likewise, when a traveler arrives in a city for a connecting flight, an agent notifies the traveler if there are any earlier connecting flights and provides both arrival and departure gates.

These innovations in travel planning and monitoring are made possible by two underlying AI technologies. The first is the Heracles interactive constraint-based planner (Knoblock *et al.* 2001), which captures the interrelationships of the data and user choices using a set of constraint rules. Using Heracles we can easily define a system for interactively planning a trip. The second is the Theseus information agent platform (Barish *et al.* 2000), which facilitates the rapid creation of information gathering and monitoring agents. These agents provide data to the Heracles planner and keep track of information changes relevant to the travel plans. Based on these technologies, we have developed a complete end-to-end travel planning and monitoring system that is in use today.

The remainder of this paper describes the travel application and underlying technology in more detail. The next section describes by example the trip planning process as well as the monitoring agents that ensure that the trip is executed smoothly. Then, we present the constraint-based planning technology that supports the trip planning. Next, we describe the information agent technology, which provides the data for the planner and the agents for monitoring the trip.

Finally, we compare with related work, and discuss our contributions and future plans.

Planning and Monitoring a Trip

In this section we describe by example the functionality and interface of our *Travel Assistant*, showing both its capabilities for interactive planning and for monitoring the travel plans.

Interactive Travel Planning

Our *Travel Assistant* starts the travel planning process by retrieving the business meetings from the user's calendar program (e.g., Microsoft Outlook). Figure 1 shows the user interface of the *Travel Assistant* with the high level information for planning a trip to attend a business meeting. The interface displays a set of boxes showing values, which we call *slots*. A slot holds a current value and a set of possible values, which can be viewed in a pull-down list by clicking the arrow at the right edge of the slot. For example, there are slots for the subject and location of the meeting with values Travel Planner Meeting and DC respectively. The user could choose to plan another meeting from the list or input meeting information directly.

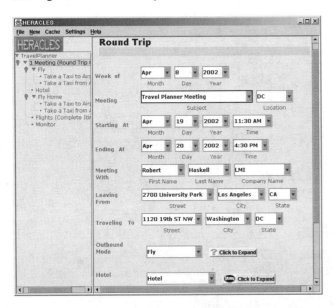

Figure 1: Planning a Meeting

Once the system has the details of the meeting, the next step is to determine how to get to the destination. There are three possible modes of transportation: Fly, Drive, or Take a Taxi. The system recommends the transportation mode based on the distance between the user's location and the meeting location. The system obtains the departure location from the user's personal profile and the meeting location from Outlook. The system computes the distance by first geocoding (determining the latitude and longitude) of the origin and destination addresses using the Mapblast Web site (www.mapblast.com). Then, using the geocoded information, a local constraint computes the distance between the

two points. In our example, the distance between Los Angeles and Washington D.C. is 2,294 miles, so the system recommends that the user Fly. Since the meeting lasts for several days, it also recommends that the user stay at a hotel. Of course, the user can always override the system suggestions.

The *Travel Assistant* organizes the process of trip planning and the associated information hierarchically. The left pane of Figure 1 shows this hierarchical structure, with the particular choices made for the current plan. In this example, the trip consists of three tasks: flying to the meeting, staying at a hotel at the meeting location, and flying back home. Some tasks are further divided into subtasks, for example, how to get to and from the aiport when flying. In Heracles these tasks are represented by related slots and constraints that are encapsulated into units called *templates*, which are organized hierarchically.

The *Travel Assistant* helps the user evaluate tradeoffs that involve many different pieces of information and calculations. For example, Figure 2 illustrates how the system recommends the mode of transportation to the departure airport. This recommendation is made by comparing the cost of parking a car at the airport for the duration of the trip to the cost of taking a taxi to and from the airport. The system computes the cost of parking by retrieving the available airport parking lots and their daily rates from the AirWise site (www.airwise.com), determining the number of days the car will be parked based on scheduled meetings, and then calculating the total cost of parking. Similarly, the system computes the taxi fare by retrieving the distance between the user's home address and the departure airport from the Yahoo Map site (maps.yahoo.com), retrieving the taxi fare from the Washington Post site (www.washingtonpost.com), and then calculating the total cost. Initially, the system recomends taking a taxi since the taxi fare is only $19.50, while the cost of parking would be $48.00 using the Terminal Parking lot (the preferred parking lot in the user's profile). However, when the user changes the selected parking lot to Economy Lot B, which is $5 per day, this makes the total parking rate cheaper than the taxi fare, so the system changes the recommendation to Drive.

The system actively maintains the dependencies among slots so that changes to earlier decisions are propagated throughout the travel planning process. For example, Figure 3 shows how the Taxi template is affected when the user changes the departure airport in the higher-level Round Trip Flights template. In the original plan, the flight departs from Los Angeles International (LAX) at 11:55 PM. The user's preference is to arrive an hour before the departure time, thus he/she needs to arrive at LAX by 10:55 PM. Since Mapblast calculates that it takes 24 minutes to drive from the user's home to LAX, the system recommends leaving by 10:31 PM. When the user changes the departure airport from LAX to Long Beach airport (LGB), the system retrieves a new map and recomputes the driving time. Changing the departure airport also results in a different set of flights. The recommended flight from LGB departs at 9:50 PM and driving to LGB takes 28 minutes. Thus, to arrive at LGB by 8:50 PM, the system now suggests leaving home by 8:22 PM.

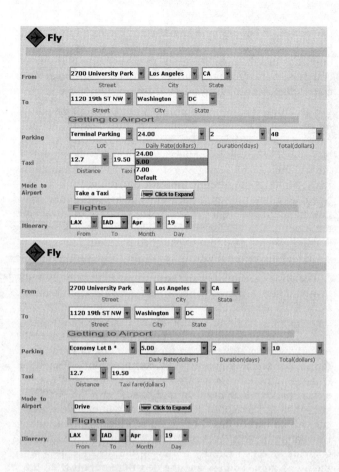

Figure 2: Comparing Cost of Driving versus Taking a Taxi

Monitoring Travel Status

There are various dynamic events that can affect a travel plan, for instance, flight delays, cancellations, fare reductions, etc. Many of these events can be detected in advance by monitoring information sources. The *Travel Assistant* is aware that some of the information it accesses is subject to change, so it delegates the task of following the evolution of such information to a set of monitoring agents. For instance, a flight schedule change is a critical event since it can have an effect not only on the user's schedule at the destination but also on the reservations at a hotel and a car rental agency. In addition to agents handling critical events, there are also monitoring agents whose purpose is to make a trip more convenient or cost-effective. For example, tracking airfares or finding restaurants near the current location of the user. In what follows, we describe the monitoring agents that we defined for travel planning. As shown in Figure 4, Heracles automatically generates the set of agents for monitoring a travel plan. Figure 5 shows some example messages sent by these agents.

The *Flight-Status* monitoring agent uses the ITN Flight Tracker site to retrieve the current status of a given flight. If the flight is on time, the agent sends the user a message to that effect two hours before departure. If the user's flight is delayed or canceled, it sends an alert through the user's

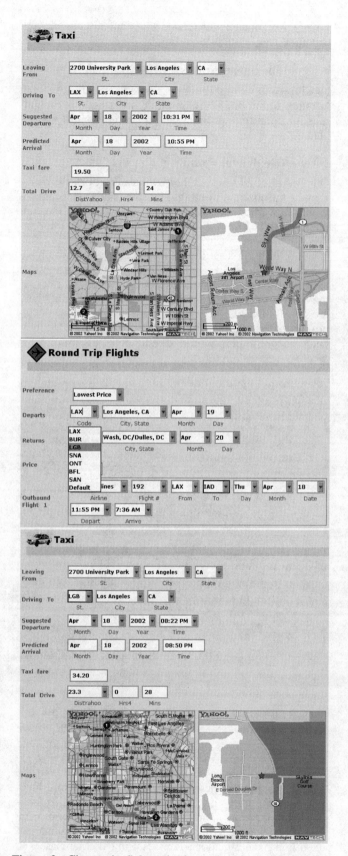

Figure 3: Change in Selected Airport Propagates to Drive Subtemplate

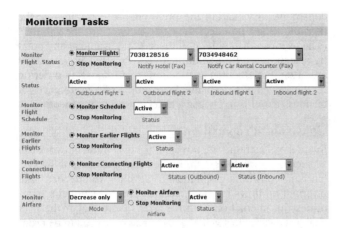

Monitoring Tasks

Figure 4: Template for Generating Monitoring Agents

(a) *Flight-Status Agent*: Flight delayed message

Your United Airlines flight 190 has been delayed. It was originally scheduled to depart at 11:45 AM and is now scheduled to depart at 12:30 PM. The new arrival time is 7:59 PM.

(b) *Flight-Status Agent*: Flight cancelled message

Your Delta Air Lines flight 200 has been cancelled.

(c) *Flight-Status Agent*: Fax to a hotel message

Attention : Registration Desk

I am sending this message on behalf of David Pynadath, who has a reservation at your hotel. David Pynadath is on United Airlines 190, which is now scheduled to arrive at IAD at 7:59 PM. Since the flight will be arriving late, I would like to request that you indicate this in the reservation so that the room is not given away.

(d) *Airfare Agent*: Airfare dropped message

The airfare for your American Airlines itinerary (IAD - LAX) dropped to $281.

(e) *Earlier-Flight Agent*: Earlier flights message

The status of your currently scheduled flight is:

190 LAX (11:45 AM) - IAD (7:29 PM) 45 minutes Late

The following United Airlines flight arrives earlier than your flight:

946 LAX (8:31 AM) - IAD (3:35 PM) 11 minutes Late

Figure 5: Actual Messages sent by Monitoring Agents

---

preferred device (e.g., a text message to a cellular phone). If the flight is delayed by more than an hour, the agent sends a fax to the car rental counter to confirm the user's reservation. If the flight is going to arrive at the destination airport after 5 PM, the agent sends another fax to the hotel so that the reserved room will not be given away. Since the probability of a change in the status of a flight is greater as the departure time gets closer, the agent monitors the status more frequently as the departure time nears.

The *Airfare* monitoring agent keeps track of current prices for the user's itinerary. The airlines change prices unpredictably, but the traveler can request a refund (for a fee) if the price drops below the purchase price. This agent gathers current fares from Orbitz (www.orbitz.com) and notifies the user if the price drops by more than a given threshold.

The *Flight-Schedule* monitoring agent keeps track of changes to the scheduled departure time of a flight (using

Orbitz) and notifies the user if there is any change. Without such an agent, a traveler often only discovers this type of schedule changes after arriving at the airport.

The *Earlier-Flight* monitoring agent uses Orbitz to find the flights that leave earlier than the scheduled flight. It shows the alternative earlier flights and their status. This information becomes extremely useful when the scheduled flight is significantly delayed or canceled.

The *Flight-Connection* agent tracks the user's current flight, and a few minutes before it lands, it sends the user the gate and status of the connecting flight.

The *Restaurant-Finder* agent locates the user based on either a Global Positioning System (GPS) device or his/her expected location according to the plan. On request, it suggests the five closest restaurants provinding cuisine type, price, address, phone number, latitude, longitude, and distance from the user's location.

In the following sections, we describe in detail the technology we have used to automate travel planning and monitoring, namely, the Heracles interactive constraint-based planning framework and the Theseus agent execution and monitoring system.

Interactive Constraint-based Planning

The critical challenge for Heracles is integrating multiple information sources, programs, and constraints into a cohesive, effective tool. We saw examples of these diverse capabilities in the *Travel Assistant*, such as retrieving scheduling information from a calendar system, computing the duration of a given meeting, and invoking an information agent to find directions to the meeting.

Constraint reasoning technology offers a clean way to integrate multiple heterogeneous subsystems in a plug-and-play approach. Our approach employs a constraint representation where we model each piece of information as a distinct variable[1] and describe the relations that define the valid values of a set of variables as constraints. A constraint can be implemented either by a local procedure within the constraint engine or by an external component. In particular, we use information agents built with Theseus to implement many of the external constraints.

Using a constraint-based representation as the basis for control has the advantage that it is a declarative representation and can have many alternative execution paths. Thus, we need not commit to a specific order for executing components or propagating information. The constraint propagation system will determine the execution order in a natural manner. The constraint reasoning system propagates information entered by the user as well as the system's suggestions, decides when to launch information requests, evaluates constraints, and computes preferences.

---

[1]In the example in the previous section we have referred to each piece of information presented to the user as a slot. We use the term slot for user interface purposes. Each slot has a corresponding variable defined in the constraint network, but there may be variables that are not presented to the user.

Constraint Network Representation

A constraint network is a set of variables and constraints that interrelate and define the valid values for the variables. Figure 6 shows the fragment of the constraint network of the *Travel Assistant* that addresses the selection of the method of travel from the user's initial location to the airport. The choices under consideration are: driving one's car (which implies leaving it parked at the airport for the duration of the trip) or taking a taxi.

Figure 6: Constraint Network: Driving Versus Taking a Taxi

In the sample network of Figure 6, the variables are shown as dark rectangles and the assigned values as white rectangles next to them. The variables capture the relevant information for this task in the application domain, such as the DepartureDate, the Duration of the trip, the ParkingTotal (the total cost of parking for the duration of the trip), the Taxi-Fare, and the ModeToAirport. The DepartureAirport has an assigned value of LAX, which is assigned by the system since it is the closest airport to the user's address.

Conceptually, a *constraint* is a n-ary predicate that relates a set of *n* variables by defining the valid combinations of values for those variables. A constraint is a computable component which may be implemented by a local table look-up, by the computation of a local function, by retrieving a set of tuples from a remote information agent, or by calling an arbitrary external program. In Heracles the constraints are directed. The system evaluates a constraint only after it has assigned values to a subset of its variables, the *input* variables. The constraint evaluation produces the set of *possible values* for the *output* variables.

In the sample network of Figure 6 the constraints are shown as rounded rectangles. For example, the compute-Duration constraint involves three variables (DepartureDate, ReturnDate, and Duration), and it's implemented by a function that computes the duration of a trip given the departure and return dates. The constraint getParkingRate is implemented by calling an information agent that accesses a web site that contains parking rates for airports in the US.

Each variable can also be associated with a preference constraint. Evaluating the preference constraint over the possible values produces the *assigned* value of the variable. (The user can manually reset the assigned value at any point by selecting a different alternative.) Preference constraints are often implemented as functions that impose an ordering on the values of a domain. An example of a preference for business travel is to choose a hotel closest to the meeting.

Constraint Propagation

Since the constraints are directed, the constraint network can be seen as a directed graph. In the current version of the system, this constraint graph must be acyclic, which means that information flows in one direction. This directionality simplifies the interaction with the user. Note that if the user changes a variable's value, this change may need to be propagated throughout the constraint graph.

The constraint propagation algorithm proceeds as follows. When a given variable is assigned a value, either directly by the user or by the system, the algorithm recomputes the possible value sets and assigned values of all its dependent variables. This process continues recursively until there are no more changes in the network. More specifically, when a variable X changes its value, the constraints that have X as input variable are recomputed. This may generate a new set of possible values for each dependent variable Y. If this set changes, the preference constraint for Y is evaluated selecting one of the possible values as the new assigned value for Y. If this assigned value is different from the previous one, it causes the system to recompute the values for further downstream variables. Values that have been assigned by the user are always preferred as long as they are consistent with the constraints.

Consider again the sample constraint network in Figure 6. First, the constraint that finds the closest airport to the user's home address assigns the value LAX to the variable DepartureAirport. Then, the constraint getParkingRate, which is a call to an information agent, fires producing a set of rates for different parking lots. The preference constraint selects terminal parking which is $16.00/day. This value is multiplied by the duration of the trip to compute the ParkingTotal of $64 (using the simple local constraint multiply). A similar chain of events results in the computation of the Taxi-Fare. Once the ParkingTotal and the TaxiFare are computed, the selectModeToAirport constraint compares the costs and chooses the cheapest means of transportation, which in this case is to take a Taxi.

Template Representation

As described previously, to modularize an application and deal with its complexity, the user interface presents the planning application as a hierarchy of templates. For example, the top-level template of the *Travel Assistant* (shown in Figure 1) includes a set of slots associated with who you are meeting with, when the meeting will occur, and where the meeting will be held. The templates are organized hierarchically so that a higher-level template representing an abstract task (e.g., Trip) may be decomposed into a set of more specific subtasks, called subtemplates (e.g., Fly, Drive, etc). This hierarchical task network structure helps to manage the complexity of the application for the user by hiding less important details until the major decisions have been achieved.

This template-oriented organization has ramifications for the constraint network. The network is effectively divided into partitions, where each partition consists of the variables and constraints that compose a single template. During the planning process the system only propagates changes to variables within the template that the user is currently working on. This strategy considerably improves performance.

Information Agents

Our system uses information agents to support both the trip planning and monitoring. While information agents are similar to other types of software agents, their plans are distinguished by a focus on gathering, integrating, and monitoring of data from distributed and remote sources. To efficiently perform these tasks we use Theseus (Barish *et al.* 2000; Barish & Knoblock 2002), which is a streaming dataflow architecture for plan execution. In this section, we describe how we use Theseus to build agents capable of efficiently gathering and monitoring information from remote data sources.

Defining an Information Agent

Building an information agent requires defining a plan in Theseus. Each plan consists of a name, a set of input and output variables, and a network of operators connected in a producer-consumer fashion. For example, the *Flight-Status* agent takes flight data (i.e., airline, flight number) as input and produces status information (i.e., projected arrival time) as output.

Each operator in a plan receives input data, processes it in some manner, and outputs the result - which is then potentially used by another operator. Operators logically process and transmit data in terms of relations, which are composed of a set of tuples. Each tuple consists of a set of attributes, where an attribute of a relation can be either a string, number, nested relation, or XML object.

The set of operators in Theseus support a range of capabilities. First, there are information gathering operators, which retrieve data from local and remote sources including web sites. Second, there are data manipulation operators, which provide the standard relational operations, such as select, project and join, as well as XML manipulation operations using *XQuery*. Third, there are monitoring-related operators, which provide scheduling and unscheduling of tasks and communication with a user through email or fax.

Plans in Theseus are just like operators: they are named and have input and output arguments. Consequently, any plan can be called as an operator from within any other plan. This subplan capability allows a developer to define new agents by composing existing ones.

Accessing Web Sources

Access to on-line data sources is a critical component of our information agents. In the *Travel Assistant* there is no data stored locally in the system. Instead, all information is accessed directly from web sources. To do this we build *wrappers* that enable web sources to be queried as structured data sources. This makes it easy for the system to manipulate the resulting data as well as integrate it with information from other data sources.

For example, a wrapper for Yahoo Weather dynamically turns the source into XML data in response to a query. Since the weather data changes frequently, it would not be practical to download this data in advance and cache it for future queries. Instead, the wrapper provides access to the live data, but provides it in a structured form.

We have developed a set of tools for semi-automatically creating wrappers for web sources (Knoblock *et al.* 2000). The tools allow a user to specify by example what the wrapper should extract from a source. The examples are then fed to an inductive learning system that generates a set of rules for extracting the required data from a site.

Once a wrapper for a site has been created, Theseus agents can programmatically access data from that site using the wrapper operator in their plans. For example, with the wrapper for Yahoo Weather, we can now send a request to get the weather for a particular city and it will return the corresponding data.

Monitoring Sources

In addition to being able to gather data from web sources, Theseus agents are capable of *monitoring* those sources and performing a set of actions based on observed changes. The monitoring is performed by retrieving data from online sources and comparing the returned results against information that was previously retreived and stored locally in a database. This provides the capability to not only check current status information (e.g., flight status), but to also determine how the information has changed over time.

There are several ways in which plans can react to a monitoring event. First, a plan can use e-mail or fax operators to asynchronously notify interested parties about important updates to monitored data. Second, a plan can schedule or unschedule other agents in response to some condition. For example, once a flight has departed, the flight monitoring agent can schedule the *Flight-Connection* agent to run a few minutes before the scheduled arrival time.

Theseus agents are managed by a scheduling system that allows agents to be run once or at a fixed interval. The agent scheduler works by maintaining a database of the tasks to run and when they are scheduled to run next. Once scheduled, agents are launched at the appropriate time. Once they are run, the database is updated to reflect the next time the task is to be run. Since the Theseus plan language supports operators that can schedule and unschedule agents, this provides the ability to run new agents at appropriate times based on events in the world.

As an example information agent that monitors a data source, consider the plan for the *Flight-Status* agent shown in Figure 7. Initially, the agent executes a wrapper operator to retrieve the current flight status information. It then uses another online source to normalize the information based on the time zone of the recipient. The resulting normalized flight status information indicates that the flight is either arrived, cancelled, departed, or pending (waiting to depart). If the flight has been cancelled, the user is notified via the email operator. In this case, the flight needs no additional monitoring and the unschedule operator is used to remove it from the list of monitored flights. For departed flights the *Flight-Connection* agent is scheduled. For each pending flight, the agent must perform two actions. First, it checks if the arrival time of the flight is later than 5pm and if so it uses the fax operator to notify the hotel (it only does this once). Second, the agent compares the current departure time with the previously retrieved departure time. If they differ by a given threshold, the agent does three things: (a) it faxes a message to the car rental agency to notify them of the delay, (b) it updates its local database with the new departure time (to track future changes) and (c) it e-mails the user.

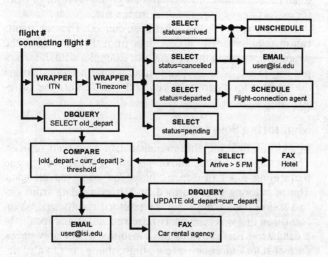

Figure 7: The Flight Status information monitoring agent

Efficiently Executing Agent Plans

Information agent plans are unique in two key respects. First, they tend to integrate data from multiple sources - for example, the *Flight-Status* agent might query multiple Internet real-time data sources to find out the in-flight status of a particular airplane. Second, they usually gather and monitor data from sources that are remote and deliver unpredictable performance - such as Internet web sites. Thus, information agent execution is often I/O-bound - with an agent spending the majority of its execution time waiting for replies from remote sources it has queried.

To efficiently execute plans that primarily integrate data from remote sources, Theseus employs a dataflow model of execution. Under this model, plan operators are arranged in a producer-consumer fashion, leading to partially ordered plans. Then, at run-time, operators can execute in parallel when their individual inputs have been received. This decentralized form of execution maximizes the amount of *horizontal parallelism*, or concurrency between independent data flows, available at run-time.

Theseus alo supports the *streaming* of data between plan operators. Streaming enables consumer operators to receive data emitted by their producers as soon as possible. This, in turn, enables these consumers to process this data immediately and communicate output to other consumers farther downstream as soon as possible. For example, consider an agent plan that fetches a large amount of data from two slow sources and joins this information together. Streaming enables the join to be executed as soon as possible on the available data, as it trickles in from either source. As a result, with streaming, producers and consumers may be processing the same logical set of data concurrently, resulting in a form of pipelined or *vertical parallelism* during execution.

Related Work

Most commercial systems for travel planning take the traditional approach of providing tools for selecting flights, hotel, and car rentals in separate steps. The only integrated approach is a system called MyTrip from XTRA On-line. Based on personal calendar information, the system automatically produces a complete plan that includes the flights, hotel and car rental. Once it has produced a plan, the user can then edit the individual selections made by the system. Unlike the *Travel Assistant*, the user cannot interactively modify the plan, such as constraining the airlines or departure airport. Also, MyTrip is limited to only the selection of flights, hotels, and car rentals. In addition to MyTrip, there exist some commercial systems (such as the one run by United Airlines) that provide basic flight status and notification. However, these systems do not actually track changes in the flight status over time (they merely notify passengers a fixed number of hours before flights) and they do not notify hotels about flight delays or suggest earlier flights or better connections when unexpected events (e.g., bad weather) occur.

In terms of constraint reasoning, there is a lot of research on constraint programming (Saraswat & van Hentenryck 1995), but not much attention has been paid to the interplay between information gathering and constraint propagation and reasoning. Bressan and Goh (1997) have applied constraint reasoning technology to information integration. They use constraint logic programming to find relevant sources and construct an evaluation plan for a user query. In our system, the relevant sources have already been identified. In dynamic constraint satisfaction (Mittal & Falkenhainer 1990), the variables and constraints present in the network are allowed to change with time. In our framework, this is related to interleaving the constraint satisfaction with the information gathering. Lamma et al. (1999) propose a framework for interactive constraint satisfaction problems (ICSP) in which the acquisition of values for each variable is interleaved with the enforcement of constraints. The information gathering stage in our constraint integration framework can also be seen as a form of ICSP. Their application domain is on visual object recognition, while our focus is on information integration

Our work on Theseus is related to two existing types of systems: *general agent executors* and *network query engines*. General agent executors, like RAPS (Firby 1994) and PRS-Lite (Myers 1996) propose highly concurrent execution models. The dataflow aspect of Theseus can be seen as another such model. The main difference is that execution in Theseus not only involves enabling operators but routing information between them as well. In this respect, Theseus shares much in common with several recently proposed network query engines (Ives *et al.* 1999; Hellerstein *et al.* 2000; Naughton *et al.* 2001). Like Theseus, these systems focus in efficiently integrating web-based data. However, network query engines have primarily focused on performance issues; while Theseus also acts as an efficient executor, it is distinguished from these other query engines by (a) its novel operators that facilitate monitoring and asynchronous notification and (b) its modular dataflow agent language that allows a wider variety of plans to be built and executed.

Discussion

The travel planning and monitoring are fully functional systems that are in use today. The planner is not yet directly connected to a reservation system, but it is a very useful tool for helping to make the myriad of decisions required for planning a trip. Likewise, the monitoring agents are able to continually monitor all aspects of a trip and provide immediate notification of changes and cancellations. There are existing commercial systems that provide small pieces of these various capabilities, but the technology and application presented here is unique in providing a complete end-to-end solution that plans and then monitors all aspects of a trip. For example, the planning process will automatically produce the fax numbers required for use by the monitoring agents to notify the hotel and car rental agency. The current system is in use at the Information Sciences Institute and we plan to make this system more widely available on the Web as part of the Electric Elves Project (Chalupsky *et al.* 2001).

One limitation of the current system is that the monitoring agents do not communicate problems or changes back to the travel planner. Ideally, if a flight is canceled one would want the system to re-book the traveler on another flight as soon as possible and then make any other needed changes to the itinerary based on the changes to the flight. Or if the price of a ticket declines to automatically rebook the ticket. The current system does not do this. We are working on the next generation of the travel planning component which will support this type of dynamic replanning of a trip based on changes in the world.

Acknowledgments

The research reported here was supported in part by the Defense Advanced Research Projects Agency (DARPA) and Air Force Research Laboratory under contract/agreement numbers F30602-01-C-0197, F30602-00-1-0504, F30602-98-2-0109, in part by the Air Force Office of Scientific Research under grant number F49620-01-1-0053, and in part by the Integrated Media Systems Center, a National Science Foundation Engineering Research Center, cooperative agreement number EEC-9529152. The U.S.Government is authorized to reproduce and distribute reports for Governmental purposes notwithstanding any copy right annotation thereon. The views and conclusions contained herein are those of the authors and should not be interpreted as necessarily representing the official policies or endorsements, either expressed or implied, of any of the above organizations or any person connected with them.

References

Barish, G., and Knoblock, C. A. 2002. Speculative plan execution for information gathering. In *Proceedings of the 6th International Conf. on AI Planning and Scheduling.*

Barish, G.; DiPasquo, D.; Knoblock, C. A.; and Minton, S. 2000. A dataflow approach to agent-based information management. In *Proceedings of the 2000 International Conference on Artificial Intelligence (IC-AI 2000).*

Bressan, S., and Goh, C. H. 1997. Semantic integration of disparate information sources over the internet using constraint propagation. In *Workshop on Constraint Reasoning on the Internet (at CP97).*

Chalupsky, H.; Gil, Y.; Knoblock, C. A.; Lerman, K.; Oh, J.; Pynadath, D. V.; Russ, T. A.; and Tambe, M. 2001. Electric elves: Applying agent technology to support human organizations. In *Proceedings of the Thirteenth Innovative Applications of Artificial Intelligence Conference.*

Firby, R. J. 1994. Task networks for controlling continuous processes. In *Proceedings of the 2nd International Conference on Artificial Intelligence Planning Systems.*

Hellerstein, J. M.; Franklin, M. J.; Chandrasekaran, S.; Deshpande, A.; Hildrum, K.; Madden, S.; Raman, V.; and Shah, M. A. 2000. Adaptive query processing: technology in evolution. *IEEE Data Engineering Bulletin* 23(2):7–18.

Ives, Z. G.; Florescu, D.; Friedman, M.; Levy, A.; and Weld, D. S. 1999. An adaptive query execution system for data integration. In *Proceedings of the ACM SIGMOD International Conference on Management of Data.*

Knoblock, C. A.; Lerman, K.; Minton, S.; and Muslea, I. 2000. Accurately and reliably extracting data from the web: A machine learning approach. *IEEE Data Engineering Bulletin* 23(4).

Knoblock, C. A.; Minton, S.; Ambite, J. L.; Muslea, M.; Oh, J.; and Frank, M. 2001. Mixed-initiative, multi-source information assistants. In *Proceedings of the Tenth International World Wide Web Conference.*

Lamma, E.; Mello, P.; Milano, M.; Cucchiara, R.; Gavanelli, M.; and Piccardi, M. 1999. Constraint propagation and value acquisition: Why we should do it interactively. In *Proceedings of the Sixteenth International Joint Conference on Artificial Intelligence.*

Mittal, S., and Falkenhainer, B. 1990. Dynamic constraint satisfaction problems. In *Proceedings of the Eighth National Conference on Artificial Intelligence*, 25–32.

Myers, K. L. 1996. A procedural knowledge approach to task-level control. In *Proceedings of the Fourth International Conference on Artificial Intelligence Planning Systems.*

Naughton, J. F.; DeWitt, D. J.; Maier., D.; et al. 2001. The niagara internet query system. *IEEE Data Engineering Bulletin* 24(2):27–33.

Saraswat, V., and van Hentenryck, P., eds. 1995. *Principles and Practice of Constraint Programming.* Cambridge, MA: MIT Press.

WhyNot: Debugging Failed Queries in Large Knowledge Bases

Hans Chalupsky and Thomas A. Russ

Information Sciences Institute

University of Southern California

4676 Admiralty Way, Marina del Rey, CA 90292

Abstract

When a query to a knowledge-based system fails and returns "unknown", users are confronted with a problem: Is relevant knowledge missing or incorrect? Is there a problem with the inference engine? Was the query ill-conceived? Finding the culprit in a large and complex knowledge base can be a hard and laborious task for knowledge engineers and might be impossible for non-expert users. To support such situations we developed a new tool called "WhyNot" as part of the PowerLoom knowledge representation and reasoning system. To debug a failed query, WhyNot tries to generate a small set of *plausible partial proofs* that can guide the user to what knowledge might have been missing, or where the system might have failed to make a relevant inference. A first version of the system has been deployed to help debug queries to a version of the Cyc knowledge base containing over 1,000,000 facts and over 35,000 rules.

Introduction

Every knowledge representation system deserving of its name has a reasoning component to allow the derivation of statements that are not directly asserted in the knowledge base but instead follow from the facts and rules that are asserted. A common approach is to use the language of some symbolic logic L as the knowledge representation (KR) language and an implementation of a proof procedure for L as the reasoning (R) engine. This results in what is usually called a knowledge representation and reasoning (KR&R) system (such as Loom, PowerLoom, Classic, Cyc, SNePS, etc.). For example, in a KR&R system based on first-order predicate logic, one can represent facts and rules like the following (we will use KIF notation (Genesereth 1991) throughout this paper):

```
(person fred)
(citizen-of fred germany)
(national-language-of germany german)

(forall (?p ?c ?l)
  (=> (and (person ?p)
           (citizen-of ?p ?c)
           (national-language-of ?c ?l))
      (speaks-language ?p ?l)))
```

When asked about the truth of (speaks-language fred german), the KR&R system can use logical inference and

answer "true". When asked about (speaks-language fred french), however, the system has to answer "unknown", since it does not have enough information to answer this question. Here and throughout the rest of this paper we make an *open world assumption*, that is, what is in a knowledge base is assumed to be an incomplete model of the world.

The larger the knowledge base grows, the more questions the system can answer; however, that set is usually small compared to the set of interesting questions within its domain that it cannot answer. Therefore, a very common query response is "unknown." While this is expected, it can be frustrating for knowledge engineers as well as non-expert users, in particular, if the system *should have known* the answer. The problem is exacerbated by the fact that the system cannot provide a good explanation for such failures beyond that everything it tried to derive an answer failed. Standard explanation techniques for logical reasoning rely on the availability or constructibility of a proof that can then be rendered and explained to a user (Chester 1976; McGuinness 1996). In this case, these techniques do not apply, since no successful proof was found among the possibly very many that were tried. Debugging such a failure manually can be very difficult and tedious.

In this paper we describe a novel query debugging tool called WhyNot, that is designed to help a human user to analyze *why* a query could *not* be answered successfully by the underlying KR&R system. It does so by trying to generate *plausible partial proofs* that approximate the correct (or expected) proof that would answer the query. The gaps in such a partial proof can then be scrutinized by the user to see whether they constitute missing knowledge or some other deficiency of the KB or query. A first version of WhyNot has been implemented and used successfully with a large Cyc knowledge base containing over a 1,000,000 facts and over 35,000 rules.

The Problem

KR&R systems can commonly answer two types of queries: (1) true/false questions such as "is it true that (speaks-language fred german)", and (2) Wh-questions such as "retrieve all ?x such that (speaks-language fred ?x)." We say that a true/false query fails, if the system can neither prove the queried fact to be true nor to be false and returns "unknown." A Wh-query fails if the system fails to generate a complete set of answers relative to the expectations of the user or using application. In this paper we are primarily concerned with failed true/false questions. Our techniques apply to Wh-queries as well, but the openness of Wh-queries introduces an extra level of difficulty; however, any one missing value can be analyzed by a corresponding true/false query.

Here are common reasons why queries fail:

Missing knowledge such as relevant facts or rules that are missing from the KB.

Limitations such as using an incomplete reasoner or an undecidable logic, resource exhaustion such as search depth cutoffs or timeouts, etc.

User misconceptions where the user chooses vocabulary missing from the KB, or asks a query that does not actually express what s/he intended to ask, or if the queried fact contradicts what is in the KB.

Bugs in the KB such as incorrect facts or rules or bugs in the inference engine or surrounding software.

A query may fail because one or more of these failure modes is to blame. Some failure modes such as using undefined vocabulary or exhaustion of inference engine resources (timeouts) can be detected by the KR&R system and communicated to the user. Others will simply lead to silent failure. All failures including exhaustion of allotted inference resources can present difficult problems to solve. The reason for this difficulty is that in such a case the KR&R system has explored a potentially very large search space to generate an answer, but everything it tried to derive an answer failed.

Standard explanation techniques to explain results of logical inference cannot be used to help a user with this problem, since they all require a data structure representing a derivation or proof for the answer to a query. Such proof structures are either generated automatically by the inference engine when the query is answered, regenerated during a rerun of the query in "explanation mode", or generated independently from how it was derived originally by the core inference engine. Which method is chosen depends on the underlying logic and performance optimizations of the inference engine. See (McGuinness 1996) for an example where proofs are generated for the sole purpose of producing explanations. Once a proof has been found, it can be rendered into an explanation for the user.

When a query fails, however, there is no relevant proof that could be explained to the user. Instead, the traditional approach to solve such a problem is to manually examine – if available – inference traces or failure nodes of search trees to see where something might have gone wrong. Since queries in logic-based systems can easily generate very large search trees due to the many different ways in which answers can be derived, this process can require a lot of analytical skills, expertise and time. Such problems are difficult for knowledge engineers, and often unsolvable for non-expert users.

To enable the use of standard proof-based explanation techniques to help with query failures, we need to generate some kind of proof despite the fact that there is not enough information in the KB to support a proof. The WhyNot tool accomplishes that by generating *plausible partial proofs*. A partial proof is a proof with some of its preconditions unsatisfied (or gaps). If the proof is plausible and close to the correct or expected proof, these gaps can pinpoint missing knowledge that when added to the KB will allow the query to succeed.

Generating plausible partial proofs within large knowledge bases poses two difficult challenges: (1) determining what it means for a proof to be *plausible* among the many possible ones, and (2) *performance*, i.e., finding plausible partial proofs without looking at too many options. How these challenges are tackled by WhyNot is described in the remainder of the paper.

The current version of the WhyNot tool primarily concentrates on the detection of missing facts. Other failures such as missing rules, incorrect knowledge, etc. might also be made easier to diagnose in some cases, but no specific support for these failure modes is available yet. For the application scenario of knowledge base development by users who are not knowledge engineers, being able to suggest potentially missing facts is an important step for helping them debug failed queries and to extend the KB.

Plausible Partial Proofs

The WhyNot tool supports the analysis of query failures by trying to generate *ranked plausible partial proofs*. Intuitively, a plausible partial proof approximates the correct proof the system would find had it all the correct knowledge and capabilities. It is an approximation, since it might not completely match the structure of the correct proof and will not have all its preconditions satisfied. We claim that if we can find a good enough approximation of the correct proof, it will allow the user to determine what pieces of knowledge are missing or what other failures might have occurred that prevented the query to succeed. By generating multiple partial proofs ranked by plausibility, we can provide explanation alternatives and enable the user to focus on the most plausible explanations among a potentially very large set of possible ones.

A *partial* proof for a queried fact q is any proof

$$P : \{p_1, \ldots, p_n\} \vdash q$$

where one or more of the premises p_i are not known to be true. A *plausible* partial proof is one where the unknown premises p_i could "reasonably" be assumed to be true. This is of course a semantic notion that can ultimately only be decided by the user.

A *good* plausible proof is one that is well entrenched in the knowledge base by applying relevant facts and rules, and that maximizes the ratio of known to unknown premises. Note that for any failed query q a minimal plausible partial proof is

$$Q : \{q\} \vdash q$$

This is akin to saying "if I had known that q is true I could have told you that q is true." This is only a good partial proof if there are no rules available to conclude q or if we cannot adequately satisfy the preconditions of any applicable rules.

Generating plausible partial proofs is a form of abductive reasoning. In abduction, q would be something that was observed (e.g., the symptoms of a disease), and the set of p_i whose truth values were not a-priori known would be the abduced explanation for q (e.g., the set of diseases that would explain the symptoms). In a standard abductive reasoner the abduced hypotheses are non-monotonic inferences that are added to the theory. In our case, they are used to generate hypothetical answers to the failed query q, for example, "if p_i and p_j were true then q would be true". This therefore is related to the work on hypothetical question answering by Burhans and Shapiro (1999).

Judging the plausibility of a partial proof is a similar problem to deciding between alternative explanations in abductive inference. In the abduction literature, many different criteria have been proposed, for example, explanations should be minimal, basic, consistent, most specific, least specific, least cost, etc. The best choice depends very much on the problem domain. For WhyNot we want a criterion that reduces the number of partial proofs for a particular query to an amount that is amenable to manual inspection without being too discriminating. For example, the strongest plausibility criterion we can apply within a logic-based framework is to require that the set of unknown premises be logically consistent with the rest of the knowledge base. However, large knowledge bases, in particular if they are under development, are often not consistent or correct; therefore, we do not want to be too aggressive about weeding out inconsistent premises, since they might indicate other problems in the KB.

Example

Before we describe the plausibility scoring and proof generation scheme, we want to give an example how the WhyNot tool can be used to analyze the failure of a query. Consider the following small knowledge base fragment:

```
(and (person fred) (person phil) (person susi))
(parent-of fred phil)
(national-language-of usa english)
(national-language-of france french)
(national-language-of germany german)
(national-language-of canada english)
(national-language-of canada french)

(forall (?p ?c ?l)
  (=> (and (person ?p)
           (citizen-of ?p ?c)
           (national-language-of ?c ?l))
      (speaks-language ?p ?l)))

(forall (?p ?c ?l)
  (=> (and (person ?p)
           (birth-place-of ?p ?c)
           (national-language-of ?c ?l))
      (native-language-of ?p ?l)))

(forall (?p ?l)
  (=> (and (person ?p)
           (native-language-of ?p ?l))
      (speaks-language ?p ?l)))

(forall (?p ?l)
  (=> (exists (?f)
         (and (parent-of ?p ?f)
              (native-language-of ?f ?l)))
      (speaks-language ?p ?l)))
```

If we ask the system whether (speaks-language fred german) is true, it returns "unknown", since at this point all that is known about Fred is that he is a person and has Phil as a parent. If we now run the WhyNot tool on the failed query

we get the following two explanations sorted by score (the plausibility score can be in the range of 1.0 for strictly true to -1.0 for strictly false):

```
Explanation #1 score=0.708:

1 (SPEAKS-LANGUAGE FRED GERMAN)
    is partially true by Modus Ponens
    with substitution ?p/FRED, ?l/GERMAN, ?f/PHIL
    since 1.1 ! (forall (?p ?l)
                      (<= (SPEAKS-LANGUAGE ?p ?l)
                          (exists (?f)
                             (and (PARENT-OF ?p ?f)
                                  (NATIVE-LANGUAGE-OF ?f ?l)))))
    and   1.2 ! (PARENT-OF FRED PHIL)
    and   1.3   (NATIVE-LANGUAGE-OF PHIL GERMAN)

1.3 (NATIVE-LANGUAGE-OF PHIL GERMAN)
    is partially true by Modus Ponens
    with substitution ?p/PHIL, ?l/GERMAN, ?c/GERMANY
    since 1.3.1 ! (forall (?p ?l)
                        (<= (NATIVE-LANGUAGE-OF ?p ?l)
                            (exists (?c)
                               (and (PERSON ?p)
                                    (BIRTH-PLACE-OF ?p ?c)
                                    (NATIONAL-LANGUAGE-OF ?c ?l)))))
    and   1.3.2 ! (PERSON PHIL)
    and   1.3.3 ? (BIRTH-PLACE-OF PHIL GERMANY)
    and   1.3.4 ! (NATIONAL-LANGUAGE-OF GERMANY GERMAN)

Explanation #2 score=0.556:

2 (SPEAKS-LANGUAGE FRED GERMAN)
    is partially true by Modus Ponens
    with substitution ?p/FRED, ?l/GERMAN, ?c/GERMANY
    since 2.1 ! (forall (?p ?l)
                      (<= (SPEAKS-LANGUAGE ?p ?l)
                          (exists (?c)
                             (and (PERSON ?p)
                                  (CITIZEN-OF ?p ?c)
                                  (NATIONAL-LANGUAGE-OF ?c ?l)))))
    and   2.2 ! (PERSON FRED)
    and   2.3 ? (CITIZEN-OF FRED GERMANY)
    and   2.4 ! (NATIONAL-LANGUAGE-OF GERMANY GERMAN)
```

In each explanation propositions that were found to be directly asserted in the KB are marked with '!' and unknown propositions are marked with '?'. Propositions without a mark such as 1.3 are supported by a further reasoning step. Each explanation describes a partial proof for the failed query. If all its unknown leafs marked with '?' would be true, the query would follow.

Despite the differences in score, both explanations above identify only a single missing fact that would allow the derivation of the expected answer. The first explanation scores higher because a larger percentage of the total number of ground facts needed in the proof tree are present. Since the plausibility scoring scheme will always be imperfect and since the system has no way to decide *a priori* which of those missing facts is more likely, we present multiple explanations for the user to consider.

By default, the WhyNot tool suppresses explanations with an absolute score of less than 0.3. If we lower the threshold to 0.0 we get the following additional explanation:

```
Explanation #3 score=0.208:

3 (SPEAKS-LANGUAGE FRED GERMAN)
    is partially true by Modus Ponens
    with substitution ?p/FRED, ?l/GERMAN, ?f/SUSI
    since 3.1 ! (forall (?p ?l)
                      (<= (SPEAKS-LANGUAGE ?p ?l)
                          (exists (?f)
                             (and (PARENT-OF ?p ?f)
                                  (NATIVE-LANGUAGE-OF ?f ?l)))))
    and   3.2 ? (PARENT-OF FRED SUSI)
    and   3.3   (NATIVE-LANGUAGE-OF SUSI GERMAN)

3.3 (NATIVE-LANGUAGE-OF SUSI GERMAN)
    is partially true by Modus Ponens
```

```
          with substitution ?p/SUSI, ?l/GERMAN, ?c/GERMANY
    since 3.3.1 ! (forall (?p ?l)
                        (<= (NATIVE-LANGUAGE-OF ?p ?l)
                            (exists (?c)
                               (and (PERSON ?p)
                                    (BIRTH-PLACE-OF ?p ?c)
                                    (NATIONAL-LANGUAGE-OF ?c ?l)))))
    and   3.3.2 ! (NATIONAL-LANGUAGE-OF GERMANY GERMAN)
    and   3.3.3 ? (BIRTH-PLACE-OF SUSI GERMANY)
    and   3.3.4 ! (PERSON SUSI)
```

This last explanation scores lower, since two additional facts would need to be added to the KB for the question to be answered true. It was generated by postulating bindings for the variable ?f in rule (3.1). In explanation 1 ?f was bound by a direct assertion. Now, in addition to Susi, there could be many other persons who might be parents of Fred. Some of them would be implausible, such as in the following suppressed partial proof:

```
4 (SPEAKS-LANGUAGE FRED GERMAN)
    is partially true by Modus Ponens
    with substitution ?p/FRED, ?l/GERMAN, ?f/FRED
    since 4.1 ! (forall (?p ?l)
                    (<= (SPEAKS-LANGUAGE ?p ?l)
                        (exists (?f)
                           (and (PARENT-OF ?p ?f)
                                (NATIVE-LANGUAGE-OF ?t ?l)))))
    and   4.2 X (PARENT-OF FRED FRED)
    and   4.3   (NATIVE-LANGUAGE-OF FRED GERMAN)
```

The explanation is suppressed, because Fred cannot be his own parent (clause 4.2), since parent-of is asserted to be ir-reflexive. In large and complex KBs, many of the dead ends pursued by the inference engine are nonsensical inferences such as the above. The primary function of the WhyNot module is to separate the wheat from the chaff and present a small number of good guesses for plausible partial inferences to the user. This allows the WhyNot module to reject the explanation on grounds of inconsistency, since (parent-of fred fred) is provably false using very simple inference. In general, however, we cannot rely on that completely, since the more ground a KB covers, the more room there is for unspecified semantic constraints; therefore, we always need a human user to make the final judgment.

Scoring Partial Proofs

A good plausible proof is one that maximizes the ratio of known to unknown premises while at the same time being well entrenched in the knowledge base. The assumed un-knowns should also not be in direct conflict with other facts in the KB. We do not require full consistency, (1) since it is not computable, and (2) since it would be much too costly to try to even approximate. Whenever we accept an unknown premise, we therefore only check for its falsity via quick lookup or shallow reasoning strategies. To implement these plausibility heuristics we use the following score computation rules:

Atomic goals p: The score of an atomic proposition p is 1.0 if it was found strictly true, -1.0 if it was found strictly false or 0.0 if it is completely unknown. If it was inferred by a rule of inference such as Modus Ponens, its score is determined by the score combination function of that rule.

AND-introduction goals (and $p_1 \ldots p_n$): the score of a conjunction is computed as a weighted average of the scores of its conjuncts: let $s(p_i)$ be the score of a conjunct and

$w(p_i)$ be its weight. The resulting score is

$$\text{score} = \frac{\sum_{i=1}^{n} w(p_i) s(p_i)}{\sum_{j=1}^{n} w(p_j)}$$

If any of the p_i is found to be strictly false, the conjunction fails strictly and the resulting score is -1.

The weights $w(p_i)$ are used to scale down the importance of certain classes of propositions. For example, a subgoal of the form (not (= ?x ?y)) has a very high likelihood to succeed for any pair of bindings. We therefore scale down the importance of the truth of such a subgoal by heuristically giving it a low weight of 0.1. Similarly, type constraints such as person in (and (person ?x) (person ?y) (father-of ?x ?y)) are given somewhat less importance, since in general they are more likely to be found true and they are often redundant. These are of course only simple heuristics in the absence of a more general scheme to determine the semantic contribu-tion of a particular conjunct (see (Hobbs *et al.* 1993)[p.84] for some more discussion of this issue). Future versions of WhyNot might perform statistical analysis of the underlying KB to determine these weights automatically.

OR-introduction goals (or $p_1 \ldots p_n$): the score of a dis-junction is the weighted score $(w(p_i) s(p_i))$ of the first dis-junct (starting from the current choice point) whose score exceeds the current minimum cutoff. A higher-scoring dis-junct can be found when we backtrack or generate the next partial proof.

Implication elimination (Modus Ponens) goals: when concluding q from p and $(\Rightarrow p\ q)$ we compute $s(q)$ as $s(p)d$ where d is a degradation factor that increases with the depth of a proof. The rationale for the degradation factor is that the longer a partial reasoning chain is, the higher the likelihood that it is incorrect. For any unknown proposition p partial support from chaining through a rule is seen as support for its truth, but that support is counted less and less the deeper we are in the proof tree.

Generating Partial Proofs

The WhyNot partial proof generator is built into the infer-ence engine of the PowerLoom KR&R system. PowerLoom uses a form of natural deduction to perform inference and it combines a forward and backward chaining reasoner to do its work. PowerLoom's inference engine is a "pragmatic" implementation. It is not a complete theorem prover for first-order logic, yet it has various reasoning services such as type level reasoning, relation subsumption, a relation classi-fier, selective closed world reasoning, etc. that go beyond the capabilities of a traditional first-order theorem prover. It also has a variety of controls for resource bounded inference to allow it to function with large knowledge bases.

The backward chainer uses depth-first search with chronological backtracking as its primary search strategy. Memoization caches successful and, if warranted, failed subgoals to avoid rederivation. The ordering of conjunc-tive goals is optimized by considering various costs such as unbound variables, goal fanout and whether a subgoal can be inferred by rules. Duplicate subgoals are detected and depth cutoffs and timeouts provide resource control. Once a solution has been found, the next one can be generated by continuing from the last choice point.

The partial proof generator is part of PowerLoom's backward chainer. Originally, it was built to overcome the general brittleness of logic-based KR&R systems by providing a partial match facility, i.e., to be able to find partial solutions to a query when no strict or full solutions can be found. The WhyNot tool extends this facility for the purposes of generating plausible partial proofs. The partial proof generator keeps trying to prove subgoals of a goal even if some other conjoined subgoals already failed. Once all subgoals have been attempted, instead of a truth value a combined score is computed to reflect the quality of the solution, and that score is then propagated to the parent goal.

To retain some pruning ability, a minimally required cutoff score is computed at each state in the proof tree and further subgoaling is avoided if it can be determined that the required cutoff score is unachievable. The top-level controller uses the cutoff mechanism to generate a set of better and better proofs by using the scores of previously found proofs as a minimal score cutoff. To avoid having high-scoring proofs found early mask out other slightly lesser scoring but equally plausible proofs, the controller accumulates at least N proofs before it uses the worst score of the current top-N proofs as the cutoff (currently, we use $N = 10$). While the WhyNot partial proof generator is running, justifications for (partially) satisfied subgoals are kept which results in a partial proof data structure for satisfied top-level goals. During normal operation of the inference engine, such justifications are not recorded for performance reasons.

Taming the Search

Generating plausible partial proofs is a form of abductive reasoning and even restricted forms of abduction are computationally intractable (cf., (Bylander *et al.* 1991; Selman & Levesque 1990)). In practice, generating partial proofs provides less opportunities to prune the search tree. For example, if we are trying to prove a conjunction as part of a strict proof, we can stop and backtrack as soon as we fail to prove one of the conjuncts. If we are looking for a partial proof we cannot do that, since the failed conjunct might be the missing knowledge we are trying to identify. We need to examine the other conjuncts to determine whether the remainder of the proof is plausible. For this reason, generating partial proofs requires different search control than generating regular proofs. Time limits are an important means to keep the effort spent under control. Additionally, the minimal cutoff score mechanism described above can reinstate some pruning opportunities, but by its nature partial proof search will be less focused. Particularly problematic can be generator subgoals as created by rules such as the following:

```
(forall (?p ?l)
  (=> (exists (?f)
        (and (person ?f)
             (parent-of ?p ?f)
             (native-language-of ?f ?l)))
      (speaks-language ?p ?l)))
```

When we are trying to prove the goal (speaks-language fred german) and backchain into the above rule, PowerLoom

tries to prove the existential by introducing a generator subgoal of the following form:

```
(and (parent-of fred ?f)
     (person ?f)
     (native-language-of ?f german))
```

The conjunctive goal optimizer reordered the subgoals to have the one that is expected to generate the least number of bindings for ?f as the first one. Once ?f is bound the remaining goals are harmless and can be solved by simple lookup or chaining. In the strict case, if the first subgoal fails to generate any binding for ?f the existential goal simply fails. If we are generating partial proofs the failed conjunct is skipped and the next conjunct is tried with ?f still unbound. This can constitute a problem, since the number of bindings generated for ?f by either of the remaining clauses might be much larger than what was estimated for the first conjunct. If we simply go on to the next clause, we would generate the set of all people in the KB which could be very large. As a first line of defense, we have to reoptimize the remaining clauses, since with ?f still unbound it might now be better to try the last clause first. If the remaining clauses are still too unconstrained, for example, if the language variable ?l was also unbound, we simply skip them and fail since the large number of unconnected bindings would probably not be useful for an explanation anyway.

Another search problem that surfaced when applying WhyNot to a very large KB such as Cyc was that not all applicable rules were tried due to query timeouts. In normal processing, this is not usually a problem, since aggressive pruning means rules often fail fairly early in their consideration. With the reduced pruning used by WhyNot, this caused certain rules not to be considered at all. We needed to change the WhyNot search strategy to "give each rule its equal chance." Now whenever it tries to prove a subgoal p and there are n applicable rules, it allocates $\frac{1}{n}$-th of the remaining available time to each rule branch. Time that wasn't fully used by one of the rules is redistributed among the remaining ones. This time-slicing ensures that we never get stuck in one subproof without any time left to explore remaining alternatives.

Explanation Post-Processing

Before explanations are presented to the user, some post-processing is required: (1) to remove unnecessary detail and make them easier to understand, (2) to remove some idiosyncrasies introduced by the partial proof search, and (3) to give some advice on how to interpret the partial proof.

How to best present a proof to a non-expert user has not been the primary focus of our work. We rely on the fact that PowerLoom's natural deduction inference can be translated fairly directly into explanations; however, some uninformative proof steps such as AND-introduction or auxiliary steps needed by the inference engine are suppressed.

A more interesting post-processing step is illustrated by the following example: suppose we ask (speaks-language fred french) in the example KB presented above. Just as before the answer will be "unknown", but WhyNot will return a slightly different explanation for the failure:

```
Explanation #1 score=0.708:

1 (SPEAKS-LANGUAGE FRED FRENCH)
     is partially true by Modus Ponens
     with substitution ?p/FRED, ?l/FRENCH, ?f/PHIL
     since 1.1 ! (forall (?p ?l)
                   (<= (SPEAKS-LANGUAGE ?p ?l)
                        (exists (?f)
                         (and (PARENT-OF ?p ?f)
                              (NATIVE-LANGUAGE-OF ?f ?l)))))
     and   1.2 ! (PARENT-OF FRED PHIL)
     and   1.3   (NATIVE-LANGUAGE-OF PHIL FRENCH)

1.3 (NATIVE-LANGUAGE-OF PHIL FRENCH)
     is partially true by Modus Ponens
     with substitution ?p/PHIL, ?l/FRENCH, ?c/[FRANCE, CANADA]
     since 1.3.1 ! (forall (?p ?l)
                     (<= (NATIVE-LANGUAGE-OF ?p ?l)
                          (exists (?c)
                           (and (PERSON ?p)
                                (BIRTH-PLACE-OF ?p ?c)
                                (NATIONAL-LANGUAGE-OF ?c ?l)))))
     and   1.3.2 ! (PERSON PHIL)
     and   1.3.3 ? (BIRTH-PLACE-OF PHIL ?c)
     and   1.3.4 ! (NATIONAL-LANGUAGE-OF ?c FRENCH)
```

The difference is that there were two countries whose national language was French. This resulted in two almost identical partial proofs that only differed in the binding for variable ?c in clauses 1.3.3 and 1.3.4. Instead of making an arbitrary choice or giving a series of almost identical explanations for each country whose national language is French, the WhyNot tool collapses those answers into one[1]. The result is an intensional explanation which might be paraphrased as "if for some ?c such that (national-language-of ?c french) it were known that (birth-place-of phil ?c), then the query could be answered. A few example individuals that were actually found to make clause 1.3.4 true are annotated in a special syntax in the variable substitution. Once a generalization has occurred, the part of the inference tree responsible for generating similar bindings is cut off to force the generation of the next structurally different proof.

Future Work

One type of post-processing not yet attempted by WhyNot is to try to give advice how to best interpret a partial proof, since gaps in a partial proof can be the result of problems other than missing knowledge. For example, consider this query given to the Cyc knowledge base: "Can Anthrax lethally infect animals?" The query fails and WhyNot produces the explanation shown in Figure 1 (this explanation is rendered for a non-expert audience and uses Cyc's natural language generation mechanism).

The partial proof found by WhyNot points to the relevant portion of the KB, but here we do not have a case of missing knowledge. Rule (1.1) is a type-level inheritance rule that says if some type of organism can lethally infect some type of host, then subtypes of the organism can infect subtypes of the host. In other words, if we know anthrax can infect mammals (fact 1.2), then anthrax can infect sheep. But instead of asking about sheep, the question was about anthrax infecting *animals*. What WhyNot could not determine in clause (1.4) was whether animal is a subtype of mammal.

This is of course not missing knowledge, but the query was asked about too general a type. One hint to that could have been that mammals actually are a subtype of animal, and that these are usually proper subtype relationships; therefore, suggesting that animal is a subtype of mammal is unlikely to be correct. At this point, however, it is not clear how to reliably make such a determination which is why it is not yet done.

Related Work

Relatively little has been done in the area of analyzing failed inferences or queries in KR&R systems. The closest is McGuinness' (1996) work on providing explanation facilities to description logics, in particular, explaining why some concept A does not subsume another concept B. Since most description logics are decidable, non-subsumption can be determined by having a complete reasoner fail on proving a subsumption relationship. To explain a non-subsumption to the user with "everything the system tried failed" is of course not a good option for the same reasons we outlined above. Since the logic is decidable, however, non-subsumption is constructively provable and explainable by generating a counter-example. McGuinness' work differs from our case where we have an (at best) semi-decidable logic and an incomplete reasoner where the answer to a query really is unknown and not derivable as opposed to false.

Kaufmann (1992) describes a utility to inspect the failed proof output of the Boyer-Moore theorem prover. He claims that inspection of such output is crucial to the successful use of the prover. The utility allows the definition of checkpoints for situations where the prover is trying some fancy strategy, since this often indicates a processing has entered a dead end. This tool does not provide automatic analysis of a failed proof and is geared towards a technical audience.

Gal (1988) and Gaasterland (1992) describe cooperative strategies for query answering in deductive databases. One of their main concerns is to provide useful answers or allow query relaxation in cases where the user has misconceptions about the content of the database. These techniques handle some query failure modes not addressed by our tool and might be useful additions in future versions.

Finally, there is a large body of work describing how to best explain the reasoning results of expert systems, planners, theorem provers, logic programs, etc. to users (see for example, (Chester 1976; Wick & Thompson 1992; McGuinness 1996)). Some of these techniques could be applied to the output of our tool. Since we wished to focus our research on generating the plausible proofs we use a relatively simple strategy to describe the partial natural deduction proofs found by the system.

Using WhyNot with Cyc

The PowerLoom WhyNot tool has been integrated into the Cyc tool suite to support the debugging of failed queries. This integration is part of DARPA's Rapid Knowledge Formation program (RKF) — an effort to research and develop new techniques and technologies to widen the knowledge

---

[1]In general, even if there were only one binding found for some variable, the choice might be arbitrary and an intensional explanation might be better; however, currently we only generate an intensional explanation if we find two or more similar bindings.

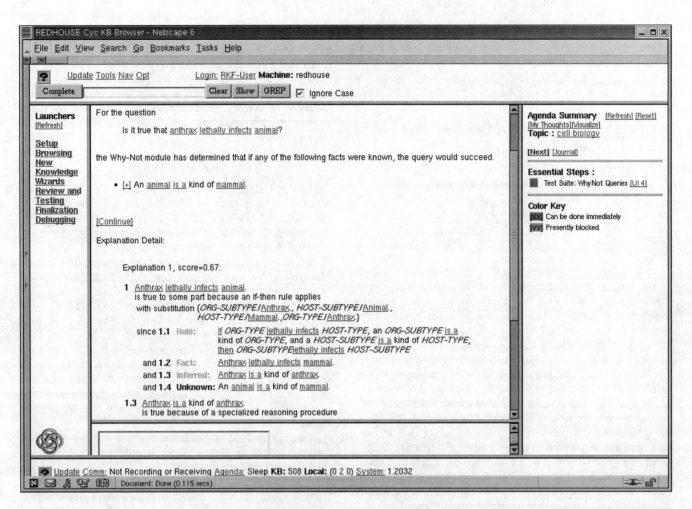

Figure 1: Showing a WhyNot Explanation in Cyc

acquisition bottleneck. The primary goal is to enable domain experts such as microbiologists who are not computer scientists to author competent knowledge bases of their field of expertise with no or only minimal help from knowledge engineers. Two teams, one led by Cycorp and one by SRI, are each developing a set of knowledge acquisition tools whose performance is repeatedly evaluated in the context of a challenge problem. Once this evaluation process is completed, we expect to be able to provide both quantitative data and qualitative feedback about the performance and usefulness of the WhyNot tool.

The tool developed by Cycorp is built around the large Cyc common sense knowledge base (Lenat 1995). The version of Cyc used within RKF contains over 1,000,000 facts and over 35,000 rules. One of the claims of Cycorp's approach is that the large amount of common sense knowledge available in Cyc makes it easier and more efficient to enter and verify new knowledge. Cycorp's tool also contains new, fairly sophisticated natural language parsing and generation components. All input from domain experts is given in natural language (in some cases constrained by templates), and any Cyc knowledge that is displayed is rendered in natural

language. The expert therefore never has to use the MELD KR language used internally by Cyc. The interface to Cyc is via a Web browser as shown in the screenshot in Figure 1.

WhyNot can be viewed as a Cyc Plug-in that can provide special reasoning services not available in Cyc. WhyNot runs as an external knowledge module connected to Cyc via the VirB[3] blackboard developed by Cycorp. It is written in our own STELLA programming language (Chalupsky & MacGregor 1999) which can be translated into Lisp, C++ and Java. In this application we used the Java translation which can be shipped as a 2 Megabyte Java Jar file. A small amount of SubLisp code was also written to provide some extensions to the Cyc API. SubLisp is a programming language developed by Cycorp that, similar to STELLA, tries to preserve a Lisp-based development environment while allowing to release code in mainstream language such as C.

When domain experts are adding knowledge or testing the knowledge they authored, they have to query the Cyc knowledge base. When a query fails and returns unknown as its result, they can ask the WhyNot module to analyze the failure. WhyNot requests are processed in the background and the user can perform other knowledge acquisition tasks while waiting for a response.

When WhyNot receives such a request on the blackboard, it first translates the failed query expression from MELD into KIF and then starts to derive plausible partial proofs. Since the WhyNot module runs in a completely separate implementation outside of Cyc, it needs to get access to all the relevant knowledge in the Cyc KB. It does so by paging in knowledge from Cyc completely dynamically on demand as it is needed by the PowerLoom inference engine. To do that a knowledge paging mechanism is used that maps PowerLoom's KB indexing and access language onto that of a foreign knowledge store such as Cyc. The Cyc API provides a rich set of access and KB indexing functions that make this fairly efficient. The connection to the Cyc API is not through the blackboard but via a dedicated TCP/IP channel to get higher throughput. Once knowledge is paged in it is cached for efficiency. Updates on the Cyc side cause relevant portions of the paging cache to be flushed. In this application large portions of the Cyc KB can be considered read-only which makes this caching scheme feasible.

Each assertion shipped from Cyc to PowerLoom is translated from MELD to KIF and back again. This is not too difficult, since the languages are fairly similar. An initial translation is performed on the Cyc side, and any remaining translations are performed by a small set of OntoMorph rewrite rules (Chalupsky 2000). Once a WhyNot explanation has been generated, it is rendered into HTML and the referenced facts and rules are run through Cyc's natural language generator. The result is then shipped back to Cyc where it appears on the agenda and can be displayed by the user (see Figure 1).

Running partial inference dynamically against a Cyc KB proved to be quite a challenging task. Cyc contains relations such as objectFoundInLocation that have hundreds of rules associated with them. Proper search and resource control as described above is therefore extremely important. Similarly, since paging in knowledge from Cyc is somewhat slow, minimizing page-in was a priority. The resulting system is not blazingly fast, but the performance is acceptable. Generating the explanation for the query in Figure 1 takes about 30 seconds the first time around including the time to page in all the relevant knowledge. Subsequent calls run in less than 5 seconds. WhyNot queries run with a timeout of three minutes which seems to be a good compromise for the queries encountered so far. Since WhyNot queries are triggered by the user and would otherwise involve time-consuming manual debugging, the reported run times and timeouts seem to be acceptable.

Acknowledgements This research was supported by the Defense Advance Research Projects Agency under Air Force Research Laboratory contract F30602-00-C-0160.

References

Burhans, D., and Shapiro, S. 1999. Finding hypothetical answers with a resolution theorem prover. In *Papers from the 1999 AAAI Fall Symposium on Question Answering Systems, Technical Report FS-99-02*, 32–38. Menlo Park, CA: AAAI Press.

Bylander, T.; Allemang, D.; Tanner, M.; and Josephson, J. 1991. The computational complexity of abduction. *Artificial Intelligence* 49(1–3):25–60.

Chalupsky, H., and MacGregor, R. 1999. STELLA – a Lisp-like language for symbolic programming with delivery in Common Lisp, C++ and Java. In *Proceedings of the 1999 Lisp User Group Meeting*. Berkeley, CA: Franz Inc.

Chalupsky, H. 2000. OntoMorph: a translation system for symbolic knowledge. In Cohn, A.; Giunchiglia, F.; and Selman, B., eds., *Principles of Knowledge Representation and Reasoning: Proceedings of the Seventh International Conference (KR2000)*. San Francisco, CA: Morgan Kaufmann.

Chester, D. 1976. The translation of formal proofs into English. *Artificial Intelligence* 7(3):261–278.

Gaasterland, T. 1992. Cooperative explanation in deductive databases. In *AAAI Spring Symposium on Cooperative Explanation*.

Gal, A. 1988. *Cooperative Responses in Deductive Databases*. Ph.D. Dissertation, University of Maryland, Department of Computer Science. CS-TR-2075.

Genesereth, M. 1991. Knowledge interchange format. In Allen, J.; Fikes, R.; and Sandewall, E., eds., *Proceedings of the 2nd International Conference on Principles of Knowledge Representation and Reasoning*, 599–600. San Mateo, CA, USA: Morgan Kaufmann Publishers.

Hobbs, J.; Stickel, M.; Appelt, D.; and Martin, P. 1993. Interpretation as abduction. *Artificial Intelligence* 63(1–2):69–142.

Kaufmann, M. 1992. An assistant for reading Nqthm proof output. Technical report 85, Computational Logic.

Lenat, D. 1995. CYC: A Large Scale Investment in Knowledge Infrastructure. *Communications of the ACM* 38(11):32–38.

McGuinness, D. 1996. *Explaining Reasoning in Description Logics*. Ph.d. dissertation, Department of Computer Science, Rutgers University, New Brunswick, New Jersey.

Selman, B., and Levesque, H. 1990. Abductive and default reasoning: A computational core. In Dietterich, T., and Swartout, W., eds., *Proceedings of the Eighth National Conference on Artificial Intelligence*, 343–348. Menlo Park, CA: AAAI Press.

Wick, M., and Thompson, W. 1992. Reconstructive expert system explanation. *Artificial Intelligence* 54(1–2):33–70.

An Analogy Ontology for Integrating Analogical Processing and First-principles Reasoning

Kenneth D. Forbus

Qualitative Reasoning Group
Northwestern University
1890 Maple Avenue
Evanston, IL, 60201, USA
forbus@northwestern.edu

Thomas Mostek

Qualitative Reasoning Group
Northwestern University
1890 Maple Avenue
Evanston, IL, 60201, USA
tmostek@naviant.com

Ron Ferguson

College of Computing
Georgia Institute of Technology
801 Atlantic Avenue
Atlanta GA 30332, USA
rwf@cc.gatech.edu

Abstract

This paper describes an *analogy ontology*, a formal representation of some key ideas in analogical processing, that supports the integration of analogical processing with first-principles reasoners. The ontology is based on Gentner's *structure-mapping* theory, a psychological account of analogy and similarity. The semantics of the ontology are enforced via procedural attachment, using cognitive simulations of structure-mapping to provide analogical processing services. Queries that include analogical operations can be formulated in the same way as standard logical inference, and analogical processing systems in turn can call on the services of first-principles reasoners for creating cases and validating their conjectures. We illustrate the utility of the analogy ontology by demonstrating how it has been used in three systems: A crisis management analogical reasoner that answers questions about international incidents, a course of action analogical critiquer that provides feedback about military plans, and a comparison question-answering system for knowledge capture. These systems rely on large, general-purpose knowledge bases created by other research groups, thus demonstrating the generality and utility of these ideas.

Introduction

There is mounting psychological evidence that human cognition centrally involves similarity computations over structured representations, in tasks ranging from high-level visual perception to problem solving, learning, and conceptual change [21]. Understanding how to integrate analogical processing into AI systems seems crucial to creating more human-like reasoning systems [12]. Yet similarity plays at best a minor role in many AI systems. Most AI systems operate on a *first-principles* basis, using rules or axioms plus logical inference to do their work. Those few reasoning systems that include analogy (cf.[1,37]) tend to treat it as a method of last resort, something to use only when other forms of inference have failed. The exceptions are case-based reasoning systems [27,28], which started out to provide computational mechanisms similar to those that people seem to use to

solve everyday problems. Unfortunately, CBR systems generally have the opposite problem, tending to use only minimal first-principles reasoning. Moreover, most of today's CBR systems also tend to rely on feature-based descriptions that cannot match the expressive power of predicate calculus. Those relatively few CBR systems that rely on more expressive representations tend to use domain-specific and task-specific similarity metrics. This can be fine for a specific application, but being able to exploit similarity computations that are more like what people do could make such systems even more useful, since they will be more understandable to their human partners.

While many useful application systems can be built with purely first-principles reasoning and with today's CBR technologies, integrating analogical processing with first-principles reasoning will bring us closer to the flexibility and power of human reasoning. This paper describes a method for doing this. The key idea is to use an *analogy ontology* that provides a formal, declarative representation of the contents and results of analogical reasoning. The semantics of this ontology is defined by the underlying theory of analogy and similarity, structure-mapping [18]. This semantics is enforced via procedural attachment, using the analogy ontology to set up computations that are solved by special-purpose analogical processing systems, and reifying the results of these programs in a way that can be used by first-principles reasoning systems.

We start by reviewing relevant aspects of structure-mapping theory. Then we present the analogy ontology, and outline its implementation. We then describe how these ideas have been used in three systems: analogical reasoning about historical precedents, critiquing military course of action sketches via cases, and answering comparison questions in knowledge capture systems. We close by discussing related and future work.

Prelude: Structure-mapping, SME, and MAC/FAC

In structure-mapping theory [18], an analogy match takes as input two structured representations (*base* and *target*) and produces as output a set of mappings. Each mapping consists of a set of *correspondences* that align base items with target items and a set of *candidate inferences*, which are surmises about the target made on the basis of the base representation plus the correspondences. The constraints that govern mappings, while originally motivated by psychological concerns [21], turn out to be equally important for the use of analogy in case-based reasoning, since they ensure that candidate inferences are well defined and that stronger arguments are preferred [11].

Two simulations based on structure-mapping are relevant to this paper. The first, the Structure-Mapping Engine (SME) [1,7,11], is a cognitive simulation of analogical matching. How SME works is described in [6,7,11]. Two characteristics are key to the work described here:

- SME operates in polynomial time, using a greedy merge algorithm to provide a small number of mappings that best satisfy the constraints of structure-mapping.

- SME's results are consistent with a large and growing body of psychological results on analogy and similarity [9], making its answers and explanations more likely to be accepted by human collaborators.

The second simulation, MAC/FAC, is a two-stage model of similarity-based retrieval that is consistent with psychological constraints [14] and has been used in a fielded application [16]. The key insight of MAC/FAC is that memory contents should be filtered by an extremely cheap match that filters a potentially huge set of candidates, followed by a structural match (i.e., SME) to select the best from the handful of candidates found by the first stage[1]. The extremely cheap match is based on *content vectors*, a representation computed from structured descriptions. Content vectors are useful because the dot product of two content vectors provides an estimate of the quality of match between the corresponding structural descriptions (see [14] for details).

The Analogy Ontology

The analogy ontology defines the types of entities and relationships used in analogical processing. The ontology can be grouped into *cases*, *matches*, *pragmatic constraints*, *mappings*, *correspondences*, *candidate inferences* and *similarities and differences*. We discuss each in turn.

Cases: Cases are collections of statements, treated as a unit. We use the relation (ist-Information ?case ?fact) to indicate that statement ?fact is in the case ?case.[2] Cases can be explicitly named in the KB, via the function explicit-case-fn, whose single argument is a term naming the case.

One important way of encoding task constraints in analogical reasoning is by specifying different collections of information about a term to be gathered from a knowledge base. In the ontology these are represented simply as additional functions. (How such functions are

---

[1] Hence the name: Many Are Called/Few Are Chosen

[2] ist-Information is drawn from the Cyc upper ontology.

implemented is described in [30], and their integration into reasoning systems described below) Here are some functions that we have found useful in several tasks:

- (minimal-case-fn ?thing) denotes all of the statements in the KB that directly mention ?thing, where ?thing can be any term. This is rarely used in isolation, instead providing a convenient starting point for defining other case functions.

- (case-fn ?thing) is the union of (minimal-case-fn ?thing) and attribute information about all of the ground terms occurring in (minimal-case-fn ?thing), e.g., in the case of Cyc, the attribute information consists of the isa statements involving the ground terms. When ?thing is an event, all causal links between the terms are included in addition to attribute information. When ?thing is an agent, all facts whose ground terms are those in (minimal-case-fn ?thing) are included. This is useful when a quick comparison is required, to see if the match is worth pursuing further.

- (recursive-case-fn ?thing) denotes the union of case-fn applied to ?thing and to all of its subparts, recursively. What constitutes a subpart depends on the KB's ontology. For instance, if ?thing is an event, its subparts are subevents.

- (in-context-case-fn ?thing ?case) denotes the subset of (case-fn ?thing) that intersects the case ?case. This is used for more focused queries, e.g., Alabama in the context of the US Civil War.

- (no-postlude-case-fn ?thing) denotes (case-fn ?thing) with all causal consequences of ?thing removed. This is useful in reasoning about alternative outcomes of a situation, since it suppresses knowledge of the actual outcomes.

The particular definitions for agent, event, causal consequences, and subparts depend on the KB used. In the KB's we have worked with to date (Cyc, SAIC, and KM) it has sufficed to enumerate short lists of predicates used to identify these concepts. For instance, in using Cyc, members of the collections Event and Agent are treated as events and agents respectively, and short lists of relationships were identified as expressing causal and mereological consequences. We expect that this technique will work for any knowledge base that includes some version of these concepts.

Matches: Matches represent a comparison between a base and target. They consist of a set of *correspondences* and *mappings*, which are described shortly. The relation (match-between ?base ?target ?match) indicates that ?match is the result of SME comparing the cases ?base and ?target. There are two variations that are like match-between, except that the process they specify is slightly different. recursive-match-between dynamically expands the cases to resolve competing entity matches. This is useful in dealing with large, complex cases. seeking-match-between only considers matches that reflect required or excluded correspondences derived from task constraints. The procedural semantics of recursive-match-between and seeking-match-between are detailed in [30].

Mappings: In structure-mapping, a mapping consists of three things: A structurally consistent set of correspondences, a set of candidate inferences, and a structural evaluation score [6,7,11]. How correspondences and candidate inferences are represented in this ontology is described below. The structural evaluation score is an estimate of match quality. The function `structural-evaluation-score` denotes the score computed by SME for the mapping. The relation (`mapping-of ?mapping ?match`) indicates that mapping `?mapping` is part of match `?match`, i.e., that it is one of the solutions SME found to the comparison. The relation (`best-mapping ?match ?mapping`) indicates that `?mapping` has the highest structural evaluation score of `?match`'s mappings. Typically this is the mapping that is preferred, so it is worth being able to specify it concisely.

Correspondences: A correspondence relates an item in the base to an item in the target. Items can be entities, expressions, or functors. Correspondences have a structural evaluation score[3]. The relation (`correspondence-between ?c ?b ?t`) indicates that item `?b` corresponds to item `?t` according to correspondence `?c`. (`has-correspondence ?m ?c`) indicates that mapping `?m` contains the correspondence `?c`. (Not all correspondences participate in mappings, and only do so under specific constraints: See [6,7] for details.)

The *parallel connectivity* constraint of structure-mapping states that if a correspondence involving two expressions is in a mapping then so must correspondences involving its aligned arguments [19]. This constraint induces a structural dependency relationship between correspondences which is reified in our ontology. The relation (`structurally-supported-by ?c1 ?c2`) indicates that correspondence `?c2` links a pair of arguments in the statements linked by correspondence `?c1`. This information is used in constructing dependency networks during first-principles reasoning, so that explanations (and backtracking) will take account of analogical processing results. For example, correspondences implicated in a contradiction can be identified by a TMS, and used to formulate constraints (described next) which push SME into seeking an alternate solution.

Pragmatic constraints: Some task constraints can be expressed in terms of restrictions on the kinds of correspondences that are created during the matching process. Such statements can be inserted into the knowledge base or used in queries. The analogy ontology incorporates three kinds of constraints:

1. (`required-correspondence ?Bitem ?Titem`) indicates that its arguments must be placed in correspondence within any valid mapping. This is useful when the task itself implies correspondences whose consequences are to be explored (e.g., "If Saddam Hussein is Hitler, then who is Churchill?")

---

[3] The structural evaluation score of the mapping is the sum of the structural evaluation score for its correspondences. See [7] for details.

2. (`Excluded-correspondence ?Bitem ?Titem`) indicates that its arguments may not be placed in correspondence within any valid mapping. This is useful when a mapping has been ruled out due to task constraints, and alternate solutions are sought. Excluding an otherwise attractive correspondence will cause SME to look for other solutions.

3. (`required-target-correspondence ?Titem`) indicates that there must be a correspondence for target item `?Titem`, but does not specify what that must be. (`required-base-correspondence` is the equivalent in the other direction.) This is useful when seeking an analogy that sheds light on a particular individual or relationship, because being placed in correspondence with something is a necessary (but not sufficient) requirement for generating candidate inferences about it.

Candidate inferences: A candidate inference is a statement in the base that, based on the correspondences in a mapping, might be brought over into the target as a consequence of the analogy [7]. Candidate inferences have the following properties:

• *Propositional Content.* The statement about the target that has been imported from the base by substituting the correspondences from the mapping into the base statement.
• *Support.* The base statement it was derived from.
• *Support score.* The degree of structural support derived from the correspondences in the mapping.
• *Extrapolation score.* The degree of novelty of the candidate inference, derived from the fraction of it that is not in the mapping.

The support and extrapolation scores are defined in [13]. The binary relationships `candidate-inference-content`, `candidate-inference-support`, `candidate-inference-support-score`, and `candidate-inference-extrapolation-score` express the relationships between a candidate inference and these properties. Candidate inferences can postulate new entities in the target, due to the existence of unmapped entities in the support statement. Such terms are denoted using the function `analogy-skolem`, whose argument is the base entity that led to the suggestion.

Similarities and differences: Summarizing similarities and differences is an important part of many analogy tasks [21]. The main source of information about similarity is of course the set of correspondences that comprise a mapping. However, it is often useful to extract a subset of similarities and differences relevant to a particular correspondence of interest. (`similarities ?mh ?m ?exact ?dim ?other`) states that the structural support for correspondence `?mh` of mapping `?m` consists of three sets: `?exact`, representing exact matches differing only in `?mh`, `?dim`, correspondences where the entities involved vary along some dimension (e.g., different in color), and `?other`, correspondences that are neither of the other two. (The set bound to `?other` are candidates for rerepresentation, to improve the alignment.) Similarly, (`differences ?mh ?m ?1only ?2only`) indicates that with respect to correspondence `?mh` of mapping `?m`, `?1only` are statements only holding in the base and `?2only` are statements only holding in the target.

Integrating 1st principles and analogical reasoning

The analogy ontology provides the glue between 1st principles reasoning and analogical processing. It provides a language for the entities and relationships of structure-mapping, so that they can be used along with other theories in logic-based reasoning systems. The intended semantics of the analogy ontology is that of structure-mapping. Just as predicates involving arithmetic typically have their semantics enforced via code, we use procedural attachment [22,38] to enforce the semantics of the analogy ontology. This is crucial because special-purpose software is needed for efficient large-scale analogical processing, where descriptions involving hundreds to thousands of relational propositions are matched. These procedural attachments provide the means for analogical processing software to be seamlessly used during first-principles reasoning. Matches and retrievals are carried out via queries, whose result bindings include entities such as matches, mappings, and correspondences, as defined above. Subsequent queries involving these entities, using other relationships from the analogy ontology, provide access to the results of analogical processing. Next we outline how this works.

Procedural attachment requires two-way communication between the reasoning system and the attached software. The reasoning system must have some means for recognizing predicates with procedural attachments and carrying out the appropriate procedures when queries involving them are made. For instance, in our FIRE reasoning system[4], *reasoning sources* provide a registration mechanism that ties procedures to particular signatures of predicate/argument combinations. For instance, (`match-between :known :known :unknown`) invokes SME, binding the result variable (third argument) to a term which can be used in subsequent queries to access the consequences of the match. The reasoning source maintains a table that translates between terms added to the reasoning system and the internal datastructures of the analogical processing system. Thus to the reasoning system, a standard unification-based query mechanism provides transparent access to analogical processing facilities.

Communication in the other direction, from analogy software to reasoning system, is handled by using the reasoner's query software from within the analogy subsystem. There are three kinds of information needed from 1st principles reasoning during an analogical query. First, SME needs basic information about the functors used in statements (e.g., are they relations, attributes, functions, or logical connectives?). This information is gathered by queries to the KB, e.g., in Cyc such questions reduce to membership in specific collections. Second, the terms

denoting cases must be evaluated to gather the statements that comprise the case. This is implemented via a method dispatch, based on the case function (e.g., `case-fn`) using the techniques described in [30]. Third, the cases that comprise a case library must be collected. This is handled by querying the KB for the members of the case library.

Let us step through the process with a simple (albeit abstract) example, to see how these mechanisms work together. Consider a goal of the form (`match-between ?base ?target ?match`). When `?base` and `?target` are bound, this goal invokes SME to match the value of `?base` against the value of `?target`. When `?base` is unbound, this goal invokes MAC/FAC, with the value of `?target` as the probe and the current case library as the memory. If `?target` is unbound, the query is considered to be an error, and the goal fails. The values of `?base` and `?target` determine how the case information fed to the software is derived. If the value is a non-atomic term whose functor is one of the case-defining functions, further reasoning is invoked to derive the contents of the case [30]. Otherwise, the value is construed as the name of a case and the appropriate facts are retrieved using queries involving `case-description`.

A successful `match-between` query results in the creation of a new term in the reasoning system to represent the match. `?match` is bound to this new term as part of the bindings produced by the goal, and the new term is linked the analogical processing data structure to support future queries. In addition, the mappings associated with the match are reified as new terms in the reasoning system, with the appropriate `mapping-of`, `best-mapping`, and structural evaluation score information asserted.

Analogical matches and retrievals involving large descriptions can result in hundreds to tens of thousands internal data structures, any of which is potentially relevant, depending on the task. Blind reification can easily bog down a reasoning session. Consequently, we use a *lazy reification* strategy. Because of the designs of SME and MAC/FAC, there can at most be only a handful of mappings created by any query[5], reifying mappings always makes sense. Correspondences and candidate inferences are reified on demand, in response to goals involving them (e.g., `correspondence-of`, `candidate-inference-of`).

We have implemented these ideas in two reasoning systems, DTE[6] and FIRE. DTE used ODBC-compliant databases to store its knowledge base, a logic-based TMS reasoning engine [10] as its working memory, a general-purpose mechanism for procedural attachments (including hooks for GIS systems and a diagrammatic reasoner) and a prolog-style query system which provides access to all of these facilities for application systems. FIRE is the

---

[4] FIRE = Integrated Reasoning Engine. The F is either Flexible or Fast, and we hope both.

[5] SME's greedy merge algorithm with its usual parameter settings only produces the top interpretation plus at most two more close interpretations. MAC/FAC's default settings allow it to return at most three candidates from the MAC stage, which means there can be at most nine mappings created in the FAC stage.

[6] DTE = Domain Theory Environment.

successor to DTE, using a higher-performance knowledge base created in collaboration with Xerox PARC, and with a streamlined mechanism for integrating other reasoning sources.

Examples

We have used the analogy ontology in a variety of systems. For concreteness, we briefly summarize how it is being used in three of them: A crisis management analogical reasoner, an analogical critiquer for military courses of action, and answering comparison questions in a knowledge capture system. We focus on showing how the analogy ontology enabled the smooth integration of analogical and first-principles reasoning in these systems.

Crisis management analogical reasoner. When reasoning about international crises, analysts commonly rely on analogy (cf. [24,32,33]). In the DARPA HPKB Crisis Management challenge problems, *parameterized questions* were introduced to express some typical types of queries [4]. Seeing how the analogy ontology enables such queries to be expressed and answered is a good illustration of its utility. We use two examples for illustration.

```
PQ226   Who/what is <SituationItem> in
{<EventSpec1> <ContextSpec1>, <SituationSpec1>}
similar to in {<EventSpec2> <ContextSpec2>,
<SituationSpec2>}?  How so, and how are they
different?
```
The terms in a parameterized question are specified according to the knowledge base used. Treating the first event as the base and the second as the target, this parameterized question is answered by using the following template:
```
(and (required-target-correspondence
        <SituationItem>)
     (recursive-match-between ?base ?target
                      ?match)
     (best-mapping ?match ?mapping)
     (has-correspondence ?mh ?mapping)
     (correspondence-between ?mh ?x
                    <SituationItem>)
     (similarities ?mh ?mapping ?exact
                 ?dimensional ?other)
     (differences ?mh ?mapping ?other
              ?obj1-only ?obj2-only))
```
For example, using the Cyc KB, the question
```
SQ226: Who/what is IRAN in Y2-SCENARIO-CONFLICT
similar to in PERSIAN-GULF-WAR?
```
yields the answer
```
IRAN in The Facts concerning Y2-SCENARIO-CONFLICT
case corresponds to IRAQ in the PERSIAN-GULF-WAR
case.
```
where the supporting structural justifications include that both were involved in hostile actions, both were in conflict with other nation states in hostile-social-actions, and so on.

Our second example:
```
PQ228 How does the analogy between
{<SituationSpec1>, <PropositionConj1>
```
```
<ContextSpec1>} and {<SituationSpec2>,
<PropositionConj2> <ContextSpec2>} [where
<AnalogyMappingSpecConj>] suggest that the latter
will turn out, and how do differences between
them affect the answer?
```
Assuming that ?bstart and ?tstart are the starting points for the base and target, the initial query uses the template
```
(and (required-correspondence ?bstart ?tstart)
     (seeking-match-between
        (case-fn ?bstart)
        (no-postlude-case-fn ?tstart)
         ?match)
     (best-mapping ?match ?mapping)
     (has-correspondence ?mh ?mapping)
     (correspondence-between ?mh ?bstart ?tstart)
     (similarities ?mh ?mapping ?exact
                ?dimensional ?other)
     (differences ?mh ?mapping ?other
               ?obj1-only ?obj2-only))
```
The follow-up query finds what candidate inferences of the mapping make predictions about what might happen after ?tstart based on its analogy with ?bstart:
```
(and (candidate-inference-of ?ci ?mapping)
     (candidate-inference-content ?ci
     (<CausalConnective> ?tstart
             (analogy-skolem ?prediction))))
```
Notice the use of the `analogy-skolem` function, whose argument is bound to the base event being projected. The set *<CausalConnective>* varies with the particular structure of the knowledge base; for instance, there were 9 such relations in the Cycorp KB and 5 in the SAIC KB.

For example, using the SAIC KB, the question
```
TQF228b: How does the analogy between Iran oppose
Saudi Arabia's influence in OPEC in the Y1
Scenario and Iran oppose Saudi Aramco influence
in the Azerbaijan International Operating Company
in the Y2 Scenario suggest that the latter will
turn out, and how do differences between them
affect the answer?
```
yields four predictions, based on Iran's responses to a relevant Saudi action in the base case: An attack on an embassy, injury of Saudi citizens in a terrorist attack, student protest marches, and demanding an explanation of the Saudi ambassador.

Our Crisis Management Analogical Reasoner was used by both teams in the HPKB program. For SAIC, we used an automatic translator to load their KB files into a DTE knowledge base. We formulated queries, and our system's explanatory hypertext was used as the team's answer on the questions we tackled. For Cycorp, we supplied them with a server version of our system, which could either interact with the Cyc IKB directly, or could be used with DTE assimilating the Cyc IKB knowledge base. The details of the evaluation process and results can be found elsewhere [34]; suffice it to say that we got a "B" which, given the difficulty of the problems, we view as a success.

Battlespace Analogical Critiquer: Military courses of action (COAs) are plans outlining how an operation is to

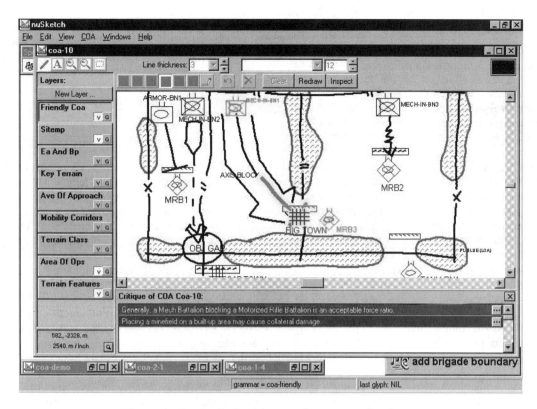

Figure 1: Analogical critiques of a course of action

be carried out. The early part of generating a COA concentrates on the *COA sketch*, a graphical depiction of the plan expressed through a graphical symbology representing military units, tasks and other relevant entities. The other challenge problem in HPKB was aimed at supporting military planners by critiquing COAs. Critiquing a sketch involves looking for violations of doctrine, ideas that might be unwise given prior experiences with the opponent, or just plain violate common sense, given that such plans are sometimes drafted in the field by people who haven't slept for days.

We created an *analogical critiquer* that provides feedback, both positive and negative, about a COA sketch based on *critique cases* authored by military personnel. The KB used is from Cyc, augmented with domain theories for spatial and geographic reasoning. Critique cases are generated by first using the same sketching tool (nuSketch COA Creator [8]) to generate a COA sketch, then using a special interface to select subsets of that COA to be encoded in cases. (A COA sketch can be used to create multiple cases, if different points can be illustrated by various aspects of it.) Each case must have a *critique point*, a proposition that is the key idea that that aspect of the case is making. Critique points are marked as positive or negative, with explanatory text added to phrase the idea in military terms. The author must also select (graphically) a subset of the sketch's propositions to be included in case. This *reminds-me* subset is what drives retrieval. A subset of that, in turn, is identified as the necessary conditions for the critique to be valid. The authoring tool installs a

justification of the critique point based on the necessary antecedents. This justification will provide the candidate inference that raises the suggestion of the critique point on retrieval.

The critiquer can be invoked by a planner as desired when using the nuSketch COA Creator to create a COA sketch. Internally the critiquer uses the current sketch as a probe to retrieve critiques via the following query:

```
(and (match-between ?critique <current sketch>
                      ?match)
     (mapping-of ?mapping ?match)
     (candidate-inference-of ?ci ?mapping)
     (candidate-inference-content ?ci
       (causes-prop-prop ?antecedents
                         ?critique)))
```

This query retrieves all critiques that are potentially relevant to the current sketch, since the only `causes-prop-prop` statement in the case is inserted by the authoring environment. The final relevance check (not shown) evaluates `?antecedents`, ensuring that they do not contain any skolems (indicating a serious mismatch) and that they are true in the current sketch. The results are presented visually to the user, as shown in Figure 1.

While this critiquer was not completed in time to be used in the official HPKB evaluations, reviews of a preliminary version by military officers not involved in its creation have led to its continued development as a component in training systems and performance support systems to be used by the US military [35].

Comparison questions in knowledge capture

One of the bottlenecks in the creation of AI systems is the difficulty of creating large knowledge bases. Research in the DARPA Rapid Knowledge Formation program is tackling this problem by creating systems that can be "taught" interactively by domain experts, without AI experts or knowledge engineers in the loop. Two end-to-end systems have been constructed. Cycorp's KRAKEN system uses a combination of natural language and forms, controlled via a dialogue manager, to interact with experts. SRI's SHAKEN system [3] uses concept maps. Our group provides analogical processing services for both teams. So far this has focused on providing answers to comparison questions (e.g., "How is *X* similar to *Y*?" and "How are *X* and *Y* different?), which are used both by users to figure out what needs to be added and to assess the KB.

SHAKEN uses the KM representation system [3], which is frame-based, and it is written in Common Lisp. These factors, plus the fact that we were generating output for users directly, led to the decision to implement a special-purpose KM interface rather than using the analogy ontology directly in the implementation. On the other hand, for interfacing with KRAKEN we created an Analogy Server, using our FIRE reasoning engine and a simple KQML vocabulary of messages for controlling it. The Analogy Server's knowledge base was kept up to date by routines in KRAKEN, and called by it when users wanted to ask comparison questions.

While these systems are still very much in progress, in Summer 2001 there was an independent evaluation carried out where domain experts (biology graduate students) used these systems to create knowledge bases for a chapter of a biology textbook. The evaluation details can be found in [35]. For this paper, the key thing to note is that the analogy ontology successfully enabled KRAKEN to use analogical processing facilities, as intended.

Related Work

There have been a number of systems that capture some aspects of reasoning by analogy. Winston [39] describes a system that extracts rules from precedents, but was only tested with very small (10 or so propositions) examples. Special-purpose matchers and retrievers have been used for exploiting analogy in problem solving and planning (cf. [1,37]), but such systems lack the flexibility to deal with large knowledge bases and cover the range of phenomena that SME and MAC/FAC handle. Other cognitive simulations of analogical processing, including ACME and ARCS [31], LISA[25], IAM [26], have only been tested with small examples, and some are known to fail when tested with descriptions even one-tenth the size of what was needed to handle the problems described here. No previous analogy systems have been successfully used with multiple, large general-purpose knowledge bases created by other research groups.

While the majority of today's CBR systems have moved to feature-vector representations, there are a number of systems that still use relational information. Some examples include [2,17,28,29]. We believe that the ideas described here could be used in these systems, and that using psychologically realistic matchers, retrievers, and similarity metrics could add value to them.

Discussion

The analogy ontology provides a key advance in creating general-purpose reasoning systems that are closer to providing human-like flexibility. By providing formal representations for concepts used in analogical reasoning, first-principles reasoning systems can use analogical matching and retrieval as resources for tackling complex problems, and analogical processing systems can in turn use first-principles reasoning to extract knowledge from general knowledge bases to create cases and test the validity of candidate inferences. We have shown that this analogy ontology enables the creation of systems that simply were not possible before, systems that can tackle complex problems, involving cases that are literally an order of magnitude larger than found in the rest of the analogy literature (involving thousands of propositions per case), and interoperating with general-purpose, large-scale knowledge bases created by other research groups.

While the analogy ontology here relies on structure-mapping theory, it does not depend at all on the details of our current simulations of structure-mapping. Most cognitive simulations of analogy today are consistent with structure-mapping to the extent needed by this ontology [20], so if more capable matchers or retrievers were created, they could be used instead. There are a number of limitations of the ontology as it stands, the most significant being that it currently does not capture the ideas of *alignable* and *non-alignable* differences [21] appropriately. Formalizing these concepts has proven to be quite subtle, but we continue to work on it.

Acknowledgements

This research was supported by the DARPA High Performance Knowledge Bases and Rapid Knowledge Formation programs, and by the Artificial Intelligence program of the Office of Naval Research.

References

1. Blythe, J. and Veloso, M. (1997) Analogical replay for efficient conditional planning, *Proceedings of AAAI-97*, pages 668-673.
2. Branting, K. L. 1999. *Reasoning with Rules and Precedents – A Computational Model of Legal Analysis.* Kluwer.
3. P. Clark, J. Thompson, K. Barker, B. Porter, V. Chaudhri, A. Rodriguez, J. Thomere, S. Mishra, Y. Gil, P. Hayes, T. Reichherzer. Knowledge Entry as the Graphical

Assembly of Components. *First International Conference on Knowledge Capture*, October 21-23, 2001.

4. Cohen, P., Schrag, R., Jones, E., Pease, A., Lin, A., Starr, B., Gunning, D., and Burke, M. 1998. The DARPA High Performance Knowledge Bases Project. *AI Magazine*, Winter, 1998.

5. Cohn, A. (1996) Calculi for Qualitative Spatial Reasoning. In Artificial Intelligence and Symbolic Mathematical Computation, LNCS 1138, eds: J Calmet, J A Campbell, J Pfalzgraf, Springer Verlag, 124-143, 1996.

6. Falkenhainer, B., Forbus, K., and Gentner, D. (1986, August) The Structure-Mapping Engine. Proceedings of AAAI-86, Philadelphia, PA

7. Falkenhainer, B., Forbus, K., Gentner, D. (1989) The Structure-Mapping Engine: Algorithm and examples. Artificial Intelligence, 41, pp 1-63.

8. Ferguson, R., Rasch, R., Turmel, B., and Forbus, K. 2000. Qualitative spatial interpretation of course-of-action diagrams. *Proceedings of QR-2000*. Morelia, Mexico.

9. Forbus, K. 2001. Exploring analogy in the large. In Gentner, D., Holyoak, K. and Kokinov, B. (Eds) *Analogy: Perspectives from Cognitive Science.* Cambridge, MA: MIT Press.

10. Forbus, K. and de Kleer, J., *Building Problem Solvers*, MIT Press, 1993.

11. Forbus, K., Ferguson, R. and Gentner, D. (1994) Incremental structure-mapping. *Proceedings of the Cognitive Science Society,* August.

12. Forbus, K., & Gentner, D. (1997). Qualitative mental models: Simulations or memories? *Proceedings of the Eleventh International Workshop on Qualitative Reasoning*, Cortona, Italy.

13. Forbus, K., Gentner, D., Everett, J. and Wu, M. 1997. Towards a computational model of evaluating and using analogical inferences. *Proceedings of CogSci97*.

14. Forbus, K., Gentner, D. and Law, K. (1995) MAC/FAC: A model of Similarity-based Retrieval. *Cognitive Science*, 19(2), April-June, pp 141-205.

15. Forbus, K. and Usher, J. 2002. Sketching for knowledge capture: A progress report. *Proceedings of IUI-2002*, ACM Publications, January, San Francisco.

16. Forbus, K.D., Whalley, P., Everett, J., Ureel, L., Brokowski, M., Baher, J. and Kuehne, S. (1999) CyclePad: An articulate virtual laboratory for engineering thermodynamics. *Artificial Intelligence.* **114**, 297-347.

17. Friedrich Gebhardt, Angi Voß, Wolfgang Gräther, Barbara Schmidt-Belz. 1997. *Reasoning with complex cases.* Kluwer, Boston, 250 pages. March.

18. Gentner, D. (1983). Structure-mapping: A theoretical framework for analogy. Cognitive Science, 7, 155-170.

19. Gentner, D. (1989). The mechanisms of analogical learning. In S. Vosniadou & A. Ortony (Eds.), *Similarity and analogical reasoning* (pp. 199-241). London: Cambridge University Press. (Reprinted in *Knowledge acquisition and learning*, 1993, 673-694.)

20. Gentner, D., & Holyoak, K. J. (1997). Reasoning and learning by analogy: Introduction. *American Psychologist, 52,* 32-34.

21. Gentner, D., & Markman, A. B. (1997). Structure mapping in analogy and similarity. *American Psychologist, 52,* 45-56. (To be reprinted in *Mind readings: Introductory selections on cognitive science,* by P. Thagard, Ed., MIT Press)

22. Greiner, R. and Lenat, D. 1980. A representation language language. *Proceedings of AAAI-80.*

23. Gross, M. and Do, E. (1995) Drawing Analogies - Supporting Creative Architectural Design with Visual References. in *3d International Conference on Computational Models of Creative Design*, M-L Maher and J. Gero (eds), Sydney: University of Sydney, 37-58.

24. Heuer, R. J. 1999. *Psychology of Intelligence Analysis.* Center for the Study of Intelligence. Government Printing Office, US Government.

25. Hummel, J. E., & Holyoak, K. J. (1997). LISA: A computational model of analogical inference and schema induction. *Psychological Review.*

26. Keane, M. T. (1990). Incremental analogising: Theory & model. In K. J. Gilhooly, M. T. G. Keane, R. H. Logie, & G. Erdos (Eds.), *Lines of thinking* (Vol. 1, pp. XX). Chichester, England: Wiley.

27. Kolodner, J. L. (1994). Case-based reasoning. San Mateo, CA: Morgan Kaufmann Publishers.

28. Leake, D. (Ed.) 1996. *Case-Based Reasoning: Experiences, Lessons, and Future Directions*, MIT Press.

29. Lenz, M., Bartsch-Spörl, B., Burkhard, H.-D., Wess, S. (Eds.), *Case Based Reasoning Technology – from Foundations to Applications.* Lecture Notes in Artificial Intelligence 1400, Springer, 1998

30. Mostek, T., Forbus, K. and Meverden, C. 2000. Dynamic case creation and expansion for analogical reasoning. *Proceedings of AAAI-2000.* Austin, Texas.

31. Thagard, P., Holyoak, K. J., Nelson, G., & Gochfeld, D. (1990). Analog retrieval by constraint satisfaction. Artificial Intelligence, 46, 259-310.

32. Neustad, R. and May, E. 1988. *Thinking in time: The uses of History for Decision Makers.* Free Press.

33. IET, Inc. and PSR Corp. 1999. HPKB Year 2 Crisis Management End-to-end Challenge Problem Specification. http://www.iet.com/Projects/HPKB/Y2/Y2-CM-CP.doc

34. http://www.iet.com/Projects/HPKB/

35. Rasch, R., Kott, A. and Forbus, K. 2002. AI on the battlefield: An experimental exploration. *Proceedings of IAAI 2002.*

36. Schrag, Robert. http://www.iet.com/Projects/RKF/

37. VanLehn, K., & Jones, R. M. (1993). Integration of analogical search control and explanation-based learning of correctness. In S. Minton (Ed.), Machine learning methods for planning (pp. 273-315). San Mateo, CA: Morgan Kaufman.

38. Weyhrauch, R. 1978. Prolegomena to a theory of formal reasoning. Stanford CS Department CS-TR-78-687, December, 1978

39. Winston, P. 1982. Learning New Principles from Precedents and Exercises," *Artificial* Intelligence **19**, 321-350

Applying Perceptually Driven Cognitive Mapping
To Virtual Urban Environments

Randall W. Hill, Jr.   Changhee Han   Michael van Lent

USC Institute for Creative Technologies
13274 Fiji Way, Suite 600, Marina del Rey, CA 90292-7008
{hill, changhee, vanlent}@ict.usc.edu

Abstract

This paper describes a method for building a cognitive map of a virtual urban environment. Our routines enable virtual humans to map their environment using a realistic model of perception. We based our implementation on a computational framework proposed by Yeap and Jefferies (Yeap & Jefferies 1999) for representing a local environment as a structure called an Absolute Space Representation (ASR). Their algorithms compute and update ASRs from a 2-1/2D [1] sketch of the local environment, and then connect the ASRs together to form a raw cognitive map. Our work extends the framework developed by Yeap and Jefferies in three important ways. First, we implemented the framework in a virtual training environment, the Mission Rehearsal Exercise (Swartout et al. 2001). Second, we describe a method for acquiring a 2-1/2D sketch in a virtual world, a step omitted from their framework, but which is essential for computing an ASR. Third, we extend the ASR algorithm to map regions that are partially visible through exits of the local space. Together, the implementation of the ASR algorithm along with our extensions will be useful in a wide variety of applications involving virtual humans and agents who need to perceive and reason about spatial concepts in urban environments.

Introduction

Our goal is to develop virtual humans with believable perceptual and spatial behaviors. For a growing number of computer games, military training simulations, and immersive learning environments, the willingness of the participant to suspend disbelief hinges on the realism of the behavior of the virtual humans. Behaviors such as self-location and way-finding have been investigated extensively in mobile robot applications, but there are numerous other spatial tasks more human in nature that need to be simulated in these applications. Interesting examples include communicating spatial information in natural language and social conventions such as initially blocking a doorway with your body and then stepping back to invite the visitor in. In military training simulations these include coordinated tactical movements, crowd control, avoiding snipers and ambushes, selecting helicopter landing zones, and establishing a security perimeter, to name a few. Underlying all these behaviors is the ability to perceive and build a spatial representation of the environment.

Humans are quite good at remembering the layout of the places they inhabit or have visited and using this information to reason about everyday tasks such as finding the local grocery store and locating a parking space in spite of the traffic jam at one end of the parking lot. Becoming familiar with the configuration of a place like a town is a process that involves walking around, looking at buildings, landmarks, streets and other details of the environment that are subsequently encoded into memories that make the place recognizable and easily navigated. The process of forming these spatial memories is called cognitive mapping (Chown & Kaplan & Kortenkamp 1995; Kuipers 1978; 2000; Yeap 1988; Yeap & Jefferies 1999). The ability to build a cognitive map is useful for any agent that has a need for tracking its location, navigating, and determining where places are located with respect to one another (Chown & Kaplan & Kortenkamp 1995; Kortenkamp & Bonasso & Murphy 1998; Kuipers 1978; 2000; Levitt & Lawton 1990).

This paper describes a method for building a cognitive map of a synthetic urban setting based on the realistic limits of human visual perception. Humans have a limited field of view and cannot see through solid objects like walls and these same limitations are imposed on our virtual agents. Only by making a series of observations from different perspectives over time can a cognitive map be built.

We based our implementation on a computational framework proposed by Yeap and Jefferies (Yeap & Jefferies 1999) that represents a local environment as a structure called an Absolute Space Representation (ASR). Building an ASR involves perceiving the local surroundings, the area immediately visible to the viewer, and computing the boundaries and exits of this space. The boundaries are obstacles that prohibit movement through the space such as walls. Exits are gaps in the boundaries that permit the agents to leave one local space and enter

---

[1] Marr (1982) defines a 2-1/2D sketch to be a list of surfaces and their spatial layout. The sketch only includes the visible portions of the surfaces in the agent's field of view.

another. For example, a room would be a single ASR with a number of boundaries (walls) and a single exit (the door). The exit would connect to another ASR (the hallway) with a number of boundaries and exits (doors) connecting to more ASRs representing other offices. By exploring a series of local spaces, representing them as ASRs, and connecting them together via their exits, a viewer builds a raw cognitive map[2]. We have taken this framework and extended it in a number of ways:

- We applied a theoretical computational framework of cognitive mapping to a training application that includes virtual humans in a virtual environment. To date most cognitive theories have been implemented in mobile robots, whose perceptual abilities are somewhat different than a human's, and whose purpose is not to exhibit human-like behavior. Yeap tested his theory with a simulated robot in a 2D world. Our cognitive mapping is done in the urban environment of the Mission Rehearsal Exercise (Swartout et al. 2001). Urban environments are of particular interest to game developers and the military simulation community.

- We extract a 2-1/2D sketch from a scene in a graphically rendered virtual world. Yeap finesses the issue of perception by assuming that a 2-1/2D map is going to be available. Computer games and military simulations generally also avoid the perception step by using a database of 3D models.

- We extended Yeap and Jefferies' cognitive mapping algorithms (Yeap & Jefferies 1999). Instead of limiting the agent to only building one ASR at a time, focusing only the immediate surroundings, we save the residue of what has been perceived through the exits in the local environment and begin the construction of the new ASRs before the areas are visited. This particular extension was made because we believe that cognitive mapping must not be limited to places that have been physically explored. Virtual humans need to build cognitive maps in anticipation of the next space they will enter.

Figure 1: View of a street in a virtual urban environment

Motivation

As previously stated, we are developing virtual humans for an immersive military training environment called the Mission Rehearsal Exercise (MRE) System. In the MRE the participants interact with virtual soldiers to perform missions involving tasks such as securing an area from attack, controlling an angry crowd, tending to an injured child, and securing a landing zone for a medevac helicopter. To perform these tasks the virtual soldiers must explore their surroundings, locate a suitable clear space, identify the potential lanes of attack into that space, and position themselves to block these lanes of attack. Performing these tasks requires spatial knowledge about landing zones and lanes of attack as well as perception of the environment to locate regions and exits that match those spatial concepts.

Many current applications finesse perception and spatial reasoning as much as possible. Computer games (Liden 2001) and military simulations (Reece & Kraus & Dumanoir 2000; Stanzione et al. 1996) often require a designer to annotate the environment with invisible spatial references to help virtual humans behave believably. Another approach is to give agents omniscient perception, giving them a complete map of the static environment and the current location of every dynamic entity. The alternative, demonstrated by the research presented here and the research of Terzopoulos and Rabie (Terzopoulos & Rabie 1995), is to give virtual humans realistic perception of their environment. Perception would be realistic both in the types of information sensed (no invisible spatial cues, no map) and the limitations on that sensing (no 360 degree field of view, no seeing through walls). As the virtual human moves around and views the environment from different perspectives, it constructs a cognitive map of its surroundings and uses that map for spatial reasoning.

Creating a cognitive map of the virtual environment, based on realistic perception, has a number of advantages over annotating the environment with spatial references. Different virtual humans can represent the environment with different cognitive maps based on their roles and knowledge. While the underlying ASR representation may be the same, the annotations placed on the spatial map would depend on the role and knowledge of the virtual human. A local resident's cognitive map of their home city, including street names and friend's houses, would be very different from the cognitive map of a soldier sent to defend that city which might include lines of attack and defensive strong points. Different map representations, based on different roles, will have far-reaching implications on the behavior of the virtual humans, affecting everything from natural language understanding and generation to movement and goal selection. In addition, cognitive mapping doesn't require the environment designer to embed spatial information in the environment, which can be a time consuming process. When spatial knowledge is encoded in the model, the designer must anticipate every behavior that could be potentially associated with a feature, leaving little for the agent to decide.

A cognitive map built from realistically limited perception also has a number of advantages over giving agents omniscient perception. At first it might seem that omniscient agents are simpler since they don't require a realistic model of perception. However, for their behavior

---

[2] A raw cognitive map contains just information about the local environment without the addition of semantic interpretation (Yeap 1988; Yeap & Jefferies 1999).

to be believable, omniscient agents must pretend to ignore the sensory information they wouldn't realistically perceive. Differentiating between the information they should and should not pretend to ignore requires a model of realistic perception at some level. In fact, realistically limited perception can help to guarantee that a virtual human is behaving believably by not allowing behavior to be affected by information a real human won't know. Realistic perception will lead to virtual humans that explore the environment and look around realistically to map their environment. In addition, these agents will get lost and make realistic mistakes based on their limited knowledge of the environment.

Building A Cognitive Map

Based on the Absolute Space Representation (ASR) algorithm developed by Yeap and Jefferies (Yeap & Jefferies 1999), our virtual human maps the local environment by continuously perceiving a scene, constructing a 2-1/2 D sketch of the surfaces, building a local map, and connecting it with other local maps that it has already constructed in the process of exploring a virtual town.

The basic idea behind Yeap's theory of cognitive maps (Yeap 1988) is to build a representation of the open space around the viewer. As previously mentioned this space is defined by the boundaries and exits that surround the viewer. The key to Yeap's construction of a raw cognitive map is the identification of the exits, which are defined as gaps between obstacles. This is the commonsense definition of an exit. But how does one compute it? We need to start by looking for gaps in the surfaces surrounding the viewer, beginning by looking for occluded edges. An exit is a way of leaving a local space. It is also a signal to compute a new ASR. Exits serve another important purpose in that they identify places in the space that have not been uncovered yet. These are places that are occluded and the viewer is not sure of. It may not actually be an exit, merely a place that has not been explored yet. If the goal is to build a complete raw cognitive map of an area, then the exits may actually be areas one needs to explore more fully, thus guiding the mapping process.

Figure 2: Detecting the edges in the urban scene

Constructing a 2-1/2D sketch

Yeap and Jefferies' cognitive mapping algorithm takes as input a 2-1/2D sketch of the scene (Marr 1982; Yeap & Jefferies 1999). The sketch is the set of boundary surfaces, including depth information, currently perceived by the viewer. These surfaces are represented as an ordered list of edges (with vertices), as they appear from left to right in the

field of view. But how is this sketch constructed? The answer depends on the domain of the application. Yeap tested the algorithm in a relatively simple 2D simulated domain but gives no details about how the sketch was derived. In a mobile robot domain, the sensors and computer vision system detect the edges and surfaces and recognizes objects in an effort to determine that the obstacles are indeed buildings or other real things. Much progress has been made in this area (e.g., see Kortenkamp & Bonasso & Murphy 1998 on mobile robotics), but it still remains a significant challenge. One of the contributions in this paper is an approach to building a 2-1/2D sketch in graphically rendered virtual environments.

We took a hybrid approach to building the 2-1/2D sketch that combines the use of the graphical model (known as the scene graph), which is represented as a graph of nodes corresponding to the objects in the scene, a graphics-rendering engine, and visual routines for edge detection. Each of the buildings and other objects in Figure 1 are represented as nodes in the scene graph that will be rendered in real time. Rather than relying on computer vision to recognize that these are buildings, we simplify the process by using this aspect of the model to tell us that these are buildings. But this only takes us part of the way toward building a 2-1/2D sketch. To do this, we take the following steps:

1. Traverse the scene graph and assign a unique number to each node corresponding to a building. This is done by taking advantage of the node pre-draw callback function in the graphics routines. The advantage of this is that each of the buildings, which are fairly simple boxes underneath the texture maps, will be assigned a unique number, which will be used later for edge detection.

2. Cull the nodes, leaving only the visible ones. This step creates the occlusions that the viewer would experience in the real world. Without this step the model would be transparent to the viewer, enabling the virtual human to see through solid walls. This step is essential for creating a 2-1/2D sketch. Without the occlusions the viewer would have be able to create a full 3D model.

3. Draw each node with its assigned number (color). The result of this step can be seen in Figure 2, where the buildings appear as different colors, corresponding to the unique numbers that were assigned.

4. Find the edges between the ground and the buildings using standard edge detection techniques.

➤ Use the graphics z-buffer to get the depth into the picture—we need the (x,y,z) positions of the points.

➤ Assume you know the color / # of the ground. Scan from the sky downward to find the ground edge. Do this across the image.

The result is a set of line segments along the boundaries between the buildings and the ground. Pixelation may result in short line segments that have to be joined together to form longer lines. These longer lines are smoothed out using standard edge detection techniques.

The output from this step is a 2-1/2D sketch, which is a set of edges and vertices in a format that can be used for Yeap's ASR algorithm, which we will describe in the next section[3].

Mapping the local space

Once a 2-1/2D sketch has been built, the key to computing an ASR is detecting where the boundaries and exits are located in the local space. Exits serve not only the obvious functional role of providing egress from a local space, but passing through an exit also triggers the construction of a new local map, which is represented as an ASR (Yeap & Jefferies 1999). Exits serve as the connections between the maps of local spaces (ASRs), and the raw cognitive map ends up being a network of exit nodes connecting local maps. Finding the boundaries of the local space is important for defining the extent of the area. Locating the exits is essential, both as a way of indicating how to leave a local space, and as a way of connecting pieces of the cognitive map together into a whole.

Exits are detected by looking for places in the scene where one surface partially occludes another. The gap between the two surfaces is what Yeap and Jefferies (Yeap & Jefferies 1999) call an occluded edge. An occluded edge has a visible vertex, which is also called the occluding vertex and is closest to the viewer, and an occluded vertex, which is where the occluded edge intersects with the backmost surface. An exit is the shortest span between the occluding vertex and another surface. It is the gap that must be crossed in order to reach the occluded edge.

To identify an exit, the surfaces from the current 2-1/2D sketch are scanned in order, from left to right, in a search for occluding vertices. Since the exit is the gap that must be crossed in order to reach an occluded edge, identifying the exit starts with the occluded edge. The ordered list of visible surfaces is divided into two groups around the occluded edge, which is done by placing one of the occluded edge's vertices in one group and the other into the second group. One of the occluded edge's vertices is unoccluded. Choose this vertex and look for the closest point on a surface contained in the opposite group. The exit is the edge formed by the unoccluded vertex and the closest point. Once identified, it is then inserted into the list of surfaces in its logical place adjacent to the surfaces contributing the vertices. The surfaces beyond the exit are trimmed from the ASR. They are no longer taken into consideration for mapping local space since they have been determined to be outside the exit. Yeap discards the trimmings—but in our implementation this residue is saved and used to map spaces outside of one's local space. This will be discussed in more detail in the section on mapping outside the local space.

Updating the local map

Since the viewer's perspective changes over time the ASR must continually be updated. Even a simple shift in gaze will uncover more details about the environment. Moving through the environment will cause some occlusions to be uncovered and others to be formed, so the question is how to incorporate this information into the raw cognitive map.

Figure 3: This is a top-down perspective of an ASR of the street scene from Figure 1. The building boundaries are shown as dark lines and the doubtless exits as thin lines. The viewer's path is shown with arrows. There are no doubtful exits in this ASR.

Yeap and Jefferies (Yeap & Jefferies 1999) distinguish between two kinds of exits: *doubtful* and *doubtless*. A *doubtless* exit is one that takes the viewer out of the local space. It consists of two unoccluded vertices—they must both have been visible sometime during the mapping process. In determining a doubtless exit, it is the shortest possible span between two surfaces. Once Yeap's algorithm has determined that an exit is doubtless it not longer needs to be updated.

When one of an exit's vertices is occluded, it is a *doubtful* exit. As the viewer moves through the environment, this type of exit must be updated. This is because as one's perspective changes, more of the occluded edge may be uncovered and the location of the occluded vertex will also change to be the shortest distance spanning the gap. This goes on until one of two things happens: either the exit is identified as doubtless (i.e., both vertices are unoccluded) or the occluded surface is completely uncovered and it is discovered that there is no exit.

The ASR is updated once per frame, where the rate may be as high as 20-30 frames per second. This may prove to be excessive in the long run, but it works for now. Each update involves taking the following steps[4]:

1. Sense the environment and construct a 2-1/2D sketch. Call this perspective CURRENT-VIEW.

---

[3] For the details of the algorithm see Yeap and Jeffires.

[4] These steps are based on the extend-ASR algorithm in Yeap and Jefferies (1999).

2. Check whether the viewer is still inside the current ASR. This can be achieved with a simple intersection test: draw a line from the viewer's current location to the initial position in the ASR and check whether this line intersects with the surface of the ASR.

3. If an exit has NOT been crossed, update the doubtful exits based on the CURRENT-VIEW. If the change in perspective uncovers an occlusion, this will cause the size of the corresponding doubtless exit to decrease. For each doubtful exit:
   a. Label the two surfaces that contribute vertices to the doubtful exit as S1 and S2.
   b. If CURRENT-VIEW includes S1 and S2, then replace the doubtful exit with the surfaces that lie between S1 and S2. Note: We found that we had to relax this condition somewhat because there are cases where the vertices of the doubtful exit are outside of the field of view of the agent.

4. Else, if an exit has been crossed, this means that the viewer is no longer in the local space represented by the current ASR. The next section deals with this situation, which involves extending the raw cognitive map with the current ASR and either starting a new ASR or using a previously computed one.

Extending the Cognitive Map

As new areas are mapped they are added to a network of ASRs that comprise the raw cognitive map. Whenever the viewer crosses an exit and enters a previously unexplored area, a new ASR is computed. Figure 4 shows a raw cognitive map with three ASRs. In this example the viewer starts where the arrows begin and proceeds up the street, turns left at an alley, goes between two buildings, and enters an open area surrounded by some buildings. The first ASR maps the street and ends when the street enters an intersection with another street, the second ASR represents the alleyway between the buildings, and the third ASR is still being formed for the open area as shown on the left side of figure 4. Note that the third ASR contains doubtful exits on the left and right sides of the viewer. This indicates that the area has not yet been completely mapped. Once the viewer's perspective has been rotated, these areas will be filled in with surfaces and doubtless exits. Figure 5 shows a more complete map of the third ASR overlaid onto the image of the town.

Extending a raw cognitive map requires the ability to recognize that an area that has previously been visited, otherwise areas would be re-mapped every time they were visited. The recognition routine is triggered when the viewer crosses an exit.

When the viewer crosses an exit, there are three possible cases:

1. The newly entered space was previously mapped and the exit is a known connector between the two ASRs. When this is the case, no updates to the raw cognitive map are required. Use the ASR from the raw cognitive map as a map of the local space.

2. The newly entered space was previously mapped, but it was not known that this exit connected these two ASRs. In this case update the raw cognitive map to reflect the fact that this exit is a connector, and use the ASR from the raw cognitive map.

3. The newly entered space is unexplored, so the viewer must begin mapping it. The steps in mapping this space are: (1) place the just exited ASR into the raw cognitive map, (2) create a new ASR, and (3) connect the ASR the viewer just departed with the new ASR at the exit point.

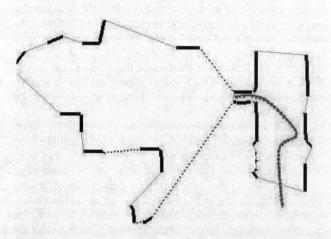

Figure 4: Three ASRs are shown connected together. The third ASR contains both doubtless (thin lines) and doubtful (dotted lines) exits.

Mapping Outside the Local Space

We developed an extension to Yeap and Jefferies' algorithm that enables the viewer to map spaces outside the current ASR. In their version, the ASR algorithm maps the local space by iteratively identifying exits and trimming off the surfaces beyond the exit. The only thing that is mapped is what is in the current local space as they define it. Our extension to Yeap's approach is to use the surfaces beyond exits to create a preliminary map of spaces that aren't local to the agent.

We do not believe that humans discard what they see on the other side of an exit. The cognitive mapping process is not confined to one's local space. A person walking around in an unfamiliar building will probably focus their attention on perceiving and mapping the local space, but it seems highly improbable that they would ignore the layout of a room that happens to be on the other side of a door or down a hallway. In fact, what is seen down the hallway (or down the street), which is a different local space, may provide important information that will impact the behavior of the viewer even before that space is entered.

An example of this arises in the context of an application that we have been working on for a military peacekeeping operation training exercise. Some virtual soldiers are looking for an open area that would be suitable for a medevac helicopter to land. A quick glance down an alley or street may reveal that there is no open space in the immediately adjacent spaces, but further down the street there is a major intersection where it may be possible for a helicopter to land. The intersection can be observed and partially mapped without physically leaving the current local space. If we restricted the cognitive mapping to only areas that had been physically visited, then the soldiers would have to behave unrealistically to acquire knowledge that is literally right before their eyes. For example, a soldier standing on the upper end of the first ASR shown in Figure 5 would be able to see into the intersection that is covered by the gray shading. But according to Yeap & Jefferies 1999 this would not be mapped and therefore would not be accessible unless the soldier took a step out of the current ASR toward the intersection.

To map areas outside of the current local space, we modified the ASR algorithm so that the areas outside the exits are not discarded. These are saved to form partial ASRs of the adjacent local spaces.

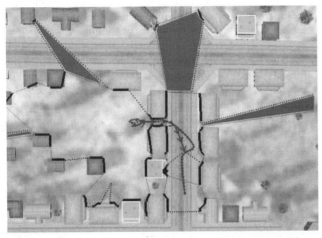

Figure 5: A raw cognitive map, including residual-ASRs (shaded regions) constructed from the residue of local computations.

The basic idea is to not only compute an ASR of the current local space, but at the same time also map the perceivable surroundings outside the local space. We call this set of surroundings outside the local space *residual-ASRs* since they are built by trimming the residue off of the current ASR. Residual-ASRs are updated every perception cycle, and their composition relies completely on the successive visual perspectives of the viewer. Computing a residual-ASR involves the following steps:

1. Each perception cycle create a 2-1/2D sketch of the area in the agent's field of view[5]. We refer to this sketch as the CURRENT-VIEW.

2. Subtract the current ASR from the CURRENT-VIEW. Call the remainder the *residue*. This computation involves two steps:
   a. For each currently visible exit in the ASR, identify the surfaces and gaps in the CURRENT-VIEW that appear through that exit. Designate these surfaces and spaces as the *residue* for that exit.
   b. Once the residue for an exit has been identified, use it to compute an ASR, i.e., identify the exits (doubtless and doubtful) and the surfaces using the same algorithm described previously. The result is the *current-residual-ASR* for that exit.

3. After each perception cycle, update the cumulative *residual-ASR* for each of the exits. The *current-residual-ASR* is only a snapshot. Its results are used to update the cumulative *residual-ASR*. The updating may involve adding new surfaces, changing exits from doubtful to doubtless, or reducing the size of doubtless exits where occlusions are uncovered.

With this extension to the basic ASR algorithm, a virtual human can map the perceivable areas outside of the local space while retaining the spatial interpretation afforded by the ASR. But what happens to these residual ASRs as the viewer travels from one local space to another? There are three cases we have considered:

1. As the viewer moves from one local space (ASR) to another, all of the residual-ASRs are saved and indexed by the location of the exit through which the residue was collected. An ASR may have multiple residual-ASRs, one for each exit. When the viewer re-enters an ASR, the residual-ASRs become available again.

2. When a viewer goes through an exit into an area that was not previously visited, it will likely have a residual-ASR that it computed for that space. At this point the residual-ASR is discarded and an ASR is computed. In our future work we will use the residual-ASR as a starting point for computing a new ASR.

3. When the viewer looks through an exit into a local space that has already been visited, then the viewer will recognize the space as having already being mapped, so it will not create a residual-ASR. It recognizes the space by taking the coordinates of the exit and indexing into the raw cognitive map, which contains all the exits and their locations.

This extension to Yeap and Jefferies' theory and algorithms provides the viewer with the ability to map areas outside of its local space. Figure 5 shows three residual-ASRs shaded in gray. For example, on the right hand side of the diagram there is a residual-ASR for the exit between the two buildings, looking out to the space beyond. In some cases phantom edges were detected due in part to the occlusions in the environment.

---

[5] This is the same 2-1/2D sketch that is used as input to the ASR-update algorithm.

Applications Of Cognitive Maps

Once a cognitive map of an area of the environment has been generated, the virtual human who generated that map can use it in a number of ways. In the Mission Rehearsal Exercise (Swartout 2001) mentioned in Section 2, many of the predicates used by the virtual human's planner involve spatial concepts. These predicates represent concepts such as individuals or groups occupying a specific region (medic-at-injury-site, crowd-in-landing-zone) and exits/entrances to a region being covered (landing-zone-secure, injury-site-secure). Currently the status of these predicates is updated through the script that drives the exercise. However, we are currently updating how these predicates are calculated within the virtual human's perception and spatial reasoning. In the new approach the virtual human will create a cognitive map that includes ASRs corresponding to regions such as the landing zone and injury site. Updating a predicate such as medic-at-injury-site will involve visually locating the medic and comparing the medic's location to the boundaries of the injury site ASR. Updating the landing-zone-secure predicate will involve visually inspecting each exit of the landing zone ASR to ensure that friendly soldiers are protecting the exits.

In addition to updating spatial predicates, a cognitive map can also be used to implement spatially oriented strategies. For example, a flanking maneuver might involve locating the ASR the enemy is in and attacking through two of that ASR's exits simultaneously. Inherent in this strategy are the concepts of scouting, examining many ASRs to locate the enemy, and desirable defensive positions, ASRs that have a small number of exits. An ASR with a single exit may not be desirable, as it leaves no escape route.

Cognitive maps will also be useful in communicating spatial information between agents. If both agents have similar cognitive maps then, once a common set of names for ASRs and exits has been negotiated, the agents can reference features of each other's cognitive maps. Furthermore, one agent can add to another agent's cognitive map (at an abstract level) by communicating spatial information about areas that the second agent hasn't seen. For example, a sergeant might report to his lieutenant "We've located a suitable space for a landing zone. It's an open area through the west exit of this area. It has three lanes of approach which have been secured."

Related Work

Cognitive mapping research has been applied in the areas of mobile robotics, military simulations, and computer games. We briefly summarize the relationship of the research in these three areas to our own research (Hill & Han & van Lent 2002).

Kuipers (Kuipers 1978) did some of groundbreaking work in cognitive mapping. He recently proposed a spatial semantic hierarchy (Kuipers 2000) as a way of representing knowledge of large-scale space. The spatial semantic hierarchy is actually a set of distinct but related ways of describing space, including sensory, control, causal, topological and metrical representations. He and Remolina recently also developed a formal logic for causal and topological maps (Remolina & Kuipers 2001). Kuipers has tested his approach on simulated robots. There are numerous other researchers in mobile robotics who have also developed and implemented cognitive mapping techniques, e.g., see (Kortenkamp & Bonasso & Murphy 1998; Levitt & Lawton 1990). Chown et al. (Chown & Kaplan & Kortenkamp 1995) developed the PLAN system, which also uses viewer-based information to build a cognitive map. PLAN was implemented with a connectionist network with the purpose of integrating wayfinding with cognitive mapping. While the research in mobile robotics has a lot in common with our domain, one of the chief differences is that many of their methods were developed to deal with noisy sensors and the difficulty of discerning one's location. Our emphasis is somewhat different in that we are trying to build agents with believable human-like behaviors. The sensors are not noisy, but they do operate with limitations. The end use of our cognitive maps is also somewhat different in that we are not just concerned about wayfinding but also about spatial awareness for a wide variety of tasks that robots are not normally concerned about.

Computer game characters commonly have perceptual omniscience. Their perception is not modeled after human capabilities and limitations. To achieve human-like behavior the designers have to give the appearance of limited perception. Alternatively their superhuman capabilities are either attributed to superior ability or to cheating, which can be disheartening for human players. Spatial reasoning is frequently programmed into the environment rather than into the game's characters (Liden 2001). The game map consists of nodes linked together into a graph structure, which are then used as paths for the characters. For the characters to exhibit intelligent behavior, knowledge is encoded into the nodes and links about what behavior is appropriate at those locations. So a node or link may have information saying that a location is good for an ambush or that the character should crawl when traversing this link to remain undercover. As we mentioned earlier in this paper, the designers have to encode everything into the environment. While this is efficient in terms of runtime computation, it does not address the issue of generality. It is a labor-intensive process that must be done for each new game environment. An alternative to real-time spatial reasoning is to automatically pre-compute and store information about the environment using the methods described here. This would avoid the problem of having to analyze and hand encode the spatial characteristics of the environment into the map representation. Laird (Laird 2001) is the one exception in the computer games world. He combines the use of simulated perception (to trace the walls) and mapping to support more sophisticated AI-based behaviors such as ambushing and trapping.

Military simulations generally require a lot of spatial reasoning. Research on virtual humans for military simulations has addressed the issue of spatial reasoning more broadly than in games. For example, Reece et al. (Reece & Kraus & Dumanoir 2000) have built on the work in path planning from AI and robotics. For areas outside of buildings they use A* search and represent the space with cell decomposition, and graph planning (which is somewhat similar to what games do.) But the characters are not limited to the graph when moving through most environments. Forbus et al. (Forbus & Mahoney & Dill 2001) are striving to apply qualitative spatial reasoning to both military simulations and to strategy games. They are currently looking at ways to improve path planning to take into consideration trafficability, visibility, and fields of fire. They use a hybrid approach that combines the representations from cell decomposition and skeletonization. Up until now, however, they have focused on analyzing terrain rather than urban environments.

Acknowledgments

The work described in this paper was supported in part by the U.S. Army Research Office under contract #DAAD19-99-C-0046. The content of this article does not necessarily reflect the position or the policy of the US Government.

References

Chown, E., Kaplan, S., and Kortencamp, D. 1995. Prototypes, location, and associative networks (PLAN): Towards a unified theory of cognitive maps. *Cognitive Science* 19:1-51.

Forbus, K., Mahoney, J., and Dill, K. 2001. How qualitative spatial reasoning can improve strategy game AIs. In *Proceedings of the 2001 AAAI Spring Symposium on Artificial Intelligence and Interactive Entertainment*: AAAI Press.

Hill, R., Han, C., and van Lent, M. 2002. Perceptually driven cognitive mapping of urban environments. In *Proceedings of the First International Conference on Autonomous Agents and Multiagent Systems*.

Kortenkamp, D., Bonasso, R.P., and Murphy, R., (editors). 1998. *Artificial Intelligence and Mobile Robots*. Menlo Park, CA: AAAI Press.

Kuipers, B. 1978. Modeling spatial knowledge. *Cognitive Science* 2:129-153.

Kuipers, B. 2000. The spatial semantic hierarchy. *Artificial Intelligence* 119:191-233.

Laird, J. 2001. It knows what you are going to do: Adding anticipation to a Quakebot. In *Proceedings of the Fifth International Conference on Autonomous Agents*. Montreal, Canada, May 28-June 1.

Laird, J. and van Lent, M. 2001. Human Level AI's killer application: Interactive computer games. *AI Magazine*, Volume 22, Issue 2, Summer.

Levitt, T. and Lawton, D. 1990. Qualitative Navigation for Mobile Robots. *Artificial Intelligence* 44(3): 305-361.

Liden, L. 2001. Using nodes to develop strategies for combat with multiple enemies. In *Proceedings of the 2001 AAAI Spring Symposium on Artificial Intelligence and Interactive Entertainment*: AAAI Press.

Marr, D. 1982 *Vision*: A computational investigation into the human representation and processing of visual information: W.H. Freeman and Company.

Reece, D., Kraus, M., and Dumanoir, P. 2000. Tactical movement planning for individual combatants. In *Proceedings of the 9th Conference on Computer Generated Forces and Behavior Representation*. Orlando, FL.

Remolina, E. and Kuipers, B. 2001. A logical account of causal and topological maps. In *Proceedings of International Joint Conference on Artificial Intelligence (IJCAI-01)*. Seattle, WA.

Stanzione, T., Evans, A., Chamberlain, F., Buettner, C., Mabius, L., Fisher, J., Sousa, M., and Lu, H. 1996. Multiple Elevation Structures in the Improved Computer Generated Forces Terrain Database. In *Proceedings of the 6th Computer Generated Forces and Behavioral Representation Conference*. University of Central Florida.

Swartout, W., Hill, R., Gratch, J., Johnson, L., Kyriakakis, C., LaBore, C., Lindheim, R., Marsella, S., Miraglia, D., Moore, B., Morie, J., Rickel, J., Thiebaux, M., Tuch, L., Whitney, R., and Douglas, J. 2001. Toward the Holodeck: Integrating Graphics, Sound, Character and Story. In *Proceedings of the Fifth International Conference on Autonomous Agents*. Montreal, Canada, May 28-June 1.

Terzopoulos, D. and Rabie, T. 1995. Animat Vision: Active Vision in Artificial Animals. In *Proceedings of the Fifth International Conference on Computer Vision (ICCV '95)*. 801-808. Cambridge, MA, June.

Yeap, W.K. 1988. Towards a computational theory of cognitive maps. *Artificial Intelligence* 34:297-360.

Yeap, W.K. and Jefferies, M.E. 1999. Computing a representation of the local environment. *Artificial Intelligence* 107:265-301.

Toward Practical Knowledge-Based Tools
for Battle Planning and Scheduling

Alexander Kott
Larry Ground
Ray Budd

BBN Technologies

11 Stanwix St., Ste 1410

Pittsburgh, PA 15222

{akott,lground,rbudd}@bbn.com

Lakshmi Rebbapragada

U.S. ArmyCECOM/RDEC/C2D

Ft. Monmouth, NJ 07703

Lakshmi.Rebbapragada@mail1.
monmouth.army.mil

John Langston

Austin Information Systems

Whispering Woods Cove

Parkville, MO 64152

Langstoj@swbell.net

Abstract

Use of knowledge-based decision aids can help alleviate the challenges of planning complex military operations. We describe the CADET system, a knowledge-based tool capable of producing automatically (or with human guidance) Army battle plans with realistic degree of detail and complexity. In ongoing experiments, it compared favorably with human planners. Tight interleaving of planning, adversary estimates, scheduling, routing, attrition and consumption processes comprise the computational approach of this tool. Although originally developed for Army large-unit operations, the technology is generic. In this paper, we focus particularly on the engineering tradeoffs in the design of the tool, and on the experimental comparative evaluation of the tool's performance.

The Problem and the Motivation

Influential voices in the US Army community argue for significant computerization of the military planning process (Wass de Czege and Biever 2001): "...the Army must create fast new planning processes that establish a new division of labor between man and machine. ... Decision aids will quickly offer suggestions and test alternative courses of actions."

The reasons for exploring potential benefits of such decision aids are multifaceted. The process of planning an Army operation remains relatively cumbersome, inflexible and slow. The planning process frequently involves significant disagreements on estimation of outcomes, attrition, consumption of supplies, and enemy reactions. There is a fundamental complexity of synchronization and effective utilization of multiple heterogeneous assets performing numerous, inter-dependent, heterogeneous tasks.

For the last several years our team was working on one such decision aid, called the Course of Action Development and Evaluation Tool (CADET), a tool for producing automatically (or with human guidance) Army battle plans. Our primary focus was on a particularly time-consuming phase of the Military Decision Making Process (MDMP), called the Course of Action (COA) analysis (Department of the Army 1997). More specifically, we focused on the COA analysis performed for relatively large and complex units of the US Army, such as a Division or a Brigade.

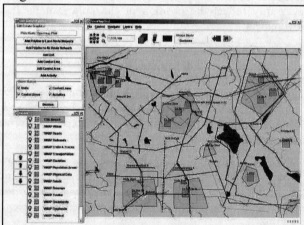

Figure 1. A COA sketch developed in one of several COA-editing tools that have been used as data-entry interfaces to CADET.

Done properly, in a setting such as an Army divisional or brigade planning cell, a detailed analysis of a tactical course of action involves a staff of 3-4 persons with in-depth knowledge of both friendly and enemy tactics.

The input for their effort comes usually from the unit Commander in the form of a sketch and a statement -- a

Views expressed in this paper are those of the authors and do not necessarily reflect those of the U. S. Army or any agency of the U.S. government.

high-level specification of the operation. In effect, such a sketch and statement comprise a set of high-level actions, goals, and sequencing, referring largely to movements and objectives of the friendly forces, e.g., "Task Force Arrow attacks along axis Bull to complete the destruction of the 2nd Red Battalion."

With this input, working as a team for several hours (typically 2 to 8 hours), the members of the planning staff examine the elements of a friendly COA in minute detail. The process involves planning and scheduling of the detailed tasks required to accomplish the specified COA; allocation of tasks to the diverse forces comprising the Division or the Brigade; assignment of suitable locations and routes; estimates of friendly and enemy battle losses (attrition); predictions of enemy actions or reactions, etc.

The outcome of the process is usually recorded in a synchronization matrix format (Department of the Army 1997), a type of Gantt chart. Time periods constitute the columns. Functional classes of actions, such as the Battlefield Operating Systems (BOS), are the rows (see Fig. 3). Examples of BOS include Maneuver, Combat Service Support (e.g., logistics), Military Intelligence, etc. The content of this plan, recorded largely in the cells of the matrix, includes the tasks and actions of the multiple sub-units and assets of the friendly force; their objectives and manner of execution, expected timing, dependencies and synchronization; routes and locations; availability of supplies, combat losses, enemy situation and actions, etc.

How CADET is Used

It is in this complex, difficult and time-consuming COA analysis process that CADET assists military planners by rapidly translating an initial, high-level COA into a detailed battle plan, and wargaming the plan to determine if it is feasible.

In brief, the human planner defines the high-level COA via a user interface that enables him to enter the information comparable to the conventional COA sketch and statement (e.g., Fig. 1). As a collection of formal assertions and/or objects, including typically on the order of 2-20 high-level tasks, this definition of the COA is transferred to CADET, which proceeds to expand this high-level specification into a detailed plan/schedule of the operation.

Within this expansion process, CADET decomposes friendly tasks into more detailed actions; determines the necessary supporting relations, allocates / schedules tasks to friendly assets; takes into account dependencies between tasks and availability of assets; predicts enemy actions and reactions; devises friendly counter-actions; and estimates paths of movements, timing requirements, attrition and risk. The resulting detailed, scheduled and wargamed plan often consists of up to 500 detailed actions with a wealth of supporting detail.

Having completed this process (largely automatically, in about 20 seconds on a mid-level modern laptop PC), CADET displays the results to the user (e.g., Fig. 3) as a synchronization matrix and sometimes as animated

movements on the map-based interface. The user then reviews the results and may either change the original specification of the COA or directly edit the detailed plan.

Overview of CADET's Algorithm

Inputs: An initial set of activities (*Acts*). An initial battlefield state (*S*), including units, and geographic information.

Outputs: The initial set of activities (*Acts*) with addition of derived activities, timing, routes and allocated resources. The new battlefield state S′ that includes effects of the added activities.

Procedure expand (*Acts*, *S*)

1. If an activity exists that is eligible for expansion then find the highest priority activity, using a set of scheduling heuristics.

2. Call the highest priority activity's expansion method to create supporting activities

   - Analyze the battlefield state using the domain specific knowledge within the task definition. Based on the analysis, generate the derived activities that are required for the successful completion of the expanding activity.

   - Calculate Resource candidates appropriate to each derived activity (including routes). Knowledge base rules specific to the activity provide the type and amount of resources needed.

   - Generate temporal constraints between the derived activities. Update *Acts*.

3. Propagate time constraints among the new activities.

4. If the newly expanded activity is ready for allocation, perform resource allocation and scheduling for this activity.

   - Use the knowledge base rules specific to the activity to compute the duration of the activity, depending on the resource and battlefield environments.

   - Use scheduling heuristics to assign resources and the time window to the activity.

   - Compute the effects of the activity, including battle losses, supply consumption, changes in geo-locations. Update *S* to reflect the effects.

5. Go to 1.

Once a satisfactory product is reached (typically within 5 to 30 minutes), the user utilizes it to present the analysis of the COA(s) to the Commander, and to produce operational orders.

Recently, there were several efforts to utilize the planning capability introduced by CADET. Battle Command Battle Lab-Leavenworth (BCBL-L) chose CADET as a key element for its Integrated COA Critiquing and Evaluation System (ICCES) program (Rasch, Kott, and Forbus, 2002), including the nuSketch system (Ferguson et al. 2000). DARPA used CADET for its Command Post of the Future (CPoF) program as a tool to provide a maneuver course of action. There, CADET was integrated with the FOX-GA system (Hayes and Schlabach 1998) to provide a more detailed planner to couple with FOX's COA generation capability. Battle Command Battle Lab-Huachuca (BCBL-H) integrated CADET with All Source Analysis System-Light (ASAS-L) to provide a planner for intelligence assets and to wargame enemy COAs against friendly COAs. The Agile Commander program of Army CECOM selected CADET-based Task Expansion Engine (TEE) as a technology for a key decision-support element within the larger framework of the program.

At this time, CADET is apparently the first and so far the only tool that was demonstrated to generate Army battle plans with realistic degree of detail and completeness, for multiple battle operating systems, and for the large scale and scope associated with such large, complex organizations as an Army Division or a Brigade. In the related domain of small-unit operations, (Tate et al. 2000) has described a very mature work.

Although originally developed for Army large-unit operations, the CADET technology is largely generic and can be applied to a broad range of tasks that require interleaving of planning, resource scheduling and spatial movements. Being a knowledge-based tool, CADET is adapted to a new application domain by changing its knowledge base. In particular, we have already built exploratory demonstrations for such tasks as intelligence collection using scouts and Unmanned Aerial Vehicles; tasks of Special Operations Forces; combat tasks of robotic forces such as the Army's forthcoming Future Combat System; and responses to terrorism incidence in an urban environment.

Key Requirements and Challenges of the Problem Domain

The needs of the problem domain clearly do not allow one to focus a useful decision aid on a narrow slice of the problem, e.g., only planning or only scheduling or only routing. Strong dependencies, for example, between scheduling of resources and hierarchical decomposition in planning as well as the route chosen for a task, indicate that a strong integration (perhaps the word unification might be even better) of all these processes is required (Wilkins and Desimone 1994, Kott and Saks 1998).

Further, as part of this tightly integrated process, the decision aid must perform elements of adversarial reasoning such as determination of enemy actions and reactions to friendly actions.

Also significant is the breadth of coverage in terms of the functional classes of tasks (BOS) that must be explored and planned by the decision aid. While maneuver tasks are central to the battle, other BOS, such as logistics or military intelligence are interdependent with the maneuver BOS and must be all analyzed in close integration.

In spite of the complexity implicit in these multiple interdependent problem aspects, speed is extremely important. It is most reasonable for a user in field conditions to expect an extremely fast response measured in seconds.

Because of rapidly changing elements of tactics, often evolving as operations unfold, and the differences in styles and procedures of different units and commanders, it is also imperative to provide a decision aid with the means to modify its Knowledge Base literally in field conditions, by end user, non-programmer.

Given that a decision aid of this type is most likely to be used in a framework of a larger deployed system, with its own style and implementation of the user interface, it is important to make the decision aid largely independent of the user interface assumptions.

The Technologies and the Engineering Tradeoffs

Perhaps the most fundamental engineering choice had to do with the basic functional focus and concept of user operation of the tool. We elect to focus CADET on the most time-consuming aspect of the MDMP, on its COA analysis phase. Other researchers (e.g., Kewley and Embrecht 2002, Atkin et al. 1999, Hayes and Schlabach 1998) are addressing a different (and preceding) phase of MDMP, the very interesting and challenging problem of generating the high-level maneuver COA. In addressing the style of interactions between the human and the decision aid, we prefer to de-emphasize the mixed-initiative, incremental style (even though CADET allows such a style) in favor of a rapid style of generating a complete plan from a high-level COA, followed by manual modifications.

The integration of planning and scheduling is achieved via an algorithm for tightly interleaved incremental planning and scheduling (see side box). The HTN-like planning step produces an incremental group of tasks by applying domain-specific "expansion" rules to those activities in the current state of the plan that require hierarchical decomposition. This process is controlled by a mechanism that leads the algorithm to focus on most significant and most constrained tasks first, and to limit the decomposition to a limited incremental set of tasks. The scheduling step performs temporal constraint propagation (both lateral and vertical within the hierarchy, a fairly complex and partially domain-knowledge driven process) and schedules the newly added activities to the available resources and time periods. This interleaving approach descends conceptually from (Kott, Agin and Fawcett 1992) where similar interleaving applied to a design domain.

Although we originally planned to use a version of Constrained Heuristic Search (e.g., Kott, Saks and Mercer 1999; Kott and Saks 1998) for the scheduling step, we were led eventually to prefer computationally inexpensive scheduling heuristics. These combine domain-independent estimate of the degree to which an activity is constrained, the "earliest-first" rule, and the domain-specific ranking of activity priorities. This choice was driven partly by the rigorous performance requirements, and partly by the fact that the simpler approach tended to produce results more understandable to the users. No-backtracking approach (with a few minor exceptions) was chosen largely for the same reasons. More generally, we feel that given the compound complexity imposed by the need for tight interleaving of multiple, diverse problem-solving processes in CADET, it is prudent to avoid any unnecessary complexity within each of these individual processes.

The same interleaving mechanism is also used to integrate incremental steps of routing, attrition and consumption estimate. A simplified, fast version of a Dijkstra routing mechanism is used to search for suitable routes over the terrain represented efficiently as a parameterized network of trafficable terrain. Optimization can be specified with respect to a number of factors, such as the overall speed of movement or cover and concealment, etc. For estimates of attrition, we developed a special version of the Dupuy algorithm (Dupuy 1990) that was calibrated with respect to estimates of military professionals, Army officers (Kott, Ground and Langston, 1999).

The adversarial aspects of planning-scheduling problems are addressed via the same incremental decomposition mechanism. CADET accounts for adversarial activity in several ways. First, it allows the commander and staff to specify the likely actions of the enemy. The automated planning then proceeds taking into account, in parallel, both the friendly and enemy actions. Further, the tool automatically infers (using its knowledge base and using the same expansion technique used for HTN planning) possible reactions and counteractions, and provides for resources and timing necessary to incorporate them into the overall plan. In effect, this follows the traditional MDMP's action/reaction/counter-action analysis (Department of the Army 1997).

In the object-oriented fashion, the knowledge base of CADET is a hierarchy of classes of Activities. A class of activities contains a number of procedures (methods) responsible for: computing conditions of applicability of a decomposition method; generating sub-activities of an activity depending on such factors as the available assets, the terrain or the location and type of the enemy forces; adding temporal constraints; estimating timing and resources required for the activity; finding suitable routes and locations; etc.

In practice, the most expensive (in terms of development and maintenance costs) part of the KB is the rules responsible for expansion (decomposition) of activities. We find a great variability in the procedures used to

evaluate preconditions of decomposition and the decomposition itself. Some of them, for example, refer to qualitative geographic relations between units of force and features of the battlefield, similar to the type described in (Ferguson et al, 2000). Others, however, are unique to each activity, require significant computations using general-purpose programming operators, and do not appear particularly amenable to generalization and formalization. This was one of the reasons we elected to use a general-purpose programming language, Java, rather than a specialized representational framework such as those of (Wilkins and Desimone1994, Tate et al. 2000). Other reasons had to do with the programmatic necessity to use a broadly popular language for which experienced programmers are readily available on the labor market.

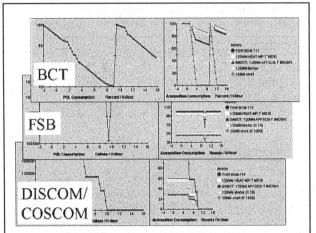

Figure 2. CADET performs detailed logistical analysis including projected ordnance and POL consumption and re-supply planning at several echelons.

On the other hand, CADET includes a module for KB maintenance that allows a non-programmer to add new units of knowledge or over-write the old ones, in a very simple point-and-click fashion. Although necessarily limited by our decision to eliminate any direct programming features, the KB maintenance tool does allow an end-user to enter potentially a majority of the required activity classes.

As a part of our developmental strategy, we elected to de-emphasize user interfaces and to develop no more than bare-bones, minimally necessary user interface features. These consisted mainly of an interface patterned after the synchronization matrix (Fig. 3), allowing the user to click on any cell (activity) and browse through the related network of domain-relevant objects (e.g., the units performing the activity, the location of the unit, etc.). This frugality with respect to user interfaces allowed us to devote a much greater fraction of the available funding to the primary functionality of CADET. Another reason is that we do not expect CADET to be deployed with a stand-alone user interface, but rather as a part of a larger framework with an existing interface.

Experimental Evaluation

Although several different experiments have explored applicability of CADET technology in the context of practical work of a brigade staff, e.g., (Rasch, Kott and Forbus 2002), here we discuss a particular experiment focused on evaluation of CADET-assisted planning process as compared to a conventional, manual one.

The experiment involved five different scenarios and nine judges (active duty officers of US military, mainly of colonel and lieutenant colonel ranks). The five scenarios were obtained from several exercises conducted by US Army, and were all brigade-sized and offensive, but still differed significantly in terrain, mix of friendly forces, nature of opposing forces, and scheme of maneuver. For each scenario/COA we were able to locate the COA sketches assigned to each planning staff, and the synchronization matrices produced by each planning staff. The participants, experienced observers of many planning exercises, estimated that these typically are performed by a team of 4-5 officers, over the period of 3-4 hours, amounting to a total of about 16 person-hours per planning product.

Using the same scenarios and COAs, we used the

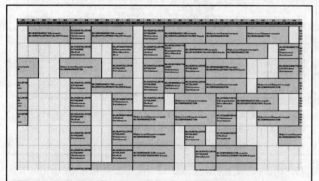

Figure 3. In this fragment of a CADET's synchronization matrix yellow blocks describe tasks and their timing (note the horizontal scale). A typical plan-schedule of a brigade-sized operation may include hundreds of significant tasks.

CADET tool to generate a detailed plan and to express it in the form of a synchronization matrices. The matrices were then reviewed and edited by a surrogate user, a retired US Army officer. This reflected the fact that CADET is to be used in collaboration with a human decision-maker. The editing was rather light – in all cases it involved changing or deleting no more than 2-3% of entries on the matrix. The time to generate these products involved less than 2 minutes of CADET execution, and about 20 minutes of review and post-editing, for a total of about 0.4 person-hours per product. The resulting matrices were transferred to the Excel spreadsheet and "disguised," i.e., given the same visual style at that of human-generated sets.

The products of both the CADET system and of human staff were organized into a total of 20 packages and submitted to the nine judges, four packages to a judge.

Each package consisted of a sketch, statement, synchronization matrix and a questionnaire with grading instructions. The judges were not told whether any of the planning products were produced by the traditional manual process or with the use of any computerized aids. To avoid evaluation biases, assignments of packages to judges were fully randomized. Each judge was asked to review a package and grade the products contained in the package.

Not unexpectedly, data showed a significant scatter. While mean values for several experimental series ranged from 3.9-5.0, standard deviations ranged from 1.6-2.4. Judges comments also demonstrated significant differences of opinion regarding the same product.

Overall, however, the results demonstrated that CADET performed on par with the human staff - the difference between CADET's and human performance was statistically insignificant. Thus, based on the mean of grades, CADET lost in two of the five scenarios, won in two, and one was an exact draw. Taking the mean of grades for all five scenarios, CADET earned 4.2, and humans earned 4.4, with standard deviation of about 2.0, a very insignificant difference. Finally, comparing the "undisguised" series, we see that CADET earned the mean grade of 4.4 and humans earned 3.9, although the difference is still rather small.

The conclusion: CADET helps produce complex planning products dramatically (almost two orders of magnitude) faster yet without loss of quality, as compared to the conventional, manual process.

Strengths, Limitations and Future Directions

CADET shows a promise of reaching the state where a military decision-maker, a commander or a staff planner, uses it in field conditions, to perform planning of tactical operations, to issue operational plans and orders, and to monitor and modify the plans as the operation is executed and the situation evolves.

CADET generates Army battle plans with realistic degree of detail and completeness, for multiple battle operating systems, for the large scale and scope associated with such complex organizations as an Army Division or a Brigade, performing dramatically faster than a conventional human-only planning staff, with comparable quality of planning products.

Although originally developed for Army large-unit operations, the CADET technology is largely generic and can be applied to a broad range of domains that involve planning, resource scheduling and spatial movements.

CADET achieves its capabilities via a combination of approaches:

- Adopting a simple and transparent concept of user operation, which assumes literally no training;
- Using tightly interleaved incremental planning and scheduling, also integrated with route and attrition and consumption calculations;
- Adhering to computationally inexpensive algorithms that often trade optimality for speed and thereby assure an almost instantaneous response to the user;

- Integrating adversarial considerations into the solution process via the action-reaction-counteraction paradigm;

CADET's current state of capabilities also points toward several key gaps that must be overcome to realize the full potential of such tools:

Military decision-making commonly requires collaboration of multiple officers with distinct functions, responsibilities and expertise. In the near-future warfare, these officers will often collaborate while dispersed over the battlefield, communicating over the tactical Internet, possibly in asynchronous mode. Tools like CADET must support such forms of collaboration.

Presentation of CADET's products requires qualitatively different user interfaces and visualization mechanisms. Our experiments suggest that the users had difficulties comprehending a synchronization matrix generated by the computer tool, even though it was presented in a very conventional, familiar manner.

It is often said "no tactical plan survives first contact with the enemy intact." Combat planners must be able to plan rapidly, communicate orders to subordinates clearly and react without delay to changes in the situation. Planning tools like CADET should give the commander the ability to accelerate this cycle of recognition, re-planning and reaction, i.e., the capability of continuous re-planning during execution.

Ongoing work on CADET technology focuses on closing these gaps.

Acknowledgements

The work described in this paper was supported by funding from US Army CECOM (DAAB 07-96-C-D603 - CADET SBIR Phase I, DAAB 07-97-C-D313 – CADET SBIR Phase II and DAAB 07-99-C-K510 - CADET Enhancements); DARPA (DAAB07-99-C-K508 Command Post of the Future); and TRADOC BCBL-H (GS-35-0559J/DABT63-00-F-1247). TRADOC BCBL-L provided additional funding under DAAB 07-99-C-K510. MAJ R. Rasch of the US Army BCBL-L provided important advice.

References

Atkin, M. S.; Westbrook, D. L.; and Cohen, P. R. 1999. Capture the Flag: Military simulation meets computer games. In Proceedings of AAAI Spring Symposium Series on AI and Computer Games, 1-5.

Bohman, W. E. 1999. STAFFSIM, An Interactive Simulation for Rapid, Real Time Course of Action Analysis by U.S. Army Brigade Staffs. Thesis, Naval Postgraduate School, Monterey, CA.

Department of the Army 1997. *Field Manual 101-5, Staff Organization and Operations*, Washington, D.C.

Dupuy, Trevor N. 1990. *Attrition: Forecasting Battle Casualties and Equipment Losses in Modern War,* Hero Books, Fairfax, Va.

Ferguson, R.W., Rasch, R.A., Turmel, W., and Forbus, K.D. June, 2000. Qualitative Spatial Interpretation of Course-of-Action Diagrams. In Proceedings of the 14th International Workshop on Qualitative Reasoning. Morelia, Mexico.

Hayes, C. C., and Schlabach, J. 1998. FOX-GA: A Planning Support Tool for assisting Military Planners in a Dynamic and Uncertain Environment. In Integrating Planning, Scheduling and Execution in Dynamic and Uncertain Environments, R. Bergmann and A. Kott, eds. AAAI Press, Madison, Wisconsin.

Kewley, R. and Embrecht, M. 1998. Fuzzy-Genetic Decision Optimization for Positioning of Military Combat Units. In Proceedings SMC'98, pp. 3658 – 3664, 1998 IEEE International Conference on Systems, Man, and Cybernetics, October 11-14, La Jolla, California

Kott, A., Ground, L., and Langston, J. 1999. Estimation of Battlefield Attrition in a Course Of Action Analysis Decision Support System. 67th Military Operations Research Society Symposium, West Point Military Academy.

Kott, A., Saks, V. and Mercer, A. 1999. A New Technique Enables Dynamic Replanning of Aeromedical Evacuation, *AI Magazine*, v.2, n.1, pp.43-54.

Kott, A. and Saks, V. 1998. A Multi-Decompositional Approach to Integration of Planning and Scheduling – an Applied Perspective. In Integrating Planning, Scheduling and Execution in Dynamic and Uncertain Environments, R. Bergmann and A. Kott, eds. AAAI Press, Madison, Wisconsin.

Kott, A., Agin, G., and Fawcett, D. 1992. Configuration Tree Solver. A Technology for Automated Design and Configuration, *ASME Journal of Mechanical Design* 114(1): 187- 195.

Rasch, R., Kott, A., and Forbus, K. 2002. AI on the Battlefield: an Experimental Exploration. In Proceedings of the IAAI 2002 Conference, Edmonton, Canada.

Tate, A., Levine, J., Jarvis, P., and Dalton, J. 2000. Using AI Planning Technology for Army Small Unit Operations. In Proceedings of the Fifth International Conference on Artificial Intelligence Planning Systems (AIPS_2000).

Wass de Czege, H. and Biever, J. D. 2001. Six Compelling Ideas On the Road to a Future Army, *Army Magazine*, Vol.51, No.2, , pp. 43-48.

Wilkins, D. E. and Desimone, R. V. 1994. Applying an AI planner to military operations planning. In Fox, M. and Zweben, M., eds. *Intelligent Scheduling*, 685--709. Calif.: Morgan Kaufmann.

Knowledge Formation and Dialogue Using the KRAKEN Toolset

Kathy Panton, Pierluigi Miraglia, Nancy Salay, Robert C. Kahlert, David Baxter, Roland Reagan
Cycorp, Inc.
3721 Executive Center Drive
Austin, Texas 78731
{panton,miraglia,nancy,rck,baxter,roland}@cyc.com

Abstract

The KRAKEN toolset is a comprehensive interface for knowledge acquisition that operates in conjunction with the Cyc knowledge base. The KRAKEN system is designed to allow subject-matter experts to make meaningful additions to an existing knowledge base, without the benefit of training in the areas of artificial intelligence, ontology development, or logical representation. Users interact with KRAKEN via a natural-language interface, which translates back and forth between English and the KB's logical representation language. A variety of specialized tools are available to guide users through the process of creating new concepts, stating facts about those concepts, and querying the knowledge base. KRAKEN has undergone two independent performance evaluations. In this paper we describe the general structure and several of the features of KRAKEN, focussing on key aspects of its functionality in light of the specific knowledge-formation and acquisition challenges they are intended to address.

Introduction

The goal of the KRAKEN effort is to develop a set of tools to support knowledge base expansion. In particular, the KRAKEN system is designed to allow subject-matter experts (SMEs) to make meaningful additions to the Cyc knowledge base, without the benefit of training in the areas of artificial intelligence, ontology development and analysis (Gangemi et al. 2001), or logical representation languages.

To fulfill these requirements, KRAKEN relies principally on natural language interactions with the user. The interface's metaphor is that of a conversation between a subject-matter expert and a non-expert; both use ordinary English, possibly containing specialized vocabulary. Consequently, two major challenges faced the project designers at the outset:

- To make the user's conversation with KRAKEN as smooth as possible, which meant development and enhancement of every aspect of Cyc-based NL processing;

- To drive the knowledge formation process in such a way that user-entered knowledge would be at a high level of logical and representational quality.

The second challenge is in effect a consequence of working in a large, comprehensive knowledge base, using a powerful logical language such as CycL. The magnitude of the KB raises non-trivial issues of navigation through the concept space, traversal of the taxonomic hierarchies, and so on.

It is worth emphasizing that both challenges are indeed familiar to experienced ontologists and knowledge engineers. We chose not to attempt to simplify the KE task by artificially restricting the knowledge base and expressive capabilities of Cyc, but to take on the very challenging problem of creating a powerful "assistant" that would allow the SME to work with all the resources made available by Cyc (Cohen et al. 1999).

This paper is organized as follows. First, we provide a brief introduction to the Cyc Knowledge Base. Next, we introduce the natural language processing components used in KRAKEN. We then give an overview of the KRAKEN system, along with an in-depth look at a few selected tools. An example of a user dialogue with the system is presented. Finally, we discuss our results to date, and our plans for future refinements of the system.

The Cyc Knowledge Base

The Cyc KB is currently the largest general knowledge base in the world, housing roughly 1.4 million hand-entered rules interrelating 100k+ concepts. Concepts are denoted in the KB with Cyc constants; these may be individuals, intensionally defined collections, extensionally defined collections, relations that obtain between terms, or functions which can be used to refer to many more individuals without having to reify a term for each (e.g. "gander" is represented in the KB by the nonatomic term *(MaleFn Goose)*). Currently, the KB has knowledge of a wide range of topics, from microbiology to pop music, and has an extensive knowledge infrastructure, including multiple treatments of causality and temporal and modal reasoning. Knowledge is clustered into context-specific domains (or "microtheories") with epistemic access determined by specialised predicates. Consequently, the system has an ability to differentiate between and accommodate logically conflicting bodies of knowledge, including hypothetical and counterfactual contexts.

Over the last fifteen years, our representational language, CycL, has evolved—as needed—into a highly expressive one, comparable to higher-order logic. The hurdle of combinatorial explosion in inference is overcome in two ways:

1. By using its partitioning of knowledge into contexts so that inferences occur within one small subset of the overall KB; and

2. By having a set of special-purpose inference modules that recognize commonly-occurring special cases and handle them efficiently.

The KRAKEN Natural Language Processing System

A crucial design feature of the KRAKEN system is its natural language interface. Primarily, the NLI was intended to allow users to interact with the system using simple English statements and queries. It was required to parse sentences and questions, and to generate English paraphrases for CycL statements. Furthermore, the interface had to be capable of immediately processing new lexical information corresponding to knowledge being entered by a user. For example, if a user introduced a new concept, such as *Clostridium-BotulinumToxin*, into the knowledge base, the system should prompt the user to supply natural language terms (such as "botulinum toxin" or "botulism toxin") that could refer to the new concept.

These design considerations, along with the need for quick parsing and generation, led us to create a system that combines features of principled, theory-driven approaches as well as more practical, less theoretical approaches. While we have, for example, decided against using an HPSG parser for this application, we still recognize the need for utilizing detailed lexical and syntactic knowledge. The KRAKEN natural language processing system consists of several subcomponents, including the lexicon, generation system, parsing system, and the iCycL (intermediate CycL) representation language, each of which is described briefly below.

The lexicon (Burns and Davis 1999) contains syntactic, semantic, and pragmatic information for about 27,000 English root words. Inflectional morphology is handled by a separate code component. Each root word is represented as a term in the KB, with assertions providing information about the word's part of speech, subcategorization patterns, and semantics. Semantic information in the lexicon provides a mapping between word senses and corresponding KB concepts or formulae.

The natural language generation system produces a word-, phrase-, or sentence-level paraphrase of KB concepts, rules, and queries. The NLG system relies on information contained in the lexicon, and is driven by generation templates stored in the KB. These templates are not solely string-based; they contain linguistic data that allows, for example, correct grammatical agreement to be generated. The NLG system is capable of providing two levels of paraphrase, depending on the demands of the application. One type of generated text is terse but potentially ambiguous, and the other is precise but potentially wordy and stilted. Through the KRAKEN Dictionary Assistant Tool, users can add parsing and generation templates for new terms as soon as they are introduced into the knowledge base.

Depth of parsing from natural language to CycL can range from very shallow (i.e. concept mapping) to deep (i.e. text understanding). For KRAKEN, deep interpretation is a requirement. However, earlier generations of parsing tools developed by our team, including an HPSG-based parser, proved much too slow to be used with KRAKEN. In order to balance demands of speed vs. depth, a hybrid top-down/bottom-up system was developed. This involves a template-matching parser for sentence-level parses, along with a chart parser and semantic templates for key sub-constituents (noun phrases and verb phrases).

Our natural language understanding system parses input strings into fully-formed semantic formulas. Design criteria for the parsing system included that it (1) be fast; (2) produce parses of adequate semantic detail; (3) ask the user for clarification only in cases where the system could not itself resolve ambiguities; and (4) support parsing into underspecified formulas, and then rely on some of the other KRAKEN tools, such as the Reformulator, to determine the best semantic translation.

The Text Processor controls the application of the various parsing subcomponents, using a heuristic best-first search mechanism that has information about the individual parsers, including their applicability to coarse syntactic categories and cost. This information is used to perform a syntax-driven search over the parse space, applying relevant parsers to the sub-constituents until all are resolved, or until the parsing options have been exhausted. The parsers at the disposal of the Text Processor are the Template parser, the Noun Compound parser, and the Phrase Structure parser.

The Template parser is essentially a string-matching mechanism driven by a set of templates compiled into an efficient internal format. These templates, like those used for generation, employ a simple format so that users can add templates as they are entering new knowledge into the system. The template parser is relatively fast, but is of limited flexibility. It tabulates semantic constraints during a parse, but does not attempt to verify them; that task is passed along to the next processing layer.

The Noun Compound parser uses a set of semantic templates combined with a generic chart-parsing approach to construct representations for noun compounds such as "anthrax vaccine stockpile". Unlike other parsing components, it makes heavy use of the Cyc ontology, and can therefore resolve many ambiguities that are impossible to handle on a purely syntactic level (e.g. "Mozart symphonies" vs. "Mozart expert").

The Phrase Structure parser takes a similar bottom-up approach to constructing parses. After completing a syntactic parse, it uses semantic constraints gleaned from the KB to perform pruning and to build the semantic representation. Specialized sub-parsers are used to parse noun phrases and verb phrases; resulting constituent parses are combined to produce a complete semantic translation.

In order for parsing to be successful in the current application, some decisions about semantic meaning needed to be deferred. In particular, radically vague or underspecified words such as "is" or "contains", which can map onto many distinct relations in the KB, introduce ambiguities which are not handled well by producing all possible interpretations in parallel. To deal with such cases, strings are parsed into an intermediate CycL (iCycL) layer that conflates relevant ambiguities into a single parse, by using very general predicates such as is-Underspecified. Another level of processing reformulates iCycL representations into final, more specific CycL representations, often with the user's help.

In addition to handling underspecification, the iCycL layer is also well-suited for other types of semantic processing, such as interpretation of quantification and negation, and type-shifting. The interpretation of quantifiers, for example, consists in a transformation from iCycL expressions into CycL logical forms performed by a dedicated "reformulation" component. Although CycL representations are modelled on first-order logic, the language itself allows the definition of higher-order constants. We exploit this capability to represent a wide range of NL quantifiers (*most, many, few, no*, etc.) formally as generalized quantifiers, i.e., as higher-order relations between collections.

Overview of KRAKEN

The KRAKEN system consists of an integrated set of tools for adding to the Cyc KB, accessed via an HTML interface. The tools already deployed include:

- Creators, selectors, and modifiers for all of the categories distinguished by the Cyc system (concepts, statements and rules, predicates) and the categories identified by analysis of the KE process (scenarios and queries).

- Tools for determining the quality and consistency of the statements made to the knowledge base, i.e. checkers for contradiction and redundancy, precision manipulators for improving generality or specificity, and tools for providing feedback on the quality of the KE done in terms of rule and query critiquers.

- Tools that leverage existing knowledge to elicit new knowledge, such as the Concept Differentiator, the Analogy Developer, and, for ensuring breadth, the Salient Descriptor.

- Lexifiers, such as the Dictionary Assistant, that allow users to enter natural-language words and phrases for concepts they are describing.

The UIA: the User Interface to KRAKEN

The User Interaction Agenda (UIA) interface is a message-based HTML system that uses the HTML REFRESH capabilities of the browser to simulate real-time updating. It consists of four areas on the user's screen:

1. A menu of tools that is organized according to the recommended steps of the KE process (i.e. browsing what is there, creating what is missing, testing it via rules, finalizing the information, and debugging).

2. A type-in box that sends the entered text or query to KRAKEN's NL processing system, to interpret the text as either a command for an action, a question to be run as a query, or a sentence to be parsed as a new statement of fact.

3. An interactive center pane that is used as the render space for the currently active tool. Most of the user and system interaction takes place here, from the selection of initial topics, to clarification dialogues in which KRAKEN asks the user to select among possible interpretations of an ambiguous utterance.

4. An agenda summary pane, where the essential steps to completing an interaction are displayed. These steps are color-coded to indicate whether the action in question is currently possible, or is blocked.

Specialized KRAKEN Knowledge Entry Tools

The process of entering or modifying knowledge in Cyc typically consists of several steps:

1. Creating basic concepts: types (collections), individuals, predicates, and so on.

2. Classifying concepts at the appropriate level of generality, by placing them in proper taxonomic relationships to existing concepts.

3. Identifying relations and slots applicable to the new concepts.

4. Formulating rules establishing the proper use (and thus expressing the meaning) of such concepts in reasoning.

Normally these tasks are performed by knowledge engineers and ontologists. The intended user of KRAKEN, however, is untrained in these areas. For this reason, KRAKEN includes a series of tools and assistants designed to ensure the quality of the knowledge acquired. These tools operate essentially by eliciting new knowledge from the user, or querying the user about optional additions (automatically generated) to the KB.

Given space limitations, we can describe here only a few among the tools that are currently implemented:

Precision Suggestor

Whenever a new concept is created, it must find its place in the taxonomic structure of the existing KB. Considering the size of the Cyc ontological hierarchy, this is of course much more easily said than done.

The Precision Suggestor helps the user place new concepts at the appropriate level of generality/specificity in the ontology. After the user has entered a concept and formulated a basic or "initial" fact about it (e.g., *Rudy Giuliani is a person* or *Botulin is a kind of toxin*), the Suggestor identifies a suitable number of possible generalizations and specializations that might be suggested for the concept entered. It then queries the user whether any of the suggestions would lead to a more accurate statement than the one originally entered. These suggestions are heuristically determined from the current state of the KB. The selection can be tuned by Cycorp ontologists using specific "KE facilitation" flags in the KB.

Salient Descriptor

A more complex task is to ensure both *breadth* and *depth* of knowledge representation. This requirement might be expressed by the question: once a concept is added, what is the minimal set of features (properties, facts, rules, ...) that should be specified about it?

Put in different terms, a robust (sufficiently broad and deep) representation should include the *salient* features of the concept. The problem of course is that salience is heavily context-dependent. The Salient Descriptor is the KRAKEN component that queries the user with suggestions about additional knowledge; it identifies such knowledge as salient on the basis of special "facilitation" rules in the KB. One such rule, for instance, might be that if X is a type of biological organ, then it makes sense to specify the biological function of X; or that if X is a particular eating event, it makes sense to specify what food was consumed in it, or who (what animal) took part in it, and so on.

On this basis, KRAKEN can query the user with additional clauses and facts that are *prima facie* salient with respect to the concept(s) the user has entered. Note, furthermore, that rules such as the ones above are quite general, because they ultimately derive from conceptual analysis. One side benefit of Cyc is that it contains the accumulated results of years of ontological analysis of ordinary concepts. In effect, the Salient Descriptor leverages this accumulated patrimony in order to foster better knowledge formation practices on the part of subject-matter experts.

Process Descriptor

The representation of *processes* as complexes of events with multiple participants playing various roles receives special focus in many domains of knowledge representation. It has figured prominently in the microbiology and biochemistry domains in which KRAKEN has been tested by SMEs. On the other hand, the representation of processes as reified "objects" in an ontology is a complex task, generally presupposing a certain degree of logical sophistication on the part of the knowledge enterer (consider, for instance, the problems of constraining and preserving the identity of participants throughout the unfolding of a complex event, well described in (Aitken 2001a)).

Cyc has a very rich vocabulary for describing processes as complex events or "scripts." A script is an event constituted by a temporally ordered sequence of subevents. Both scripts and their individual subevents are related to things and individuals playing some role in them (agent, patient, etc.) by "actor slots." Additional relations specify the temporal ordering of subevents in a script. Furthermore, the expressive power of CycL is used by casting much of the relevant vocabulary at the type level. Thus, instead of asserting that an individual event of type *Paying* follows an individual event of type *OrderingFood* in a typical instance of the script *GoingOutToEat* (at least in the context of *UnitedStatesSocialLifeMt*) by a complex rule, we can state succinctly

(startsAfterEndOfInScript Paying OrderingFood).

The type-level description, however, requires that specific constraints be added about the identity of the participants: it's easy to assert, in type-level vocabulary, that the agent in the *Paying* subevent type, as well as the agent in *OrderingFood* is a person, but less obvious how to express that

the same agent is involved in both the paying and the ordering event (in this example, actually, the precise constraint is even more complex than this: most times there are multiple agents ordering food in a particular restaurant visit, but not all of them need be the payers). In any case, it seems clear that the KRAKEN user would need to be guided through the proper steps.

This guidance is provided by a separate process description tool. It allows the user to construct the description of a process, specifying the participants by roles (at the type level, we indicate what is true of an entire class of complex or simple events), constraining their identity through the main process and its subevents, and articulating the temporal structure of the process, namely its subevents (by type) and their relative ordering within the main process.

Example of an Interaction with KRAKEN

The user begins an interaction with KRAKEN by providing his name to the system, and selecting a topic to converse about. Suppose that a user wants to teach the system about a new disease. The user has multiple means for determining whether a concept is already known to Cyc. For one, he can use the Concept Browser to navigate the ontology. For another, he can type a question such as "What do you know about Endemic Relapsing Fever?" into the interaction box. Having determined that Cyc does not yet know anything about this disease, he types into the interaction box:

Endemic Relapsing Fever is an infectious disease.

KRAKEN parses the input sentence, but does not recognize the name of the new disease. Thus, only a partial CycL representation can be created at this point. KRAKEN responds:

I do not know what *Endemic Relapsing Fever* means in this context.
[Describe now] [Search KB] [Describe later] [Continue] [Forget it]

The user selects the [Describe now] button. KRAKEN asks the user what "Endemic Relapsing Fever" is a more specific kind of, and the user responds with "infection". KRAKEN also supplies a box in which the user can enter a concept similar to Endemic Relapsing Fever, but which is already known to Cyc. The user opts to do so, entering "Rocky Mountain Spotted Fever" as a similar concept.

Since the Noun Phrase parser finds two potentially relevant meanings for "infection", KRAKEN asks for clarification of its meaning: whether it refers to an ailment, or to the process of contaminating something. The user selects the first interpretation.

The Precision Suggestor tool is then automatically invoked, to ensure that the new knowledge is presented at the appropriate level of specificity. KRAKEN asks:

In the sentence
Endemic Relapsing Fever is a kind of infection
could you replace the phrase *infection* with any of the following?
bacterial infection
viral infection

fever infection
fungal infection
parasitic infection
inhalational infection
[...]

The user, knowing that Endemic Relapsing Fever is a febrile illness that is caused by a bacterium, selects "bacterial infection" and "fever infection".

Having been supplied with a basic definition of "Endemic Relapsing Fever", KRAKEN can fully parse the user's original statement into a CycL formula. KRAKEN now invokes the Analogy Developer tool. This tool selects relevant statements about Rocky Mountain Spotted Fever, which the user claimed was similar to Endemic Relapsing Fever, and allows the user to modify those statements to fit the concept he is describing. KRAKEN scans the KB for facts about Rocky Mountain Spotted Fever. For each relevant CycL assertion, an English paraphrase is generated. These sentences are then presented to the user:

Which of the following things I know about the disease Rocky Mountain Spotted Fever are also true of Endemic Relapsing Fever?

Only R. ricketsii causes cases of Endemic Relapsing Fever

People typically acquire Endemic Relapsing Fever through biting by a tick

The risk of mortality for people afflicted with Endemic Relapsing Fever is 0.2

The incubation period for Endemic Relapsing Fever in people is usually between 3 and 14 days

There is no risk of Endemic Relapsing Fever spreading directly from people to people

The user edits the first statement to refer to Borellia recurrentis, the bacterium that causes the fever. The second statement is true as is; Endemic Relapsing Fever is indeed tickborne. The user does not know what the mortality rate and incubation periods for this infection are, so he does not select the next two statements. Finally, the last statement is correct as is. The user then submits this edited page of assertions for processing. The Salient Descriptor tool is then activated, prompting the user to give more facts about the new disease. It states:

Yes/No Question

Is the following sentence true?
Endemic Relapsing Fever has distinct stages.

The user selects "Yes", and the Salient Descriptor continues:

Here is one way in which you are encouraged to refine Endemic Relapsing Fever :

Please enter something to fill in the blank(s) in the sentence
Endemic Relapsing Fever primarily afflicts _____.
with something that is a kind of organism part.

The user enters "nervous system". Another question is then posed by KRAKEN:

Yes/No Question

Is the following sentence true?
The different stages of an instantiation of Endemic Relapsing Fever do not involve different bacteria.

The user selects Yes, since only B. recurrentis is implicated in this disease. The Salient Decriptor then prompts:

Please enter something to fill in the blank(s) in the sentence
In Endemic Relapsing Fever, fever is likely to have a onset rate.
with something that is a rate of change attribute.

Examples:
gradual
moderate
sudden

The user selects "sudden". KRAKEN processes this choice, and the initial teaching session regarding Endemic Relapsing Fever comes to an end. At this point, the user can ask KRAKEN to summarize what it has learned, by typing "What do you know about Endemic Relapsing Fever?" into the interaction box. KRAKEN collects its new knowledge about the disease, and generates English paraphrases:

Here's everything I've been told about Endemic Relapsing Fever :

[+] Endemic Relapsing Fever is a type of infection.
[+] Endemic Relapsing Fever is an infectious disease.
[+] Endemic Relapsing Fever has distinct stages.
[+] A case of Endemic Relapsing Fever is a kind of fever infection.
[+] A case of Endemic Relapsing Fever is a kind of bacterial infection.
[+] Only B. recurrentis causes cases of Endemic Relapsing Fever.
[+] Ticks are an infection vector of Endemic Relapsing Fever.
[+] Endemic Relapsing Fever is similar to the disease Rocky Mountain Spotted Fever.
[+] Endemic Relapsing Fever primarily afflicts nervous systems.
[+] The different stages of an instantiation of Endemic Relapsing Fever do not involve different bacteria.
[+] In Endemic Relapsing Fever, fever is likely to have a sudden onset rate.
[+] People typically acquire Endemic Relapsing Fever through biting by a tick.
[+] There is no risk of Endemic Relapsing Fever spreading directly from people to people.

Results and Future Plans

KRAKEN's performance was evaluated in the Summer of 2001 in an independent experiment (results for which will be published elsewhere). A team of SMEs unfamiliar with Cyc used the system to enter new knowledge in the domain of cell biology. The system's responses were rated on a 0-3 point scale in terms of correctness, quality of representation, and quality of explanation. KRAKEN's average score in the cell biology domain was 1.91 (with scores as high as 2.54 on some sections of the experiment). These results, especially since they were produced with a very early version of the system, are encouraging.

A further evaluation of KRAKEN in January, 2002 showed that knowledge entry rates of the SMEs had increased significantly, compared to the evaluation six months earlier. Improvements in tools at this stage allowed users to more rapidly create knowledge, and led users through more complex entry sequences. Most importantly, perhaps, the SMEs had caught up to the logic experts in terms of quality of representation.

From a qualitative standpoint, the KB segments produced by the SMEs using KRAKEN warranted positive marks in many areas. In some respects, the KRAKEN products compared favorably to standard practice by Cycorp knowledge engineers. Assertions were mostly introduced at the proper level of generality and specificity; logical and conceptual soundness seemed generally respected. Overall, these seem to have been the most successful aspects:

- Taxonomic relations: by and large, concepts are defined at the right level of generality and the relations of generalization and specialization between collections are well-chosen and informative.

- Articulation of events and processes in subevents, and specification of participants' roles in same (users seemed quite capable of navigating Cyc's vast stock of role-representing relations).

- Ability to insert "exception" statements (e.g.: not every transcription has a nucleolytic proofreading as subevent), by using "natural" assertions involving ordinary quantification.

Aspects that seemed less successfully developed:

- Guiding the user through stating the temporal ordering of subevents in complex events (i.e., "scripts").

- Use of complex predicates, especially to describe similarities and differences between concepts and entities; and creation of new predicates.

We believe that developments both in KRAKEN design and further engineering of the ontology should soon improve performance in these problem areas.

In the coming months, along with improvements to tools like the Process Descriptor and Analogy Developer, larger and more ambitious versions of the User Modeller will be designed. We would like to be able to use context to realize when a term can be used profitably in conversation, to determine saliency of a term description given the context, and to organize some of the answers returned by the system.

The bigger issues in the background remain challenging. In order to achieve optimal performance in User Modelling, the KRAKEN system would have to introduce an abstraction layer between itself and the SME, just as a doctor takes the layman's description of an illness and translates it opaquely into a scientific medical description without ever confronting the patient with the medical terminology. Much ontological engineering research and work will have to be done to reach this long-term goal, but there are some gains which can be made in the shorter term.

A number of refinements to the NL system are planned for the coming months. For generation, the system will move from a focus on generating isolated sentences and questions to rendering multi-sentence-level text. We will be incorporating indexicals, pronouns, and other intersentential anaphors in order to create natural-sounding interactions. Future work on the parsers will emphasize increasing their speed, and on extending coverage to include more complex structures, such as adjectival and adverbial phrases.

Acknowledgements

KRAKEN is being built as part of DARPA's Rapid Knowledge Formation (RKF) project (DARPA, 2000). The authors are indebted to the work and contributions of the Knowledge Formation and Dialogue group at Cycorp: Michael Witbrock, Dave Schneider, Keith Goolsbey, Jon Curtis, John Jantos, Matt Smith, Matthew Olken, Doug Foxvog, Fred Hoyt, Jennifer Sullivan, Kim Loika, Bjørn Aldag, Stefano Bertolo, Peter Wagner, Ben Rode and Michael Wakoff.

References

Aitken, S. 2001. Participants, Conditions and Identity in Scripts. Technical Report, Artificial Intelligence Applications Institute, University of Edinburgh.

Burns, K. J., and Davis, A. R. 1999. Building and maintaining a semantically adequate lexicon using Cyc. In Viegas, E. ed. *Breadth and depth of semantic lexicons*. Dordrecht: Kluwer.

Cohen, P., Chaudri, V., Pease, A., and Schrag, R. 1999. Does prior knowledge facilitate the development of knowledge-based systems? *Proceedings of the AAAI-99*, pp. 221-226. Menlo Park, CA.

DARPA. The Rapid Knowledge Formation Project (main website). http://reliant.teknowledge.com/RKF/, 2000.

Gangemi, A., Guarino, N., Masolo, C., and Oltramari, A. 2001. Understanding top-level ontological distinctions. To appear in *Proceedings of IJCAI 2001 Workshop on Ontologies and Information Sharing*.

AI on the Battlefield: an Experimental Exploration

Robert Rasch
Battle Command Battle Lab
ATTN: ATZL-FD-BC
415 Sherman
Ft. Leavenworth, KS 66027
raschr@leavenworth.army.mil

Alexander Kott
BBN Technologies
11 Stanwix St., Suite 1410
Pittsburgh, Pa 15222
akott@bbn.com

Kenneth D. Forbus
Northwestern University
CS Department
1890 Maple Avenue
Evanston, IL 60201
forbus@northwestern.edu

Abstract

The US Army Battle Command Battle Lab conducted an experiment with the ICCES system -- an integrated decision aid for performing several critical steps of a US Army Brigade Military Decision Making Process: from capturing a high-level Course of Action to producing a detailed analysis and plan of tasks. The system integrated several available technologies based largely on AI techniques, ranging from qualitative spatial interpretation of course-of-action diagrams to interleaved adversarial planning and scheduling. The experiment dispelled concerns about potential negative impacts of such tools on the creative aspects of the art of war, showed a potential for dramatic time savings in the MDMP process, and confirmed the maturity and suitability of the technologies for near-future deployment.

Decision Making at a Brigade Command Post

A US Army Brigade includes an impressive range of assets and capabilities: thousands of professional soldiers and officers, hundreds of combat and support vehicles, helicopters, sophisticated intelligence and communication equipment and specialists, artillery and missiles, engineers, medical units, repair shops, and much more. In a battle, these assets may perform hundreds of complex tasks of multiple types: collection of intelligence, movements, direct and indirect fires, construction of roads, bridges, and obstacles, transportation and handling of supplies, managing civilian population, command and control, and so on.

Detailed planning of a military operation -- whether a battle with an enemy or a peacekeeping operation -- requires an intensive effort of highly trained professionals, the Brigade planning staff. To accomplish this effort, the Army teaches and uses a methodologically rigorous process called the Military Decision Making Process (MDMP) (Department of the Army 1997).

The process is typically performed by a primary staff of 4-5 officers, typically ranging in ranks from captains to lieutenant colonels, with the support of a considerable sized subordinate staff, over a period of several hours. The

physical environment often consists of a tent extended from the back of one or several Army's light trucks, or armored command and control vehicles, folding tables, maps hung on the walls of the tent and covered with acetate sheets on which the officers draw symbols of units and arrows of movements.

To describe the process for the purposes of this paper, let's focus on a few salient aspects of it. The input for their effort comes usually from the unit Commander in the form of the commander's intent, concept of operation and desired end-state for the operation-- a high-level specification of the operation. This information is then used to develop COA (Course of Action) sketches and statements. In effect, such sketches and statements comprise a set of high-level actions, goals, and sequencing, referring largely to movements and objectives of the friendly forces, e.g., "Task Force Arrow attacks along axis Bull to complete the destruction of the 2nd Red Battalion." With this input, working as a team for several hours (typically ranging from to 2 to 8 hours), the members of the planning staff examine the most critical elements of the friendly COAs in minute detail. The process involves planning and scheduling of the detailed tasks required to accomplish the specified COA; allocation of tasks to the diverse forces comprising the Brigade; assignment of suitable locations and routes; estimates of friendly and enemy battle losses (attrition); predictions of enemy actions or reactions, etc. This latter process is referred to as the wargaming process.

The outcome of the process is usually recorded in a synchronization matrix format (FM 101-5 1997), a type of Gantt chart. Time periods constitute the columns and functional classes of actions, such as the Battlefield Operating Systems (BOS), are the rows (see Fig. 3). Examples of BOS include Maneuver, Combat Service Support (e.g., logistics), Military Intelligence, etc. The content of this plan, recorded largely in the cells of the matrix, includes the tasks and actions of the multiple sub-units and assets of the friendly force; their objectives and manner of execution, expected timing, dependencies and synchronization; routes and locations; availability of supplies, combat losses, enemy situation and actions, etc.

How Decision Aids Can Help MDMP

It is easy to see a number of areas in which dramatic improvements are desired and might be affected by a judicious introduction of computer aids (Wass de Czege and Biever 2001).

Currently, manual products cannot be reused downstream in the process. Multiple re-entry of information, hand-jamming, and just the fact of creating multiple overlays take time. Even when the products are produced in an ostensibly "electronic" format, e.g., a PowerPoint presentation, it is not a true digitization – it lacks semantic content and cannot be readily reused in the downstream processes and tools. Could a better set of tools, capable of capturing the semantics of the digital information, address this deficiency?

Remaining essentially manual, the current process is time and manpower consuming (Bohman 1999, Paparone 2001). Much of this consumption of man-hours is directed toward computational tasks such as logistics consumption, time/space analysis, etc., which could be at least in theory allocated to a computer aid.

The time demands of the manual process force the staff into drastically limiting the number and diversity of options they are able to explore and analyze (Banner 1997). Perhaps, an intelligent computer aid could explore a greater range of options, enabling the staff to analyze more possible options in the same amount of time, or possibly conducting deeper analysis of the same number of options that the current process allows.

The dichotomy of planning and execution remains pervasive. The gulf separating the two is unacceptably wide, and could be explained at least in part by the fact that today's planning process is far too slow to be merged effectively into execution decision-making. If computer aids make fast, real-time planning and re-planning possible, would it enable a major step toward the integration of planning and execution?

The Army's corporate knowledge continuously evolves, and the rate of this evolution and adaptation has increased under the pressure of multiple factors: new military-political realities, the threat of asymmetric warfare, and the rise in operations other than conventional war, to name just a few. The effective mechanisms for capture and transmission of such knowledge are elusive. Could it be that computer decision aids (which by necessity must contain some of the warrior's knowledge, continuously updated) can become one of such mechanisms?

Fighting by the Book and by Numbers?

In spite of potential benefits of decision aids in MDMP, their roles, limitations and concept of operations in military environments are justifiably open to a number of serious questions and concerns. These questions and concerns include:

Will they inhibit agility and dynamics of command, forcing greater reliance on slow and bureaucratic processes, command-by-plan and reduced latitude afforded to the tactical commanders?

Will such computer aids impose extensive training and specialization requirements, turning warriors into narrow-focused computer tool operators?

Will they encourage excessive fixation on analytical aspects of command, by the book and by numbers? And detract from intuitive, adaptive, art-like aspects of the military command decision making?

Will they engender undue dependence of future commanders and staff on technology that may be vulnerable in a combat environment? After all, isn't it often said with a great justification that "a map with a hole in it is still a map, but a computer with a hole in it is a doorstop?"

Will it make the plans and actions more predictable to the enemy?

The Motivation and Focus of the Experimental Exploration

Some of these questions and arguments can be clarified, if not necessarily answered with opportunities and promise of experimental investigation. That was the rationale behind the Integrated Course of Action Critiquing and Elaboration System (ICCES) experiment, conducted by the Battle Command Battle Laboratory – Leavenworth (BCBL-L) as a result of a TRADOC sponsored Concept Experimentation Program (CEP) during the Government fiscal year 2000. In this experiment, several promising and representative prototype technologies were inexpensively "lashed together" to produce a necessarily crude but sufficiently useable suite of decision aids. The resulting ICCES system was then placed in the hands of several Army officers in controlled experiments. The key question was: can such tools provide value to Army decision-making?

For the purposes of the ICCES experiment we focused on the course of action planning and analysis steps of the MDMP: from documenting and communicating a high-level COA to producing a detailed analysis and plan of tasks. A highly creative step of inventing a high-level COA, currently explored by a number of researchers (Hayes and Schlabach 1998, Atkin et al. 1999, Tate et al. 2001, Kewley and Embrecht) was left outside the scope of this effort. To further circumscribe the scope of the experiment (subject as always to budgetary constraints) we focused on the planning process at the Army Brigade echelon.

The Experimental Rig

To provide computer-aided support to the selected aspects of MDMP, we identified several existing, advanced R&D prototype tools, modified them lightly and integrated them loosely and inexpensively into a conceptually seamless suite of decision aids (Fig. 1). The resulting "rig" offered a basis for conducting practical experiments structured around the key tasks of the staff process.

COA Creator, developed by the Qualitative Reasoning Group at Northwestern University, is a tool that allows a user to sketch a COA into the computer (Ferguson et al. 2000). Although superficially similar to familiar drawing tools like MS PowerPoint, COACreator is fundamentally different in that there are semantic knowledge based representations stored into the computer for each item added to the COA sketch. Additionally, this tool uses an "overlay" approach to graphics which allows the user to switch graphics on and off easily in a fashion which is analogous to taking acetate graphics on and off a map, which is the current practice. Finally, the system is doctrinally based, to allow the military user to work in a domain environment that is familiar to him. The tool is also speech enabled, but for the purpose of the ICCES experiment, the users used drag-and-drop functionalities instead.

The COA statement tool, a product of Alphatech, Inc., was modified under the ICCES experiment to allow the staff planner to enter the COA statement. Unlike a word processor that captures words but not the semantics of the text entered, this tool presented the users with an interface that allowed them to produce natural language sentences to construct their COA statement. Additionally, this system was linked to the sketch tool to, in a sense, "auto-fill"

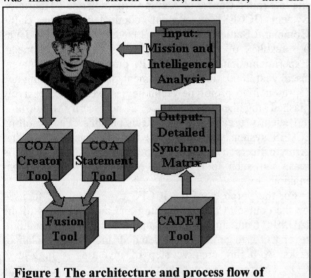

Figure 1 The architecture and process flow of ICCES.

portions of the COA statement that could be derived automatically from the sketch (e.g. units, tasks, etc.). Some examples of the sentences that can be constructed with the system are:

Close: TF 1-8, a mechanized infantry task force (Supporting Effort 1) attacks to destroys REDARCAVBN2 in order to prevent REDINBN17 and REDARCAVBN2 from engages in offensive operations. Fires: Fires will suppress OBJ CUB, then suppress OBJ ROYALS, then suppress OBJ BRAVES, then suppress OBJ BREWERS.

The sketch and statement of today's staff process during COA development reflect different aspects of the course of action. Although they go hand-in-hand, they each contain some unique information that cannot be gleaned from the other ("purpose" for example, cannot be easily inferred from a COA sketch but is usually clearly defined in the statement). These two distinct aspects also reflected themselves in the fact that we had to use two different tools

– COACreator and the COA statement tool – that capture the content of the COA from two distinct prospective. Thus, we needed a mechanism that could merge the digital representations of sketch and statement in a unified product – that was the task of the Fusion Engine. It was developed by Teknowledge, Inc. and generated a single information file from the two separate sources as well as eliminating inconsistencies between the information. Additionally, Teknowledge built an XML translator to translate the knowledge fragments into the XML schema needed for the next system in the experiment.

Once the digital representation of the sketch and statement information is properly fused and translated, it goes to the next tool called CADET, developed by Carnegie Group, Inc. (now owned by BBN Technologies) as an SBIR program, under the sponsorship of CECOM RDEC. This tool transforms the sketch and statement into a detailed plan/schedule of the operation. CADET expands friendly tasks, determines the necessary supporting relations, allocates/schedules tasks to friendly assets, takes into account dependencies between tasks and availability of assets, predicts enemy actions and reactions, devises friendly counter-actions, estimates paths of movements, timing requirements, logistics consumption, attrition and risk. The resulting digital product can be then displayed in a number of different forms – as a traditional synchronization matrix or as an animated map. Although the resulting plan still requires careful review and editing by the planning cell officers, it was our expectation that it could serve as a good starting point for further analysis by the officers, and potentially a major time saver. A detailed discussion of CADET is found in (Kott et al. 2002, Ground, Kott and Budd 2002).

Once the COA is truly digitized, a tool like CADET can automatically (or with human guidance) perform the detailed planning, including the traditionally time-consuming tasks such as time-distance analysis, logistics calculations, and potential attrition calculations for the plan.

These tools were linked together mainly via file transfer, crudely but sufficient for exercising a carefully controlled experiment. The overall "rig" supported a logical concept of operation for the end-users, a group of staff planners:

- enter the COA sketch into the COA Creator, discuss and modify (e.g., Fig. 2);
- enter the COA statement into the Statement Tool, discuss and modify;
- review the detailed plan produced by CADET (e.g., Fig. 3), modify it as desired or return to the sketch and statement to produce a new or modified COA;
- use the detailed plan product to generate the OPLAN/OPORD.

Potentially, the entire process could be accomplished in a few minutes (minus the manual generation of the textual OPLAN/OPORD). However, only experiments could determine whether it would work at all.

The Experiment

The experiment was conducted over a 3-day period and involved eight Army officers (majors and lieutenant colonels) at BCBL-L facilities in Fort Leavenworth, Kansas. All the subjects were from combat arms branches and had a variety of tactical experience, with 11-23 years of Active Service. None of the users had prior technical backgrounds, but all possessed basic computer skills with MS Office products like PowerPoint, Word, etc.

The first day of the experiment consisted of training all the officers on how to use the system. The training consisted of walking the users through a complete scenario of COA development (sketch and statement) and COA expansion within the ICCES system. The training occurred over a 4-hour period and included a description of each system within the experiment, and then a sample COA was developed by the instructor with the students following along on their own machine. Given limited resources, the users worked in pairs during training, but were each given opportunities to manipulate the software. Observers noted the users performances, and at the end of the training, the users were broken into two roughly equivalent groups of four based on their tactical skills/experience and their demonstrated technical skills during the training.

On Day Two of the experiment, each group of four officers conducted the MDMP process given a tactical scenario. One group (control group) was to use the traditional, manual process. The other group was to use the ICCES system to conduct their planning. Each group received the same plan and briefing from their simulated higher headquarters, and both groups were allowed to ask questions in order to ensure their understanding of the plan (similar to how military units request additional information in order to ensure their understanding of orders from higher). Once the groups were confident in their understanding of the high-level plan and their requirements, they were allowed to organize and conduct their planning activities. Each group was informed that their deliverable products at the end of the day were three COA sketches and statements, and one COA synchronization matrix that reflected the one COA they had chosen internally as their "best" COA with a level of detail that would allow execution of the plan. The groups were not given a specific time limit to complete their planning, but observers monitored times for post-experiment analysis.

Day Three of the experiment would involve the same procedures as Day Two, but the roles of the groups would reverse. The control group assumed the role of the automated group and vice-versa. The scenario was slightly different, but similar enough to be comparable with the Day Two scenario with regards to complexity of the plan, etc. Both groups were tasked to provide the same products as generated in Day 2 for the new scenario in their new roles (automated or manual).

Although the experiment would provide valuable data and insights into the issues of focus, there are several considerations that prevent us from claiming statistical relevance to our results. First, given the limited time availability of the user groups, we were unable to conduct enough iterations of the experiment to provide statistically valid results. Second, although the groups were broken out in order to attempt to achieve parity with regards to their tactical and technical abilities, human factors such as personalities could not be completely accounted for. Finally, by switching roles of the groups from Day Two to Day Three in the experiment, we introduced several other uncontrollable variables into the experiment, such as team

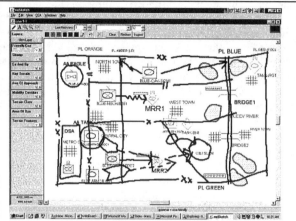

Figure 2 The users entered the high-level COA using the COA Creator tool.

building within the groups and the ability of the initial control group to retain their training from Day One to Day Three with regards to manipulating the software.

Observations and Lessons Learned

Significant observations began in the training phase. In spite of a very modest time allocated to the training session, users did not exhibit any hesitation or difficulties in operating the system that could be attributed to a need for additional training. This was all the more notable in view of the fact that most of the training focused on the workarounds necessitated by the limited integration of the system. E.g., we had to train the users how to pass files between the components of the system, how to avoid crash-prone situation, etc. None of this should be necessary in a mature, fully-developed system. Even with this overhead, we were able to complete the training session in four hours. Without the overhead, we estimate that the training could be accomplished in less than an hour.

A key factor allowing the low training requirements and rapid, easy learning curve was the use of a sketch-based multimodal interface. The nuSketch approach to multimodal interfaces (Forbus et.al. 2001, 2002) used in the COA Creator, like other multimodal interface systems such as QuickSet (Cohen et.al 1997), exploits the naturalness of drawing and visual annotations for communicating with software. While QuickSet has shown itself to be very useful, the nuSketch approach had several advantages for this task over QuickSet. The QuickSet such as QuickSet (Cohen et.al 1997), exploits the naturalness of drawing and visual annotations for communicating with software. While QuickSet has shown itself to be very useful, the nuSketch approach had several advantages for this task over QuickSet. The QuickSet approach focuses on providing recognition services as interfaces to legacy computer systems; its "smarts" are in statistical recognizers for visual symbols, speech and natural language understanding, and integrating these information sources into commands for the underlying software system. By contrast, nuSketch-based systems focus on rich conceptual understanding of the domain, spatial reasoning about the user's ink, and clever interface design instead of recognition. These differences were important for this task in several ways. First, the conceptual understanding of the domain used in the COA creator provided the representational framework needed for CADET to do its work. Second, extensive pre-training of speech vocabularies and grammars was not needed, as it would be with QuickSet or any system using existing speech recognition technology[1]. Instead, officers used the software equivalent of push-buttons (organized in layer-specific glyph bars) to indicate the intended meaning of their ink as they drew. This allows them to draw complex shapes (which cannot be handled by today's statistical recognition technologies) and deal with interruptions such

Figure 3 A typical output - plan/schedule of a brigade-sized offensive operation may include hundreds of significant tasks. A fragment of such a plan is shown here.

as conversations with fellow officers (which would cause problems for most multimodal interfaces, which interpret

---

[1] While speech recognition is useful in many applications, today's technology has severe limitations for battlefield use, including sensitivity to environmental noise and operator stress, user-specific training of the software, and training operators to work with limited vocabularies and grammars. Technology advances will change this over time, but it is worth being wary about near-future applications of speech recognition in battlefield systems.

pauses or lifting the pen as a signal that what the person is drawing is finished).

At the output side of the system, the users generally did not express dissatisfaction with the quality of the planning products generated with the ICCES system. The group that used ICCES elected to make only a small number of changes to the automatically generated product i.e., the highly detailed synchronization matrix (Fig. 3). Only about 10-15 % of the entries in the matrix were manually edited, indicating that the users were in agreement with the overwhelming majority of the plan produced by ICCES. After the editing, the products compared favorably with the products produced by the control group. For example, the COA's produced by both groups when analyzed/wargamed either through the ICCES system or manually, all resulted in roughly the same estimates for time to complete the mission and overall attrition of friendly forces. This observation was later confirmed by a different experiment reported in (Kott, Ground and Budd 2002) with regard to the CADET module of ICCES, where a larger number of test cases and multiple unbiased judges were used to compare the products of manual and the computerized processes.

Further, there was no evidence that the computer-assisted process resulted in less imaginative, more cook-book type products. This can be simply explained by the fact that the overall COA inputted into the system came directly from the user and was not constrained in any way by the software. By allowing the user to free-hand a COA sketch into the system, there was complete freedom of tactical actions for the user.

On the other hand, there were discouraging observations with regard to the presentation aspect of the products. Synchronization matrix is an accepted way of recording the results of COA analysis. However, in the ICCES experiment we found that the users had difficulties comprehending the synchronization matrix generated by the computer tool, even though it was presented in a very conventional, presumably familiar manner. Perhaps, the synchronization matrix functions well only as a mechanism for short-hand recording of one's own mental process. However, the same synchronization matrix is not nearly as useful when used to present the results of someone else's, e.g., a computer tool's, reasoning process. In effect, the synchronization matrix serves as a textual representation of a visual process. The problem was further exacerbated by the fact that ICCES-generated matrices were unusually detailed and therefore large, making it difficult for the users to navigate within this large volume of information. It appeared a system like ICCES requires a qualitative simulation/animation capability to visually present the expanded plan to the user.

Another factor contributing to the low training requirements appeared to be the intentionally simple, straightforward process flow and the concept of user-system interactions. These consisted of the sequence of steps outlined earlier in section "The Experimental Rig," and the users readily accepted them as natural and consistent with their prior training and experience in the manual MDMP process.

In fact, the users displayed preferences for further simplification of the process. For example, the users stated that they would prefer a single process of entering sketch and statement, rather than the two sequential steps that they had to perform in ICCES. Their desire for a simple and straightforward concept of operations was further demonstrated in their use of the COA Statement tool – they consistently looked and asked for one, simple way to enter the statement, and shied away from the rich, flexible, but necessarily complex approach offered by the tool. We will return to this issue in the conclusions.

Consistent with the preference for a simple concept of operations were the users' requests for a mechanism that would allow them to perform easy modifications and iterations within the process. In particular, the users wanted to make changes in the synchronization matrix produced in CADET and see it automatically reflected in the COA sketch and statement. Although such a capability is technically feasible to develop, the ICCES system did not have it at the time of the experiment.

Of the greatest practical significance were those observations that confirmed a potential for major reduction in time and manpower required for performing a typical MDMP cycle. In particular, the COA analysis/wargaming process could potentially be shortened by several hours. Significantly, the savings were realized primarily in the downstream tasks, particularly in the step that generates a detailed plan/schedule of the operation. This is hardly surprising. The upstream processes of capturing the digitized information, such as was done in our experiment in the COA Creator tool, may not be any less time-consuming than a manual counterpart. However, once the information is captured in a digitized form, great time-savings accrue in the downstream processes. To put it differently, none of the ICCES components alone can deliver time-savings; but a system of such components can.

Conclusions

This study suggests evidence for several important conclusions. To start with, AI techniques can be used to create natural sketch-based interfaces that domain experts can use with little training. The nuSketch approach to multimodal interfaces, with its emphasis on visual understanding of the user's ink tied to a rich conceptual understanding of the domain, provides a practical method of expressing COA sketches with today's technology. One important limitation noted was the desire expressed for a single tool that captures COA sketches and statements simultaneously. This approach could be extended to provide a unified map-based interface to do both tasks, but it would require additional research to apply advances in natural language understanding and dialogue management to supply this capability. Another research opportunity is to use the rich representations in the COA Creator as inputs to other support tools, such as critiquers and pattern completion (for hypotheses about Red intent) and access to

previous plans via analogy (Forbus, 2001). Such capabilities could be incrementally added to near-future deployed systems as they became available, given a stable semantic framework.

With a semantically-rich input provided by a tool like the COA Creator, techniques of tightly interleaved adversarial planning and scheduling, such as those applied in the CADET component of ICCES, can be used to create thoroughly detailed plans comparable in quality to manually generated, but dramatically faster. Decision aids that combine both natural COA sketch interfaces and a full-functionality COA expansion mechanism can indeed contribute greatly into dramatic increase in speed and agility of the staff planning process, potentially bringing it into an integrated execution-planning cycle.

With regard to the concerns that decision aids of such nature might adversely impact the creative aspects of art of war, the experiment illustrated the fact that such a suite of computer aids is merely a tool. No tool is a substitute for training, doctrine and personal qualities of the decision makers, and regardless of tools, it is ultimately up to the decision-makers to define their approach and style of decision making. Although tools do lead to changes in the details and form of the process, the experiment offered no evidence that the substantive aspects of the decision making processes will be either inhibited or dictated by any such tools. Different commanders and staffs, with different styles, will use such tools to leverage their own preferences and strengths.

Currently, there is no evidence that a tool like ICCES would in any way increase predictability of the plans, or to encourage cook-book approach. To the contrary, because it allows the staff planners to explore rapidly a broader range of possible COAs, including those that are more unconventional and out-of-the-box, there is a potential for such tools to encourage greater ingenuity, creativity and adaptivity.

Overall, the experiment suggests that the ICCES concept is a practical paradigm for a planning staff decision aid, with near-future deployment potential. Staff officers would have such a tool available on a rugged, light-weight, highly portable device, such as a PDA, linked to other such devices via tactical internet. The decision-aid tool, in keeping with ICCES lessons, would be tightly integrated, capable of producing complex operational plans and orders rapidly and with minimal manual input, with simple, straightforward and natural operation concept, easy to learn and easy to use even in stressful field conditions. An officer would use it routinely to perform planning of tactical operations, to collaborate with others while on the move and dispersed over the battlefield, to issue operational plans and orders, and to monitor and modify the plans as the operation is executed and the situation evolves. Furthermore, as demonstrated in ICCES, the current AI technology is not far from being directly transitioned into a practical tool of such nature.

Acknowledgements

The US Army CEP program, sponsored by TRADOC, provided the funding for this work. LTC's Eugene Stockel, John Duquette, and Brooks Lyles from BCBL-L provided valuable advice and guidance. Mr. Murray Burke (DARPA) made invaluable contributions to the preparation and execution of the experiment. Several of the tools used in ICCES were developed with support by DARPA through the High Performance Knowledge Bases and Command Post of the Future programs.

References

Atkin, M. S., Westbrook, D. L., and Cohen, P. R. 1999. Capture the Flag: Military simulation meets computer games. In Proceedings of AAAI Spring Symposium Series on AI and Computer Games, 1-5.

Banner, G. T. 1997. Decision Making - A Better Way, Military Review, Headquarters, Department of the Army, vol.LXXVII, no.5.

Bohman, W. E. 1999. STAFFSIM, An Interactive Simulation for Rapid, Real Time Course of Action Analysis by U.S. Army Brigade Staffs, Thesis, Naval Postgraduate School, Monterey, CA.

Department of the Army 1997. *Field Manual 101-5. Staff Organization and Operations*, Headquarters, Washington, D.C.

Cohen, P. R., Johnston, M., McGee, D., Oviatt, S., Pittman, J., Smith, I., Chen, L., and Clow, J. 1997. QuickSet: Multimodal interaction for distributed applications. In Proceedings of the Fifth Annual International Multimodal Conference (Multimedia '97), Seattle, WA, ACM Press, pp 31-40.

Ferguson, R.W., Rasch, R.A., Turmel, W., and Forbus, K.D. 2000. Qualitative Spatial Interpretation of Course-of-Action Diagrams. In Proceedings of the 14th International Workshop on Qualitative Reasoning. Morelia, Mexico.

Forbus, K., Ferguson, R. and Usher, J. 2001. Towards a computational model of sketching. In Proceedings of IUI'01, January 14-17, 2001, Santa Fe, New Mexico.

Forbus, K. 2001. Exploring analogy in the large. In Gentner, D., Holyoak, K., and Kokinov, B. eds., Analogy: Perspectives from Cognitive Science. MIT Press.

Forbus, K. and Usher, J. 2002. Sketching for knowledge capture: A progress report. In Proceedings of IUI'02, San Francisco, California.

Ground, L., Kott, A., and Budd, R. 2002. A Knowledge-Based Tool for Planning of Military Operations: the Coalition Perspective. In Proceedings of the Second International Conference on Knowledge Systems for Coalition Operations, Toulouse, France.

Hayes, C. C., and Schlabach, J. L. 1998. FOX-GA: A Planning Support Tool for assisting Military Planners in a Dynamic and Uncertain Environment. In Integrating Planning, Scheduling and Execution in Dynamic and Uncertain Environments, R. Bergmann and A. Kott, eds., AAAI Press, Madison, Wisconsin.

Kewley, R. and Embrecht, M. 1998 Fuzzy-Genetic Decision Optimization for Positioning of Military Combat Units. In Proceedings SMC'98, pp. 3658 – 3664, 1998 IEEE International Conference on Systems, Man, and Cybernetics, October 11-14, La Jolla, California

Kott, A., Ground, L., Budd, R., Rebbapragada, L., and Langston, J. 2002. Toward Practical Knowledge-Based Tools for Battle Planning and Scheduling. In Proceedings of IAAI 2002 Conference, Edmonton, Alberta, Canada.

Paparone, C. R. 2001. US Army Decisionmaking: Past, Present and Future, Military Review, Headquarters, Department of the Army, vol.LXXXI, no.4.

Tate, A., Levine, J., Jarvis, P., and Dalton, J. 2000, Using AI Planning Technology for Army Small Unit Operations. In Proceedings of the Fifth International Conference on Artificial Intelligence Planning Systems.

Wass de Czege, H. and Biever, J. D. 2001. Six Compelling Ideas On the Road to a Future Army, Army Magazine, Vol.51, No.2, pp. 43-48..

Intelligent Control of Auxiliary Ship Systems

David Scheidt, Christopher McCubbin, Michael Pekala, Shon Vick and David Alger

The Johns Hopkins University Applied Physics Laboratory
11100 Johns Hopkins Road
Laurel Maryland 20723-6099

Abstract

The Open Autonomy Kernel (OAK) is an architecture for autonomous distributed control. OAK addresses control as a three-step process: diagnosis, planning and execution. OAK is specifically designed to support "hard" control problems in which the system is complex, sensor coverage is incomplete, and distribution of control is desired. A unique combination of model-based reasoning and autonomous agents are used. Model-based reasoning is used to perform diagnosis. Observations and execution are distributed using autonomous intelligent agents. Planning is performed with simple script or graph-spanning planners. A prototype OAK system designed to control the chilled water distribution system of a Navy surface ship has been developed and is described.

Introduction

Next generation ship engineering plant designs must incorporate a variety of increasingly sophisticated propulsion and auxiliary subsystems while reducing the overall requirement for human monitoring, maintenance and control. In order to meet these objectives, new levels of subsystem interoperability and autonomy must be achieved. The *Open Autonomy Kernel* (OAK) addresses critical infrastructure requirements for next generation autonomous and semi-autonomous systems, including fault detection and recovery, and goal-directed control. OAK brings together the Artificial Intelligent (AI) technologies of agent-based systems, and qualitative model-based reasoning to enable a new generation of integrated auxiliary subsystem autonomy.

Efforts to automate the control of engineering plants aboard naval vessels have emphasized the infrastructure and diagnostic aspects of plant management, i.e. monitoring vessel subsystems via sensors and presenting sensor data to human operators. Interpretation of and response to the data remain largely manual tasks. This interpretation and response function, especially in damage control scenarios, is a significant factor in determining ship-manning levels. If the incident assessment and response loop can be closed with a reliable autonomous reasoning process, significant relief in overall manning levels can be realized. Successful automation efforts to date have been based on expert diagnostic knowledge in the form of coded rules or procedures that

are interpreted by the system at runtime to detect, predict, or diagnose fault conditions. The OAK architecture and working prototype extend this automated reasoning paradigm in a number of important ways. First, OAK uses goal-directed commanding at the system component level. This shifts the control paradigm from one of sending commands to subsystems, to that of sending goals and resources to intelligent subsystem management agents that require no direct operator interaction. Secondly, OAK's subsystem management agents are loosely coupled and distributed across a networked infrastructure. This results in a dynamic and adaptable coordination capability. Finally, OAK uses qualitative model-based reasoning as an extension to current rule- and procedure-based formalisms in the agent control loop. Model-based reasoning is used to perform real-time detection and identification of unanticipated fault conditions.

Motivating Example

The motivating example used for the existing prototype is the control of auxiliary systems on capital ships. The specific target domain is the electrical, chilled water, low-pressure air and fire main systems on US Navy Arleigh Burke class Aegis destroyers. These systems are complex, inter-dependent, distributed, redundant, embedded, and contain numerous components that are unobservable. Currently high level control is the primary responsibility of dozens of sailors on each ship. Effective automation of these systems will allow the Navy to significantly reduce its manning requirements.

The auxiliary systems on the Arleigh Burke contain thousands of interdependent controllable nodes. One of the auxiliary systems, the chilled water distribution system, consists of a dozen complex machines, such as pumps and chiller plants, approximately four hundred valves, and twenty-three service loads. Behavior of components within an auxiliary system is dependent upon the components to which they are connected, often recursively. The auxiliary systems themselves are inter-dependent; for example, the chilled water system runs on electrical power provided by the electrical system while the electrical system is kept cool by the chilled water system. Behavior of the auxiliary systems is also dependent upon other ship systems such as the HVAC, combat, and fire support systems. These dependencies combine to generate a complex super-system; no portion of which may be controlled in isolation. The size of the auxiliary systems, combined with their interdependency, prevents the effective use of traditional control system software. The auxiliary systems are designed with redundant supply and distribution mechanisms for critical resources. This redundancy presents the possibility of multiple valid configurations for a goal system-state pair, introducing control optimization in addition to control satisfaction.

Survivability, the justification for redundancy within auxiliary systems, demands that auxiliary control mechanisms avoid single points of failure. Therefore, the control mechanism must be fault tolerant.

The auxiliary Arleigh Burke control systems are only sparsely instrumented. The vast majority of system components do not have sensors that provide direct feedback on the behavior of the component. Comprehensive sensor coverage incurs additional cost, resource utilization and introduces additional points of failure. Without the availability of complete sensor coverage system states must be inferred from indirectly observable behavior.

Model-Based Reasoning

Model-Based Reasoning is an overloaded term. The Model-based reasoning used in OAK refers to a "reasoning from first principles" approach to diagnosis (Kuipers 1994). The theoretical basis for model-based reasoning is Discrete Event System theory, specifically Partially Observable Markov Decision Processes (POMDP).

Discrete Event System theory shows that systems may be modeled discretely using the automaton $G = (X, E, f, \Gamma, x_o, X_m)$ (Cassandras & Lafortune 1999) in which X is the discrete state space; E is the finite set of events associated with the transitions in Γ; f is the transition function; Γ is the active event function; x_o is the initial state; and X_m is the set of marked states. Control of Γ is provided by a control policy S that includes a set of control actions $S(s)$.

Automata that are memoryless (i.e. all past state information, and how long the process has been in the current state, is irrelevant), are considered *Markov Processes*. Association of control actions for state transitions, cost for such transitions, and transition probabilities, allows us to derive Markov Decision Processes (MDP). MDP are defined by the tuple (X_S, E_A, f_T, R) in which: X_S is the finite set of states of the system being tracked; A is the set of commands; E_A is a finite set of actions; and f_T is a state transition model of the environment which is a function mapping $X_S \times E_A$ into discrete probability distributions over X_S. The actions are non-deterministic, so we write $f_T(x, e)$ for the probability that transition e will occur given the state x. R is the cost of action. Our use of model-based reasoning is limited to diagnosis; therefore we are not concerned with R.

POMDP are MDP that have been extended to include a finite set of observations. POMDP are represented by the tuple $\mathrm{M} = (X_S, E_A, O, f_T, R)$ in which O is the observation function that maps the finite set of observations into X_S. The probability of making an observation o from state x is denoted as $O(o, x)$.

The tuple M is capable of representing the behavior of systems that are composed of independent subsystems. This may be generated by creating a supermodel M_S whose states, events and function are the cross product of the subsystem models; $M_S = M_1 \times M_2 \times \ldots \times M_N$. This approach to modeling complex systems is impractical for two reasons: first, the state space quickly becomes unwieldy; second, the majority of complex systems of interest are composed of dependent subsystems. Model-based Control solves this dilemma by modeling the system as concurrent constraint automata, separately enumerated component models that are constrained by shared attributes (Williams & Nayak 1996).

This representation scheme is beneficial when constructing large complex systems. By encapsulating component behavior within a single logical model and by constraining components through context independent attributes the components themselves become context independent models. This provides for model replication and reuse.

Model-based reasoning is a three-step process: (1) Propagation of control action effects through a system. Propagation generates a predicted state for the system, including controlled and uncontrolled components. Observations of system behavior are compared to the predicted state; if observations match predictions then the system is assumed to be behaving nominally. The existence of conflicts between observed and predicted states indicate the existence of one of more failures within the system. (2) Identification of candidate failure scenarios that most effectively resolve the conflicts. The strategy used to resolving these conflicts is *Conflict-directed best first search* (CBFS), loosely based on De Kleer and Williams' General Diagnostic Engine (de Kleer & Williams 1987) and described in detail by Kurien (Kurien 2001). (3) Selection of the most probable scenario from the identified candidates. The fitness criteria used by CBFS to select the most probable solution is a system-wide candidate probability based upon the probabilities of individual component states $f_T(X_i, E_i) \forall M$; by using a general diagnostic algorithm, implementation effort is limited to the model upon which the algorithm operates. System design and maintenance do not require software modifications. In addition, because of the encapsulation of the component models, model maintenance is limited to those components modified in the controlled system and their immediate neighbors.

Autonomous Agents

Within the context of OAK, an agent is a software process that can reason about and act upon its environment. Four sets of characteristics that may be used to describe agents and agent systems are: Intrinsic Agent Characteristics; Extrinsic Agent Characteristics; System Characteristics; and Agent and Environment-Agent characteristics. OAK agents are intrinsically permanent, stationary, exhibit both reactive and deliberative behavior, and are declaratively constructed. Agents are reactive in their ability to reconfigure the systems within their control in the context of an existing plan. Agents are deliberative in their ability to create a plan in response to observed states and defined goals. OAK agent's extrinsic characteristics include proximity to the controlled system, social independence, and both awareness of and co-operativeness with goals and states of other agents. Systems of OAK agents consist of nearly homogeneous agents, and are independently executed yet contain unique models of the system for which the agent is responsible. OAK agents are environmentally aware and behavior of the environment is predictable through each agent's model.

Application Description

OAK is a distributed, multiagent system. The system can have varying topology based on the application. OAK has two major use-cases that almost fully describe the operation of the system: OAK's reaction to user-input goals; and OAK's reaction to system state change. The primary intelligent components that enable OAK to accomplish these use-cases are the model-based reasoning engine and the planner. In the sections that follow, the OAK application is described in detail.

The Multiagent System

To perform the diagnostic phase of the control cycle, OAK agents continually update their states using the model-based reasoning engine, and pass these state updates to other agents that are interested so that these agents may update their states. In response to these states, or to the system's environment, an external actor or an OAK agent will provide goals to the OAK system, which are distributed for further processing. A hierarchical agent topology was used for testing. However, the OAK architecture does not preclude other topologies.

Agent Communication Framework and Language
Each agent has an associated Agent Communication Broker (ACB), which is responsible for handling all of the agent's communication with the Agent Communication Framework (ACF). The ACB maintains a queue of messages coming into the agent. Additionally, each agent that has direct communication with hardware has a control mediator (CM) to handle the hardware level goals that are generated by these agents for the hardware associated with it, and to receive updates about this hardware. These messages are not handled by the ACF.

The ACF of OAK is built using the Control of Agent Based Systems (CoABS) Grid, a "flexible information infrastructure" built by Global InfoTek, Incorporated. CoABS allows OAK to have a dynamic, heterogeneous agent membership, facilitates agent replication to remove single points of failure, and supplies utilities for ACF visualization.

The Agent Communication Language (ACL) of OAK provides several message templates, including messages for queries, state updates, subscription requests, goals, exceptions, and agent coordination. The ACF allows any agent to communicate directly with any other agent. Thus, communication between agents is not restricted to any particular logical framework.

User-determined Goals One of the major use-cases of OAK is to react to goals entered by an external actor. These are system-level goals which have the potential of transition-ing the entire multiagent system from one state to another.

Goals that are entered from an external actor, such as a human operator, through this interface are sent directly to the root level agent using a *goal message*. This agent develops a plan with goals that apply to the domains of its child agents. Goals have a priority associated with them, which is used for goal preemption.

After the root node develops a plan and directs a goal to one of its child agents, the goal is received by the child agent's ACB, sorted into its queue, and eventually accepted by the agent for processing. This agent develops a plan to implement the goal. Since this agent is a root of its own tree, the goals developed by the planner are passed to its child agents. This propagation continues until leaf agents receive goals for their specific domains.

Once goals are received at the leaf level, a similar process occurs, in that a plan is developed and goals are passed out of the agent. The only difference is that the goals are now passed to the agent's CM, which translates the goal into commands that a hardware driver can understand. Since the CM is the only component that has direct interaction with the hardware drivers, it is the only component that has to be updated when hardware itself is changed or when hardware drivers are updated.

Successful goal implementation implies a state change, so an agent does not have to set up callbacks with the hardware to confirm that a command was successful. Leaf agents are already required to monitor the hardware they control for changes in order to accomplish the second major use-case of OAK. Therefore, the leaf agents wait for reactions from hardware monitors to indicate that the command has been successful. The agent is then free to pass out goals that were order dependent on the goal just implemented. Since state changes are propagated up the hierarchy, agents at higher levels are also informed that their goals were implemented and they can then pass out goals that had to be put in a wait state. To an implementer of OAK, this means that the incoming goal use case and the state change use case, which comprise the two major functions of OAK, are decoupled.

Reacting to State Changes To appropriately handle changes in the state of the system, OAK uses a model-based reasoning engine (MBRE)(Kurien & Nayak 2000). In this section, we follow the sequence of events that are implied by a state change in OAK.

State change events are transmitted through the use of a *fact message*. This message contains a representation of the knowledge contained in an agent. When states change, all subscribed agents are informed, and propagation of state changes begins. Note that since many agents may subscribe to an event, state changes may be propagating in several subtrees at any given time.

One of OAK's strengths is an agent's ability to determine the state of its model, compare that state to a knowledge base, and reactively plan. Thus, an agent can autonomously control its domain until an agent that is higher in the hierarchy (or in the case of the root agent, the external actor's agent) preempts its control. The component of OAK that controls reactive planning is called the *reactive manager*.

There are two types of information in the reactive manager: persistent goals and emergency conditions.

Persistent goals are simply goals that are desired true for the duration of the agent.

We define an emergency condition as a state that cannot be reversed and requires OAK to act immediately to protect the resident system. When OAK detects an emergency, it will preempt the external actor's goal and go to a predetermined goal that will minimize damage to the system being modeled. From this point on, goals from the user are implemented as completely as possible based on the damage to the system.

Planning

OAK agents must be able to plan in order to achieve specified goals. The plan format is an ordered sequence of fragments. Each fragment consists of one or more subgoals. The idea is that, within a fragment, each subgoal may be accomplished in parallel, while subgoals in a prior fragment must be completed before the current fragment may be attempted. OAK executes a plan once it has been developed by transmitting each subgoal at the appropriate time to the appropriate agent or piece of hardware and waiting until those subgoals are accomplished or fail.

Different planners may be appropriate for different agents depending on the domain being planned. Therefore, the planner is instantiated at run-time differently for each agent from a group of developed planners. So far, two planners have been developed. The deployed planners are the *Scripted Planner* and the highly specialized *Graph-Based Planner*.

The scripted planner is extremely simple but useful for simple agents, such as leaf agents. The scripted planner matches on the incoming goal and a propositional logic expression about the current world-state, producing a predefined response. Different propositional expressions, and therefore plans, may be associated with each incoming goal. Also, since the scripts are checked in a specific predefined order, a simple priority of plans can be imposed.

The graph-based planner was written specifically for the test domain described below. Planning consisted of determining how to move flow from a source to several sinks through a dynamic pipe network, with many operational constraints. The problem representation was a digraph, with weights on each edge according to the constraints. The planner operated by performing Prim's Minimum Spanning Tree (Prim 1957) algorithm on the graph to determine how to get flow to as many of the desired sinks as possible. The planner determined the actions that each agent would need to take and would generate a plan based on the actions determined.

Implementation

OAK has been implemented on the Chilled Water Reduced Scale Advanced Demonstrator (RSAD) at the Naval Surface Warfare Center (NSWC) Philadelphia. The RSAD, seen in Figure 1, is a reduced scale model of the Arleigh Burke Chilled Water system. The RSAD is a physical implementation of two Arleigh Burke chilled water zones using reduced

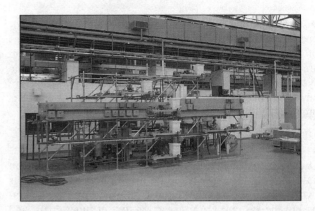

Figure 1: Reduced Scale Advanced Demonstrator (RSAD)

scale equipment. The RSAD contains four pumps, two chiller plants, two expansion tanks and approximately one hundred controllable valves. In-line tanks containing controllable heaters simulate equipment that is directly cooled by the chilled water system. The units of equipment cooled by the chilled water system are known as *loads*. The RSAD includes sixteen simulated loads.

The RSAD control prototype uses twenty OAK agents to control the RSAD's pumps, plants and valves. Each agent contains its own diagnostic engine, planning engine(s), execution managers, and the ability to receive and propagate goals and facts. The agents are organized hierarchically with agents controlling individual hardware components, small aggregations of components, system level abstractions, and the ship.

The *L2* inference engine was used within the OAK agents as the diagnostic engine. L2 is NASA AMES Research Center's second generation model-based reasoning engine. L2, and its predecessor Livingstone, are based on Williams' model-based reasoning approach.(Williams & Nayak 1996) Livingstone was demonstrated as a diagnostic tool for fault analysis of satellites in a 1998 experiment on NASA's Deep Space One(Muscettola *et al.* 1998). Models processed by L2 are written in the Java-Based Model Programming Language (JMPL). L2 provides multiple candidate identification and resolution strategies. The strategy used for the RSAD prototype is CBFS(Kurien 2001). The L2 CBFS implementation uses constraint satisfaction to identify candidate system states. The candidate states are then maintained as hypothetical belief states over time. Each successive observation is used to update the stored belief states and to generate new hypothetical belief states. L2 provides a likelihood rank associated with each belief state. OAK reconfigures the RSAD based upon the current most likely belief state while maintaining other trajectories. The reasoning system is non-monotonic, as active belief states will be abandoned if future observations provide support to other previously less likely possible belief states.

Each OAK agent contains a JMPL model of the real-world system or subsystem for which it is responsible. The model includes POMDP representations of components within the agent's system or subsystem.

The ship agent's planner accepts high-level goals from the ship's Command Center. The ship agent also accepts inferred facts from the intermediate agents that express the believed state of the ship systems. The ship agent planner generates goals for the intermediate agents.

The Chilled Water agent is the only intermediate level agent currently implemented in the RSAD prototype. The model used for diagnosis in the chilled water agent consists of twenty-one components. Each component represents a small cluster of machinery within the RSAD. The Chilled Water Agent directly controls eleven of these components.

Beneath the Chilled water agent in the hierarchy are eighteen low-level agents. These agents manage the two cooling units with their supporting valves and regional valve-pipe aggregate components within the chilled water system.

Results

Three test sets were performed for the RSAD implementation of OAK. The first round of testing was performed for and by the development team. The second round of testing was performed with control systems engineers from the Naval Surface Warfare Center Carderock Division Advanced Auxiliary Controls and Automation Group (NSWC-CD Code 825) who are familiar with the Arleigh Burke auxiliary systems. The third round of testing was performed for representatives of the ship construction industry. All three sets of testing followed the same format. All tests were performed with the RSAD hardware. Four types of test scenarios were performed during each test set. The first three scenarios were designed to provide basic coverage of the primary OAK capabilities. The final portion of testing was ad hoc, and provided the testers an opportunity to game the system. During the second and third test sets, hardware faults were instigated by either physically disconnecting a component from its power supply or by physically disconnecting a component from the control network.

The first test scenario was used to demonstrate OAK's ability to reconfigure the RSAD based on high level operator goals. During this test scenario the RSAD was given consecutive commands from a Command and Control simulator to move from one "ship state" to another. The four ship states each have a unique combination of desired states and fitness criteria.

The second test scenario consisted of inducing a series of sequential component failures that initially force OAK to reconfigure the system in order to satisfy the high-level goals and eventually degrade the RSAD so that the RSAD's stated goals are no longer achievable. The second scenario was also specifically designed to test the non-monotonic capability of the reasoning engine. An improbable component failure that was observationally indistinguishable from a probable failure was generated resulting in a misdiagnosis. Subsequent failures generated observations that re-enforced the correct belief state and caused a change of hypothesis within the inference engine.

The third scenario consisted of inducing simultaneous failures to multiple components within the RSAD.

Throughout the testing OAK consistently demonstrated the ability to plan, execute, and propagate facts and goals between agents. During the first test set, the test team found in OAK the propensity to select a legitimate yet unlikely candidate from a set of possible candidate diagnosis. This problem was addressed by modifying the agent topology for the RSAD implementation. After modifications were made, all three test sets were successfully completed. In total, fourteen separate multi-stage tests were conducted. During these fourteen tests, OAK performed thirty-four diagnose-plan-execute cycles. OAK was able to identify the most probable failure scenario when insufficient observables presented multiple indistinguishable situations: also, OAK demonstrated the ability to retroactively update its belief state when evidence was provided to support what had been a less probable candidate solution.

In some cases, equivalent "best fit" reconfigurations were available. In these cases the observing mechanical engineers noted that OAK's reconfiguration was occasionally "unusual" or "not what I would have selected". However, upon inspection, the selected reconfiguration was always consistent with the reconfiguration goals and fitness criteria, and considered reasonable by the observing engineers.

In addition to planned testing, twice during the third test set the RSAD experienced unexpected hardware failures. One failure consisted of a chiller plant unexpectedly failing to the OFF state. Another failure consisted of a valve unexpectedly failing to STUCK_SHUT. During both of these unexpected failures, OAK correctly diagnosed the failures and successfully reconfigured the RSAD.

OAK's planning and execution capabilities succeeded in performing a successful reconfiguration of the RSAD in all test cases. In all cases where a complete solution was available, a solution was found. In cases where multiple solutions were available, OAK was able to determine and select the solution deemed optimal in accordance with the fitness criteria expressed in the script-planner rule base. When no complete solution was available, the "best fit" partial solution was identified and executed.

Difficulties Distributing Diagnosis in Strongly Coupled Systems

Each OAK agent maintains the ability to obtain observations and perform diagnostics on components that the agent controls. Individual agents use observations to infer component states within the agent's sphere of influence. Information on component states are propagated throughout the agent community by disseminating facts that represent the belief state of the agent-modeled subsystem. The model and diagnostic engines within individual agents are independent and, by design, capable of performing diagnosis in isolation from other agents. When an observation is made that conflicts with the model's current belief state (indicating a fault within the system), the reasoning engine attempts to resolve the conflict internally. When the observation and faulty component(s) are both contained within the same agent/model, OAK was found to correctly diagnose component failures. However, when a conflicting observation is observed by one agent and the failed component is within the sphere of influence of another agent, and a candidate failure within the observing agent's model exists, the observing agent will attempt to resolve the conflict prior to disseminating observations. Since a candidate solution does exist, the observing agent will resolve that its internal solution is correct and disseminate the belief that its internal component is faulty. This can result in OAK selecting a less likely candidate state for the system over a more likely candidate.

The potential to select unlikely candidate failure states was mitigated by removing the diagnostic portion of the control loop from those agents that did not have access to observables either directly or through subordinate agents. Diagnostic responsibility for components that did not have access to observables was the undertaken by the lowest parent agent in the hierarchy that did have access to the necessary observations. In the RSAD implementation, this involved moving the diagnostic responsibility for the chiller plant agents into the Chilled Water agent. All agents retained the ability to make observations, plans and execute commands. Thus modified, OAK was able to successful complete all three sets of tests.

Future Work

While the principle of OAK has been demonstrated in a real world setting, additional non-AI related steps are necessary for OAK's acceptance into ship construction. A partial list of future non-AI activities include the creation of a mature set of modeling tools, development tools, and testing upon actual ships.

Future AI related activities involve the extension of the modeling capability (and corresponding model-based reasoning) to include more diverse and sophisticated representations. The most straightforward modeling extension involves the detailed modeling of the other auxiliary ship systems; namely the electrical and low pressure air distribution systems. Slightly more sophisticated is the ability to incorporate a model of the control system itself into the ship systems model. By modeling the control network and the computing infrastructure, the control system becomes capable of reasoning with an inability to command otherwise functional components. Particularly interesting is the possibility that operating agents could jointly control a system through observing each other's behavior should their communications become severed.

In addition to extending the modeling capabilities laterally, more comprehensive control may be found by extending the modeling vertically as well. In the RSAD implementation, the ship model above the chilled water system was limited to a simple finite-state model of the basic ship operating modes. Complex models of ship operating practices and policies have been developed. Extending OAK's modeling capability upward to incorporate both fluid control and operational models within a common reasoning system would further improve OAK's effectiveness. OAK may be improved by extending modeling downward as well. JMPL lacks the sophistication to represent detailed fluid systems normally modeled by ordinary differential equations. Hybrid modeling involving discrete and continuous models is a large vibrant community.

Finally, distributed non-monotonic reasoning should be investigated. Recall that while facts and goals are shared between agents, reasoning is performed in isolation. The inability to send out tentative facts limits diagnosis to encapsulated systems that have co-located components and observables.

Conclusions

OAK has successfully demonstrated the ability to autonomously control complex, sparsely observable systems with social distributed agents that use model-based reasoning for system diagnosis. Specifically OAK has been demonstrated on a reduced scale version of a US Navy destroyer's chilled water distribution system. The design of OAK is not ship system specific, and OAK has the potential to improve the autonomous control of real-world systems that exhibit similar traits. Systems OAK should be effective in controlling include electrical utilities, water utilities and communications systems.

Acknowledgments

We conducted this work as part of the Office of Naval Research "Machinery Systems and Automation to Reduce Manning" program under contract N00014-00-C-0050. The RSAD and low-level control software was developed and provided by the Naval Surface Warfare Center Carderock Division Advanced Auxiliary Controls and Automation Group. Don Dalessandro, Brian Callahan, Richard Avila and William Basil provided substantial insight into the Arleigh Burke auxiliary control system design and Naval doctrine. John Bracy contributed to the editing of this paper.

References

Cassandras, C., and Lafortune, S. 1999. *Introduction to Discrete Event Systems*. Kluwer Academic Publishers.

de Kleer, J., and Williams, B. 1987. Diagnosing multiple faults. *Artificial Intelligence* 32:97–130.

Kuipers, B. 1994. *Qualitative Reasoning*. The MIT Press, Cambridge MA.

Kurien, J., and Nayak, P. 2000. Back to the future for consistency-based trajectory tracking. In *Proceedings of AAAI-2000*.

Kurien, J. 2001. *Model-Based Monitoring, Diagnosis and Control*. Ph.D. Dissertation, Brown University Dept. of Computer Science.

Muscettola, N.; Nayak, P.; Pell, B.; and Williams, B. 1998. Remote agent: to boldly go where no AI system has gone before. *Artificial Intelligence* 103:5–47.

Prim, R. 1957. Shortest connection networks and some generalizations. *Bell System Technical Journal* 36:1389–1401.

Williams, B., and Nayak, P. 1996. A model-based approach to reactive self-configuring systems. In *Proceedings of AAAI-1996*.

Computational Vulnerability Analysis for Information Survivability *

Howard Shrobe

NE43-839
Artificial Intelligence Laboratory
Massacusetts Institute of Technology
Cambridge, MA 02139
hes@ai.mit.edu

Abstract

The Infrastructure of modern society is controlled by software systems. These systems are vulnerable to attacks; several such attacks, launched by "recreation hackers" have already led to severe disruption. However, a concerted and planned attack whose goal *is* to reap harm could lead to catastrophic results (for example, by disabling the computers that control the electrical power grid for a sustained period of time). The survivability of such information systems in the face of attacks is therefore an area of extreme importance to society.

This paper is set in the context of self-adaptive survivable systems: software that judges the trustworthiness of the computational resources in its environment and which chooses how to achieve its goals in light of this trust model. Each self-adaptive survivable system detects and diagnoses compromises of its resources, taking whatever actions are necessary to recover from attack. In addition, a long-term monitoring system collects evidence from intrusion detectors, fire-walls and all the self-adaptive components, building a composite trust-model used by each component. Self-adaptive survivable systems contain models of their intended behavior, models of the required computational resources, models of the ways in which these resources may be compromised and finally, models of the ways in which a system may be attacked and how such attacks can lead to compromises of the computational resources.

In this paper we focus on Computational Vulnerability Analysis: a system that, given a description of a computational environment, deduces all of the attacks that are possible. In particular its goal is to develop multi-stage attack models in which the compromise of one resource is used to facilitate the compromise of other, more valuable resources. Although our ultimate aim is to use these models online as part of a self-adaptive system, there are other offline uses as well which we are deploying first to help system administrators assess the vulnerabilities of their computing environment .

*This article describe research conducted at the Artificial Intelligence Laboratory of the Massachusetts Institute of Technology. Support for this research was provided by the Information Technology Office of the Defense Advanced Research Projects Agency (DARPA) under Space and Naval Warfare Systems Center - San Diego Contract Number N66001-00-C-8078. The views presented are those of the author alone and do not represent the view of DARPA or SPAWAR.

Background and Motivation

The infrastructure of modern society is controlled by computational systems that are vulnerabile to information attacks. A skillful attack could lead to consequences as dire as those of modern warfare. There is a pressing need for new approaches to protect our computational infrastructure from such attacks and to enable it to continue functioning even when attacks have been successfully launched.

Our presmise is that to protect the infrastructure we need to restructure these software systems as *Self-Adaptive Survivable Systems*. Such software systems must be informed by a *trust-model* that indicates which resources are to be trusted. When such a system starts a task, it chooses that method which the trust-model indicates is most likely to avoid compromised resources. In addition, such a system must be capable of detecting its own malfunction, it must be able to *diagnose* the failure and it must be capable of repairing itself after the failure. For example, a system might notice through self-monitoring that it is running much slower than expected. It might, therfore, deduce that the scheduler of the computer it is running on has been compromised and that the compromise resulted from the use of a buffer overflow attack that gained root access to the system and used this priviledge to change the scheduler policy. The buffer overflow attack in turn might have exploited a vulnerability of a web server (as for example happened in the "code-red" attack). Given this diagnosis, the trust model should be updated to indicate that the computer's operating system was compromised and should be avoided in the future if possible. Techniques for this type of diagnosis are described in (Shrobe 2001).

The trust model is also influenced by collating evidence from many available sources over a long period of time. In our lab, for example, we notice several alerts from our intrusion detection system over a couple a days. This was followed by a period in which nothing anomalous happened. But then we began to notice that the consumption of disk space and the amount of network traffic from outside the lab were increasing and this continued for some time. Then the load leveled off. What had happened is that a user password had been stolen and that a public ftp site had been set up for the use of the friends of the password thief. This incident is an instance of a very common *attack plan*. Such attack plans have multiple stages, temporal constraints between the stages, and constraints within each stage on values and their derivatives (e.g. the rate of growth of disk space consumption). These can, thefore, be used as "trend templates" for collating and analyzing the alerts from intrusion detection systems and the data in common system logs. This provides perspective over a longer period of time than the intrusion detection systems themselves possess, allowing detection of attacks that are intentionally subtle. Long-term monitoring systems capable of conducting trend template driven attack plan recognition are described in (Doyle *et al.* 2001a; 2001b).

Trust modeling thus depends both on attack plan recognition as well as on the self-diagnosis of self-adaptive software systems. The resulting trust model includes models of what computational resources have been *compromised*, what *attacks* were used to effect this attack and what *vulnerability* was exploited by the attack. Key to all these tasks is having a comprehensive set of attack models.

This paper focuses on Computational Vulnerability Analysis, a systematic method for developing attack models used both in attack plan recognition and self-diagnosis of adaptive systems. All current systems are driven either by *signatures* of specific exploits (e.g. the tell-tales of a password scan) or by *anomaly profiling* (e.g. detecting a difference in behavior between the current process and a statistical norm). Neither of these alone is capable of dealing with a skillful attacker who would stage his attack slowly to avoid detection, would move in stages and would use a compromise at one stage to gain access to more valuable resources later on. The systematic nature of Computation Vulnerability Analysis and the use of its attack plans in both long-term monitoring and in self-diagnosing adaptive systems leads to increased precision in trust modeling and greater survivability of critical systems.

Contributions of this Work

We develop a model-based technique, which we call Computational Vulnerability Analysis, for analyzing vulnerabilities and attacks. Rather than relying on a catalog of known specific attacks we instead reason from first principles to develop a much more comprehensive analysis of the vulnerabilities. Furthermore, the attacks developed in this analysis include both single stage attacks as well as multi-stage attacks. These are crucial issues when failure is caused by a concerted attack by a malicious opponent who is attempting to avoid detection.

We develop a unified framework for reasoning about the failures of computations, about how these failures are related to compromises of the underlying resources, about the vulnerabilities of these resources and how these vulnerabilities enable attacks. We then extend previous work in Model-Based diagnosis (Davis & Shrobe 1982; deKleer & Williams 1987; 1989; Hamscher & Davis 1988; Srinivas 1995) to enable systems capable of self-diagnosis, recovery and adaptation. We also use this framework in building long term monitoring systems (Doyle *et al.* 2001a; 2001b) capable of attack plan recognition. Both attack plan recognition and self-diagnosis lead to updated estimates of

the trustability of the computational resources. These estimates, which form the trust model, inform all future decision making about how to achieve goals.

In addition to its role in Survivable Systems, Computational Vulnerability Analysis can also be used offline to assess the vulnerability of and to identify weak links in a computational environment. This can help system administrators improve the security and robustness of their network, often by instituting simple changes. We are currently using the system, in a limited way, to assess the vulnerabilities of our lab's computing environment; as the system matures we plan to apply it more systematically to the entire lab. We are also in the process of connecting the computation vulnerability analysis system to our long-term monitoring system, and of connecting the monitoring system to a commercial instrusion detector. We plan to begin deploying this monitoring system within the next six months.

This paper first describes the modeling framework and reasoning processes used in computational vulnerability analysis and shows its application to a small section of our lab's computing environment. We conclude by explaing how attack plans fit within the self-diagnostic and the long-term monitoring frameworks.

Computational Vulnerability Analysis

In this section we examine the core issue of this paper which is how to make the modeling of attacks and vulnerabilities systematic.

We do this by grounding the analysis in a comprehensive ontology that covers:

- System properties
- System Types
- System structure
- The control and dependency relationships between system components.

.

This ontology covers what types of computing resources are present in the environment, how the resources are composed from components (e.g. an operating system has a scheduler, a file system, etc.), how the components control one another's behavior, and what vulnerabilities are known to be present in different classes of these components. Finally, the models indicate how desirable properties of such systems depend on the correct functioning of certain components of the system (for example, predicatable performance of a computer system depends on the correct functioning of its scheduler).

A relatively simple reasoning process (encoded in a rule-based system) then explores how a desirable property of a system can be impacted (e.g. you can impact the predictability of performance by affecting the scheduler, which in turn can be done by changing its input parameters which in turn can be done by gaining root access which finally is enabled by a buffer overflow attack on a process running with root priviledges). The output of this reasoning is a set of multi-stage attacks, each of which is capable of affecting the property of interest.

We also provide a structural model of the entire computing environment under consideration, including:

- Network structure and Topology
  - How is the network decomposed into subnets
  - Which nodes are on which subnets
  - Which routers and switches connect the subnets
  - What types of filters and firewalls provide control of the information flow between subnets
- System types:
  - What type of hardware is in each node
  - How is the hardware decomposed into sub-systems
  - What type of operating system is in each node
  - How is the operating system decomposed into subsystems
- Server and user software suites: What software functionality is deployed on each node.
- What are the access rights to data and how are they controlled
- What are the places in which data is stored or transmitted

The next step is to model dependencies. To do this we begin with a list of desirable properties that the computational resources are supposed to deliver. Typical properties include:

- Reliable Performance
- Privacy of Communications
- Integrity of Communications
- Integrity of Stored Data
- Privacy of Stored Data

Within the diagnostic framewok each such property corresponds to a normal behavioral mode of some (or several) computational resource(s). For example, reliable computational performance is a property to which the scheduler contributes while data privacy is a property contributed by the access-control mechanisms.

Control Relationships

We now turn our attention to a rule-base that uses this ontology to reason about how one might affect a desirable property. Our goal is to make this rule base as abstract and general as possible. For example, one such abstract rule says (this is a paraphrase of the actual rule, which is coded in a Lisp-based rule system):

```
If the goal is to affect the
  reliable-performance
  property of some component ?x
Then find a component ?y of ?x that
  contributesto the delivery
  of that property
 and find a way to control ?y
```

This puts the notion of control and dependency at the center of the reasoning process. There are several rules about how to gain control of components, which are quite general. The following are examples of such general and abstract rules:

```
If the goal is to control a compo-
nent ?x
Then find an input ?y to ?x
 and find a way to modify ?y

If the goal is to control a compo-
nent ?x
Then find a component ?y of ?x
 and find a way to control ?y

If the goal is to control a compo-
nent ?x
Then find a vulnerability ?y
     of the component ?x
 and find a way to exploit ?y
     to take control of ?x.
```

At the leaves of this reasoning chain is specific information about vulnerabilities and how to exploit them. For example:

- Microsoft IIS web-servers below a certain patch level are vulnerable to buffer overflow attacks.
- Buffer overflow attacks are capable of taking control of the components that are vulnerable.

One of the rules shown above indicates that one can control a component by modifying its inputs. The following rules describe how this can be done:

```
If the goal is to modify an input ?x of
    component ?y
then find a component ?z which control
    the input ?x
 and find a way to gain control of ?z

If the goal is to modify an input ?x
   of component ?y
then find a component ?z of the in-
put ?x
 and find a way to modify ?z
```

Access Rights

Within most computer systems the ability to read or modify data depends on obtaining access rights to that data. We model access rights in a more general way than is used in many actual systems:

- For each type of object we enumerate the *operations* that can be performed on objects of that type.
- For each operation we specify the *capabilities* that are required to perform the operation

- The capabilities are related by a subsumption relationship that forms a DAG.

- For each agent (i.e. a user or a process) we enumerate the capabilities that the agent possesses at any time.

- An agent is assumed to be able to perform an operation on an object only if it possesses a capability at least as strong as that required for the operation.

- Typically groups of machines manages access rights collectively (e.g. workgroups in MS Windows, NIS in Unix environments). We refer to such a collection of machines as an *access pool*.

- The structure of access pools may be orthogonal to the network topology. Machines in different subnets may be parts of the same access pool, while machines on a common subnet may be members of different access pools.

Given this framework we provide rules that describe how to gain access to objects:

```
If the goal is to gain access to opera-
tion ?x
   on object ?y
and operation ?x on ?y requires capil-
ity ?z
then find a process ?p whose capabil-
ity ?w
      subsumes ?z
 and find a way to take control of ?p.

If the goal is to gain access to opera-
tion ?x
   on object ?y
and operation ?x on ?y requires capil-
ity ?z
then find a user ?u whose capability ?w
      subsumes ?z
 and find a way to log in as ?u
 and launch a process ?p with capa-
bilty ?w
```

Knowledge of Secrets

Logging on to a system typically requires knowledge of a secret (e.g. a password). A set of rules describes how to obtain knowledge of a password:

- To obtain knowledge of a password, find it by guessing, using a guessing attack.

- To obtain knowledge of a password, Sniff it.

  - To sniff a piece of data place a parasitic virus on the user's machine
  - To sniff a piece of data monitor network traffic that might contain the datam
  - To sniff a piece of data find a file containing the data and gain access to it.

- To obtain knowledge of a password, gain write access to the password file and change it.

Network Structure

The next section of rules deal with networks. As mentioned above, networks are described in terms of the decomposition into subnets and the connections of subnets by routers and switches. In addition, for each subnet we provide a description of the media type; some subnets are shared media, for example coaxial-cable based ethernet and wireless ethernet. In such subnets, any connected computer can monitor any of the traffic. Other subnets are switched media (e.g. 10, 100, and 1000 base-T type ethernet); in these network only the switch sees all the traffic (although it is possible to direct the switch to reflect all traffic to a specific port). Switches and routers are themselves computers that have presence on the network; this means that, like any other computer, there are exploits that will gain control of them. However, it is typical that the switches and routers are members of a special access pool, using separate capabilities and passwords.

Given this descriptive machinery it now becomes possible to provide another rule:

```
To gain knowledge of some information
 gain the ability to monitor net-
work traffic.
```

Residences and Format Transformations

The last set of modeling issues have to do with the various places in which data live and how data is transformed between various representations. The following issues are modeled:

- Data elements reside in many places
- Executable code resides in many place
  - Main memory
  - Boot files
  - Paging files
- Data elements and code move between their various residences
  - Data migrations go through peripheral controllers
  - Data migrations go thorugh networks

Given these representations we then provide the following rules:

- To modify or observe a data element find a residence of the element and find a way to modify or observe it in that residence.

- To modify or observe a data element find a migration path and find a way to modify or observe it during the transmission.

Further rules provide details of how one might gain control of a peripheral controller or of a network segment so as to modify data during transmission. For example:

- To control traffic on a network segment launch "A man in the middle attack" by gaining control of a machine on the network and then finding a way to redirect traffic to that machine rather than to the router or switch.

- To observe network traffic get control of a switch or router and a user machine and the reflect the traffic to the user machine.
- To modify network traffic, launch an "inserted packet" attack. To do this get control of machine on the network and then send a packet from that machine with the correct serial number but wrong data before the real sender sends the correct data.

A somewhat analogous issue has to do with the various formats that data and code take on and the processes that transform data and code between these formats. In particular, code can exist in at least the following formats: Source, compiled, linked executable images. In many systems there are other representations as well (e.g. JAR files for Java code). In addition, processes such as compilation and linking transform code between these formats. This leads to the following rules:

- To modify a software component find an upstream representation of that component and then find a way to modify that representation and to cause the transformation between representations to happen.
- To modify a software component gain control of the processes that perform the transformation from upstream to downstrem representation.

An Example

The following example illustrate how these representations and rules interact to analyze the vulnerabilities of a computer. Suppose we are interested in affecting the performance of a specific computer. The rule-base would then generate the following plan:

- One goal is to control the scheduler of the computer because the scheduler is a component that impacts performance.
- One way to do that is to modify the scheduler's policy parameters because the policy parameters are inputs to the scheduler.
- One way to do that is by gaining root access to the computer because root access is required to modify these parameters.
- One way to do that is to use a buffer overflow attack on a web server because the web-server possesses root capabilities and the web-server is vulnerable to buffer-overflow attacks.

For this attack to succeed in impacting performance every step of the plan must succeed. Each of these steps has an *a apriori* probability based on its inherent difficulty.

The analysis process must take into account not just the general strategies but also the specific features of individual machines, network segments, routers, fire-walls, packet-filters etc. The attack plans include only those which satisfy all these constraints. A computer may be vulnerable to an exploit but if there is a fire-wall isolating it from the attacker, the analysis will not develop an attack plan exploiting that vulnerability.

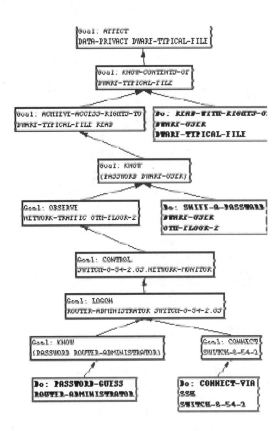

Figure 1: A Plan for Affecting Privacy

Figures 1 and 2 show 2 attack plans that our system developed to attack privacy. Other plans developed are more complex. Each plan is an And-Or tree (Goal nodes are Or nodes, they may have several incoming links from Plan nodes; all that is required is that one of the plans work. Plan nodes are And nodes; each sub-goal must be fulfilled for a plan to be valid) The leaves of the tree are primitive actions, i.e. actual attack steps. The figures show one slice through the and-or tree for simplicity.

For the given system description our vulnerability analyzer generated 7 attack plans for the privacy property and 9 plans for attacking performance.

We now turn briefly to the question of how the attack plans are utilitzed in diagnostic reasoning and in long term

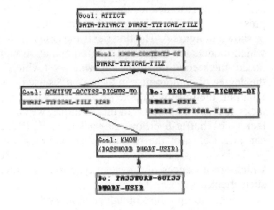

Figure 2: A Second Plan for Affecting Privacy

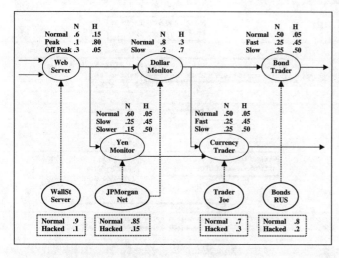

Figure 3: An Example of the Extended System Modeling Framework

monitoring. In both cases, the attack plans are transformed: for diagnostic reasoning they are converted into components of a Bayesian network. In this form they help explain why a computation has failed and they also deduce what resources are therefore likely to have been compromised. For long-term monitoring they are transformed into "trend-templates". In this format they function as a timeline for how a skillful attacker would stage an assault on the analyzed network. The monitoring system accepts and collates inputs from intrusion detectors, fire-walls, and self-monitoring applications in an attempt to detect more pernicious, multistage attacks.

We will briefly describe each use in the next two sections.

Application to Diagnosis

Figure 3 shows a model of a fictitious distributed financial system which we use to illustrate the reasoning process. The system consists of five interconnected software modules (Web-server, Dollar-Monitor, Bond-Trader, Yen-Monitor, Currency-Trader) utilizing four underlying computational resources (i.e. the computers WallSt-Server, JPMorgan, BondRUs, Trader-Joe). We use computational vulnerability analysis to deduce that one or more attack types are present in the environment, leading to a three-tiered model as shown in figure 4. The first tier is the *computational* level which models the behavior of the computation being diagnosed; the second tier is the *resource* level which monitors the degree of compromise in the resources used in the computation; the third tier is the *attack* layer which models attacks and vulnerabilities. In this example, we show two attack types, buffer-overflow and packet-flood. Packet-floods can affect each of the resources because they are all networked systems; buffer-overflows affect only the 2 resources which are instances of a system type that is vulnerable to such attacks.

A single compromise of an operating system component, such as the scheduler, can lead to anomalous behavior in several application components. This is an example of a

common mode failure; intuitively, a common mode failure occurs when a single fault (e.g. an inaccurate power supply), leads to faults at several observable points in the systems (e.g. several transistors misbehave because their biasing power is incorrect). Formally, there is a common mode failure whenever the probabilities of the failure modes of two (or more) components are dependent.

We deal with common mode failures as follows: Our modeling framework includes three kinds of objects: computational components (represented by a set of input-output relationships and delay models one for each behavioral mode), infrastructural resources (e.g. computers) and attacks. Connecting the first two kinds of models are conditional probability links; each such link states how likely a particular behavioral mode of a computational component would be if the infrastructural component that supports that component were in a particular one of its modes (e.g. normal or abnormal). We next observe that resources are compromised by attacks that are enabled by vulnerabilities. An attack is capable of compromising a resource in a variety of ways; for example, buffer overflow attacks are used both to gain control of a specific component and to gain root access to the entire system. But the variety of compromises enabled by an attack are not equally likely (some are much more difficult than others). We therefore have a third tier in our model describing the ensemble of attacks assumed to be available in the environment and we connect the attack layer to the resource layer with conditional probability links that state the likelikhood of each mode of the compromised resource once the attack has been successful. The attack plans generated by computational vulnerability analysis constitute this third tier. However a transformation is required for them to fulfill this role. Attack plans are And-Or trees. However, it is possible (and in fact likely) that different attack plans share sub-plans (e.g. lots of multi-stage attacks begin with a buffer-overflow attack being used to gain root priviledge). Therefore, all the attack plans are merged into a single And-Or tree which constitutes the third tier of the model. The top-level nodes of this tree, which model the desirable properties of the computational resources, are then connected to the second tier (the resource layer) of the model.

We will next briefly describe how the diagnostic and monitoring processes use attack plans.

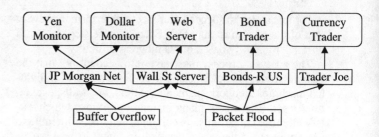

Figure 4: An Example of the Three Tiered System Modeling Framework

Diagnostic Reasoning

Diagnosis is initiated when a discrepancy is detected between the expected and actual behaviors of a computation. We use techniques similar to (deKleer & Williams 1989; Srinivas 1995). We first identify all *conflict sets* (a choice of behavior modes for each of the computational components that leads to a contradiction) and then proceed to calculate the posterior probabilities of the modes of each of the components. Conflicts are detected by choosing a behavioral mode for each computational component and then running each of the selected behavioral models. If this leads to a contradiction, then the choice of models is a conflict set. Otherwise it is a consistent diagnosis.

Whenever the reasoning process discovers a conflict it use dependency tracing (i.e. its Truth Maintenance System) to find the subset of the models in the conflict set that actually contributed to the discrepancy. At this point a new node is added to the Bayesian network representing the conflict. This node has an incoming arc from every node that participates in the conflict. It has a conditional probability table corresponding to a pure "logical and" i.e. its true state has a probability of 1.0 if all the incoming nodes are in their true states and it otherwise has probability 1.0 of being in its false state. Since this node represents a logical contradiction, it is pinned in its false state.

We continue until all possible minimal conflicts are discovered, extending the Bayesian network with a new node for each. At this point any remaining set of behavioral models is a consistent diagnosis; we choose the minimal such sets (i.e we discard any diagnosis that is a superset of some other diagnosis). For each of these we create a node in the Bayesian network which is the logical-and of the nodes corresponding to the behavioral modes of the components. This node represents the probability of this particular diagnosis. The Bayesian network is then solved giving us updated probabilities.

The sample system shown in Figure 3 was run through several analyses including both those in which the outputs are within the expected range and those in which the outputs are unexpected. Figure 5 shows the results of the analysis. There are four runs for each case, each with a different attack model developed by Computational Vulnerability Analysis. In the first, there are no attacks present and the *a priori* values are used for the probabilities of the different modes of each resource. The second run takes place in an environment in which only a buffer-overflow attack is possible; the third run includes only a packet-flood attack. The fourth run is in an environment in which both types of attacks are possible. Note that the posterior probabities are different in each case. This is because each set of attack models couples the resource models in a unique manner. These posterior probabilities may be then used to update the overall trust model, as each run provides some evidence about compromises to the resources involved. Futhermore, it is possible that a successful attack would have affected additional resources that were not used in the computation being diagnosed; this suspicion is propagated by the Bayesian network. In effect, the reasoning is: the failure of the computation is evidence that a resource has been compromised; this, in turn, is evidence that an attack has succeeded. But if the attack has succeeded, then other resources sharing the vulnerability might also have been compromised and should be trusted somewhat less in the future.

Slow Fault on both outputs 25 "Diagnoses"
34 Minimal Conflicts
Output of Bond-Trader Observed at 35
Output of Current-trader Observed at 45

Name	Prior	Posterior			
Wallst	.1	.27	.58	.75	.80
JPMorgan	.15	.45	.62	.74	.81
Bonds-R-Us	.20	21	.20	.61	.50
Trader-Joe	.30	.32	.31	.62	.50

Computations Using Each Resource					
Web-Server	Off-Peak	.03	.02	.02	.02
	Peak	.54	.70	.78	.80
	Normal	.43	.28	.20	.18
Dollar-Monitor	Slow	.74	.76	.73	.76
	Normal	.26	.24	.27	.24
Yen-Monitor	Really-Slow	.52	.54	.56	.58
	Slow	.34	.35	.34	.34
	Normal	.14	.11	.10	.08
Bond-Trader	Slow	.59	.57	.76	.70
	Fast	0	0	0	0
	Normal	.41	.43	.24	.30
Currency-Trader	Slow	.61	.54	.62	.56
	Fast	.07	.11	.16	.16
	Normal	.32	.35	.22	.28

Attack Types		Attacks Possible			
Name	Prior	None	Buffer-Overflow	Packet-Flood	Both
Buffer-Overflow	.4	0	.82	0	.58
Packet-Flood	.5	0	0	.89	.73

Figure 5: Updated Probabilities

Application to Long Term Monitoring

The long term monitoring system accepts inputs from intrusion-detectors, fire-walls, system logs, and self-diagnostic application systems and attempts to recognize multi-stage concerted attacks that would otherwise escape attention. Skillful attackers move slowly, first scoping out the structure and weaknesses of a computational environment, then slowly gaining access to resources. Often the process is staged: access to one resource is used to gain more information about the environment and more access to other resources within it. Computational Vulnerability analysis produces attack plans very much like those developed by such skillful attackers (in particular, "Red-Teamers" people who simulate attackers as part of exercises, report thought processes very similar to those developed by our tool).

The monitoring system performs many low level filtering, collating and conditioning functions on the data. Once these operations have been performed, the system attempts to match the data streams to a "trend template" a model of how a process evolves over time. A trend template is broken along one dimension into data segments, each representing a particular input or the product of applying some filter (i.e smoothing, derivate) to some other data segment. On another dimension, the template is broken into temporal intervals with landmark points separating them. There are constraints linking the data values within the segments (e.g. during this period disk consumption on system-1 is growing rapidly while network traffic is stable). There are also constraints on the length of time in each interval and on the relative placement of the landmark points (e.g. the period of disk consumption must be between 3 days and 2 weeks; the start of disk consumption must follow the start of network traffic growth).

Trend template recognition is a difficult process. It involves making (usually multiple) assumptions about where each interval begins and then tracking the data as it arrives to determine which hypothesis best matches the data. Within each interval regression analysis is used to determine degree of fit to the hypothesis. More details are provided in (Doyle *et al.* 2001b).

One source of trend templates is computational vulnerability analysis. Each attack plan actually constitutes a set of trend-templates; this is because the attack plans are developed as And-Or trees. In contrast to the diagnostic application where the plans are merged, here we unfold each individual attack plan into a set of individual plans by removing the Or nodes. Each unfolded plan, therefore, consists of a goal-node supported by a single plan-node which, in turn, is supported by a set of goal-nodes all of which must be satisfied for the plan to succeed (these goal-nodes are, in turn, supported by individual plan nodes; the recursion continues until terminated by a primitive action node). This tree represents a set of constraints on the temporal ordering: a goal is achieved after all the steps in the plan are achieved, but the plan steps may happen in parallel. Each step is characterized by expectations on the various data streams; we are currently developing the mappings between the attack plan steps and features of data streams that would be indicative of the plan step.

At any point in time, the Trend template matcher has an estimate for how well each template matches the data. These estimates are evidence that specific attacks have been launched against specific resources and are therefore also evidence about the degree and type of compromise present in each resource. Thus, this process too contributes to the overall trust model.

Conclusions and Future Work

We have shown how Computational Vulnerability Analysis can model an attack scenario, how such a model can drive both long-term monitoring and diagnostic processes that extract maximum information from the available data. In the case of diagnosis this means carefully analyzing how unexpected behavior might have arisen from compromises to the resources used in the computation. For long term monitoring, this means recognizing the signs of a multi-stage attack by collating evidence from many sources. Both processes contribute to an overall Trust Model.

The purpose of the Trust Model is to aid in recovering from a failure and to help avoid compromised resources in the future. The Trust Model functions at the levels of 1) observable behavior 2) the compromises to the underlying

computational resources and 3) the vulnerabilities and the attacks that exploit them.

Computational Vulnerability Analysis is an important part of this process. However, it has value beyond its contribution to self-adaptivity. Vulnerability assessments are a useful tool for system administrators as they attempt to keep their environments functioning. Often such an assessment can spot problems that can be corrected easily, for example by changing filtering rules or by adding a fire-wall. We have begun to use the tool in our own lab for such assessments and hope to use it more systematically as the coverage grows.

Computational Vulnerability Analysis can also be a valuable adjunct to intrusion detection systems, helping to collate events over a longer period into systematic attack plans. We have already begun to use this tool in a limited way in our lab to examine and prevent vulnerabilities in various subspaces. We are planning to add more expertise to the system and use it more widely in the future. We are also planning to integrate this tool with the lab's intrusion detection system.

References

Davis, R., and Shrobe, H. 1982. Diagnosis based on structure and function. In *Proceedings of the AAAI National Conference on Artificial Intelligence*, 137–142. AAAI.

deKleer, J., and Williams, B. 1987. Diagnosing multiple faults. *Artificial Intelligence* 32(1):97–130.

deKleer, J., and Williams, B. 1989. Diagnosis with behavior modes. In *Proceedings of the International Joint Conference on Artificial Intelligence*.

Doyle, J.; Kohone, I.; Long, W.; Shrobe, H.; and Szolovits, P. 2001a. Event recognition beyond signature and anomaly. In *Proceedings of the Second IEEE Information Assurance Workshop*. IEEE Computer Society.

Doyle, J.; Kohone, I.; Long, W.; Shrobe, H.; and Szolovits, P. 2001b. Agile monitoring for cyber defense. In *Proceedings of the Second Darpa Information Security Conference and Exhibition (DISCEX-II)*. IEEE Computer Society.

Hamscher, W., and Davis, R. 1988. Model-based reasoning: Troubleshooting. In Shrobe, H., ed., *Exploring Artificial Intelligence*. AAAI. 297–346.

Shrobe, H. 2001. Model-based diagnosis for information survivability. In Laddaga, R.; Robertson, P.; and Shrobe, H., eds., *Self-Adaptive Software*. Springer-Verlag.

Srinivas, S. 1995. Modeling techinques and algorithms for probablistic model-based diagnosis and repair. Technical Report STAN-CS-TR-95-1553, Stanford University, Stanford, CA.

A Web-based Ontology Browsing and Editing System

Jérôme Thoméré[1], Ken Barker[3,] Vinay Chaudhri[1], Peter Clark[2], Michael Eriksen[1], Sunil Mishra[1], Bruce Porter[3] and Andres Rodriguez[1]

[1]SRI International
333 Ravenswood Ave
Menlo Park, CA 94025
{thomere, acr, chaudhri, smishra, eriksen}
@ai.sri.com

[2]Boeing Research and Technology
P.O. Box 37070
Seattle, WA 98124
clarkp@redwood.rt.cs.boeing.com

[3]University of Texas
At Austin
Austin, TX 78712
{kbarker, porter}@cs.utexas.edu

Abstract

Making logic-based AI representations accessible to ordinary users has been an ongoing challenge for the successful deployment of knowledge bases. Past work to meet this objective has resulted in a variety of ontology editing tools and task-specific knowledge-acquisition methods. In this paper, we describe a Web-based ontology browsing and editing system with the following features: (a) well-organized English-like presentation of concept descriptions and (b) use of graphs to enter concept relationships, add/delete lists, and analogical correspondences. No existing tool supports these features. The system is Web-based and its user interface uses a mixture of HTML and Java. It has undergone significant testing and evaluation in the context of a real application.

Keywords: knowledge acquisition, expert systems, HTML, WWW.

Introduction

Our goal is to develop tools that enable domain experts to build knowledge bases (KBs) without relying on AI scientists and engineers. The KBs we envision are ones that support automated reasoning, not just string matching and information retrieval. That is, the KBs are written in a logical formalism, not a natural language.

Achieving this goal is essential for the efficacy of knowledge-based systems. Decades of research on knowledge representation and reasoning have produced the basic technology for knowledge-based systems, so knowledge capture is evermore the bottleneck. Three invariants are responsible for this bottleneck: significant KBs are required, domain experts lack the knowledge engineering skills to build them, and knowledge engineers lack the domain expertise to replace the experts.

Tools can help, and many have been built. Frame-based representation systems have included specialized editors such

as Protégé (Noy, Sintek et al. 2001), OntoEdit (Maedche 2000), Ontosaurus (Swartout, Patil et al. 1998), WebOnto (Domingue, Motta et al. 1999), and the Java Ontology Editor (Mahalingam and Huhns 1997). Graphical KB editors, such as the GKB-Editor (Paley and Karp 1996), use directed graphs as the primary means of interaction. Another approach is taken by task-specific knowledge-acquisition systems, such as EXPECT (Blythe, Kim et al. 2001), which is aimed at acquiring process knowledge. However, most of these tools are targeted toward users with significant experience of how knowledge is represented in a knowledge base.

Our research focuses on building a new class of tools for building and using KBs, ones that are used by domain experts with very little training. The new tools should enable domain experts to browse, create/edit, and query KBs—all without knowing logical formalisms and without assistance.

This paper describes one such tool: SHAKEN, built under the auspices of DARPA's Rapid Knowledge Formation (RKF) project. SHAKEN is a collection of modules for different KB interaction tasks: browsing, editing, and querying. Making SHAKEN usable by domain experts presented challenges for each of these modules.

The layout of the paper reflects these three major KB interaction tasks. We also describe an evaluation of SHAKEN by domain experts tasked with building KBs in a domain of biology.

Design Goals

SHAKEN was designed to satisfy the following criteria:

- It should be accessible to users not familiar with any formal logic notation.

- All the operations and interactions should be as simple as possible, and should not require more than a simple introduction.

- The presentation of the concepts, both graphical and textual, should be natural.

- The logical representations coming from the knowledge representation system should be transparent to the user.
- The editor should be accessible through a Web browser and should not require any installation at the user end.

Architecture

SHAKEN is implemented as a client-server system. The KB is stored in the Knowledge Machine (KM) representation system (Clark and Porter 1999). KM is object oriented and has the expressive power of full first-order logic. In addition, it supports a STRIPS representation of actions and a situation mechanism to represent different states of a KB. Knowledge analysis and analogy methods are reasoning services implemented on top of KM.

Most of the inference is done on the server side. It includes explanation design plans to describe concepts, analogy methods, and knowledge simulation to test the knowledge entered.

The server functionality is implemented using the allegro server from Allegro Common Lisp. The server is responsible for querying and modifying the KB, managing the interaction between the different components, and presenting the results to the user. The output is presented using HTML and XML. XML is used for representing the concepts, which are then parsed by the Java applet and rendered into graphs, akin to semantic networks.

The client can be an Internet browser. Most of the client functionality was implemented using HTML and JavaScript. The graphical editing was implemented using a Java applet.

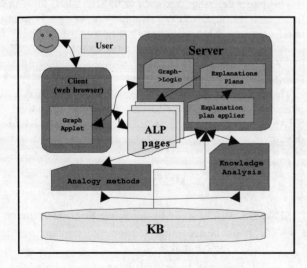

Figure1: SHAKEN architecture

To facilitate writing and debugging functions that generate HTML pages, we implemented a mechanism called Active Lisp Pages (ALP) (Rodriguez 2000), analogous to

Microsoft's ASP (Active Server pages). This mechanism allows the developers to mix HTML code and Lisp code.

On the client side, most of the user interaction takes place in the graph-editing tool, and the Graph→Logic module ensures the translation between graphs and the KB representation.

Browsing a Knowledge Base

From the user's point of view, there are two sides to browsing a KB: finding concepts and understanding the content of those concepts.

Finding Concepts

SHAKEN provides two tools for finding concepts in a KB: a taxonomy browser and a search facility.

The taxonomic view of a KB presents the class taxonomy, which can be incrementally expanded and contracted at the request of a user.

Using the search facility, the user can type a partial character string, and the system will return concept names that match that string.

SHAKEN also provides semantic searching—a function that traverses the WordNet (Al-Halimi, Berwick et al. 1998) hierarchy for terms semantically related to concepts in the KB. As part of the documentation for each concept in our core KB, we have identified the WordNet entries that most closely match the semantics of the concept. SHAKEN's WordNet-based search tool finds the search term in WordNet, and then climbs the hierarchy of hypernyms (more general terms), finding all concepts listing those hypernyms in their documentation.

One of the advantages of semantic searching is that results are sorted according to the WordNet distance between the search term and the concept, and to the depth of the concept in the hierarchy. This gives preference to more specific concepts, meaning that the user is more likely to choose a more specific (and therefore more semantically loaded) concept than when browsing top-down through the tree.

If at any point during the user interaction, a user needs to select a concept, an entry point to the browsing facility is provided. To get more information about the concepts in the taxonomy or returned by search, the user can inspect the concept, either as a formatted description or as a graph.

Showing the Content of Concepts

The formatted concept description view presented here has two novel aspects:
- Well-organized display of information
- English-like text generation

Here, we describe these novel aspects in more detail.

Concept Description

The concept description view uses the notion of explanation design plans (EDPs) to organize the presentation of information. The explanation design plan idea comes originally from a work by James Lester (Lester and Porter 1997) aimed at generating automatic English explanation of the contents of a KB. An explanation plan encodes the contents and the organization of an explanation. Every explanation plan is a tree, and the nodes at a particular level in the tree represent topics. A node n_1 is a parent of a node n_2 if n_2 is a subtopic of n_1. Explanation plans employ three basic types of node:

- Exposition node: primary topic of an explanation
- Topic node: subtopic of an explanation
- Content specification node: specification of the content to include

Explanation plans are rooted at exposition nodes. An exposition node constitutes the highest-level grouping of content, and the children of exposition nodes are topic nodes. The children of topic nodes are content specification nodes, which name KB accessors. The child of a content specification node is a view, which is constructed by applying a KB accessor(Acker and Porter 1994). The realization system generates one or a small number of sentences for each view. In short, explanation plans store a formal representation of an explanation's content and organization.

Here are three examples corresponding to the three types of node used:

Exposition node: Process

```
Process Overview
   Text Description
   Type
   Participants
Process Details
   Qualitative Description
      Subevents
   Location Description
   Condition Description
   Temporal Information
   Object Function
      Telic Description
```

Topic node: Location description

```
Location Description
   Location
   Origination
   Destination
```

Content specification node: Location

```
Location
   Make-location-view
```

Each content specification node corresponds to a view in the KB: a view is simply a subset of slots of an object. For instance, the slot "is-between" is associated with the *Location* view. To display a view, we assemble the values of the slots associated with this view. In the above example, *make-location-view* is the name of the function that computes the values of this view.

Implementation of Explanation Design Plans. The EDPs are implemented in a single KB using an OKBC server. Each one of the nodes is represented by a frame in the KB. The KB contains two main EDPs: explain-process and explain-object. The hierarchical structure of the explanation plans is naturally represented as a hierarchy of frames.

For example, 'Exposition node' is represented as a class with two slots: 'Display name' and 'Children'. 'Display name' records the label used for displaying the heading of the information appearing under the exposition node, and 'Children' are the subheadings—for example, 'Qualitative description' and 'Location description'. 'Location description' is itself represented as a frame with two slots: 'Display name' and the name of the function used to compute the location information.

Displaying Knowledge Base Contents in English

Within the concept description defined above, the problem is to describe values of slots in the KB in a form that is as close as possible to the English an expert is used to, while not getting too far from the structure of the KB itself.

To achieve this objective, we have used a simple rule-based module that translates an expression from the KB formalism to an English sentence. This allows us to take into account both the general cases of common KB structures and some particular cases that otherwise would lead to clumsy sentences.

In full generality, displaying the contents of a KB in English would involve dealing with arbitrary logical sentences. As an initial simplification of this complexity, to display a concept, we create an example instance of it and compute various slot values by applying the relevant rules. As a result, we show only those slot values and never expose the actual rules to a user.

While some of the slot values are classes, many of them are Skolem individuals. Classes can be represented to a user simply by their names. But for Skolem individuals, we need a friendly mechanism for presentation. Since KM KBs also contain STRIPS representation of actions, we also need some way of displaying the add/delete precondition and negated condition lists. Here, we discuss how we generate English for each of those types of KB content.

Displaying Skolem Individuals. In the simplest case, a Skolem individual is displayed as "a <CLASS>" where <CLASS> is the direct type of that individual.

For individuals that are instances of abstract classes, it is not very friendly to display text such as "a Tangible-Entity" or "a Place". Therefore, we instead display how this Skolem individual is related to the concept that is being currently displayed. For example "a Place" may be replaced by "the location of the object of the Invasion". In other words, we need to find a path of slots between the Skolem individual and the concept being displayed.

Here is a brief description of the algorithm we use to find the path. We start from the concept being displayed (the root) and loop over its children (the set of its slot values) and recurse until we hit the target.

```
Find-path(nd, tgt):
  if path{nd, tgt}
    then return it
    else
    for slot ∈ get-frame-slots(nd)
     ∃ find-path(get-slot-value(nd, slot), tgt)
    path{nd, tgt} ← slot & path-found
```

We also want to avoid paths that are overly complex and not easily understood. For example, "the location of the object of the next-event of the first-subevent of the Invasion" can naturally be further simplified. To keep the paths meaningful, we use the following two techniques:

- Look only for the shortest path.
- Stop searching for a path as soon as we encounter a class that is not too general.

These two heuristics proved sufficient in practice.

Displaying conditions: add- and delete-lists. SHAKEN uses a STRIPS-style representation for encoding change. Actions are events that change the state of the world. Thus, the application of an action in a situation is modeled by the creation of a new situation, reflecting the new world state after the action has been performed.

Actions are described using four lists, namely, the 'pcs_list' (preconditions list), the 'ncs_list' (negated preconditions list), the 'add_list' (add list), and the 'del_list' (delete list). The pcs_list (resp. ncs-list) contains a list of ground literals that are necessarily true (resp false) before an action is performed; the add_list (resp del-list) contains propositions that are necessarily true (resp false) after the action is performed. These lists are stored as slot values, on the frame representing the action. A proposition is a reified expression (i.e., an expression represented as an object), and allows us to make statements about that proposition P—for example, "Fred believes P"— or, for our purposes here, "the result of doing X is P"'.

A proposition is represented in KM by the structure `(:triple frame slot value)`, which denotes the assertion that `frame`'s `slot` includes `value`.

For instance, the class Move will have in its add list the triple `(:triple (the object of Self) location (the destination of Self))`, which means that when the action Move is simulated, a new situation is created where the value of the slot location for the object of the Move is the same as the value of the slot destination of this instance of Move.

To get the results shown on the second column, we used a recursive rule-based pattern matcher that translates KM expressions into lists of words.

Form	Display

`(:triple`
`(the object of Self)`
`location`
`(the destination of Self)`
`)`
	The location of the object of the action must be the destination of the action

`(:triple`
`_Breach12`
`result`
`(a Be-Broken with`
`(object  Membrane13))`
	The result of the Breach is that the Membrane is broken

The second example illustrates a need to be able to generate meaningful text for specific objects, in this case a specific Be-Broken whose object is a particular Membrane. When a fuller description of such a concept is desired, SHAKEN can generate an English description that includes selected slots of a concept. The slots relevant in a concise description depend on which concept is being described.

Displaying Axioms. In SHAKEN's core KB we have encoded relevant English phrases and the grammar rules for combining them. The phrases and rules are distributed throughout the KB, allowing text generation particular to each concept. Rules and phrases inherit, but may be overridden by more specific concepts in the taxonomy. New concepts inherit default text generation rules.

Here are some examples of the description generated for particular concepts:

Form	Display
`(a Move)`	Something moves.

`(a Move with`
`(object _Car5)`
`(agent *Wilma))`
	Wilma moves the car.

`(a Be-Touching with`
`(object _Wire6 _Terminal7`
`)`
	The wire and the terminal are touching

`(a Deliver          with`
`(object _Mail9)`
`(recipient *Stacy))`
	The mail gets delivered to Stacy

Editing a Knowledge Base

A comprehensive solution for editing a KB should support the editing of several kinds of knowledge, such as class-subclass, slot values, constraints on slot values, axioms, and process knowledge. Our previous work on GKB-Editor was directed at editing class hierarchies, slots, slot values, and slot constraints. The focus in the present work is on editing axioms. The editing system described here enables the knowledge entry of an interesting class of axioms by abstraction from the example graphical description of a concept. The technical details of the abstraction process and mapping from directed graphs to logical form are described elsewhere (Clark, Thompson et al. 2001) and are not a primary subject of discussion here. Instead, we focus on the graphical aspects of the tool, and assuming the availability of a module to convert graphs to logic, show how graphs can be used for entering add/delete lists, for analogical correspondences, and for asking questions.

From Graphs to Axioms

To use graphs for editing axioms, we need a scheme that, given an axiom, defines its graphical presentation and vice versa. To present the axioms about a concept, the raw axioms are not presented directly, but through an example of the concept, as a set of ground facts. Ground facts are graphable and provide a summary of the concept.

For instance, suppose the user wants to build a representation of how a virus invades a cell. To display this concept to the user, the system creates an instance of this class, and for each slot of these classes creates Skolem individuals corresponding to the value of that slot. This process is recursive, and is initially applied to a fixed depth limit. The user can later selectively expand portions of the graph.

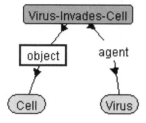

Figure 2: Early graph of VirusInvadesCell

Then, a graph is displayed, representing the concept VirusInvadesCell. Each node of the graph represents one of the Skolem individuals created. Each oriented link represents a slot, the end of the link being the value of the slot.

For such a graph, axioms could be synthesized as follows: first, the axiom is rephrased to mention only the "root" Skolem individual. For instance "Tangible-Entity3 is a Cell" becomes "the object of VirusInvadesCell1 is a Cell". This means that a path of relationships from the root to the instance replaces every "non root" individual. Then, it is generalized to hold for all instances of the Concept being defined. The final axiom thus has the form:

```
∀r isa (r , VirusInvadesCell) ⇒
(∀v objectr(r, v) ⇒isa (v, Cell))
```

Look and Feel of the Interface. The graphical interface to manipulate graphs is flexible enough to allow the subject matter expert (or end user) to feel like he is using a drawing application, but at the same time to allow construction of only "meaningful" and "correct" graphs. A tool called Concept Maps (Novak 2001) has been built by research members of the team at the University of West Florida. The goal of Concept Maps is to allow people to represent, organize, and share knowledge, knowledge being described as

relationships between concepts and being communicated in terms of graphs. The Concept Maps tool allows arbitrary graphs without any logical semantics. The graphical interface in SHAKEN is designed to feel as nonrestrictive as possible, while at the same time allowing only operations that have rigorous declarative semantics.

Since we are dealing with graphs, we have many helpful mechanisms other than written text with which to convey information to the user. A list of such mechanisms would include color and size of elements, distance between them, and horizontal/vertical order. The interface allows the user the use of such mechanisms to facilitate the construction of knowledge.

Operations to Manage the Graph. Most graphs representing concepts are virtually infinite, since for a KB to be useful, all the concepts are linked together in one sense or another. Therefore, we limit the graph we present to the user, but in the meantime, she has the ability to explore deeply into the structure of a concept. We achieve that by first limiting the depth of the initial display that is presented to the user to one or two levels, and second by managing two types of slot according to their importance. The initial display of a component shows only the abridged description. The user can then expand each one of the display nodes and also decide to view the full description. Nodes can be further expanded or contracted.

Layout Scheme. In essence, the display of graphs is hierarchical, since it starts from the concept being represented (shown in a different color), and then displays the values of its slots. Each of these values is itself a concept, so, it can be represented the same way. That does not mean that the graphs represented are trees or even directed acyclic graphs, since some of the nodes being expanded could point to nodes already present in the graphs.

The first time a concept map is drawn, the layout is automatically generated by the system, using a simple tree drawing algorithm. Assuming all the edges "cost" the same, the minimal spanning tree is calculated and the position for each node is determined. Then, all the edges from the original graph are added, completing the initial representation of the graph. Because the nodes are text, the original tree-drawing algorithm tends to generate excessively wide graphs. To resolve this, we stack nodes having the exact same edge to their parent. This approach shows trees that are more balanced in the vertical and horizontal directions.

Once the starting tree is drawn, the user is in complete control of how things will look. The user can move nodes around, organize them, and display or undisplay selectively. The user can drill down into the concepts, or add more nodes to the graph. The rendering engine must find space in the panel to fit in the nodes in a way that is intuitive and as unobtrusive as possible, so as to not interfere with the nodes that are already in the panel. This type of graph drawing algorithm is called "incremental layout algorithms". SHAKEN takes the following approach to an incremental layout: whenever it encounters a node that has not been rendered, it finds the first ancestor that existed in the original graph, and uses the tree drawing algorithm locally, starting from that existing node. The local tree drawing must respect position for preexisting nodes; otherwise, a new node pointing back to some original node might reorganize the whole graph. This approach might overlap certain nodes, but under the presumption that the user will reorganize things as she sees fit, this is not a big issue.

Implementation of the Interface. The graphical tool is implemented as a Java applet that is embedded in an HTML page. The use of a Java applet is important because, since SHAKEN is a geographically distributed research application, we are able to deliver ongoing developments to the rest of the team and potential end users. The applet can then communicate to the server by using XML messaging over HTTP. The communication between the applet and its context page (the browser) is kept at a minimum.

The typical interaction between a user and SHAKEN's graphical toolkit is for the user to open a concept (for construction or browsing). The applet is given, as a parameter, the name and nature of that concept. Then, the conversation between the applet and the server begins: the applet sends a message requesting the concept, and the server responds by sending an XML representation of the graph (loosely based on GraphXML (Herman 2000)). The applet then must parse the XML message and take appropriate action. All communication between the applet and the server occurs in this fashion. To avoid a potentially big communication overhead, the applet accumulates state (i.e., position of nodes) about the graph at the client end. It communicates with the server only when absolutely necessary.

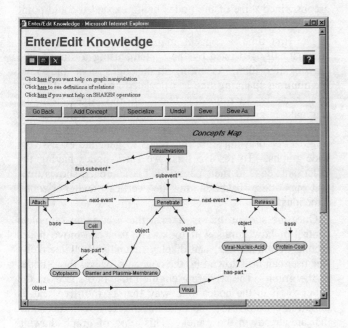

Figure 3: View of the graphical interface

Graphs for Knowledge Entry

Graphical editing operations were described in detail in a previous paper (Clark, Thompson et al. 2001). Here, we summarize those operations.

Add Concept. This operation consists in selecting any existing concept and adding it to the graph being edited. This does not link the user to any other node of the graph.

Specialize. This means selecting an existing node and changing its class by selecting one of its subclasses.

Connect. This is probably the most important operation: it allows the user to draw a relation between two concepts of the graph: she simply draws a line between two nodes, and then the system asks her to select a relation from a list of relations compatible with the two concepts being connected.

Unify. The user drags one of the nodes and drops it on top of another node. After confirmation, the two concepts are now considered to be the same object.

Querying a Knowledge Base

SHAKEN has a Question Answering facility that enables a user to ask questions about concepts in the KB. The question-answering interface is designed as a collection of fill-in-the-blank templates. Here are some example question templates:

- What is the <relation> of a <concept>?
- How does <event> occur in <concept> after <subevent>?

These questions may be instantiated by picking the values of the template variables. For example, the above two questions may be instantiated to

- What is the agent of Virus Invasion?
- How does a Copy occur in a DNA Transcription after a Move?

The user can choose the relation names from a menu, and choose the concept names by using the search facility. Very often, the variables in a parameterized question are not concept names, but logical expressions. For example, one may want to ask, "what is the agent of the Penetrate subevent of a Virus Invasion?" There is no stand-alone concept in the KB that represents the Penetrate subevent of Virus invasion. The graphical interface can be used to select such concepts. To do so, the user first selects a base concept, which in this case is Virus Invasion. He then opens the concept of Virus Invasion, and chooses the Penetrate subevent.

This choice returns to the question answering system the logical expression representing Penetrate that serves as the basis for question answering. The questions will then be titled: "Questions about a Penetrate as subevent of the Virus Invasion"

Expected Effects

The knowledge analysis module, called KANAL, allows a user to test the representation of a process (Kim and Gil 2001). KANAL functions by running an *animation* of the process and reports whether the preconditions of every step in the process hold true and also reports the changing slot values. The user can refine this testing by specifying which properties are expected to be true as a result of executing the process. For example, when testing a Virus Invasion process, a user may want to say that after the process is executed, the viral nucleic acid is inside the cell. A complete specification requires us to choose objects involved. To do so the user opens the graph representing the Virus Invasion, selects the Viral-Nucleic-Acid, then the Cell, and finally chooses a relation from a list compatible with the two objects selected.

Evaluation

During the summer of 2001, SHAKEN was extensively evaluated by IET (Information Extraction and Transport, Inc., www.iet.com). IET hired four biologists (three graduate students and one senior undergraduate) who had no background in computer science or knowledge representation. We trained the biologists to use SHAKEN, but training was limited to four days and our subsequent interactions with them were through an IET intermediary and restricted to fixing bugs in the system.

During the next four weeks, each biologist, working independently, was asked to build a KB to represent an n-page section of a college-level text on cell biology (Alberts, Bray et al. 1997). Along the way, IET asked each biologist to pose a set of questions to that biologist's own KB. The questions were drawn from standard test banks, and were presented in English. Each biologist "translated" the questions into SHAKEN's templates, and IET evaluated the responses.

Meanwhile, a pair of knowledge engineers, with significant training in knowledge representation and some background in biology, performed the same tasks by using SHAKEN. (These two people helped design and build SHAKEN.) This enabled IET to compare the biologists' KBs with those of knowledge engineers, as measured by the quality of the answers they produced.

This evaluation yielded a substantial body of data, which was then analyzed and summarized (Cohen, Chaudhri et al. 1999). The results that are most relevant to this paper examine the difference in answering ability between the KBs built by biologists and the ones built by knowledge engineers. Again, our goal is to develop tools, such as SHAKEN, that enable domain experts to build good KBs, whose quality is at least comparable to ones built by knowledge engineers.

IET hired another biologist to grade SHAKEN's answers to the questions posed by the KB builders. Each answer was assigned a score of 0 (lowest) to 3 (highest) on each of three criteria: answer correctness, quality of the representation, and quality of the explanation. These scores were averaged to give an *overall* score.

The mean overall score for answers generated from the biologists' KBs was 2.07, compared with 2.35 for knowledge engineers. This difference is small, but statistically significant ($F=69.32$, $p\sim0$). Moreover, there was considerable variance in overall scores across the set of six KBs:

KB creator	overall score
biologist 1	2.48
knowledge engineer 1	2.44
knowledge engineer 2	2.26
biologist 2	2.12
biologist 3	2.02
biologist 4	1.66

Table 1: Overall scores of knowledge bases built by biologists and knowledge engineers, sorted in descending order

The best-performing biologist was comparable with the best knowledge engineer, but the other three biologists performed less well than the second-ranked knowledge engineer. However, the overall result is most encouraging: SHAKEN can enable a domain expert to build a competent KB, and one that is comparable to one built by an experienced knowledge engineer.

Future Work

In the near future, we envision extending the editor in several directions: (1) entering analogical knowledge, (2) displaying changing fluents, (3) managing incremental layouts, and (4) showing axioms over and above a group of Skolem individuals.

Analogical Knowledge

Analogy is a powerful medium for communication used by humans. We plan to extend the current interface so that it could show two concept maps side by side and draw correspondences between the two. By using a partial specification of correspondences, the system would use the analogy engine to infer new relationships, thus greatly speeding the knowledge entry rate.

Fluents

While showing a process as a graph, the current interface shows properties of various concepts as of the beginning of the process. Currently, there is no way to show the properties as they change with the execution of the process. We plan to extend the interface so that time changing properties could be shown.

Other Axioms

As we explained earlier, the only axioms that the user can graphically view and edit are the ones that can be translated into relationships between Skolem instances. Basically, most of these axioms are of the form

$\forall x$ isa(x Class1) $\rightarrow \exists y$ isa (y Class2) $\wedge$ slot(x y)

or more generally axioms of the form

$\forall x$ isa(x Class1) $\rightarrow \exists y$ isa (y Class2) p(x y ...)

Furthermore, the current system shows only binary relations. We plan to expand the class of axioms that can be graphically represented.

Conclusion

We have described a system that enables domain experts, unassisted by AI technologists to construct competent knowledge bases. We described in detail two components of this system that helped us achieve this goal.

The first component is a well-organized English-like presentation of KB content, which makes use of Explanation Design Plans, combined with an English generation tool built on a recursive rule-based pattern matcher. The second component is a graphical interface to enter knowledge and query the KB, extending the notion of Concept Maps.

We evaluated the system in a controlled experiment with domain experts, which suggests that these tools indeed enable domain experts to build KBs comparable to those built by knowledge engineers.

Acknowledgments

This work was supported by DARPA's Rapid Knowledge Formation project. We thank all the members of the SRI team who have helped implementing SHAKEN: Boeing, ISI, KSL Stanford, NWU, UT Austin, and UWF.

References

Acker, L. and B. Porter (1994). Extracting Viewpoints from Knowledge bases. National Conference on Artificial Intelligence.

Alberts, B., D. Bray, et al. (1997). Essential Cell Biology: An Introduction to the Molecular Biology of the Cell.

Al-Halimi, R., R. C. Berwick, et al. (1998). Wordnet, and Electronic Lexical Datbase, MIT Press.

Blythe, J., J. Kim, et al. (2001). An Integrated Environment for Knowledge Acquisition. International Conference on Intelligent User Interfaces.

Clark, P. and B. Porter (1999). KM The Knowledge Machine 1.4 - Users Manual. Austin, TX, University of Texas.

Clark, P., J. Thompson, et al. (2001). Knowledge Entry as the Graphical Assembly of Components. First International Conference on Knowledge Capture.

Cohen, P., V. K. Chaudhri, et al. (1999). Does Prior Knowledge Facilitate the Development of Knowledge-based Systems. National Conference on Artificial Intelligence.

Domingue, J., E. Motta, et al. (1999). Knowledge Modelling in WebOnto and OCML.

Herman, D. I. (2000). GraphXML - An XML Based Graph Interchange Format.

Kim, J. and Y. Gil (2001). Knowledge Analysis on Process Models. IJCAI.

Lester, J. and B. Porter (1997). Developing and Empirically Evaluating Robust Explanation Generators: The KNIGHT Experiments.

Maedche, A. (2000). Ontology Engineering Environment OntoEdit.

Mahalingam, K. and M. N. Huhns (1997). An Ontology Tool for Query Formulation in an Agent-Based Context. Center for Information Technology - Department of Electrical and Computer Engineering - University of South Carolina.

Novak, J. D. (2001). The Theory Underlying Concept Maps and How To Construct Them, University of West Florida.

Noy, N. F., M. Sintek, et al. (2001). Creating Semantic Web Contents with Protege-2000. IEEE Intelligent Systems.

Paley, S. and P. Karp (1996). GKB Editor User Manual, SR International.

Rodriguez, A. (2000). Active Lisp Pages (ALP), SRI International.

Swartout, B., R. Patil, et al. (1998). Ontosaurus: A Tool for Browsing and Editing Ontologies.

The 2001 Trading Agent Competition

Michael P. Wellman[*]
University of Michigan
wellman@umich.edu

Amy Greenwald
Brown University
amygreen@cs.brown.edu

Peter Stone
AT&T Labs — Research
pstone@research.att.com

Peter R. Wurman
North Carolina State University
wurman@csc.ncsu.edu

Abstract

The 2001 Trading Agent Competition was the second in a series of events aiming to shed light on research issues in automating trading strategies. Based on a challenging market scenario in the domain of travel shopping, the competition presents agents with difficult issues in bidding strategy, market prediction, and resource allocation. Entrants in 2001 demonstrated substantial progress over the prior year, with the overall level of competence exhibited suggesting that trading in online markets is a viable domain for highly autonomous agents.

Introduction

Automated trading in online markets is increasingly recognized as a promising domain for agent technology. Programmed trading is nothing new, but the emergence of electronic marketplaces has dramatically increased the opportunities for such trading. The trading task may be particularly well-suited for automation, as the interfaces are relatively simple. For example, messages from agents are typically limited to offers to exchange quantities of standardized goods for standardized currency using standardized exchange protocols. Although decisions about desirable trades may be based on a multitude of factors, specifying reasonable strategies seems often quite feasible with normal levels of effort.

As researchers we would like to make that last statement more precise, and develop an understanding of just how effective agent strategies can be, and how automated traders might affect the conduct of electronic markets. Understanding behaviors of other agents is clearly an advantage in designing one's own, as well as in designing the market itself.

Unfortunately, data about real-world trading agents is difficult to obtain. Designers of successful trading agents are naturally reluctant to compromise their proprietary advantages by revealing their strategies. Designers of unsuccessful agents seem equally reluctant to discuss their experience, for perhaps different reasons. This has led interested researchers to study their own designs, leading in some cases

to useful observations, but all conclusions from such investigations must be qualified by questions of realism. Since the effectiveness of one agent's strategy depends on the strategies of others, having one designer choose all strategies introduces a great source of fragility to the research exercise.

One natural approach is for researchers to cooperate, by addressing their design energy to a common problem. The Trading Agent Competition (TAC) is an attempt to induce this cooperation, by organizing an event providing infrastructure, and promising external attention to the results. The first TAC (Wellman et al. 2001) was held in July 2000 in Boston, in conjunction with the International Conference on Multiagent Systems (ICMAS-00). TAC-00 attracted 18 participants from six countries, several of whom based on this experience contributed to the research literature on trading agents (Fornara & Gambardella 2001; Greenwald & Boyan 2001; Stone & Greenwald to appear; Stone et al. 2001). The competition can also claim spinoff contributions to research on visualizing real-time market data (Healey, St. Amant, & Chang 2001). Based on the success of that event, we held a sequel in October 2001 in Tampa, as part of the ACM Conference on Electronic Commerce (EC-01).

One positive result of the second TAC was the possibility of measuring actual progress, through performance and through the transfer of ideas from one competition to the next. The TAC-01 experience provides a wealth of lessons for trading agent designers, and designers of competitions.

TAC Market Game

To enter the competition, TAC participants developed software agents to play a challenging market game. Entries in the game play the role of travel agents, striving to arrange itineraries for a group of clients who wish to travel from TACTown to TAC's host city and back again during a five-day period. Travel goods are traded at simultaneous on-line auctions that run for twelve minutes (reduced from 15 minutes in the 2000 competition). An agent's objective is to secure goods serving the particular desires of its clients, but to do so as inexpensively as possible. An agent's score is the difference between the utility it earns for its clients and its net expenditure. In this section, we summarize the TAC game, noting differences between 2000 and 2001 rules; for further details, visit http://tac.eecs.umich.edu.

---

[*]Contact author. University of Michigan AI Laboratory, 1101 Beal Av, Ann Arbor, MI 48109-2110, USA.

Trading Travel Goods

Agents trade three types of travel goods: (1) flights to and from the host city, (2) room reservations at two available hotels–one considered higher quality than the other, and (3) entertainment tickets for three kinds of events. Each type is traded according to distinct market rules, with separate auctions corresponding to every combination of good type and day, yielding 28 auctions in total: eight flight auctions (there are no inbound flights on the fifth day, and there are no outbound flights on the first day), eight hotel auctions (two hotel types and four nights), and twelve entertainment ticket auctions (three entertainment event types and four nights). All 28 auctions operate simultaneously and asynchronously on the Michigan Internet AuctionBot server (Wurman, Wellman, & Walsh 1998). We describe the auctions rules for each good type in turn.

Flights. An effectively infinite supply of flights is offered by the "TAC seller" at continuously clearing auctions. No resale or exchange of flights is permitted. The seller's offers follow a random walk, setting prices initially between $250 and $400, and perturbing them every 30-40 seconds by a random value uniformly selected in the range $[-10, x(t)]$, where t is the number of seconds from game start. All prices were confined within bounds: $150 to $600 in 2000, and $150 to $800 in 2001. In 2000, price changes followed an unbiased random walk; that is, $x(t) = 10$ for all times t. Most of the entrants therefore waited until near the end of the game to purchase flights. Waiting avoided a commitment pending revelation of other relevant information (e.g., hotel prices), at zero expected cost (modulo the boundary effects). To present agents with a meaningful tradeoff, we changed the policy in 2001 so that prices were biased to drift upwards: for each flight auction a, a number x_a was uniformly drawn in the range $[10, 90]$, and $x(t) = 10 + (x_a - 10)(t/720)$.

Hotels. The TAC seller also makes available 16 rooms per hotel per night, which are sold in ascending, multi-unit, sixteenth-price auctions. In other words, the winning bidders are those who place the top sixteen bids, and these bidders uniformly pay the sixteenth-highest price. No bid withdrawal or resale in hotel auctions is permitted. There is a tendency in such auctions (observed, for example, in the Santa Fe Double Auction Tournament (Rust, Miller, & Palmer 1994)) to wait until the end to bid, both to avoid undue commitment and to withold strategic information from competing bidders. In an attempt to encourage agents to bid early, in 2000 we subjected hotel auctions to early closing after random periods of inactivity; otherwise, the auctions closed simultaneously at the end of the game. However, this countermeasure proved ineffective, as agents merely entered minimal increments at measured intervals in order to ensure the auctions stayed alive. Much of the meaningful price movements occurred as hotel prices skyrocketed near the end. In 2001, we induced early bidding through more drastic means: closing hotel auctions randomly at one-minute intervals. Specifically, one randomly selected hotel would close after four minutes, a second after five minutes, and so on, until the last auction closed after eleven minutes. From the agents' point of view, the order of auction closings was unknown and unpredictable.

Entertainment. TAC agents buy and sell entertainment tickets in continuous double auctions. Each agent receives an initial endowment of tickets. In 2000, for each event on each night, each agent received the following number of tickets: zero with probability 1/4, one with probability 1/2, and two with probability 1/4. Trading entertainment was not a major factor in 2000, as the symmetric distribution meant that agents could usually do reasonably well by keeping its initial endowment. In 2001, to promote trade, each agent received exactly 12 tickets, partitioned as follows: for day 1 or day 4, four tickets of one type and two tickets of a second type; and, for day 2 or day 3, four tickets of one type and two tickets of a second type.

Trip Utility

Eight trading agents compete for travel goods in a TAC game instance, with each agent representing eight clients. The market demand is thus determined by the sixty-four clients' preferences, which are randomly generated from specified probability distributions. A client's preference is characterized by (1) ideal arrival and departure dates (IAD and IDD, respectively, which range over days 1 through 4, and days 2 through 5, respectively), (2) value for staying in the premium quality hotel (HV, which takes integer values between 50 and 150), and (3) values for each of the three types of entertainment events (integers between 0 and 200). The three available entertainment events in 2001 were Amusement Park (AP), Alligator Wrestling (AW), and Museum (MU).

A TAC travel *package* is characterized by arrival and departure dates (AD and DD, respectively), a hotel type (H, which takes on value G for good or F for fair), and entertainment tickets (I_X is an indicator variable that represents whether or not the package includes a ticket for event X). In order to obtain positive utility for a client, a TAC agent must construct a *feasible* package for that client; otherwise, the client's utility is zero. A feasible package is one in which (1) the arrival date is strictly less than the departure date, (2) the same hotel is reserved during all intermediate nights, (3) at most one entertainment event per night is included, and (4) at most one of each type of entertainment ticket is included.

A client's utility for a feasible package is given by:

$$\text{utility} = 1000 - \text{travelPenalty} + \text{hotelBonus} + \text{funBonus}$$

where

$$\text{travelPenalty} = 100(|\text{IAD} - \text{AD}| + |\text{IDD} - \text{DD}|)$$

$$\text{hotelBonus} = \begin{cases} \text{HV} & \text{if H} = \text{G} \\ 0 & \text{otherwise} \end{cases}$$

$$\text{funBonus} = I_{\text{AP}}\text{AP} + I_{\text{AW}}\text{AW} + I_{\text{MU}}\text{MU}.$$

Allocating Goods to Clients

In 2000, TAC agents were responsible for assigning goods to clients, reporting their allocations at the end of the game. By 2001, this problem was considered well-understood; thus, we had the TAC server compute and report each agent's optimal allocation.

Themes in Agent Design

Although each TAC entry exhibited its own special features, it is possible to identify some common structures and general themes. Points of comparison can be organized into the common decisions the agents face, which we collect into the canonical agent "bidding cycle" of Table 1. Different agents may naturally frame the questions somewhat differently, or in an implicit way. Nevertheless, this skeletal structure provides a convenient organization for a discussion of characteristic strategic features.

REPEAT

1. For each good, do I want to bid now or later?

2. For each good that I want to bid on now, what quantity do I want to buy or sell?

3. For each exchange quantity, what price should I offer?

UNTIL game over

Table 1: Trading agent bidding cycle: a skeletal view.

When to Bid

The three TAC auction types present agents with distinct timing concerns. Flights are offered continuously on a posted-price take-it-or-leave-it basis, so the agent's decision is simply whether to commit at a given time. Since flight prices are expected to increase over time, agents face the tradeoff of buying early for less, or paying more with benefit of gaining information about other goods (e.g., hotel prices and winnings). Different agents approached this problem in different ways. For example, Caisersose and livingagents always acquired all their flights immediately, on average about one minute into the game. Urlaub01 was even faster on average (46 seconds), even though it occasionally picked up some extra flights late into the game. ATTac makes its flight bidding decisions based on a cost-benefit analysis: if the cost of postponing a bid on a particular flight exceeds the benefit of winning that flight under multiple scenarios, then ATTac bids. This led to some immediate purchases and others spread later in the game, with an overall mean time of about two minutes. The remaining agents in the finals deliberated further, with Tacsman getting its flights on average over four minutes after game start.

Hotels, in contrast, are exchanged through ascending auctions with periodic revelation of price quotes and one-time clearing. Once per minute, each hotel auction would release a price quote and one was randomly selected to clear and close. Since no information was revealed during these one-minute intervals, bidding was effectively organized into discrete rounds.[1] Agents typically spent the bulk of each round calculating their bidding decisions, placing the bids at round end. Exactly what time constituted the "end", though, depended on an agent's assessment of network latency and the risk of placing a late bid. Note that all agents were compelled to maintain active bids for all open hotels, since the next hotel to close was unknown and unpredictable.

Like flights, entertainment is exchanged in continuous auctions, giving agents the opportunity to time their offers based on strategic considerations. Some agents (e.g., livingagents, ATTac, 006) explicitly maintained separate control threads for entertainment bidding decisions. Most agents in TAC-01 bid on all goods only once per minute (after the first three minutes), since this timing strategy was appropriate for the sequentially closing hotel auctions.

What to Bid On

One of the key problems that a TAC agent faces is the so-called *completion* problem (Boyan & Greenwald 2001):

Given my current holdings, and given (expected) market prices, what goods would I choose to buy or sell at these prices?

We observed two general approaches in TAC-01:

- Agents such as whitebear solved the completion problem using global optimization techniques employed by TAC-00 participants, including integer linear programming (Stone *et al.* 2001) and heuristic search (Greenwald & Boyan 2001).

- TacsMan constructed travel packages by optimizing utility client-by-client, rather than globally.

Most agents used completion to choose a limited set of goods to bid on. However, ATTac always bid on all open hotel rooms, based on independent assessments of each room's predicted marginal utility.

How Much to Bid

The decision about what price to offer for a given good was typically decomposed into the problems of first establishing a reservation value, and then determining a strategic bidding policy based on that value. It is not straightforward to assign reservation values to individual goods, however, due to the interdependences among them. Perfectly complementary goods (e.g., an inflight and outflight for a particular client) are worthless in isolation, and perfectly substitutable goods (e.g., rooms in different hotels for the same client and day) provide added value only in isolation. Nonetheless, most agents employed marginal utility—ignoring interdependencies–at least as a baseline reservation value. Note that taken literally, each good necessary for trip feasibility (e.g., a hotel room on a particular night, once flights have been committed and no alternative rooms are available) has a marginal utility equal to the value of the

---

[1]This is in contrast with TAC-00, where all price information was revealed continually, and hotel auctions cleared at the end. As a result, most TAC-00 agents placed their serious hotel bids at or near the end, and prices often rose dramatically at that point.

whole trip. In TAC-00 several agents entered bids on this basis, causing hotel prices to escalate wildly.

Price Prediction

At several points in its bidding cycle (Table 1), an agent must solve a version of the completion problem. Determining what to bid on directly poses the question, and marginal utility calculations employed in pricing require that it be calculated twice—once each with and without the good included. The completion problem in turn requires a set of market prices as input. But before closing, actual prices are unknown. TAC agents employed a variety of statistical estimation techniques to predict market clearing prices.

For flights, TAC participants employed maximum likelihood estimation, least squares regression, and other simple prediction methods. For entertainment tickets, historical data suggested that most traded at or near 80. One agent (livingagents) therefore placed all its offers at this value, and another (Urlaub01), used the prediction to set upper and lower bounds on its entertainment bids.

Predicting hotel clearing prices was a central element of trading strategy in TAC-01. (In TAC-00, little information relevant to clearing prices was revealed during the course of a game.) There are many possible approaches to this hotel price estimation problem. Among those we observed in TAC-01 are the following, associated in some cases with agents that seemed to exemplify that approach.

1. Just use the current price quote, p_t.

2. Adjust based on historic data. For example, if Δ_t is the average historical difference between clearing price and price at time t, then the predicted clearing price is $p_t + \Delta_t$.

3. Predict by fitting a curve to the price points seen in the current game (polimi_bot).

4. Predict based on closing price data for that hotel in past games (livingagents). 006 combined this approach with extrapolation from current prices.

5. Same as above, but condition on hotel closing time, recognizing that the closing sequence will influence relative prices (Retsina, which also conditioned on current prices).

6. Same as above, but condition on full ordering of hotel closings (Tacsman), or which hotels are open or closed at a particular point (RoxyBot, Urlaub01).

7. Learn a mapping from features of the current game (including current prices) to closing prices based on historic data (ATTac).

8. Hand-construct rules based on observations about associations between abstract features (SouthamptonTAC).

Some agents, rather than using a point estimate of prices, took into account *distributions* of prices, solving the completion problem repeatedly for various prices sampled from this distribution. This kind of analysis reveals the sensitivity to the estimates of the conclusions drawn from them, and also permits some accounting for correlation of prices across

goods. The challenge to agents that employed such sampling techniques was to combine the results of their sampling. Simple averaging is not necessarily correct, as the appropriate action when prices are equally likely to be p or p' may be entirely different from the appropriate action when the price is certainly $(p + p')/2$.

TAC 2001 Tournament

TAC-01 was organized as a series of four competition phases, culminating with the semifinals and finals at the EC-01 conference. First, the qualifying round served to select the 16 agents that would participate in the semifinals. Second, the seeding round was used to divide these agents into two groups of eight. After the semifinals, on the morning of the 14th, four teams from each group were selected to compete in the finals, which took place that same afternoon.

Preliminary Rounds

The qualifying round ran from 10-17 September and included 28 agents, each of which were randomly selected to play in about 270 games. The main purpose of the qualifying round was to encourage competitors to create functional agents well in advance of the finals, thus ensuring a competitive field by the main event. Later scores were weighted more heavily, thus encouraging teams to experiment early on but create a stable agent by the end of the round.

Several groups entered more than one agent in the qualifying round. However only one agent per group was allowed to proceed to the seeding round. The top twelve agents automatically qualified, and all others with positive scores were invited to participate in the finals contingent on attendance at the workshop.

For the resulting field of 16 teams, a seeding round was held from 24 September until 5 October to determine how the semifinal groups would be formed. The top four and bottom four teams from the seeding round formed one group, with the rest of the teams (places 5-12) forming the other. The extensive seeding round offered a consequential testing scenario for agents during this period of intensive agent development. As a side effect, the seeding round provided a source of realistic game data for designers taking a statistical approach. Again, the scores were weighted such that those later in the round counted more.

In addition to the 16 qualifying teams, two additional agents were included in the seeding rounds for calibration purposes. First, ATTac-2000 (Stone *et al.* 2001) is a copy of the highest-scoring agent from the TAC-00 finals. To account for the rule changes between TAC-00 and TAC-01, ATTac-2000 was modified with a one-line change that caused it to place all of its bids before the first hotel closed as opposed to during the last minute of the game.

Second, dummy_buyer is included in this round's pool as a benchmark from the qualifying round. dummy_buyer is the agent provided by the TAC team to play in test games that do not have a full slate of agents. Whereas most of the other agents' behaviors were modified between (and during) the qualifying and seeding round, the dummy was left unchanged. Indeed, we observed substantial deterioration in

Agent	Affiliation	Score
SouthamptonTAC	U Southampton	3164
whitebear	Cornell U	3120
Urlaub01	Penn State U	3076
livingagents	Living Systems AG	3012
TacsMan	Stanford U	2984
CaiserSose	U Essex	2870
polimi_bot	Politecnico di Milano	2858
umbctac	U Maryland Baltimore Cty	2765
RoxyBot	Brown U	2732
ATTac	AT&T Research	2686
Retsina	Carnegie Mellon U	2675
PainInNEC	NEC Research	2575
ATTac-2000		2412
harami	Bogazici U	2156
dummy_buyer		1673
jboadw	McGill U	1307
bang	NCST Bangalore	1306
006	Swedish Inst Comp Sci	1115
arc-2k	Chinese U Hong Kong	-36

Table 2: Scores during the seeding round.

Heat 1		Heat 2	
Agent	Score	Agent	Score
livingagents	3660	Retsina	3294
SouthamptonTAC	3615	ATTac	3249
Urlaub01	3485	CaiserSose	3038
whitebear	3470	TacsMan	2966
006	3241	PainInNEC	2906
arc-2k	1746	polimi_bot	2835
jboadw	1717	umbctac	2773
harami	94	RoxyBot	2112

Table 3: Scores for the two semifinal heats. Each agent played 11 games.

the dummy's standing as the preliminary rounds progressed. Results of the seeding round are displayed in Table 2.

The Main Event

The semifinals and finals were held together on a single day, 14 October. This format severely limited the number of games that could be played. On the other hand, the single-day format allowed the culmination of the tournament to take place in a workshop environment with most of the participants present. It also ensured that agents would remain more or less unchanged during these rounds.

Each of the semifinal heats consisted of eleven games among identical agents. The top four teams from each heat advanced to the finals. The results of the semifinals are shown in Table 3.

The finals consisted of 24 games among the same eight agents. Right from the beginning, it became clear that livingagents was the team to beat in the finals. They jumped to an early lead in the first two games, and by eight games into

Agent	Final score	Client pref adjust
livingagents	3670	-66
ATTac	3622	42
whitebear	3513	-72
Urlaub01	3421	-2
Retsina	3352	-30
SouthamptonTAC	3254*	-64
CaiserSose	3074	202
TacsMan	2859	-11

Table 4: Scores during the finals. Each agent played 24 games. *SouthamptonTAC's score was adversely affected by a crash in one game. Discounting that game would have led to an average score of 3531.

the round, they were more than 135 points per game ahead of the next team (SouthamptonTAC). After another eight games, they were more than 250 points ahead of their two closest competitors (ATTac and whitebear).

At that point, ATTac began making a comeback. With one game to be played, ATTac was only an average of 22 points per game behind. It thus needed to beat livingagents by 514 points in the final game to overtake it, well within the margins observed in individual game instances.

As the game completed, ATTac's score of 3979 was one of the first to be posted by the server. The other agents' scores were reported one by one, until only the livingagents score was left. After agonizing seconds, the TAC server posted a final game score of 4626, enough for livingagents to retain the lead. Final scores are posted in Table 4.

Influence of Client Preferences

Because they determine the scoring function, randomly generated client requests for a particular game can have a significant bearing on scores. Whereas this effect can be expected to wash out over a large number of games, it may not in a smaller set (e.g., the TAC finals).

To try to assess the affect of this factor on TAC results, we identified a small number of statistics on client parameters that we would expect to be correlated with performance. We tested these for significance over the seeding round games, employing the variables in a linear regression along with indicator 0-1 variables for each of the agent identities. After a very small amount of trial-and-error, we came up with the following significant measures:

1. total client preferred travel days

2. total entertainment values

3. ratio of "easy" days (1 and 4) to hard (2 and 3) in preferred trip intervals

Applying the resulting regression model to the finals data yields an "adjustment factor" that accounts for the chance effect of client preference parameters. These values (normalized) are displayed in the final column of Table 4.

If the scores were adjusted based on these factors, there would be two changes in the rankings. First, livingagents had somewhat more favorable client data than did ATTac, and so in the adjusted rankings ATTac would come out in front. Caisersose had by far the least favorable inputs, and so it too would rise by one spot. Adjustment would result in several ranking changes within the semifinals, but no change in the top four selection for either heat.

Strategy: Livingagents vs. ATTac

A sharper contrast in agent strategy can be drawn by examining more specifically the approaches of the two particular agents that finished at the top of the standings in the finals.

ATTac uses a predictive, data-driven approach to bid based on expected marginal values of all available goods. A price-predictor based on boosting techniques (Schapire *et al.* 2002) is at the heart of the algorithm. This price-predictor generates distributions over expected hotel closing prices. ATTac then samples from these distributions in an effort to compute the expected marginal utility of each good. It then bids exactly these expected marginal utilities. As the game proceeds, the price distributions change in response to the observed price trajectories, thus causing the agent to continually revise its bids. Note that by using this strategy, provided that the price is right, ATTac automatically buys contingency goods to guard against the possibility of the most desired goods becoming too expensive.

In terms of the skeletal bidding cycle of Table 1, ATTac focuses mainly on step 3. On every cycle it determines prices for every available hotel room and entertainment ticket. For flights, like most other agents, it does determine a single coherent set of candidate flights before performing its expected marginal utility calculations to determine whether it is worth it to buy now or to wait for additional price information to reduce uncertainty.

The strategy of livingagents (Fritschi & Dorer 2002) is strikingly different. livingagents takes the initial flight prices and calculates optimal client trips, assuming hotel prices will be at historical averages.[2] It then purchases flights immediately, and bids for the required hotels at prices high enough to ensure successful acquisition. These choices are not reconsidered, and indeed the flight and hotel auctions are not monitored at all. livingagents similarly makes a fixed decision about which entertainment to attempt to buy or sell, assuming they will be priced at their historical average of $80. It does monitor the entertainment auctions, taking acceptable offers opportunistically until putting in final reservation prices at the seven-minute mark.

At first blush, it is quite surprising that an effectively open-loop strategy such as that employed by livingagents could be so successful. In general, the optimal configuration of trips will depend on hotel prices, yet the open-loop strategy ignores all the predictive information about them that is revealed as the game progresses. Moreover, the behavior is quite risky. If the initial hotel buy offers are not high enough, the agent will fail to complete some trips and

---

[2]For this estimate, livingagents used data from the preliminary rounds. As the designers note (Fritschi & Dorer 2002), hotel prices in the finals turned out to be significantly lower than during the preliminary rounds, presumably because the more successful agents in the finals were better at keeping these prices down.

thus lose substantial value. But if they are placed sufficiently high to ensure purchase, there is a danger that the agent will have to pay a price such that the trip is unprofitable (or less profitable than an alternative).

In particular, it is quite clear that if all agents followed the strategy of livingagents, the result would have been disastrous. With all eight agents placing very high bids for the hotels, the prices will skyrocket and most of the trips will be unprofitable. Indeed, experiments with analogous behaviors for a version of the ATTac-2000 agent bear out this result (Stone *et al.* 2001).

But of course, livingagents was *not* competing with copies of itself. Most of the other agents, like ATTac, employed closed-loop, adaptive strategies that condition their behaviors on the evolution of prices. By steering away from goods that are becoming expensive (or predicted to become so), they also attenuate the forces raising those prices. Thus, these agents effectively "stabilize" the system, keeping the prices lower, and less variable, than they would be without such tight monitoring. This benefits all agents, whether or not they are monitoring.

The open-loop strategy has several advantages. It is simple, and avoids the expected tangible costs of waiting (e.g., letting flight prices rise) and hedging (e.g., buying contingency goods that may not be used). Whether it is worthwhile to monitor the markets and adapt bidding behavior depends pivotally on predictability of closing prices.

- If the prices are perfectly predictable from the start of the game, then there is no benefit to an adaptive strategy. (Indeed, the optimal closed-loop strategy would degenerate to an open-loop behavior.)

- With large price variances, a closed-loop strategy should do better. Typically, it will place mid-range bids in all the auctions and end up buying the cheapest goods. In the end, it may have to pay some high prices to complete itineraries, but it should largely avoid this necessity. The open-loop strategy picks its goods up front and ends up paying whatever price they end up at, which in some cases will be quite high.

- With small price variances, an *optimal* closed-loop strategy would in principle still be as good as any open-loop strategy. Nevertheless, the increase in complexity may be great for a small potential benefit, and even small miscalculations (e.g., underconfidence in predicted values, leading to excessive waiting and hedging) can prevent the agent from achieving this benefit. Thus, the relative simplicity of the open-loop approach may more than compensate for its suboptimality.

The foregoing argument suggests that there is some natural equilibrium between adaptive and open-loop behavior in the TAC game. Exactly what this equilibrium is, and whether the configuration of agents participating in TAC-01 achieved a close balance, are subjects for further analysis and empirical study.

Discussion

All told, a tremendous amount of effort has gone into organizing and competing in TAC. Is this effort justified?

Although not entirely realistic, the TAC game incorporates more realistic elements than most models previously studied in research on economically motivated agents. TAC has provided a platform on which to demonstrate new technologies (e.g., the livingagents development platform (Fritschi & Dorer 2002)), and to apply favorite techniques (e.g., fuzzy rules used by SouthamptonTAC, constraint programming by 006 (Aurell *et al.* 2002)). In addition, it serves as a benchmark problem against which comparisons can be drawn between competing techniques.

It seems clear that TAC has been instrumental in focusing a wide variety of researchers' attention on the trading agent problem domain. However, it is still too early to tell if the agent architectures developed by the competitors will influence the technologies that are eventually deployed in commercial settings. While the game is more complex than most other research models, it is far less so than real e-commerce settings, and the abstraction may well create incentives that are not aligned with real market conditions. The game design was influenced by the desire to make it interesting and challenging, which sometimes ran counter to the desire to keep it realistic. For example, the periodic closing of randomly selected hotel auctions is a reasonable measure to promote early bidding, but one not typically seen in real-world market mechanisms.

We are encouraged that the research will remain relevant by the fact that much of the focus of 2001 competition was on price prediction and timing of bid decisions, two topics that we think will be widely relevant in commercial applications. In addition, the TAC servers have been under almost constant use since the competition by several of the participants running ongoing experiments. Indeed the two servers which host TAC-01 logged more than 25 million bids in the last six months of 2001. About 1/4 of that load came after the official competition.

Whether the research efforts succeed or not, we have been amply rewarded by the success that instructors have had using TAC in education. The design of a TAC agent incorporates many central AI and e-commerce concepts, and provides a valuable framework around which to struture many related lessons. The game has been used as a class project in AI and e-commerce courses at several universities in the United States and Europe.

The Swedish Institute of Computer Science (SICS) will organize the next TAC event, to be held in Edmonton, Canada in July 2002. SICS has released an open-source version of the TAC server, developed using SICStus Prolog. Although TAC-02 will follow the same rules as TAC-01, we expect that future events will address domains—particularly business-to-business scenarios—that present other types of challenges to trading agents.

Acknowledgments

The 2001 Trading Agent Competition was the product of dedicated effort by the Michigan TAC Team: Kevin O'Malley, Christopher Kiekintveld, Daniel Reeves, Sowmya Swaminathan, and William Walsh. The research value of the event is attributable to the energies devoted by the entrants. This account was informed by presentations from the entrants at the TAC-01 workshop, as well as their comments on earlier drafts of this paper (but please blame the authors for remaining inaccuracies). The research was supported in part by NSF grant IIS-9988715. TAC-01 also benefited from the generous sponsorship of Net Exchange, and the E-Commerce Learning Center at North Carolina State University.

References

Aurell, E.; Boman, M.; Carlsson, M.; Eriksson, J.; Finne, N.; Janson, S.; Kreuger, P.; and Rasmusson, L. 2002. A trading agent built on constraint programming. In *Eighth International Conference of the Society for Computational Economics: Computing in Economics and Finance.*

Boyan, J., and Greenwald, A. 2001. Bid determination in simultaneous auctions: An agent architecture. In *Third ACM Conference on Electronic Commerce*, 210–212.

Fornara, N., and Gambardella, L. M. 2001. An autonomous bidding agent for simultaneous auctions. In *Fifth International Workshop on Cooperative Information Agents*, number 2182 in Lecture Notes on Artificial Intelligence, 130–141.

Fritschi, C., and Dorer, K. 2002. Agent-oriented software engineering for successful TAC participation. In *First International Joint Conference on Autonomous Agents and Multi-Agent Systems.*

Greenwald, A., and Boyan, J. 2001. Bidding algorithms for simultaneous auctions: A case study. In *Third ACM Conference on Electronic Commerce*, 115–124.

Healey, C. G.; St. Amant, R.; and Chang, J. 2001. Assisted visualization of e-commerce auction agents. In *Graphics Interface*, 201–208.

Rust, J.; Miller, J. H.; and Palmer, R. 1994. Characterizing effective trading strategies: Insights from a computerized double auction tournament. *Journal of Economic Dynamics and Control* 18:61–96.

Schapire, R. E.; Stone, P.; McAllester, D.; Littman, M. L.; and Csirik, J. A. 2002. Modeling auction price uncertainty using boosting-based conditional density estimation. In *Nineteenth International Conference on Machine Learning.*

Stone, P., and Greenwald, A. to appear. The first international trading agent competition: Autonomous bidding agents. *Journal of Electronic Commerce Research.*

Stone, P.; Littman, M. L.; Singh, S.; and Kearns, M. 2001. Attac-2000: An adaptive autonomous bidding agent. *Journal of Artificial Intelligence Research* 15:189–206.

Wellman, M. P.; Wurman, P. R.; O'Malley, K.; Bangera, R.; Lin, S.-d.; Reeves, D.; and Walsh, W. E. 2001. Designing the market game for a trading agent competition. *IEEE Internet Computing* 5(2):43–51.

Wurman, P. R.; Wellman, M. P.; and Walsh, W. E. 1998. The Michigan Internet AuctionBot: A configurable auction server for human and software agents. In *Second International Conference on Autonomous Agents*, 301–308.

Student Abstracts

Multiple Instance Learning with Generalized Support Vector Machines

Stuart Andrews, Thomas Hofmann and Ioannis Tsochantaridis
Department of Computer Science, Brown University
Providence, Rhode Island 02912, {stu,th,it}@cs.brown.edu

Multiple Instance Learning

In pattern classification it is usually assumed that a training set of labeled patterns is available. Multiple-Instance Learning (MIL) generalizes this problem setting by making weaker assumptions about the labeling information. While each pattern is still believed to possess a true label, training labels are associated with sets or *bags* of patterns rather than individual patterns.

More formally, given is a set of patterns $\mathbf{x}_1, ..., \mathbf{x}_n$ grouped into bags $X_1, ..., X_m$, with $X_j = \{\mathbf{x}_i : i \in I_j\}$ and $I_j \subseteq \{1, ..., n\}$. With each bag X_j is associated a label $Y_j \in \{-1, 1\}$. These labels are interpreted in the following way: if a bag has a negative label $Y_j = -1$, all patterns in that bag inherit the negative label. If on the other hand, $Y_j = 1$, then at least one pattern $\mathbf{x}_i \in X_j$ is a positive example of the underlying concept.

The MIL scenario has many interesting applications: One prominent application is the classification of molecules in the context of drug design (Dietterich, Lathrop, & Lozano-Perez 1997). Here, each molecule is represented by a bag of possible conformations. Another application is in image retrieval where images can be viewed as bags of local image patches (Maron & Ratan 1998) or image regions.

Algorithms for the MIL problem were first presented in (Dietterich, Lathrop, & Lozano-Perez 1997; Auer 1997; Long & Tan 1996). These methods (and analytical results) are based on hypothesis classes consisting of axis-aligned rectangles. Similarly, methods developed subsequently (e.g., (Maron & Lozano-Pérez 1998; Zhang & Goldman 2002)) have focused on specially tailored machine learning algorithms that do not compare favorably in the limiting case of bags of size 1 (the standard classification setting). A notable exception is (Ramon & Raedt 2000).

Generalized Support Vector Machines

We propose to generalize Support Vector Machines (SVMs) (Vapnik 1998) to take into account weak labeling information of the type found in MIL.

SVMs are based on the theory of linear classifiers, more precisely the idea of the *maximum margin hyperplane*. For linearly separable data, the maximum margin hyperplane is

defined by parameters $\mathbf{w}^*, b^*$ with

$$(\mathbf{w}^*, b^*) = \underset{(\mathbf{w},b), \|\mathbf{w}\|=1}{\arg\max} \ \min_i \gamma_i, \quad \gamma_i \equiv y_i (\langle \mathbf{w}, \mathbf{x}_i \rangle + b) \quad (1)$$

The minimum $\gamma^* = \min_i \gamma_i$ is called the (geometric) *margin* and the patterns $\mathbf{x}_i$ with $\gamma_i = \gamma^*$ are called *support vectors*. The so-called soft-margin generalization of SVMs with L_1 penalties on margin violations amounts to solving the following convex quadratic program:

$$\text{minimize} \quad H(w, b, \eta) = \frac{1}{2}\|\mathbf{w}\|^2 + C\sum_{i=1}^{n} \eta_i \quad (2)$$

$$\text{s.t. } \forall i \quad y_i(\langle \mathbf{w}, \mathbf{x}_i \rangle + b) \geq 1 - \eta_i, \quad \eta_i \geq 0$$

where the scalar C controls the trade-off between margin violation and regularization. What makes SVMs particularly powerful is the generalization to arbitrary kernel functions K. A kernel function implicitly maps patterns to a new high dimensional feature space in which an inner product is computed. Since this mapping needs not to be performed explicitly, this results in a very efficient non-linear classification algorithm.

To generalize SVMs for MIL, labels of patterns that only occur in positive bags are treated as unknown integer variables. Each bag with a positive label imposes an inequality constraint on the labels of the contained patterns; for negative bags, the pattern labels are known to be negative. These constraints can be incorporated in a generalized version of SVM learning as follows:

$$\text{if} \quad Y_j = 1, \quad \text{then} \sum_{i \in I_j} \frac{1 + y_i}{2} \geq 1 \quad (3)$$

$$\text{if} \quad Y_j = -1, \quad \text{then } y_i = -1, \quad \forall i \in I_j$$

The resulting problem, MIL-SVM, is a mixed integer program that bears some similarity to the transductive version of SVMs (Joachims 1999; Demirez & Bennett 2000). The goal is thus to minimize (2) jointly over the continuous parameters $(\mathbf{w}, b)$ and over the integer variables (labels of patterns in positive bags).

We propose a heuristic approach in order to find an approximation to this mixed integer program which cannot be solved exactly with current optimization methods for large problem sizes. After initializing all positive bag pattern labels to $+1$, one alternates solving the quadratic program in

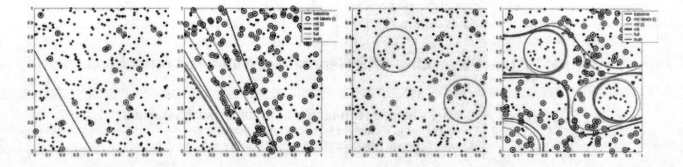

Figure 1: SVM (black), SVM with true labels (yellow), intermediate MIL-SVM (blue), MIL-SVM final (green) and correct (magenta) solutions on two synthetic data sets. Red and blue circles depict one positive bag and one negative bag on the left-hand images. On the right, blue circles indicate examples from positive bags that have been re-labeled $y_i = -1$.

(2) using the given labels, with a re-labeling step where the labels of patterns in positive bags are updated. Alternating these two steps defines a convergent procedure which will lead to a local optimum. Our current implementation swaps the label of a positive bag pattern that leads to the largest decrease in the objective (2) while not violating constraints in (3).

Results

We have experimentally verified the proposed generalization of SVMs on synthetic data, by comparing it with a naive baseline application of SVMs (labeling all patterns with the label of the bag they belong to) and with an optimal application of SVMs (labeling all patterns with the true concept label). A proof of concept on synthetic data is shown in Fig. 1 which shows that the MIL generalization of SVMs is able to identify superior discriminant functions, which is also reflected in a significantly reduced error rate.

A second preliminary series of experiments has been performed on a data set of 1000 images from the Corel image data base, preprocessed with the Blobworld system (Carson *et al.* 1999). In this representation, an image consists of a set of segments (or blobs), each characterized by color, texture and shape descriptors. Although standard SVMs already perform quite well, we have been able to achieve relative improvements in average precision in the range of 10% (e.g., from 25.3% to 30.3% for the "tiger" and from 43.2% to 46.0% for the "elephant" category). We are currently investigating ways to find better optimization heuristics and are conducting benchmark experiments on a larger scale.

Acknowledgments

Thanks to Chad Carson and the Blobworld team for making the Blobworld Matlab code publically available.

References

Auer, P. 1997. On learning from multi-instance examples: Empirical evaluation of a theoretical approach. In *Proc. 14th International Conference on Machine Learning*, 21–29. Morgan Kaufmann.

Carson, C.; Thomas, M.; Belongie, S.; Hellerstein, J. M.; and Malik, J. 1999. Blobworld: A system for region-based image indexing and retrieval. In *Third International Conference on Visual Information Systems*. Springer.

Demirez, A., and Bennett, K. 2000. Optimization approaches to semisupervised learning. In Ferris, M.; Mangasarian, O.; and Pang, J., eds., *Applications and Algorithms of Complementarity*. Kluwer Academic Publishers, Boston.

Dietterich, T. G.; Lathrop, R. H.; and Lozano-Perez, T. 1997. Solving the multiple instance problem with axis-parallel rectangles. *Artificial Intelligence* 89(1-2):31–71.

Joachims, T. 1999. Transductive inference for text classification using support vector machines. In *Proc. 16th International Conf. on Machine Learning*, 200–209. Morgan Kaufmann, San Francisco, CA.

Long, P., and Tan, L. 1996. PAC learning axis aligned rectangles with respect to product distributions from multiple-instance examples. In *Proceedings of the Conference on Computational Learning Theory*, 228–234.

Maron, O., and Lozano-Pérez, T. 1998. A framework for multiple-instance learning. In Jordan, M. I.; Kearns, M. J.; and Solla, S. A., eds., *Advances in Neural Information Processing Systems*, volume 10. The MIT Press.

Maron, O., and Ratan, A. L. 1998. Multiple-instance learning for natural scene classification. In *Proc. 15th International Conf. on Machine Learning*, 341–349. Morgan Kaufmann, San Francisco, CA.

Ramon, J., and Raedt, L. D. 2000. Multi instance neural networks. In *Proceedings of IMCL-2000 Workshop on Attribute-Value and Relational Learning*.

Vapnik, V. 1998. *Statistical Learning Theory*. Wiley.

Zhang, Q., and Goldman, S. A. 2002. EM-DD: An improved multiple-instance learning technique. In *Advances in Neural Information Processing Systems*.

Toward A Framework for Assembling Broken Pottery Vessels

Stuart Andrews and David H. Laidlaw
Department of Computer Science, Brown University
Providence, Rhode Island 02912 {stu,dhl}@cs.brown.edu

This paper addresses how to automatically reconstruct pottery vessels from a collection of sherds using a variety of features and their comparisons. To solve the problem, we designed a computational framework that is founded on the primitive operations of "match" proposal and evaluation. A match defines the geometric relationship between a pair of sherds. This framework affords a natural decomposition of the computation required by an automatic assembly process and provides a concrete basis to evaluate the utility of different features and feature comparisons for assembly. Pairwise matches are proposed and subsequently evaluated by a series of independent feature similarity modules. Assembly strategies are abstracted from the feature-specific sherd details and operate solely in terms of the probabilistic output of pair-wise proposals and evaluations.

Our framework, which is modular and extensible, paves the way for a system to automatically reconstruct pottery vessels. We demonstrate a greedy assembly strategy that predicts likely pairs and triples of sherds using a handful of proposal and evaluation modules.

Previous attempts to automate the task of reconstructing pottery vessels have relied on a single feature, and sometimes user intervention, to direct the search (Ucoluk & Toroslu 1999), (Papaioannou, Karabassi, & Theoharis 2001), (da Gama Leito & Stolfi 1998). While (Cooper *et al.* 2001) accounts for more than one feature using complex parametric models, we propose a conceptually simpler and modular system for integration akin to (Pankanti, Jain, & Tuceryan 1994) and (Keim *et al.* 1999; Keim, Shazeer, & Littman 1999). Our framework and assembly strategy are similar to (Jepson & Mann 1999) where they search for a plausible scene interpretation.

Methods

Our framework is centered around pair-wise comparison of sherds. It performs two types of comparisons: proposals, which propose a "match" or relative placement of the two sherds; and evaluations, which evaluate the likelihood of a given relative placement. These primitive operations can be realized using many different geometric features – we demonstrate only a few. Assembly modules build on top

of these primitive operations.

Proposal: Given an input pair of sherds, a proposal module generates a list of matches for the pair. The example we implemented generates a list of matches where each has a corner from each sherd coincident and one adjacent edge aligned.

Evaluation: An evaluative module produces a $\mathcal{X}^2$ statistic which - as a sum of independent and normally distributed squared residuals - provides a well-known way to evaluate the match likelihood and to form a joint likelihood from an ensemble of evaluative modules (Press *et al.* 1986). We implemented four evaluative modules. Assuming rotational symmetry of the vessels, the first two modules measure individual residuals using the axis of rotation for the respective sherds:

E₁ Alignment of the axes: the residual is the angle between the axes.

E₂ Overlap of the axes: the residual is the perpendicular distance between the axes.

The next two modules measure the alignment of the inside and outside break curves of the sherds. These curves delineate the break on the inside and outside surface of the vessel. The residuals that comprise the $\mathcal{X}^2$ are measured at closest-point pairs. For a given point A_i on one sherd's break curve, the closest-point pair is formed by the closest point $\tilde{A}_i$ on the other sherd's break curve. Points are sampled at intervals coarse enough to justify the independence of residuals.

E₃ Distance between break curves: the residuals are $\| A_i - \tilde{A}_i \|$.

E₄ Alignment of tangent vectors: the residuals are defined by the angle between tangent vectors to the break curves at A_i and $\tilde{A}_i$.

Assembly: Our prototype assembly algorithm uses the modules defined above to search for the original correct configuration of sherds. Our strategy starts by generating a set of match candidates for each pair using the proposal module. Then, we adjust the relative placement of each candidate match to maximize the ensemble likelihood and thereby improve the alignment of all features. This step is performed using a quasi-Newton algorithm for continuous function optimization (NAG 1993). The resulting optimized

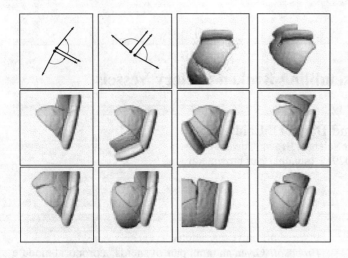

Figure 1: (by row) match proposals, ranked matches and best triples.

matches are then ranked according to their maximized ensemble likelihood values. Finally, we use a greedy strategy to select pair-wise matches to form triples. These are optimized in a similar fashion as the pairs by defining a three-way match likelihood as the sum of the three measurable pair-wise match likelihoods.

Results

The following section documents the results of our assembly algorithm when applied to a subset of 8 neighboring sherds from a 16 sherd test vessel. Of the 28 possible pairs, there are only 13 valid pair-wise matches in the correct reconstruction. The first row of the Figure depicts the geometry of two corner alignments and two examples of proposed matches. Next, we show the top four optimized matches for one pair of sherds from the vessel rim ranked by decreasing ensemble likelihood [0.999, 0.863, 0.574, 0.548]. For this pair, the ensemble likelihood identifies the correct match. In the same way, this procedure correctly identifies 6 out of the 13 valid matches. Nine correct matches are ranked among the top three matches per pair. In the last row, we show the most likely triples found by merging pairs and evaluating according to the 3-way likelihood described above; only the last one is incorrect.

Discussion and Conclusions

Our framework paves the way for a completely automated reconstruction system. There still remains several unresolved issues such as how to automate feature segmentation and how to deal with missing or faulty data. While our framework provides a foundation for the development and testing of reconstruction algorithms, an efficient working system has yet to be developed.

The main contribution of this work is the design of a modular and extensible framework for vessel assembly. We validate this framework by demonstrating a prototype reconstruction algorithm that identifies likely pairs and triples of sherds. Our strategy utilizes a multi-feature match likelihood computed by independent evaluation modules and demonstrates how one can extend pair-wise match likelihoods to handle triples and larger configurations of sherds.

References

Cooper, D.; Willis, A.; Cao, Y.; Han, D.; Leymarie, F.; Orriols, X.; Mumford, D.; et al. 2001. Assembling virtual pots from 3D measurements of their fragments. In *VAST International Symposium on Virtual Reality Archaeology and Cultural Heritage*.

da Gama Leito, H. C., and Stolfi, J. 1998. Automatic reassembly of irregular fragments. In *Universidade Fedral Fluminense (Estadual de Campinas), Technical Report IC-98-06*.

Jepson, A., and Mann, R. 1999. Qualitative probabilities for image interpretation. In *ICCV (2)*, 1123–1130.

Keim, G.; Shazeer, N.; Littman, M.; Agarwal, S.; Cheves, C.; Fitzgerald, J.; Grosland, J.; Jiang, F.; Pollard, S.; and Weinmeister, K. 1999. PROVERB: The probabilistic cruciverbalist. In *AAAI / IAAI*, 710–717.

Keim, G.; Shazeer, N.; and Littman, M. 1999. Solving crossword puzzles as probabilistic constraint satisfaction. In *AAAI / IAAI*, 156–162.

NAG. 1993. *NAG Fortran Library*. 1400 Opus Place, Suite 200, Downers Grove, Illinois 60515: Numerical Algorithms Group.

Pankanti, S.; Jain, A. K.; and Tuceryan, M. 1994. On integration of vision modules. In *CVPR*, 316–322.

Papaioannou, G.; Karabassi, E. A.; and Theoharis, T. 2001. Virtual archaeologist: Assembling the past. In *IEEE Computer Graphics and Applications*, volume 21, 53–59.

Press, W. H.; Flannery, B. P.; Teukolsky, S. A.; and Vetterling, W. T. 1986. *Numerical Recipes: The Art of Scientific Computing*. Cambridge, UK: Cambridge University Press.

Ucoluk, G., and Toroslu, I. H. 1999. Automatic reconstruction of broken 3-d surface objects. *Computers & Graphics* 23(4):573–582.

Mixed-Initiative Exception-Based Learning for

Knowledge Base Refinement

Cristina Boicu, Gheorghe Tecuci, Mihai Boicu

Learning Agents Laboratory, Computer Science Department, MS 4A5,
George Mason University, 4400 University Dr, Fairfax, VA 22030, Phone (703) 993-4669
{ccascava, tecuci, mboicu}@gmu.edu, http://lalab.gmu.edu, http://lalab.gmu.edu/cristina

Introduction

Over the years we have developed the Disciple approach for the rapid development of knowledge bases and knowledge-based agents, by subject matter experts, with limited assistance from knowledge engineers (Tecuci 1998). This approach relies on a Disciple learning agent that can be trained to solve problems by an expert. First, however, a knowledge engineer has to work with the expert to define the object ontology of Disciple. This ontology consists of hierarchical descriptions of objects and features from the application domain. Then, the expert can teach Disciple to solve problems in a way that resembles how the expert would teach a student. For instance, the expert defines a specific problem, helps the agent to understand each reasoning step toward the solution, and supervises and corrects the agent's behavior, when it attempts to solve new problems. During such mixed-initiative interactions, the agent learns general problem solving rules from individual problem solving steps and their explanations of success or failure. A critical role in this multistrategy rule learning process is played by the object ontology, which is used as the generalization hierarchy.

Mixed-Initiative Exception-Based Learning

The Disciple approach was successfully used in an agent training experiment at the US Army War College, where experts succeeded to teach personal Disciple agents their own problem solving expertise in military center of gravity (COG) determination (Boicu et al. 2001). This experiment, however, revealed that the rules learned from subject matter experts have a significant number of negative exceptions. A negative exception is a negative example that is covered by the rule, because the current object ontology does not contain any object concept or feature-value pair that distinguishes between all the positive examples of the rule, on one side, and this negative example, on the other side (Wrobel 1989). Therefore, in the context of the current ontology, the rule cannot be specialized to uncover the negative example, which is kept as a negative exception.

Such rule exceptions provide valuable information on how the ontology should be extended to represent the subtle distinctions that real experts make in their domain.

We are developing a suite of mixed-initiative multistrategy methods for learning new object concepts and features that extend the object ontology, allowing the elimination of the rule's exceptions. The first type of methods involves only the Disciple agent and the expert, and considers one rule with its exceptions at a time. The second class of methods considers again one rule with its exceptions at a time, but requires also the participation of a knowledge engineer in the mixed-initiative learning process. Finally, the third and most complex type of methods are global, considering all the exceptions from the knowledge base, and involving both the expert and the knowledge engineer. All the methods have four major phases: a candidates discovery phase, a selection phase, an ontology refinement phase, and a rule refinement phase. In the candidates discovery phase, the Disciple agent generates an ordered set of candidates that have the potential of removing the exceptions. Each candidate is a new ontology piece (for instance, a new value of an existing feature, a new object feature, or even a new object concept) that has the potential of distinguishing between the positive examples and the negative exceptions. To generate these candidates and to order them by their plausibility, Disciple uses analogical reasoning heuristics, ontology design principles, and hints from the user. In the candidate selection phase, Disciple interacts with the user to test the most plausible candidates, and to select one of them. In the ontology refinement phase, Disciple elicits additional knowledge from the expert, related to the selected candidate. For instance, if the selected candidate is a new type of feature, then Disciple will attempt to elicit from the expert which other objects from the knowledge base have that feature, and will also learn a general definition of the feature. This definition includes a domain concept (which represents the set of objects that can have that feature), and a range concept (which represents the set of possible values of that feature). Finally, in the rule refinement phase, the rule is updated based on the refined ontology. Because of the central role of the object ontology as the generalization hierarchy for learning, an ontology change may potentially affect any rule from the knowledge base, not only those with exceptions. We have therefore developed methods for rapid rule relearning in the context of the updated ontology. These methods maintain the relevant knowledge from which an individual rule was learned, such as generalized explanations and prototypical examples, and automatically regenerate the rule.

We will illustrate the first type of exception handling methods, in which the expert collaborates with Disciple to analyze a rule with a negative exception. Figure 1 shows an example of a task reduction step from the Center of Gravity analysis domain (Boicu et al. 2001). It consists of a problem solving task, a question relevant to the reduction of this task, the answer to the question, and the subtask resulted from this answer.

IF the task is
Identify a strategic COG candidate for Japan_1944 with respect to other sources of strength and power
Question: What is a source of strength and power of Japan_1944?
Answer: Japanese_army_forces_on_Luzon
THEN
Japanese_army_forces_on_Luzon is a strategic COG candidate for Japan_1944

Figure 1: A problem solving episode

Based on this problem solving episode, Disciple learns a general task reduction rule. This rule, however, generates the wrong solution "Japanese_expectation_for_negotiation is a strategic COG candidate for Japan_1944," which is rejected by the expert. Because the ontology does not contain any element that distinguishes between "Japanese_army_forces_on_Luzon" and "Japanese_expectation_for_negotiation," the incorrect reasoning step is kept as a negative exception of the rule. The expert can invoke the Exception-Based Learning module, attempting to extend the ontology by himself. First, Disciple proposes him candidate extensions that have the potential of removing the exception. For instance, Disciple looks for an existing feature that may be associated with "Japanese_army_forces_on_Luzon" (the positive example), without being associated with "Japanese_expectation_for_negotiation" (the negative exception), and finds "is_a_strategically_important_military_capability_for." The domain of this feature is "Military_factor", which includes the positive example without including the negative exception. The expert accepts this feature and specifies that its value for the positive example is Japan_1944. Next, Disciple guides the expert to also specify this feature for other instances of Military_factor, such as "Japanese_concentration_of_naval_assets." Then, it refines the object ontology with this new knowledge acquired from the expert, as shown in Figure 2. Disciple refines also the rule based on this knowledge, transforming the negative exception into a negative example that is no longer covered by the rule.

As illustrated above, the first class of methods discovers limited extensions of the ontology (such as an additional feature of an object when the feature definition is already present in the ontology). The second class of methods leads to more complex refinements, such as the definition of new types of objects or the restructuring of the object hierarchy. For instance, Disciple may elicit from the expert an explanation of why the negative exception of a rule is an incorrect problem solving episode, explanation represented by a new type of object that is placed in the object hierarchy. The methods from the third and most complex class first hypothesize knowledge pieces for all the rules with exceptions. Then, they analyze these hypotheses to define an ordered set of hypotheses, each one eliminating or reducing the exceptions from more than one rule.

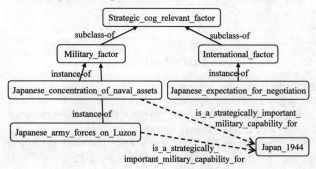

Figure 2: A fragment of the refined object ontology

Conclusions

Some of the above methods are already implemented in the Exception-Based Learning module of Disciple-RKF/COG. With these methods we are proposing a solution to the complex problem of learning with an evolving representation language, as represented by the object ontology.

Acknowledgements. This research was sponsored by DARPA, AFRL, AFMC, USAF, under agreement number F30602-00-2-0546, by the AFOSR under grant no. F49620-00-1-0072, and by the US Army War College.

References

Boicu, M.; Tecuci, G.; Stanescu, B.; Marcu, D.; and Cascaval (now Boicu), C. 2001. Automatic Knowledge Acquisition from Subject Matter Experts. In *Proceedings of the Thirteenth International Conference on Tools with Artificial Intelligence*, 69-78. Los Alamitos, California: IEEE Computer Society.

Tecuci, G. 1998. *Building Intelligent Agents: An Apprenticeship Multistrategy Learning Theory, Methodology, Tool and Case Studies*. London, England: Academic Press.

Wrobel, S. 1989. Demand-driven concept formation. In Morik, K. ed. *Knowledge Representation and Organization in Machine Learning. Lecture Notes in Artificial Intelligence* 347: 289-319. New York: Springer-Verlag.

Fuzzy Numbers for the Improvement of Causal Knowledge Representation in Fuzzy Cognitive Maps

Otto X. Cordero and Enrique Peláez

Information Technology Center - ESPOL
Edificio 37, Campus Gustavo Galindo, Km 30.5 via Perimetral.
ocordero@cti.espol.edu.ec

Abstract

We present an extension of the fuzzy cognitive map knowledge representation, based on fuzzy numbers, to improve the management of uncertainty related to linguistic expressions. In this regard, we also review the fuzzy causal algebra and outline the opportunities for applications.

Introduction

Fuzzy cognitive maps (FCM) are fuzzy directed graphs where nodes represent concepts; edges are labeled with a plus, '+', to denote causal increase and a minus, '-', to denote causal decrease. In FCMs causal relationships are assessed with linguistic terms.

FCMs are used to graphically model a system's behavior through its cause and effect relationships. However, current approaches to the management of FCMs, miss valuable information related to the uncertainty of linguistic estimations about causality. As an attempt to solve this problem, we present an extension of the FCM knowledge representation based on fuzzy numbers.

Causal Knowledge Representation with Fuzzy Numbers

Gradual association between a cause and an effect is expressed as a causal strength in the cause-effect relationship. This notion could be induced by partial or gradual occurrence of effects, or by the uncertainty of observations [Dubois and Prade, 1995]. Expressing the concept of causal strength in terms of fuzzy sets theory, we can say that having a fuzzy set $\tilde{C} = \{c_1, c_2, \ldots c_n\}$ of causes for some effect e, the degree of membership of a given cause c_i in $\tilde{C}$, denoted as $u_e(c_i)$, is the degree of sufficiency for the occurrence of e given the causality imparted by c_i.

A fuzzy set of causes for an effect is the theoretical framework that supports the FCM causal knowledge representation. However, the estimation about the degree

of causation is in many cases the result of subjective perception. To extend and improve the knowledge representation it would be useful to use fuzzy degrees of membership representing an uncertain estimation, possibly linguistic, of the degree of sufficiency. Consequently, the fuzzy set of causes will be a type-2 fuzzy set [Zadeh, 1975] where, having a set of causes C, causal relationships will be expressed by membership functions of the form:

$$A : C \rightarrow F([0,1]) \qquad (1)$$

Where F([0,1]) is the fuzzy power set of [0,1] [Klir and Yuan, 1995]. Applying this concept to the FCM knowledge representation, causal edges are represented by fuzzy numbers with membership functions associated to linguistic terms.

The Fuzzy Causal Algebra

Fuzzy causal algebra deals with the calculation of the indirect and total causal effect [Axelrod, 1976]. The indirect effect that some concept node Ci imparts to some concept node Cj is the causality that Ci imparts to Cj via the causal path that links both nodes. On the other hand, to assess the total causal effect we have to combine all causal paths leading to the node.

The operations for indirect and total causal effects are interpreted as fuzzy intersection and union respectively, defined on a partially ordered set of causal values [Peláez, 1994].

The problem is to find operators for the fuzzy intersection and union that resembles our intuition about causality. We will base our analysis on two arguments provided by [Zimmermann, 1981] that gain special relevance in the causal reasoning context.

Compensation. An operator is compensatory if a change in the resulting membership degree due to a change in one of the operands can be counteracted by a change in another operand.

Aggregative Behavior. An operation holds aggregative behavior if the resulting membership degree depends on the number of membership functions combined.

In the context of causal reasoning, both concepts describe our intuition about a causal system. For example, compensation is present in causal chaining, where the causality that Ci imparts to Cj declines as the causal path $Ci \rightarrow Cj$ gets more populated by intermediate causes. The aggregative behavior is present in causal confluence, where the causality imparted to an effect gets higher as the number of causes of the same sign increases.

We will use the standard algebraic product as indirect-effect operator and the generalized algebraic sum for total effect. Both operators are compliant with the arguments previously discussed [Zimmermann, 1987]. Hence, the indirect-effect operator will be:

$$\mu_{\cap} = \prod_{i=1}^{m} \mu_i \qquad (2)$$

Where $\mu_{\cap}$ stands for the fuzzy intersection such that $\mu_{\cap} \in F([0,1])$, being $F([0,1])$ the fuzzy power set of $[0,1]$. μ_i is the marginal causality and m is the number of nodes in the causal path.

For the total effect operator, in order to offset positive and negative causes, the algebraic sum will consider the sign label representing positive or negative causality as an algebraic sign. Therefore, for causal combination we will have the following operation:

$$\mu_{\cup} = 1 - \prod_{i=1}^{m}(1-(-1)^{\alpha}\mu_i^+) \cdot \prod_{j=1}^{n}(1-(-1)^{1-\alpha}\mu_j^-);$$

$$\alpha = \begin{cases} 0; \sum_{i=1}^{m}\mu_i^+ \geq \sum_{j=1}^{n}\mu_j^- \\ 1; \sum_{i=1}^{m}\mu_i^+ < \sum_{j=1}^{n}\mu_j^- \end{cases} \qquad (3)$$

Where μ_i^+ and μ_j^- stands for marginal positive and negative causality respectively, while $\mu_{\cup}$ is the total causality; m and n are the number of positive and negative causes linked to the effect, in that order. The α parameter used in (3) helps us to assure that $\mu_{\cup} \in F([0, 1])$.

Improving Interpretation with Linguistic Approximation

Using a simple algorithm for linguistic approximation we can convert fuzzy-numeric results, representing the activation value of concepts, into linguistic sentences that combine the terms selected for causality assessment.

Furthermore, the membership function shape can be analyzed to obtain conclusions about the uncertainty that affects the calculated activation value. For example, disperse membership functions reflect a balance between opposite sign causes. This can also be interpreted as a low degree of consensus, if we are combining FCMs designed by several experts. To perform this analysis we must use a similarity measure based on the fuzzy set shape, as for example the Hamming distance [Klir and Yuan, 1995], in combination with heuristics about significant patterns of the membership function shape.

Conclusions and Further Work

We have presented an extension of the FCM knowledge representation using fuzzy numbers to represent causal strength, and reviewing the fuzzy causal algebra for FCMs and fuzzy numbers. We have also suggested the use of linguistic approximation as an approach that allows us to revert the flow of uncertainty-based information, providing a linguistic description of the results.

FCMs can be used to build causal expert systems in controversial domains, using its graphical representation to acquire knowledge from discussions and collaborative meetings. At the moment we are applying this tool to the acquisition of knowledge and production of diagnoses about shrimp diseases such as the WSSV syndrome. We are also exploring the application of FCMs to decision-making automation, where the use of fuzzy numbers can allow us to connect the FCM with fuzzy IF-THEN rules.

References

Axelrod, R. 1976. *Structures of Decision, The Cognitive Maps of Political Elites*. Princeton University Press, NJ.

Dubois, D., and Prade, H. 1995. Fuzzy relation equations and causal reasoning. *Fuzzy Sets and Systems*, 119-134.

Dvorak, A. 1997. On Linguistic Approximation in the Frame of LFLC. *In Proceedings of the Seventh IFSA World Congress Prague* 1:413-417.

Hisdal, H. 1981. The IF THEN ELSE statement and interval-valued fuzzy sets of higher type. *The Int. J. of Man-Machine Studies* 15: 385-455.

Klir, G., and Yuan, B. 1995. *Fuzzy Sets and Fuzzy Logic: Theory and Applications*. Prentice Hall.

Kosko, B. 1992. *Fuzzy Associative Memory Systems. Fuzzy Expert Systems*. CRC Press.

Peláez, C. E. 1994. *A Fuzzy Cognitive Map Knowledge Representation for Failure Modes and Effects Analysis*. Ph.D. diss., University of South Carolina.

Zadeh, L. A. 1975. The concept of a linguistic variable and its application to approximate reasoning - I. *Information Sciences* 8:199-249.

Zimmermann, H. J. 1987. *Fuzzy Sets, Decision Making and Expert Systems*. Kluwer Academic Publishers.

A Genetic Algorithm for Tuning Variable Orderings
in Bayesian Network Structure Learning

Haipeng Guo   **Benjamin B. Perry**   **Julie A. Stilson**   **William H. Hsu**

Laboratory for Knowledge Discovery in Databases, Kansas State University
234 Nichols Hall, Manhattan, KS 66506-2302
{hpguo | bhsu | bbp9857 | jas3466}@cis.ksu.edu   http://www.kddresearch.org

1. Introduction

In the last two decades or so, Bayesian networks (BNs) [Pe88] have become a prevalent method for uncertain knowledge representation and reasoning. BNs are directed acyclic graphs (DAGs) where nodes represent random variables, and edges represent conditional dependence between random variables. Each node has a conditional probabilistic table (CPT) that contains probabilities of that node being a specific value given the values of its parents. The problem of learning a BN from data is important but hard. Finding the optimal structure of a BN from data has been shown to be *NP*-hard [HGC95], even without considering unobserved or irrelevant variables. In recent years, many Bayesian network learning algorithms have been developed. Generally these algorithms fall into two groups, score-based search and dependency analysis (conditional independence tests and constraint solving). Many previous approaches require that a node ordering is available before learning. Unfortunately, this is usually not the case in many real-world applications. To make greedy search usable when node orderings are unknown, we have developed a permutation genetic algorithm (GA) wrapper to tune the variable ordering given as input to *K2* [CH92], a score-based BN learning algorithm. In our continuing project, we have used a probabilistic inference criterion as the GA's fitness function and we are also trying some other criterion to evaluate the learning result such as the learning fixed-point property.

2. K2 and GA Wrapper

K2 uses a Bayesian score and a greedy search method to construct a Bayesian network from a database of records [CH92]. It can find structures quickly given a reasonable variable, or node, ordering. Given an ordering, only "upstream" nodes of a node are considered as its candidate

parents. *K2* is very sensitive to the ordering because of its limitation of greediness. The search scheme we have implemented is to use a permutation genetic algorithm as a wrapper to explore the ordering space by randomly generating, selecting, and recombining node orderings. This GA applies *K2* using each node ordering, and estimates which among the BN structures output by *K2* is most probable. To develop a GA for permutation problems, we need to select the proper crossover and mutation operations. We use order crossover (*OX*) for this task. *OX* exchanges subsequences of two permutations, displacing duplicated indices with holes. It then shifts the holes to one side, possibly displacing some indices, and replaces the original subsequence in these holes. Mutation is implemented by swapping uniformly selected indices.

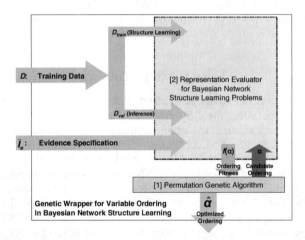

Figure 1. System Design Overview.

After the GA produces a random ordering, we validate it via inference using the BN produced by *K2*. The problem of BN inference is to compute *P(Q|E)*, the posterior probabilities of query nodes given states of evidence nodes. BN inference is also *NP*-hard [Co90]. For small and sparse networks, we can use exact inference algorithm to compute *P(Q|E)*. The Lauritzen-Spiegelhalter (*LS*) algorithm, or clique-tree propagation, is one efficient exact BN inference algorithm [LS88]. For large and

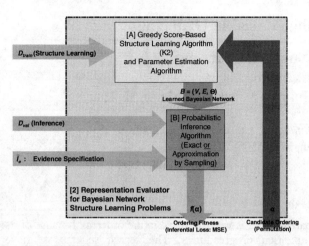

Figure 2. Probabilistic reasoning environment, Module [2] from Figure 1.

complex BNs, we apply approximate inference. Stochastic simulation algorithms are the most often used approximate inference methods, which include logic sampling, likelihood weighting, backward sampling, self-importance sampling, and adaptive importance sampling *(AIS)*. We divide the input data into training data D_{train} and validation data D_{val}. D_{train} is used to learn the BN and D_{val} is used to validate the learned BN. We first compute $P(Q|E)$ from D_{val}, and $P'(Q|E)$ from the BN produced by K2, using either LS or AIS. We then compute a loss function (RMSE) between $P(Q|E)$ and $P'(Q|E)$, and use it as the GA's fitness function. Figure 1 shows the system overview.

3. Result & Discussion

System components implemented so far include *K2* for learning BNs, the LS algorithm and several stochastic sampling algorithms for inference, and the GA wrapper for tuning the node ordering. We implemented an elitist permutation GA using OX. Our initial experiments were conducted on an eight nodes BN whose permutation space contains 8! = 40320 different orderings. The result shows the GA (10 populations, 100 generations) improves the ordering to within 0.01 of the optimal RMSE (about 0.95 calculated by LS algorithm on the standard BN). Our work is closely related to [LPYM+96] in which they also applied a GA to Bayesian network learning. But they only focused on structure learning. They used the same Bayesian score as *K2* to evaluate a learned network structure and they used GA to directly operate on the network structure itself. Our scheme uses a different fitness function and the GA operates on a smaller space, i.e., the variables ordering space. Although our initial result is promising, we feel that it could be further improved by trying better fitness functions for the GA wrapper. The problem we need to overcome is the same as discussed in [NK00]: "In case where the amount of data is small relative to the size of the model, there are likely to be many models that explain the data reasonably well". This makes us less confident about that the learned model is a true representation to the underlying process. To improve confidence we are considering sample complexity issues in the learning process. We are also trying to use the fixed-point property of the learning process as a fitness function to evaluate the learned model. Our conjecture is that a good initial model shall converge in probability to a fixed point under a learning and stochastic data generation process while a bad model shall not. Our preliminary result shows that this may be a promising direction in the future.

Acknowledgements

Support for this research was provided in part by the Army Research Lab under grant ARL-PET-IMT-KSU-07 and by the Office of Naval Research under grant N00014-01-1-0519.

References

[CD00] J. Cheng and M. J. Druzdzel. AIS-BN: An adaptive importance sampling algorithm for evidential reasoning in large Bayesian networks. *Journal of Artificial Intelligence Research (JAIR)*, 13:155-188, 2000.

[CH92] G. F. Cooper and E. Herskovits. A Bayesian Method for the Induction of Probabilistic Networks from Data. *Machine Learning*, **9**(4):309-347, 1992.

[Co90] G. F. Cooper. The computational complexity of probabilistic infernece using bayesian belief networks. *Artificial Intelligence*, 42(2-3):393-405. Elsevier, 1990.

[HGC95] D. Heckerman, D. Geiger, and D. Chickering, Learning Bayesian networks: The combination of knowledge and statistical data. *Machine Learning*, 20(3):197-243, Kluwer, 1995.

[LPYM+96] P. Larranaga, M. Poza, Y. Yurramendi, R. H. Murga and C.M.H. Kuijpers. Structure Learning of Bayesian Networks by Genetic Algorithms: A Performance Analysis of Control Parameters. *IEEE Journal on Pattern Analysis and Machine Intelligence* 18(9): 912-926, 1996.

[LS88] S. L. Lauritzen and D. J. Spiegelhalter. Local computations with probabilities on graphical structures and their application to expert systems. *Journal of the Royal Statistical Society, Series B* 50, 1988.

[NK00] N. Friedman and D. Koller. Being Bayesian About Network Structure: A Bayesian Approach to Structure Discovery in Bayesian Networks. In UAI00.

[Pe88] J. Pearl. *Probabilistic Reasoning in Intelligent Systems: Networks of Plausible Inference*, Morgan Kaufmann, San Mateo, CA, 1988.

A Model Checker for Verifying ConGolog Programs

Leila Kalantari and **Eugenia Ternovska**
Department of Computing Science
Simon Fraser University, Burnaby, BC, Canada, V5A 1S6
{lkalanta,ter}@cs.sfu.ca

Abstract

We describe our work in progress on a model checker for verifying ConGolog programs. ConGolog is a novel high-level programming language for robot control which incorporates a rich account of concurrency, prioritized execution, interrupts, and changes in the world that are beyond robot's control. The novelty of this language requires new methods of proving correctness. We apply the techniques from XSB tabling and the μ-calculus, to overcome the challenge of verifying complex non-terminating programs, in a terminating time.

This note describes our work on a model checker (Clarke Jr., Grumberg, & Peled 1999) for verifying ConGolog programs. ConGolog is a programming language for high-level control of robots (De Giacomo, Lespérance, & Levesque 2000). The language is based on the situation calculus, a formal language for representing effects of actions (cf. (Reiter 2001)). ConGolog includes facilities for executing prioritized non-terminating concurrent processes, as well as facilities for dealing with interrupts and exogenous actions. This language differs from other concurrent languages in that the initial state does not have to be specified completely; also it allows the user to define primitive actions using axioms of the situation calculus. Due to the complex features of ConGolog that we stated above, manual error checking for ConGolog programs becomes almost an impossible task. This fact necessitates the automatic verification of ConGolog programs and also shows the difficulty of implementing it.

Let us consider two simple examples. Imagine an elevator controller program, called $Ctrl_1$, which picks a random floor, tests whether there is an outstanding request from that floor; and if so, it proceeds to serve that request. Another simple elevator controller program is called $Ctrl_2$. The elevator goes up as long as there is any unserved requests for the upper floors; and if not, it goes down as long as there is an outstanding request from a lower floor. On its way, the elevator tests whether there is an unserved request from the current floor; and if so, it serves it. For $Ctrl_1$, it is possible that some requests will be ignored forever since the floor to serve is picked randomly. If this happens, we say that *starvation* occurs. Notice that starvation does not happen for $Ctrl_2$, and any request will be served eventually. Our model

checker should be able to discover the behavior of these two controllers. For $Ctrl_1$, it should detect the starvation property; and for $Ctrl_2$, it should verify that starvation will never occur.

The biggest challenge of verification of ConGolog programs is how to verify properties of non-terminating processes in terminating time. As pointed out in (De Giacomo, Lespérance, & Levesque 2000), this task is especially difficult in the presence of non-deterministic choice.

There are several approaches to formal verification. One of the most common ones uses branching time temporal modal logics for writing specifications. For the verification of ConGolog programs, we also use the branching time approach, which we need in order to deal with non-determinism of ConGolog programs. We use greatest and least least fixed points constructions, similar to those used in the propositional μ-calculus (cf. (Emerson 1990)) to express properties of non-terminating and non-deterministic processes. For example, the starvation property mentioned above can be formulated in the μ-calculus as

$$\mu Z_2 \left(\exists n \exists s' \left(now = do(reqElevator(n), s') \wedge \phi\right) \vee \Diamond Z_2\right),$$

where
$$\phi := \nu Z_1 \left(ButtonOn(n, now) \wedge \Diamond Z_1\right),$$

and now represents the current situation. This property expresses negation of the fairness requirement that every request is eventually served.

We were inspired by the ideas of (Ramakrishna *et al.* 1997) for dealing with non-termination because the abstract language for describing computational processes in (Ramakrishna *et al.* 1997) and ConGolog are both based on process algebra (Bergstra, Ponse, & Smolka 2001). We have exploited the tabling power of XSB logic programming system (cf. (XSB)) to deal with this challenge. We define a special program for exogenous (i.e., outside of robot's control) actions to model the environment. The program non-deterministicly chooses an action a, tests whether it is an exogenous action, and if so, it will execute it. To perform verification, we run each controller concurrently with a program which models the environment.

While designing the model checker, we faced the following difficulty. Along the computational tree, which represents all possible executions of a ConGolog program, the term representing the current situation grows and never repeats itself. This fact makes it difficult to use XSB tabling to handle model checking for non-terminating programs.

Let us describe our approach to how to deal with this problem. All possible executions of a non-terminating program compose an infinite computational tree. We observed that, when trying to verify a property of a non-terminating program, it is enough to verify that property for an initial finite fragment of this tree. If the property holds in that fragment, we can conclude that it will hold for the whole infinite computational tree. Our justification of this observation relies on a repetition pattern which occurs in the computational tree — the state of the system, and the state of the program. The first repetition factor is the repletion of the state of the system along a computational path. Clearly, when the number of states is finite, the only way to obtain infinite computations is by looping through the transition system. So, there must be at least one state that repeats itself. The second repetition factor is related to the execution of ConGolog programs. There are two main constructs in the language of ConGolog by which we can obtain infinite computations. The first one is δ^*, which means that program δ is being repeated zero or more times. Clearly, after executing δ once, what is left to execute is, again, δ^*. So, the program repeats itself at some point in the tree of situations. This fact is reflected in the axiomatization of the predicates $trans$ and $trans^*$ (cf. (De Giacomo, Lespérance, & Levesque 2000)). The same argument applies to the $while$ construct, which is evident from the same axiomatization.

Our model checker works on the computational tree by using recursion on the subtrees. XSB tabling is used to terminate this recursion. When the same state of the system and state of the program is encountered, instead of going on with computation, XSB will make use of the results stored in its table. This way, we verify properties of non-terminating ConGolog programs in terminating time. At the moment, our model checker is restricted to non-terminating programs.

At the time of writing this note, we have not completed testing of the model checker on large programs. Occasionally, we obtain unexpected and contradictory results, and some of them seem to coincide with the known bugs of XSB system (Refer to the section "Restrictions and Current Known Bugs" of "The XSB Programmers' Manual"). We are trying to obtain a better understanding of the XSB system to find the origin of the occasional misbehavior. As soon as we get around these problems, we will proceed to prove the correctness of our implementation. We will also study to what extend we can eliminate any of our restrictions, most notably, the requirement of finite number of fluents (i.e., properties of the world which change with performing actions).

Acknowledgments

The first author is grateful to Dr. David Warren and Luis Fernando Pias de Castro for their help with the XSB system.

References

Bergstra, J.; Ponse, A.; and Smolka, S. 2001. *Handbook of Process Algebra*. Elsevier Science.

Clarke Jr., E. M.; Grumberg, O.; and Peled, D. A. 1999. *Model Cheking*. MIT Press.

De Giacomo, G.; Lespérance, Y.; and Levesque, H. 2000. ConGolog, a concurrent programming language based on the situation calculus. *Artificial Intelligence* 121:109–169.

Emerson, I. 1990. Temporal and modal logic. In van Leeuwen, J., ed., *Handbook of Theoretical Computer Science*. 996–1072.

Ramakrishna, Y.; Ramakrishnan, C.; Ramakrishnan, I.; Smolka, S.; Swift, T.; and Warren, D. S. 1997. Efficient model checking using tabled resolution. In *Proceedings of the 9th International Conference on Computer-Aided Verification (CAV'97)*, Lecture Notes in Computer Science. Haifa, Israel: Springer-Verlag.

Reiter, R. 2001. *Knowledge in Action: Logical Foundations for Describing and Implementing Dynamical Systems*. MIT Press.

The XSB, a logic programming system developed at the State University of New York at Stony Brook. http://xsb.sourceforge.net.

Analogical Inference over a Common Sense Database

Thomas Lin

MIT Media Laboratory
410 Memorial Drive
Cambridge, MA 02139
tlin@mit.edu

Introduction

This paper shows that by applying analogical inference techniques to a large natural language common sense database, we can generate new, plausible common sense facts. Two systems that do this are described. Being able to generate new facts in this manner allows quick augmentation of the common sense database.

The role of analogical inference in common sense reasoning has been discussed before (Carbonell 1983), but only recently have large common sense databases become publicly available. We used the Open Mind Common Sense (OMCS) database, which contains several hundred thousand English common sense statements (Singh 2002).

The OMCS database is built by internet users who are prompted to enter common sense facts at a website. The reason we use the OMCS database instead of the CYC common sense database (Lenat and Guha 1994) is because this analogical inference work is concurrently being integrated into OMCS's data collection mechanism.

The idea is that an internet user can enter a fact at the OMCS website, then the system uses techniques described by this paper to respond with 30 plausible deductions based off the fact. Then, the user decides whether each deduction is true or false. True deductions become additional database facts, while false ones become negative expertise. Doing this allows for much faster data input by users.

To carry out the analogical inference, we first represent the OMCS database as a set of concepts and a set of relations. A concept is a noun phrase or an adjective. A relation looks like "A ? is for playing ?". Each original sentence becomes a relation after its concepts are replaced by question marks.

Analogies over Concepts and Relations

The first system finds "analogies over concepts and relations." It takes a sentence as input, and outputs a list of inferences.

Analogy over concepts starts by finding all other relations connecting an original sentence's set of concepts. It then finds all other sets of concepts that these relations connect. It substitutes each new set of concepts into the original relation to form deductions. Here is an example:

1. A user enters: "A mother can have a baby."
2. The system parses this into "A ? can have a ?" with concepts "mother" and "baby"
3. The system finds all other relations in the database for "mother" and "baby," such as "A ? will feed her ?"
4. Then it finds all other sets of concepts connected by each such relation. For instance, "girl" and "small dog" from "A girl will feed her small dog."
5. It substitutes each new set of concepts back into the original relation. In our example, this gives "A girl can have a small dog." This new sentence is added to the inferences list.

Analogy over relations starts by finding all other sets of concepts connected by the relation present in the original sentence. It then finds all other relations connecting each such set of concepts and substitutes the concepts from the original sentence into the new relations. Here is an example:

1. A user enters: "A mother can have a baby."
2. The program parses this as "A ? can have a ?"
3. Now it finds all other sets of concepts that are connected by this relation, such as "A child can have a goldfish."
4. For each such set of concepts, it finds the other relations that connect the set. For example, "child" and "goldfish" are also connected by "A child can take care of a goldfish."
5. This has the pattern "A ? can take care of a ?"
6. Each of these patterns is then filled with the original concepts. Here, we get "A mother can take care of a baby." This new sentence is added to the inferences list.

This system has used "Hawks eat rabbits" to deduce "There is more rabbits than there are hawks" by relating (hawks, rabbits) to (cows, grass) and finding "There is more grass than there are cows."

Analogies as Inference Rules

The second system does analogical inference by generating a list of inference rules. First, the original database is organized into a graph where the nodes are concepts and the edges are relations. Then, it finds all cycles in the graph where three 2-part relations connect three concepts. (A 2-part relation is a relation over exactly 2 variables). This could look like,

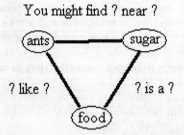

Figure 1: In this graph, "ants," "sugar," and "food" are in a cycle. The three original sentences are: "You might find ants near sugar," "Ants like food," and "Sugar is a food."

Each cycle is an inference rule. The rule here is: "(?a like ?b) (?c is a ?b) (You might find ?a near ?b)." For each rule, the system finds all other places in the graph where any two of the three elements in the inference rule are instantiated. It then forms what a third element needs to look like to be consistent with the first two, and presents it as an inference. Inference rules with more occurrences in the database are "better."

The input to the system is a sentence, and the output is all inferences that can be made with it. If the user enters "Bats like darkness" and "You might find bats near cave interiors" is already in the database, then the system matches: ?a = "bats," ?b = "darkness," and ?c = "cave interiors" to deduce "Cave interiors is a darkness" from the earlier example. This expresses a new idea that is not in the original database.

This system has used "Seeing requires that your eyes are open" to deduce "If you want to read a newspaper then you should have eyes."

Analysis

"Analogy over concepts and relations" is O(# of relations that connect any set of concepts) x O(# of concept sets that are connected by any relation) running time. "Analogies as inference rules" is O(# of inference rules that include the user's sentence's relation) x O(# of concept sets that are connected by any relation) running time. Both systems usually run within a second on a 800 MHz machine with 512 MB RAM, although "analogies as inference rules" take several seconds for certain input.

To test the validity of the inferences, 40 random sentences from the original database that had 2-part relations were used as input to both systems, and we analyzed the results.

55% of sentences produced output from "analogies over concepts and relations." 25% of overall sentences had matches from "analogy over concepts," while 40% had matches from "analogy over relations." The average sentence with matches from "analogy over concepts" had 66% of its results express new, true statements. The average sentence with matches from "analogy over relations" had 64.8% of its results express new, true statements.

67.5% of sentences had results from analogy with inference rules. The average such sentence had 35.6% of its results express new, true statements.

Sometimes the systems will make analogies that do not fit well. The probability of meaningful output can be increased by using systems of negative expertise, probability, and plausibility.

Conclusion

Two new analogical inference systems have been developed, implemented, and tested. The first one works by matching and substituting concepts and relations. The second one works by automatically generating a list of inference rules, then using these rules to make deductions.

The systems described in this paper work over large, noisy databases, not just toy examples. They will output deductions when fed new or existing sentences, and people can manually identify good and bad deductions to quickly augment the original database.

I would like to thank Push Singh for his guidance and encouragement with this work.

References

Carbonell, J. G. and Minton, S. 1983. Metaphor and Common-Sense Reasoning, Technical Report, CMU-CS-110, Carnegie-Mellon University.

Lenat, D. B. and R. V. Guha. 1994. Enabling Agents to Work Together. *Communications of the ACM* 37, no. 7.

Singh, P. 2002. The Public Acquisition of Commonsense Knowledge. In *Proceedings of AAAI Spring Symposium*. Menlo Park, Calif.: American Association of Artificial Intelligence, Inc.

MAKEBELIEVE: Using Commonsense Knowledge to Generate Stories

Hugo Liu, Push Singh

MIT Media Laboratory
20 Ames Street 320D
Cambridge, MA, 02139 USA
{hugo, push}@media.mit.edu

Introduction

This paper introduces MAKEBELIEVE, an interactive story generation agent that uses commonsense knowledge to generate short fictional texts from an initial seed story step supplied by the user. A subset of commonsense describing causality, such as the sentence "a consequence of drinking alcohol is intoxication," is selected from the ontology of the Open Mind Commonsense Knowledge Base (Singh, 2002). Binary causal relations are extracted from these sentences and stored as crude trans-frames (Minsky, 1988). By performing fuzzy, creativity-driven inference over these frames, creative "causal chains" are produced for use in story generation. The current system has mostly local pair-wise constraints between steps in the story, though global constraints such as narrative structure are being added.

Our motivation for this project stems from two questions: Can a large-scale knowledge base of commonsense benefit the artificial intelligence community by supplying new knowledge and methods to tackle difficult AI problems? And given that full commonsense reasoning has yet to mature, can we demonstrate any success with a more "fail-soft" approach? We picked story generation because we feel it is a classic AI problem that can be approached with a creative use of commonsense knowledge. Compared to problem solving or question answering, story generation is a "softer" problem where there is no wrong solution per se, and that solution is evaluated subjectively.

This paper is organized as follows. In the first section we frame our approach in the context of previous work in story generation. In the second section, we present the system's representation of commonsense and techniques for fuzzy, creativity-driven inference. The third section presents an overview of the story generation architecture of MAKEBELIEVE. We conclude with an evaluation of the system followed by some discussion.

Previous Work

Previous work on story generation has generally taken one of two approaches: structuralist, and transformationalist.

Structuralists such as Klein (1973, 1975) use real-world story structures such as canned story sequences and story grammars to generate stories. In contrast, transformationalists believe that story-telling expertise can be encoded by rules (Dreizin et al, 1978), or narrative goals (Dehn, 1981), which are applied to story elements such as setting and characters. The best example of this approach is TALE-SPIN (Meehan, 1977), which treats story generation as being analogous to problem solving. A story TALE-SPIN produces is essentially a description of the steps taken in the course of solving one or more problems.

MAKEBELIEVE inherits from both the structuralist and transformationalist traditions. First, MAKEBELIEVE is essentially a transformational story generator in its assumption that story generation is the result of simulation guided by rules manifested as local and global constraints. On the other hand, the commonsense facts about causality used in our simulation exhibit the property of being real-world story structures preferred by structuralists. The chief advantage of this is that the causal relationship between two events in a piece of commonsense is not bounded by any small set of simulation rules, but are instead bounded by the much greater variety of events and causal relations describable by commonsense knowledge.

Techniques for Using Commonsense

There are two large-scale knowledge bases of commonsense that we are aware of: Lenat's CYC (1995) and Open Mind Commonsense (OMCS). CYC contains over a million hand-crafted assertions, expressed in formal logic while OMCS has over 400,000 semi-structured English sentences, gathered through a web community of collaborators. Our current implementation uses Open Mind but CYC will be considered in the future. Sentences in OMCS are semi-structured, due to the use of sentence templates in the acquisition of knowledge, so it is relatively easy to extract relations and arguments. Compared with a logic representation, there is more semantic ambiguity associated with English sentences, but our fail-soft approach to commonsense inference is rather tolerant to ambiguity.

From the OMCS ontology, we selected a subset of 9,000 sentences that describe causation, such as the following:

- A consequence of bringing in a verdict is that the defendant is nervous

- Something that might happen when you act in a play is you forget your lines
- A consequence of eating in a fast food restaurant may be constipation

Before inference can be performed, we normalize the English sentences into a consistent form, for which we chose crude trans-frames, each with a before (cause) and after (effect) event, further decomposed into verb-object form with the help of a constituent structure parser. An example of sentence and its corresponding frame follows:

"The effect of keeping things orderly and tidy is living a better life." → {VERB: "keep" OBJS: "thing" MANNER: ("orderly", "tidy") EFFECT: "living a better life"}

Fuzzy, creativity-driven inference. Once we have a repository of trans-frames, we perform inference by trying to match the EFFECT of one frame to the CAUSE of some other frame. The heuristic for fuzzy matching is a scoring function that assigns points based on how closely the verb, object, and manner of two events are related through lexical semantics. We used WordNet nymic relations (Fellbaum, 1998) to measure semantic proximity between non-verbs, and Levin's verb classes (1993) in a similar way for verbs. While not perfect, using lexical semantics to connect related, but not identical ideas overcomes some of the brittleness associated with precise inference, and also has the effect of lending creativity to the storyline.

MAKEBELIEVE Architecture

For brevity, our system's architecture for story generation can be summarized into the following processing steps:

1. The user enters the first sentence of the story.

2. The sentence is parsed into verb-object form and fuzzy inference matches this initial event to the CAUSE slot of some trans-frame in the repository.

3. The EFFECT slot of the same trans-frame is parsed and inference continues, generating a whole chain of events.

4. After each step of inference, elements of the current story step are modified by analogous or synonymous elements taken from lexical semantic resources. This is to make sure that story steps deviate somewhat from the sometimes too logical causality that is characteristic of commonsense knowledge.

4. A global manager evaluates the chain of events to make sure it is free of cycles and contradictions, and if necessary it can backtrack to explore other storylines. Other global constraints such as narrative structure will be added here.

5. In cases where the inference chain is completely stuck, users may be asked to enter the next line in the story.

6. Frames of the inference chain and their corresponding sentences are used to generate English sentences, with the main character from the seed sentence being inserted. The structure and syntax of sentences are kept very simple in our current implementation.

An example. For brevity we present only one short story, which is typical of stories generated by MAKEBELIEVE.

John became very lazy at work. John lost his job. John decided to get drunk. He started to commit crimes. John went to prison. He experienced bruises. John cried. He looked at himself differently.

Conclusion

We have built MAKEBELIEVE, an interactive story generation agent that can generate short fictional texts of 5 to 20 lines when the user supplies the first line of the story. Our fail-soft approach to story generation represents a hybrid approach inheriting from both the structuralist and transformationalist traditions. It also incorporates a novel knowledge source, commonsense, which unlike other story knowledge bases, is not specifically purposed for story telling. Using a subset of knowledge in Open Mind, which describes causation, MAKEBELIEVE performs fuzzy and creative inference to generate casual chains, which become the basis for a storyline.

What sorts of limitations were encountered? The ambiguity inherent in any natural language representation makes it difficult to resolve the bindings of agents to actions when more than one agent is involved. For example, in this sentence from OMCS, "the effect of kicking someone is pain", we do not know enough to bind "pain" to the kicker or the kicked. This ambiguity precludes our current system from being able to tell multiple character stories.

A preliminary evaluation of MAKEBELIEVE was completed to serve as a baseline for future studies. 18 users were asked to judge the creativity, quality, and coherence of several five-line stories, generated as they interacted with the agent. On average, users scored the stories 10 out of a possible 15 points.

It was a pleasant surprise that despite being assembled out of commonsense knowledge, stories turned out to be much more interesting and dramatic from the user's perspective than we might have imagined. Furthermore, even though we did not add plot devices to the system such as motifs, climax, tension, etc., many users in our evaluation nonetheless felt that these devices were present in the generated stories. Where the generated story leaves off, the imagination of the reader seems ready to pick up.

Selected References

Klein, S. et al. 1973. *Automatic Novel Writing: A Status Report.* Wisconsin University

Meehan, J.R. 1977. TALE-SPIN, An interactive program that writes stories in *Proceedings of IJCAI-77*, pp. 91-98

Singh, P. (2002). The public acquisition of commonsense knowledge. *In Proceedings of AAAI Spring Symposium: Acquiring (and Using) Linguistic (and World) Knowledge for Information Access.* Palo Alto, CA, AAAI.

Localizing while Mapping: A Segment Approach

Andrew J. Martignoni III and **William D. Smart**
Department of Computer Science
Washington University
One Brookings Drive
St. Louis, MO 63130
United States of America
{ajm7, wds}@cs.wustl.edu
http://www.cs.wustl.edu/~ajm7/map

Localization in mobile robotics is a well studied problem in many environments (Thrun *et al.* 2000; Hinkel & Knieriemen 1988; Burgard *et al.* 1999; Rencken 1993). Map building with occupancy grids (probabilistic finite element maps of the environment) is also fairly well understood. However, trying to accomplish both localization and mapping at once has proven to be a difficult task. Updating a map with new sensor information before determining the correct adjustment for the starting point and heading can be disastrous, since it changes parts of the map which were not meant to be changed, thus the next iteration is using an incorrect map to determine the adjustment to the pose, which results in greater error, and the cycle continues.

This research hopes to solve this problem by performing localization on higher-level objects computed from the raw sensor readings. Initially these higher-level objects are line segments and common structures, such as office doors, but any object which can be detected from a single sensor reading can be used to help the localization process. Objects which require more complex analysis can be found and placed in the map, but will not be used for localization. The higher-level features provide for better localization in an unknown environment, through simpler correspondence with existing map objects. In addition, once the data from the robot's sensors have been turned into a map with human-identifiable features, the map can easily be augmented with additional information.

Much of the previous work in this area uses occupancy grids (Moravec & Elfes 1985; Elfes 1987), or pixel based maps. Pixels in occupancy grids represent a certain size area of the environment, and represents the probability that the area contains an object. Other work (Park & Kender 1995; Kuipers & Byun 1991) uses a topological system where landmarks are picked out of the environment and added as nodes on a graph which is then used for navigation.

Pixel-based maps tend to limit the size of the area that can be covered, and the actual data in the image tends to be sparse because the map representations are a fixed size and shape and do not necessarily match the size and shape of the area to be mapped. An object map (of line segments or other detected features) has no such bounds since only the end points of a segment (or similar real-valued data for other

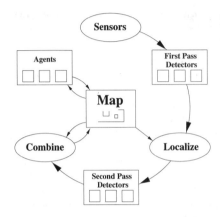

Figure 1: Architecture of the object map framework.

features) are stored. A topological map needs very accurate detections of high-level concepts or features, whereas the line segments are fairly simple to pull out of the available sensor data, and combine well with previous sensor readings.

We propose using line segments for mapping and localization because they (1) are easy to detect, (2) smooth out the noise from the sensors, (3) take little memory to store, (4) provide simple transformation constraints which are useful for localization on very little or very noisy data, and (5) are faster because measuring distance in the map becomes a line intersection instead of ray-tracing. By using line segments, we must assume that most structures in the environment are linear, and that most of the lines are static. This fits well with the office environment used in the experiments.

To extract the segments, we use the distances returned from the laser range finder to generate contact points. The points are added to a Hough Transform (Hough 1962), which allows us to calculate where the most likely line is in the data. We then take the points on the most likely line and perform a regression to get a more accurate line through the points. The line is segmented based on the contiguous sets of points in the reading. This process is repeated (with the used points removed) until the most recognizable lines are pulled out.

The lines derived from the laser scan simplify the view of the world, but it must then be integrated with previously

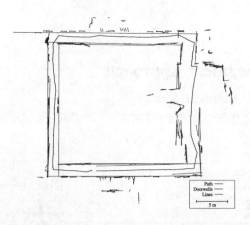

Figure 2: An object map generated from sensor data.

acquired data which is represented in the map. The lines detected in the first reading are simply added to the map at the origin. Subsequent readings must be registered with the existing map before adding. As the robot moves, the wheels may slip and cause the heading to vary by several degrees over the course of a hallway. The line segments in the new reading are matched with their closest matching line segments in the existing map. The final heading correction is determined by histogramming angle differences. This method has proven to be very robust in our experiments. Once the heading is determined, the robot's 2D location must be determined. To accomplish this, observe that the matched line segments are all within a few degrees of parallel. To move these lines together with the corresponding line in the map, we wish to move the midpoint of the new line onto the line in the map there are infinitely many possible vectors (corrections) which move the midpoint to any point on the map line, we add a constraint on the vector to a system of equations and solve it in a least squared error fashion. Solving the system yields the best-fit values of u_x and u_y which represent a 2D location adjustment. This localization relies on the position estimate being close enough to the real position that the new line segments match up with their counterparts in the map. This assumption holds for a reasonable range of speeds with our hardware. Without a somewhat accurate estimate of the motion of the robot, this method would have to rely on global searches, and would be much slower and prone to error in environments with a lot of similarities (such as office buildings). Once the pose has been updated, the new reading's line segments are merged with the existing map. The current combination method tends to weight new readings and the map line segments equally.

Currently, the system will find and detect lines and doors in an office environment. We are currently adding agents which look for other types of objects, such as people, trash cans, or other important features, especially when they may be built on the features which are already detected. Each new type of object will also improve the localization, because the distance metric uses object type to improve matching performance.

We hope to introduce better update methods, including those which may split line segments based on new information, or tracking moving objects in the environment. Also, finding features could be automated by carrying around points from laser readings which were not used for any objects in a "point bag" object which could later be matched against other objects using a clustering algorithm. This could make additional feature detectors simply a matter of giving a name for a set of objects that were already discovered and categorized.

The advantage of a direct object representation is that each object can be tagged with information, such as "Mike's Office" or "Door001", which could also lead to logic based reasoning and navigation.

References

Burgard, W.; Fox, D.; Jans, H.; Matenar, C.; and Thrun, S. 1999. Sonar-based mapping of large-scale mobile robot environments using EM. In *Proceedings of the Sixteenth International Conference on Machine Learning (ICML)*. McGraw-Hill.

Elfes, A. 1987. Sonar-based real-world mapping and navigation. *IEEE Journal on Robotics and Automation* 3(3):249–265.

Hinkel, R., and Knieriemen, T. 1988. Environment perception with a laser radar in a fast moving robot. In *Proceedings of Symposium on Robot Control*, 68.1–68.7.

Hough, P. 1962. Methods and means for recognizing complex patterns. U.S. Patent 3069654.

Kuipers, B. J., and Byun, Y.-T. 1991. A robot exploration and mapping strategy based on a semantic hierarchy of spatial representations. *Robotics and Autonomus Systems* 8:46–63.

Moravec, H. P., and Elfes, A. 1985. High-resolution maps from wide angle sonar. In *Proceedings of IEEE International Conference on Robotics and Automation*, 116–121.

Park, I., and Kender, J. 1995. Topological direction-giving and visual navigation in large environments. *Artificial Intelligence* 78(1-2):355–395.

Rencken, W. D. 1993. Concurrent localisation and map building for mobile robots using ultrasonic sensors. In *Proceedings of the IEEE/RSJ International Conference on Intelligent Robots and Systems*, 2129–2197.

Thrun, S.; Fox, D.; Burgard, W.; and Dellaert, F. 2000. Robust monte carlo localization for mobile robots. *Artificial Intelligence* 101:99–141.

Multi-Player Game Approach to Solving Multi-Entity Problems

Wee-Chong Oon and Andrew Lim

School of Computing, National University of Singapore
3 Science Drive 2, Singapore 117543, Singapore
{oonwc, alim}@comp.nus.edu.sg

Introduction

Many real-world problems involve the allocation of limited resources to competing consumers with dissimilar objective functions. Current techniques that handle such problems usually examine the problem domain as a whole in order to find a solution that maximizes a single overall performance metric (commonly expressed as a weighted sum of the utility of all consumers and some global measures). For example, stochastic search techniques such as Simulated Annealing and Genetic Algorithm all generally use this single-metric approach.

There are some drawbacks to this modeling scheme. Firstly, a solution that achieves a high score based on this single performance metric may not be good in the practical sense. For instance, such a solution may involve alienating one or two consumers while favoring others greatly. In real life, the alienated consumers may not take such treatment kindly. Secondly, such techniques fail to take advantage of the natural division of the problem domain into the subsets belonging to the different consumers. The items within these subsets generally contain some sort of interrelation, especially in real-life instances. Therefore, it may be better to tailor the allocation strategies to each subset. Thirdly, the problem may be too large to solve as a whole, but becomes more manageable if divided into smaller sub-problems.

In an ideal setting, multi-entity problems should be solved by sitting all the consumers together and negotiating the allocation of resources in a fair and diplomatic manner. Such a model can be thought of as a multi-player competitive cum collaborative game, where each consumer is a player in the game. It is competitive since each player seeks primarily to maximize his own utility; it is collaborative since all consumers must take the feasibility and quality of the overall solution into account. This research examines this Multi-Player Game Approach (MPGA).

The Multi-Player Game Approach

MPGA comprises several iterations, each with a *bidding phase* followed by an *arbitration phase*, and finally a *negotiation phase*. In the bidding phase, each consumer would bid for the available resources. After all bids have been placed, any uncontested resources would be awarded to the bidding consumer. In the arbitration phase, the initial destiny of the contested resources would be decided. In the negotiation phase, the players would attempt to improve the allocations by trading resources with each other in mutually beneficial ways. The ideal makeup of the bidding, arbitration and negotiation phases is one of the focuses of this research, and is likely to be problem-dependent.

Possible bidding schemes include letting each consumer rank all the resources; having each consumer select only their desired resources; and giving each consumer a limited number of bidding points to allocate each round. Possible arbitration schemes include highest ranking / points bid wins, and awarding the contested resource to the consumer who would benefit most. Possible negotiation schemes include exchanging previously allocated resources or ceding bidding points for future iterations.

University Exam Timetabling

MPGA was inspired by work done in the development of an automated exam-timetabling program for the National University of Singapore (NUS) (Lim et al. 2000, Lim et al. 2002). The exam-timetabling problem (ETTP) is a constraint satisfaction optimization problem, where a set of exams must be scheduled within a set of venue-session slots, subject to hard and soft constraints. A feasible schedule satisfies all hard constraints, while the quality of the solution is given by a weighted sum of the soft constraints satisfied. For the ETTP, the hard constraints are: the total number of students within a venue cannot exceed its capacity; two exams taken by the same student cannot be scheduled at the same time. This problem is NP-Hard (Garey and Johnson, 1979).

Our initial attempt to solve this problem was to schedule all the exams for the entire university. Unfortunately, this task proved too difficult for the automated scheduler, resulting in an infeasible timetable with over 200 (of 1,350) exams that could not be scheduled due to hard constraint violations. There was also great resistance from the individual faculty timetable administrators, who disliked the lack of personal control of a centrally scheduled timetable. As a result, a partially distributed strategy was adopted, where each faculty was given a copy of the scheduling program and allocated a partition of the time slots. The faculties then scheduled their own exams within their allotted partitions, and the central authority would merge these timetables into a collated whole and resolve the conflicts. Paradoxically, even though the same scheduling engine was used, this partition-merge approach achieved a solution where only 12 exams were left unscheduled (Lim et al. 2002).

MPGA is the logical extension of this partition-merge approach. The problem with the allocation of slot partitions to the different faculties is that artificial constraints are added. Using MPGA, each faculty is a player in a game, and all faculties are given access to all the available slots. One possible implementation of MPGA is as follows. In the bidding phase, each faculty bids for the slots by placing their exams into ideal slots. In the arbitration phase, the central authority would first attempt to merge the ideal schedules together as far as possible. Then, each contested slot is allocated to the exam that is "obviously most suitable" as determined by some measure. Ambiguous contested slots are not allocated. In the negotiation phase, the faculties attempt to improve their allocation by exchanging slots with each other in mutually beneficial trades. The next iteration begins with each faculty attempting to place their exams in the remaining slots if possible. If not, the unscheduleable exams may bid to be in a filled slot, and may replace the existing exam if the former is deemed "obviously most suitable". This is repeated until no more improvements occur.

Research Issues

The division of a problem into separate interrelated processes is similar to the concept of Multi-Agent Systems (MAS) (Lesser 1995, Sycara 1998), even though MPGA can be implemented centrally. Common MAS issues like the prevention of looping behavior, control of information flow and the increased complexity of implementation (when compared to single-agent systems) must also be addressed in MPGA.

Since MPGA is a natural approach to solving multi-entity optimization, it presents some distinct advantages. MPGA avoids using a single performance metric, instead relying on a logical process to produce the result. This idea is also seen in the area of market-based control (Clearwater 1996). Each player in the game can use different approaches, which may be guided by ideas of achieving Nash equilibrium (Osborne and Rubinstein 1994), but more likely in the form of simple rule-based heuristics. Furthermore, a log of the entire process can be kept as a step-by-step report of the bidding and arbitration process, which can be used to convince the human consumers that the final solution is fair and just. In real-life problems, this political aspect is an important factor.

In essence, MPGA simulates a community of experts, each attempting to achieve their best possible solution. Ideally, the heuristics used for the bidding and negotiation phases can be obtained from actual human experts. Unfortunately, these experts are seldom computer science professionals, and translating their strategies into algorithmic form may be problematic. This is a common problem in the domain of expert systems (Jackson 1999).

Conclusion

MPGA models complex multi-entity problems as a multi-player game, where each entity in the problem is a player in the game. A fair and just set of rules is imposed for the game, which is played in several iterations of bidding, arbitration and negotiation phases, and each player can employ a different customized strategy. Not only does MPGA have the advantage of being instinctive and understandable, such that actual human consumers can be more easily convinced of the fairness of the final solution, experiments on the university examination timetabling problem suggests that MPGA may produce better solutions than traditional centralized methods.

References

Clearwater, S. ed. 1996, *Market-Based Control: A Paradigm for Distributed Resource Allocation*, World Scientific.

Garey, M. R. and Johnson, D. S. 1979. *Computers and Intractability: A Guide to the Theory of NP-Completeness.*

Jackson, P. 1999. *Introduction to Expert Systems, 3rd Edition*, Harlow England: Addison-Wesley Longman.

Lesser, V. R. 1995. Multiagent Systems: An Emerging Subdiscipline of AI, *ACM Computing Surveys* 27(3), vol. 27, no. 3: 340-342.

Lim, A.; Ang, J. C.; Ho, W. K.; and Oon, W. C. 2000. A Campus-Wide University Examination Timetabling Application, in *Innovative Applications in Artificial Intelligence (AAAI/IAAI) 2000*: 1020-1025.

Lim, A.; Ang, J. C.; Ho, W. K.; and Oon, W. C. UTTSExam: A Campus-Wide University Exam-Timetabling System, accepted to *Innovative Applications in Artificial Intelligence (AAAI/IAAI) 2002*.

Osborne, M. J. and Rubinstein, A. 1994, *A Course in Game Theory*, Cambridge Mass., MIT Press.

Sycara, K. 1998. Multiagent Systems, *AI Magazine* 19(2): 79-92.

BN-Tools: A Software Toolkit for Experimentation in BBNs

Benjamin Perry ~ Julie Stilson

Laboratory for Knowledge Discovery in Database, Kansas State University
234 Nichols Hall
Manhattan, KS 66506-2302
bbp9857@ksu.edu ~ jas3466@ksu.edu

Abstract

In this paper, I describe BN-Tools, an open-source, Java-based library for experimental research in Bayesian belief networks (BBNs) that implements several popular algorithms for estimation (approximate inference) and learning along with a graphical user interface for interactive display and editing of graphical models.

Introduction

BBNs are one of the most widely-studied and applied family of knowledge representations for learning reasoning in uncertain environments. As a result, we are interested in developing efficient software toolkits in Java that implement known algorithms for exact and approximate inference, in a modular library that facilitates experimentation. Over the last two years, I have developed several tools in Java that help manipulate BBNs and extrapolate important information from them. Our toolkit consists of core BBN representation classes, the Lauritzen-Spiegelhalter (LS) [LS88] algorithm, an optimized implementation of the *K2* algorithm for structure learning [CH92], a genetic algorithm (GA) wrapper for *K2*, a genetic algorithm to find the *most probable explanation* (MPE), an adaptive importance sampling (AIS) [CD00] algorithm for approximate inference, and several other format conversion, viewing, and editing utilities, including a data simulator.

Implementation

Core classes

The core classes for dealing with a BBN consist of ways to represent each individual node, the network itself, and instantiation managers that allow manipulation of node values while protecting the internal network from changes. These classes are used throughout all of our BBN tools and provide a standard interface for manipulating the network. The network can be built at run-time or loaded from the XML *Bayesian Network Interchange Format* developed by Microsoft (or one of several commercial formats including those for the BBN software packages *Hugin, Netica, SPI,* and *IDEAL*).

Lauritzen-Spiegelhalter algorithm.

The purpose of the LS algorithm is to find the posterior probabilities of nodes in a BBN with or without some nodes being set to a pre-defined value (evidence nodes). The LS first triangulates the BBN into cliques based on the existing arcs. These cliques are then used in message propagation to pass various probability values to each clique's children and parent(s). Once the algorithm has completed its initial run, all instantiated nodes are removed and the algorithm is repeated, starting with the values computed from the first run. When the algorithm is finished, we will be able to query any node to see how likely any state is given the evidence we specified. Our implementation is multi-threaded for parallel computation of the probability propagation. Due to the overhead of threads with JAVA, the performance takes a hit on multi-processor machines with smaller networks. Larger networks (100+ nodes) do see a slight performance boost.

Adaptive importance sampling algorithm.

Approximate inference algorithms that use sampling techniques to determine the posterior probabilities of nodes are extremely important because they directly model the real-life situations that BBNs represent better than any inference algorithm. One such approximation algorithm is Adaptive Importance Sampling (AIS), where the probabilities of each node are updated several times during probabilistic sampling of the network. These repeated updates help find the importance function for the network, which is an updated version of the conditional probability tables that corrects probabilities of states given that the states of certain nodes have already been set as evidence. This importance function is described as:

$$P^{k+1}(x_i \mid Pa(X_i), \mathbf{e}) =$$
$$P^k(x_i \mid Pa(X_i), \mathbf{e}) +$$
$$\eta(k) \cdot \left(P'(x_i \mid Pa(X_i), \mathbf{e}) - P^k(x_i \mid Pa(X_i), \mathbf{e}) \right) \quad (1)$$

where P^{k+1} is the new importance function, P^k is the importance function in the last step, P' is an estimated probability based on the samples taken in the last step, η is the pre-determined learning rate, and k is the number of updates that have been made to the importance function.

e corresponds to the pre-defined evidence you set prior to running the network through AIS. AIS also employs two heuristics which adapt the conditional probability tables for unlikely evidence and extremely low probabilities by setting the parents of unlikely evidence nodes to a uniform distribution and by raising low probabilities to a set threshold. These two heuristics allow the posterior probabilities be learned properly despite very low prior probabilities. Because the heuristic initializations and the learned importance function allow AIS to learn the true probabilities better than traditional sampling, we currently use it as a fitness function for evaluating learned structures of BBNs based on different orderings.

K2 algorithm

The *K2* algorithm, developed by Cooper and Herskovits [CH92], learns the structure of a BBN based on a collection of training examples and a specific ordering of the nodes. It is a greedy-search algorithm and only considers nodes previous to the current node when building the list of parents (thus, the order is very important). To evaluate the output of *K2*, the LS algorithm is used to compute each node's probabilities. We then compute root-mean-square-error (RMSE) between the probabilities learned from the samples and the probabilities computed by some inference method with the K2-produced network. RMSE values closest to 0.0 are the best outcomes of the network. We are using other means of judging the fitness of the network as well: adaptive importance sampling and forward sampling. Both are approximates to LS, which will be a little less accurate, but (theoretically) much faster for large networks.

K2 Genetic Algorithm Wrapper.

Finding the optimal ordering is *NP*-hard, so we have designed a genetic algorithm to avoid exhaustively searching all possibilities. RMSE values of the various orderings are used as the fitness. Each chromosome in our genetic algorithm corresponds to an ordering used in K2. We use an order-crossover operator as well as an order swap operator for mutation. The order-crossover's purpose is to maintain the order of the nodes while still swapping out with another chromosome. There are other methods of crossover that we will implement and test in order to improve the performance of our genetic algorithm. We have utilized *GAJIT* as the main genetic algorithm driver. GAJIT is an elitist GA. It allows the user to specify the cull rate (the percentage of chromosomes that make the cut to the next generation). It also allows the user to add self-designed crossover and mutation operators. There are some issues within GAJIT that we will attempt to address in the future, most notably the crowding affect. When selecting two chromosomes to crossover, GAJIT does not care if a chromosome crossovers with itself. Applying the order-crossover technique on two identical chromosomes will yield two identical children, thus filling the population with clones, making it difficult to get out of a local

optimum at times. We have developed a job-farm that allows several computers to work on the same generation simultaneously. The job farm utilizes TCP to communicate and is tolerant to lag or dropped connections. Because we use java, we can employ several machines, regardless of their platform. The server manages the genetic algorithm. When a client connects, the server sends important session parameters. Once the client is initialized, the server simply sends an ordering to the client. The client then runs the K2 algorithm on the ordering, runs the specified fitness function on the learned network, and finally sends back to the server the final fitness. The job farm is also capable of running an exhaustive permutation run on smaller networks. We have begun experiments with the K2 GA wrapper by comparing the fitness values among the gold standard Asia and Alarm networks, the canonical ordering (or any topologically sorted ordering), and the best ordering obtained through the wrapper. Our initial findings are very encouraging; the GA wrapper usually produces a network that differs from the gold standard by a small percentage of graph errors (missing, added, or reversed edges).

Genetic algorithm for finding the MPE.

Finding the Most Probable Explanation (MPE) of a network is very useful, although it is *NP*-hard. We have employed a GA to speed up the process by 'stacking the deck' as each generation progresses. A chromosome represents node value instantiations for all nodes in the network. Using *GAJIT* [Fa00] as our main GA driver, we have developed a Markov-blanket crossover and chromosome (sparse state coding) rotation as a mutation operator. The Markov blanket of radius n consists of a node's children, mates, parents, and the node itself, recursively computed n times for all nodes. We use a default radius of 1 in our GA. Although it is not guaranteed to find the MPE, the GA performs well given a sufficient number of generations and population size.

References

[CD00] Cheng, J. and Druzdel, M. J. 2000. AIS-BN: An adaptive importance sampling algorithm for evidential reasoning in large Bayesian networks. *Journal of Artificial Intelligence Research (JAIR)*, 13:155-188

[CH92] Cooper, G. F. and Herskovits, E, 1992.. A Bayesian Method for the Induction of Probabilistic Networks from Data. Machine Learning, **9**(4):309-347.

[LS88] Lauritzen, S. L. and Spiegelhalter , D. J, 1988. Local computations with probabilities on graphical structures and their application to expert systems. *Journal of the Royal Statistical Society, Series B* 50.

Optimizing Parameter Learning using Temporal Differences

James F. Swafford II

Department of Computer Science
East Carolina University
Greenville, NC 27858
jfs0301@mail.ecu.edu

Abstract

Temporal difference algorithms are useful when attempting to predict outcome based on some pattern, such as a vector of evaluation parameters applied to the leaf nodes of a state space search. As time progresses, the vector begins to converge towards an optimal state, in which program performance peaks. Temporal difference algorithms continually modify the weights of a differentiable, continuous evaluation function. As pointed out by De Jong and Schultz, expert systems that rely on experience-based learning mechanisms are more useful in the field than systems that rely on growing knowledge bases (De Jong and Schultz 1988). This research focuses on the application of the TDLeaf algorithm to the domain of computer chess. In this poster I present empirical data showing the evolution of a vector of evaluation weights and the associated performance ratings under a variety of conditions.

The playing strength of modern chess playing programs is really a function of the quality of its search and its evaluation of leaf nodes. The search defines the shape of the search space, and the manner in which the program navigates through that space. The evaluation function attempts to quantitatively measure the value of a chess position, and therefore assign values to the search tree's leaf nodes. Given that computer chess programs must assign values to positions, it becomes necessary to break a chess position down into tiny parts, giving points for some attributes, and penalizing for others. The more evaluation terms included in the evaluation function, the more capable the evaluator is to distinguish between positions. This precision comes at a cost, and that cost is complexity. The more terms in the evaluator, the more difficult it becomes to properly tune a new weight relative to existing weights.

$$w := w + \alpha \sum_{i=1}^{N-1} \nabla r(x_i^l, w) \left[\sum_{j=i}^{N-1} \lambda^{j-i} d_i \right]$$

Figure 1: The TDLeaf Algorithm

Traditional (non-learning) methods of tuning evaluation parameters become increasingly impractical as the number of parameters increases. Consequently, a great deal of research has been done to find methods for the self tuning of evaluation parameters, particularly in the domain of a state space search. One such algorithm is TDLeaf (Figure 1), first introduced by Beal (Beal 1997), and applied to chess by Baxter et al. with "Knightcap" (Baxter, Tridgell, and Weaver 2000). While conventional prediction learning methods are driven by the error between predicted and actual outcomes, TD methods are driven by the error between temporally successive predictions (Sutton 1998). One advantage to this approach is that learning is applied incrementally, once per searched move. The learning is applied to the leaf node of the principal variation, adjusting the evaluation vector at that node "towards" the vector of another principal variation leaf node occurring later in the game. The algorithm allows for some tailoring with the λ value (a decay rate parameter) and α (a scaling factor). Setting λ close to one tends to adjust the vector towards the final position's vector. This could be useful if the evaluator can not be trusted. Conversely, a λ close to zero causes the vector to be adjusted towards the next position's vector.

Temporal difference algorithms have had some success in game playing. Despite the overall success of temporal difference algorithms, none of the top ranked computer chess programs utilize them, suggesting they are still unable to produce a set of evaluation parameters superior to a set of carefully hand tuned parameters. Though Schaeffer reports promising results with "Chinook" (a world class checkers program), it should be noted that Chinook contains relatively few evaluation parameters compared to a competitive chess program. The most promising results reported of temporal differences applied to chess are those of "Knightcap", which is far below the grandmaster level in playing strength. (Schaeffer, Hlynka, and Jussila 2001). Perhaps by better understanding the conditions under which temporal difference algorithms are able to converge the parameter vector to an optimal state, we will be able to use temporal difference algorithms more effectively and in a wider variety of applications.

Figure 2: Ratings Progression Beginning with a Material only Vector

Initial data, though showing TDLeaf to be effective, suggest limits to the algorithm's ability to adjust the evaluation vector to an optimal state. Figure 2 plots the ratings progression beginning from a vector in which only the values of the pieces are nonzero. To get a baseline, the engine first played online (against human opponents) with the material-only vector without learning. After 340 games the engine's mean rating was 1504. A separate run of 265 games with learning on (shown in Figure 2) ended with a mean rating of 1558 – substantially higher than the previous non-learning run. The results of a subsequent experiment were, unfortunately, not as promising. Figure 3 illustrates the progression of a separate run of games that was started using a hand-tuned vector of evaluation parameters. After another 265 games the engine had achieved a mean rating of 1715. This is substantially lower than the 1775 mean rating from a previous run of a non-learning engine using the same hand-tuned vector. In this case, the learning was not only ineffective, but was harmful. The vector was moving *away* from optimal.

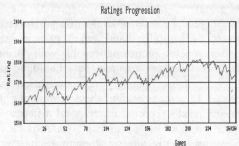

Figure 3: Ratings Progression Beginning with a Hand-Tuned Vector

There are a number of conditions that may delay or even prevent convergence. Shallow searches, for example, leave the program vulnerable to the horizon effect, eventually causing the program to lose for tactical rather than positional reasons. In these cases it is likely the TD algorithm is adjusting the vector *to predict tactical blunders,* and consequently limiting the effectiveness of the program's ability to predict outcome based strictly on positional features. The idea that search depth adversely affects the algorithm's ability to converge to optimality can be tested by running several series of training sessions, each session beginning with an engine that plays at a higher caliber than the last, using the hand tuned vector. Evaluation complexity, distance from the optimal vector, quality of opponents, or length of training games may also delay convergence. Tesauro reported continually improving performance with TD-Gammon after hundreds of thousands of games (Tesauro 1995). Other dynamic or nondeterministic aspects of the program may also confound the algorithm's ability to converge to optimality. Examples include null-move forward pruning, aspiration windows, and principal variation search.

Acknowledgements

The author wishes to acknowledge Dr. Ronnie Smith and Dr. Mike Spurr of East Carolina University for their guidance and helpful insight, and his wife Amy for her support and unending patience.

References

Beal, D. 1997. Learning Piece Values Using Temporal Differences. *International Computer Chess Association Journal,* 20:147-151

Baxter, J., Tridgell, A., and Weaver, L. 2000. Learning to Play Chess using Temporal Differences, in *Machine Learning,* 40:243-263.

Sutton, R. 1998. *Learning to Predict by the Methods of Temporal Differences,* Boston, Kluwer Academic Publishers

Schaeffer J., Hlynka M., and Jussila V. 2001. Temporal Difference Learning Applied to a High-Performance Game-Playing Program, in *Proceedings of the 2001 International Joint Conference on Artificial Intelligence (IJCAI-2001),* 529-534.

De Jong, K. and Schultz, Alan C. 1988. Using Experience-Based Learning in Game Playing, in *Proceedings of the Fifth International Machine Learning Conference,* 284-290.

Tesauro G. 1995. Temporal Difference Learning and TD-Gammon, in *Communications of the ACM,* 38:58-68.

Student Modeling for a Web-based Learning Environment: a Data Mining Approach

Tiffany Y. Tang and Gordon McCalla

Department of Computer Science
University of Saskatchewan
57 Campus Drive, Saskatoon, SK S7N 5A9 CANADA
{yat751@mail.usask.ca; mccalla@cs.usask.ca}

Introduction

This ongoing research focuses on how data mining techniques, if incorporated into web learning environments, can enhance the overall qualities of learning.

In a web-based learning environment, where both the tutors and learners are separated spatially and physically, student modeling is one of the biggest challenges. Traditional student modeling techniques are inapplicable in these systems when tutors are overwhelmed by the huge volumes of sequential data (Agrawal and Srikant 1995) generated as learners browse through the web pages. Web mining techniques, including clustering and association rules mining, could be applied to extract *hidden* and *interesting* knowledge to facilitate instructional planning and student diagnosis. Web mining in education is not new. It has been applied to mine aggregate paths for learners engaged in a distance education environment (Ha, Bae and Park 2000); to recommend relevant words to students based on text mining from their browsed documents (Ochi et al. 1998); to recommend e-articles for students based on key-word-driven text mining (Tang et al. 2000), and to analyze learners' learning behaviors (Zaiane and Luo 2001). The research proposed here will go beyond *usage* mining to consider the content of the pages that have been visited. In an e-learning system, both learners' browsing behaviors and course content are important to derive learners' learning levels, intentions, goals, interests, or abilities. Incorporating course content can aid in an understanding of learners' browsing habits. In particular, understanding the learners' browsing behaviors can facilitate, say, the personalization of course contents delivered.

Artificial intelligence in education (AIED) systems typically employ a knowledge base, a student model, and instructional plans. For a web-based AIED system, web mining becomes part of student modeling. Traditional usage data (Cooley 2000) keeps a lot of information that is not needed. But we do need the knowledge of content and complexity of each page. Finding and using such knowledge is *tractable* in our domain since we can

annotate course web pages with metadata and the knowledge base, and instructional plan also give context for the properties of each page. The system can relate its mined knowledge of page contents and student navigation patterns to students' level of understanding (Tang et al. 2001) to decide upon appropriate feedback to them.

Data Clustering for Web Learning

Among mining techniques of particular interest in web-based learning environments is data clustering. It can, for example:

• Promote group-based collaborative learning
Traditionally, learning systems focus more on how to individualize course contents and delivery. However, in web-based learning environments where both the number of students and the size of the information can be huge, to reduce the cost and the computational burdens on the system, group-based learning will also be useful.

Data clustering is a powerful tool to find clusters of students with similar learning characteristics based on their path traversal patterns and the content of each page they have visited. The clusters of students can be used to promote effective group learning, e.g., assigning students from different clusters so as to form effective learning groups for collaboration. In addition, after we find a cluster of learners with similar browsing paths, we could extract course contents along the paths to create fragmented contents (group-based course content delivery). These fragmented course contents can also be selected for recommendation, and the clustered paths can be used to sequence the curriculum for other students in the future (group-based instructional planning).

• Provide incremental learner diagnosis
Incremental clustering can be performed to help diagnose learners as they browse through the system. This is consistent with the "just-in-time" modeling proposed by (McCalla, Vassileva and Bull 2000).

A Clustering Algorithm Based on Large Generalized Sequences

We briefly describe a clustering algorithm that should be useful in clustering data for web-based learning environments. This algorithm is based on the notion of *large generalized items*. Consider a collection of transactions $\{T_1, T_2, \ldots T_n\}$, where each transaction T_i is a set of sequences $\{t_1, t_2, \ldots t_p\}$. According to (Gaul and Schmidt-Thieme 2000), *generalized sequences* are defined as:

$$T^{gen} = \left\{ t \in \left(T \cup \{*\}\right)^* \mid \exists i \in N \ \text{such that} \ t_i = t_{i+1} = * \right\}$$

where $*$ represents wildcard.

The idea behind this notion is that the navigation paths of different users might not be completely or even partially matched on a one-to-one mapping. Generalized sequences allow path deviations and retain path orders. However, among all the generalized sequences, we are only interested in those large ones. A *large* generalized sequence is the sequence whose frequency of occurrence is larger than a user specified *minimum support* θ. Formally, it is defined as:

$$T_l^{gen} = \left\{ T^{gen} \subseteq T \mid Support \left(T^{gen}\right) > \theta \right\}$$

In the context of our domain, adopting generalized sequences is more viable to derive traversal patterns than *maximal forward sequences* (Chen, Park and Yu 1998) or *longest repeated sub-sequences* (Pitkow and Pirolli 1999).

A general algorithm for finding all frequent generalized subsequences is proposed in (Gaul and Schmidt-Thieme 2000). The research proposed here will go a step further by first searching for all generalized subsequences among learners' traversal paths (i.e. path fragments). Then these path fragments will be further clustered based on course contents of each page so as to characterize learners' browsing behaviors. For example, we might find the following two large generalized sequences:

$B * D * H * I$ and
$B * DH * I$

They might belong to either two different clusters or one cluster, depending on what other pages lie in between page D and H for the first fragment and the contents of page D and H. If the pages in between D and H are those which can be regarded as additional readings for the topic covered in page D, then for learners who take the first path, we might infer that they are interested in more knowledge concerning these topics. Thus, course contents would be used to further cluster all these frequent path fragments and actions could then be taken accordingly such as recommending further readings for students, assigning collaborative work for them, etc.

Future Works

We are constructing a web-based learning environment as a test bed for our research. More data mining algorithms will be designed for our domain, since data mining algorithms are known to be dependent on application areas (Han and Kamber 2000). In the context of the proposed systems, we will also quantify the interestingness and usefulness of discovered knowledge.

Acknowledgments. This work is supported through a research assistantship from the Canadian Natural Sciences and Engineering Research Council.

References

Agrawal, R., and Srikant, R. 1995. Mining Sequential Patterns. In *Proc. of the Eleventh International Conference on Data Engineering (ICDE)*, 3-14, Taiwan.

Chen, M.S.; Park, J.S.; and Yu, P.S. 1998. Efficient Data Mining for Path Traversal Patterns. *IEEE Trans. Knowledge and Data Engineering* 10(2): 209-221.

Cooley, R. 2000. Web Usage Mining: Discovery and Application of Interesting Patterns from Web Data. Ph.D diss., Dept. of Computer Science, University of Minnesota.

Gaul, W., and Schmidt-Thieme, L. 2000. Mining Web Navigation Path Fragments. In *Proc. of 2000 Workshop on Web Mining for E-Commerce—Challengers and Opportunities*, Boston.

Ha, S.H.; Bae, S.M.; and Park, S.C. 2000. Web Mining for Distance Education. 2000. In *Proc. of IEEE International Conference on Management of Innovation and Technology (ICMIT)*, vol.2, 715-219.

Han, J.W., and Kamber, M. 2000. *Data Mining: Concepts and Techniques*. Morgan Kaufmann Publishers.

McCalla, G.; Vassileva, J.; and Bull, S. 2000. Active Learner Modeling. In *Proc. of the Fifth International Conference on Intelligent Tutoring Systems*, 53-62.

Ochi, Y.; Yano, Y.; Hayashi, T.; and Wakita, R. 1998. JUPITER: a Kanji Learning Environment Focusing on a Learner's Browsing. In *Proc. of the Third Asia Pacific Conference on Computer Human Interaction*, 446-451.

Pitkow, J., and Pirolli, P. 1999. Mining Longest Repeating Subsequences to Predict World Wide Web Surfing. In *Proc. of the USENIX Symposium on Internet Technologies and Systems*, 139-150.

Tang, C.; Lau, R.W.H.; Li, Q.; Yin, H.; Li, T.; and Kilis, D. 2000. Personalized Courseware Construction Based on Web Data Mining. In *Proc. of the First International Conference on Web Information Systems Engineering (WISE 2000)* vol.2, 204-211.

Tang, T.Y.; Chan, K.C.; Winoto, P.; and Wu, A. 2001. Forming Student Clusters Based on Their Browsing Behaviors. In *Proc. of the Ninth International Conference on Computers in Education*, vol. 3, 1229-1235.

Zaiane, O., and Luo, J. 2001. Towards Evaluating Learners' Behavior in a Web-based Distance Learning Environment. In *Proc. of IEEE International Conference on Advanced Learning Technologies*, 357-360, Madison, WI.

An Extended Alternating-Offers Bargaining Protocol for Automated Negotiation in Multi-agent Systems

Pinata Winoto, Gordon McCalla and Julita Vassileva

Department of Computer Science
University of Saskatchewan
57 Campus Drive, Saskatoon, SK S7N 5A9 CANADA
{piw410@mail.usask.ca; mccalla@cs.usask.ca; jiv@cs.usask.ca}

Introduction

Depending on the protocol type, a negotiation can be categorized as an auction, a contract-net protocol, or a voting or bargaining scheme. While most research focuses on auctions because the strategy is simple, bargaining is still an important way of negotiation. This is because
- auctions only allow negotiation for price, not other attributes (delivery time, payment method, delivery method, etc.);
- auctions usually are scheduled in advance and with time restrictions, but some buyers/sellers may not want to wait until an auction opens or finalizes;
- in some cases, many social factors are important, e.g., trusteeships, friendships, etc., which auctions cannot easily accommodate;
- most auctions extract the surplus for the benefit of the auctioneer, especially if there is a significant number of bidders.

Generally, the bargaining model in Multi-Agent Systems (MAS) adopts the classical alternating-offers model. Currently, there are many variants of this model, such as a model with time deadline (Krauss, Wilkenfeld and Zlotkin 1995; Sandholm and Vulkan 1999), with various information levels (complete/incomplete, symmetric/asymmetric), with risk of breakdown (one party walks out before negotiation ends), etc. Most of the theoretical foundations have been studied by game theorists (Nash 1950; Rubinstein 1982). However, there is one important limitation of the game-theoretic approach, i.e., searching the solution in exhaustive fashion. Considering the limitation of computational power, many heuristic techniques are adopted to develop new models, namely heuristic-based negotiation models, characterized by learning mechanisms such as Bayesian learning (Zeng and Sycara 1998), influence diagrams (Mudgal and Vassileva 2000), evolutionary algorithm (van Bragt, Gerding and LaPoutre 2000). Using these models, the negotiators can make decisions faster to find a *good* solution, although not necessarily the *best* one. In addition, some researchers have proposed an argumentation-based model that focuses on natural-language-like negotiation (Hulstijn, Dastani and van der Torre 2001; Jennings et al. 2001; Sycara 1989). The main idea of this work is to provide more flexibility in the negotiation process, such as to allow a negotiator to persuade their opponents to change their perceptions.

Proposed Approach

This project is motivated by similar goals as the research above, that is, to modify the traditional alternating-offer model and then to study its advantages/ disadvantages. The proposed modifications include:
- Allowing bargaining without revealing the negotiators' preferences. For example, in the bargaining between seller S and buyer B, the following negotiations would be allowed:
  - (1) S: I offer you $500 per unit.
    B: Give me a lower price.
  - (2) S: I will not sell for less than $500.
    B: I cannot afford more than $400.

In case (1), S sets the upper bound, and B asks for a reduction without revealing a minimum willingness to pay. In case (2), neither side reveals their exact valuations, but a range of them.
- Allowing bargaining using *strategic delay*. A strategic delay is especially important at the beginning of the bargaining since it could serve as a signal of the negotiators' valuation. The less gain a negotiator expects from the bargaining, the more patient she or he is (Crampton 1992).
- Allowing arbitrary revisions of the proposal before agreement is reached. Intuitively, during negotiations, agents may revise their valuation dynamically due to external factors (e.g. the average price increases, or the demand for the same good increases, etc.).
- Allowing negotiators to try to stimulate changes in each other's beliefs. In almost all literature, it is assumed that bargaining is only in regard to the price. However, many real bargaining situations do not involve price, and in fact often implicitly or explicitly involve trying to change attitudes of the other bargainer.

In this extended proposal, eight actions are considered: offer, counter-offer, re-offer, argue, counter-argue, strategic delay, accept and reject. And many factors influencing an agent's decision may be considered, such as private valuation, discount rate, bargaining time, unresolved disagreements, convergence rate, the likelihood of breakdown, etc.

Current and Future Work

In order to evaluate the performance of the new protocols, an agent-based simulation will be designed. The experiments will consist of two conditions: a conventional alternating-offer model (control) and a modified model designed using some or all of the modifications described earlier. There are three criteria used in the measurement of the protocol's efficiency: percentage of failure, length of bargaining, and computational costs. And there are also two metrics that are used to assess the protocol's effectiveness: fairness and participation rate.

The measurement of these five criteria is as follows:
- Ratio of failure = number of failures (walkouts)/ number of bargaining sessions.
- Length of bargaining = number of alterations until negotiation concluded.
- Computational costs = time needed for each decision.
- Fairness = % difference between buyer and seller's surplus, i.e. how much they had to concede relative to their expectations.
- Participation rate = proportion of participants in extended alternating-offer bargaining compared to participants in classical alternating-offer bargaining.

Agents used in the experiments are assumed to be bounded rational and learning agents. For instance, buyer agents will maximize their utility U_B based on the following parameters: their private valuation, time deadline, belief about market price, belief about a seller's time deadline, belief about the probability of a seller to walkout, probability to find other sellers, the price offered/counter offered by a seller, perceived probability that a seller will accept their offer, the weight (importance) assigned to the market price, and their belief about the trustworthiness of a seller's statement. Moreover, agents choose the action that yields a higher expected return in their view. For example, by indicating that the market price will be very low in the near future, a buyer can persuade a seller to sell with a lower price today, since if the buyer walks out, the seller will get less from the market.

Up to now, two steps in the research have been carried out:
- The characteristics of the bargaining protocols have been analytically studied to find the answer to some basic questions such as: will the bargaining always converge? in what conditions do bargaining solutions exist? what happens if two agents use different criteria to update their beliefs? There are, of course, many other questions which need to be studied.
- The experimental design of an agent-based simulation has been proposed, which could serve as a test-bed of the protocol design. However, there are still many unsolved problems, such as what kind of learning mechanism is appropriate? should agents trust the arguments made by their opponent? should every agent maintain a history of interactions and a model of other agents?

Acknowledgements

This work is funded through a research assistantship from the Canadian Natural Sciences and Engineering Research Council.

References

Crampton, P. C. 1992. Strategic Delay in Bargaining with Two-Sided Uncertainty. *Review of Economic Studies* 59(1): 205-225.

Hulstijn, J.; Dastani, M.; and van der Torre, L. 2001. Negotiation Protocols and Dialogue Games. In *Proceedings of the Fifth International Conference on Autonomous Agents*, 180-181, Montreal, Canada.

Jennings, N. R.; Faratin, P.; Lomuscio, A. R.; Parsons, S.; Sierra, C.; and Wooldridge, M. 2001. Automated Negotiation: Prospects, Methods and Challenges. *International Journal of Group Decision and Negotiation* 10(2): 199-215.

Krauss, S.; Wilkenfeld, K.; and Zlotkin, G. 1995. Multiagent Negotiation under Time Constraints. *Artificial Intelligence Journal* 75(2): 297-345.

Mudgal, C., and Vassileva, J. 2000. Bilateral Negotiation with Incomplete and Uncertain Information: A Decision-Theoretic Approach Using a Model of the Opponent. In Klusch and Kerschberg (Eds.) *Cooperative Information Agents IV, LNAI vol. 1860*, 107-118, Springer-Verlag.

Nash, J. F. 1950. The Bargaining Problem. *Econometrica* 18(2): 155-162.

Rubinstein, A. 1982. Perfect Equilibrium in a Bargaining Model. *Econometrica* 50(1): 97-110.

Sandholm, T. W., and Vulkan, N. 1999. Bargaining with Deadlines. In *Proceedings of the Sixteenth National Conference on Artificial Intelligence*, 44-51, Orlando, FL.

Sycara, K. 1989. Argumentation: Planning other Agents' Plans. In Proceedings of the Eleventh International Joint Conference on Artificial Intelligence, 517-523.

van Bragt, D.D.B.; Gerding, E.H.; and La Poutre, J.A. 2000. Equilibrium Selection in Alternating-Offers Bargaining Models: The Evolutionary Computing Approach. *CWI Technical Report* available at http://www.cwi.nl/projects/ASTA/2000Q3.html

Zeng, D., and Sycara, K. 1998. Bayesian Learning in Negotiation. *International Journal Human-Computer Studies* 48: 125-141.

Consistency and Set Intersection

Yuanlin Zhang and Roland H.C. Yap

School of Computing, National University of Singapore
3 Science Drive 3, 117543, Singapore
Email: {zhangyl, ryap}@comp.nus.edu.sg

Introduction

The study of local and global consistencies is an important topic in Constraint Networks (CN). For example, there are many results which relate different levels of consistency in a CN (Freuder 1982; Van Beek and Dechter 1995; Van Beek and Dechter 1997; Jeavons, Cohen and Gyssens 1997). In this paper, we present a new framework to study consistency purely in terms of general properties of set intersection.

Given a collection of l finite sets, under what conditions is the intersection of all these l sets not empty.

The significance of such set intersection results is that they can be lifted directly to a constraint network setting to obtain consistency results. We give such a proof schema to lift these results.

An example is the well known result on set intersection – any l intervals on real numbers intersect if and only if every two of them intersect. Our work is motivated by the observation from the example that local information on the intersection of two sets implies global information on the intersection of all sets. In the study of CN, it is desirable to derive global consistency from a certain level of local consistency because we would like to have an efficient consistency method, such as that from some local consistency while attaining global consistency where possible. Along these lines, several classes of special constraints have been identified in the work of van Beek and Dechter. For example, for a CN with binary *row-convex* constraints, *path consistency* is the local consistency property sufficient to guarantee global consistency. In our framework, the above result can be directly obtained from a property of the intersection of *convex* sets.

The other contribution of this paper is to present new results on finite set intersections. Based on these results and the new framework, the consistency results in (Van Beek and Dechter 1995; Van Beek and Dechter 1997) are immediate.

Set Intersection Results

Given a collection of sets $\{E_1, E_2, \cdots, E_l\}$. Van Beek and Dechter (1995) generalized the example on real intervals given in the introduction to discrete sets.

Lemma 1 (Convex Set Intersection) (Van Beek and Dechter 1995) *Let* $D = \bigcup_{i \in 1..l} E_i$. *Assume there exists a total ordering* $\preceq$ *on* D *such that for all* i, $E_i = \{v \in D \mid \min E_i \preceq v \preceq \max E_i\}$ *(set* E_i *is* convex*).* $\bigcap_{i \in 1..l} E_i \neq \emptyset$ *if and only if for any* i *and* j, $E_i \bigcap E_j \neq \emptyset$.

Lemma 1 imposes a strong restriction on the structure of the sets such that all sets are dense under a given total ordering. Motivated by the observation in (Van Beek and Dechter 1997), we have this result on unstructured sets where the only restriction is on the cardinality of the sets.

Lemma 2 (Small Set Intersection) *Assume* E_i *is finite and* $|E_i| \leq m \; (< l)$ *for all* i. $\bigcap_{i \in 1..l} E_i \neq \emptyset$ *if and only if every* $m + 1$ *sets intersect.*

Consider the sets: $E_1 = \{1, 3, 5\}$, $E_2 = \{5, 7\}$, $E_3 = \{3, 5, 7\}$, $E_4 = \{5, 7, 9\}$. Lemma 1 is applicable (and also lemma 2) as the sets are convex under the order $(1, 3, 5, 7, 9)$. Consider instead: $E'_1 = \{1, 9\}, E'_2 = \{3, 9\}, E'_3 = \{5, 9\}, E'_4 = \{7, 9\}$. Now the sets are not convex, lemma 1 doesn't apply, but lemma 2 is applicable.

Lemma 3 (Large Set Intersection) *Assume* E_i *is finite and* $|E_i| \geq m$ *for all* i, *and* $|\bigcup_{i \in 1..l} E_i| = d$. $\bigcap_{i \in 1..l} E_i \neq \emptyset$ *if* $l \leq \lceil d/(d - m) \rceil - 1$.

Set Intersection and Consistency

We now relate set intersection and consistency in constraint networks. A *constraint network* $\mathcal{R}$ is defined as a set of variables $\{x_1, x_2, \cdots, x_n\}$, a set of domains $\{D_1, D_2, \cdots, D_n\}$ where $\forall i$, D_i is the domain of x_i, and a set of constraints $\{R_{S_1}, R_{S_2}, \cdots, R_{S_e}\}$ where $\forall i$, $S_i \subseteq \{x_1, x_2, \cdots, x_n\}$. Given a constraint R_{S_i}, a variable $x \in S_i$ and any instantiation $\bar{a}$ of $S_i - \{x\}$, the *extension set* of $\bar{a}$ to x with respect to R_{S_i} is defined as $E_{i,x}(\bar{a}) = \{b \in D_x \mid (\bar{a}, b) \; satisfies \; R_{S_i}\}$.

With the notion of extension set we have the following lemma on k-consistency [see (Freuder 1978) for motivations and more information].

Lemma 4 (Set Intersection and Consistency) *A constraint network* $\mathcal{R}$ *is* k-consistent *if and only if for any consistent instantiation* $\bar{a}$ *of any* $(k-1)$ *distinct variables*

$Y = \{x_1, x_2, \cdots, x_{k-1}\}$, and for any new variable x_k, $\bigcap_{j \in 1..l} E_{i_j} \neq \emptyset$ where E_{i_j} is the extension set of $\bar{a}$ to x_k with respect to $R_{S_{i_j}}$ where $R_{S_{i_1}}, \ldots, R_{S_{i_l}}$ are those constraints which involve only x_k and a subset of variables from Y.

Example. We use c_{ij} to denote a constraint between variables x_i and x_j. Consider $c_{13} = \{(1,5),(1,7),(2,9), c_{23} = \{(3,1),(3,5),(5,9)\}, c_{43} = \{(5,7),(5,9),(8,9)\}$. Given an instantiation $\bar{a} = (1,3,5)$ of three variables (x_1, x_2, x_4). For x_3, there are totally three constraints involving it and other instantiated variables. The extension set of $\bar{a}$ to x_3 wrt c_{13} is $\{5,7\}$ because x_1 takes value of 1 in $\bar{a}$. The other extension sets of $\bar{a}$ to x_3 are $\{1,5\}$ (from c_{23}) and $\{7,9\}$ (from c_{43}). The intersection of the three extension sets of x_3 is empty. Thus the constraint network is not 3 consistent.

The insight behind this lemma is simply a view of consistency from the perspective of set intersection. The results on set intersection, including those in section 2, can be *lifted* to give various consistency results through the following *proof schema* (thus lemma 4 can also be called the *lifting* lemma).

Proof Schema

1. (*Consistency to Set*) From a certain level of consistency *in* the constraint network, we derive intersection information on the extension sets (according to lemma 4).

2. (*Set to Set*) From the *local* intersection information of sets, information may be obtained on intersection of more sets (according to set intersection results, for example the lemmas given in section 2).

3. (*Set to Consistency*) From the new information on set intersection, higher level of consistency is obtained (again according to lemma 4).

4. (*Formulate conclusion on the consistency of the constraint network*).

Applications to Consistency

The notion of *extension set* plays the role of a bridge between restrictions to set(s) and properties of the constraint network. Set restrictions, such as *convexity and cardinality*, can be translated to properties on constraint (through the extension set), like *row-convexity, tightness* and *looseness*. See (Van Beek and Dechter 1995; Van Beek and Dechter 1997) for these properties. The proof schema can be used with lemmas 1, 2 and 3 on set intersection to obtain more direct proofs for theorems 1, 2 and 3 below.

Theorem 1 (Tightness) (Van Beek and Dechter 1997) *If a constraint network $\mathcal{R}$ with constraints that are m-tight and of arity at most r is strongly $((m+1)(r-1)+1)$-consistent, then it is globally consistent.*

Theorem 2 (Row Convex) (Van Beek and Dechter 1995) *Let $\mathcal{R}$ be a network of constraints whose arity at most r is strongly $2(r-1)+1$ consistent. If there exists an ordering of the domains $D_1, \cdots, D_n$ of $\mathcal{R}$ such that all constraints are row convex, $\mathcal{R}$ is globally consistent.*

Theorem 3 (Looseness) (Van Beek and Dechter 1997) *A constraint network with domains that are of size at most d and constraints that are m-loose and of arity at least r, $r \geq 2$, is strongly k-consistent, where k is the maximum value*

such that the following inequality holds, $binomial(k-1, r-1) \leq \lceil d/(d-m) \rceil - 1$.

The above theorem statement differs slightly from the original one (Zhang and Yap (manuscript)).

We note that the consistency lemma (lemma 4) can be migrated to *relational consistency* directly from the definition of relational consistency, and the proof schema is unchanged. The set intersection results can then be directly *lifted* to consistency results for relational consistency.

Discussion and Conclusion

We have introduced a new perspective of studying consistency using the lifting lemma and properties of set intersection. The relation between set intersection and consistency can be illustrated with reference to results of a binary CN. Suppose lemma 1 applies, then all sets will intersect if we know the *local* intersection information on every *two* sets. The consistency result is that given a corresponding constraint network, local (2+1)-consistency (or path consistency) in such a restricted network implies global consistency. Lemma 2 tells us that the intersection information on k sets induces intersection on *all* sets, which results in an observation (theorem 1) that global consistency follows $(k+1)$ consistency for those kinds of networks. In lemma 3, *all* large sets with cardinality ($\geq m$) simply intersect without local intersection information. Hence, a certain level of consistency depending on m is inherent in the related constraint network.

Our work suggests that more consistency results may be obtained by purely inspecting certain set intersection problems. One possible direction is to get a lower requirement on the local intersection information identified in lemma 2 by imposing some additional structure on the sets. We believe that our framework shows potential as a general technique for obtaining more results on consistency in constraint networks from a study on properties of set intersection.

Acknowledgement

The first author is grateful to Peter van Beek for discussion and help.

References

Freuder, E. C. 1978. Synthesizing constraint expression. *Commun. of the ACM* 21(11):958–966.

Freuder, E. C. 1982. A sufficient condition for backtracking-free search. *Comm. of the ACM* 29(1):24–32.

Jeavons, P.; Cohen, D.A.; and Gyssens, M. 1998 Closure properties of constraints. *J. ACM* 44: 527–548.

van Beek, P. and Dechter, R. 1995. On the Minimality and Global Consistency of Row-Convex Constraint Networks. *J. ACM* 42(3): 543–561.

van Beek, P. and Dechter, R. 1997. Constraint Tightness and Looseness versus Local and Global Consistency. *J. ACM* 44(4): 549–566.

Zhang, Y. and Yap, R.H.C. (manuscript). Erratum: P. van Beek and R. Dechter's Theorem on Constraint Looseness and Local Consistency.

Incrementally Solving Functional Constraints

Yuanlin Zhang and Roland H.C. Yap

School of Computing, National University of Singapore
3 Science Drive 3, 117543, Singapore
Email: {zhangyl, ryap}@comp.nus.edu.sg

Introduction

Binary functional constraints represent an important constraint class in Constraint Satisfaction Problems (CSPs). They have been studied in different contexts [for example (van Hentenryck et al. 1992; Kirousis 1993; van Beek and Dechter 1995; David 1995; Zhang et al. 1999)]. Functional constraints are also a primitive in Constraint Programming (CP) systems. In a CP system (Jaffar and Maher 1994), constraints are incrementally added to and removed from its constraint store which can be modeled as a CSP. The success of CP systems illustrates the need to have efficient incremental CSP algorithms. Existing work on functional constraints deals mainly with static CSPs where all constraints are known a priori. We show that an incremental CSP with pure functional constraints can be solved in *almost* the same time complexity as a static one. To solve more constraints (not only pure functional constraints) in a *mixed* CSP with both functional and non-functional constraints, we propose an algorithm with complexity comparable to the cost of enforcing arc consistency.

Notation A *Constraint Satisfaction Problem* (N, D, C) consists of a finite set of variables $N = \{1, \cdots, n\}$, a set of domains $D = \{D_1, \cdots, D_n\}$, where D_i is the set of values that i can take, and a set of constraints $C = \{c_{ij} \mid i, j \in N\}$, where each constraint c_{ij} is a binary relation between variables i and j. We require that $(x, y) \in c_{ij}$, iff $(y, x) \in c_{ji}$. It is convenient to view a CSP as a graph whose nodes are variables and edges are constraints. When we say a CSP is *solved*, we mean either a solution of the CSP is found or it is unsatisfiable. Throughout this paper, n denotes the number of variables, d the size of the largest domain, e the number of constraints. A constraint c_{ij} is *functional* iff for all $v \in D_i$ (respectively $w \in D_j$) there exists at most one $w \in D_j$ (respectively $v \in D_i$) such that $c_{ij}(v, w)$. This definition means that c_{ij} is a function from D_i to D_j and vice versa. A CSP is *functional* if all its constraints are functional. Otherwise it is *mixed*. A *functional block* of a mixed CSP is the maximal connected sub graph of the graph of the CSP which has a spanning tree containing only functional constraints. For example, Figure 1(a) is a functional CSP and

Figure 1 (b) is a functional block.

Solving Incremental Functional CSP

Arc consistency can be enforced on a static functional CSP in time $\mathcal{O}(ed)$ (van Hentenryck et al. 1992). (Zhang et al. 1999) shows that it can be solved in the same time complexity by introducing *variable elimination*. In this section we further show that an incremental functional CSP can be solved in almost the same time complexity.

An obvious application of the static elimination algorithm will lead to an algorithm with $\mathcal{O}(e^2 d)$ time. Here we want a more incremental and efficient algorithm. A key observation is that it is not necessary to apply the complete elimination algorithm every time a new constraint is added when solving the system. It is only necessary to do so when the newly added constraint forms a circuit with those already in the system. Consider example (a) in Figure 1. There

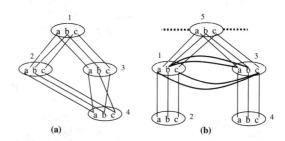

(a) (b)

Figure 1: (a) A Functional CSP; (b) A Functional Block

are four variables $\{1, 2, 3, 4\}$ with the domain $\{a, b, c\}$ in the system. Constraints are added into the system in the following order. Firstly, $c_{12} = \{(a, a), (b, b), (c, c)\}$. We need to mark a variable, say 2, with respect to c_{12} as *eliminated*. Then we mark 1 as *free* and *revise* the domain of 1 with respect to c_{21}, i.e. remove values in D_1 which are not allowed by c_{21}. Secondly, $c_{34} = \{(a, a), (b, c), (c, b)\}$. Mark 4 as eliminated and 3 as free, revising D_3. Thirdly, $c_{13} = \{(a, a), (b, b), (c, c)\}$. Both 1 and 3 are free variables. The property we want is that in any connected component of the constraint graph, there is only one free variable. Thus, we keep, say 1, as free and eliminate 3. Then revise D_1 with respect to c_{31}. So far, no real elimination has occurred but we can verify that there is a solution for the current CSP since D_1 is not empty. Lastly,

$c_{24} = \{(a,a),(b,c),(c,b)\}$. But both variables 2 and 4 have been eliminated. Here we want to ensure that a new constraint is only on free variables and not eliminated ones. Since an eliminated variable is marked with respect to a particular constraint, we can follow this until a free variable is found. From 4 we get 3 and from 3 we get 1 which is free. Elimination also occurs during this tracing. A new constraint $c_{14} = \{(a,a),(b,c),(c,b)\}$ is obtained by composing c_{13} and c_{34}, and 4 is marked as eliminated with respect to c_{14}. Discard c_{34} from the system. Similarly we trace 2 to 1. The fact that 2 and 4 share the same free variable 1, implies a circuit is formed. We can further eliminate 2 and 4 (compose c_{12}, c_{24}, and c_{41}) in sequence resulting in a new unary constraint $c_{11} = \{(a,a),(b,c),(c,b)\}$. We cannot assign variable b and c simultaneously to variable 1. Revising D_1 with respect to c_{11} gives $D_1 = \{a\}$. Discard constraint c_{24} and c_{11} from the system. Now the system contains $\{c_{12}, c_{14}, c_{13}\}$ and is satisfiable.

The above example of incremental solving can be implemented efficiently by disjoint set union algorithms (Tarjan 1975):

Theorem 1 *Given at time t, a total of e constraints are added into an incremental functional CSP which has n variables. Using disjoint set union with* union by rank *and* path compression, *the satisfiability of the incremental system can be determined in worst case time complexity of* $\mathcal{O}(ed\alpha(2e,n))$, *where α is the inverse Ackerman function.*

Solving the Functional Block in a Mixed CSP

In a mixed CSP, the algorithm described in previous section does not prune as much as it could given the presence of non-functional constraints. Consider the example (b) from Figure 1. There are variables $\{1,2,3,4,5,\ldots\}$ with domain $\{a,b,c\}$ in the CSP. Constraints are added into the system as follows. Firstly, $c_{12} = \{(a,a),(b,b),(c,c)\}$. Secondly, $c_{34} = \{(a,a),(b,c),(c,b)\}$. They are processed as before. Thirdly, a non-functional constraint, $c_{13} = \{(a,c),(b,b),(b,a),(c,c)\}$, so ignore. Fourthly, some other constraints on 5 are added. Fifthly, $c_{15} = \{(a,a),(b,b),(c,c)\}$. Because of the other functional constraints on 5, we mark 5 as free and 1 as eliminated. Lastly, $c_{53} = \{(a,a),(b,b),(c,c)\}$. Mark 5 as free and 3 as eliminated.

In this example, nothing is pruned although c_{13} could have be actively used to prune D_5. To get better pruning, we propose an algorithm which eliminates a variable as soon as possible. Consider the same example again.

Firstly, c_{12}. Revise D_1 with respect to c_{21}. Secondly, c_{34}. Repeat first step. Thirdly, c_{13}. Fourthly, some other constraints on 5. Fifthly, c_{15}. Eliminate 1 immediately. As a consequence two new constraints are added. The first is $c_{52} = \{(a,a),(b,b),(c,c)\}$, the composition of c_{51} and c_{12}. The second is $c_{53} = \{(a,c),(b,b),(b,a),(c,c)\}$ (composition of c_{51} and c_{13}). Revise D_5 with respect to the two new constraints. Discard c_{12} and c_{13}. Sixthly, $c'_{53} = \{(a,a),(b,b),(c,c)\}$. Eliminate 3. Add $c_{54} = \{(a,a),(b,b),(c,c)\}$ (composition of c'_{53} and c_{34}) and $c_{55} = \{(a,c),(b,b),(b,a),(c,c)\}$ (composition of c_{53} and c'_{35}).

D_5 is revised to be $\{b,c\}$. Discard c_{53} (non-functional) and c_{55}. Now the final system has constraints $\{c_{51}, c_{52}, c_{53}, c_{54}\}$ and is satisfiable.

Theorem 2 *Given at time t, a total of e constraints are added into an incremental functional CSP which has n variables. By appropriate choice of elimination variable, any functional block of a CSP can be solved in a worst case time complexity of $\mathcal{O}(ed^2 \log e)$.*

When adding a functional constraint, the rule is that we choose to eliminate the variable with more constraints incident on it.

Discussion and Conclusion

The most related work in CSP is bucket elimination (Dechter 1999), which is designed for a general CSP (NP-complete) and thus the complexities of corresponding algorithms are high. It may not directly lead to efficient algorithms for both static and incremental functional systems. The effort here may motivate work on more efficient bucket elimination algorithms for special classes of constraints.

Two algorithms are proposed to solve functional constraints in an incremental system. They are especially useful for CP systems (Jaffar and Maher 1994). When applied to a CP system, the first algorithm is more efficient while the second may achieve more pruning than the first. The choice of the two algorithms in a CP system will depend on the tradeoff between efficiency and pruning ability.

References

van Beek, P. and Dechter, R. 1995. On the Minimality and Global Consistency of Row-Convex Constraint Networks. *Journal of the ACM*, 42(3):543–561.

David, P. 1995. Using Pivot Consistency to Decompose and Solve Functional CSPs. *Journal of Artificial Intelligence Research*, 2:447–474.

Dechter, R. 1999. Bucket Elimination: A unifying framework for reasoning. *Artificial Intelligence* 113:41–85.

Jaffar, J. and Maher, M.J. 1994. Constraint Logic Programming. *Journal of Logic Programming* 19/20:503–581.

van Hentenryck, P., Deville, Y., and Teng, C.M. 1992. A Generic Arc-Consistency Algorithm and its Specializations. *Artificial Intelligence* 58:291–321.

Kirousis, L.M. 1993. Fast Parallel Constraint Satisfaction. *Artificial Intelligence* 64:147–160.

Tarjan, R.E. 1975. Efficiency of a good but not linear set union algorithm. *Journal of the ACM*, 22(2):146–160.

Zhang, Y., Yap, R.H.C., and J. Jaffar 1999. Functional Elimination and 0/1/All Constraints. *Proceedings of the 16th AAAI*, 275–281.

Multiple Sequence Alignment using Anytime A*

Rong Zhou and Eric A. Hansen
Computer Science Department
Mississippi State University
Mississippi State, MS 39762
{rzhou,hansen}@cs.msstate.edu

Alignment of multiple DNA or protein sequences is a central problem in computational biology. To create an alignment, gaps are inserted into sequences to shift characters to matching positions and a scoring function is used to rank the biological plausibility of alignments. Multiple sequence alignments are used to identify homologies among different species that reveal evolutionary history from a common ancestor. They are also used to discover genetic causes of certain diseases and to predict protein structure, which has significant importance in the design of drugs.

The multiple sequence alignment problem can be formalized as a shortest-path problem through a d-dimensional lattice, where d is the number of sequences to be aligned (Gusfield 1997). Dynamic programming is the traditional approach to constructing optimal alignments. Improved performance has recently been achieved using A*. However, the multiple alignment problem presents a difficulty for the classic A* algorithm. Its branching factor of $2^d - 1$ is so large that the size of the open list dramatically exceeds the number of nodes A* must expand to find an optimal solution.

Two solutions to this problem have been proposed in the literature. Yoshizumi et al. (2000) describe an extension of A*, called *A* with Partial Expansion* (PEA*). Instead of generating all successors of a node when it is expanded, PEA* inserts only the most promising successors into the open list. The "partially expanded" node is re-inserted into the open list with a revised f-cost equal to the least f-cost of its unexpanded successors, so that it can be re-expanded later. Use of this technique dramatically reduces the size of the open list, and PEA* can solve larger multiple sequence alignment problems than A*. Unfortunately, the reduced space complexity of PEA* is achieved at the cost of node re-expansion overhead. The tradeoff between space and time complexity is adjusted by setting a "cutoff value" C, which determines which successor nodes to add to the open list.

Another way to reduce the size of the open list is to prune nodes from the open list if their f-cost is equal to or greater than a previously established upper bound, since such nodes will never be expanded by A*. This approach was first proposed by Ikeda and Imai (1999), who called it *enhanced A** (EA*). One way to obtain an upper bound is to use the solution found by weighted A* search using a weight $w > 1$ in the node evaluation function $f(n) = g(n) + wh(n)$. Ikeda and Imai suggested this method of obtaining an upper bound, but did not report experimental results for it.

In this abstract, we describe a third approach to reducing the size of the open list. In this approach, we also use weighted A* search to quickly find a solution that provides an upper bound that can be used to prune the open list. But because the first solution found may not be optimal, we continue the weighted search in order to find a sequence of improved solutions that eventually converges to an optimal solution. This also provides a sequence of improved upper bounds that can further prune the open list. We call this strategy *Anytime A** (Hansen & Zilberstein 1996). Anytime A* refines both an upper bound, corresponding to the cost of the best solution found so far, and a lower bound, given by the unexpanded node with the least unweighted f-cost. Both bounds approach each other until convergence to a provably optimal solution. Before convergence, the difference between the two bounds gives an error bound on the quality of the currently available solution. Pseudocode for the algorithm is given at the end of the paper. The open list is pruned in lines 10 through 12.

Figures 1 and 2 compare the performance of Anytime A* (ATA*) to A* with Partial Expansion and Enhanced A* (where Enhanced A* uses the first solution found by weighted A* as an upper bound to prune the open list). The PAM250 cost matrix is used with a gap cost of 8. All three algorithms require dramatically less memory than conventional A* in solving the multiple sequence alignment problem, allowing a larger number of sequences to be aligned.

Figure 1 compares their performance in aligning eight sequences from a highly similar set of sequences used in earlier experiments (Ikeda & Imai 1999; Yoshizumi, Miura, & Ishida 2000). On average, Anytime A* runs more than 7 times faster and stores only 26% more nodes than PEA* using a cutoff of $C = 0$. When PEA* uses a cutoff of $C = 50$, it stores 40% more nodes than Anytime A* and still runs 18% slower on average. Enhanced A* performs best on this test set. It runs 20% faster than Anytime A* and stores 4% fewer nodes.

Figure 3 compares the performance of the algorithms in aligning five sequences from a set of dissimilar sequences used in earlier experiments (Kobayashi & Imai 1998). For

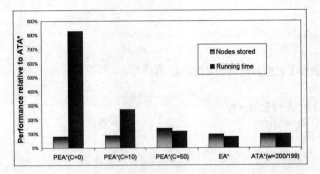

Figure 1: Average performance in aligning 8 similar sequences from (Yoshizumi, Miura, & Ishida 2000).

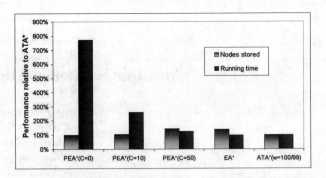

Figure 3: Average performance in aligning 5 dissimilar sequences from (Kobayashi & Imai 1998).

this test set, Anytime A* is only 2.4% slower than enhanced A* and stores 40% fewer nodes. Its better performance on the second test set is explained as follows. Because the sequences in the first test set are very similar and the heuristic is extremely accurate, the first solution found by weighted A* is optimal or close to it – a best-case scenario for Enhanced A*. Because the sequences in the second set are dissimilar and the heuristic is less accurate, the first solution found by weighted A* is usually not optimal. Anytime A* continues to find better solutions that improve the upper bound, which in turn improves memory-efficiency. Figure 2 illustrates its anytime behavior by showing how the upper and lower bounds gradually converge.

Our experimental results show that the sequence of improved solutions found by Anytime A* provide a dynamic upper bound that keeps its memory requirements close to the minimum number of nodes that must be expanded to find an optimal solution. Anytime A* is more memory-efficient than PEA* unless the latter uses the most aggressive cutoff of $C = 0$, in which case the node re-expansion overhead of PEA* slows it considerably. Anytime A* is also more memory-efficient than Enhanced A* when aligning dissimilar sequences. Anytime A* has an additional advantage over both algorithms. Because it finds a sub-optimal alignment quickly and continues to improve the alignment with additional computation time, it offers a tradeoff between solution quality and computation time that can prove useful when finding an optimal alignment is infeasible.

Pseudocode of Anytime A*

```
1   g(s) ← 0, f(s) ← g(s) + w × h(s)
2   OPEN ← {s}, CLOSED ← ∅, bound ← ∞
3   while OPEN ≠ ∅ do
4       n ← arg min_x{f(x) | x ∈ OPEN}
5       OPEN ← OPEN \ {n}
6       CLOSED ← CLOSED ∪ {n}
7       if n is a goal node then
8           bound ← g(n) + h(n)
9           Output solution and bound
10          for each x ∈ OPEN and
                    g(x) + h(x) ≥ bound do
11              OPEN ← OPEN \ {x}
12      for each n_i ∈ {x | x ∈ Successors(n),
                    g(n) + c(n,x) + h(x) < bound} do
13          if n_i ∉ OPEN ∪ CLOSED or
                    g(n_i) > g(n) + c(n,n_i) then
14              g(n_i) ← g(n) + c(n,n_i)
15              f(n_i) ← g(n_i) + w × h(n_i)
16              OPEN ← OPEN ∪ {n_i}
17              if n_i ∈ CLOSED then
18                  CLOSED ← CLOSED \ {n_i}
```

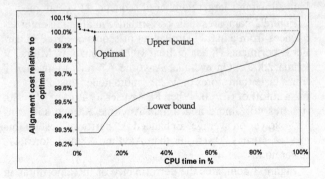

Figure 2: Convergence of bounds for Anytime A*.

References

Gusfield, D. 1997. *Algorithms on Strings, Trees, and Sequences: Computer Science and Computational Biology.* Cambridge University Press.

Hansen, E., and Zilberstein, S. 1996. Anytime heuristic search: Preliminary report. In *AAAI-96 Fall Symposium on Flexible Computation in Intelligent Systems: Results, Issues, and Opportunities*, 55–59.

Ikeda, T., and Imai, H. 1999. Enhanced A* algorithms for multiple alignments: optimal alignments for several sequences and k-opt approximate alignments for large cases. *Theoretical Computer Science* (210):341–374.

Kobayashi, H., and Imai, H. 1998. Improvement of the A* algorithm for multiple sequence alignment. *Genome Informatics* 9:120–130.

Yoshizumi, T.; Miura, T.; and Ishida, T. 2000. A* with partial expansion for large branching factor problems. In *Proceedings of the 17th National Conference on Artificial Intelligence (AAAI-2000)*, 923–929.

SIGART/AAAI Doctoral Consortium

Decision-Theoretic Planning for Intelligent User Interfaces

Thorsten Bohnenberger

Department of Computer Science, Saarland University
P.O. Box 15 11 50, D-66041 Saarbrücken, Germany
bohnenberger@cs.uni-sb.de, http://w5.cs.uni-sb.de/~bohne

The course of interaction between a system and a user cannot in general be predicted with certainty. An interface that is able to anticipate the user's actions several steps ahead can better adapt to the situation at hand, steer the interaction in a promising direction, and protect the user from possible pitfalls. Decision-theoretic planning (DTP) (see, e.g., Boutilier, Dean & Hanks, 1999) provides methods for considering the potential future consequences of available actions. The possible courses of interaction are modeled with a Markov decision process (MDP). Instead of a plan, DTP provides the interface with a policy, which specifies the optimal next step (maximizing the expected utility) for each possible state of the system's interaction with the user.

We have studied two problems in detail: (1) the presentation of location-aware navigation recommendations (Bohnenberger *et al.* 2002) and (2) the presentation of situation-dependent operating instructions for a technical device (Jameson *et al.* 2001). In both scenarios, the interaction between the user and the interface is modeled with a fully observable Markov decision process (FOMDP). Time is considered as a cost factor of the interaction. Important forms of adaptation include the selection of adequate output modalities and the degree of information detail.

Location-Aware Navigation Recommendations

A PDA-based airport guide presents to a user navigation information about how to get to their gate. If possible, the user wants to pass by some shops and buy, for example, a present for their child along the way. The guide obtains feedback about the user's current location and purchasing actions.

DTP enables the interface to adapt the navigation recommendations according to the relative importance of getting to the gate quickly vs. buying a present. The approach was evaluated in a user study with 20 subjects.

Situation-Dependent Operating Instructions

A PDA-based assistance system presents to a user operating instructions for a credit card phone. The instructions are designed to be concise (no annoying delays caused by foolproof dialog strategies) but also sufficiently comprehensive (to avoid mistakes by the user). The system makes use of

inferences about the user's cognitive load and possible time pressure.

DTP enables the interface to adapt the operating instructions to the relative importance of getting the user through the dialog efficiently vs. minimizing the likelihood of the user making a mistake.

Focus of Future Work

The consideration of uncertain feedback about the current state of the interaction requires the use of partially observable Markov decision processes (POMDPs). The serious computational complexity problems associated with POMDPs are well known. A major focus of the rest of this PhD research will be on ways of dealing with this computational complexity (e.g., the approximative technique of Roy, Pineau & Thrun, 2000) that are suitable for typical scenarios faced by intelligent user interfaces.

Acknowledgements

This research is being supported by the German Science Foundation (DFG) in its Collaborative Research Center on Resource-Adaptive Cognitive Processes, SFB 378, Project B2 (READY).

References

Bohnenberger, T.; Jameson, A.; Krüger, A.; and Butz, A. 2002. User acceptance of a decision-theoretic, location-aware shopping guide. In Gil, Y., ed., *IUI 2002: International Conference on Intelligent User Interfaces*. New York: ACM. 178–179.

Boutilier, C.; Dean, T.; and Hanks, S. 1999. Decision-theoretic planning: Structural assumptions and computational leverage. *Journal of Artificial Intelligence Research* 11:1–94.

Jameson, A.; Großmann-Hutter, B.; March, L.; Rummer, R.; Bohnenberger, T.; and Wittig, F. 2001. When actions have consequences: Empirically based decision making for intelligent user interfaces. *Knowledge-Based Systems* 14:75–92.

Roy, N.; Pineau, J.; and Thrun, S. 2000. Spoken dialogue management using probabilistic reasoning. In *Proceedings of the Thirty-Eighth Meeting of the Association for Computational Linguistics*.

Efficient Modeling of Temporally Variable User Properties
With Dynamic Bayesian Networks

Boris Brandherm

Department of Computer Science, Saarland University
P.O. Box 15 11 50, D-66041 Saarbrücken, Germany
brandherm@cs.uni-sb.de, http://w5.cs.uni-sb.de/~borisbra

The overall goal of the project that I am working within is the automatic adaptation of the behavior of a mobile assistance system to a user's *resource limitations* in order to realize a situationally appropriate presentation of instructions and information. Specifically, our assistance system models the temporally variable user properties of cognitive load, time pressure, and affective states. Because these properties are not directly observable, they have to be estimated on the basis of indirect evidence. Such evidence can be found, for example, in the user's speech and motor behavior, in data from physiological sensors, and in knowledge about possible causes of resource limitations, such as the system's own behavior or the user's activities. The system needs to track the user's state from moment to moment, taking into account previous states as well as new evidence.

Dynamic Bayesian networks (DBNs) are a suitable computational framework for this problem, but they raise serious problems of computational complexity. Rollup methods must be applied that cut off older time slices but incorporate their impact on the remaining time slices of the DBN.

There are two lines of research that I will first pursue in parallel and then bring together. One of these lines is to investigate relevant ways of increasing efficiency and the other one is to construct and test DBNs using relevant data.

Increasing Efficiency

I have designed transformations that make DBN structures specified by a human designer computationally more tractable. For example, in a DBN in which not all time slices have the same structure, it can be natural to specify static nodes, which do not lie inside any one time slice; or to specify an edge between the nth and the $n + 2$nd time slice. The above-mentioned transformations embed time-slice-skipping edges in the skipped time slice and convert static nodes into dynamic ones so that the rollup methods mentioned above can be applied directly.

I have extended the polynomial-based framework suggested by Darwiche (2000) to handle DBNs, in particular with regard to forward and backward propagation over time slices (see Kjærulff, 1995). I plan to develop new approximation techniques within the polynomial-based framework, which I will then compare and combine with other existing

approximation techniques to achieve greater efficiency in the processing of DBNs.

Constructing DBNs for Modeling Temporally Variable User Properties

I have combined two already existing Bayesian networks, one to handle speech symptoms and another to handle manual input behavior, to yield an overall network which enables the interpretation of speech and motor symptoms in multimodal input.

I have compiled causal relationships between diverse physiological variables (e.g., heart rate and muscle activity) and environmental variables (e.g., speed of movement) on the basis of a literature study, which also resulted in plausible structures for a DBN that processes this type of evidence.

The next step is to acquire suitable example data for testing (speech symptom data is already available) through cooperation with other institutions. For example, from the Evaluation Center of the German Research Center for Artificial Intelligence (DFKI), we will obtain eye tracker data showing the pupil dilations of subjects working at a computer, which can be used as an index of their cognitive load.

To make these data suitable as input to DBNs, I will have to develop appropriate methods for preprocessing the input data. One possibility, for example, is to average pupil dilations over certain windows (time-directed instantiation) instead of instantiating whenever new evidence arrives (event-directed instantiation). But because not everything can be meaningfully averaged over time (e.g., infrequently occurring but significant speech symptoms), both time-directed and event-directed instantiation have to be supported. I have worked out theoretical considerations as to how these types of instantiation can be combined.

References

Darwiche, A. 2000. A differential approach to inference in Bayesian networks. In Boutilier, C., and Goldszmidt, M., eds., *Uncertainty in Artificial Intelligence: Proceedings of the Sixteenth Conference.* San Francisco: Morgan Kaufmann.

Kjærulff, U. 1995. dHugin: A computational system for dynamic time-sliced Bayesian networks. *International Journal of Forecasting* 11:89–111.

Learning in Open-Ended Dynamic Distributed Environments

Doina Caragea
Artificial Intelligence Research Laboratory
Department of Computer Science
Iowa State University, Ames, IA 50011
dcaragea@cs.iastate.edu

In some domains (e.g., molecular biology), data repositories are large in size, dynamic, and physically distributed. Consequently, it is neither desirable nor feasible to gather all the data in a centralized location for analysis. Hence, efficient distributed learning algorithms that can operate across multiple data sources without the need to transmit large amounts of data and cumulative learning algorithms that can cope with data sets that grow at rapid rate are needed.

The problem of *learning from distributed data* can be summarized as follows: data is distributed across multiple sites and the learner's task is to discover useful knowledge from all the available data. For example, such knowledge might be expressed in the form of a decision tree or a set of rules for pattern classification. A distributed learning algorithm L_D is said to be *exact* with respect to the hypothesis inferred by a learning algorithm L, if the hypothesis produced by L_D, using distributed data sets D_1 through D_n is the same as that obtained by L when it is given access to the complete data set D, which can be constructed (in principle) by combining the individual data sets D_1 through D_n.

Our approach to distributed learning is based on a decomposition of the learning task into *information extraction* and *hypothesis generation* components. This involves identifying the information requirements of a learning algorithm and designing efficient means of providing the needed information to the hypothesis generation component, while avoiding the need to transmit large amounts of data. This offers a general strategy for transforming a batch or centralized learning algorithm into an exact distributed algorithm. In this approach to distributed learning, only the information extraction component has to effectively cope with the distributed nature of data in order to guarantee provably exact learning in the distributed learning.

We have used this approach to construct provably exact distributed algorithms for support vector machines and also for decision tree learning from horizontally as well as vertically distributed data by gathering sufficient information used further to generate the hypothesis (Caragea, Silvescu, and Honavar, 2000). Our definition of *sufficient information* for a data set is relative to a specific learning algorithm, e.g. a decision tree that implements a particular search strategy through the space of decision trees; or an algorithm that

chooses a maximal margin hyperplane for a binary classification task as in the case of SVM algorithm. Thus, the relative frequencies of instances that satisfy certain constraints on the values of their attributes represent sufficient information for decision tree algorithm, while the weight vector (expressed in terms of support vectors) that defines the maximal margin hyperplane represents sufficient information for SVM algorithm. Note that we are interested in characterizing the minimal information requirements of a learning algorithm, i.e. *minimal sufficient information* that needs to be extracted in order to determine the output of the learning algorithm.

We have formalized the treatment of distributed learning outlined above by introducing a family of learning, information extraction and information composition operators and establishing sufficient conditions for provably exact distributed and cumulative learning in terms of general algebraic properties of the operators (Caragea, Silvescu and Honavar, 2001). This theoretical framework provides a basis for a unified treatment of a diverse body of recent work related to: distributed learning approaches based on combining multiple models learned from disjoint data sets; parallel formulation of learning algorithms; techniques for scaling up distributed learning algorithms; algorithms based on distributed computation of sufficient information etc.

We plan to build up on our preliminary results mentioned above to design, implement, and analyze distributed and cumulative learning algorithms. New algorithms and software for distributed and cumulative learning will not only advance the state of the art in information technology, but also contribute to advances in emerging data-rich disciplines such as biological sciences where data available is huge, distributed and rapidly evolving.

References

Caragea, D., Silvescu, A., and Honavar, V., 2000. Agents that Learn from Distributed Dynamic Data Sources. In: *Proc. of the Workshop on Learning Agents, Agents 2000*.

Caragea, D., Silvescu, A., and Honavar, V., 2001. Invited Chapter. Towards a Theoretical Framework for Analysis and Synthesis of Agents That Learn from Distributed Dynamic Data Sources. In: *Emerging Neural Architectures Based on Neuroscience*. Berlin: Springer-Verlag.

Dynamic Bayesian Networks for Automatic Speech Recognition

Murat Deviren

INRIA-LORIA, Speech Group B.P. 101 - 54602 Villers les Nancy, France
e-mail : deviren@loria.fr

State-of-the-art automatic speech recognition (ASR) systems are based on probabilistic modelling of the speech signal using Hidden Markov Models (HMM). These models lead to the best recognition performances in ideal "lab" conditions or for easy tasks. However, in real word conditions of speech processing, the performances of HMM-based ASR systems can decrease drastically and their use becomes very limited. For this reason, the conception of robust and viable ASR systems has been a tremendous scientific and technological challenge in the field of ASR for the last decades.

The scope of this thesis is to address this challenge by attacking the core of the problem what we believe is the *robustness* in speech modelling. Precisely, our strategy is to conceive ASR systems for which robustness relies on:

- the fidelity and the flexibility in speech modelling rather than (ad-hoc) tuning of HMMs,

- a better exploitation of the information contained in the available statistical data.

A family of models which seems to be an ideal candidate to achieve this goal is *probabilistic graphical models* (PGMs). Indeed, in last decade, PGMs have emerged as a powerful formalism unifying many concepts of probabilistic modelling widely used in statistics, artificial intelligence, signal processing and other fields. However, the use of PGMs in ASR has gained attention only very recently (Bilmes 1999; Zweig 1998; Daoudi, Fohr, & Antoine 2001). In this thesis, we propose to explore the formalism of PGM thoroughly, from a theoretical and practical point of view, with the aim of developing reliable models of speech and of developing robust ASR systems.

So far, we have concentrated on the way to exploit the information contained in the statistical data to build acoustic models. We formulate the modelling problem in the dynamic Bayesian networks DBNs formalism. As a subset of PGMs, DBNs are able to encode complex independence assertions for dynamic processes. We developed a methodology in which we do not make any *a priori* dependence assumptions between the observed and hidden processes in speech. Rather, we give data a relative freedom to dictate the appropriate dependencies. In other words, we learn the dependencies *from data*. We develop this methodology using

the structure learning approach in Bayesian networks. Our approach has the advantage to *guaranty* that the resulting model represents speech with higher fidelity than HMMs. Moreover, we provide a *control mechanism* to specify the maximal dependency structure and hence to make a trade-off between modelling accuracy and model complexity. We evaluated this approach in an isolated word recognition task and presented the results in (Deviren & Daoudi 2001). A more detailed report of the approach is described in (Deviren 2001). The promising results on this simple task encouraged us to consider a more complicated application and we validated our results in continuous speech recognition in (Deviren & Daoudi 2002a). Recently, in (Deviren & Daoudi 2002b), we present a fast decoding algorithm that takes advantage of the set of DBNs we consider.

For future work, one of our objectives is to construct an operational ASR system based on the developed algorithm and compare its performance with the state-of-the-art systems. Another objective is to develop new and fast learning algorithms in order to use the DBN formalism in other fields of speech processing, such as multi-band speech recognition, natural language modelling and denoising.

References

Bilmes, J. A. 1999. *Natural Statistical Models for Automatic Speech Recognition.* Ph.D. Dissertation, U.C., Berkeley.

Daoudi, K.; Fohr, D.; and Antoine, C. 2001. Dynamic Bayesian networks for multi-band automatic speech recognition. *submitted to CSL.*

Deviren, M., and Daoudi, K. 2001. Structural learning of dynamic Bayesian networks in speech recognition. In *Eurospeech.*

Deviren, M., and Daoudi, K. 2002a. Continuous speech recognition using structural learning of dynamic Bayesian networks. In *EUSIPCO.*

Deviren, M., and Daoudi, K. 2002b. Continuous speech recognition using structural learning of dynamic Bayesian networks: A fast decoding algorithm. Forthcoming.

Deviren, M. 2001. Structural learning of dynamic Bayesian networks in speech recognition. Technical report, Loria.

Zweig, G. 1998. *Speech Recognition with Dynamic Bayesian Networks.* Ph.D. Dissertation, U.C., Berkeley.

Combining Inference and Search for the Propositional Satisfiability Problem[*]

Lyndon Drake and **Alan Frisch**
{lyndon,frisch}@cs.york.ac.uk
Computer Science Department
University of York
Heslington, York YO10 5DD
United Kingdom

Toby Walsh
tw@4c.ucc.ie
Cork Constraint Computation Centre
University College Cork
Cork
Ireland

Abstract

The most effective complete method for testing propositional satisfiability (SAT) is backtracking search. Recent research suggests that adding more inference to SAT search procedures can improve their performance. This paper presents two ways to combine neighbour resolution (one such inference technique) with search.

Introduction

Davis-Putnam (DP) (Davis & Putnam 1960) was the first practical complete algorithm for solving propositional satisfiability (SAT) problems. DP uses resolution to determine whether a SAT problem instance is satisfiable. However, resolution is generally impractical, as it can use exponential space and time. The most important refinement to DP was DLL (Davis, Logemann, & Loveland 1962), which replaced the resolution in DP with backtracking search. Backtracking search still uses exponential time in the worst case, but only needs linear space. As time is more readily available than space, the use of search was essential.

Since then, the DLL algorithm has been used almost exclusively in complete SAT solvers (Gu *et al.* 1997). However, Rish and Dechter (2000) recently showed that a hybrid complete solver which used ordered resolution along with backtracking search often outperformed pure DLL. Van Gelder and Tsuji (1995) have also shown that another hybrid resolution and search method, 2cl, outperforms standard DLL. Cha and Iwama (1996) separately described a local search algorithm that used resolution between similar (or neighbouring) clauses to improve performance. We have investigated the use of this neighbour resolution in a complete DLL-based SAT solver.

Neighbour resolution with complete search

We have completed two implementations of neighbour resolution:

During search. In the first, neighbour resolution was carried out during search. This method was not cost-effective: while it sometimes pruned the search tree by one or two orders of magnitude, the time cost of doing the resolutions outweighed the benefits to the search algorithm.

The time cost is primarily due to the expensive algorithm used to identify possible neighbour resolutions during search. We have designed an incrementally updated data structure that we plan to use in an improved implementation.

Before search. The second method emulates neighbour resolution by using binary resolution as a preprocessing step. Preliminary results show that on many problems, emulating neighbour resolution before search provides substantial improvements in performance over pure DLL, both in the number of search nodes explored and in the runtime used.

The emulation of neighbour resolution during search is imperfect. We plan to make the preprocessing implementation a closer emulation by reducing the number of resolvents generated, and by checking subsumptions due to resolutions.

References

Cha, B., and Iwama, K. 1996. Adding new clauses for faster local search. In *Proceedings of AAAI-96*, 332–337.

Davis, M., and Putnam, H. 1960. A computing procedure for quantification theory. *Journal of the ACM* 7:201–215.

Davis, M.; Logemann, G.; and Loveland, D. 1962. A machine program for theorem-proving. *Communications of the ACM* 5:394–397.

Gu, J.; Purdon, P. W.; Franco, J.; and Wah, B. W. 1997. Algorithms for the satisfiability (SAT) problem: A survey. In *Satisfiability Problem: Theory and Applications*, DIMACS Series in Discrete Mathematics and Theoretical Computer Science. American Mathematical Society. 19–152.

Rish, I., and Dechter, R. 2000. Resolution versus search: Two strategies for SAT. In Gent, I.; van Maaren, H.; and Walsh, T., eds., *SAT2000: Highlights of Satisfiability Research in the Year 2000*, volume 63 of *Frontiers in Artificial Intelligence and Applications*. IOS Press. 215–259.

van Gelder, A. 1995. Satisfiability testing with more reasoning and less guessing. In Johnson, D. S., and Trick, M., eds., *Cliques, Coloring, and Satisfiability: Second DIMACS Implementation Challenge*, DIMACS Series in Discrete Mathematics and Theoretical Computer Science. American Mathematical Society.

[*]This research is supported by EPSRC grant GR/N16129.

A Bayesian Metareasoner for Algorithm Selection for Real-time Bayesian Network Inference Problems

Haipeng Guo

Laboratory for Knowledge Discovery in Databases
Department of Computing and Information Sciences, Kansas State University
hpguo@cis.ksu.edu   http://www.kddresearch.org

1. Motivation

Bayesian network (BN) inference has long been seen as a very important and hard problem in AI. Both exact and approximate BN inference are NP-hard [Co90, Sh94]. To date researchers have developed many different kinds of exact and approximate BN inference algorithms. Each of these has different properties and works better for different classes of inference problems. Given a BN inference problem instance, it is usually hard but important to decide in advance which algorithm among a set of choices is the most appropriate. This problem is known as the algorithm selection problem [Ri76]. The goal of this research is to design and implement a meta-level reasoning system that acts as a "BN inference expert" and is able to quickly select the most appropriate algorithm for any given Bayesian network inference problem, and then predict the run time performance.

2. A Bayesian Metareasoner for Algorithm Selection for Bayesian Network Inference

I address this problem with a scheme based mainly on Bayesian methods [HRGK01]. Knowledge of dependencies among the characteristic of BN inference problem instances and the performance of the inference algorithms can be considered as dome kind of uncertain knowledge. This knowledge can be represented by a Bayesian network that we call the "inference expert network", or the metareasoner. The metareasoner is automatically learned from some training data with the guidance of some domain knowledge. To create a representative training data that contains the knowledge we are seeking, we are developing a controllable random BN inference problem generator. It could randomly generate BNs and inference problem instances from a description of the BN's characteristic. By controlling the characteristic parameters, we can generate many random representative BNs for both training and testing. Once we have synthetic real world BNs and synthetic instances of BN inference problems, we can then run the selected inference algorithms on these instances to generate the training data. These training data records the characteristic parameters of the problems, the algorithms being used, and the run time performance of the algorithms. They contain the knowledge of how well each algorithm matches each class of problems. The inference expert network, or the metareasoner, can be learned from the training data using some BNs learning algorithm such as K2 [CH92]. Having this inference expert network, we can then use it to select the right algorithm for a given Bayesian network inference problem instance and predict the run time performance of the algorithm on this problem instance. It can serve as a meta-level reasoner to selecting the "right" algorithm for real-time Bayesian network inference problems. The system should be easily extended in the future to include new characteristic parameters and new inference algorithms. The problem instances' characteristic parameters I consider include the size of the network, topology of the network, the extreme probabilities and the average skewness of the CPTs, the ratio of number of query nodes and evidence nodes, and so on. My library of candidate BN inference algorithms includes polytree algorithm, clique tree propagation algorithm, various stochastic sampling algorithms, genetic algorithms for inference, and a newly-designed search-based anytime inference algorithm.

References

[Co90] G. F. Cooper. The computational complexity of probabilistic infernece using bayesian belief networks. Artificial Intelligence, 42(2-3):393-405. Elsevier, 1990.

[HRGK01] E. Horvitz, Y. Ruan, C. Gomes, H. Kautz, B. Selman, D. M. Chickering. A Bayesian Approach to Tackling Hard Computational Problems. In UAI01, 2001.

[Ri76] Rice, J. R. The algorithm selection problem. Advances in computers 15:65-118, 1976.

[Sh94] Shimony, Solomon, E., "Finding MAPs for Belief Networks is NP-hard," Artificial Intelligence, 68, pp 399-410, 1994.

An Agent Approach to Security in Pervasive Environments

Lalana Kagal

Department of Computer Science and Electrical Engineering
University of Maryland Baltimore County
email : lkagal1@cs.umbc.edu

Research Overview

Information technology is slowly becoming invisible and will eventually be completely integrated into the environment. Computers will soon become part of a network, connecting all devices from lamps, projectors, and printers to laptops, PDAs and cellphones. The number of computationally enabled devices will increase exponentially and people will be able to access these resources and perform computing operations anytime, and anywhere, through this integrated network known as ubiquitous/pervasive computing (Weiser 1991) (Satyanarayanan 2001). In these loosely coupled, highly dynamic environments, users will be able to move around and still be connected to this network of resources, which themselves will be constantly changing. As resources will be mutable, frequently changing their parameters like location, functionality, interoperability, accessing them uniformly will be difficult. Users will also be dynamic; moving in and out of range, using different devices for accessing the environment, and using different identities. Traditionally, stand-alone computers and small networks rely on user authentication and access control to provide security. These physical methods use system-based controls to verify the identity of a person or process, explicitly enabling or restricting the ability to use, change, or view a computer resource. However the existing security mechanisms fail to meet the requirements of pervasive systems, which include authenticating foreign users and providing authorization to a large number of entities in the absence of a central control or repository. Our research proposes to model pervasive systems using agent technologies and to use principles of distributed trust management as an alternative to traditional authentication and access control schemes.

Pervasive systems suffer from several problems like service description and discovery, and negotiation for services, which have elegant interpretations in agent technologies. We believe that pervasive systems will greatly benefit from the adoption of these interpretations, as it will not only reduce development time, but also provide comprehensive and sophisticated solutions.

Distributed trust management is similar to the way security is handled in human societies, where people are judged on their abilities, assets and relationships. The basis for

trust differs from person to person, leading to trust being distributed, as every entity has its own parameters for establishing and managing trust. In terms of computing, trust management handles authorization by verifying whether an entity has the credentials that comply with the security policy governing the requested resource (Blaze, Feigenbaum, & Lacy 1996). These credentials include properties of the entities, for example, membership in a certain organization, graduate of a certain school, and recommendations by other entities. This proposal extends some of our earlier work with trust-based security (Kagal, Finin, & Peng 2001) (Kagal *et al.* 2002) by incorporating additional delegation schemes, prohibition and request for permission, all of which are common in human interactions. Another frequent occurrence among humans is the need for justification. This proposed research work enables agents to request reasons for a certain security decision or belief, and to receive in return a proof, that describes the facts and rules that lead to that decision or belief. An ontology, grounded in a semantic language, DAML+OIL (Horrocks I. et al. 2001), is used to represent security information constituting credentials, policies, beliefs, and proofs.

This research proposes an approach to security in pervasive computing environments based on agent methodologies and trust management.

References

Blaze, M.; Feigenbaum, J.; and Lacy, J. 1996. Decentralized Trust Management. *IEEE Proceedings of the 17th Symposium.*

Horrocks I. et al. 2001. DAML+OIL Language Specifications. http://www.daml.org/2000/12/daml+oil-index.

Kagal, L.; Undercoffer, J.; Perich, F.; Joshi, A.; and Finin, T. 2002. A Security Architecture Based on Trust Management for Pervasive Computing Systems. In *Proceedings of Grace Hopper Celebration of Women in Computing 2002.*

Kagal, L.; Finin, T.; and Peng, Y. 2001. A Framework for Distributed Trust Management. In *Proceedings of IJCAI-01 Workshop on Autonomy, Delegation and Control.*

Satyanarayanan, M. 2001. Pervasive Computing: Vision and Challenges. *IEEE Communications.*

Weiser, M. 1991. The Computer for the Twenty-First Century. *Scientific American, pp. 94-10, September 1991.*

Generalized Features. Their Application to Classification.

Svetlana Kiritchenko and Stan Matwin

SITE, University of Ottawa, Ottawa, Canada
{svkir, stan}@site.uottawa.ca

Classification learning algorithms in general, and text classification methods in particular, tend to focus on features of individual training examples, rather than on the relationships between the examples. However, in many situations a set of items contains more information than just feature values of individual items. For example, taking into account the articles that are cited by or cite an article in question would increase our chances of correct classification. We propose to recognize and put in use generalized features (or set features), which describe a training example, but depend on the dataset as a whole, with the goal of achieving better classification accuracy. Although the idea of generalized features is consistent with the objectives of relational learning (ILP), we feel that instead of using the computationally heavy and conceptually general ILP methods, there may be a benefit in looking for approaches that use specific relations between texts, and in particular, between emails.

Generalized features are the way to capture the information that lies beyond a particular item, the information that combines the dataset in some sort of structure. Different datasets have different structures, but we could guess what kind of information would be useful for classification. It is similar to the process of choosing relevant features. For example, we can guess that the references are relevant to the topic of an article, but the relative length is not.

There have been some attempts to include additional information about a dataset to the standard classification process based on plain features. One example is using references to classify technical articles and hyperlinks to classify web pages. This research shows that some links could be confusing while others are very helpful. Another example is character recognition. The recognition process can be based not only on the shape of a character, but also on preceding characters and even preceding words.

Our attention is focused on the email classification problem. Nowadays, when a typical user receives about 40-50 email messages daily, there is a great need in automatic classification systems that could sort, archive, and filter messages accurately. Typically, people work with emails as with general texts and base the classification decisions on the words that appear in the header and in the body of an email (the *bag of words* approach). But emails have other important sources of information, and one of them is particularly interesting for us: the time they are received. Time can be useful even as a plain feature. For example, a message received in the middle of the night is probably a junk message or has been sent from the other part of the world. Besides that, we could notice a pattern that a Java newsletter is sent every Friday morning. However, more important than plain time is a temporal sequence in which the messages arrive and/or are sent. Messages are not independent of each other. In fact, once a user has sent a message, he or she would expect to receive a reply. At the office when a working group is discussing a problem, users are likely to receive a bunch of messages on the same topic during a day or two. This information can help classification dramatically, though only a small part of it has been used in previous research. Messages that form threads "message – reply" have been investigated. We want to go further and extract all possible patterns that are present in a given email sequence and use these patterns to increase classification accuracy.

The proposed learning process can be divided into the following phases:

1. To discover all temporal patterns in data;
2. To analyze the patterns and choose the most predictive ones;
3. To employ the best patterns as generalized features in the classification process.

As the first phase, we have developed an algorithm MINTS (MINing Temporal Sequential patterns) that can find frequently occurring temporal patterns in an email sequence. The important feature of the algorithm is that it finds frequently occurring patterns consisting not only of event sequences, but also of the time intervals between the events. Therefore, the approach predicts not only the expected event in a sequence, but also when the event is likely to happen. The algorithm is general, so it can be applied to any domain where temporal relations are present. Having found the patterns, we choose the most predictive ones and discard the noise. Then, we develop the generalized features based on pattern predictions and incorporate them into the classical word-based classification.

Organizations of Self-Interested Agents

Foster McGeary
Computer and Information Sciences
University of Delaware

Existing agent-based systems apply the productive power of Multi-Agent Systems (MAS) and Distributed Artificial Intelligence (DAI) techniques. However, little work has demonstrated agents autonomous enough to form concurrently operating non-trivial, non-predetermined organizations where agents form such organizations specifically to improve their individual welfare through improving their collective productivity.

In my work, organizations are defined as sets of autonomous agents that reach, and generally abide by, agreements to exchange, over periods of time, computational services for value, and where such agreements are voluntary by each agent. The dissertation[1] identifies and explores techniques by which autonomous agents may form organizations that persist over time, in dynamic environments, and interact with agents outside the organization.

Curiosity about the computational basis of persistent organizations is a driving force behind this work. Extensive writings in Economics, Sociology, and Political Science purport to explain why certain human organizations operate the way they do. From a computational view, and in particular from an Artificial Intelligence perspective, there is no well-developed modeling approach that supports building models with the large number of agents necessary to model human social behavior using the terms of these other areas of study when they appeal to methodological individualism on a large scale. If we project recent rates of advancement in computational power, we find we can project the power to support detailed and explicit models of the behavior of each of the individual agents within an organization or society. My dissertation addresses the methods needed to harness that growing power to the creation of large-scale, detailed, models of interrelationships among large numbers of individual decision units, which decision units are "agents" in Distributed Artificial Intelligence work.

My thesis is that the formation and operation of organizations is rational and computable, and can be modeled using Artificial Intelligence tools. I extend Multi-Agent Systems technologies by introducing procedures by which sovereign computational agents may form organizations. A sovereign agent is a computational agent with its own motives — an agent that cannot be forced to abide by any convention to which it is not a willing party. Organizations of sovereign agents are expected to occur in a variety of forms and, to the extent these organizational forms are viable, the terms of traditional organizational theory will be used to catalog them. Organizations formed with the intention to sell products at a profit (and thus to enrich the agents owning the organization) are taken to be firms, a principal interest of the research.

I develop the agent environment sequentially. First, domain-level (Virtual Food Court) technologies are created to make products when properly instantiated with the skills and resources (raw materials or other products) they require. Second, agents are endowed with skills that, when applied within technologies, have value derived from the products of the technology. Third, agents negotiate compensation for the application of their skills. Fourth, agents are provided with computable preferences for products and the desire to acquire products to maximize their private welfare. Finally, the agents are permitted to act in accordance with these components and the data they collect themselves.

Agent welfare (products consumed) is expected to be enhanced by certain behaviors. Sovereign agents require basic protocols simply to engage in barter transactions. More elaborate protocols facilitate contracting for services through time. Still other methods allow each agent to identify other agents, to determine what information it is helpful to acquire from or disseminate to other agents, and thus permit agents to engage in useful "social" behavior.

Organizations are to be contingent entities, but with their form, size, and activities traceable to (and computable from) particular sets of technologies, agents, and agent preferences for products. Organizations will also be mildly contingent upon non-deterministic elements in their environments, such that a given set of initial conditions can result in slightly different organizations, depending on uncontrolled activities on the computers on which the agents operate.

The computational procedures under which sovereign agents exchange data, negotiate the application of and compensation for their skills, and make reciprocal commitments are the structures supporting the organization of firms among sovereign computational agents. This form of computational organization is original with my dissertation.

---

[1] Based in part on work supported by National Science Foundation Grant Nos. IIS-9733004 and IIS-9812764.

Distributed Constraint Optimization and its Application to Multiagent Resource Allocation

Pragnesh Jay Modi

University of Southern California/Information Sciences Institute
4676 Admiralty Way, Marina del Rey, CA 90292, USA
{modi}@isi.edu

Abstract

Distributed optimization requires the optimization of a global objective function that is distributed among a set of autonomous, communicating agents and is unknown by any individual agent. The problem is inherently distributed and the solution strategy has no control over the given distribution. Constraint based techniques offer a promising approach for these types of problems. However, previous work has either limited representation to binary good/nogood constraints or relied on synchronous sequential computation to find optimal solutions. Asynchronous methods have previously lacked any guarantees of optimality. This work proposes *Adopt*, an asynchronous, distributed, complete method for solving distributed constraint optimization problems. The fundamental ideas in Adopt are to represent constraints as discrete functions (or valuations) — instead of binary good/nogood values — and to use the evaluation of these constraints to measure progress towards optimality. In addition, Adopt uses a sound and complete partial solution combination method to allow non-sequential, asychronous computation. Adopt is applied to a real-world distributed resource allocation problem. Distributed resource allocation is a general problem in which a set of agents must optimally assign their resources to a set of tasks with respect to certain criteria. It arises in many real-world domains such as distributed sensor networks, disaster rescue, hospital scheduling, and others.

Thesis Proposal

Distributed Constraint Optimization Problem consists of n variables $V = \{x_1, x_2, ...x_n\}$, each assigned to an agent, where the values of the variables are taken from finite, discrete domains $D_1, D_2, ..., D_n$, respectively. Only the agent who is assigned a variable has control of its value and knowledge of its domain. The objective is to choose values for variables such that some criterion function over all possible assignments is at an extremum. In general optimization problems, one can imagine any arbitrarily complex criterion function. In this work, we restrict ourselves to functions that can be decomposed into the sum of a set of binary (and/or unary) functions. Thus, for each pair of variables x_i, x_j, we are given a *cost function* $f_{ij} : D_i \times D_j \rightarrow N \cup \infty$. Intuitively, one can think of the cost function as quantifing the degree to which a particular assignment of values to a

pair of variables is "deficient", or less than optimal. The objective is to find a complete assignment $\mathcal{A}^*$ of values to variables such that the total deficiency is minimized. (An assignment is *complete* if all variables in V are assigned some value.) More formally, let $\mathcal{C} = \{\mathcal{A} \mid \mathcal{A} \text{ is a complete}$ assignment of values to variables in V }. We wish to find $\mathcal{A}^*$ such that $\mathcal{A}^* = \arg\min_{\mathcal{A} \in \mathcal{C}} F(\mathcal{A})$, where

$$F(\mathcal{A}) = \sum_{x_i, x_j \in V} f_{ij}(d_i, d_j) \quad , where\ x_i = d_i,$$
$$x_j = d_j\ in\ \mathcal{A}$$

A general distributed resource allocation problem consists of a set of agents that can each perform some set of operations and a set of weighted tasks to be completed. In order to be completed, a task requires some subset of agents to perform the necessary operations. Thus, we can define tasks by the operations that agents must perform in order to complete them. The problem to be solved is an allocation of operations to tasks such that all tasks are performed, or if resources are limited, the sum of the performed tasks is maximized. More formally, a Distributed Resource Allocation Problem is a structure $<\mathcal{Ag}, \mathcal{O}, \mathcal{T}, w>$ where

- $\mathcal{Ag}$ is a set of agents, $\mathcal{Ag} = \{A_1, A_2, ..., A_n\}$.

- $\mathcal{O} = \{O_1^1, O_2^1, ..., O_p^i, ..., O_q^n\}$ is a set of operations, where operation O_p^i denotes the p'th operation of agent A_i. An agent can only perform one operation at a time.

- $\mathcal{T}$ is a set of tasks, where a task is a collection of sets of operations. Let T be a task in $\mathcal{T}(T \subseteq$ power set of $\mathcal{O})$. $t_r \in T$ is a set of operations called a *minimal set* because it represents the minimal resources necessary to complete the task. There may be alternative minimal sets that can be used to complete a given task. Minimal sets from two different tasks *conflict* if they contain operations belonging to the same agent.

- $w: \mathcal{T} \rightarrow N \cup \infty$ is a *weight function* that quantifies the cost of not completing a given task.

A *solution* to a resource allocation problem involves choosing non-conflicting minimal sets for tasks such that all task are completed or the cost of ignored tasks is minimized when resources are limited. This work addresses the resource allocation problem by modelling it as a distributed constraint optimization problem and new algorithms are presented for solving distributed constraint optimization.

Generating Trading Agent Strategies

Daniel Reeves
Advisor: Michael Wellman
University of Michigan Artificial Intelligence Lab.
1101 Beal Av, Ann Arbor, MI 48109-2110 USA
`http://ai.eecs.umich.edu/people/dreeves/`
dreeves@umich.edu

My thesis work concerns the generation of trading agent strategies—automatically, semi-automatically, and manually. Automatic generation of an agent strategy means creating a system that can read the description of some mechanism (i.e., a game) and output a strategy for a participating agent—i.e., a mapping from percepts to actions in the environment defined by the mechanism. To make this more concrete, consider an extremely simple auction mechanism: a two-player first-price sealed-bid auction. This is a game in which two players each have one piece of private information—their valuations for the good being auctioned. Each agent also has a continuum of possible actions—its bid amount. The payoff to an agent is its valuation minus its bid, if its bid is highest, and zero otherwise. My current system can take such a game description and output the optimal strategy, i.e., the Nash equilibrium. (In this case, that strategy is to bid half of your valuation.) Existing game solvers (Gambit and Gala) can only solve games with an enumerated (finite) set of actions, and this limitation makes it impossible to even approximate (i.e., by discretizing) the solution to games with a continuum of actions because the size of the game tree quickly explodes. Of course, the optimal strategy for the first-price sealed-bid auction was computed before game solvers existed; however, my algorithm can automatically solve any of a class of games (with certain caveats) that current solvers can't. In addition to this algorithm for exact solutions, I have an approximation algorithm using monte carlo simulation that can handle a more general class of games (e.g., arbitrary payoff functions and any number of players) albeit at high computational cost.

Both of the above methods are only tractable for quite simple games. For example, almost any mechanism that involves iterated bidding and multiple auctions is likely not to be tractable for strictly game-theoretic analysis, regardless of whether exact or approximate solutions are sought. An example of such a mechanism that we are analyzing is a simultaneous ascending auction for scheduling resources among a group of agents. In this domain, every agent has certain preferences for acquiring time slots (say, for use of a resource in a factory) and simultaneous English auctions are held for every slot until bidding stops and the slots are allocated. Since this mechanism is too complicated for the fully automatic techniques described above, we are attempting to generate strategies semi-automatically. We started with a baseline strategy and generalized it via a set of parameters, defining a restricted space of agent strategies. Our current work involves automating the search over that space by co-evolving strategies until an evolutionarily stable profile of strategies emerges. Such a profile will be a Nash equilibrium for the restricted game in which agents can only choose from a limited number of strategies.

Finally, there are domains in which even the semi-automatic method for generating strategies is not yet feasible. These include many real-world market scenarios, but also a particular structured domain—the Trading Agent Competition (TAC). This competition was created by our research group and first held in 2000. It will be held this year for the third time, in July in Edmonton. The domain involves shopping for travel packages for a group of hypothetical clients with varying preferences over length of trip, hotel quality, and entertainment options. The shopping involves participating in a myriad of auctions of different types. For example, hotels are sold in multi-unit English auctions while entertainment tickets are bought and sold in continuous double auctions (like the stock market). An agent's payoff is the total utility it achieves for its clients, minus its net expenditure. After hosting this competition for two years, this year we will be submitting our own agent to compete in TAC. Past competitors have made many worthwhile research advances in automated trading, and we hope our efforts will contribute as well, especially as another test for the methodology I'm developing in my thesis work. We believe this work in designing trading agent strategies for very rich domains will shed light on how to extend our results on the automatic generation of trading agent strategies.

A Reputation-Oriented Reinforcement Learning Approach for Agents in Electronic Marketplaces

Thomas Tran

Computer Science Department, University of Waterloo
Waterloo, ON, Canada N2L 3G1
tt5tran@math.uwaterloo.ca

The problem of how to design personal, intelligent agents for e-commerce applications is a subject of increasing interest from both the academic and industrial research communities. In our research, we consider the agent environment as an open marketplace which is populated with economic agents (buyers and sellers), freely entering or leaving the market. The problem we are addressing is how best to model the electronic marketplace, and what kinds of learning strategies should be provided, in order to improve the performance of buyers and sellers in electronic exchanges.

Our strategy is to introduce a reputation-oriented reinforcement learning algorithm for buyers and sellers. We take into account the fact that multiple sellers may offer the same good with different qualities. In our approach, buyers learn to maximize their expected value of goods and to avoid the risk of purchasing low quality goods by dynamically maintaining sets of reputable sellers. Sellers learn to maximize their expected profits by adjusting product prices and by optionally altering the quality of their goods.

In our buying algorithm, a buyer b uses an expected value function f^b, where $f^b(g, p, s)$ represents buyer b's expected value of buying good g at price p from seller s. Buyer b maintains reputation ratings for sellers, and chooses among its set of reputable sellers S_r^b a seller $\hat{s}$ that offers good g at price p with maximum expected value. After paying seller $\hat{s}$ and receiving good g, buyer b can examine the quality q of g. It then calculates the true value $v^b(p, q)$ of good g. The expected value function f^b is incrementally learned in a reinforcement learning framework:

$$f^b(g, p, \hat{s}) \leftarrow f^b(g, p, \hat{s}) + \alpha(v^b(p, q) - f^b(g, p, \hat{s}))$$

where α is called the *learning rate* ($0 \leq \alpha \leq 1$). The reputation rating of $\hat{s}$ is then updated based on whether or not the true value of good g is greater than or equal to the desired value. The set of reputable sellers S_r^b is also re-calculated based on the updated reputation rating of $\hat{s}$.

In our selling algorithm, seller s tries to sell good g to buyer b to maximize its expected profit h^s, where $h^s(g, p, b)$ represents the expected profit for seller s if it sells good g at price p to buyer b. The expected profit function h^s is learned incrementally using reinforcement learning:

$$h^s(g, p, b) \leftarrow h^s(g, p, b) + \alpha(Profit^s(g, p, b) - h^s(g, p, b))$$

where $Profit^s(g, p, b)$ is the actual profit of seller s when it sells good g at price p to buyer b. $Profit^s(g, p, b)$ is defined as follows:

$$Profit^s(g, p, b) = \begin{cases} p - c^s(g, b) & \text{if } s \text{ is able to sell } g \text{ to } b, \\ 0 & \text{otherwise.} \end{cases}$$

where $c^s(g, b)$ is the cost of seller s to produce good g for buyer b. Our selling algorithm also allows sellers to alter the quality of their goods, depending on the success of previous sales with buyers.

The work of (Vidal & Durfee 1996) on modeling buying and selling agents in an information economy motivates our work. Instead of focusing on having agents maintain recursive models of other agents, we believe that reputation is an important factor for buyers to exploit, and that it is important to allow for sellers to alter the quality of their goods to satisfy buyers' needs.

We feel that our approach should lead to improved satisfaction for buyers and sellers, since buyers should be less at risk of receiving low quality goods when maintaining sets of reputable sellers, and sellers are allowed to adjust both price and quality to meet buyers' needs. In addition, it should lead to improved performance for buyers (in terms of computational cost), since buyers are focusing on the subset of reputable sellers.

For future work, we plan to conduct some experimentation to measure the value of our model. Our plan is to compare the proposed algorithm with a simplified version where buyers do not use a reputation mechanism and sellers do not consider altering the quality of their products.

Other extensions of the model that we are considering exploring are: *(i)* sellers not tracking individual buyers' behaviour; *(ii)* sellers dividing buyers into groups and tracking groups of buyers' behaviour; and *(iii)* allowing buyers to receive advice from other buyers in their neighbourhoods.

Our work aims to demonstrate that reputation mechanisms can be used in combination with reinforcement learning to design intelligent learning agents that participate in market environments. We also hope to provide some general guidelines for AI-systems designers in building effective economic agents.

References

Vidal, J. M., and Durfee, E. H. 1996. The impact of nested agent models in an information economy. In *Proceedings of the Second International Conference on Multi-Agent Systems*, 377–384.

A Dialogue System with Digression Handling
- An Ontology-Based Approach

Tzong-Han Tsai

Department of CSIE
National Taiwan University
thtsai@iis.sinica.edu.tw

Introduction

Dialogue models fall into two categories. Structural approaches are based on finite state models or dialogue grammar models. They do not emphasize the contextual nature of communication. Plan-based approaches, on the other hand, attempt to recognize users' goals and plans, and produce corresponding effects.

These two approaches are effective as long as users follow the pre-planned scripts closely. However, in certain applications such as computer aided learning, digressive dialogue can be of benefit to the user. For example, Abrams has demonstrated that digressive dialogue between teachers and students may spur students on to ask for additional readings on related topics of interest. On the other hand, digression too far from the syllabi could inhibit the learning process. Therefore, a dialogue system should adapt its strategy according to the range of digression suitable to the task at hand.

It is difficult to implement an intelligent tutoring system due to the rigid nature of finite state machines and grammar rules. A plan-based approach would incur the high cost of frequently replanning and discourse context switching. We shall deal with these issues using an ontology-based approach.

Proposed Work

In this section, we describe our dialogue and digression handling mechanism based on an ontology framework, InfoMap (Hsu et al. 2001).

InfoMap can be treated as an ontology that has a tree-like structure. Generally, nodes in InfoMap fall into two categories: concept nodes and function nodes. Concept nodes represent entities, attributes, states, and events; and function nodes show how these concepts are interrelated. Usually, a root is the name of a domain such as mathematics and physics. Subclass relations organize categories into a taxonomy or taxonomic hierarchy. These nodes help to represent and identify query events. An event in InfoMap usually consists of a path from the root to a node, though it could also be a cluster of nodes. The path can include nouns, verbs, and their attributes and synonyms, provided that they form a meaningful event.

Given a natural language query, the system matches the words in the query against nodes in InfoMap to identify candidate events. A weighting scheme is then used to select the most probable event.

One can imagine that a response to a high level query could simply be a strategy that guides the user to a deeper event. Such a strategy can vary based on the user profile and the dialogue history. Our InfoMap uses "Dialogue" nodes to accommodate the implementation of these strategies. Within each dialogue node, there are ask-back questions, each associated with profile conditions and expected actions. Each profile condition specifies when a particular ask-back question should be returned. The expected actions let the user focus on predefined actions so that a controlled dialogue can continue. Each strategy can be described by a network whose nodes are the dialogue nodes whose activity sequences are controlled by the profile conditions under each dialogue node.

When the user digresses from expected actions, a dialogue system should continue the conversation rather than quit the session. Litman and Allen introduce an algorithm to recognize the current goal and use the replanning results to update the stack of discourse plans after every utterance which is time consuming. In our approach, there are two steps. First, the system allows different strategies for each level of digression. If the extracted event has a digressive level that is too high, the system will not replan. If it has a lower digressive level, the system will move to a related topic. Second, the system measures the level of digression as follows. Consider the taxonomy relation in InfoMap. Since related concepts (ex. mathematics and physics) are placed under the same parent node (science), we can use the distance between the ongoing script and the extracted event in the ontology network as a heuristic measure to calculate the level of digression. Our InfoMap can serve as a knowledge source to identify similar events in the user's utterances and to measure the level of digression. This approach potentially is very robust and requires less replanning.

Reference

Hsu, W. L., Chen, Y. S., and Wu, S. H. 2001. Concept Structure Identification Based on the Information Map - INFOMAP. In *Proceedings of the First International Workshop on Natural Language Processing and Knowledge Engineering*.

AAAI-02
Edmonton/Alberta
IAAI-02

Intelligent Systems Demonstrations

Disciple-RKF/COG: Agent Teaching by Subject Matter Experts

Mihai Boicu[1], Gheorghe Tecuci[1,2], Dorin Marcu[1], Bogdan Stanescu[1], Cristina Boicu[1], Catalin Balan[1], Marcel Barbulescu[1] and Xianjun Hao[1]

[1]Learning Agents Laboratory, Department of Computer Science, MSN 4A5, George Mason University, Fairfax, VA 22030
{mboicu, tecuci, dmarcu, bstanesc, ccascava, gbalan, mbard, xhao}@gmu.edu
[2]Center for Strategic Leadership, US Army War College, 650 Wright Ave, Carlisle Barracks, PA 17013

Introduction

We are addressing the knowledge acquisition bottleneck in the development of knowledge-based systems by elaborating the Disciple theory and methodology that enables subject matter experts to build such systems by themselves, with limited assistance from knowledge engineers (Tecuci 1998). The investigated solution consists of developing a very capable learning agent shell that can perform many of the functions of a knowledge engineer. As an expert system shell, the learning agent shell includes a general problem solving engine that can be reused for multiple applications. In addition, it includes a multistrategy learning engine for building its knowledge base (KB) which has two main components: an object ontology that defines the concepts from a specific application domain, and a set of task reduction rules expressed with these concepts. The subject matter expert and the agent engage into a mixed-initiative reasoning process during which the expert is teaching the agent his problem solving expertise, and the agent learns from the expert, building, verifying, and improving its KB.

Over the years we have developed a series of increasingly more capable learning agent shells from the Disciple family. The most recent family member, Disciple-RKF/COG, represents a significant advancement over its predecessors. It implements a more powerful plausible version space representation that allows all the types of knowledge from the KB (not only the rules, but also the objects and the tasks) to be learned with similar methods. Moreover, the partially learned knowledge pieces are represented at several levels of formalization, from natural language to formal logic, facilitating expert-agent communication, mixed-initiative problem solving, and learning. As a consequence, Disciple-RKF/COG incorporates new tools that allow a subject matter expert to perform additional knowledge engineering tasks, such as scenario specification, modeling of his problem solving process, and task formalization.

Disciple-RKF/COG was used and evaluated in several courses at the US Army War College, with very promising results, being made part of their regular syllabi.

Mixed-Initiative KB Development

The top part of Figure 1 shows the complex knowledge engineering activities that are generally required to build a KB. The knowledge engineer (KE) has to develop a model of the application domain that makes explicit the way the subject matter expert (SME) solves problems. Then the knowledge engineer has to develop the object ontology. He also needs to define general problem solving rules and to debug them.

The main idea of the theory implemented in the Disciple-RKF/COG learning agent shell is to replace these complex KB development activities performed by a knowledge engineer and a subject matter expert, with equivalent ones performed by the expert and a learning agent (Agent), through mixed-initiative reasoning, as shown in the lower part of Figure 1. The knowledge engineer is still needed to help the subject matter expert to define an initial domain model and to develop an initial object ontology. After that, however, the domain model and the ontology can be extended and refined by the expert and the Agent, with limited assistance from the knowledge engineer. For the complex activities of defining, verifying and updating the problem solving rules, the assistance needed from the knowledge engineer is much more limited. The subject matter expert can teach the Agent how to solve problems, through examples and explanations, and the Agent can learn and refine the rules by itself.

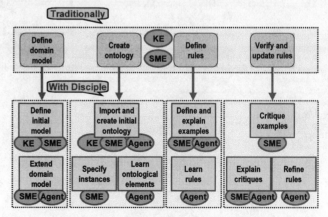

Figure 1: Complex knowledge engineering activities replaced with simpler mixed-initiative activities.

Disciple teaching by a subject matter expert

An important feature of the Disciple agent development approach is that it distinguishes very clearly the phases where the knowledge engineer plays a critical role, from those that are primarily performed by the subject matter expert.

First, the knowledge engineer has to work with the subject matter expert to develop an initial model of how the expert solves problems, based on the task reduction paradigm. This model identifies also the object concepts that need to be present in Disciple's ontology so that it can perform this type of reasoning. These object concepts represent a specification of the needed ontology, specification that guides the process of importing ontological knowledge from existing knowledge repositories. Then the knowledge engineer and the subject matter expert extend the imported ontology and define the scripts for elicitation of specific scenarios.

After the object ontology has been developed, the subject matter expert can teach the Disciple-RKF/COG agent how to solve problems, with very limited assistance from a knowledge engineer. Figure 2 shows the main steps of the agent teaching process. During Scenario specification Disciple guides the subject matter expert to describe a scenario and creates a formal representation of it consisting of instances in the object ontology. Then, in the modeling phase, the expert shows Disciple how to solve problems, by using the task reduction paradigm. The expert has to formulate an initial problem solving task. Then he has to successively reduce this task to simpler tasks, until a solution is found. This entire problem solving process is expressed in English. In the task and rule learning phase Disciple learns general tasks and rules from the task reduction steps defined in the modeling phase. In the refinement phase Disciple uses the partially learned tasks and rules in problem solving and refines them based on the expert's feedback. While this is the normal sequence of the teaching phases, there is also a need to return to a previous phase when, during problem solving, the expert needs to define a new reduction, thus performing modeling, task formalization and rule learning.

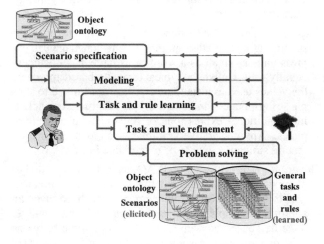

Figure 2: The main phases of the agent training

Final remarks

The Disciple-RKF/COG instructable agent is used in a sequence of two courses taught regularly at the US Army War College, "Case Studies in Center of Gravity Analysis," and "Military Applications of Artificial Intelligence" (Tecuci et al. 2002). In the first course the students use a Disciple agent that was already taught the expertise of the course's instructor in center of gravity analysis (Department of the Army 2001). During the course, the students become familiar with Disciple-RKF/COG as end-users, using it as an aid for learning about center of gravity analysis, and for developing a report containing a case study analysis. 9 of the 13 students in the Winter 2002 session of this course agreed, and the other 4 strongly agreed with the statement "The use of Disciple is an assignment that is well suited to the course's learning objectives."

In the "Military Applications of Artificial Intelligence" course, each student uses a Disciple-RKF/COG agent that does not contain any reasoning rule, and teaches it his own problem solving expertise in center of gravity analysis. The Spring 2001 session of this course ended with a final agent teaching experiment. At the end of the experiment 7 out of the 10 experts (which are high ranking military officers) agreed, 1 expert strongly agreed and 2 experts were neutral with respect to the statement: "I think that a subject matter expert can use Disciple to build an agent, with limited assistance from a knowledge engineer." To our knowledge, this is the first time that subject matter experts have trained an agent their own problem solving expertise, with very limited assistance from a knowledge engineer. This experimental result supports our long term vision of developing a capability that will allow typical computer users to build and maintain their own assistants, as easily as they now use personal computers for text processing.

Acknowledgments. This research was sponsored by DARPA, AFRL, AFMC, USAF, under agreement number F30602-00-2-0546, by AFOSR under grant no. F49620-00-1-0072, and by the US Army War College. Jerry Comello, Mike Bowman, Chip Cleckner, Jim Donlon, and Tony Lopez have contributed to the application of Disciple RKF/COG at the US Army War College.

References

Department of the Army 2001. *Field Manual 3-0, Operations*. Washington, D.C.: U.S. Gov. Printing Office.

Tecuci, G. 1998. *Building Intelligent Agents: An Apprenticeship Multistrategy Learning Theory, Methodology, Tool and Case Studies*. London, England: Academic Press.

Tecuci G.; Boicu M.; Marcu D.; Stanescu B.; Boicu C.; Comello J.; Lopez T.; Donlon J.; and Cleckner C. 2002. Development and Deployment of a Disciple Agent for Center of Gravity Analysis. In *Proceedings of the Fourteenth Annual Conference on Innovative Applications of Artificial Intelligence*. Menlo Park, Calif.: AAAI Press.

JYAG & IDEY:
A Template-Based Generator and Its Authoring Tool[*]

Songsak Channarukul and **Susan W. McRoy** and **Syed S. Ali**

{songsak, mcroy, syali}@uwm.edu

Natural Language and Knowledge Representation Research Group
Electrical Engineering and Computer Science Department
University of Wisconsin-Milwaukee

JYAG (**J**ava 2.0 Platform **YAG**) is the Java implementation of a real-time, general-purpose, template-based generation system (**YAG**, **Y**et **A**nother **G**enerator) (Channarukul 1999; McRoy, Channarukul, & Ali 2000). JYAG enables interactive applications to adapt natural language output to the interactive context without requiring developers to write all possible output strings ahead of time or to embed extensive knowledge of the grammar of the target language in the application. Currently, designers of interactive systems who might wish to include dynamically generated text face a number of barriers; for example designers must decide (1) How hard will it be to link the application to the generator? (2) Will the generator be fast enough? (3) How much linguistic information will the application need to provide in order to get reasonable quality output? (4) How much effort will be required to write a generation grammar that covers all the potential outputs of the application? The design and implementation of our template-based generation system, JYAG, is intended to address each of these concerns.

A template-based approach to text realization requires an application developer to define templates to be used at generation time; therefore, the tasks of designing, testing, and maintaining templates are inevitable. JYAG provides a set of pre-defined templates. Developers may also define their own templates to fit the requirements of a domain-specific application. Those templates might be totally new or they can be a variation of existing templates.

Even though developers can author a template by manually editing its textual definition in a text file (in YAG's declarative format or XML), it is more convenient and efficient if they can perform such tasks in a graphical, integrated development environment. A developer might have to spend a substantial amount of time dealing with syntax familiarization, authoring templates, testing their natural language output, and managing them. IDEY (**I**ntegrated **D**evelopment **E**nvironment for **YAG**) provides these services as a tool for JYAG's templates authoring, testing, and managing. IDEY's graphical interface reduces the amount of time needed for syntax familiarization through direct manipulation and template visualization. It also allows a developer to test newly constructed templates easily. The interface helps prevent errors by constraining the way in which templates may be constructed or modified. For example, values of slots in templates are constrained by context-sensitive pop-up menu choices.

In addition, JYAG and IDEY offer the following benefits to applications and application designers:

Speed: JYAG has been designed to work in real-time. The JYAG template processing engine does not use search to realize text, thus the speed of generation depends on the complexity of the template that the application selects, not on the size of the grammar. Short, simple texts are always realized faster than longer ones. (In many other approaches, speed is a function of the grammar size, because it is searched during realization (Elhadad 1992; 1993; Mann 1983; McKeown 1982; 1985).)

Robustness: In JYAG, the realization of a template cannot fail. Even if there are inconsistencies in its input (such as subject-verb disagreement), the generator will produce an understandable (if not grammatical) output. Applications that need to enforce grammaticality can use the JYAG preprocessor to detect missing or conflicting features and to supply acceptable values. The preprocessor makes use of a declarative specification of slot constraints, based on an attribute grammar (Channarukul, McRoy, & Ali 2000). This specification is modifiable and extensible by the application designer.

Expressiveness: JYAG offers an expressive language for specifying a generation grammar. This language can express units as small as a word or as large as a document equally well. Unlike the typical template-based approach, the values used to instantiate slots are not limited to simple strings, but can include a variety of structures, including conditional expressions or references to other templates. Any declarative grammar, such as one based on feature structures, would be expressible in JYAG.

Coverage: The coverage of JYAG depends on the number of templates that have been defined in its specification language. In theory, any sentence may be realized given an appropriate template. In practice, an application builder must be concerned with whether it is possible to re-use existing templates or whether it is necessary to create new

[*]This work has been supported by the National Science Foundation, under grants IRI-9701617 and IRI-9523666, and by Intel Corporation.

ones. JYAG simplifies the task of specifying a generation grammar in several ways:

- It provides an expressive, declarative language for specifying templates. This language supports template re-use by allowing template slots to be filled by other templates.

- It includes a general-purpose, template-based grammar for a core fragment of English. These templates include default values for many of the slots, so an application may omit a feature if it has no information about it. Currently, the JYAG distribution includes about 30 domain-independent syntactic templates, along with some semantic templates.

- As mentioned, IDEY helps people edit templates and see what text would be realized from a template, given a set of values for its slots.

Easy deployment: IDEY collects all resources necessary for text realization (such as templates, lexicons, morphology functions), and saves them into a single file. This file contains an instantiation of the JYAG's container class called **Generator** (using Java's serialization technique). Applications only need to add a few lines of code to create a **Generator** object and load it from the saved file. To generate a text, applications create an input as a feature structure (an object of the **FeatureStructure** class), and pass it as an argument to a generator.

JYAG and IDEY are 100% Java implementation, therefore they can run on virtually any platform that supports Java. Its original implementation (YAG, implemented in CLISP) runs on both Linux and Windows 95/98. More details can be found in (Channarukul 1999; McRoy, Channarukul, & Ali 2000; Channarukul, McRoy, & Ali 2001). YAG is a part of our ongoing research on intelligent dialog systems that collaborate with users (McRoy *et al.* 1999).

References

Channarukul, S.; McRoy, S. W.; and Ali, S. S. 2000. Enriching Partially-Specified Representations for Text Realization using An Attribute Grammar. In *Proceedings of The First International Natural Language Generation Conference*.

Channarukul, S.; McRoy, S. W.; and Ali, S. S. 2001. YAG: A Template-Based Text Realization System for Dialog. *The Internation Journal of Uncertainty, Fuzziness, and Knowledge-based Systems*. Forthcoming.

Channarukul, S. 1999. YAG: A Natural Language Generator for Real-Time Systems. Master's thesis, University of Wisconsin-Milwaukee.

Elhadad, M. 1992. *Using argumentation to control lexical choice: A functional unification-based approach.* Ph.D. Dissertation, Computer Science Department, Columbia University.

Elhadad, M. 1993. FUF: The universal unifier - user manual, version 5.2. Technical Report CUCS-038-91, Columbia University.

Grosz, B. J.; Sparck-Jones, K.; and Webber, B. L. 1986. *Readings in Natural Language Processing.* Los Altos, CA: Morgan Kaufmann Publishers.

Mann, W. C. 1983. An overview of the Penman text generation system. In *Proceedings of the Third National Conference on Artificial Intelligence (AAAI-83)*, 261–265. Also appears as USC/Information Sciences Institute Tech Report RR-83-114.

McKeown, K. R. 1982. The TEXT system for natural language generation : An overview. In *Proceedings of the 20th Annual Meeting of the ACL*, 113–120.

McKeown, K. R. 1985. Discourse strategies for generating natural-language text. *Artificial Intelligence* 27(1):1–42. Also appears in (Grosz, Sparck-Jones, & Webber 1986), pages 479-499.

McRoy, S. W.; Ali, S. S.; Restificar, A.; and Channarukul, S. 1999. Building intelligent dialog systems. *intelligence: New Visions of AI in Practice* 10(1):14–23. The Association of Computing Machinery.

McRoy, S. W.; Channarukul, S.; and Ali, S. S. 2000. Text Realization for Dialog. In *Proceedings of the 2000 International Conference on Intelligent Technologies*. Also appears in *Building Dialogue Systems for Tutorial Application*. Technical Report FS-00-01, American Association for Artificial Intelligence, North Falmouth, Massachusetts.

Research Applications of the MAGNET Multi-Agent Contracting Testbed*

John Collins[†] and **Maria Gini**
Department of Computer Science and Engineering
University of Minnesota

What is MAGNET?

MAGNET is a testbed for exploring decision processes and agent interactions in the domain of multi-agent contracting. We are interested in learning how a community of heterogeneous, self-interested agents, can operate to discover resources, make commitments, and carry out plans that involve multiple tasks and require coordination among agents. We assume that this community of agents contains some agents who have goals that they themselves cannot fully satisfy. They may lack the abilities, or they may lack the resources, to carry out at least some of the operations in their plans. There are also other self-interested agents in the community who have resources to offer, and who are willing to make those resources available to other agents in a way that maximizes their value to the agents that control them.

The MAGNET system (Collins *et al.* 2001) consists of Customer agents, Supplier agents, and a market infrastructure that mediates interactions among agents and provides them with ontological and statistical information in support of planning, negotiation, and decision-making activities. MAGNET provides support for a variety of types of transactions, from simple buying and selling of goods and services to complex multi-agent contract negotiations. In the latter case, MAGNET is designed to negotiate contracts based on temporal and precedence constraints, as well as price.

Experimental research in this area requires a simulation environment that is sufficiently rich to be easily adapted to a variety of experimental purposes, while being sufficiently straightforward to support clear conclusions. MAGNET is not a complete simulation of a working market environment. Instead, it is focused on the process of determining the form and content of Requests for Quotations (RFQs), on the management of the bidding process, and on the evaluation of bids submitted by potential suppliers. It has the ability to generate plans with well-defined statistics, or to accept hand-built plans or plans extracted from real-world data. Bids are generated by a community of abstract suppliers, again with well-defined statistics. All the major decision processes are driven by plug-in components, with documented APIs and a great wealth of configuration parameters. Data collection capabilities are well-suited to statistical studies.

The MAGNET Customer Agent framework is being released to the research community in 2002. This demonstration will explore the types of experimental work that can be carried out with this framework.

MAGNET Architecture

Agents may fulfill one or both of two roles with respect to the MAGNET architecture, as shown in Figure 1. Customer agents pursue their goals by formulating and presenting Requests for Quotations (RFQs) to Supplier agents through a market infrastructure (Collins *et al.* 1998). The RFQ specifies a task network that includes task descriptions, a precedence network, and possibly other time constraints. Customer agents attempt to satisfy their goals for the least net cost, where cost factors can include not only bid prices, but also goal completion time and risk factors. More precisely, these agents are attempting to maximize the utility function of some user, as discussed in detail in (Collins *et al.* 2000).

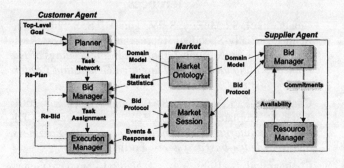

Figure 1: The MAGNET architecture

Supplier agents attempt to maximize the value of the resources under their control by submitting bids in response to those RFQs, specifying what tasks they are able to undertake, when they are available to perform those tasks, and at what price. Suppliers may submit multiple bids to specify different combinations of tasks, with prices and time constraints.

*This work was supported in part by the National Science Foundation, awards NSF/IIS-0084202 and NSF/EIA-9986042

[†]jcollins@cs.umn.edu

One of the important problems the Customer's Bid Manager component must solve is the allocation of time to the various stages of the negotiation process. The timeline in Figure 2 shows an abstract view of the progress of a single negotiation. At the beginning of the process, the Customer agent must allocate deliberation time for its own planning, for supplier bid preparation, and for its own bid evaluation process. Two of these time points, the Bid deadline and the Bid Award deadline, must be commumicated to suppliers as part of the RFQ. The Bid deadline is the latest time a supplier may submit a bid, and the Bid Award deadline is the earliest time a supplier may expire a bid. The interval between these two time points is available to the customer to determine the winners of the auction.

Figure 2: Typical Agent Interaction Timeline

In order to support the allocation of deliberation time, we have used the MAGNET testbed to run a series of experiments aimed at determining the time required to solve the Winner Determination problem (Collins & Gini 2001) given estimates of the problem complexity that are available prior to receiving bids.

The Demonstration

The demonstration environment will include a Customer agent and a set of abstract Supplier agents. User interfaces will allow inspection and manipulation of each component. The demonstrations will focus on activities and decision processes within the Customer agent, including planning, composing a Request for Quotes, managing the bidding process, and determining auction winners.

The first demonstration will help visitors visualize the components of the MAGNET system, their interactions, and their decision processes. Using the Customer agent's interface, visitors will be able to work through a "typical" contracting scenario, consisting of a series of steps:

1. Choose a plan to accomplish some goal from a library of plans, or compose a new plan from a set of task types supported by the market. The plan may be composed and/or viewed using a Gantt-chart user interface.

   To assist in composing the plan, the market will provide statistics on the various types of tasks, such as typical task duration and cost, the number of suppliers who typically bid on that type of task, and resource availability data that will impact lead time and the probability of finding resources within a specified time window.

2. Compose a Request for Quotes (RFQ) from the plan. With the help of decision support from the agent, the user will develop an RFQ that specifies the plan, the time limits for the tasks making up the plan, and a timeline for the bidding process. The user interface will show timelines graphically.

3. Submit the RFQ to the market for bids. The market will distribute the RFQ to all suppliers who have registered interest in one or more of the task types specified in the plan.

4. View the status of outstanding RFQ's. This will query the market to obtain information on number of suppliers who have been notified, and will show progress of the bidding process.

5. View incoming bids. Each bid will specify a set of tasks, a price, and resource availability times. They may be overlaid graphically on the original RFQ schedule to help spot feasibility conflicts.

6. Evaluate bids. Users will use the Agent's decision support tools to search for sets of bids that minimize cost, compose feasibly together, and meet the user's risk tolerance levels. Several different Winner Determination search methods are available.

7. Award bids. The user may select a set of bids that covers the plan and composes a feasible plan (or not, if desired), and award them to their respective suppliers.

The second demonstration will focus on the process of setting up and running experiments using the MAGNET framework. One experiment will show how we measure the performance of various winner determination methods. The second will show how the details of the RFQ generation process affect the suppliers' ability to bid, and the impact of the resulting bids on the customer's bid evaluation process.

References

Collins, J., and Gini, M. 2001. An integer programming formulation of the bid evaluation problem for coordinated tasks. In Dietrich, B., and Vohra, R. V., eds., *Mathematics of the Internet: E-Auction and Markets*, volume 127 of *IMA Volumes in Mathematics and its Applications*. New York: Springer-Verlag. 59–74.

Collins, J.; Tsvetovat, M.; Mobasher, B.; and Gini, M. 1998. MAGNET: A multi-agent contracting system for plan execution. In *Proc. of SIGMAN*, 63–68. AAAI Press.

Collins, J.; Bilot, C.; Gini, M.; and Mobasher, B. 2000. Mixed-initiative decision support in agent-based automated contracting. In *Proc. of the Fourth Int'l Conf. on Autonomous Agents*, 247–254.

Collins, J.; Bilot, C.; Gini, M.; and Mobasher, B. 2001. Decision processes in agent-based automated contracting. *IEEE Internet Computing* 61–72. special issue on Virtual Markets.

SpeechWeb: A Web of Natural-Language Speech Applications

R. A. Frost

Department of Computer Science, University of Windsor,
Windsor, Ontario, Canada N9B 3P4
richard@uwindsor.ca

Abstract

SpeechWeb consists of a collection of hyperlinked natural-language interfaces to applications which can be accessed through the Internet from speech browsers running on PCs. The applications contain hyperlinks which the browser uses to navigate SpeechWeb. The natural-language interfaces have been constructed as executable specifications of attribute grammars using a domain–specific programming language built for this purpose. The approach to natural-language processing is based on a new efficient compositional semantics that accommodates arbitrarily-nested quantification and negation. The user-independent speech browser is grammar based, and novel techniques have been developed to improve recognition accuracy.

SpeechWeb

SpeechWeb currently consists of several hyperlinked applications, including "solar man" who can answer questions about the solar system, "Judy" who knows some poems, and "Monty" who claims to be a student at the University of Windsor in Ontario. The following is an example of the spoken user-input component of a session with SpeechWeb.

```
can I talk to solar man?
what do you know?
which moons orbit earth or jupiter?
was every moon that orbits mars
                  discovered by Hall?
does something orbit no planet?
not every planet is orbited by phobos.
does every thing that orbits no planet
 and is not a person or a planet spin?
which moon that was discovered by hall
                  does not orbit mars?
can I talk to monty?


THE BROWSER IS REDIRECTED TO MONTY
hi monty
who is the president of the university
                      of windsor?
```

The Evolution of SpeechWeb

An earlier version of SpeechWeb was demonstrated at AAAI 1999 (Frost, 1999). Since then, SpeechWeb has been enhanced in the following ways: 1) The approach to natural-language processing has been extended to include arbitrarily-nested quantification and negation, thereby enhancing the expressive power of the interfaces, 2) techniques have been developed which significantly improve speech-recognition accuracy, and 3) SpeechWeb can now be accessed through wireless microphones communicating with PCs which are themselves connected through wireless to the Internet. Although this last enhancement is technically trivial, it provides true hands-free/eyes-free access to the web from remote locations.

In addition to access through a speech browser, the solar man application can also be accessed through an html web page, which contains a full listing of the executable specification and a paper describing the executable specification language.

```
www.cs.uwindsor.ca/users/r/
  richard/miranda/wage_demo.html
```

The Approach to Natural-Language Processing

The approach to natural-language processing which is used in SpeechWeb is based on a small first-order non-modal non-intentional subset of Montague Semantics (Montague, 1974) and (Dowty, Wall and Peters, 1981). To achieve computational tractability, Montague's characteristic functions are replaced by relations and operators of a higher-order relational algebra that includes partial application. A novel technique has been developed that allows arbitrarily-nested quantification and negation. Efficiency is achieved by representing the denotations of constructs involving negation by enumerating the members of complement sets.

This approach to negation, which is described in detail in Frost and Boulos (2002), is very simplistic compared to the comprehensive treatment of negation developed by other researchers (e.g. Iwanska, 1992), but is adequate for many questions to be answered with respect to a first-order knowledge source.

W/AGE: An Attribute-Grammar Programming Language

The natural-language interfaces are constructed as executable specifications of attribute grammars (Paaki, 1995) using the Windsor Attribute Grammar Programming Environment W/AGE (Frost, 1994). This language was built to enable the rapid construction of language processors that are based on compositional semantics.

The URL given earlier provides access to the W/AGE code for the "solar man" application. In summary, the program consists of a set of attribute type declarations, a dictionary defining the syntactic types and denotations of basic words (and the definition of other words as having the same meaning as a given phrase), a set of attribute-grammar productions in which syntax rules are augmented with semantic rules showing how the attributes of a compound phrase are computed from the attributes of the components of that phrase, and finally a set of definitions of semantic functions which provide links to the knowledge source.

Improving Speech-Recognition Accuracy

The SpeechWeb browser is constructed as a Java program linked to IBM's ViaVoice speech-recognition engine. This engine is grammar based in that it requires a "recognition grammar" to constrain the search space. The browser begins by downloading the recognition grammar from the remote location. The recognition engine is then specialized with this grammar. When an utterance is recognized, it is sent to the remote application for processing. If a hyperlink is returned, the browser is redirected to another location and a new grammar is downloaded from that site.

Recognition accuracy is improved if the recognition grammars define small languages. Rather than use conventional techniques for constraining the size of the input language (for example by restricting the vocabulary or range of syntactic constructs) we use an alternative technique which involves modifying the recognition grammar so that semantic constraints are "implemented" in the syntax. For example, the semantic constraint that a person cannot orbit anything (with respect to the solar-man database) is integrated into the syntax of the recognition grammar. This, and other similar restrictions on what can be recognized, has minimal impact on the user-friendliness of the interface, but results in significant improvement in recognition accuracy.

Future Research

Surprisingly little work has been done on the development of rules to assist in the design of hyperlinked speech applications. Constructing an application as a large collection of hyperlinked units, each having a small input language, can improve recognition accuracy if the user knows what s/he is allowed to say at each application. However, this approach complicates navigation, and makes it harder for the user to learn the scope of the input language. Guidelines need to be developed to help achieve a good compromise between recognition accuracy and ease of navigation. Also, very few guidelines are available which help in the design of recognition grammars.

In addition to the development of design guidelines to improve navigation and recognition accuracy, current work is directed at developing formal systems for the analysis and reformulation of queries, and for answer justification.

Acknowledgments

Many people at the University of Windsor have contribute to SpeechWeb. In particular, the author would like to thank Sanjay Chitte, Barbara Szydlowski, Tarek Haddad, Stephen Karamatos, Walid Mnaymneh, and Kunal Bhatia. The author acknowledges the support provided by NSERC in the form of an individual research grant.

References

Dowty, D. R., Wall, R. E. and Peters, S. 1981. *Introduction to Montague Semantics*. D. Reidel Publishing Company, Dordrecht, Boston, Lancaster, Tokyo.

Frost, R. A., and Boulos, P. 2002. An Efficient Compositional Semantics for Natural-Language Database Queries with Arbitrarily-Nested Quantification and Negation. Accepted for presentation at *the Fifteenth Canadian Conference on Artificial Intelligence*, AI'2002, to be held in Calgary in May 2002.

Frost, R. A. 1999. A Natural-Language Speech Interface Constructed Entirely as a Set of Executable Specifications. In *Proceedings of the Intelligent Systems Demonstrations, of the Eleventh National Conference on Artificial Intelligence, 908–909. AAAI'99* , Orlando, Florida: AAAI Press.

Frost, R. A. 1994. W/AGE The Windsor Attribute Grammar Programming Environment. *Schloss Dagstuhl International Workshop on Functional programming in the Real World*.

Iwanska, L. 1992 *A General Semantic Model of Negation in Natural Language: Representation and Inference*. Doctoral Thesis, Computer Science, University of Illinois at Urbana-Champaign.

Paaki, J. 1995. Attribute grammar paradigms — a high-level methodology in language implementation, *ACM Computing Surveys* 27(2) 196–255.

An Automated Negotiator for an International Crisis

Penina Hoz-Weiss,[1] **Sarit Kraus,**[1,3] **Jonathan Wilkenfeld,**[2,3] **and Tara E. Santmire**[2]

[1] Dept. of Computer Science
Bar-Ilan University, Ramat Gan 52900

[2] Dept. of Government and Politics   [3] Institute for advanced Computer Studies
Univ. of Maryland, College Park MD 20742

sarit@cs.biu.ac.il

Introduction

This demo presents an automated agent that negotiates efficiently with human players in a simulated bilateral international crisis. The agent negotiates in a situation characterized by time constraints, deadlines, full information, and the possibility of opting out of negotiation. The specific scenario that we focus on in this demo concerns a crisis between Spain and Canada over access to a fishery in the North Atlantic. Canada blames Spain for over-fishing near its territorial waters and thereby damaging the flatfish stock. The countries have agreed to meet and negotiate over the fishery dispute. If an agreement is not reached by the beginning of the next fishing season, a status quo outcome will be implemented. The status quo outcome is not equally advantageous to both parties.

We developed an automated agent that can play the role of either side in such negotiations. The negotiation is conducted using a semi-formal negotiation language. The language consists of seven types of messages, including detailed offers and counteroffers, threats and promises. The human players are provided with a decision support system that helps them to analyze the scenario and to compare the utility points associated with various outcomes. They are also provided with a language editor to facilitate the composition of messages during the negotiation. The model used in constructing the automated agent is based on a formal analysis of the fishing dispute scenario using game theoretic methods and heuristics for argumentation.

The Fishing Dispute Scenario

Canada and Spain have agreed to meet in an attempt to negotiate an agreement regarding the fishery dispute. Each party must consider five possible ways of ending the crisis: (1) An agreement on Total Allowable Catch (TAC) for the season. The TAC can be between 1 ton and 54 tons. (2) An agreement on limiting the length of the fishing season. (3)

Canada enforces conservation measures with military force against Spain. This can result in either success, partial success or failure. (4) Spain enforces its right to fish throughout the fishery with military force against Canada. This can result in either success, partial success or failure. (5) Status quo. The following are world state parameters that are also negotiable and affect the players' utilities: (a) Canada subsidizes the removal of Spain's ships (0, 5, 10, 15, 20 ships). (b) Spain reduces the amount of pollution caused by the fishing fleet (0%, 15%, 25%, 50%). (c) Canada imposes trade sanctions on Spain. (d) Spain imposes trade sanctions on Canada. The negotiation takes time and is divided into time periods. If the negotiation does not end by the beginning of the fishing season, then the status quo will be implemented. During the negotiation, each of the parties has the capability to make requests, threats, offers, conditional offers and counteroffers, as well as to comment on the negotiation. See (Hoz-Weiss 2001, Hoz-Weiss et. al) for the values and examples of the utility functions of the players in the fishing dispute.

Agent Design

The automated agent is a program written in FCC that handles a negotiation process. The agent is programmed to play in simulations of the fishing dispute. It can play either side in the process of negotiation. During the simulation the agent receives messages sent by humans, analyzes them and responds. It also initiates a discussion on one or more parameters of the agreement.

The agent is based on a simultaneous negotiation model. At the beginning of the crisis it computes by backward induction the subgame perfect equilibrium (Osborne & Rubinstein 1990, Kraus 2001, Hoz-Weiss 2001). It stores the offers that it should make in each time period according to the equilibrium strategy in an array, referred to as the strategy array.

We demonstrate the way the agent computes the equilibrium strategy in the case where the deadline for the negotiations is 16 time periods and the world state parameters are not taken into consideration. If Canada makes the last offer at period 15, it will offer TAC = 1, since the expected utility for Spain from opting out is 477.1 and the expected utility for Spain if Canada opts out is 379.2. If TAC=1 is accepted Canada will attain 630 and Spain 560. This is better for Spain than opting out and the best possible outcome for Canada. If Spain makes the last offer, it will offer TAC = 39 since Spain would attain 940 and Canada 440, and the expected utility for Canada from opting out is 438.8. Thus, TAC=39 is better for Canada than opting out and the best possible outcome for Spain. When going backward to t= 14 each country that will make an offer has to offer an agreement that will provide the other party a utility which is higher than the expected utility from opting out and higher than the expected utility in period 15. Both Canada and Spain, if they make an offer at t = 14, will offer TAC = 21. Continuing the backward induction, at the first time period the agreement that will be offered by a country will be TAC = 34 which gives Spain a utility of 750 and Canada a utility of 535. The other country will accept the agreement.

If the agent was playing against a rational opponent, who has the ability to identify the subgame perfect equilibrium, this would be sufficient. In particular when one version of the agent plays against another version, the agreement is reached in the first time period in the array. However, humans do not necessarily follow equilibrium strategies, and when the automated agent follows its equilibrium strategy the human negotiators become frustrated and often the negotiation ends with no agreement. Therefore, the formal theory is not enough and we added heuristics and argumentation to complete the formal model and make the agent an effective negotiator with humans.

There are two main activities that the agent performs during the negotiations: (a) Responding to incoming messages, and sending counteroffers that serve the interests of the automated agent: The specific message depends on the incoming messages, the strategy array, the world state and the agent's parameters that are specified below. The agent maintains the state of the world during the negotiation. (b) Sending messages regarding issues that have not yet been discussed: Every three minutes the agent checks which parameter was not negotiated recently and then it sends a message regarding that parameter. The specific heuristics can be found in (Hoz-Weiss 2001).

As part of the heuristics we used there is a set of parameters that influences the agent's behavior. These parameters are instantiated before the beginning of the negotiations: (i) A parameter that indicates whether the agent sends the first message in the negotiation or waits for the opponent to make the first offer. (ii) A parameter that determines if the agent will use the full offer message or will use partial offers to negotiate each issue separately. (iii) The number of negotiation units (tons of fish in the fishing dispute) the agent will increase or decrease its offer by. (iv) The agent agrees to an agreement that yields a utility that is lower than the desired utility by at most the number of points specified by this parameter.

The agent is sensitive to the risk level of its human opponent and will change its view of the human's utility function accordingly. The agent begins with the assumption that its opponent is risk neutral. We use a heuristic method to decide whether to change the estimation of the risk attitude of the opponent. When the agent decides that its opponent is risk prone, it changes the opponent's utility function. This leads the agent to a recalculation of the strategy array.

Experiments

In order to evaluate the agent's performance in negotiation situations and to compare it to the performance of humans, we conducted simulations with Computer Science students at Bar Ilan University. The students were introduced to the Generalized Decision Support System (GDSS) for the Fishing Dispute simulation, by which they could evaluate different outcomes in terms of utility point values. A total of 45 simulations were run: 15 simulations were human against human, and 30 simulations were human against the agent. In 14 simulations the agent played Spain and in 16 simulations the agent played Canada (Hoz-Weiss 2001). Comparing the results of the humans to those of the agents for those simulations that ended with an agreement, the agent plays Spain's role significantly better than the human does (agent's average utility: 845; humans' average utility: 723; t=-5.957, p<0.01) and the role of Canada just as well as a human (agent's average utility: 607; humans' average utility: 612). When looking at the results that include all the outcomes, again, the agent playing Spain played significantly better than the human playing Spain (t=-2.51, p<0.05). The results for Canada did not show a significant difference between the agent and human players.

In addition, the average sum of utility points in simulations where agreements were reached with only humans was 1336 and the average sum of the simulations where an agent was involved was 1439. We conclude that when an agent participates in a negotiation the sum of the utilities was significantly higher than when two humans played (t=-4.916, p<0.01).

References

P. Hoz-Weiss. An Automated Negotiator for a Fishing Dispute, Master thesis, Bar-Ilan Univ., Ramat-Gan 2001.

P. Hoz-Weiss, S. Kraus, J. Wilkenfeld and T. E. Santmire. An Automated Agent for Bilateral Negotiations with Humans, in M. Huget editor, Communication in MAS Springer-Verlag. (To appear).

S. Kraus, Strategic Negotiation in Multiagent Environments. MIT Press, 2001.

Osborne, M. J. and A. Rubinstein 1990. Bargaining and Markets, Academic Press.

FlexBot, Groo, Patton and Hamlet :
Research using Computer Games as a Platform

Aaron Khoo, Robin Hunicke, Greg Dunham, Nick Trienens and Muon Van

Computer Science Department, Northwestern University
1890 Maple Avenue
Evanston, IL 60201
{khoo, hunicke}@cs.northwestern.edu, {gdunham, n-trienens, van}@northwestern.edu
Fax : (847) 491-5258

Abstract

This paper describes four systems we intend to demonstrate at the AAAI-02 Conference. The first system is FlexBot – a software agent research platform built using the Half-Life game engine. The remaining three systems are research applications that were developed on top of the FlexBot architecture:

- Groo – an efficient bot constructed using behavior-based techniques.
- Patton – a system for monitoring and controlling bots through remote, possibly mobile, devices.
- Hamlet – the first part of a system for monitoring players and dynamically adjusting gameplay to promote dramatic/narrative immersion.

This demonstration is designed to show FlexBot in action and to exhibit the flexibility, efficiency and overall ease with which the FlexBot architecture supports a variety of AI research tasks.

FlexBot

In the last few years, there has been a surge of interest in using games as platforms for software agent research (Laird and van Lent 00). This is not surprising since computer games provide a rich, dynamic environment for AI research and experimentation. We were similarly interested in using computer games as a test-bed for our work on cooperative robotics and software agents. To this end, we constructed an architecture, codenamed FlexBot, that was designed to be flexible and efficient. We chose Half-Life (a popular first-person shooter game developed by Valve Studios) as a foundation for the work. The engine's open-source status provided an accessibility of code and a broad online community of veteran programmers/mentors, making it an obvious choice.

Our first step was to develop an NPC or 'bot' SDK for the Half-Life game. This SDK, written in C++, provides a 'fake client' interface for creating NPCs. The interface includes a set of sensors and actuators for programming bots, which reside in a DLL that talks to the Half-Life engine. FlexBot coders are responsible for writing control programs – separate DLLs that talk to the FlexBot interface DLL. This SDK was used to create Groo, our resident NPC, which is described below.

After the completion of Groo, we decided to add a set of development tools to FlexBot. Again, each tool is stored in a separate DLL:

- FlexDebug – Outputs debugging messages
- FlexStat – Provides statistical in-game information
- FlexMonitor – Provides player/NPC information
- FlexControl – Sends remote commands to NPCs

These development tools are being used extensively in both the Patton and Hamlet projects, described below.

In addition to its role as a development platform for independent research, FlexBot was used as a simulator in the Behavior-Based Robotics class at Northwestern University. About thirty students used the system to successfully construct their own bots, which then competed in a head-to-head tournament run on a single CPU. Not once during the tournament did the system crash.

Groo

Groo is a recent bot implementation that uses behavior-based techniques (Khoo et al 02). In their purest form, behavior-based systems divide sensing, modeling, and control between many parallel task-achieving modules called behaviors. Each behavior contains its own task-specific sensing, modeling, and control processes. Because behaviors are usually simple enough to implement as feed-forward circuits or simple finite-state machines, they can completely recompute sensor, model, and control decisions from moment to moment, responding immediately to changes in the environment. Thus, behavior-based bots are particularly suited to dealing with dynamic, complex, real-time environments.

In our system, Groo bots run concurrently with the Half-Life game server on the same physical machine. They are both efficient and stable. We have successfully run up to 31 bots on a server; the game engine itself placed a limited of 32 players in a game total, and the final spot had to be reserved for the sole human player.

While we have yet to run empirical studies similar to (Laird and Duchi 00), but anecdotal evidence indicates that our system has succeeded in presenting bots with realistic adversarial behavior. The Ledgewalker and Groo bots have been playtested at Northwestern by people familiar with first-person shooters, and during demonstrations at IJCAI-2001. In general, the reaction was positive, and most players felt that the bots exhibited behaviors associated with human death-match players.

Patton

Patton is an effort to develop a system for controlling and monitoring FlexBot from a remote device. The idea here is that the user is now a commander in charge of dispensing team- into the system at appropriate times.

At present, Patton augments the development tools provided by FlexBot with four new HTML-driven components:

- StatServer –Displays a set of in-game statistics, such as number of enemy kills, friendly kills, suicides, etc. Statistics can be sorted by individual bots, team or behavior type.
- BigBrother – Provides the user with an overhead 2D view of the current map, with player positions updated in real-time. Information is available by simply clicking on a particular player.
- RemoteConsole – Allows the commander to create/remove bots in Half-Life, set their skill levels, and switch their behaviors dynamically.
- VirtualJoystick – Allows users to directly control the movements of a bot in the game. Although primitive, this proof of concept shows that we can command the bots from a remote device.

Because Patton is entirely HTML-driven, any browser-enabled device will be able to utilize Patton's functions. We have successfully used Patton on a number of mobile devices as well as desktops, and continue to develop and refine the system. Our goal is an integrated demonstration of high-level control, in which a commander can make tactical-level decisions for bots to carry out autonomously.

Hamlet

Hamlet is a decision-theoretic system designed to manage the flow of gameplay experiences by supplying "just-in-time" aid to a player. Using techniques drawn from probability and utility theory, the Hamlet system examines the player's inventory and strategically places aid (health, weapons, armor and ammo) within reach at critical points during the action.

Our aim is to create an environment that is both responsive and responsible: a game should never be so difficult that it becomes impossible, nor should it be so easy that it becomes boring. This means lowering player frustration (needless hunting for ammo or health, repeated death at the same point) while maintaining the dramatic tension of the game (the player's experience of challenge, struggle and triumph at the controls).

Many commercial games already have some type of difficulty adjustment – most often the traditional "easy/medium/hard" setup options. Our system is designed to explore the advantages and disadvantages of different techniques for representing and reasoning about uncertainty in game environments, to see how these approaches can be extended and combined to create flexible, interactive experiences that adjust on the fly.

In its current form, the Hamlet system is responsible for altering only the physical interactions of a game environment. Future work will extend the system's capabilities for managing the strategic and narrative elements of gameplay, such as the placement of enemies, obstacles and information within the game world. Our ultimate goal is a system that combines local and global changes to create a responsive game environment where every action has a measured and dramatic consequence.

Reference

R.C. Arkin(1998) Behavior-based Robotics. MIT Press. Cambridge, MA.

A. Khoo, G. Dunham , N. Trienens , S. Sood (2002) *Efficient, Realistic NPC Control Systems using Behavior-Based Techniques.* To appear in 2002 AAAI Spring Symposium on Artificial Intelligence and Interactive Entertainment.

J. Bates(1994) The Role of Emotion in Believable Agents. Communications of the ACM, vol. 37, no. 7, pp. 122-125

J.E. Laird and J.C. Duchi(2000) Creating Human-Like Synthetic Characters with Multiple Skill Levels: A Case Study Using the Soar Quakebot AAAI 2000 Fall Symposium Series : Simulating Human Agents, November 2000 : AAAI Technical Report FS-00-03

J.E. Laird and M. van Lent(2000) Human-level AI's Killer Application : Interactive Computer Games. AAAI Fall Symposium Technical Report, North Falmouth, Massachusetts, 2000, 80-97.

UTTSExam: A University Examination Timetable Scheduler

Andrew Lim, Juay-Chin Ang, Wee-Kit Ho, Wee-Chong Oon

School of Computing, National University of Singapore
3 Science Drive 2
Singapore 117543, Singapore
{alim, angjc, howk, oonwc}@comp.nus.edu.sg

Abstract

UTTSExam is a university examination timetable-scheduling program that was successfully employed to create the examination timetable for semester 1 of the 2001/2002 academic year in the National University of Singapore. This demonstration provides insight on the various components of the system, including the hybrid centralized cum de-centralized scheduling strategy, the Combined Method scheduling algorithm and the overall process required to create the final timetable.

Introduction

The scheduling of the examination timetable for a major university is a complicated and often expensive affair. While most universities still schedule their examination timetables manually, this process can take weeks, is error-prone and is unable to easily cater for the inevitable last-minute changes. Coupled with the increasing popularity of cross-faculty modules (modules that may be taken by students from different faculties), much can be gained by automating the examination timetabling process.

UTTSExam (Lim et al. 2000, Lim et al. 2002) is one such automated university examination timetabling program. It began development in 1999 in the National University of Singapore, and was recently deployed to schedule the timetable for semester 1 of the 2001/2002 academic year for NUS. The program is split into two versions: the Registrar Version allows unlimited access to all portions of the program, while the Faculty Version allows only access to the information pertaining to the relevant faculty. A divide-and-conquer methodology is employed, whereby the individual faculties first schedule their own timetables using the Faculty Version. These faculty timetables are then uploaded to the Registrar Version to be merged into the collated timetable.

This demonstration shows *UTTSExam* in action, including the data input modules, the scheduling process and the final timetable generated. In order to allow full appreciation of the system, we also explain the hybrid

centralized cum de-centralized scheduling strategy and the Combined Method scheduling algorithm.

Demonstration

Both the full-fledged Registrar Version and the stripped-down Faculty Version of *UTTSExam* will be on display. The actual, real-life data and constraints from semester 1 of the 2001/2002 academic year in NUS will be loaded into the system to show the magnitude of an actual timetabling problem of a major university.

Scheduling Strategy

One of the most important aspects of university timetabling is the scheduling strategy. In general, there are two possible strategies, each with their own advantages and disadvantages. The *centralized* strategy has a central authority perform the entire scheduling task. While this allows the greatest global view of the problem, the sheer amount of data that a real-life examination timetabling problem of a large university makes it difficult to produce a good solution. The *de-centralized* strategy lets each faculty schedule their own timetables. While this is ideal if all the faculty timetables are entirely disjoint, modern universities offer several cross-faculty modules. The increasing necessity of communication between faculties makes the de-centralized strategy clumsy and infeasible.

As a result, a hybrid approach is adopted (Ho, Lim and Oon 2002). Before student registration, each faculty is assigned a number of seats in each session (called a *venue partition*) based on their examinations' enrolment estimates. Each faculty would then schedule their exams according to their venue partitions, using the Faculty Version, which are then merged into a campus-wide tentative timetable. After student registration, the tentative timetable is updated with the finalized information. The exams are then allocated to their actual venues, verified by the individual faculties and published.

Scheduling Algorithm

The scheduling algorithm used by *UTTSExam* is the Combined Method (Ho and Lim 2001). This method makes use of a stochastic search technique to first find a solution that may not be entirely feasible (i.e. some hard constraints may be violated) but is of high quality in terms of a weighted sum of the different constraints satisfied. This solution is then used to guide a selection algorithm with consistency checking to create a feasible timetable that still retains most of the quality of the initial solution.

UTTSExam employs the Genetic Algorithm (Marin 1998) as its stochastic search technique, with Tabu Search (Rayward-Smith et al. 1996) post-optimization. This guides the Variable Ordering Method with AC-3 (Mackworth 1977) consistency checking.

Application Modules

The *UTTSExam* program is made up of several parts. Several modules allow the input of information, including examination, student, venue and session information. Of particular interest is the input on constraint information, which is a crucial part of any timetabling system. The system allows:

- Unary constraints (e.g. paper X is to be held in venue V),
- Binary constraints (e.g. paper X must be at least 3 sessions before paper Y),
- Inter-group constraints (e.g. all papers in group A must be before all papers in group B), and
- Intra-group constraints (e.g. the papers in group A must be at least 2 sessions apart).

Additionally, *UTTSExam* allows output of all the internal information in the form of html files for ready display on the university web pages. There are also tools for defining the venue layouts and the assignment of seat numbers to each candidate.

Benefits

When compared to the only alternative of manual scheduling, automated timetable scheduling offers tremendous benefits.

- Manual scheduling usually takes several weeks to complete. *UTTSExam* takes only a few minutes.
- The timetable generated by *UTTSExam* required fewer days and sessions than those created using the previous manual system. Since some of the examinations are held in commercial venues that require rental, this translates to a substantial monetary saving.
- Previous manual timetables often contain overlooked constraint conflicts. The automated timetable is conflict-free.
- *UTTSExam* can easily handle last-minute changes to the data.
- In the future, administrators can use the system to test the feasibility of possible policy changes, like the shortening of the examination period.

Conclusion

UTTSExam is a university examination timetable scheduler that has been successfully used to create the timetable for a major university. This demonstration seeks to reveal how the various techniques employed have been incorporated into a coherent whole. Admittedly, university examination timetabling is an immensely complex and tedious process to automate, but the potential benefits are similarly tremendous. We hope to show that the automation of university examination timetabling is well worth the effort.

References

Ho, W. K. and Lim, A. *A Hybrid-Based Framework for Constraint Satisfaction Optimization Problems*, in International Conference on Information Systems (ICIS) 2001, pg. 65-76.

Ho, W. K.; Lim, A.; and Oon, W. C. *UTTSExam: A University Examination Timetabling System*, submitted to IEEE Intelligent Systems 2002.

Lim, A.; Ang, J. C.; Ho, W. K.; and Oon, W. C. *A Campus-Wide University Examination Timetabling Application*, in Innovative Applications in Artificial Intelligence (AAAI/IAAI) 2000, pg. 1020-1025

Lim, A.; Ang, J. C.; Ho, W. K.; and Oon, W. C. *UTTSExam: A Campus-Wide University Examination-Timetabling System*, submitted to Innovative Applications in Artificial Intelligence (AAAI/IAAI) 2002

Mackworth, A. K. *Consistency in Networks of Relations*, in Artificial Intelligence 8 (1977): 88-119

Marin, H. T. "Combinations of GA and CSP Strategies for Solving the Examination Timetabling Problem", *Ph.D. thesis, Instiuto Technologico y de Estudios Superiores de Menterrey*, 1998.

Rayward-Smith, V. J.; Osman, I. H.; Reeves, C. R.; and Smith, G. D. *Modern Heuristic Search Methods*, 1996.

Multi-ViewPoint Clustering Analysis (MVP-CA) Tool

Mala Mehrotra
Pragati Synergetic Research, Inc.
922 Liberty Ct.
Cupertino, CA 95014
mm@pragati-inc.com

Dmitri Bobrovnikoff
Intelligent Software Solutions
450 Redwood Ave.
Redwood City, CA 94061
dmitrib@cs.stanford.edu

Abstract

The MVP-CA tool clusters a knowledge base into related rule sets thus allowing the user to comprehend the knowledge base in terms of conceptually meaningful clusters of rules. The tool is eventually meant to aid knowledge engineers and subject matter experts to author, understand and manage the KB for its maximal utilization.

Introduction

Software engineering of knowledge bases is difficult because they tend to be large, complex and dynamic. In order to build reliable knowledge-based systems, it is important that the knowledge be abstracted, structured, and partitioned in a manner that facilitates its understanding, maintenance, management, verification, and validation. We provide a demo of the Multi-ViewPoint-Clustering Analysis (MVP-CA) tool, which is a semi-automated tool to support these objectives. The MVP-CA tool clusters a knowledge base into related rule sets thus allowing the user to comprehend the knowledge base in terms of conceptually meaningful clusters of rules. The tool is eventually meant to aid knowledge engineers and subject matter experts to author, understand and manage the KB for its maximal utilization.

The MVP-CA tool has been applied to analyze knowledge bases from a number of different application domains(Mehrotra et.al 1999, Mehrotra and Wild 1993). It is currently being used for assuring the quality of large knowledge bases, such as Kraken (Cycorp-led) and Shaken (SRI-led) KB authoring systems in the DARPA RKF program, as well as for evaluating logistic ontologies underlying NAVY multi-agent command and control systems, such as IMMACCS, SEAWAY, etc. in an ONR supported project.

Tool Description

The MVP-CA tool is an analysis tool that exposes knowledge base developers and ontology designers to the semantics of a knowledge-based system through semi-automatic clustering of its rules. The MVP-CA tool consists of three stages: *parsing, cluster generation,* and *cluster analysis*. In the parsing phase, a front-end parser

translates a knowledge base's axioms from their original form into an internal representation. The user can specify numerous filtering options at this stage, including rule and pattern transformations and the elimination of noise such as comments, duplicate rules, etc. The cluster generation phase applies a hierarchical agglomerative clustering algorithm to the filtered rules. This pattern of merging forms a hierarchy of clusters as shown in the dendrogram in Figure 1. Similarity between rules is defined by a set of heuristic distance metrics (Mehrotra and Wild 1995), which the user chooses based on the nature of the task performed by the rule base (e.g., classification, diagnosis, control, etc.) (Chandrasekharan, B 1986). For example, a data-flow metric is appropriate for classification systems in which information flows from the consequent of one rule to antecedents of other rules. Similarly, for a monitoring system application, the *antecedent* distance metric captures information only from the antecedents of rules, resulting in groupings based on the different conditions that trigger actions. These and other heuristic-based distance metrics have evolved from our experiences with different types of knowledge bases. The cluster generation phase also provides a filter to suppress user-specified patterns that can interfere with the generation of well-defined clusters.

In the cluster analysis phase, the user interacts with the tool to pinpoint the relevant clusters from the generated pool of clusters. A cluster's "relevance" depends entirely on the objective of the analysis. If one is trying to verify the correctness of the knowledge base, clusters that expose errors such as conflicts or circular conditions are relevant. The tool provides support to detect such problem clusters automatically. If the objective is to find recurring patterns in rules, the tool provides support by flagging clusters with similar repeating clauses. However, the main objective of the tool is to act as a comprehension aid. In this role, MVP-CA provides support for honing in on clusters that provide insight into the important conceptual regions in the knowledge base. In order to identify such emergent concepts, the tool generates information about patterns and clusters, such as, pattern frequency, cluster size, the dominant patterns of a cluster, etc. The user can utilize this information to assess the quality and relevance of the clusters. Graphical representations of the clustering process, such as the dendrogram view shown in Figure 1, further aid the user in establishing links across various concept terms in the knowledge base. In addition, the tool

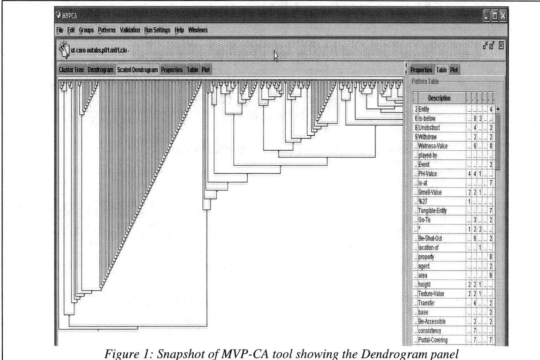

Figure 1: Snapshot of MVP-CA tool showing the Dendrogram panel

provides several views of the clusters at the pattern, rule, and cluster levels to aid the user in identifying the relevant clusters. Once a cluster is chosen, the properties of the cluster including its rules can also be examined.

In addition to the user-driven mode of navigating a knowledge base, heuristically-formulated detection routines automatically flag interesting clusters that should be examined by the user. However, a more sophisticated user of the tool can still control the types of clusters he/she wants to see by visualizing the cluster characteristics on a plot panel and identifying the relevant clusters in that manner. The dendrogram is displayed in several different ways to allow the user flexibility to navigate and explore the concepts in the knowledge base in a focused manner. Note that the dendrogram exposes the knowledge base concepts in terms of its usage as opposed to the declared taxonomic hierarchy of the KB ontology (Guha 1990).

In our demo we will lead the user through several scenarios of finding interesting patterns in the knowledge bases we have analyzed. It will be taking place in an interactive manner since a novice user may need some guidance in understanding the various measures that facilitate navigating through the knowledge base. We will present the different ways in which we first understand the knowledge base and how we extract meaningful patterns in the KB for potential reuse scenarios. In addition, detection of faceting issues will be demonstrated when the ontological placement of certain terms in the taxonomic hierarchy sits at odds with the suggested placement based on usage in the rules. This has an impact on the maintenance and management of the ontologies in the KB. We will demonstrate how we can extract templates from recurring patterns in the KB. Also we will demonstrate how we detect lexically close but semantically different terms, lexically distant but semantically close terms, complementary terms, and single and composite terms exhibiting polysemy.

References

Chandrasekharan, B 1986. Generic tasks in knowledge-based reasoning: High-level building blocks for expert systems design. IEEE Expert, Fall 1986.

Guha, R.V. 1990. Micro-theories and Contexts in Cyc Part I: Basic issues. MCC Technical Report ACT-CYC-129-9, MCC.

Mehrotra, M., Alvarado, S., and. Wainwright R. 1999. Laying a Foundation for Software Engineering of Knowledge Bases in Spacecraft Ground Systems. In *Proceedings of FLAIRS-99 Conference*, 73-77. Menlo Park, CA: AAAI Press.

Mehrotra, M. and Wild, C. 1993. Multi-View Point Clustering Analysis. In *Proceedings of 1993 Goddard Conference on Space Applications of Artificial Intelligence*. 217-231. Greenbelt, MD:.NASA Conference Publications.

Mehrotra, M. and Wild, C. 1995. Analyzing Knowledge-Based Systems Using Multi-ViewPoint Clustering Analysis. Journal of Systems and Software 29:235-249.

Fuzzy Neural Networks in a Palm Environment

Samuel Moyle and Michael Watts

Department of Information Science
University of Otago School of Business
PO Box 56
Dunedin, New Zealand
smoyle@infoscience.otago.ac.nz, mike@kel.otago.ac.nz

Abstract

This paper outlines the achievements made in the area of small expert systems, in particular the use of multiple Fuzzy Neural Networks (FuNN) within a single application implemented on a PDA. Also discussed is the opportunity for using the architecture as a generic problem solving method – if a Neural Network is an appropriate solution to a problem then a PDA based implementation becomes possible.

Introduction

This paper commences with an overview of the problem addressed. The proposed solution is outlined, as is the use of Fuzzy Neural Networks in the building of a small expert system. The generic architecture implemented, and the reasons for using such a structure, is discussed. Finally, the options for future development are outlined, as proposed by expert evaluators and system developers.

The Problem

Determining the condition of a roof can be difficult, especially for those not having a technical background. Deciding the most appropriate course of maintenance for a roof is dependent on a number of factors, dependent upon the roof type under assessment. The combination and severity of factors is used to determine what maintenance is recommended to the property owner. Often there is not a sufficiently high correlation for any one condition to be used, making the final decision complex.

In some instances input values may be contradictory to the result expected. This complexity makes training new staff difficult, especially where the staff member has little building, technical or engineering background. It is likely that more than one result is valid and it is often difficult to establish which is to be the primary decision.

Currently, maintenance experts need to climb onto the roof to be assessed. The expert must have a folder, pen, and often a tape measure. This makes the act of climbing onto

the roof hazardous, an issue identified by OSH[1] (2000). Ideally, an expert need only take a palm-sized device able to accept input. This device can be stored in a pocket until needed thus freeing hands for more important purposes (like climbing ladders).

The proposed solution

To enable novice maintenance staff to quickly become trained, it is useful for the tool to make decisions given the available inputs. Before climbing onto the roof, the expert knows:

- Where the roof is (location)
- How old the roof is (age)
- The roof profile

With this information the system should be able to 'guess' what the roof maintenance expert will see.

The expert should also have opportunity to alter the parameters to reflect what is actually found, should they be different from that expected by the system. The system should be able to take the new parameters and use them to make an assessment of preferred maintenance.

Determining Suitable Results – the underlying expert system

Having determined that a palm-sized tool is appropriate, and that the user interface can be created in a compact manner, the underlying expert system needed to be developed.

Fuzzy Neural Networks (FuNN) (Kasabov et al, 1997) are excellent tools for divining rules from a data set. As there were no initial rules, accurate training of the network was imperative. Rules were extracted and assessed by an expert to confirm suitability. Another advantage is the FuNN is capable of providing clear secondary results. Priority is established by mathematical ranking. For this work the FuNN found in FuzzyCOPE 3 as developed by the

---

[1] OSH is the Occupational Safety and Health division of the Department of Labour. They are charged with ensuring that New Zealand businesses comply with workplace safety standards.

University of Otago (Watts, Woodford and Kasabov, 1999) was used

An expert was engaged to determine expected input and results. The test values consisted of a set of randomly generated numbers that were assigned results by the expert. This data set (inputs and expected results) was used for training and testing of the FuNN. The total set was divided into two sets – 75% used as for training, 25% for testing.

Why a generic structure?

An important factor in this development is that the use of new technologies should simplify work done. In this instance we wish to take advantage of Palm technologies in creating a small, real-time, expert system.

Palm devices are small, not just in physical size, but processor power and screen size. Memory is a constraint, as memory code chunks are 32k in size. This means that, where possible, work is broken into small pieces and allowed to reside in separate memory areas. There is a limitation in the relative distance that memory calls can be made within dynamic memory – also 32k. Note that devices with more than 2mb RAM may be implicitly instructed to use a larger memory chunk size.

This memory allocation problem was overcome through allocating the generic work to layers - allowing calls to be made between chunks. The system developed uses 4 layers. The visible outer layer is the User Interface (UI). Any PDA User Interface should reflect the work being done and, wherever possible, be simple, intuitive and fast.

The next layer is a translation layer. The translation layer has two tasks. The first is to convert raw values from the UI layer into numeric values appropriate for the neural network. The values returned from the FuNN are translated into sentence form, which are returned to the UI layer for display.

The next layer, the neural network layer, is responsible for taking the neural network input values, bundling them with the relevant connection weight information and passing them on to the generic neural network layer.

The generic FuNN Structure layer is based on the CBIS code-base (Ward et al, 1997), as utilised by FuzzyCOPE3. This accepts the connection weight information and input values, processes them and returns the numeric results to the neural network layer.

In the PalmOS prototype constructed, these layers are in the form of code classes placed in separate code chunks.

This widens the appeal and possible applications that can be built using neural networks. The generic use of components becomes advantageous when there are a number of small, highly specialised, applications sharing resources in a single PDA.

Further Development

After evaluation of the PalmOS prototype, experts have identified areas of development that would make the tool even more useful. These include:

- Saving data for a specific property to a database for future visits.
- Combining the existing tool with a Global Positioning System (GPS) tool. Gathering of data points should enable automatic calculation of the surface area of the roof. This would also eliminate the need for the location to be entered, resulting in better location specific training of the Neural Network.
- Linking in of costing components – automating the creation of quotes.

From a development perspective, it would be beneficial to further separate the underlying expert system from the front end. PalmOS allows this through the ability to store the underlying FuNN structure in the form of a pre-compiled library. The use of libraries enables many applications to use a single library. Code optimisation can further reduce memory use and improve application speed. Only the recall components need be included in the PDA as training can be undertaken on the desktop computer.

The connection weight files can be stored in an independent PDA database. There are a number of advantages in doing this. The desktop computer can update weight files, the Palm database updated when next connected to the desktop. Connection weight files can be updated on the palm device without having to re-compile any application(s) using them. As many connection weight files as are needed can be stored on the palm – enhancing memory efficiency.

For small applications, the translation layer may be combined in the main program component as methods or classes. In order to maintain a generic structure separate classes are used in the PalmOS prototype. Separation provides the advantage that classes can be modified, added, or removed with minimal programming effort.

References

N Kasabov, J Kim, M Watts, and A Gray, 1997. *FuNN - A Fuzzy Neural Network Architecture for Adaptive Learning and Knowledge Acquisition in Multi-modular Distributed Environments,* Information Sciences – Applications, 101:3-4:155-175.

Occupational Safety and Health (OSH), 2000. Guidelines for the prevention of Falls, Department of Labour, NZ Government.

R Ward, M Purvis, R Raykov, F Zhang, and M Watts, 1997. An Architecture for Distributed Connectionist Computation, In *Progress in Connectionist-Based Information Systems, Proceedings of the ICONIP / ANZIIS / ANNES '97*, pages 721-724, Springer Verlag, Singapore.

M Watts, B Woodford, and N Kasabov, 1999. FuzzyCOPE - A Software Environment for Building Intelligent Systems - the Past, the Present and the Future. In *Emerging Knowledge Engineering and Connectionist-based Systems, Proceedings of the ICONIP/ANZIIS/ANNES Workshop "Future directions for intelligent systems and information sciences"*, 188-192, University of Otago, New Zealand.

CAUI* Demonstration
— Composing Music Based on Human Feelings

Masayuki Numao, Shoichi Takagi, and **Keisuke Nakamura**

Department of Computer Science, Tokyo Institute of Technology

2-12-1 O-okayama, Meguro-ku, Tokyo 152-8552, Japan

numao@cs.titech.ac.jp

Abstract

We demonstrate a method to locate relations and constraints between a music score and its impressions, by which we show that machine learning techniques may provide a powerful tool for composing music and analyzing human feelings. We examine its generality by modifying some arrangements to provide the subjects with a specified impression. This demonstration introduces some user interfaces, which are capable of predicting feelings and creating new objects based on seed structures, such as spectra and their transition for sounds that have been extracted and are perceived as favorable by the test subject.

Introduction

Music is a flow of information among its composer, player and audience. A composer writes a score that players play to create a sound to be listened by its audience. Since a score, a performance or MIDI data denotes a section of the flow, we can know a feeling caused by a piece of score or performance. A feeling consists of a very complex elements, which depend on each person, and are affected by a historical situation. Therefore, rather than clarifying what a human feeling is, we would like to clarify only musical structures that cause a specific feeling. Based on such structures, the authors constructed an automatic arrangement and composition system producing a piece causing a specified feeling on a person.

The system first collects person's feelings for some pieces, based on which it extracts a common musical structure causing a specific feeling. It arranges an existing song or composes a new piece to fit such a structure causing a specified feeling. In the following sections, we describe how to extract a musical structure, some methods for arrangement or composition, and the results of experiments.

Melody and Chords

We attempt to extract a musical structure based on melody and chords as shown in Figure 1. In a musical piece, a function — *tonic* (T), *dominant* (D), *subdominant* (S) or *subdominant minor* (SDm) — is assigned to each chord. This

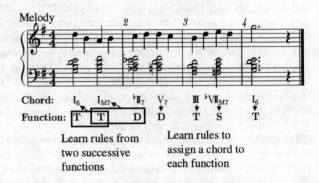

Figure 1: Melody and Chords

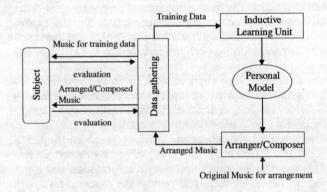

Figure 2: Demonstration Diagram

paper discusses the extraction of two aspects of the structure (i.e., each chord and a sequence of functions) from which the system derives constraints for assigning chords to a melody (supplemented by functions).

An arranger can assign chords based on the general theory of harmony, even though they are mediocre. Mimicking human arrangements (Numao, Kobayashi, & Sakaniwa 1997) introduces some *decorations* to the chords, refines the techniques used in the training examples, and improves the arrangement.

Figure 3: A Created Favorite Piece of Subject A

Figure 4: A Created Favorite Piece of Subject B

Arrangement and Composition

Figure 2 shows a diagram of the demonstration. The authors prepared 75 well-known music pieces without modulation[1], from which they extracted 8 or 16 successive bars. For automatic arrangement they prepared other three pieces. The subject evaluated each piece as one of 5 grades for 6 pairs of adjectives: *bright - dark, stable - unstable, favorable - unfavorable, beautiful - ugly, happy - unhappy, heartrending - no heartrending.* For each adjective pair the system constructed a personal model of feeling, based on which it tried to arrange the prepared three pieces into ones causing a specified feeling. It was supplied 3 original pieces, and alternatively specified 6 adjective pairs, i.e., 12 adjectives. Therefore, it produced $3 * 12 = 36$ arranged pieces.

After the experiments in (Numao, Kobayashi, & Sakaniwa 1997), the system has been improved in collecting evaluation of each bar, introducing `triplet/3` and `frame/1`, and the search mechanism for chord progression. The above results support their effects.

Based on a collection of conditions ILP derives, we have obtained a personal model to evaluate a chord progression. A genetic algorithm (GA) produces a chord progression by using the model for its fitness function. Such a chord progression utilizes a melody generator to compose a piece from scratch rather than to arrange a given piece.

This system is profoundly different from other composing systems in that it composes based on a personal model extracted from a subject by using a machine learning method. A composing system using an interactive genetic algorithm (IGA) may be similar method to ours in that it creates a piece based on the user interaction. However, IGA requires far more interactions than ours, which reduces the number of

---

[1]39 Japanese *JPOP* songs and 36 pieces from classic music or textbooks for harmonics.

interactions by utilizing a personal model generalized from examples. Other advantages are that we can recycle a personal model in many compositions, and manually tailor a predicate in the system to improve its performance.

Conclusion

Figure 3 and 4 show created pieces. Figure 3 is a piece the system tried to make favorite of subject A. Figure 4 is one it tried to make favorite of subject B. These examples show that the system composes a favorite piece without handcrafted background knowledge on favorite songs of each subject and by automatically acquiring his/her favorite musical structures.

Our method extends the concept of adaptive user interfaces (Langley 1998) in a sense that it constructs a new description adaptively. That is why we call our system CAUI (a *constructive* adaptive user interface), whose detail is described in (Numao, Takagi, & Nakamura 2002).

References

Langley, P. 1998. Machine learning for adaptive user interfaces. In *CSLI-Stanford University IAP Spring Tutorials*, 155–164.

Numao, M.; Kobayashi, M.; and Sakaniwa, K. 1997. Acquisition of human feelings in music arrangement. In *Proc. IJCAI 97*, 268–273. Morgan Kaufmann.

Numao, M.; Takagi, S.; and Nakamura, K. 2002. Constructive adaptive user interfaces — composing music based on human feelings. In *Proc. AAAI 2002*. AAAI Press.

Invited Talks

Perspectives on Artificial Intelligence Planning

Héctor Geffner

Departamento de Tecnología
Universitat Pompeu Fabra – ICREA
08003 Barcelona, Spain
hector.geffner@tecn.upf.es

Abstract

Planning is a key area in Artificial Intelligence. In its general form, planning is concerned with the automatic synthesis of action strategies (plans) from a description of actions, sensors, and goals. Planning thus contrasts with two other approaches to intelligent behavior: the programming approach, where action strategies are defined by hand, and the learning approach, where action strategies are inferred from experience. Different assumptions about the nature of actions, sensors, and costs lead to various forms of planning: planning with complete information and deterministic actions (classical planning), planning with non-deterministic actions and sensing, planning with temporal and concurrent actions, etc. Most work so far has been devoted to classical planning, where significant changes have taken place in the last few years. On the methodological side, the area has become more empirical, on the technical side, approaches based on heuristic or constrained-based search have become common.

In this paper, I try to provide a coherent picture of Planning in AI, making emphasis on the mathematical models that underlie various forms of planning and the ideas that have been found most useful computationally.

Introduction

The development of *general problem solvers* has been one of the main goals in Artificial Intelligence. A general problem solver is a program that accepts high-level descriptions of problems and automatically computes their solution (Newell & Simon 1963). The motivations for such solvers are two. On the cognitive side, humans are general problem solvers, and thus understanding, reconstructing, or simply emulating such behavior poses a key challenge. On the technical side, modeling problems at a high level is most often simpler than procedurally encoding their solutions, thus an effective GPS tool can be very useful in practice.

A general problem solver must provide the user with a suitable *general modeling language* for describing problems, and *general algorithms* for solving them. While the solutions obtained may not be as good or as fast as those obtained by more specialized methods, the approach will still pay off if the performance of the two methods is not too far

apart, or if implementing the specialized solution is just too cumbersome.

In order to develop a general problem solver, its *scope* must be clearly defined. Otherwise, it is not possible to device neither the language nor the algorithms. Indeed, different problems have solutions whose *forms* are often different. For example, the solution of a problem like the Rubik's cube is a *sequence of actions,* while the solution of a diagnostic problem may be an *action strategy* determining the tests to be performed as a function of the observations gathered.

The scope of a general problem solver can be defined by means of a suitable class of mathematical models. The mathematical model that underlies the work in *classical planning* for example, is the familiar *state model* where actions deterministically map one state into another and the task is to find an action sequence that maps the initial state into a goal state. In *conformant planning* (Smith & Weld 1998), on the other hand, an action maps a state into a set of possible successor states, and the task is to find a sequence of actions that lead to the goal for any possible transition and initial state. As *uncertainty* in the state transitions or the initial state is introduced, *feedback* also becomes important, affecting drastically the form of plans. In the absence of feedback, as in classical or conformant planning, a plan is a fixed *sequence of actions*, yet in the presence of full-state feedback, the actions depend on the state observed, and thus plans become *functions mapping states into actions*.

AI Planning is general problem solving over a class of models. Models define the scope of a planner, the types of problems it is supposed to handle, the form of the solutions, and the solutions that are best or optimal. Planning, from this perspective, is about the convenient representation and effective solution of a certain class of mathematical models.

In this paper, I try to provide a coherent picture of AI Planning as a combination of three elements:

1. **representation languages** for describing problems conveniently,
2. **mathematical models** for making the different planning tasks precise, and
3. **algorithms** for solving these models effectively (often making use of information available in their representation)

I also make emphasis on the ideas that have been found most

useful computationally, in particular in the area of classical planning, where most of the work has been made. In recent years, this area has undergone significant changes in both methodology and techniques. On the methodological side, the area has become more experimental, on the technical side, approaches based on heuristic or constrained-based search have become common. These changes have been brought about by some key publications (in particular (Blum & Furst 1995)), and events like the Planning Competition (McDermott 2000; Bacchus 2001).

The paper is not a survey on planning but a personal appraisal of part of the field. In particular, I won't say much about knowledge-based planning (Wilkins & des Jardins 2001), where the statement of the planning problem is extended with handcrafted domain-dependent knowledge relevant for solving it. While this is probably the preferred approach in practice and a lot of work in AI has been devoted to it, knowledge-based and domain-independent planning are complementary approaches, and progress in domain-independent planning will eventually translate into more robust knowledge-based planners, that rely less critically on user-provided control information (see (Long & Fox 2000) for a different integration).

It should be mentioned that AI Planning is not the only area concerned with the development of general problem solvers. E.g., work in Linear and Integer Programming (Wolsey 1998) and Constraint Programming (Marriot & Stuckey 1999) is also concerned with the development of problem solvers but over a *different class of models*: linear integer programs, in the first case; constraint satisfaction problems in the second. More interestingly, in both of these areas there has also been a trend to distinguish the *models* from the *languages* used to represent them. For example, AMPL is a recent high-level language for describing linear and integer programs (Fourer, Gay, & Kernighan 1993), while OPL is a recent language for describing such programs and CSPs (Van Hentenryck 1999).

The rest of the paper is organized as follows. We discuss planning models, planning languages, and some key computational aspects in planning in that order, and end with a brief discussion. The presentation aims to be coherent but is definitively not exhaustive.

Models

We consider first the models that make the semantics of various common planning tasks precise.

Classical Planning

Classical planning can be understood in terms of deterministic *state models* characterized by the following elements (Newell & Simon 1972; Nilsson 1980):

S1. A finite and discrete state space S,

S2. an initial situation given by a state $s_0 \in S$,

S3. a goal situation given by a non empty set $S_G \subseteq S$,

S4. actions $A(s) \subseteq A$ applicable in each state $s \in S$,

S5. a deterministic state transition function $f(a, s)$ for $a \in A(s)$

S6. positive action costs $c(a, s)$ for doing action a in s.

A *solution* to state models of this type is a sequence of actions $a_0, a_1, \ldots, a_n$ that generates a state trajectory s_0, $s_1 = f(s_0), \ldots, s_{n+1} = f(s_i, a_i)$ such that each action a_i is applicable in s_i and s_{n+1} is a goal state, i.e., $a_i \in A(s_i)$ and $s_{n+1} \in S_G$. The solution is *optimal* when the total cost $\sum_{i=0}^{n} c(s_i, a_i)$ is minimal. In classical planning, it is also assumed that all costs $c(a, s)$ are equal and thus that the optimal plans are the ones with minimal *length*.

Classical planning can be formulated as a deterministic state model that can be solved by *searching* the state-space S1–S6. This is the approach taken by heuristic search planners such as HSP (Bonet & Geffner 2001) and FF (Hoffmann & Nebel 2001). Classical planning, however, can be formulated and solved in a number of other ways; e.g., as a SAT problem (Kautz & Selman 1996), as a Constraint Satisfaction Problem (Do & Kambhampati 2000), as an Integer Programming problem (Vossen *et al.* 1999), etc. These other formulations, however, appear to yield a better pay off when other forms of planning are considered such as parallel planning or planning with resources. The success of heuristic search planners in the classical setting, as seen for example in the last AIPS Planning Competition (Bacchus 2001), lies in the use of good *heuristic functions* which are automatically extracted from the problem representation.

Planning with Uncertainty

Classical planning assumes that the initial state of the system is known and that state transitions are deterministic. When these assumptions are removed, the state of the world is no longer known. In order to define the planning task in the resulting setting it is necessary to to define how *uncertainty* is modeled, and how *sensing* or *feedback* (that reduce uncertainty) are taken into account.

Uncertainty in planning can be modeled in a number of ways. The two most common approaches are *pure non-determinism* and *probabilities*. In the first case, uncertainty about the state of the world is represented by the *set of states* $S' \subseteq S$ that are deemed possible, in the second, by a *probability distribution* over S. In both cases, we refer to the state of uncertainty as a *belief state* and distinguish it from the *actual* but potentially *unknown* state of the world.

In a similar way, uncertainty in state transitions is modeled by a function F that maps an action a and a state s into a non-empty set of states $F(a, s) \subseteq S$ in the non-deterministic setting, and by a distribution $P_a(s'|s)$ for all $s' \in S$ in the probabilistic setting. In either case, an action a *deterministically* maps a belief state b into a new belief state b_a. The formula for the non-deterministic case is

$$b_a = \{ s \mid s \in F(a, s') \text{ and } s' \in b \} \quad (1)$$

while the analogous formula for the probabilistic case is

$$b_a(s) = \sum_{s' \in S} P_a(s|s') \cdot b(s') \quad (2)$$

What is important is that in both cases the problem of *planning under uncertainty without feedback* reduces to a *deterministic search problem* in *belief space*, a space which can be characterized as the space S1–S6 above by the following elements:

C1. A space B of *belief states* over S,

C2. an initial situation given by a belief state $b_0 \in B$,

C3. a goal situation given by a set of target beliefs B_G

C4. actions $A(b) \subseteq A$ applicable in each belief state b

C5. deterministic transitions b to b_a for $a \in A(b)$ given by (1) and (2) above, and

C6. positive action costs $c(a, b)$.

In this space, it is common to define the target beliefs B_G as the ones that make a given goal condition G certain, the set of applicable actions $A(b)$ in b, as the actions a whose preconditions are certain in b, and the costs $c(a, b)$ to be uniform. In the non-deterministic case, this results in the model that underlies *conformant planning* (Smith & Weld 1998), namely planning that leads to the goal for any possible initial state or transition. In general, some of these choices can be relaxed without affecting the nature of the problem; in particular, the target belief states B_G and the action preconditions $A(b)$ can be extended to include epistemic conditions like the truth value of an atom p being known (see below for the relation between propositions and states). In the probabilistic setting, additional options are available, e.g., the target belief states b may be defined as the ones that set the probability of the goal above a threshold ($B_G = \{b \mid \sum_{s \in S_G} b(s) > Th\}$) as in the Buridan planner (Kushmerick, Hanks, & Weld 1995), action costs $c(a, b)$ can be defined as expected costs ($c(a, b) = \sum_{s \in S} c(a, s) b(s)$), etc.

Planning with Sensing

Classical and conformant planning are forms of *open-loop* planning. The resulting plans prescribe the sequences of actions that need to be executed assuming that no additional information is available at execution time. With the ability to sense the world, the choice of the actions depends on the observation gathered and thus the *form* of the plans changes. Of course, sensing only makes sense in a state of uncertainty; if there is no uncertainty, sensing provides no useful information and can be ignored.[1]

In the presence of sensing, the choice of the action a_i at time i depends on all observations $o_0, o_1, \ldots, o_{i-1}$ gathered up to that point. In the case known as *full-state observability*, observations are assumed to reveal the true state of the world, and through standard markovian assumptions, the last observation (state) summarizes the information of all previous states and observations. The choice of the next action in that case becomes a *function* mapping states into actions. Such models are known as Markovian Decision Problems or MDPs (Bertsekas 1995; Dean *et al.* 1993; Boutilier, Dean, & Hanks 1995; Russell & Norvig 1994).

In the general case, observations reveal *partial* information about the true state of the world and it is necessary to model how the two are related. The solution then takes the form of functions mapping *belief states* into actions, as states are no longer known and belief states summarize all the information from previous belief states and partial observations (Astrom 1965; Bertsekas 1995). In the probabilistic case, such models are known as Partially Observable Markovian Decision Problems or POMDPs (Sondik 1971; Kaebling, Littman, & Cassandra 1998).

In the presence of feedback, the effects of actions on belief states is no longer deterministic. Let $[o]$ stand for the set of states compatible with an observation o and, for the non-deterministic case, let $O(a, s)$ stand for the (noisy) sensor model, i.e. for the set of observations that are possible when an action a is done and the (hidden) state s is reached. Then the belief states b_a^o that can follow an action a in a belief state b are:

$$b_a^o = \{s \mid s \in b_a \text{ and } s \in [o]\} \tag{3}$$

with b_a defined as in (1) and $o \in O(a, s)$ for $s \in b_a$. The analogous equation in the probabilistic case is

$$b_a^o(s) = P_a(o|s) b_a(s) / b_a(o) \tag{4}$$

with b_a defined as in (2), $b_a(o) \neq 0$ (this is the probability of obtaining observation o after doing action a in b), and $P_a(o|s)$ representing the probabilistic sensor model (the probability of obtaining o after doing action a and ending up in s).

In either case, the problem of planning with uncertainty and *partial feedback*, becomes a search problem in a non-deterministic *belief space*, while the problem of planning with uncertainty and *full state feedback* is a search problem in a non-deterministic *state space*. In both cases the solutions are not action sequences but *policies*: policies mapping belief states into actions, in the first case, and policies mapping world states into actions in the second. Furthermore, the optimal policies are the ones that minimize the worst possible cost to the goal in the purely non-deterministic formulation, and the expected cost to the goal in the probabilistic formulation. The worst possible cost however is often infinite and thus other notions of success in purely non-deterministic planning have been proposed such as the notion of *strong cyclic plans* (Daniele, Traverso, & Vardi 1999).

State and belief-state policies are the mathematical objects that constitute the solutions of problems involving full and partial feedback respectively. These policies, however, can be represented in a number of ways such as conditional plans or situation-action rules. Moreover, in large problems, it is often not necessary to define such policies over all (belief) states, but only over the initial (belief) state and the (belief) states that are reachable through the policy.

Temporal Planning

Temporal models extend classical planning in a different direction. We consider here a simple but general model where actions have durations and their execution can overlap in

---

[1]Sensing, however, is useful in the classical setting too if the model used is not guaranteed to be completely accurate (model uncertainty). Indeed, it is standard practice in Control Engineering to obtain a closed-loop control assuming a deterministic model of a non-deterministic system, treating model inaccuracies as noise that gets corrected through the control loop.

time. More precisely, we assume a duration $d(a) > 0$ for each action a, and a predicate $comp(A)$ that defines when a set of actions A can be executed concurrently. For example, in the presence of unary resources, $comp(A)$ will be false if A contains a pair of actions using the same resource (Beck & Fox 1998). Similarly, $comp(A)$ can be defined to be false when A includes pairs of actions having interacting effects or preconditions (Blum & Furst 1995), etc.

A state model for *temporal planning* can be obtained from model S1–S6 by two simple transformations. First we need to replace the single actions a in that model by *sets* of legal actions. Temporal plans thus become sequences A_0, A_1, A_2 of legal sets of actions in which all actions in each set A_i start their execution at the same time t_i. The end or completion time of an action a in A_i is thus $t_i + d(a)$ where $d(a)$ is the duration of a. The start times t_i are defined implicitly in the plan as follows: $t_0 = 0$ and t_{i+1} is given by the end time of the first action in $A_0, \ldots, A_i$ that completes after t_i. The states s_i are defined in a similar way. The initial state s_0 is given, while s_{i+1} is a function of the state s_i at time t_i and the set of actions A^i in the plan that complete exactly at time $t + 1$; i.e., $s_{i+1} = f_T(A^i, s_i)$. The state transition function f_T is obtained from the representation of the individual actions; e.g., if actions are represented in Strips and actions with conflicting adds and deletes are not legal, then s_{i+1} will be obtained by 'adding' to s_i all the atoms in the add lists of the actions in A^i and deleting all the atoms in the delete lists. Clearly, $s_{i+1} = s_i$ if A_i is empty.

The representation of temporal plans above is not complete, as for example, it cannot represent a plan in which some arbitrary slack is inserted between two actions. Yet the representation is complete 'enough' as if there is a plan that achieves the goal, for most reasonable optimality criteria, there is a plan in this representation that achieves the goal and is as good. A similar temporal model is used in (Bacchus & Ady 2001) while a regressed version of this model is used in (Haslum & Geffner 2001).

The definitions above provide a state model for temporal planning along the lines of model S1–S6 for classical planning with primitive actions replaced by *legal sets of actions*. Namely, a (valid) temporal plan is a sequence of legal sets of actions mapping the initial state into a goal state. For the rest, the models are the same, except for the cost structure which we haven't yet defined. In sequential planning, the overall cost of a plan $P = a_0, a_1, \ldots, a_n$ is defined as the sum $\sum_{i=0,n} c(a_i, s_i)$ where s_i is either the initial state ($i = 0$) or the state that follows action a_{i-1} ($i > 0$). This cost structure is much more flexible than the one used in classical planning where $c(a, s) = 1$, and it's often quite adequate in the sequential setting. In the temporal setting, on the other hand, this cost structure is not adequate for capturing standard optimality criteria such as the minimization of the *makespan* of a plan, the makespan being the max completion time of all actions in the plan. Indeed, the makespan of a plan cannot be obtained by adding up action costs of the form $c(A_i, s_i)$ for the sets of actions A_i in the plan, as the contribution of the actions in A_i to the makespan depends on the actions taken at the previous steps $A_0, \ldots, A_{i-1}$. Nonetheless, it is sufficient to define the action costs

as $c(A_i, s_i | A_0, \ldots, A_{i-1})$ and then minimize the total cost $c(A_0, s_0) + \sum_{i=1,n} c(A_i, s_i | A_0, \ldots, A_{i-1})$. Then, if we denote the last completion time of an action in $A_0, \ldots, A_i$ as E_i, the makespan minimization criterion results from setting $c(A_i, s_i | A_0, \ldots, A_{i-1})$ to $E_i - E_{i-1}$, for $i > 0$, and $c(A_0, s_0)$ to E_0. The makespan minimization criterion ignores the state component in the action costs, yet this can be used to define more complex optimality criteria such as those taking into account the value of some variables or the use of resources.

While from the similarity between the model for sequential planning and the model for temporal planning both tasks appear to be close from a *mathematical point of view*, they are quite different from a *computational point of view*. Indeed, while heuristic search is probably the best current approach for optimal and non-optimal sequential planning, it does *not* represent the best approach for parallel planning (temporal planning with actions of unit durations only) or temporal planning (yet see (Haslum & Geffner 2001; Do & Kambhampati 2001)). The problem is the *branching factor*: indeed, if there are n primitive actions applicable in a state, the branching factor of the sequential space is n, while the branching factor of the temporal or parallel space is 2^n (namely, there are up to 2^n possible legal sets of primitive actions). SAT and CSP approaches branch in a different way, and through suitable constraints and constraint propagation rules may be able to integrate the pruning afforded by heuristic functions in the heuristic search framework with a more convenient exploration of the space of plans (see the discussion on branching below). Similarly, while partial order planners (POP) have lost favor in recent years to heuristic and SAT/CSP approaches, they are likely to be suitable for parallel and temporal planning if extended with suitable heuristic estimators and propagation rules. See (Nguyen & Kambhampati 2001) for a recent heuristic POP planner, (Jonsson *et al.* 2000) for a constraint-based temporal POP planner, and (Geffner 2001) for a general formulation of temporal planning as 'branch and bound' that connects heuristic and POP approaches in classical planning to constraint-based approaches used in scheduling. For more on the relation between planning and scheduling see (Smith, Frank, & Jonsson 2000).

Languages

The models above provide a mathematical characterization of the basic planning tasks, their solutions, and their optimal solutions. These models however do not provide a convenient *language* for encoding planning problems. This is because the explicit characterization of the state space and state transitions is feasible only in small problems. In large problems, the state space and state transitions need to be represented *implicitly* in a logical *action language*, normally through a set of (state) variables and action rules. A good action language is one that supports compact encodings of the models of interest. In AI Planning, the standard language for many years has been the Strips language introduced in (Fikes & Nilsson 1971). While from a logical point of view, Strips is a very limited language, Strips is well known and will help us to illustrate the relationship between planning *languages* and planning *models*, and to motivate some of the extensions that have been proposed.

The Strips language comprises two parts: a language for describing the world and a language for describing how the world changes. The first is called the *state language* or simply the *language*, and the second, the *operator language*. We consider the Strips language as used currently in planning (e.g., the Strips subset of PDDL (Fox & Long 2001)), rather than the original version of Strips that is more complex.

The Strips language $\mathcal{L}$ is a simple logical language made up of two types of symbols: relational and constant symbols. In the expression $on(a, b)$, on is a relational symbol of arity 2, and a and b are constant symbols. In Strips, there are no functional symbols and the constant symbols are the only *terms*. The *atoms* are defined in a standard way from the combination $p(t_1, \ldots, t_k)$ of a relational symbol p and a tuple of terms t_i of the same arity as p. Similarly the Strips *formulas* are obtained by closing the set of atoms under the standard propositional connectives. In Strips, only conjunctions are used and they are identified with sets of atoms.

A main difference between relational and constant symbols in Strips is that the former are used to keep track of aspects of the world that may change as a result of the actions (e.g., the symbol on in $on(a, b)$), while the latter are used to refer to objects in the domain (e.g., the symbols a and b in $on(a, b)$). More precisely, actions in Strips affect the denotation of relational symbols but not the denotation of constant symbols. For this reason, the former are said to be *fluent* symbols, and the latter, *fixed* symbols or *constants*.

The *operators* in Strips are defined over the set of atoms in $\mathcal{L}$. Each operator op has a precondition, add, and delete lists $Prec(op)$, $Add(op)$, and $Del(op)$ given by sets of atoms. Operators are normally defined by means of *schemas;* here we assume that such schemas have been grounded.

A Strips planning problem $P = \langle A, O, I, G \rangle$ consists of a tuple where A stands for the set of all atoms (boolean variables) in the domain, O is the set of operators, and I and G are sets of atoms defining the *initial* and *goal* situations. The problem P defines a deterministic state model $\mathcal{S}(P)$ like S1–S6 above where

A1. the states s are sets of atoms from A

A2. the initial state s_0 is I

A3. the goal states are the states s such that $G \subseteq s$

A4. $A(s)$ is the set of operators $o \in O$ s.t. $Prec(o) \subseteq s$

A5. the state transition function f is such that $f(a, s) = s + Add(a) - Del(a)$ for $a \in A(s)$

A6. costs $c(a, s)$ are all equal to 1

This mapping defines the semantics of a Strips planning problem P, whose solution is given by the solution of the state model $\mathcal{S}(P)$.

Strips allows for compact encodings of state models yet in many cases these encodings could be improved substantially by moving Strips in the direction of a truly first-order logical language with negated literals, conditional effects, quantification, function symbols, etc. (Pednault 1989). Actually, the changes needed to accommodate these extensions

are relatively minor once the logical relationship between the state language $\mathcal{L}$ and the states s in the model is made explicit.[2] Basically, *the states are suitable, finite representations of the logical interpretations of the state language* $\mathcal{L}$ (Geffner 2000). A logical interpretation must assign a denotation to every constant, function, and relational symbol in $\mathcal{L}$, and implicitly, through the standard composition rules, a denotation to every term and formula. Furthermore, if the denotation of non-fluent symbols, is fixed, states must encode the denotation of fluent symbols only. In Strips, the only fluent symbols are the relational symbols and a state s encodes their denotation by enumerating all the atoms that are true (it is also implicitly assumed that the constant symbols denote different objects in the domain and that there are no other objects). Actually, any first-order formula involving these constant and relational symbols can be evaluated in a state provided that no other non-logical symbols are used. Function symbols, whether fluent or not, can be added in a similar way provided that their denotation can be represented finitely. This can be achieved by forcing their arguments to take values in a finite domain.

If states are suitable representations of the denotation of fluent symbols, expressions in the *action language* (the operators in Strips) prescribe how these denotations change as a result of the actions. In general terms, an action a is characterized by a precondition and several effect expressions. The precondition is an arbitrary formula which must be true in the state for the action to be applicable. In Strips, preconditions are sets (conjunctions) of atoms, yet in more expressive state languages they can be arbitrary formulas. Effect expressions are more subtle, and each effect prescribes how the denotation of a fluent symbol changes as a result of the action. For a relational fluent symbol p, an effect of an action a will have the general form:

$$\text{if } A, \text{ then } p(t) := true/false$$

meaning that in the next state the denotation of p must be updated to make $p(t)$ true (false) when the denotation of A is true in s. In Strips, A is empty, the term t only contains non-fluent symbols, and atoms made true go into the add list and atoms made false into the delete list. In the more general case, t itself may contain fluent symbols and it makes sense to evaluate this tuple of terms in the state s where the action is executed. For functional fluent symbols f (including constant fluent symbols), an effect expression will thus have the general form

$$\text{if } A, \text{ then } f(t) := t'$$

meaning that in the next state the denotation of f must updated so that f maps the value of the term t into the value of the term t', both obtained in the state s. For example, an effect like

$$\text{if } x < 10, \text{ then } x := x + 1$$

says that the value of x should be increased by one in the next state if x is currently smaller than 10. For fluent sym-

---

[2]The relationship between action languages and the semantical structures that they describe has been clarified along the years by work in the area of Reasoning about Change; e.g., see (Gelfond & Lifschitz 1993; Sandewall 1994).

bols which are not affected by any action, their denotation is assumed to persist.

Domain-independent planners with expressive state and action languages of this type, include GPT (Bonet & Geffner 2000) and MBP (Bertoli *et al.* 2001), both of which provide additional constructs for expressing non-determinism and sensing. Most knowledge-based planners provide very rich modeling languages, often including facilities for representing time and resources; see (Wilkins 1988; Currie & Tate 1991; Levesque *et al.* 1997; Bacchus & Kabanza 2000; Jonsson *et al.* 2000; Chien *et al.* 2000; Kvarnström, Doherty, & Haslum 2000). For the last version of the standard PDDL language see (Fox & Long 2001), while for complexity issues that arise as the basic Strips language is extended, see (Nebel 1999)

Computation

While models and languages are key aspects in planning research, the current excitement in the field is to a large extent the result of recent advances in the resolution of Strips planning problems. Most of these advances followed the work on Graphplan, a planner introduced in (Blum & Furst 1995) which was shown to be more powerful than other approaches at the time, namely partial and total ordered planners like (Penberthy & Weld 1992; Fink & Veloso 1996). Graphplan was followed by Satplan (Kautz & Selman 1996; 1999), a SAT-based planner and HSP (Bonet, Loirincs, & Geffner 1997; Bonet & Geffner 2001), an heuristic search planner (see also (McDermott 1996)). In the Strips track of the first 1998 AIPS Planning Competition (McDermott 2000), all the planners were based on either Graphplan, SAT-Plan, or HSP, and they all were shown to be solve much larger problems than could be solved previously. The same remained true for the Strips track of the second 2000 AIPS Planning Contest (Bacchus 2001), that attracted 13 planners. In this last contest, heuristic search planners did best, with four out of the top five planners doing heuristic search one way or the other, and with FF (Hoffmann & Nebel 2001) doing best of all. The contest, however, is basically concerned with sequential planning, and thus these results do not carry much meaning for parallel or temporal planning, aspects that are expected to be addressed in the next planning contest.

In this section, we will review some of the ideas exploited by some of these recent planners, and then we'll move to temporal and uncertainty planning. We'll focus mostly on *optimal planning*. The reason is methodological; while there is always room for new, smarter non-optimal search algorithms, optimal search, an in particular optimal search in linear space (Korf 1993), is mostly the result of two operations: the branching scheme, defining how the space of solutions is searched, and the pruning scheme, defining how partial solutions are pruned. At the same time, ideas useful in optimal planning can often be used in non-optimal planning, while the opposite is seldom true.

From this perspective, an heuristic search planner like HSPr* (Haslum & Geffner 2000) does branching by regression and prunes a partial solution (a plan tail) when the accumulated cost plus the remaining cost (as estimated by an admissible heuristic) exceeds a bound. Similarly, a planner

like Satplan does branching by selecting a variable and trying each of its values, pruning a 'partial plan' when a suitable form of constraint propagation (unit resolution) detects a contradiction. In the middle, partial-order planners offer an alternative branching scheme, their weakness lying in the lack of good pruning criteria.

Heuristic Search

Heuristic search planners map planning problems into search problems that are solved with an heuristic function derived automatically from the problem representation. Then they use this heuristic to guide the search for plans either forward from the initial state (progression planners) or backward from the goal (regression planners) using algorithms such as A*, IDA*, or others. The derivation and use of these heuristic functions is the key element and the main novelty in these planners. Different types of heuristic functions have been formulated in planning and all of them correspond to optimal cost functions of relaxed problems or suitable approximations (Pearl 1983).

The first type of heuristics are based on a relaxation in which the delete lists of all operators is ignored (i.e., they are assumed empty). This simplification, however, does not make the problem of finding optimal plans tractable, thus additional simplifications are needed. The heuristic in planners like Unpop and HSP further assumes that atoms are independent and thus that the cost of achieving a set of atoms corresponds to the sum of the costs of achieving each atom in the set. The resulting heuristic, called the *additive heuristic,* is quite informative and can be computed reasonably fast for each new node. It can be formally defined by a fixed point equation of the form

$$h_+(p) \stackrel{\text{def}}{=} \begin{cases} 0 & \text{if } p \in s \\ \min_{a \in O(p)}[1 + h_+(Prec(a))] & \text{otherwise} \end{cases}$$

$$(5)$$

where $O(p)$ stands for the set of operators that add p and $h_+(C)$ is defined for sets of atoms C as

$$h_+(C) \stackrel{\text{def}}{=} \sum_{q \in C} h_+(q) \qquad (6)$$

The heuristic $h_+(s)$ of a state is $h_+(G)$ where G is the goal, and is obtained by solving (5) above with single-source shortest path algorithms. The additive heuristic, however, is not *admissible* (i.e., it is not a lower bound) and hence it's not useful for optimal planning. A different (non-admissible) heuristic based also on the delete-list relaxation is the FF heuristic. FF does not assume that atoms are independent but rather solves the relaxation suboptimally, and in the way, extracts useful information for guiding a hill-climbing search. For a detailed comparison between FF and HSP, see (Hoffmann & Nebel 2001).

A different relaxation is used in (Haslum & Geffner 2000) for defining a family of polynomial and admissible heuristics h^m for $m = 1, 2, \ldots$. These heuristics take positive and negative interactions into account, and follow from a relaxation in which the cost of a set of atoms C with size $|C| > m$ is approximated (recursively) by the cost of the mostly costly set D in C of size m. This relaxation can be formalized by a set of fixed point equations like (5) which can also be solved by shortest path algorithms. Indeed, for $m = 1$, i.e., when the cost of a set of atoms is assumed to be given by the cost of the most costly atom in the set, the resulting equations for h^m are like (5)–(6) with the summation in (6) replaced by maximization. For $m > 1$, the resulting equations and their computation are more complex. The planner HSPr* uses the heuristic h^2, which is computed only once, within an IDA* regression search. (Haslum & Geffner 2000) also develops h^m estimators por *parallel planning*. While in (Bonet & Geffner 1999) the point is made that Graphplan can be understood as an heuristic search planner doing IDA* regression search with an heuristic function h_G implicitly encoded in the plan graph, in (Haslum & Geffner 2000) it is shown that the h_G heuristic corresponds precisely to the h^m heuristic for parallel planning with $m = 2$.

A more recent relaxation model used for deriving heuristics in planning is based on the idea of pattern databases (Culberson & Schaeffer 1998). Pattern databases have been proposed in the context of the 15-puzzle and have also been used for solving the Rubik's cube optimally (Korf 1998). The general idea of pattern databases is to project the state space S of a problem into a smaller state space $\hat{S}$ that can be solved optimally and exhaustively. Then the heuristic $h(s)$ for the original state space is obtained from the solution cost $\hat{h}^*(\hat{s})$ of the projected state $\hat{s}$ in the relaxed space $\hat{S}$. For example, if S comprises the possible values of a given set of multi-valued variables, then the projected space $\hat{S}$ can be obtained by treating several values as the *same* value, thus collapsing a potentially large collection of states into a single state (Holte & Hernadvolgyi 1999). Alternatively, we can perform abstraction in the set of variables rather than in the set of values. In the Strips setting, projected state spaces can be obtained by removing a number of atoms from the model; i.e., removing them from the initial state, the goal, and the operators. Then the projected problem, if sufficiently small, can be solved optimally from all initial states, and the resulting costs can be stored in a table providing lower bounds for the original problem. Heuristics resulting from different projections (pattern dbs) can be combined with the max operator to provide still more informed heuristics. See (Edelkamp 2001) for a more elaborated scheme that uses pattern databases in planning.

Pattern databases are just one of a number of novel and powerful ideas that have been recently developed in the area of problem solving and that are likely to have influence in planning. See (Korf 2000) and (Junghanns & Schaeffer 1999).

Branching

Optimal planning and search is mostly branching and pruning. While the importance of lower bounds or admissible heuristics for pruning is well understood in AI, the importance of good branching rules is seldom mentioned. Indeed, the index of standard AI textbooks, for example, have entries for 'branching factor' but not for branching itself. Still the way the space of solutions is explored has a strong influence on performance. In AI problem solving, branch-

ing has been, for the most part, applying all possible actions. This type of forward branching, as well as its opposite, backward branching, where solutions are constructed backward from the goal, works quite well in problems like the 15-puzzle, Rubik's cube, and most sequential planning problems. Yet, for other domains like the Travelling Salesman Problem (Balas & Toth 1985), the Job Shop Scheduling Problem (Beck & Fox 1998), and others, more convenient branching schemes have been developed, which are likely to be necessary in tasks like temporal planning where the branching factor of progression and regression planners blows up. For example in the TSP, one can perform branching by selecting an edge connecting a city i to a city j, then creating two subproblems, one in which city i is followed by city j in the tour, the other in which is not. This branching rule, along with a suitable lower bound estimator for the partial tours, works much better for larger TSPs than the most straightforward approach of starting in one city and then connecting the last visited city with each non-visited city.

In AI Planning, the issue of branching has been considered but in a different form: as the choice of the space in which to perform the search. State-space planners, namely progression and regression planners, search in the space of states, while partial-order planners search in the space of plans (Weld 1994). This is a useful distinction yet it does not show what the two approaches have in common and what they have in common with SAT and CSP approaches. All planners indeed search in the space of plans. It just happens that state-space planners are designed to build plans from the head or the tail only, and as a result, the resulting partial plan heads or tails can be suitably summarized by the information obtained by progressing the initial state through the plan head or regressing the goal through the plan tail. This is useful for computing the estimated cost $f(p)$ of the best complete plans that extend a given partial plan p. In state-based or directional planners this estimated cost can be split into two: the accumulated cost of the plan $g(p)$ that depends on p only, and the estimated cost of the remaining plan $h(s)$ that depends only on the state s obtained by progression or regression and which summarizes the partial plan p completely. In partial-order and SAT/CSP planners this split of the cost function $f(p)$ for a 'partial' plan p is not possible. On the other hand, state-based planners, as we have seen, suffer from a high-branching factor in temporal planning, where the set of parallel macro actions is exponential in the number of primitive actions, and in a number of sequential domains like Sokoban (Junghanns & Schaeffer 1999), where the number of applicable actions is just too large.

There is no reason, however, for choosing between directional heuristic planners and non-directional non-heuristic planners. As in other combinatorial problems, it should be possible to combine informative lower bounds and effective branching rules, thus allowing us to prune partial solutions p whose estimated completion cost $f(p)$ exceeds a bound B. One option is to devise good admissible estimators $f(p)$ for non-directional plans. Indeed the failure of partial-order planning in relation to Graphplan and other modern approaches is that POP is a smart but blind search (branching) scheme, and hence, cannot compete with informed search algorithms such as Graphplan or HSP. The situation for SAT and CSP approaches is different. First of all, SAT and CSP approaches such as (Kautz & Selman 1999; Rintanen 1998; Do & Kambhampati 2000; M. Baioletti & Milani 2000) are not blind as they are all built on top of the plan graph constructed by Graphplan or a suitable SAT or CSP translation of it. The plan graph, as we have seen, encodes an informative and admissible heuristic function. In addition, these systems explicitly represent the condition $f(p) \leq B$ that the estimated completion cost $f(p)$ of a partial plan p has not to exceed a bound B. This is accomplished through suitable clauses or constraints that are checked for consistency in every node. For example, if the goal is $G = \{q, r\}$ and the bound B is 10, then a planner like Blackbox will force the constraint that q and r must be true at time 10 by adding the clauses q_{10} and r_{10}. Thus while SAT and CSP approaches do not perform explicit lower bound computations, they check the pruning condition $f(p) \leq B$ implicitly by constraint propagation and consistency checking. Whether explicit lower bound computations or consistency checking through suitable constraint propagation rules is the best approach for reasoning with non-directional plans depends on which of the two strategies yields more pruning. Actually, the best method will probably emerge from an integration of the two approaches as can be seen from recent work in constraint programming (Caseau & Laburthe 1994; Focacci, Lodi, & Milano 1999).

Search in Non-Deterministic Spaces

Heuristic and constraint-based approaches, so powerful in the deterministic setting, are not directly applicable to problems involving non-determinism and feedback, as the solution of these problems is not a sequence of actions but a function mapping states into actions. The standard methods for solving such problems are not based on heuristic or constraint-based search but on dynamic programming (Bellman 1957; Bertsekas 1995). Dynamic programming (DP) methods compute a value function over *all* states, and use this function to define the policy. The greedy policy $\pi_V(s)$ relative to a given value function V corresponds to the function that maps states s into actions a that minimize the worst cost or the expected cost of reaching the goal from s

$$\pi_V(s) \stackrel{\text{def}}{=} \operatorname{argmin}_{a \in A(s)} \left(c(a, s) + \max_{s' \in F(a,s)} V(s') \right)$$

$$\pi_V(s) \stackrel{\text{def}}{=} \operatorname{argmin}_{a \in A(s)} \left(c(a, s) + \sum_{s' \in S} P_a(s'|s) V(s') \right)$$

according to whether state transitions are modeled non-deterministically or probabilistically. While standard heuristic search methods like A* or IDA* cannot be used to search for policies, any heuristic function h determines a greedy policy π_V for $V = h$. Moreover, one of the basic results in DP is that this greedy policy is *optimal* when V is the optimal cost function. DP methods like value iteration thus aim to compute the optimal cost function or a suitable approximation of it, and plug that function into the greedy policy. The optimal cost function is the solution of the Bellman

equation

$$V(s) = \min_{a \in A(s)} \left(c(a, s) + \max_{s' \in F(a,s)} V(s') \right)$$

$$V(s) = \min_{a \in A(s)} \left(c(a, s) + \sum_{s' \in S} P_a(s'|s) V(s') \right)$$

for the non-deterministic and stochastic cases respectively, in both cases with $V(s) = 0$ for all goal states. Value iteration solves the Bellman equation by plugging an estimate V_i function on the right hand side, and obtaining a new value function V_{i+1} on the left hand side. This process is iterated until a fixed point is reached (in the probabilistic case, the convergence is defined in a slightly different way, see (Bertsekas 1995)). In asynchronous DP, a single vector V is used on the left and right, and the iterations are updates on this vector. Moreover, rather than performing a parallel update over all states in V, some arbitrary subset of states is selected for update in each iteration. The same convergence guarantees exist, as long as all states are updated sufficiently often (Bertsekas 1995).

DP methods work well for spaces containing hundreds of thousands of states, or even few millions. For larger spaces, the time and space requirements of pure DP methods is prohibitive. This is in contrast to heuristic search methods for deterministic problems that can deal with huge state spaces provided a good heuristic function is used for avoiding consideration of most states.

In the last few years, promising strategies that integrate DP and heuristic search methods have been proposed. Real time dynamic programming (Barto, Bradtke, & Singh 1995) is one such strategy. As an heuristic search method, RTDP performs iterated greedy searches using an heuristic function that is adjusted dynamically. More precisely, in every non-goal state s, the best action a according to the heuristic is selected (i.e., $a = \pi_h(s)$) and the heuristic value $h(s)$ of the state s is updated using Bellman equation. Then a random successor state of s and a is selected using the transition function or transition probabilities, and this process is repeated until the goal is reached. Barto et al. show two key results that generalize those proved earlier by Korf in the deterministic setting for the LRTA* algorithm (Korf 1990) (see also (Koenig & Simmons 1995)). First, that this dynamic greedy search cannot be trapped into loops forever, and thus, that it eventually reaches the goal (provided the space is suitably 'connected'). This is what's called a single trial of the algorithm. Second, that consecutive trials of the RTDP algorithm using the heuristic (value) function resulting from the previous trials, eventually results in a greedy policy that is optimal (provided that the heuristic used in the first trial is admissible). The importance of these results is that DP updates in the RTDP algorithm are focused on the states visited in the search, and that this set of states can be very small in comparison with the whole state space if the initial heuristic is sufficiently informed. In particular this may result in some states never being visited, something that makes RTDP different from other (asynchronous) DP algorithms and more similar to heuristic search algorithms in AI.

A more recent heuristic DP algorithm is LAO* (Hansen & Zilberstein 2001). LAO* is an extension of the well known AO* algorithm (Nilsson 1980; Pearl 1983) that replaces the backward induction step in AO*, which is suitable for acyclic graphs, into a full DP step. While different on the surface, LAO* and RTDP are similar and both can be seen as variations of a best-first algorithm in which a state in the best *partial* policy is selected for expansion in each step until the best partial policy becomes 'complete'. In the next few years, we are likely to get a better theoretical and empirical understanding of these and other heuristic DP algorithms, and of the heuristics that are needed to make them work in large non-deterministic spaces.

Belief Space

Planning problems involving uncertainty but no feedback can be mapped into deterministic search problems in *belief space* (Section 2). These are the so-called conformant planning problems. The two key problems from a computational point of view, are the derivation of good heuristic functions in belief space, and the effective representation and update of belief states in large state spaces. In principle, any admissible heuristic resulting from assuming complete observability can be 'lifted' into an admissible heuristic for conformant planning, yet the resulting heuristics can be very poor. Other ideas are necessary for scaling up; a promising alternative is the use of *state projections* as found in pattern databases and the heuristics h^m. Non-admissible heuristics for guiding a greedy search in belief space have been recently proposed in (Bertoli & Cimatti 2002) which also deals with the problem of efficiently representing and updating belief states through the use of OBDDs. For other approaches to conformant planning, see (Rintanen 1999; Ferraris & Giunchiglia 2000).

For Planning with uncertainty *and* partial observability, the same problems need to be faced, and in the addition, the search in belief space becomes non-deterministic. There are very few planners that handle both uncertainty and partial observability. Probably the best current such planners are GPT (Bonet & Geffner 2000), an RTDP planner, and MBP (Bertoli *et al.* 2001), a model checking planner. While planning with uncertainty and feedback is very hard, both systems can model and solve non-trivial problems. Both are available in the web and interested readers are encouraged to give them a try.

Conclusions

We have approached the problem of planning from a perspective that makes a clear distinction between planning languages, models, and algorithms. AI Planning, from this point of view, is about the representation and resolution of certain classes of models. We have also discussed some of the ideas that we think are most important from a computational point of view: heuristic functions, branching and constraint propagation rules, search in non-deterministic spaces, and search in belief spaces.

It is an exciting time to be doing research in planning. New approaches and empirical standards have opened up the field and progress in the last few years has been very fast. There is also a convergence at many levels with other areas concerned with modeling and problem solving like Constraint Programming and Combinatorial Optimization. More complex problems can now be modeled and solved, and this trend is likely to continue over the next few years. This is likely to have an impact on the use of planning tools outside of academia which is still limited.

Acknowledgments

Most of my work in planning has been in collaboration with Blai Bonet while I was at the Universidad Simón Bolívar in Caracas, Venezuela. I've also collaborated with Patrik Haslum from Linköping University and have benefited from conversations with many other people, too many to mention here.

References

Astrom, K. 1965. Optimal control of markov decision processes with incomplete state estimation. *J. Math. Anal. Appl.* 10:174–205.

Bacchus, F., and Ady, M. 2001. Planning with resources and concurrency: A forward chaining approach. In *Proc. IJCAI-01*, 417–424.

Bacchus, F., and Kabanza, F. 2000. Using temporal logics to express search control knowledge for planning. *Artificial Intelligence* 116:123–191.

Bacchus, F. 2001. The 2000 AI Planning Systems Competition. *Artificial Intelligence Magazine* 22(3).

Balas, E., and Toth, P. 1985. Branch and bound methods. In *et al.*, E. L. L., ed., *The Traveling Salesman Problem*. Essex: John Wiley and Sons. 361–401.

Barto, A.; Bradtke, S.; and Singh, S. 1995. Learning to act using real-time dynamic programming. *Artificial Intelligence* 72:81–138.

Beck, J., and Fox, M. 1998. A generic framework for constraint-directed scheduling. *AI Magazine* 19(4).

Bellman, R. 1957. *Dynamic Programming*. Princeton University Press.

Bertoli, P., and Cimatti, A. 2002. Improving heuristics for planning as search in belief space. In *Proc. AIPS-2002*.

Bertoli, P.; Cimatti, A.; Roveri, M.; and Traverso, P. 2001. Planning in nondeterministic domains under partial observability via symbolic model checking. In *Proc. IJCAI-01*.

Bertsekas, D. 1995. *Dynamic Programming and Optimal Control, Vols 1 and 2*. Athena Scientific.

Blum, A., and Furst, M. 1995. Fast planning through planning graph analysis. In *Proceedings of IJCAI-95*, 1636–1642. Morgan Kaufmann.

Bonet, B., and Geffner, H. 1999. Planning as heuristic search: New results. In *Proceedings of ECP-99*, 359–371. Springer.

Bonet, B., and Geffner, H. 2000. Planning with incomplete information as heuristic search in belief space. In *Proc. of AIPS-2000*, 52–61. AAAI Press.

Bonet, B., and Geffner, H. 2001. Planning as heuristic search. *Artificial Intelligence* 129(1–2):5–33.

Bonet, B.; Loerincs, G.; and Geffner, H. 1997. A robust and fast action selection mechanism for planning. In *Proceedings of AAAI-97*, 714–719. MIT Press.

Boutilier, C.; Dean, T.; and Hanks, S. 1995. Planning under uncertainty: structural assumptions and computational leverage. In *Proceedings of EWSP-95*.

Caseau, Y., and Laburthe, F. 1994. Improved CLP scheduling with task intervals. In *Proc. ICLP-94*, 369–383. MIT Press.

Chien *et al.*, S. 2000. Aspen – automating space mission operations using automated planning and scheduling. In *Proc. SpaceOps2000*.

Culberson, J., and Schaeffer, J. 1998. Pattern databases. *Computational Intelligence* 14(3):319–333.

Currie, K., and Tate, A. 1991. O-Plan: the open planning architecture. *Artificial Intelligence* 52(1):49–86.

Daniele, M.; Traverso, P.; and Vardi, M. Y. 1999. Strong cyclic planning revisited. In *Proceedings of ECP-99*, 35–48. Springer.

Dean, T.; Kaebling, L.; Kirman, J.; and Nicholson, A. 1993. Planning with deadlines in stochastic domains. In *Proceedings AAAI93*, 574–579. MIT Press.

Do, M. B., and Kambhampati, S. 2000. Solving planning-graph by compiling it into CSP. In *Proc. AIPS-00*, 82–91.

Do, M. B., and Kambhampati, S. 2001. Sapa: A domain-independent heuristic metric temporal planner. In *Proc. ECP 2001*, 82–91.

Edelkamp, S. 2001. Planning with pattern databases. In *Proc. ECP 2001*.

Ferraris, P., and Giunchiglia, E. 2000. Planning as satisfiability in nondeterministic domains. In *Proceedings AAAI-2000*, 748–753.

Fikes, R., and Nilsson, N. 1971. STRIPS: A new approach to the application of theorem proving to problem solving. *Artificial Intelligence* 1:27–120.

Fink, E., and Veloso, M. 1996. Formalizing the PRODIGY planning algorithm. In Ghallab, M., and Milani, A., eds., *New Directions in AI Planning*. IOS Press (Amsterdam). 261–272.

Focacci, F.; Lodi, A.; and Milano, M. 1999. Solving TSPs with time windows with constraints. In *Proc. ICLP-99*. MIT Press.

Fourer, R.; Gay, D.; and Kernighan, B. W. 1993. *AMPL: A Modeling Language for Mathematical Programming*. The Scientific Press.

Fox, M., and Long, D. 2001. PDDL2.1: An extension to PDDL for expressing temporal planning domains. At www.dur.ac.uk/d.p.long/competition.html.

Geffner, H. 2000. Functional strips. In Minker, J., ed., *Logic-Based Artificial Intelligence*. Kluwer. 187–205.

Geffner, H. 2001. Planning as branch and bound and its relation to constraint-based approaches. Tech-nical report, Universidad Simón Bolívar. Available at www.ldc.usb.ve/~hector.

Gelfond, M., and Lifschitz, V. 1993. Representing action and change by logic programs. *J. of Logic Programming* 17:301–322.

Hansen, E., and Zilberstein, S. 2001. Lao*: A heuristic search algorithm that finds solutions with loops. *Artificial Intelligence* 129:35–62.

Haslum, P., and Geffner, H. 2000. Admissible heuristics for optimal planning. In *Proc. of the Fifth International Conference on AI Planning Systems (AIPS-2000)*, 70–82.

Haslum, P., and Geffner, H. 2001. Heuristic planning with time and resources. In *Proc. ECP-01*.

Hoffmann, J., and Nebel, B. 2001. The FF planning system: Fast plan generation through heuristic search. *Journal of Artificial Intelligence Research* 2001:253–302.

Holte, R., and Hernadvolgyi, I. 1999. A space-time trade-off for memory-based heuristics. In *Proceedings AAAI-99*, 704–709. Mit Press.

Jonsson, A.; Morris, P.; Muscettla, N.; and Rajan, K. 2000. Planning in interplanetary space: Theory and practice. In *Proc. AIPS-2000*.

Junghanns, A., and Schaeffer, J. 1999. Domain-dependent single-agent search enhancements. In *Proc. IJCAI-99*. Morgan Kaufmann.

Kaebling, L.; Littman, M.; and Cassandra, T. 1998. Planning and acting in partially observable stochastic domains. *Artificial Intelligence* 101(1–2):99–134.

Kautz, H., and Selman, B. 1996. Pushing the envelope: Planning, propositional logic, and stochastic search. In *Proceedings of AAAI-96*, 1194–1201. AAAI Press / MIT Press.

Kautz, H., and Selman, B. 1999. Unifying SAT-based and Graph-based planning. In Dean, T., ed., *Proceedings IJCAI-99*, 318–327. Morgan Kaufmann.

Koenig, S., and Simmons, R. 1995. Real-time search in non-deterministic domains. In *Proceedings IJCAI-95*, 1660–1667. Morgan Kaufmann.

Korf, R. 1990. Real-time heuristic search. *Artificial Intelligence* 42:189–211.

Korf, R. 1993. Linear-space best-first search. *Artificial Intelligence* 62:41–78.

Korf, R. 1998. Finding optimal solutions to Rubik's cube using pattern databases. In *Proceedings of AAAI-98*, 1202–1207. AAAI Press / MIT Press.

Korf, R. 2000. Recent progress on the design and analysis of admissible heuristic functions. In *Proc. AAAI-2000*, 1165–1750.

Kushmerick, N.; Hanks, S.; and Weld, D. 1995. An algorithm for probabilistic planning. *Artificial Intelligence* 76:239–286.

Kvarnström, J.; Doherty, P.; and Haslum, P. 2000. Extending TALplanner with concurrency and resources. In *Proc. ECAI-2000*, 501–505.

Levesque, H.; Reiter, R.; Lespérance, Y.; Lin, F.; and Scherl, R. 1997. GOLOG: A logic programming language for dynamic domains. *J. of Logic Programming* 31:59–83.

Long, D., and Fox, M. 2000. Automatic synthesis and use of generic types in planning. In *Proceedings AIPS 2000*, 196–206.

M. Baioletti, S. M., and Milani, A. 2000. DPPlan: An algorithm for fast solution extraction from a planning graph. In *Proc. AIPS-2000*.

Marriot, K., and Stuckey, P. 1999. *Programming with Constraints*. MIT Press.

McDermott, D. 1996. A heuristic estimator for meansends analysis in planning. In *Proc. Third Int. Conf. on AI Planning Systems (AIPS-96)*.

McDermott, D. 2000. The 1998 AI Planning Systems Competition. *Artificial Intelligence Magazine* 21(2):35–56.

Nebel, B. 1999. Compilation schemes: A theoretical tool for assessing the expressive power of planning formalisms. In *KI-99: Advances in Artificial Intelligence*, 183–194. Springer-Verlag.

Newell, A., and Simon, H. 1963. GPS: a program that simulates human thought. In Feigenbaum, E., and Feldman, J., eds., *Computers and Thought*. McGraw Hill. 279–293.

Newell, A., and Simon, H. 1972. *Human Problem Solving*. Englewood Cliffs, NJ: Prentice–Hall.

Nguyen, X. L., and Kambhampati, S. 2001. Reviving partial order planning. In *Proc. IJCAI-01*.

Nilsson, N. 1980. *Principles of Artificial Intelligence*. Tioga.

Pearl, J. 1983. *Heuristics*. Addison Wesley.

Pednault, E. 1989. ADL: Exploring the middle ground between Strips and the situation calcules. In Brachman, R.; Levesque, H.; and Reiter, R., eds., *Proc. KR-89*, 324–332. Morgan Kaufmann.

Penberthy, J., and Weld, D. 1992. Ucpop: A sound, complete, partiall order planner for adl. In *Proceedings KR'92*.

Rintanen, J. 1998. A planning algorithm not based on directional search. In *Proceedings KR'98*, 617–624. Morgan Kaufmann.

Rintanen, J. 1999. Constructing conditional plans by a theorem prover. *J. of AI Research* 10:323–352.

Russell, S., and Norvig, P. 1994. *Artificial Intelligence: A Modern Approach*. Prentice Hall.

Sandewall, E. 1994. *Features and Fluents. The Representation of Knowledge about Dynamical Systems*. Oxford Univ. Press.

Smith, D., and Weld, D. 1998. Conformant graphplan. In *Proceedings AAAI-98*, 889–896. AAAI Press.

Smith, D.; Frank, J.; and Jonsson, A. 2000. Bridging the gap between planning and scheduling. *Knowledge Engineering Review* 15(1).

Sondik, E. 1971. *The Optimal Control of Partially Observable Markov Processes*. Ph.D. Dissertation, Stanford University.

Van Hentenryck, P. 1999. *The OPL Optimization Programming Language*. MIT Press.

Vossen, T.; Ball, M.; Lotem, A.; and Nau, D. 1999. On the use of integer programming models in AI planning. In *Proceedings IJCAI-99*.

Weld, D. S. 1994. An introduction to least commitment planning. *AI Magazine* 15(4):27–61.

Wilkins, D. E., and des Jardins, M. 2001. A call for knowledge-based planning. *AI Magazine* 22(1):99–115.

Wilkins, D. 1988. *Practical Planning: Extending the classical AI paradigm*. M. Kaufmann.

Wolsey, L. 1998. *Integer Programming*. Wiley.

Most Informative Dimension Reduction

Amir Globerson and **Naftali Tishby**
School of Computer Science and Engineering and
The Interdisciplinary Center for Neural Computation
The Hebrew University, Jerusalem 91904, Israel

Abstract

Finding effective low dimensional features from empirical co-occurrence data is one of the most fundamental problems in machine learning and complex data analysis. One principled approach to this problem is to represent the data in low dimension with minimal loss of the information contained in the original data. In this paper we present a novel information theoretic principle and algorithm for extracting low dimensional representations, or feature-vectors, that capture as much as possible of the mutual information between the variables. Unlike previous work in this direction, here we do not cluster or quantize the variables, but rather extract continuous feature functions directly from the co-occurrence matrix, using a converging iterative projection algorithm. The obtained features serve, in a well defined way, as approximate sufficient statistics that capture the information in a joint sample of the variables. Our approach is both simpler and more general than clustering or mixture models and is applicable to a wide range of problems, from document categorization to bioinformatics and analysis of neural codes.

Introduction

The problem of complex data analysis can be understood as the search for a most compact representation, or model, which *explains* a given set of observations. One explicit view of data *explanation* stems from the notion of sufficient statistics in parameter estimation. Sufficient statistics are functions of samples that capture *all* the information about the parameters of a distribution. Every bit of information that can be extracted from the sample about the parameters is captured by such finite dimensional statistics. One may say that sufficient statistics 'explain', or encode, the *relevant* part of the sample with respect to the parameters. This analogy between sufficient statistics and features in pattern recognition and learning has been noticed before. Here we take this analogy much further and propose a general information theoretic approach for extracting features as approximate sufficient statistics. Exact sufficient statistics in the original statistical sense exist, in general, only for very special distributions - exponential parametric families (Degroot 1986). We first extend this narrow sense of sufficiency

by considering general joint distributions of two variables. We then relax the requirement of *exact* sufficiency by introducing a variational approximation that enables us to calculate functions that approximately preserve the information, in any given dimension. For doing this we also consider the basic problem of "the information in an observation" and suggest a general and concrete answer to this question.

The following example can illustrate our motivation. Consider the familiar dice with unknown distribution of its six possible outcomes. What is the information provided by expected outcome of a dice roll about, say, the probability to obtain 6 in rolling this dice? One possible answer to this question was given by Jayens using the "maximum entropy principle", which argues that the "most probable" (or "least informative") distribution of outcome is the one which maximizes the entropy, subject to the known observation as a constraint (Jaynes 1957). This notion, however, does not tell us *which observation* is most efficient, or most informative, about the unknown value. The answer to the latter question can be obtained directly by considering the mutual information between the observation - in this case the expected dice outcome - and the value of the probability to get 6 as an outcome. Interestingly, this value can be expressed as the mutual information of a very special joint distribution, for which the specific observations (expected outcome) and corresponding functions of the relevant unknowns (probability to obtain 6) capture all its mutual information. This (unique) distribution is the one of exponential form in those functions. This exponential distribution also solves an important variational problem - it is the joint distribution with minimal mutual information subject to the observations as constraints - given the marginal distributions. This provides us with the same exponential form given by the maximum entropy principle, but the rational stems directly from the requirement to preserve mutual information. We now develop this new notion of *most informative observations*, or features, and introduce an algorithm for finding them from experimental data.

Consider a joint probability distribution, $p(x, y)$ over the variables X and Y. We say that the d-dimensional vector function $\vec{\psi}(Y) = (\psi_1(Y), ..., \psi_d(Y))$ is *sufficient* for the variable X if $I(X; Y) = I(X; \vec{\psi}(Y))$, where $I(X; Y) = \sum_{x,y} p(x, y) \log \frac{p(x,y)}{p(x)p(y)}$ is Shannon's mutual information between X and Y (Cover & Thomas 1991).[1] In this case the information about X in *a sample* of Y, for a given value $X = x$, is completely captured by the empirical expectation of $\vec{\psi}(Y)$, namely, by $\langle \vec{\psi}(Y) \rangle_{p(Y|x)}$. Similarly, one can say that the functions $\vec{\phi}(X) = (\phi_1(X), ..., \phi_d(X))$ are sufficient for Y if $I(X; Y) = I(\vec{\phi}(X); Y)$. In that case the dual problem of the information about a given $Y = y$ from a sample of X is captured by $\langle \vec{\phi}(X) \rangle_{p(X|y)}$. The interesting question we address in this work is if we can find such *dual* sets of functions, $\vec{\psi}(Y)$ and $\vec{\phi}(X)$, simultaneously.

A complete simultaneous dimensionality reduction, that preserves *all* the information in the original joint distribution, is possible in general only for special classes of $p(x, y)$, that are of an exponential form. However, these observations motivate a variational approach that finds such a reduction if one exists, but extracts functions $\vec{\psi}(Y)$ and $\vec{\phi}(X)$ that approximate such a reduction in a well defined information theoretic sense. The duality of these two function sets is a key component of our approach. We further show that this variational principle has other suggestive interpretations which make it a viable candidate for a general principled dimensionality reduction or feature extraction technique.

Problem formulation

We assume that we are given a joint distribution of two variables $p(x, y)$. In most practical cases we are in fact given only a finite sample from such a distribution, as a co-occurrence matrix. This empirical joint distribution enables us to estimate expectation values of functions of x and y. We also assume that the marginal distributions, $p(x)$ and $p(y)$, are known or can be well estimated. This latter assumption simplifies our analysis and algorithm, but can be relaxed. We first deal with just one of the two dual problems: finding the set $\vec{\psi}(Y)$. We later show that the resulting algorithm in fact solves the two problems simultaneously, and this apparent asymmetry will be removed.

We look for a set of d functions (or features) of the variable y, denoted by $\psi_i(y)$ for $i = 1 \ldots d$, whose expectations can capture the information in the joint distribution in the following information theoretic sense.

The functions $\psi_i(y)$ should satisfy two complementary requirements. On the one hand their expectation should capture all the information about the values of x, thus no other information on y can be assumed. This means that we should *minimize* the information, subject to the known expected values, $\langle \psi_i(y) \rangle_{p(y|x)}$ for every x, as constraints. On the other hand, the functions $\psi_i(y)$ should be *selected* such that these expectations provide the maximum possible information on the variable X.

Given a candidate set of d functions ψ_i, we denote by $\tilde{p}(x, y)$ the distribution with *minimal* information under the expectation constraints. Namely

$$\tilde{p}(x, y) = \arg \min_{q(x,y) \in \mathcal{P}(\psi_i(y), p)} I[q(x, y)] \quad (1)$$

where $I[q(x, y)] = \sum_{x,y} q(x, y) \log \frac{q(x,y)}{p(x)p(y)}$ and the set $\mathcal{P}(\psi_i(y), p)$ is the set of distributions that satisfy the constraints, defined by

$$\mathcal{P}(\psi_i(y), p) = \left\{ \tilde{p}(x, y) : \begin{array}{ll} \langle \psi_i \rangle_{\tilde{p}(y|x)} = \langle \psi_i \rangle_{p(y|x)} & \forall x \\ \tilde{p}(x) = p(x) \\ \tilde{p}(y) = p(y) \end{array} \right\}. \quad (2)$$

The second requirement should select the best possible candidate functions ψ_i, by *maximizing* this information over all possible d functions ψ.

Together this can be written as a single Max-Min problem for the optimal functions $\psi_i^*(y)$,

$$\psi_i^*(y) = \arg \max_{\psi_i(y)} \min_{\tilde{p}(x,y) \in \mathcal{P}(\psi_i(y), p)} I(\tilde{p}(x, y)). \quad (3)$$

Notice that this variational principle *does not* define a generative statistical model for the data and is in fact a model independent approach. As we show later, however, the resulting distribution $\tilde{p}(x, y)$ can be interpreted as a generative model in a class of exponential form. But there is no need to make any assumption about the validity of such a model for the data. The data distribution $p(x, y)$ is needed only to estimate the expectations $\langle \vec{\psi}(y) \rangle$ for every x, given the candidate features.

In what follows we present an iterative projection algorithm, which finds a local solution of this variational problem, and prove its convergence using information geometrical tools. We also show that this asymmetric variational problem for finding the functions $\psi_i(y)$ is in fact equivalent to the dual problem of finding the functions $\phi_i(x)$ and in fact the two problems are solved simultaneously. Our iterative algorithm uses any MaxEnt algorithm, such as "iterative scaling"(Darroch & Ratcliff 1972), as its inner component. Using it we perform alternating projections between two (infinite) sets of linearly constrained distributions.

The problem as formulated provides a tool for data dimensionality reduction, and as such is applicable for a wide range of problems, from natural language processing to neural code analysis and bioinformatics. An illustrative document classification application will be presented. As we discuss further, this variational problem is similar in structure to the fundamental problem of the capacity of an unknown channel which suggests other interesting interpretations for our procedure. It is also related to the recently proposed *Information Bottleneck Method* (Tishby, Pereira, & Bialek 1999) as well as to other dimensionality reduction algorithms, such as LSA(Deerwester *et al.* 1990), LLE(Roweis & Saul 2000) and non-negative matrix factorization (Lee & Seung 1999).

The nature of the solution

We first show that the problem as formulated in Eq. 3 is equivalent to the problem of minimizing the KL divergence between the empirical distribution $p(x, y)$ and a large (parametric) family of distributions of an exponential form.

To simplify notation, we sometimes omit the suffix of (x, y) from the distributions. Thus $\tilde{p}_t$ stands for $\tilde{p}_t(x, y)$ and p for $p(x, y)$

---

[1] In the conventional notation of parameter estimation X is a d dimensional parameter vector Θ, and Y is an n dimensional i.i.d sample from $p(y|\Theta)$.

Minimizing the mutual information in Eq. 1 under the linear constraints on the expectations $\langle\vec{\psi}(y)\rangle$ is equivalent to maximizing the joint entropy, $H[\tilde{p}(x,y)] = -\sum_{x,y}\tilde{p}(x,y)\log\tilde{p}(x,y)$, under these constraints, with the additional requirement on the marginals, $\tilde{p}(x) = p(x)$ and $\tilde{p}(y) = p(y)$. Due to the concavity of the entropy and the convexity of the linear constraints, there exists a unique maximum entropy distribution (for compact domains of x and y) which has the exponential form,

$$p^*_{\vec{\psi}(y)}(x,y) = \frac{1}{Z}\exp\left(\sum_{i=1}^d \phi_i(x)\psi_i(y) + A(x) + B(y)\right),$$
(4)

where $Z = \sum_{x,y}\exp\left(\sum_{i=1}^d \phi_i(x)\psi_i(y) + A(x) + B(y)\right)$ is the normalization (partition) function [2].

The functions $\phi_i(x)$ are uniquely determined as Lagrange multipliers from the expectation values $\langle\psi_i(y)\rangle$. This exponential form is also directly linked to our interpretation of the functions ψ_i and ϕ_i as conjugate sufficient statistics.

One key property of the exponential form, Eq. 4, is that it is the only joint distribution for which the mutual information between x and y is completely captured by the dual function vectors, $\psi_i(y), \phi_i(x)$. Namely, it is the only joint distribution $\tilde{p}(x,y)$ for which the following equality holds,

$$I[\tilde{p}(x,y)] = I(\psi;\phi).$$
(5)

This property manifests the fact that the reduced description of the x and y by ϕ and ψ indeed catures the relevant structure of the joint distribution. It makes it clear why one would like to find a good approximation to the given joint distribution, which is of this form.

The set of distributions of the exponential form in Eq. 4 can also be considered as a parametric family, parametrized by the infinite family of functions $\Theta = [\psi_i(y), \phi_i(x), A(x), B(y)]$ (note we treat ψ and ϕ symmetrically).

We denote this family by P_Θ and a member of the family by p_Θ. Naturally, $p^*_{\vec{\psi}(y)} \in P_\Theta$.

We define the set of distributions $\mathcal{P}_\Psi \subset P_\Theta$:

$$\mathcal{P}_\Psi = \left\{\tilde{p} \in P_\Theta : \begin{array}{l} \langle\psi_i\rangle_{\tilde{p}(y|x)} = \langle\psi_i\rangle_{p(y|x)} \quad \forall x \\ \tilde{p}(x) = p(x) \\ \tilde{p}(y) = p(y) \end{array}\right\}.$$
(6)

The problem presented above (Eq. 3) is then equivalent to finding the information maximizing distribution in $\mathcal{P}_\Psi$,

$$\tilde{p}^* = \arg\max_{\tilde{p}\in\mathcal{P}_\Psi} I[\tilde{p}].$$
(7)

We now return to the information maximization problem, i.e. the selection of the feature candidates $\vec{\psi}(y)$. For every $\tilde{p} \in \mathcal{P}_\Psi$ one can easily show that

$$I[\tilde{p}] = I[p] - D_{KL}[p|\tilde{p}],$$
(8)

where $D_{KL}[p|q] = \sum_{x,y} p\log\frac{p}{q}$. The above expression has two important consequences. The first is that maximizing

---

[2]Note that the unique distribution can actually be on the closure of such exponential forms. We do not address this detail here.

$I[\tilde{p}]$ for $\tilde{p} \in \mathcal{P}_\Psi$ is equivalent to minimizing $D_{KL}[p|\tilde{p}]$ for $\tilde{p} \in \mathcal{P}_\Psi$:

$$\tilde{p}^* = \arg\min_{\tilde{p}\in\mathcal{P}_\Psi} D_{KL}[p|\tilde{p}].$$
(9)

In addition, Eq. 8 shows that the information in $I[\tilde{p}^*]$ can not be larger than the information in the original data. This supports the intuition that the model $\tilde{p}^*$ maintains only properties present in the original distribution that are captured by the selected features $\psi_i^*(y)$, for any value of x.

The problem in Eq. 9 is a maximization of a function over a subset of P_Θ, namely $\mathcal{P}_\Psi$. The following proposition shows that this is in fact equivalent to maximizing the same function over all of P_Θ.

Proposition 1 $\arg\min_{\tilde{p}\in\mathcal{P}_\Psi} D_{KL}[p|\tilde{p}] = \arg\min_{\tilde{p}\in P_\Theta} D_{KL}[p|\tilde{p}]$

Proof: We need to show that the distribution which minimizes the right hand side is in $\mathcal{P}_\Psi$. Indeed, by taking the (generally functional) derivative of $D_{KL}[p(x,y)|\tilde{p}]$ w.r.t. the parameters Θ in $\tilde{p}$, one obtains the following conditions:

$$\begin{array}{ll} \forall x, i & \langle\psi_i(y)\rangle_{\tilde{p}(y|x)} = \langle\psi_i(y)\rangle_{p(y|x)} \\ \forall y, i & \langle\phi_i(x)\rangle_{\tilde{p}(x|y)} = \langle\phi_i(x)\rangle_{p(x|y)} \\ \forall x & \tilde{p}(x) = p(x) \\ \forall y & \tilde{p}(y) = p(y). \end{array}$$
(10)

Clearly, this distribution satisfies the constraints in $\mathcal{P}(\psi_i(y), p)$ and is therefore in $\mathcal{P}_\Psi$. □

Our problem is thus equivalent to the minimization problem:

$$p^* = \arg\min_{\tilde{p}\in P_\Theta} D_{KL}[p|\tilde{p}].$$
(11)

Equation 11 is symmetric with respect to ϕ and ψ, thus removing the asymmetry between X and Y in the formulation of Eq. 3.

Notice that this minimization problem can be viewed as a Maximum Likelihood fit to the given $p(x,y)$ in the class P_Θ, but since nothing on its own guarantees the quality of this fit, nor justifies the class P_Θ, we prefer the information theoretic, model independent, interpretation of our approach.

An Iterative Projection Algorithm

Our main result is an iterative algorithm for solving the Max-Min variational problem, Eq. 3, which provably converges to a minimum of Eq. 11. We describe the algorithm using the information geometric notion of *I-projections* (Csiszar 1975).

The *I-projection* of a distribution $q(x)$ on a set of distributions $\mathcal{P}$ is defined as the distribution $p^*(x)$ in $\mathcal{P}$ which minimizes the KL-divergence $D_{KL}[p|q]$.

$$p^*(x) = \arg\min_{p\in\mathcal{P}} D_{KL}[p|q].$$
(12)

We shall use the notation $p^*(x) = IPR(q,\mathcal{P})$.

An important property of the *I-projection* is the, so called, Pythagorean property (Cover & Thomas 1991). For every distribution p in $\mathcal{P}$ the following holds:

$$D_{KL}[p|q] \leq D_{KL}[p|p^*] + D_{KL}[p^*|q].$$
(13)

We now focus on the case where the set $\mathcal{P}$ is a convex set determined by expectation values. Given a set of d functions $f_i(x)$ and a distribution $p(x)$, we denote the set of distributions which agree with $p(x)$ on the expectation values of $f_i(x)$, by $\mathcal{P}(f_i(x), p(x))$. Namely,

$$\mathcal{P}(f_i(x), p(x)) = \left\{ \tilde{p}(x) : \langle f_i(x) \rangle_{\tilde{p}(x)} = \langle f_i(x) \rangle_{p(x)} \right\} \tag{14}$$

The *I-projection* in this case has the exponential form

$$IPR(q(x), \mathcal{P}(f_i(x), p(x))) = \frac{1}{Z^*} q(x) \exp \sum_i \lambda_i^* f_i(x) , \tag{15}$$

where λ_i^* is the Lagrange multiplier corresponding to $\langle f_i(x) \rangle_{p(x)}$. In addition, for this special set, the Pythagorean inequality actually becomes an equality (Csiszar 1975).

Before describing the algorithm, we need some additional notations:

- $\tilde{p}_t(x, y)$ - the distribution after t iterations.
- $\psi_{i,t}(y)$ - the $\psi_i(y)$ functions for $\tilde{p}_t(x, y)$, Lagrange multipliers for $\langle \phi_{i,t-1}(x) \rangle$.
- $\phi_{i,t+1}(x)$ - the $\phi_i(x)$ functions for $\tilde{p}_{t+1}(x, y)$, Lagrange multipliers for $\langle \psi_{i,t}(y) \rangle$.
- Θ_t - the full parameter set for $\tilde{p}_t(x, y)$.

The iterative projection algorithm is outlined in figure 1. In this figure the algorithm is described through iterated *I-projections* of (exponential) distributions, once for fixed $\psi_i(y)$ and their expectations, and then for fixed $\phi_i(x)$ and their expectations. Interestingly, during the first projection, the functions $\phi_i(x)$ are modified as Lagrange multipliers for $\langle \psi_i(y) \rangle$, and vice-versa in the second projection. The iteration can thus be viewed as alternating mapping between the two sets of d-dimensional functions, ψ_i and ϕ_i. This is also the direct goal of the variational problem.

We proceed to prove the convergence of the algorithm. We first show that every step reduces $D_{KL}[p(x, y) | \tilde{p}_t(x, y)]$.

Proposition 2 $D_{KL}(p(x, y), \tilde{p}_{t+1}(x, y)) \leq D_{KL}(p(x, y), \tilde{p}_t(x, y))$.

Proof: For each x, the following is true:

- $\tilde{p}_{t+1}(y|x)$ is the *I-projection* of $\tilde{p}_t(y|x)$ on the set $\mathcal{P}(\psi_{i,t}(y), p(y|x))$.
- $p(y|x)$ is also in $\mathcal{P}(\psi_{i,t}(y), p(y|x))$.

Using the Pythagorean property, (which is an equality here) we have that $D_{KL}[p(y|x) | \tilde{p}_t(y|x)]$ is equal to:

$$D_{KL}[p(y|x) | \tilde{p}_{t+1}(y|x)] + D_{KL}[\tilde{p}_{t+1}(y|x) | \tilde{p}_t(y|x)] . \tag{16}$$

Multiplying by $p(x)$ and summing over all x values, we obtain:

$$D_{KL}[p | \tilde{p}_t] = D_{KL}[p | \tilde{p}_{t+1}] + D_{KL}[\tilde{p}_{t+1} | \tilde{p}_t] . \tag{17}$$

where we have used $\tilde{p}_t(x) = p(x)$. Note that the summation resulted in the term $D_{KL}[p(x) | \tilde{p}_{t+1}(x)]$ on both sides of the equation.

Using the non-negativity of $D_{KL}[\tilde{p}_{t+1} | \tilde{p}_t]$ we have:

$$D_{KL}[p | \tilde{p}_t] \geq D_{KL}[p | \tilde{p}_{t+1}] . \tag{18}$$

Note that equality is obtained iff $D_{KL}[\tilde{p}_{t+1} | \tilde{p}_t]$. $\square$

Input: Joint (empirical) distribution $p(x, y)$

Output: $2d$ feature functions: $\psi_i(y)$ $\phi_i(x)$ that result from $\tilde{p}^*$, a solution of the variational problem Eq. 3 and a (local) minimum of Eq. 9.

Initialization:

- Initialize $\tilde{p}_0(x, y) \in P_\Theta$ randomly

Iterate:

- For all x, set:

$$\begin{aligned} \tilde{p}_{t+1}(y|x) &= IPR(\tilde{p}_t(y|x), \mathcal{P}(\psi_{i,t}(y), p(y|x))) \\ \tilde{p}_{t+1}(x, y) &= \tilde{p}_{t+1}(y|x) p(x). \end{aligned}$$

The functions $\phi_{i,t+1}(x)$ are determined as the Lagrange multipliers

- For all y, set:

$$\begin{aligned} \tilde{p}_{t+2}(x|y) &= IPR(\tilde{p}_{t+1}(x|y), \mathcal{P}(\phi_{i,t+1}(x), p(x|y))) \\ \tilde{p}_{t+2}(x, y) &= \tilde{p}_{t+2}(x|y) p(y). \end{aligned}$$

The functions $\psi_{i,t+1}(y)$ are determined as Lagrange multipliers

- Halt on convergence (when small enough change in $\tilde{p}_t(x, y)$).

Figure 1: The iterative projection algorithm.

An analogous argument proves that:

$$D_{KL}[p | \tilde{p}_{t+2}] \leq D_{KL}[p | \tilde{p}_{t+1}] . \tag{19}$$

The following easily provable proposition states that the stationary points of the algorithm coincide with extremum points of the target function $D_{KL}[p | p_\Theta]$. Its proof uses the properties of the projections in the algorithm, and the characterization of the extremum point in Eq. 10.

Proposition 3 *If $\tilde{p}_t = \tilde{p}_{t+2}$ then the corresponding Θ_t satisfies $\frac{\partial}{\partial \Theta} D_{KL}[p | p_\Theta] = 0$.*

It is now easy to prove convergence of the algorithm to a local minimum of $D_{KL}[p | p_\Theta]$ using continuity arguments and the improvement at each iteration given in Eq. 17. We will give a detailed proof in a separate paper.

Implementation - Partial I-projections

The description of the iterative algorithm assumes the existence of a module which calculates I-projections on linear constraints. Because no closed form solution for such a projection is known, it is found by successive iterations which asymptotically converge to the solution. It is straightforward to show that even if our projection algorithm uses such a "Partial I projection" algorithm as its IPR module, it still converges to a minimum.

In this work we use as an IPR algorithm the Generalized Iterative Scaling (GIS) procedure (Darroch & Ratcliff 1972), described in figure 2. Alternative algorithms such as

Improved Iterative Scaling (Pietra & Lafferty 1997) or conjugate gradient methods, can also be used and may improve convergence rate.

Input: Distributions $q(x), p(x)$, d functions $f_i(x)$

Output: $IPR(q(x), \mathcal{P}(f_i(x), p(x)))$

Initialize: $p_0(x) = q(x)$

Iterate:

- $p_{t+1}(x) = \frac{1}{Z_t} p_t(x) \exp \sum_{i=1}^{d} f_i(x) \log \frac{\langle f_i(x)\rangle_{p(x)}}{\langle f_i(x)\rangle_{p_t(x)}}$
- Z_t is a normalization constant

Figure 2: The Generalized Iterative Scaling Algorithm.

Discussion

Our proposed method is a new dimensionality reduction technique. It is nonlinear, unlike PCA or ICA, and it aims directly at preserving mutual information in a given empirical co-occurrence matrix. We achieved that through an information variation principle that enables us to calculate simultaneously informative feature functions for *both* random variables. In addition we obtain an exponential model approximation to the given data which has precisely these features as *dual sets* of sufficient statistics. We described an alternating projection algorithm for finding these features and proved its convergence to a (local) optimum. This is in fact an algorithm for extracting optimal sets of constraints from statistical data. We briefly address now several other important issues that our procedure raises.

Finite samples The basic assumption behind our problem formulation is that we have the joint distribution of the variables x and y, $p(x, y)$. For the machine learning community this assumption may look strange, but one should remember that the goal is *not* to learn the mapping from X to Y, but rather to extract good features of X w.r.t. Y. In fact, $p(x, y)$ is not needed explicitly, but only to estimate the expectation values $\langle \vec{\psi}(y)\rangle$ and $\langle \vec{\phi}(x)\rangle$. These can be estimated *uniformly well* from a finite sample under the standard uniform convergence conditions. In other words, standard learning theoretical techniques can give us the sample complexity bounds, given the dimensions of X and Y and the reduced dimension d. For continuous x and y further assumptions must be made, such as the VC dimension of the features, etc.

Uniqueness of the solution Interestingly, while the goal of the algorithm are features that preserve information, the information in the functions $\vec{\psi}(y)$ and $\vec{\phi}(x)$ is not estimated directly at any point. Furthermore, there is a freedom in selecting the features that stems from the fact that only the dot-product $\vec{\phi}(x) \cdot \vec{\psi}(y)$ appears in the distribution $\tilde{p}(x, y)$. Any invertible matrix R can be applied such that $\vec{\phi}(x)R^{-1}$ and $R\vec{\psi}(y)$ are equally good features. One can remove this ambiguity by orthogonalization and scaling of the feature

functions, for example by applying SVD to $\log \tilde{p}(x, y)$. Notice, however, that our procedure is very different from direct application of SVD to $\log p(x, y)$. These two coincide *only* when the original joint distribution is already of the exponential form of Eq.(4). In all other cases SVD based approximations (LSA included) will not preserve information as well as our features at the same dimension reduction. The resulting functions $\vec{\psi}(y)$ and $\vec{\phi}(x)$ thus depend on the initial point of the iterations, but the information extracted does not (for the same optimum).

Information theoretic interpretation Our information MaxMin principle is close in its formal structure to the problem of channel capacity with some channel uncertainty (see e.g. (Lapidoth & Narayan 1998)). This suggests the interesting interpretation for the features as channel characteristics. If the channel only enables the reliable transmission of d expected values, then our $\vec{\psi}(y)$ exploit this channel in an optimal way. The channel decoder of this case is provided by the dual vector $\vec{\phi}(x)$ and the decoding is performed through a dot-product in of these two vectors. This intriguing interpretation of our algorithm obviously requires further analysis.

Relations to other algorithms

Dimension reduction algorithms have become a fundamental component in unsupervised large scale data analysis, together with clustering. While linear methods, as PCA and ICA, provide very useful first steps, they do not provide a principled method for statistical co-occurrence data, where such linear assumptions about the matrix are unjustified. Several interesting non-linear methods have been proposed in the past years. Of particular interest are

LLE(Roweis & Saul 2000) and non-negative matrix factorization (Lee & Seung 1999). We feel that none of these new algorithms directly address the question of information preserving as we suggest here. Furthermore, preliminary comparisons of our algorithm with LSA (Deerwester *et al.* 1990) for document indexing are very encouraging and justify our non-linear approach. A closely related idea is the *Information Bottleneck Method* (Tishby, Pereira, & Bialek 1999) which aims at a clustering that preserves information. However, clustering may not be the correct answer for many problems where the relationship between the variables comes from some hidden low dimensional continuous structures. In such cases clustering tends to quantize the data in a rather arbitrary way, while low dimensional features are simpler and easier for interpretation. The resulting algorithm is also computationally simpler, with no need for complicated splitting or merging of clusters.

Acknowledgement

We thank Noam Slonim and Gal Chechik for helpful discussions and comments and for the help with experimental data. This work is partly supported by a grant from the Israeli Academy of Science. A.G. is supported by the Eshkol Foundation.

References

Cover, T., and Thomas, J. 1991. *Elements of information theory.* Wiley.

Csiszar, I. 1975. I-divergence geometry of probability distributions and minimization problems. *Annals of Probability* 3(1):146–158.

Darroch, J., and Ratcliff, D. 1972. Generalized iterative scaling for log-linear models. *Ann. Math. Statist.* 43:1470–1480.

Deerwester, S.; Dumais, S.; Landauer, T.; Furnas, G.; and Harshman, R. 1990. Indexing by latent semantic analysis. *Journal of the American Society of Information Science* 41(6):391–407.

Degroot, M. 1986. *Probability and Statistics.* Addison-Wesley.

Jaynes, E. 1957. Information theory and statistical mechanics. *Physical Review* 106:620.

Lapidoth, A., and Narayan, P. 1998. Reliable communication under channel uncertainty. *IEEE Transactions on Information Theory* 44(6):2148–2177.

Lee, D., and Seung, H. 1999. Learning the parts of objects by non-negative matrix factorization. *Nature* 401(6755):788–791.

Pietra, S. D., and Lafferty, V. D. P. J. 1997. Inducing features of random fields. *IEEE Transactions on PAMI* 19(4):380–393.

Roweis, S., and Saul, L. 2000. Nonlinear dimensionality reduction by locally linear embedding. *Science* 290(5500):2323–6.

Tishby, N.; Pereira, F.; and Bialek, W. 1999. The information bottleneck method. In *Proc. of the 37-th Annual Allerton Conference on Communication, Control and Computing*, 368–377.

Index